THE BANTAM NEW COLLEGE
GERMAN & ENGLISH DICTIONARY

The Best Low-Priced Dictionary You Can Own

With more entries than any other compact paper-bound dictionary—including thousands of new words—*The Bantam New College German & English Dictionary* is the most complete budget dictionary available today.

Whether you need it at home, the office, school, or in the library, this one indispensable, authoritative volume will prove its value over and over again, every time you use it.

D0018190

JOHN C. TRAUPMAN received his B.A. in German and in Latin at Moravian College and his M.A. and Ph.D. in Classics at Princeton University. He is chairman emeritus of the Department of Classical Languages at St. Joseph's University (Philadelphia). He served as president of the Philadelphia Classical Society, of the Pennsylvania Classical Association, and of the Classical Association of the Atlantic States. He has published widely in learned journals and is the author of a textbook for middle schools *Latin is Fun* (AMSCO, 1989) as well as of *The New College Latin & English Dictionary* (Bantam Books, 1966) and an associate editor of *The Scribner-Bantam English Dictionary* (Scribner's 1977; Bantam Books, 1979).

THE BANTAM NEW COLLEGE
GERMAN & ENGLISH
DICTIONARY

JOHN C. TRAUPMAN, Ph.D.
St. Joseph's University, Philadelphia

BANTAM BOOKS
NEW YORK · TORONTO · LONDON · SYDNEY · AUCKLAND

THE BANTAM NEW COLLEGE
GERMAN & ENGLISH DICTIONARY

A Bantam Book / February 1981
Bantam reissue / September 1991

ISBN 0-553-28088-0

Published simultaneously in the United States and Canada

Bantam Books are published by Bantam Books, a division of Bantam
Doubleday Dell Publishing Group, Inc. Its trademark, consisting of the
words "Bantam Books" and the portrayal of a rooster, is Registered in U.S.
Patent and Trademark Office and in other countries. Marca Registrada.
Bantam Books, 666 Fifth Avenue, New York, New York 10103.

PRINTED IN THE UNITED STATES OF AMERICA

RAD   20 19 18 17 16 15 14 13

CONTENTS

I wish to express my appreciation to the many persons on whose help I relied in researching and compiling this Dictionary. I am particularly indebted to Edwin B. Williams, Walter D. Glanze, Donald Reis, Rudolf Pillwein, and Helmut Kreitz.

J. C. T.

HOW TO USE THIS DICTIONARY

HINWEISE FÜR DEN BENUTZER

All entry words are treated in a fixed order according to the parts of speech and the functions of verbs. On the German-English side: past participle, adjective, adverb, pronoun, preposition, conjunction, interjection, transitive verb, reflexive verb, reciprocal verb, intransitive verb, impersonal verb, auxiliary verb, substantive; on the English-German side: adjective, substantive, pronoun, adverb, preposition, conjunction, transitive verb, intransitive verb, auxiliary verb, impersonal verb, interjection.

Alle Stichwörter werden in einheitlicher Reihenfolge gemäß der Wortart und der Verbfunktion behandelt. Im deutsch-englischen Teil: Partizip Perfekt, Adjektiv, Adverb, Pronomen, Präposition, Konjunktion, Interjektion, transitives Verb, reflexives Verb, reziprokes Verb, intransitives Verb, unpersönliches Verb, Hilfsverb, Substantiv; im englisch-deutschen Teil: Adjektiv, Substantiv, Pronomen, Adverb, Präposition, Konjunktion, transitives Verb, intransitives Verb, Hilfsverb, unpersönliches Verb, Interjektion.

The order of meanings within an entry is as follows: first, the more general meanings; second, the meanings with usage labels; third, the meanings with subject labels in alphabetical order; fourth, illustrative phrases in alphabetical order.

Die verschiedenen Bedeutungen sind innerhalb eines Stichwortartikels in folgender Anordnung gegeben: zuerst die allgemeinen Bedeutungen; dann die Bedeutungen mit Bezeichnung der Sprachgebrauchsebene; dann die Bedeutungen mit Bezeichnung des Sachgebietes, in alphabetischer Reihenfolge; zuletzt die Anwendungsbeispiele, in alphabetischer Reihenfolge.

Subject and usage labels (printed in roman and in parentheses) refer to the preceding entry word or illustrative phrase in the source language (printed in boldface), e.g.,

Die Bezeichnungen der Sprachgebrauchsebene und des Sachgebiets (in Antiqua und in Klammern) beziehen sich auf das vorangehende Stichwort oder Anwendungsbeispiel in der Ausgangssprache (halbfett gedruckt), z.B.

mund′tot *adj*—**j-n m. machen** (fig) silence s.o.
Pinke [′pɪŋkə] *f* (—;) (coll) dough

Words in parentheses and in roman coming after a meaning serve to clarify that meaning, e.g.,

Kursiv gedruckte Wörter in Klammern, die nach einer Bedeutung stehen, sollen diese Bedeutung illustrieren, z.B.

überschau′en *tr* look over, survey; overlook (*a scene*)

Words in parenthese and in roman type coming after or before a meaning are optional additions to the word in the target language, e.g.,	In Antiqua gedruckte Wörter in Klammern, die nach oder vor einer Bedeutung stehen, sind wahlfreie Erweiterungen des Wortes der Zielsprache, z.B.

Tanne ['tanə] *f* (-;-n) fir (tree)
Pap'rikaschote *f* (green) pepper

Meaning discriminations are given in the source language and are in italics, e.g.,	Bedeutungsdifferenzierungen sind in der Ausgangssprache angegeben und kursiv gedruckt, z.B.

überrei'zen *tr* overexcite; (*Augen, Nerven*) strain
earn [ʌrn] *tr* (*money*) verdienen; (*interest*) einbringen

Since vocabulary entries are not determined on the basis of etymology, homographs are listed as a single entry.	Da die Etymologie bei der Anführung der Stichwörter unberücksichtigt bleibt, sind gleichgeschriebene Wörter als ein und dasselbe Stichwort verzeichnet.

The entry word is represented within the entry by its initial letter followed by a period (if the entry word contains more than three letters), provided the form is identical. The same applies to a word that follows the parallels. The entry word is not abbreviated within the entry when associated with suspension points, e.g.,	Innerhalb eines Stichwortartikels wird das Stichwort (wenn es mehr als drei Buchstaben enthält) durch seinen Anfangsbuchstaben angegeben, vorausgesetzt, daß die betreffende Form mit dem Stichwort identisch ist. Das Gleiche gilt für ein Wort, das nach den Vertikalstrichen steht. Wenn ein Stichwort innerhalb eines Stichwortartikels in Verbindung mit Auslassungspunkten angegeben ist, wird es nicht abgekürzt, z.B.

weder ... noch

Parallels are used (a) to separate parts of speech, (b) to separate transitive, reflexive, reciprocal, intransitive, impersonal, and auxiliary verbs, (c) to separate verbs taking HABEN from those taking SEIN, (d) to indicate a change in pronunciation of the entry word, depending on the meaning, e.g.,	Es ist der Zweck der Vertikalstriche, (a) Wortarten voneinander zu trennen, (b) transitive, reflexive, reziproke, intransitive, unpersönliche Verben und Hilfsverben zu trennen, (c) Verben mit dem Hilfsverb HABEN von Verben mit dem Hilfsverb SEIN zu trennen, (d) verschiedene Aussprachen des Stichwortes je nach Bedeutung anzuzeigen, z.B.

bow [bau] *s* Verbeugung *f*; (naut) Bug *m* ...
‖ [bo] *s* (*weapon*) Bogen *m*; ...

(e) to show change from a strong verb to a weak verb and vice versa, (f) to show a change in the case governed by	(e) den Wechsel von einem starken zu einem schwachen Verb und umgekehrt anzuzeigen, (f) den Wechsel in einem

a preposition where the entry word is a preposition, (g) to show a shift of accent, e.g.,	von einer Präposition regierten Fall anzuzeigen, wo das Stichwort selbst eine Präposition ist, (g) unterschiedliche Stellungen des Akzents anzuzeigen, z.B.

ü′bergießen *tr* . . . ‖ **übergie′ßen** *tr* . . .

The centered period in the English word on the German-English side marks the point at which the following letters are dropped before irregular plural endings are added. The centered period in the entry word on the English-German side marks the point at which the following letters are dropped before irregular plural endings are added to nouns and inflections are added to verbs. The centered period in the phonetic spelling indicates diaeresis, e.g.,	Der auf Mitte stehende Punkt im Stichwort des deutsch-englischen Teils zeigt die Stelle an, wo die nachfolgenden Buchstaben abzutrennen sind, bevor unregelmäßige Pluralendungen angefügt werden können. Der auf Mitte stehende Punkt im Stichwort des englisch-deutschen Teils zeigt die Stelle an, wo die nachfolgenden Buchstaben abzutrennen sind, bevor unregelmäßige Pluralendungen an Hauptwörter and Flexionen an Verben angefügt werden können. Der auf Mitte stehende Punkt in der Lautschrift zeigt Diärese an, z.B.

befähigt [bə′fe·ɪçt]

On the German-English and the English-German side, in the case of a transitive verb, the meaning discrimination in parentheses before the target word is always the object of the verb. On the German-English side, in the case of an intransitive verb, the meaning discrimination in parentheses before the target word is always the subject of the verb. On the English-German side, the suggested subject of a verb is prefaced by the words "said of".	Im deutsch-englischen und im englisch-deutschen Teil ist die bei transitiven Verben in Klammern vor dem Wort in der Zielsprache angegebene Bedeutungsdifferenzierung immer das Objekt des Verbs. Im deutsch-englischen Teil ist bei intransitiven Verben die vor dem Wort in der Zielsprache angegebene Bedeutungsdifferenzierung immer das Subjekt des Verbs. Im englisch-deutschen Teil stehen vor dem beabsichtigten Subjekt eines Verbs die Worte "said of."

Inflections are generally not shown for compound entry words, since the inflections have been shown where the components are entry words. However, when the last component of a compound noun on the German-English side has various inflections depending on meaning, the inflection is shown for the compound, e.g.,	Bei zusammengesetzten Stichwörtern ist die Flexion im Allgemeinen nicht angegeben, da sie unter den als Stichwörter angeführten Teilen des Kompositums angegeben ist. Falls jedoch der letzte Teil eines deutschen Kompositums je nach der Bedeutung verschieden flektiert wird, ist die Flexion für das Kompositum angegeben, z.B.

Ton′band *n* (–[e]s;ǟer) . . .

German verbs are regarded as reflexive regardless of whether the reflexive pronoun is the direct or indirect object of the verb.	Deutsche Verben gelten als reflexiv ohne Rücksicht darauf, ob das Reflexivpronomen das direkte oder indirekte Objekt des Verbs ist.

On the English-German side, when the pronunciation of an entry word is not given, stress in the entry word is shown as follows: a high-set primary stress mark ′ follows the syllable that receives the primary stress, and a high-set secondary stress mark ′ follows the syllable that receives the secondary stress. When the pronunciation of an entry word *is* provided [given in brackets], a high-set primary stress mark ˈ *precedes* the syllable that receives the primary stress, and a *low*-set secondary stress mark ˌ *precedes* the syllable that receives the secondary stress.

On the German-English side, when the pronunciation of an entry word is not given, a high-set primary stress mark ′ follows the syllable of the entry word that receives the primary stress. When the pronunciation of the entry *is* provided [given in brackets], a high-set primary stress mark ˈ *precedes* the syllable that receives the primary stress. (Because opinions on the system of secondary stress in German differ widely, secondary stress marks are not employed in this Dictionary.)

Wo die Aussprache des Stichwortes im englisch-deutschen Teil nicht angegeben ist, wird die Betonung des Stichwortes folgendermaßen angedeutet: Das stärkere, obere graphische Zeichen ′ steht nach der Silbe mit dem Haupttonakzent, und das schwächere, obere Zeichen ′ steht nach der Silbe mit dem Nebentonakzent. Wo hingegen die Aussprache des Stichwortes im englisch-deutschen Teil [in eckigen Klammern] angegeben ist, steht das stärkere, obere Zeichen ˈ *vor* der Silbe mit dem Haupttonakzent und das schwächere, *untere* Zeichen ˌ *vor* der Silbe mit dem Nebentonakzent.

Wo die Aussprache das Stichwortes im deutsch-englischen Teil nicht angegeben ist, steht das starke Zeichen ′ nach der Stichwortsilbe mit dem Haupttonakzent. Wo hingegen die Aussprache des Stichwortes im deutschenglischen Teil [in eckigen Klammern] angegeben ist, steht das starke Zeichen ˈ *vor* der Silbe mit dem Haupttonakzent. (Wegen der widersprüchlichen Theorien, die die Frage des Nebentonakzents im Deutschen umgeben, wendet dieses Wörterbuch keine Nebentonzente für die deutschen Wörter an.)

Proper nouns and general abbreviations are listed in their alphabetical position in the main body of the Dictionary.

Eigennamen und allgemeine Abkürzungen sind in den beiden Hauptteilen des Wörterbuches in alphabetischer Reihenfolge angegeben.

This Dictionary contains approximately 75,000 "entries." As entries are counted (a) nonindented boldface headwords and (b) elements that could have been set nonindented as separate headwords, too, but that for reasons of style and typography are grouped under the nonindented headwords, namely, separate parts of speech and boldface idioms and phrases.

Dieses Wörterbuch enthält ungefähr 75.000 "Stichwörter." Die folgenden Elemente gelten als Stichwörter: (a) die nicht eingerückten fettgedruckten Wörter am Anfang eines Stichwortartikels und (b) Elemente, die man auf dieselbe Weise hatte drucken können, die aber aus Stil- und Typographiegründen eingerückt wurden, nämlich die unterschiedlichen Wortarten und die fettgedruckten Redewendungen.

PART ONE

German-English

GERMAN—ENGLISH

A

A, a [ɑ] *invar n* A, a; (mus) A; **das A und O** the beginning and the end; (*das Wichtigste*) the most important thing

Aal [ɑl] *m* (-[e]s;-e) eel; (nav) torpedo

aal′glatt′ *adj* (fig) sly as a fox

Aas [ɑs] *n* (-es;-e) carrion; (sl) louse

ab [ap] *adv* off; away; down; on, e.g., **von heute ab** from today on; (theat) exit, exeunt, e.g., **Hamlet ab** exit Hamlet; **ab und zu** now and then || *prep* (*dat*) from, e.g., **ab Frankfurt** from Frankfurt; minus, e.g., **ab Skonto** minus discount

ab′ändern *tr* alter; (*völlig*) change; (*mildern*) modify; (parl) amend

Ab′änderung *f* (-;-en) alteration; change; modification; (parl) amendment

Ab′änderungsantrag *m* (parl) (proposed) amendment

ab′arbeiten *tr* work off || *ref* work hard

Ab′art *f* variety, type

ab′arten *intr* (SEIN) deviate from type

Ab′bau *m* (-[e]s;) demolition; reduction; cutback; layoff; (chem) decomposition; (min) exploitation

ab′bauen *tr* demolish; (*Maschinen, Fabriken*) dismantle; (*Steuern, Preise, Truppen*) reduce; (*Zelt*) take down; (*Lager*) break; (*Angestellte*) lay off; (chem) decompose; (min) work, exploit

ab′beißen §53 *tr* bite off || *intr* take a bite

ab′bekommen §99 *tr* (*seinen Teil*) get; (*Schmutz*) get out; (*Deckel*) get off; **du wirst was a.!** you're going to get it!

ab′berufen §122 *tr* (dipl) recall

ab′bestellen *tr* cancel

ab′betteln *tr*—**die ganze Straße a.** beg up and down the street; **j-m etw a.** chisel s.th. from s.o.

ab′biegen §57 *tr* bend, twist off; (*Gefahr*) avert; (*Plan*) thwart; **das Gespräch a.** change the subject || *intr* (SEIN) branch off; (fig) get off the track; **in e-e Seitenstraße a.** turn down a side street; **nach links a.** turn left; **von e-r Straße a.** turn off a road

Ab′bild *n* picture, image

ab′bilden *tr* represent

Ab′bildung *f* (-;-en) illustration, figure

ab′binden §59 *tr* untie; (*Kalb*) wean; (*Arm*) apply a tourniquet to; (surg) tie off || *intr* (*Zement*) set

Ab′bitte *f* apology; **A. tun wegen** apologize for

ab′bitten §60 *tr* apologize for || *intr* apologize

ab′blasen §61 *tr* blow off; (fig) call off || *intr* (mil) sound the retreat

ab′blättern *intr* (SEIN) shed leaves; (*Farben, Haut*) flake, peel

ab′blenden *tr* dim; (cin) fade out; (phot) stop down || *intr* (aut) dim the lights; (nav) darken ship; (phot) stop down the lens

Ab′blendlicht *n* (aut) low-beam lights

ab′blitzen *intr* (SEIN) be unsuccessful; **j-n a. lassen** snub s.o.

ab′blühen *intr* stop blooming || *intr* (SEIN) fade

ab′böschen *tr* slope; (*Mauer*) batter

ab′brausen *tr* hose down || *ref* shower off || *intr* (SEIN) (coll) roar off

ab′brechen §64 *tr* break off; (*Belagerung*) raise; (*Gebäude*) demolish; (*Zelt*) take down; (sport) call; **das Lager a.** break camp || *intr* (SEIN) (& fig) break off

ab′bremsen *tr* slow down; (*Streik*) prevent; (*Motoren*) (aer) rev || *intr* put on the brakes; (aer) fishtail

ab′brennen §97 *tr* burn off; (*Feuerwerk*) set off; (*Geschütz*) fire; (chem) distil out; (metal) refine; (naut) bream; **ich bin vollkommen abgebrannt** (coll) I'm dead broke || *intr* (SEIN) burn down

ab′bringen §65 *tr* (*Fleck*) remove; (*gestrandetes Schiff*) refloat; **davon a. zu** (*inf*) dissuade from (*ger*); **vom rechten Weg a.** lead astray; **vom Thema a.** throw off; von der Spur a. throw off the scent; **von e-r Gewohnheit a.** break of the habit

ab′bröckeln *intr* crumble; (*Farbe*) peel (off); (*Preis, Aktie*) go slowly down; (*Mitglieder*) fall off

Ab′bruch *m* (-s Zweiges, der Beziehungen) breaking off; (*e-s Gebäudes*) demolition; (*Schaden*) damage; **A. des Spiels** (sport) calling of the game; **A. tun** (*dat*) harm, spoil; **auf A. verkaufen** sell at demolition value; (*Maschinen*) sell for junk

ab′brühen *tr* (culin) scald

ab′brummen *tr* (*Strafe*) (coll) serve, do || *intr* (SEIN) (coll) clear out

ab′buchen *tr* (*abschreiben*) write off; (acct) debit

ab′bürsten *tr* brush off

ab′büßen *tr* atone for; **e-e Strafe a.** serve time; **er hat es schwer a. müssen** (coll) he had to pay for it dearly

Abc [abeˈtse] *n* (-;-) ABC's

Abc′-Schütze *m* (-n;-n) pupil

ab′danken *tr* dismiss; (*pensionieren*)

retire ‖ *intr* resign; (*Herrscher*) abdicate; (mil) get a discharge

ab'decken *tr* uncover; (*Tisch*) clear; (*Bett*) turn down; (*Vieh*) skin; (*e-e Schuld*) pay back; (mil) camouflage; (phot) mask

ab'dichten *tr* seal (off); (*Loch*) plug up; (*mit weichem Material*) pack; (naut) caulk

ab'dienen *tr* (*Schuld*) work off; (mil) serve (*one's term*)

ab'drehen *tr* twist off; (*Gas, Licht, Wasser*) turn off ‖ *intr* turn away

ab'dreschen §67 *tr* thrash

Ab'druck *m* (-s;-e) reprint; offprint; copy; (*Abguß*) casting; (phot, typ) proof ‖ *m* (-s;-e) impression, imprint

ab'drucken *tr* print

ab'drücken *tr* (*abformen*) mold; (*Gewehr*) fire; (*Pfeil*) shoot; (*umarmen*) hug; **den Hahn a.** pull the trigger ‖ *ref* leave an impression ‖ *intr* pull the trigger

ab'duschen *ref* shower off

Abend ['ɑbənt] *m* (-s;-e) evening; **am A.** in the evening; **bunter A.** social; (tvlv) variety show; **des Abends** in the evening(s); **zu A. essen** eat dinner

A'bendblatt *n* evening paper

A'bendbrot *n* supper, dinner

A'benddämmerung *f* twilight, dusk

A'bendessen *n* supper, dinner

abendfüllend ['ɑbəntfʏlənt] *adj* full-length (*movie*)

A'bendgesellschaft *f* party (*in the evening*)

A'bendland *n* West, Occident

abendländisch ['ɑbəntlɛndɪʃ] *adj* occidental

a'bendlich *adj* evening ‖ *adv* evenings

A'bendmahl *n* supper; **das Heilige A.** Holy Communion

abends ['ɑbənts] *adv* in the evening

Abenteuer ['ɑbəntɔɪˌər] *s* (-s;-) adventure; **galantes A.** (love) affair

a'benteuerlich *adj* adventurous; (*Unternehmen*) risky

aber ['ɑbər] *adv* yet, however; (before adjectives and adverbs) really, indeed; **a. und abermals** over and over again; **hundert und a.** hundert hundreds and hundreds of ‖ *conj* but ‖ *interj*—aber, aber! now, now! ‖ **Aber** *n* (-s;-s) but; **hier gibt es kein A.!** no ifs and buts

A'berglaube *m* superstition

abergläubisch ['ɑbərglɔɪbɪʃ] *adj* superstitious

ab'erkennen §97 *tr*—j—m etw a. deny s.o. s.th.; (jur) dispossess s.o. of s.th.

Ab'erkennung *f* (-;-en) denial; (jur) dispossession

abermalig ['ɑbərmɑlɪç] *adj* repeated

abermals ['ɑbərmɑls] *adv* once more

ab'ernten *tr* reap, harvest

ab'fahren §71 *tr* cart away; (*Strecke*) cover; (*Straße*) wear out; (*Reifen*) wear down ‖ *intr* (SEIN) depart; drive off

Ab'fahrt *f* departure

Ab'fall *m* (*der Blätter*) falling; (*Bö-*

schung) steep slope; (*von e-m Glauben*) falling away; (*von e-r Partei*) defection; (*Sinken*) drop, decrease; **Abfälle** garbage, trash; chips, shavings

ab'fallen §72 *intr* (SEIN) fall off; (*von e-r Partei*) defect; (*vom Glauben*) fall away; (*abnehmen*) decrease, fail; (*Kunden*) stay away; (sport) fall behind; **a. gegen** compare badly with; **es wird etw für dich a.** there'll be s.th. in it for you; **körperlich a.** lose weight; **steil a.** drop away

abfällig ['ɑpfɛlɪç] *adj* disparaging

Ab'fallprodukt *n* by-product

ab'fangen §73 *tr* catch; (*Angriff*) foil; (*Brief*) intercept; (aer) pull out of a dive; (*U-Boot*) (nav) trim; (sport) catch (up with); **j—m die Kunden a.** steal s.o.'s customers

ab'färben *intr* (*Farben*) run; (*Stoff*) fade; **a. auf** (*acc*) stain; (fig) rub off on

ab'fassen *tr* compose, draft; (*erwischen*) catch

Ab'fassung *f* (-;-en) wording; composition

ab'faulen *intr* (SEIN) rot away

ab'fegen *tr* sweep off, whisk off

abfertigen ['ɑpfɛrtɪgən] *tr* get ready for sending off; (*Gepäck*) check; (*Zöllgüter*) clear; (*Kunden*) wait on; (*abweisen*) snub; (*verwaltungsmäßig*) (adm) process;

Ab'fertigung *f* (-;-en) dispatch; snub; zollamtliche A. clearance

ab'feuern *tr* fire; (rok) launch

ab'finden §59 *tr* (*Gläubiger*) satisfy; (*Partner*) buy off; (*entschädigen*) (für) compensate (for) ‖ *ref*—sich a. lassen settle for a lump-sum payment; **sich a. mit** put up with; come to terms with

Ab'findung *f* (-;-en) satisfaction; lump-sum settlement

Ab'findungsvertrag *m* lump-sum settlement

abflachen ['ɑpflɑxən] *tr* level; (*abschrägen*) bevel ‖ *ref* flatten out

abflauen ['ɑpflɑu-ən] *intr* (SEIN) slack off; (*Interesse*) flag; (*Preis*) go down; (st. exch.) ease off

ab'fliegen §57 *intr* (SEIN) take off

ab'fließen §76 *intr* (SEIN) flow off, drain off

Ab'flug *m* takeoff, departure

Ab'fluß *m* discharge; drain, gutter, gully; **See ohne A.** lake without outlet

Ab'flußrinne *f* drainage ditch

Ab'flußrohr *n* drainpipe; soil pipe; (*vom Dach*) downspout

ab'fordern *tr*—j—m etw a. demand s.th. from s.o.

ab'fragen *tr*—j—n etw a. question s.o. about s.th.; quiz s.o. on s.th.

ab'fressen §70 *tr* eat up; crop, chew off; (*Metall*) corrode

ab'frieren §77 *intr* (SEIN) be nipped by the frost; **abgefroren** frostbitten

Abfuhr ['ɑpfur] *f* (-;-en) removal; (*Abweisung*) (coll) cold shoulder, snub

ab'führen *tr* lead away; *(festnehmen)* arrest; *(fencing)* defeat ‖ *intr* cause the bowels to move

Abführmittel ['apfyrmɪtəl] *n* laxative

ab'füllen *tr (Wein, Bier)* bottle

Ab'gabe *f (Auslieferung)* delivery; *(Verkauf)* sale; *(Steuer)* tax; *(Zoll)* duty; *(der Wahlstimme)* casting; *(e-s Urteils)* pronouncing; *(e-r Meinung)* expressing; (fb) pass; **Abgaben** taxes, fees

ab'gabenfrei *adj* tax-free, duty-free

abgabenpflichtig ['apgabənpflɪçtɪç] *adj* taxable, subject to duty

Ab'gang *m* departure; *(von e-m Amt)* retirement; *(von der Schule)* dropping out; graduation; *(Verlust)* loss; *(Abnahme)* decrease; (gym) finish; (pathol) discharge; (pathol) miscarriage; (theat) exit; **guten A. haben** sell well

abgängig ['apgɛŋɪç] *adj* lost, missing; (com) marketable

Ab'gangsprüfung *f* final examination

Ab'gangspunkt *m* point of departure

Ab'gas *n* (aut) exhaust; (indust) waste gas

ab'geben §80 *tr (Paß)* hand over; *(Gepäck)* check; *(abliefern)* deliver; *(Schulheft)* hand in; *(Urteil)* pass; *(Meinung)* express; *(Gutachten)* give; *(Amt)* lay down; *(gute Ernte)* yield; *(Schuß)* fire; *(Wahlstimme)* cast; *(Waren)* sell, let go; *(sich eignen als)* act as, serve as; **be cut out to be;** (elec) deliver; (fb) pass; (phys) give off; **e-e Offerte a.** (jur) make an offer; **e-n Narren a.** play the fool; **er würde e-n guten Vater a.** he would make a good father; **|—m eins a.** (coll) let s.o. have it; **|—m von etw a.** share s.th. with s.o. ‖ *ref*—**sich a. mit** bother with; associate with; spend time on

abgebrannt ['apgəbrant] *adj* (coll) broke

abgebrüht ['apgəbryt] *adj* (fig) hardened

abgedroschen ['apgədrɔʃən] *adj* trite, hackneyed; *(Witz)* stale

abgefeimt ['apgəfaɪmt] *adj* cunning, out-and-out

abgegriffen ['apgəgrɪfən] *adj* well-thumbed

abgehackt ['apgəhakt] *adj* jerky

abgehärmt ['apgəhɛrmt] *adj* careworn, drawn

ab'gehen §82 *intr* (SEIN) leave, depart; *(Brief)* go off; *(Knopf)* come off; *(Schuß)* go off; *(Farbe)* fade; *(Seitenweg)* branch off; *(vom Gesprächsgegenstand)* digress, go off; *(vom rechten Wege)* stray; *(aus e-m Amt)* resign, retire; *(von der Bühne)* retire; *(von der Schule)* drop out; graduate; (com) sell; (theat) exit; **bei Barzahlung gehen fünf Prozent ab** you get a five-percent reduction for paying cash; **davon kann ich nicht a.** I must insist on it; **er geht mir sehr ab** I miss him a lot; **nicht a. von** stick to; **reißend a.** sell like hotcakes; ‖ *ref*—**sich** [dat] **nichts a.**

lassen deny oneself nothing ‖ *impers* —**es geht ihm nichts ab** he lacks for nothing; **es gehen mir zehn Dollar ab** I am ten dollars short; **es ist alles glatt abgegangen** everything went well

ab'gehend *adj (Post, Beamte)* outgoing; *(Zug)* departing

abgekämpft ['apgəkɛmpft] *adj* exhausted

abgekartet ['apgəkartət] *adj (Spiel)* fixed; **abgekartete Sache** put-up job

abgeklappert ['apgəklapərt] *adj* hackneyed

abgeklärt ['apgəklɛrt] *adj* mellow, wise

abgelebt ['apgəlept] *adj* decrepit

abgelegen ['apgəlegən] *adj* out-of-the-way, outlying

ab'gelten §83 *tr* meet, satisfy

abgemacht ['apgəmaxt] *adj* settled ‖ *interj* agreed!

abgemagert ['apgəmagərt] *adj* emaciated

abgemessen ['apgəmesən] *adj* measured; *(genau)* exact; *(Rede)* deliberate; *(Person)* stiff, formal

abgeneigt ['apgənaɪkt] *adj* reluctant; *(dat)* averse to; **ich bin durchaus nicht a.** (coll) I don't mind if I do

Ab'geneigtheit *f* (−;) aversion

abgenutzt ['apgənutst] *adj* worn out

Abgeordnete ['apgə-ɔrdnətə] §5 *mf* delegate; (pol) representative, deputy *(member of the Bundestag)*; (Brit) Member of Parliament

Ab'geordnetenhaus *n* House of Representatives; (Brit) House of Commons

abgerissen ['apgərɪsən] *adj* torn; *(zerlumpt)* ragged; *(ohne Zusammenhang)* incoherent, disconnected

Abgesandte ['apgəzantə] §5 *mf* envoy

abgeschieden ['apgəʃidən] *adj* secluded; *(verstorben)* deceased, late

Ab'geschiedenheit *f* (−;) seclusion

abgeschliffen ['apgəʃlɪfən] *adj* polished

abgeschlossen ['apgəʃlɔsən] *adj* isolated; *(Leben)* secluded; *(Ausbildung)* completed

abgeschmackt ['apgəʃmakt] *adj* tactless, tasteless; (fig) insipid

abgesehen ['apgəze-ən] *adj*—**a. davon, daß** not to mention that; **a. von** aside from, except for

abgespannt ['apgəʃpant] *adj* tired out

abgestanden ['apgəʃtandən] *adj* stale

abgestorben ['apgəʃtɔrbən] *adj (Pflanze, Gewebe)* dead; *(Glied)* numb

abgestumpft ['apgəʃtumpft] *adj* blunt; *(Kegel)* truncated; (fig) dull; *(gegen)* indifferent (to)

abgetakelt ['apgətakəlt] *adj (Person)* seedy; *(Schiff)* unrigged

abgetan ['apgətan] *adj* settled

abgetragen ['apgətragən] *adj* threadbare

abgetreten ['apgətretən] *adj* worndown

ab'gewinnen §52 *tr* win; **e-r Sache Geschmack a.** acquire a taste for s.th.; **e-r Sache Vergnügen a.** derive pleasure from s.th.; **j-m e-n Vorteil a.** gain an advantage over s.o.

abgewirtschaftet [ˈapgəvɪrt/aftət] *adj* run-down

ab'gewöhnen *tr*—**ich kann es mir nicht a.** I can't get it out of my system; **j-m etw a.** break s.o. of s.th.

abgezehrt [ˈapgətsert] *adj* emaciated

ab'gießen §76 *tr* pour off; (*Statue*) cast; (chem) decant; (culin) strain off

Ab'glanz *m* reflection

ab'gleiten §86 *intr* (SEIN) slip off; (an *dat*) glance off (*s.th.*); (aer, aut) skid; (st. exch.) decline

Ab'gott *m* idol

Abgötterei [apgœtəˈraɪ] *f* (-;-en) idolatry; **A. treiben** worship idols; **mit j-m A. treiben** idolize

abgöttisch [ˈapgœtɪ/] *adj* idolatrous || *adv*—**a. lieben** idolize

Ab'gottschlange *f* boa constrictor

ab'graben §87 *tr* (*Bach*) divert; (*Feld*) drain; (*Hügel*) level

ab'grämen *ref* eat one's heart out

ab'grasen *tr* (*Wiese*) graze on; (fig) scour, search

ab'greifen §88 *tr* wear out (*by constant handling*); (*Buch*) thumb

ab'grenzen *tr* mark off, demarcate; delimit; (fig) differentiate

Ab'grund *m* abyss; precipice

abgründig [ˈapgrYndɪç] *adj* precipitous; (fig) deep, unfathomable

ab'gucken *tr* (coll) copy, crib; (coll) pick up a habit from || *intr* (coll) copy, crib

Ab'guß *m* (sculp) cast; **A. in Gips** plaster cast

ab'hacken *tr* chop off; (*Baum*) chop down

ab'haken *tr* unhook, undo; (*in e-r Liste*) check off; (telp) take off (*the receiver*)

ab'halftern *tr* unharness; (fig) sack

ab'halten §90 *tr* hold off; (*Vorlesung*) give; (*Regen*) keep out; (*Versammlung, Parade*) hold; (**von**) keep (from)

Ab'haltung *f* (-;-en) hindrance; (*e-r Versammlung*) holding; (*e-s Festes*) celebration

ab'handeln *tr* (*Thema*) treat; (*erörtern*) discuss; **er läßt sich nichts a.** he won't come down (*in price*); **etw vom Preise a.** get s.th. off the price (*by bargaining*)

abhanden [apˈhandən] *adv*—**a. kommen** get lost; **a. sein** be missing

Ab'handlung *f* (-;-en) essay; (*Vortrag in e-m gelehrten Verein*) paper; (*Doktorarbeit*) thesis, dissertation; (*mündlich*) discourse, discussion

Ab'hang *m* slope

ab'hängen *tr* (*vom Haken*) take off; (*e-n Verfolger*) shake off; (rr) uncouple || *intr* (telp) hang up; **a. von** depend on; be subject to (*s.o.'s approval*)

abhängig [ˈaphɛnɪç] *adj* (*Stellung*) subordinate; (*Satz*) dependent; (*Rede*) indirect; (*Kasus*) oblique; (**von**) dependent (on), contingent (upon)

Ab'hängigkeit *f* (-;-en) dependence; (gram) subordination; **gegenseitige A.** interdependence

ab'härmen *ref* pine away; **sich a. wegen** (or **über** *acc*) fret about

ab'härten *tr* harden; (**gegen**) inure (to) || *ref* (**gegen**) become hardened (to)

ab'hauen §93 *tr* cut off; chop off || §109 *intr* (SEIN) (coll) scram, get lost

ab'häuten *tr* skin, flay

ab'heben §94 *tr* lift off; (*Rahm*) skim; (*Geld*) withdraw; (*Dividende*) collect; (*Haut*) (surg) strip off || *ref* become airborne; (**von**) contrast (with)

Ab'hebung *f* (-;-en) lifting; (*vom Bankkonto*) withdrawal; (cards) cutting

Ab'hebungsformular *n* withdrawal slip

ab'heften *tr* (*Briefe*) file; (sew) tack

ab'heilen *intr* (HABEN & SEIN) heal up

ab'helfen §96 *intr* (*dat*) (*e-m Unrecht*) redress; (*e-r Schwierigkeit*) remove; (*e-m Mangel*) relieve; **dem ist nicht abzuhelfen** that can't be helped

ab'hetzen *tr* drive hard, work to death; (hunt) hunt down || *ref* rush; tire oneself out

Ab'hilfe *f* remedy, redress; **A. schaffen** take remedial measures; **A. schaffen für** remedy, redress

ab'hobeln *tr* plane (down)

abhold [ˈaphɔlt] *adj* (*dat*) ill-disposed (towards), averse (to)

Abholdienst [ˈapholdinst] *m* pickup service

ab'holen *tr* fetch, call for, pick up

ab'holzen *tr* clear (of trees), deforest

Abhörapparat [ˈaphøraparat] *m* (mil, nav) listening device

ab'horchen *tr* overhear; (med) sound; (rad, telp) monitor

ab'hören *tr* overhear, eavesdrop on; (*Studenten*) quiz; (*Schallplatte, Tonband*) listen to; (mil) intercept; (telp) monitor

Ab'hörgerät *n* bugging device

Ab'hörraum *m* (rad, telv) control room

Ab'irrung *f* (-;-en) deviation; (opt) aberration

Abitur [abɪˈtur] *n* (-s;-e) final examination (*at end of junior college*); **das A. bestehen** graduate

Abiturient –in [abɪturɪˈent(ɪn)] §7 *mf* graduate (*of a junior college*)

Abitur'zeugnis *n* diploma (*from senior high school or junior college*)

ab'jagen *tr* drive hard; **j-m etw a.** recover s.th. from s.o. || *ref* run one's head off

abkanzeln [ˈapkantsəln] *tr* (coll) give (*s.o.*) a good talking to

ab'kauen *tr* chew off || *ref*—**sich** [*dat*] **die Nägel a.** bite one's nails

ab'kaufen *tr*—**j-m etw a.** buy s.th. from s.o.

Abkehr [ˈapker] *f* (-;) turning away; estrangement; (*Verzicht*) renunciation

ab'kehren *tr* turn away, avert; (**mit dem Besen**) sweep off || *ref* turn away; become estranged

ab'klappern *tr* (coll) scour, search

ab′klatschen *tr* imitate slavishly; make an exact copy of; (*beim Tanzen*) cut in on; (typ) pull (*a proof*)

ab′klingen §142 *intr* (SEIN) (*Farbe*) fade; (*Töne*) die away; (*Schmerz*) ease of

ab′klopfen *tr* beat off, knock off; (*Teppich*) beat; (med) tap, percuss ‖ *intr* stop the music (*with the rap of the baton*)

ab′knabbern *tr* (coll) nibble off

ab′knallen *tr* fire off; (sl) bump off

ab′knicken *tr* snap off ‖ *intr* (SEIN) snap off

ab′knipsen *tr* pinch off, snip off; (*Film*) use up

ab′knöpfen *tr* unbutton; **j-m Geld a.** squeeze money out of s.o.

ab′knutschen *tr* (coll) pet

ab′kochen *tr* boil; (*Obst*) stew; (*Milch*) scald ‖ *intr* cook out

ab′kommandieren *tr* detach, detail

ab′kommen §99 *intr* (SEIN) (**von**) get away (from); (*Mode*) go out of style; (naut) become afloat (again); **auf zwei Tage a.** get away for two days; **gut** (or **schlecht**) **a.** (sport) get off to a good (or bad) start; **hoch** (or **tief**) **a.** aim too high (or low); **vom Kurs a.** go off course; **vom Boden a.** become airborne; **vom Thema a.** get off the subject; **vom Wege a.** lose one's way, stray; **von der Wahrheit a.** deviate from the truth; **von e-r Ansicht a.** change one's views ‖ **Abkommen** *n* (-s;-) (com, pol) agreement; (jur) settlement

abkömmlich [′apkœmlɪç] *adj*—**a. sein** be able to get away

Abkömmling [′apkœmlɪŋ] *m* (-s;-e) descendant, scion

ab′koppeln *tr* uncouple

ab′kratzen *tr* scratch off; (*Schuhe*) scuff up ‖ *intr* (*sterben*) (sl) croak; (*abhauen*) (sl) beat it; **kratz ab!** drop dead!

ab′kriegen *tr* (coll) get off or out

ab′kühlen *tr*, *ref* & *intr* cool off

Abkunft [′apkunft] *f* (-;) lineage

ab′kürzen *tr* shorten; (*Inhalt*) abridge; (*Wort*) abbreviate; (math) reduce

Ab′kürzung *f* (-;-en) shortening; abridgement; abbreviation; (*kürzerer Weg*) shortcut

ab′küssen *tr* smother with kisses

ab′laden §103 *tr* unload; (*Schutt*) dump

Ab′ladeplatz *m* dump; (mil) unloading point

Ab′lage *f* (*für Kleider*) cloakroom; (*Lagerhaus*) depot, warehouse; (*abgelegte Akten*) files; (mil) dump

ab′lagern *tr* (*Wein, usw.*) age; (geol) deposit ‖ *ref* (geol) be deposited ‖ *intr*—**a. lassen** age, season

Ab′laß *m* (-lasses;-lässe) outlet, drain; (com) deduction; (eccl) indulgence

ab′lassen §104 *tr* leave off; (*Bier*) tap; (*Dampf*) let off; (*Teich, Faß*) drain; (*Waren*) sell; **etw vom Preise a.** knock s.th. off the price; **j-m etw billig a.** (com) let s.o. have s.th. cheaply ‖ *intr* desist, stop; **a. von** let go of, give up

Ablativ [′ablatif] *m* (-s;-e) ablative

Ab′lauf *m* overflow; (*e-r Frist, e-s Vertrags*) expiration; (*der Ereignisse*) course; (sport) start

ab′laufen §105 *tr* (*Strecke*) run; (*Stadt*) scour; (*Schuhe*) wear out; **j-m den Rang a.** get the better of s.o.; outrun s.o. ‖ *intr* (SEIN) run away; (*Zeit*) expire; (*ausfallen*) turn out; (com) fall due; (sport) start

Ab′laut *m* ablaut

Ab′leben *n* demise, decease

ab′lecken *tr* lick (off)

ab′legen *tr* (*Last, Waffen*) lay down; (*ausziehen*) take off; (*Schwert*) lay aside; (*die alte Haut*) slough; (*Karten*) discard; (*Akten, Dokumente*) file; (*Briefe*) sort; (*Namen*) drop, stop using; (*Sorgen, Kummer*) put away; (*Prüfung, Gelübde, Eid*) take; (*Predigt*) deliver; (*Gewohnheit*) give up; (*Rechenschaft*) render, give; **Bekenntnis a.** make a confession; **die Maske a.** (fig) throw off all disguise; **die Trauer a.** come out of mourning; **ein volles Geständnis a.** come clean; **Probe a.** furnish proof; **seine Fehler a.** mend one's ways; **Zeugnis a.** (für or gegen) testify (for or against) ‖ *intr* take off one's coat or hat and coat); **bitte, legen Sie ab!** please take your things off

Ab′leger *m* (-s;-) (bot) shoot; (com) subsidiary; (hort) slip, cutting

ab′lehnen *tr* refuse, turn down; (*Antrag*) reject; (*Zeugen*) challenge; (*Erbschaft*) renounce; **durch Abstimmung a.** vote down

ab′lehnend *adj* negative

Ab′lehnung *f* (-;-en) refusal

ab′leiern *tr* recite mechanically

ab′leisten *tr* (*Eid*) take; **den Militärdienst a.** (mil) serve one's time

ab′leiten *tr* lead away; (*Herkunft*) trace back; (*Fluß, Blitz*) divert; (*Wasser*) drain off; (*Wärme*) conduct; (chem) derive; (elec) shunt; (gram, math) derive; **abgeleitetes Wort** derivative ‖ *ref* (aus, von) be derived (from)

Ab′leitung *f* (-;-en) (*e-s Flusses*) diversion; (*des Wassers*) drainage; (elec, phys) conduction; (gram, math) derivation; (phys) convection

ab′lenken *tr* turn away, divert; (*Gefahr, Verdacht*) ward off; (fencing) parry; (opt, phys) deflect

Ab′lenkung *f* (-;-en) diversion; distraction; (opt) refraction

ab′lernen *tr*—**j-m etw a.** learn s.th. from s.o.

ab′lesen §107 *tr* read off; (*Zähler*) read; (*Obst*) pick; **es j-m vom Gesicht a.**, **daß** tell by looking at s.o. that

ab′leugnen *tr* deny, disown; (*Glauben*) renounce

Ab′leugnung *f* (-;-en) denial, disavowal

ab′liefern *tr* deliver, hand over, surrender

Ab′lieferung *f* (-;-en) delivery; (*der Schußwaffen*) surrender

ab'liegen §108 *intr* (*Wein*) mature; (*Obst*) ripen || *intr* (SEIN) be remote

ab'löschen *tr* extinguish; (*Stahl*) temper; (*Tinte*) blot; (*Kalk*) slake

ab'lösen *tr* loosen, detach; (*Posten*) relieve; (*Schuld*) discharge; (*Pfand*) redeem; (*Haut*) peel off || *ref* (bei) take turns (at)

Ab'lösung *f* (-;-en) loosening; relief; discharge

ab'machen *tr* undo, untie; (*erledigen*) settle, arrange; (*Vertrag*) conclude; (*Rechnung*) close

Ab'machung *f* (-;-en) settlement

abmagern ['apmagərn] *intr* (SEIN) grow thin, thin down

Ab'magerung *f* (-;) emaciation

ab'mähen *tr* mow

ab'malen *tr* portray; (fig) depict

Ab'marsch *m* departure

ab'marschieren *intr* (SEIN) march off

Ab'mattung *f* (-;) fatigue

ab'melden *tr* (*Besuch*) (coll) call off; der ist bei mir abgemeldet (coll) I've had it with him; j—n bei der Polizei a. give notice to the police that s.o. is leaving town || *ref* (mil) report off duty

ab'messen §70 *tr* measure (off); (*Worte*) weigh; (*Land*) survey

ab'montieren *tr* dismantle; (*Geschütz*) disassemble; (*Reifen*) take off || *ref* (aer) (coll) disintegrate in the air

ab'mühen *ref* exert oneself, slave

ab'murksen *tr* (sl) do in

ab'nagen *tr* gnaw (off); (*Knochen*) pick

Ab'nahme *f* (-;-n) (*Verminderung*) (an *dat*) reduction (in), drop (in); (*des Gewichts*) loss; (*des Mondes*) waning; (*des Tages*) shortening; (*e-s Eides*) administering; (*e-r Rechnung*) auditing; (indust) final inspection; (surg) amputation; A. der Geschäfte decline in business; A. e-r Parade reviewing of the troops; A. finden be sold; in A. geraten decline, wane

ab'nehmen §116 *tr* take off, remove; (*Wäsche*) take down; (*Schnurrbart*) shave off; (*wegnehmen*) take away; (*Hörer*) lift, unhook; (*Strom*) use; (*Obst*) pick; (*Eid*) administer; (*Waren*) purchase; (*Rechnung*) audit; (*prüfen*) inspect and pass; (*Verband*) remove; (phot) take; (surg) amputate; aus Berichten a. gather from reports; das kann ich dir nicht a. I can't accept what you are saying; die Parade a. inspect the troops; j—m die Arbeit a. take the work off s.o.'s shoulders; j—m die Beichte a. hear s.o.'s confession; j—m die Maske a. unmask s.o., expose s.o.; j—m die Verantwortung a. relieve s.o. of responsibility; j—m ein Versprechen a. make s.o. make a promise; j—m zuviel a. charge s.o. too much || *intr* diminish; (*Preise*) drop; (*Wasser*) recede; (*Kräfte*) fail; (*Mond*) be on the wane; an Dicke a. taper; an Gewicht a. lose weight; an Kräften a. lose strength || **Abnehmen**

n (-s;) decrease; im A. sein be on the decrease

Ab'nehmer —in §6 *mf* buyer, consumer; (*Kunde*) customer; (*Hehler*) fence

Ab'neigung *f* (-;-en) (gegen, vor *dat*) aversion (to, for), dislike (of)

abnorm [ap'nɔrm] *adj* abnormal

Abnormität [apnɔrmi'tɛt] *f* (-;-en) abnormity, monstrosity

ab'nötigen *tr* (*dat*) extort (from)

ab'nutzen, ab'nützen *tr* wear out || *ref* wear out, become worn out

Ab'nutzung *f* (-;-en) wear and tear; (*Abrieb*) abrasion; (mil) attrition

Ab'öl *n* (-s;-e) used oil

Abonnement [abɔn(ə)'mã] *n* (-s;-s) (auf *acc*) subscription (to)

Abonnements'karte *f* commutation ticket

Abonnent —in [abɔ'nɛnt(ɪn)] §7 *mf* subscriber

abonnieren [abɔ'nirən] *tr* subscribe to; abonniert sein auf (*acc*) have a subscription to || *intr* (auf *acc*) subscribe (to)

ab'ordnen *tr* delegate, deputize

Ab'ordnung *f* (-;-en) delegation

Abort [a'bɔrt] *m* (-s;-e) toilet || [a'bɔrt] *m* (-s;-e) abortion

ab'passen *tr* measure, fit; (*abwarten*) watch for; (*auflauern*) waylay

ab'pfeifen §88 *tr* (sport) stop

ab'pflücken *tr* pluck (off)

ab'placken, ab'plagen *ref* work oneself to death, slave

ab'platzen *intr* (SEIN) come loose

Abprall ['apral] *m* rebound; (*Geschoß*) richochet

ab'prallen *intr* (SEIN) rebound; ricochet

ab'pressen *tr* extort

ab'putzen *tr* clean (off); (*polieren*) polish; (*Mauer*) roughcast, plaster

ab'raten §63 *intr*—j—m von etw a. advise s.o. against s.th.

Ab'raum *m* (-es;) rubble; (min) overburden

ab'räumen *tr* clear away; (*Tisch*) clear

ab'reagieren *tr* (*Spannung, Erregung*) work off || *ref* (coll) calm down

ab'rechnen *tr* subtract; (*Spesen*) account for; (com) deduct || *intr* settle accounts

Ab'rechnung *f* (-;-en) (*von Konten*) settlement; (*Abzug*) deduction; A. halten balance accounts

Ab'rede *f* agreement, arrangement; in A. stellen deny

ab'reden *intr*—j—m von etw a. dissuade s.o. from s.th.

ab'reiben *tr* rub off; (*Körper*) rub down

Ab'reise *f* departure

ab'reisen *intr* (SEIN) (nach) depart (for)

ab'reißen §53 *tr* tear off; (*Haus*) tear down; (*Kleid*) wear out || *intr* (SEIN) tear off

ab'richten *tr* (*Tier*) train; (*Pferd*) break in; (*Brett*) dress

Ab'richter —in §6 *mf* trainer

ab'riegeln *tr* (*Tür*) bolt; (mil) seal off

ab'ringen §142 *tr*—j-m etw a. wrest s.th. from s.o.

ab'rinnen §121 *intr* (SEIN) run off, run down

Ab'riß *m* summary, outline; (*Skizze*) sketch

ab'rollen *tr & ref* unroll, unwind || *intr* (SEIN) unroll, unwind

ab'rücken *tr* push away, move back || *intr* (SEIN) clear out; (fig) dissociate oneself; (mil) march off

Ab'ruf *m* recall; auf A. on call

ab'rufen §122 *tr* call away; (*Zug*) call out, announce

ab'runden *tr* round off

ab'rupfen *tr* pluck (off)

ab'rüsten *tr & intr* disarm

Ab'rüstung *f* (-;) disarmament

ab'rutschen *intr* (SEIN) slip (off)

absacken ['apzakən] *intr* (SEIN) sink; (*Flugzeug*) pancake

Ab'sage *f* cancellation; (*Ablehnung*) refusal

ab'sagen *tr* cancel || *intr* decline; (*dat*) renounce, repudiate

ab'sägen *tr* saw off

ab'sahnen *tr* (& fig) skim (off)

Ab'satz *m* stop, pause, break; (*Zeileneinrückung*) indentation; (*Abschnitt*) paragraph; (*des Schuhes*) heel; (*der Treppen*) landing; (*Vertrieb*) market, sale(s); ohne A. without a break

Ab'satzfähig *adj* marketable

Ab'satzgebiet *n* territory (*of a salesman*)

Ab'satzmarkt *m* (com) outlet

Ab'satzstockung *f* slump in sales

ab'saugen *tr* suck off; (*Teppich*) vacuum

Ab'saugventilator *m* exhaust fan

ab'schaben *tr* scrape off

ab'schaffen *tr* abolish, do away with; (*Mißbrauch*) redress; (*Diener*) dismiss

ab'schälen *tr* peel

ab'schalten *tr* switch off

ab'schätzen *tr* (*Wert*) estimate; (*für die Steuer*) assess, appraise

abschätzig ['apʃɛtsɪç] *adj* disparaging

Ab'schaum *m* (-[e]s;) (& fig) scum

ab'scheiden §112 *tr* part, sever; (physiol) excrete; (physiol) secrete || *intr* (SEIN) pass away, pass on

Ab'scheu *m* (-[e]s;) (vor *dat*, gegen) abhorrence (of), disgust (at)

ab'scheuern *tr* scrub off, scour; (*Haut*) scrape; (*abnutzen*) wear out

abscheu'lich *adj* atrocious

ab'schicken *tr* send away; (*Post*) mail

ab'schieben §130 *tr* shove off; deport

Abschied ['ap/it] *m* (-[e]s;-e) (*Weggang*) departure; (*Entlassung*) dismissal; (mil) discharge; A. nehmen von take leave of; (e-m *Amt*) resign, retire from

Ab'schiedsfeier *f* farewell party

Ab'schiedsrede *f* valediction

Ab'schiedsschmaus *m* farewell dinner

ab'schießen §76 *tr* (*Gewehr*) fire, shoot; (*Flugzeug*) shoot down; (*Panzer*) knock out; (rok) launch; j-n a. bring about s.o.'s downfall

ab'schinden §167 *tr* skin || *ref* slave

ab'schirmen *tr* screen (off); (gegen) guard (against)

ab'schlachten *tr* butcher; (fig) massacre

Ab'schlag *m* discount; (golf) tee shot; auf A. in part payment, on account

ab'schlagen §132 *tr* knock off; (*Baum*) fell; (*Angriff*) repel; (*Bitte*) refuse; das Wasser a. pass water || *intr* (golf) tee off

abschlägig ['ap/lɛgɪç] *adj* negative; a. bescheiden turn down

Ab'schlagszahlung *f* installment

ab'schleifen §88 *tr* grind off; (fig) refine, polish || *ref* become refined

ab'schleppen *tr* drag away, tow away

Ab'schleppwagen *m* tow truck

ab'schleudern *tr* fling off, catapult

ab'schließen §76 *tr* lock (up); (*Straße*) close off; (*Rechnung*) close, settle; (*Bücher*) balance; (*Vertrag*) conclude; (*Rede*) wind up; (*Wette*) wager || *ref* seclude oneself, shut oneself off || *intr* conclude

ab'schließend *adj* definitive; (*Worte*) concluding || *adv* definitively; (*schließlich*) in conclusion

Ab'schluß *m* completion; (e-s *Vertrags*) conclusion; (*Geschäft*) transaction, deal; (*Verkauf*) sale; (*Rechnungs-, Konto-, Buch-*) closing; (mach) seal

ab'schmeicheln *tr*—j-m etw a. coax s.th. out of s.o.

ab'schmelzen §133 *tr* (*Erz*) smelt; (*Schnee*) melt || *intr* (SEIN) melt

ab'schmieren *tr* copy carelessly; (coll) beat up; (aut) lubricate || *intr* (SEIN) (aer) (coll) crash

ab'schnallen *tr* unbuckle, unstrap

ab'schnappen *intr* (SEIN) (coll) stop dead; (coll) die

ab'schneiden §106 *tr* cut (off); (*Hecke*) trim; den Weg. a. take a shortcut; j-m das Wort a. cut s.o. short; j-m die Ehre a. steal s.o.'s good name || *intr*—gut a. do well

Ab'schnitt *m* cut, cutting; (*Teilstück*) part, section; (im *Scheckbuch*) stub; (*Kapitel*) section, paragraph; (math) segment; (mil) sector

ab'schnüren *tr* untie; (surg) ligature; j-m den Atem a. choke s.o.

ab'schöpfen *tr* skim off

ab'schrägen *tr & ref* slant, slope

ab'schrauben *tr* unscrew

ab'schrecken §134 *tr* scare off; (abbringen) deter

ab'schreiben §62 *tr* copy; (*Schularbeit*) crib; (*uneinbringliche Forderung*) write off; (*Literaturwerk*) plagiarize; (*Wert*) depreciate || *intr* send a refusal

Ab'schreiber –in §6 *mf* plagiarist

Ab'schreibung *f* (-;-en) write-off

ab'schreiten §86 *tr* pace off; (mil) review; die Front a. review the troops

Ab'schrift *f* copy, transcript; (com, jur) duplicate

ab'schriftlich *adj & adv* in duplicate

ab'schuften *ref* work oneself to death

ab'schürfen *ref*—sich [*dat*] die Haut a. skin oneself

Ab′schürfung f (–;–en) abrasion
Ab′schuß m (e–r Waffe) firing; (e–r Rakete) launching; (e–s Panzers) knocking out; (e–s Flugzeugs) downing, kill; (hunt) kill
abschüssig ['apʃʏsɪç] adj sloping; (steil) steep
Ab′schußrampe f launch pad
ab′schütteln tr shake off
ab′schwächen tr weaken; (vermindern) diminish, reduce; (Farben) tone down ‖ ref (Preis) decline
ab′schweifen intr (SEIN) stray, digress
Ab′schweifung f (–;–en) digression
ab′schwellen §119 intr (SEIN) go down; (Lärm, Gesang) die down
ab′schwenken intr (SEIN) swerve
ab′schwören intr (dat) (dem Glauben) deny; (dem Trunk) swear off
ab′segeln intr (SEIN) set sail
absehbar ['apzeːbɑr] adj foreseeable
ab′sehen §138 tr foresee; es abgesehen haben auf (acc) be out to get ‖ intr—a. von disregard; refrain from
ab′seifen tr soap down
abseits ['apzaɪts] adv aside; (sport) offside ‖ prep (genit) off
ab′senden §140 tr send (off), dispatch; (Post) mail; (befördern) forward
Ab′sender –in §6 mf sender, dispatcher
Ab′sendung f (–;–en) sending, dispatching; mailing, shipping
ab′sengen tr singe off
Absentismus [apzɛn'tɪsmʊs] m (–;) absenteeism
ab′setzen tr (Betrag) deduct; (Last) set down; (entwöhnen) wean; (Beamten) remove; (König) depose; (Fallschirmtruppen, Passagiere) drop; (com) sell; (typ) set up ‖ ref settle, set; (mil) disengage ‖ intr stop, pause
Absetzung f (–;–en) dismissal
Ab′sicht f intention, purpose; in der A. with the intention; mit A. on purpose; ohne A. unintentionally
ab′sichtlich adj intentional ‖ adv on purpose, intentionally
ab′sitzen §144 tr (Strafzeit) serve, do ‖ intr (SEIN) (vom Pferde) dismount; a. lassen (chem) let settle
absolut [apzo'luːt] adj
absolvieren [apzɔl'viːrən] tr absolve; (Studien) finish; (Hochschule) graduate from; (Prüfung) pass
abson′derlich adj peculiar, strange
ab′sondern tr separate, segregate; (Kranken) isolate; (physiol) secrete ‖ ref keep aloof
absorbieren [apzɔr'biːrən] tr absorb
ab′speisen tr feed; j–n mit schönen Worten a. put s.o. off with polite words
abspenstig ['apʃpɛnstɪç] adj—a. machen lure away; j–m a. werden desert s.o.
ab′sperren tr shut off, block off; (Tür) lock; (Strom) cut off; (Gas) turn off
ab′spielen tr play through to the end; (Schallplatte, Tonband) play; (Tonbandaufnahme) play back ‖ ref take place
ab′sprechen §64 tr dispute, deny; (ab-

machen) arrange; j–m das Recht a. zu (inf) dispute s.o.'s right to (inf)
ab′sprechend adj (Urteil) unfavorable; (Kritik) adverse; (tadelnd) disparaging
ab′springen §142 intr (SEIN) jump down, jump off; (Ball) rebound; (Glasur) chip; (abschweifen) digress; (aer) bail out, jump; a. von quit, desert
Ab′sprung m jump; (ins Wasser) dive; (des Balles) rebound
ab′spulen tr unwind, unreel
ab′spülen tr rinse (off)
ab′stammen intr (SEIN) (von) be descended (from); (von) be derived (from)
Abstammung f (–;–en) descent, extraction; (gram) derivation
Ab′stand m distance; (räumlich und zeitlich) interval; A. nehmen von refrain from; A. zahlen pay compensation
abstatten ['apʃtatən] tr (Besuch) pay; (Bericht) file; (Dank) give, return
ab′stauben tr dust off; (sl) swipe
ab′stechen §64 tr (töten) stab; (Rasen) cut; (Hochofen) tap; (Karten) trump ‖ intr—gegen (or von) etwa a. contrast with s.th.
Ab′stecher m (–s;–) side trip; (Umweg) detour; (fig) digression
ab′stecken tr (Haar) unpin, let down; (Kleid) pin, fit; (surv) mark off
ab′stehen §146 intr (entfernt sein) (von) be, stand away (from); (Ohren, usw.) stick out ‖ intr (HABEN & SEIN) (von) refrain (from)
ab′steigen §148 intr (SEIN) get down, descend; in e–m Gasthof a. stay at a hotel
ab′stellen tr (Last) put down; (Radio, Gas, usw.) turn off; (Motor) switch off; (Auto) park; (Mißstand) redress; (mil) detach, assign; a. auf (acc) gear to
Ab′stellraum m storage room
ab′stempeln tr stamp
ab′sterben §149 intr (SEIN) die off; (Pflanzen) wither; (Glieder) get numb
Abstieg ['apʃtik] m (–[e]s;) descent
ab′stimmen tr tune; (com) balance; a. auf (acc) (fig) atune (to) ‖ intr (über acc) vote (on)
Abstinenzler –in [apstɪ'nɛntslər(ɪn)] §6 mf teetotaler
ab′stoppen tr stop; (sport) clock
ab′stoßen §150 tr push off; (Waren) get rid of, sell; (Schulden) pay off; (Geweih) shed; (fig) disgust, sicken; (phys) repel ‖ ref—sich (dat) die Hörner a. (fig) sow one's wild oats ‖ intr (SEIN) shove off
ab′stoßend adj repulsive
abstrakt [ap'ʃtrakt] adj abstract
ab′streichen tr (abwischen) wipe off; (Rasiermesser) strop; (abhaken) check off; (bact) swab; (com) deduct
ab′streifen tr (Handschuh, usw.) take off; (Haut) slough off; (Gewohnheit) break ‖ intr (SEIN) deviate, stray
ab′streiten §86 tr contest, dispute

Ab'strich *m* (*beim Schreiben*) down-stroke; (*Abzug*) cut; (bact) swab

ab'stufen *tr* (*Gelände*) terrace; (*Farben*) shade off

abstumpfen ['apstumpfən] *tr* blunt

Ab'sturz *m* fall; (*Abhang*) precipice; (aer) crash

abstürzen *intr* (SEIN) fall down; (aer) crash

ab'suchen *tr* (*Gebiet*) scour, comb

Ab·szeß [ap'stses] *m* (–szesses; –szesse) abscess

Abt [apt] *m* (–[e]s;–̈e) abbot

ab'takeln *tr* unrig; (coll) sack, fire

ab'tasten *tr* probe; (rad) scan

Abtei [ap'taɪ] *f* (–;–en) abbey

Ab'teil *m* compartment

ab'teilen *tr* divide, partition

Ab'teilung *f* (–;–en) department, division; (*im Krankenhaus*) ward; (arti) battery; (mil) detachment, unit

Ab'teilungsleiter –in §6 *mf* department head, section head

Ab'teilungszeichen *n* hyphen

Äbtissin [ep'tɪsɪn] *f* (–;–nen) abbess

ab'tönen *tr* tone down, shade off

ab'töten *tr* (*Bakterien*) kill; (*das Fleisch*) mortify

Abtrag ['aptrak] *m* (–[e]s;–̈e)—**j–m A. leisten** compensate s.o.; **j–m A. tun** hurt s.o.

ab'tragen §132 *tr* carry away; (*Gebäude*) raze; (*Kleid*) wear out; (*Schuld*) pay

abträglich ['aptreklɪç] *adj* detrimental

ab'treiben §62 *tr* drive away; (*Leibesfrucht*) abort ‖ *intr* (SEIN) drift away; **vom Kurs a.** drift off course

Ab'treibung *f* (–;–en) abortion

ab'trennen *tr* separate, detach; (*Glied*) sever; (*Genähtes*) unstitch

ab'treten §152 *tr* wear out (*by walking*); (*aufgeben*) cede, turn over ‖ *intr* (SEIN) retire, resign; (theat) exit

Ab'treter *m* (–s;–) doormat

Ab'tretung *f* (–;–en) (*von Grundeigentum*) transfer; (pol) cession

ab'trocknen *tr* dry ‖ *intr* (SEIN) dry

ab'tropfen *intr* (SEIN) trickle, drip

ab'trudeln *intr* (SEIN) go into a tailspin; (coll) toddle off, saunter off

abtrünnig ['aptrynɪç] *adj* unfaithful; (eccl) apostate; **a. werden** defect

Ab'trünnigkeit *f* (–;–) desertion, defection; (eccl) apostasy

ab'tun §154 *tr* (*ablegen*) take off; (*beiseite schieben*) get rid of; (*töten*) kill; (*erledigen*) settle; **a. als** dismiss as; **kurz a.** make short work of; **mit e–m Achselzucken a.** shrug off

ab'urteilen *tr* pass final judgment on

ab'verlangen *tr*—**j–m etw a.** demand s.th. of s.o.

ab'wägen §156 *tr* weigh

ab'wälzen *tr* roll away; (*Schuld*) shift

ab'wandeln *tr* (*Thema*) vary; (*Hauptwort*) (gram) decline; (*Zeitwort*) (gram) conjugate

ab'wandern *intr* (SEIN) wander off; (*Bevölkerung*) migrate; (*Arbeitskräfte*) drift away

Ab'wanderung *f* (–;–en) exodus, migration

Ab'wandlung *f* (–;–en) variation; (*e–s Hauptwortes*) declension; (*e–s Zeitwortes*) conjugation

ab'warten *tr* wait for; (*Anweisung*) await; **das bleibt abzuwarten!** that remains to be seen! **s–e Zeit a.** bide one's time ‖ *intr* wait and see

abwärts ['apverts] *adv* down, downwards; **mit ihm geht es a.** (coll) he's going downhill

ab'waschen §158 *tr* wash (off)

ab'wechseln *tr & intr* alternate

ab'wechselnd *adj* alternate

Ab'wechs(e)lung *f* (–;–en) variation; (*Mannigfaltigkeit*) variety; (*Zerstreuung*) diversion, entertainment

Ab'weg *m* wrong way; **auf Abwege führen** mislead; **auf Abwege geraten** go wrong

Ab'wehr *f* (–;–en) defense; (*e–s Stoßes, usw.*) warding off; (mil) counter-espionage service

ab'wehren *tr* ward off, avert

ab'weichen §85 *intr* (SEIN) deviate, diverge; (*verschieden sein*) differ

Ab'weichung *f* (–;–en) deviation; difference; (math) divergence

ab'weiden *tr* graze on

ab'weisen §118 *tr* refuse, turn down; (*Angriff*) repel; (*Berufung*) deny

ab'weisend *adj* (gegen) unfriendly (to)

Ab'weisung *f* (–;–en) refusal; (jur) denial; (mil) repulse

ab'wenden *tr* turn away, turn aside; (*Augen*) avert; (*Aufmerksamkeit*) divert; (*Krieg, Gefahr*) prevent ‖ §140 & 120 *ref* (von) turn away (from)

ab'werfen §160 *tr* throw off; (*Bomben*) drop; (*Blätter, Geweih*) shed; (*Gewinn*) bring in, yield; (*Zinsen*) bear; (*Karten*) discard; (*Joch*) shake off

ab'werten *tr* devaluate

Ab'wertung *f* (–;–en) devaluation

abwesend ['apvezənt] *adj* absent, missing; (fig) absent-minded

Ab'wesenheit *f* (–;–) absence; (fig) absent-mindedness

ab'wickeln *tr* unwind, unroll; (*Geschäfte*) transact; (*Schulden*) settle; (*Aktiengesellschaft*) liquidate ‖ *ref* unwind; (fig) develop **sich gut a.** (com) turn out well

ab'wiegen §57 *tr* weigh

ab'wischen *tr* wipe off, wipe clean

Abwurf ['apvurf] *m* drop(ping); (*Bomben*) release; (*Ertrag*) yield

ab'würgen *tr* wring the neck of; (aut) stall

ab'zahlen *tr* pay off

ab'zählen *tr* count off

Ab'zahlung *f* (–;–en) payment in installments; (*Rate*) installment; **auf A.** on terms

Ab'zahlungsgeschäft *n* deferred-payment system

ab'zapfen *tr* (*Bier*) tap; (*Blut*) draw

Ab'zehrung *f* emaciation; consumption

Ab'zeichen *n* distinguishing mark; badge; (mil) decoration

ab'zeichnen *tr* copy, draw, sketch;

(*Dokument*) initial || *ref* become apparent; (*gegen*) stand out (against)

Ab'ziehbild *n* decal

ab'ziehen §163 *tr* pull off; (*Kunden*) lure away; (*Reifen*) take off; (*Bett*) strip; (*vom Preise*) deduct, knock off; (*vervielfältigen*) run off; (*Abziehbild*) transfer; (*Schlüssel vom Loch*) take out; (*Rasiermesser*) strop; (*Wein*) draw; (*Truppen*) withdraw; (*Aufmerksamkeit*) divert; (arith) deduct; (phot) print; (typ) pull || *intr* (SEIN) depart; (*abmarschieren*) march off; (*Rauch*) disperse

Ab'zug *m* (*e-r Summe*) deduction; (*Rabatt*) rebate, allowance; (*Skonto*) discount; (*am Gewehr*) trigger; (*Weggang*) departure; (*für Wasser*) outlet; (*für Rauch*) escape; (mil) withdrawal; (phot) print; (typ) proof sheet

abzüglich ['aptsyklɪç] *prep* (*genit* or *acc*) less, minus

Ab'zugsbogen *m* proof sheet

Ab'zugspapier *n* duplicating paper; (phot) printing paper

Ab'zugsrohr *n* drainpipe

ab'zweigen *tr* divert || *intr* (SEIN) branch off

ach [ax] *interj* oh!; ah!; **ach so!** oh, I see!; **ach was!** nonsense!; **ach wo!** of course not!

Achse ['aksə] *f* (–;–n) axis; (*am Wagen*) axle; (mach) shaft; **auf der A.** on the move; **per A.** by truck; by rail

Achsel ['aksəl] *f* (–;–n) shoulder; **auf die leichte A. nehmen** make light of; **mit den Achseln zucken** shrug one's shoulders; **über die Achseln ansehen** look down on

Ach'selbein *n* shoulder blade

Ach'selgrube *f*, **Ach'selhöhle** *f* armpit

Ach'selträger *m* §6 *mf* opportunist

acht [axt] *adj* eight; **alle a. Tage** once a week; **in a. Tagen** within a week; **über a. Tage** a week from today || **Acht** *f* (–;–en) eight || *f* (–;) (*Bann*) outlawry; (*Obacht*) care, attention; **in die A. erklären** outlaw; (fig) ostracize; **sich in a. nehmen vor** (*dat*) watch out for

achtbar ['axtbar] *adj* respectable

achte ['axtə] §9 *adj & pron* eight

achteckig ['axtekɪç] *adj* octagonal

Achtel ['axtəl] *n* (–;–) eighth (*part*)

achten ['axtən] *tr* (*beachten*) respect; (*schätzen*) esteem; (*erachten*) consider || *intr*—**a. auf** (*acc*) pay attention to; **a. darauf, daß** see to it that

ächten ['eçtən] *tr* outlaw, proscribe; (*gesellschaftlich*) ostracize

ach'tenswert *adj* respectable

achter(n) ['axtər(n)] *adv* aft, astern

acht'geben §80 *intr* (**auf** *acc*) pay attention (*to*); **gib acht!** watch out!

acht'los *adj* careless

Acht'losigkeit *f* (–;) carelessness

acht'sam ['axtzam] *adj* cautious; (**auf** *acc*) attentive (*to*); (**auf** *acc*) careful (*of*)

Acht'samkeit *f* (–;) carefulness

achttägig ['axttegɪç] *adj* eight-day; eight-day old; one-week

Ach'tung *f* (–;) attention; (**vor** *dat*) respect (*for*); **A.!** watch out!; (mil) attention!

ach'tungsvoll *adj* respectful; (*als Briefschluß*) Yours truly

acht'zehn *adj & pron* eighteen || **Achtzehn** *f* (–;–en) eighteen

acht'zehnte §9 *adj & pron* eighteenth

achtzig ['axtsɪç] *adj* eighty

achtziger ['axtsɪgər] *invar adj* of the eighties; **die a. Jahre** the eighties || **Achtziger –in** §6 *mf* octogenarian

achtzigste ['axtsɪçstə] §9 *adj* eightieth

ächzen ['eçtsən] *intr* groan, moan

Acker ['akər] *m* (–s;–) soil, (arable) land, field; (*Maß*) acre

Ackerbau (Ak'kerbau) *m* farming

ackerbautreibend ['akərbautraɪbənt] *adj* agricultural

Ackerbestellung (Ak'kerbestellung) *f* cultivation, tilling

Ackerland (Ak'kerland) *n* arable land

ackern ['akərn] *tr & intr* plow

addieren [a'dirən] *tr & intr* add

Addiermaschine [a'dirmaʃinə] *f* adding machine

Addition [adɪ'tsjon] *f* (–;–en) addition

ade [a'de] *interj* farewell!; bye-bye!

Adel ['adəl] *m* (–s;) nobility, noble birth; (*edle Gesinnung*) noblemindedness

ad(e)lig ['ad(ə)lɪç] *adj* noble, titled; nobleman's || **Ad(e)lige** §5 *m* nobleman || §5 *f* noblewoman

A'delsstand *m* nobility

Ader ['adər] *f* (–;–n) vein

adieu [a'djø] *interj* adieu!

Adjektiv ['atjektif] *n* (–s;–e) adjective

Adjutant –in [atju'tant(ɪn)] §7 *mf* adjutant; (*e-s Generals*) aide-(de-camp)

Adler ['adlər] *m* (–s;–) eagle

Ad'lernase *f* aquiline nose

Admiral [atmi'ral] *m* (–[e]s;–e) admiral

Admiralität [atmiralɪ'tet] *f* (–;) admiralty

adoptieren [adɔp'tirən] *tr* adopt

Adoption [adɔp'tsjon] *f* (–;–en) adoption

Adoptiv– [adɔp'tif] *comb. fm.* adoptive

Adressat –in [adre'sat(ɪn)] §7 *mf* addressee; (*e-r Warensendung*) consignee

Adresse [a'dresə] *f* (–;–n) address; **an die falsche A. kommen** (fig) bark up the wrong tree; **per A.** care of

adressieren [adre'sirən] *tr* address; (*Waren*) consign

adrett [a'dret] *adj* smart, neat

Advent [at'vent] *m* (–s;–e) Advent

Adverb [at'verp] *n* (–[e]s;–ien [–1.ən]) adverb

Advokat –in [atvo'kat(ɪn)] §7 *mf* lawyer

Affäre [a'ferə] *f* (–;–n) affair

Affe ['afə] *m* (–n;–n) ape, monkey; **e-n Affen haben** (sl) be drunk

Affekt [a'fekt] *m* (–[e]s;–e) emotion; (*Leidenschaft*) passion

affektiert [afek'tirt] *adj* affected

Affektiert'heit *f* (-;-en) affectation
äffen ['ɛfən] *tr* ape, mimic
Af'fenliebe *f* doting
Af'fenpossen *pl* monkeyshines
Af'fenschande *f* crying shame
Af'fentheater *n* farce, joke
affig ['afɪç] *adj* affected; (*geckenhaft*) foppish
Äffin ['ɛfɪn] *f* (-;-nen) female ape, female monkey
Afrika ['afrɪka] *n* (-s;) Africa
afrikanisch [afrɪ'kanɪʃ] *adj* African
After ['aftər] *m* (-s;-) anus
AG, A.G., A.-G. *abbr* (**Aktiengesellschaft**) stock company
ägäisch [ɛ'ge·ɪʃ] *adj* Aegean
Agende [a'gendə] *f* (-;-n) memo pad
Agent -in [a'gent(ɪn)] §7 *mf* agent, representative; (*Geheim-*) secret agent
Agentur [agen'tur] *f* (-;-en) agency
aggressiv [agre'sif] *adj* aggressive
Ägide [ɛ'gidə] *f* (-;-n) aegis
Agio ['aʒɪ·o] *n* (-s;-s) premium
Agitation [agita'tsjon] *f* (-;-en) agitation, rabble-rousing
Agi•tator [agɪ'tator] *m* (-s;-tatoren [ta'torən] (*& mach*) agitator
agitatorisch [agita'torɪʃ] *adj* inflammatory
agitieren [agɪ'tirən] *intr* agitate
Agraffe [a'grafə] *f* (-;-n) clasp
agrarisch [a'grarɪʃ] *adj* agrarian
Ägypten [ɛ'gyptən] *n* (-s;) Egypt
Ägypter -in [ɛ'gyptər(ɪn)] §6 *mf* Egyptian
ägyptisch [ɛ'gyptɪʃ] *adj* Egyptian
ah [ɑ] *interj* ah!
Ahle ['alə] *f* (-;-n) awl, punch
Ahn [an] *m* (-(e)s & -en;-en) ancestor
ahnden ['andən] *tr* (*strafen*) punish; (*rächen*) avenge
Ahn'dung *f* (-;) revenge
ähneln ['ɛnəln] *intr* (*dat*) resemble
ahnen ['anən] *tr* have a premonition of, suspect; (*erfassen*) divine
Ah'nentafel *f* family tree
ähnlich ['ɛnlɪç] *adj* alike; (*dat*) similar (to), analogous (to): **das sieht ihm ä.** that's just like him; **j-m ä sehen** look like s.o.
Ähn'lichkeit *f* (-;-en) (*mit*) resemblance (to)
Ah'nung ['anuŋ] *f* (-;-en) (*Vorgefühl*) presentiment, hunch; (*böse*) misgiving; (*Argwohn*) suspicion; **keine A. haben** have no idea
ah'nungslos *adj* unsuspecting
ah'nungsvoll *adj* full of misgivings
Ahorn ['ahorn] *m* (-[e]s;-e) maple
Ähre ['ɛrə] *f* (-;-n) (*Korn*) ear; (*e-r Blume*) spike; **Ähren lesen** glean
Ais ['a·ɪs] *n* (-;-) (mus) A sharp
Akade•mie [akadə'mi] *f* (-;-mien ['mi·ən]) academy; university
Akademiker -in [aka'demɪkər(ɪn)] §6 *mf* university graduate
akademisch [aka'demɪʃ] *adj* academic; university
Akazie [a'katsjə] *f* (-;-n) acacia
akklimatisieren [aklimatɪ'zirən] *tr* acclimate || *refl* become acclimated
Akkord [a'kort] *m* (-[e]s;-e) chord;

(*Vereinbarung*) accord; (com) settlement; **im A. arbeiten** do piecework
Akkord'arbeit *f* piecework
Akkordeon [a'kordeɔn] *n* (-s;-s) accordion
akkreditieren [akredɪ'tirən] *tr* accredit; open an account for
Akkreditiv [akredɪ'tif] *n* (-[e]s;-e) (*Beglaubigungsschreiben*) credentials; (com) letter of credit
Akkumula•tor [akumu'lator] *m* (-s; -toren ['torən]) storage battery
akkurat [aku'rat] *adj* accurate
Akkusativ ['akuzatif] *m* (-[e]s;-e) accusative (case)
Akrobat [akro'bat] §7 *m* acrobat
Akrobatik [akro'batɪk] *f* (-;) acrobatics
Akrobatin [akro'batɪn] §7 *f* acrobat
Akt [akt] *m* (-[e]s;-e) act, action; (paint) nude; (theat) act
Akte ['aktə] *f* (-;-n) document; record, file; (jur) instrument; **zu den Akten legen** file; (fig) shelve
Ak'tendeckel *m* file folder
Ak'tenklammer *f* paper clip
Ak'tenmappe *f* brief case, portfolio
ak'tenmäßig *adj* documentary
Ak'tenschrank *m* file cabinet
Ak'tentasche *f* brief case
Ak'tenzeichen *n* file number
Aktie ['aktsjə] *f* (-;) stock
Ak'tienbesitzer -in §6 *mf* stockholder
Ak'tienbörse *f* stock exchange
Ak'tiengesellschaft *f* corporation
Ak'tieninhaber -in §6 *mf* stockholder
Ak'tienmakler -in §6 *mf* stockbroker
Ak'tienmarkt *m* stock market
Ak'tienschein *m* stock certificate
Aktion [ak'tsjon] *f* (-;-en) action; (*Unternehmung*) campaign, drive; (*polizeiliche*) raid; (mil) operation; **Aktionen** activity
Aktionär -in [aktsjo'ner(ɪn)] §8 *mf* stockholder
aktiv [ak'tif] *adj* active; (*Bilanz*) favorable; (chem) activated; (gram) active; **a. werden** become a member (*of a student club*) || **Aktiv** *n* (-s;) (gram) active voice
Aktiva [ak'tiva] *pl* assets; **A. und Passiva** assets and liabilities
Aktiv'posten *m* asset
aktuell [aktu'el] *adj* current, topical || **Aktuelle** *pl* (journ) newsbriefs
Akustik [a'kustɪk] *f* (-;) acoustics
akustisch [a'kustɪʃ] *adj* acoustic(al)
akut [a'kut] *adj* acute
Akzent [ak'tsent] *m* (-[e]s;-e) accent (mark); (*Nachdruck*) emphasis; (phonet) stress
akzentuieren [aktsentu'irən] *tr* accent; (fig) stress, accentuate
akzeptieren [aktsep'tirən] *tr* accept
Alabaster [ala'bastər] *m* (-s;) alabaster
Alarm [a'larm] *m* (-[e]s;-e) alarm; **A. blasen (or schlagen)** (mil & fig) sound the alarm; **blinder A.** false alarm
Alarm'anlage *f* alarm system; warning system (*in civil defense*)
alarm'bereit *adj* on the alert

Alarm′bereitschaft f (state of) readiness; **in A.** on the alert

alarmieren [alar′mirən] tr alert; alarm

Alaun [a′laun] m (-s;-e) alum

Alaun′stift m steptic pencil

Albanien [al′banjən] n (-s;) Albania

albanisch [al′banɪʃ] adj Albanian

albern [′albərn] adj silly

Al·bum [′album] n (-s;-ben [bən]) album

Alchimist [alçɪ′mɪst] §7 m alchemist

Alge [′algə] f (-;-n) alga; seaweed

Algebra [′algebra] f (-;) algebra

algebraisch [alge′bra·ɪʃ] adj algebraic

Algerien [al′gerjən] n (-s;) Algeria

algerisch [al′gerɪʃ] adj Algerian

Algier [′alʒir] n (-s;) Algiers

Alibi [′alɪbɪ] n (-s;-s) alibi

Alimente [alɪ′mentə] pl child support

alimentieren [alɪmen′tirən] tr pay alimony to; (Kind) support

Alkohol [′alkohol] m (-s;-e) alcohol

al′koholfrei adj non-alcoholic

Alkoholiker –in [alko′holikər(ɪn)] §6 mf alcoholic

alkoholisch [alko′holɪʃ] adj alcoholic

all [al] adj all; (jeder) every; (jeder beliebige) any; **alle beide** both (of them); **alles Gute!** take care!; (im Brief) best wishes; **alle zehn Minuten** every ten minutes; **alle zwei Tage** every other day; **auf alle Fälle** in any case || indef pron each, each one; everyone, everything; all; **aller und jeder** each and every one; **in allem** all told; **vor allem** above all, first of all

alle [′alə] adv all gone; **a. machen** finish off; **a. sein** be all gone; **a. werden** run low

Allee [a′le] f (-;-n) (tree-lined) avenue; (tree-lined) walk

Allego·rie [alego′ri] f (-;-rien [′ri·ən]) allegory

allegorisch [ale′gorɪʃ] adj allegoric(al)

allein [a′laɪn] adj alone || adv alone; only; however; no fewer than, no less than; **schon a. der Gedanke** the mere thought

Allein′berechtigung f exclusive right

Allein′flug m solo flight

Allein′handel m monopoly

Allein′herrschaft f autocracy

Allein′herrscher –in §6 mf autocrat

allei′nig adj (ausschließlich) sole, exclusive; (einzig) only

allein′stehend adj alone in the world; (unverheiratet) single; (Gebäude) detached

Allein′verkauf m, **Allein′vertrieb** m franchise

al′lemal adv every time; **ein für a.** once and for all

al′lenfalls adv if need be; (vielleicht) possibly; (höchstens) at most

allenthalben [′alənt′halbən] adv everywhere

al′lerart invar adj all kinds of

al′lerbe′ste §9 adj very best; **aufs a.** in the best possible manner

al′lerdings′ adv (gewiß) certainly (strong affirmative answer); (zugestehend) admittedly, I must admit

al′lerer′ste §9 adj very first, first … of all

Aller·gie [alɛr′gi] (-;-gien [′gi·ən]) allergy

allergisch [a′lɛrgɪʃ] adj allergic

al′lerhand′ invar adj all kinds of; (viel) a lot of || indef pron —**das ist a.!** that's great!; **das ist doch a.!** the nerve!

Allerhei′ligen invar n All Saints' Day

allerlei [′alər′laɪ] invar adj all kinds of || **Allerlei** n (-s;-s) hotchpotch; (mus) medley

al′lerletz′te §9 adj very last, last of all; latest

al′lerliebste [′alər′lipstə] §9 adj dearest … of all; (Kind) sweet

al′lermei′ste §9 adj most; **am allermeisten** most of all; chiefly

al′lernäch′ste §9 adj very next

al′lerneu′este §9 adj latest, newest

Allersee′len invar n All Souls' Day

allesamt [alə′zamt] adv all together

al′lezeit adv always

Allge′genwart f omnipresence

all′gemein adj general, universal

Allgemeinheit f universality; (Öffentlichkeit) public

Allheil′mittel n cure-all

Allianz [alɪ′ants] f (-;-en) alliance

alliieren [alɪ′irən] ref—**sich a. mit** ally oneself with

alliiert [alɪ′irt] adj allied || **Alliierte** §5 mf ally

alljähr′lich adj annual, yearly

All′macht f omnipotence

allmäch′tig adj omnipotent, almighty

allmählich [al′melɪç] adj gradual

allnächt′lich adj nightly

allseitig [′alzaɪtɪç] adj all-round || adv from all sides, on all sides

All′tag m daily routine

alltäg′lich adj daily; (fig) everyday

all′tags adv daily; (wochentags) weekdays

All′tags– comb.fm. everyday; (fig) commonplace

All′tagsmensch m common man

All′tagswort n (-[e]s;-̈er) household word

allwissend [al′vɪsənt] adj omniscient

allwö′chentlich adj & adv weekly

allzu– comb.fm. all too

all′zumal adv one and all, all together

all′zusammen adv all together

Alm [alm] f (-;-en) Alpine meadow

Almanach [′almanax] m (-[e]s;-e) almanac

Almosen [′almozen] n (-s;-) alms

Alp [alp] m (-[e]s;-e) elf, goblin; (Alptraum) nightmare

Alp′druck m (-[e]s;), **Alp′drücken** n (-s;) nightmare

Alpen [′alpən] pl Alps

Alphabet [alfa′bet] n (-[e]s;-e) alphabet

alphabetisch [alfa′betɪʃ] adj alphabetical

alpin [al′pin] adj alpine

als [als] adv as, like || conj than; when, as; but, except; **als ob** as if

alsbald′ adv presently, immediately

alsdann′ adv then, thereupon

also ['alzo] *adv* so, thus; therefore, consequently; na a.! well then!

alt [alt] *adj* (älter ['eltər], älteste ['eltəstə] §9) *adj* old; (*bejahrt*) aged; (*gebraucht*) second-hand; (*abgestanden*) stale; (*antik*) antique; (*Sprache*) ancient || **Alt** *m* (-[e]s;-e) contralto || **Alte** §5 *m* (coll) old man; **die Alten** the ancients; **mein Alter** (coll) my husband || **Alte** §5 *f* (coll) old woman; **meine Alte** (coll) my wife

Altan [al'tan] *m* (-[e]s;-e), **Altane** [al'tanə] *f* (-;-n) balcony, gallery

Altar [al'tar] *m* (-[e]s;-e) altar

alt′bewährt *adj* long-standing

Alt′eisen *n* scrap iron

Alt′eisenhändler *m* junk dealer

Alter ['altər] *n* (-s;-) age; (*Greisen-*) old age; (*Zeit-*) epoch; (*Dienst-*) seniority; **er ist in meinem A.** he is my age; **im A. von** at the age of; **mittleren Alters** middle-aged

altern ['altərn] *intr* (SEIN) age

Alternative [alterna'tivə] *f* (-;-n) alternative

Al′tersgrenze *f* age limit; (*für Beamte*) retirement age

Al′tersheim *n* home for the aged

Al′tersrente *f* old-age pension

al′tersschwach *adj* decrepit; senile

Al′tersschwäche *f* (feebleness of) old age

Al′tersversorgungskasse *f* old-age pension fund

Altertum ['altərtum] *n* (-s;) antiquity

altertümlich ['altərtymlıç] *adj* ancient; (*Möbel*) antique; (*veraltet*) archaic

Al′tertumsforscher **-in** §6 *mf* archaeologist; (*Antiquar*) antiquarian

Al′tertumskunde *f*, **Al′tertumswissenschaft** *f* study of antiquity; classical studies

althergebracht ['alt'hergəbraxt] *adj* long-standing, traditional

alther′kömmlich *adj* ancient, traditional

Altist [al'tıst] §7 *m* alto (*singer*)

Altistin [al'tıstın] §7 *f* contralto (*female singer*)

alt′klug *adj* precocious

ältlich ['eltlıç] *adj* elderly

Alt′meister *m* past master; (sport) ex-champion

alt′modisch *adj* old-fashioned

Alt′stadt *f* old (part of the) city

Alt′stadtsanierung *f* urban renewal

Alt′stimme *f* alto; contralto (*female voice*)

altväterlich ['altfetərlıç], **altväterisch** ['altfetərıʃ] *adj* old-fashioned; old-time

Alt′warenhändler **-in** §6 *mf* second-hand dealer

Altweibersommer [alt'vaıbərzɔmər] *m* Indian summer; (*Spinnweb*) gossamer

Aluminium [alu'minjum] *n* (-s;) aluminum

am [am] *contr* an dem

amalgamieren [amalga'mirən] *tr* amalgamate

Amateur [ama'tør] *m* (-s;-e) amateur

Amazone [ama'tsonə] *f* (-;-n) Amazon

Am·boß ['ambɔs] *m* (-bosses;-bosse) anvil

ambulant [ambu'lant] *adj* ambulatory || *adv*—a. **Behandelte** out-patient

Ambulanz [ambu'lants] *f* (-;-en) out-patient clinic; (*Krankenwagen*) ambulance

Ameise ['amaızə] *f* (-;-n) ant

Amerika [a'merıka] *n* (-s;) America

Amerikaner **-in** [amerı'kanər(ın)] §6 *mf* American

amerikanisch [amerı'kanıʃ] *adj* American

Ami ['ami] *m* (-s;-s) (sl) Yank || *f* (-;-s) American cigarette

Amme ['amə] *f* (-;-n) nurse, wet-nurse

Amnes·tie [amnes'ti] *f* (-;-tien ['ti·ən]) amnesty

amnestieren [amnes'tirən] *tr* pardon

A·mor ['amɔr] *m* (-s;-moren ['morən]) (myth) Cupid

Amortisation [amɔtıza'tsjon] *f* (-;-en) amortization

Amortisations′kasse *f* sinking fund

amortisieren [amɔrtı'zirən] *tr* amortize

Ampel ['ampəl] *f* (-;-n) hanging lamp; (*Verkehrs-*) traffic light

Ampere [am'per] *n* (-s;-) ampere

Amphibie [am'fibjə] *f* (-;-n) amphibian

Amphi′bienpanzerwagen *m* amphibious tank

Amphitheater [am'fite·atər] *n* (-s;-) amphitheater

Ampulle [am'pulə] *f* (-;-n) phial

Amputation [amputa'tsjon] *f* (-;-en) amputation

amputieren [ampu'tirən] *tr* amputate

Amputierte [ampu'tirtə] §5 *mf* amputee

Amsel ['amzəl] *f* (-;-n) blackbird

Amt [amt] *n* (-[e]s;-er) office; (*Pflicht*) duty, function; (dipl) post; (eccl) divine service; (telp) exchange

amtieren [am'tirən] *intr* be in office, hold office; (eccl) officiate

amt′lich *adj* official

Amts- *comb.fm.* official, of (an) office

Amts′antritt *m* inauguration

Amts′befugnis *f* competence

Amts′bereich *m* jurisdiction

Amts′bewerber **-in** §6 *mf* office seeker

Amts′bezirk *m* jurisdiction

Amts′blatt *n* official bulletin

Amts′eid *m* oath of office

Amts′enthebung *f* dismissal

Amts′führung *f* administration

amts′gemäß *adj* official || *adv* officially

Amts′gericht *n* district court

Amts′gerichtsrat *m* (official rank of) district-court judge

Amts′geschäfte *pl* official duties

Amts′gewalt *f* (official) authority

Amts′handlung *f* official act

Amts′niederlegung *f* resignation

Amts′schimmel *m* bureaucracy; (coll) red tape

Amts′siegel *n* seal of office

Amts′sprache *f* official language; (coll) officialese, gobbledygook

Amts′tracht *f* robes

Amts′träger –in §6 *mf* officeholder

Amts′verletzung *f* misconduct in office

Amts′weg *m*—auf dem Amtswege through official channels

Amts′zeichen *n* (telp) dial tone

Amulett [amu′lɛt] *n* (-[e]s;-e) amulet

amüsant [amy′zant] *adj* amusing

amüsieren [amy′zirən] *tr* amuse, entertain ‖ *ref* amuse oneself; (*sich gut unterhalten*) enjoy oneself

an [an] *adv* on; onward ‖ *prep* (*dat*) at, against, on, upon, by, to; (*Grad, Maß*) in; **an sich** per se; **an und für sich** properly speaking; **es ist an dir zu** (*inf*) it's up to you to (*inf*) ‖ *prep* (*acc*) at, on, upon, against, to

analog [ana′lok] *adj* analogous

Analo·gie [analo′gi] *f* (-;-gien [′gi·ən]) analogy

Analphabet –in [analfa′bet(in)] §7 *mf* illiterate

Analphabetentum [analfa′betəntum] *n* (-s;), **Analphabetismus** [analfabe′tismus] *m* (-s) illiteracy

analphabetisch [analfa′betiʃ] *adj* illiterate

Analyse [ana′lyzə] *f* (-;-n) analysis; (gram) parsing; **durch A.** analytically

analysieren [analy′zirən] *tr* analyze; (gram) parse

Analy·sis [a′nɑlyzɪs] *f* (-;-sen [ana-′lyzən]) (math) analysis

Analytiker –in [ana′lytikər(in)] §6 *mf* analyst

analytisch [ana′lytiʃ] *adj* analytic(al)

Anämie [anɛ′mi] *f* (-;) anemia

anämisch [an′ɛmiʃ] *adj* anemic

Ananas [′ananas] *f* (-;-se) pineapple

Anarchie [anar′çi] *f* (-;) anarchy

anästhesieren [anɛstɛ′zirən] *tr* anesthetize

Anästheti·kum [anɛs′tetikum] *n* (-s; -ka [ka]) anesthetic

an′atmen *tr* breathe on

Anato·mie [anatɔ′mi] *f* (-;-mien [′mi·ən]) anatomy

anatomisch [ana′tomiʃ] *adj* anatomical

an′backen §50 *tr* bake gently ‖ *intr* (HABEN & SEIN) cake on

an′bahnen *tr* pave the way for

anbandeln [′anbandəln] *intr*—a. mit flirt with

An′bau *m* (-[e]s;) cultivation ‖ *m* (-[e]s;-bauten) annex, new wing

an′bauen *tr* cultivate; (*Gebäudeteil*) add on

An′baufläche *f* (arable) acreage

An′baumöbel *pl* sectional furniture

An′beginn *m* outset

an′behalten §90 *tr* keep (*garment*) on

anbei [an′baɪ] *adv* enclosed (herewith)

an′beißen §53 *tr* bite into, take the first bite of ‖ *intr* nibble at the bait; (fig) bite

an′belangen *tr*—was mich anbelangt as far as I am concerned, as for me

an′bellen *tr* bark at

anberaumen [′anbəraumən] *tr* schedule

an′beten *tr* (& fig) worship

An′betracht *m*—in A. (*genit*) in consideration of, in view of

an′betteln *tr* bum, chisel

An′betung *f* (-;) worship

an′betungswürdig *adj* adorable

an′bieten §58 *tr* offer ‖ *ref* offer one's services

an′binden §59 *tr* tie (up) ‖ *intr*—mit j–m a. pick a quarrel with s.o.

an′blasen §61 *tr* blow at, blow on

An′blick *m* look, view, sight

an′blicken *tr* look at; (*besehen*) view; (*mustern*) eye

an′blinzeln *tr* wink at

an′brechen §64 *tr* (*Vorräte*) break into; (*Flasche, Kiste*) open ‖ *intr* (SEIN) (*Tag*) dawn; (*Nacht*) come on

an′brennen §97 *tr* light ‖ *intr* (SEIN) catch fire; (*Speise*) burn

an′bringen §65 *tr* bring, fetch; (*befestigen*) (an *acc*) attach (to): (*Bitte*) make; (*Klage*) lodge; (*Geld*) invest; (*Tochter*) marry off; (*Waren*) sell, get rid of; (*Bemerkung*) insert; (*Licht, Lampe*) install; (*Geld*) (coll) blow

An′bruch *m* break; **bei A. der Nacht** at nightfall; **bei A. des Tages** at daybreak

an′brüllen *tr* roar at

Andacht [′andaxt] *f* (-;-en) devotion; (*Gottesdienst*) devotions

andächtig [′andɛçtiç] *adj* devout

an′dauern *intr* continue, last; (*hartnäckig sein*) persist

An′denken *n* (-s;-) remembrance; souvenir; **zum A. an** (*acc*) in remembrance of

andere [′andərə] §9 *adj & pron* other; (*folgend*) next; **ein anderer** another; **another one; kein anderer** no one else

ändern [′ɛndərn] *tr* change; (*Wortlaut*) modify ‖ *ref* change

andernfalls [′andərn′fals] *adv* (or) else

anders [′andərs] *adj* else; (als) different (from); **a. werden** change ‖ *adv* otherwise differently

an′dersartig *adj* of a different kind

anderseits [′andər′zaits] *adv* on the other hand

an′derswo *adv* somewhere else

anderthalb [′andərt′halp] *invar adj* one and a half

Än′derung *f* (-;-n) change, variation; modification

Än′derungsantrag *m* amendment

anderwärts [′andər′verts] *adv* elsewhere

anderweitig [′andər′vaitiç] *adj* other, further ‖ *adv* otherwise; elsewhere

an′deuten *tr* indicate, suggest; (*anspielen*) hint at, allude to; (*zu verstehen geben*) imply, intimate

an′deutungsweise *adv* by way of suggestion

an′dichten *tr*—j–m etw a. impute s.th. to s.o.

An′drang *m* rush; crowd; heavy traffic; (*von Arbeit*) pressure

an′drehen *tr* turn on; **j–m etw a.** palm s.th. off on s.o.

an'drohen *tr*—j-m etw a. threaten s.o.
with s.th.

an'drücken *tr*—etw a. an (*acc*) press
s.th. against

an'eignen *ref*—sich [*dat*] a. appropriate; (*Gewohnheit*) acquire; (*Meinungen*) adopt; (*Sprache*) master;
(*widerrechtlich*) appropriate, usurp

aneinan'der *adv* together

aneinan'dergeraten §63 *intr* (SEIN)
come to blows

Anekdote [anɛk'do:tə] *f* (-;-n) anecdote

an'ekeln *tr* disgust, nauseate

an'empfehlen §147 *tr* recommend

An'erbieten *n* (-s;-) offer, proposal

an'erkennbar *adj* recognizable

an'erkennen §97 *tr* (als) recognize (as);
(als) acknowledge (as); (*Schuld*) admit; (*billigen*) approve; (*lobend*) appreciate; (*Anspruch*) allow; **nicht a.**
repudiate, disown; (sport) disallow

An'erkennung *f* (-;-en) acknowledgement; recognition; appreciation; admission; **lobende A.** honorable mention

anfachen ['anfaxən] *tr* (*Feuer*) fan;
(*Gefühle*) stimulate; (*Haß*) stir up

an'fahren §71 *tr* (*herbeibringen*) carry,
convey; (*anstoßen*) run into; (fig)
snap at; (naut) run afoul of ‖ *intr*
(SEIN) drive up; (*losfahren*) start off

An'fall *m* attack

an'fallen §72 *tr* attack, assail ‖ *intr*
(SEIN) accumulate, accrue

anfällig ['anfɛlɪç] *adj* (für) susceptible
(to)

An'fang *m* beginning, start; **von A. an**
from the very beginning

an'fangen §73 *tr* & *intr* begin, start

Anfänger –in ['anfɛŋər(ɪn)] §6 *mf* beginner; (*Neuling*) novice

anfänglich ['anfɛŋlɪç] *adj* initial

an'fangs *adv* at the start, initially

An'fangsbuchstabe *m* initial (letter)

An'fangsgründe *pl* rudiments, elements

an'fassen *tr* take hold of; (*behandeln*)
handle, touch ‖ *intr* lend a hand

an'faulen *intr* (SEIN) begin to rot

anfechtbar ['anfɛçtbar] *adj* debatable,
questionable; (jur) contestable

an'fechten §74 *tr* (*Richtigkeit*) contest; (*beunruhigen*) trouble; (jur)
challenge

An'fechtung *f* (-;-en) (eccl) temptation; (jur) challenge

an'fertigen *tr* make, manufacture

an'feuchten *tr* moisten, wet

an'feuern *tr* inflame; (sport) cheer

an'flehen *tr* implore

an'fliegen §57 *tr* (aer) approach

An'flug *m* (*Anzeichen*) suggestion,
trace; (*oberflächliche Kenntnis*) smattering; (*dünner Überzug*) film; **A.
von Bart** down; **leichter A. von slight
case of**

an'fordern *tr* call for, demand; (mil)
requisition

an'fragen *intr* (über *acc*, wegen, nach)
ask (about *s.th.*); (bei) inquire (of
s.o.)

an'fressen §70 *tr* gnaw; (*Metall*) corrode

anfreunden ['anfrɔɪndən] *ref* (mit)
make friends (with)

an'frieren §77 *intr* (SEIN) begin to
freeze; **a. an** (*acc*) freeze onto

an'fügen *tr* (an *acc*) join (to)

an'fühlen *tr* & *ref* feel

Anfuhr ['anfu:r] *f* (-;-en) delivery

an'führen *tr* lead; (*Worte*) quote;
(*Grund*) adduce; (*täuschen*) take in,
fool; (mil) lead, command

An'führer –in §6 *mf* leader; (mil)
commander; (pol) boss

An'führung *f* quotation

An'führungszeichen *n* quotation mark

an'füllen *tr* & *ref* fill up

An'gabe *f* (*Erklärung*) statement;
(*beim Zollamt*) declaration; (coll)
showing off; **Angaben** data; directions; **nähere Angaben machen** give
particulars; **wer hat die A.?** whose
serve is it?

an'geben §80 *tr* (*mitteilen*) state; (*bestimmen*) appoint; (*anzeigen*) inform
against; (*vorgeben*) pretend; (*Preis*)
quote ‖ *intr* (coll) show off; (cards)
deal first; (tennis) serve

An'geber –in §6 *mf* informer; (*Prahler*) show-off

angeblich ['angepliç] *adj* alleged

an'geboren *adj* innate, natural

An'gebot *n* offer; (*bei Auktionen*)
bid; **A. und Nachfrage** supply and
demand

angebracht ['angəbraxt] *adj* advisable;
es für a. halten zu (*inf*) see fit to
(*inf*); **gut a.** appropriate; **schlecht a.**
ill-timed

angegossen ['angəgɔsən] *adj*—**wie a.
sitzen** fit like a glove

angeheiratet ['angəharratət] *adj* related by marriage

angeheitert ['angəhartərt] *adj* tipsy

an'gehen §82 *tr* charge, attack; (*Problem*) tackle; **das geht dich gar
nichts an** that's none of your business; **j-n um etw a.** approach s.o. for
s.th. ‖ *intr* (SEIN) begin; (*zulässig
sein*) be allowable; (*leidlich sein*) be
tolerable; **das geht nicht an** that
won't do

an'gehend *adj* future, prospective

an'gehören *intr* (dat) be a member
(of)

Angehörige ['angəhørɪgə] §5 *mf* member; **nächste Angehörigen** next of kin;
seine Angehörigen his relatives

Angeklagte ['angəklʌktə] §5 *mf* defendant; (*wenn verhaftet*) suspect

Angel ['aŋəl] *f* (-;-n) fishing tackle;
(*e-r Tür*) hinge; **aus den Angeln
heben** (& fig) unhinge

an'gelangen *intr* (SEIN) (an dat, bei)
arrive (at)

an'gelegen *adj*—**sich** [*dat*] **etw a. sein
lassen** make s.th. one's business

An'gelegenheit *f* (-;-en) affair, business

angelehnt ['angəlent] *adj* ajar

An'gelgerät *n* fishing tackle

An'gelhaken *m* fish(ing) hook

angeln ['aŋəln] *intr* (nach) fish (for)

An'gelpunkt *m* pivot, central point

An'gelrute *f* fishing rod

angelsächsisch [ˈaŋəlzɛksɪʃ] *adj* Anglo-Saxon

An'gelschnur *f* fishing line

angemessen [ˈaŋəmɛsən] *adj* suitable *(ausreichend)* adequate; *(annehmbar)* reasonable; *(Benehmen)* proper; *(dat)* in keeping (with); **für a. halten** think fit

angenehm [ˈaŋənɛm] *adj* pleasant; **sehr a!** pleased to meet you!

angeregt [ˈaŋərɛkt] *adj* lively

angeschlagen [ˈaŋəʃlaːgən] *adj* chipped; *(Boxer)* groggy; (mil) hard-hit

angesehen [ˈaŋəze-ən] *adj* respected; *(ausgezeichnet)* distinguished

An'gesicht *n* countenance, face; **von A.** by sight

an'gesichts *prep (genit)* in the presence of; (fig) in view of

angestammt [ˈaŋəʃtamt] *adj* hereditary

Angestellte [ˈaŋəʃtɛltə] §5 *mf* employee; **die Angestellten** the staff

angetan [ˈaŋətaːn] (mit) clad (in); **a. sein von** have a liking for; **ganz danach a. zu** (*inf*) very likely to (*inf*)

angetrunken [ˈaŋətrʊŋkən] *adj* tipsy

angewandt [ˈaŋəvant] *adj* applied

angewiesen [ˈaŋəviːzən] *adj—***a. sein auf** (*acc*) have to rely on

an'gewöhnen *tr—***j—m etw a.** accustom s.o. to s.th.

An'gewohnheit *f* (-;-en) habit

an'gleichen §85 *tr* adapt, adjust

Angler –**in** [ˈaŋlər(ɪn)] §6 *mf* fisher

an'gliedern *tr* link, attach; *(Gesellschaft)* affiliate

an'greifen §88 *tr (anfassen)* handle; *(Vorräte)* draw on, dip into; *(Körper)* affect; (mil) attack

an'greifend *adj* aggressive, offensive

An'greifer –**in** §6 *mf* aggressor

an'grenzen *intr* (an *acc*) be adjacent (to), border (on)

An'griff *m* attack

An'griffskrieg *m* war of aggression

an'griffslustig *adj* aggressive

Angst [aŋst] *f* (-;⁻e) fear, anxiety

ängstigen [ˈɛŋstɪgən] *tr* alarm || *ref* (vor) be afraid (of); (um) be alarmed (about)

ängstlich [ˈɛŋstlɪç] *adj* uneasy, jittery; *(besorgt)* anxious; *(sorgfältig)* scrupulous; *(schüchtern)* timid

Angst'zustände *pl* jitters

an'haben §89 *tr* have on; **j—m etw a.** have s.th. on. s.o.; **j—m etw a. können** be able to harm s.o.

an'haften *intr (dat)* stick (to)

an'haken *tr* check off; (an *acc*) hook (onto)

an'halten §90 *tr* stop; *(Atem, Ton)* hold; || *intr* stop; *(andauern)* continue, last

an'haltend *adj* continuous

An'halter *m—***per A. fahren** hitch-hike

An'haltspunkt *m* clue, lead

An'hang *m* (-[e]s;⁻e) appendix; *(Gefolgschaft)* following; (jur) codicil

an'hängen §92 & §109 *tr (Hörer)* hang up; *(hinzufügen)* add on; **j—m e-e Krankheit a.** infect s.o. with a disease; **j—m e—n Prozeß a.** bring suit

against s.o.; **j—m etw a.** pin s.th. on s.o. || §92 *intr* (an *dat*) adhere (to)

An'hänger –**in** §6 *mf* follower || *m (Schmuck)* pendant; (aut) trailer

anhänglich [ˈanhɛŋlɪç] *adj* (an *acc*) attached (to), devoted (to)

Anhängsel [ˈanhɛŋzəl] *m* (-s;-) appendage, adjunct

an'hauchen *tr* breathe on

an'häufen *tr & ref* pile up

An'häufung *f* (-;-en) accumulation

an'heben §94 *tr* lift (up); *(Lied)* strike up; (aut) jack up

an'heften *tr* fasten; *(annähen)* stitch

an'heilen *tr & intr* heal up

anheim'fallen §72 *intr* (SEIN) *(dat)* devolve (upon)

anheim'stellen *tr (dat)* leave (to)

An'höhe *f* rise, hill

an'hören *tr* listen to, hear || *ref —***sich gut a.** sound good

Anilin [anɪˈliːn] *n* (-s;) aniline

Animier'dame *f* B-girl

animieren [anɪˈmiːrən] *tr* encourage

Anis [aˈniːs] *m* (-es;-e) anise

an'kämpfen *intr* (gegen) struggle (against)

An'kauf *m* purchase

an'kaufen *tr* purchase

Anker [ˈaŋkər] *m* (-s;-) anchor; (elec) armature; **vor A. gehen** drop anchor

ankern [ˈaŋkərn] *intr* anchor

an'ketten *tr* (an *acc*) chain (to)

An'klage *f* accusation, charge; (jur) indictment; **A. erheben** prefer charges; **die A. vertreten** be counsel for the prosecution; **unter A. stellen** indict

an'klagen *tr* (wegen) accuse (of), charge (with), indict (for)

An'kläger –**in** §6 *mf* accuser; (jur) prosecutor

An'klageschrift *f* (bill of) indictment

an'klammern *tr* (an *acc*) clip (to) || *ref* (an *acc*) cling (to)

An'klang *m* (an *acc*) reminiscence (of), trace (of); **A. finden** be well received, catch on

an'kleben *tr* (an *acc*) paste (on), stick (on) || *intr* (HABEN & SEIN) stick

an'kleiden *tr & ref* dress

an'klingeln *tr* ring, call up || *intr—***bei j—m a.** ring s.o.'s doorbell

an'klopfen *intr* (an *acc*) knock (on)

an'knipsen *tr* switch on

an'knüpfen *tr* tie, attach; *(Gespräch)* start || *intr* (an *acc*) link up (with)

an'kommen §99 *intr* (SEIN) (in *dat*) arrive (at); **(bei)** be well received (by); (bei) get a job (with); **es darauf a. lassen** take one's chances; **es kommt ganz darauf an, ob** it (all) depends on whether

Ankömmling [ˈankœmlɪŋ] *m* (-s;-e) newcomer, arrival

an'kündigen *tr* announce, proclaim; **j—m etw a.** notify s.o. of s.th.

An'kündigung *f* (-;-en) announcement

Ankunft [ˈankunft] *f* (-;⁻e) arrival

an'kurbeln *tr* crank up; **die Wirtschaft a.** prime the economy

an'lachen *tr* laugh at

An'lage *f* *(Anordnung)* plan, layout;

(Bau) construction; (Errichtung) installation; (Fabrik) plant, works; (Garten) park, grounds; (Fähigkeit) ability, aptitude (im Brief) enclosure; **in der A.** enclosed

An'lagekapital n invested capital; permanent assets

an'langen tr—**was mich anlangt** as far as I'm concerned ‖ intr (SEIN) arrive

An·laß ['anlas] m (—lasses;-lässe) occasion; (Grund) reason, motive; **A. geben zu** give rise to; **ohne allen A.** without any reason

an'lassen §104 tr (Kleid) keep on; (Motor) start (up); (Wasser) turn on; (Pumpe) prime; (Stahl) temper; **j–n hart a.** rebuke s.o. sharply ‖ ref **sich gut a.** shape up

Anlasser ['anlasər] m (—s;—) starter

anläßlich ['anleslıç] prep (genit) on the occasion of

An'lauf m run, start

an'laufen §105 tr run at; (Hafen) put into ‖ intr (SEIN) (Motor) start up; (Brille) fog up; (Metall) tarnish; (anwachsen) accumulate; (Schulden) mount up; (Film) start, come on; **angelaufen kommen** come running up; **ins Rollen a.** (fig) get rolling; **rot a.** blush

an'legen tr (an acc) put (on), lay (on); (Garten; Geld) lay out; (Kapital) invest; (Leitung) install; (Verband) apply; (Kolonie) found ‖ ref—**sich a. mit** have a run-in with ‖ intr put ashore; moor

An'legeplatz m pier

an'lehnen tr (an acc) lean (against); (Tür) leave ajar ‖ ref (an acc) lean (against); (fig) be based (on), rely (on)

Anleihe ['anlar·ə] f (—;-n) loan

an'leiten tr (zu) guide (to); **a. in** (dat) instruct in

An'leitung f (—;-en) guidance; (Lehre) instruction

an'lernen tr train, break in

an'liegen §108 intr (passen) fit; (an dat) lie near, be adjacent (to); **eng a.** fit tight; **j–m a.** pester s.o. ‖ **Anliegen** n (—s;—) request; **ein A. an j–n haben** have a request to make of s.o.

an'liegend adj adjacent; (Kleid) tight-fitting; (im Brief) enclosed

an'locken tr lure (on)

an'machen tr (Licht) switch on; (Feuer) light; (zubereiten) prepare; (an acc) attach (to)

an'malen tr paint

an'marschieren intr (SEIN) approach

anmaßen ['anmasən] ref—**sich** [dat] **etw a.** usurp s.th.; **sich** [dat] **a., etw zu sein** pretend to be s.th.

an'maßend adj arrogant

An'meldeformular n registration form

an'melden tr announce; report; (Anspruch, Berufung) file; (Konkurs) declare; (Patent) apply for; (educ) register; (sport) enter ‖ ref (bei) make an appointment (with); (zu) enroll (in); (mil) report in

an'merken tr note down; **j–m etw a.** notice s.th. in s.o.

an'messen §70 tr—**j–m etw a.** measure s.o. for s.th.

An'mut f (—;) charm, attractiveness

an'mutig adj charming

an'nageln tr (an acc) nail (to)

an'nähen tr (an acc) sew on (to)

annähernd ['annε·ərnt] adj approximate

an'näherung f (—;-en) approach

An'näherungsversuch m (romantic) pass; attempt at reconciliation

an'näherungsweise adv approximately

An'nahme f (—;-n) acceptance; (Vermutung) assumption

annehmbar ['annembar] adj acceptable

an'nehmen §116 tr accept, take; (vermuten) assume, suppose, guess; (Glauben) embrace; (Gewohnheit) acquire; (Gesetz) pass; (Kind) adopt; (Arbeiter) hire; (Farbe, Gestalt) take on; (Titel) assume; **etw als erwiesen a.** take s.th. for granted ‖ ref (genit) take care of

annektieren [anek'tirən] tr annex

Annexion [ane'ksjon] f (—;-en) annexation

Annonce [a'nõsə] f (—;-n) advertisement

annoncieren [anõ'sirən] tr advertise

anöden [a'nødən] tr bore to death

anonym [ano'nym] adj anonymous

an'ordnen tr arrange; (befehlen) order

an'packen tr grab hold of, seize; (Problem) tackle

an'passen tr fit; (Worte) adapt; ‖ ref (dat or an acc) adapt oneself (to)

an'passungsfähig adj adaptable

an'pflanzen tr plant, cultivate

an'pflaumen tr (coll) kid

anpöbeln ['anpøbəln] tr mob

an'pochen tr (an acc) knock (on)

An'prall m impact; (e–s Angriffs) brunt

an'prallen intr (SEIN) (gegen, an acc) collide (with), run (into)

an'preisen tr praise; **j–m etw a.** recommend s.th. to s.o.

An'probe f fitting, trying on

an'probieren tr try on

an'pumpen tr—**j–n a. um** hit s.o. for

an'quatschen tr talk the ears off

an'raten §63 tr advise, recommend

an'rechnen tr charge; **hoch a.** appreciate; **j–m etw a.** charge s.o. for s.th.

An'recht n (auf acc) right (to)

An'rede f address

an'reden tr address, speak to

an'regen tr stimulate; suggest

An'reiz m incentive

an'reizen tr stimulate; spur on

an'rennen §97 intr (SEIN) (gegen) run (into); **angerannt kommen** come running

an'richten tr (Schaden) cause, do; (culin) prepare

anrüchig ['anrʏçıç] adj disreputable

an'rücken intr (SEIN) approach

An'ruf m (telephone) call

an'rufen §122 tr call; (Gott) invoke; (Schiff) hail; (jur) appeal to; (mil) challenge; (telp) call up

an'rühren tr touch; (Thema) touch on; (mischen) stir

An'sage f announcement

an'sagen *tr* announce; (*Trumpf*) declare

An'sager –in §6 *mf* announcer

an'sammeln *tr* gather; (*anhäufen*) amass; (*Truppen*) concentrate ‖ *ref* gather; (*Zinsen*) accumulate

ansässig ['anzɛsɪç] *adj* residing; a. werden (or sich a. machen) settle ‖ Ansässige §5 *mf* resident

An'satz *m* start; (*Mundstück*) mouthpiece; (*Spur*) trace; (*in e–r Rechnung*) charge; (*Schätzung*) estimate; (geol) deposit; (mach) attachment; (math) statement

an'saugen §125 *tr* suck in; (*Pumpe*) prime

an'schaffen *tr* procure; (*kaufen*) get, purchase; Kinder a. (coll) have kids

an'schalten *tr* switch on

an'schauen *tr* look at

an'schaulich *adj* graphic

An'schauung *f* outlook, opinion; (*Vorstellung*) perception; (*Auffassung*) conception; (*Erkenntnis*) intuition; (*Betrachtung*) contemplation

An'schauungsbild *n* mental image

An'schauungsmaterial *n* visual aids

an'schein *m* appearance

an'scheinend *adj* apparent, seeming

an'scheinlich *adv* apparently

an'schicken *ref* get ready

an'schieben §130 *tr* give (s.th.) a push

anschirren ['anʃɪrən] *tr* harness

An'schlag *m* (an acc, gegen) striking (against); (*Anprall*) impact; (*Attentat*) attempt; (*Bekanntmachung*) notice; (*e–r Uhr*) stroke; (*e–r Taste*) hitting; (*Berechnung*) calculation; (*e–s Gewehrs*) firing position; (*Komplott*) plot; (mach) stop (*for arresting motion*); (mus) touch; (tennis) serve; A. spielen play tag

An'schlagbrett *n* bulletin board

an'schlagen §132 *tr* (an acc) fasten (to); (*Plakat*) post; (*Gewehr*) level; (*Tasse, usw.*) chip; (*Taste*) hit; (*einschätzen*) estimate; (*Gegner*) thrash; have in trouble; e–n anderen Ton a. (fig) change one's tune ‖ *ref* bump oneself ‖ *intr* (*Wellen*) (an acc) beat against; (*Hund*) let out a bark; (*Arznei*) work

An'schlagzettel *m* notice; poster

an'schließen §76 *tr* padlock; (*anketten*) chain; (*verbinden*) connect; (*anfügen*) join; (com) affiliate; (elec) plug in ‖ *ref* (*dat*, an acc) join, side with ‖*intr* (*Kleid*) be tight

an'schließend *adj* (an acc) subsequent (to); adjacent (to) ‖ *adv* next, then

An'schluß *m* connection; (pol) annexation, union; sie sucht A. (coll) she is looking for a man

An'schlußbahn *f* (rr) branch line

An'schlußdose *f* (elec) receptacle

An'schlußschnur *f* (elec) cord

An'schlußzug *m* connection, connecting train

an'schmachten *tr* make eyes at

an'schmiegen *ref* (an acc) nestle up (to); (*Kleid*) (an acc) cling (to)

anschmiegsam ['anʃmiːkzam] *adj* accommodating; cuddly

an'schmieren *tr* smear; (coll) bamboozle

an'schnallen *tr* buckle ‖ *ref* fasten one's seat belt

an'schnauzen *tr* snap at, bawl out

an'schneiden §106 *tr* cut into; (*Thema*) take up

An'schnitt *m* first cut

an'schrauben *tr* (an acc) screw on (to)

an'schreiben §62 *tr* write down; (*Spielstand*) mark; (*dat*) charge (to): (com) write to; etw a. lassen buy s.th. on credit

An'schreiber –in §6 *mf* scorekeeper

An'schreibtafel *f* scoreboard

an'schreien §135 *tr* yell at

An'schrift *f* address

An'schriftenmaschine *f* addressograph

anschuldigen ['anʃʊldɪgən] *tr* accuse

an'schwärzen *tr* blacken, disparage

an'schwellen *tr* cause to swell; (*Unkosten, usw.*) swell ‖ §119 *intr* (SEIN) swell up, puff up; increase

an'schwemmen *tr* wash (*s.th.*) ashore; (geol) deposit

an'sehen §138 *tr* look at; (fig) regard ‖ Ansehen *n* (–s;–) appearance; (*Achtung*) reputation; (*Geltung*) prestige, authority; von A. by sight; of high repute

ansehnlich ['anzeːnlɪç] *adj* good-looking; (*beträchtlich*) considerable; (*eindrucksvoll*) imposing

An'sehung *f* (–;)—in A. (genit) in consideration of

anseilen ['anzailən] *tr* rope together

an'setzen *tr* (an acc) put (on), apply (to): (*zum Kochen*) put on; (*Frist, Preis*) set; (*abschätzen*) rate; (*berechnen*) charge; (*Knospen*) put forth ‖ *intr* begin; (*fett werden*) get fat

An'sicht *f* view; (*Meinung*) opinion; zur A. on approval

an'sichtig *adj*—a. werden (genit) catch sight of

An'sichtspostkarte *f* picture postcard

An'sichtssache *f* matter of opinion

An'sichtsseite *f* frontal view, façade

An'sichtssendung *f* article(s) sent on approval

ansiedeln *tr* & *ref* settle

An'siedler –in §6 *mf* settler

An'siedlung *f* (–;–en) settlement

An'sinnen *n* (–s;–) unreasonable demand

an'spannen *tr* stretch; (*Pferd*) hitch up; (fig) exert, strain

An'spannung *f* (–;–en) exertion, strain

an'speien §135 *tr* spit on

an'spielen *tr* (cards) lead with ‖ *intr* (auf acc) allude (to); (mus) start playing; (sport) kick off, serve, break

An'spielung *f* (–;–en) allusion, hint

an'spitzen *tr* sharpen (*to a point*)

An'sporn *m* spur, stimulus

an'spornen *tr* spur

An'sprache *f* (an acc) address (to); e–e A. halten deliver an address

an'sprechen §64 *tr* speak to, address; (*Ziel, Punkt*) make out; a. als regard as; j–n a. um ask s.o. for ‖ *intr* (dat) appeal to, interest; (auf acc) respond (to)

an'sprechend *adj* appealing
an'springen §142 *tr* leap at ‖ *intr* (SEIN) (*Motor*) start (up); angesprungen kommen come skipping along
an'spritzen *tr* sprinkle, squirt
An'spruch *m* (*claim*); A. haben auf (*acc*) be entitled to; A. machen (or erheben) auf (*acc*), in A. nehmen demand, require, claim; große Ansprüche stellen ask too much
an'spruchslos *adj* unpretentious
an'spruchsvoll *adj* pretentious; (*wählerisch*) choosey, hard to please
an'spucken *tr* spit on
an'spülen *tr* wash ashore; (geol) deposit
an'stacheln *tr* goad on
Anstalt ['an'talt] *f* (-;-en) institution, establishment; Anstalten treffen zu make preparations for
An'stand *m* (*Schicklichkeit*) decency; (*Bedenken*) hesitation; (*Einwendung*) objection; (hunt) blind
anständig ['an'tendɪç] *adj* decent
An'standsbesuch *m* formal call
An'standsdame *f* chaperone
An'standsgefühl *n* tact
an'standshalber *adv* out of politeness, out of human decency
an'standslos *adv* without fuss
an'starren *tr* stare at, gaze at
anstatt [an'ʃtat] *prep* (genit) instead of
an'stauen *tr* dam up ‖ *ref* pile up
an'staunen *tr* gaze at (in astonishment)
an'stecken *tr* stick on; (*Ring*) put on; (*anzünden*) set on fire; (*Zigarette, Feuer*) light; (pathol) infect ‖ *ref* become infected
an'steckend *adj* infectious; (*durch Berührung*) contagious
An'steckung *f* (-;-en) infection; (*durch Berührung*) contagion
an'stehen §146 *intr* (nach) line up (for); (*zögern*) hesitate; j–m gut a. fit s.o. well, become s.o.
an'steigen §148 *intr* (SEIN) rise, ascend; (*zunehmen*) increase, mount up
an'stellen *tr* (an *acc*) place (against); (*beschäftigen*) hire; (*Versuch, usw.*) (*Vergleich*) draw; (*Heizung, Radio*) turn on ‖ *ref* (nach) line up (for); sich a., als ob act as if; stell dich nicht so dumm a.! don't play dumb!
anstellig ['an'telɪç] *adj* skillful
An'stellung *f* (-;-en) hiring; job
an'steuern *tr* steer for
Anstieg ['an'tik] *m* (-[e]s;-e) rise; (*e-s Weges*) grade
an'stieren *tr* stare at, glower at
an'stiften *tr* instigate
An'stifter -in §6 *mf* instigator
an'stimmen *tr* (*Lied*) strike up; (*Geheul*) let out
An'stoß *m* impact; (*Antrieb*) impulse; (*Ärgernis*) offense; (sport) kickoff; den A. geben zu start
an'stoßen §150 *tr* bump against; (*Ball*) kick off; (*Wagen*) give a push; (*mit dem Ellbogen*) nudge, poke ‖ *intr* clink glasses; a. an (*acc*) adjoin; bei j–m a. shock s.o.; mit den Gläsern a. clink glasses; mit der Zunge a. lisp ‖

intr (SEIN)—mit dem Kopf a. an (*acc*) bump one's head against
an'stoßend *adj* adjoining
anstößig ['an'tøsɪç] *adj* shocking
an'strahlen *tr* beam on; (fig) beam at; (*mit Scheinwerfern*) floodlight
an'streben *tr* strive for
an'streichen §85 *tr* paint; (*Fehler*) underline; (*anhaken*) check off
An'streicher *m* house painter
an'streifen *tr* brush against, graze
an'strengen *tr* exert; (*Geist*) tax; e–n Prozeß a. file suit ‖ *intr* be a strain
an'strengend *adj* strenuous, trying
An'strengung *f* (-;-en) exertion, effort
An'strich *m* (*Farbe*) paint; (*Überzug*) coat (of *paint*); (fig) tinge
An'sturm *m* assault, charge
antarktisch [ant'arktɪʃ] *adj* antarctic
an'tasten *tr* touch, finger
An'teil *m* share, portion; (*Quote*) quota; (st. exch.) share; A. nehmen an (*dat*) take part in; (fig) sympathize with
an'teilmäßig *adj* proportional
An'teilnahme *f* (-;) (an *dat*) participation (in); (*Mitleid*) sympathy
Antenne [an'tenə] *f* (-;-n) antenna, aerial; (ent) antenna, feeler
Antibioti-kum [antɪbɪ'otɪkum] *n* (-s; -ka [ka]) antibiotic
antik [an'tik] *adj* ancient; classical ‖
Antike *f* (-;-n) (classical) antiquity; (*Kunstwerk*) antique
Anti'kenhändler -in §6 *mf* antique dealer
Antilope [antɪ'lopə] *f* (-;-n) antelope
Antipa-thie [antɪpa'ti] *f* (-;-thien ['ti-ən]) antipathy
an'tippen *tr & intr* tap
Antiqua [an'tikva] *f* (-;) roman (type)
Antiquar -in [antɪ'kvar(ɪn)] §8 *mf* antique dealer; second-hand bookdealer
Antiquariat [antɪkva'rjat] *n* (-[e]s;-e) second-hand bookstore
antiquarisch [antɪ'kvarɪʃ] *adj* secondhand
Antiquität [antɪkvɪ'tet] *f* (-;-en) antique
Antlitz ['antlɪts] *m* (-es;-e) (Bib, poet) countenance
Antrag ['antrak] *m* (-[e]s;ː-e) (*Angebot*) offer; (*Vorschlag*) proposal; (*Gesuch*) application; (pol) motion
an'tragen §132 *tr* offer; (*vorschlagen*) propose ‖ *intr*—a. auf (*acc*) make a motion for; propose, suggest
An'tragsformular *n* application form
Antragsteller -in ['antrak/telər(-ɪn)] §6 *mf* applicant; (parl) mover
an'treffen §151 *tr* meet; find at home
an'treiben §62 *tr* drive on, urge on; (*Schiff*) propel; (*anreizen*) egg on ‖ *intr* (SEIN) wash ashore
an'treten §152 *tr* (*Amt, Erbschaft*) enter (upon); (*Reise*) set out on; (*Motorrad*) start up ‖ *intr* (SEIN) take one's place; (mil) fall in; (sport) enter
An'trieb *m* (-s;-e) (*Beweggrund*) motive; (*Anreiz*) incentive; (mech) drive, impetus; aus eigenem A. on

one's own initiative; **neuen A. ver-leihen** (*dat*) give fresh impetus to

An'tritt *m* (-[e]s;-e) beginning, start; (*e-s Amtes*) entrance upon

an'tun §154 *tr* (*Kleid*) put on; **j-m etw a.** do s.th. to s.o.

Antwort ['antvɔrt] *f* (-;-en) answer

antworten ['antvɔrtən] *intr* (**auf** *acc*) reply (to); answer; **j-m a.** answer s.o.

an'vertrauen *tr* entrust; (*mitteilen*) tell, confide

an'verwandt *adj* related ‖ **Anverwandte** §5 *mf* relative

an'wachsen §155 *intr* (SEIN) begin to grow; grow together; (*Wurzel schlagen*) take root; (*zunehmen*) increase

Anwalt ['anvalt] *m* (-[e]s;-̈e) attorney

An'waltschaft *f* legal profession, bar

an'wandeln *tr*—**mich wandelte die Lust an zu** (*inf*) I got a yen to (*inf*); **was wandelte dich an?** what got into you?

An'wandlung *f* (-;-en) impulse, sudden feeling; (*von Zorn*) fit

An'wärter -in §6 *mf* candidate; (*mil*) cadet, officer candidate

Anwartschaft ['anvartʃaft] *f* (-;) expectancy; (*Aussicht*) prospect

an'wehen *tr* blow on ‖ *intr* (SEIN) drift

an'weisen §118 *tr* (*beauftragen*) instruct; (*zuteilen*) assign; (*Geld*) remit

An'weisung *f* (-;-en) instruction; assignment; (*fin*) money order

anwendbar ['anvɛntbar] *adj* (**auf** *acc*) applicable (to); (**für, zu**) that can be used (for)

an'wenden §140 *tr* (**auf** *acc*) apply (to); (**für, zu**) use (for)

An'wendung *f* (-;-en) application; use

an'werben §149 *tr* recruit

an'werfen §160 *tr* (*Motor*) start up

An'wesen *n* estate, property; presence

anwesend ['anvezənt] *adj* present ‖ **Anwesende** §5 *mf* person present; **verehrte Anwesende!** ladies and gentlemen!

An'wesenheit *f* (-;) presence

an'wurzeln *ref & intr* (SEIN) take root; **wie angewurzelt** rooted to the spot

An'zahl *f* (-;) number, quantity

an'zahlen *tr* pay down ‖ *intr* make a down payment

an'zapfen *tr* tap

An'zeichen *n* indication, sign; (*Vorbedeutung*) omen; (*pathol*) symptom

Anzeige ['antsaɪgə] *f* (-;-n) (*Ankündigung*) announcement; notice; (*Reklame*) ad; (*med*) advice; **kleine Anzeigen** classified ads

an'zeigen *tr* announce; notify; (*Symptome, Fieber*) show, indicate; (*bei der Polizei*) report, inform against; (*inserieren*) advertise

An'zeigenvermittlung *f* advertising agency

an'zetteln *tr* (*Verschwörung*) hatch

an'ziehen §163 *tr* pull; (& *fig*) attract; (*Kleid*) put on; (*e-e Person*) dress; (*Riemen, Schraube*) tighten; (*Bremse*) apply; (*Beispiele, Quellen*) quote ‖

intr pull, start pulling; (*Preis*) go up; (chess) go first

An'ziehung *f* (-;-en) attraction; (*Zitat*) quotation

An'ziehungskraft *f* appeal; (& *phys*) attraction; (astr) gravitation

An'zug *m* suit; (mil) uniform; **in A. sein** (*Armee*) be approaching; (*Sturm*) be gathering; (*Gefahr*) be imminent

anzüglich ['antsyːlɪç] *adj* offensive; **a. werden** become personal

an'zünden *tr* set on fire; (*Feuer*) light

an'zweifeln *tr* doubt, question

apart [a'part] *adj* charming; (coll) cute

Apathie [apa'tiː] *f* (-;) apathy

apathisch [a'paːtɪʃ] *adj* apathetic

Apfel [ˈapfəl] *m* (-s;-̈) apple

Ap'felkompott *n* stewed apples

Ap'felmus *n* applesauce

Ap'felsaft *m* apple juice

Apfelsine [apfəl'ziːnə] *f* (-;-n) orange

Ap'feltorte *f* apple tart; **gedeckte A.** apple pie

Ap'felwein *m* cider

Apostel [a'pɔstəl] *m* (-s;-) apostle

Apostroph [apɔ'stroːf] *m* (-[e]s;-e) apostrophe

Apotheke [apɔ'teːkə] *f* (-;-n) pharmacy

Apotheker -in [apɔ'teːkər(ɪn)] §6 *mf* druggist

Apothe'kerwaren *pl* drugs

Apparat [apa'raːt] *m* (-[e]s;-e) apparatus, device; (phot) camera; (rad, telv) set; (telp) telephone; **am A.!** speaking

Appell [a'pɛl] *m* (-[e]s;-e) appeal; (mil) roll call; (mil) inspection

appellieren [apɛ'liːrən] *intr* (& *jur*) (**an** *acc*) appeal (to)

Appetit [ape'tiːt] *m* (-[e]s;-e) appetite

Appetit'brötchen *n* canapé

appetit'lich *adj* appetizing; (*Mädchen*) attractive

applaudieren [aplau'diːrən] *tr & intr* applaud

Applaus [a'plaus] *m* (-es;-e) applause

Appretur [apre'tuːr] *f* (-;-en) (tex) finish

Aprikose [apri'koːzə] *f* (-;-n) apricot

April [a'prɪl] *m* (-[s];-e) April

Aquarell [akva'rɛl] *n* (-[e]s;-e) watercolor; watercolor painting

Aqua·rium [a'kvaːrjum] *n* (-s;-rien [rɪ·ən]) aquarium

Äqua·tor [ɛ'kvaːtor] *m* (-s;-toren [ˈtoːrən]) equator

Ära ['ɛra] *f* (-;-Ären [ˈɛːrən]) era

Araber -in ['araber(ɪn)] §6 *mf* Arab

Arabien [a'raːbjən] *n* (-s) Arabia

arabisch [a'raːbɪʃ] *adj* Arabian; (*Ziffer*) Arabic

Arbeit ['arbaɪt] *f* (-;-en) work

arbeiten ['arbaɪtən] *tr & intr* work

Arbeiter ['arbaɪtər] *m* (-s;-) worker; **A. und Unternehmer** *pl* labor and management

Ar'beiterausstand *m* walkout, strike

Ar'beitergewerkschaft *f* labor union

Arbeiterin ['arbaɪtərɪn] *f* (-;-nen) working woman, working girl

Ar'beiterschaft *f* (-;) working class
Arbeitertum ['arbaɪtǝrtum] *n* (-s;) working class, workers
Ar'beitgeber –in §6 *mf* employer
Ar'beitnehmer –in §6 *mf* employee
arbeitsam ['arbaɪtzam] *adj* industrious
Ar'beitsanzug *m* overalls; (mil) fatigue clothes, fatigues
Ar'beitseinkommen *n* earned income
Ar'beitseinstellung *f* work stoppage
ar'beitsfähig *adj* fit for work
Ar'beitsgang *m* process; operation (*single step of a process*)
Ar'beitsgemeinschaft *f* team; (educ) workshop
Ar'beitsgerät *n* equipment, tools
Ar'beitskommando *n* (mil) work detail
Ar'beitskraft *f* labor force; Arbeitskräfte personnel
Ar'beitslager *n* work camp
Ar'beitsleistung *f* (work) quota; (*e-r Maschine, Fabrik*) output
Ar'beitslohn *m* wages, pay
ar'beitslos *adj* unemployed
Ar'beitslosenunterstützung *f* unemployment compensation
Ar'beitslosigkeit *f* unemployment
Ar'beitsmarkt *m* labor market
Ar'beitsminister *m* secretary of labor
Ar'beitsministerium *n* department of labor
Ar'beitsnachweis *m*, Ar'beitsnachweisstelle *f* employment agency
Ar'beitsniederlegung *f* walkout, strike
ar'beitsparend *adj* labor-saving
Ar'beitspause *f* break, rest period
Arbeitspferd *n* (& *fig*) workhorse
Ar'beitsplatz *m* job, place of employment
Ar'beitsrecht *n* labor law
ar'beitsscheu *adj* work-shy, lazy
Ar'beitsschicht *f* shift
Ar'beitsstätte *f* place of employment; workshop; yard
Ar'beitsstelle *f* job, position
Ar'beitstag *m* workday
Ar'beitsvermittlung *f* employment agency
Ar'beitsversäumnis *n* absenteeism
Ar'beitszeug *n* tools
Ar'beitszimmer *n* study; workroom
archaisch [ar'çaɪʃ] *adj* archaic
Archäologe [arçe·ɔ'logǝ] *m* (-n;-n) archaeologist
Archäologie [arçe·ɔlɔ'gi] *f* (-;) archaeology
Archäolog'in [arçe·ɔ'login] *f* (-;-nen) archaeologist
archäologisch [arçe·ɔ'logɪʃ] *adj* archaeological
Architekt –in [arçɪ'tekt(ɪn)] §7 *mf* architect
Architektur [arçɪtek'tur] *f* (-;-en) architecture
Ar·chiv [ar'çif] *n* (-[e]s;-chive ['çivǝ]) archives; (*für Zeitungen*) morgue
Areal [are·al] *n* (-s;-e) area
Are·na [a'rena] *f* (-;-nen [nǝn]) arena
arg [ark] *adj* (ärger ['ergǝr]; ärgste ['erkstǝ] §9) bad, evil, wicked; (coll) awful; (*schlimm*) grave; (*Raucher*) heavy ‖ **Arg** *n* (-s;) malice, cunning ‖ **Arge** §5 *m* Evil One ‖ §5 *n* evil
Argentinien [argen'tinjǝn] *n* (-s;) Argentina
Argentinier –in [argen'tinjǝr(ɪn)] §6 *mf* Argentinean
Ärger ['ergǝr] *m* (-s;) irritation; mit j-m Ä. haben have trouble with s.o.
är'gerlich *adj* (auf *acc* or über *acc*) annoyed (at); irritating, annoying
ärgern ['ergǝrn] *tr* annoy ‖ *ref* (über *acc*) be annoyed (at)
Ärgernis ['ergǝrnɪs] *n* (-ses;-se) scandal, offense; (*Mißstand*) nuisance
Arg'list *f* craft, cunning
arg'listig *adj* crafty, cunning
arg'los *adj* guileless; (*nichtsahnend*) unsuspecting
Argwohn ['arkvon] *m* (-s;) suspicion
argwöhnen ['arkvønǝn] *tr* suspect
argwöhnisch ['arkvønɪʃ] *adj* suspicious
Arie ['arjǝ] *f* (-;-n) aria
Arier –in ['arjǝr(ɪn)] §6 Aryan
arisch ['arɪʃ] *adj* Aryan
Aristokrat [arɪstǝ'krat] *m* (-en;-en) aristocrat
Aristokra·tie [arɪstǝkra'ti] *f* (-;-tien ['ti·ǝn]) aristocracy
Aristokratin [arɪstǝ'kratɪn] *f* (-;-nen) aristocrat
Arithmetik [arɪt'metɪk] *f* (-;) arithmetic
Arktis ['arktɪs] *f* (-;) Arctic
arktisch ['arktɪʃ] *adj* arctic
arm [arm] *adj* (ärmer ['ermǝr]; ärmste ['ermstǝ] §9 (an *dat*) poor in) ‖ **Arm** *m* (-[e]s;-e) arm; (*e-s Flusses*) branch
Armatur [arma'tur] *f* (-;-en) armature; Armaturen fittings, mountings
Armatu'renbrett *n* instrument panel; (aut) dashboard
Arm'band *n* (-[e]s;-̈er) bracelet; watchband; (*Armabzeichen*) brassard
Arm'banduhr *f* wrist watch
Arm'binde *f* brassard; (med) sling
Ar·mee [ar'me] *f* (-;-meen ['me·ǝn]) army
Ärmel ['ermǝl] *m* (-s;-) sleeve
Är'melaufschlag *m* cuff
Är'melkanal *m* English Channel
är'mellos *adj* sleeveless
Armen– [armǝn] *comb.fm.* for the poor
Ar'menhaus *n* poorhouse
Armenien [ar'menjǝn] *n* (-s;) Armenia
armenisch [ar'menɪʃ] *adj* Armenian
Ar'menpflege *f* public assistance
Ar'menunterstützung *f* public assistance, welfare
Armesün'dermiene *f* hangdog look
Arm'lehne *f* arm, armrest
Arm'leuchter *m* candelabrum
ärmlich ['ermlɪç] *adj* poor, humble
arm'selig *adj* poor, wretched; (*kläglich*) paltry
Armut ['armut] *f* (-;) poverty
Arm'zeichen *n* semaphore
Aro·ma [a'roma] *n* (-s;-men [mǝn], -mata [mata]) aroma
aromatisch [aro'matɪʃ] *adj* aromatic
Arrest [a'rest] *m* (-[e]s;-e) arrest;

(in der Schule) detention; (jur) impounding, seizure

Arsch [arʃ] *m* (-es;⁴e) (sl) ass

Arsch′backe *f* (sl) buttock

Arsch′kriecher *m* (sl) brown-noser

Arsch′lecker *m* (sl) brown-noser

Arsen [ar′zen] *n* (-s;) arsenic

Arsenal [arze′nɑl] *n* (-s;-e) arsenal

Art [ɑrt] *f* (-;-en) sort, kind; nature; *(Rasse)* race, breed; species; *(Weise)* manner; *(Verfahren)* procedure; *(Muster)* model; **das ist keine Art!** that's no way to behave!

art′eigen *adj* true to type

arten [′ɑrtən] *intr* (SEIN)—**a. nach** take after

Arterie [ar′terjə] *f* (-;-n) artery

artig [′ɑrtɪç] *adj (brav)* good, well-behaved; *(höflich)* polite

Artikel [ar′tikəl] *m* (-s;-) (com, gram, journ) article

Artillerie [artɪləˈriː] *f* (-;) artillery

Artillerie′aufklärer *m* artillery spotter

Artischocke [artɪˈʃɔkə] *f* (-;-n) artichoke

Artist -in [ar′tɪst(ɪn)] §7 *mf* artist; *(beim Zirkus)* performer

Arznei [arts′naɪ] *f* (-;-en) medicine, medication, drug

Arznei′kraut *n* herb, medicinal plant

Arznei′kunde *f*, **Arznei′kunst** *f* pharmaceutics; pharmacology

Arznei′mittel *n* medication

Arzt [artst] *m* (-[e]s;⁴e) doctor

Ärztin [′ertstɪn] *f* (-;-nen) doctor

ärztlich [′ertstlɪç] *adj* medical

As [as] *n* (Asses; Asse) ace ‖ *n* (-;-) (mus) A flat

Asbest [as′best] *m* (-[e]s;-e) asbestos

asch′bleich *adj* ashen, pale

Asche [′aʃə] *f* (-;-n) ash(es), cinders

Aschen- *comb.fm.* ash; cinder; funerary

A′schenbahn *f* cinder track

A′schenbecher *m* ashtray

Aschenbrödel [′aʃənbrødəl] *n* (-s;-) Cinderella; drudge

Aschermittwoch [aʃər′mɪtvɔx] *m* (-s;-e) Ash Wednesday

asch′fahl *adj* ashen, pale

äsen [′ezen] *intr* graze, feed

asiatisch [azi′atɪʃ] *adj* Asiatic

Asien [′ɑzjən] *n* (-s;) Asia

Asket [as′ket] *m* (-en;-en) ascetic

asketisch [as′ketɪʃ] *adj* ascetic

Asphalt [as′falt] *m* (-[e]s;) asphalt

asphaltieren [asfal′tirən] *tr* asphalt

Asphalt′pappe *f* tar paper

aß [as] *pret* of essen

Assistent -in [asɪs′tent(ɪn)] §7 *mf* assistant

Assistenz [asɪs′tents] *f* (-;-en) assistance

Assistenz′arzt *m*, **Assistenz′ärztin** *f* intern

Ast [ast] *m* (-es;⁴e) bough, branch; *(im Holz)* knot, knob

ästhetisch [es′tetɪç] *adj* esthetic(al)

Asthma [′astma] *n* (-s;) asthma

ast′rein *adj* free of knots; **nicht ganz a.** (coll) not quite kosher

Astrologe [astro′logə] *m* (-n;-n) astrologer

Astrologie [astrolɔ′gi] *f* (-;) astrology

Astronaut [astro′naut] *m* (-en;-en) astronaut

Astronom [astro′nom] *m* (-en;-en) astronomer

Astronomie [astronɔ′mi] (-;) astronomy

astronomisch [astro′nomɪʃ] *adj* astronomic(al)

Astrophysik [astrofy′zik] *f* (-;) astrophysics

Asyl [a′zyl] *n* (-[e]s;-e) asylum, sanctuary; *(Obdach)* shelter; **ohne A.** homeless

Atelier [ate′lje] *n* (-s;-s) studio

Atem [′ɑtəm] *m* (-s;) breath

A′tembeklemmung *f* shortness of breath

A′temholen *n* (-s;) respiration

a′temlos *adj* breathless

A′temnot *f* breathing difficulty

A′tempause *f* breathing spell

a′temraubend *adj* breath-taking

A′temzug *m* breath

Atheismus [ate′ɪsmus] *m* (-;) atheism

Atheist -in [ate′ɪst(ɪn)] §7 *mf* atheist

Äther [′etər] *m* (-s;) ether

Athlet [at′let] *m* (-en;-en) athlete

Athletik [at′letɪk] *f* (-;) athletics

Athletin [at′letɪn] *f* (-;-nen) athlete

athletisch [at′letɪʃ] *adj* athletic

Atlantik [at′lantɪk] *m* (-s;) Atlantic

At-las [′atlas] *m* (-′;) (myth) Atlas ‖ *m* (-lasses; -lanten [′lantən] & -lasse) atlas ‖ *m* (- & -lasses;-lasse) satin

atmen [′atmən] *tr & intr* breathe

Atmosphäre [atmo′sferə] *f* (-;-n) (& fig) atmosphere

atmosphärisch [atmo′sferɪʃ] *adj* atmospheric; **atmosphärische Störungen** (rad) static

At′mung *f* (-;) breathing

Atom [a′tom] *n* (-s;-e) atom

Atom- *comb. fm.* atom, atomic

Atom′abfall *m* fallout; atomic waste

atomar [ato′mar] *adj* atomic

Atom′bau *m* atomic structure

atom′betrieben *adj* atomic-powered

Atom′bombe *f* atomic bomb

Atom′bombenversuch *m* atomic test

Atom′-Epoche *f* atomic age

Atom′kern *m* atomic nucleus

Atom′müll *m* atomic waste

Atom′regen *m* fallout

Atom′schutt *m* atomic waste

ätsch [etʃ] *interj* (to express gloating) serves you right!, good for you!

Attentat [aten′tat] *n* (-s;-e) attempt *(on s.o.'s life)*; assassination

Attentäter -in [aten′tetər(ɪn)] §6 *mf* assailant, would-be assassin; assassin

Attest [a′test] *n* (-es;-e) certificate

attestieren [ates′tirən] *tr* attest (to)

Attrappe [a′trapə] *f* (-;-n) dummy

Attribut [atri′but] *n* (-[e]s;-e) attribute; (gram) attributive

atzen [′atsən] *tr* feed

ätzen [′etsən] *tr* corrode; (med) cauterize (typ) etch

ät′zend *adj* corrosive; caustic

Au [au] *f* (-;-en) (poet) mead, meadow

au *interj* owl, ouch!; oh!

Aubergine [ober'ʒin(ə)] *f* (-;-n) eggplant

auch [aux] *adv* also, too; (*selbst*) even

Audienz [au'djents] *f* (-;-en) audience; (*jur*) hearing

auf [auf] *adv* up; **auf und ab** up and down; **von Kind auf** from childhood on ‖ *prep* (*dat*) on, upon; **auf der ganzen Welt** in the whole world; **auf der Universität** at the university ‖ *prep* (*acc*) on; up; to; **auf den Bahnhof gehen** go to the station; **auf deutsch** in German; **drei aufs Dutzend** three to a dozen; **es geht auf vier Uhr zu** it's going on four; **Monat auf Monat** verging month after month passed ‖ *interj* get up! ‖ **Auf** *n*—**das Auf und Nieder** the ups and downs

auf'arbeiten *tr* (*Rückstände*) catch up on; (*verbrauchen*) use up; (*erneuern*) renovate; (*mach*) recondition ‖ *ref* work one's way up

auf'atmen *intr* breathe a sigh of relief

aufbahren ['aufbɑːrən] *tr* lay out

Auf'bau *m* (-[e]s;) construction; structure; organization; (*Anlage*) arrangement, setup; (*chem*) synthesis ‖ *m* (-[e]s;-ten) structure; (*aer*) framework; (*aut*) body; (*naut*) superstructure

auf'bauen *tr* erect; (*Organization*) establish; (*chem*) synthesize; (*mach*) assemble ‖ *ref*—**er baute sich vor mir auf** he planted himself in front of me; **sich** [*dat*] **e-e Existenz a.** make a life for oneself

auf'bäumen *ref* rear; (fig) rebel

auf'bauschen *tr* puff up; (fig) exaggerate

auf'begehren *intr* flare up; (gegen) protest (against), rebel (against)

auf'behalten §90 *tr* keep on; keep open

auf'bekommen §99 *tr* (*Tür*) get open; (*Knoten*) loosen; (*Hausaufgabe*) be assigned

auf'bereiten *tr* prepare, process

auf'bessern *tr* (*Gehalt*) improve, raise

auf'bewahren *tr* keep, store; **das Gepäck a. lassen** check one's baggage

auf'bieten §58 *tr* summon; (*Brautpaar*) announce the banns of; (mil) call up

auf'binden §58 *tr* tie up; (*lösen*) untie; **j-m etw a.** put s.th. over on s.o.

auf'blähen *tr* inflate, distend

auf'blasen §61 *tr* inflate ‖ *ref* get puffed up

auf'bleiben §62 *intr* (SEIN) (*Tür*) stay open; (*wachen*) stay up

auf'blenden *intr* turn on the high beam

auf'blicken *intr* glance up

auf'blitzen *intr* (HABEN & SEIN) flash

auf'blühen *intr* (SEIN) begin to bloom

auf'bocken *tr* (aut) jack up

auf'brauchen *tr* use up

auf'brausen *intr* (HABEN & SEIN) bubble, seethe; (*Wind*) roar; (fig) flare up

auf'brausend *adj* effervescent; irascible

auf'brechen §64 *tr* break up; break open; (hunt) eviscerate ‖ *intr* (SEIN) burst open; (*fortgehen*) (nach) set out (for)

auf'bringen §65 *tr* bring up; (*Geld, Truppen*) raise; (*Schiff*) capture; (*Kraft*) gather; (*Mut*) get up; (*erzürnen*) infuriate

Auf'bruch *m* departure

auf'brühen *tr* bring to a boil

auf'bügeln *tr* iron, press; refresh (*one's knowledge of s.th.*)

aufbürden ['aufbʏrdən] *tr*—**j-m etw a.** saddle s.o. with s.th.

auf'decken *tr* uncover; (*Bett*) turn down; (*Tischtuch*) spread

auf'drängen *tr* force open; **j-m etw a.** force s.th. on s.o.

auf'drehen *tr* turn up; (*Uhr*) wind; (*Hahn*) turn on; (*Schraube*) unscrew; (*Strick*) untwist ‖ *intr* (*Wagen*) increase speed; (coll) step on it, get a move on

auf'dringlich *adj* pushy; (*Farben*) gaudy

Auf'druck *m* print, imprint

auf'drücken *tr* impress, imprint, affix; (*öffnen*) squeeze open

aufeinan'der *adv* one after the other

Aufeinan'derfolge *f* succession; series

aufeinan'derfolgen *intr* (SEIN) follow one another

aufeinan'derfolgend *adj* successive

Aufenthalt ['aufenthalt] *m* (-[e]s;-e) holdup, delay; ohne A. nonstop

Auf'enthaltsgenehmigung *f* residence permit

Auf'enthaltsort *m* (*Wohnsitz*) residence; (*Verbleib*) whereabouts

Auf'enthaltsraum *m* lounge

auf'erlegen *tr* impose ‖ *ref*—**sich** [*dat*] **die Pflicht a.** zu (*inf*) make it one's duty to (*inf*); **sich** [*dat*] **Zwang a.** müssen have to restrain oneself

auf'erstehen §146 *intr* (SEIN) rise (from the dead)

Auf'erstehung *f* (-;) resurrection

auf'erwecken *tr* raise from the dead

auf'erziehen §163 *tr* bring up, raise

auf'essen §70 *tr* eat up

auf'fädeln *tr* (*Perlen*) string

auf'fahren §71 *tr* (*Fahrzeuge*) park; (*Geschütze*) bring up; (*Wein, Speisen*) serve up ‖ *intr* (SEIN) rise, mount; (*im Auto*) pull up; (*in Erregung*) jump (up); (*arti*) move into position; **a. auf** (*acc*) run into

Auf'fahrt *f* ascent; (*Zufahrt*) driveway

auf'fallen §72 *intr* (SEIN) be conspicuous; **j-m a.** strike s.o.

auf'fallend, auf'fällig *adj* striking; noticeable; (*Farben*) loud, gaudy

auf'fangen §73 *tr* (*Ball, Worte*) catch; (*Briefe, Nachrichten*) intercept

auf'fassen *tr* comprehend; (*deuten*) interpret; (*Perlen*) string

Auf'fassung *f* (-;-en) understanding; interpretation; (*Meinung*) view

auf'finden §59 *tr* find (*after searching*)

auf'fliegen §57 *intr* (SEIN) fly up; (*Tür*) fly open; (*scheitern*) fail; **a. lassen** break up (*e.g., a gang*)

auf'fordern *tr* call upon, ask

Auf'forderung *f* (-;-en) invitation; (jur) summons

auf′frischen *tr* freshen up, touch up
auf′führen *tr* (Bau) erect; (Schauspiel) present; (eintragen) enter; (Zeugen) produce; (anführen) cite; (mil) post; **einzeln a.** itemize ‖ *ref* behave, act
Auf′führung *f* (-;-en) erection; performance; entry; specification; behavior
auf′füllen *tr* fill up
Auf′gabe *f* task, job; (e-s Briefes) mailing; (des Gepäcks) checking; (e-r Bestellung) placing; (e-s Amtes, e-s Geschäfts) giving up; (educ) homework; (jur) waiver; (math) problem; (mil) assignment
auf′gabeln *tr* (& coll) pick up
Auf′gang *m* ascent; (Treppe) stairs; (astr) rising
auf′geben §80 *tr* give up; (Amt) resign; (Post) mail; (Gepäck) check in; (Anzeige) place; (Preis) quote; (Arbeit) assign; (Telegramm) send
auf′geblasen *adj* (fig) uppity
Auf′gebot *n* public notice; (eccl) banns; (mil) call-up
auf′gebracht *adj* angry, irate
auf′gedonnert *adj* (coll) dolled up
auf′gehen §82 *intr* (SEIN) rise; (Tür) open; (Pflanzen) come up; (arith) go into; **genau a.** come out exactly
auf′geklärt *adj* enlightened
auf′geknöpft *adj* (coll) chatty
auf′gekratzt *adj* (coll) chipper
Auf′geld *n* surcharge; premium
auf′gelegt *adj* (zu) disposed (to)
auf′geräumt *adj* (fig) good-humored
auf′geschlossen *adj* open-minded; (für) receptive (to)
auf′geschmissen *adj* (coll) stuck
auf′gestaut *adj* pent-up
auf′geweckt *adj* smart, bright
auf′geworfen *adj* (Lippen) pouting; (Nase) turned-up
auf′gießen §76 *tr* (auf acc) pour (on); (Tee, Kaffee) make, brew
auf′graben §87 *tr* dig up
auf′greifen §88 *tr* pick up; (Dieb) catch; (fig) take up
auf′haben §89 *tr* (Hut) have on; (Tür, Mund) have open; (Aufgabe) have to do
auf′hacken *tr* hoe up
auf′haken *tr* unhook
auf′halten §90 *tr* hold up; (Tür) hold open; (anhalten) stop, delay ‖ *ref* stay; (wohnen) live; **sich über etw a.** find fault with s.th.
Auf′hängeleine *f* clothesline
auf′hängen §92 *tr* hang up; **j-m etw a.** push s.th. on s.o.; (Wertloses) palm s.th. off on s.o.
auf′häufen *tr* & *ref* pile up
auf′heben §94 *tr* lift up, pick up; (bewahren) preserve; (ungültig machen) cancel; (Gesetz) repeal; (ausgleichen) cancel out, offset; (Strafe, Belagerung) lift; **gut aufgehoben sein** be in good hands
auf′heitern *tr* cheer up ‖ *ref* cheer up; (Gesicht) brighten; (Wetter) clear up
auf′hellen *ref* & *intr* brighten
auf′hetzen *tr* incite, egg on

auf′holen *tr* hoist; (Verspätung) make up for ‖ *intr* catch up
auf′horchen *intr* prick up one's ears
auf′hören *intr* stop, quit
auf′jauchzen *intr* shout for joy
auf′kaufen *tr* buy up; (Markt) corner
auf′klären *tr* clear up; enlighten; (mil) reconnoitre ‖ *ref* clear up; (Gesicht) light up, brighten
Auf′klärer *m* (-s;-) (aer) reconnaissance plane; (mil) scout
Auf′klärung *f* (-;-en) explanation; enlightenment; (mil) reconnaissance
Auf′klärungsbuch *n* sex-education book
Auf′klärungsspähtrupp *m* reconnaissance patrol
auf′kleben *tr* (auf acc) paste (onto)
auf′klinken *tr* unlatch
auf′knacken *tr* crack open
auf′knöpfen *tr* unbutton
auf′knüpfen *tr* (lösen) untie; (hängen) (coll) string up
auf′kochen *tr* & *intr* boil
auf′kommen §99 *intr* (SEIN) come up, rise; (Gedanke) occur; (Mode) come into fashion; (Schiff) appear on the horizon; **a. für** answer for; (Kosten) defray; **a. gegen** stand up against, cope with; **a. von** recover from ‖ **Aufkommen** *n* (-s;) rise; recovery
auf′krempeln *tr* roll up
auf′kreuzen *intr* (coll) show up
auf′lachen *intr* burst out laughing
auf′laden §103 *tr* load up; (Batterie) charge ‖ *ref*—**sich** [dat] **etw a.** saddle oneself with s.th.
Auf′lage *f* edition, printing; (e-r Zeitung) circulation; (Steuer) tax; (Stütze) rest, support
auf′lassen §104 *tr* leave open; (Fabrik, Bergwerk) abandon
Auf′lauf *m* gathering, crowd; (Tumult) riot; (com) accumulation; (culin) soufflé
auf′laufen §105 *intr* (SEIN) rise; (anwachsen) accrue; (Schiff) get stranded; (Panzer) get stuck
auf′leben *intr* (SEIN) revive
auf′lecken *tr* lick up
auf′legen *tr* (auf acc) put (on); (Steuer) impose; (Hörer) hang up; (Buch) publish; (Karten) lay on the table; (Liste) make available for inspection; (Anleihe) float; (Faß Bier) put on ‖ *intr* (telp) hang up
auf′lehnen *tr* (auf acc) lean (on) ‖ *ref* (auf acc) lean (on); (gegen) rebel (against)
Auf′lehnung *f* (-;-en) rebellion; resistance
auf′lesen §107 *tr* pick up, gather
auf′liegen §108 *intr* (auf dat) lie (on); (zur Ansicht) be displayed
auf′lockern *tr* loosen; (Eintönigkeit, Vortrag) break (up)
auf′lösbar *adj* soluble; solvable
auf′lösen *tr* untie; (öffnen) loosen; (entwirren) disentangle; (Versammlung) break up; (Heer) disband; (Ehe) dissolve; (Verbindung) sever; (Firma) liquidate; (Rätsel) solve;

(*zerlegen*) break down; dissolve; (*entziffern*) decode; **ganz aufgelöst** all out of breath

Auf′lösung f (-;-en) solution; disentanglement; (*e-r Versammlung, Ehe*) breakup; (*Zerfall*) disintegration; (*von Beziehungen*) severance; (com) liquidation

auf′machen tr open (up); (*Geschäft*) open; (*Dampf*) get up; (coll) do up (*e.g., big, tastefully*) || ref (*Wind*) rise; (nach) set out (for)

Auf′machung f (-;-en) layout, format; (*Kleidung*) outfit

Auf′marsch m parade; (mil) concentration; (*zum Gefecht*) (mil) deployment

auf′marschieren intr (SEIN) parade; (*strategisch*) assemble; (*taktisch*) deploy

auf′merken tr (auf acc) pay attention (to)

aufmerksam [′aufmerkzam] adj (auf acc) attentive (to)

Auf′merksamkeit f (-;) attention

auf′möbeln tr (coll) dress up; (*anherrschen*) (sl) chew out; (*aufmuntern*) (coll) pep up || ref (coll) doll up

auf′muntern tr cheer up

Auf′nahme f (-;-n) taking up; (*Empfang*) reception (*Zulassung*) admission; (*von Beziehungen*) establishment; (*Inventur*) stock-taking; (electron) recording; (phot) photograph

Auf′nahmeapparat m camera; recorder

Auf′nahmegerät n camera; recorder

Auf′nahmeprüfung f entrance exam

auf′nehmen §116 tr take up; (*erfassen*) grasp; (*Diktat*) take down; (*Gast*) receive; (*Inventar*) take; (*Geld*) borrow; (*Anleihe*) float; (*Spur*) pick up; (*Beziehungen*) establish; (*eintragen*) enter; (*durch Tonband, Schallplatte*) record; (geog) map out; (phot) take

auf′opfern tr offer up, sacrifice

auf′päpeln tr spoon-feed

auf′passen intr pay attention; look out; **paß auf!** watch out!

auf′pflanzen tr set up; (*Seitengewehr*) fix

auf′platzen intr (SEIN) burst (open)

auf′polieren tr polish up

auf′prägen tr (auf acc) (& fig) impress (on)

auf′prallen intr (auf acc) crash (into)

auf′pumpen tr pump up

auf′putschen tr incite; (coll) pep up

auf′putzen tr dress up; clean up || ref dress up

auf′raffen tr pick up || ref stand up; (fig) pull oneself together

auf′ragen intr tower, stand high

auf′räumen tr (*Zimmer*) straighten up; (*wegräumen*) clear away || intra—a. **mit** do away with, get rid of

Auf′räumungsarbeiten pl clearance

auf′rechnen tr add up; (acct) balance

auf′recht adj upright, erect

auf′rechterhalten §90 tr maintain

auf′regen tr excite, stir up; (*unruhig machen*) disturb, upset

Auf′regung f (-;-en) excitement

auf′reiben §62 tr rub off; (*wundreiben*) rub sore; (*vertilgen*) destroy; (*Heer*) grind up; (*Kräfte*) sap; (*Nerven*) fray || ref worry onself to death

auf′reibend adj wearing, exhausting

auf′reihen tr string, thread

auf′reißen §53 tr tear open; (*Straße*) tear up; (*Tür*) fling open; (*Augen*) open wide; (*zeichnen*) sketch || intr (SEIN) split open, crack

auf′reizen tr provoke, incite; (*stark erregen*) excite

auf′reizend adj provoking, annoying; (*Rede*) inflammatory; (*Anblick*) sexy

auf′richten tr erect, set up; (*trösten*) comfort || ref sit up

auf′richtig adj upright, sincere

Auf′richtigkeit f sincerity

auf′riegeln tr unbolt

Auf′riß m front view

auf′rollen tr roll up; (*entfalten*) unroll (to)

auf′rücken intr (SEIN) advance; (zu) be promoted (to)

Auf′ruf m (*Aufschrei*) outcry; (*Aufforderung*) call; (mil) call-up

auf′rufen §122 tr call on; (*appellieren an*) appeal to; (*Banknoten*) call in

Auf′ruhr m uproar; (*Tumult*) riot

auf′rühren tr stir up

aufrührerisch [′aufryːrərɪʃ] adj inflammatory, rebellious; (mil) mutinous

auf′runden tr round out

auf′rüsten tr & intr arm; rearm

Auf′rüstung f (-;-en) rearmament

auf′rütteln tr wake up (*by shaking*)

auf′sagen tr recite; (*ein Ende machen mit*) terminate

auf′sammeln tr gather up

aufsässig [′aufzesɪç] adj hostile; (*widerspenstig*) rebellious

Auf′satz m superstructure; (*auf dem Tische*) centerpiece; (*Schularbeit*) essay, composition; (*in der Zeitung*) article; (golf) tee; (mil) gun sight

auf′saugen §125 tr suck up; absorb

auf′schauen intr look up

auf′scheuchen tr scare up

auf′scheuern tr scrape

auf′schichten tr stack (up), pile (up)

auf′schieben §130 tr push up; (*Tür*) push open; (*verschieben*) postpone

auf′schießen §76 intr (SEIN) shoot up

Auf′schlag m (auf acc) striking (upon), impact (on); (*an Kleidung*) cuff, lapel; (*Steuer-*) surtax; (*Preis-*) price hike; (tennis) service, serve

auf′schlagen §132 tr (*öffnen*) open; (*Ei*) crack; (*Karte, Ärmel*) turn up; (*Zelt*) pitch; (*Wohnung*) take up; (*Preis*) raise; (*Knie, usw.*) bruise; (*Ball*) serve || intr (SEIN) (*Tür*) fly open; (*Flugzeug*) crash; (*Ball*) bounce; (tennis) serve

auf′schließen §76 tr unlock, open || ref (dat) pour out one's heart (to) || intr (mil) close ranks

auf′schlitzen tr slit open

Auf′schluß m information; (chem) decomposition

auf′schlußreich adj informative

auf′schnallen tr buckle; unbuckle

auf′schnappen tr snap up; (*Nachricht*) pick up

Auf′schneidemaschine *f* meat slicer
auf′schneiden §106 *tr* cut open;
  (*Fleisch*) slice ‖ *intr* (coll) talk big
Auf′schnelder *m* boaster
Auf′schnitt *m*—kalter A. cold cuts
auf′schnüren *tr* untie, undo
auf′schrauben *tr* unscrew; (auf *acc*)
  screw (on)
auf′schrecken §134 *tr* startle; (*Wild*)
  scare up ‖ *intr* (SEIN) be startled
Auf′schrei *m* scream, yell; (fig) outcry
auf′schreiben §62 *tr* write down
auf′schreien §135 *intr* scream, yell
Auf′schrift *f* inscription; (*Anschrift*)
  address; (*e-r Flasche*) label
Auf′schub *m* deferment, postponement; (*Verzögerung*) delay; (jur) stay
auf′schürfen *tr* scrape; (*Bein*) skin
auf′schwellen §119 *intr* (SEIN) swell
  up; (*Fluß*) rise
auf′schwemmen *tr* bloat
auf′schwingen §142 *ref* (& fig) soar;
  sich a., etw zu tun bring oneself to
  do s.th.
Auf′schwung *m* (& fig) upswing
auf′sehen §138 *intr* look up ‖ **Aufse-**
  hen *n* (–s) sensation, stir
auf′sehenerregend *adj* sensational
Auf′seher –in §6 *mf* supervisor; (*im
  Museum*) guard; (*im Geschäft*) floorwalker
auf′sein §139 *intr* (SEIN) be up; (*Tür*)
  be open
auf′setzen *tr* put on; (*aufrichten*) set
  up; (*schriftlich*) compose, draft ‖
  ref sit up ‖ *intr* (aer) touch down;
  (rok) splash down
Auf′sicht *f* inspection, supervision
Auf′sichtsbeamte *m*, **Auf′sichtsbeam-**
  tin *f* inspector, supervisor
Auf′sichtsbehörde *f* control board
Auf′sichtsdame *f* floorwalker
Auf′sichtsherr *m* floorwalker
Auf′sichtsrat *m* board of trustees;
  (*Mitglied*) trustee
auf′sitzen §144 *intr* (SEIN) sit up; (auf
  dat) sit (on), rest (on); j-m a. be
  taken in by s.o.; j-n a. lassen stand
  s.o. up
auf′spannen *tr* stretch, spread; (*Regenschirm*) open
auf′sparen *tr* save (up)
auf′speichern *tr* store (up)
auf′sperren *tr* unlock; (*Augen, Tür*)
  open wide
auf′spielen *tr* strike up ‖ *ref* (mit)
  show off (with) ‖ *intr* play dance
  music
auf′spießen *tr* spear, pierce
auf′sprengen *tr* force open; (mit
  Sprengstoff) blow up
auf′springen §142 *intr* (SEIN) jump up;
  (*Tür*) fly open; (*Ball*) bounce;
  (*Haut*) chap, crack
auf′spritzen *tr* (*Farbe*) spray on; (sl)
  shoot up ‖ *intr* (SEIN) squirt up
auf′sprudeln *intr* (SEIN) bubble (up)
auf′spulen *tr* wind up
auf′spüren *tr* track down, ferret out
auf′stacheln *tr* goad; (fig) stir up
auf′stampfen *intr*—mit dem Fuß a.
  stamp one's foot
Auf′stand *m* insurrection, uprising

aufständisch [′aʊfʃtɛndɪʃ] *adj* insurgent ‖ **Aufständischen** *pl* insurgents
auf′stapeln *tr* stack up, pile up
auf′stechen §64 *tr* puncture; (surg)
  lance
auf′stecken *tr* (*Flagge*) plant; (*Haar*)
  pin up; (coll) give up; j-m ein Licht
  a. enlighten s.o.
auf′stehen §146 *intr* (HABEN) stand
  open ‖ *intr* (SEIN) stand up, get up;
  (*gegen*) revolt (against)
auf′steigen §148 *intr* (SEIN) climb;
  (*Reiter*) mount; (*Rauch*) rise; (*Gewitter*) come up; (*Tränen*) well up;
  a. auf (*acc*) get on
auf′stellen *tr* set up, put up; (*Beispiel*)
  set; (*Behauptung*) make; (*Wachposten*) post; (*Bauten*) erect; (*Leiter*)
  raise (*Waren*) display; (*Maschine*)
  assemble; (*als Kandidaten*) nominate;
  (*Regel, Problem*) state; (*Lehre*) propound; (*Rekord*) set; (*Liste*) make
  out; (*Rechnung*) draw up, make out;
  (*Stühle*) arrange; (*Falle*) set; (*Bedingungen, Grundsätze*) lay down;
  (*Beweis*) furnish ‖ *ref* station oneself
Auf′stellung *f* (–;–en) erection; assertion; list, schedule; (mil) formation;
  (pol) nomination; (sport) lineup
auf′stemmen *tr* pry open ‖ *ref* prop
  oneself up
Auf′stieg *m* climb; (*Steigung*) slope;
  (fig) advancement
auf′stöbern *tr* ferret out; (fig) unearth
auf′stoßen §150 *tr* push open ‖ *ref*—
  sich [*dat*] das Knie a. skin one's
  knee ‖ *intr* (HABEN) (sl) belch ‖ *intr*
  (HABEN & SEIN) bump, touch; (*Schiff*)
  touch bottom ‖ *intr* (SEIN)—j-m a.
  strike s.o., cross s.o.'s mind
auf′streichen §85 *tr* (*Butter*) spread
auf′streuen *tr* (auf *acc*) sprinkle (on)
Auf′strich *m* upstroke; (*auf Brot*)
  spread
auf′stützen *tr* prop up
auf′suchen *tr* search for; (*nachschlagen*) look up; (*Ort*) visit; (*aufsam-
  meln*) pick up; (*Arzt*) go to see
Auf′takt *m* upbeat; (fig) prelude
auf′tauchen *intr* (SEIN) turn up, appear; (*Frage*) crop up; (*U-Boot*) surface; (*Gerücht*) arise
auf′tauen *tr* & *intr* (SEIN) thaw
auf′teilen *tr* divide up
Auftrag [′aʊftrak] *m* (–[e]s;⁔e) (*Anweisung*) orders, instructions; (*Bestellung*) order, commission; (*Sendung*)
  mission; in A. von on behalf of
auf′tragen §132 *tr* instruct, order;
  (*Speise*) serve; (*Farben, Butter*) put
  on; (*Kleidungsstück*) wear out;
  (surv) plot; j-m etw a. impose s.th.
  on s.o. ‖ *intr*—dick (or stark) a. (sl)
  put it on thick
Auf′traggeber –in §6 *mf* employer;
  (*Besteller*) client, customer
Auf′tragsformular *n* order blank
auf′tragsgemäß, auf′trag(s)mäßig *adv*
  as ordered, according to instructions
auf′treffen §151 *intr* (SEIN) strike
Auf′treffpunkt *m* point of impact
auf′treiben §62 *tr* (*Staub; Geld*) raise;

(*Wild*) flush; (*aufblähen*) distend; (*Teig*) cause to rise

auf'trennen *tr* rip, undo, unstitch

auf'treten §152 *tr* (*Tür*) kick open ‖ *intr* (SEIN) step, tread; (*erscheinen*) appear; (*handeln*) act, behave; (*eintreten*) occur, crop up; (*pathol*) break out; (*theat*) enter ‖ **Auftreten** *n* (-s;) appearance; occurrence; behavior; **sicheres A.** poise

Auf'trieb *m* drive; buoyancy; (aer & fig) lift; (agr) cattle drive; **j—m A. geben** encourage s.o.

Auf'tritt *m* (*Streit*) scene, row; (theat) entrance (*of an actor*); (theat) scene

auf'trumpfen *intr* play a higher trump; **gegen j—n** a. go to s.o. better

auf'tun §154 *tr* & *ref* open

auf'türmen *tr* & *intr* pile up

auf'wachen *intr* (SEIN) awaken, wake up

auf'wachsen §155 *intr* (SEIN) grow up

auf'wallen *intr* (SEIN) boil, seethe; (fig) surge, rise up

Auf'wallung *f* (-;-en) (fig) outburst

Aufwand ['aufvant] *m* (-[e]s;⸚e) (an *dat*) expenditure (of); (*Prunk*) show

auf'wärmen *tr* warm up; (fig) drag up

Auf'wartefrau *f* cleaning woman

auf'warten *intr* (*dat*) wait on; a. **mit** oblige with, offer

Auf'wärter -in §6 *mf* attendant ‖ *f* cleaning woman

aufwärts ['aufverts] *adv* upward(s)

Auf'wärtshaken *m* (box) uppercut

Auf'wartung *f* (-;) attendance; (*bei Tisch*) service; (*Besuch*) call; **j—m seine A. machen** pay one's respects to s.o.

Aufwasch ['aufvaʃ] *m* (-es;) washing; dirty dishes

auf'waschen §158 *tr* & *intr* wash up

auf'wecken *tr* wake (up)

auf'weichen *tr* soften; soak ‖ *intr* (SEIN) become soft; become sodden

auf'weisen §118 *tr* produce, show

auf'wenden §140 *tr* spend, expend; **Mühe a.** take pains

auf'werfen §160 *tr* throw up; (*Tür*) fling open; (*Graben*) dig; (*Frage*) raise ‖ *ref*—**sich a.** zu set oneself up as

auf'wickeln *tr* wind up; (*Haar*) curl; (*loswickeln*) unwind

aufwiegeln ['aufvigəln] *tr* instigate

Aufwiegler -in ['aufviglər(ɪn)] §6 *mf* instigator

aufwieglerisch ['aufviglərɪʃ] *adj* inflammatory

Auf'wind *m* updraft

auf'winden §59 *tr* wind up; (*Anker*) weigh ‖ *ref* coil up

auf'wirbeln *tr* (*Staub*) raise; **viel Staub a.** (coll) make quite a stir

auf'wischen *tr* wipe up

auf'wühlen *tr* dig up; (*Wasser*) churn up; (fig) stir up

auf'zählen *tr* enumerate, itemize

auf'zäumen *tr* bridle

auf'zehren *tr* consume

auf'zeichnen *tr* make a sketch of; (*notieren*) write down, record

aufzeigen *tr* point out

auf'ziehen §163 *tr* pull up; (*öffnen*) pull open; (*Uhr*) wind; (*Saite*) put on; (*Perlen*) string; (*Kind*) bring up; (*Tier*) breed; (*Pflanzen*) grow; (*Flagge, Segel*) hoist (*Anker*) weigh; (*Veranstaltung*) arrange, organize; (coll) kid ‖ *intr* (SEIN) approach, pull up

Auf'zucht *f* breeding, raising

Auf'zug *m* elevator; (e-r *Uhr*) winder; (*Aufmarsch*) parade, procession; (gym) chin-up; (theat) act

auf'zwingen §142 *tr*—**j—m etw a.** force s.th. on s.o.; **j—m seinen Willen a.** impose one's will on s.o.

Augapfel ['aukapfəl] *m* eyeball; (fig) apple of the eye

Auge ['augə] *n* (-s;-n) eye; (*auf Würfeln*) dot; (hort) bud; (typ) face

äugeln ['ɔɪgəln] *intr.*—**ä. mit** wink at

Augen- [augən] *comb.fm.* eye, of the eye(s), in the eye(s); visual; (anat) ocular, optic(al)

Au'genblick *m* moment, instant

au'genblicklich *adj* momentary; (*sofortig*) immediate, instantaneous

Au'genblicksmensch *m* hedonist; impulsive person

Au'genbraue *f* eyebrow

Au'genbrauenstift *m* eyebrow pencil

au'genfällig *adj* conspicuous, obvious

Au'genhöhle *f* eye socket

Au'genlicht *n* eyesight

Au'genlid *n* eyelid

Au'genmaß *n* sense of proportion; **ein gutes A. haben** have a keen eye; **nach dem A.** by eye

Au'genmerk *n* attention

Au'gennerv *m* optic nerve

Au'genschein *m* inspection; (*Anschein*) appearances; **in A. nehmen** inspect

au'genscheinlich *adj* obvious

Au'genstern *m* pupil; iris

Au'gentäuschung *f* optical illusion

Au'gentrost *m* sight for sore eyes

Au'genwasser *n* eyewash

Au'genweide *f* sight for sore eyes

Au'genwimper *f* eyelash

Au'genwinkel *m* corner of the eye

Au'genzeuge *m*, **Au'genzeugin** *f* eyewitness

-äugig [ɔɪgɪç] *comb.fm.* -eyed

August [au'gust] *m* (-[e]s & -;-e) August

Auktion [auk'tsjon] *f* (-;-en) auction

Auktio·nator [auktsjo'nator] *m* (-s; -natoren [na'torən]) auctioneeer

auktionieren [auktsjo'nirən] *tr* auction off, put up for auction

Au·la ['aula] *f* (-;-s & -len [lən]) auditorium

aus [aus] *adv* out; **von ... aus** from, e.g., **vom Fenster aus** from the window ‖ *prep* (*dat*) out of, from; because of

aus'arbeiten *tr* elaborate; finish ‖ *ref* work out, take physical exercise

Aus'arbeitung *f* (-;-en) elaboration; (*schriftlich*) composition; (*körperlich*) workout; (tech) finish

aus'arten *intr* (SEIN) get out of hand; (in *acc*) degenerate (into)

aus'atmen *tr* exhale

aus′baden tr (coll) take the rap for

aus′baggern tr dredge

Aus′bau m (-[e]s;) completion; expansion, development

aus′bauen tr complete; (erweitern) expand, develop

aus′bedingen tr stipulate

aus′bessern tr repair; (Kleid) mend; (Bild) retouch

aus′beulen tr take the dents out of

Aus′beute f (Ertrag) output; (Gewinn) profit, gain

ausbeuten ['ausbɔɪtən] tr exploit

aus′biegen §57 tr bend out ‖ intr (SEIN) curve; (dat, vor dat) make way (for)

aus′bilden tr develop; (lehren) train, educate; (mil) drill ‖ ref train

Aus′bilder m (mil) drill instructor

aus′bitten §60 ref—sich [dat] etw a. ask for s.th.; insist on s.th.

aus′bleiben §62 intr (SEIN) stay out; stay away; be missing

aus′bleichen §85 tr & intr (SEIN) bleach; fade

aus′blenden tr (cin, rad) fade-out

Aus′blick m (auf acc) view (of); (fig) outlook

aus′bohren tr bore (out), drill (out)

aus′borgen ref—sich [dat] etw a. von borrow s.th. from

aus′brechen §64 tr break off ‖ intr (SEIN) (aus) break out (of)

aus′breiten tr & ref spread; extend

aus′brennen §97 tr burn out, gut; (Sonne) parch; (med) cauterize ‖ intr (SEIN) burn out; (Haus) be gutted

Aus′bruch m outbreak; (e-s Vulkans) eruption; (e-s Gefangenen) breakout; (des Gelächters) outburst

aus′brüten tr incubate; hatch

Ausbuchtung ['ausbuxtuŋ] f (-;-en) bulge

ausbuddeln ['ausbudəln] tr (coll) dig out

aus′bügeln tr iron out

Aus′bund m (von) very embodiment (of)

ausbürgern ['ausbʏrgərn] tr expatriate

aus′bürsten tr brush out

Aus′dauer f perseverance

aus′dauern intr persevere, persist

aus′dauernd adj persevering; (bot) perennial

aus′dehnen tr & ref stretch, expand; (Organ) dilate

aus′denken §66 tr think out; think up; nicht auszudenken inconceivable

aus′deuten tr interpret, explain

aus′dienen intr serve one's time

aus′dorren intr (SEIN) dry up; wither

aus′dörren tr dry up, parch

aus′drehen tr turn out; turn off

Aus′druck m expression

aus′drücken tr squeeze out; (fig) express

ausdrücklich ['ausdryklɪç] adj express, explicit

aus′druckslos adj expressionless

aus′drucksvoll adj expressive

Aus′drucksweise f way of speaking

aus′dünsten tr exhale, give off ‖ intr evaporate; (schwitzen) sweat

auseinan′der adv apart; separately

auseinan′derfallen §72 intr (SEIN) fall apart

auseinan′dergehen §82 intr (SEIN) part; (Versammlung) break up; (Meinungen) differ; (Wege) branch off; (auseinanderfallen) come apart

auseinan′derhalten §90 tr keep apart

auseinan′derlaufen §105 intr (SEIN) (Menge) disperse; (Wege) diverge

auseinan′dernehmen §116 tr take apart

auseinan′dersetzen tr explain ‖ ref—sich mit etw a. come to grips with s.th.; sich mit j–m a. have it out with s.o.; (gütlich) come to an understanding with s.o.

Auseinan′dersetzung f explanation; (Erörterung) discussion, controversy; (Übereinkommen) arrangement

aus′erkoren adj chosen; predestined

aus′erlesen adj choice ‖ §107 tr choose, select

aus′ersehen §138 tr destine

aus′erwählen tr pick out, choose

aus′fahren §71 tr (Straße, Gleis) wear out; (aer) let down; den Motor a. (coll) open it up; die Kurve a. not cut the corner ‖ intr (SEIN) drive out; (naut) put to sea; (rr) pull out

Aus′fahrt f departure; exit; (Spazierfahrt) ride, drive; (Torweg) gateway

Aus′fall m falling out; (Ergebnis) result; (Verlust) loss; (fencing) lunge; (mach) breakdown; (mil) sally

aus′fallen §72 intr (SEIN) fall out; (nicht stattfinden) fail to take place; (ausgelassen werden) be omitted; (versagen) go out of commission; (Ergebnis) turn out; (mil) sortie

aus′fallend adj aggressive, insulting

aus′fechten §74 tr (Kampf) fight; (Streit) settle (by fighting)

aus′fegen tr sweep (out)

aus′fertigen tr finish; (Paß) issue; (Scheck) write out; (Schriftstück) draw up, draft; doppelt a. draw up in duplicate

aus′findig adj—a. machen find out; (aufspüren) trace

aus′fliegen §57 intr (SEIN) fly out; (wegfliegen) fly away; (von Hause wegziehen) leave home; go on a trip

aus′fließen §76 intr (SEIN) flow out

Aus′flucht f evasion; Ausflüchte machen dodge, beat around the bush

aus′fluchten tr align

Aus′flug m trip, outing

Ausflügler ['ausflyglər] m (-s;-) tourist, vacationer

Aus′fluß m outflow; (Eiter) discharge; (Ergebnis) outcome; (Mündung) outlet

aus′folgen tr hand over

aus′forschen tr investigate; sound out

aus′fragen tr interrogate, quiz

aus′fressen §70 tr empty (by eating); (chem) corrode; (geol) erode; was hast du denn ausgefressen? (coll) what were you up to?

Ausfuhr ['ausfur] f (-;-en) export

Aus′fuhrabgabe f export duty

ausführbar ['ausfyrbar] adj feasible

aus′führen *tr* carry out; export, ship; *(Auftrag)* fill; *(darlegen)* explain

Aus′fuhrhändler –in §6 *mf* exporter

ausführlich [′ausfyrlıç] *adj* detailed ‖ *adv* in detail, in full

Aus′führung *f* (-ʒ-en) carrying out, performance; *(Qualität)* workmanship; *(Darlegung)* explanation; *(e-s Gesetzes, Befehls)* implementation; *(Fertigstellung)* completion; *(e-s Verbrechens)* perpetrations; *(typ)* type, model; copy

Aus′fuhrwaren *pl* exports

aus′füllen *tr* fill out; *(Zeit)* occupy; *(Lücke; Stellung)* fill

Aus′gabe *f* *(Verteilung)* distribution; *(von Geldern)* expenditure; *(von Briefen)* delivery; *(e-s Buches)* edition; *(von Aktien)* issue

Aus′gang *m* exit; *(Auslaß)* outlet; *(Ergebnis)* result; *(Ende)* close, end; (aer) gate

Aus′gangspunkt *m* starting point

Aus′gangssprache *f* source language

aus′geben §80 *tr* give out, distribute; *(Aktien, Befehl)* issue; *(Geld)* spend; *(Briefe)* deliver; *(Karten)* deal ‖ *ref*—sich a. für pass oneself off as

ausgebeult [′ausɡəbɔılt] *adj* baggy

Aus′geburt *f* figment

aus′gedehnt *adj* extensive

aus′gedient *adj* retired; (educ) emeritus

aus′gefallen *adj* (fig) eccentric, odd

aus′gefeilt *adj* (fig) flawless

aus′geglichen *adj* *(Person)* well-balanced; *(Styl)* balanced

aus′gehen §82 *intr* (SEIN) go out; *(Vorräte, Geld, Geduld)* run out; *(Haar)* fall out; *(Farbe)* fade; a. auf *(acc)* aim at, be bent on; a. von proceed from; die Sache ging von ihm aus it was his idea; frei a. get off scot-free; gut a. turn out well; leer a. come away empty-handed; wenn wir davon a., daß going on the assumption that

Aus′gehverbot *n* curfew

aus′gekocht *adj* *(Lügner)* out-and-out; *(Verbrecher)* hardened

aus′gelassen *adj* boisterous

aus′geleiert *adj* trite; worn-out; *(Gewinde)* stripped

aus′gemacht *adj* settled; downright

ausgenommen *prep* *(acc)* except; niemand a. bar none

aus′gepicht *adj* inveterate

aus′gerechnet *adv* just, of all ...; a. Sie! you of all people!

aus′geschlossen *adj* out of the question, impossible

Ausgesiedelte [′ausɡəzidəltə] §5 *mf* evacuee, displaced person

aus′gestalten *tr* make arrangements for

aus′gesucht *adj* choice

aus′gezeichnet *adj* excellent

ausgiebig [′ausɡibıç] *adj* abundant; *(ergiebig)* productive

aus′gießen §76 *tr* pour out, pour away

Aus′gleich *m* (-ʒ-e) *(Ersatz)* compensation; *(Vergleich)* compromise; (acct) settlement; (tennis) deuce

aus′gleichen §85 *tr* level, smooth out; *(Konten)* balance; *(Verlust)* compensate for ‖ *ref* cancel one another out

Ausgleichs– *comb.fm.* balancing, compensating

Aus′gleichung *f* (-ʒ-en) equalization; settlement; compensation

aus′gleiten §86 *intr* (SEIN) slip

aus′graben §87 *tr* dig out, dig up; *(Leiche)* exhume; (archeol) excavate

aus′greifen §88 *intr* reach out; weit ausgreifend far-reaching

Ausguck [′ausɡuk] *m* (-sʒ-e) lookout

aus′gucken *intr* (nach) be on the lookout (for)

Aus′guß *m* sink; *(Tülle)* spout, nozzle

aus′haken *tr* unhook

aus′halten §90 *tr* endure, stand ‖ *intr* persevere, stick it out

aus′handeln *tr* get by bargaining

aushändigen [′aushendıɡən] *tr* hand over, surrender

Aus′hang *m* notice, shingle

Aus′hängeschild *n* (-[e]sʒ-er) sign board, shingle; (fig) front, cover

aus′harren *intr* hold out, last

aus′hauchen *tr* breathe out, exhale

aus′heben §94 *tr* lift out; *(Tür)* lift off its hinges; *(Truppen)* recruit

aushecken [′aushekən] *tr* (fig) hatch

aus′heilen *tr* heal completely ‖ *intr* (SEIN) heal up

aus′helfen §96 *intr* (dat) help out

Aus′hilfe *f* (temporary) help; (temporary) helper; makeshift

Aushilfs– *comb.fm.* temporary, emergency

Aus′hilfsarbeit *f* part-time work

Aus′hilfslehrer –in §6 *mf* substitute teacher

aus′hilfsweise *adv* temporarily

aus′höhlen *tr* hollow out

aus′holen *tr* *(ausfragen)* sound out ‖ *intr* *(beim Schwimmen)* stroke; mit dem Arm a. raise the arm *(before striking)*; weit a. start from the beginning

aus′horchen *tr* sound out, pump

aus′hülsen *tr* *(Bohnen, usw.)* shell

aus′hungern *tr* starve (out)

aus′husten *tr* cough up

aus′kehlen *tr* groove

Aus′kehlung *f* (-ʒ-en) groove

aus′kehren *tr* sweep (out)

aus′kennen §97 *ref* know one's way; *(in e-m Fach)* be well versed

Aus′klang *m* end, close

aus′klappen *tr* pull out *(a fold-away bed)*

aus′kleiden *tr* line, panel; *(ausziehen)* undress ‖ *ref* undress

aus′klopfen *tr* beat the dust out of

ausklügeln [′ausklyɡəln] *tr* figure out (ingeniously)

aus′kneifen §88 *intr* (SEIN) bolt

aus′knipsen *tr* (coll) switch off

ausknobeln [′ausknobəln] *tr* figure out

aus′kochen *tr* boil out; boil clean

aus′kommen §99 *intr* (SEIN) come out, get out; *(ausreichen)* manage ‖ Auskommen *n* (-sʒ) livelihood

auskömmlich [′auskœmlıç] *adj* adequate

aus′kosten *tr* relish

aus′kramen [′auskramən] *tr* *(aus Schubladen)* drag out; (fig) show off

aus′kratzen *tr* scratch out; (surg) curette

aus′kriechen §102 *intr* (SEIN) be hatched

aus′kugeln *ref*—sich [*dat*] den Arm a. dislocate the shoulder

aus′kundschaften *tr* explore; (mil) scout

Auskunft [′auskunft] *f* (–;⸚e) information, piece of information

Auskunftfei [′auskunftˈtaɪ] *f* (–;–en) private detective agency

Aus′kunftschalter *m* information desk

aus′kuppeln *tr* uncouple; (die Kupplung) release ‖ *intr* disengage the clutch

aus′lachen *tr* laugh at ‖ *ref* have a good laugh

aus′laden §103 *tr* unload; (Gast) put off ‖ *intr* project, jut out ‖ **Ausladen** *n* (–s;) unloading; projection

Aus′lage *f* (von Geld) outlay; (Unkosten) expenses; (von Waren) display; (Schaufenster) display window

Aus′land *n* foreign country, foreign countries; im A. leben live abroad; ins A. gehen go abroad

Ausländer –in [′auslendər(ɪn)] §6 *mf* foreigner, alien

aus′ländisch *adj* foreign, alien

Auslands– *comb.fm.* foreign

Aus′laß [′auslas] *m* (–lasses;–lässe) outlet

aus′lassen §104 *tr* let out; (weglassen) omit; (Wut) (an *dat*) vent (on) ‖ *ref* express one's opinion

Aus′lassung *f* omission; (Bemerkung) remark

Aus′lassungszeichen *n* (gram) apostrophe; (typ) caret

Aus′lauf *m* sailing; room to run

aus′laufen §105 *intr* (SEIN) run out; (Schiff) put out to sea; (Farbe) run; a. in (acc) end in; (Straße) run into

Aus′läufer *m* (geol)) spur; (hort) runner

aus′leben *tr* live out ‖ *ref* make the most of one's life ‖ *intr* die

aus′lecken *tr* lick clean

aus′leeren *tr* empty ‖ *ref* have a bowel movement

aus′legen *tr* lay out; (Waren) display; (erklären) construe; (Geld) advance; (Fußboden) cover (with carpeting); (Minen) lay; (Schlinge) set; falsch a. misconstrue, misinterpret

Aus′leger –in §6 *mf* interpreter ‖ *m* outrigger; (e–s Krans) boom

aus′leihen §81 *tr* lend (out) ‖ *ref*—sich [*dat*] etw a. borrow s.th.

aus′lernen *intr* finish one's apprenticeship; man lernt nie aus one never stops learning

Aus′lese *f* pick, choice

aus′lesen §107 *tr* pick out; (Buch) finish reading

aus′liefern *tr* deliver, turn over; (verteilen) distribute; (Verbrecher) extradite; j–m ausgeliefert sein be at s.o.'s mercy

aus′liegen §108 *intr* (SEIN) be on display

aus′löffeln *tr* spoon out; etw a. zu ha-

ben have to face the consequences of s.th.

aus′löschen *tr* (Feuer) extinguish; (Licht) put out; (Schreiben) erase

aus′losen *tr* draw lots for

aus′lösen *tr* loosen, release; (Gefangegen) ransom; (Pfand) redeem

Aus′löser *m* (–s;–) release

aus′loten *tr* (naut & fig) plumb

aus′lüften *tr* air, ventilate

aus′machen *tr* (Feuer) put out; (sichten) make out; (betragen) amount to; (Fleck) remove; (Licht) turn out; (bilden) constitute; (vereinbaren) agree upon; es macht nichts aus it doesn't matter

aus′malen *tr* paint ‖ *ref*—sich [*dat*] etw a. picture s.th.

aus′marschieren *intr* (SEIN) march out

Aus′maß *n* measurement; dimensions; in großem A. on a large scale; (fig) to a great extent

ausmergeln [′ausmergəln] *tr* exhaust

ausmerzen [′ausmertsən] *tr* reject; (ausrotten) eradicate

aus′messen §70 *tr* measure; survey

aus′misten *tr* (Stall) clean; (fig) clean up

aus′mustern *tr* discard; (mil) discharge

Aus′nahme *f* (–;–n) exception

aus′nahmslos *adj & adv* without exception

aus′nahmsweise *adv* by way of exception

aus′nehmen §116 *tr* take out; (Fisch, Huhn) clean; (ausschließen) exclude; (sl) clean out (of money) ‖ *ref*—sich gut a. look good

aus′nutzen, aus′nützen *tr* utilize; (Gelegenheit) take advantage of

aus′packen *tr* unpack; (Geheimnis) disclose ‖ *intr* (coll) unburden oneself, open up

aus′pfeifen §88 *tr* hiss (off the stage)

aus′plappern *tr* blurt out, blab out

aus′plaudern *tr* blab out

aus′plündern *tr* ransack; (coll) clean out (of money)

aus′polstern *tr* stuff, pad

aus′posaunen *tr* (coll) broadcast

aus′probieren *tr* try out, test

Aus′puff *m* (–[e]s;–e) exhaust

Aus′puffleitung *f* (aut) manifold

Aus′puffrohr *n* exhaust pipe

Aus′pufftopf *m* (aut) muffler

aus′pumpen *tr* pump out; ausgepumpt (coll) exhausted

aus′putzen *tr* (reinigen) clean out; (schmücken) adorn ‖ *ref* dress up

aus′quartieren *tr* put out (of s.o.'s room)

aus′radieren *tr* erase

aus′rangieren *tr* (coll) scrap

aus′rauben *tr* rob, ransack

aus′räumen *tr* (Schrank) clear out; (Möbel) remove; (med) clean out

aus′rechnen *tr* figure out

aus′recken *tr* stretch ‖ *ref*—sich [*dat*] den Hals a. crane one's neck

Aus′rede *f* evasion, excuse

aus′reden *tr*—j–m etw a. talk s.o. out

of s.th. || *ref* make excuses || *intr* finish speaking

aus′reiben §62 *tr* rub out; (**mach**) ream

aus′reichen *tr* suffice, be enough

aus′reichend *adj* sufficient

Aus′reise *f* departure; way out

aus′reißen §53 *tr* tear out || *ref—er reißt sich* [*dat*] *dabei kein Bein aus* he's not exactly killing himself || *intr* (SEIN) run away

Aus′reißer *m* runaway

aus′renken *tr* dislocate

aus′richten *tr* straighten; (*in e-e Linie bringen*) align; (*vollbringen*) accomplish; (*Botschaft, Gruß*) convey

aus′roden *tr* root out; (*Wald*) clear

aus′rollen *tr* roll out || *intr* (SEIN) (aer) taxi to a standstill

ausrotten [′ausrɔtən] *tr* root out; (*Volk, Tierrasse*) exterminate; (*Übel*) eradicate

aus′rücken *tr* (*Kupplung*) disengage || *intr* (SEIN) march off; run away

Aus′ruf *m* outcry; (*öffentlich*) proclamation; (*gram*) interjection

aus′rufen §122 *tr* call out; exclaim; a. **als** (or **zum**) proclaim

Aus′rufungszeichen *n* exclamation point

aus′ruhen *ref & intr* rest

aus′rupfen *tr* pluck

aus′rüsten *tr* equip, fit out; arm

aus′rutschen *intr* (SEIN) slip (out)

Aus′saat *f* sowing; (& *fig*) seed(s)

aus′säen *tr* sow; (*fig*) disseminate

Aus′sage *f* statement; (*gram*) predicate; (jur) affidavit

aus′sagen *tr* state || *intr* give evidence, make a statement

Aus′sagesatz *m* declarative sentence

Aus′sageweise *f* (gram) mood

Satz *m* leprosy

Aussätzige [′aussetsɪgə] §5 *mf* leper

aus′saugen §125 *tr* suck dry; (*fig*) bleed white

Aus′sauger **-in** §6 *mf* (coll) bloodsucker

aus′schalten *tr* (*Licht, Radio, Fernseher*) turn off; (*fig*) shut out

Aus′schalter *m* circuit breaker

Aus′schank *m* sale of alcoholic drinks; (*Kneipe*) bar, taproom

aus′scharren *tr* dig up

Aus′schau *f—A.* **halten nach** be on the lookout for

aus′schauen *intr—a.* **nach** look out for; look like; **gut schaust du aus!** what a mess you are!

aus′scheiden §112 *tr* eliminate; (physiol) excrete, secrete || *intr* (SEIN) retire, resign; (sport) drop out; **das scheidet aus!** that's out!

Aus′scheidung *f* (-;-en) elimination; retirement; (physiol) excretion, secretion

Aus′scheidungskampf *m* elimination bout

aus′schelten §83 *tr* scold, berate

aus′schenken *tr* pour (*drinks*)

aus′scheren *intr* (aus) veer away (from)

aus′schiffen *tr* disembark; (*Ladung*) unload || *ref* disembark

aus′schimpfen *tr* scold, take to task

aus′schirren *tr* unharness

aus′schlachten *tr* cut up; (*Flugzeuge, usw.*) cannibalize; (*ausnutzen*) make the most of

aus′schlafen §131 *tr* sleep off || *ref & intr* get enough sleep

Aus′schlag *m* rash; (*e-s Zeigers*) deflection; **den A.** geben turn the scales

aus′schlagen §132 *tr* knock out; (*Feuer*) beat out; (*Metall*) hammer out; (*Innenraum*) line; (*Angebot*) refuse || *intr* bud; sprout; (*Pferd*) kick; (*Pendel*) swing; (*Zeiger*) move || *intr* (SEIN) turn out

aus′schlaggebend *adj* decisive

aus′schließen §76 *tr* lock out; (*von der Schule*) expel; (*ausscheiden*) exclude; (sport) disqualify

aus′schließlich *adj* exclusive, sole || *adv* exclusively, only || *prep* (genit) exclusive of

aus′schlürfen *tr* sip

aus′schmieren *tr* grease; (**mit**) smear (with); (*fig*) pull a fast one on; (mas) point

aus′schmücken *tr* adorn, decorate; (*Geschichte*) embellish

aus′schnaufen *intr* get one's wind

aus′schneiden §106 *tr* cut out; **tief ausgeschnitten** low-cut, low-necked

Aus′schnitt *m* cut; (*Zeitungs-*) clipping; (*Kleid-*) neckline; (*literarisch*) extract; (geom) sector

aus′schreiben §62 *tr* write out (in full); finish writing; (*ankündigen*) announce; (*Formular*) fill out; (*Rezept*) make out

aus′schreiten §86 *tr* pace off || *intr* (SEIN) walk briskly

Aus′schreitung *f* (-;-en) excess

Aus′schuß *m* waste, scrap; (*Komitee*) committee

Aus′schußware *f* (indust) reject

aus′schütten *tr* pour out, spill; (*Dividende*) pay || *ref—sich* **vor Lachen a.** split one's sides laughing

aus′schwärmen *intr* (SEIN) swarm out; (*Truppen*) deploy

aus′schwatzen *tr* blab out, blurt out

aus′schweifend *adj* (*Phantasie*) wild; (*liederlich*) wild, dissolute

Aus′schweifung *f* (-;-en) excess; curve; digression

aus′schwemmen *tr* rinse out; wash out

aus′schwenken *tr* rinse

aus′schwitzen *tr* sweat out; exude

aus′sehen §138 *intr* look; **nach j-m a.** look out for s.o.; **nach Regen a.** look like rain; **wie sieht er aus?** what does he look like? || **Aussehen** *n* (-s;) look(s); appearance(s)

außen [′ausən] *adv* outside; **nach a.** out(wards)

außen-, Außen- *comb.fm.* external; outer; exterior; outdoor; foreign

Au′ßenaufnahme *f* (phot) outdoor shot

Au′ßenbahn *f* (sport) outside lane

aus′senden §140 *tr* send out

Au′ßenfläche *f* outer surface

Au′ßenminister *m* Secretary of State; (Brit) Foreign Secretary

Au′ßenpolitik *f* foreign policy

Au′ßenseite *f* outside

Außenseiter ['ausənzaɪtər] *m* (-s;-) dark horse, long shot; (*Einzelgänger*) loner; (*Nichtfachmann*) layman

Außenstände ['ausənʃtɛndə] *pl* accounts receivable

Au′ßenstelle *f* branch office

außer ['ausər] *prep* (*genit*)—a. Landes abroad ‖ *prep* (*dat*) outside, out of; except, but; besides, in addition to; **a. Hause** not at home; **a. sich sein** be beside oneself

au′ßeramtlich *adj* unofficial, private

außerdem ['ausərdem] *adv* also, besides; moreover, furthermore

au′ßerdienstlich *adj* unofficial, private; (*mil*) off duty

äußere ['ɔɪsərə] §9 *adj* outer, exterior, external ‖ **Äußere** §5 *n* exterior

au′ßerehelich *adj* extra-marital; (*Kind*) illegitimate

au′ßergewöhnlich *adj* extraordinary

außerhalb ['ausərhalp] *prep* (*genit*) outside, out of

äußerlich ['ɔɪsərlɪç] *adj* external, outward; (*oberflächlich*) superficial

Äu′ßerlichkeit *f* superficiality; (*Formalität*) formality; **Äußerlichkeiten** externals; formalities

äußern ['ɔɪsərn] *tr* express ‖ *ref* (*über acc*) express one's views (about); (*in dat*) be manifested (in)

au′ßerordentlich *adj* extraordinary; **außerordentlicher Professor** associate professor

äußerst ['ɔɪsərst] *adj* outermost; (*fig*) extreme, utmost ‖ *adv* extremely, highly ‖ **Äußerste** §5 *n* extremity, extreme(s); **aufs Ä.** to the utmost; **bis zum Äußersten** to extremes; to the bitter end

außerstande ['ausərʃandə] *adj* unable

Äu′ßerung *f* (-;-en) (*Ausdruck*) expression; (*Bemerkung*) remark

aus′setzen *tr* set out, put out; (*an der Küste*) maroon; (*Kind; dem Wetter*) expose; (*Boot*) lower; (*Wachen*) post; (*Belohnung*) hold out, promise; (*Tätigkeit*) discontinue; **auszusetzen haben an** (*dat*) find fault with ‖ *intr* stop, halt

Aus′sicht *f* (auf *acc*) view (of); (fig) (auf *acc*) hope (of); **in A. nehmen** consider, plan

aus′sichtslos *adj* hopeless

Aus′sichtspunkt *m* vantage point

aus′sichtsreich *adj* promising

Aus′sichtsturm *m* lookout tower

aussichtsvoll *adj* promising

aus′sieben *tr* sift out; (fig) screen

aus′siedeln *tr* evacuate by force

Aus′siedlung *f* (-;-en) forced evacuation

aus′sinnen §121 *tr* think up, devise

aussöhnen ['auszønən] *tr* reconcile

aus′sondern *tr* (*trennen*) separate; (*auswählen*) single out; (*physiol*) excrete

aus′spähen *tr* spy out ‖ *intr* (*nach*) keep a lookout (for), reconnoiter

aus′spannen *tr* stretch; extend; (*Zugtiere*) unhitch ‖ *intr* relax

Aus′spannung *f* (-;) relaxation

aus′speien §135 *tr* spit out

aus′sperren *tr* lock out, shut out

aus′spielen *tr* (*Karten*) lead with; (*Preis*) play for ‖ *intr* lead off

aus′spionieren *tr* spy out

Aus′sprache *f* pronunciation; (*Erörterung*) discussion, talk

aus′sprechen §64 *tr* pronounce; (*deutlich*) articulate; (*ausdrücken*) express ‖ *ref* (*über acc*) speak one's mind (about); (*für; gegen*) declare oneself (for; against); **sich mit j-m über etw a.** talk s.th. over with s.o. ‖ *intr* finish speaking

Aus′spruch *m* statement

aus′spülen *tr* rinse

aus′spüren *tr* trace (down)

aus′staffieren *tr* fit out, furnish

aus′stampfen *tr* stamp out

Aus′stand *m* walkout

aus′ständig *adj* on strike, striking; (fin) in arrears, outstanding

ausstatten ['ausʃtatən] *tr* furnish, equip; (*Tochter*) give a dowry to

Aus′stattung *f* (-;-en) furnishings; equipment; trousseau

aus′stechen §64 *tr* cut out; (*Auge*) poke out; (fig) outdo

aus′stehen §146 *tr* endure, stand ‖ *intr* still be expected, be overdue

aus′steigen §148 *intr* (SEIN) get out, get off

aus′stellen *tr* exhibit; (*Wache*) post; (*Quittung, Scheck*) make out; (*Paß*) issue

Aus′stellung *f* (-;-en) exhibit; issuance; criticism

Aus′stelungsdatum *n* date of issue

aus′sterben §149 *intr* (SEIN) die out

Aus′steuer *f* hope chest, dowry

aus′stopfen *tr* stuff, pad

Aus′stoß *m* (indust) output

aus′stoßen §150 *tr* knock out; (*vertreiben*) eject; (*Seufzer, Schrei, Fluch*) utter; (*Torpedo*) launch; (math) eliminate; (phonet) elide; (phys) emit

Aus′stoßrohr *n* torpedo tube

Aus′stoßung *f* (-;-en) ejection; utterance; (gram) elision

Aus′stoßzahlen *pl* (indust) production figures

aus′strahlen *tr & intr* radiate

aus′strecken *tr & ref* stretch out

aus′streichen §85 *tr* cross out; (*glätten*) smooth out; (*Bratpfanne*) grease

aus′streuen *tr* strew, scatter, spread

aus′strömen *tr & intr* (SEIN) pour out

aus′studieren *tr* study thoroughly

aus′suchen *tr* pick out

Aus′tausch *m* exchange

aus′tauschbar *adj* exchangeable; interchangeable

aus′tauschen *tr* exchange; interchange

Aus′tauschstoff *m* substitute

Aus′tauschstück *n* spare part

aus′teilen *tr* distribute, deal out

Auster ['austər] *f* (-;-n) oyster

aus′tilgen *tr* exterminate, wipe out

aus′toben *tr* give vent to ‖ *ref* (*Person*) let one's hair down; (*Kinder*) raise a rumpus; (*Gewitter*) stop raging

aus′tollen *ref* make a racket

Austrag ['austrak] *m* (-[e]s;)—**bis zum A. der Sache** until the matter is decided; **zum A. bringen** bring to a head; (jur) settle; **zum A. kommen** come up for a decision

aus′tragen §132 *tr* carry out; (*Briefe*) deliver; (*Kleider*) wear out; (*Meisterschaft*) decide; (*Klatschereien*) spread; (acct) cancel

Aus′träger *m* deliveryman

Australien [aus′trɑljən] *n* (-s;) Australia

Australier –in [aus′trɑljər(ɪn)] §6 *mf* Australian

aus′treiben §62 *tr* drive out; exorcise

aus′treten §152 *tr* (*Feuer*) tread out; (*Schuhe, Treppen*) wear out || *intr* (SEIN) step out; (*Blut*) come out; (coll) go to the bathroom; **a. aus** leave (*school, a company, club*)

aus′trinken §143 *tr* drink up, drain

Aus′tritt *m* withdrawal

aus′trocknen *tr & intr* (SEIN) dry up

aus′tüfteln *tr* puzzle out

aus′üben *tr* (*Aufsicht, Macht*) exercise; (*Beruf*) practice; (*Pflicht*) carry out; (*Einfluß, Druck*) exert; (*Verbrechen*) commit; **ausübende Gewalt** executive power

Aus′verkauf *m* clearance sale

aus′verkaufen *tr* sell out; close out

aus′wachsen §155 *tr* outgrow

Aus′wahl *f* choice, selection

aus′wählen *tr* select, pick out

Aus′wanderer –in §6 *mf* emigrant

aus′wandern *intr* (SEIN) emigrate

auswärtig [′ausvɛrtɪç] *adj* out-of-town; (*ausländisch*) foreign

auswärts [′ausvɛrts] *adv* outward(s); out, away from home; (*außer der Stadt*) out of town; (*im Ausland*) abroad

Aus′wärtsspiel *n* away game

aus′wechselbar *adj* interchangeable

aus′wechseln *tr* exchange, interchange; (*ersetzen*) replace

Aus′weg *m* way out; escape

Ausweich– *comb.fm.* evasive; alternate; substitute; emergency; reserve

aus′weichen §85 *intr* (SEIN) (*dat*) make way (for), get out of the way (of); (*dat*) evade; **a. auf** (*acc*) switch to

aus′weichend *adj* evasive

Aus′weichklausel *f* escape clause

Aus′weichlager *n* emergency store

Aus′weichstelle *f* passing zone

Aus′weichstraße *f* bypass

Aus′weichziel *n* secondary target

aus′weinen *ref* have a good cry || *intr* stop crying

Ausweis [′ausvais] *m* (-s;-e) identification (card); (com) statement

aus′weisen §118 *tr* expel; (*aus Besitz*) evict; (*verbannen*) banish, deport; (*zeigen*) show || *ref* prove one's identity

Aus′weispapiere *pl* identification papers

Aus′weisung *f* (-;-en) expulsion; eviction; deportation

aus′weiten *tr & ref* widen, expand

auswendig [′ausvɛndɪç] *adj* outer || *adv* outside; outwardly; by heart

aus′werfen §160 *tr* throw out; (*Graben*) dig; (*Summe*) allocate; (*Lava*) eject; (*Blut, Schleim*) spit up; (angl) cast

aus′werten *tr* evaluate; (*ausnützen*) utilize; (*Statistik*) interpret

aus′wickeln *tr* unwrap

aus′wiegen §57 *tr* weigh out

aus′wirken *tr* knead || *ref* take effect; **sich a. auf** (*acc*) affect; **sich** [*dat*] **etw bei j–m a.** obtain s.th. from s.o.

Aus′wirkung *f* (-;-en) effect

aus′wischen *tr* wipe out; wipe clean; **j–m eins a.** play a dirty joke on s.o.

aus′wittern *tr* season || *intr* weather

aus′wringen §142 *tr* wring out

Aus′wuchs *m* outgrowth; (pathol) tumor

Aus′wurf *m* throwing out; (fig) scum; (mach) ejection

aus′zacken *tr* indent; (*wellenförmig*) scallop

aus′zahlen *tr* pay out; pay off || *ref*— **es zahlt sich nicht aus** it doesn't pay

aus′zählen *tr* count out

aus′zanken *tr* scold

aus′zehren *tr* consume, waste

Aus′zehrung *f* (-;) consumption

aus′zeichnen *tr* mark, tag; (*ehren*) honor; (fig) distinguish

Aus′zeichnung *f* (-;-en) labeling; decoration, honor; distinction

aus′ziehen §163 *tr* pull out; (*Kleid*) take off; (*Stelle*) excerpt; (*Zeichnung*) ink in; (chem) extract || *ref* undress || *intr* (SEIN) set out; (*aus e–r Wohnung*) move out

aus′zischen *tr* hiss off the stage

Aus′zug *m* departure; moving; excerpt; (*Abriß*) summary; (Bib) Exodus; (chem) extract; (com) statement

aus′zugsweise *adv* in summary form

aus′zupfen *tr* pluck out

authentisch [au′tɛntɪʃ] *adj* authentic

Auto [′auto] *n* (-s;-s) auto(mobile)

Au′tobahn *f* superhighway

Au′tobus *m* bus

Autodidakt [autodɪ′dakt] *m* (-en;-en) self-educated person

Au′todroschke *f* taxi

Au′tofahrer –in §6 *mf* motorist

Au′tofahrschule *f* driving school

Au′tofahrt *f* car ride, drive

Au′tofalle *f* speed trap

Autogramm [auto′gram] *n* (-[e]s;-e) autograph

Autogramm′jäger –in §6 *mf* autograph hound

Au′tokino *n* drive-in movie

Au′tokolonne *f* motorcade

Autokrat [auto′krat] *m* (-en;-en) autocrat

autokratisch [auto′kratɪʃ] *adj* autocratic

Automat [auto′mat] *m* (-en;-en) vending machine; (*Musik–*) jukebox; (*Spiel–*) slot machine

Automa′tenrestaurant *n* automat

automatisch [auto′matɪʃ] *adj* automatic

Automobil [automo′bil] *n* (-[e]s;-e) automobile

autonom [auto′nom] *adj* autonomous

Autonomie [autono′mi] *f* (-;) autonomy

Au·tor [′autor] *m* (-s;-toren* [′torən]) author

Autoreparatur'werkstatt *f* auto repair shop, garage
Autorin [auˈtoːrɪn] *f* (-;-nen) authoress
autorisieren [autoriˈziːrən] *tr* authorize
autoritär [autoriˈtɛːr] *adj* authoritarian
Autorität [autoriˈtɛːt] *f* (-;-en) authority
Au'toschlosser *m* automobile mechanic
Au'toschuppen *m* carport

Au'tounfall *m* automobile accident
avancieren [avãˈsiːrən] *intr* (SEIN) advance; (zu) be promoted (to)
avisieren [aviˈziːrən] *tr* advise, notify
Axt [akst] *f* (-;⸚e) ax
Azalee [atsaˈleːə] *f* (-;-n) azalea
Azetat [atseˈtaːt] *n* (-[e]s;-e) acetate
Azeton [atseˈtoːn] *n* (-s;) acetone
Azetylen [atsetyˈleːn] *n* (-s;) acetylene
azurn [aˈtsuːrn] *adj* azure, sky-blue

B

B, b [beː] *invar n* B, b; (mus) B flat
babbeln [ˈbabəln] *intr* babble
Baby [ˈbeːbi] *n* (-s;-s) baby
Babysitter [ˈbeːbɪzɪtər] *m* (-s;-) baby-sitter
Bach [bax] *m* (-[e]s;⸚e) brook, creek
Backe [ˈbakə] *f* (-;-n) cheek; jaw (*of a vise*); (mach) die
backen [ˈbakən] §50 (& *pret* **backte**) *tr* bake; (*in der Pfanne*) fry ‖ (*pret* **backte**; *pp* **gebacken**) *intr* bake ‖ §109 *intr* (HABEN & SEIN) cake; stick
Backenbart (**Bak'kenbart**) *m* side whiskers
Backenstreich (**Bak'kenstreich**) *m* slap
Backenzahn (**Bak'kenzahn**) *m* molar; kleiner (or vorderer) **B.** bicuspid
Bäcker [ˈbɛkər] *m* (-s;-) baker
Bäckerei [bɛkəˈraɪ] *f* (-;-en) bakery
Back'fett *n* shortening
Back'fisch *m* fried fish; (fig) teenager
Back'fischalter *n* teens (*of girls*)
Back'form *f* cake pan
Back'hähnchen *n* fried chicken
Back'hendel *n* (Aust) fried chicken
Back'huhn *n* fried chicken
Back'obst *n* dried fruit
Back'ofen *m* baking oven
Back'pfeife *f* slap in the face, smack
Back'pflaume *f* prune
Back'pulver *n* baking powder
Back'stein *m* brick
Back'trog *m* kneading trough
Back'waren *pl* baked goods
Back'werk *n* pastries
Bad [baːt] *n* (-[e]s;⸚er) bath; bathroom; (*Badeort*) spa
Ba'deanstalt *f* public baths; public pool
Ba'deanzug *m* swim suit
Ba'dehaube *f* bathing cap
Ba'dehose *f* bathing trunks
Ba'dekappe *f* bathing cap
Ba'demantel *m* bathrobe
baden [ˈbaːdən] *tr & ref* bathe ‖ *intr* take a bath; **b. gehen** go swimming
Ba'deort *m* bathing resort; spa
Ba'destrand *m* bathing beach
Ba'detuch *n* bath towel
Ba'dewanne *f* bathtub
Badende [ˈbaːdəndə] §5 *mf* bather
Ba'dewärter -in §6 *mf* lifeguard; bath-house attendant
Ba'dezimmer *n* bathroom
baff [baf] *adj* dumbfounded

Bagage [baˈgaːʒə] *f* (-;) (fig) rabble; (mil) baggage
Bagatelle [bagaˈtɛlə] *f* (-;-n) trifle
Bagatell'lesache *f* petty offense
bagatellisieren [bagatɛliˈziːrən] *tr* minimize, make light of
Bagger [ˈbagər] *m* (-s;-) dredge
baggern [ˈbagərn] *tr & intr* dredge
bähen [ˈbɛːən] *intr* bleat
Bahn [baːn] *f* (-;-en) way, path; (aer) runway; (astr) orbit; (aut) lane; (rr) railroad; (sport) course, track; (*Eis-*) (sport) rink; **auf die schiefe B. geraten** go astray; **B. brechen** (*dat*) pave the way (for); **mit der B. fahren** travel by train
bahn'brechend *adj* pioneering, epoch-making
Bahn'brecher -in §6 *mf* pioneer
Bahn'damm *m* railroad embankment
bahnen [ˈbaːnən] *tr*—**e-n Weg. b.** clear a path, open up a path
Bahn'fahrt *f* train trip
bahn'frei *adj* free on board, f.o.b.
Bahn'hof *m* railroad station
Bahn'hofshalle *f* concourse
Bahn'hofsvorsteher *m* stationmaster
Bahn'linie *f* railroad line
Bahn'schranke *f* (rr) barrier
Bahn'steig *m* (rr) platform
Bahn'strecke *f* (rr) line, track
Bahn'übergang *m* railroad crossing
Bahn'wärter *m* (rr) signalman
Bahre [ˈbaːrə] *f* (-;-n) stretcher; bier
Bahr'tuch *n* pall
Bai [baɪ] *f* (-;-en) bay
Baiser [beˈzeː] *m & n* (-s;-s) meringue cookie
Baisse [ˈbɛsə] *f* (-;-n) (com) slump
Bais'sestimmung *f* downward trend
Baissier [bɛsˈjeː] *m* (-s;-s) (st.exch.) bear
Bajonett [bajoˈnɛt] *n* (-s;-e) bayonet
Bake [ˈbaːkə] *f* (-;-n) beacon
Bakterie [bakˈteːrjə] *f* (-;-n) bacterium
Bakte'rienforscher -in §6 *mf* bacteriologist
Bakte'rienkunde *f* bacteriology
Balance [baˈlãsə] *f* (-;-n) balance
balancieren [balãˈsiːrən] *tr & intr* balance
bald [balt] *adv* (**eher** [ˈeːər]; **eheste** [ˈeːəstə] §9 soon; (*beinahe*) nearly
baldig [ˈbaldɪç] *adj* speedy; (*Antwort*) early

baldigst ['baldıgst] *adv* very soon; at the earliest possible moment

Balg [balk] *m* (-[e]s;≃e) skin, pelt; (*Hülse*) shell, husk; **Bälge** bellows; **j–m den B. abziehen** fleece s.o. || *m & n* (-[e]s;≃er) (coll) brat

balgen ['balgən] *ref* roll around, romp; (*raufen*) scuffle || **Balgen** *m* (-s;-) (phot) bellows

Balgerei ['balgə'raı] *f* (-;-en) scuffle

Balken ['balkən] *m* (-s;-) beam, rafter

Bal'kenwerk *n* framework

Balkon [bal'kon] *m* (-s;-e) balcony

Ball [bal] *m* (-[e]s;≃e) ball; (*Tanz*) ball

Ballade [ba'ladə] *f* (-;-n) ballad

Ballast ['balast] *m* (-[e]s;-e) ballast; (fig) drag; (coll) padding

ballen ['balən] *tr*—**die Faust b.** clench one's fist || *ref* form a cluster || **Ballen** *m* (-s;-) (anat) ball; (com) bale; (pathol) bunion

ballern ['balərn] *intr* (coll) bang away

Ballett [ba'let] *n* (-[e]s;-e) ballet

Ballistik [ba'lıstık] *f* (-;) ballistics

Ballon [ba'lon] *m* (-s;-s) balloon

Ball'saal *m* ballroom

Ball'schläger *m* (sport) bat

Ball'spiel *n* ball game

Bal'lung *f* (-;-en) (mil) massing (of troops)

Balsam ['balzam] *m* (-s;-e) balm, balsam; (fig) balm

balsamieren [balza'mirən] *tr* embalm

balzen ['baltsən] *intr* perform a mating dance

Bambus ['bambus] *m* (-; & -ses;-se) bamboo

Bam'busrohr *n* bamboo, bamboo cane

banal [ba'nal] *adj* banal

Banane [ba'nanə] *f* (-;-n) banana

Banause [ba'nauzə] *f* (-n;-n) philistine

banausisch [ba'nauzıʃ] *adj* narrow-minded

Band [bant] *m* (-[e]s;≃e) volume; (*Einband*) binding || *n* (-[e]s;-e) bond, tie; **Bande** chains, shackles || *n* (-[e]s;≃er) (e–s Hutes, usw.) band; (*Bindfaden*) string; (*zum Schmuck*) ribbon; tape; (anat) ligament; (electron) recording tape; (rad) band; **am laufenden B.** continuously

Bandage [ban'daʒə] *f* (-;-n) bandage

bandagieren [banda'ʒirən] *tr* bandage

Bande ['bandə] *f* (-;-n) band, gang, crew; (billiards) cushion

Ban'denkrieg *m* guerilla war(fare)

Ban'denmitglied *n* gangster; (mil) guerilla

Ban'denunwesen *n* gangsterism; partisan activities

bändigen [bendigən] *tr* tame; (fig) subdue, overcome, master

Bandit [ban'dit] *m* (-en;-en) bandit

Band'maß *n* tape measure

Band'säge *f* band saw

Band'scheibe *f* (anat) disk

Band'scheibenquetschung *f* slipped disk

Band'wurm *m* tapeworm

bang(e) [baŋ(ə)] *adj* scared, anxious; (*Gefühl*) disquieting; **j–m b. machen** scare s.o. || **Bange** *f* (-;) fear

Bangigkeit ['baŋıçkaıt] *f* (-;) fear

Bank [baŋk] *f* (-;≃e) bench; pew; (geol) layer, bed || *f* (-;-en) bank

Bank'anweisung *f* check

Bank'ausweis *m* bank statement

Bank'einlage *f* bank deposit

Bankett [baŋ'ket] *n* (-s;-e) banquet

bank'fähig *adj* negotiable

Bank'guthaben *n* bank balance

Bank'halter **-in** §6 *mf* banker (in games)

Bankier [baŋk'je] *m* (-s;-s) banker

Bank'konto *n* bank account

bank'mäßig *adj* by check

bankrott [baŋk'rot] *adj* bankrupt || *m* (-[e]s;-e) bankruptcy

Bank'verkehr *m* banking (activity)

Bank'wesen *n* banking

Bann [ban] *m* (-[e]s;-e) ban; (Zauber) spell; (eccl) excommunication

bannen ['banən] *tr* banish; (Geister) exorcize; (eccl) excommunicate

Banner ['banər] *n* (-s;-) banner; standard

Ban'nerträger *m* standard-bearer

Bann'fluch *m* anathema

Bann'kreis *m* spell; **in j–s B. geraten** come under s.o.'s spell

Bann'meile *f* (fig) city limits

Bann'ware *f* contraband

bar [bar] *adj* bare; (rein) pure, sheer; (fin) cash || *adv* cash || *prep* (genit) devoid of, lacking || **Bar** *f* (-s;-s) bar, taproom

Bär [ber] *m* (-en;-en) bear; (astr) Dipper; **j–m e–n B. aufbinden** tell s.o. a fish story

Bar- *comb.fm.* cash

Baracke [ba'rakə] *f* (-;-n) barrack; (wooden) hut

Barbar **-in** [bar'bar(ın)] §7 *mf* barbarian

Barbarei [barba'raı] *f* (-;) barbarism; (Grausamkeit) barbarity

barbarisch [bar'barıʃ] *adj* barbarous; barbaric, primitive

bärbeißig ['berbaısıç] *adj* surly

Bar'bestand *m* cash on hand

Barbier [bar'bir] *m* (-s;-e) barber

barbieren [bar'birən] *tr* shave; (fig) fleece

Barett [ba'ret] *n* (-[e]s;-e) beret

barfuß ['barfus] *adv* barefoot

barfüßig ['barfysıç] *adj* barefooted

barg [bark] *pret* **of bergen**

Bar'geld *n* cash

barhäuptig ['barhoıptıç] *adj* bareheaded

Bar'hocker *m* bar stool

Bariton ['barıton] *m* (-s;-e) baritone

Barkasse [bar'kasə] *f* (-;-n) launch

Bärme ['bermə] *f* (-;) yeast, leaven

barmherzig [barm'hertsıç] *adj* merciful

Bar'mittel *pl* cash

barock [ba'rok] *adj* baroque || **Barock** *m & n* (-s;) baroque; baroque period

Barometer [baro'metər] *n* (-s;-) barometer

Baron [ba'ron] *m* (-s;-e) baron

Baronin [ba'ronın] *f* (-;-nen) baroness

Barre [ˈbarə] f (-;-n) bar

Barren [ˈbarən] m (-s;-) bar; ingot; (gym) parallel bars

Barriere [barˈjerə] f (-;-n) barrier

barsch [barʃ] adj gruff, rude ‖ **Barsch** m (-es;-e) (ichth) perch

Barschaft [ˈbarʃaft] f (-;-) cash

barst [barst] pret of **bersten**

Bart [bart] m (-[e]s;ᵃ) beard; (e-r Katze) whiskers; (e-s Fisches) barb; **der B. ist ab!** the jig is up!; sich [dat] **e-n B. wachsen lassen** grow a beard

bärtig [ˈbertɪç] adj bearded

bart′los adj beardless

Bar′verlust m straight loss

Basalt [baˈzalt] m (-[e]s;-e) basalt

Basar [baˈzar] m (-s;-e) bazaar

Ba·sis [ˈbazɪs] f (-;-sen [zən]) basis; (archit, math, mil) base

Baß [bas] m (Basses;Bässe) (mus) bass

Baß′geige f bass viol, contrabass

Bassin [baˈsɛ̃] n (-s;-s) reservoir; swimming pool; (naut) dock, basin

Baß′schlüssel m bass clef

Baß′stimme f bass (voice), basso

basta [ˈbasta] interj—**und damit b.!** and that's that!

Bastard [ˈbastart] m (-[e]s;-e) bastard; (bot) hybrid

Bastei [basˈtaɪ] f (-;-en) bastion

basteln [ˈbasteln] intr tinker

Bast′ler –in §6 mf hobbyist

bat [bat] pret of **bitten**

Bataillon [batalˈjon] n (-s;-e) battalion

Batte·rie [batəˈri] f (-;-rien [ˈri·ən] battery

Bau [bau] m (-[e]s;) erection, construction, building; (Bauart) structure, design; (Körper–) build; **er ist beim Bau** he is in the building trade; **in Bau** under construction ‖ m (-[e]s;-ten) building; **auf dem Bau** at the construction site ‖ m (-[e]s;-e) burrow, hole; (min) mine **–bau** m comb.fm. –construction, –building; –culture; –mining

Bau′abnahme f building inspection

Bau′arbeiter m construction worker

Bau′art f build; structure; type, model

Bauch [baux] m (-[e]s;ᵃe) belly, stomach; (Leib) bowels; (coll) pot-belly

Bauch– comb.fm. abdominal

bauchig [ˈbauxɪç] adj bulging; convex

Bauch′klatscher m belly flop

Bauch′laden m vendor's tray

Bauch′landung f belly-landing

Bauch′redner –in §6 mf ventriloquist

Bauch′speicheldrüse f pancreas

Bauch′weh n stomach ache, bellyache

bauen [ˈbau·ən] tr build; erect; make, manufacture; (ackern) till; (anbauen) grow ‖ intr build; (an dat) work (at); (auf acc) depend (on), trust

Bauer [ˈbau·ər] m (-s & -n;-n) farmer; (cards) jack; (chess) pawn ‖ m (-s;-) builder ‖ m & n (-s;-) bird-cage

Bäuerchen [ˈbɔɪ·ərçən] n (-s;-) small farmer; (baby's) burp

Bäuerin [ˈbɔɪ·ərɪn] f (-;-nen) farmer's wife

bäuerisch [ˈbɔɪ·ərɪʃ] adj boorish

Bau′erlaubnis f building permit

bäuerlich [ˈbɔɪ·ərlɪç] adj rural

Bau′ernbursche m country lad

Bau′erndirne f country girl

Bauernfänger [ˈbau·ərnfɛŋər] m (-s;-) confidence man

Bau′erngut n, **Bau′ernhof** m farm

Bau′fach n architecture

bau′fällig adj dilapidated

Bau′genhemigung f building permit

Bau′gerüst n scaffold(ing)

Bau′gewerbe n building trade

Bau′gewerkschule f school of architecture and civil engineering

Bau′grundstück n building site

Bau′holz n lumber

Bau′kasten m building set

Bau′kunst f architecture

bau′lich adj architectural; structural; **in gutem baulichen Zustand** in good repair

Baum [baum] m (-[e]s;ᵃe) tree; (mach) shaft, axle; (naut) boom

Bau′meister m building contractor, builder; architect

baumeln [ˈbauməln] intr dangle

bäumen [ˈbɔɪmən] ref rear

Baum′garten m orchard

Baum′grenze f timber line

Baum′krone f treetop

Baum′schere f pruning shears

Baum′schule f nursery (of saplings)

Baum′stamm m tree trunk

baum′stark′ adj strong as an ox

Baum′muster n model (number)

Baum′wolle f cotton

Baum′wollkapsel f cotton boll

Baum′wollsamt m velveteen

Bau′plan m ground plan

Bau′platz m building lot

Bau′rat m (-[e]s;ᵃe) building inspector

Bausch [bauʃ] m (-[e]s;-e) pad. wad; (e-s Segels) bulge, belly; **in B. und Bogen** wholesale

bauschen [ˈbauʃən] tr, ref & intr bulge, swell

bauschig [ˈbauʃɪç] adj puffy; baggy

Bau′schule f school of architecture and civil engineering

Bau′sparkasse f building and loan association

Bau′stahl m structural steel

Bau′stein m building stone; brick

Bau′stelle f building site; road construction

Bau′stoff m building material

Bau′techniker m construction engineer

Bau′unternehmer m contractor

Bau′unternehmung f building firm, building contractors

Bau′werk n building, edifice

Bau′wesen n building industry

Bau′zaun m hoarding

Bau′zeichnung f blueprint

Bayer –in [ˈbaɪ·ər(ɪn)] §6 mf Bavarian

bayerisch [ˈbaɪ·ərɪʃ] adj Bavarian

Bayern [ˈbaɪ·ərn] n (-s;) Bavaria

Bazillenträger [baˈtsɪləntrɛgər] m germ carrier

Bazil·lus [ba'tsɪlʊs] *m* (-;-len [lən]) bacillus

be- [bə] *insep pref*

beabsichtigen [bə'apzɪçtɪgən] *tr* intend; (mit) mean (by)

beach'ten *tr* pay attention to; (*merken*) note, notice; (*befolgen*) observe; (*berücksichtigen*) consider

beach'tenswert *adj* noteworthy

Beach'tung *f* (-;) attention; notice; observance; consideration

Beamte [bə'amtə] *m* (-n;-n) official

Beam'tenherrschaft *f* bureaucracy

Beam'tenlaufbahn *f* civil service career

Beamtentum [bə'amtəntum] *n* (-[e]s;) officialdom, bureaucracy

Beamtin [bə'amtɪn] *f* (-;-nen) official

beäng'stigen *tr* make anxious, alarm

beanspruchen [bə'an/pruxən] *tr* claim; (*Zeit, Raum*) require; **zu stark beansprucht werden** be worked too hard

beanstanden [bə'an/tandən] *tr* object to, find fault with; (*Waren*) reject; (*Wahl*) contest; (*Recht*) challenge

Bean'standung *f* (-;-en) objection; complaint

bean'tragen *tr* propose; (**bei**) apply for (to)

beant'worten *tr* answer

Beant'wortung *f* (-;-en) answer

bear'beiten *tr* work; (*Land*) cultivate; (*Buch, Text*) revise; (*Wörterbuch*) compile; (*für die Bühne*) adapt; (*ein Manuskript*) prepare; (*Thema; Kunden*) work on; (*Person*) try to influence; (chem) treat; (*Auftrag*) (com) handle; (*Fall*) (jur) handle; (metal) machine, tool; (mus) arrange

bearg'wöhnen *tr* be suspicious of

beaufsichtigen [bə'aufzɪçtɪgən] *tr* supervise; (*Arbeiten*) superintend; (*Kinder*) look after; (educ) proctor; **streng b.** keep a sharp eye on

beauf'tragen *tr* commission, appoint; (mit) entrust (with)

Beauftragte [bə'auftraktə] §5 *mf* representative; (com) agent

bebau'en *tr* cultivate; (*Gelände*) build up

beben ['bebən] *intr* (**vor**) tremble (with), shake (with); (*Erde*) quake

bebrilt [bə'brɪlt] *adj* bespectacled

Becher ['beçər] *m* (-s;-) cup, mug

bechern ['beçərn] *intr* (coll) booze

Becken ['bekən] *n* (-s;-) basin, bowl; (anat) pelvis; (mus) cymbal

bedacht [bə'daxt] *adj* (**auf** *acc*) intent (on); **auf alles b. sein** think of everything; **darauf b. sein zu** (*inf*) be anxious to (*inf*) ‖ **Bedacht** *m*—**B. nehmen auf** (*acc*) take into consideration; **mit B.** deliberately; with caution

bedächtig [bə'deçtɪç], **bedachtsam** [bə'daxtzam] *adj* cautious, deliberate

bedan'ken *ref*—ich würde mich bestens b., wenn (iron) I would be most indignant if; **sich b. bei j-m für** thank s.o. for

Bedarf [bə'darf] *m* (-[e]s;) demand; requirement; (**an** *dat*) need (of); **bei B.** if required; **den B. decken** meet the demand; **nach B.** as required;

seinen B. decken an (*dat*) get one's supply of

Bedarfs'artikel *pl* needs, supplies

Bedarfs'fall *m*—**im B.** in case of need

Bedarfs'güter *pl* consumer goods

Bedarfs'haltestelle *f* optional bus or trolley stop

Bedarfs'träger *m* consumer

bedauerlich [bə'dau·ərlɪç] *adj* regrettable

bedau'erlicherweise *adv* unfortunately

bedauern [bə'dau·ərn] *tr* pity, feel sorry for; regret, deplore ‖ **Bedauern** *n* (-s;) (**über** *acc*) regret (over); (*Mitleid*) (mit) pity (for)

bedau'ernswert *adj* pitiful, pitiable

bedecken (**bedek'ken**) *tr* cover; **bedeckt** overcast

Bedeckung (**Bedek'kung**) *f* (-;-en) cover; escort; (mil) escort; (nav) convoy

beden'ken §66 *tr* consider; (*beachten*) bear in mind; (*im Testament*) provide for ‖ *ref* deliberate, think a matter over; **sich e-s anderen b.** change one's mind ‖ **Bedenken** *n* (-s;—) (*Erwägung*) consideration, reflection; (*Einwand*) objection; (*Zweifel*) doubt, scruple

bedenk'lich *adj* (*ernst*) serious, critical; (*gefährlich*) risky; (*heikel*) ticklish; (*Charakter*) questionable

bedeu'ten *tr* mean; **das hat nichts zu b.** that doesn't matter; **j-m b., daß** make it clear to s.o. that

bedeu'tend *adj* important; (*beträchtlich*) considerable

bedeutsam [bə'dɔɪtzam] *adj* significant; (*Blick*) meaningful

Bedeu'tung *f* (-;-en) meaning; (*Wichtigkeit*) importance

bedeu'tungsvoll *adj* significant

bedeu'tungsweise *adv* conditionally

bedie'nen *tr* wait on, serve; (*Maschine*) operate ‖ *ref* (*genit*) make use of; **bedienen Sie sich** help yourself ‖ *intr* wait on people; (cards) follow suit

Bedie'nung *f* (-;) service; servants; waitresses

Bedienungs- *comb.fm.* control

Bedie'nungsanweisung *f* instructions

Bedie'nungsmannschaft *f* gun crew

bedingen [bə'dɪŋən] *tr* condition, stipulate; (*in sich schließen*) imply; **bedingt** conditioned, conditional

bedin'gungsweise *adv* conditionally

bedrän'gen *tr* press hard; (*beunruhigen*) pester; **bedrängte Lage** state of distress; **bedrängte Verhältnisse** financial difficulties

Bedrängnis [bə'drɛŋnɪs] *f* (-;-se) distress; **in ärgster B.** in dire straits

bedro'hen *tr* threaten, menace

bedroh'lich *adj* threatening

bedrucken (**bedruk'ken**) *tr* print on; (*Stoff*) print

bedrücken (**bedrük'ken**) *tr* oppress

bedür'fen §69 *intr* (*genit*) require

Bedürfnis [bə'dyrfnɪs] *n* (-ses;-se) need, requirement; (*Wunsch*) desire; **Bedürfnisse** necessities; **das dringende B. haben zu** (*inf*) have the urge to (*inf*)

Bedürf'nisanstalt f comfort station

bedürf'nislos adj having few needs

bedürftig [bə'dyrftıç] adj needy; **b. sein** (genit) be in need of

Beefsteak ['bifstek] n (-s;-s) steak; **Deutsches B.** hamburger

beehren [bə'erən] tr honor || **ref—sich b. zu** (inf) have the honor of (ger)

beei'len ref hurry (up)

beein'drucken tr impress

beeinflussen [bə'aınflusən] tr influence

Beein'flussung f (-;) (genit) influence (on), effect (on); (pol) lobbying

beeinträchtigen [bə'aıntrɛçtıgən] tr (Ruf) damage; (Wert) detract from; (Rechte) encroach upon; (Aussichten) hurt, spoil

been'den, been'digen tr end, conclude; (Arbeit) complete

beengen [bə'ɛŋən] tr confine, cramp; **sich beengt fühlen** feel cramped; (fig) feel restricted

beer'ben tr—j—n b. inherit s.o.'s estate

beerdigen [bə'erdigən] tr bury, inter

Beer'digung f (-;-en) burial

Beere ['berə] f (-;-n) berry

Beet [bet] n (-[e]s;-e) (agr) bed

befähigen [bə'fe·ıgən] tr enable, qualify

befähigt [bə'fe·ıçt] adj able, capable

Befä'higung f (-;-en) qualification; (Fähigkeit) ability

befahl [bə'fal] pret of **befehlen**

befahrbar [bə'farbar] adj (Weg) passable; (Wasser) navigable

befah'ren §71 tr travel; (Meer) sail; (Fluß) navigate; (Küste) sail along; (Schacht) go down into

befal'len §72 tr strike, attack; infest

befan'gen adj embarrassed; (schüchtern) shy; (voreingenommen) prejudiced; (parteiisch) partial

befas'sen tr touch, handle || **ref—sich b. mit** concern oneself with

befehden [bə'fedən] tr make war on

Befehl [bə'fel] m (-s;-e) order, command; **auf B.** (genit) by order of

befeh'len §51 tr order, command; **was b. Sie?** what is your pleasure?

befehligen [bə'feligən] tr command, be in command of

Befehls'form f imperative mood

Befehlshaber [bə'felshabər] m (-s;-) (mil) commanding officer; (nav) commander in chief; **oberster B.** supreme commander

befehlshaberisch [bə'felshabərɪʃ] adj imperious

Befehls'stelle f command post

befe'stigen tr (an dat) fasten (to), attach (to); (mil) fortify

Befe'stigung f (-;-en) fortification

befeuchten [bə'fɔıçtən] tr moisten, wet

befeu'ern tr (aer, naut) mark with lights; (mil) fire on, shoot at

befin'den §59 tr deem || ref be, feel || **Befinden** n (-s;) judgment, view; (state of) health; **je nach B.** according to taste

befindlich [bə'fıntlıç] adj present, to

be found; **all die im Hafen befindlichen Schiffe** the ships (present) in the harbor; **b. sein** happen to be

beflecken (beflek'ken) tr stain, taint

beflissen [bə'flısən] adj (genit) keen (on), interested (in) || **Beflissene** §5 mf (genit) student (of)

befohlen [bə'folən] pp of **befehlen**

befol'gen tr obey, comply with

Befol'gung f (-;) observance

beför'dern tr ship; (spedieren) forward; (im Rang) promote; (fördern) further

Beför'derungsmittel n means of transportation

befra'gen tr question, interrogate; poll; (um Rat) consult

befrakt [bə'frakt] adj in tails

befrei'en tr free; liberate; (vom Militärdienst) exempt; (von e-r Aufgabe) excuse; (von Sorgen, e-r Last) relieve

Befrei'ung f (-;-en) freeing; liberation; exemption; rescue

befremden [bə'frɛmdən] tr surprise, astonish; strike as odd || **Befremden** n (-s;) surprise, astonishment

befreunden [bə'frɔındən] ref—sich mit etw b. reconcile oneself to s.th.; **sich mit j—m b.** make friends with s.o.

befrieden [bə'fridən] tr pacify

befriedigen [bə'fridigən] tr satisfy

befrie'digend adj satisfactory

befristen [bə'frıstən] tr set a time limit on

Befri'stung f (-;-en) time limit

befruchten [bə'fruxtən] tr (Land) make fertile; (schwängern) impregnate; (Ei) fertilize; **künstlich b.** inseminate; (bot) pollinate

befugt [bə'fukt] adj authorized

befüh'len tr feel, touch

Befund m (-[e]s;-e) findings, facts

befürch'ten tr fear, be afraid of

Befürch'tung f (-;-en) apprehension

befürworten [bə'fyrvɔrtən] tr support; (anraten) recommend

begabt [bə'gapt] adj gifted, talented

Bega'bung f (-;-en) aptitude; (natural) gift, talent

Bega'bungsprüfung f intelligence test

begann [bə'gan] pret of **beginnen**

begatten [bə'gatən] tr mate with || ref copulate, mate

bege'ben §80 tr (Anleihen) float, place; (Wertpapiere) sell || ref go; occur; **es begab sich** (Bib) it came to pass; **sich an die Arbeit b.** set to work; **sich auf die Flucht b.** take to flight; **sich auf die Reise b.** set out on a trip; **sich b.** (genit) renounce; **sich in Gefahr b.** expose oneself to danger

Bege'benheit f (-;-en) event, incident

begegnen [bə'gegnən] intr (dat) meet, come upon; (Schwierigkeiten, Feind) encounter; (Gefahr) face

bege'hen §82 tr walk on; walk along; (Verbrechen, Irrtum) commit; (Fest) celebrate

Begehr [bə'ger] m & n (-s;) desire; request; (econ) demand

begehren [bə'gerən] tr wish for; crave;

(Bib) covet; **etw von j-m b.** ask s.o. for s.th. ‖ *intr* (**nach**) yearn (for)
begeh'renswert *adj* desirable
begehr'lich *adj* covetous
begehrt [bə'ge:rt] *adj* in demand
begeistert [bə'gaɪstərt] *adj* enthusiastic
Begei'sterung *f* (-;) enthusiasm
Begier [bə'gi:r] *f* (-;) var of **Begierde**
Begierde [bə'gi:rdə] *f* (-;-n) desire; (fleshly) appetite; eagerness; craving
begierig [bə'gi:rɪç] *adj* eager; (*Augen*) hungry; (**nach, auf** *acc*) desirous (of); **b. zu** (*inf*) eager to (*inf*)
begie'ßen §76 *tr* water; (culin) baste; **das wollen wir b.** we want to celebrate it (*by drinking*)
Beginn [bə'gɪn] *m* (-[e]s;) beginning; (*Ursprung*) origin
beginnen [bə'gɪnən] §52 *tr & intr* begin
beglaubigen [bə'glaʊbɪgən] *tr* certify, authenticate; (*Gesandten*) accredit
Beglau'bigung *f* (-;) authentication; accreditation
Beglau'bigungsschreiben *n* (dipl) credentials
beglei'chen §85 *tr* balance; (*Rechnung*) pay in full; (*Streit*) settle
begleiten [bə'glaɪtən] *tr* accompany; escort; see (*e.g., off, home*); **hinaus b.** see to the door
Beglei'ter *-in* §6 *mf* companion
Beglei'terscheinung *f* concomitant
Beglei'tmusik *f* background music
Beglei'tschreiben *s* covering letter
Beglei'tung *f* (-;-en) company; escort; (*Gefolge*) retinue; (mus) accompaniment
beglück'wünschen *tr* (**zu**) congratulate (**on**)
Beglück'wünschung *f* (-;-en) congratulation
begnadet [bə'gna:dət] *adj* highly gifted
begnadigen [bə'gna:dɪgən] *tr* pardon; (pol) grant amnesty to
Begna'digung *f* (-;-en) pardon; amnesty
begnügen [bə'gny:gən] *ref* (**mit**) content oneself (with), be satisfied (with)
begonnen [bə'gɔnən] *pp* of **beginnen**
begra'ben §87 *tr* bury
Begräbnis [bə'grɛpnɪs] *n* (-ses;-se) burial; funeral
Begräb'nisfeier *f* funeral
Begräb'nisstätte *f* burial place
begradigen [bə'gra:dɪgən] *tr* straighten; (tech) align
begrei'fen §88 *tr* touch, handle; (*verstehen*) grasp; (*enthalten*) comprise
begreif'lich *adj* understandable
begreif'licherweise *adv* understandably
begren'zen *tr* bound; limit, restrict
Begren'zung *f* (-;-en) limitation
Begriff [bə'grɪf] *m* (-[e]s;-e) idea, notion; (*Ausdruck*) term; (philos) concept; **im B. sein zu** (*inf*) be on the point of (*ger*)
begriffen [bə'grɪfən] *adj*—**b. sein in** (*dat*) be in the process of
begrün'den *tr* found, establish; (*Behauptung*) substantiate, prove
Begrün'der *-in* §6 *mf* founder

Begrün'dung *f* (-;-en) establishment; proof; (*Grund*) ground, reason
begrüßen *tr* greet; welcome
begünstigen [bə'gynstɪgən] *tr* favor; (*fördern*) promote, support; (jur) aid and abet
Begün'stiger *m* (-s;-) accessory after the fact
Begünstigte [bə'gynstɪçtə] §5 *mf* (ins) beneficiary
Begün'stigung *f* (-;-en) promotion, encouragement; support, backing; (jur) aiding and abetting
begut'achten *tr* give an expert opinion on; **b. lassen** obtain expert opinion on
begütert [bə'gy:tərt] *adj* well-to-do
begütigen [bə'gy:tɪgən] *tr* appease
behaart [bə'ha:rt] *adj* hairy
behäbig [bə'hɛbɪç] *adj* comfort-loving; (*beleibt*) portly
behaftet [bə'haftət] *adj* afflicted
behagen [bə'ha:gən] *intr* (dat) please, suit ‖ **Behagen** *n* (-s;) pleasure
behaglich [bə'ha:klɪç] *adj* pleasant; (*traulich*) snug, cozy
behal'ten §90 *tr* keep, retain; **Recht b.** turn out to be right
Behälter [bə'hɛltər] *m* (-s;-) container; box; (*für Öl, usw.*) tank
behan'deln *tr* treat; deal with; handle
behän'gen §92 *tr* hang; deck out
beharren [bə'harən] *intr* remain (unchanged); (**in** *dat*) persevere (in); (**auf** *dat*) persist (in), stick (to)
beharrlich [bə'harlɪç] *adj* steadfast
behau'en §93 *tr* hew
behaupten [bə'haʊptən] *tr* declare, assert; (*festhalten*) maintain, retain; allege ‖ *ref* stand one's ground; (*Preise*) remain steady
behausen [bə'haʊzən] *tr* lodge, house
Behau'sung *f* (-;-en) dwelling
behe'ben §94 *tr* (*Schwierigkeiten*) remove; (*Zweifel*) dispel; (*Schaden*) repair; (*Lage*) remedy; (*Geld*) withdraw; (*Schmerzen*) eliminate
beheimatet [bə'haɪmatət] *adj*—**b. sein in** (*dat*) reside in; come from
Behelf [bə'hɛlf] *m* (-[e]s;-e) expedient; makeshift
behel'fen §96 *ref* (**mit**) make do (with)
Behelfs- *comb.fm.* temporary
behelfs'mäßig *adj* temporary, makeshift
behelligen [bə'hɛlɪgən] *tr* bother
Behel'ligung *f* (-;-en) bother, trouble
behende [bə'hɛndə] *adj* agile, quick; (*gewandt*) handy; (*geistig*) smart
beherbergen [bə'hɛrbərgən] *tr* take in, put up (*as guest*)
beherr'schen *tr* (*Land*) rule; (*Sprache*) master; (*Gefühle*) control; (*überragen*) tower over; **den Luftraum b.** (mil) have air supremacy
Beherr'scher *-in* §6 *mf* ruler ‖ *m* master ‖ *f* mistress
beherzigen [bə'hɛrtsɪgən] *tr* take to heart, remember
beherzt [bə'hɛrtst] *adj* courageous
behe'xen *tr* bewitch; (fig) captivate
behilflich [bə'hɪlflɪç] *adj* helpful
behin'dern *tr* hinder; hamper; block
behor'chen *tr* overhear

Behörde [bə'hørdə] *f* (-;-n) authority, board; *die Behörden* the authorities
behördlich [bə'hørtlɪç] *adj* official
behüten *tr* (vor *dat*) protect (against); **Gott behüte!** God forbid!
behutsam [bə'hutzɑm] *adj* wary
bei [baɪ] *prep* (*dat*) by, beside, at, with, in; (*in Anschriften*) in care of, c/o; (*Zeit, Umstände*) at, by, during, on; (*Zustände, Eigenschaften*) at, while, in; **bei mir haben** have on me; **bei meiner Ehre** upon my honor; **bei Schiller** in the works of Schiller; **bei uns** at our house; **bei weitem** by far
bei'behalten §90 *tr* retain, keep
Bei'blatt *n* supplement
bei'bringen §65 *tr* obtain, procure; (*Beweise, Zeugen*) produce; (*Arznei, Gift*) administer; (*Wunde, Niederlage, Schlag, Verluste*) inflict; **j-m die Nachricht schonend b.** break the news gently to s.o.; **j-m etw b.** teach s.o. s.th., make s.th. clear to s.o.
Beichte ['baɪçtə] *f* (-;-n) confession
beichten ['baɪçtən] *tr* (eccl) confess
Beicht'kind *n* (eccl) penitent
Beicht'stuhl *m* (eccl) confessional
beide ['baɪdə] *adj* both; two || *pron* both; two; **keiner von beiden** neither of them
beiderlei ['baɪdər'laɪ] *invar adj* both kinds of
beiderseitig ['baɪdər'zaɪtɪç] *adj* bilateral; (*gemeinsam*) mutual
beiderseits ['baɪdər'zaɪts] *adv* on both sides; mutually, reciprocally || *prep* (*genit*) on both sides of
beieinan'der *adv* together; **gut b. sein** (coll) be in good shape
Bei'fahrer –in §6 *mf* relief driver; passenger (*next to the driver*)
Bei'fall *m* approval; applause
bei'fällig *adj* approving; (*Bericht*) favorable || *adv* approvingly
Bei'fallklatschen *n* clapping, applause
Bei'fallsgeschrei *n* loud cheering
Bei'fallsruf *m* cheer
Bei'film *m* (cin) second feature
bei'folgend *adj* enclosed
bei'fügen *tr* add; (*e-m Brief*) enclose
bei'fügend *adj* (gram) attributive
Bei'fügung *f* (-;-en) addition; enclosure; (gram) attributive
Bei'gabe *f* extra; funerary gift
bei'geben §80 *tr* add; assign || *intr* give in; **klein b.** knuckle under
Bei'geschmack *m* taste, flavor; tinge
Bei'hilfe *f* aid; (*Stipendium*) grant; (*Unterstützung*) subsidy; allowance; (jur) aiding and abetting
bei'kommen § 99 *intr* (SEIN) (*dat*) get the better of; (*dat*) reach; **e-r Schwierigkeit** overcome
Beil [baɪl] *n* (-[e]s;-e) hatchet
Bei'lage *f* (*im Brief*) enclosure; (*e-r Zeitung*) supplement; **Fleisch mit B.** meat and vegetables
beiläufig ['baɪlɔɪfɪç] *adj* incidental; casual || *adv* by the way, incidentally; **b. erwähnen** mention in passing
bei'legen *tr* add; (*Titel*) confer; (*Wichtigkeit*) attach; (*Streit*) settle; **etw**

e-m Brief b. enclose s.th. in a letter || *intr* heave to
Bei'leid *n* (-s;) condolence(s)
bei'liegen §108 *intr*—**e-m Brief b.** be enclosed in a letter; **j-m b.** lie with s.o
beim *abbr* **bei dem**
bei'messen §70 *tr* attribute, impute
bei'mischen *tr* mix in
Bein [baɪn] *n* (-[e]s;-e) leg; (*Knochen*) bone; (fig) foot; **j-m ein B. stellen** trip s.o.
beinahe ['baɪnɑ•ə], [baɪ'nɑ•e] *adv* almost, nearly
Bei'name *m* appellation; (*Spitzname*) nickname
Bein'bruch *m* fracture, broken leg
Bein'schiene *f* (surg) splint; (sport) shin guard
Bein'schützer *m* (sport) shin guard
Bein'stellen *n* (sport) tripping
bei'ordnen *tr* assign, appoint (*s.o.*) as assistant; (*dat*) place (*s.th.*) on a level (with)
beipflichten ['baɪpflɪçtən] *intr* (*dat*) agree with (*s.o.*), agree to (*s.th.*)
Bei'programm *n* (cin) second feature
Bei'rat *m* (-s;-e) adviser, counselor; (*Körperschaft*) advisory board
beir'ren *tr* mislead
beisammen [baɪ'zamən] *adv* together
Beisam'mensein *n* (-s;) being together; gathering, reunion; **geselliges B.** social; informal reception
Bei'satz *m* addition; (*bei Legierung*) alloy; (gram) appositive
Bei'schlaf *m* sexual intercourse
bei'schließen §76 *tr* enclose
Bei'schluß *m*—**unter B. von allen Dokumenten** with all documents attached
bei'schreiben §62 *tr* write in the margin; add as a postscript
Bei'schrift *f* postscript
Bei'sein *n* (-s;) presence
beisei'te *adv* aside; **b. schaffen** remove; (coll) do (*s.o.*) in
bei'setzen *tr* bury, inter
Bei'sitzer *m* associate judge
Bei'spiel *n* example; **zum B.** for example
bei'spielhaft *adj* exemplary
bei'spiellos *adj* unparalleled
bei'spielsweise *adv* by way of example
bei'springen §142 *intr* (*dat*) come to the aid of
beißen ['baɪsən] §53 *tr & intr* bite
bei'ßend *adj* biting; stinging, pungent, acrid; sarcastic; (*Reue*) bitter
Beiß'korb *m* muzzle
Beiß'zahn *m* (anat) incisor
Beiß'zange *f* pincers, nippers
Bei'stand *m* aid, support; (*Person*) assistant
bei'stehen §146 *intr* (*dat*) stand by, back, support
Bei'steuer *f* contribution
bei'steuern *tr* contribute
bei'stimmen *intr* (*dat*) agree with
Bei'stimmung *f* (-;) approval
Bei'strich *m* comma
Beitrag ['baɪtrak] *m* (-[e]s;-e) contribution; (*e-s Mitglieds*) dues

bei'tragen §132 tr & intr contribute

bei'treiben §62 tr collect; (Abgaben) exact; (mil) commandeer, requisition

bei'treten §152 intr (SEIN) (dat) join; (j–s Meinung) concur in

Bei'tritt m joining; concurrence

Bei'wagen m (aut) sidecar

Bei'werk n (–[e]s;) accessories

bei'wohnen intr (dat) attend; (e–m Ereignis) be witness to; (j–m) have intercourse with (s.o.)

Bei'wort n (–[e]s;ӥer) epithet; (gram) adjective

Beize ['bartsə] f (–;–n) corrosive; (wood) stain; (Falken–) falconry; (culin) marinade

beizeiten [bar'tsartən] adv on time; (frühzeitig) early

beizen ['bartsən] tr (ätzen) corrode; (Holz) stain; (Wunde) cauterize; (hunt) go hawking

bejahen [bə'ja·ən] tr say 'yes' to

beja'hend adj affirmative

bejahrt [bə'jart] adj aged

bekämp'fen tr fight, oppose

bekannt [bə'kant] adj known; familiar; (berühmt) well-known || Bekannte §5 mf acquaintance

Bekannt'gabe f announcement

bekannt'geben §80 tr announce

bekannt'lich adv as is well known

bekannt'machen tr announce; (Gesetz) promulgate

Bekannt'machung f (–;–en) publication, announcement; (Plakat) poster

Bekannt'schaft f (–;) acquaintance; (coll) acquaintances

bekeh'ren tr convert || ref (zu) become a convert (to)

Bekehrte [bə'kertə] §5 mf convert

beken'nen §97 tr (Sünde) confess; (zugestehen) admit; Farbe b. follow suit; (fig) put one's cards on the table || ref—sich schuldig b. plead guilty; sich zu e–r Religion b. profess a religion; sich zu e–r Tat b. own up to a deed; sich zu j–m b. stand by s.o., believe in s.o.

Bekennt'nis n (eccl) confession; (Konfession) denomination

bekla'gen tr deplore; (Tod) mourn || ref (über acc) complain (about), find fault (with)

bekla'genswert adj deplorable

Beklagte [bə'klaktə] §5 mf defendant

beklat'schen tr applaud

bekle'ben tr paste; (mit Etiketten) label; e–e Mauer mit Plakaten b. paste posters on a wall

beklei'den tr clothe, dress; (Mauer) face, cover; (Amt) hold

beklem'men tr stifle, oppress

Beklem'mung f (–;–en) worry, anxiety; Beklemmungen claustrophobia

beklommen [bə'kləmən] adj uneasy

bekom'men §99 tr get; obtain; receive; (Schnupfen) catch; (Risse) develop || intr (dat) do good; (Speise) b. do s.o. harm; wohl bekomm's! to your health!

bekömmlich [bə'kœmlıç] adj digestible; (gesund) healthful; (zuträglich) wholesome

beköstigen [bə'kœstıgən] tr board, feed || ref—sich selbst b. do one's own cooking

bekräf'tigen tr (Vorschlag) support; (bestätigen) substantiate; mit e–m Eid b. seal with an oath

bekrän'zen tr wreath, crown

bekreu'zen, bekreu'zigen ref cross oneself, make the sign of the cross

bekrie'gen tr make war on

bekrit'teln tr criticize, pick at

bekrit'zeln tr scribble on, doodle on

beküm'mern tr worry, trouble || ref (um) concern onself (with), bother (about)

beküm'mert adj (über acc) worried (about)

bekunden [bə'kundən] tr manifest, show; (öffentlich) state publicly

bela'den §103 tr load; (fig) burden

Belag [bə'lak] m (–[e]s;ӥe) covering; coat(ing); flooring; layer; surface

bela'gern tr besiege, beleaguer

Bela'gerung f (–;–en) siege

Belang [bə'laŋ] m (–[e]s;e) importance, consequence; Belange interests

belan'gen tr (jur) sue; was mich belangt as far as I am concerned

belang'los adj unimportant

bela'sten tr load (down); (Grundstück) encumber; (fig) burden; (acct) charge; (jur) incriminate

belästigen [bə'lestıgən] tr annoy, bother; (mit Fragen) pester; (unabsichtlich) inconvenience

Bela'stung f (–;–en) load; encumbrance; (fig) burden; (acct) debit; die Zeiten größter B. the peak hours

Bela'stungsprobe f (fig) acid test

Bela'stungszeuge m witness for the prosecution

belau'fen §105 ref—sich b. auf (acc) amount to, come to

belau'schen tr overhear

bele'ben tr animate; (Getränk) spike; wieder b. revive

belebt [bə'lept] adj animated, lively

Bele'bungsmittel n stimulant

Beleg [bə'lek] m (–s;–e) (Beweisstück) evidence; (Unterlage) voucher; (Beispiel) example; (jur) exhibit

bele'gen tr cover; (Platz) take, occupy; (bemannen) man; (beweisen) verify; (Vorlesung) register for; ein Brötchen mit Schinken b. make a ham sandwich; mit Beispielen b. exemplify; mit Fliesen b. tile; mit Steuern b. tax; mit Teppichen b. carpet || ref become coated

Beleg'schaft f (–;–en) crew; personnel; shift

Beleg'schein m voucher; receipt

Beleg'stelle f reference

belegt [bə'lekt] adj (Platz) reserved; (Zunge) coated; (Stimme) husky; (telp) busy; belegtes Brot sandwich

beleh'ren tr instruct || ref—sich b. lassen listen to reason

beleh'rend adj instructive

Beleh'rung f (–;–en) instruction; (Lehre) lesson; (Rat) advice; zu Ihrer B. for your information

beleibt [bə'laɪpt] *adj* stout
beleidigen [bə'laɪdɪgən] *tr* offend
belei'digend *adj* offensive
bele'sen *adj* well-read
beleuch'ten *tr* light (up), illuminate; (fig) throw light on
Beleuch'ter *m* (aer) pathfinder; (theat) juicer
Beleuch'tung *f* (-;-en) lighting, illumination; (fig) elucidation
Beleuch'tungskörper *m* lighting fixture
Belgien ['bɛlgjən] *n* (-s;) Belgium
Belgier **-in** ['bɛlgjər(ɪn)] §6 *mf* Belgian
belgisch ['bɛlgɪʃ] *adj* Belgian
belichten [bə'lɪçtən] *tr* (phot) expose
Belich'tung *f* (-;-en) exposure
belie'ben *intr* please || *impers* (*dat*)—wenn es Ihnen beliebt if you please || **Belieben** *n* (-s;) liking; es steht in Ihrem B. it's up to you; nach B. as you like
beliebig ['bə'libɪç] *adj* any (you please) || *adv* as ... as you please
beliebt [bə'lipt] *adj* favorite; (bei) popular (with)
Beliebt'heit *f* (-;) popularity
belie'fern *tr* supply, furnish
bellen ['bɛlən] *intr* bark
belob(ig)en [bə'lob(ɪg)ən] *tr* praise; commend; (mil) cite
beloh'nen *tr* reward
belü'gen §111 *tr* lie to, deceive
belustigen [bə'lʊstɪgən] *tr* amuse
bemächtigen [bə'mɛçtɪgən] *intr* (*genit*) seize, get hold of; (mil) seize
bemä'keln *tr* criticize, carp at
bema'len *tr* paint; decorate
bemängeln [bə'mɛŋəln] *tr* criticize
bemannen [bə'manən] *tr* man
Beman'nung *f* (-;-en) (nav) crew
bemänteln [bə'mɛntəln] *tr* gloss over; (*Fehler, Fehltritt*) cover up
bemei'stern *tr* master || *ref* control oneself; (*genit*) get hold of
bemerk'bar *adj* perceptible
bemer'ken *tr* notice; (*äußern*) remark
bemer'kenswert *adj* remarkable
Bemer'kung *f* (-;-en) note; remark
bemes'sen §70 *tr* measure; proportion
bemit'leiden *tr* pity, feel sorry for
bemittelt [bə'mɪtəlt] *adj* well-to-do
bemogeln [bə'mogəln] *tr* cheat
bemü'hen *tr* trouble, bother; bemüht sein zu (*inf*) take pains to (*inf*) || *ref* bother, exert oneself; sich für j-n b. intervene for s.o.; sich um etw b. make an effort to obtain s.th.; sich um j-n b. attend to s.o.; sich zu j-m b. go to s.o.
Bemü'hung *f* (-;-en) bother; effort
bemüßigt [bə'mysɪçt] *adj*—sich b. fühlen zu (*inf*) feel obliged to (*inf*)
bemu'stern *tr*—ein Angebot b. (com) send samples of an offer
bemuttern [bə'mʊtərn] *tr* mother
benachbart [bə'naxbart] *adj* neighboring; (*Fachgebiet*) related, allied
benachrichtigen [bə'naxrɪçtɪgən] *tr* notify; put on notice
Benach'richtigung *f* (-;-en) notification; notice
benachteiligen [bə'naxtaɪlɪgən] *tr*

place at a disadvantage, handicap; discriminate against
benebelt [bə'nebəlt] *adj* covered in mist; (fig) groggy
benedeien [bene'daɪ·ən] *tr* bless
beneh'men §116 *tr*—j-m etw b. take s.th. away from s.o. || *ref* behave || **Benehmen** *n* (-s;) behavior
beneiden [bə'naɪdən] *tr*—j-n um etw b. begrudge s.o. s.th.
benei'denswert *adj* enviable
benen'nen §97 *tr* name, term
Bengel ['bɛŋəl] *m* (-s;-) rascal
benommen [bə'nɔmən] *adj* dazed
benö'tigen *tr* need
benutz'bar *adj* usable
benut'zen, benüt'zen *tr* use, make use of
Benut'zerkarte *f* library card
Benzin [bɛnt'sin] *n* (-s;-e) gasoline
Benzin'behälter *m* gas tank
beobachten [bə'obaxtən] *tr* observe; (*polizeilich*) keep under surveillance; (med) keep under observation
Beob'achtung *f* (-;-en) observation; (*e–s Gesetzes*) observance
beor'dern *tr* order (*to go to a place*)
bepacken (bepak'ken) *tr* load (down)
bepflan'zen *tr* plant
bequem [bə'kvem] *adj* comfortable; cozy; (*Stellung*) soft; (*Raten, Lösung*) easy; (*faul*) lazy; b. zur Hand haben have handy
berappen [bə'rapən] *tr* (coll) shell out
bera'ten §63 *tr* (über *acc*) advise (on); discuss || *ref & intr* (über *acc*) confer (about), deliberate (on)
bera'tend *adj* advisory, consulting
beratschlagen [bə'ratʃlagən] *intr* (über *acc*) consult (on); mit j–m b. consult s.o., confer with s.o.
berat'schlagend *adj* advisory
Bera'tung *f* (-;-en) advice; (jur, med) consultation; in B. sein be under consideration
Bera'tungsstelle *f* counseling center
berau'ben *tr* (*genit*) rob (of); (*genit*) dispossess (of); (*genit*) deprive (of); (*genit*) bereave (of)
berech'nen *tr* calculate, figure out; (*schätzen*) estimate; (com) charge
berech'nend *adj* calculating
Berech'nung *f* (-;-en) calculation
berechtigen [bə'rɛçtɪgən] *tr* authorize; justify, warrant; (zu) entitle (to)
Berech'tigung *f* (-;-en) right, authorization; justification; (zu) title (to)
bereden [bə'redən] *tr* talk over, discuss; j–n zu etw b. talk s.o. into s.th. || *ref*—sich mit j–m über etw b. confer with s.o. on s.th.
beredsam [bə'retzam] *adj* eloquent
beredt [bə'ret] *adj* eloquent
Bereich *m & n* ·(-[e]s;-e) region; range; (fig) field, sphere; es fällt nicht in meinen B. it's not within my province
bereichern [bə'raɪçərn] *tr* enrich
berei'fen *tr* cover with frost; (aut) put tires on
berei'nigen *tr* (*Streit, Konto*) setttle; (*Mißverständnis*) clear up
berei'sen *tr* tour

bereit [bə'raɪt] *adj* ready

bereiten [bə'raɪtən] *tr* prepare; *(Kaffee)* make; *(Freude)* give

Bereit'schaft *f* (-;) readiness; team, squad; (mil) alert

bereit'stellen *tr* make available

Berei'tung *f* (-;-en) preparation; *(Herstellung)* manufacture

bereit'willig *adj* ready, willing

bereu'en *tr* rue, regret

Berg [bɛrk] *m* (-[e]s;-e) mountain; *(Hügel)* hill; **über alle Berge sein** be off and away; **zu Berge stehen** stand on end

bergab' *adv* downhill, down the mountain

bergauf' *adv* uphill; up the mountain

Berg'bahn *f* mountain railroad

Berg'bau *m* (-[e]s;) mining

Berg'bewohner **-in** §6 *mf* mountaineer

bergen ['bɛrgən] §54 *tr* rescue; *(enthalten)* hold; *(Gefahr)* involve; *(Segel)* take in; (naut) salvage; (poet) conceal; (rok) recover || *ref*—**in sich b. involve**

bergig ['bɛrgɪç] *adj* mountainous

Berg'kessel *m* gorge

Berg'kette *f* mountain range

Berg'kluft *f* ravine, gully

Berg'kristall *m* rock crystal, quartz

Berg'land *n* hill country

Berg'mann *m* (-[e]s;-leute) miner

Berg'predigt *f* Sermon on the Mount

Berg'recht *n* mining law

Berg'rücken *m* ridge

Berg'rutsch *m* landslide

Berg'schlucht *f* gorge, ravine

Berg'spitze *f* mountain peak

Berg'steiger **-in** §6 *mf* mountain climber

Berg'steigerei *f* mountain climbing

Berg'sturz *m* landslide

Ber'gung *f* (-;-en) rescue; (naut) salvage; (rok) recovery

Ber'gungsarbeiten *pl* salvage operations

Ber'gungsschiff *n* salvage vessel; (rok) recovery ship

Berg'wacht *f* mountain rescue service

Berg'werk *n* mine

Berg'wesen *n* mining

Bericht [bə'rɪçt] *m* (-[e]s;-e) report

berichten [bə'rɪçtən] *tr & intr* report

Berichterstatter **-in** [bə'rɪçtɛr/tatər (ɪn)] §6 *mf* reporter; correspondent; (rad) commentator

Bericht'erstattung *f* (-;) reporting

berichtigen [bə'rɪçtɪgən] *tr* rectify; *(Text)* emend; *(Schuld)* pay off

berie'chen §102 *tr* sniff at; (fig) size up || *recip* (coll) sound each other out

Berlin [bɛr'lin] *n* (-s;) Berlin

Bernstein ['bɛrn/taɪn] *m* amber

bersten ['bɛrstən] §55 *intr* (SEIN) *(vor dat)* burst (with)

berüchtigt [bə'rʏçtɪçt] *adj* notorious

berücken (berük'ken) *tr* captivate

berücksichtigen [bə'rʏksɪçtɪgən] *tr* *(erwägen)* consider; *(in Betracht ziehen)* make allowance for

Berück'sichtigung *f* (-;-en) consideration

Beruf' *m* (-[e]s;-e) vocation; profession; *(Gewerbe)* trade; *(Tätigkeit)* occupation; *(Laufbahn)* career

beru'fen *adj* called; authorized || §122 *tr* call; *(ernennen)* appoint; *(Geister)* conjure up || *ref*—**sich auf ein Gesetz b.** quote a law *(in support)*; **sich auf j—n b.** use s.o.'s name as a reference

beruf'lich *adj* professional; vocational

Berufs– *comb.fm.* professional; vocational

Berufs'diplomat *m* career diplomat

Berufs'genossenschaft *f* professional association; trade association

Berufs'heer *n* regular army

Berufs'schule *f* vocational school

Berufs'sportler **-in** §6 *mf* professional

berufs'tätig *adj* working

Beru'fung *f* (-;-en) call; vocation; appointment; (jur) appeal; **B. einlegen** (jur) appeal; **unter B. auf** *(acc)* referring to

Beru'fungsgericht *n* appellate court

beru'hen *intr* (auf *dat*) be based (on); (auf *dat*) be due (to); **e-e Sache auf sich b. lassen** let a matter rest

beruhigen [bə'ru·ɪgən] *tr* calm; appease

beru'higend *adj* soothing; reassuring

Beru'higung *f* (-;) calming; appeasement, pacification; reassurance; *(der Lage)* stabilization; **zu meiner großen B.** much to my relief

Beru'higungsmittel *n* sedative

berühmt [bə'rymt] *adj* **(wegen)** famous (for)

Berühmt'heit *f* (-;-en) renown; *(berühmte Persönlichkeit)* celebrity

berüh'ren *tr* touch; *(erwähnen)* touch on; *(wirken auf)* affect; *(Zug)* pass through || *ref* come in contact, meet

Berüh'rung *f* (-;-en) touch; contact

besä'en *tr* sow; *(bestreuen)* strew; **mit Sternen besät** star-spangled

besa'gen *tr* say; *(bedeuten)* mean

besagt [bə'zakt] *adj* aforesaid

besänftigen [bə'zɛnftɪgən] *tr* calm; appease || *ref* calm down

Besatz' *m* trimming

Besat'zung *f* (-;-en) garrison; occupation; army of occupation; (aer, nav) crew

Besat'zungsarmee *f* army of occupation

Besat'zungsbehörde *f* military government

besau'fen §124 *ref* (coll) get drunk

beschä'digen *tr* damage || *ref* injure oneself

beschaf'fen *adj*—**ich bin eben so b.** that's the way I am; **übel b. sein** be in bad shape || *tr* get, procure; *(Geld)* raise

Beschaf'fenheit *f* (-;-en) quality, property; *(Zustand)* state; *(Art)* nature; *(Anlage)* design

Beschaf'fung *f* (-;-en) procuring; *(Erwerb)* acquisition

beschäftigen [bə'ʃɛftɪgən] *tr* occupy; keep busy; *(anstellen)* employ; **beschäftigt sein** be work for *(a company)*; **beschäftigt sein mit** be busy with

beschä′men *tr* shame, make ashamed; beschämt sein be ashamed

Beschau′ *f* inspection

beschau′en *tr* look at; inspect

beschau′lich *adj* contemplative

Bescheid [bə′ʃaɪt] *m* (-[e]s;-e) answer; (*Anweisung*) instructions, directions; (*Auskunft*) information; (jur) decision; **B. hinterlassen bei** leave word with; **B. wissen** be well-informed; **j-m B. geben** (or sagen) give s.o. information or directions

beschei′den *adj* modest; (*Preise*) moderate; (*Auswahl*) limited; (*einfach*) simple, plain ‖ §112 *tr* inform; (*beordern*) order, direct; (*vorladen*) summon; (*zuteilen*) allot; **abschlägig b.** turn down; **es ist mir beschieden** it fell to my lot ‖ *ref* be satisfied

Beschei′denheit *f* (-;) modesty

bescheinigen [bə′ʃaɪnɪgən] *tr* (*Empfang*) acknowledge; (*bezeugen*) certify

Beschei′nigung *f* (-;-en) acknowledgement; certification; (*Schein*) certificate; (*im Brief*) to whom it may concern

beschei′ßen §53 *tr* (sl) cheat

beschen′ken *tr*—j-n b. mit present s.o. with

bescheren [bə′ʃerən] *tr* give gifts to

Besche′rung *f* (-;-en) distribution of gifts (*especially at Christmas*); **e-e schöne B.** (coll) a nice mess

beschicken (beschik′ken) *tr* (*mit Waren*) supply; (*Messe*) exhibit at, send exhibits to; (*Kongreß*) send delegates to; (*Hochofen*) feed, charge

beschie′ßen §76 *tr* shoot up; (mil, phys) bombard

beschimp′fen *tr* insult, call (*s.o.*) names

beschir′men *tr* shield, protect

beschla′fen *tr* (*e-e Frau*) sleep with; (*e-e Sache*) sleep on

Beschlag′ *m* (-s;-̈e) hardware; (*Huf-*) horse shoes; (*auf Fensterscheiben*) steam, vapor; (*Überzug*) thin coating; **in B. nehmen** confiscate; (*Schiff*) seize; (*Gehalt*) attach

beschla′gen *adj*—b. in (*dat*) well-versed in ‖ §132 *tr* cover, coat; (*Metallverzierungen*) fit, mount; (*Pferd*) shoe ‖ *ref & intr* steam up; (*Mauer*) sweat; (*Metall*) oxidize

beschlagnahmen (beschlak′nahmen) *tr* confiscate; (*Schuldnervermögen*) attach; (mil) requisition; (naut) seize

beschlei′chen §85 *tr* stalk, creep up on

beschleunigen [bə′ʃlɔɪnɪgən] *tr* accelerate, speed up

Beschleu′niger *m* (-s;-) accelerator

beschlie′ßen §76 *tr* end, wind up; (*sich entschließen*) decide

Beschluß′ *m* conclusion; decision; resolution; (jur) order; **unter B.** under lock and key; **zum B.** in conclusion

beschluß′fähig *adj*—b. sein have a quorum; **beschlußfähige Anzahl** quorum

beschmie′ren *tr* smear, coat; grease

beschmut′zen *tr* soil, dirty

beschnei′den §106 *tr* clip, trim; (fig) curtail; (surg) circumcise

beschneit [bə′ʃnaɪt] *adj* snow-covered

beschönigen [bə′ʃønɪgən] *tr* (*Fehler*) whitewash, cover up, gloss over

beschrän′ken *tr* limit

beschränkt′ *adj* limited; (*Verhältnisse*) straitened; (*geistig*) dense

beschrei′ben §62 *tr* describe; use up (*in writing*)

Beschrei′bung *f* (-;-en) description

beschrei′ten §86 *tr* walk on; **den Rechtsweg b.** take legal action

beschriften [bə′ʃrɪftən] *tr* inscribe; (*Kisten*) mark; (*mit Etikett*) label

Beschrif′tung *f* (-;-en) inscription; lettering; (*erläuternde*) caption

beschuldigen [bə′ʃʊldɪgən] *tr* (*genit*) accuse of, charge (with)

beschummeln [bə′ʃʊməln] *tr* (coll) (um) cheat (out of)

Beschuß′ *m* test firing

beschüt′zen *tr* protect, defend

beschwat′zen *tr* gossip about; **j-n dazu b. zu** (*inf*) talk s.o. into (*ger*)

Beschwerde [bə′ʃverdə] *f* (-;-n) trouble; (*Klage, Krankheit*) complaint

beschweren [bə′ʃverən] *tr* burden ‖ *ref* (*über acc*) complain (about)

beschwer′lich *adj* troublesome

beschwichtigen [bə′ʃvɪçtɪgən] *tr* appease; (*Hunger*) satisfy; (*Gewissen*) soothe

beschwin′deln *tr* (um) swindle (out of)

beschwingt [bə′ʃvɪŋt] *adj* lively

beschwipst [bə′ʃvɪpst] *adj* tipsy, high

beschwö′ren *tr* swear to; (*Geister*) conjure up; (*bitten*) implore, entreat

Beschwö′rungsformel *f* incantation

beseelen [bə′zelən] *tr* inspire, animate

beseelt′ *adj* animated; (*von Hoffnungen*) filled; (*Spiel*) inspired

bese′hen §138 *tr* look at; inspect

beseitigen [bə′zaɪtɪgən] *tr* eliminate, remove, clear away; (*Übel, Fehler*) redress; (*Schwierigkeit*) overcome; (*töten*) do away with; (pol) purge

Besen [′bezən] *m* (-s;-) broom

Be′senstiel *m* broomstick

besessen [bə′zesən] *adj* (von) obsessed (by); (*vom Teufel*) possessed

Beses′senheit *f* (-;-en) obsession; (*vom Teufel*) possession

beset′zen *tr* occupy; (*mit Juwelen*) set off; (*Amt, Rolle*) fill; (*Hut*) trim

besetzt′ *adj* (*Platz, Abort*) occupied; (*Stelle*) filled; (*Kleid*) trimmed, set off; (telp) busy

Besetzt′zeichen *n* (telp) busy signal

Beset′zung *f* (-;-en) decoration; (*e-r Stelle*) filling; (mil) occupation; (theat) cast

besichtigen [bə′zɪçtɪgən] *tr* view; tour; inspect; (mil) inspect, review

Besich′tigung *f* (-;-en) sightseeing; inspection; (mil) inspection, review

besie′deln *tr* colonize; populate

besie′geln *tr* seal

besie′gen *tr* defeat; (*Widerstand*) overcome; (*Gefühle*) master

besin′nen §121 *ref* consider; (auf *acc*) think (of); **sich anders b.** change one's mind; **sich e-s Besseren b.** think better of it

besinn'lich *adj* reflective

Besin'nung *f* (-;) consciousness; reflection; **j-n zur B. bringen** bring s.o. to his senses

besin'nungslos *adj* unconscious; (*unüberlegt*) senseless

Besitz' *m* (-es;-e) possession; **in B. nehmen** take possession of

bestiz'anzeigend *adj* possessive

besit'zen §144 *tr* own, possess

Besit'zer -in §6 *mf* possessor, owner

Besitz'ergreifung *f* (-;-en) occupancy; seizure

Besitz'stand *m* ownership; (fin) assets

Besitztum ['bəˈzɪtstum] *n* (-s;-̈er) possession

Besit'zung *f* (-;-en) possession, property; (*Landgut*) estate

besoffen [bəˈzɔfən] *adj* (coll) soused

besohlen [bəˈzolən] *tr* sole

besolden [bəˈzɔldən] *tr* pay

Besol'dung *f* (-;-en) pay, salary

beson'dere §9 *adj* particular, special

Beson'derheit *f* (-;-en) peculiarity; (com) specialty

beson'ders *adv* especially; separately

besonnen [bəˈzɔnən] *adj* prudent; (*bedacht*) considerate; level-headed

besor'gen *tr* take care of; (*beschaffen*) procure, get; (*befürchten*) fear

Besorgnis [bəˈzɔrknɪs] *f* (-;-se) concern; (*Furcht*) fear

besorg'niserregend *adj* alarming

besorgt [bəˈzɔrkt] *adj* (um) worried (about), anxious (for)

Besor'gung *f* (-;-en) care; procurement; (*Auftrag*) errand; **Besorgungen machen** run errands

bespre'chen §64 *tr* discuss; (*Buch*) review; **e-e Schallplatte b.** make a recording || *ref* confer

Bespre'cher -in §6 *mf* reviewer, critic

bespren'gen *tr* sprinkle

besprit'zen *tr* splash; spray

besser ['bɛsər] *adj & adv* better

bessern ['bɛsərn] *tr* better, improve || *ref* improve

Bes'serung *f* (-;-en) improvement; **baldige B.** speedy recovery

Bes'serungsanstalt *f* reform school

Bestand' *m* (-[e]s;-̈e) existence; (*Vorrat*) stock, inventory; (*Kassen-*) cash on hand; (*Baum-*) stand; **B. an** (dat) number of; **B. an kampffähigen Truppen** effective strength; **B. haben, von B. sein** have endurance, be lasting

bestän'dig *adj* constant, steady

Bestands'aufnahme *f* inventory

Bestand'teil *m* component; ingredient

bestär'ken *tr* strengthen, fortify

bestätigen [bəˈʃtɛtɪgən] *tr* confirm; (*Zeugnis*) corroborate; (*Empfang*) acknowledge; (*Vertrag*) ratify || *ref* prove true, come true

bestatten [bəˈʃtatən] *tr* bury, inter

Bestat'tungsinstitut *n* funeral home

bestau'ben, bestäuben [bəˈʃtɔɪbən] *tr* cover with dust; sprinkle; (bot) pollinate

beste ['bɛstə] §9 *adj* best; **am besten**

best (of all); **auf dem besten Weg sein zu** be well on the way to; **aufs b.** in the best way; **der erste b.** anybody

beste'chen §64 *tr* bribe; (fig) impress

beste'chend *adj* fascinating, charming

bestech'lich *adj* open to bribery

Beste'chung *f* (-;) bribery

Beste'chungsgeld *n* bribe

Besteck [bəˈʃtek] *n* (-[e]s;-e) kit; (*Tisch-*) single service; (aer, naut) reckoning, position; (med) set of instruments

bestecken (bestek'ken) *tr* stick; (culin) garnish

beste'hen §146 *tr* undergo; (*Prüfung*) pass || *intr* exist, be; (gegen) hold one's own (against); (*in e-r Prüfung*) pass; **b. auf** (dat) insist on; **b. aus** consist of; **b. in** (dat) consist in

beste'hend *adj* existing, extant; present

beste'hen §147 *tr* (um) rob (of)

bestei'gen §148 *tr* climb; (*Schiff*) board; (*Pferd*) mount; (*Thron*) ascend

Bestell'buch *n* order book

bestel'len *tr* order; (*Zimmer*) reserve; (*Zeitung*) subscribe to; (*ernennen*) appoint; (*Briefe*) deliver; (*Feld*) till; (*kommen lassen*) send for

Bestell'zettel *m* order slip

be'stenfalls *adv* at best

besteu'ern *tr* tax

bestialisch [bɛstˈjɑlɪʃ] *adj* beastly

Bestie ['bɛstjə] *f* (-;-n) beast

bestim'men *tr* determine; (*Zeit, Preis*) set; (*ernennen*) appoint; (*Begriff*) define; (gram) modify; (math) find; **j-n b. zu** (or für) destine s.o. for; **talk s.o. into** || *intr* decree; **b. in** (dat) have a say in; **b. über** (acc) dispose of

bestimmt' *adj* determined; definite; particular || *adv* definitely

Bestim'mung *f* (-;-en) determination; (*e-r Zeit, e-s Preises*) setting; destination; mission, goal; (*e-s Begriffs*) definition; (*Schicksal*) fate; (*Vorschrift*) regulation; (*e-s Vertrags*) provision; (gram) modifier; **mit B. nach** (naut) heading for; **seiner B. übergeben** dedicate, open

bestra'fen *tr* punish

bestrah'len *tr* irradiate; (med) give radiation treatment to

bestre'ben *ref* strive, endeavor || **Bestreben** *n* (-s;) tendency

Bestre'bung *f* (-;-en) effort

bestrei'chen §85 *tr* spread; (*mit Feuer*) rake; **mit Butter b.** butter

bestrei'ken *tr* strike

bestrei'ten §86 *tr* contest; fight; (*Ausgaben*) defray; (*Recht*) challenge; (*leugnen*) deny; **e-e Unterhaltung allein b.** do all the talking

bestreu'en *tr* (mit) strew (with)

bestricken (bestrik'ken) *tr* (fig) charm

besticken [bəˈʃtɪkən] *tr* arm, equip

bestür'men *tr* storm; (fig) bombard

Bestür'mung *f* (-;-en) storming

bestür'zen *tr* dismay

Besuch [bəˈzux] *m* (-[e]s;-e) visit; (*Besucher*) visitor(s), company;

(*genit*) visit (to); **auf B. gehen** pay a visit

besu'chen *tr* visit; (*Gasthaus, usw.*) frequent; (*Schule, Versammlung*) attend; (*Kino*) go to

Besu'cher **–in** §6 *mf* visitor, caller

Besuchs'zeit *f* visiting hours

besudeln *tr* soil, stain

betagt [bə'takt] *adj* advanced in years

beta'sten *tr* finger, touch, handle

betätigen [bə'tetɪgən] *tr* set in operation; (*Maschine*) operate; (*Bremse*) apply ‖ *ref*—**sich nützlich b.** make oneself useful; **sich politisch b.** be active in politics

betäuben [bə'tɔɪbən] *tr* deafen; stun; (*Schmerz*) deaden; (*durch Rauschgift*) drug, dope; (*med*) anesthetize

Betäu'bungsmittel *n* drug; painkiller; (*med*) anesthetic

Bete ['betə] *f* (–;–n) beet

beteiligen [bə'taɪlɪgən] *tr* (**an** *dat*, **bei**) give (*s.o.*) a share (in) ‖ *ref* (**an** *dat*) participate (in)

Betei'ligung *f* (–;–en) participation; (*Teilhaberschaft*) partnership; (*Teilnehmerzahl*) attendance

beten ['betən] *tr & intr* pray

beteuern [bə'tɔɪ·ərn] *tr* affirm

betiteln [bə'titəln] *tr* entitle

Beton [be'tɔn] *m* (–s;) concrete

betonen [bə'tonən] *tr* (*Silbe*) stress, accent; (*nachdrücklich*) emphasize

betonieren [bətə'nirən] *tr* cement

Betonmisch'maschine *f* cement mixer

betören [bə'tørən] *tr* infatuate

Betracht' *m* (–[e]s;) consideration; **außer B. lassen** rule out; **es kommt nicht in B.** it is out of the question; **in B. ziehen** take into account, consider

betrachten [bə'traxtən] *tr* look at; consider

beträchtlich [bə'trɛçtlɪç] *adj* considerable

Betrach'tung *f* (–;–en) observation; consideration; meditation; **Betrachtungen anstellen über** (*acc*) reflect on

Betrag [bə'trak] *m* (–[e]s;ːe) amount; **über den B. von** in the amount of

betra'gen §132 *tr* amount to ‖ *ref* behave ‖ **Betragen** *n* (–s;) behavior

betrau'en *tr* entrust

betrau'ern *tr* mourn for

Betreff' [bə'trɛf] *m* (–[e]s;) (*am Briefanfang*) re; **in B.** (*genit*) in regard to

betref'fen §151 *tr* befall; (*berühren*) affect, hit; (*angehen*) concern; **betrifft** (*acc*) re; **was das betrifft as far** that is concerned; **was mich betrifft** I for one

betreffs [bə'trɛfs] *prep* (*genit*) concerning

betrei'ben §62 *tr* carry on; (*leiten*) manage; (*Beruf*) practice; (*Studien*) pursue; (*Maschine*) operate

betre'ten *adj* embarrassed ‖ §152 *tr* step on; set foot on or in; (*Raum*) enter; (*unbefugt*) trespass on

betreuen [bə'trɔɪ·ən] *tr* look after

Betrieb [bə'trip] *m* (–s;–e) operation,

running; (*Unternehmen*) business; (*Anlage*) plant; (*Werkstatt*) workshop; (fig) rush, bustle; **aus dem B. ziehen** take out of service; **außer B.** out of order; **großer B.** hustle and bustle; **in vollem B.** in full swing

betriebsam [bə'tripzam] *adj* enterprising, active

Betriebs'amkeit *f* (–;) hustle

betriebs'fähig *adj* in working order

betriebs'fertig *adj* ready for use

Betriebs'ingenieur *m* production engineer

Betriebs'kosten *pl* operating costs

Betriebs'leiter *m* superintendent

Betriebs'material *n* (rr) rolling stock

Betriebs'prüfer **–in** §6 *mf* auditor

Betriebs'ruhe *f*—**heute B.** (public sign) closed today

Betriebs'stoff *m* fuel

Betriebs'störung *f* breakdown

Betriebs'wirtschaft *f* industrial management

betrin'ken §143 *ref* get drunk

betroffen [bə'trɔfən] *adj* shocked, stunned; (*heimgesucht*) afflicted

betrü'ben *tr* sadden, distress

betrüb'lich *adj* sad, distressing

betrübt [bə'trypt] *adj* sad, sorrowful

Betrug [bə'truk] *m* (–[e]s;) fraud, swindle; **frommer B.** white lie

betrü'gen §111 *tr* cheat, swindle

Betrügerei [batryɡə'raɪ] *f* (–;–en) deceit, cheating

betrü'gerisch *adj* deceitful; fraudulent

betrunken [bə'truŋkən] *adj* drunk

Bett [bɛt] *n* (–[e]s;–en) bed

Bett'decke *f* bedspread

Bettelei [bɛtə'laɪ] *f* (–;) begging

betteln ['bɛtəln] *intr* (**um**) beg (for)

betten ['bɛtən] *tr* put to bed ‖ *ref* **make onself a bed; bed down**

Bett'genosse *m* bedfellow

Bett'gestell *n* bedstead

Bett'himmel *m* canopy (*over a bed*)

bettlägerig ['bɛtlɛgərɪç] *adj* bedridden

Bett'laken *n* bed sheet

Bettler **–in** ['bɛtlər(ɪn)] §6 *mf* beggar

Bett'stelle *f* bedstead

Bettuch [bɛt'tuːh] *n* sheet

Bet'tung *f* (–s;) bedding; (mil) emplacement; (rr) bed

Bett'vorleger *m* bedside rug

Bett'wäsche *f* bed linen

Bett'zeug *n* bedding

betupfen [bə'tupfən] *tr* dab (at); (surg) swab

beugen ['bɔɪgən] *tr* bend; (fig) humble; (gram) inflect ‖ *ref* bend; bow

Beu'gung *f* (–;–en) bending; bowing; (gram) inflection

Beule ['bɔɪlə] *f* (–;–n) lump; (*Geschwür*) boil; (*kleiner Blechschaden*) dent

beunruhigen [bə'unru·ɪgən] *tr* make uneasy, worry, disturb

Beun'ruhigung *f* (–;–en) anxiety, uneasiness; disturbance

beurkunden [bə'urkundən] *tr* authenticate

beurlauben [bə'urlaubən] *tr* grant leave of absence to; (*vom Amt*) suspend; (mil) furlough; **sich b. lassen**

ask for time off || *ref* (**bei**) take one's leave (of)

beur'teilen *tr* evaluate; (**nach**) judge (by); **falsch b.** misjudge

Beute ['bɔɪtə] *f* (–;) booty, loot; **zur B. fallen** (*dat*) fall prey to

Beutel ['bɔɪtəl] *m* (–s;–) bag, pouch; purse; (billiards) pocket

beu'telig *adj* baggy

Beu'tezug *m* raid

bevölkern [be'fœlkərn] *tr* populate

Bevöl'kerung *f* (–;–en) population

bevollmächtigen [be'fɔlmɛçtɪgən] *tr* authorize; (*jur*) give (*s.o.*) power of attorney

Bevoll'mächtigte §5 *mf* authorized agent; proxy; (*pol*) plenipotentiary

bevor [bə'for] *conj* before; **bevor . . . nicht** until

bevormunden [be'formundən] *tr* treat in a patronizing manner

bevor'raten *tr* stock; stockpile

bevorrechtet [bə'fɔrrɛçtət] *adj* privileged

bevor'stehen §146 *intr* be imminent, be on hand; **bevorstehend** forthcoming; **j–m b.** be in store for s.o.

bevorzugen [bə'fortsugən] *tr* prefer

bevor'zugt *adj* preferential; high-priority; privileged; favorite

bewa'chen *tr* guard, watch over

bewach'sen §155 *tr* overgrow, cover

Bewa'chung *f* (–;–en) guard, custody

bewaff'nen *tr* arm

Bewaff'nung *f* (–;) armament, arms

Bewahr'anstalt *f* detention home

bewah'ren *tr* keep, preserve; (**vor** *dat*) save (from), protect (against)

bewäh'ren *tr* prove || *ref* prove one's worth; **sich nicht b.** prove a failure

Bewah'rer –in §6 *mf* keeper

bewahrheiten [bə'varhaɪtən] *tr* verify || *ref* come true

bewährt [bə'vert] *adj* tried, trustworthy

Bewah'rung *f* (–;) preservation

Bewäh'rung *f* (–;–en) testing, trial; (*jur*) probation

Bewäh'rungsfrist *f* (*jur*) probation; **j–m B. zubilligen** put s.o. on probation

Bewäh'rungsprobe *f* test

bewaldet [bə'valdət] *adj* woody

bewältigen [bə'vɛltɪgən] *tr* (*Hindernis*) overcome; (*Lehrstoff*) master

bewandert [bə'vandərt] *adj* experienced

Bewandtnis [bə'vantnɪs] *f* (–;) circumstances, situation

bewäs'sern *tr* water, irrigate

bewegen [bə'vegən] *tr* move, stir || *ref* move, stir; (*von der Stelle*) budge; (*Temperatur*) vary; (*exerzieren*) take exercise; (*astr*) revolve || §56 *tr* prompt, induce

Beweg'grund *m* motive; incentive

beweg'lich *adj* movable; (*behend*) agile; (*Geist*) versatile; (*Zunge*) glib

Beweg'lichkeit *f* (–;) mobility; agility; versatility

bewegt [bə'vekt] *adj* agitated; (*ergreifend*) stirring; (*Stimme*) trembling; (*Unterhaltung*) lively; (*Leben*) eventful; (*unruhig*) turbulent

Bewe'gung *f* (–;–en) movement; mo-

tion; move; (*Gebärde*) gesture; (*fig*) emotion; **in B. setzen** set in motion

Bewe'gungsfreiheit *f* room to move; (*fig*) leeway, freedom of action

bewe'gungslos *adj* motionless

beweh'ren *tr* arm; (*Beton*) reinforce

beweihräuchern [bə'vaɪrɔɪçərn] *tr* (*fig*) flatter; (*eccl*) incense

bewei'nen *tr* mourn, shed tears over

Beweis [bə'vaɪs] *m* (–es;–e) (**für**) proof (of), evidence (of)

beweisen [bə'vaɪzən] §118 *tr* prove, demonstrate; (*bestätigen*) substantiate

Beweis'führung *f* argumentation

Beweis'grund *m* argument

Beweis'kraft *f* cogency, force

beweis'kräftig *adj* convincing

Beweis'last *f* burden of proof

Beweis'stück *n* exhibit

bewen'den *intr*—**es dabei b. lassen** leave it at that || **Bewenden** *n*—**damit hat es sein B.** there the matter rests

bewer'ben §149 *ref*—**sich b. um** apply for; (*kandidieren*) run for; (*Vertrag*) bid for; (*Preis*) compete for; (*Frau*) court

Bewer'ber –in §6 *mf* applicant; candidate; bidder; competitor || *m* suitor

Bewer'bungsformular *n* application form

Bewer'bungsschreiben *n* written application

bewer'fen §160 *tr* pelt; (*Mauer*) plaster

bewerkstelligen [bə'verk/telɪgən] *tr* manage, bring off

bewer'ten *tr* (*auf acc*) value (at), appraise (at); **b. mit fünf Punkten** give five points to (e.g., *a performance*); **zu hoch b.** overrate

Bewer'tung *f* (–;–en) valuation

bewilligen [bə'vɪlɪgən] *tr* approve, grant

Bewil'ligung *f* (–;–en) approval; permit

bewillkommnen [bə'vɪlkɔmnən] *tr* welcome

bewir'ken *tr* cause, occasion, effect

bewir'ten *tr* entertain

bewirt'schaften *tr* (*Acker*) cultivate; (*Betrieb*) manage; (*Mangelware*) ration

Bewir'tung *f* (–;) hospitality

bewitzeln [bə'vɪtsəln] *tr* poke fun at

bewog [bə'vok] *pret* of **bewegen**

bewogen [bə'vogən] *pp* of **bewegen**

bewoh'nen *tr* inhabit, occupy

Bewoh'ner –in §6 *mf* (*e–s Landes*) inhabitant; (*e–s Hauses*) occupant

bewölken [bə'vœlkən] *tr* cloud || *ref* cloud over, get cloudy

bewölkt *adj* cloudy, overcast

Bewöl'kung *f* (–;) clouds

bewun'dern *tr* admire

bewun'dernswert, **bewun'dernswürdig** *adj* admirable

bewußt [bə'vust] *adj* conscious; **die bewußte Sache** the matter in question

bewußt'los *adj* unconscious

Bewußt'sein *n* consciousness; **bei B. sein** be conscious

Bewußt'seinsspaltung *f* schizophrenia

bezah'len *tr* pay; (*Gekauftes*) pay for

Bezah′lung *f* (-;-en) payment; (*Lohn*) pay

bezäh′men *tr* tame; (fig) control

bezau′bern *tr* bewitch; (fig) fascinate

bezeich′nen *tr* (*zeichnen*) mark; (*bedeuten*) signify; (*benennen*) designate; (*kennzeichnen*) characterize; (*zeigen*) point out

bezeich′nend *adj* characteristic

Bezeich′nung *f* (-;-en) marking, mark; (*Name*) name; (*Ausdruck*) term

bezei′gen *tr* show, manifest, express

bezeu′gen *tr* attest; (jur) testify to

bezichtigen [bəˈtsɪçtɪgən] *tr* accuse

bezieh′bar *adj* (*Ware*) obtainable; (*Wohnung*) ready for occupancy; (auf *acc*) referable (to)

bezie′hen §163 *tr* (*Polstermöbel*) cover; (*Wohnung*) move into; (*Universität*) go to; (*geliefert bekommen*) get; (*Gehalt*) draw; (auf *acc*) relate (to), refer (to); **das Bett frisch b.** change the bed linens; **die Stellung b.** (mil) occupy the position; **die Wache b.** (mil) go on guard duty ‖ *ref* become overcast; **sich auf j-n b.** use s.o.'s name as a reference

Bezie′hung *f* (-;-en) relation, connection, respect; **in B. auf** (*acc*) in respect to; **in guten Beziehungen stehen zu** be on good terms with

bezie′hungslos *adj* unrelated; irrelevant

Bezie′hungssatz *m* relative clause

bezie′hungsweise *adv* respectively

Bezie′hungswort *n* [-[e]s; ̈er] (gram) antecedent

beziffern [bəˈtsɪfərn] *tr* (auf *acc*) estimate (at) ‖ *ref*—**sich b. auf** (*acc*) amount to, number

Bezirk [bəˈtsɪrk] *m* (-s;-e) district, ward, precinct; (*Bereich*) sphere

Bezug′ *m* (-[e]s; ̈e) cover, case; (*von Waren*) purchase; (*von Zeitungen*) subscription; (*Auftrag*) order; **Bezüge** earnings; **B. nehmen auf** (*acc*) refer to; **in B. auf** (*acc*) in reference to

bezüglich [bəˈtsyklɪç] *adj* (auf *acc*) relative (to); **bezügliches Fürwort** relative pronoun ‖ *prep* (*genit*) concerning, as to, with regard to

Bezugnahme [bəˈtsuknɑmə] *f*—**unter B. auf** (*acc*) with reference to

Bezugs′anweisung *f* delivery order

bezugs′berechtigt *adj* entitled to receive ‖ **Bezugsberechtigte** §5 *mf* (ins) beneficiary

bezwecken [bəˈtsvekən] *tr* aim ′at, have in mind; (mit) intend (by)

bezwei′feln *tr* doubt, question

bezwin′gen §142 *tr* conquer; (fig) control, master

Bibel [ˈbibəl] *f* (-;-n) Bible

Bi′belforscher -in §6 *mf* Jehovah's Witness

Biber [ˈbibər] *m* (-s;-) beaver

Bibliothek [bɪblɪˈo′tek] *f* (-;-en) library

Bibliothekar -in [bɪblɪˈo′tɛˈkar(ɪn)] §8 *mf* librarian

biblisch [ˈbiblɪʃ] *adj* biblical

bieder [ˈbidər] *adj* honest; (*leichtgläubig*) gullible

Bie′dermann *m* (-[e]s; ̈er) honest man

biegen [ˈbigən] §57 *tr* bend; (gram) inflect ‖ *ref*—**sich vor Lachen b.** double up with laughter ‖ *intr* (SEIN) bend; **um die Ecke b.** go around the corner

biegsam [ˈbikzɑm] *adj* flexible

Bie′gung *f* (-;-en) bend, bending; (gram) inflection

Biene [ˈbinə] *f* (-;-n) bee

Bie′nenfleiß *m*—**mit B. arbeiten** work like a bee

Bie′nenhaus *n* beehive

Bie′nenkorb *m* beehive

Bie′nenstich *m* bee sting; (culin) almond pastry

Bie′nenstock *m* beehive

Bie′nenzucht *f* beekeeping

Bier [bir] *n* (-[e]s;-e) beer

bie′ten [ˈbitən] §58 *tr* offer; **b. auf** (*acc*) bid for ‖ *ref* present itself; **das läßt er sich nicht b.** he won't stand for it

Bigamie [bɪgaˈmi] *f* (-;) bigamy

bigott [bɪˈgɔt] *adj* bigoted

Bigotterie [bɪgɔtəˈri] *f* (-;) bigotry

Bilanz [bɪˈlants] *f* (acct) balance; (acct) balance sheet

Bilanz′abteilung *f* auditing department

bilanzieren [bɪlanˈtsirən] *intr* balance

Bild [bɪlt] *n* (-[e]s;-er) picture; image; (*Bildnis*) portrait; (in e-m Buch) illustration; (*Vorstellung*) idea; (rhet) metaphor, figure of speech; **im Bilde sein** be in the know

Bild′band *m* [-[e]s;-e) picture book ‖ *n* (-[e]s;- ̈er) (telv) video tape

Bild′bandgerät *n* video tape recorder

Bild′betrachter *m* slide viewer

Bildchen [ˈbɪltçən] *n* (-s;-) small picture; (cin) frame

Bild′einstellung *f* (-;-en) focusing

bilden [ˈbɪldən] *tr* form, fashion, create; (*entwerfen*) design; (*gründen*) establish; (*Geist*) educate, develop; (*Gruppe*) constitute ‖ *ref* form, be produced; develop; educate oneself

bil′dend *adj* instructive; **bildende Künste** fine arts, plastic arts

bil′derreich *adj* (*Buch*) richly illustrated; (*Sprache*) picturesque, ornate

Bil′derschrift *f* picture writing

Bil′dersprache *f* imagery

Bil′derstürmer *m* iconoclast

Bild′frequenz *f* camera speed

Bild′funk *m* television

bild′haft *adj* pictorial; graphic

Bildhauer [ˈbɪlthau′ər] *m* (-s;-) sculptor

Bildhauerei [ˈbɪlthau′ərai] *f* (-;) sculpture

Bildhauerin [ˈbɪlthau′ərɪn] *f* (-;-nen) sculptress

bild′hübsch *adj* pretty as a picture

Bild′karte *f* photographic map; (cards) face card

bild′lich *adj* pictorial; figurative

Bildner -in [ˈbɪldnər(ɪn)] §6 *mf* sculptor ‖ *m* (fig) molder ‖ *f* sculptress

Bildnis [ˈbɪltnɪs] *n* (-ses;-se) portrait

Bild′röhre *f* picture tube, TV tube

bildsam [ˈbɪltzɑm] *adj* plastic; (fig) pliant

Bild'säule *f* statue
Bild'schirm *m* television screen
bild'schön *adj* very beautiful
Bild'schriftzeichen *n* hieroglyph
Bild'seite *f* head, obverse
Bild'signal *n* video signal
Bild'stock *m* wayside shrine
Bild'streifen *m* filmstrip; (journ) comic strip
Bild'sucher *m* (phot) viewfinder
Bild'teppich *m* tapestry
Bild'ton'kamera *f* sound-film camera
Bil'dung *f* (-;-en) formation; shape; education, culture
Bil'dungsanstalt *f* educational institution
Bild'werfer *m* projector
Bild'werk *n* sculpture; imagery
Billard ['bɪljart] *n* (-s;) billiards
Bil'lardkugel *f* billiard ball
Bil'lardloch *n* pocket
Bil'lardstab, Bil'lardstock *m* cue
Billett [bɪl'jet] *m* (-s;-e) ticket
Billett'ausgabe *f*, **Billett'schalter** *m* ticket office; (theat) box office
billig ['bɪlɪç] *adj* cheap; (*Preis*) low; (*Ausrede, Trost*) poor
billigen ['bɪlɪgən] *tr* approve
Bil'ligung *f* (-;) approval
Billion [bɪl'jon] *f* (-;-en) trillion; (Brit) billion
bimbam ['bɪm'bam] *interj* ding-dong || **Bimbam** *m*—**heiliger B.!** holy smokes!
bimmeln ['bɪməln] *intr* (coll) jingle; (telp) ring
Bimsstein ['bɪms/taɪn] *m* (-s;-e) pumice stone
Binde ['bɪndə] *f* (-;-n) band; (*Krawatte*) tie; (*Armschlinge*) sling; (*für Frauen*) sanitary napkin; (med) bandage
Bin'deglied *n* link; (fig) bond, tie
binden ['bɪndən] §59 *tr* bind, tie
Bin'destrich *m* hyphen; **mit B. schreiben** hyphenate
Bin'dewort *n* (-[e]s;-²er) conjunction
Bind'faden *m* string, twine; **es regnet Bindfäden** it's raining cats and dogs
Bin'dung *f* (-;-en) binding; tie, bond; obligation; (mus) ligature
binnen ['bɪnən] *prep* (*genit & dat*) within; **b. kurzem** before long
Binnen- *comb.fm.* inner; internal; inland; domestic, home
Bin'nengewässer *n* inland water
Bin'nenhandel *m* domestic trade
Bin'nenland *n* inland; interior; **im B.** inland
Binse ['bɪnzə] *f* (-;-n) rush, reed; **in die Binsen gehen** (coll) go to pot
Bin'senwahrheit *f* truism
Biochemie [bɪ·oçe'mi] *f* (-;) biochemistry
Biogra·phie [bɪ·ogra'fi] (-;-phien ['fi·ən] biography
biographisch [bɪ·o'grafɪʃ] *adj* biographic(al)
Biologie [bɪ·olo'gi] *f* (-;) biology
biologisch [bɪ·o'logɪʃ] *adj* biological
Biophysik [bɪ·ofy'zik] *f* (-;) biophysics
Birke ['bɪrkə] *f* (-;-n) birch
Birma ['bɪrma] *n* (-s;) Burma

Birne ['bɪrnə] *f* (-;-n) pear; (elec) bulb; (*Kopf*) (sl) bean
bis [bɪs] *prep* (acc) (*zeitlich*) till, until; (*örtlich*) up to, to; **bis an** (acc) up to; **bis auf** (acc) except for; **bis nach** as far as || *conj* until, till
Bisamratte ['bizamratə] *f* (-;-n) muskrat
Bischof ['bɪʃof] *m* (-;-²e) bishop
bischöflich ['bɪʃøflɪç] *adj* episcopal
Bi'schofsamt *n* episcopate
Bi'schofsmütze *f* miter
Bi'schofssitz *m* episcopal see
Bi'schofsstab *m* crosier
bisher [bɪs'her] *adv* till now
bisherig [bɪs'herɪç] *adj* former, previous; (*Präsident*) outgoing
Biskuit [bɪs'kvit] *m & n* (-[e]s;-e) biscuit
bislang *adv* till now
biß [bɪs] *pret* of **beißen** || **Biß** *m* (Bisses; Bisse) bite; sting
bißchen ['bɪsçən] *n* (also used as *invar adj & adv*) bit, little bit
Bissen ['bɪsən] *m* (-s;-) bit, morsel
bissig ['bɪsɪç] *adj* biting, snappish
Bistum ['bɪstum] *n* (-s;-²er) bishopric
bisweilen [bɪs'vaɪlən] *adv* sometimes
Bitte ['bɪtə] *f* (-;-n) request; **e-e B. einlegen bei** intercede with
bitten ['bɪtən] §60 *tr* ask || *intr* **b. für** intercede for; **b. um** ask for; **wie bitte?** I beg your pardon? || *interj* please!; you are welcome!
bitter ['bɪtər] *adj* bitter
bit'terböse *adj* (coll) furious
Bit'terkeit *f* (-;) bitterness
bit'terlich *adv* bitterly; deeply
Bit'tersalz *n* Epsom salts
Bittgang ['bɪtgaŋ] *m* (-[e]s;-²e) (eccl) procession
Bittsteller ['bɪtʃtelər] *m* (-s;-) petitioner, suppliant
Biwak ['bivak] *n* (-s;-s) bivouac
biwakieren [biva'kirən] *intr* bivouac
bizarr [bɪ'tsar] *adj* bizarre
blähen ['blɛ·ən] *tr* inflate, distend || *ref* swell || *intr* cause gas
blaken ['blakən] *intr* smolder
Blamage [bla'maʒə] *f* (-;-n) disgrace
blamieren [bla'mirən] *tr* embarrass || *ref* make a fool of oneself
blank [blaŋk] *adj* bright; (*Schuh*) shiny; (*bloß*) bare; (*Schwert*) drawn; (sl) broke; **blanke Waffe** side arms; **b. ziehen** draw one's sword
Blankett [blaŋ'ket] *n* (-s;-e) blank
blanko ['blaŋko] *adv*—**b. lassen** leave blank; **b. verkaufen** sell short
Blan'koscheck *m* blank check
Blan'kovollmacht *f* blanket authority
Blank'vers *m* blank verse
Bläschen ['blɛsçən] *n* (-s;-) small blister; small bubble
Blase ['blazə] *f* (-;-n) blister; bubble; (coll) gang; (anat) bladder; **Blasen werfen** (*Farbe*) blister; **Blasen ziehen** (*Haut*) blister
Bla'sebalg *m* pair of bellows
blasen ['blazən] *tr* blow; (*Instrument*) play || *intr* blow
Bla'senleiden *n* bladder trouble
Bläser ['blezər] *m* (-s;-) blower

blasiert [bla'zirt] *adj* blasé

blasig ['blɑzɪç] *adj* blistery; bubbly

Blas'instrument *n* wind instrument

Blasphe·mie [blasfe'mi] *f* (-;-mien ['mi·ən]) blasphemy

blasphemieren [blasfe'mirən] *intr* blaspheme

Blas'rohr *n* blowpipe; peashooter

blaß [blas] *adj* pale; **keine blasse Ahnung** not the foggiest notion

Blässe ['blesə] *f* (-;) paleness, pallor

Blatt [blat] *n* (-s;⸚er) leaf; (*Papier-*) sheet; (*Gras-*) blade

Blatter ['blatər] *f* (-;-n) pustule; **die Blattern** smallpox

blätterig ['bletərɪç] *adj* leafy; scaly

blättern ['bletərn] *intr*—**in e-m Buch b.** page through a book

Blat'ternarbe *f* pockmark

Blät'terwerk *n* foliage

Blatt'gold *n* gold leaf, gold foil

Blatt'laus *f* aphid

Blatt'pflanze *f* house plant

blättrig ['bletrɪç] *adj var of* blätterig

Blatt'zinn *n* tin foil

blau [blau] *adj* (& *fig*) blue; (coll) drunk; **blaues Auge** black eye; **keinen blauen Dunst haben** (coll) not have the foggiest notion; **mit e-m blauen Auge davonkommen** (coll) get off easy ‖ **Blau** *n* (-s;-s) blue; blueness

blau'äugig *adj* blue-eyed

Blau'beere *f* blueberry

Bläue ['blɔɪ·ə] *f* (-;) blue; blueness

bläuen ['blɔɪ·ən] *tr* dye blue

bläulich ['blɔɪlɪç] *adj* bluish

blau'machen *intr* (coll) take off from work

Blech [bleç] *n* (-[e]s;-e) sheet metal; (sl) baloney; (mus) brass

Blech'büchse *f* tin can

blechen ['bleçən] *tr* (coll) pay out ‖ *intr* (coll) cough up the dough

Blech'instrument *n* brass instrument

blecken ['blekən] *tr*—**die Zähnen b.** bare one's teeth

Blei [blaɪ] *n* (-[e]s;) lead

Bleibe ['blaɪbə] *f* (-;-n) place to stay

bleiben ['blaɪbən] §62 *intr* (SEIN) remain, stay; **am Leben b.** survive; **bei etw b.** stick to s.th.; **dabei bleibt es!** that's final!; **für sich b.** keep to oneself; **sich** [*dat*] **gleich b.** never change; **und wo bleibe ich?** (coll) and where do I come in?

blei'bend *adj* lasting, permanent

bleich [blaɪç] *adj* pale ‖ **Bleiche** *f* (-;) bleaching; paleness

blei'chen *tr* bleach; make pale ‖ *intr* (SEIN) bleach; (*verblassen*) fade

Bleich'gesicht *n* paleface

Bleich'mittel *n* bleach

bleiern ['blaɪ·ərn] *adj* leaden

Blei'soldat *m* tin soldier

Blei'stift *m* pencil

Bleistiftspitzer ['blaɪ/tɪft/pɪtsər] *m* (-s;-) pencil sharpener

Blende ['blendə] *f* (-;-n) window blind; shutter; (phot) diaphragm

blen'den *tr* blind; (*bezaubern*) dazzle

blen'dend *adj* fabulous

Blen'der *m* (-s;-) (coll) fourflusher

Blendling ['blentlɪŋ] *m* (-s;-e) (*Mischling*) mongrel; (bot) hybrid

Blick [blɪk] *m* (-[e]s;-e) glance, look; (*auf acc*) view (of)

blicken [blɪk'ken] *intr* (**auf** *acc*, **nach**) glance (at), look (at); **sich b. lassen** show one's face

Blick'fang *m* (coll) eye catcher

blieb [blip] *pret of* bleiben

blies [blis] *pret of* blasen

blind [blɪnt] *adj* (**für, gegen**) blind (to); (*Spiegel*) clouded; (*trübe*) dull; (*Alarm*) false; (*Patrone*) blank; **blinder Passagier** stowaway

Blind'band *m* (-[e]s;⸚e) (typ) dummy

Blind'boden *m* subfloor

Blind'darm *m* appendix

Blind'darmentzündung *f* appendicitis

Blind'darmoperation *f* appendectomy

Blin'denheim *n* home for the blind

Blin'denhund *m* Seeing-Eye dog

Blin'denschrift *f* braille

Blind'flug *m* blind flying

Blind'gänger *m* (mil) dud

Blind'landung *f* instrument landing

blindlings ['blɪntlɪŋs] *adv* blindly

Blind'schreiben *n* touch typing

blinken ['blɪŋkən] *intr* blink, twinkle; (*Sonne*) shine; (mil) signal

Blin'ker *m*, **Blink'licht** *n* (aut) blinker

blinzeln ['blɪntsəln] *intr* blink, wink

Blitz [blɪts] *m* (-es;-e) lightning; (fig & phot) flash

Blitz'ableiter *m* lightning rod

blitz'blank *adj* shining; spick and span

Blitz'krieg *m* blitzkrieg

Blitz'licht *n* (phot) flash

Blitz'lichtaufnahme *f* (phot) flash shot

Blitz'lichtbirne *f* (phot) flash bulb

Blitz'lichtgerät *n* flash gun

Blitz'lichtröhre *f* (phot) electronic flash tube

Blitz'schlag *m* stroke of lightning

blitz'schnell *adj* quick as lightning

Blitz'strahl *m* flash of lightning

Block [blɔk] *m* (-s;-e) block, log; (*Stück Seife*) cake; (*von Schokolade*) bar; (*von Löschpapier*) pad; (geol) boulder; (metal) ingot; (pol) bloc

Blockade [blɔ'kadə] *f* (-;-n) blockade

Blocka'debrecher *m* blockade runner

blocken [blɔk'ken] *tr* (sport) block

Block'haus *n* log cabin

blockieren [blɔ'kirən] *tr* block up; (mil) blockade

Block'kalender *m* tear-off calendar

Block'schrift *f* block letters

blöd(e) ['blød(ə)] *adj* stupid, idiotic; feeble-minded; (*schüchtern*) shy

Blöd'heit *f* (-;) stupidity, idiocy

Blö'digkeit *f* (-;) shyness

Blöd'sinn *m* idiocy; nonsense

blöd'sinnig *adj* idiotic ‖ *adv* idiotically; (*sehr*) (coll) awfully

blöken ['bløkən] *intr* bleat; (*Kuh*) moo

blond [blɔnt] *adj* blond, fair ‖ **Blonde** §5 *m* blond ‖ *f* blonde

blondieren [blɔn'dirən] *tr* bleach

Blondine [blɔn'dinə] *f* (-;-n) blonde

bloß [blos] *adj* bare; (*nichts als*) mere *adv* only; barely

Blöße ['bløsə] *f* bareness; nakedness; (fig) weak point

bloß'legen *tr* lay bare
bloß'stellen *tr* expose
blühen ['bly·ən] *intr* blossom, bloom; (*Backen*) be rosy; (fig) flourish
Blume ['blumə] *f* (-;-n) flower; (*des Weins*) bouquet; (*des Biers*) head
Blu'menbeet *n* flower bed
Blu'menblatt *n* petal
Blu'mengewinde *n* garland, festoon
Blu'menhändler –in §6 *mf* florist
Blu'menkelch *m* calyx
Blu'menkohl *m* cauliflower
Blu'menstaub *m* pollen
Blu'mentopf *m* flowerpot
Bluse ['bluzə] *f* (-;-n) blouse
Blut [blut] *n* (-[e]s;) blood; bis aufs B. almost to death; B. lecken taste blood; heißes B. hot temper
Blut'andrang *m* (pathol) congestion
blut'arm *adj* anemic
Blut'armut *f* anemia
Blut'bahn *f* bloodstream
Blut'bild *n* blood count
blut'dürstig *adj* bloodthirsty
Blüte ['blytə] *f* (-;-n) blossom, flower, bloom; (fig) prime
Blut'egel *m* leech
bluten ['blutən] *intr* bleed
Blü'tenblatt *n* petal
Blü'tenstaub *m* pollen
Blut'erguß *m* bruise
Blu'terkrankheit *f* hemophilia
Blü'tezeit *f* blooming period; (fig) hey-day
Blut'farbstoff *m* hemoglobin
Blut'gerinnsel *n* blood clot
Blut'hund *m* bloodhound
blutig ['blutɪç] *adj* bloody
blut'jung' *adj* very young, green
Blut'körperchen *n* corpuscle
Blut'kreislauf *m* blood circulation
blut'leer, blut'los *adj* bloodless
Blut'pfropfen *m* blood clot
Blut'probe *f* blood test
Blut'rache *f* blood feud
Blut'rausch *m* mania to kill
blutrünstig ['blutrʏnstɪç] *adj* gory
Blut'sauger *m* bloodsucker, leech
Blut'schande *f* incest
blutschänderisch ['blutʃendərɪʃ] *adj* incestuous
Blut'spender –in §6 *mf* blood donor
blut'stillend *adj* coagulant
Blut'sturz *m* hemorrhage
Bluts'verwandte §5 *mf* blood relation
Blut'übertragung *f* blood transfusion
blut'unterlaufen *adj* bloodshot
Blut'vergießen *n* (-s;) bloodshed
blut'voll *adj* lively, vivid
Blut'wasser *n* lymph
Blut'zeuge *m*, Blut'zeugin *f* martyr
Bö [bø] *f* (-;-en) gust, squall
Bob [bɔb] *m* (-s;-s) bobsled
Bock [bɔk] *m* (-[e]s; ≃e) buck; ram; he-goat; (*Kutsch-*) driver's seat; (tech) horse; B. springen play leap-frog; e–n B. schießen pull a boner
bockbeinig ['bɔkbaɪnɪç] *adj* stubborn
bocken ['bɔkən] *intr* buck; (*sich auf-bäumen*) rear; (*ausschlagen*) kick; (*brunsten*) be in heat; (aut) hesitate
bockig ['bɔkɪç] *adj* thickheaded
Bock'sprung *m* caper; leapfrog

Boden ['bodən] *m* (-s;≃) (*Erd-*) ground, soil; (*Meeres-*) bottom; (*Fuß-*) floor; (*Dach-*) attic; (*Trocken-*) loft; B. fassen get a firm footing; zu B. drücken crush
Bo'denertrag *m* (agr) yield
Bo'denfenster *n* dormer window
Bo'denfläche *f* floor space; (agr) acre-age
Bo'denfliese *f* floor tile
Bodenfräse ['bodənfrezə] *f* (-;-n) Rotortiller
Bo'denhaftung *f* roadability
Bo'denkammer *f* attic
bo'denlos *adj* bottomless; (fig) unmiti-gated
Bo'denmannschaft *f* (aer) ground crew
Bo'denreform *f* agrarian reform
Bo'densatz *m* grounds, sediment
Bodenschätze ['bodənʃetsə] *pl* mineral resources
Bo'densee *m* (-s;) Lake Constance
bo'denständig *adj* native, indigenous
bog [bok] *pret* of biegen
Bogen ['bogən] *m* (-s;≃) bow; (*Kurve*) curve; (*Papier-*) sheet; (*beim Schi-laufen*) turn; (*beim Eislaufen*) circle; (archit) arch; (math) arc; den B. raushaben have the hang of it; den B. überspannen (fig) go too far; e–n großen B. um j–n machen give s.o. wide berth
Bo'genfenster *n* bow window
bo'genförmig *adj* arched
Bo'gengang *m* arcade; archway
Bo'genschießen *n* (-s;) archery
Bo'genschütze *m* archer
Bo'gensehne *f* bowstring
Bohle ['bolə] *f* (-;-n) plank
Böhme ['bø̈mə] *m* (-s;) Bohemian
Böhmen ['bø̈mən] *n* (-s;) Bohemia
Bohne ['bonə] *f* (-;-n) bean; blaue Bohnen bullets; grüne Bohnen string beans
Boh'nermasse *f* polish; floor polish
bohnern ['bonərn] *tr* wax, polish
Boh'nerwachs *n* floor wax
Bohr– [bor] *comb.fm.* drill, drilling, bore, boring
bohren ['borən] *tr* drill, bore
Bohrer *m* (-s;-) drill; (ent) borer
Bohr'insel *f* offshore drilling platform
Bohr'presse *f* drill press
Bohr'turm *m* derrick
bög ['bø̈·ɪç] *adj* gusty; (aer) bumpy
Boje ['bojə] *f* (-;-n) buoy
Böller ['bœlər] *m* (-s;-) mortar
böllern ['bœlərn] *intr* fire a mortar
Bollwerk ['bɔlverk] *n* (-s;-e) bulwark
Bolzen ['bɔltsən] *m* (-s;-) bolt; dowel
Bombardement [bɔmbardə'mã] *n* (-s; -s) bombardment
bombardieren [bɔmbar'dirən] *tr* bom-bard
Bombe ['bɔmbə] *f* (-;-n) bomb, bomb-shell; (coll) smash hit
Bomben– *comb.fm.* bomb, bombing; huge
Bom'benabwurf *m* bombing; gezielter B. precision bombing
Bom'benerfolg *m* (theat) smash hit
bom'benfest *adj* bombproof
Bom'benflugzeug *m* bomber

Bom'bengeschäft n (coll) gold mine

Bom'benpunktzielwurf m precision bombing

Bom'benreihenwurf m stick bombing

Bom'bensache f (coll) humdinger

Bom'benschacht m bomb bay

Bom'benschütze m bombardier

Bom'bentrichter m bomb crater

Bom'benzielanflug m bombing run

Bom'benzielgerät n bombsight

Bon [bõ] m (-s;-s) sales slip; (Gut-schein) credit note

Bonbon [bõ'bõ] m & n (-s;-s) piece of candy; Bonbons candy

Bonbonniere [bõbɔnɪ'erə] f (-;-n) box of candy

Bonze ['bɔntsə] m (-;-n) (coll) big shot, bigwig; (pol) boss

Boot [bot] n (-[e]s;-e) boat

Boots'mann m (-es;-leute) boatswain; (nav) petty officer

Bord [bɔrt] m (-es;e) edge; bookshelf; (naut) board, side; an B. aboard, on board; von B. gehen leave the ship

Bordell [bɔr'dɛl] n (-s;-e) brothel

Bord'karte f boarding pass

Bord'schütze m aerial gunner

Bord'schwelle f curb

Bord'stein m curb

Bord'waffen pl (aer, mil) armament

Bord'wand f ship's side

Borg [bɔrk] m (-s;) borrowing; auf B. on credit; on loan

borgen ['bɔrgən] tr (von, bei) borrow (from); loan out, lend

Borke ['bɔrkə] f (-;-n) bark

Born [bɔrn] m (-es; -e) (poet) fountain

borniert [bɔr'nirt] adj narrow-minded

Borsäure ['bɔrzɔɪrə] f (-;) boric acid

Börse ['bœrzə] f (-;-n) purse; stock exchange

Bör'senkurs m market price; quotation

Bör'senmakler –in ['bœrzən] §6 mf stockbroker

Bör'senmarkt m stockmarket

Bör'sennotierung f (st.exch.) quotation

Bör'senpapiere pl stocks, shares, securities

Borste ['bɔrstə] f (-;-n) bristle

borstig ['bɔrstɪç] adj birstly; (fig) crusty

Borte ['bɔrtə] f (-;-n) trim; braid; (Saum) hem

bös [bøs] var of böse

bös'artig adj nasty; (Tier) vicious; (pathol) malignant

Böschung ['bœɛ/ʊŋ] f (-;-en) slope; (e-s Flusses) bank; (rr) embankment

böse ['bøzə] adj bad, evil, nasty; angry || Böse §5 mf wicked person || m devil || n evil; harm

Bösewicht ['bøzəvɪçt] m (-s;-e) villain

boshaft ['bɔshaft] adj malicious, wicked; (tückisch) spiteful

bossieren [bɔ'sirən] tr emboss

bös'willig adj malicious, willful

bot [bot] pret of bieten

Botanik [bo'tanɪk] f (-;) botany

Botaniker –in [bo'tanɪkər] §6 mf botanist

botanisch [bo'tanɪʃ] adj botanic(al)

Bote ['botə] m (-n;-n) messenger

Bo'tengang m errand

Botin ['botɪn] f (-;-nen) messenger

Bot'schaft f (-;-en) message, news; (Amt) embassy; (Auftrag) mission

Botschafter –in ['bot/aftər(ɪn)] §6 ambassador

Bottich ['bɔtɪç] m (-s;-e) tub; vat

Bouillon [bul'jõ] f (-;-s) bouillon

Bowle ['bolə] f (-;-n) punch

boxen ['bɔksən] tr & intr box

Bo'xer m (-s;-) boxer

Box'kampf m boxing match

Boykott [bɔɪ'kɔt] m (-s;-e) boycott

boykottieren [bɔɪkɔ'tirən] tr boycott

brach [brɑx] pret of brechen || adj fallow

brachte ['brɑxtə] pret of bringen

brackig ['brɑkɪç] adj brackish

Branche ['brɑ̃/ə] f (-;-n) line of business; (com) branch

Brand [brant] m (-[e]s;-e) burning; fire; (coll) thirst; (agr) blight; (pathol) gangrene in B. geraten catch fire; in B. setzen (or stecken) set on fire

Brand'blase f blister

Brand'bombe f incendiary bomb

Brand'brief m urgent letter

Brand'direktor m fire chief

branden ['brandən] intr surge, break

Brand'fackel f firebrand

brandig ['brandɪç] adj (agr) blighted; (pathol) gangrenous

Brand'mal n brand; (fig) moral stigma

brand'marken tr stigmatize

Brand'mauer f fire wall

brandschatzen ['brant/atsən] tr sack

Brand'stifter –in §6 mf arsonist

Bran'dung f (-;) breakers

Bran'dungswelle f breaker

Brand'wunde f burn

Brand'zeichen n brand

brannte ['brantə] pret of brennen

Branntwein ['brantvaɪn] m brandy

Brasilien [bra'ziljən] n (-s;) Brazil

Bratapfel ['brɑtapfəl] m baked apple

braten ['brɑtən] §63 tr & intr roast; (im Ofen) bake; (auf dem Rost) broil, grill; (in der Pfanne) fry || Braten m (-s;-) roast

Bra'tensoße f gravy

Brat'fisch m fried fish

Brat'huhn n broiler

Brat'kartoffeln pl fried potatoes

Brat'pfanne f frying pan, skillet

Bratsche ['brat/ə] f (-;-n) viola

Bräu [brɔɪ] m & n (-[e]s;) brew

Brauch [brɑux] m (-[e]s;-e) custom

brauchbar ['brɑuxbar] adj useful

brauchen ['brɑuxən] tr need; (Zeit) take; (gebrauchen) use

Brauchtum ['brɑuxtum] n (-s;) tradition

Braue ['brɑu·ə] f (-;-n) eyebrow

brauen ['brɑu·ən] tr brew

Brau'er m (-s;-) brewer

Brauerei [brɑu·ə'raɪ] f (-;-en), Brau'-haus n brewery

braun [brɑun] adj brown; (Pferd) bay

Bräune ['brɔɪnə] f (-;) brown; sun tan; (pathol) diphtheria

bräunen ['brɔɪnən] tr tan; (culin) brown || ref & intr tan

bräunlich ['brɔɪnlɪç] adj brownish

Braus [brɑus] m (-es;) noise; revelry

Brause ['brauzə] *f* (-;-n) soda, soft drink; (*Duschbad*) shower; (*an Gieß-kannen*) nozzle
Brau′sebad *n* shower
Brau′sekopf *m* hothead
Brau′selimonade *f* soda, soft drink
brau′sen *tr* spray, water || *intr* bubble; (*toben*) roar || *intr* (SEIN) rush
Braut [braut] *f* (-;¨e) fiancée; bride
Braut′ausstattung *f* trousseau
Braut′führer *m* usher
Bräutigam ['brɔıtıgam] *m* (-s;-e) fiancé; bridegroom
Braut′jungfer *f* (-;-n) bridesmaid; **erste B.** maid of honor
Braut′kleid *n* bridal gown
Braut′leute *pl* engaged couple
bräutlich ['brɔıtlıç] *adj* bridal; nuptial
Braut′schatz *m* dowry
Braut′werber **–in** §6 *mf* matchmaker
Braut′werbung *f* courting
Braut′zeit *f* period of engagement
Braut′zeuge *m* best man
brav [braf] *adj* well-mannered, good, honest
Brav′heit *f* good behavior
Bravour [bra′vur] *f* (-;) bravado
Brech′eisen *n* crowbar, jimmy
brechen ['breçən] §64 *tr* break; (*Papier*) fold; (*Steine*) quarry; (*Blumen*) pick; (*coll*) vomit; (*opt*) refract; **die Ehe b.** commit adultery || *ref* break; (*opt*) be refracted || *intr* (SEIN) break; (*coll*) vomit
Brech′reiz *m* nausea
Brech′stange *f* crowbar
Bre′chung *f* (-;-en) (*opt*) refraction
Brei [braı] *m* (-[e]s;-e) paste; pap, gruel; **zu B. schlagen** beat to a pulp
breit [braıt] *adj* broad, wide
breitbeinig ['braıtbaınıç] *adv* with legs outspread
breit′drücken *tr* flatten (out)
Brei′te *f* (-;-n) width; latitude
Brei′tengrad *m* degree of latitude
breit′machen *ref* take up (too much) room; (*fig*) throw one's weight around
breit′schlagen §132 *tr* (*coll*) persuade
breitschulterig ['braıtʃultərıç] *adj* broad-shouldered
breitspurig ['braıtʃpurıç] *adj* (*coll*) pompous; (*rr*) broad-gauge
breit′treten §152 *tr* belabor
Breit′wand *f* (*cin*) wide screen
Bremsbelag ['bremsbəlak] *m* brake lining
Bremse ['bremzə] *f* (-;-n) brake; (*ent*) horsefly
bremsen ['bremzən] *tr* brake; (*fig*) curb; (*atom phys*) slow down || *intr* brake
Brem′ser *m* (-s;-) brakeman
Brems′flüssigkeit *f* brake fluid
Brems′fußhebel *m* brake pedal
Brems′klotz *m* wheel chock
Bremsleuchte ['bremslɔıçtə] *f*, **Brems′licht** *n* (aut) brake light
Brems′rakete *f* (rok) retrorocket
Brems′schuh *m* brake shoe
brems′sicher *adj* skidproof
Brems′spur *f* skid mark
Brems′wagen *m* (rr) caboose

Brems′weg *m* braking distance
Brennapparat ['brenaparat] *m* still
brennbar ['brenbar] *adj* inflammable, combustible
brennen §97 *tr* burn; (*Branntwein*) distil; (*Kaffee*) roast; (*Haar*) curl; (*Ziegel*) fire || *intr* burn; smart
Bren′ner *m* (-s;-) burner; distiller
Brennerei [brenə′raı] *f* (-;-en) distillery
Brenn′holz *n* firewood
Brenn′material *n* fuel
Brenn′ofen *m* kiln
Brenn′punkt *m* focus; **im B. stehen** be the focal point
Brenn′schere *f* curler
Brenn′schluß *m* (rok) burnout
Brenn′spiegel *m* concave mirror
Brenn′stoff *m* fuel
brenzlig ['brentslıç] *adj* (*Geruch*) burnt; (*Situation*) precarious
Bresche ['breʃə] *f* (-;-n) breach; **e-e B. schlagen** make a breach
Brett [bret] *n* (-[e]s;-er) board; plank; (*für Bücher, Geschirr*) shelf; **Bretter** (coll) skis; (theat) stage; **Schwarzes B.** bulletin board
Bret′terbude *f* shack
Bret′terverschlag *m* wooden partition
Brett′säge *f* ripsaw
Brezel ['bretsəl] *f* (-;-n) pretzel
Brief [brif] *m* (-[e]s;-e) letter; **Briefe wechseln** correspond
Brief′ausgabe *f* mail delivery
Briefbeschwerer ['brifbə/verər] *m* (-s; -) paperweight
Brief′bestellung *f* mail delivery
Brief′beutel *m* mail bag
Brief′bogen *m* piece of notepaper
Brief′bote *m* mailman, postman
Briefchen ['brifçən] *n* (-s;-) note; **B. Streichhölzer** book of matches
Brief′einwurf *m* slot in a mailbox; letterdrop; mailbox
Brief′fach *n* pigeonhole; post-office box
Brief′freund **–in** §8 *mf* pen pal
Brief′hülle *f* envelope
Brief′kasten *m* mailbox
Brief′klammer *f* paper clip
Brief′kopf *m* letterhead
Brief′kurs *m* (st.exch.) selling price
brief′lich *adj* written; **brieflicher Verkehr** correspondence || *adv* by letter
Brief′mappe *f* folder
Brief′marke *f* postage stamp
Brief′markenautomat *m* stamp machine
Brief′ordner *m* ring binder
Brief′papier *n* stationery; note paper
Brief′porto *n* postage
Brief′post *f* first-class mail
Brief′schaften *pl* correspondence
Brief′stempel *m* postmark
Brief′tasche *f* billfold, wallet
Brief′taube *f* carrier pigeon
Brief′träger *m* mailman, postman
Brief′umschlag *m* envelope
Brief′verkehr *m* correspondence
Brief′waage *f* postage scales
Brief′wahl *f* absentee ballot
Brief′wechsel *m* correspondence
briet [brit] *pret of* **braten**

Brigade [brɪ'gɑdə] *f* (–;–n) brigade
Briga'degeneral *m* brigadier general; (Brit) brigadier
Brikett [brɪ'ket] *n* (–[e]s;–s) briquette
brillant [brɪl'jant] *adj* brilliant || **Brillant** *m* (–en;–en) precious stone (esp. diamond)
Brille ['brɪlə] *f* (–;–n) eyeglasses; (*für Pferde*) blinkers; (*Toilettenring*) toilet seat; **B. mit doppeltem Brennpunkt** bifocals
Bril'lenbügel *m* sidepiece (*of glasses*)
Bril'lenfassung *f* eyeglass frame
Bril'lenschlange *f* cobra
bringen ['brɪŋən] §65 *tr* bring, take; **an sich b.** acquire; **es mit sich b.,** **daß** bring it about that; **es zu etw b.** achieve s.th.; **etw hinter sich b.** get s.th. over and done with; **etw über sich** (or **übers Herz**) **b.** be able to bear s.th.; **j–n auf etw b.** put s.o. on to s.th.; **j–n außer sich b.** enrage s.o.; **j–n dazu b. zu** (*inf*) get s.o. to (*inf*); **j–m um etw b.** deprive s.o. of s.th.; **j–n zum Lachen b.** make s.o. laugh; **unter die Leute b.** circulate
brisant [brɪ'zant] *adj* high-explosive
Brise ['brizə] *f* (–;–n) breeze
Britannien [brɪ'tanjən] *n* (–s) Britain
Brite ['brɪtə] *m* (–n;–n) Briton, Britisher; **die Briten** the British
Britin ['brɪtɪn] *f* (–;–nen) Briton, British woman
britisch ['brɪtɪʃ] *adj* British
Broché [bro'ʃe] *n* (–s) broché; brocaded fabric
Bröckchen ['brœkçən] *n* (–s;–) bit; morsel, crumb; fragment
bröck(e)lig ['brœk(ə)lɪç] *adj* crumbly
bröckeln ['brœkəln] *tr* & *intr* crumble
brocken ['brɔkən] *tr*—**Brot in die Suppe b.** break bread into the soup || **Brocken** *m* (–s;–) piece, bit; lump; **Brocken** *pl* scraps, bits and pieces; **harter B.** (coll) tough job
brockenweise (brok'kenweise) *adv* bit by bit
brodeln ['brodəln] *intr* bubble, simmer
Brokat [bro'kat] *m* (–s;–e) brocade
Brombeere ['brɔmberə] *f* (–;–n) blackberry
Bromid [bro'mit] *n* (–[e]s;–e) bromide
Bronchitis [brɔn'çitis] *f* (–) bronchitis
Bronze ['brõsə] *f* (–;–n) bronze
Brosche ['broʃə] *f* (–;–n) brooch
broschieren [bro'ʃirən] *tr* stitch; brocade; **broschiert** with stapled binding
Broschüre [bro'ʃyrə] *f* (–;–n) brochure
Brösel ['brøzəl] *m* (–s;–) crumb
Brot [brot] *n* (–[e]s;–e) bread; loaf; **geröstetes B.** toast
Brot'aufstrich *m* spread
Brötchen ['brøtçən] *n* (–s;–) roll
Brot'erwerb *m* livelihood, living
Brot'geber *m,* **Brot'herr** *m* employer
Brot'kasten *m* breadbox
brot'los *adj* unemployed; unprofitable
Brot'neid *m* professional jealousy
Brot'röster *m* (–s;–) toaster
Brot'schnitte *f* slice of bread
Brot'studium *n* bread-and-butter courses
Brot'zeit *f* breakfast

Bruch [brux] *m* (–[e]s;∺e) breaking; break, crack; breakage; (aer) crash; (geol) fault; (math) fraction; (min) quarry; (pathol) hernia; (surg) fracture; **B. machen** crash-land; **in die Brüche gehen** go to pot; **zu B. gehen** break || [brux] *m & n* (–s;∺e) bog
Bruch'band *n* (–s;∺er) (surg) truss
Bruch'bude *f* shanty
brüchig ['brʏçɪç] *adj* fragile, brittle
Bruch'landung *f* crash landing
Bruch'rechnung *f* fractions
Bruch'stück *n* fragment, chip; **Bruchstücke** (fig) scraps, snatches
bruch'stückhaft *adj* fragmentary
Bruch'teil *m* fraction; **im B. e–r Sekunde** in a split second
Bruch'zahl *f* fractional number
Brücke ['brʏkə] *f* (–;–n) bridge; (*Teppich*) small (narrow) rug; (gym) backbend
Brückenkopf (Brük'kenkopf) *m* bridgehead
Brückenpfeiler (Brük'kenpfeiler) *m* pier of a bridge
Brückenwaage (Brük'kenwaage) *f* platform scale
Brückenzoll (Brük'kenzoll) *m* bridge toll
Bruder ['brudər] *m* (–s∺) brother; (*Genosse*) companion; (eccl) lay brother
brüderlich ['brydərlɪç] *adj* brotherly
Brüderschaft ['brydərʃaft] *f* (–;–en) brotherhood; fraternity
Brühe ['bry.ə] *f* (–;–n) broth; (*Fleisch–*) gravy; **in der B. stecken** be in a jam
brühen ['bry.ən] *tr* boil; scald
brüh'heiß *adj* piping hot
Brüh'kartoffeln *pl* potatoes boiled in broth
Brüh'würfel *m* bouillon cube
brüllen ['brylən] *tr* & *intr* roar, bellow; (*Sturm*) howl; (*Ochse*) low; **b. vor Lachen** roar with laughter
Brummbär ['brumber] *m* (–en;–en) grouch
brummen ['brumən] *tr* mumble; grumble; growl || *intr* mumble; grumble; growl; (*summen*) buzz, hum; (*Orgel*) boom; (*im Gefängnis*) do time, do a stretch
brummig ['brumɪç] *adj* grouchy
brünett [bry'net] *adj* brunet(te) || **Brünette** §5 brunette
Brunft [brunft] *f* (–;) rut
Brunft'zeit *f* rutting season
Brunnen ['brunən] *m* (–s;–) well; (*Spring–*) spring
Brunnenkresse ['brunənkresə] *f* (–;–n) watercress
Brunst [brunst] *f* (–;) rut, heat; (fig) ardor, passion
brunsten ['brunstən] *intr* be in heat
brünstig ['brʏnstɪç] *adj* in heat; (fig) passionate
brüsk [brʏsk] *adj* brusque
brüskieren [brʏs'kirən] *tr* snub
Brust [brust] *f* (–;∺e) breast, chest
Brust'bein *n* breastbone, sternum
Brust'bild *n* portrait; (sculp) bust
brüsten ['brʏstən] *ref* show off

Brust′fellentzündung f pleurisy
Brust′kasten m, **Brust′korb** m thorax
Brust′schwimmen n breast stroke
Brust′stück n (culin) brisket
Brust′ton m —**im B. der Überzeugung** with utter conviction
Brust′umfang m chest measurement; (*bei Frauen*) bust measurement
Brü′stung f (-;-en) balustrade
Brust′warze f nipple
Brust′wehr f breastwork
Brut [brut] f (-;-en) brood; (pej) scum
brutal [bru′tal] adj brutal
Brut′apparat m, **Brut′ofen** m incubator
brüten [′brytən] tr hatch; (fig) plan || intr incubate; **b. auf** (*dat*) (fig) sit on; **b. über** (*dat*) brood over; pore over
brutto [′bruto] adj (com) gross
Brut′tosozialprodukt n gross national product
Bube [′bubə] m (-n;-n) boy; (*Schurke*) rascal; (cards) jack
Bu′benstreich m, **Bu′benstück** n prank; dirty trick
bübisch [′bybɪʃ] adj rascally
Buch [bux] n (-[e]s;⁻er) book; (cards) straight
Buch′besprechung f book review
Buchbinderei [′buxbɪndəraɪ] f (-;-en) bookbindery; (*Gewerbe*) bookbinding
Buch′binderleinwand f buckram
Buch′deckel m book cover
Buch′drama n closet drama
Buch′druck m printing, typography
Buch′drucker m printer
Buch′druckerei f print shop; (*Gewerbe*) printing
Buche [′buxə] f (-;-n) beech
Buchecker [′buxɛkər] f (-;-n) beechnut
buchen [′buxən] tr book, reserve; (com) enter
Bücher- [byçər] *comb.fm.* book
Bü′cherabschluß m balancing of books
Bücherausgabe f circulation desk
Bü′cherbrett n bookshelf
Bücherei [byçə′raɪ] f (-;-en) library
Bü′cherfreund m bibliophile
Bü′chergestell n bookrack, bookcase
Bü′cherregal n bookshelf; bookcase
Bü′cherrevision f audit
Bü′cherrevisor m auditor; accountant
Bü′cherschrank m bookcase
Bü′cherstütze f book end
Buch′führung f bookkeeping, accounting
Buch′halter -in §6 mf bookkeeper
Buch′haltung f bookkeeping; accounting department
Buch′händler -in §6 mf book dealer
Buch′handlung f bookstore
Büchlein [′byçlaɪn] n (-s;-) booklet
Buch′macher m bookmaker
Buch′prüfer -in §6 mf auditor
Buchsbaum [′buksbaum] m boxwood
Buchse [′buksə] f (-;-n) (mach) bushing
Büchse [′byksə] f (-;-n) box, case; (*Dose*) can; (*Gewhr*) rifle
Büch′senfleisch n canned meat

Büch′senöffner m can opener
Buchstabe [′bux/tabə] m (-n;-n) letter
buchstabieren [bux/ta′birən] ,tr & intr spell
buchstäblich [′bux/tepliç] adj literal
Bucht [buxt] f (-;-en) bay
Buch′umschlag m book jacket
Bu′chung f (-;-en) booking; (acct) entry
Buckel [′bukəl] m (-s;-) hump; (coll) back; **B. haben** be hunchback; **e-n B. machen** arch its back
buck(e)lig [′buk(ə)lɪç] adj hunchbacked || **Buck(e)lige** §5 mf hunchback
bücken [′bykən] tr & ref bow (down)
Bückling [′byklɪŋ] m (-s;-e) bow
Bude [′budə] f (-;-n) booth, stall; (coll) shanty; (coll) hole in the wall
Budget [by′dʒe] n (-s;-s) budget
Büfett [by′fe], [by′fet] n (-s;-s) buffet, sideboard; counter; (*Schanktisch*) bar; **kaltes B.** cold buffet
Büffel [′byfəl] m (-s;-) buffalo
Büffelei [byfə′laɪ] f (-;-en) cramming
büffeln [′byfəln] intr (für) cram (for)
Bug [buk] m (-[e]s;-e) (aer) nose; (naut) bow; (zool) shoulder, withers
Bügel [′bygəl] m (-s;-) handle; (*Kleider-*) coat hanger; (*Steig-*) stirrup; (*e-r Säge*) frame
Bü′gelbrett n ironing board
Bü′geleisen n iron, flatiron
Bü′gelfalte f crease
bü′gelfrei adj drip-dry
bügeln [′bygəln] tr iron, press
Bü′gelsäge f hacksaw
bugsieren [buk′sirən] tr tow
Buhldirne [′buldɪrnə] f (-;-n) bawd
buhlen [′bulən] intr have an affair; **um j-s Gunst b.** curry favor with s.o.
Bühne [′bynə] f (-;-n) stage; platform
Büh′nenanweisung f stage direction
Büh′nenaussprache f standard pronunciation
Büh′nenausstattung f, **Büh′nenbild** n set
Büh′nenbildner -in §6 mf stage designer
Büh′nendeutsch n standard German
Büh′nendichter -in §6 mf playwright
Büh′nendichtung f drama, play
Büh′nenkünstler m actor
Büh′nenkünstlerin f actress
Büh′nenleiter -in §6 mf stage manager
Büh′nenstück n play, stage play
buk [buk] *pret* of **backen**
Bukarest [′bukarest] n (-s) Bucharest
Bulette [bu′letə] f (-;-n) meatball
Bulgarien [bul′gɑrjən] n (-s;) Bulgaria
Bullauge [′bulaugə] n (-s;-en) porthole
Bulldogge [′buldɔgə] f (-;-n) bulldog
Bulle [′bulə] m (-n;-n) bull; brawny fellow; (sl) cop || f (-;-n) (eccl) bull
bullern [′bulərn] intr bubble, boil; (*Feuer*) roar; (*Sturm*) rage
Bummel [′buməl] m (-s) stroll
Bummelei [bumə′laɪ] f (-;-en) dawdling; loafing; sloppiness
bummelig [′buməlɪç] adj slow; sloppy
bummeln [′buməln] intr loaf; dawdle; (*Autos*) crawl || intr (SEIN) stroll

Bum′melstreik *m* slowdown
Bum′melzug *m* (coll) slow train, local
Bumm̄ler [ˈbʊmlər] *m* (-s;-) loafer, bum; slowpoke; gadabout
Bums [bʊms] *m* (-es;-e) thud, thump, bang || *interj* boom!; bang!
bumsen [ˈbʊmsən] *intr* thud, thump, bump; (sl) have intercourse
Bums′lokal *n* (coll) dive, joint
Bund [bʊnt] *m* (-[e]s;ᴗ) union, federation; (*Schlüssel-*) ring; (*Rand an Hose*) waistband; (*Ehe-*) bond; (mach) flange; (mus) fret; (pol) federal government; **im Bunde mit** with the cooperation of || *n* (-[e]s;- & -e) bunch, bundle
Bündel [ˈbʏndəl] *n* (-s;-) bunch, bundle; (phys) beam
Bundes- *comb.fm.* federal
Bun′desgenosse *m* ally, confederate
Bun′desgerichtshof *m* federal supreme court
Bun′deslade *f* ark of the covenant
bun′desstaatlich *adj* state; federal
Bun′destag *m* lower house
bündig [ˈbʏndɪç] *adj* binding; (*überzeugend*) convincing; (*treffend*) succint; **b. liegen** be flush
Bündnis [ˈbʏntnɪs] *n* (-ses;-se) agreement, pact, alliance
Bunker [ˈbʊŋkər] *m* (-;-) bin; (agr) silo; (aer) air-raid shelter; (mil) bunker; (nav) submarine pen
bunt [bʊnt] *adj* colored; (*mehrfarbig*) multicolored; (*gefleckt*) dappled; (*gemischt*) varied, motley; (*Farbe*) bright, gay; (*Wiese*) gay with flowers; **bunter Abend** variety show; **buntes Durcheinander** complete muddle
Bunt′metall *n* nonferrous metal
Bunt′stift *m* colored pencil, crayon
Bürde [ˈbʏrdə] *f* (-;-n) burden
Burg [bʊrk] *f* (-;-en) fortress, stronghold; citadel; castle
Bürge [ˈbʏrgə] *m* (-;-n) bondsman, guarantor, surety; **B. sein für** (or **als B. haften für**) stand surety for (*s.o.*); vouch for (*s.th.*)
bürgen [ˈbʏrgən] *intr*—**b. für** put up bail for (*s.o.*); vouch for (*s.th.*)
Bürger –**in** [ˈbʏrgər(ɪn)] §6 *mf* citizen; member of the middle class; commoner
Bür′gerkrieg *m* civil war
bür′gerlich *adj* civic; civil; middle-class; (*nicht überfeinert*) plain
Bür′germeister *m* mayor
Bür′gerrecht *n* civil rights
Bür′gerschaft *f* (-;) citizens

Bür′gersteig *m* sidewalk
Bürgschaft [ˈbʏrk/aft] *f* (-;-en) security, guarantee; (jur) bail; **gegen B. freilassen** release on bail
Büro [bʏˈro] *n* (-s;-s) office
Büro′angestellte §5 *mf* clerk
Büro′bedarf *m* office supplies
Büro′klammer *f* paper clip
Büro′kraft *f* office worker; **Bürokräfte** office personnel
Bürokrat [bʏroˈkrat] *m* (-en;-en) bureaucrat
Bürokra·tie [bʏrokraˈti] *f* (-;-tien [ˈti·ən]) bureaucracy; (fig) red tape
bürokratisch [bʏroˈkratɪʃ] *adj* bureaucratic
Bursch(e) [ˈbʊrʃ(ə)] *m* (-[e]n;-[e]n) boy, fellow; (mil) orderly; **ein übler B.** a bad egg
burschikos [bʊrʃɪˈkos] *adj* tomboyish; devil-may-care
Bürste [ˈbʏrstə] *f* (-;-n) brush; (coll) crewcut
bürsten [ˈbʏrstən] *tr* brush
Bürzel [ˈbʏrtsəl] *m* (-s;-) rump (*of bird*)
Bus [bʊs] *m* (-ses;-se) bus
Busch [bʊʃ] *m* (-es;ᴗe) bush; forest
Büschel [ˈbʏʃəl] *m* & *n* clump, bunch, cluster; (*Haar-*) tuft; (elec) brush
Busch′holz *n* brushwood
buschig [ˈbʊʃɪç] *adj* bushy; shaggy
Busch′klepper *m* bushwacker
Busch′messer *n* machete
Busch′werk *n* bushes, brush
Busen [ˈbuzən] *m* (-s;-) bosom, breast; (*Bucht*) bay, gulf; (fig) bosom
Bussard [ˈbʊsart] *m* (-s;-e) buzzard
Buße [ˈbusə] *f* (-;-n) penance; (*Sühne*) atonement; (*Strafgeld*) fine
büßen [ˈbysən] *tr* atone for, pay for
Büßer –**in** [ˈbʏsər(ɪn)] §6 *mf* penitent
Busserl [ˈbʊsərl] *n* (-s;-n) kiss
buß′fertig *adj* repentant
Bussole [bʊˈsolə] *f* (-;-n) compass
Büste [ˈbʏstə] *f* (-;-n) bust
Bü′stenhalter *m* brassière, bra
Bütte [ˈbʏtə] *f* (-;-n) tub; vat
Butter [ˈbʊtər] *f* (-;) butter
But′terbrot *n* bread and butter
But′terdose *f* butter dish
But′termilch *f* buttermilk
buttern [ˈbʊtərn] butter || *intr* make butter
byzantinisch [bytsanˈtinɪʃ] *adj* Byzantine
Byzanz [bʏˈtsants] *n* (-';) Byzantium
bzw. *abbr* (**beziehungsweise**) respectively

C

C, c [tze] *invar n* C, c; (meteor) centigrade; (mus) C
Café [kaˈfe] *n* (-s;-s) café; coffee shop
Camping [ˈkɛmpɪŋ] *n* (-s;-s) camping
Canaille [kaˈnaljə] *f* (-;-n) scoundrel
Cäsar [ˈtsezar] *m* (-s;) Caesar
Cellist –**in** [t/eˈlɪst(ɪn)] §7 *mf* cellist

Cello [ˈt/elo] *n* (-s;-s) cello
Cellophan [tselɔˈfan] *n* (-s;) cellophane
Celsius [ˈtselzjus] centigrade
Cembalo [ˈt/ɛmbalo] *n* (-s;-s) harpsichord
Ces [tses] *n* (-;-) (mus) C flat

Champagner [ʃamˈpanjər] *m* (-s;-) champagne

Champignon [ˈʃampɪnjõ] *m* (-s;-s) mushroom

Chance [ˈʃ̃ansə] *f* (-;-n) chance

Chaos [ˈkaːɔs] *n* (-;) chaos

chaotisch [kaˈoːtɪʃ] *adj* chaotic

Charak·ter [kaˈraktər] *m* (-s;-tere [ˈteːrə]) character; (mil) honorary rank

Charak′terbild *n* character sketch

Charak′tereigenschaft *f* trait

charak′terfest *adj* of a strong character

charakterisieren [karaktɛˈziːrən] *tr* characterize

Charakteristik [karaktɛˈrɪstɪk] *f* (-;-en) characterization

Charakteristi·kum [karaktɛˈrɪstɪkum] *n* [-s;-ka [ka]) characteristic

charakteristisch [karaktɛˈrɪstɪʃ] *adj* (für) characteristic (of)

charak′terlich *adj* of character || *adv* in character

charak′terlos *adj* wishy-washy

Charak′terzug *m* characteristic, trait

Charge [ˈʃ̃arʒə] *f* (-;-n) (metal) charge; (mil) rank; **Chargen** (mil) non-coms

charmant [ʃarˈmant] *adj* charming

Charme [ʃarm] *m* (-s;) charm, grace

Chas·sis [ʃaˈsi] *n* (-sis [ˈsi[s]]; -sis [ˈsis]) chassis

Chaus·see [ʃɔˈse] *f* (-;-seen [ˈseːən]) highway

Chef [ʃɛf] *m* (-s;-s) chief, head; (com) boss; (culin) chef; **C. des Generalstabs** chief of staff; **C. des Heeresjustizwesens** judge advocate general

Chemie [çeˈmiː] *f* (-;) chemistry; **technische C.** chemical engineering

Chemie′faser *f* synthetic fiber

Chemikalien [çemiˈkaljən] *pl* chemicals

Chemiker -in [ˈçemɪkər(ɪn)] §6 *mf* chemist; student of chemistry

chemisch [ˈçemɪʃ] *adj* chemical; **chemische Reinigung** dry cleaning

Chemotechniker -in [çemoˈtɛçnɪkər(ɪn)] §6 *mf* chemical engineer

Chiffre [ˈʃɪfər] *f* (-;-n) cipher; code; (in Anzeigen) box number

Chif′freschrift *f* code

chiffrieren [ʃɪˈfriːrən] *tr* code

China [ˈçina] *n* (-s;) China

Chinese [çiˈneːzə] *m* (-n;-n), **Chinesin** [çiˈneːzɪn] *f* (-;-nen) Chinese

chinesisch [çiˈneːzɪʃ] *adj* Chinese

Chinin [çiˈnin] *n* (-s;) quinine

Chirurg [çiˈrʊrk] *m* (-en;-en) surgeon

Chirurgie [çirʊrˈgi] *f* (-;) surgery

chirurgisch [çiˈrʊrgɪʃ] *adj* surgical

Chlor [klor] *n* (-s;) chlorine

chloren [ˈkloːrən] *tr* chlorinate

Chlorid [kloˈrit] *n* (-[e]s;-e) chloride

Chloroform [kloːrɔˈfɔrm] *n* (-s;) chloroform

chloroformieren [kloːrɔfɔrˈmiːrən] *tr* chloroform

Cholera [ˈkoləra] *f* (-;) cholera

cholerisch [koˈleːrɪʃ] *adj* choleric

Chor [kor] *m* (-s;⁔e) choir; chorus

Choral [koˈral] *m* (-s;⁔e) Gregorian chant; (Prot) hymn

Chor′altar *m* high altar

Chor′anlage *f* (archit) choir

Chor′bühne *f* choir loft

Choreograph –in [kɔre·ɔˈɡrɑf(ɪn)] §7 *mf* choreographer

Chor′hemd *n* surplice

Chor′stuhl *m* choir stall

Christ [krɪst] *m* (-s;) Christ || *m* (-en; -en) Christian

Christ′abend *m* Christmas Eve

Christ′baum *m* Christmas tree

Chri′stenheit *f* (-;) Christendom

Christentum [ˈkrɪstəntum] *n* (-s;) Christianity

Christin [ˈkrɪstɪn] *f* (-;-nen) Christian

Christ′kind *m* Christ child

christ′lich *adj* Christian

Christ′nacht *f* Holy Night

Chri·stus [ˈkrɪstus] *m* (-sti [sti];) Christ; **nach Christi Geburt A.D.**; **vor Christus B.C.**

Chri′stusbild *n* crucifix; picture of Christ

Chrom [krom] *n* (-s;) chromium, chrome

chromatisch [kroˈmatɪʃ] *adj* chromatic

Chromosom [kroməˈzom] *n* (-s;-en) chromosome

Chronik [ˈkronɪk] *f* (-;-en) chronicle

chronisch [ˈkronɪʃ] *adj* chronic

Chronist –in [kroˈnɪst(ɪn)] §7 *mf* chronicler

Chronolo·gie [kronələˈgi] *f* (-;-gien [ˈgi·ən]) chronology

chronologisch [kronəˈlogɪʃ] *adj* chronological

circa [ˈtsɪrka] *adv* approximately

Cis [tsɪs] *n* (-;-) (mus) C sharp

Clique [ˈklɪkə] *f* (-;-n) clique

Cocktail [ˈkɔktel] *m* (-s;-s) cocktail

Conferencier [kõferäˈsje] *m* (-s;-s) master of ceremony

Couch [kautʃ] *f* (-;-s) couch

Countdown [ˈkauntdaun] *m* (-s;-s) (rok) countdown

Couplet [kuˈple] *n* (-s;-s) song (in a musical)

Coupon [kuˈpõ] *m* (-s;-s) coupon

Courage [kuˈraʒə] *f* (-;) courage

Courtage [kurˈtaʒə] *f* (-;-n) brokerage

Cousin [kuˈzɛ̃] *m* (-s;-s) cousin

Cousine [kuˈzina] *f* (-;-n) cousin

Cowboy [ˈkaubɔi] *m* (-s;-s) cowboy

creme [krɛm] *adj* cream-colored || **Creme** [ˈkrɛm(ə)] *f* (-;) cream; custard

Crew [kru] *f* (-;) crew; (nav) cadets (of the same year)

Cut [kœt] *m* (-s;-s) cutaway

D

D, d [de] *invar n* D, d; (mus) D
da [da] *adv* there; then; in that case, **da und da** at such and such a place; **wieder da** back again || *conj* since, because; when
dabei [da'baɪ] *adv* nearby; besides, moreover; at that; at the same time; (*trotzdem*) yet; **d. bleiben** stick to one's point; **d. sein** be present, take part; **d. sein zu** (*inf*) be on the point of (*ger*); **es ist nichts d.** there's nothing to it
da capo [da'kapo] *interj* encore!
Dach [dax] *n* (–[e]s;ꞏer) roof; (fig) shelter; **unter D. und Fach** under cover
Dach'boden *m* attic
Dach'decker *m* roofer
Dach'fenster *n* dormer window; skylight
Dach'first *m* ridge of a roof
Dach'geschoß *n* top floor
Dach'gesellschaft *f* holding company
Dach'kammer *f* attic room
Dach'luke *f* skylight
Dach'organisation *f* parent company
Dach'pappe *f* roofing paper
Dach'pfanne *f* roof tile
Dach'rinne *f* rain gutter; eaves
Dach'röhre *f* downspout
Dachs [daks] *m* (–es;–e) badger; **ein frecher D.** a young whippersnapper
Dachs'hund *m* dachshund
Dach'sparren *m* rafter
Dach'stube *f* attic, garret
Dach'stuhl *m* roof framework
dachte ['daxtə] *pret* of **denken**
Dach'traufe *f* rain gutter
Dach'werk *n* roof
Dach'ziegel *m* roof tile
dadurch [da'dʊrç] *adv* through it; thereby; by this means; **dadurch, daß** by (*ger*)
dafür [da'fyr] *adv* for it or them; in its place; that's why; therefore
Dafür'halten *n*—**nach meinem D.** in my opinion
dagegen [da'gegən] *adv* against it or them; in exchange for it or them; in comparison; on the other hand; **etw d. haben** have an objection; **ich bin d.** I'm against it
daheim [da'haɪm] *adv* at home
daher [da'her] *adv* from there; therefore; (bei Verben der Bewegung) along || ['daher] *adv* that's why
dahin [da'hɪn] *adv* there, to that place; (*vergangen*) gone; (bei Verben der Bewegung) along; **bis d.** that far, up to there; until then; **es steht mir bis d.** I'm fed up with it
da'hinauf *adv* up there
da'hinaus *adv* out there
dahin'geben §80 *tr* give away; give up
dahin'gehen §82 *intr* (SEIN) walk along; pass; (*sterben*) pass away; **dahingehend, daß** to the effect that
dahingestellt [da'hɪngəʃtelt] *adj*—**d.**

sein lassen, ob leave the question open whether
dahin'leben *intr* exist from day to day
dahin'raffen *tr* carry off
dahin'scheiden §112 *intr* (SEIN) pass on
dahin'schwinden *intr* (SEIN) dwindle away; fade away; pine away
dahin'stehen §146 *impers*—**es steht dahin** it is uncertain
dahin'ten *adv* back there
dahin'ter *adv* behind it or them
dahinterher' *adv*—**d. sein, daß** be insistent that
dahin'terkommen §99 *intr* (SEIN) find out about it; get behind the truth of it
dahin'tersetzen *tr* put (*s.o.*) to work on it
dahin'welken §113 *intr* (SEIN) fade away
dahin'ziehen §163 *intr* (SEIN) move along
Dakapo [da'kapo] *n* (–s;–s) encore
da'lassen §104 *tr* leave behind
dalli ['dalɪ] *interj*—**mach d.!** step on it!
damalig ['damalɪç] *adj* of that time
damals ['damals] *adv* then, at that time
Damast [da'mast] *m* (–es;–e) damask
Dame ['damə] *f* (–;–n) lady; (beim Tanz) partner; (cards, chess) queen; (checkers) king; **e-e D. machen** crown a checker; **meine D.!** madam!; **meine Damen und Herrn!** ladies and gentlemen!
Da'mebrett *n* checkerboard
Da'menbinde *f* sanitary napkin
Da'mendoppelspiel *n* (tennis) women's doubles
Da'meneinzelspiel *n* (tennis) women's singles
Da'mengesellschaft *f* hen party
da'menhaft *adj* ladylike
Da'menhemd *n* chemise
Da'menschneider **–in** §6 *mf* dressmaker
Da'menwäsche *f* lingerie
Da'mespiel *n* checkers
damisch ['damɪʃ] *adj* dopey
damit [da'mɪt] *adv* with it or them; by it; thereby; **d. hat's noch Zeit** that can wait; **es ist nichts d.** it is useless || *conj* in order that, to
dämlich ['demlɪç] *adj* dopey
Damm [dam] *m* (–[e]s;ꞏe) dam; dike; embankment; causeway; breakwater; pier; (fig) barrier; (anat) perineum; **auf dem D. sein** feel up to it; **wieder auf dem D. sein** be on one's feet again
Dämmer ['demər] *m* (–s;) (poet) twilight
dämmerig ['de'mərɪç] *adj* dusky, dim
Däm'merlicht *n* dusk, twilight
dämmern ['demərn] *intr* dawn, grow light; (am Abend) grow dark; become twilight

Däm′merung *f* (-;-en) (*Morgenrot*) dawn; (*am Abend*) dusk, twilight

Dämmplatte ['dɛmplatə] *f* acoustical tile

Dämmstoff ['dɛmʃtɔf] *m* insulation

Damm′weg *m* causeway

Dämon ['dɛmon] *m* (-s; Dämonen [de'monən] demon

dämonisch [dɛ'moniʃ] *adj* demoniacal

Dampf [dampf] *m* (-[e]s;⸗e) steam; vapor; (*Angst*) (coll) fear; (*Hunger*) (coll) hunger; (vet) broken wind; **D. dahinter machen** (coll) step on it

dampfen ['dampfən] *intr* steam || *intr* (SEIN) steam along, steam away

dämpfen ['dɛmpfən] *tr* (*dünsten*) steam; (*Lärm*) muffle; (*Farben, Gefühle, Lichter*) subdue; (*Stoß*) absorb; (*Begeisterung*) dampen; **mit gedämpfter Stimme** under one's breath

Dampfer ['dampfər] *m* (-s;-) steamer

Dämpfer ['dɛmpfər] *m* (-s;-) (culin) steamer, boiler; (mach) baffle; (mus) mute; (*beim Klavier*) (mus) damper; **e-n D. aufsetzen** (*dat*) put a damper on

Dampf′heizung *f* steam heat

Dampf′kessel *m* steam boiler, boiler

Dampf′maschine *f* steam engine

Dampf′schiffahrtslinie *f* steamship line

Dämp′fungsfläche *f* (aer) stabilizer

Dampf′walze *f* steam roller

Damspiel ['dam/pil] *n* var of **Damespiel**

danach [da'nax] *adv* after it or them; accordingly; according to it or them; afterwards; **d. fragen** ask about it; **d. streben** strive for it; **d. sieht er auch aus** that's just what he looks like

Däne ['dɛnə] *m* (-n;-n) Dane

daneben [da'nebən] *adv* next to it or them || *adv* in addition

dane′bengehen §82 *intr* (SEIN) go amiss

dane′benhauen *intr* miss; (fig) be wrong

Dänemark ['denəmark] *n* (-s;) Denmark

dang [daŋ] *pret* of **dingen**

danniederliegen [da'nidərligən] §108 *intr* (fig) be down; **d. an** (*dat*) be laid up with

Dänin ['denin] *f* (-;-nen) Dane

dänisch ['deniʃ] *adj* Danish

dank [daŋk] *prep* (*dat*) thanks to || **Dank** *m* [-(e)s;] thanks; gratitude; **Gott sei D.!** thank God!, thank heaven!

dankbar ['daŋkbar] *adj* thankful; (*lohnend*) rewarding, profitable

Dank′barkeit *f* (-;) gratitude

danken ['daŋkən] *intr* (*dat*) thank; **danke!** thanks!; (*bei Ablehnung*) no, thanks!; **danke schön!** thank you!; **nichts zu d.!** you are welcome!

dan′kenswert *adj* meritorious; rewarding

dank′sagen *intr* return thanks

Danksagung ['daŋkzaguŋ] *f* (-;) thanksgiving

Dank′sagungstag *m* Thanksgiving Day

Dank′schreiben *n* letter of thanks

dann [dan] *adv* then; **d. und wann** now and then

dannen ['danən] *adv*—**von d.** away

daran [da'ran] *adv* on, at, by, in, onto it or them; **das ist alles d.!** that's great!; **er ist gut d.** he's well off; **er tut gut d. zu** (*inf*) he does well to (*inf*); **es ist nichts d.** there's nothing to it; **ich will wissen, wie ich d. bin** I want to know where I stand; **jetzt bin ich d.** it's my turn; **nahe d. sein zu** (*inf*) be on the point of (*ger*); **was liegt d.?** what does it matter?

daran′gehen §82 *intr* (SEIN) go about it; **d. gehen zu** (*inf*) proceed to (*inf*)

daran′setzen *tr*—**alles d. zu** (*inf*) do one's level best to (*inf*)

darauf [da'rauf] *adv* on it or them; after that; **d. kommt es an** that's what matters; **gerade d. zu** straight towards; **gleich d.** immediately afterwards; **ich lasse es d. ankommen** I'll risk it

daraufhin [darauf'hin] *adv* thereupon

daraus [da'raus] *adv* of it, from it; from that; from them; hence; **d. wird nichts!** nothing doing!; **es wird nichts d.** nothing will come of it

darben ['darbən] *intr* live in poverty

darbieten ['darbitən] §58 *tr* present

Dar′bietung *f* (-;-en) presentation; (theat) performance

dar′bringen §65 *tr* present, offer

Dardanellen [darda'nelən] *pl* Dardanelles

darein [da'rain] *adv* into it or them

darein′reden *intr* interrupt; **er redet mir in alles d.** he interferes in all that I do

darin [da'rin] *adv* in it or them

dar′legen *tr* explain; state

Dar′legung *f* (-;-en) explanation

Darlehen ['darle(ə)n] *n* (-s;-) loan

Dar′leh(e)nskasse *f* loan association

Darm [darm] *m* (-[e]s;⸗e) intestine, gut; (*Wursthaut*) skin

Darm— *comb.fm.* intestinal

Darm′entzündung *f* enteritis

Darm′fäule *f* dysentery

dar′stellen *tr* describe; show, depict, portray; represent; mean; plot, chart; (indust) produce; (theat) play the part of

Dar′steller –in §6 *mf* performer

Dar′stellung *f* (-;-en) representation; portrayal; account, version; (indust) production; (theat) performance

dar′tun §154 *tr* prove; demonstrate

darüber [da'rybər] *adv* over it or them; (*querüber*) across it; (*betreffs*) about that; **d. hinaus** beyond it; moreover; **ich bin d. hinweg** I've gotten over it

darum [da'rum] *adv* around it or them; (*deshalb*) therefore; **er weiß d.** he's aware of it; **es ist mir nur d. zu tun, daß** all I ask is that

darunter [da'runtər] *adv* below it or them; among them; (*weniger*) less; **d. leiden** suffer from it; **zehn Jahre und d.** ten years and under

das [das] §1 *def art* the || §1 *dem adj* & *dem pron* this, that; **das und das**

such and such || §11 *rel pron* which, that, who

da'sein §139 *intr* (SEIN) be there; be present; exist; **es ist schon alles mal dagewesen** there's nothing new under the sun; **noch nie dagewesen** unprecedented || **Dasein** *n* (-s;) being, existence, life

Da'seinsberechtigung *f* raison d'être

daselbst [da'zɛlpst] *adv* just there; ibidem; **wohnhaft d.** address as above

dasjenige ['dasjenɪɡə] §4,3 *dem adj* that || *dem pron* the one

daß [das] *conj* that; **daß du nicht vergißt!** be sure not to forget!; **daß er doch käme!** I wish he'd come; **es sei denn, daß** unless

dasselbe [das'zɛlbə] §4,3 *dem adj & dem pron* the same

da'stehen §146 *intr* stand there; **einzig d.** be unrivaled; **gut d.** be well-off; **wie stehe ich nun da!** how foolish I look now!

Daten ['datən] *pl* data

Da'tenverarbeitung *f* data processing

datieren [da'tirən] *tr & intr* date

Dativ ['datif] *m* (-s;-e) dative (case)

dato ['dato] *adv*—**bis d.** to date

Dattel ['datəl] *f* (-;-n) (bot) date

Da·tum ['datum] *n* (-s;-ten [tən]) date; **Daten** data, facts; **heutigen Datums** of today; **neueren Datums** of recent date; **welches D. haben wir heute?** what's today's date?

Daube ['daubə] *f* (-;-n) (barrel) stave

Dauer ['dau·ər] *f* (-;) length, duration; permanence; **auf die D.** in the long run; **für die D. von** for a period of; **von D. sein** last, endure

Dau'erauftrag *m* standing order

Dau'erbelastung *f* constant load

Dau'erertrag *m* constant yield

Dau'erfeuer *n* (mil) automatic fire

Dau'erflug *m* endurance flight

Dau'ergeschwindigkeit *f* cruising speed

dau'erhaft *adj* lasting, durable; (*Farbe*) fast

Dau'erkarte *f* season ticket; (rr) commutation ticket

Dau'erlauf *m* (long-distance) jogging

dauern ['dau·ərn] *tr*—**er dauert mich** I feel sorry for him || *intr* last, continue; **die Fahrt dauert fünf Stunden** the trip takes five hours; **es wird nicht lange d.,** dann it won't be long before; **lange d.** take a long time

Dau'erplissee *n* permanent pleat

Dau'erprobe *f* endurance test

Dau'erschmierung *f* self-lubrication

Dau'erstellung *f* permanent job

Dau'erton *m* (telp) dial tone

Dau'erversuch *m* endurance test

Dau'erwelle *f* permanent wave

Dau'erwirkung *f* lasting effect

Dau'erwurst *f* hard salami

Dau'erzustand *m* permanent condition; **zum D. werden** get to be a regular thing

Daumen ['daumən] *m* (-s;-) thumb; **D. halten!** keep your fingers crossed!; **die D. drehen** twiddle one's thumbs; **über den D. peilen** (or **schätzen**) give a rough estimate of

Dau'menabdruck *m* thumb print

Dau'menindex *m* thumb index

Daune ['daunə] *f* (-;-n) downy feather; **Daunen** down

Dau'nenbett *n* feather bed

Davit ['devit] *m* (-s;-s) (naut) davit

davon [da'fɔn] *adv* of it or them; from it or them; about it or them; away

davon'kommen §99 *intr* (SEIN) escape

davon'laufen §105 *intr* (SEIN) run away; || **Davonlaufen** *n*—**es ist zum D.** (coll) it's enough to drive you insane

davon'machen *ref* take off, go away

davon'tragen §132 *tr* carry off; win

davor [da'for] *adv* in front of it or them; of it or them; from it or them

dawider [da'vidər] *adv* against it

dazu [da'tsu] *adv* thereto; to it or them; in addition to that; for that purpose; about it or them; with it or them

dazu'gehörig *adj* belonging to it; proper, appropriate

da'zumal *adv* at that time

dazu'tun §154 *tr* add || **Dazutun** *n*—**ohne sein D.** without any effort on his part

dazwischen [da'tsviʃən] *adv* in between; among them

dazwi'schenfahren §71 *intr* (SEIN) jump in to intervene

dazwi'schenfunken *intr* (coll) butt in

dazwi'schenkommen §99 *intr* (SEIN) intervene

Dazwischenkunft [da'tsviʃənkunft] *f* (-;) intervention

dazwi'schentreten §152 *intr* (SEIN) intervene

Debatte [de'batə] *f* (-;-n) debate, discussion; **zur D. stehen** be under discussion; **zur D. stellen** open to discussion

debattieren [deba'tirən] *tr & intr* debate, discuss

Debet ['debɛt] *n* (-s;-s) debit; **im D. stehen** be on the debit side

Debüt [de'by] *n* (-s;-s) debut

Debütantin [deby'tantɪn] *f* (-;-nen) debutante

debütieren [deby'tirən] *intr* make one's debut

Dechant [de'çant] *m* (-en;-en) (educ, R.C.) dean

dechiffrieren [deʃɪf'rirən] *tr* decipher

Deck [dɛk] *n* (-s;-s) deck

Deck'anstrich *m* final coat

Deck'bett *n* feather bed

Deck'blatt *n* overlay

Decke ['dɛkə] *f* (-;-n) cover, covering; (*Bett*-) blanket; (*Tisch*-) tablecloth; (*Zimmer*-) ceiling; (*Schicht*) layer; **mit j-m unter e-r D. stecken** be in cahoots with s.o.; **sich nach der D. strecken** make the best of it

Deckel ['dɛkəl] *m* (-s;-) lid, cap; (*Buch*-) cover; **j-m eins auf den D. geben** (coll) chew s.o. out

decken ['dɛkən] *tr* cover; (sport) set; **das Tor d.** guard the goal || *ref* coincide || *intr* cover

Deckenbeleuchtung (Deck'kenbeleuchtung) *f* (-;) ceiling lighting

Deckenlicht (Dek'kenlicht) *n* ceiling light; skylight; (aut) dome light

Deck·farbe *f* one-coat paint

Deck·konto *n* secret account

Deck'mantel *m* pretext, pretense

Deck name *m* pseudonym; alias; (mil) code name, cover name

Deck'offizier *m* (nav) warrant officer

Deck'plane *f* awning; tarpaulin

Deckung (Dek'kung) *f* (–;-en) covering; protection; roofing; (box) defense; (com) security, surety; collateral

deckungsgleich (dek'kungsgleich) *adj* congruent

defekt [de'fekt] *adj* defective ‖ **Defekt** *m* (–[e]s;-e) defect

defensiv [defen'zif] *adj* defensive ‖ **Defensive** [defen'zivə] *f* (–;-n) defensive

definieren [defi'nirən] *tr* define

definitiv [defini'tif] *adj* (*endgültig*) definitive; (*bestimmt*) definite

Defizit ['defitsit] *n* (–s;-e) deficit

Degen ['degən] *m* (–s;-) sword; (poet) warrior; (typ) compositor

degradieren [degra'dirən] *tr* demote

Degradie'rung *f* (–;-en) demotion

dehnbar ['denbar] *adj* elastic; (*Metall*) ductile; (fig) vague, loose

dehnen ['denən] *tr* stretch; extend; expand; (*Worte*) drawl out; (*Vokal*) lengthen; (mus) sustain ‖ *ref* stretch out; expand

Deh'nung *f* (–;-en) extension; expansion; dilation; (ling) lengthening

Deich [daiç] *m* (–[e]s;-e) dike; (*Damm*) bank, embankment

Deichsel ['daiksəl] *f* (–;-n) pole

deichseln ['daiksəln] *tr* (coll) manage

dein [dain] §2 *poss adj* your, thy

deinerseits ['dainər'zaits] *adv* on your part

deinesgleichen ['dainəs'glaiçən] *invar pron* your own kin, your equals, the likes of you

deinethalben ['dainət'halbən], **deinetwegen** ['dainət'vegən], **deinetwillen** ['dainət'vilən] *adv* for your sake; because of you, on your account

deinige ['dainigə] *poss pron* yours

Dekan [de'kan] *m* (–s;-e) dean

deklamieren [dekla'mirən] *tr & intr* declaim; recite

Deklination [deklina'tsjon] *f* (–;-en) declension

deklinieren [dekli'nirən] *tr* decline

dekolletiert [dekɔlə'tirt] *adj* low-necked; (*Dame*) bare-necked

Dekorateur [dekɔra'tør] *m* (–s;-e) decorator, interior decorator

Dekoration [dekɔra'tsjon] *f* (–;-en) decoration; (theat) scenery

dekorieren [dekɔ'rirən] *tr* decorate

Dekret [de'kret] *n* (–[e]s;-e) decree

delikat [deli'kat] *adj* delicate; (*lecker*) delicious

Delikt [de'likt] *n* (–[e]s;-e) offense

Delle ['delə] *f* (–;-n) dent; dip

Delphin [del'fin] *m* (–s;-e) dolphin

Delta ['delta] *n* (–s;-s) delta

dem [dem] §1 *def art, dem adj & dem pron* ‖ §11 *rel pron*

Demagoge [dema'gogə] *m* (–n;-n) demagogue

Dementi [de'menti] *n* (–s;-s) official denial

dementieren [demen'tirən] *tr* deny (officially)

dem'entsprechend *adj* corresponding ‖ *adv* correspondingly, accordingly

dem'gegenüber *adv* in contrast

dem'gemäß *adv* accordingly

dem'nach *adv* therefore; accordingly

dem'nächst *adv* soon, before long; (theat) (public sign) coming soon

demobilisieren [demɔbili'zirən] *tr & intr* demobilize

Demokrat [demo'krat] *m* (–en;-en) democrat

Demokra·tie [demokra'ti] *f* (–;-tien ['ti·ən]) democracy

Demokratin [demo'kratin] *f* (–;-nen) democrat

demokratisch [demo'kratiʃ] *adj* democratic

demolieren [demo'lirən] *tr* demolish

Demonstrant -in [demɔn'strant(in)] §7 *mf* demonstrator

demonstrieren [demɔn'strirən] *tr & intr* demonstrate

Demontage [demɔn'taʒə] *f* (–;) dismantling

demontieren [demɔn'tirən] *tr* dismantle

demselben [dem'zelbən] §4,3 *dem adj & dem pron*

Demut ['demut] *f* (–;) humility

demütig ['demytiç] *adj* humble

demütigen ['demytigən] *tr* humble; (*beschämen*) humiliate

De'mütigung *f* (–;-en) humiliation

de'mutsvoll *adj* submissive

dem'zufolge *adv* accordingly

den [den] §1 *def art, dem adj & dem pron* ‖ §11 *rel pron* whom

denen ['denən] §11 *rel pron* to whom

Denkarbeit ['deŋkarbait] *f* (–;) brain-work

Denkart ['deŋkart] *f var of* **Denkungsart**

Denkaufgabe ['deŋkaufgabə] *f* brain twister, problem

denkbar ['deŋkbar] *adj* conceivable; (*vorstellbar*) imaginable

denken ['deŋkən] §66 *tr* think, consider; **was d. Sie zu tun?** what do you intend to do? ‖ *ref*—**bei sich** (or **für sich**) **d.** think to oneself; **denke dir e–e Zahl** think of a number; **d. Sie sich in ihre Lage** imagine yourself in her place; **sich** [*dat*] **etw d.** imagine s.th.; **was denkst du dir eigentlich?** what do you think you're doing? ‖ *intr* think; **das gibt mir zu d.** that set me thinking; **d. an** (*acc*) think about

denk'faul *adj* mentally lazy

Denk'fehler *m* fallacy, false reasoning

Denk'mal *n* (–s;-e & ⸚er) monument

Denk'schrift *f* (pol) memorandum

Denkungsart ['deŋkuŋsart] *f* way of thinking, mentality

Denk'weise *f* way of thinking, mentality

denk'würdig *adj* memorable

Denk'zettel *m*—**j-m e-n D. geben** teach s.o. a lesson

denn [den] *adv* then; **es sei denn, daß** unless || *conj* for

dennoch [ˈdɛnɔx] *adv* nevertheless, all the same, (but) still

Dentist **-in** [denˈtɪst(ɪn)] §7 *mf* dentist

Denunziant **-in** [denunˈtsjant(ɪn)] §7 *mf* informer

denunzieren [denunˈtsiːrən] *tr* denounce

Depesche [deˈpɛʃə] *f* (**-;-n**) dispatch

De·ponens [deˈpoːnens] *n* (**-;-ponenzien** [poˈnɛntsjən]) (gram) deponent

deponieren [depoˈniːrən] *tr* (com) deposit

deportieren [depɔrˈtiːrən] *tr* deport

Depot [deˈpoː] *n* (**-s;-s**) depot; warehouse; storage; safe; safe deposit

Depp [dɛp] *m* (**-s;-e**) (coll) dope

Depression [deprɛˈsjoːn] *f* (**-;-en**) depression

der [der] §1 *def art* the || §1 *dem adj* & *dem pron* this, that; **der und der** such and such, so and so || §11 *rel pron* who, which, that; (to) whom

der'art *adv* so, in such a way; (coll) that

der'artig *adj* such, of that kind

derb [dɛrp] *adj* coarse; tough; rude

Derb'heit *f* (**-;-en**) coarseness; toughness; crude joke

dereinst' *adv* some day

deren [ˈdeːrən] §11 *rel pron* whose

derenthalben [ˈdeːrəntˈhalbən], **derentwegen** [ˈdeːrəntˈveːgən], **derentwillen** [ˈdeːrəntˈvɪlən] *adv* for her sake, for their sake

dergestalt [ˈdeːrgəˈʃtalt] *adv* so

dergleichen [ˈdeːrˈglaɪçən] *invar dem adj* such; similar; of that kind || *invar dem pron* such a thing; **und d. and the like; und d. mehr** and so on

derjenige [ˈdeːrjeːnɪgə] §4,3 *dem adj* that || *dem pron* the one; he

dermaßen [der ˈmaːsən] *adv* so, in such a way

derselbe [der ˈzɛlbə] §4,3 *dem adj* & *dem pron* the same

derweilen [ˈdeːrˈvaɪlən] *adv* meanwhile

derzeit [ˈdeːrˈtsaɪt] *adv* at present

derzeitig [ˈdeːrˈtsaɪtɪç] *adj* present; then, of that time

des [dɛs] *n* (**-;-**) (mus) D flat

Desaster [deˈzastər] *n* (**-s;-**) disaster

Deserteur [dezɛrˈtøːr] *m* (**-s;-e**) deserter

desertieren [dezɛrˈtiːrən] *intr* (SEIN) desert

desgleichen [ˈdɛsˈglaɪçən] *invar dem pron* such a thing || *invar rel pron* the likes of which || *adv* likewise

deshalb [ˈdɛshalp] *adv* therefore

Desinfektion [dɛsɪnfɛkˈtsjoːn] *f* (**-;-en**) disinfection

Desinfektions'mittel *n* disinfectant

desinfizieren [dɛsɪnfɪˈtsiːrən] *tr* disinfect

Despot [dɛsˈpoːt] *m* (**-en;-en**) despot

despotisch [dɛsˈpoːtɪʃ] *adj* despotic

Dessin [deˈsɛ̃] *n* (**-s;-s**) design

destillieren [dɛstɪˈliːrən] *tr* distill

desto [ˈdɛsto] *adv* the; **d. besser** the better, all the better

deswegen [ˈdɛsˈveːgən] *adv* therefore

Detail [deˈtaɪ(l)] *n* (**-s;-s**) detail; (com) retail

Detail'geschäft *n* retail store

Detail'händler **-in** §6 *mf* retail dealer

detaillieren [detaˈjiːrən] *tr* relate in detail; specify; itemize

Detek·tiv [detɛkˈtiːf] *m* (**-s;-tive** [ˈtiːvə]) private investigator; (coll) private eye

detonieren [detoˈniːrən] *intr* detonate; **etw. d. lassen** detonate s.th.

deuchte [ˈdɔɪçtə] *pret* of **dünken**

Deutelei [dɔɪtəˈlaɪ] *f* (**-;-en**) quibble

deuteln [ˈdɔɪtəln] *intr* (**an** *dat*) quibble (about), split hairs (over)

deuten [ˈdɔɪtən] *tr* interpret; **falsch d.** misinterpret || *intr* (**auf** *acc*) (& fig) point (to)

deutlich [ˈdɔɪtlɪç] *adj* clear, distinct

deutsch [dɔɪtʃ] *adj* German || **Deutsche** §5 *mf* German

Deu'tung *f* (**-;-en**) interpretation

Devise [deˈviːzə] *f* (**-;-n**) motto; **Devisen** foreign currency

Devi'senbestand *m* foreign-currency reserve

Devi'senbilanz *f* balance of payments

Devi'senkurs *m* rate of exchange

Dezember [deˈtsɛmbər] *m* (**-s;-**) December

dezent [deˈtsɛnt] *adj* unobtrusive; (*Licht, Musik*) soft; (*anständig*) decent

Dezernat [detsɛrˈnaːt] *n* (**-[e]s;-e**) (administrative) department

dezimal [detsiˈmaːl] *adj* decimal || **Dezimale** [detsiˈmaːlə] *f* (**-;-n**) decimal

Dezimal'bruch *m* decimal fraction

Dezimal'zahl *f* decimal

dezimieren [detsiˈmiːrən] *tr* decimate

Dia [ˈdiːa] *n* (**-s;-s**) (coll) slide

Diadem [diaˈdeːm] *n* (**-s;-e**) diadem

Diagnose [diaˈgnoːzə] *f* (**-;-n**) diagnosis

diagnostizieren [diagnɔstiˈtsiːrən] *tr* diagnose

diagonal [diagoˈnaːl] *adj* diagonal || **Diagonale** *f* (**-;-n**) diagonal

Diagramm [diaˈgram] *n* (**-[e]s;-e**) diagram; graph

Diakon [diaˈkoːn] *m* (**-s;-e** & **-en;-en**) deacon

Dialekt [diaˈlɛkt] *m* (**-[e]s;-e**) dialect

dialektisch [diaˈlɛktɪʃ] *adj* dialectical

Dialog [diaˈloːk] *m* (**-s;-e**) dialogue

Diamant [diaˈmant] *m* (**-en;-en**) diamond

Diaposi·tiv [diapoziˈtiːf] *n* (**-s;-tive** [ˈtiːvə]) slide, transparency

Diät [diˈɛːt] *f* (**-;-en**) diet (*under medical supervision*); **Diäten** daily allowance; **diät leben** be on a diet

Diät- *comb.fm.* dietary

diätetisch [diɛˈteːtɪʃ] *adj* dietetic

dich [dɪç] §11 *pers pron* you, thee || *reflex pron* yourself, thyself

dicht [dɪçt] *adj* dense; thick; heavy; leakproof; tight || **Dichte** [ˈdɪçtə] *f* (**-;-en**) density

dichten ['dıçtən] *tr* tighten; caulk; compose, write || *intr* write poetry
Dichter ['dıçtər] *m* (-s;-) (important) writer; poet
Dichterin ['dıçtərın] *f* (-;-nen) poetess
dichterisch ['dıçtərıʃ] *adj* poetic(al)
dicht'gedrängt *adj* tightly packed
dicht'halten §90 *intr* keep mum
Dicht'heit *f* (-;), **Dich'tigkeit** *f* (-;) density; compactness; tightness
Dich'kunst *f* poetry
dicht'machen *tr* (coll) close up
Dich'tung *f* (-;-en) gasket; packing; imagination; fiction; poetry; poem;
Dich'tungsring *m*, **Dich'tungsscheibe** *f* washer; gasket
dick [dık] *adj* thick; fat; big; (Luft, Freunde) close; **dicke Luft!** (coll) cheese it!; **sich d. tun** talk big || **Dicke** *f* (-;) thickness, stoutness
Dick'darm *m* (anat) colon
dickfellig ['dıkfɛlıç] *adj* thick-skinned
dick'flüssig *adj* viscous
Dickicht ['dıkıçt] *n* (-[e]s;-e) thicket
Dick'kopf *m* thick head
dickköpfig ['dıkkœpfıç] *adj* thick-headed
dickleibig ['dıklaıbıç] *adj* stout, fat
Dick'schädel *m* thick head
dick'schädelig ['dık/edəlıç] *adj* thick-headed
die [di] §1 *def art* the || §1 *dem adj & dem pron* this, that; **die und die** such and such || §11 *rel pron* who, which, that
Dieb [dip] *m* (-[e]s;-e) thief
Dieberei [dibə'raɪ] *f* (-;-en) thievery; (Diebstahl) theft
Diebesbande ['dibəsbandə] *f* pack of thieves
Diebin ['dibın] *f* (-;-nen) thief
diebisch ['dibıʃ] *adj* thievish || *adv*— **sich d. freuen** be tickled pink
Diebstahl ['dip/tal] *m* (-[e]s;⸚) theft, larceny; **leichter D.** petty larceny; **schwerer D.** grand larceny
diejenige ['dijənıgə] §4,3 *dem adj* that || *dem pron* the one; she
Diele ['dilə] *f* (-;-n) floorboard; (breiter Flur) entrance hall; **Dielen** flooring
dienen ['dinən] *intr* (dat) serve; **damit ist mir nicht gedient** that doesn't help me any; **womit kann ich d.?** may I help you?
Diener -in ['dinər(ın)] §6 *mf* servant
die'nerhaft *adj* servile
dienern ['dinərn] *intr* bow and scrape
Die'nerschaft *f* (-;) domestics, help
dienlich ['dinlıç] *adj* useful
Dienst [dinst] *m* (-es;-e) service; job; employment; (adm, mil) grade; **außer D.** retired; **im. D.** on duty; **j-m e-n D. tun** do s.o. a favor
Dienstag ['dinstak] *m* (-[e]s;-e) Tuesday
Dienst'alter *n* seniority
dienstbar ['dinstbar] *adj* subservient
Dienst'barkeit *f* (-;) servitude, bondage; (jur) easement
dienst'beflissen *adj* eager to serve || *adv* eagerly

Dienst'bote *m* servant, domestic
Dienst'boteneingang *m* service entrance
Dienst'eid *m* oath of office
dienst'eifrig *adj* eager to serve || *adv* eagerly
Dienst'einteilung *f* work schedule; (mil) duty roster
Dienst'fahrt *f* official trip
dienst'frei *adj*—**d. haben** be off duty
Dienst'gebrauch *m*—**nur zum D.** for official use only
Dienst'gespräch *n* business call
Dienst'grad *m* (mil) rank, grade; (nav) rating
dienst'habend *adj* on duty
Dienst'herr *m* employer; (hist) lord
Dienst'leistung *f* service
dienst'lich *adj* official || *adv* officially; on official business
Dienst'mädchen *n* maid
Dienst'pflicht *f* official duty; compulsory military service
Dienst'plan *m* work schedule; (mil) duty roster
Dienst'sache *f* official business
dienst'tauglich *adj* fit for active service
dienstuend ['dinsttu-ənt] *adj* on duty; active; in charge
Dienst'weg *m* official channels
Dienst'wohnung *f* official residence
dies [dis] *dem adj & dem pron* var of **dieses**
diese ['dizə] §3 *dem adj* this || *dem pron* this one
dieselbe [di'zɛlbə] §4,3 *dem adj & dem pron* the same
Dieselmotor ['dizəlmotər] *m* diesel engine
dieser ['dizər] §3 *dem adj* this || *dem pron* this one
dieses ['dizəs] §3 *dem adj* this || *dem pron* this one
diesig ['dizıç] *adj* hazy, misty
dies'jährig *adj* this year's
dies'mal *adv* this time
diesseits ['diszaıts] *prep* (genit) on this side of
Dietrich ['ditrıç] *m* (-s;-e) skeleton key; (Einbrecherwerkzeug) picklock
Differential [dıfɛren'tsjal] *n* (-s;-e) (aut, math) differential
Differential- *comb.fm.* (econ, elec, mach, math, phys) differential
Differenz [dıfɛ'rɛnts] *f* (-;-en) difference
Diktaphon [dıkta'fon] *n* (-[e]s;-e) dictaphone
Diktat [dık'tat] *n* (-s;-e) dictation; **nach D. schreiben** take dictation
Dik·tator [dık'tatər] *m* (-s;-tatoren) [ta'torən] dictator
diktatorisch [dıkta'torıʃ] *adj* dictatorial
Diktatur [dıkta'tur] *f* (-;-en) dictatorship
diktieren [dık'tirən] *tr & intr* dictate
Dilettant -in [dılɛ'tant(ın)] §7 *mf* dilettante, amateur
Diner [dı'ne] *n* (-s;-s) dinner
Ding [dıŋ] *n* (-[e]s;-e) thing; **ein D. drehen** (coll) pull a job
dingen ['dıŋən] §109 & §142 *tr* hire

ding′fest *adj*—**j—n d. machen** arrest s.o.
ding′lich *adj* real
Dings [dɪŋs] *n* (-s;) (coll) thing, doo-
dad, thingamajig
Dings′bums *m* & *n* (-;) var of **Dingsda**
Dings′da *mfn* (-s;) what-d′ye-call-it
Diözese [dɪˈøˈtseːzə] *f* (-;-n) diocese
Diphtherie [dɪfteˈriˈ] *f* (-;) diphtheria
Dipl.-Ing. *abbr* (**Diplom-Ingenieur**) en-
gineer holding a degree
L..plom [dɪˈploːm] *n* (-s;-e) diploma
Diplom- *comb.fm.* holding a degree
Diplomat [dɪploˈmaːt] *m* (-en;-en) diplomat
Diplomatie [dɪploməˈtiˈ] *f* (-;) diplo-
macy
Diplomatin [dɪploˈmaːtɪn] *f* (-;-nen)
diplomat
diplomatisch [dɪploˈmaːtɪʃ] *adj* diplomatic
dir [dɪr] §11 *pers pron* to or for you,
to or for thee || *reflex pron* to or for
yourself, to or for thyself
direkt [dɪˈrɛkt] *adj* direct
Direktion [dɪrɛkˈtsjoːn] *f* (-;) direction; (*Verwaltung*) management
Direk·tor [dɪˈrɛktɔr] *m* (-s;-toren
[ˈtoːrən]) director; (*e-r Bank*) president; (*e-r Schule*) principal; (*e-s
Gefängnisses*) warden
Direktorat [dɪrɛktoˈraːt] *n* (-[e]s;-e)
directorship
Direktorin [dɪrɛkˈtoːrɪn] *f* (-;-nen) director; (educ) principal
Direkto·rium [dɪrɛkˈtoːriˈum] *n* (-s;
-rien [rɪ·ən]) board of directors; executive committee
Direktrice [dɪrɛkˈtriːsə] *f* (-;-n) direc-
tress, manager
Dirigent –in [dɪrɪˈgɛnt(ɪn)] §7 *mf*
(mus) conductor
dirigieren [dɪrɪˈgiːrən] *tr* direct, manage; (mus) conduct
Dirnd(e)l [ˈdɪrndəl] *n* (-s;-) girl;
(*Tracht*) dirndle
Dirne [ˈdɪrnə] *f* (-;-n) girl; (pej) prostitute
Dis [dɪs] *n* (-;-) D sharp
disharmonisch [dɪsharˈmoːnɪʃ] *adj* dis-
cordant
Diskont [dɪsˈkɔnt] *m* (-[e]s;-e) discount
diskontieren [dɪskɔnˈtiːrən] *tr* discount
Diskothek [dɪskoˈteːk] *f* (-;-en) discotheque
diskret [dɪsˈkreːt] *adj* discreet
Diskretion [dɪskreˈtsjoːn] *f* (-;-en)
discretion
Diskussion [dɪskuˈsjoːn] *f* (-;-en) discussion
diskutieren [dɪskuˈtiːrən] *tr* discuss ||
intr—**d. über** (*acc*) discuss
disponieren [dɪspoˈniːrən] *intr* (**über**
acc) dispose (of)
Disposition [dɪspoˈzɪˈtsjoːn] *f* (-;-en)
disposition; arrangement; disposal
Distanz [dɪsˈtants] *f* (-;-en) distance
distanzieren [dɪstanˈtsiːrən] *tr* (**mit**)
beat (by, *e.g.*, *one meter*) || *ref* (**von**)
dissociate oneself (from)
distanziert′ *adj* (fig) d·tached
Distel [ˈdɪstəl] *f* (-;-n) thistle
Dis′telfink *m* goldfinch

Distrikt [dɪsˈtrɪkt] *m* (-[e]s;-e) district
Disziplin [dɪstsɪˈpliˈn] *f* (-;-en) discipline
disziplinarisch [dɪstsɪplɪˈnarɪʃ] *adj*
disciplinary
dito [ˈdito] *adv* ditto || **Dito** *n* (-s;-s)
ditto
Dividend [dɪvɪˈdɛnt] *m* (-en;-en)
Dividende [dɪvɪˈdɛndə] *f* (-;-n) dividend
dividieren [dɪvɪˈdiːrən] *tr* divide
Division [dɪvɪˈzjoːn] *f* (-;-en) division
Diwan [ˈdiːvan] *m* (-s;-e) divan
D-Mark [ˈdeːmark] *f* (-;-) mark (*monetary unit of West Germany*)
doch [dɔx] *adv* yet; of course
Docht·[dɔxt] *m* (-[e]s;-e) wick
Dock [dɔk] *n* (-[e]s;-s & -e) dock
docken [ˈdɔkən] *tr* & *intr* (naut, rok)
dock
Dogge [ˈdɔgə] *f* (-;-n) mastiff; **deut-
sche D.** Great Dane
Dog·ma [ˈdɔgma] *n* (-s;-men [mən])
dogma
Dohle [ˈdoːlə] *f* (-;-n) jackdaw
Dok·tor [ˈdɔktɔr] *m* (-s;-toren
[ˈtoːrən]) doctor
Dok′torarbeit *f* dissertation
Dok′torvater *m* adviser (*for a doctoral
dissertation*)
Dokument [dɔkuˈmɛnt] *n* (-[e]s;-e)
document; (jur) instrument, deed
Dokumentarfilm [dɔkumɛnˈtarfɪlm] *m*
documentary
dokumentarisch [dɔkumɛnˈtarɪʃ] *adj*
documentary
Dolch [dɔlç] *m* (-[e]s;-e) dagger
Dolch′stoß *m* (pol) stab in the back
Dollar [ˈdɔlar] *m* (-s;-) dollar
dolmetschen [ˈdɔlmɛtʃən] *tr* & *intr* in-
terpret
Dol′metscher –in §6 *mf* interpreter
Dom [dom] *m* (-[e]s;-e) cathedral;
dome
Domäne [doˈmɛːnə] *f* (-;-n) domain
Domino [ˈdomino] *n* (-s;-s) domino
Donau [ˈdonau] *f* (-;) Danube
Donner [ˈdɔnər] *m* (-s;-) thunder
Don′nerkeil *m* thunderbolt
donnern [ˈdɔnərn] *intr* thunder
Don′nerschlag *m* clap of thunder
Don′nerstag *m* (-[e]s;-e) Thursday
Don′nerwetter *n* thunderstorm; **zum
D.!** confound it! || *interj* geez!
doof [dof] *adj* (coll) goofy
dopen [ˈdopən] *tr* dope (*a racehorse*)
Doppel [ˈdɔpəl] *n* (-s;-) duplicate;
(tennis) doubles
Doppel- *comb.fm.* double, two, bi-,
twin
Dop′pelbelichtung *f* double exposure
Dop′pelbild *n* (telv) ghost
Dop′pelbruch *m* compound fracture
Dop′peIehe *f* bigamy
Dop′pelgänger *m* double;·second self
Dop′pellaut *m* diphthong
doppeln [ˈdɔpəln] *tr* double
Dop′pelprogramm *n* double feature
Dop′pelpunkt *m* (typ) colon
doppelreihig [ˈdɔpəlrai·ɪç] *adj* double-
breasted
Dop′pelrendezvous *n* double date

dop′pelseitig *adj* reversible; (*Lungenentzündung*) double
Dop′pelsinn *m* double entendre
dop′pelsinnig *adj* ambiguous
Dop′pelspiel *n* (fig) double-dealing; (sport) double-header; (tennis) doubles
doppelt [′dɔpəlt] *adj* double; **doppelter Boden** false bottom; **ein doppeltes Spiel spielen mit** doublecross; **in doppelter Ausführung in duplicate** ‖ *adv* twice; **ein Buch d. haben** have two copies of a book
Dop′pelverdiener **–in** §6 *mf* moonlighter
Dop′pelvokal *m* diphthong
doppelzüngig [′dɔpəltsɣŋɪç] *adj* two-faced
Dorf [dɔrf] *n* (–[e]s;̈er) village
Dorf′bewohner **–in** §6 *mf* villager
Dörfchen [′dœrfçən] *n* (–s;–) hamlet
Dorn [dɔrn] *m* (–[e]s;–en) thorn; tongue (*of a buckle*); (mach) pin; (sport) spike
Dorn′busch *m* briar, bramble
dornig [′dɔrnɪç] *adj* thorny
Dornröschen [′dɔrnrøsçən] *n* (–s;) Sleeping Beauty
Dörr– [dœr] *comb.fm.* dried
dorren [′dɔrən] *intr* (SEIN) dry (up)
dörren [′dœrən] *tr* dry
Dorschlebertran [′dɔrʃlebərtran] *m* (–[e]s;) cod-liver oil
dort [dɔrt] *adv* there, over there
dort′her *adv* from there
dort′hin *adv* there, to that place
dor′tig *adj* in that place, there
Dose [′dozə] *f* (–;–n) can; box
dösen [′døzən] *intr* doze
Do′senöffner *m* can opener
dosieren [do′zirən] *tr* prescribe (the correct dosage of)
Dosie′rung *f* (–;–en) dosage
Do·sis [′dozɪs] *f* (–;–sen [zən]) dose
dotieren [do′tirən] *tr* endow; **ein Preis mit 100 Mark dotiert** a prize worth 100 marks
Dotter [′dɔtər] *m & n* (–s;–) yolk
Double [′dubəl] *m & n* (–s;–s) (cin, theat) stand-in
Dozent **–in** [do′tsent(ɪn)] §7 (university) instructor, lecturer
Drache [′draxə] *m* (–n;–n) dragon; (*böses Weib*) battle-ax
Drachen [′draxən] *m* (–s;–) kite
Dra′chenfliegen *n* (–s;) hang gliding
Draht [drat] *m* (–[e]s;̈e) wire; **auf D. sein** (coll) be on the beam
drahten [′dratən] *tr* telegraph, wire
draht′haarig *adj* wire-haired
Draht′hindernis *n* (mil) wire entanglement, barbed wire
drahtig [′dratɪç] *adj* wiry
draht′los *adj* wireless
Draht′seil *n* cable
Draht′seilbahn *f* cable car, funicular
Draht′zaun *m* wire fence
drall [dral] *adj* plump; (*Faden*) sturdy ‖ **Drall** *m* (–s;–e) rifling
Dra·ma [′drama] *n* (–s;–men [mən]) drama
Dramatiker **–in** [dra′matɪkər(ɪn)] §6 *mf* dramatist, playwright

dramatisch [dra′matɪʃ] *adj* dramatic
dran [dran] *adv* var of **daran**
drang [draŋ] *pret of* **dringen** ‖ **Drang** *m* (–[e]s;̈e) pressure; urge
drängeln [′drɛŋəln] *tr & intr* shove
drängen [′drɛŋən] *tr & intr* push, shove; (*drücken*) press ‖ *ref* crowd, crowd together; force one's way
Drangsal [′draŋzal] *f* (–;–e) distress, anguish; hardship
drangsalieren [draŋza′lirən] *tr* vex
drastisch [′drastɪʃ] *adj* drastic
drauf [drauf] *adv* var of **darauf**
Drauf′gänger *m* (–s;–) go-getter
drauf′gehen §82 *intr* (SEIN) (coll) go down the drain
drauflos′ *adv*—**d. arbeiten an** (*dat*) work away at
drauflos′gehen §82 *intr* (SEIN)—**d. auf** (*acc*) make straight for
drauflos′reden *intr* ramble on
drauflos′schlagen §132 *intr* (**auf** *acc*) let fly (at)
draußen [′drausən] *adv* outside; out of doors; (*in der Fremde*) abroad
drechseln [′drɛksəln] *tr* work (on a lathe); (fig) embellish
Dreck [drɛk] *m* (–[e]s;) dirt; mud; excrement; (*Abfälle*) trash
dreckig [′drɛkɪç] *adj* dirty; muddy
Dreh– [dre] *comb.fm.* revolving, rotary
Dreh′arbeiten *pl* (cin) shooting
Dreh′aufzug *m* dumb waiter
Dreh′bank *f* (–;̈e) lathe
drehbar [′drebar] *adj* revolving
Dreh′buch *n* (mov) script, scenario
drehen [′dre·ən] *tr* turn; (*Zigaretten*) roll; (coll) wangle; (cin) shoot ‖ *ref* turn; rotate
Dreh′kreuz *n* turnstile
Dreh′orgel *f* hurdy-gurdy
Dreh′orgelspieler *m* organ grinder
Dreh′punkt *m* fulcrum; (fig) pivotal point
Dreh′scheibe *f* potter's wheel; (rr) turntable
Dreh′stuhl *m* swivel chair
Dre′hung *f* (–;–en) turn
Dreh′zahl *f* revolutions per minute
Dreh′zahlmesser *m* tachometer
drei [drai] *adj & pron* three ‖ **Drei** *f* (–;–en) three; (educ) C
dreidimensional [′draɪdɪmenzjonal] *adj* three-dimensional
Dreieck [′draɪ·ɛk] *n* (–[e]s;–e) triangle
drei′eckig *adj* triangular
drei′fach *adj* threefold, triple
dreifältig [′draɪfɛltɪç] *adj* threefold, triple
Dreifaltigkeit [draɪ′faltɪçkaɪt] *f* (–;) Trinity
Drei′fuß *m* tripod
Dreikäsehoch [draɪ′kezəhoç] *m* (–s;–) (coll) shrimp, runt
drei′mal *adv* three times, thrice
Drei′rad *n* tricycle
Drei′sprung *m* hop, step, and jump
dreißig [′draɪsɪç] *adj & pron* thirty ‖ **Dreißig** *f* (–;– & –en) thirty
dreißiger [′draɪsɪgər] *invar adj* of the thirties, in the thirties
dreißigste [′draɪsɪçstə] §9 *adj & pron* thirtieth

dreist [draɪst] *adj* brazen, bold
dreistimmig ['draɪ/tɪmɪç] *adj* for three voices
drei'zehn *adj & pron* thirteen || **Dreizehn** *f* (-;-) thirteen
drei'zehnte §9 *adj & pron* thirteenth
dreschen ['drɛ/ən] §67 *tr* thresh; (coll) thrash
Dresch'flegel *m* flail
Dresch'tenne *f* threshing floor
dressieren [drɛ'siːrən] *tr* train; (*Pferd*) break in
Dressur [drɛ'suːr] *f* (-;) training
dribbeln ['drɪbəln] *intr* (sport) dribble
drillen ['drɪlən] *tr* drill; train
Drillich ['drɪlɪç] *m* (-s;-e) denim
Dril'lichanzug *m* dungarees; (mil) fatigue uniform, fatigues
Dril'lichhosen *pl* dungarees, jeans
Drilling ['drɪlɪŋ] *m* (-s;-e) triplet
drin [drɪn] *adv* var of **darin**
dringen ['drɪŋən] §142 *intr* (auf *acc*) press (for), insist (on); (in *acc*) pressure, urge || *intr* (SEIN) (aus) break forth (from); (**durch**) penetrate, pierce; (**durch**) force one's way (through); (in *acc*) penetrate (into), get (into); **in die Öffentlichkeit d.** leak out; **in j-n d.** press the point with s.o.; **d. bis zu** get as far as
drin'gend *adj* urgent; (*Gefahr*) imminent; (*Verdacht*) strong
dring'lich *adj* urgent
Dring'lichkeit *f* (-;-en) urgency; priority
Drink [drɪŋk] *m* (-s;-s) alcoholic drink
drinnen ['drɪnən] *adv* inside
dritt [drɪt] *adv*—**zu d.** the three of
dritte ['drɪtə] §9 *adj & pron* third; **ein Dritter** a disinterested person; (com, jur) a third party
Drittel ['drɪtəl] *n* (-s;-) third (*part*)
drittens ['drɪtəns] *adv* thirdly
dritt'letzt *adj* third from last
droben ['droːbən] *adv* above; up there
Droge ['droːgə] *f* (-;-n) drug
Droge-rie [droːgə'riː] *f* (-;-rien ['riːən]) drugstore
Drogist –in [droː'gɪst(ɪn)] §7 *mf* druggist
Droh'brief *m* threatening letter
drohen ['droːən] *intr* (*dat*) threaten
dro'hend *adj* threatening; impending
Drohne ['droːnə] *f* (-;-n) drone
dröhnen ['drøːnən] *intr* boom, roar; (*Kopf, Motor*) throb
Dro'hung *f* (-;-en) threat
drollig ['drɔlɪç] *adj* amusing, funny
Dromedar [droːme'daːr] *n* (-s;-e) dromedary
drosch [drɔ/] *pret* of **dreschen**
Droschke ['drɔ/kə] *f* (-;-n) cab, hackney; taxi
Drosch'kenkutscher *m* coachman
Drossel ['drɔsəl] *f* (-;-n) thrush; (aut) throttle
Dros'selhebel *m* (aut) throttle
drosseln ['drɔsəln] *tr* (coll) curb, cut; (aut) throttle; (elec) choke
drüben ['dryːbən] *adv* over there
Druck [druk] *m* (-[e]s;ːe) (& fig) pressure; (*der Hand*) squeeze; (phys)

compression, pressure || *m* (-[e]s;-e) printing; print, type; (tex) print
Druck'anzug *m* (aer) pressurized suit
Druck'bogen *m* (printed) sheet
druck'dicht *adj* pressurized
Drückeberger ['drykəbɛrgər] *m* (-s;-) shirker; absentee; (mil) goldbrick
drucken ['drukən] *tr* print
drücken ['drykən] *tr* press; squeeze; imprint; (*Preise*) lower; (cards) discard; **die Stimmung d.** be a kill-joy; **j-m die Hand d.** shake hands with s.o. || *intr* (*Schuh*) pinch
Druck'entlastung *f* decompression
Drucker ['drukər] *m* (-s;-) printer
Drücker ['drykər] *m* (-s;-) push button; (*e-s Schlosses*) latch, latch key; (*e-s Gewehrs*) trigger
Druckerei [drukə'raɪ] *f* (-;-en) print shop, press
Druckerschwärze (**Druk'kerschwärze**) *f* printer's ink
Druck'fehler *m* misprint
druck'fertig *adj* ready for the press
druck'fest *adj* pressurized
Druck'kabine *f* pressurized cabin
Druck'knopf *m* push button; (*am Kleid*) snap
Druck'knopfbetätigung *f* push-button control
Druck'luft *f* compressed air
Druckluft– *comb.fm.* pneumatic, air
Druck'luftbremse *f* air brake
Druck'lufthammer *m* jackhammer
Druck'messer *m* pressure gauge
Druck'sache *f* printed matter; **Drucksachen** (com) literature
Druck'schrift *f* type; block letters; publication, printed work; leaflet
drucksen ['druksən] *intr* hem and haw
drum [drum] *adv* var of **darum**
Drüse ['dryːzə] *f* (-;-n) gland
Drüsen– *comb.fm.* glandular
Dschungel ['dʒuŋəl] *m* (-s;-) jungle
du [du] §11 *per pron* you, thou
Dübel ['dyːbəl] *m* (-s;-) dowel
Dublette [du'blɛtə] *f* (-;-n) duplicate; imitation stone
ducken ['dukən] *tr* (*den Kopf*) duck; (coll) take down a peg or two || *ref* duck
Duckmäuser ['dukmɔɪzər] *m* (-s;-) pussyfoot
dudeln ['duːdəln] *tr* hum || *intr* hum, drone; (mus) play the bagpipe
Dudelsack ['duːdəlzak] *m* bagpipe
Duell [du'ɛl] *n* (-s;-e) duel
duellieren [du-ə'liːrən] *recip* duel
Duett [du'ɛt] *n* (-[e]s;-e) duet
Duft [duft] *m* (-[e]s;ːe) fragrance
duften ['duftən] *intr* be fragrant
duf'tend *adj* fragrant
duftig ['duftɪç] *adj* flimsy, dainty
dulden ['duldən] *tr* (*ertragen*) bear; (*leiden*) suffer; (*zulassen*) tolerate || *intr* suffer
duldsam ['duldzam] *adj* tolerant
Duld'samkeit *f* (-;) tolerance
dumm [dum] *adj* stupid, dumb; foolish
Dumm'heit *f* (-;-en) stupidity; foolishness; (*Streich*) foolish prank
Dumm'kopf *m* dunderhead
dumpf [dumpf] *adj* dull, muffled;

(*schwül*) muggy; (*moderig*) musty, moldy; (*Ahnung*) vague

dumpfig ['dʊmpfɪç] *adj* musty, moldy; muggy

Düne ['dynə] *f* (–;–n) sand dune

Dung [dʊŋ] *m* (–[e]s;) dung; (*künstlicher*) fertilizer

düngen ['dyŋən] *tr* manure; fertilize

Dünger ['dyŋər] *m* (–s;) var of **Dung**

dunkel ['dʊŋkəl] *adj* dark; vague; obscure || **Dunkel** *n* (–s;) darkness

Dünkel ['dyŋkəl] *m* (–s;) conceit

dün'kelhaft *adj* conceited

Dun'kelheit *f* (–;) darkness; obscurity

Dun'kelkammer *f* (phot) darkroom

Dun'kelmann *m* (–[e]s;–er) shady character

dünn [dyn] *adj* thin

Dunst [dʊnst] *m* (–es;–e) vapor, mist, haze; (*Rauch*) smoke; (*Dampf*) steam; **in D. und Rauch aufgehen** (fig) go up in smoke; **sich in (blauen) D. auflösen** vanish in thin air

dünsten ['dynstən] *tr & intr* stew; steam

dunstig ['dʊnstɪç] *adj* steamy; (*Wetter*) misty, hazy

Duplikat [dʊplɪ'kɑt] *n* (–[e]s;–e) duplicate; copy

Dur [dur] *invar n* (mus) major

durch [dʊrç] *adv* throughout; **d. und d.** through and through || *prep* (*acc*) through, by, by means of

durch'arbeiten *tr* work through || *ref* (durch) work one's way (through); elbow one's way (through)

durchaus' *adv* throughout; entirely; quite, absolutely; **d. nicht** by no means

durch'backen §50 *tr* bake through and through

durch'blättern *tr* thumb through

durch'bleuen *tr* beat up

Durch'blick *m* vista

durch'blicken *intr* be apparent; (durch) look (through); **d. lassen** intimate

durchblutet [dʊrç'blutət] *adj* supplied with blood

durch'bohren *tr* bore through || **durchboh'ren** *tr* pierce

durch'braten §63 *tr* roast thoroughly

durchbre'chen §64 *tr* break through; (*Vorschriften*) violate; (mil) breach || **durch'brechen** *tr* cut (*a hole*); break in half || *intr* (SEIN) break through

durch'brennen §97 *tr* burn through; (*e–e Sicherung*) blow || *intr* (SEIN) run away; (*Sicherung*) blow

durch'bringen §65 *tr* get through; (*Gesetz*) pass; (*Geld*) spend; (med) pull (*a patient*) through || *ref* support oneself; **sich ehrlich d.** make an honest living

Durch'bruch *m* breakthrough; (*Öffnung*) breach, gap; (*der Zähne*) cutting

durch'denken §66 *tr* think through || **durchden'ken** *tr* think out, think over

durch'drängen *ref* push one's way through

durch'drehen *tr* grind; (*Wäsche*) put

through the wringer || *intr* (SEIN) (coll) go mad

durchdrin'gen §142 *tr* penetrate; pervade, imbue || **durch'dringen** *intr* (SEIN) get through; penetrate

durch'drucken *tr* (parl) push through

durchdrungen [dʊrç'drʊŋən] *adj* imbued

durchei'len *tr* rush through || **durch'eilen** *intr* (SEIN) (durch) rush through

durcheinan'der *adj & adv* in confusion ||**Durcheinander** *n* (–s;–) mess, muddle

durcheinan'derbringen §65 *tr* muddle

durcheinan'dergeraten §63 *intr* (SEIN) get mixed up

durcheinan'derlaufen §105 *intr* (SEIN) mill about

durcheinan'derreden *intr* speak all at once

durcheinan'derwerfen §160 *tr* throw into confusion, turn upside down

durchfah'ren §71 *tr* travel through; (*Gedanke, Schreck*) strike || **durch'fahren** §71 *intr* (SEIN) go through without stopping

Durch'fahrt *f* passage; **keine D.!** no thoroughfare

Durch'fahrtshöhe *f* clearance

Durch'fall *m* diarrhea; (coll) flop; (educ) flunk, failure

durch'fallen §72 *intr* (SEIN) fall through; (educ) flunk; (theat) flop

durch'fechten §74 *tr* fight through

durch'finden §59 *ref* find one's way

durchflech'ten *tr* interweave

durchfor'schen *tr* examine, make an exhaustive study of

Durchfor'schung *f* exploration; search; thorough research

durch'fressen §70 *tr* eat through; corrode || *ref* (bei) sponge (on); (durch) work one's way (through)

Durchfuhr ['dʊrçfur] *f* (–;–en) transit

durchführbar ['dʊrçfyrbɑr] *adj* feasible

durch'führen *tr* lead through or across; (*Auftrag*) carry out; (*Gesetz*) enforce

Durch'gang *m* passage; aisle; (fig) transition; (astr, com) transit; **D. verboten!** no thoroughfare, no trespassing

Durch'gänger *m* (–s;–) runaway

Durch'gangslager *n* transit camp

Durch'gangsverkehr *m* through traffic

Durch'gangszug *m* through train

durch'geben §80 *tr* pass on

durch'gebraten *adj* (culin) well done

durch'gehen §82 *tr* (SEIN) go through; (*durchlesen*) go over || *intr* (SEIN) go through; (*Pferd*) bolt; (*heimlich davonlaufen*) run away; abscond; (*Vorschlag*) pass

durch'gehend(s) *adv* generally; (*durchaus*) throughout

durchgeistigt [dʊrç'gaɪstɪçt] *adj* highly intellectual

durch'greifen §88 *intr* reach through; (fig) take drastic measures

durch'greifend *adj* vigorous; drastic

durch'halten §90 *tr* keep up || *intr* hold out, stick it out

durch'hauen §93 *tr* chop through;

knock a hole through; (coll) thrash, beat

durch'hecheln *tr* (coll) run down

durch'helfen §96 *intr* (*dat*) (**durch**) help (through) || *ref* get by, manage

durch'kämmen *tr* (& fig) comb through

durch'kochen *tr* boil thoroughly

durch'kommen §99 *intr* (SEIN) come through; (*durch Krankheit*) pull through; (*sich durchhelfen*) get by; (educ) pass

durchkreu'zen *tr* cross; (*durchstreichen*) cross out; (fig) frustrate

Durch·laß ['dʊrçlas] *m* (**-lasses;-lässe**) passage; outlet; culvert

durch'lassen §104 *tr* let through, let pass; (*Licht*) transmit; (educ) pass

durchlässig ['dʊrçlɛsɪç] *adj* permeable

Durch'laßschein *m* pass

durchlau'fen §105 *tr* run through; look through; (*Schule*) go through; **seine Bahn d.** run its course || **durch'laufen** §105 *ref*—**sich** [*dat*] **die Schuhe d.** wear out one's shoes || §105 *intr* (SEIN) run through

durchle'ben *tr* live through

durch'lesen §107 *tr* read over, peruse

durchleuch'ten *tr* illuminate; (*Gesicht*) light up; (*Ei*) test; X-ray

durch'liegen §108 *ref* develop bedsores || **Durchliegen** *n* (**-s;**) bedsores

durchlo'chen *tr* punch

durch'löchern *tr* perforate; pierce; (*mit Kugeln*) riddle

durch'machen *tr* go through, undergo

Durch'marsch *m* marching through; (coll) diarrhea, runs

Durch'messer *m* diameter

durchnäs'sen *tr* soak, drench

durch'nehmen §116 *tr* (*in der Klasse*) do, have

durch'pausen *tr* trace

durch'peitschen *tr* whip soundly; (*Gesetzentwurf*) rush through

durchque'ren *tr* cross, traverse

durch'rechnen *tr* check, go over

Durch'reise *f* passage; **auf seiner D.** on his way through

durch'reisen *intr* (SEIN) travel through

Durch'reisende §5 *mf* transient, transit passenger

durch'reißen §53 *tr* tear in half || *intr* (SEIN) tear, break, snap

Durch'sage *f* special announcement

durch'sagen *tr* announce

durchschau'en *tr* (fig) see through || **durch'schauen** *intr* look through

durch'scheinen §128 *intr* shine through; show through; be seen

durch'scheuern *tr* rub through

durchschie'ßen §76 *tr* shoot through, riddle; (typ) lead || **durch'schießen** §76 *intr* (**durch**) shoot (through) || *intr* (SEIN) dash through

Durch'schlag *m* carbon copy; (*Sieb*) (large) strainer, separator; (elec) breakdown; (tech) punch

durchschla'gen §132 *tr* penetrate || **durch'schlagen** §132 *tr* knock a hole through; (*Holz*) split; (*Fensterscheibe*) smash; (*Nagel*) drive through; (*Kartoffeln, Früchte*) strain; (*mit Kohlepapier*) make a carbon copy of

|| *ref* fight one's way through; (*sich durchhelfen*) manage || *intr* come through; penetrate; take effect; show up || *intr* (SEIN) (*Sicherung*) blow

durch'schlagend *adj* effective; striking

Durch'schlagpapier *n* carbon paper

durch'schleichen §85 *ref* & *intr* (SEIN) creep through

durchschleu'sen *tr* pass (*a ship*) through a lock; (*Passagiere, Rekruten, usw.*) process; (fig) sneak (*s.o.*) through

durch'schneiden §106 *tr* cut through; cut in half || **durchschnei'den** §106 *tr* cut through, cut across || *ref* cross, intersect

Durch'schnitt *m* cutting through; average; cross section; **der große D. der Menschen** the majority of people; **im D.** on an average

durch'schnittlich *adj* average || *adv* on the average

Durchschnitts- *comb.fm.* average; mean

Durch'schnittsmensch *m* average person

durch'schreiben §62 *tr* make a carbon copy of

durch'sehen §138 *tr* look over, examine; (*flüchtig anschauen*) scan; (*Papiere, Post*) check || *intr* see through

durch'seihen *tr* filter; percolate

durchset'zen *tr* intersperse; penetrate || **durch'setzen** *tr* carry through; **d., daß** bring it about that, succeed in (ger) || *ref* get one's way

Durch'sicht *f* examination, inspection; (*auf acc*) view (of)

durch'sichtig *adj* transparent; clear

durch'sickern *intr* (SEIN) seep out; (*Wahrheit, Gerücht*) leak out

durch'sieben *tr* sift

durch'sprechen §64 *tr* talk over

durchste'chen §64 *tr* pierce || **durch'stechen** §64 *tr* (*Nadel*) stick through

durch'stehen §146 *tr* go through

durchstö'bern *tr* rummage through

durch'stoßen §150 *tr* push (*s.th.*) through; (*Tür*) knock down; (*Scheibe*) smash in; (*Ellbogen*) wear through; (mil) penetrate || **durchsto'ßen** §150 *tr* break through || **durch'stoßen** §150 *intr* (SEIN) break through

durchstrei'chen §85 *tr* roam through || **durch'streichen** §85 *tr* cross out

durchstrei'fen *tr* wander through

durchsu'chen *tr* go through, search

durch'treten §152 *tr* (*Sohle*) wear a hole in; (*Gashebel*) floor || *intr* (SEIN) go through, pass through

durchtrieben [dʊrç'tribən] *adj* sly

durchwa'chen *tr* remain awake through

durchwach'sen *adj* gristly

durch'wählen *tr* & *intr* dial direct

durchwan'dern *tr* travel or walk through || **durch'wandern** *intr* (SEIN) (**durch**) walk (through), hike (through)

durchwe'ben *tr* interweave

durch'weg(s) *adv* throughout

durchwei'chen, durch'weichen *tr* soak

durchwüh'len *tr* burrow through; (*Ge-*

päck, Schränke) rummage through ||
durch·wühlen *ref* burrow through;
(fig) work one's way through

durch·wursteln *ref* muddle through

durchzie·hen §163 *tr* pass through,
cross; *(Zimmer)* permeate, fill;
streak; (sew) interweave || **durch·-
ziehen** §163 *tr* pull through || *intr*
(SEIN) pass through; flow through

durchzucken (**durchzuk·ken**) *tr* flash
through the mind of

Durch·zug *m* passage; *(Luftzug)* draft

durch·zwängen *tr* force through || *ref*
squeeze through

dürfen ['dyrfən] §69 *aux* be allowed;
be likely; **darf ich?** may I?; **ich darf
nicht** I must not; **man darf wohl erwarten** it is to be expected

durfte ['durftə] *pret* of **dürfen**

dürftig ['dyrftɪç] *adj* needy; poor,
wretched, miserable, scanty

dürr [dyr] *adj* dry; *(Boden)* arid, barren; *(Holz)* dead, dry; *(Mensch)*
skinny || **Dürre** ['dyrə] *f* (–;) dry-
ness; barrenness; leanness; drought

Durst [durst] *m* (–[e]s;) **(nach)** thirst
(for); **D. haben** be thirsty

dursten ['durstən], **dürsten** ['dyr-
stən] *intr* be thirsty; **(nach)** thirst
(for)

durstig ['durstɪç] *adj* thirsty

Dusche ['du/ə] *f* (–;–n) shower

duschen ['du/ən] *intr* take a shower

Düse ['dyzə] *f* (–;–n) nozzle, jet

Dusel ['duzəl] *m* (–s;–) (coll) fluke

Düsen– *comb.fm.* jet

Dü·senantrieb *m* jet propulsion

Dü·senjäger *m* jet fighter

düster ['dystər] *adj* gloomy; sad; dark
|| **Düster** *n* (–s;) gloom; darkness

Dutzend ['dutsənt] *n* (–s;– & –e) dozen

dut·zendmal *adv* a dozen times

dut·zendweise *adv* by the dozen

Duzbruder ['dutsbrudər] *m* buddy

duzen ['dutsən] *tr* say **du** to, be on intimate terms with

Dynamik [dy'namɪk] *f* (–s;) dynamics

dynamisch [dy'namɪ/] *adj* dynamic

Dynamit [dyna'mit] *n* (–s;–e) dyna-
mite

Dynamo ['dynamo] *m* (–s;–s) dynamo

Dyna·stie [dynas'ti] *f* (–;–stien
['sti·ən] dynasty

D'-Zug *m* through train, express

E

E, e [e] *invar n* E, e; (mus) E

Ebbe ['ɛbə] *f* (–;–n) ebb tide

eben ['ɛbən] *adj* even, level, flat; **zu
ebener Erde** on the ground floor ||
adv just; a moment ago; exactly
|| *interj* exactly!; that's right!

E'benbild *n* image, exact likeness

ebenbürtig ['ɛbənbyrtɪç] *adj* of equal
rank, equal

ebenda ['ɛbən'da] *adv* right there;
(beim Zitieren) ibidem

ebendersel'be §4,3 *adj* self-same

ebendes'wegen *adv* for that very reason

Ebene ['ɛbənə] *f* (–;–n) plain; (fig)
level; (geom) plane

e'benerdig *adj* ground-floor

e'benfalls *adv* likewise, too

E'benholz *n* ebony

E'benmaß *n* right proportions

e'benmäßig *adj* well-proportioned

e'benso *adv* just as; likewise

e'bensogut *adv* just as well

e'bensoviel *adv* just as much

e'bensowenig *adv* just as little

Eber ['ɛbər] *m* (–s;–) boar

E'beresche *f* mountain ash

ebnen ['ɛbnən] *tr* level, even; smooth

Echo ['ɛço] *n* (–s;–s) echo

echoen ['ɛço·ən] *intr* echo

echt [ɛçt] *adj* genuine, real, true

Eck [ɛk] *n* (–[e]s;–e) corner; end

Eck– *comb.fm.* corner; end

Ecke ['ɛkə] *f* (–;–n) corner; edge

Ecker ['ɛkər] *f* (–;–n) beechnut

eckig ['ɛkɪç] *adj* angular; (fig) awkward; **eckige Klammer** bracket

Eck'stein *m* cornerstone; (cards) dia-
monds

Eck'stoß *m* (fb) corner kick

Eck'zahn *m* canine tooth

Eclair [ɛ'klɛr] *n* (–s;–s) éclair

edel ['edəl] *adj* noble; *(Metall)* precious; *(Pferd)* thoroughbred; **edle
Teile** vital organs

e'deldenkend *adj* noble-minded

e'delgesinnt *adj* noble-minded

E'del·mann *m* (–[e]s;–leute) noble

e'delmütig *adj* noble-minded

E'delstahl *m* high-grade steel

E'delstein *m* precious stone, gem

E'delweiß *n* (–[e]s;–e) edelweiss

Edikt [ɛ'dɪkt] *n* (–[e]s;–e) edict

Edle ['ɛdlə] §5 *mf* noble

Efeu ['efo/] *m* (–s;) ivy

Effekt [ɛ'fɛkt] *m* (–[e]s;–e) effect

Effekten [ɛ'fɛktən] *pl* property; effects; (fin) securities, stocks

Effek'tenmakler –in §6 *mf* stock broker

Effekthascherei [ɛfɛktha/ə'raɪ] *f* (–;)
showiness

effektiv [ɛfɛk'tif] *adj* effective; *(wirklich)* actual

Effektiv'lohn *m* take-home pay

Effet [ɛ'fe] *n* (–s;) spin, English

egal [ɛ'gal] *adj* equal; all the same

Egge ['ɛgə] *f* (–;–n) harrow

eggen ['ɛgən] *tr* harrow

Ego ['ego] *n* (–s;) ego

Egoismus [ego'ɪsmus] *m* (–;) egoism

Egoist –in [ego'ɪst(ɪn)] §7 *mf* egoist

egoistisch [ego'ɪstɪ/] *adj* egoistic

Egotist –in [ego'tɪst(ɪn)] §7 *mf* egotist

eh [e] *adv* (Aust) anyhow, anyway

ehe ['e·ə] *conj* before || **Ehe** *f* (–;–n)
marriage; matrimony

E'hebrecher *m* (–s;–) adulterer·

E'hebrecherin *f* (–;-nen) adulteress
e'hebrecherisch *adj* adulterous
E'hebruch *m* adultery, infidelity
ehedem ['e·ə'dem] *adv* formerly
E'hefrau *f* wife
E'hegatte *m* spouse
E'hegattin *f* spouse
E'hegelöbnis *n* marriage vow
E'hehälfte *f* (coll) better half
E'heleute *pl* married couple
e'helich *adj* marital; (*Kind*) legitimate
e'helos *adj* unmarried, single
E'helosigkeit *f* (–;) celibacy
ehemalig ['e·əmaliç] *adj* former; ex–;
(*verstorben*) late
ehemals ['e·əmals] *adv* formerly
E'hemann *m* husband
E'hepaar *n* married couple
eher ['e·ər] *adv* sooner; rather
E'hering *m* wedding band
ehern ['e·ərn] *adj* brass; (fig) unshak-
able
E'hescheidung *f* divorce
E'hescheidungsklage *f* divorce suit
E'heschließung *f* marriage
E'hestand *m* married state, wedlock
ehestens ['e·əstəns] *adv* at the earliest;
as soon as possible
E'hestifter –in §6 *mf* matchmaker
E'heversprechen *n* promise of mar-
riage
Ehrabschneider –in ['erap/ʃnaɪdər(ɪn)]
§6 *mf* slanderer
ehrbar ['erbar] *adj* honorable, respect-
able
Ehr'barkeit *f* (–;) respectability
Ehre ['erə] *f* (–;-n) honor; glory
ehren ['erən] *tr* honor; **Sehr geehrter
Herr** Dear Sir
eh'renamtlich *adj* honorary
Eh'rendoktor *m* honorary doctor
Eh'renerklärung *f* apology
eh'renhaft *adj* honorable
ehrenhalber ['erənhalbər] *invar adj*—
Doktor e. Doctor honoris causa
Eh'renmitglied *n* honorary member
Eh'renrechte *pl*—bürgerliche E. civil
rights
Eh'rensache *f* point of honor
eh'renvoll *adj* honorable, respectable
eh'renwert *adj* honorable
Eh'renwort *n* word of honor; **auf E.
entlassen** put on parole
ehrerbietig ['ererbitɪç] *adj* respectful,
reverent, deferential
Ehrerbietung ['ererbitʊŋ] *f* (–;), **Ehrfurcht** ['erfʊrçt] *f* (–;) respect, reverence; (**vor** *dat*) awe (of)
ehrfürchtig ['erfyrçtɪç], **ehrfurchtsvoll**
['erfʊrçtsfɔl] *adj* respectful
Ehr'gefühl *n* sense of honor
Ehr'geiz *m* ambition
ehr'geizig *adj* ambitious
ehrlich ['erlɪç] *adj* honest; sincere;
fair; **j–n e. machen** restore s.o.'s
good name
Ehr'lichkeit *f* (–;) honesty; candor
ehr'los *adj* dishonorable; (*Frau*) of
easy virtue; infamous
Ehr'losigkeit *f* (–;) dishonesty; infamy
ehrsam ['erzam] *adj* respectable
Ehr'sucht *f* (–;) ambition
ehr'süchtig *adj* ambitious

Ehr'verlust *m* loss of civil rights
ehr'würdig *adj* venerable; (eccl) rever-
end
ei [aɪ] *interj* oh!; ah!; ei,ei! oho!; ei je!
oh dear!; ei was! nonsense! || **Ei** *n*
(–[e]s;-er) egg
Eiche ['aɪçə] *f* (–;-n) oak
Eichel ['aɪçəl] *f* (–;-n) acorn; (cards)
club
Ei'chenlaub *n* oak leaf cluster
eichen ['aɪçən] *adj* oak || *tr* gauge
Eichhörnchen ['aɪçhœrnçən] *n* (–s;-),
Eichkätzchen ['aɪçkɛtsçən] *n* (–s;-)
squirrel
Eichmaß ['aɪçmas] *n* gauge; standard
Eid [aɪt] *m* (–[e]s;-e) oath
Eid'bruch *m* perjury
eid'brüchig *adj* perjured
Eidechse ['aɪdɛksə] *f* (–;-n) lizard
Eiderdaunen ['aɪdərdaunən] *pl* eider
down
eidesstattlich ['aɪdəs/tatlɪç] *adj* in lieu
of an oath, solemn
eid'lich *adj* sworn || *adv* under oath
Ei'dotter *m* egg yolk
Ei'erkrem *f* custard
Ei'erkuchen *m* omelet; pancake
Ei'erlandung *f* three-point landing
Ei'erlikör *m* eggnog
Ei'erschale *f* eggshell
Ei'erstock *m* ovary
Eifer ['aɪfər] *m* (–;) zeal, eagerness
Eiferer –in ['aɪfərər(ɪn)] §6 *mf* zealot
Ei'fersucht *f* jealousy
ei'fersüchtig *adj* (auf *acc*) jealous (of)
eifrig ['aɪfrɪç] *adj* zealous; ardent
Ei'gelb *n* (–[e]s;-e) egg yolk
eigen ['aɪgən] *adj* own; of (my, your,
etc.) own; (*dat*) peculiar (to), char-
acteristic (of) || *invar pron*—**etw
mein e. nennen** call s.th. my own
ei'genartig *adj* peculiar; odd, queer
Eigenbrötler ['aɪgənbrøtlər] *m* (–s;-)
(coll) lone wolf, loner; crank
Ei'gengewicht *n* dead weight
eigenhändig ['aɪgənhɛndɪç] *adj* & *adv*
with or in one's own hand
Ei'genheit *f* (–;-en) peculiarity
Ei'genliebe *f* self-love, egotism
Ei'genlob *n* self-praise
ei'genmächtig *adj* arbitrary, high-
handed
Ei'genname *m* proper name
Ei'gennutz *m* self-interest
ei'gennützig *adj* selfish
eigens ['aɪgəns] *adv* expressly
Ei'genschaft *f* (–;-en) quality, property; **in seiner E. als** in his capacity
as
Ei'genschaftswort *n* (–[e]s;-̈er) adjective
Ei'gensinn *m* stubbornness
ei'gensinnig *adj* stubborn
eigentlich ['aɪgəntlɪç] *adj* actual || *adv*
actually, really
Eigentum ['aɪgəntum] *n* (–[e]s;-̈er)
property, possession; ownership
Eigentümer –in ['aɪgəntymər(ɪn)] §6
mf (legal) owner || *m* proprietor || *f*
proprietress
eigentümlich ['aɪgəntymlɪç] *adj* odd;
(*dat*) peculiar (to)
Ei'gentümlichkeit *f* (–;-en) peculiarity

Ei'gentumsrecht n ownership, title
Ei'genwechsel m promissory note
ei'genwillig adj independent; (Stil) original
eignen ['aignən] ref (für) be suited (to); (als) be suitable (as); (zu) be cut out (for)
Eig'nung f (–;-en) qualification, aptitude
Ei'gnungsprüfung f aptitude test
Eilbrief ['aɪlbriːf] m special delivery
Eile ['aɪlə] f (–;) hurry; **E. haben** or **in E. sein** be in a hurry
eilen ['aɪlən] ref hurry (up) || intr be urgent || intr (SEIN) hurry; **eilt!** (Briefaufschrift) urgent! || impers—**es eilt mir nicht damit** I'm in no hurry about it
eilends ['aɪlənts] adv hurriedly
Eilgut ['aɪlguːt] n express freight
eilig ['aɪlɪç] adj quick, hurried; urgent || adv hurriedly; **es e. haben** be in a hurry
Eilpost ['aɪlpost] f special delivery
Eilzug ['aɪltsuːk] m (rr) limited
Eimer ['aɪmər] m (–s;–) bucket, pail
ein [aɪn] §2,1 indef art a, an || §2,1 num adj one || adv in; **ein und aus** in and out; **nicht ein und aus wissen** not know which way to turn || **einer** indef pron & num one **einer** indef pron & num pron one || **Einer** m (–s;–) (math) unit
ein–, Ein– comb.fm. one–, single
einan'der invar recip pron each other; (unter mehreren) one another
ein'arbeiten tr train (for a job); (in acc) work (into) || ref (in acc) become familiar (with), get the hang (of)
einarmig ['aɪnarmɪç] adj one-armed
einäschern ['aɪnɛʃərn] tr reduce to ashes, incinerate; (Leiche) cremate
ein'atmen tr & intr inhale
ein'äugig adj one-eyed
einbahnig ['aɪnbaːnɪç] adj single-lane; single-line; one-way
Ein'bahnstraße f one-way street
ein'balsamieren tr embalm
Ein'band m (–[e]s;-e) binding; cover
ein'bauen tr build in, install
einbegriffen ['aɪnbəgrɪfən] adj included, inclusive
ein'behalten §90 tr retain; (Lohn) withhold
ein'berufen §122 tr call, convene; (mil) call up, draft || **Einberufene** §5 mf draftee
Ein'berufung f (–;-en) (mil) induction
ein'betten tr embed
ein'beziehen §163 tr include
ein'bilden ref—**sich** [dat] **etw e.** imagine s.th.
ein'binden §59 tr (bb) bind
ein'blenden tr (cin) fade in
Ein'blick m view; (fig) insight
ein'brechen §64 tr break in || intr (SEIN) collapse; (Nacht) fall; (Kälte) set in; (Dieb) break in
Ein'brecher –in §6 mf burglar
ein'bringen §65 tr bring in; earn; yield
Ein'bruch m break-in, burglary; invasion; **E. der Nacht** nightfall
Ein'bruchsdiebstahl m burglary
ein'bruchssicher adj burglarproof

einbürgern ['aɪnbʏrgərn] tr naturalize || ref (fig) take root, become accepted
Ein'bürgerung f (–;) naturalization
Ein'buße f loss, forfeiture
ein'büßen tr lose, forfeit
ein'dämmen tr check, contain
ein'decken tr cover || ref (mit) stock up (on)
Eindecker ['aɪndɛkər] m (–s;–) monoplane
ein'deutig adj unequivocal, clear
eindeutschen ['aɪndɔɪtʃən] tr Germanize
ein'drängen ref squeeze in; interfere
ein'dringen §142 intr (SEIN) penetrate, come in; **e. auf** (acc) crowd in on; **e. in** (acc) rush into; penetrate; infiltrate; (mil) invade
ein'dringlich adj urgent
Eindringling ['aɪndrɪŋlɪŋ] m (–s;-e) intruder, interloper; gate-crasher
Ein'druck m imprint; impression
ein'drücken tr press in; crash, flatten; imprint; (Fenster) smash in
Ein'druckskunst f impressionism
ein'drucksvoll adj impressive
ein'engen tr narrow; (fig) limit
einer ['aɪnər] §2,4 indef pron & num pron one || **Einer** m (–s;–) (math) unit
einerlei ['aɪnərlaɪ] invar adj (nur attributiv) one kind of; (nur prädikativ) all the same || **Einerlei** n (–;) monotony
einerseits ['aɪnərzaɪts], **einesteils** ['aɪnəstaɪls] adv on the one hand
ein'fach adj single; simple || adv simply
einfädeln ['aɪnfɛːdəln] tr thread; (fig) engineer
ein'fahren §71 tr (Auto) break in; (Ernte) bring in; (aer) retract || ref get driving experience; **die Sache hat sich gut eingefahren** it's off to a good start || intr (SEIN) drive in; (rr) arrive
Ein'fahrt f entrance; gateway
Ein'fall m inroad; (fig) idea; (mil) invasion
ein'fallen §72 intr (SEIN) fall in; cave in, collapse; (in die Rede) butt in; join in; **e. in** (acc) invade; **j–m e.** occur to s.o.; **sich** [dat] **etw e. lassen** take s.th. into one's head; think up s.th.; **sich** [dat] **nicht e. lassen** not dream of; **was fällt dir ein?** what's the idea?
ein'fallslos adj unimaginative
ein'fallsreich adj imaginative
Ein'falt f simplicity; simple-mindedness
einfältig ['aɪnfɛltɪç] adj (pej) simple
Ein'faltspinsel m sucker, simpleton
ein'farbig adj one-colored; plain
ein'fassen tr edge, trim; (einschließen) enclose; (Edelstein) set
Ein'fassung f (–;-en) border; mounting
ein'fetten tr grease
ein'finden §59 ref show up
ein'flechten tr plait; (Haar) braid; (fig) insert
ein'fliegen §57 tr (Truppen) fly in;

(Flugzeug) flight-test || *intr* (SEIN) fly in

ein′fließen §76 *intr* (SEIN) flow in; e. in *(acc)* flow into; **einige Bemerkungen e.** lassen slip in a few remarks

ein′flößen *tr* infuse, instill

Ein′fluß *m* influx; (fig) influence

ein′flußreich *adj* influential

ein′förmig *adj* monotonous

einfried(ig)en [′aɪnfrid(ɪg)ən] *tr* enclose, fence in

ein′frieren §77 *tr* (& fin) freeze || *intr* (SEIN) freeze (up) || **Einfrieren** *n* (-s;) (fin) freeze

ein′fügen *tr* insert, fit || *ref* fit in; (in *acc*) adapt oneself (to)

ein′fühlen *ref* (in *acc*) relate (to)

Einfuhr [′aɪnfur] *f* (-;-en) importation; **Einfuhren** imports

ein′führen *tr* import; introduce; (in ein *Amt*) install

Ein′führung *f* (-;-en) introduction

Ein′fuhrwaren *pl* imports

Ein′fuhrzoll *m* import duty

ein′füllen *tr*—e. in *(acc)* pour into

Ein′gabe *f* petition; application

Ein′gang *m* entrance; entry; beginning; introduction; *(von Waren)* arrival; **Eingänge** (com) incoming goods; incoming mail; (fin) receipts

ein′geben §80 *tr* suggest, prompt; (med) administer, give

eingebildet [′aɪngəbɪldət] *adj* imaginary; self-conceited

eingeboren [′aɪngəborən] *adj* native; only-begotten; *(Eigenschaft)* innate || **Eingeborene** §5 *mf* native

Ein′gebung *f* (-;-en) suggestion; *(höhere)* inspiration

eingedenk [′aɪngədɛŋk] *adj (genit)* mindful (of)

ein′gefallen *adj (Backen, Augen)* sunken

eingefleischt [′aɪngəflaɪʃt] *adj* inveterate

ein′gefroren *adj* icebound

ein′gehen §82 *tr* (HABEN & SEIN) enter into; *(Verpflichtungen)* incur; *(Wette, Geschäft)* make; *(Chance)* take; *(Versicherung)* take out; **e−n Vergleich e.** come to an agreement || *intr* (SEIN) come in; arrive; *(aufhören)* come to an end; fizzle out; *(Stoff)* shrink; (bot, zool) die off; (com) close down; **e. auf** *(acc)* go into, consider; consent to; **e. lassen** drop, discontinue; **es geht mir nicht ein, daß** I can't accept the fact that

ein′gehend *adj* thorough

eingelegt [′aɪngəlegt] *adj* inlaid

Eingemachte [′aɪngəmaxtə] §5 *n* (-n;) preserves

eingemeinden [′aɪngəmaɪndən] *tr (Vorort)* incorporate

eingenommen [′aɪngənɔmən] *adj* prejudiced; **von sich e.** self-conceited

eingeschnappt [′aɪngəʃnapt] *adj* (coll) peeved

eingeschneit [′aɪngəʃnaɪt] *adj* snowed in

Eingesessene [′aɪngəzesənə] §5 *mf* resident

Ein′geständis *n* (-ses;-se) confession

ein′gestehen §146 *tr* confess, admit

Eingeweide [′aɪngəvaɪdə] *pl* viscera; intestines; *(von Vieh)* entrails

Eingeweihte [′aɪngəvaɪtə] §5 *mf* insider

ein′gewöhnen *tr* (in *acc*) accustom (to) || *ref* (in *acc*) become accustomed (to)

eingewurzelt [′aɪngəvurtsəlt] *adj* deep-rooted

ein′gießen §76 *tr* pour in, pour out

eingleisig [′aɪnglaɪzɪç] *adj* single-track

ein′gliedern *tr* integrate; annex

ein′graben §87 *tr* bury; engrave || *ref* burrow; (mil) dig in

ein′greifen §88 *intr* take action; interfere; (in *j−s Rechte*) encroach; (mach) mesh, be in gear || **Eingreifen** *n* (-s;) interference; (mach) meshing

Ein′griff *m* interference; encroachment; (mach) meshing; (surg) operation

ein′hacken *tr*—e. auf *(acc)* peck at; (fig) pick at

ein′haken *tr* (in *acc*) hook (into) || *ref* —sich bei j−m e. link arms with s.o. || *intr* (fig) cut in

Ein′halt *m* (-[e]s;) stop, halt; **E. gebieten** *(dat)* put a stop to

ein′halten §90 *tr* stick to; *(Verabredung)* keep; *(Zahlungen)* keep up; **die Zeit e.** be punctual || *intr* stop

ein′händigen *tr* hand over

ein′hängen §92 *tr (Türe)* hang; (in *acc*) hook (into); (telp) hang up || *ref*—sich bei j−m e. link arms with s.o. || *intr* (telp) hang up

ein′heften *tr* sew in; baste on

ein′heimisch *adj* domestic; local; home-grown; **e. in** *(dat)* native to

einheimsen [′aɪnhaɪmzən] *tr* reap

Einheit [′aɪnhaɪt] *f* (-;-en) oneness, unity; (math, mil) unit

ein′heitlich *adj* uniform

Einheits− *comb.fm.* standard, uniform; unit; united

ein′heizen *tr* start a fire; **j−m tüchtig e.** (fig) burn s.o. up

einhellig [′aɪnhelɪç] *adj* unanimous

ein′holen *tr* bring in; *(Flagge)* hawl down; *(Segel)* hawl down; (im *Wettlauf*) catch up with; *(Erkundigungen)* make; *(Rat, Nachricht, Erlaubnis)* get; *(Verlust)* make good; *(abholen und geleiten)* escort; *(Schiff, Tau)* tow in || *intr* shop

ein′holen *tr* bring in; *(Flagge, Segel)* lower, hawl down; (im *Wettlauf*) catch up with; *(Erkundigungen)* lauf) catch up with; *(Erkundigungen)* make; *(Rat, Nachricht, Erlaubnis)* get; *(Verlust)* make good; *(abholen und geleiten)* escort; *(Schiff, Tau)* tow in || *intr* shop

Ein′horn *n* (myth) unicorn

ein′hüllen *tr* wrap up; enclose

einig [′aɪnɪç] *adj* united; of one mind; **sich** *[dat]* **e. sein** be in agreement

einige [′aɪnɪgə] §9 *indef adj & indef pron* some

einigen [′aɪnɪgən] *tr* unite || *ref* come to terms, agree

einigermaßen [′aɪnɪgərmasən] *adv* to some extent; *(ziemlich)* somewhat

ein′niggehen §82 *intr* (SEIN) concur

Ei′nigkeit *f* (-;) unity; harmony; agreement

Ei′nigung f (-;-en) unification; agreement, understanding

ein′impfen tr—j-m Impfstoff e. inoculate s.o. with vaccine; **j-m e., daß** (fig) drive it into s.o. that

ein′jagen tr (dat) put (e.g., a scare) into

ein′jährig adj one-year-old; (bot) annual

ein′kassieren tr collect

Ein′kauf m purchase; **Einkäufe machen** go shopping

ein′kaufen tr purchase; **e. gehen** go shopping

Ein′käufer –in §6 mf shopper

Ein′kaufspreis m purchase price

Ein′kehr f—E. bei sich halten search one's conscience; **E. halten** stop off

ein′kehren intr (SEIN) stay overnight; (im Gasthaus) stop off, stay

ein′keilen tr wedge in

ein′kerben tr notch, cut a notch in

einkerkern [′aɪnkɛrkərn] tr imprison

einkesseln [′aɪnkɛsəln] tr encircle

ein′klagen tr sue for (a bad debt)

ein′klammern tr bracket, put in parentheses

Ein′klang m unison; accord

Ein′klebebuch n scrap book

ein′kleben tr (in acc) paste (into)

ein′kleiden tr clothe; vest; (mil) issue uniforms to

ein′klemmen tr jam in, squeeze in

ein′klinken tr & intr engage, catch

ein′knicken tr fold

ein′kochen tr thicken (by boiling); can || intr thicken

ein′kommen §99 intr (SEIN)—**bei j-m um etw e.** apply to s.o. for s.th. || **Einkommen** n (-s;) income, revenue

Ein′kommensteuer f income tax

Ein′kommensteuererklärung f income-tax return

Ein′kommenstufe f income bracket

ein′kreisen tr encircle

Einkünfte [′aɪnkʏnftə] pl revenue

ein′kuppeln tr let out the clutch

ein′laden §103 tr load; invite

Ein′ladung f (-;-en) invitation

Ein′lage f (-;-n) (im Brief) enclosure; (im Schuh) insole; arch support; (Zwischenfutter) padding; (Kapital-) investment; (Sparkassen-) deposit; (beim Spiel) bet; (culin) solids (in soup); (dent) temporary filling; (mus) musical extra

ein′lagern tr store, store up

Ein·laß [′aɪnlas] m (-lasses;) admission; admittance; (tech) intake

ein′lassen §104 tr let it, admit; (tech) (in acc) sink (into) || ref (auf acc, in acc) let oneself get involved (in)

Ein′laßkarte f admission ticket

Ein′lauf m incoming mail; (e-s Schiffes) arrival; **j-m e-n E. machen** give s.o. an enema

ein′laufen §105 intr (SEIN) come in, arrive; (Stoff) shrink; **das Badewasser e. lassen** run the bath; **j-m das Haus e.** keep running to s.o.'s house || ref warm up (by running)

ein′leben ref (in acc) accustom oneself (to)

Ein′legearbeit f inlaid work

Ein′legebrett n (e-s Tisches) leaf

ein′legen tr put in; (Fleisch, Gurken) pickle; (Geld) deposit; (in e-n Brief) enclose; (Film, Kassette) insert; (Veto) interpose; (Beschwerde) lodge; (Protest) enter; (Berufung) (jur) file; **Busse e.** put on extra buses

ein′leiten tr introduce; (Buch) write a preface to; (beginnen, eröffnen) start, open; **ein Verfahren e. gegen** institute proceedings against s.o.

Ein′leitung f (-;-en) introduction; initiation

ein′lenken intr (fig) give in

ein′leuchten intr be evident; (coll) sink in

ein′liefern tr deliver; (ins Gefängnis) put, commit; **ins Krankenhaus e.** take to the hospital

ein′lösen tr ransom; redeem; (Scheck) cash

ein′machen tr can, preserve

ein′mal adv once; (künftig) one day; **auf e.** suddenly; all at the same time; **einmal...einmal** now...now; **nicht e.** (unstressed) not even; (stressed) not even once

Ein′maleins′ n multiplication table

ein′malig adj unique

Einmann– comb.fm. one-man

Ein′marsch m entry

ein′marschieren intr (SEIN) march in

ein′mauern tr wall in

ein′mengen ref, **ein′mischen** ref (in acc) meddle (with), interfere (with)

Ein′mischung f (-;-en) interference

einmotorig [′aɪnmə′torɪç] adj single-engine

einmummen [′aɪnmumən] ref bundle up

ein′münden intr (in acc) empty (into); (Straßen) run (into)

Ein′mündung f (-;-en) (e-s Flusses) mouth; (e-r Straße) junction

ein′mütig adj unanimous

ein′nähen tr sew in; (Kleid) take in

Ein′nahme f (-;-n) taking; capture; (fin) receipts; **Einnahmen** income

ein′nehmen §116 tr take; capture; (Essen) eat; (Geld) earn; (Steuern) collect; (Stellung) fill; (sew) take in; **e-e Haltung e.** assume an attitude; **e-e hervorragende Stelle e.** rank high; **j-n für sich e.** captivate s.o.; **j-n gegen sich e.** prejudice s.o. against oneself; **seinen Platz e.** take one's seat

ein′nicken intr (SEIN) doze off

ein′nisten ref (in dat) settle (in); (fig) find a home (at)

Ein′öde f desert, wilderness

ein′ordnen tr put in its place; file; classify || ref fit into place; (sich anstellen) get in line; **sich rechts** (or **links**) **e.** get into the right (or left) lane

ein′packen tr pack up

ein′passen tr (in acc) fit (into)

ein′pauken tr—j-m etw e. drum s.th. into s.o.'s head

ein′pferchen tr pen up; (fig) crowd together

ein′pflanzen tr plant; implant
ein′pökeln tr pickle; salt
ein′prägen tr imprint, impress
ein′quartieren tr billet, quarter
ein′rahmen tr frame
ein′rammen tr ram in, drive in
ein′räumen tr (Recht, Kredit) grant; (zugeben) concede, admit; **e. in** (acc) put into
ein′rechnen tr include, comprise
Ein′rede f objection; (jur) plea
ein′reden tr—**j-m etw e.** talk s.o. into s.th; **das lasse ich mir nicht e.** I can't believe that || intr—**auf j-n e.** badger s.o.
ein′reiben §62 tr rub
ein′reichen tr hand in, file; (Rechnung) present; (Abschied) tender; (Gesuch) submit; (Beschwerde, Klage) file
ein′reihen tr file; rank; enroll; (Bücher) shelve || ref fall into place; fall in line
ein′reihig adj single-breasted
Ein′reise f entry
ein′reißen §53 tr tear; demolish || intr (SEIN) tear; (fig) spread
ein′renken tr (Knochen) set; (fig) set right
ein′richten tr arrange; establish; (Wohnung) furnish; (surg) set || ref settle down; economize, make ends meet; (auf acc) make arrangements (for); (nach) adapt oneself (to)
Ein′richtung f (–;-en) setup; establishment; furniture; equipment
Ein′richtungsgegenstand m piece of furniture, piece of equipment
ein′rosten intr (SEIN) get rusty
ein′rücken tr (Zeile) indent; (Anzeige) put in || intr (SEIN) march in; **in j-s Stelle e.** succeed s.o.; **zum Militär e.** enter military service
Ein′rückung f (–;-en) indentation
ein′rühren tr (in acc) stir (into)
eins [aɪns] pron one; one o'clock; **es ist mir eins it's all the same to me** || **Eins** f (–;-en) one; (auf Würfeln) ace; (educ) A
einsam [′aɪnzam] adj lonely, lonesome
ein′sammeln tr gather; (Geld) collect
Ein′satz m insert, insertion; (Wette) bet; (Risiko) risk; (Verwendung) use; (für Flaschen) deposit; (aer) sortie; (mil) action; (mus) starting in, entry; **im E. stehen** be in action; **im vollen E.** in full operation; **unter E. seines Lebens** at the risk of one's life; **zum E. bringen** employ, use; (Maschinen) put into operation; (Polizei) call out; (mil) throw into action
ein′satzbereit adj combat-ready
Ein′satzstück n insert
ein′saugen tr suck in; (fig) imbibe
ein′säumen tr (sew) hem
ein′schalten tr insert; (elec) switch on, turn on || ref intervene
ein′schärfen tr—**j-m etw e.** impress s.th. on s.o.
ein′schätzen tr appraise, value
ein′schenken tr pour
ein′schicken tr send in
ein′schieben §130 tr push in; insert

ein′schießen §76 tr (Gewehr) test; (Geld) contribute; (Brot in den Ofen) shove; (fb) score || ref (auf acc) zero in (on)
ein′schiffen tr & intr embark
Ein′schiffung f (–;-en) embarkation
ein′schlafen §131 intr (SEIN) fall asleep; (Glied) go to sleep
ein′schläf(e)rig adj single (bed)
einschläfern [′aɪn/lefərn] tr lull to sleep; (vet) put to sleep
Ein′schlag m striking; impact; explosion; (Umschlag) wrapper; (fig) admixture, element; (golf) putt; (sew) tuck; (tex) weft, woof
ein′schlagen §132 tr (Nagel) drive in; (zerbrechen) smash, bash in; (einwickeln) wrap; (Weg) take; (Laufbahn) enter upon; (Pflanzen) stick in the ground; (golf) putt; **die Richtung e. nach** go in the direction of || intr (Blitz) strike; (Erfolg haben) be a success; **nicht e.** fail
einschlägig [′aɪn/legɪç] adj relevant
Ein′schlagpapier n wrapping paper
ein′schleichen §85 ref (in acc) creep (into), slip (into); (in j-s Gunst) worm one's way
ein′schleppen tr tow in; (e–e Krankheit) bring in (from abroad)
ein′schleusen tr (Schmuggelwaren) sneak in; (Spionen) plant
ein′schließen §76 tr lock up; (in e–m Brief) enclose; (fig) include; (mil) encircle, surround
ein′schließlich adv inclusive(ly) || prep (genit) inclusive of
ein′schlummern intr (SEIN) doze off
Ein′schluß m encirclement; **mit E.** (genit) including
ein′schmeicheln ref (bei) ingratiate oneself (with)
ein′schmeichelnd adj ingratiating
ein′schmuggeln tr smuggle in
ein′schnappen intr (SEIN) snap shut; (fig) take offense
ein′schneidend adj (fig) incisive
Ein′schnitt m cut, incision; (Kerbe) notch; (geol) gorge; (pros) caesura
ein′schnüren tr tie up; pinch
ein′schränken tr (auf acc) restrict (to), confine (to); (Ausgaben) cut; (Behauptung) qualify || ref economize
Ein′schränkung f (–;-en) restriction; **ohne jede E.** without reservation
Ein′schreibebrief m registered letter
ein′schreiben §62 tr enroll; (Brief) register; (eintragen) enter; **e–n Brief e. lassen** send a letter by registered mail || ref register
ein′schreiten §86 intr (SEIN) step in, intervene; (gegen) take action (against)
ein′schrumpfen intr (SEIN) shrivel up
ein′schüchtern tr intimidate, overawe
Ein′schüchterung f (–;) intimidation
ein′schulen tr enroll in school
Ein′schuß m hit (of a bullet)
ein′schütten tr pour in
ein′segnen tr (neues Gebäude) consecrate; (konfirmieren) confirm
ein′sehen §138 tr inspect; (Akten) consult; (fig) realize; (mil) observe ||

Einsehen *n*—**ein E. haben** show (some) consideration
ein'seifen *tr* soap; (coll) softsoap
ein'seitig *adj* one-sided
ein'senden §140 *tr* send in, submit
Ein'sender *–in* §6 *mf* sender
ein'senken *tr* (in *acc*) sink (into)
ein'setzen *tr* insert, put in; (*Geld*) bet; (*Leben*) risk; (*Polizei*) call out; (*Truppen*) commit; (*Kräfte*) muster; (*Einfluß*) use; (*Beamten*) install; (*ernennen*) appoint; (*einpflanzen*) plant; (*Artillerie, Tanks, Bomber*) employ; (*Edelsteine*) mount ‖ *ref* (**für**) stand up (for) ‖ *intr* set in, begin; (*mus*) come in
Ein'sicht *f* inspection; (fig) insight
ein'sichtig *adj* understanding
ein'sichtsvoll *adj* understanding
ein'sickern *intr* (SEIN) seep in; (mil) infiltrate
Einsiedelei [aɪnziˈdəˈlaɪ] *f* (–;–en) hermitage
Einsiedler *–in* [ˈaɪnzidlər(ɪn)] §6 *mf* hermit, recluse
einsilbig [ˈaɪnzɪlbɪç] *adj* monosyllabic; (fig) taciturn
ein'sinken §143 *intr* (SEIN) sink in; (*Erdboden*) subside
ein'sparen *tr* economize on, save
ein'sperren *tr* lock up
ein'springen §142 *intr* (SEIN) jump in; (**für**) substitute (for); (tech) catch
ein'spritzen *tr* inject
Ein'spritzung *f* (–;–en) injection
Ein'spruch *m* objection; (jur) appeal
einspurig [ˈaɪnʃpurɪç] *adj* single-track
einst [aɪnst] *adv* once; (*künftig*) someday; **e. wie jezt** (now) as ever
Ein'stand *m* (tennis) deuce
ein'stecken *tr* insert, put in; stick in, pocket; (*Schwert*) sheathe; (*hinnehmen*) take; (coll) lock up, jail
ein'stehen §146 *intr* (SEIN) (**für**) vouch (for), stand up (for); **für die Folgen e.** take the responsibility
ein'steigen §148 *intr* (SEIN) get in; **alle e.!** all aboard!
Ein'steigkarte *f* (aer) boarding pass
Ein'steigloch *n* manhole
einstellbar [ˈaɪnʃtɛlbaɾ] *adj* adjustable
ein'stellen *tr* put in; (*Arbeiter*) hire; (*Gerät*) set, adjust; (*beenden*) stop, quit; (*Sender*) tune in on; (*Fernglas, Kamera*) focus; **die Arbeit e.** go on strike; **etw bei j–m e.** leave s.th. at s.o.'s house; **in die Garage e.** put into the garage; **zum Heeresdienst e.** induct ‖ *ref* show up, turn up; **sich e. auf** (*acc*) attune oneself to
Ein'stellung *f* (–;–en) adjustment; setting; focusing; stoppage; (*der Feindseligkeiten, Zahlungen*) suspension; hiring; (mil) timing; (mil) induction; **E. des Feuers** cease-fire; **geistige E.** mental attitude
einstig [ˈaɪnstɪç] *adj* former; (*verstorben*) late; (*künftig*) future
ein'stimmen *intr* join in; **e. in** (*acc*) agree to, consent to
einstimmig [ˈaɪnʃtɪmɪç] *adj* unanimous
ein'studieren *tr* study; rehearse
ein'stufen *tr* classify

ein'stürmen *intr* (SEIN) (**auf** *acc*) rush (at); (mil) charge
Ein'sturz *m* (–es;) collapse
ein'stürzen *intr* (SEIN) collapse; **e. auf** (*acc*) (fig) overwhelm
einstweilen [ˈaɪnstvaɪlən] *adv* for the present; temporarily
einstweilig [ˈaɪnstvaɪlɪç] *adj* temporary
Ein'tänzer *m* gigolo
ein'tauschen *tr* trade in; **e. gegen** exchange for
ein'teilen *tr* divide; (*austeilen*) distribute; (*einstufen*) classify; (*Geld, Zeit*) budget; (*Arbeit*) plan
eintönig [ˈaɪntøːnɪç] *adj* monotonous
Ein'tönigkeit *f* (–;) monotony
Ein'topf *m*, **Ein'topfgericht** *n* one-dish meal
Ein'tracht *f* (–;) harmony, unity
einträchtig [ˈaɪntrɛçtɪç] *adj* harmonious
Eintrag [ˈaɪntrak] *m* (–[e]s;–e) entry; **E. tun** (*dat*) hurt
ein'tragen §132 *tr* enter, register; (*Gewinn*) bring in, yield; **j–m etw e.** bring down s.th. on s.o. ‖ *ref* register
einträglich [ˈaɪntrɛklɪç] *adj* profitable, lucrative
Ein'tragung *f* (–;–en) entry
ein'treffen §151 *intr* (SEIN) arrive; (*in Erfüllung gehen*) come true
ein'treiben §62 *tr* drive in; (*Geld*) collect ‖ *intr* (SEIN) drift in, sail in
ein'treten §152 *tr* smash in ‖ *ref—sich* [*dat*] **e–n Nagel e.** step on a nail ‖ *intr* (SEIN) enter; (*geschehen*) occur; (*Fieber*) develop; (*Fall, Not*) arise; (*Dunkelheit*) fall; **e. für** stand up for, champion; **e. in** (*acc*) join, enter
Ein'tritt *m* (–s;) entry; (*Einlaß*) admittance; (*Anfang*) beginning, onset; (rok) re-entry; **E. frei** free admission; **E. verboten** no admittance
Ein'trittsgeld *n* admission fee
Ein'trittskarte *f* admission ticket
ein'trocknen *intr* (SEIN) dry up
ein'trüben *ref* become overcast
ein'tunken *tr* (in *acc*) dip (into)
ein'verleiben *tr* incorporate
Einvernahme [ˈaɪnfɛrnaːmə] *f* (–;–n) interrogation
Ein'vernehmen *n* (–s;) agreement; **sich mit j–m ins E. setzen** try to come to an understanding with s.o.
einverstanden [ˈaɪnfɛrˌʃtandən] *adj* in agreement ‖ *interj* agreed!
Ein'verständnis *n* agreement; approval
ein'wachsen *tr* wax ‖ *intr* (SEIN) (in *acc*) grow (into)
Ein'wand *m* (–s;–e) objection
Ein'wanderer *–in* §6 *mf* immigrant
ein'wandern *intr* (SEIN) immigrate
Ein'wanderung *f* (–;) immigration
ein'wandfrei *adj* unobjectionable; (*tadellos*) flawless; (*Alibi, Zustand*) perfect; (*Quelle*) unimpeachable
einwärts [ˈaɪnvɛrts] *adv* inward(s)
Einweg– *comb.fm.* disposable
ein'weichen *tr* soak
ein'weihen *tr* consecrate, dedicate; **e. in** (*acc*) initiate into; let in on

Ein'weihung *f* (-;-en) dedication; initiation

ein'weisen §118 *tr* install; (*Verkehr*) direct; **e. in** (*acc*) assign to; **j-n in seine Pflichten e.** brief s.o. in his duties; **j-n ins Krankenhaus e.** have s.o. admitted to the hospital

ein'wenden §140 *tr*—**etw e. gegen** raise an objection to; **nichts einzuwenden haben gegen** have no objections to

Ein'wendung *f* (-;-en) objection

ein'werfen §160 *tr* throw in; (*Fenster*) smash; (*Brief*) mail; (*Münze*) insert; (fig) interject

ein'wickeln *tr* wrap (up); (fig) trick

ein'willigen *intr* (**in** *acc*) agree (to)

ein'wirken *intr* (**auf** *acc*) have an effect (on), exercise infuence (on)

Ein'wirkung *f* (-;-en) effect, influence

Ein'wohner –in §6 *mf* inhabitant

Ein'wurf *m* (*Schlitz*) slot; (*e-r Münze*) insertion; (*Einwand*) objection

ein'wurzeln *ref* take root

Ein'zahl *f* (-;) singular

ein'zahlen *tr* pay in; (**in e-e Kasse**) deposit

Ein'zahlung *f* (-;-en) payment; deposit

Ein'zahlungsschein *m* deposit slip

einzäunen ['aɪntsɔɪnən] *tr* fence in

Einzel ['aɪntsəl] *n* (-s;-) singles

**Einzel– ** *comb.fm.* individual; single; isolated; detailed; retail

Ein'zelbild *n* (cin) frame; (phot) still

Ein'zelfall *m* individual case

Ein'zelgänger *m* (coll) lone wolf

Ein'zelhaft *f* solitary confinement

Ein'zelhandel *m* retail trade

Ein'zelheit *f* (-;-en) item; detail, particular; **wegen näherer Einzelheiten** for further particulars

einzellig ['aɪntsɛlɪç] *adj* single-cell

einzeln ['aɪntsəln] *adj* single; particular, individual; separate

Ein'zelperson *f* individual

Ein'zelspiel *n* singles (match)

Ein'zelwesen *n* individual

Ein'zelzimmer *n* single room; (*im Krankenhaus*) private room

ein'ziehen §163 *tr* draw in; retract; (*Flagge*) hawl down; (*Segel*) take in; (*Münzen*) call in; (*eintreiben*) collect; (mil) draft || *intr* (SEIN) move in; **e. in** (*acc*) enter; penetrate

einzig ['aɪntsɪç] *adj & adv* only; **e. darstellen** be unique || *indef pron*— **ein einziger** one only; **kein einziger** not a single one

ein'zigartig *adj* unique; extraordinary

Ein'zug *m* entry; moving in; (*Beginn*) start; (typ) indentation; **seinen E. halten** make one's entry

ein'zwängen *tr* (**in** *acc*) squeeze (into)

Eis [aɪs] *n* (-es;) ice; (*Speise*–) ice cream || ['eˑɪs] *n* (-;-s) (mus) E sharp

Eis'bahn *f* ice-skating rink

Eis'bär *m* polar bear

Eis'bein *n* (culin) pigs feet

Eis'berg *m* iceberg

Eis'beutel *m* (med) ice pack

Eis'blume *f* window frost

Eis'creme *f* ice cream

Eis'diehle *f* ice cream parlor

Eisen ['aɪzən] *n* (-s;-) iron; **altes E.** scrap iron; **heißes E.** (fig) hot potato; **zum alten E. werfen** (fig) scrap

Ei'senbahn *f* railroad; **mit der E.** by train, by rail

Ei'senbahndamm *m* railroad embankment

Ei'senbahner *m* (-s;-) railroader

Ei'senbahnknotenpunkt *m* railroad junction

Ei'senblech *n* sheet iron

Ei'senerz *n* iron ore

Ei'senhütte *f* ironworks

Ei'senwaren *pl* hardware, ironware

Ei'senwarenhandlung *f* hardware store

Ei'senzeit *f* iron age

eisern ['aɪzərn] *adj* iron; (*Fleiß*) unflagging; (*Rationen*) emergency

Eis'glätte *f* icy road conditions

eis'grau *adj* hoary

eisig ['aɪsɪç] *adj* icy; icy-cold

Eis'kappe *f* ice cap

Eis'kunstlauf *m* figure skating

Eis'lauf *m* ice skating

Eis'laufbahn *f* ice-skating rink

eis'laufen §105 *intr* (SEIN) ice-skate

Eis'läufer –in §6 *mf* skater

Eis'meer *n*—**Nördliches E.** Arctic Ocean; **Südliches E.** Antarctic Ocean

Eis'pickel *m* ice axe

Eis'schnellauf *m* speed skating

Eis'scholle *f* ice floe

Eis'schrank *m* icebox

Eis'vogel *m* kingfisher

Eis'würfel *m* ice cube

Eis'würfelschale *f* ice-cube tray

Eis'zapfen *m* icicle

Eis'zeit *f* ice age, glacial period

eitel ['aɪtəl] *adj* (*nutzlos*) vain, empty; (*selbstgefällig*) vain; || *invar adj* pure || *adv* merely

Ei'telkeit *f* (-;) vanity

Eiter ['aɪtər] *m* (-s;) pus

Ei'terbeule *f* boil, abscess

eitern ['aɪtərn] *intr* fester, suppurate

Ei'terung *f* (-;-en) festering

eitrig ['aɪtrɪç] *adj* pussy

Ei'weiß *n* (-es;-e) egg white; albumen

Ekel ['ekəl] *m* (-s;) (**vor** *dat*) disgust (at) || *n* (-s;) (coll) pest

ekelerregend ['ekələregənt] *adj* sickening, nauseating

e'kelhaft *adj* disgusting

ekeln ['ekəln] *impers*—**es eket mir** or **mich** I am disgusted || *ref* (**vor** *dat*) feel disgusted (at)

eklig ['eklɪç] *adj* disgusting, revolting; nasty, beastly

Ekzem [ɛk'tsem] *n* (-s;-e) eczema

elastisch [e'lastɪʃ] *adj* elastic

Elch [ɛlç] *m* (-[e]s;-e) elk, moose

Elefant [ele'fant] *m* (-en;-en) elephant

Elefan'tentreiber *m* mahout

Elefan'tenzahn *m* elephant's tusk

elegant [ele'gant] *adj* elegant

Eleganz [ele'gants] *f* (-;) elegance

Elektriker [ɛ'lɛktrɪkər] *m* (-s;-) electrician

elektrisch [ɛ'lɛktrɪʃ] *adj* electric(al)

elektrisieren [ɛlɛktri'zirən] *tr* electrify

Elektrolyse [ɛlɛktro'lyzə] *f* (-;-) electricity

Elektrizitäts– *comb.fm.* electric, electro–

Elektro– [ɛlɛktrə] *comb.fm.* electrical, electro–

Elektrode [ɛlɛk'trodə] *f* (–;–n) electrode

Elek'trogerät *n* electrical appliance

Elektrizität [ɛlɛktrɪtsɪ'tɛt] *f* (–;) electricity

Elek·tron [ɛ'lɛktrɔn] *n* (–s;–tronen ['trɔnən]) electron

Elektronen– [ɛlɛktrɔnən–] *comb.fm.* electronic

Elektronik [ɛlɛk'trɔnɪk] *f* (–;) electronics

Elektrotechnik *f* (–;) electrical engineering

Elektrotech'niker *m* (–s;–) electrical engineer

Element [ɛle'mɛnt] *n* (–[e]s;–e) element; (elec) cell

elementar [ɛlemɛn'tɑr] *adj* elementary

Elementar'buch *n* primer

Elen ['elen] *m & n* (–s;–) elk

elend ['elənt] *adj* miserable ‖ **Elend** *n* (–[e]s;) misery; extreme poverty; **das graue E.** the blues

E'lendsviertel *n* slums

elf [ɛlf] *adj & pron* eleven ‖ **Elf** *f* (–;–en) eleven

Elfe ['ɛlfə] *m* (–n;–n), *f* (–;–n) elf

Elfenbein ['ɛlfənbaɪn] *n* (–s;) ivory

elfte ['ɛlftə] §9 *adj & pron* eleventh

Elftel ['ɛlftəl] *n* (–s;–) eleventh (*part*)

Elite [e'litə] *f* (–;) elite, flower

Ellbogen ['ɛlbogən] *m* (–s;–) elbow

Ell'bogenfreiheit *f* elbowroom

Elsaß ['ɛlzas] *n* (–;) Elsace

elsässisch ['ɛlzɛsɪʃ] *adj* Alsatian

Elster ['ɛlstər] *f* (–;–n) magpie

elterlich ['ɛltərlɪç] *adj* parental

Eltern ['ɛltərn] *pl* parents; **nicht von schlechtern E.** (coll) terrific

El'ternbeirat *m* Parent-Teacher Association

El'ternhaus *n* home

el'ternlos *adj* orphaned; **elternlose Zeugung** spontaneous generation

El'ternschaft *f* parenthood

El'ternteil *m* parent

Email [ɛ'maj] *n* (–s;), **Emaille** [ɛ'maljə] *f* (–;) enamel

Email'geschirr *n* enamelware

Email'lack *m* enamel paint

emaillieren [ema(l)'jirən] *tr* enamel

Email'waren *pl* enamelware

emanzipieren [ɛmantsɪ'pirən] *tr* emancipate

Embargo [ɛm'bargo] *n* (–s;–s) embargo

Embo·lie [ɛmbɔ'li] *f* (–;–lien ['li·ən]) embolism

Embry·o ['ɛmbry·o] *m* (–s;–onen ['onən]) embryo

Emigrant –in [ɛmɪ'grant(ɪn)] §7 *mf* emigrant

Emigration –in [ɛmɪ'sjon] *f* (–;–en) emission; (fin) issuance; (rad) broadcasting

empfahl [ɛm'pfal] *pret* of **empfehlen**

Empfang [ɛm'pfaŋ] *m* (–[e]s;–̈e) reception; (*Erhalten*) receipt; (*im Hotel*) reception desk

empfangen [ɛm'pfaŋən] §73 *tr* receive; (*Kind*) conceive

Empfänger –in (ɛm'pfɛŋər(ɪn)] §6 *mf* receiver, recipient; addressee

empfänglich [ɛm'pfɛŋlɪç] *adj* (**für**) susceptible (to)

Empfängnis [ɛm'pfɛŋnɪs] *f* (–;) conception

empfäng'nisverhütend *adj* contraceptive; **empfängnisverhütendes Mittel** contraceptive

Empfäng'nisverhütung *f* contraception

Empfangs'chef *m* desk clerk

Empfangs'dame *f* receptionist; (*im Restaurant*) hostess

Empfangs'schein *m* (com) receipt

empfehlen [ɛm'pfelən] §147 *tr* recommend; **e. Sie mich** (*dat*) remember me to ‖ *ref* say goodbye

empfeh'lenswert *adj* commendable

Empfeh·lung *f* (–;–en) recommendation; (*Gruß*) compliments

empfinden [ɛm'pfɪndən] §59 *tr* feel

empfindlich [ɛm'pfɪntlɪç] *adj* sensitive; delicate, touchy; (*Kälte*) bitter; (gegen) susceptible (to)

Empfind'lichkeit *f* (–;–en) sensitivity, touchiness; susceptibility

empfindsam [ɛm'pfɪntzam] *adj* sensitive, touchy; sentimental

Empfind'samkeit *f* (–;–en) sensibility; sentimentality

Empfin·dung *f* (–;–en) sensation; feeling, sentiment

empfin'dungslos *adj* numb; (fig) callous

Empfin'dungswort *n* (gram) interjection

Emphysem [ɛmfy'zem] *n* (–s;) emphysema

empor [ɛm'por] *adv* up, upwards

empören [ɛm'pørən] *tr* anger, shock ‖ *ref* rebel, revolt; (mil) mutiny

empor'fahren §71 *intr* (SEIN) jump up

empor'kommen §99 *intr* (SEIN) rise up; (*in der Welt*) get ahead

Emporkömmling [ɛm'pørkœmlɪŋ] *m* (–s;–e) upstart, parvenu

empor'ragen *intr* tower, rise

empor'steigen §148 *intr* (SEIN) rise

empor'streben *intr* (SEIN) rise, soar; (fig) aspire

Empö'rung *f* (–;–en) revolt; (**über** *acc*) indignation (at)

emsig ['ɛmzɪç] *adj* industrious, busy

Em'sigkeit *f* (–;) industry; activity

End– [ɛnt] *comb.fm.* final, ultimate

Ende ['ɛndə] *n* (–s;–n) end; ending; outcome; **letzten Endes** in the final analysis; **zu E. gehen** end; **zu E. sein** be over

enden ['ɛndən] *tr & intr* end; **nicht e. wollend** unending

End'ergebnis *n* final result, upshot

End'gerade *f* (–;) home stretch

end'gültig *adj* final, definitive

endigen ['ɛndɪgən] *tr & intr* end; **e. auf** (*acc*) (gram) terminate in

Endivie [ɛn'divjə] *f* (–;–n) endive

End'lauf *m* (sport) final heat

end'lich *adj* final; limited, finite ‖ *adv* finally, at last

end'los *adj* endless

End'runde *f* final round, finals

End'station *f* final stop, terminus
End'summe *f* sum total
End'termin *m* final date; closing date
En'dung *f* (-;-en) ending
Ener-gie [ɛnɛr'giː] *f* (-;-gien ['giːən]) energy
energisch [ɛ'nɛrgɪʃ] *adj* energetic
eng [ɛŋ] *adj* narrow; tight; (*Freunde*) close; (*innig*) intimate; **im engeren Sinne** strictly speaking
engagieren [ãga'ziːrən] *tr* engage, hire || *ref* commit oneself
Enge ['ɛŋə] *f* (-;-n) narrowness; tightness; (*Meer-*) strait; (*fig*) tight spot
Engel ['ɛŋəl] *m* (-s;-) angel
en'gelhaft *adj* angelic
eng'herzig *adj* stingy; petty
England ['ɛŋlant] *n* (-s;) England
Engländer ['ɛŋlɛndər] *m* (-s;-) Englishman; **die E.** the English
Engländerin ['ɛŋlɛndərɪn] *f* (-;-nen) Englishwoman
englisch ['ɛŋlɪʃ] *adj* English
Eng'paß *m* pass, defile; (*fig*) bottleneck
engros [ã'groː] *adv* wholesale
engstirnig ['ɛŋʃtɪrnɪç] *adj* narrow-minded
Enkel ['ɛŋkəl] *m* (-s;-) grandson
Enkelin ['ɛŋkəlɪn] *f* (-;-nen) granddaughter
En'kelkind *n* grandchild
enorm [ɛ'nɔrm] *adj* enormous
Ensemble [ã'sãbl(ə)] *n* (-s;-s) (*mus*) ensemble; (*theat*) company, cast
ent- [ɛnt] *insep pref*
entarten [ɛnt'artən] *intr* (SEIN) degenerate
entartet [ɛnt'artət] *adj* degenerate; (*fig*) decadent
entäu'ßern *ref* (*genit*) divest oneself of
entbehren [ɛnt'beːrən] *tr* lack, miss; do without; (*spare*) dispense with
entbehr'lich *adj* dispensable; needless, superfluous
Entbeh'rung *f* (-;-en) privation, need
entbin'den §59 *tr* release, absolve; (*Frau*) deliver || *intr* give birth
Entbin'dung *f* (-;-en) dispensation; (*Niederkunft*) delivery, childbirth
Entbin'dungsanstalt *f* maternity hospital
entblät'tern *tr* defoliate || *ref* defoliate; (*coll*) strip
entblößen [ɛnt'bløːsən] *tr* bare; uncover; (*mil*) expose || *ref* strip; remove one's hat
entbren'nen §97 *intr* (SEIN) flare up
entdecken (**entdek'ken**) *tr* discover || *ref*—**sich j-m e.** confide in s.o.
Entdeckung (**Entdek'kung**) *f* (-;-en) discovery
Ente ['ɛntə] *f* (-;-n) duck; (*coll*) hoax
enteh'ren *tr* dishonor; (*Mädchen*) violate, deflower
enteh'rend *adj* disgraceful
Enteh'rung *f* (-;-en) disgrace; rape
enteig'nen *tr* dispossess
enteisen [ɛnt'aɪzən] *tr* defrost; deice
enter'ben *tr* disinherit
Enterich ['ɛntərɪç] *m* (-s;-e) drake
entern ['ɛntərn] *tr* (naut) board
entfachen [ɛnt'faxən] *tr* kindle; (*fig*) provoke

entfah'ren §71 *intr* (SEIN) (*dat*) slip out (on)
entfal'len §72 *intr* (SEIN) (*dat*) slip (from); **auf j-n e.** fall to s.o.'s share; **entfällt** not applicable
entfal'ten *tr* unfold; display; (*mil*) deploy || *ref* unfold; develop
entfernen [ɛnt'fɛrnən] *tr* remove || *ref* withdraw, move away; deviate
entfernt [ɛnt'fɛrnt] *adj* distant; **nicht weit davon e. zu** (*inf*) far from (*ger*)
Entfer'nung *f* (-;-en) removal; range; distance; absence
Entfer'nungsmesser *m* (phot) range finder
entfes'seln *tr* unleash
entflam'men *tr* inflame || *intr* (SEIN) ignite; flash; (*fig*) flare up
entflech'ten *tr* disentangle; (*Kartell*) break up; (*mil*) disengage
entflie'hen §75 *intr* (SEIN) flee, escape; (*Zeit*) fly
entfremden [ɛnt'fremdən] *tr* alienate
entfrosten [ɛnt'frɔstən] *tr* defrost
entfüh'ren *tr* abduct; kidnap; (*Flugzeug*) hijack; (hum) steal
Entfüh'rer *-in* §6 *mf* abductor, kidnaper; (aer) hijacker
Entfüh'rung *f* (-;-en) abduction; kidnaping; (aer) hijacking
entge'gen *prep* (*dat*) contrary to; in the direction of, towards
entge'gengehen §82 *intr* (SEIN) (*dat*) go to meet; (*dat*) face, confront
entge'gengesetzt *adj* contrary, opposite
entge'genhalten §90 *tr* hold out; point out, say in answer
entge'genkommen §99 *intr* (SEIN) (*dat*) approach; (*dat*) come to meet; (*dat*) meet halfway || **Entgegenkommen** *n* (-s;) courtesy
entge'genkommend *adj* on-coming; (fig) accommodating
entge'genlaufen §105 *intr* (SEIN) (*dat*) run towards; (*dat*) run counter to
entge'gennehmen §116 *tr* accept, receive
entge'gensehen §138 *intr* (*dat*) look forward to; (*dat*) await; (*dat*) face
entge'gensetzen *tr* put up, offer
entge'genstehen §146 *intr* (*dat*) oppose
entge'genstellen *tr* set in opposition || *ref* (*dat*) oppose, resist
entge'genstrecken *tr* (*dat*) stretch out (toward)
entge'gentreten §152 *intr* (SEIN) (*dat*) walk toward; (fig) (*dat*) confront
entgegnen [ɛnt'geːgnən] *tr* & *intr* reply
Entgeg'nung *f* (-;-en) reply
entge'hen §82 *intr* (SEIN) (*dat*) escape; elude; **sich** [*dat*] **etw e. lassen** let s.th. slip by
Entgelt [ɛnt'gelt] *n* (-[e]s;) compensation, payment
entgel'ten §83 *tr* pay for
entgeistert [ɛnt'gaɪstərt] *adj* aghast
entgleisen [ɛnt'glaɪzən] *intr* (SEIN) jump the track; (fig) make a slip
Entglei'sung *f* (-;-en) derailment; (fig) slip
entglei'ten §86 *intr* (SEIN) (*dat*) slip away (from)
entgräten [ɛnt'greːtən] *tr* bone (*a fish*)

enthaaren [ɛnt'hɑːrən] *tr* remove the hair from

Enthaa'rungsmittel *n* hair remover

enthal'ten §90 *tr* contain; comprise ‖ *ref* (*genit*) refrain (from); **sich der Stimme e.** (parl) abstain

enthaltsam [ɛnt'haltzɑm] *adj* abstinent

Enthalt'samkeit *f* (-;) abstinence

Enthal'tung *f* (-;-en) abstention

enthär'ten *tr* (*Wasser*) soften

enthaupten [ɛnt'hauptən] *tr* behead

enthäuten [ɛnt'hɔitən] *tr* skin

enthe'ben §94 *tr* (*genit*) exempt (from), relieve (of); (*e-s Amtes*) remove (*from office*)

enthei'ligen *tr* desecrate, profane

enthül'len *tr* unveil; reveal, expose

Enthül'lung *f* (-;-en) unveiling; (fig) exposé

enthül'sen *tr* shell; (*Mais*) husk

Enthusiasmus [ɛntuzi'asmus] *m* (-;) enthusiasm

enthusiastisch [ɛntuzi'astiʃ] *adj* enthusiastic

entjungfern [ɛnt'juŋfərn] *tr* deflower

entkei'men *tr* sterilize; (*Milch*) pasteurize ‖ *intr* (SEIN) sprout

entkernen [ɛnt'kɛrnən] *tr* (*Obst*) pit

entklei'den *tr* undress; (*genit*) strip (of), divest (of) ‖ *ref* undress

Entklei'dungsnummer *f* striptease act

Entklei'dungsrevüe *f* striptease show

entkom'men §99 *intr* (SEIN) (*dat*) escape (from) ‖ **Entkommen** *n* (-s;) escape

entkor'ken *tr* uncork, open

entkräften [ɛnt'krɛftən] *tr* weaken; (*Argument*) refute

entla'den §103 *tr* unload; (*Batterie*) discharge ‖ *ref* (*Gewehr*) go off; (*Sturm*) break; (elec) discharge; **sein Zorn entlud sich** he vented his anger

Entla'dung *f* (-;-en) unloading; discharge; explosion; **zur E. bringen** detonate

entlang' *adv* along ‖ *prep* (*dat* or *acc* or **an** *dat*; or after *genit* or *dat*) along

entlarven [ɛnt'larfən] *tr* expose

entlas'sen §104 *tr* dismiss, fire; set free; (mil) discharge

Entlas'sungspapiere *pl* discharge papers

entla'sten *tr* unburden; (**von**) relieve (of); (jur) exonerate

Entla'stungsstraße *f* bypass

Entla'stungszeuge *m* witness for the defense

entlauben [ɛnt'laubən] *tr* defoliate

entlaubt' *adj* leafless

entlau'fen §105 *intr* (SEIN) (*dat*) run away (from); (*mit e-m Liebhaber*) elope

entlausen [ɛnt'lauzən] *tr* delouse

entledigen [ɛnt'ledigən] *tr* (*genit*) release (from) ‖ *ref* (*genit*) get rid (of), rid oneself (of)

entlee'ren *tr* empty; drain

entle'gen *adj* distant, remote

entleh'nen *tr* borrow

entlei'hen §81 *tr* borrow

entlo'ben *ref* break the engagement

entlocken (entlok'ken) *tr* elicit

entloh'nen *tr* pay, pay off

entlüf'ten *tr* ventilate

entmannen [ɛnt'manən] *tr* castrate

entmilitarisieren [ɛntmilitari'ziːrən] *tr* demilitarize

entmutigen [ɛnt'mutigən] *tr* discourage

entneh'men §116 *tr* (*dat*) take (from); (*Geld*) (**aus**) withdraw (from); (*dat* or **aus**) infer (from), gather (from)

entnerven [ɛnt'nɛrfən] *tr* enervate

entpuppen [ɛnt'pupən] *ref* emerge from the cocoon; **sich e. als** (fig) turn out to be

enträtseln [ɛnt'rɛtsəln] *tr* solve; (*Schriftzeichen*) decipher

entrei'ßen §53 *tr* (*dat*) wrest (from)

entrich'ten *tr* pay

entrin'nen §121 *intr* (SEIN) escape (from)

entrol'len *tr* unroll; unfurl ‖ *ref* unroll ‖ *intr* (SEIN) roll down

entrüsten [ɛnt'rystən] *tr* anger ‖ *ref*— **sich e. über** (*acc*) become incensed at; be shocked at

Entrü'stung *f* (-;) anger, indignation

entsa'gen *intr* (*dat*) renounce, forego; **dem Thron e.** abdicate

Entsatz' *m* (-es;) (mil) relief

entschä'digen *tr* compensate; reimburse

Entschä'digung *f* (-;) compensation

Entschä'digungsanspruch *m* damage claim

entschär'fen *tr* defuse

Entscheid [ɛnt'ʃait] *m* (-[e]s;-e) (jur) decision

entschei'den §112 *tr, ref & intr* decide

entschei'dend *adj* decisive

Entschei'dung *f* (-;-en) decision

Entschei'dungsbefugnis *f* jurisdiction

Entschei'dungskampf *m* (sport) finals

Entschei'dungsspiel *n* (cards) rubber game; (sport) finals

Entschei'dungsstunde *f* moment of truth

entschei'dungsvoll *adj* critical

entschieden [ɛnt'ʃidən] *adj* decided; decisive; firm, resolute

entschla'fen §131 *intr* (SEIN) fall asleep; (*sterben*) pass away, die

entschlei'ern *tr* unveil; (fig) reveal

entschlie'ßen §76 *ref* (**zu**) decide (on)

Entschlie'ßung *f* (-;-en) (parl) resolution

entschlossen [ɛnt'ʃlosən] *adj* resolute

entschlüp'fen *intr* (SEIN) (*dat*) slip away (from); (*dat*) slip out (on)

Entschluß' *m* resolve, decision

entschlüs'seln *tr* decipher

Entschluß'kraft *f* will power

entschulden [ɛnt'ʃuldən] *tr* free of debt

entschuldigen [ɛnt'ʃuldigən] *tr* excuse; exculpate ‖ *ref* apologize; **es läßt sich e.** it's excusable; **sich e. lassen** beg to be excused; **sich mit Unwissenheit e.** plead ignorance

entschul'digend *adj* apologetic

Entschul'digung *f* (-;-en) excuse; apology; **ich bitte um E.** I beg your pardon

Entschul'digungsgrund *m* excuse

entseelt [ɛnt'zelt] *adj* lifeless, dead

entsen'den §140 *tr* send off

entset'zen *tr* horrify; (mil) relieve ‖

ref (über *acc*) be horrified (at) || **Ent-setzen** *n* (-s;) horror

entsetz'lich *adj* horrible, appalling || *adv* (coll) awfully

Entset'zung *f* (-;) dismissal; (mil) relief

entsi'chern *tr* take (*a gun*) off safety

entsie'geln *tr* unseal

entsin'nen §121 *ref* (*genit*) recall

entspan'nen *tr* & *ref* relax

Entspan'nung *f* (-;) relaxation; (pol) detente

entspre'chen §64 *intr* (*dat*) correspond (to); (*dat*) meet, suit; (*dat*) be equivalent (to); (*dat*) answer (*a description*)

entspre'chend *adj* corresponding; adequate; equivalent || *adv* accordingly || *prep* (*dat*) according to

entsprin'gen §142 *intr* (SEIN) rise, originate; (*entlaufen*) escape

entstaatlichen [ent'ʃtɑːtlɪçən] *tr* free from state control, denationalize

entstam'men *intr* (SEIN) (*dat*) descend (from), originate (from)

entste'hen §146 *intr* (SEIN) originate

Entste'hung *f* (-;) origin

entstel'len *tr* disfigure; deface; (*Tatsachen*) distort

enttäu'schen *tr* disappoint

entthronen [ent'troːnən] *tr* dethrone

entvölkern [ent'fœlkərn] *tr* depopulate

entwach'sen §155 *intr* (SEIN) (*dat*) outgrow

entwaff'nen *tr* disarm

entwar'nen *intr* sound the all-clear

entwäs'sern *tr* drain; dehydrate

entweder [ent'veːdər] *conj*—**entweder ... oder** either ... or

entwei'chen §85 *intr* (SEIN) escape

entwei'hen *tr* desecrate, profane

entwen'den *tr* steal

entwer'fen §160 *tr* sketch; draft

entwer'ten *tr* (*Geld*) depreciate; (*Briefmarke*) cancel; (*Karten*) punch

entwickeln (entwik'keln) *tr* develop; evolve; (mil) deploy || *ref* develop

Entwick'lung *f* (-;-en) development; evolution; (mil) deployment

Entwick'lungsland *n* developing country

Entwick'lungslehre *f* theory of evolution

entwin'den §59 *tr* (*dat*) wrest (from) || *ref* extricate oneself

entwirren [ent'vɪrən] *tr* & *ref* unravel

entwi'schen *intr* (SEIN) escape; (*dat or aus*) slip away (from)

entwöhnen [ent'vøːnən] *tr* wean; **j-n e.** (*genit*) break s.o. of || *ref* (*genit*) give up

Entwurf' *m* (-s;̈e) sketch; draft

entwur'zeln *tr* uproot

entzau'bern *tr* disenchant

entzie'hen §163 *tr* (*dat*) withdraw (from), take away (from); (*dat*) extract; **j-m das Wort e.** (parl) rule s.o. out of order || *ref* (*dat*) shirk, elude

Entzie'hungsanstalt *f* rehabilitation center

entziffern [ent'tsɪfərn] *tr* decipher

entzücken (entzük'ken) *tr* delight

Entzückung (Entzük'kung) *f* (-;-en) delight, rapture

Entzug' *m* (-[e]s;) deprivation

entzündbar [ent'tsʏntbɑr] *adj* inflammable

entzün'den *tr* set on fire; (fig) inflame || *ref* catch fire; (pathol) become inflamed

Entzün'dung *f* (-;) kindling; (pathol) inflammation

entzwei' *adv* in two, apart

entzwei'brechen §64 *tr* & *intr* break in two, snap

entzweien [ent'tsvaɪ.ən] *tr* divide

Enzykli-ka [ɛn'tsyklɪkɑ] *f* (-;-ken [kən]) encyclicle

Enzyklopä-die [entsyklopɛ'diː] *f* (-;-dien ['diː.ən]) encyclopedia

Enzym [ɛn'tsyːm] *n* (-[e]s;-e) enzyme

Epaulette [epɔ'lɛtə] *f* (-;-n) epaulet

ephemer [ɛfe'meːr] *adj* ephemeral

Epide-mie [epɪde'miː] *f* (-;-mien ['miː.ən] epidemic

epidemisch [epɪ'deːmɪʃ] *adj* epidemic

Epigramm [epɪ'gram] *n* (-s;-e) epigram

Epik ['eːpɪk] *f* (-;) epic poetry

Epilog [epɪ'loːk] *m* (-s;-e) epilogue

episch ['eːpɪʃ] *adj* epic

Episode [epɪ'zoːdə] *f* (-;-n) episode

Epoche [e'pɔxə] *f* (-;-n) epoch

Epos ['eːpɔs] *n* (-;Epen ['eːpən]) epic

Equipage [ek(v)ɪ'paːʒə] *f* (-;-n) carriage; (naut) crew; (sport) team

Equipe [ɛ'k(v)ɪp(ə)] *f* (-;-n) team; group

er [er] §11 *pers pron* he; it

er- [er] *insep pref*

erach'ten *tr* think || **Erachten** *n* (-s;) opinion; **meines Erachtens** in my opinion

erar'beiten *tr* acquire (*by working*)

Erb- [ɛrp] *comb.fm.* hereditary

Erb'anfall *m* inheritance

Erb'anlage *f* (biol) gene

erbarmen [ɛr'barmən] *tr* move to pity || *ref* (*genit*) pity; **erbarme Dich unser** have mercy on us || **Erbarmen** *n* (-s;) pity, mercy

erbar'menswert, erbar'menswürdig *adj* pitiable

erbärmlich [ɛr'bɛrmlɪç] *adj* pitiful; wretched, miserable || *adv* awfully

erbar'mungslos *adj* pitiless

erbau'en *tr* erect; (fig) edify || *ref* (*dat*) be edified (by)

Erbau'er *m* (-s;-) builder

erbau'lich *adj* edifying

Erbau'ung *f* (-;) building; edification

Erbau'ungsbuch *n* book of devotions

erb'berechtigt *adj* eligible as heir

Erbe ['ɛrbə] *m* (-n;-n) heir; **ohne Leibliche Erben** without issue || *n* (-s;) inheritance, heritage; **väterliches E.** patrimony

erbe'ben *intr* (SEIN) tremble

erb'eigen *adj* hereditary

erben ['ɛrbən] *tr* inherit

erbet'teln *tr* get (by begging)

erbeuten [ɛr'bɔɪtən] *tr* capture

Erb'feind *m* traditional enemy

Erb'folge *f* succession

erbie'ten §58 *ref* volunteer

Erbin ['ɛrbɪn] f (-;-nen) heiress
erbit'ten §60 ref—sich [dat] etw e. ask for s.th., request s.th.
erbittern [ɛr'bɪtərn] tr embitter
Erb'krankheit f hereditary disease
erblassen [ɛr'blasən] intr (SEIN) turn pale
Erblasser –in ['ɛrplasər(ɪn)] §6 mf testator
erbleichen [ɛr'blaɪçən] §85 & §109 intr (SEIN) turn pale; (poet) die
erb'lich adj hereditary
Erb'lichkeit f (-;) heredity
erblicken (erblik'ken) tr spot, see
erblinden [ɛr'blɪndən] intr (SEIN) go blind
Erblin'dung f (-;) loss of sight
Erb'onkel m (coll) rich uncle
erbre'chen §64 tr break open || ref vomit
erbrin'gen §65 tr produce
Erb'schaft f (-;-en) inheritance
Erbse ['ɛrpsə] f (-;-n) pea
Erb'stück n heirloom
Erb'sünde f original sin
Erb'tante f (coll) rich aunt
Erb'teil m share (in an inheritance)
Erd– [ɛrt] comb.fm. earth, of the earth; geo–; ground
Erd'anschluß m (elec) ground
Erd'arbeiten pl excavation work
Erd'bahn f orbit of the earth
Erd'ball m globe
Erd'beben n (-s;-) earthquake
Erd'bebenmesser m seismograph
Erd'beere f strawberry
Erd'boden m ground, earth; dem E. gleichmachen raze (to the ground)
Erde ['ɛrdə] f (-;-n) earth; ground, soil, land; (elec) ground wire; zu ebener E. on the ground floor
erden ['ɛrdən] tr (elec) ground
erden'ken §66 tr think up
erdenk'lich adj imaginable
Erd'gas n natural gas
Erd'geschoß n ground floor
erdich'ten tr fabricate, think up
Erdich'tung f (-;-en) fabrication
erdig ['ɛrdɪç] adj earthy
Erd'innere §5 n interior of the earth
Erd'klumpen m clod
Erd'kreis m earth, world
Erd'kugel f globe, sphere; world
Erd'kunde f geography
Erd'leitung f (elec) ground wire
Erd'nuß f peanut
Erd'nußbutter f peanut butter
Erd'öl n petroleum, oil; auf E. stoßen strike oil
erdolchen [ɛr'dɔlçən] tr stab
Erd'reich n soil
erdreisten [ɛr'draɪstən] ref have the nerve, have the audacity
Erd'rinde f crust of the earth
erdros'seln tr strangle
erdrücken (erdrük'ken) tr crush to death
erdrückend (erdrük'kend) adj overwhelming
Erd'rutsch m land slide
Erd'schicht f stratum
Erd'spalte f fissure; chasm
Erd'teil m continent

erdul'den tr suffer
ereifern [ɛr'aɪfərn] ref get excited
ereignen [ɛr'aɪgnən] ref happen, occur
Ereignis [ɛr'aɪgnɪs] n (-ses;-se) event, occurrence
ereig'nislos adj uneventful
ereig'nisvoll adj eventful
Erektion [ɛrɛk'tsjon] f (-;-en) erection
Eremit [ɛrе'mit] m (-en;-en) hermit
erer'ben tr inherit
erfah'ren adj experienced || §71 tr find out; (erleben) experience; (Pflege) receive
Erfah'rung f (-;-en) experience
erfas'sen tr grasp; understand; include; register, list
erfin'den §59 tr invent
Erfin'der –in §6 mf inventor
erfinderisch [ɛr'fɪndərɪʃ] adj inventive
Erfin'dung f (-;-en) invention
Erfin'dungsgabe f inventiveness
erfle'hen tr obtain (by entreaty)
Erfolg [ɛr'fɔlk] m (-[e]s;-e) success; (Wirkung) result
erfol'gen intr (SEIN) ensue; occur
erfolg'los adj unsuccessful || adv in vain
erfolg'reich adj successful
Erfolgs'mensch m go-getter
erfolg'versprechend adj promising
erforderlich [ɛr'fɔrdərlɪç] adj required, necessary
erfor'derlichenfalls adv if need be
erfordern [ɛr'fɔrdərn] tr require
Erfordernis [ɛr'fɔrdərnɪs] n (-ses;-se) requirement; exigency
erfor'schen tr investigate; (Land) explore
Erfor'scher –in §6 mf explorer
Erfor'schung f (-;-en) investigation, exploration
erfra'gen tr ask for; find out
erfreu'en tr delight || ref (an dat) be delighted (at); sich e. (genit) enjoy
erfreulich [ɛr'frɔɪlɪç] adj delightful; (Nachricht) welcome, good
erfreut [ɛr'frɔɪt] adj (über acc) glad (about); e. zu (inf) pleased to (inf)
erfrie'ren §77 intr (SEIN) freeze to death; (Pflanzen) freeze
Erfrie'rung f (-;-en) frostbite
erfrischen [ɛr'frɪʃən] tr refresh
Erfri'schung f (-;-en) refreshment
erfül'len tr fill; fulfill; (Aufgabe) perform; (Bitte) comply with; (Hoffnungen) live up to || ref materialize
Erfül'lung f (-;) fulfillment; accomplishment; in E. gehen come true
erfunden [ɛr'fundən] adj made-up
ergänzen [ɛr'gɛntsən] tr complete; complement; (Statue) restore
ergän'zend adj complementary
ergattern [ɛr'gatərn] tr (coll) dig up
ergau'nern tr—etw von j–m e. cheat s.o. out of s.th.
erge'ben adj devoted || §80 tr yield; amount to; show || ref surrender; (dat) devote oneself (to); (aus) result (from); sich dem Trunk e. take to drinking; sich e. in (acc) resign oneself to
Erge'benheit f (-;) devotion; resignation

ergebenst [ɛr'ge:bənst] *adv* respectfully

Ergebnis [ɛr'ge:pnɪs] *n* (–ses;–se) result, outcome; (*Punktzahl*) score

Erge'bung *f* (–;) submission, resignation; (mil) surrender

erge'hen §82 *intr* (SEIN) come out, be published; **e.** lassen issue, publish; **etw über sich e.** lassen put up with s.th.; **Gnade vor Recht e.** lassen show leniency ‖ *ref* take a stroll; **sich e.** in (*acc*) indulge in; **sich e.** über (*acc*) expatiate on ‖ *impers*—**es ist ihm gut ergangen** things went well for him ‖ **Ergehen** *n* (–s;) state of health

ergiebig [ɛr'gi:bɪç] *adj* productive, fertile; rich, abundant

ergie'ßen §76 *ref* flow; pour out

ergötzen [ɛr'gœtsən] *tr* amuse ‖ *ref* (**an** *dat*) take delight (in)

ergötz'lich *adj* delightful

ergrau'en *intr* (SEIN) turn gray

ergrei'fen §88 *tr* seize; (*Verbrecher*) apprehend; (*Gemüt*) move; (*Beruf, Waffen*) take up; (*Maßnahmen*) take

Ergrei'fung *f* (–;) seizure

ergriffen [ɛr'grɪfən] *adj* moved; **e. von** seized with

Ergrif'fenheit *f* (–;) emotion

ergrün'den *tr* get to the bottom of

Erguß' *m* discharge; (fig) flood of words

erha'ben *adj* elevated, lofty; **erhabene Arbeit** relief work; **e. sein über** (*acc*) be above

Erhalt' *m* (–es;) receipt

erhal'ten §90 *tr* get, receive; keep, keep up, maintain; conserve; (*Familie*) support; (*Gesundheit*) preserve; **Betrag dankend e.** (*stamped on bills*) paid; **gut e.** well preserved; **noch e. sein** survive ‖ *ref* survive; (**von**) subsist (on)

erhältlich [ɛr'heltlɪç] *adj* obtainable

Erhal'tung *f* (–;) preservation; maintenance; support; (*der Energie, usw.*) conservation

erhän'gen *tr* hang

erhär'ten *tr* harden; (fig) substantiate ‖ *intr* (SEIN) harden

erha'schen *tr* catch; **e–n Blick von ihr e.** catch her eye

erhe'ben §94 *tr* raise; (*erhöhen*) elevate; (*preisen*) exalt; (*Steuern*) collect; (*Anklage*) bring; (math) raise ‖ *ref* get up, rise, start; arise

erheblich [ɛr'he:plɪç] *adj* considerable

Erhe'bung *f* (–;–en) elevation; promotion; uprising, revolt; **Erhebungen machen** make inquiries

erheitern [ɛr'haɪtərn] *tr* amuse ‖ *ref* cheer up

erhellen [ɛr'helən] *tr* light up; (fig) shed light on ‖ *ref* grow light(er); light up ‖ *impers*—**es erhellt** it appears

erhitzen [ɛr'hɪtsən] *tr* heat; (fig) inflame ‖ *ref* grow hot; get angry

erhöhen [ɛr'hø:ən] *tr* raise; (fig) heighten ‖ *ref* increase; be enhanced

Erhö'hung *f* (–;–en) rise

erho'len *ref* recover; relax

Erho'lung *f* (–;–en) recovery; relaxation; recreation

erho'lungsbedürftig *adj* in need of rest

Erho'lungsheim *n* convalescent home

erhö'ren *tr* (*Gebet*) hear; (*Bitte*) grant

erinnerlich [ɛr'ɪnərlɪç] *adj*—**das ist mir nicht e.** it slipped my mind; **soviel mir e. ist** as far as I can remember

erinnern [ɛr'ɪnərn] *tr* (**an** *acc*) remind (of) ‖ *ref* (**an** *acc*) remember

Erin'nerung *f* (–;–en) recollection, remembrance; (*Mahnung*) reminder; **zur E. an** (*acc*) in memory of

Erin'nerungsvermögen *n* memory

erkalten [ɛr'kaltən] *intr* (SEIN) cool off; (fig) grow cool

erkälten [ɛr'kɛltən] *ref* catch cold

Erkäl'tung *f* (–;–en) cold

erkennbar [ɛr'kɛnba:r] *adj* recognizable

erkennen [ɛr'kɛnən] §97 *tr* make out; recognize; detect; realize; **j–n e. für** (com) credit s.o. with; **sich zu e. geben** disclose one's identity; **zu e. geben, daß** indicate that ‖ *intr*—**auf e–e Geldstrafe e.** impose a fine; **gegen j–n e.** judge against s.o.

erkenntlich [ɛr'kɛntlɪç] *adj* grateful

Erkennt'lichkeit *f* (–;) gratitude

Erkenntnis [ɛr'kɛntnɪs] *f* (–;–se) insight, judgment, realization, knowledge; (philos) cognition ‖ *n* (–ses; –se) decision, finding

Erker ['ɛrkər] *m* (–s;–) (archit) oriel

Er'kerfenster *n* bay window

erklären [ɛr'klɛrən] *tr* explain, account for; (*aussprechen*) state

Erklä'rer –in §6 *mf* commentator

erklär'lich *adj* explicable

Erklä'rung *f* (–;–en) explanation; statement; commentary; (jur) deposition

erklin'gen §142 *intr* (SEIN) sound; (*widerhallen*) resound

erkor (ɛr'ko:r) *pret of* **erkiesen**

erkoren [ɛr'ko:rən] *adj* chosen

erkranken [ɛr'kraŋkən] *intr* (SEIN) get sick; (*Pflanzen*) become diseased

erkühnen [ɛr'ky:nən] *ref* dare, venture

erkunden [ɛr'kundən] *tr* & *intr* reconnoiter

erkundigen [ɛr'kundigən] *ref* inquire

Erkun'digung *f* (–;–en) inquiry

Erkun'dung *f* (–;) reconnaissance

erlahmen [ɛr'la:mən] *intr* (SEIN) tire; (*Kraft*) give out

erlangen [ɛr'laŋən] *tr* reach; (*sich verschaffen*) get; **wieder e.** recover

Er.laß [ɛr'las] *m* (–lasses;–lässe) remission; exemption; edict, order

erlas'sen §104 *tr* release; (*Schulden*) cancel; (*Strafe*) remit; (*Sünden*) pardon; (*Verordnung*) issue; **e. Sie es mir zu** (*inf*) allow me not to (*inf*), don't ask me to (*inf*)

erläßlich [ɛr'leslɪç] *adj* pardonable

erlauben [ɛr'laubən] *tr* allow ‖ *ref*—**sich** [*dat*] **e. zu** (*inf*) take the liberty to (*inf*); **sich** [*dat*] **nicht e.** not be able to afford

Erlaubnis [ɛr'laupnɪs] *f* (–;–se) permission

Erlaub'nisschein *m* permit, license

erlaucht [ɛr'lauxt] *adj* illustrious

erläutern [ɛr'lɔɪtərn] *tr* explain

Erläu'terung *f* (–;–en) explanation

Erle ['ɛrlə] f (-;-n) (bot) alder
erle'ben tr live to see; experience
Erlebnis [ɛr'lepnɪs] n (-ses;-se) experience, adventure; occurrence
erledigen [ɛr'ledɪgən] tr settle; (Post, Einkäufe, Gesuch) attend to, take care of; **j-n e.** (coll) do s.o. in
erledigt [ɛr'ledɪçt] adj (& fig) finished; (Stellung) open; (coll) bushed
erle'gen tr pay down; (töten) kill
erleichtern [ɛr'laɪçtərn] tr lighten; make easy; (Not) relieve, ease
Erleich'terung f (-;) alleviation
erlei'den §106 tr suffer
erler'nen tr learn
erle'sen adj choice || §107 tr choose
erleuch'ten tr light up; enlighten
erlie'gen §108 intr (SEIN) (dat) succumb (to), fall victim (to)
erlogen [ɛr'logən] adj false
Erlös [ɛr'løs] m (-es;) proceeds
erlosch [ɛr'lɔʃ] pret of erlöschen
erloschen [ɛr'lɔʃən] pp of erlöschen
erlöschen [ɛr'lœʃən] §110 intr (SEIN) go out; (Vertrag) expire; (fig) become extinct
erlö'sen tr redeem; free; get (by sale)
Erlö'ser m (-s;-) deliverer; (relig) Redeemer
Erlö'sung f (-;) redemption
ermächtigen [ɛr'mɛçtɪgən] tr authorize
Ermäch'tigung f (-;-en) authorization
ermah'nen tr admonish
Ermah'nung f (-;-en) admonition
ermangeln [ɛr'maŋəln] intr (genit) lack; **es an nichts e. lassen** spare no pains; **nicht e. zu** (inf) not fail to (inf)
Erman'gelung f—**in E.** (genit) in default of
ermä'ßigen tr reduce
ermatten [ɛr'matən] tr tire || intr (SEIN) tire; grow weak; slacken
Ermat'tung f (-;) fatigue
ermes'sen §70 tr judge, estimate; realize; **e. aus** infer from || **Ermessen** n (-s;) judgment, opinion; **nach freiem E.** at one's discretion
ermitteln [ɛr'mɪtəln] tr ascertain || intr conduct an investigation
Ermitt'lung f (-;-en) ascertainment; Ermittlungen investigation
Ermitt'lungsausschuß m fact-finding committee
Ermitt'lungsbeamte m investigator
Ermitt'lungsverfahren n judicial inquiry
ermöglichen [ɛr'møklɪçən] tr enable, make possible
ermorden [ɛr'mɔrdən] tr murder
ermüden [ɛr'mydən] tr tire || intr (SEIN) tire, get tired
Ermü'dung f (-;) fatigue
ermuntern [ɛr'muntərn] tr cheer up; encourage || ref cheer up
Ermun'terung f (-;) encouragement
ermutigen [ɛr'mutɪgən] tr encourage
ernäh'ren tr nourish; (fig) support
Ernäh'rer —in §6 mf supporter
Ernäh'rung f (-;) nourishment; support; (physiol) nutrition
ernen'nen §97 tr nominate, appoint
erneuern [ɛr'nɔɪ-ərn] tr renew; reno-

vate; (Gemälde) restore; (Öl) change; (Reifen) retread; (mach) replace
Erneu'ert adj repeated || adv anew
Erneu'erung f (-;-en) renewal; renovation; restoration; replacement
erniedrigen [ɛr'nidrɪgən] tr lower; (demütigen) humble; (im Rang) degrade || ref humble oneself; debase oneself
ernst [ɛrnst] adj earnest; serious || **Ernst** m (-[e]s;) seriousness; **im E.** in earnest
Ernst'fall m—**im E.** in case of emergency; (mil) in case of war
ernst'haft adj earnest, serious
ernst'lich adj earnest; serious
Ernte ['ɛrntə] f (-;-n) harvest; crop
ernten ['ɛrntən] tr reap, harvest
ernüch'tern tr sober; disallusion || ref sober up; be disallusioned
Ero'berer —in §6 mf conqueror
erobern [ɛr'obərn] tr conquer
Ero'berung f (-;-en) conquest
eröff'nen tr open; (feierlich) inaugurate; disclose || ref open; present itself; **sich j-m e.** unburden oneself to s.o.
Eröff'nung f (-;-en) (grand) opening; inauguration; announcement
erörtern [ɛr'œrtərn] tr discuss
erotisch [e'rotɪʃ] adj erotic
Erpel ['ɛrpəl] m (-s;-) drake
erpicht [ɛr'pɪçt] adj—**e. auf** (acc) keen on, dead set on, hell bent on
erpres'sen tr extort; (Person) blackmail
Erpres'sung f (-;-en) extortion; blackmail
erpro'ben tr test, try out
erquicken [ɛr'kvɪkən] tr refresh
erquick'lich adj refreshing; agreeable
erra'ten §63 tr guess
errech'nen tr calculate
erregbar [ɛr'rekbar] adj excitable; irritable
erregen [ɛr'regən] tr excite; cause || ref get excited, get worked up
Erre'gung f (-;) excitation; agitation; excitement; **E. öffentlichen Ärgernisses** disorderly conduct
erreichbar [ɛr'raɪçbar] adj reachable; available
errei'chen tr reach, attain; get to; (Zug, Bus) catch; **e., daß** bring it about that
erret'ten tr save, rescue
Erret'tung f (-;-en) rescue; (relig) Salvation
errich'ten tr erect; found
errin'gen §142 tr get; attain, achieve
errö'ten intr (SEIN) redden; blush
Errungenschaft [ɛr'ruŋənʃaft] f (-;-en) achievement; acquisition
Ersatz' m (-es;) substitute; replacement; compensation; (mil) recruitment
Ersatz- comb.fm. substitute, replacement; spare; alternative; recruiting
Ersatz'mann m substitute; alternate
Ersatz'stück n, **Ersatz'teil** n spare part, spare
erschaf'fen §126 tr create
Erschaf'fer —in §6 mf creator
Erschaf'fung f (-;-en) creation

erschal'len §127 *intr* (SEIN) begin to sound; ring out; resound

erschau'ern *intr* (SEIN) shudder

erschei'nen §128 *intr* (SEIN) appear; (*Buch*) come out, be published

Erschei'nung *f* (–;–en) appearance; apparition; phenomenon

erschie'ßen §76 *tr* shoot (dead)

Erschie'ßung *f* (–;–en) shooting, execution

Erschie'ßungskommando *n* firing squad

erschlaffen [er'/laf ən] *tr* relax; enervate || *intr* (SEIN) relax; weaken

erschla'gen §132 *tr* slay; **wie e.** dead tired

erschlie'ßen §76 *tr* open up; develop; **e. aus** infer from; derive from || *ref* —**sich j–m e.** unburden oneself to s.o.

erschöp'fen *tr* exhaust; (*fig*) deplete

erschrak [er'/rak] *pret of* **erschrecken**

erschrecken (**erschrek'ken**) *tr* startle; shock || *ref* get scared || §134 *intr* (SEIN) be startled

erschreckend (**erschrek'kend**) *adj* terrifying; alarming; dreadful

erschüt'ten *tr* shake, upset; move deeply

Erschüt'terung *f* (–;–en) tremor; vibration; deep feeling; concussion

erschweren [er'/verən] *tr* make more difficult; hamper, impede

erschwin'deln *tr*—**etw von j–m e.** cheat s.o. out of s.th.

erschwin'gen §142 *tr* afford

erschwing'lich *adj* within one's means

erse'hen §138 *tr* (aus) gather (from)

erseh'nen *tr* long for

ersetzbar [er'zetsbar] *adj* replaceable

erset'zen *tr* replace; (*Schaden*) compensate for; (*Kräfte*) renew; **j–m etw e.** reimburse s.o. for s.th.; **sie ersetzte ihm die Eltern** she was mother and father to him

ersetz'lich *adj* replaceable

ersicht'lich *adj* evident

ersin'nen §121 *tr* think up

erspa'ren *tr* save

Ersparnis [er'/sparnıs] *f* (–;–se) (an *dat*) saving (in)

ersprießlich [er'/prislıç] *adj* useful

erst [erst] *adv* first; at first; just; only; not until; **e. recht** really; **e. recht nicht** most certainly not

erstar'ren *intr* (SEIN) grow stiff; (*Finger*) grow numb; (*Blut*) congeal; (*Zement*) set; (fig) run cold; **vor Schreck e.** be paralyzed with fear

erstatten [er'/tatən] *tr* refund, repay; (*Bericht*) file; **Meldung e.** report

Erstat'tung *f* (–;–en) refund; reimbursement; compensation

Erst'aufführung *f* primiere

erstau'nen *tr* astonish || *intr* (SEIN) (*über acc*) be astonished (at) || **Erstaunen** *n* (–s;) astonishment; **in E. setzen** astonish

erstaun'lich *adj* astonishing

Erst'ausfertigung *f* original

erste ['ersta] §9 *adj* first; **der erste beste** the first that comes along; **fürs e.** for the time being; **zum ersten, zum zweiten, zum dritten** going, going, gone

erste'chen §64 *tr* stab

erste'hen §146 *tr* buy, get || *intr* (SEIN) rise; (*Städte*) spring up

erstei'gen §148 *tr* climb

erstel'len *tr* provide, supply; erect

erstens ['erstəns] *adv* first; in the first place

erst'geboren *adj* first-born

ersticken [er'/tıkən] *tr* choke, stifle, smother; **im Keim e.** nip in the bud || *intr* (SEIN) choke; **in Arbeit e.** be snowed under

erstklassig ['erstklasıç] *adj* first-class

Erstling ['erstlıŋ] *m* (–s;–e) first-born child; (fig) first fruits

Erstlings– *comb.fm.* first

Erst'lingsausstattung *f* layette

erstmalig ['erstmalıç] *adj* first

erstre'ben *tr* strive for

erstrecken (**erstrek'ken**) *ref* extend

ersu'chen *tr* request, ask

ertappen [er'tapən] *tr* surprise, catch

ertei'len *tr* give; confer; (*Auftrag*) place; (*Audienz, Patent*) grant

ertö'nen *intr* (SEIN) sound; resound

ertö'ten *tr* (fig) stifle

Ertrag [er'trak] *m* (–[e]s;–̈e) yield; proceeds; produce

erträglich [er'treklıç] *adj* bearable

ertränken [er'treŋkən] *tr* drown

erträu'men *tr* dream of

ertrin'ken §143 *intr* (SEIN) drown

ertüchtigen [er'tyçtıgən] *tr* train

erübrigen [er'ybrıgən] *tr* save; (*Zeit*) spare || *ref* be superfluous

erwa'chen *intr* (SEIN) wake up

erwach'sen *adj* adult || §155 *intr* (SEIN) grow, grow up; arise || **Erwachsene** §5 *mf* adult, grown-up

erwä'gen §156 *tr* weigh, consider

Erwä'gung *f* (–;–en) consideration

erwäh'len *tr* choose

erwäh'nen *tr* mention

erwäh'nenswert *adj* worth mentioning

Erwäh'nung *f* (–;) mention

erwär'men *tr* warm, warm up

erwar'ten *tr* expect, await; **etw zu e. haben** be in for s.th.

Erwar'tung *f* (–;–en) expectation

erwar'tungsvoll *adj* expectant

erwecken (**erwek'ken**) *tr* wake; (*Hoffnungen*) raise; (*Gefühle*) awaken; **den Anschein e.** give the impression

erweh'ren *ref* (genit) ward off; (*genit*) refrain from; (*der Tränen*) hold back

erwei'chen *tr* soften; (fig) move, touch; **sich e. lassen** relent

erwei'sen §118 *tr* prove; show; (*Achtung*) show; (*Dienst*) render; (*Ehre, Gunst*) do || *ref*—**sich e. als** prove

erweitern [er'vaıtərn] *tr & ref* widen; (*vermehren*) increase; extend; expand

Erwerb [er'verp] *m* (–[e]s;–e) acquisition; (*Verdienst*) earnings; (*Unterhalt*) living

erwer'ben §149 *tr* acquire; gain; (*verdienen*) earn; (*kaufen*) purchase

erwerbs'behindert *adj* disabled

Erwerbs'betrieb *m* business enterprise

erwerbs'fähig *adj* capable of earning a living

erwerbs'los *adj* unemployed

Erwerbs'quelle f source of income
Erwerbs'sinn m acquisitiveness
erwerbs'tätig adj gainfully employed
erwerbs'unfähig adj unable to earn a living
Erwerbs'zweig m line of business
Erwer'bung f (–;–en) acquisition
erwidern [er'vidərn] tr reply; reciprocate, return
Erwi'derung f (–;–en) reply; return; retaliation
erwir'ken tr secure, obtain
erwi'schen tr catch; **ihn hat's erwischt!** (coll) he's had it!
erwünscht [er'vyn/t] adj desired; welcome; (wünschenswert) desirable
erwür'gen tr strangle
Erz [erts] n (–es;–e) ore; brass; bronze
Erz-, erz- comb.fm. ore; bronze; utterly; (fig) arch–
erzählen [er'tselən] tr tell, narrate
Erzäh'lung f (–;–en) story, narrative
Erz'bischof m archbishop
Erz'engel m archangel
erzeu'gen tr beget; manufacture; produce; generate
Erzeugnis [er'tsɔɪknɪs] n (–ses;–se) product; produce
Erzeu'gung f (–;–en) production; manufacture
erzie'hen §163 tr bring up, rear; (geistig) educate
Erzieher [er'tsi·ər] m (–s;–) educator; private tutor
Erzieherin [er'tsi·ərɪn] f (–;–nen) educator; governess
erzieherisch [er'tsi·ərɪʃ] adj educational, pedagogical
Erzie'hung f (–;) upbringing; education; (Lebensart) breeding
Erzie'hungslehre f (educ) education
Erzie'hungswesen n educational system
erzie'len tr achieve, reach; (Gewinn) realize; (sport) score
Erz'lager n ore deposit
Erz'probe f assay
erzür'nen tr anger || ref get angry
erzwin'gen §142 tr force; wring, obtain by force; (Gehorsam) exact
es [es] adv (as expletive) there; **es gibt** there is, there are || §11 pers pron it; he; she || **Es** n (–;–) (mus) E flat; (psychol) id
Esche ['ɛʃə] f (–;–n) ash tree
Esel ['ezəl] m (–s;–) donkey, ass
Eselei [ezə'laɪ] f (–;–en) foolish act, foolish remark
E'selsbrücke f (educ) pony
E'selsohr n dog's-ear
eskalieren [eska'lirən] tr & intr escalate
Eskimo ['ɛskɪmo] m (–s;–s) Eskimo
Espe ['ɛspə] f (–;–n) (bot) aspen
eßbar ['ɛsbar] adj edible, eatable
Eßbesteck ['ɛsbəʃtɛk] n knife, fork, and spoon
Esse ['ɛsə] f (–;–n) chimney; forge
essen ['ɛsən] §70 tr & intr eat; **zu Mittag e.** eat lunch || **Essen** n (–s;) eating; food, meal
Essenz [ɛ'sɛnts] f (–;–en) essence
Eßgeschirr ['ɛsgə/ɪr] n (–s;) tableware; table service; (mil) mess kit

Eßgier ['ɛsgir] f (–;) gluttony
Essig ['ɛsɪç] m (–s;–e) vinegar
Es'siggurke f pickle, gherkin
Es'sigsäure f acetic acid
Eßlöffel ['ɛslœfəl] m (–s;–) tablespoon
Eßnapf ['ɛsnapf] m dinner pail
Eßsaal ['ɛszal] m dining room
Eßstäbchen ['ɛs/tɛpçən] n chopstick
Eßwaren ['ɛsvarən] pl food, victuals
Eßzimmer ['ɛstsɪmər] n (–s;–) dining room
Estland ['ɛstlant] n (–s;) Estonia
Estrade [ɛs'tradə] f (–;–n) dais
etablieren [ɛta'blirən] tr establish
Etablissement [ɛtablɪs(ə)'mã] n (–s; –s) establishment
Etage [ɛ'taʒə] f (–;–n) floor, story
Eta'genbett n bunk bed
Eta'genwohnung f apartment
Etappe [ɛ'tapə] f (–;–n) (Teilstrecke) leg, stage; (mil) rear echelon, rear
Etat [ɛ'ta] m (–s;–s) budget
Etats'jahr n fiscal year
etepetete [ɛtəpe'tetə] adj overly particular
Ethik ['ɛtɪk] f (–;) ethics
ethisch ['ɛtɪ/] adj ethical
ethnisch ['ɛtnɪ/] adj ethnic
Ethnologie [ɛtnolo'gi] f (–;) ethnology
Etikett [ɛtɪ'kɛt] n (–s;–e) tab, label
Etikette [ɛtɪ'ketə] f (–;) etiquette
etikettieren [ɛtɪke'tirən] tr label
etliche ['ɛtlɪçə] adj & pron a few
Etui [ɛ'tvi] n (–s;–s) case (for spectacles, cigarettes, etc.)
etwa ['ɛtva] adv about, around; perhaps; by chance; for example
etwaig [ɛt'va·ɪç] adj eventual
etwas ['ɛtvas] adj some, a little || adv somewhat || pron something; anything || **Etwas** n—**ein gewißes E.** a certain something
euch [ɔɪç] pers pron you; to you || reflex pron yourselves
euer ['ɔɪ·ər] adj your
Eukalyp·tus [ɔɪka'lɪptus] m (–; & –ten [tən]) eucalyptus
Eule ['ɔɪlə] f (–;–n) owl
Euphorie [ɔɪfo'ri] f (–;) euphoria
euphorisch [ɔɪ'fori/] adj euphoric
eurige ['ɔɪrɪgə] §2,5 pron yours
Europa [ɔɪ'ropa] n (–s;) Europe
Europäer -in [ɔɪro·pe·ər(ɪn)] §6 mf European
europäisch [ɔɪro'pe·ɪ/] adj European
Euter ['ɔɪtər] n (–s;–) udder
evakuieren [evaku'irən] tr evacuate
evangelisch [evan'geli/] adj evangelical; Protestant
Evangelist [evange'lɪst] m (–en;–en) Evangelist
Evange·lium [evan'geljum] n (–s;–lien [ljən]) gospel
eventuell [ɛventu'ɛl] adj eventual || adv possibly
ewig ['eviç] adj eternal; perpetual
E'wigkeit f (–;–en) eternity
e'wiglich adv forever
exakt [ɛ'ksakt] adj exact
Exa·men [ɛ'ksamən] n (–s;–s & –mina [mɪna]) examination
examinieren [ɛksami'nirən] tr examine
exekutiv [ɛkseku'tif] adj executive

Exempel [ε'ksεmpəl] *n* (-s;-) example; ein E. statuieren an (*dat*) make an example of

Exemplar [εksεm'plɑr] *n* (-s;-e) sample, specimen; (*e-s Buches*) copy

exerzieren [εksεr'tsirən] *tr & intr* exercise

Exil [ε'ksil] *n* (-s;-e) exile

Existenz [εksi'stεnts] *f* (-;-en) existence; livelihood; personality

Existenz'minimum *n* living wage

existieren [εksis'tirən] *intr* exist

exklusiv [εkslu'zif] *adj* exclusive

Exkommunikation [εkskɔmunika'tsjon] *f* (-;-en) excommunication

exkommunizieren [εkskɔmuni'tsirən] *tr* excommunicate

Exkrement [εkskre'mεnt] *n* (-[e]s;-e) excrement

exmittieren [εksmi'tirən] *tr* evict

exotisch [ε'ksotiʃ] *adj* exotic

expedieren [εkspe'dirən] *tr* send, ship

Expedition [εkspedi'tsjon] *f* (-;-en) forwarding; (mil) expedition

Experiment [εkspεri'mεnt] *n* (-[e]s; -e) experiment

experimentieren [εkspεrimεn'tirən] *intr* experiment

explodieren [εksplo'dirən] *intr* (SEIN) explode; blow up

Explosion [εksplo'zjon] *f* (-;-en) explosion

exponieren [εkspo'nirən] *tr* expose; (*darlegen*) expound, set forth

Export [εks'pɔrt] *m* (-[e]s;-e) export

exportieren [εkspɔr'tirən] *tr* export

Ex-preß [εks'prεs] *m* (-presses; -presse) express

Expreß'zug *m* express train

extra ['εkstra] *adv* extra; (coll) on purpose, for spite

Ex'trablatt *n* (journ) extra

extrahieren [εkstra'hirən] *tr* extract

Extrakt [εks'trakt] *m* (-[e]s;-e) extract; (*aus Büchern*) excerpt

extravagant [εkstrava'gant] *adj* luxurious; wild, fantastic

Extravaganz [εkstrava'gants] *f* (-;-en) luxury

extrem [εks'trem] *adj* extreme ‖ **Extrem** *n* (-s;-e) extreme

Exzellenz [εkstse'lεnts] *f* (-;-en) Excellency

exzentrisch [εks'tsεntriʃ] *adj* eccentric

Ex-zeß [εks'tsεs] *m* (-zesses;-zesse) excess

F

F, f [εf] *invar n* F, f; (mus) F

Fabel ['fɑbəl] *f* (-;-n) fable; story; (*e-s Dramas*) plot

fa'belhaft *adj* fabulous

fabeln ['fɑbəln] *intr* tell stories

Fabrik [fa'brik] *f* (-;-en) factory, mill

Fabrik'anlage *f* manufacturing plant

Fabrikant -in [fabri'kant(in)] §7 *mf* manufacturer, maker

Fabrikat [fabri'kat] *n* (-[e]s;-e) product; brand, make

Fabrikation [fabrika'tsjon] *f* (-;) manufacture, manufacturing

Fabrikations'fehler *m* flaw, defect

Fabrikations'nummer *f* serial number

Fabrik'marke *f* trademark

fabrik'mäßig *adj* mass

Fabrik'nummer *f* serial number

Fabrik'waren *pl* manufactured goods

Fabrik'zeichen *n* trademark

fabrizieren [fabri'tsirən] *tr* manufacture

fabulieren [fabu'lirən] *tr* make up ‖ *intr* tell yarns

fabulös [fabu'løs] *adj* fabulous

Facette [fa'sεtə] *f* (-;-n) facet

Fach [fax] *n* (-[e]s;⁻er) compartment; (*im Schreibtisch*) pigeonhole; (*Bücherbrett*) shelf; (fig) field, department; line, business; (educ) subject; vom F. sein be an expert

Fach'arbeiter -in §6 *mf* specialist

Fach'arzt *m*, **Fach'ärztin** *f* (med) specialist

Fach'ausbildung *f* professional training

Fach'ausdruck *m* technical term

fächeln ['fεçəln] *tr* fan

Fächer ['fεçər] *m* (-s;-) fan

Fä'cherpalme *f* palmetto

Fach'gebiet *n* field, line; department

Fach'gelehrte §5 *mf* expert

fach'gemäß *adj* expert, professional

Fach'genosse *m* colleague

Fach'kenntnisse *pl* specialized knowledge

Fach'kreis *m* experts, specialists

fach'kundig *adj* expert, experienced

fach'lich *adj* professional; technical, specialized

Fach'mann *m* (-es;⁻er & -leute) expert, specialist

fachmännisch ['faxmεniʃ] *adj* expert

Fach'schule *f* vocational school

Fachsimpelei [faxzimpə'lai] *f* (-;-en) shoptalk

fachsimpeln ['faxzimpəln] *intr* talk shop

Fach'werk *n* framework; specialized book

Fach'zeitschrift *f* technical journal

Fackel ['fakəl] *f* (-;-n) torch

fackeln ['fakəln] *intr* flare; (fig) hesitate, dilly-dally

Fackelschein (**Fak'kelschein**) *m* torchlight

Fackelzug (**Fak'kelzug**) *m* torchlight procession

fade ['fɑdə] *adj* stale; (fig) dull

Faden ['fɑdən] *m* (-s;⁻) (& fig) thread; filament; (naut) fathom; keinen guten F. lassen an (*dat*) tear apart

Fa'denkreuz *n* crosshairs

Fa'dennudeln *pl* vermicelli

fadenscheinig [ˈfadən/aɪnɪç] *adj* threadbare

Fagott [faˈgɔt] *n* (-[e]s;-e) bassoon

fähig [ˈfɛ·ɪç] *adj* capable, able

Fä'higkeit *f* (-;-en) ability; talent

fahl [fal] *adj* pale; faded, washed-out

fahnden [ˈfandən] *intr* (nach) search (for), hunt (for)

Fahn'dung *f* (-;-en) search, hunt

Fahne [ˈfanə] *f* (-;-n) flag; pennant; (mil) colors; (typ) galley proof

Fah'nenabzug *m* galley proof

Fah'neneid *m* (mil) swearing in

Fah'nenflucht *f* desertion

fah'nenflüchtig *adj*—f. werden desert ‖ Fahnenflüchtige §5 *mf* deserter

Fah'nenmast *m* flagpole

Fah'nenträger -in §6 *mf* standard bearer

Fähnrich [ˈfenrɪç] *m* (-s;-e) officer cadet; F. zur See midshipman

Fahrbahn [ˈfarban] *f* (traffic) lane

fahrbar [ˈfarbar] *adj* passable; navigable; mobile

fahrbereit [ˈfarbəraɪt] *adj* in running order

Fahr'bereitschaft *f* (-;-en) motor pool

Fähre [ˈferə] *f* (-;-n) ferry

fahren [ˈfarən] §71 *tr* haul; (*lenken*) drive; (*Boot*) sail ‖ *intr* (SEIN) go; travel, drive; ride; es fuhr mir durch den Sinn it flashed across my mind; f. lassen run (*a boat, train*); let go; (fig) abandon, renounce; gut f. bei do well in; mit der Hand f. über (*acc*) run one's hand over; rechts f. (public sign) keep right; was ist in ihn gefahren? what's gotten into him?

fah'renlassen §104 *tr* let go of

Fah'rer -in §6 *mf* driver

Fah'rerflucht *f* hit-and-run case

Fahrgast [ˈfargast] *m* passenger

Fahrgeld [ˈfargelt] *n* fare

Fahrgelegenheit [ˈfargəleɡənhaɪt] *f* transportation (facilities)

Fahrgestell [ˈfargə/tel] *n* (-[e]s;-e) (aer) landing gear; (aut) chassis

fahrig [ˈfarɪç] *adj* fidgety

Fahrkarte [ˈfarkartə] *f* ticket

Fahr'kartenausgabe *f*, Fahr'kartenschalter *m* ticket window

fahrlässig [ˈfarlesɪç] *adj* negligent; fahrlässige Tötung involuntary manslaughter

Fahr'lässigkeit *f* (-;) negligence

Fahrlehrer -in [ˈfarlerər(ɪn)] §6 *mf* driving instructor

Fahrnis [ˈfarnɪs] *f* (-;-se) movables

Fährnis [ˈfernɪs] *f* (-;-se) (poet) danger

Fahrplan [ˈfarplan] *m* schedule

fahr'planmäßig *adj* scheduled ‖ *adv* on schedule, on time

Fahrpreis [ˈfarpraɪs] *m* fare

Fahrprüfung [ˈfarpryfʊŋ] *f* driver's test

Fahrrad [ˈfarrad] *n* bicycle

Fahrrinne [ˈfarrɪnə] *f* channel

Fahrschein [ˈfar/aɪn] *m* ticket

Fahrstuhl [ˈfar/tul] *m* elevator; (med) wheel chair

Fahr'stuhlführer -in §6 *mf* elevator operator

Fahr'stuhlschacht *m* elevator shaft

Fahrstunde [ˈfar/tundə] *f* driving lesson

Fahrt [fart] *f* (-;-en) ride, drive; trip; auf F. gehen go hiking; F. verlieren lose speed; freie F. haben have the green light; in F. kommen pick up speed; (fig) swing into action; in F. sein (coll) be keyed up; (coll) be on the warpath; (naut) be under way

Fährte [ˈfertə] *f* (-;-n) track, scent

Fahrt'unterbrechung *f* (-;-en) stopover

Fahrwasser [ˈfarvasər] *n* navigable water; (& fig) wake

Fahrwerk [ˈfarverk] *n* see Fahrgestell

Fahrzeug [ˈfartsɔɪk] *n* vehicle; vessel, craft

Fahr'zeugpark *m* (aut) fleet; (rr) rolling stock

fair [fer] *adj* fair

Fairneß [ˈfernes] *f* (-;) fairness

Fäkalien [feˈkaljən] *pl* feces

faktisch [ˈfaktɪ/] *adj* actual, factual

Fak-tor [ˈfaktɔr] *m* (-s;-toren [ˈtorən]) factor; foreman; (com) agent

Faktu-ra [fakˈtura] *f* (-;-ren [rən]) invoice

Fakultät [fakʊlˈtet] *f* (-;-en) (educ) department, school

falb [falp] *adj* claybank (*horse*)

Falke [ˈfalkə] *m* (-;-n) falcon; (pol) hawk

Fal'kenjagd *f* falconry

Falkner [ˈfalknər] *m* (-s;-) falconer

Fall [fal] *m* (-[e]s;ˉe) fall, drop; downfall; case; auf alle Fälle in any case; auf keinen F. in no case; auf jeden F. in any case; gesetzt den F. supposing; im besten F. at best; im schlimmsten F. if worst comes to worst; von F. zu F. according to circumstances; zu F. bringen; (fig) ruin; (parl) defeat; zu F. kommen (fig) collapse

Fall'brücke *f* drawbridge

Falle [ˈfalə] *f* (-;-n) (& fig) trap; (fig) pitfall; (*Bett*) (coll) sack

fallen [ˈfalən] §72 *intr* (SEIN) fall, drop; (*Schuß*) be heard; (mil) fall in battle; j-m ins Wort f. interrupt s.o. ‖ Fallen *n* (-s;) fall, drop; (fig) downfall

fällen [ˈfelən] *tr* (*Bäume*) fell; (*Urteil*) pass; (chem) precipitate

Fallensteller [ˈfalən/telər] *m* (-s;-) trapper

Fall'grube *f* trap, pit; (fig) pitfall

fällig [ˈfelɪç] *adj* due; payable

Fäl'ligkeit *f* (-;-en) due date

Fall'obst *n* windfall

Fall'rohr *n* soil pipe; (*e-r Dachrinne*) down spout

falls [fals] *conj* in case, if

Fall'schirm *m* parachute

Fall'schirmabsprung *m* parachute jump

Fall'schirmjäger *m* paratrooper

Fall'schirmspringer -in §6 *mf* parachutist, sky diver

Fall'strick *m* snare

Fall'sucht *f* (pathol) epilepsy

fall'süchtig *adj* (pathol) epileptic

Fall'tür *f* trapdoor

falsch [falʃ] *adj* false; *(verkehrt)* wrong; *(unecht)* counterfeit; **falsches Spiel** double-dealing ‖ *adv* wrongly; **f. gehen** (horol) be off; **f. schreiben** misspell; **f. schwören** perjure oneself; **f. singen** sing off key; **f. spielen** cheat; **f. verbunden** wrong number ‖ **Falsch** *m*—**ohne F.** without guile

fälschen ['fɛlʃən] *tr* falsify; *(Geld)* counterfeit; *(Urkunde)* forge

Fäl'scher –in §6 *mf* forger; counterfeiter

Falsch'geld *n* counterfeit money

Falsch'heit *f* (–;–en) falsity; deceitfulness

fälschlich ['fɛlʃlɪç] *adv* falsely

Falsch'münzer *m* counterfeiter

Falsch'spieler –in §6 *mf* card sharp

Fäl'schung *f* (–;–en) falsification; forgery; fake

Faltboot ['faltboːt] *n* collapsible boat

Falte ['faltə] *f* (–;–n) fold; *(Plissee)* pleat, crease; *(Runzel)* wrinkle

fälteln ['fɛltəln] *tr* pleat

falten ['faltən] *tr* fold; wrinkle

Fal'tenrock *m* pleated skirt

Falter ['faltər] *m* (–s;–) butterfly; *(Nacht-)* moth

faltig ['faltɪç] *adj* creased; wrinkled

Falz [falts] *m* (–es;–e) fold; *(Kerbe)* notch; (carp) rabbet

familiär [famɪ'ljeːr] *adj* intimate; familiar

Familie [fa'miːljə] *f* (–;–n) family

Fami'lienangehörige §5 *mf* member of the family

Fami'lienanschluß *m*—**F. haben** live as one of the family

Fami'lienname *m* last name

Fami'lienstand *m* marital status

Fami'lienstück *n* family heirloom

Fami'lienzuwachs *m* addition to the family

famos [fa'moːs] *adj* excellent, swell

Fan [fɛn] *m* (–s;–s) (sport) fan

Fanatiker –in [fa'naːtɪkər(ɪn)] §6 *mf* fanatic; (sport) fan

fanatisch [fa'naːtɪʃ] *adj* fanatic

fand [fant] *pret* of **finden**

Fanfare [fan'faːrə] *f* (–;–n) (mus) fanfare

Fang [faŋ] *m* (–[e]s;–e) capture; *(Fisch-)* haul, catch; *(Falle)* trap; *(Kralle)* claw

Fang'arm *m* tentacle

Fang'eisen *n* steel trap

fangen ['faŋən] §73 *tr* catch; trap; *(Ohrfeige)* get ‖ *ref* get caught ‖ **Fangen** *n*—**F. spielen** play catch

Fang'frage *f* loaded question

Fang'messer *n* hunting knife

Fang'zahn *m* fang; tusk

Farb– [farp] *comb.fm.* color

Farb'abzug *m* (phot) color print

Farb'aufnahme *f* color photograph

Farb'band *n* (–[e]s;–er) typewriter ribbon

Farbe ['farbə] *f* (–;–n) color; dye; *(zum Malen)* paint; *(Gesichts–)* complexion; (cards) suit; **F. bekennen** folow suit; (fig) lay one's cards on the table

färben ['fɛrbən] *tr* color, dye, tint ‖

ref take on color; change color; **sich rot f.** turn red; blush

far'benprächtig *adj* colorful

Fär'ber –in §6 *mf* dyer

Farb'fernsehen *n* color television

Farb'film *m* color film

farbig ['farbɪç] *adj* colored; colorful

Farb'kissen *n* ink pad

Farb'körper *m* pigment

farb'los *adj* colorless

Farb'spritzpistole *f* paint sprayer

Farb'stift *m* colored pencil; crayon

Farb'stoff *m* dye

Farb'ton *m* tone, hue, shade

Fär'bung *f* (–;–en) coloring; hue

Farm [farm] *f* (–;–en) farm

Farmer –in ['farmər(ɪn)] §6 *mf* farmer

Farn [farn] *m* (–[e]s;–e) fern

Farn'kraut *n* fern

Fasan [fa'zaːn] *m* (–s;–e & –en) pheasant

Fasching ['faʃɪŋ] *m* (–s;) carnival

Faschismus [fa'ʃɪsmus] *m* (–;) fascism

Faschist –in [fa'ʃɪst(ɪn)] §7 *mf* fascist

Faselei [fazə'laɪ] *f* (–;–en) drivel

Faselhans ['faːzəlhans] *m* (–';–e & ⁼e) blabberer; scatterbrain

faseln ['faːzəln] *intr* talk nonsense

Faser ['faːzər] *f* (–;–n) fiber; *(im Holz)* grain; *(Fädchen)* thread, string

Fa'serholzplatte *f* fiberboard

fasern ['faːzərn] *tr* unravel ‖ *ref* fray ‖ *intr* unravel

Fa'serschreiber *m* felt pen

Faß [fas] *n* (Fasses;Fässer) barrel, keg; *(Bütte)* vat, tub

Fassade [fa'saːdə] *f* (–;–n) façade

faßbar ['fasbaːr] *adj* comprehensible

Faß'bier *n* draft beer

fassen ['fasən] *tr* *(packen)* seize; *(erwischen)* apprehend; *(begreifen)* grasp; *(Edelstein)* mount; *(enthalten können)* hold, seat; *(Essen)* (mil) draw; **e–n Gedanken f.** form an idea; **in Worte f.** put into words; **j–n bei der Ehre f.** appeal to s.o.'s honor; **Tritt fassen** fall in step ‖ *ref* get hold of oneself; **in sich f.** include; **sich f. an** *(acc)* put one's hand to, touch; **sich in Geduld f.** exercise patience; **sich kurz f.** be brief ‖ *intr* take hold; *(nach)* grab (for); **es ist nicht zu f.** it is incomprehensible

Faß'hahn *m* tap, faucet

faß'lich *adj* conceivable

Fasson [fa'sõ] *f* (–;–en) style, cut

Fas'sung *f* (–;–en) composure; *(schriftlich)* draft; *(für Edelsteine)* setting, mounting; *(Brillenrand)* frame; *(Wortlaut)* wording; *(Lesart)* version; (elec) socket; **aus der F. bringen** upset; **außer F. sein** be beside onself

Fas'sungskraft *f* comprehension

fas'sungslos *adj* disconcerted, shaken

Fas'sungsvermögen *n* capacity; *(geistliches)* (powers of) comprehension

fast [fast] *adv* almost, nearly

fasten ['fastən] *intr* fast ‖ **Fasten** *n* (–s;) fasting

Fa'stenzeit *f* Lent, Lenten season

Fast'nacht *f* carnival

Fast'tag *m* day of fasting, fast day

faszinieren [fastsɪ'niːrən] *tr* fascinate
fatal [fa'tɑl] *adj* disastrous; (*unangenehm*) unpleasant
fauchen ['fauxən] *intr* hiss; (*Person*) snarl; (*Katze*) spit
faul [faul] *adj* rotten; lazy; bad, nasty; (*verdächtig*) fishy; (*Ausrede, Witz*) lame, poor; (sport) foul || **Faul** *n* (-s;-s) (sport) foul
Fäule ['foilə] *f* (-;) rot, decay
faulen ['faulən] *intr* rot, decay
faulenzen ['faulentsən] *intr* loaf
Faulenzer ['faulentsər] *m* (-s;-) loafer; (*Liegestuhl*) chaise longue; (*Linienblatt*) ruled sheet of paper
Faul′heit *f* (-;) laziness
faulig ['faulɪç] *adj* rotten, putrid
Fäulnis ['foilnɪs] *f* (-;) rot; **in F. übergehen** begin to rot
Faul′pelz *m* (coll) loafer
Faust [faust] *f* (-;ˮe) fist; **auf eigene F.** on one's own
faust′dick *adj* (coll) whopping
Faust′handschuh *m* mitten
Faust′kampf *m* boxing match
Fäustling ['foistlɪŋ] *m* (-[e]s;-e) mitten
Faust′schlag *m* punch, blow
Favorit –in [favo'riːt(ɪn)] §7 *mf* favorite
Faxen ['faksən] *pl* antics; faces; **F. machen** fool around; make a fuss; **F. schneiden** make faces
Fazit ['fɑtsɪt] *n* (-s;-e & -s) result; **das F. ziehen** sum it up
Feber ['feːbər] *m* (-[s];-) (Aust) February
Februar ['februːɑr] *m* (-[s];-e) February
fechten ['feçtən] §74 *intr* fence; fight; (*betteln*) beg
Feder ['feːdər] *f* (-;-n) feather; pen; quill; (mach) spring; **F. und Nut** (carp) tongue and groove
Fe′derball *m* shuttlecock
Fe′derballspiel *n* badminton
Fe′derbett *n* feather bed
Fe′derbusch *m* plume
Fe′derdecke *f* feather quilt
Federfuchser ['feːdərfuksər] *m* (-s;-) scribbler; hack writer
fe′derführend *adj* in charge
Fe′dergewicht *n* featherweight division
Federgewichtler ['feːdərgəvɪçtlər] *m* (-s;-) featherweight (boxer)
Fe′derhubtor *n* overhead door
Fe′derkernmatratze *f* innerspring mattress
Fe′derkiel *m* quill
Fe′derkraft *f* springiness; tension
Fe′derkrieg *m* paper war, war of words
fe′derleicht *adj* light as a feather
Fe′derlesen *n*—**ohne viel Federlesen(s)** without much ado
Fe′dermesser *n* penknife
federn ['feːdərn] *tr* fit with springs || *intr* be springy; (*Vogel*) moult; (gym) bounce
Fe′derring *m* lock washer
Fe′derstrich *m* stroke of the pen
Fe′derung *f* (-;) (aut) suspension
Fe′derzug *m* stroke of the pen
Fee [feː] *f* (-;Feen ['feːən]) fairy

Feg(e)feuer ['feːg(ə)foiˌər] *n* (-s;) purgatory
fegen ['feːgən] *tr* sweep; (*Laub*) tear off || *intr* (SEIN) tear along
Fehde ['feːdə] *f* (-;-n) feud
Feh′dehandschuh *m* gauntlet
fehl [feːl] *adj*—**f. am Ort** out of place || **Fehl** *m* (-[e]s;-e) blemish; fault
fehl– *comb.fm.* wide of the mark; mis-, incorrectly, wrongly || **Fehl**– *comb. fm.* missing; vain, unsuccessful; incorrect, wrong; faulty; negative
Fehl′anzeige *f* negative report
Fehl′ball *m* (tennis) fault
fehlbar ['feːlbɑr] *adj* fallible
Fehl′betrag *m* shortage, deficit
Fehl′bitte *f* vain request; **e–e F. tun** meet with a refusal
fehlen ['feːlən] *tr* miss || *intr* be absent; be missing; be lacking; fail, be unsuccessful; sin, err; (*dat*) miss, e.g., **er fehlt mir sehr** I miss him very much; (*dat*) lack, e.g., **ihm fehlt die Zeit** he lacks the time; **was fehlt Ihnen?** what's wrong with you? || *impers*—**es fehlte nicht viel, und ich wäre gefallen** I came close to falling
Fehler ['feːlər] *m* (-s;-) mistake, error; flaw, imperfection; blunder
feh′lerfrei *adj* faultless, flawless
feh′lerhaft *adj* faulty
feh′lerlos *adj* faultless, flawless
Fehl′geburt *f* miscarriage
fehl′gehen §82 *intr* (SEIN) go wrong; (*Schuß*)
Fehl′gewicht *n* short weight
fehl′greifen §88 *intr* miss one's hold; (fig) make a mistake
Fehl′griff *m* mistake, blunder
Fehl′leistung *f* (Freudian) slip
fehl′leiten *tr* (& fig) misdirect
Fehl′schlag *m* miss; failure, disappointment; (baseball) foul
Fehl′schluß *m* false inference; fallacy
Fehl′spruch *m* miscarriage of justice
Fehl′start *m* false start
Fehl′tritt *m* false step; (fig) slip
Fehl′wurf *m* (*beim Würfeln*) crap
fehl′zünden *intr* backfire
feien ['faiən] *tr*—**gefeit sein gegen** be immune to; **j–n f. gegen** make s.o. immune to
Feier ['faiˌər] *f* (-;-n) celebration; ceremony
Fei′erabend *m* closing time
fei′erlich *adj* solemn
Fei′erlichkeit *f* (-;-en) solemnity; **Feierlichkeiten** festivities; ceremonies
feiern ['faiˌərn] *tr* celebrate, observe; honor || *intr* rest from work
Fei′erstunde *f* commemorative ceremony
Fei′ertag *m* holiday; holy day
feig [faik] *adj* cowardly
feige ['faigə] *adj* cowardly || **Feige** *f* (-;-n) fig
Feig′heit *f* (-;) cowardice
feig′herzig *adj* faint-hearted
Feigling ['faiklɪŋ] *m* (-s;-e) coward
feil [fail] *adj* for sale
feil′bieten §58 *tr* offer for sale
Feile ['failə] *f* (-;-n) file

feilen [´faɪlən] *tr* file

feilschen [´faɪlʃən] *intr* (**um**) haggle (over), dicker (about)

Feilspäne [´faɪlʃpɛnə] *pl* filings

fein [faɪn] *adj* fine; delicate; fancy

feind [faɪnt] *adj* hostile || **Feind** *m* (-[e]s;-e) enemy, foe

Feind- *comb.fm.* enemy, hostile; against the enemy

Feind´fahrt *f* (nav) operation against the enemy

Feind´flug *m* (aer) combat mission

Feindin [´faɪndɪn] *f* (-;-nen) enemy

feind´lich *adj* hostile

Feind´schaft *f* (-;-en) enmity

feind´selig *adj* hostile

Feind´seligkeit *f* (-;-en) hostility, animosity; hostile action

fein´fühlend, fein´fühlig *adj* sensitive

Fein´gefühl *n* sensitivity

Fein´heit *f* (-;-en) fineness, fine quality; delicacy; subtlety

Fein´mechanik *f* precision engineering

Feinschmecker [´faɪnʃmɛkər] *m* (-s;-) gourmet, epicure

fein´sinnig *adj* sensitive; subtle

feist [faɪst] *adj* fat, plump

Feld [fɛlt] *n* (-[e]s;-er) field; panel, compartment; (checkers, chess) square; **auf dem Felde** in the field(s); **auf freiem Felde** in the open; **aufs F. gehen** go to (work in) the fields; **das F. behaupten** stand one's ground; **ins F. ziehen** take the field

Feld´bau *m* agriculture

Feld´becher *m* collapsible drinking cup

Feld´bett *n* army cot; camping cot

Feld´blume *f* wild flower

Feld´bluse *f* army jacket

feld´dienstfähig *adj* fit for active duty

Feld´flasche *f* canteen

Feld´geistliche *m* (-n;-n) army chaplain

Feld´gendarm *m* military police

Feld´gendarmerie *f* military police

Feld´geschrei *n* battle cry

Feld´geschütz *n* field gun, field piece

Feld´herr *m* general; commander in chief

Feld´lager *n* bivouac, camp

Feld´lazarett *n* evacuation hospital

Feld´lerche *f* skylark

Feld´marschall *m* field marshal

feld´marschmäßig *adj* with full field pack

Feld´messer *m* surveyor

Feld´meßkunst *f* (-;) surveying

Feld´mütze *f* (mil) overseas cap

Feld´postamt *n* army post office

Feld´schlacht *f* battle

Feld´stecher *m* field glasses

Feldwebel [´fɛltvebəl] *m* (-s;-) sergeant

Feld´zeichen *n* ensign, standard

Feld´zug *m* campaign

Felge [´fɛlgə] *f* (-;-n) rim

Fell [fɛl] *n* (-[e]s;-e) pelt; skin; fur; **ein dickes F. haben** be thick-skinned

Fels [fɛls] *m* (-es & -en;-en) rock; cliff; **zackige Felsen** crags

Fels´block *m* boulder

Felsen [´fɛlzən] *m* (-s;-) rock; cliff

fel´senfest *adj* firm as a rock

Fel´sengebirge *n* Rocky Mountains

Fel´senklippe *f* cliff

Fel´senriff *n* reef

felsig [´fɛlzɪç] *adj* rocky

Fenster [´fɛnstər] *n* (-s;-) window

Fen´sterbrett *n* window sill

Fen´sterflügel *m* casement

Fen´sterladen *m* window shutter

Fen´sterleder *n* chamois

Fen´sterplatz *m* (rr) window seat

Fen´sterrahmen *m* window frame; sash

Fen´sterrosette *f* rose window

Fen´sterscheibe *f* windowpane

Ferien [´ferjən] *pl* vacation; (parl) recess

Fe´rienreisende §5 *mf* vacationer

Fe´rienstimmung *f* holiday spirit

Ferkel [´fɛrkəl] *n* (-s;-) piglet

Ferkelei [fɛrkə´laɪ] *f* (-;-en) obscenity

fern [fɛrn] *adj* far, distant; (*entlegen*) remote; (*weit fort*) far away

Fern´amt *n* long-distance exchange

Fern´anruf *m* long-distance call

Fern´aufklärung *f* long-range reconnaissance

Fern´bedienung *f* remote control

fern´bleiben §62 *intr* (SEIN) (*dat*) stay away (from) || **Fernbleiben** *n* (-s;) absence; absenteeism

Fern´blick *m* distant view, vista

Ferne [´fɛrnə] *f* (-;-n) distance

ferner [´fɛrnər] *adj* remote, distant || *adv* further; moreover

Fern´fahrer *m* long-distance trucker

Fern´fahrt *f* long-distance trip

Fern´gang *m* (aut) overdrive

Fern´geschoß *n* long-range missile

Fern´geschütz *n* long-range gun

Fern´gespräch *n* long-distance call; toll call

Fern´glas *n* binoculars

fern´halten §90 *tr & ref* keep away

Fern´heizung *f* heating from a central heating plant

Fern´kursus *m* correspondence course

Fern´laster *m* long-distance truck

fern´lenken *tr* guide by remote control

Fern´lenkrakete *f* guided missile

Fern´lenkung *f* (-;-en) remote control

Fern´lenkwaffe *f* guided missile

Fern´licht *n* (aut) high beam

fern´liegen §108 *impers*—**es liegt mir fern zu** (*inf*) I'm far from (*ger*)

Fernmelde- [fɛrnmɛldə] *comb.fm.* communications, signal

Fern´meldetruppen *pl* signal corps

Fern´meldewesen *n* telecommunications system

fern´mündlich *adj & adv* by telephone

Fern´objektiv *n* telephoto lens

Fernost- *comb.fm.* Far Eastern

fern´östlich *adj* Far Eastern

Fern´rohr *n* telescope

Fern´rohraufsatz *m* telescopic gun sight

Fern´ruf *m* telephone call; telephone number

Fern´schnellzug *m* long-distance express

Fern´schreiber *m* teletype, telex

Fernseh- [fɛrnze] *comb.fm.* television

Fern´sehansager **-in** §6 *mf* television announcer

Fern´sehapparat *m* television set

Fern′sehbildröhre f picture tube
fern′sehen §138 intr watch television
|| **Fernsehen** n (-s;) television
Fern′seher m (-s;-) television set; television viewer
Fern′sehgerät n television set
Fern′sehkanal m television channel
Fern′sehschau f television show
Fern′sehsendung f telecast
Fern′sehteilnehmer –in §6 mf televiewer
Fern′sehübertragung f telecast
Fern′sicht f view, vista; panorama
fern′sichtig adj far-sighted
Fernsprech– [fern/pre̜ç] comb.fm. telephone
Fern′sprechauftragsdienst m answering service
Fern′sprechautomat m pay phone
Fern′sprecher m telephone
Fern′sprechzelle f telephone booth
fern′stehen §146 intr (dat) have no personal contact (with); (dat) not be close (to)
Fern′stehende §5 mf outsider; disinterested observer
fern′steuern tr guide by remote control
Fern′studium n correspondence course
Ferse [′fɛrzə] f (-;-n) heel
Fer′sengeld n—F. geben take to one's heels
fertig [′fɛrtɪç] adj finished; ready; (kaputt) ruined, done for
fertig–, Fertig– comb.fm. final; finished; finishing; prefabricated
fer′tigbringen §65 tr finish, get done; bring about; **es glatt f. zu** (inf) be capable of (ger); **es nicht f., ihm das zu sagen** not have the heart to tell him that
fertigen [′fɛrtɪgən] tr manufacture
Fer′tigkeit f (-;-en) skill
Fer′tigrasen m sod
fer′tigstellen tr complete; get ready
Fer′tigung f (-;-en) manufacture, production; copy, draft
Fes [fɛs] n (mus) F flat
fesch [fɛʃ] adj smart, chic
Fessel [′fɛsəl] f (-;-n) fetter, bond; (anat) ankle; (vet) fetlock
Fes′selballon m captive balloon
fesseln [′fɛsəln] tr chain, tie; (bezaubern) captivate, arrest; (mil) contain; **ans Bett gefesselt** confined to bed, bedridden
fes′selnd adj fascinating, gripping; (Personalität) magnetic
fest [fɛst] adj firm; solid; tight; stationary; steady; (Preis, Kost, Einkommen, Gehalt) fixed; (Schlaf) sound; (mil) fortified; **feste Straße** improved road || **Fest** n (-es;-e) feast; festival
fest′backen intr (SEIN) cake (on)
fest′besoldet adj with a fixed salary
fest′binden §59 tr (an dat) tie (to)
Fest′essen n banquet
fest′fahren §71 tr run aground || ref come to a standstill
fest′halten §90 tr hold on to || ref (an dat) cling (to); hold on (to)
festigen [′fɛstɪgən] tr strengthen; consolidate || ref grow stronger

Fe′stigkeit f (-;-en) firmness; steadiness; strength
Fe′stigung f (-;) strengthening; consolidation; stabilization
Fest′land n continent
fest′legen tr fix, determine, set; (Anordnung) lay down; (fin, naut) tie up; **j–n f. auf** (acc) pin s.o. down on || **ref** (auf acc) commit oneself (to)
fest′lich adj festive
Fest′lichkeit f (-;-en) festivity
fest′liegen §108 intr be stranded
fest′machen tr fix; (fig) settle || intr (naut) moor
Fest′mahl n feast
Fest′nahme f (-;-n) arrest
fest′nehmen §116 tr arrest, apprehend
Fest′rede f ceremonial speech
Fest′saal m grand hall, banquet hall
fest′schnallen tr buckle up || ref fasten one's seat belt
Fest′schrift f homage volume
fest′setzen tr fix, set || ref settle down (in a town, etc.)
fest′sitzen intr fit tight; be stuck
Fest′spiel n play for a festive occasion; **Festspiele** (mus, theat) festival
fest′stehen §146 intr stand firm; (Tatsache) be certain || impers—**es steht fest** it is a fact
fest′stehend adj stationary; (Achse) fixed; (Tatsache) established
feststellbar [′fɛst/tɛlbar] adj ascertainable
Fest′stellbremse f hand brake
fest′stellen tr ascertain; (unbeweglich machen) lock, secure; (Tatbestand) find out, establish; (angeben) state; (Schaden) assess; (Kurs) (fin) set, fix
Fest′stellschraube f set screw
Fest′tag m feastday; holiday
Fe′stung f (-;-en) fortress
Fe′stungsgraben m moat
Fest′wagen m float
Fest′wert m standard value; (math, phys) constant
Fest′wiese f fairground
fest′ziehen §163 tr pull tight
Fest′zug m procession
Fetisch [′fetɪ/] m (-[e]s;-e) fetish
fett [fɛt] adj fat; (Boden, Milch, Gemisch) rich; (Zeiten, Leben) of plenty || **Fett** n (-[e]s;-e) fat; (Schmalz) lard; (Pflanzen–) shortening; (Schmier–) grease
Fett′auge n speck of fat
Fett′druck m boldface type
fetten [′fɛtən] tr grease, lubricate
Fett′fleck m grease spot
fettig [′fɛtɪç] adj fatty, greasy, oily
Fett′kloß m (coll) fatso
Fett′kohle f bituminous coal
fettleibig [′fɛtlaɪbɪç] adj stout
Fettnäpfchen [′fɛtnɛpfçən] n—**bei j–m ins F. treten** hurt s.o.'s feelings; **ins F. treten** put one's foot in it
Fett′presse f (aut) grease gun
Fett′spritze f (aut) grease gun
Fett′sucht f obesity
Fett′wanst m (sl) fatso
Fetzen [′fɛtsən] m (-s;-) rag; bit, scrap; (Aust) dishcloth; **daß die F. fliegen** violently
feucht [fɔɪçt] adj moist, damp, humid

feuchten ['fɔɪçtən] tr moisten, dampen
Feuch'tigkeit f (-;) moisture, damp-
ness, humidity
feudal [fɔɪ'dɑl] adj feudal; (fig) mag-
nificent
Feudalismus [fɔɪda'lɪsmʊs] m (-;)
feudalism
Feuer ['fɔɪ·ər] n (-s;-) fire
Feu'eralarm m fire alarm
Feu'eralarmübung f fire drill
feu'erbeständig adj fireproof
Feu'erbestattung f cremation
Feu'erbrand m firebrand
Feu'ereifer m enthusiasm, zeal
Feu'ereinstellung f cease-fire
feu'erfest adj fireproof
Feu'erfliege f firefly
feu'erflüssig adj molten
Feu'ergefährlich adj inflammable
Feu'erhahn m hydrant, fireplug
Feu'erhaken m poker
Feu'erherd m fireplace
Feu'erkampf m fire fight, gun battle
Feu'erkraft f (mil) fire power
Feu'erleiter f fire ladder; (Nottreppe)
fire escape
Feu'erlinie f firing line
Feu'erlöscher m fire extinguisher
Feu'ermelder m fire alarm
Feu'ermeldung f fire alarm
feuern ['fɔɪ·ərn] tr fire; (coll) fire,
sack || intr fire, shoot
Feu'erprobe f ordeal by fire; acid test
Feu'ersalve f fusillade
Feu'erschneise f firebreak
Feu'erspritze f fire engine
Feu'erstein m flint
Feu'ertaufe f baptism of fire
Feu'erversicherung f fire insurance
Feu'erwache f firehouse
Feu'erwalze f (mil) creeping barrage
Feu'erwehr f fire department
Feu'erwehrmann m (-[e]s;ᵘer &
-leute) fireman
Feu'erwerk n fireworks
Feu'erwerkskörper m firecracker
Feu'erzange f fire tongs
Feu'erzeug n cigarette lighter
Feu'erzeugbenzin n lighter fluid
feurig ['fɔɪrɪç] adj fiery; ardent
Fiasko [fɪ'asko] n (-s;-s) fiasco
Fibel ['fibəl] f (-;-n) primer; (archeol)
fibula
Fiber ['fibər] f (-;-n) fiber
Fichte ['fɪçta] f (-;-n) spruce; pine
Fich'tennadel f pine needle
fidel [fɪ'del] adj jolly, cheerful
Fieber ['fibər] n (-s;-) fever; das F.
messen take the temperature
fie'berhaft adj feverish
fieberig ['fibərɪç] adj feverish
fie'berkrank adj running a fever
fiebern ['fibərn] intr be feverish
Fie'berphantasie f delirium
Fie'bertabelle f temperature chart
Fiedel ['fidəl] f (-;-n) fiddle
Fie'delbogen m fiddlestick
fiel [fil] pret of fallen
Figur [fɪ'gur] f (-;-en) figure; (cards)
face card
figürlich [fɪ'gyrlɪç] adj figurative
fiktiv [frk'tif] adj fictitious
Filet [fɪ'le] n (-s;-s) (culin) fillet

Filiale [fɪl'jɑlə] f (-;-n) branch
Filia'lengeschäft n chain store
Filigran [fɪlɪ'grɑn] n (-s;-e), Fili-
gran'arbeit f filigree
Film [fɪlm] m (-s;-e) film; (cin) movie
Film'atelier n motion-picture studio
Film'empfindlichkeit f film speed
Film'kulisse f (cin) movie set
Film'leinwand f movie screen
Film'probe f screen test
Film'regisseur m (cin) director
Film'wesen n motion-picture industry
Filter ['fɪltər] m & n (-s;-) filter
Fil'teranlage f filtration plant
Fil'terkaffee m drip-grind coffee
Fil'termundstück n filter tip
filtern ['fɪltərn] tr filter, strain
filtrieren [fɪl'triran] tr filter
Filz [fɪlts] m (-es;-e) felt; (coll)
miser, skinflint
Filz'schreiber m felt pen
Fimmel ['fɪməl] m (-s;-) craze, fad
-fimmel m comb.fm. mania for
Finanz [fɪ'nants] f (-;-en) finance
Finanz- comb.fm. financial, fiscal
Finanz'amt n internal revenue service
Finanz'ausschuß m (adm) ways and
means committee
Finanzen [fɪ'nantsən] pl finances
finanziell [fɪnan'tsjel] adj financial
finanzieren [fɪnan'tsiran] tr finance
Finanz'minister m secretary of the
treasury
Finanz'ministerium n treasury department
Finanz'wesen n finances
Finanz'wirtschaft f public finances
Findelkind ['fɪndəlkɪnt] n foundling
finden ['fɪndən] §59 tr find; f. Sie
nicht? don't you think so? || ref be
found; ach, das wird sich schon f.
oh, we'll see about that; es fanden
sich there were; es findet sich it
happens, it turns out; sich f. in (acc)
resign oneself to; sie haben sich ge-
funden they were united || intr find
one's way
findig ['fɪndɪç] adj resourceful
Findling ['fɪntlɪŋ] m (-s;-e) foundling;
(geol) boulder
fing [fɪŋ] pret of fangen
Finger ['fɪŋər] m (-s;-) finger
Fin'gerabdruck m fingerprint
fin'gerfertig adj deft
Fin'gerhut m thimble; (bot) foxglove
fingern ['fɪŋərn] tr finger
Fin'gerspitze f finger tip; bis in die
Fingerspitzen through and through
Fin'gerspitzengefühl n sensitivity
Fin'gersprache f sign language
Fingerzeig ['fɪŋərtsaɪk] m (-s;-e) hint
fingieren [fɪŋ'giran] tr feign
fingiert [fɪŋ'girt] adj fictitious
Fink [fɪŋk] m (-en;-en) finch
Finne ['fɪna] m (-n;-n) Finn || f (-;
-n) fin; (Ausschlag) pimple
Fin'nenausschlag m acne
Finnin ['fɪnɪn] f (-;-nen) Finn
finnisch ['fɪnɪʃ] adj Finnish
Finnland ['fɪnlant] n (-s;) Finland
finster ['fɪnstər] adj dark; gloomy
Finsternis ['fɪnstərnɪs] f (-;) dark-
ness; gloom

Finte ['fɪntə] f (-;-n) feint; trick

Firlefanz ['fɪrləfants] m (-es;) junk; F. treiben fool around

Fir·ma ['fɪrma] f (-;-men [mən]) firm

Firmament [fɪrma'ment] n (-[e]s;-e) firmament

firmen ['fɪrmən] tr (Cath) confirm

Fir'menschild n (com) name plate

Fir'menwert m (com) good will

Firmling ['fɪrmlɪŋ] m (-s;-e) (Cath) person to be confirmed

Fir'mung f (-;-en) (Cath) confirmation

Fir·nis ['fɪrnɪs] m (-ses;-se) varnish; mit F. streichen varnish

firnissen ['fɪrnɪsən] tr varnish

First [fɪrst] m (-es;-e) (archit) ridge (of roof); (poet) mountain ridge

Fis [fɪs] n (-;-) (mus) F sharp

Fisch [fɪʃ] m (-es;-e) fish

fischen ['fɪʃən] tr fish for, catch || intr (nach) fish (for)

Fi'scher m (-s;-) fisherman

Fischerei [fɪʃə'raɪ] f (-;-en) fishing; fishery; fishing trade

Fi'schergerät n fishing tackle

Fisch'fang m catch, haul

Fisch'gräte f fishbone

Fisch'grätenmuster n (tex) herringbone

Fisch'händler –in §6 mf fishmonger

fischig ['fɪʃɪç] adj fishy

Fisch'kunde f ichthyology

Fisch'laich m spawn, fish eggs

Fisch'otter m & f otter

Fisch'rogen m roe

Fisch'schuppe f scale (of a fish)

Fisch'zug m (& fig) catch

fiskalisch [fɪs'kalɪʃ] adj fiscal

Fis·kus ['fɪskus] m (-;-kusse & -ken [kən]) treasury

Fistelstimme ['fɪstəl'tɪmə] f falsetto

Fittich ['fɪtɪç] m (-es;-e) (poet) wing

fix [fɪks] adj (Idee, Preis) fixed; (flink) smart, sharp; fix und fertig all set; all in; done for; fix und fertig mit through with; mach fix! make it snappy!

fixen ['fɪksən] intr sell short

fixieren [fɪ'ksirən] tr fix, decide upon; stare fixedly at; (phot) fix

Fixier'mittel n (phot) fixer

flach [flax] adj flat, level; shallow; (Relief) low; (fig) dull

Fläche ['flɛçə] f (-;-n) surface; plain; expanse; facet; (geom) area

Flä'cheninhalt m (geom) area

Flä'chenraum m surface area

flach'fallen §72 intr (SEIN) (coll) fall flat, flop

Flach'heit f (-;) flatness; shallowness

Flach'land n lowland

Flach'relief n low relief, bas-relief

Flach'rennen n flat racing

Flachs [flaks] m (-es;-e) flax

flachsen ['flaksən] intr (coll) kid

flächse(r)n ['flɛksə(r)n] adj flaxen

Flach'zange f pliers

flackern ['flakərn] intr flicker; (Stimme) quaver, shake

Flagge ['flagə] f (-;-n) flag (esp. for signaling or identification)

Flag'genmast m flagpole

Flag'genstange f flagstaff

Flagg'schiff n flagship

Flak [flak] abbr (Flugzeugabwehrkanone) anti-aircraft gun

Flak'feuer n flak

Flakon [fla'kõ] m & n (-s;-s) perfume bottle

Flamme ['flamə] f (-;-n) flame

flammen ['flamən] intr blaze; be in flames

flam'mend adj passionate

Fla'mmenwerfer m flame thrower

Flandern ['flandərn] n (-s;) Flanders

flandrisch ['flandrɪʃ] adj Flemish

Flanell [fla'nel] m (-s;-e) flannel

Flanke ['flaŋkə] f (-;-n) flank

Flan'kenfeuer n (mil) enfilade; mit F. bestreichen enfilade

flankieren [flaŋ'kirən] tr flank

Flansch [flanʃ] m (-es;-e) flange

Flasche ['flaʃə] f (-;-n) bottle; (coll) flop; (mach) pulley

Fla'schengranate f Molotov cocktail

Fla'schenzug m block and tackle; (coll) pulley

Flaschner ['flaʃnər] m (-s;-) plumber

flatterhaft ['flatərhaft] adj fickle

flattern ['flatərn] intr flutter, flap

flau [flau] adj stale; (schwach) feeble, faint; (fade) dull, lifeless; (com) slack; (phot) overexposed; mir ist f. (im Magen) I feel queezy

Flaum [flaum] m (-[e]s;) down; (am Gesicht, am Pfirsich) fuzz

flaumig ['flaumɪç] adj downy, fluffy

Flause ['flauzə] f (-;-n) fib; Flausen funny ideas, nonsense

Flaute ['flautə] f (-;-n) (com) slack period; (naut) dead calm

fläzen ['flɛtsən] ref sprawl out

Flechse ['flɛksə] f (-;-n) (dial) sinew, tendon

Flechte ['flɛçtə] f (-;-n) plait; (bot) lichen; (pathol) ringworm

flechten ['flɛçtən] §74 tr braid, plait; (Körbe) weave

Fleck [flek] m (-[e]s;-e & -en) spot; blemish; (Flicken, Landstück) patch

Flecken ['flekən] m (-s;-) spot; piece of land; (Markt–) market town

fleckenlos ['flek'kenlos] adj spotless

Fleck'fieber n spotted fever

fleckig ['flekɪç] adj spotty; splotchy

fleddern ['fledərn] tr (sl) rob

Fledermaus ['fledərmaus] f bat

Flegel ['flegəl] m (-s;-) flail; (coll) lout, boor

Flegelei [flegə'laɪ] f (-;) rudeness

fle'gelhaft adj uncouth, boorish

Fle'geljahre pl awkward age

flehen ['fleən] intr plea; zu j-m f. implore s.o. || Flehen n (-s;-) supplication

Fleisch [flaɪʃ] n (-es;) flesh; meat; sich ins eigene F. schneiden cut one's own throat; wildes F. proud flesh

Fleisch'bank f (-;̈-e) meat counter

Fleisch'beil n cleaver

Fleisch'beschau f meat inspection

Fleisch'brühe f broth

Flei'scher m (-s;-) butcher

Flei'scheslust f (-;) lust

Fleisch'farbe f flesh color

fleisch'fressend adj carnivorous

Fleisch'hacker (-s;-) *m*, **Fleisch'hauer** *m* (-s;-) butcher

fleischig ['flaɪʃɪç] *adj* fleshy; meaty

fleisch'lich *adj* carnal

Fleisch'markt *m* meat market

Fleisch'pastete *f* meat pie

Fleisch'saft *m* meat juice, gravy

Fleisch'salat *m* diced-meat salad

Fleisch'speise *f* meat course

Fleisch'spieß *m* skewer

Fleischwerdung ['flaɪʃverdʊŋ] *f* (-;) incarnation

Fleisch'wolf *m* meat grinder

Fleisch'wunde *f* flesh wound, laceration

Fleisch'wurst *f* pork sausage

Fleiß [flaɪs] *m* (-es;) diligence, industry; **mit F.** intentionally

fleißig ['flaɪsɪç] *adj* diligent, hardworking

flektieren [flɛk'tirən] *tr* inflect

fletschen ['flɛtʃən] *tr* bare (*teeth*)

Flexion [flɛk'sjon] *f* (-;-en) (gram) inflection

flicken ['flɪkən] *tr* patch, repair || **Flicken** *m* (-s;-) patch

Flick'schuster *m* cobbler

Flick'werk *n* patchwork; hotchpotch; (*Pfuscherei*) bungling job

Flick'zeug *n* repair kit

Flieder ['flidər] *m* (-s;-) lilac

Fliege ['fligə] *f* (-;-n) fly; (coll) bow tie

fliegen ['fligən] §57 *tr* fly, pilot || *intr* (SEIN) fly; (coll) get sacked; **in die Luft f.** blow up

Flie'genfenster *n* window screen

Flie'gengewicht *n* flyweight division

Fliegengewichtler ['fligəngəvɪçtlər] *m* (-s;-) flyweight (boxer)

Flie'gengitter *n* screen

Flie'genklappe *f*, **Flie'genklatsche** *f* fly swatter

Flie'genpilz *m* toadstool

Flie'ger *m* (-s;-) flyer

Flieger– *comb.fm.* air-force; air, aerial; flying; airman's

Flie'gerabwehr *f* anti-aircraft defense

Flie'geralarm *m* air-raid alarm

Flie'gerangriff *m* air raid

Flie'gerheld *m* (aer) ace

Flie'gerhorst *m* air base

Flie'gerin *f* (-;-nen) flyer

Flie'gerschaden *m* air-raid damage

fliehen ['fli-ən] §75 *tr* run away from; avoid || *intr* (SEIN) flee

Flieh'kraft *f* (-;) centrifugal force

Fliese ['flizə] *f* (-;-n) tile

Flie'senleger *m* tiler, tile man

Fließband ['flisbant] *n* (-[e]s;-er) assembly line

fließen ['flisən] §76 *intr* (SEIN) flow

flie'ßend *adj* (*Wasser*) running; (fig) fluent

Fließheck ['flishɛk] *n* (aut) fastback

Fließpapier ['flispapir] *n* blotting paper

flimmern ['flɪmərn] *intr* glimmer; glisten, shimmer; flicker

flink [flɪŋk] *adj* nimble, quick; **mach mal f.!** get a move on!

Flinte ['flɪntə] *f* (-;-n) shotgun; gun

Flin'tenlauf *m* gun barrel

flirren ['flɪrən] *intr* shimmer

Flirt [flɪrt] *m* (-s;-s) flirtation; boyfriend, girlfriend

flirten ['flɪrtən] *intr* flirt

Flitter ['flɪtər] *m* (-s;-) sequins; (*Scheinglanz*) flashiness

Flit'terglanz *m* flashiness

Flit'tergold *m* gold tinsel

Flit'terkram *m* trinkets

Flit'terstaat *m* flashy clothes

Flit'terwochen *pl* honeymoon

flitzen ['flɪtsən] *intr* (SEIN) flit

flocht [flɔxt] *pret* of flechten

Flocke ['flɔkə] *f* (-;-n) flake; tuft

flog [flok] *pret* of fliegen

floh [flo] *pret* of fliehen || **Floh** *m* (-s;ˑe) flea; **j-m e-n F. ins Ohr setzen** put a bug in s.o.'s ear

Floh'hüpfspiel *n* tiddlywinks

Flor [flor] *m* (-s;-e) bloom || *m* (-s;-e & ˑe) gauze; (tex) nap, pile

Flor'band *n* (-[e]s;-er) crepe; mourning band

Florett [flo'rɛt] *n* (-s;-e) foil

florieren [flo'rirən] *intr* flourish

Floskel ['flɔskəl] *f* (-;-n) rhetorical ornament, flowery phrase

Floß [flos] *n* (-es;ˑe) raft

Flosse ['flɔsə] *f* (-;-n) fin; (aer) stabilizer

flößen ['fløsən] *tr* float

Flöte ['fløtə] *f* (-;-n) flute; (cards) flush

flöten ['fløtən] *tr* play on the flute || *intr* play the flute; **f. gehen** (fig) go to the dogs

flott [flɔt] *adj* afloat; brisk, lively; gay; chic, dashing

Flotte ['flɔtə] *f* (-;-n) fleet

Flot'tenstützpunkt *m* naval base

flott'gehend *adj* (com) brisk, lively

Flottille [flɔ'tɪljə] *f* (-;-n) flotilla

flott'machen *tr* set afloat; (fig) get going again

Flöz [fløts] *n* (-es;-e) (min) seam

Fluch [flux] *m* (-[e]s;ˑe) curse

fluchen ['fluxən] *intr* curse

Flucht [fluxt] *f* (-;-en) flight; escape; straight line, alignment; (*Häuser-*) row; (*Spielraum*) space, leeway; (*Zimmer-*) suite; **außerhalb der F.** out of line; **in die F. schlagen** put to flight

flüchten ['flʏçtən] *ref* (an *acc*, in *acc*) take refuge (in), have recourse (to) || *intr* (SEIN) flee; escape; (vor *dat*) run away (from)

flüchtig ['flʏçtɪç] *adj* fugitive; fleeting; cursory, superficial; hurried; (chem) volatile; **f. sein** be on the run; **f. werden** escape, flee

Flüch'tigkeitsfehler *m* oversight, slip

Flüchtling ['flʏçtlɪŋ] *m* (-s;-e) fugitive; refugee

Flücht'lingslager *n* refugee camp

Flug [fluk] *m* (-[e]s;ˑe) flight

Flug'abwehr *f* anti-aircraft defense

Flugabwehr– *comb.fm.* anti-aircraft

Flug'anschluß *m* plane connection

Flug'aufgabe *f*, **Flug'auftrag** *m* (aer) mission

Flug'bahn *f* line of flight; trajectory

Flug'blatt *n* leaflet, flyer

Flügel ['flygəl] m (-s;-) wing; (e-r Doppeltür) leaf; (mus) grand piano

Flü'geladjutant m aide-de-camp

Flü'gelfenster n casement window

Flü'gelmutter f wing nut

Flü'gelschlag m flap of the wings

Flü'gelschraube f thumb screw

Flü'geschraubenmutter f wing nut

Flü'geltür f folding door

Flug'gast m (aer) passenger

flügge ['flygə] adj (Vogel) fledged; (fig) ready to go on one's own

Flug'gesellschaft f airline company

Flug'hafen m airport

Flug'hafenbefeuerung f airport lights

Flug'kapitän m captain, pilot

Flug'karte f plane ticket; aeronautical chart

flug'klar adj ready for take-off

Flug'körper m missile; space vehicle

Flug'leitung f air-traffic control

Flug'linie f air route; airline

Flug'meldesystem n air-raid warning system

Flug'motor m aircraft engine

Flug'ortung f (aer) navigation

Flug'plan m flight schedule

Flug'platz m airfield, airport

Flug'post f air mail

Flug'preis m air fare

flugs [fluks] adv quickly; at once

Flug'schein m plane ticket

Flug'schneise f air lane

Flug'schrift f pamphlet

Flug'strecke f flying distance

Flug'stützpunkt m air base

flug'tauglich, flug'tüchtig adj airworthy

Flug'techniker –in §6 mf aeronautical engineer

Flug'verbot n (aer) grounding

Flug'verkehr m air traffic

Flug'wesen n aviation; aeronautics

Flug'wetter n flying weather

Flug'zeug n airplane, aircraft

Flug'zeugabwehrgeschütz n, **Flug'zeugabwehrkanone** f anti-aircraft gun

Flug'zeugführer m pilot; zweiter F. copilot, second officer

Flug'zeugführerschein m pilot's license

Flug'zeuggeschwader n wing (consisting of 3 squadrons of 9 planes each)

Flug'zeugkreuzer m, **Flug'zeugmutterschiff** n seaplane tender, seaplane carrier

Flug'zeugrumpf m fuselage

Flug'zeugstaffel f squadron (consisting of 9 planes)

Flug'zeugträger m aircraft carrier

Flug'zeugwerk n aircraft factory

Flunder ['flundər] f (-;-n) flounder

Flunkerer ['fluŋkərər] m (-s;-) fibber

flunkern ['fluŋkərn] intr fib

Flunsch [flunʃ] m (-es;-e) face; e-n F. ziehen (or machen) make a face

Fluor ['flu·ər] n (-s;) fluorine

Fluoreszenz [flu·ɔres'tsents] f (-;) fluorescence; fluorescent light

Fluorid [flu·o'rit] n (-[e]s;-e) fluoride

Flur [flur] m (-[e]s;-e) entrance hall; hallway || f (-;-en) open farmland; meadow; community farmland

Flur'garderobe f hallway closet

Fluß [flus] m (Flusses; Flüsse) river; flow; (metal) fusion; (phys) flux

flußab'wärts adv downstream

flußauf'wärts adv upstream

Fluß'bett n riverbed, channel

Flüßchen ['flYsçən] n (-s;-) rivulet

flüssig ['flYsɪç] adj liquid; fluid; (Gelder) ready; f. machen convert into cash || adv fluently

Flüs'sigkeit f (-;-en) liquid, fluid; (fig) fluency; (fin) liquidity

Flüs'sigkeitsmaß n liquid measure

Fluß'pferd n hypopotamus

flüstern ['flYstərn] tr & intr whisper

Flü'sterparole f rumor

Flut [flut] f (-;-en) flood; waters; high tide

fluten ['flutən] tr flood || intr (SEIN) flow, pour

Flut'grenze f high-water mark

Flut'licht n floodlight

Flut'linie f high-water mark

Flut'wasser n tidewater

Flut'welle f tidal wave

Flut'zeit f flood tide, high tide

focht [foxt] pret of fechten

Focksegel ['fɔkzegəl] n (-s;-) foresail

fohlen ['folən] intr foal || **Fohlen** n (-s;-) foal

Folge ['fɔlgə] f (-;-n) sequence; consequence; succession; series; (e-s Romans) continuation; (e-r Zeitschrift) number; die Folgen tragen take the consequences; in der F. subsequently

folgen ['fɔlgən] intr (dat) obey || intr (SEIN) (dat) follow; (dat) succeed; (aus) ensue (from)

folgendermaßen ['fɔlgəndərmasən] adv in the following manner, as follows

fol'genschwer adj momentous, grave

fol'gerichtig adj logical, consistent

folgern ['fɔlgərn] tr infer, conclude

Fol'gerung f (-;-en) inference, conclusion

Fol'gesatz m (gram) result clause

fol'gewidrig adj inconsistent

Fol'gezeit f—in der F. in subsequent times

folglich ['fɔlklɪç] adv consequently

folgsam ['fɔlkzam] adj obedient

Foliant [fol'jant] m (-en;-en) folio

Folie ['foljə] f (-;-n) (metal) foil

Folter ['fɔltər] f (-;-n) torture; rack; auf die F. spannen put to the rack; (fig) keep in suspense

Fol'terbank f (-;:-e) rack

foltern ['fɔltərn] tr torture

Fol'terqual f torture

Fol'terverhör n third degree

Fön [føn] m (-[e]s;-e) hand hairdryer

Fond [fõ] m (-s;-s) background; rear, back; (culin) gravy

Fonds [fõ] m (-s [fõs];-s [fõs]) fund

Fontäne [fon'tenə] f (-;-n) fountain

foppen ['fɔpən] tr tease; bamboozle

Fopperei [fɔpə'raɪ] f (-;-en) teasing

forcieren [fɔr'sirən] tr force; speed up

Förderband ['fœdərbant] n (-;:-er) conveyor belt

För'derer m (-s;-) promoter; patron

för'derlich adj useful; (dat) conducive (to)

fordern ['fɔrdərn] tr demand; (Recht) claim; (zum Zweikampf) challenge; (vor Gericht) summon

fördern ['fœrdərn] tr promote, back; (Kohle) produce; **förderndes Mitglied** social member; **zutage f.** bring to light

For'derung f (-;-en) demand, claim; debt; (zum Zweikampf) challenge

För'derung f (-;-en) promotion; support; encouragement; (min) output

Forelle [fo'rɛlə] f (-;-n) trout

Forke ['fɔrkə] f (-;-n) pitchfork

Form [fɔrm] f (-;-en) form; shape; mold; condition; (gram) voice; **die F. wahren** keep up appearances

formal [fɔr'mal] adj formal

Formalität [fɔrmalɪ'tet] f (-;-en) formality

Format [fɔr'mat] n (-[e]s;-e) size, format; distinction, stature

Formel ['fɔrməl] f (-;-n) formula

for'melhaft adj (Wendung, Gebet) set

formell [fɔr'mɛl] adj formal

formen ['fɔrmən] tr form, shape, mold

For'menlehre f morphology

Form'fehler m defect; flaw; (jur) irregularity

formieren [fɔr'mirən] tr & ref line up

-förmig [fœrmɪç] comb.fm. -shaped

förmlich ['fœrmlɪç] adj formal || adv virtually; literally; formally

form'los adj shapeless; informal; unconventional; rude; (chem) amorphous

form'schön adj well-shaped, beautiful

Formular [fɔrmu'lar] n (-s;-e) form, blank

formulieren [fɔrmu'lirən] tr formulate; word, phrase

Formulie'rung f (-;-en) formulation; wording

form'vollendet adj perfectly shaped

forsch [fɔrʃ] adj dashing || adv briskly

forschen ['fɔrʃən] intr do research; (nach) search (for)

For'scher -in §6 mf researcher; scholar; explorer

For'schung f (-;-en) research

For'schungsanstalt f research center

Forst [fɔrst] m (-[e]s;-e) forest

Förster ['fœrstər] m (-s;-) forester; forest ranger

Forst'fach n forestry

Forst'mann m (-es;-leute) forester

Forst'revier n forest range

Forst'wesen n, **Forst'wirtschaft** f forestry

fort [fɔrt] adv away; gone, lost; (weiter) on; (vorwärts) forward; **ich muß f.** I must be off; **in e-m f.** continuously; **und so f.** and so forth || **Fort** [for] n (-s;-s) (mil) fort

fortan' adv from now on, henceforth

Fort'bestand m continued existence

fort'bestehen §146 intr continue

fort'bewegen §56 tr move along || ref get about

fort'bilden ref continue one's studies

Fort'bildung f continuing education

fort'bleiben §62 intr (SEIN) stay away

Fort'dauer f continuance

fort'dauern intr continue; last

fort'fahren §71 tr hawl away; continue (to say); **f. zu** (inf) continue to (inf), go on (ger) || intr continue, go on || intr (SEIN) drive off, leave

Fort'fall m omission; discontinuation; **in F. kommen** be discontinued

fort'fallen §72 intr (SEIN) drop out; be omitted; be discontinued

fort'führen tr lead away; continue; (Geschäft) carry on; (Linie) extend

Fort'gang m departure; continuation; progress

fort'gehen §82 intr (SEIN) go away

fort'geschritten adj advanced; late

fort'gesetzt adj incessant

fort'kommen §99 intr (SEIN) go on, make progress; get away; **in der Welt f.** get ahead in the world || **Fortkommen** n (-s;) progress

fort'lassen §104 tr allow to go; omit

fort'laufen §105 intr (SEIN) run away

fort'laufend adj continuing; (Nummer) consecutive

fort'leben intr live on

fort'pflanzen tr propagate; spread || ref reproduce; propagate; spread

Fort'pflanzung f (-;) propagation

fort'reißen §53 tr tear away; carry || **sich f.** sweep s.o. off his feet; **sich f. lassen** be caried away

fort'schaffen tr remove

fort'scheren ref (coll) scram

fort'schreiten §86 intr (SEIN) progress, advance

Fort'schritt m progress; improvement

fort'schrittlich adj progressive

fort'setzen tr continue; resume

Fort'setzung f (-;-en) continuation; sequel; installment; **F. folgt** to be continued

fort'während adj continual; lasting, permanent || adv all the time, always

Fossil [fɔ'sil] n (-s;-ien [jən]) fossil

foul [faul] adj foul, dirty || **Foul** n (-s;-) (sport) foul; **ein F. begehen an** (dat) commit a foul against

foulen ['faulən] tr (sport) foul

Foyer [fwa'je] n (-s;-s) foyer; (im Hotel) lobby

Fracht [fraxt] f (-;-en) freight, cargo

Fracht'brief m bill of lading

Frachter ['fraxtər] m (-s;-) freighter

Fracht'gut n freight, goods

Fracht'raum m cargo compartment; cargo capacity

Fracht'stück n package

Frack [frak] m (-[e]s;ːe & -s) tails

Frack'schoß m coattail

Frage ['fragə] f (-;-n) question; **außer F. stehen** be out of the question; **e-e F. stellen** ask a question; **in F. stellen** call in question; **kommt nicht in F.!** nothing doing!

Fra'gebogen m questionnaire

fragen ['fragən] tr ask; **j-n f. nach** ask s.o. about; **j-n nach der Zeit f.** ask s.o. the time; **j-n f. um** ask s.o. for || ref wonder || impers ref—**es fragt sich, ob** the question is whether || intr ask

Fra'gesatz m interrogative sentence; **abhängiger F.** indirect question

Fragesteller ['fragə'tɛlɐr] m (-s;-) questioner

Fra'gewort n (-es;≠er) interrogative

Fra'gezeichen n question mark

fraglich ['fraːklɪç] adj questionable

fraglos ['fraːkloːs] adv unquestionably

Fragment [frag'ment] n (-[e]s;-e) fragment

frag'würdig adj questionable

Fraktion [frak'tsjoːn] f (-;-en) (chem) fraction; (pol) faction

fraktionell [fraktsɔ'nɛl] adj factional

Fraktur [frak'tuːr] f (-;-en) fracture; Gothic type, Gothic lettering; **mit j-m F. reden** talk turkey with s.o.

frank [fraŋk] adv—**f. und frei** quite frankly

Franke ['fraŋkə] m (-n;-n) Franconian; (hist) Frank

Franken ['fraŋkən] m (-[e]s;-) (Swiss) franc ‖ n (-s;) Franconia

frankieren [fraŋ'kiːrən] tr frank, put postage on

Fränkin ['frɛŋkɪn] f (-;-nen) Frank

franko ['fraŋko] adv postage paid; **f. Berlin** freight paid to Berlin; **f. verzollt** free of freight and duty

Frank'reich n (-s;) France

Franse ['franzə] f (-;-n) fringe

fransen ['franzən] intr fray

Franzband ['frantsbant] m (-[e]s;≠e) leather binding

Franz'branntwein m rubbing alcohol

Franzose [fran'tsoːzə] m (-n;-n) Frenchman; **die Franzosen** the French

Französin [fran'tsøːzɪn] f (-;-nen) Frenchwoman

französisch [fran'tsøːzɪʃ] adj French

frappant [fra'pant] adj striking

frappieren [fra'piːrən] tr strike, astonish; (Wein) put on ice

fräsen ['frɛːzən] tr mill

fraß [fraːs] pret of fressen ‖ **Fraß** m (-es;) fodder, food; (pel) garbage

Fratz [frats] m (-es;-e) brat

Fratze ['fratsə] f (-;-n) grimace; (coll) face; **e-e F. schneiden** make a face

frat'zenhaft adj grotesque

Frau [frau] f (-;-en) woman; lady; wife; (vor Namen) Mrs; **zur F. geben** give in marriage

Frauen- comb.fm. of women

Frau'enarzt m, **Frau'enärztin** f gynecologist

Frau'enheld m ladykiller

Frau'enkirche f Church of Our Lady

Frau'enkleidung f women's wear

Frau'enklinik f women's hospital

Frau'enleiden n gynecological disorder

Frau'enzimmer n (pej) woman, female

Fräulein ['frɔɪlaɪn] n (-s;-) young lady; (vor Namen) Miss

frau'lich adj womanly

frech [frɛç] adj brazen; fresh, smart

Frech'dachs m smart aleck

Frech'heit f (-;-en) impudence

Fregatte [fre'gatə] f (-;-n) frigate

frei [fraɪ] adj free; (Feld) open; (offen) frank; **auf freien Fuß setzen** release; **auf freier Strecke** (rr) outside the station; **die freien Berufe** the professions; **freie Fahrt** (public sign) resume speed; **freies Spiel haben** have a free hand; **frei werden** (chem) be released; **ich bin so frei** thank you, I will have some; **sich frei machen** take off one's clothes ‖ **Freie** §5 n—**im Freien** out of doors; **ins Freie** out of doors, into the open

Frei'bad n outdoor swimming pool

Frei'bank f (-;≠e) cheap-meat counter

frei'beruflich adj freelance

Frei'betrag m allowable deduction

Frei'brief m charter; (fig) license

Freier ['fraɪ·ɐr] m (-s;-) suitor

Frei'frau f baroness

Frei'gabe f release

frei'geben §80 tr release; **für den Verkehr f.** open to traffic ‖ intr—**j-m f.** give s.o. (time) off

freigebig ['fraɪgeːbɪç] adj generous

Frei'gebigkeit f (-;) generosity

Frei'geist m freethinker

frei'geistig adj open-minded

frei'gestellt adj optional

frei'haben intr be off

Frei'hafen m free port

frei'halten §90 tr keep open; **j-n f. pay** the tab for s.o.

Frei'heit f (-;-en) freedom; **dichterische F.** poetic license

Frei'heitskrieg m war of liberation

Frei'heitsstrafe f imprisonment

Frei'herr m baron

Frei'karte f free ticket; (theat) complimentary ticket

Frei'korps n volunteer corps

frei'lassen §104 tr release, set free

Frei'lauf m coasting

frei'legen tr lay open, expose

frei'lich adv of course

Freilicht- comb.fm. open-air

frei'machen tr (Platz) vacate; (Straße) clear; (Brief) stamp; **den Arm f.** roll up one's sleeves ‖ ref undress

Frei'marke f postage stamp

Frei'maurer m Freemason

Frei'maurerei f freemasonry

Frei'mut m frankness

frei'mütig adj frank, outspoken

frei'schaffend adj freelance

Frei'sinn m (pol) liberalism

frei'sinnig adj (pol) liberal

frei'sprechen §64 tr acquit

Frei'spruch m acquittal

frei'stehen §146 intr—**es steht Ihnen frei zu** (inf) you are free to (inf)

frei'stehend adj free-standing; (Gebäude) detached

Frei'stelle f scholarship

frei'stellen tr exempt; **j-m etw f.** leave it to s.o.'s discretion

Frei'stoß m (fb) free kick

Frei'tag m Friday

Frei'tod m suicide

Frei'treppe f outdoor stairway

Frei'wild n (& fig) fair game

frei'willig adj voluntary ‖ **Freiwillige** §5 mf (& mil) volunteer

Frei'zeichen n (telp) dial tone

Frei'zeit f spare time, leisure

Frei'zeitgestaltung f planning one's leisure time

freizügig ['fraɪtsyːgɪç] adj unhampered

fremd [fremt] *adj* foreign; strange; someone else's; (*Name*) assumed

fremd′artig *adj* strange, odd

Fremde ['fremdə] §5 *mf* foreigner; stranger || *f*—aus der F. from abroad; in der F. far from home; in die F. gehen go far from home; go abroad

Frem′denbuch *n* visitors' book

Frem′denführer –in §6 *mf* tour guide; (*Buch*) guidebook

Frem′denheim *n* boarding house

Frem′denlegion *f* foreign legion

Frem′denverkehr *m* tourism

Frem′denzimmer *n* guest room; spare room

Fremd′herrschaft *f* foreign domination

Fremd′körper *m* foreign body; (pol) alien element

fremdländisch ['fremtlendɪʃ] *adj* foreign

Fremdling ['fremtlɪŋ] *m* (**-s;-**) stranger

Fremd′sprache *f* foreign language

Fremd′wort *n* (**-es;=er**) foreign word

frequentieren [frekven'tirən] *tr* frequent

Frequenz [fre'kvɛnts] *f* (**-;-en**) frequency; (*Besucherzahl*) attendance

Freske ['freska] *f* (**-;-n**), **Fres·ko** ['fresko] *n* (**-s;-ken** [kən]) fresco

Freßbeutel ['frɛsbɔɪtəl] *m* feed bag

Fresse ['fresə] *f* (**-;-n**) (sl) puss

fressen ['fresən] §70 *tr* (*von Tieren*) eat; feed on; (sl) devour; (*ätzen*) corrode, pit; (tech) freeze || *ref*—sich satt f. stuff oneself || *intr* (sl) eat; (an *dat*) gnaw (at)

Fresserei [fresə'raɪ] *f* (**-;**) gluttony

Freude ['frɔɪdə] *f* (**-;-n**) joy, pleasure

Freu′denbotschaft *f* glad tidings

Freu′denfeier *f*, **Freu′denfest** *n* celebration, happy occasion

Freu′denhaus *n* brothel

Freu′denmädchen *n* prostitute

freudig ['frɔɪdɪç] *adj* joyful, happy

freud′los *adj* joyless, sad

freuen ['frɔɪ·ən] *tr* please || *ref* be happy; (an *dat*) be delighted (by); (auf *acc*) look forward to (to); (über *acc*) be glad (about) || *impers*—es freut mich I am glad

Freund [frɔɪnt] *m* (**-[e]s;-e**) friend; boyfriend; F. der Musik music lover

Freundin ['frɔɪndɪn] *f* (**-;-nen**) friend; girlfriend

freund′lich *adj* friendly; cheerful

Freund′lichkeit *f* (**-;**) friendliness

Freund′schaft *f* (**-;-en**) friendship

Frevel ['frefəl] *m* (**-s;-**) outrage; crime; sacrilege

fre′velhaft *adj* wicked

freveln ['frefəln] *intr* commit an outrage; am Gesetz f. violate the law

Fre′veltat *f* outrage

Friede ['fridə] *m* (**-ns;**), **Frieden** ['fridən] *m* (**-s;**) peace

Frie′densrichter *m* justice of the peace

Frie′densschluß *m* conclusion of peace

Frie′densstifter –in §6 *mf* peacemaker

Frie′densverhandlungen *pl* peace negotiations

Frie′densvertrag *m* peace treaty

friedfertig ['fritfertɪç] *adj* peaceable

Friedhof ['frithof] *m* cemetery

friedlich ['fritlɪç] *adj* peaceful

friedliebend ['fritlibənt] *adj* peace-loving

frieren ['frirən] §77 *intr* be cold; freeze || *impers*—es friert mich I'm freezing

Fries [fris] *m* (**-es;-e**) frieze

Frikadelle [frika'dɛlə] *f* (**-;-n**) meatball

frisch [frɪʃ] *adj* fresh; (*kühl*) cool; (*munter*) brisk || *adv* freshly; f. gestrichen (public sign) wet paint; f. zu! on with it! || **Frische** *f* (**-;**) freshness; coolness; briskness

Frisch′haltepackung *f* vacuum package

Friseur [frɪ'zør] *m* (**-s;-e**) barber

Friseur′laden *m* barbershop

Friseur′sessel *m* barber chair

Friseuse [frɪ'zøzə] *f* (**-;-n**) hairdresser

frisieren [frɪ'zirən] *tr* (*Dokumente*) doctor; (aut) soup up; j–m die Haare f. do s.o.'s hair

Frisier′haube *f* hair dryer; hair net

Frisier′kommode *f*, **Frisier′tisch** *m* dresser

Frist [frɪst] *f* (**-;-en**) time, period, term; (com, jur) grace; die F. einhalten meet the deadline

fristen ['frɪstən] *tr*—das Leben f. eke out a living

Frisur [frɪ'zur] *f* (**-;-en**) hairstyle

frivol [frɪ'vol] *adj* frivolous

froh [fro] *adj* glad, happy, joyful

froh′gelaunt *adj* cheerful

fröhlich ['frølɪç] *adj* gay, merry

froh′locken *intr* rejoice

Froh′sinn *m* good humor

fromm [from] *adj* pious, devout

Frömmelei [fromə'laɪ] *f* (**-;-en**) sanctimoniousness; sanctimonious act

frommen ['fromən] *intr* (dat) profit

Frömmigkeit ['frœmɪçkaɪt] *f* (**-;**) piety

Frömmler –in ['frœmlər–ɪn] §6 *mf* hypocrite

Fron [fron] *f* (**-;**) drudgery; (hist) forced labor

frönen ['frønən] *intr* (dat) gratify

Fron′leichnam *m* Corpus Christi

Front [front] *f* (**-;-en**) (& mil) front

Front′abschnitt *m* (mil) sector

fror [fror] *pret* of **frieren**

Frosch [frɔʃ] *m* (**-es;=e**) frog; (*Feuerwerkkörper*) firecracker; sei kein F.! don't be a party pooper

Frost [frɔst] *m* (**-es;=e**) frost

Frost′beule *f* chilblain

frösteln ['frœstəln] *intr* feel chilly

Frosterfach ['frɔstərfax] *n* freezer compartment (of *refrigerator*)

frostig ['frɔstɪç] *adj* frosty; chilly

Frost′schutzmittel *n* antifreeze

Frottee [fro'te] *m* & *n* (**-s;-s**) terry cloth

frottieren [frɔ'tirən] *tr* rub down

Frottier′tuch *n* Turkish towel

Frucht [fruxt] *f* (**-;=e**) fruit; foetus

fruchtbar ['fruxtbar] *adj* fruitful

frucht′bringend *adj* productive

Früch′tebecher *m* fruit cup (as *dessert*)

fruchten ['fruxtən] *intr* bear fruit; have effect; be of use

Frucht′folge f rotation of crops
Frucht′knoten m (bot) pistil
frucht′los adj fruitless
Frucht′saft m fruit juice
Frucht′wechsel m rotation of crops
frugal [fru′gɑl] adj frugal
früh [fry] adj early || adv early; in the morning; **von f. bis spät** from morning till night || **Frühe** f (-;) early morning; **in aller F.** very early
früher [′fry·ər] adj earlier; former || adv earlier; sooner; formerly
frühestens [′fry·əstəns] adv at the earliest
Früh′geburt f premature birth
Früh′jahr n, **Frühling** [′fryliŋ] m (-s; -e) spring
Früh′lingsmüdigkeit f spring fever
früh′reif adj precocious
Früh′schoppen m eye opener (beer, wine)
Früh′stück n breakfast; **zweites F.** lunch
frühstücken [′fryʃtykən] intr eat breakfast
früh′zeitig adj & adv (too) early
Fuchs [fuks] m (-es;ːe) fox; (Pferd) sorrel, chestnut; (educ) freshman
Fuchsie [′fuksjə] f (-;-n) fuchsia
fuchsig [′fuksɪç] adj red; (fig) furious, wild
Fuchs′jagd f fox hunt(ing)
fuchs′rot adj sorrel
Fuchs′schwanz m foxtail; (bot) amaranth; (carp) hand saw (with tapered blade)
fuchs′teufelswild′ adj hopping mad
Fuge [′fugə] f (-;-n) joint; (mus) fugue; **aus allen Fugen gehen** come apart; go to pieces, go to pot
fügen [′fygən] tr join; (verhängen) decree; (carp) joint || ref give in; **es fügte sich** it so happened
fügsam [′fykzam] adj compliant; (Haar) manageable
Fü′gung f (-;-en) (gram) construction; **F. des Himmels, F. Gottes** divine providence; **F. des Schicksals** stroke of fate; **göttliche F.** divine providence
fühlbar [′fylbɑr] adj tangible; noticeable; **sich f. machen** make itself felt
fühlen [′fylən] tr feel, touch; sense || ref feel; feel big || intr—f. mit feel for (s.o.); **f. nach** feel for, grope for
–fühlig [fylɪç] comb.fm. –feeling
Füh′lung f (-;) touch, contact; **F. nehmen** mit get in touch with
fuhr [fur] pret of **fahren**
Fuhre [′furə] f (-;-n) wagon load
führen [′fyrən] tr lead; guide; (Artikel) carry, sell; (Besprechungen) hold, conduct; (Bücher) keep; (Geschäft) run, manage; (Krieg) carry on; (Sprache) use; (Titel) bear; (Truppen) command; (Waffe) wield; (Fahrzeug) drive; (aer) pilot; **den Beweis f.** prove; **die Aufsicht f. über** (acc) superintend; **j-m den Haushalt f.** keep house for s.o. || ref conduct oneself || intr lead; (sport) be in the lead
Füh′rer –in §6 mf leader, guide; (aer)

pilot; (aut) driver; (com) manager; (sport) captain
Füh′rerschaft f (-;) leadership
Füh′rerschein m driver's license
Füh′rerscheinentzug m suspension of driver's license
Führhund [′fyrhunt] m Seeing Eye dog
Fuhr′park m (aut) fleet
Füh′rung f (-;-en) guidance; leadership; management; guided tour; behavior; (mil) command; (sport) lead
Füh′rungskraft f executive; **die Führungskräfte** management; (pol) authorities; **untere F.** junior executive
Füh′rungsschicht f (com) management
Füh′rungsspitze f top echelon
Fuhr′unternehmen n trucking
Fuhr′werk n cart, wagon; vehicle
Füllbleistift [′fylblaɪʃtɪft] m mechanical pencil
Fülle [′fylə] f (-;) fullness; abundance, wealth; (Körper-) plumpness
füllen [′fylən] tr fill || ref fill up || **Füllen** n (-s;-) foal, colt, filly
Fül′ler m (-s;-) fountain pen
Füll′federhalter m fountain pen
Füll′horn n cornucopia
Füllsel [′fylzəl] n (-s;-) stopgap; (beim Schreiben) padding; (culin) stuffing
Fül′lung f (-;-en) (Zahn-) filling; (Tür-) panel; (culin) stuffing
Fund [funt] m (-[e]s;-e) find; discovery
Fundament [funda′ment] n (-[e]s;-e) foundation
fundamental [fundamen′tɑl] adj fundamental
Fund′büro n lost-and-found department
Fund′grube f (fig) mine, storehouse
fundieren [fun′dirən] tr lay the foundations of; found; establish; (Schuld) fund; **fundiertes Einkommen** unearned income; **gut fundiert** well-established
fünf [fynf] adj & pron five || **Fünf** f (-;-en) five
Fünf′eck n pentagon
fünfte [′fynftə] §9 adj & pron fifth
Fünftel [′fynftəl] n (-s;-) fifth (part)
fünf′zehn adj & pron fifteen || **Fünf-zehn** f (-;-en) fifteen
fünf′zehnte §9 adj & pron fifteenth
Fünf′zehntel n (-s;-) fifteenth (part)
fünf′zig [′fynftsɪç] adj fifty
fünf′ziger invar adj of the fifties; **die f. Jahre** the fifties
fünfzigste [′fynftsɪçstə] §9 adj & pron fiftieth
fungieren [fuŋ′girən] intr function; **f. als** function as, act as
Funk [funk] m (-s;) radio
Funk′amateur m (rad) ham
Funk′bastler –in §6 mf (rad) ham
Fünkchen [′fyŋkən] n (-s;-) small spark; **kein F.** (fig) not an ounce
Funke [′funkə] m (-ns;-n), **Funken** [′fyŋkən] m (-s;-) spark
funkeln [′fuŋkəln] intr sparkle; (Sterne) twinkle
fun′kelnagelneu′ adj brand-new

funken ['fuŋkən] *tr* radio, broadcast
|| *intr* spark
Fun'ker *m* (-s;-) radio operator
Funk'feuer *n* (aer) radio beacon
Funk'leitstrahl *m* radio beam
Funk'meßanlage *f* radar installation
Funk'meßgerät *n* radar
Funk'netz *n* radio network
Funk'peilung *f* radio direction finding
Funk'spruch *m* radiogram
Funk'streifenwagen *m* squad car
Funktionär –in [fuŋktsjə'ner(ɪn)] §8
mf functionary
für [fyr] *prep* (*acc*) for || **Für** *n*—das
Für und Wider the pros and cons
Für'bitte *f* intercession
Furche ['furçə] *f* (-;-n) furrow; (*Run-
zel*) wrinkle; (*Wagenspur*) rut
furchen ['furçən] *tr* furrow; wrinkle
Furcht [furçt] *f* (-;) fear, dread
furchtbar ['furçtbar] *adj* terrible
fürchten ['fyrçtən] *tr* fear, be afraid
of || *ref* (*vor dat*) be afraid (of)
fürchterlich ['fyrçtərlɪç] *adj* terrible,
awful
furcht'erregend *adj* awe-inspiring
furcht'los *adj* fearless
furchtsam ['furçtzam] *adj* timid, shy
Furie ['furjə] *f* (-;-n) (myth) Fury
Furnier [fur'nir] *n* (-s;-e) veneer
Furore [fu'rorə] *f* (-;) & *n* (-s;) stir;
F. machen cause a stir, be a big hit
Für'sorge *f* care; welfare
Für'sorgeamt *n* welfare department
Fürsorger –in ['fyrzorgər(ɪn)] §6 *mf*
social worker; welfare officer
fürsorglich ['fyrzorklɪç] *adj* thought-
ful
Für'sprache *f* intercession; F. einlegen
intercede
Für'sprecher –in §6 *mf* intercessor
Fürst [fyrst] *m* (-en;-en) prince
Fürstentum ['fyrstəntum] *n* (-s;⁻er)
principality
Fürstin ['fyrstɪn] *f* (-;-nen) princess
fürst'lich *adj* princely
Furt [furt] *f* (-;-en) ford
Furunkel [fu'runkəl] *m* (-s;-) boil
Für'wort *n* (-[e]s;⁻er) pronoun

Furz [furts] *m* (-es;⁻e) (vulg) fart
Fusel ['fuzəl] *m* (-s;) (coll) booze
Fusion [fu'sjon] *f* (-;-en) (com) merger
Fuß [fus] *m* (-es;⁻e) foot; auf freien
Fuß setzen set free; zu Fuß on foot;
zu Fuß gehen walk
Fuß'abdruck *m* footprint
Fuß'ball *m* soccer; football
Fuß'bank *f* (-;⁻e) footstool
Fuß'bekleidung *f* footwear
Fuß'boden *m* floor; flooring
Fussel ['fusəl] *f* (-;-n) fuzz
fußen ['fusən] *intr*—f. auf (*dat*) be
based on; rely on
Fuß'fall *m* prostration
fuß'fällig *adv* on one's knees
fuß'frei *adj* ankle-length
Fuß'freiheit *f* leg room
Fuß'gänger *m* (-s;-) pedestrian
Fuß'gelenk *n* ankle joint
Fuß'gestell *n* pedestal
–füßig [fysɪç] *comb.fm.* -footed
Fuß'knöchel *m* ankle
Fuß'leiste *f* baseboard, washboard
Füßling ['fyslɪŋ] *m* (-s;-e) foot (*of
stocking, sock, etc.*)
Fuß'note *f* footnote
Fuß'pfad *m* footpath
Fuß'pilz *m* athlete's foot
Fuß'spur *f* footprint(s)
Fuß'stapfe *f* footstep
Fuß'steg *m* footbridge; footpath
Fuß'steig *m* footpath; sidewalk
Fuß'tritt *m* step; (*Stoß*) kick
futsch [futʃ] *adj* (coll) gone; (coll)
ruined
Futter ['futər] *n* (-s;) fodder, feed;
(*e–s Mantels*) lining
Futteral [futə'ral] *n* (-s;-e) case
Fut'terkrippe *f* crib; (sl) gravy train
Fut'terkrippensystem *n* (pol) spoils
system
futtern ['futərn] *intr* (coll) eat heart-
ily
füttern ['fytərn] *tr* feed; (*Kleid, Man-
tel, Pelz*) line
Fut'terneid *m* jealousy
Fut'terstoff *m* lining
Fut'tertrog *m* feed trough

G

G, g [ge] *invar n* G, g; (mus) G
gab [gap] *pret of* geben
Gabardine [gabar'dinə] *m* (-s;-) (tex)
gabardine
Gabe ['gabə] *f* (-;-n) gift; donation;
talent; (med) dose; milde G. alms
Gabel ['gabəl] *f* (-;-n) fork; (arti)
bracket; (telp) cradle
Ga'belbein *n* wishbone
Ga'belbissen *m* tidbit
Ga'belfrühstück *n* brunch
gabelig ['gabəlɪç] *adj* forked
gabeln ['gabəln] *tr* pick up with a fork
|| *ref* divide, branch off
Ga'belstapler *m* forklift
Ga'belung *f* (-;-en) fork (*in the road*)

gackeln ['gakəln], **gackern** ['gakərn],
gacksen ['gaksən] *intr* cackle, cluck
Gage ['gaʒə] *f* (-;-n) salary, pay
gähnen ['genən] *intr* yawn
gaffen ['gafən] *intr* gape; stare
Gala ['gala] *invar f* gala, Sunday best
galant [ga'lant] *adj* courteous; galantes Abenteuer love affair
Galante·rie [galantə'ri] *f* (-;-rien
['ri·ən]) courtesy; flattering word
Gala·xis [ga'laksɪs] *f* (-;-xien [ksjən])
galaxy
Galeere [ga'lerə] *f* (-;-n) galley
Gale·rie [galə'ri] *f* (-;-rien ['ri·ən])
gallery
Galgen ['galgən] *m* (-s;-) gallows

Gal′genfrist f (coll) brief respite
Gal′genhumor m grim humor
Gal′genstrick m, **Gal′genvogel** m (coll) good-for-nothing
gälisch [ˈgɛlɪʃ] adj Gaelic
Galle [ˈgalə] f (-;) gall, bile; (fig) bitterness
Gal′lenblase f gall bladder
Gal′lenstein m gallstone
Galiert [ˈgalɛrt] n -[e]s;-e), **Gallerte** [gaˈlɛrtə] f (-;-n) gelatine; jelly
gallig [ˈgalɪç] adj bitter; grouchy
Gallone [gaˈlonə] f (-;-n) gallon
Galopp [gaˈlɔp] m (-[e]s;-s & -e) gallop; **im G. reiten** gallop; **in gestrecktem G.** at full gallop; **in kurzem G.** at a canter
galoppieren [galoˈpirən] intr (SEIN) gallop
galt [galt] pret of **gelten**
galvanisieren [galvanɪˈzirən] tr galvanize; electroplate
Gambe [ˈgambə] f (-;-n) bass viol
gammeln [ˈgaməln] intr bum around
Gammler [ˈgamlər] m (-s;-) hippie
Gamsbart [ˈgamsbart] m goatee
gang [gaŋ] adj—g. **und gäbe** customary || **Gang** m (-[e]s;ˈˑ) walk, gait; (e-r Maschine) running, operation; (im Hause) hallway; (zwischen Reihen) aisle; (Botengang) errand; (Röhre) conduit; (e-r Schraube) thread; (anat) duct, canal; (aut) gear; (box) round; (culin) course; (min) vein, lode; (min) gallery; (mus) run; **außer G. setzen** stop; (aut) put in neutral; **erster G.** low gear; **es ist etw im G.** there is s.th. afoot; **im G. sein** be in operation; be in progress; **in G. bringen** (or **setzen**) set in motion; **in vollem G.** in full swing
Gang′art f gait
gangbar [ˈgaŋbar] adj passable; (Münze) current; (com) marketable
Gängelband [ˈgɛŋəlbant] n—**am G. führen** (fig) lead by the nose, dominate
-gänger [gɛŋər] comb.fm., e.g., **Fußgänger** pedestrian
gängig [ˈgɛŋɪç] adj see **gangbar**
Gang′schaltung f (aut) gear shift
Gangster [ˈgɛŋstər] m (-s;-s) gangster
Ganove [gaˈnovə] m (-s;-n) crook
Gans [gans] f (-;ˈˑe) goose
Gänseblümchen [ˈgɛnzəblymçən] n (-s;-) daisy
Gänsehaut [ˈgɛnzəhaut] f (coll) goose flesh, goose pimples
Gänseklein [ˈgɛnzəklain] n (-s;) (culin) giblets
Gänsemarsch [ˈgɛnzəmarʃ] m single file
Gänserich [ˈgɛnzərɪç] m (-s;-e) gander
ganz [gants] adj whole; all; total; intact; **im ganzen** in all || adv entirely, quite; **g. und gar** completely; **g. und gar nicht** not at all || **Ganze** §5 n whole; **aufs G. gehen** go all the way
Ganz′aufnahme f full-length photograph
Gänze [ˈgɛntsə] f (-;)—**in G.** in its entirety; **zur G.** entirely
Ganz′fabrikat n finished product

Ganz′leinenband m (-[e]s;ˈˑe) clothbound volume
gänzlich [ˈgɛntslɪç] adj entire, total
ganz′seitig adj full-page
ganz′tägig adj full-time
gar [gar] adj (culin) well done; (metal) refined || adv even, very; (sogar) even; **gar nicht** not at all
Garage [gaˈraʒə] f (-;-n) garage
Garan-tie [garanˈti] f (-;-tien [ˈti-ən]) guarantee
garantieren [garanˈtirən] tr guarantee || intr—**g. dafür, daß** guarantee that
Garaus [ˈgaraus] m (-;) finishing blow
Garbe [ˈgarbə] f (-;-n) sheaf, shock
Garde [ˈgardə] f (-;-n) guard
Gardenie [garˈdenjə] f (-;-n) gardenia
Garderobe [gardəˈrobə] f (-;-n) wardrobe; (Kleiderablage) cloakroom; (theat) dressing room
Gardero′benmarke f hat or coat check
Gardero′benständer m coatrack, hatrack
Garderobiere [gardəroˈbjɛrə] f (-;-n) cloakroom attendant
Gardine [garˈdinə] f (-;-n) curtain
Gardi′nenhalter m tieback
Gardi′nenpredigt f (coll) dressing down
Gardi′nenstange f curtain rod
gären [ˈgerən] §78 intr ferment; bubble
Gärmittel [ˈgermɪtəl] n ferment; leaven
Garn [garn] n (-[e]s;-e) yarn; thread; snare; (fig) trap; (fig) yarn
Garnele [garˈnelə] f (-;-n) shrimp
garnieren [garˈnirən] tr garnish; trim
Garnison [garnɪˈzon] f (-;-en) garrison
Garnitur [garnɪˈtur] f (-;-en) trimming; set (of matching objects); (mach) fittings, mountings; (mil) uniform
garstig [ˈgarstɪç] adj ugly; nasty
Garten [ˈgartən] m (-s;ˈˑ) garden
Gar′tenanlage f gardens, grounds
Gar′tenarbeit f gardening
Gar′tenarchitekt m landscape gardener
Gar′tenbau m gardening; horticulture
Gar′tenlaube f arbor
Gar′tenmesser n pruning knife
Gärtner [ˈgertnər] m (-s;-) gardener
Gärtnerei [gertnəˈrai] f (-;-en) gardening; truck farm; nursery
Gä′rung f (-;) fermentation
Gas [gas] n (-es;-e) gas; **Gas geben** step on the gas
Gas′anstalt f gasworks
gas′artig adj gaseous
Gas′behälter m gas tank
gas′förmig adj gaseous
Gas′hebel m (aut) accelerator
Gas′heizung f gas heat(ing)
Gas′herd m gas range
Gas′krieg m chemical warfare
Gas′leitung f gas main
Gas′messer m gas meter
Gasse [ˈgasə] f (-;-n) side street; **über die G. verkaufen** sell takeouts
Gas′sendirne f streetwalker
Gas′senhauer m popular song
Gas′senjunge m urchin

Gast [gast] m (-[e]s;⸚e) guest; boarder; (com) customer; (theat) guest performer; **zu Gast bitten** invite

Gästebuch ['gɛstəbux] n guest book; visitors' book

Gast'freund m guest

gast'freundlich adj hospitable

Gast'freundschaft f hospitality

Gast'geber m host

Gast'geberin f hostess

Gast'haus n, **Gast'hof** m inn

Gast'hörer –in §6 mf (educ) auditor

gastieren [gas'tirən] intr (telv, theat) appear as a guest

gast'lich adj hospitable

Gast'mahl n feast; banquet

Gast'professor m visiting professor

Gast'rolle f guest performance; **e-e G. geben** pay a flying visit

Gast'spiel n (theat) guest performance

Gast'stätte f restaurant

Gast'stube f dining room

Gast'wirt m innkeeper

Gast'wirtschaft f restaurant

Gas'uhr f gas meter

Gas'werk n gas works

Gas'zähler m gas meter

Gatte ['gatə] m (-n;-n) husband; **Gatten** married couple

Gatter ['gatər] n (-s;-) grating; latticework; iron gate

Gattin ['gatɪn] f (-;-nen) wife

Gattung ['gatuŋ] f (-;-en) kind, type, species; family; (biol) genus

Gat'tungsname m generic name; (gram) common noun

Gau [gau] m (-[e]s;-e) district

Gaukelbild ['gaukəlbɪlt] n illusion

gaukeln ['gaukəln] intr flit, flutter; perform hocus-pocus

Gau'kelspiel n, **Gau'kelwerk** n sleight of hand; delusion

Gaul [gaul] m (-[e]s;⸚e) horse; nag

Gaumen ['gaumən] m (-s;-) palate

Gauner ['gaunər] m (-s;-) rogue; swindler

Gaunerei [gaunə'raɪ] f (-;-en) swindling, cheating

gaunern ['gaunərn] intr swindle

Gau'nersprache f thieves' slang

Gaze ['gazə] f (-;-n) gauze; cheesecloth

Gazelle [ga'tselə] f (-;-n) gazelle

Geächtete [gə'ɛçtətə] §5 mf outlaw

Geächze [gə'ɛçtsə] n (-s;) moaning

geartet [gə'artət] adj—**anders g. sein** be of a different disposition

Gebäck [gə'bɛk] n (-s;) baked goods, cookies

geballt [gə'balt] adj concentrated; dense; (Schnee) hardened; (Faust) clenched; (Stil) succinct

gebannt [gə'bant] pp spellbound

gebar [gə'bar] pret of **gebären**

Gebärde [gə'bɛrdə] f (-;-n) gesture

gebärden [gə'bɛrdən] ref behave

Gebär'denspiel n gesticulation

gebaren [gə'barən] ref behave, act ‖ **Gebaren** n (-s;) behavior

gebären [gə'bɛrən] §79 tr bear ‖ **Gebären** n (-s;) childbirth; labor

Gebär'mutter f (anat) uterus

Gebär'mutterkappe f diaphragm

Gebäude [gə'bɔɪdə] n (-s;-) building

gebefreudig ['gebəfrɔɪdɪç] adj openhanded

Gebein [gə'baɪn] n (-[e]s;-e) bones; **Gebeine** bones; mortal remains

Gebell [gə'bɛl] n (-[e]s;), **Gebelle** [gə'bɛlə] n (-s;) barking

geben ['gebən] §80 tr give; yield; (Gelegenheit) afford; (Laut) utter; (Karten) deal; **Feuer g.** give (s.o.) a light; (mil) open fire; **viel g. auf** (acc) set great store by; **von sich g.** utter; throw up; (Rede) deliver; (chem) give off ‖ ref give; (Kopfweh, usw.) get better; **sich g. als** pretend to be; **sich gefangen g.** surrender ‖ impers—**es gibt** there is, there are; **es wird Regen geben** it's going to rain

Ge'ber –in §6 mf giver, donor

Gebet [gə'bet] n (-[e]s;-e) prayer

gebeten [gə'betən] pp of **bitten**

Gebiet [gə'bit] n (-[e]s;-e) district, territory; (Fläche) area; (Fach) line; (Bereich) field, sphere

gebieten [gə'bitən] §58 tr (Stillschweigen) impose; (Ehrfurcht) command; (verlangen) demand; **j-m g., etw zu tun** order s.o. to do s.th. ‖ intr (über acc) have control (over); (dat) control

Gebieter [gə'bitər] m (-s;-) master; ruler; commander; governor

Gebieterin [gə'bitərɪn] f (-;-nen) mistress; (des Hauses) lady

gebieterisch [gə'bitərɪʃ] adj imperious

Gebilde [gə'bɪldə] n (-s;-) shape, form; structure; (geol) formation

gebildet [gə'bɪldət] adj educated

Gebirge [gə'bɪrgə] n (-s;-) mountain range, mountains; **festes G.** bedrock

gebirgig [gə'bɪrgɪç] adj mountainous

Gebirgs– [gəbɪrks] comb.fm. mountain

Gebirgs'bewohner –in §6 mf mountaineer

Gebirgs'kamm m, **Gebirgs'rücken** m mountain ridge

Gebirgs'zug m mountain range

Ge·biß [gə'bɪs] n (-bisses;-bisse) teeth; false teeth; (am Zaum) bit

gebissen [gə'bɪsən] pp of **beißen**

Gebläse [gə'blezə] n (-s;-) bellows; blower; (aut) supercharger

geblieben [gə'blibən] pp of **bleiben**

Geblök [gə'blœk] n (-[e]s;) bleating

geblümt [gə'blymt] adj flowered

Geblüt [gə'blyt] n (-[e]s;) (& fig) blood

geboren [gə'borən] pp of **gebären** ‖ adj born; native; **geborene nee**

geborgen [gə'bɔrgən] pp of **bergen** ‖ adj safe

Gebor'genheit f (-;) safety, security

geborsten [gə'bɔrstən] pp of **bersten**

Gebot [gə'bot] n (-[e]s;-e) order, command; commandment; (Angebot) bid

geboten [gə'botən] pp of **bieten** ‖ adj requisite; **dringend g.** imperative

Gebr. abbr. (Gebrüder) Brothers

gebracht [gə'braxt] pp of **bringen**

gebrannt [gə'brant] pp of **brennen**

Gebräu [gə'brɔɪ] *n* (-[e]s;-e) brew

Gebrauch [gə'braux] *m* (-s;-̈e) use; usage; (*Sitte*) custom

gebrauchen [gə'brauxən] *tr* use, employ

gebräuchlich [gə'brɔɪçlɪç] *adj* usual; in use; (*gemein*) common

Gebrauchs'anweisung *f* directions

gebrauchs'fertig *adj* ready for use; (*Kaffee, usw.*) instant

Gebrauchs'graphik *f* commercial art

Gebrauchs'gut *n* commodity

Gebrauchs'muster *n* registered pattern

gebraucht [gə'brauxt] *adj* second-hand

Gebraucht'wagen *m* used car

Gebrechen [gə'breçən] *n* (-s;-) physical disability, infirmity

gebrech'lich *adj* frail, weak; rickety

gebrochen [gə'brɔxən] *pp* of brechen

Gebrüder [gə'brydər] *pl* brothers

Gebrüll [gə'bryl] *n* (-[e]s;) roaring; bellowing; lowing

Gebühr [gə'byr] *f* (-;-en) charge, fee; due, what is due; nach G. deservedly; über G. excessively; zu ermäßigter G. at a reduced rate

gebühren [gə'byrən] *intr* (*dat*) be due to || *impers ref*—es gebührt sich it is proper

gebüh'rend *adj* due; (*entsprechend*) appropriate || *adv* duly

gebüh'renfrei *adj* free of charge

gebüh'renpflichtig *adj* chargeable

gebunden [gə'bundən] *pp* of binden || *adj* bound; (*Hitze*) latent; (*Preise*) controlled; (*Kapital*) tied-up; g. an (*acc*) (chem) combined with; gebundene Rede verse

Geburt [gə'burt] *f* (-;-en) birth

Gebur'tenbeschränkung *f* birth control

Gebur'tenregelung *f* birth control

Gebur'tenrückgang *m* decline in births

gebürtig [gə'byrtɪç] *adj* native

Geburts'anzeige *f* announcement of birth; registration of birth

Geburts'fehler *n* congenital defect

Geburts'helfer -in §6 *mf* obstetrician || *f* midwife

Geburts'hilfe *f* obstetrics

Geburts'mal *n* birth mark

Geburts'recht *n* birthright

Geburts'schein *m* birth certificate

Geburts'tag *m* birthday

Geburts'tagskind *n* person celebrating his or her birthday

Geburts'wehen *pl* labor pains

Geburts'zange *f* forceps

Gebüsch [gə'by/] *n* (-es;-e) thicket, underbrush; clump of bushes

Geck [gɛk] *m* (-en;-en) dude

geckenhaft [gɛk'kenhaft] *adj* flashy

gedacht [gə'daxt] *pp* of denken

Gedächtnis [gə'dɛçtnɪs] *n* (-ses;) memory; aus dem G. by heart; im G. behalten bear in mind; zum G. (*genit* or an *acc*) in memory of

Gedächt'nisfehler *m* lapse of memory

Gedächt'nisrede *f* memorial address

gedämpft [gə'dɛmpft] *adj* muffled; hushed, quiet; (*Licht, Stimme*) subdued; (culin) stewed

Gedanke [gə'daŋkə] *m* (-ns;-n) thought; notion, idea; etw in Ge-

danken tun do s.th. absent-mindedly; in Gedanken sein be preoccupied; sich ⌊*dat*⌋ Gedanken machen über (*acc*) worry about

Gedan'kenblitz *m* (iron) brain wave

Gedan'kenfolge *f*, Gedan'kengang *m* train of thought

gedan'kenlos *adj* thoughtless; absent-minded; irresponsible

Gedan'kenpunkt *m* suspension point

Gedan'kenstrich *m* (typ) dash

Gedan'kenübertragung *f* telepathy

gedank'lich *adj* mental; intellectual

Gedärme [gə'dermə] *pl* intestines

Gedeck [gə'dɛk] *n* (-[e]s;-e) cover; table setting; menu

gedeihen [gə'daɪ·ən] §81 *intr* (SEIN) thrive; succeed || Gedeihen *n* (-s;) prosperity; success

Gedenk- [gədɛŋk] *comb.fm.* memorial, commemorative

gedenken [gə'dɛŋkən] §66 *intr* (*genit*) think of, be mindful of; remember; mention; g. zu (*inf*) intend to (*inf*) || Gedenken *n* (-s;) memory

gedeucht [gə'dɔɪçt] *pp* of dünken

Gedicht [gə'dɪçt] *n* (-[e]s;-e) poem; (fig) dream

gediegen [gə'digən] *adj* (*Gold*) solid; (*Silber*) sterling; (*Arbeit*) excellent; (*Kenntnisse*) thorough; (*Möbel*) solidly made; (*Charakter*) sterling; (coll) very funny

gedieh [gə'di] *pret* of gedeihen

gediehen [gə'di·ən] *pp* of gedeihen

Gedränge [gə'drɛŋə] *n* (-s;-) pushing; crowd; difficulties; (fb) scrimmage

gedrängt [gə'drɛŋt] *adj* crowded, packed; (*Sprache*) concise

gedroschen [gə'drɔ/ən] *pp* of dreschen

gedrückt [gə'drykt] *adj* depressed

gedrungen [gə'druŋən] *pp* of dringen || *adj* compact; stocky; squat; (*Sprache*) concise

Geduld [gə'dult] *f* (-;) patience

gedulden [gə'duldən] *ref* wait (patiently)

Geduld'spiel *n* puzzle

geduldig [gə'duldɪç] *adj* patient

gedungen [gə'duŋən] *pp* of dingen

gedunsen [gə'dunzən] *adj* bloated

gedurft [gə'durft] *pp* of dürfen

geehrt [gə'ert] *adj*—Sehr geehrte Herren! Dear Sirs; Sehr geehrter Herr X! Dear Mr. X

geeignet [gə'aɪgnət] *adj* suitable, right; qualified; appropriate

Gefahr [gə'far] *f* (-;-en) danger; (*Wagnis*) risk; G. laufen zu (*inf*) run the risk of (ger)

gefährden [gə'ferdən] *tr* jeopardize

gefährlich [gə'ferlɪç] *adj* dangerous

gefahr'los *adj* safe

Gefährt [gə'fert] *n* (-[e]s;-e) carriage

Gefährte [gə'fertə] *m* (-n;-n), Gefährtin [gə'fertɪn] *f* (-;-nen) companion; spouse

Gefälle [gə'fɛlə] *n* (-s;-) pitch; slope

gefallen [gə'falən] *pp* of fallen; (mil) killed in action || §72 *ref*—sich g. in (*dat*) take pleasure in || *intr* please; das gefällt mir I like this; das lasse ich mir nicht g. I won't stand for this ‖ **Gefallen** *m* (-;-) favor ‖ *n* (-s;) (an *dat*) pleasure (in); j-m etw zu U. **tun** do s.th. to please s.o.; **nach G.** as one pleases; at one's descretion

gefällig [gə'fɛlɪç] *adj* pleasing; obliging; kind; j-m g. **sein** do s.o. a favor; **Kaffee g.?** would you care for coffee?; **was ist g.?** what can I do for you?; **würden Sie so g. sein zu** (*inf*)? would you be so kind as to (*inf*)?

Gefäl'ligkeit *f* (-;-en) favor

gefälligst [gə'fɛlɪçst] *adv* if you please; please

gefangen [gə'faŋən] *pp of* **fangen** ‖ *adj* captive; g. **nehmen** take prisoner ‖ **Gefangene** §5 *mf* captive, prisoner

Gefan'genenlager *n* prison camp; (mil) prisoner-of-war camp

Gefan'gennahme *f* (-;) capture; arrest

gefan'gennehmen §116 *tr* take prisoner

Gefan'genschaft *f* (-;) captivity; imprisonment; **in G. geraten** be taken prisoner

gefan'gensetzen *tr* imprison

Gefängnis [gə'fɛŋnɪs] *n* (-ses;-se) prison, jail; imprisonment

Gefäng'nisdirektor *m* warden

Gefäng'nisstrafe *f* prison term

Gefäng'niswärter -in §6 *mf* guard

Gefäß [gə'fɛs] *n* (-es;-e) vessel; jar

gefaßt [gə'fast] *adj* calm, composed; **g. auf** (*acc*) ready for

Gefecht [gə'fɛçt] *n* (-[e]s;-e) fight, battle, action

Gefechts'auftrag *m* (mil) objective

Gefechts'kopf *m* warhead

Gefechts'lage *f* tactical situation

Gefechts'stand *m* command post

gefeit [gə'faɪt] *adj* (**gegen**) immune (from), proof (against)

Gefieder [gə'fidər] *n* (-s;-) plumage

gefleckt [gə'flɛkt] *adj* spotted

geflissentlich [gə'flɪsəntlɪç] *adj* intentional, willful

geflochten [gə'flɔxtən] *pp of* **flechten**

geflogen [gə'flogən] *pp of* **fliegen**

geflohen [gə'flo-ən] *pp of* **fliehen**

geflossen [gə'flɔsən] *pp of* **fließen**

Geflügel [gə'flygəl] *n* (-s;) fowl; (*Federvieh*) poultry

Geflü'gelmagen *m* gizzard

Geflunker [gə'fluŋkər] *m* (-s;) (coll) fibbing

Geflüster [gə'flystər] *n* (-s;) whisper

Gefolge [gə'fɔlgə] *n* (-s;-) retinue; **in seinem G.** in its wake

Gefolgschaft [gə'fɔlk/aft] *f* (-;-en) allegiance; followers

gefräßig [gə'frɛsɪç] *adj* gluttonous

Gefrä'ßigkeit *f* (-;) gluttony

Gefreite [gə'fraɪtə] §5 *m* private first class; lance corporal (Brit)

gefressen [gə'frɛsən] *pp of* **fressen**

Gefrieranlage [gə'friranlagə] *f* **Gefrierapparat** [gə'friraparat] *m* freezer

gefrieren [gə'frirən] §77 *intr* (SEIN) freeze

Gefrie'rer *m* (-s;-) freezer; deepfreeze

Gefrier'fach *n* freezing compartment

Gefrier'punkt *m* freezing point

Gefrier'schutz *m*, **Gefrier'schutzmittel** *n* antifreeze

gefroren [gə'frorən] *pp of* **frieren** ‖ **Gefrorene** §5 *n* ice cream

Gefüge [gə'fygə] *n* (-s;-) structure, make-up; arrangement; texture

gefügig [gə'fygɪç] *adj* pliant, pliable

Gefühl [gə'fyl] *n* (-[e]s;-e) feeling; feel; touch; sense; sensation

gefühl'los *adj* numb; callous

gefühls-, Gefühls- [gəfyls] *comb.fm.* of the emotions; emotional; sentimental; (anat) sensory

gefühls'betont *adj* emotional

Gefühlsduselei [gə'fylsduzəlaɪ] *f* (-;) sentimentalism, mawkishness

gefühls'selig *adj* mawkish

gefühl'voll *adj* sensitive; tender-hearted ‖ *adv* with feeling

gefunden [gə'fundən] *pp of* **finden**

gefurcht [gə'furçt] *adj* furrowed

gegangen [gə'gaŋən] *pp of* **gehen**

gegeben [gə'gebən] *pp of* **geben** ‖ *adj* given; (*Umstände*) existing; **gegebene Methode** best approach; **zu gegebener Zeit** at the proper time

gege'benfalls *adv* if necessary

gegen ['gegən] *prep* (*acc*) towards; against; about, approximately; compared with; contrary to; in exchange for

gegen-, Gegen- *comb.fm.* anti-; counter-; contrary; opposite; back; in return

Ge'genantwort *f* rejoinder

Ge'genbeschuldigung *f* countercharge

Ge'genbild *n* counterpart

Gegend ['gegənt] *f* (-;-en) neighborhood, vicinity; region, district

gegeneinan'der *adv* against one another; towards one another

Ge'gengerade *f* back stretch

Ge'gengewicht *n* counterbalance; (am *Rad*) (aut) weight; **das G. halten** (*dat*) counterbalance

Ge'gengift *n* antidote

Ge'genkandidat -in §7 *mf* rival candidate

Ge'genklage *f* countercharge; counterclaim

Ge'genmittel *n* (**gegen**) remedy (for), antidote (against)

Ge'genrede *f* reply, rejoinder

Ge'gensatz *m* contrast; opposite, antithesis; (*Widerspruch*) opposition

gegensätzlich ['gegənzɛtslɪç] *adj* contrary, opposite, antithetical

Ge'genschlag *m* counterplot

ge'genseitig *adj* mutual, reciprocal

Ge'genstand *m* object, thing; subject

gegenständlich ['gegən/tɛntlɪç] *adj* objective; (fa) representational; (log) concrete

ge'genstandslos *adj* baseless; without purpose; irrelevant; (fa) non-representational

Ge'genstoß *m* (box) counterpunch; (mil) counterthrust

Ge'genstück *n* counterpart

Ge'genteil *n* contrary, opposite; **im G.** on the contrary

ge'genteilig *adj* contrary, opposite

gegenü'ber *prep* (*dat*) opposite to; across from; with regard to; compared with

gegenü'berstellen *tr* (*dat*) place opposite to; (*dat*) confront with; (*dat*) contrast with

Gegenü'berstellung *f* confrontation; comparison; (*auf e–r Wache*) line-up

Gegenwart [ˈgeːɡənvart] *f* (–;) present; present time; (*gram*) present tense

gegenwärtig [ˈgeːɡənvɛrtɪç] *adj* present, current || *adv* at present; nowadays

Ge'genwehr *f* defense, resistance

Ge'genwind *m* head wind

Ge'genwirkung *f* (auf *acc*) reaction (to)

ge'genzeichnen *tr* countersign

Ge'genzug *m* countermove

geglichen [ɡəˈɡlɪçən] *pp* of gleichen

geglitten [ɡəˈɡlɪtən] *pp* of gleiten

Gegner –in [ˈɡeːɡnər(ɪn)] §6 *mf* opponent, rival || *m* (mil) enemy

gegnerisch [ˈɡeːɡnərɪʃ] *adj* adverse; antagonistic; opposing; (mil) enemy

gegolten [ɡəˈɡɔltən] *pp* of gelten

gegoren [ɡəˈɡoːrən] *pp* of gären

gegossen [ɡəˈɡɔsən] *pp* of gießen

gegriffen [ɡəˈɡrɪfən] *pp* of greifen

Gehabe [ɡəˈhaːbə] *n* (–s;) affectation

gehaben [ɡəˈhaːbən] *ref* fare; gehab dich nicht so! stop putting on!; gehab dich wohl! farewell!

Gehackte [ɡəˈhaktə] §5 *n* hamburger

Gehalt [ɡəˈhalt] *m* (–[e]s;–e) contents; capacity; standard; G. an (*dat*) percentage of || *n* (–[e]s;⸚er) salary

Gehalts'stufe *f* salary bracket

Gehalts'zulage *f* increment, raise

gehalt'voll *adj* substantial; profound

Gehänge [ɡəˈhɛŋə] *n* (–s;–) slope; pendant; festoon; (*e–s Degens*) belt

gehangen [ɡəˈhaŋən] *pp* of hängen

gehässig [ɡəˈhɛsɪç] *adj* spiteful, nasty

Gehäuse [ɡəˈhɔɪzə] *n* (–s;–) case, box; housing; (*e–r Schnecke*) shell; (*e–s Apfels*) core

Gehege [ɡəˈheːɡə] *n* (–s;–) enclosure

geheim [ɡəˈhaɪm] *adj* secret; streng g. top-secret

geheim'halten §90 *tr* keep secret

Geheimnis [ɡəˈhaɪmnɪs] *n* (–ses;–se) secret, mystery

geheim'nisvoll *adj* mysterious

Geheim'schrift *f* code; coded message

Geheim'tinte *f* invisible ink

Geheim'vorbehalt *m* mental reservation

Geheiß [ɡəˈhaɪs] *n* (–es;) bidding

gehen [ˈɡeːən] §82 *intr* (SEIN) go; walk; leave; (*Teig*) rise; (*Maschine*) work; (*Uhr*) go; (*Ware*) sell; (*Wind*) blow; das geht nicht that will not do; das geht schon it will be all right; sich g. lassen take it easy; wieviel Zoll g. auf einen Fuß? how many inches make a foot? || *impers* es geht mir gut I am doing well; es geht nichts über (*acc*) there is nothing like; es geht um... is at stake; wie geht es Ihnen? how are you?

geheuer [ɡəˈhɔɪ.ər] *adj*—mir war nicht recht g. zumute I didn't feel quite at ease; nicht g. spooky; suspicious; risky

Geheul [ɡəˈhɔɪl] *n* (–s;) howling; loud sobbing

Gehilfe [ɡəˈhɪlfə] *m* (–n;–n), Gehilfin [ɡəˈhɪlfɪn] *f* (–;–nen) assistant

Gehirn [ɡəˈhɪrn] *n* (–[e]s;–e) brains, mind; (anat) brain; sein G. anstrengen rack one's brain

Gehirn– *comb.fm.* brain; cerebral

Gehirn'erschütterung *f* concussion

Gehirn'schlag *m* (pathol) stroke

Gehirn'wäsche *f* brainwashing

gehoben [ɡəˈhoːbən] *pp* of heben || *adj* (*Stellung*) high; (*Stil*) lofty; gehobene Stimmung high spirits

Gehöft [ɡəˈhøːft] *n* (–[e]s;–e) farm

geholfen [ɡəˈhɔlfən] *pp* of helfen

Gehölz [ɡəˈhœlts] *n* (–es;–e) grove; thicket

Gehör [ɡəˈhøːr] *n* (–s;) hearing; ear

Gehör– *comb.fm.* of hearing; auditory

gehorchen [ɡəˈhɔrçən] *intr* (dat) obey

gehören [ɡəˈhøːrən] *ref* to be proper, be right || *intr* (dat or zu) belong to; (in *acc*) go into, belong in

gehörig [ɡəˈhøːrɪç] *adj* proper, due; (*dat* or zu) belonging to || *adv* properly; duly; thoroughly

Gehörn [ɡəˈhœrn] *n* (–s;–e) horns; Gehörne sets of horns

gehorsam [ɡəˈhorzam] *adj* obedient || *adv* obediently; gehorsamst respectfully || Gehorsam *m* (–s;) obedience

Gehor'samverweigerung *f* disobedience

gehren [ˈɡeːrən] *tr* (carp) miter

Gehrlade [ˈɡeːrlaːdə] *f* (–;–n) miter box

Gehrock [ˈɡeːrɔk] *m* Prince Albert

Geh'rung *f*—auf G., nach der G. on the slant; auf G. verbinden miter

Geh'rungslade *f* (–;–n) miter box

Gehsteig [ˈɡeːʃtaɪk] *m* sidewalk

Gehweg [ˈɡeːvek] *m* sidewalk; footpath

Gehwerk [ˈɡeːvɛrk] *n* clockwork, works

Geier [ˈɡaɪ.ər] *m* (–s;–) vulture; zum Geier! what the devil!

Geifer [ˈɡaɪfər] *m* (–s;) drivel; froth, slaver, foam; (fig) venom

geifern [ˈɡaɪfərn] *intr* slaver

Geige [ˈɡaɪɡə] *f* (–;–n) violin, fiddle

geigen [ˈɡaɪɡən] *intr* play the violin

Gei'genbogen *m* bow, fiddlestick

Gei'genharz *n* rosin

Gei'ger –in §6 *mf* violinist

geil [ɡaɪl] *adj* lustful, in heat; (*Boden*) rich; (*üppig*) luxuriant

Geisel [ˈɡaɪzəl] *f* (–;–n) hostage

Geiser [ˈɡaɪzər] *m* (–s;–) geyser

Geiß [ɡaɪs] *f* (–;–en) she-goat

Geißel [ˈɡaɪsəl] *f* (–;–n) scourge

geißeln [ˈɡaɪsəln] *tr* scourge; (fig) castigate

Geist [ɡaɪst] *m* (–es;–er) spirit; (*Gespenst*) ghost; (*Verstand*) mind, intellect; im Geiste in one's imagination; in spirit

Gei'sterbeschwörung *f* (–;) necromancy

Gei'sterstadt *f* ghost town

Gei'sterstunde *f* witching hour

geistes– [ˈɡaɪstəs] *comb.fm.* spiritually; mentally, intellectually || Geistes– *comb.fm.* spiritual; mental, intellectual

gei'stesabwesend *adj* absent-minded

Gei'stesanlagen *pl* natural gift

Gei'stesarbeit *f* brainwork

Gei'stesarmut *f* dullness, stupidity

Gei'stesblitz *m* brain wave; aphorism

Gei'stesflug *m* flight of the imagination

Gei'stesfreiheit *f* intellectual freedom

Gei'stesfrucht *f* brainchild

Gei'stesgegenwart *f* presence of mind

gei'stesgegenwärtig *adj* mentally alert

geistesgestört [ˈgaɪstəsgəˌʃtørt] *adj* mentally disturbed

Gei'steshaltung *f* mentality

gei'steskrank *adj* insane

gei'stesschwach *adj* feeble-minded

Gei'stesstörung *f* mental disorder

Gei'stes- und Natur'wissenschaften *pl* arts and sciences

Gei'stesverfassung *f* frame of mind

gei'stesverwandt *adj* (**mit**) spiritually akin (to); (**mit**) congenial (with)

Gei'stesverwirrung *f* derangement

Gei'steswissenschaften *pl* humanities

gei'steswissenschaftlich *adj* humanistic

Gei'steszustand *m* state of mind

geistig [ˈgaɪstɪç] *adj* mental, intellectual; spiritual

geist'lich *adj* spiritual; (*Orden*) religious; (*kirchlich*) sacred, ecclesiastical; **der geistliche Stand** holy orders; the clergy ‖ **Geistliche §5** *m* clergyman

Geist'lichkeit *f* (–;) clergy

geist'los *adj* spiritless; dull; stupid

geist'reich *adj* witty; ingenious

Geiz [gaɪts] *m* (–es;) stinginess; avarice

geizen [ˈgaɪtsən] *intr*—g. **mit** be sparing with; **nicht g. mit** show freely

Geiz'hals *m* (coll) tightwad

geizig [ˈgaɪtsɪç] *adj* stingy, miserly

Geiz'kragen *m* (coll) tightwad

Gejammer [gəˈjamər] *n* (–s;) wailing

gekannt [gəˈkant] *pp* of **kennen**

Geklapper [gəˈklapər] *n* (–s;) rattling

Geklatsche [gəˈklatʃə] *n* (–s;) clapping; gossiping

Geklirr [gəˈklɪr] *n* (–[e]s;) rattling

geklommen [gəˈkləmən] *pp* of **klimmen**

geklungen [gəˈkluŋən] *pp* of **klingen**

gekniffen [gəˈknɪfən] *pp* of **kneifen**

gekonnt [gəˈkənt] *pp* of **können**

Gekreisch [gəˈkraɪʃ] *n* (–es;) screaming; screeching

Gekritzel [gəˈkrɪtsəl] *n* (–s;) scribbling

gekrochen [gəˈkrəxən] *pp* of **kriechen**

Gekröse [gəˈkrøzə] *n* (–s;) tripe

gekünstelt [gəˈkynstəlt] *adj* affected

Gelächter [gəˈlɛçtər] *n* (–s;) laughter

Gelage [gəˈlɑːgə] *n* (–s;) carousing

Gelände [gəˈlɛndə] *n* (–s;–) terrain; site, lot; (educ) campus; (golf) fairway

Gelän'delauf *m* crosscountry running

Gelän'depunkt *m* landmark

Geländer [gəˈlɛndər] *n* (–s;–) railing; guardrail; banister; parapet

gelang [gəˈlaŋ] *pret* of **gelingen**

gelangen [gəˈlaŋən] *intr* (SEIN) (**an** *acc*, **in** *acc*, **zu**) attain, reach

gelassen [gəˈlasən] *pp* of **lassen** ‖ *adj* composed, calm

Gelatine [ʒelaˈtinə] *f* (–;) gelatin

geläufig [gəˈləɪfɪç] *adj* fluent; (*gemein*) common; (*Zunge*) glib

---

gelaunt [gəˈlaunt] *adj*—**gut gelaunt in good humor; zu etw g. sein** be in the mood for s.th.

Geläut [gəˈləɪt] *n* (–es;), **Geläute** [gəˈləɪtə] *n* (–s;) ringing; chimes

gelb [gelp] *adj* yellow ‖ **Gelb** *n* (–s;) yellow

gelb'lich *adj* yellowish

Gelb'sucht *f* jaundice

Geld [gelt] *n* (–[e]s;) money; **bares G.** cash

Geld- *comb.fm.* money, financial

-geld *n comb.fm.* money; fee(s); tax, toll; allowance

Geld'anlage *f* investment

Geld'anleihe *f* loan

Geld'anweisung *f* money order; draft

Geld'ausgabe *f* expense; expenditure

Geld'beutel *m* pocketbook

Geld'bewilligung *f* (parl) appropriation

Geld'buße *f* fine

Geld'einlage *f* deposit

Geld'einwurf *m* coin slot

Geld'entwertung *f* inflation

Geld'erwerb *m* moneymaking

Geld'geber *m* investor; mortgagee

Geld'gier *f* avarice

Geld'mittel *pl* funds, resources

Geld'onkel *m* sugar daddy

Geld'schein *m* bank note, bill

Geld'schrank *m* safe

Geld'schublade *f* till (*of cash register*)

Geld'sendung *f* remittance

Geld'sorte *f* (fin) denomination

Geld'spende *f* contribution, donation

Geld'strafe *f* fine

Geld'stück *n* coin

Geld'überhang *m* surplus (of money)

Geld'währung *f* currency; monetary standard

Geld'wechsel *m* money exchange

Geld'wesen *n* financial system, finance

Gelee [ʒeˈle] *m & n* (–s;–s) jelly

gelegen [gəˈlegən] *pp* of **liegen** ‖ *adj* located; convenient; opportune; **du kommst mir gerade g.** you're just the person I wanted to see; **es kommt mir gerade gelegen** that suits me just fine; **mir ist daran g. zu** (*inf*) I'm anxious to (*inf*); **was ist daran g.?** what of it?

Gele'genheit *f* (–;–en) occasion; opportunity, chance; (com) bargain

Gelegenheits- *comb.fm.* occasional

Gele'genheitsarbeit *f* odd job

Gele'genheitskauf *m* good bargain

gele'gentlich *adj* occasional; casual; chance ‖ *adv* occasionally ‖ *prep* (*genit*) on the occasion of

gelehrig [gəˈleːrɪç] *adj* teachable; intelligent

gelehrsam [gəˈleːrzam] *adj* erudite

gelehrt [gəˈleːrt] *adj* learned, erudite ‖ **Gelehrte §5** *mf* scholar

Geleise [gəˈlaɪzə] *n* (–s;–) rut; (rr) track; **totes G.** blind alley, deadlock

Geleit [gəˈlaɪt] *n* (–[e]s;) escort; **freies** (or **sicheres**) **G.** safe-conduct; **j-m das G. geben** escort s.o., accompany s.o.; **zum G.** forward

geleiten [gəˈlaɪtən] *tr* escort, accompany; **j-n zur Tür g.** see s.o. to the door

Geleit′zug *m* convoy
Geleit′zugsicherung *f* convoy escort
Gelenk [gə'leŋk] *n* (-[e]s;-e) joint
Gelenk′entzündung *f* arthritis
gelenkig [gə'leŋkiç] *adj* jointed; flexible; agile
gelernt [gə'lernt] *adj* skilled
Gelichter [gə'liçtər] *n* (-s;) riffraff
Geliebte [gə'liptə] §6 *mf* beloved, sweetheart
geliehen [gə'li·ən] *pp* of **leihen**
gelieren [ʒe'lirən] *intr* jell, gel
gelinde [gə'lində] *adj* soft; gentle, mild ‖ *adv* gently, mildly; g. gesagt to put it mildly
gelingen [gə'liŋən] §142 *intr* (SEIN) succeed ‖ *impers* (SEIN)—es gelingt mir I succeed ‖ **Gelingen** *n* (-s;) success
gelitten [gə'litən] *pp* of **leiden**
gell [gel] *adj* shrill ‖ *interj* say!
gellen ['gelən] *intr* ring out; yell
gel′lend *adj* shrill, piercing
geloben [gə'lobən] *tr* solemnly promise, vow; take the vow of ‖ *ref*—sich [*dat*] g. vow to oneself
gelogen [gə'logən] *pp* of **lügen**
gelt [gelt] *interj* say!
gelten ['geltən] §83 *tr* be worth; wenig g. mean little ‖ *intr* be valid; (*Münze*) be legal tender; (*Gesetz*) be in force; (*Grund*) hold true; (*Regel*) apply; (*Mittel*) be allowable; (*beim Spiel*) count; g. als or für have the force of; be ranked as; pass for, be considered; g. lassen acknowledge as correct; j–m g. be aimed at s.o. ‖ *impers*—es gilt (*acc*) be at stake; be a matter of; be worth (*s.th.*); es gilt mir gleich, ob it's all the same to me whether; es gilt zu (*inf*) it is necessary to (*inf*); jetzt gilt's! here goes!
Gel′tung *f* (-;) validity; value, importance; zur G. bringen make the most of; zur G. kommen show off well
Gel′tungsbedürfnis *n* need for recognition
Gelübde [gə'lypdə] *n* (-s;-) vow
gelungen [gə'luŋən] *pp* of **gelingen** ‖ *adj* successful; (*Wendung*) well-turned; funny
Gelüst [gə'lyst] *n* (-[e]s;-e) desire
gelüsten [gə'lystən] *impers*—es gelüstet mich nach I could go for
gemach [gə'max] *adv* slowly, by degrees ‖ **Gemach** *n* (-[e]s;-er) room; apartment; chamber
gemächlich [gə'meçliç] *adj* leisurely; comfortable
Gemahl [gə'mal] *m* (-[e]s;-e) husband
Gemahlin [gə'malin] *f* (-;-nen) wife
Gemälde [gə'meldə] *n* (-s;-) painting
gemäß [gə'mes] *prep* (*dat*) according to
gemäßigt [gə'mesiçt] *adj* moderate
gemein [gə'main] *adj* common; mean, vile; sich g. machen mit associate with ‖ **Gemeine** §5 *m* (mil) private
Gemeinde [gə'maində] *f* (-;-n) community; municipality; (eccl) parish
Gemein′deabgaben *pl* local taxes
Gemein′deanleihen *pl* municipal bonds

Gemein′dehaus *n* town hall
gemein′frei *adj* in the public domain
gemein′gefährlich *adj* constituting a public danger, dangerous
gemein′gültig *adj* generally accepted
Gemein′heit *f* (-;-en) meanness; dirty trick; vulgarity
gemein′hin *adv* commonly, usually
Gemein′kosten *pl* overhead
Gemein′nutz *m* public interest
gemein′nützig *adj* non-profit
Gemein′platz *m* platitude
gemeinsam [gə'mainzam] *adj* common, joint; mutual
Gemein′schaft *f* (-;-en) community; close association
gemein′schaftlich *adj* common, joint; mutual
Gemein′schaftsanschluß *m* (telp) party line
Gemein′schaftsarbeit *f* teamwork
Gemein′schaftsgeist *m* esprit de corps
Gemein′sinn *m* public spirit
gemein′verständlich *adj* popular; g. darstellen popularize
Gemein′wesen *n* community
Gemein′wohl *n* commonweal
Gemenge [gə'meŋə] *n* (-s;-) mixture; (*Kampfgewühl*) scuffle, melee
gemessen [gə'mesən] *pp* of **messen** ‖ *adj* deliberate; precise; dignified; g. an (*dat*) compared with
Gemetzel [gə'metsəl] *n* (-s;-) massacre
gemieden [gə'midən] *pp* of **meiden**
Gemisch [gə'miʃ] *n* (-es;-e) mixture
Gemischt′warenhandlung *f* general store
Gemme ['gemə] *f* (-;-n) gem
gemocht [gə'mɔxt] *pp* of **mögen**
gemolken [gə'mɔlkən] *pp* of **melken**
Gemse ['gemzə] *f* (-;-n) chamois
Gemunkel [gə'muŋkəl] *n* (-s;-) gossip, whispering
Gemurmel [gə'murməl] *n* (-s;) murmur
Gemüse [gə'myzə] *n* (-s;-) vegetable; vegetables
Gemü′sebau *m* (-[e]s;) vegetable gardening
Gemü′sekonserven *pl* canned vegetables
gemüßigt [gə'mysiçt] *adj*—sich g. fühlen feel compelled
gemußt [gə'must] *pp* of **müssen**
Gemüt [gə'myt] *n* (-[e]s;-er) mind; disposition; person, soul; warmth of feeling; j–m etw zu Gemüte führen bring s.th. home to s.o.
gemütlich [gə'mytliç] *adj* good-natured, easy-going; (*Wohnung*) cosy
Gemüt′lichkeit *f* (-;) easy-going nature; cosiness
Gemüts′art *f* disposition, nature
Gemüts′bewegung *f* emotion
gemüts′krank *adj* melancholy
Gemüts′mensch *m* warm-hearted person
Gemüts′ruhe *f*—in (aller) G. in peace and quiet
Gemüts′stimmung *f* mood
Gemüts′verfassung *f* state of mind
Gemüts′zustand *m* frame of mind

gemüt'voll adj emotional

gen [gen] prep (acc) (poet) towards ‖ **Gen** [gen] n (-s;-e) (biol) gene

genannt [gə'nant] pp of **nennen**

genau [gə'naʊ] adj exact; fussy

genau'genommen adv strictly speaking

Genau'igkeit f (-;) exactness, accuracy; meticulousness

Gendarm [ʒā'darm] m (-en;-en) policeman

Gendarme•rie [ʒādarmə'ri] f (-;-rien ['ri.ən]) rural police; rural police station

Genealo•gie [genε.alə'gi] f (-;-gien ['gi.ən]) genealogy

genehm [gə'nem] adj agreeable; acceptable; (dat) convenient (for)

genehmigen [gə'nemɪgən] tr grant; approve; **sich** [dat] **etw g.** (coll) treat oneself to s.th.; **genehmigt** O.K.

Geneh'migung f (-;-en) grant; approval; permission; permit

geneigt [gə'naɪkt] adj sloping; (zu) inclined (to); (dat) well-disposed (towards)

Geneigt'heit f inclination; good will

General [gene'ral] m (-[e]s;-e & *e) general

General'feldmarschall m field marshal

General'inspekteur m chief of the joint chiefs of staff

Generalität [generalɪ'tet] f (-;) body of generals

General'konsul m consul general

General'leutnant m lieutenant general; (aer) air marshal

General'major m major general

General'nenner m common denominator

General'probe f dress rehearsal

General'stabskarte f strategic map

General'vollmacht f full power of attorney

Generation [genera'tsjon] f (-;-en) generation

generell [gene'rel] adj general, blanket

genesen [gə'nezən] §84 intr (SEIN) convalesce; (von) recover (from)

Gene'sung f (-;-en) convalescence

Gene'sungsheim n convalescent home

genetisch [ge'netɪʃ] adj genetic

Genf [genf] n (-s;) Geneva

Gen'forscher –in §6 mf genetic engineer

Gen'forschung f (-;) genetic engineering

genial [ge'njal] adj brilliant, gifted

Genick [gə'nɪk] n (-s;-e) nape of the neck

Genick'bruch m broken neck

Genick'schlag m (box) rabbit punch

Genie [ʒe'ni] n (-s;-s) (man of) genius

genieren [ʒe'nirən] tr bother; embarrass ‖ ref feel embarrassed

genießbar [gə'nisbar] adj edible; drinkable; (fig) agreeable

genießen [gə'nisən] §76 tr enjoy; eat; drink

Genie'streich m stroke of genius

Genitalien [genɪ'taljən] pl genitals

Geni•tiv ['genɪtif] m (-s;-tive ['tivə]) genitive

genommen [gə'nɔmən] pp of **nehmen**

genoß [gə'nɔs] pret of **genießen**

Genosse [gə'nɔsə] m (-n;-n) companion, buddy; (pol) comrade –**genosse** m comb.fm. fellow-, -mate

Genos'senschaft f (-;-en) association; coöperative

Genossin [gə'nɔsɪn] f (-;-nen) companion, buddy; (pol) comrade

genug [gə'nuk] invar adj & adv enough

Genüge [gə'nygə] f—j–m **G. tun** give s.o. satisfaction; **zur G.** enough; only too well

genügen [gə'nygən] intr suffice, do ‖ ref—**sich** [dat] **g. lassen an** (dat) be content with

genü'gend adj sufficient

genügsam [gə'nykzam] adj easily satisfied; frugal

genug'tun §154 intr (dat) satisfy

Genugtuung [gə'nuktu·ʊŋ] f (-;) satisfaction

Ge•nuß [gə'nʊs] m (-nusses;-nüsse) enjoyment; pleasure; (Nutznießung) use; (von Speisen) consumption

Genuß'mittel n semi-luxury (as coffee, tobacco, etc.)

genuß'reich adj thoroughly enjoyable

genuß'süchtig adj pleasure-seeking

Geographie [ge.ɔgra'fi] f (-;) geography

geographisch [ge.ɔ'grafɪʃ] adj geographical

Geologe [ge.ɔ'logə] m (-n;-n) geologist

Geologie [ge.ɔlɔ'gi] f (-;) geology

Geometer [ge.ɔ'metər] m (-s;-) surveyor

Geometrie [ge.ome'tri] f (-;) geometry

Geophysik [ge.ɔfy'zik] f (-;) geophysics

Geopolitik [ge.ɔpɔlɪ'tik] f (-;) geopolitics

Georgine [ge.ɔr'ginə] f (-;-n) dahlia

Gepäck [gə'pek] n (-[e]s;) luggage

Gepäck'abfertigung f luggage check-in; luggage counter

Gepäck'ablage f luggage rack

Gepäck'anhänger m tag; luggage trailer

Gepäck'aufbewahrung f baggage room

Gepäck'netz n baggage rack (net type)

Gepäck'raum m luggage compartment

Gepäck'schein m luggage check

Gepäck'träger m porter; (aut) roof rack

Gepäck'wagen m (rr) baggage car

gepanzert [gə'pantsərt] adj armored

gepfeffert [gə'pfefərt] adj peppered; (Worte) sharp; (Preis) exorbitant

Gepfeife [gə'pfaɪfə] n (-s;) whistling

gepfiffen [gə'pfɪfən] pp of **pfeifen**

geflogen [gə'pflogən] pp of **pflegen**

Gepflo'genheit f (-;-en) custom, practice

Geplänkel [gə'plɛŋkəl] n (-s;) skirmish; (fig) exchange of words

Geplapper [gə'plapər] n (-s;) jabber

Geplärr [gə'plɛr] n (-s;) bawling

Geplauder [gə'plaʊdər] n (-s;) small talk, chat

Gepolter [gə'pɔltər] n (-s;) rumbling

Gepräge [gə'pregə] n (-s;) impression; stamp, character

Gepränge [gə'prɛŋə] n (-s;) pomp

gepriesen [gə'pri:zən] *pp* of **preisen**
gequollen [gə'kvɔlən] *pp* of **quellen**
gerade [gə'ra:də] *adj* straight; even; direct; (*Haltung*) erect; (*aufrichtig*) straightforward || *adv* straight; exactly; just; just now || **Gerade** *f* (*-n*; *-n*) straight line; straightaway; (box) straight; **rechte G.** straight right
gerade(n)wegs [gə'ra:də(n)veks] *adv* immediately, straightaway
geradezu/ *adv* downright
Geranie [ge'ra:njə] *f* (*-*;*-n*) geranium
gerannt [gə'rant] *pp* of **rennen**
Gerassel [gə'rasəl] *n* (*-s*;) clanking
Gerät [gə'rɛt] *n* (*-[e]s*;*-e*) device, instrument; tool; (rad, telv) set
geraten [gə'ra:tən] *pp* of **raten** || *adj* successful; (*ratsam*) advisable || §63 *intr* (SEIN) (*gut*, *schlecht*, *usw.*) turn out; **außer sich g.** be beside oneself; **g. an** (*acc*) come by; **g. auf** (*acc*) get into; get on to; **g. hinter** (*acc*) get behind; find out about; **g. in** (*acc*) get into, fall into; **g. nach** take after; **g. über** (*acc*) come across; **in Bewegung g.** begin to move; **in Brand g.** catch fire; **ins Schleudern g.** begin to skid; **ins Stocken g.** come to a standstill
Gerä/teschuppen *m* tool shed
Geratewohl [gə'ra:təvol] *n* (*-s*;)—**aufs G.** at random
geraum [gə'raum] *adj* considerable
geräumig [gə'rɔımıç] *adj* spacious
Geräusch [gə'rɔıʃ] *n* (*-[e]s*;*-e*) noise
gerben ['gerbən] *tr* tan
Gerberei [gerbə'raı] *f* (*-*;*-en*) tannery
gerecht [gə'rɛçt] *adj* just, fair; justified; **g. werden** (*dat*) do justice to
Gerech/tigkeit *f* (*-*;) justice; fairness
Gerede [gə're:də] *n* (*-s*;) talk; hearsay
gereichen [gə'raıçən] *intr*—**es gereicht ihm zur Ehre** it does him justice; **es gereicht ihm zum Vorteil** it is to his advantage; **es gereicht mir zur Freude** it gives me pleasure
gereizt [gə'raıtst] *adj* irritable; irritated
gereuen [gə'rɔı·ən] *tr* cause (*s.o.*) regret || *ref*—**sich keine Mühe g. lassen** spare no trouble || *impers*—**es gereut mich** I regret
Geriatrie [gerı·a'tri] *f* (*-*;) geriatrics
Gericht [gə'rıçt] *n* (*-[e]s*;*-e*) court; courthouse; judgment; (culin) dish; **das Jüngste G.** the Last Judgment
gericht/lich *adj* legal, judicial, court
Gerichtsbarkeit [gə'rıçtsbarkaıt] *f* (*-*;) jurisdiction
Gerichts/bote *m* (jur) bailiff
Gerichts/hof *m* law court; **Oberster G.** Supreme Court
Gerichts/medizin *f* forensic medicine
Gerichts/saal *m* courtroom
Gerichts/schreiber —in §6 *mf* (jur) clerk
Gerichts/stand *m* (jur) venue
Gerichts/verhandlung *f* hearing; trial
Gerichts/vollzieher *m* (jur) marshal
Gerichts/wesen *n* judicial system
gerieben [gə'ri:bən] *pp* of **reiben** || *adj* cunning, smart
Geriesel [gə'ri:zəl] *n* (*-s*;) purling
gering [gə'rıŋ] *adj* slight, trifling;

small; (*niedrig*) low; (*ärmlich*) poor; (*minderwertig*) inferior; **nicht im geringsten** not in the least
gering/achten *tr* think little of
gering/fügig *adj* insignificant
gering/schätzen *tr* look down on
Gering/schätzung *f* contempt, disdain
gerinnen [gə'rınən] §121 *intr* coagulate, clot; (*Milch*) curdle
Gerinnsel [gə'rınzəl] *n* (*-s*;) clot
Gerippe [gə'rıpə] *n* (*-s*;) skeleton; (*Gerüst*) framework
gerippt [gə'rıpt] *adj* ribbed; (*Säule*) fluted; (*Stoff*) corded
gerissen [gə'rısən] *pp* of **reißen** || *adj* sly
geritten [gə'rıtən] *pp* of **reiten**
gern(e) ['gern(ə)] *adv* gladly; **g. haben** or **mögen** like; **ich rauche g.** I like to smoke
gerochen [gə'rɔxən] *pp* of **riechen**
Geröll [gə'rœl] *n* (*-s*;) pebbles
geronnen [gə'rɔnən] *pp* of **gerinnen** & **rinnen**
Gerste ['gerstə] *f* (*-*;*-n*) barley
Ger/stenkorn *n* grain of barley; (pathol) sty
Gerte ['gertə] *f* (*-*;*-n*) switch, rod
Geruch [gə'rux] *m* (*-[e]s*;*-e*) smell
geruch/los *adj* odorless
Gerücht [gə'rʏçt] *n* (*-[e]s*;*-e*) rumor
geruhen [gə'ru·ən] *intr* deign
geruhsam [gə'ruzam] *adj* quiet; relaxed
Gerümpel [gə'rʏmpəl] *n* (*-s*;) junk
gerungen [gə'ruŋən] *pp* of **ringen**
Gerüst [gə'rʏst] *n* (*-s*;*-e*) scaffold; (*Tragewerk*) frame; (fig) outline
Ges [ges] *n* (*-*;*-*) (mus) G flat
gesamt [gə'zamt] *adj* entire, total
gesamt-, Gesamt- *comb.fm.* total, overall; all-; joint; collective
gesandt [gə'zant] *pp* of **senden**
Gesand/te §5 *mf* envoy
Gesandt/schaft *f* (*-*;*-en*) legation
Gesang [gə'zaŋ] *m* (*-[e]s*;*-e*) singing; song; (lit) canto
Gesang/verein *m* glee club
Gesäß [gə'zes] *n* (*-es*;*-e*) buttocks; (coll) behind
Geschäft [gə'ʃeft] *n* (*-[e]s*;*-e*) business; deal, bargain; shop, store
Geschäftemacherei [gə'ʃeftəmaxəraı] *f* (*-*;) commercialism
geschäftig [gə'ʃetıç] *adj* busy
Geschäf/tigkeit *f* (*-*;) hustle, bustle
geschäft/lich *adj* business || *adv* on business
Geschäfts/abschluß *m* contract; deal
Geschäfts/aufsicht *f* receivership
Geschäfts/bedingungen *pl* terms
geschäfts/führend *adj* managing; executive; **geschäftsführende Regierung** caretaker government
Geschäfts/führer —in §6 *mf* manager
Geschäfts/haus *n* firm; office building
Geschäfts/inhaber —in §6 *mf* proprietor
geschäfts/kundig *adj* with business experience
Geschäfts/lokal *n* business premises; (*Laden*) shop; (*Büro*) office
Geschäfts/mann *m* (*-[e]s*;*-leute*) businessman

geschäfts'mäßig adj business-like

Geschäfts'ordnung f rules of procedure; **zur G.!** point of order!

Geschäfts'reise f business trip

Geschäfts'schluß m closing time

Geschäfts'stelle f office; branch

Geschäfts'träger m agent, representative; (pol) chargé d'affaires

geschäfts'tüchtig adj sharp

Geschäfts'verbindung f business connections

Geschäfts'verkehr m business transactions

Geschäfts'viertel n business district

Geschäfts'wert m (com) good will

Geschäfts'zweig m line of business

geschah [gə'/ɑ] pret of geschehen

geschehen [gə'/eːən] §138 intr (SEIN) happen; take place; be done; **das geschieht dir recht!** serves you right! || **Geschehen** n (-s;) events

Geschehnis n (-ses;-se) event

gescheit [gə'/ɑɪt] adj clever; bright; sensible; **er ist wohl nicht ganz g.** he's not all there

Geschenk [gə'/ɛŋk] n (-[e]s;-e) gift

Geschichte [gə'/ɪçtə] f (-;-n) story; history; (coll) affair, thing

geschicht'lich adj historical

Geschichts'forscher –in §6 mf, **Geschichts'schreiber** –in §6 mf historian

Geschick [gə'/ɪk] n (-[e]s;-e) fate, destiny; dexterity, skill

Geschick'lichkeit f (-;) skillfulness

geschickt [gə'/ɪkt] adj skillful

geschieden [gə'/iːdən] pp of scheiden

geschienen [gə'/iːnən] pp of scheinen

Geschirr [gə'/ɪr] n (-[e]s;-e) dishes; china; pot; (e-s Pferdes) harness

Geschirr'schrank m kitchen cabinet

Geschirrspülmaschine [gə'/ɪr/pyːlmaʃinə] f dishwasher

Geschirr'tuch n dishtowel

geschissen [gə'/ɪsən] pp of scheißen

Geschlecht [gə'/lɛçt] n (-[e]s;-er) sex; race; family, line; generation; (gram) gender

geschlecht'lich adj sexual

Geschlechts'krankheit f venereal disease

Geschlechts'teile pl genitals

Geschlechts'trieb m sexual instinct

Geschlechts'verkehr m intercourse

Geschlechts'wort n (-[e]s;-̈er) (gram) article

geschlichen [gə'/lɪçən] pp of schleichen

geschliffen [gə'/lɪfən] pp of schleifen || adj (Glas) cut; (fig) polished

geschlissen [gə'/lɪsən] pp of schleißen

geschlossen [gə'/losən] pp of schließen || adj closed; enclosed; (Front) united; (Gesellschaft) private; (ling) close; (telv) closed-circuit || adv unanimously; **g. hinter j—m stehen** be solidly behind s.o.

geschlungen [gə'/luŋən] pp of schlingen

Geschmack [gə'/mak] m (-s;-̈e & -̈er) taste

Geschmacks'richtung f vogue

geschmeidig [ge'/maɪdɪç] adj pliant; flexible; lithe; (Haar) manageable

Geschmeiß [gə'/maɪs] n (-es;) vermin; rabble

geschmissen [gə'/mɪsən] pp of schmeißen

geschmolzen [gə'/moltsən] pp of schmelzen

Geschnatter [gə'/natər] n (-s;) cackle

geschniegelt [gə'/niːgəlt] adj spruce

geschnitten [gə'/nɪtən] pp of schneiden

geschnoben [gə'/noːbən] pp of schnauben

geschoben [gə'/oːbən] pp of schieben

gescholten [gə'/oltən] pp of schelten

Geschöpf [gə'/œpf] n (-[e]s;-e) creature

geschoren [gə'/oːrən] pp of scheren

Ge'schoß [gə'/os] n (-schosses;-schosse) shot; missile; shell; floor, story

Geschoß'bahn f trajectory

geschossen [gə'/osən] pp of schießen

geschraubt [gə'/raubt] adj affected; (Stil) stilted

Geschrei [gə'/raɪ] n (-[e]s;) shouting

Geschreibsel [gə'/raɪpsəl] n (-s;) scribbling, scrawl

geschrieben [gə'/riːbən] pp of schreiben

geschrieen [gə'/riːən] pp of schreien

geschritten [gə'/rɪtən] pp of schreiten

geschunden [gə'/undən] pp of schinden

Geschütz [gə'/yts] n (-es;-e) gun

Geschütz'bedienung f gun crew

Geschütz'legierung f gun metal

Geschütz'stand m gun emplacement

Geschwader [gə'/vadər] n (-s;-) (aer) group (consisting of 27 aircraft); (nav) squadron

Geschwätz [gə'/vɛts] n (-es;) chatter

geschweige [gə'/vaɪgə]—**g. denn** let alone, much less

geschwiegen [gə'/viːgən] pp of schweigen

geschwind [gə'/vɪnt] adj quick

Geschwin'digkeit f (-;-en) speed; velocity; **mit der G. von** at the rate of

Geschwin'digkeitsbegrenzung f speed limit

Geschwin'digkeitsmesser m speedometer

Geschwind'schritt m (mil) double time

Geschwister [gə'/vɪstər] pl brother and sister, brothers, sisters, brothers and sisters; siblings

geschwollen [gə'/volən] pp of schwellen || adj turgid

geschwommen [gə'/voːmən] pp of schwimmen

geschworen [gə'/voːrən] pp of schwören || **Geschworene** §5 mf juror; **die Geschworenen** the jury

Geschwo'renengericht n jury

Geschwulst [gə'/vulst] f (-;-̈e) swelling; tumor

geschwunden [gə'/vundən] pp of schwinden

geschwungen [gə'/vuŋən] pp of schwingen

Geschwür [gə'/vyr] n (-s;-e) ulcer

Geselle [gə'zelə] *m* (-n;-n) journey-man; companion; lad, fellow
gesellen [gə'zelən] *ref*—**sich zu j-m g.** join s.o.
gesellig [gə'zelɪç] *adj* gregarious, sociable
Gesell'schaft *f* (-;-en) society; company; (pej) bunch; (com) company; **j-m G. leisten** keep s.o. company
Gesell'schafter –in §6 *mf* companion; shareholder; (com) partner
gesell'schaftlich *adj* social
Gesell'schaftsspiel *n* party game
Gesell'schaftswissenschaft *f* social science; sociology
gesessen [gə'zesən] *pp of* **sitzen**
Gesetz [gə'zets] *n* (-es;-e) law
Gesetz'buch *n* legal code
Gesetz'entwurf *m* (parl) bill
Gesetzes– [gəzetsəs] *comb.fm.* legal, of law, of the law
Geset'zesantrag *m*, **Geset'zesvorlage** *f* (parl) bill
gesetz'gebend *adj* legislative
Gesetz'geber –in §6 *mf* legislator
Gesetz'gebung *f* (-;) legislation
gesetz'lich *adj* legal
gesetz'los *adj* lawless
gesetz'mäßig *adj* legal; legitimate
Gesetz'sammlung *f* code of laws
gesetzt [gə'zetst] *adj* sedate; (*Alter*) mature; **g. den Fall, daß** assuming that || *adv* in a dignified manner
gesetz'widrig *adj* illegal, unlawful
Gesicht [gə'zɪçt] *n* (-es;-er) face; sight; eyesight; (*Aussehen*) look
Gesichts'farbe *f* complexion
Gesichts'kreis *m* horizon; outlook
Gesichts'punkt *m* point of view, angle
Gesichts'spannung *f* face lift
Gesichts'zug *m* feature
Gesims [gə'zɪms] *n* (-es;-e) molding
Gesindel [gə'zɪndəl] *n* (-s;) rabble; **lichtscheues G.** shady characters
gesinnt [gə'zɪnt] *adj* disposed; –minded
Gesinnung [gə'zɪnʊŋ] *f* (-;-en) mind; character; convictions
gesin'nungslos *adj* without definite convictions
gesin'nungsmäßig *adv* according to one's convictions
gesin'nungstreu, gesin'nungstüchtig *adj* staunch
gesittet [gə'zɪtət] *adj* polite; civilized
gesoffen [gə'zofən] *pp of* **saufen**
gesogen [gə'zogən] *pp of* **saugen**
gesonnen [gə'zonən] *pp of* **sinnen** || *adj*—**g. sein zu** (*inf*) have a mind to (*inf*), be inclined to (*inf*)
gesotten [gə'zotən] *pp of* **sieden**
Gespann [gə'ʃpan] *n* (-[e]s;-e) team; pair, combination
gespannt [gə'ʃpant] *adj* stretched; tense; (*Aufmerksamkeit*) close; (*Beziehungen*) strained; **ich bin g.** (coll) I wonder, I am anxious to know
Gespenst [gə'ʃpenst] *n* (-[e]s;-er) ghost, specter
gespen'sterhaft *adj* ghostly; spooky
gespenstisch [gə'ʃpenstɪʃ] *adj* ghostly
gespie(e)n [gə'ʃpi(ə)n] *pp of* **speien**
Gespiele [gə'ʃpilə] *m* (-n;-n), **Gespielin** [gə'ʃpilɪn] *f* (-;-nen) playmate

Gespinst [gə'ʃpɪnst] *n* (-es;-e) yarn; (*Gewebe*) web
gesponnen [gə'ʃpɔnən] *pp of* **spinnen**
Gespött [gə'ʃpœt] *n* (-[e]s;) ridicule; laughing stock
Gespräch [gə'ʃpreç] *n* (-[e]s;-e) conversation; (telp) call; **Gespräche** (pol) talks; **G. mit Voranmeldung** person-to-person call
gesprächig [gə'ʃpreçɪç] *adj* talkative
gespreizt [gə'ʃpraɪtst] *adj* outspread; affected || *adv*—**g. tun** act big
gesprenkelt [gə'ʃprenkəlt] *adj* spotted
gesprochen [gə'ʃprɔçən] *pp of* **sprechen**
gesprossen [gə'ʃprɔsən] *pp of* **sprießen**
gesprungen [gə'ʃprʊŋən] *pp of* **springen**
Gestade [gə'ʃtadə] *n* (-s;-) (river) bank; (sea)shore
Gestalt [gə'ʃtalt] *f* (-;-en) shape; figure; (*Wuchs*) stature
gestalten [gə'ʃtaltən] *tr* shape; form; arrange || *ref* take shape; turn out
Gestal'tung *f* (-;-en) formation; development; arrangement; design
gestanden [gə'ʃtandən] *pp of* **stehen**
geständig [gə'ʃtendɪç] *adj*—**g. sein** admit one's guilt
Geständnis [gə'ʃtentnɪs] *n* (-ses;-se) confession, admission
Gestank [gə'ʃtaŋk] *m* (-[e]s;) stench
Gestapo [gə'ʃtapo] *f* (-;) (**Geheime Staatspolizei**) secret state police
gestatten [gə'ʃtatən] *tr* permit, allow
Geste ['gestə] *f* (-;-n) gesture
gestehen [gə'ʃte·ən] §146 *tr* admit
Gestein [gə'ʃtaɪn] *n* (-[e]s;-e) rock
Gestell [gə'ʃtel] *n* (-[e]s;-e) frame; rack; mounting; (coll) beanpole
Gestel'lungsbefehl *m* (mil) induction orders
gestern ['gestərn] *adv* yesterday; **g. abend** last evening, last night
gestiefelt [gə'ʃtifəlt] *adj* in boots
gestiegen [gə'ʃtigən] *pp of* **steigen**
gestikulieren [gestiku'lirən] *intr* gesticulate
Gestirn [gə'ʃtɪrn] *n* (-[e]s;-e) star; (*Sternbild*) constellation
gestirnt [gə'ʃtɪrnt] *adj* starry
gestoben [gə'ʃtobən] *pp of* **stieben**
Gestöber [gə'ʃtøbər] *n* (-s;-) snow flurry
gestochen [gə'ʃtɔxən] *pp of* **stechen**
gestohlen [gə'ʃtolən] *pp of* **stehlen**
gestorben [gə'ʃtorbən] *pp of* **sterben**
gestoßen [gə'ʃtosən] *pp of* **stoßen**
Gesträuch [gə'ʃtrɔɪç] *n* (-[e]s;) bushes, shrubbery
gestreift [gə'ʃtraɪft] *adj* striped
gestrichen [gə'ʃtrɪçən] *pp of* **streichen**
gestrig ['gestrɪç] *adj* yesterday's
gestritten [gə'ʃtrɪtən] *pp of* **streiten**
Gestrüpp [gə'ʃtryp] *n* (-[e]s;) underbrush
gestunken [gə'ʃtʊŋkən] *pp of* **stinken**
Gestüt [gə'ʃtyt] *n* (-[e]s;-e) stud farm
Gestüt'hengst *m* stallion, studhorse
Gesuch [gə'zux] *n* (-[e]s;-e) request; application; (jur) petition
gesucht [gə'zuxt] *adj* wanted; in demand; studied; (*Vergleich*) far-fetched
Gesudel [gə'zudəl] *n* (-s;) messy job

Gesumme [gə'zumə] n (-s;) humming
gesund [gə'zunt] adj healthy; sound;
  wholesome; **g. werden** get well
Gesund'beter –in §6 mf faith healer
Gesund'brunnen m mineral spring
gesunden [gə'zundən] intr (SEIN) get
  well again, recover
Gesund'heit f (-;) health; **auf Ihre G.!**
  to your health!; **G.!** (God) bless you!
Gesund'heitslehre f hygiene
Gesund'heitspflege f hygiene
Gesund'heitsrücksichten pl—**aus G.**
  for reasons of health
Gesund'heitswesen n public health
gesungen [gə'zuŋən] pp of **singen**
gesunken [gə'zuŋkən] pp of **sinken**
Getäfel [gə'tefəl] n (-s;) wainscoting
getä'felt adj inlaid
getan [gə'tan] pp of **tun**
Getöse [gə'tøzə] n (-s;) din, noise
getragen [gə'tragən] pp of **tragen** ‖ adj
  solemn
Getrampel [gə'trampəl] n (-s;) trample
Getränk [gə'treŋk] n (-[e]s;-e) drink
getrauen [gə'trau-ən] ref dare
Getreide [gə'traidə] n (-s;-) grain
Getrei'deboden m granary
Getrei'despeicher m grain elevator
getreu [gə'trɔɪ] adj faithful, true
getreu'lich adv faithfully
Getriebe [gə'tribə] n (-s;-) hustle and
  bustle; (adm) machinery; (aut) transmission
getrieben [gə'tribən] pp of **treiben**
getroffen [gə'trɔfən] pp of **treffen**
getrogen [gə'trogən] pp of **trügen**
getrost [gə'trost] adj confident
getrunken [gə'truŋkən] pp of **trinken**
Getto ['geto] n (-s;-s) ghetto
Getue [gə'tu-ə] n (-s;) fuss
Getümmel [gə'tyməl] n (-s;) turmoil
getupft [gə'tupft] adj polka-dot
Geviert [gə'firt] n (-[e]s;-e) square
Gewächs [gə'veks] n (-es;-e) growth;
  plant
gewachsen [gə'vaksən] adj—**g. sein**
  (dat) be equal to, be up to
Gewächs'haus n greenhouse, hothouse
gewagt [gə'vakt] adj risky; off-color
gewählt [gə'velt] adj choice; refined
gewahr [gə'var] adj—**g. werden** (genit)
  become aware of
Gewähr [gə'ver] f (-;) guarantee
gewahren [gə'varən] tr notice
gewähren [gə'verən] tr grant
gewähr'leisten tr guarantee, ensure
Gewähr'leistung f (-;-en) guarantee
Gewahrsam [gə'varzam] m (-[e]s;)
  safekeeping, custody ‖ n (-[e]s;-e)
  prison
Gewährs'mann m (-[e]s;̈-er & -leute)
  informant, source
Gewährs'pflicht f warranty
Gewalt [gə'valt] f (-;-en) force; violence; authority; (Aufsicht) control
Gewalt'haber m (-s;-) ruler; tyrant
Gewalt'herrschaft f tyranny
Gewalt'herrscher m tyrant
gewal'tig adj powerful; huge; (coll)
  awful ‖ adv terribly
Gewalt'kur f drastic measure; (coll)
  crash program
gewalt'los adj nonviolent

Gewalt'marsch m forced march
Gewalt'mensch m brute, tyrant
gewaltsam [gə'valtzam] adj violent;
  forcible; drastic ‖ adv by force
Gewalt'samkeit f (-;) violence
Gewalt'streich m bold stroke
Gewalt'tat f act of violence
gewalt'tätig adj violent, brutal
Gewalt'verbrechen n felony
Gewalt'verbrecher –in §6 mf felon
Gewand [gə'vant] n (-[e]s;̈-er) robe;
  appearance, guise; (eccl) vestment
gewandt [gə'vant] pp of **wenden** ‖ adj
  agile; clever
gewann [gə'van] pret of **gewinnen**
gewärtig [gə'vertiç] adj—**g. sein**
  (genit) be prepared for
Gewäsch [gə'veʃ] n (-es;) nonsense
Gewässer [gə'vesər] n (-s;-) body of
  water; waters
Gewebe [gə'vebə] n (-s;-) tissue; (tex)
  fabric
geweckt [gə'vekt] adj bright, sharp
Gewehr [gə'ver] n (-[e]s;-e) rifle
Geweih [gə'vai] n (-[e]s;-e) antlers
Gewerbe [gə'verbə] n (-s;-) trade,
  business; calling, profession; industry
Gewer'bebetrieb m business enterprise
Gewer'beschule f trade school
gewerblich [gə'verpliç] adj industrial;
  commercial, business
gebwerbs'mäßig adj professional
Gewerkschaft [gə'verkʃaft] f (-;-en)
  labor union
gewerk'schaftlich adj union ‖ adv—
  sich g. organisieren unionize
Gewerk'schaftsbeitrag m union dues
gewesen [gə'vezən] pp of **sein**
gewichen [gə'viçən] pp of **weichen**
Gewicht [gə'viçt] n (-[e]s;-e) (& fig)
  weight
gewichtig [gə'viçtiç] adj weighty
gewiegt [gə'vigt] adj experienced,
  smart, shrewd
gewiesen [gə'vizən] pp of **weisen**
gewillt [gə'vilt] adj willing
Gewimmel [gə'viməl] n (-s;) swarm;
  (Menschen–) throng
Gewimmer [gə'vimər] n (-s;) whim-
  pering; whining
Gewinde [gə'vində] n (-s;-) thread
  (of a screw); (Kranz) garland; skein
Gewinn [gə'vin] m (-[e]s;-e) win-
  nings; profit; (Vorteil) advantage
Gewinn'anteil m dividend
Gewinn'aufschlag m (com) markup
Gewinn'beteiligung f profit sharing
gewinn'bringend adj profitable
gewinnen [gə'vinən] §121 tr win, gain;
  reach ‖ intr win; make a profit;
  improve; **g. an** (dat) gain in; **g. von**
  or **durch** profit by
gewin'nend adj engaging
Gewinn'spanne f margin of profit
Gewinn'sucht f greed; profiteering
Gewinsel [gə'vinzəl] n (-s;) whim-
  pering
Gewirr [gə'vir] n (-[e]s;-e) tangle;
  entanglement; maze
gewiß [gə'vis] adj sure, certain ‖ adv
  certainly; **aber g.!** of course!
Gewissen [gə'visən] n (-s;-) conscience

gewis'senhaft *adj* conscientious

gewis'senlos *adj* unscrupulous

Gewis'sensbisse *pl* pangs of conscience

Gewis'sensnot *f* moral dilemma

gewis'sermaßen *adv* to some extent; so to speak

Gewiß'heit *f* (-;-en) certainty

gewiß'lich *adv* certainly

Gewitter [gə'vɪtər] *n* (-s;-) thunderstorm

gewittern [gə'vɪtərn] *impers*—es ge-wittert a storm is brewing

Gewit'terregen *m* thundershower

gewitzigt [gə'vɪtsɪçt] *adj*—g. sein to have learned from experience

gewitzt [gə'vɪtst] *adj* bright, smart

gewoben [gə'vobən] *pp* of weben

gewogen [gə'vogən] *pp* of wägen & wiegen || *adj* well disposed

Gewo'genheit *f* (-;) favorable attitude

gewöhnen [gə'vønən] *tr* (an *acc*) accus-tom (to) || *ref* (an *acc*) get used (to)

Gewohnheit [gə'vonhaɪt] *f* (-;-en) habit, custom

gewohn'heitsmäßig *adj* habitual

Gewohn'heitsmensch *m* creature of habit

gewöhnlich [gə'vønlɪç] *adj* usual; nor-mal; common, ordinary

gewohnt [gə'vont] *adj* usual; g. sein (*acc*) be used to

Gewölbe [gə'vœlbə] *n* (-s;-) vault; arch

gewölbt [gə'vœlpt] *adj* vaulted

Gewölk [gə'vœlk] *n* (-[e]s;) clouds

gewonnen [gə'vonən] *pp* of gewinnen

geworben [gə'vorbən] *pp* of werben

geworden [gə'vordən] *pp* of werden

geworfen [gə'vorfən] *pp* of werfen

gewrungen [gə'vruŋən] *pp* of wringen

Gewühl [gə'vyl] *n* (-[e]s;) milling crowd

gewunden [gə'vundən] *pp* of winden

gewürfelt [gə'vyrfəlt] *adj* checkered

Gewürm [gə'vyrm] *n* (-[e]s;) vermin

Gewürz [gə'vyrts] *n* (-[e]s;-e) spice

Gewürz'nelke *f* clove

gewußt [gə'vust] *pp* of wissen

Geysir ['gaɪzɪr] *m* (-s;-) geyser

gezackt [gə'tsakt] *adj* jagged; (bot) serrated

gezähnt [gə'tsɛnt] *adj* toothed; (*Rand*) perforated; (bot) dentated

Gezänk [gə'tsɛŋk] *n* (-[e]s;) squab-bling

Gezeiten [gə'tsaɪtən] *pl* tides

Gezeiten– *comb.fm.* tidal

Gezeter [gə'tsetər] *n* (-s;) yelling

geziehen [gə'tsi-ən] *pp* of zeihen

geziemen [gə'tsimən] *intr* (*dat*) be proper for || *impers ref*—es geziemt sich für j–n it is right for s.o.

geziert [gə'tsirt] *adj* affected, phoney

Gezisch [gə'tsɪʃ] *n* (-es;) hissing

gezogen [gə'tsogən] *pp* of ziehen

Gezücht [gə'tsʏçt] *n* (-[e]s;-e) riff-raff

Gezwitscher [gə'tsvɪtʃər] *n* (-s;) chirping

gezwungen [gə'tsvuŋən] *pp* of zwingen || *adj* forced; (*Stil*) labored || *adv* stiffly

Gicht [gɪçt] *f* (-;-en) gout

Giebel ['gibəl] *m* (-s;-) gable

Gier [gir] *f* (-;) greed

gierig ['gɪrɪç] *adj* (nach) greedy (for)

Gießbach ['gisbax] *m* torrent

gießen ['gisən] §76 *tr* pour; (*Blumen usw.*) water; (metal) cast, found || *impers*—es gießt it is pouring

Gießer ['gisər] *m* (-s;-) foundryman

Gießerei [gisə'raɪ] *f* (-;-en) foundry

Gieß'form *f* casting mold; (typ) matrix

Gieß'kanne *f* sprinkling can

Gift [gɪft] *n* (-[e]s;-e) poison

giftig ['gɪftɪç] *adj* poisonous; malicious

Gigant [gɪ'gant] *m* (-en;-en) giant

Gilde ['gɪldə] *f* (-;-n) guild

Gimpel ['gɪmpəl] *m* (-s;-) (coll) sucker

ging [gɪŋ] *pret* of gehen

Gipfel ['gɪpfəl] *m* (-s;-) top; peak

Gip'felkonferenz *f* summit meeting

Gips [gɪps] *m* (-es;-e) gypsum; plas-ter of Paris; (surg) cast

Gips'arbeit *f* plastering

Gips'diele *f* plasterboard

gipsen ['gɪpsən] *tr* plaster

Gips'verband *m* (surg) cast

Giraffe [gɪ'rafə] *f* (-;-n) giraffe

girieren [ʒɪ'rirən] *tr* endorse

Girlande [gɪr'landə] *f* (-;-n) garland

Giro ['ʒiro] *n* (-s;-s) endorsement

girren ['gɪrən] *intr* coo

Gis [gɪs] *n* (-;-) (mus) G sharp

Gischt [gɪʃt] *m* (-es;) foam; spray

Gitarre [gɪ'tarə] *f* (-;-n) guitar

Gitter ['gɪtər] *n* (-s;-) grating, grille; bars; lattice; railing; trellis; (elec-tron) grid

Git'terbett *n* baby crib

Git'ternetz *n* grid (on *map*)

Git'tertor *n* wrought-iron gate

Git'terwerk *n* latticework

Glacéhandschuhe [gla'sehant∫u·ə] *pl* (& *fig*) kid gloves

Gladi-ator [gladi'atər] *m* (-s;-atoren [a'torən]) gladiator

Glanz [glants] *m* (-es;) shine; polish; luster; brilliance

glänzen ['glentsən] *tr* polish || *intr* shine; durch Abwesenheit g. be con-spicuous by one's absence

glän'zend *adj* bright; glossy; polished; (*fig*) splendid, brilliant

Glanz'leder *n* patent leather

Glanz'licht *n* (paint) highlight

glanz'los *adj* dull; lackluster

Glanz'punkt *m* highlight

Glanz'stück *n* master stroke

glanz'voll *adj* brilliant, splendid

Glanz'zeit *f* heyday, golden age

Glas [glas] *n* (-es;=er) glass

Glaser ['glazər] *m* (-s;-) glazier

gläsern ['glezərn] *adj* glass; glassy

Glas'hütte *f* glassworks

glasieren [gla'zirən] *tr* glaze; (*Kuchen*) frost, ice

glasig ['glazɪç] *adj* glassy; vitreous

Glas'jalousie *f* jalousie window

Glas'scheibe *f* pane of glass

Glasur [gla'zur] *f* (-;-en) enamel (on *pots*); glaze; (culin) icing

glatt [glat] *adj* smooth; (*eben*) even; (*poliert*) glossy; (*schlüpfrig*) slippery; (*Absage*) flat; (*Lüge*) downright || *adv* smoothly; directly; entirely

Glätte ['glɛtə] f (-;) smoothness; slipperiness; (*Politur*) polish

Glatt'eis n sheet of ice; **bei G. fahren** drive in icy conditions

glätten ['glɛtən] tr smooth; smooth out || ref smooth out; become calm

glatt'streichen §85 tr smooth out

glatt'weg adv outright, point-blank

glattzüngig ['glatsʏnɪç] adj smooth-talking

Glatze ['glatsə] f (-;-n) bald head

glatz'köpfig adj baldheaded

Glaube ['glaubə] m (-ns;), **Glauben** ['glaubən] m (-s;) belief; faith

glauben ['glaubən] tr believe; (*annehmen*) suppose || intr (dat) believe; **g. an** (acc) believe in; **j-m aufs Wort glauben** take s.o.'s word

Glau'bensbekenntnis n profession of faith; creed

Glau'benslehre f Christian doctrine

Glau'benssatz m dogma

gläubig ['glɔɪbɪç] adj believing || **Gläubige** §5 mf believer || **Gläubiger** –in §6 mf creditor

glaublich ['glauplɪç] adj credible

glaub'würdig adj credible; reliable; plausible

Glaukom [glau'kom] n (-s;-e) glaucoma

gleich [glaɪç] adj (dat) like; (an dat) equal (in); **es ist mir ganz g.** it's all the same to me || adv equally; immediately

gleichaltrig ['glaɪçaltrɪç] adj of the same age

gleich'artig adj similar, homogeneous

gleich'bedeutend adj synonymous

Gleich'berechtigung f (pol) equality

gleichen ['glaɪçən] §85 intr (dat) resemble, look like, be like

glei'chermaßen adv equally, likewise

gleich'falls adv likewise; as well

gleich'förmig adj uniform; regular; monotonous

gleich'gesinnt adj like-minded

Gleich'gewicht n equilibrium

gleich'gültig adj indifferent; **es ist mir g.** it's all the same to me

Gleich'heit f (-;-en) equality; (*Ähnlichkeit*) likeness

Gleich'klang m consonance; unison

gleich'kommen §99 intr (SEIN) (dat) equal; (dat) be tantamount to

gleich'laufend adj (mit) parallel (to)

gleich'machen tr make equal; standardize; **dem Erdboden g.** raze

Gleich'maß n regularity; evenness; balance, equilibrium; proportion

gleich'mäßig adj symmetrical; regular

Gleich'mut m equanimity, calmness

gleich'mütig adj calm

gleichnamig ['glaɪçnamɪç] adj of the same name; (phys) like

Gleichnis ['glaɪçnɪs] n (-ses;-se) parable; figure of speech; simile

Gleich'richter m (elec) rectifier

gleichsam ['glaɪçzam] adv so to speak; more or less, practically

gleichschenklig ['glaɪçʃɛŋklɪç] adj isosceles

Gleich'schritt m—**im G.** in cadence; **im G. marsch!** forward, march!

gleich'seitig adj equilateral

gleich'setzen tr (dat or mit) equate (with)

Gleich'setzung f (-;), **Gleich'stellung** f (-;) equalization

Gleich'strom m direct current

gleich'tun §154 tr—es **j-m g.** emulate s.o.

Glei'chung f (-;-en) (math) equation

gleichviel' adv—**g. wer** not matter who

gleich'wertig adj evenly matched

gleichwohl' adv nevertheless

gleich'zeitig adj simultaneous

gleich'ziehen §163 intr (mit) catch up (with or to)

Gleis [glaɪs] n (-es;-e) (rr) track

Gleitboot ['glaɪtbot] n hydrofoil

gleiten ['glaɪtən] §86 intr (SEIN) glide; slip, slide

Gleitfläche ['glaɪtflɛçə] f (aer) hydroplane

Gleitflugzeug ['glaɪtfluktsɔɪk] n (aer) glider

Gleitschutz– comb.fm. skid-proof

Gleit'zeit f flexitime

Gletscher ['glɛtʃər] m (-s;-) glacier

glich [glɪç] pret of gleichen

Glied [glit] n (-[e]s;-er) limb; member; joint; link; (anat) penis; (log, math) term; (mil) rank, file

glie'derlahm adj paralyzed

gliedern ['glidərn] tr arrange; plan; divide, break down || ref (in acc) consist of

Glie'derung f (-;-en) arrangement; construction; division; organization

Gliedmaßen ['glitmasən] pl limbs

glimmen ['glɪmən] intr §136 & §109 intr glimmer; glow

Glim'mer m (-s;) glimmer; (min) mica

glimpflich ['glɪmpflɪç] adj gentle; (*Strafe*) light, lenient

glitschen ['glɪtʃən] intr (SEIN) slip

glitschig ['glɪtʃɪç] adj slippery

glitt [glɪt] pret of gleiten

glitzern ['glɪtsərn] intr glitter

global [glo'bal] adj global

Glo·bus ['globus] m (-bus & –busses; –busse & –ben [bən]) globe

Glöckchen ['glœkçən] n (-s;-) small bell

Glocke ['glɔkə] f (-;-n) bell; (e-s *Rocks*) flare

Glockenspiel (Glok'kenspiel) n carillon

Glockenstube (Glok'kenstube) f, **Glockenturm (Glok'kenturm)** m belfry

Glockenzug (Glok'kenzug) m bell rope

Glöckner ['glœknər] m (-s;-) bell ringer; sexton

glomm [glɔm] pret of glimmen

Glorie ['glorjə] f (-;-n) glory

Glo'rienschein m halo

glorreich ['glorraɪç] adj glorious

glotzäugig ['glɔtsɔɪgɪç] adj popeyed

glotzen ['glɔtsən] intr stare, goggle

Glück [glʏk] n (-[e]s;) luck; fortune; happiness; **auf gut G.** at random; **zum G.** luckily

glucken ['glukən] intr cluck

glücken ['glʏkən] intr (SEIN) succeed || impers—**es glückt mir** I succeed

gluckern ['glukərn] intr gurgle

glück′lich *adj* lucky, fortunate; happy; (*günstig*) auspicious

glück′licherweise *adv* fortunately

glück′selig *adj* blissful; blessed; joyful

Glück′seligkeit *f* (–;) bliss; joy

glucksen [′gluksən] *intr* gurgle; chuckle

Glücks′fall *m* stroke of luck; windfall

Glücks′güter *pl* earthly possessions

Glücks′hafen *m* raffle drum

Glücks′pilz *m* (coll) lucky dog

Glücks′spiel *n* game of chance

Glücks′topf *m* grab bag

glück′verheißend *adj* auspicious

Glück′wunsch *m* good wishes, congratulations

Glück′wunschkarte *f* greeting card

Glühbirne [′glybɪrnə] *f* light bulb

glühen [′gly-ən] *tr* make red-hot; (metal) anneal || *intr* glow

glü′hendheiß *adj* red-hot

Glühfaden [′glyfadən] *m* filament

Glühwurm [′glyvurm] *m* firefly

Glut [glut] *f* (–;) embers; fire; scorching heat; (fig) ardor

Glyzerin [glytsə′rin] *n* (–s;) glycerine

GmbH *abbr* (**Gesellschaft mit beschränkter Haftung**) Inc.; Ltd. (Brit)

Gnade [′gnadə] *f* (–;–n) grace; favor; mercy; **von eigenen Gnaden** self-styled

Gna′denbeweis *m* token of favor

Gna′denbrot *n*—**bei j–m das G. essen** to live on s.o.'s charity

Gna′denfrist *f* grace, e.g., **e–e G. von zwei Monaten** two months' grace

Gna′dengesuch *n* plea for mercy

Gna′denstoß *m* coup de grâce, deathblow

gnädig [′gnedɪç] *adj* gracious, kind; merciful; **gnädige Frau** madam; **Sehr verehrte gnädige Frau** Dear Madam

Gold [gɔlt] *n* (–[e]s;) gold

Gold′blech *n* gold foil

Gold′fink *m* (orn) goldfinch

goldig [′gɔldɪç] *adj* (coll) cute

Gold′plombe *f* (dent) gold filling

Gold′schmied *m* goldsmith

Gold′schnitt *m* gilt edging

Golf [gɔlf] *m* (–[e]s;–e) gulf; bay || *n* (–s;) golf

Golf′platz *m* golf course

Golf′schläger *m* golf club

Gondel [′gɔndəl] *f* (–;–n) gondola

Gon′delführer *m* gondolier

gönnen [′gœnən] *tr* not begrudge; allow; **j–m etw nicht g. begrudge** s.o. s.th.

Gön′ner –**in** §6 *mf* patron

gön′nerhaft *adj* patronizing

Gön′nerschaft *f* (–;) patronage

gor [gor] *pret of* **gären**

Gorilla [gə′rɪla] *m* (–s;–s) gorilla

goß [gɔs] *pret of* **gießen**

Gosse [′gɔsə] *f* (–;–n) gutter

Gote [′gotə] *m* (–n;–n) Goth

gotisch [′gotɪʃ] *adj* Gothic

Gott [gɔt] *m* (–[e]s;⸚er) god; God

gottbegnadet [′gɔtbəgnadət] *adj* gifted

gott′ergeben *adj* resigned to God's will

Got′tesdienst *m* divine service; Mass

got′tesfürchtig *adj* God-fearing

Got′tesgabe *f* godsend

got′teslästerlich *adj* blasphemous

Got′teslästerung *f* blasphemy

Got′tesurteil *n* ordeal

gott′gefällig *adj* pleasing to God

Gott′heit *f* (–;–en) deity, divinity

Göttin [′gœtɪn] *f* (–;–nen) goddess

göttlich [′gœtlɪç] *adj* godlike, divine; (fig) heavenly

gottlob′ *interj* thank goodness!

Gott′mensch *m* God incarnate

gott′selig *adj* godly

gott′verlassen *adj* godforsaken

Götze [′gœtsə] *m* (–n;–n) idol

Göt′zenbild *n* idol

Göt′zendiener –**in** §6 *mf* idolater

Göt′zendienst *m* idolatry

Gouvernante [guvɛr′nantə] *f* (–;–n) governess

Gouverneur [guvɛr′nør] *m* (–s;–e) governor

Grab [grap] *n* (–[e]s;⸚er) grave; tomb

graben [′grabən] §87 *tr* dig; burrow || **Graben** *m* (–s;⸚) ditch; trench; moat

Grab′geläute *n* death knell

Grab′gesang *m* funeral dirge

Grab′hügel *m* burial mound

Grab′inschrift *f* epitaph

Grab′mal *n* tombstone; tomb, sepulcher

Grab′stätte *f* burial place

Grab′stelle *f* burial plot

Grad [grat] *m* (–[e]s;–e) degree; grade; (mil) rank

grade [′gradə] *adv* var of **gerade**

Grad′einteilung *f* gradation

Grad′messer *m* graduated scale; (fig) yardstick

grad′weise *adv* by degrees

Graf [graf] *m* (–en;–en) count; earl (Brit)

Gräfin [′grefɪn] *f* (–;–nen) countess

gräflich [′greflɪç] *adj* count's; earl's

Graf′schaft *f* (–;–en) county

gram [gram] *adj*—**j–m g. sein** be cross with s.o. || **Gram** *m* (–[e]s;) grief

grämen [′gremən] *tr* sadden, distress || *ref* (**über** *acc*) grieve (over)

grämlich [′gremlɪç] *adj* glum; crabby

Gramm [gram] *n* (–s;– & –e) gram

Grammatik [gra′matɪk] *f* (–;–en) grammar

grammatisch [gra′matɪʃ] *adj* grammatical

Gran [gran] *n* (–[e]s;) (fig) bit, jot

Granat [gra′nat] *m* (–[e]s;–e) garnet

Granat′apfel *m* pomegranate

Granate [gra′natə] *f* (–;–n) (arti) shell; (mil) grenade

Granat′feuer *n* shelling

Granat′hülse *f* shell case

Granat′splitter *m* shrapnel

Granat′werfer *m* (mil) mortar

grandios [grandɪ′os] *adj* grandiose

Granit [gra′nit] *m* (–[e]s;–e) granite

Graphik [′grafɪk] *f* (–;–en) graphic arts; print; engraving; woodcut

graphisch [′grafɪç] *adj* graphic

Graphit [gra′fit] *m* (–[e]s;–e) graphite

Gras [gras] *n* (–es;⸚er) grass

grasen [′grazən] *intr* graze

Gras′halm *m* blade of grass

Grashüpfer [′grashypfer] *m* (–s;–) grasshopper

grasig ['grɑzɪç] adj grassy
Gras'mäher m lawn mower; grass cutter
Gras'mähmaschine f lawn mower
Gras'narbe f sod, turf
grassieren [gra'sirən] intr rage
gräßlich ['grɛslɪç] adj grisly
Gras'weide f pasture
Grat [grat] m (-[e]s;-e) ridge; edge
Gräte ['grɛtə] f (-;-n) fishbone
Gratifikation [gratɪfɪka'tsjon] f (-;-en) bonus
grätig ['gretɪç] adj full of fishbones; (mürrisch) crabby
gratis ['grɑtɪs] adv gratis; g. und franko (coll) for free
Gratulation [gratula'tsjon] f (-;-en) congratulations
gratulieren [gratu'lirən] intr—j-m g. zu congratulate s.o. on
grau [grau] adj gray; (Vorzeit) remote || Grau n (- & -s;-s) gray
Grau'bär m grizzly bear
grauen ['grau.ən] intr dawn || impers—es graut day is breaking; es graut mir vor (dat) I shudder at || Grauen n (-s;) (vor dat) horror (of)
grau'enhaft, grau'envoll adj horrible
gräulich ['grɔɪlɪç] adj grayish
Graupe ['graupə] f (-;-n) peeled barley
graupeln ['graupəln] impers—es graupelt it is sleeting || Graupeln pl sleet
Graus [graus] m (-es;) dread, horror
grausam ['grauzam] adj cruel; (coll) awful
Grau'schimmel m gray horse
grausen ['grauzən] impers—es graust mir vor (dat) I shudder at
grausig ['grauzɪç] adj gruesome
Graveur [gra'vør] m (-s;-e) engraver
gravieren [gra'virən] tr engrave
gravie'rend adj aggravating
gravitätisch [gravɪ'tetɪʃ] adj stately
Grazie ['grɑtsjə] f (-;-n) grace, charm
graziös [gra'tsjøs] adj graceful
Greif [graif] m (-[e]s;-e) griffin
greifbar ['graifbar] adj tangible; at hand
greifen ['graifən] §88 tr grasp; seize; (Note) strike || intr (Anker) catch; (Zahnrad) engage; ans Herz g. touch deeply; an j-s Ehre g. attack s.o.'s honor; g. in (acc) reach into; g. nach reach for; try to seize; g. zu reach for; (fig) resort to; um sich g. grope about; (Feuer) spread; zu den Waffen g. take up arms
Greis [grais] m (-es;-e) old man
Grei'senalter n old age
grei'senhaft adj aged; senile
Greisin ['graizɪn] f (-;-nen) old lady
grell [grɛl] adj (Ton) shrill; (Farbe, Kleider) flashy; (Licht) glaring
Gre·mium ['gremjum] n (-s;-mien [mjən]) group, body; committee; corporation
Grenze ['grɛntsə] f (-;-n) boundary; frontier; borderline; limit
grenzen ['grɛntsən] intr an (an acc) adjoin, border (on); (fig) verge (on)
gren'zenlos adj limitless
Grenz'fall m borderline case

Grenz'linie f boundary line
Grenz'sperre f ban on border traffic; frontier barricade
Grenz'stein m boundary stone
Greuel ['grɔɪ.əl] m (-s;-) abhorrence; horror, abomination
Greu'eltat f atrocity
greulich ['grɔɪlɪç] adj horrible
Griebs ['grips] m (-es;-e) core
Grieche ['griçə] m (-n;-n) Greek
Grie'chenland n (-s;) Greece
Griechin ['griçɪn] f (-;-nen) Greek
griechisch ['griçɪʃ] adj Greek
Griesgram ['grisgram] m (-[e]s;-e) (coll) grouch
Grieß [gris] m (-es;-e) grit; gravel
Grieß'mehl n farina
griff [grif] pret of greifen || Griff m (-[e]s;-e) grip; handle; hilt; (mus) touch
Grill [gril] m (-s;-s) grill; broiler
Grille ['grilə] f (-;-n) cricket; (fig) whim
grillen ['grilən] tr grill; broil
gril'lenhaft adj whimsical
Grimasse [grɪ'masə] f (-;-n) grimace
Grimm [grim] m (-[e]s;) anger, fury
grimmig ['grimɪç] adj furious
Grind [grint] m (-[e]s;-e) scab
grinsen ['grinzən] intr grin
Grippe ['gripə] f (-;) grippe
grob [grop] adj coarse, rough; crude
Grobian ['grobjan] m (-s;-e) boor
gröblich ['grøplɪç] adj gross
grölen ['grølən] intr shout raucously
Groll [grɔl] m (-[e]s;) resentment
grollen ['grɔlən] intr rumble; (über acc) be resentful (about); j-m g. have a grudge against s.o.
Grönland ['grønlant] n (-s;) Greenland
Gros [grɔs] n (-ses;-) gross || [gro] n (-;-) bulk; (mil) main forces
Groschen ['grɔʃən] m (-s;-) (Aust) penny (one hundredth of a shilling)
groß [gros] adj big, large; tall; great
groß'artig adj grand; magnificent
Groß'aufnahme f (phot) close-up
groß'äugig adj wide-eyed
Groß'betrieb m big company
Großbritan'nien n Great Britain
Größe ['grøsə] f (-;-n) size, greatness; celebrity; (astr) magnitude; (math) quantity
Groß'eltern pl grandparents
Groß'enkel m great-grandson
Groß'enkelin f great-granddaughter
großenteils ['grosəntails] adv largely
Größenwahn ['grøsənvan] f megalomania
Groß'grundbesitz m large estate
Groß'handel m wholesale trade; im G. kaufen buy wholesale
Großhandels– comb.fm. wholesale
Groß'händler –in §6 mf wholesaler
Groß'handlung f (-;-en) wholesale business
groß'herzig adj big-hearted
Grossist [grɔ'sɪst] m (-en;-en) wholesaler
groß'jährig adj of legal age
Groß'maul n bigmouth
Groß'mut m magnanimity

groß'mütig *adj* big-hearted
Groß'mutter *f* grandmother
Groß'onkel *m* great-uncle
Groß'schreibung *f* capitalization
Groß'segel *n* main sail
Groß'sprecher *m* braggart
großspurig ['grosʃpurɪç] *adj* pompous
Groß'stadt *f* large city (*with over 100,000 inhabitants*)
Großstädter ['grosʃtɛtər] *m* (**-s;-**) (coll) city slicker
Groß'tat *f* achievement
Groß'teil *m* major part
größtenteils ['grøstəntaɪls] *adv* mainly
groß'tun §154 *intr* brag; put on the dog
Groß'vater *m* grandfather
Groß'wild *n* big game
groß'ziehen §163 *tr* bring up, raise
großzügig ['grostsygɪç] *adj* broad-minded, liberal; generous; large-scale
grotesk [gro'tesk] *adj* grotesque
Grotte ['grɔtə] *f* (**-;-n**) grotto
grub [grup] *pret of* **graben**
Grübchen ['grypçən] *n* (**-s;-**) dimple
Grube ['grubə] *f* (**-;-n**) pit; mine
Grübelei [grybə'laɪ] *f* (**-;-en**) brooding
grübeln ['grybəln] *intr* brood
Gruben– [gruban] *comb.fm.* mine, miner's
Gruft [gruft] *f* (**-;⁻e**) tomb, vault
grün [gryn] *adj* green; **Grüne Minna** (sl) paddy wagon ‖ **Grün** *n* (**-s;**) green
Grün'anlage *f* public park
Grund [grunt] *m* (**-[e]s;⁻e**). ground; land; bottom; foundation, basis; cause, ground; **auf G. von** on the strength of; **G. und Boden** property; **im Grunde genommen** after all; in **G. und Boden** outright
–grund *m comb.fm.* bottom of; –ground; grounds for, reasons for
Grund'anstrich *m* first coat
Grund'ausbildung *f* (mil) basic training
Grund'bedeutung *f* primary meaning
Grund'begriff *m* fundamental principle
Grund'besitz *m* real estate
Grund'buch *n* land register
grund'ehr'lich *adj* thoroughly honest
gründen ['gryndən] *tr* found; **g. auf** (*acc*) base on ‖ *ref* (**auf** *acc*) be based (on)
Gründer –in ['gryndər(ɪn)] §6 *mf* founder
grund'falsch' *adj* absolutely false
Grund'farbe *f* primary color
Grund'fläche *f* area; (geom) base
grundieren [grun'dirən] *tr* prime; size
Grundier'farbe *f* primer coat
Grundier'schicht *f* primer coat
Grund'kapital *n* capital stock
Grund'lage *f* basis, foundation
grund'legend *adj* basic, fundamental
Grund'legung *f* founding, foundation
gründlich ['gryntlɪç] *adj* thorough
Grund'linie *f* (geom) base; **Grundlinien** basic features, outlines
Gründon'nerstag *m* Holy Thursday
Grund'riß *m* floor plan; outline

Grund'satz *m* principle
grundsätzlich ['grunttsetslɪç] *adj* basic ‖ *adv* as a matter of principle
Grund'schule *f* primary school
Grund'stein *m* cornerstone
Grund'stellung *f* position of attention; **die G. einnehmen** come to attention
Grund'steuer *f* real-estate tax
Grund'stoff *m* raw material; (chem) element
Grund'strich *m* downstroke
Grund'stück *n* lot, property
Grund'ton *m* (fig) prevailing mood; (mus) keynote; (paint) ground shade
Grün'dung *f* (**-;-en**) foundation
grund'verschie'den *adj* entirely different
Grund'wasserspiegel *m* water table
Grund'zahl *f* cardinal number
Grund'zug *m* main feature; **Grundzüge** fundamentals, essentials
Grüne ['grynə] *n*—**ins G.** into the country
grün'lich *adj* greenish
Grün'schnabel *m* know-it-all
Grünspan ['grynʃpan] *m* (**-[e]s;**) verdigris
Grün'streifen *m* grass strip; (*auf der Autobahn*) median strip
grunzen ['gruntsən] *tr & intr* grunt
Gruppe ['grupə] *f* (**-;-n**) group; (mil) squad
Grup'penführer *m* group leader; (hist) lieutenant general (*of S.S. troops*); (mil) squad leader
gruppieren [gru'pirən] *tr & ref* group
Gruppie'rung *f* (**-;-en**) grouping
gruselig ['gruzəlɪç] *adj* creepy
gruseln ['gruzəln] *intr*—**j–n g. machen** give s.o. the creeps ‖ *ref* have a creepy feeling ‖ *impers*—**es gruselt mir** (or **mich**) it gives me the creeps
Gruß [grus] *m* (**-es;⁻e**) greeting; salute; greetings, regards; **mit freundlichem Gruß, Ihr . . .** Sincerely yours
grüßen ['grysən] *tr* greet; salute; **grüß Gott!** hello!; **j–n g. lassen** send best regards to s.o.
Grütze ['grytsə] *f* (**-;-n**) groats; (coll) brains
gucken ['gukən] *intr* look; peep
Guck'loch *n* peephole
Guerilla [ge'rɪlja] *m* (**-s;-s**) guerilla
Gulasch ['gula∫] *n* (**-[e]s;**) goulash
gültig ['gyltɪç] *adj* valid; legal
Gummi ['gumi] *m & n* (**-s;-s**) gum; rubber
gum'miartig *adj* gummy; rubbery
Gum'miband *n* (**-[e]s;⁻er**) rubber band; elastic
Gum'mibaum *m* rubber plant
Gum'mibonbon *m & n* gumdrop
gummieren [gu'mirən] *tr* gum; rubberize
Gum'miknüppel *m* truncheon; billy club
Gummilinse *f* (phot) zoom lens
Gum'mimantel *m* mackintosh
Gum'mireifen *m* tire
Gum'mischuhe *pl* rubbers
Gum'mizelle *f* padded cell
Gunst [gunst] *f* (**-;**) favor, goodwill; kindness, good turn

Gunst′bezeigung f expression of good-will

günstig ['gʏnstɪç] adj favorable; (Be-dingungen) easy

Günstling ['gʏnstlɪŋ] m (-s;-e) favorite; (pej) minion

Gurgel ['gurgəl] f (-;-n) gullet

gurgeln ['gurgəln] intr gurgle; gargle

Gurke ['gurkə] f (-;-n) cucumber

Gurt [gurt] m (-[e]s;-e) belt, strap

Gürtel ['gʏrtəl] m (-s;-) girdle; belt; (geog) zone

gürten ['gʏrtən] tr gird

Guß [gus] m (Gusses; Güsse) gush; (Regen) downpour; (Gießen) casting; (culin) icing; (typ) font

gut [gut] adj good; es ist schon gut it's all right; mach's gut! so long! || adv well || Gut n (-[e]s;-er) good; possessions; estate; (com) commodity; Güter goods; assets

Gut′achten n (-s;-) expert opinion

gut′artig adj good-natured; (pathol) benign

gut′aussehend adj good-looking

Gut′dünken n (-s;) judgment; discretion; nach G. at will, as one pleases; (culin) to taste

Gute ['gutə] §5 n good; alles G! best of everything; sein Gutes haben have its good points

Güte ['gytə] f (-;) goodness

Güter- [gytər] comb.fm. freight; property; (com) of goods

Gü′terabfertigung f freight office

Gü′terbahnhof m (rr) freight yard

gut′erhalten adj in good condition

Gü′terwagen m freight car; geschlossener G. boxcar; offener G. gondola car

Gü′terzug m freight train

gut′gelaunt adj good-humored

gut′gesinnt adj well-disposed

gut′haben §89 tr have to one's credit || Guthaben n (-s;-) credit balance

gut′heißen §95 tr approve of

gut′herzig adj good-hearted

gütig ['gytɪç] adj kind, good

gütlich ['gytlɪç] adj amicable

gut′machen tr—wieder g. make good for

gut′mütig adj good-natured

gut′sagen intr—für j—n g. vouch for s.o.

Gut′schein m coupon; credit note

gut′schreiben §62 tr—j—m e-n Betrag g. credit s.o. with a sum

Gut′schrift f credit entry; credit item

Gut′schriftsanzeige f credit note

Guts′herr m landowner

gut′tun §154 intr do good; behave

gut′willig adj willing, obliging

Gymnasiast –in [gʏm′nazjast(ɪn)] §7 mf high school student

Gymna·sium [gʏm′nazjum] n (-s;-sien [zjən]) high school (with academic course)

Gymnastik [gʏm′nastɪk] f (-;) gymnastics

Gynäkologe [gʏnɛkə′logə] m (-n;-n), **Gynäkologin** [gʏnɛkə′login] f (-;nen) gynecologist

Gynäkologie [gʏnɛkələ′gi] f (-;) gynecology

H

H, h [ha] invar n H, h; (mus) B

Haar [har] n (-[e]s;-e) hair; (tex) nap, pile; aufs H. exactly; um ein H. by a hair's breadth

Haar′büschel n tuft of hair

haaren ['harən] intr lose hair

Haarfärbmittel ['harfɛrpmɪtəl] n hair dye

Haar′feder f hairspring

haar′genau adj exact, precise

haarig ['harɪç] adj hairy

haar′klein adj (coll) in detail

Haar′locke f lock of hair

Haar′nadel f hairpin

haar′scharf adj razor-sharp

Haar′schneider m barber

Haar′schnitt m haircut

Haar′spange f barrette

Haarspray ['harspre] m (-s;-s) hair spray

haar′sträubend adj hair-raising

Haar′teil m hair piece

Haar′tolle f loose curl

Haar′tracht f hairdo

Haar′trockner m, **Haar′trockenhaube** f hair dryer

Haar′wäsche f shampoo

Haar′wasser n hair tonic

Haar′wickler m curler; hair roller

Haar′zwange f tweezers

Hab [hap] invar n—Hab und Gut possessions

Habe ['habə] f (-;) possessions

haben ['habən] §89 tr & aux have || Haben n (-s;) credit side

Habe′nichts m (-es;-e) have-not

Hab′gier f greed, avarice

hab′haft adj—h. werden (genit) get hold of; (Diebes) apprehend

Habicht ['habɪçt] m (-[e]s;-e) hawk

Ha′bichtsnase f aquiline nose

Habilitation [habɪlɪta′tsjon] f (-;-en) accreditation as a university lecturer

habilitieren [habɪlɪ′tirən] ref be accredited as a university lecturer

Hab′seligkeiten pl belongings

Hab′sucht f greed, avarice

hab′süchtig adj greedy, avaricious

Hackbeil ['hakbaɪl] n cleaver

Hacke ['hakə] f (-;-n) heel; hoe; pick; pickax; hatchet; mattock

hacken ['hakən] tr hack, chop; peck || intr (nach) peck (at)

Häckerling ['hɛkərlɪŋ] m (-s;) chaff

Hackfleisch ['hakflaɪʃ] n ground meat

Häcksel ['hɛksəl] n (-s;) chaff

Hader ['hadər] *m* (-s;) strife ‖ *m* (-s; -n) rag

hadern ['hadərn] *intr* quarrel

Hafen ['hafən] *m* (-s;^{..}) harbor; port; (fig) haven

Ha'fenamt *n* port authority

Ha'fenanlagen *pl* docks

Ha'fenarbeiter *m* longshoreman

Ha'fendamm *m* jetty, mole

Ha'fensperre *f* blockade

Ha'fenstadt *f* seaport

Ha'fenviertel *n* dock area, waterfront

Hafer ['hafər] *m* (-s;-) oats; **ihn sticht der H.** he's feeling his oats

Ha'fergrütze *f*, **Ha'fermehl** *n* oatmeal

Hafner ['hafnər] *m* (-s;-) potter

Haft [haft] *f* (-;) arrest; custody; imprisonment; **in H.** under arrest; **in custody; in prison**

haftbar ['haftbar] *adj* (jur) liable

Haft'befehl *m* warrant for arrest

haften ['haftən] *intr* (**an** *dat*) cling (to), stick (to); **h. für** vouch for; (jur) be held liable for; (jur) put up bail for

Haft'fähigkeit *f*, **Haft'festigkeit** *f* adhesion

Häftling ['heftlɪŋ] *m* (-s;-e) prisoner

Haft'lokal *n* (mil) guardhouse

Haft'pflicht *f* liability

haft'pflichtig *adj* (**für**) liable (for)

Haft'pflichtversicherung *f* liability insurance

Haft'richter *m* (jur) magistrate

Haft'schale *f* contact lens

Haf'tung *f* (-;-en) liability

Hag [hak] *m* (-[e]s;-e) enclosure; (*Hain*) grove; (*Buschwerk*) bushes

Hagedorn ['hagədorn] *m* hawthorn

Hagel ['hagəl] *m* (-s;) hail

Ha'gelkorn *n* hailstone

hageln ['hagəln] *intr* (SEIN) (fig) rain down ‖ *impers*—**es hagelt** it is hailing

Ha'gelschauer *m* hailstorm

hager ['hagər] *adj* gaunt, haggard

Hagestolz ['hagəʃtɔlts] *m* (-es;-e) confirmed bachelor

Häher ['he.ər] *m* (-s;-) (orn) jay

Hahn [han] *m* (-[e]s;^{..}e) rooster; (*Wasser*-) faucet; **den H. spannen** cock the gun; **H. im Korbe sein** rule the roost

Hähnchen ['hençən] *n* (-s;-) young rooster

Hah'nenkamm *m* cockscomb

Hah'nenkampf *m* cock fight

Hah'nenschrei *m* crow of the cock

Hahnrei ['hanraɪ] *m* (-s;-e) cuckold

Hai [haɪ] *m* (-[e]s;-e), **Hai'fisch** *m* shark

Hain [haɪn] *m* (-[e]s;-e) grove

Haiti [ha'iti] *n* (-s;) Haiti

Häkelarbeit ['hekəlarbaɪt] *f* crocheting

häkeln ['hekəln] *tr & intr* crochet ‖ **Häkeln** *n* (-s;) crocheting

Haken ['hakən] *m* (-s;-) hook; (*Spange*) clasp; (fig) snag, hitch

Ha'kenkreuz *n* swastika

Ha'kennase *f* hooknose

halb [halp] *adj & adv* half

halb-, Halb- *comb.fm.* half-, semi-

Halb'blut *n* half-breed

–halber [halbər] *comb.fm.* for the sake of; owing to

halb'fett *adj* (typ) bold

Halb'franzband *m* (bb) half leather

halb'gar *adj* (culin) (medium) rare

Halb'gott *m* demigod

Halbheit ['halphaɪt] *f* (-;) half-

Halb'kugel *f* hemisphere

halbieren [hal'birən] *tr* halve, bisect

Halb'insel *f* peninsula

Halb'kettenfahrzeug *n* half-track

Halb'kugel *f* hemisphere

halb'lang *adj* half-length; **halblange Ärmel** half sleeves

halb'laut *adj* low ‖ *adv* in a low voice

Halb'leiter *m* (elec) semiconductor

halb'mast *adv* at half-mast; **auf h.** at half-mast

Halb'messer *m* radius

halbpart ['halppart] *adv*—**mit j–m h. machen** go fifty-fifty with s.o.

Halb'schuh *m* low shoe

Halb'schwergewicht *n* light-heavyweight division

Halb'schwergewichtler *m* light-heavyweight

halb'stündig *adj* half-hour

halb'stündlich *adj* half-hourly ‖ *adv* every half hour

Halb'vers *m* hemistich

halbwegs ['halpveks] *adv* halfway

Halb'welt *f* demimonde

halbwüchsig ['halpvyksɪç] *adj* teenage ‖ **Halbwüchsige** §5 *mf* teenager

Halb'zug *m* (mil) section

Halde ['haldə] *f* (-;-n) slope; (*Schutt*-) slag pile

half [half] *pret* of **helfen**

Hälfte ['helftə] *f* (-;-n) half

Halfter ['halftər] *f* (-;-n) holster ‖ *n* (-s;-) halter

Hall [hal] *m* (-[e]s;-e) sound; clang

Halle ['halə] *f* (-;-n) hall; (*e-s Hotels*) lobby; (aer) hangar; (rr) concourse

hallen ['halən] *intr* sound, resound

Hal'lenbad *n* indoor pool

Hallo [ha'lo] *n* (-s;) hullabaloo ‖ *interj* (to attract attention) hey!; (telp) hello

Halm [halm] *m* (-[e]s;-e) stem, stalk; blade (*of grass*)

Hals [hals] *m* (-es;^{..}e) neck; throat; **H. über Kopf** head over heels

Hals'abschneider *m* cutthroat

hals'abschneiderisch *adj* cutthroat

Hals'ader *f* jugular vein

Hals'ausschnitt *m* neckline, neck

Hals'band *n* (-[e]s;^{..}er) necklace, choker; (*e-s Hundes*) collar

halsbrecherisch ['halsbreçərɪʃ] *adj* breakneck

Hals'entzündung *f* sore throat

Hals'kette *f* necklace, chain

Hals'kragen *m* collar

Hals'krause *f* frilled collar

hals'starrig *adj* stubborn

Hals'weh *n* sore throat

halt [halt] *adv* just, simply ‖ *interj* stop!; (mil) halt! ‖ **Halt** *m* (-[e]s; -e) hold; foothold; support; stability; stop, halt

haltbar ['haltbar] *adj* durable; tenable

halten ['haltən] §90 *tr* hold; keep; detain; (*Rede*) deliver; (*Vorlesung*) give; (*feiern*) celebrate; **es h. mit do with; have an affair with; etw auf sich h.** have self-respect; **j–n h. für** take s.o. for; **viel h. von** think highly of || *ref* keep, last; hold ones own; **an sich h.** restrain oneself; **auf sich h.** be particular about one's appearance; **sich an etw h.** (fig) stick to s.th.; **sich an j–n h.** hold s.o. liable; **sich gesund h.** keep healthy; **sich links h.** keep to the left || *intr* stop; last; **h. auf** (*acc*) pay attention to; **h. nach** head for; **h. zu** stick by; **was das Zeug hält** with might and main
Hal′ter *m* (–s;–) holder; rack; owner
Hal′teriemen *m* strap (*on bus or trolley*)
Hal′testelle *f* bus stop, trolley stop; (rr) stop
Hal′teverbot *n* (public sign) no stopping
–haltig [haltɪç] *comb.fm.* containing
halt′los *adj* without support; helpless; unprincipled
halt′machen *intr* stop, halt
Hal′tung *f* (–;–en) pose, posture; attitude
Halte′zeichen *n* stop sign
Halunke [ha′lʊŋkə] *m* (–;–n) rascal
hämisch ['hɛmɪʃ] *adj* spiteful, malicious
Hammel ['haməl] *m* (–s;–e & ꞏꞏ) wether; (coll) mutton-head; (culin) mutton
Ham′melkeule *f* leg of mutton
Hammer ['hamər] *m* (–s;ꞏꞏ) hammer; gavel; **unter den H. kommen** be auctioned off
hämmern ['hɛmərn] *tr & intr* hammer
Hämorrhoiden [hɛmɔrɔ′idən] *pl* hemorroids, piles
Hampelmann ['hampəlman] *m* (–[e]s; ꞏꞏer) jumping jack
hamstern ['hamstərn] *tr* hoard
Hand [hant] *f* (–;ꞏꞏe) hand; **an H. von** with the help of; **auf eigene H.** of one's own accord; **aus erster H.** (*bei Verkauf*) one-owner; **aus erster H. haben** hear first-hand; **aus erster H. kaufen** buy directly; **bei der H.** at hand, handy; **die letzte H. (fig) finishing touches; die öffentliche H.** the state, public authorities; **es liegt auf der H.** it is obvious; **H. ans Werk legen** get down to work; **H. aufs Herz!** cross my heart! **Hände hoch!** hands up!; **H. und Fuß haben** make sense; **in die H. (or Hände) bekommen** get one's hands on; **j–m an die H. gehen** lend s.o. a hand; **j–m die H. drücken** shake hands with s.o.; **j–m etw an (die) H. geben** quote s.o. a price on s.th.; **j–m zur H. gehen** lend s.o. a hand; **unter der H.** underhandedly; unofficially; **von der H. weisen** reject; **zu Händen Herrn X** Attention Mr. X; **zur H.** at hand, handy
Hand′arbeit *f* manual labor; needlework
Hand′aufheben *n,* **Hand′aufhebung** *f* show of hands

Hand′ausgabe *f* abridged edition
Hand′bedienung *f* manual control
Hand′betrieb *m*—**mit (or für) H.** hand-operated
Hand′bibliothek *f* reference library
hand′breit *adj* wide as a hand || **Hand′breit** *f* (–;–) hand's breadth
Hand′bremse *f* (aut) hand brake
Hand′buch *n* handbook, manual
Händedruck ['hɛndədrʊk] *m* handshake
Händeklatschen ['hɛndəklatʃən] *n* clapping
Handel ['handəl] *m* (–s;ꞏꞏ) trade; deal, bargain; business; affair; **e–n H. eingehen** conclude a deal; **e–n H. treiben** carry on business; **H. und Gewerbe** trade and industry; **Händel suchen** pick a quarrel; **im H. sein** be on the market; **in den H. bringen** put on the market
–handel *m comb.fm.* –trade, –business
handeln ['handəln] *intr* act; take action; proceed; **gegen das Gesetz h.** go against the law; **gut an j–m h.** treat s.o. well; **h. über** (*acc*) or **von** deal with; **h. mit** do business with; **im großen h.** do wholesale business || *impers ref*—**es handelt sich um** it is a matter of; **darum handelt es sich nicht** that's not the point
Han′delsabkommen *n* trade agreement
Han′delsartikel *m* commodity
Han′delsbetrieb *m* commercial enterprise; business; firm
Han′delsbilanz *f* balance of trade; **aktive H.** favorable balance of trade
Han′delsdampfer *m* (naut) merchantman
han′delseinig *adj*—**h. werden mit** come to terms with
Han′delsgärtner *m* truck farmer
Han′delskammer *f* chamber of commerce
Han′delsmarine *f* merchant marine
Han′delsmarke *f* trademark
Han′delsminister *m* secretary of commerce
Han′delsministerium *n* department of commerce
Han′delsplatz *m* trade center
Han′delsschiff *n* merchantman
Han′delssperre *f* trade embargo
händelsüchtig ['hɛndəlzʏçtɪç] *adj* quarrelsome
Han′delsvertrag *m* commercial treaty
Han′delswert *m* trade-in value
Han′delszeichen *n* trademark
Hand′exemplar *n* desk copy
Hand′fertigkeit *f* manual dexterity
Hand′fessel *f* handcuff
hand′fest *adj* sturdy; well-founded
Hand′fläche *f* palm of the hand
Hand′geld *n* advance payment; deposit
Hand′gelenk *n* wrist; **aus (or mit) dem H.** (coll) easy as pie
hand′gemein *adj*—**h. werden** come to blows
Hand′gemenge *n* scuffle
Hand′gepäck *n* hand luggage
Hand′gepäckschließfach *n* locker
Hand′granate *f* hand grenade
hand′greiflich *adj* tangible; obvious;

j-m etw h. machen make s.th. clear to s.o.; h. werden come to blows

Hand'griff m grip; handle; keinen H. tun not lift a finger

Hand'habe f (-;-n) handle; pretext; occasion; er hat keine H. gegen mich he has nothing on me

hand'haben tr handle; (Maschine) operate; (Rechtspflege) administer; (fig) manage

-händig [hɛndɪç] comb.fm. -handed

Hand'karren m hand cart, push cart

Hand'koffer m suitcase; attaché case

Hand'langer ['hantlaŋər] m (-s;-) handyman; (pej) underling

Händler -in ['hɛndlər(ɪn)] §6 mf dealer, merchant; storekeeper

Hand'lesekunst f palmistry

Hand'leserin f (-;-nen) palm reader

hand'lich adj handy

Hand'lung f (-;-en) shop; act, action

-handlung f comb.fm. business; shop

Hand'lungsgehilfe m clerk, salesman

Hand'lungsweise f conduct

Hand'pflege f manicure

Hand'pflegerin f (-;-nen) manicurist

Hand'rücken m back of the hand

Hand'schaltung f manual shift

Hand'schelle f handcuff

Hand'schlag m handshake

Hand'schreiben n hand-written letter

Hand'schrift f handwriting; manuscript; (sl) slap, box on the ear

Hand'schriftenkunde f paleography

hand'schriftlich adj hand-written

Hand'schuh m glove

Hand'schuhfach n (aut) glove compartment

Hand'streich m (mil) raid

Hand'tasche f handbag, purse

Hand'tuch n towel; schmales H. (sl) beanpole

Hand'tuchhalter m towel rack

Hand'umdrehen n—im. H. in a jiffy

Hand'voll f (-;-) handful

Hand'werk n craft, trade; j-m ins H. pfuschen (sl) stick one's nose in s.o. else's business

Hand'werker m craftsman

Hand'werkszeug n tool kit

Hand'wörterbuch n pocket dictionary

Hand'wurzel f wrist

Hand'zettel m handbill

hanebüchen ['hanəbyçən] adj (coll) incredible; (coll) monstrous

Hanf [hanf] m (-[e]s;) hemp

Hang [haŋ] m (-[e]s;꞉e) slope; hillside; (fig) inclination, tendency

Hangar ['haŋgar] m (-s;-s) hangar

Hängebacken ['hɛŋəbakən] pl jowls

Hängebauch ['hɛŋəbaux] m potbelly

Hängebrücke ['hɛŋəbrykə] f suspension bridge

Hängematte ['hɛŋəmatə] f hammock

hängen ['hɛŋən] tr hang || ref—sich an j-n h. hang on to s.o.; sich ans Telephon h. be on the telephone || §92 intr hang; cling, stick

hän'genbleiben §62 intr (SEIN) stick; be detained, get stuck; (an dat) get caught (on); (educ) stay behind

Hans [hans] m (-' & -ens;) Johnny, Jack

Hans'dampf m (-[e]s;꞉e) busybody; H. in allen Gassen jack-of-all trades

Hänselei [hɛnzə'laɪ] f (-;-en) teasing

hänseln ['hɛnzəln] tr tease

Hans'narr m fool

Hans'wurst m (-es;꞉e & ꞉꞉e) clown

Hantel ['hantəl] f (-;-n) dumbbell

hantieren [han'tirən] intr (an acc) be busy (with); mit etw h. handle s.th.

hapern ['hapərn] impers—bei mir hapert es an (dat) (or mit) I am short of; bei mir hapert es in (dat) (or mit) I am weak in; damit hapert's that's the hitch

Happen ['hapən] m (-s;-) morsel; mouthful; (fig) good opportunity; fetter H. (coll) big hawl

happig ['hapɪç] adj greedy; (Preis) steep

Härchen ['herçən] n (-s;-) tiny hair

Harem ['harɛm] m (-s;-s) harem

Häre·sie [herɛ'zi] f (-;-sien ['zi·ən]) heresy

Häretiker [he'retikər] m (-s;-) heretic

Harfe ['harfə] f (-;-n) harp

Harke ['harkə] f (-;-n) rake

harken ['harkən] tr & intr rake

Harm [harm] m (-[e]s;) harm; grief

härmen ['hermən] ref (um) grieve (over)

harm'los adj harmless

Harmo·nie [harmo'ni] f (-;-nien ['ni·ən]) harmony

harmonieren [harmo'nirən] intr harmonize

Harmoni·ka [har'monika] f (-;-kas & -ken [kən]) accordion; harmonica

harmonisch [har'monɪʃ] adj harmonious

Harn [harn] m (-[e]s;꞉e) urine; H. lassen pass water

Harn'blase f (anat) bladder

harnen ['harnən] intr urinate

Harn'glas n urinal

Harn'grieß m (pathol) gravel

Harnisch ['harnɪʃ] m (-es;-e) armor; in H. geraten über (acc) fly into a rage over; j-n in H. bringen get s.o. hopping mad

Harn'leiter m (anat) ureter; (surg) catheter

Harn'röhre f urethra

harn'treibend adj diuretic

Harpune [har'punə] f (-;-n) harpoon

harpunieren [harpu'nirən] tr harpoon

harren ['harən] intr tarry; hope; (genit or auf acc) wait (for)

harsch [harʃ] adj harsh || Harsch m (-es;), Harsch/schnee m crushed snow

hart [hart] adj hard; severe || adv—h. an (dat) close to, hard by

Härte ['hertə] f (-;) hardness; severity

härten ['hertən] tr, ref & intr harden

Hart'faserplatte f fiber board

Hart'geld n coins

hartgesotten ['hartgəzotən] adj hardboiled; (Verbrecher) hardened

hart'herzig adj hard-hearted

hart'köpfig adj thick-headed

hart'leibig adj constipated

Hart'leibigkeit f (-;) constipation

hart'löten tr braze

hartnäckig ['hartnɛkɪç] *adj* stubborn
Hart'platz *m* (tennis) hard court
Harz [harts] *n* (-es;-e) resin; rosin
harzig ['hartsɪç] *adj* resinous
Hasardspiel [ha'zart/pil] *n* gambling game; gamble
haschen ['haʃən] *tr* snatch, grab ‖ *intr* (**nach**) try to catch, snatch (at)
Hase ['hazə] *m* (-n;-n) hare; **alter H.** old-timer, veteran
Ha'selnuß ['hazəlnus] *f* hazelnut
Hasenfuß *m* (coll) coward
Ha'senherz *n* (coll) yellow belly
Ha'senmaus *f* chinchilla
Hasenpanier ['hazənpanir] *n*—**das H. ergreifen** take to ones heels
ha'senrein *adj*—**nicht ganz h.** (fig) a bit fishy, rather shady
Ha'senscharte *f* harelip
Haspe ['haspə] *f* (-;-n) hasp
Haspel ['haspəl] *f* (-;-n) & *m* (-s;-) reel, spool; winch, windlass
haspeln ['haspəln] *tr* reel, spool
Haß *m* (Hasses) hatred
hassen ['hasən] *tr* hate
has'senswert, has'senswürdig *adj* hateful
häßlich ['heslɪç] *adj* ugly; nasty
Hast [hast] *f* (-;) haste
hasten ['hastən] *intr* be in a hurry, act quickly ‖ *intr* (SEIN) hasten, rush
hastig ['hastɪç] *adj* hasty
hätscheln ['hetʃəln] *tr* caress, cuddle; (*verzärteln*) coddle, spoil
hatte ['hatə] *pret* of **haben**
Haube ['haubə] *f* (-;-n) cap; (aer) cowling; (aut) hood; (orn) crest
Haubitze [hau'bɪtsə] *f* (-;-n) howitzer
Hauch [haux] *m* (-[e]s;-e) breath; breeze; (*Schicht*) thin layer; (*Spur*) trace
hauch'dünn' *adj* paper-thin
hauchen ['hauxən] *tr* whisper; (ling) aspirate ‖ *intr* breathe
Hauch'laut *m* (ling) aspirate
Haue ['hau·ə] *f* (-;-n) hoe; adze; **H. kriegen** get a spanking
hauen ['hau·ən] §93 *tr* hack, cut; strike; (*Baum*) fell; (*Stein*) hew ‖ §109 *tr* beat (up) ‖ *intr*—**h. nach** lash out at; **um sich h.** flail
Hauer ['hau·ər] *m* (-s;-) tusk
häufeln ['hɔɪfəln] *tr* hill
häufen ['hɔɪfən] *tr* & *ref* pile up
Haufen ['haufən] *m* (-s;-) pile, heap
Hau'fenwolke *f* cumulus cloud
häufig ['hɔɪfɪç] *adj* frequent ‖ *adv* frequently
Häu'figkeit *f* (-;) frequency
Häu'fung *f* (-;-en) accumulation
Haupt [haupt] *n* (-[e]s;-er) head; top; chief, leader **aufs H. schlagen** vanquish
Haupt- *comb.fm.* head; chief; major; most important; prime; primary, leading
Haupt'altar *m* high altar
haupt'amtlich *adj* full-time
Haupt'bahnhof *m* main train station
Haupt'darsteller *m* leading man
Haupt'darstellerin *f* leading lady
Häuptel ['hɔɪptəl] *n* (-s;-) head
Haupt'fach *n* (educ) major

Haupt'farbe *f* primary color
Haupt'feldwebel *m* first sergeant
Haupt'film *m* (cin) feature
Haupt'gefreite §5 *m* private first class; lance corporal (Brit); seaman; airman second class
Haupt'geschäftsstelle *f* head office
Haupt'gewinn *m* first prize
Haupt'haar *n* hair (*on the head*)
Häuptling ['hɔɪptlɪŋ] *m* (-s;-e) chief
häuptlings ['hɔɪptlɪŋs] *adv* head first
Haupt'linie *f* (rr) trunk line
Haupt'mann *m* (-[e]s;-leute) captain
Haupt'masse *f* bulk
Haupt'mast *m* mainmast
Hauptnenner ['hauptnɛnər] *m* (-s;-) (math) common denominator
Haupt'probe *f* dress rehearsal
Haupt'quartier *n* headquarters; **Großes H.** general headquarters
Haupt'rolle *f* leading role, lead
Haupt'sache *f* main thing; (jur) point at issue
haupt'sächlich *adj* main, principal
Haupt'satz *m* (gram) main clause; (phys) principle, law
Haupt'schalter *m* master switch
Haupt'schiff *n* (archit) nave
Haupt'schlagader *f* aorta
Haupt'schlüssel *m* master key, pass key
Haupt'schriftleiter *m* editor in chief
Haupt'spaß *m* great fun; great joke
Haupt'stadt *f* capital
Haupt'straße *f* main street; highway
Haupt'strecke *f* (rr) main line
Haupt'stütze *f* mainstay
Haupt'ton *m* primary accent
Haupt'treffer *m* first prize; jackpot
Haupt'verkehr *m* peak-hour traffic
Haupt'verkehrsstraße *f* main artery
Haupt'verkehrszeit *f* rush hour
Haupt'wort *n* (-[e]s;-er) noun
Haus [haus] *n* (-es;-er) house; **ein großes H. führen** do a lot of entertaining; **H. und Hof** house and home; **öffentliches H.** brothel; **nach Hause** home; **sich zu Hause fühlen** feel at home; **von zu Hause** from home
Haus'angestellte §5 *mf* domestic
Haus'apotheke *f* medicine cabinet
Haus'arbeit *f* housework; (educ) homework
Haus'arzt *m* family doctor
Haus'aufgabe *f* homework
haus'backen *adj* homemade; (*Frau*) plain; (fig) provincial
Haus'bedarf *m* household needs; **für den H.** for the home
Haus'brand *m* domestic fuel
Haus'bursche *m* porter
Haus'diener *m* porter
hausen ['hauzən] *intr* reside; (coll) make a mess; **schlimm h.** wreak havoc
Häuserblock ['hɔɪzərblɔk] *m* block of houses
Häusermakler **-in** ['hɔɪzərmaklər(ɪn)] §6 *mf* realtor
Haus'flur *m* entrance hall; hallway
Haus'frau *f* housewife; landlady
Haus'freund *m* friend of the family; (coll) wife's lover

Haus′gebrauch *m* family custom; household use

Haus′gehilfin *f* domestic

Haus′genosse *m*, **Haus′genossin** *f* occupant of the same house

Haus′gesinde *n* domestics

Haus′glocke *f* doorbell

Haus′halt *m* household; budget; **den H. führen** keep house

haus′halten §90 *intr* keep house; economize

Haushälter –in [′haʊshɛltər(ɪn)] §6 *mf* housekeeper

haushälterisch [′haʊshɛltərɪʃ] *adj* economical

Haus′haltsausschuß *m* ways and means committee

Haus′haltsgerät *n* household utensil

Haus′haltsjahr *n* fiscal year

Haus′haltsplan *m* budget

Haus′haltung *f* housekeeping; household; family budget; management

Haus′haltungslehre *f* home economics

Haus′herr *m* master of the house; landlord

Haus′herrin *f* lady of the house; landlady

haus′hoch′ *adj* very high; vast

Haus′hofmeister *m* steward

hausieren [haʊ′zirən] *intr*—**mit etw h.** peddle s.th.; go around telling everyone about s.th.

Hausierer [haʊ′zirər] *m* (–s;–) door-to-door salesman

Haus′lehrer –in §6 *mf* private tutor

häuslich [′hɔɪslɪç] *adj* home, domestic; homey; thrifty

Häus′lichkeit *f* (–;) family life; home

Haus′mädchen *n* maid

Haus′meister *m* caretaker, janitor

Haus′mittel *n* home remedy

Haus′mutter *f* mother of the family

Haus′pflege *f* home nursing

Haus′schlüssel *m* front-door key

Haus′schuh *m* slipper

Hausse [′hosə] *f* (–;–n) (econ. st. exch.) boom

Haus′sespekulant *m* (st. exch.) bull

Haussier [hos′je] *m* (–s;–) (st. exch.) bull

haussieren [ho′sirən] *tr* (fin) raise ‖ *intr* (fin) go up, rise

Haus′stand *m* household

Haus′suchungsbefehl *m* search warrant

Haus′tier *n* domestic animal; pet

Haus′vater *m* father of the family

Haus′verwalter *m* superintendent

Haus′wesen *n* household

Haus′wirt *m* landlord

Haus′wirtin *f* landlady

Haus′wirtschaft *f* housekeeping

haus′wirtschaftlich *adj* domestic; household

Haus′wirtschaftslehre *f* home economics

Haus′zins *m* house rent

Haut [haʊt] *f* (–;ːe) skin; hide; **aus der H. fahren** fly off the handle

Haut′abschürfung *f* skin abrasion

Haut′arzt *m* dermatologist

Haut′ausschlag *m* rash

Häutchen [′hɔɪtçən] (–s;–) membrane; pellicle; film

häuten [′hɔɪtən] *tr* skin ‖ *ref* slough the skin

haut′eng *adj* skin-tight

Haut′farbe *f* complexion

Haut′plastik *f* skin graft

Haut′reizung *f* skin irritation

Haut′transplantation *f*, **Haut′verpflanzung** *f* skin grafting

havariert [hava′rirt] *adj* damaged

H′-Bombe *f* H-bomb

Hebamme [′hepamə] *f* (–;–n) midwife

Hebebaum [′hebəbaum] *m* lever

Hebebühne [′hebəbynə] *f* car lift

Hebeeisen [′hebə·aizən] *n* crowbar

Hebel [′hebəl] *m* (–s;–) lever

heben [′hebən] §94 *tr* lift, raise; (*steigern*) increase; (*fördern*) further; (aut) jack up ‖ *ref* rise

Heber [′hebər] *m* (–s;–) siphon; (aut) jack

Hebeschiff [′hebə·ʃɪf] *n* salvage ship

Hebräer –in [he′bre·ər(ɪn)] §6 *mf* Hebrew

hebräisch [he′bre·ɪʃ] *adj* Hebrew

He′bung *f* (–;–en) lifting; increase; improvement; (mus, pros) stress

Hecht [hɛçt] *m* (–[e]s;–e) (ichth) pike

hechten [′hɛçtən] *intr* dive

Hecht′sprung *m* flying leap; jacknife dive

Heck [hɛk] *n* (–[e]s;–e & –s) stern; (aer) tail; (aut) rear

Heck′antrieb *m* (aut) rear drive

Hecke [′hɛkə] *f* (–;–n) hedge; brood, hatch

hecken [′hɛkən] *tr & intr* breed

Heckenhüpfen (Hek′kenhüpfen) *n* (–s;) (aer) hedgehopping

Heckenschütze (Hek′kenschütze) *m* sniper

Heck′fenster *n* (aut) rear window

Heck′licht *n* (aer, aut) tail light

Heck′motor *m* rear engine

Heck′pfennig *m* lucky penny

Heck′schütze *m* (aer) tail gunner

heda [′heda] *interj* hey there!

Heer [her] *n* (–[e]s;–e) army; host

Heeres– [herəs] *comb.fm.* army

Hee′resbericht *m* official army communiqué

Hee′resdienst *m* military service

Hee′resdienstvorschriften *pl* army regulations

Hee′resgeistliche §5 *m* army chaplain

Hee′resmacht *f* armed forces; army

Hee′reszug *m* (mil) campaign

Heer′lager *n* army camp; (pol) faction

Heer′schar *f* host, legion

Heer′zug *m* (mil) campaign

Hefe [′hefə] *f* (–;–n) yeast; dregs

He′feteig *m* leavened dough

Heft [hɛft] *n* (–[e]s;–e) haft, handle; notebook; (*e–r Zeitschrift*) issue

heften [′hɛftən] *tr* fasten together; sew, stitch; tack, baste; (*Blick*) ‖ *ref* (**an** *acc*) stick close (to)

heftig [′hɛftɪç] *adj* violent; (*Regen*) heavy; (*Fieber*) high; **h. werden** lose one's temper

Heft′klammer *f* paper clip; staple

Heft′maschine *f* stapler

Heft′stich *m* (sew) tack

Heft′zwecke *f* thumbtack

hegen ['heːgən] *tr* (*Wild*) preserve; (*Zweifel, Gedanken*) have; **h. und pflegen** lavish care on

Hehl [heːl] *n* (-[e]s;) secret

hehlen ['heːlən] *intr* receive stolen goods

Heh′ler –in §6 *mf* fence

hehr [heːr] *adj* sublime, noble

Heide ['haɪdə] *m* (-n;-n) heathen; (*Bib*) gentile || *f* (-;-n) heath

Hei′dekraut *n* heather

Heidelbeere ['haɪdəlbeːrə] *f* blueberry

Hei′denangst *f* (coll) jitters

Hei′dengeld *n* (coll) piles of money

Hei′denlärm *m* hullabaloo

hei′denmäßig *adv*—**h. viel** tremendous amount of

Hei′denspaß *m* (coll) great fun

Heidentum ['haɪdəntum] *n* (-s;) heathendom

heidi [haɪ′diː] *adj* gone; lost; **h. gehen** get lost; be all gone || *interj* quick!

Heidin ['haɪdɪn] *f* (-;-nen) heathen

heidnisch ['haɪdnɪʃ] *adj* heathen

heikel ['haɪkəl] *adj* particular, fastidious; (*Sache*) ticklish

heil [haɪl] *adj* safe, sound; undamaged || **Heil** *n* (-[e]s;) welfare, benefit; salvation || **Heil** *interj* hail!

Heiland ['haɪlant] *m* (-[e]s;) Saviour

Heil′anstalt *f* sanitarium

Heil′bad *n* spa

heilbar ['haɪlbar] *adj* curable

heil′bringend *adj* beneficial, healthful

Heilbutt ['haɪlbut] *m* (-[e]s;-e) (ichth) halibut

heilen ['haɪlən] *tr* heal || *intr* (HABEN & SEIN) heal

Heil′gehilfe *m* male nurse

Heil′gymnastik *f* physical therapy

heilig ['haɪlɪç] *adj* holy, sacred || **Heilige** §5 *mf* saint

Hei′ligabend *m* Christmas Eve

heiligen ['haɪlɪgən] *tr* hallow

Hei′ligenschein *m* halo

Hei′ligkeit *f* (-;) holiness, sanctity

hei′ligsprechen §64 *tr* canonize

Heiligtum ['haɪlɪçtum] *n* (-[e]s;ː-er) sanctuary; shrine; sacred relic

Hei′ligung *f* (-;) sanctification

Heil′kraft *f* healing power

Heil′kraut *n* medicinal herb

Heil′kunde *f* medical science

heil′los *adj* wicked; (coll) awful

Heil′mittel *n* remedy; medicine

Heil′mittellehre *f* pharmacology

heilsam ['haɪlzam] *adj* healthful

Heils′armee *f* Salvation Army

Heil′stätte *f* sanitarium

Hei′lung *f* (-;-en) cure

heim [haɪm] *adv* home || **Heim** *n* (-[e]s;-e) home; (*Alters-*) old-age home

Heimat ['haɪmat] *f* (-;-en) home; hometown; homeland

hei′matlich *adj* native

hei′matlos *adj* homeless

Hei′matort *m* hometown, home village

Hei′matstadt *f* hometown, native city

heim′begeben §80 *ref* head home

Heimchen ['haɪmçən] *n* (-s;-) cricket

Heim′computer *m* home computer

Heim′fahrt *f* homeward journey

heim′finden §59 *intr* find one's way home

Heim′gang *m* going home; passing on

heimisch ['haɪmɪʃ] *adj* local; locally-produced; domestic; **heimische Sprache** vernacular; **h. werden** settle down; become established; **sich h. fühlen** feel at home

Heimkehr ['haɪmker] *f* (-;) homecoming

heim′kehren *intr* (SEIN) return home

Heim′kunft *f* homecoming

heim′leuchten *intr* (sl) (dat) tell (*s.o.*) where to get off

heim′lich *adj* secret

Heim′lichkeit *f* (-;-en) secrecy; (*Geheimnis*) secret

Heim′reise *f* homeward journey

heim′suchen *tr* afflict, plague

Heim′tücke *f* treachery

heim′tückisch *adj* treacherous

heimwärts ['haɪmverts] *adv* homeward

Heim′weh *n* homesickness; nostalgia

heim′zahlen *tr*—j—m etw h. (coll) pay s.o. back for s.th.

Heini ['haɪni] *m* (-s;) Harry; guy

Heinzelmännchen ['haɪntsəlmençən] *pl* (myth) little people

Heirat ['haɪrat] *f* (-;-en) marriage

heiraten ['haɪratən] *tr & intr* marry

Hei′ratsantrag *m* marriage proposal

hei′ratsfähig *adj* marriageable

Hei′ratsgut *n* dowry

Hei′ratskandidat *m* eligible bachelor

Hei′ratsurkunde *f* marriage certificate

Hei′ratsvermittler –in §6 *mf* marriage broker

heischen ['haɪʃən] *tr* demand; beg

heiser ['haɪzər] *adj* hoarse

heiß [haɪs] *adj* hot; (fig) ardent

heißen ['haɪsən] §95 *tr* call; ask, bid; mean || *intr* be called; **das heißt** that is, i.e.; **wie h. Sie?** what is your name?

heiß′geliebt *adj* beloved

heiter ['haɪtər] *adj* cheerful; hilarious; serene; (*Wetter*) clear

Heiz– [haɪts–] *comb.fm.* heating

Heiz′anlage *f* heating system

Heiz′apparat *m* heater

heizen ['haɪtsən] *tr* heat; **den Ofen mit Kohle h.** burn coal in the stove || *intr* give off heat; heat; turn on the heating; light the fire (or stove)

Hei′zer *m* (-s;) boilerman; (naut) stoker; (rr) fireman

Heiz′faden *m* (elec) filament

Heiz′kissen *n* heating pad

Heiz′körper *m* radiator; heater

Heiz′material *n* fuel

Heiz′platte *f* hot plate

Heiz′raum *m* boiler room

Heiz′schlange *f* heating coil

Heiz′ung *f* (-;) heating; (coll) central heating; radiator

Hei′zungskessel *m* boiler

Hei′zungsrohr *n* radiator pipe

Held [hɛlt] *m* (-en;-en) hero

Hel′denalter *n* heroic age

Hel′dengedicht *n* epic

Hel′dengeist *m* heroism

hel′denhaft *adj* heroic

Hel′denmut *m* heroism

hel′denmütig *adj* heroic
Hel′dentat *f* heroic deed, exploit
Heldentum [′hɛldəntum] *n* (-[e]s;) heroism
Heldin [′hɛldɪn] *f* (-;-nen) heroine
helfen [′hɛlfən] *intr* (*dat*) help; **es hilft nichts** it's of no use
Hel′fer –in §6 *mf* helper
Hel′fershelfer *m* accomplice
Helikopter [helɪ′kɔptər] *m* (-s;-) helicopter
hell [hɛl] *adj* clear; bright; lucid; (*Haar*) fair; (*Bier*) light; (*Wahnsinn, usw.*) sheer || **Helle** §5 *f* brightness; lightness; clarity || *n* light; **ein Helles** a glass of light beer
hellenisch [he′lenɪʃ] *adj* Hellenic
Heller [′hɛlər] *m* (-s;-) penny
hellhörig [′hɛlhøːrɪç] *adj* having sharp ears; **h. werden** prick up one's ears
hellicht [′hɛlɪçt] *adj*—**hellichter Tag** broad daylight
Hel′ligkeit *f* (-;-en) brightness; (*astr*) magnitude
hell′sehen §138 *intr* be clairvoyant || **Hellsehen** *n* (-s;) clairvoyance
Hell′seher –in §6 *mf* clairvoyant; (coll) mind reader
hell′sichtig *adj* clear-sighted
hell′wach′ *adj* wide awake
Helm [hɛlm] *m* (-[e]s;-e) helmet; (archit) dome, spire; (naut) helm
Helm′busch *m* crest, plume
Hemd [hɛmt] *n* (-[e]s;-en) shirt
Hemd′brust *f* dickey, shirt front
Hemd′hose *f* union suit
hemmen [′hɛmən] *tr* slow up; stop; **gehemmt** inhibited
Hemmnis [′hɛmnɪs] *n* (-ses;-se) hindrance
Hemmschuh [′hɛmʃu] *m* (fig) hindrance; (rr) brake
Hem′mung *f* (-;-en) inhibition
hem′mungslos *adj* uninhibited
Hengst [hɛŋst] *m* (-es;-e) stallion
Henkel [′hɛŋkəl] *m* (-s;-) handle
henken [′hɛŋkən] *tr* hang (*s.o.*)
Henker [′hɛŋkər] *m* (-s;-) hangman
Henne [′hɛnə] *f* (-;-n) hen
her [her] *adv* hither, here; ago
herab [he′rap] *adv* down, downwards
herab– *comb.fm.* down; down here
herab′drücken *tr* press down; force down; **die Kurse h.** bear the market
herab′lassen §104 *ref* condescend
Herab′lassung *f* (-;) condescension
herab′sehen §138 *intr* (auf *acc*) look down (on)
herab′setzen *tr* put down; reduce; belittle, disparage
herab′steigen §148 *intr* (SEIN) climb down; (*vom Pferd*) dismount
herab′würdigen *tr* demean
Heraldik [he′raldɪk] *f* (-;) heraldry
heran [he′ran] *adv* near; up
heran′arbeiten *ref* work one's way (towards)
heran′bilden *tr* (zu) train (as)
heran′brechen §64 *intr* (SEIN) (*Tag*) dawn, break; (*Nacht*) fall, come on
heran′gehen §82 *intr* (SEIN) go close; **h. an** (*acc*) approach, go up to
heran′kommen §99 *intr* (SEIN) come

near; **h. an** (*acc*) approach; get at; **h. bis an** (*acc*) reach as far as
heran′machen *ref*—**h. an** (*acc*) apply oneself to; approach
heran′nahen *intr* (SEIN) approach
heran′wachsen §155 *intr* (SEIN) (zu) grow up (to be)
heran′wagen *ref* (an *acc*) dare to approach
heran′ziehen §163 *tr* pull closer; call on for help; (*Quellen*) consult; (*zur Beratung*) call in; (*Pflanzen*) grow; (*Nachwuchs*) train || *intr* (SEIN) approach
herauf [he′rauf] *adv* up, up here; upstairs
herauf′arbeiten *ref* work one's way up
herauf′bemühen *ref* take the trouble to come up (or upstairs)
herauf′beschwören §137 *tr* conjure up; (*verursachen*) bring on, provoke
herauf′kommen §99 *intr* (SEIN) come up
herauf′setzen *tr* raise, increase
herauf′steigen §148 *intr* (SEIN) climb up; (*Tag*) dawn
herauf′ziehen §163 *tr* pull up || *intr* (SEIN) move upstairs; (*Sturm*) come up
heraus [he′raus] *adv* out, out here
heraus′bekommen §99 *tr* (aus) get out (of); (*Wort*) utter; (*Geld*) get back in change; (*Problem*) figure out
heraus′bringen §65 *tr* bring out; (*Wort*) utter; (*Lösung*) work out; (*Buch*) publish; (*Fabrikat*) bring out
heraus′drücken *tr* squeeze out; (*die Brust*) throw out
heraus′fahren §71 *intr* (SEIN) drive out; (*aus dem Bett*) jump out; (*Bemerkung*) slip out
heraus′finden §59 *tr* find out || *ref* (aus) find one's way out (of)
heraus′fordern *tr* challenge, call on
heraus′fordernd *adj* defiant || *adv* defiantly; **sich h. anziehen** dress provocatively
Heraus′forderung *f* (-;-en) challenge
heraus′fühlen *tr* sense
Heraus′gabe *f* surrender; (*e–s Buches*) publication; (jur) restitution
heraus′geben §80 *tr* surrender; give back; (*Buch*) publish || *intr* (*dat*) give (*s.o.*) his change; **h. auf** (*acc*) give change for
Heraus′geber *m* publisher; (*Redakteur*) editor
heraus′greifen §88 *tr* single out
heraus′haben §89 *tr* have (*s.th.*) figured out; **er hat den Bogen heraus** (coll) he has the knack of it
heraus′halten §90 *tr* hold out || *ref* (aus) keep out (of)
heraus′hängen §92 *tr* & *intr* hang out
heraus′kommen §99 *intr* (SEIN) come out
heraus′lesen §107 *tr* pick out; deduce; **zu viel aus e–m Gedicht h.** read too much into a poem
heraus′machen *tr* (*Fleck*) get out || *ref* (*Kinder*) turn out well; (*Geschäft*) make out well
heraus′nehmen §116 *tr* take out || *ref*

—sich [*dat*] **zu viel** (or **Freiheiten**) **h.** take liberties
heraus′platzen *intr* (SEIN)—**mit etw h.** blurt out s.th.
heraus′putzen *ref* dress up
heraus′reden *ref* (**aus**) talk one's way out (of)
heraus′rücken *tr* move out (here); (**coll**) (*Geld*) shell out ‖ *intr* (SEIN) —**mit dem Geld h.** shell out money; **mit der Sprache h.** reveal it, admit it
heraus′schälen *ref* become apparent
heraus′stehen §146 *intr* protrude
heraus′steigen §148 *intr* (SEIN) (**aus**) climb out (of), step out (of)
heraus′stellen *tr* put out; **groß h.** give a big build-up to; **klar h.** present clearly ‖ *ref* emerge, come to light; **sich h. als** prove to be
heraus′streichen §85 *tr* delete; (*fig*) praise
heraus′suchen *tr* pick out
heraus′treten §152 *intr* (SEIN) come out, step out; bulge, protrude
heraus′winden §59 *ref* extricate oneself
heraus′wirtschaften *tr* manage to save; (*Profit*) manage to make
heraus′ziehen §163 *tr* pull out
herb [herp] *adj* harsh; (*sauer*) sour; (*zusammenziehend*) tangy; (*Wein*) dry; (*Worte*) bitter; (*Schönheit*) austere ‖ **Herbe** *f* (–;) harshness; tang; bitterness; austerity
herbei′ *adv* here (*toward the speaker*)
herbei– *comb.fm.* up, along, here (*toward the speaker*)
herbei′bringen §65 *tr* bring along
herbei′eilen *intr* (SEIN) hurry here
herbei′führen *tr* bring here; cause
herbei′kommen §99 *intr* (SEIN) come up
herbei′lassen §104 *ref* condescend
herbei′rufen §122 *tr* call over; summon
herbei′schaffen *tr* bring here; procure; (*Geld*) raise
herbei′sehnen *tr* long for
herbei′strömen *intr* (SEIN) come flocking, flock
herbei′winken *tr* beckon (*s.o.*) to come over
herbei′wünschen *tr* long for, wish for
Herberge [′hɛrbɛrgə] *f* (–;–n) lodging, shelter; hostel; (*obs*) inn
her′beten *tr* say mechanically
Herb′heit *f* (–;), **Her′bigkeit** *f* (–;) harshness; tang; bitterness; austerity
her′bringen §65 *tr* bring here
Herbst [herpst] *m* (–es;–e) autumn
herbst′lich *adj* autumn, fall
Herd [hert] *m* (–[e]s;–e) hearth, fireplace; home; kitchen range; center
Herde [′herdə] *f* (–;–n) herd, flock
herein [he′raɪn] *adv* in, in here; **h.!** come in!
herein– *comb.fm.* in, in here (*toward the speaker*)
herein′bemühen *tr* ask (*s.o.*) to come in ‖ *ref* trouble oneself to come in
herein′bitten §60 *tr* invite in
Herein′fall *m* disappointment, letdown
herein′fallen §72 *intr* (SEIN) fall in; **h. auf** (*acc*) fall for; **h. in** (*acc*) fall into

herein′legen *tr* fool, take in
herein′platzen *intr* (SEIN) burst in
her′fallen §72 *intr* (SEIN)—**h. über** (*acc*) fall upon, attack
her′finden §59 *ref* & *intr* find one's way here
Her′gang *m* background details
her′geben §80 *tr* hand over; give up ‖ *ref*—**sich h. zu** be a party to
her′halten §90 *tr* hold out, extend ‖ *intr*—**h. müssen** (*Person*) be the victim; (*Sache*) have to do (*as a makeshift*)
Hering [′herɪŋ] *m* (–s;–e) herring; **sitzen wie die Heringe** be packed in like sardines
her′kommen §99 *intr* (SEIN) come here; (*Wort*) originate; **wo kommst du denn her?** where have you come from? ‖ **Herkommen** *n* (–s;–) origin; custom, tradition, convention
herkömmlich [′herkœmlɪç] *adj* customary, usual; traditional, conventional
Herkunft [′herkunft] *f* (–;) origin; birth, family
her′laufen §105 *intr* (SEIN) walk here; **hinter j–m h.** follow s.o.
her′leiten *tr* derive; deduce, infer
Her′leitung *f* (–;–en) derivation
her′machen *tr*—**viel h. von** make a fuss over ‖ *ref*—**sich h. über** (*acc*) attack; (*fig*) tackle
Hermelin [hermə′lin] *m* (–s;–e) ermine ‖ *n* (–s;–e) (zool) ermine
hermetisch [her′metɪʃ] *adj* hermetic
hernach′ *adv* afterwards
her′nehmen §116 *tr* get; **j–n scharf h.** give s.o. a good talking-to
hernie′der *adv* down, down here
Heroin [hero′in] *n* (–s;) (pharm) heroin
Heroine [hero′inə] *f* (–;–n) heroine
heroisch [he′ro·ɪʃ] *adj* heroic
Heroismus [hero′ɪsmus] *m* (–;) heroism
Herold [′herəlt] *m* (–[e]s;–e) herald
Heros [′heros] *m* (–;) **Heroen** [he′ro·ən] hero
Herr [her] *m* (–n;–en) lord; master; gentleman; (*als Anrede*) Sir; (*vor Eigennamen*) Mr.; (*Gott*) Lord; **meine Herren!** gentlemen!
her′reichen *tr* hand, pass
Herren– [′herən] *comb.fm.* man's, men's; gentlemen's
Her′renabend *m* stag party
Her′renbegleitung *f*—**in H.** accompanied by a gentleman
Her′rendoppel(spiel) *n* (tennis) men's doubles
Her′reneinzel(spiel) *n* (tennis) men's singles
Her′renfahrer *m* (aut) owner-driver
Her′renfriseur *m* barber
Her′rengesellschaft *f* male company; stag party
Her′rengröße *f* men's size
Her′rengut *n* domain, manor
Her′renhaus *n* mansion; House of Lords
Her′renhof *m* manor
Her′renleben *n* life of Riley

her'renlos adj ownerless

Her'renmensch m born leader

Her'renschnitt m woman's very short hairstyle

Herr'renzimmer n study

Herr'gott m Lord, Lord God

her'richten tr arrange; get ready

Herrin ['hɛrɪn] f (–;-nen) lady

herrisch ['hɛrɪʃ] adj masterful

herr'lich adj splendid

Herr'lichkeit f (–;-en) splendor

Herr'schaft f (–;-en) rule, domination; mastery; control; lord, master; estate; **meine Herrschaften!** ladies and gentlemen!

herr'schaftlich adj ruler's; gentleman's; high-class

herrschen ['hɛrʃən] intr rule; prevail; exist

Herr'scher –in §6 mf ruler

Herrschsucht ['hɛrʃzʊçt] f (–;) thirst for power; bossiness

herrsch'süchtig adj power-hungry; autocratic; domineering

her'rühren intr—h. von come from, originate with

her'sagen tr recite, say

her'schaffen tr get (here)

her'stammen intr—h. von come from, be descended from; (gram) be derived from

her'stellen tr put here; (erzeugen) produce; **fabrikmäßig h.** mass-produce; **Verbindung h.** establish contact; (telp) put a call through

Her'steller m (–s;–) manufacturer

Her'stellung f (–;-en) production

Her'stellungsbetrieb m factory

Her'stellungsverfahren n manufacturing process

herüber [hɛ'rybər] adv over, over here, in this direction (toward the speaker)

herum [hɛ'rʊm] adv around; about

herum'bringen §65 tr bring around; (Zeit) spend

herum'drehen tr, ref & intr turn around

herum'fragen intr make inquiries

herumfuchteln [hɛ'rʊmfʊxtəln] intr—mit den Händen h. wave one's hands about

herum'führen tr show around

herum'greifen §88 intr—h. um reach around

herum'hacken intr—h. auf (dat) pick on, criticize

herum'kauen intr (an dat, auf dat) chew away (on)

herum'kommen §99 intr (SEIN) get around; **h. um** get around; evade

herum'lungern intr loaf around

herum'reiten §86 intr (SEIN) ride around; **h. auf** (dat) harp on (s.th.); pick on (s.o.)

herum'schnüffeln intr snoop around

herum'streichen §85 intr (SEIN) prowl about

herum'streiten §86 ref squabble

herum'treiben §62 tr drive around ‖ ref roam around, knock about

Herum'treiber m (–s;–) loafer, tramp

herum'ziehen §163 tr pull around; **h. um** draw (s.th.) around ‖ ref—**sich h. um** surround ‖ intr (SEIN) wander around; run around; **h. um** march around

herunter [hɛ'rʊntər] adv down, down here (towards the speaker); downstairs; **den Berg h.** down the mountain; **ins Tal h.** down into the valley

herun'terbringen §65 tr bring down; (fig) lower, reduce

herun'tergehen §82 intr (SEIN) go down; (Preis, Temperatur) fall, drop

herun'terhandeln tr (Preis) beat down

herun'terhauen §93 tr chop off; (Brief) dash off; **j–m eins h.** clout s.o.

herun'terkommen §99 intr (SEIN) come down; come downstairs; deteriorate

herun'terlassen §104 tr let down, lower

herun'terleiern tr drone

herun'terlesen §107 tr (Liste) read down; rattle off

herun'termachen tr take down; turn down; (coll) chew out; (coll) pan

herun'terschießen §76 tr shoot down

herun'tersein §139 intr (SEIN) be run-down

herun'terwirtschaften tr ruin (through mismanagement)

herun'terwürgen tr choke down

hervor [hɛr'for] adv out; forth

hervor'bringen §65 tr bring out; engender, produce; (Wort) utter

hervor'dringen §142 intr (SEIN) emerge

hervor'gehen §82 intr (SEIN)—**h. aus** come from; emerge from; to have been trained at

hervor'heben §94 tr highlight

hervor'holen tr produce

hervor'kommen §99 intr (SEIN) come out

hervor'lugen intr peep out

hervor'ragen intr jut out; be prominent; **h. über** (acc) tower over

hervor'ragend adj prominent

hervor'rufen §122 tr evoke, cause; (Schauspieler) recall

hervor'stechen §64 intr stick out; be conspicuous; be prominent

hervor'treten §152 intr (SEIN) emerge; come to the fore; become apparent; (Augen) bulge; (Ader) protrude

hervor'tun §154 ref distinguish oneself

hervor'wagen ref dare to come out; **sich mit e-r Antwort h.** venture an answer

hervor'zaubern tr produce by magic; **ein Essen h.** whip up a meal

Herweg ['hɛrvek] m way here; way home

Herz [hɛrts] n (–ens;-en) heart; (als Anrede) darling; (cards) heart(s); **ich bringe es nicht übers H. zu** (inf) I haven't the heart to (inf); **sich** [dat] **ein H. fassen** get up the courage; **seinem Herzen Luft machen** give vent to one's feelings

Herz– comb.fm. heart, cardiac

Herz'anfall m heart attack

Herz'beschwerden pl heart trouble

Herz'blume f (bot) bleeding heart

herzen ['hɛrtsən] tr hug, embrace

Her'zensgrund m bottom of one's heart

her'zensgut adj good-hearted

Her′zenslust f—**nach H.** to one's heart's content
herz′ergreifend adj moving, touching
Herz′geräusch n heart murmur
herz′haft adj hearty
herzig [′hɛrtsɪç] adj sweet, cute
–herzig comb.fm. **–hearted**
Herzinfarkt [′hɛrtsɪnfarkt] m (-[e]s; -e) cardiac infarction
herz′innig adj heartfelt
herz′inniglich adv sincerely
Herz′klappe f cardiac valve
Herz′klopfen n palpitations
Herz′kollaps m heart failure
herz′lich adj cordial; sincere ‖ adv very; **h. wenige** precious few
herz′los adj heartless
Herzog [′hɛrtsɔk] m (-[e]s;⸗e) duke
Herzogin [′hɛrtsɔgɪn] f (-;-nen) duchess
Herzogtum [′hɛrtsɔktum] n (-[e]s;⸗er) dukedom; duchy
Herz′schlag m heartbeat; heart failure
Herz′stück n heart, central point
Herz′verpflanzung f heart transplant
Herz′weh n (& fig) heartache
Hetzblatt [′hɛtsblat] n scandal sheet
Hetze [′hɛtsə] f (-;-n) hunting; hurry, rush; vicious campaign; baiting
hetzen [′hɛtsən] tr hunt; bait; rush; (fig) hound; **e-n Hund auf j–n h.** sic a dog on s.o. ‖ ref rush ‖ intr stir up trouble; **h. gegen** conduct a vicious campaign against ‖ intr (SEIN) race, dash
Het′zer –in §6 mf agitator
Hetz′hund m hound, hunting dog
Hetz′jagd f hunt; baiting; hurry
Hetz′rede f inflammatory speech
Heu [hɔɪ] n (-[e]s;) hay
Heu′boden m hayloft
Heuchelei [hɔɪçə′laɪ] f (-;-en) hypocrisy; piece of hypocrisy
heucheln [′hɔɪçəln] tr feign ‖ intr be hypocritical
Heuch′ler –in §6 mf hypocrite
heuchlerisch [′hɔɪçlərɪʃ] adj hypocritical
heuen [′hɔɪ-ən] intr make hay
heuer [′hɔɪ-ər] adv this year
heuern [′hɔɪ-ərn] tr hire
Heu′fieber n hayfever
Heu′gabel f pitchfork
heulen [′hɔɪlən] intr bawl; (Wind) howl
heurig [′hɔɪrɪç] adj this year's ‖ **Heurige** §5 m new wine
Heu′schnupfen m (-s;) hayfever
Heuschober [′hɔɪʃobər] m (-s;-) haystack
Heu′schrecke f (-;-n) locust
heute [′hɔɪtə] adv today; **h. abend** this evening; **h. früh** (or **h. morgen**) this morning; **h. vor acht Tagen** a week ago today; **h. in acht Tagen** today a week
heutig [′hɔɪtɪç] adj today's; present-day; **am heutigen Tage** (or **der heutige Tag** or **mit dem heutigen Tag**) today
heutzutage [′hɔɪttsutagə] adv nowadays
Hexe [′hɛksə] f (-;-n) witch; hag

hexen [′hɛksən] intr practice witchcraft
He′xenkessel m chaos, inferno
He′xenmeister m wizard; sorcerer
He′xenschuß m lumbago
Hexerei [hɛksə′raɪ] f (-;) witchcraft
Hiatus [hɪ′atus] m (-;-) (& pros) hiatus
Hibis·kus [hɪ′bɪskus] m (-;-ken [kən]) hibiscus
hieb [hip] pret of **hauen** ‖ **Hieb** m (-[e]s;-e) blow, stroke; **Hiebe** thrashing
hieb′–undstich′fest adj (fig) watertight
Hieb′wunde f gash
hielt [hɪlt] pret of **halten**
hier [hir] adv here
hieran′ adv at (by, in, on, to) it or them
Hierar·chie [hɪ·erar′çi] f (-;-chien [′çi·ən]) hierarchy
hierauf′ adv on it, on them; then
hieraus′ adv out of it (or them); from this (or these)
hierbei′ adv near here; here; in this case; in connection with this
hierdurch′ adv through it (or them); through here; hereby
hierfür′ adv for it (or them)
hierge′gen adv against it
hierher′ adv hither, here
hier′herum adv around here
hierhin′ adv here; **bis h.** up to here
hierin′ adv herein, in this
hiermit′ adv herewith, with it
hiernach′ adv after this, then; about this; according to this
Hieroglyphe [hɪ·ero′glyfə] f (-;-n) hieroglyph
hierorts [′hirɔrts] adv in this town
hierü′ber adv over it (or them); about it (or this)
hierzu′ adv to it; in addition to it; concerning this
hiesig [′hizɪç] adj local
hieß [his] pret of **heißen**
Hilfe [′hɪlfə] f (-;-n) help, aid; **zu H. nehmen** make use of
Hil′feleistung f assistance
Hil′feruf m cry for help
hilf′los adj helpless
hilf′reich adj helpful
Hilfs– [hɪlfs] comb.fm. auxiliary
Hilfs′arbeiter –in §6 mf unskilled laborer
Hilfs′arzt m, **Hilf′ärztin** f intern
hilfs′bedürftig adj needy
hilfs′bereit adj ready to help
Hilfs′dienst m help, assistance
Hilfs′gerät n labor-saving device
Hilfs′kraft f assistant, helper; (mach) auxiliary power
Hilfs′kraftbremse f power brake
Hilfs′kraftlenkung f power steering
Hilfs′lehrer –in §6 mf student teacher
Hilfs′maschine f auxiliary engine
Hilfs′mittel n aid, device; remedy; financial aid
Hilfs′quellen pl material; sources
Hilfs′rakete f booster rocket
Hilfs′schule f school for the mentally slow

Hilfs′truppen pl auxiliaries
Hilfs′werk n welfare organization
Hilfs′zeitwort n (-[e]s;⁼er) (gram) auxiliary (verb)
Himbeere [′hɪmbərə] f (-;-n) raspberry
Himmel [′hɪməl] m (-s;-) sky, skies; heaven(s); firmament; (eccl) baldachin; **ach du lieber H.!** good heavens!; **aus heiterem H.** out of the blue; **in den H. heben** praise to the skies
himmelan′ adv skywards; heavenwards
him′melangst invar adj—**mir wird h.** I feel frightened to death
Him′melbett n canopy bed
him′melblau adj sky-blue
Him′melfahrt f ascension; assumption
Him′melfahrtstag m Ascension Day
Him′melreich n kingdom of heaven
Himmels- comb.fm. celestial
him′melschreiend adj atrocious
Him′melsgegend f region of the sky; point of the compass
Him′melskörper m celestial body
Him′melsrichtung f point of the compass; direction
Him′melsschrift f skywriting
Him′melswagen m (astr) Great Bear
Him′melszelt n canopy of heaven
himmelwärts [′hɪməlverts] adv skywards; heavenwards
himmlisch [′hɪmlɪʃ] adj heavenly, celestial; divine; (coll) gorgeous
hin [hɪn] adv there (away from the speaker); **ganz hin** (coll) bushed; (coll) quite carried away; **hin ist hin** what's done is done; **hin und her** up and down, back and forth; **hin und wieder** now and then; **vor sich hin** to oneself
hinab′ adv down
hinan′ adv up; **bis an etw h.** up to s.th., as far as s.th.
hinauf′ adv up, up there; upstairs; **den Fluß h.** up the river
hinauf′reichen tr hand (s.th.) up || intr reach up
hinauf′schrauben tr (Preis) jack up
hinauf′setzen tr raise, increase
hinauf′steigen §148 tr (SEIN) (Treppe, Berg) climb || intr (SEIN) climb up; (Temperatur) rise
hinaus′ adv out, out there; **auf viele Jahre h.** for many years to come
hinaus′beißen §53 tr (coll) edge out
hinaus′gehen §82 intr (SEIN) go out; **h. auf** (acc) look out over; lead to; drive at, imply; **h. über** (acc) exceed
hinaus′kommen §99 intr (SEIN) come out; **es kommt auf eins** (or **aufs gleiche**) **hinaus** it amounts to the same thing; **h. über** (acc) get beyond
hinaus′laufen §105 intr (SEIN) run out; **es läuft aufs eins** (or **aufs gleiche**) **hinaus** it amounts to the same thing
hinaus′schieben §130 tr push out; (Termin, usw.) postpone
hinaus′werfen §160 tr throw out; fire
hinaus′wollen §162 intr want to go out; **h. auf** (acc) be driving at; **hoch h.** aim high, be ambitious
hinaus′ziehen §163 tr prolong || ref

take longer than expected || intr (SEIN) go out; move out
Hin′blick m—**im H. auf** (acc) in view of
hin′bringen §65 tr bring (there); take (there); (Zeit) pass
hinderlich [′hɪndərlɪç] adj in the way
hindern [′hɪndərn] tr block; **h. an** (dat) prevent from (ger)
Hindernis [′hɪndərnɪs] n (-ses;-se) hindrance; obstacle
Hin′dernisbahn f obstacle course
Hin′dernislauf m (sport) hurdles
Hin′dernisrennen n steeplechase; hurdles
hin′deuten intr (auf acc) point (to)
hindurch′ adv through; **den ganzen Sommer h.** throughout the summer
hinein′ adv in, in there
hinein′arbeiten ref—**sich h. in** (acc) work one's way into
hinein′denken §66 ref—**sich h. in** (acc) imagine oneself in
hinein′geraten §63 intr (SEIN)—**h. in** (acc) get into, fall into
hinein′leben intr—**in den Tag h.** live for the moment
hinein′tun §154 tr put in
Hin′fahrt f journey there, out-bound passage
hin′fallen §72 intr (SEIN) fall down
hinfällig [′hɪnfɛlɪç] adj frail; (Gesetz) invalid
hinfort′ adv henceforth
hing [hɪŋ] pret of **hängen**
Hin′gabe f (an acc) devotion (to)
hin′geben §80 tr give up || ref (dat) abandon oneself (to)
Hin′gebung f (-;) devotion
hinge′gen adv on the other hand
hin′gehen §82 intr (SEIN) go there; pass
hin′halten §90 tr hold out; (Person) keep waiting, string along; **den Kopf h.** (fig) take the rap
hinken [′hɪŋkən] intr limp; **der Vergleich hinkt** that's a poor comparison || intr (SEIN) limp
hin′länglich adj sufficient
hin′legen tr put down || ref lie down
hin′nehmen §116 tr accept; take, put up with
hin′raffen tr snatch away
hin′reichen tr (dat) pass to, hand to || intr reach; suffice
hin′reißen §53 tr enchant, carry away
hin′richten tr execute; **h. auf** (acc) direct towards
Hin′richtung f (-;-en) execution
Hin′richtungsbefehl m death warrant
hin′setzen tr put down || ref sit down
Hin′sicht f respect, way; **in H. auf** (acc) regarding, in regard to
hin′sichtlich prep (genit) regarding
hin′stellen tr put there; put down
hintan′setzen, hintan′stellen tr put last, consider last
hinten [′hɪntən] adv at the back, in the rear; **h. im Zimmer** at the back of the room; **nach h.** to the rear; backwards; **von h.** from the rear
hinter [′hɪntər] prep (dat) behind; **h. j-m her sein** be after s.o. || prep (acc) behind; **h. etw kommen** find

out about s.th., get to the bottom of s.th.

Hin′terachse f rear axle

Hin′terbacke f buttock

Hin′terbein n hind leg; **sich auf die Hinterbeine setzen** strain oneself

Hinterbliebene [ˈhɪntərblibənə] §5 mf survivor (*of a deceased*); **H.** pl next-of-kin

hinterbrin′gen §65 tr—j—m etw h. let s.o. in on s.th.

Hin′terdeck n quarter deck

hinterdrein [hɪntərˈdraɪn] adv after; subsequently, afterwards

hin′tere §9 adj back, rear ‖ **Hintere** §5 m (coll) behind

hintereinan′der adv one behind the other; in succession; one after the other

Hin′terfuß m hind foot

Hin′tergaumen m soft palate, velum

Hin′tergedanke m ulterior motive

hinterge′hen §82 tr deceive

Hin′tergrund m background

Hin′terhalt m ambush

hinterhältig [ˈhɪntərhɛltɪç] adj under-handed

Hin′terhand f hind quarters (*of horse*)

Hin′terhaus n rear building

hinterher′ adv behind; afterwards

Hin′terhof m backyard

Hin′terkopf m back of the head

Hin′terland n hinterland

hinterlas′sen §104 tr leave behind

Hinterlas′senschaft f (-;-en) inheritance

Hin′terlauf m hind leg

hinterle′gen tr deposit

Hinterle′gung f (-;-en) deposit

Hin′terlist f deceit; trick, ruse

Hin′termann m (-[e]s;-̈er) instigator; wheeler-dealer; (pol) backer

Hintern [ˈhɪntərn] m (-s;-) (coll) behind

Hin′terradantrieb m rear-wheel drive

hinterrücks [ˈhɪntərryks] adv from behind; (fig) behind one's back

Hin′tertreffen n—ins H. geraten fall behind; **im H. sein** be at a disadvantage

hintertrei′ben §62 tr frustrate

Hintertrei′bung f (-;-en) frustration

Hin′tertreppe f backstairs

Hin′tertür f backdoor

Hinterwäldler [ˈhɪntərvɛltlər] m (-s;-) hillbilly

hin′terwäldlerisch adj hillbilly

hinterzie′hen §163 tr evade

Hinterzie′hung f (-;) tax evasion

hinü′ber adv over, over there; across

hinun′ter adv down

hinun′tergehen §82 tr (SEIN) (*Treppe*) go down ‖ intr (SEIN) go down

hinweg [hɪnˈwɛk] adv away; **über etw h.** over s.th., across s.th. ‖ **Hinweg** [ˈhɪnvek] m way there

hinweg′kommen §99 intr (SEIN)—h. über (*acc*) get over

hinweg′sehen §138 intr—h. über (*acc*) look over; overlook, ignore

hinweg′setzen ref—sich h. über (*acc*) ignore, disregard

hinweg′täuschen tr mislead, blind

Hinweis [ˈhɪnvaɪs] m (-es;-e reference; hint; announcement

hin′weisen §118 tr—j—n h. auf (*acc*) point s.th. out to s.o. ‖ intr—h. auf (*acc*) point to; point out

hin′werfen §160 tr throw down; (coll) dash off, jot down

hin′wirken intr—h. auf (*acc*) work toward(s)

hin′ziehen §163 tr attract protract ‖ ref drag on; **sich h. an** (*dat*) run along; **sich h. bis zu** extend to

hin′zielen intr—h. auf (*acc*) aim at

hinzu′ adv there, thither; in addition

hinzu′fügen tr add

hinzu′kommen §99 intr (SEIN) come (upon the scene); be added; **es kamen noch andere Gründe hinzu** besides, there were other reasons

hinzu′setzen tr add

hinzu′treten §152 intr (SEIN) (zu) walk up (to); **es traten noch andere Gründe hinzu** besides, there were other reasons

hinzu′tun §154 tr add

hinzu′ziehen §163 tr (*Arzt*) call in

Hirn [hɪrn] n (-[e]s;-e) brain; brains; **sein H. anstrengen** rack one's brains

Hirn- comb.fm. brain; cerebral; intellectual

Hirn′anhang m pituitary gland

Hirn′gespinst n figment of the imagination

Hirn′hautentzündung f meningitis

hirn′los adj brainless

Hirn′rinde f (anat) cortex

Hirn′schale f cranium

hirn′verbrannt adj (coll) crazy

Hirsch [hɪrʃ] m (-es;-e) deer, stag

Hirsch′fänger m hunting knife

Hirsch′kalb n fawn, doe

Hirsch′kuh f hind

Hirsch′leder n deerskin, buckskin

Hirt [hɪrt] m (-en;-en) shepherd –hirte [ˈhɪrtə] m (-n;-n) –herd

Hir′tenbrief m (eccl) pastoral letter

Hirtin [ˈhɪrtɪn] f (-;-nen) shepherdess

His [hɪs] n (-;) (mus) B sharp

hissen [ˈhɪsən] tr hoist

Historie [hɪsˈtorjə] f (-;-n) history; story

Historiker –in [hɪsˈtorɪkər(ɪn)] §6 mf historian

historisch [hɪsˈtorɪʃ] adj historical

Hitze [ˈhɪtsə] f (-;-n) heat

hit′zebeständig adj heat-resistant

Hit′zeferien pl school holiday (*because of hot weather*)

Hit′zeschild m (rok) heat shield

Hit′zewelle f heat wave

hitzig [ˈhɪtsɪç] adj hot-tempered

Hitz′kopf m hothead

hitz′köpfig adj hot-headed

Hitz′schlag m heatstroke

hob [hop] pret of heben

Hobel [ˈhobəl] m (-s;-) (carp) plane

Ho′belbank f carpenter's bench

hobeln [ˈhobəln] tr (carp) plane

hoch [hox], (**hohe** [ˈho·ə] §9) adj (**höher** [ˈhø·ər]; **höchste** [ˈhø̈çstə] §9) high; noble; (*Alter*) advanced; **das ist mir zu h.** that's beyond me; **hohes Gericht!** your honor!; members of the jury!; **in höchster Not** in dire need || *adv* high; highly, very; (math) to the ... power || **Hoch** *n* (-s;-s) (*Trinkspruch, Heilruf*) cheer; (meteor) high

hoch– *comb.fm.* up; upwards; highly, very; high, as high as

hoch'achten *tr* esteem

Hoch'achtung *f* (-;) esteem; **mit vorzüglicher H., Ihr ... or Ihre ...** Very truly yours, Respectfully yours

hoch'achtungsvoll *adj* respectful || *adv* —h., Ihr ... or Ihre ... Very truly yours, Respectfully yours

Hoch'amt *n* (eccl) High Mass

Hoch'antenne *f* outdoor antenna

hoch'arbeiten *ref* work one's way up

hoch'aufgeschossen *adj* tall, lanky

Hoch'bahn *f* el., elevated train

Hoch'bauingenieur *m* structural engineer

hoch'bäumen *ref* rear up

Hoch'behälter *m* water tower; reservoir

Hochbeiner ['hoxbaɪnər] *m* (-s;-) (ent) daddy-long-legs

hoch'beinig *adj* long-legged

hoch'betagt *adj* advanced in years

Hoch'betrieb *m* bustle, big rush

Hoch'blüte *f* high bloom; (fig) heyday

hoch'bringen §65 *tr* restore to health; (*Geschäft*) put on its feet; **es h.** (sport) get a high score

Hoch'burg *f* fortress, citadel

hoch'denkend *adj* noble-minded

hoch'deutsch *adj* High German

Hoch'druck *m* high pressure; (fig) great pressure; (meteor) high; **mit H.** (fig) full blast

Hoch'druckgebiet *n* (meteor) high, high-pressure area

Hoch'ebene *f* plateau

hoch'fahrend *adj* high-handed

hoch'fein *adj* very refined; high-grade

Hoch'flut *m* high tide; (fig) deluge

Hoch'form *f* top form

hochfrequent ['hoxfrɛkvɛnt] *adj* high-frequency

Hoch'frequenz *f* high-frequency

Hoch'frisur *f* upsweep

Hoch'gefühl *n* elation

hoch'gemut *adj* cheerful

Hoch'genuß *m* great pleasure

Hoch'gericht *n* place of execution

hoch'gesinnt *adj* noble-minded

hoch'gespannt *adj* (*Hoffnungen*) high; (elec) high-voltage

hoch'gestellt *adj* high-ranking

Hoch'glanz *m* high polish, high gloss

Hoch'haus *n* high rise (building)

hoch'herzig *adj* generous

hoch'jagen *tr* (*Wild*) ferret out; (*Motor*) race; (coll) blow up

hochkant ['hoxkant] *adv* on end

Hoch'konjunktur *f* (econ) boom

Hoch'land *n* highlands; plateau

Hoch'leistung *f* (-;-en) high output; (sport) first-class performance

Hochleistungs– *comb.fm.* high-powered; high-capacity; high-speed; heavy-duty

Hoch'mut *m* haughtiness, pride

hoch'mütig *adj* haughty, proud

hochnäsig ['hoxnɛzɪç] *adj* snooty

Hoch'ofen *m* blast furnace

hoch'ragend *adj* towering

hoch'rappeln *ref* (coll) get on one's feet again, pick up again

hoch'rollen *tr* roll up

Hoch'ruf *m* cheer

Hoch'saison *f* height of the season

Hoch'schule *f* university, academy

Hoch'schüler –in §6 *mf* university student

Hoch'seefischerei *f* deep-sea fishing

hoch'selig *adj* late, of blessed memory

Hoch'spannung *f* high voltage

Hoch'spannungsleitung *f* high-tension line

hoch'spielen *tr* play up; put into the limelight

Hoch'sprache *f* standard language; **(die) deutsche H.** standard German

höchst *adv* see hoch

Höchst– *comb.fm.* maximum, top

Hochstapelei [hox/tɑpə'laɪ] *f* (-;) false pretenses; fraud

Hochstapler ['hox/tɑplər] *m* (-s;) confidence man; imposter, swindler

Hoch'start *m* (sport) standing start

Höchst'belastung *f* (-;-en) maximum load; (elec) peak load

höchstens ['høçstəns] *adv* at best, at the very most

Höchst'form *f* (sport) top form

Höchst'frequenz *f* ultrahigh frequency

Höchst'geschwindigkeit *f* top speed; **zulässige H.** speed limit

Höchst'leistung *f* (-;-en) maximum output; highest achievement; (sport) record

Hoch'straße *f* overpass

Hoch'ton *m* (ling) primary stress

hoch'tönend *adj* bombastic

hochtourig ['hoxturɪç] *adj* high-revving

hoch'trabend *adj* pompous

Hoch'–und Tief'bau *m* (-[e]s;) civil engineering

hoch'verdient *adj* of great merit

Hoch'verrat *m* high treason

Hoch'verräter –in §6 *mf* traitor

Hoch'wasser *n* flood(s); **der Fluß führt H.** the river is swollen

hoch'wertig *adj* high-quality

Hoch'wild *n* big game

Hoch'würden *pl* (*als Anrede*) Reverend; **Seine H. ...** the Reverend ...

Hoch'zeit *f* wedding

hoch'zeitlich *adj* bridal; nuptial

Hoch'zeitsfeier *f* wedding ceremony; wedding reception

Hoch'zeitspaar *n* newly-weds

Hoch'zeitsreise *f* honeymoon

Hocke ['hokə] *f* (-;-n) crouch

hocken ['hokən] *ref & intr* squat; (coll) sit down

Hocker ['hokər] *m* (-s;-) stool

Höcker ['hœkər] *m* (-s;-) hump; bump

höckerig ['hœkərɪç] *adj* hunchbacked; (*Weg*) bumpy

Hockey ['hoki] *n* (-s;) hockey

Ho'ckeyschläger *m* hockey stick

Hode ['hodə] *f* (-;-n) testicle

Ho'densack *m* (anat) scrotum

Hof [hof] *m* (-[e]s;-̈e) courtyard;

yard; barnyard; (e–s Königs) court; (astr) halo; corona; **e–m Mädchen den Hof machen** court a girl

Hoffart ['hɔfart] f (–;) haughtiness

hoffärtig ['hɔfɛrtɪç] adj haughty

hoffen ['hɔfən] tr—**das Beste h.** hope for the best ‖ intr (auf acc) hope (for); **auf j–n h.** put one's hopes in s.o

hoffentlich ['hɔfəntlɪç] adv as I hope; **h. kommt er bald** I hope he comes soon

Hoffnung ['hɔfnʊŋ] f (–;-en) hope

hoff'nungslos adj hopeless

hoff'nungsvoll adj hopeful; promising

Hof'hund m watchdog

hofieren [ha'firən] tr court

höfisch ['høfɪʃ] adj court, courtly

höflich ['høflɪç] adj polite, courteous

Höf'lichkeit f (–;-en) politeness, courtesy

Höf'lichkeitsformel f complimentary close (in a letter)

Höfling ['høflɪŋ] m (–[e]s;-e) courtier

Hof'meister m steward; tutor

Hof'narr m court jester

Hof'staat m royal household; retinue

hohe ['ho·ə] adj see **hoch**

Höhe ['hø·ə] f (–;-en) height; altitude; (Anhöhe) hill; (mus) pitch; **auf der H.** in good shape; **das ist die H.!** that's the limit!; **in der H. von** in the amount of; **in die H.** up; **in die H. fahren** jump up; **wieder in die H. bringen** (com) put back on its feet

Hoheit ['hohart] f (–;-en) sovereignty; (als Titel) Highness

Ho'heitsbereich m (pol), **Ho'heitsgebiet** n (pol) territory

Ho'heitsgewässer pl territorial waters

Ho'heitsrechte pl sovereign rights

ho'heitsvoll adj regal, majestic

Ho'heitszeichen n national emblem

Höhenmesser m altimeter

Höh'enruder n (aer) elevator

Höh'ensonne f ultra-violet lamp

Höh'enstrahlen pl cosmic rays

Höh'enzug m mountain range

Hö'hepriester m high priest

Hö'hepunkt m climax; height; acme

höher ['hø·ər] adj see **hoch**

hohl [hol] adj hollow

Höhle ['hø·lə] f (–;-n) cave; grotto; lair, den; hollow, cavity; socket

Höh'lenmensch m caveman

hohl'geschliffen adj hollow-ground

Hohl'heit f (–;) hollowness

Hohl'maß n dry measure; liquid measure

Hohl'raum m hollow, cavity

Hohl'saum m hemstitch

Hohl'weg m defile, narrow pass

Hohn [hon] m (–[e]s;) scorn; sarcasm; **etw j–m Hohn tun** do s.th. in defiance of s.o.

höhnen ['hø·nən] intr jeer; sneer

höhnisch ['hø·nɪʃ] adj scornful

hohn'sprechen §64 intr (dat) treat with scorn; defy; make a mockery of

Höker -in ['hø·kər(ɪn)] §6 mf huckster

hold [hɔlt] adj kindly; lovely; sweet

hold'selig adj lovely, sweet

holen ['ho·lən] tr fetch; get; (Atem, Luft) draw; **h. lassen** send for; **sich** [dat] **etw h.** (coll) catch s.th.

Holland ['hɔlant] n (–s;) Holland

Holländer ['hɔlɛndər] m (–s;–) Dutchman

Holländerin ['hɔlɛndərɪn] f (–;-nen) Dutch woman

holländisch ['hɔlɛndɪʃ] adj Dutch

Hölle ['hœlə] f (–;) hell

Höl'lenangst f mortal fear

höllisch ['hœlɪʃ] adj hellish

Holm [hɔlm] m (–[e]s;-e) islet; (Stiel) handle; (aer) spar; (gym) parallel bar

holp(e)rig ['hɔlp(ə)rɪç] adj bumpy

holpern ['hɔlpərn] intr jolt, bump along; (beim Lesen) stumble

Holunder [ho'lundər] m (–s;–) (bot) elder

Holz [hɔlts] n (–es;ˮer) wood; lumber; timber, trees; **ins H. gehen** go into the woods

Holz'apfel m crab apple

Holz'arbeit f woodwork; lumbering

Holz'arbeiter m woodworker; lumberjack

holz'artig adj woody

Holz'blasinstrumente pl wood winds

Holz'brei m wood pulp

holzen ['hɔltsən] tr fell; deforest; (coll) spank ‖ intr cut wood

hölzern ['hœltsərn] adj wooden; (fig) clumsy

Holzfäller ['hɔltsfɛlər] m (–s;–) lumberjack, logger

Holz'faser f wood fiber; wood pulp; grain; **gegen die H.** against the grain

Holz'faserstoff m wood pulp

Holzhacker ['hɔltshakər] m (–s;–), **Holzhauer** ['hɔltshau·ər] m (–s;–) lumberjack; wood chopper

holzig ['hɔltsɪç] adj woody, wooded; (Gemüse) stringy

Holz'knecht m lumberjack

Holz'kohle f charcoal

Holz'nagel m wooden peg

Holz'platz m lumber yard

holz'reich adj wooded

Holz'schnitt m woodcut; wood engraving

Holz'schuh m wooden shoe

Holz'schuppen m woodshed

Holz'wolle f excelsior

Homi-lie [homɪ'li] f (–;-lien ['li·ən]) homily

homogen [homo'gen] adj homogeneous

Homosexualität [homozeksu·alɪ'tet] f (–;) homosexuality

homosexuell [homozeksu'ɛl] adj homosexual ‖ **Homosexuelle** §5 mf homosexual

Honig ['honɪç] m (–s;) honey

Ho'nigkuchen m gingerbread

ho'nigsüß adj sweet as honey

Ho'nigwabe f honeycomb

Honorar [hono'rar] n (–s;-e) fee

Honoratioren [honoratsɪ'orən] pl dignitaries

honorieren [hono'rirən] tr give an honorarium to; pay royalties to; (Scheck) honor

Hopfen ['hɔpfən] m (–s;) hops

hopp [həp] *interj* up!; quick!; hopp, los! get going!

hoppla ['həplə] *interj* whoops!; **jetzt aber h.!** come on!; look sharp!

hops [həps] *adj*—**h. gehen** go to pot; **h. sein** be done for

hopsasa ['həpsasa] *interj* upsy-daisy

hopsen ['həpsən] *intr* (SEIN) hop

Hop'ser *m* (-s;-) hop

Hörapparat ['hørapa·rat] *m* hearing aid

hörbar ['hørbar] *adj* audible

hörbehindert ['hørbəhindərt] *adj* hard of hearing

Hörbericht ['hørbərɪçt] *m* radio report; radio commentary

horchen ['hərçən] *intr* listen; eavesdrop

Hor'cher –in §6 *mf* eavesdropper

Horch'gerät *n* sound detector; (nav) hydrophone

Horch'posten *m* (mil) listening post

Horde ['hərdə] *f* (-;-n) horde

hören ['hørən] *tr* hear; listen to; (*Vorlesung*) attend ‖ *intr* hear; **h. auf** (acc) pay attention to, obey

Hö'rer *m* (-s;-) listener; member of an audience; student; (telp) receiver

Hö'rerbrief *m* letter from a listener

Hö'rerkreis *m* listeners

Hö'rerschaft *f* (-;-en) audience; (educ) enrollment

Hör'folge *f* radio serial

Hör'gerät *n* hearing aid

hörig ['hørɪç] *adj* in bondage ‖ **Hörige** §5 *mf* serf, thrall

Horizont [hərɪ'tsənt] *m* (-[e]s;-e) horizon

horizontal [hərɪtsən'tal] *adj* horizontal ‖ **Horizontale** §5 *f* horizontal line

Horn [hərn] *n* (-[e]s;-̈er) horn; (mil) bugle; (mus) horn, French horn

Hörnchen ['hœrnçən] *n* (-s;-) crescent roll

Horn'haut *f* (anat) cornea

Hornisse [hər'nɪsa] *f* (-;-n) hornet

Hornist [hər'nɪst] *m* (-en;-en) bugler

Horn'ochse *f* (coll) dumb ox

Horoskop [hərə'skop] *n* (-[e]s;-e) horoscope

horrend [hə'rent] *adj* (coll) terrible

Hör'rohr *n* stethoscope

Hör'saal *m* lecture room

Hör'spiel *n* radio play

Horst [hərst] *m* (-[e]s;-e) (eagle's) nest

Hort [hərt] *m* (-[e]s;-e) hoard, treasure; (place of) refuge; protector

Hör'weite *f*—**in H.** within earshot

Hose ['hozə] *f* (-;-n), **Hosen** ['hozən] *pl* pants, trousers; (*Unterhose*) shorts; panties; **sich auf die Hosen setzen** buckle down

Ho'senboden *m* seat (of trousers)

Ho'senklappe *f*, **Ho'senlatz** *m* fly

Ho'senrolle *f* (theat) male role

Ho'senträger *pl* suspenders

Hospitant [həspɪ'tant] *m* (-en;-en) (educ) auditor

hospitieren [həspɪ'tirən] *intr* (educ) audit a course

Hospiz [həs'pits] *n* (-es;-e) hospice

Hostie ['həstjə] *f* (-;-n) host, wafer

Hotel [hə'tel] *n* (-s;-s) hotel

Hotel'boy *m* bellboy, bellhop

Hotel'diener *m* hotel porter

Hotel'fach *n*, **Hotel'gewerbe** *n* hotel business

Hub [hup] *m* (-[e]s;-̈e) (mach) stroke

hübsch [hyp/] *adj* pretty; handsome; (coll) good-sized

Hubschrauber ['hup/raubər] *m* (-s;-) helicopter

huckepack ['hukəpak] *adv* piggyback

hudeln ['hudəln] *intr* be sloppy

Huf [huf] *m* (-[e]s;-e) hoof

Huf'eisen *n* horseshoe

Huf'schlag *m* hoofbeat

Hüfte ['hyftə] *f* (-;-n) hip; **die Arme in die Hüften gestemmt** with arms akimbo

Hüft'gelenk *n* hip joint

Hüft'gürtel *m*, **Hüft'halter** *m* garter belt

Hügel ['hygəl] *m* (-s;-) hill; mound

hügelab' *adv* downhill

hügelauf' *adv* uphill

hügelig ['hygəlɪç] *adj* hilly

Huhn [hun] *n* (-[e]s;-̈er) fowl; hen, chicken

Hühnchen ['hynçən] *n* (-s;-) young chicken; **ein H. zu rupfen haben mit** (fig) have a bone to pick with

Hüh'nerauge *n* (pathol) corn

Hüh'nerdraht *m* chicken wire

Hüh'nerhund *m* bird dog

Huld [hult] *f* (-;) grace, favor

huldigen ['huldɪgən] *intr* (dat) pay homage to

Hul'digung *f* (-;) homage

Hul'digungseid *m* oath of allegiance

huld'reich, huld'voll *adj* gracious

Hülle ['hylə] *f* (-;-n) cover; case; wrapper; envelope; (*e–s Buches*) jacket; (fig) cloak; **in H. und Fülle** in abundance; **sterbliche H.** mortal remains

hüllen ['hylən] *tr* cover; veil; wrap

Hülse ['hylzə] *f* (-;-n) pod, hull; cartridge case, shell case

Hül'senfrucht *f* legume

human [hu'man] *adj* humane

humanistisch [huma'nɪstɪ/] *adj* humanistic; classical

humanitär [humanɪ'ter] *adj* humanitarian

Humanität [humanɪ'tet] *f* (-;) humanity; humaneness

Humanitäts'duselei *f* sentimental humanitarianism

Humanitäts'verbrechen *n* crime against humanity

Hummel ['huməl] *f* (-;-n) bumblebee

Hummer ['humər] *m* (-s;-) lobster

Humor [hu'mor] *m* (-s;) humor

humoristisch [humo'rɪstɪ/] *adj* humorous

humpeln ['humpəln] *intr* (SEIN) hobble

Hund [hunt] *m* (-[e]s;-e) dog

Hündchen ['hyntçən] *n* (-s;-) small dog; puppy

Hun'deangst *f*—**e–e H. haben** (coll) be scared stiff

Hun'dearbeit *f* drudgery

Hun'dehütte *f* doghouse

Hun'dekälte *f* severe cold

Hun′demarke *f* dog tag
hun′demü′de *adj* (coll) dog-tired
hundert [′hʊndərt] *invar adj & pron* hundred ‖ **Hundert** *n* (-s;-e) hundred; **drei von H.** three percent; **im H. by the hundred** ‖ *f* (-;-en) hundred
hun′dertfach *adj* hundredfold
Hundertjahr′feier *f* centennial
Hun′dertsatz *m* percentage
hundertste [′hʊndərtstə] §9 *adj & pron* hundredth
Hun′deschau *f* dog show
Hun′dezwinger *m* dog kennel
Hündin [′hʏndɪn] *f* (-;-nen) bitch
hündisch [′hʏndɪʃ] *adj* (*Benehmen*) servile; (*Angst*) deadly
hunds′gemein *adj* beastly
hunds′miserabel *adj* (sl) lousy
Hunds′stern *m* Dog Star
Hunds′tage *pl* dog days
Hüne [′hynə] *m* (-n;-n) giant
hü′nenhaft *adj* gigantic
Hunger [′hʊŋər] *m* (-s;) hunger; **H. haben** be hungry
Hun′gerkur *f* starvation diet
Hun′gerlohn *m* starvation wages
hungern [′hʊŋərn] *intr* be hungry; go without food; **h. nach** yearn for ‖ *impers*—**es hungert mich** I am hungry
Hun′gersnot *f* famine
Hun′gertod *m* death from starvation
Hun′gertuch *n*—**am H. nagen** go hungry; live in poverty
hungrig [′hʊŋrɪç] *adj* hungry; (*Jahre*) lean
Hunne [′hʊnə] *m* (-n;-n) (hist) Hun
Hupe [′hupə] *f* (-;-n) (aut) horn
hupen [′hupən] *intr* blow the horn
hüpfen [′hʏpfən], **hupfen** [′hʊpfən] *intr* (SEIN) hop, jump
Hürde [′hʏrdə] *f* (-;-n) hurdle
Hure [′hura] *f* (-;-n) whore
huren [′hurən] *intr* whore around
hurtig [′hʊrtɪç] *adj* nimble, swift
huschen [′hʊʃən] *intr* (SEIN) scurry
hüsteln [′hystəln] *intr* clear the throat
husten [′hʊstən] *tr* cough up ‖ *intr* cough; **h. auf** (*acc*) (coll) not give a rap about

Hut [hut] *m* (-[e]s;ˮe) hat ‖ *f* (-;) protection, care; **auf der Hut sein** be on guard
hüten [′hytən] *tr* guard, protect; tend; **das Bett h.** be confined to bed; **das Haus h.** stay indoors; **Kinder h.** baby-sit ‖ *ref* (**vor** *dat*) be on guard (against), beware (of); **ich werde mich schön h.** (coll) I'll do no such thing
Hü′ter –in §6 *mf* guardian
Hut′krempe *f* brim of a hat
hut′los *adj* hatless
Hütte [′hytə] *f* (-;-n) hut; cabin; doghouse; glassworks; (Bib) tabernacle; (metal) foundry
Hüt′tenkunde *f*, **Hüt′tenwesen** *n* metallurgy
Hyäne [hy′ɛnə] *f* (-;-n) hyena
Hyazinthe [hya′tsɪntə] *f* (-;-n) hyacinth
Hydrant [hy′drant] *m* (-en;-en) hydrant
Hydraulik [hy′draulɪk] *f* (-;) hydraulics; hydraulic system
hydraulisch [hy′draulɪʃ] *adj* hydraulic
hydrieren [hy′drirən] *tr* hydrogenate
Hygiene [hy′gjenə] *f* (-;) hygiene
hygienisch [hy′gjenɪʃ] *adj* hygienic
Hymne [′hymnə] *f* (-;-n) hymn; anthem
Hyperbel [hy′pɛrbəl] *f* (-;-n) (geom) hyperbola; (rhet) hyperbole
Hypnose [hyp′nozə] *f* (-;-n) hypnosis
hypnotisch [hyp′notɪʃ] *adj* hypnotic
Hypothese [hflpo′tezə] *f* (-;-n) hypothesis
Hypochonder [hypo′xɔndər] *m* (-s;-) hypochondriac
Hypothek [hypo′tek] *f* (-;-en) mortgage
Hypothe′kengläubiger *m* mortgagee
Hypothe′kenschuldner *m* mortgagor
Hypothese [hypo′tezə] *f* (-;-n) hypothesis
hypothetisch [hypo′tetɪʃ] *adj* hypothetical
Hysterektomie [hysterektoˈmi] *f* (-;) hysterectomy
Hysterie [hystəˈri] *f* (-;) hysteria
hysterisch [hysˈteriʃ] *adj* hysterical

I, i [i] *invar n* I, i
iah [ˈiˈɑ] *interj* heehaw!
iahen [ˈiˈɑ-ən] *intr* heehaw, bray
iberisch [ɪˈberɪʃ] *adj* Iberian
ich [ɪç] §11 *pers pron* I
ichbezogen [ˈɪçbətsogən] *adj* self-centered, egocentric
Ich′sucht *f* egotism
ideal [ɪdeˈal] *adj* ideal ‖ **Ideal** *n* (-s;-e) ideal
idealisieren [ɪdeˌalɪˈzirən] *tr* idealize
Idealismus [ɪdeˌaˈlɪsmus] *m* (-;) idealism
Idealist –in [ɪdeˌaˈlɪst(ɪn)] §7 *mf* idealist

idealistisch [ɪdeˌaˈlɪstɪʃ] *adj* idealistic
I·dee [ɪˈde] *f* (-;-deen [ˈde-ən]) idea
Iden [ˈidən] *pl* Ides
identifizieren [ɪdɛntɪfɪˈtsirən] *tr* identify ‖ *ref*—**i. mit** identify with
identisch [ɪˈdɛntɪʃ] *adj* identical
Identität [ɪdɛntɪˈtɛt] *f* (-;-en) identity
Ideolo·gie [ɪdeˌoloˈgi] *f* (-;-gien [ˈgiən]) ideology
Idiom [ɪˈdjom] *n* (-s;-e) idiom, dialect, language
idiomatisch [ɪdjoˈmɑtɪʃ] *adj* idiomatic
Idiosynkra·sie [ɪdjozynkraˈzi] *f* (-;-sien [ˈzi-ən]) idiosyncrasy
Idiot [ɪˈdjot] *m* (-en;-en) idiot

Idio·tie [ɪdjo'ti] *f* (-;-tien ['ti·ən]) idiocy

Idiotin [ɪdjotɪn] *f* (-;-nen) idiot

Idol [ɪ'dol] *n* (-s;-e) idol

idyllisch [i'dʏlɪʃ] *adj* idyllic

Igel ['igəl] *m* (-s;-) hedgehog

Ignorant [ɪgno'rant] *m* (-en;-en) ignoramus

ignorieren [ɪgno'rirən] *tr* ignore

ihm [im] §11 *pers pron* (dative of **er** and **es**) (to) him; (to) it

ihn [in] §11 *pers pron* (accusative of **er**) him

ihnen ['inən] §11 *pers pron* (dative of **sie**) (to) them || **Ihnen** §11 *pers pron* (dative of **Sie**) (to) you

ihr [ir] §2,2 *poss adj* her; their || §11 *pers pron* (dative of **sie**) (to) her || **Ihr** §2,2 *poss adj* your

ihrerseits ['irərzaɪts] *adv* on her (or their) part; **Ihrerseits** on your part

ihresgleichen ['irəs'glaɪçən] *pron* the likes of her (or them); her (or their) equal(s); **Ihresgleichen** the likes of you; your equal(s)

ihrethalben ['irət'halbən] *adv* var of **ihretwegen**

ihretwegen ['irət'vegen] *adv* because of her (or them); for her (or their) sake; **Ihretwegen** because of you, for your sake

ihretwillen ['irət'vɪlən] *adv* var of **ihretwegen**

ihrige ['irɪgə] §2,5 *poss pron* hers; theirs; **Ihrige** yours

Ikone [ɪ'konə] *f* (-;-n) icon

illegal [ɪle'gal] *adj* illegal

illegitim [ɪlegɪ'tim] *adj* illegitimate

illuminieren [ɪlumi'nirən] *tr* illuminate

Illusion [ɪlu'zjon] *f* (-;-en) illusion

illustrieren [ɪlus'trirən] *tr* illustrate

Illustrierte [ɪlus'trirtə] §5 *f* (illustrated) magazine

Iltis ['ɪltɪs] *m* (-ses;-se) polecat

im [ɪm] *contr* in dem

Image ['ɪmɪdʒ] *n* (-s;-s) (fig) image

imaginär [ɪmagɪ'ner] *adj* imaginary

Im·biß ['ɪmbɪs] *m* (-bisses;-bisse) snack

Im'bißhalle *f* luncheonette

Im'bißstube *f* snack bar

Imitator [ɪmi'tator] *m* (-s;-tatoren [ta'torən]) imitator; impersonator

Imker ['ɪmkər] *m* (-s;-) beekeeper

immateriell [ɪmate'rjel] *adj* immaterial, spiritual

immatrikulieren [ɪmatrɪku'lirən] *tr & intr* register; **sich i. lassen** get registered

immens [ɪ'mens] *adj* immense

immer ['ɪmər] *adv* always; **auf i. und ewig** for ever and ever; **für i.** for good; **i. langsam!** steady now!; **i. mehr** more and more; **i. wieder** again and again; **noch i.** still; **nur i. zu!** keep trying!; **was auch i.** whatever

immerdar' *adv* (Lit) forever

immerfort' *adv* all the time

im'mergrün *adj* evergreen || **Immergrün** *n* (-s;-e) evergreen

immerhin' *adv* after all, anyhow

immerwäh'rend *adj* perpetual

immerzu' *adv* all the time, constantly

Immobilien [ɪmo'biljen] *pl* real estate

Immobi'lienmakler **-in** §6 *mf* real-estate broker

immun [ɪ'mun] *adj* (gegen) immune (to)

immunisieren [ɪmuni'zirən] *tr* immunize

Imperativ [ɪmpera'tif] *m* (-s;-e) (gram) imperative

Imperfek·tum [ɪmper'fektum] *n* (-s; -ta [ta]) (gram) imperfect

Imperialismus [ɪmperi·a'lɪsmus] *m* (-;) imperialism

impfen ['ɪmpfen] *tr* vaccinate; inoculate

Impfling ['ɪmpflɪŋ] *m* (-s;-e) person to be vaccinated or inoculated

Impf'schein *m* vaccination certificate

Impf'stoff *m* vaccine

Imp'fung *f* (-;-en) vaccination; inoculation

imponieren [ɪmpo'nirən] *intr* (dat) impress

Import [ɪm'port] *m* (-[e]s;-e) import

importieren [ɪmpor'tirən] *tr* import

imposant [ɪmpo'zant] *adj* imposing

imprägnieren [ɪmpreg'nirən] *tr* waterproof; creosote

Impresario [ɪmpre'zarjo] *m* (-s;-s) agent, business manager

Impres·sum [ɪm'presum] *n* (-s;-sen [sən]) (journ) masthead

imstande [ɪm'ʃtandə] *adv*—**i. sein zu** (*inf*) be in a position to (*inf*)

in [ɪn] *prep* (*position*) (*dat*) in, at; (*direction*) (*acc*) in, into

Inangriffnahme [ɪn'angrɪfnamə] *f* (-;) starting; putting into action

Inanspruchnahme [ɪn'an/pruxnamə] *f* (-;) laying claim; demands; utilization

In'begriff *m* essence; embodiment

in'begriffen *adj* included

Inbrunst ['ɪnbrunst] *f* (-;) ardor

inbrünstig ['ɪnbrʏnstɪç] *adj* ardent

indem [ɪn'dem] *conj* while, as; by (*ger*)

Inder **-in** ['ɪndər(ɪn)] §6 *mf* Indian (*inhabitant of India*)

indes [ɪn'des], **indessen** [ɪn'desən] *adv* meanwhile; however || *conj* while; whereas

Indianer **-in** [ɪn'djanər(ɪn)] §6 *mf* Indian (*of North America*)

Indien ['ɪndjən] *n* (-s;) India

Indio ['ɪndi·o] *m* (-s;-s) Indian (*of Central or South America*)

indisch ['ɪndɪʃ] *adj* Indian

indiskret [ɪndɪs'kret] *adj* indiscreet

indiskutabel [ɪndɪsku'tabəl] *adj* out of the question

individuell [ɪndɪvɪdu'el] *adj* individual

Individu·um [ɪndɪ'vidu·um] *n* (-s;-en [ən]) individual; (pej) character

Indizienbeweis [ɪn'ditsjənbevaɪs] *m* (piece of) circumstantial evidence

Indossament [ɪndosa'ment] *n* (-[e]s; -e) indorsement

Indossant [ɪndo'sant] *m* (-en;-en) indorser

indossieren [ɪndo'sirən] *tr* indorse

industrialisieren [ɪndustri·ali'zirən] *tr* industrialize

Indus·trie [ɪndʊsˈtri] *f* (–;–trien [ˈtriən]) industry
Industrie′anlage *f* industrial plant
Industrie′betrieb *m* industrial establishment
Industrie′kapitän *m* tycoon
industriell [ɪndʊstriˈel] *adj* industrial || **Industrielle** §5 *m* industrialist
ineinan′der *adv* into one another; **i. übergehen** merge
ineinan′derfügen *tr* dovetail
ineinan′dergreifen §88 *intr* mesh
ineinan′derpassen *intr* dovetail
infam [ɪnˈfam] *adv* (coll) frightfully
Infante·rie [ɪnfantəˈri] *f* (–;–rien [ˈriən]) infantry
Infanterist [ɪnfantəˈrɪst] *m* (–en;–en) infantryman
infantil [ɪnfanˈtil] *adj* infantile
Infektion [ɪnfekˈtsjon] *f* (–;–en) infection
Infini·tiv [ɪnfɪnɪˈtif] *m* (–s;–tive [ˈtivə]) infinitive
infizieren [ɪnfiˈtsirən] *tr* infect
infolge [ɪnˈfɔlgə] *prep* (*genit*) in consequence of, owing to; according to
infolgedes′sen *adv* consequently
Information [ɪnfɔrmaˈtsjon] *f* (–;–en) (piece of) information
informieren [ɪnfɔrˈmirən] *tr* inform
infrarot [ɪnfraˈrot] *adj* infrared || **Infrarot** *n* (–s;–) infrared
Ingenieur [ɪnʒenˈjør] *m* (–s;–e) engineer
Ingenieur′bau *m* (–[e]s;) civil engineering
Ingenieur′wesen *n* engineering
ingeniös [ɪngeˈnjøs] *adj* ingenious
Ingrimm [ˈɪngrɪm] *m* inner rage
Ingwer [ˈɪnvər] *m* (–s;) ginger
Ing′werplätzchen *n* gingersnap
Inhaber [ˈɪnhabər(ɪn)] §6 *mf* owner; bearer; occupant; holder
inhaftieren [ɪnhafˈtirən] *tr* arrest
Inhalierapparat [ɪnhaˈliraparat] *m* (med) inhalator
inhalieren [ɪnhaˈlirən] *tr & intr* inhale
Inhalt [ˈɪnhalt] *m* (–[e]s;–e) contents; subject matter; (geom) area; volume
In′haltsangabe *f* summary; list of contents
in′haltsarm, in′haltsleer *adj* empty
in′haltsreich *adj* substantive; (*Leben*) full
in′haltsschwer *adj* pregnant with meaning; momentous
In′haltsverzeichnis *n* table of contents
in′haltsvoll *adj* full of meaning
inhibieren [ɪnhiˈbirən] *tr* inhibit
Initiative [ɪnɪtsjaˈtivə] *f* (–;–en) initiative
Injektion [ɪnjekˈtsjon] *f* (–;–en) injection
Injektions′nadel *f* hypodermic needle
injizieren [ɪnjɪˈtsirən] *tr* inject
Inkasso [ɪnˈkaso] *n* (–s;–s) bill collecting
Inkas′sobeamte *m* bill collector
inklusive [ɪnkluˈzivə] *adj* inclusive || *prep* (*genit*) including
inkonsequent [ˈɪnkɔnzekvɛnt] *adj* inconsistent; illogical
Inkraft′treten *n* going into effect

In′land *n* (–[e]s;) home country; interior
Inländer –in [ˈɪnlendər(ɪn)] §6 *mf* native
inländisch [ˈɪnlendɪʃ] *adj* home, domestic; inland
In′landspost *f* domestic mail
Inlett [ˈɪnlet] *n* (–[e]s;–e) bedtick
in′liegend *adj* enclosed
inmit′ten *prep* (*genit*) in the middle of, among
innehaben [ˈɪnəhabən] §89 *tr* (*Amt*) hold; (*Wohnung*) occupy, own
innehalten [ˈɪnəhaltən] §90 *intr* stop
innen [ˈɪnən] *adv* inside; indoors; **nach i.** inwards; **tief i.** deep down
Innen– comb.fm. inner, internal; inside, interior; home, domestic
In′nenarchitekt –in §7 *mf* interior decorator
In′nenaufnahme *f* (phot) indoor shot
In′nenhof *m* quadrangle
In′nenleben *n* inner life
In′nenminister *m* Secretary of the Interior; Secretary of State for Home Affairs (Brit)
In′nenpolitik *f* domestic policy
In′nenraum *m* interior (*of building*)
In′nenstadt *f* center of town, inner city
inner– [ɪnər] comb.fm. internal; intra-
innere [ˈɪnərə] §9 *adj* inner, internal; inside; inward; domestic || **Innere** §5 *n* inside, interior
in′nerhalb *adv* on the inside; **i. von** within || *prep* (*genit*) inside, within
in′nerlich *adj* inner, inward || *adv* inwardly; mentally, emotionally
In′nerlichkeit *f* (–;–en) introspection; inner quality
innerste [ˈɪnərstə] §9 *adj* innermost
innesein [ˈɪnəzaɪn] §139 *intr* (SEIN) (*genit*) be aware of
innewerden [ˈɪnəverdən] §159 *intr* (SEIN) (*genit*) become aware of
innig [ˈɪnɪç] *adj* close; deep, heartfelt || *adv* deeply
In′nigkeit *f* (–;) intimacy; deep feeling; tender affection
Innung [ˈɪnʊŋ] *f* (–;–en) guild
inoffiziell [ˈɪnɔfɪtsjel] *adj* unofficial
ins *contr* **in das**
Insasse [ˈɪnzasə] *m* (–n;–n), **Insassin** [ˈɪnsasɪn] *f* (–;–nen) occupant; (*e–s Gefängnisses*) inmate; (*e–s Autos*) passenger
insbesondere [ɪnsbəˈzɔndərə] *adv* in particular, especially
In′schrift *f* inscription
Insekt [ɪnˈzekt] *n* (–[e]s;–en) insect
Insek′tenbekämpfungsmittel *n* insecticide
Insek′tenkunde *f* entomology
Insek′tenstich *m* insect bite
Insektizid [ɪnzektɪˈtsit] *n* (–[e]s;–e) insecticide
Insel [ˈɪnzəl] *f* (–;–n) island
Inserat [ɪnzəˈrat] *n* (–es;–e) classified advertisement, ad
inserieren [ɪnzəˈrirən] *tr* insert || *intr* (in *dat*) advertise (in)
insgeheim [ɪnsgəˈhaɪm] *adv* secretly
insgemein [ɪnsgəˈmaɪn] *adv* as a whole; in general, generally

insgesamt [ɪnsgə'zamt] *adv* in a body, as a unit; in all, altogether

inso'fern *adv* to this extent || **insofern/ conj** in so far as

insoweit' *adv & conj* var of **insofern**

Inspek·tor [ɪn'spektor] *m* (-s;-toren ['torən]) inspector

inspirieren [ɪnspɪ'rirən] *tr* inspire

inspizieren [ɪnspɪ'tsirən] *tr* inspect

Installation [ɪnstala'tsjon] *f* (-;-en) installation

installieren [ɪnsta'lirən] *tr* install

instand [ɪn'/tant] *adv*—**i. halten** keep in good condition; **i. setzen** repair

Instand'haltung *f* upkeep, maintenance

inständig [ɪn'/tendɪç] *adj* insistent

Instand'setzung *f* repair, renovation

Instanz [ɪn'stants] *f* (-;-en) (adm) authority; **e-e höhere I. anrufen** appeal to a higher court; **Gericht der ersten I.** court of primary jurisdiction; **Gericht der zweiten I.** court of appeal; **höchste I.** court of final appeal

Institut [ɪnstɪ'tut] *n* (-[e]s;-e) institute

instruieren [ɪnstru'irən] *tr* instruct

Instruktion [ɪnstruk'tsjon] *f* (-;-en) instruction

Instrument [ɪnstru'ment] *n* (-[e]s;-e) instrument

Instrumentalist –in [ɪnstrumenta'lɪst (ɪn)] §7 *mf* instrumentalist

Insulaner –in [ɪnzu'lanər(ɪn)] §6 *mf* islander

insular [ɪnzu'lar] *adj* insular

Insulin [ɪnzu'lin] *n* (-s;) insulin

inszenieren [ɪnstse'nirən] *tr* stage

Intellekt [ɪnte'lekt] *m* (-[e]s;) intellect

intellektuell [ɪntelektu'el] *adj* intellectual || **Intellektuelle** §5 *mf* intellectual

intelligent [ɪntelɪ'gent] *adj* intelligent

Intelligenzler [ɪntelɪ'gentslər] *m* (-s;-) (pej) egghead

Intendant [ɪnten'dant] *m* (-en;-en) (theat) director

intensiv [ɪnten'zif] *adj* intense; intensive

–intensiv *comb.fm.*, e.g., **lohnintensive Güter** goods of which wages constitute a high proportion of the cost

interessant [ɪntere'sant] *adj* interesting

Interesse [ɪnte'resə] *n* (-s;-n) (an *dat*, **für**) interest (in)

interes'selos *adj* uninterested

Interes'sengemeinschaft *f* community of interest; (com) syndicate

Interessent –in [ɪntere'sent(ɪn)] §7 *mf* interested party

interessieren [ɪntere'sirən] *tr* (für) interest (in) || **ref—sich i. für** be interested in

interimistisch [ɪnterɪ'mɪstɪʃ] *adj* provisional

intern [ɪn'tern] *adj* internal

Internat [ɪnter'nat] *n* (-[e]s;-e) boarding school

international [ɪnternatsjə'nal] *adj* international

Internat(s)'schüler –in §6 *mf*, **Interne** [ɪn'ternə] §5 *mf* boarding student

internieren [ɪnter'nirən] *tr* intern

Internist –in [ɪnter'nɪst(ɪn)] §7 *mf* (med) internist

Interpret [ɪnter'pret] *m* (-en;-en) interpreter; exponent

interpunktieren [ɪnterpuŋk'tirən] *tr* punctuate

Interpunktion [ɪnterpuŋk'tsjon] *f* (-;-en) punctuation

Interpunktions'zeichen *n* punctuation mark

Intervall [ɪnter'val] *n* (-s;-e) interval

intervenieren [ɪnterve'nirən] *intr* intervene

Interview ['ɪntervju] *n* (-s;-s) interview

interviewen [ɪnter'vju·ən] *tr* interview

intim [ɪn'tim] *adj* intimate

Intimität [ɪntimɪ'tet] *f* (-;-en) intimacy

intolerant [ɪntole'rant] *adj* intolerant

intonieren [ɪntə'nirən] *tr* intone

intransitiv ['ɪntransitif] *adj* intransitive

intravenös [ɪntrave'nøs] *adj* intravenous

intrigant [ɪntrɪ'gant] *adj* intriguing, scheming || **Intragant –in** §7 *mf* intriguer, schemer

Intrige [ɪn'trigə] *f* (-;-n) intrigue

introspektiv [ɪntrospek'tif] *adj* introspective

Introvertierte [ɪntrover'tirtə] §5 *mf* introvert

invalide [ɪnva'lidə] *adj* disabled || **Invalide** §5 *mf* invalid

Invalidität [ɪnvalidɪ'tet] *f* (-;) disability

Invasion [ɪnva'zjon] *f* (-;-en) invasion

Inventar [ɪnven'tar] *n* (-s;-e) inventory

Inventur [ɪnven'tur] *f* (-;-en) stock taking; **I. machen** take stock

inwärts ['ɪnverts] *adv* inwards

inwendig ['ɪnvendɪç] *adj* inward, inner

inwiefern' *adv* how far; in what way

inwieweit' *adv* var of **inwiefern**

In'zucht *f* inbreeding

inzwi'schen *adv* meanwhile

Ion [ɪ'on] *n* (-s;-en) (phys) ion

ionisieren [ɪ·onɪ'zirən] *tr* ionize

Irak [ɪ'rak] *m* (-s;) Iraq

Iraker –in [ɪ'rakər(ɪn)] §6 *mf* Iraqi

irakisch [ɪ'rakɪʃ] *adj* Iraqi

Iran [ɪ'ran] *m* (-s;) Iran

Iraner –in [ɪ'ranər(ɪn)] §6 *mf* Iranian

iranisch [ɪ'ranɪʃ] *adj* Iranian

irden ['ɪrdən] *adj* earthen

irdisch ['ɪrdɪʃ] *adj* earthly, worldly || **Irdische** §5 *n* earthly nature

Ire ['irə] *m* (-n;-n) Irishman; **die Iren** the Irish

irgend ['ɪrgənt] *adv*—**i. etwas** something, anything; **i. jemand** someone, anyone; **nur i.** possibly

ir'gendein *adj* some, any || **ingendeiner** *indef pron* someone, anyone

ir'gendeinmal *adv* at some time or other

ir'gendwann *adv* at some time or other

ir'gendwelcher *adj* any; any kind of

ir'gendwer *indef pron* someone

ir'gendwie *adv* somehow or other

ir'gendwo *adv* somewhere or other; anywhere

ir'gendwoher *adv* from somewhere or other

ir'gendwohin *adv* somewhere or other

Irin ['ɪrɪn] *f* (-;-nen) Irish woman

Iris ['ɪrɪs] *f* (-;-) (anat, bot) iris

irisch ['ɪrɪʃ] *adj* Irish

Irland ['ɪrlant] *n* (-s;) Ireland

Iro·nie [ɪro'ni] *f* (-;-nien ['ni·ən]) irony

ironisch [ɪ'ronɪʃ] *adj* ironic(al)

irre ['ɪrə] *adj* stray; confused; mad; **i. werden** go astray; get confused; **i. werden an** (*dat*) lose faith in || **Irre** §5 *mf* lunatic || *f* maze; wrong track; **in die I. führen** put on the wrong track; **in die I. gehen** go astray

ir'refahren §71 *intr* (SEIN) lose one's way, go wrong

ir'reführen *tr* mislead

ir'regehen §82 *intr* (SEIN) lose one's way; (fig) go wrong

ir'remachen *tr* confuse; **j–n i. an** (*dat*) make s.o. lose faith in

irren ['ɪrən] *intr* go astray; err || *ref* (**in** *dat*) be mistaken (about); **sich in der Straße i.** take the wrong road; **sich in der Zeit i.** misjudge the time

Ir'renanstalt *f*, **Ir'renhaus** *n* insane asylum

Ir'renhäusler ['ɪrənhɔɪzlər] *m* (-s;-) inmate of an insane asylum

ir'rereden *intr* rave; talk deliriously

Irrfahrt ['ɪrfart] *f* odyssey

Irrgang ['ɪrgaŋ] *m* (-[e]s;) winding path

Irrgarten ['ɪrgartən] *m* labyrinth

Irrglaube ['ɪrglaubə] *m* heresy

irrgläubig ['ɪrglɔɪbɪç] *adj* heretical

irrig ['ɪrɪç] *adj* mistaken

Irri·gator [ɪrɪ'gatər] *m* (-s;-gatoren [ga·torən]) douche

irritieren [ɪrɪ'tirən] *tr* irritate; (coll) confuse

Irrlehre ['ɪrlerə] *f* false doctrine

Irrlicht ['ɪrlɪçt] *n* jack-o'-lantern

Irrsinn ['ɪrzɪn] *m* insanity

irr'sinnig *adj* insane

Irrtum ['ɪrtum] *m* (-s;-̈er) error

irrtümlich ['ɪrtymlɪç] *adj* erroneous

Irrweg ['ɪrvek] *m* wrong track

Irrwisch ['ɪrvɪʃ] *m* (-es;-e) jack-o'-lantern; (coll) fireball

Islam [ɪs'lam] *m* (-s;) Islam

Island ['ɪslant] *n* (-s;) Iceland

Iso·lator [ɪzo'latər] *m* (-s;-latoren [la'torən]) (elec) insulator

Isolier– [ɪzo'lir] *comb.fm.* isolation; insulating; insulated

Isolier'band *n* (-[e]s;-̈er) friction tape

isolieren [ɪzo'lirən] *tr* (*Kranke*) isolate; (*abdichten*) insulate

Isolier'haft *f* solitary confinement

Insolier'station *f* isolation ward

Isolie'rung *f* (-;-en) isolation; (elec) insulation

Isotop [ɪzo'top] *n* (-[e]s;-e) isotope

Israel ['ɪsra·el] *n* (- & -s;) Israel

Israeli [ɪsra'eli] *m* (-s;-s) Israeli

israelisch [ɪsra'eliʃ] *adj* Israeli

Israelit –**in** [ɪsra·e'lit(ɪn)] §7 *mf* Israelite

israelitisch [ɪsra·e'litɪʃ] *adj* Israelite

Ist– [ɪst] *comb.fm.* actual

Ist–'Bestand *m* actual stock; (fin) actual balance; (mil) actual stockpile

Ist–'Stand *m*, **Ist–'Stärke** *f* (mil) effective strength

Italien [ɪ'taljən] *n* (-s;) Italy

Italiener –**in** [ɪtal'jenər(ɪn)] §6 *mf* Italian

italienisch [ɪtal'jenɪʃ] *adj* Italian

J

J, j [jɔt] *invar n* J, j

ja [ja] *adv* yes; indeed, certainly; of course || **Ja** *n* (-s;-s) yes

Jacht [jaxt] *f* (-;-en) yacht

Jacke ['jakə] *f* (-;-n) jacket, coat

Jackenkleid (**Jak'kenkleid**) *n* lady's two-piece suit

Jackett [ʒa'ket] *n* (-s;-s) jacket

Jagd [jakt] *f* (-;-en) hunt(ing); **auf die J. gehen** go hunting; **J. machen auf** (*acc*) hunt for

Jagd'abschirmung *f* (aer) fighter screen

Jagd'aufseher *m* gamewarden

jagdbar ['jaktbar] *adj* in season, fair (*game*)

Jagd'bomber *m* (aer) fighter-bomber

Jagd'flieger *m* fighter pilot

Jagd'flugzeug *n* (aer) fighter plane

Jagd'gehege *n* game preserve

Jagd'geleit *n* (aer) fighter escort

Jagd'hund *m* hunting dog, hound

Jagd'rennen *n* steeplechase

Jagd'revier *n* hunting ground

Jagd'schein *m* hunting license

Jagd'schutz *m* (aer) fighter protection

Jagd'verband *m* (aer) fighter unit

Jagd'wild *n* game; game bird

jagen ['jagən] *tr* hunt; pursue; chase; (fig) follow close on; **in die Luft j.** blow up || *intr* go hunting; **j. nach** pursue || *intr* (SEIN) rush

Jäger ['jegər] *m* (-s;-) hunter; (aer) fighter plane; (mil) rifleman

Jägerei [jegə'raɪ] *f* (-;) hunting

Jä'gerlatein *n* (coll) fish story

Jaguar ['jagu·ar] *m* (-s;-e) jaguar

jäh [je] *adj* sudden; steep || **Jähe** *f* (-;) suddenness; steepness

jählings ['jelɪŋs] *adv* suddenly; steeply

Jahr [jar] *n* (-[e]s;-e) year

jahraus' *adv*–**j. jahrein** year in year out, year after year

Jahr'buch *n* almanac; yearbook; annual

jahrelang ['jarəlaŋ] *adj* long-standing || *adv* for years

jähren ['jerən] *ref* be a year ago

Jahres– ['jarəs] *comb.fm.* annual, yearly, of the year

Jah'resfeier f anniversary
Jah'resfrist f period of a year
Jah'resrente f annuity
Jah'restag m anniversary
Jah'reszahl f date, year
Jah'reszeit f season
jah'reszeitlich adj seasonal
Jahr'gang m age group; class, year; crop; vintage; **er gehört zu meinem J.** he was born in the same year as I
Jahrhun'dert n century
–jährig [jerıç] comb.fm. –year-old
jährlich ['jerlıç] adj yearly, annual
Jahr'markt m fair
Jahr'marktplatz m fairground
Jahrtau'send n millennium
Jahrzehnt [jar'tsent] n (–[e]s;–e) decade
Jäh'zorn m fit of anger; hot temper
jäh'zornig adj quick-tempered
Jalou·sie [ʒalu'zi] f (–;–sien ['zi·ən]) louvre; Venetian blind
Jammer ['jamər] m (–s;) misery; wailing; **es ist ein J., daß** it's a pity that
Jam'merlappen m (pej) jellyfish
jämmerlich ['jemərlıç] adj miserable, pitiful; (*Anblick*) sorry
jammern ['jamərn] tr move to pity || intr (**über** acc, **um**) moan (about); **j. nach** (or **um**) whimper for
jam'merschade adj deplorable
Jänner ['jenər] m (–s & –;–) (Aust) January
Januar ['janu·ar] m (–s & –;–e) January
Japan ['japan] n (–s;) Japan
Japaner –in [ja'panər(ın)] §6 mf Japanese
japanisch [ja'panıʃ] adj Japanese
jappen ['japən] intr pant, gasp
Jasager ['jazagər] m (–s;–) yes-man
jäten ['jetən] tr weed; **das Unkraut j.** pull out weeds || intr weed
Jauche ['jauxə] f (–;–n) liquid manure; (sl) slop
jauchen ['jauxən] tr manure
Jau'chegrube f cesspool
jauchzen ['jauxtsən] intr rejoice; **vor Freude j.** shout for joy || **Jauchzen** n (–s;) jubilation
Jauch'zer m (–s;–) shout of joy
jawohl [ja'vol] interj yes, indeed!
Ja'wort n (–[e]s;) consent
Jazz [dʒɛz], [jats] m (–;) jazz
je [je] adv ever; **denn je** than ever; **je länger, je** (or desto) **besser** the longer the better; **je nach** according to, depending on; **je nachdem, ob** according to whether; **je Pfund** per pound; **je zwei** two each; two by two, in twos; **seit je** always
Jeans [dʒinz] pl jeans
jedenfalls ['jedənfals] adv at any rate; **ich j.** I for one
jeder ['jedər] §3 indef adj each, every || indef pron each one, everyone
jederlei ['jedər'lai] invar adj every kind of
je'dermann indef pron everyone, everybody
je'derzeit adv at all times, at any time
je'desmal adv each time, every time
jedoch [je'dox] adv however

jeglicher ['jeklıçər] §3 indef adj each, every || indef pron each one, everyone
je'her adv—**von j.** since time immemorial
Jelän'gerjelie'ber m & n honeysuckle
jemals ['jemals] adv ever
jemand ['jemant] indef pron someone, somebody; anyone, anybody
jener ['jenər] §3 dem adj that || dem pron that one
jenseitig ['jenzaıtıç] adj opposite, beyond, otherworldly
jenseits ['jenzaıts] prep (genit) on the other side of; beyond || **Jenseits** n (–;) beyond
jetzig ['jetsıç] adj present, current
jetzt [jetst] adv now
jeweilig ['jevaılıç] adj at that time
jeweils ['jevaıls] adv at that time
jiddisch ['jıdıʃ] adj Yiddish
Joch [jox] n (–[e]s;–e) yoke; yoke of oxen; (*e–r Brücke*) span; (*e–s Berges*) saddleback
Joch'bein n cheekbone
Joch'brücke f pile bridge
Jockei ['dʒoki] m (–s;–s) jockey
Jod [jot] n (–s;) iodine
jodeln ['jodəln] intr yodel
Jodler –in ['jodlər(ın)] §6 mf yodeler || m yodel
Jodtinktur ['jottıŋktur] f (–;) (pharm) iodine
Johannisbeere [jo'hanısberə] f currant
johlen ['jolən] intr yell, boo
jonglieren [ʒoŋ'(g)lirən] tr & intr juggle
Journalist –in [ʒurna'lıst(ın)] §7 mf journalist
jovial [jo'vjal] adj jovial
Jubel ['jubəl] m (–s;) jubilation
Ju'belfeier f, **Ju'belfest** n jubilee
Ju'beljahr n jubilee year
jubeln ['jubəln] intr rejoice; shout for joy
Jubilä·um [jubı'le·um] n (–s;–en [ən]) jubilee
juche [jux'he] interj hurray!
juchei [jux'hai] interj hurray!
juchzen ['juxtsən] intr shout for joy
jucken ['jukən] tr itch; scratch || ref scratch || intr itch || impers—**es juckt mich** I feel itchy; **es juckt mir** (or **mich**) **in den Fingern zu** (inf) I am itching to (inf); **es juckt sie in den Beinen** she is itching to dance
Jude ['judə] m (–n;–n) Jew
Ju'denschaft f (–;) Jewry
Ju'denstern m star of David
Judentum ['judəntum] n (–s;) Judaism; **das J.** the Jews
Jüdin ['jydın] f (–;–nen) Jewish woman
jüdisch ['jydıʃ] adj Jewish
Jugend ['jugənt] f (–;) youth
Ju'gendalter n youth; adolescence
Ju'gendgericht n juvenile court
Ju'gendherberge f youth hostel
Ju'gendkriminalität f juvenile delinquency
jugendlich ['jugəntlıç] adj youthful || **Jugendliche** §5 mf youth, teenager
Ju'gendliebe f puppy love
Ju'gendstrich m youthful prank

Jugoslawien [jugə'slavjən] *n* (-s;) Yugoslavia

jugoslawisch [jugə'slavɪʃ] *adj* Yugoslav

Juli ['juli] *m* (-[s];-s) July

jung [juŋ] *adj* (**jünger** ['jyŋər]; **jüngste** ['jyŋstə] §9) young; (*Erbsen*) green; (*Wein*) new ‖ **Junge** §5 *m* boy ‖ *n* newly born; young

jungen ['juŋən] *intr* produce young

jun'genhaft *adj* boyish

Jünger ['jyŋər] *m* (-s;-s) disciple

Jungfer ['juŋfər] *f* (-;-n) maiden; virgin

jüngeferlich ['jyŋfərlɪç] *adj* maidenly

Jung'fernfahrt *f* maiden voyage

Jung'fernhäutchen *n* hymen

Jung'fernkranz *m* bridal wreath

Jung'fernschaft *f* virginity

Jung'frau *f* virgin

jungfräulich ['juŋfrɔɪlɪç] *adj* maidenly; virgin

Jung'fräulichkeit *f* virginity

Jung'geselle *m* bachelor

Jung'gesellenstand *m* bachelorhood

Jung'gesellin *f* single girl

Jüngling ['jyŋlɪŋ] *m* (-s;-e) young man

jüngst [jyŋst] *adv* recently

jüng'ste *adj* see jung

Juni ['juni] *m* (-[s];-s) June

Junker ['juŋkər] *m* (-s;-) young nobleman; nobleman

Jura ['jura] *pl*—**J. studieren** study law

Jurist –in [ju'rɪst(ɪn)] §7 *mf* lawyer; (*educ*) law student

Juristerei [jurɪstə'raɪ] *f* (-;) jurisprudence

juristisch [ju'rɪstɪʃ] *adj* legal, law; **juristische Person** legal entity, corporation

just [just] *adv* just, precisely

justieren [jus'tirən] *tr* adjust

Justiz [jus'tits] *f* (-;) justice; administration of justice

Justiz'irrtum *m* miscarriage of justice

Justiz'minister *m* minister of justice; attorney general; Lord Chancellor (Brit)

Jutesack ['jutəzak] *m* gunnysack

Juwel [ju'vel] *n* (-s;-en) jewel, gem; **Juwelen** jewelry

Juwe'lenkästchen *n* jewel box

Juwelier –in [juvɛ'lir(ɪn)] §6 *mf* jeweler

Juwelier'waren *pl* jewelry

Jux [juks] *m* (-es;-e) spoof, joke; **aus Jux** as a joke; **sich** [*dat*] **e-n Jux mit j–m machen** play a joke on s.o.

K

K, k [ka] *invar n* K, k

Kabale [ka'balə] *f* (-;-n) intrigue

Kabarett [kaba'ret] *n* (-[e]s;-e) cabaret; floor show; (*drehbare Platte*) lazy Suzan

Kabel ['kabəl] *n* (-s;-) cable

Ka'belgramm *n* (-es;-e) cablegram

Kabeljau ['kabəljau] *m* (-s;-e) codfish

kabeln ['kabəln] *tr* cable

Kabine [ka'binə] *f* (-;-n) cabin; booth; (aer) cockpit

Kabinett [kabi'net] *n* (-s;-e) closet; small room; (& pol) cabinet

Kabriolett [kabri•o'let] *n* (-[e]s;-e) (aut) convertible

Kachel ['kaxəl] *f* (-;-n) glazed tile

kacken ['kakən] *intr* (sl) defecate

Kadaver [ka'davər] *m* (-s;-) cadaver

Kada'vergehorsam *m* blind obedience

Kadenz [ka'dents] *f* (-;-en) cadence

Kader ['kadər] *m* (-s;-) cadre

Kadett [ka'det] *m* (-en;-en) cadet

Käfer ['kefər] *m* (-s;-) beetle

Kaffee ['kafe] *m* (-s;-s) coffee

Kaf'feebohne *f* coffee bean

Kaf'feeklatsch *m* coffee klatsch

Kaf'feemaschine *f* coffee maker

Kaf'feepflanzung *f*, **Kaf'feeplantage** *f* coffee plantation

Kaf'feesatz *m* coffee grounds

Kaf'feetante *f* coffee fiend

Käfig ['kefɪç] *m* (-[e]s;-e) cage

kahl [kal] *adj* bald; (*Baum*) bare; (*Landschaft*) bleak, barren

kahl'köpfig *adj* bald-headed

Kahm [kam] *m* (-[e]s;-e) mold; scum

kahmig ['kamɪç] *adj* moldy; scummy

Kahn [kan] *m* (-[e]s;-e) boat; barge

Kai [kaɪ], [ke] *m* (-s;-s) quay, wharf

Kaiser ['kaɪzər] *m* (-s;-) emperor

Kaiserin ['kaɪzərɪn] *f* (-;-nen) empress

kai'serlich *adj* imperial

Kai'serreich *n*, **Kaisertum** ['kaɪzərtum] *n* (-[e]s;-er) empire

Kai'serschnitt *m* Caesarian operation

Kai'serzeit *f* (*hist*) Empire

Kajüte [ka'jytə] *f* (-;-n) (naut) cabin

Kajü'tenjunge *m* cabin boy

Kajü'tentreppe *f* (naut) companionway

Kakao [ka'ka•o] *m* (-s;-) cocoa; **j–n durch den K. ziehen** pull s.o.'s leg

Kaktee [kak'te•ə] *f* (-;-n), **Kaktus** ['kaktus] *m* (-;-se) cactus

Kalauer ['kalau•ər] *m* (-s;-) pun

Kalb [kalp] *n* (-[e]s;-er) calf

Kalbe ['kalbə] *f* (-;-n) heifer

kalbern ['kalbərn] *intr* be silly

Kalb'fell *n* calfskin

Kalb'fleisch *n* veal

Kalbs'braten *m* roast veal

Kalbs'kotelett *n* veal cutlet

Kalbs'schnitzel *n* veal cutlet

Kaleidoskop [kalaɪdə'skop] *n* (-s;-e) kaleidoscope

Kalender [ka'lendər] *m* (-s;-) calendar

Kali ['kalɪ] *n* (-s;) potash

Kaliber [ka'libər] *n* (-s;-) caliber

kalibrieren [kalɪ'brirən] *tr* calibrate; gauge

Kaliko ['kalɪko] *m* (-s;-s) calico

Kalium ['kaljum] *n* (-s;) potassium

Kalk [kalk] m (-[e]s;-e) lime; calcium
kalken ['kalkən] tr whitewash; lime
kalkig ['kalkıç] adj limy
Kalk'ofen m limekiln
Kalk'stein m limestone
Kalk'steinbruch m limestone quarry
Kalkül [kal'kyl] m & n (-s;-e) calculation; (math) calculus
kalkulieren [kalku'lirən] tr calculate
Kal·mar ['kalmar] m (-s;-mare
['marə]) squid
Kalo·rie [kalo'ri] f (-;-rien ['ri·ən])
calorie
Kalotte [ka'lɔtə] f (-;-n) skullcap
kalt [kalt] adj (kälter ['keltər]; käl-
teste ['keltəstə] §9) cold
kaltblütig ['kaltblytıç] adj cold-
blooded
Kälte ['keltə] f (-;) cold, coldness
käl'tebeständig adj cold-resistant
Käl'tegrad m degree below freezing
kälten ['keltən] tr chill
Käl'tewelle f (meteor) cold wave
Kalt'front f cold front
kalt'herzig adj cold-hearted
kalt'machen tr (sl) bump off
kaltschnäuzig ['kalt/nɔitsıç] adj (coll)
callous; (coll) cool, unflappable
kalt'stellen tr render harmless
kam [kam] pret of kommen
Kambodscha [kam'bɔtʒa] n (-s;) Cam-
bodia
kambodschanisch [kambo'dʒanı/] adj
Cambodian
Kamel [ka'mel] n (-[e]s;-e) camel
Kamel'garn n mohair
Kamera ['kamera] f (-s;-s) camera
Kamerad [kame'rat] m (-en;-en), Ka-
meradin [kame'radın] f (-;-nen)
comrade
Kamerad'schaft ((-;-en) comradeship
Kamin [ka'min] m (-s;-e) chimney;
fireplace
Kamin'platte f hearthstone
Kamin'sims n mantelpiece
Kamm [kam] m (-[e]s;ːe) comb; (e-s
Gebirges) ridge; (e-r Welle) crest
kämmen ['kemən] tr comb; (Wolle)
card
Kammer ['kamər] f (-;-n) chamber;
(adm) board; (anat) ventricle
Kam'merdiener m valet
Kämmerer ['kemərər] m (-s;-) cham-
berlain; (Schatzmeister) treasurer
Kam'mermusik f chamber music
Kamm'garn n (tex) worsted
Kamm'rad n cogwheel
Kampagne [kam'panjə] f (-;-n) cam-
paign
Kämpe ['kempə] m (-n;-n) warrior
Kampf [kampf] m (-[e]s;ːe) fight
Kampf'bahn f (sport) stadium, arena
kämpfen ['kempfən] tr & intr fight
Kampfer ['kampfər] m (-s;) camphor
Kämpfer -in ['kempfər(ın)] §6 mf
fighter
kämpferisch ['kempfərı/] adj fighting
kampf'erprobt adj battle-tested
kampf'fähig adj fit to fight; (mil) fit
for active service
Kampf'hahn m gamecock; (fig) scrap-
per
Kampf'handlung f (mil) action

Kampf'müdigkeit f combat fatigue
Kampf'parole f (pol) campaign slogan
Kampf'platz m battleground
Kampf'raum m battle zone
Kampf'richter m referee, umpire
Kampf'schwimmer m (nav) frogman
Kampf'spiel n (sport) competition
Kampf'staffel f tactical squadron
kampf'unfähig adj disabled; k. machen
put out of action
Kampf'veranstalter m (sport) promo-
tor
Kampf'verband m combat unit
Kampf'wert m fighting efficiency
Kampf'ziel n (mil) objective
kampieren [kam'pirən] intr camp
Kanada ['kanada] n (-s;) Canada
Kanadier -in [ka'nadjər(ın)] §6 mf
Canadian || m canoe
kanadisch [ka'nadı/] adj Canadian
Kanaille [ka'naljə] f (-;-n) bum;
(Pöbel) riffraff
Kanal [ka'nal] m (-s;ːe) canal; (für
Abwasser) drain, sewer; (agr) irri-
gation ditch; (anat, elec) duct; (geol,
telv) channel
Kanalisation [kanalıza'tsjon] f (-;)
drainage; sewerage system
Kanalräumer [ka'nalrɔimər] m (-s;-)
sewer worker
Kanal'wähler m (telv) channel selector
Kanapee ['kanape] n (-s;-s) sofa
Kanarienvogel [ka'narjənfogəl] m ca-
nary
Kandare [kan'darə] f (-;-n) bit, curb;
j-n an die K. nehmen take s.o. in
hand
Kanda'renkette f curb chain
Kandelaber [kande'labər] m (-s;-)
candelabrum
Kandidat -in [kandı'dat(ın)] §7 mf
candidate
Kandidatur [kandıda'tur] f·(-;-en)
candidacy
kandideln [kan'didəln] ref get drunk
kandidieren [kandı'dirən] intr be a
candidate, run for office
Kandis ['kandıs] m (-;) rock candy
Kaneel [ka'nel] m (-s;-e) cinnamon
Känguruh ['keŋguru] n (-s;-s) kangaroo
Kaninchen [ka'ninçən] n (-s;-) rabbit
Kanister [ka'nıstər] m (-s;-) canister
Kanne ['kanə] f (-;-n) can; pot; jug
Kannelüre [kanə'lyrə] f (-;-n) (archit)
flute
Kannibale [kanı'balə] m (-n;-n), Kan-
nibalin [kanı'balın] f (-;-nen) can-
nibal
kannte ['kantə] pret of kennen
Ka·non ['kanɔn] m (-s;-s) (Maßstab;
Gebet bei der Messe) canon; (mus)
round || m (-s;-nones ['nonəs] canon
(of Canon Law)
Kanone [ka'nonə] f (-;-n) (arti) gun;
(hist) canon; (coll) expert; unter
aller K. indescribably bad
Kano'nenboot n gunboat
Kano'nenrohr n gun barrel; heiliges
K.! holy smokes!
kanonisieren [kanɔnı'zirən] tr canonize
Kante ['kantə] f (-;-n) edge

kanten ['kantən] *tr* set on edge; (*beim Schifahren*) cant ‖ **Kanten** *m* (-s;-) end of a loaf, crust

Kanthaken ['kanthɑkən] *m* grappling hook

kantig ['kantɪç] *adj* angular; squared

Kantine [kan'tinə] *f* (-;-n) canteen; (mil) post exchange

Kanton [kan'ton] *m* (-s;-e) canton

Kan·tor ['kantɔr] *m* (-s;-toren ['torən]) choir master; organist

Kanu [ka'nu] *n* (-s;-s) canoe

Kanzel ['kantsəl] *f* (-;-n) pulpit; (aer) cockpit

Kanzlei [kants'laɪ] *f* (-;-en) office; chancellery

Kanzlei′papier *n* official foolscap

Kanzlei′sprache *f* legal jargon

Kanzler ['kantslər] *m* (-s;-) chancellor

Kap [kap] *n* (-s;-s) cape, headland

Kapaun [ka'paun] *m* (-s;-e) capon

Kapazität [kapatsɪ'tet] *f* (-;-en) capacity; (*Können*) authority

Kapelle [ka'pelə] *f* (-;-n) chapel; (mus) band

Kapell′meister *m* band leader; orchestra conductor

kapern ['kapərn] *tr* capture; (coll) nab

kapieren [ka'pirən] *tr* get, understand ‖ *intr* get it; **kapiert?** got it?

kapital [kapɪ'tal] *adj* excellent ‖ **Kapital** *n* (-s;-e & -ien [jən]) (fin) capital; **K. schlagen aus** capitalize on; **K. und Zinsen** principal and interest

Kapital′anlage *f* investment

Kapital′ertragssteuer *f* tax on unearned income

kapitalisieren [kapɪtalɪ'zirən] *tr* (fin) capitalize

Kapitalismus [kapɪta'lɪsmus] *m* (-s;) capitalism

Kapitalist –in [kapɪta'lɪst(ɪn)] *m* §7 capitalist

Kapital′verbrechen *n* capital offense

Kapitän [kapɪ'ten] *m* (-s;-e) captain, skipper; **K. zur See** (nav) captain

Kapitän′leutnant *m* (nav) lieutenant

Kapitel [ka'pɪtəl] *n* (-s;-) chapter

Kapitell [kapɪ'tel] *n* (-s;-e) (archit) capital

kapitulieren [kapɪtu'lirən] *intr* capitulate, surrender; reenlist

Kaplan [ka'plan] *m* (-s;ːe) chaplain; (R.C.) assistant (pastor)

Kapo ['kapo] *m* (-s;-s) prisoner overseer; (mil) (coll) N.C.O.

Kappe ['kapə] *f* (-;-n) cap; hood, cover; **etw auf seine eigene K. nehmen** take the responsibility for s.th.

Käppi ['kepɪ] *n* (-s;-s) garrison cap

Kaprice [ka'prisə] *f* (-;-n) caprice

Kapriole [kaprɪ'olə] *f* (-;-n) caper

kaprizieren [kaprɪ'tsirən] *ref*—**sich k. auf** (*acc*) be dead set on

kapriziös [kaprɪ'tsjøs] *adj* capricious

Kapsel ['kapsəl] *f* (-;-n) capsule; (*e-r Flasche*) cap; (*e-s Sprengkörpers*) detonator

kaputt [ka'put] *adj* (sl) broken; (sl) ruined; (sl) exhausted; (sl) dead

kaputt′gehen §82 *intr* (SEIN) get ruined

kaputt′machen *tr* ruin

Kapuze [ka'putsə] *f* (-;-n) hood; (eccl) cowl

Kapuziner [kapu'tsinər] *m* (-s;-) Capuchin

Kapuzi′nerkresse *f* Nasturtium

Karabiner [kara'binər] *m* (-s;-) carbine

Karabi′nerhaken *m* snap

Karaffe [ka'rafə] *f* (-;-n) carafe

Karambolage [karambo'laʒə] *f* (-;-n) (coll) collision

karambolieren [karambo'lirən] *intr* (coll) collide

Karamelle [kara'melə] *f* (-;-n) caramel

Karat [ka'rat] *n* (-[e]s;) carat

-karätig [karetɪç] *comb.fm. -carat*

Karawane [kara'vanə] *f* (-;-n) caravan

Karbid [kar'bit] *n* (-[e]s;-e) carbide

Karbolsäure [kar'bɔlzɔɪrə] *f* (-;) carbolic acid

Karbon [kar'bon] *n* (-s;) (geol) carbon

Karbunkel [kar'buŋkəl] *n* (-s;-) carbuncle

Kardinal– [kardinal] *comb.fm.* cardinal, principal ‖ **Kardinal** *m* (-s;ːe) (eccl, orn) cardinal

Karenzzeit [ka'rentstsaɪt] *f* (ins) waiting period

Karfreitag [kar'fraɪtak] *m* Good Friday

karg [kark] *adj* (**karger & kärger** ['kergər]; **kargste & kärgste** ['kerstə] §9) (*ärmlich*) meager; (*Boden*) poor; (*Landschaft*) bleak

kargen ['kargən] *intr* be sparing

Karg′heit *f* (-;) bleakness; meagerness; frugality

kärglich ['kerlɪç] *adj* meager, poor

kariert [ka'rirt] *adj* checked, squared

Karikatur [karɪka'tur] *f* (-;-en) caricature; cartoon

karikieren [karɪ'kirən] *tr* caricature

Karl [karl] *m* (-s;) Charles; **Karl der Große** Charlemagne

Karmeliter [karme'litar] *m* (-s;-) Carmelite Friar

Karmelitin [karme'litɪn] *f* (-;-nen) Carmelite nun

karmesinrot [karme'zinrot], **karminrot** [kar'minrot] *adj* crimson

Karneval ['karnəval] *m* (-s;-s & -e) carnival

Karnickel [kar'nɪkəl] *n* (-s;-) (coll) rabbit; (*Sündenbock*) (coll) scapegoat; (*Einfaltspinsel*) simpleton

Karo ['karo] *n* (-s;-s) diamond; check, square; (cards) diamond(s)

Karosse [ka'rosə] *f* (-;-n) state carriage

Karosse·rie [karosə'ri] *f* -;-rien ['ri·ən] (aut) body

Karotte [ka'rotə] *f* (-;-n) carrot

Karpfen ['karpfən] *m* (-s;-) carp

Karre ['karə] *f* (-;-n), **Karren** ['karən] *m* (-s;-) cart; wheelbarrow; **die alte K.** the old rattletrap

Karriere [ka'rjerə] *f* (-;-n) career; gallop; **K. machen** get ahead

Karte ['kartə] *f* (-;-n) card; ticket; (*Landkarte*) map; (*Speise-*) menu

Kartei [kar'taɪ] *f* (-;-en) card file

Kartei′karte *f* index card

Kartell [kar'tɛl] *n* (-s;-e) cartel

Kar'tenkunststück *n* card trick

Kartenlegerin ['kartənlegərɪn] *f* (-; -nen) fortuneteller

Kar'tenstelle *f* ration board

Kartoffel [kar'tɔfəl] *f* (-;-n) potato

Kartof'felbrei *m* mashed potatoes

Kartof'felpuffer [kar'tɔfəlpufər] *m* (-s; -) potato pancake

Karton [kar'ton] *m* (-s;-s) cardboard; carton; (paint) cartoon

Kartonage [karto'naʒə] *f* (-;-n) cardboard box

kartoniert [karto'nirt] *adj* (bb) softcover

Karton'papier *n* (thin) cardboard

Kartothek [karto'tek] *f* (-;-en) card index; card filing system

Kartothek'ausgabe *f* loose-leaf edition

Karussell [karu'sɛl] *n* (-s;-e) merry-go-round

Karwoche ['karvɔxə] *f* Holy Week

Karzer ['kartsər] *m* (-s;-) (educ) detention room; **K. bekommen** get a detention

Kaschmir ['kaʃmɪr] *m* (-s;-e) cashmere

Käse ['kezə] *m* (-s;-) cheese; (sl) baloney

Kaserne [ka'zɛrnə] *f* (-;-n) barracks

käsig ['keziç] *adj* cheesy; (*Gesichtsfarbe*) pasty

Kasino [ka'zino] *n* (-s;-s) casino; (mil) officer's mess

Kas'pisches Meer' ['kaspiʃəs] *n* Caspian Sea

Kassa ['kasa] *f*—per **K. in cash**

Kassa— *comb.fm.* cash, spot

Kasse ['kasə] *f* (-;-n) money box; till; cash register; cashiers desk; (*Bargeld*) cash; (adm) finance department; (educ) bursars office; (sport) ticket window; (theat) box office; **gegen** (or per) **K.** cash, for cash; **gut bei K. sein** (coll) be flush

Kas'senabschluß *m* balancing of accounts

Kas'senbeamte *m* cashier; teller

Kas'senbeleg *m* sales slip

Kas'senbestand *m* cash on hand

Kas'senerfolg *m* (theat) hit

Kas'senführer **–in** §6 *mf* cashier

Kas'senschalter *m* teller's window

Kas'senschrank *m* safe

Kas'senzettel *m* sales slip

Kasserolle [kasə'rɔlə] *f* (-;-n) casserole

Kassette [ka'sɛtə] *f* (-;-n) base, box; (cin, phot) cassette

kassieren [ka'sirən] *tr* (*Geld*) take in; get; (*Urteil*) annul; (coll) confiscate; (coll) arrest; (mil) break

Kassie'rer **–in** §6 *mf* cashier; teller

Kastagnette [kastan'jetə] *f* (-;-n) castanet

Kastanie [kas'tanjə] *f* (-;-n) chestnut

Kästchen ['kɛstçən] *n* (-s;-) case, box

Kaste ['kastə] *f* (-;-n) caste

kasteien [kas'tai-ən] *tr & ref* mortify; **sein Leib k.** mortify the flesh

Kastell [kas'tɛl] *n* (-s;-e) small fort

Kasten ['kastən] *m* (-s;⸗ & -) chest, case, box; cupboard, cabinet; (*Auto*

(coll) crate; (*Boot*) (coll) tub; (*Gefängnis*) (coll) jug

Ka'stengeist *m* snobbishness

Ka'stenwagen *m* (aut) panel truck; (rr) boxcar

Ka'stenwesen *n* caste system

Kastrat [kas'trat] *m* (-en;-en) eunuch

kastrieren [kas'trirən] *tr* castrate

Katakomben [kata'kɔmbən] *pl* catacombs

Katalog [kata'lok] *m* (-[e]s;-e) catalogue

katalogisieren [katalɔgi'zirən] *tr* catalogue

Katapult [kata'pult] *m & n* (-[e]s;-e) catapult

katapultieren [katapul'tirən] *tr* catapult

Katarakt [kata'rakt] *m* (-[e]s;-e) cataract, rapids; (pathol) cataract

Katasteramt [ka'tastəramt] *n* landregistry office

katastrophal [katastro'fal] *adj* catastrophic, disastrous

Katastrophe [kata'strofə] *f* (-;-n) catastrophe, disaster

Katastro'phengebiet *m* disaster area

Kate·go·rie [katego'ri] *f* (-;-rien ['ri·ən] category

kategorisch [kate'goriʃ] *adj* categorical

Kater ['katər] *m* (-s;-) tomcat; (coll) hangover

Katheder [ka'tedər] *n & m* (-s;-) teacher's desk

Kathe'derblüte *f* teacher's blunder

Kathedrale [kate'dralə] *f* (-;-n) cathedral

Kathode [ka'todə] *f* (-;-n) cathode

Katholik **–in** [kato'lik(ɪn)] §7 *mf* Catholic

katholisch [ka'toliʃ] *adj* Catholic

Kattun [ka'tun] *m* (-s;-e) calico

Kätzchen ['kɛtsçən] *n* (-s;-) kitten

Katze ['katsə] *f* (-;-n) cat; **für die K.** (coll) for the birds

kat'zenartig *adj* cat-like, feline

Kat'zenbuckel *m* cat's arched back; **vor j-m K. machen** lick s.o.'s boots

kat'zenfreundlich *adj* overfriendly

Kat'zenjammer *m* hangover; blues

Kat'zenkopf *m* (coll) cobblestone; (box) rabbit punch

Kat'zensprung *m* stone's throw

Kauderwelsch ['kaudərvelʃ] *n* (-es;) gibberish

kauen ['kau-ən] *tr* chew

kauern ['kau-ərn] *ref & intr* cower

Kauf [kauf] *m* (-[e]s;⸗e) purchase; **in K. nehmen** (fig) take, put up with; **leichten Kaufes davonkommen** get off cheaply; **zum K. stehen** be for sale

Kauf'auftrag *m* (com) order

kaufen ['kaufən] *tr* purchase, buy

Käufer **–in** ['kɔifər(ɪn)] §6 *mf* buyer

Kauf'haus *n* department store

Kauf'kraft *f* purchasing power

käuflich ['kɔiflɪç] *adj* for sale; (*bestechlich*) open to bribes

Kauf'mann *m* (-[e]s;-leute) businessman; salesman

kaufmännisch ['kaufmɛnɪʃ] *adj* commercial, business
Kauf'mannsdeutsch *n* business German
Kauf'zwang *m* obligation to buy
Kaugummi ['kaugumɪ] *m* chewing gum
kaukasisch [kau'kɑzɪʃ] *adj* Caucasian
Kaulquappe ['kaulkvapə] *f* (-;-n) tadpole, polliwog
kaum [kaum] *adv* hardly, scarcely
Kautabak ['kautabak] *m* chewing tobacco
Kaution [kau'tsjon] *f* (-;-en) (jur) bond; (*Bürgschaft*) (jur) bail; **gegen K.** on bail
Kautschuk ['kautʃuk] *m* (-s;-e) rubber
Kauz [kauts] *m* (-es;-e) owl; (sl) crackpot
Kavalier [kava'lir] *m* (-s;-e) cavalier, gentleman; beau
Kavalkade [kaval'kɑdə] *f* (-;-n) cavalcade
Kavalle·rie [kavalə'ri] *f* (-;-rien ['ri·ən]) cavalry
Kavallerist [kavalə'rɪst] *m* (-en;-en) cavalryman, trooper
Kaviar ['kavjar] *m* (-[e]s;-e) caviar
keck [kɛk] *adj* bold; impudent; cheeky
Kegel ['kegəl] *m* (-s;-) tenpin; (geom) cone; **K. schieben** bowl
Ke'gelbahn *f* bowling alley
kegeln ['kegəln] *intr* bowl
Keg'ler –in §6 *mf* bowler
Kehle ['kelə] *f* (-;-n) throat
kehlig ['kelɪç] *adj* throaty
Kehlkopf ['kelkɔpf] *m* larynx
Kehl'kopfentzündung *f* laryngitis
Kehre ['kerə] *f* (-;-n) turn, bend
kehren ['kerən] *tr* sweep; (*wenden*) turn; **alles zum besten k.** make the best of it; **j–m den Rücken k.** turn one's back on s.o. || *ref* turn; **in sich gekehrt sein** be lost in thought; **sich an nichts k.** not care about anything; **sich k. an** (*acc*) *intr* sweep
Kehricht ['kerɪçt] *m & n* (-[e]s;) sweepings; trash, rubbish
Keh'richteimer *m* trash can
Keh'richtschaufel *f* dustpan
Kehr'maschine *f* street cleaner
Kehr'reim *m* refrain, chorus
Kehr'seite *f* reverse; (fig) seamy side
kehrtmachen ['kertmaxən] *intr* turn around; (mil) about-face
Kehrt'wendung *f* about-face
keifen ['kaifən] *intr* nag
Keiferei [kaifə'rai] *f* (-;-en) nagging; squabble
Keil [kail] *m* (-[e]s;-e) wedge
keilen ['kailən] *tr* wedge; (*coll*) recruit || *recip* scrap
Keilerei [kailə'rai] *f* (-;-en) scrap
keil'förmig *adj* wedge-shaped; tapered
Keil'hammer *m* sledgehammer
Keil'hose *f* tapered trousers
Keil'schrift *f* cuneiform writing
Keim [kaim] *m* (-[e]s;-e) germ; embryo; (fig) seeds; (bot) bud, sprout; **im K. ersticken** nip in the bud; **im K. vorhanden** at an embryonic stage; **Keime treiben** germinate
keimen ['kaimən] *intr* germinate;

sprout || **Keimen** *n*—**zum K. bringen** cause to germinate
keim'frei *adj* germ-free, sterile
Keimling ['kaimlɪŋ] *m* (-s;-e) embryo; sprout; seedling
keimtötend ['kaimtøtənt] *adj* germicidal; antiseptic, sterilizing
Keim'zelle *f* germ cell, sex cell
kein [kain] §2,2 *adj* no, not any
keiner [kain] §2,4 *indef pron* none; no one, nobody, not one; **k. von beiden** neither of them
keinerlei ['kainər'lai] *invar adj* no... of any kind, no...whatsoever
keineswegs ['kainəs'veks] *adv* by no means, not at all
Keks [keks] *m & n* (-es;-e) biscuit, cracker; cookie
Kelch [kɛlç] *m* (-[e]s;-e) cup; (bot) calyx; (eccl) chalice
Kelch'blatt *n* (bot) sepal
Kelle ['kɛlə] *f* (-;-n) ladle; (hort, mas) trowel
Keller ['kɛlər] *m* (-s;-) cellar
Kel'lergeschoß *n* basement
Kel'lergewölbe *n* underground vault
Kellner ['kɛlnər] *m* (-s;-) waiter
Kellnerin ['kɛlnərɪn] *f* (-;-nen) waitress
Kelte ['kɛltə] *m* (-n;-n) Celt
Kelter ['kɛltər] *f* (-;-n) wine press
keltern ['kɛltərn] *tr* press
Keltin ['kɛltɪn] *f* (-;-nen) Celt
keltisch ['kɛltɪʃ] *adj* Celtic
kennbar ['kɛnbar] *adj* recognizable
kennen ['kɛnən] §97 *tr* be acquainted with, know
ken'nenlernen *tr* get to know, meet
Ken'ner –in §6 *mf* expert
Ken'nerblick *m* knowing glance
Ken'ner –in §6 *mf* expert
Kennkarte ['kɛnkartə] *f* identity card
kenntlich ['kɛntlɪç] *adj* identifiable, recognizable; conspicuous
Kenntnis ['kɛntnɪs] *f* (-;-se) knowledge; **gute Kenntnisse haben in** (*dat*) be well versed in; **j–n von etw in K. setzen** apprise s.o. of s.th.; **Kenntnisse** knowledge; skills; know-how; **oberflächliche Kenntnisse** a smattering; **von etw K. nehmen** take note of s.th.; **zur K. nehmen** take note of s.th.
Kennwort ['kɛnvɔrt] *n* (-[e]s;-er) code word; (mil) password
Kennzeichen ['kɛntsaiçən] *n* distinguishing mark; hallmark; criterion; (aer) marking; (aut) license number
kennzeichnen ['kɛntsaiçnən] *tr* characterize; identify; brand
Kennziffer ['kɛntsɪfər] *f* code number
kentern ['kɛntərn] *intr* (SEIN) capsize
Keramik [ke'ramɪk] *f* (-;) ceramics; pottery
keramisch [ke'ramɪʃ] *adj* ceramic
Kerbe ['kɛrbə] *f* (-;-n) notch, groove
kerben ['kɛrbən] *tr* notch, nick; make a groove in; serrate
Kerbholz ['kɛrphɔlts] *n*—**etw auf dem K. haben** have a crime chalked up against one
Kerbtier ['kɛrptir] *n* insect
Kerker ['kɛrkər] *m* (-s;-) jail

Kerl [kɛrl] *m* (-s;-e) fellow, guy; (*Mädchen*) lass

Kern [kɛrn] *m* (-[e]s;-e) kernel; (*im Obst*) pit, stone, pip; hard core; (*e-s Problems*) crux; (phys) nucleus

Kern- *comb.fm.* core; central, basic; through and through; (phys) nuclear

Kern′aufbau *m* nuclear structure

kern′deutsch′ *adj* German through and through

Kern′energie *f* nuclear energy

Kern′fächer *pl* core curriculum

kern′gesund′ *adj* perfectly sound

Kern′holz *n* heartwood

kernig [ˈkɛrnɪç] *adj* full of seeds; robust, vigorous

Kern′los *adj* seedless

Kern′physik *f* nuclear physics

Kern′punkt *m* gist, crux; focal point

Kern′schußweite *f*—**auf K.** at point-blank range

Kern′spaltung *f* nuclear fission

Kern′truppen *pl* crack troops

Kern′verschmelzung *f* nuclear fusion

Kern′waffe *f* nuclear weapon

Kerosin [kero'zin] *n* (-s;) kerosene

Kerze [ˈkɛrtsə] *f* (-;-n) candle; (aut) plug

ker′zengera′de *adj* straight as an arrow ‖ *adv* bolt upright

Kessel [ˈkɛsəl] *m* (-s;-) kettle; cauldron; boiler; (geog) basin-shaped valley; (mil) pocket

Kes′selpauke *f* kettledrum

Kes′selraum *m* boiler room

Kes′selschmied *m* boilermaker

Kes′selwagen *m* (aut) tank truck; (rr) tank car

Kette [ˈkɛtə] *f* (-;-n) chain; (*e-s Panzers*) track

ketten [ˈkɛtən] *tr* (an *acc*) chain (to)

Ket′tengeschäft *n* chain store

Ket′tenglied *n* chain link

Ket′tenhund *m* watch dog

Ket′tenrad *n* sprocket

Ket′tenraucher –in §6 *mf* chain smoker

Ket′tenstich *m* chain stitch, lock stitch

Ketzer –in [ˈkɛtsər(ɪn)] §6 *mf* heretic

Ketzerei [kɛtsə'raɪ] *f* (-;-en) heresy

ketzerisch [ˈkɛtsərɪʃ] *adj* heretical

keuchen [ˈkɔɪçən] *intr* pant, gasp

Keuch′husten *m* (-s;) whooping cough

Keule [ˈkɔɪlə] *f* (-;-n) club; (culin) leg, drumstick

keusch [kɔɪʃ] *adj* chaste

Keusch′heit *f* (-;) chastity

KG *abbr* (**Kommanditgesellschaft**) Ltd.

Khaki [ˈkaki] *m* (-;) (tex) khaki

kichern [ˈkɪçərn] *intr* giggle

kicken [ˈkɪkən] *tr* (fb) kick

Kicker [ˈkɪkər] *m* (-s;-) soccer player

Kiebitz [ˈkibɪts] *m* (-[e]s;-e) (orn) lapwing; (*Zugucker*) kibitzer

kiebitzen [ˈkibɪtsən] *intr* kibitz

Kiefer [ˈkifər] *m* (-s;-) jaw(bone) ‖ *f* (-;-n) pine; gemeine **K.** Scotch pine

Kiel [kil] *m* (-[e]s;-e) (Feder) quill; (naut) keel

Kiel′raum *m* hold

Kiel′wasser *n* wake

Kieme [ˈkimə] *f* (-;-n) gill

Kien [ˈkin] *m* (-[e]s;-e) pine cone

Kien′span *m* pine torch

Kiepe [ˈkipə] *f* (-;-n) basket (*carried on one's back*)

Kies [kis] *m* (-es;-e) gravel

Kiesel [ˈkizəl] *m* (-s;-) pebble

Kilo [ˈkilo] *n* (-s;-s & –) kilogram

Kilogramm [kilo'gram] *n* (-s;-e & –) kilogram

Kilometer [kilo'metər] *m & n* (-s;-) kilometer

Kilome′terfresser *m* (coll) speedster

Kilowatt [kilo'vat] *n* (-s;-) kilowatt

Kimm [kɪm] *m* (-es;-e) horizon ‖ *f* (-;-e) (naut) bilge

Kimme [ˈkɪmə] *f* (-;-n) notch; groove; (*e-s Gewehrs*) sight

Kind [kɪnt] *n* (-[e]s;-er) child; baby

Kinder- [ˈkɪndər] *comb.fm.* child's, children's

Kin′derarzt *m*, **Kin′derärztin** *f* pediatrician

Kinderei [kɪndə'raɪ] *f* (-;-en) childish behavior, childish prank

Kin′derfrau *f* nursemaid

Kin′derfräulein *n* governess

Kin′derfürsorge *f* child welfare

Kin′dergarten *m* nursery school, play-school

Kin′dergärtnerin *f* nursery school attendant

Kin′dergeld *n* see **Kinderzulage**

Kin′derheilkunde *f* pediatrics

Kin′derheim *n* children's home

Kin′derhort *m* day nursery

Kin′derlähmung *f* polio

kin′derleicht *adj* easy as pie

Kin′derlied *n* nursery rhyme

kin′derlos *adj* childless

Kin′dermädchen *n* nursemaid

Kin′derpuder *m* baby powder

Kin′derreim *m* nursery rhyme

Kin′derschreck *m* bogeyman

Kin′dersportwagen *m* stroller

Kin′derstube *f* nursery; (*Erziehung*) upbringing

Kin′derstuhl *m* highchair

Kin′derwagen *m* baby carriage

Kin′derzulage *f* family allowance (*paid by the employer*)

Kin′desalter *n* childhood; infancy

Kin′desannahme *f* adoption

Kin′desbeine *pl*—**von Kindesbeinen an** from childhood on

Kin′desentführer –in §6 *mf* kidnaper

Kin′desentführung *f*, **Kin′desraub** *m* kidnaping

Kind′heit *f* (-;) childhood

kindisch [ˈkɪndɪʃ] *adj* childish

kindlich [ˈkɪntlɪç] *adj* childlike

Kinetik [kɪ'netɪk] *f* (-;) kinetics

kinetisch [kɪ'netɪʃ] *adj* kinetic

Kinkerlitzchen [ˈkɪŋkərlɪtsçən] *pl* trifles; gimmicks

Kinn [kɪn] *n* (-[e]s;-e) chin

Kinn′backen *m* jawbone

Kinn′haken *m* (box) uppercut

Kinn′kette *f* curb chain

Kino [ˈkino] *n* (-s;-s) movie theater

Ki′nobesucher –in §6 *mf* moviegoer

Ki′nokamera *f* movie camera

Ki′nokasse *f* box office

Kiosk [kɪ'ɔsk] *m* (-[e]s;-e) stand

Kipfel [ˈkɪpfəl] *n* (-s;-) (Aust) (culin) crescent roll

Kippe ['kɪpə] *f* (–;–n) edge; (*Zigarettenstummel*) butt; **auf der K. stehen** stand on edge; (fig) be touch and go

kippen ['kɪpən] *tr* tilt, tip over; dump || *intr* (SEIN) tilt; overturn

Kipper ['kɪpər] *m* (–s;–) dump truck

Kirche ['kɪrçə] *f* (–;–n) church

Kirchen– ['kɪrçən] *comb.fm.* church, ecclesiastical

Kir'chenbann *m* excommunication; **in den K. tun** excommunicate

Kir'chenbau *m* (–[e]s;) building of churches || *m* (–[e]s;–ten) church

Kir'chenbesuch *m* church attendance

Kir'chenbuch *n* parish register

Kir'chendiener *m* sacristan, sexton

Kir'chengut *n* church property

Kir'chenlied *n* hymn

Kir'chenschändung *f* desecration of a church

Kir'chenschiff *n* (archit) nave

Kir'chenspaltung *f* schism

Kir'chenstaat *m* Papal States

Kir'chenstuhl *m* pew

Kir'chentag *m* Church congress

Kirchgang ['kɪrçgaŋ] *m* going to church

Kirch'gänger –in §6 *mf* church-goer

Kirch'hof *m* churchyard

kirch'lich *adj* church, ecclesiastical

Kirch'spiel *n* parish

Kirch'turm *m* steeple

Kirch'turmpolitik *f* (pej) parochialism

Kirch'turmspitze *f* spire

Kirchweih ['kɪrçvaɪ] *f* (–;–en) church picnic

Kirch'weihe *f* dedication of a church

Kirch'weihfest *n* church picnic

Kirsch [kɪrʃ] *m* (–es;–) cherry brandy

Kirsche ['kɪrʃə] *f* (–;–n) cherry

Kirsch'wasser *n* cherry brandy

Kissen ['kɪsən] *n* (–s;–) cushion, pillow; (*Polster*) pad

Kis'senbezug *m* pillowcase

Kiste ['kɪstə] *f* (–;–n) box, crate, case; (aer) crate; (aut) rattletrap; (naut) tub

Kitsch [kɪtʃ] *m* (–es;) kitsch

kitschig ['kɪtʃɪç] *adj* trashy; mawkish

Kitt [kɪt] *m* (–[e]s;–e) putty; cement; **der ganze Kitt** the whole caboodle

Kittchen ['kɪtçən] *n* (–s;–) (coll) jail

Kittel ['kɪtəl] *m* (–s;–) smock, coat; (Aust) skirt

Kit'telkleid *n* house dress

kitten ['kɪtən] *tr* putty; cement, glue; (fig) patch up

Kitzel ['kɪtsəl] *m* (–s;) tickle; (fig) itch

kitzeln ['kɪtsəln] *tr* tickle

kitzlig ['kɪtslɪç] *adj* ticklish

Kladderadatsch [kladəra'datʃ] *m* (–es) crash, bang; mess, muddle

klaffen ['klafən] *intr* gape, yawn

kläffen ['klɛfən] *intr* yelp

Klafter ['klaftər] *f* (–;– & –n), *m* & *n* (–s;–) fathom; (*Holz–*) cord

klagbar ['klakbar] *adj* (jur) actionable

Klage ['klagə] *f* (–;–n) complaint; (jur) (civil) suit

Kla'gelied *n* dirge, threnody

klagen ['klagən] *tr—j-m seinen Kummer k.* pour out one's troubles to s.o.

|| *intr* complain; **auf Scheidung k.** sue for divorce; **k. über** (*acc*) complain about; **k. um** lament

Kläger –in ['klɛgər(ɪn)] §6 *mf* (jur) plaintiff

Kla'geweib *n* hired mourner

kläglich ['klɛklɪç] *adj* plaintive, pitiful; (*Zustand*) sorry; (*Ergebnis, Ende*) miserable

klaglos ['klaklos] *adv* uncomplainingly

klamm [klam] *adj* (*erstarrt*) numb; (*feuchtkalt*) clammy; **k. an Geld** (coll) short of dough || **Klamm** *f* (–;–en) gorge

Klammer ['klamər] *f* (–;–n) clamp; clip; paper clip; (*Schließe*) clasp; clothespin; hair clip, bobby pin; **eckige K.** bracket; **runde K.** parenthesis

klammern ['klamərn] *tr* clamp; clasp || *ref—sich k. an* (*acc*) cling to

Klamotte [kla'mɔtə] *f* (–;–n)—**alte K.** oldy; (aer, aut) old crate; **Klamotten** things, clothes

Klampfe ['klampfə] *f* (–;–n) guitar

klang [klaŋ] *pret of* klingen || **Klang** *m* (–[e]s;-̈e) tone, sound

Klang'farbe *f* timbre

klang'getreu *adj* high-fidelity

Klang'regler *m* (rad) tone-control knob

Klang'taste *f* tone-control push button

klang'voll *adj* sonorous

Klappe ['klapə] *f* (–;–n) flap; (*Mund*) (sl) trap; (anat, mach) valve; **in die K. gehen** (sl) hit the sack

klappen ['klapən] *tr* flip || *intr* flap, fold || *impers*—**es klappt** (coll) it clicks, it turns out well

Klapper ['klapər] *f* (–;–n) rattle

klap'perdürr *adj* skinny

Klap'pergestell *n* (coll) beanpole; (*Kiste*) (coll) rattletrap

klappern ['klapərn] *intr* rattle, clatter; (*Zähne*) chatter

Klap'perschlange *f* rattlesnake

Klap'perstorch *m* stork

Klappflügel ['klapflygəl] *m* (aer) folding wing (*of carrier plane*)

Klappmesser ['klapmɛsər] *n* jackknife

klapprig ['klaprɪç] *adj* rickety

Klappstuhl ['klaptul] *m* folding chair

Klapptisch ['klaptɪʃ] *m* drop-leaf table

Klapptür ['klaptyr] *f* trap door

Klaps [klaps] *m* (–es;–e) smack, slap; **e-n K. kriegen** (sl) go nuts

klapsen ['klapsən] *tr* smack, slap

Klaps'mühle *f* (coll) booby hatch

klar [klar] *adj* clear; **klar zum Start** ready for take-off

Kläranlage ['klɛranlagə] *f* sewage-disposal plant

klären ['klɛrən] *tr* clear; (*Mißverständnis*) clear up || *ref* become clear

Klar'heit *f* (–;) clearness, clarity

Klarinette [klari'nɛtə] *f* (–;–n) clarinet

klar'legen, klar'stellen *tr* clear up

Klärung ['klɛruŋ] *f* (–;) clarification

Klasse ['klasə] *f* (–;–n) class; (educ) grade, class

Klas'senarbeit *f* test

Klas'senaufsatz *m* composition (*written in class*)

klas'senbewußt *adj* class-conscious

Klas'seneinteilung f classification
Klas'senkamerad -in §7 mf classmate
Klas'sentreffen n (-s;-) class reunion
klassifizieren [klasıfı'tsirən] tr classify
Klassifizie'rung f (-;-en) classification
-klassig [klasıç] comb.fm. -class, -grade
Klassik ['klasık] f (-;) classical antiquity, classical period
Klas'siker -in §6 mf classical author
klassisch ['klasıʃ] adj classic(al)
Klatsch [klatʃ] m (-es;) clap; gossip
Klatsch'base f gossipmonger; tattletale
Klatsch'blatt n scandal sheet
Klatsche ['klatʃə] f (-;-n) fly swatter; tattletale; (educ) pony
klatschen ['klatʃən] tr smack, slap; **dem Lehrer etw k.** tattletale to the teacher about s.th.; **j-m Beifall k.** applaud s.o. || intr clap; (Regen) patter; (fig) gossip; **in die Hände (or mit den Händen) k.** clap the hands
Klatscherei [klatʃə'raı] f (-;-en) gossip
klatsch'naß' adj soaking wet
Klatsch'spalte f glossip column
klauben ['klaubən] tr pick
Klaue ['klau·ə] f (-;-n) claw, talon; (Spalthuf) hoof; (coll) scrawl
klauen ['klau·ən] tr (coll) snitch
Klause ['klauzə] f (-;-n) hermitage; (Schlucht) defile; (coll) den, pad
Klausel ['klauzəl] f (-;-n) clause; (Abmachung) stipulation
Klausner ['klauznər] m (-s;-) hermit
Klausur [klau'zur] f (-;-en) seclusion; (educ) final examination
Klausur'arbeit f final examination
Klaviatur [klavja'tur] f (-;-en) keyboard
Klavier [kla'vir] n (-[e]s;-e) piano
Klavier'auszug m piano score
Klebemittel ['klebəmıtəl] n (-s;-) adhesive, glue
kleben ['klebən] tr & intr stick
Kleberolle ['klebərələ] f roll of gummed tape
Klebestreifen ['klebə/traıfən] m adhesive tape; Scotch tape (trademark)
Klebezettel ['klebətsetəl] m label, sticker
klebrig ['klebrıç] adj sticky
Klebstoff ['klep/təf] m adhesive
Klecks [kleks] m (-es;-e) stain; dab
klecksen ['kleksən] tr splash || intr make blotches
Kleckser -in ['kleksər(ın)] §6 mf scribbler; dauber
Klee [kle] m (-s;) clover
Klee'blatt n cloverleaf; (fig) trio
Kleid [klaıt] n (-[e]s;-er) garment; dress; robe; **Kleider** clothes
kleiden ['klaıdən] tr dress; **j-n gut k.** look good on s.o.
Klei'derablage f cloakroom; (Kleiderständer) clothes rack
Klei'derbestand m wardrobe
Klei'derbügel m coat hanger
Klei'dersack m (mil) duffle bag
Klei'derschrank m clothes closet
Klei'derständer m clothes rack
kleidsam ['klaıtzam] adj well-fitting, becoming

Klei'dung f (-;) clothing
Kleie ['klaı·ə] f (-;-n) bran
klein [klaın] adj small, little; short; **ein k. wenig** a little bit || **Kleine** §5 m little boy || f little girl || n little one
Klein'anzeigen pl classified ads
Klein'arbeit f detailed work
Klein'asien n Asia Minor
Klein'bahn f narrow-gauge railroad
Klein'bauer m small farmer
Klein'betrieb m small business
Kleinbild- comb.fm. (phot) 35mm
klein'bürgerlich adj lower middle-class
Klein'geld n change
klein'gläubig adj of little faith
Klein'handel m retail business
Klein'händler -in §6 mf retailer
Klein'hirn n (anat) cerebellum
Klein'holz n kindling; **K. aus j-m machen** (coll) beat s.o. to a pulp
Klei'nigkeit f small object; trifle, minor detail; small matter
Klei'nigkeitskrämer m fusspot
kleinkalibrig ['klaınkalibrıç] adj small-bore
Klein'kind n infant
Klein'kinderbewahranstalt f day care center
Klein'kram m odds and ends; details
klein'laut adj subdued
klein'lich adj stingy; (Betrag) paltry; (engstirnig) narrow-minded, pedantic
Klein'mut m despondency; faintheartedness
klein'mütig adj despondent; faint-hearted
Klei'nod ['klaınot] n (-[e]s;-node & -nodien ['nodjən] jewel, gem
klein'schneiden §106 tr chop up
Klein'schreibmaschine f portable typewriter
Kleister ['klaıstər] m (-s;-) paste
Klemme ['klemə] f (-;-n) clamp, clip; (coll) tight spot, fix; (elec) terminal; (surg) clamp
klemmen ['klemən] tr tuck, put; (stehlen) pinch, swipe || ref—**sich** [dat] **den Finger k.** smash one's finger; **sich hinter die Arbeit k.** get down to business; **sich k. hinter** (acc) get after || intr be stuck
Klempner ['klempnər] m (-s;-) tinsmith; plumber
Klempnerei [klempnə'raı] f (-;) plumbing
Kleptomane [klepto'manə] §5 mf kleptomaniac
klerikal [klerı'kal] adj clerical
Kleriker ['klerıkər] m (-s;-) clergyman, priest
Klerus ['klerus] m (-;) clergy
Klette ['kletə] f (-;-n) (bot) burr; (coll) pain in the neck
Klet'tergarten m training area (for mountain climbing)
klettern ['kletərn] intr (SEIN) climb
Klet'terpflanze f (bot) creeper
Klet'terrose f rambler
Klet'tertour f climbing expedition
Klient [klı'ent] m (-en;-en) client
Klientel [klı·en'tel] f (-;-en) clientele (of a lawyer)

Klientin [klɪˈɛntɪn] *f* (-;-nen) client
Klima [ˈklima] *n* (-s;-s) climate
Kli'maanlage *f* air conditioner
kli'magerecht *adj* air-conditioned
klimatisch [klɪˈmatɪʃ] *adj* climatic
klimatisieren [klɪmatɪˈzirən] *tr* air-condition
Klimatisie'rung *f* (-;) air conditioning
Klimbim [klɪmˈbɪm] *m* (-s;) (coll) junk; (coll) racket; (coll) fuss
klimmen [ˈklɪmən] §164 *intr* (SEIN) climb
klimpern [ˈklɪmpərn] *intr* jingle; (auf der Gitarre) strum; **mit den Wimpern k.** flutter one's eyelashes
Klinge [ˈklɪŋə] *f* (-;-n) blade; sword, saber; **über die K. springen lassen** put to the sword
Klingel [ˈklɪŋəl] *f* (-;-n) bell
Klin'gelbeutel *m* collection basket
Klin'gelknopf *m* doorbell button
klingeln [ˈklɪŋəln] *intr* ring, tinkle; (Vers, Reim) jingle || *impers*—es **klingelt** the doorbell is ringing; there goes the (school) bell; the phone is ringing
kling'klang *interj* ding-dong!
Klinik [ˈklinɪk] *f* (-;-en) teaching hospital (of a university); private hospital; nursing home
klinisch [ˈklinɪʃ] *adj* clinical; hospital
Klinke [ˈklɪŋkə] *f* (-;-n) door handle; (telp) jack; **Klinken putzen** beg or peddle from door to door
Klippe [ˈklɪpə] *f* (-;-n) rock, reef
klirren [ˈklɪrən] *intr* rattle, clang; (Gläser) clink; (Waffen) clash
Klischee [klɪˈʃe] *n* (-s;-s) cliché
Klistier [klɪsˈtir] *n* (-s;-e) enema
klistieren [klɪsˈtirən] *tr* give an enema to
klitschig [ˈklɪtʃɪç] *adj* doughy
Klo [klo] *n* (-s;-s) (coll) john
Kloake [kloˈakə] *f* (-;-n) sewer
Kloben [ˈkloban] *m* (-s;-) pulley; (Holz) block; (Schraubenstock) vise
klobig [ˈklobɪç] *adj* clumsy; bulky
klomm [klɔm] *pret* of **klimmen**
klopfen [ˈklɔpfən] *tr* (Nagel) drive; (Teppich) beat; (Fleisch) pound || *intr* knock; (Herz) beat, pound; (Motor) ping; **j-m auf die Schulter k.** pat s.o. on the back || *impers*—es **klopft** s.o. is knocking
klopffest [ˈklɔpffɛst] *adj* antiknock
Klöppel [ˈklœpəl] *m* (-s;-) bobbin; (e-r Glocke) clapper; (mus) mallet
klöppeln [ˈklœpəln] *tr* make (lace) with bobbins
Klops [klɔps] *m* (-es;-e) meatball
Klosett [kloˈzet] *n* (-s;-e & -s) (flush) toilet
Klosett'becken *n* toilet bowl
Klosett'brille *f* toilet seat
Klosett'deckel *m* toilet-seat lid
Klosett'papier *n* toilet paper
Kloß [klos] *m* (-es;-e) dumpling; **e-n K. im Hals haben** have a lump in one's throat
Kloster [ˈklostər] *n* (-s;-) monastery; convent
Kloster- *comb.fm.* monastic
Klo'sterbruder *m* lay brother, friar

Klo'sterfrau *f* nun
klösterlich [ˈkløstərlɪç] *adj* monastic
Klotz [klɔts] *m* (-es;-e) block; toy building block; (coll) blockhead; **ein K. am Bein** (coll) a drag; **wie ein K. schlafen** sleep like a log
klotzig [ˈklɔtsɪç] *adj* clumsy; uncouth || *adv*—**k. reich** filthy rich
Klub [klup] *m* (-s;-s) club
Klub'jacke *f* blazer
Klub'sessel *m* easy chair
Kluft [kluft] *f* (-;-e) gorge, ravine; (fig) gulf; (poet) chasm || *f* (-;-en) outfit, uniform
klug [kluk] *adj* (klüger [ˈklygər]; klügste [ˈklygstə] §9) clever, bright; wise; **aus Schaden k. werden** learn the hard way; **nicht k. werden können aus** be unable to figure out
klügeln [ˈklygəln] *intr* quibble
Klug'heit *f* (-;) cleverness; intelligence; wisdom
klüglich [ˈklyklɪç] *adv* wisely
Klug'redner *m* wise guy, know-it-all
Klumpen [ˈklumpən] *m* (-s;-) lump, clod; (Haufen) heap; (min) nugget
Klumpfuß [ˈklumpfus] *m* clubfoot
klumpig [ˈklumpɪç] *adj* lumpy
Klüngel [ˈklyŋəl] *m* (-s;-) clique
knabbern [ˈknabərn] *intr* nibble
Knabe [ˈknabə] *m* (-n;-n) boy
Kna'benalter *n* boyhood
kna'benhaft *adj* boyish
knack [knak] *interj* crack!; snap!; click!
knacken [ˈknakən] *tr* crack || *intr* crack; (Schloß) click; (Feuer) crackle
Knacks [knaks] *m* (-es;-e) crack; snap; click; **e-n K. kriegen** get a crack; **e-n K. weg haben** be badly hit; **sich** [dat] **e-n K. holen** suffer a blow
Knack'wurst *f* pork sausage; smoked sausage
Knall [knal] *m* (-[e]s;-e) crack, bang; **K. und Fall** on the spot, at once
Knallblättchen [ˈknalblɛtçən] *n* (-s;-) cap (for a toy pistol)
Knall'bonbon *m* & *n* noise maker
Knall'büchse *f* popgun
Knall'dämpfer *m* silencer
Knall'effekt *m* big surprise
knall'rot *adj* fiery red
knapp [knap] *adj* (eng) close, tight; (Mehrheit) bare; (Zeit) short; (fig) concise; **k. werden** run short, run low
Knappe [ˈknapə] *m* (-n;-n) (hist) squire; (min) miner
Knapp'heit *f* (-;) closeness, tightness; shortage; conciseness
Knapp'schaft *f* (-;-en) miner's union
Knapp'schaftskasse *f* miner's insurance
knarren [ˈknarən] *intr* creek
Knaster [ˈknastər] *m* (-s;-) tobacco
knattern [ˈknatərn] *intr* crackle; (Maschinengewehr) rattle || *intr* (SEIN) put-put along
Knäuel [ˈknɔɪ-əl] *m* & *n* (-s;-) (Garn-) ball; (Menschen-) throng
Knauf [knauf] *m* (-[e]s;-e) knob
Knauser -in [ˈknauzər(ɪn)] §6 *mf* tightwad

Knauserei [knauzə'raɪ] ƒ (-;) stinginess
knauserig ['knauzərɪç] adj stingy
knausern ['knauzərn] intr be stingy
knautschen ['knautʃən] tr crumple || intr crumple; (coll) wimper
Knebel ['knebəl] m (-s;-) gag
Kne'belbart m handlebar moustache
knebeln ['knebəln] tr gag; (fig) muzzle
Kne'belpresse ƒ tourniquet
Kne'belung ƒ—K. der Presse muzzling of the press
Knecht [knɛçt] m (-[e]s;-e) servant; farmhand; serf; slave
knechten ['knɛçtən] tr enslave; oppress
knechtisch ['knɛçtɪʃ] adj servile
Knecht'schaft ƒ (-;) servitude
kneifen ['knaɪfən] §88 & §109 tr pinch || §88 intr (Kleid) be too tight; back out, back down; (fencing) retreat; **k. vor** (dat) shirk, dodge
Kneifzange ['knaɪftsaŋə] ƒ (pair of) pincers
Kneipe ['knaɪpə] ƒ (-;-n) saloon
kneipen ['knaɪpən] intr (coll) booze
Knei'penwirt m saloon keeper
Kneiperei [knaɪpə'raɪ] ƒ (-;-en) drinking bout
kneten ['knetən] tr knead; massage
Knick [knɪk] m (-[e]s;-e) bend; (Bruch) break; (Falte) fold, crease
knicken ['knɪkən] tr bend; break; fold; (Hoffnungen) dash || intr (SEIN) snap
Knicker ['knɪkər] m (-s;-) tightwad
Knicks [knɪks] m (-es;-e) curtsy
knicksen ['knɪksən] intr curtsy
Knie [kni] n (-s;- ['kni·ə]) knee
Knie'beuge ƒ knee bend
Knie'beugung ƒ genuflection
knie'fällig adj on one's knees
knie'frei adj above-the-knee
Knie'freiheit ƒ legroom
Knie'kehle ƒ hollow of the knee
knien ['kni·ən] intr kneel
Knie'scheibe ƒ kneecap
Knie'schützer m (sport) kneepad
kniff [knɪf] pret of **kneifen** || **Kniff** m (-[e]s;-e) crease, fold; (Kunstgriff) knack
kniff(e)lig ['knɪf(ə)lɪç] adj tricky
kniffen ['knɪfən] tr crease, fold
Knigge ['knɪgə] m (-;) (fig) Emily Post
knipsen ['knɪpsən] tr (Karte) punch; (phot) snap || intr snap a picture; **mit den Fingern k.** snap one's fingers
Knirps [knɪrps] m (-es;-e) (coll) shrimp
knirschen ['knɪrʃən] intr crunch; **mit den Zähnen k.** gnash one's teeth
knistern ['knɪstərn] intr crackle; (Seide) rustle
knitterfest ['knɪtərfɛst] adj wrinkle-proof
knittern ['knɪtərn] tr wrinkle; crumple
knobeln ['knobəln] intr play dice; **an e-m Problem k.** puzzle over a problem
Knoblauch ['knoblaux] m (-[e]s) garlic
Knöchel ['knœçəl] m (-s;-) knuckle, joint; ankle
Knochen ['knɔxən] m (-s;-) bone

Kno'chenbruch m fracture
Kno'chengerüst n skeleton
Kno'chenmark n marrow
Kno'chenmühle ƒ (coll) sweat shop
knöchern ['knœçərn] adj bone; bony
knochig ['knɔxɪç] adj bony
Knödel ['knødəl] m (-s;-) dumpling; **e-n K. im Hals haben** have a lump in one's throat
Knolle ['knɔlə] ƒ (coll) bulbous nose; (bot) tuber
Knollen ['knɔlən] m (-s;-) lump; (coll) bulbous nose
knollig ['knɔlɪç] adj bulbous
Knopf [knɔpf] m (-[e]s;ːe) button; knob; (e-r Stechnadel) head; **alter K.** old fogey
knöpfen ['knœpfən] tr button
Knopf'loch n buttonhole
knorke ['knɔrkə] adj (coll) super
Knorpel ['knɔrpəl] m (-s;-) cartilage
Knorren ['knɔrən] m (-s;-) knot, gnarl
knorrig ['knɔrɪç] adj gnarled, knotty
Knospe ['knɔspə] ƒ (-;-n) bud
knospen ['knɔspən] intr bud
knoten ['knotən] tr & intr knot || **Knoten** m (-s;-) knot; (Schwierigkeit) snag; (Haarfrisur) chignon; (Seemeile) knot; (astr, med, phys) node; (theat) plot
Kno'tenpunkt m intersection, interchange; (rr) junction
knotig ['knotɪç] adj knotty
Knuff [knuf] m (-[e]s;ːe) (coll) poke
knuffen ['knufən] tr (coll) poke
knüllen ['knʏlən] tr crumple
Knüller ['knʏlər] m (-s;-) (coll) hit
knüpfen ['knʏpfən] tr tie, knot; (Teppich) weave; (Bündnis) form; (befestigen) fasten; **k. an** (acc) tie in with || ref—**sich k. an** (acc) be tied in with
Knüppel ['knʏpəl] m (-s;-) cudgel; (e-s Polizisten) blackjack; (aer) control stick
knurren ['knurən] intr growl, snarl; (Magen) rumble; (fig) grumble
knurrig ['knurɪç] adj grumpy
knusprig ['knusprɪç] adj crisp; (Mädchen) attractive
Knute ['knutə] ƒ (-;-n) whip; (Gewalt) power; (Gewaltherrschaft) tyranny
knutschen ['knutʃən] tr, recip & intr (coll) neck, pet
Knüttel ['knʏtəl] m (-s;-) cudgel
Knüt'telvers m doggerel
k.o. ['ka'o] adj knocked out || **adv—k.o. schlagen** knock out || **K.O.** m (-[s];-s) knockout
Koalition [ko·alɪ'tsjon] ƒ (-;-en) coalition
Kobalt ['kobalt] n (-es;) cobalt
Koben ['kobən] m (-s;-) pigsty
Kobold ['kobɔlt] m (-[e]s;-e) goblin
Kobolz [ko'bɔlts] m—**e-n K. schießen** do a somersault
Koch [kɔx] m (-[e]s;ːe) cook
Koch'buch n cookbook
kochen ['kɔxən] tr & intr cook; boil
Kocher ['kɔxər] m (-s;-) cooker; boiler

Köcher ['kœçər] m (-s;-) quiver; golf bag
Koch'fett n shortening
Koch'geschirr n (mil) mess kit
Koch'herd m kitchen range
Köchin ['kœçɪn] f (-;-nen) cook
Koch'löffel m wooden spoon
Koch'salz n table salt
Köder ['kødər] m (-s;-) bait; lure
ködern ['kødərn] tr bait; lure
Kodex ['kodɛks] m (-es;-e) codex; (jur) code
kodifizieren [kodifɪ'tsirən] tr codify
Koffein [kɔfɛ'in] n (-s;) caffeine
Koffer ['kɔfər] m (-s;-) suitcase; trunk; case (for portable items)
Kof'ferfernseher m portable television
Kof'fergerät n (rad, telv) portable set
Kof'ferraum m (aut) trunk
Kof'ferschreibmaschine f portable typewriter
Kognak ['kɔnjak] m (-s;-e) cognac
Kohl [kol] m (-s;) cabbage; nonsense
Kohle ['kolə] f (-;-n) coal; (Holz-kohle) charcoal
Kohlehydrat ['kolehYdrat] n (-[e]s; -e) carbohydrate
kohlen ['kolən] tr & intr carbonize
Koh'lenbergbau m coal mining
Koh'lenbergwerk n coal mine
Koh'lendioxyd n carbon dioxide
Koh'lenoxyd n carbon monoxide
Koh'lenrevier n coal field
Koh'lensäure f carbonic acid
Koh'lenstoff m carbon
Koh'lenwagen m coal truck; (rr) coal car
Koh'lepapier n carbon paper
Koh'leskizze f charcoal sketch
kohl'ra'benschwarz' adj jet black
Koitus ['ko·ɪtus] m (-;) coitus
Koje ['kojə] f (-;-n) bunk, berth
Kojote [ko'jotə] m (-;-n) coyote
Kokain [koka'in] n (-s;) cocaine
Kokerei [koka'raɪ] f (-;-en) coking plant
kokett [ko'kɛt] adj flirtatious || **Kokette** f (-;-n) flirt
kokettieren [koke'tirən] intr flirt
Kokon [ko'kõ] m (-s;-s) cocoon
Kokosnuß ['kokosnus] f coconut
Kokospalme ['kokospalmə] f coconut palm, coconut tree
Koks [koks] m (-es;-e) coke; (coll) nonsense; (Geld) (coll) dough
Kolben ['kɔlbən] m (-s;-) butt; (Keule) mace; (Löt-) soldering iron; (aut) piston; (chem) flask; (culin) cob; (elec) bulb
Kol'benhub m piston stroke
Kol'benring m piston ring
Kol'benstange f piston rod
Kolchose [kɔl'çozə] f (-;-n) collective farm
Kolibri ['kolibrɪ] m (-s;-s) humming bird
Kolik ['kolik] f (-;-en) colic
Kolkrabe ['kɔlkrabə] m (-n;-n) raven
Kollaborateur [kɔlabora'tør] m (-s;-) collaborator (with the enemy)
kollaborieren [kɔlabo'rirən] intr collaborate
Kollaps [ko'laps] m (-es;-e) collapse

kollationieren [kɔlatsjo'nirən] tr collate
Kol·leg [ko'lek] n (-s;-s & –legien ['legjən]) lecture; course of lectures; theological college
Kollege [ko'legə] m (-n;-n) colleague
Kolleg'heft n lecture notes
Kollegin [ko'legɪn] f (-;-nen) colleague
Kollekte [ko'lektə] f (-;-n) collection; (eccl) collect
Kollektion [kɔlek'tsjon] f (-;-en) collection
kollektiv [kɔlek'tif] adj collective || **Kollektiv** n (-s;-e) collective
Koller ['kɔlər] m (-s;) rage, temper
kollern ['kɔlərn] ref roll about; (vor Lachen) double over || intr (Puter) gobble; (Magen) rumble || intr (SEIN) roll
kollidieren [kɔlɪ'dirən] intr (SEIN) collide
Kollier [ko'lir] n (-s;-s) necklace
Kollision [kɔlɪ'zjon] f (-;-en) collision
Köln [kœln] n (-s;) Cologne
Kölnischwasser [kœlnɪʃ'vasər] n cologne
kolonial [kolo'njal] adj colonial
Kolonial'waren pl groceries
Kolonial'warengeschäft n grocery store
Kolo·nie [kolo'ni] f (-;-nien ['ni·ən]) colony
Kolonnade [kolo'nadə] f (-;-n) colonnade
Kolonne [ko'lonə] f (-;-n) column; (mil) convoy (of vehicles)
kolorieren [kolo'rirən] tr color
Kolorit [kolo'rit] n (-[e]s;-e) coloring
Ko·loß [ko'los] m (-losses;-losse) colossus; giant
kolossal [kolo'sal] adj colossal
Kolportage [kɔlpor'taʒə] f (-;-n) trashy literature; spreading of rumors
kolportieren [kɔlpor'tirən] tr peddle; (Gerüchte) spread
Kolumnist –in [kɔlum'nɪst(ɪn)] §7 mf columnist
Kombi ['kɔmbi] m (-s;-s) (coll) station wagon
Kombination [kɔmbɪna'tsjon] f (-; -en) combination; (Flieger-) flying suit; (e-s Monteurs) coveralls; sport suit; reasoning, deduction; conjecture
kombinieren [kɔmbɪ'nirən] tr combine || intr reason
Kom'biwagen m station wagon
Kombüse [kɔm'byzə] f (-;-n) (naut) galley, kitchen
Komik ['komɪk] f (-;) humor
Komiker ['komɪkər] m (-s;-) comedian
Komikerin ['komɪkərɪn] f (-;-nen) comedienne
komisch ['komɪʃ] adj funny
Komitee [komɪ'te] n (-s;-s) committee
Komma ['kɔma] n (-s;-s) comma; (Dezimalzeichen) decimal point
Kommandant [kɔman'dant] m (-en; -en) commanding officer; commandant

Kommandantur [kɔmandan'tur] *f* (–; –en) headquarters

Kommandeur [kɔman'dør] *m* (–s;–e) commanding officer, commander

kommandieren [kɔman'dirən] *tr* command, order; be in command of; (mil) detail; (mil) detach || *intr* command, be in command

Kommanditgesellschaft [kɔman'ditgəzel/aft] *f* limited partnership; **K. auf Aktien** partnership limited by shares

Kommando [kɔ'mando] *n* (–s;–s) command, order; (mil) command; (mil) detachment, detail; **K. zurück!** as you were!

Komman′dobrücke *f* (nav) bridge

Komman′doraum *m* control room

Komman′dostab *m* baton

Komman′dostand *m*, **Komman′dostelle** *f* command post; (nav) bridge

Komman′dotruppe *f* commando unit

Komman′doturm *m* conning tower; control tower (*of an aircraft carrier*)

kommen ['kɔmən] §99 *intr* (SEIN) come; (*geschehen*) happen; **auf etw** [*acc*] **k.** hit on s.th.; **auf jeden k. drei Mark** each one gets three marks; **das kommt bloß daher, daß** that's entirely due to; **dazu k.** get around to it; get hold of it; **hinter etw** [*acc*] **k.** find s.th. out; **j–m grob k.** be rude to s.o.; **k. lassen** send for; **nichts k. lassen auf** (*acc*) defend; **so weit k., daß** reach the point where; **ums Leben k.** lose one's life; **wenn Sie mir so k.** if you talk like that to me; **weit k.** get far; **wieder zu sich k.** come to, regain consciousness; **wie kam er denn dazu?** how come he did it? **wie komme ich zum Bahnhof?** how do I get to the train station?

Kommentar [kɔmen'tar] *m* (–s;–e) commentary; **kein K.!** no comment!

Kommen·tator [kɔmen'tator] *m* (–s; –tatoren [ta'torən]) commentator

kommentieren [kɔmen'tirən] *tr* comment on

Kommers [kɔ'mers] *m* (–es;–e) drinking party

Kommers′buch *n* students' song book

kommerziell [kɔmer'tsjel] *adj* commercial

Kommilitone [kɔmili'tonə] *m* (–n;–n) fellow student

Kom·mis [kɔ'mi] *m* (–mis ['mis; –mis ['mis]) clerk

Kom·miß [kɔ'mɪs] *m* (–misses;) (coll) army; (coll) army life

Kommissar [kɔmɪ'sar] *m* (–s;–e) commissioner; (pol) commissar

kommissarisch [kɔmɪ'sarɪʃ] *adj* provisional, temporary

Kommission [kɔmɪ'sjon] *f* (–;–en) commission, board; **in K.** (com) on consignment; **on a commission basis**

Kommissionär [kɔmɪsjə'ner] *m* (–s;–e) agent; wholesale bookseller

Kommissions′gebühr *f* (com) commission

kommissions′weise *adv* on a commission basis

Kommiß′stiefel *m* army boot

kommod [kɔ'mot] *adj* comfortable

Kommode [kɔ'modə] *f* (–;–n) bureau, chest of drawers

kommunal [kɔmu'nɑl] *adj* municipal, local

Kommunal′politik *f* local politics

Kommune [kɔ'munə] *f* (–;–n) municipality; **die K.** the Commies

Kommunikant –in [kɔmunɪ'kant(ɪn)] §7 *mf* communicant

Kommunion [kɔmu'njon] *f* (–;–en) Communion

Kommuniqué [kɔmynɪ'ke] *n* (–s;–s) communiqué

Kommunismus [kɔmu'nɪsmus] *m* (–;) communism

Kommunist –in [kɔmu'nɪst(ɪn)] §7 *mf* communist

kommunistisch [kɔmu'nɪstɪʃ] *adj* communist(ic)

Komödiant [kɔmø'djant] *m* (–en;–en) comedian; (pej) ham

Komödie [kɔ'mødjə] *f* (–;–n) comedy; **K. spielen** (coll) put on an act

Kompagnon [kɔmpan'jõ] *m* (–s;–s) (business) partner; associate

kompakt [kɔm'pakt] *adj* compact

Kompa·nie [kɔmpa'ni] *f* (–;–nien ['ni·ən]) company

Kompanie′chef *m* company commander

komparativ [kɔmpara'tif] *adj* comparative || **Komparativ** *m* (–s;–e) comparative

Komparse [kɔm'parzə] *m* (–n;–n) (theat) extra

Kom·paß ['kɔmpas] *m* (–passes; –passe) compass

Kompen·dium [kɔm'pendjum] *n* (–s; –dien [djən]) compendium

Kompensation [kɔmpenza'tsjon] *f* (–; –en) compensation

Kompensations′geschäft *n* fair-value exchange

kompensieren [kɔmpen'zirən] *tr* compensate for, offset

Kompetenz [kɔmpe'tents] *f* (–;–en) (jur) jurisdiction

komplementär [kɔmplemen'ter] *adj* complementary

Komplet [kɔ'ple] *n* (–s;–s) dress with matching coat

komplett [kɔm'plet] *adj* complete; everything included

komplex [kɔm'pleks] *adj* complex || **Komplex** *m* (–es;–e) complex

Komplice [kɔm'plitsə] *m* (–n;–n) accomplice

komplizieren [kɔmpli'tsirən] *tr* complicate

Komplott [kɔm'plɔt] *n* (–[e]s;–e) plot

Komponente [kɔmpə'nentə] *f* (–;–n) component

komponieren [kɔmpə'nirən] *tr* compose

Komponist –in [kɔmpə'nɪst(ɪn)] §7 *mf* composer

Komposition [kɔmpəzɪ'tsjon] *f* (–;–en) composition

Komposi·tum [kɔm'pozitum] *n* (–s; –ta [ta] & –ten [tən]) compound (word)

Kompott [kɔm'pɔt] *n* (–[e]s;–e) stewed fruit

Kompres·sor [kɔm'presɔr] *m* (**-s;** **-soren** ['soːrən]) compressor; (aut) supercharger

komprimieren [kɔmprɪ'miːrən] *tr* compress

Kompro·miß [kɔmprə'mɪs] *m* (**-mis·ses; -misse**) compromise

kompromittieren [kɔmprɔmɪ'tiːrən] *tr* compromise

kondensieren [kɔndɛn'ziːrən] *tr, ref & intr* (SEIN) condense

Kondensmilch [kɔn'dɛnsmɪlç] *f* evaporated milk

Kondens′streifen [kɔn'dɛns∫traɪfən] *m* contrail

Konditorei [kɔndɪtoˈraɪ] *f* (**-;-en**) pastry shop

Konfekt [kɔn'fɛkt] *n* (**-[e]s;**) candy, chocolates; fancy cookies

Konfektion [kɔnfɛk'tsjoːn] *f* (**-;**) ready-made clothes; manufacture of ready-made clothes

Konfektionär [kɔnfɛktsjə'nɛr] *m* (**-s; -e**) clothing manufacturer; clothing retailer

konfektionieren [kɔnfɛktsjə'niːrən] *tr* manufacture (*clothes*)

Konferenz [kɔnfe'rɛnts] *f* (**-;-en**) conference

konferieren [kɔnfe'riːrən] *intr* confer, hold a conference

Konfession [kɔnfe'sjoːn] *f* (**-;-en**) religious denomination; (eccl) confession; confession of faith, creed

konfessionell [kɔnfɛsjə'nɛl] *adj* denominational

konfessions′los *adj* nondenominational

Konfessions′schule *f* denominational school, parochial school

konfirmieren [kɔnfɪr'miːrən] *tr* (eccl) (Prot) confirm

konfiszieren [kɔnfɪs'tsiːrən] *tr* confiscate

Konfitüre [kɔnfɪ'tyːrə] *f* (**-;-n**) jam

Konflikt [kɔn'flɪkt] *m* (**-[e]s;-e**) conflict

konform [kɔn'fɔrm] *adj* concurring; **mit j-m k. gehen** agree with s.o.

Konfrontation [kɔnfrɔnta'tsjoːn] *f* (**-; -en**) confrontation

konfrontieren [kɔnfrɔn'tiːrən] *tr* confront

konfus [kɔn'fuːs] *adj* confused, puzzled

Kongruenz [kɔngru'ɛnts] *f* (**-;**) (geom) congruence; (gram) agreement

König ['køːnɪç] *m* (**-[e]s;-e**) king

Königin ['køːnɪgɪn] *f* (**-;-nen**) queen

kö′niglich *adj* kingly, royal

Kö′nigreich *n* kingdom

Kö′nigsadler *m* golden eagle

Kö′nigsrose *f* (bot) peony

Kö′nigsschlange *f* boa constrictor

kö′nigstreu *adj* royalist

Kö′nigswürde *f* kingship

Königtum ['køːnɪçtum] *n* (**-s;**) royalty, kinship; monarchy

konisch ['koːnɪ∫] *adj* conical

konjugieren [kɔnju'giːrən] *tr* conjugate

Konjunktion [kɔnjuŋk'tsjoːn] *f* (**-;-en**) conjunction

Konjunktiv ['kɔnjuŋk'tiːf] *m* (**-s;-e**) subjunctive mood

Konjunktur [kɔnjuŋk'tuːr] *f* (**-;-en**) economic situation; business trend; (*Hochstand*) boom

konkav [kɔn'kaːf] *adj* concave

konkret [kɔn'kreːt] *adj* concrete

Konkurrent -in [kɔnku'rɛnt(ɪn)] §7 *mf* competitor

Konkurrenz [kɔnku'rɛnts] *f* (**-;-en**) competition; **K. machen** (dat) compete with

konkurrenz′fähig *adj* competitive

konkurrieren [kɔnku'riːrən] *intr* compete

Konkurs [kɔn'kurs] *m* (**-es;-e**) bankruptcy; **in K. gehen** (or **geraten**) go bankrupt; **K. anmelden** declare bankruptcy

Konkurs′masse *f* bankrupt company's assets

können ['kœnən] §100 *tr* able to do; know; **ich kann nichts dafür** I can't help it ‖ *intr*—**ich kann nicht hinein** I can't get in ‖ *mod aux* be able to; know how to; be allowed; **das kann sein** that may be; **ich kann nicht sehen** I can't see ‖ **Können** *n* (**-s;**) ability

Könner ['kœnər] *m* (**-s;-**) expert

konnte ['kɔntə] *pret* of **können**

konsequent [kɔnze'kvɛnt] *adj* consistent

Konsequenz [kɔnze'kvɛnts] *f* (**-;-en**) consistency; (*Folge*) consequence

konservativ [kɔnzerva'tiːf] *adj* conservative

Konservato·rium [kɔnzerva'toːrjum] *n* (**-s;-rien** [rjən]) conservatory

Konserve [kɔn'zɛrvə] *f* (**-;-n**) canned food

Konser′venbüchse *f*, **Konser′vendose** *f* can

Konser′venfabrik *f* cannery

Konser′venöffner *m* can opener

konservieren [kɔnzɛr'viːrən] *tr* preserve

Konservie′rung *f* (**-;**) preservation

Konsisto·rium [kɔnzɪs'toːrjum] *n* (**-s; -rien** [rjən]) (eccl) consistory

Konsole [kɔn'zoːlə] *f* (**-;-n**) bracket; (archit) console

konsolidieren [kɔnzolɪ'diːrən] *tr* consolidate

Konsonant [kɔnzo'nant] *m* (**-en;-en**) consonant

Konsorte [kɔn'zɔrtə] *m* (**-n;-n**) (pej) accomplice; (fin) member of a syndicate

Konsor·tium [kɔn'zɔrtjum] *n* (**-s;-tien** [tjən]) (fin) syndicate

konstant [kɔn'stant] *adj* constant ‖ **Konstante** §5 *f* (math, phys) constant

konstatieren [kɔnsta'tiːrən] *tr* ascertain; state; (med) diagnose

konsterniert [kɔnster'nirt] *adj* stunned

konstituieren [kɔnstɪtu'iːrən] *tr* constitute ‖ *ref* be established; **sich als Ausschuß k.** form a committee of the whole

konstitutionell [kɔnstɪtutsjə'nɛl] *adj* constitutional

konstruieren [kɔnstru'iːrən] *tr* construct; (*entwerfen*) design; (gram) construe

Konsul ['kɔnzul] *m* (**-s;-n**) consul

konsularisch [kɔnzu'lɑrɪʃ] *adj* consular

Konsulat [kɔnzu'lɑt] *n* (-[e]s;-e) consulate; (hist) consulship

Konsulent -in [kɔnzu'lent(ɪn)] §7 *mf* (jur) counsel

konsultieren [kɔnzul'tirən] *tr* consult

Konsum [kɔn'zum] *m* (-s;-s) cooperative store; (com) consumption

Konsument -in [kɔnzu'ment(ɪn)] §7 *mf* consumer

Konsum'güter *pl* consumer goods

konsumieren [kɔnzu'mirən] *tr* consume

Konsum'verein *m* cooperative society

Kontakt [kɔn'takt] *m* (-[e]s;-e) contact

Kontakt'glas *n*, **Kontakt'schale** *f* contact lens

Konteradmiral ['kɔntəratmɪrɑl] *m* rear admiral

Konterfei [kɔntər'faɪ] *n* (-s;-e) portrait, likeness

kontern ['kɔntərn] *tr* counter

Kontinent ['kɔntɪnənt] *m* (-[e]s;-e) continent

Kontingent [kɔntɪŋ'gent] *n* (-[e]s;-e) quota; (mil) contingent

Kon·to ['kɔnto] *n* (-s;-s & -ten [tən]) account

Kon'toauszug *m* bank statement

Kontor [kɔn'tor] *n* (-s;-e) (com) office

Kontorist -in [kɔnto'rɪst(ɪn)] §7 *mf* clerk (*in an office*)

Kontrahent [kɔntra'hent] *m* (-en;-en) contracting party; dueller

kontrahieren [kɔntra'hirən] *tr & intr* contract

Kontrakt [kɔn'trakt] *m* (-[e]s;-e) contract

Kontrapunkt ['kɔntrapuŋkt] *m* (mus) counterpoint

konträr [kɔn'trer] *adj* contrary

Kontrast [kɔn'trast] *m* (-[e]s;-e) contrast

konstrastieren [kɔntras'tirən] *intr* contrast

Kontrast'regelung *f* (telv) contrast button

Kontroll– [kɔn'trɔl] *comb.fm.* checking; control

Kontroll'abschnitt *m* stub (*of ticket*)

Kontrolle [kɔn'trɔlə] *f* (-;-n) control, check, inspection

Kontrolleur -in [kɔn'trɔ'lør] *m* (-s;-e) inspector, supervisor; (aer) air-traffic controller; (indust) timekeeper

kontrollieren [kɔntrɔ'lirən] *tr* control; check, inspect; (*Bücher*) audit

Kontroll'kasse *f* cash register

Kontroll'leuchte *f* (aut) warning light (*on dashboard*)

Kontroll'turm *m* (aer) control tower

Kontroverse [kɔntra'verzə] *f* (-;-n) controversy

Kontur [kɔn'tur] *f* (-;-en) contour

Konvent [kɔn'vent] *m* (-[e]s;-e) convent; monastery; (*Versammlung*) convention

Konvention [kɔnven'tsjon] *f* (-;-en) convention

konventionell [kɔnventsjɔ'nel] *adj* conventional

Konversation [kɔnverza'tsjon] *f* (-;-en) conversation

Konversations'lexikon *n* encyclopedia; **wandelndes K.** (coll) walking encyclopedia

konvertieren [kɔnver'tirən] *tr* convert || *intr* be converted

Konvertit -in [kɔnver'tit(ɪn)] §7 *mf* convert

konvex [kɔn'veks] *adj* convex

Konvikt [kɔn'vɪkt] *n* (-s;-e) minor seminary

Konvoi ['kɔnvɔɪ] *m* (-s;-s) convoy

Konvolut [kɔnvə'lut] *n* (-[e]s;-e) bundle, roll

Konzentration [kɔntsentra'tsjon] *f* (-;-en) concentration

Konzentrations'lager *n* concentration camp

konzentrieren [kɔntsen'trirən] *tr & ref* (**auf** *acc*) concentrate (*on*)

konzentrisch [kɔn'tsentrɪʃ] *adj* concentric

Konzept [kɔn'tsept] *n* (-[e]s;-e) rough draft; **aus dem K. bringen** confuse, throw off; **aus dem K. kommen** lose one's train of thought

Konzept'papier *n* scribbling paper

Konzern [kɔn'tsern] *m* (-s;-e) (com) combine

Konzert [kɔn'tsert] *n* (-[e]s;-e) concert

Konzert'flügel *m* grand piano

Konzession [kɔntse'sjon] *f* (-;-en) concession; license

konzessionieren [kɔntsesjɔ'nirən] *tr* (com) license

Kon·zil [kɔn'tsil] *n* (-[e]s;-e & -zilien ['tsiljən]) (eccl) council

konziliant [kɔntsɪ'ljant] *adj* conciliatory; understanding

konzipieren [kɔntsɪ'pirən] *tr* conceive

koordiniren [kɔ·ɔrdɪ'nirən] *tr* coordinate

Kopf [kɔpf] *m* (-es;⁻e) head; **aus dem Kopfe** by heart; **j–m über den K. wachsen** be taller than s.o.; (fig) be too much for s.o.; **mit dem K. voran** head first; **seinen eigenen K. haben** have a mind of one's own; **seinen K. lassen müssen** lose one's life

Kopf'bedeckung *f* headgear, head wear

Kopf'brett *n* headboard

köpfen ['kœpfən] *tr* behead; (*Baum*) top; (fb) head

Kopf'ende *n* head (*of bed, etc.*)

Kopf'geld *n* reward (*for capture of criminal*)

Kopf'haut *f* scalp

Kopf'hörer *m* headset, earphones

–köpfig [kœpfɪç] *comb.fm.* –headed; –man

Kopf'kissen *n* pillow

Kopf'kissenbezug *m* pillowcase

kopf'lastig *adj* top-heavy

Kopf'lehne *f* headrest

Kopf'rechnen *n* (-s;) mental arithmetic

Kopf'salat *m* head lettuce

kopf'scheu *adj* (*Pferd*) nervous; (*Person*) shy; **k. werden** become alarmed

Kopf'schmerzen *pl* headache

Kopf'schuppen *pl* dandruff

Kopf'sprung m dive; **e-n K. machen** dive

Kopf'stand m handstand; **e-n K. machen** (aer) nose over

Kopf'stärke f (mil) strength

kopf'stehen §146 intr stand on one's head; (fig) be upside down

Kopf'steinpflaster n cobblestones

Kopf'steuer f poll tax

Kopf'stimme f falsetto

Kopf'stoß m butt; (fb) header

Kopf'tuch n kerchief, babushka

kopfü'ber adv head over heels

kopfun'ter adv—**kopfüber k.** head over heels

Kopf'weh n headache

Kopf'wellenknall m sonic boom

Ko·pie [kə'pi] f (–;-pien ['pi·ən]) copy, duplicate; (phot) print

kopieren [kə'pirən] tr copy; (phot) print

Kopier'maschine f copier, photocopying machine

Kopier'papier n tracing paper; carbon paper; (phot) printing paper

Kopier'stift m indelible pencil

Koppel ['kɔpəl] f (–;-n) leash; (Gehege) enclosure, paddock || n (–;s;–) (mil) belt

koppeln ['kɔpəln] tr tie together, yoke; (fig) tie in; (elec) connect; (rad, rr) couple; (rok) dock || **Koppeln** n (–s;) (aer, naut) dead reckoning; (rok) docking

Kopplungsgeschäft ['kɔpluŋsgəʃɛft] n package deal

Koralle [kə'ralə] f (–;-n) coral

Korb [kɔrp] m (–[e]s;–̈e) basket; **j-m den K. geben** (fig) give s.o. the brush-off

Korb'ball m basketball

Körbchen ['kœrpçən] n (–s;–) little basket; (e-s Büstenhalters) cup

Korb'flasche f demijohn

Korb'geflecht n wickerwork

Korb'möbel pl wicker furniture

Korb'weide f (bot) osier

Kordel ['kɔrdəl] f (–;-n) cord

Kordon [kɔr'dõ] m (–s;-s) cordon; (Ordensband) ribbon

Korea [ko're·a] n (–s;) Korea

koreanisch [kore'aniʃ] adj Korean

Korinthe [ko'rintə] f (–;-n) currant

Kork [kɔrk] m (–[e]s;-e) cork

Korken ['kɔrkən] m (–s;–) cork, stopper

Korkenzieher ['kɔrkəntsi·ər] m (–s;–) corkscrew

Korn [kɔrn] n (–[e]s;–̈er) grain; seed; (am Gewehr) bead; (Getreide) rye; (e-r Münze) fineness; (phot) graininess; **j-n aufs K. nehmen** draw a bead on s.o.

Korn'ähre f ear of grain

Korn'branntwein m whiskey

Kornett [kɔr'net] n (–[e]s;-e) (mus) cornet

körnig ['kœrniç] adj granular

Korn'kammer f granary; (fig) breadbasket

koronar [koro'nar] adj coronary

Körper ['kœrpər] m (–s;–) body; (geom, phys) solid

Kör'perbau m (–[e]s;) build, physique

kör'perbehindert adj physically handicapped

Kör'perbeschaffenheit f constitution

Körperchen ['kœrpərçən] n (–s;–) corpuscle

Kör'perfülle f plumpness, corpulence

Kör'pergeruch m body odor

Kör'perhaltung f posture, bearing

Kör'perkraft f physical strength

kör'perlich adj physical; (stofflich) corporeal

Kör'perpflege f personal hygiene

Kör'perpuder m talcum powder

Kör'perschaft f (–;-en) body (of persons); corporation

Kör'perverletzung f bodily injury

Korporation [kɔrpora'tsjon] f (–;-en) corporation

Korps [kor] n (– [kors];– [kors]) corps

Korps'geist m esprit de corps

Korps'student m member of a fraternity

korrekt [kɔ'rekt] adj correct, proper

Korrek·tor [kɔ'rektor] m (–s;-toren ['toren]) proofreader

Korrektur [kɔrek'tur] f (–;-en) correction; proofreading

Korrektur'bogen m page proof

Korrektur'fahne f galley proof

Korrelat [kɔre'lat] n (–[e]s;-e) correlative

Korrespondent –in [kɔrespɔn'dent(in)] §7 mf correspondent

Korrespondenz [kɔrespɔn'dents] f (–;-en) correspondence

Korrespondenz'karte f (Aust) postcard

Korridor ['kɔridor] m (–s;-e) corridor

korrigieren [kɔri'girən] tr correct

korrodieren [kɔro'dirən] tr & intr corrode

Korse ['kɔrzə] m (–n;-n) Corsican

Korsett [kɔr'zet] n (–[e]s;-e & –s) corset

Korsika ['kɔrzika] n (–s;) Corsica

Korvette [kɔr'vetə] f (–;-n) corvette

Kosak [ko'zak] m (–en;-en) Cossack

K.-o.-Schlag [ka'o'ʃlak] m knockout punch

kosen ['kozən] tr fondle, caress

Kosename ['kozənamə] m pet name

Kosmetik [kɔs'metik] f (–;) beauty treatment; **chirurgische K.** cosmetic surgery, plastic surgery

Kosme'tikartikel m cosmetic

Kosmeti·kum [kɔs'metikum] n (–s;-ka [ka]) cosmetic

kosmisch ['kɔzmiʃ] adj cosmic

kosmopolitisch [kɔsmopo'litiʃ] adj cosmopolitan

Kosmos ['kɔsmos] m (–;) cosmos

Kost [kɔst] f (–;) food, board

kostbar ['kɔstbar] adj valuable; costly

Kost'barkeit f (–;-en) costliness; (fig) precious thing

kosten ['kɔstən] tr cost; taste, sip || **Kosten** pl costs; **auf K.** (genii) at the expense of; **auf seine K. kommen** get one's money's worth; **sich in K. stürzen** go to great expense

Ko'stenanschlag m estimate

Ko'stenaufwand m expenditure, outlay

Ko'stenberechnung f cost accounting

Ko'stenersatz *m*, **Ko'stenerstattung** *f* reimbursement of expenses
ko'stenlos *adj* free of charge
Ko'stenvoranschlag *m* estimate
Kost'gänger –in §6 *mf* boarder
köstlich ['kœstlɪç] *adj* delicious; delightful || *adv*—**sich k. amüsieren** have a grand time
Kost'probe *f* sample (*to taste*)
kostspielig ['kɔst/piːlɪç] *adj* expensive
Kostüm [kɔs'tyːm] *n* (**–s;–e**) costume; woman's suit; fancy dress
kostümieren [kɔsty'miːrən] *tr & ref* dress up
Kostüm'probe *f* dress rehearsal
Kot [kot] *m* (**–[e]s;**) mud, dirt; (*tierischer*) dirt, dung; excrement
Kotelett [kɔtə'lɛt] *n* (**–[e]s;–e & –s**) pork chop; cutlet
Köter ['køːtər] *m* (**–s;–**) mut, mongrel
Kot'flügel *m* (aut) fender
kotig ['kotɪç] *adj* muddy, dirty
kotzen ['kɔtsən] *intr* (sl) puke || **Kotzen** *n*—**es ist zum K.** it's enough to make you throw up
Krabbe ['krabə] *f* (**–;–n**) crab; shrimp; (*niedliches Kind*) little darling
krabbeln ['krabəln] *tr & intr* tickle || *intr* (SEIN) crawl
Krach [krax] *m* (**–[e]s;–s & –e**) crash, bang; (*Lärm*) racket; (*Streit*) row; (fin) crash; **K. machen** kick up a row
krachen ['kraxən] *intr* crash, crack
krächzen ['krɛçtsən] *intr* croak, caw
kraft [kraft] *prep* (*genit*) by virtue of || **Kraft** *f* (**–;–e**) strength, power, force; **außer K. setzen** repeal; **in K. sein** be in force; **in K. treten** come into force
Kraft'anlage *f* (elec) power plant
Kraft'anstrengung *f* strenuous effort
Kraft'aufwand *m* effort
Kraft'ausdruck *m* swear word; **Kraftausdrücke** strong language
Kraft'brühe *f* concentrated broth
Kraft'fahrer –in §6 *mf* motorist
Kraft'fahrzeug *n* motor vehicle
kräftig ['krɛftɪç] *adj* strong, powerful; (*Speise*) nutritious || *adv* hard; heartily
kräftigen ['krɛftɪgən] *tr* strengthen
Kraft'leistung *f* feat of strength
kraft'los *adj* powerless; weak
Kraft'meier *m* (coll) bully; (coll) muscle man
Kraft'probe *f* test of strength
Kraft'protz *m* (coll) powerhouse
Kraft'rad *n* motorcycle
Kraft'stoff *m* fuel
Kraft'stoffleitung *f* fuel line
kraftstrotzend ['kraft/trɔtsənt] *adj* strapping
Kraft'übertragung *f* (aut) transmission
Kraft'wagen *m* motor vehicle
Kraft'werk *n* generating plant
Kraft'wort *n* (**–[e]s;–er**) swear word
Kragen ['kraːgən] *m* (**–s;–**) collar
Krähe ['krɛːə] *f* (**–;–n**) crow
krähen ['krɛːən] *intr* crow
Krähenfüße ['krɛːənfyːsə] *pl* crow's feet (*wrinkles*)
Krakeel [kra'keːl] *m* (**–s;–e**) (coll) rumpus; (*lauter Streit*) brawl

krakeelen [kra'keːlən] *intr* (coll) kick up a storm
Kralle ['kralə] *f* (**–;–n**) claw
Kram [kraːm] *m* (**–[e]s;**) (coll) things, stuff; (coll) business, affairs
kramen ['kraːmən] *intr* rummage
Krämer –in ['krɛːmər(ɪn)] §6 *mf* shopkeeper || *m* (pej) philistine
Krä'merseele *f* philistine
Kram'laden *m* general store
Krampe ['krampə] *f* (**–;–n**) staple
Krampf [krampf] *m* (**–[e]s;–e**) cramp, spasm; convulsion; (*Unsinn*) nonsense
Krampf'ader *f* varicose vein
krampf'artig *adj* spasmodic
krampf'haft *adj* convulsive
Kran [kraːn] *m* (**–[e]s;–e & –e**) (mach) crane
Kranich ['kraːnɪç] *m* (**–s;–e**) (orn) crane
krank [kraŋk] *adj* sick, ill || **Kranke** §5 *mf* patient
–krank *comb.fm.* suffering from
kränkeln ['krɛŋkəln] *intr* be sickly
kranken ['kraŋkən] *intr*—**k. an** (*dat*) suffer from
kränken ['krɛŋkən] *tr* hurt, offend || *ref* (*über acc*) feel hurt (at)
Kran'kenanstalt *f* hospital
Kran'kenbahre *f* stretcher
Kran'kenbett *n* sickbed
Kran'kenfahrstuhl *m* wheel chair
Kran'kengeld *n* sick benefit
Kran'kenhaus *n* hospital; **ins K. einweisen** hospitalize
Kran'kenkasse *f* medical insurance plan
Kran'kenlager *n* sickbed
Kran'kenpflege *f* nursing
Kran'kenpfleger –in §6 *mf* nurse
Kran'kenrevier *n* (mil) sick quarters; (nav) sick bay
Kran'kensaal *m* hospital ward
Kran'kenschwester *f* nurse
Kran'kenstube *f* infirmary
Kran'kenstuhl *m* wheel chair
Kran'kenurlaub *m* sick leave
Kran'kenversicherung *f* health insurance
Kran'kenwagen *m* ambulance
krank'feiern *intr* (coll) play sick
krank'haft *adj* morbid, pathological
Krank'heit *f* (**–;–en**) sickness, disease
Krank'heitsbericht *m* medical bulletin
Krank'heitserscheinung *f* symptom
kränklich ['krɛŋklɪç] *adj* sickly
Kränk'lichkeit *f* (**–;**) poor health
Kränkung ['krɛŋkʊŋ] *f* (**–;–en**) offense
Kran'wagen *m* (aut) wrecker, tow truck
Kranz [krants] *m* (**–[e]s;–e**) wreath
Kränzchen ['krɛntsçən] *n* (**–s;–**) small wreath; ladies' circle; informal dance
kränzen ['krɛntsən] *tr* wreathe
Krapfen ['krapfən] *m* (**–s;–**) doughnut
kraß [kras] *adj* crass, gross
Krater ['kraːtər] *m* (**–s;–**) crater
Kratzbürste ['kratsbyrstə] *f* wire brush; (fig) stand-offish woman
Krätze ['krɛtsə] *f* (**–;**) itch, scabies
kratzen ['kratsən] *tr & intr* scratch
Krat'zer *m* (**–s;–**) scratch; scraper

krauen ['krau·ən] *tr* scratch gently
kraus [kraus] *adj* (*Haar*) frizzy; (*Gedanken*) confused; **die Stirn k. ziehen** knit one's brows
Krause ['krauzə] *f* (–;–n) ruffle
kräuseln ['krɔɪzəln] *tr & ref* curl
Krau'seminze *f* (bot) spearmint
Kraus'haar *n* frizz
Kraut [kraut] *n* (–[e]s;–er) herb, plant; leafy top; (*Kohl*) cabbage; **ins K. schießen** run wild
Krawall [kra'val] *m* (–[e]s;–e) riot; (coll) rumpus
Krawatte [kra'vatə] *f* (–;–n) necktie
Krawat'tenhalter *m* tie clip
kraxeln ['kraksəln] *intr* (SEIN) climb
Kreatur [kre·a'tur] *f* (–;–en) creature
Krebs [kreps] *m* (–es;–e) crawfish, crab; (pathol) cancer
krebs'artig *adj* (pathol) cancerous
Kredenz [kre'dɛnts] *f* (–;–en) buffet, credenza, sideboard
kredenzen [kre'dɛntsən] *tr* (*Wein*) serve
Kredit [kre'dit] *m* (–[e]s;–e) credit
Kredit'bank *f* commercial bank
kreditieren [kredɪ'tirən] *tr* credit || *intr* give credit
Kredit'karte *f* credit card
Kredit'würdigkeit *f* trustworthiness; (com) credit rating
Kreide ['kraɪdə] *f* (–;–n) chalk, piece of chalk, crayon
kreieren [kre'irən] *tr* create
Kreis [kraɪs] *m* (–es;–e) circle; (*Bereich*) field; (*Bezirk*) district; (adm) county; (elec) circuit
Kreis'abschnitt *m* segment
Kreis'amt *n* district office
Kreis'ausschnitt *m* sector
Kreis'bahn *f* orbit
Kreis'bogen *m* (geom) arc
kreischen ['kraɪ̯ən] *intr* shriek
Kreisel ['kraɪzəl] *m* (–s;–) gyroscope; top (toy)
Krei'selbewegung *f* gyration
Krei'selhorizont *m* artificial horizon
kreiseln ['kraɪzəln] *intr* spin, rotate, gyrate; spin the top
Krei'selpumpe *f* centrifugal pump
kreisen ['kraɪzən] *intr* circle; revolve; (*Blut*) circulate
kreis'förmig *adj* circular
Kreis'lauf *m* circulation; cycle
Kreis'laufstörung *f* circulatory disorder
kreis'rund *adj* circular
Kreis'säge *f* circular saw, buzz saw
kreißen ['kraɪsən] *intr* be in labor
Kreißsaal ['kraɪsʒal] *m* delivery room
Kreis'stadt *f* (rural) county seat
Kreis'umfang *m* circumference
Kreis'verkehr *m* traffic circle
Krem [krem] *f* (–;–s) & *m* (–s;–s) cream
Kreml ['kreməl] *m* (–[e]s;) Kremlin
Krempe ['krempə] *f* (–;–n) brim, rim
Krempel ['krempəl] *m* (–s;) (coll) stuff, junk || *f* (–;–n) (tex) card
Kren [kren] *m* (–[e]s;) horseradish
krepieren [kre'pirən] *intr* (SEIN) (*Tiere*) die; (*Granate*) explode, burst; (sl) kick the bucket

Krepp [krep] *m* (–s;–s) crepe
Kreta ['kreta] *n* (–s;) Crete
Kretonne [kre'tɔnə] *f* (–;–n) cretonne
kreuz [krɔɪts] *adv*—**k. und quer** crisscross || **Kreuz** *n* (–es;–e) cross; (anat) small of the back; (cards) club(s)
Kreuz'abnahme *f* deposition
Kreuz'band *n* (–[e]s;–er) mailing wrapper (*for newspapers, etc.*)
kreuz'brav' *adj* (coll) very honest; (coll) very well-behaved
kreuzen ['krɔɪtsən] *tr* cross || *recip* cross; interbreed || *intr* cruise
Kreuzer ['krɔɪtsər] *m* (–s;–) penny; (nav) cruiser
Kreuz'fahrer *m* crusader
Kreuz'fahrt *f* cruise; (hist) crusade
Kreuz'feuer *n* crossfire
kreuz'fidel' *adj* very cheerful
Kreuz'gang *m* (archi) cloister(s)
kreuzigen ['krɔɪtsɪgən] *tr* crucify
Kreu'zigung *f* (–;–en) crucifixion
Kreuz'otter *f* adder
Kreuz'ritter *m* crusader; Knight of the Teutonic Order
Kreuz'schiff *n* transept (*of church*)
Kreuz'schlitzschraubenzieher *m* Phillips screwdriver
Kreu'zung *f* (–;–en) intersection; cross-breeding; hybrid; (rr) crossing
Kreuz'verhör *n* cross-examination; **j-n ins K. nehmen** cross-examine s.o.
Kreuz'verweis *m* cross reference
Kreuz'weg *m* crossroad; (eccl) stations of the cross
Kreuz'worträtsel *n* crossword puzzle
Kreuz'zeichen *n* (eccl) sign of the cross; (typ) dagger
Kreuz'zug *m* crusade
kribbelig ['krɪbəlɪç] *adj* irritable; (nervös) edgy, on edge
kribbeln ['krɪbəln] *intr* tickle
kriechen ['kriçən] §102 *intr* (SEIN) creep, crawl
kriecherisch ['kriçərɪʃ] *adj* fawning
Kriechtier ['kriçtir] *n* reptile
Krieg [krik] *m* (–[e]s;–e) war
kriegen ['krigən] *tr* (coll) get, catch
Krie'ger *m* (–s;–) warrior
kriegerisch ['krigərɪʃ] *adj* warlike; (*Person*) belligerent
krieg'führend *adj* warring
Kriegs'akademie *f* war college
Kriegs'bemalung *f* war paint
Kriegs'berichter *m*, **Kriegs'berichterstatter** *m* war correspondent
Kriegs'dienst *m* military service
Kriegs'dienstverweigerer *m* conscientious objector
Kriegs'einsatz *m* (mil) action
Kriegs'entschädigung *f* reparations
Kriegs'fall *m*—**im K.** in case of war
Kriegs'flotte *f* fleet; naval force
Kriegs'fuß *m*—**mit j-m auf K. stehen** be at loggerheads with s.o.
Kriegs'gebiet *n* war zone
Kriegs'gefangene §5 *mf* prisoner of war
Kriegs'gericht *n* court martial
Kriegsgewinnler ['kriksgəvɪnlər] *m* (–s;–) war profiteer
Kriegs'hafen *m* naval base
Kriegs'hetzer *m* warmonger

Kriegs′kamerad m fellow soldier
Kriegs′lazarett n base hospital
Kriegs′list f stratagem
Kriegs′marine f navy
Kriegs′ministerium n war department
Kriegs′opfer n war victim
Kriegs′pfad m warpath
Kriegs′rat m council of war
Kriegs′recht n martial law
Kriegs′rüstung f arming for war; war production
Kriegs′schauplatz m theater of war
Kriegs′schuld f war debt; war guilt
Kriegs′teilnehmer m combatant; (*ehemaliger*) ex-serviceman, veteran
Kriegs′verbrechen n war crime
Kriegs′versehrte §5 m disabled veteran
kriegs′verwendungsfähig adj fit for active duty
Kriegs′wesen n warfare, war
Kriegs′zug m (mil) campaign
Kriegs′zustand m state of war
Krim [krɪm] f (–;) Crimea
Krimi [′krimi] m (–s;–s) & (–;–) (coll) murder mystery; (telv) thriller
kriminal [krɪmɪ′nɑl] adj criminal
Kriminal– comb.fm. criminal, crime
Kriminal′beamte m criminal investigator
Kriminal′roman m detective novel
Kriminal′stück n (telv) thriller
kriminell [krɪmɪ′nɛl] adj criminal ||
Kriminelle §5 mf criminal
Krimskrams [′krɪmskrams] m (–es;) (coll) junk
Kripo [′kripo] abbr (**Kriminalpolizei**) crime squad
Krippe [′krɪpə] f (–;–n) crib, manger; day nursery (*for infants up to 3 years*)
Krise [′krizə] f (–;–n) crisis
kriseln [′krizəln] impers—es **kriselt** there's a crisis, trouble is brewing
Kristall [krɪs′tal] m (–s;–e) crystal
Kristalleuchter (**Kristall′leuchter**) m crystal chandelier
Kristall′glas n crystal
kristallisieren [krɪstalɪ′zirən] ref & intr crystallize
Kristall′zucker m granulated sugar
Krite·rium [krɪ′terjum] n (–s;–rien [rjən]) criterion
Kritik [krɪ′tik] f (–;–en) criticism; critique; **unter aller K.** abominable
Kritikaster [krɪtɪ′kastər] m (–s;–) (pej) faultfinder
Kritiker –in [′kritikər(ɪn)] §6 mf critic; reviewer
kritik′los adj uncritical
kritisch [′kritɪʃ] adj critical
kritisieren [krɪtɪ′zirən] tr criticize; (*werten*) review
Krittelei [krɪtə′laɪ] f (–;–en) faultfinding; petty criticism
kritteln [′krɪtəln] intr (**an** dat) find fault (with), grumble (about)
Kritzelei [krɪtsə′laɪ] f (–;–en) scribbling, scrawling; scribble, scrawl
kritzeln [′krɪtsəln] tr & intr scribble
kroch [krɔx] pret of **kriechen**
Krokodil [krokə′dil] n (–[e]s;–e) crocodile
Krokus [′krokʊs] m (–;– & –se) crocus

Krone [′kronə] f (–;–n) crown
krönen [′krønən] tr crown
Kronerbe [′kronɛrbə] m, **Kronerbin** [′kronɛrbɪn] f heir apparent
Kronleuchter [′kronlɔɪçtər] m chandelier
Kronprinz [′kronprɪnts] m crown prince
Kronprinzessin [′kronprɪntsɛsɪn] f crown princess
Krö′nung f (–;–en) coronation
Kropf [krɔpf] m (–[e]s;–e) crop (*of bird*); (pathol) goiter
Kröte [′krøtə] f (–;–n) toad; **Kröten** (coll) coins, coppers
Krücke [′krʏkə] f (–;–n) crutch
Krückstock [′krʏkʃtɔk] m walking stick
Krug [kruk] m (–[e]s;–e) jar, jug; mug; pitcher; (*Wirtshaus*) tavern
Krume [′krumə] f (–;–n) crumb; topsoil
Krümel [′kryməl] m (–s;–) crumb
krümeln [′kryməln] tr & intr crumble
krumm [krum] adj (**krummer** & **krümmer** [′krʏmər]; **krummste** & **krümmste** [′krʏmstə] §9) bent, stooping; crooked
krumm′beinig adj bowlegged
krümmen [′krʏmən] tr bend, curve || ref (*vor Schmerzen*) writhe; (*vor Lachen*) double up; (*Wurm*) wriggle; (*Holz*) warp; (*Fluß, Straße*) wind
Krümmer [′krʏmər] m (–s;–) (tech) elbow
krumm′nehmen §116 tr (coll) take the wrong way, take amiss
Krumm′stab m (eccl) crozier
Krüm′mung f (–;–en) bend, curve; winding
krumpeln [′krumpəln] tr & intr (coll) crumple, crease
Krüppel [′krʏpəl] m (–s;–) cripple; **zum K. machen** cripple
krüp′pelhaft adj deformed
krüp′pelig adj crippled; stunted
Kruste [′krustə] f (–;–n) crust
Kru′stentier n crustacean
krustig [′krustɪç] adj crusty
Kruzifix [krutsɪ′fɪks] n (–es;–e) crucifix
Kryp·ta [′krypta] f (–;–ten [tən]) crypt
Kübel [′kybəl] m (–s;–) tub; bucket
Kü′belwagen m jeep
kubieren [ku′birən] tr (math) cube
Kubik– [kubik] comb.fm. cubic
Kubik′maß n cubic measure
kubisch [′kubɪʃ] adj cubic
Kubismus [ku′bismus] m (–;) cubism
Küche [′kʏçə] f (–;–n) kitchen; (culin) cuisine
Kuchen [′kuxən] m (–s;–) cake, pie
Ku′chenblech n cookie sheet
Küchenchef m chef
Kü′chendienst m (mil) K.P.
Ku′chenform f cake pan
Kü′chengerät n kitchen utensil
Kü′chengeschirr n kitchen utensils
Kü′chenherd m kitchen range, stove
Kü′chenmaschine f electric kitchen appliance
Kü′chenmeister m chef

Kü'chenzettel *m* menu
Küchlein ['kyçlaın] *n* (-s;-) chick; (culin) small cake
Kuckuck ['kukuk] *m* (-s;-e) cuckoo; **zum K. gehen** (coll) go to hell
Kufe ['kufə] *f* (-;-n) vat; (*Schlitten-*) runner
Küfer ['kyfər] *m* (-s;-) cooper
Kugel ['kugəl] *f* (-;-n) ball; sphere; (*Geschoß*) bullet; (sport) shot
ku'gelfest *adj* bulletproof
ku'gelförmig *adj* spherical
Ku'gelgelenk *n* (mach) ball-and-socket joint; (anat) socket joint
Ku'gellager *n* ball bearing
kugeln ['kugəln] *tr* roll || *ref* roll around; **sich vor Lachen k.** double over with laughter || *intr* (SEIN) roll
Ku'gelregen *m* hail of bullets
ku'gelrund *adj* round; (coll) tubby
Ku'gelschreiber *m* ball-point pen
Ku'gelstoßen *n* (sport) shot put
Kuh [ku] *f* (-;-e) cow
Kuh'dorf *n* hick town
Kuh'fladen *m* cow dung
Kuh'handel *m* (pol) horse trading
Kuh'haut *f* cowhide; **das geht auf keine K.** but that's a long story
kühl [kyl] *adj* cool
Kühl'anlage *f* refrigerator; cooling system; cold storage (room)
Kühle ['kylə] *f* (-;) cool, coolness
kühlen ['kylən] *tr* cool; (*Wein*) chill
Küh'ler *m* (-s;-) cooler; (aut) radiator
Küh'lerverschluß *m* radiator cap
Kühl'mittel *n* coolant
Kühl'schrank *m* refrigerator
Kühl'truhe *f* freezer
Kühl'wagen *m* refrigerator truck; (rr) refrigerator car
Kuh'magd *f* milkmaid
Kuh'mist *m* cow dung
kühn [kyn] *adj* bold, daring
Kühn'heit *f* (-;) boldness, daring
Kuhpocken ['kupɔkən] *pl* cowpox
Kuh'stall *m* cowshed, cow barn
Kujon [ku'jon] *m* (-s;-e) (pej) louse
kujonieren [kujo'nirən] *tr* bully
Küken ['kykən] *n* (-s;-) chick
Kukuruz ['kukuruts] *m* (-es;) (Aust) corn
kulant [ku'lant] *adj* obliging; generous
Kuli ['kulı] *m* (-s;-s) coolie
kulinarisch [kulı'narıʃ] *adj* culinary
Kulisse [ku'lısə] *f* (-;-n) (theat) wing; **hinter den Kulissen** behind the scenes; **Kulissen** scenery
Kulis'senfieber *n* stage fright
kullern ['kulərn] *intr* (SEIN) roll
kulminieren [kulmı'nirən] *intr* culminate
Kult [kult] *m* (-[e]s;-e) cult
kultivieren [kultı'virən] *tr* cultivate
Kultur [kul'tur] *f* (-;-en) culture, civilization; (agr) cultivation; (bact, chem) culture
Kultur'austausch *m* cultural exchange
kulturell [kultu'rel] *adj* cultural
Kultur'erbe *n* cultural heritage
Kultur'film *m* educational film
Kultur'geschichte *f* history of civilization; cultural history
Kultur'volk *n* civilized people

Kul·tus ['kultus] *m* (-;-te [tə]) cult
Kümmel ['kyməl] *m* (-s;-) caraway seed; caraway brandy
Küm'melbrot *n* seeded rye bread
Kummer ['kumər] *m* (-s) grief, sorrow; worry, concern, trouble; **j-m großen K. bereiten** cause s.o. a lot of worry; **sich** [*dat*] **K. machen über** (*acc*) worry about
kümmerlich ['kymərlıç] *adj* wretched; (*dürftig*) needy
Kümmerling ['kymərlıŋ] *m* (-s;-e) stunted animal; stunted plant
kümmern ['kymərn] *tr* trouble, worry; concern || *ref*—**sich k. um** worry about; take care of; **sich nicht k. um** not bother about; neglect
Kümmernis ['kymərnıs] *f* (-;-se) worry, trouble
kum'mervoll *adj* grief-stricken
Kumpan [kum'pan] *m* (-s;-e) companion; buddy
Kumpel ['kumpəl] *m* (-s;-) buddy, sidekick; (min) miner
kund [kunt] *adj* known
kündbar ['kyntbar] *adj* (*Vertrag*) terminable; (fin) redeemable
Kunde ['kundə] *m* (-n;-n) customer; **übler K.** (fig) tough customer || *f* (-;) news, information; lore
–**kunde** *f* *comb.fm.* –ology; –graphy; science of; guide to, study of
Kun'dendienst *m* customer service; warranty service
Kun'denkreis *m* clientele
kund'geben §80 *tr* make known, announce
Kundgebung ['kuntgebuŋ] *f* (-;-en) manifestation; (pol) rally
kundig ['kundıç] *adj* well-informed; **k. sein** (genit) know
–**kundig** *comb.fm.* well versed in; able to
kündigen ['kyndıgən] *tr* (*Vertrag*) give notice to terminate; (*Wohnung*) give notice to vacate; (*Stellung*) give notice of quitting; (*Kapital*) call in; (*Hypothek*) foreclose on; **j-n fristlos k.** (coll) sack s.o. || *intr* (*dat*) given notice to, release
Kün'digung *f* (-;-en) (*seitens des Arbeitnehmers*) resignation; (*seitens des Arbeitgebers*) notice (*of termination*); **mit monatlicher K.** subject to a month's notice
Kün'digungsfrist *f* period of notice
kund'machen *tr* make known, announce
Kund'machung *f* (-;-en) announcement
Kund'schaft *f* (-;) clientele, customer(s); (mil) reconnaissance
kundschaften ['kunt/aftən] *intr* go on reconnaissance, scout
Kund'schafter *m* (-s;-) scout, spy
kund'tun §154 *tr* make known, announce
kund'werden §159 *intr* (SEIN) become known
künftig ['kynftıç] *adj* future, to come, next || *adv* in the future, from now on
künf'tighin' *adv* from now on, hereafter

Kunst [kʊnst] *f* (-;-ᵉe) art; skill; **das ist keine K.** it's easy
Kunstbanause ['kʊnstbanauzə] *m* (-n; -n) philistine
Kunst′dünger *m* chemical fertilizer
Künstelei [kynstə'lai] *f* (-;-en) affectation
Kunst′faser *f* synthetic fiber
Kunst′fehler *m*—ärztlicher **K.** malpractice
kunst′fertig *adj* skillful, skilled
Kunst′flieger *m* stunt pilot
Kunst′flug *m* stunt flying
Kunst′freund –in §8 *mf* art lover; patron of the arts
Kunst′gegenstand *m* objet d'art
kunst′gerecht *adj* skillful; expert
Kunst′gewerbe *n* arts and crafts
Kunst′glied *n* artificial limb
Kunst′griff *m* trick
Kunst′händler –in §6 *mf* art dealer
Kunst′kenner –in §6 *mf* art connoisseur
Kunst′laufen *n* figure skating
Künstler –in ['kynstlər(ɪn)] §6 *mf* artist; performer
künstlerisch ['kynstlərɪʃ] *adj* artistic
künstlich ['kynstlɪç] *adj* artificial; (chem) synthetic
Kunst′liebhaber –in §6 *mf* art lover
kunst′los *adj* unaffected
Kunst′maler –in §6 *mf* painter, artist
Kunst′pause *f* pause for effect
kunst′reich *adj* ingenious
Kunst′reiter *m* equestrian
Kunst′seide *f* rayon
Kunst′springen *n* (sport) diving
Kunst′stoff *m* plastic material; synthetic material; (tex) synthetic fiber
Kunststoff– *comb.fm.* plastic; plastics
Kunst′stopfen *n* invisible mending
Kunst′stück *n* trick, feat
Kunst′tischler *m* cabinet maker
Kunstverständige ['kunstfer/tendɪgə] §5 *mf* art expert
kunst′voll *adj* elaborate, ornate
Kunst′werk *n* work of art
kunterbunt ['kʊntərbʊnt] *adj* chaotic
Kupfer ['kʊpfər] *n* (-s;) copper
kupfern ['kʊpfərn] *adj* copper
kupieren [ku'piːrən] *tr* (Schwanz, Ohren) cut off; (Spielkarten) cut; (Fahrkarten) punch
Kuppe ['kʊpə] *f* (-;-n) top, summit
Kuppel ['kʊpəl] *f* (-;-n) cupola
Kuppelei [kʊpə'lai] *f* (-;) procuring
kuppeln ['kʊpəln] *tr* couple, connect ‖ *intr* be a pimp; be a procuress; (aut) operate the clutch
Kuppler ['kʊplər] *m* (-s;-) pimp
Kupplerin ['kʊplərɪn] *f* (-;-nen) procuress
Kupplung ['kʊplʊŋ] *f* (-;-en) (aut) clutch; (rr) coupling
Kur [kur] *f* (-;-en) cure (at a spa); **j–n in die Kur nehmen** give s.o. a talking to
Kuratel [kura'tel] *f* (-;) guardianship; **j–n unter K. stellen** appoint a guardian for s.o.
Ku·rator [ku'rator] *m* (-s;-ratoren [ra'toren]) (e–s Museums) curator; (educ) trustee; (jur) guardian

Kurato·rium [kura'torjʊm] *n* (-s;-rien [rjən]) (educ) board of trustees
Kurbel ['kʊrbəl] *f* (-;-n) crank, handle, winch
Kurbelei [kʊrbə'lai] *f* (-;-en) shooting a film; (aer) dogfight
Kur′belgehäuse *n* (aut) crankcase
kurbeln ['kʊrbəln] *tr* crank; (Film) shoot ‖ *intr* engage in a dogfight
Kur′belstange *f* (mach) connecting rod
Kur′belwelle *f* (mach) crankshaft
Kürbis ['kyrbɪs] *m* (-ses;-se) pumpkin; (Kopf) (sl) bean
küren ['kyrən] §165 & §109 *tr* elect
Kurfürst ['kurfyrst] *m* (-en;-en) elector (of the Holy Roman Empire)
Kur′haus *n* spa; hotel
Kurie ['kurjə] *f* (-;-n) (eccl) curia
Kurier [ku'rir] *m* (-s;-e) courier
kurieren [ku'rirən] *tr* cure
kurios [ku'rjos] *adj* odd, curious
Kuriosität [kurjozi'tet] *f* (-;-en) quaintness; curio, curiosity
Kur′ort *m* health resort, spa
Kurpfuscher ['kurpfuʃər] *m* (-s;-) quack
Kurrentschrift [ku'rɛnt/rɪft] *f* cursive script
Kurs [kurs] *m* (-es;-e) (educ) course; (fin) rate of exchange; (fin) circulation; (naut) course; (st. exch.) price; **außer K. setzen** take out of circulation; **hoch im K. stehen** be at a premium; (fig) rate high; **zum Kurse von** at the rate of
Kurs′bericht *m* (st. exch.) market report
Kurs′buch *n* (rr) timetable
Kürschner ['kyr/nər] *m* (-s;-) furrier
Kurs′entwicklung *f* price trend
Kurs′gewinn *m* (st. exch.) gain
kursieren [kur'ziːrən] *intr* circulate
Kursive [kur'zivə] *f* (-;), **Kursivschrift** [kur'zif/rɪft] *f* (-;) italics
Kurs′stand *m* (st. exch.) price level
Kur·sus ['kurzʊs] *m* (-;-se [zə]) (educ) course
Kurs′veränderung *f* (fin) change in exchange rates; (naut) change of course; (pol) change of policy; (st. exch.) price change
Kurs′wert *m* (st. exch.) market value
Kurve ['kurvə] *f* (-;-n) curve; **in die K. gehen** (aer) bank
kurz [kurts] *adj* (kürzer ['kyrtsər]; kürzeste ['kyrtsəstə] §9) short, brief; **auf das kürzeste** very briefly; **binnen kurzem** within a short time; **in kurzem** before long; **k. und gut in a word**; **seit kurzem** for the last few days or weeks; **über k. oder lang** sooner or later; **zu k. kommen** (coll) get the short end of it ‖ *adv* shortly; briefly; curtly
kurzatmig ['kurtsatmɪç] *adj* short-winded; (Pferd) broken-winded
Kürze ['kyrtsə] *f* (-;) shortness; brevity; **in K.** shortly; briefly
kürzen ['kyrtsən] *tr* shorten; (Gehalt) cut; (math) reduce
kurzerhand′ *adv* offhand
Kurz′fassung *f* abridged version
Kurz′film *m* (cin) short

kurzfristig [ˈkurtsfrɪstɪç] *adj* short-term

Kurz′geschichte *f* short story

kurzlebig [ˈkurtslebɪç] *adj* short-lived

kürzlich [ˈkyrtslɪç] *adj* lately, recently

Kurz′meldung *f* news flash

Kurz′nachrichten *pl* news summary

kurz′schließen §76 *tr* short-circuit

Kurz′schluß *m* short circuit

Kurz′schlußbrücke *f* (elec) jumper

Kurz′schrift *f* shorthand

kurz′sichtig *adj* near-sighted; (fig) short-sighted

Kurz′streckenlauf *m* sprint

Kurz′streckenläufer –in §6 *mf* sprinter

kurzum′ *adv* in short, in a word

Kür′zung *f* (–;–en) reduction; curtailment; (*e–s Buches*) abridgment

Kurz′waren *pl* sewing supplies

kurz′weg *adv* bluntly, flatly

Kurzweil [ˈkurtsvaɪl] *f* (–;) pastime

kurzweilig [ˈkurtsvaɪlɪç] *adj* amusing

kusch [kuʃ] *interj* lie down! (*to a dog*)

kuschen [ˈkuʃən] *ref* lie down; crouch || *intr* lie down; crouch, cringe; (*Person*) knuckle under, submit

Kusine [kuˈzinə] *f* (–;–n) female cousin

Kuß [kus] *m* (**Kusses; Küsse**) kiss; **kalter K.** popsicle

küssen [ˈkysən] *tr & intr* kiss

Kuß′hand *f*—**j–m e–e K. zuwerfen** throw s.o. a kiss; **mit K.** with pleasure

Küste [ˈkystə] *f* (–;–n) coast, shore

Kü′stenfahrer *m* coasting vessel

Kü′stenfischerei *f* inshore fishing

Kü′stengewässer *n* coastal waters

Kü′stenlinie *f* coastline, shoreline

kü′stennah *adj* offshore; coastal

Kü′stenschiffahrt *f* coastal shipping

Kü′stenstreife *f* shore patrol

Küster [ˈkystər] *m* (–s;–) sexton

Kustos [ˈkustɔs] *m* (–; **Kustoden** [kusˈtodən]) custodian

Kutsche [ˈkutʃə] *f* (–;–n) coach

Kut′scher *m* (–s;–) coachman

kutschieren [kuˈtʃirən] *intr* drive a coach || *intr* (SEIN) ride in a coach

Kutte [ˈkutə] *f* (–;–n) (eccl) cowl

Kutteln [ˈkutəln] *pl* tripe

Kutter [ˈkutər] *m* (–s;–) (naut) cutter

Kuvert [kuˈvert] *n* (–s;–s) & (–[e]s;–e) envelope; table setting

kuvertieren [kuverˈtirən] *tr* put into an envelope

Kux [kuks] *m* (–es;–e) mining share

Kyklon [kyˈklon] *m* (–s;–e) cyclone

Kyniker [ˈkynɪkər] *m* (–s;–) (philos) cynic

L

L, l [ɛl] *invar n* L, l

laben [ˈlabən] *tr* refresh

Labial [laˈbjal] *m* (–s;–e) labial

labil [laˈbil] *adj* unstable

Labor [laˈbor] *n* (–s;–s) (coll) lab

Laborant [labɔˈrant] (in) §7 *mf* laboratory technician

Laborato·rium [labɔraˈtorjum] *n* (–s; **rien** [rjən]) laboratory

laborieren [labɔˈrirən] *intr* experiment; **l. an** (*dat*) suffer from

Labsal [ˈlapzal] *n* (–[e]s;–e) refreshment

La′bung *f* (–;–en) refreshment

Labyrinth [labyˈrɪnt] *n* (–[e]s;–e) labyrinth

Lache [ˈlaxə] *f* (–;–n) puddle, pool; laugh; **e–e gellende L. anschlagen** break out in laughter

lächeln [ˈlɛçəln] *intr* (**über** *acc*) smile (at) || **Lächeln** *n* (–s;) smile; **höhnisches L.** sneer

lachen [ˈlaxən] *intr* laugh; **daß ich nicht lache!** don′t make me laugh! || **Lachen** *n* (–s;) laugh, laughter; **du hast gut L.!** you can laugh!

lächerlich [ˈlɛçərlɪç] *adj* ridiculous; **l. machen** ridicule; **sich l. machen** make a fool of oneself

lachhaft [ˈlaxhaft] *adj* ridiculous

Lachkrampf [ˈlaxkrampf] *m* fit of laughter

Lachs [laks] *m* (–es;–e) salmon

Lachsalve [ˈlaxzalvə] *f* (–;–n) peal of laughter

Lachs′schinken *m* raw, lightly smoked ham

Lack [lak] *m* (–[e]s;–e) lacquer, varnish

Lackel [ˈlakəl] *m* (–s;–) (coll) dope

lackieren [laˈkirən] *tr* lacquer, varnish; (*Autos*) paint

Lack′leder *n* patent leather

Lackmuspapier [ˈlakmuspapir] *n* litmus paper

Lack′schuhe *pl* patent-leather shoes

Lade [ˈladə] *f* (–;–n) box, case; (*Schublade*) drawer

La′dearbeiter *m* loader

La′debaum *m* derrick

La′defähigkeit *f* loading capacity

La′dehemmung *f* jamming (*of a gun*); **L. haben** jam

La′deklappe *f* tailgate

La′delüke *f* (naut) hatch

laden [ˈladən] §103 *tr* load; (*Gast*) invite; (elec) charge; (jur) summon; **geladen sein** (coll) be burned up || **Laden** *m* (–s;–) store, shop; (*Fenster*-) shutter; **den L. schmeißen** pull it off, lick it

La′dendieb *m*, **La′dendiebin** *f* shoplifter

La′dendiebstahl *m* shoplifting

La′denhüter *m* drug on the market

La′deninhaber –in §6 *mf* shopkeeper

La′denkasse *f* till

Lä′denmädchen *n* salesgirl

La′denpreis *m* retail price

La′denschluß *m* closing time

La'denschwengel m (pej) stupid shop clerk
La'dentisch m counter
La'derampe f loading platform
La'deschein m bill of lading
La'destock m ramrod
La'dung f (-;-en) loading; load; (Güter) freight; (elec) charge; (jur) summons; shell, charge; (naut) cargo
Lafette [la'fɛtə] f (-;-n) gun mount
Laffe ['lafə] m (-n;-n) jazzy dresser
lag [lɑk] pret of liegen
Lage ['lɑgə] f (-;-n) site, location; situation; (Zustand) condition, state; (Haltung) posture; (Schicht) layer, deposit; (Salve) volley; (Bier) round; (bb) quire; (mil) position; (mus) pitch; **mißliche L.** predicament; **versetzen Sie sich in meine L.** put yourself in my position
Lager ['lɑgər] n (-s;-) bed; (e-s Wildes) lair; (Stapelplatz) dump; (Partei) side, camp; (von Waffen) cache; (Vorrat) stock; (Warenlager) stockroom; (geol) stratum, vein; (mach) bearing; (mil) camp; **auf L.** in stock; (fig) up one's sleeve; **ein L. halten von** keep stock of
La'geraufnahme f inventory
La'gerbier n lager beer
La'gerfähigkeit f shelf life
La'gerfeuer n campfire
La'gergebühr f storage charges
La'gerhalter m stock clerk
La'gerhaus n warehouse
Lagerist -in [lɑgə'rɪst(ɪn)] §7 mf warehouse clerk
La'gerleben n camp life
lagern ['lɑgərn] tr lay down; (Waren) stock, store; (altern) season; (mach) mount on bearings || ref lie down, rest || intr lie down, rest; (Waren) be stored; (Wein) season; (geol) be deposited; (mil) camp
La'gerort m, **La'gerplatz** m resting place; (Stapelplatz) dump; (mil) camp site
La'gerraum m storeroom, stockroom
La'gerstand m stock on hand, inventory
La'gerstätte f, **La'gerstelle** f resting place; (geol) deposit; (mil) camp site
La'gerung f (-;-en) storage; (Alterung) seasoning; (geol) stratification
La'gervorrat m stock, supply
Lagune [la'gunə] f (-;-n) lagoon
lahm [lɑm] adj lame; paralyzed || **Lahme** §5 mf paralytic
lahmen ['lɑmən] intr be lame, limp
lähmen ['lɛmən] tr paralyze; (Verkehr) tie up; (fig) cripple
lahm'legen tr cripple, paralyze; (mil) neutralize
Läh'mung f (-;-en) paralysis
Laib [laɪp] m (-[e]s;-e) loaf
Laich [laɪç] m (-[e]s;-e) spawn
laichen ['laɪçən] intr spawn
Laie ['laɪə] m (-n;-n) layman; **Laien** laity
Lai'enbruder m lay brother
lai'enhaft adj layman's
Lakai [la'kaɪ] m (-en;-en) lackey

Lake ['lɑkə] f (-;-n) brine, pickle
Laken ['lɑkən] n (-s;-) sheet
lakonisch [la'konɪʃ] adj laconic
Lakritze [la'krɪtsə] f (-;-n) licorice
Lakune [la'kunə] f (-;-n) lacuna
lallen ['lalən] tr & intr stammer
lamellenförmig [la'mɛlənfœrmɪç] adj laminate
lamentieren [lamɛn'tirən] intr wail
Lametta [la'mɛta] n (-s;) tinsel
Lamm [lam] n (-[e]s;̈er) lamb
Lamm'braten m roast lamb
Lämmerwolke ['lɛmərvɔlkə] f cirrus
Lamm'fleisch n (culin) lamb
lamm'fromm' adj meek as a lamb
Lampe ['lampə] f (-;-n) lamp; light
Lam'penfieber n stage fright
Lam'penschirm m lamp shade
Lampion [lam'pjõ] m (-s;-s) Chinese lantern
lancieren [lã'sirən] tr launch, promote; (Kandidaten) (pol) groom
Land [lant] n (-[e]s;̈er & -e) land; (Ackerboden) ground, soil; (Staat) country; (Provinz) state; (Gegensatz: Stadt) country; **ans L.** ashore; **auf dem Lande** in the country; **aufs L.** into the country; **aus aller Herren Ländern** from everywhere; **außer Landes gehen** go abroad; **zu Lande** by land
Land'arbeiter m farm hand
Land'armee f land forces
Land'bau m farming, agriculture
Land'besitz m landed property
Land'besitzer -in §6 mf landowner
Landebahn ['landəban] f runway
Landedeck ['landədɛk] n flight deck
Land'edel·mann m (-es;-leute) country gentleman
Landefeuer ['landəfɔɪ·ər] n runway lights
land'einwärts adv inland
Landekopf ['landəkopf] m beachhead
landen ['landən] tr & intr (SEIN) land
Land'enge f isthmus, neck of land
Landeplatz ['landəplats] m wharf; (aer) landing field
Länderei [lɛndə'raɪ] f (-;-en) or **Ländereien** pl lands, estates
Länderkunde ['lɛndərkundə] f geography
Landes- ['landəs] comb.fm. national, native, of the land
Lan'desaufnahme f land survey
Lan'desbank f national bank
Lan'desbeschreibung f topography
lan'deseigen adj state-owned
Lan'deserzeugnis n domestic product
Lan'desfarben pl national colors
Lan'desfürst m sovereign
Lan'desgesetz n law of the land
Lan'desherr m sovereign
Lan'desherrschaft f, **Lan'deshoheit** f sovereignty
Lan'dessprache f vernacular
Lan'destracht f national costume
Lan'destrauer f public mourning
lan'desüblich adj customary
Lan'desvater m sovereign
Lan'desverrat m high treason
Lan'desverräter -in §6 mf traitor
Lan'desverteidigung f national defense

Land'flucht f rural exodus
land'flüchtig adj exiled, fugitive
Land'friedensbruch m disturbance of the peace
Land'gericht n district court, superior court
Land'gewinnung f land reclamation
Land'gut n country estate
Land'haus n country house
Land'jäger m rural policeman; (culin) sausage
Land'junker m country squire
Land'karte f map
Land'kreis m rural district
land'läufig adj customary
Ländler ['lɛntlər] m (-s;-) waltz
Land'leute pl country folk
ländlich ['lɛntlɪç] adj rural, rustic
Land'luft f country air
Land'macht f land forces
Land'mann m (-[e]s;-leute) farmer
Land'marke f landmark (for travelers and sailors)
Land'maschinen pl farm machinery
Land'messer m surveyor
Land'partie f outing, picnic
Land'plage f nation-wide plague; (coll) big nuisance
Land'rat m regional governor
Land'ratte f (fig) landlubber
Land'recht n common law
Land'regen m steady rain
Land'rücken m ridge
Land'schaft f (-;-en) landscape, scenery; (Bezirk) district, region
land'schaftlich adj scenic; regional
Landser ['lantsər] m (-s;-) G.I.
Lands'knecht m mercenary
Lands'mann m (-[e]s;-leute) fellow countryman
Land'spitze f promontory
Land'straße f highway
Land'streicher m (-s;-) tramp, hobo
Land'strich m tract of land
Land'sturm m home guard
Land'tag m state assembly
landumschlossen ['lantʊm/lɔsən] adj landlocked
Lan'dung f (-;-en) landing
Lan'dungsboot n landing craft
Lan'dungsbrücke f jetty, pier
Lan'dungsgestell n landing gear
Lan'dungssteg m gangplank
Land'vermessung f surveying
Land'volk n country folk
Land'weg m overland route
Land'wehr f militia, home guard
Land'wirt m farmer
Land'wirtschaft f agriculture; **L. betreiben** farm
land'wirtschaftlich adj farm, agricultural
Land'zunge f spit of land
lang [laŋ] adj (länger ['lɛŋər]; längste ['lɛŋstə] §9) long; (Person) tall ||
adv—**die ganze Woche l.** all week; **e–e Stunde l.** for an hour
langatmig ['laŋatmɪç] adj long-winded
lang'beinig adj long-legged
lange ['laŋə] adv long, a long time; **es ist noch l. nicht fertig** it is far from ready; **schon l. her** long ago; **schon l. her, daß** a long time since;

so l. bis until; **so l. wie** as long as; **wie l.?** how long?
Länge ['lɛŋə] f (-;-n) length; long syllable; (geog) longitude; (pros) quantity; **auf die L.** in the long run; **der L. nach** lengthwise; **in die L. ziehen** drag out
langen ['laŋən] tr reach, hand; **j–m eine l.** (coll) give s.o. a smack || intr be enough; **l. nach** reach for || impers—**es langt mir** I have enough; **jetzt langt's mir aber!** I've had it!
Län'gengrad m degree of longitude
Län'genkreis m meridian
Län'genmaß n linear measure
Lan'geweile f boredom; **sich** [dat] **die L. vertreiben** (coll) kill time
Lang'finger m pickpocket
langfingerig ['laŋfɪŋərɪç] adj (fig) thievish
langfristig ['laŋfrɪstɪç] adj long-term
lang'jährig adj long-standing
Lang'lauf m crosscountry skiing
langlebig ['laŋlebɪç] adj long-lived
Lang'lebigkeit f (-;) longevity
lang'legen ref lie down, stretch out
länglich ['lɛŋlɪç] adj oblong
läng'lichrund adj oval, elliptical
Lang'mut f patience
Lang'mütigkeit f patience
lang'mütig adj patient
längs [lɛŋs] prep (genit or dat) along
langsam ['laŋzam] adj slow
Lang'spielplatte f long-playing record
längst [lɛŋst] adv long since, long ago
längstens ['lɛŋstəns] adv at the latest; (höchstens) at the most
Langstrecken– comb.fm. long-range; (sport) long-distance
langweilen ['laŋvaɪlən] tr bore || ref feel bored
Lang'weiler m (-s;-) slowpoke
langweilig ['laŋvaɪlɪç] adj boring
langwierig ['laŋvirɪç] adj lengthy
Lanolin [lano'lin] n (-s;) lanolin
Lanze ['lantsə] f (-;-n) lance, spear
Lan'zenstechen n (-s;) jousting
Lanzette [lan'tsetə] f (-;-n) lancet
Lappalie [la'paljə] f (-;-n) trifle
Lappen ['lapən] m (-s;-) rag; washrag; (Flicken) patch; (anat) lobe
läppisch ['lɛpɪ/] adj silly, trifling
Lappland ['laplant] n (-s;) Lapland
Lärche ['lɛrçə] f (-;-n) (bot) larch
Lärm [lɛrm] m (-[e]s;) noise; **L. schlagen** (fig) make a fuss
lärmen ['lɛrmən] intr make noise
lär'mend adj noisy
Larve ['larfə] f (-;-n) mask; larva
las [las] pret of **lesen**
lasch [la/] adj limp; (Speise) insipid
Lasche ['la/ə] f (-;-n) (Klappe) flap; (Schuh–) tongue; (rr) fishplate
lasieren [la'zirən] tr glaze
lassen ['lasən] §104 tr let; (erlauben) allow; (bewirken) have, make; leave (behind, undone, open, etc.); **den Film entwickeln l.** have the film developed; **etw fallen l.** drop s.th.; **ich kann es nicht l.** I can't help it; **j–n warten l.** keep s.o. waiting; **kommen l.** send for; **laß den Lärm!** stop

the noise!; **laß es!** cut it out!; **läßt uns gehen** let us go; **sein Leben l.** lose one's life; **sein Leben l. für** sacrifice one's life for || *ref*—**das läßt sich denken** I can imagine; **das läßt sich hören!** now you're talking!; **es läßt sich nicht beschreiben** it defies description; **es läßt sich nicht leugnen, daß** it cannot be denied that; **sich** (*dat*) **Zeit l.** take one's time

lässig ['lɛsɪç] *adj* (*faul*) lazy; (*träge*) sluggish; (*nachlässig*) remiss

Läs'sigkeit *f* (*–;*) laziness; negligence

läßlich ['lɛslɪç] *adj* venial

Last [last] *f* (*–;-en*) load, weight; (*Bürde*) burden; (*Hypotek*) encumbrance; (*aer, naut*) cargo, freight; **j–m etw zur L. legen** blame s.o. for s.th.; **L. der Beweise** weight of evidence; **ruhende L.** dead weight; **zur L. fallen** (*dat*) become a burden for

Last'auto *n* truck

lasten ['lastən] *intr* (**auf** *dat*) weigh (on)

la'stenfrei *adj* unencumbered

La'stensegler *m* transport glider

Laster ['lastər] *m* (*–s;-*) (*coll*) truck || *n* (*–s;-*) vice

Lästerer –**in** ['lɛstərər(ɪn)] §6 *mf* slanderer; blasphemer

la'sterhaft *adj* vicious

La'sterleben *n* life of vice

lästerlich ['lɛstərlɪç] *adj* slanderous; blasphemous

Lästermaul ['lɛstərmaʊl] *n* scandalmonger

lästern ['lɛstərn] *tr* slander; blaspheme

Lä'sterung *f* (*–;-en*) slander; blasphemy

lästig ['lɛstɪç] *adj* troublesome; **j–m l. fallen** bother s.o.

Last'kahn *m* barge

Last'kraftwagen *m* truck

Last'schrift *f* (*acct*) debit

Last'tier *n* beast of burden

Last'träger *m* porter

Last'wagen *m* truck

Last'zug *m* tractor-trailer (*consisting of several trailers*)

Lasur [la'zur] *f* (*–;*) glaze

Latein [la'taɪn] *n* (*–s;*) Latin

lateinisch [la'taɪnɪʃ] *adj* Latin

Laterne [la'tɛrnə] *f* (*–;-n*) lantern; lamp

Latrine [la'trinə] *f* (*–;-n*) latrine

Latri'nenparole *f* scuttlebut

Latsche ['lɑtʃə] *f* (*–;-n*) (*coll*) slipper || *f* (*–;-n*) (*bot*) dwarf pine

latschen ['lɑtʃən] *intr* (SEIN) shuffle along

Latte ['latə] *f* (*–;-n*) lath

Lat'tenkiste *f* crate

Lat'tenzaun *m* picket fence

Lattich ['latɪç] *m* (*–s;-e*) lettuce

Latz [lats] *m* (*–es;̈e*) bib; (*Klappe*) flap; (*Schürzchen*) pinafore

Lätzchen ['lɛtsçən] *n* (*–s;-*) bib

lau [laʊ] *adj* lukewarm; (*Wetter*) mild; (*fig*) half-hearted

Laub [laʊp] *n* (*–[e]s;*) foliage

Laub'baum *m* deciduous tree

Laube ['laʊbə] *f* (*–;-n*) arbor; (*Säulen-*

gang) portico; (*Bogengang*) arcade; (*theat*) box

Lau'bengang *m* arcade

Laub'säge *f* fret saw

Laub'sägearbeit *f* fretwork

Laub'werk *n* foliage

Lauer ['laʊ·ər] *f* (*–;*) ambush; **auf der L. liegen** lie in wait

lauern ['laʊ·ərn] *intr* lurk; **l. auf** (*acc*) lie in wait for, watch for

lau'ernd *adj* (*Blick*) wary; (*Gefahr*) lurking

Lauf [laʊf] *m* (*–[e]s;̈e*) running; run; (*e–s Flusses*) course; (*Strömung*) current; (*Wettlauf*) race; (*astr Gewehrs*) barrel; (*astr*) path, orbit; **den Dingen freien L. lassen** let things take their course; **im Laufe der Zeit** in the course of time; **im vollen Laufe** at full speed

Lauf'bahn *f* career; (*astr*) orbit; (*sport*) lane

Lauf'bursche *m* errand boy; office boy

laufen ['laʊfən] §105 *intr* (SEIN) run; (*zu Fuß gehen*) walk; (*leck sein*) leak; (*Zeit*) pass; **die Dinge l. lassen** let things slide; **j–n l. lassen** let s.o. go; (*strafles*) let s.o. off

lau'fend *adj* (*ständig*) steady; (*Jahr, Preis*) current; (*Nummern*) consecutive; (*Wartung, Geschäft*) routine; (*Meter, usw.*) running; **auf dem laufenden** up to date; **laufendes Band** conveyor belt; assembly line

Läufer ['lɔɪfər] *m* (*–s;-*) runner; (*Teppich*) runner; (*chess*) bishop; (*fb*) halfback; (*mach*) rotor; (*mus*) run

Lauferei [laʊfə'raɪ] *f* (*–;-en*) running around

Lauf'feuer *n* (*–s;*) wildfire

Lauf'fläche *f* tread (*on tire*)

Lauf'gewicht *n* sliding weight

Lauf'gitter *n* playpen

Lauf'graben *m* trench

läufig ['lɔɪfɪç] *adj* in heat

Läu'figkeit *f* (*–;*) heat

Lauf'junge *m* errand boy; office boy

Lauf'kran *m* (mach) traveling crane

Lauf'kunde *m* chance customer

Lauf'masche *f* run (*in stocking*)

lauf'maschenfrei *adj* runproof

Lauf'paß *m* (*coll*) walking papers; (*coll*) brush-off

Lauf'planke *f* gangplank

Lauf'rad *n* (*e–r Turbine*) rotor; (aer) landing wheel

Lauf'schritt *m* double-quick time

Lauf'steg *m* footbridge

Laufställchen ['laʊf/tɛlçən] *n* (*–s;-*) playpen

Lauf'zeit *f* rutting season; (*e–s Vertrags*) term; (*cin*) running time; (mach) (service) life

Lauge ['laʊgə] *f* (*–;-n*) lye; (*Salzlauge*) brine; (*Seifenlauge*) suds

Lau'gensalz *n* alkali

lau'gensalzig *adj* alkaline

Laune ['laʊnə] *f* (*–;-n*) mood, humor; (*Grille*) whim

lau'nenhaft *adj* capricious

launig ['laʊnɪç] *adj* humorous, witty

lau'nisch *adj* moody

Laus [laʊs] *f* (*–;̈e*) louse

Laus′bub m rascal
lauschen [′lauʃən] intr listen; eaves-drop; **l. auf** (acc) listen to
Lau′scher –in §6 mf eavesdropper
lauschig [′lauʃɪç] adj cosy, peaceful
Lausebengel m, **Lau′sejunge** m, **Lau′-sekerl** m (coll) rascal, brat
lausen [′lauzən] tr pick lice from; **ich denke, mich laust der Affe** (coll) I couldn't believe my eyes
lausig [′lauzɪç] adj lousy
laut [laut] adj loud; (lärmend) noisy; **l. werden** become public; **l. werden lassen** divulge || prep (genit & dat) according to; (com) as per; **l. Be-richt** according to the report || **Laut** m (–[e]s;–e) sound
Laute [′lautə] f (–;–n) lute
lauten [′lautən] intr sound; (Worte) read, go, say; **das Urteil lautet auf Tod** the sentence is death
läuten [′lɔɪtən] tr & intr ring, toll || impers—**es läutet** the bell is ringing || **Läuten** n (–s;) toll
lauter [′lautər] adj pure; (aufrecht) sincere || invar adj (nichts als) noth-ing but
Lau′terkeit f (–;) purity; sincerity
läutern [′lɔɪtərn] tr purify; (Metall, Zucker) refine; (veredeln) ennoble
Laut′gesetz n phonetic law
Laut′lehre f phonetics, phonology
laut′lich adj phonetic
laut′los adj soundless
Laut′malerei f onomatopoeia
Laut′schrift f phonetic spelling
Laut′sprecher m loudspeaker
Laut′sprecheranlage f public address system
Laut′sprecherwagen m sound truck
Laut′stärke f volume
Laut′stärkeregler m volume control
Laut′system n phonetic system
Laut′zeichen n phonetic symbol
lau′warm adj lukewarm
Lava [′lava] f (–;) lava
Lavendel [la′vɛndəl] m (–s;) (bot) lavender
laven′delfarben adj lavender
lavieren [la′virən] intr (fig) maneuver; (naut) tack
Lawine [la′vinə] f (–;–n) avalanche
lax [laks] adj lax
Lax′heit f (–;) laxity
Laxiermittel [la′ksirmɪtəl] n laxative
Layout [′le.aut] n (–s;–s) layout
Lazarett [latsa′rɛt] n (–[e]s;–e) (mil) hospital
Lebedame [′lebədamə] f woman of lei-sure
Lebehoch [lebə′hox] n (–s;–s) cheer; toast; **ein dreimaliges L.** three cheers
Lebemann [′lebəman] m playboy
leben [′lebən] tr & intr live || **Leben** n (–s;–) life; existence; **am L. blei-ben** survive; **am L. erhalten** keep alive; **ins L. rufen** bring into being; **sein L. lang** all his life; **ums L. kom-men** lose one's life
lebendig [le′bɛndɪç] adj living, alive; (lebhaft) lively; (Darstellung) vivid
Le′bensalter n age, period of life
Le′bensanschauung f outlook on life
Le′bensart f manners
Le′bensaufgabe f mission in life
Le′bensbaum m (bot) arbor vitae
Le′bensbedingungen pl living condi-tions
Le′bensbeschreibung f biography
Le′bensdauer f life span
Le′benserwartung f life expectancy
le′bensfähig adj viable
Le′bensfrage f vital question
Le′bensgefahr f mortal danger
le′bensgefährlich adj perilous
Le′bensgefährte m, **Le′bensgefährtin** f life companion, spouse
le′bensgroß adj life-size
Le′benshaltung f standard of living
Le′benshaltungskosten pl cost of living
Le′bensinteressen pl vital interests
Le′benskraft f vitality
Le′benskünstler m—er ist ein L. noth-ing can get him down
lebenslänglich [′lebənsleŋlɪç] adj life
Le′benslauf m curriculum vitae
Le′bensmittel pl groceries
Le′bensmittelgeschäft n grocery store
Le′bensmittelkarte f food ration card
Le′bensmittellieferant m caterer
le′bensmüde adj weary of life
le′bensnotwendig adj vital, essential
Le′bensprozeß m vital function
Le′bensstandard m standard of living
Le′bensstellung f lifetime job; tenure
Le′bensstil m life style
Le′bensunterhalt m livelihood
le′bensuntüchtig adj impractical
Le′bensversicherung f life insurance
Le′benswandel m conduct; life
Le′bensweise f way of life
Le′bensweisheit f worldly wisdom
le′benswichtig adj vital, essential
Le′benszeichen n sign of life
Le′benszeit f lifetime; **auf L.** for life
Leber [′lebər] f (–;–n) liver; **frei von der L. weg reden** speak frankly
Le′berfleck m mole
Leberkäs [′lebərkɛs] m (–es;) meat loaf (made with liver)
Le′bertran m cod-liver oil
Lebewesen [′lebəvezən] n living being
Lebewohl [lebə′vol] n (–[e]s;–e) fare-well
lebhaft [′lephaft] adj lively; full of life; (Farbe) bright; (Straße) busy; (Börse) brisk; (Interesse) keen
Lebkuchen [′lepkuxən] m gingerbread
leblos [′leplos] adj lifeless
Lebtag [′leptak] m—**mein L.** in all my life
Lebzeiten [′leptsaɪtən] pl—**zu meinen L.** in my lifetime
lechzen [′leçtsən] intr (nach) thirst (for)
leck [lek] adj leaky || **Leck** n (–[e]s;–e) leak; **ein L. bekommen** spring a leak
lecken [′lekən] tr lick || intr leak; (naut) have sprung a leak
lecker [′lekər] adj dainty; (köstlich) delicious
Leckerbissen (Lek′kerbissen) m deli-cacy, dainty
Leckerei [leka′raɪ] f (–;–en) daintiness; sweets
leckerhaft (lek′kerhaft) adj dainty

Leckermaul (Lek′kermaul) *n*—ein L. sein have a sweet tooth
Leder [′ledər] *n* (-s;) leather
ledern [′ledərn] *adj* leather; (fig) dull, boring
ledig [′ledɪç] *adj* single; (Kind) illegitimate; **l.** (genit) free of; **lediger Stand** single state; celibacy
le′diglich *adv* merely, only
leer [ler] *adj* empty, void; (fig) vain ‖ **Leere** *f* (-;) emptiness, void; vacuum ‖ *n*—**der Schlag ging ins L.** the blow missed; **ins L. starren** stare into space
leeren [′lerən] *tr* empty
Leer′gut *n* empties (bottles, cases)
Leer′lauf *m* (aut) idling, idle; (Gang) (aut) neutral
leer′laufen §105 *intr* (SEIN) idle
leer′stehend *adj* unoccupied, vacant
Leer′taste *f* (typ) space bar
legal [le′gɑl] *adj* legal
legalisieren [legalɪ′zirən] *tr* legalize
Legat [le′gɑt] *m* (-en;-en) legate ‖ *n* (-[e]s;-e) legacy, bequest
legen [′legən] *tr* lay, put; **auf die Kette l.** chain, tie up; **j-m ans Herz l.** recommend warmly to s.o.; **Nachdruck l. auf** (acc) emphasize; **Wert l. auf** (acc) attach importance to ‖ *ref* lie down; go to bed; (Wind) die down; **die Krankheit hat sich ihm auf die Lungen gelegt** his sickness affected his lungs
legendär [legen′der] *adj* legendary
Legende [le′gendə] *f* (-;-n) legend
legieren [le′girən] *tr* alloy
Legie′rung *f* (-;-en) alloy
Legion [le′gjon] *f* (-;-en) legion
Legionär [legjo′ner] *m* (-s;-e) legionnaire, legionary
legislativ [legɪsla′tif] *adj* legislative ‖ **Legislative** [legɪsla′tivə] *f* (-;-n) legislature
Legis·lator [legɪs′lɑtor] *m* (-s;-latoren [la′torən]) legislator
Legislatur [legɪsla′tur] *f* (-;-en) legislature
legitim [legɪ′tim] *adj* legitimate
Legitimation [legɪtima′tsjon] *f* (-;-en) proof of identity
legitimieren [legɪti′mirən] *tr* legitimize; (berechtigen) authorize ‖ *ref* prove one's identity
Lehen [′le·ən] *n* (-s;-) (hist) fief
Le′hensherr *m* liege lord
Le′hens·mann *m* (-[e]s;-leute) vassal
Lehm [lem] *m* (-[e]s;-e) clay, loam
lehmig [′lemɪç] *adj* clayey, loamy
Lehne [′lenə] *f* (-;-n) support; (e-s Stuhls) arm, back; (Abhang) slope
lehnen [′lenən] *tr, ref & intr* lean
Lehnsessel [′lenzesəl] *m*, **Lehnstuhl** [′len/tul] *m* armchair, easy chair
Lehn′wort [′lenvɔrt] *n* (-[e]s;-ˮer) loan word
Lehramt [′leramt] *n* teaching profession; professorship
Lehranstalt [′leran/talt] *f* educational institution
Lehrbrief [′lerbrif] *m* apprentice's diploma
Lehrbube [′lerbubə] *m* apprentice

Lehrbuch [′lerbux] *n* textbook
Lehrbursche [′lerbur/ə] *m* apprentice
Lehre [′lerə] *f* (-;-n) doctrine, teaching; (Wissenschaft) science; (Theorie) theory; (Unterweisung) instruction; (Warnung) lesson; (e-r Fabel) moral; (Richtschnur) rule, precept; (e-s Lehrlings) apprenticeship; (tech) gauge; **in der L. sein** be serving one's apprenticeship
lehren [′lerən] *tr* teach, instruct
Lehrer –in [′lerər(ɪn)] §6 *mf* teacher
Leh′rerbildungsanstalt *f* teacher's college
Leh′rerkollegium *n* teaching staff
Lehrfach [′lerfax] *n* subject
Lehrfilm [′lerfɪlm] *m* educational film
Lehrgang [′lergaŋ] *m* (educ) course
Lehrgedicht [′lergədɪçt] *n* didactic poem
Lehrgegenstand [′lergegən/tant] *m* (educ) subject
Lehrgeld [′lergelt] *n*—L. zahlen (fig) learn the hard way
lehrhaft [′lerhaft] *adj* didactic
Lehrjunge [′lerjuŋə] *m* apprentice
Lehrkörper [′lerkœrpər] *m* teaching staff; faculty (of a university)
Lehrling [′lerlɪŋ] *m* (-s;-e) apprentice
Lehrmädchen [′lermetçən] *n* girl apprentice
Lehrmeister [′lermaɪstər] *m* master, teacher, instructor
Lehrmittel [′lermɪtəl] *n* teaching aid
Lehrplan [′lerplan] *m* curriculum
lehrreich [′lerraɪç] *adj* instructive
Lehrsaal [′lerzal] *m* lecture hall
Lehrsatz [′lerzats] *m* (eccl) dogma; (math) theorem
Lehrspruch [′ler/prux] *m* maxim
Lehrstelle [′ler/telə] *f* position as an apprentice
Lehrstoff [′ler/tɔf] *m* subject matter
Lehrstuhl [′ler/tul] *m* (educ) chair
Lehrstunde [′ler/tundə] *f* lesson
Lehrzeit [′lertsaɪt] *f* apprenticeship
Leib [laɪp] *m* (-[e]s;-er) body; (Bauch) belly, abdomen; (Taille) waist; (Mutterleib) womb; **am ganzen L. zittern** tremble all over; **bleib mir nur damit vom Leibe!** (coll) don't bother me with that: **e-n harten L. haben** be constipated; **gesegneten Leibes** with child; **L. und Leben** life and limb; **mit L. und Seele** through and through; **sich** [dat] **j-n vom Leibe halten** keep s.o. at arm's length; **zu Leibe gehen** (dat) tackle (s.th.), attack (s.o.)
Leib′arzt *m* personal physician
Leibchen [′laɪpçən] *n* (-s;-) bodice; vest
leib′eigen *adj* in bondage ‖ **Leibeigene** §5 *mf* serf
Leib′eigenschaft *f* (-;) serfdom, bondage
Lei′besbeschaffenheit *f* (-;-en) constitution
Lei′beserbe *m* (-n;-n) offspring
Lei′beserziehung *f* physical education
Lei′besfrucht *f* fetus
Lei′beskräfte *pl*—aus **Leibeskräften**

schreien scream at the top of one's lungs

Lei′besübungen *pl* physical education

Lei′besvisitation *f* body search

Leib′garde *f* bodyguard

Leibgardist [ˈlaɪpgardɪst] *m* (−en;−en) bodyguard

Leib′gericht *n* favorite dish

leibhaft(ig) [ˈlaɪphaft(ɪç)] *adj* incarnate, real

leib′lich *adj* bodily, corporal; **leiblicher Vetter** first cousin; **sein leiblicher Sohn** his own son

Leib′rente *f* annuity for life

Leib′schmerzen *pl*, **Leib′schneiden** *n* abdominal pains

Leibstandarte [ˈlaɪpʃtandartə] *f* (−;−n) (hist) SS bodyguard

Leib′wache *f* bodyguard

Leib′wäsche *f* underwear

Leiche [ˈlaɪçə] *f* (−;−n) corpse, body; carcass; (dial) funeral

Leichenbegängnis [ˈlaɪçənbəgɛŋnɪs] *n* (−ses;−se) funeral, interment

Leichenbeschauer [ˈlaɪçənbəʃau·ər] *m* (−s;−) coroner

Leichenbestatter [ˈlaɪçənbəʃtatər] *m* (−s;−) undertaker

Lei′chenbittermiene *f* woe-begone look

Leichenfledderer [ˈlaɪçənfledərər] *m* (−s;−) body stripper

Lei′chengift *n* ptomaine poison

lei′chenhaft *adj* corpse-like

Lei′chenhalle *f* mortuary

Lei′chenöffnung *f* autopsy

Lei′chenräuber *m* body snatcher

Lei′chenrede *f* eulogy

Lei′chenschau *f* post mortem

Lei′chenschauhaus *m* morgue

Lei′chenstarre *f* rigor mortis

Lei′chenträger *m* pallbearer

Lei′chentuch *n* shroud

Lei′chenverbrennung *f* cremation

Lei′chenwagen *m* hearse

Lei′chenzug *m* funeral cortege

Leichnam [ˈlaɪçnam] *m* (−[e]s;−e) corpse

leicht [laɪçt] *adj* light; (*nicht schwierig*) easy; (*gering*) slight; **leichten Herzens** light-heartedly

Leicht′atletik *f* track and field

Leicht′bauweise *f* lightweight construction

Leicht′benzin *n* cleaning fluid

leichtbeschwingt [ˈlaɪçtbəʃvɪŋt] *adj* gay

leicht′blütig *adj* light-hearted

leicht′entzündlich *adj* highly flammable

Leichter [ˈlaɪçtər] *m* (−s;−) (naut) lighter

leicht′fertig *adj* frivolous, flippant; careless

leicht′flüchtig *adj* highly volatile

leicht′flüssig *adj* thin

Leicht′gewicht *n* lightweight division

Leichtgewichtler [ˈlaɪçtgəvɪçtlər] *m* (−s;−) lightweight boxer

leicht′gläubig *adj* gullible

leicht′hin′ *adv* lightly, casually

Leich′tigkeit *f* (−;) ease

leichtlebig [ˈlaɪçtlebɪç] *adj* easygoing

Leicht′sinn *m* frivolity, irresponsibility;

(*Sorglosigkeit*) carelessness; (*Unbedachtsamkeit*) imprudence

leicht′sinnig *adj* frivolous, irresponsible

leicht′verdaulich *adj* easy to digest

leicht′verderblich *adj* perishable

leid [laɪt] *adj*—**er tut mir l. I** feel sorry for him; **es tut mir l., daß I** am sorry that; **es ist (or tut) mir l. um I** feel sorry for, **I** regret; **ich bin es l. I'm** fed up with it ‖ **Leid** *n* (−[e]s;) (*Betrübnis*) sorrow; (*Schaden*) harm; (*Unrecht*) wrong; **j−m ein L. antun** harm s.o.

Leideform [ˈlaɪdəfɔrm] *f* (gram) passive voice

leiden [ˈlaɪdən] §106 *tr* suffer; (*ertragen*) stand ‖ *intr* (**an** *dat*) suffer (*from*) ‖ **Leiden** *n* (−s;−) suffering; (*Krankheit*) ailment

Lei′denschaft *f* (−;−en) passion

lei′denschaftlich *adj* passionate

lei′denschaftslos *adj* dispassionate

Lei′densgefährte *m*, **Lei′densgefährtin** *f* fellow sufferer

Lei′densgeschichte *f* tale of woe; (relig) Passion

Lei′densweg *m* way of the cross

leider [ˈlaɪdər] *adv* unfortunately

leiderfüllt [ˈlaɪterfʏlt] *adj* sorrowful

leidig [ˈlaɪdɪç] *adj* tiresome

leidlich [ˈlaɪtlɪç] *adv* tolerable; (*halbwegs gut*) passable ‖ *adj* so-so

leidtragend [ˈlaɪttragənt] *adj* in mourning ‖ **Leidtragende** §5 *mf* mourner; **er ist der L. dabei** he is the one that suffers for it

Leid′wesen *n*—**zu meinem L.** to my regret

Leier [ˈlaɪ·ər] *f* (−;−n) (mus) lyre

Lei′erkasten *m* hand organ, hurdy-gurdy

Lei′ermann *m* (−[e]s;−̈er) organ grinder

leiern [ˈlaɪ·ərn] *tr* (*winden*) crank; (*Gebete, Verse*) drone ‖ *intr* drone

Leih− [laɪ] *comb.fm.* loan, rental

Leih′amt *n*, **Leih′anstalt** *f* loan office

Leih′bibliothek *f* rental library

leihen [ˈlaɪ·ən] *tr* lend, loan out; (*entleihen*) (**von**) borrow (*from*)

Leih′gebühr *f* rental fee

Leih′haus *n* pawnshop

Leim [laɪm] *m* (−[e]s;−e) glue; birdlime; **aus dem L. gehen** fall apart; **j−m auf den L. gehen** be taken in by s.o.

leimen [ˈlaɪmən] *tr* glue; (*betrügen*) take in, fool

Leim′farbe *f* distemper

leimig [ˈlaɪmɪç] *adj* gluey

Lein [laɪn] *m* (−[e]s;−e) flax

Leine [ˈlaɪnə] *f* (−;−n) line, cord; (*Hunde−*) leash

Leinen [ˈlaɪnən] *n* (−s;−) linen

Lei′neneinband *m* (−[e]s;−̈e) (bb) cloth binding

Lei′nenschuh *m* sneaker, canvas shoe

Lei′nenzeug *n* linen fabric

Lein′öl *n* linseed oil

Lein′tuch *n* sheet

Lein′wand *f* linen cloth; canvas; (cin) screen

leise [ˈlaɪzə] *adj* soft, low; (*sanft*) gentle; (*gering*) faint; (*Schlaf*) light

lei'sestellen tr (rad) turn down

Lei'setreter m (-s;-) pussyfoot

Leiste ['laɪstə] f (-;-n) (Rand) border; (anat) groin; (carp) molding

leisten ['laɪstən] tr do, perform, accomplish; (Dienst) render; (Eid) take; (Abbitte, Hilfe, Widerstand) offer; Bürgschaft l. für put up bail for; Folge l. (dat), Gehorsam l. (dat) obey; Genüge l. (dat) satisfy; j-m Gesellschaft l. keep s.o. company; sich [dat] etw l. können be able to afford s.th. ǁ Leisten m (-s;-) last; alles über e-n L. schlagen (fig) be undiscriminating

Lei'stenbruch m hernia, rupture

Lei'stung f (-;-en) performance; efficiency; ability; feat, achievement; (Ergebnis) result; (Erzeugung) production; (Abgabe, Ausstoß) output; (Beitrag) contribution; (Dienstleistungen) services rendered; (elec) power, wattage; (indust) output, production; (insur) benefits; (mach) capacity

Lei'stungsanreiz m incentive

lei'stungsfähig adj (Person) efficient; (Motor) powerful; (Fabrik) productive; (phys) efficient

Lei'stungsfähigkeit f efficiency; proficiency; (e-s Autos) performance; (e-s Motors) power; (mach) output

lei'stungsgerecht adj based on merit

Lei'stungsgrenze f peak of performance

Leis'tungslohn m pay based on performance

Lei'stungszulage f bonus

Leit- [laɪt] comb.fm. leading, dominant, guiding

Leit'artikel m editorial

Leit'bild n (good) example, ideal

leiten ['laɪtən] tr lead, guide; (Verkehr) route; (Betrieb) direct, run; (Versammlung) preside over; (arti) direct; (elec, mus, phys) conduct

Lei'ter m (-s;-) leader; director; (educ) principal; (elec, mus) conductor ǁ f (-;-n) ladder

Lei'terin f (-;-nen) leader; director

Leit'faden m manual, guide

Leit'fähigkeit f conductivity

Leit'gedanke m main idea, main theme

Leit'hammel m (fig) boss, leader

Leit'motiv n keynote; (mus) leitmotiv

Leit'satz m basic point

Leit'spruch m motto

Leit'stelle f head office

Leit'stern m polestar, lodestar

Lei'tung f (-;-en) direction, guidance; (Beaufsichtigung) management; (Rohr) pipeline; (für Gas, Wasser) main; (elec) lead; (phys) conduction; (telp) line; e-e lange L. haben rather dense; L. besetzt! line is busy!

Lei'tungsdraht m (elec) lead

Lei'tungsmast m telephone pole

Lei'tungsnetz n (elec) power lines

Lei'tungsrohr n pipe, main

Lei'tungsvermögen n conductivity

Lei'tungswasser n tap water

Leit'werk n (aer) tail assembly

Leit'zahl f code number

Lektion [lɛk'tsjon] f (-;-en) lesson; (fig) lecture, rebuke

Lek·tor ['lɛktər] m (-s;-toren ['torən]) lecturer; (e-s Verlags) reader

Lektüre [lɛk'tyrə] f (-;) reading matter, literature

Lende ['lɛndə] f (-;-n) loin; (Hüfte) hip

Len'denbraten m roast loin, sirloin

len'denlahm adj stiff; (Ausrede) lame

Len'denschurz m loincloth

Len'denstück n tenderloin, sirloin

lenkbar ['lɛŋkbar] adj manageable; steerable, maneuverable; lenkbares Luftschiff dirigible

lenken ['lɛŋkən] tr guide, control; (Wagen) drive; (wenden) turn; (steuern) steer; Aufmerksamkeit l. auf (acc) call attention to

Len'ker -in $6 mf ruler; (aut) driver

Lenkrad ['lɛŋkrat] n steering wheel

Lenksäule ['lɛŋkzɔɪlə] f steering column

Lenkstange ['lɛŋkʃtaŋə] f handlebar; (aut) connecting rod

Len'kung f (-;-en) guidance, control; (aut) steering mechanism

Lenz [lɛnts] m (-es;-e) (fig) prime of life; (poet) spring

Lenz'pumpe f bilge pump

Lepra ['lepra] f (-;) leprosy

Lerche ['lɛrçə] f (-;-n) (orn) lark

lernbegierig ['lɛrnbəgiriç] adj eager to learn, studious

lernen ['lɛrnən] tr & intr learn; study

Lesart ['lezart] f version

lesbar ['lezbar] adj legible; readable

Lesbierin ['lɛsbɪ·ərɪn] f (-;-nen) lesbian

lesbisch ['lɛsbɪʃ] adj lesbian; lesbische Liebe lesbianism

Lese ['lezə] f (-;-n) gathering, picking; (Wein-) vintage

Lese- [lezə] comb.fm. reading; lecture

Le'sebrille f reading glasses

Le'sebuch n reader

Le'sehalle f reading room

lesen ['lezən] §107 tr read; gather; (Messe) say ǁ intr read; lecture; l. über (acc) lecture on

le'senswert adj worth reading

Le'seprobe f specimen from a book; (theat) reading rehearsal

Le'ser -in $6 mf reader; picker

Le'seratte f (coll) bookworm

le'serlich adj legible

Le'serzuschrift f letter to the editor

Le'sestoff m reading matter

Le'sezeichen n bookmark

Le'sung f (-;-en) reading

Lette ['lɛtə] m (-n;-n), Lettin ['lɛtɪn] f (-;-nen) Latvian

lettisch ['lɛtɪʃ] adj Latvian

Lettland ['lɛtlant] n (-[e]s;) Latvia

letzte ['lɛtstə] §9 adj last; (endgültig) final, ultimate; (neueste) latest; (Ausweg) last; bis ins l. to the last detail; in den letzten Jahren in recent years; in der letzten Zeit lately; letzten Endes in the final analysis ǁ Letzte §5 pron last, last one; am Letzten on the last of the month; sein Letztes hergeben do one's utmost; **zu guter Letzt** finally, last but not least

letztens ['lɛtstəns] *adv* lately

letztere ['lɛtstərə] §5 *mfn* latter

letzthin [lɛtst'hɪn] *adv* lately

letztlich ['lɛtstlɪç] *adv* lately, recently; in the final analysis

letztwillig ['lɛtstvɪlɪç] *adj* testamentary

Leucht– [lɔɪçt] *comb.fm.* luminous; illuminating

Leucht'bombe *f* flare bomb

Leuchte ['lɔɪçtə] *f* (–;–n) light, lamp; lantern; (fig) luminary

leuchten ['lɔɪçtən] *intr* shine

leuch'tend *adj* shining, bright; luminous

Leuchter ['lɔɪçtər] *m* (–s;–) candlestick; chandelier

Leucht'farbe *f* luminous paint

Leucht'feuer *n* (aer) flare; (naut) beacon

Leucht'käfer *m* lightning bug

Leucht'körper *m* light bulb; light fixture

Leucht'kugel *n* tracer bullet; flare

Leucht'pistole *f* Very pistol

Leucht'rakete *f* (aer) flare

Leucht'reklame *f* neon sign

Leucht'röhre *f* fluorescent lamp

Leucht'spurgeschoß *n* tracer bullet

Leucht'turm *m* lighthouse

Leucht'zifferblatt *n* luminous dial

leugnen ['lɔɪgnən] *tr* deny; disclaim

Leukoplast [lɔɪko'plast] *n* (–[e]s;–e) adhesive tape

Leumund ['lɔɪmunt] *m* (–[e]s;) reputation

Leu'mundszeugnis *n* character reference

Leute ['lɔɪtə] *pl* people, persons, men; (*Dienstleute*) servants

Leu'teschinder *m* oppressor; slave driver

Leutnant ['lɔɪtnant] *m* (–s;–s) lieutenant

Leut'priester *m* secular priest

leut'selig *adj* affable

Lexikograph [lɛksɪko'graf] *m* (–en;–en) lexicographer

Lexikon ['lɛksɪkon] *n* (–s;–s) encyclopedia

Libanon ['libanon] *n* (–s;) Lebanon

Libelle [lɪ'bɛlə] *f* (–;–n) dragonfly; (carp) level

liberal [lɪbe'ral] *adj* liberal

Liberalismus [lɪbera'lɪsmus] *m* (–s;) liberalism

Libyen ['liby·ən] *n* (–s;) Libya

licht [lɪçt] *adj* light, bright; (*durchsichtig*) clear ‖ **Licht** *n* (–[e]s;–er) light; (*Kerze*) candle

licht'beständig *adj* non-fading

Licht'bild *n* photograph

Licht'bildervortrag *m* illustrated lecture

licht'blau *adj* light-blue

Licht'blick *m* (fig) bright spot

Licht'bogen *m* (elec) arc

Licht'bogenschweißung *f* arc welding

Licht'brechung *f* (–;–en) refraction of light

Licht'druck *m* phototype

licht'durchlässig *adj* translucent

licht'echt *adj* non-fading

licht'empfindlich *adj* sensitized; **l. machen** sensitize

Licht'empfindlichkeit *f* (phot) speed

lichten ['lɪçtən] *tr* clear; thin; (*Anker*) weigh

lichterloh ['lɪçtərlo] *adv* ablaze; **l. brennen** be ablaze

Licht'hof *m* (archit) light well, inner court; (phot) halo

Licht'kegel *m* beam of light

Licht'maschine *f* generator, dynamo

Licht'pause *f* blueprint

Licht'punkt *m* (fig) ray of hope

Licht'schacht *m* light well

Licht'schalter *m* light switch

licht'scheu *adj*—**lichtscheues Gesindel** shady characters

Licht'schirm *m* lamp shade

Licht'seite *f* (fig) bright side

Licht'spiele *pl*, **Licht'spielhaus** *n*, **Licht'spieltheater** *n* movie theater

licht'stark *adj* (*Objektiv*) high-powered; (phot) high-speed

Lich'tung *f* (–;–en) clearing

Lid [lit] *n* (–[e]s;–er) eyelid

Lid'schatten *m* eye shadow

lieb [lip] *adj* dear; (*nett*) nice; **der liebe Gott** the good Lord; **es ist mir l., daß** I am glad that; **seien Sie so l. und** please; **sich lieb Kind machen bei** ingratiate oneself with

lieb'äugeln *intr*—**l. mit** (& fig) flirt with

Liebchen ['lipçən] *n* (–s;–) darling

Liebe ['libə] *f* (–;) (zu) love (for, of)

liebedienerisch ['libədinərɪʃ] *adj* fawning

Liebelei [libə'laɪ] *f* (–;–en) flirtation

lieben ['libən] *tr* love, be fond of

lie'bend *adj* loving ‖ *adv*—**l. gern** gladly ‖ **Liebende** §5 *mf* lover

lie'benswert *adj* lovable

lie'benswürdig *adj* lovable; charming; **das ist sehr l. von Ihnen** that's very kind of you

lieber ['libər] *adv* rather, sooner; **l. haben** prefer

Liebes– [libəs] *comb.fm.* love, of love

Lie'besdienst *m* favor, good turn

Lie'beserlebnis *n* romance

Lie'besgabe *f* charitable gift

Lie'beshandel *m* love affair

Lie'besmahl *n* love feast

Lie'besmühe *f*—**verlorene L.** wasted effort

Lie'bespaar *n* couple (of lovers)

Lie'bespfand *n* token of love

Lie'bestrank *m* love potion

Lie'beswerben *n* advances

lie'bevoll *adj* loving, affectionate

Lieb'frauenkirche *f* Church of Our Lady

lieb'gewinnen §121 *tr* grow fond of

lieb'haben §89 *tr* love, be fond of

Liebhaber ['liphabər] *m* (–s;–) lover, beau; amateur; fan, buff; **erster L.** leading man

lieb'kosen *tr* caress, fondle

lieb'lich *adj* lovely, sweet; charming

Liebling ['liplɪŋ] *m* (–s;–e) darling; (*Haustier*) pet; (*Günstling*) favorite

Lieblings– *comb.fm.* favorite

Lieb′lingsgedanke *m* pet idea
Lieb′lingswunsch *m* dearest wish
lieb′los *adj* unkind
lieb′reich *adj* kind, affectionate
Lieb′reiz *m* charm, attractiveness
lieb′reizend *adj* charming
Lieb′schaft *f* (-;-en) love affair
liebste [′lipstə] §9 *adj* favorite; **am liebsten trinke ich Wein** I like wine best of all
Lied [lit] *n* (-[e]s;-er) song; **er weiß ein L. davon zu singen** he can tell you all about it; **geistliches L.** hymn
liederlich [′lidərlɪç] *adj* dissolute; (*unordentlich*) disorderly
lief [lif] *pret* of **laufen**
Lieferant -in [lifə′rant(ɪn)] §7 *mf* supplier; (*Verteiler*) distributor; (*von Lebensmitteln*) caterer
Lieferauto [′lifərauto] *n* delivery truck
lieferbar [′lifərbar] *adj* available, deliverable
Liefergebühr [′lifərgə′byr] *f* delivery charge
liefern [′lifərn] *tr* deliver; (*beschaffen*) supply, furnish; (*Ertrag*) yield; **ich bin geliefert** (coll) I'm done for
Lieferschein [′lifərʃain] *m* delivery receipt
Lie′ferung *f* (-;-en) delivery, shipment; supply; (*e-s Werkes*) installment, number; **zahlbar bei L.** cash on delivery
Lieferwagen [′lifərvagən] *m* delivery truck
Liege [′ligə] *f* (-;-n) couch
Lie′gekur *f* rest cure
liegen [′ligən] §108 *intr* lie, be situated; **gut auf der Straße l.** hug the road; **l. an** (*dat*) lie near; (fig) be due to; **wie die Sache jetzt liegt** as matters now stand ‖ *impers*—**es liegt an ihm zu** (*inf*) it's up to him to (*inf*); **es liegt auf der Hand** it is obvious; **es liegt mir nichts daran** it doesn't matter to me; **es liegt mir (sehr viel) daran** it matters (a great deal) to me
lie′genbleiben §62 *intr* (SEIN) stay in bed; (*Waren*) remain unsold; (*stekkenbleiben*) have a breakdown; (*Arbeit*) be left undone
lie′genlassen §104 *tr* let lie; leave alone; (*Arbeit*) leave undone
Lie′genschaft *f* (-;-en) real estate
Lie′gestuhl *m* deck chair
Lie′gestütz *m* (gym) pushup
lieh [li] *pret* of **leihen**
ließ [lis] *pret* of **lassen**
Li-ga [′liga] *f* (-;-gen [gən]) league
Liguster [lɪ′gustər] *m* (-s;-) privet
liieren [lɪ′irən] *ref*—**sich l. mit** ally oneself with
Likör [lɪ′kø̈r] *m* (-s;-e) liqueur
lila [′lila] *adj* lilac
Lilie [′liljə] *f* (-;-n) lily
Limonade [lɪmə′nadə] *f* (-;-n) soft drink, soda
lind [lɪnt] *adj* mild, gentle
Linde [′lɪndə] *f* (-;-n) (bot) linden
lindern [′lɪndərn] *tr* alleviate; (*Übel*) mitigate; (*mildern*) soften

Lindwurm [′lɪntvurm] *m* dragon
Lineal [lɪne′al] *n* (-s;-e) ruler
Linguist -in [lɪŋgu′ɪst(ɪn)] §7 *mf* linguist
Linie [′linjə] *f* (-;-n) line; **auf gleicher L. mit** on a level with; **in erster L.** in the first place
Li′nienpapier *n* lined paper
Li′nienrichter *m* (sport) linesman
Li′nienschiff *n* ship of the line
li′nientreu *adj*—**l. sein** follow the party line
linieren [lɪ′nirən] *tr* line, rule
linke [′lɪŋkə] §9 *adj* left; (*Seite*) wrong, reverse ‖ §5 **Linke** *m* (box) left ‖ §5 *f* left side; left hand; **die L.** (pol) the left
linkisch [′lɪŋkɪʃ] *adj* clumsy, awkward
links [lɪŋks] *adv* left; to the left; on the left; (*verkehrt*) inside out; **l. liegenlassen** bypass, ignore; **links um!** left, face!
links′drehend *adj* counterclockwise
linksgängig [′lɪŋksgɛŋɪç] *adj* counterclockwise
Linkshänder [′lɪŋkshɛndər] *m* (-s;-) left-hander
links′läufig *adj* counterclockwise
links′stehend *adj* (pol) leftist
Linnen [′lɪnən] *n* (-s;) linen
Linse [′lɪnzə] *f* (-;-n) (bot) lentil; (opt) lens
Lippe [′lɪpə] *f* (-;-n) lip; **e-e L. riskieren** (fig) speak out of turn
Lip′penbekenntnis *n* lip service
Lip′penlaut *m* labial
Lip′penstift *m* lipstick
liquid [lɪ′kvit] *adj* (*Geldmittel*) liquid; (*Gesellschaft*) solvent
Liquidation [lɪkvida′tsjon] *f* (-;-en) liquidation; (*Kostenrechnung*) bill
liquidieren [lɪkvi′dirən] *tr* liquidate; (*Geschäft*) wind up; (*Honorar*) charge
lispeln [′lɪspəln] *tr* & *intr* lisp; (*flüstern*) whisper
Lissabon [′lɪsa′bən] *n* (-s) Lisbon
List [lɪst] *f* (-;-en) cunning; trick
Liste [′lɪstə] *f* (-;-n) list; **schwarze L.** blacklist
Li′stenwahl *f* block voting
listig [′lɪstɪç] *adj* cunning, sly
Litanei [lita′nai] *f* (-;-en) litany
Litauen [′litau·ən] *n* (-s;) Lithuania
litauisch [′litau·ɪʃ] *adj* Lithuanian
Liter [′litər] *m* & *n* (-s;-) liter
literarisch [lɪta′rarɪç] *adj* literary
Literatur [lɪtera′tur] *f* (-;-en) literature
Litfaßsäule [′lɪtfaszɔilə] *f* advertising pillar
Litur·gie [lɪtur′gi] *f* (-;-gien [′gi·ən]) liturgy
Litze [′lɪtsə] *f* (-;-n) cord; (elec) strand
Li·vree [lɪ′vre] *f* (-;-vreen [′vre·ən]) uniform, livery
Lizenz [lɪ′tsɛnts] *f* (-;-en) license
Lob [lop] *n* (-[e]s;) praise
loben [′lobən] §109 *tr* praise
lo′benswert *adj* praiseworthy
Lobhudelei [lophudə′lai] *f* (-;-en) flattery

lob'hudeln *tr* heap praise on
löblich ['løpliç] *adj* commendable
lob'preisen *tr* extol, praise
Lob'rede *f* panegyric
Loch [lɔx] *n* (-es;⁼er) hole
Loch'bohrer *m* auger
lochen ['lɔxən] *tr* punch, perforate
Locher ['lɔxər] *m* (-s;-) punch
löcherig ['lœçəriç] *adj* full of holes
Loch'karte *f* punch card
Lo'chung *f* (-;-en) perforation
Locke ['lɔkə] *f* (-;-n) lock, curl
locken ['lɔkən] *tr* allure, entice; decoy; (*Hund*) whistle to
locker ['lɔkər] *adj* loose; (*nicht straff*)
slack; spongy; (*moralisch*) loose
lockern ['lɔkərn] *tr* loosen
lockig ['lɔkiç] *adj* curly, curled
Lock'mittel *n*, **Lock'speise** *f* (& fig)
bait
Lockspitzel ['lɔkʃpitsəl] *m* stoolpigeon
Lo'ckung *f* (-;-en) allurement
Lock'vogel *m* (& fig) decoy
Loden ['lodən] *m* (-s;-) coarse woolen
cloth
lodern ['lodərn] *intr* blaze; (fig) glow
Löffel ['lœfəl] *m* (-s;-) spoon; (culin)
spoonful; (coll & hunt) ear; **über
den L. balbieren** hoodwink
Löf'felbagger *m* power shovel
löffeln ['lœfəln] *tr* spoon out
log [lok] *pret of* **lügen**
Logbuch ['lɔkbux] *n* logbook
Loge ['loʒə] *f* (-;-n) (*der Freimau-
rer*) lodge; (theat) box
Lo'genbruder *m* freemason
Logierbesuch [lo'ʒirbəzux] *m* house-
guest(s)
logieren [lo'ʒirən] *intr* (bei) stay (with)
Logik ['logik] *f* (-;) logic
Logis [lo'ʒi] *invar n* lodgings
logisch ['logiʃ] *adj* logical
Lohe ['lo·ə] *f* (-;-n) blaze, flame
Lohgerber ['logerbər] *m* (-s;-) tanner
Lohn [lon] *m* (-[e]s;⁼e) pay, wages;
(fig) reward
Lohn'abbau *m* wage cut
lohnen ['lonən] *tr* compensate, reward;
(*Arbeiter*) pay; **j-m etw l.** reward
s.o. for s.th. || *ref* pay, be worth-
while
löhnen ['lønən] *tr* pay, pay wages to
Lohn'erhöhung *f* raise, wage increase
Lohn'gefälle *n* wage differential
Lohn'herr *m* employer
lohn'intensiv *adj* with high labor costs
Lohn'liste *f* payroll
Lohn'satz *m* pay rate
Lohn'stopp *m* wage freeze
Lohn'tag *m* payday
Lohn'tüte *f* pay envelope
Löh'nung *f* (-;-en) payment
lokal [lo'kal] *adj* local || **Lokal** *n*
(-[e]s;-e) locality, premises; (*Wirts-
haus*) restaurant, pub, inn
lokalisieren [lokali'zirən] *tr* localize
Lokalität [lokali'tet] *f* (-;-en) locality
Lokomotive [lokomo'tivə] *f* (-;-n) lo-
comotive
Lokomotiv'führer *m* (rr) engineer
Lokus ['lokus] *m* (-;-se) (coll) john
Lorbeer ['lɔrbər] *m* (-s;-en) laurel

los [los] *adj* loose; **es ist etw los** there
is s.th. going on; **es ist nichts los**
there is nothing going on; **etw los
haben** have s.th. on the ball; **j-n**
(or **etw**) **los sein** be rid of s.o. (or
s.th.); **los! go on!, scram!;** (*sprich*)
fire away!; (*mach schnell!*) let's go!;
(sport) play ball!; **mit ihm ist nicht
viel los** he's no great shakes; **was
ist los?** what's the matter? || **Los** *n*
(-[e]s;-e) lot; (*Lotterie*) ticket;
(*Anteil*) lot, portion; (*Schicksal*)
fate; **das Große Los** first prize; **das
Los ziehen** draw lots; **die Lose sind
gefallen** the die is cast
los- *comb.fm.* un-, e.g., **losmachen**
undo
los'arbeiten *tr* extricate || *ref* get
loose, extricate oneself || *intr* (**auf**
acc) work away (at)
lösbar ['løsbar] *adj* solvable
los'binden §59 *tr* loosen, untie
los'brechen §64 *tr* break off || *intr*
(SEIN) break loose
Löschblatt ['lœʃblat] *n* blotter
Löscheimer ['lœʃaimər] *m* fire bucket
löschen ['lœʃən] *tr* put out; (*Durst*)
quench; (*Schuld*) cancel; (*Schrift*)
blot; (*Bandaufnahme*) erase; (*Firma*)
liquidate; (*Hypotek*) pay off; (naut)
unload
Lö'scher *m* (-s;-) blotter; (*Feuer-*)
fire extinguisher
Löschgerät ['lœʃgəret] *n* fire extinguisher
Löschmannschaft ['lœʃmanʃaft] *f* fire
brigade
Löschpapier ['lœʃpapir] *n* blotting
paper
Lö'schung *f* (-;-en) extinction; (*Tilgung*) cancellation; (naut) unloading
los'drehen *tr* unscrew, twist off
los'drücken *tr* fire || *intr* pull the
trigger
lose ['lozə] §9 *adj* loose
Lösegeld ['løzəgelt] *n* ransom
loseisen ['losaizən] *tr*—**Geld l. von**
wangle money out of; **j-n l. aus** get
s.o. out of; **j-n l. von** get s.o. away
from || *ref* (**von**) worm one's way
(out of)
losen ['lozən] *intr* draw lots
lösen ['løzən] *tr* loosen, untie; (*abtrennen*) sever; (*Bremse*) release;
(*Fahrkarte*) buy; (*loskaufen*) ransom;
(*lossprechen*) absolve; (*Rätsel*) solve;
(*Schuß*) fire; (*Verlobung*) break off
|| *ref* come loose, come undone; dis-
solve; (*sich befreien*) free oneself
los'fahren §71 *intr* (SEIN) drive off; **l.
auf** (*acc*) head for; rush at; attack
(verbally)
los'gehen §82 *intr* (SEIN) (coll) begin;
(*Gewehr*) go off; (*sich lösen*) come
loose; **auf j-n l.** attack s.o.
los'haken *tr* unhook
los'kaufen *tr* ransom
los'ketten *tr* unchain
los'kommen §99 *intr* (SEIN) come loose,
come off; **ich komme nicht davon
los** I can't get over it; **l. von** get
away from; get rid of
los'lachen *intr* burst out laughing

los'lassen §104 *tr* let go; release; **den Hund l. auf** (*acc*) sic the dog on

los'legen *intr* (coll) start up, let fly; (*reden*) (coll) open up; **leg los!** (*coll*) fire away!

löslich ['løːslɪç] *adj* soluble

los'lösen *tr* detach

los'machen *tr* undo, untie; (*freimachen*) free || *ref* disengage onself

los'platzen *intr* (SEIN) burst out laughing; **l. mit** blurt out

los'reißen §53 *tr* & *ref* break loose

los'sagen *ref*—**sich l. von** renounce

los'schlagen §132 *tr* knock off; (*verkaufen*) dispose of, sell cheaply || *intr* open the attack; **l. auf** (*acc*) let fly at

los'schnallen *tr* unbuckle

los'schrauben *tr* unscrew

los'sprechen §64 *tr* absolve

los'steuern *intr*—**l. auf** (*acc*) head for

Lo'sung *f* (–;–en) (*Kot*) dung; (mil) password; (pol) slogan

Lö'sung *f* (–;–en) solution

Lö'sungsmittel *n* solvent; thinner

los'werden §159 *tr* (SEIN) get rid of

los'ziehen §163 *intr* (SEIN) set out, march away; **l. auf** (*acc*) talk about, run down

Lot [loːt] *n* (–[e]s;–e) plummet; plumb line; (*Lötmetall*) solder; (geom) perpendicular; **im Lot** perpendicular; (fig) in order; **ins Lot bringen** (fig) set right

Löteisen ['løːtaɪzən] *n* soldering iron

loten ['loːtən] *tr* (naut) plumb || *intr* (naut) take soundings

löten ['løːtən] *tr* solder

Lötkolben ['løːtkɔlbən] *m* soldering iron

Lötlampe ['løːtlampə] *f* blowtorch

Lötmetall ['løːtmetal] *n* solder

lot'recht *adj* perpendicular

Lotse ['loːtsə] *m* (–n;–n) (aer) air traffic controller; (naut) pilot

lotsen ['loːtsən] *tr* (*Flugzeuge*) guide in; (naut) pilot

Lotte·rie [lɔtə'riː] *f* (–;–rien ['riːən]) lottery, sweepstakes

Lotterie'los *n* lottery ticket

lotterig ['lɔtərɪç] *adj* sloppy

Lotterleben ['lɔtərleːbən] *n* dissolute life

Lotto ['lɔto] *n* (–s;–s) state-owned numbers game

Löwe ['løːvə] *m* (–n;–n) lion

Lö'wenanteil *m* lion's share

Lö'wenbändiger **–in** §6 *mf* lion tamer

Lö'wengrube *f* lion's den

Lö'wenmaul *n* (bot) snapdragon

Lö'wenzahn *m* (bot) dandelion

Löwin ['løːvɪn] *f* (–;–nen) lioness

loyal [lɔa'jal] *adj* loyal

Luchs [luks] *m* (–es;–e) lynx

Lücke ['lʏkə] *f* (–;–n) gap, hole; (*Mangel*) deficiency; (*im Gesetz*) loophole; (*Zwischenraum*) interval; **auf L. stehend** staggered

Lückenbüßer ['lʏkənbysər] *m* (–s;–) stop-gap

lückenhaft (lük'kenhaft) *adj* defective, fragmentary

Luder ['luːdər] *n* (–s;–) carrion; (coll)

cad; (*Weibsbild*) slut; **das arme L.!** the poor thing!; **dummes L.!** fathead!

Lu'derleben *n* dissolute life

ludern ['luːdərn] *intr* lead a dissolute life

Luft [luft] *f* (–;=e) air; (*Atem*) breath; (*Brise*) breeze; **die L. ist rein** the coast is clear; **es ist dicke L.** there is trouble brewing; **es liegt etw in der L.** (fig) there's s.th. in the air; **frische L. schöpfen** get a breath of fresh air; **in die L. fliegen** be blown up; **in die L. gehen** blow one's top; **in die L. sprengen** blow up; **j–n an die L. setzen** give s.o. the air; **nach L. schnappen** gasp for breath; **seinem Zorn L. machen** give vent to one's anger; **tief L. holen** take a deep breath

Luft'alarm *m* air-raid alarm

Luft'angriff *m* air raid

Luft'ansicht *f* aerial view

Luft'aufklärung *f* air reconnaissance

Luft'bild *n* aerial photograph

Luft'bremse *f* air brake

Luft'brücke *f* airlift

Lüftchen ['lʏftçən] *n* (–s;–) gentle breeze

luft'dicht *adj* airtight

Luft'druck *m* atmospheric pressure; (*e–r Explosion*) blast; (aut) air pressure

Luft'druckbremse *f* air brake

Luft'druckmesser *m* barometer

Luft'druckprüfer *m* tire gauge

Luft'düse *f* air nozzle, air jet

lüften ['lʏftən] *tr* air, ventilate; **den Hut l.** tip one's hat

Luft'fahrt *f* aviation

Luft'fahrzeug *n* aircraft

Luft'flotte *f* air force

luft'förmig *adj* gaseous

Luft'hafen *m* airport

Luft'heizung *f* hot-air heating

Luft'herrschaft *f* air supremacy

Luft'hülle *f* atmosphere

luftig ['luftɪç] *adj* airy; (*windig*) windy; (*Person*) flighty; (*Kleidung*) loosely woven, light

Luftikus ['luftɪkus] *m* (–;–se) lightheaded person

Luft'klappe *f* air valve

luft'krank *adj* airsick

Luft'kurort *m* mountain resort

Luft'landetruppen *pl* airborne troops

luft'leer *adj* vacuous; **luftleerer Raum** vacuum

Luft'linie *f* beeline; **fünfzig Kilometer L.** 50 kilometers as the crow flies

Luft'loch *n* vent; (aer) air pocket

Luft'parade *f* flyover

Luft'post *f* airmail

Luft'raum *m* atmosphere; air space

Luft'reifen *m* tire

Luft'reklame *f* sky writing

Luft'röhre *f* (anat) windpipe

Luft'schiff *n* airship

Luft'schiffahrt *f* aviation

Luft'schloß *n* castle in the air

Luft'schutz *m* air-raid protection

Luft'schutzkeller *m* air-raid shelter

Luft'schutzwart *m* air-raid warden

Luft'spiegelung *f* mirage

Luft′sprung *m* caper
Luft′streitkräfte *pl* air force
Luft′strom *m* air current
Luft′strudel *m* (aer) wash
Luft′stützpunkt *m* air base
luft′tüchtig *adj* air-worthy
Lüf′tung *f* (-;) airing, ventilation
Luft′veränderung *f* change of climate
Luft′verkehrsgesellschaft *f*, Luft′ver-
kehrslinie *f* airline
Luft′vermessung *f* aerial survey
Luft′verpestung *f* (-;), Luft′ver-
schmutzung *f* (-;), Luft′verunreini-
gung *f* (-;) air pollution
Luft′waffe *f* air force
Luft′warnung *f* air-raid warning
Luft′weg *m* air route; auf dem Luft-
wege by air
Luft′widerstand *m* (phys) air resistance
Luft′zug *m* draft
Lug [luk] *m* (-[e]s;) lie; Lug und Trug
pack of lies
Lüge [′lygə] *f* (-;-n) lie; fromme L.
white lie; j-n Lügen strafen prove
s.o. a liar
lugen [′lugən] *intr* peep
lügen [′lygən] §111 *tr*—das Blaue vom
Himmel herunter l. lie like mad ‖
intr lie, tell a lie
Lügendetek·tor [′lygəndetektɔr] *m* (-s;
-toren [′torən] lie detector
Lü′gengeschichte *f* cock-and-bull story
Lü′gengespinst *n*, Lü′gengewebe *n* tissue of lies
lü′genhaft *adj* (*Person*) dishonest, lying; (*Nachricht*) untrue
Lügner -in [′lygnər(ın)] §6 *mf* liar
lügnerisch [′lygnərıʃ] *adj* dishonest
Luke [′lukə] *f* (-;-n) (*am Dach*) dormer window; (naut) hatch
Lümmel [′lyməl] *m* (-s;-) lout
Lump [lump] *m* (-en;-en) scoundrel
lumpen [′lumpən] *intr* lead a wild life;
sich nicht l. lassen (coll) be generous ‖ Lumpen *m* (-s;-) rag
Lum′pengeld *n* measly sum; für ein L.
dirtcheap
Lum′pengesindel *n* mob, rabble
Lum′penhändler *m* ragman
Lum′penkerl *m* (coll) bum
Lum′penpack *n* rabble, riffraff
Lumperei [lumpə′raɪ] *f* (-;-en) shady
deal; dirty trick; (*Kleinigkeit*) trifle
lumpig [′lumpıç] *adj* ragged; shabby

Lunge [′luŋə] *f* (-;-n) lung
Lungen– *comb.fm.* pulmonary
Lun′genentzündung *f* pneumonia
Lun′genflügel *m* lung
lun′genkrank *adj* consumptive ‖ Lun-
genkranke §5 *mf* consumptive
Lun′genschwindsucht *f* tuberculosis
lungern [′luŋərn] *intr* (HABEN & SEIN)
loiter about, lounge about
Lunte [′luntə] *f* (-;-n) fuse; L. riechen
smell a rat
Lupe [′lupə] *f* (-;-n) magnifying glass;
unter die L. nehmen examine closely
lüpfen [′lypfən] *tr* lift gently
Lust [lust] *f* (-;=e) pleasure; (*Verlangen*) desire; (*Wollust*) lust; L.
haben zu (*inf*) feel like (*ger*); mit
L. und Liebe with heart and soul
Lust′barkeit *f* (-;-en) amusement, entertainment
Lüster [′lystər] *m* (-s;-) luster
lüstern [′lystərn] *adj* (nach) desirous
(*of*); lustful; (*Bilder, Späße*) lewd
Lü′sternheit *f* (-;) greediness; lustful-
ness; lewdness
Lust′fahrt *f* pleasure ride
lustig [′lustıç] *adv* gay, jolly; (*belu-
stigend*) amusing; du bist vielleicht
l.! you must be joking!; l. sein have
a gay time; sich l. machen über
(*acc*) poke fun at
Lüstling [′lystlıŋ] *m* (-s;-e) lecher
lust′los *adj* listless; (*Börse*) inactive
Lustmolch [′lustmɔlç] *m* (-[e]s;-e)
sex fiend
Lust′mord *m* sex murder
Lust′reise *f* pleasure trip
Lust′seuche *f* venereal disease
Lust′spiel *n* comedy
lust′wandeln *intr* (SEIN) stroll
Lutheraner -in [lutə′ranər(ın)] §6 *mf*
Lutheran
lutherisch [′lutərıʃ] *adj* Lutheran
lutschen [′lutʃən] *tr & intr* suck
Lut′scher *m* (-s;-) nipple, pacifier
Luxus [′luksus] *m* (-;) luxury
Lu′xusausgabe *f* deluxe edition
Luzerne [lu′tsernə] *f* (-;-n) alfalfa
Lymphe [′lymfə] *f* (-;-n) lymph
lynchen [′lynçən] *tr* lynch
Lyrik [′lyrık] *f* (-;) lyric poetry
lyrisch [′lyrıʃ] *adj* lyric(al)
Lyze·um [ly′tse·um] *n* (-s;-en [ən])
girls' high school

M

M, m [ɛm] *invar n* M, m
M *abbr* (Mark) (fin) mark
Maar [mar] *n* (-[e]s;-e) crater lake
Maat [mat] *m* (-[e]s;-e) (naut) mate
Machart [′maxart] *f* make, type
Mache [′maxə] *f* (-;) (coll) make-believe; er hat es schon in der M. he is
working on it
machen [′maxən] *tr* make; (*tun*) do;
(*bewirken*) produce; (*verursachen*)
cause; (*Prüfung, Reise, Spaziergang*)

take; (*Begriff*) form; (*Besuch*) pay;
(*Freude*) give; (*Holz*) chop; (*Konkurrenz*) offer; das macht mir zu
schaffen that causes me trouble; das
macht nichts it doesn't matter; never
mind; das macht Spaß that's fun;
Dummheiten m. behave foolishly;
Ernst m. be in earnest; gemacht!
right!; O.K.!; Geschäfte m. do business; Geschichten m. make a fuss;
Hochzeit m. get married; ich mache

Spaß I'm joking; **mach dir nichts daraus!** don't worry about it; **mach's gut!** so long!; **wieviel macht es?** how much is it? || *ref* make progress, do all right; **sich auf den Weg m.** set out; **sich** [*dat*] **etw m. lassen** have s.th. made to order; **sich m. an** (*acc*) get down to; **sich** [*dat*] **nichts daraus m.** not care for (or about) || *intr*— **laß mich nur m.!** just leave it to me; **mach, daß . . . !** see to it that . . . !; **m. in** (*dat*) deal in; dabble in; **mach schon** (or **zu**)**!** get going!; **nichts zu m!** (coll) nothing doing! no dice!

Machenschaften ['maxənʃaftən] *pl* intrigues

Macher ['maxər] *m* (-s;-) instigator; (coll) big shot

Macht [maxt] *f* (-;⁻e) might, power; (*Kraft*) force, strength; **aus eigener M.** on one's own responsibility; **an der Macht** in power; **an die M. kommen** come to power

Macht′ausgleich *m* balance of power

Macht′befugnis *f* authority

Machthaber ['maxthabər] *m* (-s;-) ruler; dictator

machthaberisch ['maxthabərɪʃ] *adj* dictatorial

mächtig ['mɛçtɪç] *adj* mighty, powerful; (*riesig*) huge

macht′los *adj* powerless

Macht′losigkeit *f* (-;) impotence

Macht′politik *f* power politics

Macht′vollkommenheit *f* absolute power; **aus eigener M.** on one's own authority

Macht′wort *n* (-[e]s;-e)—**ein M. sprechen** put one's foot down

Machwerk ['maxverk] *n* bad job

Mädchen ['mɛtçən] *n* (-s;-) girl; maid

mäd′chenhaft *adj* girlish; maidenly

Mäd′chenhandel *m* white slavery

Mäd′chenname *m* maiden name; girl's name

Made ['madə] *f* (-;-n) maggot

Mädel ['mɛdəl] *n* (-s;-) (coll) girl

madig ['madɪç] *adj* wormy

Magazin [maga'tsin] *n* (-s;-e) warehouse; (*Zeitschrift; Fernsehprogramm; am Gewehr*) magazine

Magd [makt] *f* (-;⁻e) maid; (poet) maiden

Magen ['magən] *m* (-s;⁻ & -) stomach; **auf nüchternem M.** on an empty stomach

Ma′genbeschwerden *pl* stomach trouble

Ma′gengrube *f* pit of the stomach

Ma′gensaft *m* gastric juice

Ma′genweh *n* stomach ache

mager ['magər] *adj* lean; (*Ernte*) poor

Magie [ma'gi] *f* (-;) magic

Magier –**in** ['magjər(ɪn)] §6 *mf* magician

magisch ['magɪʃ] *adj* magic(al)

Magister [ma'gɪstər] *m* (-s;-) school teacher; **M. der freien Künste** Master of Arts

Magistrat [magɪs'trat] *m* (-[e]s;-e) city council; (hist) magistracy

Magnat [mag'nat] *m* (-en;-en) magnate

Magnet [mag'net] *m* (-[e]s;-e) or (-en;-en) magnet

magnetisch [mag'netɪʃ] *adj* magnetic

magnetisieren [magneti'zirən] *tr* magnetize

Magnetismus [magne'tɪsmʊs] *m* (-;) magnetism

Mahagoni [maha'goni] *n* (-s;) mahogony

Mahd [mat] *f* (-;-en) mowing

Mähdrescher ['medrəʃər] *m* (agr) combine

mähen ['me·ən] *tr* mow; (*Getreide*) reap

Mä′her *m* (-s;-) mower; reaper

Mahl [mal] *n* (-[e]s;⁻er) meal

mahlen ['malən] (*pp* **gemahlen**) *tr* grind || *intr* spin

Mahl′zahn *m* molar

Mahl′zeit *f* meal; **prost M.!** that's a nice mess!

Mähmaschine ['mema∫inə] *f* reaper; (*Rasen–*) lawn mower

Mähne ['menə] *f* (-;-n) mane

mahnen ['manən] *tr* (an *acc*) remind (of); (an *acc*) warn (about or of)

Mahnmal ['manmal] *n* (-s;-e) monument

Mah′nung *f* (-;-en) admonition; (com) reminder, notice

Mähre ['merə] *f* (-;-n) old nag

Mähren ['merən] *n* (-s;) Moravia

Mai [maɪ] *m* (-[e]s;-e) May

Mai′baum *m* maypole

Mai′blume *f* lily of the valley

Maid [maɪt] *f* (-;-en) (poet) maiden

Mai′glöckchen *n* lily of the valley

Mai′käfer *m* June bug

Mailand ['maɪlant] *n* (-[e]s;) Milan

Mais [maɪs] *m* (-es;) Indian corn

Maische ['maɪʃə] *f* (-;-) mash

Mais′hülse *f* corn husk

Mais′kolben *m* corncob

Majestät [majɛs'tet] *f* (-;-en) majesty

majestätisch [majɛs'tetɪʃ] *adj* majestic

Major [ma'jor] *m* (-s;-e) major

Majoran [majo'ran] *m* (-s;-e) marjoram

majorenn [majo'ren] *adj* of age

Majorität [majorɪ'tet] *f* (-;-en) majority

Makel ['makəl] *m* (-s;-) spot, stain

Mäkelei [mekə'laɪ] *f* (-;-en) carping

mäkelig ['mekəlɪç] *adj* critical; (*im Essen*) picky

ma′kellos *adj* spotless; (fig) impeccable

mäkeln ['mekəln] *intr* (an *dat*) carp (at), find fault (with)

Makkaroni [maka'roni] *pl* macaroni

Makler –**in** ['maklər(ɪn)] §6 *mf* agent, broker

Mäkler –**in** ['meklər(ɪn)] §6 *mf* faultfinder

Mak′lergebühr *f* brokerage

Makrele [ma'krelə] *f* (-;-n) mackerel

Makrone [ma'kronə] *f* (-;-n) macaroon

Makulatur [makula'tur] *f* (-;) waste

mal [mal] *adv* (coll) once; (arith) times; **komm mal her!** come here once!; **zwei mal drei** two times three; **zwei mal Spinat** two (orders) of spinach || **Mal** n (-[e]s;-e) mark, sign; (*Mutter-*) birthmark, mole; (*Fleck*) stain; time; **dieses Mal** this time; **manches liebe Mal** many a time; **mit e-m Male** all at once

Malbuch ['mɑlbux] n coloring book

malen ['mɑlen] tr & intr paint

Ma'ler –in §6 mf painter

Malerei [mɑlǝ'raɪ] f (-;-en) painting

malerisch ['mɑlǝrɪʃ] adj picturesque

Ma'lerleinwand f canvas

Malkunst ['mɑlkunst] f art of painting

Malstrom ['mɑl/trom] m maelstrom

malträtieren [mɑltrɛ'tirǝn] tr maltreat

Malve ['mɑlvǝ] f (-;-n) mallow

Malz [mɑlts] n (-es;) malt

Malz'bonbon m cough drop

Mal'zeichen n multiplication sign

Mama [mɑ'mɑ], ['mɑmɑ] f (-;-s) mom, ma

Mamsell [mɑm'zɛl] f (-;-en) miss; (*Wirtschafterin*) housekeeper

man [mɑn] indef pron one, they, people, you; **man hat mir gesagt** I have been told

manch [mɑnç] invar adj—**manch ein** many a || **mancher** §3 adj many a; **manche** pl some, several || pron many a person; many a thing

mancherlei ['mɑnçǝrlaɪ] invar adj all sorts of, various

Manchester [mɑn'/ɛstǝr] m (-s;) corduroy

manch'mal adv sometimes

Mandant –in [mɑn'dɑnt(ɪn)] §7 mf client

Mandarine [mɑndɑ'rinǝ] f (-;-n) tangerine

Mandat [mɑn'dɑt] n (-[e]s;-e) mandate

mandatieren [mɑndɑ'tirǝn] tr mandate

Mandel ['mɑndǝl] f (-;-n) almond; (15 *Stück*) fifteen; (anat) tonsil

Man'delentzündung f tonsilitis

Mandoline [mɑndǝ'linǝ] f (-;-n) mandolin

Mandschurei [mɑnt/u'raɪ] f (-;) Manchuria

Mangan [mɑn'gɑn] n (-s;) manganese

Mangel ['mɑnǝl] m (-s;:) lack, deficiency; (*Knappheit*) shortage; (*Fehler*) shortcoming; **aus M. an** (dat) for lack of; **M. haben an** (dat) be deficient in; **M. leiden an** (dat) be short of || f (-;-n) mangle

Mangel- comb.fm. in short supply

Man'gelberuf m undermanned profession

man'gelhaft adj defective; faulty; unsatisfactory, deficient

Man'gelkrankheit f nutritional deficiency

mangeln ['mɑnǝln] tr (*Wäsche*) mangle || intr (**an** dat) be short of, lack || impers—**es mangelt mir an** (dat) I lack

Mängelrüge ['mɛnǝlrygǝ] f (-;-n) (com) complaint (*about a shipment*)

mangels ['mɑnǝls] prep (genit) for want of, for lack of

Ma·nie [mɑ'ni] f (-;-nien ['ni·ǝn]) mania

Manier [mɑ'nir] f (-;-en) manner

manieriert [mɑnɪ'rirt] adj affected

Manieriert'heit f (-;-en) mannerism

manier'lich adj mannerly, polite

Manifest [mɑnɪ'fɛst] n (-es;-e) (aer, naut) manifest; (pol) manifesto

Maniküre [mɑnɪ'kyrǝ] f (-;-n) manicure; manicurist

maniküren [mɑnɪ'kyrǝn] tr manicure

manipulieren [mɑnɪpu'lirǝn] tr manipulate

manisch ['mɑnɪʃ] adj maniacal

Manko ['mɑnko] n (-s;-s) deficit; (com) shortage

Mann [mɑn] m (-[e]s;:er) man; (*Gatte*) husband; **an den M. bringen** manage to get rid of; **der M. aus dem Volke** the man in the street; **seinen M. stehen** hold one's own

mannbar ['mɑnbar] adj marriageable

Mann'barkeit f (-;) puberty; marriageable age (*of girls*)

Männchen ['mɛnçǝn] n (-s;-) little man; (*Ehemann*) hubby; (zool) male; **M. machen** sit on its hind legs

Männerchor ['mɛnǝrkor] m men's choir

Mannesalter ['mɑnǝsɑltǝr] n manhood

Manneszucht ['mɑnǝstsuxt] f discipline

mann'haft adj manly, valiant

mannigfaltig ['mɑnɪçfɑltɪç] adj manifold

Man'nigfaltigkeit f (-;) diversity

männlich ['mɛnlɪç] adj male; (fig) manly; (gram) masculine

Männ'lichkeit f (-;) manhood; virility

Mannsbild ['mɑnsbɪlt] n (pej) man

Mann'schaft f (-;-en) crew; (sport) team, squad; **Mannschaften** (mil) enlisted men

Mann'schaftsführer –in §6 mf (sport) captain

Mann'schaftswagen m (mil) personnel carrier

Mannsleute ['mɑnslɔɪtǝ] pl menfolk

mannstoll ['mɑnstol] adj man-crazy

Manns'tollheit f (-;) nymphomania

Mann'weib n mannish woman

Manometer [mɑnǝ'metǝr] n pressure gauge

Manöver [mɑ'nøvǝr] n (-s;-) maneuver

manövrieren [mɑnø'vrirǝn] intr maneuver

manövrier'fähig adj maneuverable

Mansarde [mɑn'zɑrdǝ] f (-;-n) attic

manschen ['mɑn/ǝn] tr & intr splash

Manschette [mɑn'/etǝ] f (-;-n) cuff

Manschet'tenknopf m cuff link

Mantel ['mɑntǝl] m (-s;:) overcoat; (*Fahrrad-*) tire; (*e-s Kabels*) sheathing; (*Geschoß-*) jacket, case; (geol, orn) mantle

manuell [mɑnu'ɛl] adj manual

Manufaktur [mɑnufɑk'tur] f (-;-en) manufacture

Manufaktur'waren pl manufactured goods

Manuskript [mɑnu'skrɪpt] n (-[e]s;-e) manuscript

Mappe ['mɑpǝ] f (-;-n) briefcase; (*Aktendeckel*) folder

Märchen ['mɛrçǝn] n (-s;-) fairy tale

mär'chenhaft adj legendary; (fig) fabulous

Mär'chenland n fairyland
Marchese [mar'kezə] m (-ʒ-n) marquis
Marder ['mardər] m (-s;-) marten; (fig) thief
Margarine [marga'rinə] f (-;) margarine
Marienbild [ma'ri·ənbɪlt] n image of the Virgin
Marienfäden [ma'ri·ənfedən] pl gossamer(s)
Marienglas [ma'ri·ənglas] n mica
Marienkäfer [ma'ri·ənkefər] m ladybug
Marine [ma'rinə] f (-;-n) (Kriegs-) navy; (Handels-) merchant marine
mari'neblau adj navy-blue
Mari'neflugzeug n seaplane
Mari'neinfanterie f marines
Mari'neminister m secretary of the navy
Mari'neoffizier -in §6 mf naval officer
Mari'nesoldat m marine
marinieren [marɪ'nirən] tr marinate
Marionette [marɪ·ə'netə] f (-;-n) puppet
Marionet'tentheater n puppet show
Mark [mark] f (-;-) (fin) mark; (hist) borderland, march || n (-[e]s;-) marrow; (im Holz) pith; **bis ins M.** to the quick; **er hat M.** (fig) he has guts; **j-m durch M. und Bein gehen** (fig) go right through s.o.
markant [mar'kant] adj (einprägsam) marked; (außergewöhnlich) striking; (Geländepunkt) prominent
Marke ['markə] f (-;-n) mark; (Brief-) stamp; (Handelszeichen) trademark; (Sorte) brand; (Fabrikat) make; (Spiel-) counter
mark'erschütternd adj piercing
Marketenderei [markətendə'raɪ] f (-;-en) post exchange, PX
Marketing ['markɪtɪŋ] n (-s;) (com) marketing
markieren [mar'kirən] tr mark; (spielen) pretend to be
Markise [mar'kizə] f (-;-n) awning
Mark'stein m landmark
Markt [markt] m (-[e]s;⁓e) market; (Jahrmarkt) fair
Markt'bude f booth, stall
markten ['marktən] intr (um) bargain (for)
markt'fähig adj marketable
Markt'flecken m market town
marktgängig ['marktgeŋɪç] adj marketable
Markt'platz m market place
Markt'schreier m quack
Marmelade [marmə'ladə] f (-;-n) jam
Marmor ['marmər] m (-s;-e) marble
Mar'morbruch m marble quarry
marmorn ['marmorn] adj marble
marode [ma'rodə] adj (coll) tired out
Marodeur [marə'dør] m (-s;-e) marauder
marodieren [marə'dirən] intr maraud
Marone [ma'ronə] f (-;-n) chestnut
Maroquin [marə'kẽ] m (-s;) morocco
Marotte [ma'rɔtə] f (-;-n) whim
marsch [marʃ] interj march!; be off!; **m., m.!** on the double || **Marsch** m (-es; ⁓e) march; **in M. setzen** get going; **j-m den M. blasen** (coll) chew s.o. out; **(sich) in M. setzen** set out
Marschall ['marʃal] m (-s;⁓e) marshal
Mar'schallstab m marshal's baton
Marsch'gepäck n full field pack
marschieren [mar'ʃirən] intr (SEIN) march
Marsch'kompanie f replacement company
Marsch'lied n marching song
Marsch'verpflegung f field rations
Marter ['martər] f (-;-n) torture
martern ['martərn] tr torture, torment
Mar'terpfahl m stake
Märtyrer -in ['mertyrər(ɪn)] §6 mf martyr
Märtyrertum ['mertyrərtum] n (-s;) martyrdom
März [merts] m (-[es];-e) March
Masche ['maʃə] f (-;-n) mesh; stitch; (fig) trick
Ma'schendraht m chicken wire; screen; wire mesh
ma'schenfest adj runproof
Maschine [ma'ʃinə] f (-;-n) machine; (aer) airplane
maschinell [maʃɪ'nel] adj mechanical || adv by machine
Maschi'nenantrieb m—**mit M.** machine-driven
Maschi'nenbau m (-[e]s;) mechanical engineering
Maschi'nengewehr n machine gun
Maschi'nengewehrschütze m machine gunner
maschi'nenmäßig adj mechanical
Maschi'nenpistole f tommy gun
Maschi'nenschaden m engine trouble
Maschi'nenschlosser m machinist
maschi'nenschreiben tr type || **Maschinenschreiben** n (-s;-) typing; typewritten letter
Maschi'nenschrift f typescript
Maschi'nensprache f computer language
Maschinerie [maʃɪnə'ri] f (-;) (& fig) machinery
Maschinist -in [maʃɪ'nɪst(ɪn)] §7 mf machinist
Masern ['mazərn] pl measles
Maserung ['mazərʊŋ] f (-;) grain (in wood)
Maske ['maskə] f (-;-n) mask; (fig) disguise; (theat) make-up
Ma'skenball m masquerade
Maskerade [maskə'radə] f (-;-n) masquerade
maskieren [mas'kirən] tr mask
Maskotte [mas'kɔtə] f (-;-n) mascot
maskulin [masku'lin] adj masculine
Maskuli·num [masku'linum] n (-s;-na [na]) masculine noun
maß [mas] pret of **messen** || **Maß** n (-es;-e) measure; (Messung) measurement; (Ausdehnung) extent, dimension; (Verhältnis) rate, proportion; (Grad) degree; (Mäßigung) moderation; **das Maß ist voll!** I've had it!; **das Maß überschreiten** go too far; **er hat sein gerütteltes Maß an Kummer gehabt** he had his full share of trouble; **in gewissem Maße** to a certain extent; **in hohem Maße**

highly; **j-m Maß nehmen zu** take s.o.'s measurements for; **Maß halten** observe moderation; **mit Maße** in moderation; **nach Maß angefertigt** custom-made; **ohne Maß und Ziel** without limit; **weder Maß noch Ziel kennen** know no bounds; **zweierlei Maß** double standard ‖ *f* (-; & -e) quart (*of beer*), stein

massakrieren [masaˈkriːrən] *tr* massacre

Maß'anzug *m* tailor-made suit

Maß'arbeit *f* work made to order

Masse [ˈmasə] *f* (-;-n) mass; bulk; (*Menge*) volume; (*Volk*) crowd; (*Hinterlassenschaft*) estate; (elec) ground; **die breite M.** the masses; the rank and file; **e-e Masse...**(coll) lots of

Maß'einheit *f* unit of measure

Masseleisen [ˈmasəlaɪzən] *n* pigiron

Massen– *comb.fm.* mass, bulk, wholesale

Mas'senabsatz *m* wholesale selling

Mas'senangriff *m* mass attack

Mas'senanziehung *f* gravitation

mas'senhaft *adj* in large quantities

Maß'gabe *f*—**mit der M.**, **daß** with the understanding that; **nach M.** (*genit*) in proportion to; according to; (*jur*) as provided in

maß'gebend, maßgeblich [ˈmasɡeplɪç] *adj* standard; authoritative; (*Kreise*) leading, influential; **das ist nicht maßgebend für** that is no criterion for

maß'gerecht *adj* to scale

maß'halten §90 *intr* observe moderation

maß'haltig *adj* precise

massieren [maˈsiːrən] *tr* massage; (*Truppen*) mass

massig [ˈmasɪç] *adj* bulky; solid; (*Person*) stout ‖ *adv*—**m. viel** (coll) very much

mäßig [ˈmɛsɪç] *adj* moderate; frugal; (*Leistung*) mediocre

mäßigen [ˈmɛsɪɡən] *tr* moderate, tone down ‖ *ref* control oneself

Mä'ßigkeit *f* moderation; frugality; temperance

Mä'ßigung *f* (-;) moderation

massiv [maˈsiːf] *adj* massive; solid

Maß'krug *m* beer mug, stein

Maß'liebchen *n* daisy

maß'los *adj* immoderate ‖ *adv* extremely

Maß'nahme *f* (-;-n), **Maß'regel** *f* (-; -n) measure, step, move

maß'regeln *tr* reprimand

Maß'schneider *m* custom tailor

Maß'stab *m* ruler; (fig) yardstick, standard; (*auf Landkarten*) scale; **jeden M. verlieren** lose all sense of proportion

maß'voll *adj* moderate; (*Benehmen*) discreet

Mast [mast] *m* (-es;-en & -e) pole; (naut) mast ‖ *f* (-;) (*Schweinefutter*) mast

Mast'baum *m* (naut) mast

Mast'darm *m* rectum

mästen [ˈmɛstən] *tr* fatten

Mast'korb *m* masthead, crow's nest

Material [materiˈɑl] *n* (-s;-ien [ɪ-ən]) material

Materialismus [materiˈaˈlɪsmʊs] *m* (-;) materialism

materialistisch [materiaˈlɪstɪʃ] *adj* materialistic

Material'waren *pl* (Aust) medical supplies

Materie [maˈteriːə] *f* (-;-n) matter

materiell [materiˈɛl] *adj* material; (*Schwierigkeiten*) financial; (*Recht*) substantive

Mathe [ˈmatə] *f* (-;) (coll) math

Mathematik [matemaˈtik] *f* (-;) mathematics

Mathematiker –in [mateˈmɑtikər(ɪn)] §6 *mf* mathematician

mathematisch [mateˈmɑtɪʃ] *adj* mathematical

Matratze [maˈtratsə] *f* (-;-n) mattress

Mätresse [mɛˈtresə] *f* (-;-n) mistress

Matrize [maˈtritsə] *f* (-;-n) stencil; (*Stempel*) die, matrix

Matrone [maˈtronə] *f* (-;-n) matron

matro'nenhaft *adj* matronly

Matrose [maˈtrozə] *m* (-n;-n) sailor

Matro'senanzug *m* sailor's uniform

Matro'senjacke *f* (nav) peacoat

Matsch [matʃ] *m* (-es) (*Brei*) mush; (*Schlamm*) mud; (*halbgetauter Schnee*) slush

matschig [ˈmatʃɪç] *adj* mushy; muddy; slushy

matt [mat] *adj* dull; weak; limp; (*Glas, Birne*) frosted; (*Börse*) slack; (*erschöpft*) exhausted; (*Kugel*) spent; (*Licht*) dim; (*Metall*) tarnished; (phot) matt; **m. machen** dull; tarnish; **m. setzen** checkmate

Matte [ˈmatə] *f* (-;-n) mat; (*Wiese*) Alpine meadow; (poet) mead

Matt'glas *n* frosted glass

Matt'gold *n* dull gold

Matt'heit *f* dullness; fatigue

matt'herzig *adj* faint-hearted

Mat'tigkeit *f* (-;) fatigue

Matura [maˈtura] *f* (-;) (Aust) final examination (*before graduation*)

Mätzchen [ˈmɛtsçən] *n* (-s;-) trick; **M. machen** play tricks; put on airs

Mauer [ˈmaʊ.ər] *f* (-;-n) wall

Mau'erblümchen *n* (fig) wallflower

Mau'erkalk *m* mortar

mauern [ˈmaʊ.ərn] *tr* build (*in stone or brick*)

Mau'erstein *m* brick

Mau'erwerk *n* brickwork; masonry

Mau'erziegel *m* brick

Maul [maʊl] *n* (-[e]s;⸚er) mouth; maw; **halt's M.!** (sl) shut up!

Maul'affe *m* gaping fool

Maul'beerbaum *m* mulberry tree

Maul'beere *f* mulberry

maulen [ˈmaʊlən] *intr* gripe

Maul'esel *m* mule

maul'faul *adj* too lazy to talk

Maul'held *m* braggart

Maul'korb *m* muzzle

Maul'schelle *f* slap in the face

Maul'sperre *f* lock jaw

Maul'tier *n* mule

Maul'trommel *f* Jew's-harp

Maul'– und Klau'enseuche f hoof and mouth disease
Maul'werk n—**ein großes M. haben** have the gift of gab
Maul'wurf m (zool) mole
Maul'wurfshaufen m, **Maul'wurfshügel** m molehill
Maure ['maurə] m (-n;-n) Moor
Maurer ['maurər] m (-s;-) mason; bricklayer
Mau'rerkelle f trowel
Mau'rerpolier m bricklayer foreman
Maus [maus] f (-;¨e) mouse
Mäuschen ['mɔisçən] n (-s;-) little mouse; (fig) pet, darling; wench
Mau'sefalle f mousetrap
mausen ['mauzən] tr pilfer, swipe || intr catch mice
Mauser ['mauzər] f (-;) molting season; **in der M. sein** be molting
mausern ['mauzərn] ref molt
mau'setot' adj dead as a doornail
mausig ['mauzıç] adj—**sich m. machen** put on airs, be stuck-up
Mauso·leum [mauzo'le·um] n (-s; –leen ['le·ən]) mausoleum
Maxime [ma'ksimə] f (-;-n) maxim
Mayonnaise [majo'nezə] f (-;) mayonnaise
Mechanik [me'çanık] f (-;-en) mechanics; (Triebwerk) mechanism
Mechaniker [me'çanıkər] m (-s;-) mechanic
mechanisch [me'çanıʃ] adj mechanical; power-
mechanisieren [meçanı'zirən] tr mechanize
Mechanis·mus [meça'nısmus] m (-; –men [mən]) mechanism; (Uhrwerk) works
Meckerer ['mɛkərər] m (-s;-) (coll) grumbler
meckern ['mekərn] intr bleat; (coll) grumble
Medaille [me'daljə] f (-;-n) medal
Medaillon [medal'jɔ̃] n (-s;-s) medallion; locket
Medikament [medıka'ment] n (-s;-e) medication
Meditation [medıta'tsjon] f (-;-en) meditation
meditieren [medı'tirən] intr meditate
Medizin [medı'tsin] f (-;-en) medicine
Medizinalassistant [medıtsı'nalasıstant(ın)] §7 mf intern
Medizinalbeamte [medıtsı'nalbə·amtə] m health officer
Medizinalbehörde [medıtsı'nalbəhørdə] f board of health
Mediziner -in [medı'tsinər(ın)] §6 mf physician; medical student
medizinisch [medı'tsinıʃ] adj medical, medicinal; medicated; **medizinische Fakultät** medical school
Meer [mer] n (-[e]s;-e) sea; **am Meere** at the seashore; **übers M.** overseas
Meer'busen m bay, gulf
Meer'enge f straits
Meeres– [merəs] comb.fm. sea, marine
Mee'resarm m inlet
Mee'resboden m bottom of the sea
Mee'resbucht f bay

Mee'resgrund m bottom of the sea
Mee'reshöhe f sea level
Mee'resküste f seacoast
Mee'resleuchten n phosphorescence
Mee'resspiegel m sea level
meer'grün adj sea-green
Meer'rettich m horseradish
Meer'schaum m meerschaum
Meer'schwein n porpoise
Meer'schweinchen n guinea pig
Meer'ungeheuer n sea monster
Meer'weib n mermaid
Mehl [mel] n (-[e]s;) (grobes) meal; (feines) flour; (Staub) dust, powder
Mehl'kloß m dumpling
Mehl'speise f pastry; pudding
Mehl'suppe f gruel
Mehl'tau m mildew
mehr [mer] invar adj & adv more; **immer m.** more and more; **kein Wort m.!** not another word!; **m. oder weniger** more or less, give or take; **nicht m.** no more, no longer; **nie m.** never again || **Mehr** n (-s;) majority; (Zuwachs) increase; (Überschuß) surplus
Mehr'arbeit f extra work; (Überstunden) overtime
Mehr'aufwand m, **Mehr'ausgabe** f additional expenditure
Mehr'betrag m surplus; extra charge
mehr'deutig adj ambiguous
mehren ['merən] tr & ref increase
mehrere ['merərə] adj & pron several
mehr'fach adj manifold; repeated, multiple
mehr'farbig adj multicolored
Mehr'gebot n higher bid
Mehr'gepäck n excess luggage
Mehr'gewicht n excess weight
Mehr'heit f (-;-en) majority; (pol) plurality
Mehr'heitsbeschluß m, **Mehr'heitsentscheidung** f plurality vote
mehr'jährig adj (bot) perennial
Mehr'kosten pl extra charges
Mehr'ladegewehr n repeater
Mehr'leistung f increased performance; (ins) extended benefits
mehrmalig ['mermalıç] adj repeated
mehrmals ['mermals] adv several times, on several occasions; repeatedly
Mehr'porto n additional postage
Mehr'preis m extra charge
mehr'seitig adj multilateral; many-sided; (Brief) of many pages
mehrsilbig ['merzılbıç] adj polysyllabic
mehrsprachig ['merʃpraxıç] adj polyglot
mehrstöckig ['merʃtœkıç] adj multistory
mehrstufig ['merʃtufıç] adj multistage
Meh'rung f (-;) increase, multiplication
Mehr'verbrauch m increased consumption
Mehr'wertsteuer f added value tax
Mehr'zahl f majority; (gram) plural
meiden ['maidən] §112 tr avoid, shun
Meier ['mai·ər] m (-s;-) tenant farmer; dairy farmer
Meierei [mai·ə'rai] f (-;-en) dairy

Mei′ergut n, **Mei′erhof** m dairy farm

Meile [ˈmaɪlə] f (−;−n) mile

mei′lenweit adj extending for miles, miles and miles of || adv far away; **m. auseinander** miles apart

Mei′lenzahl f mileage

mein [maɪn] §2,2 poss adj my || §2,4,5 pron mine; **das Meine** my share; my due; **die Meinen** my family

Meineid [ˈmaɪnaɪt] m (−[e]s;) perjury; **e−n M. schwören** (or **leisten**) commit perjury

meineidig [ˈmaɪnaɪdɪç] adj perjured; **m. werden** perjure oneself

meinen [ˈmaɪnən] tr think; (im Sinne haben) mean, intend; **das will ich m.** I should think so; **die Sonne meint es heute gut** the sun is very warm to-day; **es ehrlich m.** have honorable intentions; **es gut m.** mean well; **ich meinte dich im Recht** I thought you were in the right; **m. Sie das ernst** (or **im Ernst**)? do you really mean it?; **was m. Sie damit?** what do you mean by that?; **was m. Sie dazu?** what do you think of that? || intr think; **w. Sie?** do you think so?; **m. Sie nicht auch?** don't you agree?; **wie m. Sie?** I beg your pardon?

meinerseits [ˈmaɪnərˈzaɪts] adv for my part

meinesgleichen [ˈmaɪnəsˈɡlaɪçən] pron people like me, the likes of me

meinethlben [ˈmaɪnətˈhalbən], **meinetwegen** [ˈmaɪnətˈveːɡən] adv for my sake, on my account; for all I care

meinetwillen [ˈmaɪnətˈvɪlən] adv—**um m.** for my sake, on my behalf

meinige [ˈmaɪnɪɡə] §2,5 pron mine

Mei′nung f (−;−en) opinion; **anderer M. mit j−m sein über** (acc) disagree with s.o. about; **der M. sein** be of the opinion; **geteilter M. sein** be of two minds; **j−m die** (or **seine**) **M. sagen** give s.o. a piece of one's mind; **meiner M. nach** in my opinion; **vorgefaßte M.** preconceived idea

Mei′nungsäußerung f expression of opinion

Mei′nungsaustausch m exchange of views

Mei′nungsbefragung f, **Mei′nungsforschung** f public opinion poll

Mei′nungsumfrage f public opinion poll

Mei′nungsverschiedenheit f difference of opinion, disagreement

Meise [ˈmaɪzə] f (−;−n) titmouse

Meißel [ˈmaɪsəl] m (−s;−) chisel

meißeln [ˈmaɪsəln] tr & intr chisel

meist [maɪst] adj most; **am meisten** most; **das meiste** the most; **die meisten Menschen** most people; **die meiste Zeit** most of the time; **die meiste Zeit des Jahres** most of the year || adv usually, generally

Meist′begünstigungsklausel f most-favored nation clause

Meist′bietende §5 mf highest bidder

meistens [ˈmaɪstəns] adv mostly

Meister [ˈmaɪstər] m (−s;−) master; boss; (im Betrieb) foreman; (sport) champion

mei′sterhaft adj masterly

Meisterin [ˈmaɪstərɪn] f (−;−nen) master's wife; (sport) champion

mei′sterlich adj masterly

meistern [ˈmaɪstərn] tr master

Mei′sterschaft f (−;−en) mastery; (sport) championship

Mei′sterstück n, **Mei′sterwerk** n masterpiece

Mei′sterzug m master stroke

Melancholie [melaŋkoˈliː] f (−;) melancholy

melancholisch [melaŋˈkoːlɪʃ] adj melancholy

Melasse [meˈlasə] f (−;−n) molasses

Meldeamt [ˈmɛldəˌamt] n. **Meldebüro** [ˈmɛldəˌbyro] n registration office

Meldefahrer [ˈmɛldəˌfarər] m (mil) dispatch rider

Meldegänger [ˈmɛldəˌɡɛŋər] m (mil) messenger, runner

melden [ˈmɛldən] tr report; (polizeilich) turn (s.o.) in; **den Empfang m.** (genit) acknowledge the receipt of; **er hat nichts zu m.** he has nothing to say in the matter; **gemeldet werden zu** (sport) be entered in; **j−m m. lassen, daß** send s.o. word that || ref report; (Alter) begin to show; (Gläubiger) come forward; (Kind) cry; (Magen) growl; (polizeilich) register; (Winter) set in; (telp) answer; **sich auf e−e Anzeige m.** answer an ad; **sich krank m.** (mil) go on sick call; **sich m. zu** apply for; (freiwillig) volunteer for; (mil) enlist in; (sport) enter; **sich zum Dienst m.** (mil) report for duty; **sich zum Wort m.** ask to speak; (in der Schule) hold up the hand

Mel′der m (−s;−) (mil) runner

Meldezettel [ˈmɛldətsɛtəl] m registration form

Mel′dung f (−;−en) report; message, notification; (Bewerbung) application

Melkeimer [ˈmɛlkaɪmər] m milk pail

melken [ˈmɛlkən] §113 tr milk

Melo·die [meloˈdiː] f (−;−dien [ˈdiːən] melody

melodisch [meˈloːdɪʃ] adj melodious

Melone [meˈloːnə] f (−;−n) melon; (coll) derby

Meltau [ˈmɛltau] m (−[e]s;) honeydew

Membran [memˈbran] f (−;−en), **Membrane** [memˈbranə] f (−;−n) membrane

Memme [ˈmɛmə] f (−;−n) coward

Memoiren [memoˈarən] pl memoirs

memorieren [memoˈriːrən] tr memorize

Menge [ˈmɛŋə] f (−;−n) quantity, amount; crowd; **e−e M.** a lot of

mengen [ˈmɛŋən] tr mix || ref (unter acc) mingle (with); (in acc) meddle (in)

Men′genlehre f (math) theory of sets

men′genmäßig adj quantitative

Mengsel [ˈmɛŋzəl] n (−s;−) hodgepodge

Mennige [ˈmɛnɪɡə] f (−;) rust-preventive paint

Mensch [menʃ] m (−en;−en) human being, man; person, individual; **die Menschen** the people; **kein M.** no one || n (−es; −er) hussy, slut

Menschen– [mɛnʃən] *comb.fm.* man, of men; human
Men'schenalter *n* generation, age
Men'schenfeind –in §8 *mf* misanthropist
Men'schenfresser *m* cannibal
Men'schenfreund –in §8 *mf* philanthropist
men'schenfreundlich *adj* philanthropic, humanitarian
Men'schengedenken *n*—**seit M.** since time immemorial
Men'schengeschlecht *n* mankind
Men'schengewühl *n* milling crowd
Men'schenglück *n* human happiness
Men'schenhandel *m* slave trade
Men'schenhaß *m* misanthropy
Men'schenjagd *f* manhunt
Men'schenkenner –in §6 *mf* judge of human nature
Men'schenkind *n* human being; **armes M.** poor soul
men'schenleer *adj* deserted
Men'schenliebe *f* philanthropy
Men'schenmaterial *n* manpower
men'schenmöglich *adj* humanly possible
Men'schenraub *m* kidnaping
Men'schenräuber –in §6 *mf* kidnaper
Men'schenrechte *pl* human rights
men'schenscheu *adj* shy, unsociable
Men'schenschinder *m* oppressor, slave driver
Men'schenschlag *m* race
Men'schenseele *f* human soul; **keine M.** not a living soul
Men'schenskind *interj* man alive!
Men'schensohn *m* (Bib) Son of man
men'schenunwürdig *adj* degrading
Men'schenverächter –in §6 *mf* cynic
Men'schenverstand *m*—**guter M.** common sense
Men'schenwürde *f* human dignity
men'schenwürdig *adj* decent
Mensch'heit *f* (–;) mankind, humanity
mensch'lich *adj* human; (*human*) humane
Mensch'lichkeit *f* (–;) humanity
Menschwerdung ['mɛn/vɛrduŋ] *f* (–;) incarnation
Menstruation [mɛntru·a'tsjon] *f* (–;-en) menstruation
Mensur [mɛn'zur] *f* (–;-en) measure; (*Meßglas*) measuring glass; students' duel
Mentalität [mɛntalɪtɛt] *f* (–;) mentality
Menuett [menu'ɛt] *n* (–[e]s;-e) minuet
Meridian [merɪ'djan] *m* (–s;-e) (astr) meridian
merkbar ['mɛrkbar] *adj* noticeable
Merkblatt ['mɛrkblat] *n* instruction sheet
Merkbuch ['mɛrkbux] *n* notebook
merken ['mɛrkən] *tr* notice; realize; **etw m. lassen** show s.th., betray s.th.; **man merkte es sofort an ihrem Ausdruck, daß** one noticed immediately by her expression that || *ref*—**m. Sie sich** [*dat*], **was ich sage!** mark my word!; **sich** [*dat*] **etw m.** bear s.th. in mind; **sich** [*dat*] **nichts m. lassen** not give oneself away || *intr*—**m. auf** (*acc*) pay attention to, heed
merk'lich *adj* noticeable

Merkmal ['mɛrkmal] *n* (–[e]s;-e) mark, feature, characteristic
Merkur [mɛr'kur] *m & n* (–s;) mercury
Merk'wort *n* (–[e]s;-̈er) catchword; (theat) cue
merk'würdig *adj* remarkable; (*seltsam*) curious, strange
merkwürdigerweise ['mɛrkvʏrdɪgər-vaɪzə] *adv* strange to say
Merk'würdigkeit *f* (–;-en) strange thing
Merk'zeichen *n* mark
meschugge [me'ʃuɡə] *adj* (coll) nuts
Mesner ['mɛsnər] *m* (–s;-) sexton
Meß– [mɛs] *comb.fm.* measuring; (eccl) mass
Meß'band *n* (–[e]s;-̈er) measuring tape
meßbar ['mɛsbar] *adj* measurable
Meß'buch *n* (relig) missal
Meß'diener *m* acolyte
Messe ['mɛsə] *f* (–;-n) fair; (eccl) mass; (nav) officers' mess
messen ['mɛsən] §70 *tr* measure; (*Zeit*) time, clock; (*mustern*) size up || *ref* —**sich m. mit** cope with; (*geistig*) match wits with; **sich nicht m. können mit** be no match for || *intr* measure
Messer ['mɛsər] *m* (–s;-) gauge; meter || *n* (–s;-) knife; (surg) scalpel; **bis aufs M.** to the death
Mes'serheld *m* (coll) cutthroat
mes'serscharf *adj* razor-sharp
Mes'serschmied *m* cutler
Messerschmiedewaren ['mɛsər/midəva-rən] *pl* cutlery
Mes'serschneide *f* knife edge
Meß'gewand *n* (eccl) vestment; chasuble
Meß'hemd *n* (eccl) alb
Messias [mɛ'si·as] *invar m* Messiah
Messing ['mɛsɪŋ] *n* (–s;) brass
messingen ['mɛsɪŋən] *adj* brass
Meß'opfer *n* sacrifice of the mass
Mes'sung *f* (–;-en) measurement
Metall [me'tal] *n* (–s;-e) metal
Metall'baukasten *m* erector set
metallen [me'talən], **metallisch** [me-'talɪʃ] *adj* metallic
Metall'säge *f* hacksaw
Metallurgie [metalur'gi] *f* (–;) metallurgy
metall'verarbeitend *adj* metal-processing
Metall'waren *pl* hardware
Metapher [me'tafər] *f* (–;-n) metaphor
Meteor [mɛtɛ'or] *m* (–s;-e) meteor
Meteorologe [mɛtɛ·oro'loɡə] *m* (–n;-n) meteorologist
Meteorologie [mɛtɛ·orolo'gi] *f* (–;) meteorolgy
Meteorologin [mɛtɛ·oro'loɡɪn] *f* (–;-nen) meteorologist
meteorologisch [mɛtɛ·oro'loɡɪʃ] *adj* meteorological
Meteor'stein *m* meteorite, aerolite
Meter ['metər] *m & n* (–s;-) meter
Me'termaß *n* tape measure
Methode [me'todə] *f* (–;-n) method
methodisch [me'todɪʃ] *adj* methodical
Metrik ['metrɪk] *f* (–;) metrics
metrisch ['metrɪʃ] *adj* metrical

Metropole [metrə'polə] *f* (-;-n) metropolis

Mette ['metə] *f* (-;-n) matins

Mettwurst ['metvurst] *f* soft sausage

Metzelei [metsə'laɪ] *f* (-;-en) massacre, slaughter

metzeln ['metsəln] *tr* massacre

Metzger ['metsgər] *m* (-s;-) butcher

Metzgerei [metsgə'raɪ] *f* (-;-en) butcher shop

Meuchelmord ['mɔɪçəlmɔrt] *m* assassination

Meuchelmörder –in ['mɔɪçəlmœrdər (ɪn)] §6 *mf* assassin

meucheln ['mɔɪçəln] *tr* murder

meuchlerisch ['mɔɪçlərɪʃ] *adj* murderous

meuchlings ['mɔɪçlɪŋs] *adv* treacherously

Meute ['mɔɪtə] *f* (-;-n) pack (*of hounds*); (fig) horde, gang

Meuterei [mɔɪtə'raɪ] *f* (-;-en) mutiny

meuterisch ['mɔɪtərɪʃ] *adj* mutinous

meutern ['mɔɪtərn] *intr* mutiny

Mexikaner –in [meksɪ'kanər(ɪn)] §6 *mf* Mexican

mexikanisch [meksɪ'kanɪʃ] *adj* Mexican

Mexiko ['meksɪko] *n* (-s;) Mexico

miauen [mɪ'au.ən] *intr* meow

mich [mɪç] *pers pron* me ‖ §11 *reflex pron* myself

mied [mit] *pret of* **meiden**

Mieder ['midər] *n* (-s;-) bodice

Mie'derwaren *pl* foundation garments

Mief [mif] *n* (-s;) foul air

Miene ['minə] *f* (-;-n) mien; facial expression; **M. machen zu** (*inf*) make a move to (*inf*); **ohne die M. zu verziehen** without flinching

mies [mis] *adj* (coll) miserable, lousy

Mies'macher *m* (-s;-) alarmist

Miet– [mit] *comb.fm.* rental, rented; rent

Miet'auto *n* rented car

Miete ['mitə] *f* (-;-n) rent; (*Zins*) rental; (*Erd-*) pit (*for storing vegetables*); **in M. geben** rent out; **in M. nehmen** rent; **kalte M.** rent not including heat; **zur M. wohnen** live in a rented apartment (or home)

mieten ['mitən] *tr* rent, hire; (*Flugzeug*),charter

Miet'entschädigung *f* allowance for house rent

Mie'ter –in §6 *mf* tenant

Miet'ertrag *m* rent, rental

Miet'kontrakt *m* lease

Mietling ['mitlɪŋ] *m* (-s;-e) hireling

Miets'haus *n* apartment building

Miets'kaserne *f* tenement house

Miet'vertrag *m* lease

Miet'wagen *m* rented car

Miet'wohung *f* apartment

Miet'zins *m* rent

Mieze ['mitsə] *f* (-;-n) pussy

Migräne [mɪ'grɛnə] *f* (-;-n) migraine

Mikrobe [mɪ'krobə] *f* (-;-n) microbe

Mikrofilm ['mikrofɪlm] *m* microfilm

Mikrophon [mɪkrə'fon] *n* (-s;-e) microphone

Mikroskop [mɪkrə'skop] *n* (-s;-e) microscope

mikroskopisch [mɪkrə'skopɪʃ] *adj* microscopic

Milbe ['mɪlbə] *f* (-;-n) (ent) mite

Milch [mɪlç] *f* (-;) milk

Milch'bart *m* sissy

Milch'brot *n*, **Milch'brötchen** *n* French roll

Milch'bruder *m* foster brother

Milch'drüse *f* mammary gland

Milch'eimer *m* milk pail

Milch'geschäft *n* creamery, dairy

Milch'glas *m* milk glass

milchig ['mɪlçɪç] *adj* milky

Milch'mädchen *n* milkmaid

Milch'mädchenrechnung *f* oversimplification

Milch'mixgetränk *n* milkshake

Milch'pulver *n* powdered milk

Milch'reis *m* rice pudding

Milch'schwester *f* foster sister

Milch'straße *f* Milky Way

Milch'tüte *f* carton of milk

Milch'wirtschaft *f* dairy

Milchzähne ['mɪlçtsɛnə] *pl* baby teeth

mild [mɪlt] *adj* mild; (*nicht streng*) lenient; (*Stiftung*) charitable; (*Wein*) smooth; (*Lächeln*) faint ‖ **Milde** *f* (-;) mildness; leniency; kindness

mildern ['mɪldərn] *tr* soften, alleviate; **mildernde Umstände** extenuating circumstances

Mil'derung *f* (-;) softening, alleviation, mitigation

mild'herzig, mild'tätig *adj* charitable

Militär [mɪlɪ'tɛr] *n* (-s;) military, army; **zum M. gehen** join the army ‖ *m* (-s;-s) professional soldier

Militär'dienst *m* military service

Militär'geistliche §5 *m* chaplain

Militär'gericht *n* military court

militärisch [mɪlɪ'tɛrɪʃ] *adj* military

Militarismus [mɪlɪta'rɪsmus] *m* (-;) militarism

Miliz [mɪ'lits] *f* (-;) militia

Miliz'soldat *m* militiaman

Milliardär –in [mɪljar'dɛr(ɪn)] §8 *mf* multimillionaire

Milliarde [mɪl'jardə] *f* (-;-n) billion

Milligramm [mɪlɪ'gram] *n* milligram

Millimeter [mɪlɪ'metər] *n* & *m* millimeter

Millime'terpapier *n* graph paper

Million [mɪl'jon] *f* (-;-en) million

Millionär –in [mɪljo'ner(ɪn)] §8 *mf* millionaire

millionste [mɪl'jonstə] §9 *adj* & *pron* millionth

Milz [mɪlts] *f* (-;) spleen

Mime ['mimə] *m* (-n;-n) mime

Mimiker –in ['mimɪkər(ɪn)] §6 *mf* mimic

Mimose [mɪ'mozə] *f* (-;-n) mimosa

minder ['mɪndər] *adj* lesser, smaller; (*geringer*) minor, inferior ‖ *adv* less; **m. gut** inferior; **nicht m.** likewise

min'derbedeutend *adj* less important

min'derbegabt *adj* less talented

min'derbemittelt *adj* of moderate means

Min'derbetrag *m* shortage, deficit

Min'derheit *f* (-;-en) minority

min'derjährig *adj* underage ‖ **Minderjährige** §5 *mf* minor

mindern ['mɪndərn] *tr* lessen, diminish
Min'derung *f* (-;-en) diminution
min'derwertig *adj* inferior
Min'derwertigkeit *f* inferiority
Min'derwertigkeitskomplex *m* inferiority complex
Min'derzahl *f* minority
Mindest– [mɪndəest] *comb.fm.* minimum
mindeste ['mɪndəstə] §9 *adj* least; (*kleinste*) smallest; **nicht die mindesten Aussichten** not the slightest chance; **nicht im mindesten** not in the least; **zum mindesten** at the very least
mindestens ['mɪndəstəns] *adv* at least
Min'destgebot *n* lowest bid
Min'destlohn *m* minimum wage
Mine ['minə] *f* (-;-n) (*im Bleistift*) lead; (mil, min) mine; **alle Minen springen lassen** (fig) pull out all the stops
Minenleger ['minənlegər] *m* (-s;-) minelayer
Minenräumboot ['minənrɔɪmbot] *n* minesweeper
Mineral [minə'ral] *n* (-s;-e & -ien [jən]) mineral
mineralisch [minə'ralɪʃ] *adj* mineral
Mineralogie [minəralo'gi] *f* (-;) mineralogy
Miniatur [mɪnja'tur] *f* (-;-en) miniature
minieren [mɪ'nirən] *tr* (fig) undermine; (mil) mine
minimal [mɪnɪ'mal] *adj* minimal
Minirock ['mɪnɪrɔk] *m* miniskirt
Minister [mɪ'nɪstər] *m* (-s;-) minister, secretary
Ministe∙rium [mɪnɪs'terjum] *n* (-s; -rien [rjən]) ministry, department
Mini'sterpräsident *m* prime minister
Mini'sterrat *m* (-[e]s;-̈e) cabinet
Ministrant [mɪnɪs'trant] *m* (-en;-en) altar boy, acolyte
Minne ['mɪnə] *f* (-;) (obs) love
Min'nesänger *m* minnesinger; troubadour
minorenn [mɪno'rɛn] *adj* underage
minus ['minʊs] *adv* minus ‖ **Minus** *n* (-;-) minus; (com) deficit
Minute [mɪ'nutə] *f* (-;-n) minute
Minu'tenzeiger *m* minute hand
–minutig [mɪnutɪç] *comb.fm.* –minute
Minze ['mɪntsə] *f* (-;-n) (bot) mint
mir [mir] §11 *pers pron* me, to me, for me; **mir ist kalt** I am cold; **mir nichts, dir nichts** suddenly; **von mir aus** for all I care ‖ §11 *reflex pron* myself, to myself, for myself
Mirabelle [mira'belə] *f* (-;-n) yellow plum
Mirakel [mɪ'rakəl] *n* (-s;-) miracle
Mira'kelspiel *n* miracle play
Mischehe ['mɪʃ·eə] *f* mixed marriage
mischen ['mɪʃən] *tr* mix, blend; (cards) shuffle
Mischling ['mɪʃlɪŋ] *m* (-es;-e) halfbreed; mongrel
Mischmasch ['mɪʃmaʃ] *m* (-es;-e) hodgepodge
Mischpult ['mɪʃpʊlt] *n* (rad, telv) master console

Mischrasse ['mɪʃrasə] *f* cross-breed
Mi'schung *f* (-;-en) mixture, blend
Misere [mɪ'zerə] *f* (-;-n) misery
Miß–, miß– [mɪs] *comb.fm.* mis–, dis–, amiss; bad, wrong, false
mißach'ten *tr* disregard; (*geringschätzen*) slight
mißartet [mɪs'artət] *adj* degenerate
miß'behagen *intr* (*dat*) displeasure ‖ **Mißbehagen** *n* (-s;) displeasure
miß'bilden *tr* misshape, deform
Miß'bildung *f* (-;-en) deformity
miß'billigen *tr* disapprove
Miß'billigung *f* (-;-en) disapproval
Miß'brauch *m* abuse; (*falsche Anwendung*) misuse
mißbrau'chen *tr* abuse; misuse
mißbräuchlich ['mɪsbrɔɪçlɪç] *adj* improper
mißdeu'ten *tr* misinterpret
missen ['mɪsən] *tr* miss; do without
Miß'erfolg *m* failure, flop
Miß'ernte *f* bad harvest
Missetat ['mɪsətat] *f* misdeed; (*Verstoß*) offense; (*Verbrechen*) felony; (*Sünde*) sin
Missetäter –in ['mɪsətetər(ɪn)] §6 *mf* wrongdoer; offender; felon; sinner
mißfal'len §72 *intr* (*dat*) displease ‖ **Mißfallen** *n* (-s;) displeasure
miß'fällig *adj* displeasing; (*anstößig*) shocking; (*verächtlich*) disparaging
miß'farben, miß'farbig *adj* discolored
Miß'geburt *f* freak
mißgelaunt ['mɪsgəlaunt] *adj* in bad humor, sour
Miß'geschick *n* (-s;) mishap; misfortune
Miß'gestalt *f* deformity; monster
miß'gestaltet *adj* deformed, misshapen
mißgestimmt ['mɪsgə·tɪmt] *adj* grumpy
mißglücken (mißglük'ken) *intr* (SEIN) fail, not succeed
mißgön'nen *tr* begrudge
Miß'griff *m* mistake
Miß'gunst *f* grudge, jealousy
mißhan'deln *tr* mistreat
Miß'heirat *f* mismarriage
Mißhelligkeit ['mɪshelɪçkaɪt] *f* (-;-en) friction, disagreement
Mission [mɪ'sjon] *f* (-;-en) mission
Missionar [mɪsjo'nar] *m*, **Missionär** [mɪsjo'ner] *m* (-s;-e) missionary
Miß'klang *m* dissonance; (fig) sour note
Miß'kredit *m* discredit, disrepute
mißlang [mɪs'laŋ] *pret* of **mißlingen**
miß'lich *adj* awkward; (*gefährlich*) dangerous; (*bedenklich*) critical
miß'liebig *adj* unpopular
mißlingen [mɪs'lɪŋən] §142 *intr* (SEIN) go wrong, misfire, prove a failure ‖ **Mißlingen** *n* (-s;) failure
Miß'mut *m* bad humor; discontent
miß'mutig *adj* sullen; discontented
mißra'ten §63 *intr* (SEIN) go wrong, misfire; **mißratene Kinder** spoiled children
Miß'stand *m* bad state of affairs; **Mißstände abschaffen** remedy abuses
Miß'stimmung *f* dissension; (*Mißmut*) bad humor
Miß'ton *m* dissonance; (fig) sour note

mißtrau'en *intr* (*dat*) mistrust, distrust || **Miß'trauen** *n* (–s;) mistrust

mißtrauisch ['mɪstrau·ɪʃ] *adj* distrustful

Miß'vergnügen *n* displeasure

miß'vergnügt *adj* cross; discontented

Miß'verhältnis *n* disproportion

Miß'verständnis *n* misunderstanding

miß'verstehen §146 *tr* & *intr* misunderstand

Miß'wirtschaft *f* mismanagement

Mist [mɪst] *m* (–es;) dung, manure; (*Schmutz*) dirt; (fig) mess, nonsense; **M. machen** (coll) blow the job; (*Spaß machen*) (coll) horse around; **viel M. verzapfen** talk a lot of nonsense

Mist'beet *n* hotbed

Mistel ['mɪstəl] *f* (–;–n) mistletoe

misten ['mɪstən] *tr* (*Stall*) muck; (*Acker*) fertilize

Mist'fink *m* (coll) dirty brat

Mist'haufen *m* manure pile

mistig ['mɪstɪç] *adj* dirty; (*sehr unangenehm*) very unpleasant

mit [mɪt] *adv* along; also, likewise; simultaneously || *prep* (*dat*) with; **mit 18 Jahren** at the age of eighteen

Mit'angeklagte §5 *mf* codefendant

Mit'arbeit *f* cooperation, collaboration

mit'arbeiten *intr* cooperate, collaborate; **m. an** (*dat*) contribute to

Mit'arbeiter –in §6 *mf* co-worker

Mit'arbeiterstab *m* staff

mit'bekommen §99 *tr* receive when leaving; (*verstehen*) get, catch

mit'benutzen *tr* use jointly

Mit'bestimmung *f* share in decision making

mit'bewerben *ref* (um) compete (for)

Mit'bewerber –in §6 *mf* competitor

mit'bringen §65 *tr* bring along

Mitbringsel ['mɪtbrɪŋzəl] *n* (–s;–) little present

Mit'bürger –in §6 *mf* fellow citizen

Mit'eigentümer –in §6 *mf* co-owner

miteinan'der *adv* together

mit'empfinden §59 *tr* sympathize with

Mit'erbe *m*, **Mit'erbin** *f* coheir

Mitesser ['mɪtesər] *m* (–s;–) pimple, blackhead

mit'fahren §71 *intr* (SEIN) ride along; **j–n m. lassen** give s.o. a lift

mit'fühlen *tr* share, sympathize with

mit'fühlend *adj* sympathetic

mit'gehen §82 *intr* (SEIN) (mit) go along (with)

Mit'gift *f* dowry

Mit'giftjäger *m* fortune hunter

Mit'glied *n* member; **M. auf Lebenszeit** life member

Mit'gliederversammlung *f* general meeting

Mit'gliederzahl *f* membership

Mit'gliedsbeitrag *m* dues

Mit'gliedschaft *f* (–;–en) membership

Mit'gliedskarte *f* membership card

Mit'gliedstaat *m* member nation

Mit'haftung *f* joint liability

mit'halten §90 *intr* be one of a party; **ich halte mit** I'll join you

mit'helfen §96 *intr* help along, pitch in

Mit'helfer –in §6 *mf* assistant

Mit'herausgeber –in §6 *mf* coeditor

Mit'hilfe *f* assistance

mithin' *adv* consequently

mit'hören *tr* listen in on; (*zufällig*) overhear; (rad, telp) monitor

Mit'inhaber –in §6 *mf* copartner

Mit'kämpfer –in §6 *mf* fellow fighter

mit'klingen §142 *intr* resonate

mit'kommen §99 *intr* (SEIN) come along; (fig) keep up

mit'kriegen *tr* (coll) see **mitbekommen**

Mit'läufer –in §6 *mf* (pol) fellow traveler

Mit'laut *m* consonant

Mit'leid *n* compassion, pity

Mit'leidenschaft *f—j–n* in M. ziehen affect s.o.

mit'leidig *adj* compassionate; pitiful

Mit'leidsbezeigung *f* condolences

mit'leidslos *adj* pitiless

mit'leidsvoll *adj* full of pity

mit'machen *tr* participate in, join in on; (*ertragen*) suffer, endure

Mit'mensch *m* fellow man

mit'nehmen §116 *tr* take along; (*erschöpfen*) wear out, exhaust; (*abholen*) pick up; (*Ort, Museum*) visit, take in; **j–n arg m.** treat s.o. roughly

mitnichten [mɪt'nɪçtən] *adv* by no means, not at all

mit'rechnen *tr* include || *intr* count

mit'reden *tr—ein Wort mitzureden haben bei** have a say in || *intr* join in a conversation

Mit'reisende §5 *mf* travel companion

mit'reißen §53 *tr* (& fig) carry away

mit'reißend *adj* stirring

mitsamt [mɪt'zamt] *prep* (*dat*) together with

mit'schreiben §62 *intr* take notes

Mit'schuld *f* (an *dat*) complicity (in)

mit'schuldig *adj* (an *dat*) accessory (to) || **Mitschuldige** §5 *mf* accomplice

Mit'schüler –in §6 *mf* schoolmate

mit'singen §142 *intr* sing along

mit'spielen *intr* play along; (fig) be involved; **j–m arg (or übel) m. play** s.o. dirty

Mit'spieler –in §6 *mf* partner

Mit'spracherecht *n* right to share in decision making

mit'sprechen §64 *tr* say with (s.o.) || *intr* be involved; (*an e–r Entscheidung beteiligt sein*) share in decision making

Mit'tag *m* noon; (poet) South; **M. machen** stop for lunch; **zu M. essen** eat lunch

Mittag– *comb.fm.* midday, noon; lunch

Mit'tagbrot *n*, **Mit'tagessen** *n* lunch

mit'täglich *adj* midday, noontime

mittags ['mɪtaks] *adv* at noon

Mit'tagskreis *m*, **Mit'tagslinie** *f* meridian

Mit'tagsruhe *f* siesta

Mit'tagsstunde *f* noon; lunch hour

Mit'tagstisch *m* lunch table; lunch; **gut bürglicher M.** good home cooking

Mit'tagszeit *f* noontime; lunch time

Mit'täter –in §6 *mf* accomplice

Mit'täterschaft *f* complicity

Mitte ['mɪtə] ƒ (-;-n) middle, midst; (*Mittelpunkt*) center; **ab durch die M.!** (coll) scram!; **aus unserer M.** from among us; **die goldene M.** the golden mean; **die richtige M. treffen** hit a happy medium; **er ist M. Vierzig** he is in his mid-forties; **in die M. nehmen** take by both arms; (sport) sandwich in; **j-m um die M. fassen** put one's arms around s.o.'s waist

mit′teilbar *adj* communicable

mit′teilen *tr* tell; (*im Vertrauen*) intimate; **ich muß Ihnen leider m.,** **daß** I regret to inform you that

mitteilsam ['mɪttaɪlzam] *adj* communicative

Mit′teilung ƒ (-;-en) communication; information; (*amtliche*) communiqué; (*an die Presse*) release

mittel ['mɪtəl] *adj* medium, average ‖ **Mittel** *n* (-s;-) middle; means; (*Heil-*) remedy; (*Maßnahme*) measure;. (*Ausweg*) expedient; (*Durchschnitt*) average; (math) mean; (phys) medium; **im M.** on the average; **ins M. treten** (or **sich ins M. legen**) intervene, intercede; **letztes M.** last resort; **mit allen Mitteln** by every means; **Mittel** *pl* resources, means; funds; **M. und Wege** ways and means; **M. zum Zweck** means to an end; **sicheres M.** reliable method

Mit′telalter *n* Middle Ages

mittelalterlich ['mɪtəlaltərlɪç] *adj* medieval

Mit′telamerika *n* Central America

mittelbar ['mɪtəlbar] *adj* indirect

Mit′telgang *m* center aisle

Mit′telgebirge *n* highlands

Mit′telgewicht *n* (box) middleweight class

Mittelgewichtler ['mɪtəlgəvɪçtlər] *m* (-s;-) middleweight boxer

Mit′telgröße ƒ medium size

mit′telhochdeutsch *adj* Middle High German ‖ **Mittelhochdeutsch** *n* (-es;) Middle High German

Mit′tellage ƒ central position; (mus) middle range

mittelländisch ['mɪtəllendɪʃ] *adj* Mediterranean

Mit′telläufer *m* (fb) center halfback

mit′tellos *adj* penniless, destitute

Mit′telmaß *n* medium; balance; average

mitt′telmäßig *adj* medium, mediocre; (*leidlich*) indifferent, so-so

Mit′telmäßigkeit ƒ mediocrity

Mit′telmast *m* mainmast

Mit′telmeer *n* Mediterranean

Mit′telohr *n* middle ear

Mit′telpreis *m* average price

Mit′telpunkt *m* center

mittels ['mɪtəls] *prep* (*genit*) by means of

Mit′telschiff *n* (archit) nave

Mit′telschule ƒ secondary school

Mit′tels·mann *m* (-[e]s;-er & -leute) go-between; (com) middleman

Mit′telsorte ƒ medium quality

Mit′telsperson ƒ see **Mittelsmann**

Mit′telstand *m* middle class

Mit′telstürmer *m* (fb) center forward

Mit′telweg *m* middle course; **der goldene M.** the golden mean; **e-n M. einschlagen** steer a middle course

Mit′telwort *n* (-[e]s;-er) (gram) participle

mitten ['mɪtən] *adv*—**m. am Tage** in broad daylight; **m. auf dem Wege** well on the way; **m. auf der Straße,** right in the middle of the street; **m. aus** from the midst of, from among; **m. darin** right in the very center (of it, of them); **m. entzwei brechen** break right in two; **m. im Winter** in the dead of winter; **m. in der Luft** in midair; **m. ins zwanzigste Jahrhundert** well into the twentieth century

Mitternacht ['mɪtərnaxt] ƒ midnight

mitternächtig ['mɪtərneçtɪç], **mitternächtlich** ['mɪtərneçtlɪç] *adj* midnight

Mittler -in ['mɪtlər(ɪn)] §6 *mf* mediator; (com) middleman

mittlere ['mɪtlərə] §9 *adj* middle, central; (*durchschnittlich*) average; (*mittelmäßig*) medium; (math) mean; **der Mittlere Osten** the Middle East; **in mittleren Jahren sein** be middle-aged; **von mittlerer Größe** medium-sized

mitt′lerweile *adv* in the meantime

mittschiffs ['mɪt/ɪfs] *adv* amidships

Mittwoch ['mɪtvɔx] *m* (-[e]s;-e) Wednesday

mitun′ter *adv* now and then

mit′unterzeichnen *tr & intr* countersign

mit′verantwortlich *adj* jointly responsible

Mit′verantwortung ƒ joint responsibility

Mit′verschworene §5 *mf* co-conspirator

Mit′welt ƒ present generation; our (his, etc.) contemporaries

mit′wirken *intr* (an *dat* or bei) cooperate (in)

Mit′wirkung ƒ cooperation

Mit′wissen *n*—**ohne mein M.** without my knowledge

Mitwisser -in ['mtvɪsər(ɪn)] §6 *mf* accessory; one in the know

mit′zählen *tr* include ‖ *intr* count along

mixen ['mɪksən] *tr* mix

Mixgetränk ['mɪksgətreŋk] *n* mixed drink

Mixtur [mɪks′tur] ƒ (-;-en) mixture

Möbel ['møbəl] *n* (-s;-) piece of furniture; **Möbel** *pl* furniture

Mö′belstück *n* piece of furniture

Möbeltransporteur ['møbəltranspɔrtør] *m* (-s;-e) mover

Mö′belwagen *m* moving van

mobil [mo′bil] *adj* movable; (*flink*) chipper; (mil) mobile

Mobiliar [mobɪ′ljar] *n* (-[e]s;) furniture

Mobilien [mo′biljən] *pl* movables

mobilisieren [mobɪlɪ′zirən] *tr* mobilize

Mobilisierung [mobɪlɪ′zirʊŋ] ƒ (-;) mobilization

mobil'machen *tr* mobilize

Mobilmachung [mɔ'bilmaxuŋ] *f* (-;) mobilization

möblieren [mø'bliːrən] *tr* furnish; **möbliert wohnen** (coll) live in a furnished room; **neu m.** refurnish

mochte ['mɔxtə] *pret* of **mögen**

Mode ['moːdə] *f* (-;-n) fashion, style

Mo'debild *n* fashion plate

Modell [mɔ'dɛl] *n* (-[e]s;-e) model; (*Muster*) pattern; (fig) prototype; **M. stehen zu** (*dat*) model for

modellieren [mɔdɛ'liːrən] *tr* fashion, shape

Modell'puppe *f* mannequin

modeln ['moːdəln] *tr* fashion, shape; (*nach*) model (on) || *ref*—**zu alt sein, um sich m. zu lassen** be too old to change

Mo'dengeschäft *n* dress shop

Mo'denschau *f* fashion show

Mo'denzeitung *f* fashion magazine

Moder ['moːdər] *m* (-;) mold; mustiness; (*Schlamm*) mud

Mo'derduft *m*, **Mo'dergeruch** *m* musty smell

moderig ['moːdərɪç] *adj* moldy, musty

modern [mo'dɛrn] *adj* modern || ['moːdərn] *intr* rot, decay || **Modern** *n* (-s;) decay

modernisieren [mɔdɛrnɪ'ziːrən] *tr* modernize; bring up to date

Mo'deschmuck *m* costume jewelry

Mo'deschriftsteller **-in** §6 *mf* popular writer

Mo'dewaren *pl* (com) novelties

modifizieren [mɔdifi'tsiːrən] *tr* modify

modisch ['moːdɪʃ] *adj* fashionable

Modistin [mo'dɪstɪn] *f* (-;-nen) milliner

modrig ['moːdrɪç] *adj* moldy

modulieren [mɔdu'liːrən] *tr* modulate; (*Stimme*) inflect

Mo·dus ['moːdus] *m* (-;-di [di]) mode, manner; (gram) mood

mogeln ['moːgəln] *intr* cheat || **Mogeln** *n* (-s;) cheating

mögen ['møːgən] §114 *tr* like, care for; **ich mag lieber** I prefer || *mod aux* may; can; care to; **er mag nicht nach Hause gehen** he doesn't care to go home; **ich möchte lieber bleiben** I'd rather stay; **ich möchte wissen** I should like to know; **mag kommen was da will** come what may; **wer mag das nur sein?** who can that be?; **wie mag das geschehen sein?** how could this have happened?

möglich ['møːklɪç] *adj* possible; (*ausführbar*) feasible; **sein möglichstes tun** do one's utmost || **Mögliche** §5 *n* possibility; **er muß alles Mögliche bedenken** he must consider every possibility; **im Rahmen des Möglichen** within the realm of possibility

möglichenfalls ['møːklɪçənfals], **möglicherweise** ['møːklɪçərvaɪzə] *adv* possibly, if possible

Mög'lichkeit *f* (-;-en) possibility; potentiality; **ist es die M.!** well, I never!; **finanzielle Möglichkeiten** financial means; **nach M.** as far as possible

möglichst ['møːklɪçst] *adv* as ... as possible

Mohn [moːn] *m* (-[e]s;-e) poppyseed; (bot) poppy

Mohn'samen *m* poppyseed

Mohr [moːr] *m* (-en;-en) Moor

Möhre ['møːrə] *f* (-;-n) carrot

Mohr'rübe *f* carrot

Mokka ['mɔka] *m* (-s;-s) mocha (*coffee*)

Molch [mɔlç] *m* (-[e]s;-e) salamander

Mole ['moːlə] *f* (-;-n) mole, breakwater

Molekül [mɔle'kyːl] *n* (-s;-e) molecule

molekular [mɔlekuˈlɑːr] *adj* molecular

Molke ['mɔlkə] *f* (-;) whey

Molkerei [mɔlkə'raɪ] *f* (-;-en) dairy

Moll [mɔl] *invar n* (mus) minor

mollig ['mɔlɪç] *adj* plump; (*Frau*) buxom; (*behaglich*) snug, cozy

Moll'tonart *f* (mus) minor key

Moment [mɔ'mɛnt] *m* (-[e]s;-e) moment || *n* (-[e]s;-e) momentum; (*Antrieb*) impulse, impetus; (*Faktor*) factor, point; (*Beweggrund*) motive

momentan [mɔmɛn'taːn] *adj* momentary

Moment'aufnahme *f* snapshot; (*Bewegungsaufnahme*) action shot

Monarch [mo'narç] *m* (-en;-en) monarch

Monar·chie [mɔnar'çiː] *f* (-;-chien ['çiː-ən]) monarchy

Monat ['moːnat] *m* (-[e]s;-e) month

monatelang ['moːnatəlaŋ] *adj* lasting for months || *adv* for months

mo'natlich *adj* monthly

Mo'natsbinde *f* sanitary napkin

Mo'natsfluß *m* menstruation

mo'natsweise *adv* monthly

Mönch [mœnç] *m* (-[e]s;-e) monk, friar

Mönchs'kappe *f* monk's cowl

Mönchs'kloster *n* monastery

Mönchs'kutte *f* monk's habit

Mönchs'orden *m* monastic order

Mönchs'wesen *n* monasticism

Mond [moːnt] *m* (-[e]s;-e) moon; **abnehmender M.** waning moon; **zunehmender M.** waxing moon

mondän [mɔn'dɛːn] *adj* sophisticated

Mond'fähre *f* (rok) lunar lander

Mond'finsternis *f* lunar eclipse

mond'hell *adj* moonlit

Mond'jahr *n* lunar year

Mond'kalb *n* (fig) born fool

Mond'schein *m* moonlight

Mond'sichel *f* crescent moon

Mond'sucht *f* lunacy; somnambulism

mond'süchtig *adj* moonstruck

Moneten [mo'neːtən] *pl* (coll) dough

monieren [mo'niːrən] *tr* criticize; remind

Monogramm [mɔno'gram] *n* (-s;-e) monogram

Monolog [mɔno'loːk] *m* (-s;-e) monologue

Monopol [mɔno'poːl] *n* (-s;-e) monopoly

monopolisieren [mɔnopɔli'ziːrən] *tr* monopolize

monoton [mɔno'toːn] *adj* monotonous

Monotonie [mɔnoto'niː] *f* (-;) monotony

Monsterfilm ['mɔnstərfɪlm] *m* (cin) spectacular
Monstranz [mɔn'strants] *f* (-;-en) monstrance
monströs [mɔn'strøs] *adj* monstrous
Monstrosität [mɔnstrɔzɪ'tet] *f* (-;-en) monstrosity
Mon·strum ['mɔnstrum] *n* (-;-stra [stra]) monster
Monsun [mɔ'zun] *m* (-s;-e) monsoon
Montag ['mɔntak] *m* (-[e]s;-e) Monday
Montage [mɔn'taʒə] *f* (-;-n) mounting, fitting; (mach) assembly
Monta'gebahn *f*, **Monta'geband** *n* assembly line
Monta'gehalle *f* assembly room
montags ['mɔntaks] *adv* Mondays
Montan– [mɔntan] *comb.fm.* mining
Monteur [mɔn'tør] *m* (-s;-e) assemblyman, mechanic
Monteur'anzug *m* coveralls
montieren [mɔn'tirən] *tr* mount, fit; (*zusammenbauen*) assemble; (*einrichten*) install; (*aufstellen*) set up
Montur [mɔn'tur] *f* (-;-en) uniform
Moor [mor] *n* (-[e]s;-e) swamp
Moor'bad *n* mud bath
moorig ['morɪç] *adj* swampy
Moos [mos] *n* (-es;) moss; (*Geld*) (coll) dough
Mop [mɔp] *m* (-s;-s) mop
Moped ['moped] *n* (-s;-s) motor bike, moped
moppen ['mɔpən] *tr* mop
mopsen ['mɔpsən] *tr* (coll) swipe || *ref* be bored stiff; be upset
Moral [mo'ral] *f* (-;) morality; (*Nutzwendung*) moral; (mil) morale
moralisch [mo'ralɪ] *adj* moral
moralisieren [moralɪ'zirən] *intr* moralize
Moralität [moralɪ'tet] *f* (-;) morality
Morast [mo'rast] *m* (-es;-e & ⁼e) mire; morass, quagmire
Mord [mɔrt] *m* (-[e]s;-e) murder
Mord'anschlag *m* murder attempt; (pol) assassination attempt
Mord'brennerei *f* arson and murder
Mord'bube *m* murderer, assassin
morden ['mɔrdən] *tr & intr* murder
Mörder –in ['mœrdər(ɪn)] §6 murderer
möderisch ['mœrdərɪʃ] *adj* murderous; (coll) awful, terrible
mord'gierig *adj* bloodthirsty
Mord'kommission *f* homicide squad
mord'lustig *adj* bloodthirsty
Mords– [mɔrts] *comb.fm.* huge; terrible, awful; fantastic, incredible
Mords'angst *f* mortal fear
Mords'geschichte *f* tall story
Mords'geschrei *n* loud shouting
Mords'kerl *m* (coll) great guy
mords'mäßig *adv* (coll) awfully
Mords'spektakel *n* awful din
Mord'tat *f* murder
Mord'waffe *f* murder weapon
Mores ['mores] *pl*—j–n M. lehren teach s.o. manners
morgen ['mɔrgən] *adv* tomorrow; m. abend tomorrow evening (or night); m. früh tomorrow morning; m. in

acht Tagen (or über acht Tage) a week from tomorrow; **m. mittag** tomorrow noon || **Morgen** *m* (-s;-) morning; acre; **des Morgens** in the morning || *n* (-;) tomorrow
Mor'genblatt *n* morning paper
Mor'gendämmerung *f* dawn, daybreak
mor'gendlich *adj* morning
Mor'gengabe *f* wedding present
Mor'gengrauen *n* dawn, daybreak
Mor'genland *n* Orient
Morgenländer –in ['mɔrgənlendər(ɪn)] §6 *mf* Oriental
Mor'genrock *m* house robe
Mor'genrot *n*, **Mor'genröte** *f* dawn, sunrise; (fig) dawn, beginning
morgens ['mɔrgəns] *adv* in the morning
Mor'genstern *m* morning star
Mor'genstunde *f* morning hour
Mor'genzeitung *f* morning paper
morgig ['mɔrgɪç] *adj* tomorrow's
Morphium ['mɔrfjum] *n* (-s;) morphine
morsch [mɔrʃ] *adj* rotten; (*baufällig*) dilapidated; (*brüchig*) brittle; (fig) decadent
Morsealphabet ['mɔrzə·alfabet] *n* Morse code
Mörser ['mœrzər] *m* (-s;-) (& mil) mortar
Mör'serkeule *f* pestle
Mörtel ['mœrtəl] *m* (-s;-) mortar; plaster; **mit M. bewerfen** roughcast
Mör'telkelle *f* trowel
Mör'teltrog *m* hod
Mosaik [moza'ik] *n* (-s;-en) mosaic
mosaisch [mo'za·ɪʃ] *adj* Mosaic
Moschee [mɔ'ʃe] *f* (-;-n) mosque
Moskau ['mɔskau] *n* (-s;) Moscow
Moslem ['mɔsləm] *m* (-s;-s) Moslem
moslemisch [mɔs'lemɪʃ] *adj* Moslem
Most [mɔst] *m* (-es;-e) must, grape juice; new wine
Mostrich ['mɔstrɪç] *m* (-[e]s;-e) mustard
Motel [mo'tel] *n* (-s;-s) motel
Motiv [mo'tif] *n* (-[e]s;-e) (*Beweggrund*) motive; (mus, paint) motif
motivieren [motɪ'virən] *tr* justify
Mo·tor ['motor], [mo'tor] *m* (-s; -toren** ['torən] & **-tore** ['torə]) motor
Mo'tordefekt *m* motor trouble
Mo'torhaube *f* (aer) cowl; (aut) hood
–motorig [motorɪç] *comb.fm.* –motor, –engine
Mo'torpanne *f* (aut) breakdown
Mo'torpflug *m* tractor plow
Mo'torrad *n* motorcycle
Mo'torradfahrer –in §6 *mf* motorcyclist
Mo'torrasenmäher *m* power mower
Mo'torroller *m* motor scooter
Mo'torsäge *f* power saw
Mo'torschaden *m* engine trouble
Motte ['mɔtə] *f* (-;-n) moth
mot'tenfest *adj* mothproof
Mot'tenkugel *f* mothball
Motto ['mɔto] *n* (-s;-s) motto
moussieren [mu'sirən] *intr* fizz; (*Wein*) sparkle
Möwe ['møvə] *f* (-;-n) sea gull

Mucke ['mʊkə] f (-;-n) whim; (dial) gnat; **Mucken haben** have moods

Mücke ['mʏkə] f (-;-n) gnat; mosquito; (dial) fly

Mucker ['mʊkər] m (-s;-) hypocrite; bigot; grouch; (coll) awkward guy

Muckerei [mʊkə'raɪ] f (-;) hypocrisy

muckerhaft ['mʊkərhaft] adj hypocritical, bigoted

Mucks [mʊks] m (-es;-e) faint sound; **keinen M. mehr!** not another sound!

mucksen ['mʊksən] ref & intr stir, say a word; **nicht gemuckst!** stay pat!

müde ['mydə] adj tired; **zum Umfallen m.** ready to drop

Mü'digkeit f (-;) weariness

Muff [mʊf] m (-[e]s;-e) (Handwärmer) muff; (Schimmel) mold; musty smell

Muffe ['mʊfə] f (-;-n) (mach) sleeve

muffeln ['mʊfəln] intr sulk, be grouchy; (anhaltend kauen) munch; mumble

muffig ['mʊfɪç] adj musty; (Person) sulky; (Luft) stale, frowzy

Mühe ['my·ə] f (-;-n) trouble, pains; (Anstrengung) effort; **geben Sie sich keine M.!** don't bother; **j-m M. machen** cause s.o. trouble; **mit M.** with difficulty; **mit M. und Not** barely; **nicht der M. wert** not worthwhile; **sich** [dat] **große M. machen** go to great pains; **verlorene M.** wasted effort

mü'helos adj easy, effortless

muhen ['mu·ən] intr moo, low

mühen ['my·ən] ref take pains

mü'hevoll adj hard, troublesome

Mühewaltung ['my·əvaltʊŋ] f (-;) trouble, efforts; **für Ihre M. dankend, verbleiben wir ... thanking you for your cooperation, we remain ...**

Mühle ['mylə] f (-;-n) mill

Mühlrad ['mylraːt] n water wheel

Mühlstein ['mylʃtaɪn] m millstone

Muhme ['mumə] f (-;-n) aunt; cousin

Mühsal ['myzaːl] f (-;-e) trouble

mühsam ['myzaːm] adj wearisome; (Leben) hard; (Arbeit) painstaking || adv with effort, with difficulty

mühselig ['myzeːlɪç] adj (Arbeit) hard; (Leben) miserable, tough

Mulatte [mu'latə] m (-n;-n), **Mulattin** [mu'latɪn] f (-;-nen) mulatto

Mulde ['mʊldə] f (-;-n) trough; (geol) depression, basin

Mull [mʊl] m (-[e]s;) gauze

Müll [mʏl] m (-[e]s;) dust, ashes; (Abfälle) trash, garbage

Müll'abfuhr f garbage disposal

Müll'abfuhrwagen m garbage truck

Müll'eimer m trash can, garbage can

Müller ['mʏlər] m (-s;-) miller

Müllerin ['mʏlərɪn] f (-;-nen) miller's wife; miller's daughter

Müll'fahrer m garbage man

Müll'haufen m scrap heap

Müll'platz m garbage dump

Müll'schaufel f dustpan

Mulm [mʊlm] m (-[e]s;) rotten wood

mul'mig adj rotten; dusty; (Luft) sticky; (Lage) ticklish

Multiplikation [mʊltɪplɪka'tsjon] f (-;) multiplication

multiplizieren [mʊltɪplɪ'tsirən] tr multiply

Mumie ['mumjə] f (-;-n) mummy

Mumm [mʊm] m (-s;) (coll) drive, grit

Mummelgreis ['mʊməlgraɪs] m (coll) old fogey

mummeln ['mʊməln] tr & intr mumble

Mund [mʊnt] m (-[e]s;⁼er) mouth; **den M. aufreißen** brag; **den M. halten** shut up; **den M. vollnehmen** talk big; **e-n losen M. haben** answer back; **sich** [dat] **den Mund verbrennen** put one's foot into it; **wie auf den M. geschlagen** dumbfounded

Mund'art f dialect

Mündel ['mʏndəl] m & n (-s;-) & f (-;-n) ward

Mündelgelder ['mʏndəlgeldər] pl trustfund

mün'delsicher adj gilt-edged; absolutely safe

munden ['mʊndən] intr taste good

münden ['mʏndən] intr—**m. in** (acc) empty into, flow into

mund'faul adj too lazy to talk

mund'gerecht adj palatable

Mund'geruch m halitosis

Mund'harmonika f mouth organ

Mund'höhle f oral cavity

mündig ['mʏndɪç] adj of age

Mün'digkeit f (-;) majority, full age

mündlich ['mʏntlɪç] adj oral, verbal

Mund'pflege f oral hygiene

Mund'sperre f lockjaw

Mund'stück n mouthpiece; (Zigaretten-) tip; (Düse) nozzle

mund'tot adj—**j-n m. machen** (fig) silence s.o.

Mund'tuch n table napkin

Mün'dung f (-s Flusses) mouth; (e-r Feuerwaffe) muzzle

Mün'dungsfeuer n muzzle flash

Mün'dungsweite f (arti) bore

Mund'vorrat m provisions

Mund'wasser n mouthwash

Mund'werk n (fig) mouth, tongue

Mund'winkel m corner of the mouth

Munition [muni'tsjon] f (-;) ammunition

Munitions'lager n ammunition dump

munkeln ['mʊŋkəln] tr & intr whisper

Münster ['mʏnstər] n (-s;-) cathedral

munter ['mʊntər] adj awake; (lebhaft) lively; (rüstig) vigorous; gay

Münz- [mʏnts] comb.fm. monetary; of the mint; coin; coinage; coin-operated

Münz'anstalt f mint

Münze ['mʏntsə] f (-;-n) coin; change; (Münzanstalt) mint; (Denkmünze) medal; **bare M.** hard cash; **für bare Münze nehmen** take at face value

Münz'einheit f monetary unit

Münz'einwurf m coin slot

münzen ['mʏntsən] tr coin, mint; **das ist auf ihn gemünzt** that is meant for him || **Münzen** n (-s;) mintage, coinage

Münz'fälscher m counterfeiter

Münz'fernsprecher m public telephone

Münz′kunde *f* numismatics
Münz′wesen *n* monetary system
Münz′wissenschaft *f* numismatics
mürb [myrp], **mürbe** [′myrbə] *adj*
(*Fleisch*) tender; (*sehr reif*) mellow;
(*gut durchgekocht*) well done; (*Gebäck*) crisp and flaky; (*brüchig*)
brittle; (*erschöpft*) worn out; (mil)
demoralized; **j-n mürbe machen** (fig)
break s.o. down; **mürbe werden**
soften, give in
Murks [murks] *m* (**-es;**) bungling job
murksen [′murksən] *intr* bungle
Murmel [′murməl] *f* (**-;-n**) marble
murmeln [′murməln] *tr & intr* murmur
Mur′meltier *n* ground hog, woodchuck
murren [′murən] *intr* grumble
mürrisch [′myrɪʃ] *adj* grouchy, crabby
Mus [mus] *n* (**-es;-e**) purée; sauce
Muschel [′muʃəl] *f* (**-;-n**) mussel;
(*Schale*) shell; (anat) concha
Muse [′muzə] *f* (**-;-n**) (myth) Muse
Muse·um [mu′ze·um] *n* (**-s;-en**) mu-
seum
Musik [mu′zik] *f* (**-;**) music
Musikalien [muzɪ′kaljən] *pl* music
book
musikalisch [muzɪ′kalɪʃ] *adj* musical
Musikant [muzɪ′kant] *m* (**-en;-en**)
musician
Musikan′tenknochen *m* funny bone
Musik′automat *m*, **Musikbox** [′mjuzɪk-
bɔks] *f* (**-;-en**) juke box
Musiker –in [′muzɪkər(ɪn)] §6 *mf*
musician
Musik′hochschule *f* conservatory
Musik′kapelle *f* band
Musik′korps *n* military band
Musik′pavillon *n* bandstand
Musik′schrank *m*, **Musik′truhe** *f* radio-
phonograph console
Musi·kus [′muzɪkus] *m* (**-;-zi** [tsi])
(hum) musician
Musik′wissenschaft *f* musicology
musisch [′muzɪʃ] *adj* artistic
musizieren [muzɪ′tsirən] *intr* play
music
Muskat [mus′kat] *m* (**-[e]s;-e**) nut-
meg
Muskateller [muska′telər] *m* (**-s;**)
muscatel
Muskat′nuß *f* nutmeg
Muskel [′muskəl] *m* (**-s;-n**) muscle
Mus′kelkater *m* (coll) charley horse
Mus′kelkraft *f* brawn
Mus′kelriß *m* torn muscle
Mus′kelschwund *m* muscular distrophy
Mus′kelzerrung *f* pulled muscle
Muskete [mus′ketə] *f* (**-;-n**) musket
Muskulatur [muskula′tur] *f* (**-;-en**)
muscles, muscular system
muskulös [musku′løs] *adj* muscular
Muß [mus] *invar n* must, necessity
Muße [′musə] *f* (**-;**) leisure; **mit M.**
at leisure
Muß′ehe *f* shotgun wedding
Musselin [musə′lin] *m* (**-s;-e**) muslin
müssen [′mysən] *intr*—**ich muß nach
Hause** I must go home ‖ *mod aux*—
ich muß (*inf*) I must (*inf*), I have to
(*inf*); **ich muß nicht** I don't have to;
muß das wirklich sein? is it really
neecessary?; **sie hätten hier sein m.**

they ought to have been here; **sie
müssen bald kommen** they are bound
to come soon
müßig [′mysɪç] *adj* idle; (*unnütz*) unprofitable; (*zwecklos*) useless; (*überflüssig*) superfluous
Mü′ßiggang *m* idleness
Müßiggänger *m* loafer
mußte [′mustə] *pret* of **müssen**
Muster [′mustər] *n* (**-s;-**) pattern;
(*Probestück*) sample; (*Vorbild*) example, model; **das M. e-r Hausfrau**
a model housewife; **nach dem M.
von** along the lines of; **sich** [*dat*]
ein M. nehmen an (*dat*) model oneself on
Mu′sterbeispiel *n* typical example
Mu′sterbild *n* ideal, paragon
Mu′stergatte *m* model husband
Mu′stergattin *f* model wife
mu′stergültig *adj* model, ideal
Mu′stergut *n* model farm
mu′sterhaft *adj* model, ideal
Mu′sterknabe *m* (pej) sissy
Mu′sterkollektion *f* (kit of) samples
mustern [′mustərn] *tr* examine, eye,
size up; (mil) inspect, review
Mu′sterprozeß *m* test case
Mu′sterschüler –in §6 *mf* model pupil
Mu′sterstück *n* specimen, sample
Mu′sterstudent –in §7 *mf* model stu-
dent
Mu′sterung *f* (**-;-en**) inspection; ex-
amination; (mil) review
Mu′sterungsbescheid *m* induction no-
tice
Mu′sterungskommission *f* draft board
Mu′sterwerk *n* standard work
Mu′sterwort *n* (**-[e]s;–er**) (gram) paradigm
Mut [mut] *m* (**-[e]s;**) courage; **den
Mut sinken lassen** lose heart; **guten
Mutes sein** feel encouraged; **j-m
den Mut nehmen** discourage s.o.;
nur Mut! cheer up!
Mutation [muta′tsjon] *f* (**-;-en**) (biol)
mutation, sport
Mütchen [′mytçən] *n*—**sein M. kühlen
an** (*dat*) take it out on
mutieren [mu′tirən] *intr* (*Stimme*)
change
mutig [′mutɪç] *adj* courageous, brave
-mütig [mytɪç] *comb.fm.* -minded,
-feeling
mut′los *adj* discouraged
Mut′losigkeit *f* (**-;**) discouragement
mutmaßen [′mutmasən] *tr* suppose,
conjecture
mutmaßlich [′mutmaslɪç] *adj* supposed, alleged; **mutmaßlicher Erbe**
heir presumptive ‖ *adv* presumably
Mut′maßung *f* (**-;-en**) conjecture,
guesswork; **Mutmaßungen anstellen**
conjecture
Mutter [′mutər] *f* (**-;–**) mother; **werdende M.** expectant mother ‖ *f* (**-;
-n**) nut
Mut′terboden *m* rich soil
Mütterchen [′mytərçən] *n* (**-s;-**)
mummy; little old lady
Mut′tererde *f* rich soil; native soil
Mut′terfürsorge *f* maternity welfare
Mut′terkuchen *m* (anat) placenta

Mut′terleib m womb
Mütterlich [′mʏtərlɪç] adj motherly, maternal; **m. verwandt** related on the mother's side
mut′terlos adj motherless
Mut′termal n birthmark
Mut′terpferd n mare
Mut′terschaf n ewe
Mut′terschaft f (-;) motherhood, maternity
Mut′terschlüssel m (mach) wrench
mut′terseelenallein′ adj all alone
Muttersöhnchen [′mutərzønçən] n (-s;-) mamma's boy
Mut′tersprache f mother tongue
Mut′terstelle f—bei j-m die M. vertreten be a mother to s.o.
Mut′terstute f mare
Mut′tertier n (zool) dam
Mut′terwitz m common sense
Mutti [′muti] f (-;-s) (coll) mom
mut′voll adj courageous
Mut′wille m mischievousness

mut′willig adj mischievous, willful
Mütze [′mʏtsə] f (-;-n) cap
Myriade [mʏri′adə] f (-;-n) myriad
Myrrhe [′mʏrə] f (-;-n) myrrh
Myrte [′mʏrtə] f (-;-n) myrtle
Mysterienspiel [mʏs′terjən/pil] n (theat) mystery play
mysteriös [mʏste′rjøs] adj mysterious
Myste·rium [mʏs′terjum] n (-s;-rien [rjən]) mystery
mystifizieren [mʏstifr′tsirən] tr mystify; (täuschen) hoax
Mystik [′mʏstɪk] f (-;) mysticism
My′stiker –in §6 mf mystic
mystisch [′mʏstɪ/] adj mystic(al)
Mythe [′mytə] f (-;-n) myth
mythisch [′mytɪ/] adj mythical
Mytholo·gie [mytolə′gi] f (-;-gien [′gi·ən]) mythology
mythologisch [mytə′logɪ/] adj mythological
My·thus [′mytus] m (-;-then [tən]) myth

N

N, n [ɛn] invar n N, n
na [na] interj well!; **na also!** there you are!; **na, so was!** don't tell me!; **na, und ob!** I'll say!; **na, warte!** just you wait!
Nabe [′nabə] f (-;-n) hub
Nabel [′nabəl] m (-s;-) navel
Na′belschnur f umbilical cord
nach [nax] adv after; **n. und n.** little by little; **n. wie vor** now as ever ‖ prep (dat) (Zeit) after; (Reihenfolge) after, behind; (Ziel, Richtung) to, towards, for; (Art, Maß, Vorbild, Richtschnur) according to, after
Nach–, nach– comb.fm. subsequent, additional, supplementary; post–; over, over again, re–; after
nach′äffen tr ape, imitate
nachahmen [′naxamən] tr imitate, copy
Nach′ahmer –in §6 mf imitator
Nach′ahmung f (-;-en) imitation, copy
nach′arbeiten tr copy; (ausbessern) touch up; (Versäumtes) make up for
nach′arten intr (SEIN) (dat) take after
Nachbar [′naxbar] m (-s & -n;-n), **Nachbarin** [′naxbarɪn] f (-;-nen) neighbor
nach′barlich adj neighborly; neighboring
Nach′barschaft f (-;-en) neighborhood; **gute N. halten** be on friendly terms with neighbors
Nach′bau m (-s;) imitation, duplication; licensed manufacture; **unerlaubter N.** illegal manufacture
Nach′behandlung f (med) follow-up treatment
nach′bestellen tr reorder, order more of
Nach′bestellung f (-;-en) repeat order
nach′beten tr & intr repeat mechanically

nach′bezahlen tr pay afterwards; pay the rest of ‖ intr pay afterwards
Nach′bild n copy
nach′bilden tr copy
Nach′bildung f (-;-en) copying; (Kopie) copy, reproduction; (Modell) mock-up; (Attrappe) dummy
nach′bleiben §62 intr (SEIN) remain behind; (educ) stay in; **hinter j–m n.** lag behind s.o.
nach′blicken intr (dat) look after
nach′brennen §97 intr smolder ‖ Nach′brennen n (-s;) (rok) afterburn
Nach′brenner m (aer) afterburner
nach′datieren tr postdate
nachdem [nax′dem] adv afterwards; **je n.** as the case may be, it all depends ‖ conj after, when; **je n.** according to how, depending on how
nach′denken §66 intr think it over; **n. über** (acc) think over, reflect on ‖ Nachdenken n (-s;) reflection; **bei weiterem N.** on second thought
nach′denklich adj reflective, thoughtful; (Buch) thought-provoking; (abwesend) lost in thought
Nach′dichtung f (-;-en) free poetical rendering
nach′drängen intr (SEIN) (dat) crowd after; pursue
nach′dringen §142 intr be in hot pursuit; (dat) pursue
Nach′druck m (Betonung) stress, emphasis; energy; (Raubdruck) pirated edition; (typ) reprint; **mit N.** emphatically; **N. verboten** all rights reserved
nach′drucken tr reprint
nach′drücklich adj emphatic; **n. betonen** emphasize
nach′dunkeln intr get darker
nach′eifern intr (dat) emulate

nach'eilen *intr* (SEIN) (*dat*) hasten after, rush after

nacheinan'der *adv* one after another

nach'empfinden §59 *tr* have a feeling for; **j-m etw n.** sympathize with s.o. about s.th.

Nachen ['naxən] *m* (-s;-) (poet) boat

nach'erzählen *tr* repeat, retell

Nachfahr ['naxfar] *m* (-s;-en) descendant

nach'fahren §71 *intr* (SEIN) (*dat*) drive after, follow

nach'fassen *tr* (mil) get a second helping of || *intr* (econ) do a follow-up

Nach'folge *f* succession

nach'folgen *intr* (*dat*) succeed, follow; follow in the footsteps of

nach'folgend *adj* following, subsequent

Nach'folger -in §6 *mf* follower; successor

nach'fordern *tr* charge extra; claim subsequently

nach'forschen *intr* (*dat*) investigate

Nach'frage *f* inquiry; (com) demand

nach'fragen *intr* (nach) ask (about)

Nach'frist *f* time extension

nach'fühlen *tr*—**j-m etw n.** sympathize with s.o. about s.th.

nach'füllen *tr* refill, fill up

nach'geben §80 *tr* give later; (*beim Essen*) give another helping of; **j-m nichts an Eifer n.** not be outdone by s.o. in zeal || *intr* give way, give; (*schlaff werden*) slacken, give; (*dat*) give in to, yield to

nach'geboren *adj* younger; posthumous

Nach'gebühr *f* postage due

nach'gehen §82 *intr* (SEIN) (*dat*) follow; (*Geschäften*) attend to; (*untersuchen*) investigate, check on

nachgemacht ['naxgəmaxt] *adj* false, imitation; (*künstlich*) artificial

nachgeordnet ['naxgə·ɔrdnət] *adj* subordinate

nach'gerade *adv* by now; (*allmählich*) gradually; (*wirklich*) really

Nach'geschmack *m* aftertaste, bad taste

nachgewiesenermaßen ['naxgəvizənərmasən] *adv* as has been shown (or proved)

nachgiebig ['naxgibɪç] *adj* elastic, yielding, compliant; (*nachsichtig*) indulgent; (st. exch.) declining

nach'gießen §76 *tr* fill up, refill || *intr* add more

nach'glühen *tr* (tech) temper || *intr* smolder

nach'grübeln *intr* (dat or über *acc*) mull (over), ponder (on)

Nach'hall *m* echo, reverberation

nach'hallen *intr* echo, reverberate

nachhaltig ['naxhaltɪç] *adj* lasting

nach'hängen §92 *intr* (*dat*) give free rein to || *impers*—**es hängt mir nach** I still feel the effects of it

nach'helfen §96 *intr* (*dat*) help along

nach'her *adv* afterwards, later, then; **bis n.!** so long!

nachherig ['naxherɪç] *adj* later

Nach'hilfe *f* assistance, help

Nach'hilfelehrer -in §6 *mf* tutor

Nach'hilfestunde *f* tutoring lesson

Nach'hilfeunterricht *m* tutoring

nach'hinken *intr* (*dat*) lag behind

Nachholbedarf ['naxholbədarf] *m* backlog of unsatisfied demands

nach'holen *tr* make up for

Nach'hut *f* (mil) rear guard

nach'jagen *tr*—**j-m etw n.** send s.th. after s.o. || *intr* (SEIN) (*dat*) pursue

Nach'klang *m* echo; (fig) reminiscence

nach'klingen §142 *intr* reecho, resound

Nachkomme ['naxkəmə] *m* (-n;-n) offspring, descendant

nach'kommen §99 *intr* (SEIN) (*dat*) follow; join (*s.o.*) later; (*Vorschriften, e-m Gesetz*) obey; (*e-m Versprechen*) keep; (*e-r Pflicht*) live up to

Nach'kommenschaft *f* (-;) posterity

Nachkömmling ['naxkœmlɪŋ] *m* (-s; -e) offspring, descendant

nach'laß ['naxlas] *m* (-lasses;-lässe) remission; (*am Preis*) reduction; (*Erbschaft*) estate; **literarischer N.** unpublished works

nach'lassen §104 *tr* leave behind; (*lockern*) slacken; **j-m 15% vom Preise n.** give s.o. a fifteen percent reduction in price || *intr* (*sich lockern*) slacken; (*sich vermindern*) diminish; (*milder werden*) relent; (*Regen*) let up; (*Kräfte*) give out; (*Wind, Sturm*) go down; (*schlechter werden*) get worse

Nach'laßgericht *n* probate court

nach'lässig *adj* careless, negligent

Nach'lässigkeit *f* carelessness, negligence

nach'laufen §105 *intr* (SEIN) (*dat*) run after, pursue

nach'leben *intr* (*dat*) live up to || **Nach'leben** *n* afterlife

Nach'lese *f* gleanings

nach'lesen §107 *tr* glean; (*Stelle im Buch*) reread, look up

nach'liefern *tr* deliver subsequently

nach'machen *tr* imitate; (*fälschen*) counterfeit; **j-m alles n.** imitate s.o. in everything

nach'malen *tr* copy

nachmalig ['naxmalɪç] *adj* later

nachmals ['naxmals] *adv* afterwards

nach'messen §70 *tr* measure again

Nach'mittag *m* afternoon

Nach'mittags *adv* in the afternoon

Nach'mittagsvorstellung *f* matinée

Nach'nahme *f* (-;) C.O.D.

Nach'name *m* last name, family name

nach'plappern *tr* repeat mechanically

Nach'porto *n* postage due

nachprüfbar ['naxpryfbar] *adj* verifiable

nach'prüfen *tr* verify, check out

nach'rechnen *tr* (acct) check

Nach'rede *f* epilogue; **j-n in üble N. bringen** bring s.o. into bad repute; **üble N.** slander; **üble N. verbreiten** spread nasty rumors

nach'reden *tr*—**j-m etw n.** say s.th. behind s.o.'s back

Nachricht ['naxrɪçt] *f* (-;-en) news; (*Bericht*) report; (*kurzer Bericht*) notice; (*Auskunft*) information; **e-e N. verbreiten** spread the news; **geben Sie mir von Zeit zu Zeit N.!** keep me advised; **Nachrichten** (rad, telv) news, news report; **Nachrichten einholen** make inquiries; **Nachrichten einziehen** gather information; **zur N.!** for your information

Nach′richtenabteilung *f* (mil) intelligence section

Nach′richtenagentur *f* news agency

Nach′richtenbüro *n* news room; news agency

Nach′richtendienst *m* news service; (mil) army intelligence

Nach′richtensatellit *m* communications satellite

Nach′richtensendung *f* newscast

Nach′richtenwesen *n* communications

nach′rücken *intr* (SEIN) (*im Rang*) move up; (mil) (*dat*) follow up; **j–m n.** move up into s.o.'s position

Nach′ruf *m* obituary

nach′rufen §122 *tr* (*dat*) call after

Nach′ruhm *m* posthumous fame

nach′rühmen *tr*—**j–m etw n.** say s.th. nice about s.o.

nach′sagen *tr*—**j–m etw n.** repeat s.th. after s.o.; say s.th behind s.o.'s back; **das lasse ich mir nicht n.** I won't let that be said of me

Nach′satz *m* concluding clause

nach′schaffen *tr* replace

nach′schauen *intr* (*dat*) gaze after

nach′schicken *tr* forward

Nachschlagebuch [′nɑxʃlɑgəbux] *n* reference book

nach′schlagen §132 *tr* look up; (*Buch*) consult ‖ *intr* (box) counter

Nachschlagewerk [′nɑxʃlɑgəverk] *n* reference work

Nach′schlüssel *m* skeleton key

nach′schreiben §62 *tr* copy; take down from dictation

Nach′schrift *f* postscript

Nach′schub *m* (mil) supply, fresh supplies; (mil) supply lines

Nach′schublinie *f* (mil) supply line

Nach′schubstützpunkt *m* (mil) supply base

Nach′schubweg *m* supply line

nach′sehen §138 *tr* (*nachschlagen*) look up; (*nachprüfen*) check; (acct) audit; (mach) overhaul; **j–m vieles n.** overlook much in s.o. ‖ *intr* (*dat*) gaze after ‖ **Nachsehen** *n*—**das N. haben** get the short end

nach′senden §140 *tr* send after, forward

nach′setzen *intr* (*dat*) run after

Nach′sicht *f* patience; **mit j–m N. üben** have patience with s.o.

nach′sichtig, nach′sichtsvoll *adj* lenient, considerate

Nach′silbe *f* suffix

nach′sinnen §121 *intr* (*über acc*) reflect (on), muse (over)

nach′sitzen *intr* be kept in after school

Nach′sommer *m* Indian summer

Nach′speise *f* dessert

Nach′spiel *n* (fig) sequel

nach′spüren *intr* (*dat*) track down

nächst [neçst] *prep* (*dat*) next to

nächst′beste §9 *adj* second-best

nächstdem′ *adv* thereupon

nächste [′neçstə] §9 *adj* (*super* of

nahe) next; (*Weg*) shortest; (*Beziehungen*) closest ‖ **Nächste** §5 *mf* neighbor, fellow man, fellow creature

nach′stehen §146 *intr* (*dat*) be inferior to

nach′stehend *adj* following ‖ *adv* (mentioned) below

nach′stellen *tr* (*Schraube*) reset, adjust; (*Uhr*) set back ‖ *intr* (*dat*) be after; (*e–m Mädchen*) run after

Nach′stellung *f* (–;–en) persecution; ambush; (gram) postposition

nächsten [′neçstən] *adv* one of these days, before long; next time

Näch′stenliebe *f* charity

nächst′liegend *adj* nearest

nach′stöbern *intr* (*dat*) rummage about

nach′stoßen §150 *intr* (SEIN) (*dat*) (mil) follow up

nach′streben *intr* (*dat*) strive after; (*e–r Person*) emulate

nach′strömen, nach′strümen, nach′stürzen *intr* (SEIN) (*dat*) crowd after

nach′suchen *tr* search for ‖ *intr*—**n. um** apply for

Nach′suchung *f* (–;–en) search, inquiry; petition

Nacht [naxt] *f* (–;ːe) night; **bei N. und Nebel** under cover of night

Nacht′ausgabe *f* final (edition)

Nacht′teil *m* disadvantage

nach′teilig *adj* disadvantageous

Nacht′essen *n* supper

Nacht′eule *f* night owl

Nacht′falter *m* (ent) moth

Nacht′geschirr *n* chamber pot

Nacht′gleiche *f* equinox

Nacht′hemd *n* nightgown

Nachtigall [′naxtɪgal] *f* (–;–n) nightingale

nächtigen [′neçtɪgən] *intr* pass the night

Nacht′tisch *m* dessert

Nacht′klub *m*, **Nacht′lokal** *n* nightclub

Nacht′lager *n* accommodations for the night

nächtlich [′neçtlɪç] *adj* night, nightly

Nacht′mal *n* supper

Nacht′musik *f* serenade

nach′tönen *intr* resound; (*Note*) linger

Nacht′quartier *n* accommodations for the night

Nachtrag [′naxtrak] *m* (–[e]s;ːe) supplement, addition

nach′tragen §132 *tr* add; **j–m etw n.** carry s.th. after s.o.; (fig) hold s.th. against s.o.

nachträgerisch [′naxtregərɪʃ] *adj* resentful. vindictive

nachträglich [′naxtreklɪç] *adj* supplementary; (*später*) subsequent

Nachtrags– *comb.fm.* supplementary

Nacht′trupp *m* (–;ː) rear guard

nachts [naxts] *adv* at night

Nacht′schicht *f* night shift

nacht′schlafend *adj*—**bei** (or **zu**) **nacht′schlafender Zeit** late at night

Nacht′schwärmer *m*—**in** §6 *mf* reveler

Nacht′tisch *m* night table

Nacht′topf *m* chamber pot

nach′tun §154 *tr*—**j–m etw n.** imitate s.o. in s.th.

Nacht′wache *f* night watch, vigil

Nacht′wächter *m* night watchman

Nachtwandler –in ['naxtvandlər(ɪn)] §6 *mf* sleepwalker, somnambulist

Nacht'zeug *n* overnight things

Nach'urlaub *m* extended leave

nach'wachsen §155 *intr* (SEIN) grow again

Nach'wahl *f* special election

Nachwehen ['naxve·ən] *pl* afterpains; (fig) painful consequences

nach'weinen *tr*—**keine Tränen n.** (*dat*) waste no tears over || *intr* (*dat*) cry over

Nachweis ['naxvaɪs] *m* (–es;–e) proof; **den N. bringen** (or **führen**) furnish proof

nach'weisbar *adj* demonstrable

nach'weisen §118 *tr* point, show; (*beweisen*) prove; (*begründen*) substantiate; (*verweisen*) refer to

nach'weislich *adj* demonstrable

Nach'welt *f* posterity

nach'wiegen §57 *tr* verify the weight of

nach'wirken *intr* have an aftereffect

Nach'wirkung *f* (–;–en) aftereffect

Nach'wort *n* (–[e]s;–e) epilogue

Nach'wuchs *m* younger generation; younger set; children

nach'zahlen *tr & intr* pay extra

nach'zählen *tr* count over, check

nach'zeichnen *tr* draw a copy of || *intr* copy

nach'ziehen §163 *tr* drag; tow; (*Linien*) trace; (*Schraube*) tighten || *intr* (SEIN) (*dat*) follow after

nach'zoteln *intr* (SEIN) (coll) trot after

Nachzügler –in ['naxtsyklər(ɪn)] §6 *mf* straggler; latecomer

Nackedei ['nakədaɪ] *m* (–[e]s;–e) naked child; nude

Nacken ['nakən] *m* (–s;–) nape of the neck

nackend ['nakənt] *adj* var of **nackt**

Nackenschlag (Nak'kenschlag) *m* rabbit punch; (fig) hard blow

–nackig [nakɪç] *comb.fm.* **–necked**

nackt [nakt] *adj* nude, bare; (*Tatsache*) hard; **sich n. ausziehen** strip bare

Nackt'heit *f* (–;) nudity, nakedness

Nadel ['nadəl] *f* (–;–n) needle; pin; **wie auf Nadeln sitzen** be on pins and needles

Na'delbaum *m* coniferous tree

Na'delkissen *n* pin cushion

Nadelöhr ['nadəlør] *n* (–s;–e) eye of a needle

Na'delstich *m* pinprick; (sew) stitch

Nagel ['nagəl] *m* (–s;⸚) nail; **an den N. hängen** (fig) shelve; **an den Nägeln kauen** bite one's nails

Na'gelhaut *f* cuticle

nageln ['nagəln] *tr & intr* nail

na'gelneu' *adj* brand-new

nagen ['nagən] *tr* gnaw; **das Fleisch vom Knochen n.** pick the meat off the bone || *intr* (an *dat*) gnaw (at), nibble (at); (fig) (an *dat*) rankle

Nagetier ['nagətir] *n* rodent

Nah– [na] *comb.fm.* close-range, short-range

Näh– [ne] *comb.fm.* sewing, needlework

Näh'arbeit *f* sewing, needlework

Näh'aufnahme *f* (phot) close-up

nahe ['na·ə] *adj* (näher ['ne·ər]; nächste ['neçstə] §9) near, close; nearby; (*bevorstehend*) forthcoming; (*Gefahr*) imminent || *adv*—**j—m zu n. treten** hurt s.o.'s feelings; **n. an.** (*dat* or *acc*), **n. bei** close to; **n. daran sein zu** (*inf*) be on the point of (*ger*)

Nähe ['ne·ə] *f* (–;–n) nearness; vicinity; **in der N.** close by

na'hebei *adv* nearby

na'hebringen §65 *tr* drive home

na'hegehen §82 *intr* (SEIN) (*dat*) affect, touch, grieve

na'hekommen §99 *intr* (SEIN) approach; (*dat*) come near to; **der Wahrheit n.** get at the truth

na'helegen *tr* suggest

na'heliegen §108 *intr* be close by; be obvious; be easy

na'heliegend *adj* obvious

nahen ['na·ən] *ref & intr* (SEIN) approach; (*dat*) draw near to

nähen ['ne·ən] *tr & intr* sew, stitch

näher ['ne·ər] *adj* (comp of **nahe**) nearer; **bei näherer Betrachtung** upon further consideration || *adv* closer; **immer n. kommen** close in; **treten Sie n.!** this way, please! || **Nähere** §5 *n* details, particulars; **das N. auseinandersetzen** explain fully; **Näheres erfahren** learn further particulars; **sich des Näheren entsinnen** remember all particulars; **wenn Sie Näheres wissen wollen** if you want details

Näherin ['ne·ərɪn] *f* (–;–nen) seamstress

nähern ['ne·ərn] *ref* approach; (*dat*) draw near to, approach

Nä'herungswert *m* approximate value

na'hestehen §146 *intr* (*dat*) share the view of

na'hetreten §152 *intr* (SEIN) (*dat*) come into close contact with

na'hezu *adv* almost, nearly

Näh'garn *n* thread

Nah'kampf *m* hand-to-hand fighting; (box) in-fighting

nahm [nam] *pret* of **nehmen**

Näh'maschine *f* sewing machine

–nahme [namə] *f* (–;–n) *comb.fm.* taking

Nähr– [ner] *comb.fm.* nutritive

Nähr'boden *m* rich soil; (fig) breeding ground; (biol) culture medium

nähren ['nerən] *tr* nourish, feed; (*Kind*) nurse || *ref* make a living; **sich n. von** subsist on || *intr* be nutritious

nahrhaft ['narhaft] *adj* nourishing, nutritious, nutritive

Nähr'mittel *pl* (*Teigwaren*) noodles; (*Hülsenfrüchte*) beans and peas

Nahrung ['narʊŋ] *f* (–;) nourishment; (*Kost*) diet; (*Unterhalt*) livelihood

Nah'rungsmittel *pl* food

Nah'rungsmittelvergiftung *f* food poisoning

Nah'rungssorgen *pl* difficulty in making ends meet

Nähr'wert *m* nutritive value

Näh'stube *f* sewing room

Naht [nat] *f* (–;⸚e) seam

Nah′verkehr *m* local traffic

Näh′zeug *n* sewing kit

naiv [na′if] *adj* naive

Name [′namə] *m* (-ns;-n), **Namen** [′namən] *m* (-s;-) name

na′menlos *adj* nameless; (*unsäglich*) indescribable

namens [′namens] *adv* named, called ‖ *prep* (*genit*) in the name of, on behalf of

Na′mensschild *n* nameplate

Na′menstag *m* name day

Na′mensvetter *m* namesake

namentlich [′namentliç] *adj*—**namentliche Abstimmung** roll-call vote ‖ *adv* by name, individually; (*besonders*) especially

Na′menverzeichnis *n* index of names; nomenclature

namhaft [′namhaft] *adj* distinguished; (*beträchtlich*) considerable; **n. machen** name, specify

nämlich [′nemliç] *adv* namely, that is; (*coll*) you know, you see

nannte [′nantə] *pret* of **nennen**

nanu [na′nu] *interj* gee!

Napf [napf] *m* (-es;:-e) bowl

Narbe [′narbə] *f* (-;-n) scar; (*des Leders*) grain; (*agr*) topsoil

narbig [′narbiç] *adj* scarred

Narkose [nar′kozə] *f* (-;-n) anesthesia

Narkoti•kum [nar′kotikum] *n* (-s;-ka [ka]) narcotic, dope

narkotisch [nar′kotiʃ] *adj* narcotic

Narr [nar] *m* (-en;-en) fool; (hist) jester; **j-n zum Narren halten** make a fool of s.o.

Närrchen [′nerçən] *n* (-s;-) silly little goose

narren [′narən] *tr* make a fool of

Narrenfest [′narənfest] *n* masquerade

Narrenhaus [′narənhaus] *n* madhouse

Narrenkappe [′narənkapə] *f* cap and bells

narrensicher [′narənziçər] *adj* (coll) foolproof

Narren(s)possen [′narən(s)posən] *pl* horseplay; **laß die N.!** stop horsing around!

Narr′heit *f* (-;-en) folly

närrisch [′neriʃ] *adj* foolish; (*verrückt*) crazy; (*Kauz*) eccentric; **n. sein auf** (*acc*) be crazy about

Narzisse [nar′tsisə] *f* (-;-n) (bot) narcissus; **gelbe N.** daffodil

naschen [′naʃən] *tr* nibble at ‖ *intr* (an *dat*, von) nibble (on); **gern n.** have a sweet tooth

Näscher -in [′neʃər(in)] §6 *mf* nibbler

Näscherei [neʃə′rai] *f* (-;-en) snack

naschhaft [′naʃhaft] *adj* sweet-toothed

Naschkatze [′naʃkatsə] *f* nibbler

Naschmaul [′naʃmaul] *n* nibbler

Naschwerk [′naʃverk] *n* sweets, tidbits

Nase [′nazə] *f* (-;-n) nose; **auf der N. liegen** be laid up in bed; **aufgeworfene N.** turned-up nose; **das sticht ihm in die N.** it annoys him; he's itching to have it; **daß du die N. im Gesicht behältst!** keep your shirt on!; **dem Kind die N. putzen** wipe the child's nose; **die N. läuft ihm blau an** his nose is getting red; **die N. rüm-**

pfen über (*acc*) turn up one's nose at; **die N. voll haben von** be fed up with; **e-e tüchtige N. voll bekommen** (or **einstecken müssen**) get chewed out; **faß dich an deine eigene N.!** mind your own business!; **feine N. für** flair for; **immer der N. nach!** follow your nose!; **in der N. bohren** poke one's nose; **j-m e-e lange N. machen** thumb one's nose at s.o.; **j-m e-e N. drehen** outwit s.o.; **j-m die Würmer aus der N. ziehen** worm it out of s.o.; **j-m etw auf die N. binden** divulge s.th. to s.o.; **j-m in die N. fahren** (or **steigen**) annoy s.o.; **j-n an der N. herumführen** lead s.o. by the nose; **man kann es ihm an der N. ansehen** it's written all over his face; **mit langer N. abziehen** be the loser; **pro N.** per head; **sich** [*dat*] **die N. begießen** wet one's whistle

näseln [′nezəln] *intr* speak through the nose ‖ **Näseln** *n* (-s;) nasal twang

nä′seind *adj* nasal

Na′senbein *n* nasal bone

Na′senbluten *n* (-s;) nosebleed

na′senlang *adv*—**alle n.** constantly

Na′senlänge *f*—**um e-e N.** by a nose

Na′senlaut *m* (phonet) nasal

Na′senloch *n* nostril

Na′senrücken *m* bridge of the nose

Na′senschleim *m* mucus

Na′senschleimhaut *f* mucous membrane

Nasenspray [′nazənʃpre] *m* (-s;-s) nose spray

Na′sentropfen *m* nose drop

na′seweis *adj* fresh, wise ‖ **Naseweis** *m* (-es;-e) wise guy

Na′seweisheit *f* freshness

nasführen [′nasfyrən] *tr* lead by the nose; (*foppen*) fool

Nashorn [′nashorn] *n* (-[e]s;:-er) rhinoceros

naß [nas] *adj* (**nasser** [′nasər] or **nässer** [′nesər]; **nasseste** [′nasəstə] or **nässeste** [′nesəstə] §9) wet; (*feucht*) moist ‖ **Naß** *n* (Nasses;) (poet) liquid

Nassauer [′nasau•ər] *m* (-s;-) sponger, chiseler

nassauern [′nasau•ərn] *intr* (coll) sponge

Nässe [′nesə] *f* (-;) wetness; moisture

nässen [′nesən] *tr* wet; moisten ‖ *intr* ooze

naß′forsch *adj* rash, bold

naß′kalt *adj* raw, cold and damp

Nation [na′tsjon] *f* (-;-en) nation

national [natsjo′nal] *adj* national

National′hymne *f* national anthem

nationalisieren [natsjonali′zirən] *tr* nationalize

Nationalismus [natsjona′lismus] *m* (-;) nationalism

Nationalität [natsjonali′tet] *f* (-;-en) nationality; ethnic minority

National′sozialismus *m* national socialism, Nazism

National′sozialist -in §7 *mf* national socialist, Nazi

National′tracht *f* national costume

Nativität [nativi′tet] *f* (-;-en) horoscope

Natrium ['nɑtrɪ·ʊm] *n* (-s;) sodium
Natter ['natər] *f* (-;-n) adder, viper
Natur [na'tur] *f* (-;-en) nature; (*Körperbeschaffenheit*) constitution; (*Gemütsart*) disposition; (*Art*) character; (*Person*) creature; **von N.** by nature
Natura [na'tura] *f*—in N. in kind
Naturalien [natu'raljən] *pl* produce
naturalisieren [naturalɪ'zirən] *tr* naturalize ‖ *ref*—**sich n. lassen** become naturalized
Natur'anlage *f* disposition
Natur'arzt *m* naturopath
Naturell [natu'rɛl] *n* (-[e]s;-e) nature, temperament
Natur'erscheinung *f* phenomenon
Natur'forscher —**in** §6 *mf* naturalist
Natur'gabe *f* natural gift, talent
natur'gemäß *adv* naturally
Natur'geschichte *f* natural history
Natur'gesetz *n* natural law
natur'getreu *adj* life-like
Natur'kunde *f*, **Natur'lehre** *f* natural science
natürlich [na'tyrlɪç] *adj* natural; (*echt*) real; (*ungezwungen*) natural; **das geht aber nicht mit natürlichen Dingen zu** there is s.th. fishy about it; **das geht ganz n. zu** there is nothing strange about it ‖ *adv* naturally, of course
Natur'mensch *m* primitive man; nature enthusiast
Natur'philosoph *m* natural philosopher
Natur'recht *n* natural right
Natur'schutz *m* preservation of natural beauty
Natur'schutzgebiet *n* wildlife preserve
Natur'schutzpark *m* national park
Natur'spiel *n* freak of nature
Natur'theater *n* outdoor theater
Natur'trieb *m* instinct
Natur'verehrung *f* natural religion
Natur'volk *n* primitive people
natur'widrig *adj* contrary to nature
Natur'wissenschaft *f* natural science
Natur'wissenschaftler —**in** §6 *mf* scientist
naturwüchsig [na'turvyksɪç] *adj* unspoiled by civilization
Natur'zustand *m* natural state
nautisch ['nautɪʃ] *adj* nautical
Navigation [naviga'tsjon] *f* (-;) navigation
navigieren [navɪ'girən] *intr* navigate
Nazi ['natsi] *m* (-s;-s) Nazi
Nazismus [na'tsɪmʊs] *m* (-;) Nazism
nazistisch [na'tsɪstɪʃ] *adj* Nazi
Nebel ['nebəl] *m* (-s;-) fog, mist; (*Dunst*) haze
Ne'belbank *f* (-;⁚e) fog bank
Ne'belfeld *n* patch of fog
Ne'belferne *f* hazy distance; (fig) dim future
Ne'belfleck *m* (astr) nebula
ne'belhaft *adj* foggy, hazy; (*Ferne*) dim
Ne'belhorn *n* foghorn
nebeln ['nebəln] *intr* be foggy
Ne'belscheinwerfer *m* (aut) fog light
Ne'belschicht *f* fog bank
Ne'belschirm *m* smoke screen
Ne'belvorhang *m* smoke screen
neben ['nebən] *prep* (*dat* & *acc*) by,

beside; side by side with, alongside, close to, next to; (*verglichen mit*) compared with; (*außer*) besides, aside from; in addition to; extra
Neben— *comb.fm.* secondary, accessory, by-, side-, subordinate
Ne'benabsicht *f* ulterior motive
Ne'benaltar *m* side altar
Ne'benamt *n* additional duties
nebenan' *adv* close by; next-door
Ne'benanschluß *m* (telp) extension; (telp) party line
Ne'benarbeit *f* extra work
Ne'benarm *m* tributary, branch
Ne'benausgaben *pl* incidentals, extras
Ne'benausgang *m* side exit
Ne'benbahn *f* (rr) branch line
Ne'benbedeutung *f* (-;-en) secondary meaning
nebenbei' *adv* close by; (*außerdem*) besides, on the side; (*beiläufig*) incidentally
Ne'benberuf *m* sideline, side job
ne'benberuflich *adj* sideline, spare-time
Ne'benbeschäftigung *f* sideline
Nebenbuhler —**in** ['nebənbulər(ɪn)] §6 *mf* competitor, rival
ne'benbuhlerisch *adj* rival
Ne'benbuhling *n* secondary matter
nebeneinan'der *adv* side by side; neck and neck; (*gleichzeitig*) simultaneously; **n. bestehen** coexist
Nebeneinan'derleben *n* coexistence
nebeneinan'derstellen *tr* juxtapose
Ne'beneingang *m* side entrance
Ne'beneinkünfte *pl*, **Ne'beneinnahmen** *pl* extra income
Ne'benerzeugnis *n* by-product
Ne'benfach *n* (educ) minor; **als N. studieren** minor in
Ne'benflügel *m* (archit) wing
Ne'benfluß *m* tributary
Ne'benfrage *f* side issue
Ne'benfrau *f* concubine
Ne'bengang *m* side aisle
Ne'bengasse *f* side street, alley
Ne'bengebäude *n* annex, wing
Ne'bengedanke *m* ulterior motive
Ne'bengericht *n* side dish
Ne'bengeschäft *n* (com) branch
Ne'bengleis *n* (rr) siding, sidetrack
Ne'benhandlung *f* (-;-en) subplot
nebenher' *adv* on the side; besides; along
nebenhin' *adv* incidentally, by the way
Ne'benkosten *pl* incidentals, extras
Ne'benlinie *f* (rr) branch line
Ne'benmann *m* (-[e]s;⁚er) neighbor
Ne'benprodukt *n* by-product
Ne'benpunkt *m* minor point
Ne'benrolle *f* supporting role
Ne'bensache *f* side issue
ne'bensächlich *adj* subordinate; incidental; (*unwesentlich*) unimportant
Ne'bensächlichkeit *f* unimportance; triviality
Ne'bensatz *m* subordinate clause
Ne'benschaltung *f* (-;-en) (elec) shunt
Ne'benschluß *m* (elec) shunt
Ne'benspesen *pl* additional charges
ne'benstehend *adj* marginal, in the margin ‖ **Nebenstehende** §5 *mf* bystander

Ne'benstelle *f* branch; (telp) extension
Ne'benstraße *f* side street
Ne'bentisch *m* next table
Ne'bentür *f* side door
Ne'benverdienst *m* extra pay; side job
Ne'benvorstellung *f* side show
Ne'benweg *m* road
Ne'benwirkung *f* (-;-en) side effect
Ne'benzimmer *n* adjoining room
Ne'benzweck *m* secondary aim
neblig ['neblɪç] *adj* foggy, misty
nebst [nepst] *prep* (dat) including
necken ['nekən] *tr & recip* tease, kid
Neckerei [nekə'raɪ] *f* (-;-en) teasing
neckisch ['nekɪʃ] *adj* fond of teasing;
(coll) cute
nee [ne] *adv* (dial) no
Neffe ['nefə] *m* (-n;-n) nephew
Negation [nega'tsjon] *f* (-;-en) negation
negativ [nega'tif] *adj* negative || Neg-
ativ *n* (-s;-e) negative
Neger –in ['negər(ɪn)] §6 *mf* black,
Negro
Negligé [negli'ʒe] *n* (-s;-s) negligee
nehmen ['nemən] §116 *tr* take; (weg-)
take away; (anstellen) take on, hire;
(Anwalt) retain; (Hindernis) clear,
take; (Kurve) negotiate; (Schaden)
suffer; **Anfang n.** begin; **Anstand n.**
hesitate; **an sich n.** pocket, misappropriate; collect; retrieve; **Anstoß n.**
an (dat) take offense at; **auf sich n.**
assume, take upon oneself; **das Wort**
n. begin to speak; **den Mund voll n.**
(coll) talk big; **die Folgen auf sich**
n. bear the consequences; **ein Ende**
n. come to an end; **ein gutes Ende n.**
turn out all right; **er versteht es, die**
Kunden richtig zu n. he knows how
to handle customers; **etw genau n.**
take s.th. literally; **ich lasse es mir**
nicht n. zu (inf) I insist on (ger); **im**
Grunde genommen basically; **in An-**
griff n. begin; **in Arbeit n.** start making; **in die Hand n.** pick up; (fig) take
in hand; **j-m etw n.** take s.th. away
from s.o.; **deprive s.o. of s.th.; kein**
Ende n. go on endlessly; **man nehme**
zwei Eier, usw. (im Kochbuch) take
two eggs, etc.; **n. Sie bitte Platz!**
please sit down; **n. wir den Fall, daß**
let's suppose that; **Rücksicht n. auf**
(acc) show consideration for; **sich**
[dat] **das Leben n.** take one's life;
sich [dat] **nichts von seinen Rechten**
n. lassen insist on one's rights; **streng**
genommen strictly speaking; **Stunden**
n. take lessons; **Urlaub n.** take a vacation; (mil) go on furlough; **wie**
man's nimmt it all depends; **zu Hilfe**
n. use; **zur Ehe n.** marry; **zu sich**
[dat] **n.** put into one's pocket;
(Speise) eat; (Kind) take charge of
Neid [naɪt] *m* (-es) envy; **blasser (or**
gelber) N. pure envy; **vor N. ver-**
gehen die of envy
neiden ['naɪdən] *tr*—**j-m etw n.** envy
s.o. for s.th.
Neid'hammel *m* envious person
nei'dig *adj* (dial) var of neidisch
neidisch ['naɪdɪʃ] *adj* (auf acc) envious (of)

neid'los *adj* free of envy
Neid'nagel *m* hangnail
Neige ['naɪgə] *f* (-;-n) slope; (Abnahme) decline; (Überbleibsel) sediment, dregs; **zur N. gehen** (Geld,
Vorräte) run low; (Sonne) go down;
(Tag, Jahr) draw to a close
neigen ['naɪgən] *tr* incline, bend; ge-
neigt sloping; (fig) friendly, favor-
able || *ref* (vor dat) bow (to); (Ab-
hang) slope; **sich zum Ende n.** draw
to a close || *intr*—**n. zu** be inclined to
Nei'gung *f* (-;-en) slope, incline; (des
Hauptes) bowing; (e-s Schiffes) list;
(in der Straße) dip; (Gefälle) gra-
dient; (Hang) inclination; (Anlage)
tendency; (Vorliebe) taste, liking;
(Zuneigung) affection; **e-e N. nach**
rechts haben lean towards the right;
N. fassen zu take (a fancy) to
nein [naɪn] *adv* no || Nein *n* (-s;) no
Nein'stimme *f* (parl) nay
Nekrolog [nekro'lok] *m* (-[e]s;-e)
obituary
Nektar ['nektar] *m* (-s;) nectar
Nelke ['nelkə] *f* (-;-n) carnation; (Ge-
würz) clove
Nel'kenöl *n* oil of cloves
Nel'kenpfeffer *m* allspice
Nemesis ['nemezɪs] *f* (-;) Nemesis
nennbar ['nenbar] *adj* mentionable
nennen ['nenən] §97 *tr* name, call; (er-
wähnen) mention; (benennen) term
|| *ref* be called, be named
nen'nenswert *adj* worth mentioning
Nenner ['nenər] *m* (-s;-) (math) de-
nominator; **auf e-n gemeinsamen N.**
bringen reduce to a common denomi-
nator
Nennform ['nenform] *f* (gram) infini-
tive
Nenngeld ['nengelt] *n* entry fee
Nen'nung *f* (-;) naming; mentioning
Nennwert ['nenvert] *m* face value
Neologismus [ne-olo'gismus] *m* (-;
-men [mən]) neologism
Neon ['ne-on] *n* (-s;) neon
Ne'onlicht *n* neon light
Nepotismus [nepo'tismus] *m* (-;) nepotism
neppen ['nepən] *tr* (coll) gyp, clip
Nepplokal ['neplokal] *n* (sl) clip joint
Neptun [nep'tun] *m* (-s;) Neptune
Nerv [nerf] *m* (-s;-en) nerve; **die Ner-**
ven behalten keep cool; **die Nerven**
verlieren lose one's head; **j-m auf**
die Nerven gehen get on s.o.'s nerves;
mit den Nerven herunter sein be a
nervous wreck
Nerven-, nerven- ['nerfən] *comb.fm.*
nervous, neuro-, of nerves
ner'venaufreibend *adj* nerve-racking
Ner'venarzt *m*, Ner'venärztin *f* neurol-
ogist
Ner'venberuhigungsmittel *n* sedative
Ner'venbündel *n* (fig) bundle of nerves
Ner'venentzündung *f* neuritis
Ner'venfaser *f* nerve fiber
Ner'venheilanstalt *f* mental institution
Ner'venheilkunde *f* neurology
Ner'venkitzel *m* thrill, suspense
Ner'venknoten *m* ganglion
ner'venkrank *adj* neurotic

Ner'venkrieg *m* war of nerves
Ner'venlehre *f* neurology
Ner'vensäge *f* (coll) pain in the neck
Ner'venschmerz *m* neuralgia
Ner'venschwäche *f* nervousness
Ner'venzentrum *n* (fig) nerve center
Ner'venzusammenbruch *m* nervous breakdown
nervig ['nɛrvɪç], ['nɛrfɪç] *adj* sinewy
nervös [nɛr'vøs] *adj* nervous
Nervosität [nɛrvozɪ'tet] *f* (-;) nervousness
Nerz [nɛrts] *m* (-es;-e) (zool) mink
Nerz'mantel *m* mink coat
Nessel ['nɛsəl] *f* (-;-n) nettle; **sich in die Nesseln setzen** (fig) get oneself into hot water
Nest [nɛst] *n*. (-es;-er) nest; (*Schlupfwinkel*) hideout; small town; dead town; (*Bett*) (coll) bed
nesteln ['nɛstəln] *tr* lace, tie || *intr* —n. an (*dat*) fiddle with, fuss with
Nesthäkchen ['nɛsthɛkçən] *n* (-s;-), **Nestküken** ['nɛstkykən] *n* (-s;-) baby (*of the family*)
nett [nɛt] *adj* nice; (*sauber*) neat; (*niedlich*) cute; **das kann ja n. werden!** (iron) that's going to be just dandy!
netto ['nɛto] *adv* net; clear
Net'togewicht *n* net weight
Net'togewinn *m* clear profit
Net'tolohn *m* take-home pay
Net'topreis *m* net price
Netz [nɛts] *n* (-es;-e) net; network; grid
netzen ['nɛtsən] *tr* wet, moisten
Netz'haut *f* retina
Netz'werk *n* netting, webbing
neu [nɔɪ] *adj* new; (*frisch*) fresh; (*unlängst geschehen*) recent; **aufs neue** anew; **neuere Geschichte** modern history; **neuere Sprachen** modern languages; **von neuem** all over again || *adv* newly; recently; anew; afresh || **Neue** §5 *mf* newcomer || §5 *n*— **was gibt es Neues?** what's new?
Neu-, neu- *comb.fm.* new–, newly; re–; neo–
Neu'anlage *f* new installation; (fin) reinvestment
Neu'anschaffung *f* recent acquisition
neu'artig *adj* novel; modern
Neu'aufführung *f* (-;-en) (theat) revival
Neu'ausgabe *f* new edition, republication; (*Neudruck*) reprint
Neu'bau *m* (-[e]s;-bauten) new building
neu'bearbeiten *tr* revise
Neubelebung ['nɔɪbelebʊŋ] *f* (-;-en) revival
Neu'bildung *f* (-;-en) new growth; (gram) neologism
Neu'druck *m* reprint
neuerdings ['nɔɪ·ɛrdɪŋs] *adv* recently; (*vom neuem*) anew
Neuerer –in ['nɔɪ·ərər(ɪn)] §6 *mf* innovator
Neuerung ['nɔɪ·ərʊŋ] *f* (-;-en) innovation
neuestens ['nɔɪ·əstəns] *adv* recently
Neu'fassung *f* revision

Neufundland [nɔɪ'fʊntlant] *n* (-s;) Newfoundland
neu'gebacken *adj* fresh-baked; brand-new
neu'geboren *adj* new-born
neu'gestalten *tr* reorganize
Neu'gier *f*, **Neugierde** ['nɔɪgɪrdə] *f* (-;) curiosity, inquisitiveness
neu'gierig *adj* curious, nosey
Neu'gründung *f* (-;-en) reestablishment
Neu'gruppierung *f* (-;-en) regrouping; reshuffling
Neu'heit *f* (-;-en) novelty
neu'hochdeutsch *adj* modern High German
Neu'igkeit *f* (-;-en) news, piece of news
Neu'jahr *n* New Year
Neu'land *n* virgin soil; (fig) new ground
neu'lich *adv* lately
Neuling ['nɔɪlɪŋ] *m* (-[e]s;-e) beginner
neu'modisch *adj* fashionable; new-fangled
neun [nɔɪn] *invar adj & pron* nine || **Neun** *f* (-;-en) nine
Neunmalkluge ['nɔɪnmalklugə] §5 *mf* wiseacre
neunte ['nɔɪntə] §9 *adj & pron* ninth
Neuntel ['nɔɪntəl] *n* (-s;-) ninth
neun'zehn *invar adj & pron* nineteen || **Neunzehn** *f* (-;-en) nineteen
neun'zehnte §9 *adj & pron* nineteenth
neunzig ['nɔɪntsɪç] *invar adj & pron* ninety || **Neunzig** *f* (-;-en) ninety
neunziger ['nɔɪntsɪgər] *invar adj* of the nineties; **die n. Jahre** the nineties || **Neunziger –in** §6 *mf* nonagenarian
neunzigste ['nɔɪntsɪçstə] §9 *adj & pron* ninetieth
Neu'ordnung *f* (-;-en) reorganization
Neural·gie [nɔɪral'gi] *f* (-;-gien ['gi·ən]) neuralgia
Neu'regelung *f* (-;-en) rearrangement
Neu·ron ['nɔɪron] *n* (-;-ronen ['ro-nən]) neuron
Neurose [nɔɪ'rozə] *f* (-;-n) neurosis
Neurotiker –in [nɔɪ'rotɪkər(ɪn)] §6 *mf* neurotic
neurotisch [nɔɪ'rotɪʃ] *adj* neurotic
Neusee'land *n* (-s;) New Zealand
Neu'silber *n* German silver
Neusprachler –in ['nɔɪʃpraxlər(ɪn)] §6 *mf* modern-language teacher
Neu'stadt *f* new section of town
Neu'steinzeit *f* neolithic age
neu'steinzeitlich *adj* neolithic
neutral [nɔɪ'tral] *adj* neutral
neutralisieren [nɔɪtralɪ'zirən] *tr* neutralize
Neutralität [nɔɪtralɪ'tet] *f* (-;) neutrality
Neu·tron ['nɔɪtrən] *n* (-;-tronen ['tronən]) neutron
Neu·trum ['nɔɪtrʊm] *n* (-s;-tra [tra] & -tren [trən]) (gram) neuter
neuvermählt ['nɔɪfɛrmelt] *adj* newly married || **Neuvermählte** §5 *pl* newlyweds
Neu'zeit *f* recent times
Nibelung ['nibəlʊŋ] *m* (-s;) (myth)

(King) Nibelung ‖ *m* (-en;-en) Nibelung

nicht [nɪçt] *adv* not; **auch...nicht** not ...either; **n. doch!** please don't; **n. einmal** not even, not so much as; **n. mehr** no longer, no more; **n. um die Welt** not for the world; **n. wahr?** isn't it so?, no?, right?

Nicht-, nicht- comb.fm. in-, im-, un-, non-

Nicht'achtung *f* disregard, disrespect; **N. des Gerichts** contempt of court

nicht'amtlich *adj* unofficial

Nicht'angriffspakt *m* nonaggression pact

Nicht'annahme *f* nonacceptance

Nichte ['nɪçtə] *f* (-;-n) niece

Nicht'einmischung *f* noninterference

Nicht'eisenmetall *n* nonferrous metal

nichtig ['nɪçtɪç] *adj* invalid; void; (*eitel*) vain; (*vergänglich*) transitory; **für n. erklären** annul

Nich'tigkeit *f* (-;-en) invalidity; futility; (*Kleinigkeit*) trifle; **Nichtigkeiten** trivia

Nich'tigkeitserklärung *f* annulment

Nicht'kämpfer *m* noncombatant

nicht'öffentlich *adj* private; (*Sitzung*) closed

nicht'rostend *adj* rustproof; (*Stahl*) stainless

nichts [nɪçts] *indef pron* nothing; **gar n.** nothing at all; **n. als** nothing but; **n. mehr davon!** not another word about it!; **n. und wieder n.** absolutely nothing; **soviel wie n.** next to nothing; **um n.** for nothing, to no avail; **weiter n.?** is that all?; **wenn es weiter n. ist** if it's nothing worse than that ‖ **Nichts** *n* (-s;) nothingness; nonentity; (*Leere*) void; (*Kleinigkeit*) trifle; **vor dem N. stehen** be faced with utter ruin

nichtsdestowe'niger *adv* nevertheless

Nichts'könner *m* incompetent person; ignoramus

Nichts'nutz *m* good-for-nothing

nichts'nutzig *adj* good-for-nothing

nichts'sagend *adj* insignificant; (*Antwort*) vague; noncommittal; (*Gesicht*) vacuous; (*Redensart*) trite

Nichts'tuer –*m* ;*m* loafer

Nichts'wisser –*m* ;*m mf* ignoramus

nichts'würdig *adj* contemptible

Nicht'zutreffende §5 *n*—**Nichtzutreffendes streichen!** delete if not applicable

Nickel ['nɪkəl] *n* (-s;-) (metal) nickel

nicken ['nɪkən] *intr* nod; (*schlummern*) nap

Nickerchen ['nɪkərçən] *n* (-s;-) nap

nie [ni] *adv* never, at no time

nieder ['nidər] *adj* low; (*gemein*) base ‖ *adv* down

nie'derbrechen §64 *tr & intr* (SEIN) break down

nie'derbrennen §97 *tr & intr* (SEIN) burn down

nie'derdeutsch *adj* Low German ‖ **Niederdeutsch** *n* Low German ‖ **Niederdeutsche** §5 *mf* North German

nie'derdonnern *tr* (coll) shout down ‖ *intr* go (or come) crashing down

Nie'derdruck *m* low pressure

nie'derdrücken *tr* press down (fig) weigh down; (*unterdrücken*) oppress; (*entmutigen*) depress

nie'derfallen §72 *intr* (SEIN) fall down

Nie'derfrequenz *f* low frequency; audio frequency

Nie'dergang *m* descent; (*der Sonne*) setting; (fig) decline, fall

nie'dergehen §82 *intr* (SEIN) go down; (*Flugzeug*) land; (*Regen*) fall; (*Vorhang*) drop

nie'dergeschlagen *adj* dejected

nie'derhalten §90 *tr* hold down, keep down

nie'derholen *tr* lower, haul down

Nie'derholz *n* underbrush

nie'derkämpfen *tr* (& fig) overcome

nie'derkommen §99 *intr* (SEIN) (**mit**) give birth (to)

Niederkunft ['nidərkunft] *f* (-;) confinement, childbirth

Nie'derlage *f* defeat; (*Lager*) warehouse; (*Filiale*) branch

Niederlande, die ['nidərlandə] *pl* The Netherlands, Holland

Niederländer ['nidərlendər] *m* (-s;-) Dutchman

niederländisch ['nidərlendɪʃ] *adj* Dutch

nie'derlassen §104 *tr* let down ‖ *ref* sit down, recline; (*Wohnsitz nehmen*) settle; (*ein Geschäft eröffnen*) set oneself up in business; (*Vogel, Flugzeug*) land

Nie'derlassung *f* (-;-en) settlement, colony; establishment; (*e-r Bank*) branch; (com) plant

nie'derlegen *tr* lay down, put down; (*Amt*) resign; (*Geschäft*) give up; (*Krone*) abdicate; (*schriftlich*) set down in writing; **die Arbeit n.** go on strike ‖ *ref* lie down; go to bed

nie'dermachen *tr* butcher, massacre

nie'dermähen *tr* mow down

nie'dermetzeln *tr* butcher, massacre

Nie'derschlag *m* (*Bodensatz*) sediment; (box) knockdown; (chem) precipitate; (meteor) precipitation; **radioaktiver N.** fallout

nie'derschlagen §132 *tr* knock down; (*Augen*) cast down; (*Aufstand*) put down; (*vertuschen*) hush up; (*Verfahren*) quash; (*Forderung*) waive; (*Hoffnungen*) dash; (chem) precipitate

nie'derschmettern *tr* knock to the ground; (fig) crush

nie'derschreiben §62 *tr* write down

nie'dersetzen *tr* set down ‖ *ref* sit down

nie'dersinken §143 *intr* (SEIN) sink down

nie'derstimmen *tr* vote down

Nie'dertracht *f* nastiness, meanness

nie'derträchtig *adj* nasty; underhand

Nie'derung *f* (-;-en) low ground, depression

niederwärts ['nidərverts] *adv* downward

nie'derwerfen §160 *tr* knock down; (*Aufstand*) put down ‖ *ref* fall down

Nie'derwild *n* small game

niedlich ['nitlɪç] *adj* nice, cute

Niednagel ['nitnagəl] *m* hangnail

niedrig ['niːdrɪç] *adj* low; *(Herkunft)* humble; *(gemein)* mean, base
niemals ['niːmals] *adv* never
niemand ['niːmant] *indef pron* no one, nobody
Nie'mandsland *n* no man's land
Niere ['niːrə] *f* (–;–n) kidney; **das geht mir an die Nieren** (fig) that cuts me deep
nieseln ['niːzəln] *impers*—**es nieselt** it is drizzling
Nie'selregen *m* drizzle
niesen ['niːzən] *intr* sneeze
Niet [niːt] *m* (–[e]s;–e) rivet
Niete ['niːtə] *f* (–;–n) rivet; *(in der Lotterie)* blank; *(Versager)* flop
nieten ['niːtən] *tr* rivet
niet–/ und na'gelfest *adj* nailed down
Nihilismus [nihɪ'lɪsmɪs] *m* (–;) nihilism
Nikotin [nikə'tiːn] *n* (–s;) nicotine
nikotin'arm *adj* low in nicotine
Nil [nil] *m* (–s;) Nile
Nil'pferd *n* hippopotamus
Nimbus ['nɪmbus] *m* (–;–se) halo; aura; *(Ansehen)* prestige; *(meteor)* nimbus
nimmer ['nɪmər] *adv* never; *(dial)* no more
nim'mermehr *adv* never more; by no means
Nippel ['nɪpəl] *m* (–s;–) *(mach)* nipple
nippen ['nɪpən] *tr & intr* sip
Nippsachen ['nɪpzaxən] *pl* knicknacks
nirgends ['nɪrgənts] *adv* nowhere
nirgendwo ['nɪrgəntvoː] *adv* nowhere
Nische ['niːʃə] *f* (–;–n) niche
nisten ['nɪstən] *intr* nest
Nitrat [ni'traːt] *n* (–[e]s;–e) nitrate
Nitrid [ni'triːt] *n* (–[e]s;–e) nitride
Nitroglyzerin [nitroglytsə'riːn] *n* (–s;) nitroglycerin
Niveau [ni'voː] *n* (–s;–s) level; **N. haben** have class; **unter dem N. sein** be substandard
Niveau'übergang *m* (rr) grade crossing
nivellieren [nivɛ'liːrən] *tr* level
nix [nɪks] *indef pron* (dial) nothing ‖ **Nix** *m* (–[e]s;–e) water sprite
Nixe ['nɪksə] *f* (–;–n) water nymph
nobel ['noːbəl] *adj* noble; elegant; *(freigebig)* generous
noch [nɔx] *adv* still, yet; even; else; **heute n.** this very day; **n. besser** even bettter; **n. dazu** over and above that; **n. einer** one more, still another; **n. einmal** once more; **n. einmal so viel** twice as much; **n. etwas** one more thing; **n. etwas?** anything else?; **n. heute** even today; **n. immer** still; **n. nicht** not yet; **n. nie** never before; **n. und n.** (coll) over and over; **sei es n. so klein** now matter how small it is; **was denn n. alles?** what next? **wer kommt n.?** who else is coming?
noch'mal *adv* once more
nochmalig ['nɔxmaːlɪç] *adj* repeated
nochmals ['nɔxmaːls] *adv* once more
Nocke ['nɔkə] *f* (–;–n) *(mach)* cam
Nockenwelle (Nok'kenwelle) *f* camshaft
Nockerl ['nɔkərl] *n* (–s;– & –n) (Aust) dumpling

Nomade [no'maːdə] *m* (–n;–n) nomad
nominell [nomɪ'nɛl] *adj* nominal
nominieren [nomɪ'niːrən] *tr* nominate
Nonne ['nɔnə] *f* (–;–n) nun
Non'nenkloster *n* convent
Noppe ['nɔpə] *f* (–;–n) (tex) nap
Nord [nɔrt] *m* (–[e]s;) North; (poet) north wind
Norden ['nɔrdən] *m* (–s;) North; **im N. von** north of
nordisch ['nɔrdɪʃ] *adj* northern; *(Rasse)* Nordic; *(skandinavisch)* Norse
nördlich ['nœrtlɪç] *adj* northern
Nord'licht *n* northern lights
nordwärts ['nɔrtvɛrts] *adv* northward
Nörgelei [nœrgə'laɪ] *f* (–;–en) griping
nörgelig ['nœrgəlɪç] *adj* nagging
nörgeln ['nœrgəln] *intr*—**n. an** (dat) gripe about, kick about
Norm [nɔrm] *f* (–;–en) norm, standard
normal [nɔr'maːl] *adj* normal, standard
normalisieren [nɔrmalɪ'ziːrən] *tr* normalize
Normal'zeit *f* standard time
Normanne [nɔr'manə] *m* (–n;–n) Norman
normen ['nɔrmən], **normieren** [nɔr'miːrən] *tr* normalize, standardize
Norwegen ['nɔrveːgən] *n* (–s;) Norway
Norweger –in ['nɔrveːgər(ɪn)] §6 *mf* Norwegian
norwegisch ['nɔrveːgɪʃ] *adj* Norwegian
Not [noːt] *f* (–;̈e) need, want; *(Notlage)* necessity; *(Gefahr)* distress; *(Dringlichkeit)* emergency; **es hat keine Not** there's no hurry about it; **es tut not** it is necessary; **in der Not** in a pinch; **in Not geraten** fall upon hard times; **j–m große Not machen** give s.o. a lot of trouble; **j–m seine Not klagen** cry on s.o.'s shoulders; **mit knapper Not** narrowly; **mit Not** scarcely; **Not haben zu** (*inf*) be scarcely able to (*inf*); **Not leiden** suffer want; **ohne Not** needlessly; **seine liebe Not haben mit** have a lot of trouble with; **sie haben Not auszukommen** they have difficulty making ends meet; **zur Not** if need be, in a pinch
Nota ['noːta] *f* (–;–s) note; **etw in N. geben** place an order for s.th.; **etw in N. nehmen** make a note of s.th.
Notar –in [no'taːr(ɪn)] §8 *mf* notary public
Notariat [nota'rjaːt] *n* (–[e]s;–e) notary office
notariell [nota'rjɛl] *adv*—**n. beglaubigen** notarize
Not'ausgang *m* emergency exit
Not'ausstieg *m* escape hatch
Not'behelf *m* makeshift, stopgap
Not'bremse *f* (rr) emergency brake
Not'durft ['noːtdurft] *f* (–;) want; necessities of life; **seine N. verrichten** relieve oneself
not'dürftig *adj* scanty, poor; hard up; *(behelfsmäßig)* temporary
Note ['noːtə] *f* (–;–n) note; *(Banknote)* bill; *(Eigenart)* trait; (educ) mark; (mus) note; **in Noten setzen** set to music; **nach Noten** (fig) thoroughly; **persönliche Note** personal

touch; **wie nach Noten** like clock-work

No′tenblatt n sheet music

No′tenbuch n, **No′tenheft** n music book

No′tenlinie f (mus) line

No′tenschlüssel m (mus) clef

No′tenständer m music stand

No′tensystem n (mus) staff

Not′fall m emergency

notfalls [′notfals] adv if necessary

notgedrungen [′notgədruŋən] adj compulsory ǁ adv of necessity

notieren [no′tirən] tr note down; jot down; (Preise) quote

Notie′rung f (-; -en) noting; (st. exch.) quotation

nötig [′nøtiç] adj necessary; **das habe ich nicht n.!** I don′t have to stand for that!; n. **haben** need

nötigen [′nøtigən] tr urge; (zwingen) force ǁ ref—**lassen Sie sich nicht n.!** don′t wait to be asked; **sich genötigt sehen zu** (inf) feel compelled to (inf)

nö′tigenfalls adv in case of need

Nö′tigung f (-;) compulsion; urgent request; (jur) duress

Notiz [no′tits] f (-; -en) notice; (Vermerk) note, memorandum; **keine N. nehmen von** take no notice of; **sich** [dat] **Notizen machen** jot down notes

Notiz′block m scratch pad

Not′lage f predicament; emergency

Not′landung f emergency landing

Not′lüge f white lie

Not′maßnahme f emergency measure

Not′nagel m (fig) stopgap

notorisch [no′torif] adj notorious

Not′pfennig m savings; **sich e-n N. aufsparen** save up for a rainy day

Not′ruf m (telp) emergency

Not′signal n distress signal

Not′stand m state of emergency

Not′standsgebiet n disaster area

Not′treppe f fire escape

Not′wehr f—**aus N.** in self-defense

notwendig [′notvendiç] adj necessary

Not′wendigkeit f (-; -en) necessity

Not′zeichen n distress signal

Not′zucht f rape

not′züchtigen tr rape, ravish

Nougat [′nugat] m & n (-s; -s) nougat

Novelle [no′velə] f (-; -n) short story; (parl) amendment, rider

November [no′vembər] m (-s; -) November

Novität [novi′tet] f (-; -en) novelty

Novize [no′vitsə] m (-n; -n), **Novizin** [no′vitsin] f (-; -nen), novice

Noviziat [novi′tsjat] n (-[e]s; -e) novitiate

Nu [nu] invar m—**im Nu** in a jiffy

Nuance [ny′ãsə] f (-; -n) nuance

nüchtern [′nyçtərn] adj fasting; not having had breakfast; (Magen) empty; (nicht betrunken) sober; (leidenschaftslos) cool; (geistlos) dry, dull; (unsentimental) matter-of-fact

Nudel [′nudəl] f (-; -n) noodle; **e-e komische N.** (coll) a funny person

Nu′delholz n rolling pin

nudeln [′nudəln] tr force-feed

Nugat [′nugat] m (-s; -s) nougat

nuklear [nukle′ar] adj nuclear

Nukle-on [′nukle·on] n (-s; -onen [′onən]) nucleon

null [nul] adj null; n. **und nichtig** null and void; n. **und nichtig machen** annul ǁ **Null** f (-; -en) naught; zero; (fig) nobody; **in weniger als N. Komma nichts** in less than no time, in no time

Null′punkt m zero; freezing point; **auf dem N. angekommen sein** hit bottom

Numera-le [nume′ralə] n (-s; -lien [ljən] & -lia [lja]) numeral

numerieren [nume′rirən] tr number; **numerierten Platz** reserved seat

numerisch [nu′merif] adj numerical

Nummer [′numər] f (-; -n) number; (Größe) size; (e-r Zeitung) issue; **auf N. Sicher sitzen** (sl) be in jail; **bei j-m e-e gute N. haben** (coll) be in good with s.o.; **e-e bloße N.** a mere figurehead; **er ist e-e N.** he′s quite a character; **laufende N.** serial number; **N. besetzt!** line is busy!

Num′mernfolge f numerical order

Num′mernscheibe f (telp) dial

Num′mernschild n (aut) license plate

nun [nun] adv now; **nun?** well?; **nun aber** now; **nun also!** well now!; **nun gut!** all right then!; **nun und nimmer(mehr)** never more; **von nun ab** from now on; **wenn er nun käme?** what if he came?

nun′mehr′ adv now; from now on

nur [nur] adv only, merely, but; (lauter) nothing but; **nicht nur …** sondern auch not only … but also; **nur daß** except that; **nur eben** scarcely; (zeitlich) a moment ago; **nur zu!** go to it!; **wenn nur** if only, provided that

Nürnberg [′nyrnberk] n (-s;) Nuremberg

nuscheln [′nuʃəln] intr (coll) mumble

Nuß [nus] f (-; **Nüsse**) nut

nuß′braun adj nut-brown; (Augen) hazel

Nuß′kern m kernel

Nußknacker [′nusknakər] m (-s; -) nutcracker

Nuß′schale f nutshell

Nüster [′nystər] f (-; -n) nostril

Nut [nut] f (-; -en), **Nute** [′nutə] f (-; -n) groove, rabbet

Nutte [′nutə] f (-; -n) whore

nutz [nuts] adj useful; **zu nichts n. sein** be good for nothing ǁ **Nutz** m (-es;) use; benefit; profit; **zu j-s N. und Frommen** for s.o.′s benefit

Nutz′anwendung f utilization

nutzbar [′nutsbar] adj useful; **sich** [dat] **etw n. machen** utilize s.th.

nutz′bringend adj useful, profitable

nütze [′nytsə] adj useful; **nichts n.** of no use; **zu nichts n. sein** be good for nothing

Nutz′effekt m efficiency

nutzen [′nutsən], **nützen** [′nytsən] tr make use of; **das kann mir viel (wenig, nichts) n.** this can do me much (little, no) good; **was nützt das**

alles? what's the good of all this? ‖ *intr* do good ‖ *impers*—es nützt nichts it's no use ‖ **Nutzen** *m* (-s;-) use; benefit; (*Gewinn*) profit; (*Vorteil*) advantage; **von N. sein** be of use
Nutz′fahrzeug *n* commercial vehicle
Nutz′garten *m* vegetable garden
Nutz′holz *n* lumber
Nutz′leistung *f* (mech) output

nützlich [′nʏtslɪç] *adj* useful
nutz′los *adj* useless
Nutz′losigkeit *f* (-;) uselessness
Nutz′schwelle *f* break-even point
Nut′zung *f* (-;) use
Nylon [′naɪlɔn] *n* (-s;) nylon
Nymphe [′nʏmfə] *f* (-;-n) nymph
Nymphomanin [nʏmfo′manɪn] *f* (-; -nen) nymphomaniac

O

O, o [o] *invar n* O, o
Oase [o′azə] *f* (-;-n) oasis
ob [ɔp] *prep* (*dat*) above; (*genit*) on account of ‖ *conj* whether; **als ob** as if; **na ob!** rather!; **und ob!** and how!
Obacht [′obaxt] *f* (-;)—**in O. nehmen** take care of; **O.!** watch out!; **O. geben auf** (*acc*) pay attention to; take care of
Obdach [′ɔpdax] *n* (-[e]s;) shelter
ob′dachlos *adj* homeless
Obduktion [ɔpduk′tsjon] *f* (-;-en) autopsy
obduzieren [ɔpdu′tsirən] *tr* perform an autopsy on
O-Beine [′obaɪnə] *pl* bow legs
O′-beinig *adj* bowlegged
Obelisk [obe′lɪsk] *m* (-en;-en) obelisk
oben [′obən] *adv* above; (*in der Höhe*) up; (*im Himmelsraum*) on high; (*im Hause*) upstairs; (*auf der Spitze*) at the top; (*auf der Oberfläche*) on the surface; (*Aufschrift auf Kisten*) this side up; **da o.** up there; **nach o. gehen** go up, go upstairs; **o. am Tische sitzen** sit at the head of the table; **o. auf** (*dat*) at the top of, on the top of; **von o.** from above; **von o. bis unten** from top to bottom; from head to foot; **von o. herab** (fig) condescendingly; **wie o. angegeben** as stated above
obenan′ *adv* at the top, at the head
obenauf′ *adv* on top; **immer o. sein** be always in top spirits
obendrein [obən′draɪn] *adv* on top of it, into the bargain
o′benerwähnt, o′bengenannt *adj* above-mentioned
o′bengesteuert *adj* (aut) overhead
obenhin′ *adv* superficially; perfunctorily
obenhinaus′ *adv*—**o. wollen** have big ideas
o′ben-oh′ne *adj* (coll) topless
o′benstehend *adj* given above
Ober [′obər] *m* (-s;-) (coll) waiter; **Herr O.!** waiter!
Ober- *comb.fm.* upper, higher; superior; chief, supreme, head; southern
O′berägypten *n* Upper Egypt
O′berarm *m* upper arm
O′beraufseher *m* inspector general; superintendent
O′beraufsicht *f* superintendence

O′berbau *m* (-[e]s;-ten) superstructure
O′berbefehl *m* supreme command; **O. führen** have supreme command
O′berbefehlshaber *m* commander in chief
O′berbegriff *m* wider concept
O′berdeck *n* upper deck
O′berdeckomnibus *m* double-decker bus
o′berdeutsch *adj* of southern Germany
obere [′obərə] §9 *adj* higher, upper; chief, superior; supreme ‖ **Obere** §5 *m* (eccl) father superior ‖ *n* top
o′berfaul *adj* (fig) fishy
O′berfeldwebel *m* sergeant first class
O′berfläche *f* surface
o′berflächlich *adj* superficial
O′bergefreite §5 *m* corporal
O′bergeschoß *n* upper floor
O′bergewalt *f* supreme authority
o′berhalb *prep* (*genit*) above
O′berhand *f* (fig) upper hand; **die O. gewinnen über** (*acc*) get the better of
O′berhaupt *n* head, chief
O′berhaus *n* upper house
O′berhaut *f* epidermis
O′berhemd *n* shirt, dress shirt
O′berherr *m* sovereign
O′berherrschaft *f* sovereignty; supremacy
O′berhirte *m* prelate
O′berhofmeister *m* Lord Chamberlain
O′berhoheit *f* supreme authority
Oberin [′obərɪn] *f* (-;-nen) mother superior; (med) head nurse
O′beringenieur *m* chief engineer
o′berirdisch *adj* above-ground; overhead
O′berkellner *m* head waiter
O′berkiefer *m* upper jaw
O′berkleidung *f* outer wear
O′berkommando *n* general headquarters
O′berkörper *m* upper part of the body
O′berland *n* highlands
Oberländer -in [′obərlendər(ɪn)] §6 *mf* highlander
o′berlastig *adj* top-heavy
O′berleder *n* uppers
O′berlehrer -in §6 *mf* secondary school teacher, high school teacher
O′berleitung *f* supervision; (elec) overhead line (*of trolley, etc.*)
O′berleutnant *m* first lieutenant

O′berlicht n skylight
O′berliga f (sport) upper division
O′berlippe f upper lip
O′berpostamt n general post office
O′berprima f senior class
Obers ['ɔbərs] m (-;) (Aust) cream
O′berschenkel m thigh
O′berschicht f upper layer; (der Be-völkerung) upper classes; **geistige O.** intelligentsia
O′berschule f high school
O′berschwester f (med) head nurse
O′berseite f topside, right side
Oberst ['obərst] m (-en;-en) colonel
O′berstaatsanwalt m attorney general
oberste ['obərstə] §9 adj (super of obere) uppermost, highest, top || **Oberste** §5 mf senior, chief
O′berstimme f treble, soprano
O′berstleutnant m lieutenant colonel
O′berstock m upper floor
O′berwasser n—**O. haben** (fig) have the upper hand
O′berwelt f upper world
O′berwerk n upper manual (of organ)
obgleich′ conj though, although
Ob′hut f (-;) care, protection
obig ['obɪç] adj above, above-men-tioned
Objekt [ɔp'jekt] n (-[e]s;-e) object
objektiv [ɔpjek'tif] adj objective; (un-parteiisch) impartial || **Objektiv** n (-s;-e) objective lens
Objektivität [ɔpjektivɪ'tet] f (-;) ob-jectivity; impartiality
Objekt′träger m slide (of microscope)
Oblate [ɔ'blɑtə] f (-;-n) wafer; (eccl) host
obliegen [ɔp'ligən] §108 intr (dat) ap-ply oneself to, devote oneself to; (dat) be incumbent upon || impers—**es obliegt mir zu** (inf) it's up to me to (inf)
Ob′liegenheit f (-;-en) obligation
obligat [ɔblɪ'gat] adj obligatory; (uner-läßlich) indispensable; (unvermeid-lich) inevitable
Obligation [ɔblɪga'tsjon] f (-;-en) bond; obligation
obligatorisch [ɔblɪga'torɪʃ] adj obliga-tory
Ob·mann ['ɔpman] m (-[e]s;-̈er & -leute) chairman; (jur) foreman
Oboe [ɔ'boə] f (-;-n) oboe
Obrigkeit ['obrɪçkart] f (-;-en) author-ity; (coll) authorities
o′brigkeitlich adj government(al)
obschon′ conj though, although
Observato·rium [ɔpzerva'torjum] n (-s;-rien) [rjən] observatory
obsiegen ['ɔpzigən] intr be victorious; (dat) triumph over
obskur [ɔps'kur] adj obscure
Obst [opst] n (-es;) (certain kinds of) fruit (mainly central-European, e.g., apples, plums; but not bananas, oranges); **O. und Südfrüchte** Euro-pean and (sub)tropical fruit
Obst′garten m orchard
Obst′kern m stone; seed, pip
Obstruktion [ɔpstruk'tsjon] f (-;-en) obstruction; (pol) filibuster; **O. trei-ben** filibuster

obszön [ɔps'tsøn] adj obscene
Obszönität [ɔpstsønɪ'tet] f (-;-en) ob-scenity
ob′walten, obwal′ten intr exist; pre-vail; hold sway
obwohl′ conj though, although
Ochse ['ɔksə] m (-n;-n) ox
ochsen ['ɔksən] intr (educ) cram
O′chsenfleisch n beef
O′chsenfrosch m bullfrog
öde ['øːdə] adj bleak || **Öde** f (-;-n) wasteland; (fig) bleakness
Ödem [ø'dem] n (-s;-e) edema
oder ['odər] conj or
Öd·land ['øtlant] n (-[e]s;-ländereien [lendə'rar·ən]) wasteland
Ofen ['ofən] m (-s;̈-) stove; (Back-) oven; (Hoch-) furnace; (Brenn-, Dürr-) kiln
O′fenklappe f damper
O′fenrohr n stovepipe
O′fenröhre f warming oven
offen ['ɔfən] adj open; (öffentlich) public; (fig) frank, open
offenbar ['ɔfənbar] adj obvious, mani-fest
offenbaren [ɔfən'barən] tr reveal
Offenba′rung f (-;-en) revelation
Of′fenheit f (-;) openness
of′fenherzig adj forthright; (Kleid) (hum) low-cut
of′fenkundig adj well-known; (offen-sichtlich) obvious; (Beweis) clear
of′fensichtlich adj obvious
offensiv [ɔfen'zif] adj offensive || **Of-fensive** [ɔfen'zivə] f (-;-n) offen-sive
öffentlich ['œfəntlɪç] adj public; (Dienst) civil; **öffentliches Haus** brothel
Öf′fentlichkeit f (-;) public; publicity; **an die Ö. treten** appear in public; **im Licht der Ö.** in the limelight; **in aller Ö.** in public; **sich in die Ö. flüchten** rush into print
offerieren [ɔfə'rirən] tr offer
Offerte [ɔ'fertə] f (-;-n) offer
Offerto·rium [ɔfer'torjum] n (-s;-rien [rjən]) offertory
Offiziant [ɔfɪ'tsjant] m (-en;-en) of-ficiating priest
offiziell [ɔfɪ'tsjel] adj official
Offizier [ɔfɪ'tsir(in)] §6 mf officer
Offiziers′anwärter -in §6 mf officer candidate
Offiziers′bursche m orderly
Offiziers′deck n quarter deck
Offiziers′kasino n officers' club
Offiziers′patent n officer's commission
Offizin [ɔfɪ'tsin] f (-;-en) drugstore; (Druckerei) print shop, press
offiziös [ɔfɪ'tsjøs] adj semiofficial
öffnen ['œfnən] tr & ref open
Öff′ner m (-s;-) opener
Öff′nung f (-;-en) opening
oft [ɔft], **öfter(s)** ['œftər(s)] adv often
oftmals ['ɔftmals] adv often(times)
oh [o] interj oh!, O!
Oheim ['oharm] m (-s;-e) uncle
Ohm [om] m (-s;-e) (poet) uncle || n (-s;-) (elec) ohm
ohne ['onə] prep (acc) without; **o. daß** (ind) without (ger); **o. mich!** count

me out!; **o. weiteres** right off; **o. zu** (*inf*) without (*ger*)

ohnedies' *adv* anyhow, in any case

ohneglei'chen *adj* unequaled

ohnehin' *adv* anyhow, as it is

Ohnmacht ['ɔnmaxt] *f* (-;) faint, unconsciousness; helplessness; **in O. fallen** (or **sinken**) faint, pass out

ohnmächtig ['ɔnmɛçtɪç] *adj* unconscious; helpless; **o. werden** faint

Ohr [or] *n* (-[e]s;-en) ear; (*im Buch*) dog-ear; **die Ohren spitzen** prick up the ears; **es dick hinter den Ohren haben** be sly; **ganz Ohr sein** be all ears; **j–m in den Ohren liegen** keep dinning it into s.o.'s ears; **j–n hinter die Ohren hauen** box s.o.'s ears; **j–n übers Ohr hauen** cheat s.o.; **sich aufs Ohr legen** take a nap; **zum e–n Ohr hinein, zum anderen wieder hinaus** in one ear and out the other

Öhr [ør] *n* (-(e)s;-e) eye (*of needle*); ax hole, hammer hole

ohrenbetäubend *adj* earsplitting

Oh'renklingen *n* ringing in the ears

Oh'rensausen *n* buzzing in the ear

Oh'renschmalz *n* earwax

Oh'renschmaus *m* treat for the ears

Ohrenschützer *m* earmuff

Ohr'feige *f* (-;-n) box on the ear

ohrfeigen ['orfaɪgən] *tr* box on the ear

Ohrläppchen ['orlɛpçən] *n* (-s;-) earlobe

Ohr'muschel *f* auricle

okkult [ɔ'kʊlt] *adj* occult

Ökologie [økɔlɔ'gi] *f* (-;) ecology

ökologisch [økɔ'logiʃ] *adj* ecological

Ökonom [økɔ'nom] *m* (-en;-en) economist

Ökono·mie [økɔnɔ'mi] (-;-mien ['miən]) economy; economics

ökonomisch [økɔ'nomiʃ] *adj* economical

Oktav [ɔk'taf] *n* (-s;-e) octavo

Oktave [ɔk'tavə] *f* (-;-n) octave

Oktober [ɔk'tobər] *m* (-s;-) October

oktroyieren [ɔktrwa'jirən] *tr* impose

Okular [ɔku'lar] *n* (-s;-e) eyepiece

okulieren [ɔku'lirən] *tr* inoculate

Ökumene [øku'menə] *f* (-;) ecumenism

ökumenisch [øku'meniʃ] *adj* ecumenical

Okzident ['ɔktsɪdɛnt] *m* (-s;) Occident

Öl [øl] *n* (-[e]s;-e) oil; **Öl ins Feuer gießen** (fig) add fuel to the fire

Öl'baum *m* olive tree

Öl'berg *m* Mount of Olives

Oleander [ɔle'andər] *m* (-s;-) oleander

ölen ['ølən] *tr* oil; (mach) lubricate

Öl'götze *m* (coll) dummy, lout

Öl'heizung *f* oil heat

ölig ['øliç] *adj* oily

Oligar·chie [ɔligar'çi] *f* (-;-chien ['çiən]) oligarchy

Olive [ɔ'livə] *f* (-;-n) olive

Oli'venöl *n* olive oil

Öl'leitung *f* pipeline

Öl'quelle *f* oil well

Öl'schlick *m* oil slick

Öl'stand *m* (aut) oil level

Öl'standanzeiger *m* oil gauge

Öl'standmesser *m* (aut) oil gauge; dip stick

Ö'lung *f* (-;-en) oiling; anointing; **die Letzte Ö.** extreme unction

Olymp [ɔ'lʏmp] *m* (-s;) Mt. Olympus

Olympiade [ɔlʏm'pjadə] *f* (-;-n) olympiad

olympisch [ɔ'lʏmpiʃ] *adj* Olympian; Olympic; **die Olympischen Spiele** the Olympics

Öl'zweig *m* olive branch

Oma ['oma] *f* (-;-s) (coll) grandma

Omelett [ɔm(ə)'let] *n* (-[e]s;-e & -s) omelette

O·men ['omen] *n* (-s;-mina [mina]) omen

ominös [ɔmi'nøs] *adj* ominous

Omnibus ['ɔmnibus] *m* (ses;-se) bus

Onanie [ɔna'ni] *f* (-;) masturbation

ondulieren [ɔndu'lirən] *tr* (*Haar*) wave

Onkel ['ɔŋkəl] *m* (-s;- & -s) uncle; **der große O.** (coll) the big toe

Opa ['opa] *m* (-s;-s) (coll) grandpa

Oper ['opər] *f* (-;-n) opera

Operateur [ɔpera'tør] *m* (-s;-s) operator; (cin) projectionist; (surg) operating surgeon

Operation [ɔpera'tsjon] *f* (-;-en) operation

Operations'gebiet *n* theater of operations

Operations'saal *m* operating room

operativ [ɔpera'tif] *adj* surgical; operational, strategic

operieren [ɔpe'rirən] *tr* operate on; **sich o. lassen** undergo an operation

O'pernglas *n*, **O'perngucker** *m* opera glasses

O'pernhaus *n* opera house, opera

Opfer ['ɔpfər] *n* (-s;-) sacrifice; victim; **zum O. fallen** (*dat*) fall victim to

op'ferfreudig *adj* self-sacrificing

Op'fergabe *f* offering

Op'ferkasten *m* poor box

Op'ferlamm *n* sacrificial lamb; **Lamb of God**; (fig) victim

Op'fermut *m* spirit of sacrifice

opfern ['ɔpfərn] *tr* sacrifice, offer up

Op'ferstock *m* poor box

Op'fertier *n* victim

Op'fertod *m* sacrifice of one's life

Op'fertrank *m* libation

Op'ferung *f* (-;-en) offering, sacrifice

op'ferwillig *adj* willing to make sacrifices

opponieren [ɔpo'nirən] *intr* (*dat*) oppose

opportun [ɔpɔr'tun] *adj* opportune

optieren [ɔp'tirən] *intr—o. für** opt for

Optik ['ɔptik] *f* (-;) optics

Optiker -in ['ɔptikər(ɪn)] §6 *mf* optician

optimistisch [ɔpti'mistiʃ] *adj* optimistic

optisch ['ɔptiʃ] *adj* optic(al)

Orakel [o'rakəl] *n* (-s;-) oracle

ora'kelhaft *adj* oracular

orange [o'rãʒə] *adj* orange ‖ **Orange** *f* (-;-n) orange

oran'genfarben, oran'genfarbig *adj* orange-colored

oratorisch [ɔra'toriʃ] *adj* oratorical

Orchester [ɔr'kɛstər] *n* (-s;-) orchestra

orchestral [ɔrçɛs'trɑl] *adj* orchestral

orchestrieren [ɔrkɛs'triːrən] *tr* orchestrate

Orchidee [ɔrçi'deːə] *f* (-;-n) orchid

Orden ['ɔrdən] *m* (-s;-) medal, decoration; (eccl) order

Or'densband *n* (-[e]s;⁼er) ribbon

Or'densbruder *m* monk, friar

Or'denskleid *n* (eccl) habit

Or'densschwester *f* nun, sister

ordentlich ['ɔrdəntlɪç] *adj* orderly; (*aufgeräumt*) tidy; (*anständig*) decent, respectable; (*regelrecht*) regular; (*tüchtig*) sound; (*Frühstück*) solid; (*Mitglied*) active; (*Professor*) full; **e-e ordentliche Leistung** a pretty good job; **in ordentlichem Zustand** in good condition || *adv* thoroughly, properly; (*sehr*) (coll) awfully, very; really

Order ['ɔrdər] *f* (-;-n) (com, mil) order

ordinär [ɔrdɪ'nɛr] *adj* ordinary; vulgar; rude

Ordina·rius [ɔrdɪ'narjʊs] *m* (-;-rien [rjən]) professor; (eccl) ordinary

Ordinär'preis *m* retail price

ordinieren [ɔrdɪ'niːrən] *tr* ordain || *intr* (med) have office hours

ordnen ['ɔrdnən] *tr* arrange; (*regeln*) put in order; (*säubern*) tidy up

Ord'nung *f* (-;-en) order, arrangement; classification; system; class; rank; regulation; (mil) formation; **aus der O. bringen** disturb; **in bester O.** in tiptop shape; **in O. bringen** set in order; **in O. sein** be all right; **nicht in O. sein** be out of order; be wrong; be out of sorts

ord'nungsgemäß *adv* duly

Ord'nungsliebe *f* tidiness, orderliness

ord'nungsmäßig *adj* orderly, regular || *adv* duly

Ord'nungsruf *m* (parl) call to order

Ord'nungssinn *m* sense of order

Ord'nungsstrafe *f* fine

ord'nungswidrig *adj* irregular, illegal

Ord'nungszahl *f* ordinal number

Ordonnanz [ɔrdɔ'nants] *f* (-;-en) (mil) orderly

Organ [ɔr'gɑn] *n* (-s;-e) organ

Organisation [ɔrganiza'tsjoːn] *f* (-;-en) organization

organisch [ɔr'gɑnɪʃ] *adj* organic; (*Gewebe*) structural || *adv* organically

organisieren [ɔrganɪ'ziːrən] *tr* organize; (mil) scrounge || *ref* unionize; **organisierter Arbeiter** union worker

Organis·mus [ɔrga'nɪsmʊs] *m* (-;-men [mən]) organism

Organist -in [ɔrga'nɪst(ɪn)] §7 *mf* organist

Orgas·mus [ɔr'gasmʊs] *m* (-;-men [mən]) orgasm

Orgel ['ɔrgəl] *f* (-;-n) organ

Or'gelzug *m* organ stop

Orgie ['ɔrgjə] *f* (-;-n) orgy

Orient ['oːrjɛnt] *m* (-s;) Orient

Orientale [ɔrjɛn'talə] *m* (-n;-n) **Orientalin** [ɔrjɛn'talɪn] *f* (-;-nen) Oriental

orientalisch [ɔrjɛn'talɪʃ] *adj* oriental

orientieren [ɔrjɛn'tiːrən] *tr* orient; (fig) inform, instruct; (mil) brief

Orientie'rung *f* (-;-en) orientation; information, instruction; **die O. verlieren** lose one's bearings

Orientie'rungssinn *m* sense of direction

original [ɔrigi'nɑl] *adj* original || **Original** *n* (-s;-e) original; (typ) copy

Original'ausgabe *f* first edition

Originalität [ɔriginali'tɛt] *f* (-;) originality

Original'sendung *f* live broadcast

originell [ɔrigi'nɛl] *adj* original

Orkan [ɔr'kɑn] *m* (-[e]s;-e) hurricane

Ornament [ɔrna'mɛnt] *n* (-[e]s;-e) ornament

Ornat [ɔr'nɑt] *m* (-[e]s;-e) robes

Ort [ɔrt] *m* (-[e]s;-e) place, spot; (*Örtlichkeit*) locality; (*Dorf*) village; **am Ort sein** be appropriate; **an allen Orten** everywhere; **an Ort und Stelle** on the spot; **an Ort und Stelle gelangen** reach one's destination; **höheren Ortes** at higher levels; **Ort der Handlung** scene of action; **vor Ort** on location; **vor Ort arbeiten** (min) work at the face || *m* (-[e]s; ⁼er) position, locus

Örtchen ['œrtçən] *n* (-s;-) toilet

orten ['ɔrtən] *tr* get the bearing on, locate || *intr* take a bearing

orthodox [ɔrto'dɔks] *adj* orthodox

Orthographie [ɔrtogra'fiː] *f* (-;) orthography

Orthopäde [ɔrto'pɛːdə] *m* (-n;-n) **Orthopädin** [ɔrto'pɛːdɪn] *f* (-;-nen) orthopedist

orthopädisch [ɔrto'pɛːdɪʃ] *adj* orthopedic

örtlich ['œrtlɪç] *adj* local, topical

Ört'lichkeit *f* (-;-en) locality

Orts-, orts- [ɔrts] *comb.fm.* local

Orts'amt *n* (telp) local exchange

Orts'angabe *f* address

orts'ansässig *adj* resident || **Ortsansässige** §5 *mf* resident

Orts'behörde *f* local authorities

Orts'beschreibung *f* topography

Ort'schaft *f* (-;-en) place; (*Dorf*) village

orts'fremd *adj* nonlocal, out-of-town

Orts'gespräch *n* (telp) local call

Orts'kenntnis *f* familiarity with a place

orts'kundig *adj* familiar with the locality

Orts'name *m* place name

Orts'sinn *m* sense of direction

Orts'veränderung *f* change of scenery

Orts'verkehr *m* local traffic

Orts'zeit *f* local time

Orts'zustellung *f* local delivery

Or'tung *f* (-;-en) (aer, naut) taking of bearings, navigation

Öse ['øːzə] *f* (-;-n) loop, eye; (*des Schuhes*) eyelet

Ost [ɔst] *m* (-es;-e) East; (poet) east wind

Ost- *comb.fm.* eastern, East

Osten ['ɔstən] *m* (-s;) East; **der Ferne O.** the Far East; **der Nahe O.** the Near East; **nach O.** eastward

ostentativ [ɔstɛnta'tiːf] *adj* ostentatious

Oster– ['ostər] *comb.fm.* Easter
O'sterei *n* Easter egg
O'sterfest *n* Easter
O'sterhase *m* Easter bunny
O'sterlamm *m* paschal lamb
Ostern ['ostərn] *n* (–;–) & *pl* Easter
Österreich ['østəraɪç] *n* (–s;) Austria
Österreicher –in ['østəraɪçər(ɪn)] §6 *mf* Austrian
österreichisch ['østəraɪçiʃ] *adj* Austrian
O'sterzeit *f* Eastertide
Ost'front *f* eastern front
Ost'gote *m* Ostrogoth
östlich ['œstlɪç] *adj* eastern, easterly; Oriental; **ö. von** east of
Ost'mark *f* East-German mark
Ost'see *f* Baltic Sea
ostwärts ['ostverts] *adv* eastward

Otter ['ɔtər] *m* (–s;–) otter ‖ *f* (–;–n) (*Schlange*) adder
Ouvertüre [uver'tyrə] *f* (–;–n) (mus) overture
oval [o'val] *adj* oval ‖ **Oval** *n* (–s;–e) oval
Ovar [o'var] *n* (–s;–e & –ien [jən]) ovary
Overall ['ovərol] *m* (–s;–s) overalls
Oxyd [ɔ'ksyt] *n* (–[e]s;–e) oxide
Oxydation [ɔksyda'tsjon] *f* (–;) oxidation
oxydieren [ɔksy'dirən] *tr & intr* (SEIN) oxidize
Ozean ['otse.an] *m* (–s;–e) ocean; **der Große** (or **Stille**) **O.** the Pacific
Ozeanographie [otse.anogra'fi] *f* (–;) oceanography
Ozon [o'tson] *n* (–s;) ozone

P, p [pe] *invar n* P, p
paar [par] *adj* even ‖ *invar adj*—**ein p.** a couple of, a few ‖ **Paar** *n* (–[e]s; –e) pair, couple; **zu Paaren treiben** rout
paaren ['parən] *tr* match, mate ‖ *ref* mate
paarig ['parɪç] *adj* in pairs
paar'laufen §105 *intr* (SEIN) skate as a couple
paar'mal *adv*—**ein p.** a couple of times
Paa'rung *f* (–;) pairing, matching; (*Begattung*) mating
Paa'rungszeit *f* mating season
paar'weise *adv* in pairs, two by two
Pacht [paxt] *f* (–;–en) lease; (*Geld*) rent; **in P. geben** lease out; **in P. nehmen** lease, rent
Pacht'brief *m* lease
pachten ['paxtən] *tr* take a lease on
Pächter –in ['peçtər(ɪn)] §6 *mf* tenant
Pacht'ertrag *m*, **Pacht'geld** *n* rent
Pacht'gut *n*, **Pacht'hof** *m* leased farm
Pacht'kontrakt *m* lease
Pach'tung *f* (–;–en) leasing, leasehold
Pacht'vertrag *m* lease
Pacht'zeit *f* term of lease
Pacht'zins *m* rent
Pack [pak] *m* (–[e]s;–e & ⁔e) pack; (*Paket*) parcel; (*Ballen*) bale; **ein P. Spielkarten** a pack of cards ‖ *n* (–[e]s;) rabble; **ein P. von Lügnern** a pack of liars
Päckchen ['pekçən] *n* (–s;–) small package; (*Zigaretten*–) pack
packen ['pakən] *tr* pack, pack up; (*fassen*) seize, grab; (fig) grip, thrill; **pack dich!** scram! ‖ **Packen** *m* (–s;–) pack; (*Ballen*) bale ‖ *n* (–s;) packing
Pack'esel *m* (fig) drudge
Pack'papier *n* wrapping paper
Pack'pferd *n* packhorse
Pack'tier *n* pack animal
Packung (Pak'kung) *f* (–;–en) packing; (*Paket*) packet; **P. Zigaretten** pack of cigarettes

Pack'wagen *m* (rr) baggage car
Pädadoge [peda'gogə] *m* (–n;–n) pedagogue
Pädagogik [peda'gogɪk] *f* (–;) pedagogy
pädagogisch [peda'gogiʃ] *adj* pedagogical, educational
Paddel ['padəl] *n* (–s;–) paddle
Pad'delboot *n* canoe
paddeln ['padəln] *intr* paddle, canoe
Pädiatrie [pedi.a'tri] *f* (–;) pediatrics
paff [paf] *interj* bang!
paffen ['pafən] *tr & intr* puff
Page ['paʒə] *m* (–n;–n) page
Pa'genfrisur *f*, **Pa'genkopf** *m* pageboy
Pagode [pa'godə] *f* (–;–n) pagoda
Pair [per] *m* (–s;–s) peer
Pak [pak] *f* (–;–& –s) (Panzerabwehrkanone) antitank gun
Paket [pa'ket] *n* (–[e]s;–e) parcel; (*Bücher*–, *Post*–) bundle
Paket'adresse *f* gummed label
Paket'post *f* parcel post
Pakt [pakt] *m* (–[e]s;–e) pact
paktieren [pak'tirən] *intr* make a pact
Paläontologie [pale.ontolo'gi] *f* (–;) paleontology
Palast [pa'last] *m* (–es;⁔e) palace
palast'artig *adj* palatial
Palästina [pale'stina] *n* (–s;) Palestine
Palette [pa'letə] *f* (–;–n) palette
Palisade [palɪ'zadə] *f* (–;–n) palisade
Palme ['palmə] *f* (–;–n) palm tree; palm branch; **j–n auf die P. bringen** (coll) drive s.o. up the wall
Palm'wedel *m*, **Palm'zweig** *m* palm branch
Pampelmuse ['pampəlmuzə] *f* (–;–n) grapefruit
Pamphlet [pam'flet] *n* (–[e]s;–e) lampoon
Panama ['panama] *n* (–s;) Panama
Paneel [pa'nel] *n* (–s;–e) panel
paneelieren [pane'lirən] *tr* panel
Panier [pa'nir] *n* (–s;–e) slogan
panieren [pa'nirən] *tr* (culin) bread

Panik [´panɪk] *f* (-;) panic
panisch [´panɪʃ] *adj* panic-stricken
Panne [´panə] *f* (-;-n) breakdown; (*Reifenpanne*) blowout; (fig) mishap
Panora·ma [panɔ´rama] *n* (-s;-men [mən]) panorama
panschen [´panʃən] *tr* adulterate, water down ‖ *intr* splash about; mix
Panther [´pantər] *m* (-s;-) panther
Pantine [pan´tinə] *f* (-;-n) clog
Pantoffel [pan´tɔfəl] *m* (-s;-n) slipper; **unter dem P. stehen** be henpecked
Pantof'felheld *m* henpecked husband
Panzer [´pantsər] *m* (-s;-) armor; armor plating; (mil) tank; (zool) shell
Pan'zerabwehrkanone *f* antitank gun
pan'zerbrechend *adj* armor-piercing
Pan'zerfalle *f* tank trap
Pan'zerfaust *f* bazooka
Pan'zergeschoß *n*, **Pan'zergranate** *f* armor-piercing shell
Pan'zerhandschuh *m* gauntlet
Pan'zerhemd *n* coat of mail
Pan'zerkreuzer *m* battle cruiser
panzern [´pantsərn] *tr* armor ‖ *ref* arm oneself
Pan'zerschrank *m* safe
Panzerspähwagen [´pantsər/pevagən] *m* (mil) armored car
Pan'zersperre *f* antitank obstacle
Pan'zerung *f* (-;-en) armor plating
Pan'zerwagen *m* armored car
Papagei [papa´gaɪ] *m* (-en;-en) & (-[e]s;-e) parrot
Papier [pa´pir] *n* (-[e]s;-e) paper
Papier'bogen *m* sheet of paper
Papier'brei *m* paper pulp
papieren [pa´pirən] *adj* paper
Papier'fabrik *f* paper mill
Papier'format *n* size of paper
Papier'korb *m* wastebasket
Papier'krieg *m* (fig) red tape
Papier'mühle *f* paper mill
Papier'schlange *f* paper streamer
Papier'tüte *f* paper bag
Papier'waren *pl* stationery
Papp [pap] *m* (-[e]s;-e) (*Brei*) pap; (*Kleister*) paste
Papp- [pap] *comb.fm.* sticky; cardboard
Papp'band *m* (-[e]s;ːe) paperback
Papp'deckel *m* piece of cardboard
Pappe [´papə] *f* (-;) cardboard
Pappel [´papəl] *f* (-;-n) poplar
päppeln [´pepəln] *tr* feed lovingly
pappen [´papən] *tr* paste, glue ‖ *intr* stick
Pap'penstiel *m* (coll) trifle; **das ist keinen P. wert** (coll) this isn't worth a thing
papperlapapp [papərla´pap] *interj* nonsense!
pap'pig *adj* sticky
Papp'karton *m*, **Papp'schachtel** *f* cardboard box, cardboard carton
Papp'schnee *m* sticky snow (*for skiing*)
Paprika [´paprika] *m* (-s;) paprika
Pap'rikaschote *f* (green) pepper
Papst [papst] *m* (-es;ːe) pope
päpstlich [´pepstlɪç] *adj* papal
Papsttum [´papsttum] *n* (-s;) papacy
Papy·rus [pa´pyrus] *m* (-;-ri) [rɪ]) papyrus

Parabel [pa´rabəl] *f* (-;-n) parable; (geom) parabola
Parade [pa´radə] *f* (-;-n) parade; (fencing) parry; (mil) review; (fb) save
Para'deanzug *m* (mil) dress uniform
Paradeiser [para´daɪzər] *m* (-s;-) (Aust) tomato
Para'depferd *n* (fig) show-off
Para'deplatz *m* parade ground
Para'deschritt *m* goose step
paradieren [para´dirən] *intr* parade; (fig) show off
Paradies [para´dis] *n* (-es;-e) paradise
Paradies'apfel *m* tomato
paradox [para´dɔks] *adj* paradoxical ‖ **Paradox** *n* (-es;-e) paradox
Paraffin [para´fin] *n* (-s;-e) paraffin
Paragraph [para´graf] *m* (-en & -s; -en) paragraph; (jur) section
parallel [para´lel] *adj* parallel ‖ **Parallele** *f* (-;-n) parallel
Paralyse [para´lyzə] *f* (-;-n) paralysis
paralysieren [paraly´zirən] *tr* paralyze
Paralytiker **-in** [para´lytikər(ɪn)] §6 *mf* paralytic
Paranuß [´paranus] *f* Brazil nut
Parasit [para´zit] *m* (-en;-en) parasite
parat [pa´rat] *adj* ready
Pardon [par´dõ] *m* (-s;) pardon; **keinen P. geben** (mil) given no quarter
Parenthese [paren´tezə] *f* (-;-n) parenthesis
Parfüm [par´fym] *n* (-[e]s;-e) perfume
Parfüme·rie [parfymə´ri] *f* (-;-rien [´ri·ən]) perfume shop
parfümieren [parfy´mirən] *tr* perfume
pari [´pari] *adv* at par ‖ **Pari** *m* (-[s];) par; **auf P. at par**
Paria [´parja] *m* (-s;-s) pariah
parieren [pa´rirən] *tr* (*Pferd*) rein in; (*Hieb*) parry ‖ *intr* (*dat*) obey
Pa'rikurs *m* (com) parity
Paris [pa´ris] *n* (-;) Paris
Pariser **-in** [pa´rizər(ɪn)] §6 *mf* Parisian
Parität [parɪ´tet] *f* (-;) equality; (fin, st. exch.) parity
paritätisch [parɪ´tetɪʃ] *adj* on a footing of equality
Park [park] *m* (-s;-s & -e) park
Park'anlage *f* park; **Parkanlagen** grounds
parken [´parkən] *tr* & *intr* park
Parkett [par´ket] *n* (-[e]s;-e) (*Fußboden*) parquet; (theat) parquet
Parkett'fußboden *m* parquet flooring
Park'licht *n* parking light
Park'platz *m* parking lot
Park'platzwärter *m* parking lot attendant
Park'uhr *f* parking meter
Parlament [parla´ment] *n* (-[e]s;-e) parliament
Parlamentär [parlamen´ter] *m* (-s;-e) truce negotiator
parlamentarisch [parlamen´tarɪʃ] *adj* parliamentary
parlamentieren [parlamen´tirən] *intr* (coll) parley
Paro·die [parɔ´di] *f* (-;-dien [´di·ən]) parody
parodieren [parɔ´dirən] *tr* parody

Parole [paˈrolə] f (-;-n) (mil) password; (pol) slogan
Partei [parˈtaɪ] f (-;-en) party; (Mieter) tenant(s); (jur, pol) party;
(sport) side; j–s P. ergreifen or P.
nehmen für j–n side with s.o.
Partei′bonze m (pol) party boss
Partei′gänger –in §6 mf (pol) party
sympathizer
Partei′genosse m, **Partei′genossin** f
party member
Partei′grundsatz m party plank
parteiisch [parˈtaɪ·ɪʃ] adj partial, bi-
ased; (pol) partisan
partei′lich adj partisan
Partei′lichkeit f (-;) partiality
partei′los adj (pol) independent ‖ **Par-
teilose** §5 mf independent
Partei′losigkeit f (-;) impartiality; political independence
Partei′nahme f (-;) taking sides
Partei′programm n party platform
Partei′tag m party rally
Partei′zugehörigkeit f party affiliation
Parterre [parˈter] n (-s;-s) ground
floor; (theat) parterre
Par•tie [parˈti] f (-;-tien [ˈti·ən]) part;
(Gesellschaft) party; (Spiel) game;
(Ausflug) outing; (com) lot; (theat)
role; e–e gute P. machen (coll) marry
rich; ich bin mit von der P.! count
me in!
partiell [parˈtsjel] adj partial ‖ adv
partly, partially
Partikel [parˈtikəl] f (-;-n) particle
Partisan –in [partɪˈzan(ɪn)] §7 mf partisan
Partitur [partɪˈtur] f (-;-en) (mus)
score
Partizip [partɪˈtsip] n (-s;-ien [jən])
participle
Partner –in [ˈpartnər(ɪn)] §6 mf partner
Part′nerschaft f (-;-en) partnership
Parzelle [parˈtselə] f (-;-n) lot
parzellieren [partseˈlirən] tr parcel out,
allot
paschen [ˈpaʃən] tr smuggle ‖ intr
smuggle; (würfeln) play dice
Paß [pas] m (Passes; Pässe) pass;
passport; (geog) mountain pass
passabel [paˈsabəl] adj tolerable
Passage [paˈsaʒə] f (-;-n) passage;
(mus) run
Passagier [pasaˈʒir] m (-s;-e) passenger; blinder P. stowaway
Passagier′dampfer m passenger liner
Passagier′gut n luggage
Passah [ˈpasa] n (-s;), **Pas′sahfest** n
Passover
Paß′amt n passport office
Passant –in [paˈsant(ɪn)] §7 mf passer-
by
Paß′ball m (sport) pass
Paß′bild n passport photograph
passen [ˈpasən] ref be proper ‖ intr
fit; (dat) suit; (cards, fb) pass; p. auf
(acc) watch for, wait for; p. zu suit,
fit; sie p. zueinander they are a good
match
pas′send adj suitable; convenient;
(Kleidungsstück) matching; für p.
halten think it proper

Paß′form f—e–e gute P. haben be
form-fitting
passierbar [paˈsirbar] adj passable
passieren [paˈsirən] tr pass, cross;
(culin) sift, sieve ‖ intr (SEIN)
happen
Passier′schein m pass, permit
Passion [paˈsjon] f (-;-en) passion
passioniert [pasjoˈnirt] adj ardent
Passions′spiel n passion play
passiv [paˈsif] adj passive; (Handels-
bilanz) unfavorable; passives Wahlrecht eligibility ‖ **Passiv** n (-s;-e)
(gram) passive
Passiva [paˈsiva] pl, **Passiven** [pa-
ˈsiven] pl debts, liabilities
Paß′kontrolle f passport inspection
Paste [ˈpastə] f (-;-n) paste
Pastell [paˈstel] n (-s;-e) pastel;
crayon
pastell′farben adj pastel
Pastell′stift m crayon
Pastete [pasˈtetə] f (-;-n) meat pie,
fish pie
pasteurisieren [pastœriˈzirən] tr pasteurize
Pastille [paˈstilə] f (-;-n) lozenge
Pa•stor [ˈpastər] m (-s;-storen
[ˈtorən]) pastor, minister, vicar
Pate [ˈpatə] m (-n;-n) godfather ‖ f
(-;-n) godmother
Pa′tenkind n godchild
patent [paˈtent] adj neat; smart; ein
patenter Kerl quite a fellow ‖ **Patent**
n (-[e]s;-e) patent; (mil) commission; P. angemeldet patent pending
Patent′amt n patent office
patentieren [patenˈtirən] tr patent
Pater [ˈpatər] m (-s; Patres [ˈpatres])
(eccl) Father
pathetisch [paˈtetɪʃ] adj impassioned;
solemn
Pathologe [patoˈlogə] m (-n;-n) pathologist
Pathologie [patoloˈgi] f (-;) pathology
Pathologin [patoˈlogin] f (-;-nen)
pathologist
Patient –in [paˈtsjent(ɪn)] §7 mf pa-
tient
Patin [ˈpatɪn] f (-;-nen) godmother
Patriarch [patriˈarç] m (-en;-en) pa-
triarch
Patriot –in [patriˈot(ɪn)] §7 mf patriot
patriotisch [patriˈotɪʃ] adj patriotic
Patrize [paˈtritsə] f (-;-n) die, stamp
Patrizier –in [paˈtritsjər(ɪn)] §6 mf
patrician
Patron [paˈtron] m (-s;-e) patron;
(pej) guy
Patronat [patroˈnat] n (-[e]s;-e) pa-
tronage
Patrone [paˈtronə] f (-;-n) cartridge
Patro′nengurt m cartridge belt
Patro′nenhülse f cartridge case
Patronin [paˈtronin] f (-;-nen) pa-
troness
Patrouille [paˈtruljə] f (-;-n) patrol
patrouillieren [patruˈjirən] tr & intr
patrol
Patsche [ˈpatʃə] f (-;-en) (Pfütze) pud-
dle; (coll) jam, scrape; in der P.
lassen leave in a lurch; in e–e P.
geraten get into a jam

patschen ['patʃən] *tr* slap || *intr* splash; in die Hände p. clap hands

patsch'naß *adj* soaking wet

patzig ['patsɪç] *adj* snappy, sassy

Pauke ['paukə] *f* (-;-n) kettledrum; j-m e-e P. halten give s.o. a lecture

pauken ['paukən] *tr* (educ) cram || *intr* beat the kettledrum; (educ) cram

Pau'ker *m* (-s;-) (coll) martinet

pausbackig ['pausbakɪç], pausbäckig ['pausbɛkɪç] *adj* chubby-faced

pauschal [pau'ʃal] *adj* (Summe) flat

Pauschal'betrag *m* flat rate

Pauscha·le [pau'ʃalə] *n* (-s;-lien [ljən]) lump sum

Pauschal'preis *m* package price

Pauschal'reise *f* all-inclusive tour

Pauschal'summe *f* flat sum

Pause ['pauzə] *f* (-;-n) pause; (Pauszeichnung) tracing; (educ) recess, break; (mus) rest; (theat) intermission; e-e P. machen take a break

pausen ['pauzən] *tr* trace

pau'senlos *adj* continuous

Pau'senzeichen *n* (rad) station identification

pausieren [pau'zirən] *intr* pause; rest

Pauspapier ['pauzpapir] *n* tracing paper

Pavian ['pɑvjɑn] *m* (-s;-e) baboon

Pavillon ['pavɪljɔ] *m* (-s;-s) pavilion

Pazifik [pa'tsifɪk] *m* (-s;) Pacific

pazifisch [pa'tsifɪʃ] *adj* Pacific

Pazifist -in [patsɪ'fɪst(ɪn)] §7 *mf* pacifist

Pech [peç] *n* (-[e]s;-e) pitch; P. haben (coll) have tough luck

Pech'fackel *f* torch

Pech'kohle *f* bituminous coal

pech'ra'benschwarz' *adj* pitch-black

pech'schwarz' *adj* pitch-dark

Pech'strähne *f* streak of bad luck

Pech'vogel *m* (coll) unlucky fellow

Pedal [pe'dal] *n* (-s;-e) pedal

Pedant [pe'dant] *m* (-en;-en) pedant

pedantisch [pe'dantɪʃ] *adj* pedantic

Pegel ['pegəl] *m* (-s;-) water gauge

Pe'gelstand *m* water level

Peil- [paɪl] *comb.fm.* direction-finding, sounding

peilen ['paɪlən] *tr* take the bearings of; (Tiefe) sound; über den Daumen p. (coll) estimate roughly || *intr* take bearings

Pei'lung *f* (-;-en) bearings; taking of bearings; sounding

Pein [paɪn] *f* (-;) pain, torment

peinigen ['paɪnɪgən] *tr* torment

pein'lich *adj* painful; embarrassing; (genau) painstaking; (sorgfältig) scrupulous || *adv* scrupulously; carefully

Peitsche ['paɪtʃə] *f* (-;-n) whip; mit der P. knallen crack the whip

peitschen ['paɪtʃən] *tr* whip

Peit'schenhieb *m* whiplash

Peit'schenknall *m* crack of the whip

Pelerine [pelə'rinə] *f* (-;-n) cape

Pelikan ['pelɪkan] *m* (-s;-e) pelican

Pelle ['pelə] *f* (-;-n) peel, skin

pellen ['pelən] *tr* peel, skin

Pellkartoffeln ['pelkartɔfəln] *pl* potatoes in their jackets

Pelz [pelts] *m* (-es;-e) fur; (Fell) pelt; fur coat

Pelz'besatz *m* fur trimming

Pelz'futter *n* fur lining

Pelz'händler -in §6 *mf* furrier

pel'zig *adj* furry; (Gefühl im Mund) cottony

Pelz'tier *n* fur-bearing animal

Pelz'tierjäger *m* trapper

Pelz'werk *n* furs

Pendel ['pendəl] *n* (-s;-) pendulum

pendeln ['pendəln] *intr* swing, oscillate; (zwischen zwei Orten) commute

Pen'deltür *f* swinging door

Pen'delverkehr *m* commuter traffic; shuttle service

Pen'delzug *m* shuttle train

Pendler ['pentlər] *m* (-s;-) commuter

Penizillin [penɪtsɪ'lin] *n* (-s;) penicillin

Pension [pen'zjon] *f* (-;-en) pension, retirement pay; (Fremdenhaus) boarding house; (Unterkunft und Verpflegung) room and board; (Pensionat) girls' boarding school; in P. gehen go on pension

Pensionär [penzjo'ner] *m* (-s;-e) pensioner; boarder

Pensionat [penzjo'nat] *n* (-[e]s;-e) girls boarding school

pensionieren [penzjo'nirən] *tr* put on pension; (mil) retire on half pay; sich p. lassen retire

Pensions'kasse *f* pension fund

Pensions'preis *m* price of room and board

Pen·sum ['penzum] *n* (-s;-sen [zən] & -sa [za]) task, assignment; quota

per [per] *prep* (acc) per, by, with; (zeitlich) by, until; per Adresse care of, c/o; per sofort at once

perfekt [per'fekt] *adj* perfect; concluded || Perfekt *n* (-[e]s;-e) perfect

Pergament [perga'ment] *n* (-[e]s;-e) parchment

Periode [per'jodə] *f* (-;-n) period

periodisch [per'jodɪʃ] *adj* periodic

Periphe·rie [perɪfe'ri] *f* (-;-rien ['ri-ən]) periphery

Periskop [perɪ'skop] *n* (-s;-e) periscope

Perle ['perlə] *f* (-;-n) pearl; (aus Glas) bead; (Tropfen) drop, bead; (Bläschen) bubble; (fig) gem

perlen | 'perlən] *intr* sparkle

Per'lenauster *f* pearl oyster

Per'lenkette *f*, Per'lenschnur *f* pearl necklace, string of pearls

Perlhuhn ['perlhun] *n* guinea fowl

perlig | 'perlɪç] *adj* pearly

Perl'muschel *f* pearl oyster

Perlmutt ['perlmut] *n* (-s;), Perl'mutter *f* mother of pearl

perplex [per'pleks] *adj* perplexed

Persenning [per'zenɪŋ] *f* (-;-en) tarpaulin

Persien ['perzjən] *n* (-s;) Persia

persisch [perzɪʃ] *adj* Persian

Person [per'zon] *f* (-;-en) person; (theat) character; ich für meine P. I for one; klein von P. small of stature

Personal [perzo'nal] *n* (-s;) personnel

Personal'akte *f* personal file, dossier

Personal'angaben *pl* personal data
Personal'aufzug *m* passenger elevator
Personal'ausweis *m* identity card
Personal'chef *m* personnel manager
Personalien [perzɔ'naljən] *pl* personal data, particulars
Personal'pronomen *n* personal pronoun
Perso'nengedächtnis *n* good memory for names
Perso'nenkraftwagen *m* passenger car
Perso'nenschaden *m* personal injury
Perso'nenverzeichnis *n* list of persons; (theat) dramatis personae, cast
Perso'nenwagen *m* passenger car
Perso'nenzug *m* passenger train; (rr) local
personifizieren [perzɔnifɪ'tsirən] *tr* personify
persönlich [per'zønlɪç] *adj* personal || *adv* personally, in person
Persön'lichkeit *f* (-;-en) personality
Perspektiv [perspek'tif] *n* (-s;-e) telescope
Perücke [pɛ'rykə] *f* (-;-n) wig
pervers [per'vers] *adj* perverse
pessimistisch [pesɪ'mɪstɪʃ] *adj* pessimistic
Pest [pest] *f* (-;) plague
pest'artig *adj* pestilential
Pestilenz [pestɪ'lents] *f* (-;-en) pestilence
Petersilie [petər'ziljə] *f* (-;) parsley
Petroleum [pe'trolɛ-um] *n* (-s;) petroleum
Petschaft ['petʃaft] *n* (-s;-e) seal
Petting ['petɪŋ] *n* (-s;) petting
petto ['peto]—in p. haben have in reserve; (coll) have up one's sleeve
Petunie [pe'tunjə] *f* (-;-n) petunia
Petze ['petsə] *f* (-;-n) tattletale
petzen ['petsən] *intr* tattle, squeal
Pfad [pfat] *m* (-[e]s;-e) path, track
Pfadfinder ['pfatfɪndər] *m* (-s;-) boy scout
Pfadfinderin ['pfatfɪndərɪn] *f* (-;-nen) girl scout
Pfaffe ['pfafə] *m* (-n;-n) (pej) priest
Pfahl [pfal] *m* (-[e]s;:e) stake; post
Pfahl'bau *m* (-[e]s;-bauten) lake dwelling
Pfahl'werk *n* palisade, stockade
Pfahl'wurzel *f* taproot
Pfahl'zaun *m* palisade, stockade
Pfälzer –in | 'pfeltsər(ın)] §6 *mf* inhabitant of the Palatinate
Pfand [pfant] *n* (-[e]s;:er) pledge; deposit; (*Bürgschaft*) security, pawn (*auf Immobilien*) mortgage; **zum Pfande geben** (or **setzen**) pawn, mortgage
pfändbar ['pfentbar] *adj* (jur) attachable
Pfand'brief *m* mortgage papers
pfänden ['pfendən] *tr* attach, impound
Pfand'geber *m* mortgagor
Pfand'gläubiger *m* mortgagee
Pfand'haus *n*, **Pfand'leihe** *f* pawnshop
Pfand'leiher –in §6 *mf* pawnbroker
Pfand'recht *n* lien
Pfand'schein *m* pawn ticket
Pfand'schuldner *m* mortgagor
Pfän'dung *f* (-;-en) attachment, confiscation

Pfanne ['pfanə] *f* (-;-n) pan; (anat) socket; **etw auf der P. haben** (fig) have s.th. up one's sleeve; **in die P. hauen** (fig) make mincemeat of
Pfan'nenstiel *m* panhandle
Pfann'kuchen *m* pancake; **Berliner P.** doughnut
Pfarr- [pfar] *comb.fm.* parish, parochial
Pfarr'amt *n* rectory
Pfarr'bezirk *m* parish
Pfarr'dorf *n* parish seat
Pfarre ['pfarə] *f* (-;-n) parish; (*Pfarrhaus*) rectory
Pfarrei [pfa'rai] *f* (-;-en) parish; (*Pfarrhaus*) rectory
Pfarrer ['pfarər] *m* (-s;-) pastor
Pfarr'gemeinde *f* parish
Pfarr'haus *n* rectory
Pfarr'kind *n* parishioner
Pfarr'kirche *f* parish church
Pfarr'schule *f* parochial school
Pfau [pfau] *m* (-[e]s;-en) peacock
Pfau'enhenne *f* peahen
Pfeffer ['pfefər] *m* (-s;) pepper
pfefferig ['pfefərɪç] *adj* peppery
Pfef'ferkorn *n* peppercorn
Pfef'ferkuchen *m* gingerbread
Pfef'ferminze *f* (bot) peppermint
Pfef'ferminzplätzchen *n* peppermint cookie
pfeffern ['pfefərn] *tr* pepper
Pfef'fernuß *f* ginger nut
Pfeife ['pfaifə] *f* (-;-n) whistle; (*Orgel-*) pipe; (*zum Rauchen*) (tobacco) pipe
pfeifen ['pfaifən] *tr* whistle; **ich pfeife ihm was** he can whistle for it || *intr* whistle; (*Schiedsrichter*) blow the whistle; (*Maus*) squeak; (*Vogel*) sing; (*dat*) whistle for or to; **auf dem letzten Loche p.** be on one's last legs; **ich pfeife darauf!** I couldn't care less!
Pfei'fenkopf *m* pipe bowl
Pfei'fenrohr *n* pipestem
Pfei'fer –in §6 *mf* whistler; (mus) piper, fife player
Pfeif'kessel *m*, **Pfeif'topf** *m* whistling kettle
Pfeil [pfail] *m* (-[e]s;-e) arrow, dart; **P. und Bogen** bow and arrow
Pfei'ler *m* (-s;-) (& fig) pillar; (*e-r Brücke*) pier
pfeil'gera'de *adj* straight as an arrow
pfeil'schnell' *adj* swift as an arrow || *adv* like a shot
Pfeil'schütze *m* archer
Pfeil'spitze *f* arrowhead
Pfennig ['pfenɪç] *m* (-[e]s;-e & -) pfennig, penny (*one hundredth of a mark*)
Pfennigfuchser ['pfenɪçfuksər] *m* (-s; -) penny pincher
Pferch [pferç] *m* (-[e]s;-e) fold, pen
pferchen ['pferçən] *tr* herd together, pen in
Pferd [pfert] *n* (-[e]s;-e) horse; **zu Pferde** on horseback
Pferde- [pferdə] *comb.fm.* horse
Pfer'deapfel *m* horse manure
Pfer'debremse *f* horsefly
Pfer'dedecke *f* horse blanket

Pfer'defuß m (*Kennzeichen des Teufels*) cloven hoof; (pathol) clubfoot
Pfer'degeschirr n harness
Pfer'degespann n team of horses
Pfer'deknecht m groom
Pfer'dekoppel f corral
Pfer'delänge f (*beim Rennen*) length
Pfer'derennbahn f race track
Pfer'derennen n horse racing
Pfer'destärke f horsepower
Pfer'dezucht f horse breeding
pfiff [pfɪf] *pret* of **pfeifen** || **Pfiff** m (-[e]s;-e) whistle; **den P. heraushaben** (fig) know the ropes
Pfifferling ['pfɪfərlɪŋ] m (-s;-e (bot) chanterelle; **keinen P. wert** not worth a thing
pfiffig ['pfɪfɪç] *adj* shrewd, sharp
Pfiffikus ['pfɪfɪkʊs] m (-;-), (-ses;-se) (coll) sly fox
Pfingsten ['pfɪnstən] n (-s;) Pentecost
Pfingst'rose f (bot) peony
Pfingst'sonntag m Whitsunday
Pfirsich ['pfɪrzɪç] m (-[e]s;-e) peach
Pflanze ['pflantsə] f (-;-n) plant
pflanzen ['pflantsən] *tr* plant
Pflan'zenfaser f vegetable fiber
Pflan'zenfett n vegetable shortening
pflan'zenfressend *adj* herbivorous
Pflan'zenkost f vegetable diet
Pflan'zenkunde f botany
Pflan'zenleben n plant life, vegetation
Pflan'zenlehre f botany
Pflan'zenöl n vegetable oil
Pflan'zenreich n vegetable kingdom
Pflan'zensaft m sap, juice
Pflan'zenschutzmittel n pesticide
Pflan'zenwelt f flora
Pflan'zer -in §6 mf planter
pflanz'lich *adj* vegetable
Pflanz'schule f, **Pflanz'stätte** f nursery; (fig) hotbed
Pflan'zung f (-;-en) plantation
Pflaster ['pflastər] n (-s;-) pavement; (*Fleck*) patch; (med) Band-Aid; **als P.** (fig) in compensation; **ein teueres P.** (fig) an expensive place; **P. treten** (fig) pound the sidewalks
Pflasterer ['pflastərər] m (-s;-) paver
pfla'stermüde *adj* tired of walking the streets
pflastern ['pflastərn] *tr* pave
Pfla'sterstein m paving stone; (*Kopfstein*) cobblestone
Pfla'stertreter m (-s;-) loafer
Pfla'sterung f (-;) paving
Pflaume ['pflaumə] f (-;-n) plum; (*spitze Bemerkung*) dig
pflaumen ['pflaumən] *intr* (coll) tease
pflau'menweich *adj* (fig) spineless
Pflege ['pflegə] f (-;-n) care; (*e-s Krankenn*) nursing; (*Wartung*) tending; (*e-s Gartens, der Künste*) cultivation; **gute P. haben** be well cared for; **in P. nehmen** take charge of
Pflegebefohlene ['pflegəbəfolənə] §5 mf charge; fosterchild
Pfle'geeltern pl foster parents
Pfle'geheim n nursing home
Pfle'gekind n foster child
pflegen ['pflegən] *tr* take care of, look after; (*Kranken*) nurse; (*Garten, Kunst*) cultivate; (*Freundschaft*) fos-

ter; **Gesellligkeit p.** lead an active social life; **Umgang p. mit** associate with || *intr*—**p. zu** (*inf*) be wont to (*inf*), be in the habit of (*ger*); **sein Vater pflegte zu sagen** his father used to say; **sie pflegt morgens zeitig aufzustehen** she usually gets up early in the morning || *intr* (*pp* **gepflegt & gepflogen**) (*genit*) carry on; **der Liebe p.** enjoy the pleasures of love; **der Ruhe p.** take a rest; **Rats p. mit** consult with
Pfle'ger -in §6 mf nurse; (jur) guardian
Pfle'gesohn m foster son
Pfle'gestelle f foster home
Pfle'getochter f foster daughter
Pfle'gevater m foster father
pfleglich ['pfleklɪç] *adj* careful
Pflegling ['pfleklɪŋ] m (-s;-e) foster child; (*Pflegebefohlenen*) charge
Pflegschaft ['pflek∫aft] f (-;-en) (jur) guardianship
Pflicht [pflɪçt] f (-;-en) duty; **sich seiner P. entziehen** evade one's duty
pflicht'bewußt *adj* conscientious
Pflicht'bewußtsein n conscientiousness
Pflicht'eifer m zeal
pflicht'eifrig *adj* zealous
Pflicht'erfüllung f performance of duty
Pflicht'fach n (educ) required course
Pflicht'gefühl n sense of duty
pflicht'gemäß *adj* dutiful
-pflichtig [pflɪçtɪç] *comb.fm.* obligated, e.g., **schulpflichtig** obligated to attend school
pflicht'schuldig *adj* duty-bound
pflicht'treu *adj* dutiful, loyal
pflicht'vergessen *adj* forgetful of one's duty; (*untreu*) disloyal
Pflicht'vergessenheit f dereliction of duty; disloyalty
Pflicht'verletzung f, **Pflicht'versäumnis** n neglect of duty
Pflock [pflɔk] m (-[e]s;ˉe) peg; e-n **P. zurückstecken** (fig) come down a peg
pflog [pflɔk] *pret* of **pflegen**
pflücken ['pflʏkən] *tr* pluck, pick
Pflug [pfluk] m (-[e]s;ˉe) plow
pflügen ['pflygən] *tr & intr* plow
Pflug'schar f plowshare
Pforte ['pfɔrtə] f (-;-n) gate
Pförtner -in ['pfœrtnər(ɪn)] §6 mf gatekeeper || m doorman; (anat) pylorus
Pfosten ['pfɔstən] m (-s;-) post; (carp) jamb
Pfote ['pfotə] f (-;-n) paw; **j-m eins auf die Pfoten geben** rap s.o.'s knuckles
Pfriem [pfrim] m (-[e]s;-e) awl
Pfropf [pfrɔpf] m (-[e]s;-e) stopper, plug, cork
pfropfen ['pfrɔpfən] *tr* cork, plug; (*stopfen*) cram; (hort) graft || **Pfropfen** m (-s;-) stopper, plug, cork
Pfrop'fenzieher m corkscrew
Pfropf'reis n (hort) graft
Pfründe ['pfrʏndə] f (-;-n) benefice; (*ohne Seelsorge*) sinecure; **fette P.** (fig) cushy, well-paying job
Pfuhl [pful] m (-[e]s;-e) pool, puddle; (fig) pit

Pfühl [pfyl] *m* (-[e]s;-e) (poet) cushion
pfui ['pfu·ɪ] *interj* phooey!; **p. über dich!** shame on you!
Pfund [pfunt] *n* (-[e]s;-e) pound
pfundig ['pfʊndɪç] *adj* (coll) great
-**pfündig** [pfyndɪç] *comb.fm.* –pound
Pfundskerl ['pfʊntskerl] *m* (coll) great guy
pfund'weise *adv* by the pound
Pfuscharbeit ['pfu·arbaɪt] *f* bungling
pfuschen ['pfu·ən] *tr* & *intr* bungle; **j–m ins Handwerk p.** meddle in s.o.'s business
Pfuscherei [pfu·ə'raɪ] *f* (-;-en) bungling
Pfütze ['pfʏtsə] *f* (-;-n) puddle
Phänomen [fɛnə'men] *n* (-s;-e) phenomenon
phänomenal [fɛnəme'nal] *adj* phenomenal
Phanta·sie [fanta'zi] *f* (-;-sien ['zi·ən]) imagination
Phantasie'gebilde *n* daydream
phantasieren [fanta'zirən] *intr* daydream; (mus) improvise; (pathol) be delirious
phantasie'voll *adj* imaginative
Phantast –in [fan'tast(ɪn)] §7 *mf* visionary
phantastisch [fan'tastɪʃ] *adj* fantastic
Phantom [fan'tom] *n* (-s;-e) phantom
Pharisäer [farɪ'zɛ·ər] *m* (-s;-) Pharisee; (fig) pharisee
pharmazeutisch [farma'tsɔɪtɪʃ] *adj* pharmaceutical
Pharmazie [farma'tsi] *f* (-;) pharmacy
Phase ['fazə] *f* (-;-n) phase
Philantrop –in [filan'trop(ɪn)] §7 *mf* philanthropist
philanthropisch [filan'tropɪʃ] *adj* philanthropic
Philister [fɪ'lɪstər] *m* (-s;-) Philistine
Phiole [fɪ'olə] *f* (-;-n) vial, phial
Philologe [fɪlo'logə] *m* (-n;-n) philologist
Philologie [fɪlolo'gi] *f* (-;) philology
Philologin [fɪlo'login] *f* (-;-nen) philologist
Philosoph [filo'zof] *m* (-en;-en) philosopher
Philoso·phie [fɪlozo'fi] *f* (-;-fien ['fi·ən]) philosophy
philosophieren [fɪlozo'firən] *intr* philosophize
philosophisch [fɪlo'zofɪʃ] *adj* philosophic(al)
Phlegma ['flegma] *n* (-s;) indolence
Phonetik [fo'netɪk] *f* (-;) phonetics
phonetisch [fo'netɪʃ] *adj* phonetic
Phönix ['fønɪks] *m* (-[e]s;-pe] phoenix
Phönizien [fø'nitsjən] *n* (-s;) Phoenicia
Phönizier –in [fø'nitsjər(ɪn)] §6 *mf* Phoenician
Phosphor ['fosfər] *m* (-s;) phosphorus
phos'phorig *adj* phosphorous
Photo ['foto] *n* (-s;-) photo
Pho'toapparat *m* camera
photogen [foto'gen] *adj* photogenic
Photograph [foto'graf] *m* (-en;-en) photographer
Photogra·phie [fotogra'fi] *f* (-;-fien ['fi·ən]) photography

photographieren [fotogra'firən] *tr* & *intr* photograph; **sich p. lassen** have one's photograph taken
Photographin [foto'grafɪn] *f* (-;-nen) photographer
photographisch [foto'grafɪʃ] *adj* photographic
Photokopie' *f* photocopy
photokopie'ren *tr* photocopy
Pho'tozelle *f* photoelectric cell
Phrase ['frazə] *f* (-;-n) phrase; (fig) platitude; **das sind nur Phrasen** that's just talk
phra'senhaft *adj* empty, trite; windy
Physik [fy'zik] *f* (-;) physics
physikalisch [fyzɪ'kalɪʃ] *adj* physical
Physiker –in ['fysɪkər(ɪn)] §6 *mf* physicist
Physiogno·mie [fyzɪɔgno'mi] *f* (-;-mien ['mi·ən]) physiognomy
Physiologie [fyzɪɔlɔ'gi] *f* (-;) physiology
physiologisch [fyzɪɔ'logɪʃ] *adj* physiological
physisch ['fyzɪʃ] *adj* physical
Pianino [pi·a'nino] *n* (-s;-s) small upright piano
Pianist –in [pi·a'nɪst(ɪn)] §7 *mf* pianist
picheln ['pɪçəln] *tr* & *intr* tipple
pichen ['pɪçən] *tr* pitch, cover with pitch
Pichler –in ['pɪçlər(ɪn)] §6 *mf* tippler
Picke ['pɪkə] *f* (-;-n) pickax
Pickel ['pɪkəl] *m* (-s;-) pimple; (*Picke*) pickax; (*Eispicke*) ice ax
Pickelhaube (Pik'kelhaube) *f* spiked helmet
Pickelhering (Pik'kelhering) *m* pickled herring
pickelig (pik'kelig) *adj* pimply
picken ['pɪkən] *tr* & *intr* peck
picklig ['pɪklɪç] *adj* var of pickelig
Picknick ['pɪknɪk] *n* (-s;-s) picnic
pieken ['pikən] *tr* sting; (coll) prick
piekfein ['pik'faɪn] *adj* tiptop
pieksauber ['pik'zaubər] *adj* spick and span
piepen ['pipən] *intr* chirp; (*Maus*) squeal; **bei dir piept's wohl?** are you quite all there? || **Piepen** *n*— **das ist zum P.!** that's ridiculous
Pier [pir] *m* (-s;-e) pier
piesacken ['pizakən] *tr* (coll) pester
Pietät [pi·e'tet] *f* (-;) piety
pietät'los *adj* irreverent
pietät'voll *adj* reverent(ial)
Pigment [pɪg'ment] *n* (-[e]s;-e) pigment
Pik [pik], [pɪk] *m* (-s;-s & -e) (*Bergspitze*) peak || *m* (-s;-e) (coll) grudge; **e-n Pik auf j–n haben** hold a grudge against s.o. || *n* (-s;-e) (cards) spade(s)
pikant [pi'kant] *adj* piquant, pungent; (*Bemerkung*) suggestive
Pikante·rie [pɪkantə'ri] *f* (-;-rien ['ri·ən]) piquancy; spicy story, suggestive remark
Pike ['pikə] *f* (-;-n) pike, spear; **von der P. auf dienen** (fig) rise through the ranks
pikiert [pi'kirt] *adj* (über *acc*) piqued (at)

Pikkolo ['pɪkɔlo] *m* (-s;-s) apprentice waiter; (mus) piccolo

Pik'koloflöte *f* (mus) piccolo

Pilger ['pɪlgər] *m* (-s;-) pilgrim

Pil'gerfahrt *f* pilgrimage

Pilgerin ['pɪlgərɪn] *f* (-;-nen) pilgrim

pilgern ['pɪlgərn] *intr* (SEIN) go on a pilgrimage, make a pilgrimage

Pille ['pɪlə] *f* (-;-n) pill; **P. danach** morning-after pill

Pilot –in [pɪ'lot(ɪn)] §7 *mf* pilot

Pilz [pɪlts] *m* (-es;-e) fungus; mushroom

pimp(e)lig ['pɪmp(ə)lɪç] *adj* sickly, delicate; (*verweichlicht*) effeminate

Pinguin ['pɪngu'ɪn] *m* (-s;-e) penguin

Pinie ['pɪnjə] *f* (-;-n) umbrella pine

Pinke ['pɪŋkə] *f* (-;) (coll) dough

Pinkel ['pɪŋkəl] *m* (-s;-) (coll) dude

pinkeln ['pɪŋkəln] *intr* (sl) pee

Pinne ['pɪnə] *f* (-;-n) pin; tack; (naut) tiller

Pinscher ['pɪnʃər] *m* (-s;-) terrier

Pinsel ['pɪnzəl] *m* (-s;-) brush; (fig) simpleton, dope

Pinselei [pɪnzə'laɪ] *f* (-;-en) daubing; (*schlechte Malerei*) daub

pinseln ['pɪnzəln] *tr & intr* paint

Pinzette [pɪn'tsetə] *f* (-;-n) pair of tweezers, tweezers

Pionier [pi·ə'nir] *m* (-s;-e) (fig) pioneer; (mil) engineer

Pionier'arbeit *f* (fig) spadework

Pionier'truppe *f* (mil) engineers

Pirat [pɪ'rat] *m* (-en;-en) pirate

Piraterie [pɪratə'ri] *f* (-;) piracy

Pirol [pɪ'rol] *m* (-s;-e) oriole

Pirsch [pɪrʃ] *f* (-;) hunt

pirschen ['pɪrʃən] *intr* stalk game

Pirsch'jagd *f* hunt

Pistazie [pɪs'tatsjə] *f* (-;-n) pistachio

Piste ['pɪstə] *f* (-;-n) beaten track; ski run; toboggan run; (aer) runway

Pistole [pɪs'tolə] *f* (-;-n) pistol

Pisto'lentasche *f* holster

pitsch(e)naß ['pɪtʃ(ə)'nas] *adj* soaked to the skin

pittoresk [pɪtə'resk] *adj* picturesque

Pkw., PKW *abbr* (**Personenkraftwagen**) passenger car

placieren [pla'sirən] *tr* place

placken ['plakən] *tr* pester, plague ‖ *ref* toil, drudge

Plackerei [plakə'raɪ] *f* (-;) drudgery

plädieren [plɛ'dirən] *intr* plead

Plädoyer [pledwa'je] *n* (-s;-s) plea

Plage ['plagə] *f* (-;-n) trouble, bother; torment; (*Seuche*) plague

Pla'gegeist *m* pest, pain in the neck

plagen ['plagən] *tr* trouble, bother; (*mit Fragen, usw.*) pester

Plagiat [pla'gjat] *n* (-[e]s;-e) plagiarism

Pla'giator [pla'gjatər] *m* (-s;-giatoren [gja'torən]) plagiarist

Plakat [pla'kat] *n* (-[e]s;-e) poster

Plakat'träger *m* sandwich man

Plakette [pla'ketə] *f* (-;-n) plaque

plan [plan] *adj* plain, clear; (*eben*) level ‖ **Plan** *m* (-[e]s;-e) plan; (*Stadt*-) map; (poet) battlefield; **auf den P. treten** appear on the scene

Plane ['planə] *f* (-;-n) tarpaulin

Plänemacher ['plenəmaxər] *m* (-s;-) schemer

planen ['planən] *tr* plan

Pläneschmied ['plenə/mit] *m* schemer

Planet [pla'net] *m* (-en;-en) planet

Planeta·rium [plane'tarjum] *n* (-s; -rien [rjən]) planetarium

Planeten– [planetən] *comb.fm.* planetary

Plane'tenbahn *f* planetary orbit

plan'gemäß *adv* according to plan

planieren [pla'nirən] *tr* level, grade

Planier'raupe *f* bulldozer

Planimetrie [planime'tri] *f* (-;) plane geometry

Planke ['plaŋkə] *f* (-;-n) plank

Plänkelei [plɛŋkə'laɪ] *f* (-;-en) skirmish, skirmishing

plänkeln ['plɛŋkəln] *intr* skirmish

plan'los *adj* aimless; indiscriminate

plan'mäßig *adj* systematic; fixed, regular; (*Verkehr*) scheduled ‖ *adv* according to plan

planschen ['planʃən] *intr* splash

Plantage [plan'taʒə] *f* (-;-n) plantation

Pla'nung *f* (-;) planning

plan'voll *adj* systematic, methodical

Plan'wagen *m* covered wagon

Plan'wirtschaft *f* planned economy

Plapperei [plapə'raɪ] *f* (-;) chatter

Plappermaul ['plapərmaʊl] *n* chatterbox

plappern ['plapərn] *intr* chatter; prattle

plärren ['plerən] *intr* (coll) bawl

Plas·ma ['plasma] *n* (-s;-men [mən]) plasma

Plastik ['plastɪk] *f* (-;-en) (*Bildwerk*) sculpture; (surg) plastic surgery ‖ *n* (-s;) plastic

plastisch ['plastɪʃ] *adj* plastic; (*anschaulich*) graphic

Platane [pla'tanə] *f* (-;-n) sycamore

Plateau [pla'to] *n* (-s;-s) plateau

Plateau'schuhe *pl* platform shoes

Platin [pla'tin] *n* (-s;) platinum

platin'blond *adj* platinum-blonde

Platoniker [pla'tonɪkər] *m* (-s;-) Platonist

platonisch [pla'tonɪʃ] *adj* Platonic

plätschern ['pletʃərn] *intr* splash; (*Bach*) babble

platt [plat] *adj* flat; (*nichtssagend*) trite; (coll) flabbergasted

Plättbrett ['pletbret] *n* ironing board

platt'deutsch *adj* Low German

Platte ['platə] *f* (-;-n) plate; top, surface; slab; (*Präsentierteller*) tray; (*Speise*) dish; (fig) pate, bean; (mus) record; (phot) plate

Plätteisen ['pletaɪzən] *n* flatiron

plätten ['pletən] *tr & intr* iron

Plat'tenjockey *m* disc jockey

Plat'tenspieler *m* record player

Plat'tenteller *m* turntable

Plat'tenwechsler *m* record changer

Platt'form *f* platform

Platt'fuß *m* (aut) flat; **Plattfüße** flat feet

platt'füßig *adj* flat-footed

Platt'heit *f* (-;-en) flatness; (fig) banality

plattieren [pla'tirən] *tr* plate

Plättwäsche ['plɛtvɛ/ə] *f* ironing

Platz [plats] *m* (-es;ᵉe) place; spot; locality; square; (*Sitz*) seat; (*Raum*) room, space; (*Stellung*) position; (sport) ground, field; (tennis) court; **auf die Plätze, fertig, los!** on your marks, get set, go! **fester P.** (mil) fortified position; **freier P.** open space; **immer auf dem Platze sein** be always on the alert; **nicht am P. sein** be out of place; be irrelevant; **P. da!** make way; **P. greifen** (fig) take effect, gain ground; **P. machen** make room; **P. nehmen** sit down; **seinen P. behaupten** stand one's ground

Platz'anweiser **-in** §6 *mf* usher

Plätzchen ['plɛtsçən] *n* (-s;-) little place; little square; (*Süßware*) candy wafer; (*Gebäck*) cookie, cracker

platzen ['platsən] *intr* (SEIN) burst; split; crack; (*Granate*) explode; (*Luftreifen*) blow out; (fig) come to nothing; **da platzte ihm endlich der Kragen** he finally blew his top; **der Wechsel ist geplatzt** the check bounced

Platz'karte *f* reserved-seat ticket

Platz'kommandant *m* commandant

Platz'konzert *n* open-air concert

Platz'patrone *f* blank cartridge; **mit Platzpatronen schießen** fire blanks

Platz'regen *m* cloudburst

Platz'runde *f* (aer) circuit of a field

Platz'wechsel *m* change of place; (sport) change in lineup

Platz'wette *f* betting on a horse to finish in first, second, or third place, bet to place

Plauderei [plaudə'raɪ] *f* (-;-en) chat; small talk

Plau'derer **-in** §6 *mf* talker, chatterer

plaudern ['plaudərn] *intr* chat, chatter; **aus der Schule p.** tell tales out of school

Plaudertasche ['plaudərtaʃə] *f* chatterbox

Plauderton ['plaudərton] *m* conversational tone

plausibel [plau'zibəl] *adj* plausible

plauz [plauts] *interj* crash!

pleite ['plaɪtə] *adj* (coll) broke || *adv* **—p. gehen** go broke || **Pleite** *f* (-;) (coll) bankruptcy; **P. machen** (coll) go broke

Plenarsitzung [ple'narzɪtsuŋ] *f* (-;-en) plenary session

Plenum ['plenum] *n* (-s;) plenary session

Pleuelstange ['plɔɪ·əl/taŋə] *f* (mach) connecting rod

Plexiglas ['plɛksɪglas] *n* (-es;) plexiglass

Plinse ['plɪnzə] *f* (-;-n) pancake; fritter

Plissee [plɪ'se] *n* (-s;-s) pleat

Plissee'rock *m* pleated skirt

plissieren [plɪ'sirən] *tr* pleat

Plombe ['plɔmbə] *f* (-;-n) lead seal; (dent) filling

plombieren [plɔm'birən] *tr* seal with lead; (dent) fill

plötzlich ['plœtslɪç] *adj* sudden || *adv* suddenly, all of a sudden

plump [plump] *adj* (*unförmig*) shapeless; (*schwerfällig*) heavy, slow; (*derb*) coarse; (*unbeholfen*) ungainly; (*taktlos*) tactless, blunt

plumps [plumps] *interj* plop! thump!

plumpsen ['plumpsən] *intr* (HABEN & SEIN) plop, flop

Plunder ['plundər] *m* (-s;) junk

plündern ['plyndərn] *tr* & *intr* plunder

Plural ['plural] *m* (-s;-e) plural

plus [plus] *adv* plus || **Plus** *n* (-;-) plus; (*Überschuß*) surplus; (*Vorteil*) advantage, edge

Plus'pol *m* (elec) positive pole

Plutokrat [pluto'krat] *m* (-en;-en) plutocrat

Plutonium [plu'tonjum] *n* (-s;) plutonium

pneumatisch [pnɔɪ'matɪʃ] *adj* pneumatic

Pöbel ['pøbəl] *m* (-s;) mob, rabble

pö'belhaft *adj* rude, rowdy

Pö'belherrschaft *f* mob rule

pochen ['pɔxən] *tr* (min) crush || *intr* knock; (*Herz*) pound; **p. an** (*dat*) knock on; **p. auf** (*acc*) pound on; (fig) insist on

Pochmüle ['pɔxmylə] *f*, **Pochwerk** ['pɔxvɛrk] *n* crushing mill

Pocke ['pɔkə] *f* (-;-n) pockmark; **Pocken** (pathol) smallpox

Pockennarbe [Pɔk'kennarbe] *f* pockmark

pockennarbig (pɔk'kennarbig) *adj* pockmarked

Podest [po'dest] *m* & *n* (-es;-e) pedestal; (*Treppenabsatz*) landing; podium

Po·dium ['podjum] *n* (-s;-dien [djən]) podium, platform

Poesie [po·e'zi] *f* (-;) poetry

Poet [po'et] *m* (-en;-en) poet

Poetik [po'etɪk] *f* (-;) poetics

poetisch [po'etɪʃ] *adj* poetic

Pointe [po'ɛ̃tə] *f* (-;) point (*of joke*)

Pokal [po'kal] *m* (-s;-e) goblet; (sport) cup

Pökel ['pøkəl] *m* (-s;) brine

Pö'kelfleisch *n* salted meat

Pö'kelhering *m* pickled herring

pökeln ['pøkəln] *tr* pickle, salt

Poker ['pokər] *n* (-s;) poker

Pol [pol] *m* (-s;-e) pole

Polar- [polar] *comb.fm.* polar

polarisieren [polarɪ'zirən] *tr* polarize

Polarität [polarɪ'tet] *f* (-;-en) polarity

Polar'kreis *m* polar circle; **nördlicher P.** Arctic Circle; **südlicher P.** Antarctic Circle

Polar'licht *n* polar lights

Polar'stern *m* polestar

Polar'zone *f* frigid zone

Pole ['polə] *m* (-n;-n) Pole

Polemik [po'lemɪk] *f* (-;) polemics

polemisch [po'lemɪʃ] *adj* polemical

Polen ['polən] *n* (-s;) Poland

Police [po'lisə] *f* (-;-n) (ins) policy

Polier [po'lir] *m* (-s;-e) foreman

polieren [po'lirən] *tr* polish

Polin ['polɪn] *f* (-;-nen) Pole

Politik [polɪ'tik] *f* (-;-en) policy; (*Staatsangelegenheiten*) politics

Politiker –in [pɔ'litɪkər(ɪn)] §6 *mf* politician

Politi·kum [pɔ'litɪkum] *n* (–s;-ka [ka]) political issue, political matter

politisch [pɔ'litɪʃ] *adj* political

politisieren [pɔlɪti'zirən] *intr* talk politics

Politur [pɔlɪ'tur] *f* (–;-en) polish

Polizei [pɔlɪ'tsaɪ] *f* (–;) police

Polizei'aufgebot *n* posse

Polizei'aufsicht *f*—unter P. stehen have to report periodically to the police

Polizei'beamte §5 *m* police officer

Polizei'büro *n*, **Polizei'dienststelle** *f* police station

Polizei'knüppel *m* billy club

Polizei'kommissar *m* police commissioner

polizei'lich *adj* police

Polizei'präsident *m* chief of police

Polizei'revier *n* police station

Polizei'spion *m*, **Polizei'spitzel** *m* stoolpigeon

Polizei'streife *f* raid; police patrol

Polizei'streifenwagen *m* squad car

Polizei'stunde *f* closing time; curfew

Polizei'wache *f* police station

polizei'widrig *adj* against police regulations

Polizist [pɔlɪ'tsɪst] *m* (–en;-en) policeman

Polizistin [pɔlɪ'tsɪstɪn] *f* (–;-nen) policewoman

Polizze [pɔ'lɪtsə] *f* (–;-n) (Aust) insurance policy

Polka ['pɔlka] *f* (–;-s) polka

polnisch ['pɔlnɪʃ] *adj* Polish

Polo ['pɔlo] *n* (–s;) (sport) polo

Polster ['pɔlstər] *m & n* (–s;-) cushion

Pol'stergarnitur *f* living-room suite

Pol'stermöbel *pl* upholstered furniture

polstern ['pɔlstərn] *tr* upholster

Pol'stersessel *m* upholstered chair

Pol'sterstuhl *m* padded chair

Pol'sterung *f* (–;) padding, stuffing

Polterabend ['pɔltərabənt] *m* eve of the wedding day

Poltergeist ['pɔltərgaɪst] *m* poltergeist

poltern ['pɔltərn] *intr* make noise; (*rumpeln*) rumble; (*zanken*) bluster

Polyp [po'lyp] *m* (–en;-en) (pathol, zool) polyp; (*Polizist*) (sl) cop

Polytechni·kum [poly'teçnɪkum] *n* (–s; -ka [ka]) polytechnic institute

Pomade [po'madə] *f* (–;-n) pomade

Pomeranze [pomə'rantsə] *f* (–;-n) bitter orange

Pommern ['pɔmərn] *n* (–s;) Pomerania

Pommes frites [pɔm'frit] *pl* French fries

Pomp [pɔmp] *m* (–es;) pomp

Pompadour ['pɔmpadur] *m* (–s;-e & -s) lady's string-drawn bag

pomp'haft, **pompös** [pɔm'pøs] *adj* pompous

pontifikal [pɔntɪfɪ'kal] *adj* pontifical

Pontifikat [pɔntɪfɪ'kat] *n* (–s;) pontificate

Pontius ['pɔntsjus] *m*—von P. zu Pilatus geschickt werden (coll) get the run-around

Pony ['pɔni] *m* (–s;-s) (*Damenfrisur*) pony ‖ *n* (–s;-s) (*Pferd*) pony

Popo [po'po] *m* (–s;-s) (coll) backside

populär [popu'lɛr] *adj* popular

Popularität [populari'tɛt] *f* (–;) popularity

Pore ['porə] *f* (–;-n) pore

porig ['poriç] *adj* porous

Pornofilm ['pɔrnofɪlm] *m* (coll) smoker, pornographic movie

Pornoladen ['pɔrnoladən] *m* (coll) porn shop

Pornographie [pɔrnogra'fi] *f* (–;) pornography

poros [po'ros] *adj* porous

Porphyr ['pɔrfyr] *m* (–s;) porphyry

Porree ['pɔre] *m* (–s;-s) (bot) leek

Portal [pɔr'tal] *n* (–s;-e) portal

Portemonnaie [pɔrtmo'ne] *n* (–s;-s) wallet

Portier [pɔr'tje] *m* (–s;-s) doorman

Portion [pɔr'tsjon] *f* (–;-en) portion; (culin) serving, helping; **halbe P.** (coll) half pint; **zwei Portionen Kaffee** two cups of coffee

Por·to ['pɔrto] *n* (–s;-ti [ti]) postage

Por'togebühren *pl* postage

Por'tokasse *f* petty cash

Porträt [pɔr'trɛt] *n* (–s;-s), (–[e]s;-e) portrait

porträtieren [pɔrtrɛ'tirən] *tr* portray

Portugal ['pɔrtugal] *n* (–s;) Portugal

Portugiese [pɔrtu'gizə] *m* (–n;-n), **Portugiesin** [pɔrtu'gizɪn] *f* (–;-nen) Portuguese

portugiesisch [pɔrtu'giziʃ] *adj* Portuguese

Porzellan [pɔrtsə'lan] *n* (–s;-e) porcelain; china; **Meißener Porzellan** Dresden china

Porzellan'brennerei *f* porcelain factory

Posament [poza'ment] *n* (–[e]s;-en) trimming, lace

Posaune [po'zaunə] *f* (–;-n) trombone

posaunen [po'zaunən] *intr* play the trombone

Pose ['pozə] *f* (–;-n) pose

posieren [po'zirən] *intr* pose

Position [pozi'tsjon] *f* (–;-en) position

Positions'lampe *f* **Positions'licht** *n* (aer, naut) navigation light

positiv [pozi'tif] *adj* (*bejahend*) affirmative; (*Kritik*) favorable; (elec, math, med) positive ‖ *adv* in the affirmative; (coll) for certain ‖ **Positiv** *m* (–s;-e) (gram) positive degree ‖ *n* (–s;-e) (mus) small organ; (phot) positive

Positur [pozi'tur] *f* (–;-en) posture, attitude; **sich in P. setzen** (or **stellen** or **werfen**) strike a pose

Posse ['posə] *f* (–;-n) (theat) farce

Possen ['posən] *m* (–s;-) trick, practical joke; **j-m e-n P. spielen** play a practical joke on s.o.; **laß die P.!** cut out the nonsense; **P. treiben** (or **reißen**) crack jokes

pos'senhaft *adj* farcical, comical

Possenreißer ['posənraɪsər] *m* (–s;-) joker

Pos'senspiel *n* farce, burlesque

possierlich [po'sirlɪç] *adj* funny

Post [pɔst] *f* (–;-en) mail; (*Postgebäude*) post office

postalisch [pɔs'talɪʃ] *adj* postal

Postament [posta'ment] *n* (-[e]s;-e) pedestal
Post'amt *n* post office
Post'anweisung *f* money order
Post'auto *n* mail truck
Post'beamte *m* postal clerk
Post'beutel *m* mailbag
Post'bote *m* mailman
Post'direktor *m* postmaster
Posten ['postən] *m* (-s;-) post; (*Stellung*) position; (acct) entry, item; (com) line, lot; (mil) guard, sentinel; **auf dem P. sein** (fig) be on guard; **auf verlorenem P. kämpfen** (coll) play a losing game; **nicht recht auf dem P. sein** be out of sorts; **P. aufstellen** post sentries; **P. stehen** stand guard; **ruhiger P.** (mil) soft job
Po'stenjäger –in *§6 mf* job hunter
Po'stenkette *f* line of outposts
Post'fach *n* post-office box
Post'gebühr *f* postage
posthum [post'hum] *adj* posthumous
postieren [pos'tirən] *tr* post, place
Postille [pos'tilə] *f* (-;-n) devotional book
Post'karte *f* post card
Post'kasten *m* mail box
Post'kutsche *f* stagecoach
post'lagernd *adj* general-delivery || *adv* general delivery
Postleitzahl ['postlaɪtsal] *f* zip code
Post'minister *m* postmaster general
Post'nachnahme *f* (-;-n) C.O.D.
Post'sack *m* mailbag
Post'schalter *m* post-office window
Post'scheck *m* postal check
Postschließfach ['post/lisfax] *n* post-office box
Postskript [post'skript] *n* (-[e]s;-e) postscript
Post'stempel *m* postmark
Post'überweisung *f* money order
post'wendend *adj* & *adv* by return mail
Post'wertzeichen *n* postage stamp
Post'wesen *n* postal system
potent [po'tent] *adj* potent
Potential [poten'tsjal] *n* (-s;-e) potential
Potenz [po'tents] *f* (-;-en) potency; (math) power; **dritte P.** (math) cube; **zweite P.** (math) square
potenzieren [poten'tsirən] *tr* raise to a higher power; (fig) intensify
Pottasche ['pota/ə] *f* (-;) potash
Pottwal ['potval] *m* sperm whale
potz [pots] *interj*—**p. Blitz!** holy smoke!
potztau'send *interj* holy smoke!
poussieren [pu'sirən] *tr* (coll) flirt with; (coll) butter up || *intr* flirt
Pracht [praxt] *f* (-;) splendor, magnificence
Pracht'ausgabe *f* deluxe edition
Pracht'exemplar *n* beauty, beaut
prächtig ['prɛçtɪç] *adj* splendid
Pracht'kerl *m* (coll) great guy
Pracht'stück *n* (coll) beauty, beaut
pracht'voll *adj* gorgeous
Pracht'zimmer *n* stateroom (*in palace*)
Prädikat [predɪ'kat] *n* (-[e]s;-e) title; (educ) mark, grade; (gram) predicate

Prädikatsnomen [predɪ'katsnomən] *n* (-s;-s) (gram) complement
Präfix [pre'fɪks] *n* (-es;-e) prefix
Prag [prak] *n* (-s;) Prague
Prägeanstalt ['pregə-anstalt] *f* mint
prägen ['pregən] *tr* stamp, coin || *ref*—**das hat sich mir tief in das Gedächtnis geprägt** that made a lasting impression on me
Prä'gestempel *m* (mach) die
pragmatisch [prag'matɪʃ] *adj* pragmatic
prägnant [pre'gnant] *adj* pithy, terse
Prä'gung *f* (-;-en) coining, minting; (fig) coinage
prahlen ['pralən] *intr* (mit) brag (about); (mit) show off (with)
Prah'ler *m* (-s;-) braggart; show-off
Prahlerei [pralə'raɪ] *f* (-;-en) bragging, boasting; (*Prunken*) showing off
Prah'lerin *f* (-;-nen) braggart; show-off
prahlerisch ['pralərɪʃ] *adj* bragging
Prahlhans ['pralhans] *m* (-es;⁻e) braggart
Prahm [pram] *m* (-[e]s;-e) flat-bottomed lighter
Praktik ['praktɪk] *f* (-;-en) practice; (*Kniff*) trick
Praktikant –in [praktɪ'kant(ɪn)] *§7 mf* student in on-the-job training
Praktiker ['praktɪkər] *m* (-s;-) practical person
Prakti-kum ['praktɪkum] *n* (-s;-ka [ka]) practical training
Praktikus ['praktɪkus] *m* (-;-se) old hand
praktisch ['praktɪʃ] *adj* practical; **praktischer Arzt** general practitioner
praktizieren [praktɪ'tsirən] *tr* practice; **etw in die Tasche p.** manage to slip s.th. into the pocket
Prälat [pre'lat] *m* (-en;-en) prelate
Praline [pra'linə] *f* (-;-n) chocolate
prall [pral] *adj* (*straff*) tight; (*Brüste*) full; (*Backen*) chubby; (*Arme, Beine*) shapely; (*Sonne*) blazing || **Prall** *m* (-[e]s;-e) impact; collision
prallen ['pralən] *intr* (SEIN) bounce, rebound; (*Sonne*) beat down
Prämie ['premjə] *f* (-;-n) award, prize; premium; bonus
prämiieren [premɪ'irən] *tr* award a prize to
prangen ['praŋən] *intr* shine; look beautiful
Pranger ['praŋər] *m* (-s;-) pillory
Pranke ['praŋkə] *f* (-;-n) claw
pränumerando [prenumə'rando] *adv* in advance, beforehand
Präparat [prepa'rat] *n* (-[e]s;-e) preparation
präparieren [prepa'rirən] *tr* prepare
Präposition [prepozɪ'tsjon] *f* (-;-en) preposition
Prä-rie [pre'ri] *f* (-;-rien ['ri-ən]) prairie
Präsens ['prezens] *n* (-; Präsentia [pre'zentsɪ-a]) (gram) present
präsent [pre'zent] *adj* present || **Präsent** *n* (-[e]s;-e) present, gift
präsentieren [prezen'tirən] *tr* present
Präsentier'teller *m* tray

Präsenzstärke [prɛˈzɛnts/tɛrkə] *f* effective strength
Präservativ [prezɛrvaˈtiːf] *m* (-s;-e) prophylactic, condom
Präsident [prɛziˈdɛnt] *m* (-en;-en) president
Präsidenten– [prɛzidɛntən] *comb.fm.* presidential
Präsident/schaft *f* (-;-en) presidency
präsidieren [prɛziˈdiːrən] *intr* preside
Präsi·dium [prɛˈziːdjum] *n* (-s;-dien [djən]) presidency; chairmanship
prasseln [ˈprasəln] *intr* crackle; *(Regen)* patter
prassen [ˈprasən] *intr* lead a dissipated life
Prasserei [prasəˈraɪ] *f* (-;) luxurious living, high life
Prätendent [pretɛnˈdɛnt] *m* (-en;-en) *(auf acc)* pretender (to)
Pra·xis [ˈpraksɪs] *f* (-;-xen [ksən]) practice; experience; doctor's office; law office; (jur) clientele; (med) patients
Präzedenzfall [pretseˈdɛntsfal] *m* precedent
präzis [preˈtsiːs] *adj* precise
Präzision [pretsiˈzjoːn] *f* (-;) precision
predigen [ˈpreːdɪɡən] *tr & intr* preach
Prediger [ˈpreːdɪɡər] *m* (-s;-) preacher
Predigt [ˈpreːdɪçt] *f* (-;-en) sermon
Preis [praɪs] *m* (-es;-e) price, rate, cost; (poet) praise, glory; äußerster P. (coll) rock-bottom price; um jeden P. (fig) at all costs; um keinen P. (fig) on no account; zum P. von at the rate of
Preis/aufgabe *f* project in a competition
Preis/aufschlag *m* extra charge
Preis/ausschreiben *n* competition
Preisdrückerei [ˈpraɪsdrʏkəraɪ] *f* (-;-en) price cutting
Preiselbeere [ˈpraɪzəlbeːrə] *f* cranberry
preisen [ˈpraɪzən] *tr* praise
Preis/ermäßigung *f* price reduction
Preis/frage *f* question in a competition; question of price (coll) sixty-four-dollar question
Preis/gabe *f* abandonment, surrender
preis/geben §80 *tr* abandon, surrender; *(Geheimnis)* betray; j–n dem Spott p. hold s.o. up to ridicule
preisgekrönt [ˈpraɪsɡəkrønt] *adj* prize-winning
Preis/gericht *n* jury
Preis/grenze *f* price limit; obere P. ceiling; untere P. minimum price
preis/günstig *adj* worth the money
Preis/lage *f* price range
Preis/niveau *n* price level
Preis/notierung *f* rate of exchange
Preis/richter *m* judge (in competition)
Preis/schießen *n* shooting competition
Preis/schild *n* price tag
Preis/schlager *m* bargain price
Preis/schrift *f* prize-winning essay
Preis/stopp *m* price freezing
Preis/sturz *m* drop in prices
Preis/träger –in §6 *mf* prize winner
Preistreiberei [praɪstraɪbəˈraɪ] *f* (-;) price rigging
Preis/überwachung *f* price control

Preis/verzeichnis *n* price list
preis/wert, preis/würdig *adj* worth the money, reasonable
Preis/zuschlag *m* markup
prekär [preˈkɛːr] *adj* precarious
Prellbock [ˈprɛlbok] *m* (rr) buffer
prellen [ˈprɛlən] *tr* bump; bounce; toss up *(in a blanket)*; (um) cheat (out of) ‖ *ref—sich [dat]* den Arm p. bruise one's arm
Prel/ler *m* (-s;-) bump; ricochet; bilker, cheat
Prellerei [prɛləˈraɪ] *f* (-;-en) (act of) cheating
Prell/schuß *m* ricochet
Prell/stein *m* curbstone
Prel/lung *f* (-;-en) bruise
Premier [prəˈmjeː] *m* (-s;-s) premier
Premiere [prəˈmjɛːrə] *f* (-;-n) (theat) premiere, first night, opening
Premier/minister *m* prime minister
Presbyterianer –in [prɛsbytəˈrjanər (ɪn)] §6 *mf* Presbyterian
presbyterianisch [prɛsbytəˈrjanɪʃ] *adj* Presbyterian
preschen [ˈprɛʃən] *intr* charge
pressant [prɛˈsant] *adj* pressing
Presse [ˈprɛsə] *f* (-;-n) (& journ) press; (educ) cram class
Pres/seagentur *f* press agency
Pres/seamt *n* public-relations office
Pres/seausweis *m* press card
Pres/sebericht *m* press report
Pres/sechef *m* press secretary
Pres/sekonferenz *f* press conference
Pres/semeldung *f* news item
Pres/sestelle *f* public-relations office
Pres/severtreter *m* reporter; public-relations officer
Preßkohle [ˈprɛskoːlə] *f* briquette
Preßluft [ˈprɛsluft] *f* compressed air
Preß/lufthammer *m* jackhammer
Preuße [ˈprɔɪsə] *m* (-n;-n) Prussian
Preußen [ˈprɔɪsən] *n* (-s;) Prussia
Preußin [ˈprɔɪsɪn] *f* (-;-nen) Prussian
preußisch [ˈprɔɪsɪʃ] *adj* Prussian
prickeln [ˈprɪkəln] *intr* tingle
Priem [priːm] *m* (-[e]s;-e) plug *(of tobacco)*
priemen [ˈpriːmən] *intr* chew tobacco
pries [priːs] *pret* of **preisen**
Priester [ˈpriːstər] *m* (-s;-) priest
Prie/steramt *n* priesthood
Priesterin [ˈpriːstərɪn] *f* (-;-nen) priestess
prie/sterlich *adj* priestly
Prie/sterrock *m* cassock
Priestertum [ˈpriːstərtum] *n* (-s;) priesthood
Prie/sterweihe *f* (eccl) ordination
prima [ˈpriːma] *invar adj* first-class; terrific, swell
primär [prɪˈmɛːr] *adj* primary ‖ *adv* primarily
Primat [prɪˈmaːt] *m & n* (-[e]s;-e) primacy, priority ‖ *m* (-en;-en) primate
Primel [ˈpriːməl] *f* (-;-n) primrose
primitiv [prɪmiˈtiːf] *adj* primitive
Prinz [prɪnts] *m* (-en;-en) prince
Prinzessin [prɪnˈtsɛsɪn] *f* (-;-nen) princess
Prinz/gemahl *m* prince consort

Prin·zip [prɪn'tsip] *n* (-s;-zipien ['tsipjən]) principle
prinzipiell [prɪntsɪ'pjɛl] *adj* in principle, fundamentally
Prinzi'pienreiter *m* (coll) pedant
prinz'lich *adj* princely
Pri·or ['pri·ɔr] *m* (-s;-oren ['orən]) (eccl) prior
Priorität [prɪ·ɔrɪ'tɛt] *f* (-;-en) priority
Prise ['prizə] *f* (-;-n) pinch (*of salt, etc.*); (nav) prize
Pris·ma ['prɪsma] *n* (-s;-men [mɛn]) prism
privat [prɪ'vat] *adj* private; personal
Privat'adresse *f*, **Privat'anschrift** *f* home address
Privat'dozent **–in** §7 *mf* non-salaried university lecturer
Privat'druck *m* private printing
Privat'eigentum *n* private property
Privat'gespräch *n* (telp) personal call
privatim [prɪ'vatɪm] *adv* privately; confidentially
privatisieren [privatɪ'zirən] *intr* be financially independent
Privat'lehrer **–in** §6 *mf* tutor
Privat'recht *n* civil law
privat'rechtlich *adj* (jur) civil
Privi·leg [privɪ'lek] *n* (-[e]s;-legien ['legjən]) privilege
privilegiert [privɪle'girt] *adj* privileged
probat [pro'bat] *adj* tried, tested
Probe ['probə] *f* (-;-n) (*Versuch*) trial, experiment; (*Prüfung*) test; (*Muster*) sample; (*Beweis*) proof; (theat) rehearsal; **auf die P. stellen** put to the test; **auf** (or **zur**) **P.** on approval
Pro'beabdruck *m*, **Pro'beabzug** *m* (typ) proof
Pro'bebild *n* (phot) proof
Pro'bebogen *m* proof sheet
Pro'bedruck *m* (typ) proof
Pro'befahrt *f* road test, trial run
Pro'beflug *m* test flight
Pro'belauf *m* trial run; dry run
Pro'besendung *f* sample sent on approval
probieren [pro'birən] *tr* try out, test; try, taste; (metal) assay
Probier'glas *n* test tube
Probier'stein *m* touch-stone
Problem [pro'blem] *n* (-s;-e) problem
Produkt [pro'dukt] *n* (-[e]s;-e) product; (*des Bodens*) produce
Produktion [produk'tsjon] *f* (-;-en) production; (indust) output
produktiv [produk'tif] *adj* productive
Produzent [produ'tsent] *m* (-en;-en) (& cin) producer
produzieren [produ'tsirən] *tr* produce || *ref* perform; (pej) show off
profan [pro'fan] *adj* profane
profanieren [profa'nirən] *tr* profane
Profession [profe'sjon] *f* (-;-en) profession
Professional [profesjo'nal] *m* (-s;-e) (sport) professional
professionell [profesjo'nɛl] *adj* professional
Profes·sor [pro'fɛsɔr] *m* (-s;-soren

['sorən]), **Professorin** [profe'sorɪn] *f* (-;-nen) professor; **außerordentlicher P.** associate professor; **ordentlicher P.** full professor
Professur [profe'sur] *f* (-;-en) professorship
Profi ['profi] *m* (-s;-s) (coll) pro
Profil [pro'fil] *n* (-s;-e) profile; (aut) tread; **im P.** in profile
profiliert [profi'lirt] *adj* outstanding
Profit [pro'fit] *m* (-[e]s;-e) profit
profitabel [profi'tabəl] *adj* profitable
Profit'gier *f* profiteering
profitieren [profi'tirən] *tr* & *intr* profit
Prognose [pro'gnozə] *f* (-;-n) (med) prognosis; (meteor) forecast
Programm [pro'gram] *n* (-s;-e) program; (pol) platform
programmieren [progra'mirən] *tr* (data proc) program
Projekt [pro'jekt] *n* (-[e]s;-e) project
Projektil [projek'til] *n* (-s;-e) projectile
Projektion [projek'tsjon] *f* (-;-en) projection
Projektions'apparat *m*, **Projektions'gerät** *n*, **Projek·tor** [pro'jektɔr] *m* (-s;-toren ['torən]) projector
projizieren [proji'tsirən] *tr* project
proklamieren [prokla'mirən] *tr* proclaim
Prokura [pro'kura] *f* (-;-) power of attorney; **per P.** by proxy
Prolet [pro'let] *m* (-en;-en) (pej) cad
Proletariat [proleta'rjat] *n* (-[e]s;-e) proletariat
Proletarier **–in** [prole'tarjər(ɪn)] §6 *mf* proletarian
proletarisch [prole'tarɪʃ] *adj* proletarian
Prolog [pro'lok] *m* (-[e]s;-e) prologue
prolongieren [prolon'girən] *tr* extend; (cin) hold over
Promenade [promə'nadə] *f* (-;-n) avenue; (*Spaziergang*) promenade
promenieren [promə'nirən] *intr* stroll
prominent [promɪ'nent] *adj* prominent
Promotion [promo'tsjon] *f* (-;-en) awarding of the doctor's degree
promovieren [promo'virən] *intr* attain a doctor's degree
prompt [prompt] *adj* prompt, quick
Prono·men [pro'nomən] *n* (-s;-mina [mina]) pronoun
Propaganda [propa'ganda] *f* (-;) propaganda
propagieren [propa'girən] *tr* propagate
Propeller [pro'pelər] *m* (-s;-) propeller
Prophet [pro'fet] *m* (-en;-en) prophet
Prophetin [pro'fetɪn] *f* (-;-nen) prophetess
prophetisch [pro'fetɪʃ] *adj* prophetic
prophezeien [profe'tsai·ən] *tr* prophesy
Prophezei'ung *f* (-;-en) prophecy
Proportion [propor'tsjon] *f* (-;-en) proportion
proportional [proportsjo'nal] *adj* proportional
proportioniert [proportsjo'nirt] *adj* proportionate
Propst [propst] *m* (-es;ᵘe) provost

Prosa ['proza] f (-;) prose
prosaisch [pro'za·ıʃ] adj prosaic
prosit ['prozıt] interj to your health!
 || **Prosit** n (-s;-s) toast
Prospekt [pro'spekt] m (-[e]s;-e)
 prospect, view; brochure, folder
prostituieren [prostıtu'irən] tr prostitute
Prostituierte [prostıtu'irtə] §5 f prostitute
protegieren [prote'girən] tr patronize;
 (schützen) protect
Protektion [protek'tsjon] f (-;) pull,
 connections
Protest [pro'test] m (-es;-e) protest
Protestant –in [protes'tant(ın)] §7 mf
 Protestant
protestantisch [protes'tantıʃ] adj Protestant
protestieren [protes'tirən] tr & intr
 protest
Protokoll [proto'kɔl] n (-s;-e) protocol; record, minutes; P. führen take
 the minutes; zu P. nehmen take down
Protokoll'führer –in §6 mf recording
 secretary; (jur) clerk
protokollieren [protoko'lirən] tr record
Pro-ton ['proton] n (-s;-tonen
 ['tonən]) (phys) proton
Protz [prots] m (-en;-en) show-off
protzen ['protsən] intr show off
prot'zenhaft, protzig ['protsıç] adj
 show-offish
Prozedur [protse'dur] f (-;-en) procedure; (jur) proceeding
Prozent [pro'tsent] n (-[e]s;-e) percent
Prozent'satz m percentage
Pro-zeß [pro'tses] m (-zesses;-zesse)
 process; (jur) case, suit; (jur) proceedings; e–en P. anstrengen (or
 führen) gegen sue; kurzen P. machen
 mit make short work of
Prozeß'akten pl (jur) record
Prozeß'führer –in §6 mf litigant
prozessieren [protse'sirən] intr go to
 court; p. gegen sue
Prozession [protse'sjon] f (-;-en) procession
Prozeß'kosten pl (jur) court costs
Prozeß'vollmacht f power of attorney
prüde ['prydə] adj prudish
prüfen ['pryfən] tr test; (nachprüfen)
 check, verify; (untersuchen) examine;
 (kosten) taste; (acct) audit
Prüfer –in §6 mf examiner; (acct) auditor
Prüfling ['pryflıŋ] m (-s;-e) examinee
Prüfstein ['pryfʃtaın] m touchstone
Prü'fung f (-;-en) test; examination;
 check, verification; (acct) audit; (jur)
 review
Prü'fungsarbeit f test paper
Prü'fungsausschuß m, **Prü'fungskom-
 mission** f examining board
Prügel ['prygəl] m (-s;-) stick, cudgel;
 Prügel pl whipping
Prügelei [prygə'laı] f (-;-en) brawl;
 free-for-all
Prü'gelknabe m whipping boy, scape-
 goat
prügeln ['prygəln] tr beat, whip || ref
 have a fight

Prü'gelstrafe f corporal punishment
Prunk [pruŋk] m (-[e]s;) pomp, show
prunken ['pruŋkən] intr show off
Prunk'gemach n stateroom
prunk'haft adj showy
Prunk'sucht f ostentatiousness
prunk'süchtig adj ostentatious
prunk'voll adj gorgeous
Prunk'zimmer n stateroom
prusten ['prustən] intr snort
Psalm [psalm] m (-s;-en) psalm
Psalter ['psaltər] m (-s;-) psalter
Pseudonym [psɔıdo'nym] n (-s;-e)
 pseudonym
Psychiater (psyçı'atər] m (-s;-) psychiatrist
Psychiatrie [psyçı·a'tri] f (-;) psychiatry
psychiatrisch [psyçı'atrıʃ] adj psychi-
 atric
psychisch ['psyçıʃ] adj psychic(al)
Psychoanalyse [psyço·ana'lyzə] f (-;)
 psychoanalysis
Psychoanalytiker –in [psyço·ana'lytı-
 kər(ın)] §6 mf psychoanalyst
Psychologe [psyço'logə] m (-n;-n) psychologist
Psychologie [psyçolo'gi] f (-;) psychology
Psychologin [psyço'login] f (-;-nen)
 psychologist
psychologisch [psyço'logıʃ] adj psy-
 chological
Psychopath –in [psyço'pat(ın)] §7 mf
 psychopath
Psychose [psy'çozə] f (-;-n) psychosis
Psychotherapie [psyçotera'pi] f (-;)
 psychotherapy
Pubertät [puber'tet] f (-;) puberty
publik [pub'lik] adj public
Publi·kum ['publıkum] n (-s;-ka
 [ka]) public; (theat) audience
publizieren [publı'tsirən] tr publish
Publizist –in [publı'tsıst(ın)] §7 mf
 (journ) writer on public affairs;
 teacher or student of journalism
Publizität [publıtsı'tet] f (-;) publicity
Pudel ['pudəl] m (-s;-) poodle; des
 Pudels Kern (fig) gist of the matter
Pu'delmütze f fur cap; woolen cap
pu'delnaß adj (coll) soaking wet
Puder ['pudər] m (-s;) powder
Pu'derdose f powder box; compact
Pu'derquaste f powder puff
Pu'derzucker m powdered sugar
Puff [puf] m (-[e]s;-e & -e) (Stoß)
 poke; (Knall) pop; (Bausch) puff;
 || m (-s;-s) (coll) brothel
Puff'ärmel m puffed sleeve
puffen ['pufən] tr poke; (coll) prod ||
 intr puff; (knallen) pop, bang away
Puffer ['pufər] m (-s;-) buffer; pop-
 gun; (culin) potato pancake
Puf'ferbatterie f booster battery
Puf'ferstaat m buffer state
Puff'mais m popcorn
Puff'reis m (-es;) puffed rice
Pulli ['puli] m (-s;-s) (coll) sweater
Pullover [pu'lovər] m (-s;-) sweater
Puls [puls] m (-es;-e) pulse
Puls'ader f artery
pulsieren [pul'zirən] intr pulsate
Puls'schlag m pulse beat

Pult [pʊlt] *n* (-[e]s;-e) desk
Pulver ['pʊlfər] *n* (-s;-) powder; (*Schieß*-) gunpowder; (coll) dough
pul'verig *adj* powdery
pulverisieren [pʊlfərɪ'zirən] *tr* pulverize
Pul'verschnee *m* powdery snow
Pummel ['pʊməl] *m* (-s;-) butterball (*chubby child*)
pummelig ['pʊməlɪç] *adj* (coll) chubby
Pump [pʊmp] *m*—**auf P.** (coll) on tick
Pumpe ['pʊmpə] *f* (-;-n) pump
pumpen ['pʊmpən] *tr* pump; (coll) give on tick; (coll) get on tick || *intr* pump
Pum'penschwengel *m* pump handle
Pumpernickel ['pʊmpərnɪkəl] *m* (-s; -) pumpernickel
Pump'hosen *f* pair of knickerbockers
Punkt [pʊŋkt] *m* (-[e]s;-e) point; (*Tüpfelchen*) dot; (*Stelle*) spot; (*Einzelheit*) item; (gram) period; **der tote P. a** deadlock; **dunkler P.** (fig) skeleton in the closet; **nach Punkten siegen** win on points; **P. sechs Uhr** at six o'clock sharp; **springender P.** crux; **strittiger P.** point at issue; **wunder P.** (fig) sore spot
Punkt'gleichheit *f* (sport) tie
punktieren [pʊŋk'tirən] *tr* dot, stipple; **punktierte Linie** dotted line
pünktlich ['pʏŋktlɪç] *adj* punctual
Punkt'sieg *m* (box) winning on points
punktum ['pʊŋktum] *interj*—**und damit p.!** and that's it!; period!
Punkt'zahl *f* (sport) score
Punsch [pʊn/] *m* (-es;) punch (*drink*)
Punze ['pʊntsə] *f* (-;-n) punch, stamp
punzen ['pʊntsən] *tr* punch, stamp
Pupille [pu'pɪlə] *f* (-;-n) (anat) pupil
Puppe ['pʊpə] *f* (-;-n) doll; puppet; (*Schneider*-) dummy; (zool) pupa
Pup'penspiel *n* puppet show
Pup'penwagen *m* doll carriage
pur [pur] *adj* pure, sheer

Püree [pʏ're] *n* (-s;-s) mashed potatoes; puree
purgieren [pur'girən] *tr & intr* purge
Purpur ['purpur] *m* (-s;) purple
pur'purfarben *adj* purple
purpurn [purpurn] *adj* purple
Purzelbaum ['pʊrtsəlbaum] *m* somersault; **e-en P. schlagen** do a somersault
purzeln ['pʊrtsəln] *intr* (SEIN) tumble
pusselig ['pʊsəlɪç] *adj* fussy
Puste ['pustə] *f* (-s) (coll) breath
Pustel ['pʊstəl] *f* (-;-n) pustule
pusten ['pustən] *tr*—**ich puste dir was!** (coll) you may whistle for it! || *intr* puff, pant
Pu'sterohr *n* peashooter
Pute ['putə] *f* (-;-n) turkey (hen)
Puter ['putər] *m* (-s;-) turkey (cock)
Putsch [put/] *m* (-es;-e) putsch, uprising
Putz [pʊts] *m* (-es;) finery; trimming; ornaments; plaster
putzen ['pʊtsən] *tr* (*reinigen*) clean; (*Schuhe*) polish; (*Zähne*) brush; (*Person*) dress; (*schmücken*) adorn || *ref* dress; **sich** [*dat*] **die Nase p.** blow one's nose
Put'zer *m* (-s;-) cleaner; (mil) orderly
Putzerei [pʊtsə'rai] *f* (-;-en) (Aust) dry cleaner's; (Aust) laundry
Putz'frau *f* cleaning woman
putzig ['pʊtsɪç] *adj* funny
Putz'lappen *m* cleaning cloth
Putz'mittel *n* cleaning agent
Putz'wolle *f* cotton waste
Putz'zeug *n* cleaning things
Pygmäe [pyg'me-ə] *m* (-n;-n) pygmy
Pyjama [pɪ'dʒɑma] *m* (-s;-s) pajamas
Pyramide [pʏra'midə] *f* (-;-n) pyramid; (mil) stack
Pyrenäen [pʏre'nɛ-ən] *pl* Pyrenees
Pyrotechnik [pʏro'tɛçnɪk] *f* (-;) pyrotechnics
Pythonschlange ['python/laŋə] *f* python

Q

Q, q [ku] *invar n* Q, q
quabbelig ['kvabəlɪç] *adj* flabby; quivering, jelly-like
quabbeln ['kvabəln] *intr* quiver
Quackelei [kvakə'lai] *f* (-;-en) silly talk; (*unnützes Zeug*) rubbish
Quacksalber ['kvakzalbər] *m* (-s;-) quack
Quader ['kvadər] *m* (-s;-) ashlar
Quadrant [kva'drant] *m* (-en;-en) quadrant
Quadrat [kva'drat] *n* (-[e]s;-e) square; **e-e Zahl ins Q. erheben** square a number; **zwei Fuß im Q.** two feet square
quadratisch [kva'dratɪ/] *adj* square; quadratic
Quadrat'meter *n* square meter
Quadrat'wurzel *f* square root
quadrieren [kva'drirən] *tr* square

quaken ['kvakən] *intr* (*Ente*) quack; (*Frosch*) croak
quäken ['kvɛkən] *intr* bawl
Qual [kval] *f* (-;-en) torment, agony
quälen ['kvɛlən] *tr* torment; worry; (*ständig bedrängen*) pester || *ref*—**sich mit e-r Arbeit q.** slave at a job; **sich umsonst q.** labor in vain; **sich zu Tode q.** worry oneself to death
Quälgeist ['kvɛlgaɪst] *m* pest
Qualifikation [kvalɪfɪka'tsjon] *f* (-; -en) qualification
qualifizieren [kvalɪfɪ'tsirən] *tr & ref* (zu) qualify (for)
Qualität [kvalɪ'tɛt] *f* (-;-en) quality
Qualitäts- *comb.fm.* high-quality, high-grade, quality
Qualle ['kvalə] *f* (-;-n) jellyfish
Qualm [kvalm] *m* (-[e]s;) smoke; vapor

qualmen ['kvalmən] *tr* smoke || *intr* smoke; (coll) smoke like a chimney

qual'mig *adj* smoky

qual'voll *adj* agonizing

Quantentheorie ['kvantənte·ori] *f* quantum theory

Quantität [kvanti'tɛt] *f* (-;-en) quantity

Quan·tum ['kvantum] *n* (-s;-ten [tən]) quantum; quantity; (*Anteil*) portion

Quappe ['kvapə] *f* (-;-n) tadpole

Quarantäne [kvaran'tɛnə] *f* (-;-n) quarantine

Quark [kvark] *m* (-[e]s) curds; cottage cheese; (fig) nonsense

Quark'käse *m* cottage cheese

quarren ['kvarən] *intr* (*Frosch*) croak; (fig) groan

Quart [kvart] *n* (-s;-e) quart; quarto || *f* (-s;-en) (mus) fourth

Quartal [kvar'tal] *n* (-s;-e) quarter (*of a year*)

Quartals'abrechnung *f* (fin) quarterly statement

Quartals'säufer *m* periodic drunkard

Quart'band *m* (-[e]s;⸗e) quarto volume

Quarte ['kvartə] *f* (-;-n) (mus) fourth

Quartett [kvar'tet] *n* (-[e]s;-e) quartet

Quart'format *n* quarto

Quartier [kvar'tir] *n* (-s;-e) (*Stadtviertel*) quarter; (*Unterkunft*) quarters; (mil) quarters, billet

Quartier'meister *m* (mil) quartermaster

Quarz [kvarts] *m* (-es;-e) quartz

quasseln ['kvasəln] *tr* (coll) talk || *intr* talk nonsense

Quast [kvast] *m* (-[e]s;-e) brush

Quaste ['kvastə] *f* (-;-n) tassel

Quatsch [kvatʃ] *m* (-es;) (coll) baloney

quatschen ['kvatʃən] *intr* chatter; talk nonsense; (*durch Schlamm*) slog

Quecksilber ['kvekzilbər] *n* mercury

queck'silbrig *adj* fidgety

Quell [kvel] *m* (-[e]s;-e) (poet) var of Quelle

Quelle ['kvelə] *f* (-;-n) fountainhead; source; spring

quellen ['kvelən] §119 *tr* cause to swell; soak || *intr* (SEIN) spring, gush; (*Tränen*) well up; (*anschwellen*) swell; ihm quollen die Augen fast aus dem Kopf his eyes almost popped out

Quel'lenangabe *f* citation; bibliography

quel'lenmäßig *adj* according to the best authorities, authentic

Quel'lenmaterial *n* source material

Quel'lenstudium *n* original research

Quell'fluß *m* source

Quell'gebiet *n* headwaters

Quell'wasser *n* spring water

Quengelei [kveŋə'lai] *f* (-;-en) nagging

quengeln ['kveŋəln] *intr* nag

quer [kver] *adj* cross, transverse || *adv* crosswise; q. über (*acc*) across

Quer'balken *m* crossbeam

Quere ['kverə] *f* (-;) diagonal direction; j–m in die Q. kommen run across s.o.; (fig) disturb s.o.

queren ['kverən] *tr* traverse, cross

querfeldein' *adv* cross-country

Quer'kopf *m* contrary person

quer'köpfig *adj* contrary

Quer'pfeife *f* (mus) fife

Quer'ruder *n* (aer) aileron

Quer'schiff *n* (archit) transept

Quer'schläger *m* ricochet

Quer'schnitt *m* cross section

Quer'treiber *m* schemer, plotter

querü'ber *adv* straight across

Querulant –in [kveru'lant(ın)] §7 *mf* grumbler, grouch

Quetsche ['kvetʃə] *f* (-;-n) squeezer; (pej) joint

quetschen ['kvetʃən] *tr* squeeze, pinch; bruise; (*zerquetschen*) crush, mash

Quetsch'kartoffeln *pl* mashed potatoes

Quet'schung *f* (-;-en) bruise, contusion

Quetsch'wunde *f* bruise

quick [kvık] *adj* brisk, lively

quick'lebendig *adj* (coll) very lively

quieken ['kvikən] *intr* squeal, squeak

quietschen ['kvitʃən] *intr* (*Tür*) creak; (*Ferkel*) squeal; (*Bremsen*) screech

Quintessenz ['kvıntesents] *f* (-;) quintessence

Quintett [kvın'tet] *n* (-[e]s;-e) quintet

Quirl [kvırl] *m* (-[e]s;-e) (fig) fidgeter; (culin) whisk, mixer

quirlen ['kvırlən] *tr* beat, mix

quitt [kvıt] *adj* even, square

Quitte ['kvıtə] *f* (-;-n) quince

quittieren [kvı'tirən] *tr* give a receipt for; (*aufgeben*) quit

Quit'tung *f* (-;-en) receipt

Quiz [kvıs] *n* (-;) quiz

quoll [kvɔl] *pret* of quellen

Quotation [kvota'tsjon] *f* (-;-en) (st. exch.) quotation

Quote ['kvotə] *f* (-;-en) quota

Quotient [kvo'tsjent] *m* (-en;-en) quotient

quotieren [kvo'tirən] *tr* quote

R

R, r [er] *invar n* R, r

Rabatt [ra'bat] *m* (-[e]s;-e) reduction, discount

Rabatt'marke *f* trading stamp

Rabatz [ra'bats] *m*—R. machen (coll) raise Cain

Rab·bi ['rabi] *m* (-[s];-s & -binen ['binən]), **Rabbiner** [ra'binər] *m* (-s;-) rabbi

Rabe ['rabə] *m* (-n;-n) raven; weißer R. (fig) rare bird

Ra'benaas *n* (coll) beast

Ra'benmutter *f* hard-hearted mother

ra'benschwarz' *adj* jet-black

rabiat [ra'bjɑt] *adj* rabid, raving
Rache ['raxə] *f* (-;) revenge
Rachen ['raxən] *m* (-s;-) throat; mouth; (fig) jaws
rächen ['rɛçən] *tr* avenge ‖ *ref* (an *dat*) avenge oneself (on)
Ra'chenhöhle *f* pharynx
Ra'chenkatarrh *m* sore throat
Rä'cher –in §6 *mf* avenger
Rachgier ['raxgir] *f* revengefulness
rach'gierig, rach'süchtig *adj* vengeful
Rad [rɑt] *n* (-[e]s;̈er) wheel; bike; **ein Rad schlagen** turn a cartwheel; (*Pfau*) fan the tail
Radar ['rɑdɑr], [ra'dɑr] *n* (-s;) radar
Ra'dargerät *n* radar
Ra'darschirm *m* radarscope
Radau [ra'dau] *m* (-s;-) (coll) row
Radau'macher *m* rowdy
Rädchen ['rɛtçən] *n* (-s;-) little wheel
Rad'dampfer *m* river boat
radebrechen ['rɑdəbrɛçən] §64 *tr* murder (*a language*)
radeln ['rɑdəln] *intr* (SEIN) (coll) ride a bike
Rädelsführer ['rɛdəlsfyrər] *m* ringleader
rädern ['rɛdərn] *tr* torture; **wie gerädert sein** (coll) be bushed
Räderwerk ['rɛdərvɛrk] *n* gears; (fig) clockwork
rad'fahren §71 *intr* (SEIN) ride a bicycle
radieren [ra'dirən] *tr* erase; etch
Radie'rer *m* (-s;-) eraser; etcher
Radier'gummi *m* eraser
Radier'kunst *f* art of etching
Radier'messer *n* scraper, eraser
Radie'rung *f* (-;-en) erasure; etching
Radieschen [ra'disçən] *n* (-s;-) radish
radikal [radɪ'kɑl] *adj* radical ‖ **Radikale** §5 *mf* radical, extremist
Radio ['rɑdjo] *n* (-s;-s) radio; **im R.** on the radio; **R. hören** listen to the radio
Ra'dioamateur *m* (rad) ham
Ra'dioapparat *m*, **Ra'diogerät** *n* radio set
Radiologe [radjə'logə] *m* (-n;-n) radiologist
Radiologie [radjələ'gi] *f* (-;) radiology
Ra'dioröhre *f* radio tube
Ra'diosender *m* radio transmitter
Radium ['rɑdjum] *n* (-s;) radium
Ra·dius ['rɑdjus] *m* (-;-dien [djən]) radius
Rad'kappe *f* hubcap
Rad'kranz *m* rim
Radler –in ['rɑdlər(ɪn)] §6 *mf* cyclist
Rad'nabe *f* hub
Rad'rennen *n* bicycle race
–rädrig [rɛdrɪç] *comb.fm.* –wheeled
rad'schlagen §132 *intr* turn a cartwheel
Rad'spur *f* rut, track
Rad'stand *m* wheelbase
Rad'zahn *m* cog
raffen ['rafən] *tr* snatch up, gather up; (sew) take up
Raffgier ['rafgir] *f* rapacity
raffgierig ['rafgirɪç] *adj* rapacious
Raffine·rie [rafinə'ri] *f* (-;-rien ['ri·ən]) refinery
raffinieren [rafɪ'nirən] *tr* refine

raffiniert [rafɪ'nirt] *adj* refined; (fig) shrewd, cunning
Raffzahn ['raftsɑn] *m* canine tooth
ragen ['rɑgən] *intr* tower, loom
Ragout [ra'gu] *n* (-s;-s) (culin) stew
Rahe ['rɑ·ə] *f* (-;-n) (naut) yard
Rahm [rɑm] *m* (-[e]s;) cream
Rahmen ['rɑmən] *m* (-s;-) frame; (*Gefüge*) framework; (*Bereich*) scope, limits; (fig) setting; (aut) chassis; **aus dem R. fallen** be out of place; **e–n R. abgeben für** form a setting for; **im R.** (*genit*) in the course of; **im R. von** (or *genit*) within the scope of; **within the framework of**
Rah'menerzählung *f* story within a story
rahmig ['rɑmɪç] *adj* creamy
Rakete [ra'ketə] *f* (-;-n) rocket
Rake'tenabschußrampe *f* launch pad
Rake'tenbunker *m* silo
Rake'tenstart *m* rocket launch
Rake'tenwerfer *m* rocket launcher
Rake'tenwesen *n* rocketry
Rakett [ra'ket] *n* (-[e]s;-e & -s) (tennis) racket
Rammbär ['rambɛr] *m*, **Rammbock** ['rambɔk] *m*, **Ramme** ['ramə] *f* (-;-n) rammer; pile driver
rammeln ['raməln] *tr* shove; (*zusammenpressen*) pack; (*belegen*) copulate with ‖ *intr* copulate
rammen ['ramən] *tr* ram; (*Beton*) tamp
Rampe ['rampə] *f* (-;-n) ramp; (rok) launch pad; (rr) platform; (theat) apron
Ram'penlicht *n* footlights; (fig) limelight
Ramsch [ram/] *m* (-es;) odds and ends; junk; (com) rummage
Ramsch'verkauf *m* rummage sale
Ramsch'waren *pl* junk
Rand [rant] *m* (-[e]s;̈er) edge, border; (*e–s Druckseite*) margin; **am Rande bemerken** note in passing; **außer R. und Band** completely out of control; **bis zum Rande** to the brim; **e–n R. hinterlassen** leave a ring (*e.g., from a wet glass*); **Ränder unter den Augen** circles under the eyes
Rand'auslöser *m* (typ) margin release
Rand'bemerkung *f* marginal note; (fig) snide remark
rändeln ['rɛndəln], **rändern** ['rɛndərn] *tr* border, edge; (*Münzen*) mill
Rand'gebiet *n* borderland; (*e–r Stadt*) outskirts
rand'los *adj* rimless
Rand'staat *m* border state
Ranft [ranft] *m* (-[e]s;̈e) crust
rang [raŋ] *pret of* **ringen** ‖ **Rang** *m* (-[e]s;̈e) rank; (theat) balcony; **j–m den R. ablaufen** (fig) run rings around s.o.
Rang'abzeichen *n* insignia of rank
Rang'älteste §5 *mf* ranking officer
Range ['raŋə] *m* (-n;-n) & *f* (-;-n) brat
Rangier'bahnhof *m* (rr) marshaling yard
rangieren [rɑ̃'ʒirən] *tr* rank; (rr) shunt, switch ‖ *intr* rank

Rang'ordnung f order of precedence

Rang'stufe f rank

rank [raŋk] adj slender

Ranke ['raŋkə] f (-;-n) tendril

Ränke ['rɛŋkə] pl schemes; **R. schmieden** scheme

ranken ['raŋkən] ref & intr creep, climb; **sich r. um** wind around

rän'kevoll adj scheming

rann [ran] pret of **rinnen**

rannte ['rantə] pret of **rennen**

Ranzen ['rantsən] m (-s;-) knapsack; school bag; (Bauch) belly; (mil) field pack

ranzig ['rantsɪç] adj rancid

rapid [ra'pit], **rapide** [ra'pidə] adj rapid

Rappe ['rapə] m (-n;-n) black horse

rar [rar] adj rare, scarce

Rarität [rarɪ'tɛt] f (-;-en) rarity

rasant [ra'zant] adj grazing, point-blank (fire); (fig) impetuous

Rasanz [ra'zants] f (-;) flat trajectory; (fig) impetuosity

rasch [raʃ] adj quick; (hastig) hasty

rascheln ['raʃəln] intr rustle

Rasch'heit f (-;) haste, speed

rasen ['razən] intr rage, rave || (SEIN) rush; (aut) speed || **Rasen** m (-s;-) lawn, grass

ra'send adj raging, raving; wild, mad; (Hunger) ravenous; (Wut) towering; (Tempo) break-neck; **r. werden** see red

Ra'sendecke f turf

Ra'senmäher m lawn mower

Ra'senplatz m lawn

Ra'sensprenger m lawn sprinkler

Raserei [razə'raɪ] f (-;) rage, madness; (aut) reckless driving

Rasier- [razir] comb.fm. shaving, razor

Rasier'apparat m safety razor

rasieren [ra'zirən] tr & ref shave

Rasier'klinge f razor blade

Rasier'messer n straight razor

Rasier'napf m shaving mug

Rasier'pinsel m shaving brush

Rasier'wasser n after-shave lotion

Rasier'zeug n shaving outfit

Raspel ['raspəl] f (-;-n) rasp; (culin) grater

raspeln ['raspəln] tr rasp; grate

Rasse ['rasə] f (-;-n) race; (Zucht) breed, blood, stock; (fig) good breeding

Rassel ['rasəl] f (-;-n) rattle

rasseln ['rasəln] intr rattle; **durchs Examen r.** (coll) flunk the exam

Rassen- [rasən] comb.fm. racial

Ras'senfrage f racial problem

Ras'senhaß m racism, race hatred

Ras'senkreuzung f miscegenation; crossbreeding

Ras'senkunde f ethnology

ras'senmäßig adj racial

Ras'senmerkmal n racial characteristic

Ras'sentrennung f segregation

Ras'senunruhen pl racial disorders

Ras'sepferd n thoroughbred (horse)

ras'serein adj racially pure; thoroughbred

Ras'sevieh n purebred cattle

rassig ['rasɪç] adj racy; thoroughbred

rassisch ['rasɪʃ] adj racial

Rast [rast] f (-;-en) rest; station, stage; (mach) notch, groove; (mil) halt; **e-e R. machen** take a rest

rasten ['rastən] intr rest; (mil) halt

rast'los adj restless

Rast'losigkeit f (-;) restlessness

Rast'platz m, **Rast'stätte** f resting place

Rast'tag m day of rest

Rasur [ra'zur] f (-;-en) shave

Rat [rat] m (-[e]s; **Ratschläge** ['rat-ʃlɛgə]) advice, piece of advice, counsel; (Beratung) deliberation; (Ausweg) means, solution; **auf e-n Rat hören** listen to reason; **sich [dat] keinen Rat mehr wissen** be at one's wits' end; **zu Rate ziehen** consult (a person, dictionary, etc.) || m (-[e]s; ˶e) council, board; (Person) councilor, alderman; advisor; (jur) counsel

Rate ['ratə] f (-;-n) installment; **auf Raten** on the installment plan

raten ['ratən] §63 tr guess (Rätsel) solve; **das will ich dir nicht geraten haben!** you had better not!; **geraten!** you guessed it!; **j–m etw r.** advise s.o. about s.th.; **komm nicht wieder. das rate ich dir!** take my advice and don't come back! || intr guess; give advice; (dat) advise; **gut r.** take a good guess; **hin und her r.** make random guesses; **j–m gut r.** give s.o. good advice; **j–m zu etw r.** recommend s.th. to s.o. || **Raten** n (-s;) guesswork; advice

ra'tenweise adv by installments

Ra'tenzahlung f payment in installments; **auf R.** on the installment plan

Räterepublik ['retərepublik] f Soviet Union, Soviet Republic

Rat'geber –in §6 mf adviser, counselor

Rat'haus n city hall

ratifizieren [ratɪfɪ'tsirən] tr ratify

Ratifizie'rung f (-;-en) ratification

Ration [ra'tsjon] f (-;-en) ration

rational [ratsjo'nal] adj rational

rationalisieren [ratsjonalɪ'zirən] tr streamline (operations in industry)

rationell [ratsjo'nel] adj rational

rationieren [ratsjo'nirən] tr ration

rätlich ['retlɪç] adj advisable

rat'los adj helpless, perplexed

ratsam ['ratzam] adj advisable

Ratsche ['ratʃə] f (-;-n) rattle; (coll) chatterbox; (tech) ratchet

ratschen ['ratʃən] intr make noise with a rattle; (coll) chat

Rat'schlag m advice, piece of advice

rat'schlagen §132 intr deliberate, consult

Rat'schluß m decision, decree, resolution

Rätsel ['retsəl] n (-s;-) puzzle; (fig) riddle, enigma, mystery

rät'selhaft adj puzzling; mysterious

Ratte ['ratə] f (-;-n) rat

Rat'tenschwanz m rat tail; (fig) tangle; (coll) whole string (of questions, etc.); (Haarzopf) (coll) pigtail

rattern ['ratərn] intr rattle

ratzekahl ['ratsə'kal] adj (Person)

completely bald; (*Landschaft*) completely barren || *adv* completely
Raub [raup] *m* (-[e]s;) robbery; plunder; (*Beute*) prey, spoils; **zum Raube fallen** fall prey, fall victim
Raub- *comb.fm.* predatory, rapacious
Raub′bau *m* (-[e]s;) excessive exploitation (*of natural resources*)
rauben [′raubən] *tr—j-m etw* r. rob s.o. of s.th.; **e-m Mädchen die Unschuld** r. seduce a girl; **e-n Kuß** r. steal a kiss || *intr* rob
Räuber [′rɔɪbər] *m* (-s;-) robber; **R. und Gendarm spielen** play cops and robbers
Räu′berbande *f* gang of robbers
Räu′berhauptmann *m* gang leader
räuberisch [′rɔɪbərɪʃ] *adj* predatory
Raub′fisch *m* predatory fish
Raub′gesindel *n* gang of robbers
Raub′lust *f* rapacity
raub′gierig *adj* rapacious
Raub′lust *f* rapacity
Raub′mord *m* murder with robbery
Raub′mörder *m* robber and murderer
Raub′schiff *n* corsair, pirate ship
Raub′tier *n* beast of prey
Raub′überfall *m* holdup, robbery
Raub′vogel *m* bird of prey
Raub′zug *m* plundering raid
Rauch [raux] *m* (-[e]s;) smoke
rauchen [′rauxən] *tr & intr* smoke
Raucher [′rauxər] *m* (-s;-) smoker
Räucher- [rɔɪxər] *comb.fm.* smoked
Rau′cherabteil *n* smoking section
Räu′cherfaß *n* (eccl) censer
Räu′cherhering *m* smoked herring
Rau′cherhusten *m* cigarette cough
Räu′cherkammer *f* smokehouse
räuchern [′rɔɪxərn] *tr* smoke, cure; (*desinzieren*) fumigate
Räu′cherschinken *m* smoked ham
Räu′cherung *f* (-;) smoking; fumigation
Rau′cherwagen *m* (rr) smoker
Rauch′fahne *f* trail of smoke
Rauch′fang *m* (*über dem Herd*) hood; (*im Schornstein*) flue
Rauch′fleisch *n* smoked meat
rauchig [′rauxɪç] *adj* smoky
rauch′los *adj* smokeless
Rauch′schleier *m* (mil) smoke screen
Rauch′waren *pl* (Pelze) furs; (*Tabakwaren*) tobacco supplies
Räude [′rɔɪdə] *f* (-;) mange
räudig [′rɔɪdɪç] *adj* mangy; **räudiges Schaf** (fig) black sheep
Raufbold [′raufbɔlt] *m* (-[e]s;-e) roughneck, bully
Raufe [′raufə] *f* (-;-n) hayrack
raufen [′raufən] *tr* tear, pull out || *recip & intr* fight, brawl, scuffle
Rauferei [raufə′raɪ] *f* (-;-en) fight, scuffle
Rauf′handel *m* fight, scuffle
rauf′lustig *adj* scrappy, belligerent
rauh [rau] *adj* rough; (*Hals*) hoarse; (*Behandlung*) harsh; **rauhe Wirklichkeit** hard facts
Rauh′bein *n* (fig) roughneck, churl
rauh′beinig *adj* tough, churlish
Rauh′heit *f* (-;) roughness; hoarseness
rauhen [′rau·ən] *tr* roughen

Rauh′futter *n* roughage
rauh′haarig *adj* shaggy, hirsute
Rauh′reif *m* hoarfrost
Raum [raum] *m* (-[e]s;-̈e) room, space; (*Zimmer*) room; (*Bereich*) area; (*e-s Schiffes*) hold; **am Rande R. lassen** (typ) leave a margin; **freier R.** open space; **gebt R.!** make way! **luftleerer R.** vacuum; **R. bieten für** accommodate; **R. einnehmen** take up space; **R. geben** (*dat*) give way to; comply with
Raum′anzug *m* space suit
Räumboot [′rɔɪmbot] *n* minesweeper
Raum′dichte *f* (phys) density by volume
räumen [′rɔɪmən] *tr* clear; (*Wohnung*) vacate; (*Minen*) sweep; (mil) evacuate; **den Saal** r. clear the room; **das Lager** r. (com) clear out the stock; **j-n aus dem Wege** r. (fig) finish s.o. off
Raum′ersparnis *f* economy of space; **der R. wegen** to save space
Raum′fahrer *m* spaceman
Raum′fahrt *f* space travel
Raum′flug *m* space flight
Raum′gestaltung *f* interior decorating
Raum′inhalt *m* volume, capacity
Raum′kunst *f* interior decorating
Raum′lehre *f* geometry
räumlich [′rɔɪmlɪç] *adj* spatial
Räum′lichkeit *f* (-;-en) room
Raum′mangel *m* lack of space
Raum′medizin *f* space medicine
Raum′meter *n* cubic meter
Raum′schiff *n* space ship
Raum′schiffart *f* space travel
Raum′schiffkapsel *f* space capsule
Raum′sonde *f* unmanned space explorer
Raum′ton *m* stereophonic sound
Räu′mung *f* (-;-en) clearing, removal; (com) clearance; (mil) evacuation
Räu′mungsausverkauf *m* clearance sale
Räu′mungsbefehl *m* eviction notice; (mil) evacuation order
raunen [′raunən] *tr & intr* whisper
raunzen [′rauntsən] *intr* grumble
Raupe [′raupə] *f* (-;-n) (ent, mach) caterpillar
Rau′penfahrzeug *n* full-track vehicle
Rau′penkette *f* caterpillar track
Rau′penschlepper *m* caterpillar tractor
Rausch [rauʃ] *m* (-es;-e) drunkenness; (fig) intoxication, ecstasy; **e-n R. haben** be drunk; **sich** [*dat*] **e-n R. antrinken** get drunk
rauschen [′rauʃən] *intr* (*Blätter, Seide*) rustle; (*Bach*) murmur; (*Brandung, Sturm*) roar || *intr* (SEIN) strut; rush
rau′schend *adj* rustling; (*Fest*) uproarious; (*Beifall*) thunderous
Rausch′gift *n* drug, dope
Rausch′gifthandel *m* drug traffic
Rausch′giftschieber –**in** §6 *mf* pusher
Rausch′giftsucht *f* drug addiction
Rausch′giftsüchtige §5 *mf* dope addict
Rausch′gold *n* tinsel
räuspern [′rɔɪspərn] *ref* clear one's throat
Rausschmeißer [′raus/maɪsər] *m* (-s;-) (coll) bouncer

Raute ['rautə] *f* (-;-n) (cards) diamond; (geom) rhombus

Rayon [re'jõ] *m* (-s;-s) (*Bezirk*) district, region; (*im Warenhaus*) department

Raz·zia ['ratsja] *f* (-;-zien [tsjən]) police raid

Reagenzglas [re·a'gɛntsglas] *n* test tube

reagieren [re·a'girən] *intr* (auf *acc*) react (to)

Reaktion [re·ak'tsjon] *f* (-;-en) reaction

reaktionär [re·aktsjo'nɛr] *adj* reactionary ‖ **Reaktionär** *m* (-s;-e) reactionary

Reak·tor [re'aktɔr] *m* (-s;-toren ['torən]) (phys) reactor

real [re'al] *adj* real

Real'gymnasium *n* high school (*where modern languages, mathematics, or sciences are stressed*)

Realien [re'aljən] *pl* real facts, realities; exact sciences

realisieren [re·alɪ'zirən] *tr* realize

Realist -in [re·a'lɪst(ɪn)] §7 *mf* realist

realistisch [re·a'lɪstɪʃ] *adj* realistic

Realität [re·alɪ'tɛt] *f* (-;-en) reality; **Realitäten** real property

Real'lexikon *n* encyclopedia

Real'lohn *m* purchasing power of wages

Real'schule *f* non-classical secondary school

Rebe ['rebə] *f* (-;-n) vine; tendril

Rebell [re'bɛl] *m* (-en;-en) rebel

rebellieren [rebe'lirən] *intr* rebel

Rebellin [re'bɛlɪn] *f* (-;-nen) rebel

Rebellion [rɛbɛl'jon] *f* (-;-en) rebellion

rebellisch [re'bɛlɪʃ] *adj* rebellious

Re'bensaft *m* (poet) juice of the grape

Rebhuhn ['rephun] *n* partridge

Rebstock ['rep/tok] *m* vine

rechen ['reçən] *tr* rake ‖ **Rechen** *m* (-s;-) rake; grate

Re'chenaufgabe *f* arithmetic problem

Re'chenautomat *m* computer

Re'chenbrett *n* abacus

Re'chenbuch *n* arithmetic book

Re'chenexemplar *n* arithmetic problem

Re'chenkunst *f* arithmetic

Re'chenmaschine *f* calculator

Re'chenpfennig *m* counter

Re'chenschaft *f* (-;) account; **j-n zur R. ziehen** call s.o. to account

Re'chenschaftsbericht *m* report

Re'chenschieber *m* slide rule

rechnen ['reçnən] *tr* reckon, calculate, figure out ‖ *intr* reckon; calculate; **falsch r.** miscalculate; **r. auf** (*acc*) count on; **r. mit** be prepared for; expect; take into account; **r. zu** be counted among ‖ **Rechnen** *n* (-s;) arithmetic; calculation

Rech'ner *m* (-s;-) calculator, computer; **er ist ein guter R.** he is good at numbers

rechnerisch ['reçnərɪʃ] *adj* arithmetical

Rech'nung *f* (-;-en) calculation; account; bill; (*Warenrechnung*) invoice; (*im Restaurant*) check; **auf j-s R. setzen** (or **stellen**) charge to s.o.'s

account; **auf R. kaufen** buy on credit; **auf seine R. kaufen** get one's money's worth; **außer R. lassen** overlook; **das geht auf meine R.** this is on me; **die R. begleichen** settle an account (or bill); **j-m in R. stellen** charge to s.o.'s account; **in R. ziehen** take into account; **R. tragen** (*dat*) make allowance for

Rech'nungsabschluß *m* closing of accounts

Rech'nungsauszug *m* (com) statement

Rech'nungsführer -in §6 *mf* accountant

Rech'nungsführung *f* accounting

Rech'nungsjahr *n* fiscal year

Rech'nungsprüfer -in §6 *mf* auditor

Rech'nungswesen *n* accounting

recht [reçt] *adj* right; (*richtig*) correct; (*echt*) real; (*gerecht*) all right; right; (*geziemend*) suitable, proper; **es ist mir nicht r.** I don't like it; **es ist schon r.** that's all right; **mir soll's r. sein** I don't mind; **zur rechten Zeit** at the right moment ‖ *adv* right; quite; (*sehr*) very; **das kommt mir gerade r.** that comes in handy; **erst r.** all the more; **es j-m r. machen** please s.o.; **es geschieht ihm r.** it serves him right; **j-m r. geben** agree with s.o.; **nun erst r. nicht** now less than ever; **r. daran tun zu** (*inf*) do right to (*inf*); **r. haben** be right ‖ **Recht** *n* (-[e]s;-e) right; (*Vorrecht*) privilege; (jur) law; **alle Rechte vorbehalten** all rights reserved; **die Rechte studieren** study law; **mit R.** with good reason; **R. sprechen** dispense justice; **sich** [*dat*] **selbst R. verschaffen** take the law into one's hands; **von Rechts wegen** by rights; **wieder zu seinem Rechte kommen** come into one's own again; **zu R. bestehen** be justified ‖ **Rechte** §5 *mf* right person; **an den Rechten kommen** meet one's match; **du bist mir der R.!** you're a fine fellow! ‖ *f* right hand; (box) right; **die R.** (pol) the right ‖ *n* right; **er dünkt sich** [*dat*] **was Rechtes** he thinks he's somebody; **nach dem Rechten sehen** look after things

Recht'eck *n* rectangle, oblong

recht'eckig *adj* rectangular

recht'fertigen *tr* justify, vindicate

Recht'fertigung *f* (-;-en) justification

recht'gläubig *adj* orthodox

rechthaberisch ['reçthabərɪʃ] *adj* dogmatic

recht'lich *adj* legal, lawful; (*ehrlich*) honest, honorable

Recht'lichkeit *f* (-;) legality; (*Redlichkeit*) honesty

recht'los *adj* without rights

recht'mäßig *adj* legal; legitimate

Recht'mäßigkeit *f* (-;) legality; legitimacy

rechts [reçts] *adv* on the right; right, to the right

Rechts- *comb.fm.* legal

Rechts'angelegenheit *f* legal matter

Rechts'anspruch *m* legal claim

Rechts'anwalt *m* lawyer, attorney

Rechts'ausdruck *m* legal term
Rechts'auskunft *f* legal advice
Rechts'außen *m* (-;-) (fb) right wing
recht'schaffen *adj* honest
Recht'schaffenheit *f* (-;) honesty
Recht'schreibung *f* orthography
Rechts'fall *m* case, legal case
Rechts'gang *m* legal procedure
Rechts'gefühl sense of justice
Rechts'gelehrsamkeit *f* jurisprudence
Rechts'grund *m* legal grounds; (*Anspruch*) title, claim
rechts'gültig *adj* legal, valid
Rechts'gültigkeit *f* legality
Rechts'gutachten *n* legal opinion
Rechts'handel *m* lawsuit
rechtshändig ['reçtshɛndɪç] *adj* right-handed
rechts'herum *adv* clockwise
Rechts'kraft *f* legal force
rechts'kräftig *adj* valid
Rechts'lage *f* legal status
Rechts'lehre *f* jurisprudence
Rechts'mittel *n* legal remedy
Rechts'pflege *f* administration of justice
Recht'sprechung *f* (-;) administration of justice; **die R.** (coll) the judiciary
Rechts'schutz *m* legal protection
Rechts'spruch *m* verdict
Rechts'streit *m* legal dispute; pending case; difference of opinion in the interpretation of the law
rechtsum' *interj* (mil) right face!
rechts'ungültig *adj* illegal, invalid
rechts'verbindlich *adj* legally binding
Rechtsverdreher **-in** ['reçtsfɛrdreər(ɪn)] §6 *mf* pettifogger
Rechts'verletzung *f* (-;-en) violation of the law; infringement of another's rights
Rechts'weg *m* recourse to the law; **auf dem Rechtswege** by the courts; **den R. beschreiten** take legal action
Rechts'wissenschaft *f* jurisprudence
Reck [rek] *n* (-[e]s;-e) horizontal bar
recken ['rekən] *tr* stretch; **den Hals r.** crane one's neck
Redakteur [redak'tør] *m* (-s;-e) editor
Redaktion [redak'tsjon] *f* (-;-en) editorship; (*Arbeitskräfte*) editorial staff; (*Arbeitsraum*) editorial office
redaktionell [redaktsjo'nel] *adj* editorial
Redaktions'schluß *m* press time, deadline
Rede ['redə] *f* (-;-n) speech; (*Gespräch*) conversation; (*Gerücht*) rumor; **das ist nicht der R. wert** that is not worth mentioning; **davon kann keine R. sein** that's out of the question; **die in R. stehende Person** the person in question; **e-e R. halten** give a speech; **es geht die R., daß** it is rumored that; **gebundene R.** verse; **gehobene R.** lofty language; **j-m in die R. fallen** interrupt s.o.; **j-m R. und Antwort stehen** explain oneself to s.o.; **j-n zur R. stellen** take s.o. to task; **keine R.!** absolutely not!; **lose Reden führen** engage in loose talk; **ungebundene R.** prose

Re'defigur *f* figure of speech
Re'defluß *m* flow of words
Re'defreiheit *f* freedom of speech
Re'degabe *f* eloquence, fluency
re'degewandt *adj* fluent; (iron) glib
Re'degewandtheit *f* fluency, eloquence
Re'dekunst *f* eloquence
reden ['redən] *tr* speak, talk || **ref**— **mit sich r. lassen** listen to reason; **sich heiser r.** talk oneself hoarse; **von sich r. machen** cause a lot of talk || *intr* speak, talk; converse; **du hast gut r.!** it's easy for you to talk; **j-m ins Gewissen r.** appeal to s.o.'s conscience; **j-m nach dem Munde r.** humor s.o.; **mit j-m deutsch r.** (fig) talk turkey to s.o.
Re'densart *f* phrase, expression; idiom
Rederei [redə'raɪ] *f* (-;-en) empty talk
Re'deschwall *m* verbosity
Re'deteil *m* part of speech
Re'deweise *f* style of speaking
Re'dewendung *f* phrase, expression
redigieren [redi'girən] *tr* edit
redlich ['retlɪç] *adj* upright, honest || *adv*—**es r. meinen** mean well; **sich r. bemühen** make an honest effort
Red'lichkeit *f* (-;) honesty, integrity
Redner **-in** ['rednər(ɪn)] §6 *mf* speaker
Red'nerbühne *f* podium, platform
Red'nergabe *f* (gift of) eloquence
rednerisch ['rednərɪʃ] *adj* rhetorical
Redoute [re'dutə] *f* (-;-n) masquerade; (mil) redoubt
redselig ['retzelɪç] *adj* talkative
Reduktion [reduk'tsjon] *f* (-;-en) reduction
reduplizieren [redupli'tsirən] *tr* reduplicate
reduzieren [redu'tsirən] *tr* (**auf** *acc*) reduce (to)
Reede ['redə] *f* (-;-n) (naut) roadstead
Reeder ['redər] *m* (-s;-) shipowner
Reederei [redə'raɪ] *f* (-;-en) shipping company; shipping business
reell [re'el] *adj* honest; (*Preis*) fair; (*Geschäft*) sound || *adv*—**r. bedient werden** get one's money's worth
Reep [rep] *n* (-[e]s;-e) (naut) rope
Referat [refə'rat] *n* (-[e]s;-e) report; (*Vortrag*) paper; **ein R. halten** give a paper
Referendar [referen'dar] *m* (-s;-e) junior lawyer; in-service teacher
Referent **-in** [refe'rent(ɪn)] §7 *mf* reader of a paper; (*Berichterstatter*) reporter; (*Gutachter*) official adviser
Referenz [refe'rents] *f* (-;-en) reference; **j-n als R. angeben** give s.o. as a reference; **über gute Referenzen verfügen** have good references
referieren [refe'rirən] *intr* (**über** *acc*) give a report (on); (**über** *acc*) read a paper (on)
reffen ['refən] *tr* (naut) reef
reflektieren [reflek'tirən] *tr* reflect || *intr* reflect; **r. auf** (*acc*) reflect on; (com) think of buying
Reflek·tor [re'flektor] *m* (-s;-toren [-'torən]) reflector
Reflex [re'fleks] *m* (-es;-e) reflex
Reflex'bewegung *f* reflex action

Reflexion [rɛfle'ksjon] *f* (–;–en) reflection

reflexiv [rɛfle'ksif] *adj* reflexive

Reform [re'fɔrm] *f* (–;–en) reform

Reformation [reforma'tsjon] *f* (–;–en) reformation

Refor·mator [refor'mator] *m* (–s; [ma'toren]) reformer

Reform'haus *n* health-food store

reformieren [refor'miren] *tr* reform

Reform'kost *f* health food

Refrain [rə'frɛ̃] *m* (–s;–s) refrain; **den R. mitsingen** join in the refrain

Regal [re'gal] *n* (–s;–e) shelf

Regat·ta [re'gata] *f* (–;–ten [tən]) regatta

rege ['rege] *adj* brisk, lively

Regel ['regəl] *f* (–;–n) rule, regulation; (pathol) menstruation; **in der R. as a rule**

re'gellos *adj* irregular; disorderly

Re'gellosigkeit *f* (–;–en) irregularity

re'gelmäßig *adj* regular

Re'gelmäßigkeit *f* regularity

regeln ['regəln] *tr* regulate; arrange; control

re'gelrecht *adj* regular; downright

Re'gelung *f* (–;–en) regulation; control

re'gelwidrig *adj* against the rules; (sport) foul

regen ['regən] *tr* & *ref* move, stir ‖ **Regen** *m* (–s;–) rain; **vom R. unter die Traufe kommen** jump out of the frying pan into the fire

re'genarm *adj* rainless, dry

Re'genbö *f* rain squall

Re'genbogen *m* rainbow

Re'genbogenhaut *f* (anat) iris

re'gendicht *adj* rainproof

Re'genfall *m* rainfall

re'genfest *adj* rainproof

Re'genguß *m* downpour

Re'genhaut *f* oilskin coat

Re'genmantel *m* raincoat

Re'genmenge *f* amount of rainfall

Re'genmesser *m* rain gauge

Re'genpfeifer *m* (orn) plover

Re'genschauer *m* shower

Re'genschirm *m* umbrella

Regent –in [re'gent(ɪn)] §7 *mf* regent

Re'gentag *m* rainy day

Re'gentropfen *m* raindrop

Re'genumhang *m* cape

Re'genwetter *n* rainy weather

Re'genwurm *m* earthworm

Re'genzeit *f* rainy season

Re·gie [re'ʒi] *f* (–;–gien ['ʒi·ən]) management, administration; (com) state monopoly; (cin, theat) direction

Regie'assistent –in §7 *mf* (cin, theat) assistant director

Regie'pult *n* (rad) control console

Regie'raum *m* (rad) control room

regieren [re'girən] *tr* govern, rule; (gram) govern, take ‖ *intr* reign; (fig) predominate

Regie'rung *f* (–;–en) government, rule; administration; reign

Regie'rungsanleihe *f* government loan

Regie'rungsantritt *m* accession

Regie'rungsbeamte §5 *m* government official

Regie'rungssitz *m* seat of government

Regie'rungszeit *f* reign; administration

Regime [re'ʒim] *n* (–s;–s) regime

Regiment [regɪ'ment] *n* (–[e]s;–e) rule, government ‖ *n* (–[e]s;–er) (mil) regiment

Regiments– *comb.fm.* regimental

Regiments'kommandeur *m* regimental commander

Region [re'gjon] *f* (–;–en) region

regional [regjo'nal] *adj* regional

Regisseur [reʒɪ'sør] *m* (–s;–e) (cin, theat) director

Register [re'gɪstər] *n* (–s;–) file clerk; (*Inhaltsverzeichnis*) index; (*Orgel–*) stop

Regi·strator [regɪs'trator] *m* (–s; –stratoren [stra'toren]) registrar

Registratur [regɪstra'tur] *f* (–;–en) filing; filing cabinet

registrieren [regɪs'trirən] *tr* register; (*Betrag*) ring up

Registrier'kasse *f* cash register

Registrie'rung *f* (–;–en) registration

Reglement [reglə'mã] *n* (–s;–s) regulation(s), rule(s)

Regler ['reglər] *m* (–s;–) regulator; (mach) governor

reglos ['reklos] *adj* motionless

regnen ['regnən] *impers*—**es regnet** it is raining; **es regnet Bindfäden** it's raining cats and dogs; **es regnete Püffe** blows came thick and fast

regnerisch ['regnərɪʃ] *adj* rainy

Re·greß [re'gres] *m* (–gresses;–gresse) recourse, remedy; **R. nehmen zu** have recourse to

regsam ['rekzam] *adj* lively; quick

regulär [regu'ler] *adj* regular

regulierbar [regu'lirbar] *adj* adjustable

regulieren [regu'lirən] *tr* regulate; adjust

Regung ['regun] *f* (–;–en) motion, stirring; emotion; impulse

Reh [re] *n* (–[e]s;–e) deer

rehabilitieren [rehabɪlɪ'tirən] *tr* rehabilitate

Rehabilitie'rung *f* (–;–en) rehabilitation

Reh'bock *m* roebuck

Reh'braten *m* roast venison

Reh'kalb *n* fawn

Reh'keule *f* leg of venison

Rehkitz ['rekɪts] *n* (–es;–e) fawn

Reh'leder *n* doeskin

Reibahle ['raɪpalə] *f* (–;–n) reamer

Reibe ['raɪbə] *f* (–;–n) (coll) grater

Reibeisen ['raɪpaɪzən] *n* (culin) grater

reiben ['raɪbən] §62 *tr* rub; grate; grind ‖ *ref*—**sich r. an** (*dat*) take offense at ‖ *intr* rub

Reiberei ['raɪbə'raɪ] *f* (–;–en) (coll) friction, squabble

Rei'bung *f* (–;–en) friction

rei'bungslos *adj* frictionless; (fig) smooth

reich [raɪç] *adj* wealthy; (**an** *dat*) rich (in); (*Fang*) big; (*Phantasie*) fertile; (*Mahlzeit*) lavish ‖ **Reich** *n* (–[e]s; –e) empire, realm; kingdom

reichen ['raɪçən] *tr* reach; hand, pass ‖ *intr* reach, extend; do, manage; **das reicht!** that will do!

reich'haltig *adj* rich; abundant

reich'lich adj plentiful, abundant || adv pretty, fairly
Reichs'kanzlei f chancellery
Reichs'kanzler m chancellor
Reichs'mark f reichsmark
Reichs'tag m (hist) diet; (hist) Reichstag (lower house)
Reichtum ['raɪçtum] n (-s;ⁿer) riches
Reich'weite f reach, range
reif [raɪf] adj ripe; (fig) mature || **Reif** m (-[e]s;) frost
Reife ['raɪfə] f (-;) ripeness; (fig) maturity
reifen ['raɪfən] intr (SEIN) ripen; mature || impers—es reift there is frost || **Reifen** m (-s;-) tire; hoop
Rei'fendruckmesser m tire gauge
Rei'fenpanne f, **Rei'fenschaden** m flat tire, blowout
Rei'feprüfung f final examination (as prerequisite for entering university)
Rei'fezeugnis n high school diploma
reif'lich adj careful
Reigen ['raɪgən] m (-s;-) square dance
Reihe ['raɪ·ə] f (-;-n) row, string; set, series; rank, file; turn; **an der R. sein** be next; **an die R. kommen** get one's turn; **aus der R. tanzen** (fig) go one's own way; **die R. ist an mir** it's my turn; **nach der R.** in succession
reihen ['raɪ·ən] tr range, rank; (Perlen) string
Rei'hendorf n one-street village
Rei'henfabrikation f assembly-line production
Rei'henfolge f succession, sequence
Rei'henhaus n row house
Rei'henschaltung f (elec) series connection
reih'enweise adv in rows
Reiher ['raɪ·ər] m (-s;-) heron
Reim [raɪm] m (-[e]s;-e) rhyme
reimen ['raɪmən] tr (auf acc) make rhyme (with) || ref rhyme; (fig) make sense; (auf acc) rhyme (with) || intr rhyme
reim'los adj unrhymed, blank
rein [raɪn] adj pure; (sauber) clean; (klar) clear; (Gewinn) net; (Wahrheit) simple; (Wahnsinn) sheer, absolute; **etw ins reine bringen** clear up s.th.; **etw ins reine schreiben** write (or type) a final copy of s.th.; **mit j—m ins reine kommen** come to an understanding with s.o. || adv quite, downright; **r. alles** almost everything || **Rein** f (-;-en) pan
Reindl ['raɪndəl] n (-s;- & -n) pan
Rei'nemachen n (-s;) housecleaning
Rein'ertrag m clear profit
Rein'gewicht n net weight
Rein'gewinn m net profit
Rein'heit f (-;) purity; cleanness
reinigen ['raɪnɪgən] tr clean, cleanse; (fig) purify, refine
Rei'nigung f (-;-en) cleaning; purification; dry cleaning
Rei'nigungsanstalt f dry cleaner's
Rei'nigungsmittel n cleaning agent
Reinmachefrau ['raɪnmaxəfrau] f cleaning woman
Rein'schrift f final copy

reinweg ['raɪn'vɛk] adv (coll) flatly, absolutely
rein'wollen adj all-wool
Reis [raɪs] m (-es;) rice || n (-es;-er) twig; (fig) scion
Reis'brei m rice pudding
Reise ['raɪzə] f (-;-n) trip, tour; (aer) flight; (naut) voyage; **auf der R.** while traveling; **auf Reisen sein** be traveling
Rei'sebericht m travelogue
Rei'sebeschreibung f travel book
Rei'sebüro n travel agency
rei'sefertig adj ready to leave
Rei'seführer m guidebook
Rei'segefährte m, **Rei'segefährtin** f travel companion
Rei'segenehmigung f travel permit
Rei'segepäck n luggage; (rr) baggage
Rei'segesellschaft f tour operator(s); travel group
Rei'sehandbuch n guidebook
Rei'seleiter –in §6 mf courier, guide
rei'selustig adj fond of traveling
reisen ['raɪzən] intr (SEIN) travel
Reisende ['raɪzəndə] §5 mf traveler
Rei'sepaß m passport
Rei'seplan m itinerary
Rei'seprospekt m travel folder
Rei'seroute f itinerary
Rei'sescheck m traveler's check
Rei'seschreibmaschine f portable typewriter
Rei'sespesen pl travel expenses
Rei'setasche f overnight bag, flight bag
Rei'seziel n destination
Reisig ['raɪzɪç] n (-s;) brushwood
Rei'sigbündel n faggot
Reisige ['raɪzɪgə] §5 m cavalryman
Reißaus [raɪs'aus] n—**R. nehmen** (coll) take to one's heels
Reißbrett ['raɪsbret] n drawing board
reißen ['raɪsən] §53 tr tear, rip; (ziehen) pull, yank; (wegschnappen) wrest, snatch || intr tear; pull, tug; break, snap; (sich spalten) split, burst; **das reißt ins Geld** this is running into money; **mir reißt die Geduld** I am losing all patience || ref—an sich r. seize; (com) monopolize; **die Führung an sich r.** take the lead; **sich an e–m Nagel r.** scratch oneself on a nail; **sich um etw r.** scramble for s.th. || **Reißen** n (-s;) tearing; bursting; sharp pains; rheumatism
rei'ßend adj rapid; (Schmerz) sharp; (Tier) rapacious; **reißenden Absatz finden** (coll) sell like hotcakes
Reißer ['raɪsər] m (-s;-) bestseller; (cin) box-office hit; (com) good seller
Reißfeder ['raɪsfedər] f drawing pen
Reißleine ['raɪslaɪnə] f rip cord
Reißnagel ['raɪsnagəl] m thumbtack
Reißschiene ['raɪsʃinə] f T-square
Reißverschluß ['raɪsfer/lus] m zipper
Reißzahn ['raɪstsan] m canine tooth
Reißzeug ['raɪstsɔɪk] n mechanical-drawing tools
Reißzwecke ['raɪstsvekə] f thumbtack
Reit– [raɪt] comb.fm. riding
Reit'anzug m riding habit

Reit'bahn f riding ring

reiten ['raɪtən] §86 tr ride; **e-n Weg r.** ride along a road; **ihn reitet der Teufel** (coll) he is full of the devil; **krumme Touren r.** (coll) pull shady deals; **Prinzipien r.** (fig) stick rigidly to principles; **über den Haufen r.** knock down || intr (SEIN) go horseback riding; **geritten kommen** come on horseback; **vor Anker r.** ride at anchor

Rei'ter –in §6 mf rider

Rei'terstandbild n equestrian statue

Reit'gerte f riding crop

Reit'hose f riding breeches

Reit'knecht m groom

Reit'kunst f horsemanship

Reit'peitsche f riding crop

Reit'pferd n saddle horse

Reit'schule f riding academy

Reit'stiefel m riding boot

Reit'weg m bridle path

Reiz [raɪts] m (-es;-e) charm, appeal; (Erregung) irritation; (physiol, psychol) stimulus; **e-n R. ausüben auf** (acc) attract; **sie läßt ihre Reize spielen** she turns on the charm

reizbar ['raɪtsbar] adj irritable; (empfindlich) sensitive, touchy

reizen ['raɪtsən] tr (entzünden, ärgern) irritate; (locken) allure; (anziehen) attract; (anregen) excite, stimulate; (aufreizen) provoke; (Appetit) whet || intr (cards) bid || impers—**es reizt mich zu** (inf) I'm itching to (inf)

rei'zend adj charming; cute, sweet; (pathol) irritating

Reiz'entzug m sensory deprivation

Reiz'husten m (-s;) constant cough

reiz'los adj unattractive; (Kost) bland

Reiz'mittel n stimulant; (fig) incentive

Reiz'stoff m irritant

Rei'zung f (-;-en) irritation; (Lokkung) allurement; (Anregung) stimulation; (Aufreizung) provocation

reiz'voll adj charming, attractive; fascinating; (verlockend) tempting

rekeln ['rekəln] ref (coll) lounge

Reklamation [reklama'tsjon] f (-;-en) complaint, protest

Reklame [re'klamə] f (-;-n) advertisement, ad; publicity; **R. machen für** advertise

Rekla'mebüro n advertising agency

Rekla'mefeldzug m advertising campaign

reklamieren [rekla'mirən] tr claim || intr (gegen) protest (against); (wegen) complain (about)

rekognoszieren [rekɔs'tsirən] tr & intr reconnoiter

Rekonvaleszent –in [rekɔnvales'tsent (ɪn)] §7 mf convalescent

Rekonvaleszenz [rekɔnvales'tsents] f (-;) convalescence

Rekord [re'kɔrt] m (-[e]s;-e) record

Rekord'ernte f bumper crop, record crop

Rekordier –in [re'kɔrtlər(ɪn)] §6 mf (coll) record holder

Rekord'versuch m attempt to break the record

Rekrut [re'krut] m (-en;-en) recruit

Rekru'tenausbildung f basic training

Rekru'tenaushebung f recruitment

rekrutieren [rekru'tirən] tr recruit || ref—**sich r. aus** be recruited from

Rek·tor ['rektor] m (-s;-toren ['torən]) principal; (e-r Universität) president

Relais [rə'le] n (-lais ['le(s)];-lais ['les]) relay

relativ [rela'tif] adj relative

Relegation [relega'tsjon] f (-;-en) expulsion

relegieren [rele'girən] tr expel

Relief [re'ljef] n (-s;-s & -e) relief

Religion [reli'gjon] f (-;-en) religion

Religions'ausübung f practice of religion

Religions'bekenntnis n religious denomination

religiös [reli'gjøs] adj religious

Reling ['relɪŋ] f (-s;-s) (naut) rail

Reliquie [re'likvjə] f (-;-n) relic

Reli'quienschrein m reliquary

remis [rə'mi] adj (cards) tied || **Remis** n (-;-) (chess) tie, draw

remittieren [remɪ'tirən] tr (Geld) remit; (Waren) return || intr (Fieber) go down

rempeln ['rempəln] tr bump, jostle || intr (fb) block

Remter ['remtər] m (-s;-) refectory; assembly hall

Ren [ren] (-s;-e) reindeer

Renaissance [rənə'sãs] f (-;-n) renaissance

Rendite [ren'ditə] f (-;-n) return

Renn- [ren] comb.fm. race, racing

Renn'bahn f race track; (aut) speedway

Renn'boot n racing boat

rennen ['renən] §97 tr run; **j-m den Degen durch den Leib r.** run s.o. through with a sword; **über den Haufen r.** run over; **zu Boden r.** knock down || intr (SEIN) run; race || **Rennen** n (-s;-) running; race; (Einzelrennen) heat; **das R. machen** win the race; **totes R.** dead heat, tie

Ren'ner m (-s;-) (good) race horse

Renn'fahrer m (aut) race driver

Renn'pferd n race horse

Renn'platz m race track; (aut) speedway

Renn'rad n racing bicycle, racer

Renn'sport m racing

Renn'strecke f race track; distance (to be raced); (aut) speedway

Renn'wagen m racing car, racer

Renommee [reno'me] n (-s;-s) reputation

renommieren [reno'mirən] intr (mit) brag (about), boast (about)

renommiert' adj (wegen) renowned (for)

Renommist [reno'mɪst] m (-en;-en) braggart

renovieren [reno'virən] tr renovate; redecorate

rentabel [ren'tabəl] adj profitable

Rentabilität [rentabili'tet] f (-;-en) (e-r Investition) return; (fin) productiveness

Rente ['rɛntə] *f* (-;-n) income, revenue; pension; annuity
Ren'tenbrief *m* annuity bond
Ren'tenempfänger –in §6 *mf* pensioner
Rentier [ren'tje] *m* (-s;-s) person of independent means || ['rentir] *n* (-s;-s;) reindeer
rentieren [ren'tirən] *ref* pay
Rentner –in ['rɛntnər(ɪn)] §6 *mf* person on pension
Reparatur [repara'tur] *f* (-;-en) repair
Reparatur'werkstatt *f* repair shop; (aut) garage
reparieren [repa'rirən] *tr* repair, fix
Reportage [repɔr'taʒə] *f* (-;-n) report; coverage
Reporter –in [re'pɔrtər(ɪn)] §6 *mf* reporter
Repräsentant –in [reprezen'tant(ɪn)] §7 *mf* representative
repräsentieren [reprezen'tirən] *tr* represent || *intr* be a socialite
Repressalie [repre'saljə] *f* (-;-n) reprisal
Reprise [re'prizə] *f* (-;-n) (cin) rerun; (mus) repeat; (theat) revival
reproduzieren [reprodu'tsirən] *tr* reproduce
Reptil [rep'til] *n* (-s;-ien [jən] & –e) reptile
Republik [repu'blik] *f* (-;-en) republic
Republikaner –in [republɪ'kanər(ɪn)] §6 *mf* republican
republikanisch [republɪ'kanɪʃ] *adj* republican
Requisit [rekvɪ'zit] *n* (-[e]s;-en) requisite; **Requisiten** (theat) props
Reservat [rezer'vat] *n* (-[e]s;-e) reservation
Reserve [re'zervə] *f* (-;-n) reserve
Reser'vebank *f* (-;-e) (sport) bench
Reser'vereifen *m* spare tire
Reser'veteil *m* spare part
Reser'vetruppen *pl* (mil) reserves
reservieren [rezer'virən] *tr* reserve
Reservie'rung *f* (-;-en) reservation
Residenz [rezi'dents] *f* (-;-en) residence
Residenz'stadt *f* capital
residieren [rezi'dirən] *intr* reside
resignieren [rezig'nirən] *intr* resign
Respekt [re'spekt] *m* (-[e]s;)
respektabel [respek'tabəl] *adj* respectable
respektieren [respek'tirən] *tr* respect
respekt'los *adj* disrespectful
respekt'voll *adj* respectful
Ressort [re'sɔr] *n* (-s;-s) department
Rest [rest] *m* (-es;-e & -er) rest; (*Stoff*–) remnant; (*Zahlungs*–) balance; (*Bodensatz*) residue; (math) remainder; **irdische** (or **sterbliche**) **Reste** earthly (or mortal) remains; **j–m den R. geben** (coll) finish s.o. off
Rest'auflage *f* remainders
Restaurant [resto'rã] *n* (-s;-s) restaurant
Restauration [restaura'tsjon] *f* (-;-en) restoration; (Aust) restaurant
Rest'bestand *m* remainder
Rest'betrag *m* balance, remainder
Re'steverkauf *m* remnant sale

rest'lich *adj* remaining
rest'los *adj* complete
Resultat [rezul'tat] *n* (-[e]s;-e) result; upshot; (sport) score
retten ['retən] *tr* save, rescue
Ret'ter *m* (-s;-) rescuer; (*Heiland*) Savior
Rettich ['retɪç] *m* (-s;-e) radish
Ret'tung *f* (-;-en) rescue; salvation
Ret'tungsaktion *f* rescue operation
Ret'tungsboot *n* lifeboat
Ret'tungsfloß *n* life raft
Ret'tungsgürtel *m* life preserver
Ret'tungsleine *f* life line
ret'tungslos *adj* irretrievable
Ret'tungsmannschaft *f* rescue party
Ret'tungsring *m* life preserver
Ret'tungsstation *f* first-aid station
retuschieren [retu'ʃirən] *tr* retouch
Reue ['rɔɪə] *f* (-;) remorse
reu'elos *adj* remorseless, impenitent
reuen ['rɔɪən] *tr*—**die Tat reut mich** I regret having done it; **die Zeit reut mich** I regret wasting the time || *impers*—**es reut mich, daß I** regret that, I am sorry that
reu'evoll *adj* repentant, contrite
Reugeld ['rɔɪgelt] *n* forfeit
reumütig ['rɔɪmytɪç] *adj* repentant
Revanche [re'vãʃə] *f* (-;) revenge
Revan'chekrieg *m* punitive war
revan'chelustig *adj* vengeful
Revan'chepartie *f* (sport) return game
revanchieren [revã'ʃirən] *ref* (an *dat*) take revenge (on); **sich für e–en Dienst r.** return a favor
Revers [re'vers] *m* (-es;-e) (*e–r Münze*) reverse; (*Erklärung*) statement || (re'ver] *m* (Aust) & *n* (-;-) lapel; cuff
revidieren [revɪ'dirən] *tr* revise; (*nachprüfen*) check; (com) audit
Revier [re'vir] *n* (-s;-e) district; quarter; hunting ground; police station; (mil) sick quarters
Revier'stube *f* (mil) sickroom
Revision [revɪ'zjon] *f* (-;-en) revision; (com) audit; (jur) appeal
Re'visor [re'vizɔr] *m* (-s;-visoren [vɪ'zorən]) reviser; (com) auditor
Revolte [re'vɔltə] *f* (-;-n) revolt
revoltieren [revɔl'tirən] *intr* revolt
Revolution [revolu'tsjon] *f* (-;-en) revolution
revolutionär [revolutsjo'ner] *adj* revolutionary || **Revolutionär** –in §8 *mf* revolutionary
Revolver [re'vɔlvər] *m* (-s;-) revolver
Revol'verblatt *n* (coll) scandal sheet
Revol'verschnauze *f* (coll) lip, sass
Re-vue [re'vy] *f* (-;-vuen ['vy-ən]) review; (theat) revue
Rezensent –in [retsen'zent(ɪn)] §7 *mf* reviewer, critic
rezensieren [retsen'zirən] *tr* review
Rezension [retsen'zjon] *f* (-;-en) review
Rezept [re'tsept] *n* (-[e]s;-e) (culin) recipe; (med) prescription
rezitieren [retsɪ'tirən] *tr* recite
Rhabarber [ra'barbər] *m* (-s;) rhubarb
Rhapso-die [rapso'di] *f* (-;-dien ['di-ən]) rhapsody

Rhein [raɪn] *m* (-[e]s;) Rhine

Rhesusfaktor [ˈrezusˌfaktər] *m* (-s;) Rh factor

Rhetorik [reˈtoːrɪk] *f* (-;) rhetoric

rhetorisch [reˈtoːrɪʃ] *adj* rhetorical

rheumatisch [rɔɪˈmaːtɪʃ] *adj* rheumatic

Rheumatismus [rɔɪmaˈtɪsmus] *m* (-;) rheumatism

rhythmisch [ˈrʏtmɪʃ] *adj* rhythmical

Rhyth-mus [ˈrʏtmus] *m* (-;-men [mən]) rhythm

Richtbeil [ˈrɪçtbaɪl] *n* executioner's ax

Richtblei [ˈrɪçtblaɪ] *n* plummet

richten [ˈrɪçtən] *tr* arrange, adjust; put in order; (*lenken*) direct; (*Waffe, Fernrohr*) (auf *acc*) point (at), aim (at); (*Bitte, Brief, Frage, Rede*) (an *acc*) address (to); (*Augenmerk, Streben*) (auf *acc*) concentrate (on), focus (on); (*Bett*) make; (*Essen*) prepare; (*ausbessern*) fix; (*gerade biegen*) straighten; (*jur*) judge, sentence; (*mil*) dress; **zugrunde r.** ruin || *ref* (auf *acc*, gegen) be directed (at); **das richtet sich ganz danach, ob** it all depends on whether; **sich** [*dat*] **die Haare r.** do one's hair; **sich r. nach** follow the example of; **sich selbst r.** commit suicide || *intr* judge, sit in judgment

Rich'ter *m* (-s;-) judge

Rich'teramt *n* judgeship

Rich'terin *f* (-;-nen) judge

Rich'terkollegium *n* (jur) bench

rich'terlich *adj* judicial

Rich'terspruch *m* judgment; sentence

Rich'terstand *m* judiciary

Rich'terstuhl *m* tribunal, bench

richtig [ˈrɪçtɪç] *adj* right, correct; (*echt*) real, genuine; (*genau*) exact; (*Zeit*) proper || *adv* right, really, downright; **die Uhr geht r.** the clock keeps good time; **und r., da kam sie!** and sure enough, there she was!

rich'tiggehend *adj* (Uhr) keeping good time; (fig) regular

Rich'tigkeit *f* (-;) correctness; accuracy

rich'tigstellen *tr* rectify

Richtlinien [ˈrɪçtlinjən] *pl* guidelines

Richtlot [ˈrɪçtloːt] *n* plumbline

Richtmaß [ˈrɪçtmaːs] *n* standard, gauge

Richtplatz [ˈrɪçtplats] *m* place of execution

Richtpreis [ˈrɪçtpraɪs] *n* standard price

Richtschnur [ˈrɪçtˌnuːr] *f* plumbline; (fig) guiding principle

Richtschwert [ˈrɪçtˌvɛrt] *n* executioner's sword

Richtstätte [ˈrɪçtˌtɛtə] *f* place of execution

Rich'tung *f* (-;-en) direction; (*Weg*) course; (*Entwicklung*) trend; (*Einstellung*) slant, view

Rich'tungsanzeiger *m* (aut) direction signal

Richtwaage [ˈrɪçtˌvaːgə] *f* level

rieb [rip] *pret* of **reiben**

riechen [ˈriçən] §102 *tr* smell; (fig) stand; **kein Pulver r. können** have no guts || *intr* smell; **r. an** (*dat*) sniff at; **r. nach** smell of

Riechsalz [ˈriçzalts] *n* smelling salts

rief [rif] *pret* of **rufen**

Riefe [ˈrifə] *f* (-;-n) groove; (archit) flute

Riege [ˈrigə] *f* (-;-n) (gym) squad

Riegel [ˈrigəl] *m* (-s;-) bolt; (*Seife*) cake; (*Schokolade*) bar

riegeln [ˈrigəln] *tr* bolt, bar

Riemen [ˈrimən] *m* (-s;-) strap; (*Leib-, Trieb-*) belt; (*Ruder*) oar; (*e-s Gewehrs*) sling

Rie'menscheibe *f* pulley

Ries [ris] *n* (-es;-e) ream (*of one thousand sheets*)

Riese [ˈrizə] *m* (-;-n) giant

rieseln [ˈrizəln] *intr* (HABEN & SEIN) trickle; (*Bach*) purl || *impers*—**es rieselt** it is drizzling

Rie'selregen *m* drizzle

Rie'senbomber *m* superbomber

Rie'senerfolg *m* smash hit

rie'sengroß *adj* gigantic

rie'senhaft *adj* gigantic

Rie'senrad *n* Ferris wheel

Rie'senschlange *f* boa constrictor

Rie'sentanne *f* (bot) sequoia

riesig [ˈrizɪç] *adj* gigantic, huge || *adv* (coll) awfully

Riesin [ˈrizɪn] *f* (-;-nen) giant

riet [rit] *pret* of **raten**

Riff [rɪf] *n* (-[e]s;-e) reef

Rille [ˈrilə] *f* (-;-n) groove; small furrow; (archit) flute

Rimesse [rɪˈmɛsə] *f* (-;-n) (com) remittance

Rind [rɪnt] *n* (-[e]s;-er) head of cattle; **Rinder** cattle

Rinde [ˈrɪndə] *f* (-;-n) rind; (*Baum-*) bark; (*Brot-*) crust; (anat) cortex

Rin'derbraten *m* roast beef

Rin'derbremse *f* horsefly

Rin'derherde *f* herd of cattle

Rin'derhirt *m* cowboy

Rind'fleisch *n* beef

Rinds'leder *n* cowhide

Rinds'lendenstück *n* rump steak, tenderloin

Rinds'rückenstück *n* sirloin of beef

Rind'vieh *n* cattle; (sl) idiot

Ring [rɪŋ] *m* (-[e]s;-e) ring; (*Kreis*) circle; (*Kettenglied*) link; (*Kartell*) combine; (astr) halo

Ringel [ˈrɪŋəl] *m* (-s;) small ring; (*Locke*) ringlet, curl

Rin'gelblume *f* marigold

ringeln [ˈrɪŋəln] *tr* & *ref* curl

Rin'gelreihen *m* ring-around-the-rosy

Rin'gelspiel *n* merry-go-round

ringen [ˈrɪŋən] §142 *tr* wrestle; (*Wäsche, Hände*) wring; (*herauswinden*) wrest || *intr* wrestle; (fig) struggle

Rin'ger –in §6 *mf* wrestler

Ring'kampf *m* wrestling match

Ring'mauer *f* town wall, city wall

Ring'richter *m* (box) referee

rings [rɪŋs] *adv* around; **r. um** all around

Ring'schlüssel *m* socket wrench

rings'herum', rings'um', rings'umher' *adv* all around

Rinne [ˈrinə] *f* (-;-n) groove; (*Strombett*) channel; (*Leitung*) duct; (*Gosse*) gutter; (*Erdfurche*) furrow

rinnen ['rɪnən] §121 *intr* (SEIN) run, flow; trickle || *intr* (HABEN) leak

Rinnsal ['rɪnzal] *n* (-[e]s;-e) little stream

Rinn'stein *m* gutter; *(Ausgußbecken)* sink; *(unterirdisch)* culvert

Rippchen ['rɪpçən] *n* (-s;-) cutlet

Rippe ['rɪpə] *f* (-;-n) rib; *(Schokolade)* bar; (archit) groin

rippen ['rɪpən] *tr* rib, flute

Rip'penfellentzündung *f* pleurisy

Rip'penstoß *m* nudge (in the ribs)

Rip'penstück *n* loin end

Risi-ko ['riziko] *n* (-s;-s & -ken [kən]) risk; **ein R. eingehen** take a risk

riskant [rɪs'kant] *adj* risky

riskieren [rɪs'kirən] *tr* risk

riß [rɪs] *pret of* **reißen** || **Riß** *m* (Risses; Risse) tear, rip; *(Bruch)* fracture; *(Lücke)* gap; *(Kratzer)* scratch; *(Spalt)* split, cleft; *(Spaltung)* fissure; *(Sprung)* crack; *(Zeichnung)* sketch; (eccl) schism; (geol) crevasse

rissig ['rɪsɪç] *adj* torn; cracked; split; *(Haut)* chapped

Rist [rɪst] *m* (-es;-e) wrist; *(des Fußes)* instep

ritt [rɪt] *pret of* **reiten** || **Ritt** *m* (-[e]s; -e) ride

Ritter ['rɪtər] *m* (-s;-) knight; cavalier; **zum R. schlagen** knight

Rit'tergut *n* manor

Rit'terkreuz *n* (mil) Knight's Cross (of the Iron Cross)

rit'terlich *adj* knightly; (fig) chivalrous

Rit'terlichkeit *f* (-;) chivalry

Rit'terzeit *f* age of chivalry

rittlings ['rɪtlɪŋs] *adv*—**r. auf** (dat or acc) astride

Ritual [ritu'al] *n* (-s;-e & -ien [jən]) ritual

rituell [rɪtu'ɛl] *adj* ritual

Ri-tus ['ritus] *m* (-;-ten [tən]) rite

Ritz [rɪts] *m* (-es;-e), **Ritze** ['rɪtsə] *f* (-;-en) crack, crevice; *(Schlitz)* slit; *(Schramme)* scratch

ritzen ['rɪtsən] *tr* scratch; *(Glas)* cut

Rivale [ri'valə] *m* (-n;-n), **Rivalin** [ri'valɪn] *f* (-;-nen) rival

rivalisieren [rivali'zirən] *intr* be in rivalry; **r. mit** rival

Rivalität [rivali'tɛt] *f* (-;-en) rivalry

Rizinusöl ['ritsinusøl] *n* castor oil

Robbe ['rɔbə] *f* (-;-n) seal

robben ['rɔbən] *intr* (HABEN & SEIN) (mil) crawl *(using one's elbows)*

Rob'benfang *m* seal hunt

Robe ['robə] *f* (-;-n) robe, gown

Roboter ['robotər] *m* (-s;-) robot

robust [ro'bust] *adj* robust

roch [rɔx] *pret of* **riechen**

röcheln ['rœçəln] *tr* gasp out || *intr* rattle *(in one's throat)*

rochieren [rɔ'ʃirən] *intr* (chess) castle

Rock [rɔk] *m* (-[e]s;-e) skirt; jacket

Rock'schoß *m* coattail

Rodel ['rodəl] *m* (-s;-) & *f* (-;-n) toboggan; *(mit Steuerung)* bobsled

Ro'delbahn *f* toboggan slide

rodeln ['rodəln] *intr* (HABEN & SEIN) toboggan

Ro'delschlitten *m* toboggan; bobsled

roden ['rodən] *tr* root out; *(Wald)* clear; *(Land)* make arable

Rogen ['rogən] *m* (-s;) roe, spawn

Roggen ['rɔgən] *m* (-s;) rye

roh [ro] *adj* raw; crude; *(Steine)* unhewn; *(Dielen)* bare; (fig) uncouth, brutal

Roh'bau *m* (-[e]s;-ten) rough brickwork

Roh'diamant *m* uncut diamond

Roh'einnahme *f* gross receipts

Roh'eisen *n* pig iron

Ro'heit *f* (-;) rawness, raw state; crudeness; brutality

Roh'entwurf *m* rough sketch

Roh'gewicht *n* gross weight

Roh'gewinn *m* gross profit

Roh'gummi *m* crude rubber

Roh'haut *f* rawhide

Roh'kost *f* uncooked vegetarian food

Rohling ['rolɪŋ] *m* (-s;-e) blank; slug; (fig) thug, hoodlum

Roh'material *n* raw material

Roh'öl *n* crude oil

Rohr [ror] *n* (-[e]s;-e) reed, cane; *(Röhre)* pipe, tube; *(Kanal)* duct, channel; *(Gewehrlauf)* barrel

Rohr'anschluß *m* pipe joint

Rohr'bogen *m* pipe elbow

Röhre ['rørə] *f* (-;-n) tube, pipe; (electron) tube

Röh'renblitz *m* electronic flash

Röh'renblitzgerät *n* electronic flash unit

Rohr'leger *m* pipe fitter

Rohr'leitung *f* pipeline, main

Rohr'schäftung *f* sleeve joint

Rohr'schelle *f* pipe clamp

Rohr'zange *f* pipe wrench

Rohr'zucker *m* cane sugar

Roh'stoff *m* raw material

Rolladen (**Roll'laden**) *m* sliding shutter; sliding cover

Rollbahn ['rɔlban] *f* (aer) runway; (mil) road leading up to the front

Röllchen ['rœlçən] *n* (-s;-) caster

Rolldach ['rɔldax] *n* (aut) sun roof

Rolle ['rɔlə] *f* (-;-n) roll; *(Walze)* roller; *(Flaschenzug)* pulley; *(Spule)* spool, reel; *(unter Möbeln)* caster; *(Mangel)* mangle; *(Liste)* list, register; (theat) role; **aus der R. fallen** (fig) misbehave; **spielt keine R.!** never mind!, forget it!

rollen ['rɔlən] *tr* roll; *(auf Rädern)* wheel; *(Wäsche)* mangle; || *ref* curl up || *intr* (HABEN & SEIN) roll; *(Flugzeug)* taxi; *(Geschütze)* roar || **Rollen** *n*—**ins. R. kommen** get going

Rol'lenbesetzung *f* (theat) cast

Rol'lenlager *n* roller bearing

Rol'lenzug *m* block and tackle

Rol'ler *m* (-s;-) scooter; motor scooter

Roll'feld *n* (aer) runway

Roll'kragen *m* turtleneck

Roll'mops *m* pickled herring

Rollo ['rolo] *n* (-s;-s) (coll) blind, shade

Roll'schuh *m* roller skate; **R. laufen** roller-skate

Roll'schuhbahn *f* roller-skating rink

Roll'stuhl *m* wheelchair

Roll'treppe *f* escalator

Roll'wagen *m* truck
Rom [rom] *n* (-s;) Rome
Roman [ro'man] *m* (-s;-e) novel
Roman'folge *f* serial
roman'haft *adj* fictional
romanisch [ro'manıʃ] *adj* (*Sprache*) Romance; (*archit*) Romanesque
Romanist —in [roma'nıst(ın)] §7 *mf* scholar of Romance languages
Roman'schriftsteller —in §6 *mf* novelist
Romantik [ro'mantık] *f* (-;) Romanticism
romantisch [ro'mantıʃ] *adj* romantic
Romanze [ro'mantsə] (-;-n) romance
Römer —in ['rø̞mər(ın)] §6 *mf* Roman
römisch ['rø̞mıʃ] *adj* Roman
rö'misch-katho'lisch *adj* Roman Catholic
röntgen ['rœntgən] *tr* x-ray
Rönt'ansicht *f* rear view
Rönt'genapparat *m* x-ray machine
Rönt'genarzt *m*, Rönt'genärztin *f* radiologist
Rönt'genaufnahme *f*, Rönt'genbild *n* x-ray
Rönt'genstrahlen *pl* x-rays
rosa ['roza] *adj* pink ‖ Rosa *n* (-s; & -s) pink
Rose ['rozə] *f* (-;-n) rose
Ro'senkohl *m* Brussels sprouts
Ro'senkranz *m* (eccl) rosary
ro'senrot *adj* rosy, rose-colored
ro'senstock *m* rosebush
rosig ['rozıç] *adj* (& fig) rosy; (*Laune*) happy
Rosine [ro'zinə] *f* (-;-n) raisin
Roß [ros] *n* (Rosses; Rosse) horse; (sl) jerk; (poet) steed
Rost [rost] *m* (-es;) rust; mildew ‖ (-es;-e) grate; grill; auf dem R. braten grill
Rost'braten *m* roast beef
Röstbrot ['rø̞stbrot] *n* toast
rosten ['rostən] *intr* rust
rösten ['rø̞stən] *tr* (*auf dem Rost*) grill; (*in der Pfanne*) roast; (*Brot*) toast; (*Mais*) pop; (*Kaffee*) roast
Rö'ster *m* (-s;-) roaster; toaster
Rost'fleck *m* rust stain
rost'frei *adj* rust-proof; (*Stahl*) stainless
rosig ['rostıç] *adj* rusty, corroded
rot [rot] *adj* (röter ['rø̞tər]; röteste ['rø̞təstə]) §9 red ‖ Rot *n* (-es;) red; (*Schminke*) rouge
Rotation [rota'tsjon] *f* (-;-en) rotation
Rotations'maschine *f* rotary press
rotbäckig ['rotbekıç] *adj* red-cheeked
Rot'dorn *m* (bot) pink hawthorn
Röte ['rø̞tə] *f* (-;) red(ness); blush
Röteln ['rø̞təln] *pl* German measles
rotieren [ro'tirən] *intr* rotate
Rotkäppchen ['rotkepçən] *n* (-s;) Little Red Riding Hood
Rotkehlchen ['rotkelçən] *n* (-s;-) robin
rötlich ['rø̞tlıç] *adj* reddish
Ro·tor ['rotor] *m* (-s;-toren ['torən]) (aer) rotor; (elec) armature
Rot'schimmel *m* roan (horse)
Rot'tanne *f* spruce
Rotte ['rotə] *f* (-;-n) gang, mob
Rotz [rots] *m* (-es;-e) (sl) snot
rot'zig *adj* (sl) snotty

Rouleau [ru'lo] *n* (-s;-s) window shade
Route ['rutə] *f* (-;-n) route
Routine [ru'tinə] *f* (-;) routine; practice, experience
routiniert [ruti'nirt] *adj* experienced
Rübe ['rybə] *f* (-;-n) beet; gelbe R. carrot; weiße R. turnip
Rubin [ru'bin] *m* (-s;-e) ruby
Rubrik [ru'brik] *f* (-;-en) rubric; heading; (*Spalte*) column
ruchbar ['ruxbar] *adj* known, public
ruchlos ['ruxlos] *adj* wicked
Ruck [ruk] *m* (-[e]s;-e) jerk; yank; jolt; auf e-n R. at once; mit e-m R. in one quick move
Rück-, rück- [ryk] *comb.fm.* re-, back, rear; return
Rück'antwort *f* reply; Postkarte mit R. prepaid reply postcard
rück'bezüglich *adj* (gram) reflexive
Rück'bleibsel *n* remainder
rücken ['rykən] *tr* move, shove ‖ *intr* (SEIN) move; (*Platz machen*) move over; (*marschieren*) march; höher r. be promoted; näher r. approach ‖ Rücken *m* (-s;-) back; (*Rückseite*) rear; (*der Nase*) bridge
Rückendeckung (Rük'kendeckung) *f* (fig) backing, support
Rückenlehne (Rük'kenlehne) *f* back rest
Rückenmark (Rük'kenmark) *n* spinal cord
Rückenschwimmen (Rük'kenschwimmen) *n* backstroke
Rückenwind (Rük'kenwind) *m* tail wind
Rückenwirbel (Rük'kenwirbel) *m* (anat) vertebra
rück'erstatten *tr* reimburse, refund
Rück'fahrkarte *f*, Rück'fahrschein *m* round-trip ticket
Rück'fahrt *f* return trip
Rück'fall *m* relapse
rück'fällig *adj* habitual, relapsing
rück'federnd *adj* resilient
Rück'flug *m* return flight
Rück'frage *f* further question
Rück'führung *f* repatriation
Rück'gabe *f* return, restitution
Rück'gang *m* return; regression; (*der Preise*) drop; (econ) recession
rückgängig ['rykgeŋıç] *adj* retrogressive; dropping; r. machen cancel
rück'gewinnen §121 *tr* recover
Rück'grat *n* backbone, spine
Rück'griff *m* (auf *acc*) recourse (to)
Rück'halt *m* backing; (mil) reserves; e-n R. an j—m haben have s.o.'s backing; ohne R. without reservation
rück'haltlos *adj* frank, unreserved ‖ *adv* without reserve
Rück'handschlag *m* (tennis) back-hand stroke
Rück'kauf *m* repurchase
Rück'kehr *f* return; (fig) comeback
Rück'kopplung *f* (electron) feedback
Rück'lage *f* reserves, savings
Rück'lauf *m* reverse; (mil) recoil
Rück'läufer *m* letter returned to sender
rückläufig ['rykloıfıç] *adj* retrograde

Rück'licht n (aut) taillight
rücklings ['rʏklɪŋs] adv backwards
Rück'nahme f withdrawal, taking back
Rück'porto n return postage
Rück'prall m bounce, rebound, recoil
Rück'reise f return trip
Ruck'sack m knapsack
Rück'schau m—**R. halten auf** (acc) look back on
Rück'schlag m back stroke; (e-s Balles) bounce; (fig) setback
Rück'schluß m conclusion, inference
Rück'schritt m backward step; (fig) falling off, retrogression
Rück'seite f back; reverse; wrong side
Rück'sicht f regard, respect, consideration; **aus R. auf** (acc) out of consideration for; **in** (or **mit**) **R. auf** (acc) in regard to; **ohne R. auf** (acc) irrespective of; **R. nehmen auf** (acc) take into account, show consideration for
rück'sichtlich prep (genit) considering
rück'sichtslos adj inconsiderate; reckless; ruthless
rück'sichtsvoll adj considerate
Rück'sitz m (aut) rear seat
Rück'spiegel m (aut) rear-view mirror
Rück'spiel n return match
Rück'sprache f discussion; conference; **R. nehmen mit** consult with
Rück'stand m arrears; (Satz) sediment; (Rest) remainder; (von Aufträgen, usw.) backlog; (chem) residue
rück'ständig adj behind, in arrears; (Geld) outstanding; (Raten) delinquent; (altmodisch) backward
Rück'stau m back-up water
Rück'stelltaste f backspace key
Rück'stoß m repulsion; recoil, kick
Rückstrahler ['rʏkʃtrɑːlər] m (-s;-) reflector
Rück'strahlung f reflection
Rück'tritt m resignation
Rück'trittbremse f coaster brake
Rück'umschlag m return envelope
rückwärts ['rʏkvɛrts] adv backward(s)
Rück'wärtsgang m (aut) reverse
Rück'weg m way back, return
ruck'weise adv by fits and starts
rück'wirken intr react
rück'wirkend adj retroactive
Rück'wirkung f (-;-en) reaction; repercussion
rück'zahlen tr repay, refund
Rück'zug m withdrawal; retreat; **zum R. blasen** sound the retreat
Rück'zugsgefecht n running fight
rüde ['rʏdə] adj rude, coarse ‖ **Rüde** m (-n;-n) male (wolf, fox, etc.)
Rudel ['ruːdəl] n (-s;-) herd; flock; (von Wölfen, U-Booten) wolf pack
Ruder ['ruːdər] n (-s;-) (aer, naut) rudder; (naut) oar
Ru'derblatt n blade of an oar
Ru'derboot n rowboat
Ru'derer –in §6 mf rower
Ru'derklampe f oarlock
rudern ['ruːdərn] tr & intr row
Ru'derschlag m stroke of the oar
Ru'dersport m (sport) crew
Ruf [ruːf] m (-[e]s;-e) call; shout, yell; (Berufung) vocation; (Nach-

rede) reputation; appointment; (com) credit
rufen ['ruːfən] §122 tr call; shout; **r. lassen** send for ‖ intr call; shout
Ruf'mord m character assassination
Ruf'name m first name
Ruf'nummer f telephone number
Ruf'weite f—**in R.** within earshot
Ruf'zeichen n (rad) station identification; (telp) call sign
Rüge f ['ryːgə] f (-;-n) reprimand
rügen ['ryːgən] tr reprimand
Ruhe f ['ruːə] f (-;) rest; quiet, calm; (Frieden) peace; (Stille) silence; **immer mit der R.!** (coll) take it easy!
ru'hebedürftig adj in need of rest
Ru'hegehalt n pension
Ru'hekur f rest cure
ru'helos adj restless
ruhen ['ruːən] intr rest; sleep
Ru'hepause f pause, break
Ru'heplatz m resting place
Ru'hestand m retirement
Rü'hestätte f resting place
Ru'hestörer –in §6 mf disturber of the peace
Ru'hetag m day of rest, day off
Ru'hezeit f leisure
ruhig ['ruːɪç] adj still, quiet; calm
Ruhm [ruːm] m (-[e]s;) glory, fame
rühmen ['ryːmən] tr praise ‖ ref (genit) boast (about)
rühmlich ['ryːmlɪç] adj praiseworthy
ruhm'los adj inglorious
ruhmredig ['ruːmreːdɪç] adj vainglorious
ruhm'reich adj glorious
ruhm'voll adj famous, glorious
ruhm'würdig adj praiseworthy
Ruhr [ruːr] f (-;) dysentery; **Ruhr** (river)
Rührei ['ryːraɪ] n scrambled egg
rühren ['ryːrən] tr stir; touch, move; (Trommel) beat; **alle Kräfte r.** exert every effort ‖ ref stir, move; get a move on; **rührt euch!** (mil) at ease! ‖ intr stir, move; **r. an** (acc) touch; (fig) mention; **r. von** originate in
rührig ['ryːrɪç] adj active; agile
Rührlöffel ['ryːrlœfəl] m ladle
rührselig ['ryːrzeːlɪç] adj sentimental
Rührstück ['ryːrʃtʏk] n soap opera
Rüh'rung f (-;-en) emotion
Ruin [ruˈiːn] m (-s;) ruin; decay
Ruine [ruˈiːnə] f (-;-n) ruins; (fig) wreck
rui'nenhaft adj ruinous
ruinieren [ruˑiˈniːrən] tr ruin
Rülps [rʏlps] m (-es;-e) belch
rülpsen ['rʏlpsən] intr belch
Rülp'ser m (-s;-) belch
Rum [ruːm] m (-s;-s) rum
Rumäne [ruˈmɛnə] m (-n;-n) Rumanian
Rumänien [ruˈmɛnjən] n (-s;) Rumania
Rumänin [ruˈmɛnɪn] f (-;-nen) Rumanian
rumänisch [ruˈmɛnɪʃ] adj Rumanian
Rummel ['rʊməl] m (-s;) junk; racket; hustle and bustle; **auf den R. gehen** go to the fair; **den ganzen R. kaufen** (coll) buy the works
Rum'melplatz m amusement park, fair
Rumor [rʊˈmoːr] m (-s;) noise, racket

Rumpel ['rumpəl] f (-;-n) scrub board

Rum'pelkammer f storage room, junk room

Rum'pelkasten m (aut) jalopy

rumpeln ['rumpəln] tr (Wäsche) scrub || intr rumble, rattle

Rumpf [rumpf] m (-[e]s;ⁿe) trunk, body; torso; (aer) fuselage; (naut) hull

rümpfen ['rʏmpfən] tr—die Nase r. über (acc) turn up one's nose at

rund [runt] adj round; (Absage) flat || adv around; about, approximately; r. um around

Rund'blick m panorama

Rund'brief m circular letter

Runde ['rundə] f (-;-n) round; (box) round; (beim Rennsport) lap

runden ['rundən] tr make round; round off || ref become round

Rund'erlaß m circular

rund'erneuern tr (aut) retread; runderneuerter Reifen m retread

Rund'fahrt f sightseeing tour

Rund'flug m (aer) circuit

Rund'frage f questionnaire, poll

Rund'funk m radio; im R. on the radio

Rund'funkansage f radio announcement

Rund'funkansager –in §6 mf radio announcer

Rund'funkgerät n radio set

Rund'funkgesellschaft f broadcasting company

Rund'funkhörer –in §6 mf listener

Rund'funknetz n radio network

Rund'funksender m broadcasting station

Rund'funksendung f radio broadcast

Rund'funksprecher –in §6 mf announcer

Rund'funkwerbung f (rad) commercial

Rund'gang m tour; stroll

rund'heraus' adv plainly, flatly

rundherum' adv all around

rund'lich adj round; (dick) plump

Rund'reise f sightseeing tour

Rund'schau f panorama; (journ) news in brief

Rund'schreiben n circular letter

rundweg ['runt'vek] adv bluntly, flatly

Runzel ['runtsəl] f (-;-n) wrinkle

runzelig ['runtseliç] adj wrinkled

runzeln ['runtsəln] tr wrinkle; die Brauen r. knit one's brows; die Stirn r. frown || ref wrinkle

Rüpel ['rʏpəl] m (-s;-) boor

rü'pelhaft adj rude, boorish

rupfen ['rupfən] tr pluck; (fig) fleece

ruppig ['rupiç] adj shabby; (fig) rude

Ruprecht ['rupreçt] m (-s;)—Knecht R. Santa Claus

Ruß [rus] m (-es;) soot

Russe ['rusə] m (-n;-n) Russian

Rüssel ['rʏsəl] m (-s;-) snout; (Elephanten-) trunk; (coll) snout; (ent) proboscis

rußig ['rusiç] adj sooty

Russin ['rusin] f (-;-nen) Russian

russisch ['rusi/] adj Russian

Rußland ['ruslant] n (-s;) Russia

Rüst- [rʏst] comb.fm. scaffolding; armament, munition

rüsten ['rʏstən] tr arm, equip; prepare || ref get ready || intr (zu) get ready (for); zum Krieg r. mobilize

Rüster ['rʏstər] f (-;-n) elm

rüstig ['rʏstiç] adj vigorous; alert

Rüst'kammer f armory, arsenal

Rü'stung f (-;-en) preparation; equipment; armament; mobilization; armor; implements; (archit) scaffolding

Rü'stungsbetrieb m munitions factory

Rü'stungsfertigung f war production

Rü'stungsindustrie f war industry

Rü'stungskontrolle f arms control

Rü'stungsmaterial n war materiel

Rü'stungsstand m state of preparedness

Rüst'zeug n kit; (fig) knowledge

Rute ['rutə] f (-;-n) rod; twig; tail; (anat) penis

Rutsch [rut/] m (-es;-e) slip, slide

Rutsch'bahn f slide; chute

Rutsche ['rutə] f (-;-n) slide; chute

rutschen ['rut/ən] intr (SEIN) slip, slide; (aut) skid

rutschig ['rut/iç] adj slippery

rütteln ['rʏtəln] tr shake; jolt; (Getreide) winnow; (aus dem Schlafe) rouse || intr—r. an (acc) cause to rattle; (fig) try to undermine

S

S, s [es] invar n S, s

SA abbr (mil) (Sturmabteilung) storm troopers

Saal [zal] m (-[e]s; Säle ['zelə]) hall

Saat [zat] f (-;-en) seed; (Säen) sowing; (Getreide auf dem Halm) crop(s); die S. bestellen sow

Saat'bestellung f sowing

Saat'kartoffel f seed potato

Sabbat ['zabat] m (-s;-e) Sabbath

Sabberei [zabə'rar] f (-;-en) drooling; (Geschwätz) drivel

sabbern ['zabərn] intr drool, drivel

Säbel ['zebəl] m (-s;) saber; mit dem S. rasseln (pol) rattle the saber

säbeln ['zebəln] tr (coll) hack

Sä'belbeinig adj bowlegged

Sä'belrasseln n (pol) saber rattling

Sabotage [zabo'taʒə] f (-;-n) sabotage

Saboteur [zabo'tør] m (-s;-e) saboteur

sabotieren [zabo'tirən] tr sabotage

Saccharin [zaxa'rin] n (-s;) ·saccharin

Sach- [zax] comb.fm. of facts, factual

Sach'anlagevermögen n tangible fixed assets

Sach'bearbeiter –in §6 mf specialist

Sach′beschädigung f property damage
Sach′bezüge pl compensation in kind
Sach′buch n nonfiction (work)
Sach′darstellung f statement of facts
sach′dienlich adj relevant, pertinent
Sache [ˈzaxə] f (–;–n) thing, matter; cause; (jur) case; **bei der S. sein** be on the ball; **beschlossene S.** foregone conclusion; **die S. der Freiheit** the cause of freedom; **große S.** big affair; **gute S.** good cause; **heikle S.** delicate point; **in eigner S.** on one's own behalf; **in Sachen X gegen Y** (jur) in the case of X versus Y; **meine sieben Sachen** all my belongings; **nicht bei der S. sein** not be with it; **nicht zur S. gehörig** irrelevant; **von der S. abkommen** get off the subject; **zur S.!** come to the point! (parl) question!
sach′gemäß adj proper, pertinent ‖ adv in a suitable manner
Sach′kenner –in §6 mf expert
Sach′kenntnis f, **Sach′kunde** f expertise
sach′kundig adj expert ‖ **Sach′kundige** §5 mf expert
Sach′lage f state of affairs, circumstances
Sach′leistung f payment in kind
sach′lich adj (treffend) to the point; (gegenständlich) objective; (tatsächlich) factual; (unparteiisch) impartial; (nüchtern) matter-of-fact ‖ adv to the point
sächlich [ˈzɛçlɪç] adj (gram) neuter
Sach′lichkeit f (–;) objectivity; reality; impartiality; matter-of-factness
Sach′register n index
Sach′schaden m property damage
Sach′schadenersatz m indemnity (for property damage)
Sachse [ˈzaksə] m (–n;–n) Saxon
Sachsen [ˈzaksən] n (–s;) Saxony
sächsisch [ˈzɛksɪʃ] adj Saxon
sacht(e) [ˈzaxt(ə)] adj soft, gentle; (langsam) slow ‖ adv gingerly; **immer sacht!** easy does it!
Sach′verhalt m facts of the case
Sach′vermögen n real property
sach′verständig adj experienced ‖ **Sachverständige** §5 mf expert
Sach′wert m actual value; **Sachwerte** material assets
Sach′wörterbuch n encyclopedia
Sack [zak] m (–[e]s;–̈e) sack, bag; pocket; **j–n in den S. stecken** (coll) be way above s.o.; **mit S. und Pack** bag and baggage
Säckel [ˈzɛkəl] m (–s;–) little bag; pocket; purse
sacken [ˈzakən] tr bag ‖ ref be baggy ‖ intr (SEIN) sag; (archit) settle; (naut) founder
Sack′gasse f blind alley, dead end; (fig) stalemate, dead end
Sack′leinwand f burlap
Sack′pfeife f bagpipe
Sack′tuch n handkerchief
Sadist –in [zaˈdɪst(ɪn)] §7 mf sadist
sadistisch [zaˈdɪstɪʃ] adj sadistic
säen [ˈzɛ·ən] tr & intr sow
Saffian [ˈzafjɑn] m (–s;) morocco

Safran [ˈzafrɑn] m (–s;–e) saffron
Saft [zaft] m (–[e]s;–̈e) juice; sap; (culin) gravy
saftig [ˈzaftɪç] adj juicy; (Witze) spicy
saft′los adj juiceless; (fig) wishy-washy
saft′reich adj juicy, succulent
Sage [ˈzagə] f (–;–n) legend, saga
Säge [ˈzɛgə] f (–;–n) saw
Sä′geblatt n saw blade
Sä′gebock m sawhorse, sawbuck
Sä′gefisch m sawfish
Sä′gemehl n sawdust
sagen [ˈzagən] tr say; (mitteilen) tell; **das hat nichts zu s.** that's neither here nor there; **das will nicht s.** that is not to say; **gesagt, getan** no sooner said than done; **j–m s. lassen** send s.o. word; **laß dir gesagt sein** let it be a warning to you; **sich** [dat] **nichts s. lassen** not listen to reason
sägen [ˈzɛgən] tr saw ‖ intr saw; (coll) snore, cut wood
sa′genhaft adj legendary
Sägespäne [ˈzɛgəˌpɛnə] pl sawdust
Sä′gewerk n sawmill
sah [zɑ] pret of sehen
Sahne [ˈzɑnə] f (–;) cream
Saison [sɛˈzõ] f (–;–s) season
Saison– comb.fm. seasonal
saison′bedingt, saison′mäßig adj seasonal
Saite [ˈzaɪtə] f (–;–n) string, chord
Sai′teninstrument n string instrument
Sakko [ˈzako] m & n (–s;–s) suit coat
Sak′koanzug m sport suit
Sakrament [zakraˈment] n (–[e]s;–e) sacrament; **das S. des Altars** the Eucharist ‖ interj (sl) dammit!
Sakrileg [zakriˈlek] n (–s;–e) sacrilege
Sakristan [zakrɪsˈtan] m (–s;–e) sacristan
Sakristei [zakrɪsˈtaɪ] f (–;–en) sacristy
Säkular– [zɛkuˈlar] comb.fm. secular; centennial
säkularisieren [zɛkularɪˈzirən] tr secularize
Salami [zaˈlɑmi] f (–;–s) salami
Salat [zaˈlat] m (–[e]s;–e) salad; lettuce; **gemischter S.** tossed salad
Salat′soße f salad dressing
salbadern [zalˈbadərn] intr talk hypocritically, put on the dog
Salbe [ˈzalbə] f (–;–n) salve
salben [ˈzalbən] tr put salve on; anoint
Sal′bung f (–;–en) anointing
sal′bungsvoll adj unctuous
saldieren [zalˈdirən] tr (com) balance
Sal·do [ˈzaldo] m (–s;–s & di [di]) (acct) balance; **e–n S. aufstellen** (or ziehen) strike a balance; **e–n S. ausweisen** show a balance
Saline [zaˈlinə] f (–;–n) saltworks
Salmiak [zalˈmjak] m (–s;) ammonium chloride, sal ammoniac
Salmiak′geist m ammonia
Salon [zaˈlõ] m (–s;–s) salon; parlor, living room
salon′fähig adj (Aussehen) presentable; (Ausdruck) fit for polite company
Salon′held m, **Salon′löwe** m ladies' man
salopp [zaˈlɔp] adj sloppy; (ungezwungen) casual
Salpeter [zalˈpetər] m (–s;) saltpeter

salpeterig [zal'petərɪç] *adj* nitrous
Salpe'tersäure *f* nitric acid
Saito ['zalto] *m* (-s;-s) somersault
Salut [za'lut] *m* (-[e]s;-e) salute; **S. schießen** fire a salute
salutieren [zalu'tirən] *tr & intr* salute
Salve ['zalvə] *f* (-s;-n) volley, salvo
Salz [zalts] *n* (-es;-e) salt
Salz'bergwerk *n* salt mine
Salz'brühe *f* brine
salzen ['zaltsən] *tr* salt
Salz'faß *n* salt shaker
Salz'fleisch *n* salted meat
Salz'gurke *f* pickle
salz'haltig *adj* saline
Salz'hering *m* pickled herring
salzig ['zaltsɪç] *adj* salty; saline
Salz'kartoffeln *pl* boiled potatoes
Salz'lake *f* brine
Salz'säure *f* hydrochloric acid, muriatic acid
Salz'sole *f* brine
Salz'werk *n* salt works
Samariter –in [zama'ritər(ɪn)] §6 *mf* Samaritan
Same ['zamə] *m* (-ns;-n), **Samen** ['zamən] *m* (-s;-) seed; (biol) semen
Sa'menkorn *n* grain of seed
Sa'menstaub *m* pollen
Samentierchen ['zaməntirçən] *n* (-s;-) spermatozoon
sämig ['zemɪç] *adj* (culin) thick, creamy
Sämischleder ['zemɪ/ledər] *n* chamois
Sämling ['zemlɪŋ] *m* (-s;-e) seedling
Sammel- [zaməl] *comb.fm.* collecting, collective
Sam'melbatterie *f* storage battery
Sam'melbecken *n* reservoir; storage tank
Sam'melbegriff *m* collective noun
Sam'melbüchse *f* poor box
Sam'mellinse *f* convex lens
sammeln ['zaməln] *tr* gather; collect; (*Aufmerksamkeit, Truppen*) concentrate ‖ *ref* gather; compose oneself; **sich wieder s.** (mil) reassemble
Sam'melname *m* collective noun
Sam'melplatz *m* collecting point; meeting place; (mil) rendezvous
Sam'melverbindung *f* conference call
Sam'melwerk *n* compilation
Sammler ['zamlər] *m* (-s;-) collector; compiler; (elec) storage cell
Samm'lung *f* (-;-en) collection; (*Zusammenstellung*) compilation; (*Fassung*) composure; concentration
Samstag ['zamstak] *m* (-[e]s;-e) Saturday
samt [zamt] *adv*—**s. und sonders** each and everyone, without exception ‖ *prep* (*dat*) together with ‖ **Samt** *m* (-[e]s;-e) velvet
samt'artig *adj* velvety
sämtlich ['zemtlɪç] *adj* all, complete ‖ *adv* all together
Sanato-rium [zana'torjʊm] *n* (-s;-rien [rjən]) sanitarium
Sand [zant] *m* (-[e]s;-e) sand; **im Sande verlaufen** (fig) peter out
Sandale [zan'dalə] *f* (-;-n) sandal
Sand'bahn *f* (sport) dirt track
Sand'bank *f* (-;ːe) sandbank

Sand'boden *m* sandy soil
Sand'düne *f* sand dune
Sand'grube *f* sand pit
sandig ['zandɪç] *adj* sandy
Sand'kasten *m* sand box
Sand'korn *n* grain of sand
Sand'mann *m* (-[e]s;) (*fig*) sandman
Sand'papier *n* sandpaper; **mit S. abschleifen** sand, sandpaper
Sand'sack *m* sandbag
Sand'stein *m* sandstone
Sand'steingebäude *n* brownstone
sand'strahlen *tr* sandblast
Sand'sturmgebiet *n* dust bowl
sandte ['zantə] *pret* of **senden**
Sand'torte *f* sponge cake
Sand'uhr *f* hour glass
Sand'wüste *f* sandy desert
sanft [zanft] *adj* soft, gentle
Sänfte ['zenftə] *f* (-;-n) sedan chair
Sanft'mut *f* gentleness, meekness
sanft'mütig *adj* gentle, meek, mild
sang [zaŋ] *pret* of **singen** ‖ **Sang** *m* (-[e]s;ːe) song; **mit S. und Klang** (fig) with great fanfare
sang–und klang'los *adv* unceremoniously
Sänger ['zeŋər] *m* (-s;-) singer
Sän'gerchor *m* glee club
Sängerin ['zeŋərɪn] *f* (-;-nen) singer
Sanguiniker [zaŋ'gwinɪkər] *m* (-s;-) optimist
sanguinisch [zaŋ'gwinɪ/] *adj* sanguine
sanieren [za'nirən] *tr* cure; improve the sanitary conditions of; disinfect; (fin) put on a firm basis
Sanie'rung *f* (-;-en) restoration; reorganization
sanitär [zanɪ'ter] *adj* sanitary
Sanitäter [zanɪ'tetər] *m* (-s;-) first-aid-man; (mil) medic
Sanitäts– [zanɪtets] *comb.fm.* first-aid, medical
Sanitäts'korps *n* army medical corps
Sanitäts'soldat *m* medic
Sanitäts'wache *f* first-aid station
Sanitäts'wagen *m* ambulance
Sanitäts'zug *m* hospital train
sank [zaŋk] *pret* of **sinken**
Sanka ['zaŋka] *m* (-s;-s) (**Sanitätskraftwagen**) field ambulance
Sankt [zaŋkt] *invar mf* Saint
Sanktion [zaŋk'tsjon] *f* (-;-en) sanction
sanktionieren [zaŋktsjo'nirən] *tr* sanction
sann [zan] *pret* of **sinnen**
Saphir ['zafɪr] *m* (-s;-e) sapphire
sapperment [zapər'ment] *interj* the deuce!
Sardelle [zar'delə] *f* (-;-n) anchovy
Sardine [zar'dinə] *f* (-;-n) sardine
Sardinien [zar'dinjən] *n* (-s) Sardinia
sardinisch [zar'dinɪ/] *adj* Sardinian
Sarg [zark] *m* (-[e]s;ːe) coffin
Sarg'tuch *n* pall
Sarkasmus [zar'kasmʊs] *m* (-;) sarcasm
sarkastisch [zar'kastɪ/] *adj* sarcastic
Sarkophag [zarko'fak] *m* (-s;-e) sarcophagus
saß [zas] *pret* of **sitzen**
Satan ['zatan] *m* (-s;-e) Satan

satanisch [za'tɑːnɪʃ] *adj* satanic(al)
Satellit [zate'liːt] *m* (-en;-en) satellite
Satin [sa'tɛ̃] *m* (-s;-s) satin
Satire [za'tiːrə] *f* (-;-n) satire
Satiriker –in [za'tiːrɪkər(ɪn)] §6 *mf* satirist
satirisch [za'tiːrɪʃ] *adj* satirical
satt [zat] *adj* satisfied; satiated; (*Farben*) deep, rich; (chem) saturated; etw s. bekommen (or haben) be fed up with s.th.; ich bin s. I've had enough; sich s. essen eat one's fill
Sattel ['zatəl] *m* (-s;ːe) saddle
sat'telfest *adj* (fig) well-versed
Sat'telgurt *m* girth
satteln ['zatəln] *tr* saddle
Sat'telschlepper *m* semi-trailer
Sat'teltasche *f* saddlebag
Satt'heit *f* (-;) saturation; (der Farben) richness
sättigen ['zɛtɪɡən] *tr* satisfy, satiate; saturate
Sät'tigung *f* (-;) satiation; saturation
Sattler ['zatlər] *m* (-s;-) harness maker
sattsam ['zatzam] *adv* sufficiently
saturieren [zatu'riːrən] *tr* saturate
Satz [zats] *m* (-es;ːe) sentence; clause; phrase; (*Behauptung*) proposition; (*Bodensatz*) grounds; sediment; (*Betrag*) amount; (*Tarif*) rate; (*Gebühr*) fee; (*Garnitur*) set; (*Sprung*) leap; (*Wette*) stake; (*Menge*) batch; (math) theorem; (mus) movement; (tennis) set; (typ) typesetting, composition; e-n S. machen jump; e-n S. aufstellen set down an article of faith; einfacher S. simple sentence; hauptwörtlicher S. substantive clause; in S. gehen go to press; verkürzter S. phrase; zum S. von at the rate of; zusammengesetzter S. compound sentence
Satz'aussage *f* (gram) predicate
Satz'bau *m* (-[e]s;) (gram) construction
Satz'gefüge *n* complex sentence
Satz'gegenstand *m* (gram) subject
Satz'lehre *f* syntax
Satz'teil *m* (gram) part of speech
Sat'zung *f* (-;-en) rule, regulation; (*Vereins-*) bylaw; statute
sat'zungsgemäß, sat'zungsmäßig *adj* statutory, according to the bylaws
Satz'zeichen *n* punctuation mark
Sau [zau] *f* (-;ːe) sow; (pej) pig; wie e-e gesengte Sau fahren drive like a maniac
Sau'arbeit *f* (coll) sloppy work; (coll) tough job; (coll) dirty job
sauber ['zaubər] *adj* clean; exact
säuberlich ['zɔɪbərlɪç] *adj* clean, neat; (anständig) decent
sau'bermachen *tr* clean, clean up
säubern ['zɔɪbərn] *tr* clean; (freimachen) clear; (Buch) expurgate; (mil) mop up; (pol) purge
Säu'berungsaktion *f* (mil) mopping-up operation; (pol) purge
Sau'borste *f* hog bristle
Sauce ['zoːsə] *f* (-;-n) sauce; gravy; (Salat-) dressing
sau'dumm *adj* (coll) awfully dumb
sauer ['zauər] *adj* sour

Sau'erbraten *m* braised beef soaked in vinegar
Sauerei [zau·ə'raɪ] *f* (-;-en) filth, filthy joke
Sau'erkohl *m*, **Sau'erkraut** *n* sauerkraut
säuerlich ['zɔɪ·ərlɪç] *adj* sourish, acidulous; (Lächeln) forced
säuern ['zɔɪ·ərn] *tr* sour; (Teig) leaven || *intr* turn sour, acidify
Sau'erstoff *m* (-[e]s;) oxygen
Sau'erstofflasche *f* oxygen tank
Sau'erteig *m* leaven
Sau'ertopf *m* (coll) sourpuss
Sau'erwasser *n* sparkling water
Saufaus ['zaufaus] *m* (-;-), **Saufbold** ['zaufbɔlt] *m* (-[e]s;-e), **Saufbruder** ['zaufbruːdər] *m* (coll) booze hound
saufen ['zaufən] §124 *tr* drink, guzzle || *intr* drink; (sl) booze
Säufer –in ['zɔɪfər(ɪn)] §6 *mf* drunkard
Saufgelage ['zaufɡəlaːɡə] *n* booze party
Sau'fraß *m* terrible food, slop
Säugamme ['zɔɪkamə] *f* wet nurse
saugen ['zauɡən] §109 & §125 *tr* suck || *ref—sich* [dat] etw aus den Fingern s. invent s.th., make up s.th.
säugen ['zɔɪɡən] *tr* suckle, nurse
Sauger ['zauɡər] *m* (-s;-) sucker; nipple; pacifier
Säuger ['zɔɪɡər] *m*, **Säugetier** ['zɔɪɡətiːr] *n* mammal
Saug'flasche *f* baby bottle
Säugling ['zɔɪklɪŋ] *m* (-s;-e) baby
Säug'lingsausstattung *f* layette
Säug'lingsheim *n* nursery
Sau'glück *n* (coll) dumb luck
Saug'napf *m* suction cup
Saug'pumpe *f* suction pump
Saug'watte *f* absorbent cotton
Saug'wirkung *f* suction
Sau'hund *m* (sl) louse, dirty dog
Sau'igel *m* (sl) dirty guy
sauigeln ['zau·iɡəln] *intr* (sl) tell dirty jokes
Sau'kerl *m* (sl) cad, skunk
Säule ['zɔɪlə] *f* (-;-n) column; (& fig) pillar; (elec) dry battery; (phys) pile
Säu'lenfuß *m* base of a column
Säu'lengang *m* colonnade, peristyle
Säu'lenhalle *f* portico, gallery
Säu'lenkapitell *n*, **Säu'lenknauf** *m*, **Säu'lenknopf** *m* (archit) capital
Säu'lenschaft *m* shaft of a column
Säu'lenvorbau *m* portico, (front) porch
Saum [zaum] *m* (-[e]s;ːe) seam, hem; (Rand) border; (e-r Stadt) outskirts
säumen ['zɔɪmən] *tr* hem; border; (Straßen) line || *intr* tarry
Sau'mensch *n* (sl) slut
säumig ['zɔɪmɪç] *adj* tardy
Säumnis ['zɔɪmnɪs] *f* (-;-nisse) dilatoriness; (Verzug) delay; (Nichterfüllung) default
Saum'pfad *m* mule track
Saum'tier *n* beast of burden
Sau'pech *n* (coll) rotten luck
Säure ['zɔɪrə] *f* (-;-n) sourness; acidity; tartness; (chem) acid
Sauregur'kenzeit *f* slack season
Säu'remesser *m* (aut) battery tester
Saures ['zaurəs] *n—gib ihm S.* (coll) give it to 'im!

Saus [zaʊs] *m*—**in S. und Braus leben** live high
säuseln [ˈzɔɪzəln] *intr* rustle; **mit säuselnder Stimme** in whispers
sausen [ˈzaʊsən] *intr* (*Wind, Kugel*) whistle; (*Wasser*) gush ‖ *intr* (SEIN) rush, whiz ‖ *impers*—**mir saust es in den Ohren** my ears are ringing ‖ **Sausen** *n* (**–s;**) rush and roar; humming, ringing (*in the ears*)
Sau'stall *m* pigsty; (fig) terrible mess
Sau'wetter *n* (coll) nasty weather
Sau'wirtschaft *f* (coll) helluva mess
sau'wohl' *adj* (coll) in great shape
Saxophon [zaksɔˈfon] *n* (**–s;–e**) saxophone
Schabe [ˈʃɑbə] *f* (**–;–n**) cockroach
Schabeisen [ˈʃɑpaɪzən] *n* scraper
schaben [ˈʃɑbən] *tr* scrape; grate, rasp
Scha'ber *m* (**–s;–**) scraper
Schabernack [ˈʃɑbərnak] *m* (**–[e]s;–e**) practical joke
schäbig [ˈʃebɪç] *adj* shabby; (fig) mean
Schablone [ʃaˈblonə] *f* (**–;–n**) (*Muster*) pattern, model; (*Matrize*) stencil; (*mechanische Arbeit*) routine; **nach der S.** mechanically
schablo'nenhaft, schablo'nenmäßig *adj* mechanical; (*Arbeit*) routine
Schach [ʃax] *n* (**–[e]s;**) chess; **in S. halten** (fig) keep in check; **S. bieten** (or **geben**) check; (fig) defy; **S. dem König!** check!
Schach'brett *n* chessboard
Schacher [ˈʃaxər] *m* (**–s;**) haggling; **S. treiben** haggle, huckster
Schach'feld *n* (chess) square
Schach'figur *f* chessman; (fig) pawn
schach'matt' *adj* checkmated; (fig) beat
Schach'partie *f*, **Schach'spiel** *n* game of chess
Schacht [ʃaxt] *m* (**–[e]s;⸚e**) shaft; manhole
Schacht'deckel *m* manhole cover
Schachtel [ˈʃaxtəl] *f* (**–;–n**) box; (*von Zigaretten*) pack; (fig) frump
Schach'zug *m* (chess & fig) move
schade [ˈʃɑdə] *adj* too bad
Schädel [ˈʃedəl] *m* (**–s;–**) skull; **mir brummt** (or **dröhnt**) **der S.** my head is throbbing
Schä'delbruch *m*, **Schä'delfraktur** *f* skull fracture
Schä'delhaut *f* scalp
Schä'delknochen *m* cranium
Schä'dellehre *f* phrenology
schaden [ˈʃɑdən] *intr* do harm; (*dat*) harm, damage; **das wird ihr nichts s.** it serves her right; **ein Versuch kann nichts s.** there's no harm in trying ‖ *impers*—**es schadet nichts** it doesn't matter ‖ **Schaden** *m* (**–s;⸚**) damage, injury; (*Verlust*) loss; (*Nachteil*) disadvantage; **er will deinen S. nicht** he means you no harm; **j–m S. zufügen** inflict loss on s.o.; (coll) give s.o. a black eye; **mit S. verkaufen** sell at a loss; **S. nehmen** come to grief; **zu meinem S.** to my detriment
Scha'denersatz *m* compensation, damages; (*Wiedergutmachen*) reparation; **S. leisten** pay damages; make amends
Scha'denersatzklage *f* damage suit
Scha'denfreude *f* gloating
scha'denfroh *adj* gloating, malicious
Scha'denversicherung *f* comprehensive insurance
schadhaft [ˈʃɑthaft] *adj* damaged; (*Material*) faulty; (*Zähne*) decayed; (*baufällig*) dilapidated
schädigen [ˈʃedɪgən] *tr* inflict financial damage on; (*benachteiligen*) wrong; (*Ruf*) damage; (*Rechte*) infringe on
Schä'digung *f* (**–;**) damage
schädlich [ˈʃetlɪç] *adj* harmful; (*nachteilig*) detrimental; (*verderblich*) noxious; (*Speise*) unwholesome
Schädling [ˈʃetlɪŋ] *m* (**–s;–e**) (*Person*) parasite; (ent) pest; **Schädlinge** vermin
Schäd'lingsbekämpfung *f* pest control
schadlos [ˈʃɑtlos] *adj*—**sich an j–m s. halten** make s.o. pay (*for an injury done to oneself*); **sich für etw s. halten** compensate oneself for s.th., make up for s.th.
Schaf [ʃɑf] *n* (**–[e]s;–e**) sheep; (fig) blockhead, dope
Schaf'bock *m* ram
Schäfchen [ˈʃefçən] *n* (**–s;–**) lamb; (*Wolken*) fleecy clouds
Schäf'chenwolke *f* fleecy cloud
Schäfer [ˈʃefər] *m* (**–s;–**) shepherd
Schä'ferhund *m* sheep dog; **deutscher S.** German shepherd
Schaf'fell *n* sheepskin
schaffen [ˈʃafən] **§109** *tr* do; get; put; manage, manage to do; (*erreichen*) accomplish; (*liefern*) supply; (*erschaffen*) bring, cause; (*wegbringen*) take; **auf die Seite s.** put aside; (*betrügerisch*) embezzle; **ich schaffe es noch, daß** I'll see to it that; **Rat s.** know what to do; **vom Halse s.** get off one's neck ‖ **§126** *tr* create; produce; **wie geschaffen sein für** cut out for ‖ **§109** *intr* do; (*arbeiten*) work; **j–m viel zu s. machen** cause s.o. a lot of trouble; **sich zu s. machen** be busy, putter around
schaf'fend *adj* working; (*schöpferisch*) creative; (*produktiv*) productive
Schaf'fensdrang *m* creative urge
Schaf'fenskraft *f* creative power
Schaffner [ˈʃafnər] *m* (**–s;–**) (rr) conductor
Schaf'fung *f* (**–;–en**) creation
Schaf'hirt *m* shepherd
Schaf'pelz *m* sheepskin coat
Schaf'pferch *m* sheepfold
Schafs'kopf *m* (sl) mutton-head
Schaf'stall *m* sheepfold
Schaft [ʃaft] *m* (**–[e]s;⸚e**) shaft; (*e–r Feder*) stem; (*e–s Gewehrs*) stock; (*e–s Ankers*) shank; (bot) stem, stalk
Schaft'stiefel *m* high boot
Schaf'zucht *f* sheep raising
Schakal [ʃaˈkɑl] *m* (**–s;–e**) jackal
schäkern [ˈʃekərn] *intr* joke around; flirt
schal [ʃɑl] *adj* stale; insipid; (fig) flat ‖ **Schal** *m* (**–s;–e & –s**) scarf; shawl
Schale [ˈʃɑlə] *f* (**–;–n**) bowl; (*Tasse*) cup; (*von Obst*) peel, skin; (*Hülse*) shell; (*Schote*) pod; (*Rinde*) bark;

(Waagschale) scale; (zool) shell; **sich in S. werfen** (coll) doll up

schälen [ˈʃɛlən] *tr* peel; *(Mais)* husk; *(Baumrinde)* bark || *ref* peel off

Scha′lentier *n* (zool) crustacean

Schalk [ʃalk] *m* (–[e]s;-e & ⸚e) rogue

schalk′haft *adj* roguish

Schall [ʃal] *m* (–[e]s;-e & ⸚e) sound; *(Klang)* ring; *(Lärm)* noise

Schall′boden *m* sounding board

Schall′dämpfer *m* *(an Schußwaffen)* silencer; (aut) muffler; (mus) soft pedal

schall′dicht *adj* soundproof

Schall′dose *f* (electron) pickup

Schall′druck *m* sonic boom

Schallehre (Schall′lehre) *f* acoustics

schallen [ˈʃalən] *intr* sound, resound

Schall′grenze *f* sound barrier

Schall′mauer *f* sound barrier

Schall′meßgerät *n* sonar

Schall′pegel *m* sound level

Schall′platte *f* phonograph record

Schall′plattenaufnahme *f* recording

Schall′wand *f* baffle

Schall′welle *f* sound wave

Schalotte [ʃaˈlɔtə] *f* (–;-n) (bot) scallion

schalt [ʃalt] *pret of* **schelten**

Schalt– *comb.fm.* switch; connecting; breaking; shifting

Schalt′bild *n* circuit diagram

Schalt′brett *n* switchboard; control panel; (aut) dashboard

Schalt′dose *f* switch box

schalten [ˈʃaltən] *tr* switch; *(anlassen)* start; *(Gang)* (aut) shift || *intr* switch; *(regieren)* be in command; (aut) shift gears; **s. und walten mit** do as one pleases with

Schal′ter *m* (–s;-) switch; *(Ausschalter)* circuit breaker; *(für Kundenverkehr)* window, ticket window

Schal′terdeckel *m* switch plate

Schalt′hebel *m* (aut) gearshift; (elec) switch lever

Schalt′jahr *n* leap year

Schalt′kasten *m* switch box

Schalt′pult *n* (rad, telv) control desk

Schalt′tafel *f* switchboard, instrument panel; (aut) dashboard

Schalt′uhr *f* timer

Schal′tung *f* (–;-en) switching; (elec) connection; (elec) circuit

Schaluppe [ʃaˈlupə] *f* (–;-n) sloop

Scham [ʃam] *f* (–;) shame; (anat) genitals

Scham′bein *n* (anat) pubis

schämen [ˈʃɛmən] *ref* *(über acc)* feel ashamed (of)

Scham′gefühl *n* sense of shame

Scham′haar *n* pubic hair

scham′haft *adj* modest, bashful

scham′los *adj* shameless

Schampun [ʃamˈpun] *n* (–s;-s) shampoo

schampunieren [ʃampuˈnirən] *tr* shampoo

scham′rot *adj* blushing; **s. werden** blush

Scham′teile *pl* genitals

Schand– [ʃant] *comb.fm.* of shame

schandbar [ˈʃantbar] *adj* shameful; infamous

Schande [ˈʃandə] *f* (–;) shame, disgrace

schänden [ˈʃɛndən] *tr* disgrace; *(entweihen)* desecrate; *(Mädchen)* rape

Schän′der *m* (–s;-) violator; rapist

Schand′fleck *m* stain; (fig) blemish; (fig) good-for-nothing; **der S. der Familie** the disgrace of the family

schändlich [ˈʃɛntlɪç] *adj* shameful, disgraceful; scandalous || *adv* (coll) awfully

Schand′mal *n* stigma

Schand′tat *f* shameful deed, crime

Schän′dung *f* (–;-en) desecration; disfigurement; rape

Schank [ʃaŋk] *m* (–[e]s;⸚e) bar, saloon

Schank′bier *n* draft beer

Schank′erlaubnis *f*, **Schank′gerechtigkeit** *f*, **Schank′konzession** *f* liquor license

Schank′stätte *f* bar, tavern

Schank′tisch *m* bar

Schank′wirt *m* bartender

Schank′wirtschaft *f* bar, saloon

Schanzarbeit [ˈʃantsarbaɪt] *f* earthwork; **Schanzarbeiten** entrenchments

Schanze [ˈʃantsə] *f* (–;-n) entrenchments, trenches; (naut) quarter-deck; (sport) take-off ramp *(of ski jump)*

Schanz′gerät *n* entrenching tool

Schar [ʃar] *f* (–;-en) group, bunch; crowd; *(von Vögeln)* flock, flight

Scharade [ʃaˈradə] *f* (–;-n) charade

scharen [ˈʃarən] *ref* (um) gather (around)

scharf [ʃarf] *adj* (schärfer [ˈʃɛrfər] schärfste [ˈʃɛrfstə] §9) sharp; *(Tempo)* fast; *(Bemerkung)* cutting; *(Blick)* hard; *(Brille)* strong; *(Fernrohr)* powerful; *(Geruch)* pungent; *(Munition)* live; *(Pfeffer, Senf)* hot; *(streng)* severe; *(genau)* exact; *(Ton)* shrill; *(wahrnehmend)* keen; **s. machen** sharpen; **s. sein auf** (acc) be keen on || *adv* hard; fast; **s-n s. nehmen** be very strict with s.o.; **s. ansehen** look hard at; **s. geladen** loaded; **s. schießen** shoot with live ammunition; **s. umreißen** define clearly

Scharf′blick *m* (fig) sharp eye

Schärfe [ˈʃɛrfə] *f* (–;-n) sharpness; keenness; pungency; severity; accuracy

Scharf′einstellung *f* (phot) focusing

schärfen [ˈʃɛrfən] *tr* sharpen, whet; make pointy; (fig) intensify

scharf′kantig *adj* sharp-edged

scharf′machen *tr* stir up; *(Bomben)* arm; *(Zünder)* activate

Scharf′macher *m* demagogue, agitator

Scharf′richter *m* executioner

Scharf′schütze *m* (mil) sharpshooter

scharf′sichtig *adj* sharp-eyed; (fig) clear-sighted

Scharf′sinn *m* sagacity, acumen

scharf′sinnig *adj* sharp, sagacious

Scharlach [ˈʃarlax] *m* (–s;-e) scarlet; (pathol) scarlet fever

schar′lachfarben *adj* scarlet

schar′lachrot *adj* scarlet

Scharlatan [ˈʃarlatan] *m* (–s;-e) charlatan, quack

scharmant [ʃar'mant] *adj* charming

Scharmützel [ʃar'mʏtsəl] *n* (-s;-) skirmish

Scharnier [ʃar'niːr] *n* (-s;-e) hinge; joint

Schärpe ['ʃɛrpə] *f* (-;-n) sash

Scharre ['ʃarə] *f* (-;-n) scraper

Scharreisen ['ʃaraɪzən] *n* scraper

scharren ['ʃarən] *tr* scrape, paw || *intr* scrape; (an *acc*) scratch (on); **auf den Boden** s. paw the ground; **mit den Füßen** scrape the feet (*in disapproval*)

Scharte ['ʃartə] *f* (-;-n) nick, dent; (*Kerbe*) notch; (*Kratzer*) scratch; (*Riß*) crack; (*Bergsattel*) gap; (fig) mistake; **e-e S. auswetzen** (fig) make amends

Scharteke [ʃar'teːkə] *f* (-;-n) worthless old book; (fig) frump

schartig ['ʃartɪç] *adj* jagged; notched

Schatten ['ʃatən] *m* (-s;-) shade; shadow; **in den S. stellen** throw into the shade

Schat′tenbild *n* silhouette; (fig) phantom

Schat′tendasein *n* shadowy existence

Schat′tengestalt *f* shadowy figure

schat′tenhaft *adj* shadowy

Schat′tenriß *m* silhouette

Schat′tenseite *f* shady side; dark side; (fig) seamy side

schattieren [ʃa'tiːrən] *tr* shade; (*schraffieren*) hatch; (*abtönen*) tint

Schattie′rung *f* (-;-en) shading; (*Farbton*) shade, tint

schattig ['ʃatɪç] *adj* shadowy; shady

Schatulle [ʃa'tʊlə] *f* (-;-n) cash box; (*für Schmuck*) jewelry box; (hist) private funds (*of a prince*)

Schatz [ʃats] *m* (-es;̈-e) treasure; (*Vorrat*) store; (fig) sweetheart

Schatz′amt *n* treasury department

Schatz′anweisung *f* treasury bond

schätzbar ['ʃɛtsbaːr] *adj* valuable

schätzen ['ʃɛtsən] *tr* (*Grundstücke, Häuser, Schaden*) estimate, appraise; (*urteilen, vermuten*) guess; (*achten*) esteem, value; (*würdigen*) appreciate; **er schätzte mich auf 20 Jahre** he took me for 20 years old; **zu hoch** s. overestimate, overrate; **zu s. wissen** appreciate || *ref*—sich [*dat*] **es zu Ehre** s. consider it an honor; **sich glücklich** s. consider oneself lucky || *recip*—**sie s. sich nicht** there's no love lost between them

schät′zenswert *adj* valuable

Schät′zer -in §6 *mf* appraiser; (*zur Besteuerung*) assessor

Schatz′kammer *m* treasury; (fig) storehouse

Schatz′meister -in §6 *mf* treasurer

Schät′zung *f* (-;-en) estimate; (*Meinung*) estimation; (*Hochachtung*) esteem; (*Hochschätzung*) appreciation; (*zur Besteuerung*) assessment

schät′zungsweise *adv* approximately

Schät′zungswert *m* estimated value; assessed value; (*des Schadens*) appraisal

Schatz′wechsel *m* treasury bill

Schau [ʃaʊ] *f* (-;-en) view; (*Ausstel-*

lung) exhibition, show; (mil) review; (telv) show; **zur S. stehen** be on display; **zur S. stellen** put on display; **zur S. tragen** feign

Schau′bild *n* diagram, chart

Schauder ['ʃaʊdər] *m* (-s;-) shudder, shiver; (*Schrecken*) horror, terror

schauderbar ['ʃaʊdərbar] *adj* terrible

schau′dererregend *adj* horrifying

schau′derhaft *adj* horrible, awful

schaudern ['ʃaʊdərn] *intr* shudder || *impers*—**es schaudert mich** I shudder

schauen ['ʃaʊ.ən] *tr* look at; (*beobachten*) observe || *intr* look

Schauer ['ʃaʊ.ər] *m* (-s;-) shower, downpour; (*Schauder*) shudder, chill; thrill; (*Anfall*) fit, attack; **einzelne S.** scattered showers

Schau′erdrama *n* (theat) thriller

schau′erlich *adj* dreadful, horrible

schauern ['ʃaʊ.ərn] *intr* shudder || *impers*—**es schauert** it is pouring; **es schauert mich** (or **mir**) **vor** (*dat*) **I** shudder at; **I** shiver with

Schau′erroman *m* thriller

Schaufel ['ʃaʊfəl] *f* (-;-n) shovel; scoop; (*Rad-*) paddle; (*Turbinen-*) blade, vane

schaufeln ['ʃaʊfəln] *tr* shovel; (*Grab*) dig || *intr* shovel

Schau′felrad *n* paddle wheel

Schau′fenster *n* display window; **die S. ansehen** go window-shopping

Schau′fensterauslage *f* window display

Schau′fensterbummel *m* window-shopping

Schau′fensterdekoration *f* window dressing

Schau′fliegen *n* stunt flying

Schau′flug *m* air show

Schau′gepränge *n* pageantry

Schau′gerüst *n* grandstand

Schau′kampf *m* (box) exhibition fight

Schau′kasten *m* showcase

Schaukel ['ʃaʊkəl] *f* (-;-n) swing

Schau′kelbrett *n* seesaw

schaukeln ['ʃaʊkəln] *tr* swing; rock || *intr* swing; rock; sway

Schau′kelpferd *n* rocking horse

Schau′kelreck *n* trapeze

Schau′kelstuhl *m* rocking chair

Schau′loch *n* peephole

Schaum [ʃaʊm] *m* (-[e]s;̈-e) foam, froth; (*Abschaum*) scum; (*Geifer*) slaver; **zu S. schlagen** whip; **zu S. werden** (fig) come to nothing

Schaum′bad *n* bubble bath

schäumen ['ʃɔɪmən] *intr* foam; (*Wein*) sparkle; (*aus Wut*) fume, boil

Schaum′gummi *n & m* foam rubber

Schaum′haube *f* head (*on beer*)

schaumig ['ʃaʊmɪç] *adj* foamy

Schaum′krone *f* whitecap (*on wave*)

Schau′modell *n* mock-up

Schaum′wein *m* sparkling wine

Schau′platz *m* scene, theater

Schau′prozeß *m* mock trial

schaurig ['ʃaʊrɪç] *adj* horrible

Schau′spiel *n* play, drama; spectacle

Schau′spieler *m* actor

Schau′spielerin *f* actress

schau′spielerisch *adj* theatrical

schauspielern ['ʃauʃpilərn] *intr* act; (*schwindeln*) act, make believe
Schau'spielhaus *n* theater
Schau'spielkunst *f* dramatic art
Schau'stück *n* show piece; (*Muster*) sample
Scheck [ʃɛk] *m* (-s;-s & -e) check; e-n S. ausstellen an (*acc*) über (*acc*) write out a check to (*s.o.*) in the amount of; e-n S. einlösen cash a check; e-n S. sperren lassen stop payment on a check; offener S. blank check
Scheck'abschnitt *m* check stub
Scheck'formular *n* blank check
Scheck'heft *n* check book
scheckig ['ʃɛkɪç] *adj* dappled
Scheck'konto *n* checking account
scheel [ʃel] *adj* squinting; squint-eyed; (*fig*) envious, jealous
Scheffel ['ʃɛfəl] *m* (-s;-) bushel
scheffeln ['ʃɛfəln] *tr* amass
Scheibe ['ʃaɪbə] *f* (-;-n) disk; sheet; plate; (*Glas-*) pane; (*Honig-*) honeycomb; (*Ziel*) target; (*Schnitte*) slice; (*astr*) orb, disk; (*mach*) washer; (*telp*) dial
Schei'benbremse *f* disk brake
Schei'benkönig *m* top marksman
Schei'benschießen *n* target practice
Schei'benwäscher *m* windshield washer
Schei'benwischer *m* windshield wiper
Scheide ['ʃaɪdə] *f* (-;-n) sheath; border, boundary; (*anat*) vagina
Schei'debrief *m* farewell letter
Schei'degruß *m* goodbye
scheiden ['ʃaɪdən] §112 *tr* separate, divide; (*zerlegen*) decompose; (*Ehe*) dissolve; (*Eheleute*) divorce; (*chem*) analyze; (*chem*) refine || *ref* part; sich s. lassen get a divorce || *intr* (SEIN) part; depart; (*aus dem Amt*) resign, retire
schei'dend *adj* (*Tag*) closing; (*Sonne*) setting
Schei'dewand *f* partition
Schei'deweg *m* fork, crossroad; (*fig*) moment of decision
Schei'dung *f* (-;-en) separation; (*Ehe-*) divorce
Schein [ʃaɪn] *m* (-[e]s;-e) shine; (*Licht*) light; (*Schimmer*) gleam, glitter; (*Strahl*) flash; (*Erscheinung*) appearance; (*Anschein*) pretense, show; (*Urkunde*) certificate, papers, license, ticket; (*Geldschein*) bill; (*Quittung*) receipt; dem Scheine nach apparently; den äußeren S. wahren save face; sich [*dat*] den S. geben make believe; zum S. pro forma
Schein- *comb.fm.* sham, mock, make-believe
scheinbar ['ʃaɪnbar] *adj* seeming, apparent; likely; (*vorgeblich*) make-believe
Schein'bild *n* illusion; phantom
scheinen ['ʃaɪnən] §128 *intr* shine; seem, appear || *impers*—es scheint it seems
Schein'grund *m* pretext
schein'heilig *adj* sanctimonious, hypocritical
Schein'tod *m* suspended animation

Schein'werfer *m* flashlight; (aer) beacon; (aut) headlight
Scheit [ʃaɪt] *n* (-[e]s;-e) piece of chopped wood; Holz in Scheite hakken chop wood
Scheitel ['ʃaɪtəl] *m* (-s;-) apex, top; top of the head; (*des Haares*) part; e-n S. ziehen make a part
scheiteln ['ʃaɪtəln] *tr* & *ref* part
Schei'telpunkt *m* (fig) summit; (astr) zenith; (math) vertex
Schei'telwinkel *m* opposite angle
Scheiterhaufen ['ʃaɪtərhaufən] *m* funeral pile; auf dem S. sterben die at the stake
scheitern ['ʃaɪtərn] *intr* (SEIN) run aground, be wrecked; (*Plan*) miscarry || Scheitern *n* (-s;) shipwreck; (fig) failure
Schelle ['ʃɛlə] *f* (-;-n) bell; (*Fessel*) handcuff; (*Ohrfeige*) box on the ear
schellen ['ʃɛlən] *tr* & *intr* ring
Schel'lenkappe *f* cap and bells
Schellfisch ['ʃɛlfɪʃ] *m* haddock
Schelm [ʃɛlm] *m* (-[e]s;-e) rogue; (*Lit*) knave; armer S. poor devil
Schel'menstreich *m* prank
schelmisch ['ʃɛlmɪʃ] *adj* roguish, impish
Schelte ['ʃɛltə] *f* (-;-n) scolding
schelten ['ʃɛltən] *tr* & *intr* scold
Scheltwort ['ʃɛltvɔrt] *n* (-[e]s;-e & ̈-er) abusive word; word of reproof
Sche·ma ['ʃema] *n* (-s;-s & -mata [mata] & -men [mən]) scheme; diagram; (*Muster*) pattern, design
Schemel ['ʃeməl] *m* (-s;-) stool
Schemen ['ʃemən] *m* (-s;-) phantom, shadow
sche'menhaft *adj* shadowy
Schenk [ʃɛŋk] *m* (-en;-en) bartender
Schenke ['ʃɛŋkə] *f* (-;-n) bar, tavern
Schenkel ['ʃɛŋkəl] *m* (-s;-) thigh; (*e-s Winkels*) side; (*e-r Schere*) blade; (*e-s Zirkels*) leg
schenken ['ʃɛŋkən] *tr* give, offer, pour (out); (*Aufmerksamkeit*) pay; (*Schuld*) remit; das ist geschenkt that's dirt cheap; das kann ich mir s. I can pass that up; das kannst du dir s.! keep it to yourself! j-m Beifall s. applaud s.o.; j-m das Leben s. grant s.o. pardon
Schenk'stube *f* taproom, barroom
Schenk'tisch *m* bar
Schen'kung *f* (-;-en) donation
Schenk'wirt *m* bartender
scheppern ['ʃɛpərn] *intr* (coll) rattle
Scherbe ['ʃɛrbə] *f* (-;-n), **Scherben** ['ʃɛrbən] *m* (-s;-) broken piece; potsherd; in Scherben gehen go to pieces
Scher'bengericht *n* ostracism
Scherbett [ʃɛr'bɛt] *m* (-[e]s;-e) sherbe(r)t
Schere ['ʃerə] *f* (-;-n) (pair of) scissors; shears; (*Draht-*) cutter; (zool) claw
scheren ['ʃerən] *tr* bother; was schert dich das? what's that to you? || §129 *tr* cut, clip, trim; (*Schafe*) shear; || §109 *ref*—scher dich ins Bett! off to bed with you!; scher dich zum Teu-

fel! the devil with you!; **sich um etw s.** trouble oneself about s.th.

Schererei [ʃɛrə'raɪ] f (-;-en) trouble

Scherflein ['ʃɛrflaɪn] n (-s;-) bit; **sein S. beitragen** contribute one's bit

Scherz [ʃɛrts] m (-es;-e) joke; **im (or zum) S.** for fun; **S. treiben mit** make fun of

scherzen ['ʃɛrtsən] intr joke, kid

scherz/haft adj joking, humorous

Scherz/name m nickname

scherz/weise adv in jest, as a joke

scheu [ʃɔʏ] adj shy; **s. machen** frighten; startle || **Scheu** f (-;) shyness

Scheuche ['ʃɔʏçə] f (-;-n) scarecrow

scheuchen ['ʃɔʏçən] tr scare (away)

scheuen ['ʃɔʏən] tr shun; shrink from; fear; (Mühen, Kosten) spare; **ohne die Kosten zu s.** regardless of expenses || ref (vor dat) be afraid (of); **ich s. mich zu** (inf) I am reluctant to (inf) || intr—**s. vor** (dat) shy at

Scheuer ['ʃɔʏər] f (-;-n) barn

Scheu/erbürste f scrub brush

Scheu/erfrau f scrubwoman

Scheu/erlappen m scrub rag

scheuern ['ʃɔʏərn] tr scrub, scour; (reiben) rub

Scheu/erpulver n scouring powder

Scheu/klappe f blinder (for horses)

Scheune ['ʃɔʏnə] f (-;-n) barn

Scheu/nendrescher m—**er ißt wie ein S.** (coll) he eats like a horse

Scheusal ['ʃɔʏzal] n (-s;-e) monster

scheußlich ['ʃɔʏslɪç] adj dreadful, atrocious; (coll) awful, rotten

Scheuß/lichkeit f (-;-en) hideousness; (Tat) atrocity

Schi [ʃiː] m (-s;- & -er) ski; **Schi fahren (or laufen)** ski

Schicht [ʃɪçt] f (-;-en) layer, film; (Farb-) coat; (Arbeiter-) shift; (Gesellschafts-) class; (geol) stratum; (phot) emulsion; **Leute aus allen Schichten** people from all walks of life; **S. machen** (coll) knock off from work

Schicht/arbeit f shift work

schichten ['ʃɪçtən] tr arrange in layers; laminate; (Holz) stack (up); (in Klassen einteilen) classify; (geol) stratify; (Ladung) (naut) stow

Schich/tenaufbau m, **Schich/tenbildung** f (geol) stratification

-schichtig [ʃɪçtɪç] comb.fm. -layer, -ply

Schicht/linie f contour line

Schicht/linienplan m contour map

Schicht/meister m shift foreman

schicht/weise adv in layers; in shifts

schick [ʃɪk] adj chic, swank || **Schick** m (-[e]s;) stylishness; (Geschick) skill; (Geschmack) tact, taste; **S. haben für** have a knack for

schicken ['ʃɪkən] tr send || ref—**sich s. für** (or zu) be suitable for; **sich s. in** (acc) adapt oneself to; resign oneself to || intr—**nach j-m s.** send for s.o. || impers—**es schickt sich** it is proper; (sich ereignen) come to pass

schick/lich adj proper; decent

Schick/lichkeit f (-;) propriety

Schick/lichkeitsgefühl ·n sense of propriety

Schicksal ['ʃɪkzal] n (-[e]s;-e) destiny, fate

Schick/salsgefährte m fellow sufferer

Schick/salsglaube m fatalism

Schick/salsgöttinnen pl (myth) Fates

Schick/salsschlag m stroke of fate

Schickung (Schik/kung) f (-;-en) (divine) dispensation

Schiebe- ['ʃiːbə] comb.fm. sliding, push

Schie/beleiter f extension ladder

schieben ['ʃiːbən] §130 tr push, shove; traffic in; **auf die lange Bank s.** put off; **e-e ruhige Kugel s.** have a cushy job; **Kegel s.** bowl; **Wache s.** (mil) pull guard duty || ref move, shuffle || intr shuffle along; profiteer

Schieber ['ʃiːbər] m (-s;-) slide valve; (Riegel) bolt; (am Schornstein) damper; (fig) racketeer

Schie/bergeschäft f (com) racket

Schiebertum ['ʃiːbərtum] n (-s;) (com) racketeering

Schie/betür f sliding door

schied [ʃiːt] pret of **scheiden**

Schieds- [ʃiːts] comb.fm. of arbitration

Schieds/gericht n board of arbitration; **an ein S. verweisen** refer to arbitration

Schieds/mann m (-[e]s;-̈er) arbitrator

Schieds/richter m arbitrator; (sport) referee, umpire

schieds/richterlich adj of an arbitration board || adv by arbitration

Schieds/spruch m decision; **e-n S. fällen** render a decision

schief [ʃiːf] adj (abfallend) slanting; (krumm) crooked; (einseitig) lopsided; (geneigt) inclined; (Winkel) oblique; (falsch) false, wrong; **auf die schiefe Ebene geraten** (fig) go downhill; **schiefe Lage** (fig) tight spot; **schiefes Licht** (fig) bad light || adv at an angle; awry; obliquely; wrong; **s. ansehen** look askance at; **s. halten** tip, tilt; **s. nehmen** take amiss

Schiefer ['ʃiːfər] m (-s;-) slate; (Splitter) splinter

Schie/ferbruch m slate quarry

Schie/feröl n shale oil

Schie/fertafel f (educ) slate

schief/gehen §82 intr (SEIN) go wrong

schief/treten §152 tr—**die Absätze s.** wear down the heels

schieläugig ['ʃiːlɔɪgɪç] adj squint-eyed; cross-eyed

schielen ['ʃiːlən] intr squint; **s. nach** squint at; leer at

schie/lend adj squinting; cross-eyed; furtive

schien [ʃiːn] pret of **scheinen**

Schienbein ['ʃiːnbaɪn] n shinbone, tibia

Schien/beinschützer m shinguard

Schiene ['ʃiːnə] f (-;-n) (rr) rail, track; (surg) splint; **aus den Schienen springen** jump the track

schienen ['ʃiːnən] tr put in splints

Schie/nenbahn f track, rails; streetcar; railroad

Schie/nenfahrzeug n rail car

Schie/nengleis n track

schier [ʃir] *adj* sheer || *adv* almost
Schierling [ˈʃirlɪŋ] *m* (-s;-e) (bot) hemlock
Schieß– [ʃis] *comb.fm.* shooting
Schieß'baumwolle *f* guncotton
Schieß'bedarf *m* ammunition
Schieß'bude *f* shooting gallery
Schieß'eisen *n* (hum) shooting iron
schießen [ˈʃisən] §76 *tr* shoot, fire; e–n **Bock** s. (coll) pull a boner; ein **Tor** s. make a goal || *intr* (auf *acc*) shoot (at); aus dem **Hinterhalt** s. snipe; gut s. be a good shot; **scharf** s. shoot with live ammunition || *intr* (SEIN) shoot up; spurt; zig, fly; das **Blut** schoß ihm ins **Gesicht** his face got red; in **Samen** s. go to seed; ins **Kraut** s. sprout || **Schießen** *n* (-s;) shooting; das ist ja zum s.! (coll) that's a riot!
Schießerei [ʃisəˈraɪ] *f* (-;-en) gun fight; pointless firing
Schieß'gewehr *n* firearm
Schieß'hund *m* (hunt) pointer
Schieß'lehre *f* ballistics
Schieß'platz *m* firing range
Schieß'prügel *m* (hum) shooting iron
Schieß'pulver *n* gunpowder
Schieß'scharte *f* loophole
Schieß'scheibe *f* target
Schieß'stand *m* shooting gallery; (mil) firing range, rifle range
Schieß'übung *f* firing practice
Schi'fahrer –in §6 *mf* skier
Schiff [ʃɪf] *n* (-[e]s;-e) ship; (archit) nave; (typ) galley
Schiffahrt (**Schiff'fahrt**) *f* navigation
Schiffahrtslinie (**Schiff'fahrtslinie**) *f* steamship line
Schiffahrtsweg (**Schiff'fahrtsweg**) *m* shipping lane
schiffbar [ˈʃɪfbar] *adj* navigable
Schiff'bau *m* (-[e]s;) shipbuilding
Schiff'bruch *m* shipwreck
schiff'brüchig *adj* shipwrecked
Schiff'brücke *f* pontoon bridge; (naut) bridge
Schiffchen [ˈʃɪfçən] *n* (-s;-) little ship; (mil) overseas cap; (tex) shuttle
schiffen [ˈʃɪfən] *intr* (vulg) pee || *impers*—es schifft (vulg) it's pouring
Schiffer [ˈʃɪfər] *m* (-s;-) seaman; skipper; (Schiffsführer) navigator
Schif'ferklavier *n* (coll) concertina
Schiffs'journal *n* log, logbook
Schiffs'junge *m* cabin boy
Schiffs'küche *f* galley
Schiffs'ladung *f* cargo
Schiffs'luke *f* hatch
Schiffs'mannschaft *f* crew
Schiffs'ortung *f* dead reckoning
Schiffs'raum *m* hold; tonnage
Schiffs'rumpf *m* hull
Schiffs'schraube *f* propeller
Schiffs'tau *n* hawser
Schiffs'taufe *f* christening of a ship
Schiffs'werft *f* shipyard, dockyard
Schiffs'winde *f* winch, capstan
Schiffs'zimmermann *m* ship's carpenter; (bei e–r Werft) shipwright
Schikane [ʃɪˈkanə] *f* (-;-n) chicanery; mit allen **Schikanen** with all the frills; (aut) fully loaded

schikanieren [ʃɪkaˈnirən] *tr* harass
schikanös [ʃɪkaˈnøs] *adj* annoying
Schi'langlauf *m* cross-country skiing
Schi'lauf *m* skiing
schi'laufen §105 *intr* (SEIN) ski || **Schilaufen** *n* (-s;) skiing
Schi'läufer –in §6 *mf* skier
Schild [ʃɪlt] *m* (-[e]s;-e) shield; (heral) coat of arms; etw im **Schilde** führen have s.th. up one's sleeve || *n* (-[e]s;-er) sign; road sign; nameplate; (e–s Arztes, usw.) shingle; (Etikett) label; (Mützenschirm) visor, shade
Schild'bürger *m* (fig) dunce
Schild'bürgerstreich *m* boner
Schild'drüse *f* thyroid gland
Schilderhaus [ˈʃɪldərhaus] *n* sentry box
Schil'dermaler *m* sign painter
schildern [ˈʃɪldərn] *tr* depict, describe
Schil'derung *f* (-;-en) description
Schild'kröte *f* tortoise, turtle
Schildpatt [ˈʃɪltpat] *n* (-[e]s;) tortoise shell, turtle shell
Schilf [ʃɪlf] *n* (-[e]s;-e) reed
Schilf'rohr *n* reed
Schi'lift *m* ski lift
Schiller [ˈʃɪlər] *m* (-s;) luster; iridescence
schillern [ˈʃɪlərn] *intr* be iridescent
Schil'lerwein *m* bright-red wine
Schilling [ˈʃɪlɪŋ] *m* (-s;- & -e) shilling; (Aust) schilling
Schimäre [ʃɪˈmɛrə] *f* (-;-n) chimera
Schimmel [ˈʃɪməl] *m* (-s;-) white horse; mildew, mold
schimmelig [ˈʃɪmlɪç] *adj* moldy
schimmeln [ˈʃɪməln] *intr* (HABEN & SEIN) get moldy
Schimmer [ˈʃɪmər] *m* (-s;) glimmer
schimmern [ˈʃɪmərn] *intr* glimmer
schimmlig [ˈʃɪmlɪç] *adj* moldy
Schimpanse [ʃɪmˈpanzə] *m* (-n;-n) chimpanzee
Schimpf [ʃɪmpf] *m* (-[e]s;-e) insult, abuse
schimpfen [ˈʃɪmpfən] *tr* scold, abuse || *intr* be abusive; (über *acc* or auf *acc*) curse (at), swear (at)
schimpf'lich *adj* disgraceful
Schimpf'name *m* nickname; **j–m Schimpfnamen geben** call s.o. names
Schimpf'wort *n* (-[e]s;-e & -̈er) swear word
Schindaas [ˈʃɪntas] *n* carrion
Schindel [ˈʃɪndəl] *f* (-;-n) shingle
schindeln [ˈʃɪndəln] *tr* shingle
schinden [ˈʃɪndən] §167 *tr* skin; torment; oppress; exploit; **Eindruck** s. try to make an impression; **Eintrittsgeld** s. crash the gate; **Zeilen** s. pad the writing; **Zigaretten** s. bum cigarettes || *ref* break one's back
Schin'der *m* (-s;-) slave driver
Schinderei [ʃɪndəˈraɪ] *f* (-;-en) drudgery, grind
Schindluder [ˈʃɪntludər] *n* carrion; mit **j–m** S. treiben treat s.o. outrageously
Schindmähre [ˈʃɪntmɛrə] *f* old nag
Schinken [ˈʃɪŋkən] *m* (-s;-) ham; (hum) tome; (hum) huge painting
Schinnen [ˈʃɪnən] *pl* dandruff

Schippe [ˈʃɪpə] f (-;-n) shovel, scoop; (cards) spade(s); e-e S. machen (or ziehen) pout; j-n auf die S. nehmen (coll) pull s.o.'s leg

schippen [ˈʃɪpən] tr & intr shovel

Schirm [ʃɪrm] m (-[e]s;-e) screen; umbrella; x-ray screen; lampshade; visor; (fig) protection, shelter; (hunt) blind

Schirm'bild n x-ray

Schirm'bildaufnahme f x-ray

Schirm'dach n lean-to

schirmen [ˈʃɪrmən] tr protect

Schirm'futteral n umbrella case

Schirm'herr m protector, patron

Schirm'herrin f protectress, patroness

Schirm'herrschaft f protectorate; patronage

Schirm'ständer m umbrella stand

Schir'mung f (-;-n) (elec) shielding

schirren [ˈʃɪrən] tr harness

Schis·ma [ˈʃɪsma] n (-;-mata [mata] & -men |mən] schism

Schi'sprung m ski jump

Schi'stock m ski pole

schizophren [ʃçɪtsoˈfren] adj schizophrenic

Schizophrenie [ʃçɪtsofreˈni] f (-;) schizophrenia

schlabbern [ˈʃlabərn] tr lap up || intr (geifern) slobber; (fig) babble

Schlacht [ʃlaxt] f (-;-en) battle; die S. bei the battle of

schlachten [ˈʃlaxtən] tr slaughter

Schlach'tenbummler m camp follower; (sport) fan

Schlächter [ˈʃlɛçtər] m (-s;-) butcher

Schlacht'feld n battlefield

Schlacht'flieger m combat pilot; close-support fighter

Schlacht'geschrei n battle cry

Schlacht'haus n slaughterhouse

Schlacht'kreuzer m heavy cruiser

Schlacht'opfer n sacrifice; (fig) victim

Schlacht'ordnung f battle array

Schlacht'roß n (hist) charger

Schlacht'ruf m battle cry

Schlacht'schiff n battleship

Schlach'tung f (-;-en) slaughter

Schlacke [ˈʃlakə] f (-;-n) cinder; lava; (metal) slag, dross

schlackig [ˈʃlakɪç] adj sloppy (weather)

Schlaf [ʃlaf] m (-[e]s;) sleep

Schlaf'abteil n sleeping compartment

Schlaf'anzug m pajamas

Schläfchen [ˈʃlɛfçən] n (-s;-) nap; ein S. machen take a nap

Schläfe [ˈʃlɛfə] f (-;-n) temple

schlafen [ˈʃlafən] §131 tr sleep || intr sleep; sich s. legen go to bed

Schla'fenszeit f bedtime

Schläfer -in [ˈʃlɛfər(ɪn)] §6 mf sleeper

schläfern [ˈʃlɛfərn] impers—es schläfert mich I'm sleepy

schlaff [ʃlaf] adj slack; limp; flabby; (locker) loose

Schlaf'gelegenheit f sleeping accommodations

Schlaf'kammer f bedroom

Schlaf'krankheit f sleeping sickness

schlaf'los adj sleepless

Schlaf'losigkeit f (-;) sleeplessness

Schlaf'mittel n sleeping pill

Schlaf'mütze f nightcap; (fig) sleepyhead

schläfrig [ˈʃlefrɪç] adj sleepy, drowsy

Schläf'rigkeit f (-;) sleepiness, drowsiness

Schlaf'rock m housecoat

Schlaf'saal m dormitory

Schlaf'sack m sleeping bag

Schlaf'stätte f, **Schlaf'stelle** f place to sleep

Schlaf'stube f bedroom

Schlaf'trunk m (hum) nightcap

schlaf'trunken adj still half-asleep

Schlaf'wagen m (rr) sleeping car

schlaf'wandeln intr (SEIN) walk in one's sleep

Schlafwandler -in [ˈʃlafvandlər(ɪn)] §6 mf sleepwalker

Schlaf'zimmer n bedroom

Schlag [ʃlak] m (-[e]s;⸚e) blow; stroke; (Puls-) beat; (Faust-) punch; (Hand-) slap; (Donner-) clap; (Tauben-) loft; (Art, Sorte) kind, sort, breed; (e-s Taues) coil; (der Vögel) song; (vom Pferd) kick; (e-r Kutsche) door; (Holz-) cut; (Pendel) swing; (agr) field; (elec) shock; (mil) scoop; ladleful; (pathol) stroke; ein S. ins Wasser a vain attempt; Leute seines Schlages the likes of him; S. zwölf Uhr at the stroke of twelve; von gutem S. of the right sort

Schlag'ader f artery

Schlag'anfall m (pathol) stroke

schlag'artig adj sudden, surprise; (heftig) violent || adv all of a sudden: with a bang

Schlag'baum m barrier

Schlag'besen m eggbeater

Schlag'bolzen m firing pin

Schlägel [ˈʃlegəl] m (-s;-) sledge hammer

schlagen [ˈʃlagən] §132 tr hit; strike; beat; (besiegen) defeat; (strafen) spank; (Alarm) sound; (Brücke) build; (Eier) beat; (Geld) coin; (Holz) fell; (Saiten) strike; (Schlacht) fight; die Augen zu Boden s. cast down the eyes; durch ein Sieb s. strain, sift; e-e geschlagene Stunde (coll) a solid hour; in die Flucht s. put to flight; in Fesseln s. put in chains; in Papier s. wrap in paper; Wurzel s. take root; zu Boden s. knock down || ref come to blows; fight a duel; fence; sich gut s. stand one's ground; sich s. zu side with; um sich s. flail about || intr strike; beat; (Pferd) kick; (Vogel) sing; mit den Flügeln s. flap the wings; nach j-m s. take a swing at s.o.; (fig) be like s.o., take after s.o.

schla'gend adj striking, impressive; convincing; schlagende Verbindung dueling fraternity; schlagende Wetter firedamp

Schla'ger m (-s;-) (tolle Sache) hot item; (mus, theat) hit

Schläger [ˈʃleger] m (-s;-) beater; hitter; batter; baseball bat; golf club; tennis racket; eggbeater; mallet; (Singvogel) warbler; (Raufbold) bully

Schlägerei [ʃlɛgəˈraɪ] f (-;-en) fight; fighting; brawl

Schla'gerpreis m rock-bottom price

Schla'gersänger -in §6 mf pop singer

schlag'fertig adj quick with an answer; (Antwort) ready

Schlag'holz n club, bat

Schlag'instrument n percussion instrument

Schlag'kraft f striking power

schlag'kräftig adj (Armee) powerful; (Beweis) conclusive

Schlag'licht n strong light; glare

Schlag'loch n pothole

Schlag'mal n (baseball) home plate

Schlag'ring m brass knuckles

Schlag'sahne f whipped cream

Schlag'schatten m deep shadow

Schlag'seite f (naut) list; **S. haben** have a list; (hum) be drunk

Schlag'uhr f striking clock

Schlag'weite f striking distance

Schlag'welle f breaker, comber

Schlag'wetter pl (min) firedamp

Schlag'wort n (-[e]s;ᵘᵉʳ & -e) slogan; key word, subject (in cataloguing); (Phrasendrescherei) claptrap

Schlag'wörterkatalog m (libr) subject index

Schlag'zeile f headline

Schlag'zeug n percussion instruments

Schlaks [ʃlaks] m (-es;-e) lanky person

schlaksig [ˈʃlaksɪç] adj lanky

Schlamassel [ʃlaˈmasəl] m & n (-s;-) (coll) jam, pickle, mess

Schlamm [ʃlam] m (-[e]s;-e) mud, slime; (im Motor) sludge; (fig) mire

Schlamm'bad n mud bath

schlämmen [ˈʃlɛmən] tr dredge; (metal) wash

schlammig [ˈʃlamɪç] adj muddy

Schlampe [ˈʃlampə] f (-;-n) frump; (sl) slut

Schlamperei [ʃlampəˈraɪ] f (-;-en) slovenliness; untidiness, mess

schlampig [ˈʃlampɪç] adj sloppy

schlang [ʃlaŋ] pret of schlingen

Schlange [ˈʃlaŋə] f (-;-n) snake; queue, waiting line; (Wasser-schlauch) hose; **Schlange stehen** nach line up for

schlängeln [ˈʃlɛŋəln] ref wind; (Fluß) meander; (sich krümmen) squirm; wriggle; (fig) worm one's way

Schlan'genbeschwörer -in §6 mf snake charmer

Schlan'genlinie f wavy line

schlank [ʃlaŋk] adj slender, slim; im schlanken Trabe at a fast clip

Schlank'heit f (-;) slenderness

Schlank'heitskur f—e—e **S. machen** diet

schlankweg [ˈʃlaŋkvɛk] adv flatly; downright

schlapp [ʃlap] adj slack, limp; flabby; (müde) washed out || **Schlappe** f (-;-n) setback; (Verlust) loss

schlappen [ˈʃlapən] intr flap; shuffle along || **Schlappen** m (-s;-) slipper

schlappern [ˈʃlapərn] tr lap up

schlapp'machen intr (zusammenbre-chen) collapse; (ohnmächtig werden) faint; (nicht durchhalten) call it quits

Schlapp'schwanz m (coll) weakling; sissy; (Feigling) coward

Schlaraffenland [ʃlaˈrafənlant] n paradise

Schlaraffenleben [ʃlaˈrafənlebən] n life of Riley

schlau [ʃlaʊ] adj sly; clever

Schlauch [ʃlaʊx] m (-[e]s;ᵘᵉ) hose; tube; (fig) souse; (aut) inner tube; (educ) pony

Schlauch'boot n rubber dinghy

schlauchen [ˈʃlaʊxən] tr drive hard; (mil) drill mercilessly

Schlauch'ventil n (aut) valve

Schläue [ˈʃlɔɪə] f (-;) slyness

schlau'erweise adv prudently

Schlaufe [ˈʃlaʊfə] f (-;-n) loop

Schlau'kopf m, **Schlau'meier** m sly fox

schlecht [ʃlɛçt] adj bad, poor; mir wird s. I'm getting sick; schlechter werden get worse; s. werden so bad || adv poorly; **die Uhr geht s.** the clock is off; **s. daran sein** be badly off; s. und recht somehow; s. zu sprechen sein auf (acc) have it in for

schlechterdings [ˈʃlɛçtərdɪŋs] adv utterly, absolutely

schlecht'gelaunt adj in a bad mood

schlecht'hin' adv simply, downright

schlecht'machen tr talk behind the back of

schlechtweg [ˈʃlɛçtvɛk] adv simply, downright

schlecken [ˈʃlɛkən] tr lick || intr eat sweets, nibble

Schleckerei [ʃlɛkəˈraɪ] f (-;-en) sweets

schleckern [ˈʃlɛkərn] intr have a sweet tooth || impers—mich schleckert es nach I have a yen for

Schlegel [ˈʃlegəl] m (-s;-) sledge hammer; (Holz-) mallet; (culin) leg; (mus) drumstick

schleichen [ˈʃlaɪçən] §85 ref & intr (SEIN) sneak

schlei'chend adj creeping; furtive; (Krankheit) lingering; (Gift) slow

Schlei'cher m (-s;-) sneak, hypocrite

Schleicherei [ʃlaɪçəˈraɪ] f (-;-en) sneaking; underhand dealing

Schleich'gut n contraband

Schleich'handel m underhand dealing; smuggling; black-marketing

Schleich'weg m secret path; **auf Schleichwegen** in a roundabout way

Schleier [ˈʃlaɪ.ər] m (-s;-) veil; haze; gauze

schlei'erhaft adj hazy; mysterious; (fig) veiled; **das ist mir s.** I don't know what to make of it

Schleif- [ʃlaɪf] comb.fm. sliding; grinding, abrasive

Schleif'bürste f (elec) brush

Schleife [ˈʃlaɪfə] f (-;-n) (am Kleid, im Haar) bow; (in Schnüren) slip-knot; (e-r Straße) hairpin curve; (e-s Flusses) bend; (Wende-) loop; (mit langen Bändern) streamer; (Rutschbahn) slide, chute; (aer) loop

schleifen [ˈʃlaɪfən] tr drag; (Kleid) trail along; demolish; raze; (mus) slur || §88 tr grind; whet; polish; (Glas, Edelstein) cut; (mil) drill hard || §109 intr drag, trail

Schleif′mit′tel n abrasive
Schleif′papier n sandpaper
Schleif′rad n emery wheel
Schleif′stein m whetstone
Schleim |/laim| m (-[e]s;-e) slime; mucus, phlegm
Schleim′haut f mucous membrane
schleimig |′/laimiç| adj slimy; mucous
schleißen |′/laisən| §53 tr split; slit; (Federkiele) strip || intr wear out
Schlemm |/lɛm| m (-s;-e) (cards) slam
schlemmen |′/lɛmən| intr carouse; gorge oneself; live high
Schlem′mer –in §6 mf glutton, guzzler; gourmet
schlem′merhaft adj gluttonous; (üppig) plentiful, luxurious
Schlem′merlokal n gourmet restaurant
Schlempe |′/lɛmpə| f (-;-n) slop
schlendern |′/lɛndərn| intr (SEIN) stroll
Schlendrian |′/lɛndri·an| m (-s;) routine
schlenkern |′/lɛŋkərn| tr dangle, swing || intr dangle; **mit den Armen s.** swing the arms
Schlepp– |/lɛp| comb.fm. towing, drag
Schlepp′dampfer m tugboat
Schlepp′dienst m towing service
Schleppe |′/lɛpə| f (-;-n) train
schleppen |′/lɛpən| tr drag; lug, tote; (aer, naut) tow || ref drag along; **sich mit etw s.** be burdened with s.th.
Schlep′penkleid n dress with a train
Schlep′per m (-s;-) hauler; tractor; tugboat; tender, lighter
Schlepp′fischerei f trawling
Schlepp′netz n dragnet, dredge; trawling net
Schlepp′netzboot n trawler
Schlepp′schiff n tugboat
Schlepp′tau n towline; **ins S. nehmen** take in tow
Schleuder |′/lɔidər| f (-;-n) sling; slingshot; (aer) catapult; (mach) centrifuge
Schleu′derpreis m cutrate price
Schleu′dersitz m (aer) ejection seat
schleunig |′/lɔiniç| adj speedy || adv **in all haste**; (sofort) at once
schleunigst |′/lɔiniçst| adv as soon as possible; right away
Schleuse |′/lɔizə| f (-;-n) lock, sluice, sluice way; drain, sewer
schleusen |′/lɔizən| tr (fig) maneuver
schlich |/liç| pret of **schleichen** ||
Schlich |/liç| m (-[e]s;-e) trick; **alle Schliche kennen know all the ropes**; **j–m auf die Schliche (or hinter j–s Schliche) kommen** be on to s.o.
schlicht |/liçt| adj smooth; plain
schlichten |′/liçtən| tr smooth; (fig) settle, arbitrate
Schlich′ter –in §6 mf arbitrator
Schlich′tung f (-;-en) arbitration; settlement
schlief |/lif| pret of **schlafen**
Schließe |′/lisə| f (-;-n) clasp; pin
schließen |′/lisən| §76 tr shut, close; lock; end, conclude; (Betrieb) shut

down; (Bücher) balance; (Konto; Klammer) close; (Bündnis) form; (Frieden; Rede) conclude; (Kompromiß) reach; (Heirat) form; (Geschäft, Handel) strike; (Versammlung) adjourn; (Wette) make; (Reihen) (mil) close; **ans Herz s.** press to one's heart; **aus etw. s., daß** conclude from s.th. that; **den Zug s.** (mil) bring up the rear; **e–n Vergleich s.** come to an agreement; **ins Herz s.** take a liking to; **kurz s.** (elec) short || ref shut, close; **in sich s.** comprise, include; (bedeuten) imply; (umfassen) involve; **von sich auf andere s.** judge others by oneself || intr shut, close; end
Schließ′fach n post office box; safe-deposit box
schließlich |′/lislɪç| adj final, eventual || adv finally
schliff |/lif| pp of **schleifen** || **Schliff** m (-[e]s;-e) polish; (e–s Diamanten) cut; (fig) polish; (mil) rigorous training
schlimm |/lim| adj bad; (bedenklich) serious; (traurig) sad; (wund) sore; (eklig) nasty; **am schlimmsten** worst; **immer schlimmer** worse and worse; **s. daran sein** be badly off
schlimmstenfalls |′/limstənfals| adv at worst
Schlinge |′/liŋə| f (-;-n) loop; coil; (fig) trap, difficulty; (bot) tendril; (hunt) snare; (surg) sling; **in die S. gehen** (fig) fall into a trap
Schlingel |′/liŋəl| m (-s;-) rascal; **fauler S.** lazybones
schlingen |′/liŋən| §142 tr tie; twist; wind; wrap; gulp || ref wind, coil; climb, creep || intr gulp down food
Schlingerbewegung |′/liŋərbəveguŋ| f (naut) roll
schlingern |′/liŋərn| intr (naut) roll
Schlinggewächs |′/liŋgəveks| n, **Schlingpflanze** |′/liŋpflantsə| f climber
Schlips |/lips| m (-es;-e) necktie
Schlitten |′/litən| m (-s;-) sled; (an der Schreibmaschine) carriage
schlit′tenfahren §71 intr go sleigh riding; **mit j–m s.** make life miserable for s.o.
schlittern |′/litərn| intr (HABEN & SEIN) slide; (Wagen) skid
Schlittschuh |′/lit/u| m ice skate; **S. laufen** skate, go ice-skating
Schlitt′schuhläufer –in §6 mf ice skater
Schlitz |/lits| m (-es;-e) slit, slot; (Hose, pr.) fly
schlit′zäugig adj slit-eyed, sloe-eyed
schlitzen |′/litsən| tr slit; rip
Schloß |/los| n (Schlosses; Schlösser) castle; country mansion; lock; snap, clasp; **hinter S. und Riegel** behind bars; **unter S. und Riegel** under lock and key
Schloße |′/losə| f (-;-n) hailstone
Schlosser |′/losər| m (-s;-) mechanic, locksmith
Schloß′graben m moat
Schlot |/lot| m (-[e]s;-e & ″e) chimney, smokestack; (fig) louse

Schlot'baron m (coll) tycoon
Schlot'feger m chimney sweep
schlotterig ['ʃlɔtərɪç] adj loose, dangling; wobbly; (*liederlich*) slovenly
schlottern ['ʃlɔtərn] intr fit loosely; (*baumeln*) dangle; (*zittern*) tremble; (*wackeln*) wobble
Schlucht [ʃluçt] f (-;-en) gorge; ravine
schluchzen ['ʃluxtsən] intr sob
Schluck [ʃluk] m (-[e]s;-e) gulp; sip
Schluck'auf m (-s;) hiccups
schlucken ['ʃlukən] tr & intr gulp
Schlucker ['ʃlukər] m (-s;)—**armer S.** (coll) poor devil
schlucksen ['ʃluksən] intr have the hiccups
schluderig ['ʃludərɪç] adj slipshod
schludern ['ʃludərn] intr do slipshod work
Schlummer ['ʃlumər] m (-s;) slumber
Schlum'merlied n lullaby
schlummern ['ʃlumərn] intr slumber
schlum'mernd adj latent
Schlum'merrolle f cushion
Schlund [ʃlunt] m (-[e]s;-e) gullet; pharynx; (*e-s Vulcans*) crater; (fig) abyss
Schlund'röhre f esophagus
Schlupf [ʃlupf] m (-[e]s;⸚e) hole; (elec, mach) slip
schlüpfen ['ʃlʏpfən] intr (SEIN) slip; sneak
Schlüp'fer m (-s;-) (pair of) panties; (pair of) bloomers
Schlupf'jacke f sweater
Schlupf'loch n hiding place; loophole
schlüpfrig ['ʃlʏpfrɪç] adj slippery; (*obszön*) off-color
Schlupf'winkel m hiding place; haunt
schlurfen ['ʃlurfən] intr (SEIN) shuffle
schlürfen ['ʃlʏrfən] tr slurp; lap up
Schluß [ʃlus] m (Schlusses; Schlüsse) end, close; (*Ablauf*) expiration; (*Folgerung*) conclusion; **S. damit!** time!; cut it out!; **S. folgt** to be concluded; **S. machen mit** put an end to; knock off from (*work*); break up with (*s.o.*); **zum S.** in conclusion
Schluß'effekt m upshot
Schlüssel ['ʃlʏsəl] m (-s;-) key; wrench; quota; code key; (fig) key, clue
Schlüs'selbein n collarbone, clavicle
Schlüs'selblume f cowslip; **helle S.** primrose
Schlüs'selbrett n keyboard
Schlüs'selbund m bunch of keys
schlüs'selfertig adj ready for occupancy
Schlüs'selloch n keyhole
Schluß'ergebnis n final result
Schluß'folge f, **Schluß'folgerung** f conclusion, deduction
Schluß'formel f complimentary close
schlüssig ['ʃlʏsɪç] adj determined; logical; (*Beweis*) conclusive; **sich** [*dat*] **noch nicht s. sein, ob** be undecided whether
Schluß'licht n (aut) taillight
Schluß'linie f (typ) dash
Schluß'rennen n (sport) final heat
Schluß'runde f (sport) finals
Schluß'schein m sales agreement

Schluß'verkauf m clearance sale
Schmach [ʃmax] f (-;) disgrace, shame; insult; humiliation
schmachten ['ʃmaxtən] intr (vor dat) languish (with); **s. nach** long for
Schmacht'fetzen ['ʃmaxtfetsən] m sentimental song or book; melodrama
schmächtig ['ʃmɛçtɪç] adj scrawny
Schmacht'riemen ['ʃmaxtrimən] m—**den S. enger schnallen** (fig) tighten one's belt
schmach'voll adj disgraceful; humiliating
schmackhaft ['ʃmakhaft] adj tasty
schmähen ['ʃmɛ·ən] tr revile, abuse; speak ill of
schmählich ['ʃmɛlɪç] adj disgraceful, scandalous; humiliating
Schmä'hrede ['ʃmɛredə] f abuse; diatribe
Schmäh'schrift ['ʃmɛʃrɪft] f libel
schmähsüchtig ['ʃmɛzʏçtɪç] adj abusive
Schmä'hung f (-;-en) abuse; slander
schmal [ʃmal] adj narrow; slim; meager
schmälern ['ʃmɛlərn] tr curtail; belittle
Schmal'spurbahn f narrow-gauge railroad
Schmalz [ʃmalts] n (-[e]s;) lard, grease; (fig) schmaltz
schmalzen ['ʃmaltsən] tr lard, grease
schmalzig ['ʃmaltsɪç] adj greasy; fatty; (fig) schmaltzy
schmarotzen [ʃma'rɔtsən] intr (bei) sponge (on)
Schmarot'zer m (-s;-) sponger; (zool) parasite
schmarotzerisch [ʃma'rɔtsərɪʃ] adj sponging; (zool) parasitic(al)
Schmarre ['ʃmarə] f (-;-n) scar; scratch
schmarrig ['ʃmarɪç] adj scary
Schmatz [ʃmats] m (-es;-e) hearty kiss
schmatzen ['ʃmatsən] tr (coll) kiss loudly ‖ intr smack one's lips
Schmaus [ʃmaus] m (-es;⸚e) feast; treat
schmausen ['ʃmauzən] intr (von) feast (on)
schmecken ['ʃmɛkən] tr taste, sample; (fig) stand ‖ intr taste good; **s. nach** taste like
Schmeichelei [ʃmaiçə'lai] f (-;-en) flattery; coaxing
schmeichelhaft ['ʃmaiçəlhaft] adj flattering
schmeicheln ['ʃmaiçəln] ref—**sich** [*dat*] **s. zu** (*inf*) pride oneself on (*ger*) ‖ intr be flattering; (*dat*) flatter
Schmeich'ler m —in §6 mf flatterer
schmeichlerisch ['ʃmaiçlərɪʃ] adj flattering; complimentary; fawning
schmeißen ['ʃmaisən] §53 tr (coll) throw; (coll) manage; **e-e Runde Bier s.** set up a round of beer ‖ ref—**mit Geld um sich s.** throw money around
Schmelz [ʃmɛlts] m (-es;-e) enamel; glaze; melodious ring; (fig) bloom
schmelzen ['ʃmɛltsən] §133 tr melt; smelt ‖ intr (SEIN) melt; (fig) soften

schmel'zend *adj* mellow; melodious

Schmelzerei [ˌʃmɛltsə'raɪ] *f* (-;-en) foundry

schmelz'flüssig *adj* molten

Schmelz'hütte *f* foundry

Schmelz'käse *m* soft cheese

Schmelz'ofen *m* smelting furnace

Schmelz'punkt *m* melting point

Schmelz'tiegel *m* crucible, melting pot

Schmer [ʃmer] *m & n* (-s;) fat, grease

Schmer'bauch *m* (coll) potbelly

Schmerz [ʃmɛrts] *m* (-es;-en) pain, ache; **mit Schmerzen** (coll) anxiously, impatiently

schmerzen [ʃmɛrtsən] *tr & intr* hurt

schmer'zend *adj* aching, sore

Schmer'zensgeld *n* damages (*for pain or anguish*)

Schmer'zenskind *n* problem child

schmerz'haft *adj* painful, aching

schmerz'lich *adj* painful, severe

schmerz'lindernd *adj* soothing

schmerz'los *adj* painless

Schmerz'schwelle *f* threshold of pain

Schmetterling [ʃmɛtərlɪŋ] *m* (-s;-e) butterfly

Schmet'terlingsstil *m* (sport) butterfly

schmettern [ʃmɛtərn] *tr* smash; **zu Boden s.** knock down || *intr* (*Trompete*) blare; (*Vogel*) warble

Schmied [ʃmit] *m* (-[e]s;-e) smith

Schmiede [ʃmidə] *f* (-;-n) forge; blacksmith shop

Schmie'deeisen *n* wrought iron

Schmie'dehammer *m* sledge hammer

schmieden [ʃmidən] *tr* forge; hammer; (*Pläne, usw.*) devise, concoct

schmiegen [ʃmigən] *tr—das Kinn* (or **die Wange**) **in die Hand s.** prop one's chin (or cheek) in one's hand || *ref* (**an** *acc*) snuggle up (to); **sich s. und biegen vor** (*dat*) bow and scrape before

schmiegsam [ʃmikzam] *adj* flexible

Schmier– [ʃmir] *comb.fm.* grease, lubricating; smearing

Schmiere [ʃmirə] *f* (-;-n) grease; lubricant; salve; (*Schmutz*) muck; (fig) mess; (fig) spanking; (theat) barnstormers; **S. stehen** be the lookout man

schmieren [ʃmirən] *tr* grease, lubricate; smear; (*Butter*) spread; (*Brot*) butter; (*bestechen*) bribe; **j—m e-e s.** (coll) paste s.o.; **wie geschmiert** like greased lightning || *ref—sich* [*dat*] **die Kehle s.** (coll) wet one's whistle || *intr* scribble

Schmie'renkomödiant –in §7 *mf* (theat) barnstormer, ham

Schmiererei [ʃmirə'raɪ] *f* (-;-en) greasing; smearing; scribbling

Schmier'fink *m* scrawler; (*Schmutzkerl*) dirty fellow

Schmier'geld *n* (coll) bribe; (coll) hush money; (pol) slush fund

schmierig [ʃmirɪç] *adj* smeary, greasy; oily; (*Geschäfte*) dirty

Schmier'käse *m* cheese spread

Schmier'mittel *n* lubricant

Schmier'pistole *f*, **Schmier'presse** *f* grease gun

Schmie'rung *f* (-;-en) lubrication

Schminke [ʃmɪŋkə] *f* (-;-n) rouge; make-up

schminken [ʃmɪŋkən] *tr* apply make-up to; rouge; **die Lippen s.** put on lipstick || *ref* put on make-up

Schminkunterlage [ʃmɪŋkʊntərlagə] *f* base

Schmirgel [ʃmɪrgəl] *m* (-s;) emery

Schmir'gelleinen *n*, **Schmir'gelleinwand** *f* emery cloth

Schmir'gelpapier *n* emery paper

Schmir'gelscheibe *f* emery wheel

Schmiß [ʃmɪs] *m* (Schmisses; Schmisse) (coll) stroke, blow; (coll) gash; (coll) dueling scar; (coll) zip

schmissig [ʃmɪsɪç] *adj* (coll) snazzy

schmollen [ʃmɔlən] *intr* pout, sulk

schmolz [ʃmɔlts] *pret* of **schmelzen**

Schmorbraten [ʃmorbratən] *m* braised meat

schmoren [ʃmorən] *tr* braise, stew || *intr* (fig) swelter; **laß ihn s.!** let him stew!

Schmuck [ʃmʊk] *adj* nice, cute; smart, dapper; (*sauber*) neat || **Schmuck** *m* (-[e]s;) ornament; decoration; trimmings; trinket(s); jewelry

schmücken [ʃmʏkən] *tr* adorn; decorate, trim; (*Aufsatz*) embellish || *ref* spruce up, dress up

Schmuck'kästchen *n* jewel box

schmuck'los *adj* unadorned, plain

Schmuck'waren *pl* jewelry

Schmuddel [ʃmʊdəl] *m* (-s;-) slob

schmuddelig [ʃmʊdəlɪç] *adj* dirty

Schmuggel [ʃmʊgəl] *m* (-s;), **Schmuggelei** [ʃmʊgə'laɪ] *f* (-;-en) smuggling

schmuggeln [ʃmʊgəln] *tr & intr* smuggle

Schmug'gelware *f* contraband

Schmuggler –in [ʃmʊglər(ɪn)] §6 *mf* smuggler

schmunzeln [ʃmʊntsəln] *intr* grin || **Schmunzeln** *n* (-s;) big grin

Schmutz [ʃmʊts] *m* (-es;) dirt, filth; (*Zote*) smut

schmutzen [ʃmʊtsən] *tr & intr* soil

Schmutz'fink *m* (coll) slob

Schmutz'fleck *m* stain, smudge, blotch

schmut'zig *adj* dirty

Schnabel [ʃnabəl] *m* (-s;⁼) beak, bill; **halt den S.!** (sl) shut up!

Schna'belhieb *m* peck

schnäbeln [ʃnebəln] *tr & intr* peck; (fig) kiss

Schnalle [ʃnalə] *f* (-;-n) buckle; (vulg) whore

schnallen [ʃnalən] *tr* buckle, fasten

schnalzen [ʃnaltsən] *intr—mit den Fingern s.** snap one's fingers; **mit der Zunge s.** click one's tongue

schnapp [ʃnap] *interj* snap!

schnappen [ʃnapən] *tr* grab; (*Dieb*) nab || *intr* snap; **ins Schloß s.** snap shut; **mit den Fingern s.** snap one's fingers; **nach Luft s.** gasp for air; **s. nach** snap at

Schnapp'messer *n* jackknife

Schnapp'schuß *m* (phot) snapshot

Schnaps [ʃnaps] *m* (-es;⁼e) hard liquor

Schnaps'brennerei *f* distillery

Schnaps'bruder *m* (coll) booze hound

Schnaps'idee f (coll) crazy idea

schnarchen [ˈʃnarçən] intr snore

Schnarre [ˈʃnarə] f (-;-n) rattle

schnarren [ˈʃnarən] intr rattle; (Säge) buzz; (Insekten) drone, buzz

schnattern [ˈʃnatərn] intr (Enten) cackle; (Zähne) chatter; (fig) gab

schnauben [ˈʃnaubən] intr pant, puff; (Pferd) snort; **nach Rache s.** breathe revenge; **vor Wut s.** fume with rage || ref blow one's nose

schnaufen [ˈʃnaufən] intr pant; wheeze

Schnau'fer m (-s;-) (coll) deep breath

Schnauzbart [ˈʃnautsbart] m mustache

Schnauze [ˈʃnautsə] f (-;-n) snout, muzzle; spout; (sl) snoot; (sl) big mouth

Schnauzer [ˈʃnautsər] m (-s;-) schnauzer

schnauzig [ˈʃnautsɪç] adj rude

Schnecke [ˈʃnɛkə] f (-;-n) snail; (Nacht-) slug; (e-r Säule) volute; spiral; (anat) cochlea; (mach) worm; (e-r Violine) (mus) scroll

Schneckenhaus (Schnek'kenhaus) n snail shell

Schneckentempo (Schnek'kentempo) n (fig) snail's pace

Schnee [ʃne] m (-s;) snow; whipped egg white

Schnee'besen m eggbeater

Schnee'brett n snow slide, avalanche

Schnee'brille f snow goggles

Schnee'decke f blanket of snow

Schnee'flocke f snowflake

Schnee'gestöber n snow flurry

schneeig [ˈʃne-ɪç] adj snowy

Schnee'matsch m slush

Schnee'pflug m snowplow

Schnee'schaufel f, **Schnee'schippe** f snow shovel

Schnee'schläger m eggbeater

Schnee'schmelze f thaw

Schnee'treiben n blizzard

schneeverweht [ˈʃnefervet] adj snowbound

Schnee'verwehung f snowdrift

Schnee'wehe f snowdrift

Schneewittchen [ˈʃnevɪtçən] n (-s;) Snow White

Schneid [ʃnaɪt] m (-[e]s;) (coll) pluck; (Mut) (coll) guts

Schneid'brenner m cutting torch

Schneide [ˈʃnaɪdə] f (-;-n) (cutting) edge; (e-s Hobels) blade; **auf des Messers S.** (fig) on the razor's edge

Schnei'debrett n cutting board

Schnei'demaschine f cutter, slicer

Schnei'demühle f sawmill

schneiden [ˈʃnaɪdən] §106 tr cut; (Baum) prune; (Fingernägel) pare; (Hecke) trim; (nicht grüßen) snub; (surg) operate on; (tennis) slice; **Gesichter s.** make faces; **klein s.** cut up || ref (fig) be mistaken; (fig) be disappointed; (math) intersect; **sich in den Finger s.** cut one's finger || intr cut

Schnei'der (-s;-) m cutter; tailor

Schneiderei [ʃnaɪdəˈraɪ] f (-;-en) tailoring; (Werkstatt) tailorshop

Schnei'derin f (-;-nen) dressmaker

schneidern [ˈʃnaɪdərn] tr make || intr do tailoring; be a dressmaker

Schnei'derpuppe f dummy

Schnei'dezahn m incisor

schneidig [ˈʃnaɪdɪç] adj sharp-edged; energetic; smart, sharp

schneien [ˈʃnaɪ-ən] impers—es schneit it is snowing

Schneise [ˈʃnaɪzə] f (-;-n) lane (between rows of trees)

schnell [ʃnɛl] adj fast, quick

Schnellauf (Schnell'lauf) m race; sprint; speed skating

Schnell'bahn f high-speed railroad

Schnelle [ˈʃnɛlə] f (-;-n) speed; (Strom-) rapids; **auf die S.** (coll) in a hurry, very briefly

schnellen [ˈʃnɛlən] tr let fly || intr (SEIN) spring, jump up; (Preise) shoot up; **mit dem Finger s.** snap one's fingers

Schnell'gang m (aut) overdrive

Schnellhefter [ˈʃnɛlheftər] m (-s;-) folder, file

Schnell'imbiß m snack

Schnell'kraft f elasticity

schnellstens [ˈʃnɛlstəns] adv as fast as possible

Schnell'verfahren n quick process; (jur) summary proceeding

Schnell'zug m express train

Schneppe [ˈʃnɛpə] f (-;-n) spout; (sl) prostitute

schneuzen [ˈʃnɔɪtsən] ref blow one's nose

schniegeln [ˈʃnigəln] ref dress up; **geschniegelt und gebügelt** dressed to kill

schnipfeln [ˈʃnɪpfəln] tr & intr snip

Schnippchen [ˈʃnɪpçən] n—**j-m ein S. schlagen** (coll) pull a fast one on s.o.; outwit s.o.

Schnippel [ˈʃnɪpəl] m & n (-s;-) chip

schnippeln [ˈʃnɪpəln] tr & intr snip

schnippen [ˈʃnɪpən] intr—**mit den Fingern s.** (coll) snap one's fingers

schnippisch [ˈʃnɪpɪʃ] adj fresh || adv pertly; **s. erwidern** snap back

schnitt [ʃnɪt] pret of **schneiden** || **Schnitt** m (-[e]s;-e) cut, incision; (Kerbe) notch; (Schnitte) slice; (Quer-) profile, cross section; (Durch-) average; (e-s Anzuges) cut, style; (Gewinn) cut; (agr) reaping; (bb) edge; (cin) editing; (geom) intersection; **weicher Schnitt** (cin) dissolve

Schnitt'ansicht f sectional view

Schnitt'ball m (tennis) slice

Schnitt'blumen pl cut flowers

Schnitt'bohnen pl string beans

Schnittchen [ˈʃnɪtçən] n (-s;-) thin slice; sandwich

Schnitte [ˈʃnɪtə] f (-;-n) slice

Schnit'ter **–in** §6 mf reaper, mower

Schnitt'fläche f (geom) plane

Schnitt'holz n lumber

schnittig [ˈʃnɪtɪç] adj smart-looking; (aut) streamlined

Schnitt'lauch [ˈʃnɪtlaux] m (-[e]s;) (bot) chive

Schnitt'linie f (geom) secant

Schnitt'meister m (cin) editor

Schnitt′muster n pattern (of dress, etc.)

Schnitt′punkt m intersection

Schnitt′waren pl dry goods

Schnitt′wunde f cut, gash

Schnitz [ʃnɪts] m (—es;—e) cut; slice; chop; chip

Schnitzel [′ʃnɪtsəl] n (—s;—) chip; slice; shred; (Abfälle) parings; (culin) cutlet

schnitzeln [′ʃnɪtsəln] tr cut up; shred; (Holz) whittle

schnitzen [′ʃnɪtsən] tr carve

Schnit′zer m (—s;—) carver; (Fehler) blunder; grober S. boner

Schnitzerei [ʃnɪtsə′raɪ] f (—;—en) wood carving, carved work

schnob [ʃnop] pret of schnauben

schnodderig [′ʃnɔdərɪç] adj brash

schnöde [′ʃnøːdə] adj vile; disdainful; (Gewinn) filthy

Schnorchel [′ʃnɔrçəl] m (—s;—) snorkel

Schnörkel [′ʃnœrkəl] m (—s;—) (beim Schreiben) flourish; (fig) frills; (archit) scroll

schnorren [′ʃnɔrən] tr (coll) chisel, bum || intr (coll) sponge, chisel

Schnösel [′ʃnøːzəl] m (—s;—) wise guy

schnüffeln [′ʃnʏfəln] intr snoop around; (an dat) sniff (at)

Schnüff′ler —in §6 mf (coll) snoop

Schnuller [′ʃnʊlər] m (—s;—) pacifier

Schnultze [′ʃnʊltsə] f (—;—n) (coll) tear-jerker

schnultzig [′ʃnʊltsɪç] adj (coll) corny, mawkish

schnupfen [′ʃnʊpfən] tr snuff || intr take snuff || **Schnupfen** m (—s;—) cold; den S. bekommen catch a cold

Schnupftabak [′ʃnʊpftabak] m snuff

schnuppe [′ʃnʊpə] adj—das ist mir s. it's all the same to me || **Schnuppe** f (—;—n) shooting star; (e—r Kerze) snuff

Schnur [ʃnuːr] f (—:—e & —en) string; (Band) braid; (elec) flexible cord; nach der S. regularly

Schnürband [′ʃnyːrbant] n (—[e]s;—er) shoestring; corset lace

Schnürchen [′ʃnyːrçən] n (—s;—) string; etw am S. haben have at one's fingertips; wie am S. like clockwork

schnüren [′ʃnyːrən] tr tie; lace; (Perlen) string || ref put on a corset

schnur′gerade adj straight || adv straight, as the crow flies

schnurr [ʃnʊr] interj purr!; buzz!

Schnurrbart [′ʃnʊrbart] m mustache

schnurren [′ʃnʊrən] intr (Katze) purr; (Rad) whir; (Maschine) hum; (schnorren) sponge, chisel

schnurrig [′ʃnʊrɪç] adj funny; queer

Schnürschuh [′ʃnyːrʃuː] m oxford shoe

Schnürsenkel [′ʃnyːrzɛŋkəl] m shoestring

schnurstracks [′ʃnʊrʃtraks] adv right away; directly; s. entgegengesetzt diametrically opposite; s. losgehen auf (acc) make a beeline for

schob [ʃop] pret of schieben

Schober [′ʃoːbər] m (—s;—) stack

Schock [ʃɔk] m (—[e]s;—s) shock || n (—[e]s;—e) threescore

schockant [ʃɔ′kant] adj shocking

schockieren [ʃɔ′kiːrən] tr shock

schofel [′ʃoːfəl] adj mean; miserable; (schäbig) shabby; (geizig) stingy

Schöffe [′ʃœfə] m (—n;—n) juror

Schokolade [ʃoko′laːdə] f (—;—n) chocolate

schokoladen [ʃokoʹlaːdən] adj chocolate

Schokola′dentafel f chocolate bar

scholl [ʃɔl] pret of schallen

Scholle [′ʃɔlə] f (—;—n) clod; sod; stratum; ice floe; (ichth) sole; heimatliche S. native soil

schon [ʃon] adv already; as early as; yet, as yet; (sogar) even; (bloß) the bare, the mere; ich komme s.! all right, I'm coming!; s. am folgenden Tage on the very next day; s. der Gedanke the mere thought; s. früher before now; s. gut! all right!; s. immer always; s. lange long since, for a long time; s. wieder again

schön [ʃøːn] adj beautiful; nice; (Künste) fine; (Mann) handsome; (Summe) nice round; (Geschlecht) fair; schönen Dank! many thanks!; schönen Gruß an (acc) best regards to || adv nicely; der Hund macht s. the dog sits up and begs; s. warm nice and warm

schonen [′ʃoːnən] tr spare; take it easy on; treat with consideration || ref take care of oneself

scho′nend adj careful; considerate

schön′färben tr gloss over

Schon′frist f period of grace

Schon′gang m (aut) overdrive

Schön′heit f (—;—en) beauty

Schön′heitsfehler m flaw

Schön′heitskönigin f beauty queen

Schön′heitspflege f beauty treatment

schön′tun §154 intr (dat) flatter; (dat) flirt (with)

Scho′nung f (—;—en) care, careful treatment; mercy; consideration; tree nursery; wild-game preserve

scho′nungslos adj unsparing; merciless; relentless

scho′nungsvoll adj considerate

Schon′zeit f (hunt) closed season

Schopf [ʃɔpf] m (—[e]s;—e) tuft of hair; (orn) crest

schöpfen [′ʃœpfən] tr draw; bail; scoop, ladle; (frische Luft) breathe; (Mut) take; Verdacht s. become suspicious; wieder Atem (or Luft) s. (fig) breathe freely again

Schöp′fer m (—s;—) creator; author; composer; painter; sculptor; dipper, ladle

schöpferisch [′ʃœpfərɪʃ] adj creative

Schöp′ferkraft f creative power

Schöpf′kelle f scoop

Schöpf′löffel m ladle

Schöp′fung f (—;—en) creation

Schoppen [′ʃɔpən] m (—s;—) pint; glass of beer, glass of wine

schor [ʃoːr] pret of scheren

Schorf [ʃɔrf] m (—[e]s;—e) scab

Schornstein [′ʃɔrnʃtaɪn] m chimney; smokestack

Schorn′steinfeger m chimney sweeper

Schoß [ʃoːs] m (Schosses; Schosse)

sprout ‖ [ʃos] m (-es;⁼e) lap; womb; (fig) bosom; **die Hände in den S. legen** cross one's arms; (fig) be idle
Schößling [ˈʃœslɪŋ] m (-s;-e) shoot
Schote [ˈʃoːtə] f (-;-n) pod, shell
Schotte [ˈʃotə] m (-n;-n) Scotchman ‖ f (-;-n) (naut) bulkhead
Schotter [ˈʃotər] m (-s;-) gravel; macadam, crushed stone; (rr) ballast
Schottin [ˈʃotɪn] f (-;-nen) Scotchwoman
schottisch [ˈʃotɪʃ] adj Scotch
schraffieren [ʃraˈfiːrən] tr hatch
schräg [ʃrɛk] adj oblique; (abfallend) slanting, sloping; diagonal ‖ adv obliquely; **s. gegenüber von** diagonally across from; **s. geneigt** sloping
Schräg′linie f diagonal
schrak [ʃrak] pret of **schrecken**
Schramme [ˈʃramə] f (-;-n) scratch, abrasion; scar
schrammen [ˈʃramən] tr scratch; skin
Schrank [ʃraŋk] m (-[e]s;⁼e) closet
Schranke [ˈʃraŋkə] f (-;-n) barrier; (fig) bounds, limit; (jur) bar; (rr) gate; (sport) starting gate
schran′kenlos adj boundless; exaggerated
Schran′kenwärter m (rr) signalman
Schrank′fach n compartment
Schrank′koffer m wardrobe trunk
Schrapnell [ʃrapˈnɛl] n (-s;-e & -s) shrapnel, piece of shrapnel
Schraubdeckel [ˈʃraupdɛkəl] m screw-on cap
Schraube [ˈʃraubə] f (-;-n) screw; bolt; (aer, naut) propeller
schrauben [ˈʃraubən] tr screw; **in die Höhe s.** raise ‖ ref—**sich in die Höhe s.** circle higher and higher
Schrau′benflügel m propeller blade
Schrau′bengang m, **Schrau′bengewinde** n thread (of a screw)
Schrau′benmutter f (-;-n) nut
Schrau′benschlüssel m wrench; **verstellbarer S.** monkey wrench
Schrau′benstrahl m, **Schrau′benstrom** m (aer) slipstream
Schraubenzieher [ˈʃraubəntsiˑər] m (-s;-) screwdriver
Schraubstock [ˈʃraupʃtok] m vice
Schrebergarten [ˈʃreːbərgartən] m garden plot (at edge of town)
Schreck [ʃrɛk] m (-[e]s;-e) var of **Schrecken**
Schreck′bild n frightful sight; boogeyman
schrecken [ˈʃrɛkən] tr frighten, scare ‖ **Schrecken** m (-s;-) fright, fear
Schreckensbotschaft (**Schrek′kensbotschaft**) f alarming news
Schreckensherrschaft (**Schrek′kensherrschaft**) f reign of terror
Schreckenskammer (**Schrek′kenskammer**) f chamber of horrors
Schreckensregiment (**Schrek′kensregiment**) n reign of teror, terrorism
Schreckenstat (**Schrek′kenstat**) f atrocity
schreck′haft adj timid
schreck′lich adj frightful, terrible
Schrecknis [ˈʃrɛknɪs] n (-ses;-se) horror

Schreck′schuß m warning shot
Schreck′sekunde f reaction time
Schrei [ʃrai] m (-[e]s;-e) cry, shout; **letzter S.** latest fashion
Schreib- [ʃraip] comb.fm. writing
Schreib′art f style; spelling
Schreib′bedarf m stationery
Schreib′block m writing pad, note pad
schreiben [ˈʃraibən] §62 tr write; spell; type; **ins Konzept s.** make a rough draft of; **ins reine s.** make a clean copy; **Noten s.** copy music ‖ ref spell one's name ‖ intr write; spell; type ‖ **Schreiben** n (-s;-) writing; (com) letter
Schrei′ber m (-s;-) writer; clerk; recording instrument, recorder
schreib′faul adj too lazy to write
Schreib′feder f pen
Schreib′fehler m slip of the pen
Schreib′heft n copybook, exercise book
Schreib′mappe f portfolio
Schreib′maschine f typewriter; **mit der S. geschrieben** typed; **S. schreiben** type
Schreib′maschinenfarbband n (-[e]s; ⁼er) typewriter ribbon
Schreib′maschinenschreiber –in §6 mf typist
Schreib′maschinenschrift f typescript
Schreib′materialien pl, **Schreib′papier** n stationery
Schreib′schrift f (typ) script
Schreib′stube f (mil) orderly room
Schreib′tisch m desk
Schrei′bung f (-;-en) spelling
Schreib′unterlage f desk pad
Schreib′waren pl stationery
Schreib′warenhandlung f stationery store
Schreibweise f style; spelling
Schreib′zeug n writing materials
schreien [ˈʃraiˑən] §135 tr cry, shout, scream, howl ‖ ref—**sich heiser s.** shout oneself hoarse; **sich tot s.** yell one's lungs out ‖ intr cry, shout, scream, howl; (Esel) bray; (Eule) screech; (Schwein) squeal; **s. nach** clamor for; **s. über** (acc) cry out against; **s. vor** (dat) shout for (joy); cry out in (pain); roar with (laughter) ‖ **Schreien** n (-s;) shouting; **das ist zum S.!** that's a scream!
schrei′end adj shrill; (Farbe) loud; (Unrecht) flagrant
Schrei′hals m (coll) crybaby
Schrei′krampf m crying fit
Schrein [ʃrain] m (-[e]s;-e) reliquary
Schreiner [ˈʃrainər] m (-s;-) carpenter; cabinetmaker
schreiten [ˈʃraitən] §86 intr (SEIN) step; stride; **zur Abstimmung s.** proceed to vote; **zur Tat s.** proceed to act
schrie [ʃri] pret of **schreien**
schrieb [ʃriːp] pret of **schreiben**
Schrift [ʃrɪft] f (-;-en) writing; handwriting; letter, character; document; book; publication; periodical; (auf Münzen) legend; (typ) type, font; **die Heilige S.** Holy Scripture; **nach der S. sprechen** speak standard German

Schrift′art f type, font
Schrift′auslegung f exegesis
Schrift′bild n type face
Schrift′deutsch n literary German
Schrift′führer –in §6 mf secretary
Schrift′leiter –in §6 mf editor
schrift′lich adj written || adv in writing; s. wiedergeben transcribe
Schrift′satz m (jur) brief; (typ) composition
Schrift′setzer m typesetter
Schrift′sprache f literary language
Schriftsteller –in [ˈʃrɪftʃtelər(ɪn)] §6 mf writer, author
Schrift′stück n piece of writing; document
Schrifttum [ˈʃrɪfttum] n (–s;) literature
Schrift′verkehr m, **Schrift′wechsel** m correspondence
Schrift′zeichen n letter, character
schrill [ʃrɪl] adj shrill
schrillen [ˈʃrɪlən] intr ring loudly
schritt [ʃrɪt] pret of schreiten ||
Schritt m (–[e]s;–e) step; pace; stride; (e–r Hose) crotch; (fig) step
Schritt′macher m pacemaker
schritt′weise adv gradually; step by step
schroff [ʃrɔf] adj steep; rugged; rude, uncouth; rough, harsh; (Ablehnung, Widerspruch) flat
schröpfen [ˈʃrœpfən] tr (fig) milk, fleece; (med) bleed, cup
Schrot [ʃrot] m & n (–[e]s;–e) scrap; (Getreide) crushed grain, grits; (zum Schießen) buckshot
Schrot′brot n whole grain bread
Schrot′flinte f shotgun
Schrot′korn n, **Schrot′kugel** f pellet
Schrott [ʃrɔt] m (–[e]s;) scrap metal
Schrott′platz m junk yard
schrubben [ˈʃrʊbən] tr scrub
Schrulle [ˈʃrʊlə] f (–;–n) (coll) nutty idea
schrul′lenhaft, schrullig [ˈʃrʊlɪç] adj whimsical
schrumpelig [ˈʃrʊmpəlɪç] adj crumpled; wrinkled, shriveled
schrumpeln [ˈʃrʊmpəln] intr shrivel
schrumpfen [ˈʃrʊmpfən] intr (SEIN) shrink; shrivel; (pathol) atrophy
Schub [ʃup] m (–[e]s;–e) shove, push; batch; (phys) thrust
Schub′fach n drawer
Schub′karre f, **Schub′karren** m wheelbarrow
Schub′kasten m drawer
Schub′kraft f thrust
Schub′lade f drawer
Schub′leistung f thrust
Schubs [ʃups] m (–es;–e) (coll) shove
schubsen [ˈʃupsən] tr & intr shove
Schub′stange f (aut) connecting rod
schüchtern [ˈʃʏçtərn] adj shy, bashful
schuf [ʃuf] pret of schaffen
Schuft [ʃuft] m (–[e]s;–e) cad
schuften [ˈʃuftən] intr drudge, slave
Schufterei [ʃuftəˈraɪ] f (–;) drudgery; (Schuftigkeit) meanness
schuftig [ˈʃuftɪç] adj (fig) rotten
Schuh [ʃu] m (–[e]s;–e) shoe; boot
Schuh′band n (–[e]s;–er) shoestring

Schuhflicker [ˈʃuflɪkər] m (–s;–) shoe repairman, shoemaker
Schuh′krem m shoe polish
Schuh′laden m shoe store
Schuh′leisten m last
Schuh′löffel m shoehorn
Schuh′macher m shoemaker
Schuhplattler [ˈʃuplatlər] m (–s;–) Bavarian folk dance
Schuh′putzer m shoeshine boy
Schuh′sohle f sole
Schuhspanner [ˈʃuʃpanər] m (–s;–) shoetree
Schuh′werk n footwear
Schuh′wichse f shoe polish
Schuh′zeug n footwear
Schul– [ʃul] comb.fm. school
Schul′amt n school board
Schul′arbeit f homework; (Aust) classroom work
Schul′aufsicht f school board
Schul′bank f (–;–e) school desk
Schul′behörde f school board; board of education
Schul′beispiel n (fig) test case
Schul′besuch m attendance at school
Schul′bildung f schooling, education
Schuld [ʃult] adj at fault, to blame ||
Schuld f (–;–en) debt; fault; guilt
schuld′bewußt adj conscious of one's guilt
schulden [ˈʃʊldən] tr owe
schuld′haft adj culpable || **Schuld′haft** f imprisonment for debt
Schul′diener m school janitor
schuldig [ˈʃʊldɪç] adj guilty; responsible; j–m etw s. sein owe s.o. s.th. ||
Schuldige §5 mf culprit; guilty party
Schul′digkeit f (–;–en) duty, obligation; seine S. tun do one's duty
Schul′direktor –in §7 mf principal
schuld′los adj innocent
Schuld′losigkeit f (–;) innocence
Schuldner –in [ˈʃʊldnər(ɪn)] §6 mf debtor
Schuld′schein m promissory note, IOU
Schuld′spruch m verdict of guilty
Schuld′verschreibung f promissory note, IOU; (Obligation) bond
Schule [ˈʃulə] f (–;–n) school; auf der S. in school; S. machen (fig) set a precedent; von der S. abgehen quit school
schulen [ˈʃulən] tr train; (pol) indoctrinate
Schüler [ˈʃylər] m (–s;–) pupil (in grammar school or high school); trainee; (Jünger) disciple
Schü′leraustausch m student exchange
Schülerin [ˈʃylərɪn] f (–;–nen) pupil
Schul′film m educational film
Schul′flug m training flight
schul′frei adj—schulfreier Tag holiday; s. haben have off
Schul′gelände n school grounds; campus
Schul′geld n tuition
Schul′gelehrsamkeit f book learning
Schul′hof m schoolyard, playground
Schul′kamerad m school chum
Schul′lehrer –in §6 mf schoolteacher
Schul′mappe f schoolbag
Schul′meister m schoolmaster; pedant
schul′meistern intr criticize

Schul'ordnung f school regulation
Schul'pflicht f compulsory school attendance
schul'pflichtig adj of school age; **schulpflichtiges Alter** school age
Schul'plan m curriculum
Schul'ranzen m schoolbag
Schul'rat m (-[e]s;:e) (educ) superintendent
Schul'reise f field trip
Schul'schiff n training ship
Schul'schluß m close of school
Schul'schwester f teaching nun
Schul'stunde f lesson, period
Schul'tasche f schoolbag
Schulter ['ʃʊltər] f (-;-n) shoulder
Schul'terblatt n shoulder blade
schul'terfrei adj off-the-shoulder; (trägerfrei) strapless
schultern ['ʃʊltərn] tr shoulder
Schul'terstück n epaulet
Schul'unterricht m instruction; schooling; **im S.** in school
Schul'wesen n school system
Schul'zeugnis n report card
Schul'zimmer n classroom
Schul'zwang m compulsory education
schummeln ['ʃʊməln] intr (coll) cheat
schund [ʃʊnt] pret of **schinden** ‖ **Schund** m (-[e]s;) junk, trash
Schund'literatur f trashy literature
Schund'roman m dime novel
Schupo ['ʃupo] m (-s;-s) (Schutzpolizist) policeman, copy ‖ f (-;) (Schutzpolizei) police
Schuppe ['ʃʊpə] f (-;-n) scale; **Schuppen** dandruff
schuppen ['ʃʊpən] tr scale; scrape ‖ **Schuppen** m (-s;-) shed; (aer) hangar; (aut) garage
schuppig ['ʃʊpɪç] adj scaly, flaky
Schups [ʃʊps] m (-es;-e) shove
schupsen ['ʃʊpsən] tr shove
Schüreisen ['ʃyraɪzən] n poker
schüren ['ʃyrən] tr poke, stir; (fig) stir up, foment
schürfen ['ʃʏrfən] tr scratch, scrape; dig for ‖ intr (nach) prospect (for)
schurigeln ['ʃurɪgəln] tr (coll) bully
Schurke ['ʃʊrkə] m (-n;-n) bum, punk
Schur'kenstreich m, **Schur'kentat** f, **Schurkerei** [ʃʊrkə'raɪ] f (-;-en) mean trick
schurkisch ['ʃʊrkɪʃ] adj mean, lowdown
Schürze ['ʃʏrtsə] f (-;-n) apron
schürzen ['ʃʏrtsən] tr tuck up; tie
Schür'zenband n (-[e]s;:er) apron
Schür'zenjäger m skirt chaser, wolf
Schuß [ʃus] m (Schusses; Schüsse) shot; (Ladung) round; (Schußwunde) gunshot wound; (rasche Bewegung) rush; (Brot) batch; (bot) shoot; (culin) dash; (sport) shot; **blinder S.** blank; etw. **abgeben** fire a shot; **ein S. ins Blaue** a wild shot; **ein S. ins Schwarze** a bull's-eye; **im S. haben** have under control; **im vollen S.** in full swing; **in S. bekommen** get going; **in S. bringen** get (s.th.) going; **j–m vor den S. kommen** come within s.o.'s range; (fig) come across s.o.; **scharfer S.**

live round; **weit vom S.** out of harm's way
Schüssel ['ʃʏsəl] f (-;-n) bowl; (fig) dish
schuß'fest, schuß'sicher adj bulletproof
Schuß'waffe f firearm
Schuß'weite f range
Schuster ['ʃustər] m (-s;-) shoemaker; (fig) bungler
schustern ['ʃustərn] intr bungle
Schutt [ʃʊt] m (-es;) rubbish; rubble
Schutt'abladeplatz m dump
Schüttboden ['ʃʏtbodən] m granary
Schüttelfrost ['ʃʏtəlfrɔst] m shivers
schütteln ['ʃʏtəln] tr shake; **j–m die Hand s.** shake hands with s.o.
schütten ['ʃʏtən] tr pour, spill ‖ impers —es schüttet it is pouring
Schutz [ʃʊts] m (-es;) protection, defense; (Obdach) shelter; (Deckung) cover; (Schirm) screen; (Schutzgeleit) safeguard; **zu S. und Trutz** defensive and offensive
Schutz'brille f safety goggles
Schütze ['ʃʏtsə] m (-n;-n) marksman, shot; (astr) Sagittarius; (mil) rifleman ‖ f (-;-n) sluice gate
schützen ['ʃʏtsən] tr (gegen) protect (against), defend (against); (vor dat) preserve (from) ‖ **Schützen** m (-s;-) tex) shuttle
schüt'zend adj protective; tutelary
Schutz'engel m guardian angle
Schüt'zengraben m (mil) foxhole
Schüt'zenkompanie f rifle company
Schüt'zenkönig m crack shot
Schüt'zenloch n (mil) foxhole
Schüt'zenmine f anti-personnel mine
Schutz'geleit n escort; safe conduct; (aer) air cover; (nav) convoy
Schutz'glocke f (aer) umbrella
Schutz'gott m, **Schutz'göttin** f tutelary deity
Schutz'haft f protective custody
Schutzheilige §5 mf patron saint
Schutz'herr m protector; patron
Schutz'herrin f protectress; patroness
Schutz'impfung f immunization
Schutz'insel f traffic island
Schützling ['ʃʏtslɪŋ] m (-s;-e) ward
schutz'los adj defenseless
Schutz'mann m (-[e]s;:er & -leute) policeman
Schutz'marke f trademark
Schutz'mittel n preservative; preventive
Schutz'patron –in §8 mf patron saint
Schutz'polizei f police
Schutz'polizist m policeman, cop
Schutz'scheibe f (aut) windshield
Schutz'staffel f SS troops
Schutz'umschlag m dust jacket
Schutz–'und–Trutz–'Bündnis f defensive and offensive alliance
Schutz'waffe f defensive weapon
Schutz'zoll m protective tariff
Schwabe ['ʃvabə] m (-n;-n) Swabian
Schwaben ['ʃvabən] n (-s;) Swabia
Schwäbin ['ʃvebɪn] f (-;-nen) Swabian
schwäbisch ['ʃvebɪʃ] adj Swabian; **das Schwäbische Meer** Lake Constance
schwach [ʃvax] adj (schwächer ['ʃveçər]; schwächste ['ʃveçstə] §9)

weak; (*Hoffnung, Ton, Licht*) faint; (*unzureichend*) scanty; sparse; (*armselig*) poor

Schwäche ['ʃvɛçə] *f* (-;-n) weakness

Schwach'kopf *m* dunce; sap, dope

schwächlich ['ʃvɛçlɪç] *adj* feeble, delicate

Schwächling ['ʃvɛçlɪŋ] *m* (-s;-e) weakling

schwach'sinnig *adj* feeble-minded || **Schwachsinnige** §5 *mf* dimwit, moron

Schwach'strom *m* low-voltage current

Schwaden ['ʃvadən] *m* (-s;-) swath; cloud (*of smoke, etc.*)

Schwadron [ʃva'dron] *f* (-;-en) squadron

schwadronieren [ʃvadro'nirən] *intr* (coll) brag

schwafeln ['ʃvafəln] *intr* talk nonsense

Schwager ['ʃvagər] *m* (-s;⁼) brother-in-law

Schwägerin ['ʃvɛgərɪn] *f* (-;-nen) sister-in-law

Schwalbe ['ʃvalbə] *f* (-;-n) swallow

Schwal'bennest *n* (aer) gun turret

Schwal'benschwanz *m* (*Frack*) tails; (carp) dovetail

Schwall [ʃval] *m* (-[e]s;-e) flood; (*von Worten*) torrent

schwamm [ʃvam] *pret of* **schwimmen** || **Schwamm** *m* (-[e]s;⁼e) sponge; mushroom; fungus; dry rot; **S. darüber!** skip it!

schwammig ['ʃvamɪç] *adj* spongy

Schwan [ʃvan] *m* (-[e]s;⁼e) swan

schwand [ʃvant] *pret of* **schwinden**

schwang [ʃvaŋ] *pret of* **schwingen**

schwanger ['ʃvaŋər] *adj* pregnant

schwängern ['ʃvɛŋərn] *tr* make pregnant; (fig) impregnate

Schwan'gerschaft *f* (-;-en) pregnancy

Schwan'gerschaftsverhütung *f* contraception

schwank [ʃvaŋk] *adj* flexible; unsteady || **Schwank** *m* (-[e]s;⁼e) prank; joke; funny story; (theat) farce

schwanken ['ʃvaŋkən] *intr* stagger; (*schaukeln*) rock; (*schlingern*) roll; (*stampfen*) pitch; (*Flamme*) flicker; (*pendeln*) oscillate; (*vibrieren*) vibrate; (*wellenartig*) undulate; (*zittern*) shake; (*Preise*) fluctuate; (*zögern*) vacillate, hesitate

Schwanz [ʃvants] *m* (-es;⁼e) tail; (*Gefolge*) train; (vulg) pecker; **kein S.** not a living soul; **mit dem S. wedeln** (or **wippen**) wag its tail

schwänzeln ['ʃvɛntsəln] *intr* wag its tail; **s. um** fawn on

schwänzen ['ʃvɛntsən] *tr*—**die Schule s.** play hooky from school; **e-e Stunde s.** cut a class || *intr* play hooky

schwappen ['ʃvapən] *intr* slosh around; **s. über** (acc) spill over

schwapps [ʃvaps] *interj* slap!; splash!

Schwäre ['ʃvɛrə] *f* (-;-n) abscess

schwären ['ʃvɛrən] *intr* fester

Schwarm [ʃvarm] *m* (-[e]s;⁼e) swarm; flock, herd; (*von Fischen*) school; (fig) idol; (fig) craze; (aer) flight of five aircraft; **sie ist mein S.** (coll) I have a crush on her

schwärmen ['ʃvɛrmən] *intr* swarm; stray; daydream; go out on the town; **s. für** (or **über** acc or **von**) rave about

Schwär'mer *m* (-s;-) enthusiast; reveler; daydreamer; firecracker; (religious) fanatic; (ent) hawk moth

Schwärmerei [ʃvɛrmə'raɪ] *f* (-;-en) enthusiasm; daydreaming; revelry; fanaticism

schwärmerisch ['ʃvɛrmərɪʃ] *adj* enthusiastic; gushy; fanatic; fanciful

Schwarte ['ʃvartə] *f* (-;-n) rind, skin; (coll) old book

schwarz [ʃvarts] *adj* black; dark; (*ungesetzlich*) illegal; (*schmutzig*) dirty; (*düster*) gloomy; (*von der Sonne*) tanned; **schwarze Kunst** black magic; **schwarzes Brett** bulletin board || *adv* illegally

Schwarz'arbeit *f* moonlighting; non-union work; illicit work

Schwarz'brenner *m* moonshiner

Schwärze ['ʃvɛrtsə] *f* (-;-n) blackness; darkness; printer's ink

schwärzen ['ʃvɛrtsən] *tr* darken; blacken

schwarz'fahren §71 *intr* (SEIN) drive without a license; ride without a ticket

Schwarz'fahrer –in §6 *mf* unlicensed driver; rider without a ticket

Schwarz'fahrt *f* joy ride; ride without a ticket

Schwarz'handel *m* black-marketing

Schwarz'händler –in §6 *mf* black marketeer; (*mit Eintrittskarten*) scalper

schwärzlich ['ʃvɛrtslɪç] *adj* blackish

Schwarz'markt *m* black market

Schwarz'seher –in §6 *mf* pessimist

Schwarz'sender *m* illegal transmitter

schwatzen ['ʃvatsən], **schwätzen** ['ʃvɛtsən] *tr* (coll) talk || *intr* (coll) yap, talk nonsense; (coll) gossip

Schwät'zer –in §6 *mf* windbag; gossip

schwatz'haft *adj* talkative

Schwatz'maul *n* blabber mouth

Schwebe ['ʃvebə] *f* (-;) suspense; **in der S. sein** be undecided; be pending

Schwe'bebahn *f* cablecar

Schwe'beflug *m* hovering, soaring

schweben ['ʃvebən] *intr* (HABEN & SEIN) be suspended; hang; float; (*Hubschrauber*) hover; (*Segelflugzeug*) soar; glide; (fig) waver, be undecided; **in Gefahr s.** be in danger; **in Ungewißheit s.** be in suspense

Schwede ['ʃvedə] *m* (-n;-n) Swede

Schweden ['ʃvedən] *n* (-s;) Sweden

Schwedin ['ʃvedɪn] *f* (-;-nen) Swede

schwedisch ['ʃvedɪʃ] *adj* Swedish

Schwefel ['ʃvefəl] *m* (-s;) sulfur

Schwe'felsäure *f* sulfuric acid

Schweif [ʃvaɪf] *m* (-[e]s;-e) tail; (fig) train

schweifen ['ʃvaɪfən] *tr* curve; (*spülen*) rinse || *intr* (SEIN) roam, wander

Schweigegeld ['ʃvaɪgəgɛlt] *n* hush money

schweigen ['ʃvaɪgən] §148 *intr* be silent, keep silent; (*aufhören*) stop; **ganz zu s. von** to say nothing of; **s. zu** make no reply to

schwei′gend *adj* silent ‖ *adv* in silence
schweigsam [′ʃvaɪkzəm] *adj* taciturn
Schwein [ʃvaɪn] *n* (-[e]s;-e) pig, hog; **S. haben** be lucky, have luck
Schwei′nebraten *m* roast pork
Schwei′nefleisch *n* pork
Schwei′nehund *m* (pej) filthy swine
Schwei′nekoben *m* pigsty, pig pen
Schweinerei [ʃvaɪnə′raɪ] *f* (-;-en) mess; dirty business
Schwei′nerippchen *pl* pork chops
Schwei′newirtschaft *f* dirty mess
Schweins′kotelett *n* pork chop
Schweiß [ʃvaɪs] *m* (-es;) perspiration
schweißen [′ʃvaɪsən] *tr* weld ‖ *intr* begin to melt, fuse; (hunt) bleed
Schwei′ßer –in §6 *mf* welder
Schweißfüße [′ʃvaɪsfysə] *pl* sweaty feet
schweißig [′ʃvaɪsɪç] *adj* sweaty; (hunt) bloody
Schweiß′perle *f* bead of sweat
Schweiz [ʃvaɪts] *f* (-;)—**die S.** Switzerland
Schwei′zer *m* Swiss; dairyman
schweizerisch [′ʃvaɪtsərɪʃ] *adj* Swiss
schwelen [′ʃveːlən] *intr* smolder
schwelgen [′ʃvɛlgən] *intr* feast; **s. in** (*dat*) (fig) revel in; wallow in
Schwelgerei [ʃvɛlgə′raɪ] *f* (-;-en) feasting, carousing
schwelgerisch [′ʃvɛlgərɪʃ] *adj* riotous; luxurious
Schwelle [′ʃvɛlə] *f* (-;-n) sill; doorstep; (fig) verge; (psychol) threshold; (rr) railroad tie
schwellen [′ʃvɛlən] §119 *tr* swell ‖ *intr* (SEIN) swell; (*Wasser*) rise; (*anwachsen*) increase
Schwel′lung *f* (-;-en) swelling
Schwemme [′ʃvɛmə] *f* (-;-n) watering place; (coll) taproom; (com) glut
schwemmen [′ʃvɛmən] *tr* wash off, rinse; (*Vieh*) water; (*Holz*) float
Schwengel [′ʃvɛŋəl] *m* (-s;-) pump handle; (*e-r Glocke*) hammer
schwenkbar [′ʃvɛŋkbar] *adj* rotating
schwenken [′ʃvɛŋkən] *tr* swing; shake; (*drohend*) brandish; (*Hut*) wave; (*spülen*) rinse ‖ *intr* (SEIN) turn; swivel, pivot; (*Geschütz*) traverse; (mil) wheel; (pol) change sides
Schwen′kung *f* (-;-en) turn; wheeling; traversing; (fig) change of mind
schwer [ʃveːr] *adj* heavy; difficult, hard; serious; (*schwerfällig*) ponderous; (*Strafe*) severe; (*Wein*) strong; (*Speise*) rich; (*unbeholfen*) clumsy; (*Kompanie*) heavy-weapons; **drei Pfund s. sein** weigh three pounds; **schweres Geld bezahlen** pay a stiff price ‖ *adv* hard; with difficulty; (coll) very
Schwere [′ʃveːrə] *f* (-;) weight; seriousness; (*des Weines*) body; difficulty; significance; (phys) gravity
schwe′relos *adj* weightless
schwer′fällig *adj* heavy; clumsy, slow
Schwer′gewicht *n* heavyweight class; (*Nachdruck*) emphasis
Schwergewichtler –in [′ʃveːrgəvɪçtlər (ɪn)] §6 *mf* (sport) heavyweight
schwer′hörig *adj* hard of hearing

Schwer′industrie *f* heavy industry
Schwer′kraft *f* gravity
schwer′lich *adv* hardly
Schwer′mut *f* melancholy, depression
schwer′mütig *adj* melancholy, depressed
schwer′nehmen §116 *tr* take hard
Schwer′punkt *m* center of gravity; crucial point, focal point
Schwert [ʃveːrt] *n* (-[e]s;-er) sword
Schwer′verbrecher –in §6 *mf* felon
schwer′verdient *adj* hard-earned
schwer′wiegend *adj* weighty
Schwester [′ʃvɛstər] *f* (-;-n) sister; nurse; nun
Schwe′sterleferin *f* nurse's aide
schwieg [ʃviːk] *pret* of **schweigen**
Schwieger– [′ʃviːgər] *comb.fm.* -in-law
Schwie′germutter *f* mother-in-law
Schwie′gersohn *m* son-in-law
Schwie′gertochter *f* daughter-in-law
Schwie′gervater *m* father-in-law
Schwiele [′ʃviːlə] *f* (-;-n) callus
schwielig [′ʃviːlɪç] *adj* callous
schwierig [′ʃviːrɪç] *adj* hard, difficult
Schwie′rigkeit *f* (-;-en) difficulty
Schwimm– [ʃvɪm] *comb.fm.* swimming
Schwimm′anstalt *f*, **Schwimm′bad** *n*, **Schwimm′bassin** *n*, **Schwimm′becken** *n* swimming pool
schwimmen [′ʃvɪmən] §136 *intr* (HABEN & SEIN) swim; float
Schwimm′gürtel *m* life belt
Schwimm′haut *f* web
Schwimm′hose *f* bathing trunks
Schwimm′kraft *f* buoyancy
Schwimm′panzer *m* amphibious tank
Schwimm′weste *f* life jacket
Schwindel [′ʃvɪndəl] *m* (-s;-) dizziness; swindle, gyp; (*Unsinn*) bunk; (pathol) vertigo; **der ganze S.** the whole caboodle
Schwin′delanfall *m* dizzy spell
Schwin′delfirma *f* fly-by-night
schwin′delhaft *adj* fraudulent, bogus
schwindelig [′ʃvɪndəlɪç] *adj* dizzy
schwindeln [′ʃvɪndəln] *tr* swindle ‖ *intr* fib ‖ *impers*—**mir schwindelt** I feel dizzy
Schwin′delunternehmen *n* fly-by-night
schwinden [′ʃvɪndən] §59 *intr* (SEIN) dwindle; decline; (*Farbe*) fade
Schwind′ler –in §6 *mf* swindler; fibber
schwindlig [′ʃvɪntlɪç] *adj* dizzy
Schwindsucht [′ʃvɪntzuçt] *f* tuberculosis
Schwinge [′ʃvɪŋə] *f* (-;-n) wing; fan; winnow; (poet) pinion
schwingen [′ʃvɪŋən] §142 *tr* swing; wave; brandish; (agr) winnow; (tex) swingle ‖ *ref* vault; soar ‖ *intr* swing; sway; oscillate; vibrate
Schwin′ger *m* (-s;-) oscillator; (box) haymaker
Schwin′gung *f* (-;-en) oscillation; vibration; swinging
Schwips [ʃvɪps] *m*—**e-n S. haben** (coll) be tight, be tipsy
schwirren [′ʃvɪrən] *intr* (HABEN & SEIN) whiz, whir; buzz; (*Gerüchte*) fly
Schwitzbad [′ʃvɪtsbat] *n* Turkish bath
schwitzen [′ʃvɪtsən] *tr & intr* sweat

schwoll [ʃvɔl] *pret of* **schwellen**
schwor [ʃvor] *pret of* **schwören**
schwören [ˈʃvøːrən] §137 *tr & intr* swear; **auf j-n** (*or* **etw**) **s.** swear by s.o. (*or* s.th.)
schwul [ʃvuːl] *adj* (vulg) homosexual
schwül [ʃvyːl] *adj* sultry, muggy
Schwulität [ʃvuliˈtɛt] *f* (*-;-en*) trouble
Schwulst [ʃvulst] *m* (*-es;⁻e*) bombast
schwülstig [ˈʃvylstɪç] *adj* bombastic
schwummerig [ˈʃvumərɪç] *adj* (coll) shaky
Schwund [ʃvunt] *m* (*-[e]s;*) dwindling; shrinkage; loss; leakage; (*des Haares*) falling out; (rad) fading; (pathol) atrophy
Schwung [ʃvuŋ] *m* (*-[e]s;⁻e*) swing; vault; (*Tatkraft*) zip, go; (*der Phantasie*) flight; **in S. bringen** start; **S. bekommen** gather momentum
schwung'haft *adj* brisk, lively
Schwung'kraft *f* centrifugal force; (fig) zip, pep; (phys) momentum
Schwung'rad *n* (mach) flywheel
schwung'voll *adj* enthusiastic, lively
schwur [ʃvur] *pret of* **schwören** ‖ **Schwur** *m* (*-[e]s;⁻e*) oath
Schwur'gericht *n* jury
sechs [zeks] *invar adj & pron* six ‖ **Sechs** *f* (*-;-en*) six
Sechs'eck *n* hexagon
Sechser [ˈzeksər] *m* (*-s;-*) six; (*in der Lotterie*) jackpot
Sechsta'gerennen *n* six-day bicycle race
sechste [ˈzekstə] §9 *adj & pron* sixth
Sechstel [ˈzekstəl] *n* (*-s;-*) sixth
sech'zehn *invar adj & pron* sixteen ‖ **Sech'zehn** *f* (*-;-en*) sixteen
sech'zehnte §9 *adj & pron* sixteenth
Sech'zehntel *n* (*-s;-*) sixteenth
sechzig [ˈzeçtsɪç] *invar adj & pron* sixty ‖ **Sechzig** *f* (*-;-en*) sixty
sechziger [ˈzeçtsɪɡər] *invar adj* of the sixties; **die s. Jahre** the sixties ‖ **Sechziger** *m* (*-s;-*) sexagenarian
sechzigste [ˈzeçtsɪçstə] §9 *adj & pron* sixtieth
See [zeː] *m* (**Sees; Seen** [ˈzeːən] lake ‖ *f* (**See; Seen** [ˈzeːən]) sea; ocean; **an der See** at the seashore; **an die See gehen** go to the seashore; **auf See** at sea; **in See gehen** (*or* **stechen**) put out to sea; **in See sein** to be in open water; **Kapitän zur See** navy captain; **zur See gehen** go to sea
See'bad *n* seashore resort
See'bär *m* (fig) sea dog
see'fähig *adj* seaworthy
See'fahrer *m* seafarer
See'fahrt *f* seafaring; voyage
see'fest *adj* seaworthy; **s. werden** get one's sea legs
See'gang *m* **—hoher** (*or* **schwerer** *or* **starker**) **S.** heavy seas
See'hafen *m* seaport
See'handel *m* maritime trade
See'hund *m* (zool) seal
See'jungfer *f*, **See'jungfrau** *f* mermaid
See'kadett *m* naval cadet
See'karte *f* (naut) chart
see'krank *adj* seasick
See'krebs *m* lobster
Seele [ˈzeːlə] *f* (*-;-n*) soul; mind; (*Ein-*

wohner) inhabitant, soul; (*e-s Geschützes*) bore; (*e-s Kabels*) core
See'lenangst *f* mortal fear
See'lenfriede *m* peace of mind
See'lenheil *n* salvation
See'lennot *f* mental distress
See'lenpein *f*, **See'lenqual** *f* mental anguish
See'lenruhe *f* peace of mind; composure
see'lensgut *adj* good-hearted
seelisch [ˈzeːlɪʃ] *adj* mental, psychic
Seel'sorge *f* (*-;*) ministry
Seel'sorger *m* (*-s;-*) minister, pastor
See'macht *f* sea power
See'mann *m* (*-[e]s;-leute*) seaman
See'meile *f* nautical mile
See'möwe *f* sea gull
See'not *f* (naut) distress
See'ratte *f* (fig) old salt
See'raub *m* piracy
See'räuber *m* pirate; corsair
See'räuberei *f* piracy
See'recht *n* maritime law
See'reise *f* voyage; cruise
See'sperre *f* naval blockade
See'stadt *f* seaport town; coastal town
See'straße *f* shipping lane
See'streitkräfte *pl* naval forces
See'tang *m* seaweed
see'tüchtig *adj* seaworthy
See'warte *f* oceanographic institute
See'weg *m* sea route; **auf dem S. by sea**
See'wesen *n* naval affairs
Segel [ˈzeːɡəl] *n* (*-s;-*) sail
Se'gelboot *n* sailboat; (sport) yacht
Se'gelfliegen *n* gliding
Se'gelflieger –in §6 *mf* glider pilot
Se'gelflug *m* glide, gliding
Se'gelflugzeug *n* glider
Se'gelleinwand *f* sailcloth, canvas
segeln [ˈzeːɡəln] *intr* (HABEN & SEIN) sail; (aer) glide
Se'gelschiff *n* sailing vessel
Se'gelsport *m* sailing
Se'geltuch *n* sailcloth, canvas
Se'geltuchhülle *f*, **Se'geltuchplane** *f* tarpaulin
Segen [ˈzeːɡən] *m* (*-s;-*) blessing
se'gensreich *adj* blessed, blissful
Segler [ˈzeːɡlər] *m* (*-s;-*) yachtsman; (aer) glider; (naut) sailing vessel
segnen [ˈzeːɡnən] *tr* bless
Seh- [zeː] *comb.fm.* visual, of vision
sehen [ˈzeːən] §138 *tr* see ‖ *intr* see; look; **s. auf** (*acc*) look at; take care of; face (*a direction*); **s. nach** look for, look around for; **schlecht s. have poor eyes** ‖ **Sehen** *n* (*-s;*) sight; eyesight, vision; **vom S. by sight**
se'henswert *adj* worth seeing
Se'henswürdigkeit *f* object of interest; **Sehenswürdigkeiten** sights
Seher [ˈzeːər] *m* (*-s;-*) seer, prophet
Se'hergabe *f* gift of prophecy
Seh'feld *n* field of vision
Seh'kraft *f* eyesight
Sehne [ˈzeːnə] *f* (*-;-n*) tendon, sinew; (*Bogen-*) string; (geom) secant
sehnen [ˈzeːnən] *ref—sich s. nach* long for, crave ‖ **Sehnen** *n* (*-s;*) longing
Seh'nerv *m* optic nerve**

sehnig ['zeːnɪç] *adj* sinewy; (*Fleisch*) stringy

sehnlich ['zeːnlɪç] *adj* longing; ardent

Sehnsucht ['zeːnzʊxt] *f* (–;) yearning

sehr [zer] *adv* very; very much

Seh'rohr *n* periscope

Seh'vermögen *n* sight, vision

Seh'weite *f* visual range; **in S.** within sight

seicht [zaɪçt] *adj* (& *fig*) shallow

Seide ['zaɪdə] *f* (–;–n) silk

seiden ['zaɪdən] *adj* silk, silky

Sei'denatlas *m* satin

Sei'denpapier *n* tissue paper

Sei'denraupe *f* silkworm

Sei'denspinnerei *f* silk mill

Sei'denstoff *m* silk cloth

seidig ['zaɪdɪç] *adj* silky

Seife ['zaɪfə] *f* (–;–n) soap

Sei'fenblase *f* soap bubble

Sei'fenbrühe *f* soapsuds

Sei'fenflocken *pl* soap flakes

Sei'fenlauge *f* soapsuds

Sei'fenpulver *n* soap powder

Sei'fenschale *f* soap dish

Sei'fenschaum *m* lather

seifig ['zaɪfɪç] *adj* soapy

seihen ['zaɪ-ən] *tr* strain, filter

Sei'her *m* (–s;–) strainer, filter

Seil [zaɪl] *n* (–[e]s;–e) rope; cable

Seil'bahn *f* cable railway; cable car

seil'springen *intr* jump rope

Seil'tänzer –in §6 *mf* ropewalker

sein [zaɪn] §139 *intr* be; exist; **es ist mir, als wenn** I feel as if; **es sei denn, daß** unless; **lassen Sie das s.!** stop it!; **wenn dem so ist** if that is the case; **wie dem auch sein mag** however that may be ‖ *aux* (to form compound past tenses of intransitive verbs of motion, change of condition, etc.) have, e.g., **ich bin gegangen** I have gone, I went ‖ §2,2 *poss adj* his; its; one's; her ‖ §2,4,5 *poss pron* his; hers; **die Seinen** his family; **er hat das Seine getan** he did his share; **jedem das Seine** to each his own ‖ **Sein** *n* (–s;) being; existence; being

seinerseits ['zaɪnər'zaɪts] *adv* for his part

seinerzeit ['zaɪnər'tsaɪt] *adv* in its time; in those days; in due time

seinesgleichen ['zaɪnəs'glaɪçən] *pron* people like him, the likes of him

seinethalben ['zaɪnət'halbən], **seinet- wegen** ['zaɪnət'veːgən] *adv* for his sake; on his account; (*von ihm aus*) for all he cares

seinetwillen ['zaɪnət'vɪlən] *adv*—**um s.** for his sake, on his behalf

Seinige ['zaɪnɪgə] §2,5 *pron* his; das **S.** his property, his own; his due; his share; **die Seinigen** his family

seit [zaɪt] *prep* (*dat*) since, for; **s. e–m Jahr** for one year; **s. einiger Zeit** for some time past; **s. kurzem** lately; **s. langem** for a long time; **s. wann** since when ‖ *conj* since

seitdem [zaɪt'dem] *adv* since that time ‖ *conj* since

Seite ['zaɪtə] *f* (–;–n) side; page; di- rection; (*Quelle*) source; (*mil*) flank

Sei'tenansicht *f* side view, profile

Sei'tenbau *m* (–[e]s;–ten) annex

Sei'tenblick *m* side glance

Sei'tenflosse *f* (aer) horizontal stabil- izer

Sei'tenflügel *m* (archit) wing

Sei'tengang *m* side aisle

Sei'tengeleise *n* sidetrack

Sei'tenhieb *m* snide remark, dig

sei'tenlang *adj* pages of

Sei'tenriß *m* profile

sei'tens *prep* (*genit*) on the part of

Sei'tenschiff *n* (archit) aisle

Sei'tenschwimmen *n* sidestroke

Sei'tensprung *m* (fig) escapade

Sei'tenstück *n* (fig) counterpart

Sei'tenwind *m* cross wind

seither [zaɪt'her] *adv* since then

–seitig [zaɪtɪç] *comb.fm.* –sided

seit'lich *adj* lateral

seitwärts ['zaɪtverts] *adv* sideways, sidewards; aside

Sekretär –in [zekre'ter(ɪn)] §8 *mf* secretary

Sekt [zekt] *m* (–[e]s;–e) champagne

Sekte ['zektə] *f* (–;–n) sect

Sek•tor ['zektɔr] *m* (–s;–toren ['torən]) sector; (fig) field

Sekundant [zekun'dant] *m* (–en;–en) (box) second

sekundär [zekun'der] *adj* secondary

Sekunde [ze'kundə] *f* (–;–n) second

Sekun'denbruchteil *m* split second

Sekun'denzeiger *m* second hand

Sekurit [zeku'rit] *n* (–s;) safety glass

selber ['zelbər] *invar pron* (coll) var of selbst

selbst [zelpst] *invar pron* self; in per- son, personally; (*sogar*) even; by one- self; **ich s. I** myself; **von s.** voluntar- ily; spontaneously; automatically ‖ *adv* even; **s. ich** even I; **s. wenn** even if, even when

Selbst'achtung *f* self-respect

selbständig ['zelp/tendɪç] *adj* inde- pendent

Selbst'bedienung *f* self-service

Selbst'beherrschung *f* self-control

Selbst'beobachtung *f* introspection

Selbst'bestimmung *f* self-determination

Selbst'betrug *m* self-deception

Selbst'bewußt *adj* self-confident

Selbst'binder *m* necktie; (agr) combine

Selbst'erhaltung *f* self-preservation

selbst'gebacken *adj* homemade

selbst'gefällig *adj* complacent, smug

Selbst'gefühl *n* self-confidence

selbst'gemacht *adj* homemade

selbst'gerecht *adj* self-righteous

Selbst'gespräch *n* soliloquy

selbst'gezogen *adj* home-grown

selbst'herrlich *adj* high-handed

Selbst'herrschaft *f* autocracy

Selbst'herrscher *m* autocrat

Selbst'kosten *pl* production costs

Selbst'kostenpreis *m* factory price; **zum S. abgeben** sell at-cost

Selbstlader ['zelpstlaːdər] *m* (–s;–) automatic (weapon)

Selbst'laut *m* vowel

selbst'los *adj* unselfish

Selbst'mord *m* suicide

selbst'sicher *adj* self-confident

Selbst'steuer *n* automatic pilot

Selbst'sucht f egotism, selfishness
selbst'süchtig adj egotistical
selbst'tätig adj automatic
Selbst'täuschung f self-deception
Selbstüberhebung [ˈzɛlpstyɔrhebʊŋ] f (-;) self-conceit, presumption
Selbst'verbrennung f spontaneous combustion; self-immolation
Selbst'verlag m—**im S.** printed privately
Selbst'verleugnung f self-denial
Selbst'versorger m (-s;-) self-supporter
selbst'verständlich adj obvious; natural || adv of course
Selbst'verständlichkeit f foregone conclusion, matter of course
Selbst'verteidigung f self-defense
Selbst'vertrauen n self-confidence
Selbst'verwaltung f autonomy
Selbst'wähler m (-s;-) dial telephone
Selbst'zucht f self-discipline
selbst'zufrieden adj self-satisfied
Selbst'zufriedenheit f self-satisfaction
Selbst'zweck m end in itself
selig [ˈzeːlɪç] adj blessed; (verstorben) late; (fig) ecstatic; (fig) tipsy; **seligen Angedenkens** of blessed memory; **s. werden** attain salvation, be saved
Se'ligkeit f (-;) happiness; salvation
Se'ligpreisung f (Bib) beatitude
se'ligsprechen §64 tr beatify
Sellerie [ˈzɛləri] m (-s;) & f (-;) celery (bulb)
selten [ˈzɛltən] adj rare, scarce || adv seldom, rarely
Selterswasser [ˈzɛltərsvasər] n seltzer, soda water
seltsam [ˈzɛltzam] adj odd, strange
Semester [zeˈmɛstər] n (-s;-) semester
Semikolon [ˈzemikolɔn] n semicolon
Seminar [zɛmɪˈnaːr] n (-s;-e) seminary; (educ) seminar
Seminarist [zɛmɪnaˈrɪst] m (-en;-en) seminarian
semitisch [zeˈmiːtɪʃ] adj Semitic
Semmel [ˈzɛməl] f (-;-n) roll
Senat [zeˈnaːt] m (-[e]s;-e) senate
Se·nator [zeˈnaːtor] m (-s;-natoren [naˈtoːrən]) senator
Sende- [zɛndə] comb.fm. transmitting, transmitter, broadcasting
senden [ˈzɛndən] tr & intr transmit, broadcast; telecast || §120 & §140 tr send || intr—**s. nach** send for
Sen'der m (-s;-) (rad, telv) transmitter; (rad) broadcasting station
Sen'deraum m broadcasting studio
Sen'dezeichen n station identification
Sen'dezeit f air time
Sen'dung f (-;-en) sending; (fig) mission; (com) shipment; (rad) broadcast; (telv) telecast
Senf [zɛnf] m (-[e]s;-e) mustard
sengen [ˈzɛŋən] tr singe, scorch
seng(e)rig [ˈzɛŋ(ə)rɪç] adj burnt; (fig) suspicious, fishy
senil [zeˈniːl] adj senile
Senilität [zenɪliˈtɛt] f (-;) senility
senior [ˈzeːnjor] adj senior
Senkblei [ˈzɛŋkblaɪ] n plummet; (naut) sounding lead
Senke [ˈzɛŋkə] f (-;-n) depression
senken [ˈzɛŋkən] tr lower; sink; (Kopf)

bow || ref sink, settle; dip, slope; (Mauer) sag
Senkfüße [ˈzɛŋkfysə] pl flat feet, fallen arches
Senk'fußeinlage f arch support
Senkgrube [ˈzɛŋkgrubə] f cesspool
Senkkasten [ˈzɛŋkkastən] m caisson
senkrecht [ˈzɛŋkrɛçt] adj vertical; (geom) perpendicular
Sen'kung f (-;-en) sinking; depression; dip, slope; sag; (der Preise) lowering
Sensation [zɛnzaˈtsjon] f (-;-en) sensation
sensationell [zɛnzatsjɔˈnɛl] adj sensational
Sensations'blatt n (pej) scandal sheet
Sensations'lust f sensationalism
Sensations'meldung f, **Sensations'nachricht** f (journ) scoop
Sensations'presse f yellow journalism
Sense [ˈzɛnzə] f (-;-n) scythe
sensibel [zɛnˈzibəl] adj sensitive; (Nerven) sensory
Sensibilität [zɛnzɪbiliˈtɛt] f (-;) sensitivity, sensitiveness
sentimental [zɛntɪmɛnˈtal] adj sentimental
separat [zepaˈraːt] adj separate
September [zɛpˈtɛmbər] m (-[s];) September
Serenade [zereˈnaːdə] f (-;-n) serenade
Serie [ˈzerjə] f (-;-n) series; line
Se'rienanfertigung f, **Se'rienbau** m, **Se'rienfabrikation** f, **Se'rienherstellung** f mass production
se'rienmäßig adj—**serienmäßige Herstellung** mass production || adv—**s. herstellen** mass-produce
Se'riennummer f serial number
Se'rienproduktion f mass production
seriös [zeˈrjøs] adj serious; reliable
Se·rum [ˈzerum] n (-s;-ren [rən] & -ra [ra]) serum
Service [ˈzɔrvɪs] m (**Services** [ˈzɔrvɪs(əs)];) (Kundendienst) service || [zerˈvis] n (**Services** [zerˈvis]; **Service** [zerˈvis(ə)]) (Tafelgeschirr) service
Servierbrett [zerˈvirbret] n tray
servieren [zerˈviːrən] tr serve; **es ist serviert!** dinner is ready! || intr wait at table
Serviertisch [zerˈvirtɪʃ] m sideboard
Servierwagen [zerˈvirvagən] m serving cart
Serviette [zerˈvjetə] f (-;-n) napkin
Servo- [zervə] comb.fm. booster, auxiliary, servo, power, automatic
Ser'vobremsen pl power brakes
Ser'vokupplung f automatic transmission
Ser'volenkung f power steering
Servus [ˈzervus] interj (Aust) hello!; (coll) so long!
Sessel [ˈzesəl] m (-s;-) easy chair
Ses'sellift m chair lift
seßhaft [ˈzeshaft] adj settled; **sich s. machen** settle down
Setzei [ˈzɛtsaɪ] n fried egg
setzen [ˈzɛtsən] tr set, put, place; seat; (beim Spiel) bet; (Denkmal) erect; (Frist) fix; (Junge) breed; (Fische) stock; (Pflanzen) plant; (mus) com-

pose; (typ) set ‖ *ref* sit down; (*Kaffee*) settle ‖ *intr* set type; **s. auf** (*acc*) bet on ‖ *intr* (SEIN)—**s. über** (*acc*) jump over

Set′zer *m* (–s;–) typesetter, compositor

Setz′fehler *m* typographical error

Seuche [′zɔɪçə] *f* (–;–n) epidemic

seufzen [′zɔɪftsən] *intr* sigh

Seuf′zer *m* (–s;–) sigh

Sex [zɛks] *m* (–es;) sex

Sex-Appeal [′zɛks ə′pil] *m* (–s;) sex appeal

Sex′-Bombe *f* (coll) sex pot

Sexual– [zɛksual] *comb.fm.* sex

sexuell [zɛksu′ɛl] *adj* sexual

Sexus [′zɛksus] *m* (–;–) sex

sezieren [ze′tsirən] *tr* dissect

Shampoo [′ʃam′pu] *n* (–s;–s) shampoo

Sibirien [zɪ′birjən] *n* (–s;) Siberia

sich [zɪç] §11 *reflex pron* oneself; himself; herself; itself; themselves; **an (und für) s.** in itself; **außer s. sein** be beside oneself ‖ *recip pron* each other, one another

Sichel [′zɪçəl] *f* (–;–n) sickle

sicher [′zɪçər] *adj* sure; positive; reliable; (*vor dat*) safe (from), secure (from) ‖ *adv* surely, certainly

Si′cherheit *f* (–;–en) safety, security; (*Gewißheit*) certainty; (*Zuverlässigkeit*) reliability; (*im Auftreten*) assurance; (com) security; (jur) bail

Si′cherheitsgurt *m*, **Si′cherheitsgürtel** *m* (aer, aut) seat belt

Si′cherheitsnadel *f* safety pin

Si′cherheitspolizei *f* security police

Si′cherheitsspielraum *m* margin of safety, leeway

si′cherlich *adv* surely, certainly

sichern [′zɪçərn] *tr* secure; fasten; guarantee; (*Gewehr*) put on safety

Si′cherstellung *f* safekeeping; guarantee

Si′cherung *f* (–;–en) protection; guarantee; (*an Schußwaffe*) safety catch; (elec) fuse; **durchgebrannte S.** blown fuse

Si′cherungskasten *m* fuse box

Sicht [zɪçt] *f* (–;) sight; (*Aussicht*) view; (*Sichtigkeit*) visibility; **auf kurze S.** short-range; **auf S.** at sight

sichtbar [′zɪçtbar] *adj* visible

sichten [′zɪçtən] *tr* sight; (fig) sift

sichtig [′zɪçtɪç] *adj* clear

sicht′lich *adj* visible

Sicht′vermerk *m* visa

sickern [′zɪkərn] *intr* (HABEN & SEIN) trickle, seep, leak

sie [zi] §11 *pers pron* she, her; it; they, them ‖ §11 **Sie** *pers pron* you

Sieb [zip] *n* (–[e]s;–e) sieve, colander; screen; (rad) filter

sieben [′zibən] *invar adj & pron* seven ‖ *tr* sift, strain; (fig) screen; (rad) filter ‖ **Sieben** *f* (–;–en) seven

siebente [′zibəntə] §9 *adj & pron* seventh

Siebentel [′zibəntəl] *n* (–s;–) seventh

siebte [′ziptə] §9 *adj & pron* seventh

Siebtel [′ziptəl] *n* (–s;–) seventh

siebzehn [′ziptsen] *invar adj & pron* seventeen ‖ **Siebenzehn** *f* (–;–en) seventeen

siebzehnte [′ziptsentə] §9 *adj & pron* seventeenth

Siebzehntel [′ziptsentəl] *n* (–s;–) seventeenth

siebzig [′ziptsɪç] *invar adj & pron* seventy ‖ **Siebzig** *f* (–;–en) seventy

siebziger [′ziptsɪgər] *invar adj & pron* of the seventies; **die s. Jahre** the seventies ‖ **Siebziger** *m* (–s;–) septuagenarian

siebzigste [′ziptsɪçstə] §9 *adj & pron* seventieth

siech [ziç] *adj* sickly

siechen [′ziçən] *intr* be sickly

Siechtum [′ziçtum] *n* (–s;) lingering illness

siedeheiß [′zidə′haɪs] *adj* piping hot

siedeln [′zidəln] *intr* settle

sieden [′zidən] §141 *tr & intr* boil

Siedepunkt [′zidəpuŋkt] *m* boiling point

Siedler –in [′zidlər(ɪn)] §6 *mf* settler

Sied′lerstelle *f* homestead

Sied′lung *f* (–;–en) settlement; colony; housing development

Sieg [zik] *m* (–[e]s;–e) victory

Siegel [′zigəl] *n* (–s;–) seal

siegeln [′zigəln] *tr* seal

Sie′gelring *m* signet ring

siegen [′zigən] *intr* win, be victorious

Sie′ger –in §6 *mf* winner, victor; **zweiter Sieger** runner-up

Sieges– [zigəs] *comb.fm.* victory, of victory, triumphal

Sie′gesbogen *m* triumphal arch

sieg′reich *adj* victorious

Signal [zɪ′gnal] *n* (–s;–e) signal

signalisieren [zɪgnalɪ′zirən] *tr* signal

Silbe [′zɪlbə] *f* (–;–n) syllable

Sil′bentrennung *f* syllabification

Silber [′zɪlbər] *n* (–s;) silver

silbern [′zɪlbərn] *adj* silver, silvery

Sil′berzeug *n* silver, silverware

Silhouette [zɪlu′ɛtə] *f* (–;–n) silhouette

Silo [′zilo] *m* (–s;–s) silo

Silvester [zɪl′vɛstər] *m* (–s;–), **Silve′sterabend** *m* New Year's Eve

simpel [′zɪmpəl] *adj* simple ‖ **Simpel** *m* (–s;–) simpleton

Sims [zɪms] *m & n* (–es;–e) ledge; (*Fenster–*) sill; (*Kamin–*) mantelpiece

Simulant –in [zɪmu′lant(ɪn)] §7 *mf* faker; (mil) goldbrick

simulieren [zɪmu′lirən] *tr* simulate, fake ‖ *intr* loaf

simultan [zɪmul′tan] *adj* simultaneous

Sinfo·nie [zɪnfo′ni] *f* (–;–nien [′ni·ən]) symphony

singen [′zɪŋən] §142 *tr & intr* sing

Singsang [′zɪŋzaŋ] *m* (–[e]s;) singsong

Sing′spiel *n* musical comedy, musical

Sing′stimme *f* vocal part

Singular [′zɪŋgular] *m* (–s;–e) singular

sinken [′zɪŋkən] §143 *intr* (SEIN) sink slump, sag; (*Preise*) drop; **s. lassen** lower; (*Mut*) lose

Sinn [zɪn] *m* (–[e]s;–e) sense; mind; meaning; liking, taste

Sinn′bild *n* emblem, symbol

sinn′bildlich *adj* symbolic(al) ‖ *adv* symbolically; **s. darstellen** symbolize

sinnen [′zɪnən] §121 *tr* plan; plot ‖ *intr* (**auf** *acc*) plan, plot; (**über** *acc*)

think (about) ‖ **Sinnen** n (-s;) reflection, meditation, reverie
sin′nend adj pensive, reflective
Sin′nenlust f sensuality
Sin′nenmensch m sensualist
Sin′nenwelt f material world
Sin′nesänderung f change of mind
Sin′nesart f character, disposition
Sin′nestäuschung f illusion, hallucination, mirage
sinn′lich adj sensual; material
sinn′los adj senseless
sinn′reich adj ingenious, bright
sinn′verwandt adj synonymous
sinn′voll adj meaningful; sensible
Sintflut [′zɪntfluːt] f deluge, flood
Sippe [′zɪpə] f (-;-n) kin; clan
Sipp′schaft f (-;-en) clique, set
Sirup [′ziːrʊp] m (-s;-e) syrup
Sitte [′zɪtə] f (-;-n) custom; habit; usage; **die Sitten** the morals
Sit′tenbild n, **Sit′tengemälde** n description of the manners (of an age)
Sit′tengesetz n moral law
Sit′tenlehre f ethics
sit′tenlos adj immoral
Sit′tenpolizei f vice squad
sit′tenrein adj chaste
Sit′tenrichter m censor
sit′tenstreng adj puritanical, prudish
Sittich [′zɪtɪç] m (-s;-e) parakeet
sittlich [′zɪtlɪç] adj moral, ethical
Sittlichkeit f (-;) morality
Sitt′lichkeitsverbrechen n indecent assault
sittsam [′zɪtzam] adj modest, decent
Situation [zɪtuˈaˈtsjoːn] f (-;-en) situation
situiert [zɪtuˈiːrt] adj—**gut s.** well-to-do
Sitz [zɪts] m (-es;-e) seat; residence; (e-s Kleides) fit; (eccl) see
sitzen [′zɪtsən] §144 intr sit; dwell; (Vögel) perch; (Kleider) fit; (Hieb) hit home; (coll) be in jail
sit′zenbleiben §62 intr (SEIN) remain seated; (beim Tanzen) be a wallflower; (bei der Heirat) remain unmarried; (educ) stay behind, flunk
sit′zenlassen §104 tr leave, abandon; (Mädchen) jilt
Sitz′gelegenheit f seating accommodation
Sitz′ordnung f seating arrangement
Sitz′platz m seat
Sitz′streik m sit-down strike
Sitz′ung f (-;-en) session
Sitz′ungsbericht m minutes
Sitz′ungsperiode f session; (jur) term
Sizilien [zɪˈtsiːljən] n (-s;) Sicily
Ska·la [′skaːla] f (-;-len [lən]) scale
Skandal [skanˈdaːl] m (-s;-e) scandal
skandalös [skandaˈløːs] adj scandalous
Skandinavien [skandiˈnaːvjən] n (-s;) Scandinavia
Skelett [skeˈlɛt] n (-[e]s;-e) skeleton
Skepsis [′skɛpsɪs] f (-;) skepticism
Skeptiker –in [′skɛptɪkər(ɪn)] §6 mf skeptic
skeptisch [′skɛptɪʃ] adj skeptical
Ski [ʃiː] m (-s;) **Skier** [′ʃiːər]) ski
Skizze [′skɪtsə] f (-;-n) sketch
skizzieren [skɪˈtsiːrən] tr & intr sketch
Sklave [′sklaːvə] m (-n;-n) slave

Sklaverei [sklaːvəˈraɪ] f (-;) slavery
sklavisch [′sklaːvɪʃ] adj slavish
Skonto [′skɔnto] m & n (-s;-s) discount
Skrupel [′skruːpəl] m (-s;-) scruple
skru′pellos adj unscrupulous
skrupulös [skrupuˈløːs] adj scrupulous
Skulptur [skʊlpˈtuːr] f (-;-en) sculpture
Slalom [′slaːlɔm] m & n (-s;-s) slalom
Slawe [′slaːvə] m (-n;-n), **Slawin** [′slaːvɪn] f (-;-nen) Slav
slawisch [′slaːvɪʃ] adj Slavic
Smaragd [smaˈrakt] m (-[e]s;-e) emerald
Smoking [′smoːkɪŋ] m (-s;-s) tuxedo
so [zo] adv so; this way, thus; **so ein** such a; **so oder so** by hook or by crook; **so...wie so...as**
sobald′ conj as soon as
Socke [′zɔkə] f (-;-n) sock
Sockenhalter (Sok′kenhalter) m garter
Soda [′zoːda] f (-;) & n (-s;) soda
sodann′ adv then
Sodbrennen [′zoːtbrɛnən] n (-s;) heartburn
soeben [zoˈeːbən] adv just now, just
Sofa [′zoːfa] n (-s;-s) sofa
sofern′ conj provided, if
soff [zɔf] pret of **saufen**
sofort′ adv at once, right away
sofortig [zoˈfɔrtɪç] adj immediate
sog [zoːk] pret of **saugen** ‖ **Sog** m (-[e]s;) suction; undertow; (aer) wash
sogar′ adv even
so′genannt adj so-called; would-be
sogleich′ adv at once, right away
Sohle [′zoːlə] f (-;-n) sole; bottom
Sohn [zoːn] m (-[e]s;-e) son
solan′ge conj as long as
solch [zɔlç] adj such
Sold [zɔlt] m (-[e]s;-e) pay
Soldat [zɔlˈdaːt] m (-en;-en) soldier
Söldner [′zœldnər] m (-s;-) mercenary
Sole [′zoːlə] f (-;-n) brine
solid [zoˈliːt] adj solid; sound; reliable; steady; respectable; (Preis) reasonable; (com) sound, solvent
solide [zoˈliːdə] adj var of **solid**
Solist –in [zoˈlɪst(ɪn)] §7 mf soloist
Soll [zɔl] n (-s;-e) quota; (acct) debit side; **S. und Haben** debit and credit
Soll– comb.fm. estimated; debit
sollen [′zɔlən] §145 mod (inf) be obliged to (inf), have to (inf); (inf) be supposed to (inf); (inf) be said to (inf)
Soll′wert m face value
solo [′zoːlo] adv (mus) solo ‖ **So·lo** n (-s;-s & -li [li]) solo
somit′ adv so, consequently
Sommer [′zɔmər] m (-s;-) summer
Som′merfrische f health resort; **in die S. fahren** go to the country
Sommerfrischler [′zɔmərfrɪʃlər] m (-s;-) vacationer
som′merlich adj summery
Som′mersprosse f freckle
sonach′ adv consequently, so
Sonate [zoˈnaːtə] f (-;-n) sonata
Sonde [′zɔndə] f (-;-n) probe
Sonder– [zɔndər] comb.fm. special, extra; separate

sonderbar ['zɔndərbɑr] *adj* strange, odd; peculiar

son'derlich *adj* special, particular

Sonderling ['zɔndərlɪŋ] *m* (-s;-e) odd person, strange character

sondern ['zɔndərn] *tr* separate; sever; part; sort out; classify ‖ *conj* but

Son'derrecht *n* privilege

Son'derung *f* (-;-en) separation; sorting, sifting; classifying

Son'derverband *m* (mil) task force

Son'derzug *m* (rr) special

sondieren [zɔn'dirən] *tr* probe; (fig) sound out; (naut) sound

Sonnabend ['zɔnɑbənt] *m* (-s;-e) Saturday

Sonne ['zɔnə] *f* (-;-n) sun

sonnen ['zɔnən] *tr* sun ‖ *ref* sun oneself

Son'nenaufgang *m* sunrise

Son'nenbad *n* sun bath

Son'nenblende *f* (aut) sun visor; (phot) lens shade

Sonnenbrand *m* sunburn

Son'nenbräune *f* suntan

Son'nenbrille *f* (pair of) sun glasses

Son'nendach *n* awning

Son'nenenergie *f* solar energy

Son'nenfinsternis *f* eclipse of the sun

Son'nenfleck *m* sunspot

Son'nenjahr *n* solar year

son'nenklar' *adj* sunny; (fig) clear as day

Son'nenlicht *n* sunlight

Son'nenschein *m* sunshine

Son'nenschirm *m* parasol

Son'nensegel *n* awning

Son'nenseite *f* sunny side

Son'nenstich *m* sunstroke

Son'nenstrahl *m* sunbeam

Son'nensystem *n* solar system

Son'nenuhr *f* sundial

Son'nenuntergang *m* sunset

son'nenverbrannt *adj* sunburnt, tanned

Son'nenwende *f* solstice

sonnig ['zɔnɪç] *adj* sunny

Sonntag ['zɔntɑk] *m* (-s;-e) Sunday

sonn'tags *adv* on Sundays

Sonn'tagsfahrer –in §6 *mf* Sunday driver

Sonn'tagskind *n* person born under a lucky star

Sonn'tagsstaat *m* Sunday clothes

sonor [zo'nor] *adj* sonorous

sonst [zɔnst] *adv* otherwise; else; (*ehemals*) formerly; s. etw something else; s. keiner no one else; s. nichts nothing else; s. noch was? anything else?; wie s. as usual; wie s. was (coll) like anything

sonstig ['zɔnstɪç] *adj* other

sonst'wer *pron* someone else

sonst'wie *adv* in some other way

sonst'wo *adv* somewhere else

Sopran [zo'prɑn] *m* (-s;-e) soprano; treble

Sopranist –in [zɔprɑ'nɪst(ɪn)] §7 *mf* soprano

Sorge ['zɔrgə] *f* (-;-n) care; worry; außer S. sein be at ease; keine S.! don't worry; sich [*dat*] Sorgen machen über (*acc*) or um be worried about

sorgen ['zɔrgən] *intr*—dafür s., daß take care that, see to it that; s. für take care of ‖ *ref* be uneasy; sich s. über (*acc*) grieve over; sich s. um be worried about

sor'genfrei *adj* carefree; untroubled

Sor'genkind *n* problem child

sor'genlos *adj* carefree

sor'genvoll *adj* uneasy, anxious

Sor'gerecht *n* (für) custody (of)

Sorgfalt ['zɔrkfalt] *f* (-;) care, carefulness; accuracy

sorgfältig ['zɔrkfeltɪç] *adj* careful

sorglich ['zɔrklɪç] *adj* careful

sorglos ['zɔrklos] *adj* careless; thoughtless; carefree

sorgsam ['zɔrkzam] *adj* careful; cautious

Sorte ['zɔrtə] *f* (-;-n) sort, kind

sortieren [zɔr'tirən] *tr* sort out

Sortiment [zɔrti'ment] *n* (-[e]s;-e) assortment

Soße ['zosə] *f* (-;-n) sauce; gravy

sott [zɔt] *pret* of sieden

Souffleur [zu'flør] *m* (-s;-s), **Souffleuse** [zu'fløzə] *f* (-;-n) prompter

soufflieren [zu'flirən] *intr* (*dat*) prompt

Soutane [zu'tanə] *f* (-;-n) cassock

Souvenir [zuvə'nir] *n* (-s;-s) souvenir

souverän [zuvə'ren] *adj* sovereign ‖ **Souverän** *m* (-s;-e) sovereign

Souveränität [zuvərenɪ'tet] *f* (-;) sovereignty

soviel' *adv* so much; noch einmal s. twice as much ‖ *conj* as far as

soweit' *conj* as far as

sowie' *conj* as well as

sowieso' *adv* in any case, anyhow

Sowjet [zɔv'jet] *m* (-s;-s) Soviet

sowjetisch [zɔv'jetɪʃ] *adj* Soviet

sowohl' *conj*—sowohl...als auch as well as, both...and

sozial [zo'tsjal] *adj* social

Sozial'fürsorge *f* social welfare

sozialisieren [zɔtsjalɪ'zirən] *tr* nationalize

Sozialismus [zɔtsja'lɪsmus] *m* (-;) socialism

Sozialist –in [zɔtsja'lɪst(ɪn)] §7 *mf* socialist

sozialistisch [zɔtsja'lɪstɪʃ] *adj* socialistic

Sozial'wissenschaft *f* social science

Soziologie [zɔtsjolo'gi] *f* (-;) sociology

Sozius ['zotsjus] *m* (-;-se) associate, partner; (*auf dem Motorrad*) rider

sozusa'gen *adv* so to speak, as it were

Spachtel ['ʃpaxtəl] *m* (-s;-) & *f* (-;-n) spatula; putty knife

Spach'telmesser *n* putty knife

Spagat [ʃpa'gat] *m* (-[e]s;-e) (gym) split; (dial) string

spähen ['ʃpe·ən] *intr* peer; spy

Spä'her *m* (-s;-) lookout; (mil) scout

Spä'herblick *m* searching glance

Spähtrupp ['ʃpetrup] *m* reconnaissance squad

Späh'wagen *m* reconnaissance car

Spalier [ʃpa'lir] *n* (-s;-e) trellis; double line (*of people*)

Spalt [ʃpalt] *m* (-[e]s;-e) split; crack; slit; (geol) cleft

Spalte ['ʃpaltə] *f* (-;-n) split; crack; slit; (typ) column

spalten ['ʃpaltən] *tr* (*pp* **gespaltet** or **gespalten**) split; slit; crack; (*Holz*) chop

Spal'tung *f* (-;-en) split; (*der Meinungen*) division; (chem) decomposition; (eccl) schism; (phys) fission

Span [ʃpan] *m* (-[e]s;-e) chip; splinter; **Späne** shavings

Span'ferkel *n* suckling pig

Spange ['ʃpaŋə] *f* (-;-n) clasp; hair clip; (*Schnalle*) buckle

Spanien ['ʃpanjən] *n* (-s;) Spain

Spanier -in ['ʃpanjər(ɪn)] §6 *mf* Spaniard

spanisch ['ʃpanɪʃ] *adj* Spanish; **das kommt mir s. vor** (coll) that's Greek to me; **spanischer Pfeffer** paprika; **spanische Wand** folding screen

spann [ʃpan] *pret* of **spinnen** ‖ **Spann** *m* (-s;-e) instep

Spanne ['ʃpanə] *f* (-;-n) span; (com) margin

spannen ['ʃpanən] *tr* stretch; strain; make tense; (*Bogen*) bend; (*Feder*) tighten; (*Flinte*) cock; (*Erwartungen*) raise; (*Pferde*) hitch; **straff s.** tighten; ‖ *intr* be (too) tight; **s. auf** (*acc*) wait eagerly for; listen closely to

span'nend *adj* tight; exciting

Spann'kraft *f* tension; elasticity; (fig) resiliency

spann'kräftig *adj* elastic

Span'nung *f* (-;-en) stress; strain; pressure; close attention; suspense; excitement; strained relations; (elec) voltage

Spar- [ʃpar] *comb.fm.* savings

Spar'buch *n* bank book, pass book

Spar'büchse *f* piggy bank

sparen ['ʃparən] *tr & intr* save

Spar'flamme *f* pilot light

Spargel ['ʃpargəl] *m* (-s;-) asparagus

Spar'kasse *f* savings bank

Spar'konto *n* savings account

spärlich ['ʃperlɪç] *adj* scanty; scarce; sparse; frugal; (*Haar*) thin ‖ *adv* poorly; scantily; sparsely

Sparren ['ʃparən] *m* (-s;-) rafter

sparsam ['ʃparzam] *adj* thrifty

Spaß [ʃpas] *m* (-es;¨e) joke; fun; **aus S.** in fun; **S. beiseite!** all joking aside; **S. haben an** (*dat*) enjoy; **S. machen** be joking; be fun; **viel S.!** have fun!; **zum S.** for fun

spaß'haft, spaßig ['ʃpasɪç] *adj* funny, facetious

Spaß'macher *m* joker

Spaßverderber ['ʃpasverderbər] *m* (-s;-) (coll) kill-joy

Spaß'vogel *m* joker

spät [ʃpet] *adj* late; **wie s. ist es?** what time is it? ‖ *adv* late

Spaten ['ʃpatən] *m* (-s;-) spade

später ['ʃpetər] *adv* later

späterhin *adv* later on

spätestens ['ʃpetəstəns] *adv* at the latest

Spät'jahr *n* autumn, fall

Spatz [ʃpats] *m* (-es & -en;-en) sparrow

spazieren [ʃpa'tsirən] *intr* (SEIN) stroll, take a walk

spazie'renfahren §71 *intr* (SEIN) go for a drive

spazie'renführen *tr* walk (*e.g., a dog*)

spazie'rengehen §82 *intr* (SEIN) go for a walk

Spazier'fahrt *f* drive

Spazier'gang *m* stroll, walk; **e-n S. machen** take a walk

Spazier'gänger -in §6 *mf* stroller

Spazier'weg *m* walk

Specht [ʃpeçt] *m* (-[e]s;-e) woodpecker

Speck [ʃpek] *m* (-[e]s;) fat; bacon; (*beim Wal*) blubber

Speck'bauch *m* (coll) potbelly

speckig ['ʃpekɪç] *adj* greasy, dirty

spedieren [ʃpe'dirən] *tr* dispatch, ship

Spediteur [ʃpedɪ'tør] *m* (-s;-e) shipper; furniture mover

Spedition [ʃpedɪ'tsjon] *f* (-;-en) shipment; moving company, movers

Speer [ʃper] *m* (-[e]s;-e) spear; (sport) javelin

Speiche ['ʃpaiçə] *f* (-;-n) spoke

Speichel ['ʃpaiçəl] *m* (-s;) saliva

Spei'chellecker *m* brown-noser

speicheln ['ʃpaiçəln] *intr* drool

Speicher ['ʃpaiçər] *m* (-s;-) warehouse; grain elevator; attic, loft

speichern ['ʃpaiçərn] *tr* store

speien ['ʃpaiən] §135 *tr* vomit; spit; (*Feuer*) belch; (*Wasser*) spurt ‖ *intr* vomit, throw up; spit

Speise ['ʃpaizə] *f* (-;-n) food; meal; (*Gericht*) dish

Spei'seeis *n* ice cream

Spei'sekammer *f* pantry

Spei'sekarte *f* menu

speisen ['ʃpaizən] *tr* feed; (fig) supply ‖ *intr* eat; **auswärts s.** dine out

Spei'senfolge *f* menu

Spei'sereste *pl* leftovers

Spei'serohr *n* (mach) feed pipe

Spei'seröhre *f* esophagus

Spei'sesaal *m* dining room

Spei'seschrank *m* cupboard

Spei'sewagen *m* (rr) diner

Spei'sezimmer *n* dining room

Spektakel [ʃpek'takəl] *m* (-s;-) noise, racket

Spekulant -in [ʃpeku'lant(ɪn)] §7 *mf* speculator

Spekulation [ʃpekula'tsjon] *f* (-;-en) speculation; venture

spekulieren [ʃpeku'lirən] *intr* speculate, reflect; (fin) speculate

Spelunke [ʃpe'luŋkə] *f* (-;-n) (coll) drive, joint

Spende ['ʃpendə] *f* (-;-n) donation

spenden ['ʃpendən] *tr* give; donate; (*Sakramente*) administer; (*Lob*) bestow; **j-m Trost s.** comfort s.o.

spendieren [ʃpen'dirən] *tr*—**j-m etw s.** treat s.o. to s.th.

Sperling ['ʃperlɪŋ] *m* (-s;-e) sparrow

Sperr- [ʃper] *comb.fm.* barrage; barred

Sperr'baum *m* barrier, bar

Sperre ['ʃperə] *f* (-;-n) shutting; close; blockade; embargo; barricade; catch; lock; (rr) gate

sperren ['ʃperən] *tr* shut; (*Gas, Licht*) cut off; (*Straße*) block off; cordon off; (blockieren) blockade; (mit Schloß) lock; (verriegeln) bolt; (Konto, Gelder) freeze; (Scheck) stop payment on; (verbieten) stop; (sport) block; (sport) suspend; (typ) space || intr jam, be stuck

Sperr′feuer n barrage

Sperr′gebiet n restricted area

Sperr′holz n plywood

sperrig [′pɛrɪç] adj bulky

Sperr′sitz m (im Kino) rear seat; (im Zirkus) front seat

Sperr′stunde f closing time; curfew

Sper′rung f (–;–en) stoppage; blocking; blockade; embargo; suspension (of telephone service, etc.)

Spesen [′ʃpezən] pl costs, expenses

Spezi [′ʃpetsi] m (–s;–s) (coll) buddy

spezial [ʃpe′tsjal] adj special

Spezial′arzt m, **Spezial′ärztin** f specialist

Spezial′fach n specialty

Spezial′geschäft n specialty shop

spezialisieren [ʃpetsjalɪ′zirən] ref (auf acc) specialize (in)

Spezialist –in [ʃpetsja′lɪst(ɪn)] §7 mf specialist

Spezialität [ʃpetsjalɪ′tet] f (–;–en) specialty

speziell [ʃpe′tsjɛl] adj special

spezifisch [ʃpe′tsifɪʃ] adj specific

Sphäre [′sferə] f (–;–n) sphere

sphärisch [′sferɪʃ] adj spherical

Spickaal [′ʃpɪkal] m smoked eel

spicken [′ʃpɪkən] tr lard; (fig) bribe

spie [ʃpi] pret of speien

Spiegel [′ʃpigəl] m (–s;–) mirror

Spie′gelbild n reflection (in mirror)

spie′gelblank′ adj spick and span

Spie′gelei n fried egg

spie′gelglatt′ adj glassy

spiegeln [′ʃpigəln] tr reflect; mirror || ref be reflected || intr shine

Spiel [ʃpil] n (–[e]s;–e) game; play; set (of chessmen or checkers); (cards) deck; (mach) play; (mus) playing; (sport) match; (theat) acting, performance; **auf dem S. stehen** be at stake; **aufs S. setzen** risk; **bei etw im S. sein** be at the bottom of s.th.; **leichtes S. haben mit** have an easy time with; **S. der Natur** freak of nature

Spiel′art f (biol) variety

Spiel′automat m slot machine

Spiel′bank f (–;–en) gambling table; gambling casino

Spiel′dose f music box

spielen [′ʃpilən] tr & intr play

Spielerei [ʃpilə′raɪ] f (–;–en) fooling around; child's play

Spiel′ergebnis n (sport) score

spielerisch [′ʃpilərɪʃ] adj playful

Spiel′feld n (sport) playing field

Spiel′film m feature film

Spiel′folge f program

Spiel′gefährte m, **Spiel′gefährtin** f playmate

Spiel′karten pl (playing) cards

Spiel′leiter m (cin, theat) director

Spiel′marke f chip, counter

Spiel′plan m program

Spiel′platz m playground; playing field

Spiel′raum m (fig) elbowroom; (mach) play

Spiel′sachen pl toys

Spiel′tisch m gambling table

Spiel′verderber m kill-joy

Spiel′verlängerung f overtime

Spiel′waren pl toys

Spiel′zeug n toy(s)

Spieß [ʃpis] m (–es;–e) spear, pike; (sl) top kick; (culin) spit; **den S. umdrehen gegen** turn the tables on

Spieß′bürger m Philistine, lowbrow

spieß′bürgerlich adj narrow-minded

spießen [′ʃpisən] tr spear; spit

Spie′ßer m (–s;–) Philistine, lowbrow

Spieß′gesell m accomplice

Spießruten [′ʃpisrutən] pl—**S. laufen** run the gauntlet

spinal [ʃpɪ′nal] adj spinal; **spinale Kinderlähmung** infantile paralysis

Spinat [ʃpɪ′nat] m (–[e]s;–e) spinach

Spind [ʃpɪnt] m & n (–[e]s;–e) wardrobe; (mil) locker

Spindel [′ʃpɪndəl] f (–;–n) spindle; (Spinnrocken) distaff

spin′deldürr′ adj skinny, scrawny

Spinne [′ʃpɪnə] f (–;–n) spider

spinnen [′ʃpɪnən] tr spin; **Ränke s.** hatch plots || intr purr; (im Gefängnis sitzen) do time; (sl) be looney

Spin′nengewebe n spider web

Spin′ner m (–s;–) spinner; (sl) nut

Spinnerei [ʃpɪnə′raɪ] f (–;–en) spinning; spinning mill

Spinn′faden m spider thread; **Spinn′fäden** gossamer

Spinn′gewebe n (–s;–) cobweb

Spinn′rad n spinning wheel

Spinn′webe f (–;–n) (Aust) cobweb

Spion [ʃpi′on] m (–[e]s;–e) spy

Spionage [ʃpi·o′naʒə] f (–;) spying, espionage

Spiona′geabwehr f counterintelligence

spionieren [ʃpi·o′nirən] intr spy

Spirale [ʃpi′ralə] f (–;–n) spiral

Spirituosen [ʃpɪrɪtu′ozən] pl liquor

Spiritus [′ʃpirɪtus] m (–;–se) alcohol

Spital [ʃpi′tal] n (–s;–er) hospital

spitz [ʃpɪts] adj pointed; sharp; (Winkel) acute

Spitz′bart m goatee

Spitz′bube m rascal; thief; swindler

Spitze [′ʃpɪtsə] f (–;–n) point; tip; top, summit; (tex) lace; **an der S. liegen** be in the lead; **auf die S. treiben** carry to extremes

Spitzel [′ʃpɪtsəl] m (–s;–) spy; stool pigeon; plain-clothes man

spitzen [′ʃpɪtsən] tr point; sharpen; (Ohren) prick up; **den Mund s.** purse the lips || ref—**sich s. auf** (acc) look forward to || intr be on one's toes

Spitzen– comb.fm. top; peak; leading; topnotch; maximum; (tex) lace

Spitzen′form f (sport) top form

Spit′zenleistung f top performance

Spit′zenmarke f (com) top brand

Spit′zer m (–s;–) pencil sharpener

spitz′findig adj subtle; sharp

Spitz′hacke f, **Spitz′haue** f pickax

spitzig [′ʃpɪtsɪç] adj pointed; (& fig) sharp

Spitz'marke f (typ) heading
Spitz'name m nickname; pet name
Spitz'nase f pointed nose
spleißen ['ʃplaisən] §53 tr splice
spliß [ʃplis] pret of spleißen
Splitter ['ʃplitər] m (-s;-) splinter; chip; fragment
split'ternackt' adj stark-naked
Split'terpartei f splinter party
split'tersicher adj shatterproof
spontan [ʃpɔn'taːn] adj spontaneous
Spore ['ʃpoːrə] f (-;-n) spore
Sporn [ʃpɔrn] m (-[e]s; Sporen ['ʃpoːrən] spur; (fig) stimulus; (aer) tail skid; (naut) ram
spornen ['ʃpɔrnən] tr spur
Sport [ʃpɔrt] m (-[e]s;-e) sport(s); S. ausüben (or treiben) play sports
Sport'freund –in §8 mf sports fan
Sport'hose f shorts, trunks
Sport'jacke f sport jacket, blazer
Sport'kleidung f sportswear
Sportler –in ['ʃpɔrtlər(ɪn)] §6 mf athlete
sport'lich adj sportsmanlike; (Figur) athletic; (Kleidung) sport
Sport'wagen m sports car; (Kinder- wagen) stroller
Sport'wart m trainer
Spott [ʃpɔt] m (-[e]s;) mockery; scorn
Spott'bild n caricature
spott'bil'lig adj dirt-cheap
Spott'drossel f mockingbird
Spöttelei [ʃpœtə'lai] f (-;-en) mockery
spotten ['ʃpɔtən] intr (über acc) scoff (at), ridicule; das spottet jeder Be- schreibung that defies description
Spötterei [ʃpœtə'rai] f (-;-en) mock- ery
Spott'gebot n (com) ridiculous offer
spöttisch ['ʃpœtɪʃ] adj mocking, satir- ical; sneering
Spott'name m nickname
Spott'schrift f satire
sprach [ʃpraːx] pret of sprechen
Sprach– comb.fm. speech; grammati- cal; linguistic; philological
Sprache ['ʃpraːxə] f (-;-n) language, tongue; speech; diction; style; idiom
Sprach'eigenheit f, Sprach'eigentüm- lichkeit f idiom, idiomatic expression
Sprach'fehler m speech defect
Sprach'forschung f linguistics
Sprach'führer m phrase book
Sprach'gebrauch m usage
Sprach'gefühl n feeling for a language
sprach'gewandt adj fluent
sprach'kundig adj proficient in lan- guages
Sprach'lehre f grammar
Sprach'lehrer –in §6 mf language teacher
sprach'lich adj grammatical; linguistic
sprach'los adj speechless
Sprach'rohr n megaphone; (fig) mouth- piece
Sprach'schatz m vocabulary
Sprach'störung f speech defect
Sprach'wissenschaft f philology; lin- guistics
sprang [ʃpraŋ] pret of springen
Sprech– [ʃprɛç] comb.fm. speaking
Sprech'art f way of speaking

Sprech'bühne f legitimate theater
sprechen ['ʃprɛçən] §64 tr speak; talk; (Gebet) say; (Urteil) pronounce; speak to, see || intr (über acc, von) speak (about), talk (about); er ist nicht zu s. he's not available
Spre'cher –in §6 mf speaker, talker
Sprech'fehler m slip of the tongue
Sprech'funkgerät n walkie-talkie
Sprech'probe f audition
Sprech'sprache f spoken language
Sprech'stunde f office hours
Sprech'stundenhilfe f receptionist
Sprech'zimmer n office (of doctor, etc.)
Spreize ['ʃpraitsə] f (-;-n) prop, strut; (gym) split
spreizen ['ʃpraitsən] tr spread, stretch out || ref sprawl out; (fig) (mit) boast (of); sich s. gegen resist
Spreng– [ʃprɛŋ] comb.fm. high-explo- sive
Sprengel ['ʃprɛŋəl] m (-s;-) diocese; parish
sprengen ['ʃprɛŋən] tr break, burst; (mit Sprengstoff) blow up; (Tür) force; (Versammlung) break up; (Mine) set off; (bespritzen) sprinkle; (Garten) water || intr (SEIN) gallop
Spreng'kommando n bomb disposal unit
Spreng'kopf m warhead
Spreng'körper m, Spreng'stoff m ex- plosive
Spreng'wagen m sprinkling truck
Sprenkel ['ʃprɛŋkəl] m (-s;-) speck
sprenkeln ['ʃprɛŋkəln] tr speckle
Spreu [ʃprɔi] f (-;) chaff
Sprichwort ['ʃprɪçvɔrt] n (-[e]s;ᵉer) proverb, saying
sprichwörtlich ['ʃprɪçvœrtlɪç] adj pro- verbial
sprießen ['ʃpriːsən] §76 intr (SEIN) sprout
Springbrunnen ['ʃprɪŋbrunən] m (-s;-) fountain
springen ['ʃprɪŋən] §142 intr (SEIN) jump; dive; burst; (Eis) crack; (coll) rush, hurry
Sprin'ger m (-s;-) jumper; (chess) knight; (sport) diver
Spring'insfeld m (-[e]s;-e) (coll) live wire
Spring'kraft f (& fig) resiliency
Spring'seil n jumping rope
Sprint [ʃprɪnt] m (-s;-s) sprint
Sprit [ʃprɪt] m (-[e]s;-e) alcohol; (coll) gasoline
Spritze ['ʃprɪtsə] f (-;-n) squirt; (Feu- erwehr) fire engine; (med) injection, shot; (med) syringe
spritzen ['ʃprɪtsən] tr squirt; splash; (sprühen) spray; (sprengen) sprinkle; (Wein) mix with soda water; (med) inject || intr spurt, spout || impers— es spritzt it is drizzling || intr (SEIN) dash, flit
Spritz'tour f (coll) side trip
spröde ['ʃprøːdə] adj brittle; (Haut) chapped; (fig) prudish, coy
sproß [ʃpros] pret of sprießen || Sproß m (Sprosses; Sprosse) offspring, de- scendant; (bot) shoot

Sprosse ['∫prɔsə] f (-;-n) rung; prong
sprossen ['∫prɔsən] intr (HABEN & SEIN) sprout
Sprößling ['∫prœslɪŋ] m (-s;-e) offspring, descendant; (bot) sprout
Spruch [∫prux] m (-[e]s;⁼e) saying; motto; text, passage; (jur) sentence; (jur) verdict; e-n S. fällen give the verdict
Spruch/band n (-[e]s;⁼er) banderole
Sprudel ['∫prudəl] m (-s;-) mineral water
sprudeln ['∫prudəln] intr bubble
sprühen ['∫pry·ən] tr emit ‖ intr spray; sparkle; (fig) flash ‖ impers—es sprüht it is drizzling
Sprüh/regen m drizzle
Sprüh/teufel m (coll) spitfire
Sprung [∫pruŋ] m (-[e]s;⁼e) jump; crack; (sport) dive
Sprung/brett n diving board; (fig) stepping stone
Spucke ['∫pukə] f (-;) (coll) spit
spucken ['∫pukən] tr spit ‖ intr spit; (Motor) sputter
Spuk [∫puk] m (-[e]s;-e) ghost, spook; (Lärm) racket; (Alptraum) nightmare
spuken ['∫pukən] intr linger on ‖ impers—es spukt hier this place is haunted
spuk/haft adj spooky
Spülabort ['∫pylabɔrt] m flush toilet
Spül/becken n sink
Spule ['∫pulə] f (-;-n) spool, reel; (elec) coil
Spüle ['∫pylə] f (-;-n) wash basin
spulen ['∫pulən] tr reel, wind
spülen ['∫pylən] tr wash, rinse; (Abort) flush; an Land s. wash ashore ‖ intr flush the toilet; undulate
Spü/ler m (-s;-) dishwasher
Spülicht ['∫pylɪçt] n (-[e]s;-e) dishwater; swill, slop
Spül/maschine f dishwasher
Spül/mittel n detergent
Spülwasser n dishwater
Spund [∫punt] m (-[e]s;⁼e) bung, plug; (carp) feather, tongue
Spur [∫pur] f (-;-en) trace; track, rut; (hunt) scent; S. Salz pinch of salt
spürbar ['∫pyrbar] adj perceptible
spüren ['∫pyrən] tr trace; track, trail; (fühlen) feel; (wahrnehmen) perceive
spur/los adj trackless ‖ adv without a trace
Spür/nase f (coll) good nose
Spür/sinn m flair
Spur/weite f (aut) tread; (rr) gauge
sputen ['∫putən] ref hurry up
SS ['ɛs'ɛs] f (-;) (Schutzstaffel) S.S.
Staat [∫tat] m (-[e]s;-en) state; government; (Aufwand) show; (Putz) finery
Staats– comb.fm. state; government; national; public; political
Staatsangehörigkeit ['∫tatsangəhøriç-kart] f (-;-en) nationality
Staats/anwalt m district attorney
Staats/bauten pl public works
Staats/beamte m civil servant

Staats/bürger –in §6 mf citizen
Staats/bürgerkunde f civics
Staats/bürgerschaft f citizenship
Staats/dienst m civil service
staats/eigen adj state-owned
Staats/feind m public enemy
staats/feindlich adj subversive
Staats/form f form of government
Staats/gewalt f supreme power
Staats/hoheit f sovereignty
staats/klug adj politic, diplomatic
Staats/klugheit f statecraft
Staats/kunst f statesmanship
Staats/mann m (-[e]s;⁼er) statesman
staats/männisch adj statesmanlike
Staats/oberhaupt n head of state
Staats/papiere pl government bonds
Staats/recht n public law
Staats/streich m coup d'état
Staats/wirtschaft f political economy
Staats/wissenschaft f political science
Stab [∫tap] m (-[e]s;⁼e) staff; rod; bar; (e-r Jalousie) slat; (eccl) crozier; (mil) staff; (mil) headquarters; (mus, sport) baton
stab/hochspringen §142 intr (SEIN) pole-vault
stabil [∫ta'bil] adj stable, steady
stabilisieren [∫tabɪli'zirən] tr stabilize
stach [∫tax] pret of stechen
Stachel ['∫taxəl] m (-s;-n) prick; quill; (bot) thorn; (ent) sting
Sta/chelbeere f gooseberry
Sta/cheldraht m barbed wire
stachelig ['∫taxəlɪç] adj prickly; (& fig) thorny
Sta/chelschwein n porcupine
Sta-dion ['∫tadjən] n (-s;-dien [djən]) stadium
Sta-dium ['∫tadjum] n (-s;-dien [djən]) stage
Stadt [∫tat] f (-;⁼e) city, town
Städtchen ['∫tetçən] n (-s;-) town
Städtebau ['∫tetəbau] m (-[e]s;) city planning
Stadt/gemeinde f township
Stadt/gespräch n talk of the town
städtisch ['∫tetɪ∫] adj municipal
Stadt/plan m map of the city
Stadt/rand m outskirts
Stadt/rat m (-[e]s;⁼e) city council; (Person) city councilor
Stadt/teil m Stadt/viertel n quarter (of the city)
Stafette [∫ta'fetə] f (-;-n) courier; (sport) relay
Staffel ['∫tafəl] f (-;-n) step, rung; (Stufe) degree; (aer) squadron (of nine aircraft); (sport) relay team
Staffelei [∫tafə'lar] f (-;-en) easel
Staf/felkeil m (aer) V-formation
Staf/fellauf m relay race
staffeln ['∫tafəln] tr graduate; (Arbeitszeit, usw.) stagger
stahl [∫tal] pret of stehlen ‖ **Stahl** m (-[e]s;⁼e) steel
Stahl/beton m reinforced concrete
stählen ['∫telən] tr temper; (fig) steel
Stahl/kammer f steel vault
Stahlspäne ['∫tal/penə] pl steel wool
stak [∫tak] pret of stecken
Stalag ['∫talak] n (-s;-s) (Stammlager) main camp (for P.O.W.'s)

Stall [ʃtal] *m* (-[e]s;⁼e) stable; shed
Stall′knecht *m* groom
Stamm [ʃtam] *m* (-[e]s;⁼e) stem; stalk; trunk; stock, race; tribe; breed
Stamm′aktie *f* common stock
Stamm′baum *m* family tree; pedigree
stammeln [′ʃtaməln] *tr & intr* stammer
Stamm′eltern *pl* ancestors
stammen [′ʃtamən] *intr* (SEIN) (aus, von) come (from); (von) date (from); (gram) (von) be derived (from)
Stamm′gast *m* regular customer
stämmig [′ʃtemɪç] *adj* stocky; husky
Stamm′kneipe *f* favorite bar
Stamm′kunde *m*, **Stamm′kundin** *f* regular customer
Stamm′personal *n* skeleton staff
Stamm′tisch *m* reserved table
Stammutter (**Stamm′mutter**) *f* ancestress
Stamm′vater *m* ancestor
stampfen [′ʃtampfən] *tr* tamp, pound; (*Kartoffeln*) mash; (*Boden*) paw ‖ *intr* stamp the ground; (*durch Schnee*) trudge; (naut) pitch
stand [ʃtant] *pret of* stehen ‖ **Stand** *m* (-[e]s;⁼e) stand; footing, foothold; level, height; condition; status, rank; class, caste; booth; profession; trade; (sport) score; **seinen S. behaupten** hold one's ground
Standard [′ʃtandart] *m* (-s;-s) standard
Standarte [ʃtan′dartə] *f* (-;-n) banner; standard
Stand′bild *n* statue
Ständchen [′ʃtentçən] *n* (-s;-) serenade; **j-m ein S. bringen** serenade s.o.
Ständer [′ʃtendər] *m* (-s;-) stand, rack; pillar; stud; (mach) column
Stan′desamt *n* bureau of vital statistics
stan′desamtlich *adj & adv* before a civil magistrate
stan′desgemäß *adj* according to rank
Stan′desperson *f* dignitary
stand′fest *adj* stable, steady, sturdy
stand′haft *adj* steadfast
stand′halten §90 *intr* hold out; (*dat*) withstand
ständig [′ʃtendɪç] *adj* permanent; steady, constant
Stand′licht *n* parking light
Stand′ort *m* position; station; (mil) base; (mil) garrison
Stand′pauke *f* (coll) lecture
Stand′punkt *m* standpoint
Stand′recht *n* martial law
Stand′uhr *f* grandfather's clock
Stange [′ʃtaŋə] *f* (-;-n) pole; rod, bar; perch, roost; **e-e S. Zigaretten** a carton of cigarettes; **von der S.** ready-made (*clothes*)
stank [ʃtank] *pret of* stinken
stänkern [′ʃteŋkərn] *intr* (coll) stink; (coll) make trouble
Stanniol [ʃta′njol] *n* (-s;-e), **Stanniol′papier** *n* tinfoil
Stanze [′ʃtantsə] *f* (-;-n) stanza; punch, die, stamp
stanzen [′ʃtantsən] *tr* (mach) punch
Stapel [′ʃtapəl] *m* (-s;-) stack; depot;

stock; (naut) slip; (tex) staple; **auf S. liegen** be in drydock; **vom S. laufen lassen** launch
Sta′pellauf *m* launching
stapeln [′ʃtapəln] *tr* stack, pile up
Sta′pelplatz *m* lumberyard; depot
stapfen [′ʃtapfən] *intr* slog
Star [ʃtar] *m* (-[e]s;-e) (orn) starling; (pathol) cataract; **grauer S.** cataract; **grüner S.** glaucoma ‖ *m* (-s;-s) (cin, theat) star
starb [ʃtarp] *pret of* sterben
stark [ʃtark] *adj* (stärker [′ʃterkər]; stärkste [′ʃterkstə] §9) strong; stout; (*Erkältung*) bad; (*Familie*) big; (*Kälte*) severe; (*Frost, Verkehr*) heavy; (*Wind*) high; (*Stunde*) full ‖ *adv* much; hard; very
Stärke [′ʃterkə] *f* (-;-n) strength; force; stoutness; thickness; might; violence; intensity; (*Anzahl*) number; (fig) forte; (chem) starch
stärken [′ʃterkən] *tr* strengthen; (*Wäsche*) starch ‖ *ref* take some refreshment
Stark′strom *m* high-voltage current
Stär′kung *f* (-;-en) strengthening; refreshment; (*Imbiß*) snack
starr [ʃtar] *adj* stiff, rigid; fixed; inflexible; obstinate; dumbfounded; numb ‖ *adv*—s. ansehen stare at
starren [′ʃtarən] *intr* (auf *acc*) stare (at); **s. von** be covered with
Starr′kopf *m* stubborn fellow
starr′köpfig *adj* stubborn
Starr′krampf *m* (-es;) tetanus
Starr′sinn *m* (-[e]s;) stubbornness
Start [ʃtart] *m* (-[e]s;-s & -e) start; (aer) take-off; (rok) launching
Start′bahn *f* (aer) runway
starten [′ʃtartən] *tr* start; launch ‖ *intr* (SEIN) start; (aer) take off; (rok) lift off, be launched
Start′rampe *f* (rok) launch pad
Station [ʃta′tsjon] *f* (-;-en) station; (med) ward; **freie S.** free room and board
statisch [′ʃtatɪʃ] *adj* static
Statist **-in** [ʃta′tɪst(ɪn)] §7 *mf* (cin) extra; (theat) supernumerary
Statistik [ʃta′tɪstɪk] *f* (-;-en) statistic; (*Wissenschaft*) statistics
statistisch [ʃta′tɪstɪʃ] *adj* statistical
Stativ [ʃta′tif] *n* (-s;-e) stand; (phot) tripod
statt [ʃtat] *prep* (*genit*) instead of; **s. zu** (*inf*) instead of (*ger*) ‖ **Statt** *f* (-;) place, stead; **an Kindes S. annehmen** adopt
Stätte [′ʃtetə] *f* (-;-n) place, spot; (*Wohnung*) abode; room
statt′finden §59 *intr* take place
statt′haft *adj* admissible; legal
Statthalter [′ʃtathaltər] *m* (-s;-) governor
statt′lich *adj* stately; imposing
Statue [′ʃtatuˑə] *f* (-;-n) statue
statuieren [ʃtatu′irən] *tr* establish; **ein Exempel s. an** (*dat*) make an example of
Statur [ʃta′tur] *f* (-;-en) stature
Statut [ʃta′tut] *n* (-[e]s;-en) statute; **Statuten** bylaws

Stau [ʃtau] *m* (-[e]s;-e) dammed-up water; updraft; (aut) tie-up
Staub [ʃtaup] *m* (-[e]s;) dust
Stau′becken *n* reservoir
stauben [′ʃtaubən] *intr* make dust
stäuben [′ʃtɔɪbən] *tr* dust; sprinkle, powder; (*Flüssigkeit*) spray ‖ *intr* make dust; throw off spray
staubig [′ʃtaubɪç] *adj* dusty
staub′saugen *tr & intr* vacuum
Staub′sauger *m* vacuum cleaner
Staub′wedel *m* feather duster
Staub′zucker *m* powdered sugar
stauchen [′ʃtauçən] *tr* knock, jolt; compress; (sl) chew out
Stau′damm *m* dam
Staude [′ʃtaudə] *f* (-;-n) perennial
stauen [′ʃtau·ən] *tr* dam up; (*Waren*) stow away; (*Blut*) stanch ‖ *ref* be blocked, jam up
Stau′er *m* (-s;-) stevedore
staunen [′ʃtaunən] *intr* (**über** *acc*) be astonished (at) ‖ **Staunen** *n* (-s;) astonishment
stau′nenswert *adj* astonishing
Staupe [′ʃtaupə] *f* (-;) (vet) distemper
Stau′see *m* reservoir
Stau′ung *f* (-;-en) damming up; block-age; (*Engpaß*) bottleneck; (*Verkehrs-*) jam-up; (pathol) congestion
stechen [′ʃteçən] §64 prick; sting, bite; (*mit e-r Waffe*) stab; (*Torf*) cut; (*Star*) remove; (*Kontrolluhr*) punch; (*Wein*) draw; (*Näherei*) stitch; (*gravieren*) engrave; (cards) trump; (cards) take (*a trick*) ‖ *intr* sting, bite; (*Sonne*) be hot; (cards) be trump; **j-m in die Augen s.** catch s.o.'s eye ‖ *impers*—**es sticht mich in der Brust I** have a sharp pain in my chest
ste′chend *adj* (*Blick*) piercing; (*Geruch*) strong; (*Schmerz*) sharp, stabbing
Stech′karte *f* timecard
Stech′schritt *m* goosestep
Stech′uhr *f* time clock
Steckbrief [′ʃtɛkbrif] *m* warrant for arrest
steck′brieflich *adv*—**s. verfolgen** put out a "wanted" notice for
Steckdose [′ʃtɛkdozə] *f* (elec) outlet
stecken [′ʃtɛkən] *tr & intr* stick ‖ **Stecken** *m* (-s;-) stick
steckenbleiben (stek′kenbleiben) §62 *intr* (SEIN) get stuck
Steckenpferd (Stek′kenpferd) hobby-horse; (fig) hobby
Stecker (Stek′ker) *m* (-s;-) (elec) plug
Steck′kontakt *m* (elec) plug
Steck′nadel *f* pin
Steg [ʃtek] *m* (-[e]s;-e) footpath; footbridge; (*e-r Brille, Geige*) bridge; (*Landungs-*) jetty; (naut) gangplank
Steg′reif *m*—**aus dem S.** extempore
stehen [′ʃte·ən] §146 *tr*—**e-m Maler Modell s.** sit for a painter; **Schlange s.** stand in line; **Schmiere s.** (coll) be a lookout; **Wache s.** stand guard ‖ *intr* (HABEN & SEIN) stand; stop; be; (gram) occur, be used; (*Kleider*) fit; **das steht bei Ihnen** that depends

on you; **gut s.** (*dat*) fit, suit; **gut s. mit** be on good terms with; **wie steht's?** (coll) how is it going?
ste′henbleiben §62 *intr* (SEIN) stop
ste′henlassen §104 *tr* leave standing; (*nicht anrühren*) leave alone; (*Fehler*) leave uncorrected; (*vergessen*) forget; (culin) allow to stand or cool
Ste′her *m* (-s;-) long-distance cyclist
Stehlampe [′ʃtelampə] *f* floor lamp
Stehleiter [′ʃtelaɪtər] *f* stepladder
stehlen [′ʃtelən] §147 *tr & intr* steal
Stehplatz [′ʃteplats] *m* standing room
steif [ʃtaɪf] *adj* stiff; rigid; (*Lächeln*) forced; (*förmlich*) formal; (*starr*) numb
steifen [′ʃtaɪfən] *tr* stiffen; (*Wäsche*) starch
Steig [ʃtaɪk] *m* (-[e]s;-e) path
Steig′bügel *m* stirrup
steigen [′ʃtaɪgən] §148 *tr* (*Treppen*) climb ‖ *intr* (SEIN) climb; rise; go up; (*Nebel*) lift; (*Blut in den Kopf*) rush ‖ **Steigen** *n* (-s;) rise; increase
steigern [′ʃtaɪgərn] *tr* raise, increase; (*verstärken*) enhance; (gram) compare ‖ *ref* increase, go up
Stei′gerung *f* (-;-en) rising; increase; intensification; (gram) comparison
Stei′gerungsgrad *m* (gram) degree of comparison
Stei′gung *f* (-;-en) rise; (*Hang*) slope; (*e-s Propellers*) pitch
steil [ʃtaɪl] *adj* steep
Stein [ʃtaɪn] *m* (-[e]s;-e) stone; rock; (horol) jewel; (pathol) stone
stein′alt′ *adj* old as the hills
Stein′bruch *m* quarry
Stein′druck *m* lithography; (*Bild*) lithograph
steinern [′ʃtaɪnərn] *adj* stone
Stein′gut *n* earthenware
steinig [′ʃtaɪnɪç] *adj* stony, rocky
steinigen [′ʃtaɪnɪgən] *tr* stone
Stein′kohle *f* hard coal
Stein′metz *m* stonemason
stein′reich′ *adj* (coll) filthy rich
Stein′salz *n* rock salt
Stein′schlag *m* (public sign) falling rocks
Stein′wurf *m* stone's throw
Stein′zeit *f* stone age
Steiß [ʃtaɪs] *m* (-es;-e) buttocks
Stelldichein [′ʃtɛldɪçaɪn] *n* (-[s]; -[s]) (coll) date
Stelle [′ʃtɛlə] *f* (-;-n) place, spot; position; job; agency, department; quotation; (math) digit; **an S. von** in place of; **auf der S.** on the spot; **auf der S. treten** (fig & mil) mark time; **freie** (or **offene**) **S.** opening; **zur S. sein** be on hand
stellen [′ʃtɛlən] *tr* put, place; set; stand; (elec) regulate, adjust; (*anordnen*) fix, arrange; (*Frage*) ask; (*Horoskop*) cast; (*Diagnose*) give; (*Falle, Wecker*) set; (*Kaution*) put up; (*Zeugen*) produce; **e-n Antrag s.** make a motion; **in Dienst s.** appoint; put into service ‖ *ref* place oneself, stand; give oneself up; **der Preis stellt sich auf…** the price is…; **sich s., als ob** act as if

Stel′lenangebot n help wanted
Stel′lenbewerber –in §6 mf applicant
Stel′lengesuch n situation wanted
Stel′lenjagd f job hunting
Stel′lennachweis m, Stel′lenvermittlungsbüro n employment agency
stel′lenweise adv here and there
–stellig [ʹtɛlɪç] comb.fm. –digit
Stell′schraube f set screw
Stel′lung f (–;–en) position; situation; job; standing; status; rank; posture; (mil) line, position; (mil) emplacement; S. nehmen zu express one's opinion on; (erklären) explain; (beantworten) answer
Stel′lungnahme f (–;–n) attitude, point of view; (Erklärung) comment; (Gutachten) opinion; (Bericht) report; (Beantwortung) answer; (Entscheid) decision; sich [dat] e–e S. vorbehalten not commit oneself
Stel′lungsgesuch n (job) application
stel′lunglos adj jobless
stell′vertretend adj acting
Stell′vertreter –in §6 mf representative; deputy; proxy; substitute
Stell′vertretung f (–;–en) representation; substitution; in S. by proxy
Stelzbein [ʹtɛltsbaɪn] n wooden leg
Stelze [ʹtɛltsə] f (–;–n) stilt
stelzen [ʹtɛltsən] intr (SEIN) stride
Stemmeisen [ʹtɛmaɪzən] n crowbar
stemmen [ʹtɛmən] tr support; (Gewicht) lift; (Loch) chisel ‖ ref—sich s. gegen oppose
Stempel [ʹtɛmpəl] m (–s;–) stamp; prop; (Kolben) piston; (bot) pistil
Stem′pelkissen n ink pad, stamp pad
stempeln [ʹtɛmpəln] tr stamp ‖ intr—s. gehen (coll) collect unemployment insurance
Stengel [ʹtɛŋəl] m (–s;–) stalk
Steno [ʹteno] f (–;) stenography
Stenograph [stenoʹɡraf] m (–en;–en) stenographer
Stenographie [stenograˈfi] f (–;) stenography, shorthand
stenographieren [stenoɡrˈfirən] tr take down in shorthand ‖ intr do shorthand
Stenographin [stenoˈɡrafɪn] f (–;–nen) stenographer
Stenotypistin [stenotʏˈpɪstɪn] f (–;–nen) stenographer
Step [tep] m (–s;–) tap dance; S. tanzen tap-dance
Steppdecke [ʹtɛpdɛkə] f comforter
Steppe [ʹtɛpə] f (–;–n) steppe
steppen [ʹtɛpən] tr quilt ‖ intr tap-dance ‖ Steppen (–s;) tap-dancing
Sterbe– [ʹtɛrbə] comb.fm. dying, death
Ster′befall m death
Ster′begeld n death benefit
Ster′behilfe f euthanasia
sterben [ʹtɛrbən] §149 intr (SEIN) (an dat) die (of)
sterb′lich adj mortal ‖ adv—s. verliebt in (acc) head over heals in love with
Sterb′lichkeit f (–;) mortality
Sterb′lichkeitsziffer f death rate
stereotyp [stereˑˈtyp] adj stereotyped
steril [teˈril] adj sterile
sterilisieren [ʃterɪlˈzirən] tr sterilize

Stern [ʃtern] m (–[e]s;–e) star; (typ) asterisk
Stern′bild n constellation
Stern′blume f aster
Sterndeuter [ʹʃterndɔɪtər] m (–s;–) astrologer
Sterndeuterei [ʃterndɔɪtəˈraɪ] f (–;) astrology
Ster′nenbanner n Stars and Stripes
stern′ha′gelvoll′ adj (sl) dead drunk
stern′hell′ adj starlit
Stern′himmel m starry sky
Stern′kunde f astronomy
Stern′schuppe f shooting star
Stern′warte f observatory
stet [tet], stetig [ʹtetɪç] adj steady
stets [tets] adv constantly, always
Steuer [ʹtɔɪ·ər] f (–;–n) tax; duty ‖ n (–s;–) rudder, helm; (aer) controls; (aut) steering wheel; am S. at the helm; (aut) behind the wheel
Steu′eramt n tax office
Steu′erbord n (naut) starboard
Steu′ererhebung f levy of taxes
Steu′ererklärung f tax return
Steu′erflosse f vertical stabilizer
Steu′erhinterziehung f tax evasion
Steu′erjahr n fiscal year
Steu′erknüppel m control stick
Steu′er·mann m (–[e]s;–er & –leute) helmsman
steuern [ʹtɔɪ·ərn] tr steer; control; regulate; (aer, naut) pilot; (aut) drive ‖ intr (dat) curb, check
steu′erpflichtig adj taxable; dutiable
Steu′errad n steering wheel
Steu′erruder n rudder, helm
Steu′ersatz m tax rate
Steu′ersäule f (aer) control column; (aut) steering column
Steu′erstufe f tax bracket
Steu′erung f (–;–en) steering; (Bekämpfung) control; (Verhinderung) prevention; (aer) piloting; (aut) steering mechanism
Steu′erveranlagung f tax assessment
Steu′erwerk n (aer) controls
Steu′erzahler –in §6 mf tax payer
Steu′erzuschlag m surtax
Steven [ʹteven] m (–s;–) (naut) stem
Stewar·deß [ˈstjuˑərdɛs] f (–;–dessen [desən]) (aer) stewardess
stibitzen [tɪˈbrtsən] tr snitch
Stich [tɪç] m (–[e]s;–e) prick; (Messer–) stab; (Insekten–) sting, bite; (Stoß) thrust; (Seitenstechen) sharp pain; (Kupfer–) engraving; (cards) trick; (naut) knot; (sew) stitch; im S. lassen abandon
Stichelei [ʃtɪçəˈlaɪ] f (–;–en) taunt
sticheln [ʹtɪçəln] intr—gegen j–n s. (fig) needle s.o.
Stich′flamme f flash
stich′haltig adj valid, sound
Stich′probe f spot check
Stich′tag m effective date; due date
Stich′wahl f run-off election
Stich′wort n (–[e]s;–er) key word; dictionary entry ‖ n (–[e]s;–e) (theat) cue
Stich′wunde f stab wound
sticken [ʹtɪkən] tr embroider ‖ intr embroider

Stickerei [ʃtɪkə'raɪ] ƒ (-;-en) embroidery
Stick'husten m whooping cough
stickig ['ʃtɪkɪç] adj stuffy, close
Stick'stoff m nitrogen
stieben ['ʃtibən] §130 intr (HABEN & SEIN) fly; (Menge) disperse
Stief [ʃtif] comb.fm. step-
Stief'bruder m stepbrother
Stiefel ['ʃtifəl] m (-s;-) boot
Stie'felknecht m bootjack
Stief'mutter ƒ stepmother
Stief'mütterchen n (bot) pansy
Stief'vater m stepfather
stieg [ʃtik] pret of steigen
Stiege ['ʃtigə] ƒ (-;-n) staircase
Stiel [ʃtil] m (-[e]s;-e) handle; (bot) stalk
stier [ʃtir] adj staring, glassy || **Stier** m (-[e]s;-e) bull; (astr) Taurus
stieren ['ʃtirən] intr (auf acc) stare (at)
Stier'kampf m bullfight
stieß [ʃtis] pret of stoßen
Stift [ʃtɪft] m (-[e]s;-e) pin; peg; pencil; crayon; (Zwecke) tack; (coll) apprentice || n (-[e]s;-e & -er) charitable foundation or institution
stiften ['ʃtɪftən] tr (gründen) found; (spenden) donate; (verursachen) cause; (Unruhe) stir up; (Frieden) make; (Brand) start; (e-e Runde Bier) set up
Stif'ter –in §6 mf founder; donor; (fig) author, cause
Stif'tung ƒ (-;-en) foundation; donation; grant; **fromme S.** religious establishment; **milde S.** charitable institution
Stif'tungsfest n founder's day
Stil [ʃtil] m (-[e]s;-e) style
stil'gerecht adj in good taste
stilisieren [ʃtili'zirən] tr word
stilistisch [ʃtɪ'lɪstɪʃ] adj stylistic
still [ʃtɪl] adj still; calm; silent; (com) slack; **im stillen** in secret; **Stiller Ozean** Pacific Ocean || **Stille** ƒ (-;) stillness; silence
still'bleiben §62 intr (SEIN) keep still
Stilleben (Still'leben) n still life
stillegen (still'legen) tr (Betrieb) shut down; (Verkehr) stop; (Schiff) put into mothballs
stillen ['ʃtɪlən] tr still; (Hunger) appease; (Durst) quench; (Blut) stanch; (Begierde) gratify
stilliegen (still'liegen) §108 intr lie still; (Betrieb) lie idle; (Verkehr) be at a standstill
still'schweigen §148 intr be silent; **s. zu** acquiesce in || **Stillschweigen** n (-s;) silence; secrecy
still'schweigend adj silent; (fig) tacit
Still'stand m standstill; (Sackgasse) stalemate, deadlock
still'stehen §146 intr stand still; (Betrieb) be idle; (mil) stand at attention; **stillgestanden!** (mil) attention!
Stil'möbel pl period furniture
stil'voll adj stylish
Stimm- [ʃtɪm] comb.fm. vocal; voting
Stimm'abgabe ƒ vote, voting
Stimm'band n (-[e]s;⸚er) vocal cord

Stimm'block m (parl) bloc
Stimm'bruch m change of voice
Stimme ['ʃtɪmə] ƒ (-;-n) voice; vote
stimmen ['ʃtɪmən] tr make feel (happy, etc.); (mus) tune || intr be right; vote; (mus) be in tune
Stim'menrutsch m (pol) landslide
Stimm'enthaltung ƒ abstention
Stimm'gabel ƒ tuning fork
Stimm'recht n right to vote, suffrage
Stim'mung ƒ (-;-en) tone; (Laune) mood; (mil) morale; (mus) tuning; (st.exch.) trend
stim'mungsvoll adj cheerful
Stimm'zettel m ballot
stinken ['ʃtɪnkən] §143 intr stink
Stink'tier n skunk
Stipen·dium [ʃtɪ'pɛndjum] n (-s;-dien [djən]) scholarship, grant
stippen ['ʃtɪpən] tr (coll) dunk
Stippvisite ['ʃtɪpvɪzitə] ƒ (-;-n) short visit
Stirn [ʃtɪrn] ƒ (-;-en), **Stirne** ['ʃtɪrnə] ƒ (-;-n) forehead, brow; (fig) insolence, gall; **die S. runzeln** frown
Stirn'runzeln n (-s;) frown(ing)
stob [ʃtop] pret of stieben
stöbern ['ʃtøbərn] tr (Wild) flush; (aus dem Bett) yank || intr poke around; browse; (Schnee) drift
stochern ['ʃtɔxərn] intr poke around; **im Essen s.** pick at one's food; **im Feuer s.** stoke the fire; **in den Zähnen s.** pick one's teeth
Stock [ʃtɔk] m (-[e]s;⸚e) stick; cane; wand; baton; stem; vine; tree stump; cleaning rod; beehive; massif; story, floor; **im ersten S.** on the second floor
Stock-, stock- comb.fm. thoroughly
stock'blind' adj stone-blind
stock'dun'kel adj pitch-dark
Stöckel ['ʃtœkal] m (-s;-) high heel
stocken ['ʃtɔkən] intr stop; (Geschäft) slack off; (Blut) coagulate; (in der Rede) get stuck; (Milch) curdle; (Stimme) falter; (schimmeln) get moldy; (Unterhandlungen) become deadlocked; (Verkehr) get tied up; (zögern) hesitate || **Stocken** n (-s;) stopping; hesitation; **ins S. bringen** tie up
stock'fin'ster adj pitch-black
Stock'fleck m mildew
stock'fleckig adj mildewy
stockig ['ʃtɔkɪç] adj moldy
-stöckig [ʃtœkɪç] comb.fm. -story
stock'nüch'tern adj dead-sober
stock'steif' adj stiff as a board
stock'taub' adj stone-deaf
Stockung (Stok'kung) ƒ (-;-en) stoppage; (des Verkehrs) tie-up; (des Blutes) congestion; (Unterbrechung) interruption; (Verlangsamung) slowdown; (Zeitverlust) delay; (Pause) pause; (Zögern) hesitation; (der Unterhandlungen) deadlock
Stock'werk n story, floor
Stoff [ʃtɔf] m (-[e]s;-e) stuff, matter; fabric, material; cloth; subject, topic; (chem) substance
stoff'lich adj material
Stoff'rest m (tex) remnant

Stoff'wechsel m metabolism
stöhnen ['ʃtøːnən] intr groan, moan
Stolle ['ʃtɔlə] f (-;-n) fruit cake
Stollen ['ʃtɔlən] m (-s;-) fruit cake; tunnel; (Pfosten) post; (Stütze) prop
stolpern ['ʃtɔlpərn] intr (SEIN) stumble, trip
stolz [ʃtɔlts] adj (auf acc) proud (of) || **Stolz** m (-es;) pride
stolzieren [ʃtɔl'tsiːrən] intr (SEIN) strut; (Pferd) prance
stopfen ['ʃtɔpfən] tr stuff, cram; (Pfeife) fill; (Strumpf) darn; (mus) mute; j-m den Mund s. shut s.o. up || intr be filling; cause constipation
Stopf'garn n darning yarn
Stoppel ['ʃtɔpəl] f (-;-n) stubble
stoppelig ['ʃtɔpəlɪç] adj stubbly
stoppeln ['ʃtɔpəln] tr glean; (fig) patch
stoppen ['ʃtɔpən] tr stop; clock, time || intr stop
Stopp'licht n tail light; stoplight
Stopp'uhr f stopwatch
Stöpsel ['ʃtœsəl] m (-s;-) stopper, cork; (coll) squirt; (elec) plug
stöpseln ['ʃtœpsəln] tr plug; cork
Storch [ʃtɔrç] m (-[e]s;̈e) stork
stören ['ʃtøːrən] tr disturb, bother; (Pläne) cross; (Vergnügen) spoil; (mil) harass; (rad) jam
Störenfried ['ʃtøːrənfriːt] m (-[e]s;-e) pain in the neck
störrig ['ʃtœrɪç], **störrisch** ['ʃtœrɪʃ] adj stubborn
Stö'rung f (-;-en) disturbance, trouble; breakdown; interruption; annoyance; intrusion; (rad) static; (rad) jamming
Stoß [ʃtoːs] m (-es;̈e) push, shove; hit, blow; nudge, poke; (Einschlag) impact; (Erschütterung) shock; (Fecht-) pass; (Feuer-) burst (of fire); (Fuß-) kick; (Haufen) pile, bundle; (Rück-) recoil; (Saum) seam, hem; (Schwimm-) stroke; (Trompeten-) blast; (Wind-) gust; (mil) thrust; (orn) tail
Stoß'dämpfer m shock absorber
Stößel ['ʃtøːsəl] m (-s;-) pestle
stoßen ['ʃtoːsən] §150 tr push, shove; hit, knock; kick; punch; jab, nudge, poke; ram; pound; pulverize; oust || ref bump oneself; sich s. an (dat) take offense at; take exception to || intr kick; (mit den Hörnen) butt; (Gewehr) recoil, kick; (Wagen) jolt (Schiff) toss; in die Trompete s. blow the trumpet; s. auf (acc) swoop down on || intr (SEIN)—s. an (acc) bump against; adjoin; be next-door to; s. auf (acc) run into; come across; (naut) dash against; s. durch (mil) smash through; vom Lande s. shove off; zu j-m s. side with s.o.
Stoß'stange f (aut) bumper
Stoß'trupp m assault party; **Stoßtruppen** shock troops; commandos, rangers
Stoß'zahn m tusk
stottern ['ʃtɔtərn] tr stutter, stammer || intr stutter, stammer; (aut) sputter
stracks [ʃtraks] adv immediately; (geradeaus) straight ahead
Straf- [ʃtraːf] comb.fm. penal; criminal

Straf'anstalt f penal institution
Straf'arbeit f (educ) extra work
Straf'aufschub m reprieve
strafbar ['ʃtraːfbaːr] adj punishable
Strafe ['ʃtraːfə] f (-;-n) punishment; penalty; (Geld-) fine; bei S. von under pain of; zur S. as punishment
strafen ['ʃtraːfən] tr punish
straff [ʃtraf] adj tight; (Seil) taut; (gespannt) tense; (aufrecht) erect; (fig) strict; s. spannen tighten
straf'fällig adj punishable; culpable
Straf'geld n fine
Straf'gesetzbuch n penal code
sträflich ['ʃtrɛːflɪç] adj culpable
Sträfling ['ʃtrɛːflɪŋ] m (-s;-e) convict
straf'los adj unpunished
Straf'porto n postage due
Straf'predigt f talking-to, lecture
Straf'raum m (sport) penalty box
Straf'recht n criminal law
Straf'stoß m (sport) penalty kick
Straf'umwandlung f (jur) commutation
Straf'verfahren n criminal proceedings
Strahl [ʃtraːl] m (-[e]s;-en) ray; beam; flash; jet; (geom) radius
Strahl'antrieb m jet propulsion
strahlen ['ʃtraːlən] intr beam, shine
Strahl'motor m, **Strahl'triebwerk** n jet engine
Strah'lung f (-;-en) radiation
Strähne ['ʃtrɛːnə] f (-;-n) strand; lock; hank, skein
strähnig ['ʃtrɛːnɪç] adj wispy
stramm [ʃtram] adj tight; (kräftig) strapping; (Zucht) strict; (Arbeit) hard; (Soldat) smart; (Mädel) buxom || adv—s. stehen stand at attention
stramm'ziehen §163 tr draw tight
strampeln ['ʃtrampəln] intr kick
Strand [ʃtrant] m (-[e]s;̈e) beach, seashore, shore
stranden ['ʃtrandən] intr (SEIN) be beached, run aground, be stranded
Strand'gut n flotsam, jetsam
Strand'gutjäger -in §6 mf beachcomber
Strand'korb m hooded beach chair
Strand'schirm m beach umbrella
Strang [ʃtraŋ] m (-[e]s;̈e) rope; (Strähne) hank; (Zugseil) trace; (rr) track; wenn alle Stränge reißen (fig) if worse comes to worst
Strapaze [ʃtra'paːtsə] f (-;-n) fatigue; exertion, strain
strapazieren [ʃtrapa'tsiːrən] tr tire out; (Kleider) wear hard
strapazier'fähig adj heavy-duty
strapaziös [ʃtrapa'tsjøːs] adj tiring
Straße ['ʃtraːsə] f (-;-n) street; road, highway; (Meerenge) strait
Stra'ßenanzug m business suit
Stra'ßenbahn f streetcar, trolley, trolley line
Stra'ßenbahnwagen m streetcar
Stra'ßendirne f streetwalker
Stra'ßengraben m ditch, gutter
Stra'ßenhändler -in §6 mf street vendor
Stra'ßenjunge m urchin
Stra'ßenkarte f street map
Stra'ßenkreuzung f intersection
Stra'ßenlage f (aut) roadability
Stra'ßenrennen n drag race

Stra′ßenrinne f gutter
Stra′ßenschild n street sign
Stra′ßensperrung f (public sign) road closed
Stra′ßenstreife f highway patrol
strategisch [ʃtra′tegɪʃ] adj strategic
sträuben [′ʃtrɔɪbən] tr ruffle ‖ ref bristle, stand on end; **sich s. gegen** resist, struggle against
Strauch [ʃtraux] m (-[e]s;⸗er) shrub
straucheln [′ʃtrauxəln] intr (SEIN) stumble, trip; (fig) go wrong
Strauß [ʃtraus] m (-[e]s;⸗e) bouquet ‖ m (-[e]s;-e) ostrich
Strebe [′ʃtrebə] f (-;-n) prop, strut
Stre′bebogen m flying buttress
streben [′ʃtrebən] intr (nach) strive (after); (nach) tend (toward) ‖ **Streben** n (-s;-) striving; pursuit; (Hang) tendency; (Anstrengung) endeavor
Stre′ber m (-s;-) go-getter, eager beaver; social climber; (in der Schule) grind
strebsam [′ʃtrepzam] adj zealous
Streb′samkeit f (-;) zeal; industry
Strecke [′ʃtrɛkə] f (-;-n) stretch; extent; distance; stage, leg; (geom) straight line; (hunt) bag; (rr) section; **zur S. bringen** catch up with; (box) defeat; (hunt) bag
strecken [′ʃtrɛkən] tr stretch; (Metalle) laminate; (Wein) dilute; (fig) make last; **die Waffen s.** lay down one's arms ‖ ref stretch (oneself)
Streich [ʃtraɪç] m (-[e]s;-e) blow; (fig) trick, prank
streicheln [′ʃtraɪçəln] tr stroke; pat
streichen [′ʃtraɪçən] §85 tr stroke; (Butter, usw.) spread; (an-) paint; (Geige) play; (Messer) whet; (Rasiermesser) strop; (Streichholz) strike; (Flagge, Segel) lower; (Armel) roll down; (Ziegel) make; (mit Ruten) flog; delete; (sport) scratch ‖ intr—**mit der Hand s. über** (acc) pass one's hand over ‖ intr (SEIN) stretch, extend; wander; pass, move; rush
Streich′holz n match
Streich′holzbrief m matchbook
Streich′instrument n stringed instrument
Streich′orchester n string band
Streich′riemen m razor strop
Streif [ʃtraɪf] m (-[e]s;-e) streak, stripe; strip
Streif′band n (-[e]s;⸗er) wrapper
Streife [′ʃtraɪfə] f (-;-n) raid; (Runde) beat; (mil) patrol
streifen [′ʃtraɪfən] tr stripe; streak; graze; skim over; (abziehen) strip; (grenzen an) verge on; (Thema) touch on ‖ intr (SEIN) roam; (mil) patrol; **s. an** (acc) brush against; (fig) verge on; **s. über** (acc) scan ‖ **Streifen** m (-s;-) stripe; streak; strip; slip; (cin) movie
Strei′fendienst m patrol duty
Strei′fenwagen m patrol car, squad car
streifig [′ʃtraɪfɪç] adj striped
Streif′licht n flash, streak of light; **S. werfen auf** (acc) shed light on
Streif′wunde f scratch

Streif′zug m exploratory trip, looksee
Streik [ʃtraɪk] m (-[e]s;-s) strike, walkout; **wilder S.** wildcat strike
streiken [′ʃtraɪkən] intr go on strike
Strei′kende §5 mf striker
Streik′posten m picket; **S. stehen** picket
Streit [ʃtraɪt] m (-[e]s;-e) fight; argument, quarrel; (jur) litigation
Streit′axt f battle-ax; **die S. begraben** (fig) bury the hatchet
streitbar [′ʃtraɪtbar] adj belligerent
streiten [′ʃtraɪtən] §86 recip & intr quarrel
Streit′frage f point at issue
streitig [′ʃtraɪtɪç] adj controversial; at issue
Streit′kräfte pl (mil) forces, troops
Streit′lustig adj belligerent, scrappy
Streit′objekt n bone of contention
Streit′punkt m issue, point at issue
streit′süchtig adj quarrelsome
streng [ʃtrɛŋ] adj severe, stern; austere; strict; (Geschmack) sharp ‖ **Strenge** f (-;) severity, sternness; austerity; strictness; sharpness
streng′genommen adv strictly speaking
streng′gläubig adj orthodox
Streu [ʃtrɔɪ] f (-;-en) straw bed
Streu′büchse f shaker
streuen [′ʃtrɔɪ-ən] tr strew, sprinkle; (ausbreiten) spread; (verbreiten) scatter ‖ intr spread, scatter
strich [ʃtrɪç] pret of streichen ‖ **Strich** m (-[e]s;-e) stroke; line; (Streif) stripe; (Landstrich) tract; (carp) grain; (tex) nap; (typ) dash; **auf den S. gehen** walk the streets (as prostitute); **gegen den S. gehen** go against the grain; (fig) rub the wrong way
Strich′mädchen n streetwalker
Strich′punkt m semicolon
Strich′regen m local shower
strich′weise adv here and there
Strick [ʃtrɪk] m (-[e]s;-e) rope, cord; (fig) rogue, good-for-nothing
stricken [′ʃtrɪkən] tr & intr knit
Strick′garn n knitting yarn
Strick′jacke f cardigan
Strick′kleid n knitted dress
Strick′leiter f rope ladder
Strick′waren pl knitwear
Strick′zeug n knitting things
Striemen [′ʃtrimən] m (-s;-) stripe, streak; (in der Haut) weal
Strippe [′ʃtrɪpə] f (-;-n) string; strap; shoestring; (telp) line
stritt [ʃtrɪt] pret of streiten
strittig [′ʃtrɪtɪç] adj controversial
Stroh [ʃtro] n (-[e]s) straw
Stroh′dach n thatched roof
Stroh′halm m straw; drinking straw
Stroh′mann m (-[e]s;⸗er) scarecrow; (cards) dummy
Stroh′puppe f scarecrow
Stroh′sack m straw mattress; **heiliger S.!** holy smokes!
Strolch [ʃtrɔlç] m (-[e]s;-e) bum
strolchen [′ʃtrɔlçən] intr bum around
Strom [ʃtrom] m (-[e]s;⸗e) river; stream; (von Worten) torrent; (& elec) current

strom·ab'wärts adv downstream
strom·auf'wärts adv upstream
Strom'ausfall m (elec) power failure
strömen ['ʃtrømən] intr (HABEN & SEIN) stream; (Regen) pour (down)
Stro'mer m (-s;-) (coll) tramp
Strom'kreis m (elec) circuit
strom'linienförmig adj streamlined
Strom'richter m (elec) converter
Strom'schnelle f rapids
Strom'spannung f voltage
Strom'stärke f (elec) amperage
Strö'mung f (-;-en) current; trend
Strom'unterbrecher m circuit breaker
Strom'wandler m (elec) transformer
Strom'zähler m electric meter
Strophe ['ʃtrofə] f (-;-n) stanza
strotzen ['ʃtrotsən] intr—s. von or vor (dat) abound in, teem with
Strudel ['ʃtrudəl] m (-s;-) eddy, whirlpool; (fig) maelstrom; (culin) strudel
strudeln ['ʃtrudəln] intr eddy, whirl
Struktur [ʃtruk'tur] f (-;-en) structure; (tex) texture
Strumpf [ʃtrumpf] m (-[e]s;ᵁe) stocking
Strumpf'band n (-[e]s;ᵁer), Strumpf'halter m garter
Strumpf'waren pl hosiery
struppig ['ʃtrupɪç] adj shaggy, unkempt
Stube ['ʃtubə] f (-;-n) room
Stu'benmädchen n chambermaid
stu'benrein adj housebroken
Stubsnase ['ʃtupsnazə] f snub nose
Stuck [ʃtuk] m (-[e]s;) stucco
Stück [ʃtyk] n (-[e]s;-e) piece; lot; plot; stretch distance; (Butter) pat; (Zucker) lump; (Seife) cake; (Vieh) head; (mus) piece, number; (theat) play, show; pro S. apiece
stückeln ['ʃtykəln] tr cut or break into small pieces; piece together
stück'weise adv piecemeal
Stück'werk n patchwork
Student [ʃtu'dent] m (-en;-en) college student
Studen'tenheim n dormitory
Studen'tenverbindung f fraternity
Studentin [ʃtu'dentɪn] f (-;-nen) college student, coed
Studie ['ʃtudjə] f (-;-n) (Lit) essay; (paint) study, sketch
Stu'diengang m (educ) course
Stu'dienplan m curriculum
Stu'dienrat m (-[e]s;ᵁe) high school teacher
Stu'dienreferendar –in §8 mf practice teacher
Stu'dienreise f (educ) field trip
studieren [ʃtu'dirən] tr & intr study (at college); examine
studiert [ʃtu'dirt] adj college-educated; (gekünstelt) affected
Studier'zimmer n study
Stu·dium ['ʃtudjʊm] n (-s;-dien [djən]) study (at college); studies
Stufe ['ʃtufə] f (-;-n) step, stair; (e–r Leiter) rung; (Grad) degree; (Niveau) level; stage; (mus) interval
Stu'fenfolge f graduation; succession
Stu'fenleiter f stepladder; (fig) gamut
stu'fenweise adv by degrees

Stuhl [ʃtul] m (-[e]s;ᵁe) chair; (Stuhlgang) stool, feces; der Heilige S. the Holy See
Stuhl'bein n leg of a chair
Stuhl'drang m urgent call of nature
Stuhl'gang m stool, feces; S. haben have a bowel movement
Stuhl'lehne f back of a chair
Stulpe ['ʃtulpə] f (-;-n) cuff
Stülpnase ['ʃtylpnazə] f snub nose
stumm [ʃtum] adj dumb, mute; (schweigend) silent; (gram) mute
Stummel ['ʃtuməl] m (-s;-) (e–s Armes, Baumes, e–r Zigarette) stump
Stümper ['ʃtympər] m (-s;-) bungler
Stümperei [ʃtympə'raɪ] f (-;-en) bungling
stüm'perhaft adj bungling
stümpern ['ʃtympərn] tr & intr bungle
stumpf [ʃtumpf] adj blunt; (& fig) obtuse || Stumpf m (-[e]s;ᵁe) stump
Stumpf'sinn m apathy, dullness
stumpf'sinnig adj dull, stupid
Stunde ['ʃtundə] f (-;-n) hour; (educ) class, lesson, period
stunden ['ʃtundən] tr grant postponement of
Stun'dengeld n tutoring fee
Stun'dengeschwindigkeit f miles per hour
Stun'denkilometer pl kilometers per hour
stun'denlang adv for hours
Stun'denlohn m hourly wage(s)
Stun'denplan m roster, schedule
stun'denweise adv by the hour
Stun'denzeiger m hour hand
–stündig [ʃtyndɪç] comb.fm. –hour
stündlich ['ʃtyntlɪç] adj hourly
Stun'dung f (-;-en) period of grace
Stunk [ʃtuŋk] m (-[e]s; (sl)) stink; S. machen (sl) raise a stink
Stups [ʃtups] m (-es;-e) nudge
stupsen ['ʃtupsən] tr nudge
Stups'nase f snub nose
stur [ʃtur] adj stubborn; (Blick) fixed
Sturm [ʃturm] m (-[e]s;ᵁe) storm; gale
Sturm'abteilung f storm troopers
stürmen ['ʃtyrmən] tr storm || intr rage, roar || intr (SEIN) rush || impers —es stürmt it is stormy
Stürmer ['ʃtyrmər] m (-s;-) (fb) forward
stürmisch ['ʃtyrmɪʃ] adj stormy; impetuous || adv—nicht so s.! not so fast!
Sturm'schritt m (mil) double time
Sturm'trupp m assault party
Sturm'welle f (mil) assault wave
Sturm'wind m gale, hurricane
Sturz [ʃturts] m (-es;-e) fall, sudden drop; overthrow; collapse; (archit) lintel; (aut) camber; (com) slump
Sturz'bach m torrent
Sturz'bomber m dive bomber
Stürze ['ʃtyrtsə] f (-;-n) lid
stürzen ['ʃtyrtsən] tr throw down; upset, overturn; overthrow; (stürzen) plunge; nicht s.! this side up! || ref rush; plunge || intr (SEIN) fall, tumble; rush; (Tränen) pour; (aer) dive
Sturz'flug m (aer) dive
Sturz'helm m crash helmet

Sturz′regen *m* downpour
Sturz′see *f* heavy seas
Stute [′∫tutə] *f* (–;–n) mare
Stütze [′∫tʏtsə] *f* (–;–n) support, prop; (fig) help, support
stutzen [′∫tutsən] *tr* cut short; (*Flügel*) clip; (*Bäume*) prune; (*Ohren*) crop; (*Bart*) trim ‖ *intr* stop short; be startled; (*Pferd*) shy
stützen [′∫tʏtsən] *tr* support; prop; shore up; (fig) support ‖ *ref*—**sich s. auf** (*acc*) lean on; (fig) depend on
Stutzer [′∫tutsər] *m* (–s;–) car coat; (coll) snazzy dresser
Stutz′flügel *m* baby grand piano
stutzig [′∫tutsɪç] *adj* suspicious
Stütz′pfeiler *m* abutment
Stütz′punkt *m* footing; (mil) base; (phys) fulcrum
Subjekt [zup′jekt] *n* (–[e]s;–e) (coll) guy, character; (gram) subject
subjektiv [zupjek′tif] *adj* subjective
Substantiv [′zupstan′tif] *n* (–[e]s;–e) (gram) substantive, noun
Substanz [zup′stants] *f* (–;–en) substance
subtil [zup′til] *adj* subtle
subtrahieren [zuptra′hirən] *tr* subtract
Subtraktion [zuptrak′tsjon] *f* (–;–en) subtraction
Subvention [zupvɛn′tsjon] *f* (–;–en) subsidy
Such– [zux] *comb.fm.* search
Such′anzeige *f* want ad
Such′büro *n*, **Such′dienst** *m* missing-persons bureau
Suche [′zuxə] *f* (–;–en) search; **auf der S. nach** in search of, in quest of
suchen [′zuxən] *tr* search for, look for; (*erstreben*) seek; want, desire; (in *der Zeitung*) advertise for; (*Gefahr*) court; **das Weite s.** run away ‖ *intr* search; **nach etw s.** look for s.th.
Sucht [zuxt] *f* (–;⸚e) passion, mania; (*nach*) addition (to)
süchtig [′zʏçtɪç] *adj* addicted ‖ **Süchtige** §5 *mf* addict
Sud [zut] *m* (–[e]s;–e) brewing; brew
Süd [zyt] *m* (–[e]s;s) south
sudelhaft [′zudəlhaft], **sudelig** [′zudəlɪç] *adj* slovenly, sloppy
sudeln [′zudəln] *tr & intr* mess up
Süden [′zydən] *m* (–s;) south
Sudeten [zu′detən] *pl* Sudeten mountains (*along northern border of Czechoslovakia*)
Süd′früchte *pl* (*tropical and subtropical*) fruit (*e.g., bananas, oranges*)
süd′lich *adj* south, southern, southerly; **s. von** south of ‖ *adv* south
Südost′ *m*, **Südo′sten** *m* southeast
südöst′lich *adj* southeast(ern)
Süd′pol *m* (–s;) South Pole
südwärts [′zytverts] *adv* southward
Südwest′ *m*, **Südwe′sten** *m* southwest
süffig [′zʏfɪç] *adj* tasty
suggerieren [zuge′rirən] *tr* suggest
suggestiv [zuges′tif] *adj* suggestive
Suggestiv′frage *f* leading question
suhlen [′zulən] *ref* wallow
Sühne [′zynə] *f* (–;) atonement
sühnen [′zynən] *tr* atone for, expiate
Sülze [′zʏltsə] *f* (–;–n) jellied meat

summarisch [zu′marɪ∫] *adj* summary
Summe [′zumə] *f* (–;–n) sum, total
summen [′zumən] *tr* hum ‖ *intr* hum; buzz
Sum′mer *m* (–s;–) buzzer
summieren [zu′mirən] *tr* sum up, total ‖ *ref* run up, pile up
Summton [′zumton] *m* (telp) dial tone
Sumpf [zumpf] *m* (–[e]s;⸚e) swamp
sumpfig [′zumpfɪç] *adj* swampy, marshy
Sünde [′zʏndə] *f* (–;–n) sin
Sün′denbock *m* scapegoat
Sün′denerlaß *m* absolution
Sün′denfall *m* original sin
Sün′der *m* (–s;–) sinner
Sünd′flut [′zʏntflut] *f* Deluge
sünd′haft, sündig [′zʏndɪç] *adj* sinful
sündigen [′zʏndɪgən] *intr* sin
Superlativ [′zuperlatif] *m* (–s;–e) (gram) superlative
Su′permarkt *m* supermarket
Suppe [′zupə] *f* (–;–n) soup
Sup′penschüssel *f* tureen
surren [′zurən] *intr* buzz
Surrogat [zurɔ′gat] *n* (–[e]s;–e) substitute
suspendieren [zuspen′dirən] *tr* suspend
süß [zys] *adj* sweet ‖ **Süße** *f* (–;) sweetness
süßen [′zysən] *tr* sweeten
Sü′ßigkeit *f* (–;–en) sweetness; **Süßigkeiten** sweets, candy
Süß′kartoffel *f* sweet potato
süß′lich *adj* sweetish; (fig) mawkish
Süß′stoff *m* artificial sweetener
Süß′waren *pl* sweets, candy
Süß′wasser *n* fresh water
Symbol [zym′bol] *n* (–s;–e) symbol
Symbolik [zym′bolik] *f* (–;) symbolism
symbolisch [zym′boli∫] *adj* symbolic(al)
Symme·trie [zymɛ′tri] *f* (–;–trien) [′tri·ən]) symmetry
symmetrisch [zy′metri∫] *adj* symmetrical
Sympa·thie [zympa′ti] *f* (–;–thien [′ti·ən]) liking
sympathisch [zym′pati∫] *adj* likeable; **er ist mir s.** I like him
sympathisieren [zympati′zirən] *intr*—**s. mit** sympathize with; like
Sympho·nie [zymfo′ni] *f* (–;–nien [′ni·ən]) symphony
Symptom [zymp′tom] *n* (–s;–e) symptom
symptomatisch [zymptɔ′mati∫] *adj* (**für**) symptomatic (of)
Synagoge [zyna′gogə] *f* (–;–n) synagogue
synchronisieren [zynkrɔni′zirən] *tr* synchronize
Syndikat [zyndi′kat] *n* (–[e]s;–e) syndicate
Syndi·kus [′zyndikus] *m* (–;–kusse & -ki [ki]) corporation lawyer
synonym [zyno′nym] *adj* synonymous ‖ **Synonym** *n* (–s;–e) synonym
Syntax [′zyntaks] *f* (–;) syntax
synthetisch [zyn′teti∫] *adj* synthetic
Syrien [′zyrjən] *n* (–s;) Syria

System [zɪs'tem] *n* (-s;-e) system
systematisch [zɪste'matɪ∫] *adj* systematic
Szene ['stsenə] *f* (-;-n) scene; **in S.**

setzen stage; **sich in S. setzen** put on an act
Sze'nenaufnahme *f* (cin) take
Szenerie [stenə'ri] *f* (-;) scenery

T

T, t [te] *invar n* T, t
Tabak [ta'bak], ['tabak] *m* (-[e]s;-e) tobacco
Tabaks'beutel *m* tobacco pouch
Tabak'trafik *f* (Aust) cigar store
Tabak'waren *pl* tobacco products
tabellarisch [tabe'larɪ∫] *adj* tabular
tabellarisieren [tabelarɪ'zirən] *tr* tabulate
Tabelle [ta'belə] *f* (-;-n) table, chart; graph
Tabernakel [taber'nakəl] *m & n* (-s;-) tabernacle
Tablett [ta'blet] *n* (-[e]s;-e) tray
Tablette [ta'bletə] *f* (-;-n) tablet, pill
tabu [ta'bu] *adj* taboo || **Tabu** *n* (-s; -s) taboo
Tachometer [taxo'metər] *n* speedometer
Tadel ['tadəl] *m* (-s;-) scolding; (Schuld) blame; (educ) demerit
ta'dellos *adj* blameless; flawless
tadeln ['tadəln] *tr* scold, reprimand; blame, find fault with
Tafel ['tafəl] *f* (-;-n) (Tisch, Diagramm) table; (Anschlag-) billboard; (Glas-, Platte) pane; (Holz-, Schalt-) panel; (Mahlzeit) meal, dinner; (Metall-) sheet, plate; (Platte) slab; (Schiefer-) slate; (Schreib-) tablet; (Schokolade) bar; (Wand-) blackboard; **bei T.** at dinner; **die T. decken** set the table; **offene T. halten** have open house
Ta'felaufsatz *m* centerpiece
Ta'felbesteck *n* knife, fork, and spoon
ta'felförmig *adj* tabular
Ta'felgeschirr *n* table service
Ta'felland *n* tableland, plateau
Ta'felmusik *f* dinner music
tafeln ['tafəln] *intr* dine, feast
täfeln ['tefəln] *tr* (Wand) wainscot, panel; (Fußboden) parquet
Ta'felöl *n* salad oil
Ta'felservice *n* tableware
Tä'felung *f* (-;-en) inlay; paneling
Taft [taft] *m* (-[e]s;-e) taffeta
Tag [tak] *m* (-[e]s;-e) day; daylight; **am Tage** by day; **am Tage nach** the day after; **an den Tag bringen** bring to light; **bei Tage** by day, in the daytime; **den ganzen Tag** all day long; **e-n Tag um den andern** every other day; **e-s Tages** someday; **es wird Tag** day is breaking; **guten Tag!** hello!; how do you do?; (bei Verabschiedung) good day!; goodby!; **Tag der offenen Tür** open house; **unter Tage** (min) underground, below the surface
tagaus', tagein' *adv* day in and day out
Tage- [tagə] *comb.fm.* day-, daily

Ta'geblatt *n* daily, daily paper
Ta'gebuch *n* diary, journal
Ta'gegeld *n* per diem allowance
ta'gelang *adv* for days
Ta'gelohn *m* daily wage
Tagelöhner –in ['tagəlønər(ɪn)] §6 *mf* day laborer
tagen ['tagən] *intr* dawn; (beraten) meet; (jur) be in session
Ta'gesanbruch *m* daybreak
Ta'gesangriff *m* (aer) daylight raid
Ta'gesbefehl *m* (mil) order of the day
Ta'gesbericht *m* daily report
Ta'geseinnahme *f* daily receipts
Ta'gesgespräch *n* topic of the day
ta'geshell *adj* as light as day
Ta'geskasse *f* (theat) box office
Ta'gesleistung *f* daily output
Ta'geslicht *n* daylight
Ta'geslichtaufnahme *f* (phot) daylight shot
Ta'gesordnung *f* agenda; (coll) order of the day
Ta'gespreis *m* market price
Ta'gespresse *f* daily press
Ta'gesschau *f* (telv) news
Ta'geszeit *f* time of day; daytime; **zu jeder T.** at any hour
Ta'geszeitung *f* daily paper
ta'geweise *adv* by the day
Ta'gewerk *n* day's work
–tägig [tegɪç] *comb.fm.* –day
täglich ['teklɪç] *adj* daily
tags [taks] *adv* –t. **darauf** the following day; **t. zuvor** the day before
Ta'gschicht *f* day shift
tags'über *adv* during the day, in the daytime
Tagung ['tagʊŋ] *f* (-;-en) convention, conference, meeting
Ta'gungsort *m* meeting place
Taifun [taɪ'fun] *m* (-s;-e) typhoon
Taille ['taljə] *f* (-;-n) waist; (Mieder) bodice
Takel ['takəl] *n* (-s;-) tackle
Takelage [takə'laʒə] *f* (-;-n) rigging
takeln ['takəln] *tr* rig
Ta'kelwerk *n* var of **Takelage**
Takt [takt] *m* (-[e]s;-e) tact; (mach) stroke; (mus) time, beat; (mus) bar; **den T. schlagen** mark time; **im T.** in time; in step; **T. halten** mark time
takt'fest *adj* keeping good time; (fig) reliable
Taktik ['taktɪk] *f* (-;-en) (& fig) tactics
Tak'tiker *m* (-s;-) tactician
taktisch ['taktɪ∫] *adj* tactical
takt'los *adj* tactless
Takt'messer *m* metronome
Takt'stock *m* baton

Takt'strich m (mus) bar
takt'voll adj tactful
Tal [tɑl] n (-[e]s;ᵘer) valley
Talar [ta'lɑr] m (-s;-e) robe, gown
Tal'boden m valley floor
Talent [ta'lɛnt] n (-[e]s;-e) talent
talentiert [talɛn'tirt] adj talented
Tal'fahrt f descent
Talg [talk] m (-[e]s;-e) suet; tallow
Talg'kerze f, Talg'licht n tallow candle
Talisman ['tɑlɪsman] m (-s;-e) talisman
Talk(um)puder ['talk(ʊm)pudər] m talcum powder
Talmi ['talmi] n (-s;) (fig) imitation
Tal'sperre f dam
Tamburin [tambu'rin] n (-s;-e) tambourine
Tampon [tɑ̃'põ] m (-s;-s) (med) tampon
Tamtam [tam'tam] n (-s;-s) gong; (fig) fanfare, drum beating
Tand [tant] m (-[e]s;) trifle; bauble
tändeln ['tɛndəln] intr trifle; flirt
Tang [taŋ] m (-[e]s;-e) seaweed
Tangente [taŋ'gɛntə] f (-;-n) (geom) tangent
tangieren [taŋ'girən] tr concern
Tango ['taŋgo] m (-s;-s) tango
Tank [taŋk] m (-[e]s;-e & -s) tank
tanken ['taŋkən] intr get gas; refuel
Tan'ker m, Tank'schiff n tanker
Tank'stelle f gas (or service) station
Tank'wagen m tank truck; (rr) tank car
Tankwart ['taŋkvart] m (-[e]s;-e) gas station attendant
Tanne ['tanə] f (-;-n) fir (tree)
Tan'nenbaum m fir tree
Tan'nenzapfen m fir cone
Tante ['tantə] f (-;-n) aunt; T. Meyer (coll) john
Tantieme [tɑ̃'tjemə] f (-;-n) dividend; (com) royalty
Tanz [tants] m (-es;ᵘe) dance
Tanz'bein n—das T. schwingen (coll) cut a rug
Tanz'diele f dance hall
tänzeln ['tɛntsəln] intr (HABEN & SEIN) skip about; (Pferd) prance
tanzen ['tantsən] tr & intr dance
Tänzer –in ['tɛntsər(ɪn)] §6 mf dancer
Tanz'fläche f dance floor
Tanz'kapelle f dance band
Tanz'lokal n dance hall
Tanz'saal m ballroom
Tanz'schritt m dance step
Tanz'stunde f dancing lesson
Tapete [ta'petə] f (-;-n) wallpaper
Tape'tenpapier n wallpaper (in rolls)
Tape'tentür f wallpapered door
Tapezierarbeit [tape'tsirarbaɪt] f paperhanging
tapezieren [tape'tsirən] tr wallpaper
Tapezie'rer m (-s;-) paperhanger
tapfer ['tapfər] adj brave, valiant
Ta'pferkeit f (-;) bravery, valor
tappen ['tapən] intr (HABEN & SEIN) grope about; t. nach grope for
täppisch ['tɛpɪʃ] adj clumsy
tapsen ['tapsən] intr (SEIN) clump along

Tara ['tɑra] f (-;) (com) tare
Tarif [ta'rif] m (-s;-e) tariff; price list; wage scale; postal rates
Tarif'lohn m standard wages
Tarif'verhandlung f collective bargaining
Tarif'vertrag m wage agreement
Tarn– [tarn] comb.fm. camouflage
tarnen ['tarnən] tr camouflage
Tarn'kappe f (myth) magic cap (rendering wearer invisible)
Tar'nung f (-;) camouflage
Tasche ['taʃə] f (-;-n) pocket; handbag; pocketbook; schoolbag; flight bag; pouch; briefcase
Ta'schenausgabe f pocket edition
Ta'schenbuch n paperback
Ta'schendieb m pickpocket
Ta'schendiebstahl m pickpocketing
Ta'schengeld n pocket money
Ta'schenlampe f flashlight
Ta'schenmesser n pocketknife
Ta'schenrechner m pocket calculator
Ta'schenspieler –in §6 mf magician
Ta'schenspielerei f sleight of hand
Ta'schentuch n handkerchief
Ta'schenuhr f pocket watch
Ta'schenwörterbuch n pocket dictionary
Tasse ['tasə] f (-;-n) cup
Tastatur [tasta'tur] f (-;-en) keyboard
Taste ['tastə] f (-;-n) key
tasten ['tastən] tr feel, touch; (telg) send ‖ ref feel one's way ‖ intr (nach) grope (for)
Tastsinn ['tastzɪn] m sense of touch
tat [tɑt] pret of tun ‖ Tat f (-;-en) deed, act; (Verbrechen) crime; auf frischer Tat ertappen catch redhanded; in der Tat in fact; in die Tat umsetzen implement
Tat'bestand m facts of the case
Tat'bestandsaufnahme f factual statement
tatenlos ['tɑtənlos] adj inactive
Ta'tenlosigkeit f (-;) inactivity
Täter –in ['tetər(ɪn)] §6 mf doer, perpetrator; culprit
Tat'form f (gram) active voice
tätig ['tetɪç] adj active; busy; t. sein bei be employed by
tätigen ['tetɪgən] tr conclude
Tä'tigkeit f (-;-en) activity; occupation, job, profession
Tä'tigkeitsbericht m progress report
Tä'tigkeitsfeld n field, line
Tä'tigung f (-;-en) transaction
Tat'kraft f energy, strength; vigor
tat'kräftig adj energetic; vigorous
tätlich ['tetlɪç] adj violent; tätliche Beleidigung (jur) assault and battery; t. werden gegen assault ‖ adv —t. beleidigen (jur) assault
Tät'lichkeit f (-;-en) (act of) violence; es kam zu Tätlichkeiten it came to blows
Tat'ort m scene of the crime
tätowieren [teto'virən] tr tattoo
Tätowie'rung f (-;-en) tattoo
Tat'sache f fact
Tat'sachenbericht m factual report
tat'sächlich adj actual, real, factual
tätscheln ['tet/əln] tr pet, stroke

Tatterich ['tatərɪç] *m* (–s;) shakes
Tatze ['tatsə] *f* (–;-n) paw
Tau [tau] *m* (–[e]s;) dew ‖ *n* (–[e]s; -e) rope; (naut) hawser
taub [taup] *adj* deaf; (*betäubt*) numb; (*unfruchtbar*) barren; (*Gestein*) not containing ore; (*Nuß*) hollow; (*Ei*) unfertile; (*Hafer*) wild; **t. gegen** deaf to; **t. vor Kälte** numb with cold
Taube ['taubə] *f* (–;-n) pigeon; (pol) dove
Tau′benhaus *n*, **Tau′benschlag** *m* dovecote
Taub′heit *f* (–;) deafness; numbness
taub′stumm *adj* deaf and dumb ‖ **Taub- stumme** §5 *mf* deaf-mute
Tauchboot ['tauxbot] *n* submarine
tauchen ['tauxən] *tr* dip, duck, immerse ‖ *intr* (HABEN & SEIN), dive, plunge; (naut) submerge, dive
Tau′cher –in §6 *mf* (& orn) diver
Tau′cheranzug *m* diving suit
Tau′chergerät *n* aqualung
Tau′cherglocke *f* diving bell
Tauch′krankheit *f* bends
Tauch′schwimmer *m* (nav) frogman
tauen ['tau-ən] *tr* thaw, melt; (*schlep- pen*) tow ‖ *intr* (HABEN & SEIN) thaw ‖ *impers*—**es taut** dew is falling ‖ *impers* (HABEN & SEIN)—**es taut** it is thawing ‖ **Tauen** *n* (–s;) thaw
Tauf– [tauf] *comb.fm.* baptismal
Tauf′becken *n* baptismal font
Tauf′buch *n* parish register
Taufe ['taufə] *f* (–;-n) baptism, christening
taufen ['taufən] *tr* baptize, christen
Täufer ['tɔɪfər] *m*—**Johannes der T.** John the Baptizer
Täufling ['tɔɪflɪŋ] *m* (–s;-e) child (or person) to be baptized
Tauf′name *m* Christian name
Tauf′pate *m* godfather
Tauf′patin *f* godmother
Tauf′schein *m* baptismal certificate
taugen ['taugən] *intr* be of use; **zu etw t.** be good for s.th.
Taugenichts ['taugənɪçts] *m* (–es;-e) good-for-nothing
tauglich ['tauklɪç] *adj* (für, zu) good (for), fit (for), suitable (for); (mil) able-bodied; **t. zu** (*inf*) able to (*inf*)
Taumel ['tauməl] *m* (–s;) giddiness; (*Überschwang*) ecstasy
taumelig ['tauməlɪç] *adj* giddy; reeling
taumeln ['tauməln] *intr* (SEIN) reel, stagger; be giddy; be ecstatic
Tausch [tauʃ] *m* (–es;-e) exchange
tauschen ['tauʃən] *tr* (gegen) exchange (for) ‖ *intr*—**mit j–m t.** exchange places with s.o.
täuschen ['tɔɪʃən] *tr* deceive, fool; (*betrügen*) cheat; (*Erwartungen*) disappoint ‖ *ref* be mistaken
täu′schend *adj* deceptive, illusory; (*Ähnlichkeit*) striking
Tausch′geschäft *n* exchange, swap
Tausch′handel *m* barter; **T. treiben** barter
Täu′schung *f* (–;-en) deception, deceit; fraud; **optische I.** optical illusion
Täu′schungsangriff *m* (mil) feint attack
Täu′schungsmanöver *n* feint

Tausch′wert *m* trade-in value
tausend ['tauzənt] *invar adj & pron* thousand ‖ **Tausend** *m*—**ei der T.!** (or **potz T.!**) holy smokes! ‖ *f* (–; -en) thousand ‖ *n* (–s;-e) thousand
Tau′sendfuß *m*, **Tausendfüß(l)er** ['tau- zəntfys(l)ər] *m* (–s;–) centipede
tausendste ['tauzəntstə] §9 *adj & pron* thousandth
Tausendstel ['tauzəntstəl] *n* (–s;–) thousandth
Tau′tropfen *m* dewdrop
Tau′werk *n* (naut) rigging
Tau′wetter *n* thaw
Tau′ziehen *n* tug of war
Taxameter [taksa′metər] *m* taxi meter
Taxe ['taksə] *f* (–;-n) tax; (*Schätzung*) appraisal; (*Gebühr*) fee; (*Taxi*) taxi
Taxi ['taksi] *n* (–s;-s) taxi, cab
taxieren [ta′ksirən] *tr* appraise; rate
Taxifahrer –in §6 *mf* taxi driver
Ta′xistand *m* taxi stand
Taxus ['taksus] *m* (–;–) (bot) yew
Team [tim] *n* (–s;-s) team
Technik ['tɛçnɪk] *f* (–;-en) technique; workmanship; technology
Tech′niker –in §6 *mf* technician; engineer
Techni·kum ['tɛçnɪkum] *n* (–s;-ka [ka] & -ken [kən]) technical school; school of engineering
technisch ['tɛçnɪʃ] *adj* technical; **tech- nische Angelegenheit** technicality; **technische Hochschule** technical institute
Technologie [tɛçnɔlə′gi] *f* (–;) technology
technologisch [tɛçnə′logɪʃ] *adj* technological
Tee [te] *m* (–s;-s) tea
Tee′gebäck *n* tea biscuit, cookie
Tee′kanne *f* teapot
Tee′kessel *m* teakettle
Tee′löffel *m* teaspoon; teaspoonful
Teenager ['tinedʒər] *m* (–s;–) teenager
Teer [ter] *m* (–[e]s;-e) tar
Teer′decke *f* tar surface, blacktop
teeren ['terən] *tr* tar
Teer′pappe *f* tar paper
Tee′satz *m* tealeaves
Teich [taɪç] *m* (–[e]s;-e) pond, pool
Teig [taɪk] *m* (–[e]s;-e) dough
teigig ['taɪgɪç] *adj* doughy
Teig′mulde *f* kneading trough
Teig′waren *pl* noodles; pastries
Teil [taɪl] *m & n* (–[e]s;-e) part; piece; portion; (*Abschnitt*) section; (jur) party; **der dritte T. von** one third of; **edle Teile des Körpers** vital parts; **zu gleichen Teilen** fifty-fifty; **zum größten T.** for the most part; **zum T.** partly, in part
Teil– *comb.fm.* partial
teilbar ['taɪlbar] *adj* divisible
Teilchen ['taɪlçən] *n* (–s;–) particle
teilen ['taɪlən] *tr* divide; (mit) share (with) ‖ *ref* (*Weg*) divide; (*An- sichten*) differ; **sich t. in** (*acc*) share
teil′haben §89 *intr* (an *dat*) participate (in), share (in)
Teilhaber –in ['taɪlhabər(ɪn)] §6 *mf* participant; (com) partner
Teil′haberschaft *f* (–;-en) partnership

–teilig [taɪlɪç] *comb.fm.* –piece
Teil'nahme *f* (–;) participation; sympathy; interest
teilnahmslos ['taɪlnɑmslos] *adj* indifferent; apathetic
Teil'nahmslosigkeit *f* (–;) indifference; apathy
teilnahmsvoll ['taɪlnɑmsfɔl] *adj* sympathetic; (*besorgt*) solicitous
teil'nehmen §116 *intr* (an *dat*) participate (in), take part (in); (an *dat*) attend; (fig) (an *dat*) sympathize (with)
Teil'nehmer –in §6 *mf* participant; (*Mitglied*) member; (sport) competitor; (telp) customer, party
teils [taɪls] *adv* partly
Teil'strecke *f* section, stage
Tei'lung *f* (–;-en) division; partition; separation; (*Grade*) graduation, scale; (*Anteile*) sharing
teil'weise *adv* partly
Teil'zahlung *f* partial payment; **auf T. kaufen** buy on the installment plan
Teint [tɛ̃] *m* (–s;-s) complexion
Telefon [tele'fon] *n* (–s;-e) telephone
Telegramm [tele'gram] *n* (–s;-e) telegram
Telegraph [tele'graf] *m* (–en;-en) telegraph
Telegra'phenstange *f* telegraph pole
telegraphieren [telegra'firən] *tr & intr* telegraph; (*nach Übersee*) cable
Teleobjektiv ['tele·objektif] *n* telephoto lens
Telephon [tele'fon] *n* (–s;-e) telephone, phone; **ans T. gehen** answer the phone
Telephon'anruf *m* telephone call
Telephon'anschluß *m* telephone connection
Telephon'gespräch *n* telephone call
Telephon'hörer *m* receiver
telephonieren [telefo'nirən] *intr* telephone; **mit j–m t.** phone s.o.
telephonisch [tele'fonɪʃ] *adj* telephone || *adv* by telephone
Telephonist –in [telefo'nɪst(ɪn)] §7 *mf* telephone operator
Telephon'vermittlung *f* telephone exchange
Telephon'zelle *f* telephone booth
Telephon'zentrale *f* telephone exchange
Teleskop [tele'skop] *n* (–s;-e) telescope
Television [televi·'zjon] *f* (–;) television
Teller ['tɛlər] *m* (–s;–) plate
Tel'lereisen *n* trap
Tel'lermine *f* antitank mine
Tel'lertuch *n* dishtowel
Tempel ['tempəl] *m* (–s;–) temple
Temperament [tempəra'ment] *n* –[e] s;-e) temperament; enthusiasm; **er hat kein T.** he has no life in him; **hitziges T.** hot temper
temperament'los *adj* lifeless, boring
temperament'voll *adj* lively, vivacious
Temperatur [tempera'tur] *f* (–;-en) temperature
Temperenzler [tempe'rentslər] *m* (–s; –) teetotaler
temperieren [tempe'rirən] *tr* temper; cool; air-condition; (mus) temper

Tem·po ['tempo] *n* (–s;-s & pi [pi]) tempo; speed; (mus) movement
Tem·pus ['tempus] *n* (–; -pora [pɔra]) (gram) tense
Tendenz [ten'dents] *f* (–;-en) tendency
Tender ['tendər] *m* (–s;–) (nav, rr) tender
Tenne ['tenə] *f* (–;-n) threshing floor
Tennis ['tenɪs] *n* (–;) tennis
Ten'nisplatz *m* tennis court
Ten'nisschläger *m* tennis racket
Ten'nistournier *n* tennis tournament
Tenor ['tenər] *m* (–s;) (*Wortlaut*) tenor, purport || [te'nor] *m* (–[e]s; ꞊e) tenor
Teppich ['tepɪç] *m* (–s;-e) rug, carpet
Teppichkehrmaschine ['tepɪçkerma-/inə] *f* carpet sweeper
Termin [ter'min] *m* (–s;-e) date, time, day; deadline; (com) due date; **er hat heute T.** he is to appear in court today; **äußerster T.** deadline
termin'gemäß *adv* on time, punctually
Termin'geschäft *n* futures
Termin'kalender *m* appointment book; (jur) court calendar
Terminolo·gie [termɪnolə'gi] *f* (–; -gien ['gi·ən]) terminology
termin'weise *adv* (com) on time
Terpentin [terpen'tin] *m* (–s;) terpentine
Terrain [te'rɛ̃] *n* (–s;-s) ground; (*Grundstück*) lot; (mil) terrain; **T. gewinnen** (fig & mil) gain ground
Terrasse [te'rasə] *f* (–;-n) terrace
terras'senförmig *adj* terraced
Terrine [te'rinə] *f* (–;-n) tureen
Territo·rium [teri'torjum] *n* (–s;-rien [rjən]) territory
Terror ['terər] *m* (–s;) terror
terrorisieren [terori'zirən] *tr* terrorize
Terrorist –in [tero'rɪst(ɪn)] §7 *mf* terrorist
Terz [terts] *f* (–;-en) (mus) third
Terzett [ter'tset] *n* (–[e]s;-e) trio
Test [test] *m* (–[e]s;-e & –s) test
Testament [testa'ment] *n* (–[e]s;-e) will; (eccl) Testament
testamentarisch [testamen'tarɪʃ] *adj* testamentary || *adv* by will; **t. bestimmen** will
Testaments'vollstrecker –in §6 *mf* executor
testen ['testən] *tr* test
teuer ['tɔɪ·ər] *adj* dear, expensive; (*Preis*) high
Teu'erung *f* (–;-en) rise in price
Teu'erungswelle *f* rise in prices
Teu'erungszulage *f* cost-of-living increase
Teufel ['tɔɪfəl] *m* (–s;–) devil; **des Teufels sein** be mad; **wer zum T.?** who the devil?
Teufelei [tɔɪfə'laɪ] *f* (–;-en) deviltry
Teufelsbanner ['tɔɪfəlsbanər] *m* (–s;–) exorcist
Teu'felskerl *m* helluva fellow
teuflisch ['tɔɪflɪʃ] *adj* devilish
Teutone [tɔɪ'tonə] *m* (–n;–n) Teuton
teutonisch [tɔɪ'tonɪʃ] *adj* Teutonic
Text [tekst] *m* (–[e]s;-e) text, words; (cin) script; (mus) libretto; (typ) double pica; **aus dem T. kommen**

lose the train of thought; **j—m den T. lesen** give s.o. a lecture
Text'buch n (mus) libretto
Texter **–in** ['tekstər(ın)] §6 mf ad writer, ad man; (mus) lyricist
Textil– [tekstil] comb.fm. textile
Textilien [teks'tiljən] pl, **Textil'waren** pl textiles
text'lich adj textual
Theater [te'atər] n (–s;–) theater; **T. machen** (fig) make a fuss; **T. spielen** (fig) make believe, put on
Thea'terbesucher **–in** §6 mf theater-goer
Thea'terdichter **–in** §6 mf playwright
Thea'terkarte f theater ticket
Thea'terkasse f box office
Thea'terprobe f rehearsal
Thea'terstück n play
Thea'terzettel m program
theatralisch [te·a'tralɪʃ] adj theater; (fig) theatrical
Theke ['tekə] f (–;–n) counter; bar
The·ma ['tema] n (–s;–men [mən] & –mata [mata]) theme, subject
Theologe [te·ɔ'logə] m (–n;–n) theologian
Theologie [te·ɔlɔ'gi] f (–;) theology
theologisch [te·ɔ'logɪʃ] adj theological
theoretisch [te·ɔ'retɪʃ] adj theoretic(al)
Theo·rie [te·ɔ'ri] f (–;–rien ['ri·ən]) theory
Thera·pie [tera'pi] f (–;–pien ['pi·ən]) therapy
Thermalbad [ter'malbat] n thermal bath
Thermometer [termə'metər] n thermometer
Thermome'terstand m thermometer reading
Thermosflasche ['tɛrməsflaʃə] f thermos bottle
Thermostat [termə'stat] m (–[e]s;–e) & (–en;–en) thermostat
These ['tezə] f (–;–n) thesis
Thrombose [trom'bozə] f (–;–n) thrombosis
Thron [tron] m (–[e]s;–e) throne
Thron'besteigung f accession to the throne
Thron'bewerber m pretender to the throne
Thron'folge f succession to the throne
Thron'folger m successor to the throne
Thron'himmel m canopy, baldachin
Thron'räuber m usurper
Thunfisch ['tunfɪʃ] m tuna
Tick [tık] m (–[e]s;–s & –e) tic; (fig) eccentricity; **e–n T. auf j–n haben** have a grudge against s.o.; **e–n T. haben** (coll) be balmy
ticken ['tıkən] intr tick
ticktack ['tık'tak] adv ticktock ‖ **Ticktack** n (–s) ticktock
tief [tif] adj deep; profound; (niedrig) low; (Schlaf) sound; (Farbe) dark; (äußerst) extreme; **aus tiefstem Herzen** from the bottom of one's heart; **im tiefsten Winter** in the dead of winter ‖ adv deeply; **zu t. singen** be flat ‖ **Tief** n (–[e]s;–e) (meteor) low
Tief'angriff m low-level attack

Tief'bau m (–[e]s;) underground engineering; underground work
tief'betrübt adj deeply grieved
Tief'druckgebiet n (meteor) low
Tiefe ['tifə] f (–;–n) depth; profundity
Tief'ebene f lowlands, plain
teif'empfunden adj heartfelt
Tie'fenanzeiger m (naut) depth gauge
Tie'fenschärfe f (phot) depth of field
Tief'flug m low-level flight
Tief'gang m (fig) depth; (naut) draft
tief'gekühlt adj deep-freeze
tief'greifend adj far-reaching; radical; deep-seated
Tief'kühlschrank m deep freeze
Tief'land n lowlands
tief'liegend adj low-lying; deep-seated; (Augen) sunken
Tief'punkt m (& fig) low point
Tief'schlag m (box) low blow
Tiefsee– [tifze] comb.fm. deep-sea
tief'sinnig adj pensive; melancholy
Tief'stand m low level
Tiegel ['tigəl] m (–s;–) saucepan; (zum Schmelzen) crucible; (typ) platen
Tier [tir] n (–[e]s;–e) animal; (& fig) beast; **großes** (or **hohes**) **T.** (coll) big shot, big wheel
Tier'art f species (of animal)
Tier'arzt m veterinarian
Tier'bändiger **–in** §6 mf wild-animal tamer
Tier'garten m zoo
Tier'heilkunde f veterinary medicine
tierisch ['tirıʃ] adj animal (fig) brutish, bestial
Tier'kreis m zodiac
Tier'kreiszeichen n sign of the zodiac
Tier'quälerei f cruelty to animals
Tier'reich n animal kingdom
Tier'schutzverein m society for the prevention of cruelty to animals
Tier'wärter m keeper (at zoo)
Tier'welt f animal kingdom
Tiger ['tigər] m (–s;–) tiger
Tigerin ['tigərın] f (–;–nen) tigress
tilgen ['tılgən] tr wipe out; (ausrotten) eradicate; (Schuld) pay off; (Sünden) expiate; (streichen) delete
Til'gung f (–;–en) eradication, extinction; payment; deletion
Til'gungsfonds m sinking fund
Tingeltangel ['tıŋəltaŋəl] m & n (–s;–) honky-tonk
Tinktur [tıŋk'tur] f (–;–en) tincture
Tinte ['tıntə] f (–;–n) ink; **in der T. sitzen** (coll) be in a pickle
Tin'tenfaß n inkwell
Tin'tenfisch m cuttlefish
Tin'tenfleck m, **Tin'tenklecks** m ink spot
Tin'tenstift m indelible pencil
Tip [tıp] m (–s;–s) tip, hint
Tippelbruder ['tıpəlbrudər] m tramp
tippeln ['tıpəl] intr (SEIN) (coll) tramp; (coll) toddle
tippen ['tıpən] tr type ‖ intr type; tap; (wetten) bet; **an j–n nicht t. können** not be able to come near s.o. (in performance); **daran kannst du nicht t.** that's beyond your reach; **t. auf** (acc) predict ‖ ref—**sich an die Stirn t.** tap one's forehead

Tippfehler ['tɪpfelər] *m* typographical error

Tippfräulein ['tɪpfrɔɪlaɪn] *n* (coll) typist

tipptopp ['tɪp'tɔp] *adj* tiptop

Tirol [tɪ'rol] *n* (–s;) Tyrol

Tiroler –in [tɪ'rolər(ɪn)] §6 *mf* Tyrolean

tirolerisch [tɪ'rolərɪʃ] *adj* Tyrolean

Tisch [tɪʃ] *m* (–es;–e) table; (*Mahlzeit*) meal, dinner, supper; **bei T.** during the meal; **nach T.** after the meal; **reinen T. machen** make a clean sweep of it; **unter den T. fallen** be ignored; **vom grünen T.** arm-chair; bureaucratic; **vor T.** before the meal; **zu T., bitte!** dinner is ready

Tisch'aufsatz *m* centerpiece

Tisch'besen *m* crumb brush

Tisch'besteck *n* knife, fork, and spoon

Tisch'blatt *n* leaf of a table

Tisch'decke *f* tablecloth

Tisch'gast *m* dinner guest

Tisch'gebet *n*—**T. sprechen** say grace

Tisch'gesellschaft *f* dinner party

Tisch'glocke *f* dinner bell

Tisch'karte *f* name plate

Tisch'lampe *f* table lamp; desk lamp

Tischler ['tɪʃlər] *m* (–s;–) cabinet maker

Tisch'platte *f* table top

Tisch'rede *f* after-dinner speech

Tisch'tennis *n* Ping-Pong

Tisch'tuch *n* tablecloth

Tisch'zeit *f* mealtime, dinner time

Tisch'zeug *n* table linen and tableware

Titan [tɪ'tɑn] *m* (–en;–en) Titan || *n* (–s;) (chem) titanium

titanisch [tɪ'tɑnɪʃ] *adj* titanic

Titel ['titəl] *m* (–s;–) title; (*Anspruch*) claim; **e–n T. innehaben** (sport) hold a title

Ti'telbild *n* frontispiece; (*e–r Illustrierten*) cover picture

Ti'telblatt *n* title page

Ti'telkampf *m* (box) title bout

Ti'telrolle *f* title role

titulieren [tɪtu'lirən] *tr* title

Toast [tost] *m* (–es;–e & –s) toast

toasten ['tostən] *tr* (*Brot*) toast || *intr* propose a toast, drink a toast; **auf j–n t.** toast s.o.

toben ['tobən] *intr* rage; (*Kinder*) raise a racket || **Toben** *n* (–s;) rage, raging; racket, noise

Tob'sucht *f* frenzy, madness

tob'süchtig *adj* raving, mad; frantic

Tochter ['tɔxtər] *f* (–;–̈) daughter

Toch'terfirma *f*, **Toch'tergesellschaft** *f* (com) subsidiary, affiliate

Tod [tot] *m* (–es;–e) death; (jur) decease; **des Todes sein** be a dead man; **sich** [*dat*] **den Tod holen** catch a death of a cold

tod'ernst *adj* dead serious

Todes– [todəs] *comb.fm.* of death; deadly

To'desanzeige *f* obituary

To'desfall *m* death

To'desgefahr *f* mortal danger

To'deskampf *m* death struggle

To'deskandidat *m* one at death's door

To'desstoß *m* coup de grâce

To'desstrafe *f* death penalty; **bei T. on pain of death**

To'destag *m* anniversary of death

To'desursache *f* cause of death

To'desurteil *n* death sentence

Tod'feind –in §8 *mf* mortal enemy

todgeweiht ['totgəvaɪt] *adj* doomed

tödlich ['tøtlɪç] *adj* deadly, fatal

tod'müde *adj* dead tired

tod'schick *adj* (coll) very chic

tod'si'cher *adj* (coll) dead sure

Tod'sünde *f* mortal sin

Toilette [twa'lɛtə] *f* (–;–n) toilet

Toilet'tentisch *m* dressing table

tolerant [tolə'rant] *adj* (**gegen**) tolerant (toward)

Toleranz [tolə'rants] *f* (–;–en) toleration; (mach) tolerance

tolerieren [tolə'rirən] *tr* tolerate

toll [tɔl] *adj* mad, crazy; fantastic; terrific; **das wird noch toller kommen** the worst is yet to come; **er ist nicht so t.** (coll) he's not so hot; **es zu t. treiben** carry it a bit too far; **t. nach** crazy about

tollen ['tɔlən] *intr* (HABEN & SEIN) romp about

Toll'haus *n* (fig) bedlam

Toll'heit *f* (–;–en) madness

Toll'kopf *m* (coll) crackpot

toll'kühn *adj* foolhardy, rash

Toll'wut *f* rabies

Tolpatsch ['tɔlpatʃ] *m* (–es;–e), **Tölpel** ['tœlpəl] *m* (–s;–) (coll) clumsy ox

töl'pelhaft *adj* clumsy

Tomate [to'matə] *f* (–;–n) tomato

Ton [ton] *m* (–[e]s;–̈e) tone; sound; tint, shade; (*Betonung*) accent, stress; (fig) fashion; **den Ton angeben** (fig) set the tone; (mus) give the keynote; **e–n anderen Ton anschlagen** change one's tune; **große Töne reden** talk big; **guter Ton** (fig) good taste; **hast du Töne!** can you beat that! || *m* (–s;–e) clay

Ton'abnehmer *m* (electron) pickup

ton'angebend *adj* leading

Ton'arm *m* pickup arm

Ton'art *f* type of clay; (mus) key

Ton'atelier *n* (cin) sound studio

Ton'band *n* (–[e]s;–̈er) (cin) sound track; (electron) tape

Ton'bandgerät *n* tape recorder

tönen ['tønən] *tr* tint, shade || *intr* sound; (*läuten*) ring

tönern ['tønərn] *adj* clay, of clay

Ton'fall *m* intonation, accent

Ton'farbe *f* timbre

Ton'film *m* sound film

Ton'folge *f* melody

Ton'frequenz *f* audio frequency

Ton'geschirr *n* earthenware

Ton'höhe *f*, **Ton'lage** *f* pitch

Ton'leiter *f* (mus) scale

ton'los *adj* voiceless; unstressed

Ton'malerei *f* onomatopoeia

Ton'meister *m* sound engineer

Tonnage [to'naʒə] *f* (–;–n) (naut) tonnage

Tonne ['tɔnə] *f* (–;–n) barrel; ton

Ton'silbe *f* accented syllable

Ton'spur *f* groove (*of record*)

Ton'streifen *m* (cin) sound track

Tonsur [tɔn'zur] *f* (-;-en) tonsure
Ton'taube *f* clay pigeon
Ton'taubenschießen *n* trapshooting
Tö'nung *f* (-;-en) tint; (phot) tone
Ton'verstärker *m* amplifier
Ton'waren *pl* earthenware
Topas [to'pas] *m* (-es;-e) topaz
Topf [tɔpf] *m* (-[e]s;ːe) pot
Topf'blume *f* potted flower
Töpfer ['tœpfər] *m* (-s;-) potter
Töpferei [tœpfə'raɪ] *f* (-;-en) potter's shop
Töp'ferscheibe *f* potter's wheel
Töp'ferwaren *pl* pottery
Topf'lappen *m* potholder
Topf'pflanze *f* potted plant
Topp [tɔp] *m* (-s;-e) (naut) masthead ‖ topp *interj* it's a deal
Tor [*tor*] *m* (-en;-en) fool ‖ *n* (-[e]s; -e) gate; gateway; (sport) goal
Torbogen *m* archway
Torf [tɔrf] *m* (-[e]s;) peat
Tor'flügel *m* door (*of double door*)
Torf'moos *n* peat moss
Tor'heit *f* (-;-en) foolishness, folly
Tor'hüter *m* gatekeeper; (sport) goalie
töricht ['tøːrɪçt] *adj* foolish, silly
Törin ['tøːrɪn] *f* (-;-nen) fool
torkeln ['tɔrkəln] *intr* (HABEN & SEIN) (coll) stagger
Tor'latte *f* (sport) crossbar
Tor'lauf *m* slalom
Tor'linie *f* (sport) goal line
Tornister [tɔr'nɪstər] *m* (-s;-) knapsack; school bag; (mil) field pack
torpedieren [tɔrpe'diːrən] *tr* torpedo
Torpedo [tɔr'peːdo] *m* (-s;-s) torpedo
Tor'pfosten *m* doorpost; (fb) goal post
Tor'schluß *m*—kurz vor T. (fig) at the eleventh hour
Torte ['tɔrtə] *f* (-;-n) cake; pie
Tortur [tɔr'tuːr] *f* (-;-en) torture
Tor'wächter *m*, Torwart ['tɔrvart] *m* (-[e]s;-e) (sport) goalie
Tor'weg *m* gateway
tosen ['toːzən] *intr* (HABEN & SEIN) rage, roar ‖ Tosen *n* (-s;) rage, roar
tot [toːt] *adj* dead; (*Kapital*) idle; (*Wasser*) stagnant; toter Punkt dead center; (fig) snag; totes Rennen dead heat; tote Zeit dead season
total [to'taːl] *adj* total; all-out
totalitär [totali'tɛːr] *adj* totalitarian
tot'arbeiten *ref* work oneself to death
Tote ['toːtə] §5 *mf* dead person
töten ['tøːtən] *tr* kill; (*Nerv*) deaden
To'tenacker *m* churchyard
To'tenbett *n* deathbed
to'tenblaß *adj* deathly pale
To'tenblässe *f* deathly pallor
to'tenbleich *adj* deathly pale
To'tengräber *m* gravedigger
To'tengruft *f* crypt
To'tenhemd *n* shroud, winding sheet
To'tenklage *f* lament
To'tenkopf *m* skull
To'tenkranz *m* funeral wreath
To'tenmaske *f* death mask
To'tenmesse *f* requiem
To'tenreich *n* (myth) underworld
To'tenschau *f* coroner's inquest
To'tenschein *m* death certificate
To'tenstadt *f* necropolis

To'tenstarre *f* rigor mortis
To'tenstille *f* dead silence
To'tenwache *f* wake
tot'geboren *adj* stillborn
Tot'geburt *f* stillbirth
tot'lachen *ref* die laughing
Toto ['toto] *m* (-s;-s) football pool
tot'schießen §76 *tr* shoot dead
Tot'schlag *m* manslaughter
tot'schlagen §132 *tr* strike dead; (*Zeit*) kill
tot'schweigen §148 *tr* hush up; keep under wraps ‖ *intr* hush up
tot'stellen *ref* feign death, play dead
tot'treten §152 *tr* trample to death
Tö'tung *f* (-;-en) killing
Tour [tur] *f* (-;-en) tour; turn; (*Umdrehung*) revolution; auf die krumme T. by hook or by crook; auf die langsame T. very leisurely; auf höchsten Touren at full spead; (fig) full blast; auf Touren bringen (aut) rev up; auf Touren kommen pick up speed; (fig) get worked up; auf Touren sein (coll) be in good shape
Tou'renzahl *f* revolutions per minute
Tourismus [tu'rɪsmʊs] *m* (-;) tourism
Tourist [tu'rɪst] *m* (-en;-en) tourist
Touri'stenverkehr *m*, Touristik [tu'rɪstɪk] *f* (-;) tourism
Touristin [tu'rɪstɪn] *f* (-;-nen) tourist
Tour-nee [tur'ne] *f* (-;-neen ['ne·ən]) (mus, theat) tour
Trab [trap] *m* (-[e]s;) trot; im T. at a trot
Trabant [tra'bant] *m* (-en;-en) satellite
traben ['traːbən] *intr* (HABEN & SEIN) trot
Tra'ber *m* (-s;-) trotter
Tra'berwagen *m* sulky
Trab'rennen *n* harness racing
Tracht [traxt] *f* (-;-en) costume; (*Last*) load; (*Ertrag*) yield
trachten ['traxtən] *intr*—t. nach strive for; t. zu (*inf*) endeavor to (*inf*)
trächtig ['trɛçtɪç] *adj* pregnant
Tradition [tradɪ'tsjoːn] *f* (-;-en) tradition
traditionell [tradɪtsjo'nɛl] *adj* traditional
traf [traf] *pret* of treffen
Trafik [tra'fɪk] *f* (-;-en) (Aust) cigar store
träg [trɛk] *adj* var of träge
Tragbahre ['traːkbarə] *f* (-;-n) stretcher, litter
Trag'balken ['traːkbalkən] *m* supporting beam; girder; joist
Tragband ['traːkbant] *n* (-[e]s;ːer) strap; shoulder strap
tragbar ['traːkbar] *adj* portable; (*Kleid*) wearable; (fig) bearable
Trage ['traːgə] *f* (-;-n) litter
träge ['trɛgə] *adj* lazy; slow; inert
tragen ['traːgən] §132 *tr* carry; bear; endure; support; (*Kleider*) wear, have on; (*hervorbringen*) produce, yield; (*Bedenken*) have; (*Folgen*) take; (*Risiko*) run; (*Zinsen*) yield; bei sich t. have on one's person; getragen sein von be based on; zur Schau t. show off ‖ *ref* dress; sich

gut t. wear well || *intr* (*Stimme*) carry; (*Schußwaffe*) have a range; (*Baum, Feld*) bear, yield; (*Eis*) be thick enough

Träger ['trɛgər] *m* (-s;-) carrier; porter; (*Inhaber*) bearer; shoulder strap; (archit) girder, beam

Trägerflugzeug *n* carrier plane

trägerlos *adj* strapless

tragfähig ['trɑːkfɛ-ɪç] *adj* strong enough, capable of carrying; **tragfähige Grundlage** (fig) sound basis

Tragfähigkeit *f* (-;-en) capacity, load limit; (naut) tonnage

Tragfläche ['trɑːkflɛçə] *f*, **Tragflügel** ['trɑːkflyɡəl] *m* airfoil

Trägheit ['trɛkhaɪt] *f* (-;) laziness; (phys) inertia

Traghimmel ['trɑːkhɪməl] *m* canopy

Tragik ['trɑːgɪk] *f* (-;) tragedy

tragisch ['trɑːgɪʃ] *adj* tragic

Tragödie [tra'gøːdjə] *f* (-;-n) tragedy

Tragriemen ['trɑːkriːmən] *m* strap

Tragsessel ['trɑːkzɛsəl] *m* sedan chair

Tragtasche ['trɑːktaʃə] *f* shopping bag

Tragtier ['trɑːktiːr] *n* pack animal

Tragweite ['trɑːkvaɪtə] *f* range; (*Bedeutung*) significance, moment

Tragwerk ['trɑːkvɛrk] *n* (aer) airfoil

Trainer ['trɛnər] *m* (-s;-) coach

trainieren [trɛ'niːrən] *tr & intr* train; coach

Training ['trɛnɪŋ] *n* (-s;) training

Trainingsanzug *m* sweat suit

traktieren [trak'tiːrən] *tr* treat; treat roughly

Trak·tor ['traktər] *m* (-s;-toren ['toːrən]) tractor

trällern ['trɛlərn] *tr & intr* hum

trampeln ['trampəln] *tr* trample

Trampelpfad *m* beaten path

Tran [trɑn] *m* (-[e]s;-e) whale oil; **im T. sein** be drowsy; be under the influence of alcohol

tranchieren [trɑ̃'ʃiːrən] *tr* carve

Träne ['trɛnə] *f* (-;-n) tear

tränen ['trɛnən] *intr* water

Tränengas *n* tear gas

frank [traŋk] *pret of* **trinken** || **Trank** *m* (-[e]s;-e) drink, beverage; potion

Tränke ['trɛŋkə] *f* (-;-n) watering hole

tränken ['trɛŋkən] *tr* give (*s.o.*) a drink; (*Tiere*) water; soak

Transfor·mator [transfɔr'mɑtor] *m* (-s; -matoren [ma'toːrən] transformer

transformieren [transfɔr'miːrən] *tr* transform; step up; step down

Transfusion [transfu'zjoːn] *f* (-;-en) transfusion

Tran·sistor [tran'zɪstər] *m* (-s;-sistoren [zɪs'toːrən]) transistor

transitiv [tranzi'tiːf] *adj* transitive

Transmission [transmɪ'sjoːn] *f* (-;-en) transmission

transparent [transpa'rɛnt] *adj* transparent || **Transparent** *n* (-[e]s;-e) transparency; (*Spruchband*) banderol

transpirieren [transpi'riːrən] *intr* perspire

Transplantation [transplanta'tsjoːn] *f* (-;-en) (surg) transplant

Transport [trans'pɔrt] *m* (-[e]s;-e) transportation

transportabel [transpɔr'tɑbəl] *adj* transportable

Transporter [trans'pɔrtər] *m* (-s;-) troopship; transport plane

transportfähig *adj* transportable

transportieren [transpɔr'tiːrən] *tr* transport, ship

Transportunternehmen *n* carrier

Trapez [tra'peːts] *n* (-es;-e) trapeze; (geom) trapezoid

trappeln ['trapəln] *intr* (SEIN) clatter; (*Kinder*) patter

Trassant [tra'sant] *m* (-en;-en) (fin) drawer

Trassat [tra'sɑt] *m* (-en;-en) drawee

trassieren [tra'siːrən] *tr* trace, lay out; **e-n Wechsel t. auf** (*acc*) write out a check to

trat [trɑt] *pret of* **treten**

Tratsch [trɑtʃ] *m* (-es;) gossip

tratschen ['trɑtʃən] *intr* gossip

Tratte ['tratə] *f* (-;-n) (fin) draft

Trau- [trau] *comb.fm.* wedding, marriage

Traube ['traubə] *f* (-;-n) grape; bunch of grapes; (fig) bunch

Traubensaft *m* grape juice

Traubenzucker *m* glucose

trauen ['trau-ən] *tr* (*Brautpaar*) marry; **sich t. lassen** get married || *ref* dare || *intr* (*dat*) trust (in), have confidence (in)

Trauer ['trau-ər] *f* (-;) grief, sorrow; mourning; (*Trauerkleidung*) mourning clothes; **T. anlegen** put on mourning clothes; **T. haben** be in mourning

Traueranzeige *f* obituary

Trauerbotschaft *f* sad news

Trauerfall *m* death

Trauerfeier *f* funeral ceremony

Trauerflor *m* mourning crepe

Trauergefolge *n*, **Trauergeleit** *n* funeral procession

Trauergottesdienst *m* funeral service

Trauerkloß *m* (coll) sad sack

Trauermarsch *m* funeral march

trauern ['trau-ərn] *intr* (um) mourn (for); (um) wear mourning (for)

Trauerspiel *n* tragedy

Trauerweide *f* weeping willow

Trauerzug *m* funeral cortege

Traufe ['traufə] *f* (-;-n) eaves

träufeln ['trɔɪfəln] *tr & intr* drip

Traufrinne *f* rain gutter

Traufröhre *f* rain pipe

traulich ['traulɪç] *adj* intimate; cozy

Traum [traum] *m* (-[e]s;-e) dream; (fig) daydream, reverie

Traumbild *n* vision, phantom

Traumdeuter **-in** §6 *mf* interpreter of dreams

träumen ['trɔɪmən] *tr & intr* dream

Träumer *m* (-s;-) dreamer

Träumerei [trɔɪmə'raɪ] *f* (-;-en) dreaming; daydream

Träumerin ['trɔɪmərɪn] *f* (-;-nen) dreamer

träumerisch ['trɔɪmərɪʃ] *adj* dreamy; absent-minded

Traumgesicht *n* vision, phantom

traumhaft *adj* dream-like

traurig ['traurɪç] *adj* sad

Trauring *m* wedding ring (or band)

Trau'schein *m* marriage certificate

traut [traut] *adj* dear; cozy; intimate

Trau'ung *f* (-;-en) marriage ceremony; **kirchliche T.** church wedding; **standesamtliche T.** civil ceremony

Trau'zeuge *m* best man

Trecker ['trɛkər] *m* (-s;-) tractor

Treff [trɛf] *n* (-s;-s) (cards) club(s)

treffen ['trɛfən] §151 *tr* hit; (*begegnen*) meet; (*betreffen*) concern ‖ *ref* meet; assemble; **sich t. mit** meet with ‖ *intr* hit home; (box) land, connect ‖ **Treffen** *n* (-s;-) meeting; (mil) encounter; (sport) meet

tref'fend *adj* pertinent; to the point; (*Ähnlichkeit*) striking

Tref'fer *m* (-s;-) hit; winner; prize

treff'lich *adj* excellent

Treff'punkt *m* rendezvous, meeting place

Treib- [traɪp] *comb.fm.* moving; driving

treiben ['traɪbən] §62 *tr* drive; propel; chase, expel; (*Beruf*) pursue; (*Blätter, Blüten*) put forth; (*Geschäft*) run, carry on; (*Metall*) work; (*Musik, Sport*) go in for; (*Sprachen*) study; (*Pflanzen*) force; **es zu weit t.** go too far; **was treibst du denn?** (coll) what are you doing? ‖ *intr* blossom; sprout; (*Teig*) ferment ‖ *intr* (SEIN) drift, float ‖ **Treiben** *n* (-s;) doings, activity; drifting, floating

Treib'haus *n* hothouse

Treib'holz *n* driftwood

Treib'kraft *f* driving force

Treib'mine *f* floating mine

Treib'rakete *f* booster rocket

Treib'riemen *m* drive belt

Treib'sand *m* drifting sand; quicksand

Treib'stange *f* connecting rod

Treib'stoff *m* fuel; propellant

Treib'stoffbehälter *m* fuel tank

trennbar ['trɛnbar] *adj* separable

trennen ['trɛnən] *tr* separate; sever; (*Naht*) undo; (*Ehe*) dissolve; (elec, telp) cut off ‖ *ref* part; separate; (*Weg*) branch off

Tren'nung *f* (-;-en) separation; parting; dissolution

Tren'nungsstrich *m* dividing line; hyphen

Trense ['trɛnzə] *f* (-;-n) snaffle

Treppe ['trɛpə] *f* (-;-n) stairs, stairway; flight of stairs; **die T. hinauffallen** (coll) be kicked upstairs; **zwei Treppen hoch wohnen** live two flights up

Trep'penabsatz *m* landing

Trep'penflucht *f* flight of stairs

Trep'pengeländer *n* banister

Trep'penhaus *n* staircase

Trep'penläufer *m* stair carpet

Trep'penstufe *f* step, stair

Tresor [tre'zor] *m* (-s;-e) safe; vault

Tresse ['trɛsə] *f* (-;-n) (mil) stripe

treten ['tretən] §152 *tr* tread; tread on; trample; (*Fußhebel*) work; (*Orgel*) pump; **mit Füßen t.** (fig) trample under foot ‖ *intr* (SEIN) step, walk; tread; **an j-s Stelle t.** succeed s.o.; **auf der Stelle t.** (mil) mark time; in

Kraft t. go into effect; **j-m zu nahe t.** offend s.o.; **t. in** (acc) enter (into)

Tretmühle ['tretmylə] *f* treadmill

treu [trɔɪ] *adj* loyal, faithful, true

Treu'bruch *m* breach of faith

Treue ['trɔɪ·ə] *f* (-s) loyalty, fidelity; allegiance; **j-m die T. halten** remain loyal to s.o.

Treu'eid *m* oath of allegiance

Treu'hand *f* (jur) trust

Treuhänder **-in** ['trɔɪhɛndər(m)] §6 *mf* trustee

Treu'handfonds *m* trust fund

treu'herzig *adj* trusting; sincere

treu'los *adj* unfaithful; (gegen) disloyal (to)

Tribüne [tri'bynə] *f* (-;-n) rostrum; (mil) reviewing stand; (sport) grandstand

Tribut [tri'but] *m* (-[e]s;-e) tribute

Trichter ['trɪçtər] *m* (-s;-) funnel; (*Bomben-*) crater, pothole; (mus) bell (*of wind instrument*); **auf den T. kommen** (coll) catch on

Trick [trɪk] *m* (-s;-s & -e) trick

Trick'film *m* animated cartoon

trieb [trip] *pret of* treiben ‖ **Trieb** *m* (-[e]s;-e) sprout, shoot; urge, drive; instinct

Trieb'feder *f* (horol) mainspring

Trieb'kraft *f* motive power

trieb'mäßig *adj* instinctive

Trieb'werk *n* motor, engine

triefäugig ['trif,ɔɪgɪç] *adj* bleary-eyed

triefen ['trifən] §153 *intr* drip; (*Augen*) water; (*Nase*) run

triezen ['tritsən] *tr* (coll) tease

Trift [trɪft] *f* (-;-en) pasture land; cattle track; log-running

triftig ['trɪftɪç] *adj* cogent; valid

Trigonometrie [trigonɔme'tri] *f* (-;) trigonometry

Trikot [tri'ko] *m & n* (-s;-s) knitted cloth; (sport) trunks, tights

Triller ['trɪlər] *m* (-s;-) trill; (mus) quaver

trillern ['trɪlərn] *intr* trill; (*Vogel*) warble

Tril'lerpfeife *f* whistle

Trink- [trɪŋk] *comb.fm.* drinking

trinkbar ['trɪŋkbar] *adj* drinkable

Trink'becher *m* drinking cup

trinken ['trɪŋkən] §143 *tr & intr* drink

Trin'ker **-in** §6 *mf* drinker

trink'fest *adj* able to hold one's liquor

Trink'gelage *n* drinking party

Trink'geld *n* tip, gratuity

Trink'glas *n* drinking glass

Trink'halm *m* straw

Trink'spruch *m* toast

Trink'wasser *n* drinking water

Trio ['tri·o] *n* (-s;-s) trio

trippeln ['trɪpəln] *intr* (SEIN) patter

Tripper ['trɪpər] *m* (-s;) gonorrhea

trist [trɪst] *adj* dreary

tritt [trɪt] *pret of* treten ‖ **m** (-[e]s;-e) step; kick; pace; footstep; footprint; small stepladder; pedal; **j-m e-n T. versetzen** give s.o. a kick

Tritt'brett *n* running board

Tritt'leiter *f* stepladder

Triumph [tri'ʊmf] *m* (-[e]s;-e) triumph

Triumph'bogen m triumphal arch
triumphieren [trɪ·umˈfiːrən] intr triumph
Triumph'zug m triumphal procession
trocken ['trɔkən] adj dry; arid; **trokkenes Brot** plain bread
Trockenbagger (**Trok'kenbagger**) m (mach) excavator
Trockendock (**Trok'kendock**) n drydock
Trockenei (**Trok'kenei**) n dehydrated eggs
Trockeneis (**Trok'keneis**) n dry ice
Trockenhaube (**Trok'kenhaube**) f hair drier
Trockenheit (**Trok'kenheit**) f (–;) dryness, aridity
trockenlegen (**trok'kenlegen**) tr (Sumpf) drain; (Säugling) change (the diapers of)
Trockenmaß (**Trok'kenmaß**) n dry measure
Trockenmilch (**Trok'kenmilch**) f powdered milk
Trockenschleuder (**Trok'kenschleuder**) f spin-drier, clothes drier
Trockenübung (**Trok'kenübung**) f dry run
trocknen ['trɔknən] tr dry || intr (SEIN) dry, dry up
Troddel ['trɔdəl] f (–;-n) tassel
Trödel ['trøːdəl] m (-s;) secondhand goods; old clothes; junk; (fig) nuisance, waste of time
Trö'delkram m junk
trödeln ['trøːdəln] intr waste time
Tröd'ler –in §6 mf secondhand dealer
troff [trɔf] pret of **triefen**
trog [troːk] pret of **trügen   Trog** m (-[e]s;⸚e) trough
Trommel ['trɔməl] f (–;-n) drum
Trom'melfell n drumhead; (anat) eardrum
trommeln ['trɔməln] tr & intr drum
Trom'melschlag m drumbeat
Trom'melschlegel m, **Trom'melstock** m drumstick
Trom'melwirbel m drum roll
Trommler ['trɔmlər] m (-s;-) drummer
Trompete [trɔmˈpeːtə] f (–;-n) trumpet
trompeten [trɔmˈpeːtən] intr blow the trumpet; (Elefant) trumpet
Trompe'ter –in §6 mf trumpeter
Tropen ['troːpən] pl tropics
Tropf [trɔpf] m (-[e]s;⸚e) simpleton; armer T. poor devil
tröpfeln ['trœpfəln] tr & intr drip || intr (SEIN) trickle || impers—es tröpfelt it is sprinkling
tropfen ['trɔpfən] tr & intr drip || intr (SEIN) trickle || tr **Tropfen** m (-s;-) drop; **ein T. auf den heißen Stein** a drop in the bucket
trop'fenweise adv drop by drop
Trophäe [troˈfɛ·ə] f (–;-n) trophy
tropisch ['troːpiʃ] adj tropical
Troß [trɔs] m (Trosses; Trosse) (coll) load, baggage; (coll) hangers-on
Trosse ['trɔsə] f (–;-n) cable; (naut) hawser
Trost [troːst] m (-es;) consolation, comfort; **geringer T.** cold comfort;

wohl nicht bei T. sein not be all there
trösten ['trøːstən] tr console, comfort || ref cheer up; feel consoled
tröstlich ['trøːstlɪç] adj comforting
trost'los adj disconsolate; bleak
Trost'preis m consolation prize
trost'reich adj comforting
Trö'stung f (–;-en) consolation
Trott [trɔt] m (-[e]s;-e) trot; (coll) routine
Trottel ['trɔtəl] m (-s;-) (coll) dope
trotten ['trɔtən] intr (SEIN) trot
Trottoir [trɔˈtwaːr] n (-s;-e & -s) sidewalk
trotz [trɔts] prep (genit) in spite of; **t. alledem** for all that || **Trotz** m (-es;) defiance; **j-m T. bieten** defy s.o.
trotz'dem adv nevertheless || conj although
trotzen ['trɔtsən] intr be stubborn; (schmollen) sulk; (dat) defy
trotzig ['trɔtsɪç] adj defiant; sulky; obstinate
Trotz'kopf m defiant child (or adult)
trüb [tryːp], trübe ['tryːbə] adj turbid, muddy; (Wetter) dreary; (glanzlos) dull; (Erfahrung) sad
Trubel ['truːbəl] m (-s;) bustle
trüben ['tryːbən] tr make turbid, muddy; dim; dull; disturb; trouble (Freude, Stimmung) spoil || ref grow cloudy; become muddy; become strained
Trübsal ['tryːpzaːl] f (–;-en) distress, misery; **T. blasen** be in the dumps
trüb'selig adj gloomy, sad
Trüb'sinn m (-[e]s;) gloom
trüb'sinnig adj gloomy
Trü'bung f (–;) muddiness; blurring
trudeln ['truːdəln] intr go into a spin || **Trudeln** n (-s;) spin; **ins T. kommen** (aer) go into a spin
trug [truːk] pret of **tragen** || **Trug** m (-[e]s;) deceit; fraud; delusion
Trug'bild n phantom; illusion
trügen ['tryːgən] §111 tr & intr deceive
trügerisch ['tryːgərɪʃ] adj deceptive, illusory; (verräterisch) treacherous
Trug'schluß m fallacy
Truhe ['truː·ə] f (–;-n) trunk, chest
Trulle ['trulə] f (–;-n) slut
Trümmer ['trymər] pl ruins; rubble
Trumpf [trumpf] m (-[e]s;⸚e) trump
Trunk [truŋk] m (-[e]s;⸚e) drinking; **im T.** when drunk
trunken ['truŋkən] adj drunk; **t. vor** (dat) elated with
Trunkenbold ['truŋkənbɔlt] m (-[e]s;-e) drunkard
Trun'kenheit f (–;) drunkenness; **T. am Steuer** (jur) drunken driving
trunk'süchtig adj alcoholic || **Trunksüchtige** §5 mf alcoholic
Trupp [trup] m (-s;-s) troop, gang; (mil) detail, detachment
Truppe ['trupə] f (–;-n) (mil) troop; (theat) troupe; **Truppen** (mil) troops
Trup'peneinheit f unit
Trup'penersatz m reserves
Trup'pengattung f branch of service
Trup'penschau f (mil) review, parade

Trup′pentransporter m (aer) troop carrier; (nav) troopship

Trup′penübung f field exercise

Trup′penverband m unit; task force

Trup′penverbandplatz m (mil) first-aid station

Trust [trʌst] m (-[e]s;-e & -s) (com) trust

Truthahn [′truthɑn] m turkey (cock)

Truthenne [′truthenə] f turkey (hen)

trutzig [′trʊtsɪç] adj defiant

Tscheche [′tʃɛçə] m (-n;-n), **Tschechin** [′tʃɛçɪn] f (-;-nen) Czech

tschechisch [′tʃɛçɪʃ] adj Czech

Tschechoslowakei [tʃɛçəsləva′kaɪ] f (-;)—die T. Czechoslovakia

Tube [′tubə] f (-;-n) tube; **auf die T. drücken** (aut) step on it

Tuberkulose [tuberkʊ′lozə] f (-;) tuberculosis

Tuch [tux] n (-[e]s;-e) cloth; fabric || n (-[e]s;-er) kerchief; shawl; scarf

tuchen [′tuxən] adj cloth, fabric

Tuch′fühlung f—T. **haben mit** (mil) stand shoulder to shoulder with; **T. halten mit** keep in close touch with

Tuch′seite f right side (of cloth)

tüchtig [′tʏçtɪç] adj able, capable, efficient; sound, thorough; excellent; good; (Trinker) hard; **t. in** (dat) good at; **t. zu** qualified for || adv very much; hard; soundly, thoroughly; (sl) awfully

Tüch′tigkeit f (-;) ability, efficiency; soundness, thoroughness; excellency

Tuch′waren pl dry goods

Tücke [′tʏkə] f (-;-n) malice; **mit List und T.** by cleverness

tückisch [′tʏkɪʃ] adj insidious

tüfteln [′tʏftəln] intr—t. **an** (dat) (coll) puzzle over

Tugend [′tugənt] f (-;-en) virtue

Tugendbold [′tugəntbɔlt] m (-[e]s;-e) (pej) paragon of virtue

tu′gendhaft adj virtuous

Tulpe [′tʊlpə] f (-;-n) tulip

tummeln [′tʊməln] tr (Pferd) exercise || ref hurry; (Kinder) romp about

Tum′melplatz m playground; (fig) arena

Tümmler [′tʏmlər] m (-s;-) dolphin; (Taube) tumbler

Tumor [′tumɔr] m (-s; **Tumoren** [tu′morən]) tumor

Tümpel [′tʏmpəl] m (-s;-) pond

Tumult [tu′mʊlt] m (-[e]s;-e) uproar; uprising

tun [tun] §154 tr do; make; take; **dazu tun** add to it; **e-n Zug tun** take a swig; **es zu tun bekommen mit** have trouble with; **j-n in ein Internat tun** send s.o. to a boarding school || intr do; be busy; **alle Hände voll zu tun haben** have one's hands full; **es ist mir darum zu tun** I am anxious about it; **groß tun** talk big; **mir ist sehr darum zu tun zu** (inf) it is very important for me to (inf); **nur so tun, als ob** pretend that; **spröde tun** be prudish; **stolz tun** be proud; **weh tun** hurt; **zu t. haben** be busy; have one's work cut out; **zu tun haben mit** have trouble with || impers—**es tut mir leid** I am sorry; **es tut nichts** it doesn't matter || **Tun** n (-s;) doings; action; **Tun und Treiben** doings

Tünche [′tʏnçə] f (-;-n) whitewash

tünchen [′tʏnçən] tr whitewash

Tunichtgut [′tunɪçtgut] m (- & -[e]s; -e) good-for-nothing

Tunke [′tʊŋkə] f (-;-n) sauce; gravy

tunken [′tʊŋkən] tr dip, dunk

tunlichst [′tunlɪçst] adv—**das wirst du t. bleiben lassen** you had better leave it alone

Tunnel [′tunəl] m (-s;- & -) tunnel

Tüpfchen [′tʏpfçən] n (-s;-) dot

Tüpfel [′tʏpfəl] m & n (-s;-) dot

tüpfen [′tʏpfən] tr dab; dot || **Tupfen** m (-s;-) dot, spot

Tür [tyr] f (-;-en) door

Tür′angel f door hinge

Tür′anschlag m doorstop

Turbine [tur′binə] f (-;-n) turbine

Turboprop [′turbɔprɔp] m (-s;-s) turboprop

Tür′drücker m latch

Tür′flügel m door (of double door)

Tür′griff m door handle; door knob

Türke [′tʏrkə] m (-n;-n) Turk

Türkei [tʏr′kaɪ] f (-;)—die T. Turkey

Türkin [′tʏrkɪn] f (-;-nen) Turk

Türkis [tʏr′kis] m (-es;-e) turquoise

türkisch [′tʏrkɪʃ] adj Turkish

türkisen [tʏr′kizən] adj turquoise

Tür′klingel f doorbell

Tür′klinke f door handle

Turm [turm] m (-[e]s;-e) tower; steeple; turret; (chess) castle

Türmchen [′tʏrmçən] n (-s;-) turret

türmen [′tʏrmən] tr & ref pile up || intr (SEIN) run away, bolt

turm′hoch′ adj towering || adv (by) far

Turm′spitze f spire

Turm′springen n high diving

Turn- [turn] comb.fm. gymnastic, gym, athletic

turnen [′turnən] intr do exercises || **Turnen** n (-s;) gymnastics

Tur′ner –in §6 mf gymnast

turnerisch [′turnərɪʃ] adj gymnastic

Turn′gerät n gymnastic apparatus

Turn′halle f gymnasium, gym

Turn′hemd n gym shirt

Turn′hose f trunks

Turnier [tur′nir] n (-s;-e) tournament

Turn′schuhe pl sneakers

Tür′pfosten m doorpost

Tür′rahmen m doorframe

Tür′schild n doorplate

Tür′schwelle f threshold

Tusche [′tʊʃə] f (-;-n) (paint) wash; **chinesische T.** India ink

tuscheln [′tʊʃəln] intr whisper

Tute [′tutə] f (-;-n) (aut) horn

Tüte [′tytə] f (-;-n) paper bag; paper cone; ice cream cone

tuten [′tutən] intr blow the horn; (coll) blare away

Twen [tvɛn] m (-s;-s) young man (in his twenties)

Typ [typ] m (-s;-en) type; (Bauart) model

Type [′typə] f (-;-n) type; (coll) strange character

Ty′pennummer f model number

Typhus ['tyfus] *m* (–;) typhoid
typisch ['typɪʃ] *adj* (für) typical (of)
Tyrann [ty'ran] *m* (–en;–en) tyrant
Tyrannei [tyra'naɪ] *f* (–;–en) tyranny

tyrannisch [ty'ranɪʃ] *adj* tyrannical
tyrannisieren [tyranɪ'zirən] *tr* tyrannize, oppress
Tz ['tetset] *n*—bis ins Tz thoroughly

U

U, u [u] *invar n* U, u
u.A.w.g. *abbr* (um Antwort wird gebeten) R.S.V.P.
U-Bahn ['uban] *f* (Untergrundbahn)
subway
übel ['ybəl] *adj* evil; (*schlecht*) bad;
(*unwohl*) queasy, sick; (*Geruch,
usw.*) nasty, foul; er ist ein übler
Geselle he's a bad egg; mir ist ü.
I feel sick; ü. daran sein have it
rough ‖ *adv* badly; est steht ü. mit
things don't look good for; ü. auslegen misconstrue; ü. deuten misinterpret; ü. ergehen fare badly; ü.
gelaunt in bad humor ‖ **Übel** *n*
(–s;–) evil; ailment
ü'belgelaunt *adj* ill-humored
ü'belgesinnt *adj* evil-minded
Ü'belkeit *f* (–;) nausea
ü'belnehmen §116 *tr* take amiss; take
offense at, resent
ü'belnehmend *adj* resentful
ü'belriechend *adj* foul-smelling
U'belstand *m* evil; bad state of affairs
Ü'beltat *f* misdeed, crime, offense
Ü'beltäter **–in** §6 *mf* wrongdoer; criminal
ü'belwollen §162 *intr* (*dat*) be ill-disposed towards ‖ **Übelwollen** *n* (–s;)
ill will, malevolence
ü'belwollend *adj* malevolent
üben ['ybən] *tr* practice, exercise;
(*e–e Kunst*) cultivate; (*Handwerk*)
pursue; (*Gewalt*) use; (*Verrat*) commit; (mil) drill; (sport) train; Barmherzigkeit ü. an (*dat*) have mercy on;
Gerechtigkeit ü. gegen be fair to;
Nachsicht ü. gegen be lenient towards; Rache ü. an (*dat*) take revenge on ‖ *ref*—sich im Schifahren
ü. practice skiing
über ['ybər] *adv*—j–m ü. sein in (*dat*)
be superior to s.o. in; ü. und ü.
over and over ‖ *prep* (*dat*) over;
above, on top of ‖ *prep* (*acc*) by way
of, via; (*bei, während*) during; (*nach*)
past; over; across; (*betreffend*)
about, concerning; **Briefe ü. Briefe**
letter after letter; **ein Scheck ü.**
10·DM a check for 10 marks; es geht
nichts ü. there is nothing better than;
heute übers Jahr a year from today;
ü. Gebühr more than was due; ü.
kurz oder lang sooner or later; ü.
Land crosscountry
überall' *adv* everywhere, all over
überall'her' *adv* from all sides
überall'hin' *adv* in every direction
Ü'berangebot *n* over-supply
überan'strengen *tr* overexert, strain ‖
ref overexert oneself, strain oneself

überar'beiten *tr* revise, touch up ‖ *ref*
—sich ü. overwork oneself
Überar'beitung *f* (–;–en) revision,
touching up; revised text
ü'beraus *adv* extremely, very
überbacken (überbak'ken) §50 *tr* bake
lightly
Ü'berbau *m* (–[e]s; -e & –ten [tən])
superstructure
ü'berbeanspruchen *tr* overwork
ü'berbelasten *tr* overload
ü'berbelegt *adj* overcrowded
ü'berbelichten *tr* (phot) overexpose
ü'berbetonen *tr* overemphasize
überbie'ten §58 *tr* outbid; (fig) outdo
Überbleibsel ['ybərblaɪpsəl] *n* (–s;–)
remains; leftovers
Überblen'dung *f* (cin) dissolve
Ü'berblick *m* survey; (fig) synopsis
überblicken (überblik'ken) *tr* survey
überbrin'gen §65 *tr* deliver; convey
Überbrin'ger –in §6 *mf* bearer
überbrücken (überbrük'ken) *tr* (& fig)
bridge
Überbrückung (Überbrük'kung) *f* (–;
–en) bridging; (rr) overpass
Überbrückungs– *comb.fm.* emergency,
stop-gap
überdachen [ybər'daxən] *tr* roof over
überdau'ern *tr* outlast
überdecken (überdek'ken) *tr* cover
überdies' *adv* moreover, besides
überdre'hen *tr* (*Uhr*) overwind
Ü'berdruck *m* excess pressure
Ü'berdruckanzug *m* space suit
Ü'berdruckkabine *f* pressurized cabin
Über-druß ['ybərdrus] *m* (–drusses;)
boredom; (*Übersättigung*) satiety;
(*Ekel*) disgust; bis zum Ü. ad nau-
seam
überdrüssig ['ybərdrysɪç] *adj* (*genit*)
sick of, disgusted with
ü'berdurchschnittlich *adj* above the
average
Ü'bereifer *m* excessive zeal
ü'bereifrig *adj* overzealous
überei'len *tr* precipitate; rush ‖ *ref*
be in too big a hurry; act rashly
übereilt [ybər'aɪlt] *adj* hasty, rash
übereinan'der *adv* one on top of the
other
übereinan'derschlagen §132 *tr* cross
überein'kommen §99 *intr* (SEIN) come
to an agreement ‖ **Übereinkommen**
n (–s;–) agreement
Überein'kunft *f* agreement
überein'stimmen *intr* be in agreement;
concur; (*Farben, usw.*) harmonize
Überein'stimmung *f* agreement; accord; (*Gleichförmigkeit*) conformity;

(Einklang) harmony; **in Ü. mit** in line with

ü′berempfindlich *adj* oversensitive

überfah′ren §71 *tr* run over, run down; *(Fluß, usw.)* cross; **ein Signal ü.** go through a traffic light; **ü. werden** (coll) be taken in ‖ **ü′berfahren** §71 *tr (über e–n Fluß, usw.)* take across ‖ *intr* (SEIN) drive over, cross

Ü′berfahrt *f* crossing

Ü′berfall *m* surprise attack, assault; *(Raubüberfall)* holdup; *(Einfall)* raid

überfal′len §72 *tr (räuberisch)* hold up; assault; (mil) surprise; (mil) invade, raid; **ü. werden** be overcome *(by sleep)*; be seized *(with fear)*

ü′berfällig *adj* overdue

Ü′berfallkommando *n* riot squad

überflie′gen §57 *tr* fly over; *(Buch)* skim through

ü′berfließen §76 *intr* (SEIN) overflow

überflügeln [ybər′flygəln] *tr* outflank; (fig) outstrip

Ü′berfluß *m* abundance; excess; **im Ü. vorhanden sein** be plentiful

ü′berflüssig *adj* superfluous

überflu′ten *tr* overflow, flood, swamp ‖ **ü′berfluten** *intr* (SEIN) overflow

überfor′dern *tr* demand too much of; overwork

Ü′berfracht *f* excess luggage

ü′berführen *tr* carry across; *(Leiche)* transport in state ‖ **überfüh′ren** *tr (genit)* convince of; *(genit)* convict of

Überfüh′rung *f* (–;–en) overpass; *(e–s Verbrechers)* conviction

Ü′berfülle *f* superabundance

überfül′len *tr* stuff, jam, pack

Ü′bergabe *f* delivery; (& mil) surrender

Ü′bergang *m* passage; crossing; transition; (jur) transfer; (mil) desertion; (paint) blending; (rr) crossing

Ü′bergangsbeihilfe *f* severance pay

Ü′bergangsstadium *n* transition stage

Ü′bergangszeit *f* transitional period

überge′ben §80 *tr* hand over; give up; *(einreichen)* submit; (& mil) surrender; **dem Verkehr ü.** open to traffic ‖ *ref* vomit, throw up

überge′hen §82 *tr* omit; overlook; **mit Stillschweigen ü.** pass over in silence ‖ **ü′bergehen** §82 *intr* (SEIN) go over, cross; *(sich verändern)* **(in** *acc)* change (into); **auf j–n ü.** devolve upon s.o.; **in andere Hände ü.** change hands; **in Fäulnis ü.** become rotten

Ü′bergewicht *n* overweight; (fig) preponderance; **das Ü. bekommen** become top-heavy; (fig) get the upper hand

ü′bergießen §76 *tr* spill ‖ **übergie′ßen** §76 *tr* pour over, pour on; *(Braten)* baste; **mit Zuckerguß ü.** (culin) ice

ü′bergreifen §88 *intr* **(auf** *acc)* spread (to); **(auf** *acc)* encroach (on)

Ü′bergriff *m* encroachment

ü′bergroß *adj* huge, colossal; oversize

ü′berhaben §89 *tr* have left; *(Kleider)* have on; (fig) be fed up with

überhand′nehmen §116 *intr* get the upper hand; run riot

ü′berhängen §92 *tr (Mantel)* put on;

(Gewehr) sling over the shoulders ‖ *intr* overhang, project

überhäu′fen *tr* overwhelm, swamp

überhaupt′ *adv* really; anyhow; *(besonders)* especially; *(überdies)* besides; at all; **ü. kein no...whatever**; **ü. nicht not at all**; **wenn ü. if...at all**; **if...really**

überheblich [ybər′heplıç] *adj* arrogant

überhei′zen, überzhit′zen *tr* overheat

überhöhen [ybər′hø·ən] *tr (Kurve)* bank; *(Preise)* raise too high

ü′berholen *tr* take across; **die Segel ü.** shift sails ‖ *intr* (naut) heel ‖ **überho′len** *tr* outdistance, outrun; *(ausbessern)* overhaul; *(Fahrzeug)* pass; (fig) outstrip

überholt [ybər′holt] *adj* obsolete, out of date; *(repariert)* reconditioned

überhö′ren *tr* not hear, miss; ignore; misunderstand

ü′berirdisch *adj* supernatural

überkandidelt [′ybərkandıdəlt] *adj* (coll) nutty, wacky

ü′berkippen *intr* (SEIN) tilt over

überkle′ben *tr* paper over; **ü. mit** cover with

Ü′berkleid *n* outer garment; overalls

ü′berklug *adj* (pej) wise, smart

ü′berkochen *intr* (SEIN) boil over

überkom′men *adj* traditional ‖ §99 *tr* overcome ‖ *intr* (SEIN) be handed down to

überla′den *adj* overdone ‖ §103 *tr* overload

Ü′berlandbahn *f* interurban trolley line

Ü′berlandleitung *f* (elec) high-tension line; (telp) long-distance line

überlas′sen §104 *tr* yield, leave, relinquish; entrust; (com) sell; **das bleibt ihm ü.** he is free to do as he pleases ‖ *ref (dat)* give way to

Ü′berlast *f* overload; overweight

überla′sten *tr* overload

überlau′fen *adj* overcrowded; (fig) swamped ‖ §105 *tr* overrun; *(belästigen)* pester; **Angst überlief ihn** fear came over him ‖ **ü′berlaufen** §105 *intr* (SEIN) run over, overflow; boil over; (fig & mil) desert; **die Galle läuft mir über** (fig) my blood boils ‖ *impers*—**mich überläuft es kalt** I shudder

Ü′berläufer -in §6 *mf* (mil) deserter; (pol) turncoat

ü′berlaut *adj* too noisy

überle′ben *tr* outlive, survive ‖ *ref* go out of style

überle′bend *adj* surviving ‖ **Überlebende** §5 *mf* survivor

ü′berlebensgroß *adj* bigger than life

überlebt [ybər′lept] *adj* antiquated

überle′gen *adj (dat)* superior (to); **(an** *dat)* superior (in) ‖ *tr* consider, think over ‖ *ref—sich [dat]* anders ü. change one's mind; **sich** *[dat]* **ü.** consider, think over ‖ *intr* think it over ‖ **ü′berlegen** *tr* lay across; *(Mantel)* put on

Überle′genheit *f* (–;) superiority

überlegt′ *adj* well considered; (jur) willful

Überle′gung f (-;-en) consideration
überle′sen §107 tr read over, peruse
überlie′fern tr deliver; hand down, transmit; (mil) surrender
Überlie′ferung f (-;-en) delivery; (fig) tradition; (mil) surrender
überli′sten tr outwit, outsmart
überma′chen tr bequeath
Ü′bermacht f superiority; (fig) predominance
ü′bermächtig adj overwhelming; predominant
überma′len tr paint over
übermannen [ybər′manən] tr overpower
Ü′bermaß n excess; bis zum Ü. to excess
ü′bermäßig adj excessive || adv excessively; overly
Ü′bermensch m superman
ü′bermenschlich adj superhuman
übermitteln [ybər′mɪtəln] tr transmit, convey, forward
Übermitt′lung f (-;-en) transmission, conveyance, forwarding
ü′bermorgen adv the day after tomorrow
übermüdet [ybər′mydət] adj overtired
Ü′bermut m exuberance, mischievousness
ü′bermütig adj exuberant; haughty
ü′bernächste §9 adj next but one; am übernächsten Tag the day after tomorrow; ü. Woche week after next
übernach′ten intr spend the night
Übernach′tung f (-;-en) accommodations for the night; spending the night
Ü′bernahme f taking over, takeover
ü′bernatürlich adj supernatural
überneh′men §116 tr take over; assume; undertake; take upon oneself; accept, receive || **ü′bernehmen** §116 tr (Mantel, Schal) put on; (Gewehr) shoulder || **überneh′men** §116 ref overreach oneself; sich beim Essen ü. overeat
ü′berordnen tr place over, set over
ü′berparteilich adj nonpartisan
Ü′berproduktion f overproduction
überprü′fen tr examine again, check; verify; (Personen) screen
Überprü′fung f (-;-en) checking; checkup
ü′berquellen §119 intr (SEIN) (Teig) run over; überquellende Freude irrepressible joy
überqueren [ybər′kverən] tr cross
überra′gen tr tower over; (fig) surpass
überraschen [ybər′raʃən] tr surprise
Überra′schung f (-;-en) surprise
überrech′nen tr count over
überre′den tr persuade; j-n zu etw ü. talk a person into s.th.
Überre′dung f (-;-) persuasion
ü′berreich adj (an dat) abounding (in) || adv-ü. ausgestattet well equipped
überrei′chen tr hand over, present
ü′berreichlich adj superabundant
ü′berreif adj overripe
überrei′zen tr overexcite; (Augen, Nerven) strain
überreizt′ adj overwrought

überren′nen §97 tr overrun; (fig) overwhelm
Ü′berrest m rest, remainder; **irdische Überreste** mortal remains
ü′berrock m topcoat, overcoat
überrum′peln tr take by surprise
Überrum′pelung f (-;-en) surprise
überrun′den tr (sport) lap
übersät [ybər′zet] adj (fig) strewn, dotted
übersät′tigen tr stuff; cloy; (chem) saturate, supersaturate
Übersät′tigung f (chem) supersaturation
Überschall- comb.fm. supersonic
überschat′ten tr overshadow
überschät′zen tr overestimate
Ü′berschau f survey
überschau′en tr look over, survey; overlook (a scene)
überschla′fen §131 tr (fig) sleep on
Ü′berschlag m rough estimate; (aer) loop; (gym) somersault
überschla′gen adj lukewarm || §132 tr skip, omit; estimate roughly; consider || ref go head over heels; do a somersault; (Auto) overturn; (Boot) capsize; (Flugzeug) do a loop; (beim Landen) nose over; (Stimme) break; (fig) (vor dat) outdo oneself (in) || **ü′berschlagen** §132 tr (Beine) cross; flip over; ü. in (acc) (fig) change suddenly to
ü′berschnappen intr (SEIN) (Stimme) squeak; (coll) flip one's lid
überschnei′den §106 ref (Linien) intersect; (& fig) overlap
überschrei′ben §62 tr sign over
überschrei′en §135 tr shout down || ref strain one's voice
überschrei′ten §86 tr cross, step over; (Kredit) overdraw; (Gesetz) violate, transgress; (fig) exceed, overstep
Ü′berschrift f heading, title
Ü′berschuh m overshoe
Ü′berschuß m surplus, excess; profit
ü′berschüssig adj surplus, excess
überschüt′ten tr shower; (& fig) overwhelm, flood
Ü′berschwang m (-[e]s;) rapture
überschwem′men tr flood, inundate
Überschwem′mung f (-;-en) flood, inundation
überschwenglich [′ybərʃvɛŋlɪç] adj effusive, gushing
Ü′bersee f (-;) overseas
Ü′berseedampfer m ocean liner
Ü′berseehandel m overseas trade
übersehbar [ybər′zebar] adj visible at a glance
überse′hen §138 tr survey, look over; (nicht bemerken) overlook; (absichtlich) ignore; (erkennen) realize
übersen′den §140 tr send, forward; transmit; (Geld) remit
Übersen′dung f (-;-en) forwarding; transmission; consignment
übersetzen tr ferry across || **über-set′zen** tr translate
Überset′zung f (-;-en) translation; (mach) gear, transmission
Ü′bersicht f survey, review; (Abriß) abstract; (Zusammenfassung) sum-

mary; (*Umriß*) outline; (*Ausblick*) perspective; **jede Ü. verlieren** lose all perspective

ü′bersichtlich *adj* clear; (*Gelände*) open

Ü′bersichtsplan *m* general plan

ü′bersiedeln *intr* (SEIN) move; emigrate

ü′bersinnlich *adj* transcendental

überspan′nen *tr* span; cover; overstrain; (fig) exaggerate

überspannt [ybər′/pant] *adj* eccentric; extravagant

Überspannt′heit *f* (-;-en) eccentricity

Überspan′nung *f* (-;-en) overstraining; (fig) exaggeration; (elec) excess voltage

überspie′len *tr* outplay; outwit; (*Tonbandaufnahme*) transcribe; (*Schüchternheit*) hide

überspitzt [ybər′/pɪtst] *adj* oversubtle

übersprin′gen §142 *tr* jump; (*auslassen*) omit, skip ‖ **ü′berspringen** §142 *intr* (SEIN) jump

ü′bersprudeln *intr* (SEIN) bubble over

ü′berständig *adj* leftover; (*Bier*) flat; (*Obst*) overripe

überste′hen §146 *tr* stand; endure; (*Krankheit, usw.*) get over; (*Operation*) pull through; (*überleben*) survive ‖ **ü′berstehen** §146 *intr* jut out

überstei′gen §148 *tr* climb over; (*Hindernisse*) overcome; (*Erwartungen*) exceed ‖ **ü′bersteigen** §148 *intr* (SEIN) step over

überstim′men *tr* vote down, defeat

überstrah′len *tr* shine upon; (*verdunkeln*) outshine, eclipse

überstrei′chen §85 *tr* paint over

ü′berstreifen *tr* slip on

überströ′men *tr* flood, inundate ‖ **ü′berströmen** *intr* (SEIN) overflow

Ü′berstunde *f* hour of overtime; **Überstunden machen** work overtime

überstür′zen *tr* rush, hurry ‖ *ref* be in too big a hurry; act rashly; (*Ereignisse*) follow one another rapidly

überstürzt [ybər′/tyrtst] *adj* hasty

überteuern [ybər′tɔɪ-ərn] *tr* overcharge

übertölpeln [ybər′tœpəln] *tr* dupe

übertö′nen *tr* drown out

Übertrag [′ybərtrak] *m* (-[e]s;⸗e) (acct) carryover, balance

übertragbar [ybər′trakbər] *adj* transferable; (pathol) contagious

übertra′gen *adj* figurative, metaphorical ‖ §132 *tr* carry over, transfer; (*Amt, Titel*) confer; (*Aufgabe*) assign; (*Vollmacht*) delegate; (*Kurzschrift*) transcribe; (in *acc*) translate (into); (acct) transfer; (pathol) spread, communicate; (rad) broadcast, transmit; (*mit Relais*) relay; (telv) televise

Übertra′gung *f* (-;-en) carrying over; transfer; assignment; delegation; conferring; transcription; translation; copy; (pathol) spread; (rad) broadcast; relay; (telv) televising

übertref′fen §151 *tr* surpass, outdo

übertrei′ben §62 *tr* overdo; exaggerate; (theat) overact

Übertrei′bung *f* (-;-en) overdoing; exaggeration; (theat) overacting

übertre′ten §152 *tr* (*Gesetz*) transgress, break ‖ *ref—sich* [*dat*] **den Fuß ü.** sprain one's ankle ‖ **ü′bertreten** §152 *intr* (SEIN) (sport) go off sides; **ü. zu** (fig) go over to; (relig) be converted to

Übertre′tung *f* (-;-en) violation

Ü′bertritt *m* change, going over; (relig) conversion

übervölkern [ybər′fœlkərn] *tr* overpopulate

Übervöl′kerung *f* (-;-) overpopulation

ü′bervoll *adj* brimful; crowded

übervorteilen [ybər′fortaɪlən] *tr* take advantage of, get the better of

überwa′chen *tr* watch over; supervise; (*kontrollieren*) inspect, check; (*polizeilich*) shadow; (rad, telv) monitor

Überwa′chung *f* (-;-en) supervision; inspection; control; surveillance

Überwa′chungsausschuß *m* watchdog committee

überwältigen [ybər′veltigən] *tr* overpower (fig) overwhelm

überwei′sen §118 *tr* (*Geld*) send; (*zu e-m Spezialisten*) refer

Überwei′sung *f* (-;-en) sending, remittance; referral

ü′berweltlich *adj* otherworldly

überwer′fen §160 *tr* throw over ‖ **überwer′fen** §160 *ref* (mit) have a run-in (with)

überwie′gen §57 *tr* outweigh ‖ *intr* prevail, preponderate ‖ **Überwiegen** *n* (-s;) prevalence, preponderance

überwie′gend *adj* prevailing; (*Mehrheit*) vast ‖ *adv* predominantly

überwin′den §59 *tr* conquer, overcome ‖ *ref—sich* **ü. zu** (*inf*) bring oneself to (*inf*)

überwintern [ybər′vɪntərn] *intr* pass the winter; (bot) survive the winter

überwu′chern *tr* overrun; (fig) stifle

Ü′berwurf *m* wrap; shawl

Ü′berzahl *f* numerical superiority; majority

überzah′len *tr & intr* overpay

überzäh′len *tr* count over, recount

überzählig [′ybərtseliç] *adj* surplus

überzeu′gen *tr* convince ‖ *ref—ü.* **Sie sich selbst davon!** go and see for yourself!

Überzeu′gung *f* (-;-en) conviction

überzie′hen §163 *tr* cover; (*mit Farbe*) coat; (*Bett*) put fresh linen on; (*Konto*) overdraw; **ein Land mit Krieg ü.** invade a country ‖ **ü′berziehen** §163 *tr* (*Mantel, usw.*) slip on; **j-m eins ü.** (coll) give s.o. a whack

Ü′berzieher *m* (-s;-) overcoat

überzuckern (überzuk′kern) *tr* (& fig) sugarcoat

Ü′berzug *m* coat, film; (*Decke*) cover; (*Hülle*) case; pillow case; (*Kruste*) crust; (*Schale, Rinde*) skin

üblich [′ypliç] *adj* usual, customary

U′-Boot *n* (*Unterseeboot*) submarine

U′-Bootbunker *m* submarine pen

U′-Bootjäger *m* (aer) antisubmarine aircraft; (nav) subchaser

U′-Bootortungsgerät *n* sonar

U′-Bootrudel *n* (nav) wolf pack

übrig [′ybrɪç] *adj* left (over), remaining, rest (of); **die übrigen** the others, the rest; **ein übriges tun** do more than is necessary; **etw ü. haben für** have a soft spot for; **im übrigen** for the rest, otherwise

ü′brigbehalten §90 *tr* keep, spare

ü′brigbleiben §62 *intr* (SEIN) be left (over) || *impers*—**es blieb mir nichts anderes ü. als zu** (*inf*) I had no choice but to (*inf*)

übrigens [′ybrɪgəns] *adv* moreover; after all; by the way

ü′briglassen §104 *tr* leave, spare

Übung [′ybuŋ] *f* (-;-en) exercise; practice; (*Gewohnheit*) use; (*Ausbildung*) training; (mil) drill

Ü′bungsbeispiel *n* practical example

Ü′bungsbuch *n* composition book; workbook

Ü′bungsgelände *n* training ground; (*für Bomben*) target area

Ü′bungshang *m* (sport) training slope

Ü′bungsheft *n* composition book; workbook

Ufer [′ufər] *n* (-s;-) (*e-s Flusses*) bank; (*e-s Meers*) shore

U′ferdamm *m* embankment, levee

u′ferlos *adj* fruitless

Uhr [ur] *f* (-;-en) clock; watch; o′clock; **um wieviel Uhr?** at what time; **um zwölf Uhr** at twelve o′clock; **wieviel Uhr ist es?** what time is it?

Uhr′armband *n* (-[e]s;⁼er) watchband

Uhr′feder *f* watch spring

Uhr′glas *n* watch crystal

Uhr′macher *m* watchmaker

Uhr′werk *n* works, clockwork

Uhr′zeiger *m* hand

Uhr′zeigerrichtung *f*—**entgegen der U.** counterclockwise; **in der U.** clockwise

Uhr′zeigersinn *m*—**im U.** clockwise

Uhu [′uhu] *m* (-s;-s) owl

Ukraine [u′krainə] *f* (-;)—**die U.** the Ukraine

ukrainisch [u′krainɪʃ] *adj* Ukrainian

UK-Stellung [u′ka/telʊŋ] *f* (-;-en) military deferment

Ulk [ulk] *m* (-[e]s;-e) joke, fun

ulken [′ulkən] *intr* (coll) make fun

ulkig [′ulkɪç] *adj* funny

Ulme [′ulmə] *f* (-;-n) elm

Ultima·tum [ultɪ′matum] *n* (-s;-ten [tən] & -ta [ta]) ultimatum

Ultra-, ultra- [ultra] *comb.fm.* ultra-

Ul′trakurzfrequenz *f* ultrashort frequency

ultramontan [ultramɔn′tan] *adj* strict Catholic

ul′trarot *adj* infrared

Ultraschall– *comb.fm.* supersonic

ul′traviolett *adj* ultraviolet

um [um] *adv*—**deine Zeit ist um** your time is up; **je. . .um so the. . .the; um so besser** all the better; **um so weniger** all the less; **um und um** round and round || *prep* (*acc*) around, about; for; at; **um die Hälfte mehr** half as much again; **um die Wette laufen** race; **um ein Jahr älter** one year older; **um etw eintauschen** exchange for s.th.; **um jeden Preis** at

any price; **um. . .Uhr** at. . .o′clock; **um. . .zu** (*inf*) in order to (*inf*)

um′ackern *tr* plow up, turn over

um′adressieren *tr* readdress

um′ändern *tr* change (around)

Um′änderung *f* (-;-en) change, alteration

um′arbeiten *tr* rework; (*Metall*) recast; (*Buch*) revise; (*Haus*) remodel; (*berichtigen*) emend, correct; (*verbessern*) improve

umar′men *tr* embrace, hug

Umar′mung *f* (-;-en) embrace, hug

Um′bau *m* (-[e]s;-e & -ten) rebuilding; alterations, remodeling; reorganization

um′bauen *tr* remodel; reorganize || **um·bau′en** *tr* build around; **umbauter Raum** floor space

um′besetzen *tr* (*Stellungen*) switch around; (pol) reshuffle; (theat) recast

um′biegen §47 *tr* bend (over); bend up, bend down

um′bilden *tr* remodel; reconstruct; (adm) reorganize, (pol) reshuffle

Um′bildung *f* (-;-en) remodeling; reconstruction; reorganization; reshuffling

um′binden §59 *tr* (*Schürze, usw.*) put on || **umbin′den** §59 *tr* (*verletztes Glied, usw.*) bandage

um′blättern *tr* turn || *intr* turn the page(s)

um′brechen §64 *tr* (*Bäume, usw.*) knock down; (*Acker*) plow up || **umbre′chen** *tr* make into page proof

um′bringen §65 *tr* kill

Um′bruch *m* upheaval; (typ) page proof

um′buchen *tr* transfer to another account; book for another date

um′denken §66 *tr* rethink

um′dirigieren *tr* redirect

um′disponieren *tr* rearrange

umdrän′gen *tr* crowd around

um′drehen *tr* turn around; (*Hals*) wring; (*f-s Worte*) twist || *ref* turn around || *intr* turn around

Umdre′hung *f* (-;-en) turn; revolution

Um′druck *m* reprint; (typ) transfer

umeinan′der *adv* around each other

um′erziehen §163 *tr* reeducate

um′fahren §71 *tr* run down || **umfah′ren** §71 *tr* drive around; sail around

um′fallen §72 *intr* (SEIN) fall over, fall down; collapse; give in

Um′fang *m* circumference; perimeter; (*Bereich*) range; (*Ausdehnung*) extent; (*des Leibes*) girth; (fig) scope; (mus) range; **im großen U.** on a large scale

umfan′gen §73 *tr* surround; embrace

um′fangreich *adj* extensive; (*körperlich*) bulky; (*geräumig*) spacious

umfas′sen *tr* embrace; clasp; comprise, cover; include; contain; (mil) envelop

umfas′send *adj* comprehensive;. extensive

Umfas′sung *f* (-;-en) embrace; clasp; enclosure, fence; (mil) envelopment

Umfas'sungsmauer *f* enclosure
umflat'tern *tr* flutter around
umflech'ten §74 *tr* braid
umflie'gen §57 *tr* fly around || **um'fliegen** §57 *intr* (SEIN) (coll) fall down
umflie'ßen §76 *tr* flow around
um'formen *tr* reshape; (elec) convert
Um'former *m* (-s;-) (elec) converter
Um'frage *f* inquiry, poll; **öffentliche U.** public opinion poll
umfrieden ['ʊm'fridən] *tr* enclose
Um'gang *m* round, circuit; revolution, rotation; (*Zug*) procession; association, company; (archit) gallery; **geschlechtlicher U.** sexual intercourse; **schlechter U.** bad company; **U. mit j–m haben** (or **pflegen**) associate with s.o.
umgänglich ['ʊmgɛnlɪç] *adj* sociable
Um'gangsformen *pl* social manners
Um'gangssprache *f* colloquial speech
um'gangssprachlich *adj* colloquial
umgar'nen *tr* (fig) trap
umge'ben §80 *tr* surround
Umgebung [ʊm'gebʊŋ] *f* (-;-en) surroundings, environs, neighborhood; company, associates; background, environment
Umgegend ['ʊmgegənt] *f* (-;) (coll) neighborhood
umgehen §82 *tr* go around; evade; bypass; (mil) outflank || **um'gehen** §82 *intr* (SEIN) go around; (*Gerücht*) circulate; **an** (or **in**) **e–m Ort u.** haunt a place; **mit dem Gedanken** (or **Plan**) **u. zu** (*inf*) be thinking of (*ger*); **u. mit** deal with, handle; manage; be occupied with; hang around with
um'gehend *adj* immediate; **mit umgehender Post** by return mail; **umgehende Antwort erbeten!** please answer at your earliest convenience || *adv* immediately
Umge'hung *f* (-;-en) going around; bypassing; (fig) evasion; (mil) flanking movement
Umge'hungsstraße *f* bypass
umgekehrt ['ʊmgəkert] *adj* reverse; contrary || *adv* on the contrary; vice versa; upside down; inside out
um'gestalten *tr* alter; remodel
um'graben §87 *tr* dig up
umgren'zen *tr* fence in; (fig) limit
Umgren'zung *f* (-;-en) enclosure; (fig) limit, boundary
um'gruppieren *tr* regroup; (pol) reshuffle
um'gucken *ref* look around
um'haben §89 *tr* have on, be wearing
Um'hang *m* wrap; cape; shawl
um'hängen *tr* put on; (*Gewehr*) sling; (*Bild*) hang elsewhere
Um'hängetasche *f* shoulder bag
um'hauen §93 *tr* cut down; (coll) bowl over
umher' *adv* around, about
umher'blicken *tr* look around
umher'fuchteln *intr* gesticulate
umher'schweifen, umher'streifen *intr* (SEIN) rove, roam about
umhin' *adv*—**ich kann nicht u.** I can't do otherwise; **ich kann nicht u. zu** (*inf*) I can't help (*ger*)

umhül'len *tr* wrap up, cover; envelop
Umhül'lung *f* (-;-en) wrapping
Umkehr ['ʊmker] *f* (-;) return; change; conversion; (elec) reversal
um'kehren *tr* turn around; overturn; (*Tasche*) turn out; (elec) reverse; (gram, math, mus) invert || *intr* (SEIN) turn back, return
Um'kehrung *f* (-;-en) overturning; reversal; conversion; inversion
um'kippen *tr* upset || *intr* (SEIN) tilt over
umklam'mern *tr* clasp; cling to; (mil) envelop; **einander u.** (box) clinch
Umklam'merung *f* (-;-en) embrace; (box) clinch; (mil) envelopment
umklei'den *tr* clothe || *ref* change around || **um'kleiden** *tr* change the clothes of
Um'kleideraum *m* dressing room
um'kommen §99 *intr* (SEIN) perish; (*Essen*) spoil
Um'kreis *m* circuit; vicinity; (geom) circumference; **5 km im U.** within a radius of 5 km
umkrei'sen *tr* circle, revolve around
um'krempeln *tr* (*Ärmel*) roll up; **völlig u.** (coll) change completely
um'laden §103 *tr* reload; transship
Um'lauf *m* circulation; (*Umdrehung*) revolution, rotation; (*Flugblatt*) circular; (*Rundschreiben*) circular letter; **in U. setzen** circulate
Um'laufbahn *f* orbit
um'laufen §105 *tr* run down || *intr* (SEIN) circulate || **umlau'fen** §105 *tr* walk around
Um'laut *m* (-es;-e) umlaut, vowel mutation; mutated vowel
umlegbar ['ʊmlekbar] *adj* reversible
um'legen *tr* lay down; turn down; (*anders legen*) shift; (*Kragen*) put on; (*gleichmäßig verteilen*) apportion; (coll) knock down; (vulg) lay
um'leiten *tr* detour, divert
Um'leitung *f* (-;-en) detour
um'lenken *tr* turn back
um'lernen *tr* relearn, learn anew
um'liegend *adj* surrounding
ummau'ern *tr* wall in
um'modeln *tr* remodel
umnachtet [ʊm'naxtət] *adj* deranged
Umnach'tung *f* (-;)—**geistige U.** mental derangement
um'nähen *tr* hem
umne'beln *tr* (fig) dull; **umnebelter Blick** glassy eyes
um'nehmen §116 *tr* put on
um'packen *tr* repack
um'pflanzen *tr* transplant || **umpflan'zen** *tr*—**etw mit Blumen u.** plant flowers around s.th.
um'pflügen *tr* plow up, turn over
umrah'men *tr* frame
umranden [ʊm'randən] *tr* edge, border
Umran'dung *f* (-;-en) edging, edge
umran'ken *tr* twine around; **mit Efeu umrankt** ivy-clad
um'rechnen *tr* convert; **umgerechnet auf** (*acc*) expressed in
Um'rechnungskurs *m* rate of exchange
Um'rechnungstabelle *f* conversion table
Um'rechnungswert *m* exchange value

um′reißen §53 *tr* pull down; knock down ‖ **umrei′ßen** §53 *tr* outline

umrin′gen *tr* surround

Um′riß *m* outline

Um′rißzeichnung *f* sketch

um′rühren *tr* stir, stir up

um′satteln *tr* resaddle ‖ *intr* change jobs; (*educ*) change one's course or major; (*pol*) switch parties

Um′satz *m* turnover, sales

Um′satzsteuer *f* sales tax

umsäu′men *tr* enclose, hem in

um′schalten *tr* switch; (*Strom*) convert ‖ *intr* (*auf acc*) switch back (to)

Um′schalter *m* (*elec*) switch; (*typ*) shift key

Um′schaltung *f* (–;–en) switching; shifting

Um′schau *f* look around; **U. halten** have a look around

um′schauen *ref* look around

um′schichten *tr* regroup, reshuffle

umschichtig [′ʊmʃɪçtɪç] *adv* alternately

umschif′fen *tr* circumnavigate; (*ein Kap*) double

Um′schlag *m* (sudden) change, shift; envelope; (*e-s Buches*) cover, jacket; cuff; hem; transshipment; (*med*) compress

um′schlagen §132 *tr* knock down; (*Ärmel*) roll up; (*Bäume*) fell; (*Saum*) turn up; (*Seite*) turn; (*umladen*) transship ‖ *intr* (SEIN) (*Laune, Wetter*) change; (*Wind*) shift; (*kentern*) capsize

Um′schlagpapier *n* wrapping paper

umschlie′ßen §76 *tr* surround, enclose

umschlin′gen §142 *tr* clasp; embrace; wind around

um′schnallen §53 *tr* (coll) throw over

um′schnallen *tr* buckle on

um′schreiben §62 *tr* rewrite; (*abschreiben*) transcribe; (*Wechsel*) re-endorse; **u. auf** (*acc*) transfer to ‖ **umschrei′ben** §62 *tr* circumscribe; paraphrase

um′schreibung *f* (–;–en) transcription; transfer ‖ **Umschrei′bung** *f* (–;–en) paraphrase

Um′schrift *f* transcription; (*e-r Münze*) legend

um′schulen *tr* retrain

um′schütteln *tr* shake (up)

um′schütten *tr* spill; pour into another container

umschwär′men *tr* swarm around; (fig) idolize

Um′schweif *m* digression; **ohne Umschweife** point-blank; **Umschweife machen** beat around the bush

umschweifig [ʊm′ʃvaɪfɪç] *adj* round-about

um′schwenken *intr* wheel around; (fig) change one's mind

Um′schwung *m* change; (*Drehung*) revolution; (*Umkehrung*) reversal; (*der Gesinnung*) revulsion

umse′geln *tr* sail around; (*Kap*) double

Umse′gelung *f* (–;–en) circumnavigation

um′sehen §138 *ref* (*nach*) look around (for); (fig) (*nach*) look out (for)

um′sein §139 *intr* (SEIN) (*Zeit*) be up; (*Ferien*) be over

um′setzen *tr* shift; transplant; (*Nährstoffe*) assimilate; (*Schüler*) switch around; (*Ware*) sell; (*verwandeln*) convert; (mus) transpose; **Geld u. in** (*acc*) spend money on; **in die Tat u.** translate into action ‖ *ref*—**sich u. in** (*acc*) (biochem) be converted into

Um′sicht *f* (–;) circumspection

umsichtig [′ʊmzɪçtɪç] *adj* circumspect

um′siedeln *tr* & *intr* (SEIN) resettle

Um′siedlung *f* (–;–en) resettlement

umsonst′ *adv* for nothing, gratis; (*vergebens*) in vain

um′spannen *tr* (*Wagenpferde*) change; (elec) transform ‖ **umspan′nen** *tr* span; encompass; include

Um′spanner *m* (–s;–) (elec) transformer

um′springen §142 *intr* (SEIN) (*Wind*) shift; **mit j-m rücksichtslos u.** (coll) treat s.o. thoughtlessly

Um′stand *m* circumstance; factor; fact; (*Einzelheit*) detail; (*Aufheben*) fuss; **in anderen Umständen** (coll) pregnant; **sich** [*dat*] **Umstände machen** go to the trouble; **Umstände machen** be formal; **unter Umständen** under certain conditions

umständehalber [′ʊm/tendəhalbər] *adv* owing to circumstances

umständlich [′ʊm/tentlɪç] *adj* detailed; (*förmlich*) formal; (*zu genau*) fussy; (*verwickelt*) complicated; (*Erzählung*) long-winded, round-about

Um′standskleid *n* maternity dress

Um′standskrämer *m* fusspot

Um′standswort *n* (–[e]s;–er) adverb

um′stehend *adj* (*Seite*) next ‖ **Umstehende** §5 *mf* bystander

Um′steige(fahr)karte *f* transfer

um′steigen §148 *intr* (SEIN) transfer

um′stellen *tr* put into a different place, shift; (*Möbel*) rearrange; (*auf acc*) convert (to) ‖ *ref* (*auf acc*) adjust (to) ‖ **umstel′len** *tr* surround

Um′stellung *f* (–;–en) change of position, shift; conversion; readjustment

um′stimmen *tr* tune to another pitch; make (*s.o.*) change his mind

um′stoßen §150 *tr* knock down; (*Pläne*) upset; (*Vertrag*) annul; (*Urteil*) reverse

umstricken (umstrik′ken) *tr* ensnare

umstritten [ʊm′ʃtrɪtən] *adj* contested; controversial

Um′sturz *m* overthrow

um′stürzen *tr* overturn; overthrow; (*Mauer*) tear down; (*Plan*) change, throw out ‖ *intr* (SEIN) fall down

Umstürzler **-in** [′ʊm/tyrtslər(ɪn)] §6 *mf* revolutionary, subversive

umstürzlerisch [′ʊm/tyrtslərɪʃ] *adj* revolutionary; subversive

Um′tausch *m* exchange

um′tauschen *tr* (gegen) exchange (for)

um′tun §154 *tr* (*Kleider*) put on ‖ *ref* —**sich u. nach** look around for

um′wälzen *tr* roll around; (fig) revolutionize ‖ *ref* roll around

umwäl′zend *adj* revolutionary

Umwäl′zung *f* (–;–en) revolution

umwandelbar ['ʊmvandəlbar] *adj* (com) convertible

um'wandeln *tr* change; (elec, fin) convert; (jur) commute

Um'wandlung *f* (-;-en) change; (elec, fin) conversion; (jur) commutation

um'wechseln *tr* exchange; (fin) convert

Um'weg *m* detour; **auf Umwegen** indirectly

um'wehen *tr* knock down || **umwe'hen** *tr* blow around

Um'welt *f* environment

Um'weltverschmutzung *f* ecological pollution

um'wenden §140 *tr* turn over || *ref* & *intr* turn around

umwer'ben §149 *tr* court, go with

um'werfen §160 *tr* throw down; upset; (*Plan*) ruin; (*Kleider*) throw about one's shoulders

umwickeln (umwik'keln) *tr* (*mit Band*) tape

umwin'den *tr* wreathe

umwölken [ʊm'vœlkən] *ref* & *intr* cloud over

umzäunen [ʊm'tsɔɪnən] *tr* fence in

um'ziehen §163 *tr* change one's clothes || *intr* (SEIN) move || **umzie'hen** §163 *ref*—**der Himmel hat sich umzogen** the sky has become overcast

umzingeln [ʊm'tsɪŋəln] *tr* encircle

Um'zug *m* procession, parade; (*Wohnungswechsel*) moving; (pol) march

un- [ʊn] *comb.fm.* un-, in-, ir-, non-

unabän'derlich *adj* unalterable

un'abhängig *adj* (von) independent (of) || **Unabhängige** §5 *mf* (pol) independent

Un'abhängigkeit *f* independence

unabkömm'lich *adj* unavailable; indispensable; (mil) essential (*on the homefront*); **ich bin augenblicklich u.** I can't get away at the moment

unabläs'sig ['ʊnaplɛsɪç] *adj* incessant

unablös'bar [ʊnap'løsbar], **unablöslich** [ʊnap'løslɪç] *adj* unpayable

unabseh'bar *adj* unforeseeable; immense

unabsetz'bar *adj* irremovable

unabsicht'lich *adj* unintentional

unabwendbar [ʊnap'vɛntbar] *adj* inevitable

un'achtsam *adj* careless, inattentive

um'ähnlich *adj* dissimilar, unlike

unanfecht'bar *adj* indisputable

un'angebracht *adj* out of place

un'angefochten *adj* undisputed

un'angemessen *adj* improper; inadequate; unsuitable

un'angenehm *adj* unpleasant, disagreeable; awkward

un'annehmbar *adj* unacceptable

Un'annehmlichkeit *f* unpleasantness; annoyance, inconvenience; **Unannehmlichkeiten** trouble

un'ansehnlich *adj* unsightly; (*unscheinbar*) plain, inconspicuous

un'anständig *adj* indecent; obscene

un'antastbar *adj* unassailable

un'appetitlich *adj* unappetizing; (*ekelhaft*) unsavory

Un'art *f* bad habit; (*Ungezogenheit*)

naughtiness; (*schlechte Manieren*) bad manners

un'artig *adj* ill-behaved, naughty

un'aufdringlich *adj* unostentatious; unobtrusive

un'auffällig *adj* inconspicuous

unauffindbar ['ʊnauffɪntbar] *adj* not to be found

unaufgefordert ['ʊnaufgəfordərt] *adj* unasked, uncalled for || *adv* spontaneously

unaufhaltbar ['ʊnaufhaltbar], **unaufhaltsam** ['ʊnaufhaltzam] *adj* irresistible; relentless

unaufhörlich ['ʊnaufhørlɪç] *adj* incessant

un'aufmerksam *adj* inattentive

un'aufrichtig *adj* insincere

unaufschiebbar ['ʊnauf'ʃipbar] *adj* not to be postponed, urgent

unausbleiblich ['ʊnausblaɪplɪç] *adj* inevitable

unausführbar ['ʊnausfyrbar] *adj* unfeasible, impracticable

unausgeglichen ['ʊnausgəglɪçən] *adj* uneven; (fig) unbalanced

unauslöschbar ['ʊnauslœ/bar], **unauslöschlich** ['ʊnauslœ/lɪç] *adj* inextinguishable; (*Tinte*) indelible

unaussprechlich ['ʊnaus/prɛçlɪç] *adj* unspeakable, ineffable

unausstehlich ['ʊnaus/teliç] *adj* intolerable, insufferable

unbändig ['ʊnbendɪç] *adj* wild

un'barmherzig *adj* unmerciful

un'beabsichtigt *adj* unintentional

un'beachtet *adj* unobserved, unnoticed

unbeanstandet ['ʊnbə-an/tandət] *adj* unopposed, unhampered

unbearbeitet ['ʊnbə-arbaɪtət] *adj* unworked; (*roh*) raw; (*Land*) untilled; (mach) unfinished

unbebaut ['ʊnbəbaʊt] *adj* uncultivated; (*Gelände*) undeveloped

unbedacht ['ʊnbədaxt] *adj* thoughtless

un'bedenklich *adj* unhesitating; unswerving; unobjectionable, harmless || *adv* without hesitation

un'bedeutend *adj* unimportant; slight

un'bedingt *adj* unconditional, unqualified; implicit

un'befahrbar *adj* impassable

un'befangen *adj* unembarrassed; (*unparteiisch*) impartial; natural, unaffected

unbefleckt ['ʊnbəflɛkt] *adj* immaculate

un'befriedigend *adj* unsatisfactory

un'befriedigt *adj* unsatisfied

un'befugt *adj* unauthorized; (jur) incompetent || **Unbefugte** §5 *mf* unauthorized person

un'begabt *adj* untalented

unbegreif'lich *adj* incomprehensible

un'begrenzt *adj* unlimited

un'begründet *adj* unfounded

Un'behagen *n* discomfort, uneasiness

un'behaglich *adj* uncomfortable

unbehelligt ['ʊnbəhɛlɪçt] *adj* undisturbed, unmolested

unbehindert ['ʊnbəhɪndərt] *adj* unhindered; unrestrained

unbeholfen ['ʊnbəhɔlfən] *adj* clumsy

unbeirrbar ['ʊnbə·ɪrbɑr] *adj* unwavering

unbeirrt ['ʊnbə·ɪrt] *adj* unswerving

un'bekannt *adj* unknown; unfamiliar; unacquainted; (*Ursache*) unexplained ‖ **Unbekannte §5** *m f* stranger ‖ *f* (math) unknown quantity

unbekümmert ['ʊnbəkʏmərt] *adj* (**um**) unconcerned (about)

un'beladen *adj* unloaded

unbelastet ['ʊnbəlɑstət] *adj* unencumbered; (*Wagen*) unloaded; carefree

un'belebt *adj* inanimate; (*Straße*) quiet; (com) slack

unbelichtet ['ʊnbəlɪçtət] *adj* (*Film*) unexposed

un'beliebt *adj* unpopular, disliked

unbemannt ['ʊnbəmant] *adj* unmanned

un'bemerkbar *adj* imperceptible

un'bemittelt *adj* poor

un'benommen *adj*—**es bleibt Ihnen u. zu** (*inf*) you are free to (*inf*); **es ist mir u., ob** it's up to me whether

unbenutzbar ['ʊnbənutsbɑr] *adj* unusable

unbenutzt ['ʊnbənutst] *adj* unused

un'bequem *adj* inconvenient; uncomfortable

unberechenbar ['ʊnbəreçənbɑr] *adj* incalculable; unpredictable

un'berechtigt *adj* unauthorized; unjustified

unbeschadet ['ʊnbəʃɑdət] *prep* (*genit*) without prejudice to

unbeschädigt ['ʊnbəʃedɪçt] *adj* unhurt; undamaged

un'bescheiden *adj* pushy

unbescholten ['ʊnbəʃɔltən] *adj* of good reputation

un'beschränkt *adj* unlimited; absolute

unbeschreiblich ['ʊnbəʃraɪplɪç] *adj* indescribable

unbesehen ['ʊnbəze·ən] *adv* sight unseen

un'besetzt *adj* unoccupied, vacant

unbesiegbar ['ʊnbəzikbɑr] *adj* invincible

unbesoldet ['ʊnbəzɔldət] *adj* unsalaried

un'besonnen *adj* thoughtless; careless; rash

un'besorgt *adj* unconcerned; carefree

un'beständig *adj* unsteady, inconstant; (*Preise*) fluctuating; (*Wetter*) changeable; (*Person*) fickle, unstable

unbestätigt ['ʊnbəʃtetɪçt] *adj* unconfirmed

un'bestechlich *adj* incorruptible

un'bestimmt *adj* indeterminate; vague; (*unsicher*) uncertain; (*unentschieden*) undecided; (gram) indefinite

unbestraft ['ʊnbəʃtraft] *adj* unpunished

unbestreit'bar *adj* indisputable

unbestritten ['ʊnbəʃtrɪtən] *adj* undisputed, uncontested

unbeteiligt ['ʊnbətaɪlɪçt] *adj* uninterested; indifferent; impartial

un'beträchtlich *adj* trifling, slight

unbeugsam ['ʊnbɔɪkzam] *adj* inflexible

unbewacht ['ʊnbəvaxt] *adj* unguarded

unbewaffnet ['ʊnbəvafnət] *adj* unarmed; (*Auge*) naked

un'beweglich *adj* immovable; motionless

unbewiesen ['ʊnbəvizən] *adj* unproved

unbewohnt ['ʊnbəvont] *adj* uninhabited

un'bewußt *adj* unconscious; involuntary

unbezähmbar [ʊnbə'tsembɑr] *adj* untamable; (fig) uncontrollable

Un'bilden *pl*—**U. der Witterung** inclement weather

Un'bildung *f* lack of education

un'billig *adj* unfair

unbotmäßig ['ʊnbotmesɪç] *adj* unruly; insubordinate

unbrauch'bar *adj* useless, of no use

un'bußfertig *adj* unrepentant

un'christlich *adj* unchristian

und [ʊnt] *conj* and; **und?** so what? **und wenn** even if

Un'dank *m* ingratitude

un'dankbar *adj* ungrateful; thankless

Un'dankbarkeit *f* ingratitude

undatiert ['ʊndatirt] *adj* undated

undenk'bar *adj* unthinkable

undenklich [ʊn'deŋklɪç] *adj*—**seit undenklichen Zeiten** from time immemorial

un'deutlich *adj* unclear, indistinct

un'deutsch *adj* un-German

un'dicht *adj* not tight; leaky

Un'ding *n* nonsense, absurdity

un'duldsam *adj* intolerant

undurchdring'lich *adj* (**für**) impervious (to); **undurchdringliche Miene** poker face

undurchführ'bar *adj* not feasible

un'durchlässig *adj* (**für**) impervious (to)

un'durchsichtig *adj* opaque; (*Beweggründe*) hidden; (*Machenschaften*) shady

un'eben *adj* uneven; bumpy; **nicht u.!** (coll) not bad!

un'echt *adj* false, spurious; artificial, imitation; (*Farbe*) fading

un'edel *adj* ignoble; (*Metall*) base

un'ehelich *adj* illegitimate

Un'ehre *f* dishonor

un'ehrenhaft *adj* dishonorable

un'ehrerbietig *adj* disrespectful

un'ehrlich *adj* dishonest; underhand

un'eigennützig *adj* unselfish

un'einig *adj* disunited; at odds

Un'einigkeit *f* disagreement

uneinnehm'bar *adj* impregnable

un'eins *adj* at odds, at variance

un'empfänglich *adj* (**für**) insusceptible (to)

un'empfindlich *adj* (**gegen**) insensitive (to); (gegen) insensible (to)

unend'lich *adj* endless; infinite; **auf u. einstellen** (phot) set at infinity ‖ *adv* endlessly; infinitely; **u. viele** an endless number of

unentbehr'lich *adj* indispensible

unentrinnbar [ʊnent'rɪnbɑr] *adj* inescapable

un'entschieden *adj* undecided; (*schwankend*) indecisive; (sport) tie ‖ **Unentschieden** *n* (-s;-) (sport) tie

Un'entschiedenheit *f* indecision

un'entschlossen *adj* irresolute

Un'entschlossenheit *f* indecision
unentschuld'bar *adj* inexcusable
unentwegt ['ʊnɛntvekt] *adj* staunch; unswerving ‖ *adv* continuously; untiringly ‖ Unentwegte §5 *mf* die-hard
unentwirrbar ['ʊnɛntvɪrbar] *adj* inextricable
unerbittlich [ʊnɛr'bɪtlɪç] *adj* inexorable; (*Tatsache*) hard
un'erfahren *adj* inexperienced
unerfindlich [ʊnɛr'fɪntlɪç] *adj* incomprehensible, mysterious
unerforschlich [ʊnɛr'fɔrʃlɪç] *adj* inscrutable
unerfreulich ['ʊnɛrfrɔɪlɪç] *adj* unpleasant
unerfüllbar [ʊnɛr'fʏlbar] *adj* unattainable
un'ergiebig *adj* unproductive
un'ergründlich *adj* unfathomable
un'erheblich *adj* insignificant; (für) irrelevant (to)
unerhört [ʊnɛr'høːrt] *adj* unheard-of, unprecedented; outrageous ‖ un'erhört *adj* (*Bitte*) unanswered
un'erkannt *adj* unrecognized ‖ *adv* incognito
unerklär'lich *adj* inexplicable
unerläßlich [ʊnɛr'lɛslɪç] *adj* indispensable
un'erlaubt *adj* illicit, unauthorized
un'erledigt *adj* unsettled, unfinished
unermeßlich [ʊnɛr'mɛslɪç] *adj* immense
unermüdlich [ʊnɛr'myːdlɪç] *adj* untiring; (*Person*) indefatigable
unerquicklich [ʊnɛr'kvɪklɪç] *adj* unpleasant
unerreich'bar *adj* unattainable, out of reach
unerreicht ['ʊnɛrraɪçt] *adj* unrivaled
unersättlich [ʊnɛr'zɛtlɪç] *adj* insatiable
unerschlossen ['ʊnɛrʃlɔsən] *adj* undeveloped; (*Boden*) unexploited
unerschöpflich [ʊnɛr'ʃøpflɪç] *adj* inhaustible
unerschrocken ['ʊnɛrʃrɔkən] *adj* intrepid, fearless
unerschütterlich [ʊnɛr'ʃʏtɛrlɪç] *adj* unshakable; imperturbable
unerschwing'lich *adj* unattainable; beyond one's means; exorbitant
unersetz'bar, unersetz'lich *adj* irreplaceable; (*Schaden*) irreparable
unerträg'lich *adj* intolerable
unerwähnt ['ʊnɛrvɛnt] *adj* unmentioned; u. lassen pass over in silence
unerwartet ['ʊnɛrvartət] *adj* unexpected, sudden
unerweis'lich *adj* unprovable
un'erwünscht *adj* undesired; unwelcome
unerzogen ['ʊnɛrtsogən] *adj* ill-bred
un'fähig *adj* incapable, unable; unqualified, inefficient
Un'fähigkeit *f* inability; inefficiency
Un'fall *m* accident, mishap
Un'fallflucht *f* hit-and-run offense
Un'fallstation *f* first-aid station
Un'falltod *m* accidental death
Un'fallversicherung *f* accident insurance
Un'fallziffer *m* accident rate

unfaß'bar, unfaß'lich *adj* incomprehensible; inconceivable
unfehl'bar *adj* infallible; unfailing
Unfehl'barkeit *f* infallibility
un'fein *adj* coarse; indelicate
un'fern *adj* near; u. von not far from ‖ *prep* (*genit*) not far from
un'fertig *adj* not ready; not finished; immature
Unflat ['ʊnflat] *m* (-s;) dirt, filth
unflätig ['ʊnflɛtɪç] *adj* dirty, filthy
un'folgsam *adj* disobedient
Un'folgsamkeit *f* disobedience
unförmig ['ʊnfœrmɪç] *adj* shapeless
un'förmlich *adj* informal
unfrankiert ['ʊnfraŋkirt] *adj* unfranked, unstamped
un'frei *adj* not free; unstamped ‖ *adv* —u. schicken send c.o.d.
un'freiwillig *adj* involuntary
un'freundlich *adj* unfriendly, unkind
Un'friede *m* dissension, discord
un'fruchtbar *adj* unfruitful, sterile; (fig) fruitless
Unfug ['ʊnfuk] *m* (-[e]s;) nuisance, disturbance; mischief; misdemeanor; U. treiben cause mischief
ungang'bar *adj* impassable; unsalable
Ungar ['ʊngar] *m* (-s;-n), Ungarin ['ʊngarɪn] *f* (-;-nen) Hungarian
ungarisch ['ʊngarɪʃ] *adj* Hungarian
Ungarn ['ʊngarn] *n* (-s;) Hungary
un'gastlich *adj* inhospitable
ungeachtet ['ʊngə'axtət] *adj* not esteemed ‖ *prep* (*genit*) regardless of
ungeahnt ['ʊngə'ant] *adj* unexpected
ungebärdig ['ʊngəbɛrdɪç] *adj* unruly
ungebeten ['ʊngəbetən] *adj* unbidden
ungebeugt ['ʊngəbɔɪkt] *adj* unbowed; (gram) uninflected
un'gebildet *adj* uneducated
un'gebräuchlich *adj* unusual; (veraltet) obsolete
un'gebraucht *adj* unused
Un'gebühr *f* indecency, impropriety
un'gebührlich *adj* indecent, improper
ungebunden ['ʊngəbʊndən] *adj* unbound; (ausschweifend) loose, dissolute; (frei) unrestrained; ungebundene Rede prose
ungedeckt ['ʊngədɛkt] *adj* uncovered; (Tisch) unset; (Haus) roofless; (Kosten) unpaid; (Scheck) overdrawn
Un'geduld *f* impatience
un'geduldig *adj* impatient
un'geeignet *adj* unfit, unsuitable; unqualified
ungefähr ['ʊngɛfɛr] *adj* approximate ‖ *adv* approximately, about; nicht von u. on purpose
ungefährdet ['ʊngɛfɛrdət] *adj* safe, unendangered
un'gefährlich *adj* not dangerous
un'gefällig *adj* discourteous
un'gefüge *adj* monstrous; clumsy
un'gefügig *adj* unyielding, inflexible
ungefüttert ['ʊngɛfʏtərt] *adj* unlined
un'gehalten *adj* (Versprechen) unkept, broken; (über acc) indignant (at)
ungeheißen ['ʊngəhaɪsən] *adv* of one's own accord
ungehemmt ['ʊngəhemt] *adj* unchecked

ungeheuer ['ungəhɔɪ.ər] *adj* huge; monstrous ‖ *adv* tremendously ‖ **Ungeheuer** *n* (-s;-) monster

un'geheuerlich *adj* monstrous ‖ *adv* (coll) tremendously

ungehobelt ['ungəhobəlt] *adj* unplaned; (fig) uncouth

un'gehörig *adj* improper; (*Stunde*) ungodly

Un'gehörigkeit *f* (-;-en) impropriety

un'gehorsam *adj* disobedient ‖ **Ungehorsam** *m* (-s;) disobedience

un'gekünstelt *adj* unaffected, natural

un'gekürzt *adj* unabridged

un'gelegen *adj* inconvenient

Un'gelegenheiten *pl* inconvenience

un'gelehrig *adj* unteachable

un'gelenk *adj* clumsy; stiff

un'gelernt *adj* (coll) unskilled

Un'gemach *n* discomfort; trouble

un'gemein *adj* uncommon

un'gemütlich *adj* uncomfortable; (*Zimmer*) dreary; (*Person*) disagreeable

un'genannt *adj* anonymous

un'genau *adj* inaccurate, inexact

ungeniert ['ʊnʒenirt] *adj* informal ‖ *adv* freely

ungenieß'bar *adj* inedible; undrinkable; (& fig) unpalatable

un'genügend *adj* insufficient; **u. bekommen** get a failing grade

ungepflastert ['ungəpflastərt] *adj* unpaved, dirt

un'gerade *adj* uneven; crooked; (*Zahl*) odd

un'geraten *adj* spoiled

un'gerecht *adj* unjust, unfair

Un'gerechtigkeit *f* injustice

ungereimt ['ungəraɪmt] *adj* unrhymed; (*unvernünft*) absurd; **ungereimtes Zeug reden** talk nonsense

un'gern *adv* unwillingly, reluctantly

ungerührt ['ungəryrt] *adj* (fig) unmoved

un'geschehen *adj* undone; **u. machen** undo

ungescheut ['ungəʃɔɪt] *adv* without fear

Un'geschick *n*, **Un'geschicklichkkeit** *f* awkwardness

un'geschickt *adj* awkward, clumsy

ungeschlacht ['ungəʃlaxt] *adj* uncouth

ungeschliffen ['ungəʃlɪfən] *adj* unpolished; (*Messer*) blunt; (*Edelstein*) uncut; (fig) rude

un'geschminkt ['ungəʃmɪŋkt] *adj* without makeup; (*Wahrheit*) unvarnished

un'gesellig *adj* unsociable

un'gesetzlich *adj* illegal

ungesittet ['ungəzɪtət] *adj* unmannerly; uncivilized

ungestört ['ungəʃtørt] *adj* undisturbed

ungestraft ['ungəʃtraft] *adj* unpunished ‖ *adv* scot-free

ungestüm ['ungəʃtym] *adj* impetuous, violent ‖ **Ungestüm** *n* (-[e]s;) impetuosity, violence

un'gesund *adj* unhealthy; unwholesome

ungeteilt ['ungətaɪlt] *adj* undivided

un'getreu *adj* disloyal, untrue

ungetrübt ['ungətrypt] *adj* cloudless; clear; (fig) untroubled

Ungetüm ['ungətym] *n* (-[e]s;-e) monster

ungeübt ['ungə.ypt] *adj* untrained; (*Arbeiter*) inexperienced

un'gewandt *adj* unskillful; clumsy

un'gewiß *adj* uncertain; **j-n im ungewissen lassen** keep s.o. in suspense

Un'gewißheit *f* uncertainty

Un'gewitter *n* storm

un'gewöhnlich *adj* unusual

un'gewohnt *adj* unusual; (*genit*) unaccustomed (to)

ungezählt ['ungətselt] *adj* countless

Ungeziefer ['ungətsifər] *n* (-s;) vermin, bugs

ungeziemend ['ungətsimənt] *adj* improper; (*frech*) impudent

un'gezogen *adj* rude; naughty

ungezügelt ['ungətsygəlt] *adj* unbridled

un'gezwungen *adj* unforced; natural, easy-going

Un'glaube *m* disbelief, unbelief

un'gläubig *adj* incredulous; (*heidnisch*) infidel ‖ **Ungläubige** §5 *mf* infidel

unglaub'lich *adj* incredible

un'glaubwürdig *adj* untrustworthy; incredible

un'gleich *adj* uneven, unequal; (*unähnlich*) unlike, dissimilar; (*Zahl*) odd ‖ *adv* much, far, by far

un'gleichartig *adj* heterogeneous

un'gleichförmig *adj* unequal; irregular

Un'gleichheit *f* inequality; difference, dissimilarity; unevenness

un'gleichmäßig *adj* disproportionate

Unglimpf ['unglɪmpf] *m* (-[e]s;-e) harshness; wrong, insult

un'glimpflich *adj* harsh

Un'glück *n* (-s;) bad luck; (*Unfall*) accident; disaster, calamity

un'glücklich *adj* unlucky; unfortunate; unhappy

un'glücklicherweise *adv* unfortunately

Un'glücksbote *m* bearer of bad news

Un'glücksbringer *m* (-s;-) jinx

un'glückselig *adj* miserable; disastrous

Un'glücksfall *m* accident, misfortune

Un'glücksmensch *m* unlucky person

Un'glücksrabe *m*, **Un'glücksvogel** *m* unlucky fellow

Un'gnade *f* (-;) disfavor, displeasure

un'gnädig *adj* ungracious; **etw u. aufnehmen** take s.th. amiss

un'gültig *adj* null and void, invalid; **für u. erklären** nullify, void

Un'gültigkeit *f* invalidity

Un'gültigkeitserklärung *f* annulment

Un'gunst *f* disfavor; **zu meinen Ungunsten** to my disadvantage

un'günstig *adj* unfavorable, bad, adverse

un'gut *adj* unkind; **nichts für u.!** no offense!; **ungutes Gefühl** misgivings

un'haltbar *adj* not durable; untenable

un'handlich *adj* unwieldy, unhandy

Un'heil *n* disaster; mischief; **U. anrichten** cause mischief; **U. heraufbeschwören** ask for trouble

unheil'bar *adj* incurable; irreparable

un'heilvoll *adj* ominous; disastrous

un'heimlich *adj* uncanny; sinister

un'höflich *adj* impolite, uncivil

Un'höflichkeit *f* impoliteness
un'hold *adj* unkind || Unhold *m* (-[e]s; -e) fiend
un'hörbar *adj* inaudible
un'hygienisch *adj* unsanitary
Uni ['uni] *f* (-;-s) (Universität) (coll) university
uniform [uni'form] *adj* uniform || Uniform *f* (;-en) uniform
Uni·kum ['unikum] *n* (-s;-s & -ka [ka]) unique example; (coll) queer duck
un'interessant *adj* uninteresting
un'interessiert *adj* (an *dat*) uninterested (in)
Union [un'jon] *f* (-;-en) union
universal [univer'zal] *adj* universal
Universal'mittel *n* panacea, cure-all
Universal'schlüssel *m* monkey wrench
Universität [universi'tet] *f* (-;-en) university
Universitäts'auswahlmannschaft *f* varsity (team)
Universum [uni'verzum] *n* (-s;) universe
Unke ['unkə] *f* (-;-n) toad
unken ['unkən] *intr* (coll) be a prophet of doom
un'kenntlich *adj* unrecognizable; u. machen disguise
Un'kenntnis *f* (-;) ignorance
Un'kenruf *m* croak
un'keusch *adj* unchaste
un'kindlich *adj* precocious; (*Verhalten*) disrespectful
un'kirchlich *adj* secular, worldly
un'klar *adj* unclear; muddy; misty; im unklaren sein über (*acc*) be in the dark about
Un'klarheit *f* obscurity
un'kleidsam *adj* unbecoming
un'klug *adj* unwise, imprudent
Un'klugheit *f* imprudence; foolish act
un'kontrollierbar *adj* unverifiable
un'körperlich *adj* incorporeal
Un'kosten *pl* expenses, costs; overhead; sich in U. stürzen go to great expense
Un'kraut *n* weed, weeds; U. jäten pull weeds
Un'krautvertilgungsmittel *n* weed killer
un'kündbar *adj* binding; (*Darlehen*) irredeemable; (*Stellung*) permanent
un'kundig *adj* (*genit*) ignorant (of), unacquainted (with)
unlängst ['unleŋst] *adv* recently, the other day
un'lauter *adj* unfair
un'leidlich *adj* intolerable
un'lenksam *adj* unruly
unles'bar, unle'serlich *adj* illegible
unleugbar ['unlɔrkbar] *adj* indisputable, undeniable
un'lieb *adj* disagreeable; es ist mir u. I am sorry
un'logisch *adj* illogical
unlös'bar *adj* (*Problem*) unsolvable; (*untrennbar*) inseparable; (chem) insoluble
unlös'lich *adj* (chem) insoluble
Un'lust *f* reluctance; listlessness
un'lustig *adj* reluctant; listless

un'manierlich *adj* impolite
un'männlich *adj* unmanly
Un'maß *n* excess; im U. to excess
Un'masse *f* (coll) vast amount, lots
un'maßgeblich *adj* unauthoritative; irrelevant; nach meiner unmaßgeblichen Meinung in my humble opinion
un'mäßig *adj* immoderate; excessive
Un'menge *f* (coll)—e e U. von lots of
Un'mensch *m* brute, monster
un'menschlich *adj* inhuman, brutal
Un'menschlichkeit *f* brutality
un'merklich *adj* imperceptible
un'methodisch *adj* unmethodical
un'mißverständlich *adj* unmistakable
un'mittelbar *adj* direct, immediate
un'möbliert *adj* unfurnished
un'modern *adj* outmoded
un'möglich, unmög'lich *adj* impossible
Un'möglichkeit *f* impossibility
Un'moral *f* immorality
un'moralisch *adj* immoral
un'mündig *adj* underage
un'musikalisch *adj* unmusical
Un'mut *m* (über *acc*) displeasure (at)
un'mutig *adj* displeased, annoyed
unnachahmlich ['unnaxamlıç] *adj* inimitable
un'nachgiebig *adj* unyielding
un'nachsichtig *adj* unrelenting, inexorable; strict
unnahbar [un'nabar] *adj* inaccessible
un'natürlich *adj* unnatural
un'nennbar *adj* inexpressible
un'nötig *adj* unnecessary
unnütz ['unnyts] *adj* useless; vain
un'ordentlich *adj* disorderly; untidy
Un'ordnung *f* disorder; mess; in U. bringen throw into disorder
un'organisch *adj* inorganic
un'paar, un'paarig *adj* unpaired, odd
un'parteiisch, un'parteilich *adj* impartial, disinterested
Un'parteilichkeit *f* impartiality
un'passend *adj* unsuitable; (*unschicklich*) improper; (*unzeitgemäß*) untimely
un'passierbar *adj* impassable
unpäßlich ['unpeslıç] *adj* indisposed, ill
un'patriotisch *adj* unpatriotic
un'persönlich *adj* impersonal
un'politisch *adj* nonpolitical
un'populär *adj* unpopular
un'praktisch *adj* impractical; (*unerfahren*) unskillful
Un'rast *f* restlessness
Un'rat *m* (-[e]s;) garbage; dirt; U. wittern (coll) smell a rat
un'rätlich, un'ratsam *adj* inadvisable
un'recht *adj* wrong || Unrecht *n* (-[e]s;) —im U. sein be in the wrong; j—m U. geben decide against s.o.; mit (or zu) U. wrongly; unjustly; illegally
un'redlich *adj* dishonest
Un'redlichkeit *f* dishonesty
un'reell *adj* unfair
un'regelmäßig *adj* irregular
Un'regelmäßigkeit *f* irregularity
un'reif *adj* unripe, green; (fig) immature
Un'reife *f* unripeness; immaturity
un'rein *adj* unclean; (& fig) impure;

ins u. schreiben make a rough copy of

un'reinheit f uncleanness; (& fig) impurity

un'reinlich adj dirty

un'rentabel adj unprofitable

un'rettbar adj irrecoverable

un'richtig adj incorrect, wrong

un'ritterlich adj unchivalrous

Un'ruh f (-;-en) (horol) balance wheel

Un'ruhe f restlessness; uneasiness; (Aufruhr) commotion, riot; (Störung) disturbance; (Besorgnis) anxiety

un'ruhig adj restless; uneasy; (laut) noisy; (Pferd) restive; (Meer) choppy; (nervös) jumpy

un'rühmlich adj inglorious

Un'ruhstifter –in §6 mf agitator, troublemaker; (Wirrkopf) screwball

uns [uns] pers pron us; to us || reflex pron ourselves; wir sind doch unter uns we are by ourselves || recip pron each other, one another; wir sehen uns später we'll meet later

un'sachgemäß adj inexpert

un'sachlich adj subjective; personal

unsagbar [un'zakbar], unsäglich [un-'zeːklɪç] adj unspeakable; (fig) immense

un'sauber adj unclean; (unlauter) unfair, dirty

un'schädlich adj harmless

un'scharf adj (Apparat) out of focus; (Bild) blurred; (Begriff) poorly defined

un'schätzbar adj inestimable, invaluable

un'scheinbar adj inconspicuous, insignificant

un'schicklich adj unbecoming; indecent

Un'schicklichkeit f impropriety

un'schlüssig adj indecisive

Un'schlüssigkeit f indecision, hesitation

un'schmackhaft adj insipid, unpalatable

un'schön adj unlovely; plain, homely; (Angelegenheit) unpleasant

Un'schuld f innocence; ich wasche meine Hände in U. I wash my hands of it

un'schuldig adj innocent; (keusch) chaste; harmless; sich für u. erklären (jur) plead not guilty

un'schwer adj not difficult

Un'segen m adversity; (Fluch) curse

un'selbständig adj dependent, helpless

un'selig adj unfortunate; (Ereignis) fatal

unser ['unzər] §2,3 poss adj our || §2,4 poss pron ours || pers pron us; of us; erinnerst du dich unser noch? do you still remember us?; es waren unser vier there were four of us

unseresgleichen ['unzərəs'glaɪçən] pron people like us; the likes of us

unserige ['unzərɪgə] §2,5 pron ours

unserthalben ['unzərt'halbən], unsertwegen ['unzərt'veːgən] adv for our sake, on our behalf, on our account

un'sicher adj unsafe; shaky; precarious

Un'sicherheit f unsafeness; shakiness; insecurity; precariousness

un'sichtbar adj invisible

Un'sinn m (-[e]s;) nonsense, rubbish; U. machen fool around

un'sinnig adj nonsensical

Un'sitte f bad habit

un'sittlich adj immoral, indecent

Un'sittlichkeit f immorality

un'solid(e) adj unsolid; (Person) loose; (Firma) unreliable, shaky

unsortiert ['unzɔrtirt] adj unsorted

un'sozial adj antisocial

un'sportlich adj unsportsmanlike

unsrerseits ['unzrər'zaɪts] adv as for us, for our part

unsrige ['unzrɪgə] §2,5 poss pron ours

un'ständig adj impermanent, temporary

un'statthaft adj inadmissible; forbidden

unsterb'lich adj immortal

Unsterb'lichkeit f immortality

Un'stern m unlucky star; (fig) disaster

un'stet adj unsteady; restless; changeable

un'stillbar adj unappeasable; (Durst) unquenchable; (Hunger) unsatiable

unstimmig ['un'ʃtɪmɪç] adj discrepant; inconsistent

Un'stimmigkeit f (-;-en) discrepancy; inconsistency; (Widerspruch) disagreement

un'sträflich adj blameless; guileless

un'streitig adj indisputable

Un'summe f enormous sum

un'symmetrisch adj asymmetrical

un'sympathisch adj unpleasant; er ist mir u. I don't like him

un'tadelhaft adj blameless; flawless

Un'tat f crime

un'tätig adj inactive

un'tauglich adj unfit, unsuitable; useless; (Person) incompetent; u. machen disqualify

un'teilbar adj indivisible

unten ['untən] adv below, beneath; downstairs; da u. down there; er ist bei ihnen u. durch they are through with him; nach u. downstairs; downwards; tief u. far below; u. am Berge at the foot of the mountain; u. an der Seite at the bottom of the page; von u. her from underneath

unter ['untər] prep (dat) under, below; beneath, underneath; (zwischen) among; (während) during; ganz u. uns gesagt just between you and me; u. aller Kritik beneath contempt; u. anderem among other things; u. diesem Gesichtspunkt from this point of view; u. Null below zero; was versteht man unter...? what is meant by...? || prep (acc) under, below; beneath, underneath; among || Unter m (-s;-) (cards) jack

Unter-, unter- comb.fm. under-, sub-; lower

Un'terabteilung f subdivision

Un'terarm m forearm

Un'terart f subspecies

Un'terausschuß m subcommittee

Un'terbau m (-[e]s;-ten) foundation

un'terbelichten tr underexpose
un'terbewußt adj subconscious
Un'terbewußtsein n subconscious
unterbie'ten §58 tr undercut, undersell; underbid
un'terbinden §59 tr tie underneath || **unterbin'den** §59 tr (Verkehr) tie up; (Blutgefäß) tie off; (verhindern) prevent; (Angriff) neutralize
Unterbin'dung f stoppage; (surg) ligature
unterblei'ben §62 intr (SEIN) remain undone; not take place; be discontinued; **das muß u.** that must be stopped
unterbre'chen §64 tr interrupt; (einstellen) suspend; (Schweigen, Stille, Kontakt) break; (Verkehr) hold up; (telp) disconnect; **die Reise in München u.** have a stopover in Munich || ref stop short
Unterbre'cher m (elec) circuit breaker
Unterbre'chung f interruption; disconnection; (e-r Fahrt) stopover
unterbrei'ten tr submit
un'terbringen §65 tr provide a place for; find room for; (Gäste) accommodate, put up; (Stapeln) store; (Anleihe) place; (Geld) invest; (Pferde) stable; (Wagen) park; (Truppe) billet; **e-n Artikel bei e-r Zeitung u.** have an article published in a newspaper; **j-n auf e-m Posten** (or **in e-r Stellung**) **u.** find s.o. a job, place s.o.
Un'terbringung f (–;-en) accommodations, housing; billet; storage; investment; placement
Un'terbringungsmöglichkeiten pl accommodations
unterdes [unter'des], **unterdessen** [unter'desen] adv meanwhile
Un'terdruck m low pressure
unterdrücken (unterdrük'ken) tr suppress; (Aufstand) quell; (bedrücken) oppress; (ersticken) stifle; (Seufzer) repress
Un'terdruckgebiet n low-pressure area
Unterdrückung (Unterdrük'kung) f (–;) oppression; suppression
untere ['untere] §9 adj lower, inferior
untereinan'der adv among one another; mutually; reciprocally
unterentwickelt ['unterentvikelt] adj underdeveloped
unterernährt ['unterernert] adj undernourished
Un'terernährung f (–;) undernourishment
Un'terfamilie f subfamily
unterfer'tigen tr sign
Unterfüh'rung f (–;-en) underpass
unterfüt'tern tr line
Un'tergang m setting; (fig) decline, fall; (naut) sinking
unterge'ben adj (dat) subject (to), inferior (to) || **Untergebene** §5 mf subordinate
un'tergehen §82 intr (SEIN) go down, sink; (fig) perish; (astr) set
untergeordnet ['untergeˌordnet] adj subordinate || **Untergeordnete** §5 mf subordinate

Un'tergeschoß n ground floor; (Kellergeschoß) basement
Un'tergestell n undercarriage
Un'tergewand n underwear
un'tergliedern tr subdivide
untergra'ben §87 tr undermine
Un'tergrund m subsoil
Un'tergrundbahn f subway
Un'tergrundbewegung f underground movement
un'terhalb prep (genit) below
Un'terhalt m –[-e]s;) support; maintenance, upkeep; livelihood
un'terhalten §90 tr hold under || **unterhal'ten** §90 tr maintain; support; (Briefwechsel) keep up; (Feuer) feed; entertain, amuse || ref enjoy oneself, have a good time; amuse oneself; **sich u. mit** talk with
unterhaltsam [unter'haltzam] adj entertaining, amusing, enjoyable
Un'terhaltsbeitrag m alimony; (für Kinder) support
Unterhaltsberechtigte ['unterhaltsbəˌreçtɪgtə] §5 mf dependent
Un'terhaltskosten pl living expenses
Unterhal'tung f (–;-en) entertainment, amusement; (Gespräch) conversation; (Aufrechterhaltung) upkeep; (Unterstützung) support
Unterhal'tungskosten pl maintenance cost, maintenance
Unterhal'tungslektüre f light reading
unterhan'deln intr negotiate
Un'terhändler –in §6 mf negotiator; (Vermittler) mediator
Unterhand'lung f (–;-en) negotiation
Un'terhaus n (parl) lower house
Un'terhemd n undershirt
unterhöh'len tr undermine
Un'terholz n undergrowth, underbrush
Un'terhose f shorts; panties; **in Unterhosen zeigen** (coll) debunk
un'terirdisch adj underground, subterranean; (myth) of the underworld
Un'terjacke f vest
unterjo'chen tr subjugate
Unterjo'chung f (–;) subjugation
Un'terkiefer m lower jaw
Un'terkinn n double chin
Un'terkleid n slip
Un'terkleidung f (–;) underwear
un'terkommen §99 intr (SEIN) find accommodations; find employment || **Unterkommen** n (–s;) accommodations; (Stellung) job
Un'terkörper m lower part of the body
un'terkriegen tr (coll) get the better of; **er läßt sich nicht u.** he won't knuckle under
Unterkunft ['unterkunft] f (–;-̈e) accommodations; apartment; (Obdach) shelter, place to stay; (mil) quarters; **U. und Verpflegung** room and board
Un'terlage f foundation; base; pad; desk pad;- rubber pad (for a bed); (Teppich–) underpad; (Beleg) voucher; (Urkunde) document; (archit) support; (geol) substratum; **keine Unterlagen haben** have nothing to go on; **Unterlagen** documentation; data
Un'terland n lowland

Unterlaß ['ʊntərlas] *m*—**ohne U.** without letup

unterlas'sen §104 *tr* omit; neglect; skip; stop, cut out

Unterlas'sung *f* (-;-en) omission; neglect; failure

Unterlas'sungssünde *f* sin of omission

unterlau'fen *adj*—**blau u.** black-and-blue; **mit Blut u.** bloodshot || **un'terlaufen** §105 *intr* (SEIN) (*Fehler*) slip in

un'terlegen *tr* lay under, put under; (*Bedeutung, Sinn*) attach; **der Musik Worte u.** set words to music || **unterle'gen** *adj* defeated; (*dat*) inferior (to) || **Unterlegene** §5 *mf* loser

Unterle'genheit *f* (-;) inferiority

Unterlegring ['ʊntərlekrɪŋ] *m*, **Unterlegscheibe** ['ʊntərlek/aɪbə] *f* washer

Un'terleib *m* abdomen

Unterleibs- *comb.fm.* abdominal

unterlie'gen §108 *intr* (SEIN) (*dat*) be beaten (by), lose (to); **e-m Rabatt u.** be subject to discount || *impers* (SEIN)—**es unterliegt keinem Zweifel, daß** there is no doubt that

Un'terlippe *f* lower lip

unterma'len *tr* put the primer on; **mit Musik u.** accompany with music

untermau'ern *tr* support

Un'termiete *f* (-;) subletting; **in U. abgeben** sublet; **in U. wohnen bei** sublet from

Un'termieter –**in** §6 *mf* subtenant

unterminie'ren *tr* (fig) undermine

unterneh'men §116 *tr* undertake; (*versuchen*) attempt; **Schritte u.** (fig) take steps || **Unternehmen** *n* (-s;-) undertaking; venture; enterprise; (mil) operation

unterneh'mend *adj* enterprising

Unterneh'mensberater *m* management consultant

Unterneh'mer –**in** §6 *mf* entrepreneur; (*Arbeitgeber*) employer; (*Bau-*) contractor

Unterneh'mung *f* (-;-en) undertaking; enterprise, business; (mil) operation

Unterneh'mungsgeist *m* initiative

unterneh'mungslustig *adj* enterprising

Un'teroffizier *m* noncommissioned officer, N.C.O.

un'terordnen *tr* (*dat*) subordinate (to) || *ref* (*dat*) submit (to)

unterre'den *ref* (mit) confer (with)

Unterre'dung *f* (-;-en) conference

Unterricht ['ʊntərrɪçt] *m* (-[e]s;-e) instruction, lessons

unterrich'ten *tr* instruct; **u. von** (or **über** *acc*) inform (of, about)

Un'terrichtsfach *n* subject, course

Un'terrichtsfilm *m* educational film; (mil) training film

Un'terrichtsministerium *n* department of public instruction

Un'terrichtsstunde *f* (educ) period

Un'terrichtswesen *n* education; teaching

Un'terrock *m* slip

untersa'gen *tr* forbid, prohibit

Un'tersatz *m* saucer; support; (*Gestell*) stand; (archit) socle; (log) minor premise

unterschät'zen *tr* underrate, underestimate; undervalue

unterschei'den §112 *tr* distinguish || *ref* (von) differ (from)

Unterschei'dung *f* (-;-en) difference, distinction

Un'terschenkel *m* shank

un'terschieben §130 *tr* shove under; (statt *genit*) substitute (for); (*dat*) impute (to), foist (on)

Unterschied ['ʊntər/it] *m* (-[e]s;-e) difference, distinction; **zum U. von** as distinct from, unlike

un'terschiedlich *adj* different; varying

un'terschiedslos *adj* indiscriminate

unterschla'gen §132 *tr* embezzle; (*Nachricht*) suppress; (*Brief*) intercept

Unterschla'gung *f* (-;-en) embezzlement; suppression; interception

Unterschlupf ['ʊntər/lʊpf] *m* (-[e]s;) shelter; hide-out

unterschrei'ben §62 *tr* sign; (fig) subscribe to, agree to

Un'terschrift *f* signature

Un'terseeboot *n* submarine

unterseeisch ['ʊntərze-ɪ/] *adj* submarine

Un'terseekabel *n* transoceanic cable

Un'terseite *f* underside

untersetzt [ʊntər'zetst] *adj* stocky

Un'tersetzung *f* (-;-en) (mech) reduction

un'tersinken §143 *intr* (SEIN) go down

Un'terstand *m* (mil) dugout

unterste ['ʊntərstə] §9 *adj* lowest, bottom

unterste'hen §146 *ref* dare; **untersteh dich!** don't you dare! || *intr* (*dat*) be under (*s.o.*) || **un'terstehen** §146 *intr* take shelter

un'terstellen *tr* place under; (*Auto*) put into the garage || *ref* take cover || **unterstel'len** *tr* assume, suppose; (*dat*) impute (to); (mil) (*dat*) put under the command (of)

Unterstel'lung *f* (-;-en) assumption; imputation

unterstrei'chen §85 *tr* underline

unterstüt'zen *tr* support, back; help

Unterstüt'zung *f* (-;-en) support, backing; assistance; (*Beihilfe durch Geld*) relief; (ins) benefit

untersu'chen *tr* examine, inspect; investigate; study, do research on; (chem) analyze

Untersu'chung *f* (-;-en) examination; inspection; investigation; study, research; (chem) analysis

Untersu'chungsausschuß *m* fact-finding committee

Untersu'chungsgericht *n* court of inquiry

Untersu'chungshaft *f* (jur) detention

Untersu'chungsrichter *m* examining judge

Untertagebau [ʊntər'tagəbau] *m* (-[e]s;) mine

Untertan ['ʊntərtan] *m* (-s & -en;-en) subject

untertänig [ʊntər'tenɪç] *adj* submissive

Un'tertasse *f* saucer; **fliegende U.** flying saucer

un'tertauchen *tr* submerge; duck ‖ *intr* (SEIN) dive; (fig) disappear ‖ **Untertauchen** *n* (-s;) dive; disappearance

Un'terteil *m & n* lower part, bottom

untertei'len *tr* subdivide

Untertei'lung *f* (-;-en) subdivision

Un'tertitel *m* subtitle; caption

Un'terton *m* undertone

un'tertreten §152 *intr* (SEIN) take cover

un'tervermieten *tr* sublet

Un'tervertrag *m* subcontract

unterwan'dern *tr* infiltrate

Un'terwäsche *f* underwear

Unterwasser– *comb.fm.* underwater, submarine

Un'terwasserbombe *f* depth charge

Un'terwasserhorchgerät *n* hydrophone

Un'terwasserortungsgerät *n* sonar

unterwegs [ʊntər'veks] *adv* on the way; (com) in transit

unterwei'sen §118 *tr* instruct

Unterwei'sung *f* (-;-en) instruction

Un'terwelt *f* underworld; (myth) lower world

unterwer'fen §160 *tr* subjugate; (*dat*) subject (to) ‖ *ref* (*dat*) submit to, subject oneself to; **sich** [*dat*] **ein Volk u.** subjugate a people

Unterwer'fung *f* (-;) subjugation; submission

unterworfen [ʊntər'vɔrfən] *adj* subject

unterwürfig ['ʊntərvʏrfɪç] *adj* submissive, subservient

unterzeich'nen *tr* sign

Unterzeich'ner –in §6 *mf* signer; signatory

Unterzeichnete [ʊntər'tsaɪçnətə] §5 *mf* undersigned

Unterzeich'nung *f* (-;-en) signing; signature

un'terziehen §163 *tr* put on underneath ‖ **unterzie'hen** §163 *tr* (*dat*) subject (to) ‖ *ref*—**sich der Mühe u. zu** (*inf*) take the trouble to (*inf*); **sich e-r Operation u.** have an operation; **sich e-r Prüfung u.** take an examination

un'tief *adj* shallow ‖ **Untiefe** *f* (-;-n) shoal

Un'tier *n* (*& fig*) monster

untilg'bar *adj* inextinguishable; (*Tinte*) indelible; (*Anleihe*) irredeemable

untrag'bar *adj* unbearable; (*Kleidung*) unwearable; (*Kosten*) prohibitive

untrenn'bar *adj* inseparable

un'treu *adj* unfaithful ‖ **Untreue** *f* unfaithfulness; infidelity

untröst'lich *adj* inconsolable

untrüg'lich *adj* unerring, infallible

un'tüchtig *adj* incapable; inefficient

Un'tugend *f* bad habit, vice

un'überlegt *adj* thoughtless; rash

unüberseh'bar *adj* vast, huge; incalculable ‖ *adv* very

unübersetz'bar *adj* untranslatable

un'übersichtlich *adj* unclear; (*Kurve*) blind

unübersteig'bar, unübersteig'lich *adj* insurmountable

unübertreff'lich *adj* unsurpassable

unübertroffen [ʊnybər'trɔfən] *adj* unsurpassed

unüberwind'lich *adj* invincible; (*Schwierigkeiten*) insurmountable

unumgäng'lich *adj* indispensable

unumschränkt ['ʊnʊm/rɛŋkt] *adj* unlimited; (pol) absolute

unumstößlich ['ʊnʊm/tøslɪç] *adj* irrefutable; (*unwiderruflich*) irrevocable

unumwunden ['ʊnʊmvʊndən] *adj* blunt

un'unterbrochen *adj* continuous

unverän'derlich *adj* unchangeable, invariable

unverant'wortlich *adj* irresponsible

unveräu'ßerlich *adj* inalienable

unverbesserlich [ʊnfɛr'bɛsərlɪç] *adj* incorrigible

unverbind'lich *adj* without obligation; (*Verhalten*) proper, formal; (*Antwort*) noncommittal

un'verblümt *adj* blunt, plain

unverbürgt [ʊnfɛr'bʏrkt] *adj* unwarranted; (*Nachricht*) unconfirmed

un'verdächtig *adj* unsuspected

un'verdaulich *adj* indigestible

unverderbt ['ʊnfɛrdɛrpt], **unverdorben** ['ʊnfɛrdɔrbən] *adj* unspoiled

un'verdient ['ʊnfɛrdint] *adj* undeserved

un'verdrossen *adj* indefatigable

unverdünnt ['ʊnfɛrdʏnt] *adj* undiluted

unverehelicht ['ʊnfɛrə·əlɪçt] *adj* unmarried, single

un'vereinbar *adj* incompatible; contradictory

unverfälscht ['ʊnfɛrfɛl/t] *adj* genuine; (*Wein*) undiluted

un'verfänglich *adj* innocent

un'verfroren *adj* brash

un'vergänglich *adj* imperishable

un'vergeßlich *adj* unforgettable

un'vergleichbar *adj* incomparable

unvergleichlich ['ʊnfɛrglaɪçlɪç] *adj* incomparable

un'verhältnismäßig *adj* disproportionate

un'verheiratet *adj* unmarried

un'vergolten ['ʊnfɛrgɔltən] *adj* unrewarded

unverhofft ['ʊnfɛrhoft] *adj* unhoped-for

unverhohlen ['ʊnfɛrholən] *adj* unconcealed; (fig) open

un'verkäuflich *adj* unsalable

unverkennbar ['ʊnfɛrkɛnbar] *adj* unmistakable

unverkürzt ['ʊnfɛrkʏrtst] *adj* unabridged

unverlangt ['ʊnfɛrlaŋt] *adj* unsolicited

un'verletzbar, un'verletzlich *adj* undamageable; (fig) inviolable

unverletzt ['ʊnfɛrlɛtst] *adj* safe and sound, unharmed; (*Sache*) undamaged

unvermeid'lich *adj* inevitable

unvermindert ['ʊnfɛrmɪndərt] *adj* undiminished

unvermittelt ['ʊnfɛrmɪtəlt] *adj* sudden

Un'vermögen *n* inability; impotence

un'vermögend *adj* poor; impotent

unvermutet ['ʊnfɛrmutət] *adj* unexpected

un'vernehmlich *adj* imperceptible

Un'vernunft *f* unreasonableness; folly

un'vernünftig *adj* unreasonable; foolish

un'verschämt *adj* brazen, shameless

unverschuldet ['ʊnfɛrʃʊldət] *adj* unencumbered; (*unverdient*) undeserved
un'versehens *adv* unawares, suddenly
unversehrt ['ʊnfɛrzeːrt] *adj* undamaged (*Person*) unharmed
unversichert ['ʊnfɛrziçərt] *adj* uninsured
unversiegbar [ʊnfɛr'ziːkbɑr] **unversieglich** [ʊnfɛr'ziːklɪç] *adj* inexhaustible
unversiegelt ['ʊnfɛrziːgəlt] *adj* unsealed
un'versöhnlich *adj* irreconcilable
unversorgt ['ʊnfɛrzɔrkt] *adj* unprovided for
Un'verstand *m* lack of judgment
un'verständig *adj* foolish
un'verständlich *adj* incomprehensible
unversucht ['ʊnfɛrzuːxt] *adj* untried
un'verträglich *adj* unsociable; quarrelsome; incompatible, contradictory
un'verwandt *adj* steady, unflinching
unverwelklich [ʊnfɛr'vɛlklɪç] *adj* unfading
un'verwendbar *adj* unusable
unverweslich ['ʊnfɛrveːzlɪç] *adj* incorruptible
unverwindbar [ʊnfɛr'vɪntbɑr] *adj* irreparable; (*Enttäuschung*) lasting
un'verwundbar *adj* invulnerable
unverwüstlich ['ʊnfɛrvyːstlɪç] *adj* indestructible; (*Stoff*) durable; (fig) irrepressible
unverzagt ['ʊnfɛrtsɑːkt] *adj* undaunted
un'verzeihlich *adj* unpardonable
unverzerrt ['ʊnfɛrtsɛrt] *adj* undistorted
unverzinslich ['ʊnfɛrtsɪnslɪç] *adj* (fin) without interest
unverzüglich ['ʊnfɛrtsyːklɪç] *adj* prompt, immediate || *adv* without delay
unvollendet ['ʊnfɔlɛndət] *adj* unfinished
un'vollkommen *adj* imperfect
Un'vollkommenheit *f* imperfection
un'vollständig *adj* incomplete; (gram) defective
un'vorbereitet *adj* unprepared; (*Rede*) extemporaneous || *adv* extempore
un'voreingenommen *adj* unbiased
un'vorhergesehen *adj* unforeseen
un'vorsätzlich *adj* unintentional
un'vorsichtig *adj* incautious; careless
un'vorteilhaft *adj* disadvantageous; unprofitable; (*Kleid*) unflattering
un'wahr *adj* untrue
un'wahrhaftig *adj* untruthful
Un'wahrheit *f* untruth, falsehood
un'wahrnehmbar *adj* imperceptible
un'wahrscheinlich *adj* unlikely, improbable
unwan'delbar *adj* unchangeable
unwegsam ['ʊnveːkzɑm] *adj* impassable
unweigerlich [ʊn'vaɪgərlɪç] *adj* unhesitating; (*Folge*) necessary || *adv* without fail
un'weit *adj*—**u. von** not far from || *prep* (*genit*) not far from
Un'wesen *n* mischief; **sein U. treiben** be up to one's old tricks
un'wesentlich *adj* unessential; unimportant; (für) immaterial (to)
Un'wetter *n* storm

un'wichtig *adj* unimportant
unwiederbringlich [ʊnviːdər'brɪŋlɪç] *adj* irretrievable, irreparable
unwiderleg'bar *adj* irrefutable
un'widerruf'lich *adj* irrevocable
unwidersteh'lich *adj* irresistible
Un'wille *m*, **Un'willen** *m* indignation, displeasure; reluctance
un'willig *adj* (über *acc*) indignant (at), displeased (at); **u. zu** (*inf*) reluctant to (*inf*)
un'willkommen *adj* unwelcome
un'willkürlich *adj* involuntary
un'wirklich *adj* unreal
un'wirksam *adj* ineffective; inefficient; (chem) inactive; (jur) null and void
Un'wirksamkeit *f* ineffectiveness; inefficiency; (chem) inactivity
unwirsch ['ʊnvɪrʃ] *adj* surly
un'wirtlich *adj* inhospitable
un'wirtschaftlich *adj* uneconomical
unwissend ['ʊnvɪsənt] *adj* ignorant
Unwissenheit ['ʊnvɪsənhaɪt] *f* (—;) ignorance
un'wissenschaftlich *adj* unscientific
un'wissentlich *adv* unwittingly
un'wohl *adj* sickish; **ich fühle mich u.** I don't feel well
un'wohnlich *adj* uninhabitable; (*unbehaglich*) uncomfortable
un'würdig *adj* unworthy
Un'zahl *f* (von) huge number (of)
unzähl'bar, **unzählig** [ʊn'tseːlɪç] *adj* countless, innumerable
un'zart *adj* indelicate
Unze ['ʊntsə] *f* (—;-n) ounce
Un'zeit *f* wrong time
un'zeitgemäß *adj* out-of-date
un'zeitig *adj* untimely; (*Obst*) unripe
unzerbrech'lich *adj* unbreakable
unzerstör'bar *adj* indestructible
unzertrennlich [ʊntsɛr'trɛnlɪç] *adj* inseparable
unziemend ['ʊntsiːmənt], **un'ziemlich** *adj* unbecoming, unseemly
Un'zucht *f* unchastity; lewdness
un'züchtig *adj* unchaste; lewd
un'zufrieden *adj* dissatisfied
un'zugänglich *adj* inaccessible; aloof
un'zulänglich *adj* inadequate
un'zulässig *adj* inadmissible; (*Beeinflussung, Einmischung*) undue
un'zurechnungsfähig *adj* unaccountable
un'zureichend *adj* inadequate
un'zusammenhängend *adj* incoherent
un'zuträglich *adj* (*dat*) bad (for)
un'zutreffend *adj* not applicable
un'zuverlässig *adj* unreliable
un'zweckmäßig *adj* inappropriate; unsuitable; impractical
un'zweideutig *adj* unambiguous
un'zweifelhaft *adj* undoubted
üppig ['ʏpɪç] *adj* luxurious, plush; (*Mahl*) sumptuous; (*Pflanzenwuchs*) luxuriant; (*sinnlich*) voluptuous
Ur-, ur- [ur] *comb.fm.* original; very
ur'alt *adj* very old, ancient
Uran [u'rɑn] *n* (—s;) uranium
Ur'aufführung *f* world première
urbar ['ʊrbɑr] *adj* arable; **u. machen** reclaim
Urbarmachung ['ʊrbɑrmɑxʊŋ] *f* (—;) reclamation

Ur′bewohner pl aborigines
Ur′bild n prototype; original
ur′deutsch adj hundred-percent German
ur′eigen adj one's very own; original
Ur′einwohner pl aborigines
Ur′eltern pl ancestors
Ur′enkel m great-grandson
Ur′geschichte f prehistory
Ur′großmutter f great-grandmother
Ur′großvater m great-grandfather
Urheber **-in** [′urhebər(ın)] §6 mf originator, author
Ur′heberrecht n copyright
Ur′heberschaft f (-;-e) authorship
Urin [u′riːn] m (-s;) urine
urinieren [urı′niːrən] intr urinate
ur′ko′misch adj very funny
Urkunde [′urkundə] f (-;-n) document; deed; (Vertrag) instrument
Ur′kundenmaterial n documentation
urkundlich [′urkuntlıç] adj documentary; (verbürgt) authentic
Urlaub [′urlaup] m (-[e]s;-e) vacation; (mil) furlough
Ur′lauber **-in** §6 mf vacationer
Ur′laubsschein m (mil) pass
Ur′laubstag m day off
Urne [′urnə] f (-;-n) urn; ballot box; **zur U. gehen** go to the polls
Ur′nengang m balloting

ur′plötz′lich adj sudden ‖ adv all of a sudden
Ur′sache f cause, reason; **keine U.!** don't mention it!
ur′sächlich adj causal
Ur′schleim m (-es;) protoplasm
Ur′schrift f original text, original
Ur′sprung m origin, source; beginning; (Ursache) cause
ursprünglich [′ur/prynlıç] adj original
Ur′stoff m primary matter; (chem) element
Ur′teil n judgment; (Ansicht) view, opinion; (jur) verdict; (Strafmaß) (jur) sentence
urteilen [′urtaılən] intr judge; **u. nach** judge by
Ur′teilskraft f discernment
Ur′teilsspruch m verdict; sentence
Ur′text m original text
Ur′tier n protozoon
Ur′volk n aborigines
Ur′wald m virgin forest; jungle
ur′weltlich adj primeval
urwüchsig [′urvyksıç] adj original; (fig) rough
Ur′zeit f remote antiquity
Utensilien [uten′ziljən] pl utensils
Uto·pie [uto′piː] f (-;-pien [′piː-ən]) utopia; pipe dream
uzen [′utsən] tr tease, kid

V

V, v [fau] invar n V, v
vag [vak] adj vague
Vagabund [vaga′bunt] m (-en;-en) vagabond, tramp, bum
vagabundieren [vagabun′diːrən] intr (HABEN & SEIN) bum around
vage [′vagə] adj vague
vakant [va′kant] adj vacant
Vakanz [va′kants] f (-;-en) vacancy
Vaku·um [′vaku·um] n (-s;-ua [u·a]) vacuum
Vakzine [vak′tsinə] f (-;-n) vaccine
vakzinieren [vaktsi′niːrən] tr vaccinate
Valet [va′leːt] n (-s;-s) farewell
Valu·ta [va′luta] f (-;-ten [tən]) value; (foreign) currency
Vampir [′vampiːr] m (-s;-e) vampire
Vandale [van′dalə] m (-n;-n) Vandal; (fig) vandal
Vanille [va′nıljə] f (-;) vanilla
Variante [varı′antə] f (-;-n) variant
Varietät [varı·e′tɛt] f (-;-en) variety
Varieté [varı·e′te] n (-s;-s) vaudeville; vaudeville stage
variieren [varı′iːrən] tr & intr vary
Vase [′vazə] f (-;-n) vase
Vaselin [vaze′liːn] n (-s;-e), **Vaseline** [vaze′linə] f (-;-n) vaseline
Vater [′fatər] m (-s;∸) father
Va′terland n (native) country
vaterländisch [′fatərlɛndı/] adj national ‖ adv-v. gesinnt patriotic
Va′terlandsliebe f patriotism
väterlich [′fetərlıç] adj fatherly

väterlicherseits [′fetərlıçər′zaıts] adv on the father's side
Va′terliebe f paternal love
Va′terschaft f (-;) fatherhood
Va′terschaftsklage f paternity suit
Va′tersname m family name, last name
Va′terstadt f home town
Va′terstelle f—**bei j-m V. vertreten** be a father to s.o.
Vaterun′ser n (-s;-) Lord's Prayer
Vati [′fati] m (-s;-s) dad, daddy
Vatikan [vatı′kan] m (-s;) Vatican
v. Chr. abbr (vor Christus) B.C.
Vegetarier **-in** [vege′tarjər(ın)] §6 mf vegetarian
Vegetation [vegeta′tsjon] f (-;) vegetation
vegetieren [vege′tiːrən] intr vegetate
Veilchen [′faılçən] n (-s;-) (bot) violet
Vene [′venə] f (-;-n) (anat) vein
Venedig [ve′nediç] n (-s;) Venice
venerisch [ve′neːrı/] adj venereal; venerisches Leiden venereal disease
Ventil [ven′til] n (-s;-e) valve; (bei der Orgel) stop; (fig) outlet
Ventilation [ventila′tsjon] f (-;) ventilation
Venti·lator [ventı′lator] m (-s;-latoren [la′toːrən]) ventilator; fan
ver- [fer] pref up, e.g., **verbrauchen** use up; away, e.g., **verjagen** chase away; mis-, wrongly, e.g., **verstellen** misplace, **verdrehen** turn the wrong

way; (to form verbs from other parts of speech) **verwirklichen** realize, **vergöttern** deify; (to express a sense opposite that of the simple verb) **verlernen** forget, **verkaufen** sell; (to indicate consumption or waste through the action of the verb) **verschreiben** use up in writing; (to indicate intensification or completion) **verhungern** die of hunger; (to indicate cessation of action) **vergären** cease to ferment; (to indicate conversion to another state) **verflüssigen** liquify

verabfolgen [fɛr'ʔpfɔlgən] *tr* hand over; deliver; (*Arznei*) give, administer

verabreden [fɛr'ʔpredən] *tr* agree upon; **schon anderweitig verabredet sein** have a prior engagement || *ref* make an appointment

Verab'redung *f* (-;-en) agreement; appointment

verabreichen [fɛr'ʔpraɪçən] *tr* give

verabsäumen [fɛr'ʔpzɔɪmən] *tr* var of **versäumen**

verabscheuen [fɛr'ʔpʃɔɪ·ən] *tr* detest, loath, abhor

verab'scheuenswert, verab'scheuenswürdig detestable

verabschieden [fɛr'ʔpʃidən] *tr* dismiss; (*Beamte*) put on pension; (*Gesetz*) pass; (mil) disband || *ref* (von) take leave (of), say goodbye (to)

Verab'schiedung *f* (-;-en) dismissal; pensioning; (mil) disbanding; (parl) passing, enactment

verach'ten *tr* despise; **nicht zu v.** not to be sneezed at

verächtlich [fɛr'ɛçtlɪç] *adj* contemptuous; (*verachtungswert*) contemptible

Verach'tung *f* (-;) contempt

veralbern [fɛr'albərn] *tr* tease

verallgemeinern [fɛralgə'maɪnərn] *tr* & *intr* generalize

Verallgemei'nerung *f* (-;-en) generalization

veralten [fɛr'altən] *intr* become obsolete; (*Kleider*) go out of style

veraltet [fɛr'altət] *adj* obsolete; out of date, old-fashioned

Veran·da [ve'randa] *f* (-;-den [dən]) veranda, porch

veränderlich [fɛr'ɛndərlɪç] *adj* changeable; (math) variable

Verän'derlichkeit *f* (-;-en) changeableness; fluctuation; instability

verän'dern [fɛr'ɛndərn] *tr* change; vary || *ref* change; look for a new job

Verän'derung *f* (-;-en) change

verängstigt [fɛr'ɛŋstɪçt] *adj* intimidated

verankern [fɛr'aŋkərn] *tr* anchor, moor

Veran'kerung *f* (-;-en) anchorage, mooring

veranlagen [fɛr'anlagən] *tr* (*zu e-r Steuer*) assess; **gut veranlagt** highly talented; **künstlerisch veranlagt** artificially inclined; **schlecht veranlagt** poorly endowed

Veran'lagung *f* (-;-en) talents; disposition; (fin) assessment

veran'lassen *tr* cause, occasion, make; (*bereden*) induce

Veran'lassung *f* (-;-en) cause, occasion; **auf V. von** at the suggestion of; **ohne jede V.** without provocation; **V. geben zu** give rise to

veranschaulichen [fɛr'anʃaʊlɪçən] *tr* make clear, illustrate

veran'schlagen §132 *tr* rate, value; (*im voraus berechnen*) estimate; **zu hoch v.** overrate

Veran'schlagung *f* (-;) estimate

veranstalten [fɛr'anʃtaltən] *tr* organize, arrange; (*Empfang*) give; (*Sammlung*) take up; (*Versammlung*) hold

Veran'stalter –in §6 *mf* organizer

Veran'staltung *f* (-;-en) organization, arrangement; affair; performance, show; meeting; (sport) event, meet

veran'tworten *tr* answer for, account for; (*verteidigen*) defend || *ref* defend oneself, justify oneself

verantwortlich [fɛr'antvʊrtlɪç] *adj* responsible, answerable; **für etw v. zeichnen** sign for s.th.

Verant'wortlichkeit *f* (-;) responsibility; (jur) liability

Verant'wortung *f* (-;-en) responsibility; (*Rechtfertigung*) justification; **auf eigene V.** at one's own risk; **die V. abwälzen auf** (*acc*) pass the buck to; **zur V. ziehen** call to account

Verant'wortungsbewußtsein *n* sense of responsibility

verant'wortungsfreudig *adj* willing to assume responsibility

verant'wortungsvoll *adj* responsible

veräppeln [fɛr'ɛpəln] *tr* (coll) tease

verar'beiten *tr* manufacture, process; (*zu*) make (into); (*verdauen*) digest; (fig) assimilate

verar'beitend *adj* manufacturing

Verar'beitung *f* (-;-en) manufacturing; digestion; (fig) assimilation

verargen [fɛr'argən] *tr—j—m etw v.** blame s.o. for s.th.

verär'gern *tr* annoy

verarmen [fɛr'armən] *intr* (SEIN) grow poor

verästeln [fɛr'ɛstəln] *ref* branch out

verausgaben [fɛr'ausgabən] *tr* pay out || *ref* run short of money

veräußern [fɛr'ɔɪsərn] *tr* sell

Verb [vɛrp] *n* (-s;-en) verb

verbal [vɛr'bal] *adj* verbal

Verband [fɛr'bant] *m* (-[e]s;⁻e) association, union, federation; (aer, nav) formation; (mil) unit; (surg) bandage, dressing; **sich aus dem V. lösen** (aer) peel off

Verband'kasten *m* first-aid kit

Verband'päckchen *n* first-aid pack

Verband'platz *m* first-aid station

Verband'stoff *m* bandage, dressing

verbannen [fɛr'banən] *tr* banish, exile

Verbannte [fɛr'bantə] §5 *mf* exile

Verban'nung *f* (-;-en) banishment; place of exile

verbarrikadie'ren *tr* barricade

verbau'en *tr* (*Gelände*) build up; use up (*in building*); (*Geld*) spend (*in building*); build poorly; **j—m den Weg v. zu** bar s.o.'s way to

verbei′ßen §53 *tr* swallow, suppress ‖ *ref* (in *acc*) stick (to)
verber′gen §54 *tr* & *ref* hide
verbes′sern *tr* improve; correct; (*Aufsatz*) grade; (*Gesetz*) amend; (*Tatsache*) rectify ‖ *ref* improve; better oneself
Verbes′serung *f* (–;–en) improvement; correction; amendment
verbeu′gen *ref* bow
Verbeu′gung *f* (–;–en) bow; curtsy
verbeulen [fɛr′bɔɪlən] *tr* dent; batter
verbie′gen §57 *tr* bend ‖ *ref* warp
verbie′ten §58 *tr* forbid
verbil′den *tr* spoil; educate badly
verbil′ligen *tr* reduce the price of
Verbil′ligung *f* (–;–en) reduction
verbin′den §59 *tr* tie, tie up; join, unite; (*verketten*) link; (*zu Dank verpflichten*) obligate; (chem) combine; (med) bandage; (telp) (mit) connect (with), put through (to); **j–m die Augen v.** blindfold s.o. ‖ *ref* unite
verbindlich [fɛr′bɪntlɪç] *adj* obliging; binding; **verbindlichsten Dank!** thank you ever so much!
Verbind′lichkeit *f* (–;–en) obligation; commitment; polite way; (*e–s Vertrags*) binding force
Verbin′dung *f* (–;–en) union; association; alliance; combination; contact; touch; (*Fuge, Gelenk*) joint; (chem) compound; (educ) fraternity; (mach, rr, telp) connection; (mil) liaison; **die V. verlieren mit** lose touch with; **e–e V. eingehen** (chem) form a compound; **er hat gute Verbindungen** he has good connections; **in V. mit** in conjunction with; **sich in V. setzen mit** get in touch with; **unmittelbare V.** (telp) direct call
Verbin′dungsbahn *f* connecting train
Verbin′dungsleitung *f* (telp) trunk line
Verbin′dungslinie *f* line of communication
Verbin′dungsoffizier *m* liaison officer
Verbin′dungspunkt *m*, **Verbin′dungsstelle** *f* joint, juncture
Verbin′dungsstück *n* joint, coupling
verbissen [fɛr′bɪsən] *adj* dogged, grim; (*Zorn*) suppressed; **v. sein in** (*dat*) stick doggedly to
Verbis′senheit *f* (–;) doggedness, grimness
verbitten [fɛr′bɪtən] §60 *ref*—**sich** [*dat*] **etw v.** not stand for s.th.
verbittern [fɛr′bɪtərn] *tr* embitter
Verbit′terung *f* (–;) bitterness
verblassen [fɛr′blasən] *intr* (SEIN) grow pale; (fig) fade
verblättern [fɛr′blɛtərn] *tr*—**die Seite v.** lose the page
Verbleib [fɛr′blaɪp] *m* (–[e]s;) whereabouts
verblei′ben §62 *intr* (SEIN) remain, be left; (bei) persist (in); **wir sind so verblieben, daß** we finally agreed that
verblei′chen §85 *intr* (SEIN) fade
verblen′den *tr* blind; dazzle; (*Mauer*) face; (*Fenster*) wall up
Verblen′dung *f* (–;–en) blindness, infatuation; (archit) facing

verblichen [fɛr′blɪçən] *adj* faded
verblödet [fɛr′blødət] *adj* idiotic
verblüffen [fɛr′blʏfən] *tr* dumbfound, flabbergast; bewilder, perplex
Verblüf′fung *f* (–;) bewilderment
verblü′hen *intr* (SEIN) wither; fade
verblümt [fɛr′blymt] *adj* euphemistic
verblu′ten *ref* & *intr* (SEIN) bleed to death
verbocken [fɛr′bɔkən] *tr* bungle
verboh′ren *ref*—**sich v. in** (*acc*) stick stubbornly to
verbohrt [fɛr′bort] *adj* stubborn; odd
verbolzen [fɛr′bɔltsən] *tr* bolt
verbor′gen *adj* secret; latent; hidden ‖ *tr* lend out ‖ **Verborgene** §5 *n*—**im Verborgenen** in secret, on the sly
Verbor′genheit *f* (–;) secrecy; concealment; seclusion
Verbot [fɛr′bot] *n* (–[e]s;–e) prohibition; (jur) injunction
verboten [fɛr′botən] *adj* forbidden; **Eintritt v.!** no admittance; **Plakatankleben v.!** post no bills!; **Stehenbleiben v.!** no loitering
verbrämen [fɛr′brɛmən] *tr* trim, edge; (fig) sugar-coat
verbrannt [fɛr′brant] *adj* burnt; torrid; **Politik der verbrannten Erde** scorched-earth policy
Verbrauch′ *m* (–[e]s;) use, consumption
verbrau′chen *tr* use up, consume; waste; (*abnutzen*) wear out
Verbrau′cher *m* (–s;–) consumer; (*Benützer*) user; (*Kunde*) customer
Verbrau′chergenossenschaft *f* co-op
Verbrauchs′güter *pl* consumer goods
verbraucht′ *adj* used up, consumed; worn out; (*Geld*) spent; (*Luft*) stale
verbre′chen §64 *tr* commit, do ‖ **Verbrechen** *n* (–s;–) crime
Verbre′cher *m* (–s;–) criminal
Verbre′cheralbum *n* rogues′ gallery
Verbre′cherin *f* (–;–nen) criminal
verbrecherisch [fɛr′breçərɪʃ] *adj* criminal
Verbre′cherkolonie *f* penal colony
verbreiten [fɛr′braɪtən] *tr* spread; (*Frieden, Licht*) shed ‖ *ref* spread; **sich v. über** (*acc*) expatiate on
verbreitern [fɛr′braɪtərn] *tr* & *ref* widen, broaden
Verbrei′terung *f* (–;) widening, broadening
Verbrei′tung *f* (–;) spreading; dissemination; diffusion
verbren′nen §97 *tr* burn; scorch; (*bräunen*) tan; (*Leichen*) cremate ‖ *ref* burn oneself; **sich** [*dat*] **die Finger v.** (& fig) burn one′s fingers
Verbren′nung *f* (–;–en) burning, combustion; cremation; (*Brandwunde*) burn
Verbren′nungskraftmaschine *f*, **Verbren′nungsmotor** *m* internal combustion engine
Verbren′nungsraum *m* combustion chamber
verbrin′gen §65 *tr* spend, pass; (*wegbringen*) take away
verbrüdern [fɛr′brydərn] *ref* (**mit**) fraternize (with)

Verbrü′derung *f* (—;) fraternizing

verbrü′hen *tr* scald

verbu′chen *tr* book; **etw als Erfolg v.** chalk s.th. up as a success

Ver·bum [′vɛrbum] *n* (—s;—ba [ba]) verb

verbunden [fɛr′bundən] *adj* connected; **falsch v.!** sorry, wrong number!; **untereinander v.** interconnected; **zu Dank v.** obligated

verbünden [fɛr′byndən] *ref*—**sich mit j-m v.** ally oneself with s.o.

Verbun′denheit *f* (—;) connection, ties; solidarity, union

Verbündete [fɛr′byndətə] §5 *mf* ally

verbür′gen *tr* guarantee, vouch for ‖ *ref*—**sich v. für** vouch for

verbürgt [fɛr′byrkt] *adj* authenticated

verbüßen [fɛr′bysən] *tr* atone for, pay for; **seine Strafe v.** serve one's time

verchromen [fɛr′kroːmən] *tr* chromeplate

Verchro′mung *f* (—;—en) chromeplating

Verdacht [fɛr′daxt] *m* (—[e]s;) suspicion; **in V. kommen** come under suspicion; **V. hegen gegen** have suspicions about; **V. schöpfen** get suspicious

verdächtig [fɛr′dɛçtɪç] *adj* suspicious; (*genit*) suspected (of)

verdächtigen [fɛr′dɛçtɪgən] *tr* cast suspicion on; (*genit*) suspect (of)

Verdäch′tigung *f* (—;—en) insinuation

verdammen [fɛr′damən] *tr* condemn; damn

Verdammnis [fɛr′damnɪs] *f* (—;) damnation, perdition

verdammt′ *adj* (sl) damn ‖ *interj* (sl) damn it!

verdamp′fen *tr* & *intr* (SEIN) evaporate

Verdamp′fung *f* (—;) evaporation

verdan′ken *tr*—**j-m etw v.** be indebted to s.o. for s.th.

verdarb [fɛr′darp] *pret of* **verderben**

verdattert [fɛr′datərt] *adj* (coll) shook up

verdauen [fɛr′dau·ən] *tr* digest

verdaulich [fɛr′daulɪç] *adj* digestible

Verdau′ung *f* (—;) digestion

Verdau′ungsbeschwerden *pl* **Verdau′ungsstörung** *f* indigestion

Verdau′ungswerkzeug *n* digestive track

Verdeck [fɛr′dɛk] *n* (—[e]s;—e) hood (*of baby carriage*); (aut) convertible top; (naut) deck

verdecken (verdek′ken) *tr* cover; hide

verden′ken §66 *tr*—**j-m etw v.** blame s.o. for s.th.

Verderb [fɛr′dɛrp] *m* (—[e]s;) ruin; decay

verderben [fɛr′dɛrbən] §149 *tr* spoil; ruin; (*Magen*) upset; (*verführen*) corrupt ‖ *intr* (SEIN) spoil, go bad; (fig) go to pot ‖ **Verderben** (—s;) ruin; **j-n ins V. stürzen** ruin s.o.

verderblich [fɛr′dɛrplɪç] *adj* ruinous; (*Lebensmittel*) perishable

Verderbnis [fɛr′dɛrpnɪs] *f* (—;) depravity

verderbt′ [fɛr′dɛrpt] *adj* depraved

Verderbt′heit *f* (—;) depravity

verdeutlichen [fɛr′dɔɪtlɪçən] *tr* make plain, explain

verdeutschen [fɛr′dɔɪtʃən] *tr* translate into (or express in) German

verdich′ten *tr* condense, thicken ‖ *ref* condense; solidify; thicken; (*Nebel, Rauch*) grow thicker; (*Verdacht*) become stronger, grow

verdicken [fɛr′dɪkən] *tr* & *ref* thicken

verdie′nen *tr* deserve; (*Geld*) earn

Verdienst [fɛr′dinst] *m* (—es;—e) earnings; gain, profit ‖ *n* (—es;—e) merit; deserts; **es ist dein V., daß** it is owing to you that; **nach V.** deservedly; **nach V. behandelt werden** get one's due; **sich** [*dat*] **als** (or **zum**) **V. anrechnen** take credit for it; **V. um** services to

Verdienst′ausfall *m* loss of wages

verdienst′lich *adj* meritorious

Verdienst′spanne *f* margin of profit

verdienst′voll *adj* meritorious

verdient [fɛr′dint] *adj*—**sich um j-n v. machen** serve s.o. well

verdol′metschen *tr* translate orally; interpret

Verdol′metschung *f* (—;) oral translation; interpretation

verdonnern [fɛr′dɔnərn] *tr* (coll) condemn

verdop′peln *tr* & *ref* double

verdorben [fɛr′dɔrbən] *adj* spoiled; (*Luft*) foul; (*Magen*) upset; (*moralisch*) depraved

verdorren [fɛr′dɔrən] *intr* (SEIN) dry up, wither

verdrän′gen *tr* push aside, crowd out; dislodge; (phys) displace; (psychol) repress, inhibit

Verdrän′gung *f* (—;—en) (phys) displacement; (psychol) repression, inhibition

verdre′hen *tr* twist; (*Augen*) roll; (*Glied*) sprain; (fig) distort; **j-m den Kopf v.** make s.o. fall in love with one

verdreht′ *adj* twisted; (fig) distorted; (fig) (*verrückt*) cracked

verdreifachen [fɛr′drɑɪfaxən] *tr* triple

verdre′schen §67 *tr* (coll) spank

verdrießen [fɛr′drisən] §76 *tr* bother, annoy, get down; **laß es dich nicht v.!** don't let it get you down; **sich keine Mühe v. lassen** spare no pains ‖ *impers*—**es verdrießt mich, daß** it bothers me that

verdrießlich [fɛr′drislɪç] *adj* glum; tiresome, depressing; annoyed

verdroß [fɛr′drɔs] *pret of* **verdrießen**

verdro′ßen *adj* cross; (*mürrisch*) surly; (*lustlos*) listless

verdrucken (verdruk′ken) *tr* misprint

verdrücken (verdrük′ken) *tr* wrinkle; (coll) eat up, polish off ‖ *ref* (coll) sneak away

Ver·druß [fɛr′drʊs] *m* (—drusses; —drusse) annoyance, vexation; **j-m etw zum V. tun** do s.th. to spite s.o.

verduften [fɛr′dʊftən] *intr* (SEIN) lose its aroma; (coll) take off, scram

verdummen [fɛr′dumən] *tr* make stupid ‖ *intr* (SEIN) become stupid

verdunkeln [fɛr′dunkəln] *tr* darken; obscure; (*Glanz*) dull; (fig) cloud; (astr) eclipse; (mil) black out ‖ *ref* darken; (*Himmel*) cloud over

Verdun'kelung *f* (-;-en) darkening; (astr) eclipse; (mil) blackout

verdünnen [fɛr'dʏnən] *tr* thin; dilute; (*Gase*) rarefy

verdun'sten *intr* (SEIN) evaporate

Verdun'stung *f* (-;) evaporation

verdur'sten *intr* (SEIN) die of thirst

verdutzen [fɛr'dutsən] *tr* bewilder

veredeln [fɛr'edəln] *tr* ennoble; (*verfeinen*) refine; (*Rohstoff*) process; (*Boden*) enrich; (*Pflanze, Tier*) improve

Vere'delung *f* (-;) refinement; processing; enrichment; improvement

verehelichen [fɛr'e·əlɪçən] *ref* get married

verehren [fɛr'erən] *tr* revere; worship; (fig) adore; **j-m etw v.** present s.o. with s.th.

Vereh'rer **-in** §6 *mf* worshiper; (*Liebhaber*) admirer

verehrt [fɛr'ert] *adj*—**Sehr verehrte gnädige Frau!** Dear Madam; **Sehr verehrter Herr!** Dear Sir; **Verehrte Anwesende** (or **Gäste**)! Ladies and Gentlemen!

Vereh'rung *f* (-;) reverence, veneration; worship, adoration

vereiden [fɛr'aɪdən], **vereidigen** [fɛr'aɪdɪgən] *tr* swear in

Verein [fɛr'aɪn] *m* (-[e]s;-e) society

vereinbar [fɛr'aɪnbar] *adj* compatible

vereinbaren [fɛr'aɪnbarən] *tr* agree to, agree upon || *ref*—**das läßt sich mit meinen Grundsätzen nicht v.** that is inconsistent with my principles

Verein'barkeit *f* (-;) compatibility

Verein'barung *f* (-;) agreement, arrangement; terms; **nur nach V.** by appointment only

vereinen [fɛr'aɪnən] *tr* unite, join

vereinfachen [fɛr'aɪnfaxən] *tr* simplify

Verein'fachung *f* (-;-en) simplification

vereinheitlichen [fɛr'aɪnhaɪtlɪçən] *tr* standardize

vereinigen [fɛr'aɪnɪgən] *tr* unite, join; (*verbinden*) combine; (*verschmelzen*) merge; (*versammeln*) assemble || *ref* unite, join; (*Flüsse*) meet; **sich v. mit** team up with; **sich v. lassen mit** be compatible with, square with

Verei'nigten Staa'ten *pl* United States

Verein'igung *f* (-;-en) union; combination; society, association

vereinnahmen [fɛr'aɪnnamən] *tr* take in

vereinsamen [fɛr'aɪnzamən] *intr* (SEIN) become lonely; become isolated

Verein'samung *f* (-;) loneliness; isolation

Vereins'meier **-in** §6 *mf* (coll) joiner

vereinzeln [fɛr'aɪntsəln] *tr* isolate

verein'zelt *adj* isolated; sporadic

vereisen [fɛr'aɪzən] *tr* (surg) freeze || *intr* (SEIN) become covered with ice; (aer) ice up

vereiteln [fɛr'aɪtəln] *tr* frustrate; baffle

verekeln [fɛr'ekəln] *tr*—**j-m etw v.** spoil s.th. for s.o.

veren'den *intr* (SEIN) die

verengen [fɛr'ɛŋən] *tr* & *ref* narrow

verer'ben *tr* bequeath, leave; (*über-*

mitteln) hand down; (*Krankheit*) transmit || *ref* run in the family

Verer'bung *f* (-;-en) inheritance; transmission; heredity

Verer'bungslehre *f* genetics

verewigen [fɛr'evɪgən] *tr* perpetuate

verewigt [fɛr'evɪçt] *adj* late, deceased

verfah'ren *adj* bungled, messed up || §71 *tr* bungle; (*Geld, Zeit*) spend (on *travel*) || *ref* lose one's way, take a track || *intr* (SEIN) proceed; act || **wrong turn;** (fig) be on the wrong **Verfahren** *n* (-s;-) procedure, method; system; (chem) process; (jur) proceedings, case

Verfall *m* (-[e]s;) deterioration, decay; decline, downfall; (*Fristablauf*) expiration; (*von Wechseln*) maturity; **in V. geraten** become delapidated

verfal'len *adj* delapidated; **e-m Rauschgift v. sein** be addicted to a drug || §72 *intr* (SEIN) decay, go to ruin, decline; (*ablaufen*) expire; (*Kranker*) waste away; (*Recht*) lapse; (*Pfand*) be forfeited; (*Wechsel*) mature

Verfall'tag *m* due date; date of maturity

verfäl'schen *tr* falsify; (*Geld*) counterfeit; (*Wein*) adulterate; (*Urkunde*) forge

Verfäl'schung *f* (-;-en) falsification; forging; adulteration

verfan'gen §73 *ref* become entangled || *intr* (bei) have an effect (on)

verfänglich [fɛr'fɛŋlɪç] *adj* (*Frage*) loaded; (*Situation*) awkward

verfär'ben *ref* change color

verfas'sen *tr* compose, write

Verfas'ser **-in** §6 *mf* author

Verfas'sung *f* (-;-en) constitution; (*Zustand*) condition; frame of mind, mood

verfas'sungsgemäß, verfas'sungsmäßig *adj* constitutional

verfas'sungswidrig *adj* unconstitutional

verfau'len *intr* (SEIN) rot

verfech'ten §74 *tr* defend, stand up for

Verfech'ter *m* (-s;-) champion

verfeh'len *tr* (*Abzweigung, Ziel, Zug*) miss; (*Wirkung*) fail to achieve, not have; **ich werde nicht v. zu** (*inf*) I will not fail to (*inf*) || *recip*—**wir haben uns verfehlt** we missed each other

verfehlt [fɛr'felt] *adj* wrong

Verfeh'lung *f* (-;-en) offense; mistake

verfeinden [fɛr'faɪndən] *recip* become enemies

verfeinern [fɛr'faɪnərn] *tr* refine, improve || *ref* become refined, improve

verfertigen [fɛr'fɛrtɪgən] *tr* manufacture, make

Verfer'tigung *f* (-;) manufacture

verfilmen [fɛr'fɪlmən] *tr* adapt to the screen, make into a movie

Verfil'mung *f* (-;-en) film version

verfilzen [fɛr'fɪltsən] *ref* get tangled

verfinstern [fɛr'fɪnstərn] *ref* get dark

verflachen [fɛr'flaxən] *tr* flatten || *ref* & *intr* (SEIN) flatten out

verflech'ten §74 *tr* interweave; (fig) implicate, involve

verflie'gen §57 *ref* (aer) lose one's

bearings || *intr* (SEIN) fly away; (*Zeit*) fly; evaporate; (fig) vanish

verflie'ßen §76 *intr* (SEIN) flow off; (*Frist*) run out, expire; (*Farben*) blend; (*Begriffe, Grenzen*) overlap

verflixt [fɛr'flɪkst] *adj* (sl) darn

verflossen [fɛr'flɔsən] *adj* past; former

verflu'chen *tr* curse, damn

verflucht' *adj* (sl) damn || *interj* (sl) damn it!

verflüchtigen [fɛr'flʏçtɪgən] *tr* volatilize || *ref* evaporate; (fig) disappear

verflüssigen [fɛr'flʏsɪgən] *tr & ref* liquefy

Verfolg [fɛr'fɔlk] *m* (-s;) course; im V. (*genit*) in pursuance of

verfol'gen *tr* pursue; follow up; persecute; haunt; (hunt) track; (jur) prosecute; **j-n steckbrieflich v.** send out a warrant for the arrest of s.o.

Verfol'ger **-in** §6 *mf* pursuer; persecutor

Verfol'gung *f* (-;-en) pursuit; persecution; (jur) prosecution

Verfol'gungswahn *m*, **Verfol'gungswahnsinn** *m* persecution complex

verfrachten [fɛr'fraxtən] *tr* ship; (coll) bundle off

Verfrach'ter **-in** §6 *mf* shipper

verfrühen [fɛr'fry.ən] *ref* be too early

verfügbar [fɛr'fykbar] *adj* available, at one's disposal

verfü'gen *tr* decree, order || *ref*—**sich v. nach** betake oneself to || *intr*—**v. über** (*acc*) have at one's disposal, have control over

Verfü'gung *f* (-;-en) decree, order; disposal; **einstweilige V.** (jur) injunction; **j-m zur V. stehen** be at s.o.'s disposal; **j-m zur V. stellen** put at s.o.'s disposal; **letztwillige V.** last will and testament

verfüh'ren *tr* mislead; (zum Irrtum) lead; (*verlocken*) seduce

Verfüh'rer **-in** §6 *mf* seducer

verführerisch [fɛr'fyrərɪʃ] *adj* seductive, tempting

Verfüh'rung *f* (-;-en) seduction

vergaffen [fɛr'gafən] *ref* (coll) (in *acc*) fall in love with

vergammeln [fɛr'gaməln] *intr* (SEIN) (coll) go to the dogs

vergangen [fɛr'gaŋən] *adj* past; (*Schönheit*) faded

Vergan'genheit *f* (-;) past; background; (gram) past tense

vergänglich [fɛr'gɛŋlɪç] *adj* transitory

vergasen [fɛr'gazən] *tr* gas

Verga'ser *m* (-s;-) carburetor

vergaß [fɛr'gas] *pret* of **vergessen**

verge'ben §68 *tr* forgive (*s.th.*); give away; (*Chance*) miss, pass up; (*Amt, freie Stelle*) fill; (*Auftrag*) place; (*Karten*) misdeal; (*verleihen*) confer; **v. sein** have a previous engagement; be engaged (*to a man*) || *ref*—**sich** [*dat*] **etw v.** compromise on s.th. || *intr* (*dat*) forgive (*s.o.*)

verge'bens [fɛr'gebəns] *adv* in vain

vergeb'lich [fɛr'geplɪç] *adj* vain, futile

Verge'bung *f* (-;) forgiveness; bestowal

vergegenwärtigen [fɛr'gegənvɛrtɪgən] *ref*—**sich** [*dat*] **etw. v.** visualize s.th.

verge'hen §82 *ref*—**sich an j-m v.** offend s.o.; (*sexuell*) violate s.o. || *intr* (SEIN) pass, go away; fade || **Verge'hen** *n* (-s;-) offense, misdemeanor

vergel'ten §83 *tr* requite; **vergelt's Gott!** (coll) thank you!

Vergel'tung *f* (-;) repayment; retaliation, reprisal

Vergel'tungswaffe *f* V-1 or V-2

vergesellschaften [fɛrgə'zɛlʃaftən] *tr* socialize; nationalize

vergessen [fɛr'gesən] §70 *tr* forget

Verges'senheit *f* (-;)—**in V. geraten** fall (or sink) into oblivion

vergeßlich [fɛr'geslɪç] *adj* forceful

Vergeß'lichkeit *f* (-;) forgetfulness

vergeuden [fɛr'gɔɪdən] *tr* waste

Vergeu'dung *f* (-;) waste, squandering

vergewaltigen [fɛrgə'valtɪgən] *tr* do violence to; (*Mädchen*) rape

Vergewal'tigung *f* (-;-en) rape

vergewerkschaften [fɛrgə'vɛrkʃaftən] *tr* unionize

vergewissern [fɛrgə'vɪsərn] *ref* (genit) make sure of, ascertain

vergie'ßen §76 *tr* spill; (*Tränen*) shed

vergiften [fɛr'gɪftən] *tr* (& fig) poison; (*verseuchen*) contaminate || *ref* take poison

Vergif'tung *f* (-;-en) poisoning; contamination

vergipsen [fɛr'gɪpsən] *tr* plaster

Vergißmeinnicht [fɛr'gɪsmaɪnnɪçt] *n* (-[e]s;-e) forget-me-not

vergittern [fɛr'gɪtərn] *tr* bar up

Vergleich [fɛr'glaɪç] *m* (-[e]s;-e) comparison; (*Verständigung*) agreement; (*Ausgleich*) settlement; **e-n V. anstellen zwischen** make a comparison between; **e-n V. treffen** reach a settlement, come to an agreement

vergleichbar [fɛr'glaɪçbar] *adj* comparable

verglei'chen [fɛr'glaɪçən] §85 *tr* (mit) compare (with, to) || *ref* (mit) come to an agreement (with)

Vergleichs'grundlage *f* basis for comparison

vergleichs'weise *adv* by way of comparison

Verglei'chung *f* (-;-en) comparison; matching; contrasting

verglü'hen *intr* (SEIN) cease to glow

vergnügen [fɛr'gnygən] *tr* amuse, delight || *ref* enjoy oneself, amuse oneself || **Vergnügen** *n* (-s;-) delight, pleasure; **mit V.** with pleasure; **V. finden an** (*dat*) take delight in; **viel V.!** (coll) have fun!; **zum V.** for fun

vergnügt [fɛr'gnykt] *adj* cheerful, gay; (*über acc*) delighted (with)

Vergnü'gung *f* (-;-en) pleasure, amusement

Vergnü'gungspark *m* amusement park

Vergnü'gungsreise *f* pleasure trip

Vergnü'gungssteuer *f* entertainment tax

vergnü'gungssüchtig *adj* pleasure-loving

vergolden [fɛr'gɔldən] *tr* gild

Vergol'dung *f* (-;-en) gilding

vergönnen [fɛr'gœnən] *tr* not begrudge

vergöttern [fɛr'gœtərn] *tr* deify; (fig) idolize

vergra'ben §87 *tr* (& fig) bury

vergrämen [fɛr'grɛmən] *tr* annoy, anger

vergrämt [fɛr'grɛmt] *adj* haggard

vergrei/fen §88 *ref* (mus) hit the wrong note; **sich v. an** (*dat*) lay violent hands on; (*fremdem Gut*) encroach on; (*Geld*) misappropriate; (*Mädchen*) assault; **sich im Ausdruck v.** express oneself poorly

vergreisen [fɛr'graizən] *intr* (SEIN) age; become senile

vergriffen [fɛr'grɪfən] *adj* sold out; (*Buch*) out of print

vergröbern [fɛr'grøbərn] *tr* roughen || *ref* become coarser

vergrößern [fɛr'grøsərn] *tr* enlarge; increase; (*ausdehnen*) expand; (opt) magnify || *ref* become larger

Vergrö/ßerung *f* (-;-en) enlargement; increase; expansion; (opt) magnification

Vergrö/ßerungsapparat *m* (phot) enlarger

Vergrö/ßerungsglas *m* magnifying glass

Vergünstigung [fɛr'gʏnstiguŋ] *f* (-; -en) privilege; (*bevorzugte Behandlung*) preferential treatment

vergüten [fɛr'gytən] *tr* make good; (*Stahl*) temper; **j-m etw v.** reimburse (or compensate) s.o. for s.th.

Vergü/tung *f* (-;-en) reimbursement, compensation; tempering

verhaften [fɛr'haftən] *tr* apprehend

Verhaf/tung *f* (-;-en) apprehension

verhal/ten *adj* (*Atem*) bated; (*Stimme*) low || §90 *tr* hold back; (*Atem*) hold; (*Lachen*) suppress; (*Stimme*) keep down; **den Schritt v.** slow down; (*stehenbleiben*) stop || *ref* behave, act; be; **A verhält sich zu B wie X zu Y** A is to B as X is to Y; **sich anders v.** be different; **sich ruhig v.** keep quiet || *impers ref*—**wenn es sich so verhält** if that's the case || **Verhalten** *n* (-s;) conduct, behavior; attitude

Verhältnis [fɛr'hɛltnɪs] *n* (-ses;-se) proportion, ratio; (*Beziehung*) relation; (*Liebes-*) love affair; **aus kleinen Verhältnissen** of humble birth; **bei sonst gleichen Verhältnissen** other things being equal; **das steht in keinem V. zu** that is all out of proportion to; **Verhältnisse** circumstances, conditions; matters; means

verhält/nismäßig *adj* proportionate || *adv* relatively, comparatively

Verhält/nismaßregeln *pl* instructions

Verhält/niswahl *f* proportional representation

verhält/niswidrig *adj* disproportionate

Verhält/niswort *n* (-[e]s;ːer) preposition

verhan/deln *tr* discuss; (*Waren*) sell || *intr* negotiate; argue; (*beraten*) confer; (jur) plead a case; **gegen j-n wegen etw v.** (jur) try s.o. for s.th.

Verhand/lung *f* (-;-en) negotiation; discussion; proceedings; trial

verhangen [fɛr'haŋən] *adj* overcast

verhän/gen *tr* (*Fenster*) put curtains on; (*Strafe*) impose; (*Untersuchung*) order; (*Belagerungszustand*) proclaim; **mit verhängtem Zügel** at full speed

Verhängnis [fɛr'hɛŋnɪs] *n* (-ses;-se) destiny, fate; (*Unglück*) disaster

verhäng/nisvoll *adj* fateful; disastrous

verhärmt [fɛr'hɛrmt] *adj* haggard

verharren [fɛr'harən] *intr* (HABEN & SEIN) remain; (**auf** *dat*, **in** *dat*, **bei**) stick (to)

verhärten [fɛr'hɛrtən] *tr & ref* harden

verhaßt [fɛr'hast] *adj* hated, hateful

verhätscheln [fɛr'hɛtʃəln] *tr* pamper

Verhau [fɛr'hau] *m* (-[e]s;-e) barbwire entanglement

verhau/en §93 *tr* lick, beat up; (*Kind*) spank; (*Auftrag, Ball, usw.*) muff || *ref* make a blunder

verheddern [fɛr'hɛdərn] *ref* get tangled up

verheeren [fɛr'herən] *tr* devastate

verhee/rend *adj* terrible; (coll) awful

Verhee/rung *f* (-;) devastation

verhehlen [fɛr'helən] *tr* conceal

verhei/len *intr* (SEIN) heal up

verheimlichen [fɛr'haimliçən] *tr* keep secret, conceal

Verheim/lichung *f* (-;) concealment

verhei/raten *tr* marry; (*Tochter*) give away || *ref* (**mit**) get married (to)

Verhei/ratung *f* (-;) marriage

verhei/ßen §95 *tr* promise

Verhei/ßung *f* (-;-en) promise

verhei/ßungsvoll *adj* promising

verhel/fen §96 *intr*—**j-m zu etw v.** help s.o. to acquire s.th.

verherrlichen [fɛr'hɛrliçən] *tr* glorify

Verherr/lichung *f* (-;) glorification

verhet/zen *tr* instigate

verhexen [fɛr'hɛksən] *tr* bewitch, hex

verhimmeln [fɛr'himəln] *tr* praise to the skies; (*Schauspieler*) idolize

verhin/dern *tr* prevent

Verhin/derung *f* (-;) prevention; **im Falle seiner V.** in case he's unavailable

verhohlen [fɛr'holən] *adj* hidden

verhöh/nen *tr* jeer at; make fun of

Verhöh/nung *f* (-;) jeering; ridicule

Verhör [fɛr'hør] *n* (-s;-e) interrogation, questioning, hearing

verhö/ren *tr* interrogate, question || *ref* hear wrong

verhudeln [fɛr'hudəln] *tr* (coll) bungle

verhüllen [fɛr'hʏlən] *tr* cover, veil; wrap up; disguise

Verhül/lung *f* (-;-en) cover; disguise

verhun/gern *intr* (SEIN) starve to death

verhunzen [fɛr'huntsən] *tr* (coll) botch

verhü/ten *tr* prevent, avert

verinnerlicht [fɛr'inərliçt] *adj* introspective

verir/ren *ref* lose one's way; (*Augen, Blick*) wander; (fig) make a mistake

verirrt [fɛr'ɪrt] *adj* stray

verja/gen *tr* chase away

verjähren [fɛr'jerən] *intr* (SEIN) fall under the statute of limitations

verjubeln [fɛr'jubəln] *tr* squander

verjüngen [fɛr'jʏŋən] *tr* rejuvenate; reduce in scale; taper || *ref* be rejuvenated; taper, narrow

Verjün/gung *f* (-;) rejuvenation; tapering; scaling down

verkatert [fɛr'katərt] *adj* suffering from a hangover

Verkauf' *m* (-[e]s;-̈e) sale

verkau'fen *tr* sell

Verkäu'fer -in §6 *mf* seller; salesclerk; vendor ‖ *m* salesman ‖ *f* salesgirl, saleswoman

verkäuf'lich *adj* salable

Verkaufs'anzeige *f* for-sale ad

Verkaufs'automat *m* vending machine

Verkaufs'leiter -in §6 *mf* sales manager

Verkaufs'schlager *m* good seller

Verkaufs'steigerung *f* sales promotion

Verkaufs'vertrag *m* agreement of sale

Verkehr [fɛr'ker] *m* (-s;) traffic; commerce; company, association; (*sexuell*) intercourse; (aer, rr) service; (fin) circulation

verkeh'ren *tr* reverse, invert; turn upside down; convert, change; (*Sinn, Worte*) twist ‖ *intr* (*Fahrzeug*) run, run regularly; **mit j–m geschlechtlich v.** have intercourse with s.o.; **mit j–m v.** associate with s.o.

Verkehrs'ader *f* main artery

Verkehrs'ampel *f* traffic light

Verkehrs'andrang *m* heavy traffic

Verkehrs'betrieb *m* public transportation company

Verkehrs'delikt *n* traffic violation

Verkehrs'flugzeug *n* airliner

Verkehrs'insel *f* traffic island

Verkehrs'mittel *n* means of transportation

Verkehrs'ordnungen *pl* traffic regulations

Verkehrs'polizist -in §7 *mf* traffic cop

verkehrs'reich *adj* crowded, congested

verkehrs'stark *adj* busy

Verkehrs'stockung *f*, **Verkehrs'störung** *f* traffic jam

Verkehrs'unfall *m* traffic accident

Verkehrs'unternehmen *n* transportation company

Verkehrs'vorschrift *f* traffic regulation

Verkehrs'wesen *n* traffic, transportation

Verkehrs'zeichen *n* traffic sign

verkehrt [fɛr'kert] *adj* reversed; upside down; inside out; wrong

verken'nen §97 *tr* misunderstand; (*Person*) misjudge, mistake

verketten [fɛr'ketən] *tr* chain together; (fig) link

Verket'tung *f* (-;) chaining; (fig) concatenation; (fig) coincidence

verkit'ten *tr* cement; putty; seal, bond

verkla'gen *tr* accuse; (jur) sue

Verklagte [fɛr'klɑktə] §5 *mf* defendant

verklat'schen *tr* (coll) slander; (educ) squeal on

verkle'ben *tr* glue, cement; **v. mit** cover with

verklei'den *tr* disguise, dress up; (*täfeln*) panel; line, face; (mil) camouflage

Verklei'dung *f* (-;-en) disguise; paneling; lining, facing; (mil) camouflage

verkleinern [fɛr'klaınərn] *tr* lessen, diminish; (fig) disparage; (math) reduce; **maßstäblich v.** scale down

Verklei'nerung *f* (-;-en) diminution, reduction; (fig) detraction

Verklei'nerungsform *f* diminutive

verklin'gen §142 *intr* (SEIN) die away

verkloppen [fɛr'klɔpən] *tr* (coll) beat up

verknacken [fɛr'knakən] *tr* (coll) sentence

verknallt [fɛr'knalt] *adj*—**in j–n v. sein** (coll) have a crush on s.o.

verknappen [fɛr'knapən] *intr* (SEIN) run short, run low

Verknap'pung *f* (-;) shortage

verknei'fen §88 *tr*—**sich** [*dat*] **etw v.** deny oneself s.th.

verkniffen [fɛr'knıfən] *adj* wry

verknip'sen *tr* (*Film*) waste

verknöchern [fɛr'knœçərn] *intr* (SEIN) ossify; (*Glieder*) become stiff

verknöchert [fɛr'knœçərt] *adj* pedantic; (*Junggeselle*) inveterate

verknoten [fɛr'knotən] *tr* snarl, tie up

verknüp'fen *tr* tie together; (fig) connect, combine, relate

verknusen [fɛr'knuzən] *tr* (coll) stand

verkohlen [fɛr'kolən] *tr* carbonize; char; **j–n v.** (coll) pull s.o.'s leg

verkom'men *adj* decayed; degenerate; (*Gebäude*) squalid ‖ §99 *intr* (SEIN) decay, spoil; (fig) go to the dogs; **v. zu** degenerate into

Verkom'menheit *f* (-;) depravity

verkop'peln *tr* couple; (*Interessen*) (com) consolidate

verkorken [fɛr'kɔrkən] *tr* cork up

verkorksen [fɛr'kɔrksən] *tr* (coll) bungle ‖ *ref*—**sich** [*dat*] **den Magen v.** (coll) upset one's stomach

verkörpern [fɛr'kœrpərn] *tr* embody, personify; (*Rolle*) play

Verkör'perung *f* (-;-en) embodiment, incarnation

verkra'chen *ref*—**sich mit j–m v.** have an argument with s.o. ‖ *intr* (SEIN) (coll) go bankrupt

verkrampft [fɛr'krampft] *adj* cramped

verkrie'chen §102 *ref* hide; (& fig) crawl into a hole; **neben ihm kannst du dich v.!** you're no match for him!

verkrümeln [fɛr'krymələn] *tr* crumble ‖ *ref* (fig) disappear

verkrüm'men *tr* & *ref* bend

Verkrüm'mung *f* (-;) bend, crookedness; curvature

verkrüppeln [fɛr'krypələn] *tr* cripple ‖ *intr* (SEIN) become crippled; (*verkümmern*) become stunted

verkrustet [fɛr'krustət] *adj* caked

verküh'len *ref* catch a cold

verküm'mern *intr* (SEIN) become stunted; (pathol) atrophy

Verküm'merung *f* (-;) atrophy

verkünden [fɛr'kyndən], **verkündigen** [fɛr'kyndıgən] *tr* announce, proclaim; (*Urteil*) pronounce

Verkün'digung *f* (-;-en), **Verkün'dung** *f* (-;-en) announcement, proclamation; pronouncement; **Mariä Verkündigung** (feast of the) Annunciation

verkup'peln *tr* couple; (*Mädchen, Mann*) procure; (*Tochter*) sell into prostitution

verkür′zen *tr* shorten; abridge; (*be-schränken*) curtail; (*Zeit*) pass

Verkür′zung *f* (–;–en) shortening; abridgement; curtailment

verla′chen *tr* laugh at

verla′den §103 *tr* load, ship

Verlag [fɛr′lɑk] *m* –[e]s;–e) publisher; **im V. von** published by

verla′gern *tr* shift; (*aus Sicherheitsgründen*) evacuate ‖ *ref* shift

Verla′gerung *f* (–;–en) shift, shifting; evacuation

Verlags′anstalt *f* publisher

Verlags′buchhandlung *f* publisher and dealer

Verlags′recht *n* copyright

verlangen [fɛr′laŋən] *tr* demand, require; want, ask ‖ *intr*—**v. nach** ask for; long for ‖ **Verlangen** *n* (–s;) demand; request; wish; claim; (*Sehnsucht*) longing, yearning; **auf V.** upon demand, upon request

verlängern [fɛr′lɛŋərn] *tr* lengthen; prolong, extend; **seinen Paß v. lassen** have one's passport renewed

Verlän′gerung *f* (–;–en) lengthening; prolongation, extension; (*sport*) overtime

Verlän′gerungsschnur *f* extension cord

verlangsamen [fɛr′laŋzamən] *tr* slow down

verläppern [fɛr′lɛpərn] *tr* (coll) fritter away

Ver•laß [fɛr′las] *m* (–lasses;) reliance; **es ist kein V. auf ihn** you can't rely on him

verlas′sen *adj* abandoned, deserted; lonesome ‖ §104 *tr* leave; forsake, desert ‖ *ref*—**sich v. auf** (*acc*) rely on

Verlas′senheit *f* (–;) loneliness

verläßlich [fɛr′lɛslɪç] *adj* reliable

verlästern [fɛr′lɛstərn] *tr* slander

Verlä′sterung *f* (–;–en) slander

Verlaub [fɛr′laup] *m*—**mit V.** with your permission; **mit V. zu sagen** if I may say so

Verlauf′ *m* (–[e]s;) course; e–n guten **V. haben** turn out well; **nach V. von** after a lapse of

verlau′fen §105 *intr* (SEIN) (*Zeit*) pass, lapse; (*ablaufen*) turn out, come off; (*vorgehen*) proceed, run ‖ *ref* lose one's way; (*Wasser*) run off; (*Menschenmenge*) disperse

verlau′ten *intr* (SEIN) become known, be reported; **kein Wort davon v. lassen** not breathe a word about it; **wie verlautet** as reported ‖ *impers*—**es verlautet** it is reported

verle′ben *tr* spend, pass

verlebt [fɛr′lept] *adj* haggard

verle′gen *adj* embarrassed; confused; um **v. um** (*e–e Antwort*) at a loss for; (*Geld*) short of ‖ *tr* move, shift; transfer; misplace; (*Buch*) publish; (*Geleise, Kabel, Rohre*) lay; (*sperren*) block; (*vertagen*) postpone ‖ *ref*—**sich v. auf** (*acc*) apply onself to; devote oneself to; resort to

Verle′genheit *f* (–;) embarrassment; difficulties; predicament; **in V. bringen** embarrass

Verle′ger *m* (–s;–) publisher

Verle′gung *f* (–;–en) move, shift; transfer; postponement; (*von Kabeln, usw.*) laying

verlei′den *tr* spoil, take the joy out of

Verleih [fɛr′laɪ] *m* (–s;–e) rental service

verlei′hen §81 *tr* lend out, loan; rent out; (*Gunst*) grant; (*Titel*) confer; (*Auszeichnung*) award

Verlei′her –in §6 *mf* lender; grantor; (*von Filmen*) distributor

Verlei′hung *f* (–;–en) lending out; rental; grant; bestowal

verlei′ten *tr* mislead; (*zur Sünde, zum Trunk*) lead; (jur) suborn

verler′nen *tr* unlearn, forget

verle′sen §107 *tr* read out; (*Namen*) read off; (*Salat*) clean; (*Gemüse*) sort out ‖ *ref* misread

verletzen [fɛr′lɛtsən] *tr* (& fig) injure, hurt; (*kränken*) offend; (*Gesetz*) break; (*Recht*) violate

verlet′zend *adj* offensive

Verletzte [fɛr′lɛtsə] §5 *mf* injured party

Verlet′zung *f* (–;–en) injury; offense; (*e–s Gesetzes*) breaking; (*e–s Rechtes*) violation

verleug′nen *tr* deny; (*Kind*) disown; (*Glauben*) renounce ‖ *ref*—**sich selbst v.** act contrary to one's nature; **sich vor Besuchern v. lassen** refuse to see visitors

Verleug′nung *f* (–;–en) denial; renunciation; disavowal

verleumden [fɛr′lɔɪmdən] *tr* slander

verleumderisch [fɛr′lɔɪmdərɪʃ] *adj* slanderous, libelous

Verleum′dung *f* (–;–en) slander

verlie′ben *ref*—**sich in j–n v.** fall in love with s.o.

verliebt [fɛr′lipt] *adj* in love

verlieren [fɛr′lirən] §77 *tr* lose ‖ *ref* lose one's way; disappear; disperse

Verlies [fɛr′lis] *n* (–es;–e) dungeon

verlo′ben *ref* (mit) become engaged (to)

Verlöbnis [fɛr′løpnɪs] *n* (–ses;–se) engagement

Verlobte [fɛr′loptə] §5 *m* fiancé; **die Verlobten** the engaged couple ‖ *f* fiancée

Verlo′bung *f* (–;–en) engagement

verlocken (verlok′ken) *tr* lure, tempt; (*verführen*) seduce

verlockend (verlok′kend) *adj* tempting

Verlockung (Verlok′kung) *f* (–;–en) allurement, temptation

verlogen [fɛr′logən] *adj* dishonest

verlohn′nen *impers ref*—**es verlohnt sich nicht** it doesn't pay ‖ *impers*—**es verlohnt der Mühe nicht** it is not worth the trouble

verlor [fɛr′lor] *pret* of **verlieren**

verloren [fɛr′lorən] *pp* of **verlieren** ‖ *adj* lost; (*hilflos*) forlorn; (*Ei*) poached; **der verlorene Sohn** the prodigal son

verlo′rengeben §80 *tr* give up for lost

verlo′rengehen §82 *intr* (SEIN) be lost

verlö′schen §110 *tr* extinguish; (*Schrift*) erase ‖ *intr* (SEIN) (*Licht, Kerze*) go out; (*Zorn*) cease

verlo′sen *tr* raffle off, draw lots for
verlö′ten *tr* solder; **e–n v.** (coll) belt one down
verlottern [fer′lɔtərn] *intr* (coll) go to the dogs
verlumpen [fer′lumpən] *tr* (coll) blow, squander || *intr* (coll) go to the dogs
Verlust [fer′lust] *m* (–[e]s;–e) loss; **in V. geraten** get lost; **Verluste** (mil) casualties
Verlust′liste *f* (mil) casualty list
verma′chen *tr* bequeath, leave
Vermächtnis [fer′meçtnɪs] *n* (–ses;–se) bequest, legacy
vermählen [fer′melən] *tr* marry || *ref* (mit) get married (to)
Vermäh′lung *f* (–;–en) marriage, wedding
vermah′nen *tr* admonish, warn
Vermah′nung *f* (–;–en) admonition
vermaledeien [fermale′daɪ·ən] *tr* curse
vermanschen [fer′manʃən] *tr* (coll) make a mess of
vermasseln [fer′masəln] *tr* (coll) bungle, muff
vermassen [fer′masən] *intr* (SEIN) lose one's individuality
vermauern [fer′mau·ərn] *tr* wall up
vermehren [fer′merən] *tr* & *ref* increase; **(an Zahl)** multiply; **vermehrte Auflage** enlarged edition
vermei′den *tr* avoid
vermeidlich [fer′maɪtlɪç] *adj* avoidable
Vermei′dung *f* (–;) avoidance
vermei′nen *tr* suppose; presume, allege
vermeintlich [fer′maɪntlɪç] *adj* supposed, alleged; **(erdacht)** imaginary
vermel′den *tr* (poet) announce
vermen′gen *tr* mix, mingle; confound || *ref* (mit) meddle (with)
Vermerk [fer′merk] *m* (–[e]s;–e) note
vermer′ken *tr* note, record
vermes′sen *adj* daring, bold || §70 *tr* measure; **(Land)** survey || *ref* measure wrong; **sich v. zu** (*inf*) have the nerve to (*inf*)
Vermes′sung *f* (–;–en) surveying
vermie′ten *tr* rent out; lease out
Vermie′ter –in §6 *mf* (jur) lessor || *m* landlord || *f* landlady
vermindern [fer′mɪndərn] *tr* diminish, lessen; **(beschränken)** reduce, cut || *ref* diminish, decrease
Vermin′derung *f* (–;–en) diminution, decrease; reduction, cut
verminen [fer′minən] *tr* (mil) mine
vermi′schen *tr* & *ref* mix
Vermi′schung *f* (–;–en) mixture
vermissen [fer′mɪsən] *tr* miss
vermißt [fer′mɪst] *adj* (mil) missing in action || **Vermißte** §5 *mf* missing person
vermitteln [fer′mɪtəln] *tr* negotiate; arrange, bring about; **(beschaffen)** get, procure || *intr* mediate; intercede
vermittels [fer′mɪtəls] *prep* (*genit*) by means of, through
Vermitt′ler –in §6 *mf* mediator, go-between; (com) agent
Vermitt′lung *f* (–;–en) negotiation; mediation; procuring; providing; intercession; **(Mittel)** means; agency;

brokerage; (telp) exchange; **durch gütige V.** (*genit*) through the good offices of
Vermitt′lungsamt *n* (telp) exchange
Vermitt′lungsgebühr *f*, **Vermitt′lungsprovision** *f* commission; brokerage
vermo′dern *intr* (SEIN) rot, decay
vermöge [fer′møɡə] *prep* (*genit*) by virtue of
vermö′gen §114 *tr* be able to do; **j–n v. zu** (*inf*) induce s.o. to (*inf*); **sie vermag bei ihm viel** (or **wenig**) she has great (or little) influence with him; **v. zu** (*inf*) be able to (*inf*), have the power to (*inf*) || **Vermögen** *n* (–s;–) ability; capacity; power; fortune, means; property; (fin) capital, assets; **nach bestem V.** to the best of one's ability
vermö′gend *adj* well-to-do, well-off
Vermö′genslage *f* financial situation
Vermö′genssteuer *f* property tax
vermorscht [fer′mɔrʃt] *adj* rotten
vermottet [fer′mɔtət] *adj* moth-eaten
vermummen [fer′mumən] *tr* disguise || *ref* disguise oneself
vermuten [fer′mutən] *tr* suppose, presume
vermutlich [fer′mutlɪç] *adj* presumable || *adv* presumably, I suppose
Vermu′tung *f* (–;–en) guess, conjecture
vernachlässigen [fer′naxlesɪɡən] *tr* neglect
Vernach′lässigung *f* (–;) neglect
verna′geln *tr* nail up; board up
vernä′hen *tr* sew up
vernarben [fer′narbən] *intr* (SEIN) heal up
vernarren [fer′narən] *ref*—**sich v. in** (*acc*) be crazy about, be stuck on
verna′schen *tr* spend on sweets; **(Mädchen)** make love to
vernebeln [fer′nebəln] *tr* (mil) screen with smoke; (fig) hide, cover over
vernehmbar [fer′nembar] *adj* perceptible
verneh′men §116 *tr* perceive; **(erfahren)** hear, learn; (jur) question; **sich v. lassen** be heard, express an opinion || **Vernehmen** *n* (–s;–)—**dem V. nach** reportedly, according to the report
vernehmlich [fer′nemlɪç] *adj* perceptible, audible; distinct
Verneh′mung *f* (–;–en) interrogation
vernei′gen *ref* bow; curtsy
Vernei′gung *f* (–;–en) bow; curtsy
verneinen [fer′naɪnən] *tr* say no to; reject, refuse; disavow
vernei′nend *adj* negative
Vernei′nung *f* (–;–en) negation; denial
vernichten [fer′nɪçtən] *tr* destroy, annihilate; **(Hoffnung)** dash
vernich′tend *adj* **(Kritik)** scathing; **(Niederlage)** crushing
Vernich′tung *f* (–;) destruction
vernickeln [fer′nɪkəln] *tr* nickel-plate
vernie′ten *tr* rivet
Vernunft [fer′nunft] *f* (–;) reason; good sense; senses; **die gesunde V.** common sense; **V. annehmen** listen to reason; **zur V. bringen** bring to one's senses

Vernunft′ehe *f* marriage of convenience

vernunft′gemäß *adj* reasonable

vernünftig [fer'nʏnftɪç] *adj* rational; reasonable; sensible, level-headed

vernunft′los *adj* senseless

vernunft′mäßig *adj* rational; reasonable

veröden [fer'ʎødən] *intr* (SEIN) become desolate

veröffentlichen [fer'œfəntlɪçən] *tr* publish; announce

Veröf′fentlichung *f* (-;-en) publication; announcement

verord′nen *tr* decree; (med) prescribe

Verord′nung *f* (-;-en) decree, order; (med) prescription

verpach′ten *tr* farm out; lease, rent out

Verpäch′ter -in §6 *mf* lessor

verpacken (verpak′ken) *tr* pack up

Verpackung (Verpak′kung) *f* (-;-en) packing (material); wrapping

verpas′sen *tr* (*Gelegenheit, Anschluß, usw.*) miss; j-m e-n Anzug v. fit s.o. with a suit; j-m e-e v. (coll) give s.o. a smack

verpatzen [fer'patsən] *tr* (coll) make a mess of

verpesten [fer'pestən] *tr* infect, contaminate

verpet′zen *tr* (coll) squeal on

verpfän′den *tr* pawn; mortgage; sein Wort v. give one's word of honor

verpflan′zen *tr* (bot, surg) transplant

Verpflan′zung *f* (-;-en) (bot, surg) transplant

verpfle′gen *tr* feed; (mil) supply

Verpfle′gung *f* (-;) feeding; board; (mil) rations, supplies

verpflichten [fer'pflɪçtən] *tr* obligate, bind; zu Dank v. put under obligation

Verpflich′tung *f* (-;-en) obligation; commitment; (jur) liability

verpfuschen [fer'pfuʃən] *tr* (coll) botch, bungle, muff

verplap′pern *ref* blab out a secret

verplau′dern *tr* waste in chatting

verpönt [fer'pønt] *adj* taboo

verprü′geln *tr* (coll) wallop, thrash

verpuf′fen *intr* (SEIN) fizzle; (fig) fizzle out

verpulvern [fer'pulfərn] *tr* (coll) waste, fritter away

verpum′pen *tr* (coll) loan

verpusten [fer'pustən] *ref* (coll) catch one's breath

Verputz [fer'puts] *m* (-es;-e) finishing coat (of plaster)

verput′zen *tr* plaster; (*aufessen*) polish off; (coll) stand

verquicken [fer'kvɪkən] *tr* interrelate

verquollen [fer'kvɔlən] *adj* (*Augen*) swollen; (*Gesicht*) puffy; (*Holz*) warped

verrammeln [fer'ramaln] *tr* barricade

verramschen [fer'ramʃən] *tr* (coll) sell dirt-cheap

verrannt [fer'rant] *adj*—v. sein in (*acc*) be stuck on

Verrat′ *m* (-[e]s;) betrayal; treason

verra′ten §63 *tr* betray

Verräter -in [fer'retər(ɪn)] §6 *mf* traitor; betrayer

verräterisch [fer'retərɪʃ] *adj* treacherous; (*Spur, usw.*) telltale

verrau′chen *tr* spend on smokes

verräu′chern *tr* fill with smoke

verrech′nen *tr* (*ausgleichen*) balance; (*Scheck*) deposit; (fin) clear || *ref* miscalculate; (fig) be mistaken

Verrech′nung *f* (-;-en) miscalculation; (fin) clearing; nur zur V. for deposit only

Verrech′nungsbank *f*, **Verrech′nungskasse** *f* clearing house

verrecken [fer'rekən] *intr* (SEIN) die; (sl) croak; verrecke! drop dead!

verreg′nen *tr* spoil with too much rain

verrei′sen *intr* (SEIN) go on a trip; v. nach depart for

verreist [fer'raɪst] *adj* out of town

verren′ken *tr* wrench, dislocate || *ref*—sich [*dat*] den Arm v. wrench one's arm; sich [*dat*] den Hals v. (coll) crane one's neck

Verren′kung *f* (-;-en) dislocation

verrich′ten *tr* do; (*Gebet*) say; seine Notdurft v. ease oneself

Verrich′tung *f* (-;-en) performance; task, duty

verrie′geln *tr* bolt, bar

verringern [fer'rɪŋərn] *tr* diminish, reduce || *ref* diminish; be reduced

Verrin′gerung *f* (-;-en) diminution; reduction

verrin′nen §121 *intr* (SEIN) run off; (*Zeit*) pass

verro′sten *intr* (SEIN) rust

verrotten [fer'rɔtən] *intr* (SEIN) rot

verrucht [fer'ruxt] *adj* wicked

verrücken (verrük′ken) *tr* move, shift

verrückt [fer'rʏkt] *adj* crazy; v. auf etw crazy about s.th.; v. nach j-m crazy about s.o. || **Verrückte** §5 *mf* lunatic

Verrückt′heit *f* (-;-en) craziness, madness; crazy action or act

Verruf′ *m* (-[e]s;) discredit, disrepute

verru′fen *adj* disreputable

verrüh′ren *tr* stir thoroughly

verrut′schen *intr* (SEIN) slip

Vers [fers] *m* (-es;-e) verse

versa′gen *tr* refuse; versagt sein have a previous engagement || *ref*—sich [*dat*] etw v. deny oneself s.th.; ich kann es mir nicht v. zu (*inf*) I can't refrain from (*ger*) || *intr* fail; (*Beine, Stimme, usw.*) give out; (*Gewehr*) misfire; (*Motor*) fail to start; bei e-r Prüfung v. flunk a test || **Versagen** *n* (-s;-) failure, flop; misfire

Versa′ger *m* (-s;-) failure, flop; (*Patrone*) dud

versal′zen *tr* oversalt; (fig) spoil

versam′meln *tr* gather together, assemble; convoke || *ref* gather, assemble

Versamm′lung *f* (-;-en) assembly, meeting

Versand [fer'zant] *m* (-[e]s;) shipment; mailing

Versand′abteilung *f* shipping department

versanden [fer'zandən] *intr* (SEIN) silt up; (fig) bog down

Versand'geschäft n, **Versand'haus** n mail-order house

versäu'men tr (*Gelegenheit, Schule, Zug*) miss; (*Geschäft, Pflicht*) neglect; **v. zu** (*inf*) fail to (*inf*)

Versäumnis [fer'zɔɪmnɪs] f (–;–se), n (–ses;–se) omission, neglect; (*educ*) absence; (jur) default

verschaf'fen tr get, obtain || *ref*—**sich** [*dat*] **etw v.** get; **sich** [*dat*] **Geld v.** raise money; **sich** [*dat*] **Respekt v.** gain respect

verschämt [fer'ʃemt] adj bashful, coy

Verschämt'heit f (–;) bashfulness

verschandeln [fer'ʃandəln] tr deface

verschan'zen tr fortify || *ref* entrench oneself; **sich v. hinter** (*dat*) (fig) hide behind

Verschan'zung f (–;–en) entrenchment

verschär'fen tr intensify; aggravate; **verschärfter Arrest** detention on a bread-and-water diet || *ref* get worse

verschei'den §112 intr (SEIN) pass away

verschen'ken tr give away

verscher'zen *ref*—**sich** [*dat*] **etw v.** throw away, lose (*frivolously*)

verscheu'chen tr scare away

verschicken (**verschik'ken**) tr send away; (*deportieren*) deport

Verschie'behahnhof m marshaling yard

verschie'ben §130 tr postpone; shift; displace; black-market; (rr) shunt, switch || *ref* shift

Verschie'bung f (–;–en) postponement; shift, shifting

verschieden [fer'ʃidən] adj different, various; distinct

verschie'denartig adj of a different kind

verschiedenerlei [fer'ʃidənərlaɪ] invar adj different kinds of

Verschie'denheit f (–;–en) difference; variety, diversity

verschiedentlich [fer'ʃidəntlɪç] adv repeatedly; at times, occasionally

verschie'ßen §76 tr (*Schießvorrat*) use up, expend || intr (SEIN) (*Farbe*) fade

verschif'fen tr ship

Verschif'fung f (–;) shipment

verschim'meln intr (SEIN) get moldy

verschla'fen adj sleepy, drowsy || §131 tr miss by sleeping; (*Zeit*) sleep away || intr oversleep

Verschla'fenheit f (–;) sleepiness

Verschlag' m partition; crate

verschla'gen adj sly; (*lau*) lukewarm || §132 tr partition off; board up; (*Kisten*) nail shut; (*Seite im Buch*) lose; (naut) drive off course; (tennis) misserve; **j–m den Atem v.** take s.o.'s breath away; **j–m die Sprache** (or **Rede, Stimme**) **v.** make s.o. speechless; **v. werden auf** (*acc*) (or **in** *acc*) be driven to || impers—**es verschlägt nichts** it doesn't matter

verschlammen [fer'ʃlamən] intr (SEIN) silt up

verschlampen [fer'ʃlampən] tr ruin (*through neglect*); (*verlegen*) misplace || intr get slovenly

verschlechtern [fer'ʃleçtərn] tr make worse || *ref* get worse, deteriorate

Verschlech'terung f (–;) deterioration

verschleiern [fer'ʃlaɪ·ərn] tr veil; (*Tatsachen*) cover up; (*Stimme*) disguise; (mil) screen; **die Bilanz v.** juggle the books || *ref* cloud up

verschleiert [fer'ʃlaɪ·ərt] adj hazy; (*Stimme*) husky; (*Augen*) misty

Verschlei'erung f (–;) coverup; camouflaging; (jur) suppression of evidence

verschlei'fen §88 tr slur, slur over

Verschleiß [fer'ʃlaɪs] m (–es;) wear and tear; (Aust) retail trade

verschlei'ßen §53 tr wear out; (Aust) retail || *ref* wear out

verschleiß'fest adj durable

verschlep'pen tr drag off; abduct; (*im Krieg*) displace; (*Verhandlungen*) drag out; (*Seuche*) spread; (*verzögern*) delay

verschleu'dern tr waste, squander; (*Waren*) sell dirt-cheap

verschlie'ßen §76 tr shut; lock; put under lock and key || *ref* (*dat*) close one's mind to

verschlimmern [fer'ʃlɪmərn] tr make worse; (fig) aggravate || *ref* get worse

verschlin'gen §142 tr devour, wolf down; (*verflechten*) intertwine

verschlissen [fer'ʃlɪsən] adj frayed

verschlossen [fer'ʃlɔsən] adj shut; (fig) reserved, tight-lipped

verschlucken (**verschluk'ken**) tr swallow || *ref* swallow the wrong way

verschlungen [fer'ʃlʊŋən] adj (*Weg*) winding; (fig) intricate

Ver·schluß' m (–schlusses;–schlüsse) fastener; (*Schnapp–*) catch; (*Schloß*) lock; (*e–r Flasche*) stopper; (*Stöpsel*) plug; (*Plombe*) seal; (*e–s Gewehrs*) breechlock; (phot) shutter; **unter V.** under lock and key

verschlüsseln [fer'ʃlysəln] tr code

Verschluß'laut m (ling) stop, plosive

verschmach'ten intr (SEIN) pine away; **vor Durst v.** be dying of thirst

verschmä'hen tr disdain

verschmel'zen §133 tr & intr (SEIN) fuse, merge; blend

Verschmel'zung f (–;–en) fusion; (com) merger

verschmer'zen tr get over

verschmie'ren tr smear; soil, dirty; (*verwischen*) blur

verschmitzt [fer'ʃmɪtst] adj crafty

verschmut'zen tr dirty || intr (SEIN) get dirty

verschnap'pen *ref* give oneself away

verschnau'fen *ref* & intr stop for breath

verschnei'den §106 tr clip, trim; cut wrong; castrate; (*Branntwein, Wein*) blend

verschneit [fer'ʃnaɪt] adj snow-covered

Verschnitt' m (–[e]s;) blend

verschnup'fen tr annoy; **verschnupft sein** have a cold; (coll) be annoyed

verschnü'ren tr tie up

verschollen [fer'ʃɔlən] adj missing, never heard of again; (jur) presumed dead

verscho'nen tr spare; **j–n mit etw v.** spare s.o. s.th.

verschönern [fer'ʃønərn] tr beautify

verschossen [fɛrˈʃɔsən] *adj* faded, discolored; (**in** *acc*) (coll) be madly in love (with)

verschränken [fɛrˈʃrɛŋkən] *tr* fold (*one's arms*)

verschrau/ben *tr* screw tight

verschrei/ben §62 *tr* use up (*in writing*); (jur) make over; (med) prescribe || *ref* make a mistake (*in writing*)

Verschrei/bung *f* (–;-en) prescription

verschrei/en §135 *tr* decry

verschrien [fɛrˈʃriːən] *adj*—**v. sein als** have the reputation of being

verschroben [fɛrˈʃroːbən] *adj* eccentric

Verschro/benheit *f* (–;-en) eccentricity

verschrotten [fɛrˈʃrɔtən] *tr* scrap

verschüch/tern *tr* intimidate

verschul/den *tr* encumber with debts; etw v. be guilty of s.th.; be the cause of s.th. || **Verschulden** *n* (–s;) fault

verschuldet [fɛrˈʃʊldət] *adj* in debt

Verschul/dung *f* (–;-en) indebtedness; encumbrance

verschüt/ten *tr* spill; (*ausfüllen*) fill up; (*Person*) bury alive

verschwägert [fɛrˈʃvɛːgərt] *adj* related by marriage

verschwei/gen §148 *tr* keep secret; **j–m etw v.** keep s.th. from s.o.

Verschwei/gung *f* (–;) concealment

verschwei/ßen *tr* weld (together)

verschwenden [fɛrˈʃvɛndən] *tr* (an *acc*) waste (on), squander (on)

Verschwen/der –in §6 *mf* spendthrift

verschwenderisch [fɛrˈʃvɛndərɪʃ] *adj* wasteful; lavish, extravagant

Verschwen/dung *f* (–;) waste; extravagance

verschwiegen [fɛrˈʃviːgən] *adj* discreet; reserved, reticent

Verschwie/genheit *f* (–;) discretion; reticence; secrecy

verschwim/men §136 *intr* (SEIN) become blurred; (fig) fade

verschwin/den §59 *intr* (SEIN) disappear; **ich muß mal v.** (coll) I have to go (to the toilet); **v. lassen** put out of the way; spirit off || **Verschwinden** *n* (–s;) disappearance

verschwistert [fɛrˈʃvɪstərt] *adj* closely related

verschwit/zen *tr* sweat up; (coll) forget

verschwollen [fɛrˈʃvɔlən] *adj* swollen

verschwommen [fɛrˈʃvɔmən] *adj* hazy, indistinct; (*Bild*) blurred

Verschwom/menheit *f* (–;) haziness

verschwö/ren §137 *tr* forswear || *ref* (gegen) plot (against); **sich zu etw v.** plot s.th.

Verschwö/rer –in §6 *mf* conspirator

Verschwö/rung *f* (–;-en) conspiracy

verse/hen §138 *tr* (*Amt, Stellung*) hold; (*Dienst, Pflicht*) perform; (*Haushalt, usw.*) look after; (mit) provide (with); (eccl) administer the last rites to; **j–s Dienst v.** fill in for s.o.; **mit e–m Saum v.** hem; **mit Giro v.** endorse; **mit Unterschrift v. sign** || *ref* make a mistake; **ehe man es sich versieht** before you know it; **sich v.** (*genit*) expect || **Versehen** *n* (–s;–) mistake, slip; oversight; **aus V. by** mistake

versehentlich [fɛrˈzeːəntlɪç] *adv* by mistake, erroneously, inadvertently

versehren [fɛrˈzeːrən] *tr* injure

Versehrte [fɛrˈzeːrtə] §5 *mf* disabled person

versen/den §140 *tr* send, ship; **ins Ausland v.** export

versen/gen *tr* scorch; (*Haar*) singe

versen/ken *tr* sink; submerge; lower; (*Kabel*) lay; (*Schraube*) countersink; (naut) scuttle || *ref*—**sich v. in** (*acc*) become engrossed in

Versen/kung *f* (–;-en) sinking; (theat) trapdoor; **in der V. verschwinden** (fig) vanish into thin air

versessen [fɛrˈzɛsən] *adj*—**v. auf** (*acc*) crazy about, obsessed with

verset/zen *tr* move, shift; (*Pflanze*) transplant; (*Schulkind*) promote; (*Beamte*) transfer; (*Schlag*) deal, give; (*verpfänden*) pawn; (*vermischen*) mix; (*Metall*) alloy; (*erwidern*) reply; (*vergeblich warten lassen*) (coll) stand up; (mus) transpose; **in Angst v.** terrify; **in Erstaunen v.** amaze; **in den Ruhestand v.** retire; **in Zorn v.** anger || *ref*—**v. Sie sich in meine Lage** put yourself in my place

Verset/zung *f* (–;-en) moving, shifting; transplanting; transfer; mixing; alloying; (educ) promotion

Verset/zungszeichen *n* (mus) accidental

verseuchen [fɛrˈzɔɪçən] *tr* infect, contaminate

Verseu/chung *f* (–;) infection; contamination

Vers/fuß *m* (pros) foot

versicherbar [fɛrˈzɪçərbɑr] *adj* insurable

versichern [fɛrˈzɪçərn] *tr* assure; assert, affirm; insure || *ref* (genit) assure oneself of

Versicherte [fɛrˈzɪçərtə] §5 *mf* insured

Versi/cherung *f* (–;-en) assurance; affirmation; insurance

Versi/cherungsanstalt *f* insurance company

Versi/cherungsbeitrag *m* premium

versi/cherungsfähig *adj* insurable

Versi/cherungsgesellschaft *f* insurance company

Versi/cherungsleistung *f* insurance benefit

Versi/cherungsmathematiker –in §6 *mf* actuary

Versi/cherungsnehmer –in §6 *mf* insured

versi/cherungspflichtig *adj* subject to mandatory insurance

Versi/cherungspolice *f*, **Versi/cherungsschein** *m* insurance policy

Versi/cherungsträger *m* underwriter

Versi/cherungszwang *m* compulsory insurance

versickern (versik/kern) *intr* (SEIN) seep out, trickle away

versie/geln *tr* seal (up); (jur) seal off

Versie/gelung *f* (–;) sealing (off)

versie/gen *intr* (SEIN) dry up

versil/bern *tr* silver-plate; (coll) sell

Versil/berung *f* (–;) silver-plating

versin'ken §143 *intr* (SEIN) (in *acc*)
sink (into); (fig) (in *acc*) lapse (into)
versinnbildlichen [fɛr'zɪnbɪltlɪçən] *tr*
symbolize
Version [vɛr'zjon] *f* (-;-en) version
versippt [fɛr'zɪpt] *adj* (mit) related
(to)
versklaven [fɛr'sklɑvən] *tr* enslave
Vers'kunst *f* versification
Vers'macher –in §6 *mf* versifier
Vers'maß *n* meter
versoffen [fɛr'zɔfən] *adj* (coll) drunk
versohlen [fɛr'zolən] *tr* (coll) give
(*s.o.*) a good licking
versöhnen [fɛr'zønən] *tr* (mit) reconcile (with) ‖ *ref* become reconciled
versöhnlich [fɛr'zønlɪç] *adj* conciliatory
Versöh'nung *f* (-;) reconciliation
Versöh'nungstag *m* Day of Atonement
versonnen [fɛr'zɔnən] *adj* wistful
versor'gen *tr* look after; provide for;
(mit) supply (with), provide (with)
Versor'ger –in §6 *mf* provider, bread-
winner
Versor'gung *f* (-;) providing, supply-
ing; (*Unterhalt*) maintenance;
(*Alters– und Validen–*) social security
Versor'gungsbetrieb *m* public utility
Versor'gungstruppen *pl* service troops
Versor'gungswege *pl* supply lines
verspan'nen *tr* guy, brace
verspäten [fɛr'pɛtən] *ref* come late;
(rr) be behind schedule
verspätet [fɛr'pɛtət] *adj* belated, late
Verspä'tung *f* (-;-en) lateness, delay;
mit e–r Stunde V. one hour behind
schedule; V. haben be late
verspei'sen *tr* eat up
verspekulie'ren *tr* lose on a gamble ‖
ref lose all through speculation
versper'ren *tr* bar, block, obstruct;
(*Tür*) lock
verspie'len *tr* lose, gamble away ‖ *intr*
—bei j–m v. lose favor with s.o.
verspielt [fɛr'pɪlt] *adj* playful; frivolous
versponnen [fɛr'pɔnən] *adj*—in Gedanken versponnen lost in thought
verspot'ten *tr* mock, deride
Verspot'tung *f* (-;) mockery, derision
verspre'chen §64 *tr* promise ‖ *ref* make
a mistake in speaking; ich verspreche
mir viel davon I expect a lot from
that ‖ Versprechen *n* (-s;-) promise;
slip of the tongue
Verspre'chung *f* (-;-en) promise
verspren'gen *tr* scatter, disperse
Versprengte [fɛr'prɛntə] §5 *mf* (mil)
straggler
versprit'zen *tr* squirt, spatter
versprü'hen *tr* spray
verspü'ren *tr* feel, sense
verstaatlichen [fɛr'tɑtlɪçən] *tr* nationalize
Verstaat'lichung *f* (-;) nationalization
verstädtern [fɛr'tɛtərn] *tr* urbanize
Verstäd'terung *f* (-;) urbanization
Verstand' *m* (-[e]s;) understanding;
intellect; intelligence, brains; (*Vernunft*) reason; (*Geist*) mind; senses;
sense; den V. verlieren lose one's

mind; gesunder V. common sense;
klarer V. clear head; nicht bei V.
sein be out of one's mind
Verstan'deskraft *f* intellectual power
verstan'desmäßig *adj* rational
Verstan'desmensch *m* matter-of-fact
person
verstän'dig *adj* intelligent; sensible,
reasonable; wise
verständigen [fɛr'tɛndɪgən] *tr* (von)
inform (about), notify (of) ‖ *ref*—
sich v. mit make oneself understood
to; come to an understanding with
Verstän'digung *f* (-;) understanding;
information; communication; (telp)
quality of reception
verständlich [fɛr'tɛntlɪç] *adj* understandable, intelligible; sich v. machen make oneself understood
Verständnis [fɛr'tɛntnɪs] *n* (-ses;-se)
(für) understanding (of), appreciation (for)
verständ'nislos *adj* uncomprehending
verständ'nisinnig *adj* with deep mutual understanding; (*Blick*) knowing
verständ'nisvoll *adj* understanding; appreciative; (*Blick*) knowing
verstär'ken *tr* stink up
verstär'ken *tr* strengthen; (*steigern*) intensify; (elec) boost; (mil) reinforce;
(rad) amplify
Verstär'ker *m* (-s;-) (rad) amplifier
Verstär'kung *f* (-;-en) strengthening;
intensification; (mil) reinforcement;
(rad) amplification
verstatten [fɛr'tɑtən] *tr* permit
verstau'ben *intr* (SEIN) get dusty
verstäu'ben *intr* atomize
verstaubt [fɛr'taupt] *adj* dusty; (fig)
antiquated
verstau'chen *tr* sprain
Verstau'chung *f* (-;-en) sprain
verstau'en *tr* stow away
Versteck [fɛr'tɛk] *m* (-[e]s;-e) hiding place; hideout; V. spielen play
hide-and-seek
verstecken (verstek'ken) *tr & ref* hide
versteckt [fɛr'tɛkt] *adj* hidden, veiled;
(*Absicht*) ulterior
verste'hen §146 *tr* understand, see;
make out; realize; (*Sprache*) know;
e–n Spaß v. take a joke; ich verstehe es zu (*inf*) I know how to (*inf*);
falsch v. misunderstand; verstanden?
get it?; v. Sie mich recht! don't get
me wrong!; was v. Sie unter (*dat*)?
what do you mean by? ‖ *ref*—(das)
versteht sich! that's understood!;
das versteht sich von selbst! that
goes without saying; sich gut v. mit
get along well with; sich v. auf (*acc*)
be skilled in; sich zu etw v. (*sich zu
etw entschließen*) bring oneself to do
s.th.; (*in etw einwilligen*) agree to
s.th. ‖ *recip* understand each other
verstei'fen *tr* stiffen; strut, brace, reinforce ‖ *ref* stiffen; sich v. auf (*acc*)
insist on
verstei'gen §148 *ref* lose one's way in
the mountain; sich dazu v., daß go
so far as to (*inf*)
Verstei'gerer *m* (-s;-) auctioneer
verstei'gern *tr* auction off

Verstei'gerung f (-;-en) auction
verstei'nern intr (SEIN) become petrified; (fig) be petrified
verstell'bar adj adjustable
verstel'len tr (regulieren) adjust; (versperren) block; (Stimme, usw.) disguise; (Weiche) throw; (Verkehrsampel) switch; (Zeiger e–r Uhr) move; misplace; j–m den Weg v. block s.o.'s way || ref put on an act
Verstel'lung f (-;-en) adjusting; disguise
versteu'ern tr pay taxes on
Versteu'erung f (-;) paying of taxes
verstiegen [fɛr'ʃtigən] adj (Idee, Plan) extravagant, fantastic
verstim'men tr put out of tune; (fig) put out of humor
verstimmt [fɛr'ʃtɪmt] adj out of tune; (Magen) upset; v. über (acc) upset over
Verstim'mung f (-;) bad humor; (zwischen zweien) bad feeling, bad blood
verstockt [fɛr'ʃtɔkt] adj stubborn; (Verbrecher) hardened; (eccl) impenitent
Verstockt'heit f (-;) stubbornness; (eccl) impenitence
verstohlen [fɛr'ʃtolən] adj furtive
verstop'fen tr stop up, clog; (Straße) block, jam; (Leib) constipate
Verstop'fung f (-;) stopping up, clogging; congestion; (pathol) constipation
verstorben [fɛr'ʃtɔrbən] adj late, deceased || Verstorbene §5 mf deceased
verstört [fɛr'ʃtørt] adj shaken, bewildered, distracted
Verstört'heit f (-;) bewilderment
Verstoß' m (gegen) violation (of), offense (against)
versto'ßen §150 tr disown || intr—v. gegen violate, break
verstre'ben tr prop, brace
verstrei'chen §85 tr (Butter) spread; (Risse) plaster up || intr (SEIN) pass, elapse; (Gelegenheit) slip by; (Frist) expire
verstreu'en tr scatter, disperse, strew
verstricken (verstrik'ken) tr use up in knitting; (fig) involve, entangle || ref get entangled
verstümmeln [fɛr'ʃtyməln] tr mutilate; (Funkspruch) garble
Verstüm'melung f (-;-en) mutilation; (rad) garbling
verstummen [fɛr'ʃtumən] intr (SEIN) become silent; (vor Erstaunen) be dumbstruck; (Geräusch) cease
Versuch [fɛr'zux] m (-[e]s;-e) try, attempt; (Probe) test, trial; (wissenschaftlich) experiment; e–n V. machen mit have a try at
versu'chen tr try; tempt; (kosten) taste
Versuchs'anstalt f research institute
Versuchs'ballon m (& fig) trial balloon
Versuchs'flieger m test pilot
Versuchs'flug m test flight
Versuchs'kaninchen n (fig) guinea pig
Versuchs'reihe f series of tests
versuchs'weise adv by way of a test; on approval
Versu'chung f (-;-en) temptation

versumpfen [fɛr'zumpfən] intr (SEIN) become marshy; (coll) go to the dogs
versün'digen ref (an dat) sin (against)
versunken [fɛr'zuŋkən] adj sunk; v. in (acc) (fig) lost in
versü'ßen tr sweeten
verta'gen tr & ref (auf acc) adjourn (till), recess (till)
Verta'gung f (-;-en) adjournment
vertändeln [fɛr'tɛndəln] tr trifle away
vertäuen [fɛr'tɔɪ-ən] tr (naut) moor
vertau'schen tr (gegen) exchange (for)
Vertau'schung f (-;-en) exchange
verteidigen [fɛr'taɪdɪgən] tr defend
Vertei'diger –In §6 mf defender; (Befürworter) advocate; (jur) counsel for the defense || m (fb) back
Vertei'digung f (-;-en) defense
Vertei'digungsbündnis n defensive alliance
Vertei'digungsminister m secretary of defense
Vertei'digungsministerium n department of defense
Vertei'digungsschrift f written defense
Vertei'digungsstellung f defensive position
vertei'len tr distribute; (zuteilen) allot; (über e–e große Fläche) scatter; (steuerlich) spread out; (Rollen) (theat) cast || ref spread out
Vertei'ler m (-s;-) distributer; (Anschriftenliste) mailing list; (von Durchschlägen) distribution; (aut) distributor
Vertei'lung f (-;-en) distribution; allotment; (theat) casting
verteuern [fɛr'tɔɪ-ərn] tr raise the price of
verteufelt [fɛr'tɔɪfəlt] adj devilish; a devil of a
vertiefen [fɛr'tifən] tr make deeper; (fig) deepen || ref—sich v. in (acc) become absorbed in
Vertie'fung f (-;-en) deepening; (Höhlung) hollow, depression; (Nische) niche; (Loch) hole; (fig) absorption
vertiert [fɛr'tirt] adj bestial
vertikal [vɛrti'kɑl] adj vertical || Vertikale f (-;-n) vertical
vertil'gen tr exterminate, eradicate; (aufessen) (coll) eat, polish off
Vertil'gung f (-;) extermination
vertip'pen tr type incorrectly || ref make a typing error
verto'nen tr set to music
Verto'nung f (-;-en) musical arrangement
vertrackt [fɛr'trakt] adj (coll) odd, strange; (coll) blooming
Vertrag [fɛr'trak] m (-[e]s;-̈e) contract, agreement; (dipl) treaty
vertra'gen §132 tr stand, take; tolerate || recip agree, be compatible; (Farben) harmonize; (Personen) get along
vertrag'lich adj contractual || adv by contract, as stipulated; sich v. verpflichten zu (inf) contract to (inf)
verträglich [fɛr'trɛklɪç] adj sociable, personable; (Speise) digestible
Vertrags'bruch m breach of contract
vertragsbrüchig [fɛr'traksbryçɪç] adj —v. werden break a contract

vertrags'gemäß *adj* contractual

vertrags'widrig *adj* contrary to the terms of a contract or treaty

vertrau'en *intr (dat)* trust; v. auf *(acc)* trust in, have confidence in || Vertrauen *n* (-s;) trust, confidence; ganz im V. just between you and me; im V. confidentially

vertrau'enerweckend *adj* inspiring confidence

Vertrau'ensbruch *m* breach of trust

Vertrau'ens•mann *m* (-[e]s;=er & -leute) confidential agent; *(Vertrauter)* confidant; *(Sprecher)* spokesman; *(Gewährsmann)* informant

Vertrau'ensposten *m*, Vertrau'ensstellung *f* position of trust

vertrau'ensvoll *adj* confident; trusting

Vertrau'ensvotum *n* vote of confidence

vertrau'enswürdig *adj* trustworthy

vertrauern [fer'trau·ərn] *tr* spend in mourning

vertraulich [fer'trauliç] *adj* confidential; intimate

Vertrau'lichkeit *f* (-;-en) intimacy, familiarity; sich *[dat]* Vertraulichkeiten herausnehmen take liberties

verträu'men *tr* dream away

verträumt [fer'trɔımt] *adj* dreamy

vertraut [fer'traut] *adj* familiar; friendly, intimate || Vertraute §5 *mf* intimate friend || *m* confidant || *f* confidante

Vertraut'heit *f* (-;) familiarity

vertrei'ben §62 *tr* drive away, expel; *(aus dem Hause)* chase out; *(aus dem Lande)* banish; *(Ware)* sell, market; *(Zeit)* pass, kill

Vertrei'bung *f* (-;) expulsion

vertre'ten §152 *tr* represent; substitute for; *(Ansicht, usw.)* advocate || *ref* —sich *[dat]* den Fuß v. sprain one's ankle; sich *[dat]* die Beine v. (coll) stretch one's legs

Vertre'ter –in §6 *mf* representative; substitute; *(Bevollmächtigte)* proxy; *(im Amt)* deputy; *(Fürsprecher)* advocate; (com) agent

Vertre'tung *f* (-;-en) representation; substitution; (com) agency; (pol) mission; in V. by proxy; in V. (genit) signed for

Vertrieb' *m* (-[e]s;-e) sale, turnover; retail trade; sales department

Vertriebs'abkommen *n* franchise agreement

Vertriebs'abteilung *f* sales department

Vertriebs'kosten *pl* distribution costs

Vertriebs'leiter –in §6 *mf* sales manager

Vertriebs'recht *n* franchise

vertrin'ken §143 *tr* drink up

vertrock'nen *intr* (SEIN) dry up

vertrödeln [fer'trødəln] *tr* fritter away

vertrö'sten *tr* string along; auf später v. put off till later

vertun' §154 *tr* waste || *ref* (coll) make a mistake

vertu'schen *tr* hush up

verübeln [fer'ybəln] *tr* take (s.th.) the wrong way; j-m etw v. blame s.o. for s.th.

verü'ben *tr* commit, perpetrate

verul'ken *tr* (coll) kid

verunehren [fer'uneːrən] *tr* dishonor

veruneinigen [fer'unaınıgən] *tr* disunite || *recip* fall out, quarrel

verunglimpfen [fer'unglımpfən] *tr* slander, defame

verunglücken [fer'unglykən] *intr* (SEIN) have an accident; (coll) fail

Verunglückte [fer'unglyktə] §5 *mf* victim, casualty

verunreinigen [fer'unraınıgən] *tr* soil, dirty; *(Luft, Wasser)* pollute

Verun'reinigung *f* (-;) pollution

verunstalten [fer'unʃtaltən] *tr* disfigure, deface

veruntreuen [fer'untrɔı·ən] *tr* embezzle

Verun'treuung *f* (-;) embezzlement

verunzieren [fer'untsiːrən] *tr* mar

verursachen [fer'urzaxən] *tr* cause

verur'teilen *tr* condemn; sentence

Verur'teilung *f* (-;-en) condemnation; sentence

vervielfachen [fer'filfaxən] *tr* multiply || *ref* increase considerably

vervielfältigen [fer'filfɛltıgən] *tr* multiply; duplicate; mimeograph; *(nachbilden)* reproduce

Verviel'fältigung *f* (-;-en) duplication; mimeographing; reproduction; (phot) printing

Verviel'fältigungsapparat *m* duplicator

vervollkommnen [fer'fɔlkɔmnən] *tr* improve on, perfect

Vervoll'kommnung *f* (-;) improvement, perfection

vervollständigen [fer'fɔlʃtɛndıgən] *tr* complete

Vervoll'ständigung *f* (-;) completion

verwach'sen *adj* overgrown; deformed; hunchbacked; mit etw v. sein (fig) be attached to s.th. || *intr* (SEIN) grow together; become deformed; *(Wunde)* heal up; zu e-r Einheit v. form a whole

Verwach'sung *f* (-;-en) deformity

verwackelt [fer'vakəlt] *adj* (phot) blurred

verwah'ren *tr* keep; v. vor *(dat)* protect against || *ref*—sich v. gegen protest against

verwahrlosen [fer'varlozən] *tr* neglect || *intr* (SEIN) *(Gebäude)* deteriorate; *(Kinder)* run wild; *(Personen)* go to the dogs

verwahrlost [fer'varlost] *adj* uncared-for; *(Person)* unkempt; *(sittlich)* degenerate; *(Garten)* overgrown with weeds

Verwahr'losung *f* (-;) neglect

Verwah'rung *f* (-;) care, safekeeping, custody; (fig) protest; etw in V. nehmen take care of s.th.; j—m in V. geben entrust to s.o.'s care

verwaisen [fer'vaızən] *intr* (SEIN) become an orphan, be orphaned

verwaist [fer'vaıst] *adj* orphaned; (fig) deserted

verwalten [fer'valtən] *tr* administer, manage

Verwal'ter –in §6 *mf* administrator, manager

Verwal'tung *f* (-;-en) administration, management

Verwal/tungsapparat *m* administrative machinery

Verwal/tungsbeamte *m* civil service worker; administrative official

Verwal/tungsdienst *m* civil service

Verwal/tungsrat *m* advisory board; (*e-r Aktiengesellschaft*) board of directors; (*e-s Instituts*) board of trustees

verwan/deln *tr* change, turn, convert; (*Strafe*) commute ‖ *ref* change, turn

Verwand/lung *f* (-;-en) change, transformation; (jur) commutation

verwandt [fer'vant] *adj* (mit) related (to); (*Wissenschaften*) allied; (*Wörter*) cognate; (*Seelen*) kindred ‖ **Verwandte §5** *mf* relative, relation

Verwandt/schaft *f* (-;-en) relationship; relatives; (chem) affinity

verwandt/schaftlich *adj* kindred

Verwand/schaftsgrad *m* degree of relationship

verwanzt [fer'vantst] *adj* (coll) full of bugs, lousy

verwar/nen *tr* warn, caution

Verwar/nung *f* (-;-en) warning, caution

verwa/schen *adj* washed-out, faded; (*verschwommen*) vague, fuzzy

verwäs/sern *tr* dilute; (fig) water down

verwe/ben §94 *tr* interweave

verwe/chseln *tr* confuse, get (*various items*) mixed up; (*Hüte, Mäntel*) take by mistake ‖ **Verwechseln** *n* (-s;)—**sie sehen sich zum V. ähnlich** they are as alike as two peas

Verwechs/lung *f* (-;-en) mix-up

verwegen [fer'vegən] *adj* bold, daring

verwe/hen *tr* (*Blätter*) blow away; (*Spur*) cover up (with snow) ‖ *intr* (SEIN) be blown in all directions; (*Spur*) be covered up; (*Worte*) drift away

verweh/ren *tr*—**j—m etw v.** refuse s.o. s.th.; prevent s.o. from getting s.th.

Verwe/hung *f* (-;-en) (snow)drift

verweichlichen [fer'vaiçliçən] *tr* make effeminate; (*Kind*) coddle ‖ *ref* & *intr* become effeminate; grow soft

verweichlicht [fer'vaiçliçt] *adj* effeminate; soft, flabby

Verweich/lichung *f* (-;) effeminacy

verwei/gern *tr* refuse, deny, turn down

Verwei/gerung *f* (-;-en) refusal

verweilen [fer'vailən] *intr* linger, tarry; (fig) dwell

verweint [fer'vaint] *adj* red with tears

Verweis [fer'vais] *m* (-es;-e) reprimand, rebuke; (*Hinweis*) reference

verwei/sen §118 *tr* banish; (*Schüler*) expel; **j—m etw v.** reprimand s.o. for s.th.; **j-n an j-n v.** refer s.o. to s.o.; **j-n auf etw v.** refer s.o. to s.th.

Verwei/sung *f* (-;-en) banishment; expulsion; (an *acc*) referral (to); (auf *acc*) reference (to)

verwel/ken *intr* (SEIN) wither, wilt

verweltlichen [fer'veltliçən] *tr* secularize

verwendbar [fer'ventbɑr] *adj* applicable; available; usable

Verwend/barkeit *f* (-;) availability; usefulness

verwen/den §140 *tr* use, employ; (auf *acc*, für) apply (to); **Zeit und Mühe v. auf** (*acc*) spend time and effort on ‖ *ref*—**sich bei j—m v. für** intercede with s.o. for

Verwen/dung *f* (-;-en) use, employment; application; **keine V. haben für** have no use for; **vielseitige V.** versatility

verwen/dungsfähig *adj* usable

verwer/fen §160 *tr* reject; (*Plan*) discard; (*Berufung*) turn down; (*Klage*) dismiss; (*Urteil*) overrule ‖ *ref* (*Holz*) warp; (geol) fault

verwerf/lich *adj* objectionable

Verwer/fung *f* (-;-en) rejection; warping; (geol) fault

verwer/ten *tr* utilize

Verwer/tung *f* (-;-en) utilization

verwesen [fer'vezən] *intr* (SEIN) rot

verweslich [fer'vezliç] *adj* perishable

Verwe/sung *f* (-;) decay

verwet/ten *tr* lose (*in betting*)

verwich/sen *tr* (coll) clobber

verwickeln (verwik/keln) *tr* snarl, entangle; complicate; (fig) involve ‖ *ref*—**sich v. in** (*acc*) get entangled in; (fig) get involved in

Verwick/lung *f* (-;-en) snarl, tangle; involvement; complexity; complication

verwil/dern *intr* become overgrown; (*Person*) become depraved; (*Kind*) run wild, go wild

verwildert [fer'vildərt] *adj* wild, savage; weed-grown

verwin/den §59 *tr* get over; (*Verlust*) recover from

verwir/ken *tr* forfeit; (*Strafe*) incur ‖ *ref*—**sich** [*dat*] **j–s Gunst v.** lose favor with s.o.

verwirklichen [fer'virkliçən] *tr* realize, make come true ‖ *ref* come true

Verwirk/lichung *f* (-;) realization

Verwir/kung *f* (-;) forfeiture

verwirren [fer'virən] *tr* throw into disorder; (*Haar*) muss up; confuse

verwirrt [fer'virt] *adj* confused

Verwir/rung *f* (-;-en) confusion; **in V.** geraten become confused

verwirt/schaften *tr* squander

verwi/schen *tr* wipe out; (*teilweise*) blur; (*verschmieren*) smear; (*Spuren*) cover ‖ *ref* become blurred

verwit/tern *intr* (SEIN) become weatherbeaten; (*zerfallen*) crumble away

verwittert [fer'vitərt] *adj* weatherbeaten

verwitwet [fer'vitvət] *adj* widowed

verwöhnen [fer'vønən] *tr* pamper, spoil

verworfen [fer'vorfən] *adj* depraved

Verwor/fenheit *f* (-;) depravity

verworren [fer'vorən] *adj* confused

verwundbar [fer'vuntbɑr] *adj* vulnerable

verwun/den *tr* wound

verwunderlich [fer'vundərliç] *adj* remarkable, astonishing

verwun/dern *tr* astonish ‖ *ref* (über *acc*) be astonished (at), wonder (at)

Verwun/derung *f* (-;) astonishment; **j–n in V. setzen** astonish s.o.

verwundet [fer'vundət] *adj* wounded

|| **Verwundete** §5 *mf* wounded person

verwunschen [fer'vunʃən] *adj* enchanted

verwün'schen *tr* damn, curse; (*in Märchen*) bewitch, put a curse on

verwünscht [fer'vynʃt] *adj* confounded, darn || *interj* darn it!

Verwün'schung *f* (–;–en) curse

verwurzelt [fer'vurtsəlt] *adj* deeply rooted

verwüsten [fer'vystən] *tr* devastate

Verwü'stung *f* (–;–en) devastation

verzagen [fer'tsagən] *intr* (SEIN) lose heart, despair; **v. an** (*dat*) give up on

verzagt [fer'tsakt] *adj* despondent

Verzagt'heit *f* (–;) despondency

verzäh'len *ref* miscount

verzärteln [fer'tsertəln] *tr* pamper

verzau'bern *tr* bewitch, charm; **v. in** (*acc*) change into

Verzehr [fer'tser] *m* (–[e]s;) consumption

verzeh'ren *tr* consume; (*Geld*) spend; (*Mahlzeit*) eat || *ref* (*in dat, vor dat*) pine away (with); (*nach*) yearn (for)

verzeh'rend *adj* (*Blick*) longing; (*Fieber*) wasting; (*Leidenschaft*) burning

Verzeh'rung *f* (–;) consumption

verzeich'nen *tr* draw wrong; make a list of; register; catalogue; (*opt*) distort

Verzeichnis [fer'tsaıçnıs] *n* (–ses;–se) list; catalogue; (*im Buch*) index; (*Inventar*) inventory; (*Tabelle*) table; (*telp*) directory

verzeihen [fer'tsaı·ən] §81 *tr* forgive, pardon (*s.th.*); condone || *intr* (*dat*) forgive, pardon (*s.o.*)

verzeihlich [fer'tsaılıç] *adj* pardonable

Verzei'hung *f* (–;) pardon

verzer'ren *tr* distort; contort

Verzer'rung *f* (–;–en) distortion; contortion; grimace

verzetteln [fer'tsetəln] *tr* fritter away; catalogue || *ref* spread oneself too thin

Verzicht [fer'tsıçt] *m* (–[e]s;) renunciation; **V. leisten auf** (*acc*) waive

verzichten [fer'tsıçtən] *intr*—**v. auf** (*acc*) do without; (*verabsäumen*) pass up; (*aufgeben*) give up, renounce; (*Rechte*) waive

verzieh [fer'tsi] *pret* of **verziehen**

verzie'hen §163 *tr* distort; (*Kind*) spoil; **den Mund v.** make a face; **ohne e–e Miene zu v.** without batting an eye || *ref* disappear; (*Schmerz*) go away; (*Menge, Wolken*) disperse; (*Holz*) warp; (*durch Druck*) buckle; (*coll*) sneak off

verzie'ren *tr* decorate

Verzie'rung *f* (–;–en) decoration; (*Schmuck*) ornament

verzinsen [fer'tsınzən] *tr* pay interest on; **e–e Summe zu 6% v.** pay 6% interest on a sum || *ref* yield interest; **sich mit 6% v.** yield 6% interest

verzinslich [fer'tsınslıç] *adj* bearing interest || *adv*—**v. anlegen** put out at interest

Verzin'sung *f* (–;) interest

verzog [fer'tsok] *pret* of **verziehen**

verzogen [fer'tsogən] *adj* distorted; (*Kind*) spoiled; (*Holz*) warped

verzö'gern *tr* delay; put off, postpone || *ref* be late

Verzö'gerung *f* (–;–en) delay; postponement

verzollen [fer'tsolən] *tr* pay duty on; (naut) clear; **haben Sie etw zu v.?** do you have anything to declare?

verzückt [fer'tsykt] *adj* ecstatic

Verzückung [fer'tsykuŋ] *f* (–;) ecstasy

Verzug' *m* (–[e]s;) delay; (**in der Leistung**) default; **in V. geraten** mit fall behind in; **ohne V.** without delay

verzwei'feln *intr* (HABEN & SEIN) (**an** dat) despair (of) || **Verzweifeln** *n*—**es ist zum V.** it's enough to drive one to despair

verzweifelt [fer'tsvaıfəlt] *adj* desperate

Verzweif'lung *f* (–;) despair

verzweigen [fer'tsvaıgən] *ref* branch out

verzweigt [fer'tsvaıkt] *adj* having many branches; (fig) complex

verzwickt [fer'tsvıkt] *adj* (coll) tricky, ticklish

Vestibül [vestı'byl] *n* (–s;–e) vestibule; (theat) lobby

Veteran [vete'ran] *m* (–en;–en) veteran, ex-serviceman

Veterinär –in [veterı'ner(ın)] §8 *mf* veterinarian

Veto ['veto] *n* (–s;–s) veto

Vetter ['fetər] *m* (–s;–) cousin

Vet'ternwirtschaft *f* nepotism

Vexierbild [ve'ksirbılt] *n* picture puzzle

vexieren [ve'ksirən] *tr* tease; pester

V-förmig ['faufœrmıç] *adj* V-shaped

vibrieren [vı'brirən] *intr* vibrate

Vieh [fi] (–[e]s;) livestock; cattle; animal, beast

Vieh'bestand *m* livestock

Vieh'bremse *f* horsefly

viehisch ['fi·ıʃ] *adj* brutal

Vieh'tränke *f* water hole

Vieh'wagen *m* (rr) cattle car

Vieh'weide *f* cow pasture

Vieh'zucht *f* cattle breeding

Vieh'züchter –in §6 *mf* rancher

viel [fil] *adj* much; many; **a lot of** || *adv* much; a lot || *pron* much; many

viel'beschäftigt *adj* very busy

viel'deutig *adj* ambiguous

Viel'eck *n* polygon

vielerlei ['filər'laı] *invar adj* many kinds of

viel'fach *adj* multiple; manifold || *adv* (coll) often

Vielfach– comb.fm. multiple

viel'fältig *adj* manifold, various

Viel'fältigkeit *f* (–;) multiplicity; variety

vielleicht' *adv* maybe, perhaps

vielmalig ['filmalıç] *adj* oft repeated

vielmals ['filmals] *adv* frequently; **danke v.!** many thanks!

vielmehr' *adv* rather, on the contrary

viel'sagend *adj* suggestive

viel'seitig *adj* many-sided, versatile

vielstufig ['fil'tufıç] *adj* multistage

viel'teilig *adj* of many parts

viel'versprechend *adj* very promising

vier [fir] *adj* four; **unter vier Augen** confidentially ‖ *pron* four; **auf allen vieren** on all fours ‖ **Vier** *f* (–;–en) four

vier′beinig *adj* four-legged

Vier′eck *n* quadrangle

vier′eckig *adj* quadrangular

viererlei ['firər'laɪ] *invar adj* four different kinds of

vier′fach, vier′fältig *adv* fourfold, quadruple

Vierfüßer ['firfysər] *m* (–s;–) quadruped

vierhändig ['firhendɪç] *adv*—**v. spielen** (mus) play a duet

Vierlinge ['firlɪŋə] *pl* quadruplets

vier′mal *adv* four times

vierschrötig ['fir/rø̞tɪç] *adj* stocky

vierstrahlig ['fir/traːlɪç] *adj* four-engine (jet)

viert [firt] *pron*—**zu v.** in fours; **wir gehen zu v.** the four of us are going

Viertakter ['firtaktər] *m* (–s;–), **Vier′taktmotor** ['firtaktmotɔr] *m* four-cycle engine

Vierte ['firtə] §9 *adj & pron* fourth

vier′teilen *tr* quarter

Viertel ['firtəl] *n* (–s;–) quarter; fourth (part); (Stadtteil) quarter, section

Vierteljahr′ *n* quarter (of a year)

vierteljäh′rig, vierteljähr′lich *adj* quarterly

vierteln ['firtəln] *tr* quarter

Vier′telnote *f* (mus) quarter note

Viertelpfund′ *n* quarter of a pound

Viertelstun′de *f* quarter of an hour

viertens ['firtəns] *adv* fourthly

vier′zehn *invar adj & pron* fourteen ‖ **Vierzehn** *f* (–;–en) fourteen

vier′zehnte §9 *adj & pron* fourteenth

Vier′zehntel *n* (–s;–) fourteenth (part)

vierzig ['firtsɪç] *invar adj & pron* forty ‖ **Vierzig** *f* (–;–en) forty

vierziger ['firtsɪɡər] *invar adj* of the forties; **die v. Jahre** the forties

vierzigste ['firtsɪçstə] §9 *adj & pron* fortieth

Vikar [vi'kar] *m* (–s;–e) vicar

Vil-la ['vɪla] *f* (–;–len [lən]) villa

violett [vi.o'let] *adj* violet

Violine [vi.o'linə] *f* (–;–n) violin

Violin′schlüssel *m* treble clef

Viper ['vipər] *f* (–;–n) viper

viril [vi'ril] *adj* virile

virtuos [virtu'os] *adj* masterly ‖ **Virtuose** [virtu'ozə] *m* (–n;–n), **Virtuosin** [virtu'ozɪn] *f* (–;–nen) virtuoso

Vi-rus ['virus] *n* (–;–ren [rən]) virus

Visage [vi'zaʒə] *f* (–;–n) (coll) mug

Visier [vi'zir] *n* (–s;–e) visor; (am Gewehr) sight

visieren [vi'zirən] *tr* (eichen) gauge; (Paß) visa

Vision [vi'zjon] *f* (–;–en) vision

visionär [vizjo'ner] *adj* visionary ‖ **Visionär** *m* (–s;–e) visionary

Visitation [vizita'tsjon] *f* (–;–en) inspection; search

Visite [vi'zitə] *f* (–;–n) formal call; **Visiten machen** (med) make the rounds

Visi′tenkarte *f* calling card

---

visuell [vizu'el] *adj* visual

Vi-sum ['vizum] *n* (–s;–sa [za]) visa

vital [vi'tal] *adj* energetic

Vitalität [vitali'tet] *f* (–;) vitality

Vitamin [vita'min] *n* (–s;–e) vitamin

Vitamin′mangel *m* vitamin deficiency

Vitrine [vi'trinə] *f* (–;–n) showcase

Vize- [fitsə], [vitsə] *comb.fm.* vice-

Vi′zekönig *m* viceroy

Vlies [flis] *n* (–es;–e) fleece

Vogel ['fogəl] *m* (–s;–̈) bird; (coll) chap, bird; **den V. abschießen** (coll) bring down the house; **du hast e–n V.!** (coll) you're cuckoo!

Vo′gelbauer *n* birdcage

Vogelbeerbaum ['fogəlberbaum] *m* mountain ash

vo′gelfrei *adj* outlawed

Vo′gelfutter *n* birdseed

Vo′gelkunde *f* ornithology

Vo′gelmist *m* bird droppings

vögeln ['fø̞gəln] *tr & intr* (vulg) screw

Vo′gelperspektive *f*, **Vo′gelschau** *f* bird's-eye view

Vo′gelpfeife *f* bird call

Vo′gelscheuche *f* scarecrow

Vo′gelstange *f* perch

Vogel-Strauß′-Politik *f* burying one's head in the sand; **V. betreiben** bury one's head in the sand

Vo′gelstrich *m*, **Vo′gelzug** *m* migration of birds

Vöglein ['fø̞glaɪn] *n* (–s;–) little bird

Vogt [fokt] *m* (–[e]s;–̈e) (obs) steward; (obs) governor, prefect, magistrate

Vokabel [vo'kabəl] *f* (–;–n) vocabulary word

Vokal [vo'kal] *m* (–s;–e) vowel

Volk [folk] *n* (–[e]s;–̈er) people, nation; lower classes; (von Bienen) swarm; (von Rebhühnern) covey

Völker- [fœlkər] *comb.fm.* international

Völ′kerbund *m* League of Nations

Völ′kerfriede *m* international peace

Völ′kerkunde *f* ethnology

Völ′kermord *m* genocide

Völ′kerrecht *n* international law

Völ′kerschaft *f* (–;–en) tribe

Völ′kerwanderung *f* barbarian invasions

volk′reich *adj* populous

Volks′abstimmung *f* plebiscite

Volks′aufwiegler *m* rabble rouser

Volks′ausdruck *m* household expression

Volks′befragung *f* public opinion poll

Volks′begehren *n* national referendum

Volks′bibliotek *f* free library

Volks′charakter *m* national character

Volks′deutsche §5 *mf* German national

Volks′dichter *m* popular poet

volks′eigen *adj* state-owned

Volks′entscheid *m* referendum

Volks′feind *m* public enemy

Volks′gunst *f* popularity

Volks′haufen *m* crowd, mob

Volks′herrschaft *f* democracy

Volks′hochschule *f* adult evening school

Volks′justiz *f* lynch law

Volks′küche *f* soup kitchen
Volks′kunde *f* folklore
Volks′lied *n* folksong
volks′mäßig *adj* popular
Volks′meinung *f* popular opinion
Volks′menge *f* populace, crowd of people
Volks′musik *f* popular music
Volks′partei *f* people's party
Volks′republik *f* people's republic
Volks′schule *f* grade school
Volks′sitte *f* national custom
Volks′sprache *f* vernacular
Volks′stamm *m* tribe; race
Volks′stimme *f* popular opinion
Volks′stimmung *f* mood of the people
Volks′tracht *f* national costume
Volkstum [′fɔlkstum] *n* (-s;) nationality
volkstümlich [′fɔlkstymlɪç] *adj* national; popular
Volks′verführer –in §6 *mf* demagogue
Volks′versammlung *f* public meeting
Volks′vertreter –in §6 *mf* representative
Volks′wirt *m* political economist
Volks′wirtschaft *f* national economy
Volks′wirtschaftslehre *f* (educ) political economy
Volks′wohl *n* public good
Volks′wohlfahrt *f* public welfare
Volks′zählung *f* census
voll [fɔl] *adj* full, filled; whole, entire; (*Tageslicht*) broad; (coll) drunk; **aus dem vollen schöpfen** have unlimited resources; **j–n für v. ansehen** (or **nehmen**) take s.o. seriously ‖ *adv* fully, in full; **v. und ganz** fully
vollauf′ *adv*—**das genügt v.** that's quite enough; **v. beschäftigt** plenty busy; **v. zu tun haben** have plenty to do
Voll′beschäftigung *f* full employment
Voll′besitz *m* full possession
Voll′blut *n,* **Voll′blutpferd** *n* thoroughbred
vollblütig [′fɔlblytɪç] *adj* full-blooded
vollbrin′gen §65 *tr* achieve
vollbusig [′vɔlbuzɪç] *adj* big-breasted
Voll′dampf *m* full steam; **mit V.** (fig) at full blast, full speed
vollenden [fɔl′ɛndən] *tr* bring to a close, finish, complete; (*vervollkommnen*) perfect; **er hat sein Leben vollendet** (poet) he died
vollendet [fɔl′ɛndət] *adj* perfect
vollends [′fɔlɛnts] *adv* completely
Vollen′dung *f* (-;) finishing, completing; (*Vollkommenheit*) perfection
Völlerei [fœlə′raɪ] *f* (-;) gluttony
voll′führen *tr* carry out, execute
voll′füllen *tr* fill up
Voll′gas *n* full throttle
Voll′gefühl *n*—**im V.** (genit) fully conscious of
Voll′genuß *m* full enjoyment
vollgepfropft [′fɔlgəprɔpft] *adj* jammed, packed
voll′gießen §76 *tr* fill up
völlig [′fœlɪç] *adj* full, complete
voll′jährig *adj* of age
Voll′jährigkeit *f* legal age, majority
vollkom′men, voll′kommen *adj* perfect ‖ *adv* (coll) absolutely

Vollkom′menheit *f* (-;) perfection
Voll′kornbrot *n* whole-grain bread
Voll′kraft *f* full vigor, prime
voll′machen *tr* fill up; (coll) dirty
Voll′macht *f* full authority; (jur) power of attorney; **in V. for...** (*prefixed to the signature of another at end of letter*)
Voll′matrose *m* able-bodied seaman
Voll′milch *f* whole milk
Voll′mond *m* full moon
Voll′pension *f* full board and lodging
voll′saftig *adj* juicy, succulent
voll′schenken *tr* fill up
voll′schlagen §132 *ref*—**sich** [*dat*] **den Bauch v.** (coll) stuff oneself
voll′schlank *adj* well filled out
Voll′sitzung *f* plenary session
Voll′spur *f* (rr) standard-gauge track
voll′ständig *adj* full; complete, entire ‖ *adv* completely, quite
Voll′ständigkeit *f* (-;) completeness
voll′stopfen *tr* stuff, cram
vollstrecken (vollstrek′ken) *tr* (*Urteil*) carry out; (*Testament*) execute; **ein Todesurteil an j–m v.** execute s.o.
Vollstreckung (Vollstrek′kung) *f.* (-;) execution
voll′tanken *tr* (aut) fill up ‖ *intr* (aut) fill it up
volltönend [′fɔltønənt] *adj* (*Stimme*) rich; (*Satz*) well-rounded
Voll′treffer *m* direct hit
Voll′versammlung *f* plenary session
Voll′waise *f* (full) orphan
voll′wertig *adj* of full value; complete, perfect
vollzählig [′fɔltselɪç] *adj* complete; **sind wir v.?** are we all here? ‖ *adv* in full force
vollzie′hen §163 *tr* execute, carry out, effect; (*Vertrag*) ratify; (*Ehe*) consummate ‖ *ref* take place
vollzie′hend *adj* executive
Vollzie′hung *f,* **Vollzug′** *m* execution, carrying out
Vollzugs′ausschuß *m* executive committee
Volontär –in [vɔlɔn′tɛr(ɪn)] §8 *mf* volunteer; trainee
volontieren [vɔlɔn′tirən] *intr* work as a trainee
Volt [vɔlt] *n* (-[e]s;-) (elec) volt
Volu·men [vo′lumən] *n* (-s;- & -mina [mina]) (*Band; Rauminhalt*) volume
vom [fɔm] *abbr* **von dem**
von [fɔn] *prep* (dat) (*beim Passiv*) by; *für den Genitiv* of; (*räumlich, zeitlich*) from; (*über*) about, of; **von...an** from...on; **von Holz** (made) of wood; **von Kindheit auf** from earliest childhood; **von mir aus** as far as I am concerned; **von selbst** automatically
voneinan′der *adv* from each other; of each other; apart
vonnöten [fɔn′nøtən] *invar adj*—**v. sein** be necessary
vonstatten [fɔn′tatən] *adv*—**gut v. gehen** go well; **v. gehen** take place
vor [for] *prep* (dat) (*örtlich*) in front of, before; (*zeitlich*) before, prior to; (*Abwehr*) against, from; (*wegen*) of,

with, for; **etw vor sich haben** face s.th.; **heute vor acht Tagen** today a week ago; **vor sich gehen** take place, occur; **vor sich hin** to oneself || *prep* (*acc*) in front of

vorab' *adv* in advance

Vor'abend *m*—**am V.** (*genit*) on the eve of

Vor'ahnung *f* (coll) hunch, idea

voran' *adv* in front, out ahead || *interj* go ahead!, go on!

voran'gehen §82 *intr* (SEIN) go on ahead, take the lead; (fig) set an example; **die Arbeit geht gut voran** the work is coming along well

voran'kommen §99 *intr* (SEIN) make progress; **gut v.** come along well

Vor'anschlag *m* rough estimate

Vor'anzeige *f* preliminary announcement; (cin) preview of coming attractions

Vor'arbeit *f* preliminary work

vor'arbeiten *intr* do the work in advance; do the preliminary work

vorauf' *adv* ahead, in front

voraus' *adv* in front; (*dat*) ahead (of) || **vor'aus** *adv*—**im v.** in advance

Voraus'abteilung *f* (mil) vanguard

voraus'bedingen §142 *tr* stipulate beforehand

voraus'bestellen *tr* reserve

voraus'bestimmen *tr* predetermine

voraus'bezahlen *tr* pay in advance

voraus'eilen *intr* (SEIN) rush ahead

vorausgesetzt [fo'rausgəzetst] *adj*—**v., daß** provided that

Voraus'sage *f* prediction; prophecy; (*des Wetters*) forecast; (*Wink*) tip

voraus'sagen *tr* predict; prophesy; (*Wetter*) forecast

Voraus'sagung *f* var of **Voraussage**

voraus'schauen *intr* look ahead

voraus'schicken *tr* send ahead; (fig) mention beforehand

voraus'sehen §138 *tr* foresee

voraus'setzen *tr* presume, presuppose

Voraus'setzung *f* assumption; prerequisite; premise

Voraus'sicht *f* foresight

voraus'sichtlich *adj* probable, presumable || *adv* probably, presumably, the way it looks

Voraus'zahlung *f* advance payment

Vor'bau *m* −[e]s;-ten) projection; balcony, porch

vor'bauen *tr* build out || *intr* (*dat*) take precautions against

vor'bedacht *adj* premeditated || **Vorbedacht** *m* (−[e]s;)—**mit V.** on purpose; **ohne V.** unintentionally

vor'bedeuten *tr* forebode

Vor'bedeutung *f* (−;-en) foreboding; omen, portent

Vor'bedingung *f* (−;-en) precondition

Vorbehalt ['forbəhalt] *m* (−[e]s;-e) reservation; proviso; **mit allem V. hinnehmen!** take it for what it's worth!; **mit** (*or* **unter**) **dem V., daß** with the proviso that; **stiller** (*or* **innerer**) **V.** mental reservation; **unter V. aller Rechte** all rights reserved

vor'behalten §90 *tr* reserve; **Änderungen v.!** subject to change without

notice || *ref*—**sich** [*dat*] **etw v.** reserve s.th. for oneself

vor'behaltlich *prep* (*genit*) subject to

vor'behaltlos *adj* unreserved, unconditional

vorbei' *adv* over, past, gone; **es ist drei Uhr v.** it's past three o'clock; **v. an** (*dat*) past, by; **v. ist v.** done is done; **v. können** be able to pass

vorbei'eilen *intr* (SEIN)—**an j-m v.** rush past s.o.

vorbei'fahren §71 *intr* (SEIN) drive by

vorbei'fliegen §57 *intr* (SEIN) fly past

vorbei'fließen §76 *intr* (SEIN) flow by

vorbei'gehen §82 *intr* (SEIN) pass; **an j-m v.** pass by s.o. || **Vorbeigehen** *n* —**im V.** in passing

vorbei'gelingen §142 *intr* (SEIN) fail

vorbei'kommen §99 *intr* (SEIN) pass by; (coll) stop in

vorbei'lassen §104 *tr* let pass

Vorbei'marsch *m* parade

vorbei'marschieren *intr* (SEIN) march by

Vor'bemerkung *f* (−;-en) preliminary remark; (parl) preamble

vorbenannt ['forbənant] *adj* aforementioned

vor'bereiten *tr* prepare || *ref* (**auf** *acc*, **für**) get ready (for)

vor'bereitend *adj* preparatory

Vor'bereitung *f* (−;-en) preparation

Vor'bericht *m* preliminary report

Vor'besprechung *f* (−;-en) preliminary discussion

vor'bestellen *tr* order in advance; (*Zimmer, usw.*) reserve

Vor'bestellung *f* (−;-en) advance order; reservation

vor'bestraft *adj* previously convicted

vor'beten *tr* keep repeating || *intr* lead in prayer

vor'beugen *ref* bend forward || *intr* (*dat*) prevent

vor'beugend *adj* preventive

Vor'beugung *f* (−;-en) prevention

Vor'beugungsmittel *n* preventive

Vor'bild *n* model; (*Beispiel*) example

vor'bildlich *adj* exemplary, model

Vor'bildung *f* (−;-en) educational background

Vor'bote *m* forerunner; (fig) harbinger

vor'bringen §65 *tr* bring forward, produce; (*Gründe*) give; (*Plan*) propose; (*Klagen*) prefer; (*Wunsch*) express

vor'buchstabieren *tr* spell out

Vor'bühne *f* apron, proscenium

vor'datieren *tr* antedate

vordem [for'dem] *adv* formerly

Vor'derachse *f* front axle

Vor'derarm *m* forearm

Vor'derbein *n* foreleg

vordere ['fordərə] §9 *adj* front

Vor'derfront *f* front; (fig) forefront

Vor'derfuß *m* front foot

Vor'dergrund *m* foreground

vor'derhand *adv* for the time being

vor'derlastig *adj* (aer) nose-heavy

Vor'derlauf *m* (hunt) foreleg

Vor'dermann *m* (−[e]s;-̈er) man in front; **j-n auf V. bringen** (coll) put s.o. straight; **V. halten** keep in line

Vor′derpfote f front paw
Vor′derrad n front wheel
Vor′derradantrieb m front-wheel drive
Vor′derreihe f front row; front rank
Vor′dersicht f front view
Vor′derseite f front side, front; (e-r Münze) obverse, heads
Vor′dersitz m front seat
vorderste [′fɔrdərstə] §9 adj farthest front
Vor′dersteven m (naut) stem
Vor′derteil m & n front section; (naut) prow
Vor′dertür f front door
Vor′derzahn m front tooth
Vor′derzimmer n front room
vor′drängen tr & ref press forward
vor′dringen §142 intr (SEIN) forge ahead, advance
vor′dringlich adj urgent
Vor′druck m printed form, blank
vor′ehelich adj premarital
Vor′eilig adj hasty, rash
Vor′eiligkeit f (–;) haste, rashness
vor′eingenommen adj biased, prejudiced
Vor′eingenommenheit f (–;-en) bias, prejudice
Vor′eltern pl ancestors, forefathers
vor′enthalten §90 tr—j–m etw v. withhold s.th. from s.o.
Vor′entscheidung f (–;-en) preliminary decision
vor′erst adv first of all; for the time being, for the present
vorerwähnt [′fɔrervent] adj aforesaid
Vorfahr [′fɔrfar] m (–en;-en) forebear
vor′fahren §71 intr (SEIN) (bei) drive up (to)
Vor′fahrt f, **Vor′fahrt(s)recht** n right of way
Vor′fall m incident; event
vor′fallen §72 intr (SEIN) happen
Vor′feld n (aer) apron (of airport); (mil) approaches
vor′finden §59 tr find there
Vor′freude f anticipation
Vor′frühling m early spring
vor′fühlen intr—bei j–m v. feel s.o. out, put out feelers to s.o.
Vorführdame [′fɔrfyrdamə] f mannequin
vor′führen tr bring forward, produce; display, demonstrate; (Kleider) model; (Film) show; (Stück) (theat) present
Vor′führer –in §6 mf projectionist
Vor′führung f (–;-en) production; demonstration; showing; show, performance
Vor′gabe f points, handicap
Vor′gaberennen n handicap (race)
Vor′gabespiel n handicap
Vor′gang m event, incident, phenomenon; (Verfahren) process, procedure; (Präzedenzfall) precedent; (in den Akten) previous correspondence
Vor′gänger –in §6 mf predecessor
Vor′garten m front yard
vor′geben §80 tr pretend; give as an excuse; j–m zehn Punkte v. give s.o. ten points odds ‖ intr—j–m v. give

s.o. odds ‖ **Vorgeben** n (–s;–) pretext
Vor′gebirge n foothills; (Kap) cape
vorgeblich [′fɔrgeplɪç] adj ostensible
vorgefaßt [′fɔrgəfast] adj preconceived
Vor′gefühl n inkling; banges V. misgivings; im V. von or genit in anticipation of
vor′gehen §82 intr (SEIN) advance; go first; act; take action, proceed; (sich ereignen) go on, happen; (Uhr) be fast; (dat) take precedence (over); die Arbeit geht vor work comes first; was geht hier vor? what's going on here? ‖ **Vorgehen** n (–s;) advance; action, proceeding; gemeinschaftliches V. concerted action
vorgelagert [′fɔrgəlagərt] adj offshore
Vor′gelände n foreground
vorgenannt [′fɔrgənant] adj aforementioned
Vor′gericht n appetizer
Vor′geschichte f previous history; (Urgeschichte) prehistory
vor′geschichtlich adj prehistoric
Vor′geschmack m foretaste
Vorgesetzte [′fɔrgəzetstə] §5 mf superior; boss; (mil) senior officer
vor′gestern adv day before yesterday
vor′gestrig adj of the day before yesterday
vorgetäuscht [′fɔrgətɔɪʃt] adj makebelieve
vor′greifen §88 intr (dat) anticipate
Vor′griff m anticipation
vor′gucken intr (Unterkleid) show
vor′haben §89 tr have in mind, plan; intend to do; (ausfragen) question; (schelten) scold; (Schürze) (coll) have on ‖ **Vorhaben** n (–s;–) intention, plan; project
Vor′halle f entrance hall; lobby
vor′halten §90 tr—j–m etw v. hold s.th. in front of s.o.; (fig) reproach s.o. with s.th. ‖ intr last
Vor′haltung f (–;-en) reproach; j–m Vorhaltungen machen über (acc) reproach s.o. for
Vor′hand f (cards) forehand; (tennis) forehand stroke; die V. haben (cards) lead off
vorhanden [for′handən] adj present, at hand, available; (com) in stock; v. sein exist
Vorhan′densein n existence; presence
Vor′hang m (–[e]s;ᴗe) curtain; (theat) (coll) curtain call; Eiserner V. iron curtain
Vorhängeschloß [′forhɛŋəʃlɔs] n padlock
Vor′hangstange f curtain rod
Vor′hangstoff m drapery material
Vor′haut f foreskin
Vor′hemd n dicky, shirt front
vor′her adv before, previously; (im voraus) in advance
vorher′bestellen tr reserve
vorher′bestimmen tr predetermine; (eccl) predestine
Vorher′bestimmung f predestination
vorher′gehend, vorherig [for′heriç] adj preceding, previous; prior
Vor′herrschaft f predominance

vor'herrschen *intr* predominate, prevail

vor'herrschend *adj* predominant, prevailing

Vorher'sage *f* prediction; forecast

vorher'sagen *tr* predict, foretell; (*Wetter*) forecast

vorhin' *adv* a little while ago

vor'historisch *adj* prehistoric

Vor'hof *m* front yard; (anat) auricle

Vor'hut *f* (mil) vanguard

vorige ['forɪgə] §9 *adj* previous, former; **voriges Jahr** last year

Vor'jahr *n* preceding year

vor'jährig *adj* last year's

Vor'kammer *f* (anat) auricle; (aut) precombustion chamber

Vor'kampf *m* (box) preliminary bout; (sport) heat

Vor'kämpfer –in §6 *mf* pioneer

Vorkehrung ['forkeruŋ] *f* (–;-en) precaution; **Vorkehrungen treffen** take precautions

Vor'kenntnis *f* (von) basic knowledge (of); **Vorkenntnisse** rudiments, basics; **Vorkenntnisse nicht erforderlich** no previous experience necessary

vor'knöpfen *ref*—**sich** [*dat*] **j–n** v. (coll) chew s.o. out

Vor'kommando *n* (mil) advance party

vor'kommen §99 *intr* (SEIN) happen; (*Fall*) come up; (*als Besucher*) be admitted; (*scheinen*) seem, look; (*sich finden*) be found; (*zu Besuch*) call on ‖ *ref*—**er kam sich** [*dat*] **dumm vor** he felt silly ‖ *impers*—**es kommt dir nur so vor** you are just imagining it; **es kommt mir vor it** seems to me ‖ **Vorkommen** *n* (–s;–) occurrence; (min) deposit

Vorkommnis ['forkɔmnɪs] *n* (–ses;–se) event, occurrence

Vorkriegs– *comb.fm.* prewar

vor'laden §103 *tr* (jur) summon; (*unter Strafandrohung*) (jur) subpoena

Vor'ladung *f* (–;-en) (jur) summons; (*unter Strafandrohung*) (jur) subpoena

Vor'lage *f* submission, presentation; proposal; (*Muster*) pattern; bedside carpet; (fb) forward pass; (parl) bill

vor'lassen §104 *tr* let go ahead; (*Auto*) let pass; (*zulassen*) admit

Vor'lauf *m* (sport) qualifying heat

Vor'läufer –in §6 *mf* forerunner

vor'läufig *adj* preliminary; temporary ‖ *adv* provisionally; temporarily, for the time being

vor'laut *adj* forward, fresh

Vor'leben *n* past life, former life

Vorlegebesteck ['forlegəbə/stɛk] *n* carving set

Vorlegegabel ['forlegəgabəl] *f* carving fork

Vor'legelöffel ['forlegəlœfəl] *m* serving spoon

Vorlegemesser ['forlegəmesər] *n* carving knife

vor'legen *tr* put forward; propose; (*Ausweis, Paß*) show; (*Essen*) serve; (*zur Prüfung, usw.*) submit, present; **den Ball** v. (fb) pass the ball; **ein scharfes Tempo** v. (coll) speed it up;

j–m e–e Frage v. ask s.o. a question ‖ *ref* lean forward

Ver'leger *m* (–s;–) throw rug

Vorlegeschloß ['forlegə/los] *n* padlock

vor'lesen §107 *tr*—**j–m etw** v. read s.th. to s.o.

Vor'lesung *f* (–;-en) reading; lecture; **e–e V. halten über** (*acc*) give a lecture on

Vor'lesungsverzeichnis *n* university catalogue

vor'letzte §9 *adj* second last; (gram) penultimate

Vor'liebe *f* preference

vorliebnehmen [for'lipnemən] §116 *intr* take pot luck; v. **mit** put up with

vor'liegen §108 *intr* be present; exist; be under consideration; **dem Richter** v. be up before the judge; **heute liegt nichts vor** there's nothing doing today; **mir liegt e–e Beschwerde vor** I have a complaint here; **was liegt gegen ihn vor?** what is the charge against him?

vor'liegend *adj* present, at hand

vor'lügen §111 *tr*—**j–m etw** v. **über** (*acc*) tell s.o. lies about

vor'machen *tr*—**du kannst mir doch nichts** v. you can't put anything over on me; **j–m etw** v. show s.o. how to do s.th. ‖ *ref*—**er läßt sich** [*dat*] **nichts** v. he's nobody's fool; **sich** [*dat*] **selbst etw** v. fool oneself

Vor'macht *f* leading power; supremacy

Vor'machtstellung *f* (position of) supremacy

vormalig ['formalɪç] *adj* former

vormals ['formals] *adv* formerly

Vor'marsch *m* advance

vor'merken *tr* note down; reserve; **sich** v. **lassen für** put in for

Vor'mittag *m* forenoon, morning

vor'mittags *adv* in the forenoon

Vor'mund *m* guardian

Vor'mundschaft *f* (–;-en) guardianship

vor'mundschaftlich *adj* guardian's

Vor'mundschaftsgericht *n* orphans' court

vorn [forn] *adv* in front; ahead; **ganz** v. all the way up front; **nach** v. forward; **nach** v. **heraus wohnen** live in the front part of the house; **nach** v. **liegen** face the front; **von** v. from the front; **von** v. **anfangen** begin at the beginning

Vor'nahme *f* undertaking

Vor'name *m* first name

vorne ['fornə] *adv* (coll) var of **vorn**

vornehm ['fornem] *adj* distinguished, high-class; **vornehme Welt** high society; **vornehmste Aufgabe** principal task ‖ *adv*—v. **tun** put on airs

vor'nehmen §116 *tr* (*umbinden*) put on; undertake, take up; (*Änderungen*) make; **wieder** v. resume ‖ *ref*—**sich** [*dat*] **ein Buch** v. take up a book; **sich** [*dat*] **etw** v. decide upon s.th.; **sich** [*dat*] **j–n** v. take s.o. to task; **sich** [*dat*] v. **zu** (*inf*) make up one's mind to (*inf*); **sich** [*dat*] **zuviel** v. bite off more than one can chew

Vor'nehmheit *f* (–;) distinction, high rank; distinguished bearing vor'nehmlich *adv* especially

vor'neigen *ref* bend forward

vorn'herein *adv*—von v. from the first

vornweg ['fɔrnvɛk], (forn'vɛk) *adv*—er ist weit v. he is way out in front; mit dem Kopf v. head first; mit dem Mund v. sein be fresh

Vor'ort *m* suburb

Vorort– *comb.fm.* suburban

Vor'ortbahn *f* (rr) suburban line

Vor'ortzug *m* commuter train

Vor'platz *m* front yard; (*Diele*) entrance hall; (*Vorfeld*) (aer) apron

Vor'posten *m* (mil) outpost

Vor'rang *m* precedence; priority; preeminence; den V. vor j–m haben have precedence over s.o.

Vor'rat *m* (–[e]s͞–⁻e) (an *dat*) stock (of), supply (of); auf V. kaufen buy in quantity; e–n V. anlegen an (*dat*) stock

vorrätig ['fɔrretɪç] *adj* in stock

Vor'ratskammer *f* pantry, storeroom

Vor'ratsraum *m* storeroom

Vor'ratsschrank *m* pantry

Vor'raum *m* anteroom

vor'rechnen *tr*—j–m etw v. figure out s.th. for s.o.; j–m seine Fehler v. enumerate s.o.'s mistakes to s.o.

Vor'recht *n* privilege, prerogative

Vor'rede *f* preface, introduction

vor'reden *tr*—j–m etw v. try to make s.o. believe s.th.

Vor'redner –in §6 *mf* previous speaker

Vor'richtung *f* (–;–en) preparation; (*Gerät*) device, appliance, mechanism; (mach) fixture

vor'rücken *tr* move forward || *intr* (SEIN) (*Truppen*) advance; (*Polizei*) move in; (*im Dienst*) be promoted

Vor'runde *f* (sport) play-offs

vors [fɔrs] *abbr* vor das

vor'sagen *tr*—j–m etw v. recite s.th. to s.o. || *intr* (*dat*) prompt

Vor'sager –in §6 *mf* prompter

Vor'satz *m* purpose, intention; (jur) premeditation; den V. fassen zu (*inf*) make up one's mind to (*inf*); mit V. on purpose; seinen V. ausführen gain one's ends

Vor'satzblatt *n* (bb) end paper

Vor'satzgerät *n* adapter

vorsätzlich ['fɔrzetslɪç] *adj* deliberate; (*Mord*) premeditated

Vor'schau *f* (cin) preview

vor'schieben §130 *tr* push forward; offer as an excuse; (fig) plead; den Riegel v. (*dat*) (fig) prevent; Truppen v. move troops forward

vor'schießen §76 *tr* (*Geld*) (coll) advance || *intr* (SEIN) dart ahead

Vor'schiff *n* (naut) forecastle

Vor'schlag *m* proposal; (*Angebot*) offer; (*Anregung*) suggestion; (*Empfehlung*) recommendation; (mus) grace note; (parl) motion; in V. bringen propose; (parl) move

vor'schlagen §132 *tr* propose; suggest; recommend; zur Wahl v. nominate

Vor'schlagsliste *f* slate of candidates

Vor'schlußrunde *f* (sport) semifinal

vor'schnell *adj* rash, hasty

vor'schreiben §62 *tr* prescribe, order;

specify; write out; ich lasse mir nichts v. I take orders from no one

vor'schreiten §86 *intr* (SEIN) step forward; advance

Vor'schrift *f* order, direction; regulation; (med) prescription

vor'schriftsmäßig *adj* & *adv* according to regulations

vor'schriftswidrig *adj* & *adv* against regulations

Vor'schub *m* assistance; (mach) feed; V. leisten (*dat*) encourage; (jur) aid and abet

Vor'schule *f* prep school; (*Elementarschule*) elementary school

Vor'schuß *m* (*Geld*–) advance; (jur) retainer

vor'schützen *tr* pretend, plead

Vor'schützung *f* (–;) pretense

vor'schweben *intr*—mir schwebte etw anderes vor I had s.th. else in mind; das schwebt mir dunkel vor I have a dim recollection of it

vor'schwindeln *tr*—j–m etw v. fool s.o. about s.th.

vor'sehen §138 *tr* schedule, plan; provide; (fin) earmark; das Gesetz sieht vor, daß the law provides that || *ref* be careful, take care; sich mit etw v. provide oneself with s.th.; sich v. vor (*dat*) be on one's guard against s.th.

Vor'sehung *f* (–;) Providence

vor'setzen *tr* put forward; (*Silbe*) prefix; j–m etw v. set s.th. before s.o. (*to eat*); j–m j–n v. set s.o. over s.o.

Vor'sicht *f* caution, care; (*Umsicht*) prudence; V.! watch out! (*auf Kisten*) handle with care!; V., Stufe! watch your step!

vor'sichtig *adj* cautious, careful

Vor'sichtigkeit *f* (–;) caution

vorsichtshalber ['fɔrzɪçtshalbər] *adv* to be on the safe side, as a precaution

Vor'sichtsmaßnahme *f*, Vor'sichtsmaßregel *f* precaution

Vor'silbe *f* prefix

vor'singen §142 *tr*—j–m etw v. sing s.th. to s.o. || *intr* lead the choir

Vor'sitz *m* chairmanship, chair; presidency; den V. haben (or führen) bei preside over; unter V. von presided over by

Vorsitzende ['fɔrzɪtsəndə] §5 *mf* chairperson; president

Vor'sorge *f* provision; V. tragen (or treffen) für make provision for, provide for

vor'sorgen *intr* (für) provide (for)

vorsorglich ['fɔrzɔrklɪç] *adv* as a precaution, just in case

Vor'spann *m* (cin) credits; (*Kurzfilm*) (cin) short

Vor'speise *f* appetizer

vor'spiegeln *tr*—j–m etw v. delude s.o. with s.th.; j–m falsche Tatsachen v. misrepresent facts to s.o.

Vor'spiegelung *f* (–;) sham; pretense; V. falscher Tatsachen misrepresentation of facts

Vor'spiel *n* prelude; (*beim Geschlechtsverkehr*) foreplay; (mus) overture; (theat) curtain raiser; das war nur das **V.**! (fig) that was only the beginning!

vor′spielen tr—j—m etw v. play s.th. for s.o.

vor′sprechen §64 tr—j—m etw v. pronounce s.th. for s.o.; teach s.o. how to pronounce s.th. || intr—bei j—m v. drop in on s.o.; j—m v. audition before s.o.

vor′springen §142 intr (SEIN) leap forward; (aus dem Versteck) jump out; (vorstehen) stick out, protrude

Vor′sprung m projection; (Sims) ledge; (Vorteil) advantage; (sport) head start; (sport) lead

Vor′stadt f suburb

vor′städtisch adj suburban

Vor′stand m board of directors; executive committee, executive board; (Person) chairman of the board

vor′stehen §146 intr protrude; (dat) be at the head of, direct, manage

Vor′steher m (-s;-) head, director, manager; (educ) principal

Vor′steherdrüse f prostate gland

Vor′steherin f (-;-nen) head, director, manager; (educ) principal

vor′stellen tr place in front, put ahead; (Uhr) set ahead; (einführen) introduce, present; (darstellen) represent; (bedeuten) mean; (hinweisen auf) point out || ref—sich [dat] etw v. imagine s.th., picture s.th.

Vor′stellung f (-;-en) introduction, presentation; (Begriff) idea; (Einspruch) remonstrance, protest; (cin) show; (theat) performance

Vor′stellungsvermögen n imagination

Vor′stoß m (fig & mil) thrust, drive

vor′stoßen §150 tr push forward || intr (SEIN) push forward, advance

Vor′strafe f previous conviction

Vor′strafenregister n previous record

vor′strecken tr stretch out; (Geld) advance

Vor′stufe f preliminary stage

Vor′tag m previous day

vor′täuschen tr pretend, put on

Vor′teil m advantage; profit; (tennis) advantage

vor′teilhaft adj advantageous; profitable

Vortrag [′fortrak] m (-[e]s;⸗e) performance; (Bericht) report; (e-s Gedichtes) recitation; (e-r Rede) delivery; (Vorlesung) lecture; (acct) balance (carried over); (mus) recital; e-n V. halten über (acc) give a lecture on

vor′tragen §132 tr perform; present

Vortragende [′fortragəndə] §5 mf performer; speaker; lecturer

vortrefflich [′fortrefliç] adj excellent

vor′treten §152 intr (SEIN) step forward; (fig) stick out, protrude

Vor′tritt m (-[e]s) precedence

vorü′ber adv past, by, along; (zeitlich) over, gone by

vorü′bergehen §82 intr (SEIN) pass; (an dat) pass by; (fig) disregard

vorü′bergehend adj passing, transitory || **Vorübergehende** §5 mf passer-by

vorü′berziehen §163 intr (SEIN) march by; (Gewitter) blow over

Vor′übung f warmup

Vor′untersuchung f preliminary investigation

Vor′urteil n prejudice

vor′urteilsfrei, vor′urteilslos adj unprejudiced

Vor′vergangenheit f (gram) past perfect

Vor′verkauf m advance sale; (theat) advance reservation

vor′verlegen tr advance, move up

Vor′wahl f (pol) primary

vor′wählen intr dial the area code

Vor′wählnummer f (telp) area code

Vor′wand m (-[e]s;⸗e) pretext; excuse

vorwärts [′forverts] adv forward, on, ahead || interj go on!

vor′wärtsbringen §65 tr bring forward; (fig) advance

vor′wärtsgehen §82 intr (SEIN) progress

vor′wärtskommen §99 intr (SEIN) go ahead; progress, make headway

vorweg [for′vek] adv beforehand; out in front

Vorweg′nahme f anticipation

vorweg′nehmen §116 tr anticipate; presuppose, assume

vor′weisen §118 tr produce, show

Vor′welt f prehistoric world

vor′weltlich adj primeval

vor′werfen §160 tr—j—m etw v. throw s.th. to s.o.; (fig) throw s.th. up to s.o.

vorwiegend [′forvigənt] adj predominant || adv predominantly, chiefly

Vor′wissen n foreknowledge

vor′witzig adj inquisitive; brash

Vor′wort n (-[e]s;-e) foreword

Vor′wurf m reproach, blame; (e-s Dramas) subject; j—m Vorwürfe machen blame s.o.

vor′wurfslos adj irreproachable

vor′wurfsvoll adj reproachful

vor′zählen tr enumerate

Vor′zeichen n omen; (math) sign; (mus) accidental; negatives V. minus sign

vor′zeichnen tr—j—m etw v. draw or sketch s.th. for s.o.

Vor′zeichnung f (-;-en) drawing; (mus) signature

vor′zeigen tr produce, show; (Wechsel) present

Vor′zeiger –in §6 mf bearer

Vor′zeigung f (-;-en) producing, showing; presentation

Vor′zeit f remote antiquity

vor′zeiten adv in days of old

vor′zeitig adj premature

vor′ziehen §163 tr draw forth; pull out; prefer; (mil) move up

Vor′zimmer n anteroom; entrance hall

Vor′zug m preference; (Vorteil) advantage; (Überlegenheit) superiority; (Vorrang) priority; (Vorrecht) privilege; (Vorzüglichkeit) excellence; e-r Sache den V. geben prefer s.th.

vorzüglich [′fortsykliç] adj excellent, first-rate || adv especially

Vor′züglichkeit f (-;) excellence

Vor′zugsaktie f preferred stock

Vor'zugsbehandlung *f* preferential treatment
Vor'zugspreis *m* special price
Vor'zugsrecht *n* priority; privilege
vor'zugsweise *adv* preferably
votieren [vɔ'tirən] *intr* vote
Votiv- [vɔtif] *comb.fm.* votive
Vo•tum ['votum] *n* (-s;-ten [tən] & -ta [ta]) vote

vulgär [vul'gɛr] *adj* vulgar
Vulkan [vul'kan] *m* (-s;-e) volcano
Vulkan'ausbruch *m* eruption
vulkanisch [vul'kanɪʃ] *adj* volcanic
vulkanisieren [vulkanı'zirən] *tr* vulcanize
Vulkan'schlot *m* volcanic vent
VW *abbr* (Volkswagen) VW
V-Waffe *f* (Vergeltungswaffe) V-1, V-2

W

W, w [ve] *invar n* W, w
Waage ['vagə] *f* (-;-n) (pair of) scales; (astr) Libra; (gym) horizontal position; **die beiden Dinge halten sich** [dat] **die W.** the two things balance each other; **die W. halten** (dat) counterbalance; **j-m die W. halten** be a match for s.o.
waa'gerecht, waagrecht ['vakreçt] *adj* horizontal, level
Waagschale ['vak/alə] *f* scale(s); **in die W. fallen** carry weight; **in die W. werfen** bring to bear
wabbelig ['vabəlɪç] *adj* (coll) flabby
Wabe ['vabə] *f* (-;-n) honeycomb
wach [vax] *adj* awake; (lebhaft) lively; (Geist) alert; **ganz w.** wide awake
Wach'ablösung *f* changing of the guard
Wach'dienst *m* guard duty
Wache ['vaxə] *f* (-;-n) guard, watch; (Wachstube) guardroom; (Wachlokal) guardhouse; (Polizei-) police station; (Wachdienst) guard duty; (Posten) guard, sentinel; **auf W.** on guard; **auf W. ziehen** mount guard; **W. schieben** (coll) pull guard duty
wachen ['vaxən] *intr* be awake; **bei j-m w.** sit up with s.o.; **w. über** (acc) watch over, guard
wach'habend *adj* on guard duty
wach'halten §90 *tr* keep awake; (fig) keep alive
Wach'hund *m* watchdog
Wach'lokal *n* guardroom; police station
Wach'mann *m* (-[e]s;-leute) (Aust) policeman
Wach'mannschaft *f* (mil) guard detail
Wacholder [va'xɔldər] *m* (-s;-) juniper
Wachol'derbranntwein *m* gin
Wach'posten *m* sentry
wach'rufen §122 *tr* wake up; (Erinnerung) bring back
Wachs [vaks] *n* (-es;-e) wax
wachsam ['vaxzam] *adj* vigilant
Wach'samkeit *f* (-;) vigilance
Wachs'bohne *f* wax bean
wachsen ['vaksən] *tr* wax || §155 *intr* (SEIN) grow; (an dat) increase (in)
wächsern ['veksərn] *adj* wax; (fig) waxy
Wachs'figurenkabinett *n* wax museum
Wachs'kerze *f*, **Wachs'licht** *n* wax candle
Wachs'leinwand *f* oilcloth

Wach'stube *f* guardroom
Wachs'tuch *n* oilcloth
Wachstum ['vaxstum] *n* (-s;) growth; increase
Wacht [vaxt] *f* (-;-en) guard, watch
Wächte ['veçtə] *f* (-;-n) snow cornice
Wachtel ['vaxtəl] *f* (-;-n) quail
Wach'telhund *m* spaniel
Wächter ['veçtər] *m* (-s;-) guard
Wacht'meister *m* police sergeant
Wach'traum *m* daydream
Wacht'turm *m* watchtower
wackelig ['vakəlɪç] *adj* wobbly; (Zahn) loose; (fig) shaky
Wackelkontakt ['vakəlkɔntakt] *m* (elec) loose connection, poor contact
wackeln ['vakəln] *intr* wobble; shake; (locker sein) be loose
wacker ['vakər] *adj* decent, honest; (tapfer) brave || *adv* heartily
wacklig ['vaklɪç] *adj* var of **wackelig**
Wade ['vadə] *f* (-;-n) (anat) calf
Wa'denbein *n* (anat) fibula
Wa'denkrampf *m* leg cramp
Wa'denstrumpf *m* calf-length stocking
Waffe ['vafə] *f* (-;-n) weapon; branch of service; **die Waffen strecken** surrender; (fig) give up; **zu den Waffen greifen** take up arms
Waffel ['vafəl] *f* (-;-n) waffle
Waf'fenbruder *m* comrade in arms
waf'fenfähig *adj* capable of bearing arms
Waf'fengang *m* armed conflict
Waf'fengattung *f* branch of service
Waf'fengewalt *f* force of arms
Waf'fenkammer *f* armory
Waf'fenlager *n* ordnance depot; **heimliches W.** cache of arms
waf'fenlos *adj* unarmed
Waf'fenruhe *f* truce
Waf'fenschein *m* gun permit
Waf'fenschmied *m* gunsmith
Waf'fenschmuggel *m* gunrunning
Waf'fen-SS *f* (-;) SS combat unit
Waf'fenstillstand *m* armistice
Wagehals ['vagəhals] *m* daredevil
Wagemut ['vagəmut] *m* daring
wagen ['vagən] *tr* dare; risk || *ref* venture, dare || **Wagen** *m* (-s;-) wagon; (Fahrzeug; Teil e-r Schreibmaschine) carriage; (aut, rr) car; **der Große Wagen** the Big Dipper; **j-m an den W. fahren** (fig) step on s.o.'s toes
wägen ['vegən] *tr* (& fig) weigh
Wa'genabteil *n* (rr) compartment

Wa'genburg f barricade of wagons
Wa'genheber m (aut) jack
Wa'genpark m fleet of cars
Wa'genpflege f (aut) maintenance
Wa'genschlag m car door, carriage door
Wa'genschmiere f (aut) grease
Wa'genspur f wheel track, rut
Wa'genwäsche f car wash
Wagestück ['vagə/tyk] n hazardous venture, daring deed
Waggon [va'gõ] m (-s;-s) railroad car
waghalsig ['vakhalzıç] adj foolhardy
Wagnis ['vaknıs] n (-ses;-se) risk
Wahl [val] f (-;-en) choice, option; (Auswahl) selection; (Alternative) alternative; (pol) election; e-e W. treffen make a choice; vor der W. stehen have the choice
wählbar ['velbar] adj eligible
Wähl'barkeit f (-;) eligibility
Wahl'beeinflussung f interference with the election process
wahl'berechtigt adj eligible to vote
Wahl'beteiligung f election turnout
Wahl'bezirk m ward
wählen ['velən] tr choose; select; (pol) elect; (telp) dial || intr vote
Wäh'ler m (-s;-) voter
Wahl'ergebnis n election returns
Wäh'lerin f (-;-nen) voter
wählerisch ['verlərıʃ] adj choosy, particular
Wäh'lerschaft f (-;-en) constituency
Wäh'lerscheibe f (telp) dial
Wahl'fach n (educ) elective
wahl'fähig adj eligible for election; having a vote
wahl'frei adj (educ) elective
Wahl'gang m ballot
Wahl'kampf m election campaign
Wahl'kreis m constituency; district
Wahl'leiter m campaign manager
Wahl'list f (pol) slate, ticket
Wahl'lokal n polling place
Wahl'lokomotive f (coll) vote getter
wahl'los adj indiscriminate
Wahl'parole f campaign slogan
Wahl'programm n (pol) platform
Wahl'recht n right to vote, suffrage
Wahl'rede f campaign speech
Wahl'spruch m motto; (com, pol) slogan
Wahl'urne f ballot box
Wahl'versammlung f campaign rally
wahl'verwandt adj congenial
Wahl'zelle f voting booth
Wahl'zettel m ballot
Wahn [van] m (-[e]s;) delusion; error; folly; madness
Wahn'bild n phantom, delusion
wähnen ['venən] tr fancy, imagine
Wahn'idee f delusion; (coll) crazy idea
Wahn'sinn m (& fig) madness
wahn'sinnig adj (vor dat) mad (with); (coll) terrible || adv madly; (coll) awfully || **Wahnsinnige** §5 mf lunatic
Wahn'vorstellung f hallucination
Wahn'witz m (& fig) madness
wahn'witzig adj mad; (unverantwortlich) irresponsible
wahr [var] adj true; (wirklich) real; (echt) genuine; nicht w.? right?

wahren ['varən] tr keep; (Anschein) keep up; (vor dat) protect (against)
währen ['verən] intr last
während ['verənt] prep (genit) during; (jur) pending || conj while; whereas
wahr'haben §89 tr admit
wahr'haft, wahr'haftig adj true, truthful; (wirklich) real || adv actually
Wahr'haftigkeit f (-;) truthfulness
Wahr'heit f (-;-en) truth; j-m die W. sagen give s.o. a piece of one's mind
wahr'heitsgemäß, wahr'heitsgetreu adj true, faithful; truthful
Wahr'heitsliebe f truthfulness
wahr'heitsliebend adj truthful
wahr'lich adv truly; (Bib) verily
wahrnehmbar ['varnembar] adj noticeable
wahr'nehmen §116 tr notice; (benutzen) make use of; (Interesse) protect; (Recht) assert
Wahr'nehmung f (-;) observation, perception; (der Interessen) safeguarding
wahr'sagen ref—sich [dat] w. lassen have one's fortune told || intr prophesy; tell fortunes
Wahr'sagerin f (-;-nen) fortuneteller
wahrscheinlich [var'ʃaınlıç] adj probable, likely || adv probably
Wahrschein'lichkeit f (-;) probability
Wahr'spruch m verdict
Wah'rung f (-;) safeguarding
Wäh'rung f (-;-en) currency; standard
Wäh'rungsabwertung f devaluation
Wäh'rungseinheit f monetary unit
Wahr'zeichen n landmark
Waise ['vaızə] f (-;-n) orphan
Wai'senhaus n orphanage
Wal [val] m (-[e]s;-e) whale
Wald [valt] m (-[e]s;¨er) forest, woods
Wald- comb.fm. forest; sylvan; wild
Wald'aufseher m forest ranger
Wald'brand m forest fire
waldig ['valdıç] adj wooded
Waldung ['valduŋ] f (-;-en) forest
Wald'wirtschaft f forestry
Wal'fang m whaling
Wal'fänger m (-s;-) whaler
walken ['valkən] tr full
Wal'ker m (-s;-) fuller
Wall [val] m (-[e]s;¨e) mound; embankment; (mil) rampart
Wallach ['valax] m (-[e]s;-e) gelding
wallen ['valən] intr (sieden) boil; (sprudeln) bubble; (Gewand, Haar) flow, fall in waves || intr (SEIN) go on a pilgrimage; travel, wander
wall'fahren insep intr (SEIN) go on a pilgrimage
Wall'fahrer -in §6 mf pilgrim
Wall'fahrt f pilgrimage
Wall'graben m moat
Wal'lung f (-;) simmering, boiling; bubbling; flow; flutter; (Blutandrang) congestion; in W. bringen enrage; in W. geraten fly into a rage; **Wallungen** hot flashes
Walnuß ['valnus] f walnut
Walroß ['valros] n walrus
Wal'speck m blubber
walten ['valtən] intr rule; hold sway;

Gnade w. lassen show mercy; seines Amtes w. attend to one's duties
Wal'tran m whale oil
Walze ['valtsə] f (-;-n) cylinder, drum; roll, roller; (der Schreib-maschine) platen
walzen ['valtsən] tr roll
wälzen ['veltsən] tr roll; (Bücher) pore over; (Gedanken) turn over in one's mind; die Schuld auf j-n w. shift the blame to s.o. else || ref roll, toss; (im Kot) wallow; (im Blut) welter
Wal'zer m (-s;-) waltz
Wäl'zer m (-s;-) (coll) thick tome
Walz'werk n rolling mill
Wamme ['vamə] f (-;-n) dewlap; (coll) potbelly
Wampe ['vampə] f (-;-n) (coll) pot-belly
wand [vant] pret of winden || Wand f (-;ːe) wall; partition; (Fels-) cliff; spanische W. folding screen
Wand'apparat m (telp) wall phone
Wand'bekleidung f wainscot
Wandel ['vandəl] m (-s;) change
wandelbar ['vandəlbar] adj changeable
Wan'delgang m, **Wan'delhalle** f lobby
wandeln ['vandəln] tr change || ref (in acc) change (into) || intr (SEIN) (poet) wander; (poet) walk
Wan'derer –in §6 mf wanderer; hiker
Wan'derlust f wanderlust, itch to travel
wandern ['vandərn] intr (SEIN) wander; hike; (Vögel) migrate
Wan'derniere f floating kidney
Wan'derpreis m challenge trophy
Wan'derschaft f (-;) travels, wander-ings
Wan'derstab m walking stick
Wan'derung f (-;-en) hike; migration
Wan'dervogel m migratory bird; (coll) rover
Wand'gemälde n mural
Wand'karte f wall map
Wand'leuchter m sconce
Wand'lung f (-;-en) change, transfor-mation; (eccl) consecration
Wand'malerei f wall painting
Wand'pfeiler m pilaster
Wand'schirm m folding screen
Wand'schrank m wall shelves
Wand'spiegel m wall mirror
Wand'steckdose f, **Wand'stecker** m (elec) wall outlet
Wand'tafel f blackboard
wandte ['vantə] pret of wenden
Wand'teppich m tapestry
Wange ['vaŋə] f (-;-n) cheek
–wangig [vaŋɪç] comb.fm. –cheeked
Wan'kelmut m fickleness
wan'kelmütig adj fickle
wanken ['vaŋkən] intr stagger; sway, rock; (fig) waver
wann [van] adv & conj when; w. im-mer anytime, whenever
Wanne ['vanə] f (-;-n) tub
Wanst [vanst] m (-es;ːe) belly, paunch
–wanstig [vanstɪç] comb.fm. –bellied
Wanze ['vantsə] f (-;-n) bedbug
Wappen ['vapən] n (-s;-) coat of arms
Wap'penkunde f heraldry

Wap'penschild m escutcheon
wappnen ['vapnən] ref arm oneself; sich mit Geduld w. have patience
war [var] pret of sein
warb [varp] pret of werben
ward [vart] pret of werden
Ware ['varə] f (-;-n) ware; article; commodity; **Waren** goods, merchan-dise
–waren [varən] pl comb.fm. –ware
Wa'renaufzug m freight elevator
Wa'renausgabe f wrapping department
Wa'renbestand m stock
Wa'renbörse f commodity market
Wa'renhaus n department store
Wa'renlager n warehouse; stockroom
Wa'renmarkt m commodity market
Wa'renmuster n, **Wa'renprobe** f sam-ple
Wa'renrechnung f invoice
Wa'renzeichen n trademark
warf [varf] pret of werfen
warm [varm] adj (wärmer ['vermər]; wärmste ['vermstə] §9) warm
Warmblüter ['varmblytər] m (-s;-) warm-blooded animal
warmblütig ['varmblytɪç] adj warm-blooded
Wärme ['vermə] f (-;) warmth, heat
wär'mebeständig adj heatproof
Wär'meeinheit f thermal unit; calory
Wär'megrad m degree of heat, tem-perature
wärmen ['vermən] tr warm, heat
Wär'meplatte f—elektrische W. hot-plate
Wärm'flasche f hot-water bottle
warm'halten §90 tr keep warm
warm'herzig adj warm-hearted
warm'laufen §105 intr—den Motor w. lassen let the motor warm up
Warmluft'heizung f hot-air heating
Warmwas'serbehälter m hot-water tank
Warmwas'serheizung f hot-water heat-ing
Warmwas'serspeicher m hot-water tank
Warn– [varn] comb.fm. warning
Warn'anlage f warning system
warnen ['varnən] tr (vor dat) warn (of), caution (against)
Warn'gebiet n danger zone
Warn'schuß m warning shot
Warn'signal n warning signal
War'nung f (-;-en) warning, caution; zur W. as a warning
War'nungsschild n, **Warn'zeichen** n danger sign
Warschau ['varʃau] n (-s;) Warsaw
Warte ['vartə] f (-;-n) watchtower, lookout
War'tefrau f attendant; nurse
War'tefrist f waiting period
warten ['vartən] tr tend, attend to; (pflegen) nurse || intr (auf acc) wait (for)
Wärter ['vertər] m (-s;-) attendant; (Pfleger) male nurse; (Aufseher) caretaker; (Gefängnis–) guard; (rr) signalman
War'teraum m waiting room
Wärterin ['vertərɪn] f (-;-nen) attend-ant; nurse

War'tesaal *m*, **War'tezimmer** *n* waiting room

War'tung *f* (-;) maintenance

warum [va'rum] *adv* why

Warze ['vartsə] *f* (-;-n) wart; (*Brust-*) nipple

was [vas] *indef pron* something; na, so was! well, I never! ‖ *interr pron* what; ach was! go on! was für ein what kind of, what sort of; was haben wir gelacht! how we laughed! ‖ *rel pron* what; which; that; was auch immer no matter what; was immer whatever

Wasch- [va∫] *comb.fm.* wash, washing

waschbar ['va∫bar] *adj* washable

Wasch'bär *m* racoon

Wasch'becken *n* sink

Wasch'benzin *n* cleaning fluid

Wasch'blau *n* bluing

Wasch'bütte *f* washtub

Wäsche ['ve∫ə] *f* (-;-n) wash, laundry; linen; underwear

Wä'schebeutel *m* laundry bag

wasch'echt *adj* washable; (fig) genuine

Wä'scheklammer *f* clothespin

Wä'schekorb *m* clothesbasket

Wä'scheleine *f* clothesline

waschen ['va∫ən] §158 *tr* wash; launder; (*Gold*) pan; (*Haar*) shampoo; (*reinigen*) purify ‖ *ref* wash; sich [*dat*] die Hände w. wash one's hands ‖ *intr* wash

Wä'scher ['ve∫ər] *m* (-s;-) washer; laundryman

Wäscherei [ve∫ə'rar] *f* (-;-en) laundry

Wäscherin ['ve∫ərɪn] *f* (-;-nen) washerwoman, laundress

Wä'scherolle *f* mangle

Wä'scheschleuder *f* spin-drier

Wä'scheschrank *m* linen closet

Wä'schezeichen *n* laundry mark

Wasch'frau *f* laundress

Wasch'haus *n* laundry

Wasch'korb *m* clothesbasket

Wasch'küche *f* laundry

Wasch'lappen *m* washcloth; (fig) wishy-washy person

Wasch'maschine *f* washmachine, washer

Wasch'mittel *n* detergent

Wasch'raum *m* washroom, lavatory

Wasch'schüssel *f* wash basin

Wasch'tisch *m* washstand

Wasch'trog *m* washtub

Wa'schung *f* (-;-en) washing; ablution

Wasch'weib *n* (coll) gossip (*woman*)

Wasch'zettel *m* laundry list; (*am Schutzumschlag*) blurb

Wasser ['vasər] *n* (-s;-) water; das W. läuft mir im Mund zusammen my mouth is watering; j-m das W. abgraben pull the rug out from under s.o.; mit allen Wassern gewaschen sharp as a needle

was'serabstoßend *adj* water-repellent

was'serarm *adj* arid

Was'serball *m* water polo

Was'serbau *m* (-[e]s;) harbor and canal construction

Was'serbehälter *m* water tank; reservoir; cistern

Was'serblase *f* bubble; (*auf der Haut*) blister

Was'serbombe *f* depth charge

Was'serbüffel *m* water buffalo

Was'serdampf *m* steam

was'serdicht *adj* watertight, waterproof

Was'sereimer *m* bucket

Was'serfall *m* waterfall, cascade

Was'serfarbe *f* watercolor

Was'serflasche *f* water bottle

Was'serflugzeug *n* seaplane

Was'sergeflügel *n* waterfowl

Was'sergraben *m* drain; moat

Was'serhahn *m* faucet, spigot

Was'serhose *f* waterspout

wässerig ['vesərɪç] *adj* watery

Was'serjungfer *f* dragonfly

Was'serkessel *m* cauldron

Was'serklosett *n* toilet

Was'serkraftwerk *n* hydroelectric plant

Was'serkrug *m* water jug, water pitcher

Was'serkur *f* spa

Was'serland'flugzeug *n* amphibian plane

Was'serland'panzerwagen *m* amphibian tank

Was'serlauf *m* watercourse

Was'serleitung *f* water main; aqueduct

Was'sermangel *m* water shortage

Was'sermann *m* (-[e]s;) (astr) Aquarius

Was'sermelone *f* watermelon

wassern ['vasərn] *intr* land on water; (rok) splash down

wässern ['vesərn] *tr* water; irrigate; (phot) wash ‖ *intr* (*Augen*, *Mund*) water

Was'serratte *f* water rat; (fig) old salt

Was'serrinne *f* gutter

Was'serrohr *n* water pipe

Was'serscheide *f* watershed, divide

was'serscheu *adj* afraid of water

Was'serschi *m* water ski

Was'serschlauch *m* hose

Wasserspeier ['vasər/par-ər] *m* (-s;-) gargoyle

Was'serspiegel *m* surface; water level

Was'sersport *m* aquatics

Was'serstand *m* water level

Was'serstiefel *m* rubber boots

Was'serstoff *m* hydrogen

was'serstoffblond *adj* peroxide-blond

Was'serstoffbombe *f* hydrogen bomb

Was'serstrahl *m* jet of water

Was'serstraße *f* waterway

Was'sersucht *f* dropsy

Was'serung *f* (-;-en) (aer) landing on water; (rok) splashdown

Wäs'serung *f* (-;) watering; irrigation

Was'serverdrängung *f* displacement

Was'serversorgung *f* water supply

Was'servogel *m* waterfowl

Was'serwaage *f* (carp) level

Was'serweg *m* waterway; auf dem W. by water

Was'serwerk *n* waterworks

Was'serzähler *m* water meter

Was'serzeichen *n* watermark

wässrig ['vesrɪç] *adj* watery

waten ['vatən] *intr* (SEIN) wade

Watsche ['vat∫ə] *f* (-;-n) slap

watscheln ['vat∫əln] *intr* (SEIN) waddle

watschen ['vat∫ən] *tr* slap

Watt [vat] n (-s;-) (elec) watt
Watte ['vatə] f (-;-en) absorbent cotton; wadding
Wat'tebausch m swab
Wat'tekugel f cotton ball
Wat'tenmeer n shallow coastal waters
Wat'testäbchen n Q-tip, cotton swab
wattieren [va'tirən] tr pad, wad
Wattie'rung f (-;-en) padding, wadding
wauwau ['vau'vau] interj bow-wow! || **Wauwau** m (-s;-s) bow-wow, doggy
weben ['vebən] §109 & §94 tr & intr weave
We'ber m (-s;-) weaver
Weberei [vebə'rai] f (-;-en) weaving
We'berin f (-;-nen) weaver
We'berknecht m daddy-long-legs
Webstuhl ['vep/tul] m loom
Webwaren ['vepvarən] pl textiles
Wechsel ['veksəl] m (-s;-) change, shift; (für Studenten) allowance; (agr) rotation (of crops); (fin) bill of exchange; (hunt) run, beaten track; **gezogener W.** draft; **offener W.** letter of credit; **trockener** (or **eigener**) **W.** promissory note
Wech'selbeziehung f correlation
Wechselfälle ['veksəlfelə] pl ups and downs, vicissitudes
Wech'selfieber n intermittent fever; malaria
Wech'selfrist f period of grace (before bill of exchange falls due)
Wech'selgeld n change, small change
Wech'selgesang m antiphony
Wech'selgespräch n dialogue
wech'selhaft adj changeable
Wech'selkurs m rate of exchange
Wech'selmakler –in §6 mf bill-broker
wechseln ['veksəln] tr change; vary; (austauschen) exchange; **den Besitzer w.** change hands; **die Zähne w.** get one's second set of teeth; **seinen Wohnsitz w.** move || intr change; vary
Wech'selnehmer m (fin) payee
Wech'selnotierung f foreign exchange rate
Wech'selrichter m (elec) vibrator (producing a.c.)
wech'selseitig adj mutual, reciprocal
Wech'selseitigkeit f (-;) reciprocity
Wech'selspiel n interplay
Wech'selsprechanlage f intercom
Wech'selstrom m alternating current
Wech'selstube f money-exchange office
Wech'seltierchen n amoeba
wech'selvoll adj (Landschaft) changing; (Leben) checkered; (Wetter) changeable
wech'selweise adv mutually; alternately
Wech'selwirkung f interaction
Wech'selwirtschaft f crop rotation
wecken ['vekən] tr wake, awaken, rouse
Wecker (**Wek'ker**) m (-s;-) alarm clock
Weck'ruf m (mil) reveille
Wedel ['vedəl] m (-s;-) brush, whisk; (Schwanz) tail; (eccl) sprinkler
wedeln ['vedəln] tr brush away || intr

—**mit dem Fächer w.** fan oneself; **mit dem Schwanz w.** wag its tail
weder ['vedər] conj—**weder...noch** neither...nor
weg [vek] adv away, off; gone; lost || **Weg** [vek] m (-[e]s;-e) way, path; road; route, course; (Art und Weise) way; (Mittel) means; **am Wege** by the roadside; **auf dem besten Wege sein** be well on the way; **auf gütlichem Wege** amicably; **auf halbem Wege** halfway; **aus dem Weg räumen** remove; (fig) bump off; **etw in die Wege leiten** prepare the way for s.th.; introduce s.th.; **j—m aus dem Wege gehen** make way for s.o.; steer clear of s.o.; **Weg und Steg kennen** know every turn in the road
weg'bekommen §99 tr (Fleck) get out; (Krankheit) catch; (verstehen) get the hang of; **e—e w.** (coll) get a crack
weg'bleiben §62 intr (SEIN) stay away; be omitted
weg'blicken intr glance away
weg'bringen §65 tr take away; (Fleck) get out
Wegebau ['vegəbau] m (-[e]s;) road building
Wegegeld ['vegəgelt] n mileage allowance; turnpike toll
wegen ['vegən] prep (genit) because of, on account of; for the sake of; (mit Rücksicht auf) in consideration of; (infolge) in consequence of; (jur) on (the charge of); **von Amts w.** officially; **von Rechts w.** by right
Wegerecht ['vegəreçt] n right of way
weg'essen §70 tr eat up
weg'fahren §71 tr remove || intr (SEIN) drive away, leave
weg'fallen §72 intr (SEIN) fall away, fall off; (ausgelassen werden) be omitted; (aufhören) cease; (abgeschafft werden) be abolished
weg'fangen §73 tr snap away, snatch
weg'fliegen §57 intr (SEIN) fly away
weg'fressen §70 tr devour
weg'führen tr lead away
Weggang ['vekgaŋ] m departure
weg'geben §80 tr give away
weg'gehen §82 intr (SEIN) go away; **w. über** (acc) pass over; **wie warme Semmeln w.** go like hotcakes
weg'haben §89 tr get rid of; (Schläge, usw.) have gotten one's share of; (verstehen) catch on to; **der hat eins weg** (sl) he has a screw loose; (sl) he's loaded
weg'jagen tr chase away
weg'kehren tr sweep away; (Gesicht) avert || ref turn away
weg'kommen §99 intr (SEIN) come away; get away (verlorengehen) get lost; **nicht w. über** (acc) not get over
weg'können §100 intr—**nicht w.** not be able to get away
Wegkreuzung ['vekkroitsuŋ] f (-;-en) crossing, intersection
weg'kriegen tr get; (Fleck) get out
weg'lassen §104 tr leave out; let go; cross out; (gram) elide; (math) cancel
weg'legen tr put aside

weg'machen *tr* take away; (*Fleck*) take out

wegmüde ['vɛkmydə] *adj* travel-weary

weg'müssen §115 *intr* have to go

Wegnahme ['vɛknɑːmə] *f* (-;-n) taking away; confiscation; (mil) capture

weg'nehmen §116 *tr* take away; (*Raum, Zeit*) take up; (*beschlagnahmen*) confiscate; (mil) capture

weg'packen *tr* pack away ‖ *ref* pack off

weg'raffen *tr* snatch away

Wegrand ['vɛkrant] *m* wayside

weg'räumen *tr* clear away

weg'reißen §53 *tr* tear off, tear away

weg'rücken *tr* move away

weg'schaffen *tr* remove; get rid of

weg'scheren §129 *tr* clip ‖ *ref* scram

weg'scheuchen *tr* scare away

weg'schicken *tr* send away

weg'schleichen §85 *ref & intr* (SEIN) sneak away, steal away

weg'schmeißen §53 *tr* (coll) throw away

weg'schneiden §106 *tr* cut away

weg'sehen §138 *intr* look away; **w. über** (*acc*) shut one's eyes to

weg'setzen *tr* put away ‖ *ref*—**sich w. über** (*acc*) not mind; feel superior to ‖ *intr* (SEIN)—**w. über** (*acc*) jump over

weg'spülen *tr* wash away; (geol) erode

weg'stehlen §147 *ref* slip away

weg'stellen *tr* put aside

weg'stoßen §150 *tr* shove aside

weg'streichen §85 *tr* cross out

weg'treten §152 *tr* (SEIN) step aside; (mil) break ranks; **weggetreten!** (mil) dismissed!; **w. lassen** (mil) dismiss

weg'tun §154 *tr* put away

Wegweiser ['vɛkvaɪzər] *m* (-s;-) roadsign; (*Buch, Reiseführer*) guide

weg'wenden §120 & §140 *tr & ref* turn away

weg'werfen §160 *tr* throw away ‖ *ref* degrade oneself

weg'werfend *adj* disparaging

weg'wischen *tr* wipe away

weg'zaubern *tr* spirit away

weg'ziehen §163 *tr* pull away ‖ *intr* (SEIN) move; (mil) pull out

weh [ve] *adj* painful, sore; **mir ist weh ums Herz** I am sick at heart ‖ *adv*—**sich** [*dat*] **weh tun** hurt oneself; **weh tun ache** ‖ *interj* **woe! weh mir!** woe is me! ‖ **Weh** *n* (-[e]s;-e) pain, ache

wehe ['ve·ə] *adj, adv, & interj* var of **weh** ‖ **Wehe** *f* (-;-n) drift

wehen ['ve·ən] *tr* blow; (*Schnee*) drift ‖ *intr* (*Wind*) blow; (*Fahne, Kerzenflamme*) flutter ‖ **Wehen** *pl* labor, labor pains; (fig) travail

Weh'geschrei *n* wails, wailing

Weh'klage *f* wail

weh'klagen *intr* (**über** *acc*) wail (over); **w. um** lament for

weh'leidig *adj* complaining, whining; **W. tun** whine

Weh'mut *f* (-;) melancholy; nostalgia

weh'mütig *adj* melancholy; nostalgic

Wehr [ver] *f* (-;-en) weapon; (*Abwehr*) defense, resistance; (*Brüstung*,

parapet; **sich zur W. setzen** offer resistance ‖ **Wehr** *n* (-[e]s;-e) dam

Wehr'dienst *m* military service

Wehr'dienstpflichtig *adj* subject to military service

Wehr'dienstverweigerer *m* (-s;-) conscientious objector

wehren ['verən] *tr*—**j-m etw w.** keep s.o. (away) from s.th. ‖ *ref* defend oneself; resist, put up a fight; **sich seiner Haut w.** save one's skin ‖ *intr* (*dat*) resist; (*dat*) check

wehr'fähig *adj* fit for military service

wehr'haft *adj* (*Person*) full of fight; (*Burg*) strong

wehr'los *adj* defenseless

Wehr'macht *f* (hist) German armed forces

Wehr'meldeamt *n* draft board

Wehr'paß *m* service record

Wehr'pflicht *f* compulsory military service; **allgemeine W.** universal military training

wehr'pflichtig *adj* subject to military service

Weib [vaɪp] *n* (-[e]s;-er) woman; wife; **ein tolles W.** a luscious doll

Weibchen ['vaɪpçən] *n* (-s;-) (*Tier*) female; (*Ehefrau*) little woman

Weiberfeind ['vaɪbərfaɪnt] *m* womanhater

Weiberheld ['vaɪbərhɛlt] *m* ladies' man

Weibervolk ['vaɪbərfɔlk] *n* womenfolk

weibisch ['vaɪbɪʃ] *adj* womanish, effeminate

weib'lich *adj* female; womanly; (& gram) feminine

Weib'lichkeit *f* (-;) womanhood; feminine nature; **die holde W.** (hum) the fair sex

Weibs'bild *n* female; (pej) wench

Weibs'stück *n* (sl) woman

weich [vaɪç] *adj* soft; (*Ei*) soft-boiled; (*zart*) tender; (*schwach*) weak; **w. machen** soften up; **w. werden** (& fig) soften; relent

Weich'bild *n* urban area, outskirts

Weiche ['vaɪçə] *f* (-;-n) (anat) side, flank; (rr) switch; **Weichen stellen** throw the switch

weichen ['vaɪçən] *tr & intr* soften; soak ‖ §85 *intr* (SEIN) yield; give ground; (*Boden*) give way; (*dat*) give in to; **j-m nicht von der Seite w.** not leave s.o.'s side; **nicht von der Stelle w.** not budge from the spot; **von j-m w.** leave s.o.

Weichensteller ['vaɪçənstɛlər] *m* (-s; -) (rr) switchman

Weich'heit *f* (-;) softness; tenderness

weich'herzig *adj* soft-hearted

Weich'käse *m* soft cheese

weich'lich *adj* soft; tender; flabby; insipid; (*weibisch*) effeminate; (*lässig*) indolent

Weichling ['vaɪçlɪŋ] *m* (-s;-e) weakling

Weich'tier *n* mollusk

Weide ['vaɪdə] *f* (-;-n) pasture; (bot) willow

Wei'deland *n* pasture land

weiden ['vaɪdən] *tr* graze; (*Augen*,

feast ‖ *ref*—**sich w. an** (*dat*) feast
one's eyes on ‖ *intr* graze
Wei′denkorb *m* wicker basket
weidlich [′vaɪtlɪç] *adv* heartily
weidmännisch [′vaɪtmɛnɪʃ] *adj* (hunt)
sportsmanlike
weigern [′vaɪgərn] *ref*—**sich w. zu** (*inf*)
refuse to (*inf*)
Wei′gerung *f* (-;-en) refusal
Weihe [′vaɪə] *f* (-;-n) consecration;
(*e-s Priesters*) ordination
weihen [′vaɪən] *tr* consecrate; (*zum
Priester*) ordain; (*widmen*) dedicate;
dem Tode geweiht doomed to death
‖ *ref* devote oneself
Wei′her *m* (-s;-) pond
wei′hevoll *adj* solemn
Weihnachten [′vaɪnaxtən] *n* (-s;) & *pl*
Christmas; **zu W.** for or at Christmas
Weih′nachtsabend *m* Christmas Eve
Weih′nachtsbaum *m* Christmas tree;
(coll) bombing markers
Weih′nachtsbescherung *f* exchange of
Christmas presents
Weih′nachtsfeier *f* Christmas celebra-
tion; (*in Betrieben*) Christmas party
Weih′nachtsfest *n* feast of Christmas
Weih′nachtsgeschenk *n* Christmas pres-
ent
Weih′nachtsgratifikation *f* Christmas
bonus
Weih′nachtslied *n* Christmas carol
Weih′nachtsmann *m* (-[e]s;) Santa
Claus
Weih′nachtsmarkt *m* Christmas fair
(*at which Christmas decorations are
sold*)
Weih′nachtag *m* Christmas day
Weih′rauch *m* incense
Weih′rauchfaß *n* censer
Weih′wasser *n* holy water
Weih′wedel *m* (eccl) sprinkler
weil [vaɪl] *conj* because, since
weiland [′vaɪlant] *adv* formerly
Weilchen [′vaɪlçən] *n* (-s;) little while
Weile [′vaɪlə] *f* (-;) while
weilen [′vaɪlən] *intr* stay, linger
Wein [vaɪn] *m* (-[e]s;-e) wine;
(*Pflanze*) vine
Wein′bau *m* (-[e]s;) winegrowing
Wein′bauer -in §6 *mf* winegrower
Wein′beere *f* grape
Wein′berg *m* vineyard
Wein′blatt *n* vine leaf
Wein′brand *m* brandy
weinen [′vaɪnən] *tr* (*Tränen*) shed ‖
intr cry, weep; **vor Freude w.** weep
for joy; **w. um** cry over
weinerlich [′vaɪnərlɪç] *adj* tearful;
(*Stimme*) whining
Wein′ernte *f* vintage
Wein′essig *m* wine vinegar
Wein′faß *n* wine barrel
Wein′händler *m* wine merchant
Wein′jahr *n* vintage year
Wein′karte *f* wine list
Wein′keller *m* wine cellar
Wein′kelter *f* wine press
Wein′kenner *m* connoisseur of wine
Wein′krampf *m* crying fit
Wein′laub *n* vine leaves
Wein′lese *f* grape picking
Wein′presse *f* wine press

Wein′ranke *f* vine tendril
Wein′rebe *f* grapevine
wein′selig *adj* tipsy, tight
Wein′stock *m* vine
Wein′traube *f* grape; bunch of grapes
weise [′vaɪzə] *adj* wise ‖ **Weise** §5 *m*
wise man, sage ‖ *f* (-;-n) way;
(*Melodie*) tune; **auf diese W.** in this
way
-weise *comb.fm.* -wise; by, e.g., **dut-
zendweise** by the dozen; -ly, e.g.,
glücklicherweise luckily
weisen [′vaɪzən] §118 *tr* point out,
show; (*aus dem Lande*) expel; (*aus
der Schule*) expel; **j-n w. an** (*acc*)
refer s.o. to; **j-n w. nach** direct s.o.
to; **j-n w. von** order s.o. off (*premises, etc.*); **j-n w. von der Hand w.** refuse;
weit von der Hand w. have nothing
to do with ‖ *ref*—**von sich w.** refuse
‖ *intr*—**w. auf** (*acc*) point to
Weis′heit *f* (-;-en) wisdom; wise saying; **Weisheiten** words of wisdom
Weis′heitszahn *m* wisdom tooth
weis′lich *adv* wisely, prudently
weismachen [′vaɪsmaxən] *tr*—**j-m etw
w.** put s.th. over on s.o.; **mach das
anderen weis!** tell it to the marines!
weiß [vaɪs] *adj* white
weissagen [′vaɪszagən] *tr* foretell
Weiß′blech *n* tin plate, tin
Weiß′blechdose *f* tincan
weiß′bluten *tr* bleed white
Weiß′brot *n* white bread
Weiß′dorn *m* (bot) hawthorn
Weiße [′vaɪsə] *f* (-;-n) whiteness;
(Berlin) ale ‖ §5 *m* white man ‖ *f*
white woman ‖ *n* (*im Auge, im Ei*)
white
weißen [′vaɪsən] *tr* whiten; (*tünchen*)
whitewash
weiß′glühend *adj* white-hot
Weiß′glut *f* white heat, incandescence
Weiß′kohl *m*, **Weiß′kraut** *n* cabbage
weiß′lich *adj* whitish
Weiß′metall *n* pewter; Babbitt metal
Weiß′waren *pl* linens
Weiß′wein *m* white wine
Wei′sung *f* (-;-en) directions, instructions; directive
weit [vaɪt] *adj* far, distant; (*ausgedehnt*) extensive; (*breit*) wide, broad;
(*geräumig*) large; (*Gewissen*) elastic;
(*Herz*) big; (*Kleid*) full, big; (*Meer*)
broad; (*Reise, Weg*) long; (*Welt*)
wide; **bei weitem besser** better by
far; **von weitem** from afar ‖ *adv* far,
way; widely; greatly; **w. besser** far
better
weit′ab′ *adv* (**von**) far away (from)
weit′aus′ *adv* by far
Weit′blick *m* farsightedness
weit′blickend *adj* farsighted
Weite [′vaɪtə] *f* (-;-n) width, breadth;
(*Ferne*) distance; (*Umfang*) size;
(*Ausdehnung*) extent; (*Durchmesser*)
diameter; (fig) range; **in die W.
ziehen** go out into the world
weiten [′vaɪtən] *tr* widen; (*Loch*) enlarge; (*Schuh*) stretch ‖ *ref* widen
weiter [′vaɪtər] *adj* farther; further;
wider; **bis auf weiteres** until further
notice; **des weiteren** furthermore;

ohne weiteres without further ado || *adv* farther; further; furthermore; *(voran)* on; **er kann nicht w.** he can't go on; **nur s. w.!** keep it up!; **und so w.** and so forth, and so on

weiter— *comb.fm.* on; keep on, continue to

wei′terbefördern *tr* forward

Wei′terbestand *m* continued existence

wei′terbestehen §146 *intr* survive

wei′terbilden *tr* develop || *ref* continue one's studies

wei′tererzählen *tr* spread *(rumors)*

wei′terfahren §71 *intr* (SEIN) drive on

wei′tergeben §80 *tr* pass on, relay

wei′tergehen §82 *intr* (SEIN) go on

wei′terhin′ *adv* furthermore; again

wei′terkommen §99 *intr* (SEIN) get ahead, make progress

wei′terkönnen §100 *intr* be able to go on; **ich kann nicht weiter** I'm stuck

wei′terleben *intr* live on, survive

wei′termachen *tr* & *intr* continue || *interj* (mil) as you were!, carry on!

weit′gehend *adj* far-reaching

weit′gereist *adj* widely traveled

weit′greifend *adj* far-reaching

weit′her′ *adv*—**von w.** from afar

weit′her′geholt *adj* far-fetched

weit′herzig *adj* broad-minded

weit′hin′ *adv* far off

weitläufig ['vartlɔɪfɪç] *adj* lengthy, detailed; complicated; *(Verwandte)* distant; *(geräumig)* roomy || *adv* at length, in detail

weit′reichend *adj* far-reaching

weitschweifig ['vart/vaifiç] *adj* detailed, lengthy; long-winded

weit′sichtig *adj* (& fig) far-sighted

Weit′sprung *m* (sport) long jump

Weit′streckenflug *m* long-distance flight

weit′tragend *adj* long-range; (fig) far-reaching

Weit′winkelobjektiv *n* wide-angle lens

Weizen ['vartsən] *m* (—s;—) wheat

Wei′zenmehl *n* wheat flour

welch [velç] *interr adj* which || *interr pron* which one; *(in Ausrufen)* what ...!; **mit welcher** (or **mit welch einer**) **Begeisterung arbeitet er!** with what enthusiasm he works! || *indef pron* any; some || *rel pron* who, which, that

welcherlei ['velçər'laɪ] *invar adj* what kind of; whatever

welk [velk] *adj* withered; *(Haut, Lippen)* wrinkled; (fig) faded

welken ['velkən] *intr* (SEIN) wither; (fig) fade

Wellblech ['velbleç] *n* corrugated iron

Well′blechhütte *f* Quonset hut

Welle ['velə] *f* (—;—n) wave; *(Wellbaum)* shaft; (gym) circle *(around horizontal bar)*; (mach) shaft

wellen ['velən] *tr* & *ref* wave

Wel′lenbereich *m* wave band

Wel′lenberg *m* crest *(of wave)*

Wel′lenbewegung *f* undulation

Wel′lenbrecher *m* breakwater

wel′lenförmig *adj* wavy

Wel′lenlänge *f* wavelength

Wel′lenlinie *f* wavy line

Wel′lenreiten §86 *intr* surf; waterski || **Wellenreiten** *n* (—s;) surfing, surfboard riding; waterskiing

Wel′lenreiter —in §6 *mf* surfer; waterskier

Wel′lenreiterbrett *n* surfboard; water ski

Wel′lental *n* trough *(of wave)*

wellig ['velɪç] *adj* wavy

Well′pappe *f* corrugated cardboard

Welt [velt] *f* (—;—en) world

Welt′all *n* universe; outer space

Welt′anschauung *f* outlook on life; ideology

Welt′ausmaß *m*—**im W.** on a global scale

Welt′ausstellung *f* world's fair

welt′bekannt, welt′berühmt *adj* world-renowned

Wel′tenbummler *m* globetrotter

welt′erfahren *adj* sophisticated

Weltergewicht ['veltərgəviçt] *n* welterweight class

Weltergewichtler ['veltərgəviçtlər] *m* (—s;—) welterweight boxer

welt′erschütternd *adj* earth-shaking

welt′fremd *adj* secluded; innocent

Welt′friede *m* world peace

Welt′geistlicher *m* secular priest

welt′gewandt *adj* worldly-wise

Welt′karte *f* map of the world

welt′klug *adj* worldly-wise

Welt′körper *m* heavenly body

Welt′krieg *m* world war

Welt′kugel *f* globe

Welt′lage *f* international situation

welt′lich *adj* worldly; secular

Welt′macht *f* world power

Welt′mann *m* (—[e]s;—er) man of the world

welt′männisch *adj* sophisticated

Welt′meer *n* ocean

Welt′meinung *f* world opinion

Welt′meister —in §6 *mf* world champion

Welt′meisterschaft *f* world championship

Welt′ordnung *f* cosmic order

Welt′postverein *m* postal union

Welt′priester *m* secular priest

Welt′raum *m* (—[e]s;) outer space

Welt′raumfahrer *m* spaceman

Welt′raumfahrt *f* space travel

Welt′raumfahrzeug *n* spacecraft

Welt′raumforschung *f* exploration of outer space

Welt′raumgeschoß *n* space shot

Welt′raumkapsel *f* space capsule

Welt′raumstation *f* space station

Welt′raumstrahlen *pl* cosmic rays

Welt′reich *n* world empire

Welt′reise *f* trip around the world

Welt′rekord *m* world record

Welt′ruf *m* world-wide renown

Welt′ruhm *m* world-wide fame

Welt′schmerz *m* world-weariness

Welt′sicherheitsrat *m* U.N. Security Council

Welt′stadt *f* metropolis *(city with more than one million inhabitants)*

Welt′teil *m* continent

welt′umfassend *adj* world-wide

Welt′weisheit *f* philosophy

wem [vem] *interr & rel pron* to whom
Wem′fall *m* dative case
wen [ven] *interr & rel pron* whom
Wende [′vendə] *f* (-;-n) turn; turning point; (gym) face vault, front vault
Wen′dekreis *m* (geog) tropic
Wendeltreppe [′vendəltrepə] *f* spiral staircase
Wen′demarke *f* (aer) pylon; (sport) turn post
wenden [′vendən] §140 *tr* turn; turn around; turn over; (*Geld, Mühe*) spend || *ref* turn; (*Wind, Wetter*) change || *intr* turn, turn around
Wen′depunkt *m* turning point
wendig [′vendɪç] *adj* maneuverable; (*Person*) versatile, resourceful
Wen′dung *f* (-;-en) turn; change; (*Redensart*) idiomatic expression
Wen′fall *m* accusative case
wenig [′venɪç] *adj* little; **ein w.** a little, a bit of; **wenige** few, a few, some || *adv* little; not very; seldom || *indef pron* little; **wenige** few, a few
weniger [′venɪgər] *adj* fewer; less; (arith) minus
We′nigkeit *f* (-;) fewness; smallness; pittance; trifle; **meine W.** (coll) poor little me
wenigste [′venɪçstə] §9 *adj* least; very few, fewest; **am wenigsten** least of all
wenigstens [′venɪçstəns] *adv* at least
wenn [ven] *conj* if, in case; (*zeitlich*) when, whenever; **auch w.** even if; **außer w.** except when, except if, unless; **w. anders** provided that; **w. auch** although, even if; **w. schon, denn schon** go all the way || **Wenn** *n* (-;-) if
wenngleich′, wennschon′ *conj* although
Wenzel [′ventsəl] *m* (-s;-) (cards) jack
wer [ver] *interr pron* who, which one; **wer auch immer** whoever; **wer da?** who goes there? || *rel pron* he who, whoever || *indef pron* somebody, anybody
Werbe- [′verbə] *comb.fm.* advertising; publicity; commercial
Wer′befernsehen *n* commercial television
Wer′befilm *m* commercial
Wer′befläche *f* advertising space
Wer′begraphik *f* commercial art
Wer′begraphiker –in §6 *mf* commercial artist
werben [′verbən] §149 *tr* (*neue Kunden*) try to get; (mil) recruit || *intr* advertise; **für e-n neuen Handelsartikel w.** advertise a new product; **um ein Mädchen w.** court a girl
Wer′beschrift *f* folder
Wer′bestelle *f* advertising agency
Wer′bung *f* (-;-en) advertising; publicity; courting; recruiting
Werdegang [′verdəgaŋ] *m* career, background; (*Entwicklung*) development; (*Wachstum*) growth; (*Ablauf der Herstellung*) process of production
werden [′verdən] §159 *intr* (SEIN) become, grow, get, turn; **w. zu** change into; **zu nichts w.** come to nought ||

aux (SEIN) (to form the future) **er wird gehen** he will go; (to form the passive) **er wird geehrt** he is being honored || **Werden** *n* (-s;) becoming, growing; (*Entstehung*) evolution; (*Wachstum*) growth; **im W. sein** be in the process of development; be in the making
wer′dend *adj* nascent; (*Mutter*) expectant; (*Arzt*) future
Werder [′verdər] *m* (-s;-) islet
Wer′fall *m* subjective case
werfen [′verfən] §160 *tr* throw, cast; (*Junge*) produce; (*Blasen*) form, blow; **Falten w.** wrinkle || *ref* (*Holz*) warp; **sich hin und her w.** toss; **sich in die Brust w.** throw out one's chest || *intr* throw; (*Tieren*) produce young
Werft [verft] *f* (-;-e) shipyard
Werft′halle *f* (aer) repair hangar
Werg [verk] *n* (-[e]s;) oakum, tow
Werk [verk] *n* (-[e]s;-e) work; (*Tat*) deed; (*Erzeugnis*) production;- (*Leistung*) performance; (*Unternehmen*) undertaking; (*Fabrik*) works, plant, mill; (horol) clockwork; **das ist dein W.** that's your doing; **gutes W.** good deed; **im Werke sein** be in the works; **zu Werke gehen** go to it
Werk′anlage *f* plant, works
Werk′bank *f* (-;-e) workbench
werk′fremd *adj* (*Personen*) unauthorized
Werk′meister *m* foreman
Werk′nummer *f* factory serial number
Werks′angehörige §5 *mf* employee
Werk′schutz *m* security force
Werks′kantine *f* factory cafeteria
Werk′statt *f*, **Werk′stätte** *f* workshop
Werk′stattwagen *m* maintenance truck
Werk′stoff *m* manufacturing material
Werk′stück *n* (indust) piece
Werk′tag *m* weekday; working day
werk′tägig *adj* workaday, ordinary
werk′tags *adv* (on) weekdays
werk′tätig *adj* working; practical
Werk′zeug *n* tool
Werk′zeugmaschine *f* machine tool
Wermut [′vermut] *m* (-[e]s;) vermouth; (bot) wormwood
wert [vert] *adj* worth; worthy; esteemed; **etw** [*genit or acc*] **w. sein** be worth s.th.; **nicht der Rede w. sein** not worth mentioning; **nichts w. sein** be good for nothing; **Werter Herr X Dear Mr. X** || **Wert** *m* (-[e]s;-e) worth, value; price, rate; (*Wichtigkeit*) importance; (chem) valence; **äußerer W.** face value; **im W. von** valued at; **innerer W.** intrinsic value; **Werte** (com) assets; (phys) data
Wert′angabe *f* valuation
wert′beständig *adj* of lasting value; (*Währung*) stable
Wert′bestimmung *f* appraisal
Wert′brief *m* insured letter
werten [′vertən] *tr* (*bewerten*) value; (*nach Leistung*) rate; (*auswerten*) evaluate
Wert′gegenstand *m* valuable article; **Wertgegenstände** valuables
–wertig [vertɪç] *comb.fm.* –value, –quality, e.g., **geringwertig** low-qual-

ity; (chem) –valent, e.g., **zweiwertig** bivalent

Wer'tigkeit *f* (–;–en) (chem) valence

wert'los *adj* worthless

Wert'papiere *pl* securities

Wert'sachen *pl* valuables

wert'voll *adj* valuable

Wert'zeichen *n* stamp; (*Briefmarke*) postage stamp; (*Banknote*) bill

Wesen ['vezən] *n* (–s;–) being, creature; entity; (*inneres Sein, Kern*) essence; (*Betragen*) conduct, way; (*Getue*) fuss; (*Natur*) nature, character; **einnehmendes W.** pleasing personality; **höchtes W.** Supreme Being –**wesen** *n comb.fm.* system

we'senhaft *adj* real; characteristic

we'senlos *adj* unreal; incorporeal

wesentlich ['vezəntlɪç] *adj* essential; (*beträchtlich*) substantial

Weser ['vezər] *f* (–;) Weser (River)

Wes'fall *m* genitive case

weshalb [vɛs'halp] *adv* why; wherefore

Wespe ['vɛspə] *f* (–;–n) wasp

wessen ['vɛsən] *interr pron* whose

West [vɛst] *m* (–s;) west; (poet) west wind

Weste ['vɛstə] *f* (–;–n) vest; **e–e reine W.** a clean slate

Westen ['vɛstən] *m* (–s;) west; **im W. von west of; nach W.** westward

Westfalen [vɛst'falən] *n* (–s;) Westphalia

westfälisch [vɛst'fɛlɪʃ] *adj* Westphalian

West'gote *m* (–n;–n) Visigoth

Westindien [vɛst'ɪndjən] *n* (–s;) the West Indies

west'lich *adj* west, western; westerly

Westmächte ['vɛstmɛçtə] *pl* Western Powers

westwärts ['vɛstvɛrts] *adv* westward

weswegen [vɛs'vegən] *adv* why; wherefore

wett [vɛt] *adj* even, quits

Wett– *comb.fm.* competitive

Wett'bewerb *m* (–s;–e) competition, contest; (*Treffen*) meet

Wett'bewerber –in §6 *mf* competitor

Wette ['vɛtə] *f* (–;–n) bet, wager; **e–e W. abschließen** (or **eingehen**) make a bet; **mit j–m um die W. laufen** race s.o.; **was gilt die W.?** what do you bet?

Wett'eifer *m* competitiveness, rivalry

wetteifern ['vɛtaɪfərn] *insep intr* compete; **w. um** compete for

Wetter ['vɛtər] *n* (–s;) weather; (min) ventilation; **alle W.!** holy smokes!

wet'terbeständig, wet'terfest *adj* weatherproof

Wet'terglas *n* barometer

wet'terhart *adj* hardy

Wet'terkunde *f* meteorology

Wet'terlage *f* weather conditions

wet'terleuchten *insep impers*—es **wetterleuchtet** there is summer lightning || **Wetterleuchten** *n* (–;) summer lightning, heat lightning

Wet'terverhältnisse *pl* weather conditions

Wet'tervorhersage *f* weather forecast

Wet'terwarte *f* meteorological station

Wet'terwechsel *m* change in the weather

wetterwendisch ['vɛtərvɛndɪʃ] *adj* moody

Wett'fahrer –in §6 *mf* racer

Wett'fahrt *f* race

Wett'kampf *m* competition, contest

Wett'kämpfer –in §6 *mf* competitor, contestant

Wett'lauf *m* race, foot race

Wett'läufer –in §6 *mf* runner

wett'machen *tr* make up for

Wett'rennen *n* race

Wett'rudern *n* boat race

Wett'rüsten *n* armaments race

Wett'schwimmen *n* swimming meet

Wett'segeln *n* regatta

Wett'spiel *n* game, match

Wett'streit *m* contest, match, game

Wett'zettel *m* betting ticket

wetzen ['vɛtsən] *tr* whet, sharpen

Wetzstein ['vɛts/taɪn] *m* whetstone

Whisky ['vɪski] *m* (–s;–s) whiskey

wich [vɪç] *pret of* weichen

Wichs [vɪks] *m* (es–;–e) gala; **in vollem W. in** full dress; **sich in W. werfen** dress up

Wichse ['vɪksə] *f* (–;–n) shoepolish || *f* (–;) (coll) spanking

wichsen ['vɪksən] *tr* polish; (coll) spank, beat up

Wicht [vɪçt] *m* (–[e]s;–e) elf; dwarf

Wichtel ['vɪçtəl] *m* (–s;–) dwarf

wichtig ['vɪçtɪç] *adj* important || *adv* —**w. tun** act important

Wich'tigkeit *f* (–;) importance

Wichtigtuer ['vɪçtɪçtu·ər] *m* (–s;–) busybody

wichtigtuerisch ['vɪçtɪçtu·ərɪ∫] *adj* officious

Wicke ['vɪkə] *f* (–;–n) (bot) vetch

Wickel ['vɪkəl] *m* (–s;–) wrapper; curler, roller; (*von Garn*) ball; (med) compress

wickeln ['vɪkəln] *tr* wrap; wind (*Haar*) curl; (*Kind*) diaper; (*Zigaretten*) roll

Widder ['vɪdər] *m* (–s;–) ram; (astr) Ram

wider ['vɪdər] *prep* (*acc*) against, contrary to

wider– *comb.fm.* re–, con–, un–, counter–, contra–, anti–, with–

wi'derborstig *adj* stubborn, contrary

widerfah'ren §71 *intr* (SEIN) (*dat*) befall, happen to

Wi'derhaken *m* barb

Wi'derhall *m* echo, reverberation; (fig) response, reaction

wi'derhallen *intr* echo, resound

Wi'derlager *n* abutment

widerle'gen *tr* refute

wi'derlich *adj* repulsive

wi'dernatürlich *adj* unnatural

widerra'ten §63 *tr*—**j–m etw w. dissuade** s.o. from s.th.

wi'derrechtlich *adj* illegal

Wi'derrede *f* contradiction

Wi'derruf *m* recall; cancellation; retraction; denial; **bis auf W.** until further notice

widerru'fen §122 *tr* revoke; (*Auftrag*)

cancel; (*Befehl*) countermand; (*Behauptung*) retract
Widersacher **–in** ['vɪdərzaxər(ɪn)] §6 *mf* adversary
Wi'derschein *m* reflection
widerset'zen *ref* (*dat*) oppose, resist
widersetz'lich *adj* insubordinate
wi'dersinning *adj* absurd, nonsensical
widerspenstig ['vidərʃpɛnstiç] *adj* refractory, contrary; (*Haar*) stubborn
wi'derspiegeln *tr* reflect || *ref* (**in** *dat*) be reflected (in)
Wi'derspiel *n* contrary, reverse
widerspre'chen §64 *intr* (*dat*) contradict; (*dat*) oppose
widerspre'chend *adj* contradictory
Wi'derspruch *m* contradiction; opposition; **auf heftigen W. stoßen bei** meet with strong opposition from
widersprüchlich ['vidərʃpryçliç] *adj* contradictory
wi'derspruchsvoll *adj* full of contradictions
Wi'derstand *m* resistance; opposition; (elec) resistance; (elec) resistor
Wi'derstandsnest *n* pocket of resistance
widerste'hen §146 *intr* (*dat*) withstand, resist; (*dat*) be repugnant to
widerstre'ben *intr* (*dat*) oppose, resist; (*dat*) be repugnant to || *impers*—es **widerstrebt mir zu** (*inf*) I hate to (*inf*)
widerstre'bend *adj* reluctant
Wi'derstreit *m* opposition, antagonism; (fig) conflict, clash
widerstrei'ten §86 *intr* (*dat*) clash with
widerwärtig ['vidərvɛrtiç] *adj* nasty
Wi'derwille *m* (**gegen**) dislike (of, for), aversion (to); (*Widerstreben*) reluctance; **mit W.** reluctantly
wi'derwillig *adj* reluctant, unwilling
widmen ['vɪtmən] *tr* dedicate, devote || *ref* (*dat*) devote oneself to
Wid'mung *f* (*–;–en*) dedication
widrig ['vidriç] *adj* contrary; (*ungünstig*) unfavorable, adverse
wid'rigenfalls *adv* otherwise, or else
wie [vi] *adv* how; (*vergleichend*) as, such as, like...so...wie as...as; und **wie! and how!; wie, bitte?** what did you say?; **wie dem auch sei** be that as it may; **wie wäre es mit...?** how about...?
wieder ['vidər] *adv* again; anew; (*zurück*) back; (*als Vergeltung*) in return
**wieder– ** *comb.fm.* re-
Wie'derabdruck *m* reprint
wiederan'knüpfen *tr* resume
Wiederauf'bau *m* (*–[e]s;*) rebuilding
wiederauf'bauen *tr* rebuild, reconstruct
wiederauf'erstehen §146 *intr* (SEIN) rise from the dead
Wiederauf'erstehung *f* resurrection
Wiederauf'führung *f* (theat) revival
wiederauf'kommen §99 *intr* (SEIN) (*Kranker*) recover; (*Mode*) come in again
Wiederauf'nahme *f* resumption; (jur) reopening
Wiederauf'nahmeverfahren *n* retrial
Wiederauf'rüstung *f* rearmament

Wie'derbeginn *m* reopening
wie'derbekommen §99 *tr* recover
wie'derbeleben *tr* revive, resuscitate
wie'derbeschaffen *tr* replace
wie'derbringen §65 *tr* bring back; restore, give back
wiederein'bringen §65 *tr* make up for
wiederein'setzen *tr* (**in** *acc*) reinstate (in); **in Rechte w.** restore to former rights
wiederein'stellen *tr* rehire; (mil) reenlist
Wie'dereintritt *m* (rok) reentry
wie'derergreifen §88 *tr* recapture
wie'dererhalten §90 *tr* get back
wie'dererkennen §97 *tr* recognize
wie'dererlangen *tr* recover, retrieve
wie'dererstatten *tr* restore; (*Geld*) refund
Wie'dergabe *f* return; reproduction; rendering
wie'dergeben §80 *tr* give back; (*Ton*) reproduce; (spielen, übersetzen) render; (*Ehre, Gesundheit*) restore
Wie'dergeburt *f* rebirth
wie'dergenesen §84 *intr* (SEIN) recover
wie'dergewinnen §52 *tr* regain
wiedergut'machen *tr* make good
Wiedergut'machung *f* (*–;–en*) reparation
wiederher'stellen *tr* restore
wie'derholen *tr* bring back; take back || **wiederho'len** *tr* repeat
wiederholt [vidər'holt] *adv* repeatedly
Wiederho'lung *f* (*–;–en*) repetition
Wiederho'lungszeichen *n* dittomarks; (mus) repeat
Wie'derhören *n*—**auf W.!** (telp) goodbye!
wie'derimpfen *tr* give (*s.o.*) a booster shot
wiederinstand'setzen *tr* repair
wiederkäuen ['vidərkɔ·ən] *tr* ruminate; (fig) repeat over and over || *intr* chew the cud
Wiederkehr ['vidərker] *f* (*–;*) return; recurrence; anniversary
wie'derkehren *intr* (SEIN) return; recur
wie'derkommen §99 *intr* (SEIN) come back
Wiederkunft ['vidərkunft] *f* (*–;*) return
wie'dersehen §138 *tr* see again || *recip* meet again || **Widersehen** *n* (*–s;–*) meeting again; **auf W.!** see you!
Wie'dertäufer *m* Baptist
wie'dertun §154 *tr* do again, repeat
wie'derum *adv* again; on the other hand
wie'dervereinigen *tr* reunite; reunify
Wie'dervereinigung *f* reunion; (pol) reunification
wie'derverheiraten *tr* & *recip* remarry
Wie'derverkäufer **–in** §6 *mf* retailer
Wie'derwahl *f* reelection
wie'derwählen *tr* reelect
wiederzu'lassen §104 *tr* readmit
Wiege ['vigə] *f* (*–;–n*) cradle
wiegen ['vigən] *tr* (schaukeln) rock || *ref*—**sich in den Hüften w.** sway one's hips; **sich w. in** (*acc*) lull oneself into || §57 *tr* & *intr* weigh
Wie'gendruck *m* incunabulum
Wie'genlied *n* lullaby

wiehern ['vi·ərn] *intr* neigh; **wiehern-des Gelächter** horselaugh

Wien [vin] *n* (–s;) Vienna

Wiener –in ['vinər(ın)] §6 *mf* Viennese

wienerisch ['vinərɪʃ] *adj* Viennese

wies [vis] *pret* of **weisen**

Wiese ['vizə] *f* (–;–n) meadow

Wiesel ['vizəl] *n* (–s;–) weasel

Wie'senland *n* meadowland

wieso' *adv* why, how come

wieviel' *adj* how much; **w. Uhr ist es?** what time is it? || *adv & pron* how much || **vieviele** *adj & pron* how many

wievielte [vi'fıltə] §9 *adj* which, what; **den wievielten haben wir?** (or **der w. ist heute?**) what day of the month is it?

wiewohl' *conj* although

wild [vɪlt] *adj* wild; savage; (*grausam*) ferocious; (*Flucht*) headlong; (*auf acc*) wild (about); **wilde Ehe** concubinage; **wilder Streik** wildcat strike || **Wild** *n* (–es;) game

Wild'bach *m* torrent

Wild'braten *m* roast venison

Wildbret ['vɪltbret] *n* (–s;) game; venison

Wild'dieb *m* poacher

Wilde ['vɪldə] §5 *mf* savage; **wie ein Wilder** like a madman

Wild'ente *f* wild duck

Wilderer ['vɪldərər] *m* (–s;–) poacher

wildern ['vɪldərn] *intr* poach

Wild'fleisch *n* game; venison

wild'fremd' *adj* completely strange

Wild'hüter *m* game warden

Wild'leder *n* doeskin, buckskin; chamois; suede

Wildnis ['vɪltnɪs] *f* (–;) wilderness

Wild'schwein *n* wild boar

Wild'wasser *n* rapids

Wildwest'film *m* western

wildwüchsig ['vɪltvyksɪç] *adj* wild

Wille ['vɪlə] §5 *mf* savage; **wie ein Wilder** like a madman, **Willen** ['vɪlən] *m* (–ns;–n), **Willen** ['vɪlən] *m* (–s;) will; (*Absicht*) intention; **mit W.** on purpose; **um j-s willen** for s.o.'s sake; **wider Willen** unwillingly; unintentionally; **willens sein zu** (*inf*) be willing to (*inf*)

wil'lenlos *adj* irresolute; unstable

Wil'lensfreiheit *f* free will

Wil'lenskraft *f* will power

wil'lensschwach *adj* weak-willed

wil'lensstark *adj* strong-willed

willfah'ren *intr* (*dat*) comply with

willig ['vɪlɪç] *adj* willing, ready

Wil'ligkeit *f* (–;) willingness

willkom'men *adj* welcome; **j-n w. heißen** welcome s.o. || **Willkommen** *m & n* (–s;) welcome

Willkür ['vɪlkyr] *f* (–;) arbitrariness

will'kürlich *adj* arbitrary

wimmeln ['vɪməln] *intr* (**von**) team (with)

wimmern ['vɪmərn] *intr* whimper

Wimpel ['vɪmpəl] *m* (–s;–) streamer; pennant

Wimper ['vɪmpər] *f* (–;–n) eyelash; **ohne mit der W. zu zucken** without batting an eye

Wim'perntusche *f* mascara

Wind [vɪnt] *m* (–[e]s;–e) wind; flatulence; (hunt) scent

Wind'beutel *m* (fig) windbag; (aer) windsock; (culin) cream puff

Winde ['vɪndə] *f* (–;–n) winch, windlass; reel; (naut) capstan

Windel ['vɪndəl] *f* (–;–n) diaper

win'delweich *adj*—**w. schlagen** (coll) beat to a pulp

winden ['vɪndən] §59 *tr* wind; twist, coil; (*Kranz*) weave, make || *ref* wriggle; (*Fluß*) wind; (*vor Schmerzen*) writhe

Wind'fang *m* storm porch

Wind'hose *f* tornado

Wind'hund *m* greyhound; (coll) windbag

windig ['vɪndɪç] *adj* windy; (fig) flighty

Wind'kanal *m* wind tunnel

Wind'licht *n* hurricane lamp

Wind'mühle *f* windmill

Wind'pocken *pl* chicken pox

Wind'sack *m* windsock

Wind'schatten *m* lee

Wind'schutzscheibe *f* windshield

Wind'stärke *f* wind velocity

wind'still *adj* calm || **Windstille** *f* calm

Wind'stoß *m* gust

Wind'strömung *f* air current

Win'dung *f* (–;–en) winding, twisting; (*Kurve*) bend; (e-r *Schlange*) coil; (e-r *Schraube*) thread, worm; (e-r *Muschel*) whorl

Wind'zug *m* air current, draft

Wink [vɪŋk] *m* (–[e]s;–e) sign; (*Zwinkern*) wink; (*mit der Hand*) wave; (*mit dem Kopfe*) nod; (*Hinweis*) hint, tip; **W. mit dem Zaunpfahl** broad hint

Winkel ['vɪŋkəl] *m* (–s;–) corner; (carp) square; (geom) angle; (mil) chevron

winkelig ['vɪŋkəlıç] *adj* angular; (*Straße*) crooked

Win'kellinie *f* diagonal

Win'kelmaß *n* (carp) square

Win'kelzug *m* subterfuge; evasion

winken ['vɪŋkən] *intr* signal; **mit der Hand** wave; (*mit dem Kopfe*) nod; (*mit dem Auge*) wink; **mit dem Taschentuch w.** wave the handkerchief

Win'ker *m* (–s;–) signalman; (aut) direction signal

winseln ['vɪnzəln] *intr* whimper, whine

Winter ['vɪntər] *m* (–s;–) winter

win'terfest *adj* winterized; (*Pflanzen*) hardy

win'terlich *adj* wintry

Win'terschlaf *m* hibernation; **W. halten** hibernate

Win'tersonnenwende *f* winter solstice

Winzer ['vɪntsər] *m* (–s;–) vinedresser; (*Traubenlese*) grape picker

winzig ['vɪntsıç] *adj* tiny

Wipfel ['vɪpfəl] *m* (–s;–) treetop

Wippe ['vɪpə] *f* (–;–n) seesaw

wippen ['vɪpən] *intr* seesaw; rock; balance oneself

wir [vir] §11 *pers pron* we

Wirbel ['vɪrbəl] *m* (–s;–) whirl; eddy; whirlpool; (*Trommel–*) roll; (*Violin–*)

peg; (anat) vertebra; **e-n W. machen** (coll) raise Cain

wirbelig ['vɪrbəlɪç] adj whirling; giddy

Wir'belknochen m (anat) vertebra

wir'bellos adj spineless, invertebrate

wirbeln ['vɪrbəln] tr warble || intr whirl; (Wasser) eddy; (Trommel) roll; (Lerche) warble; **mir wirbelt der Kopf** my head is spinning

Wir'belsäule f spinal column, spine

Wir'belsturm m hurricane, typhoon

Wir'beltier n vertebrate

Wir'belwind m whirlwind

wirken ['vɪrkən] tr work, bring about, effect; (Teig) knead; (Teppich) weave; (Pullover) knit; **Gutes w.** do good; **Wunder w.** work wonders || intr work; be active; function; look, appear; (Worte) tell, hit home; **als Arzt w.** be a doctor; **an e-r Schule (als Lehrer) w.** teach school; **anregend w.** act as a stimulant; **berauschend w. auf** (acc) intoxicate; **beruhigend w. auf** (acc) have a soothing effect on; **gut w.** work well; **lächerlich w.** look ridiculous; **stark w. auf** (acc) touch deeply; **w. auf** (acc) affect, have an effect on; **w. bei** have an effect on; **w. für** work for; **w. gegen** work against, counteract ||

Wirken n (-s;) action, performance; operation

wirk'lich adj real, actual; true || adv really, actually; truly

Wirk'lichkeit f (-;-en) reality; actual fact

Wirk'lichkeitsform f indicative mood

wirksam ['vɪrkzam] adj active; effective; (Hieb) telling; **w. für good for**

Wirk'samkeit f (-;) effectiveness

Wirk'stoff m metabolic substance (vitamin, hormone, or enzyme)

Wir'kung f (-;-en) effect; result; operation, action; influence, impression

Wir'kungsbereich m scope; effective range; (mil) zone of fire

wir'kungsfähig adj active; effective; efficient

Wir'kungskreis m domain, province

wir'kungslos adj ineffective; inefficient

wir'kungsvoll adj effective; efficacious

Wirk'waren pl knitwear

wirr [vɪr] adj confused; (verworren) chaotic; (Haar) disheveled

Wirren ['vɪrən] pl disorders, troubles

Wirr'kopf m scatterbrain

Wirrwarr ['vɪrvar] m (-s;) mix-up, mess

Wirt [vɪrt] m (-[e]s;-e) host; innkeeper; landlord; (biol) host

Wirtin ['vɪrtɪn] f (-;-nen) hostess; innkeeper, innkeeper's wife; landlady

wirt'lich adj hospitable

Wirt'schaft f (-;-en) economy; business; industry and trade; (Haushaltung) housekeeping; (Hauswesen) household; (Gasthaus) inn; (Treiben) goings-on; (Durcheinander) mess; (Umstände) fuss, trouble; **die W. besorgen (or führen)** keep house; **gelenkte W.** planned economy

wirtschaften ['vɪrtʃaftən] intr keep

house; economize; (herumhantieren) bustle about; **gut w.** manage well

Wirt'schafter –**in** §6 mf manager || f housekeeper

Wirt'schaftler –**in** §6 mf economist; economics teacher

wirt'schaftlich adj economical, thrifty; economic; industrial; (vorteilhaft) profitable

Wirt'schaftsgeld n housekeeping money

Wirt'schaftshilfe f economic aid

Wirt'schaftsjahr n fiscal year

Wirt'schaftslehre f economics

Wirt'schaftspolitik f economic policy

Wirt'schaftsprüfer –**in** §6 mf certified public accountant, CPA

Wirts'haus n inn, restaurant; bar

wischen ['vɪʃən] tr wipe

Wisch'lappen m dustcloth

Wisch'tuch n dishtowel

wispern ['vɪspərn] tr & intr whisper

Wißbegierde ['vɪsbəgirdə] f (-;) craving for knowledge; curiosity

wissen ['vɪsən] §161 tr & intr know || **Wissen** n (-s;) knowledge; learning; know-how; **meines Wissens** as far as I know

Wis'senschaft f (-;-en) knowledge; science

Wis'senschaftler –**in** §6 mf scientist

wis'senschaftlich adj scientific; scholarly; learned

Wis'sensdrang m, **Wis'sensdurst** m thirst for knowledge

Wis'sensgebiet n field of knowledge

wis'senswert adj worth knowing

wis'sentlich adj conscious; willful || adv knowingly; on purpose

wittern ['vɪtərn] tr scent, smell

Wit'terung f (-;-en) weather; (hunt) scent; **bei günstiger W.** weather permitting; **e-e feine W. haben** have a good nose

Wit'terungsverhältnisse pl weather conditions

Witwe ['vɪtvə] f (-;-n) widow

Witwer ['vɪtvər] m (-s;-) widower

Witz [vɪts] m (-es;-e) joke; wisecrack; wit; wittiness; **das ist der ganze W.** that's all; **Witze machen (or reißen)** crack jokes

Witz'blatt n comics

Witzbold ['vɪtsbɔlt] m (-[e]s;-e) joker

witzig ['vɪtsɪç] adj witty; funny

wo [vo] adv where; **wo auch (or wo immer)** wherever; **wo nicht** if not; **wo nur** wherever

woan'ders adv somewhere else

wob [vop] pret of weben

wobei' adv whereby; whereat; whereto; at which; in the course of which

Woche ['vɔxə] f (-;-n) week; **heute in e-r W.** a week from today; **in den Wochen sein** be in labor; **in die Wochen kommen** go into labor; **unter der W.** (coll) during the week

Wo'chenbeihilfe f maternity benefits

Wo'chenbett n post-natal period

Wo'chenblatt n weekly (newspaper)

Wo'chenende n weekend

Wo'chengeld n weekly allowance; (für Mütter) maternity benefits

wo'chenlang *adj* lasting many weeks ‖ *adv* for weeks

Wo'chenlohn *m* weekly wages

Wo'chenschau *f* (cin) newsreel

wöchentlich ['vœçəntlıç] *adj* weekly ‖ *adv* every week; **einmal w.** once a week

-wöchig [vœçıç] *comb.fm.* –week

Wöchnerin ['vœçnərın] *f* (–;-nen) recent mother

Wodka ['votka] *m* (–s;) vodka

wodurch' *adv* whereby, by which; how

wofern' *conj* provided that; **w. nicht** unless

wofür' *adv* wherefore, for which; what for; **w. halten Sie mich?** what do you take me for?

wog [vok] *pret of* **wägen** & **wiegen**

Woge ['vogə] *f* (–;-n) billow; **Wogen der Erregung** waves of excitement

woge'gen *adv* against what; against which; in exchange for what

wogen ['vogən] *intr* billow, surge, heave; (*Getreide*) wave; **hin und her w.** fluctuate

woher' *adv* from where; **w. wissen Sie das?** how do you know this?

wohin' *adv* whereto, where

wohinge'gen *conj* whereas

wohl [vol] *adj* well ‖ *adv* well; (*freilich*) to be sure, all right; I guess; possibly, probably; perhaps; **es sich** [*dat*] **w. sein lassen** have a good time; **nun w.!** well!; **w. daran tun zu** (*inf*) do well to (*inf*); **w. dem, der** happy he who; **w. kaum** hardly; **w. oder übel** willy-nilly ‖ **Wohl** *n* (–[e]s;) good health, well-being; (*Wohlfahrt*) welfare; (*Gedeihen*) prosperity; **auf Ihr W.!** to your health! **gemeines W.** common good

wohlan' *interj* all right then!

wohlauf' *adj* in good health, well ‖ *interj* all right then!

wohlbedacht ['volbədaxt] *adj* well-thought-out

Wohl'befinden *n* (–;) well-being

Wohl'behagen *n* comfort, contentment

wohl'behalten *adj* safe and sound

wohl'bekannt *adj* well-known

wohl'beschaffen *adj* in good condition

Wohl'ergehen *n* well-being

wohl'erzogen *adj* well-bred

Wohl'fahrt *f* (–;) welfare

Wohl'fahrtsarbeit *f* social work

wohl'feil *adj* cheap

Wohl'gefallen *n* (–s;) pleasure, satisfaction

wohl'gefällig *adj* pleasant, agreeable

wohl'gemeint *adj* well-meant

wohlgemut ['volgəmut] *adj* cheerful

wohl'genährt *adj* well-fed

wohl'geneigt *adj* affectionate

Wohl'geruch *m* fragrance, perfume

wohl'gesinnt *adj* well-disposed

wohl'habend *adj* well-to-do

wohlig ['volıç] *adj* comfortable

Wohl'klang *m* melodious sound

wohl'klingend *adj* melodious

Wohl'leben *n* good living, luxury

wohl'riechend *adj* fragrant

wohl'schmeckend *adj* tasty

Wohl'sein *n* good health, well-being

Wohl'stand *m* prosperity, wealth

Wohl'tat *f* benefit; (*Gunst*) kindness, good deed; **e–e W. sein** hit the spot

Wohl'täter **–in** §6 *mf* benefactor

wohl'tätig *adj* charitable; beneficent

Wohl'tätigkeit *f* charity

wohltuend ['voltu·ant] *adj* pleasant

wohl'tun §154 *intr* do good; (*dat*) be pleasant (to)

wohl'unterrichtet *adj* well-informed

wohl'verdient *adj* well-deserved

wohl'verstanden *interj* mark my words!

wohl'weislich *adv* very wisely

wohl'wollen §162 *intr* (*dat*) be well-disposed towards ‖ **Wollwollen** *n* (–s;) good will; (*Gunst*) favor

Wohn– [von] *comb.fm.* residential; dwelling, living

Wohn'anhänger *m* house trailer

Wohn'block *m* block of apartments

wohnen ['vonən] *intr* live, reside; (*als Mieter*) room

wohn'haft *adj* residing, living

Wohn'haus *n* dwelling; apartment house

Wohn'küche *f* efficiency apartment

Wohn'laube *f* garden house

wohn'lich *adj* livable; cozy

Wohn'möglichkeit *f* living accommodations

Wohn'ort *m* place of residence; (jur) domicile; **ständiger W.** permanent address

Wohn'raum *m* living space; room (*of a house*)

Wohn'sitz *m* place of residence

Woh'nung *f* (–;-en) dwelling, home; apartment; room; accommodations

Woh'nungsamt *n* housing authority

Woh'nungsbau *m* (–[e]s;) housing construction

Woh'nungsfrage *f* housing problem

Woh'nungsinhaber **–in** §6 *mf* occupant

Woh'nungsmangel *m*, **Woh'nungsnot** *f* housing shortage

Wohn'viertel *n* residential district

Wohn'wagen *m* mobile home

Wohn'wagenparkplatz *m* trailer camp

Wohn'zimmer *n* living room

wölben ['vœlbən] *tr* vault, arch ‖ *ref* (über *dat or acc*) arch (over)

Wöl'bung *f* (–;-en) curvature; vault

Wolf [volf] *m* (–[e]s;⁻e) wolf; (*Fleisch–*) meat grinder; (astr) Lupus; (pathol) lupus

Wolfram ['volfram] *n* (–s;) tungsten

Wolke ['volkə] *f* (–;-n) cloud

Wol'kenbildung *f* cloud formation

Wol'kenbruch *m* cloudburst

Wol'kendecke *f* cloudcover

Wol'kenfetzen *m* wispy cloud

Wol'kenhöhe *f* (meteor) ceiling

Wol'kenkratzer *m* (–s;–) skyscraper

Wol'kenwand *f* cloud bank

wolkig ['volkıç] *adj* cloudy, clouded

Wolldecke ['voldekə] *f* woolen blanket

Wolle ['volə] *f* (–;-n) wool

wollen ['volən] *adj* woolen, wool ‖ §162 *tr* want, wish; mean, intend; (*gern haben*) like ‖ *intr* wish, like; **dem sei, wie ihm wolle** be that as it may; **wie Sie w.** as you please ‖ *mod aux* want (to), wish (to), intend (to);

be going (to) || **Wollen** n (-s;) will; volition

Wollfett ['vɔlfet] n lanolin

Wollgarn ['vɔlgarn] n worsted

wollig ['vɔlɪç] adj woolly

Wolljacke ['vɔljakə] f cardigan

Wollsachen ['vɔlzaxən] pl woolens

Wollstoff ['vɔl/tɔf] m woolen fabric

Wollust ['vɔllust] f (-;ᵘe) lust

wollüstig ['vɔllystɪç] adj voluptuous; (geil) lewd, lecherous

Wollüstling ['vɔllʏstlɪŋ] m (-s;-e) voluptuary

Wollwaren ['vɔlvarən] pl woolens

womit' adv with which; with what; wherewith; **w. kann ich dienen?** (com) can I help you?

womöglich adv possibly, if possible

wonach' adv after which, whereupon; according to which

Wonne ['vɔnə] f (-;-n) delight; bliss

Won'negefühl n blissful feeling

Won'neschauer m thrill of delight

won'netrunken adj enraptured

won'nevoll, wonnig ['vɔnɪç] adj blissful

woran' adv at which; at what; **ich weiß nicht, w. ich bin** I don't know where I stand

worauf' adv on which; on what; whereupon; **w. warten Sie?** what are you waiting for?

woraus' adv out of what, from what; out of which, from which; **w. ist das gemacht?** what is this made of?

worden ['vɔrdən] pp of werden

worin' adv in what; in which

Wort [vɔrt] n (-[e]s;ᵘer) word (individual; literal) || n (-[e]s;-e) word (expression; figurative); (Ausspruch) saying; (Ehrenwort) word (of honor); **auf ein W.!** may I have a word with you!; **auf mein W.!** word of honor!; **aufs W.** implicitly, to the letter; **das W. ergreifen** begin to speak; (parl) take the floor; **das W. erhalten** (or **haben**) be allowed to speak; (parl) have the floor; **das W. führen** be the spokesman; **hast du Worte!** (coll) can you beat that!; **in Worten** in writing; **j-m das W. erteilen** allow s.o. to speak; **j-m ins W. fallen** cut s.o. short

Wort'art f (gram) part of speech

Wort'bedeutungslehre f semantics

Wort'beugung f declension

Wort'bildung f word formation

wort'brüchig adj—**w. werden** break one's word

Wörterbuch ['vœrtərbux] n dictionary

Wörterverzeichnis ['vœrtərfertsaɪçnɪs] n word index; vocabulary; glossary

Wort'folge f word order

Wort'führer -in §6 mf spokesman

Wort'gefecht n dispute

wort'getreu adj literal; verbatim

wort'karg adj taciturn

Wortklauber -in ['vɔrtklaubər(ɪn)] §6 mf quibbler, hairsplitter

Wort'laut m wording; (fig) letter

wörtlich ['vœrtlɪç] adj word-for-word; literal; (Rede) direct

wort'los adv without saying a word

Wort'register n word index

Wort'schatz m vocabulary

Wort'schwall m flood of words, verbiage

Wort'spiel n pun

Wort'stamm m stem

Wort'stellung f word order

Wort'streit m, **Wort'wechsel** m argument

worüber [vo'rybər] adv over what, over which

worum [vo'rum] adv about what, about which

worunter [vo'runtər] adv under what, under which; among which

wovon' adv from what, of what, from which, of which; **w. ist die Rede?** what are they talking about?

wovor' adv of what; before which

wozu' adv for what; why; to which

Wrack [vrak] n (-[e]s;-e & -s) (& fig) wreck

Wrack'gut n wreckage

wrang [vraŋ] pret of wringen

wringen ['vrɪŋən] §142 tr wring

Wringmaschine ['vrɪŋmaʃinə] f wringer

Wucher ['vuxər] m (-s;) profiteering; **das ist ja W.!** (coll) that's highway robbery!; **W. treiben** profiteer

Wu'cherer -in §6 mf profiteer; loan shark

Wu'chergewinn m excess profit

wu'cherhaft, wucherisch ['vuxərɪʃ] adj profiteering, exorbitant

Wu'chermiete f excessive rent

wuchern ['vuxərn] intr grow luxuriantly; (Wucher treiben) profiteer

Wu'cherung f (-;-en) (bot) rank growth; (pathol) growth

Wu'cherzinsen pl excessive interest

wuchs [vuks] pret of wachsen || **Wuchs** m (-es;) growth; groß von W. tall

-wüchsig ['vyksɪç] comb.fm. -growing, -grown

Wucht [vuxt] f (-;-en) weight, force

wuchten ['vuxtən] tr lift with effort

wuchtig ['vuxtɪç] adj heavy; massive

Wühlarbeit ['vylarbaɪt] f subversive activity

wühlen ['vylən] intr dig, burrow; (Schwein) root about; (suchend) rummage about; (pol) engage in subversive activities; **im Geld w.** be rolling in money; **in Schmutz w.** wallow in filth

Wüh'ler -in §6 mf subversive, agitator

Wulst [vulst] m (-es;ᵘe) & f (-;ᵘe) bulge; (aut) rim (of tire)

wulstig ['vulstɪç] adj bulging; (Lippen) thick

wund [vunt] adj sore; (poet) wounded

Wunde ['vundə] f (-;-n) wound; sore

Wunder ['vundər] n (-s;-) wonder; miracle; **W. wirken** work wonders

wunderbar ['vundərbar] adj wonderful; (& fig) miraculous

Wun'derding n marvel

Wun'derdoktor m faith healer

Wun'derkind n child prodigy

Wun'derkraft f miraculous power

wun'derlich adj queer, odd

wundern ['vundərn] tr amaze || ref

(über *acc*) be amazed (at) ‖ *impers*
—**es sollte mich w., wenn** I'd be surprised if; **es wundert mich, daß** I am surprised that

wun'derschön' *adv* lovely, gorgeous

Wun'dertat *f* miracle

Wun'dertäter –in §6 *mf* wonder worker

wundertätig *adj* miraculous

wun'dervoll *adj* wonderful, marvelous

Wun'derwerk *n* (& fig) miracle

Wun'derzeichen *n* omen, prodigy

Wund'klammer *f* (surg) clamp

wund'liegen §108 *ref* get bedsores

Wund'mal *n* scar, sore; (relig) wound

wund'reiten §86 *ref* become saddlesore

Wunsch [vʊnʃ] *m* (-es;⁼e) wish;
(nach) desire (for); **auf W.** upon request; **ein frommer W.** wishful thinking; **nach W.** as desired

Wünschelrute ['vʏnʃəlrutə] *f* divining rod

Wün'schelrutengänger *m* dowser

wünschen ['vʏnʃən] *tr* wish; wish for, desire; **was w. Sie?** (com) may I help you? ‖ *intr* wish, please

wün'schenswert *adj* desirable

Wunsch'form *f* (gram) optative

Wunsch'konzert *n* (rad) request program

wunsch'los *adj* contented ‖ *adv*—**w. glücklich** perfectly happy

wuppdich ['vʊpdɪç] *interj* zip!, in a flash!; all of a sudden!

wurde ['vʊrdə] *pret* of **werden**

Würde ['vʏrdə] *f* (-;-n) honor; title; dignity; post, office; **akademische W.** academic degree; **unter aller W.** beneath contempt

wür'delos *adj* undignified

Wür'denträger –in §6 *mf* dignitary

wür'devoll *adj* dignified

würdig ['vʏrdɪç] *adj* dignified; (*genit*) worthy (of), deserving (of)

würdigen ['vʏrdɪgən] *tr* appreciate, value; (*genit*) deem worthy (of)

Wurf [vʊrf] *m* (-[e]s;⁼e) throw, cast, pitch; (fig) hit, success; (zool) litter, brood

Wurf'anker *m* grapnel

Würfel ['vʏrfəl] *m* (-s;-) die; cube;

square; (geom) cube; **W. spielen** play dice

Wür'felbecher *m* dice box

würfelig ['vʏrfəlɪç] *adj* cube-shaped; (*Muster*) checkered

würfeln ['vʏrfəln] *intr* play dice

Wür'felzucker *m* cube sugar

Wurf'geschoß *n* projectile, missile

Wurf'pfeil *m* dart

würgen ['vʏrgən] *tr* choke; strangle ‖ *intr* choke; **am Essen w.** gag on food

Wurm [vʊrm] *m* (-s;⁼er) (& mach) worm

wurmen ['vʊrmən] *tr* (coll) bug

wurmig ['vʊrmɪç] *adj* wormy; wormeaten

wurmstichig ['vʊrmʃtɪçɪç] *adj* wormeaten

Wurst [vʊrst] *f* (-;⁼e) sausage; **es geht um die W.** now or never; **es ist mir W.** I couldn't care less

Würstchen ['vʏrstçən] *n* (-s;-), **Würstel** ['vʏrstəl] *n* (-s;-n) hotdog

wursteln ['vʊrstəln] *intr* muddle along

Würze ['vʏrtsə] *f* (-;-n) spice, seasoning; (fig) zest

Wurzel ['vʊrtsəl] *f* (-;-n) root; **W. fassen** (or **schlagen**) take root

wurzeln ['vʊrtsəln] *intr* (HABEN & SEIN) take root; **w. in** (*dat*) be rooted in

würzen ['vʏrtsən] *tr* spice, season

würzig ['vʏrtsɪç] *adj* spicy; aromatic

Würz'stoff *m* seasoning

wusch [vʊʃ] *pret* of **waschen**

wußte ['vʊstə] *pret* of **wissen**

Wust [vʊst] *m* (-es;) jumble, mess

wüst [vyst] *adj* desert, waste; (*roh*) coarse; (*wirr*) confused

Wüste ['vystə] *f* (-;-en) desert

Wüstling ['vystlɪŋ] *m* (-s;-e) debauchee

Wut [vʊt] *f* (-;) rage, fury; madness

Wut'anfall *m* fit of rage

wüten ['vytən] *intr* rage

wü'tend *adj* (**auf** *acc*) furious (at)

Wüterich ['vytərɪç] *m* (-s;-e) madman; bloodthirsty villain

wut'schäumend *adj* foaming with rage

wut'schnaubend *adj* in a towering rage

Wut'schrei *m* shout of anger

X

X, x [ɪks] *invar n* X, x

X'-Beine *pl* knock-knees

x'-beinig *adj* knock-kneed

x'-beliebig *adj* any, whatever ‖ **X-beliebige** §5 *m*—**jeder X.** every Tom, Dick, and Harry

x'-fach *adj* (coll) hundredfold

x'-mal *adv* umpteen times

X'-Strahlen *pl* x-rays

X'-Tag *m* D-day

x-te ['ɪkstə] §9 *adj* umpteenth; **die x-te Potenz** (math) the nth power

Xylophon [ksylo'fon] *n* (-s;-e) xylophone

Y

Y, y [ypsilon] *invar n* Y, y

Yacht [jaxt] *f* (-;-en) yacht

Yamswurzel ['jamsvʊrtsəl] *f* (-;-n) (bot) yam

Yankee ['jɛŋki] *m* (-s;-s) Yankee

Yoghurt ['jogʊrt] *m* & *n* (-s;) yogurt

Yo-Yo ['jo'jo] *n* (-s;-s) yo-yo

Ypsilon ['ypsilon] *n* (-[s];-s) y

Z

Z, z [tset] *invar n* Z, z

Zacke [ˈtsakə] *f* (-;-n) sharp point; (*Zinke*) prong; (*Fels-*) crag; (*e-s Kamms, e-r Säge*) tooth; (*am Kleid*) scallop

zacken [ˈtsakən] *tr* notch; scallop ‖ **Zacken** *m* (-s;-) var of **Zacke**

zackig [ˈtsakɪç] *adj* toothed; notched; (*Felsen*) jagged; (*spitz*) pointed; (*Kleid*) scalloped; (fig) sharp

zagen [ˈtsagən] *intr* be faint-hearted

zaghaft [ˈtsakhaft] *adj* timid

zäh [tse] *adj* tough; (*klebig*) viscous; (*beharrlich*) persistent; (*Gedächtnis*) tenacious; (*halsstarrig*) dogged

zäh'flüssig *adj* viscous

Zäh'flüssigkeit *f* (-;) viscosity

Zä'higkeit *f* (-;) toughness; tenacity; viscosity; doggedness

Zahl [tsal] *f* (-;-en) number; (*Betrag, Ziffer*) figure; **an Z. übertreffen** outnumber; **arabische Z.** Arabic numeral; **der Z. nach** in number; **ganze Z.** integer; **gebrochene Z.** fraction; **gerade Z.** even number; **in roten Zahlen stecken** be in the red; **ungerade Z.** odd number; **wenig an der Z.** few in number

zahlbar [ˈtsalbar] *adj* payable; **z. bei Lieferung** cash on delivery

zählebig [ˈtselebɪç] *adj* hardy

zahlen [ˈtsalən] *tr* pay; (*Schuld*) pay off ‖ *intr* pay

zählen [ˈtselən] *tr* count; number; amount to ‖ *intr* count; be of importance, count; **nach Tausenden z.** number in the thousands; **z. auf** (*dat*) count on; **z. zu** be numbered among, belong to

Zah'lenangaben *pl* figures

Zah'lenfolge *f* numerical order

zah'lenmäßig *adj* numerical

Zah'ler –in §6 *mf* payer

Zäh'ler (-s;-) counter; recorder; (*für Gas, Elektrizität*) meter; (math) numerator; (parl) teller; (sport) scorekeeper

Zählerableser [ˈtselərapleʐər] *m* (-s;-) meter man

Zahl'karte *f* money-order form

zahl'los *adj* countless, innumerable

Zahl'meister *m* paymaster; (mil) pay officer; (nav) purser

zahl'reich *adj* numerous

Zähl'rohr *n* Geiger counter

Zahl'stelle *f* cashier's window; (*e-r Bank*) branch office

Zahl'tag *m* payday

Zah'lung *f* (-;-en) payment; (*e-r Schuld*) settlement

Zäh'lung *f* (-;-en) counting; computation

Zah'lungsanweisung *f* draft; check; postal money order

Zah'lungsausgleich *m* balance of payments

Zah'lungsbedingungen *pl* (fin) terms

Zah'lungsbestätigung *f* receipt

Zah'lungsbilanz *f* balance of payments; **aktive** (or **passive**) **Z.** favorable (or unfavorable) balance of payments

zah'lungsfähig *adj* solvent

Zah'lungsfähigkeit *f* (-;) solvency

Zah'lungsfrist *f* due date

Zah'lungsmittel *n* medium of exchange; **gesetzliches Z.** legal tender; **bargeldloses Z.** instrument of credit

Zah'lungsschwierigkeiten *pl* financial embarrassment

Zah'lungssperre *f* stoppage of payments

Zah'lungstermin *m* date of payment; (fin) date of maturity

Zah'lungsverzug *m* (fin) default

Zähl'werk *n* meter

Zahl'wort *n* (-[e]s;ˑer) numeral

Zahl'zeichen *n* figure, cipher

zahm [tsam] *adj* tame; domesticated

zähmen [ˈtsemən] *tr* tame; domesticate; (fig) control ‖ *ref* control oneself

Zäh'mung *f* (-;) taming; domestication

Zahn [tsan] *m* (-[e]s;ˑe) tooth; (mach) tooth, cog; **j-m auf den Z. fühlen** sound s.o. out; **mit den Zähnen knirschen** grind one's teeth

Zahn'arzt *m,* **Zahn'ärztin** *f* dentist

Zahn'bürste *f* toothbrush

Zahn'creme *f* toothpaste

zahnen [ˈtsanən] *intr* cut one's teeth

Zahn'ersatz *m* denture

Zahn'fäule *f* tooth decay, caries

Zahn'fleisch *n* gum

Zahn'füllung *f* (dent) filling

Zahn'heilkunde *f* dentistry

Zahn'klammer *f* (-;-n) (dent) brace

Zahn'krem *f* toothpaste

Zahn'krone *f* (dent) crown

Zahn'laut *m* (phonet) dental

Zahn'lücke *f* gap between the teeth

Zahn'paste *f* toothpaste

Zahn'pflege *f* dental hygiene

Zahn'pulver *n* tooth powder

Zahn'rad *n* cog wheel; (*Kettenrad*) sprocket

Zahn'radbahn *f* cog railway

Zahn'schmerz *m* toothache

Zahn'spange *f* (-;-n) (dent) brace

Zahn'stein *m* (dent) tartar

Zahnstocher [ˈtsanʃtoxər] *m* (-s;-) toothpick

Zahn'techniker –in §6 *mf* dental technician

Zahn'weh *n* toothache

Zange [ˈtsaŋə] *f* (-;-en) (pair of) pliers; (pair of) tongs; (*Pinzette*) (pair of) tweezers; (dent, surg, zool) forceps; **j-n in die Z. nehmen** corner s.o. (*with tough questioning*)

Zank [ˈtsaŋk] *m* (-[e]s;) quarrel, fight

Zank'apfel *m* apple of discord

zanken [ˈtsaŋkən] *tr* scold ‖ *recip & intr* quarrel, fight

zank'haft, zänkisch [ˈtsɛŋkɪʃ], **zank'süchtig** *adj* quarrelsome

Zäpfchen ['tsɛpfçən] *n* (-s;-) little peg; (anat) uvula; (med) suppository

zapfen ['tsapfən] *tr* (*Bier*, *Wein*) tap ‖ **Zapfen** *m* (-s;-) plug, bung; (*Stift*) stud; (*Drehpunkt*) pivot; (*Eis-*) icicle; (*Tannen-*) cone; (carp) tenon; (mach) pin; (mach) journal

Zap′fenstreich *m* (mil) taps

Zapfhahn ['tsapfhan] *m* tap, spigot

Zapfsäule ['tsapfzɔɪlə] *f* (-;-n) (aut) gasoline pump

Zapfstelle ['tsapfʃtɛlə] *f* (-;-n) (aut) service station, gas station

Zapfwart ['tsapfvart] *m* (-[e]s;-e) (aut) service station attendant

zappelig ['tsapəlɪç] *adj* fidgety

zappeln ['tsapəln] *intr* fidget; squirm; (*im Wasser*) flounder

Zar [tsar] *m* (-en;-en) czar

Zarge ['tsargə] *f* (-;-n) border; frame

zart [tsart] *adj* tender; (*Farbe*, *Haut*) soft; (*Gesundheit*) delicate

zart′fühlend *adj* tender; sensitive

Zart′gefühl *n* sensitivity; tact

Zart′heit *f* (-;) tenderness

zärtlich ['tsɛrtlɪç] *adj* tender, affectionate

Zärt′lichkeit *f* (-;-en) tenderness; (*Liebkosung*) caress

Zaster ['tsastər] *m* (-s;) (coll) dough

Zauber ['tsaubər] *m* (-s;-) spell; magic; (fig) charm, glamor

Zauber- *comb.fm.* magic

Zauberei [tsaubə′raɪ] *f* (-;-en) magic; witchcraft, sorcery

Zau′berer *m* (-s;-) magician; sorcerer

Zau′berformel *f* incantation, spell

zau′berhaft *adj* magic; enchanting

Zau′berin *f* (-;-nen) sorceress, witch; enchantress

zauberisch ['tsaubərɪʃ] *adj* magic

Zau′berkraft *f* magic power

Zau′berkunst *f* magic

Zau′berkünstler –in §6 *mf* magician

Zau′berkunststück *n* magic trick

Zau′berland *n* fairyland

zaubern ['tsaubərn] *tr* produce by magic ‖ *intr* practice magic; do magic tricks

Zau′berspruch *m* incantation, spell

Zau′berstab *m* magic wand

Zau′bertrank *m* magic potion

Zau′berwerk *n* witchcraft

Zau′berwort *n* (-[e]s;-e) magic word

zaudern ['tsaudərn] *intr* procrastinate; hesitate; linger

Zaum [tsaum] *m* (-[e]s;ⁿe) bridle; im Z. halten keep in check

zäumen ['tsɔɪmən] *tr* bridle

Zaun [tsaun] *m* (-[e]s;ⁿe) fence; e–n Streit vom Z. brechen pick a quarrel

Zaun′gast *m* non-paying spectator

Zaun′könig *m* (orn) wren

Zaun′pfahl *m* fence post

zausen ['tsauzən] *tr* tug at; tousle, ruffle ‖ *recip* tug at each other

Zebra ['tsebra] *n* (-s;-s) zebra

Ze′brastreifen *m* zebra stripe; (*auf der Fahrbahn*) passenger crossing

Zech- [tsɛç] *comb.fm.* drinking

Zeche ['tsɛçə] *f* (-;-n) (*Wirtshausrechnung*) check; (min) mine die Z.

prellen (coll) sneak out without paying the bill

zechen ['tsɛçən] *intr* booze

Ze′cher –in §6 *mf* heavy drinker

Zech′gelage *n* drinking party

Zechpreller ['tsɛçprɛlər] *m* (-s;-) cheat, bilker

Zech′tour *f* binge; e–e Z. machen go on a binge

Zecke ['tsɛkə] *f* (-;-n) (ent) tick

Zeder ['tsedər] *f* (-;-n) cedar

Zehe ['tse·ə] *f* (-;-n) toe; (*Knoblauch-*) clove

Ze′hennagel *m* toenail

Ze′henspitze *f* tip of the toe; auf den Zehenspitzen (on) tiptoe

zehn [tsen] *invar adj & pron* ten ‖ **Zehn** *f* (-;-en) ten

Zehner ['tsenər] *m* (-s;-) ten; tenmark bill

zehn′fach, **zehn′fältig** *adj* tenfold

Zehnfin′gersystem *n* touch-type system

Zehn′kampf *m* decathlon

zehn′mal *adv* ten times

zehnte ['tsentə] §9 *adj & pron* tenth ‖ **Zehnte** §5 *mfn* tenth

Zehntel ['tsentəl] *n* (-s;-) tenth (*part*)

zehren ['tserən] *intr* be debilitating; an den Kräften z. drain one's strength; an der Gesundheit z. undermine one's health; z. an (*dat*) (fig) gnaw at; z. von live on, live off

Zeh′rung *f* (-;) provisions; expenses

Zeichen ['tsaɪçən] *n* (-s;-) sign; signal; token; (*Merkmal*) distinguishing mark; (*Beweis*) proof; symbol; (astr) sign; (com) brand; (med) symptom; (rad) call sign; er ist seines Zeichens Anwalt he is a lawyer by profession; zum Z., daß as proof that

Zei′chenbrett *n* drawing board

Zei′chenbuch *n* sketchbook

Zei′chengerät *n* drafting equipment

Zei′chenheft *n* sketchbook

Zei′chenlehrer –in §6 *mf* art teacher

Zei′chenpapier *n* drawing paper

Zei′chensetzung *f* punctuation

Zei′chensprache *f* sign language

Zei′chentisch *m* drawing board

Zei′chentrickfilm *m* animated cartoon

Zei′chenunterricht *m* drawing lesson

zeichnen ['tsaɪçnən] *tr* draw; sketch; (*entwerfen*) design; (*brandmarken*) brand; (*Anleihe*) take out; (*Aktien*) buy; (*Geld*) pledge; (*Wäsche*) mark; (*Brief*) sign ‖ *intr* draw; sketch; (hunt) leave a trail of blood; z. für sign for

Zeich′ner –in §6 *mf* draftsman; (*Mode-*) designer; (*e–r Anleihe*) subscriber

zeichnerisch ['tsaɪçnərɪʃ] *adj* (*Begabung*) for drawing; (*Darstellung*) graphic

Zeich′nung *f* (-;-en) drawing; sketch; design; picture, illustration; diagram; signature; (*e–r Anleihe*) subscription; (*des Holzes*) grain

zeich′nungsberechtigt *adj* authorized to sign

Zeigefinger ['tsaɪgəfɪŋər] *m* index finger

zeigen ['tsaɪgən] *tr* show, indicate;

(*in e-r Rede*) point out; (*zur Schau stellen*) display; (*beweisen*) prove; (*dartun*) demonstrate ‖ *ref* appear, show up; prove to be ‖ *intr* point; z. auf (*acc*) point to; z. nach point toward ‖ *impers ref*—es zeigt sich, daß it turns out that; es wird sich ja z., ob we shall see whether

Zei′ger *m* (*-s;-*) pointer; indicator; (*e-r Uhr*) hand

Zeigestock [′tsaɪgəʃtɔk] *m* pointer

Zeile [′tsaɪlə] *f* (*-;-n*) line; (*Reihe*) row

Zeit [tsaɪt] *f* (*-;-en*) time; auf Z. (com) on credit, on time; in der letzten Z. lately; in jüngster Z. quite recently; mit der Z. in time, in the course of time; vor Zeiten in former times; zu meiner Z. in my time; zu rechter Z. in the nick of time; on time; zur Z. at present; zur Z. (*genit*) at the time of

Zeit′abschnitt *m* period, epoch

Zeit′abstand *m* interval of time

Zeit′alter *n* age

Zeit′angabe *f* time; date; exact date and hour; ohne Z. undated

Zeit′ansage *f* (rad) (giving of) time

Zeit′aufnahme *f* (phot) time exposure

Zeit′aufwand *m* loss of time; (für) time spent (on)

Zeit′dauer *f* term, period of time

Zeit′einteilung *f* timetable; timing

Zei′tenfolge *f* sequence of tenses

Zei′tenwende *f* beginning of the Christian era

Zeit′folge *f* chronological order

Zeit′form *f* tense

Zeit′geist *m* spirit of the times

zeit′gemäß *adj* timely; up-to-date

Zeit′genosse *m*, **Zeit′genossin** *f* contemporary

zeitgenössisch [′tsaɪtgənœsɪʃ] *adj* contemporary

Zeit′geschichte *f* contemporary history

zeitig [′tsaɪtɪç] *adj* early; (*reif*) mature, ripe

zeitigen [′tsaɪtɪgən] *tr* ripen

Zeit′karte *f* commuter ticket

Zeit′lage *f* state of affairs

Zeit′lang *f*—e-c Z. for some time

Zeit′lauf *m* course of time

zeit′lebens *adv* during my (his, your, etc.) life

zeit′lich *adj* temporal; chronological ‖ *adv* in time ‖ **Zeitliche** §5 *n*—das Z. segnen depart this world

zeit′los *adj* timeless

Zeit′lupe *f* (cin) slow motion

Zeit′mangel *m* lack of time

Zeit′maß *n* (mus) tempo; (pros) quantity

Zeit′nehmer –in §6 *mf* timekeeper

Zeit′ordnung *f* chronological order

Zeit′punkt *m* point of time, moment

Zeitraffer [′tsaɪtrafər] *m* (*-s;*) time-lapse photography

zeit′raubend *adj* time-consuming

Zeit′raum *m* space of time, period

Zeit′rechnung *f* era

Zeit′schaltgerät *n* timer

Zeit′schrift *f* periodical, magazine

Zeit′spanne *f* span (of time)

Zeit′tafel *f* chronological table

Zei′tung *f* (*-;-en*) newspaper; journal

Zei′tungsarchiv *n* (journ) morgue

Zei′tungsartikel *m* newspaper article

Zei′tungsausschnitt *m* newspaper clipping

Zei′tungsbeilage *f* supplement

Zei′tungsdeutsch *n* journalese

Zei′tungsente *f* (journ) hoax, spoof

Zei′tungskiosk *m* newsstand

Zei′tungsmeldung *f*, **Zei′tungsnotiz** *f* newspaper item

Zei′tungspapier *n* newsprint

Zei′tungsverkäufer –in §6 *mf* newsvendor

Zei′tungswesen *n*—das Z. the press

Zeit′vergeudung *f* waste of time

zeit′verkürzend *adj* entertaining

Zeit′verlust *m* loss of time

Zeit′vermerk *m* date

Zeit′verschwendung *f* waste of time

Zeit′vertreib *m* pastime

zeitweilig [′tsaɪtvaɪlɪç] *adj* temporary; periodic ‖ *adv* temporarily; at times, from time to time

Zeit′wende *f* beginning of a new era

Zeit′wert *m* current value

Zeit′wort *n* (*-[e]s;=er*) verb

Zeit′zeichen *n* time signal

Zeit′zünder *m* time fuse

Zelle [′tsɛlə] *f* (*-;-n*) cell; (aer) fuselage; (telp) booth

Zel′lenlehre *f* cytology

Zellophan [tsɛlo′fan] *n* (*-s;*) cellophane

Zellstoff [′tsɛlʃtɔf] *m* cellulose

Zelluloid [tsɛlu′lɔɪt] *n* (*-s;*) celluloid

Zellulose [tsɛlu′lozə] *f* (*-;*) cellulose

Zelt [tsɛlt] *n* (*-[e]s;-e*) tent

zelten [′tsɛltən] *intr* camp out

Zelt′leinwand *f* canvas

Zelt′pfahl *m* tent pole

Zelt′pflock *m* tent peg, tent stake

Zelt′stange *f*, **Zelt′stock** *m* tent pole

Zement [tse′mɛnt] *m* (*-[e]s;*) cement

zementieren [tsɛmɛn′tirən] *tr* cement

Zenit [tse′nit] *m* (*-[e]s;*) zenith

zensieren [tsɛn′zirən] *tr* censor; (educ) mark, grade

Zen·sor [′tsɛnzor] *m* (*-s;-soren* [′zorən]) censor

Zensur [tsɛn′zur] *f* (*-;-en*) censorship; (educ) grade, mark

Zentimeter [tsɛntɪ′metər] *m & n* centimeter

Zentner [′tsɛntnər] *m* (*-s;-*) hundredweight

Zent′nerlast *f* (fig) heavy load

zentral [tsɛn′tral] *adj* central

Zentral′behörde *f* central authority

Zentrale [tsɛn′tralə] *f* (*-;-n*) central office; telephone exchange, switchboard; (elec) power station

Zentral′heizung *f* central heating

Zen·trum [′tsɛntrum] *m* (*-s;-tren* [trən]) center

Zephir [′tsefɪr] *m* (*-s;-e*) zephyr

Zepter [′tsɛptər] *n* (*-s;-*) scepter

zer- [tser] *pref* up, to pieces, apart

zerbei′ßen §53 *tr* bite to pieces

zerber′sten §55 *intr* (SEIN) split apart

zerbre′chen §64 *tr* break to pieces, shatter, smash ‖ *ref*—**sich** [*dat*] **den**

Kopf z. über (acc) rack one's brains over || intr (SEIN) shatter

zerbrech'lich adj fragile, brittle

zerbröckeln (zerbrök'keln) tr & intr (SEIN) crumble

zerdrücken (zerdrük'ken) tr crush; (Kleid) wrinkle; (Kartoffeln) mash

Zeremonie [tseremo'ni] f (-;-nien ['ni-ən]) ceremony

zeremoniell [tseremo'njel] adj ceremonial || **Zeremoniell** n (-s;-e) ceremonial

Zeremo'nienmeister m master of ceremonies

zerfah'ren adj (Weg) rutted; (zerstreut) absent-minded; (konfus) scatterbrained

Zerfall' m (-s;) decay, ruin; disintegration; (geistig) decadence

zerfal'len adj—z. sein mit to be at variance with || §72 intr (SEIN) fall into ruin; decay; disintegrate; z. in (acc) divide into; z. mit fall out with

zerfa'sern tr unravel || intr fray

zerfet'zen tr tear to shreds

zerflei'schen tr mangle; lacerate

zerflie'ßen §76 intr (SEIN) melt; (Farben) run

zerfres'sen §70 tr eat away, chew up; erode, eat a hole in; corrode

zerge'hen §82 intr (SEIN) melt

zerglie'dern tr dissect; analyze

zerhacken (zerhak'ken) tr chop up

zerkau'en tr chew well

zerkleinern [tser'klaınərn] tr cut into small pieces; chop up

zerklop'fen tr pound

zerklüftet [tser'klYftət] adj jagged

zerknirscht [tser'knırʃt] adj contrite

Zerknir'schung f (-;) contrition

zerknit'tern tr (Papier) crumple; (Kleider) rumple

zerknül'len tr crumple up

zerko'chen tr overcook

zerkrat'zen tr scratch up

zerkrü'meln tr & intr (SEIN) crumble

zerlas'sen §104 tr melt, dissolve

zerlegbar [tser'lekbar] adj collapsible; (chem) decomposable; (math) divisible

zerle'gen tr take apart; (zerstückeln) cut up; (Braten) carve; (Licht) disperse; (anat) dissect; (chem) break down; (geom, mus) resolve; (gram & fig) analyze; (mach) tear down

zerle'sen adj well-thumbed

zerlö'chern tr riddle with holes

zerlumpt [tser'lumpt] adj tattered

zermah'len tr grind

zermal'men tr crush

zermür'ben tr wear down

Zermür'bung f (-;) attrition, wear

zerna'gen tr gnaw, chew up; (chem) corrode

zerplat'zen intr (SEIN) burst; explode

zerquet'schen tr crush; (culin) mash

Zerrbild ['tserbılt] n distorted picture; caricature

zerrei'ben §62 tr grind, pulverize

zerrei'ßen §95 tr tear; tear up; (zerfleischen) mangle; (fig) split; (pathol) rupture; j-m das Herz z. break s.o.'s heart || ref—sich z. für

(fig) knock oneself out for || intr (SEIN) tear

zerren ['tserən] tr drag; (Sehne) pull || intr (an dat) tug (at)

zerrin'nen §121 intr (SEIN) melt away

zerrissen [tser'rısən] adj torn

Zer'rung f (-;-en) strain, muscle pull

zerrütten [tser'rYtən] tr disorganize; (Geist) unhinge; (Gesundheit) undermine; (Nerven) shatter; (Ehe) wreck

zersä'gen tr saw up

zerschel'len intr (SEIN) be wrecked; (Schiff) break up

zerschie'ßen §76 tr shoot up

zerschla'gen adj battered, broken; exhausted, beat || §132 tr beat up; break to pieces; smash; batter

zerschmel'zen tr & intr (SEIN) melt

zerschmet'tern tr smash, crush

zerschnei'den §106 tr cut up; mince

zerset'zen tr decompose; electrolyze; (fig) undermine || ref decompose, disintegrate

zerspal'ten tr split

zersplit'tern tr split up; splinter; (Menge) disperse; (Kraft, Zeit) fritter away || ref spread oneself thin

zerspren'gen tr blow up; (Kette) break; (mil) rout

zersprin'gen §142 intr (SEIN) break, burst; (Glas) crack; (Saite) snap; (Kopf) split; (vor Wut) explode; (vor Freude) burst

zerstamp'fen tr crush, pound; trample

zerstäu'ben tr pulverize, spray

Zerstäu'ber m (-s;-) sprayer; (für Parfüm) atomizer

zerste'chen §64 tr sting; bite

zerstie'ben intr §130 intr (SEIN) scatter

zerstö'ren tr destroy; (Fernsprechleitung) disrupt; (Leben, Ehe, usw.) ruin; (Illusionen) shatter

Zerstö'rer m (-s;-) (& nav) destroyer

Zerstö'rung f (-;-en) destruction; ruin; disruption

Zerstö'rungswerk n work of destruction

Zerstö'rungswut f vandalism

zerstoßen §150 tr pound, crush

zerstreu'en tr scatter, disperse; (Bedenken, Zweifel) dispel; (ablenken) distract; (Licht) diffuse || ref scatter; amuse oneself

zerstreut' adj dispersed; (Licht) diffused; (fig) absent-minded

Zerstreut'heit f (-;) absent-mindedness

Zerstreu'ung f (-;) scattering; diffusion; diversion; absent-mindedness

zerstückeln [tser'ʃtYkəln] tr chop up; (Körper) dismember; (Land) parcel out

zertei'len tr divide; (zerstreuen) disperse; (Braten, usw.) cut up || ref divide, separate

Zertifikat [tsertıfı'kat] n (-[e]s;-e) certificate

zertren'nen tr sever

zertre'ten §152 tr trample, squash; (Feuer) stamp out

zertrümmern [tser'trYmərn] tr smash, demolish; (Atome) split

zerwüh'len tr root up; (Haar) dishevel; (Bett, Kissen) rumple

Zerwürfnis [tsɛrˈvʏrfnɪs] n (-ses;-se) disagreement, quarrel

zerzau′sen tr (Haar) muss; (Federn) ruffle

Zeter [ˈtsetər] n (-s;)—**Z. und Mordio schreien** (coll) cry bloody murder

zetern [ˈtsetərn] intr cry out, raise an outcry

Zettel [ˈtsetəl] m (-s;-) slip of paper; note; (Anschlag) poster; (zum Ankleben) sticker; (zum Anhängen) tag

Zet′telkartei f, **Zet′telkasten** m, **Zet′-telkatalog** m card file

Zeug [tsɔɪk] n (-[e]s;-e) stuff, material; (Stoff) cloth, fabric; (Sachen) things; (Waren) goods; (Geräte) tools; (Plunder) junk; **dummes Z.** silly nonsense; **er hat das Z.** he has what it takes

–zeug n comb.fm. stuff; tools; equipment; tackle; instrument; things; –wear

Zeuge [ˈtsɔɪgə] m (-n;-n) witness; **als Z. aussagen** testify

zeugen [ˈtsɔɪgən] tr beget; (fig) produce, generate || intr produce offspring; testify; **z. für** testify in favor of; **z. von** bear witness to

Zeu′genaussage f deposition
Zeu′genbank f witness stand
Zeu′genbeeinflussung f suborning of witnesses
Zeu′genstand m witness stand

Zeugin [ˈtsɔɪgɪn] f (-;-nen) witness

Zeugnis [ˈtsɔɪknɪs] n (-ses;-se) evidence, testimony; proof; (Schein) certificate; (educ) report card; **j-m ein Z. ausstellen** (or **schreiben**) write s.o. a letter of recommendation; **Z. ablegen** testify; **zum Z. dessen** in witness whereof

Zeu′gung f (-;) procreation; breeding
Zeu′gungstrieb m sexual drive
zeu′gungsunfähig adj impotent

Zicke [ˈtsɪkə] f (-;-n) (pej) old nanny goat; **Zicken machen** (coll) play tricks

Zicklein [ˈtsɪklaɪn] n (-s;-) kid
Zickzack [ˈtsɪktsak] m (-[e]s;-e) zigzag; **im Z. laufen** run zigzag
Zick′zackkurs m—**im Z. fahren** zigzag
Ziege [ˈtsigə] f (-;-n) she-goat
Ziegel [ˈtsigəl] m (-s;-) brick; (Dach-) tile
Zie′gelbrenner m brickmaker; tilemaker
Zie′gelbrennerei f brickyard; tileworks
Zie′geldach n tiled roof
Zie′gelstein m brick
Zie′genbart m goatee
Zie′genbock m billy goat
Zie′genhirt m goatherd
Zie′genpeter m (pathol) mumps
Zieh– [tsi] comb.fm. draw; tow–; foster
Zieh′brunnen m well
ziehen [ˈtsi-ən] §163 tr pull; (Folgerung, Kreis, Linie, Los, Schwert, Seitengewehr, Vorhang, Wechsel) draw; (Glocke) ring; aus der Tasche) pull out; (Zahn) extract, pull; (züchten) grow, breed; (Kinder) raise; (beim Schach) move; (den

Hut) tip; (Graben) dig; (Mauer) build; (Schiff) tow; (Blasen) raise; (Vergleich) make; (Gewehrlauf) rifle; (math) extract; **auf Fäden z.** string (pearls); **auf Flaschen z.** bottle; **auf seine Seite z.** win over to one's side; **den kürzeren z.** get the short end of it; **die Bilanz z.** balance accounts; **die Stirn kraus z.** knit the brows; **Grimassen z.** make faces; **ins Vertrauen z.** take into confidence; **j–n auf die Seite z.** take s.o. aside; **Nutzen z.** derive benefit; **Wasser z.** leak || ref (Holz) warp; (Stoff) stretch; (geog) extend, run; **an sich** (or **auf sich**) **z.** attract; **sich in die Länge z.** drag on || intr ache; (an dat) pull (on); (theat) (coll) pull them in; **an e–r Zigarette z.** puff on a cigarette || intr (SEIN) go; march; (Vögel) migrate; (Wohnung wechseln) move || impers—**es zieht** there is a draft; **es zieht mich nach I feel drawn to** || **Ziehen** n (-s;) drawing; cultivation; growing; raising; breeding; migration

Zieh′harmonika f accordion
Zieh′kind n foster child
Zie′hung f (-;-en) drawing (of lots)
Ziel [tsil] n (-[e]s;-e) aim; mark; goal; (beim Rennsport) finish line; (e–r Reise) destination; (beim Schießen) target; (Grenze) limit, boundary; (Zweck) end, object; (des Spottes) butt; (Frist) term; (mil) objective; **auf Z.** (com) on credit; **durchs Z. gehen** pass the finish line; **gegen zwei Jahre Z.** (or **mit zwei Jahren Z.**) with two years to pay; **j–m zwei Jahre Z. gewähren** give s.o. two years to pay; **seinem Ehrgeiz ein Z. setzen** set a limit to one's ambition

Ziel′anflug m (aer) bomb run
Ziel′band n (-[e]s;-er) (sport) tape
ziel′bewußt adj purposeful; singleminded
zielen [ˈtsilən] intr take aim; **z. auf** (acc) or **nach** aim at
Ziel′fernrohr n telescopic sight
Ziel′gerade f homestretch
Ziel′gerät n gunsight; (aer) bombsight
Ziel′landung f pinpoint landing
Ziel′linie f (sport) finish line
ziel′los adj aimless
Ziel′photographie f photo finish
Ziel′punkt m objective; bull's-eye
Ziel′scheibe f target; (fig) butt
Ziel′setzung f objective, target
ziel′sicher adj steady, unerring
Ziel′sprache f target language
zielstrebig [ˈtsil′trebɪç] adj singleminded, determined
Ziel′sucher m (rok) homing device
Ziel′vorrichtung f gunsight; bombsight
ziemen [ˈtsimən] ref be proper; **sich für j–n z.** become s.o. || intr (dat) be becoming to
ziemlich [ˈtsimlɪç] adj fit, suitable; (leidlich) middling; (mäßig) fair; (beträchtlich) considerable || adv pretty, rather, fairly; (fast) almost, practically

Zier [tsir] f (—;), **Zierat** ['tsirɑt] m (—s;) ornament, decoration

Zierde ['tsirdə] f (—;—n) ornament decoration; (fig) credit, honor

zieren ['tsirən] tr decorate, adorn || ref be affected, be coy; (beim Essen) need to be coaxed; **zier dich doch nicht so!** don't be coy!

Zier'leiste f trim(ming)

zier'lich adj delicate; (nett) nice

Zier'pflanze f ornamental plant

Zier'puppe f glamour girl

Ziffer ['tsɪfər] f (—;—n) digit, figure

Zif'ferblatt n face (of a clock)

zig [tsɪç] invar adj (coll) umpteen

Zigarette [tsɪga'retə] f (—;—n) cigarette

Zigaret'tenautomat m cigarette machine

Zigaret'tenetui n cigarette case

Zigaret'tenspitze f cigarette holder

Zigaret'tenstummel m cigarette butt

Zigarre [tsɪ'garə] f (—;—n) cigar

Zigeuner –in [tsɪ'gɔɪnər(ɪn)] §6 mf gipsy

Zimbel ['tsɪmbəl] f (—;—n) cymbal

Zimmer ['tsɪmər] n (—s;—) room

Zim'merantenne f indoor antenna

Zim'merarbeit f carpentry

Zim'merdienst m room service

Zim'mereinrichtung f furniture

Zim'merer m (—s;—) carpenter

Zim'merflucht f suite

Zim'mermädchen n chambermaid

Zim'mer-mann m (—[e]s;—leute) carpenter

zimmern ['tsɪmərn] tr carpenter, build || intr carpenter

Zim'mervermieter m landlord

–zimmrig [tsɪmrɪç] comb.fm. –room

zimperlich ['tsɪmpərlɪç] adj prudish; fastidious; (gegen Kälte) oversensitive

Zimt [tsɪmt] m (—[e]s;) cinnamon

Zink [tsɪŋk] m & n (—[e]s;) zinc

Zinke ['tsɪŋkə] f (—;—n) prong; (e–s Kammes) tooth; (carp) dovetail

zinken ['tsɪŋkən] tr dovetail; (Karten) mark || **Zinken** m (—s;—) (sl) schnozzle

–zinkig [tsɪŋkɪç] comb.fm. –pronged

Zinn [tsɪn] n (—[e]s;) tin

Zinne ['tsɪnə] f (—;—n) pinnacle; battlement

zinnoberrot [tsɪ'nobərrot] adj vermilion

Zins [tsɪns] m (—es;—) interest; (Miete) rent; **auf Zinsen anlegen** put out at interest; **j–m mit Zinsen (und Zinseszinsen) heimzahlen** (coll) pay s.o. back in full; **Zinsen berechnen** charge interest

zins'bringend adj interest-bearing

Zin'senbelastung f interest charge

Zinseszinsen ['tsɪnzəstsɪnzən] pl compound interest

zins'frei adj rent-free; interest-free

Zins'fuß m, **Zins'satz** m rate of interest

Zins'schein m (interest) coupon; dividend warrant

Zionismus [tsɪ-ɔ'nɪsmʊs] m (—;) Zionism

Zipfel ['tsɪpfəl] m (—s;—) tip, point;

edge; (Ecke) corner; (e–r Wurst) end piece

Zip'felmütze f nightcap, tasseled cap

zirka ['tsɪrka] adv approximately

Zirkel ['tsɪrkəl] m (—s;) circle; (Reißzeug) compass; (fig) circle

Zir'kelschluß m vicious circle

Zirkon [tsɪr'kon] m (—s;—e) zircon

zirkulieren [tsɪrku'lirən] intr (SEIN) circulate; **z. lassen** circulate

Zirkus ['tsɪrkʊs] m (—;—se) circus

zirpen ['tsɪrpən] intr chirp

zischeln ['tsɪʃəln] tr & intr whisper

zischen ['tsɪʃən] intr hiss; sizzle; (schwirren) whiz || **Zischen** n (—s;) hissing; sizzle; whiz

Zisch'laut m hissing sound; (phonet) sibilant

ziselieren [tsɪze'lirən] tr chase

Zisterne [tsɪs'ternə] f (—;—n) cistern

Zitadelle [tsɪta'delə] f (—;—n) citadel

Zitat [tsɪ'tat] n (—[e]s;—e) quotation

Zither ['tsɪtər] f (—;—n) zither

zitieren [tsɪ'tirən] tr quote; **j–n vor Gericht z.** issue s.o. a summons

Zitronat [tsɪtro'nat] n (—[e]s;—e) candied lemon peel

Zitrone [tsɪ'tronə] f (—;—n) lemon

Zitro'nenlimonade f lemonade; (mit Sodawasser) lemon soda

Zitro'nenpresse f lemon squeezer

Zitro'nensaft m lemon juice

Zitro'nensäure f citric acid

zitterig ['tsɪtərɪç] adj shaky

zittern ['tsɪtərn] intr quake, tremble; quiver; (flimmern) dance; (vor dat) shake (with), shiver (with); **beim dem Gedanken an etw** [acc] **z.** shudder at the thought of s.th.

Zit'terpappel ['tsɪtərpapəl] f aspen

Zitze ['tsɪtsə] f (—;—n) teat

zivil [tsɪ'vil] adj civil; civilian; (Preise) reasonable || **Zivil** n (—s;) civilians; **in Z.** in plain clothes

Zivil'courage f courage of one's convictions, moral courage

Zivil'ehe f civil marriage

Zivilisation [tsɪvɪliza'tsjon] f (—;—en) civilization

zivilisieren [tsɪvɪli'zirən] tr civilize

Zivilist –in [tsɪvɪ'lɪst(ɪn)] §7 mf civilian

Zivil'klage f (jur) civil suit

Zivil'kleidung f civilian clothes

Zivil'person f civilian

Zobel ['tsobəl] m (—s;—) (zool) sable

Zofe ['tsofə] f (—;—n) lady-in-waiting

zog [tsok] pret of **ziehen**

zögern ['tsøgərn] intr hesitate; delay || **Zögern** n (—s;) hesitation; delay

Zögling ['tsøklɪŋ] m (—s;—e) pupil

Zölibat [tsøli'bat] m & n (—[e]s;) celibacy

Zoll [tsɔl] m (—[e]s;—e) duty, customs; (Brückenzoll) toll; (Maß) inch

Zoll'abfertigung f customs clearance

Zoll'amt n customs office

Zoll'beamte §5 m customs official

zollen ['tsɔlən] tr give, pay; **j–m Achtung z.** show s.o. respect; **j–m Beifall z.** applaud s.o.; **j–m Dank z.** thank s.o.; **j–m Lob z.** praise s.o.

Zoll'erklärung f customs declaration

zoll′frei *adj* duty-free
Zoll′grenze *f* customs frontier
–zöllig [tsœlɪç] *comb.fm.* –inch
Zoll′kontrolle *f* customs inspection
zoll′pflichtig *adj* dutiable
Zoll′schein *m* customs clearance
Zoll′schranke *f* customs barrier
Zoll′stab *m*, **Zoll′stock** *m* foot rule
Zoll′tarif *m* tariff
Zone [′tsonə] *f* (–;–n) zone; **blaue Z.** limited-parking area; **Z. der Windstille** doldrums
Zoo [tso] *m* (– & –s;–s) zoo
Zoologe [tsɔ·ɔ′logə] *m* (–n;–n) zoologist
Zoologie [tsɔ·ɔlɔ′gi] *f* (–;) zoology
Zoologin [tsɔ·ɔ′login] *f* (–;–nen) zoologist
zoologisch [tsɔ·ɔ′logiʃ] *adj* zoological
Zopf [tsɔpf] *m* (–[e]s;–ᵉe) plait of hair; pigtail; twisted (bread) roll; **alter Z.** outdated custom
zopfig [′tsɔpfɪç] *adj* pedantic; old-fashioned
Zorn [tsɔrn] *m* (–[e]s;) anger, rage
Zorn′anfall *m* fit of anger
Zorn′ausbruch *m* outburst of anger
zornig [′tsɔrnɪç] *adj* (**auf** *acc*) angry (at)
zorn′mütig *adj* hotheaded
Zote [′tsotə] *f* (–;–n) obscenity; dirty joke; **Zoten reißen** crack dirty jokes; talk dirty
zo′tenhaft, zotig [′tsotɪç] *adj* obscene, dirty
Zotte [′tsotə] *f* (–;–n) tuft of hair; strand of hair
Zottel [′tsotəl] *f* (–;–n) strand of hair
Zot′telhaar *n* stringy hair
zottelig [′tsotəlɪç] *adj* stringy (*hair*)
zotteln [′tsotəln] *intr* (SEIN) (coll) saunter
zottig [′tsotɪç] *adj* shaggy; matted
zu [tsu] *adj* closed, shut || *adv* too; **immer zu!** (or **nur zu!**) go on! || *prep* (*dat*) at, in, on; to; along with; in addition to; beside, near; **zu Anfang** at the beginning; **zu dritt** in threes; **zu Wasser und zu Lande** by land and by sea
zuallererst [tsu·alər′erst] *adv* first of all
zuallerletzt [tsu·alər′lɛtst] *adv* last of all
zuballern [′tsubalərn] *tr* (coll) slam
zu′bauen *tr* wall up, wall in
Zubehör [′tsubəhør] *m & n* (–s;) accessories; fittings; trimmings; **Wohnung mit allem Z.** apartment with all utilities
Zu′behörteil *m* accessory, attachment, component
zu′beißen §53 *intr* bite; snap at people
zu′bekommen §99 *tr* get in addition; (*Tür, usw.*) manage to close
zu′bereiten *tr* prepare; (*Speise*) cook; (*Getränk*) mix
Zu′bereitung *f* (–;–en) preparation
zu′billigen *tr* grant, allow, concede
zu′binden §59 *tr* tie up; **j–m die Augen z.** blindfold s.o.
zu′bleiben §62 *intr* (SEIN) remain closed

zu′blinzeln *intr* (*dat*) wink at
zu′bringen §65 *tr* (*Zeit*) spend; (coll) manage to shut; (tech) feed
Zu′bringer *m* (–s;–) (tech) feeder
Zu′bringerdienst *m* shuttle service
Zu′bringerstraße *f* access road
Zucht [tsuxt] *f* (–;) breeding; rearing; (*Rasse*) race, stock; (*Pflanzen-*) cultivation; (*Schul-*) education; discipline; training, drill; **Z. halten** maintain discipline
züchten [′tsyçtən] *tr* breed; rear, raise; (bot) grow, cultivate
Züch′ter –in §6 *mf* breeder; grower
Zucht′haus *n* penitentiary, hard labor; **lebenslängliches Z.** life imprisonment
Zuchthäusler –in [′tsuxthɔyslər(ɪn)] §6 *mf* convict, prisoner at hard labor
Zucht′hengst *m* studhorse
züchtig [′tsyçtɪç] *adj* modest, chaste
züchtigen [′tsyçtɪgən] *tr* chastise
zucht′los *adj* undisciplined
Zucht′losigkeit *f* (–;) lack of discipline
Zucht′meister *m* disciplinarian
Zucht′perle *f* cultured pearl
Züch′tung *f* (–;) breeding; rearing; growing, cultivation
zucken [′tsukən] *tr* (*Achseln*) shrug || *intr* twitch, jerk; (*Blitz*) flash; (*vor Schmerzen*) wince; **mit keiner Wimper z.** not bat an eye; **ohne zu z.** without wincing || *impers*—**es zuckte mir in den Fingern zu** (*inf*) my fingers were itching to (*inf*) || **Zucken** *n* (–s;) twitch
zücken [′tsykən] *tr* (*Schwert*) draw
Zucker [′tsukər] *m* (–s;) sugar
Zuckerdose (Zuk′kerdose) *f* sugar bowl
Zuckererbse (Zuk′kererbse) *f* sweet pea
Zuckerguß (Zuk′kerguß) *m* frosting
Zuckerharnruhr (Zuk′kerharnruhr) *f* diabetes
Zuckerhut (Zuk′kerhut) *m* sugar loaf
zuckerig [′tsukərɪç] *adj* sugary
zuckerkrank (zuk′kerkrank) *adj* diabetic || **Zuckerkranke** §5 *mf* diabetic
Zuckerkrankheit (Zuk′kerkrankheit) *f* diabetes
Zuckerlecken (Zuk′kerlecken) *n* (–s;) (fig) pushover, picnic
Zuckerrohr (Zuk′kerrohr) *n* sugar cane
Zuckerrübe (Zuk′kerrübe) *f* sugar beet
zuckersüß (zuk′kersüß′) *adj* sweet as sugar
Zuckerwerk (Zuk′kerwerk) *n*, **Zuckerzeug** (Zuk′kerzeug) *n* candy
Zuckung (Zuk′kung) *f* (–;–en) twitch, spasm, convulsion
Zu′decke *f* (coll) bed covering
zu′decken *tr* cover up
zudem [tsu′dem] *adv* moreover, besides
zu′denken §66 *tr*—**j–m etw z.** intend s.th. as a present for s.o.
Zu′drang *m* crowding, rush
zu′drehen *tr* turn off; **j–m den Rücken z.** turn one's back on s.o.
zu′dringlich *adj* obtrusive; **z. werden** make a pass
zu′drücken *tr* close, shut
zu′eignen *tr* dedicate
Zu′eignung *f* (–;–en) dedication

zu'erkennen §97 *tr* confer, award; (jur) adjudge, award

zuerst' *adv* first; at first

zu'erteilen *tr* award; confer, bestow

zu'fahren §71 *intr* (SEIN) drive on; z. auf (acc) drive in the direction of (s.th.); rush at (s.o.)

Zu'fahrt *f* access

Zu'fahrtsrampe *f* on-ramp

Zu'fahrtsstraße *f* access road

Zu'fall *m* chance; coincidence; accident; durch Z. by chance

zu'fallen §72 *intr* (SEIN) close, shut; j—m z. fall to s.o.'s share

zufällig ['tsufɛlɪç] *adj* chance, fortuitous; accidental; casual ‖ *adv* by chance; accidentally

zu'fälligerweise *adv* by chance

Zufalls– comb.fm. chance

zu'fassen *intr* set to work; lend a hand; (e—e Gelegenheit wahrnehmen) seize the opportunity

Zu'flucht *f* refuge; (fig) recourse; seine Z. nehmen zu take refuge in; have recourse to

Zu'fluß *m* influx; (Nebenfluß) tributary; (mach) feed

zu'flüstern *intr* (dat) whisper to

zufolge [tsu'fɔlgə] *prep* (genit & dat) in consequence of; according to

zufrieden [tsu'friːdən] *adj* satisfied; j—n z. lassen leave s.o. alone

zufrie'dengeben §80 *ref* (mit) be satisfied (with), acquiesce (in)

Zufrie'denheit *f* (–;) satisfaction

zufrie'denstellen *tr* satisfy

zufrie'denstellend *adj* satisfactory

Zufrie'denstellung *f* satisfaction

zu'frieren §77 *intr* (SEIN) freeze up

zu'fügen *tr* add; (Niederlage) inflict; (Kummer, Schaden, Schmerz) cause

Zufuhr ['tsufuːr] *f* (–;) supply; importation; supplies; (mach) feed

zu'führen *tr* convey, bring; (Waren) supply; (mach) feed

Zu'führung *f* (–;–en) conveyance; supply; importation; (elec) lead; (mach) feed

Zug [tsuk] *m* (–[e]s;–e) train; pull, tug; drawing, pulling; (Spannung) tension; strain; (beim Rauchen) puff; (beim Atmen) breath, gasp; (Schluck) drink, gulp, swig; (Luft–) draft; (Reihe) row, line; (Um–) procession, parade; (Kriegs–) campaign; (Geleit) escort; (von Vögeln) flock; flight, migration; (von Fischen) school; (Rudel) pack; (Trupp) platoon; (Gespann) team, yoke; (Gesichts–) feature; (Charakter–) trait; characteristic; (Neigung) trend, tendency; (im Gewehrlauf) groove, rifling; (Strich) stroke; (Schnörkel) flourish; (Umriß) outline; (beim Brettspiel) move; auf dem Zuge on the march; auf e–n Zug in one gulp; at one stroke; at a stretch; du bist am Zug (& fig) it's your move; e–n guten Zug haben drink like a fish; e–n Zug tun take a puff; make a move; take a drink; gut im Zuge sein (or im besten Zuge sein) be going strong; in e–m Zuge in one

gulp; in one breath; at one stroke; at a stretch; in großen Zügen in broad outlines; in vollen Zügen thoroughly; in Zug bringen start; nicht zum Zug kommen not get a chance; ohne rechten Zug half-heartedly; Zug um Zug in rapid succession

Zu'gabe *f* addition; (theat) encore

Zu'gang *m* access; approach; entrance; (Zunahme) increase; (libr) accession

zugänglich ['tsugɛnlɪç] *adj* accessible; (Person) affable; (benutzbar) available; (dat, für) open (to); nicht z. für proof against

Zug'artikel *m* (com) popular article

Zug'brücke *f* drawbridge

zu'geben §80 *tr* add; (erlauben) allow; (anerkennen) admit, concede; (eingestehen) confess; (com) throw into the bargain

zugegen [tsu'geːgən] *adj* (bei) present (at)

zu'gehen §82 *intr* (SEIN) go on; walk faster; (sich schließen) shut; auf j–n z. go up to s.o.; j–m etw z. lassen send s.th. to s.o.

zu'gehören *intr* (dat) belong to

zu'gehörig *adj* (dat) belonging to

Zu'gehörigkeit *f* (–;) (zu) membership (in)

Zügel ['tsygəl] *m* (–s;–) rein; bridle; (fig) curb

zü'gellos *adj* (& fig) unbridled; (ausschweifig) dissolute

Zü'gellosigkeit *f* (–;) licentiousness

zügeln ['tsygəln] *tr* bridle; (fig) curb

Zu'geständnis *n* admission, concession

zu'gestehen §146 *tr* admit, concede

zu'getan *adj* (dat) fond of

Zug'feder *f* tension spring

Zug'führer *m* (mil) platoon leader; (rr) chief conductor

zu'gießen §76 *tr* add

zugig ['tsuːgɪç] *adj* drafty

zügig ['tsygɪç] *adj* speedy, fast

Zug'klappe *f* damper

Zug'kraft *f* tensile force; (fig) drawing power

zug'kräftig *adj* attractive, popular

zugleich' *adv* at the same time; z. mit together with

Zug'luft *f* draft

Zug'maschine *f* tractor

Zug'mittel *n* (fig) attraction, draw

zu'graben §87 *tr* cover up

zu'greifen §88 *intr* grab hold; lend a hand; (fig) go into action; greifen Sie zu! (bei Tisch) help yourself!; (bei Reklamen) don't miss this opportunity!

Zu'griff *m* grip; (fig) clutches

zugrunde [tsu'grundə] *adv*–z. gehen go to ruin; z. legen (dat) take as a basis (for); z. liegen (dat) underlie

Zug'tier *n* draft animal

zu'gucken *intr* (coll) look on

zugunsten [tsu'gunstən] *prep* (genit) in favor of; for the benefit of

zugute [tsu'guːtə] *adv*–j–m etw z. halten make allowance to s.o. for s.th.; j–m z. kommen stand s.o. in good stead

Zug'verkehr *m* train service

Zug′vogel m migratory bird
zu′haben §89 tr (Augen) have closed; (Mantel) have buttoned up || intr (Geschäft) be closed
zu′halten §90 tr keep closed; (Ohren) shut || intr—z. auf (acc) head for
Zuhälter ['tsuheltər] m (-s;-) pimp
Zuhälterei [tsuhelte'rai] f (-;) pimping
zuhanden [tsu'handən] prep (genit) (auf Briefumschlägen) Attn:
Zuhause [tsu'hauzə] n (-s;) home
zu′heilen intr (SEIN) heal up
zu′hören intr (dat) listen (to)
Zu′hörer –in §6 mf hearer, listener; die Z. the audience
Zu′hörerschaft f (-;) audience
zu′jauchzen, zu′jubeln intr cheer
zu′klappen tr shut, slam shut
zu′kleben tr glue up, paste up
zu′knallen tr bang, slam shut
zu′kneifen §88 tr—die Augen z. blink; ein Auge z. wink
zu′knöpfen tr button up
zu′kommen §99 intr (SEIN) (dat) reach; (dat) be due to; auf j—n z. come up to s.o.; das kommt dir nicht zu you're not entitled to it; j—m etw z. lassen let s.o. have s.th.; send s.th. to s.o. || impers—mir kommt es nicht zu zu (inf) it's not up to me to (inf)
zu′korken tr put the cork on
Zu′kost f vegetables; trimmings
Zukunft ['tsukunft] f (-;) future; (gram) future (tense)
zukünftig ['tsukynftiç] adj future || adv in the future || **Zukünftige** §5 m (coll) fiancé || f (coll) fiancée
Zu′kunftsmusik f wishful thinking
Zu′kunftsroman m science fiction
zu′lächeln intr (dat) smile at; (dat) smile on
Zu′lage f extra pay; pay raise
zulande [tsu'landə] adv—bei uns z. in my (or our) country
zu′langen intr suffice, do; (bei Tisch) help oneself
zu′länglich adj adequate, sufficient
zu′lassen §104 tr admit; (erlauben) allow; (Tür) leave shut; (Fahrzeug) license; (Zweifel) admit of
zulässig ['tsulesiç] adj permissible; zulässige Abweichung allowance, tolerance
Zu′lassung f (-;-en) admission; permission; approval; license
Zu′lassungsprüfung f college entrance examination
Zu′lassungsschein m registration card
Zu′lauf m crowd, rush; Z. haben be popular; (theat) have a long run
zu′laufen §105 intr (SEIN) run on; run faster; (dat) flock to; auf j—n z. run up to s.o.; spitz z. end in a point
zu′legen tr add; etw z. up one's offer || ref—sich [dat] etw. z. (coll) get oneself s.th.
zuleide [tsu'laidə] adv—j—m etw z. tun hurt s.o., do s.o. wrong
zu′leiten intr (Wasser) (dat) let in (to); (dat) direct (s.o.) (to); (Schreiben) (dat) pass on (to); auf dem Amtsweg) channel (to); (tech) feed

Zu′leitung f (-;-en) feed pipe; (elec) lead-in wire; (elec) conductor
zuletzt [tsu'letst] adv last; at last; finally; after all
zuliebe [tsu'libə] prep (dat) for (s.o.'s) sake
zum [tsum] abbr zu dem; es ist zum ...it's enough to make one...
zu′machen tr shut; (Loch) close up; (zuknöpfen) button up
zumal [tsu'mal] adv especially; z. da all the more because
zu′mauern tr wall up
zumindest [tsu'mindəst] adv at least
zumute [tsu'mutə] adv—mir ist gut (or wohl) z. I feel good; mir ist nicht zum Lachen z. I don't feel like laughing
zumuten ['tsumutən] tr—j—m etw z. expect s.th. of s.o. || ref—sich [dat] zuviel z. attempt too much
Zu′mutung f (-;-en) imposition
zunächst [tsu'neçst] adv first, at first, first of all; (erstens) to begin with; (vorläufig) for the time being || prep (dat) next to
zu′nageln tr nail up, nail shut
zu′nähen tr sew up
Zu′nahme f (-;-n) increase; growth; rise
Zu′name m last name, family name
Zünd– (tsYnt] comb.fm. ignition
zünden ['tsyndən] tr ignite; kindle; (Sprengstoff) detonate || intr ignite, catch fire; (fig) catch on
Zün′der m (-s;-) fuse; detonator
Zünd′flamme f pilot light
Zünd′holz n match
Zünd′kerze f (aut) spark plug
Zünd′nadel f firing pin
Zünd′satz m primer
Zünd′schlüssel m ignition key
Zünd′schnur f fuse
Zünd′stein m flint
Zünd′stoff m fuel
Zün′dung f (-;-en) (aut) ignition
zu′nehmen §116 intr (an dat) increase (in); (steigen) rise; grow longer
zu′neigen tr (dat) tilt toward || ref & intr (dat) incline toward(s); sich dem Ende z. draw to a close
Zu′neigung f (-;) (für, zu) liking (for)
Zunft [tsunft] f (-;-̈e) guild
Zunge ['tsuŋə] f (-;-n) tongue
züngeln ['tsyŋəln] intr dart out the tongue; (Flamme) dart, leap up
Zun′genbrecher m tongue twister
zun′genfertig adj glib
Zun′genspitze f tip of the tongue
zunichte [tsu'niçtə] adv—z. machen destroy; (Plan) spoil; (Theorie) explode; z. werden come to nothing
zu′nicken intr (dat) nod to
zunutze [tsu'nutsə] adv—sich etw z. machen utilize s.th.
zuoberst [tsu'obərst] adv at the top
zupfen ['tsupfən] tr pull; pluck || intr (an dat) tug (at)
zu′prosten intr (dat) toast
zur [tsur] abbr zu der
zu′rechnen tr add; (dat) number among, classify with; (dat) attribute to

zu'rechnungsfähig *adj* accountable; responsible; of sound mind

Zu'rechnungsfähigkeit *f* responsibility; sound mind

zurecht– [tsu'reçt] *comb.fm.* right, in order; at the right time

zurecht'biegen §57 *tr* straighten out

zurecht'bringen §65 *tr* set right

zurecht'finden §59 *ref* find one's way; (fig) see one's way

zurecht'kommen §99 *intr* (SEIN) come on time; get on, manage; turn out all right; **mit etw nicht z.** make a mess of s.th.; **mit j–m z.** get along with s.o.

zurecht'legen *tr* lay out in order || *ref–sich* [*dat*] z. figure out

zurecht'machen *tr & ref* get ready

zurecht'schneiden §106 *tr* cut to size

zurecht'setzen *tr* set right, fix, adjust

zurecht'weisen §118 *tr* reprimand

zu'reden *intr* (*dat*) try to persuade; (*dat*) encourage

zu'reichen *tr* reach, pass || *intr* do

zu'reichend *adj* sufficient

zu'reiten §86 *tr* break in

zu'richten *tr* prepare; cook

zu'riegeln *tr* bolt

zürnen ['tsyrnən] *intr* (*dat*) be angry (with)

zurren ['tsurən] *tr* (naut) lash down

Zurschau'stellung *f* display

zurück [tsu'ryk] *adv* back; backward; behind; **ein paar Jahre z.** a few years ago || *interj* back up!

zurück– *comb.fm.* back; behind; re–

zurück'behalten §90 *tr* keep back

zurück'bekommen §99 *tr* get back

zurück'bleiben §62 *intr* (SEIN) stay behind; fall behind; (*Uhr*) lose time; (hinter *dat*) fall short (of)

Zurück'blenden *n* (cin) flashback

zurück'blicken *intr* look back

zurück'bringen §65 *tr* bring back; z. auf (*acc*) (math) reduce to

zurück'datieren *tr* antedate

zurück'drängen *tr* force back; repress

zurück'dürfen §69 *intr* be allowed to return

zurück'erobern *tr* reconquer, win back

zurück'erstatten *tr* return; (*Ausgaben*) refund; (*Kosten*) reimburse

zurück'fahren §71 *tr* drive back || *intr* (SEIN) drive back, ride back; (vor *Schreck*) recoil, start

zurück'finden §59 *tr* find one's way back

zurück'fordern *tr* reclaim, demand back

zurück'führen *tr* lead back; trace back; z. auf (*acc*) refer to; attribute to

zurück'geben §80 *tr* give back, return

zurück'gehen §82 *intr* (SEIN) go back; (*Fieber, Preise*) drop; (*Geschwulst*) go down; (mil) fall back

zurück'gezogen *adj* secluded

zurück'greifen §88 *intr–*z. auf (*acc*) (fig) fall back on

zurück'halten §90 *tr* hold back; j–n davon z. zu (*inf*) keep s.o. from (*ger*) || *intr* mit etw z. conceal s.th.

zurück'haltend *adj* reserved; shy

Zurück'haltung *f* (–;–en) reserve

zurück'kehren *intr* (SEIN) return

zurück'kommen §99 *intr* (SEIN) return; z. auf (*acc*) come back to, revert to; (*hinweisen*) refer to

zurück'können §100 *intr* be able to return

zurück'lassen §104 *tr* leave behind; outstrip, outrun

zurück'legen *tr* (*Kopf*) lean back; (*Geld*) put aside; (*Jahre*) complete; (*Strecke*) cover; (*Ware*) lay away || *ref* lean back

zurück'lehnen *ref* lean back

zurück'liegen §108 *intr* belong to the past || *impers*—**es liegt jetzt zehn Jahre zurück, daß** it's ten years now that

zurück'müssen §115 *intr* have to return

zurück'nehmen §116 *tr* take back; (*widerrufen*) revoke; (*Auftrag*) cancel; (*Vorwurf*) retract; (*Klage*) complete; (*Versprechen*) go back on; (*Truppen*) pull back; **das Gas z.** slow down

zurück'prallen *intr* (SEIN) rebound; (vor *Schreck*) start, be startled

zurück'rufen §122 *tr* call back, recall

zurück'schauen *intr* look back

zurück'schicken *tr* send back

zurück'schlagen §132 *tr* beat back, throw back || *intr* strike back

zurück'schrecken *tr* frighten away; (von) deter (from) || §109 & §134 *intr* (SEIN) (von, vor *dat*) shrink back (from)

zurück'sehnen *ref* yearn to return

zurück'sein §139 *intr* (SEIN) be back; (in dat) be behind (in)

zurück'setzen *tr* put back; (*im Preis*) reduce; (fig) snub || *ref* sit back

zurück'stecken *tr* put back

zurück'stellen *tr* (*Uhr*) set back; (*Plan*) shelve; (mil) defer

zurück'stoßen §150 *tr* push back; repel

zurück'strahlen *tr* reflect

zurück'streifen *tr* (*Ärmel*) roll up

zurück'treten §152 *intr* (SEIN) step back; (vom *Amt*) resign; (*Wasser, Berge*) recede

zurück'tun §154 *tr* put back

zurück'verfolgen *tr* (*Schritte*) retrace; (fig) trace back

zurück'verweisen §118 *tr* (an *acc*) refer back (to); (parl) remand (to)

zurück'weichen §85 *intr* (SEIN) fall back, make way; (*Hochwasser*) recede; (vor dem *Feind*) give ground; z. vor (*dat*) shrink from

zurück'weisen §118 *tr* turn back; (*ablehnen*) turn down; (*Angriff*) repel || *intr*–z. auf (*acc*) refer to

Zurück'weisung *f* (–;–en) rejection

zurück'wenden §140 *tr & ref* turn back

zurück'werfen §160 *tr* throw back; (e–n *Patienten*) set back; (*Strahlen*) reflect; (*Feind*) hurl back

zurück'wirken *intr* (auf *acc*) react (on); (*Gesetz*) be retroactive

zurück'zahlen *tr* pay back; (fin) refund

zurück'ziehen §163 *tr* draw back; (*Antrag*) withdraw; (*Geld*) call in; (*Truppen*) pull back; (sport) scratch || *ref* withdraw; (*schlafengehen*) re-

tire; (mil) pull back || intr (SEIN)
move back; (mil) fall back, retreat
Zu'ruf m call; cheer; (parl) acclamation
zu'rufen §122 tr—j—m etw z. shout
s.th. to s.o.
Zu'sage f (-;-n) assent; promise
zu'sagen tr promise || intr accept an
invitation; (dat) please; (dat) agree
(with)
zusammen [tsu'zamən] adv together;
in common; at the same time
Zusam'menarbeit f cooperation
zusam'menarbeiten intr cooperate
zusam'menballen tr (Faust) clench
zusam'menbeißen §53 tr—die Zähne z.
grit one's teeth
zusam'menbinden §59 tr tie together
zusam'menbrauen tr concoct || ref
(Sturm) brew
zusam'menbrechen §64 intr (SEIN)
break down; collapse
Zusam'menbruch m collapse; breakdown
zusam'mendrängen tr crowd together
zusam'mendrücken tr compress
zusam'menfahren §71 intr (SEIN) be
startled; (mit) collide (with)
zusam'menfallen §72 intr (SEIN) fall
in, collapse; (Teig) fall; (Person)
lose weight; (mit) coincide (with)
Zusam'menfall m coincidence
zusam'menfalten tr fold
zusam'menfassen tr (in sich fassen)
comprise; (verbinden) combine;
(Macht, Funktionen) concentrate;
(Bericht) summarize
zusam'menfassend adj comprehensive;
summary
Zusam'menfassung f (-;-en) summary,
résumé
zusam'menfinden §59 ref meet
zusam'menfügen tr join together;
(Scherben, Teile) piece together
zusam'mengehen §82 intr (SEIN) go
together; match; close; shrink
zusam'mengehören intr belong together
zusam'mengeraten §63 intr (SEIN) collide
zusammengewürfelt [tsu'zamɘngevʏr-
fɘlt] adj mixed, motely
Zusam'menhalt m cohesion; consistency
zusam'menhalten §90 tr hold together;
compare || intr stick together
Zusam'menhang m connection, relation; context; coherence
zusam'menhängend adj coherent; allied
zusam'menklappen tr fold up; die
Hacken z. click one's heels || intr
(SEIN) collapse
zusam'menkommen §99 intr (SEIN)
come together
Zusammenkunft [tsu'zamənkunft] f
(-;⸚e) meeting
zusam'menlaufen §105 intr (SEIN) run
together; come together; flock;
(Milch) curdle; (Farben) run; (ein-
schrumpfen) shrink up; (geom) converge
zusammenlegbar [tsu'zamənlekbɑr] adj
collapsible
zusam'menlegen tr put together; (fal-

ten) fold; (Geld) pool; (vereinigen)
combine, consolidate || intr pool
money
zusam'mennehmen §116 tr gather up;
(Gedanken) collect; (Kräfte, Mut)
muster; alles zusammengenommen
considering everything || ref pull one-
self together
zusam'menpacken tr pack up
zusam'menpassen tr & intr match
zusam'menpferchen tr crowd together
Zusam'menprall m collision; (fig) (mit)
impact (on)
zusam'menprallen intr collide
zusam'menraffen tr collect in haste;
(ein Vermögen) amass; (Kräfte)
summon up, marshal || ref pull one-
self together
zusam'menreißen §53 ref (coll) pull
oneself together
zusam'menrollen tr roll up
zusam'menrotten ref band together,
form a gang; (Aufrührer) riot
zusam'menrücken tr push together ||
intr (SEIN) move closer together
zusam'menschießen tr (Stadt) shoot
up; (Menschen) shoot down; (Geld)
pool
zusam'menschlagen §132 tr smash up;
(Absätze) click; (Beine, Gegen-
stände) fold; (Hände) clap; (zerschlagen)
beat up; die Hände über den Kopf z.
(fig) throw up one's hands || intr
(SEIN)—aneinander z. clash
zusam'menschließen §76 tr join; link
together || ref join together, unite
Zusam'menschluß m union; alliance
zusam'menschmelzen intr (SEIN) fuse;
melt away; (fig) dwindle
zusam'menschnüren tr tie up
zusam'menschrumpfen intr (SEIN)
shrivel; (Geld) (coll) dwindle away
zusam'mensetzen tr put together;
(mach) assemble || ref sit down to-
gether; sich z. aus consist of
Zusam'mensetzung f (-;-en) composition; (Bestandteile) ingredients;
(Struktur) structure; (chem, gram)
compound
Zusam'menspiel n teamwork
zusam'menstauchen tr browbeat, chew
out
zusam'menstellen tr put together;
(Liste) compile; (Farben) match;
organize
Zusam'menstoß m collision; (der Meinungen) clash; (Treffen) encounter;
(mil) engagement
zusam'menstoßen §150 tr knock to-
gether; (Gläser) touch || intr adjoin;
mit den Gläsern z. clink glasses ||
intr (SEIN) collide; (Gegner) clash
zusam'menstückeln tr piece together
zusam'menstürzen intr (SEIN) collapse
zusam'mentragen §132 tr collect
zusam'mentreffen §151 intr (SEIN)
meet; coincide || Zusammentreffen
n (-s;) encounter, meeting; coincidence
zusam'mentreiben §62 tr round up;
(Geld) scrape up
zusam'mentreten §152 intr (SEIN) meet
zusam'menwirken intr cooperate; col-

laborate; interact || **Zusammen-wirken** n (-s;) cooperation; inter-action

zusam'menzählen tr count up, add up

zusam'menziehen §163 tr dräw to-gether, contract; (*Lippen*) pucker; (*Brauen*) knit; (*Summe*) add up; (*kürzen*) shorten; (*Truppen*) concen-trate || ref contract; (*Gewitter*) brew || intr (SEIN)—**mit j–m z.** move in with s.o.

Zu'satz m addition; (*Ergänzung*) sup-plement; (*Anhang*) appendix; (*Nach-schrift*) postscript; (*Beimischung*) admixture; (*zu e–m Testament*) codi-cil; (parl) rider; **unter Z. von** with the addition of

Zu'satzgerät n attachment

zusätzlich ['tsuzetslɪç] adj additional, extra || adv in addition

zuschanden [tsu'ʃandən] adv—z. ma-**chen** ruin; **z. werden** go to ruin

zu'schauen intr look on; (dat) watch

Zu'schauer –in §6 mf spectator

Zu'schauerraum m auditorium

zu'schicken tr (dat) send (to)

zu'schieben §130 tr close, shut; (*Rie-gel*) push forward; **j–m die Schuld z.** push the blame on s.o.

Zu'schlag m extra charge; **den Z. er-halten** get the contract (*on a bid*)

zu'schlagen §132 tr (*Tür*) slam; (*Buch*) shut; (*auf Auktionen*) knock down; (*hinzurechnen*) add || intr hit hard

zu'schließen §76 tr shut, lock

zu'schnallen tr buckle (up)

zu'schnappen intr snap shut; **z. lassen** snap shut

zu'schneiden §106 tr cut out; (*Anzug*) cut to size

Zu'schnitt m cut; (fig) style

zu'schnüren tr lace up

zu'schrauben tr screw tight

zu'schreiben §62 tr ascribe; (*Bedeu-tung*) attach; (*Grundstück, usw.*) transfer, sign over || ref—**er hat es sich** [dat] **selbst zuzuschreiben** he has himself to thank for it

Zu'schrift f letter, communication

zuschulden [tsu'ʃʊldən] adv—**sich** [dat] **etw. z. kommen lassen** take the blame for s.th.

Zu'schuß m subsidy; grant; allowance

zu'schütten tr add; (*Graben*) fill up

zu'sehen §138 intr look on; (dat) watch; **z., daß** see to it that

zusehends ['tsuze·ənts] adv visibly

zu'senden §120 & §140 tr (dat) send to

zu'setzen tr add; (*Geld*) lose || intr (dat) pester; (dat) be hard on; (mil) (dat) put pressure on

zu'sichern tr—**j–m etw z.** assure s.o. of s.th.

Zu'sicherung f (-;-en) assurance

zu'siegeln tr seal up

Zu'speise f side dish

zu'sperren tr lock

zu'spielen tr—**j–m den Ball z.** pass the ball to s.o.; **j–m etw z.** slip s.th. to s.o.

zu'spitzen tr sharpen, make pointy || ref (*Lage*) come to a head

zu'sprechen §64 tr (& jur) award

Zu'spruch m consolation, encourage-ment; (com) customers, clientele

zu'springen §142 intr (SEIN) snap shut

Zu'stand m state, condition; **gegen-wärtiger Z.** status quo; **in gutem Z.** in good condition; **Zustände** state of affairs

zustande [tsu'ʃtandə] adv—**z. bringen** bring about; put across; get away with; **z. kommen** come about, come off; happen; be realized; (*Gesetz*) pass; (*Vertrag*) be reached

zu'ständig adj competent; (*Behörde*) proper; (*verantwortlich*) responsible

Zu'ständigkeit f (-;) jurisdiction

zustatten [tsu'ʃtatən] adv—**z. kommen** come in handy

zu'stehen §146 intr (dat) be due to

zu'stellen tr deliver; (jur) serve

Zu'stellung f (-;-en) delivery; (jur) serving

zu'steuern tr (*Geld*) contribute, kick in || intr (dat, auf acc) head for

zu'stimmen intr (dat) agree to, approve of (*s.th.*); (dat) agree with (*s.o.*)

Zu'stimmung f (-;) consent, approval

zu'stopfen tr plug up

zu'stoßen §150 tr slam || intr (SEIN) lunge; (dat) happen to

zu'streben intr (dat) strive for

zutage [tsu'tagə] adv to light; **z. liegen** be evident

Zutaten ['tsutatən] pl ingredients

zuteil [tsu'taɪl] adv—**j–m z. werden** fall to s.o.'s share

zu'teilen tr allot; ration; award; (*ge-währen*) grant; confer; (mil) assign

Zu'teilung f (-;-en) allotment, alloca-tion; rationing; (mil) assignment

zu'tragen §132 tr carry; (*Neuigkeiten*) report || ref happen

zuträglich ['tsutreklɪç] adj advanta-geous; (*Klima*) healthful; (*Nahrung*) wholesome; **j–m z. sein** agree with s.o.

zu'trauen tr—**j–m etw z.** give s.o. credit for s.th.; imagine s.o. capable of s.th. || **Zutrauen** n (-s;) (zu) con-fidence (in)

zu'traulich adj trustful; (zahm) tame

zu'treffen §151 intr (SEIN) prove right; come true; hold true, be conclusive; **z. auf** (acc) apply to

zu'treffend adj correct; to the point; (*anwendbar*) applicable

zu'trinken §143 intr (dat) drink to

Zu'tritt m access; admission, entrance; **kein Z.!** no admittance!

zu'tun §154 tr close; (*hinzufügen*) add

zu'verlässig adj reliable; **von zuverläs-siger Seite** on good authority

Zu'verlässigkeit f (-;) reliability

Zuversicht ['tsufɛrzɪçt] f (-;) confi-dence

zu'versichtlich adj confident

zuviel [tsu'fil] adv & indef pron too much; **einer z.** one too many

zuvor [tsu'for] adv before, previously; first (of all); **kurz z.** shortly before

zuvor– comb.fm. beforehand

zuvor'kommen §99 intr (SEIN) (dat) anticipate; **j–m z.** get the jump on s.o.

zuvor'kommend *adj* obliging; polite

zuvor'tun §154 *tr*—es j—m z. outdo s.o.

Zu'wachs *m* increase; growth; **auf Z.** (big enough) to allow for growth

zu'wachsen §155 *intr* (SEIN) grow together; (*Wunde*) heal up; (*dat*) accrue (to)

Zu'wachsrate *f* rate of increase

zuwege [tsu'vega] *adv*—z. bringen bring about; achieve; finish; **gut z. sein** be fit as a fiddle

zuweilen [tsu'vaɪlən] *adv* sometimes

zu'weisen §118 *tr* assign, allot

zu'wenden §120 & §140 *tr* (*dat*) turn (*s.th.*) towards; (*dat*) give (*s.th.*) to, devote (*s.th.*) to || *ref* (*dat*) devote oneself to, concentrate on

Zu'wendung *f* (—;-en) gift, donation

zuwenig [tsu'veniç] *adv* & *pron* too little

zu'werfen §160 *tr* (*Tür*) slam; (*Blick*) cast; (*Grube*) fill up; **j—m etw z.** throw s.o. s.th.

zuwider [tsu'vidər] *adj* (*dat*) distasteful (to) || *prep* (*dat*) contrary to

zuwi'derhandeln *intr* (*dat*) go against

Zuwi'derhandlung *f* (—;-en) violation

zu'winken *intr* (*dat*) wave to; beckon to

zu'zahlen *tr* pay extra

zu'zählen *tr* add

zuzeiten [tsu'tsaɪtən] *adv* at times

zu'ziehen §163 *tr* (*Vorhang*) draw; (*Knoten*) tighten; (*Arzt, Experten*) call in || *ref*—sich (*dat*) etw z. incur s.th.; contract s.th. || *intr* (SEIN) move in; move (to *a city*)

Zu'ziehung *f*—unter Z. (*genit* or *von*) in consultation with

zuzüglich ['tsutsyklıç] *prep* (*genit*) plus; including

zwang [tsvaŋ] *pret of* zwingen || **Zwang** *m* (—[e]s;) coercion, force; restraint; obligation; (*Druck*) pressure; (jur) duress; **auf j—n Z.** ausüben put pressure on s.o. || *ref*—sich (*dat*) **keinen Z. antun** (or auferlegen) relax

zwängen ['tsvɛŋən] *tr* force, squeeze || *ref* (*durch*) squeeze (through)

zwang'los *adj* free and easy; informal

Zwang'losigkeit *f* (—;) ease; informality

Zwangs— [tsvaŋs] *comb.fm.* force, compulsory

Zwangs'arbeit *f* hard labor

Zwangs'arbeitslager *n* labor camp

Zwangs'jacke *f* strait jacket

Zwangs'lage *f* tight spot

zwangs'läufig *adj* inevitable

zwangs'mäßig *adj* forced; coercive

Zwangs'maßnahme *f*—zu Zwangsmaßnahmen greifen resort to force

Zwangs'verschleppte §5 *mf* displaced person

Zwangs'verwaltung *f* receivership

Zwangs'vorstellung *f* hallucination

zwangs'weise *adv* by force

Zwangs'wirtschaft *f* (econ) government control, controlled economy

zwanzig ['tsvantsıç] *invar adj* & *pron* twenty || **Zwanzig** *f* (—;-en) twenty

zwanziger ['tsvansigər] *invar adj* of the twenties; **die z. Jahre** the twenties

zwanzigste .['tsvantsıçstə] §9 *adj* & *pron* twentieth

Zwanzigstel ['tsvantsıçstəl] *n* (—s;—) twentieth (*part*)

zwar [tsvar] *adv* indeed, no doubt, it is true; **und z.** namely, that is

Zweck [tsvɛk] *m* (—[e]s;-e) purpose, aim, object, point; **es hat keinen Z.** there's no point to it

zweck'dienlich *adj* serviceable, useful

Zwecke ['tsvɛkə] *f* (—;-n) tack; thumbtack

zweck'entfremden *tr* misuse

zweck'entsprechend *adj* appropriate

zweck'los *adj* pointless

zweck'mäßig *adj* serving its purpose; (*Möbel*) functional

zwecks [tsvɛks] *prep* (*genit*) for the purpose of

zwei [tsvaɪ] *adj* & *pron* two; **alle z.** (coll) both; **zu zweien** in twos, two by two, in pairs; **zu zweien hintereinander** in double file || **Zwei** *f* (—;-en) two

zwei'beinig *adj* two-legged

Zwei'bettzimmer *n* double room

Zweidecker ['tsvaɪdɛkər] *m* (—s;—) biplane

zweideutig ['tsvaɪdɔɪtıç] *adj* ambiguous; (*Witz*) off-color; (*schlüpfrig*) suggestive

zweierlei ['tsvaɪər'laɪ] *invar adj* two kinds of; **das ist z.** (coll) that's different

zwei'fach, zwei'fältig *adj* twofold, double; **in zweifacher Ausfertigung** in duplicate

Zweifami'lienhaus *n* duplex

zwei'farbig *adj* two-tone

Zweifel ['tsvaɪfəl] *m* (—s;—) doubt; **in Z. stellen** (or ziehen) call into question; **über allen Zweifeln erhaben** beyond reproach

zwei'felhaft *adj* doubtful; questionable; (*Persönlichkeit*) suspicious

zwei'fellos *adj* doubtless

zweifeln ['tsvaɪfəln] *intr* be in doubt; waver, hesitate; **z. an** (*dat*) doubt

Zwei'felsfall *m*—im Z. in case of doubt

Zwei'fler —in §6 *mf* skeptic

Zweig [tsvaɪk] *m* (—[e]s;-e) branch

Zweig'anstalt *f*, **Zweig'geschäft** *n* (com) branch

Zweig'gesellschaft *f* (com) affiliate

Zweig'niederlassung *f*, **Zweig'stelle** *f* (com) branch

Zwei'kampf *m* duel, single combat

zwei'mal *adj* twice

zweimalig ['tsvaɪmalıç] *adj* repeated

zweimotorig ['tsvaɪmotorıç] *adj* two-engine, twin-engine

zweireihig ['tsvaɪraɪ.ıç] *adj* (*Sakko*) double-breasted

zwei'schneidig *adj* double-edged

zwei'seitig *adj* bilateral; reversible

zweisprachig ['tsvaɪ/praxıç] *adj* bilingual

Zweis:är'kenglas *n* bifocal lens; (*Brille*) bifocals

zwei'stimmig *adj* for two voices

zweistufig ['tsvaɪ/tufıç] *adj* (rok) two-stage

zwei'stündig *adj* two-hour

zwei′stündlich adj & adv every two hours

zweit [tsvaɪt] adv—**zu z.** by twos; **wir sind zu z.** there are two of us

Zwei′taktmotor m two-cycle engine

Zweit′ausfertigung f duplicate

zweit′beste §9 adj second-best

zweite [′tsvaɪtə] §9 adj & pron second; another; **aus zweiter Hand** second-hand; **at second hand; zum zweiten** secondly ‖ **Zweite** §5 mf (sport) runner-up

zwei′teilig adj two-piece; two-part

zweitens [′tsvaɪtəns] adv secondly

zweit′klassig adj second-class

Zwerchfell [′tsvɛrçfɛl] n diaphragm

Zwerg [tsvɛrk] m (-[e]s;-e) dwarf

zwer′genhaft adj dwarfish

Zwetsche [′tsvɛtʃə] f (-;-n), **Zwetschge** [′tsvɛt/gə] f (-;-n) plum

Zwetsch′genwasser n plum brandy

zwicken [′tsvɪkən] tr pinch

Zwicker (**Zwik′ker**) m (-s;-) pince-nez

Zwickmühle [′tsvɪkmylə] f (fig) fix

zwie- [tsvi] comb.fm. dis-, two-, double

Zwieback [′tsvibak] m (-s;ːe & -e) zwieback

Zwiebel [′tsvibəl] f (-;-n) onion; (Blumen-) bulb

Zwie′gespräch n dialogue

Zwie′licht n twilight

Zwiesel [′tsvizəl] f (-;-n) fork (of tree)

Zwie′spalt m dissension; schism; discrepancy; **im Z. sein mit** be at variance with

zwiespältig [′tsvi/pɛltɪç] adj disunited, divided; divergent

Zwie′tracht f (-;) discord

Zwilling [′tsvɪlɪŋ] m (-s;-e) twin; **eineiige Zwillinge** identical twins

Zwil′lingsbruder m twin brother

Zwil′lingsschwester f twin sister

Zwinge [′tsvɪŋə] f (-;-n) ferrule; clamp; (Schraubstock) vise

zwingen [′tsvɪŋən] §142 tr force, compel; (schaffen) accomplish, swing

zwin′gend adj forceful, cogent

Zwin′ger m (-s;-) dungeon; cage; dog kennel; bear pit; lists

zwinkern [′tsvɪŋkərn] intr blink

Zwirn [tsvɪrn] m (-[e]s;-e) thread

Zwirns′faden m thread

zwischen [′tsvɪ/ən] prep (dat & acc) between, among

Zwi′schenbemerkung f interruption

Zwi′schendeck n steerage

Zwi′schending n cross, mixture

zwischendurch′ adv in between; at times

Zwi′schenergebnis n incomplete result

Zwi′schenfall m (unexpected) incident

Zwi′schenhändler **-in** §6 mf middleman

Zwi′schenlandung f stopover

Zwi′schenlauf m (sport) quarterfinal; (sport) semifinal

Zwi′schenpause f break, intermission

Zwi′schenraum m space, interval

Zwi′schenruf m boo; interruption

Zwi′schenrunde f (sport) quarterfinal; (sport) semifinal

Zwi′schenspiel n interlude

zwi′schenstaatlich adj international; interstate

Zwi′schenstation f (rr) way station

Zwi′schenstecker m (elec) adapter

Zwi′schenstellung f (-;-en) intermediate position

Zwi′schenstück n insert; (Verbindung) connection; (elec) adapter

Zwi′schenstufe f intermediate stage

Zwi′schenträger **-in** §6 mf gossip

Zwi′schenwand f partition wall

Zwi′schenzeit f interval, meanwhile

Zwist [tsvɪst] m (-es;-e) discord; quarrel; (Feindschaft) enmity

Zwi′stigkeit f (-;-en) hostility

zwitschern [′tsvɪt/ərn] tr—**e–n z.** (coll) have a shot of liquor ‖ intr chirp

Zwitter [′tsvɪtər] m (-s;-) hermaphrodite

Zwit′terfahrzeug n (mil) half-track

zwo [tsvo] adj & pron (coll) two

zwölf [tsvœlf] invar adj & pron twelve ‖ **Zwölf** f (-;-en) twelve

Zwölffin′gerdarm m duodenum

zwölfte [′tsvœlftə] §9 adj & pron twelfth

Zwölftel [′tsvœftəl] n (-s;-) twelfth (part)

Zyklon [tsy′klon] m (-s;-e), **Zyklone** [tsy′klonə] f (-;-n) cyclone

Zyk·lus [′tsyklus] m (-;-len [lən]) cycle; (Reihe) series, course

Zylinder [tsy′lɪndər] m (-s;-) cylinder (e–r Lampe) chimney; (Hut) top hat

zylindrisch [tsy′lɪndrɪ/] adj cylindrical

Zyniker [′tsynɪkər] m (-s;-) cynic; (philos) Cynic

zynisch [′tsynɪ/] adj cynical

Zypern [′tsypərn] n (-s;) Cyprus

Zypresse [tsy′prɛsə] f (-;-n) cypress

Zyste [′tsystə] f (-;-n) cyst

GRAMMATICAL EXPLANATIONS

German Pronunciation

All the German letters and their variant spellings are listed below (in column 1) with their IPA symbols (in column 2), a description of their sounds (in column 3), and German examples with phonetic transcription (in column 4).

		VOWELS	
SPELLING	SYMBOL	APPROXIMATE SOUND	EXAMPLES
a	[a]	Like *a* in English *swat*	Apfel [ˈapfəl], lassen [ˈlasən], Stadt [ʃtat]
a	[ɑ]	Like *a* in English *father*	Vater [ˈfɑtər], laden [ˈlɑdən]
aa	[ɑ]	" "	Paar [pɑr], Staat [ʃtɑt]
ah	[ɑ]	" "	Hahn [hɑn], Zahl [tsɑl]
ä	[ɛ]	Like *e* in English *met*	Äpfel [ˈɛpfəl], lässig [ˈlɛsɪç], Städte [ˈʃtɛtə]
ä	[e]	Like *e* in English *they* (without the following sound of *y*)	mäßig [ˈmesɪç], Väter [ˈfetər]
äh	[e]	" "	ähnlich [ˈenlɪç], Zähne [ˈtsenə]
e	[ə]	Like *e* in English *system*	Bitte [ˈbɪtə], rufen [ˈrufən]
e	[ɛ]	Like *e* in English *met*	Kette [ˈkɛtə], messen [ˈmɛsən]
e	[e]	Like *e* in English *they* (without the following sound of *y*)	Feder [ˈfedər], regnen [ˈregnən]
ee	[e]	" "	Meer [mer], Seele [ˈzelə]
eh	[e]	" "	Ehre [ˈerə], zehn [tsen]
i	[ɪ]	Like *i* in English *sin*	bin [bɪn], Fisch [fɪʃ]
i	[i]	Like *i* in English *machine*	Maschine [maˈʃinə], Lid [lit]
ih	[i]	" "	ihm [im], ihr [ir]
ie	[i]	" "	dieser [ˈdizər], tief [tif]
o	[ɔ]	Like *o* in English *often*	Gott [gɔt], offen [ˈɔfən]
o	[o]	Like *o* in English *note*, but without the diphthongal glide	holen [ˈholən], Rose [ˈrozə]
oo	[o]	" "	Boot [bot], Moos [mos]
oh	[o]	" "	Bohne [ˈbonə], Kohle [ˈkolə]
ö	[œ]	The lips are rounded for [ɔ] and held without moving while the sound [ɛ] is pronounced.	Götter [ˈgœtər], öffnen [ˈœfnən]

3a

SPELLING	SYMBOL	APPROXIMATE SOUND	EXAMPLES
ö	[ø]	The lips are rounded for [o] and held without moving while the sound [e] is pronounced.	böse ['bøzə], Löwe ['løvə]
öh	[ø]	" "	Röhre ['rørə], Söhne ['zønə]
u	[ʊ]	Like u in English *bush*	Busch [bʊʃ], muß [mʊs], Hund [hʊnt]
u	[u]	Like u in English *rule*	Schule ['ʃulə], Gruß [grus]
uh	[u]	" "	Uhr [ur], Ruhm [rum]
ü	[ʏ]	The lips are rounded for [ʊ] and held without moving while the sound [ɪ] is pronounced.	Hütte ['hʏtə], müssen ['mʏsən]
ü	[y]	The lips are rounded for [u] and held without moving while the sound [i] is pronounced.	Schüler ['ʃylər], Grüße ['grysə]
üh	[y]	" "	Mühle ['mylə], kühn [kyn]
y	[ʏ]	Like ü [ʏ] above	Mystik ['mʏstɪk]
y	[y]	Like ü [y] above	Mythe ['mytə]

DIPHTHONGS

SPELLING	SYMBOL	APPROXIMATE SOUND	EXAMPLES
ai	[aɪ]	Like i in English *night*	Saite ['zaɪtə], Mais [maɪs]
au	[aʊ]	Like ou in English *ouch*	kaufen ['kaufən], Haus [haus]
äu	[ɔɪ]	Like oy in English *toy*	träumen ['trɔɪmən], Gebäude [gə'bɔɪdə]
ei	[aɪ]	Like i in English *night*	Zeit [tsaɪt], nein [naɪn]
eu	[ɔɪ]	Like oy in English *toy*	heute ['hɔɪtə], Eule ['ɔɪlə]

CONSONANTS

SPELLING	SYMBOL	APPROXIMATE SOUND	EXAMPLES
b	[b]	Like b in English *boy*	Buch [bux], haben ['habən]
b	[p]	Like p in English *lap*	gelb [gelp], lieblich ['liplɪç]
c	[k]	Like c in English *car*	Clown [klaun], Café [ka'fe]
c	[ts]	Like ts in English *its*	Cäsar ['tsezar], Centrale [tsen'tralə]
ch	[x]	This sound is made by breathing through a space between the back of the tongue and the soft palate.	auch [aux], Buche ['buxə]
ch	[ç]	This sound is made by breathing through a space left when the front of the tongue is pressed close to the hard palate with the tip of the tongue behind the lower teeth.	ich [ɪç], Bücher ['byçər], Chemie [çe'mi], durch [durç]

4a

SPELLING	SYMBOL	APPROXIMATE SOUND	EXAMPLES
ch	[k]	Like *k* in English *key*	**Charakter** [ka'raktər], **Chor** [kor]
ch	[ʃ]	Like *sh* in English *shall*	**Chef** [ʃef], **Chassis** [ʃa'si]
chs	[ks]	Like *x* in English *box*	**sechs** [zɛks], **Wachs** [vaks]
ck	[k]	Like *k* in English *key* When *ck* in a vocabulary entry in this Dictionary has to be divided by an accent mark, the word is first spelled with *ck* and is then repeated in parentheses with the *ck* changed to *kk* in accordance with the principle which requires this change when the division comes at the end of the line, e.g., **Deckenlicht (Dek'ken-licht)**.	**wecken** ['vɛkən], **Ruck** [rʊk]
d	[d]	Like *d* in English *door*	**laden** ['lɑdən], **deutsch** [dɔɪtʃ]
d	[t]	Like *t* in English *time*	**Freund** [frɔɪnt], **Hund** [hʊnt]
dt	[t]	" "	**verwandt** [fer'vant], **Stadt** [ʃtat]
f	[f]	Like *f* in English *five*	**Fall** [fal], **auf** [aʊf]
g	[g]	Like *g* in English *go*	**geben** ['gebən], **Regen** ['regən]
g	[k]	Like *k* in English *key*	**Krieg** [krik], **Weg** [vek]
g	[ç]	See *ch* [ç] above	**wenig** ['venɪç], **häufig** ['hɔɪfɪç]
h	[h]	Like *h* in English *hat*	**Haus** [haʊs], **Freiheit** ['fraɪhaɪt]
j	[j]	Like *y* in English *yet*	**Jahr** [jɑr], **jener** ['jenər]
k	[k]	Like *k* in English *key*	**Kaffee** [ka'fe], **kein** [kaɪn]
l	[l]	This sound is made with the tip of the tongue against the back of the upper teeth and the side edges of the tongue against the side teeth.	**laden** ['lɑdən], **fahl** [fɑl]
m	[m]	Like *m* in English *man*	**mehr** [mer], **Amt** [amt]
n	[n]	Like *n* in English *neck*	**Nase** ['nɑzə], **kaufen** ['kaʊfən]
n	[ŋ]	Like *n* in English *sink*	**sinken** ['zɪŋkən], **Funke** ['fʊŋkə]
ng	[ŋ]	" "	**Finger** ['fɪŋər], **Rang** [raŋ]
p	[p]	Like *p* in English *pond*	**Perle** ['perlə], **Opfer** ['ɔpfər]
ph	[f]	Like *f* in English *five*	**Phase** ['fɑzə], **Graphik** ['grɑfɪk]
qu	[kv]	Does not occur in English.	**Quelle** ['kvɛlə], **bequem** [bə'kvem]
r	[r]	This sound is a trilled sound made by vibrating the tip of the tongue against the upper gums or by vibrating the uvula.	**rufen** ['rufən], **Rede** ['redə]

SPELLING	SYMBOL	APPROXIMATE SOUND	EXAMPLES
s	[s]	Like s in English *sock*	**Glas** [glɑs], **erst** [erst]
s	[z]	Like z in English *zest*	**sind** [zɪnt], **Eisen** ['aɪzən]
sch	[ʃ]	Like *sh* in English *shall*	**Schuh** [ʃu], **Schnee** [ʃne]
sp	[ʃp]	Does not occur in English in the initial position.	**sparen** ['ʃparən], **Spott** [ʃpɔt]
ss	[s]	This spelling is used only in the intervocalic position and when the preceding vowel sound is one of the following: [a], [ɛ], [ɪ], [ə], [œ], [ʊ], [ʏ]	**Klasse** ['klasə], **essen** ['esən], **wissen** ['vɪsən], **Gosse** ['gosə], **Rössel** ['rœsəl], **Russe** ['rusə], **müssen** ['mʏsən]
ß	[s]	This spelling is used instead of ss (a) when in the final position in a word or component, (b) when followed by a consonant, or (c) when intervocalic and preceded by a diphthong or one of the following vowel sounds: [ɑ], [e], [i], [o], [ø], [u], [y]	(a) **Fluß** [flʊs], **Flußufer** ['flʊsufər], (b) **läßt** [lest], (c) **dreißig** ['draɪsɪç], **Straße** ['ʃtrasə], **mäßig** ['mesɪç], **schießen** ['ʃisən], **stoßen** ['ʃtosən], **Stößel** ['ʃtøsəl], **Muße** ['musə], **müßig** ['mysɪç]
st	[ʃt]	Does not occur in English in the initial position.	**Staub** [ʃtaup], **stehen** ['ʃte·ən]
t	[t]	Like *t* in English *time*	**Teller** ['telər], **Tau** [tau]
th	[t]	" "	**Theater** [te'atər], **Thema** ['tema]
ti+ vowel	[tsj]	Does not occur in English.	**Station** [sta'tsjon], **Patient** [pa'tsjent]
tz	[ts]	Like *ts* in English *its*	**schätzen** ['ʃɛtsən], **jetzt** [jetst]
v	[f]	Like *f* in English *five*	**Vater** ['fatər], **brav** [braf]
v	[v]	Like *v* in English *vat*	**November** [nɔ'vɛmbər], **Verb** [verp]
w	[v]	" "	**Wasser** ['vasər], **wissen** ['vɪsən]
x	[ks]	Like *x* in English *box*	**Export** [eks'pɔrt], **Taxe** ['taksə]
z	[ts]	Like *ts* in English *its*	**Zahn** [tsan], **reizen** ['raɪtsən]

German Grammar References

§1. Declension of the Definite Article

| | SINGULAR | | | PLURAL |
	MASC	FEM	NEUT	MASC, FEM, NEUT
NOM	der	die	das	die
ACC	den	die	das	die
DAT	dem	der	dem	den
GENIT	des	der	des	der

§2. Declension of the Indefinite Article and the Numeral Adjective

1.

| | SINGULAR | | | PLURAL |
	MASC	FEM	NEUT	MASC, FEM, NEUT
NOM	ein	eine	ein	
ACC	einen	eine	ein	
DAT	einem	einer	einem	
GENIT	eines	einer	eines	

2. Other words that are declined like **ein** are: **kein** *no, not any* and the possessive adjectives **mein** *my;* **dein** *thy, your;* **sein** *his; her; its;* **ihr** *her; their;* **Ihr** *your;* **unser** *our;* **euer** *your.* Unlike **ein**, they have plural forms, as shown in the following paradigm.

| | SINGULAR | | | PLURAL |
	MASC	FEM	NEUT	MASC, FEM, NEUT
NOM	kein	keine	kein	keine
ACC	keinen	keine	kein	keine
DAT	keinem	keiner	keinem	keinen
GENIT	keines	keiner	keines	keiner

3. The **e** of **er** of **unser** and **euer** is generally dropped when followed by an ending, as shown in the following paradigm. And instead of the **e** of **er** dropping, the **e** of final **em** and **en** in these words may drop.

| | SINGULAR | | | PLURAL |
	MASC	FEM	NEUT	MASC, FEM, NEUT
NOM	unser	uns(e)re	unser	uns(e)re
ACC	uns(e)ren or unsern	uns(e)re	unser	uns(e)re
DAT	uns(e)rem or unserm	uns(e)rer	uns(e)rem or unserm	uns(e)ren or unsern
GENIT	uns(e)res	uns(e)rer	uns(e)res	uns(e)rer

All adjectives that follow these words are declined in the mixed declension.

4. The pronouns **einer** and **keiner**, as well as all the possessive pronouns, are declined according to the strong declension of adjectives. The neuter forms **eines** and **keines** have the variants **eins** and **keins**.

5. When the possessive adjectives are used as possessive pronouns, they are declined according to the strong declension of adjectives. When preceded by the definite article, they are declined according to the weak declension of adjectives. There are also possessive pronouns with the infix **ig** which are always preceded by the definite article and capitalized and are declined according to the declension of adjectives, e.g., **der, die, das Meinige** *mine*.

§3. Declension of the Demonstrative Pronoun

	SINGULAR			PLURAL
	MASC	FEM	NEUT	MASC, FEM, NEUT
NOM	dieser	diese	dieses or dies	diese
ACC	diesen	diese	dieses or dies	diese
DAT	diesem	dieser	diesem	diesen
GENIT	dieses	dieser	dieses	dieser

Other words that are declined like **dieser** are **jeder** *each;* **jener** *that;* **mancher** *many a;* **welcher** *which.* All adjectives that come after these words are declined in the weak declension.

§4. Declension of Adjectives.

Adjectives have three declensions: 1) the strong declension, 2) the weak declension, and 3) the mixed declension. On both sides of this Dictionary, adjectives occurring in the expressions consisting solely of an adjective and a noun are entered in their weak forms.

1. The strong declension of adjectives, whose endings are shown in the following table, is used when the adjective is not preceded by **der** or by **dieser** or any of the other words listed in §3 or by **ein** or any of the other words listed in §2.

	SINGULAR			PLURAL
	MASC	FEM	NEUT	MASC, FEM, NEUT
NOM	–er	–e	–es	–e
ACC	–en	–e	–es	–e
DAT	–em	–er	–em	–en
GENIT	–en	–er	–en	–er

2. The weak declension of adjectives, whose endings are shown in the following table, is used when the adjective is preceded by **der** or **dieser** or any of the other words listed in §3.

	SINGULAR			PLURAL
	MASC	FEM	NEUT	MASC, FEM, NEUT
NOM	–e	–e	–e	–en
ACC	–en	–e	–e	–en
DAT	–en	–en	–en	–en
GENIT	–en	–en	–en	–en

3. The **der** component of **derselbe** and **derjenige** is the article **der** and is declined like it, while the **–selbe** and **–jenige** components are declined according to the weak declension of adjectives.

4. The mixed declension of adjectives, whose endings are shown in the following table, is used when the adjective is preceded by **ein** or **kein** or any of the other words listed in §2.

	SINGULAR			PLURAL
	MASC	FEM	NEUT	MASC, FEM, NEUT
NOM	**–er**	**–e**	**–es**	**–en**
ACC	**–en**	**–e**	**–es**	**–en**
DAT	**–en**	**–en**	**–en**	**–en**
GENIT	**–en**	**–en**	**–en**	**–en**

§5. Adjectives Used as Nouns. When an adjective is used as a masculine, feminine, or neuter noun, it is spelled with an initial capital letter and is declined as an adjective in accordance with the principles set forth in §4. We have, for example, **der** or **die Fremde** the foreigner; **der** or **die Angestellte** *the employee;* **ein Angestellter** *a (male) employee,* **eine Angestelite** *a (female) employee;* **das Deutsche** *German* (i.e., *language*). These nouns are entered on both sides of this Dictionary in the weak form of the adjective and their genitives and plurals are not shown.

§6. Many masculine nouns ending in **–er** and **–ier** have feminine forms made by adding **–in.** The masculine forms have genitives made by adding **s** and remain unchanged in the plural, while the feminine forms remain unchanged in the singular and have plurals made by adding **–nen.** For example:

	MASC	FEM
NOM SG	**Verkäufer** *salesperson (salesman)*	**Verkäuferin** *salesperson (saleslady)*
GENIT SG	**Verkäufers**	**Verkäuferin**
NOM PL	**Verkäufer**	**Verkäuferinnen**

§7. Many masculine nouns ending in **–at** (e.g., **Advokat**), or in **–ant** (e.g., **Musikant**), or in **–ist** (*e.g.,* **Artist**), or in **–ent** (e.g., **Student**), or in **–graph** (e.g., **Choreograph**), or in **–ot** (e.g., **Pilot**), or in **–et** (e.g.,**Analphabet**), or in **–it** (e.g., **Israelit**), or in **–ast** (e.g., **Phantast**), etc., have feminine forms made by adding **–in.** The masculine forms have genitives and plurals made by adding **–en,** while the femine forms remain unchanged in the singular and have plurals made by adding **–nen.** For example:

	MASC	FEM
NOM SG	**Advokat** *attorney*	**Advokatin** *attorney*
GENIT SG	**Advokaten**	**Advokatin**
NOM PL	**Advokaten**	**Advokatinnen**

§8. Many masculine nouns ending in **–ar** (e.g., **Antiquar**) or in **–är** (e.g., **Milliardär**) have feminine forms made by adding **–in.** The masculine forms have genitives made by adding **–(e)s** and plurals made by adding **–e,** while the feminine forms remain unchanged in the singular and have plurals made by adding **–nen.** For example:

	MASC	FEM
NOM SG	**Antiquar** *antique dealer*	**Antiquarin** *antique dealer*
GENIT SG	**Antiquar(e)s**	**Antiquarin**
NOM PL	**Antiquare**	**Antiquarinnen**

§9. Adjectives are generally given in their uninflected form, the form in which they appear in the predicate, e.g., **billig, reich, alt.** However, those adjectives which do not occur in an uninflected form are given with the weak ending **–e,** which in the nominative is the same for all genders, e.g., **andere, besondere, beste, hohe.**

9a

§10. Adjectives which denote languages may be used as adverbs. When so used with **sprechen, schreiben, können**, and a few others, they are translated in English by the corresponding noun, and actual and immediate action is implied, e.g., **deutsch sprechen** *to speak German* (i.e., to be speaking German right now). Adjectives which denote languages may be capitalized and used as invariable nouns, and when so used with **sprechen, schreiben, können**, and a few other verbs, general action is implied, e.g., **Deutsch sprechen** *to speak German* (i.e., to know how to speak German, to be a speaker of German).

With other verbs, these adjectives used as adverbs are translated by the corresponding noun preceded by "auf" or "in", e.g., **sich auf** (or **in**) **deutsch unterhalten** *to converse in German.*

§11. Personal and Reflexive Pronouns

PERSONS	SUBJECT	PERSONAL DIRECT OBJECT	PERSONAL INDIRECT OBJECT	REFLEXIVE DIRECT OBJECT	REFLEXIVE INDIRECT OBJECT
SG					
1	ich *I*	mich *me*	mir *(to) me*	mich *myself*	mir *(to) myself*
2	du *you*	dich *you*	dir *(to) you*	dich *yourself*	dir *(to) yourself*
3 MASC	er *he; it*	ihn *him; it*	ihm *(to) him; (to) it*	sich *himself; itself*	sich *(to) himself; (to) itself*
3 FEM	sie *she; it*	sie *her; it*	ihr *(to) her; (to) it*	sich *herself; itself*	sich *(to) herself; (to) itself*
3 NEUT	es *it; she; he*	es *it; her; him*	ihm *(to) it; (to) her; (to) him*	sich *itself; herself; himself*	sich *(to) itself; (to) herself; (to) himself*
PL					
1	wir *we*	uns *us*	uns *(to) us*	uns *ourselves*	uns *(to) ourselves*
2	ihr *you*	euch *you*	euch *(to) you*	euch *yourselves*	euch *(to) yourselves*
3	sie *they*	sie *them*	ihnen *(to) them*	sich *themselves*	sich *(to) themselves*
FORMAL SG & PL					
2	Sie *you*	Sie *you*	Ihnen *(to) you*	sich *yourself; yourselves*	sich *(to) yourself; (to) yourselves*

er means *it* when it stands for a masculine noun that is the name of an animal or a thing, as **Hund, Tisch.**
sie means *it* when it stands for a feminine noun that is the name of an animal or a thing, as **Hündin, Feder.**
es means *she* when it stands for a neuter noun that is the name of a female person, as **Fräulein, Mädchen, Weib;** it means *he* when it stands for a neuter noun that is the name of a male person, as **Söhnchen, Söhnlein.**
The dative means also *from me, from you,* etc., with certain verbs expressing separation such as **entnehmen.**

11a

§12. Separable and Inseparable Prefixes. Many verbs can be compounded either with a prefix, which is always inseparable and unstressed, or with a combining form (conventionally called also a prefix), which can be separable and stressed or inseparable and unstressed. Exceptions are indicated by the abbreviations *sep* and *insep*.

1. The inseparable prefixes are be-, emp-, ent-, er-, ge-, ver-, and zer-, e.g., beglei'ten, erler'nen, verste'hen. They are never stressed.

2. The separable prefixes (i.e., combining forms) are prepositions, e.g., auf- as in auf'tragen, adverbs, e.g., vorwärts- as in vor'wärtsbringen, adjectives, e.g., tot- as in tot'schlagen, nouns, e.g., maschine- as in maschi'neschreiben, or other verbs, e.g., stehen- as in ste'henbleiben. They are always stressed except as provided for those listed in the following section.

3. The prefixes (combining forms) durch, hinter, über, um, unter, wider, and wieder, when their meaning is literal, are separable and stressed, e.g. durch'schneiden *cut through, cut in two*, and, when their meaning is figurative or derived, are inseparable and unstressed, e.g., durchschnei'den *cut across, traverse.*

4. A compound prefix is (a) inseparable if it consists of an inseparable prefix plus a separable prefix, e.g., beauf'tragen, (b) separable if it consists of a separable prefix plus an inseparable prefix, e.g.,vor'bereiten—er bereitet etwas vor, and (c) separable if it consists of two separable prefixes, e.g., vorbei'laufen—sie lief vorbei. Although verbs falling under (b) are separable, they do not take –ge– in the past participle, e.g., vor'bereitet (past participle of vorbereiten). But they do take the infix –zu– in the infinitive, e.g., vor'-zubereiten. Note that compound prefixes falling under (c) are stressed on the second of the two separable components.

§13. German verbs are regarded as reflexive regardless of whether the reflexive pronoun is the direct or indirect object of the verb.

§14. The declension of German nouns is shown by giving the genitive singular followed by the nominative plural, in parentheses after the abbreviation indicating gender. This is done by presenting the whole noun by a hyphen with which the ending and/or the umlaut may or may not be shown according to the inflection; e.g., Stadt [ʃtat] *f* (-;⸚e) means der Stadt and die Städte. If the noun has no plural, the closing parenthesis comes immediately after the semicolon following the genitive singular, e.g., Kleidung ['klaɪduŋ] *f* (-;). In loan words in which the ending changes in the plural, the centered period is used to mark off the portion of the word that has to be detached before the portion showing the plural form is added, e.g., Da·tum ['datum] *n* (-s;-ten [tən]).

When a vowel is added to a word ending in ß, the ß remains if it is preceded by a diphthong or one of the following vowel sounds: [ɑ], [e], [i], [o], [ø], [y], e.g., Stoß [ʃtos], plural: Stöße; Strauß, plural: Sträuße, but changes to ss if it is preceded by one of the following vowel sounds: [a], [ɛ], [ɪ], [ɔ], [œ], [u], [ʏ], e.g., Roß [rɔs], plural Rosses. In this Dictionary the inflection of words in which ß does not change is shown in the usual way, e.g., Stoß [ʃtos] *m* (-es;⸚e); Strauß [ʃtraus] *m* (-es;⸚e), while the inflection of words in which ß changes to ss is shown in monosyllables by repeating the full word in its inflected forms, e.g., Roß [rɔs] *n* (Rosses; Rosse) and in polysyllables by marking off with a centered dot the final syllable and then repeating it in its inflected forms, e.g., Ver·laß [fer'las] *m* (-lasses;).

§15. When a word ending in a double consonant is combined with a following word beginning with the same single consonant followed by a vowel, the resultant group of three identical consonants is shortened to two, e.g., Schiff combined with Fahrt makes Schiffahrt and Schall combined with Lehre makes

Schallehre.[1] However, when such a compound as a vocabulary entry has to be divided by an accent mark, the word is first spelled with two identical consonants and is then repeated in parentheses with three identical consonants, e.g., **Schiffahrt (Schiff′fahrt).** Furthermore, when such a compound has to be divided because the first component comes at the end of a line and is followed by a hyphen and the second component begins the following line, the three consonants are used, e.g., **Schiff–fahrt** and **Schall–lehre.**

When the medial group **ck** in a vocabulary entry has to be divided by an accent mark, the word is first spelled with **ck** and is then repeated in parentheses with the **ck** changed to **kk** in accordance with the orthographic principle which requires this change when the division comes at the end of the line, e.g., **Deckenlicht (Dek′kenlicht).**

---

[1] If the intial consonant of the following word is followed by a consonant instead of a vowel, the group of three identical consonants remains, e.g., **Fetttropfen, Rohstofffrage.**

German Model Verbs

These verbs are models for all the verbs that appear as vocabulary entries in the German-English part of this Dictionary. If a section number referring to this table is not given with an entry, it is understood that the verb is a weak verb conjugated like **loben, reden, handeln,** or **warten.** If a section number is given, it is understood that the verb is a strong, mixed, or irregular verb and that it is identical in all forms with the model referred to in its radical vowel or diphthong and the consonants that follow the radical. Thus **schneiden** is numbered §106 to refer to the model **leiden.** Such words include the model itself, e.g., **denken,** numbered §66 to refer to the model **denken,** compounds of the model, e.g., **bekommen,** numbered §99 to refer to the model **kommen,** and verbs that have the same radical component, e.g., **empfehlen,** numbered §51 to refer to the model **befehlen.**

If a strong or mixed verb in a given function (transitive or intransitive) and/or meaning may be conjugated also as a weak verb, this is indicated by the insertion of the section number of the appropriate weak verb (**loben, handeln, reden,** or **warten**) after the section number of the model strong verb, e.g., **dingen** §142 & §109.

If a strong or mixed verb in a different function is conjugated as a weak verb, this is indicated by dividing the two functions by parallels and showing the conjugation of each by the insertion of the appropriate section numbers, e.g., **hängen** §92 *tr* . . . ‖ §109 *intr*.

If a strong or mixed verb in a different meaning is conjugated as a weak verb, this is indicated by dividing the two meanings by parallels and showing the conjugation of each by the insertion of the appropriate section numbers, e.g., **bewegen** *tr* move, set in motion . . . ‖ §56 *tr* move, induce.

It is understood that verbs with inseparable prefixes, verbs with compound separable prefixes of which the first component is separable and the second inseparable, and verbs ending in –ieren do not take ge in the past participle.

No account is taken here of the auxiliary used in forming compound tenses. The use of SEIN is indicated in the body of the Dictionary.

Alternate forms are listed in parentheses immediately below the corresponding principal part of the model verb.

	INFINITIVE	3D SG PRESENT INDICATIVE	IMPERFECT INDICATIVE	IMPERFECT SUBJUNCTIVE	PAST PARTICIPLE
§50	backen	bäckt	buk	büke	gebacken
§51	befehlen	befiehlt	befahl	beföhle	befohlen
§52	beginnen	beginnt	begann	begönne (begänne)	begonnen
§53	beißen	beißt	biß	bisse	gebissen
§54	bergen	birgt	barg	bärge (bürge)	geborgen
§55	bersten	birst (berstet)	barst	bärste (börste)	geborsten
§56	bewegen	bewegt	bewog	bewöge	bewogen
§57	biegen	biegt	bog	böge	gebogen
§58	bieten	bietet	bot	böte	geboten
§59	binden	bindet	band	bände	gebunden
§60	bitten	bittet	bat	bäte	gebeten
§61	blasen	bläst	blies	bliese	geblasen
§62	bleiben	bleibt	blieb	bliebe	geblieben
§63	braten	brät	briet	briete	gebraten
§64	brechen	bricht	brach	bräche	gebrochen
§65	bringen	bringt	brachte	brächte	gebracht
§66	denken	denkt	dachte	dächte	gedacht
§67	dreschen	drischt	drosch (drasch)	drösche (dräsche)	gedroschen
§68	dünken	dünkt (deucht)	dünkte (deuchte)	dünkte (deuchte)	gedünkt (gedeucht)

15a

	INFINITIVE	3D SG PRESENT INDICATIVE	IMPERFECT INDICATIVE	IMPERFECT SUBJUNCTIVE	PAST PARTICIPLE
§69	dürfen	darf	durfte	dürfte	gedurft (dürfen)
§70	essen	ißt	aß	äße	gegessen
§71	fahren	fährt	fuhr	führe	gefahren
§72	fallen	fällt	fiel	fiele	gefallen
§73	fangen	fängt	fing	finge	gefangen
§74	fechten	ficht	focht	föchte	gefochten
§75	fliehen	flieht	floh	flöhe	geflohen
§76	fließen	fließt	floß	flösse	geflossen
§77	frieren	friert	fror	fröre	gefroren
§78	gären	gärt	gor	göre	gegoren
§79	gebären	gebiert	gebar	gebäre	geboren
§80	geben	gibt	gab	gäbe	gegeben
§81	gedeihen	gedeiht	gedieh	gediehe	gediehen
§82	gehen	geht	ging	ginge	gegangen
§83	gelten	gilt	galt	gälte (gölte)	gegolten
§84	genesen	genest	genas	genäse	genesen
§85	gleichen	gleicht	glich	gliche	geglichen
§86	gleiten	gleitet	glitt	glitte	geglitten
§87	graben	gräbt	grub	grübe	gegraben
§88	greifen	greift	griff	griffe	gegriffen
§89	haben	hat	hatte	hätte	gehabt
§90	halten	hält	hielt	hielte	gehalten

	INFINITIVE	3D SG PRESENT INDICATIVE	IMPERFECT INDICATIVE	IMPERFECT SUBJUNCTIVE	PAST PARTICIPLE
§91	handeln	handelt	handelte	handelte	gehandelt
§92	hängen	hängt	hing	hinge	gehangen
§93	hauen	haut	hieb	hiebe	gehauen
§94	heben	hebt	hob	höbe	gehoben
§95	heißen	heißt	hieß	hieße	geheißen
§96	helfen	hilft	half	hälfe	geholfen
				(hülfe)	
§97	kennen	kennt	kannte	kennte	gekannt
§98	kiesen	kiest	kor	köre	gekoren
§99	kommen	kommt	kam	käme	gekommen
§100	können	kann	konnte	könnte	gekonnt
					(können)
§101	kreischen	kreischt	kreischte	kreischte	gekreischt
			(krisch)	(krische)	(gekrischen)
§102	kriechen	kriecht	kroch	kröche	gekrochen
§103	laden	lädt	lud	lüde	geladen
§104	lassen	läßt	ließ	ließe	gelassen
§105	laufen	läuft	lief	liefe	gelaufen
§106	leiden	leidet	litt	litte	gelitten
§107	lesen	liest	las	läse	gelesen
§108	liegen	liegt	lag	läge	gelegen
§109	loben	lobt	lobte	lobte	gelobt
§110	löschen	lischt	losch	lösche	geloschen
§111	lügen	lügt	log	löge	gelogen

	INFINITIVE	3D SG PRESENT INDICATIVE	IMPERFECT INDICATIVE	IMPERFECT SUBJUNCTIVE	PAST PARTICIPLE
§112	meiden	meidet	mied	miede	gemieden
§113	melken	melkt	molk	mölke	gemolken
§114	mögen	mag	mochte	möchte	gemocht (mögen)
§115	müssen	muß	mußte	müßte	gemußt (müssen)
§116	nehmen	nimmt	nahm	nähme	genommen
§117	pflegen	pflegt	pflog	pflöge	gepflogen
§118	preisen	preist	pries	priese	gepriesen
§119	quellen	quillt	quoll	quölle	gequollen
§120	reden	redet	redete	redete	geredet
§121	rinnen	rinnt	rann	ränne (rönne)	geronnen
§122	rufen	ruft	rief	riefe	gerufen
§123	salzen	salzt	salzte	salzte	gesalzen
§124	saufen	säuft	soff	söffe	gesoffen
§125	saugen	saugt	sog	söge	gesogen
§126	schaffen	schafft	schuf	schüfe	geschaffen
§127	schallen	schallt	scholl	schölle	geschollen
§128	scheinen	scheint	schien	schiene	geschienen
§129	scheren	schert (schiert)	schor	schöre	geschoren
§130	schieben	schiebt	schob	schöbe	geschoben
§131	schlafen	schläft	schlief	schliefe	geschlafen

18a

	INFINITIVE	3d SG PRESENT INDICATIVE	IMPERFECT INDICATIVE	IMPERFECT SUBJUNCTIVE	PAST PARTICIPLE
§132	schlagen	schlägt	schlug	schlüge	geschlagen
§133	schmelzen	schmilzt	schmolz	schmölze	geschmolzen
§134	schrecken	schrickt	schrak	schräke	geschrocken
§135	schreien	schreit	schrie	schriee	geschrie(e)n
§136	schwimmen	schwimmt	schwamm	schwämme (schwömme)	geschwommen
§137	schwören	schwört	schwur (schwor)	schwüre	geschworen
§138	sehen	sieht	sah	sähe	gesehen
§139	sein	ist	war	wäre	gewesen
§140	senden	sendet	sandte	sendete	gesandt
§141	sieden	siedet	sott	sötte	gesotten
§142	singen	singt	sang	sänge	gesungen
§143	sinken	sinkt	sank	sänke	gesunken
§144	sitzen	sitzt	saß	säße	gesessen
§145	sollen	soll	sollte	sollte	gesollt (sollen)
§146	stehen	steht	stand	stände (stünde)	gestanden
§147	stehlen	stiehlt	stahl	stähle (stöhle)	gestohlen
§148	steigen	steigt	stieg	stiege	gestiegen
§149	sterben	stirbt	starb	stürbe	gestorben
§150	stoßen	stößt	stieß	stieße	gestoßen

19a

	INFINITIVE	3D SG PRESENT INDICATIVE	IMPERFECT INDICATIVE	IMPERFECT SUBJUNCTIVE	PAST PARTICIPLE
§151	treffen	trifft	traf	träfe	getroffen
§152	treten	tritt	trat	träte	getreten
§153	triefen	trieft	troff	tröffe	getroffen
§154	tun	tut	tat	täte	getan
§155	wachsen	wächst	wuchs	wüchse	gewachsen
§156	wägen	wiegt	wog	wöge	gewogen
§157	warten	wartet	wartete	wartete	gewartet
§158	waschen	wäscht	wusch	wüsche	gewaschen
§159	werden	wird	wurde (ward)	würde	geworden (worden)
§160	werfen	wirft	warf	würfe	geworfen
§161	wissen	weiß	wußte	wüßte	gewußt
§162	wollen	will	wollte	wollte	gewollt (wollen)
§163	ziehen	zieht	zog	zöge	gezogen
§164	klimmen	klimmt	klomm	klömme	geklommen
§165	küren	kürt	kor	köre	gekoren
§166	schinden	schindet	schund	schünde	geschunden

Die Aussprache des Englischen

Die nachstehenden Lautzeichen bezeichnen fast alle Laute der englischen Sprache:

VOKALE		
LAUTZEICHEN	**UNGEFÄHRER LAUT**	**BEISPIEL**
[æ]	Offener als *ä* in *hätte*	**hat** [hæt]
[ɑ]	Wie *a* in *Vater* Wie *a* in *Mann*	**father** ['fɑðər] **proper** ['prɑpər]
[ɛ]	Wie *e* in *Fett*	**met** [mɛt]
[e]	Offener als *eej* in *Seejungfrau*	**fate** [fet] **they** [ðe]
[ə]	Wie *e* in *finden*	**haven** ['hɛvən] **pardon** ['pɑrdən]
[i]	Wie *ie* in *sie*	**she** [ʃi] **machine** [mə'ʃin]
[ɪ]	Offener als *i* in *bitte*	**fit** [fɪt] **beer** [bɪr]
[o]	Offenes *o* mit anschließendem kurzem (halbvokalischem) *u*	**nose** [noz] **road** [rod] **row** [ro]
[ɔ]	Wie *o* in *oft*	**bought** [bɔt] **law** [lɔ]
[ʌ]	Wie *er* in *jeder* (umgangssprachlich)	**cup** [kʌp] **come** [kʌm] **mother** ['mʌðər]
[ʊ]	Wie *u* in *Fluß*	**pull** [pʊl] **book** [bʊk] **wolf** [wʊlf]
[u]	Wie *u* in *Fluß*	**move** [muv] **tomb** [tum]

DIPHTHONGE		
LAUTZEICHEN	**UNGEFÄHRER LAUT**	**BEISPIEL**
[aɪ]	Wie *ei* in *nein*	**night** [naɪt] **eye** [aɪ]
[aʊ]	Wie *au* in *Haus*	**found** [faʊnd] **cow** [kaʊ]
[ɔɪ]	Wie *eu* in *heute*	**voice** [vɔɪs] **oil** [ɔɪl]

KONSONANTEN		
LAUTZEICHEN	**UNGEFÄHRER LAUT**	**BEISPIEL**
[b]	Wie *b* in *bin*	**bed** [bɛd] **robber** ['rɑbər]

LAUTZEICHEN	UNGEFÄHRER LAUT	BEISPIEL
[d]	Wie *d* in *du*	**dead** [dɛd] **add** [æd]
[dʒ]	Wie *dsch* in *Dschungel*	**gem** [dʒem] **jail** [dʒel]
[ð]	*d* als Reibelaut ausgesprochen	**this** [ðɪs] **Father** [ˈfɑðər]
[f]	Wie *f* in *fett*	**face** [fes] **phone** [fon]
[g]	Wie *g* in *gehen*	**go** [go] **get** [gɛt]
[h]	Wie *h* in *Haus*	**hot** [hɑt] **alcohol** [ˈælkəˌhɔl]
[j]	Wie *j* in *ja*	**yes** [jes] **unit** [ˈjunɪt]
[k]	Wie *k* in *kann*	**cat** [kæt] **chord** [kɔrd] **kill** [kɪl]
[l]	Wie *l* in *lang*, aber mit angehobenem Zungenrücken	**late** [let] **allow** [əˈlaʊ]
[m]	Wie *m* in *mehr*	**more** [mor] **command** [kəˈmænd]
[n]	Wie *n* in *Nest*	**nest** [nest] **manner** [ˈmænər]
[ŋ]	Wie *ng* in *singen*	**king** [kɪŋ] **conquer** [ˈkɑŋkər]
[p]	Wie *p* in *Pech*	**pen** [pen] **cap** [kæp]
[r]	Im Gegensatz zum deutschen gerollten Zungenspitzen- oder Zäpfchen-r, ist das englische *r* mit retroflexer Zungenstellung und gerundeten Lippen zu artikulieren.	**run** [rʌn] **far** [fɑr] **art** [ɑrt] **carry** [ˈkæri]
[s]	Wie *s* in *es*	**send** [send] **cellar** [ˈselər]
[ʃ]	Wie *sch* in *Schule*	**shall** [ʃæl] **machine** [məˈʃin] **nation** [ˈneʃən]
[t]	Wie *t* in *Tee*	**ten** [ten] **dropped** [drɑpt]
[tʃ]	Wie *tsch* in *deutsch*	**child** [tʃaɪld] **much** [mʌtʃ] **nature** [ˈnetʃər]
[θ]	Ist als stimmloser linguadentaler Lispellaut zu artikulieren	**think** [θɪŋk] **truth** [truθ]
[v]	Wie *w* in *was*	**vest** [vest] **over** [ˈovər] **of** [ɑv]
[w]	Ist als Halbvokal zu artikulieren	**work** [wʌrk] **tweed** [twid] **queen** [kwin]
[z]	Ist stimmhaft zu artikulieren wie *s* in *so*	**zeal** [zil] **busy** [ˈbɪzi] **his** [hɪz] **winds** [wɪndz]
[ʒ]	Wie *j* in *Jalousie*	**azure** [ˈeʒər] **measure** [ˈmeʒər]

Aussprache der zusammengesetzten Wörter

Im englisch-deutschen Teil dieses Wörterbuches ist die Aussprache aller einfachen englischen Wörter in einer Neufassung der Lautzeichen des Internationalen Phonetischen Alphabets in eckigen Klammern angegeben.

Außer den mit Präfixen, Suffixen und Wortbildungselementen gebildeten Zusammensetzungen gibt es im Englischen drei Arten von zusammengesetzten Wörtern: (1) zusammengeschriebene, z.B. **bookcase** Bücherregal, (2) mit Bindestrich geschriebene, z.B. **short-circuit** kurzschließen, und (3) getrennt geschriebene, z.B. **post card** Postkarte. Die Aussprache der englischen zusammengesetzten Wörter ist nicht angegeben, sofern die Aussprache der Bestandteile an der Stelle angegeben ist, wo sie als selbständige Stichwörter erscheinen; angegeben ist jedoch die Betonung durch Haupt- und Nebentonakzent und zwar jeweils am Ende der betonten Silben, z.B. **book′case′**, **short′-cir′cuit**, **post′ card′**.

In Hauptwörtern, in denen der Nebenton auf den Bestandteilen **-man** und **-men** liegt, wird der Vokal dieser Bestandteile wie in den Wörtern **man** und **men** ausgesprochen, z.B. **mailman** ['mel͵mæn] und **mailmen** ['mel͵men]. In Hauptwörtern, in denen diese Bestandteile unbetont bleiben, wird der Vokal beider Bestandteile als schwa ausgesprochen, z.B. **policeman** [pə'lismən] und **policemen** [pə'lismən]. Es gibt Hauptwörter, in denen diese Bestandteile entweder mit dem Nebenton oder unbetont ausgesprochen werden, z.B. **doorman** ['dɔr͵mæn] oder ['dɔrmən] und **doormen** ['dɔr͵men] oder ['dɔrmən]. In diesem Wörterbuch ist die Lautschrift für diese Wörter nicht angegeben, sofern sie für den ersten Bestandteil dort angeführt ist, wo er als Stichwort erscheint; angegeben sind jedoch Haupt- und Nebenton:

> **mail′man** s (**–men′**)
> **police′man** s (**–men**)
> **door′man′** & **door′man** s (**–men′** & **–men**)

Aussprache des Partizip Perfekt

Bei Wörtern, die auf **–ed** (oder **–d** nach stummem e) enden und nach den nachstehenden Regeln ausgesprochen werden, ist die Aussprache in diesem Wörterbuch nicht angegeben, sofern sie für die endungslose Form dort angegeben ist, wo diese als Stichwort erscheint. Die Doppelschreibung des Schlußkonsonanten nach einfachem betonten Vokal hat keinen Einfluß auf die Aussprache der Endung **–ed**.

Die Endung **–ed** (oder **–d** nach stummem e) der Vergangenheit, des Partizip Perfekt und gewisser Adjektive hat drei verschiedene Aussprachen je nach dem Klang des Konsonanten am Stammende.

1) Wenn der Stamm auf einen stimmhaften Konsonanten mit Ausnahme von [d] ausgeht, nämlich [b], [g], [l], [m], [n], [ŋ], [r], [v], [z], [ʒ], oder auf einen Vokal, wird **–ed** als [d] ausgesprochen.

KLANG DES STAMMENDES	INFINITIV	VERGANGENHEIT UND PARTIZIP PERFEKT
[b]	ebb [ɛb]	ebbed [ɛbd]
	rob [rɑb]	robbed [rɑbd]
	robe [rob]	robed [robd]
[g]	egg [ɛg]	egged [ɛgd]
	sag [sæg]	sagged [sægd]
[l]	mail [mel]	mailed [meld]
	scale [skel]	scaled [skeld]
[m]	storm [stɔrm]	stormed [stɔrmd]
	bomb [bɑm]	bombed [bɑmd]
	name [nem]	named [nemd]
[n]	tan [tæn]	tanned [tænd]
	sign [saɪn]	signed [saɪnd]
	mine [maɪn]	mined [maɪnd]
[ŋ]	hang [hæŋ]	hanged [hæŋd]
[r]	fear [fɪr]	feared [fɪrd]
	care [kɛr]	cared [kɛrd]
[v]	rev [rɛv]	revved [rɛvd]
	save [sev]	saved [sevd]
[z]	buzz [bʌz]	buzzed [bʌzd]
[ð]	smooth [smuð]	smoothed [smuðd]
	bathe [beð]	bathed [beðd]
[ʒ]	massage [mə'sɑʒ]	massaged [mə'sɑʒd]
[dʒ]	page [pedʒ]	paged [pedʒd]
Klang des Vokals	key [ki]	keyed [kid]
	sigh [saɪ]	sighed [saɪd]
	paw [pɔ]	pawed [pɔd]

2) Wenn der Stamm auf einen stimmlosen Konsonanten mit Ausnahme von [t] ausgeht, nämlich: [f], [k], [p], [s], [θ], [ʃ] oder [tʃ], wird –ed als [t] ausgesprochen.

KLANG DES STAMMENDES	INFINITIV	VERGANGENHEIT UND PARTIZIP PERFEKT
[f]	loaf [lof] knife [naɪf]	loafed [loft] knifed [naɪft]
[k]	back [bæk] bake [bek]	backed [bækt] baked [bekt]
[p]	cap [kæp] wipe [waɪp]	capped [kæpt] wiped [waɪpt]
[s]	hiss [hɪs] mix [mɪks]	hissed [hɪst] mixed [mɪkst]
[θ]	lath [læθ]	lathed [læθt]
[ʃ]	mash [mæʃ]	mashed [mæʃt]
[tʃ]	match [mætʃ]	matched [mætʃt]

3) Wenn der Stamm auf einen Dentallaut ausgeht, nämlich: [t] oder [d], wird –ed als [ɪd] oder [əd] ausgesprochen.

KLANG DES STAMMENDES	INFINITIV	VERGANGENHEIT UND PARTIZIP PERFEKT
[t]	wait [wet] mate [met]	waited ['wetɪd] mated ['metɪd]
[d]	mend [mend] wade [wed]	mended ['mɛndɪd] waded ['wedɪd]

Es ist zu beachten, daß die Doppelschreibung des Schlußkonsonanten nach einem einfachen betonten Vokal die Aussprache der Endung –ed nicht beeinflußt: **batted** ['bætɪd], **dropped** [drɑpt], **robbed** [rɑbd].

Diese Regeln gelten auch für zusammengesetzte Adjektive, die auf –ed enden. Für diese Adjektive ist nur die Betonung angegeben, sofern die Aussprache der beiden Bestandteile ohne die Endung –ed dort angegeben ist, wo sie als Stichwörter erscheinen, z.B. **o'pen-mind'ed**.

Es ist jedoch zu beachten, daß bei manchen Adjektiven, deren Stamm auf einen anderen Konsonanten als [d] oder [t] ausgeht, das –ed als [ɪd] ausgesprochen wird; in diesem Fall ist die volle Aussprache in phonetischer Umschrift angegeben, z.B. **blessed** ['blesɪd], **crabbed** ['kræbɪd].

PART TWO

English-German

ENGLISH—GERMAN

A

A, a [e] *s* erster Buchstabe des englischen Alphabets; (mus) A *n*; **A flat** As *n*; **A sharp** Ais *n*

a [e], [ə] *indef art* ein ‖ *prep* pro; **once a year** einmal im Jahr

abandon [ə'bændən] *s*—**with a.** rückhaltlos ‖ *tr* (*forsake*) verlassen; (*give up*) aufgeben; (*a child*) aussetzen; (*a position*) (mil) überlassen; **a. oneself to** sich ergeben (*dat*)

abase [ə'bes] *tr* demütigen

abasement [ə'besmənt] *s* Demütigung *f*

abashed [ə'bæʃt] *adj* fassungslos

abate [ə'bet] *tr* mäßigen ‖ *intr* nachlassen

abbess ['æbɪs] *s* Äbtissin *f*

abbey ['æbi] *s* Abtei *f*

abbot ['æbət] *s* Abt *m*

abbreviate [ə'brivɪ,et] *tr* abkürzen

abbreviation [ə,brivɪ'eʃən] *s* Abkürzung *f*

ABC's [,e,bi'siz] *spl* Abc *n*

abdicate ['æbdɪ,ket] *tr* niederlegen; (*a right, claim*) verzichten auf (*acc*) ‖ *intr* abdanken

abdomen ['æbdəmən] *s* Unterleib *m*

abdominal [æb'dɑmɪnəl] *adj* Unterleibs-

abduct [æb'dʌkt] *tr* entführen

abet [ə'bet] *v* (*pret & pp* **abetted;** *ger* **abetting**) *tr* (*a person*) aufhetzen; (*a crime*) Vorschub leisten (*dat*)

abeyance [ə'be·əns] *s*—**in a.** in der Schwebe

ab·hor [æb'hɔr] *v* (*pret & pp* —**horred;** *ger* —**horring**) *tr* verabscheuen

abhorrent [æb'hɔrənt] *adj* verhaßt

abide [ə'baɪd] *v* (*pret & pp* **abode** [ə'bod] & **abided**) *intr*—**a. by** (*an agreement*) sich halten an (*acc*); (*a promise*) halten

ability [ə'bɪlɪti] *s* Fähigkeit *f*; **to the best of one's a.** nach bestem Vermögen

abject [æb'dʒɛkt] *adj* (*servile*) unterwürfig; (*poverty*) äußerst

ablative ['æblətɪv] *s* Ablativ *m*

ablaze [ə'blez] *adj* in Flammen; (**with**) glänzend (vor *dat*); (**excited**) (**with**) erregt (vor *dat*)

able ['ebəl] *adj* fähig, tüchtig; **be a. to** (*inf*) können (*inf*)

able-bodied ['ebəl'bɑdid] *adj* kräftig; (mil) wehrfähig; **a. seaman** Vollmatrose *m*

ably ['ebli] *adv* mit Geschick

abnormal [æb'nɔrməl] *adj* abnorm

abnormality [,æbnər'mælɪti] *s* Ungewöhnlichkeit *f*; (pathol) Mißbildung *f*

abnor′mal psychol′ogy *s* Psychopathologie *f*

aboard [ə'bord] *adv* an Bord; **all a.!** (*a ship*) alles an Bord! (*a bus, plane, train*) alles einsteigen! ‖ *prep* (*a ship*) an Bord (*genit*); (*a bus, train*) in (*dat*)

abode [ə'bod] *s* Wohnsitz *m*

abolish [ə'bɑlɪʃ] *tr* aufheben, abschaffen

abominable [ə'bɑmɪnəbəl] *adj* abscheulich

aborigines [,æbə'rɪdʒɪ,niz] *spl* Ureinwohner *pl*, Urvolk *n*

abort [ə'bɔrt] *tr* (rok) vorzeitig zur Explosion bringen ‖ *intr* fehlgebären; (fig) fehlschlagen

abortion [ə'bɔrʃən] *s* Abtreibung *f*

abortive [ə'bɔrtɪv] *adj* (fig) mißlungen; **prove a.** fehlschlagen

abound [ə'baund] *intr* reichlich vorhanden sein; **a. in** reich sein an (*dat*)

about [ə'baut] *adv* umher, herum; (*approximately*) ungefähr, etwa; **be a. to** (*inf*) im Begriff sein zu (*inf*) ‖ *prep* (*around*) um (*acc*); (*concerning*) über (*acc*); (*approximately at*) gegen (*acc*)

about′ face′ *interj* kehrt!

about′-face′ *s*—**do an a.** (fig) umschwenken; **complete a.** (fig) völliger Umschwung *m*

above [ə'bʌv] *adj* obig ‖ *adv* oben, droben ‖ *prep* (*position*) über (*dat*); (*direction*) über (*acc*); (*physically*) oberhalb (*genit*); **a. all** vor allem

above′ board′ *adj* & *adv* ehrlich, redlich

above′-men′tioned *adj* obenerwähnt, obig

abrasion [ə'breʒən] *s* Abschleifen *n*; (*of the skin*) Abschürfung *f*

abrasive [ə'bresɪv] *adj* abschleifend; (*character*) auf die Nerven gehend ‖ *s* Schleifmittel *n*

abreast [ə'brest] *adj* & *adv* nebeneinander; **keep a. of** Schritt halten mit

abridge [ə'brɪdʒ] *tr* verkürzen

abridgement [ə'brɪdʒmənt] *s* Verkürzung *f*

abroad [ə'brɔd] *adv* im Ausland; (*direction*) ins Ausland; (*out of doors*) draußen

abrogate ['æbrə,get] *tr* abschaffen

abrupt [ə'brʌpt] *adj* (*sudden*) jäh; (*curt*) schroff; (*change*) unvermittelt; (*style*) abgerissen

abscess ['æbsɛs] *s* Geschwür *n*, Abszeß *m*

abscond [æb'skɑnd] *intr* (**with**) durchgehen (mit)

absence ['æbsəns] *s* Abwesenheit *f*; (*lack*) Mangel *m*; **in the a. of** in Ermangelung von (or *genit*)

ab'sence without' leave' s unerlaubte Entfernung f von der Truppe

absent ['æbsənt] adj abwesend; **be a. fehlen** ‖ [æb'sent] tr—a. oneself (stay away) fernbleiben; (go away) sich entfernen

absentee [,æbsən'ti] s Abwesende mf

ab'sent-mind'ed adj geistesabwesend

absolute ['æbsə,lut] adj absolut

absolutely ['æbsə,lutlı] adj. absolut, völlig ‖ [,æbsə'lutlı] adv (coll) ganz bestimmt, jawohl; **a. not!** keine Rede!

absolve [æb'salv] tr (from sin, an obligation) lossprechen; (sins) vergeben

absorb [æb'sɔrb] tr aufsaugen; (a shock) dämpfen; (engross) ganz in Anspruch nehmen; **be absorbed in** vertieft sein in (acc)

absorbent [æb'sɔrbənt] adj aufsaugend
absor'bent cot'ton s Verbandswatte f

absorbing adj (fig) packend

abstain [æb'sten] intr (from) sich enthalten (genit); (parl) sich der Stimme enthalten

abstention [æb'stenʃən] s (from) Enthaltung f (von); (parl) Stimmenthaltung f

abstinence ['æbstınəns] s Enthaltsamkeit f; (from) Enthaltung f (von)

abstinent ['æbstınənt] adj enthaltsam

abstract ['æbstrækt] adj abstrakt ‖ s (summary) Abriß m; **in the a.** im und für sich (betrachtet) ‖ [æb'strækt] tr (the general from the specific) abstrahieren; (summarize) kurz zusammenfassen; (purloin) entwenden

abstruse [æb'strus] adj dunkel

absurd [æb'sʌrd] adj unsinnig

absurdity [æb'sʌrdıtı] s Unsinn m

abundance [ə'bʌndəns] s (of) Fülle f (von), Überfluß m (an dat, von)

abundant [ə'bʌndənt] adj reichlich; **a. in** reich an (dat)

abuse [ə'bjus] s (misuse) Mißbrauch m; (insult) Beschimpfung f; (physical ill-treatment) Mißhandlung f ‖ [ə'bjuz] tr mißhandeln; (insult) beschimpfen; (ill-treat) mißhandeln; (a girl) schänden

abusive [ə'bjusıv] adj mißbräuchlich; (treatment) beleidigend; **a. language** Schimpfworte pl; **become a.** ausfällig werden

abut [ə'bʌt] v (pret & pp abutted; ger abutting) intr—a. on grenzen an (acc)

abutment [ə'bʌtmənt] s (of arch) Strebepfeiler m; (of bridge) Widerlager m

abyss [ə'bıs] s Abgrund m

academic [,ækə'demık] adj akademisch

academ'ic gown' s Talar m

academy [ə'kædəmı] s Akademie f

accede [æk'sid] intr beistimmen; **a. to** (s.o.'s wishes) gewähren; (an agreement) beitreten (dat); **a. to the throne** den Thron besteigen

accelerate [æk'sɛlə,ret] tr & intr beschleunigen

accelerator [æk'sɛlə,retər] s Gashebel m

accent ['æksɛnt] s (stress) Betonung f; (peculiar pronunciation) Akzent m ‖ [æk'sɛnt] tr betonen

ac'cent mark' s Tonzeichen n, Akzent m

accentuate [æk'sɛntʃʊ,et] tr betonen

accept [æk'sɛpt] tr annehmen; (one's fate, blame) auf sich [acc] nehmen; (put up with) hinnehmen; (recognize) anerkennen

acceptable [æk'sɛptəbəl] adj annehmbar; (pleasing) angenehm; (welcome) willkommen

acceptance [æk'sɛptəns] s Annahme f; (recognition) Anerkennung f

access ['æksɛs] s Zugang m; (to a person) Zutritt m; (data proc) Zugriff m

accessible [æk'sɛsıbəl] adj (to) zugänglich (für)

accession [æk'sɛʃən] s (to an office) Antritt m; **a. to the throne** Thronbesteigung f

accessory [æk'sɛsərı] adj (subordinate) untergeordnet; (additional) zusätzlich ‖ s Zubehörteil n; (to a crime) Teilnehmer –in mf; (after the fact) Begünstiger –in mf; (before the fact) Anstifter –in mf

ac'cess road' s Zufahrtsstraße f; (on a turnpike) Zubringerstraße f

accident ['æksıdənt] s (mishap) Unfall m; (chance) Zufall m; **by a.** zufälligerweise; **have an a.** verunglücken

accidental [,æksı'dɛntəl] adj zufällig; **a. death** Unfalltod m ‖ s (mus) Versetzungszeichen n

acclaim [ə'klem] s Beifall m ‖ tr (e.g., as king) begrüßen, akklamieren

acclamation [,æklə'meʃən] s Beifall m

acclimate ['æklı,met] tr akklimatisieren ‖ intr (to) sich gewöhnen (an acc)

accommodate [ə'kamə,det] tr (oblige) aushelfen (dat); (have room for) Platz haben für

accom'modating adj gefällig

accommodation [ə,kamə'deʃən] s (convenience) Annehmlichkeit f; (adaptation, adjustment) Anpassung f; (willingness to please) Gefälligkeit f; (compromise) Übereinkommen n; **accommodations** (lodgings) Unterkunft f

accompaniment [ə'kʌmpənımənt] s Begleitung f

accompanist [ə'kʌmpənıst] s Begleiter –in mf

accompany [ə'kʌmpənı] v (pret & pp -nied) tr begleiten

accomplice [ə'kamplıs] m Mitschuldige mf

accomplish [ə'kamplıʃ] tr (a task) vollenden; (a goal) erreichen

accom'plished adj (skilled) ausgezeichnet

accomplishment [ə'kamplıʃmənt] s (completion) Vollendung f; (achievement) Leistung f

accord [ə'kɔrd] s Übereinstimmung f; **in a. with** übereinstimmend mit; **of**

one's own a. aus eigenem Antriebe || *tr* gewähren || *intr* übereinstimmen
accordingly [ə'kɔrdɪŋlɪ] *adv* demgemäß
accord'ing to' *prep* gemäß (*dat*), laut (*genit* or *dat*), nach (*dat*)
accordion [ə'kɔrdɪ-ən] *s* Akkordeon *n*
accost [ə'kɔst] *tr* ansprechen
account [ə'kaunt] *s* Rechnung *f*; (*narrative*) Erzählung *f*; (*report*) Bericht *m*; (*importance*) Bedeutung *f*; (com) Konto *n*; **by all accounts** nach allem, was man hört; **call to a.** zur Rechenschaft ziehen; **on a. of** wegen; **on no a.** auf keinen Fall; **render an a. of s.th. to s.o.** j-m Rechenschaft von etw ablegen; **settle accounts with** (coll) abrechnen mit; **take into a.** in Betracht ziehen
accountable [ə'kauntəbəl] *adj* (*explicable*) erklärlich; (*responsible*) (**for**) verantwortlich (für)
accountant [ə'kauntənt] *s* Rechnungsführer –in *mf*, Buchhalter –in *mf*
account'ing *s* Rechnungswesen *n*
accouterments [ə'kutərmənts] *spl* Ausrüstung *f*
accredit [ə'krɛdɪt] *tr* (e.g., *an ambassador*) beglaubigen; (*a school*) bestätigen; (*a story*) als wahr anerkennen; (*give credit for*) gutschreiben
accrue [ə'kru] *intr* anwachsen; (*said of interest*) auflaufen || *intr* sich anhäufen
accumulation [ə‚kjumjə'leʃən] *s* Anhäufung *f*
accuracy ['ækjərəsɪ] *s* Genauigkeit *f*
accurate ['ækjərɪt] *adj* genau
accursed [ə'kʌrsɪd], [ə'kʌrst] *adj* verwünscht
accusation [‚ækjə'zeʃən] *s* Anschuldigung *f*; (jur) Anklage *f*
accusative [ə'kjuzətɪv] *s* Akkusativ *m*
accuse [ə'kjuz] *tr* (of) beschuldigen (*genit*); (jur) (of) anklagen (wegen)
accustom [ə'kʌstəm] *tr* (to) gewöhnen (an *acc*); **become accustomed to** sich gewöhnen an (*acc*)
ace [es] *s* (aer, cards) As *n*
acetate ['æsɪ‚tet] *s* Azetat *n*; (tex) Azetatseide *f*
ace'tic ac'id [ə'sitɪk] *s* Essigsäure *f*
acetone ['æsɪ‚ton] *s* Azeton *n*
acet'ylene torch' ['æsɛtɪ‚lin] *s* Schweißbrenner *m*
ache [ek] *s* Schmerz *m* || *intr* schmerzen; **a. for** (coll) sich sehnen nach
achieve [ə'tʃiv] *tr* erlangen; (*success*) erzielen; (*a goal*) erreichen
achievement [ə'tʃivmənt] *s* (*something accomplished*) Leistung *f*; (*great deed*) Großtat *f*; (*heroic deed*) Heldentat *f*; (*of one's object*) Erreichung *f*
achieve'ment test' *s* Leistungsprüfung *f*
Achil'les' ten'don [ə'kɪlis] *s* Achillessehne *f*
acid ['æsɪd] *adj* sauer || *s* Säure *f*
acidity [ə'sɪdɪtɪ] *s* Säure *f*, Schärfe *f*; (*of the stomach*) Magensäure *f*
ac'id test' *s* (fig) Feuerprobe *f*
acidy ['æsɪdɪ] *adj* säuerlich, säurig
acknowledge [æk'nɑlɪdʒ] *tr* anerken-

nen; (*admit*) zugeben; (*receipt*) bestätigen
acknowledgment [æk'nɑlɪdʒmənt] *s* Anerkennung *f*; (e.g., *of a letter*) Bestätigung *f*
acme ['ækmɪ] *s* Höhepunkt *m*
acne ['æknɪ] *s* (pathol) Akne *f*
acolyte ['ækə‚laɪt] *s* Ministrant *m*
acorn ['ekɔrn] *s* Eichel *f*
acoustic(al) [ə'kustɪk(əl)] *adj* akustisch, Gehör–, Hör–
acous'tical tile' *s* Dämmplatte *f*
acoustics [ə'kustɪks] *s* & *spl* Akustik *f*
acquaint [ə'kwent] *tr*—**a. s.o. with s.th.** j-n mit etw bekanntmachen, j-m etw mitteilen; **be acquainted with** kennen; **get acquainted with** kennenlernen
acquaintance [ə'kwentəns] *s* Bekanntschaft *f*; (*person*) Bekannte *mf*
acquiesce [‚ækwɪ'ɛs] *intr* (in) einwilligen (in *acc*)
acquiescence [‚ækwɪ'ɛsəns] *s* (in) Einwilligung *f* (in *acc*)
acquire [ə'kwaɪr] *tr* erwerben, sich [*dat*] anschaffen; **a. a taste for** Geschmack gewinnen an (*dat*)
acquisition [‚ækwɪ'zɪʃən] *s* Anschaffung *f*
acquisitive [ə'kwɪzɪtɪv] *adj* gewinnsüchtig
acquit [ə'kwɪt] *v* (*pret* & *pp* **acquitted;** *ger* **acquitting**) *tr* freisprechen
acquittal [ə'kwɪtəl] *s* Freispruch *m*
acre ['ekər] *s* Acre *m*
acreage ['ekərɪdʒ] *s* Fläche *f*
acrid ['ækrɪd] *adj* beißend, scharf
acrobat ['ækrə‚bæt] *s* Akrobat –in *mf*
acrobatic [‚ækrə'bætɪk] *adj* akrobatisch || **acrobatics** *spl* Akrobatik *f*; (aer) Kunstflug *m*
acronym ['ækrənɪm] *s* Akronym *n*
across [ə'krɔs] *adv* herüber, hinüber; **a. from** gegenüber (*dat*); **ten feet a.** zehn Fuß im Durchmesser || *prep* (quer) über (*acc*); (*on the other side of*) jenseits (*genit*); **come a.** (*a person*) treffen; (*a thing*) stoßen auf (*acc*); **come a. with it!** (*say it!*) heraus damit!; (*give it!*) her damit!
across'-the-board' *adj* allgemein
acrostic [ə'krɔstɪk] *s* Akrostichon *n*
act [ækt] *s* Tat *f*, Handlung *f*; (jur) Gesetz *n*; (telv) Nummer *f*; (theat) Akt *m*, Aufzug *m*; **catch in the act** auf frischer Tat ertappen || *tr* spielen; || *intr* (stage action) handeln; (*function*) wirken; (*behave*) (*like*) sich benehmen (wie); (theat & fig) Theater spielen; **act as** dienen als; **act as if** so tun, als ob; **act on** (*follow*) befolgen; (*affect*) (ein)wirken auf (*acc*)
act'ing *adj* stellvertretend; (theat) Bühnen– || *s* (*as an art*) Schauspielkunst *f*
action ['ækʃən] *s* Tätigkeit *f*, Tat *f*; (*effect*) Wirkung *f*; (jur) Klage *f*; (mil) Gefecht *n*; (tech) Wirkungsweise *f*; **go into a.** eingreifen; **put out of a.** (mil) außer Gefecht setzen; (tech) außer Betrieb setzen; **see a.** (mil) an der Front kämpfen

activate [ˈæktɪˌvet] *tr* aktivieren; (mil) aufstellen
active [ˈæktɪv] *adj* tätig; (*member*) ordentlich; (gram, mil) aktiv
ac'tive voice' *s* Tätigkeitsform *f*
activist [ˈæktɪvɪst] *s* Aktivist –in *mf*
activity [ækˈtɪvɪti] *s* Tätigkeit *f*
act' of God' *s* höhere Gewalt *f*
act' of war' *s* Angriffshandlung *f*
actor [ˈæktər] *s* Schauspieler *m*
actress [ˈæktrɪs] *s* Schauspielerin *f*
actual [ˈæktʊˌəl] *adj* wirklich
actually [ˈæktʃʊˌəli] *adv* (*really*) wirklich; (*as a matter of fact*) eigentlich
actuary [ˈæktʃʊˌɛri] *s* Aktuar –in *mf*
actuate [ˈæktʃʊˌet] *tr* in Bewegung setzen; (*incite*) antreiben
acumen [əˈkjumən] *s* Scharfsinn *m*
acupuncture [ˈækjəˌpʌŋktʃər] *s* Akupunktur *f*
acute [əˈkjut] *adj* (*stage, appendicitis*) akut; (*pain*) scharf; (*need*) vordringlich; (*vision*) scharf; (*hearing*) fein; (*problem*) brennend; (*shortage*) bedenklich; (*angle*) spitz
A.D. *abbr* n. Chr. (*nach Christus*)
ad [æd] *s* (coll) Anzeige *f*; **put an ad in the papers** inserieren
adage [ˈædɪdʒ] *s* Sprichwort *n*
adamant [ˈædəmənt] *adj* unnachgiebig
Ad'am's ap'ple [ˈædəmz] *s* Adamsapfel *m*
adapt [əˈdæpt] *tr* (to) anpassen (*dat* or an *acc*); **a. to the stage** für die Bühne bearbeiten; **a. to the screen** verfilmen || *intr* sich anpassen
adaptation [ˌædæpˈteʃən] *s* (*adjustment*) (**to**) Anpassung *f* (an *acc*); (*reworking, rewriting*) (**for**) Bearbeitung *f* (für)
adapter [əˈdæptər] *s* Zwischenstück *n*; (elec) Zwischenstecker *m*
add [æd] *tr* hinzufügen; (math) addieren; **add** (*e.g., 10%*) **to the price** auf den Preis aufschlagen; **add up** zusammenrechnen || *intr* (math) addieren; **add to** (*in number*) vermehren; (*in size*) vergrößern; **add up** (coll) stimmen; **add up to** betragen
adder [ˈædər] *s* Natter *f*, Otter *f*
addict [ˈædɪkt] *s* Süchtige *mf* || [əˈdɪkt] *tr*—**a. oneself to** sich ergeben (*dat*)
addict'ed *adj* ergeben; **a. to drugs** rauschgiftsüchtig
addiction [əˈdɪkʃən] *s* (**to**) Sucht *f* (nach)
add'ing machine' *s* Addiermaschine *f*
addition [əˈdɪʃən] *s* Hinzufügung *f*, Zusatz *m*; (*to a family, possessions*) Zuwachs *m*; (*to a building*) Anbau *m*; (math) Addition *f*; **in a.** außerdem; **in a. to** außer
additional [əˈdɪʃənəl] *adj* zusätzlich
additive [ˈædɪtɪv] *s* Zusatz *m*
address [əˈdrɛs], [ˈædrɛs] *s* Adresse *f*, Anschrift *f* || [əˈdrɛs] *s* Rede *f*; **deliver an a.** e–e Rede halten || *tr* (*a letter*) (**to**) adressieren (an *acc*); (*words, a question*) (**to**) richten (an *acc*); (*an audience*) e–e Ansprache halten an (*acc*)
adduce [əˈd(j)us] *tr* anführen

adenoids [ˈædəˌnɔɪdz] *spl* Polypen *pl*
adept [əˈdɛpt] *adj* (**in**) geschickt (in *dat*)
adequate [ˈædɪkwɪt] *adj* angemessen; (**to**) ausreichend (für)
adhere [ædˈhɪr] *intr* (**to**) haften (an *dat*); (fig) (**to**) festhalten (an *dat*)
adherence [ædˈhɪrəns] *s* (**to**) Festhaften *n* (an *dat*); (fig) (**to**) Festhalten *n* (an *dat*), Beharren *n* (bei)
adherent [ædˈhɪrənt] *s* Anhänger –in *mf*
adhesion [ædˈhiʒən] *s* (*sticking*) Ankleben *n*; (*loyalty*) Anhänglichkeit *f*; (pathol, phys) Adhäsion *f*
adhesive [ædˈhisɪv] *adj* anklebend || *s* Klebemittel *n*, Klebstoff *m*
adhe'sive tape' *s* Heftpflaster *m*
adieu [əˈd(j)u] *s* (**adieus & adieux**) Lebewohl *n* || *interj* lebe wohl!
adjacent [əˈdʒesənt] *adj* (**to**) angrenzend (an *acc*); (*angles*) Nebenadjective** [ˈædʒɪktɪv] *s* Eigenschaftswort *n*, Adjektiv *n*
adjoin [əˈdʒɔɪn] *tr* angrenzen an (*acc*) || *intr* angrenzen, naheliegen
adjoin'ing *adj* angrenzend; **a. rooms** Nebenzimmer *pl*
adjourn [əˈdʒʌrn] *tr* vertagen || *intr* sich vertagen
adjournment [əˈdʒʌrnmənt] *s* Vertagung *f*
adjudge [əˈdʒʌdʒ] *tr* (*a prize*) zusprechen; **a. s.o. guilty** j–n für schuldig erklären
adjudicate [əˈdʒudɪˌket] *tr* gerichtlich entscheiden
adjunct [ˈædʒʌŋkt] *s* (**to**) Zusatz *m* (zu)
adjust [əˈdʒʌst] *tr* (*to the right position*) einstellen; (*to an alternate position*) verstellen; (*fit*) (**to**) anpassen (*dat* or an *acc*); (*differences*) ausgleichen; (*an account*) bereinigen; (ins) berechnen || *intr* (**to**) sich anpassen (*dat* or an *acc*)
adjustable [əˈdʒʌstəbəl] *adj* verstellbar
adjuster [əˈdʒʌstər] *s* (ins) Schadenssachverständiger –in *mf*
adjustment [əˈdʒʌstmənt] *s* (**to**) Anpassung *f* (*dat* or an *acc*); (*of an account*) Bereinigung *f*; (ins) Berechnung *f*; (mach) Einstellung *f*
adjutant [ˈædʒətənt] *s* Adjutant *m*
ad-lib [ˌædˈlɪb] *v* (*pret & pp*) **–libbed;** *ger* **–libbing** *tr & intr* improvisieren
ad·man [ˈædmæn] *s* (**–men**) Werbefachmann *m*; (*writer*) Werbetexter *m*
administer [ædˈmɪnɪstər] *tr* verwalten; (*help*) leisten; (*medicine*) eingeben; (*an oath*) abnehmen; (*punishment*) verhängen; (*a sacrament*) spenden; **a. justice** Recht sprechen || *intr*— **a. to** dienen (*dat*)
administration [ædˌmɪnɪsˈtreʃən] *s* (*of an institution*) Verwaltung *f*; (*of an official*) Amtsführung *f*; (*government*) Regierung *f*; (*period of government*) Regierungszeit *f*; (*of a president*) Amtszeit *f*; (*of tests*) Durchführung *f*; (*of an oath*) Abnahme *f*; (*of a sacrament*) Spendung *f*; **a. of justice** Rechtspflege *f*

administrator [æd'mınıs ‚tretər] s Verwalter –in *mf*

admiral ['ædmırəl] s Admiral *m*

admiration [‚ædmı'reʃən] s Bewunderung *f*

admire [æd'maır] *tr* (**for**) bewundern (wegen)

admirer [æd'maırər] s Bewunderer –in *mf*; (*of a woman*) Verehrer *m*

admissible [æd'mısıbəl] *adj* (& jur) zulässig

admission [æd'mıʃən] s (*entry*) Eintritt *m*; (*permission to enter*) Eintrittserlaubnis *f*; (*entry fee*) Eintrittsgebühr *f*; (*of facts*) Anerkennung *f*; (*of guilt*) Eingeständis *n*; (*enrollment*) (**to, into**) Aufnahme *f* (in acc); (**to**) (*a profession*) Zulassung *f* (zu)

ad·mit [æd'mıt] *v* (*pret & pp* –**mitted**; *ger* –**mitting**) *tr* (hin)einlassen; (**to**) (*a hospital, a society*) aufnehmen (in acc); (**to**) (*a profession*) zulassen (zu); (*accept*) anerkennen; (*concede*) zugeben; (*a crime, guilt*) eingestehen || *intr*—**a.** of zulassen

admittance [æd'mıtəns] s Eintritt *m*; **no a.** Eintritt verboten

admittedly [æd'mıtıdli] *adv* anerkanntermaßen

admixture [æd'mıkstʃər] s Beimischung *f*

admonish [æd'manıʃ] *tr* ermahnen

admonition [‚ædmə'nıʃən] s Ermahnung *f*

ado [ə'du] s Getue *n*; **much ado about nothing** viel Lärm um nichts; **without further ado** ohne weiteres

adobe [ə'dobi] s Lehmstein *m*

adolescence [‚ædə'lesəns] s Jugendalter *n*

adolescent [‚ædə'lesənt] *adj* jugendlich || s Jugendliche *mf*

adopt [ə'dapt] *tr* (*a child*) adoptieren; (*an idea*) annehmen

adopt′ed child′ s Adoptivkind *n*

adoption [ə'dapʃən] s (*of a child*) Adoption *f*; (*of an idea*) Annahme *f*

adorable [ə'dorəbəl] *adj* anbetungswürdig; (coll) entzückend

adore [ə'dor] *tr* anbeten; (coll) entzückend finden

adorn [ə'dorn] *tr* schmücken

adornment [ə'dornmənt] s Schmuck *m*

adrenaline [ə'drenəlın] s Adrenalin *n*

adrift [ə'drıft] *adj*—**be a.** treiben; (fig) weder aus noch ein wissen

adroit [ə'droıt] *adj* geschickt, gewandt

adulation [‚ædjə'leʃən] s Schmeichelei *f*

adult [ə'dʌlt], ['ædʌlt] *adj* erwachsen || s Erwachsene *mf*

adult′ educa′tion s Erwachsenenbildung *f*

adulterate [ə'dʌltə ‚ret] *tr* verfälschen; (*e.g., wine*) panschen

adulterer [ə'dʌltərər] s Ehebrecher *m*

adulteress [ə'dʌltərıs] s Ehebrecherin *f*

adulterous [ə'dʌltərəs] *adj* ehebrecherisch

adultery [ə'dʌltəri] s Ehebruch *m*

advance [æd'væns] s Fortschritt *m*; (*money*) Vorschuß *m*; **in a.** im voraus; **make advances to** (*e.g., a girl*) Annäherungsversuche machen bei || *tr* vorrücken; (*a clock*) vorstellen; (*money*) vorschießen; (*a date*) aufschieben; (*an opinion*) vorbringen; (*s.o.'s interests*) fördern; (*in rank*) befördern || *intr* vorrücken

advancement [æd'vænsmənt] s Fortschritt *m*; (*promotion*) Beförderung *f*; (*of a cause*) Förderung *f*

advance′ pay′ment s Voraus(be)zahlung *f*

advantage [æd'væntıdʒ] s Vorteil *m*; **be of a.** nützlich sein; **take a. of** ausnutzen; **to a.** vorteilhaft

advantageous [‚ædvən'tedʒəs] *adj* vorteilhaft

advent ['ædvent] s Ankunft *f*; **Advent** Advent *m*, Adventszeit *f*

adventure [æd'ventʃər] s Abenteuer *n*

adventurer [æd'ventʃərər] s Abenteurer *m*

adventuress [æd'ventʃərıs] s Abenteurerin *f*

adventurous [æd'ventʃərəs] *adj* (*person*) abenteuerlustig; (*undertaking*) abenteuerlich

adverb ['ædvʌrb] s Umstandswort *n*

adverbial [æd'vʌrbıəl] *adj* adverbial

adversary ['ædvər ‚seri] s Gegner –in *mf*

adverse [æd'vʌrs], ['ædvʌrs] *adj* ungünstig, nachteilig

adversity [æd'vʌrsıti] s Unglück *n*, Not *f*

advertise ['ædvər ‚taız] *tr* Reklame machen für || *intr* Reklame machen; **a. for** durch Inserat suchen

advertisement [‚ædvər'taızmənt], [æd'vʌrtısmənt] s Anzeige *f*, Reklame *f*

ad′vertising a′gency s Reklamebüro *n*

ad′vertising campaign′ s Werbefeldzug *m*

ad′vertising man′ s (*solicitor*) Anzeigenvermittler *m*; (*writer*) Werbetexter *m*

advice [æd'vaıs] s Rat *m*, Ratschlag *m*; **a piece of a.** ein Rat *m*; **get a. from s.o.** [dat] Rat holen bei; **give a. to** raten (dat)

advisable [æd'vaızəbəl] *adj* ratsam

advise [æd'vaız] *tr* raten (dat); (**of**) benachrichtigen (von); (**on**) beraten (über acc); **a. s.o. against s.th.** j-m von etw abraten

advisement [æd'vaızmənt] s—**take under a.** in Betracht ziehen

adviser [æd'vaızər] s Berater –in *mf*

advisory [æd'vaızəri] *adj* Beratungs–

advi′sory board′ s Beirat *m*

advocate ['ædvə ‚ket] s Fürsprecher –in *mf*; (jur) Advokat –in *mf* || *tr* befürworten

aeon ['i·ən], ['i·an] s Äon *m*

aerial ['erı·əl] *adj* Luft– || s Antenne *f*

aerodynamic [‚erodaı'næmık] *adj* aerodynamisch || **aerodynamics** s Aerodynamik *f*

aeronautic(al) [‚erə'natık(əl)] *adj* aeronautisch || **aeronautics** s Aeronautik *f*, Luftfahrt *f*

aerosol ['erə ‚sol] s Sprühdose *f*

aerospace ['ɛrəspes] *adj* Raum–

aesthetic [ɛs'θetɪk] *adj* ästhetisch || **aesthetics** *s* Ästhetik *f*

afar [ə'fɑːr] *adv*—**a. off** weit weg; **from a.** von weit her

affable ['æfəbəl] *adj* leutselig

affair [ə'fɛr] *s* Angelegenheit *f*; (*event, performance*) Veranstaltung *f*; (*romantic involvement*) Verhältnis *n*

affect [ə'fɛkt] *tr* (*influence*) berühren; (*injuriously*) angreifen; (*pretend*) vortäuschen

affectation [ˌæfɛk'teʃən] *s* Geziertheit *f*

affect'ed *adj* affektiert

affection [ə'fɛkʃən] *s* (*for*) Zuneigung *f* (zu); (pathol) Erkrankung *f*

affectionate [ə'fɛkʃənɪt] *adj* liebevoll

affidavit [ˌæfɪ'devɪt] *s* (schriftliche) eidesstattliche Erklärung *f*

affiliate [ə'fɪlɪˌet] *s* Zweiggesellschaft *f* || *tr* angliedern || *intr* sich angliedern

affinity [ə'fɪnɪti] *s* Verwandschaft *f*

affirm [ə'fʌrm] *tr* & *intr* behaupten

affirmation [ˌæfər'meʃən] *s* Behauptung *f*

affirmative [ə'fʌrmətɪv] *adj* bejahend || *s* Bejahung *f*; **in the a.** bejahend, positiv

affix ['æfɪks] *tr* (*a seal*) aufdrücken; **(to)** befestigen (an *dat*), anheften (an *acc*)

afflict [ə'flɪkt] *tr* plagen; **afflicted with** erkrankt an (*dat*)

affliction [ə'flɪkʃən] *s* Elend *n*, Leiden *n*; (*grief*) Betrübnis *f*

affluence ['æflu-əns] *s* Wohlstand *m*

affluent ['æflu-ənt] *adj* wohlhabend

af'fluent socie'ty *s* Wohlstandsgesellschaft *f*

afford [ə'ford] *tr* (*confer*) gewähren; (*time*) erübrigen; (*be able to meet the expense of*) sich [*dat*] leisten

affront [ə'frʌnt] *s* Beleidigung *f* || *tr* beleidigen

afire [ə'faɪr] *adj* & *adv* in Flammen

aflame [ə'flem] *adj* & *adv* in Flammen

afloat [ə'flot] *adj* flott, schwimmend; (*awash*) überschwemmt; (*at sea*) auf dem Meer; (*in circulation*) im Umlauf; **keep a.** (& fig) über Wasser halten; **stay a.** (& fig) sich über Wasser halten

afoot [ə'fut] *adj* & *adv* (*on foot*) zu Fuß; (*in progress*) im Gange

aforesaid [ə'for͵sɛd] *adj* vorerwähnt

afoul [ə'faul] *adj* (*entangled*) verwickelt || *adv*—**run a. of the law** mit dem Gesetz in Konflikt geraten

afraid [ə'fred] *adj* ängstlich; **be a. (of)** (*inf*) sich scheuen zu (*inf*)

afresh [ə'frɛʃ] *adv* aufs neue

Africa ['æfrɪkə] *s* Afrika *n*

African ['æfrɪkən] *adj* afrikanisch || *s* Afrikaner –in *mf*

aft [æft] *adv* (nach) achtern

after ['æftər] *adj* später; (naut) achter || *adv* nachher, darauf || *prep* nach (*dat*); **a. all** immerhin; **a. that** darauf; **be a. s.o.** hinter j–m her sein || *conj* nachdem

af'ter-din'ner speech' *s* Tischrede *f*

af'tereffect' *s* Nachwirkung *f*; **have an a.** nachwirken

af'terlife' *s* (*later life*) zukünftiges Leben *n*; (*life after death*) Leben *n* nach dem Tode

aftermath ['æftər͵mæθ] *s* Nachwirkungen *pl*; (agr) Grummet *n*

af'ternoon' *s* Nachmittag *m*; **in the a.** am Nachmittag, nachmittags; **this a.** heute nachmittag

af'ter-shave' lo'tion *s* Rasierwasser *n*

af'tertaste' *s* Nachgeschmack *m*

af'terthought' *s* nachträglicher Einfall *m*

afterward(s) ['æftərwərd(z)] *adv* später

af'terworld' *s* Jenseits *n*

again [ə'gɛn] *adv* wieder, noch einmal; **half as much a.** anderthalbmal so viel; **what's his name a.?** wie heißt er doch schnell?

against [ə'gɛnst] *prep* gegen (*acc*); **a. it** dagegen; **a. the rules** regelwidrig; **be up a. it** (coll) in der Klemme sein

age [edʒ] *s* Alter *n*, Lebensalter *n*; (*period of history*) Zeitalter *n*; **at the age of** mit, im Alter von; **come of age** mündig werden; **for ages** or **ages** Ewigkeit *f*; **of age** volljährig; **of the same age** gleichaltrig; **twenty years of age** zwanzig Jahre alt || *tr* alt machen; (*wine*) ablagern || *intr* altern; (*said of wine*) lagern

aged [edʒd] *adj* alt, e.g., **a. three** drei Jahre alt || ['edʒɪd] *adj* bejahrt

age' lim'it *s* Altersgrenze *f*

agency ['edʒənsi] *s* (*instrumentality*) Vermittlung *f*; (*activity*) Tätigkeit *f*; (adm) Behörde *f*; (com) Agentur *f*

agenda [ə'dʒɛndə] *s* Tagesordnung *f*

agent ['edʒənt] *s* Handelnde *mf*; (biol, chem) Agens *n*; (com) Agent –in *mf*

agglomeration [əˌglamə'reʃən] *s* Anhäufung *f*

aggravate ['ægrə͵vet] *tr* erschweren, verschärfen; (coll) ärgern

aggravation [ˌægrə've͵ʃən] *s* Erschwerung *f*, Verschärfung *f*; (coll) Ärger *m*

aggregate ['ægrɪ͵get] *adj* gesamt || *s* Aggregat *n*; **in the a.** im ganzen || *tr* anhäufen

aggression [ə'grɛʃən] *s* Agression *f*

aggressive [ə'grɛsɪv] *adj* aggressiv

aggressor [ə'grɛsər] *s* Aggressor *m*

aggrieved [ə'grivd] *adj* (*saddened*) betrübt; (jur) geschädigt

aghast [ə'gæst] *adj* entsetzt

agile ['ædʒɪl] *adj* flink; (*mind*) rege

agility [ə'dʒɪlɪti] *s* Flinkheit *f*; (*of the mind*) Regsamkeit *f*

agitate ['ædʒɪ͵tet] *tr* hin und her bewegen; (fig) beunruhigen || *intr* agitieren

agitator ['ædʒɪ͵tetər] *s* Unruhestifter –in *mf*; (*in a washer*) Rührapparat *m*

aglow [ə'glo] *adj* & *adv* (er)glühend

agnostic [æg'nɑstɪk] *adj* agnostisch || *s* Agnostiker –in *mf*

ago [ə'go] *adv* vor (*dat*), e.g., **a year ago** vor e–m Jahr; **long ago** vor langer Zeit

agog [ə'gɑg] *adv* gespannt, erpicht

agonize ['ægə͵naɪz] *intr* sich quälen

ag′onizing *adj* qualvoll

agony [′ægəni] *s* Qual *f;* (*death struggle*) Todeskampf *m*

agrarian [ə′grɛri·ən] *adj* landwirtschaftlich, agrarisch

agree [ə′gri] *intr* übereinstimmen; a. on (or upon) sich einigen über (*acc*); a. to zustimmen (*dat*); a. to (*inf*) übereinkommen zu (*inf*); a. with (& gram) übereinstimmen mit; (*affect one's health*) bekommen (*dat*)

agreeable [ə′gri·əbəl] *adj* angenehm

agreed! *interj* abgemacht!, einverstanden!

agreement [ə′grimənt] *s* Abkommen *n*, Vereinbarung *f;* (*contract*) Vertrag *m;* (& gram) Übereinstimmung *f*

agriculture [′ægrɪˌkʌltʃər] *s* Landwirtschaft *f*, Ackerbau *m*

aground [ə′graund] *adv* gestrandet; run a. stranden, auf Grund laufen

ahead [ə′hɛd] *adj* & *adv* (*in the front*) vorn; (*to the front*) nach vorn; (*in advance*) voraus; (*forward*) vorwärts; a. of vor (*dat*); get a. vorwärtskommen; go a. vorangehen; go a.! los!; go a. with fortfahren mit; look a. an die Zukunft denken

ahoy [ə′hɔɪ] *interj* ahoi!

aid [ed] *s* Hilfe *f*, Beihilfe *f* ‖ *tr* helfen (*dat*); aid and abet Vorschub leisten (*dat*)

aide [ed] *s* Gehilfe *m*

aide-de-camp [′ɛddə′kæmp] *s* (aides-de-camp) Adjutant *m*

ail [el] *tr* schmerzen; what ails you? was fehlt Ihnen? ‖ *intr* (*have pain*) Schmerzen haben; (*be ill*) erkrankt sein

ail′ing *adj* leidend, kränklich

ailment [′elmənt] *s* Leiden *n*

aim [em] *s* Ziel *n;* (fig) Ziel *n*, Zweck *m;* is your aim good? zielen Sie gut?; take aim zielen ‖ *tr* (*a gun, words*) (at) richten auf (*acc*); aim to (*inf*) beabsichtigen zu (*inf*) ‖ *intr* zielen; aim at (& fig) zielen auf (*acc*); aim for streben nach

aimless [′emlɪs] *adj* ziellos, planlos

air [ɛr] *s* Luft *f;* (mus) Melodie *f;* be on the air (*an announcer*) senden; (*a program*) gesendet werden; be up in the air (fig) in der Luft hängen; by air per Flugzeug; go off the air die Sendung beenden; go on the air die Sendung beginnen; in the open air im Freien; put on airs groß tun; walk on air sich wie im Himmel fühlen ‖ *tr* lüften

air′base′ *s* Flugstützpunkt *m*

airborne [′ɛrˌbɔrn] *adj* aufgestiegen; a. troops Luftlandetruppen *pl*

air′brake′ *s* Druckluftbremse *f*

air′-condi′tion *tr* klimatisieren

air′ condi′tioner *s* Klimaanlage *f*

air′ cov′er *s* Luftsicherung *f*

air′craft′ *s* (pl *aircraft*) Flugzeug *n*

air′craft car′rier *s* Flugzeugträger *m*

air′ cur′rent *s* Luftströmung *f*

air′ fare′ *s* Flugpreis *m*

air′field′ *s* Flugplatz *m*

air′force′ *s* Luftstreitkräfte *pl*

air′ing *s* Lüftung *f*

air′ lane′ *s* Flugschneise *f*

air′lift′ *s* Luftbrücke *f* ‖ *tr* auf dem Luftwege transportieren

air′line(s)′ *s* Luftverkehrsgesellschaft *f*

air′line pi′lot *s* Flugkapitän *m*

air′lin′er *s* Verkehrsflugzeug *n*

air′mail′ (′) *s* Luftpost *f*

air′-mail let′ter *s* Luftpostbrief *m*

air′-mail stamp′ *s* Luftpostbriefmarke *f*

air′plane′ *s* Flugzeug *n*

air′ pock′et *s* Luftloch *n*

air′ pollu′tion *s* Luftverunreinigung *f*

air′port′ *s* Flughafen *m*, Flugplatz *m*

air′ raid′ *s* Fliegerangriff *m*

air′-raid drill′ *s* Luftschutzübung *f*

air′-raid shel′ter *s* Luftschutzraum *m*

air′-raid war′den *s* Luftschutzwart *m*

air′-raid warn′ing *s* Fliegeralarm *m*

air′ recon′naissance *s* Luftaufklärung *f*

air′show′ *s* Flugvorführung *f*

air′sick′ *adj* luftkrank

air′sleeve′, **air′sock′** *s* Windsack *m*

air′strip′ *s* Start- und Landestreifen *m*

air′ suprem′acy *s* Luftherrschaft *f*

air′tight′ *adj* luftdicht

air′ time′ *s* (rad, telv) Sendezeit *f*

air′-traffic control′ *s* Flugsicherung *f*

air′waves′ *spl* Rundfunk *m*; on the a. im Rundfunk

air′way′ *s* Luft(verkehrs)linie *f*

air′wor′thy *adj* lufttüchtig

airy [′ɛri] *adj* (*room*) luftig; (*lively*) lebhaft; (*flippant*) leichtsinnig

aisle [aɪl] *s* Gang *m;* (archit) Seitenschiff *n*

ajar [ə′dʒɑr] *adj* angelehnt

akimbo [ə′kɪmbo] *adj*—with arms a. die Arme in die Hüften gestemmt

akin [ə′kɪn] *adj* verwandt; a. to ähnlich (*dat*)

alabaster [′ælə‚bæstər] *s* Alabaster *m*

alacrity [ə′lækrɪti] *s* Bereitwilligkeit *f*

alarm [ə′lɑrm] *s* Alarm *m;* (*sudden fear*) Bestürzung *f;* (*apprehension*) Unruhe *f* ‖ *tr* alarmieren

alarm′ clock′ *s* Wecker *m*

alas [ə′læs] *interj* o weh!

Albania [æl′bɛnɪ·ə] *s* Albanien *n*

Albanian [æl′bɛnɪ·ən] *adj* albanisch ‖ *s* Alban(i)er –in *mf*

albatross [′ælbə‚trɔs] *s* Albatros *m*

album [′ælbəm] *s* Album *n*

albumen [æl′bjumən] *s* Eiweiß *n*

alchemy [′ælkɪmɪ] *s* Alchimie *f*

alcohol [′ælkəˌhɔl] *s* Alkohol *m*

alcoholic [ˌælkə′hɔlɪk] *adj* alkoholisch ‖ *s* Alkoholiker –in *mf*

alcove [′ælkov] *s* Alkoven *m*

alder [′ɔldər] *s* (bot) Erle *f*

al′der·man *s* (–men) Stadtrat *m*

ale [el] *s* Ale *n*, englisches Bier *n*

alert [ə′lʌrt] *adj* wachsam ‖ *s* (*state of readiness*) Alarmbereitschaft *f;* on the a. alarmbereit; (fig) auf der Hut ‖ *tr* alarmieren

alfalfa [æl′fælfə] *s* Luzerne *f*

algae [′ældʒi] *spl* Algen *pl*

algebra [′ældʒɪbrə] *s* Algebra *f*

Algeria [æl′dʒɪrɪ·ə] *s* Algerien *n*

Algerian [æl′dʒɪrɪ·ən] *adj* algerisch ‖ *s* Algerier –in *mf*

Algiers [æl′dʒɪrz] *s* Algier *n*

alias [ˈeɪlɪ·əs] *adv* alias, sonst...genannt ‖ *s* Deckname *m*

ali·bi [ˈælɪˌbaɪ] *s* (**–bis**) Alibi *n;* (*excuse*) Ausrede *f*

alien [ˈeljən], [ˈelɪ·ən] *adj* fremd ‖ *s* Fremde *mf,* Ausländer –in *mf*

alienate [ˈeljəˌnet], [ˈelɪ·əˌnet] *tr* entfremden; (*jur*) übertragen

alight [əˈlaɪt] *v* (*pret & pp* **alighted &** **alit** [əˈlɪt]) *intr* aussteigen; (*said of a bird*) (**on**) sich niederlassen (auf *dat* or *acc*); (aer) landen

align [əˈlaɪn] *tr* (**with**) ausrichten (nach); (aut) einstellen; **a. oneself** **with** sich anschließen an (*acc*) ‖ *intr* —a. with sich ausrichten nach

alignment [əˈlaɪnmənt] *s* Ausrichten *n;* (pol) Ausrichtung *f;* **bring into** **s.** gleichschalten; **out of a.** schlecht ausgerichtet

alike [əˈlaɪk] *adj* gleich, ähnlich; **look** **a.** sich [*dat*] ähnlich sehen; (*resemble completely*) gleich aussehen

alimony [ˈælɪˌmoni] *s* Unterhaltskosten *pl*

alive [əˈlaɪv] *adj* lebendig; (*vivacious*) lebhaft; **keep a.** am Leben bleiben; **keep s.o. a.** j–n am Leben erhalten

alka·li [ˈælkəˌlaɪ] *s* (**–lis &** **–lies**) Laugensalz *n,* Alkali *n*

alkaline [ˈælkəˌlaɪn] *adj* alkalisch

all [ɔl] *adj* all, ganz; **all day long** den ganzen Tag; **all kinds of** allerlei; **all** **the time** fortwährend; **for all that** trotzdem ‖ *adv* ganz, völlig; **all along** schon immer; **all at once** auf einmal; **all gone** alle; **all in** (coll) völlig erschöpft; **all over** (*everywhere*) überall; (*ended*) ganz vorbei; **all right** gut, schön; **all the better** um so besser; **all the same** dennoch; **not be all** **there** (coll) nicht ganz richtig im Kopf sein ‖ *s*—**after all** schließlich; **all in all** im großen und ganzen; **and** **all gesamt**, e.g., **he went, family and** **all** er ging mit gesamter Familie; **in** **all insgesamt; not at all** überhaupt nicht, gar nicht ‖ *indef pron* alle; (*everything*) alles

all'-around' *adj* vielseitig

allay [əˈle] *tr* beschwichtigen; (*hunger,* *thirst*) stillen

all'-clear' *s* Entwarnung *f*

allege [əˈlɛdʒ] *tr* behaupten; (*advance* *as an excuse*) vorgeben

alleged' *adj* angeblich, mutmaßlich

allegiance [əˈlidʒəns] *s* Treue *f*

allegoric(al) [ˌælɪˈɡɔrɪk(əl)] *adj* allegorisch

allegory [ˈælɪˌɡori] *s* Allegorie *f*

allergic [əˈlʌrdʒɪk] *adj* allergisch

allergy [ˈælərdʒi] *s* Allergie *f*

alleviate [əˈlivɪˌet] *tr* lindern

alley [ˈæli] *s* Gasse *f;* (*for bowling*) Kegelbahn *f*

alliance [əˈlaɪ·əns] *s* Bündnis *n*

allied *adj* (*field*) benachbart; (*science*) verwandt; (mil, pol) alliiert

alligator [ˈælɪˌɡetər] *s* Alligator *m*

all'-inclu'sive *adj* Pauschal–

alliteration [əˌlɪtəˈreʃən] *s* Stabreim *m,* Alliteration *f*

all'-know'ing *adj* allwissend

allocate [ˈæləˌket] *tr* zuteilen

al·lot [əˈlɑt] (*pret & pp* **–lotted;** *ger* **–lotting**) *tr* zuteilen, austeilen

all'-out' *adj* vollkommen, total

allow [əˈlaʊ] *tr* erlauben, gestatten; (*admit*) zugeben; (*e.g., a discount*) gewähren; **be allowed to** (*inf*) dürfen (*inf*) ‖ *intr*—a. for bedenken

allowable [əˈlaʊ·əbəl] *adj* zulässig

allowance [əˈlaʊ·əns] *s* (*tolerance*) Duldung *f;* (*permission*) Erlaubnis *f;* (*ration*) Zuteilung *f,* Ration *f;* (*pocket money*) Taschengeld *n;* (*discount*) Abzug *m;* (*salary for a par-* *ticular expense*) Zuschuß *m,* Zulage *f;* (*for groceries*) Wirtschaftsgeld *n;* (*mach*) Toleranz *f;* **make a. for** berücksichtigen

alloy [ˈælɔɪ] *s* Legierung *f* ‖ [əˈlɔɪ] *tr* legieren

all'-pow'erful *adj* allmächtig

all' right' *adj*—**be a.** in Ordnung sein ‖ *interj* schon gut!

All' Saints'' Day' *s* Allerheiligen *n*

All' Souls'' Day' *s* Allerseelen *n*

all'spice' *s* Nelkenpfeffer *m*

all'-star' *adj* (*sport*) aus den besten Spielern bestehend

allude [əˈlud] *intr*—a. to anspielen auf (*acc*)

allure [əˈlʊr] *s* Charme *m* ‖ *tr* anlocken

allurement [əˈlʊrmənt] *s* Verlockung *f*

allur'ing *adj* verlockend

allusion [əˈluʒən] *s* (**to**) Anspielung *f* (auf *acc*)

al·ly [ˈælaɪ], [əˈlaɪ] *s* Alliierte *mf,* Verbündete *mf* ‖ [əˈlaɪ] *v* (*pret &* *pp* **–lied**) *tr*—a. oneself with sich verbünden mit

almanac [ˈɔlməˌnæk] *s* Almanach *m*

almighty [ɔlˈmaɪti] *adj* allmächtig

almond [ˈɑmənd] *s* Mandel *f*

almost [ˈɔlmost], [ɔlˈmost] *adv* fast

alms [ɑmz] *s & spl* Almosen *n*

aloft [əˈlɔft] *adv* (*position*) oben; (*direction*) nach oben; **raise a.** emporheben

alone [əˈlon] *adj* allein; **let a.** (*not to* *mention*) geschweige denn; (*not* *bother*) in Ruhe lassen ‖ *adv* allein

along [əˈlɔŋ] *adv* vorwärts, weiter; **all** **a.** schon immer; **a. with** zusammen mit; **get a. with** sich gut vertragen mit; **go a. with** mitgehen mit; (*agree* *with*) sich einverstanden erklären mit ‖ *prep* (*direction*) entlang (*acc*); (*position*) an (*dat*), längs (*genit*)

along'side' *adv* (naut) längsseits; **a. of** im Vergleich zu ‖ *prep* neben (*dat*); (naut) längsseits (*genit*)

aloof [əˈluf] *adj* zurückhaltend ‖ *adv*—**keep a. (from)** sich fernhalten (von); **stand a.** für sich bleiben

aloud [əˈlaʊd] *adv* laut

alphabet [ˈælfəˌbɛt] *s* Alphabet *n*

alphabetic(al) [ˌælfəˈbɛtɪk(əl)] *adj* alphabetisch

alpine [ˈælpaɪn] *adj* alpin, Alpen–

Alps [ælps] *spl* Alpen *pl*

already [ɔlˈrɛdi] *adv* schon, bereits

Alsace [ælˈses], [ˈælsæs] *s* Elsaß *n*

Alsatian [ælˈseʃən] *adj* elsässisch ‖ *s*

Elsässer −in *mf;* (*dog*) deutscher Schäferhund *m*
also [ˈɔlso] *adv* auch
altar [ˈɔltər] *s* Altar *m*
al'tar boy' *s* Ministrant *m*
alter [ˈɔltər] *tr* ändern; (*castrate*) kastrieren ‖ *intr* sich ändern
alteration [ˌɔltəˈreʃən] *s* Änderung *f;* **alterations** (*in construction*) Umbau *m*
alternate [ˈɔltərnɪt] *adj* abwechselnd ‖ *s* Ersatzmann *m* ‖ [ˈɔltərˌnet] *tr* (ab)wechseln; (*e.g., hot and cold compresses*) zwischen (*dat*) und (*dat*) abwechseln ‖ *intr* miteinander abwechseln
al'ternating cur'rent *s* Wechselstrom *m*
alternative [ɔlˈtʌrnətɪv] *adj* Ausweich−, Alternativ− ‖ *s* Alternative *f*
although [ɔlˈðo] *conj* obgleich, obwohl
altimeter [ælˈtɪmɪtər] *s* Höhenmesser *m*
altitude [ˈæltɪˌt(j)ud] *s* Höhe *f*
al·to [ˈælto] *s* (−tos) Alt *m*, Altstimme *f;* (*singer*) Altist *m*
altogether [ˌɔltəˈgeðər] *adv* durchaus; (*in all*) insgesamt
altruist [ˈæltru·ɪst] *s* Altruist −in *mf*
alum [ˈæləm] *s* Alaun *m*
aluminum [əˈlumɪnəm] *s* Aluminium *n*
alu'minum foil' *s* Aluminiumfolie *f*
alum·na [əˈlʌmnə] *s* (−nae [ni]) ehemalige Studentin *f*
alum·nus [əˈlʌmnəs] *s* (−ni [naɪ]) ehemaliger Student *m*
always [ˈɔlwɪz], [ˈɔlwez] *adv* immer
A.M. *abbr* (ante meridiem) vormittags; (**amplitude modulation**) Amplitudenmodulation *f*
amalgam [əˈmælgəm] *s* Amalgam *n;* (*fig*) Mischung *f*, Gemenge *n*
amalgamate [əˈmælgəˌmet] *tr* amalgamieren ‖ *intr* sich amalgamieren
amass [əˈmæs] *tr* aufhäufen, ansammeln
amateur [ˈæmətʃər] *adj* Amateur− ‖ *s* Amateur *m*, Liebhaber *m*
amaze [əˈmez] *tr* erstaunen
amaz'ing *adj* erstaunlich
Amazon [ˈæməˌzɑn] *s* (*river*) Amazonas *m;* (*fig*) Mannweib *n;* (*myth*) Amazone *f*
ambassador [æmˈbæsədər] *s* Botschafter −in §6 *mf;* (*fig*) Bote *m*
ambassadorial [æmˌbæsəˈdɔrɪəl] *adj* Botschafts−
amber [ˈæmbər] *adj* Bernstein−; (*in color*) bernsteinfarben ‖ *s* Bernstein *m*
ambiguity [ˌæmbɪˈgju·ɪti] *s* Doppelsinn *m*, Zweideutigkeit *f*
ambiguous [æmˈbɪgju·əs] *adj* doppelsinnig, zweideutig
ambit [ˈæmbɪt] *s* Bereich *m*
ambition [æmˈbɪʃən] *s* Ehrgeiz *m;* (*aim, object*) Ambition *f*
ambitious [æmˈbɪʃəs] *adj* ehrgeizig
ambivalent [æmˈbɪvələnt] *adj* (*chem*) ambivalent; (*psychol*) zwiespältig
amble [ˈæmbəl] *s* (*of a person*) gemächlicher Gang *m;* (*of a horse*) Paßgang *m* ‖ *intr* schlendern; (*said of a horse*) im Paßgang gehen

ambulance [ˈæmbjələns] *s* Krankenwagen *m*
ambulatory [ˈæmbjələˌtori] *adj* gehfähig
ambuscade [ˌæmbəsˈked] *s* Hinterhalt *m*
ambush [ˈæmbuʃ] *s* Hinterhalt *m* ‖ *tr* aus dem Hinterhalt überfallen
ameliorate [əˈmiljəˌret] *tr* verbessern ‖ *intr* besser werden
amen [ˈeˈmen], [ˈɑˈmen] *s* Amen *n* ‖ *interj* amen!
amenable [əˈmenəbəl] *adj* (*docile*) fügsam; **a. to** (*e.g., flattery*) zugänglich (*dat*); (*e.g., laws*) unterworfen (*dat*)
amend [əˈmend] *tr* (*a law*) (ver)bessern; (*one's ways*) (ab)ändern ‖ *intr* sich bessern
amendment [əˈmendmənt] *s* Änderungsantrag *m;* (*by addition*) Zusatzantrag *m;* (*to the constitution*) Zusatzartikel *m*
amends [əˈmendz] *s & spl* Genugtuung *f;* **make a. for** wiedergutmachen
amenity [əˈmenɪti] *s* (*pleasantness*) Annehmlichkeit *f;* **amenities** (*of life*) Annehmlichkeiten *pl*
America [əˈmerɪkə] *s* Amerika *n*
American [əˈmerɪkən] *adj* amerikanisch ‖ *s* Amerikaner −in *mf*
Americanize [əˈmerɪkəˌnaɪz] *tr* amerikanisieren
amethyst [ˈæmɪθɪst] *s* Amethyst *m*
amiable [ˈemi·əbəl] *adj* liebenswürdig
amicable [ˈæmɪkəbəl] *adj* freundschaftlich, gütlich
amid [əˈmɪd] *prep* inmitten (*genit*)
amidships [əˈmɪd/ɪps] *adv* mittschiffs
amiss [əˈmɪs] *adj* (*improper*) unpassend; (*wrong*) verkehrt; **there is s.th. a.** etwas stimmt nicht ‖ *adv* verkehrt; **go a.** danebengehen; **take a.** übelnehmen
amity [ˈæmɪti] *s* Freundschaft *f*
ammo [ˈæmo] *s* (sl) Muni *m*
ammonia [əˈmoni·ə] *s* (*gas*) Ammoniak *n;* (*solution*) Salmiakgeist *m*
ammunition [ˌæmjəˈnɪʃən] *s* Munition *f*
amnesia [æmˈniʒ·ə] *s* Amnesie *f*
amnes·ty [ˈæmnɪsti] *s* Amnestie *f* ‖ *v* (*pret & pp.* −tied) *tr* begnadigen
amoeba [əˈmibə] *s* Amöbe *f*
among [əˈmʌŋ] *prep* (*position*) unter (*dat*); (*direction*) unter (*acc*); **a. other things** unter anderem
amorous [ˈæmərəs] *adj* amourös
amortize [ˈæmərˌtaɪz] *tr* tilgen
amount [əˈmaunt] *s* (*sum*) Betrag *m;* (*quantity*) Menge *f* ‖ *intr*—**a. to** betragen
ampere [ˈæmpɪr] *s* Ampere *n*
amphibian [æmˈfɪbi·ən] *s* Amphibie *f*
amphibious [æmˈfɪbi·əs] *adj* amphibisch
amphitheater [ˈæmfɪˌθi·ətər] *s* Amphitheater *n*
ample [ˈæmpəl] *adj* (*sufficient*) genügend; (*spacious*) geräumig
amplifier [ˈæmplɪˌfaɪ·ər] *s* Verstärker *m*
ampli·fy [ˈæmplɪˌfaɪ] *v* (*pret & pp* −fied) *tr* (*a statement*) erweitern; (electron, rad, phys) verstärken

amplitude [ˈæmplɪˌt(j)ud] *s* Weite *f*; (electron, rad, phys) Amplitude *f*

am'plitude modula'tion *s* Amplituden-modulation *f*

amputate [ˈæmpjəˌtet] *tr* amputieren

amputee [ˌæmpjəˈti] *s* Amputierte *mf*

amuck [əˈmʌk] *adv*—**run a.** Amok laufen

amulet [ˈæmjəlɪt] *s* Amulett *n*

amuse [əˈmjuz] *tr* amüsieren, belustigen

amusement [əˈmjuzmənt] *s* Vergnügen *n*

amuse'ment park' *s* Vergnügungspark *m*

amus'ing *adj* amüsant

an [æn], [ən] *indef art* ein

anachronism [əˈnækrəˌnɪzəm] *s* Anachronismus *m*

analogous [əˈnæləgəs] *adj* (to) analog (*dat*), ähnlich (*dat*)

analogy [əˈnælədʒɪ] *s* Analogie *f*

analy·sis [əˈnælɪsɪs] *s* (**-ses** [ˌsiz]) Analyse *f*; (of a literary work) Zergliederung *f*

analyst [ˈænəlɪst] *s* Analytiker –in *mf*

analytic(al) [ˌænəˈlɪtɪk(əl)] *adj* analytisch

analyze [ˈænəˌlaɪz] *tr* analysieren

anarchist [ˈænərkɪst] *s* Anarchist –in *mf*

anarchy [ˈænərkɪ] *s* Anarchie *f*

anatomic(al) [ˌænəˈtɑmɪk(əl)] *adj* anatomisch

anatomy [əˈnætəmɪ] *s* Anatomie *f*

ancestor [ˈænsestər] *s* Vorfahr *m*, Ahne *m*

ancestral [ænˈsestrəl] *adj* angestammt, Ahnen–; (inherited) Erb–, ererbt

ancestry [ˈænsestrɪ] *s* Abstammung *f*

anchor [ˈænkər] *s* Anker *m*; **cast a.** vor Anker gehen; **weigh a.** den Anker lichten ‖ *tr* verankern ‖ *intr* ankern

anchorage [ˈænkərɪdʒ] *s* Ankerplatz *m*

anchovy [ˈæntʃovɪ] *s* Anschovis *f*

ancient [ˈentʃənt] *adj* (very old) uralt; (civilization) antik ‖ **the ancients** *spl* die alten Griechen und Römer

an'cient his'tory *s* alte Geschichte *f*

and [ænd], [ənd] *conj* und; **and how!** und ob! **and so forth** and so weiter

andiron [ˈændˌaɪ.ərn] *s* Kaminbock *m*

anecdote [ˈænɪkˌdot] *s* Anekdote *f*

anemia [əˈnimi.ə] *s* Anämie *f*

anemic [əˈnimɪk] *adj* anämisch, blutarm

anesthesia [ˌænɪsˈθiʒə] *s* Anästhesie *f*; **general a.** Vollnarkose *f*; **local a.** Lokalanästhesie *f*

anesthetic [ˌænɪsˈθetɪk] *adj* betäubend ‖ *s* Betäubungsmittel *n*; **local a.** örtliches Betäubungsmittel *n*

anesthetize [əˈnesθɪˌtaɪz] *tr* betäuben

anew [əˈn(j)u] *adv* von neuem, aufs neue

angel [ˈendʒəl] *s* Engel *m*; (financial backer) Hintermann *m*

angelic(al) [ænˈdʒelɪk(əl)] *adj* engelgleich, engelhaft

anger [ˈængər] *s* Zorn *m* ‖ *tr* erzürnen

angina pectoris [ænˈdʒaɪnəˈpektərɪs] *s* Brustbeklemmung *f*, Herzbräune *f*

angle [ˈængəl] *s* Winkel *m*; (point of view) Gesichtswinkel *m*; (ulterior motive) Hintergedanken *m*; (side) Seite *f*

angler [ˈænglər] *s* Angler –in *mf*

angry [ˈængrɪ] *adj* zornig, böse; (wound) entzündet; **a. at** (s.th.) zornig über (acc); **a. with** (s.o.) zornig auf (acc)

anguish [ˈængwɪʃ] *s* Qual *f*, Pein *f*

angular [ˈængjələr] *adj* kantig

animal [ˈænɪməl] *adj* tierisch, Tier— ‖ *s* Tier *n*

animate [ˈænɪmɪt] *adj* belebt; (lively) lebhaft ‖ [ˈænɪˌmet] *tr* beleben, beseelen; (make lively) aufmuntern

an'imated cartoon' *s* Zeichentrickfilm *m*

animation [ˌænɪˈmeʃən] *s* Lebhaftigkeit *f*; (cin) Herstellung *f* von Zeichentrickfilm

animosity [ˌænɪˈmɑstɪ] *s* Feindseligkeit *f*

anion [ˈænˌaɪ.ən] *s* Anion *n*

anise [ˈænɪs] *s* Anis *m*

anisette [ˌænɪˈset] *s* Anisett *m*

ankle [ˈænkəl] *s* Fußknöchel *m*

an'kle support' *s* Knöchelstütze *f*

anklet [ˈænklɪt] *s* (ornament) Fußring *m*; (sock) Söckchen *n*

annals [ˈænəlz] *spl* Annalen *pl*

anneal [əˈnil] *tr* ausglühen; (the mind) stählen

annex [ˈæneks] *s* (building) Anbau *m*, Nebengebäude *n*; (supplement) Zusatz *m* ‖ [əˈneks] *tr* annektieren

annexation [ˌæneksˈeʃən] *s* Einverleibung *f*; (pol) Annexion *f*

annihilate [əˈnaɪ.ɪˌlet] *tr* vernichten; (fig) zunichte machen

annihilation [əˌnaɪ.ɪˈleʃən] *s* Vernichtung *f*

anniversary [ˌænɪˈvʌrsərɪ] *s* Jahrestag *m*

annotate [ˈænəˌtet] *tr* mit Anmerkungen versehen

annotation [ˌænəˈteʃən] *s* Anmerkung *f*

announce [əˈnauns] *tr* ankündigen, anmelden; (rad) ansagen, melden

announcement [əˈnaunsmənt] *s* Ankündigung *f*; (rad) Durchsage *f*

announcer [əˈnaunsər] *s* Ansager –in *mf*

annoy [əˈnɔɪ] *tr* ärgern; **be annoyed at** sich ärgern über (acc)

annoyance [əˈnɔɪ.əns] *s* Ärger *m*

annoy'ing *adj* ärgerlich

annual [ˈænju.əl] *adj* jährlich, Jahres–; (plant) einjährig ‖ *s* (book) Jahrbuch *n*; (bot) einjährige Pflanze *f*

annuity [əˈn(j)u.ɪtɪ] *s* Jahresrente *f*

an·nul [əˈnʌl] *v* (*pret & pp* **-nulled;** *ger* **-nulling**) *tr* annullieren

annulment [əˈnʌlmənt] *s* Annullierung *f*; (of marriage) Nichtigkeitserklärung *f*

anode [ˈænod] *s* Anode *f*

anoint [əˈnɔɪnt] *tr* salben

anomaly [əˈnɑmɪlɪ] *s* Anomalie *f*

anonymous [əˈnɑnɪməs] *adj* anonym

another [əˈnʌðər] *adj* (a different) ein anderer; (an additional) noch ein; **a. Caesar** ein zweiter Cäsar ‖ *pron* (*a different one*) ein anderer; (*an additional one*) noch einer

answer ['ænsər] *s* Antwort *f*; (*to a problem*) Lösung *f* || *tr* (*a person*) antworten (*dat*); (*a question, letter*) beantworten; (*need, description*) entsprechen (*dat*); (*enemy fire*) antworten auf (*acc*); **a. an ad** sich auf e-e Anzeige melden; **a. the door** die Tür öffnen; **a. the telephone** ans Telefon gehen || *intr* antworten; (telp) sich melden; **a. back** e-n losen Mund haben; **a. for** verantworten; **a. to** (*a description*) entsprechen (*dat*)

an′swering serv′ice *s* Fernsprechauftragsdienst *m*

ant [ænt] *s* Ameise *f*

antagonism [æn′tægə‚nɪzəm] *s* Feindseligkeit *f*

antagonize [æn′tægə‚naɪz] *tr* sich [*dat*] zum Gegner machen

antarctic [ænt′ɑrktɪk] *adj* antarktisch || **the Antarctic** *s* die Antarktis

Antarc′tic Cir′cle *s* südlicher Polarkreis *m*

Antarc′tic O′cean *s* südliches Eismeer *n*

ante ['ænti] *s* (cards) Einsatz *m*; (com) Scherflein *n* || *tr* (cards) einsetzen || *intr* (*in a joint venture*) sein Scherflein beitragen; (*pay up*) (coll) blechen; (cards) einsetzen

antecedent [‚æntɪ′sidənt] *adj* vorhergehend || *s* (gram) Beziehungswort *n*; **antecedents** Antezedenzien *pl*

antechamber ['æntɪ‚tʃembər] *s* Vorzimmer *n*

antelope ['æntɪ‚lop] *s* Antilope *f*

anten·na [æn′tɛnə] *s* (*-nae* [ni]) (ent) Fühler *m* || *s* (*-nas*) (rad) Antenne *f*

antepenult [‚æntɪ′pinʌlt] *s* drittletzte Silbe *f*

anthem ['ænθəm] *s* Hymne *f*

ant′hill′ *s* Ameisenhaufen *m*

anthology [æn′θɑlədʒi] *s* Anthologie *f*

anthropology [‚ænθrə′pɑlədʒi] *s* Anthropologie *f*, Lehre *f* vom Menschen

antiaircraft [‚ænti′ɛr‚kræft] *adj* Flak-, Flugabwehr– || *s* Flak *f*

antiair′craft gun′ *s* Flak *f*

antibiotic [‚æntɪbaɪ′ɑtɪk] *s* Antibiotikum *n*

antibody ['æntɪ‚bɑdi] *s* Antikörper *m*

anticipate [æn′tɪsɪ‚pet] *tr* (*expect*) erwarten; (*remarks, criticism, etc.*) vorwegnehmen; (*trouble*) vorausahnen; (*pleasure*) vorausempfinden; (*s.o.'s wish or desire*) zuvorkommen (*dat*)

anticipation [æn‚tɪsɪ′peʃən] *s* Erwartung *f*, Vorfreude *f*

antics ['æntɪks] *spl* Possen *pl*

antidote ['æntɪ‚dot] *s* Gegengift *n*

antifreeze ['æntɪ‚friz] *s* Gefrierschutzmittel *n*

antiknock [‚æntɪ′nɑk] *adj* klopffest || *s* Antiklopfmittel *n*

antipathy [æn′tɪpəθi] *s* Abneigung *f*, Antipathie *f*

antiquarian [‚æntɪ′kwɛri‚ən] *adj* altertümlich || *s* Altertumsforscher *–in mf*

antiquated ['æntɪ‚kwetɪd] *adj* veraltet

antique [æn′tik] *adj* (ur)alt, antik || *s* Antiquität *f*

antique′ deal′er *s* Antiquitätenhändler *–in mf*

antique′ shop′ *s* Antiquitätenladen *m*

antiquity [æn′tɪkwɪti] *s* Altertum *n*, Vorzeit *f*; **antiquities** Antiquitäten *pl*, Altertümer *pl*

antirust [‚æntɪ′rʌst] *adj* Rostschutz-

anti-Semitic [‚æntɪsɪ′mɪtɪk] *adj* antisemitisch, judenfeindlich

antiseptic [‚æntɪ′septɪk] *adj* antiseptisch || *s* Antiseptikum *n*

antitank [‚æntɪ′tæŋk] *adj* Panzer–; (*unit*) Panzerjäger–

antitank′ mine′ *s* Tellermine *f*

antithe·sis [æn′tɪθɪsɪs] *s* (*-ses* [‚siz]) Gegensatz *m*, Antithese *f*

antitoxin [‚æntɪ′tɑksɪn] *s* Gegengift *n*

antitrust [‚æntɪ′trʌst] *adj* Antitrust–

antiwar [‚æntɪ′wɔr] *adj* antimilitaristisch

antler ['æntlər] *s* Geweihsprosse *f*; (**pair of**) **antlers** Geweih *n*

antonym ['æntənɪm] *s* Antonym *n*

anus ['enəs] *s* After *m*

anvil ['ænvɪl] *s* Amboß *m*

anxiety [æn′zaɪ·əti] *s* (**over**) Besorgnis *f* (um); (psycho) Beklemmung *f*

anxious ['æŋk/əs] *adj* (**about**) besorgt (um or wegen); (**for**) gespannt (auf *acc*), begierig (auf *acc*); **I am a. to** (*inf*) es liegt mir daran zu (*inf*)

any ['eni] *indef adj* irgendein, irgendwelch; (*a little*) etwas; **any** (**possible**) etwaig; **any** (**you wish**) jeder beliebige; **do you have any money on you?** haben Sie Geld bei sich?; **I do not have any money** ich habe kein Geld || *adv*—**any more** (*e.g., coffee*) noch etwas; (*e.g., apples*) noch ein paar; **not any better** keinwegs besser; **not ...any longer** nicht mehr; **not...any more** nicht mehr

an′ybod′y *indef pron* var of **anyone**

an′yhow′ *adv* sowieso, trotzdem; (*in any event*) jedenfalls

an′yone′ *indef pron* (irgend)jemand, irgendeiner; **a. but you** jeder andere als du; **a. else** sonstnochwer; **ask a.** frag wen du willst; **I don't see a.** ich sehe niemand

an′yplace′ *adv* (coll) var of **anywhere**

an′ything *indef pron* (irgend)etwas, (irgend)was; **a. but** alles andere als; **a. else?** noch etwas?, sonst etwas?; **a. you want** was du willst; **not...a.** nichts; **not for a. in the world** um keinen Preis

an′ytime′ *adv* zu jeder (beliebigen) Zeit; (*at some unspecified time*) irgendwann

an′yway′ *adv* sowieso, trotzdem

an′ywhere′ *adv* (*position*) irgendwo; (*everywhere*) an jedem beliebigen Ort; (*direction*) irgendwohin; (*everywhere*) an jeden beliebigen Ort; (*to any extent*) einigermaßen, e.g., **a. near correct** einigermaßen richtig; **get a.** (*achieve success*) es zu etwas bringen

apace [ə′pes] *adv* schnell, rasch

apart [ə′pɑrt] *adv* (*to pieces*) auseinander; (*separately*) einzeln, für sich; a. **from** abgesehen von

apartment [ə'pɑrtmənt] *s* Wohnung *f*

apart′ment house′ *s* Apartmenthaus *n*

apathetic [ˌæpə'θetɪk] *adj* apathisch, teilnahmslos

apathy ['æpəθi] *s* Apathie *f*

ape [ep] *s* Affe *m* ‖ *tr* nachäffen

aperture ['æpərtʃər] *s* Öffnung *f*; (phot) Blende *f*

apex ['epeks] *s* (**apexes** & **apices** ['æpɪˌsiz]) Spitze *f*; (fig) Gipfel *m*

aphid ['æfɪd] *s* Blattlaus *f*

aphorism ['æfəˌrɪzəm] *s* Aphorismus *m*

apiary ['epɪˌeri] *s* Bienenhaus *n*

apiece [ə'pis] *adv* pro Stück; (*per person*) pro Person

aplomb [ə'plɑm] *s* sicheres Auftreten *n*

apogee ['æpəˌdʒi] *s* Erdferne *f*

apologetic [əˌpɑlə'dʒetɪk] *adj* (*remark*) entschuldigend; (*letter, speech*) Entschuldigungs–; **be a.** (**about**) Entschuldigungen vorbringen (für)

apologize [ə'pɑləˌdʒaɪz] *intr* sich entschuldigen; **a. to s.o. for s.th.** sich bei j–m wegen etw entschuldigen

apology [ə'pɑlədʒi] *s* (*excuse*) Entschuldigung *f*; (*apologia*) Verteidigung *f*

apoplec′tic stroke′ [ˌæpə'plektɪk] *s* Schlaganfall *m*

apoplexy ['æpəˌpleksi] *s* Schlaganfall *m*

apostle [ə'pɑsəl] *s* Apostel *m*

apostolic [ˌæpəs'tɑlɪk] *adj* apostolisch

apostrophe [ə'pɑstrəfi] *s* (gram) Apostroph *m*; (rhet) Anrede *f*

apothecary [ə'pɑθɪˌkeri] *s* (*druggist*) Apotheker *m*; (*drugstore*) Apotheke *f*

appall [ə'pɔl] *tr* entsetzen

appall′ing *adj* entsetzlich

appara·tus [ˌæpə'retəs], [ˌæpə'rætəs] *s* (**-tus** & **-tuses**) Apparat *m*

apparel [ə'pærəl] *s* Kleidung *f*, Tracht *f*

apparent [ə'pærənt] *adj* (*visible*) sichtbar; (*obvious*) offenbar; (*seeming*) scheinbar

apparition [ˌæpə'rɪʃən] *s* Erscheinung *f*; (*ghost*) Gespenst *n*

appeal [ə'pil] *s* (*request*) Appell *m*, dringende Bitte *f*; (*to reason, etc.*) Appell *m*; (*charm*) Anziehungskraft *f*; (jur) (**to**) Berufung *f* (an *acc*) ‖ *tr*—a. **a case** Berufung einlegen in e–r Rechtssache ‖ *intr*—**a. to** (*entreat*) dringend bitten; (*be attractive to*) reizen; (jur) appellieren an (*acc*)

appear [ə'pir] *intr* erscheinen; (*seem*) scheinen; (*come before the public*) sich zeigen; (jur) sich stellen; (theat) auftreten; **a. as a guest** (telv) gastieren

appearance [ə'pɪrəns] *s* Erscheinen *n*; (*outward look*) Aussehen *n*; (*semblance*) Anschein *m*; (*on the stage*) Auftreten *n*; (jur) Erscheinen *n*; **for the sake of appearances** anstandshalber; **to all appearances** allem Anschein nach

appease [ə'piz] *tr* beruhigen; (*hunger*)

stillen; (*pain*) mildern; (dipl) beschwichtigen

appeasement [ə'pizmənt] *s* Beruhigung *f*; (*of hunger*) Stillung *f*; (dipl) Beschwichtigung *f*

appel′late court′ [ə'pelɪt] *s* Berufungsgericht *n*

append [ə'pend] *tr* anhängen; (*a signature*) hinzufügen

appendage [ə'pendɪdʒ] *s* Anhang *m*

appendectomy [ˌæpən'dektəmi] *s* Blinddarmoperation *f*

appendicitis [əˌpendɪ'saɪtɪs] *s* Blinddarmentzündung *f*, Appendizitis *f*

appen·dix [ə'pendɪks] *s* (**-dixes** & **-dices** [dɪˌsiz]) Anhang *m*; (anat) Appendix *m*

appertain [ˌæpər'ten] *intr* (**to**) gehören (zu), gebühren (*dat*)

appetite ['æpɪˌtaɪt] *s* (**for**) Appetit *m* (auf *acc*)

appetizer ['æpɪˌtaɪzər] *s* Vorspeise *f*

ap′petizing *adj* appetitlich

applaud [ə'plɔd] *tr* Beifall klatschen (*dat*); (*praise*) billigen ‖ *intr* Beifall klatschen

applause [ə'plɔz] *s* Beifall *m*, Applaus *m*

apple ['æpəl] *s* Apfel *m*

ap′plecart′ *s*—**upset the a.** die Pläne über den Haufen werfen

ap′ple of one′s eye′ *s* Augapfel *m*

ap′ple pie′ *s* gedeckte Apfeltorte *f*

ap′ple-pol′isher *s* (coll) Speichellecker *m*

ap′plesauce′ *s* Apfelmus *n*

ap′ple tree′ *s* Apfelbaum *m*

appliance [ə'plaɪəns] *s* Gerät *n*, Vorrichtung *f*

applicable ['æplɪkəbəl] *adj* (**to**) anwendbar (auf *acc*); **not a.** nicht zutreffend

applicant ['æplɪkənt] *s* Bewerber –in *mf*

application [ˌæplɪ'keʃən] *s* (*use*) Anwendung *f*; (*for a job*) Bewerbung *f*; (*for a grant*) Antrag *m*; (*zeal*) Fleiß *m*; (med) Anlegen *n*

applica′tion blank′ *s* (*for a job*) Bewerbungsformular *n*; (*for a grant*) Antragsformular *n*

applied′ *adj* angewandt

apply [ə'plaɪ] *v* (*pret* & *pp* **-plied**) *tr* anwenden; (med) anlegen; **a. oneself to** sich befleißigen (*genit*); **a. the brakes** bremsen ‖ *intr* gelten; **a. for** (*a job*) sich bewerben um; (*a grant*) beantragen

appoint [ə'pɔɪnt] *tr* (*a person*) ernennen; (*a time, etc.*) festsetzen

appointment [ə'pɔɪntmənt] *s* Ernennung *f*; (*post*) Stelle *f*; (*engagement*) Verabredung *f*; **by a. only** nur nach Vereinbarung; **have an a. with** (*e.g., a dentist*) bestellt sein zu

appoint′ment book′ *s* Terminkalender *m*

apportion [ə'pɔrʃən] *tr* zumessen

appraisal [ə'prezəl] *s* Abschätzung *f*

appraise [ə'prez] *tr* (ab)schätzen

appraiser [ə'prezər] *s* Schätzer –in *mf*

appreciable [ə'priʃɪ·əbəl] *adj* (*notice-*

able) merklich; (*considerable*) erheblich

appreciate [əˈpriʃɪˌet] *tr* dankbar sein für; (*danger*) erkennen; (*regard highly*) hochschätzen ‖ *intr* (im Werte) steigen

appreciation [əˌpriʃɪˈeʃən] *s* (*gratitude*) Dank *m*, Anerkennung *f*; (*for art*) Verständnis *n*; (*high regard*) Schätzung *f*; (*increase in value*) Wertzuwachs *m*

appreciative [əˈpriʃɪˌətɪv] *adj* (*of*) dankbar (für)

apprehend [ˌæprɪˈhɛnd] *tr* verhaften, ergreifen; (*understand*) begreifen

apprehension [ˌæprɪˈhɛnʃən] *s* (*arrest*) Verhaftung *f*; (*fear*) Befürchtung *f*; (*comprehending*) Begreifen *n*

apprehensive [ˌæprɪˈhɛnsɪv] *adj* (*of*) besorgt (um)

apprentice [əˈprɛntɪs] *s* Lehrling *m*

appren'ticeship' *s* Lehre *f*; **serve an a.** in der Lehre sein

apprise, apprize [əˈpraɪz] *tr* (*of*) benachrichtigen (von)

approach [əˈprotʃ] *s* Annäherung *f*; (*e.g., a road*) Zugang *m*, Zufahrt *f*; (*e.g., to a problem*) Behandlung *f*; (*tentative sexual approach*) Annäherungsversuch *m*; (aer) Anflug *m* ‖ *tr* sich nähern (*dat*); (*e.g., a problem*)—behandeln; (*perfection*) nahekommen (*dat*); (aer) anfliegen ‖ *intr* sich nähern

approachable [əˈprotʃəbəl] *adj* zugänglich

approbation [ˌæprəˈbeʃən] *s* (*approval*) Beifall *m*; (*sanction*) Billigung *f*

appropriate [əˈpropriˌɪt] *adj* (**to**) angemessen (*dat*) ‖ [əˈpropriˌet] *tr* (*take possession of*) sich [*dat*] aneignen; (*authorize*) bewilligen

approval [əˈpruvəl] *s* (*approbation*) Beifall *m*; (*sanction*) Billigung *f*; **meet with s.o.'s a.** j–s Beifall finden; **on a.** auf Probe

approve [əˈpruv] *tr* (*sanction*) genehmigen; (*judge favorably*) billigen; (*a bill*) (parl) annehmen ‖ *intr*—**a. of** billigen

approvingly [əˈpruvɪŋli] *adv* beifällig

approximate [əˈpraksɪmɪt] *adj* annähernd ‖ [əˈpraksɪˌmet] *tr* (*come close to*) nahekommen (*dat*); (*estimate*) schätzen; (*simulate closely*) täuschend nachahmen

approximately [əˈpraksɪmɪtli] *adv* ungefähr, etwa

apricot [ˈeprɪˌkɑt] *s* Aprikose *f*

ap'ricot tree' *s* Aprikosenbaum *m*

April [ˈeprɪl] *s* April *m*

A'pril fool' *interj* April, April!

A'pril Fools' Day' *s* der erste April *m*

apron [ˈeprən] *s* Schürze *f*; (aer) Vorfeld *n*; (theat) Vorbühne *f*

apropos [ˌæprəˈpo] *adj* passend ‖ *adv* —**a. of** in Bezug auf (*acc*)

apse [æps] *s* Apsis *f*

apt [æpt] *adj* (*suited to the occasion*) passend; (*suited to the purpose*) geeignet; (*metaphor*) zutreffend; **be apt to** (*inf*) (*be prone to*) dazu neigen zu

(*inf*); **he is apt to believe it** er wird es wahrscheinlich glauben

aptitude [ˈæptɪˌt(j)ud] *s* Eignung *f*

ap'titude test' *s* Eignungsprüfung *f*

aqualung [ˈækwəˌlʌŋ] *s* Tauchergerät *n*

aquamarine [ˌækwəməˈrin] *adj* blaugrün ‖ *s* Aquamarin *m*

aquari·um [əˈkwɛrɪəm] *s* (**-ums & –a** [ə]) Aquarium *n*

aquatic [əˈkwætɪk] *adj* Wasser– ‖ **aquatics** *spl* Wassersport *m*

aqueduct [ˈækwəˌdʌkt] *s* Aquädukt *n*

aq'uiline nose' [ˈækwɪˌlaɪn] *s* Adlernase *f*

Arab [ˈærəb] *adj* arabisch ‖ *s* Araber –in *mf*

Arabia [əˈrebɪ·ə] *s* Arabien *n*

Arabic [ˈærəbɪk] *adj* arabisch ‖ *s* Arabisch *n*

arable [ˈærəbəl] *adj* urbar, Acker–

arbiter [ˈɑrbɪtər] *s* Schiedsrichter *m*

arbitrary [ˈɑrbɪˌtreri] *adj* (*act*) willkürlich; (*number*) beliebig; (*person, government*) tyrannisch

arbitrate [ˈɑrbɪˌtret] *tr* schlichten ‖ *intr* als Schiedsrichter fungieren

arbitration [ˌɑrbɪˈtreʃən] *s* Schlichtung *f*

arbitrator [ˈɑrbɪˌtretər] *s* Schiedsrichter *m*

arbor [ˈɑrbər] *s* Laube *f*; (mach) Achse *f*

arbore·tum [ˌɑrbəˈritəm] *s* (**-tums & -ta** [tə]) Baumgarten *m*

arc [ɑrk] *s* (astr, geom, mach) Bogen *m*; (elec) Lichtbogen *m*

arcade [ɑrˈked] *s* Bogengang *m*, Arkade *f*

arcane [ɑrˈken] *adj* geheimnisvoll

arch [ɑrtʃ] *adj* (*liar, etc.*) abgefeimt ‖ *s* Bogen *m* ‖ *tr* wölben; (*span*) überwölben ‖ *intr* sich wölben

archaeologist [ˌɑrkɪˈalədʒɪst] *s* Archäolog(e) *m*, Archäologin *f*

archaeology [ˌɑrkɪˈalədʒi] *s* Archäologie *f*

archaic [ɑrˈke·ɪk] *adj* (*word*) veraltet; (*manner, notion*) antiquiert

archangel [ˈɑrkˌendʒəl] *s* Erzengel *m*

archbishop [ˈɑrtʃˈbɪʃəp] *s* Erzbischof *m*

archduke [ˈɑrtʃˈd(j)uk] *s* Erzherzog *m*

archenemy [ˈɑrtʃˌɛnimi] *s* Erzfeind *m*

archer [ˈɑrtʃər] *s* Bogenschütze *m*

archery [ˈɑrtʃəri] *s* Bogenschießen *n*

archipela·go [ˌɑrkɪˈpelago] *s* (**-gos & -goes**) Inselmeer *n*; (*group of islands*) Inselgruppe *f*, Archipel *m*

architect [ˈɑrkɪˌtekt] *s* Architekt –in *mf*

architecture [ˈɑrkɪˌtektʃər] *s* Architektur *f*, Baukunst *f*

archives [ˈɑrkaɪvz] *spl* Archiv *n*

arch'way' *s* Bogengang *m*, Torbogen *m*

arctic [ˈɑrktɪk] *adj* arktisch, nördlich ‖ **the Arctic** *s* die Arktis

Arc'tic Cir'cle *s* nördlicher Polarkreis *m*

arc' weld'ing *s* Lichtbogenschweißung *f*

ardent [ˈɑrdənt] *adj* feurig, eifrig

ardor [ˈɑrdər] *s* Eifer *m*, Inbrust *f*

arduous [ˈɑrdʒʊ·əs] *adj* mühsam
area [ˈɛrɪ·ə] *s* (*surface*) Fläche *f*; (*district*) Gegend *f*; (*field of enterprise*) Bereich *m*, Gebiet *n*; (*of danger*) Zone *f*
arena [əˈrinə] *s* Arena *f*, Kampfbahn *f*
Argentina [ˌɑrdʒənˈtinə] *s* Argentinien *n*
argue [ˈɑrgju] *tr* erörtern; (*maintain*) behaupten; **a. into** (*ger*) dazu überreden zu (*inf*) || *intr* (*with*) streiten (mit); **a. for** (or *against*) *s.th.* für (or gegen) etw eintreten; **don't a.!** keine Widerrede!
argument [ˈɑrgjəmənt] *s* (*discussion*) Erörterung *f*; (*point*) Beweisgrund *m*; (*disagreement*) Auseinandersetzung *f*; (*theme*) Thema *n*
argumentative [ˌɑrgjəˈmentətɪv] *adj* streitsüchtig
aria [ˈɑrɪ·ə], [ˈɛrɪ·ə] *s* Arie *f*
arid [ˈærɪd] *adj* trocken, dürr
aridity [əˈrɪdɪti] *s* Trockenheit *f*
arise [əˈraɪz] *v* (*pret* **arose** [əˈroz]; *pp* **arisen** [əˈrɪzən]) *intr* (*come into being*) (**from**) entstehen (aus); (*get out of bed*) aufstehen; (*from a seat*) sich erheben; (*occur*) aufkommen, auftauchen; (*said of an opportunity*) sich bieten; (*stem*) (**from**) stammen (von)
aristocracy [ˌærɪsˈtɑkrəsi] *s* Aristokratie *f*
aristocrat [əˈrɪstəˌkræt] *s* Aristokrat –in *mf*
aristocratic [əˌrɪstəˈkrætɪk] *adj* aristokratisch
arithmetic [əˈrɪθmətɪk] *s* Arithmetik *f*
arithmetical [ˌærɪθˈmetɪkəl] *adj* arithmetisch, rechnerisch
ark [ɑrk] *s* Arche *f*
ark′ of the cov′enant *s* Bundeslade *f*
arm [ɑrm] *s* Arm *m*; (*of a chair*) Seitenlehne *f*; (*weapon*) Waffe *f*; **keep s.o. at arm's length** sich j–m vom Leibe halten; **take up arms zu den Waffen greifen; up in arms** in Aufruhr || *tr* bewaffnen; || *intr* sich bewaffnen
armament [ˈɑrməmənt] *s* Kriegsausrüstung *f*, Bewaffnung *f*
ar′maments race′ *s* Rüstungswettlauf *m*
armature [ˈɑrmə·tʃər] *s* (*of doorbell or magnet*) Anker *m*; (*of a motor or dynamo*) Läufer *m*; (biol) Panzer *m*
arm′chair′ *s* Lehnsessel *m*; (*unpadded*) Lehnstuhl *m*
armed′ for′ces *spl* Streitkräfte *pl*
armed′ rob′bery *s* bewaffneter Raubüberfall *m*
Armenia [ɑrˈminɪ·ə] *s* Armenien *n*
armful [ˈɑrmˌfʊl] *s* Armvoll *m*
armistice [ˈɑrmɪstɪs] *s* Waffenstillstand *m*
armor [ˈɑrmər] *s* Panzer *m* || *tr* panzern
ar′mored car′ *s* Panzerwagen *m*
armor-piercing [ˈɑrmərˌpɪrsɪŋ] *adj* panzerbrechend
ar′mor plat′ing [ˈpletɪŋ] *s* Panzerung *f*
armory [ˈɑrməri] *s* (*large arms storage*) Arsenal *n*; (*arms repair and storage room of a unit*) Waffenkam-

mer *f*; (*arms factory*) Waffenfabrik *f*; (*drill hall*) Exerzierhalle *f*
arm′pit′ *s* Achselhöhle *f*
arm′rest′ *s* Armlehne *f*
army [ˈɑrmi] *adj* Armee–, Heeres– || *s* Armee *f*, Heer *n*; **join the a.** zum Militär gehen
aroma [əˈromə] *s* Aroma *n*, Duft *m*
aromatic [ˌærəˈmætɪk] *adj* aromatisch
around [əˈraʊnd] *adv* ringsherum; **be a.** in der Nähe sein; **get a.** viel herumkommen; **get a. to** (*inf*) dazukommen zu (*inf*) || *prep* um (acc) herum; (*approximately*) etwa; (*near*) bei (*dat*); **a. town** in der Stadt
arouse [əˈraʊz] *tr* aufwecken; (fig) erwecken
arraign [əˈren] *tr* (*accuse*) anklagen; (jur) vor Gericht stellen
arrange [əˈrendʒ] *tr* arrangieren; (*in a certain order*) (an)ordnen; (*a time*) festsetzen; (mus) bearbeiten || *intr*— **a. for** Vorkehrungen treffen für
arrangement [əˈrendʒmənt] *s* Anordnung *f*; (*agreement*) Vereinbarung *f*; (mus) Bearbeitung *f*; **make arrangements to** (*inf*) Vorbereitungen treffen, um zu (*inf*)
array [əˈre] *s* (*of troops, facts*) Ordnung *f*; (*large number or quantity*) Menge *f*; (*apparel*) Staat *m* || *tr* ordnen; (*dress up*) putzen
arrears [əˈrɪrz] *spl* Rückstand *m*; **in a.** rückständig
arrest [əˈrest] *s* Verhaftung *f*; **make an a.** e–e Verhaftung vornehmen; **place under a.** in Haft nehmen; **under a.** verhaftet || *tr* verhaften; (*attention*) fesseln; (*a disease, progress*) hemmen
arrival [əˈraɪvəl] *s* Ankunft *f*; (*of merchandise*) Eingang *m*; (*a person*) Ankömmling *m*
arrive [əˈraɪv] *intr* ankommen; (*said of time, an event*) kommen; **a. at** (*a conclusion, decision*) erlangen
arrogance [ˈærəgəns] *s* Anmaßung *f*
arrogant [ˈærəgənt] *adj* anmaßend
arrogate [ˈærəˌget] *tr* sich [*dat*] anmaßen
arrow [ˈæro] *s* Pfeil *m*
ar′rowhead′ *s* Pfeilspitze *f*
arsenal [ˈɑrsənəl] *s* Arsenal *n*
arsenic [ˈɑrsɪnɪk] *s* Arsen *n*
arson [ˈɑrsən] *s* Brandstiftung *f*
arsonist [ˈɑrsənɪst] *s* Brandstifter –in *mf*
art [ɑrt] *s* Kunst *f*
artery [ˈɑrtəri] *s* Pulsader *f*; (*highway*) Verkehrsader *f*
artful [ˈɑrtfəl] *adj* (*cunning*) schlau, listig; (*skillful*) kunstvoll
arthritic [ɑrˈθrɪtɪk] *adj* arthritisch, gichtisch || *s* Arthritiker –in *mf*
arthritis [ɑrˈθraɪtɪs] *s* Arthritis *f*
artichoke [ˈɑrtɪˌtʃok] *s* Artischocke *f*
article [ˈɑrtɪkəl] *s* (*object*) Gegenstand *m*; (com, gram, journ, jur) Artikel *m*
articulate [ɑrˈtɪkjəlɪt] *adj* deutlich || [ɑrˈtɪkjəˌlet] *tr & intr* deutlich aussprechen
artifact [ˈɑrtɪˌfækt] *s* Artefakt *n*
artifice [ˈɑrtɪfɪs] *s* Kunstgriff *m*
artificial [ˌɑrtɪˈfɪʃəl] *adj* Kunst–,

künstlich; (*emotion, smile*) gekünstelt

artillery [ɑr'tɪləri] *s* Artillerie *f*

artil'lery·man *s* (**-men**) Artillerist *m*

artisan ['ɑrtɪzən] *s* Handwerker –in *mf*

artist ['ɑrtɪst] *s* Künstler –in *mf*

artistic [ɑr'tɪstɪk] *adj* künstlerisch

artistry ['ɑrtɪstri] *s* Kunstfertigkeit *f*

artless ['ɑrtlɪs] *adj* (*lacking art*) unkünstlerisch; (*made without skill*) stümperhaft; (*ingenuous*) unbefangen

arts' and crafts' *spl* Kunstgewerbe *n*

arts' and sci'ences *spl* Geistes– und Naturwissenschaften *pl*

arty ['ɑrti] *adj* (coll) gekünstelt

Aryan ['ɛrɪ·ən], ['ɑrjən] *adj* arisch ‖ *s* Arier –in *mf*; (*language*) Arisch *n*

as [æz], [əz] *adv* wie; **as...as** (eben)so ...wie; **as far as Berlin** bis nach Berlin; **as far as I know** soviel ich weiß; **as far back as 1900** schon im Jahre 1900; **as for me** was mich betrifft; **as if** als ob; **as long as** solange; (*with the proviso that*) vorausgesetzt, daß; **as soon as** sobald wie; **as though** als ob; **as well** ebensogut, auch; **as yet** bis jetzt ‖ *rel pron* wie, was ‖ *prep* als; **as a rule** in der Regel ‖ *conj* wie; (*while*) als, während; (*because*) da, weil, indem; **as it were** sozusagen

asbestos [æs'bɛstəs] *adj* Asbest– ‖ *s* Asbest *m*

ascend [ə'sɛnd] *tr* (*stairs*) hinaufsteigen; (*a throne, mountain*) besteigen ‖ *intr* emporsteigen; (*said of a balloon, plane*) aufsteigen

ascendancy [ə'sɛndənsi] *s* Überlegenheit *f*

ascension [ə'sɛnʃən] *s* Aufsteigen *n*

Ascen'sion Day' *s* Himmelfahrtstag *m*

ascent [ə'sɛnt] *s* (*on foot*) Besteigung *f*; (*by vehicle*) Auffahrt *f*; (*upward slope*) Steigung *f*; (& fig) Aufstieg *m*

ascertain [ˌæsər'ten] *tr* feststellen

ascetic [ə'sɛtɪk] *adj* asketisch ‖ *s* Asket –in *mf*

ascribe [ə'skraɪb] *tr—a.* **to** zuschreiben (*dat*)

aseptic [ə'sɛptɪk] *adj* aseptisch

ash [æʃ] *s* Asche *f*; (*tree*) Esche *f*; **ashes** Asche *f*; (*mortal remains*) sterbliche Überreste *pl*

ashamed [ə'ʃemd] *adj—be* (or **feel**) **a.** (**of**) sich schämen (*genit*)

ash'can' *s* Ascheneimer *m*

ashen ['æʃən] *adj* aschgrau

ashore [ə'ʃor] *adv* (*position*) am Land; (*direction*) ans Land

ash'tray' *s* Aschenbecher *m*

Ash' Wednes'day *s* Aschermittwoch *m*

Asia ['eʒə], ['eʃə] *s* Asien *n*

A'sia Mi'nor *s* Kleinasien *n*

aside [ə'saɪd] *adv* zur Seite; **a. from** außer ‖ *s* (theat) Seitenbemerkung *f*

asinine ['æsɪˌnaɪn] *adj* eselhaft

ask [æsk] *tr* (*request*) bitten; (*demand*) auffordern; (*a high price*) fordern; (*inquire of*) fragen; **ask a question** (**of s.o.**) (j–m) e–e Frage stellen; **ask in** hereinbitten; **that is asking too much** das ist zuviel verlangt ‖ *intr*

fragen; **ask for** bitten um; **ask for trouble** sich [*dat*] selbst Schwierigkeiten machen

askance [əs'kæns] *adv—look* **a. at** schief ansehen

askew [ə'skju] *adv* schräg

ask'ing *s—for the* **a.** umsonst

asleep [ə'slip] *adj* schlafend; (*numb*) eingeschlafen; **be a.** schlafen; **fall a.** einschlafen

asp [æsp] *s* Natter *f*

asparagus [ə'spærəgəs] *s* Spargel *m*

aspect ['æspɛkt] *s* Gesichtspunkt *m*

aspen ['æspən] *s* Espe *f*

aspersion [ə'spʌrʒən] *s* (eccl) Besprengung *f*; **cast aspersions on** verleumden

asphalt ['æsfɔlt], ['æsfælt] *s* Asphalt *m* ‖ *tr* asphaltieren

asphyxiate [æs'fɪksɪˌet] *tr & intr* ersticken

aspirant [ə'spaɪrənt] *s* Bewerber –in *mf*

aspirate ['æspɪrɪt] *s* Hauchlaut *m* ‖ ['æspɪˌret] *tr* behauchen

aspire [ə'spaɪr] *intr* (*after,* **to**) streben (*nach*); **a. to** (*inf*) danach streben zu (*inf*)

aspirin ['æspɪrɪn] *s* Aspirin *n*

ass [æs] *s* Esel *m*; (*vulg*) Arsch *m*; **make an ass of oneself** (sl) sich lächerlich machen

assail [ə'sel] *tr* angreifen, anfallen; (*with questions*) bestürmen

assassin [ə'sæsɪn] *s* Meuchelmörder –in *mf*

assassinate [ə'sæsɪˌnet] *tr* ermorden

assassination [əˌsæsɪ'neʃən] *s* Meuchelmord *m*, Ermordung *f*

assault [ə'sɔlt] *s* Überfall *m*; (*rape*) Vergewaltigung *f*; (*physical violence*) (jur) tätlicher Angriff *m*; (*threat of violence*) (jur) unmittelbare Bedrohung *f*; (mil) Sturm *m* ‖ *tr* (er)stürmen, anfallen; (jur) tätlich beleidigen

assault' and bat'tery *s* schwere tätliche Beleidigung *f*

assay [ə'se], ['æse] *s* Prüfung *f* ‖ [ə'se] *tr* prüfen

assemble [ə'sɛmbəl] *tr* versammeln; (mach) montieren ‖ *intr* sich versammeln

assembly [ə'sɛmbli] *s* Versammlung *f*; (mach) Montage *f*; (pol) Unterhaus *n*

assem'bly line' *s* Fließband *n*

assent [ə'sɛnt] *s* Zustimmung *f* ‖ *intr* (**to**) zustimmen (*dat*)

assert [ə'sʌrt] *tr* behaupten; **a. oneself** sich behaupten

assertion [ə'sʌrʃən] *s* Behauptung *f*; (*of rights*) Geltendmachung *f*

assess [ə'sɛs] *tr* (*damage*) festsetzen; (*property*) (**at**) (ab)schätzen (auf *acc*); **assessed value** Schätzungswert *m*

assessment [ə'sɛsmənt] *s* (*of damage*) Festsetzung *f*; (*valuation*) Einschätzung *f*; (*of real estate*) Veranlagung *f*

assessor [ə'sɛsər] *s* Steuereinschätzer *m*

asset ['æset] *s* Vorzug *m;* (com) Aktivposten *m;* **assets** Vermögenswerte *pl;* **assets and liabilities** Aktiva und Passiva *pl*

assiduous [ə'sɪdʒʊ-əs] *adj* emsig

assign [ə'saɪn] *tr* zuweisen; *(homework)* aufgeben; *(transfer)* (jur) abtreten; (mil) zuteilen

assignment [ə'saɪnmənt] *s* Zuweisung *f; (homework)* Aufgabe *f; (task)* Auftrag *m,* Aufgabe *f; (transference)* (jur) Abtretung *f; (to a unit)* (mil) Zuteilung *f*

assimilate [ə'sɪmɪˌlet] *tr* angleichen ‖ *intr* sich angleichen

assimilation [əˌsɪmɪ'leʃən] *s* Assimilierung *f,* Angleichung *f*

assist [ə'sɪst] *s* (sport) Zuspiel *n* ‖ *tr* beistehen (dat) ‖ *intr*—**a. in** beistehen bei, behilflich sein bei

assistance [ə'sɪstəns] *s* Hilfe *f*

assistant [ə'sɪstənt] *adj* Hilfs-, Unter- ‖ *s (helper)* Gehilfe *m,* Gehilfin *f*

associate [ə'soʃɪ-ɪt] *adj* Mit-, beigeordnet; *(member)* außerordentlich ‖ *s (companion)* Gefährte *m,* Gefährtin *f; (colleague)* Kollege *m,* Kollegin *f;* (com) Partner *m* ‖ [ə'soʃɪˌet] *tr* verbinden ‖ *intr* (with) verkehren (mit)

asso'ciate profes'sor *s* außerordentlicher Professor *m*

association [əˌsoʃɪ'eʃən] *s (connection)* Verbindung *f; (social intercourse)* Verkehr *m; (society)* Verband *m; (suggested ideas, feelings)* Assoziation *f*

assonance ['æsənəns] *s* Assonanz *f*

assorted [ə'sɔrtɪd] *adj* verschieden

assortment [ə'sɔrtmənt] *s* Sortiment *n*

assuage [ə'swedʒ] *tr* (pain) lindern; *(hunger)* befriedigen; *(thirst)* stillen

assume [ə'ʃ(j)um] *tr (a fact as true; a certain shape, property, habit)* annehmen; *(a duty)* auf sich nehmen; *(office)* antreten; *(power)* ergreifen; **assuming that** vorausgesetzt, daß

assumed' *adj (feigned)* erheuchelt; **a. name** Deckname *m*

assumption [ə'sʌmpʃən] *s (supposition)* Annahme *f; (e.g., of power)* Übernahme *f*

assurance [ə'ʃʊrəns] *s* Versicherung *f*

assure [ə'ʃʊr] *tr* versichern

aster ['æstər] *s* Aster *f*

asterisk ['æstəˌrɪsk] *s* Sternchen *n*

astern [ə'stʌrn] *adv* achtern, achteraus

asthma ['æzmə] *s* Asthma *n*

astonish [ə'stɑnɪʃ] *tr* in Erstaunen setzen; **be astonished at** staunen über (acc), sich wundern über (acc)

astonishing *adj* erstaunlich

astonishment [ə'stɑnɪʃmənt] *s* Erstaunen *n,* Verwunderung *f*

astound [ə'staund] *tr* überraschen

astounding *adj* erstaunlich

astray [ə'stre] *adv*—**go a.** irregehen; **lead a.** irreführen

astride [ə'straɪd] *adv* rittlings ‖ *prep (a road)* an beiden Seiten (genit); *(a horse)* rittlings auf (dat)

astringent [əs'trɪndʒənt] *adj* stopfend ‖ *s* Stopfmittel *n*

astrology [ə'strɑlədʒɪ] *s* Astrologie *f*

astronaut ['æstrəˌnɔt] *s* Astronaut *m*

astronautics [ˌæstrə'nɔtɪks] *s* Raumfahrtwissenschaft *f,* Astronautik *f*

astronomer [ə'strɑnəmər] *s* Astronom –in *mf*

astronomic(al) [ˌæstrə'nɑmɪk(əl)] *adj* astronomisch

astronomy [ə'strɑnəmɪ] *s* Astronomie *f*

astute [ə'st(j)ut] *adj* scharfsinnig; *(cunning)* schlau

asunder [ə'sʌndər] *adv* auseinander

asylum [ə'saɪləm] *s (refuge)* Asyl *n; (for the insane)* Irrenhaus *n*

at [æt], [ət] *prep (position)* an (dat), auf (dat), in (dat), bei (dat), zu (dat); *(direction)* auf (acc), gegen (acc), nach (dat), zu (dat); *(manner, circumstance)* auf (acc), in (dat), unter (dat), bei (dat), zu (dat); *(time)* um (acc), bei (dat), auf (dat) zu (dat); **at all** *(in questions)* überhaupt; **at high prices** zu hohen Preisen; **even at that** sogar so

atheism ['eθɪˌɪzəm] *s* Atheismus *m*

atheist ['eθɪ-ɪst] *s* Atheist –in *mf*

Athens ['eθɪnz] *s* Athen *n*

athlete ['æθlɪt] *s* Sportler –in *mf*

ath'lete's foot' *s* Fußflechte *f*

athletic [æθ'letɪk] *adj* athletisch, Sport-, Turn- ‖ **athletics** *s* Athletik *f*

Atlantic [æt'læntɪk] *adj* atlantisch ‖ *s* Atlantik *m*

atlas ['ætləs] *s* Atlas *m*

atmosphere ['ætməsˌfɪr] *s* (& fig) Atmosphäre *f*

atmospheric [ˌætməs'ferɪk] *adj* atmosphärisch

atom ['ætəm] *s* Atom *n*

atomic [ə'tɑmɪk] *adj* atomisch, atomar, Atom-

atom'ic age' *s* Atomzeitalter *n*

atom'ic bomb' *s* Atombombe *f*

atom'ic pow'er *s* Atomkraft *f;* **atomic powers** (pol) Atommächte *pl*

atomizer ['ætəˌmaɪzər] *s* Zerstäuber *m*

atone [ə'ton] *intr*—**a. for** büßen

atonement [ə'tonmənt] *s* Buße *f*

atrocious [ə'troʃəs] *adj* gräßlich

atrocity [ə'trɑsɪtɪ] *s* Greueltat *f*

atrophy ['ætrəfɪ] *s* Verkümmerung *f,* Atrophie *f* ‖ *v (pret & pp* –**phied**) *tr* auszehren ‖ *intr* verkümmern

attach [ə'tætʃ] *tr (with glue, stitches, tacks)* (to) anheften (an acc); *(connect)* (to) befestigen (an acc); *(importance)* (to) beimessen (dat); *(a person)* (jur) verhaften; *(a thing)* (jur) beschlagnahmen; (mil) (to) zuteilen (dat); **a. oneself to** sich anschließen an (acc); **be attached to** festhalten an (dat); (fig) verwachsen sein mit

attaché [ˌætə'ʃe] *s* Attaché *m*

attaché' case' *s* Aktenköfferchen *n*

attachment [ə'tætʃmənt] *s* Befestigung *f; (regard)* (to) Zuneigung *f* (zu); *(device)* Zusatzgerät *n; (of a person)* (jur) Verhaftung *f; (of a thing)* (jur) Beschlagnahme *f*

attack [ə'tæk] *s* Angriff *m;* (pathol)

Anfall *m* ‖ *tr & intr* angreifen; (*pathol*) überfallen

attain [ə'ten] *tr* erreichen, erzielen ‖ *intr*—a. to erreichen

attainment [ə'tenmənt] *s* Erreichen *n*; **attainments** Fertigkeiten *pl*

attempt [ə'tempt] *s* Versuch *m*; (*assault*) Attentat *n* ‖ *tr* versuchen

attend [ə'tɛnd] *tr* beiwohnen (*dat*); (*school, church*) besuchen; (*accompany*) begleiten; (*a patient*) behandeln ‖ *intr*—a. to nachgehen (*dat*), erledigen

attendance [ə'tɛndəns] *s* Besuch *m*; (*number in attendance*) Besucherzahl *f*; (*med*) Behandlung *f*

attendant [ə'tɛndənt] *s* (*servant, waiter*) Diener –in *mf*; (*keeper*) Wärter –in *mf*; (*at a gas station*) Tankwart *m*; (*escort*) Begleiter –in *mf*

attention [ə'tɛnʃən] *s* Aufmerksamkeit *f*; Acht *f*; **a. Mr. X.** zu Händen von Herrn X; **call a. to** hinweisen auf (*acc*); **call s.o.'s a. to** j–n aufmerksam machen auf (*acc*); **pay a.** achtgeben; **pay a. to** achten auf (*acc*); **stand at a.** stillstehen ‖ *interj* (*mil*) Achtung!

attentive [ə'tɛntɪv] *adj* aufmerksam

attenuate [ə'tɛnju‚et] *tr* (*dilute, thin*) verdünnen; (*weaken*) abschwächen

attest [ə'tɛst] *tr* bezeugen ‖ *intr*—a. to bezeugen

attic ['ætɪk] *s* Dachboden *m*; (*as living quarters*) Mansarde *f*

attire [ə'taɪr] *s* Putz *m* ‖ *tr* kleiden

attitude ['ætɪ‚t(j)ud] *s* Haltung *f*; (aer, rok) Lage *f*

attorney [ə'tʌrni] *s* Rechtsanwalt *m*

attorney general *s* (**attorneys general**) Justizminister *m*

attract [ə'trækt] *tr* anziehen, reizen; (*attention*) erregen

attraction [ə'trækʃən] *s* Anziehungskraft *f*; (*that which attracts*) Anziehungspunkt *m*; (*in a circus, variety show*) Attraktion *f*; (*theat*) Zugstück *n*

attractive [ə'træktɪv] *adj* reizvoll; (*price, offer*) günstig

attribute ['ætrɪ‚bjut] *s* Attribut *n* ‖ [ə'trɪbjut] *tr* (*to*) zuschreiben (*dat*)

attrition [ə'trɪʃən] *s* Abnutzung *f*, Verschleiß *m*

attune [ə't(j)un] *tr* (*to*) abstimmen (auf *acc*)

auburn ['ɔbərn] *adj* kastanienbraun

auction ['ɔk/ən] *s* Auktion *f* ‖ *tr*—a. off versteigern; **be auctioned off** unter den Hammer kommen

auctioneer [‚ɔk/ən'ɪr] *s* Versteigerer –in *mf*

audacious [ə'deʃəs] *adj* (*daring*) kühn; (*brazen*) keck

audacity [ə'dæsɪti] *s* (*daring*) Kühnheit *f*; (*insolence*) Unverschämtheit *f*

audience ['ɔdɪ‚əns] *s* (*spectators*) Publikum *n*; (*formal hearing*) Audienz *f*; (rad) Zuhörerschaft *f*; (telv) Fernsehpublikum *n*

audio frequency ['ɔdɪ‚o] *s* Tonfrequenz *f*, Hörfrequenz *f*

audio-visual *adj* audiovisuell; **a. aids** Lehrmittel *pl*

audit ['ɔdɪt] *s* Rechnungsprüfung *f* ‖ *tr* prüfen, revidieren; (*a lecture*) als Gasthörer belegen

audition [ə'dɪ/ən] *s* Hörprobe *f* ‖ *tr* vorspielen (or vorsingen) lassen ‖ *intr* vorspielen, vorsingen

auditor ['ɔdɪtər] *s* (com) Rechnungsprüfer –in *mf*; (educ) Gasthörer –in *mf*

auditorium [‚ɔdɪ'tɔrɪ‚əm] *s* Hörsaal *m*

auger ['ɔgər] *s* Bohrer *m*

augment [og'mɛnt] *tr* (*in size*) vergrößern; (*in number*) vermehren ‖ *intr* sich vergrößern; sich vermehren

augur ['ɔgər] *s* Augur *m* ‖ *intr* weissagen; **a. well for** Gutes versprechen für

augury ['ɔgərɪ] *s* Weissagung *f*

august [ɔ'gʌst] *adj* erhaben ‖ **August** ['ɔgəst] *s* August *m*

aunt [ænt], [ɑnt] *s* Tante *f*

auricle ['ɔrɪkəl] *s* äußeres Ohr *n*; (*of the heart*) Herzohr *n*

auspices ['ɔspɪsɪz] *spl* Auspizien *pl*

auspicious [ɔs'pɪ/əs] *adj* glückverheißend

austere [ɔs'tɪr] *adj* (*stern*) streng; (*simple*) einfach; (*frugal*) genügsam; (*style*) schmucklos

Australia [ɔ'streljə] *s* Australien *n*

Australian [ɔ'streljən] *adj* australisch ‖ *s* Australier –in *mf*

Austria ['ɔstrɪ‚ə] *s* Österreich *n*

Austrian ['ɔstrɪ‚ən] *adj* österreichisch ‖ *s* Österreicher –in *mf*; (*dialect*) Österreichisch *n*

authentic [ɔ'θɛntɪk] *adj* authentisch

authenticate [ɔ'θɛntɪ‚ket] *tr* (*establish as genuine*) als echt erweisen; (*a document*) beglaubigen

author ['ɔθər] *s* (*of a book*) Autor –in *mf*; (*creator*) Urheber –in *mf*

authoritative [ɔ'θɔrɪ‚tetɪv] *adj* maßgebend

authority [ɔ'θɔrɪti] *s* (*power; expert*) Autorität *f*; (*right*) Recht *n*; (*approval*) Genehmigung *f*; (*source*) Quelle *f*; (*commanding influence*) Ansehen *n*; (*authoritative body*) Behörde *f*; **on one's own a.** auf eigene Verantwortung; **the authorities** die Behörden

authorize ['ɔθə‚raɪz] *tr* autorisieren

authorship *s* Autorschaft *f*

auto ['ɔto] *s* (-tos) Auto *n*

autobiography [‚ɔtobaɪ'ɑgrəfi] *s* Selbstbiographie *f*

autocratic [‚ɔtə'krætɪk] *adj* autokratisch

autograph ['ɔtə‚græf] *s* Autogramm *n* ‖ *tr* autographieren

automat ['ɔtə‚mæt] *s* Automaten-restaurant *n*

automatic [‚ɔtə'mætɪk] *adj* automatisch ‖ *s* Selbstladepistole *f*

automatic transmission *s* Automatik *f*

automation [‚ɔtə'me/ən] *s* Automation *f*

automaton [ɔ'tɔmə‚tɑn] *s* (-tons & -ta [tə]) Automat *m*

automobile [ˌɔtəmoˈbil] s Automobil n

automotive [ˌɔtəˈmotɪv] adj Auto—

autonomous [ɔˈtɑnəməs] adj autonom

autonomy [ɔˈtɑnəmi] s Autonomie f

autopsy [ˈɔtɑpsi] s Obduktion f

autumn [ˈɔtəm] adj Herbst– ‖ s Herbst m

autumnal [ɔˈtʌmnəl] adj herbstlich

auxiliary [ɔgˈzɪljəri] adj Hilfs– ‖ s (helper) Helfer –in mf; (gram) Hilfszeitwort n; **auxiliaries** (mil) Hilfstruppen pl

avail [əˈvel] s—to no a. nutzlos; without a. vergeblich ‖ tr nützen (dat); a. oneself of sich bedienen (genit) ‖ intr nützen

available [əˈveləbəl] adj vorhanden; (articles, products) erhältlich ‖ (gram, documents) zugänglich; be a. (for consultation, etc.) zu sprechen sein; make a. (to) zur Verfügung stellen (dat)

avalanche [ˈævəˌlæntʃ] s Lawine f

avarice [ˈævərɪs] s Habsucht f, Geiz m

avaricious [ˌævəˈrɪʃəs] adj geizig

avenge [əˈvendʒ] tr (a person) rächen; (a crime) ahnden; a. oneself on sich rächen an (dat)

avenger [əˈvendʒər] s Rächer –in mf

avenue [ˈævəˌn(j)u] s (wide street) Straße f; (fig) Weg m

average [ˈævərɪdʒ] adj Durchschnitts– ‖ s Durchschnitt m; (naut) Havarie f; on the a. im Durchschnitt ‖ tr (amount to, as a mean quantity) durchschnittlich betragen; (find the average of) den Durchschnitt berechnen von; (earn on the average) durchschnittlich verdienen; (travel on the average) durchschnittlich zurücklegen

averse [əˈvʌrs] adj (to) abgeneigt (dat)

aversion [əˈvʌrʒən] s (to) Abneigung f (gegen)

avert [əˈvʌrt] tr abwenden

aviary [ˈevɪˌeri] s Vogelhaus n

aviation [ˌevɪˈeʃən] s Flugwesen n

aviator [ˈevɪˌetər] s Flieger –in mf

avid [ˈævɪd] adj gierig

avocation [ˌævəˈkeʃən] s Nebenbeschäftigung f

avoid [əˈvɔɪd] tr (a person) meiden; (a thing) vermeiden

avoidable [əˈvɔɪdəbəl] adj vermeidbar

avoidance [əˈvɔɪdəns] s (of a person) Meidung f; (of a thing) Vermeidung f

avow [əˈvau] tr bekennen, gestehen

avowal [əˈvau·əl] s Bekenntnis n

avowed adj (declared) erklärt; (acknowledged) offen anerkannt

await [əˈwet] tr ei warten

awake [əˈwek] adj wach, munter ‖ v (pret & pp **awoke** [əˈwok] & **awaked**) tr wecken; (fig) erwecken ‖ intr erwachen

awaken [əˈweken] tr wecken; (fig) erwecken ‖ intr erwachen

awakening s Erwachen n; a rude a. ein unsanftes Erwachen

award [əˈwɔrd] s Preis m, Prämie f ‖ tr (to) zuerkennen (dat)

aware [əˈwer] adj—be a. of sich (dat) bewußt sein (genit)

awareness [əˈwernɪs] s Bewußtsein n

awash [əˈwɑʃ] adj überschwemmt

away [əˈwe] adj abwesend; (on a trip) verreist; (sport) Auswärts– ‖ adv fort, (hin)weg; do a. with abschaffen; make a. with (kill) umbringen

awe [ɔ] s (of) Ehrfurcht f (vor dat); stand in awe of s.o. vor j–m Ehrfurcht haben

awesome [ˈɔsəm] adj ehrfurchtgebietend

awful [ˈɔfəl] adj ehrfurchtgebietend; (coll) furchtbar

awfully [ˈɔfəli] adv (coll) furchtbar

awhile [əˈhwaɪl] adv eine Zeitlang

awkward [ˈɔkwərd] adj ungeschickt; (situation) peinlich

awl [ɔl] s Ahle f, Pfriem m

awning [ˈɔnɪŋ] s Markise f

awry [əˈraɪ] adv—go a. schiefgehen

ax [æks] s Axt f, Beil n

axiom [ˈæksɪəm] s Axiom n

axiomatic [ˌæksɪ·əˈmætɪk] adj axiomatisch

axis [ˈæksɪs] s (axes [ˈæksiz]) Achse f

axle [ˈæksəl] s Achse f

ay(e) [aɪ] adv (yes) ja; aye, aye, sir! zu Befehl, Herr (Leutnant, etc.) ‖ s Ja n, Jastimme f; the ayes have it die Mehrheit ist dafür

azalea [əˈzeljə] s Azalee f

azure [ˈeʒər] adj azurblau ‖ s Azur m

B

B, b [bi] zweiter Buchstabe des englischen Alphabets; (mus) H n; **B flat** B n; **B sharp** His n

babble [ˈbæbəl] s Geschwätz n; (of brook) Geplätscher n ‖ tr schwätzen ‖ intr schwätzen; (said of a brook) plätschern

babe [beb] s Kind n; (naive person) Kindskopf m; (pretty girl) Puppe f

baboon [bæˈbun] s (zool) Pavian m

baby [ˈbebi] s Baby n; (youngest child) Nesthäkchen n ‖ v (pret & pp –bied) tr verzärteln

baby bottle s Saugflasche f

baby carriage s Kinderwagen m

baby grand s Stutzflügel m

baby powder s Kinderpuder m

baby-sit v (pret & pp –sat; ger –sitting) intr Kinder hüten

baby-sitter s Babysitter m

ba'by talk' s Babysprache f
ba'by teeth' spl Milchzähne pl
baccalaureate [ˌbækəˈlɔrɪ-ɪt] s (bach-elor's degree) Bakkalaureat n; (serv-ice) Gottesdienst m bei der akade-mischen Promotion
bacchanal [ˈbækənəl] s (devotee) Bac-chantin f; (orgy) Bacchanal n
bachelor [ˈbætʃələr] s Junggeselle m
bach'elorhood' s Junggesellenstand m
Bach'elor of Arts' s Bakkalaureus m der Geisteswissenschaften
Bach'elor of Sci'ence s Bakkalaureus m der Naturwissenschaften
bacil·lus [bəˈsɪləs] s (-li [laɪ]) Ba-zillus m, Stäbchenbakterie f
back [bæk] adj Hinter-, Rück- || s (of a man, animal) Rücken m, Kreuz n; (of a hand, book, knife, mountain) Rücken m; (of a head, house, door, picture, sheet) Rückseite f; (of a fabric) linke Seite f; (of a seat) Rückenlehne f; (of a coin) Kehrseite f; (of clothing) Rückenteil m; (sport) Verteidiger m; at the b. of (e.g., a room) hinten in (dat); b. to b. (coll) nacheinander; behind s.o.'s b. hinter j-s Rücken; have one's b. to the wall an die Wand gedrückt sein; turn one's b. on s.o. (& fig) j-m den Rücken kehren || adv zurück; b. and forth hin und her; b. home bei uns (zulande); || tr (a person) den Rücken decken (dat); (a candidate, product) befürworten; (a horse) set-zen auf (acc); b. up (a car) rückwärts laufen lassen; b. water rückwärts rudern; das Schiff rückwärts fahren lassen; (fig) sich zurückziehen || intr —b. down klein beigeben; b. down from abstehen von; b. out of zurück-treten von; b. up zurückfahren; zurückgehen; (said of a sewer) zurückfließen
back'ache' s Rückenschmerzen pl
back'bit'ing s Anschwärzerei f
back'bone' s Rückgrat m; (fig) Willens-kraft f
back'break'ing adj mühsam
back' door' s Hintertür f
back'drop' s (fig & theat) Hintergrund m
backer [ˈbækər] s Förderer m, Unter-stützer m; (com) Hintermann m
back'fire' s Fehlzündung f || intr fehl-zünden; (fig) nach hinten losgehen
back'ground' adj Hintergrund- || s (& fig) Hintergrund m; (e.g., of an ap-plicant) Vorbildung f, Erfahrung f
back'hand' s (tennis) Rückhandschlag m
back'hand'ed adj Rückhand-; (compli-ment) zweideutig
back'ing s Unterstützung f; (material) versteifende Ausfütterung f
back'lash' s (& fig) Rückschlag m; (mach) toter Gang m
back'log' s Rückstand m
back' or'der s rückständiger Auftrag m
back' pay' s rückständiger Lohn m
back' seat' s Rücksitz m
back'side' s Rückseite f; (coll) Gesäß n

back'space' intr den Wagen zurück-schieben
back'space key' s Rücktaste f
back'spin' s Rückeffet m
back'stage' adv hinten auf die Bühne
back' stairs' spl Hintertreppe f
back'stop' s (baseball) Ballfang m
back' stretch' s Gegengerade f
back'stroke' s Rückenschwimmen n
back'swept' adj pfeilförmig
back' talk' s freche Antworten pl
back'track' intr denselben Weg zurück-gehen; (fig) e-n Rückzieher machen
back'up' s (stand-by) Beistand m; (in traffic) Verkehrsstauung f
back'up light' s (aut) Rückfahrschein-werfer m
backward [ˈbækwərd] adj rückwärts gerichtet, Rück-; (country) rück-ständig; (in development) zurückge-blieben; (shy) zurückhaltend || adv rückwärts, zurück; (fig) verkehrt; b. and forward vor und zurück
backwardness [ˈbækwərdnɪs] s Rück-ständigkeit f; (shyness) Zurückhal-tung f
back'wash' s zurücklaufende Strömung f
back'wa'ter s Rückstau m; (fig) Öde f
back'woods' spl Hinterwälder pl
back'yard' s Hinterhof m
bacon [ˈbekən] s Speck m; bring home the b. (sl) es schaffen
bacteria [bækˈtɪrɪ-ə] spl Bakterien pl
bacteriological [bækˌtɪrɪ-əˈlɑdʒɪkəl] adj bakteriologisch
bacteriology [bækˌtɪrɪˈɑlədʒɪ] s Bak-teriologie f, Bakterienkunde f
bacteri·um [bækˈtɪrɪ-əm] s (-a [ə]) Bakterie f
bad [bæd] adj schlecht, schlimm; (un-favorable) ungünstig; (risk) zweifel-haft; (debt) uneinbringlich; (check) ungedeckt; (blood) böse; (breath) übelriechend; (language) anstößig; (pain) stark; bad for schädlich (dat); from bad to worse immer schlimmer; I feel bad about it es tut mir leid; too bad! schade!
bad' egg' s (sl) übler Kunde m
badge [bædʒ] s Abzeichen n
badger [ˈbædʒər] s Dachs m || tr quälen
bad' luck' s Unglück n, Pech n
badly [ˈbædlɪ] adv schlecht, übel; (coll) dringend; b. wounded schwer-verwundet; be b. off übel dran sein
badminton [ˈbædmɪntən] s Federball-spiel n
bad'-tem'pered adj schlecht gelaunt
baffle [ˈbæfəl] s Sperre f; (on loud-speaker) Schallwand f || tr verwir-ren; (gas) drosseln
baf'fling adj verwirrend
bag [bæg] s Sack m; (for small items) Tüte f; (for travel) Reisetasche f; (sl) Frauenzimmer n; (hunt) Strecke f; bag and baggage mit Sack und Pack; it's in the bag das haben wir in der Tasche || v (pret & pp bagged; ger bagging) tr einsacken; (hunt) zur Strecke bringen || intr sich bauschen
baggage [ˈbægɪdʒ] s Gepäck n

bag'gage car' s Gepäckwagen m

bag'gage check' s Gepäckschein m

bag'gage count'er s Gepäckabfertigung f

bag'gage room' s Gepäckaufbewahrung f

baggy ['bægi] adj bauschig

bag'pipe' s Dudelsack m; **play the b.** dudeln

bail [bel] s Kaution f; **be out on b.** gegen Kaution auf freiem Fuß sein; **put up b. for** bürgen für || tr—b. **out** (water) aussschöpfen; (fig) retten; (jur) durch Kaution aus der Haft befreien || intr Wasser schöpfen; **b. out** (aer) abspringen

bailiff ['belɪf] s (agr) Gutsverwalter m; (jur) Gerichtsvollzieher m

bailiwick ['belɪwɪk] s (fig) Spezialgebiet n; (jur) Amtsbezirk m

bait [bet] s (& fig) Köder m || tr (traps) mit Köder versehen; (lure) ködern; (harass) quälen

bake [bek] tr (bread) backen; (meat) braten; (in a kiln) brennen || intr backen; (meat) braten

baked' goods' spl Gebäck n, Backwaren pl

baked' pota'to s gebackene Pellkartoffel f

baker ['bekər] s Bäcker –in mf

bak'er's doz'en s dreizehn Stück pl

bakery ['bekəri] s Bäckerei f

bak'ing pow'der s Backpulver n

bak'ing so'da s Backpulver n

balance ['bæləns] s (equilibrium) Gleichgewicht n; (remainder) Rest m; (scales) Waage f; (in a bank account) Bankguthaben n; (fig) Fassung f; (com) Bilanz f; || tr balancieren; (offset) abgleichen; (make come out even) ausgleichen || intr balancieren

bal'ance of pay'ments s Devisenbilanz f

bal'ance of pow'er s Gleichgewicht n der Kräfte

bal'ance sheet' s Bilanz f

bal'ance wheel' s (horol) Unruh f

balcony ['bælkəni] s Balkon m; (theat) Rang m

bald [bɔld] adj kahl; (eagle) weißköpfig; (fig) unverblümt

bald'head'ed adj kahlköpfig

baldness ['bɔldnɪs] s Kahlheit f

bald' spot' s Kahlstelle f

bale ['bæl] s Ballen m || tr in Ballen verpacken

baleful ['belfəl] adj unheilvoll

balk [bɔk] intr (at) scheuen (vor dat)

Balkan ['bɔlkən] adj Balkan– || s—**the Balkans** der Balkan

balky ['bɔki] adj störrisch

ball [bɔl] s Ball m; (dance) Ball m; (of yarn) Knäuel m & n; (of the foot) Ballen m; **be on the b.** (coll) bei der Sache sein; **have a lot on the b.** (coll) viel auf dem Kasten haben

ballad ['bæləd] s Ballade f

ball'-and-soc'ket joint' s Kugelgelenk n

ballast ['bæləst] s (aer, naut) Ballast m; (rr) Schotter m || tr (aer, naut) mit Ballast beladen; (rr) beschottern

ball' bear'ing s Kugellager n

ballerina [ˌbælə'rinə] s Ballerina f

ballet [bæ'le] s Ballett n

ball' han'dling s (sport) Balltechnik f

ballistic [bə'lɪstɪk] adj ballistisch || **ballistics** s Ballistik f

balloon [bə'lun] s Ballon m

ballot ['bælət] s Stimmzettel m || intr abstimmen

bal'lot box' s Wahlurne f

ball'-point pen' s Kugelschreiber m

ball'room' s Ballsaal m, Tanzsaal m

ballyhoo ['bælɪˌhu] s Tamtam n || tr Tamtam machen um

balm [bɑm] s (& fig) Balsam m

balmy ['bɑmi] adj mild, lind; **be b.** (coll) e–n Tick haben

baloney [bə'loni] s (sausage) (coll) Bolognawurst f; (sl) Quatsch m

balsam ['bɔlsəm] s Balsam m

Baltic ['bɔltɪk] adj baltisch || s Ostsee f

baluster ['bæləstər] s Geländersäule f

balustrade ['bæləsˌtred] s Brüstung f

bamboo [bæm'bu] s Bambus m, Bambusrohr n

bamboozle [bæm'buzəl] tr (cheat) anschmieren; (mislead) irreführen; (perplex) verwirren

ban [bæn] s Verbot n; (eccl) Bann m; || v (pret & pp banned; ger banning) tr verbieten

banal ['benəl] adj banal

banana [bə'nænə] s Banane f; (tree) Bananenbaum m

band [bænd] s (e.g., of a hat) Band n; (stripe) Steifen m; (gang) Bande f; (mus) Musikkapelle f; (rad) Band n || intr—b. **together** sich zusammenrotten

bandage ['bændɪdʒ] s Verband m || tr verbinden

Band'-Aid' s (trademark) Schnellverband m

bandit ['bændɪt] s Bandit m

band'lead'er s Kapellmeister m

band' saw' s Bandsäge f

band'stand' s Musikpavillon m

band'wag'on s—**climb the b.** mitlaufen

bane [ben] s Ruin m

baneful ['benfəl] adj verderblich

bang [bæŋ] s Knall m; **bangs** Ponyfrisur f; **with a b.** mit Krach || tr knallen lassen; (a door) zuschlagen; || intr knallen; (said of a door) zuschlagen; || interj bums! paff!

bang'-up' adj (sl) tipptopp, prima

banish ['bænɪʃ] tr verbannen

banishment ['bænɪʃmənt] s Verbannung f

banister ['bænɪstər] s Geländer n

bank [bæŋk] s Bank f; (of a river) Ufer n; (in a road) Überhöhung f; (aer) Schräglage f; (rr) Böschung f; || tr (money) in e–r Bank deponieren; (a road) überhöhen; (aer) in Schräglage bringen || intr (at) ein Bankkonto haben (bei); (aer) in die Kurve gehen; **b. on** bauen auf (acc)

bank' account' s Bankkonto n

bank' bal'ance s Bankguthaben n

bank'book' s Sparbuch n, Bankbuch n

banker ['bæŋkər] s Bankier –in mf

bank**/**ing *s* Bankwesen *n*
bank**/** note**/** *s* Geldschein *m*
bank**/**roll**/** *s* Rolle *f* von Geldscheinen
|| *tr* (sl) finanzieren
bankrupt [**'**bæŋkrʌpt] *adj* bankrott; go
b. Pleite machen || *tr* bankrott
machen
bankruptcy [**'**bæŋkrʌptsi] *s* Bankrott *m*
bank**/** state**/**ment *s* Bankausweis *m*
bank**/** tell**/**er *s* Kassierer –in *mf*
banner [**'**bænər] *s* Fahne *f*, Banner *n*
banquet [**'**bæŋkwɪt] *s* Bankett *n* || *intr*
tafeln
banter [**'**bæntər] *s* Neckerei *f* || *intr*
necken
baptism [**'**bæptɪzəm] *s* Taufe *f*
baptismal [bæp**'**tɪzməl] *adj* Tauf-
baptis**/**mal certi**/**ficate *s* Taufschein *m*
bap**/**tism of fire**/** *s* Feuertaufe *f*
Baptist [**'**bæptɪst] *s* Baptist –in *mf*,
Wiedertäufer *m*
baptistery [**'**bæptɪstəri] *s* Taufkapelle
f
baptize [bæp**'**taɪz] *tr* taufen
bar [bɑr] *s* Stange *f*; (*of a door, win-dow*) Riegel *m*; (*of gold, etc.*) Barren
m; (*of chocolate, soap*) Riegel *m*;
(*barroom*) Bar *f*; (*counter*) Schank-tisch *m*; (*obstacle*) (*to*) Schranke *f*
(*gegen*); (*jur*) Gerichtshof *m*, An-waltschaft *f*; (*bar line*) (mus) Takt-strich *m*; (*measure*) Takt *m*; (naut)
Barre *f*; be admitted to the bar zur
Advokatur zugelassen werden; be-hind bars hinter Gittern; || *prep*—
bar none ohne Ausnahme || *v* (*pret
& pp* barred; *ger* barring) *tr* (*a door*)
verriegeln; (*a window*) vergittern;
(*the way*) versperren; bar s.o. from
j–n hindern an (*dat*)
barb [bɑrb] *s* Widerhaken *m*; (fig)
Stachelrede *f*; (bot) Bart *m*
barbarian [bɑr**'**bɛrɪən] *s* Barbar *m*
barbaric [bɑr**'**bærɪk] *adj* barbarisch
barbarism [**'**bɑrbə‚rɪzəm] *s* Barbarei
f; (gram) Barbarismus *m*
barbarity [bɑr**'**bɛrɪti] *s* Barbarei *f*
barbarous [**'**bɑrbərəs] *adj* barbarisch
barbecue [**'**bɑrbɪ‚kju] *s* am Spieß (*or*
am Rost) gebratenes Fleisch *n*; (*grill*)
Bratrost *m*; (*outdoor meal*) Garten-grillfest *n* || *tr* am Spieß (*or* am Rost)
braten
barbed**/** wire**/** *s* Stacheldraht *m*
barbed**/**-wire entan**/**glement *s* Draht-verhau *m*
barber [**'**bɑrbər] *s* Friseur *m*
bar**/**ber chair**/** *s* Friseursessel *m*
bar**/**bershop**/** *s* Friseurladen *m*
bard [bɑrd] *s* Barde *m*
bare [bɛr] *adj* nackt, bloß; (*tree, wall*)
kahl; (*facts*) nackt; (*majority*) knapp
|| *tr* entblößen; (*heart, thoughts*)
offenbaren; (*teeth*) fletschen
bare**/**back**/** *adj & adv* sattellos
bare**/**faced**/** *adj* unverschämt
bare**/**foot**/** *adj & adv* barfuß
bare**/**head**/**ed *adj & adv* barhäuptig
barely [**'**bɛrli] *adv* kaum, bloß
bar**/**fly**/** *s* Kneipenhocker *m*
bargain [**'**bɑrgɪn] *s* (*deal*) Geschäft *n*;
(*cheap purchase*) Sonderangebot *n*;
into the b. obendrein; it's a b.! abge-

macht! || *tr*—b. away mit Verlust
verkaufen || *intr* handeln; b. for ver-handeln über (*acc*)
bar**/**gain price**/** *s* Preisschlager *m*
bar**/**gain sale**/** *s* Sonderverkauf *m*
barge [bɑrdʒ] *s* Lastkahn *m*; || *intr*—
b. in hereinstürzen; b. into stürzen
in (*acc*)
baritone [**'**bærɪ‚ton] *s* Bariton *m*
barium [**'**bɛrɪəm] *s* Barium *f*
bark [bɑrk] *s* (*of a tree*) Rinde *f*; (*of a
dog*) Bellen *n*, Gebell *n*; (*boat*) Barke
f; || *tr*—b. out bellend hervorstoßen
|| *intr* bellen; b. at anbellen
barker [**'**bɑrkər] *s* Anreißer *m*
barley [**'**bɑrli] *s* Gerste *f*; grain of b.
Graupe *f*
bar**/**maid**/** *s* Schankmädchen *n*, Bar-dame *f*
barn [bɑrn] *s* Scheune *f*; (*for animals*)
Stall *m*
barnacle [**'**bɑrnəkəl] *s* Entenmuschel *f*
barn**/**storm**/** *intr* auf dem Lande
Theateraufführungen veranstalten;
(pol) auf dem Lande Wahlreden hal-ten
barn**/**yard**/** *s* Scheunenhof *m*
barometer [bə**'**rɑmɪtər] *s* Barometer *n*
barometric [‚bærə**'**metrɪk] *adj* baro-metrisch
baron [**'**bærən] *s* Baron *m*
baroness [**'**bærənɪs] *s* Baronin *f*
baroque [bə**'**rok] *adj* barock || *s*
(*style, period*) Barock *m & n*
barracks [**'**bærəks] *s* (*temporary wood-en structure*) Baracke *f*; (mil) Ka-serne *f*
barrage [bə**'**rɑʒ] *s* Sperrfeuer *n*; *mov-ing b.* Sperrfeuerwalze *f*
barrel [**'**bærəl] *s* Faß *n*, Tonne *f*; (*of a
gun*) Lauf *m*; (*of money, fun*) große
Menge *f*; have over the b. (sl) in der
Gewalt haben || *intr* (coll) rasen,
sausen
barren [**'**bærən] *adj* dürr, unfruchtbar;
(*landscape*) kahl
barricade [**'**bærɪ‚ked] *s* Barrikade *f*
|| *tr* verbarrikadieren
barrier [**'**bærɪ‚ər] *s* Schranke *f*, Schlag-baum *m*; (*e.g., on a street*) Sperre *f*
bar**/**room**/** *s* Schenkstube *f*, Bar *f*
bartend [**'**bɑr‚tend] *intr* Getränke aus-schenken
bar**/**tend**/**er *s* Schankwirt *m*, Barmixer
m
barter [**'**bɑrtər] *s* Tauschhandel *m* ||
tauschen || *intr* Tauschhandel treiben
basalt [bə**'**sɔlt], [**'**bæsɔlt] *s* Basalt *m*
base [bes] *adj* gemein, niedrig; (*metal*)
unedel || *s* (*cosmetic*) Schminkunter-lage *f*; (fig) Grundlage *f*; (archit)
Basis *f*, Fundament *n*; (baseball)
Mal *n*; (chem) Base *f*; (geom) Grund-linie *f*, Grundfläche *f*; (math) Basis
f; (mil) Stützpunkt *m* || *tr* (mil) sta-tionieren; b. on stützen auf (*acc*),
gründen auf (*acc*)
base**/**ball**/** *s* Baseball *m*
base**/**board**/** *s* Wandleiste *f*
basement [**'**besmənt] *s* Kellergeschoß
n
bash [bæʃ] *s* heftiger Schlag *m*
bashful [**'**bæʃfəl] *adj* schüchtern

basic ['besɪk] *adj* grundsätzlich; (*e.g.,* *salary*) Grund–; (chem) basisch

basically ['besɪkəli] *adv* grundsätzlich

ba'sic train'ing *s* Grundausbildung *f*

basilica [bə'sɪlɪkə] *s* Basilika *f*

basin ['besɪn] *s* Becken *n;* (geol) Mulde *f;* (naut) Bassin *n*

ba·sis ['besɪs] *s* (–ses [siz]) Basis *f,* Grundlage *f;* **b. of comparison** Vergleichsgrundlage *f;* **put on a firm b.** (fin) sanieren

bask [bæsk] *intr* (& fig) sich sonnen

basket ['bæskɪt] *s* (& sport) Korb *m*

bas'ketball' *s* Basketball *m,* Korbball *m*

bas-relief [,bɑrɪ'lif] *s* Flachrelief *n*

bass [bes] *adj* Baß– || *s* (mus) Baß *m* || [bæs] *s* (ichth) Flußbarsch *m,* Seebarsch *m*

bass' clef' *s* Baßschlüssel *m*

bass' drum' *s* große Trommel *f*

bass' fid'dle *s* Baßgeige *f*

bassoon [bə'sun] *s* Fagott *n*

bass viol ['bes'var·əl] *s* Gambe *f*

bastard ['bæstərd] *adj* Bastard–; (*illegitimate in birth*) unehelich || *s* Bastard *m;* (vulg) Schweinehund *m*

baste [best] *tr* (*thrash*) verprügeln; (*scold*) schelten; (culin) begießen; (*sew*) lose (an)heften

bastion ['bæst/ən] *s* Bastion *f*

bat [bæt] *s* (sport) Schläger *m;* (zool) Fledermaus *f;* **go to bat for s.o.** (fig) für j–n eintreten || *v* (*pret & pp* **batted;** *ger* **batting**) *tr* schlagen; **without batting an eye** ohne mit der Wimper zu zucken

batch [bæt/] *s* Satz *m,* Haufen *m;* (*of bread*) Schub *m;* (*of letters*) Stoß *m* || *tr* (comp)—**b. out** stapeln

bated ['betɪd] *adj*—**with b. breath** mit verhaltenem Atem

bath [bæθ] *s* Bad *n;* **take a b.** ein Bad nehmen

bathe [beð] *tr & intr* baden

bather ['beðər] *s* Badende *mf*

bath'house' *s* Umkleideräume *pl*

bath'ing cap' *s* Baden *n,* Bad *n*

bath'ing cap' *s* Badehaube *f*

bath'ing suit' *s* Badeanzug *m*

bath'ing trunks' *spl* Badehose *f*

bath'robe' *s* Bademantel *m*

bath'room' *s* Badezimmer *n*

bath'room fix'tures *spl* Armaturen *pl*

bath'room scales *spl* Personenwaage *f*

bath' tow'el *s* Badetuch *n*

bath'tub' *s* Badewanne *f*

baton [bæ'tɑn] *s* (mil) Kommandostab *m;* (mus) Taktstock *m*

battalion [bə'tæljən] *s* Bataillon *n*

batter ['bætər] *s* Teig *m;* (baseball) Schläger –in *mf* || *tr* zerschlagen; (aer) bombardieren; **b. down** niederschlagen; **b. in** einschlagen

bat'tering ram' *s* Sturmbock *m*

battery ['bætəri] *s* Batterie *f;* (*secondary cell*) Akkumulator *m;* (arti) Batterie *f;* (nav) Geschützgruppe *f*

battle ['bætəl] *s* Schlacht *f;* (& fig) Kampf *m;* **do b.** kämpfen; **in b.** im Felde || *tr* bekämpfen || *intr* kämpfen

bat'tle array' *s* Schlachtordnung *f*

bat'tleax' *s* Streitaxt *f;* (fig) Drachen *m*

bat'tle cruis'er *s* Schlachtkreuzer *m*

bat'tle cry' *s* Schlachtruf *m;* (fig) Schlagwort *n*

bat'tle fatigue' *s* Kriegsneurose *f*

bat'tlefield' *s* Schlachtfeld *n*

bat'tlefront' *s* Front *f,* Hauptkampflinie *f*

bat'tleground' *s* Kampfplatz *m*

battlement ['bætəlmənt] *s* Zinne *f*

bat'tle scar' *s* Kampfmal *n*

bat'tleship' *s* Schlachtschiff *n*

bat'tle wag'on *s* (coll) Schlachtschiff *n*

batty ['bæti] *adj* (sl) doof

bauble ['bɔbəl] *s* Tand *m;* (*jester's staff*) Narrenstab *m*

Bavaria [bə'verɪ·ə] *s* Bayern *n*

Bavarian [bə'verɪ·ən] *adj* bayerisch || *s* Bayer –in *mf*

bawd [bɔd] *s* Dirne *f*

bawdy ['bɔdi] *adj* unzüchtig

bawl [bɔl] *s* Geplärr *n* || *tr*—**b. out** (*names, etc.*) ausschreien; (*scold*) anschnauzen || *intr* (coll) plärren

bay [be] *adj* kastanienbraun || *s* Bucht *f;* (*horse*) Rotfuchs *m;* (bot) Lorbeer *m;* **keep at bay in** Schach halten || *intr* laut bellen; **bay at** anbellen

bayo·net ['be·ənɪt] *s* Bajonett *n,* Seitengewehr *n;* **with fixed bayonets** mit aufgepflanztem Bajonett || *v* (*pret & pp* **–net(t)ed;** *ger* **–net(t)ing**) *tr* mit dem Bajonett erstechen

bay' win'dow *s* Erkerfenster *n*

bazaar [bə'zɑr] *s* Basar *m,* Markt *m*

bazooka [bə'zukə] *s* Panzerfaust *f*

be [bi] *v* (*pres am* [æm], *is* [ɪz], *are* [ɑr]; *pret was* [wɑz], [wɑz], *were* [wʌr]; *pp been* [bɪn]) *intr* sein; **be about** in der Nähe sein; **be about to** (*inf*) im Begriff sein zu (*inf*); **be after s.o.** hinter j–m her sein; **be along** hier sein; **be behind in** im Rückstand sein mit; **be behind s.o.** j–m den Rücken decken; **be from** (*a country*) stammen aus, sein aus; **be in** zu Hause sein; **be in for** zu erwarten haben; **be in for it** in der Patsche sitzen; **be in on** dabei sein bei; **be off** weggehen; **be on to s.o.** j–m auf die Schliche kommen; **be out** nicht zu Hause sein, aus sein; **be out for s.th.** auf der Suche nach etw sein; **be up** auf sein; **be up to s.th.** etw im Sinn haben; **how are you?** wie geht es Ihnen?, wie befinden Sie sich?; **how much is that?** wieviel kostet das?; **there are, there is es gibt** (*acc*) || *aux*—**he is studying** er studiert; **he is to go** er soll gehen; **he was hit** er ist getroffen worden || *impers*—**how is it that…?** wie kommt es, daß…?; **it is cold** es ist kalt; **it is to be seen that** es ist darauf zu sehen, daß

beach [bit/] *s* Strand *m;* **on the b.** am Strand, an der See || *tr* auf den Strand ziehen; **be beached** stranden

beach'comb'er *s* Strandgutjäger *m;* (*wave*) Strandwelle *f*

beach'head' *s* Landekopf *m*

beach' tow'el *s* Badetuch *n*

beach' umbrel'la *s* Strandschirm *m*

beacon ['bikən] *s* Leuchtfeuer *n,* Bake *f;* (*lighthouse*) Leuchtturm *m;* (aer)

Scheinwerfer *m* ‖ *tr* lenken ‖ *intr* leuchten

bead [bid] *(of glass, wood, sweat)* Perle *f*; *(of a gun)* Korn *n*; **beads** (eccl) Rosenkranz *m*; **draw a b. on** zielen auf *(acc)*

beagle ['bigel] *s* Spürhund *m*

beak [bik] *s* Schnabel *m*; *(nose)* (sl) Rübe *f*

beam [bim] *s (of wood)* Balken *m*; *(of light, heat, etc.)* Strahl *m*; *(fig)* Glanz *m*; *(aer)* Leitstrahl *m*; *(width of a vessel)* (naut) größte Schiffsbreite *f*; *(horizontal structural member)* (naut) Deckbalken *m*; **b. of light** Lichtkegel *m*; **off the b.** (sl) auf dem Holzweg; **on the b.** (sl) auf Draht ‖ *intr* strahlen; **b.** at anstrahlen

bean [bin] *s* Bohne *f*; *(head)* (sl) Birne *f*; **spill the beans** (sl) alles ausquatschen

bean'pole' *s* (& coll) Bohnenstange *f*

bear [ber] *adj (market)* flau, Baisse- ‖ *s* Bär *m*; (st. exch.) Baissier *m* ‖ *v (pret* bore [bor]; *pp* borne [born]) *tr (carry)* tragen; *(endure)* dulden, ertragen; *(children)* gebären; *(date)* tragen; *(a name, sword)* führen; *(a grudge, love)* hegen; *(a message)* überbringen; *(the consequences)* auf sich *[acc]* nehmen; **bear in mind** bedenken, beachten; **bear fruit** Früchte tragen; (fig) Frucht tragen; **bear out** bestätigen ‖ *intr*—**bear down** on losgehen auf *(acc)*; (naut) zufahren auf *(acc)*; **bear left** sich links halten; **bear on** sich beziehen auf *(acc)*; **bear up** (well) against gut ertragen; **bear with** Geduld haben mit

bearable ['berəbəl] *adj* erträglich

beard [bɪrd] *s* Bart *m*

beard'ed *adj* bärtig

beardless ['bɪrdlɪs] *adj* bartlos

bearer ['berər] *s* Träger –in *mf*; *(of a message)* Überbringer –in *mf*; (com) Inhaber –in *mf*

bear' hug' *s* (coll) Knutsch *m*

bear'ing *s* Körperhaltung *f*; *(mach)* Lager *n*; *(on)* Beziehung *f* (auf *acc*); **bearings** (aer, naut) Lage *f*, Richtung *f*, Peilung *f*; **lose one's bearings** die Richtung verlieren

bear'skin' *s* Bärenfell *n*

beast [bist] *s* Tier *n*; (fig) Bestie *f*

beastly ['bistli] *adj* bestialisch; **b. weather** Hundewetter *n*

beast' of bur'den *s* Lasttier *n*

beat [bit] *adj* (sl) erschöpft ‖ *s (of the heart)* Schlag *m*; *(of a policeman)* Runde *f*, Revier *n*; (mus) Takt *m* ‖ *v (pret* beat; *pp* beat & beaten) *tr (eggs, a child, record, team, etc.)* schlagen; *(a carpet)* ausklopfen; *(metal)* hämmern; *(a path)* treten; **b. it!** hau ab!; **b. one's brains out** sich *[dat]* den Kopf zerbrechen; **b. s.o. to it** j–m zuvorkommen; **b. up** verprügeln ‖ *intr* schlagen, klopfen; **b. against** peitschen gegen; **b. down** niederprallen

beati·fy [bɪ'ætɪ͵faɪ] *v (pret & pp –fied) tr* seligsprechen

beat'ing *s* Prügel *pl*

beatitude [bɪ'ætɪ͵t(j)ud] *s* Seligpreisung *f*

beau [bo] *s* (beaus & beaux [boz]) Liebhaber *m*

beautician [bju'tɪʃən] *s* Kosmetiker –in *mf*; *(hairdresser)* Friseuse *f*

beautiful ['bjutɪfəl] *adj* schön

beauti·fy ['bjutɪ͵faɪ] *v (pret & pp –fied) tr* verschönern

beauty ['bjuti] *s (quality; woman)* Schönheit *f*; (coll) Prachtexemplar *n*

beau'ty queen' *s* Schönheitskönigin *f*

beau'ty shop' *s* Frisiersalon *m*

beau'ty sleep' *s* Schönheitsschlaf *m*

beau'ty spot' *s* Schönheitsmal *n*

beaver ['bivər] *s* Biber *m*

because [bɪ'kɔz] *conj* weil, da ‖ *interj* darum!

because' of' *prep* wegen (*genit*)

beck [bek] *s* Wink *m*; **be at s.o.'s b. and call** j–m ganz zu Diensten sein

beckon ['bekən] *tr* zuwinken *(dat)*; *(summon)* heranwinken ‖ *intr* winken; **b. to s.o.** j–m zuwinken

become [bɪ'kʌm] *v (pret* –came; *pp* –come) *tr (said of clothes)* gut anstehen *(dat)*; *(said of conduct)* sich schicken für ‖ *intr* werden; **what has b. of him?** was ist aus ihm geworden?

becom'ing *adj (said of clothes)* kleidsam; *(said of conduct)* schicklich

bed [bed] *s (for sleeping; of a river)* Bett *n*; *(of flowers)* Beet *n*; *(of straw)* Lager *n*; (geol) Lager *n*; (rr) Unterbau *m*; **put to bed** zu Bett bringen

bed'bug' *s* Wanze *f*

bed'clothes' *spl* Bettwäsche *f*

bed'ding *s* Bettzeug *n*; *(for animals)* Streu *f*

bed'fel'low *s*—**strange bedfellows** ein seltsames Paar *n*

bedlam ['bedləm] *s* (fig) Tollhaus *n*; **there was b.** es ging zu wie im Tollhaus

bed' lin'en *s* Bettwäsche *f*

bed'pan' *s* Bettschüssel *f*

bed'post' *s* Bettpfosten *m*

bedraggled [bɪ'drægəld] *adj* beschmutzt

bedridden ['bed͵rɪdən] *adj* bettlägerig

bed'rock' *s* Grundgestein *n*; (fig) Grundlage *f*

bed'room' *s* Schlafzimmer *n*

bed'side' *s*—**at s.o.'s b.** an j–s Bett

bed'sore' *s* wundgelegene Stelle *f*; **get bedsores** sich wundliegen

bed'spread' *s* Bettdecke *f*, Tagesdecke *f*

bed'spring' *s (one coil)* Sprungfeder *f*; *(framework of springs)* Sprungfedermatratze *f*

bed'stead' *s* Bettgestell *n*

bed'time' *s* Schlafenszeit *f*; **it's past b.** es ist höchste Zeit, zu Bett zu gehen

bee [bi] *s* Biene *f*

beech [bitʃ] *s* Buche *f*

beech'nut' *s* Buchecker *f*

beef [bif] *s* Rindfleisch *n*; *(brawn)* (coll) Muskelkraft *f*; *(human flesh)* (coll) Fleisch *n*; *(complaint)* (sl) Gemecker *n* ‖ *tr*—**b. up** (coll) verstärken || *intr (complain)* (sl) meckern

beef' broth' *s* Kraftbrühe *f*

beef'steak' *s* Beefsteak *n*

beefy ['bifi] *adj* muskulös

bee'hive' *s* Bienenstock *m*, Bienenkorb *m*

bee'line' *s*—make a b. for schnurstracks losgehen auf *(acc)*

beer [bɪr] *s* Bier *n*

bee' sting' *s* Bienenstich *m*

beeswax ['biz‚wæks] *s* Bienenwachs *n*

beet [bit] *s* Rübe *f*

beetle ['bitəl] *s* Käfer *m*

be·fall [bɪ'fɔl] *v (pret* **-fell** ['fel]; *pp* **-fallen** ['fɔlən] *tr* betreffen, zustoßen || *intr* sich ereignen

befit'ting *adj* passend

before [bɪ'for] *adv* vorher, früher || *prep (position or time)* vor *(dat)*; *(direction)* vor *(acc)*; **b. long** binnen kurzem; **b. now** schon früher || *conj* bevor, ehe

before'hand' *adv* zuvor, vorher

befriend [bɪ'frend] *tr* sich *[dat] (j–n)* zum Freund machen, sich anfreunden mit

befuddle [bɪ'fʌdəl] *tr* verwirren

beg [beg] *v (pret & pp* begged; *ger* begging) *tr* bitten um; *(a meal)* betteln um; **beg s.o. to** *(inf)* j–n bitten zu *(inf)*; **I beg your pardon** (ich bitte um) Verzeihung! || *intr* betteln; *(said of a dog)* Männchen machen; **beg for** bitten um, flehen um; **beg off** absagen

be·get [bɪ'get] *v (pret* **-got** ['gɑt]; *pp* **-gotten & -got;** *ger* **-getting)** *tr* erzeugen

beggar ['begər] *s* Bettler –in *mf*

be·gin [bɪ'gɪn] *v (pret* **-gan** ['gæn]; *pp* **-gun** ['gʌn]; *ger* **-ginning** ['gɪnɪŋ]) *tr* beginnen, anfangen || *intr* beginnen, anfangen; **to b. with** zunächst

beginner [bɪ'gɪnər] *s* Anfänger –in *mf*

begin'ning *s* Beginn *m*, Anfang *m*

begrudge [bɪ'grʌdʒ] *tr*—b. s.o. s.th. j–m etw mißgönnen

beguile [bɪ'gaɪl] *tr (mislead)* verleiten; *(charm)* betören

behalf [bɪ'hæf] *s*—on b. of zugunsten *(genit)*, für; *(as a representative of)* im Namen *(genit)*, im Auftrag von

behave [bɪ'hev] *intr* sich benehmen

behavior [bɪ'hevjər] *s* Benehmen *n*

behead [bɪ'hed] *tr* enthaupten

behind [bɪ'haɪnd] *adj (in arrears)* (in) im Rückstand (mit); **the clock is ten minutes b.** die Uhr geht zehn Minuten nach || *adv (in the rear)* hinten, hinterher; *(to the rear)* nach hinten, zurück; **from b.** von hinten || *s* (sl) Hintern *m*, Popo *m* || *prep (position)* hinter *(dat)*; *(direction)* hinter *(acc)*; **be b. schedule** sich verspäten; **b. time** zu spät; **b. the times** hinter dem Mond

be·hold [bɪ'hold] *v (pret & pp* **-held** ['held]) *tr* betrachten || *interj* schau!

behoove [bɪ'huv] *impers*—it behooves me es geziemt mir

beige [beʒ] *adj* beige || *s* Beige *n*

be'ing *adj*—for the time b. einstweilen || *s* Dasein *n*; *(creature)* Wesen *n*; **come into b.** entstehen

belabor [bɪ'lebər] *tr* herumreiten auf *(dat)*

belated [bɪ'letɪd] *adj* verspätet

belch [beltʃ] *s* Rülpser *m* || *tr (fire)* ausspeien || *intr* rülpsen

beleaguer [bɪ'ligər] *tr* belagern

belfry ['belfri] *s* Glockenturm *m*

Belgian ['belʒən] *adj* belgisch || *s* Belgier –in *mf*

Belgium ['beldʒəm] *s* Belgien *n*

belief [bɪ'lif] *s* (in) Glaube(n) *m* (an *acc*)

believable [bɪ'livəbəl] *adj* glaublich

believe [bɪ'liv] *tr (a thing)* glauben; *(a person)* glauben *(dat)* || *intr* glauben; **b. in** glauben an *(acc)*; **I don't b. in war** ich halte nicht viel vom Kriege

believer [bɪ'livər] *s* Gläubige *mf*

belittle [bɪ'lɪtəl] *tr* herabsetzen

bell [bel] *s* Glocke *f*; *(small bell)* Klingel *f*; *(of a wind instrument)* Schalltrichter *m*; *(box)* Gong *m*

bell'boy' *s* Hotelboy *m*

bell'hop' *s* (sl) Hotelpage *m*

belligerent [bə'lɪdʒərənt] *adj* streitlustig || *s* kriegführender Staat *m*

bell' jar' *s* Glasglocke *f*

bellow ['belo] *s* Gebrüll *n*; **bellows** Blasebalg *m*; *(phot)* Balgen *m* || *tr & intr* brüllen

bell' tow'er *s* Glockenturm *m*

bel·ly ['beli] *s* Bauch *m*; *(of a sail)* Bausch *m* || *v (pret & pp* **-lied)** *intr* bauschen

bel'lyache' *s* (coll) Bauchweh *n* || *intr* (sl) jammern

bel'ly but'ton *s* Nabel *m*

bel'ly danc'er *s* Bauchtänzerin *f*

bel'ly flop' *s* Bauchklatscher *m*

bellyful ['beli‚ful] *s*—have a b. of die Nase voll haben von

bel'ly-land'ing *s* Bauchlandung *f*

belong [bɪ'lɔŋ] *intr* **b. to** *(designating ownership)* gehören *(dat)*; *(designating membership)* gehören zu; **where does this table b.?** wohin gehört dieser Tisch?

belongings [bɪ'lɔŋɪŋz] *spl* Sachen *pl*

beloved [bɪ'lʌvɪd], [bɪ'lʌvd] *adj* geliebt || *s* Geliebte *mf*

below [bɪ'lo] *adv (position)* unten; *(direction)* nach unten, hinunter || *prep (position)* unter *(dat)*, unterhalb *(genit)*; *(direction)* unter *(acc)*

belt [belt] *s* Riemen *m*, Gurt *m*, Gürtel *m*; *(geol)* Gebiet *n*; *(mach)* Treibriemen *m*; **tighten one's b.** den Riemen enger schnallen || *tr* (sl) e–n heftigen Schlag versetzen *(dat)*

belt' buck'le *s* Gürtelschnalle *f*

belt'way' *s* Verkehrsgürtel *m*

bemoan [bɪ'mon] *tr* betrauern, beklagen

bench [bentʃ] *s* Bank *f*; *(jur)* Gerichtshof *m*; *(sport)* Reservebank *f*, Bank *f*

bend [bend] *s* Biegung *f*; *(in a road)* Kurve *f*; **bends** (pathol) Taucherkrankheit *f* || *v (pret & pp* bent [bent]) *tr* biegen, beugen; *(a bow)* spannen ||

intr sich biegen, sich beugen; **b. down** sich bücken; **b. over backwards** (fig) sich [*dat*] übergroße Mühe geben

beneath [bɪ'niθ] *adv* unten ‖ *prep* (*position*) unter (*dat*), unterhalb (*genit*); (*direction*) unter (*acc*); **b. me** unter meiner Würde

benediction [͵benɪ'dɪkʃən] *s* Segen *m*

benefactor ['benɪ͵fæktər] *s* Wohltäter –in *mf*

beneficence [bɪ'nefɪsəns] *s* Wohltätigkeit *f*

beneficent [bɪ'nefɪsənt] *adj* wohltätig

beneficial [͵benɪ'fɪʃəl] *adj* heilbringend, gesund; (to) nützlich (*dat*)

beneficiary [͵benɪ'fɪʃɪ͵erɪ] *s* Begünstigte *mf*; (ins) Bezugsberechtigte *mf*

benefit ['benɪfɪt] *s* Nutzen *m;* (*fund-raising performance*) Benefiz *n;* (ins) Versicherungsleistung *f*

benevolence [bɪ'nevələns] *s* Wohlwollen *n*

benevolent [bɪ'nevələnt] *adj* wohlwollend

benign [bɪ'naɪn] *adj* gütig; (pathol) gutartig

bent [bent] *adj* krumm, verbogen; **b. on** versessen auf (*acc*) ‖ *s* Hang *m*

benzene [ben'zin] *s* Benzol *n*

bequeath [bɪ'kwið] *tr* vermachen

bequest [bɪ'kwest] *s* Vermächtnis *n*

berate [bɪ'ret] *tr* ausschelten, rügen

be·reave [bɪ'riv] *v* (*pret & pp* **–reaved & –reft** ['reft]) *tr* (of) berauben (*genit*)

bereavement [bɪ'rivmənt] *s* Trauerfall *m*

beret [bə're] *s* Baskenmütze *f*

Berlin [bər'lɪn] *adj* Berliner, berlinerisch ‖ *s* Berlin *n*

Berliner [bər'lɪnər] *s* Berliner –in *mf*

berry ['berɪ] *s* Beere *f*

berserk [bər'sʌrk] *adj* wütend ‖ *adv*— **go b.** wütend werden

berth [bʌrθ] *s* Schlafkoje *f;* (naut) Liegeplatz *m;* (rr) Bett *n;* **give s.o. wide b.** um j–n e–n weiten Bogen machen ‖ *tr* am Kai festmachen

be·seech [bɪ'sitʃ] *v* (*pret & pp* **–sought** ['sɔt] & **–seeched**) *tr* anflehen

be·set [bɪ'set] *v* (*pret & pp* **–set;** *ger* **–setting**) *tr* bedrängen, umringen

beside [bɪ'saɪd] *prep* (*position*) neben (*dat*), bei (*dat*); (*direction*) neben (*acc*); **be b. oneself with** außer sich [*dat*] sein vor (*dat*)

besides [bɪ'saɪdz] *adv* überdies, außerdem ‖ *prep* außer (*dat*)

besiege [bɪ'sidʒ] *tr* belagern

besmirch [bɪ'smʌrtʃ] *tr* beschmutzen

be·speak [bɪ'spik] *v* (*pret* **–spoke** ['spok]; *pp* **–spoken** ['spokən]) *tr* bezeigen

best [best] *adj* beste; **b. of all, very b.** allerbeste ‖ *adv* am besten; **had b. es wäre am besten, wenn** ‖ *s*—at **b.** bestenfalls; **be at one's b.** in bester Form sein; **for the b.** zum Besten; **make the b. of** sich abfinden mit; **to the b. of one's ability** nach bestem Vermögen

bestial ['bestʃəl] *adj* bestialisch

best′ man′ *s* Brautführer *m*

bestow [bɪ'sto] *tr* verleihen

bestowal [bɪ'sto·əl] *s* Verleihung *f*

best′ sel′ler *s* (*book*) Bestseller *m*

bet [bet] *s* Wette *f;* **make a bet** e–e Wette abschließen (or eingehen) ‖ *v* (*pret & pp* **bet & betted;** *ger* **betting**) *tr* (on) wetten (auf *acc*) ‖ *intr* wetten; **you bet!** aber sicher!

betray [bɪ'tre] *tr* verraten; (*a secret*) preisgeben; (*ignorance*) offenbaren; (*a trust*) mißbrauchen

betrayal [bɪ'tre·əl] *s* Verrat *m*

betrayer [bɪ'tre·ər] *s* Verräter –in *mf*

better ['betər] *adj* besser; **the b. part of** der größere Teil (*genit*) ‖ *s*— **change for the b.** sich zum Besseren wenden; **get the b. of** übervorteilen; **one's betters** die Höherstehenden *pl;* ‖ *adv* besser; **all the b.** um so besser; **b. off** besser daran; (*financially*) wohlhabender; **so much the b.** desto besser; **you had b. do it at once** am besten tust du es sofort; **you had b. not** das will ich dir nicht geraten haben ‖ *tr* verbessern; **b. oneself** sich verbessern

bet′ter half′ *s* (coll) bessere Hälfte *f*

betterment ['betərmənt] *s* Besserung *f*

bettor ['betər] *s* Wettende *mf*

between [bɪ'twin] *adv*—**in b.** dazwischen ‖ *prep* (*position*) zwischen (*dat*); (*direction*) zwischen (*acc*); **just b. you and me** ganz unter uns gesagt

bev·el ['bevəl] *adj* schräg ‖ *s* schräge Kante *f;* ‖ *v* (*pret & pp* **–el(l)ed;** *ger* **–el(l)ing**) *tr* abschrägen

beverage ['bevərɪdʒ] *s* Getränk *n*

bevy ['bevɪ] *s* Schar *f*

bewail [bɪ'wel] *tr* beklagen

beware [bɪ'wer] *intr* sich hüten; **b.! gib acht!; b. of** sich hüten vor (*dat*); **b. of imitations** vor Nachahmungen wird gewarnt

bewilder [bɪ'wɪldər] *tr* verblüffen

bewilderment [bɪ'wɪldərmənt] *s* Verblüffung *f*

bewitch [bɪ'wɪtʃ] *tr* (fig) bezaubern

beyond [bɪ'jand] *adv* jenseits ‖ *s*— **the b.** das Jenseits ‖ *prep* jenseits (*genit*), über (*acc*) hinaus; (fig) über (*acc*), außer (*dat*); **he is b. help** ihm ist nicht mehr zu helfen; **that's b. me** das geht über meinen Verstand

B′-girl′ *s* (coll) Animiermädchen *n*

bias ['baɪ·əs] *s* Voreingenommenheit *f* ‖ *tr* (*against*) einnehmen (gegen)

bi′ased *adj* voreingenommen

bib [bɪb] *s* Latz *m*, Lätzchen *n*

Bible ['baɪbəl] *s* Bibel *f*

Biblical ['bɪblɪkəl] *adj* biblisch

bibliographer [͵bɪblɪ'agrəfər] *s* Bibliograph –in *mf*

bibliography [͵bɪblɪ'agrəfɪ] *s* Bücherverzeichnis *n;* (*science*) Bücherkunde *f*

bi·ceps ['baɪseps] *s* (**–cepses** [sepsɪz] & **–ceps**) Bizeps *m*

bicker ['bɪkər] *intr* (sich) zanken

bick′ering *s* Gezänk *n*

bicuspid [baɪ'kʌspɪd] *s* kleiner Backenzahn *m*

bicycle ['baɪsɪkəl] s Fahrrad n
bid [bɪd] s Angebot n; (cards) Meldung f; (com) Kostenvoranschlag m || v (pret **bade** [bæd] & **bid**; pp **bidden** ['bɪdən]) tr (ask) heißen; (at auction) bieten; (cards) melden, reizen || intr (cards) reizen; (com) ein Preisangebot machen; **bid for** sich bewerben um
bidder ['bɪdər] s (at an auction) Bieter –in mf; **highest b.** Meistbietende mf
bid'ding s (at an auction) Bieten n; (request) Geheiß n; (cards) Reizen n
bide [baɪd] tr—**b. one's time** seine Gelegenheit abwarten
biennial [baɪ'enɪəl] adj zweijährig
bier [bɪr] s Totenbahre f
bifocals [baɪ'fokəlz] spl Zweistärkenbrille f
big [bɪg] adj (bigger; biggest) groß
bigamist ['bɪgəmɪst] s Bigamist m
bigamous ['bɪgəməs] adj bigamisch
bigamy ['bɪgəmi] s Bigamie f
big'-boned' adj starkknochig
big' busi'ness s das große Geschäft; (collectively) Großunternehmertum n
Big' Dip'per s Großer Bär m
big' game' s Hochwild n
big'-heart'ed adj großherzig
big'mouth' s (sl) Großmaul n
bigot ['bɪgət] s Fanatiker –in mf
bigoted ['bɪgɪtɪd] adj bigott, fanatisch
bigotry ['bɪgətri] s Bigotterie f
big' shot' s (coll) hohes Tier n, Bonze m
big'-time' adj groß, erstklassig; **b. operator** Großschieber –in mf
big' toe' s große Zehe f
big' top' s (coll) großes Zirkuszelt n
big' wheel' s (coll) hohes Tier n
big'wig' s (coll) Bonze m
bike [baɪk] s (coll) Rad n
bikini [bɪ'kini] s Bikini m
bilateral [baɪ'lætərəl] adj beiderseitig verbindlich
bile [baɪl] s Galle f
bilge [bɪldʒ] s Bilge f, Kielraum m
bilge' wat'er s Bilgenwasser n
bilingual [baɪ'lɪŋwəl] adj zweisprachig
bilk [bɪlk] tr (out of) prellen (um)
bill [bɪl] s Rechnung f; (paper money) Geldschein m, Schein m; (of a bird) Schnabel m; (parl) Gesetzesvorlage f; **pass a b.** ein Gesetz verabschieden || tr in Rechnung stellen
bill'board' s Anschlagtafel f
bill' collec'tor s Einkassierer –in mf
billet ['bɪlɪt] s (mil) Quartier n || tr (mil) einquartieren, unterbringen
bil'fold' s Brieftasche f
bil'liard ball' s Billardkugel f
billiards ['bɪljərdz] s Billard n
bil'liard ta'ble s Billardtisch m
billion ['bɪljən] s Milliarde f; (Brit) Billion f (million million)
bill' of exchange' s Tratte f, Wechsel m
bill' of fare' s Speisekarte f
bill' of health' s Gesundheitszeugnis n; **he gave me a clean b.** (fig) er hat mich für einwandfrei befunden
bill' of lad'ing ['ledɪŋ] s Frachtbrief m

bill' of rights' s erste zehn Zusatzartikel pl zur Verfassung (der U.S.A.)
bill' of sale' s Kaufurkunde f
billow ['bɪlo] s Woge f || intr wogen
bil'ly club' ['bɪli] s Polizeiknüppel m
bil'ly goat' s (coll) Ziegenbock m
bind [baɪnd] s—**in a b.** in der Klemme || v (pret & pp **bound** [baʊnd]) tr binden; (obligate) verpflichten; (bb) einbinden
binder ['baɪndər] s Binder –in mf; (e.g., cement) Bindemittel n; (for loose papers) Aktendeckel m; (mach) Garbenbinder m
bindery ['baɪndəri] s Buchbinderei f
bind'ing adj (on) verbindlich (für) || s Binden n; (for skis) Bindung f; (bb) Einband m
binge [bɪndʒ] s (sl) Zechtour f; **go on a b.** (sl) e–e Zechtour machen
binoculars [baɪ'nakjələrz] spl Fernglas n
biochemistry [,baɪ-ə'kemɪstri] s Biochemie f
biographer [baɪ'agrəfər] s Biograph –in mf
biographic(al) [,baɪ-ə'græfɪk(əl)] adj biographisch
biography [baɪ'agrəfi] s Biographie f
biologic(al) [,baɪ-ə'ladʒɪk(əl)] adj biologisch
biologist [baɪ'alədʒɪst] s Biologe m, Biologin f
biology [baɪ'alədʒi] s Biologie f
biophysics [,baɪ-ə'fɪzɪks] s Biophysik f
biopsy ['baɪ-əpsi] s Biopsie f
bipartisan [baɪ'partɪzən] adj Zweiparteien-
biped ['baɪped] s Zweifüßer m
bird [bɪrd] s Vogel m; **for the birds** für die Katz; **kill two birds with one stone** zwei Fliegen mit e–r Klappe schlagen
bird'cage' s Bauer n, Vogelkäfig m
bird' call' s Vogelruf m, Lockpfeife f
bird' dog' s Hühnerhund m
bird' of prey' s Raubvogel m
bird'seed' s Vogelfutter n
bird's'-eye view' s Vogelperspektive f
birth [bʌrθ] s Geburt f; (origin) Herkunft f; **give b.** to gebären
birth' certi'ficate s Geburtsurkunde f
birth' control' s Geburtenbeschränkung f
birth'day' s Geburtstag m
birth'day cake' s Geburtstagskuchen m
birth'day par'ty s Geburtstagsfeier f
birth'day pres'ent s Geburtstagsgeschenk n
birth'day suit' s (hum) Adamskostüm n
birth'mark' s Muttermal n
birth'place' s Geburtsort m
birth' rate' s Geburtenziffer f
birth'right' s Geburtsrecht n
biscuit ['bɪskɪt] s Keks m
bisect [baɪ'sɛkt] tr halbieren || intr sich teilen
bishop ['bɪʃəp] s Bischof m; (chess) Läufer m
bison ['baɪsən] s Bison m
bit [bɪt] s Bißchen n; (of food) Stück-

chen *n;* (*of time*) Augenblick *m;* (*part of a bridle*) Gebiß *n;* (*drill*) Bohrer *m;* **a bit** (*somewhat*) ein wenig; **a little bit** ein klein wenig; **bit by bit** brockenweise; **bits and pieces** Brocken *pl;* **every bit as** ganz genauso

bitch [bɪtʃ] *s* Hündin *f;* (*vulg*) Weibsbild *n*

bite [baɪt] *s* Biß *m;* (*wound*) Bißwunde *f;* (*of an insect*) Stich *m;* (*of a snake*) Biß *m;* (*snack*) Imbiß *m;* (*fig*) Bissigkeit *f;* **I have a b.** (*in fishing*) es beißt e–r an ‖ *v* (*pret* **bit** [bɪt]; *pp* **bit & bitten** ['bɪtən]) *tr* beißen; (*said of insects*) stechen; (*said of snakes*) beißen; **b. one's nails** an den Nägeln kauen ‖ *intr* beißen; (*said of fish*) anbeißen; (*said of the wind*) schneiden; **b. into** anbeißen

bit'ing *adj* (*remark*) bissig; (*cold, wind*) schneidend

bit' part' *s* kleine Rolle *f*

bitter ['bɪtər] *adj* (*& fig*) bitter; (*Person, Blick*) bitterböse

bitterly ['bɪtərli] *adv* bitterlich

bitterness ['bɪtərnɪs] *s* Bitterkeit *f*

bitters ['bɪtərz] *spl* Magenbitter *m*

bitu'minous coal' [bɪ't(j)umɪnəs] *s* Fettkohle *f*

bivouac ['bɪvwæk] *s* Biwak *n* ‖ *intr* biwakieren

bizarre [bɪ'zɑr] *adj* bizarr

blab [blæb] *v* (*pret & pp* **blabbed;** *ger* **blabbing**) *tr* ausplaudern ‖ *intr* plaudern

blabber ['blæbər] *intr* schwatzen

blab'bermouth' *s* Schwatzmaul *n*

black [blæk] *adj* schwarz ‖ *s* Schwarz *n;* (*black person*) Neger –in *mf,* Schwarze *mf* ‖ *tr* schwärzen; **b. out** (*mil*) verdunkeln ‖ *intr—***b. out** die Besinnung verlieren

black'-and-blue' *adj* blau unterlaufen; **beat s.o.** j–n grün und blau schlagen

black' and white' *s—***in b.** schwarz auf weiß, schriftlich

black'-and-white' *adj* schwarzweiß

black'ball' *tr* (*ostracize*) ausschließen; (*vote against*) stimmen gegen

black'ber'ry *s* Brombeere *f*

black'berry bush' *s* Brombeerstrauch *m*

black'bird' *s* Amsel *f*

black'board' *s* Tafel *f,* Wandtafel *f*

blacken ['blækən] *tr* schwärzen; (*a name*) anschwärzen

black' eye' *s* blaues Auge *n;* **give s.o. a b.** (*fig*) j–m Schaden zufügen

black'head' *s* Mitesser *m*

blackish ['blækɪʃ] *adj* schwärzlich

black'jack' *s* (*club*) Totschläger *m;* (*cards*) Siebzehnundvier *n* ‖ *tr* niederknüppeln

black'list' *s* schwarze Liste *f* ‖ *tr* auf die schwarze Liste setzen

black' mag'ic *s* schwarze Kunst *f*

black'mail' *s* Erpressung *f* ‖ *tr* erpressen

blackmailer ['blæk ˌmelər] *s* Erpresser –in *mf*

black' mar'ket *s* Schwarzmarkt *m*

black' marketeer' *s* Schwarzhändler –in *mf*

black'out' *s* (*fainting*) Bewußtlosigkeit *f;* (*of memory*) kurze Gedächtnisstörung *f;* (*of news*) Nachrichtensperre *f;* (*mil*) Verdunkelung *f;* (*tlv*) Sperre *f;* (*theat*) Auslöschen *n* aller Rampenlichter

black' sheep' *s* (*fig*) schwarzes Schaf *n*

black'smith' *s* Grobschmied *m;* (*person who shoes horses*) Hufschmied *m*

bladder ['blædər] *s* Blase *f*

blade [bled] *s* (*of a sword, knife*) Klinge *f;* (*of grass*) Halm *m;* (*of a saw, ax, shovel, oar*) Blatt *n;* (*of a propeller*) Flügel *m*

blame [blem] *s* Schuld *f* ‖ *tr* die Schuld geben (*dat*); **b. s.o. for** j–m Vorwürfe machen wegen; **I don't b. you for laughing** ich nehme es Ihnen nicht übel, daß Sie lachen

blameless ['blemlɪs] *adj* schuldlos

blame'wor'thy *adj* tadelnswert, schuldig

blanch [blæntʃ] *tr* erbleichen lassen; (*celery*) bleichen; (*almonds*) blanchieren ‖ *intr* erbleichen

bland [blænd] *adj* sanft, mild

blandish ['blændɪʃ] *tr* schmeicheln (*dat*)

blank [blæŋk] *adj* (*cartridge*) blind; (*piece of paper, space, expression*) leer; (*form*) unausgefüllt; (*tape*) unbespielt; (*nonplussed*) verblüfft; **my mind went b.** ich konnte mich an nichts erinnern ‖ *s* (*cartridge*) Platzpatrone *f;* (*unwritten space*) leere Stelle *f;* (*form*) Formular *n;* (*unfinished piece of metal*) Rohling *m* ‖ *tr* (*sport*) auf Null halten

blank' check' *s* Blankoscheck *m*

blanket ['blæŋkɪt] *adj* generell, umfassend ‖ *s* Decke *f*

blank' verse' *s* Blankvers *m*

blare [bler] *s* Lärm *m;* (*of trumpets*) Geschmetter *n* ‖ *intr* schmettern; (*aut*) laut hupen

blasé [blɑ'ze] *adj* blasiert; **b. attitude** Blasiertheit *f*

blaspheme [blæs'fim] *tr & intr* lästern

blasphemous ['blæsfɪməs] *adj* lästerlich

blasphemy ['blæsfɪmi] *s* Lästerung *f*

blast [blæst] *s* (*of an explosion*) Luftdruck *m;* (*of a horn, trumpet, air*) Stoß *m;* (*of air*) Luftzug *m;* **at full b.** (*fig*) auf höchsten Touren ‖ *tr* (*e.g., a tunnel*) sprengen; (*ruin*) (fig) verderben; (*criticize*) wettern gegen; (*blight*) versengen; **b. it!** verdammt! ‖ *intr—***b. off** (rok) starten

blast' fur'nace *s* Hochofen *m*

blast'-off' *s* (rok) Start *m*

blatant ['bletənt] *adj* (*lie, infraction*) eklatant; (*nonsense*) schreiend

blaze [blez] *s* Brand *m;* **b. of color** Farbenpracht *f;* **b. of glory** Ruhmesglanz *m;* **b. of light** Lichterglanz *m;* **go to blazes!** (sl) geh zum Teufel!; **like blazes** wie verrückt ‖ *tr—***b. a trail** e–n Weg markieren; (fig) e–n Weg bahnen ‖ *intr* lodern; **b. away at** drauflosschießen auf (*acc*)

blazer [ˈblezər] s Sportjacke f

blaz′ing adj (sun) prall

bleach [bliːtʃ] s Bleichmittel n ‖ tr bleichen; (hair) blondieren ‖ intr bleichen

bleachers [ˈbliːtʃərs] spl Zuschauersitze pl im Freien

bleak [bliːk] adj öde, trostlos

bleary-eyed [ˈblɪriˌaɪd] adj triefäugig

bleat [bliːt] s Blöken n ‖ intr blöken; (said of a goat) meckern

bleed [bliːd] v (pret & pp bled [blɛd]) tr (brakes) entlüften; (med) zur Ader lassen; **b. white** (fig) zum Weißbluten bringen ‖ intr bluten; **b. to death** verbluten

blemish [ˈblɛmɪʃ] s Fleck m, Makel m; (fig) Schandfleck m

blend [blɛnd] s Mischung f; (liquor) Verschnitt m ‖ v (pret & pp blended & blent [blɛnt]) tr mischen; (wine, liquor) verschneiden; (said of colors) zueinander passen, zusammenpassen

bless [blɛs] tr segnen; **God b. you!** (after a sneeze) Gesundheit!

blessed [ˈblɛsɪd] adj selig

bless′ing s Segen m, Gnade f; **b. in disguise** Glück n im Unglück

blight [blaɪt] s (fig) Gifthauch m; (agr) Brand m, Mehltau m ‖ tr (fig) verderben; (agr) schädigen

blight′ed adj brandig

blimp [blɪmp] s unstarres Luftschiff n

blind [blaɪnd] adj blind; (curve) unübersichtlich; **go b.** erblinden ‖ s Jalousie f; (hunt) Attrappe f ‖ tr blenden; (fig) verblenden

blind′ al′ley s (& fig) Sackgasse f

blind′ date′ s Verabredung f mit e-r (or e–m) Unbekannten

blinder [ˈblaɪndər] s Scheuklappe f

blind′ fly′ing s Blindflug m

blind′fold′ adj mit verbundenen Augen ‖ adv blindlings ‖ tr die Augen verbinden (dat)

blind′ man′ s Blinder m

blind′man′s′ bluff′ s Blindekuhspiel n

blindness [ˈblaɪndnɪs] s Blindheit f

blink [blɪŋk] s Blinken n; (with the eyes) Blinzeln n; **on the b.** (sl) kaputt ‖ tr—**b. one's eyes** mit den Augen zwinkern ‖ intr (said of a light) blinken; (said of the eyes) blinzeln

blinker [ˈblɪŋkər] s (for horses) Scheuklappe f; (aut) Blinker m

blip [blɪp] s (radar) Leuchtfleck m

bliss [blɪs] s Wonne f

blissful [ˈblɪsfəl] adj glückselig

blister [ˈblɪstər] s Blase f; (from a burn) Brandblase f ‖ intr (said of the skin) Blasen ziehen; (said of paint) Blasen werfen

blithe [blaɪð] adj fröhlich

blitzkrieg [ˈblɪtsˌkrig] s Blitzkrieg m

blizzard [ˈblɪzərd] s Blizzard m

bloat [blot] tr aufblähen ‖ intr anschwellen

bloc [blɑk] s (parl) Stimmblock m; (pol) Block m

block [blɑk] s (of wood) Klotz m; (toy) Bauklotz m; (for chopping) Hackklotz m; (of houses) Häuser-

block m; (of seats) Reihe f; (mach) Rolle f; (sport) Block m; **five blocks from here** fünf Straßen weiter ‖ tr versperren; (traffic, a street, a player) blockieren; (a ball) abfangen; (a hat) aufdämpfen; **be blocked** sich stauen; **b. off** (a street) absperren; **b. up** verstopfen, versperren

blockade [blɑˈked] s Blockade f, Sperre f ‖ tr blockieren, sperren

blockade′ run′ner s Blockadebrecher m

blockage [ˈblɑkɪdʒ] s Stockung f

block′ and tac′kle s Flaschenzug m

block′head′ s Klotz m, Dummkopf m

blond [blɑnd] adj blond ‖ s Blonde m

blonde [blɑnd] s Blondine f

blood [blʌd] s Blut n; (lineage) Geblüt n; **in cold b.** kaltblütig

blood′ circula′tion s Blutkreislauf m

blood′ clot′ s Blutgerinnsel n

bloodcurdling [ˈblʌdˌkɑrdlɪŋ] adj haarsträubend

blood′ do′nor s Blutspender –in mf

blood′hound′ s (& fig) Bluthund m

bloodless [ˈblʌdlɪs] adj blutlos; (revolution) unblutig

blood′ poi′soning s Blutvergiftung f

blood′ pres′sure s Blutdruck m

blood′ rela′tion s Blutsverwandte mf

blood′shed′ s Blutvergießen n

blood′shot′ adj blutunterlaufen

blood′stain′ s Blutfleck m, Blutspur f

blood′stained′ adj blutbefleckt

blood′stream′ s Blutstrom m

blood′suck′er s (& fig) Blutsauger m

blood′ test′ s Blutprobe f

blood′thirst′y adj blutdürstig

blood′ transfu′sion s Blutübertragung f

blood′ type′ s Blutgruppe f

blood′ ves′sel s Blutgefäß n

blood·y [ˈblʌdi] adj blutig; (bloodstained) blutbefleckt ‖ v (pret & pp -ied) tr mit Blut beflecken

bloom [blum] s Blüte f ‖ intr blühen

blossom [ˈblɑsəm] s Blüte f ‖ intr blühen

blot [blɑt] s Fleck m; (fig) Schandfleck m ‖ v (pret & pp blotted; ger blotting) tr (smear) beschmieren; (with a blotter) (ab)löschen; **b. out** ausstreichen; (fig) auslöschen ‖ intr (said of ink) klecksen

blotch [blɑtʃ] s Klecks m; (on the skin) Ausschlag m

blotter [ˈblɑtər] s Löscher m

blot′ting pa′per s Löschpapier n

blouse [blaus] s Bluse f

blow [blo] s Schlag m, Hieb m; (fig) Schlag m; **come to blows** handgemein werden ‖ v (pret blew [blu]; pp blown) tr blasen; (money) (sl) verschwenden; (a fuse) durchbrennen; **b. a whistle** pfeifen; **b. off steam** sich austoben; **b. one's top** (coll) hochgehen; **b. out** (a candle) ausblasen; **b. up** (inflate) aufblasen; (with explosives) sprengen; (phot) vergrößern ‖ intr blasen; **b. out** (said of a candle) auslöschen; (said of a tire) platzen; **blow over** vorüberziehen; **b. up** (& fig) in die Luft gehen

blower [ˈblo·ər] s Gebläse n, Bläser m

blow'out' s (sl) Gelage n; (aut) Reifenpanne f
blow'pipe' s Blasrohr n
blow'torch' s Lötlampe f
blubber ['blʌbər] s Tran m || intr (cry noisily) jaulen
bludgeon ['blʌdʒən] s Knüppel m || tr mit dem Knüppel bearbeiten
blue [blu] adj blau; (fig) bedrückt || s Blau n; **blues** (mus) Blues m; **have the blues** trüb gestimmt sein; **out of the b.** aus heiterem Himmel
blue'ber'ry s Heidelbeere f
blue'bird' s Blaukehlchen n
blue' chip' s (cards) blaue Spielmarke f; (fin) sicheres Wertpapier n
blue'-col'lar work'er s Arbeiter m
blue' jeans' spl Jeans pl
blue' moon' s—**once in a b.** alle Jubeljahre einmal
blue'print' s Blaupause f
blue' streak' s—**talk a b.** (coll) in e-r Tour reden
bluff [blʌf] adj schroff; (person) derb || s (coll) Bluff m; (geol) Steilküste f; **call s.o.'s b.** j–m beim Wort nehmen || tr & intr bluffen
bluffer ['blʌfər] s Bluffer m
blu'ing s Waschblau n
bluish ['blu·ɪʃ] adj bläulich
blunder ['blʌndər] s Schnitzer m; || intr e–n Schnitzer machen; **b. into** stolpern in (acc); **b. upon** zufällig geraten auf (acc)
blunt [blʌnt] adj stumpf; (fig) plump, unverblümt || tr abstumpfen
bluntly ['blʌntli] adv unverblümt
blur [blʌr] s Verschwommenheit f || v (pret & pp blurred; ger blurring) tr verwischen || intr verschwommen werden
blurb [blʌrb] s Reklametext m
blurred adj verschwommen; (vision) unscharf
blurt [blʌrt] tr—**b. out** herausplatzen
blush [blʌʃ] s Röte f, Schamröte f || intr (at) erröten (über acc)
bluster ['blʌstər] s Prahlerei f || intr (said of a person) prahlen, poltern; (said of wind) toben
blustery ['blʌstəri] adj stürmisch
boa constrictor ['bo·ə kən'strɪktər] s Abgottschlange f, Königsschlange f
boar [bor] s Eber m; (wild boar) Wildschwein n
board [bord] s Brett n; (of administrators) Ausschuß m, Behörde f, Rat m; (meals) Kost f; (educ) Schultafel f; **above b.** offen; **on b.** an Bord || tr (a ship) besteigen; (a plane, train) einsteigen in (acc); (paying guests) beköstigen; **b. up mit** Brettern vernageln || intr (with) in Kost sein (bei)
boarder ['bordər] s Kostgänger –in mf
board'inghouse' s Pension f
board'ing pass' s Bordkarte f
board'ing school' s Internat n
board'ing stu'dent s Interne mf
board' of direc'tors s Verwaltungsrat m, Aufsichtsrat m
board' of educa'tion s Unterrichtsministerium n

board' of health' s Gesundheitsbehörde f
board' of trade' s Handelskammer f
board' of trustees' s Verwaltungsrat m
board'walk' s Strandpromenade f
boast [bost] s Prahlerei f; (cause of pride) Stolz m || tr sich rühmen (genit) || intr (about) prahlen (mit)
boastful ['bostfəl] adj prahlerisch
boat [bot] s Boot n; **in the same b.** (fig) in der gleichen Lage
boat'house' s Bootshaus n
boat'ing s Bootsfahrt f; **go b.** e–e Bootfahrt machen
boat'race' s Bootrennen n
boat' ride' s Bootsfahrt f
boatswain ['bosən] s Hochbootsmann m
bob [bab] s (jerky motion) Ruck m; (hairdo) Bubikopf m; (of a fishing line) Schwimmer m; (of a plumb line) Senkblei n || v (pret & pp bobbed; ger bobbing) tr (hair) kurz schneiden || intr sich hin und her bewegen; **bob up and down** sich auf und ab bewegen
bobbin ['babın] s Klöppel m
bobble ['babəl] tr (coll) ungeschickt handhaben
bob'by pin' ['babi] s Haarklammer f
bob'sled' s Bob m, Rennschlitten m
bode [bod] tr bedeuten
bodily ['badılı] adj leiblich; **b. injury** Körperverletzung f || adv leibhaftig
body ['badi] s Körper m; (of a person or animal) Körper m; (corpse) Leiche f; (collective group) Körperschaft f; (of a plane, ship) Rumpf m; (of a vehicle) Karosserie f; (of beer, wine) Schwere f; (of a letter) Text m; **b. of water** Gewässer n; **in a b.** geschlossen
bod'yguard' s Leibgarde f
bod'y o'dor s Körpergeruch m
bog [bag] s Sumpf m || v (pret & pp bogged; ger bogging) intr—**bog down** steckenbleiben
bogey-man ['bogi ‚mæn] s (-men) Kinderschreck m
bogus ['bogəs] adj schwindelhaft
Bohemia [bo'himi·ə] s Böhmen n
Bohemian [bo'himi·ən] adj böhmisch || s (person) Böhme m, Böhmin f; (fig) Bohemien m; (language) Böhmisch n
boil [bɔɪl] s (pathol) Geschwür n; **bring to a b.** zum Sieden bringen || tr kochen, sieden || intr kochen, sieden; **b. away** verkochen; **b. over** überkochen
boiled' ham' s gekochter Schinken m
boiled' pota'toes spl Salzkartoffeln pl
boiler ['bɔɪlər] s (electrical water tank) Boiler m; (kettle) Kessel m
boil'ermak'er s Kesselschmied m
boil'er room' s Heizraum m
boil'ing adj siedend || adv—**be b. mad** vor Zorn kochen; **b. hot** siedeheiß
boil'ing point' s Siedepunkt m
boisterous ['bɔɪstərəs] adj ausgelassen
bold [bold] adj kühn, gewagt; (outlines) deutlich
bold'face' s Fettdruck m

boldness ['bəʊldnɪs] *s* Kühnheit *f*
Bolshevik ['bɒlʃəvɪk] *adj* bolsche-
wistisch || *s* Bolschewik –in *mf*
bolster ['bəʊlstər] *s* Nackenrolle *f* || *tr*
unterstützen
bolt [bəʊlt] *s* Bolzen *m*; (*door lock*)
Riegel *m*; (*of cloth*) Stoffballen *m*;
(*of lightning*) Blitzstrahl *m*; **b. out of
the blue** Blitz *m* aus heiterem Him-
mel || *tr* (*a door*) verriegeln; (*a po-
litical party*) im Stich lassen; (*food*)
hinunterschlingen || *intr* davonstür-
zen; (*said of a horse*) durchgehen
bomb [bɒm] *s* (*dropped from the air*)
Bombe *f*; (*planted*) Sprengladung *f*;
(*fiasco*) (sl) Versager *m* || *tr* (*from
the air*) bombardieren; (*blow up*)
sprengen || *intr* (sl) versagen
bombard [bɒm'bɑrd] *tr* bombardieren,
beschießen; (fig) bombardieren
bombardier [ˌbɒmbər'dɪr] *s* Bomben-
schütze *m*
bombardment [bɒm'bɑrdmənt] *s* Bombardement *n*, Beschießung *f*
bombast ['bɒmbæst] *s* Schwulst *m*
bombastic [bɒm'bæstɪk] *adj* schwülstig
bomb′ bay′ *s* Bombenschacht *m*
bomb′ cra′ter *s* Bombentrichter *m*
bomber ['bɒmər] *s* Bomber *m*
bomb′ing *s* Bombenabwurf *m*
bomb′ing run′ *s* Bomben(ziel)anflug *m*
bomb′proof′ *adj* bombenfest, bomben-
sicher
bomb′shell′ *s* (& fig) Bombe *f*
bomb′ shel′ter *s* Bombenkeller *m*
bomb′sight′ *s* Bombenzielgerät *n*
bomb′ squad′ *s* Entschärfungskom-
mando *n*
bona fide ['bɒnə ˌfaɪd] *adj* ehrlich,
echt; (*offer*) solide
bonanza [bo'nænzə] *s* Goldgrube *f*
bond [bɒnd] *s* Fessel *f*; (fin) Obligation *f*
bondage ['bɒndɪdʒ] *s* Knechtschaft *f*
bond′hold′er *s* Inhaber –in *mf* e-r Obligation
bonds·man ['bɒndzmən] *s* (–men)
Bürge *m*
bone [bɒn] *s* Knochen *m*, Bein *n*; (*of
fish*) Gräte *f*; **bones** Gebein *n*; (*mortal remains*) Gebeine *pl*; **have a b. to
pick with** ein Hühnchen zu rupfen
haben mit; **make no bones about it**
nicht viel Federlesens machen mit;
to the b. bis ins Mark || *tr* (*meat*)
ausbeinen; (*fish*) ausgräten || *intr*—
b. up for (sl) büffeln für
bone′-dry′ *adj* knochentrocken
bone′head′ *s* Dummkopf *m*
boneless ['bɒnlɪs] *adj* ohne Knochen;
(*fish*) ohne Gräten
boner ['bɒnər] *s* (coll) Schnitzer *m*;
pull a b. (coll) e-n Schnitzer machen
bonfire ['bɒnˌfaɪr] *s* Freudenfeuer *n*
bonnet ['bɒnɪt] *s* Haube *f*
bonus ['bɒnəs] *s* Gratifikation *f*
bony ['bɒni] *adj* knochig; (*fish*) grätig
boo [bu] *s* Pfuiruf *m* || *tr* niederbrüllen
|| *intr* pfui rufen || *interj* (*to jeer*)
pfui!; (*to scare someone*) huh!
boob [bub] *s* (sl) Blödkopf *m*
booby ['bubi] *s* Blödkopf *m*
boo′by hatch′ *s* (sl) Affenkasten *m*

boo′by prize′ *s* Trostpreis *m*
boo′by trap′ *s* Minenfalle *f*
boogey·man ['bugi ˌmæn], ['bogi-
ˌmæn] *s* (–men′) Schreckgespenst *n*
book [bʊk] *s* Buch *n*; (*of stamps, tickets, matches*) Heftchen *n*; **keep books**
Bücher führen || *tr* buchen; (*e.g.,
seats*) vorbestellen
book′bind′er *s* Buchbinder –in *mf*
book′bind′ery *s* Buchbinderei *f*
book′bind′ing *s* Buchbinden *n*
book′case′ *s* Bücherschrank *m*
book′ end′ *s* Bücherstütze *f*
bookie ['bʊki] *s* (coll) Buchmacher –in
mf
book′ing *s* Buchung *f*
bookish ['bʊkɪʃ] *adj* lesefreudig
book′keep′er *s* Buchhalter –in *mf*
book′keep′ing *s* Buchhaltung *f*
book′ learn′ing *s* Schulweisheit *f*
booklet ['bʊklɪt] *s* Büchlein *n*
book′mak′er *s* Buchmacher –in *mf*
book′mark′ *s* Lesezeichen *n*
book′rack′ *s* Büchergestell *n*
book′ review′ *s* Buchbesprechung *f*
book′sel′ler *s* Buchhändler –in *mf*
book′shelf′ *s* (–shelves) Bücherregal *n*
book′stand′ *s* Bücher(verkaufs)stand *m*
book′store′ *s* Buchhandlung *f*
book′worm′ *s* (& fig) Bücherwurm *m*
boom [bum] *s* (*noise*) dumpfes Dröhnen *n*; (*of a crane*) Ausleger *m*; (cin,
telv) Galgen *m*; (econ) Boom *m*,
Hochkonjunktur *f*; (naut) Baum *m*,
Spiere *f*; (st.exch.) Hausse *f* || *intr*
dröhnen; (*said of an organ*) brummen
boomerang ['bumə ˌræŋ] *s* Bumerang
m
boon [bun] *s* Wohltat *f*, Segen *m*
boon′ compan′ion *s* Zechkumpan *m*
boor [bʊr] *s* Rüpel *m*, Flegel *m*
boorish ['bʊrɪʃ] *adj* flegelhaft
boost [bust] *s* (*push*) Auftrieb *m*; (in
pay) Gehaltserhöhung *f* || *tr* fördern;
(*prices*) in die Höhe treiben; (elec)
verstärken; **b. business** die Wirtschaft ankurbeln
booster ['bustər] *s* (*backer*) Förderer
m, Förderin *f*
boost′er rock′et *s* Hilfsrakete *f*
boost′er shot′ *s* (med) Nachimpfung *f*
boot [but] *s* Stiefel *m*; (*kick*) Fußtritt
m; **to b. noch dazu; you can bet your
boots on that** (sl) darauf kannst du
Gift nehmen || *tr* (sl) stoßen; (fb)
kicken; **b. out** (sl) 'rausschmeißen
booth [buθ] *s* (*at a fair*) Marktbude *f*;
(*for telephone, voting*) Zelle *f*
boot′leg′ *adj* geschmuggelt || *v* (*pret &
pp* **–legged**; *ger* **–legging**) *tr* (*make
illegally*) illegal brennen; (*smuggle*)
schmuggeln
bootlegger ['but ˌlɛgər] *s* Alkohol-
schmuggler *m*, Bootlegger *m*
bootlicker ['but ˌlɪkər] *s* (sl) Kriecher
m
booty ['buti] *s* Beute *f*
booze [buz] *s* (coll) Schnaps *m* || *intr*
(coll) saufen
booze′ hound′ *s* Saufbold *m*, Saufaus *m*
border ['bɔrdər] *s* Rand *m*; (*of a country*) Grenze *f*; (*of a dress, etc.*) Saum

m, Borte *f* ‖ *tr* umranden, begrenzen; **be bordered by** grenzen an (*acc*) ‖ *intr*—**b. on** (& *fig*) grenzen an (*acc*)

bor′derline′ *s* Grenzlinie *f*

bor′derline case′ *s* Grenzfall *m*

bore [bor] *s* (*drill hole*) Bohrloch *n*; (*of a gun*) Bohrung *f*; (*of a cylinder*) innerer Zylinderdurchmesser *m*; (*fig*) langweiliger Mensch *m* ‖ *tr* bohren; (*fig*) langweilen

boredom [ˈbordəm] *s* Langeweile *f*

bor′ing *adj* langweilig ‖ *s* Bohren *n*

born [bɔrn] *adj* geboren; **he was b.** (*said of a living person*) er ist geboren; (*said of a deceased person*) er war geboren

borough [ˈbʌro] *s* Städtchen *n*

borrow [ˈbɔro] *tr* leihen

borrower [ˈbɔro‧ər] *s* Entleiher –in *mf*; (*fin*) Kreditnehmer –in *mf*

bor′rowing *s* Borgen *n*; (*fin*) Kreditaufnahme *f*; (*ling*) Lehnwort *n*

bosom [ˈbuzəm] *s* Busen *m*; (*fig*) Schoß *m*

bos′om friend′ *s* Busenfreund *m*

boss [bɔs] *s* (*coll*) Chef *m*, Boß *m*; (*of a shield*) Buckel *m*; (*pol*) Bonze *m* ‖ *tr* (*around*) herumkommandieren

bossy [ˈbɔsi] *adj* herrschsüchtig

botanical [bəˈtænɪkəl] *adj* botanisch

botanist [ˈbɑtənɪst] *s* Botaniker –in *mf*

botany [ˈbɑtəni] *s* Botanik *f*

botch [bɑtʃ] *tr* (*coll*) verpfuschen

both [boθ] *adj* & *pron* beide ‖ *conj*—**both...and** sowohl... als auch

bother [ˈbɑðər] *s* Belästigung *f*, Mühe *f* ‖ *tr* (*annoy*) belästigen, stören; (*worry*) bedrücken; (*said of a conscience*) quälen ‖ *intr* sich bemühen; **b. about** sich bekümmern um; **b. with** (*a thing*) sich befassen mit; (*a person*) verkehren mit

bothersome [ˈbɑðərsəm] *adj* lästig

bottle [ˈbɑtəl] *s* Flasche *f* ‖ *tr* in Flaschen abfüllen; **bottled up** aufgestaut

bot′tleneck′ *s* Flaschenhals *m*; (*fig*) Engpaß *m*, Stauung *f*

bot′tle o′pener *s* Flaschenöffner *m*

bottom [ˈbɑtəm] *adj* niedrigste, unterste ‖ *s* Boden *m*; (*of a well, shaft, river, valley*) Sohle *f*; (*of a mountain*) Fuß *m*; (*of an affair*) Grund *m*; (*buttocks*) Hintern *m*; **at the b. of the page** unten auf der Seite; **bottoms up!** prosit, ex!; **get to the b. of a problem** e–r Frage auf den Grund gehen; **reach b.** (*fig*) den Nullpunkt erreichen

bottomless [ˈbɑtəmlɪs] *adj* bodenlos

bough [bau] *s* Ast *m*

bouillon [ˈbuljɑn] *s* Kraftbrühe *f*

bouil′lon cube′ *s* Bouillonwürfel *m*

boulder [ˈboldər] *s* Felsblock *m*

bounce [bauns] *s* Aufprall *m*; (*fig*) Schwung *m* ‖ *tr* (*a ball*) aufprallen lassen; (*throw out*) (sl) ′rausschmeißen ‖ *intr* aufprallen, aufspringen; (*said of a check*) (coll) platzen

bouncer [ˈbaunsər] *s* (sl) Rausschmeißer *m*

bounc′ing *adj* (*baby*) stramm

bound [baund] *adj* gebunden, gefes-

selt; (*book*) gebunden; (*in duty*) verpflichtet; **be b. for** unterwegs sein nach; **be b. up with** eng verbunden sein mit; **I am b. to** (*inf*) ich muß (*inf*) ‖ *s* Sprung *m*, Satz *m*; **bounds** Grenzen *pl*, Schranken *pl*; **in bounds** (sport) in; **keep within bounds** in Schranken halten; **know no bounds** weder Maß noch Ziel kennen; **out of bounds** (sport) aus; **within the bounds of** im Bereich (*genit*) ‖ *tr* begrenzen ‖ *intr* aufprallen, aufspringen

boundary [ˈbaundəri] *s* Grenze *f*; (*fig*) Umgrenzung *f*

boun′dary line′ *s* Grenzlinie *f*

boun′dary stone′ *s* Grenzstein *m*

boundless [ˈbaundlɪs] *adj* grenzenlos

bountiful [ˈbauntɪfəl] *adj* (*generous*) freigebig; (*ample*) reichlich

bounty [ˈbaunti] *s* (*generosity*) Freigebigkeit *f*; (*gift*) Geschenk *n*; (*reward*) Prämie *f*

bouquet [buˈke] *s* Strauß *m*; (*aroma*) Blume *f*

bout [baut] *s* (*box*) Kampf *m*; (*fencing*) Gang *m*; (*pathol*) Anfall *m*

bow [bau] *s* Verbeugung *f*; (*naut*) Bug *m* ‖ *intr* sich verbeugen; **bow and scrape before** sich schmiegen und biegen vor (*dat*); **bow down** sich bücken; **bow out** sich geschickt zurückziehen; **bow to** sich (ver)neigen vor (*dat*) ‖ [bo] *s* (*weapon*) Bogen *m*; (*of a violin*) Geigenbogen *m*; (*bowknot*) Schleife *f*; **bow and arrow** Pfeil *m* und Bogen *m* ‖ *intr* (mus) geigen

bowel [ˈbau‧əl] *s* Darm *m*; **bowels** Eingeweide *pl*; **bowels of the earth** Erdinnere *n*

bow′el move′ment *s* Stuhlgang *m*

bowl [bol] *s* Napf *m*, Schüssel *f*; (*of a pipe*) Kopf *m*; (*washbowl, toilet bowl*) Becken *n*; (*of a spoon*) Höhlung *f*; (sport) Stadion *n* ‖ *tr* umhauen; (fig) umwerfen ‖ *intr* kegeln

bowlegged [ˈbo‧lɛg(ɪ)d] *adj* O-beinig

bowler [ˈbolər] *s* Kegler –in *mf*

bowl′ing *s* Kegeln *n*

bowl′ing al′ley *s* Kegelbahn *f*

bowl′ing ball′ *s* Kegelkugel *f*

bowl′ing pin′ *s* Kegel *m*

bowstring [ˈbo‧strɪŋ] *s* Bogensehne *f*

bow′ tie′ [bo] *s* Schleife *f*, Fliege *f*

bow′ win′dow [bo] *s* Bogenfenster *n*

bowwow [ˈbau‧wau] *interj* wauwau!

box [bɑks] *s* (*small and generally of cardboard*) Schachtel *f*; (*larger and generally of cardboard*) Karton *m*; (*generally of wood*) Kasten *m*; (*larger and generally of wood*) Kiste *f*; (*of strips of wood*) Spanschachtel *f*; (theat) Loge *f*; (typ) Kasten *m*; **box of candy** Bonbonniere *f*; **box on the ear** Ohrfeige *f* ‖ *tr* (sport) boxen; **box in** einschließen; **box s.o.'s ears** j–n ohrfeigen ‖ *intr* (sport) boxen

box′car′ *s* geschlossener Güterwagen *m*

boxer [ˈbɑksər] *s* (sport, zool) Boxer *m*

box′ing *s* Boxen *n*, Boxsport *m*

box′ing glove′ *s* Boxhandschuh *m*

box'ing match' *s* Boxkampf *m*
box' kite' *s* Kastendrachen *m*
box' of'fice *s* (cin, theat) Kasse *f*
box' seat' *s* Logenplatz *m*
box'wood' *s* Buchsbaum *m*
boy [bɔɪ] *s* Junge *m*; (*servant*) Boy *m*
boycott ['bɔɪkat] *s* Boykott *m* ‖ *tr* boykottieren
boy'friend' *s* Freund *m*
boy'hood' *s* Knabenalter *n*
boyish ['bɔɪ·ɪʃ] *adj* jungenhaft
boy' scout' *s* Pfadfinder *m*
bra [bra] *s* (coll) BH *m*
brace [bres] *s* (carp) Strebe *f*, Stütze *f*; (dent) Zahnklammer *f*, Zahnspange *f*; (hunt) Paar *n*; (med) Schiene *f*; (typ) geschweifte Klammer *f* ‖ *tr* verstreben; (fig) stärken; **b. oneself** sich zusammenreißen; **b. oneself against** sich stemmen gegen; **b. oneself for** seinen Mut zusammennehmen für; **b. up** (fig) aufpulvern
brace' and bit' *s* Bohrwinde *f*
bracelet ['breslɪt] *s* Armband *n*
brac'ing *adj* (*invigorating*) erfrischend
bracket ['brækɪt] *s* Winkelstütze *f*, Konsole *f*; (*wall bracket*) Wandarm *m*; (*mounting clip*) Befestigungsschelle *f*; (typ) eckige Klammer *f* ‖ *tr* einklammern; (arti) eingabeln
brackish ['brækɪʃ] *adj* brackig
brag [bræg] *v* (*pret & pp* **bragged**; *ger* **bragging**) *intr* (*about*) prahlen (mit)
braggart ['brægərt] *s* Prahler –in *mf*
brag'ging *adj* prahlerisch ‖ *s* Prahlerei *f*
braid [bred] *s* (*of hair*) Flechte *f*; (*flat trimming*) Tresse *f*, Litze *f*; (*round trimming*) Kordel *f* ‖ *tr* (*hair, rope*) flechten; (*trim with braid*) mit Tresse (or Borten) besetzen
braille [brel] *s* Blindenschrift *f*
brain [bren] *s* Hirn *n*; **brains** Hirn *n*; (fig) Grütze *f* ‖ *tr* (coll) den Schädel einschlagen (*dat*)
brain'child' *s* Geistesfrucht *f*
brainless ['brenlɪs] *adj* hirnlos
brain'storm' *s* (coll) Geistesblitz *m*
brain'wash' *tr* Gehirnwäsche vornehmen bei
brain'wash'ing *s* Gehirnwäsche *f*
brain' wave' *s* Hirnwelle *f*; (fig) Geistesblitz *m*
brain'work' *s* Gehirnarbeit *f*
brainy ['breni] *adj* geistreich
braise [brez] *tr* schmoren, dünsten
brake [brek] *s* Bremse *f*; **put on the brakes** bremsen ‖ *intr* bremsen
brake' drum' *s* Bremstrommel *f*
brake' light' *s* Bremslicht *n*
brake' lin'ing *s* Bremsbelag *m*
brake'man *s* (–men) Bremser *m*
brake'ped'al *s* Bremspedal *n*
brake' shoe' *s* (aut) Bremsbacke *f*
bramble ['bræmbəl] *s* Dornbusch *m*
bran [bræn] *s* Kleie *f*
branch [bræntʃ] *s* (*of a tree*) Ast *m*; (*smaller branch; of lineage*) Zweig *m*; (*of river*) Arm *m*; (*of a road, railroad*) Abzweigung *f*; (*of science, work, a shop*) Branche *f*, Unterabteilung *f*; (com) Filiale *f*, Nebenstelle

f ‖ *intr*—**b. off** abzweigen; **b. out** sich verzweigen
branch' line' *s* Seitenlinie *f*
branch' of'fice *s* Zweigstelle *f*
branch' of serv'ice *s* Truppengattung *f*
brand [brænd] *s* (*kind*) Marke *f*; (*trademark*) Handelsmarke *f*; (*on cattle*) Brandmal *n*; (*branding iron*) Brandeisen *n*; (*dishonor*) Schandfleck *m* ‖ *tr* (& fig) brandmarken
brand'ing i'ron *s* Brandeisen *n*
brandish ['brændɪʃ] *tr* schwingen; (*threateningly*) schwenken
brand'-new' *adj* nagelneu
brandy ['brændi] *s* Branntwein *m*
brash [bræʃ] *adj* schnodd(e)rig, frech
brass [bræs] *adj* Messing-‖ *s* Messing *n*; (mil) hohe Offiziere *pl*; (mus) Blechinstrumente *pl*
brass' band' *s* Blechblaskapelle *f*
brassiere [brə'zɪr] *s* Büstenhalter *m*
brass' knuck'les *spl* Schlagring *m*
brass' tacks' *spl*—**get down to b.** (coll) zur Sache kommen
brat [bræt] *s* (coll) Balg *m*
bravado [brə'vado] *s* Bravour *f*, Angabe *f*
brave [brev] *adj* tapfer, mutig ‖ *s* indianischer Krieger *m* ‖ *tr* trotzen (*dat*)
bravery ['brevəri] *s* Tapferkeit *f*
bra·vo ['bravo] *s* (–vos) Bravo *n* ‖ *interj* bravo!
brawl [brɔl] *s* Rauferei *f* ‖ *intr* raufen
brawler ['brɔlər] *s* Raufbold *m*
brawn [brɔn] *s* Muskelkraft *f*
brawny ['brɔni] *adj* muskulös, kräftig
bray [bre] *s* Eselsschrei *m* ‖ *intr* schreien, iahen
braze [brez] *tr* (*brassplate*) mit Messing überziehen; (*solder*) hartlöten
brazen ['brezən] *adj* Messing-, ehern; (fig) unverschämt ‖ *tr*—**b. it out** unverschämt durchsetzen
Brazil [brə'zɪl] *s* Brasilien *n*
Brazilian [brə'zɪljən] *adj* brasilianisch, brasilisch ‖ *s* Brasilianer –in *mf*
Brazil' nut' *s* Paranuß *f*
breach [britʃ] *s* Bruch *m*; (mil) Bresche *f* ‖ *tr* (mil) durchbrechen
breach' of con'tract *s* Vertragsbruch *m*
breach' of prom'ise *s* Verlöbnisbruch *m*
breach' of the peace' *s* Friedensbruch *m*
breach' of trust' *s* Vertrauensbruch *m*
bread [bred] *s* Brot *n*; (*money*) (sl) Pinke *f* ‖ *tr* (culin) panieren
bread' and but'ter *s* Butterbrot *n*; (*livelihood*) Lebensunterhalt *m*
bread' box' *s* Brotkasten *m*
bread' crumb' *s* Brotkrume *f*
bread'ed *adj* paniert
bread'ed veal' cut'let *s* Wiener Schnitzel *n*
bread' knife' *s* Brotmesser *n*
breadth [bredθ] *s* Breite *f*
bread'win'ner *s* Brotverdiener –in *mf*
break [brek] *s* Bruch *m*; (*split, tear*) Riß *m*; (*crack*) Sprung *m*; (*in relations*) Bruch *m*; (*in a forest*) Lichtung *f*; (*in the clouds*) Lücke *f*; (*recess*) Pause *f*; (*rest from work*)

Arbeitspause *f;* (*luck*) Glück *n;* (*chance*) Chance *f;* (*box*) Lösen *n;* **bad b.** Pech *n;* **b. in the weather** Wetterumschlag *m;* **give s.o. a b.** j-m e-e Chance geben; **make a b. for** losstürzen auf (*acc*); **take a b.** e-e Pause machen; **tough b.** Pech *n;* **without a b.** ohne Unterbrechung ‖ *v* (*pret* **broke** [brok]; *pp* **broken** ['brokən]) *tr* (& *fig*) brechen; (*snap*) zerreißen; (*a string*) durchreißen; (*a dish*) zerbrechen; (*an appointment*) nicht einhalten; (*contact*) unterbrechen; (*an engagement*) auflösen; (*a law, limb*) verletzen; (*monotony*) auflockern; (*a record*) brechen; (*a seal*) erbrechen; (*a window*) einschlagen; (*one's word, promise*) nicht halten; **b. down** (*into constituents*) zerlegen; (*s.o.'s resistance*) überwinden; (*mach*) abmontieren; **b. in** (*a horse*) zureiten; (*a car*) einfahren; (*a person*) anlernen; **b. loose** losreißen; **b. off** abbrechen, losbrechen; (*an engagement*) auflösen; **b. open** aufbrechen; **b. s.o. from s.th.** j-m etw abgewöhnen; **b. the news (to)** die Nachricht eröffnen (*dat*), die Nachricht beibringen (*dat*); **b. to pieces** zerbrechen; (*a meeting*) auflösen; (*forcibly*) sprengen; **break wind** e-n Darmwind abgehen lassen ‖ *intr* brechen; (*snap*) reißen; (*said of the voice*) mutieren; (*said of waves*) sich brechen; (*said of large waves*) sich überschlagen; (*said of the weather*) umschlagen; **b. down** zusammenbrechen; (*mach*) versagen; **b. even** gerade die Unkosten decken; **b. loose** losbrechen, sich losreißen; **b. out** (*said of fire, an epidemic, prisoner*) ausbrechen; **b. up** (*said of a meeting*) sich auflösen

breakable ['brekəbəl] *adj* zerbrechlich

breakage ['brekɪdʒ] *s* Bruch *m;* (*cost of broken articles*) Bruchschaden *m*

break'down' *s* (*of health, discipline, morals*) Zusammenbruch *m;* (*disintegration*) Zersetzung *f;* (*of costs, etc.*) Aufgliederung *f;* (*aut*) Panne *f;* (*chem*) Analyse *f;* (*elec*) Durchschlag *m;* (*of a piece of equipment*) (*mach*) Versagen *n;* (*e.g., of power supply, factory equipment*) Betriebsstörung *f*

breaker ['brekər] *s* Sturzwelle *f;* **breakers** Brandung *f*

breakfast ['brekfəst] *s* Frühstück *n* ‖ *intr* frühstücken

break'neck' *adj* halsbrecherisch

break' of day' *s* Tagesanbruch *m*

break'through' *s* Durchbruch *m*

break'up' *s* Aufbrechen *n;* (*of a meeting*) Auflösung *f*

break'wa'ter *s* Wellenbrecher *m*

breast [brest] *s* Brust *f;* (*of a woman*) Brust *f,* Busen *m;* **beat one's b.** sich an die Brust schlagen; **make a clean b. of s.th.** [*dat*] vom Herzen reden

breast'bone' *s* Brustbein *n*

breast' feed'ing *s* Stillen *n*

breast'plate' *s* Brustharnisch *m*

breast'stroke' *s* Brustschwimmen *n*

breath [brεθ] *s* Atem *m;* (*single inhalation*) Atemzug *m;* (*fig*) Hauch *m;* **b. of air** Lüftchen *n;* **gasp for b.** nach Luft schnappen; **have bad b.** aus dem Mund riechen; **in the same b.** im gleichen Atemzug; **save one's b.** sich [*dat*] seine Worte ersparen; **take a deep b.** tief Luft holen; **take one's b. away** j-m den Atem verschlagen; **waste one's b.** in den Wind reden

breathe [brið] *tr* atmen, schöpfen; **b. a sigh of relief** aufatmen; **b. life into** beseelen; **b. one's last** die Seele aushauchen; **b. out** ausatmen; **not b. a word about it** kein Wort davon verlauten lassen ‖ *intr* atmen, hauchen; **b. again** aufatmen; **b. on** anhauchen

breath'ing space' *s* Atempause *f*

breathless ['brεθlɪs] *adj* atemlos

breath'-tak'ing *adj* atemberaubend

breech [brit∫] *s* Verschlußstück *n*

breed [brid] *s* Zucht *f,* Stamm *m;* (*sort, group*) Schlag *m;* (*of animals*) Rasse *f* ‖ *v* (*pret* & *pp* **bred** [bred]) *tr* (*beget*) erzeugen; (*raise*) züchten; (*fig*) hervorrufen ‖ *intr* sich vermehren

breeder ['bridər] *s* Züchter –in *mf*

breed'ing *s* (*of animals*) Züchtung *f,* Aufzucht *f;* (*fig*) Erziehung *f*

breeze [briz] *s* Lüftchen *n,* Brise *f* ‖ *intr*—**b. by** vorbeiflitzen; **b. in** frisch und vergnügt hereinkommen

breezy ['brizi] *adj* luftig; (*fig*) keß

brevity ['breviti] *s* Kürze *f*

brew [bru] *s* Brühe *f;* (*of beer*) Bräu *m* ‖ *tr* (*tea, coffee*) aufbrühen; (*beer*) brauen ‖ *intr* ziehen; (*said of a storm*) sich zusammenbrauen; **something is brewing** etwas ist im Anzuge

brewer ['bru·ər] *s* Brauer –in *mf*

brewery ['bru·əri] *s* Brauerei *f*

bribe [braɪb] *s* Bestechungsgeld *n* ‖ *tr* bestechen

bribery ['braɪbəri] *s* Bestechung *f*

brick [brɪk] *s* Ziegelstein *m*

bricklayer ['brɪk ,le·ər] *s* Maurer *m*

brick'work' *s* Mauerwerk *n*

brick'yard' *s* Ziegelei *f*

bridal ['braɪdəl] *adj* Braut-, Hochzeits-

brid'al gown' *s* Brautkleid *n*

brid'al veil' *s* Brautschleier *m*

bride [braɪd] *s* Braut *f*

bride'groom' *s* Bräutigam *m*

brides'maid' *s* Brautjungfer *f*

bridge [brɪdʒ] *s* (*over a river*) Brücke *f;* (*of eyeglasses*) Steg *m;* (*of a nose*) Nasenrücken *m;* (*cards*) Bridge *n;* (*dent*) Zahnbrücke *f;* (*naut*) Kommandobrücke *f* ‖ *tr* (& *fig*) überbrücken

bridge'head' *s* Brückenkopf *m*

bridge'work' *s* (*dent*) Brückenarbeit *f*

bridle ['braɪdəl] *s* Zaum *m,* Zügel *m* ‖ *tr* aufzäumen, zügeln

bri'dle path' *s* Reitweg *m*

brief [brif] *adj* kurz; **be b.** sich kurz fassen ‖ *s* (*jur*) Schriftsatz *m* ‖ *tr* einweisen, orientieren

brief' case' *s* Aktentasche *f*

brief′ing s Einsatzbesprechung f

brier [′braɪ·ər] s Dornbusch m

brig [brɪg] s (naut) Brigg f; (nav) Knast m

brigade [brɪ′ged] s Brigade f

brigadier′ gen′eral [ˌbrɪgə′dɪr] s Brigadegeneral m

brigand [′brɪgənd] s Brigant m

bright [braɪt] adj hell; (color) lebhaft; (face) strahlend; (weather) heiter; (smart) gescheit, aufgeweckt ‖ adv —b. and early in aller Frühe

brighten [′braɪtən] tr aufhellen ‖ intr sich aufhellen

bright′-eyed′ adj helläugig

brightness [′braɪtnɪs] s Helle f

bright′ side′ s (fig) Lichtseite f

bright′ spot′ s (fig) Lichtblick m

brilliance [′brɪljəns], **brilliancy** [′brɪljənsi] s Glanz m

brilliant [′brɪljənt] adj (& fig) glänzend

brim [brɪm] s Rand m; (of a hat) Krempe f; **to the b.** bis zum Rande ‖ v (pret & pp **brimmed**; ger **brimming**) intr—**b.** over (with) (fig) überschäumen (vor dat)

brimful [′brɪmˌful] adj übervoll

brim′stone′ s Schwefel m

brine [braɪn] s Salzwasser n, Sole f; (for pickling) Salzlake f

bring [brɪŋ] v (pret & pp **brought** [brɔt]) tr bringen; **b. about** zustande bringen; **b. back** zurückbringen; (memories) zurückrufen; **b. down** herunterbringen; (shoot down) abschießen; **b. down the house** (fig) Lachstürme entfesseln; **b. forth** (e.g., complaints) hervorbringen; **b. forward** vorbringen; **b. it about that** es durchsetzen, daß; **b. on** herbeiführen; **b. oneself to** (inf) sich überwinden zu (inf); **b. to** wieder zu sich bringen; **b. together** zusammenbringen; **b. up** (children) erziehen; (a topic) zur Sprache bringen

bring′ing-up′ s Erziehung f

brink [brɪŋk] s (& fig) Rand m

brisk [brɪsk] adj (pace, business) flott; (air) frisch, scharf

bristle [′brɪsəl] s Borste f ‖ intr sich sträuben

bristly [′brɪsli] adj borstig

Britain [′brɪtən] s Britannien n

British [′brɪtɪʃ] adj britisch ‖ **the B.** spl die Briten pl

Britisher [′brɪtɪʃər] s Brite m, Britin f

Briton [′brɪtən] s Brite m, Britin f

Brittany [′brɪtəni] s die Bretagne f

brittle [′brɪtəl] adj brüchig, spröde

broach [brotʃ] tr zur Sprache bringen

broad [brɔd] adj breit; (outline) hellicht; (sense) weit; (view) allgemein, umfassend

broad′cast′ s Sendung f, Übertragung f ‖ v (pret & pp –cast) tr (rumors, etc.) ausposaunen ‖ (pret & pp –cast & –casted) tr & intr senden, übertragen

broadcaster [′brɔdˌkæstər] s Rundfunksprecher –in mf

broad′casting sta′tion s Sender m

broad′casting stu′dio s Senderaum m

broad′cloth′ s feiner Wäschestoff m

broaden [′brɔdən] tr verbreitern ‖ intr sich verbreitern

broad′-gauge′ adj (rr) breitspurig

broad′-mind′ed adj großzügig

broad′-shoul′dered adj breitschultrig

broad′side′ s (guns on one side of ship) Breitseite f; (fig) Schimpfkanonade f

brocade [bro′ked] s Brokat m

broccoli [′brakəli] s Spargelkohl m

brochure [bro′ʃur] s Broschüre f

broil [brɔɪl] tr am Rost braten, grillen

broiler [′brɔɪlər] s Bratrost m

broke [brok] adj (coll) abgebrannt, pleite; **go b.** (coll) pleite gehen

broken [′brokən] adj zerbrochen; (limb, spirit, English) gebrochen; (home) zerrüttet; (line) gestrichelt

bro′ken-down′ adj erschöpft; (horse) abgearbeitet

bro′ken-heart′ed adj mit gebrochenem Herzen

broker [′brokər] s Makler –in mf

brokerage [′brokərɪdʒ] s Maklergeschäft n; (fee) Maklergebühr f

bromide [′bromaɪd] s Bromid n; (coll) Binsenweisheit f

bromine [′bromin] s Brom n

bronchial [′braŋkɪ·əl] adj bronchial

bron′chial tube′ s Luftröhre f, Bronchie f

bronchitis [braŋ′kaɪtɪs] s Bronchitis f

bron·co [′braŋko] s (–cos) kleines halbwildes Pferd n

bronze [branz] adj Bronze– ‖ s Bronze f ‖ tr bronzieren ‖ intr sich bräunen

brooch [brotʃ], [brutʃ] s Brosche f

brood [brud] s Brut f, Junge pl ‖ tr ausbrüten ‖ intr brüten; (coll) sinnieren; **b. over** grübeln über (acc)

brook [bruk] s Bach m ‖ tr dulden

broom [brum] s Besen m

broom′stick′ s Besenstiel m

broth [brɔθ] s Brühe f

brothel [′brɑθəl] s Bordell n

brother [′brʌðər] s Bruder m; **brother(s) and sister(s)** Geschwister pl

broth′erhood′ s (& relig) Brüderschaft f

broth′er-in-law′ s (brothers-in-law) Schwager m

brotherly [′brʌðərli] adj brüderlich

brow [brau] s Stirn f

brow′beat′ v (pret –beat; pp –beaten) tr einschüchtern

brown [braun] adj braun ‖ s Bräune f ‖ tr & intr bräunen

brownish [′braunɪʃ] adj bräunlich

brown′-nose′ tr (sl) kriechen (dat)

brown′ sug′ar s brauner Zucker m

browse [brauz] intr grasen, weiden; (through books) schmökern, stöbern; (through a store) herumsuchen

bruise [bruz] s Quetschung f ‖ tr quetschen

brunette [bru′net] adj brünett ‖ s Brünette f

brunt [brʌnt] s Anprall m; **bear the b.** die Hauptlast tragen

brush [brʌʃ] s Bürste f; (of an artist; for shaving) Pinsel m; (brief encoun-

ter) kurzer Zusammenstoß *m;* (*light touch*) leichte Berührung *f;* (*bot*) Gebüsch *n;* (*elec*) Bürste *f;* || *tr* bürsten; **b. aside** beiseite schieben; **b. off** abbürsten; (*devour*) verschlingen; (*make light of*) abwimmeln || *intr*—**b. against** streifen; **b. up on** auffrischen

brush'-off' *s* (*coll*) Laufpaß *m*

brush'wood' *s* Unterholz *n*, Niederwald *m*

brusque [brʌsk] *adj* brüsk

Brussels ['brʌsəlz] *s* Brüssel *n*

Brus'sels sprouts' *spl* Rosenkohl *m*

brutal ['brutəl] *adj* brutal

brutality [bru'tælti] *s* Brutalität *f*

brute [brut] *adj* viehisch; (*strength*) roh || *s* Tier *n;* (*fig*) Unmensch *m*

brutish ['brutɪʃ] *adj* tierisch, roh

bubble ['bʌbəl] *s* Blase *f*, Bläschen *n* || *intr* sprudeln; **b. over** (**with**) übersprudeln (*vor dat*)

bub'ble bath' *s* Schaumbad *n*

bub'ble gum' *s* Knallkaugummi *m*

bubbly ['bʌbli] *adj* sprudelnd; (*Person*) lebhaft

buck [bʌk] *s* Bock *m;* (*sl*) Dollar *m;* **pass the b.** (*coll*) die Verantwortung abschieben || *tr* (*fig*) kämpfen gegen; **b. off** abwerfen || *intr* bocken; **b. for** (*a promotion*) sich bemühen um

bucket ['bʌkɪt] *s* Eimer *m*

buck'et seat' *s* Schalensitz *m*

buckle ['bʌkəl] *s* Schnalle *f;* (*bend*) Ausbuchtung *f* || *tr* zuschnallen || *intr* (*from heat, etc.*) zusammensacken; **b. down** sich auf die Hosen setzen

buck' pri'vate *s* gemeiner Soldat *m*

buckram ['bʌkrəm] *s* Buckram *n*

buck'shot' *s* Rehposten *m*

buck'tooth' *s* (**–teeth**) vorstehender Zahn *m*

buck'wheat' *s* Buchweizen *m*

bud [bʌd] *s* Knospe *f*, Keim *m;* **nip in the bud** (fig) im Keime ersticken || *v* (*pret & pp* **budded;** *ger* **budding**) *intr* knospen, keimen, ausschlagen

buddy ['bʌdi] *s* (*coll*) Kumpel *m*

budge [bʌdʒ] *tr* (von der Stelle) bewegen || *intr* sich (von der Stelle) bewegen

budget ['bʌdʒɪt] *s* Budget *n*, Haushaltsplan *m;* (*of a state*) Staatshaushalt *m* || *tr* einteilen, vorausplanen

budgetary ['bʌdʒɪˌteri] *adj* Budget-

buff [bʌf] *adj* lederfarben || *s* Lederfarbe *f;* (*coll*) Schwärmer –in *mf* || *tr* polieren

buffa·lo ['bʌfəˌlo] *s* (**–loes & –los**) Büffel *m*

buffer ['bʌfər] *s* Puffer *m;* (*polisher*) Polierer *m;* (rr) Prellbock *m*

buff'er state' *s* Pufferstaat *m*

buffet [bu'fe] *s* (*meal*) Büfett *n;* (*furniture*) Kredenz *f* || ['bʌfɪt] *tr* herumstoßen

buffoon [bə'fun] *s* Hanswurst *m*

bug [bʌg] *s* Insekt *n*, Käfer *m;* (*defect*) (coll) Defekt *m;* (electron) Abhörgerät *n*, Wanze *f;* **bugs** Ungeziefer *n* || *v* (*pret & pp* **bugged;** *ger* **bugging**) *tr* (*annoy*) (sl) ärgern;

(electron) (sl) Abhörgeräte einbauen in (*dat*)

bug'-eyed' *adj* (sl) mit großen Augen

buggy ['bʌgi] *adj* verwanzt; (*crazy*) (sl) verrückt || *s* Wagen *m*

bugle ['bjugəl] *s* Signalhorn *n*

bu'gle call' *s* Signal *n*

bugler ['bjuglər] *s* Hornist –in *mf*

build [bɪld] *s* Bauart *f*, Gestalt *f;* (*of a person*) Körperbau *m* || *v* (*pret & pp* **built** [bɪlt]) *tr* bauen; (*a bridge*) schlagen; (*with stone or brick*) mauern; (*a fire*) anmachen; **b. up** aufbauen; (*an area*) ausbauen; (*hopes*) erwecken

builder ['bɪldər] *s* Baumeister *m*

build'ing *s* Gebäude *n*

build'ing and loan' associa'tion *s* Bausparkasse *f*

build'ing block' *s* Zementblock *m;* (*for children*) Bauklötzchen *n*

build'ing con'tractor *s* Bauunternehmer *m*

build'ing in'dustry *s* Bauindustrie *f*

build'ing lot' *s* Bauplatz *m*, Grundstück *n*

build'ing mate'rial *s* Baustoff *m*

build'-up' *s* (coll) Propaganda *f*

built'-in' *adj* Einbau-

built'-up' *adj* bebaut

bulb [bʌlb] *s* (bot) Knolle *f*, Zwiebel *f;* (elec) Glühbirne *f;* (phot) Blitzlampe *f*

Bulgaria [bʌl'gɑrɪ·ə] *s* Bulgarien *n*

Bulgarian [bʌl'gɑrɪ·ən] *adj* bulgarisch || *s* Bulgare *m*, Bulgarin *f;* (*language*) Bulgarisch *n*

bulge [bʌldʒ] *s* Ausbauchung *f*, Beule *f;* (*of a sail*) Bausch *m;* (mil) Frontvorsprung *m* || *intr* sich bauschen; (*said of eyes*) hervortreten

bulg'ing *adj* (belly, muscles) hervorspringend; (*eyes*) hervorquellend; (*sails*) gebläht; **b. with** bis zum Platzen gefüllt mit

bulk [bʌlk] *s* Massen–, unverpackt || *s* Masse *f;* (*main part*) Hauptteil *m;* **in b.** unverpackt || *intr*—**b. large** e–e große Rolle spielen

bulk'head' *s* (aer) Spant *m;* (naut) Schott *n*

bulky ['bʌlki] *adj* sperrig

bull [bul] *s* Bulle *m*, Stier *m;* (sl) Quatsch *m;* (eccl) Bulle *f;* (st. exch.) Haussier *m;* **like a b. in a china shop** wie ein Elefant im Porzellanladen; **shoot the b.** (sl) quatschen; **take the b. by the horns** den Stier an den Hörnern packen; **throw the b.** (sl) aufschneiden

bull'dog' *s* Bulldogge *f*

bull'doze' *tr* einschüchtern; (fig) überfahren

bulldozer ['bʌlˌdozər] *s* Planierraupe *f*

bullet ['bulɪt] *s* Kugel *f*

bul'let hole' *s* Schußöffnung *f*

bulletin ['bulətɪn] *s* (*report*) Bulletin *n;* (*flyer*) Flugschrift *f*

bul'letin board' *s* Anschlagbrett *n*

bul'letproof' *adj* kugelsicher

bull'fight' *s* Stierkampf *m*

bull'fight'er *s* Stierkämpfer –in *mf*

bull'frog' *s* Ochsenfrosch *m*

bull'-head'ed adj dickköpfig
bull' horn' s Richtungslautsprecher m
bullion ['buljən] s Barren m; (mil, nav) Kordel f
bull' mar'ket s Spekulationsmarkt m
bullock ['bulək] s Ochse m
bull'pen' s Stierpferch m; (baseball) Übungsplatz m für Reservewerfer
bull'ring' s Stierkampfarena f
bull' ses'sion s (sl) zwanglose Diskussion f
bull's'-eye' s (of a target) Schwarze n; (round window) Bullauge n; **hit the b.** ins Schwarze treffen
bul·ly ['buli] adj—**b. for you!** großartig! || s Raufbold m || v (pret & pp –lied) tr tyrannisieren
bulrush ['bul‚rʌʃ] s Binse f
bulwark ['bulwərk] s Bollwerk n
bum [bʌm] (sl) Strolch m; **give s.o. the bum's rush** j–n auf den Schub bringen || v (pret & pp **bummed**; ger **bumming**) tr (sl) schinden, schnorren || intr—**bum around** bummeln
bumblebee ['bʌmbəl‚bi] s Hummel f
bump [bʌmp] s Stoß m, Bums m; (swelling) Beule f; (in the road) holp(e)rige Stelle f || tr (an)stoßen; **b. off** (sl) abknallen; **b. one's head against s.th.** mit dem Kopf gegen etw stoßen || intr zusammenstoßen; **b. against** stoßen an (acc); **b. into** stoßen gegen; (meet unexpectedly) in die Arme laufen (dat)
bumper ['bʌmpər] s Stoßstange f
bumpkin ['bʌmpkin] s Tölpel m
bumpy ['bʌmpi] adj holperig; (aer) böig
bum' steer' s—**give s.o. a b.** (coll) nasführen
bun [bʌn] s Kuchenbrötchen n; (of hair) Haarknoten m
bunch [bʌntʃ] s Bündel n; (of grapes) Traube f; (group) Schar f, Bande f; **b. of flowers** Blumenstrauß m; **b. of grapes** Weintraube f || tr—**b. together** zusammenfassen || intr—**b. together** sich zusammendrängen
bundle ['bʌndəl] s Bündel n; (heap) Stoß m; (of straw) Schütte f; **b. of nerves** Nervenbündel n || tr bündeln; **b. off** (coll) verfrachten; **b. up** sich warm anziehen
bung [bʌŋ] s Spund m || tr verspunden
bungalow ['bʌŋgə‚lo] s Bungalow m
bung'hole' s Spundloch n
bungle ['bʌŋgəl] s Pfuscherei f || tr verpfuschen || intr pfuschen
bungler ['bʌŋglər] s Pfuscher –in mf
bun'gling adj stümperhaft || s Stümperei f
bunk [bʌŋk] s Schlafkoje f; (sl) Unsinn m || intr (with) schlafen (mit)
bunk' bed' s Etagenbett n
bunker ['bʌŋkər] s Bunker m
bunny ['bʌni] s Kaninchen n
bunt'ing s (cloth) Fahnentuch n; (decoration) Fahnenschmuck m; (orn) Ammer f
buoy [bɔɪ], ['bu‚i] s Boje f || tr—**b. up** flott erhalten; (fig) Auftrieb geben (dat)

buoyancy ['bɔɪ‚ənsi] s Auftrieb m; (fig) Spannkraft f
buoyant ['bɔɪ‚ənt] adj schwimmend; (fig) lebhaft
burden ['bʌrdən] s Bürde f, Last f; (fig) Belastung f || tr belasten
bur'den of proof' s Beweislast f
burdensome ['bʌrdənsəm] adj lästig
bureau ['bjuro] s Kommode f; (office) Büro n; (department) Amt n
bureaucracy [bju'rɑkrəsi] s Bürokratie f, Beamtenschaft f
bureaucrat ['bjurə‚kræt] s Bürokrat –in mf
bureaucratic [‚bjurə'krætɪk] adj bürokratisch
burglar ['bʌrglər] s Einbrecher –in mf
bur'glar alarm' s Einbruchssicherung f
burglarize ['bʌrglə‚raɪz] tr einbrechen in (acc)
bur'glarproof' adj einbruchssicher
burglary ['bʌrgləri] s Einbruchdiebstahl m
Burgundy ['bʌrgəndi] s Burgund n; (wine) Burgunder m
burial ['berɪ‚əl] s Beerdigung f
bur'ial ground' s Begräbnisplatz m
burlap ['bʌrlæp] s Sackleinwand f
burlesque [bər'lesk] adj burlesk || s Burleske f || tr burlesk behandeln
burlesque' show' s Varieté n
burly ['bʌrli] adj stämmig, beleibt
Burma ['bʌrmə] s Birma n
Bur·mese [bər'miz] adj birmanisch || s (–mese) (person) Birmane m, Birmanin f; (language) Birmanisch n
burn [bʌrn] s Brandwunde f; || v (pret & pp **burned** & **burnt** [bʌrnt]) tr (ver)brennen; **b. be burned up** (coll) fauchen; **b. down** niederbrennen; **b. up** (coll) wütend machen || intr (ver)brennen; (said of food) anbrennen; **b. out** ausbrennen; (elec) durchbrennen; **b. up** ganz verbrennen; (during reentry) verglühen
burner ['bʌrnər] s Brenner m
burn'ing adj (& fig) brennend
burnish ['bʌrnɪʃ] tr polieren
burn'out' s (rok) Brennschluß m
burnt adj verbrannt; (smell) brenzlig
burp [bʌrp] s Rülpser m || tr rülpsen lassen || intr rülpsen
burr [bʌr] s (growth on a tree) Auswuchs m; (in metal) Grat m; (bot) Klette f
burrow ['bʌro] s Bau m || tr graben || intr sich eingraben, wühlen
bursar ['bʌrsər] s Schatzmeister m
burst [bʌrst] s Bersten n; (split) Riß m; Bruch m; **b. of gunfire** Feuerstoß m || v (pret & pp **burst**) tr (auf)sprengen, zum Platzen bringen || intr bersten, platzen; (split) reißen; (said of a boil) aufgehen; **b. into** (e.g., a room) hereinstürzen in (acc); **b. into tears** in Tränen ausbrechen; **b. open** aufplatzen; **b. out laughing** loslachen
bur·y ['beri] v (pret & pp –ied) tr beerdigen, begraben; **be buried in thought** in Gedanken versunken sein; **b. alive** verschütten
bus [bʌs] s (busses & buses) Autobus m, Bus m || v (pret & pp) **bussed &**

bused; ger bussing & busing) tr & intr mit dem Bus fahren

bus' boy' s Pikkolo m

bus' driv'er s Autobusfahrer –in mf

bush [buʃ] s Busch m; beat around the b. um die Sache herumreden

bushed adj (coll) abgeklappert

bushel ['buʃəl] s Scheffel m; by the b. scheffelweise

bush'ing s Buchse f

bushy ['buʃi] adj strauchbewachsen; (brows) buschig

business ['bɪznɪs] adj Geschäfts– || s Geschäft n; (company) Firma f, Betrieb m; (employment) Beruf m, Gewerbe n; (duty) Pflicht f; (right) Recht n; (coll) Sache f; be in b. geschäftlich tätig sein; do b. with Geschäfte machen mit; get down to b. (coll) zur Sache kommen; go about one's b. seiner Arbeit nachgehen; he means b. (coll) er meint es ernst; know one's b. seine Sache verstehen; make s.th. one's b. sich [dat] etw angelegen sein lassen; mind your own b. kümmere dich um deine eigenen Sachen; that's none of your b. das geht dich gar nichts an; the whole b. die ganze Geschichte; you have no b. here du hast hier nichts zu suchen

busi'ness call' s Dienstgespräch n

busi'ness card' s Geschäftskarte f

busi'ness cen'ter s Geschäftszentrum n

busi'ness col'lege s Handelsschule f

busi'ness dis'trict s Geschäftsviertel n

busi'ness expens'es spl Geschäftsspesen pl

busi'ness hours' s Geschäftszeit f

busi'ness let'ter s Geschäftsbrief m

busi'nesslike' adj sachlich; (pej) geschäftsmäßig

busi'ness·man' s (–men') Geschäftsmann m

busi'ness reply' card' s Rückantwortkarte f

busi'ness suit' s Straßenanzug m

busi'ness·wom'an s (–wom'en) Geschäftsfrau f

bus' line' s Autobuslinie f

bus' stop' s Autobushaltestelle f

bust [bʌst] s (chest) Busen m; (measurement) Oberweite f; (statue) Brustbild n; (blow) .(sl) Faustschlag m; (failure) (sl) Platzen n; (binge) (sl) Sauftour f || .(sl) tr (sl) kaputtmachen; (mil) degradieren || intr (break) (sl) kaputtgehen

bustle ['bʌsəl] s (activity) Hochbetrieb m, Trubel m || intr umherhasten; b. about herumsausen

bus'tling adj geschäftig

bus·y ['bɪzi] adj tätig, beschäftigt; (day, life) arbeitsreich; (street) lebhaft, verkehrsstark; (telp) belegt, besetzt; be b. (be occupied) zu tun haben; (be unavailable) nicht zu sprechen sein || v (pret & pp –ied) tr beschäftigen

bus'ybod'y s Wichtigtuer –in mf

bus'y sig'nal s (telp) Besetztzeichen n

but [bʌt] adv nur, lediglich, bloß; (just, only) erst; all but beinahe ||

prep außer (dat); (after negatives) als; all but one alle bis auf einen || conj aber; (after negatives) sondern

butcher ['butʃər] s Fleischer –in mf, Metzger –in mf; (fig) Schlächter –in mf || tr schlachten; (fig) abschlachten

butch'er knife' s Fleischermesser n

butch'er shop' s Metzgerei f

butchery ['butʃəri] s (slaughterhouse) Schlachthaus n; (fig) Gemetzel n

butler ['bʌtlər] s Haushofmeister m

butt [bʌt] s (of a gun) Kolben m; (of a cigarette) Stummel m; (with the horns, head) Stoß m; (of ridicule) Zielscheibe f || tr stoßen || intr stoßen; b. in (sl) sich einmischen, dazwischenfahren

butter ['bʌtər] s Butter f || tr mit Butter bestreichen; (bread) schmieren; b. s.o. up (coll) j–m Honig um den Mund schmieren

but'terball' s Butterkugel f; (chubby child) Pummelchen n

but'tercup' s Butterblume f, Hahnenfuß m

but'ter dish' s Butterdose f

but'terfly' s Schmetterling m; (sport) Schmetterlingsstil m

but'ter knife' s Buttermesser n

but'termilk' s Buttermilch f

buttocks ['bʌtəks] spl Hinterbacken pl

button ['bʌtən] s Knopf m || tr knöpfen; button up zuknöpfen

but'tonhole' s Knopfloch n || tr im Gespräch festhalten

buttress ['bʌtrɪs] s Strebepfeiler m; (fig) Stütze f || tr (durch Strebepfeiler) stützen; (fig) (unter)stützen

butt'-weld' tr stumpfschweißen

buxom ['bʌksəm] adj beleibt

buy [baɪ] s Kauf m || v (pret & pp bought [bɔt]) tr kaufen; (bus ticket, train ticket) lösen; (accept, believe) glauben; buy off (bribe) bestechen; buy out auskaufen; buy up aufkaufen

buyer ['baɪ·ər] s Käufer –in mf

buzz [bʌz] s Summen n, Surren n; (telp) (coll) Anruf m || tr (coll) (aer) dicht vorbeisausen an (dat); (telp) (coll) anrufen || intr summen, surren; b. around herumsausen

buzzard ['bʌzərd] s Bussard m

buzz' bomb' s Roboterbombe f, V-Waffe f

buzzer ['bʌzər] s Summer m; did the b. sound? ist der Summer ertönt

buzz' saw' s Kreissäge f, Rundsäge f

by [baɪ] adv vorüber, vorbei; by and by nach und nach; by and large im großen und ganzen || prep (agency) von (dat), durch (acc); (position) bei (dat), an (dat), neben (dat); (no later than) bis spätestens; (in division) durch (acc); (indicating mode of transportation) mit (dat); (indicating authorship) von (dat); (according to) nach (dat); (past) an (dat) vorbei; (by means of) mit (dat); by (ge) indem (ind); by an inch um e–n Zoll; by day bei Tag; by far bei weitem; by heart auswendig; by itself (automatically) von selbst; by land zu Lande; by mail per Post; **by myself** ganz allein; **by nature** von Natur aus; **by now** schon; **by the pound** per Pfund; **two by four** zwei mal vier

bye [baɪ] *s* (sport) Freilos *n*

bye'bye' *interj* Wiedersehen!

bygone ['baɪˌgɒn] *adj* vergangen ‖ *s*— **let bygones be bygones** laß(t) das Vergangene ruhen

by'law' *s* Satzung *f*; **bylaws** (*of an organization*) Statuten *pl*, Satzungen *pl*

by'-line' *s* (journ) Verfasserangabe *f*

by'pass' *s* Umgehungsstraße *f*, Umleitung *f*; (elec) Nebenschluß *m* ‖ *tr* umgehen

by'prod'uct *s* Nebenprodukt *n*

bystander ['baɪˌstændər] *s* Umstehende *mf*

by'way' *s* Seitenweg *m*

by'word' *s* Sprichwort *n*

Byzantine ['bɪzənˌtin], [bɪ'zæntin] *adj* byzantinisch ‖ *s* Byzantiner *–in mf*

Byzantium [bɪ'zænʃɪˌəm], [bɪ'zæntɪˌəm] *s* Byzanz *n*

C

C, c [si] *s* dritter Buchstabe des englischen Alphabets; (mus) C *n*; **C flat** Ces *n*; **C sharp** Cis *n*

cab [kæb] *s* Taxi *n*; (*of a truck*) Fahrerkabine *f*

cabaret [ˌkæbəˈre] *s* Kabarett *n*

cabbage ['kæbɪdʒ] *s* Kohl *m*, Kraut *n*

cab'driv'er *s* Taxifahrer *–in mf*

cabin ['kæbɪn] *s* Hütte *f*; (aer) Kabine *f*; (naut) Kajüte *f*, Kabine *f*

cab'in boy' *s* Schiffsjunge *m*

cabinet ['kæbɪnɪt] *adj* Kabinetts– ‖ *s* (*in a kitchen*) Küchenschrank *m*; (*for a radio*) Gehäuse *n*; (pol) Kabinett *n*, Ministerrat *m*

cab'inetmak'er *s* Tischler *m*

cable ['kebəl] *s* Kabel *n*, Seil *n*; (naut) Tau *m*; (telg) Kabelnachricht *f* ‖ *tr & intr* kabeln

ca'ble car' *s* Seilbahn *f*, Schwebebahn *f*

ca'blegram' *s* Kabelnachricht *f*

caboose [kəˈbus] *s* (rr) Dienstwagen *m*

cab'stand' *s* Taxistand *m*

cache [kæʃ] *s* Geheimlager *n*, Versteck *n*; **c. of arms** Waffenlager *n*

cachet [kæˈʃe] *s* Siegel *n*; (fig) Stempel *m*; (pharm) Kapsel *f*

cackle ['kækəl] *s* (*of chickens*) Gegacker *n*; (*of geese*) Geschnatter *n* ‖ *intr* gackern, gackeln; schnattern

cac·tus ['kæktəs] *s* (–tuses & –ti [taɪ]) Kaktus *m*

cad [kæd] *s* (sl) Saukerl *m*, Schuft *m*

cadaver [kəˈdævər] *s* Kadaver *m*, Leiche *f*

caddie ['kædi] *s* Golfjunge *m* ‖ *intr* die Schläger tragen

cadence ['kedəns] *s* (*rhythm*) Rhythmus *m*; (*flow of language*) Sprechrhythmus *m*; (mus) Kadenz *f*

cadet [kəˈdɛt] *s* Offizier(s)anwärter *–in mf*

cadre ['kædri] *s* Kader *m*

Caesar'ean opera'tion [sɪˈzɛrɪˌən] *s* Kaiserschnitt *m*

café [kæˈfe] *s* Cafe *n*

cafeteria [ˌkæfəˈtɪrɪˌə] *s* Selbstbedienungsrestaurant *n*

caffeine [kæˈfin] *s* Koffein *n*

cage [kedʒ] *s* Käfig *m* ‖ *tr* in e–n Käfig sperren

cagey ['kedʒi] *adj* (coll) schlau

cahoots [kəˈhuts] *s*—**be in c.** (sl) unter e–r Decke stecken

Cain [ken] *s*—**raise C.** Krach schlagen

caisson ['kesən] *s* Senkkasten *m*

cajole [kəˈdʒol] *tr* beschwatzen

cake [kek] *s* Kuchen *m*; (*round cake*) Torte *f*; (*of soap*) Riegel *m*; **he takes the c.** (coll) er schießt den Vogel ab; **that takes the c.** (coll) das ist die Höhe ‖ *intr* zusammenbacken; **c. on** anbacken

calamitous [kəˈlæmɪtəs] *adj* unheilvoll

calamity [kəˈlæmɪti] *s* Unheil *n*

calci·fy ['kælsɪˌfaɪ] *v* (*pret & pp* –fied) *tr & intr* verkalken

calcium ['kælsɪˌəm] *s* Kalzium *n*

calculate ['kælkjəˌlet] *tr* berechnen ‖ *intr* rechnen

cal'culated risk' *s*—**take a c.** ein bewußtes Risiko eingehen

cal'culating *adj* berechnend

calculation [ˌkælkjəˈleʃən] *s* Berechnung *f*; **rough c.** Überschlagsrechnung *f*

calculator ['kælkjəˌletər] *s* Rechenmaschine *f*; (data proc) Rechner *m*

calcu·lus ['kælkjələs] *s* (–luses & –li [ˌlaɪ]) (math) Differenzial– und Integralrechnung *f*; (pathol) Stein *m*

caldron ['kɔldrən] *s* Kessel *m*

calendar ['kæləndər] *s* Kalender *m*

calf [kæf] *s* (**calves** [kævz] (*of a cow*) Kalb *n*; (*of certain other mammals*) Junge *n*; (anat) Wade *f*

calf'skin' *s* Kalbleder *n*

caliber ['kælɪbər] *s* (& fig) Kaliber *n*

calibrate ['kælɪˌbret] *tr* kalibrieren

cali·co ['kælɪˌko] *s* (–coes & –cos) Kaliko *m*

calisthenics [ˌkælɪsˈθɛnɪks] *spl* Leibesübungen *pl*

calk [kɔk] *tr* abdichten, kalfatern

calk'ing *s* Kalfaterung *f*

call [kɔl] *s* Ruf *m*; (*visit*) Besuch *m*; (*reason*) Grund *m*; (com) (**for**) Nachfrage *f* (nach); (naut) Anlaufen *n*; (telp) Anruf *m*; **on c.** auf Abruf ‖ *tr* rufen; (*name*) nennen; (*wake*) wecken; (*a meeting*) einberufen; (*a game*) absagen; (*a strike*) ausrufen; (*by phone*) anrufen; (*a witness*) vorladen; (*a doctor; taxi*) kommen lassen; be **called** heißen; **c. down** (coll) herunterputzen; **c. in** (*a doctor, specialist*) hinzuziehen; (*for advice*) zu Rate ziehen; (*currency*) einziehen; (*capital*) kündigen; **c. it a day** (coll) Schluß machen; **c. off** absagen; **c. out** ausrufen; (*the police*) einsetzen; **c. s.o. names** j–n beschimpfen; **c. up** (mil) einberufen; (telp) anrufen ‖ *intr* rufen; (cards) ansagen; **c. for** (*require*) erfordern; (*fetch*) abholen; (*help*) rufen um; (*a person*) rufen nach; **c. on** (*a pupil*) aufrufen; (*visit*) e–n Besuch machen bei; **c. to s.o.** j–m zurufen; **c. upon** auffordern

call' bell' *s* Rufglocke *f*

call' boy' *s* Hotelpage *m*; (theat) Inspezientengehilfe *m*

caller ['kɔlər] *s* Besucher –in *mf*

call' girl' *s* Callgirl *n*

call'ing *s* Beruf *m*; (relig) Berufung *f*

call'ing card' *s* Visitenkarte *f*

call'ing-down' *s* (coll) Standpauke *f*

call' num'ber *s* (libr) Standortnummer *f*

callous ['kæləs] *adj* schwielig; (fig) gefühllos, abgestumpft

call'up' *s* (mil) Einberufung *f*

callus ['kæləs] *s* Schwiele *f*

calm [kɑm] *adj* ruhig ‖ *s* Ruhe *f*; (naut) Flaute *f* ‖ *tr* beruhigen; **c. down** beruhigen ‖ *intr*—**c. down** sich beruhigen

calorie ['kælərɪ] *s* Kalorie *f*

calumny ['kæləmnɪ] *s* Verleumdung *f*

Calvary ['kælvərɪ] *s* Golgatha *n*

calve [kæv] *intr* kalben

cam [kæm] *s* Nocken *m*

camel ['kæməl] *s* Kamel *n*

camellia [kə'mɪljə] *s* Kamelie *f*

cam-eo ['kæmɪ‚o] *s* (–os) Kamee *f*

camera ['kæmərə] *s* Kamera *f*

cam'era·man' *s* (–men') Kameramann *m*

camouflage ['kæmə‚flɑʒ] *s* Tarnung *f* ‖ *tr* tarnen

camp [kæmp] *s* (& fig) Lager *n* ‖ *intr* kampieren, lagern, campen

campaign [kæm'pen] *s* (& fig) Feldzug *m*; (pol) Wahlfeldzug *m* ‖ *intr* an e–m Feldzug teilnehmen; **c. for** (pol) Wahlpropaganda machen für

campaigner [kæm'penər] *s* (*for a specific cause*) Befürworter –in *mf*; (pol) Wahlredner –in *mf*

campaign' slo'gan *s* Wahlparole *f*

campaign' speech' *s* Wahlrede *f*

camper ['kæmpər] *s* Camper *m*

camp'fire' *s* Lagerfeuer *n*

camp'ground' *s* Campingplatz *m*

camphor ['kæmfər] *s* Kampfer *m*

camp'ing *s* Camping *n*

campus ['kæmpəs] *s* Universitätsgelände *n*

cam'shaft' *s* Nockenwelle *f*

can [kæn] *s* Dose *f*, Büchse *f*; (*for gasoline, water*) Kanister *m* ‖ *v* (*pret & pp* canned; *ger* canning) *tr* einmachen; (sl) 'rausschmeißen ‖ *v* (*pret & cond*) (could) *aux*—I can come ich kann kommen; I cannot come ich kann nicht kommen

Canada ['kænədə] *s* Kanada *n*

Canadian [kə'nedɪ·ən] *adj* kanadisch ‖ *s* Kanadier –in *mf*

canal [kə'næl] *s* Kanal *m*; (anat) Gang *m*

canary [kə'nerɪ] *s* Kanarienvogel *m* ‖ **the Canaries** *spl* die Kanarischen Inseln *pl*

can·cel ['kænsəl] *v* (*pret & pp* –el(l)ed; *ger* –el(l)ing) *tr* (*an event*) absagen; (*an order*) rückgängig machen; (*something written*) (aus)streichen, annulieren; (*stamps*) entwerten; (*a debt*) tilgen; (*a newspaper*) abbestellen; (math) streichen; **c. out** ausgleichen

cancellation [‚kænsə'leʃən] *s* (*of an event*) Absage *f*; (*of an order*) Annullierung *f*; (*of something written*) Streichung *f*; (*of a debt*) Tilgung *f*; (*of a stamp*) Entwertung *f*; (*of a newspaper*) Abbestellung *f*

cancer ['kænsər] *s* Krebs *m*

cancerous ['kænsərəs] *adj* krebsartig

candela·brum [‚kændə'lɑbrəm] *s* (–bra [brə] & –brums) Armleuchter *m*

candid ['kændɪd] *adj* offen

candidacy ['kændɪdəsɪ] *s* Kandidatur *f*

candidate ['kændɪ‚det] *s* (*for*) Kandidat –in *mf* (für)

candied ['kændɪd] *adj* kandiert

candle ['kændəl] *s* Kerze *f*

can'dlelight' *s* Kerzenlicht *n*

can'dlepow'er *s* Kerzenstärke *f*

can'dlestick' *s* Kerzenhalter *m*

candor ['kændər] *s* Offenheit *f*

can·dy ['kændɪ] *s* Süßwaren *pl*; **piece of c.** Bonbon *m* & *n* ‖ *v* (*pret & pp* –died) *tr* glacieren, kandieren

can'dy store' *s* Süßwarengeschäft *n*

cane [ken] *s* (*plant; stem*) Rohr *n*; (*walking stick*) Stock *m* ‖ *tr* mit e–m Stock züchtigen

cane' sug'ar *s* Rohrzucker *m*

canine ['kenaɪn] *adj* Hunde– ‖ *s* (*tooth*) Eckzahn *m*, Reißzahn *m*

canister ['kænɪstər] *s* Dose *f*

canker ['kæŋkər] *s* (bot) Brand *m*; (pathol) Mundgeschwür *n*

canned' goods' *spl* Dosenkonserven *pl*

canned' mu'sic *s* Konservenmusik *f*

canned' veg'etables *spl* Gemüsekonserven *pl*

cannery ['kænərɪ] *s* Konservenfabrik *f*

cannibal ['kænɪbəl] *s* Kannibale *m*

can'ning *adj* Konserven– ‖ *s* Konservenfabrikation *f*

cannon ['kænən] *s* Kanone *f*

cannonade [‚kænə'ned] *s* Kanonade *f*, Beschießung *f* ‖ *tr* beschießen

can'nonball' *s* Kanonenkugel *f*

can'non fod'der *s* Kanonenfutter *n*

canny ['kænɪ] *adj* (*shrewd*) schlau; (*sagacious*) klug

canoe [kə'nu] *s* Kanu *n*

canoe'ing *s* Kanufahren *n*

canoeist [kə'nu·ɪst] *s* Kanufahrer *m*

canon ['kænən] *s* Kanon *m*; (*of a cathedral*) Domherr *m*

canonical [kə'nɑnɪkəl] *adj* kanonisch ‖ **canonicals** *spl* kirchliche Amtstracht *f* canonize ['kænə‚naız] *tr* heiligsprechen

can'on law' *s* kanonisches Recht *n*

can' o/pener *s* Dosenöffner *m*

canopy ['kænəpı] *s* Baldachin *m*; (*above a king or pope*) Thronhimmel *m*; (*of a bed*) Betthimmel *m*

cant [kænt] *s* (*insincere statements*) unaufrichtiges Gerede *n*; (*jargon of thieves*) Gaunersprache *f*; (*technical phraseology*) Jargon *m*

cantaloupe ['kæntə‚lop] *s* Kantalupe *f*

cantankerous [kæn'tæŋkərəs] *adj* mürrisch, zänkisch

cantata [kən'tɑtə] *s* Kantate *f*

canteen [kæn'tin] *s* (*service club, service store*) Kantine *f*; (*flask*) Feldflasche *f*

canter ['kæntər] *s* kurzer Galopp *m* ‖ *intr* im kurzen Galopp reiten

canticle ['kæntıkəl] *s* Lobgesang *m*

canton ['kæntən] *s* Kanton *m*

canvas ['kænvəs] *s* Leinwand *f*; (naut) Segeltuch *n*; (*a painting*) Gemälde *n*

canvass ['kænvəs] *s* (econ) Werbefeldzug *m*; (pol) Wahlfeldzug *m* ‖ *tr* (*a district*) (pol) bearbeiten; (*votes*) (pol) werben

canyon ['kænjən] *s* Schlucht *f*

cap [kæp] *s* Kappe *f*, Mütze *f*; (*of a jar*) Deckel *m*; (*twist-off type*) Kapsel *f*; (*for a toy pistol*) Knallblättchen *n*; (typ) großer Buchstabe *m*; use caps (typ) großschreiben ‖ *v* (*pret & pp* capped; *ger* capping) *tr* (*a bottle*) mit e–r Kapsel versehen; (*e.g., with snow*) bedecken; (*outdo*) übertreffen; (*success*) krönen

capability [‚kepə'bılıtı] *s* Fähigkeit *f*

capable ['kepəbəl] *adj* tüchtig; **c. of** fähig (*genit*); (*ger*) fähig zu (*inf*)

capacious [kə'pe/əs] *adj* geräumig

capacity [kə'pæsıtı] *adj* maximal, Kapazitäts– ‖ *s* (*ability*) Fähigkeit *f*; (*content*) Fassungsvermögen *n*; (*of a truck, bridge*) Tragfähigkeit *f*; (tech) Kapazität *f*; **in my c. as** in meiner Eigenschaft als

cap' and gown' *s* Barett *n* und Talar *m*

cape [kep] *s* Umhang *m*; (geog) Kap *n*

Cape' of Good' Hope' *s* Kap *n* der Guten Hoffnung

caper ['kepər] *s* Luftsprung *m*; (*prank*) Schabernack *m*; (culin) Kaper *f* ‖ *intr* hüpfen

capita ['kæpıtə] *spl*—**per c.** pro Kopf, pro Person

capital ['kæpıtəl] *adj* (*importance*) äußerste, höchste; (*city*) Haupt–; (*crime*) Kapital– ‖ *s* (*city*) Hauptstadt *f*; (archit) Kapitell *n*; (fin) Kapital *n*; (typ) Großbuchstabe *m*

cap'ital gains' *spl* Kapitalzuwachs *m*

capitalism ['kæpıtə‚lızəm] *s* Kapitalismus *m*

capitalist ['kæpıtəlıst] *s* Kapitalist –in *mf*

capitalistic [‚kæpıtə'lıstık] *adj* kapitalistisch

capitalize ['kæpıtə‚laız] *tr* (fin) kapitalisieren; (typ) groß schreiben (or

drucken ‖ *intr*—**c. on** Nutzen ziehen aus

cap'ital let'ter *s* Großbuchstabe *m*

cap'ital pun'ishment *s* Todesstrafe *f*

capitol ['kæpıtəl] *s* Kapitol *n*

capitulate [kə'pıt/ə‚let] *intr* kapitulieren

capon ['kepən] *s* Kapaun *m*

caprice [kə'pris] *s* Grille *f*, Kaprice *f*

capricious [kə'prı/əs] *adj* kapriziös

capsize ['kæpsaız] *tr* zum Kentern bringen ‖ *intr* kentern

capsule ['kæpsəl] *s* Kapsel *f*

captain ['kæptən] *s* (*of police, of firemen, in the army*) Hauptmann *m*; (naut, sport) Kapitän *m*; (nav) Kapitän *m* zur See; (sport) Mannschaftsführer *m*

caption ['kæp/ən] *s* (*heading of an article*) Überschrift *f*; (*wording under a picture*) Bildunterschrift *f*; (cin) Untertitel *m*

captivate ['kæptı‚vet] *tr* fesseln

captive ['kæptıv] *adj* gefangen ‖ *s* Gefangene *mf*

cap'tive au'dience *s* unfreiwillige Zuhörerschaft *f*

captivity [kæp'tıvıtı] *s* Gefangenschaft *f*

captor ['kæptər] *s* Fänger –in *mf*

capture ['kæpt/ər] *s* Fangen *n*, Gefangennahme *f*; (naut) Kaperung *f* ‖ *tr* (*animals*) fangen; (*soldiers*) gefangennehmen; (*a ship*) kapern; (*a town*) erobern; (*a prize*) gewinnen

car [kar] *s* (aut, rr) Wagen *m*

carafe [kə'ræf] *s* Karaffe *f*

caramel ['kærəməl] *s* Karamelle *f*

carat ['kærət] *s* Karat *n*

caravan ['kærə‚væn] *s* Karawane *f*

car'away seed' ['kærə‚we] *s* Kümmelkorn *n*

carbide ['karbaıd] *s* Karbid *n*

carbine ['karbaın] *s* Karabiner *m*

carbohydrate [‚karbo'haıdret] *s* Kohlenhydrat *n*

carbol'ic ac'id [kar'balık] *s* Karbolsäure *f*

carbon ['karbən] *s* (chem) Kohlenstoff *m*; (elec) Kohlenstift *m*

carbonated ['karbə‚netıd] *adj* kohlensäurehaltig, Brause–

car'bon cop'y *s* Durchschlag *m*; **make a c. of** durchschlagen

car'bon diox'ide *s* Kohlendioxyd *n*

car'bon monox'ide *s* Kohlenoxyd *n*

car'bon pa'per *s* Kohlepapier *n*

carbuncle ['karbʌŋkəl] *s* (*stone*) Karfunkel *m*; (pathol) Karbunkel *m*

carburetor ['karb(j)ə‚retər] *s* Vergaser *m*

carcass ['karkəs] *s* Kadaver *m*, Aas *n*; (*without offal*) Rumpf *m*

car' coat' *s* Stutzer *m*

card [kard] *s* Karte *f*; (*person*) (coll) Kerl *m*; (text) Krempel *f* ‖ *tr* (text) kardätschen

card'board' *s* Kartonpapier *n*; (*thick pasteboard*) Pappe *f*; **piece of c.** Papp(en)deckel *m*

card'board box' *s* Pappkarton *m*, Pappschachtel *f*

card' cat'alogue *s* Kartothek *f*

card′ file′ s Kartei *f*
cardiac [′kɑrdɪ‚æk] *adj* Herz– ‖ s
(*remedy*) Herzmittel *n;* (*patient*)
Herzkranke *mf*
cardinal [′kɑrdɪnəl] *adj* Kardinal– ‖ *s*
(eccl, orn) Kardinal *m*
card′ in′dex s Karthotek *f,* Kartei *f*
card′sharp′ s Falschspieler –in *mf*
card′ trick′ s Kartenkunststück *n*
care [ker] *s* (*accuracy*) Sorgfalt *f;*
(*worry*) Sorge *f,* Kummer *m;* (*pru-*
dence) Vorsicht *f;* (*upkeep*) Pflege
f; **be under a doctor's c.** unter der
Aufsicht e–s Arztes stehen; **c. of** (*on*
letters) bei; **take c.** aufpassen; **take**
c. not to (*inf*) sich hüten zu (*inf*);
take c. of s.o. (*provide for s.o.*) für
j–n sorgen; (*attend to*) sich um j–n
kümmern; **take c. of s.th.** etw besorgen; (*e.g., one's clothes*) schonen
‖ *intr*—**c. about** sich kümmern um;
c. for (*like*) mögen, gern haben;
(*have concern for*) sorgen für; (*at-*
tend to) pflegen; **c. to** (*inf*) Lust
haben zu (*inf*); **for all I c.** von mir
aus
careen [kə′rin] *tr* auf die Seite legen
‖ *intr* (aut) sich in die Kurve neigen
career [kə′rɪr] *adj* Berufs– ‖ s Karriere *f*
career′ wo′man s berufstätige Frau *f*
care′free′ *adj* unbelastet, sorgenfrei
careful [′kɛrfəl] *adj* (*cautious*) vorsichtig; (*accurate*) sorgfältig; **b. c.!**
gib acht!
careless [′kɛrlɪs] *adj* (*incautious*) unvorsichtig; (*remark*) unbedacht; (*in-*
accurate) nachlässig
carelessness [′kɛrlɪsnɪs] *s* Unvorsich-
tigkeit *f;* Nachlässigkeit *f*
caress [kə′rɛs] *s* Liebkosung *f* ‖ *tr*
liebkosen
caret [′kærət] *s* Auslassungszeichen *n*
caretaker [′kɛr‚tekər] *s* Verwalter *m*
care′worn′ *adj* abgehärmt, vergrämt
car′fare′ s Fahrgeld *n*
car·go [′kɑrgo] *s* (–**goes** & –**gos**)
Fracht *f*
car′go compart′ment s Frachtraum *m*
car′go plane′ s Frachtflugzeug *n*
Caribbean [‚kærɪ′bi·ən], [kə′rɪbɪ·ən]
adj karibisch ‖ *s* Karibisches Meer *n*
caricature [′kærɪkət∫ər] *s* Karikatur *f*
‖ *tr* karikieren
caries [′kɛriz] *s* (dent) Karies *f*
carillon [′kærɪ‚lɑn] *s* Glockenspiel *n*
car′ lift′ s (aut) Hebebühne *f*
car′load′ s Wagenladung *f*
carnage [′kɑrnɪdʒ] *s* Blutbad *n*
carnal [′kɑrnəl] *adj* fleischlich
car′nal know′ledge s Geschlechtsverkehr *m*
carnation [kɑr′ne∫ən] *s* Nelke *f*
carnival [′kɑrnɪvəl] *s* Karneval *m*
carnivorous [kɑr′nɪvərəs] *adj* fleisch-
fressend
car·ol [′kærəl] *s* Weihnachtslied *n* ‖
v (*pret & pp* –**ol**(**l**)**ed;** *ger* –**l**(**l**)**ing**)
intr Weihnachtslieder singen
carom [′kærəm] *s* (*billiards*) Karambolage *f* ‖ *intr* (*fig*) zusammenstoßen; (billiards) karambolieren
carouse [kə′rauz] *intr* zechen

carp [kɑrp] *s* Karpfen *m* ‖ *intr* nörgeln
carpenter [′kɑrpəntər] *s* Zimmermann
m
carpentry [′kɑrpəntri] *s* Zimmerei *f*
carpet [′kɑrpɪt] *s* Teppich *m* ‖ *tr* mit
Teppichen belegen
car′pet sweep′er *s* Teppichkehrmaschine *f*
car′port′ s Autoschuppen *m*
car′-ren′tal serv′ice s Autovermietung
f
carriage [′kærɪdʒ] *s* Kutsche *f;* (*of a*
typewriter) Wagen *m;* (*bearing*)
Körperhaltung *f;* (econ) Transportkosten *pl*
car′ ride′ s Autofahrt *f*
carrier [′kæri·ər] *s* Träger *m;* (*com-*
pany) Transportunternehmen *n*
car′rier pig′eon s Brieftaube *f*
carrion [′kæri·ən] *s* Aas *n*
carrot [′kærət] *s* Karotte *f,* Mohrrübe
f
carrousel [‚kærə′zel] *s* Karussell *n*
car·ry [′kæri] *v* (*pret & pp* –**ried**) *tr*
tragen; (*wares*) führen; (*a message*)
überbringen; (*a tune*) halten; (*said*
of transportation) befördern; (*insur-*
ance) haben; (math) übertragen;
(*parl*) durchbringen; **be carried**
(*said of a motion, bill*) angenommen
werden; **be carried away by** (& fig)
mitgerissen werden von; **c. away** (*an*
audience) mitreißen; **c. off** (*a prize*)
davontragen; **c. on** weiterführen; (*a*
business) betreiben, führen; **c. out**
hinaustragen; (*a duty*) erfüllen;
(*measures*) durchführen; (*a sen-*
tence) vollstrecken; (*an order*) ausführen; **c. over** (*acct*) übertragen;
c. s.th. too far etw übertreiben; **c.**
through durchsetzen; ‖ *intr* (*said of*
sounds) tragen; (parl) durchgehen;
c. on (*continue*) weitermachen; (*act*
up) (coll) toben; **c. on with** ein Verhältnis haben mit
car′rying char′ges spl Kreditgebühren
pl
car′ry-o′ver s Überbleibsel *n;* (acct)
Übertrag *m*
cart [kɑrt] *s* Karren *m* ‖ *tr* mit dem
Handwagen befördern; **c. away** (or
c. off) abfahren
cartel [kɑr′tel] *s* Kartell *n*
cartilage [′kɑrtɪlɪdʒ] *s* Knorpel *m*
carton [′kɑrtən] *s* Karton *m;* **a c. of**
cigarettes e–e Stange Zigaretten
cartoon [kɑr′tun] *s* Karikatur *f;*
(*comic strip*) Karikaturenreihe *f;*
(cin) Zeichentrickfilm *m;* (paint)
Entwurf *m* natürlicher Größe ‖ *tr*
karikieren
cartoonist [kɑr′tunɪst] *s* Karikaturen-
zeichner –in *mf*
cartridge [′kɑrtrɪdʒ] *s* Patrone *f;*
(phot) Filmpatrone *f*
car′tridge belt′ s Patronengurt *m*
cart′wheel′ s Wagenrad *n;* **turn a c.**
ein Rad schlagen
carve [kɑrv] *tr* (*wood*) schnitzen;
(*meat*) tranchieren, vorschneiden;
(*stone*) meißeln; **c. out** (*e.g., a ca-*
reer) aufbauen

carver ['kɑrvər] *s* (*at table*) Vor-schneider –in *mf*

carv'ing knife' *s* Tranchiermesser *n*

car' wash' *s* Wagenwäsche *f*

cascade [kæs'ked] *s* Kaskade *f* ‖ *intr* kaskadenartig herabstürzen

case [kes] *s* (*instance*) Fall *m*; (*situation*) Sache *f*; (*box*) Kiste *f*; (*for a knife, etc.*) Hülle *f*; (*for cigarettes*) Etui *n*; (*for eyeglasses*) Futteral *n*; (*for shipping*) Schutzkarton *m*; (*of a watch*) Gehäuse *n*; (*of sickness*) Krankheitsfall *m*; (*sick person*) Pa-tient –in *mf*; (*gram*) Fall *m*; (*jur*) Fall *m*, Sache *f*, Prozeß *m*; (*typ*) Setzkasten *m*; **as the c. may be** je nachdem; **have a strong c.** schlüssige Beweise haben; **if that's the c.** wenn es sich so verhält; **in any c.** auf jeden Fall, jedenfalls; **in c.** falls; **in c. of** im Falle (*genit*); **in c. of emergency** im Notfall; **in no c.** keinesfalls ‖ *tr* (*sl*) genau ansehen; **the c. at issue** der vorliegende Fall

case' his'tory *s* Vorgeschichte *f*; (*med*) Krankengeschichte *f*

casement ['kesmənt] *s* Fensterflügel *m*

case'ment win'dow *s* Flügelfenster *n*

cash [kæʃ] *adj* Bar– ‖ *s* Bargeld *n*; (*cash payment*) Barzahlung *f*; **c. and carry** nur gegen Barzahlung und eigenen Transport; **in c.** per Kasse; **out of c.** nicht bei Kasse; **pay c. for** bar bezahlen ‖ *tr* einlösen ‖ *intr*— **c. in on** (coll) Nutzen ziehen aus

cash'box' *s* Schatulle *f*, Kasse *f*

cash' dis'count *s* Kassaskonto *n*

cashew' nut' [kæ'ʃu], [kæʃu] *s* Ka-schunuß *f*

cashier [kæ'ʃɪr] *s* Kassierer –in *mf*

cashmere ['kæ/mɪr] *s* Kaschmir *m*

cash' on deliv'ery *adv* per Nachnahme

cash' reg'ister *m* Registrierkasse *f*

cas'ing *s* (*wrapping*) Verpackung *f*; (*housing*) Gehäuse *n*; (*of a window or door*) Futter *n*; (*of a tire*) Mantel *m*; (*of a sausage*) Wurstdarm *m*

casi·no [kə'sino] *s* (*-nos*) Kasino *n*

cask [kæsk] *s* Faß *n*, Tonne *f*

casket ['kæskɪt] *s* Sarg *m*

casserole ['kæsə,rol] *s* Kasserolle *f*

cassette [kæ'set] *s* Kassette *f*

cassock ['kæsək] *s* (eccl) Soutane *f*

cast [kæst] *s* (*throw*) Wurf *m*; (*act of molding*) Guß *m*; (*mold*) Gußform *f*; (*object molded*) Abguß *m*; (*hue*) Abtönung *f*; (*surg*) Gipsverband *m*; (*theat*) Rollenbesetzung *f* ‖ *v* (*pret & pp* **cast**) *tr* werfen; (*a net, anchor*) auswerfen; (*a ballot*) abgeben; (*lots*) ziehen; (*skin, horns*) abwerfen; (*a shadow, glance*) werfen; (*metal*) gießen; (*a play or motion picture*) die Rollen besetzen in (*dat*); **be c. down** niedergeschlagen sein; **c. aside** (*reject*) verwerfen; ‖ *intr* (angl) die Angel auswerfen; **c. off** (naut) los-werfen

castanet [,kæstə'nɛt] *s* Kastagnette *f*

cast'away' *adj* verworfen; (naut) schiffbrüchig ‖ *s* (naut) Schiff-brüchige *mf*

caste [kæst] *s* Kaste *f*

caster ['kæstər] *s* (*under furniture*) Rolle *f*; (*shaker*) Streuer *m*

castigate ['kæstɪ,get] *tr* züchtigen; (fig) geißeln

cast'ing *s* Wurf *m*; (*act of casting*) (metal) Guß *m*; (*the object cast*) (metal) Gußstück *n*; (theat) Rollen-verteilung *f*

cast'ing rod' *s* Wurfangel *f*

cast' i'ron *s* Gußeisen *n*

cast'-i'ron *adj* gußeisern; (fig) eisern

castle ['kæsəl] *s* Schloß *n*, Burg, *f*; (chess) Turm *m* ‖ *intr* (chess) ro-chieren

cast'off' *adj* abgelegt ‖ *s* (*e.g., dress*) abgelegtes Kleidungsstück *n*; (*person*) Verstoßene *mf*

cas'tor oil' ['kæstər] *s* Rizinusöl *n*

castrate ['kæstret] *tr* kastrieren

casual ['kæʒʊ·əl] *adj* (*cursory*) bei-läufig; (*occasional*) gelegentlich; (*in-cidental*) zufällig; (*informal*) zwang-los; (*unconcerned*) gleichgültig

casualty ['kæʒʊ·əltɪ] *s* (*victim*) Opfer *n*; (*accident*) Unfall *m*; (*person in-jured*) Verunglückte *mf*; (*person killed*) (mil) Gefallene *mf*; (*person wounded*) (mil) Verwundete *mf*; **casualties** (*in an accident*) Verun-glückte *pl*; (*in war*) Verluste *pl*

cas'ualty list' *s* Verlustliste *f*

cat [kæt] *s* Katze *f*; (*guy*) (sl) Typ *m*; (*malicious woman*) (sl) falsche Katze *f*

catacomb ['kætə,kom] *s* Katakombe *f*

catalog(ue) ['kætə,log] *s* Katalog *m*; (*list*) Verzeichnis *n*; (*of a university*) Vorlesungsverzeichnis *n* ‖ *tr* kata-logisieren

catalyst ['kætəlɪst] *s* Katalysator *m*

catapult ['kætə,pʌlt] *s* Katapult *m* & *n* ‖ *tr* katapultieren, abschleudern

cataract ['kætə,rækt] *s* Katarakt *m*; (pathol) grauer Star *m*; **remove s.o.'s c.** j–m den Star stechen

catastrophe [kə'tæstrəfi] *s* Katastro-phe *f*

cat'call' *s* Auspfeifen *n* ‖ *tr* auspfeifen

catch [kætʃ] *s* Fang *m*; (*of fish*) Fisch-fang *m*; (*device*) Haken *m*, Klinke *f*; (*desirable partner*) Partie *f*; (fig) Haken *m*; ‖ *v* (*pret & pp* **caught** [kɔt]) *tr* fangen; (*s.o. or s.th. fall-ing*) auffangen; (*by pursuing*) ab-fangen; (*s.o. or s.th. that has es-caped*) einfangen; (*by surprise*) ertappen, erwischen; (*in midair*) aufschnappen; (*take hold of*) fassen; (*said of a storm*) überraschen; (*e.g., a train*) erreichen; **c. a cold** sich er-kälten; **c. fire** in Brand geraten; **c. hold of** ergreifen; **c. it** (coll) sein Fett kriegen; **c. one's breath** wieder Atem schöpfen; **c. one's eye** j–m ins Auge fallen; **get caught on** hängen-bleiben an (*dat*) ‖ *intr* (*said of a bolt, etc.*) einschnappen; **c. on** (*said of an idea*) Anklang finden; **c. on to** (fig) kapieren; **catch up** aufholen; **c. up on** nachholen; **c. up with** ein-holen

catch'ing *adj* (*disease*) ansteckend; (*attractive*) anziehend

catch′word′ s (*slogan*) Schlagwort n; (*actor's cue*) Stichwort n; (pol) Parteiparole f

catchy [′kætʃi] adj einschmeichelnd

catechism [′kætɪ,kɪzəm] s Katechismus m

category [′kætɪ,gori] s Kategorie f

cater [′ketər] tr Lebensmittel liefern für ‖ intr—**c. to** schmeicheln (*dat*); (*deliver food to*) Lebensmittel liefern für

cater-corner [′kætər,kornər] adj & adv diagonal

caterer [′ketərər] s Lebensmittellieferant –in mf

caterpillar [′kætər,pɪlər] s (ent, mach) Raupe f

cat′fish′ s Katzenwels m, Katzenfisch m

cat′gut′ s (mus) Darmseite f; (surg) Katgut m

cathedral [kə′θidrəl] s Dom m

catheter [′kæθɪtər] s Katheter n

cathode [′kæθod] s Kathode f

catholic [′kæθəlɪk] adj universal; **Catholic** katholisch ‖ **Catholic** s Katholik –in mf

cat′nap′ s Nickerchen n

catnip [′kætnɪp] s Baldrian m

catsup [′kætsəp], [′ketʃəp] s Ketschup m

cattle [′kætəl] spl Vieh n

cat′tle car′ s (rr) Viehwagen m

cat′tle-man s (–men) Viehzüchter m

cat′tle ranch′ s Viehfarm f

catty [′kæti] adj boshaft

cat′walk′ s Steg m, Laufplanke f

Caucasian [kɔ′keʒən] adj kaukasisch ‖ s Kaukasier –in mf

caucus [′kɔkəs] s Parteiführerversammlung f

cauliflower [′kɔlɪ,flau·ər] s Blumenkohl m

cause [kɔz] s (*origin*) Ursache f; (*reason*) Grund m; (*person*) Urheber –in mf; (*occasion*) Anlaß m; **for a good c.** für e–e gute Sache ‖ tr verursachen; **c. s.o. to** (*inf*) j–n veranlassen zu (*inf*)

cause′way′ s Dammweg m

caustic [′kɔstɪk] adj (& fig) ätzend

cauterize [′kɔtə,raɪz] tr verätzen

caution [′kɔʃən] s (*carefulness*) Vorsicht f; (*warning*) Warnung f ‖ tr (*against*) warnen (vor dat)

cautious [′kɔʃəs] adj vorsichtig

cavalcade [′kævəl,ked] s Kavalkade f

cavalier [,kævə′lɪr] adj hochmütig ‖ s Kavalier m

cavalry [′kævəlri] s Kavallerie f

cav′alry-man s (–men) Kavallerist m

cave [kev] s Höhle f ‖ intr—**c. in** (*collapse*) einstürzen

cave′-in′ s Einsturz m

cave′ man′ s Höhlenmensch m

cavern [′kævərn] s (*große*) Höhle f

caviar [′kævɪ,ar] s Kaviar m

cav·il [′kævɪl] v (*pret & pp* –l(l)ed; *ger* –l(l)ing) intr (at, about) herumnörgeln (an dat)

cavity [′kævɪti] s Hohlraum m; (anat) Höhle f; (dent) Loch n

cavort [kə′vɔrt] intr (coll) herumtollen

caw [kɔ] s Krächzen n ‖ intr krächzen

cease [sis] s—**without c.** unaufhörlich ‖ tr einstellen; (*ger*) aufhören (zu *inf*); **c. fire** das Feuer einstellen ‖ intr aufhören

cease′fire′ s Feuereinstellung f

ceaseless [′sislɪs] adj unaufhörlich

cedar [′sidər] s Zeder f

cede [sid] tr abtreten, überlassen

cedilla [sɪ′dɪlə] s Cedille f

ceiling [′silɪŋ] s Decke f; (fin) oberste Grenze f; **hit the c.** (coll) platzen

ceil′ing light′ s Deckenlicht n

ceil′ing price′ s Höchstpreis m

celebrant [′selɪbrənt] s Zelebrant m

celebrate [′selɪ,bret] tr (*a feast*) feiern; (*mass*) zelebrieren ‖ intr feiern; (eccl) zelebrieren

cel′ebrat′ed adj (for) berühmt (wegen)

celebration [,selɪ′breʃən] s Feier f; (eccl) Zelebrieren n; **in c. of** zur Feier (*genit*)

celebrity [sɪ′lebrɪti] s Berühmtheit f; (*person*) Prominente m

celery [′seləri] s Selleriestengel m

celestial [sɪ′lestʃəl] adj himmlisch; (astr) Himmels–

celibacy [′selɪbəsi] s Zölibat m & n

celibate [′selɪbɪt] adj ehelos

cell [sel] s Zelle f

cellar [′selər] s Keller m

cellist [′tʃelɪst] s Cellist –in mf

cel·lo [′tʃelo] s (–los) Cello n

cellophane [′selə,fen] s Zellophan n

celluloid [′seljə,lɔɪd] s Zelluloid n

Celt [selt], [kelt] s Kelte m, Keltin f

Celtic [′seltɪk], [′keltɪk] adj keltisch

cement [sɪ′ment] s (*glue*) Bindemittel n; (*used in building*) Zement m ‖ tr zementieren; (*glue*) kitten; (fig) (be)festigen

cement′ mix′er s Betonmischmaschine f

cemetery [′semɪ,teri] s Friedhof m

censer [′sensər] s Räucherfaß m

censor [′sensər] s (*of printed matter, films*) Zensor m; (*of morals*) Sittenrichter m ‖ tr zensieren

cen′sorship′ s Zensur f

censure [′senʃər] s Tadel m ‖ tr tadeln

census [′sensəs] s Volkszählung f

cent [sent] s Cent m

centaur [′sentɔr] s Zentaur m

centennial [sen′tenɪəl] adj hundertjährig ‖ s Hundertjahrfeier f

center [′sentər] s Zentrum n, Mittelpunkt m; (pol) Mitte f ‖ tr in den Mittelpunkt stellen; (tech) zentrieren ‖ intr—**c. on** sich konzentrieren auf (*acc*)

cen′ter aisle′ s Mittelgang m

cen′ter cit′y s Stadtmitte f

cen′terpiece′ s Tischaufsatz m

centigrade [′sentɪ,gred] s Celsius, e.g., **one degree c.** ein Grad Celsius

centimeter [′sentɪ,mitər] s Zentimeter m

centipede [′sentɪ,pid] s Hundertfüßler m

central [′sentrəl] adj zentral

Cen′tral Amer′ica s Mittelamerika n

centralize [′sentrə,laɪz] tr zentralisieren

centri'fugal force' [sɛn'trɪfjəgəl] s Fliehkraft f

centrifuge ['sentrɪ‚fjudʒ] s Zentrifuge f

century ['sentʃərɪ] s Jahrhundert n

ceramic [sɪ'ræmɪk] adj keramisch ‖ **ceramics** s (art) Keramik f; spl Töpferwaren pl

cereal ['sɪrɪ‑əl] adj Getreide– ‖ s (grain) Getreide n; (dish) Getreideflockengericht n

cerebral ['sɛrɪbrəl] adj Gehirn–

ceremonial [‚sɛrɪ'monɪ‑əl] adj zeremoniell, feierlich

ceremonious [‚sɛrɪ'monɪ‑əs] adj zeremoniös, umständlich

ceremony ['sɛrɪ‚monɪ] s Zeremonie f

certain ['sʌrtən] adj (sure) sicher, bestimmt; (particular but unnamed) gewiß; **be c.** feststehen; **for c.** gewiß; **make c. of** sich vergewissern (genit); **make c. that** sich vergewissern, daß

certainly ['sʌrtənlɪ] adv sicher(lich); (as a strong affirmative) allerdings

certainty ['sʌrtəntɪ] s Sicherheit f

certificate [sər'tɪfɪkɪt] s Schein m; (educ) Abgangszeugnis n

certification [‚sʌrtɪfɪ'keʃən] s Bescheinigung f, Beglaubigung f

cer'tified adj beglaubigt

cer'tified check' s durch Bank bestätigter Scheck m

cer'tified pub'lic account'ant s amtlich zugelassener Wirtschaftsprüfer m

certi‑fy ['sʌrtɪ‚faɪ] v (pret & pp –fied) bescheinigen, beglaubigen

cervix ['sʌrvɪks] s (cervices [sər'vaɪsɪz]) Genick n

cessation [se'seʃən] s (of territory) Abtretung f; (of activities) Einstellung f

cesspool ['sɛs‚pul] s Senkgrube f

chafe [tʃef] tr (the skin) wundscheuern ‖ intr (rub) scheuern; (become sore) sich wundreiben; (be irritated) (at) sich ärgern über (acc)

chaff [tʃæf] s Spreu f

chaff'ing dish' s Speisenwärmer m

chagrin [ʃə'grɪn] s Verdruß m ‖ tr verdrießen

chain [tʃen] s Kette f ‖ tr (to) anketten (an acc)

chain' gang' s Kettensträflinge pl

chain' reac'tion s Kettenreaktion f

chain' smok'er s Kettenraucher –in mf

chain' store' s Kettenladen m

chair [tʃer] s Stuhl m; (upholstered) Sessel m; (of the presiding officer) Vorsitz m; (presiding officer) Vorsitzende mf; (educ) Lehrstuhl m ‖ tr den Vorsitz führen von

chair'la'dy s Vorsitzende f

chair' lift' s Sessellift m

chair'man s (–men) Vorsitzende m

chair'manship' s Vorsitz m

chalice ['tʃælɪs] s Kelch m

chalk [tʃɔk] s Kreide f ‖ tr—**c. up** ankreiden; (coll) verbuchen

challenge ['tʃælɪndʒ] s Aufforderung f; (to a duel) Herausforderung f; (jur) Ablehnung f; (mil) Anruf m ‖ tr auffordern; (to a duel) herausfor

dern; (a statement, right) bestreiten; (jur) ablehnen; (mil) anrufen

chamber ['tʃembər] s Kammer f; (parl) Sitzungssaal m

chamberlain ['tʃembərlɪn] s Kammerm

cham'bermaid' s Stubenmädchen n

cham'ber of com'merce s Handelskammer f

chameleon [kə'milɪ‑ən] s Chamäleon n

chamfer ['tʃæmfər] s Schrägkante f ‖ tr abschrägen; (furrow) auskehlen

cham‑ois ['ʃæmɪ] s (–ois) Sämischleder n; (zool) Gemse f

champ [tʃæmp] s (coll) Meister m ‖ tr kauen; **champ the bit** am Gebiß kauen

champagne [ʃæm'pen] s Champagner m, Sekt m

champion ['tʃæmpɪ‑ən] s (of a cause) Verfechter –in m; (sport) Meister –in mf ‖ tr eintreten für

cham'pionship' s Meisterschaft f

chance [tʃæns] adj zufällig ‖ s (accident) Zufall m; (opportunity) Chance f, Gelegenheit f; (risk) Risiko n; (possibility) Möglichkeit f; (lottery ticket) Los n; **by c.** zufällig; **c. of a lifetime** einmalige Gelegenheit f; **chances are (that)** aller Wahrscheinlichkeit nach; **on the c. that** für den Fall, daß; **take a c.** ein Risiko eingehen; **take no chances** nichts riskiren; ‖ tr riskieren ‖ intr geschehen; **c. upon** stoßen auf (acc)

chancel ['tʃænsəl] s Altarraum m

chancellery ['tʃænsələrɪ] s Kanzlei f

chancellor ['tʃænsələr] s Kanzler m; (hist) Reichskanzler m

chandelier [‚ʃændə'lɪr] s Kronleuchter m

change [tʃendʒ] s Veränderung f; (in times, styles, etc.) Wechsel m; (in attitude, relations, etc.) Wandel m; (small coins) Kleingeld n; (of weather) Umschlag m; **c. for the better** Verbesserung f; **c. for the worse** Verschlechterung f; **for a c.** zur Abwechslung; **give c. for a dollar** auf e–n Dollar herausgeben; **need a c.** Luftveränderung brauchen ‖ tr verändern; (plans) ändern; (money, subject, oil) wechseln; (a baby) trockenlegen; (stations, channels) umschalten; **c. around** umändern; **c. hands** den Besitzer wechseln; **c. one's mind** sich anders besinnen; **c. trains (or buses, streetcars)** umsteigen ‖ intr sich verändern; (said of a mood, wind, weather) umschlagen; (said of a voice) mutieren; (change clothes) sich umziehen **change into** sich wandeln in (acc)

changeable ['tʃendʒəbəl] adj veränderlich

changeless ['tʃendʒlɪs] adj unveränderlich

change' of heart' s Sinnesänderung f

change' of life' s Wechseljahre pl

change' of scen'ery s Ortsveränderung f

change'-o'ver s Umstellung f

chan·nel [ˈtʃænəl] s (strait) Kanal m; (of a river) Fahrrinne f; (groove) Rinne f; (furrow) Furche f; (fig) Weg m; (telv) Kanal m; **through official channels** auf dem Amtswege ‖ v (pret & pp -nel(l)ed; ger -nel-(l)ing) tr lenken; (furrow) kanalisieren

chant [tʃænt] s Gesang m; (singsong) Singsang m; (eccl) Kirchengesang m ‖ tr singen

chanter [ˈtʃæntər] s Kantor m

chaos [ˈkeˑɑs] s Chaos n

chaotic [keˈɑtɪk] adj chaotisch

chap [tʃæp] s (in the skin) Riß m; (coll) Kerl m ‖ v (pret & pp chapped; ger chapping) tr (the skin) rissig machen ‖ intr rissig werden, aufspringen

chapel [ˈtʃæpəl] s Kapelle f

chaperon [ˈʃæpəˌron] s Begleiter –in mf; (of a young couple) Anstandsdame f ‖ tr als Anstandsdame begleiten

chaplain [ˈtʃæplɪn] s Kaplan m

chapter [ˈtʃæptər] s Kapitel n; (of an organization) Ortsgruppe f

char [tʃɑr] v (pret & pp charred; ger charring) tr verkohlen

character [ˈkærɪktər] s Charakter m; (letter) Schriftzeichen n; (typewriter space) Anschlag m; (coll) Kauz m; (theat) handelnde Person f; **be out of c.** nicht passen

characteristic [ˌkærɪktəˈrɪstɪk] adj (of) charakteristisch (für) ‖ s Charakterzug m, Kennzeichen n

characterize [ˈkærɪktəˌraɪz] tr charakterisieren, kennzeichnen

charade [ʃəˈred] s Scharade f

charcoal [ˈtʃɑrˌkol] s Holzkohle f; (for sketching) Zeichenkohle f

charge [tʃɑrdʒ] s (accusation) Anklage f; (fee) Gebühr f; (custody) Obhut f; (responsibility) Pflicht f; (ward) Pflegebefohlene mf; (of an explosive or electricity) Ladung f; (assault) Ansturm m; (of a judge to the jury) Rechtsbelehrung f; **be in c.** of verantwortlich sein für; **charges** Spesen pl; **take c.** of die Verantwortung übernehmen für; **there is no c.** es kostet nichts; **under s.o.'s c.** unter j–s Aufsicht ‖ tr (a battery) (auf)-laden; (with) anklagen (wegen); (a jury) belehren; (mil) stürmen; **c. s.o. ten marks for** j–m zehn Mark berechnen für; **c. s.o.'s account** auf j–s Rechnung setzen ‖ intr (mil) anrechnen für; **c. to s.o.'s account** auf j–s Rechnung setzen ‖ intr (mil) anstürmen

charge' account' s laufendes Konto n

charger [ˈtʃɑrdʒər] s (elec) Ladevorrichtung f; (hist) Schlachtroß n

chariot [ˈtʃærɪˑət] s Kampfwagen m

charitable [ˈtʃærɪtəbəl] adj (generous) freigebig; (lenient) Almosen m; **c. institution** wohltätige Stiftung f

charity [ˈtʃærɪti] s (giving of alms) Wohltätigkeit f; (alms) Almosen n; (institution) Wohlfahrtsinstitut n; (love of neighbor) Nächstenliebe f

charlatan [ˈʃɑrlətən] s Scharlatan m

Charles [tʃɑrlz] s Karl m

char'ley horse' [ˈtʃɑrli] s (coll) Muskelkater m

charm [tʃɑrm] s Charme m; (trinket) Amulett n ‖ tr verzaubern; (fig) entzücken

charm'ing adj scharmant, reizend

chart [tʃɑrt] s Karte f; (table) Tabelle f; (naut) Seekarte f ‖ tr entwerfen, auf e–r Karte graphisch darstellen

charter [ˈtʃɑrtər] adj (plane, etc.) Charter- ‖ s Freibrief m, Charter m; (of an organization) Gründungsurkunde f und Satzungen pl ‖ tr chartern

char'ter mem'ber s gründendes Mitglied n

char·woman [ˈtʃɑrˌwumən] s (–women [ˌwɪmɪn] Putzfrau f

chase [tʃes] s (pursuit) Verfolgung f; (hunt) Jagd f ‖ tr jagen; (girls) nachsteigen (dat); **c. away** verjagen; **c. out** vertreiben ‖ intr—**c. after** nachlaufen (dat)

chasm [ˈkæzəm] s (& fig) Abgrund m

chas·sis [ˈtʃæsi] s (–sis [siz]) Chassis n; (aut) Fahrgestell n

chaste [tʃest] adj keusch

chasten [ˈtʃesən] tr züchtigen

chastise [tʃæsˈtaɪz] tr züchtigen

chastity [ˈtʃæstɪti] s Keuschheit f

chat [tʃæt] s Plauderei f ‖ v (pret & pp chatted; ger chatting) intr plaudern

chattel [ˈtʃætəl] s Sklave m; **chattels** Hab und Gut n

chatter [ˈtʃætər] s (talk) Geplapper n; (of teeth) Klappern n ‖ intr (talk) plappern; (said of teeth) klappern

chat'terbox' s (coll) Plappermaul n

chauffeur [ˈʃofər], [ʃoˈfʌr] s Chauffeur m ‖ tr fahren

cheap [tʃip] adj (inexpensive) billig; (shoddy) minderwertig; (base) gemein; (stingy) geizig; **feel c.** sich verlegen fühlen ‖ adv billig; **get off c.** mit e–m blauen Auge davonkommen

cheapen [ˈtʃipən] tr herabsetzen

cheat [tʃit] s Betrüger –in mf ‖ tr (out of) betrügen (um) ‖ intr schwindeln; (at cards) mogeln; **c. on** (e.g., a wife) betrügen

cheat'ing s Betrügerei f; (at cards) Mogelei f

check [tʃek] s (of a bank) Scheck m; (for luggage) Schein m; (in a restaurant) Rechnung f; (inspection) Kontrolle f; (test) Nachprüfung f; (repulse) Rückschlag m; (restraint) (on) Hemmnis n (für); (square) Karo n; (chess) Schach n; **hold in c.** in Schach halten ‖ tr (restrain) hindern; (inspect) kontrollieren; (test) nachprüfen, überprüfen; (a hat, coat) abgeben; (luggage) aufgeben; (figures) nachrechnen; (chess) Schach bieten (dat); **c. off** abhaken ‖ intr (agree) übereinstimmen; **c. out** (of a hotel) sich abmelden; **c. up on** überprüfen; (a person) sich erkun-

digen über (acc); **c. with** (correspond to) übereinstimmen mit; (consult) sich besprechen mit ‖ interj
Schach!
check′book′ s Scheckbuch n, Scheck-
heft n
checker [′tʃɛkər] s Kontrolleur m; (in
checkers) Damestein m; **checkers**
Damespiel n
check′erboard′ s Damebrett n
check′ered adj kariert; (life, career)
wechselvoll
check′ing account′ s Scheckkonto n
check′ list′ s Kontrolliste f
check′mate′ s Schachmatt n; (fig)
Niederlage f ‖ tr (& fig) matt setzen
‖ interj schachmatt!
check′-out count′er s Kasse f
check′point′ s Kontrollstelle f
check′room′ s Garderobe f
check′up′ s Überprüfung f; (med) ärztliche Untersuchung f
cheek [tʃik] s Backe f, Wange f; (coll)
Frechheit f
cheek′bone′ s Backenknochen m
cheek′ by jowl′ adv Seite an Seite
cheeky [′tʃiki] adj (coll) frech
cheer [tʃɪr] s (applause) Beifallsruf
m; (encouragement) Ermunterung f;
(sport) Ermunterungsruf m; **three
cheers for** ein dreifaches Hoch auf
(acc) ‖ tr zujubeln (dat); **c. on** an-
feuern; **c. up** aufmuntern; **c. up!** nur
Mut!
cheerful [′tʃɪrfəl] adj heiter; (room,
surroundings) freundlich
cheer′lead′er s Anführer –in mf beim
Beifallsrufen
cheerless [′tʃɪrlɪs] adj freudlos
cheese [tʃiz] s Käse m
cheeseburger [′tʃiz‚bʌrgər] s belegtes
Brot n mit Frikadelle und über-
backenem Käse
cheese′ cake′ s Käsekuchen m
cheese′ cloth′ s grobe Baumwollgaze f
cheesy [′tʃizi] adj (sl) minderwertig
chef [ʃɛf] s Küchenchef m
chemical [′kɛmɪkəl] adj chemisch;
(fertilizer) Kunst– ‖ s Chemikalie f
chemist [′kɛmɪst] s Chemiker –in mf
chemistry [′kɛmɪstri] s Chemie f
cherish [′tʃɛrɪʃ] tr (hold dear) schätzen; (hopes, thoughts) hegen
cherry [′tʃɛri] s Kirsche f
cher′ry tree′ s Kirschbaum m
cher·ub [′tʃɛrəb] s (–ubim [əbɪm])
Cherub m ‖ s (–ubs) Engelskopf m
chess [tʃɛs] s Schach n
chess′board′ s Schachbrett n
chess′man′ s (–men′) Schachfigur f
chest [tʃɛst] s Truhe f; (anat) Brust f
chestnut [′tʃɛsnət] adj kastanienbraun
‖ s Kastanie f; (tree) Kastanien-
baum m; (horse) Rotfuchs m
chest′ of drawers′ s Kommode f
chevron [′ʃɛvrən] s (mil) Winkel m
chew [tʃu] s Kauen n; (stick of tobacco) Priem m ‖ tr kauen; **c. the
cud** wiederkäuen; **c. the rag** (sl)
schwatzen
chew′ing gum′ s Kaugummi m
chew′ing tobac′co s Kautabak m
chic [ʃik] adj schick ‖ s Schick m

chicanery [ʃɪ′kɛnəri] s Schikane f
chick [tʃɪk] s Küken n; (girl) (sl) kesse
Biene f
chicken [′tʃɪkən] adj Hühner–; (sl)
feig(e) ‖ s Huhn n, Hühnchen n
chick′en coop′ s Hühnerstall m
chick′en-heart′ed adj feig(e)
chick′en pox′ s Windpocken pl
chick′en wire′ s Maschendraht m
chick′pea′ s Kichererbse f
chicory [′tʃɪkəri] s Zichorie f
chide [tʃaɪd] v (pret & pp chided &
chid [tʃɪd]; pp chided) tr tadeln
chief [tʃif] adj Haupt–, Ober–, oberste;
(leading) leitend ‖ s Chef m, Ober-
haupt n; (of an Indian tribe) Häuptling m
chief′ exec′utive s Regierungsober-
haupt n
chief′ jus′tice s Vorsitzender m des
obersten Gerichtshofes
chiefly [′tʃifli] adv vorwiegend
chief′ of police′ s Polizeipräsident m
chief′ of staff′ s Generalstabschef m
chief′ of state′ s Staatschef m
chieftain [′tʃiftən] s Häuptling m
chiffon [ʃɪ′fɑn] s Chiffon m
child [tʃaɪld] s (children [′tʃɪldrən])
Kind n; **with c.** schwanger
child′ abuse′ s Kindermißhandlung f
child′birth′ s Niederkunft f
child′hood′ s Kindheit f
childish [′tʃaɪldɪʃ] adj kindisch
childless [′tʃaɪldlɪs] adj kinderlos
child′like′ adj kindlich
child′ prod′igy s Wunderkind n
child′s′ play′ s (fig) Kinderspiel n
child′ support′ s Alimente pl
child′ wel′fare s Jugendfürsorge f
Chile [′tʃɪli] s Chile n
chili [′tʃɪli] s Cayennepfeffer m
chil′i sauce′ s Chilisoße f
chill [tʃɪl] s (coldness) Kälte f; (sensation of cold or fear) Schau(d)er
m; **chills** Fieberschau(d)er m ‖ tr
kühlen; (hopes, etc.) dämpfen; (metals) abschrecken; **be chilled to the
bone** durchfrieren ‖ intr abkühlen
chilly [′tʃɪli] adj (& fig) frostig; **feel
chilly** frösteln
chime [tʃaɪm] s Geläut n; **chimes**
Glockenspiel n ‖ intr (said of bells)
läuten; (said of a doorbell) ertönen;
(said of a clock) schlagen; **c. in**
(coll) beipflichten
chimera [kaɪ′mɪrə] s Hirngespinst n
chimney [′tʃɪmni] s Schornstein m;
(of a lamp) Zylinder m
chimpanzee [tʃɪm′pænzi] s Schimpanse m
chin [tʃɪn] s Kinn n; **keep one's c. up**
die Ohren steifhalten; **up to the c.**
bis über die Ohren
china [′tʃaɪnə] s Porzellan n ‖ **China**
s China n
chi′na clos′et s Porzellanschrank m
chi′na·man s (–men) (pej) Chinese m
chin′aware′ s Porzellanwaren pl
Chi·nese [tʃaɪ′niz] adj chinesisch ‖ s
(–nese) Chinese m, Chinesin f; (language) Chinesisch n
Chi′nese lan′tern s Lampion m
chink [tʃɪŋk] s Ritze f; (of coins or

glasses) Klang *m* || *tr* (*glasses*) anstoßen

chin'-up' *s* Klimmzug *m*

chip [tʃɪp] *s* Span *m*, Splitter *m*; (*in china*) angestoßene Stelle *f*; (*in poker*) Spielmarke *f*; **a c. off the old block** (coll) ganz der Vater; **have a c. on one's shoulder** (coll) vor Zorn geladen sein || *v* (*pret & pp* **chipped**; *ger* **chipping**) *tr* (*e.g., a cup*) anschlagen; **c. in** (coll) beitragen; **c. off** abbrechen || *intr* (leicht) abbrechen; **c. in** (with) einspringen (mit); **c. off** (*said of paint*) abblättern

chipmunk ['tʃɪp‚mʌŋk] *s* Streifenhörnchen *n*

chipper ['tʃɪpər] *adj* (coll) munter

chiropodist [kaɪ'rapədɪst], [kɪ'rapədɪst] *s* Fußpfleger –in *mf*

chiropractor ['kaɪrə‚præktər] *s* Chiropraktiker –in *mf*

chirp [tʃʌrp] *s* Gezwitscher *n* || *intr* zwitschern

chis·el ['tʃɪzəl] *s* Meißel *m* || *v* (*pret & pp* **-el[l]ed**; *ger* **-il[l]ing**) *tr* meißeln; (sl) bemogeln || meißeln; (sl) mogeln

chiseler ['tʃɪzələr] *s* (sl) Mogler *m*

chitchat ['tʃɪt‚tʃæt] *s* Schnickschnack *m*

chivalrous ['ʃɪvəlrəs] *adj* ritterlich

chivalry ['ʃɪvəlrɪ] *s* Rittertum *n*; (*politeness*) Ritterlichkeit *f*

chive [tʃaɪv] *s* Schnittlauch *m*

chloride ['klɔraɪd] *s* Chlorid *n*

chlorine ['klorin] *s* Chlor *n*

chloroform ['klorə‚fɔrm] *s* Chloroform *n* || *tr* chloroformieren

chlorophyll ['klorəfɪl] *s* Chlorophyll *n*

chock-full ['tsak'ful] *adj* zum Bersten voll

chocolate ['tʃɔkəlɪt] *adj* Schokoladen–; (*in color*) schokoladenfarben || *s* Schokolade *f*; (*chocolate-covered candy*) Praline *f*

choc'olate bar' *s* Schokoladentafel *f*

choice [tʃɔɪs] *adj* (aus)erlesen || *s* Wahl *f*; (*selection*) Auswahl *f*

choir [kwaɪr] *s* Chor *m*; (archit) Chor *m*

choir'boy' *s* Chorknabe *m*

choir' loft' *s* Chorgalerie *f*

choir'mas'ter *s* Chordirigent *m*

choke [tʃok] *s* (aut) Starterklappe *f* || *tr* erwürgen, ersticken; **c. back** (*tears*) herunterschlucken; **c. down** herunterwürgen; **c. up** verstopfen || *intr* ersticken; **c. on** ersticken an (*dat*)

choker ['tʃokər] *s* enges Halsband *n*

cholera ['kalərə] *s* Cholera *f*

cholesterol [kə'lestə‚rol] *s* Blutfett *n*

choose [tʃuz] *v* (*pret* **chose** [tʃoz]; *pp* **chosen** ['tʃozən]) *tr & intr* wählen

choosy ['tʃuzi] *adj* (coll) wählerisch

chop [tʃap] *s* Hieb *m*; (culin) Kotelett *n*, Schnitzel *n*; **chops** (sl) Maul *n* || *v* (*pret & pp* **chopped**; *ger* **chopping**) *tr* hacken; **c. down** niederhauen; **c. off** abhacken; **c. up** zerhacken

chopper ['tʃapər] *s* (ax) Hackbeil *n*; (coll) Hubschrauber *m*

chop'ping block' *s* Hackklotz *m*

choppy ['tʃapi] *adj* (sea) bewegt

chop'stick' *s* Eßstäbchen *n*

choral ['korəl] *adj* Chor–, Sänger–

chorale [ko'ral] *s* Choral *m*

chord [kord] *s* (anat) Band *n*; (geom) Sehne *f*; (*combination of notes*) (mus) Akkord *m*; (mus & fig) Saite *f*

chore [tʃor] *s* Hausarbeit *f*

choreography [‚korɪ'agrəfɪ] *s* Choreographie *f*

chorus ['korəs] *s* Chor *m*; (*refrain*) Kehrreim *m*

cho'rus girl' *s* Revuetänzerin *f*

chowder ['tʃaudər] *s* Fischsuppe *f*

Christ [kraɪst] *s* Christus *m*

Christ' child' *s* Christkind *n*

christen ['krɪsən] *tr* taufen

Christendom ['krɪsəndəm] *s* Christenheit *f*

chris'tening *s* Taufe *f*; **c. of a ship** Schiffstaufe *f*

Christian ['krɪstʃən] *adj* christlich || *s* Christ –in *mf*

Chris'tian E'ra *s* christliche Zeitrechnung *f*

Christianity [‚krɪstɪ'ænɪtɪ] *s* (*faith*) Christentum *n*; (*all Christians*) Christenheit *f*

Chris'tian name' *s* Taufname *m*

Christmas ['krɪsməs] *adj* Weihnachts– || *s* Weihnachten *pl*, Weihnachtsfest *n*

Christ'mas card' *s* Weihnachtskarte *f*

Christ'mas car'ol *s* Weihnachtslied *n*

Christ'mas Eve' *s* Heiliger Abend *m*

Christ'mas gift' *s* Weihnachtsgeschenk *n*

Christ'mas tree' *s* Christbaum *m*

Christ'mas tree' lights' *spl* Weihnachtskerzen *pl*

Christopher ['krɪstəfər] *s* Christoph *m*

chromatic [kro'mætɪk] *adj* chromatisch

chrome [krom] *adj* Chrom– || *s* Chrom *n* || *tr* verchromen

chrome'plate' *tr* verchromen

chromium ['kromɪ‐əm] *s* Chrom *n*

chromosome ['kromə‚som] *s* Chromosom *n*

chronic ['kranɪk] *adj* chronisch

chronicle ['kranɪkəl] *s* Chronik *f* || *tr* aufzeichnen

chronicler ['kranɪklər] *s* Chronist –in *mf*

chronological [‚kranə'ladʒɪkəl] *adj* chronologisch

chronology [krə'nalədʒɪ] *s* Chronologie *f*

chronometer [krə'namɪtər] *s* Chronometer *n*

chrysanthemum [krɪ'sænθɪməm] *s* Chrysantheme *f*

chubby ['tʃʌbi] *adj* pummelig

chuck [tʃʌk] *s* (culin) Schulterstück *n*; (mach) Klemmfutter *n* || *tr* schmeißen

chuckle ['tʃʌkəl] *s* Glucksen *n* || *intr* glucksen

chug [tʃʌg] *s* Tuckern *n* || *v* (*pret & pp* **chugged**; *ger* **chugging**) *intr* tuckern; **c. along** tuckernd fahren

chum [tʃʌm] s (coll) Kumpel m ‖ v (pret & pp **chummed;** ger **chumming**) intr—**c. around with** sich eng an-schließen an (acc)

chummy ['tʃʌmi] adj eng befreundet

chump [tʃʌmp] s (coll) Trottel m

chunk [tʃʌŋk] s Klotz m, Stück n

church [tʃʌrtʃ] adj Kirchen–, kirchlich ‖ s Kirche f

churchgoer ['tʃʌrtʃ,goʊ-ər] s Kirch-gänger –in mf

church' pic'nic s Kirchweih f

church'yard' s Kirchhof m

churl [tʃʌrl] s Flegel m

churlish ['tʃʌrlɪʃ] adj flegelhaft

churn [tʃʌrn] s Butterfaß n ‖ tr (cream) buttern; **c. up** aufwühlen ‖ intr sich heftig bewegen

chute [ʃut] s (for coal, etc.) Rutsche f; (for laundry, etc.) Abwurfschacht m; (sliding board) Rutschbahn f; (in a river) Stromschnelle f; (aer) Fall-schirm m

cider ['saɪdər] s Apfelwein m

cigar [sɪ'gɑr] s Zigarre f

cigarette [,sɪgə'ret] s Zigarette f

cigarette' cough' s Raucherhusten m

cigarette' light'er s Feuerzeug n

cigar' store' s Rauchwarenladen m

cinch [sɪntʃ] s (sure thing) totsichere Sache f; (snap) (sl) Kinderspiel n; (likely candidate) tot-sicherer Kandidat m ‖ tr (sl) sich [dat] sichern

cinder ['sɪndər] s (ember) glühende Kohle f; (slag) Schlacke f; **cinders** Asche f

Cinderella [,sɪndə'relə] s Aschenbrö-del n

cin'der track' s (sport) Aschenbahn f

cinema ['sɪnəmə] s Kino n

cinematography [,sɪnəmə'tɑgrəfi] s Kinematographie f

cinnamon ['sɪnəmən] s Zimt m

cipher ['saɪfər] s Ziffer f; (zero) Null f; (code) Chiffre f ‖ tr chiffrieren

circle ['sʌrkəl] s Kreis m; **circles un-der the eyes** Ränder pl unter den Augen ‖ tr einkreisen; (go around) umkreisen ‖ intr kreisen

circuit ['sʌrkɪt] s (course) Kreislauf m; (elec) Stromkreis m; (jur) Bezirk m

cir'cuit break'er s Ausschalter m

cir'cuit court' s Bezirksgericht m

circuitous [sər'kju·ɪtəs] adj weit-schweifig

circular ['sʌrkjələr] adj kreisförmig; (saw) Kreis– ‖ s Rundschreiben n

circulate ['sʌrkjə,let] tr in Umlauf setzen; (a rumor) verbreiten; (fin) girieren ‖ intr umlaufen; (said of blood) kreisen; (said of a rumor) umgehen

circulation [,sʌrkjə'leʃən] s (of blood) Kreislauf m; (of a newspaper) Auf-lage f; (of money) Umlauf m

circumcize ['sʌrkəm,saɪz] tr beschnei-den

circumference [sər'kʌmfərəns] s Um-fang m

circumflex ['sʌrkəm,fleks] s Zirkum-flex m

circumlocution [,sʌrkəmlo'kjuʃən] s Umschreibung f

circumscribe ['sʌrkəm,skraɪb] tr (geom) umschreiben; (fig) umgren-zen

circumspect ['sʌrkəm,spekt] adj um-sichtig

circumstance ['sʌrkəm,stæns] s Um-stand m; **circumstances** (financial situation) Verhältnisse pl

cir'cumstan'tial ev'idence [,sʌrkəm-'stænʃəl] s Indizienbeweis m

circumvent [,sʌrkəm'vent] tr umgehen

circus ['sʌrkəs] s Zirkus m

cistern ['sɪstərn] s Zisterne f

citadel ['sɪtədəl] s Burg f

citation [saɪ'teʃən] s Zitat n; (jur) Vorladung f; (mil) Belobung f

cite [saɪt] tr (quote) anführen; (jur) vorladen; (mil) belobigen

citizen ['sɪtɪzən] s Bürger –in mf

cit'izenship' s Staatsangehörigkeit f

cit'rus fruit' ['sɪtrəs] s Zitrusfrucht f

city ['sɪti] s Stadt f

cit'y coun'cil s Stadtrat m

cit'y fa'ther s Stadtrat m

cit'y hall' s Rathaus n

cit'y plan'ning s Stadtplanung f

civic ['sɪvɪk] adj bürgerlich, Bürger– ‖ **civics** s Staatsbürgerkunde f

civil ['sɪvɪl] adj (life, duty) bürger-lich; (service) öffentlich; (polite) höflich; (jur) privatrechtlich

civ'il cer'emony s standesamtliche Trauung f

civ'il defense' s zivile Verteidigung f

civ'il engineer'ing s Hoch– und Tief-bau m

civilian [sɪ'vɪljən] adj bürgerlich, Zivil– ‖ s Zivilist –in mf

civilization [,sɪvɪlɪ'zeʃən] s Zivilisa-tion f, Kultur f

civilize ['sɪvɪ,laɪz] tr zivilisieren

civ'il rights' spl Bürgerrechte pl

civ'il serv'ant s Staatsbeamte m, Staatsbeamtin f

civ'il serv'ice s Staatsdienst m

civ'il war' s Bürgerkrieg m

claim [klem] s Anspruch m; (asser-tion) Behauptung f; (for public land) beanspruchtes Land n ‖ tr bean-spruchen; (assert) behaupten; (at-tention) erfordern; **c. to be** sich ausgeben für

claim' check' s Aufgabeschein m

clairvoyance [kler'vɔɪ-əns] s Hellsehen n

clairvoyant [kler'vɔɪ-ənt] adj hellse-herisch; **be c.** hellsehen ‖ s Hellse-her –in mf

clam [klæm] s eßbare Meermuschel f

clamber ['klæmər] intr klettern

clammy ['klæmi] adj feuchtkalt

clamor ['klæmər] s Geschrei n ‖ intr (for) schreien (nach)

clamorous ['klæmərəs] adj schreiend

clamp [klæmp] s Klammer f; (surg) Klemme f ‖ tr (ver)klammern ‖ intr —**c. down on** einschreiten gegen

clan [klæn] s Stamm m; (pej) Sipp-schaft f

clandestine [klæn'destɪn] adj heimlich

clang [klæŋ] s Geklirr n ‖ intr klirren

clank [klæŋk] s Geklirr n, Gerassel n || intr klirren, rasseln

clannish ['klænɪ] adj stammesbewußt

clap [klæp] s (of the hands) Klatschen n; (of thunder) Schlag m || v (pret & pp clapped; ger clapping) tr (a tax, fine, duty) (on) auferlegen (dat); **clap hands** in die Hände klatschen || intr Beifall klatschen

clapper ['klæpər] s Klöppel m

clap'trap' s Phrasendrescherei f

claque [klæk] s Claque f

clari·fy ['klærɪ‚faɪ] v (pret & pp -fied) tr erklären

clarinet [‚klærɪ'nɛt] s Klarinette f

clarity ['klærɪti] s Klarheit f

clash [klæ] s (sound) Geklirr n; (of interests, etc.) Widerstreit m || intr (conflict) kollidieren; (said of persons) aufeinanderstoßen; (said of ideas) im Widerspruch stehen; (said of colors) nicht zusammenpassen

clasp [klæsp] s (fastener) Schließe f, Spange f; (on a necktie) Klammer f; (embrace) Umarmung f; (of hands) Händedruck m || tr umklammern; **c. s.o.'s hand** j–m die Hand drücken

class [klæs] s (group) Klasse f; (period of instruction) Stunde f; (year) Jahrgang m; **have c.** (sl) Niveau haben || tr einstufen

classic ['klæsɪk] adj klassisch || s Klassiker m

classical ['klæsɪkəl] adj klassisch; **c. antiquity** Klassik f; **c. author** Klassiker m

classicist ['klæsɪsɪst] s Kenner –in mf der Klassik

classification [‚klæsɪfɪ'keʃən] s Klassifikation f, Anordnung f

clas'sified aid' geheimzuhaltend

clas'sified ad' s kleine Anzeige f

classi·fy ['klæsɪ‚faɪ] v (pret & pp -fied) tr klassifizieren

class'mate' s Klassenkamerad m

class' reun'ion s Klassentreffen n

class'room' s Klassenzimmer n

classy ['klæsi] adj (sl) pfundig

clatter ['klætər] s Geklapper n || intr klappern

clause [klɔz] s Satzteil m; (jur) Klausel f

clavicle ['klævɪkəl] s Schlüsselbein n

claw [klɔ] s Klaue f, Kralle f; (of a crab) Schere f || tr zerkratzen; (a hole) scharren || intr kratzen

clay [kle] adj tönern || s Ton m, Lehm m

clay' pig'eon s Tontaube f

clean [klin] adj sauber, rein; (cut) glatt; (features) klar || adv (coll) völlig || tr reinigen, putzen; **c. out** (clear out by force) räumen; (empty) ausleeren; (sl) ausbeuten; **c. up** (a room) aufräumen || intr putzen; **c. up** sich zurechtmachen; (in gambling) (sl) schwer einheimsen

clean'-cut' adj (person) ordentlich; (clearly outlined) klar umrissen

cleaner ['klinər] s (person, device) Reiniger m; **cleaners** (establishment) Reinigungsanstalt f

clean'ing flu'id s flüssiges Reinigungsmittel n

clean'ing wo'man s Reinemachefrau f

cleanliness ['klɛnlɪnɪs] s Sauberkeit f

cleanse [klɛnz] tr reinigen

cleanser ['klɛnzər] s Reinigungsmittel n

clean'-shav'en adj glattrasiert

clean'up' s Reinemachen n; (e.g., of vice, graft) Säuberungsaktion f

clear [klɪr] adj klar; (sky, weather) heiter; (light) hell; (profit) netto; (conscience) rein; (proof) offenkundig || adv (coll) völlig; (fin) netto || tr klären; (streets) freimachen; (the table) abräumen; (a room) räumen; (a forest) roden; (the air) reinigen; (an obstacle without touching it) setzen über (acc); (a path) bahnen; (as profit) rein gewinnen; (at customs) zollamtlich abfertigen; (one's name) reinwaschen; **c. away** wegräumen; (doubts) beseitigen; **c. up** klarlegen || intr sich klären; **c. out** (coll) sich davonmachen; **c. up** sich aufklären

clearance ['klɪrəns] s (approval) Genehmigung f; (at customs) Zollabfertigung f; (of a bridge) lichte Höhe f; (aer) Starterlaubnis f; (mach) Spielraum m

clear'ance sale' s Räumungsverkauf m

clear'-cut' adj klar, eindeutig

clear'-head'ed adj verständig

clear'ing s (in a woods) Lichtung f

clear'ing house' s Abstimmungszentrale f; (fin) Verrechnungsstelle f

clear'-sight'ed adj scharfsichtig

cleat [klit] s Stollen m

cleavage ['klivɪdʒ] s Spaltung f

cleave [kliv] v (pret & pp cleft [klɛft] & cleaved) tr zerspalten || intr (split) sich spalten; (to) kleben (an dat)

cleaver ['klivər] s Hackbeil n

clef [klɛf] s Notenschlüssel m

cleft [klɛft] s Riß m, Spalt m

clemency ['klɛmənsi] s Milde f; (jur) Begnadigung f

clement ['klɛmənt] adj mild

clench [klɛntʃ] tr (a fist) ballen; (the teeth) zusammenbeißen

clerestory ['klɪr‚stori] s Lichtgaden m

clergy ['klɛrdʒi] s Geistlichkeit f

cler'gy·man s (-men) Geistliche m

cleric ['klɛrɪk] s Kleriker m

clerical ['klɛrɪkəl] adj Schreib–, Büro–; (eccl) geistlich

cler'ical er'ror s Schreibfehler m

cler'ical staff' s Schreibkräfte pl

cler'ical work' s Büroarbeit f

clerk [klɑrk] s (in a store) Verkäufer –in mf; (in an office) Büroangestellte mf; (in a post office) Schalterbeamte m; (jur) Gerichtsschreiber –in mf

clever ['klɛvər] adj (intelligent) klug; (adroit) geschickt; (witty) geistreich; (ingenious) findig

cleverness ['klɛvərnɪs] s (intelligence) Klugheit f; (adroitness) Geschicklichkeit f; (ingeniousness) Findigkeit f

cliché [kli'ʃe] s Klischee n

click [klɪk] *s* Klicken *n;* (*of the tongue*) Schnalzen *n;* (*of a lock*) Einschnappen *n* ‖ *tr* klicken lassen; **c. one's heels** die Hacken zusammenschlagen ‖ *intr* klicken; (*said of heels*) knallen; (*said of a lock*) einschnappen ‖ *impers*—**it clicks** (coll) es klappt

client [ˈklaɪ-ənt] *s* (*customer*) Kunde *m,* Kundin *f;* (*of a company*) Auftraggeber –in *mf;* (*jur*) Klient –in *mf*

clientele [ˌklaɪ-ənˈtel] *s* Kundschaft *f;* (com, jur) Klientel *f*

cliff [klɪf] *s* Klippe *f,* Felsen *m*

climate [ˈklaɪmɪt] *s* Klima *n*

climax [ˈklaɪmæks] *s* Höhepunkt *m*

climb [klaɪm] *s* Aufstieg *m,* Besteigung *f;* (aer) Steigungsflug *m* ‖ *tr* ersteigen, besteigen; (*stairs*) hinaufsteigen; **climb a tree** auf e–n Baum klettern; ‖ *intr* steigen, klettern; (*said of a street*) ansteigen

climber [ˈklaɪmər] *s* Kletterer –in *mf;* (*of a mountain*) Bergsteiger –in *mf;* (bot) Kletterpflanze *f*

clinch [klɪntʃ] *s* (box) Clinch *m* ‖ *tr* (*settle*) entscheiden ‖ *intr* clinchen

clincher [ˈklɪntʃər] *s* (coll) Trumpf *m*

cling [klɪŋ] *v* (*pret & pp* **clung** [klʌŋ]) *intr* haften; **c. to** sich anklammern an (*acc*); (*said of a dress*) sich anschmiegen an (*acc*); (fig) festhalten an (*dat*)

clinic [ˈklɪnɪk] *s* Klinik *f*

clinical [ˈklɪnɪkəl] *adj* klinisch

clink [klɪŋk] *s* Klirren *n;* (*prison*) (sl) Kittchen *n* ‖ *tr*—**c. glasses** mit den Gläsern anstoßen ‖ *intr* klirren

clip [klɪp] *s* Klammer *f;* **go at a good c.** ein scharfes Tempo gehen ‖ *v* (*pret & pp* **clipped**) *ger* **clipping** *tr* (*a hedge*) beschneiden; (*hair*) schneiden; (*wings*) stutzen; (*sheep*) scheren; (*from newspapers, etc.*) ausschneiden; (*syllables*) verschlucken; (sl) schröpfen; **c. together** zusammenklammern

clip′board′ *s* Manuskripthalter *m*

clip′ joint′ *s* (sl) Nepplokal *n*

clipper [ˈklɪpər] *s* (aer) Klipperflugzeug *n;* (naut) Klipper *m;* **clippers** Haarschneidemaschine *f*

clip′ping *s* (act) Stutzen *n;* (*from newspapers*) Ausschnitt *m;* **clippings** (*of paper*) Schnitzel *pl;* (*scraps*) Abfälle *pl*

clique [klik] *s* Sippschaft *f*

cliquish [ˈkliki] *adj* cliquenhaft

cloak [klok] *s* Umhang *m;* (fig) Deckmantel *m;* **under the c. of darkness** im Schutz der Dunkelheit ‖ *tr* (fig) bemänteln

cloak′-and-dag′ger *adj* Spionage–

cloak′room′ *s* Garderobe *f*

clobber [ˈklɑbər] *tr* (coll) verwichsen

clock [klɑk] *s* Uhr *f* ‖ *tr* (*a runner*) abstoppen

clock′mak′er *s* Uhrmacher –in *mf*

clock′ tow′er *s* Uhrturm *m*

clock′wise′ *adv* im Uhrzeigersinn

clock′work′ *s* Uhrwerk *n;* **like c.** wie am Schnürchen

clod [klɑd] *s* Klumpen *m,* Scholle *f*

clodhopper [ˈklɑdˌhɑpər] *s* Bauerntölpel *m*

clog [klɑg] *s* Verstopfung *f;* (*shoe*) Holzschuh *m* ‖ *v* (*pret & pp* **clogged**) *ger* **clogging** *tr* verstopfen ‖ *intr* sich verstopfen

cloister [ˈklɔɪstər] *s* Kloster *n;* (*covered walk*) Kreuzgang *m*

close [klos] *adj* (*near*) nahe; (*tight*) knapp; (*air*) schwül; (*ties; friend*) eng; (*attention*) gespannt; (*game*) beinahe gleich; (*observer*) scharf; (*surveillance*) streng; (*supervision*) genau; (*inspection*) eingehend; (*resemblance; competition*) stark; (*shave*) glatt; (*translation*) wortgetreu; (*stingy*) geizig; (*order*) (mil) geschlossen; **c. to** (*position*) nahe an (*dat*), neben (*dat*); (*direction*) nahe an (*acc*), neben (*acc*) ‖ *adv* dicht, eng; **from c. up** in der Nähe ‖ [kloz] *s* Schluß *m,* Ende *n;* **bring to a c.** zu Ende bringen; **draw to a c.** zu Ende gehen ‖ *tr* schließen; (*an account, deal*) abschließen; **c. down** stillegen; **c. off** abschließen; (*a road*) sperren; **c. out** (com) ausverkaufen; **c. up** zumachen ‖ *intr* sich schließen; **c. in** immer näher kommen; **c. in on** umschließen

close-by [ˈklosˈbaɪ] *adj* nebenan

close-cropped [ˈkloskrɑpt] *adj* kurz geschoren

closed [klozd] *adj* geschlossen; **c. today** (public sign) heute Betriebsruhe

closed′ shop′ *s* Unternehmen *n* mit Gewerkschaftszwang

closefisted [ˈklosˈfɪstəd] *adj* geizig

close-fitting [ˈklosˈfɪtɪŋ] *adj* eng anliegend

close-mouthed [ˈklosˈmauðd] *adj* verschwiegen

close′ or′der drill′ [klos] *s* (mil) geschlossenes Exerzieren *n*

closeout [ˈklozˌaut] *s* Räumungsausverkauf *m*

close′ shave′ [klos] *s* glatte Rasure *f;* (fig) knappes Entkommen *n;* **have a c.** mit knapper Not davonkommen

closet [ˈklɑzɪt] *s* Schrank *m*

close-up [ˈklos ˌʌp] *s* Nahaufnahme *f*

clos′ing *adj* Schluß–; (*day*) scheidend ‖ *s* Schließung *f;* (*of an account*) Abschluß *m;* (*of a factory*) Stillegung *f;* (*of a road*) Sperrung *f*

clos′ing price′ *s* Schlußkurs *m*

clos′ing time′ *s* (*of a shop*) Geschäftsschluß *m;* (*of bars*) Polizeistunde *f*

clot [klɑt] *s* Klumpen *m;* (*of blood*) Gerinnsel *n* ‖ *v* (*pret & pp* **clotted**) *ger* **clotting** *intr* gerinnen

cloth [klɑθ] *s* Stoff *m,* Tuch *n;* (*for cleaning, etc.*) Lappen *m;* **the c.** die Geistlichkeit

clothe [kloð] *v* (*pret & pp* **clothed** & **clad** [klæd]) *tr* ankleiden, (be)kleiden; (fig) (in) einhüllen in (*acc*)

clothes [kloz], [kloðz] *spl* Kleider *pl;* **change one's clothes** sich umziehen; **put on one's clothes** sich anziehen

clothes′bas′ket *s* Wäschekorb *m*

clothes′brush′ *s* Kleiderbürste *f*

clothes′ clos′et *s* Kleiderschrank *m*

clothes′ dri′er s Wäschetrockner m
clothes′ hang′er s Kleiderbügel m
clothes′line′ s Wäscheleine f
clothes′pin′ s Wäscheklammer f
clothier [′kloðjər] s Kleiderhändler m; (cloth maker) Tuchmacher m; (cloth dealer) Tuchhändler m
clothing [′kloðɪŋ] s Kleidung f
cloud [klaud] s Wolke f; **be up in the clouds** (fig) in höheren Regionen schweben ‖ tr bewölken; (a liquid) trüben; (fig) verdunkeln ‖ intr—c. over (or up) sich bewölken
cloud′burst′ s Wolkenbruch m
cloud′-capped′ adj von Wolken bedeckt
cloudiness [′klaudɪnɪs] s Bewölktheit f
cloudless [′klaudlɪs] adj unbewölkt
cloudy [′klaudi] adj bewölkt; (liquid) trüb(e)
clout [klaut] s (blow) (coll) Hieb m; (influence) (coll) Einfluß m ‖ tr—c. s.o. (coll) j—m eins herunterhauen
clove [klov] s Gewürznelke f; c. of garlic Knoblauchzehe f
clo′ven hoof′ [′kloven] s (as a sign of the devil) Pferdefuß m
clover [′klovər] s Klee m
clo′ver-leaf′ s (-leaves) Kleeblatt n
clown [klaun] s Clown m, Hanswurst m
clownish [′klaunɪʃ] adj närrisch
cloy [klɔɪ] tr übersättigen
club [klʌb] s (weapon) Keule f; (organization) Klub m; (cards) Kreuz n; (golf) Schläger m ‖ (pret & pp **clubbed**; ger **clubbing**) tr verprügeln
club′ car′ s (rr) Salonwagen m
club′house′ s Klubhaus n
cluck [klʌk] s Glucken n ‖ intr glucken
clue [klu] s Schlüssel m, Anhaltspunkt m
clump [klʌmp] s (of earth) Klumpen m; (of hair, grass) Büschel n; (of trees) Gruppe f; (heavy tramping sound) schwerer Tritt m; c. of bushes Gebüsch n ‖ intr—c. along trapsen
clumsy [′klʌmzi] adj ungeschickt, plump; c. ox Tölpel m
cluster [′klʌstər] s (bunch growing together) Büschel n; (of grapes) Traube f; (group) Gruppe f ‖ intr—c. around sich zusammendrängen um
clutch [klʌtʃ] s Griff m; (aut) Kupplung f; **fall into s.o.'s clutches** j—m in die Klauen geraten; **let out the c.** einkuppeln; **step on the c.** auskuppeln ‖ tr packen
clutter [′klʌtər] s Durcheinander n ‖ tr—c. up vollstopfen
Co. abbr (Company) Gesellschaft f
c/o abbr (care of) per Adresse, bei
coach [kotʃ] s Kutsche f; (rr) Personenwagen m; (sport) Trainer m ‖ tr Nachhilfeunterricht geben (dat); (sport) trainieren ‖ intr (sport) trainieren
coach′ing s Nachhilfeunterricht m; (sport) Training n
coach′man s (–men) Kutscher m

coagulate [ko′ægjə‚let] tr gerinnen lassen ‖ intr gerinnen
coal [kol] s Kohle f
coal′bin′ s Kohlenkasten m
coal′-black′ adj kohlrabenschwarz
coal′ car′ s (rr) Kohlenwagen m
coal′deal′er s Kohlenhändler m
coalesce [‚ko·ə′les] intr zusammenwachsen, sich vereinigen
coalition [‚ko·ə′lɪʃən] s Koalition f
coal′ mine′ s Kohlenbergwerk n
coal′ min′ing s Kohlenbergbau m
coal′ oil′ s Petroleum n
coal′yard′ s Kohlenlager n
coarse [kors] adj (& fig) grob
coast [kost] s Küste f; **the c. is clear** (coll) die Luft ist rein ‖ intr im Leerlauf fahren; c. along (fig) sich mühelos fortbewegen
coastal [′kostəl] adj küstennah, Küsten-
coaster [′kostər] s (for a glass) Untersatz m; (naut) Küstenfahrer m
coast′guard′ s Küstenwachdienst m
coast′line′ s Küstenlinie f
coat [kot] s (of a suit) Jacke f, Rock m; (topcoat) Mantel m; (of fur) Fell n; (of enamel, etc.) Belag m; (of paint) Anstrich m ‖ tr (e.g., with teflon) beschichten; (e.g., with chocolate) überziehen; (e.g., with oil) beschmieren
coat′ed adj überzogen; (tongue) belegt
coat′ hang′er s Kleiderbügel m
coat′ing s Belag m, Überzug m
coat′ of arms′ s Wappen n
coat′rack′ s Kleiderständer m
coat′room′ s Garderobe f
coat′tail′ s Rockschoß m; (of formal wear) Frackschoß m
coauthor [′ko‚oðər] s Mitautor m
coax [koks] tr schmeicheln (dat); c. s.o. to (inf) j—n überreden zu (inf)
cob [kab] s Kolben m
cobalt [′kobolt] s Kobalt m
cobbler [′kablər] s Flickschuster m
cobblestone [′kabəl‚ston] s Pflasterstein m, Kopfstein m
cobra [′kobrə] s Kobra f
cob′web′ s Spinn(en)gewebe n
cocaine [ko′ken] s Kokain n
cock [kak] s Hahn m; (faucet) Wasserhahn m; (of a gun) Gewehrhahn m ‖ tr (one's ears) spitzen; (one's hat) schief aufsetzen; (the firing mechanism) spannen
cock-a-doodle-doo [′kakə‚dudəl′du] s Kikeriki m
cock′-and-bull′ sto′ry s Lügengeschichte f
cockeyed [′kak‚aɪd] adj (cross-eyed) nach innen schielend; (slanted to one side) (sl) schief; (drunk) (sl) blau; (absurd) (sl) verrückt
cock′fight′ s Hahnenkampf m
cock′pit′ s Hahnenkampfplatz m; (aer) Kabine f, Kanzel f
cock′roach′ s Schabe f
cock′sure′ adj todsicher
cock′tail′ s Cocktail m
cock′tail dress′ s Cocktailkleid n
cock′tail par′ty s Cocktailparty f

cock'tail shak'er s Cocktailmischgefäß n

cocky ['kaki] adj (coll) frech

cocoa ['koko] s Kakao m

coconut ['koka ,nʌt] s Kokosnuß f

co'conut palm', **co'conut tree'** s Kokospalme f

cacoon [ka'kun] s Kokon m

C.O.D., c.o.d. abbr (**cash on delivery**) per Nachnahme

cod [kad] s Kabeljau m

coddle ['kadəl] tr hätscheln

code [kod] s Geheimschrift f; (jur) Kodex m || tr verschlüsseln, chiffrieren

codefendant [,kodɪ'fendənt] s Mitangeklagte m

code' name' s Deckname m

code' of hon'or s Ehrenkodex m

code' of laws' s Gesetzsammlung f

code' word' s Kennwort n

codex ['kodɛks] s (**codices** ['kodɪ,siz]) Kodex m

cod'fish' s Kabeljau m

codicil ['kadɪsɪl] s Kodizill n

codi-fy ['kadɪ,faɪ] v (pret & pp -**fied**) tr kodifizieren

cod'-liver oil' s Lebertran m

coed, co-ed ['ko ,ɛd] s Studentin f

coeducation [,ko ,ɛdʒə'keʃən] s Koedukation f

coeducational [,ko ,ɛdʒə'keʃənəl] adj Koedukations-

coefficient [,ko·ɪ'fɪʃənt] s Koeffizient m

coerce [ko'ʌrs] tr zwingen

coercion [ko'ʌrʃən] s Zwang m

coexist [,ko·ɪg'zɪst] intr koexistieren

coexistence [,ko·ɪg'zɪstəns] s Koexistenz f

coffee ['kɔfi] s Kaffee m

cof'fee bean' s Kaffeebohne f

cof'fee break' s Kaffeepause f

cof'fee fiend' s Kaffeetante f

cof'fee grounds' spl Kaffeesatz m

cof'fee pot' s Kaffeekanne f

cof'fee shop' s Kaffeestube f

coffer ['kɔfər] s Truhe f; (archit) Deckenfeld n; **coffers** Schatzkammer f

cof'ferdam' s (caisson) Kastendamm m; (naut) Kofferdamm m

coffin ['kɔfɪn] s Sarg m

cog [kag] s Zahn m; (cogwheel) Zahnrad n

cogency ['kodʒənsi] s Beweiskraft f

cogent ['kodʒənt] adj triftig

cognac ['konjæk], ['kanjæk] s Kognak m

cognizance ['kagnɪzəns] s Kenntnis f; **take c. of s.th.** etw zur Kenntnis nehmen

cognizant ['kagnɪzənt] adj—**be c. of** Kenntnis haben von

cog'wheel' s Zahnrad m

cohabit [ko'hæbɪt] intr in wilder Ehe leben

coheir [ko'ɛr] s Miterbe m, Miterbin f

cohere [ko'hɪr] intr zusammenhängen

cohesion [ko'hiʒən] s Kohäsion f

coiffeur [kwa'fʌr] s Friseur m

coiffure [kwa'fjur] s Frisur f

coil [kɔɪl] s (something wound in a spiral) Spirale f, Rolle f; (of tubing) Schlange f; (single wind) Windung f; (elec) Spule f || tr aufrollen; (naut) aufschießen || intr—**c. up** sich zusammenrollen

coil' spring' s Spiralfeder f

coin [kɔɪn] s Münze f, Geldstück n || tr münzen, (& fig) prägen

coinage ['kɔɪnɪdʒ] s (minting) Prägen n; (coins collectively) Münzen pl; (fig) Prägung f

coincide [,ko·ɪn'saɪd] intr (**with**) zusammentreffen (mit); (in time) (**with**) gleichzeitig geschehen (mit)

coincidence [ko'ɪnsɪdəns] s Zufall m; **by mere c.** rein zufällig

coin' machine' s Münzautomat m

coin' slot' s Münzeinwurf m

coition [ko'ɪʃən], **coitus** ['ko·ɪtəs] s Koitus m, Beischlaf m

coke [kok] s Koks m; (coll) Coca-Cola n

colander ['kʌləndər] s Sieb n

cold [kold] adj kalt || s Kälte f; (in disposition) Erkältung f

cold' blood' s—**in c.** kaltblütig

cold'-blood'ed adj kaltblütig

cold' chis'el s Kaltmeißel m

cold' com'fort s (fig) geringer Trost m

cold' cream' s Cold Cream n

cold' cuts' spl kalter Aufschnitt m

cold' feet' spl—**have c.** (fig) Angst haben

cold' front' s Kaltfront f

cold'-heart'ed adj kaltherzig

coldness ['koldnɪs] s Kälte f

cold' should'er s—**give s.o. the c.** j–m die kalte Schulter zeigen

cold' snap' s plötzlicher Kälteeinbruch m

cold' stor'age s Lagerung f im Kühlraum

cold' war' s kalter Krieg m

cold' wave' s (meteor) Kältewelle f

coleslaw ['kol ,slɔ] s Krautsalat m

colic ['kalɪk] s Kolik f

coliseum [,kalɪ'si·əm] s Kolosseum n

collaborate [kə'læbə ,ret] intr mitarbeiten; (pol) kollaborieren

collaboration [kə ,læbə're ʃən] s Mitarbeit f; (pol) Kollaboration f

collaborator [kə'læbə ,retər] s Mitarbeiter –in mf; (pol) Kollaborateur m

collapse [kə'læps] s (of a bridge, etc.) Einsturz m; (com) Krach m; (pathol) Zusammenbruch m, Kollaps m || intr einstürzen; (fig) zusammenbrechen

collapsible [kə'læpsɪbəl] adj zusammenklappbar

collaps'ible boat' s Faltboot n

collar ['kalər] s Kragen m; (of a dog) Halsband n; (of a horse) Kummet n; (mach) Ring m, Kragen m

col'larbone' s Schlüsselbein n

collate [kə'let] tr kollationieren

collateral [kə'lætərəl] adj kollateral, Seiten– || s (fin) Deckung f

collation [kə'le ʃən] s Kollation f

colleague ['kalig] s Kollege m, Kollegin f

collect ['kalɛkt] s (eccl) Kollekte f || [kə'lɛkt] adj—**make a c. call** ein R–

Gespräch führen || *adv*—call c. ein
R-Gespräch führen; **send c.** gegen
Nachnahme schicken || *tr* (*money*)
(ein)kassieren; (*stamps, coins*) sammeln; (*e.g., examination papers*) ein-
sammeln; (*taxes*) abheben; (*one's
thoughts*) zusammennehmen; **c. one-
self** sich fassen || *intr* sich (ver)-
sammeln; (*pile up*) sich anhäufen
collect′ed *adj* (*works*) gesammelt;
(*self-possessed*) gefaßt
collection [kə′lek∫ən] *s* (*of stamps,
etc.*) Sammlung *f*; (*accumulation*)
Ansammlung *f*; (*of money*) Einzie-
hung *f*; (*in a church*) Kollekte *f*; (*of
mail*) Leerung *f* des Briefkastens;
(com) Kollektion *f*
collec′tion a′gency *s* Inkassobüro *n*
collec′tion bas′ket *s* Klingelbeutel *m*
collective [kə′lektɪv] *adj* kollektiv,
Sammel-, Gesamt- || *s* (pol) Kollek-
tiv *n*
collec′tive bar′gaining *s* Tarifverhand-
lungen *pl*
collec′tive farm′ *s* Kolchose *f*
collector [kə′lektər] *s* (*e.g., of stamps*)
Sammler –in *mf*; (*bill collector*) Einkassierer –in *mf*; (*of taxes*) Einneh-
mer –in *mf*; (*of tickets*) Fahrkarten-
abnehmer –in *mf*
college [′kɑlɪdʒ] *s* College *n*; (*e.g., of
cardinals*) Kollegium *n*
collide [kə′laɪd] *intr* zusammenstoßen
collie [′kɑli] *s* Collie *m*
collision [kə′lɪʒən] *s* Zusammenstoß *m*
colloquial [kə′lokwɪ·əl] *adj* umgangssprachlich, Umgangs-
colloquialism [kə′lokwɪ·ə‚lɪzəm] *s*
Ausdruck *m* der Umgangssprache
colloquy [′kɑləkwi] *s* Gespräch *n*
collusion [kə′luʒən] *s* Kollusion *f*; **be
in c.** kolludieren
colon [′kolən] *s* (anat) Dickdarm *m*;
(gram) Doppelpunkt *m*
colonel [′kʌrnəl] *s* Oberst *m*
colonial [kə′lonɪ·əl] *adj* Kolonial- || *s*
Einwohner –in *mf·*e–r Kolonie
colonialism [kə′lonɪ·ə‚lɪzəm] *s* Kolo-
nialismus *m*
colonize [′kɑlə‚naɪz] *tr* besiedeln
colonnade [‚kɑlə′ned] *s* Säulengang *m*
colony [′kɑləni] *s* Kolonie *f*
color [′kʌlər] *adj* (*film, photo, pho-
tography, slide, television*) Farb- ||
s Farbe *f*; **lend c. to** beleben; **show
one's colors** sein wahres Gesicht zeigen; **the colors** die Flagge; **with fly-
ing colors** glänzend || *tr* färben;
(fig) (schön)färben || *intr* sich ver-
färben; (*become red*) erröten
col′or-blind′ *adj* farbenblind
col′ored *adj* farbig
col′or-fast′ *adj* farbecht
colorful [′kʌlərfəl] *adj* bunt, farben-
reich; (fig) farbig
col′oring *s* Kolorit *n*, Färbung *f*
col′oring book′ *s* Malbuch *n*
colorless [′kʌlərlɪs] *adj* farblos
col′or ser′geant *s* Fahnenträger *m*
colossal [kə′lɑsəl] *adj* kolossal
colossus [kə′lɑsəs] *s* Koloß *m*
colt [kolt] *s* Füllen *n*
Columbus [kə′lʌmbəs] *s* Kolumbus *m*

column [′kɑləm] *s* Säule *f*; (*syndi-
cated article*) Kolumne *f*; (mil) Kolonne *f*; (typ) Spalte *f*, Rubrik *f*; **c.
of smoke** Rauchsäule *f*
columnist [′kɑləmɪst] *s* Kolumnist –in
mf
coma [′komə] *s* Koma *n*
comb [kom] *s* Kamm *m*; (*honeycomb*)
Wabe *f*; (*of a rooster*) Kamm *m* ||
tr kämmen; (*an area*) absuchen
com·bat [′kɑmbæt] (*e.g., pilot,
strength, unit, zone*) Kampf– || *s*
Kampf *m*, Streit *m* || [′kɑmbæt],
[kəm′bæt] *v* (*pret & pp* –bat[t]ed;
ger –bat[t]ing) *tr* bekämpfen || *intr*
kämpfen
combatant [′kɑmbətənt] *s* Kämpfer
–in *mf*
com′bat fatigue′ *s* Kriegsneurose *f*
combative [′kɑmbətɪv] *adj* streitsüchtig
comber [′komər] *s* Sturzwelle *f*
combination [‚kɑmbɪ′ne∫ən] *s* Verbindung *f*; (com) Konzern *m*
combine [′kɑmbaɪn] *s* (agr) Mähdrescher *m*; (com) Interessengemein-
schaft *f* || [kəm′baɪn] *tr* kombinie-
ren, verbinden
combustible [kəm′bʌstɪbəl] *adj* (ver)-
brennbar || *s* Brennstoff *m*
combustion [kəm′bʌst∫ən] *s* Verbrennung *f*
combus′tion cham′ber *s* Brennkammer
f
combus′tion en′gine *s* Verbrennungs-
maschine *f*
come [kʌm] *v* (*pret* **came** [kem]; *pp*
come) *intr* kommen; **c. about** geschehen, sich ereignen; **c. across**
(*discover*) stoßen auf (*acc*); (*said of
a speech, etc.*) ankommen; **c. across
with** (coll) blechen; **c. after** folgen
(*dat*); (*fetch*) holen kommen; **c.
along** mitkommen; (coll) vorwärtskommen; **c. apart** auseinanderfallen;
c. around herumkommen; (*said of a
special day*) wiederkehren; (*improve*) wieder zu sich kommen;
(*change one's view*) von e–r Ansicht
abgehen; **c. back** zurückkehren; (*recur to the mind*) wieder einfallen;
c. between treten zwischen (*acc*); **c.
by** vorbeikommen; (*acquire*) geraten
an (*acc*); **c. clean** (sl) mit der Wahrheit herausrücken; **c. down** (*said of
prices*) sinken; (& fig) herunterkom-
men; **c. down with** erkranken an
(*dat*); **c. first** (*have priority*) zuerst
an die Reihe kommen; **c. for** abholen; **c. forward** vortreten; **c. from**
herkommen; (*e.g., a rich family*)
stammen aus; (*e.g., school*) kommen
aus; **c. in** hereinkommen; **c. in for**
(coll) erhalten; **c. in second** den
zweiten Platz belegen; **c. off** (*said
of a button*) abgehen; (*come loose*)
losgehen; (*said of an event*) vorkommen; **c. on!** los!; **c. out** herauskommen; (*said of a spot*) herausgehen;
(*said of a publication*) erscheinen;
c. out against (or **for**) sich erklären
gegen (or für); **c. over** (*said of fear,
etc.*) überlaufen; **c. to** (*amount to*)

betragen; (after fainting) wieder zu sich kommen; **c. together** zusammenkommen; **c. true** in Erfüllung gehen; **c. up** (occur) vorkommen; (said of a number) herauskommen; (said of plants) aufgehen; (in conversation) zur Sprache kommen; (said of a storm) heranziehen; **c. upon** kommen auf (acc); **c. up to** entsprechen (dat); **for years to c.** auf Jahre hinaus; **how c.?** (coll) wieso?; **it comes easy to me** es fällt mir leicht

come'back' s Comeback m

comedian [kə'mɪdɪ·ən] s Komiker m; (pej) Komödiant –in mf

comedienne [kə‚mɪdɪ'ɛn] s Komikerin f

come'down' s (coll) Abstieg m

comedy ['kɑmədɪ] s Komödie f

comely ['kʌmlɪ] adj anmutig

come'-on' s (sl) Lockmittel n

comet ['kɑmɪt] s Komet m

comfort ['kʌmfərt] s (solace) Trost m; (of a room, etc.) Behaglichkeit f; (person or thing that comforts) Tröster m; (bed cover) Steppdecke f || tr trösten

comfortable ['kʌmfərtəbəl] adj behaglich, bequem; (income) ausreichend; **be (or feel) c.** sich wohl fühlen

comforter ['kʌmfərtər] s Tröster m; (bed cover) Steppdecke f

com'forting adj tröstlich

com'fort sta'tion s Bedürfnisanstalt f

comic ['kɑmɪk] adj komisch || s Komiker m; **comics** Comics pl, Witzblatt n

comical ['kɑmɪkəl] adj komisch

com'ic op'era s Operette f

com'ic strip' s Bildstreifen m

com'ing adj künftig, kommend; **c. soon** (notice at theater) demnächst || s Kommen n, Ankunft f; **c. of age** Mündigwerden n

comma ['kɑmə] s Komma n, Beistrich m

command [kə'mænd] s (order) Befehl m; (of language) Beherrschung f; (mil) Kommando n; (jurisdiction) (mil) Kommandobereich m; **at s.o.'s c.** j–s Befehl; **be in c. of** (mil) das Kommando führen über (acc); **have a good c. of** gut beherrschen; **take c. of** (mil) das Kommando übernehmen über (acc) || tr (a person) befehlen (dat); (respect, silence) gebieten; (troops) führen; (a high price) erzielen || intr (mil) kommandieren

commandant [‚kɑmən'dænt] s Kommandant m

commandeer [‚kɑmən'dɪr] tr (coll) organisieren; (mil) requirieren

commander [kə'mændər] s Truppenführer m; (of a company) Chef m; (of a military unit from battalion to corps) Kommandeur m; (of an army) Befehlshaber m; (nav) Fregattenkapitän m

comman'der in chief' s Oberbefehlshaber m

command'ing adj (appearance) eindrucksvoll; (view) weit; (position)

beherrschend; (general) kommandierend

command'ing of'ficer s Einheitsführer m

commandment [kə'mændmənt] s Gebot n

command' post' s Befehlsstand m

commemorate [kə'mɛmə‚ret] tr gedenken (genit), feiern

commemoration [kə‚mɛmə'reʃən] s Gedenkfeier f; **in c. of** zum Gedächtnis von

commence [kə'mɛns] tr & intr anfangen

commencement [kə'mɛnsmənt] s Anfang m; (educ) Schulentlassungsfeier f

commend [kə'mɛnd] tr (praise) (&
mil) belob(ig)en; (entrust) empfehlen

commendable [kə'mɛndəbəl] adj lobenswert

commendation [‚kɑmən'deʃən] s Belobigung f

comment ['kɑmənt] s Bemerkung f, Stellungnahme f; **no c.!** kein Kommentar! || intr Bemerkungen machen; **c. on** kommentieren

commentary ['kɑmən‚terɪ] s Kommentar m

commentator ['kɑmən‚tetər] s Kommentator –in mf; (of a text) Erklärer –in mf

commerce ['kɑmərs] s Handel m

commercial [kə'mʌrʃəl] adj Handels–, Geschäfts–, kommerziell || s (rad, telv) Werbesendung f

commer'cial art' s Gebrauchsgraphik f

commercialism [kə'mʌrʃə‚lɪzəm] s Handelsgeist m

commercialize [kə'mʌrʃə‚laɪz] tr kommerzialisieren

commiserate [kə'mɪzə‚ret] intr—**c. with** bemitleiden

commissar ['kɑmɪ‚sɑr] s (pol) Kommissar m

commissary ['kɑmɪ‚serɪ] s (deputy) Kommissar m; (store) Militärversorgungsstelle f

commission [kə'mɪʃən] s (order) Auftrag m; (of a crime) Begehung f; (committee) Kommission f; (percentage) Provision f; (mil) Offizierspatent n; **out of c.** außer Betrieb; || tr beauftragen; (a work) bestellen; (a ship) in Dienst stellen; (mil) ein Offizierspatent verleihen (dat)

commis'sioned of'ficer s Offizier –in mf

commissioner [kə'mɪʃənər] s Kommissar –in mf

com·mit [kə'mɪt] v (pret & pp -mitted; ger -mitting) tr (a crime) begehen; (entrust) anvertrauen; (give over) übergeben; (to an institution) einweisen; **c. oneself to** sich festlegen auf (acc); **c. to memory** auswendig lernen; **c. to writing** zu Papier bringen

commitment [kə'mɪtmənt] s (to) Festlegung f (auf acc); (to an asylum) Anstaltsüberweisung f

committee [kə'mɪtɪ] s Ausschuß m

commode [kə'mod] s Kommode f

commodious ['kə'mɒdɪ-əs] *adj* geräumig

commodity ['kə'mɒdɪtɪ] *s* Ware *f*

common ['kɒmən] *adj* (*language, property, interest*) gemeinsam; (*general*) allgemein; (*people*) einfach; (*soldier*) gemein; (*coarse, vulgar*) gemein; (*frequent*) häufig ‖ *s*—in **c.** gemeinsam

com'mon denom'inator *s* gemeinsamer Nenner *m*; **reduce to a c.** auf e-n gemeinsamen Nenner bringen

commoner ['kɒmənər] *s* Bürger –in *mf*

com'mon-law mar'riage *s* wilde Ehe *f*

Com'mon Mar'ket *s* Gemeinsamer Markt *m*

com'mon noun' *s* Gattungsname *m*

com'monplace' *adj* alltäglich ‖ *s* Gemeinplatz *m*

com'mon sense' *s* gesunder Menschenverstand *m*

com'mon stock' *s* Stammaktien *pl*

commonweal ['kɒmən,wil] *s* Gemeinwohl *n*

com'monwealth' *s* (*republic*) Republik *f*; (*state in U.S.A.*) Bundesstaat *m*

commotion [kə'moʃən] *s* Aufruhr *m*

commune ['kɒmjun] *s* Kommune *f* ‖ [kə'mjun] *intr* sich vertraulich besprechen

communicable [kə'mjunɪkəbəl] *adj* übertragbar

communicant [kə'mjunɪkənt] *s* Kommunikant –in *mf*

communicate [kə'mjunɪ,ket] *tr* mitteilen; (*a disease*) (**to**) übertragen (auf *acc*) ‖ *intr* sich besprechen

communication [kə,mjunɪ'keʃən] *s* Mitteilung *f*; (*message*) Nachricht *f*; **communications** Nachrichtenwesen *n*; (mil) Fernmeldewesen *n*

communicative [kə'mjunɪ,ketɪv] *adj* mitteilsam

communion [kə'mjunjən] *s* Gemeinschaft *f*; (Prot) Abendmahl *n*; (R. C.) Kommunion *f*

commun'ion rail' *s* Altargitter *n*

communiqué [kə,mjunɪ'ke] *s* Kommuniqué *n*

communism ['kɒmjə,nɪzəm] *s* Kommunismus *m*

communist ['kɒmjənɪst] *s* kommunistisch ‖ *s* Kommunist –in *mf*

community [kə'mjunɪtɪ] *s* Gemeinschaft *f*; (*people living together*) Gemeinde *f*

communize ['kɒmjə,naɪz] *tr* kommunistisch machen

commutation [,kɒmjə'teʃən] *s* (jur) Umwandlung *f*

commuta'tion tick'et *s* Zeitkarte *f*

commutator ['kɒmjə,tetər] *s* (elec) Kommutator *m*, Kollektor *m*

commute [kə'mjut] *tr* (jur) umwandeln ‖ *intr* pendeln

commuter [kə'mjutər] *s* Pendler –in *mf*

commut'er train' *s* Pendelzug *m*

compact [kəm'pækt] *adj* kompakt, dicht ‖ ['kɒmpækt] *s* (*for cosmetics*) Kompaktdose *f*; (*agreement*) Vertrag *m*; (aut) Kompaktwagen *m*

companion [kəm'pænjən] *s* Kumpan –in *mf*; (*one who accompanies*) Begleiter –in *mf*

companionable [kə'pænjənəbəl] *adj* gesellig

compan'ionship' *s* Gesellschaft *f*

compan'ionway' *s* Kajütstreppe *f*

company ['kʌmpənɪ] *s* (*companions*) Umgang *m*; (& com) Gesellschaft *f*; (mil) Kompanie *f*; (theat) Truppe *f*; **keep c.** with verkehren mit; **keep s.o. c.** with verkehren mit; **keep s.o. c.** j–m Gesellschaft leisten

com'pany command'er *s* Kompaniechef *m*

comparable ['kɒmpərəbəl] *adj* vergleichbar

comparative [kəm'pærətɪv] *adv* vergleichend; (gram) komparativ ‖ *s* (gram) Komparativ *m*

comparatively [kəm'pærətɪvlɪ] *adv* verhältnismäßig

compare [kəm'per] *s*—beyond **c.** unvergleichlich ‖ *tr* (**with, to**) vergleichen (**mit**); (gram) steigern; **as compared with** im Vergleich zu

comparison [kəm'pærɪsən] *s* Vergleich *m*; (gram) Steigerung *f*

compartment [kəm'partmənt] *s* Fach *n*; (rr) Abteil *n*

compass ['kʌmpəs] *s* Kompaß *m*; (geom) Zirkel *m*; **within the c. of** innerhalb (*genit*)

com'pass card' *s* Kompaßrose *f*

compassion [kəm'pæʃən] *s* Mitleid *n*

compassionate [kəm'pæʃənɪt] *adj* mitleidig

compatible [kəm'pætɪbəl] *adj* vereinbar

com·pel [kəm'pel] *v* (*pret & pp* –pelled; *ger* –pelling) *tr* zwingen, nötigen

compendious [kəm'pendɪ-əs] *adj* gedrängt

compendi·um [kəm'pendɪ-əm] *s* (–ums & –a [ə]) Abriß *m*, Kompendium *n*

compensate ['kɒmpən,set] *tr* entschädigen ‖ *intr*—c. **for** Ersatz leisten (or bieten) für

compensation [,kɒmpən'seʃən] *s* (*for damages*) Entschädigung *f*; (*remuneration*) Entgeld *n*

compete [kəm'pit] *intr* (**with**) konkurrieren (**mit**); (**for**) sich mitbewerben (**um**); (sport) am Wettkampf teilnehmen

competence ['kɒmpɪtəns] *s* (*mental state*) Zurechnungsfähigkeit *f*; (*ability*) (**in**) Fähigkeit *f* (**zu**)

competent ['kɒmpɪtənt] *adj* (*able*) fähig, tüchtig; (*witness*) zulässig

competition [,kɒmpɪ'trɪʃən] *s* Wettbewerb *m*; (com) Konkurrenz *f*; (sport) Wettkampf *m*

competitive [kəm'petɪtɪv] *adj* (*bidding*) Konkurrenz–; (*prices*) konkurrenzfähig; (*person*) ehrgeizig; (*exam*) Auslese–

competitor [kəm'petɪtər] *s* Mitbewerber –in *mf*; (com) Konkurrent –in *mf*; (sport) Wettkämpfer –in *mf*

compilation [,kɒmpɪ'leʃən] *s* Zusammenstellung *f*; (*book*) Sammelwerk *n*

compile [kəm'paɪl] *tr* zusammenstellen, kompilieren; (*Material*) zusammentragen

complacence [kəm'pleɪsəns], **complacency** [kəm'pleɪsənsi] *s* Selbstgefälligkeit *f*

complacent [kəm'pleɪsənt] *adj* selbstgefällig

complain [kəm'pleɪn] *intr* klagen; **c. to s.o. about** sich bei j–m beklagen über (*acc*)

complaint [kəm'pleɪnt] *s* Klage *f*; (*ailment*) Beschwerde *f*

complement ['kɑmplɪmənt] *s* (& gram) Ergänzung *f*; (geom) Komplement *n*; (nav) Bemannung *f* || ['kɑmplɪ,ment] *tr* ergänzen

complete [kəm'plit] *adj* ganz, vollkommen, vollständig; (*works*) sämtlich || *tr* (*make whole*) vervollständigen; (*make perfect*) vollenden; (*finish*) beenden; (*a job*) erledigen

completely [kəm'plitli] *adv* völlig

completion [kəm'pliʃən] *s* Vollendung *f*

complex [kəm'plɛks], ['kɑmplɛks] *adj* verwickelt || ['kɑmplɛks] *s* Komplex *m*

complexion [kəm'plɛkʃən] *s* Gesichtsfarbe *f*; (*appearance*) Aussehen *n*

complexity [kəm'plɛksɪti] *s* Kompliziertheit *f*

compliance [kəm'plaɪəns] *s* Einwilligung *f*; **in c. with your wishes** Ihren Wünschen gemäß

complicate ['kɑmplɪ,ket] *tr* komplizieren

com'plicat'ed *adj* kompliziert

complication [,kɑmplɪ'keʃən] *s* Verwicklung *f*; (& pathol) Komplikation *f*

complicity [kəm'plɪsɪti] *s* (in) Mitschuld *f* (an *dat*)

compliment ['kɑmplɪmənt] *s* Kompliment *n*; (*praise*) Lob *n*; **compliments** Empfehlungen *pl*; **pay s.o. a (high) c.** j–m ein (großes) Lob spenden || *tr* (on) beglückwünschen (zu)

complimentary [,kɑmplɪ'mentəri] *adj* (*remark*) schmeichelhaft; (*free*) Frei–

com·ply [kəm'plaɪ] *v* (*pret & pp* –**plied**) *intr* sich fügen; **c. with** einwilligen in (*acc*); **c. with the rules** sich an die Vorschriften halten

component [kəm'ponənt] *adj* Teil– || *s* Bestandteil *m*; (math, phys) Komponente *f*

compose [kəm'poz] *tr* (*writings*) verfassen; (*a sentence*) bilden; (mus) komponieren; (typ) setzen; **be composed of** bestehen aus; **c. oneself** sich fassen

composed' *adj* ruhig, gefaßt

composer [kəm'pozər] *s* Verfasser –in *mf*; (mus) Komponist –in *mf*

composite [kəm'pazɪt] *adj* zusammengesetzt || *s* Zusammensetzung *f*

composition [,kɑmpə'zɪʃən] *s* (chem) Zusammensetzung *f*; (educ) Aufsatz *m*; (mus, paint) Komposition *f*; (typ) Schriftsatz *m*

composi'tion book' *s* Übungsheft *n*

compositor [kəm'pazɪtər] *s* Setzer –in *mf*

composure [kəm'poʒər] *s* Fassung *f*

compote ['kɑmpot] *s* (*stewed fruit*) Kompott *n*; (*dish*) Kompottschale *f*

compound ['kɑmpaund] *adj* zusammengesetzt; (*fracture*) kompliziert || *s* Zusammensetzung *f*; (*enclosure*) umzäumtes Gelände *n*; (chem) Verbindung *f*; (gram) Kompositum *n*; (mil) Truppenlager *n* || [kəm'paund] *tr* zusammensetzen

com'pound in'terest *s* Zinseszinsen *pl*

comprehend [,kɑmprɪ'hend] *tr* auffassen

comprehensible [,kɑmprɪ'hensɪbəl] *adj* faßlich, begreiflich

comprehension [,kɑmprɪ'henʃən] *s* Auffassung *f*; (*ability to understand*) Fassungskraft *f*

comprehensive [,kɑmprɪ'hensɪv] *adj* umfassend

compress ['kɑmpres] *s* (med) Kompresse *f* || [kəm'pres] *tr* komprimieren

compressed' *adj* komprimiert; (*air*) Druck–; (fig) gedrängt

compression [kəm'preʃən] *s* Kompression *f*, Druck *m*

comprise [kəm'praɪz] *tr* umfassen; **be comprised of** bestehen aus

compromise ['kɑmprə,maɪz] *s* Kompromiß *m* || *tr* kompromittieren; (*principles*) preisgeben || *intr* (on) e–n Kompromiß schließen (über *acc*)

comptroller [kən'trolər] *s* Rechnungsprüfer *m*

compulsion [kəm'pʌlʃən] *s* Zwang *m*

compulsive [kəm'pʌlsɪv] *adj* triebhaft

compulsory [kəm'pʌlsəri] *adj* obligatorisch, Zwangs–; **c. military service** allgemeine Wehrpflicht *f*

compute [kəm'pjut] *tr* berechnen || *intr* rechnen

computer [kəm'pjutər] *s* Computer *m*

comput'er lan'guage *s* Maschinensprache *f*

comrade ['kɑmræd] *s* Kamerad *m*

con [kɑn] *v* (*pret & pp* **conned;** *ger* **conning**) *tr* beschwindeln

concave [kɑn'kev] *adj* konkav

conceal [kən'sil] *tr* verheimlichen

concealment [kən'silmənt] *s* Verheimlichung *f*; (*place*) Versteck *n*

concede [kən'sid] *tr* zugestehen, zubilligen; **c. victory** (pol) den Wahlsieg überlassen || *intr* nachgeben

conceit [kən'sit] *s* (*vanity*) Einbildung *f*, Dünkel *m*; (*witty expression*) Witz *m*

conceit'ed *adj* eingebildet

conceivable [kən'sivəbəl] *adj* denkbar

conceive [kən'siv] *tr* begreifen; (*a desire*) hegen; (*a child*) empfangen

concentrate ['kɑnsən,tret] *tr* konzentrieren; (*troops*) zusammenziehen || *intr* (on) sich konzentrieren (auf *acc*); (*gather*) sich sammeln

concentration [,kɑnsən'treʃən] *s* Konzentration *f*

concentric [kən'sentrɪk] *adj* konzentrisch

concept ['kɑnsɛpt] *s* Begriff *m*

conception [kən'sepʃən] s (idea) Vorstellung f; (design) Entwurf m; (biol) Empfängnis f

concern [kən'sʌrn] s (worry) Besorgnis f; (matter) Angelegenheit f; (com) Firma f; **that is no c. of mine** das geht mich nichts an || tr betreffen, angehen; **as far as I am concerned** von mir aus; **c. oneself about** sich bekümmern um; **c. oneself with** sich befassen mit; **to whom it may c.** Bescheinigung

concern'ing prep betreffend (acc), betreffs (genit), über (acc)

concert ['kɑnsərt] s (mus) Konzert n; **in c.** (with) im Einvernehmen (mit) || [kən'sʌrt] tr zusammenfassen

concession [kən'seʃən] s Konzession f

conciliate [kən'sɪlɪ͵et] tr versöhnen

conciliatory [kən'sɪlɪə͵tori] adj versöhnlich

concise [kən'saɪs] adj kurz, bündig

conclude [kən'klud] tr schließen; **c. from s.th. that** aus etw schließen, daß; **to be concluded** Schluß folgt || intr (with) schließen (mit)

conclusion [kən'kluʒən] s Schluß m; **draw conclusions from** Schlüsse ziehen aus; **in c.** zum Schluß; **jump at conclusions** voreilige Schlüsse ziehen

conclusive [kən'klusɪv] adj (decisive) entscheidend; (proof) schlagkräftig

concoct [kən'kɑkt] tr (brew) zusammenbrauen; (plans) schmieden

concoction [kən'kɑkʃən] s Gebräu n

concomitant [kən'kɑmɪtənt] adj begleitend || s Begleitumstand m

concord ['kɑŋkɔrd] s Eintracht f

concordance [kən'kɔrdəns] s Übereinstimmung f; (book) Konkordanz f

concourse ['kɑŋkors] s (of people) Zusammenlaufen n, Anlauf m; (of rivers) Zusammenfluß m; (rr) Bahnhofshalle f

concrete ['kɑnkrit], [kɑn'krit] adj (not abstract) konkret; (solid) fest; (evidence) schlüssig; (of concrete) Beton–; (math) benannt || s Beton m || tr betonieren

con'crete block' s Betonblock m

con'crete noun' s Konkretum n

concubine ['kɑŋkjə͵baɪn] s Nebenfrau f; (mistress) Konkubine f

con-cur [kən'kʌr] v (pret & pp) –curred; ger –curring) intr (agree) übereinstimmen; (coincide) (with) zusammenfallen (mit); **c. in** (an opinion) beistimmen (dat)

concurrence [kən'kʌrəns] s (agreement) Einverständnis n; (coincidence) Zusammentreffen n; (geom) Schnittpunkt m

condemn [kən'dem] tr verdammen; (& jur) verurteilen; (a building) für unbewohnlich erklären

condemnation [͵kɑndem'neʃən] s Verurteilung f; (of a building, ship, plane) Untauglichkeitserklärung f

condense [kən'dens] tr (make thicker) verdichten; (writing) zusammendrängen; || intr kondensieren

condenser [kən'densər] s Kondensator m

condescend [͵kɑndɪ'send] intr sich herablassen

condescend'ing adj herablassend

condescension [͵kɑndɪ'senʃən] s Herablassung f

condiment ['kɑndɪmənt] s Würze f

condition [kən'dɪʃən] s (state) Zustand m; (state of health) Verfassung f; (stipulation) Bedingung f; **conditions** (e.g. for working; of the weather) Verhältnisse pl; **on c. that** unter der Bedingung, daß || tr (impose stipulations on) bedingen; (accustom) (to) gewöhnen (an acc); (sport) in Form bringen

conditional [kən'dɪʃənəl] adj bedingt

condi'tional clause' s Bedingungssatz m

conditionally [kən'dɪʃənəli] adv bedingungsweise

condole [kən'dol] intr (with) kondolieren (dat)

condolence [kən'doləns] s Beileid n

condom ['kɑndəm] s Präservativ n

condominium [͵kɑndə'mɪnɪ-əm] s Eigentumswohnung f

condone [kən'don] tr verzeihen

conducive [kən'd(j)usɪv] adj—**c. to** förderlich (dat)

conduct ['kɑndʌkt] s (behavior) Betragen n; (guidance) Führung f || [kən'dʌkt] tr (business, a campaign, a tour) führen; (elec, phys) leiten; (mus) dirigieren; **c. oneself** sich betragen || intr (mus) dirigieren

conductor [kən'dʌktər] s (elec, phys) Leiter m; (mus) Dirigent m; (rr) Schaffner m

conduit ['kɑnd(v)ɪt] s Röhre f; (elec) Isolierrohr n

cone [kon] s (ice cream cone; paper cone) Tüte f; (bot) Zapfen m; (geom) Kegel m, Konus m

confection [kən'fekʃən] s Konfekt n

confectioner [kən'fekʃənər] s Zuckerbäcker –in mf

confec'tioner's sug'ar s Puderzucker m

confectionery [kən'fekʃə͵neri] s (shop) Konditorei f; (sweets) Zuckerwerk n

confederacy [kən'fedərəsi] s Bündnis n; (conspiracy) Verschwörung f

confederate [kən'fedərɪt] adj verbündet || s Bundesgenosse m, Bundesgenossin f; (accomplice) Helfershelfer –in mf || [kən'fedə͵ret] tr verbünden || intr sich verbünden

confederation [kən͵fedə'reʃən] s Bund m

con-fer [kən'fʌr] v (pret & pp –ferred; ger –ferring) tr (on, upon) verleihen (dat) || intr sich besprechen, konferieren

conference ['kɑnfərəns] s Konferenz f; (sport) Verband m

con'ference call' s Sammelverbindung f

confess [kən'fes] tr (ein)gestehen, bekennen; (sins) beichten || intr gestehen

confession [kən'feʃən] s Geständnis n, Bekenntnis n; (of sins) Beichte f; **go to c.** beichten

confessional [kən'feʃənəl] *s* Beichtstuhl *m*

confes'sion of faith' *s* Glaubensbekenntnis *n*

confessor [kən'fesər] *s* Beichtvater *m*

confidant [‚kɑnfɪ'dænt] *s* Vertraute *mf*

confide [kən'faɪd] *tr* (to) anvertrauen (*dat*) ‖ *intr*—c. in vertrauen (*dat*)

confidence ['kɑnfɪdəns] *s* (*trust*) (in) Vertrauen *n* (auf *acc*, zu); (*assurance*) Zuversicht *f*; in c. im Vertrauen

con'fidence man' *s* Bauernfänger *m*

confident ['kɑnfɪdənt] *adj* zuversichtlich; be c. of sich [*dat*] sicher sein (*genit*)

confidential [‚kɑnfɪ'denʃəl] *adj* vertraulich

confine ['kɑnfaɪn] *s*—the confines die Grenzen *pl* ‖ *tr* [kən'faɪn] *tr* (*limit*) (to) beschränken (auf *acc*); (*shut in*) einsperren; **be confined** (*in pregnancy*) niederkommen; **be confined to bed** bettlägerig sein

confinement [kən'faɪnmənt] *s* Beschränkung *f*; (*arrest*) Haft *f*; (*childbirth*) Niederkunft *f*

confirm [kən'fɑrm] *tr* bestätigen; (Prot) konfirmieren; (R.C.) firmen; **confirm in writing** verbriefen

confirmation [‚kɑnfər'meʃən] *s* Bestätigung *f*; (Prot) Konfirmation *f*; (R.C.) Firmung *f*

confirmed' *adj* (*e.g., report*) bestätigt; (*inveterate*) unverbesserlich; **c. bachelor** Hagestolz *m*

confiscate ['kɑnfɪs‚ket] *tr* beschlagnahmen, konfiszieren

confiscation [‚kɑnfɪs'keʃən] *s* Beschlagnahme *f*

conflagration [‚kɑnflə'greʃən] *s* Brand *m*, Feuerbrunst *f*

conflict ['kɑnflɪkt] *s* (*of interests, of evidence*) Konflikt *m*; (*fight*) Zusammenstoß *m* ‖ [kən'flɪkt] *intr* (with) im Widerspruch stehen (zu)

conflict'ing *adj* einander widersprechend

con'flict of in'terest *s* Interessenkonflikt *m*, Interessenkollision *f*

confluence ['kɑnfluəns] *s* Zusammenfluß *m*

conform [kən'fɔrm] *tr* anpassen ‖ *intr* übereinstimmen; (to) sich anpassen (*dat*)

conformity [kən'fɔrmɪti] *s* (*adaptation*) (to) Anpassung *f* (an *acc*); (*agreement*) (with) Übereinstimmung *f* (mit)

confound [kɑn'faʊnd] *tr* (*perplex*) verblüffen; (*throw into confusion*) verwirren; (*erroneously identify*) (with) verwechseln (mit) ‖ ['kɑn'faʊnd] *tr*—c. it! zum Donnerwetter!

confound'ed *adj* (coll) verwünscht

confrere ['kɑnfrer] *s* Kollege *m*

confront [kən'frʌnt] *tr* (*face*) gegenüberstehen (*dat*); (a problem, an enemy) entgegentreten (*dat*); **be confronted with** gegenüberstehen (*dat*); **c. s.o. with** j-n konfrontieren mit

confrontation [‚kɑnfrən'teʃən] *s* Konfrontation *f*; (*of witnesses*) Gegenüberstellung *f*

confuse [kən'fjuz] *tr* (*e.g., names*) verwechseln; (*persons*) verwirren

confused' *adj* konfus, verwirrt, wirr

confusion [kən'fjuʒən] *s* Verwechslung *f*; (*disorder, chaos*) Verwirrung *f*

confute [kən'fjut] *tr* widerlegen

congeal [kən'dʒil] *tr* erstarren lassen ‖ *intr* erstarren

congenial [kən'dʒinjəl] *adj* (*person*) sympathisch; (*surroundings*) angenehm

congenital [kən'dʒenɪtəl] *adj* angeboren

congen'ital de'fect *s* Geburtsfehler *m*

congest [kən'dʒest] *tr* überfüllen

congest'ed *adj* überfüllt; (*area*) übervölkert; (*with traffic*) verkehrsreich

congestion [kən'dʒestʃən] *s* Überfüllung *f*; (*of traffic*) Verkehrsstockung *f*; (*of population*) Übervölkerung *f*; (*pathol*) Blutandrang *m*

congratulate [kən'grætʃə‚let] *tr* gratulieren (*dat*); **c. s.o. on** j-m gratulieren zu

congratulations [kən‚grætʃə'leʃənz] *spl* Glückwunsch *m*; **c.!** ich gratuliere!

congregate ['kɑŋgrɪ‚get] *intr* sich (ver)sammeln, zusammenkommen

congregation [‚kɑŋgrɪ'geʃən] *s* Versammlung *f*; (eccl) Gemeinde *f*

congress ['kɑŋgres] *s* Kongreß *m*

congressional [kən'greʃənəl] *adj* Kongreß-

congress-man ['kɑŋgrɪsmən] *s* (-men) Abgeordnete *m*

con'gress-wom'an *s* (-wom'en) Abgeordnete *f*

congruent ['kɑŋgruənt] *adj* kongruent

conical ['kɑnɪkəl] *adj* kegelförmig

conjecture [kən'dʒektʃər] *s* Vermutung *f*, Mutmaßung *f* ‖ *tr & intr* vermuten

conjugal ['kɑndʒəgəl] *adj* ehelich

conjugate ['kɑndʒə‚get] *tr* abwandeln

conjugation [‚kɑndʒə'geʃən] *s* Abwandlung *f*

conjunction [kən'dʒʌŋkʃən] *s* Bindewort *n*; **in c. with** in Verbindung mit

conjure [kən'dʒur] *tr* (*appeal solemnly to*) beschwören ‖ ['kʌndʒər] *tr*—**c. away** wegzaubern; **c. up** heraufbeschwören

conk [kɑŋk] *tr* (sl) hauen ‖ *intr*—**c. out** (sl) versagen

connect [kə'nekt] *tr* verbinden; (& fig) verknüpfen; (elec) (to) anschließen (an *acc*); (telp) (with) verbinden (mit) ‖ *intr* verbunden sein; (*said of trains, etc.*) (with) Anschluß haben (an *acc*); (box) treffen

connect'ing *adj* Verbindungs-, Binde-; (*trains, buses*) Anschluß-; (*rooms*) mit Zwischentür

connect'ing rod' *s* Schubstange *f*

connection [kə'nekʃən] *s* (*e.g., of a pipe*) Verbindung *f*; (*of ideas*) Verknüpfung *f*; (*context*) Zusammenhang *m*; (*part that connects*) Verbindungsteil *m*; (elec) Schaltung *f* (mach, rr, telp) Verbindung *f;* **con-nections** Beziehungen *pl;* **in c. with** in Zusammenhang mit

con'ning tow'er ['kɑnɪŋ] *s* Kommandoturm *m*

connive [kə'naɪv] *intr*—c. at ein Auge zudrücken bei; **c. with** im geheimen Einverständnis stehen mit

connotation [‚kɑnoˈteʃən] *s* Nebenbedeutung *f*

connote [kə'not] *tr* mitbezeichnen

conquer ['kɑŋkər] *tr* (*win in war*) erobern; (*overcome*) überwinden

conquerer ['kɑŋkərər] *s* Eroberer *m*

conquest ['kɑŋkwest] *s* Eroberung *f*

conscience ['kɑnʃəns] *s* Gewissen *n*

conscientious [‚kɑnʃɪ'enʃəs] *adj* gewissenhaft, pflichtbewußt

conscien'tious objec'tor [əb'dʒektər] *s* Wehrdienstverweigerer *m*

conscious ['kɑnʃəs] *adj* bei Bewußtsein; **c. of** bewußt (*genit*)

consciousness ['kɑnʃəsnɪs] *s* Bewußtsein *n;* (*awareness*) (**of**) Kenntnis *f* (*genit* or von); **regain c.** wieder zu sich kommen

conscript ['kɑnskrɪpt] *s* Dienstpflichtige *m;* (*mil*) Wehrdienstpflichtige *m* || [kən'skrɪpt] *tr* ausheben

conscription [kən'skrɪpʃən] *s* Dienstpflicht *f;* (*draft*) Aushebung *f*

consecrate ['kɑnsɪ‚kret] *tr* weihen

consecration [‚kɑnsɪ'kreʃən] *s* Einweihung *f;* (*at Mass*) Wandlung *f*

consecutive [kən'sekjətɪv] *adj* aufeinanderfolgend

consensus [kən'sensəs] *s* allgemeine Übereinstimmung *f;* **the c. of opinion** die übereinstimmende Meinung

consent [kən'sent] *s* Zustimmung *f;* **by common c.** mit allgemeiner Zustimmung || *intr* zustimmen; **c. to** (*inf*) sich bereit erklären zu (*inf*)

consequence ['kɑnsɪ‚kwens] *s* Folge *f;* (*influence*) Einfluß *m;* **in c. of** infolge (*genit*); **it is of no c.** es hat nichts auf sich; **suffer the consequences** die Folgen tragen

consequently ['kɑnsɪ‚kwentlɪ] *adv* folglich, infolgedessen, mithin

conservation [‚kɑnsər'veʃən] *s* Bewahrung *f;* (*of energy, etc.*) Erhaltung *f;* (*supervision of natural resources*) Naturschutz *m;* (*ecology*) Umweltschutz *m*

conservatism [kən'sɑrvə‚tɪzəm] *s* Konservatismus *m*

conservative [kən'sɑrvətɪv] *adj* konservativ; (*estimate*) vorsichtig || *s* Konservative *mf*

conservatory [kən'sɑrvə‚tori] *s* Treibhaus *n;* (*mus*) Konservatorium *n*

conserve [kən'sɑrv] *tr* sparsam umgehen mit

consider [kən'sɪdər] *tr* (*take into account*) berücksichtigen; (*show consideration for*) Rücksicht nehmen auf (*acc*); (*reflect on*) sich [*dat*] überlegen; (*regard as*) halten für, betrachten als; **all things considered** alles in allem

considerable [kən'sɪdərəbəl] *adj* beträchtlich, erheblich

considerate [kən'sɪdərɪt] *adj* (**to-wards**) rücksichtsvoll (**gegen**)

consideration [kən‚sɪdə'reʃən] *s* (*taking into account*) Berücksichtigung *f;* (*regard*) (**for**) Rücksicht *f* (auf *acc*); **be an important c.** e–e wichtige Rolle spielen; **be under c.** in Betracht gezogen werden; **for a c.** entgeltlich; **in c. of** in Anbetracht (*genit*); **take into c.** in Betracht ziehen; **with c.** rücksichtsvoll

consid'ering *adv* (coll) den Umständen nach || *prep* in Anbetracht (*genit*)

consign [kən'saɪn] *tr* (*ship*) versenden; (*address*) adressieren

consignee [‚kɑnsaɪ'ni] *s* Adressat –in *mf*

consignment [kən'saɪnmənt] *s* (*act of sending*) Versand *m;* (*merchandise sent*) Sendung *f;* **on c.** in Kommission

consist [kən'sɪst] *intr*—c. in bestehen in (*dat*); **c. of** bestehen aus

consistency [kən'sɪstənsɪ] *s* Konsequenz *f;* (*firmness*) Festigkeit *f;* (*viscosity*) Dickflüssigkeit *f;* (*agreement*) Übereinstimmung *f;* (*steadfastness*) (**in**) Beständigkeit *f* (in *dat*)

consistent [kən'sɪstənt] *adj* (*performer*) stetig; (*performance*) gleichmäßig; (*free from contradiction*) konsequent; **c. with** in Übereinstimmung mit

consistory [kən'sɪstərɪ] *s* Konsistorium *n*

consolation [‚kɑnsə'leʃən] *s* Trost *m*

console ['kɑnsol] *s* (*for radio or record player*) Musiktruhe *f;* (*of an organ*) Spieltisch *m;* (*television*) Fernsehtruhe *f* || [kən'sol] *tr* trösten

consolidate [kən'sɑlɪ‚det] *tr* (*a position*) festigen; (*debts*) konsolidieren; (*combine*) zusammenlegen

consonant ['kɑnsənənt] *adj* (**with**) im Einklang (**mit**) || *s* Mitlaut *m*

consort ['kɑnsɔrt] *s* (*male*) Gemahl *m;* (*female*) Gemahlin *f* || [kən'sɔrt] *intr* (**with**) Umgang haben (**mit**)

consorti·um [kən'sɔrtɪ·əm] *s* (**–a** [ə]) Konsortium *n*

conspicuous [kən'spɪkju·əs] *adj* auffallend, auffällig; **c. for** bemerkenswert wegen

conspiracy [kən'spɪrəsɪ] *s* Verschwörung *f*

conspirator [kən'spɪrətər] *s* Verschwörer –in *mf*

conspire [kən'spaɪr] *intr* sich verschwören

constable ['kɑnstəbəl] *s* Gendarm *m*

constancy ['kɑnstənsɪ] *s* Beständigkeit *f*

constant ['kɑnstənt] *adj* (*continuous*) dauernd, ständig; (*faithful*) treu; (*resolute*) standhaft; (*element, time element*) fest; (fig & tech) konstant || *s* (math, phys) Konstante *f*

constantly ['kɑnstəntlɪ] *adv* immerfort

constellation [‚kɑnstə'leʃən] *s* Sternbild *n*

consternation [‚kɑnstər'neʃən] *s* Bestürzung *f*

constipate ['kɒnstɪˌpet] *tr* verstopfen
constipation [ˌkɒnstɪ'peʃən] *s* Verstopfung *f*
constituency [kən'stɪtʃʊˌənsi] *s* Wählerschaft *f*
constituent [kən'stɪtʃʊˌənt] *adj* wesentlich; **c. part** Bestandteil *m* ‖ *s* Komponente *f*; (pol) Wähler –in *mf*
constitute ['kɒnstɪˌt(j)ut] *tr* (*make up*) ausmachen, bilden; (*found*) gründen
constitution [ˌkɒnstɪ't(j)uʃən] *s* (*of a country or organization*) Verfassung *f*; (*bodily condition*) Konstitution *f*; (*composition*) Zusammensetzung *f*
constitutional [ˌkɒnstɪ't(j)uʃənəl] *adj* (*according to a constitution*) konstitutionell; (*crisis, amendment, etc.*) Verfassungs-
constrain [kən'stren] *tr* zwingen
constraint [kən'strent] *s* Zwang *m*; (jur) Nötigung *f*
constrict [kən'strɪkt] *tr* zusammenziehen
construct [kən'strʌkt] *tr* errichten; (eng, geom, gram) konstruieren
construction [kən'strʌkʃən] *s* (*act of building*) Errichtung *f*; (*manner of building*) Bauweise *f*; (*interpretation*) Auslegung *f*; (eng, geom, gram) Konstruktion *f*; **under c.** im Bau
constructive [kən'strʌktɪv] *adj* konstruktiv
construe [kən'stru] *tr* (*interpret*) auslegen; (gram) konstruieren
consul ['kɒnsəl] *s* Konsul *m*
consular ['kɒns(j)ələr] *adj* konsularisch
consulate ['kɒns(j)əlɪt] *s* Konsulat *n*
con′sul gen′eral *s* Generalkonsul *m*
consult [kən'sʌlt] *tr* konsultieren, um Rat fragen; (*a book*) nachschlagen ‖ *intr*—**c. with** sich beraten mit
consultant [kən'sʌltənt] *s* Berater –in *mf*
consultation [ˌkɒnsəl'teʃən] *s* Beratung *f*; (& med) Konsultation *f*
consume [kən's(j)um] *tr* verzehren; (*use up*) verbrauchen; (*time*) beanspruchen
consumer [kən's(j)umər] *s* Konsument –in *mf*, Verbraucher –in *mf*
consum′er goods′ *spl* Konsumgüter *pl*
consummate [kən'sʌmɪt] *adj* vollendet; (pej) abgefeimt ‖ ['kɒnsəˌmet] *tr* vollziehen
consumption [kən'sʌmpʃən] *s* (*of food*) Verzehr *m*; (econ) (*of*) Verbrauch *m* (an *dat*); (pathol) Schwindsucht *f*
consumptive [kə'sʌmptɪv] *adj* schwindsüchtig ‖ *s* Schwindsüchtige *mf*
contact ['kɒntækt] *s* Kontakt *m*, Berührung *f*; (fig) (*with*) Verbindung *f* (mit); (elec) Kontakt *m* ‖ *tr* (coll) sich in Verbindung setzen mit
con′tact lens′ *s* Haftschale *f*
contagion [kən'tedʒən] *s* Ansteckung *f*
contagious [kən'tedʒəs] *adj* ansteckend
contain [kən'ten] *tr* enthalten; (*an*

enemy) aufhalten; (*one's feelings*) verhalten; **c. oneself** sich beherrschen
container [kən'tenər] *s* Behälter *m*
containment [kən'tenmənt] *s* (mil, pol) Eindämmung *f*
contaminate [kən'tæmɪˌnet] *tr* verunreinigen; (fig) vergiften
contamination [kənˌtæmɪ'neʃən] *s* Verunreinigung *f*; (fig) Vergiftung *f*
contemplate ['kɒntəmˌplet] *tr* betrachten; (*intend*) beabsichtigen ‖ *intr* nachdenken
contemplation [ˌkɒntəm'pleʃən] *s* Betrachtung *f*; (*consideration*) Erwägung *f*
contemporaneous [kənˌtempə'renɪˌəs] *adj* (*with*) gleichzeitig (mit)
contemporary [kən'tempəˌreri] *adj* zeitgenössisch; (*modern*) modern ‖ *s* Zeitgenosse *m*, Zeitgenossin *f*
contempt [kən'tempt] *s* Verachtung *f*; **beneath c.** unter aller Kritik
contemptible [kən'temptɪbəl] *adj* verachtungswürdig
contempt′ of court′ *s* Mißachtung *f* des Gerichtes
contemptuous [kən'temptʃʊˌəs] *adj* verachtungsvoll, verächtlich
contend [kən'tend] *tr* behaupten ‖ *intr* (**for**) sich bewerben (um); (**with**) kämpfen (mit)
contender [kən'tendər] *s* (**for**) Bewerber –in *mf* (um)
content [kən'tent] *adj* (**with**) zufrieden (mit); **c. to** (*inf*) bereit zu (*inf*) ‖ *s* Zufriedenheit *f*; **to one's heart's c.** nach Herzenslust ‖ ['kɒntent] *s* Inhalt *m*; (chem) Gehalt *m*; **contents** Inhalt *m* ‖ [kən'tent] *tr* zufriedenstellen; **c. oneself with** sich begnügen mit
content′ed *adj* zufrieden
contention [kən'tenʃən] *s* (*strife*) Streit *m*; (*assertion*) Behauptung *f*
contest ['kɒntest] *s* (**for**) Wettkampf *m* (um); (*written competition*) Preisausschreiben *n* ‖ [kən'test] *tr* (*argue against*) bestreiten; (*a will*) anfechten; (mil) kämpfen um; **contested** umstritten
contestant [kən'testənt] *s* Bewerber –in *mf*; (sport) Wettkämpfer –in *mf*
context ['kɒntekst] *s* Zusammenhang *m*
contiguous [kən'tɪgjuˌəs] *adj* einander berührend; (**to**) angrenzend (an *acc*)
continence ['kɒntɪnəns] *s* Enthaltsamkeit *f*
continent ['kɒntɪnənt] *adj* enthaltsam ‖ *s* Kontinent *m*
continental [ˌkɒntɪ'nentəl] *adj* kontinental, Kontinental-
contingency [kən'tɪndʒənsi] *s* Zufall *m*
contingent [kən'tɪndʒənt] *adj* (**upon**) abhängig (von) ‖ *s* (mil) Kontingent *n*
continual [kən'tɪnjuˌəl] *adj* immer wiederkehrend
continuation [kənˌtɪnju'eʃən] *s* Fortsetzung *f*; (*continued existence*) Fortdauer *f*
continue [kən'tɪnju] *tr* fortsetzen; **c.**

to (*inf*) fortfahren zu (*inf*); weiter-,
e.g., **c. to read** weiterlesen; **to be
continued** Fortsetzung folgt || *intr*
fortfahren; (*said of things*) anhalten

continuity [ˌkɑntɪ'n(j)u·ɪtɪ] *s* Stetig-
keit *f*

continuous [kən'tɪnju·əs] *adj* ununterbrochen, anhaltend

contortion [kən'tɔr/ən] *s* Verzerrung *f*

contour ['kɑntur] *s* Kontur *f*

con'tour line' *s* Schichtlinie *f*

con'tour map' *s* Landkarte *f* mit
Schichtlinien

contraband [ˈkɑntrəˌbænd] *adj*
Schmuggel- || *s* Konterbande *f*,
Schmuggelware *f*

contraceptive [ˌkɑntrə'septɪv] *adj*
empfängnisverhütend || *s* Empfäng-
nisverhütungsmittel *n*

contract [ˈkɑntrækt] *s* Vertrag *m*,
Kontrakt *m*; (*order*) Auftrag *m* ||
[kən'trækt] *tr* (*marriage*) (ab)schlie-
ßen; (*a disease*) sich [*dat*] zuziehen;
(*e.g., a muscle*) zusammenziehen;
(*debts*) geraten in (*acc*); (*ling*) kon-
trahieren || *intr* (*shrink*) sich zusam-
menziehen; **c. to** (*inf*) sich vertraglich verpflichten zu (*inf*)

contract'ing *adj* vertragsschließend

contraction [kən'trækʃən] *s* (& ling)
Zusammenziehung *f*, Kontraktion *f*;
(*contracted word*) Verkürzung *f*

contractor [ˈkɑntræktər] *s* (*supplier*)
Lieferant *m*; (*builder*) Bauunternehmer *m*

contradict [ˌkɑntrə'dɪkt] *tr* widersprechen (*dat*)

contradiction [ˌkɑntrə'dɪkʃən] *s*
Widerspruch *m*

contradictory [ˌkɑntrə'dɪktərɪ] *adj*
widerspruchsvoll

contrail [ˈkɑnˌtrel] *s* Kondensstreifen
m

contral·to [kən'trælto] *s* (-tos) (*person*) Altistin *f*; (*voice*) Alt *m*

contraption [kən'træpʃən] *s* (coll)
Vorrichtung *f*; (*car*) (coll) Kiste *f*

contrary [ˈkɑntrerɪ] *adj* konträr, gegensätzlich; (*person*) querköpfig; **c.
to** entgegen (*dat*); **c. to nature** na-
turwidrig || *s* Gegenteil *n*; **on the c.**
im Gegenteil

contrast [ˈkɑntræst] *s* Gegensatz *m* ||
[kən'træst] *tr* (with) gegenüber-
stellen (*dat*) || *intr* (with) im Gegen-
satz stehen (zu)

contravene [ˌkɑntrə'vin] *tr* zuwider-
handeln (*dat*)

contribute [kən'trɪbjut] *tr* beitragen,
spenden || *intr*—**c. to** beitragen zu;
(*with help*) mitwirken an (*dat*)

contribution [ˌkɑntrɪ'bjuʃən] *s* Beitrag *m*; (*of money*) Spende *f*

contributor [kən'trɪbjutər] *s* Spender
–in *mf*; (*to a periodical*) Mitarbeiter
–in *mf*

contrite [kən'traɪt] *adj* reuig

contrition [kən'trɪʃən] *s* Reue *f*

contrivance [kən'traɪvəns] *s* (*device*)
Vorrichtung *f*; (*expedient*) Kunstgriff *m*; (*act of contriving*) Aushecken *n*

contrive [kən'traɪv] *tr* (*invent*) erfin-

den; (*devise*) ersinnen; **c. to** (*inf*) es
fertig bringen zu (*inf*) || *intr* An-
schläge aushecken

con·trol [kən'trol] *s* Kontrolle *f*, Gewalt *f*; (mach) Steuerung *f*; (mach)
(*devise*) Regler *m*; **be out of c.** nicht
zu halten sein; **be under c.** in bester
Ordnung sein; **controls** (aer) Steuer-
werk *n*; **gain c. over** die Herrschaft
gewinnen über (*acc*); **have c. over**
s.o. über j–n Gewalt haben; **keep
under c.** im Zaume halten || *v* (*pret
& pp* -**trolled**; *ger* -**trolling**) *tr* (*dominate*) beherrschen; (*verify*) kontrollieren; (*contain*) eindämmen; (*steer*)
steuern; (*regulate*) regeln; **c. oneself**
sich beherrschen

control' pan'el *s* Schaltbrett *n*

control' room' *s* Kommandoraum *m*;
(rad) Regieraum *m*

control' stick' *s* (at an airport) Steuerknüppel *m*

control' tow'er *s* (*at an airport*) Kon-
trollturm *m*; (*on an aircraft carrier*)
Kommandoturm *m*

controversial [ˌkɑntrə'vʌrʃəl] *adj* umstritten, strittig; **c. subject** Streitfrage *f*

controversy [ˈkɑntrəˌvʌrsɪ] *s* Kontroverse *f*, Auseinandersetzung *f*

controvert [ˈkɑntrəˌvʌrt] *tr* (*argue
against*) bestreiten; (*argue about*)
streiten über (*acc*)

contusion [kən't(j)uʒən] *s* Quetschung
f

convalesce [ˌkɑnvə'les] *intr* genesen

convalescence [ˌkɑnvə'lesəns] *s* Genesung *f*

convalescent [ˌkɑnvə'lesənt] *s* Gene-
sende *mf*

convales'cent home' *s* Genesungsheim
n

convene [kən'vin] *tr* versammeln ||
intr sich versammeln

convenience [kən'vinjəns] *s* Bequem-
lichkeit *f*; **at one's c.** nach Belieben;
at your earliest c. möglichst bald;
modern conveniences moderner
Komfort *m*

convenient [kən'vinjənt] *adj* gelegen

convent ['kɑnvent] *s* Nonnenkloster *n*

convention [kən'venʃən] *s* (*professional meeting*) Tagung *f*; (*political
meeting*) Konvent *m*; (*accepted usage*) Konvention *f*

conventional [kən'venʃənəl] *adj* konventionell, herkömmlich

converge [kən'vʌrdʒ] *intr* zusammenlaufen; **c. on** sich stürzen auf (*acc*)

conversation [ˌkɑnvər'seʃən] *s* Gespräch *n*

conversational [ˌkɑnvər'seʃənəl] *adj*
Gesprächs-

converse ['kɑnvʌrs] *adj* gegenteilig ||
s (of) Gegenteil *n* (von) || [kən'vʌrs]
intr sich unterhalten

conversion [kən'vʌrʒən] *s* (into) Umwandlung *f* (in *acc*); (*of a factory*)
(to) Umstellung *f* (auf *acc*); (*of a
building*) (into) Umbau *m* (zu); (*of
currency*) (into) Umwechslung *f* (in
acc); (elec) (to) Umformung *f* (in
acc); (math) Umrechnung *f*; (phys)
Umsetzung *f*; (relig) Bekehrung *f*

convert [ˈkɒnvᴧrt] *s* **(to)** Bekehrte *m/f* (zu) ‖ [kənˈvᴧrt] *tr* **(into)** umwandeln (in *acc*); (*a factory*) **(to)** umstellen (auf *acc*); (*a building*) **(into)** umbauen (zu); (*currency*) **(into)** umwechseln (in *acc*); (*biochem*) **(into)** umsetzen (in *acc*); (*chem*) **(into)** umwandeln (in *acc*), verwandeln (in *acc*); (*elec*) **(to)** umformen (in *acc*); (*math*) **(to)** umrechnen (in *acc*); (*phys*) **(to)** umsetzen (in *acc*); (*relig*) **(to)** bekehren (zu) ‖ *intr* **(to)** sich bekehren (zu)

converter [kənˈvᴧrtər] *s* (elec) Umformer *m*, Stromrichter *m*

convertible [kənˈvᴧrtɪbəl] *adj* umwandelbar; (fin) konvertierbar ‖ *s* (aut) Kabriolett *n*

convex [ˈkɒnveks], [kənˈveks] *adj* konvex

convey [kənˈve] *tr* (*transport*) befördern; (*greetings, message*) übermitteln; (*sound*) fortpflanzen; (*meaning*) ausdrücken; (*a property*) abtreten

conveyance [kənˈve·əns] *s* (*act*) Beförderung *f*; (*means*) Transportmittel *n*; (jur) Abtretung *f*

conveyor [kənˈve·ər] *s* Beförderer –in *mf*

convey'or belt' *s* Förderband *n*

convict [ˈkɒnvɪkt] *s* Sträfling *m* ‖ [kənˈvɪkt] *tr* **(of)** überführen (genit)

conviction [kənˈvɪkʃən] *s* (*of a crime*) Verurteilung *f*; (*certainty*) Überzeugung *f*; **convictions** Gesinnung *f*

convince [kənˈvɪns] *tr* **(of)** überzeugen (von)

convivial [kənˈvɪvɪ·əl] *adj* gesellig

convocation [ˌkɒnvəˈkeʃən] *s* Zusammenberufung *f*; (educ) Eröffnungsfeier *f*

convoke [kənˈvok] *tr* zusammenberufen

convoy [ˈkɒnvɔɪ] *s* (*of vehicles*) Kolonne *f*, Konvoi *m*; (nav) Geleitzug *m*

convulse [kənˈvᴧls] *tr* erschüttern

convulsion [kənˈvᴧlʃən] *s* Krampf *m*; **go into convulsions** Krämpfe bekommen

coo [ku] *intr* girren

cook [kuk] *s* Koch *m*, Köchin *f* ‖ *tr* braten, backen; (*boil*) kochen; **c. up** (fig) zusammenbrauen ‖ *intr* braten, backen; (*boil*) kochen

cook'book' *s* Kochbuch *n*

cookie [ˈkuki] *s* Plätzchen *n*, Keks *m* & *n*; **cookies** *pl* Gebäck *n*

cook'ing *s* Kochen *n*; **do one's own c.** sich selbst beköstigen

cool [kul] *adj* (& fig) kühl; **keep c.!** ruhig Blut!; **keep one's c.** (coll) ruhig Blut bewahren ‖ *s* Kühle *f* ‖ *tr* kühlen; **c. down** (fig) beruhigen; **c. off** abkühlen ‖ *intr* (& fig) sich abkühlen

cooler [ˈkulər] *s* Kühler *m*; (sl) Kittchen *n*

cool'-head'ed *adj* besonnen

coolie [ˈkuli] *s* Kuli *m*

coolness [ˈkulnɪs] *s* (& fig) Kühle *f*

coon [kun] *s* (zool) Waschbär *m*

coop [kup] *s* (*building*) Hühnerstall *m*; (*enclosure*) Hühnerhof *m*; (jail) (sl) Kittchen *n*; **fly the c.** (sl) auskneifen ‖ *tr*—**c. up** einsperren

co-op [ˈko·ɑp] *s* Konsumverein *m*

cooper [ˈkupər] *s* Küfer *m*, Böttcher *m*

cooperate [koˈɑpəˌret] *intr* (in) mitwirken (an *dat*, bei); **(with)** mitarbeiten (mit)

cooperation [koˌɑpəˈreʃən] *s* Mitwirkung *f*, Mitarbeit *f*

cooperative [koˈɑpəˌretɪv] *adj* hilfsbereit

coordinate [koˈɔrdɪnɪt] *adj* gleichrangig; (gram) beigeordnet ‖ *s* (math) Koordinate *f* ‖ [koˈɔrdɪˌnet] *tr* koordinieren

coordination [koˌɔrdɪˈneʃən] *s* Koordination *f*; (gram) Beiordnung *f*

cootie [ˈkuti] *s* (sl) Laus *f*

co-owner [ˈkoˌonər] *s* Miteigentümer –in *mf*

cop [kɒp] *s* (sl) Bulle *m* ‖ *v* (*pret & pp* **copped**; *ger* **copped**) *tr* (*catch*) (sl) erwischen; (*steal*) (sl) klauen ‖ *intr*—**cop out** (coll) auskneifen

copartner [koˈpɑrtnər] *s* Mitinhaber –in *mf*

cope [kop] *intr*—**c. with** sich messen mit, aufkommen gegen

cope'stone' *s* Schlußstein *m*

copier [ˈkɑpɪ·ər] *s* Kopiermaschine *f*

copilot [ˈkoˌpaɪlət] *s* Kopilot *m*

coping [ˈkopɪŋ] *s* Mauerkappe *f*

copious [ˈkopɪ·əs] *adj* reichlich

cop'-out' *s* (*act*) Kneifen *n*; (*person*) Drückeberger *m*

copper [ˈkɑpər] *adj* kupfern, Kupfer–; (*color*) kupferrot ‖ *s* Kupfer *n*; (*coin*) Kupfermünze *f*; (sl) Schupo *m*

cop'persmith' *s* Kupferschmied *m*

copter [ˈkɑptər] *s* (coll) Hubschrauber *m*

copulate [ˈkɑpjəˌlet] *intr* sich paaren

cop·y [ˈkɑpi] *s* Kopie *f*; (*of a book*) Exemplar *n*; (typ) druckfertiges Manuskript *n* ‖ *v* (*pret & pp* **–ied**) *tr* kopieren; (*in school*) abschreiben

cop'ybook' *s* Schreibheft *n*, Heft *n*

cop'ycat' *s* (*imitator*) Nachäffer –in *mf*

cop'yright' *s* Urheberrecht *n*, Verlagsrecht *n* ‖ *tr* urheberrechtlich schützen, verlagsrechtlich schützen

cop'ywrit'er *s* Texter –in *mf*

coquette [koˈket] *s* Kokette *f*

coquettish [koˈketɪʃ] *adj* kokett

coral [ˈkɔrəl] *adj* Korallen– ‖ *s* Koralle *f*

cor'al reef' *s* Korallenriff *n*

cord [kɔrd] *s* Schnur *f*, Strick *m*; (*of wood*) Klafter *n*; (elec) Leitungsschnur *f*

cordial [ˈkɔrdʒəl] *adj* herzlich ‖ *s* Likör *m*; (med) Herzstärkung *f*

cordiality [kɔrˈdʒælɪti] *s* Herzlichkeit *f*

cordon [ˈkɔrdən] *s* Kordon *m*, Absperrkette *f* ‖ *tr*—**c. off** absperren

corduroy [ˈkɔrdəˌrɔɪ] *s* Kordsamt *m*; **corduroys** Kordsamthose *f*

core [kɔr] *s* (*of fruit*) Kern *m*; (*of a*

cable) Seele *f;* (fig) Kern *m,* Mark *n;* (elec) Spulenkern *m*

cork [kɔrk] *s* Kork *m;* (*stopper*) Pfropfen *m,* Korken *m* ‖ *tr* verkorken

corker ['kɔrkər] *s* (sl) Schlager *m*

cork'ing *adj* (sl) fabelhaft

cork'oak', cork' tree' *s* Korkeiche *f*

cork'screw' *s* Korkenzieher *m*

corn [kɔrn] *s* (*Indian corn*) Mais *m;* (*on a foot*) Hühnerauge *n;* (*joke*) (sl) Kalauer *m*

corn'bread' *s* Maisbrot *n*

corn'cob' *s* Maiskolben *m*

corn'cob pipe' *s* Maiskolbenpfeife *f*

corn'crib' *s* Maisspeicher *m*

cornea ['kɔrnɪ-ə] *s* Hornhaut *f*

corned' beef' ['kɔrnd] *s* Pökelfleisch *n*

corner ['kɔrnər] *adj* Eck– ‖ *s* Ecke *f;* (*secluded spot*) Winkel *m;* (*curve*) Kurve *f;* **c. of the eye** Augenwinkel *m;* **from all corners of the world** von allen Ecken und Enden; **turn the c.** um die Ecke biegen ‖ *tr* (*a person*) in die Zange nehmen; (*the market*) aufkaufen

cor'nerstone' *s* Eckstein *m;* (*of a new building*) Grundstein *m*

cornet [kɔr'nɛt] *s* (mus) Kornett *n*

corn' exchange' *s* Getreidebörse *f*

corn'field' *s* Maisfeld *n;* (*grain field*) (Brit) Kornfeld *n*

corn'flakes' *spl* Maisflocken *pl*

corn' flour' *s* Maismehl *n*

corn'flow'er *s* Kornblume *f*

corn' frit'ter *s* Maispfannkuchen *m*

corn'husk' *s* Maishülse *f*

cornice ['kɔrnɪs] *s* Gesims *n*

corn' liq'uor *s* Maisschnaps *m*

corn' meal' *s* Maismehl *n*

corn' on the cob' *s* Mais *m* am Kolben

corn' silk' *s* Maisfasern *pl*

corn'stalk' *s* Maisstengel *m*

corn'starch' *s* Maisstärke *f*

cornucopia [ˌkɔrnə'kopɪ-ə] *s* Füllhorn *n*

corny ['kɔrni] *adj* (*sentimental*) rührselig; (*joke*) blöd

corollary ['kɔrəˌlɛri] *s* (**to**) Folge *f* (von)

coron·a [kə'ronə] *s* (**–nas** & **–nae** [ni]) (astr) Hof *m,* Korona *f;* (archit) Kranzleiste *f*

coronary ['kɔrəˌnɛri] *adj* koronar

coronation [ˌkɔrə'neʃən] *s* Krönung *f*

coroner ['kɔrənər] *s* Gerichtsmediziner *m*

cor'oner's in'quest *s* Totenschau *f*

coronet ['kɔrəˌnɛt] *s* Krönchen *n;* (*worn by the nobility*) Adelskrone *f;* (*worn by women*) Diadem *n*

corporal ['kɔrpərəl] *adj* körperlich ‖ *s* (mil) Obergefreite *m*

corporate ['kɔrpərɪt] *adj* korporativ

corporation [ˌkɔrpə'reʃən] *s* (fin) Aktiengesellschaft *f;* (jur) Körperschaft *f*

corpora'tion law'yer *s* Syndikus *m*

corporeal [kɔr'porɪ-əl] *adj* körperlich

corps [kor] *s* (**corps** [korz]) Korps *n*

corpse [kɔrps] *s* Leiche *f,* Leichnam *m*

corps'man *s* (**–men**) Sanitäter *m*

corpulent ['kɔrpjələnt] *adj* beleibt

corpuscle ['kɔrpəsəl] *s* Blutkörperchen *n*

cor·ral [kə'ræl] *s* Pferch *m* ‖ *v* (*pret* & *pp* **–ralled;** *ger* **–ralling**) *tr* zusammenpferchen

correct [kə'rɛkt] *adj* richtig; (*manners*) korrekt; (*time*) genau; **be c.** (*said of a thing*) stimmen; (*said of a person*) recht haben ‖ *tr* korrigieren; (*examination papers*) verbessern; (*beat*) züchtigen; (*scold*) zurechtweisen; (*an unjust situation*) ausgleichen

correction [kə'rɛkʃən] *s* Berichtigung *f;* (*of examination papers*) Verbesserung *f,* Korrektur *f;* (*punishment*) Bestrafung *f*

corrective [kə'rɛktɪv] *adj* (*measures*) Gegen–; (*lenses, shoes*) Ausgleichs–

correctness [kə'rɛktnɪs] *s* Richtigkeit *f;* (*in manners*) Korrektheit *f*

correlate ['kɔrəˌlet] *tr* in Wechselbeziehung bringen ‖ *intr* in Wechselbeziehung stehen

correlation [ˌkɔrə'leʃən] *s* Wechselbeziehung *f,* Korrelation *f*

correlative [kə'rɛlətɪv] *adj* korrelativ ‖ *s* Korrelat *n*

correspond [ˌkɔrɪ'spand] *intr* einander übereinstimmen; (**to, with**) entsprechen (*dat*); (*exchange letters*) (**with**) im Briefwechsel stehen (**mit**)

correspondence [ˌkɔrɪ'spandəns] *s* (*act of corresponding*) Übereinstimmung *f;* (*instance of correspondence*) Entsprechung *f;* (*exchange of letters; letters*) Korrespondenz *f*

correspon'dence course' *s* Fernkursus *m*

correspondent [ˌkɔrɪ'spandənt] *s* Briefpartner **–in** *mf;* (journ) Korrespondent **–in** *mf*

correspond'ing *adj* entsprechend

corridor ['kɔrɪdər] *s* Korridor *m*

corroborate [kə'rabəˌret] *tr* bestätigen

corrode [kə'rod] *tr* & *intr* korrodieren

corrosion [kə'roʒən] *s* Korrosion *f*

corrosive [kə'rosɪv] *adj* ätzend; (*influence*) schädigend ‖ *s* Ätzmittel *n*

cor'rugated card'board ['kɔrəˌgetɪd] *s* Wellpappe *f*

cor'rugated i'ron *s* Wellblech *n*

corrupt [kə'rʌpt] *adj* (*text*) verderbt; (*morally*) verdorben; (*open to bribes*) bestechlich ‖ *tr* verderben; (*bribe*) bestechen

corruption [kə'rʌpʃən] *s* Verderbtheit *f;* (*bribery*) Korruption *f*

corsage [kɔr'saʒ] *s* Blumensträußchen *n* zum Anstecken

corsair ['kɔrsɛr] *s* Korsar *m*

corset ['kɔrsɪt] *s* Korsett *n*

Corsica ['kɔrsɪkə] *s* Korsika *f*

Corsican ['kɔrsɪkən] *adj* korsisch

cortege [kɔr'tɛʒ] *s* Gefolge *n;* (*at a funeral*) Leichenzug *m*

cor·tex ['kɔr,tɛks] *s* (**–tices** [tɪˌsiz]) Rinde *f,* Kortex *m*

cortisone ['kɔrtɪˌson] *s* Cortison *n*

corvette [kɔr'vɛt] *s* (naut) Korvette *f*

cosmetic [kaz'mɛtɪk] *adj* kosmetisch ‖ *s* Kosmetikum *n;* **cosmetics** Kosmetikartikel *pl*

cosmic ['kɑzmɪk] *adj* kosmisch
cosmonaut ['kɑzmə‚nɔt] *s* Kosmonaut –in *mf*
cosmopolitan [‚kɑzə'pɑlɪtən] *adj* kosmopolitisch ‖ *s* Kosmopolit –in *mf*
cosmos ['kɑzməs] *s* Kosmos *m*
cost [kɔst] *s* Preis *m*; **at all costs** (fig) um jeden Preis; **at c.** zum Selbstkostenpreis; **at the c. of** auf Kosten (*genit*); **costs** Kosten *pl*; (jur) Gerichtskosten *pl* ‖ *v* (*pret & pp* **cost**) *intr* kosten
cost′ account′ing *s* Kostenrechnung *f*
costly ['kɔstlɪ] *adj* kostspielig; (*of great value*) kostbar
cost′ of liv′ing *s* Lebenshaltungskosten *pl*
costume ['kɑst(j)um] *s* Kostüm *n*; (*national dress*) Tracht *f*
cos′tume ball′ *s* Kostümball *m*
cos′tume jew′elry *s* Modeschmuck *m*
cot [kɑt] *s* Feldbett *n*
coterie ['kotərɪ] *s* Klüngel *m*, Koterie *f*
cottage ['kɑtɪdʒ] *s* Hütte *f*; (*country house*) Landhaus *n*
cot′tage cheese′ *s* Quark *m*, Quarkkäse *m*
cot′ter pin′ ['kɑtər] *s* Schließbolzen *m*
cotton ['kɑtən] *s* (*fiber, yarn*) Baumwolle *f*; (*unspun cotton*) Watte *f*; (*sterilized cotton*) Verbandswatte *f*
cot′ton field′ *s* Baumwollfeld *n*
cot′ton gin′ *s* Entkörnungsmaschine *f*
cot′ton mill′ *s* Baumwollspinnerei *f*
cot′ton pick′er ['pɪkər] *s* Baumwollpflücker –in *mf*; (*machine*) Baumwollpflückmaschine *f*
cot′tonseed oil′ *s* Baumwollsamenöl *n*
cot′ton waste′ *s* Putzwolle *f*
couch [kautʃ] *s* Couch *f*, Liege *f* ‖ *tr* (*words*) fassen; (*thoughts*) ausdrücken
cougar ['kugər] *s* Puma *m*
cough [kɔf] *s* Husten *m* ‖ *tr*—**c. up** aushusten; (*money*) (sl) blechen ‖ *intr* husten; (*in order to attract attention*) sich räuspern
cough′ drop′ *s* Hustenbonbon *m & n*
cough′ syr′up *s* Hustentropfen *pl*
could [kud] *aux*—**he c.** (*was able*) er konnte; **if he c.** (*were able*) wenn er könnte
council ['kaunsəl] *s* Rat *m*; (eccl) Konzil *n*
coun′cil·man *s* (**–men**) Stadtratsmitglied *n*
councilor ['kaunsələr] *s* Rat *m*
coun·sel ['kaunsəl] *s* Rat *m*; (*for the defense*) Verteidiger –in *mf*; (*for the prosecution*) Anklagevertreter –in *mf* ‖ *v* (*pret & pp* **-sel[l]ed**; *ger* **-sel[l]ing**) *tr* raten (*dat*) ‖ *intr* Rat geben
counselor ['kaunsələr] *s* Berater –in *mf*
count [kaunt] *s* Zahl *f*; (*nobleman*) Graf *m*; (jur) Anklagepunkt *m*; **lose c.** sich verzählen ‖ *tr* zählen; (*the costs*) berechnen; **c. in** einschließen; **c. off** abzählen; **c. out** (*money, a boxer*) auszählen ‖ *intr* zählen; **c. for little** (or **much**) wenig (or viel)

gelten; **c. off** (mil) abzählen; **c. on** zählen auf (*acc*)
count′down′ *s* Countdown *m & n*
countenance ['kauntɪnəns] *s* Antlitz *n* ‖ *tr* (*tolerate*) zulassen; (*approve*) billigen
counter ['kauntər] *adj* Gegen– ‖ *adv*—**c. to** wider; **run c. to** zuwiderlaufen (*dat*) ‖ *s* Zähler *m*; (*in games*) Spielmarke *f*; (*in a store*) Ladentisch *m*, Theke *f*; (*in a restaurant*) Büffet *n*; (*in a bank*) Schalter *m*; **under the c.** (fig) heimlich ‖ *tr* widerstreben (*dat*); (*in speech*) widersprechen (*dat*) ‖ *intr* Gegenmaßnahmen treffen; (box) kontern, nachschlagen
coun′teract′ *tr* entgegenwirken (*dat*)
coun′terattack′ *s* Gegenangriff *m* ‖ *tr* e–n Gegenangriff machen auf (*acc*) ‖ *intr* e–n Gegenangriff machen
coun′terbal′ance *s* Gegengewicht *n* ‖ *coun′terbal′ance* *tr* das Gegengewicht halten (*dat*)
coun′terclock′wise *adj* linksläufig ‖ *adv* entgegen der Uhrzeigerrichtung
coun′teres′pionage *s* Gegenspionage *f*
counterfeit ['kauntərfɪt] *adj* gefälscht ‖ *s* Fälschung *f*; (*money*) Falschgeld *n* ‖ *tr* fälschen
counterfeiter ['kauntər‚fɪtər] *s* Falschmünzer –in *mf*
coun′terfeit mon′ey *s* Falschgeld *n*
coun′terintel′ligence *s* Spionageabwehr *f*
countermand ['kauntər‚mænd] *s* Gegenbefehl *m* ‖ *tr* widerrufen
coun′termeas′ure *s* Gegenmaßnahme *f*
coun′teroffen′sive *s* Gegenoffensive *f*
coun′terpart′ *s* Gegenstück *n*; (*person*) Ebenbild *n*
coun′terpoint′ *s* (mus) Kontrapunkt *m*
coun′terrevolu′tion *s* Konterrevolution *f*
coun′tersign′ *s* Gegenzeichen *n* ‖ *tr & intr* mitunterzeichnen
coun′tersink′ *v* (*pret & pp* **-sunk**) *tr* (*a screw*) versenken; (*a hole*) ausfräsen
coun′terspy′ *s* Gegenspion –in *mf*
coun′terstroke′ *s* Gegenstoß *m*
coun′terweight′ *s* Gegengewicht *n*
countess ['kauntɪs] *s* Gräfin *f*
countless ['kauntlɪs] *adj* zahllos
countrified ['kʌntrɪ‚faɪd] *adj* ländlich; (*boorish*) bäu(e)risch
country ['kʌntrɪ] *adj* (*air, house, life, road*) Land– ‖ *s* (*state; rural area*) Land *n*; (*land of birth*) Heimatland *n*; **in the c.** auf dem Lande; **to the c.** aufs Land
coun′try club′ *s* exklusiver Klub *m* auf dem Lande
coun′tryfolk′ *spl* Landvolk *n*
coun′try gen′tleman *s* Landedelmann *m*
coun′try·man *s* (**–men**) Landsmann *m*
coun′tryside′ *s* Landschaft *f*, Land *n*
coun′try-wide′ *adj* über das ganze Land verbreitet (or ausgedehnt)
county ['kauntɪ] *s* Kreis *m*
coun′ty seat′ *s* Kreisstadt *f*

coup [ku] *s* Coup *m*

coup d'état [ku de 'tɑ] *s* Staatsstreich *m*

coupe [ku'pe], [kup] *s* Coupé *n*

couple ['kʌpəl] *s* Paar *n*; (*of lovers*) Liebespaar *n*; (*man and wife*) Ehepaar *n*; (*phys*) Kräftepaar *n*; **a c. of** ein paar, e.g., **a c. of days ago** vor ein paar Tagen ‖ *tr* koppeln ‖ *intr* sich paaren

couplet ['kʌplɪt] *s* Verspaar *n*

coupling ['kʌplɪŋ] *s* Verbindungsstück *n*; (rad) Kopplung *f*; (rr) Kupplung *f*

coupon ['k(j)upɑn] *s* Gutschein *m*

courage ['kʌrɪdʒ] *s* Mut *m*, Courage *f*; **get up the c. to** (inf) sich [dat] ein Herz fassen zu (inf)

courageous [kə'redʒəs] *adj* mutig

courier ['kʌrɪ·ər] *s* Eilbote *m*; (tour guide) Reiseleiter –in *mf*

course [kors] *s* (direction) Richtung *f*, Kurs *m*; (of a river, of time) Lauf *m*; (method of procedure) Weg *m*, Weise *f*, Kurs *m*; (in racing) Bahn *f*; (archit) Schicht *f*; (culin) Gang *m*; (educ) Kurs *m*; **c. of action** Handlungsweise *f*; **go off c.** (aer) sich verfliegen; **in due c.** zur rechten Zeit; **in the c. of** im Verlaufe von (or genit); (with expressions of time) im Laufe (genit); **of c.** natürlich; **run its c.** seinen Verlauf nehmen

court [kort] *s* (of a king) Hof *m*; (of justice) Gericht *n*; (yard) Hof *m*; (tennis) Platz *m*; **in c.** (or **into c.** or **to c.**) vor Gericht; **out of c.** außergerichtlich ‖ *tr* (a girl) werben um; (danger) suchen; (disaster) heraufbeschwören

courteous ['kʌrtɪ·əs] *adj* höflich

courtesan ['kɔrtɪʒən] *s* Kurtisane *f*

courtesy ['kʌrtɪsɪ] *s* Höflichkeit *f*; **by c. of** freundlicherweise zur Verfügung gestellt von

court'house' *s* Gerichtsgebäude *n*

courtier ['kortɪ·ər] *s* Höfling *m*

courtly ['kortlɪ] *adj* höfisch

court'-mar'tial *s* (**courts-martial**) Kriegsgericht *n* ‖ *v* (pret & pp –tial[l]ed; ger –tial[l]ing) *tr* vor ein Kriegsgericht stellen

court'room' *s* Gerichtssaal *m*

court'ship' *s* Werbung *f*

court'yard' *s* Hof *m*

cousin ['kʌzɪn] *s* Vetter *m*; (female) Kusine *f*

cove [kov] *s* Bucht *f*

covenant ['kʌvənənt] *s* Vertrag *m*; (Bib) Bund *m*

cover ['kʌvər] *s* Decke *f*; (lid) Deckel *m*; (wrapping) Hülle *f*; (e.g., of a bed) Bezug *m*; (of a book) Einband *m*; (protection) Schutz *m*; (mil) Deckung *f*; **from c. to c.** von vorn bis hinten; **take c.** sich unterstellen; **under c.** im Geheimen; **under c. of night** im Schutz der Dunkelheit ‖ *tr* bedecken, decken; (conceal) verdecken; (distances) zurücklegen; (a sales territory) bearbeiten; (a bet) die gleiche Summe setzen gegen; (ex-penses, losses) decken; (upholstered furniture) beziehen; (deal with) behandeln; (include) umfassen; (material in class) durchnehmen; (said of a reporter) berichten über (acc); (said of plants) bewachsen; (with insurance) versichern, decken; (protect with a gun) sichern; (threaten with a gun) in Schach halten; (have within range) beherrschen; **c. up** zudecken; (conceal) verheimlichen ‖ *intr*—**c. for** einspringen für

coverage ['kʌvərɪdʒ] *s* (area covered) Verbreitungsgebiet *n*; (of news) Berichterstattung *f*; (rad, telv) Sendebereich *m*

coveralls ['kʌvər͵ɔlz] *spl* Monteuranzug *m*

cov'ered wag'on *s* Planwagen *m*

cov'er girl' *s* Covergirl *n*

cov'ering *s* Decke *f*, Bedeckung *f*

covert ['kovərt] *adj* verborgen

cov'erup' *s* Beschönigung *f*, Bemäntelung *f*

covet ['kʌvɪt] *tr* begehren

covetous ['kʌvɪtəs] *adj* begehrlich

covetousness ['kʌvɪtəsnɪs] *s* Begehrlichkeit *f*

covey ['kʌvɪ] *s* (brood) Brut *f*; (small flock) Schwarm *m*; (bevy) Schar *f*

cow [kau] *s* Kuh *f* ‖ *tr* einschüchtern

coward ['kau·ərd] *s* Feigling *m*, Memme *f*

cowardice ['kau·ərdɪs] *s* Feigheit *f*

cowardly ['kau·ərdlɪ] *adj* feig(e)

cow'bell' *s* Kuhglocke *f*

cow'boy' *s* Cowboy *m*

cower ['kau·ər] *intr* kauern

cow'herd' *s* Kuhhirt *m*

cow'hide' *s* Rindsleder *n*

cowl [kaul] *s* (on a chimney) Schornsteinkappe *f*; (aer) Motorhaube *f*; (eccl) Kapuze *f*

cowling ['kaulɪŋ] *s* (aer) Motorhaube *f*

co-worker ['ko͵wɑrkər] *s* Mitarbeiter –in *mf*

cowpox ['kau͵pɑks] *s* Kuhpocken *pl*

coxswain ['kɑksən] *s* Steuermann *m*

coy [kɔɪ] *adj* spröde

coyote [kaɪ'otɪ], ['kaɪ·ot] *s* Kojote *m*, Präriewolf *m*, Steppenwolf *m*

cozy ['kozɪ] *adj* gemütlich

C.P.A. ['si'pi'e] *s* (**certified public accountant**) amtlich zugelassener Wirtschaftsprüfer *m*

crab [kræb] *s* Krabbe *f*; (grouch) Sauertopf *m*

crab' ap'ple *s* Holzapfel *m*

crabbed ['kræbɪd] *adj* mürrisch; (handwriting) unleserlich; (style) schwer verständlich, verworren

crabby ['kræbɪ] *adj* mürrisch, grämlich

crack [kræk] *adj* erstklassig; (troops) Elite– ‖ *s* Riß *m*, Sprung *m*; (of a whip or rifle) Knall *m*; (blow) (sl) Klaps *m*; (opportunity) (sl) Gelegenheit *f*; (try) (sl) Versuch *m*; (cutting remark) (sl) Seitenhieb *m*; **at the c. of dawn** bei Tagesanbruch; **take a c. at** (sl) versuchen ‖ *tr* spalten; (a nut, safe) knacken; (an egg) aufschlagen;

(a code) entziffern; (hit) (sl) e-n
Klaps geben (dat); (chem) spalten;
c. a joke e-n Witz reißen; **c. a smile**
lächeln || *intr (make a cracking
sound)* knacken, krachen; *(develop
a crack)* rissig werden; *(said of a
whip or rifle)* knallen; *(said of a
voice)* umschlagen; *(said of ice)*
(zer) springen; **c. down on** scharf
vorgehen gegen; **c. up** (coll) überschnappen; (aut) aufknallen

cracked *adj (split)* rissig; *(crazy)* (sl)
übergeschnappt

cracker ['krækər] *s* Keks *m & n*

crack'erjack' *adj* (coll) erstklassig || *s*
(coll) Kanone *f*

crackle ['krækəl] *s* Krakelierung *f* ||
tr krakelieren *intr* prasseln

crack'pot' *adj* (sl) verrückt || *s* (sl)
Verrückte *mf*

crack'shot' *s* Meisterschütze *m*

crack'-up' *s* (aut) Zusammenstoß *m*

cradle ['kredəl] *s* Wiege *f*; (telp) Ga-
bel *f* || *tr* in den Armen wiegen

craft [kræft] *s* Handwerk *n*, Gewerbe
n; (naut) Fahrzeug *n*; by c. durch
List || *spl* Fahrzeuge *pl*, Schiffe *pl*;
small c. kleine Schiffe *pl*

craftiness ['kræftɪnɪs] *s* List *f*

crafts·man ['kræftsmən] *s* (—men)
Handwerker *m*

crafts'manship' *s* Kunstfertigkeit *f*

crafty ['kræftɪ] *adj* arglistig

crag [kræg] *s* Felszacke *f*

cram [kræm] *v (pret & pp crammed;
ger cramming) tr* vollstopfen; **c. into**
hineinstopfen in (acc) || *intr* (educ)
büffeln, ochsen; **c. into** sich hinein-
zwängen in (acc)

cram'course' *s* Presse *f*

cramp [kræmp] *s* Krampf *m*; *(clamp)*
Klammer *f* || *tr* einschränken, been-
gen

cramped *adj* eng

cranberry ['kræn,berɪ] *s* Preiselbeere
f

crane [kren] *s* (mach) Kran *m*; (orn)
Kranich *m* ||—**c. one's neck** den Hals
recken

crani·um ['krenɪ·əm] *s* (—a [ə]) *s*
Hirnschale *f*, Schädel *m*

crank [kræŋk] *s* Kurbel *f*; (grouch)
(coll) Griesgram *m*; *(eccentric)* (coll)
Sonderling *m* || *tr* kurbeln; **c. up**
ankurbeln

crank'case' *s* Kurbelgehäuse *n*

crank'shaft' *s* Kurbelwelle *f*

cranky ['kræŋkɪ] *adj* launisch

cranny ['krænɪ] *s* Ritze *f*

crap [kræp] *s (nonsense)* (sl) Unsinn
m; **craps** Würfel *pl*; **shoot craps**
Würfel spielen

crash [kræʃ] *s* Krach *m*; (aer) Absturz
m; (aut) Zusammenstoß *m*; (econ)
Zusammenbruch *m* || *tr* zerschmet-
tern; *(a party)* hineinplatzen in
(acc); (aer) zum Absturz bringen ||
intr (produce a crashing sound)
krachen; *(shatter)* zerbrechen; *(collapse)* zusammenstürzen; (aer) abstürzen; (aut) zusammenstoßen; **c.
into** fahren gegen

crash'dive' *s* Schnelltauchen *n*

crash'-dive' *intr* schnelltauchen

crash'hel'met *s* Sturzhelm *m*

crash'land'ing *s* Bruchlandung *f*

crash'pro'gram *s* Gewaltkur *f*

crass [kræs] *adj* kraß

crate [kret] *s* Lattenkiste *f*; *(old car,
old plane)* (coll) Kiste *f* || *tr* in e-r
Lattenkiste verpacken

crater ['kretər] *s* Krater *m*; *(of a
bomb)* Trichter *m*

crave [krev] *tr* ersehnen || *intr*—**c. for**
verlangen nach

craven ['krevən] *adj* feige || *s* Feigling
m

crav'ing *s* (for) Verlangen *n* (nach)

craw [krɔ] *s* Kropf *m*

crawl [krɔl] *s* Kriechen *n* || *intr* krie-
chen; *(said of the skin)* kribbeln;
(said of a swimmer) kraulen; *(said
of cars)* schleichen; **c. along** im
Schneckentempo gehen (or fahren);
c. into a hole (& fig) sich verkrie-
chen; **c. with** wimmeln von

crayon ['kre·ən] *s (wax crayon)*
Wachsmalkreide *f*; *(colored pencil)*
Farbstift *m*; *(artist's crayon)* Zei-
chenkreide *f*

craze [krez] *s* Mode *f*, Verrücktheit *f*
|| *tr* verrückt machen

crazy ['krezɪ] *adj* verrückt; *(senseless)*
sinnlos; **c. about** verrückt nach; **c.
idea** Wahnidee *f*; **drive c.** verrückt
machen

cra'zy bone' *s* Musikantenknochen *m*

creak [krik] *s (high-pitched sound)*
Quietschen *n*; *(low-pitched sound)*
Knarren *n* || *intr* quietschen; knarren

creaky ['krikɪ] *adj* quietschend; knar-
rend

cream [krim] *adj* Sahne-, Rahm-;
(color) creme, cremefarben || *s*
Sahne *f*, Rahm *m*; *(cosmetic)* Creme
f; *(color)* Cremefarbe *f*; *(fig)* Creme
f || *tr (milk)* abrahmen; *(trounce)*
(sl) schlagen

cream'cheese' *s* Rahmkäse *m*, Sahne-
käse *m*

creamery ['krimərɪ] *s* Molkerei *f*

cream'pit'cher *s* Sahnekännchen *n*

cream'puff' *s* Windbeutel *m*

cream'sep'arator ['sepə,retər] *s*
Milchschleuder *f*, Milchzentrifuge *f*

creamy ['krimɪ] *adj* sahnig

crease [kris] *s* Falte *f*; *(in trousers)*
Bügelfalte *f* || *tr* falten; *(trousers)*
bügeln || *intr* knittern

create [krɪ'et] *tr* (er)schaffen; *(excitement, an impression)* hervorrufen;
(noise) verursachen; *(appoint)* ernennen, machen zu; *(a role, fashions)* kreieren

creation [krɪ'eʃən] *s* Schaffung *f*; *(of
the world)* Schöpfung *f*; *(in fashions)* Modeschöpfung *f*

creative [krɪ'etɪv] *adj* schöpferisch

creator [krɪ'etər] *s* Schöpfer *m*

creature ['kritʃər] *s* Kreatur *f*, Geschöpf *n*; **every living c.** jedes Lebewesen *n*

credence ['kridəns] *s* Glaube *m*

credentials [krɪ'den∫əlz] *spl* Beglaubigungsschreiben *n*, Akkreditiv *n*

credenza [krɪ'denzə] *s* Kredenz *f*

credibility [ˌkredɪˈbɪlɪti] *s* Glaub-
würdigkeit *f*
credibil'ity gap' *s* Vertrauenslücke *f*
credible [ˈkredɪbəl] *adj* glaubwürdig
credit [ˈkredɪt] *s* (*credence*) Glaube
m; (*honor*) Ehre *f*; (*recognition*)
Anerkennung *f*; (educ) Anrechnungs-
punkt *m*; (fin) Kredit *m*; (*credit
balance*) (fin) Guthaben *n*; **be a c.
to** Ehre machen (*dat*); **credits** (cin)
Vorspann *m*; **give s.o. c. for s.th.**
j–m etw hoch anrechnen; **on c.** auf
Kredit; **on thirty days' c.** auf dreißig Tage Ziel; **take c. for** sich [*dat*]
als Verdienst anrechnen; **to s.o.'s c.**
zu j–s Ehre ‖ *tr* (*believe*) glauben
(*dat*); (*an account*) gutschreiben
(*dat*); **c. s.o. with s.th.** j–m etw hoch
anrechnen
creditable [ˈkredɪtəbəl] *adj* ehrenwert
cre'dit card' *s* Kreditkarte *f*
cre'dit hour' *s* (educ) Anrechnungs-
punkt *m*
creditor [ˈkredɪtər] *s* Gläubiger –in
mf
cre'dit rat'ing *s* Bonität *f*
credulous [ˈkredʒələs] *adj* leichtgläubig
creed [krid] *s* (& fig) Glaubensbekenntnis *n*
creek [krik] *s* Bach *m*
creep [krip] *s* Kriechen *n*; (sl) Spinner
m; **it gives me the creeps** mir gruselt
‖ *v* (*pret & pp* **crept** [krept]) *intr*
kriechen, schleichen; (*said of plants*)
kriechen; **c. along** dahinschleichen;
c. up on heranschleichen an (*acc*);
it makes my flesh c. es macht mich
schaudern
creeper [ˈkripər] *s* Kletterpflanze *f*
creepy [ˈkripi] *adj* schaudererregend;
(*sensation*) gruselig; **have a c. feeling** gruseln
cremate [ˈkrimet] *tr* einäschern
cremation [krɪˈmeʃən] *s* Einäscherung
f
crematory [ˈkrimәˌtori] *s* Kremato-
rium *n*
crepe [krep] *s* Krepp *m*; (*mourning
band*) Trauerflor *m*
crepe' pa'per *s* Kreppapier *n*
crescent [ˈkresənt] *s* Mondsichel *f*
cres'cent roll' *s* Hörnchen *n*
cress [kres] *s* (bot) Kresse *f*
crest [krest] *s* (*of a hill, wave, or
rooster*) Kamm *m*; (*of a helmet*)
Helmbusch *m*; (*of a bird*) Feder-
büschel *n*
crestfallen [ˈkrestˌfɔlən] *adj* niedergeschlagen
Crete [krit] *s* Kreta *n*
crevice [ˈkrevɪs] *s* Riß *m*
crew [kru] *s* Gruppe *f*; (aer, nav) Besatzung *f*; (*of a boat*) (sport) Mannschaft *f*; (*rowing*) (sport) Rudersport
m
crew' cut' *s* Bürstenschnitt *m*
crib [krɪb] *s* (*manger*) Krippe *f*; (*for
children*) Kinderbettstelle *f*; (*bin*)
Speicher *m*; (*student's pony*) Eselsbrücke *f* ‖ *v* (*pret & pp* **cribbed**;
ger **cribbing**) *tr & intr* abbohren
cricket [ˈkrɪkɪt] *s* (*ent*) Grille *f*;

(sport) Kricketspiel *n*; **not c.** (coll)
nicht fair
crime [kraɪm] *s* Verbrechen *n*
criminal [ˈkrɪmɪnəl] *adj* verbrecherisch; (*act, case, code, court, law*)
Straf–; (*investigation, trial, police*)
Kriminal– ‖ *s* Verbrecher –in *mf*
crim'inal charge' *s* Strafanzeige *f*
crim'inal neg'ligence *s* grobe Fahrlässigkeit *f*
crim'inal offense' *s* strafbare Handlung
f
crim'inal rec'ord *s* Strafregister *n*
crimp [krɪmp] *s* Welle *f*; **put a c. in**
(coll) e–n Dämpfer aufsetzen (*dat*)
‖ *tr* wellen, riffeln
crimson [ˈkrɪmzən] *adj* karmesinrot ‖
s Karmesin *n*
cringe [krɪndʒ] *intr* sich krümmen;
(*fawn*) kriechen
crinkle [ˈkrɪŋkəl] *s* Runzel *f* ‖ *tr* runzeln; (*one's nose*) rümpfen
cripple [ˈkrɪpəl] *s* Krüppel *m* ‖ *tr* verkrüppeln; (fig) lähmen, lahmlegen
cri·sis [ˈkraɪsɪs] *s* (–ses [siz]) Krise *f*
crisp [krɪsp] *adj* (*brittle*) knusprig;
(*firm and fresh*) mürb; (*air, clothes*)
frisch; (*manner*) forsch
crisscross [ˈkrɪsˌkrɔs] *adj & adv* kreuz
und quer ‖ *tr* kreuz und quer markieren ‖ *intr* sich kreuzen
criteri·on [kraɪˈtɪrɪ·ən] *s* (–a [ə] &
–ons) Kennzeichen *n*, Kriterium *n*
critic [ˈkrɪtɪk] *s* Kritiker –in *mf*
critical [ˈkrɪtɪkəl] *adj* kritisch
criticism [ˈkrɪtɪˌsɪzəm] *s* Kritik *f*
criticize [ˈkrɪtɪˌsaɪz] *tr* kritisieren
critique [krɪˈtik] *s* (*review*) Rezension
f; (*critical discussion*) Kritik *f*
croak [krok] *s* (*of a frog*) Quaken *n*;
(*of a raven*) Krächzen *n* ‖ *intr*
quaken; krächzen; (*die*) (sl) verrecken
cro·chet [kroˈʃe] *s* Häkelarbeit *f* ‖ *v*
(*pret & pp* –**cheted** [ˈʃed]; *ger*
–**cheting** [ˈʃe·ɪŋ]) *tr & intr* häkeln
crochet' nee'dle *s* Häkelnadel *f*
crock [krak] *s* irdener Topf *m*, Krug
m
crockery [ˈkrakəri] *s* irdenes Geschirr
n
crocodile [ˈkrakəˌdaɪl] *s* Krokodil *n*
croc'odile tears' *spl* Krokodilstränen
pl
crocus [ˈkrokəs] *s* (bot) Krokus *m*
crone [kron] *s* altes Weib *n*
crony [ˈkroni] *s* alter Kamerad *m*
crook [kruk] *s* (*of a shepherd*) Hirten-
stab *m*; (sl) Gauner *m* ‖ *tr* krümmen
crooked [ˈkrukɪd] *adj* krumm; (*dishonest*) unehrlich
croon [krun] *tr & intr* schmalzig
singen
crooner [ˈkrunər] *s* Schnulzensänger *m*
crop [krap] *s* Ernte *f*; (*whip*) Peitsche
f; (*of a bird*) Kropf *m*; (*large number*) Menge *f*; **the crops** die ganze
Ernte ‖ *v* (*pret & pp* **cropped**; *ger*
cropping) *tr* stutzen; (*said of an animal*) abfressen ‖ *intr*—**c. up** auftauchen
crop' fail'ure *s* Mißerte *f*
croquet [kroˈke] *s* Krocket *n*

croquette [kro'kɛt] s (culin) Krokette f

crosier ['kroʒər] s Bischofsstab m

cross [kros] adj Quer-, Kreuz-; (biol) Kreuzungs-; (angry) (with) ärgerlich (auf acc, über acc) || s (& fig) Kreuz n; (biol) Kreuzung f || tr (arms, legs, streets, plans, breeds) kreuzen; (a mountain) übersteigen; (oppose) in die Quere kommen (dat); c. my heart! Hand aufs Herz!; c. oneself sich bekreuzigen; c. s.o.'s mind j—m durch den Kopf gehen; c. out ausstreichen || intr sich kreuzen; c. over to hinübergehen zu

cross'bones' spl gekreuzte Skelettknochen pl

cross'bow' s (hist) Armbrust f

cross'breed' v (pret & pp -bred) tr kreuzen

cross'-coun'try adj (vehicle) geländegängig || cross'-coun'try s (sport) Langlauf m

cross'cur'rent s Gegenströmung f

cross'-exam'ine tr ins Kreuzverhör nehmen

cross'-examina'tion s Kreuzverhör n

cross'-eyed' adj schieläugig

cross'fire' s Kreuzfeuer n

cross'ing s (of streets) Kreuzung f; (of the ocean) Überfahrt f, Überquerung f; (rr) Übergang m

cross'piece' s Querstück n

cross'-pur'pose s—be at cross-purposes einander entgegenarbeiten

cross' ref'erence s Querverweis m

cross'road' s Querweg m; crossroads Straßenkreuzung f; (fig) Scheideweg m

cross' sec'tion s Querschnitt m

cross'wind' s Seitenwind m

cross'wise' adj & adv quer, in die Quere

cross'word puz'zle s Kreuzworträtsel n

crotch [krɑtʃ] s (of a tree) Gabelung f; (of a body or trousers) Schritt m

crotchety ['krɑtʃɪti] adj verschroben

crouch [krautʃ] s Hocke f || intr hocken

croup [krup] s (of a horse) Kruppe f; (pathol) Halsbräune f

croupier ['krupɪ·ər] s Croupier -in mf

crouton ['krutɑn] s gerösteter Brotwürfel m

crow [kro] s (cry) Krähen n; (bird) Krähe f; as the c. flies schnurgrade; eat c. klein beigeben || intr krähen

crow'bar' s Stemmeisen n

crowd [kraud] s Menge f; (mob) Masse f; (set) Gesellschaft f || tr vollstopfen; (push) stoßen; c. out verdrängen || intr (around) sich drängen (um); c. into sich hineindrängen in (acc)

crowd'ed adj überfüllt; (street) belebt

crown [kraun] s Krone f; (dent) Zahnkrone f || tr krönen, bekränzen; (checkers) zur Dame machen; (sl) eins aufs Dach geben (dat); (dent) überkronen

crown' jew'els spl Kronjuwelen pl

crown' prince' s Kronprinz m

crown' prin'cess s Kronprinzessin f

crow's'-feet' spl (wrinkles) Krähenfüße pl

crow's'-nest' s (naut) Krähennest n

crucial ['kruʃəl] adj entscheidend; (point) springend; c. question Gretchenfrage f; c. test Feuerprobe f

crucible ['krusɪbəl] s Schmelztiegel m

crucifix ['krusɪfɪks] s Kruzifix n

crucifixion [‚krusɪ'fɪkʃən] s Kreuzigung f

cruci·fy ['krusɪ‚faɪ] v (pret & pp -fied) tr kreuzigen

crude [krud] adj (raw, unrefined) roh; (person) grob, ungeschliffen; c. joke plumper Scherz m

crudity ['krudɪti] s Roheit f

cruel ['kru·əl] adj (to) grausam (gegen)

cruelty ['kru·əlti] s Grausamkeit f; c. to animals Tierquälerei f

cruet ['kru·ɪt] s Fläschchen n; (relig) Meßkännchen n

cruise [kruz] s Kreuzfahrt f || intr (aer) mit Reisegeschwindigkeit fliegen; (aut) herumfahren; (naut) kreuzen

cruiser ['kruzər] s (nav) Kreuzer m

cruise' ship' s Vergnügungsdampfer m

cruller ['krʌlər] s Krapfen m

crumb [krʌm] s Krümel m; (& fig) Bröckchen n; (sl) Schweinehund m

crumble ['krʌmbəl] tr & intr zerbröckeln

crumbly ['krʌmbli] adj bröcklig

crummy ['krʌmi] adj (sl) schäbig

crumple ['krʌmpəl] tr zerknittern || intr (said of clothes) faltig werden; (collapse) zusammenbrechen

crunch [krʌntʃ] s Knacken n; (of snow) Knirschen n; (tight situation) Druck m || tr knirschend kauen || intr (said of snow) knirschen; c. on knirschend kauen

crusade [kru'sed] s Kreuzzug m

crusader [kru'sedər] s Kreuzfahrer m

crush [krʌʃ] s Gedränge n; have a c. on s.o. (coll) in j—n vernarrt sein || tr (zer)quetschen, zerdrücken; (grain) schroten; (stone) zerkleinern; (suppress) unterdrücken; (oppress) bedrücken; (hopes) knicken; (overwhelm) zerschmettern; (min) pochen; c. out (a cigarette) ausdrücken || intr zerdrückt werden

crush'ing adj (victory) entscheidend; (defeat) vernichtend; (experience) überwältigend

crust [krʌst] s Kruste f; (sl) Frechheit f

crustacean [krʌs'teʃən] s Krebstier n

crustaceous [krʌs'teʃəs] adj Krebs-

crusty ['krʌsti] adj krustig, rösch; (surly) mürrisch

crutch [krʌtʃ] s (& fig) Krücke f

crux [krʌks] s Kern m, Kernpunkt m

cry [kraɪ] s (cries) (shout) Schrei m, Ruf m; (weeping) Weinen n; a far cry from etw ganz anderes als; cry for help Hilferuf m; have a good cry sich ordentlich ausweinen || v (pret & pp cried) tr schreien, rufen; cry one's eyes out sich [dat] die Augen aus dem Kopf weinen || intr (weep) weinen; *(shout)* schreien; **cry for help** um Hilfe rufen; **cry on s.o.'s shoulder** j–m seine Not klagen; **cry out against** scharf verurteilen; **cry out in** *(pain)* schreien vor *(dat)*; **cry over** nachweinen *(dat)*

cry'ba'by *s* (**–bies**) Schreihals *m*

cry'ing *adj* **–c.** jag Schreikrampf *m*; **c. shame** schreiende Ungerechtigkeit *f* ‖ *s* Weinen *n*; **for c. out loud!** um Himmels willen!

crypt [krɪpt] *s* Totengruft *f*, Krypta *f*

cryptic(al) [ˈkrɪptɪk(əl)] *adj* *(secret)* geheim; *(puzzling)* rätselhaft; *(coded)* verschlüsselt

crystal [ˈkrɪstəl] *adj* Kristall– ‖ *s* Kristall *m*; *(cut glass)* Kristallglas *n*; *(of a watch)* Uhrglas *n*

crys'tal ball' *s* Kristall *m*

crystalline [ˈkrɪstəlɪn], [ˈkrɪstəˌlaɪn] *adj* kristallinisch, kristallen

crystallize [ˈkrɪstəˌlaɪz] *tr* kristallisieren ‖ *intr* kristallisieren; (fig) feste Form annehmen

cub [kʌb] *s* Junge *n*

Cuba [ˈkjubə] *s* Kuba *n*

Cuban [ˈkjubən] *adj* kubanisch ‖ *s* Kubaner –in *mf*

cubbyhole [ˈkʌbɪˌhol] *s* gemütliches Zimmerchen *n*

cube [kjub] *s* Würfel *m*; (math) dritte Potenz *f* ‖ *tr* in Würfel schneiden; (math) kubieren

cubic [ˈkjubɪk] *adj* Raum–; (math) kubisch; **c. foot** Kubikfuß *m*

cub' report'er *s* unerfahrener Reporter *m*

cub' scout' *s* Wölfling *m*

cuckold [ˈkʌkəld] *s* Hahnrei *m* ‖ *tr* zum Hahnrei machen

cuckoo [ˈkuku] *adj* (sl) verrückt ‖ *s* Kuckuck *m*

cuck'oo clock' *s* Kuckucksuhr *f*

cucumber [ˈkjukʌmbər] *s* Gurke *f*

cud [kʌd] *s*—**chew the cud** wiederkäuen

cuddle [ˈkʌdəl] *tr* herzen ‖ *intr* sich kuscheln; **c. up** sich behaglich zusammenkuscheln

cudgel [ˈkʌdʒəl] *s* Prügel *m* ‖ *v* (pret & pp **–el[l]ed**; ger **–el[l]ing**) *tr* verprügeln

cue [kju] *s* Hinweis *m*; (billiards) Billardstock *m*; (theat) Stichwort *n*; **take the cue from s.o.** sich nach j–m richten ‖ *tr* das Stichwort geben *(dat)*

cuff [kʌf] *s* *(of a shirt)* Manschette *f*; *(of trousers)* Aufschlag *m*; *(blow)* Ohrfeige *f*; **off the c.** aus dem Handgelenk

cuff' link' *s* Manschettenknopf *m*

cuisine [kwɪˈzin] *s* Küche *f*

culinary [ˈkjulɪˌneri] *adj* kulinarisch, Koch–; **c. art** Kochkunst *f*

cull [kʌl] *tr* *(choose)* auslesen; *(pluck)* pflücken

culminate [ˈkʌlmɪˌnet] *intr* (**in**) kulminieren (in *dat*), gipfeln (in *dat*)

culmination [ˌkʌlmɪˈneʃən] *s* Gipfel *m*

culpable [ˈkʌlpəbəl] *adj* schuldhaft

culprit [ˈkʌlprɪt] *s* Schuldige *mf*

cult [kʌlt] *s* Kult *m*, Kultus *m*

cultivate [ˈkʌltɪˌvet] *tr* *(soil)* bearbeiten; *(plants)* ziehen; *(activities)* betreiben; *(an art)* pflegen; *(friendship)* hegen

cul'tivat'ed *adj* kultiviert

cultivation [ˌkʌltɪˈveʃən] *s* *(of the soil)* Bearbeitung *f*; *(of the arts)* Pflege *f*; *(of friendship)* Hegen *n*; **under c.** bebaut

cultivator [ˈkʌltɪˌvetər] *s* (mach) Kultivator *m*

cultural [ˈkʌltʃərəl] *adj* kulturell, Kultur–

culture [ˈkʌltʃər] *s* Kultur *f*

cul'tured *adj* kultiviert

cul'ture me'dium *s* Nährboden *m*

culvert [ˈkʌlvərt] *s* Rinnstein *m*

cumbersome [ˈkʌmbərsəm] *adj* *(unwieldy)* unhandlich; *(slow-moving)* schwerfällig; *(burdensome)* lästig

cunning [ˈkʌnɪŋ] *adj* (arg)listig ‖ *s* List *f*, Arglist *f*, Schlauheit *f*

cup [kʌp] *s* Tasse *f*; *(of a bra)* Körbchen *n*; (fig, bot, relig) Kelch *m*; (sport) Pokal *m* ‖ *v* (pret & pp **cupped**) ger **cupping**) *tr* *(the hands)* wölben; (med) schröpfen

cupboard [ˈkʌbərd] *s* Schrank *m*

cupidity [kjuˈpɪdɪti] *s* Habgier *f*

cupola [ˈkjupələ] *s* Kuppel *f*

cur [kʌr] *s* Köter *m*; (pej) Halunke *m*

curable [ˈkjurəbəl] *adj* heilbar

curate [ˈkjurɪt] *s* Kaplan *m*

curative [ˈkjurətɪv] *adj* heilend, Heil–

curator [kjuˈretər] *s* Kustos *m*

curb [kʌrb] *s* *(of a street)* Randstein *m*; *(of a horse)* Kandare *f* ‖ *tr* (& fig) zügeln; *(a person)* an die Kandare nehmen

curb'stone' *s* Bordstein *m*

curd [kʌrd] *s* Quark *m*; **curds** Quark *m*

curdle [ˈkʌrdəl] *tr* gerinnen lassen; (fig) erstarren lassen ‖ *intr* gerinnen, stocken; (fig) erstarren

cure [kjur] *s* *(restoration to health)* Heilung *f*; *(remedy)* Heilmittel *n*; *(treatment)* Kur *f* ‖ *tr* *(a disease, evil)* heilen; *(by smoking)* räuchern; *(by drying)* trocknen; *(by salting)* einsalzen ‖ *intr* heilen

cure'-all' *s* Allheilmittel *n*

curfew [ˈkʌrfju] *s* Ausgehverbot *n*; *(enforced closing time)* Polizeistunde *f*

curio [ˈkjurɪˌo] *s* (**–os**) Kuriosität *f*

curiosity [ˌkjurɪˈɑsɪti] *s* Neugier *f*; *(strange article)* Kuriosität *f*

curious [ˈkjurɪ-əs] *adj* neugierig; *(odd)* kurios, merkwürdig

curl [kʌrl] *s* *(of hair)* Locke *f*; *(of smoke)* Rauchkringel *m* ‖ *tr* locken; *(lips)* verächtlich schürzen ‖ *intr* sich kräuseln; **c. up** sich zusammenrollen; *(said of an edge)* sich umbiegen

curler [ˈkʌrlər] *s* Haarwickler *m*

curlicue [ˈkʌrlɪˌkju] *s* Schnörkel *m*

curly [ˈkʌrli] *adj* lockig; *(leaves, etc.)* gekräuselt

currant [ˈkʌrənt] *s* *(raisin)* Korinthe *f*; (genus Ribes) Johannisbeere *f*

currency [ˈkʌrənsi] s (*money*) Währung f; (*circulation*) Umlauf m; foreign c. Devisen pl; gain c. in Gebrauch kommen

current [ˈkʌrənt] adj (*year, prices, account*) laufend; (*events*) aktuell, Tages–; be c. Gültigkeit haben; (*said of money*) gelten || s (& elec) Strom m

currently [ˈkʌrəntli] adv gegenwärtig

curricu·lum [kəˈrɪkjələm] s (–lums & –la [lə]) Lehrplan m

cur·ry [ˈkʌri] s Curry m || v (*pret & pp* –ried) tr (*a horse*) striegeln; c. favor with s.o. sich bei j–m einzuschmeicheln suchen

cur'rycomb' s Striegel m

cur'ry pow'der s Currypulver n

curse [kʌrs] s Fluch m; put a c. on verwünschen || tr verfluchen || intr (at) fluchen (auf acc)

cursed [ˈkʌrsɪd], [kʌrst] adj verflucht

curse' word' s Fluchwort n, Schimpfwort n

cursive [ˈkʌrsɪv] adj Kurrent–

cursory [ˈkʌrsəri] adj flüchtig

curt [kʌrt] adj barsch, schroff

curtail [kərˈtel] tr einschränken

curtain [ˈkʌrtɪn] s Gardine f; (*drape*) Vorhang m; (theat) Vorhang m || tr—c. off mit Vorhängen abteilen

cur'tain call' s Vorhang m, Hervorruf m

cur'tain rod' s Gardinenstange f

curt·sy [ˈkʌrtsi] s Knicks m || v (*pret & pp* –sied) intr (to) knicksen (vor dat)

curvaceous [kʌrˈveʃəs] adj kurvenreich

curvature [ˈkʌrvətʃər] s (*of the spine*) Verkrümmung f; (*of the earth*) Krümmung f

curved adj krumm

cushion [ˈkuʃən] s Kissen n, Polster m & n; (billiards) Bande f || tr polstern; (*a shock*) abfedern

cuss [kʌs] s (sl) Kerl m; (*curse*) (sl) Fluch m || tr (sl) verfluchen || intr (sl) fluchen

cussed [ˈkʌsɪd] adj (sl) verflucht

cussedness [ˈkʌsɪdnɪs] s (sl) Bosheit f

custard [ˈkʌstərd] s Eierkrem f

custodian [kəsˈtodi·ən] s (e.g., *of records*) Verwalter m; (*of inmates*) Wärter m; (*caretaker*) Hausmeister m

custody [ˈkʌstədi] s Verwahrung f, Obhut f; (jur) Gewahrsam m; c. of (*children*) Sorgerecht für; in the c. of in der Obhut (*genit*); take into c. in Gewahrsam nehmen

custom [ˈkʌstəm] s Brauch m, Sitte f; (*habit*) Gewohnheit f; customs Zollkontrolle f; pay customs on s.th. für etw Zoll bezahlen

customary [ˈkʌstə‚meri] adj gebräuchlich

cus'tom-built' adj nach Wunsch gebaut

customer [ˈkʌstəmər] s Kunde m, Kundin f; (*in a restaurant*) Gast m; (telp) Teilnehmer –in mf

cus'tom-made' adj nach Maß angefertigt

cus'toms clear'ance s Zollabfertigung f

cus'toms declara'tion s Zollerklärung f; (*form*) Abfertigungsschein m

cus'toms inspec'tion s Zollkontrolle f

cus'toms of'fice s Zollamt n

customs of'ficer s Zollbeamte m, Zollbeamtin f

cus'tom tai'lor s Maßschneider m

cut [kʌt] adj (glass) geschliffen; cut flowers Schnittblumen pl; cut out for wie geschaffen für (or zu) || s Schnitt m; (*piece cut off*) Abschnitt m; (slice) Schnitte f; (*wound*) Schnittwunde f; (*of a garment*) Schnitt m, Fasson f; (*of the profits*) Anteil m; (*in prices, pay*) Kürzung f, Senkung f; (*absence from school*) Schwänzen n; (*of meat*) Stück n; (cards) Abheben n; (tennis) Drehschlag m; a cut above e–e Stufe besser als || v (*pret & pp* cut; ger cutting) tr schneiden; (glass, precious stones) schleifen; (grass) mähen; (hedges) stutzen; (hay) machen; (*a tunnel*) bohren; (*a motor*) abstellen; (*production*) drosseln; (pay) kürzen, vermindern; (class) (coll) schwänzen; (prices) herabsetzen, kürzen; (whiskey) (coll) panschen; (cards) abheben; (tennis) schneiden; cut back (plants) stutzen; (fig) abbauen; cut down fällen; cut it out! Schluß damit!; cut off abschneiden; (*a tail*) kupieren; (gas, telephone, electricity) absperren; (troops) absprengen; cut one's finger sich in den Finger schneiden; cut out the nonsense! laß den Quatsch!; cut short (e.g., *a vacation*) abkürzen; (*a person*) das Wort abschneiden (dat); cut up zerstückeln || intr schneiden; cut down on einschränken, verringern; cut in sich einmischen; (*at a dance*) ablösen; cut in ahead of s.o. vor j–m einbiegen; cut up (sl) wild darauf losschießen

cut-and-dried [ˈkʌtənˈdraɪd] adj fix und fertig

cut'away' s Cut m

cut'back' s Einschränkung f

cute [kjut] adj (pretty) niedlich; (shrewd) (coll) klug

cut' glass' s geschliffenes Glas n

cuticle [ˈkjutɪkəl] s Nagelhaut f

cutie [ˈkjuti] s (sl) flotte Biene f

cutlass [ˈkʌtləs] s Entermesser n

cutlery [ˈkʌtləri] s Schneidwerkzeuge pl

cutlet [ˈkʌtlɪt] s Schnitzel n

cut'-off' s (turn-off) Abzweigung f; (cut-off point) (acct) gemeinsamer Endpunkt m; (elec) Ausschaltvorrichtung f; (mach) Absperrvorrichtung f

cut'-off date' s Abschlußtag m

cut'-out' s Ausschnitt m; (design to be cut out) Ausschneidemuster n; (aut) Auspuffklappe f

cut'-rate' adj (price) Schleuder–

cutter [ˈkʌtər] s (naut) Kutter m

cut'throat' adj halsabschneiderisch || s Halsabschneider –in mf

cut'ting adj schneidend; (tools)

Schneide–; (remark) scharf ‖ s Abschnitt m; (of prices) Herabsetzung f; (hort) Steckling m; cuttings Abfälle pl
cut'ting board' s Schneidebrett n
cut'ting edge' s Schnittkante f
cut'ting room' s (cin) Schneideraum m
cuttlefish ['kʌtəl‚fiʃ] s Tintenfisch m
cyanamide [saɪ'ænə‚maɪd] s (chem) Zyanamid n; (com) Kalkstickstoff m
cycle ['saɪkəl] s Kreis m; (of an internal combustion engine) Takt m; (phys) Periode f ‖ intr radeln
cyclic(al) ['sɪklɪk(əl)] adj zyklisch, kreisförmig
cyclist ['saɪklɪst] s Radfahrer –in mf
cyclone ['saɪklon] s Zyklon m
cyclotron ['saɪklə‚trɑn] s Zyklotron n, Beschleuniger m
cylinder ['sɪlɪndər] s Zylinder m
cyl'inder block' s Zylinderblock m
cyl'inder bore' s Zylinderbohrung f

cyl'inder head' s Zylinderkopf m
cylindric(al) [sɪ'lɪndrɪk(əl)] adj zylindrisch
cymbal ['sɪmbəl] s Becken n
cynic ['sɪnɪk] adj (philos) zynisch ‖ s Menschenverächter –in mf; (philos) Zyniker m
cynical ['sɪnɪkəl] adj zynisch
cynicism ['sɪnɪ‚sɪzəm] s Zynismus m; (cynical remark) zynische Bemerkung f
cypress ['saɪprəs] s Zypresse f
Cyprus ['saɪprəs] s Zypern n
Cyrillic [sɪ'rɪlɪk] adj kyrillisch
cyst [sɪst] s Zyste f
czar [zɑr] s Zar m
czarina [zɑ'rinə] s Zarin f
Czech [tʃek] adj tschechisch ‖ s Tscheche m, Tschechin f; (language) Tschechisch n
Czechoslovakia [‚tʃekəslo'væki‚ə] s die Tschechoslowakei f

D

D, d [di] s vierter Buchstabe des englischen Alphabets; (mus) D; D flat Des n; D sharp Dis n
D.A. abb (District Attorney) Staatsanwalt m
dab [dæb] s (of color) Klecks m; (e.g., of butter) Stückchen n ‖ v (pret & pp dabbed; ger dabbing) tr betupfen ‖ intr—dab at betupfen
dabble ['dæbəl] tr bespritzen ‖ intr (splash about) plantschen; d. in herumstümpern in (dat)
dachshund ['dɑks‚hund] s Dachshund m
dad [dæd] s (coll) Vati m
daddy ['dædi] s (coll) Vati m
dad'dy-long'legs' s (–legs) Weberknecht m
daffodil ['dæfədɪl] s gelbe Narzisse f
daffy ['dæfi] adj (coll) doof
dagger ['dægər] s Dolch m; (typ) Kreuzzeichen n; look daggers at s.o. j–n mit Blicken durchbohren
dahlia ['dæljə] s Georgine f, Dahlie f
daily ['deli] adj täglich, Tages– ‖ adv täglich ‖ s Tageszeitung f
dainty ['denti] adj zart; (food) lecker; (finicky) wählerisch
dairy ['dɛri] s Molkerei f
dair'y farm' s Meierei f
dair'y farm'er s Meier –in mf
dais ['de‚ɪs] s Tribüne f
daisy ['dezi] s Gänseblümchen n
dal·ly ['dæli] v (pret & pp –lied) intr (delay) herumtrödeln; (play amorously) liebäugeln
dam [dæm] s Damm m; (female quadruped) Muttertier n ‖ v (pret & pp dammed; ger damming) tr eindämmen; dam up anstauen
damage ['dæmɪdʒ] s Schaden m; damages (jur) Schadenersatz m; do d. Schaden anrichten; sue for damages

auf Schadenersatz klagen ‖ tr beschädigen; (a reputation) beeinträchtigen
dam'aging adj (influence) schädlich; (evidence) belastend
dame [dem] s Dame f; (sl) Weibsbild n
damn [dæm] adj (sl) verflucht ‖ s— I don't give a d. about it (sl) ich mache mir e–n Dreck daraus; not be worth a d. (sl) keinen Pfifferling wert sein ‖ tr verdammen; (curse) verfluchen; d. it! (sl) verflucht!
damnation [dæm'neʃən] s Verdammnis f
damned adj verdammt; (sl) verflucht ‖ adv (sl) verdammt ‖ the d. spl die Verdammten pl
damp [dæmp] adj feucht ‖ s Feuchtigkeit f ‖ tr (be)feuchten; (a fire; enthusiasm) dämpfen; (elec, mus, phys) dämpfen
dampen ['dæmpən] tr befeuchten; (fig) dämpfen
damper ['dæmpər] s (of a fireplace) Schieber m; (of a stove) Ofenklappe f; (mus) Dämpfer m; put a d. on e–n Dämpfer aufsetzen (dat)
dampness ['dæmpnɪs] s Feuchtigkeit f
damsel ['dæmzəl] s Jungfrau f
dance [dæns] s Tanz m ‖ tr & intr tanzen
dance' band' s Tanzkapelle f
dance' floor' s Tanzfläche f
dance' hall' s Tanzsaal m, Tanzlokal n
dancer ['dænsər] s Tänzer –in mf
dance' step' s Tanzschritt m
danc'ing part'ner s Tanzpartner –in mf
dandelion ['dændɪ‚laɪ-ən] s Löwenzahn m
dandruff ['dændrəf] s Schuppen pl

dandy ['dændi] *adj* (coll) pfundig, nett ‖ *s* Stutzer *m*

Dane [den] *s* Däne *m*, Dänin *f*

danger ['dendʒər] *s* (**to**) Gefahr *f* (für) **dan'ger list'** *s*—**be on the d.** in Lebensgefahr sein

dangerous ['dendʒərəs] *adj* gefährlich

dangle ['dæŋgəl] *tr* schlenkern, baumeln lassen ‖ *intr* baumeln

Danish ['denɪʃ] *adj* dänisch ‖ *s* (*language*) Dänisch *n*

Dan'ish pas'try *s* feines Hefegebäck *n*

dank [dæŋk] *adj* feucht

Danube ['dænjub] *s* Donau *f*

dapper ['dæpər] *adj* schmuck

dappled ['dæpəld] *adj* scheckig, bunt

dare [der] *s* Herausforderung *f* ‖ *tr* wagen; (*a person*) herausfordern; **d. to** (*inf*) es wagen zu (*inf*); **don't you d. go** unterstehen Sie sich, wegzugehen!; **I d. say** ich darf wohl behaupten ‖ *intr*—**don't you d.!** unterstehen Sie sich!

dare'dev'il *s* Waghals *m*, Draufgänger *m*

dar'ing *adj* (*deed*) verwegen; (*person*) wagemutig ‖ *s* Wagemut *m*

dark [dɑrk] *adj* finster; (*color, beer, complexion*) dunkel; (fig) düster ‖ *s* Finsternis *n*, Dunkel *n*; **be in the d. about** im unklaren sein über (*acc*)

Dark' A'ges *spl* frühes Mittelalter *n*

dark-complexioned ['dɑrkkəm'plekʃənd] *adj* dunkelhäutig

darken ['dɑrkən] *tr* (*a room*) verfinstern ‖ *intr* sich verfinstern; (fig) sich verdüstern

dark'-eyed' *adj* schwarzäugig

dark' horse' *s* Außenseiter *m*

darkly ['dɑrkli] *adv* geheimnisvoll

darkness ['dɑrknɪs] *s* Finsternis *f*

dark'room' *s* (phot) Dunkelkammer *f*

darling ['dɑrlɪŋ] *adj* lieb ‖ *s* Liebchen *n*

darn [dɑrn] *adj* (coll) verwünscht ‖ *adv* (coll) verdammt ‖ *s*—**I don't give a d. about** it ich pfeif drauf! ‖ *tr* (*stockings*) stopfen; **d. it!** (coll) verflixt!; **I'll be darned if** der Kukkuck soll mich holen, wenn

darn'ing nee'dle *s* Stopfnadel *f*

dart [dɑrt] *s* Wurfspieß *m*, Pfeil *m*; (sew) Abnäher *m*; **darts** (*game*) Pfeilwerfen *n*; **play darts** Pfeile werfen ‖ *intr* huschen; **d. ahead** vorschießen; **d. off** davonstürzen

dash [dæʃ] *s* (*rush*) Ansturm *m*; (*smartness*) Schneidigkeit *f*; (*spirit*) Schwung *m*; (*of solids*) Prise *f*; (*of liquids*) Schuß *m*; (sport) Kurzstreckenlauf *m*; (typ) Gedankenstrich *m*; **make a d. for** losstürzen auf (*acc*) ‖ *tr* (*throw*) schleudern; (*hopes*) niederschlagen, knicken; **d. off** (*a letter*) hinwerfen ‖ *intr* stürmen, stürzen

dash'board' *s* (aut) Armaturenbrett *n*

dash'ing *adj* schneidig, forsch

dastardly ['dæstərdli] *adj* feige

data ['detə] *s* or *spl* Daten *pl*, Angaben *pl*

da'ta proc'essing *s* Datenverarbeitung *f*

date [det] *s* Datum *n*; (*fixed time*) Termin *m*; (*period*) Zeitraum *m*; (*appointment*) (coll) Verabredung *f*; (*person on a date*) Freund –in *mf*; (bot) Dattel *f*; (jur) Termin *m*; **have a d. with** verabredet sein mit; **make a d. with** sich verabreden mit; **out of d.** veraltet; **to d.** bis heute; **what is the d. today?** der wievielte ist heute? ‖ *tr* datieren; (coll) ausgehen mit ‖ *intr*—**d. back to** zurückgehen auf (*acc*); **d. from** stammen aus

dat'ed *adj* (*provided with a date*) datiert; (*out-of-date*) zeitgebunden

date' line' *s* Datumsgrenze *f*

date'line' *s* (journ) Datumszeile *f*

date' palm' *s* Dattelpalme *f*

dative ['detɪv] *s* Dativ *m*, (grr) Wemfall *m*

daub [dɔb] *s* Bewurf *m* ‖ *tr* (*a canvas*) beschmieren; (*a wall*) bewerfen; (*e.g. mud, plaster*) (on) schmieren (auf *acc*) ‖ *intr* (paint) klecksen

daughter ['dɔtər] *s* Tochter *f*

daugh'ter-in-law' *s* (**daughters-in-law**) Schwiegertochter *f*

daunt [dɔnt] *tr* einschüchtern

dauntless ['dɔntlɪs] *adj* furchtlos

davenport ['dævən ˌpɔrt] *s* Diwan *m*

davit ['dævɪt] *s* (naut) Bootskran *m*

daw [dɔ] *s* (orn) Dohle *f*

dawdle ['dɔdəl] *intr* trödeln, bummeln

dawn [dɔn] *s* Morgendämmerung *f*; (fig) Anbeginn *m* ‖ *intr* dämmern; **d. on s.o.** j-m zum Bewußtsein kommen

day [de] *adj* Tage-, Tages- ‖ *s* Tag *m*; (*specific date*) Termin *m*; **all day long** den ganzen Tag; **by day** am Tage, bei Tage; **by the day** tageweise; **call it a day** (coll) Feierabend machen; **day after day** Tag für Tag; **day by day** Tag für Tag; **day in, day out** tagaus, tagein; **day off** Urlaubstag *m*, Ruhetag *m*; **every other day** jeden zweiten Tag; **in days of old** in alten Zeiten; **in his day** zu seiner Zeit; **in those days** damals; **one day** e–s Tages; **one of these days** demnächst; **the day after** am folgenden Tag; **the day after tomorrow** übermorgen; **the day before** am Vortag; **the day before yesterday** vorgestern; **the other day** neulich, unlängst; **these days** heutzutage; **to this very day** bis auf den heutigen Tag; **what day of the week is it?** welchen Wochentag haben wir?

day' bed' *s* Ruhebett *n*, Liege *f*

day'break' *s* Tagesanbruch *m*

day'-by-day' *adj* tagtäglich, Tag für Tag

day'-care cen'ter *s* Kindertagesstätte *f*, Kindergarten *m*

day' coach' *s* (rr) Personenwagen *m*

day'dream' *s* Träumerei *f*, Wachtraum *m*; (*wild ideas*) Phantasterei *f* ‖ *intr* mit offenen Augen träumen

day'dream'er *s* Träumer –in *mf*

day' la'borer *s* Tagelöhner –in *mf*

day'light' *adj* Tageslicht- ‖ *s* Tageslicht *n*; **in broad d.** am hellichten Tag; **knock the daylights out of** (sl) zur Sau machen

day′light-sav′ing time′ s Sommerzeit f
day′ nurs′ery s Kleinkinderbewahranstalt f
day′ of reck′oning s Jüngster Tag m
day′ shift′ s Tagschicht f
day′time′ s Tageszeit f; **in the d.** bei Tage, am Tage
daze [dez] s Benommenheit f; **be in a d.** benommen sein || tr betäuben
dazzle [′dæzəl] s Blenden n || tr (& fig) blenden
dazz′ling adj blendend
D-day [′di‚de] s X-Tag m; (hist) Invasionstag m
deacon [′dikən] s Diakon m
deaconess [′dikənıs] s Diakonisse f
dead [ded] adj tot; (plant) abgestorben, dürr; (faint, sleep) tief; (numb) gefühllos; (volcano, fire) erloschen; (elec) stromlos; (sport) tot, nicht im Spiel; **d. as a doornail** mausetot; **d. shot** unfehlbarer Schütze m; **d. stop** völliger Stillstand m; **d. silence** Totenstille f || adv völlig, tod– || s— **in the d. of night** mitten in der Nacht; **in the d. of winter** im tiefsten Winter
dead′ beat′ s (sl) Nichtstuer –in mf
dead′ bolt′ s Absteller m
dead′ calm′ s Windstille f
dead′ cen′ter s genaue Mitte f; (dead point) (mach) toter Punkt m
deaden [′dedən] tr (pain) betäuben; (a nerve) abtöten; (sound) dämpfen
dead′ end′ s (& fig) Sackgasse f
dead′head′ s Dummkopf m
dead′ heat′ s totes Rennen n
dead′-let′ter of′fice s Abteilung f für unbestellbare Briefe
dead′line′ s (letzter) Termin m; (journ) Redaktionsschluß m; **meet the d.** den Termin einhalten; **set a d. for** terminieren
dead′lock′ s Stillstand m; **break the d.** den toten Punkt überwinden; **reach a d.** steckenbleiben || tr zum völligen Stillstand bringen; **become deadlocked** stocken
deadly [′dedlı] adj (fatal) tödlich; **d. enemy** Todfeind –in mf; **d. fear** Todesangst f || adv—**d. dull** sterbenlangweilig; **d. pale** leichenblaß
dead′ly sins′ spl Todsünden pl
dead′pan′ s (sl) (look) ausdruckslos; (person) schafsgesichtig
dead′ pan′ s (coll) Schafsgesicht n
dead′ reck′oning s (naut) Koppelkurs m
dead′ ring′er [′rıŋər] s (coll) Doppelgänger m
dead′wood′ s (& fig) totes Holz n
deaf [def] adj taub; **d. and dumb** taubstumm; **d. to** (fig) taub gegen; **turn a d. ear** to taube Ohren haben für
deafen [′defən] tr betäuben
deaf′ening adj ohrenbetäubend
deaf′-mute′ adj taubstumm || s Taubstumme mf
deafness [′defnıs] s Taubheit f
deal [dil] s (business transaction) Geschäft n; (underhanded agreement) Schiebung f; (cards) Austeilen n, Geben n; **a good d. of** (coll) ziemlich viel; **a good d. worse** (coll) viel (or weit) schlechter; **a great d. of** (coll) sehr viel; **give s.o. a good d.** (be fair to s.o.) j–n fair behandeln; (make s.o. a good offer) j–m ein gutes Angebot machen; **give s.o. a raw d.** j–m übel mitspielen; **it is my d.** (cards) ich muß geben; **it's a d.!** abgemacht!; **make a d.** (coll) ein Abkommen treffen || v (pret & pp dealt [delt]) tr (a blow) versetzen; (cards) austeilen, geben || intr (cards) geben; **d. at** (a store) kaufen bei; **d. in** handeln mit; **d. with** (settle) erledigen; (occupy oneself or itself with) sich befassen mit; (treat, e.g., fairly) behandeln; (patronize) kaufen bei; (do business with) in Geschäftsbeziehungen stehen mit; **I'll d. with you later** mit Ihnen werde ich später abrechnen!
dealer [′dilər] s Geber –in mf; (com) Händler –in mf
deal′ings spl (business dealings) Handel m; (relations) Umgang m; **I'll have no d. with** ich will nichts zu tun haben mit
dean [din] s (eccl, educ) Dekan m
dean′ship′ s (eccl, educ) Dekanat n
dear [dır] adj lieb, traut; (expensive) teuer; **Dear Madam** Sehr verehrte gnädige Frau!; **Dear Mrs. X** Sehr geehrte Frau X; **Dear Mr. X** Sehr geehrter Herr X!; **Dear Sir** Sehr geehrter Herr! || s Liebling m, Schatz m || interj—**oh d.!** ach herrje!
dearie [′dırı] s (coll) Liebchen n
dearth [dʌrθ] s (of) Mangel m (an dat)
death [deθ] s Tod m; (in the family) Todesfall m; **at death's door** sterbenskrank; **catch a d. of a cold** sich [dat] den Tod holen; **he'll be the d. of me yet** er bringt mich noch ins Grab; **put to d.** hinrichten; **to the d.** bis aufs Messer; **work to d.** totarbeiten
death′bed′ s Totenbett n, Sterbebett n
death′blow′ s Gnadenstoß m; (fig) Todesstoß m
death′ certif′icate s Totenschein m
death′ house′ s Todeshaus n
death′ knell′ s Grabgeläute n
deathless [′deθlıs] adj unsterblich
deathly [′deθlı] adj tödlich, Todes–, Toten– || adv toten–
death′ mask′ s Totenmaske f
death′ pen′alty s Todesstrafe f
death′ rate′ s Sterblichkeitsziffer f
death′ rat′tle s Todesröcheln n
death′ sen′tence s Todesurteil n
death′ strug′gle s Todeskampf m
death′ trap′ s (fig) Mausefalle f
death′ war′rant s Hinrichtungsbefehl m
debacle [di′bakəl] s Zusammenbruch m
de·bar [dı′bɑr] v (pret & pp –barred; ger –barring) tr (from) ausschließen (aus)
debark [dı′bɑrk] tr ausschiffen || intr sich ausschiffen, an Land gehen
debarkation [‚dibɑr′keʃən] s Ausschiffung f

debase [dɪ'bes] *tr* entwürdigen; *(currency)* entwerten

debatable [dɪ'betəbəl] *adj* strittig

debate [dɪ'bet] *s* Debatte *f* || *tr & intr* debattieren

debauch [dɪ'bɔtʃ] *s* Schwelgerei *f* || *tr* verderben; *(seduce)* verführen; **d. oneself** verkommen

debauched *adj* ausschweifend

debauchee [ˌdɛbɔ'tʃi] *s* Wüstling *m*

debauchery [dɪ'bɔtʃəri] *s* Schwelgerei *f*

debenture [dɪ'bɛntʃər] *s (bond)* Obligation *f*; *(voucher)* Schuldschein *m*

debilitate [dɪ'bɪlɪˌtet] *tr* entkräften

debility [dɪ'bɪlɪti] *s* Schwäche *f*

debit ['dɛbɪt] *s* Debet *n*, Soll *n*; *(as entry)* Belastung *f*

de'bit bal'ance *s* Sollsaldo *n*

de'bit side' *s* Soll *n*, Sollseite *f*

debonair [ˌdɛbə'nɛr] *adj (courteous)* höflich; *(carefree)* heiter und sorglos

debris [de'bri] *s* Trümmer *pl*

debt [dɛt] *s* Schuld *f*; **be in s.o.'s d.** j–m verpflichtet sein; **run into d.** in Schulden geraten

debtor [dɛtər] *s* Schuldner –in *mf*

de-bug [dɪ'bʌg] *v pret & pp* –bugged; *ger* –bugging) *tr (remove defects from)* bereinigen; *(electron)* Abhörgeräte entfernen aus

debut [de'bju, 'debju] *s* Debüt *n*; **make one's d.** debütieren

debutante ['dɛbjuˌtɑnt] *s* Debütantin *f*

decade ['dɛked] *s* Jahrzehnt *n*, Dekade *f*

decadence ['dɛkədəns] *s* Dekadenz *f*

decadent ['dɛkədənt] *adj* dekadent; *(art)* entartet

decal ['dikæl] *s* Abziehbild *n*

decanter [dɪ'kæntər] *s* Karaffe *f*

decapitate [dɪ'kæpɪˌtet] *tr* enthaupten

decathlon [dɪ'kæθlən] *s* Zehnkampf *m*

decay [dɪ'ke] *s (rotting)* Verwesung *f*; *(fig)* Verfall *m*; *(dent)* Karies *f*; **fall into d.** *(& fig)* in Verfall geraten || *intr* verfaulen; *(fig)* verfallen

decease [dɪ'sis] *s* Ableben *n*

deceased' *adj* verstorben || *s* Verstorbene *mf*

deceit [dɪ'sit] *s* Betrügerei *f*

deceitful [dɪ'sitfəl] *adj* betrügerisch

deceive [dɪ'siv] *tr* betrügen || *intr* trügen

decelerate [di'sɛləˌret] *tr* verlangsamen || *intr* seine Geschwindigkeit verringern

December [dɪ'sɛmbər] *s* Dezember *m*

decency ['disənsi] *s* Anstand *m*; **decencies** Anstandsformen *pl*

decent ['disənt] *adj* anständig

decentralize [dɪ'sɛntrəˌlaɪz] *tr* dezentralisieren

deception [dɪ'sɛpʃən] *s (act of deceiving)* Betrug *m*; *(state of being deceived)* Täuschung *f*

deceptive [dɪ'sɛptɪv] *adj* trügerisch; *(misleading)* irreführend; *(similarity)* täuschend

decide [dɪ'saɪd] *tr* entscheiden || *intr (on)* sich entscheiden, sich entschließen (über *acc*, für)

deciduous [dɪ'sɪdʒu·əs] *adj* blattabwerfend; **d. tree** Laubbaum *m*

decimal ['dɛsɪməl] *adj* dezimal || *s* Dezimalzahl *f*

dec'imal place' *s* Dezimalstelle *f*

dec'imal point' *s (in German the comma is used to separate the decimal fraction from the integer)* Komma *n*

decimate ['dɛsɪˌmet] *tr* dezimieren

decipher [dɪ'saɪfər] *tr* entziffern

decision [dɪ'sɪʒən] *s* Entscheidung *f*, Entschluß *m*; *(jur)* Urteil *n*

decisive [dɪ'saɪsɪv] *adj* entscheidend

deck [dɛk] *s (of cards)* Spiel *n*; *(data proc)* Kartensatz *m*; *(naut)* Deck *n*, Verdeck *n* || *tr (coll)* zu Boden schlagen; **d. out** ausschmücken

deck' chair' *s* Liegestuhl *m*

deck' hand' *s* gemeiner Matrose *m*

deck' land'ing *s (aer)* Trägerlandung *f*

declaim [dɪ'klem] *tr & intr* deklamieren

declaration [ˌdɛklə'reʃən] *s* Erklärung *f*; *(at customs)* Zollerklärung *f*

declarative [dɪ'klærətɪv] *adj*—**d. sentence** Aussagesatz *m*

declare [dɪ'klɛr] *tr* erklären; *(tourist's belongings)* verzollen; *(commercial products)* deklarieren; **d. oneself against** sich aussprechen gegen

declension [dɪ'klɛnʃən] *s* Deklination *f*

declinable [dɪ'klaɪnəbəl] *adj* deklinierbar

decline [dɪ'klaɪn] *s (decrease)* Abnahme *f*; *(in prices)* Rückgang *m*; *(deterioration)* Verschlechterung *f*; *(slope)* Abhang *m*; *(fig)* Niedergang *m*; **be on the d.** in Abnahme begriffen sein || *tr (refuse)* ablehnen; *(gram)* deklinieren || *intr (refuse)* ablehnen; *(descend)* sich senken; *(sink)* sinken; *(draw to a close)* zu Ende gehen

declivity [dɪ'klɪvɪti] *s* Abhang *m*

decode [di'kod] *tr* entschlüsseln

decompose [ˌdikəm'poz] *tr* zerlegen || *intr* sich zersetzen, verwesen

decomposition [ˌdikɑmpə'zɪʃən] *s* Zersetzung *f*, Verwesung *f*

decompression [ˌdikəm'prɛʃən] *s* Dekompression *f*

decontamination [ˌdikən,tæmɪ'neʃən] *s* Entseuchung *f*

décor [de'kɔr] *s* Dekor *m*

decorate ['dɛkəˌret] *tr* dekorieren, (aus)schmücken; *(a new room)* einrichten; *(e.g., with a badge)* auszeichnen

decoration [ˌdɛkə'reʃən] *s* Schmuck *m*; *(medal)* Orden *m*, Ehrenzeichen *n*, Dekoration *f*

decorative ['dɛkərətɪv] *adj* dekorativ

decorator ['dɛkəˌretər] *s* Dekorateur –in *mf*

decorous ['dɛkərəs] *adj* schicklich

decorum ['dɛkɔrəm] *s* Schicklichkeit *f*

decoy ['dikɔɪ] *s (bird or person)* Lockvogel *m*; *(anything used as a lure)* Lockmittel *n* || [dɪ'kɔɪ] *tr* locken

decrease ['dikris] *s* Abnahme *f* ||

[dɪ'kris] *tr* verringern ‖ *intr* abnehmen

decree [dɪ'kri] *s* Dekret *n*, Verordnung *f* ‖ *tr* dekretieren, verordnen

decrepit [dɪ'krɛpɪt] *adj* (*age-worn*) altersschwach; (*frail*) gebrechlich

de·cry [dɪ'kraɪ] *v* (*pret & pp* –**cried**) *tr* (*disparage*) herabsetzen; (*censure openly*) kritisieren

dedicate ['dɛdɪ ,ket] *tr* (*a book, one's life*) (**to**) widmen (*dat*); (*a building*) einweihen

dedication [,dɛdɪ'keʃən] *s* Widmung *f*; (*of a building, etc.*) Einweihung *f*; (**to**) Hingabe *f* (an *acc*)

deduce [dɪ'd(j)us] *tr* (**from**) schließen (aus)

deduct [dɪ'dʌkt] *tr* abziehen, abrechnen

deduction [dɪ'dʌkʃən] *s* Abzug *m*; (*conclusion*) Schluß *m*, Folgerung *f*

deed [did] *s* (*act*) Tat *f*; (*jur*) Besitzurkunde *f*

deem [dim] *tr* halten für; **d. s.o. worthy of my confidence** j–n meines Vertrauens für würdig halten

deep [dip] *adj* tief; (*recondite*) dunkel; (*impression*) tiefgehend; (*color, sound*) tief, dunkel; **be d. in debt** tief in Schulden stecken; **four** (*ranks*) **d.** in Viererreihen; **in d. water** (fig) in Schwierigkeiten; **that's too d. for me** das ist mir zu hoch ‖ *adv* tief; **d. down in tief innen in** (*dat*) ‖ *s* Tiefe *f*, Meer *n*

deepen ['dipən] *tr* (& fig) vertiefen ‖ *intr* sich vertiefen

deep'-freeze' *v* (*pret* –**freezed** & –**froze**; *pp* –**freezed** & –**frozen**) *tr* tiefkühlen

deep'-fry' *v* (*pret & pp* –**fried**) *tr* fritieren

deep'-laid' *adj* schlau angelegt

deep' mourn'ing *s* tiefe Trauer *f*

deep'-root'ed *adj* tiefsitzend

**deep'-set' *adj* (*eyes*) tiefliegend

deer [dɪr] *s* Hirsch *m*, Reh *n*, Rotwild *n*

deer'skin' *s* Hirschleder *n*, Wildleder *n*

deface [dɪ'fes] *tr* (*disfigure*) verunstalten; (*make illegible*) unleserlich machen

defacement [dɪ'fesmənt] *s* Verunstaltung *f*

de facto [di'fækto] *adj & adv* tatsächlich, de facto

defamation [,dɛfə'meʃən] *s* Verleumdung *f*

defame [dɪ'fem] *tr* verleumden

default [dɪ'fɔlt] *s* (*in duties*) Unterlassung *f*; (fin) Verzug *m*; **by d.** (jur) durch Nichterscheinen; (sport) durch Nichtantreten; **in d. of** in Ermanglung (*genit*) ‖ *tr* nicht erfüllen; (fin) nicht zahlen ‖ *intr* seinen Verpflichtungen nicht nachkommen; (fin) in Verzug sein

defeat [dɪ'fit] *s* Niederlage *f*; (parl) Niederstimmen *n*; **admit d.** sich geschlagen geben ‖ *tr* besiegen, schlagen; (*frustrate*) hilflos machen; (*plans*) zunichte machen; (*a bill*) niederstimmen; **d. the purpose** den Zweck verfehlen

defeatism [dɪ'fitɪzəm] *s* Defätismus *m*

defeatist [dɪ'fitɪst] *s* Defätist –in *mf*

defecate ['dɛfɪ ,ket] *intr* Stuhl haben

defect ['difɛkt] *s* Defekt *m*; (*physical or mental defect*) Gebrechen *n*; (*imperfection*) Mangel *m*; (*in manufacture*) Fabrikationsfehler *m* ‖ [dɪ'fɛkt] *intr* (**from**) (*a religion*) abfallen (von); (*a party*) abtrünnig werden (von); (**to**) überlaufen (zu)

defection [dɪ'fɛkʃən] *s* Abfall *m*; (**to**) Übertritt *m* (zu)

defective [dɪ'fɛktɪv] *adj* fehlerhaft; (gram) unvollständig; (tech) defekt

defector [dɪ'fɛktər] *s* (pol) Abtrünnige *mf*, Überläufer –in *mf*

defend [dɪ'fɛnd] *tr* verteidigen

defendant [dɪ'fɛndənt] *s* (*in civil suit*) Beklagte *mf*; (*in criminal suit*) Angeklagte *mf*

defender [dɪ'fɛndər] *s* Verteidiger –in *mf*; (sport) Titelverteidiger –in *mf*

defense [dɪ'fɛns] *s* (& jur, sport) Verteidigung *f*; (*tactical*) (mil) Abwehr *f*; **d. against** (*e.g., disease*) Schutz *m* vor (*dat*)

defenseless [dɪ'fɛnslɪs] *adj* schutzlos

defensible [dɪ'fɛnsɪbəl] *adj* verteidigungsfähig; (*argument, claim*) verfechtbar

defensive [dɪ'fɛnsɪv] *adj* defensiv; (mil) Verteidigungs–, Abwehr– ‖ *s* Defensive *f*; (*tactical*) Abwehr *f*; **be on the d.**—sich in der Defensive befinden

de·fer [dɪ'fʌr] *v* (*pret & pp* –**ferred**; *ger* –**ferring**) *tr* verschieben; (mil) zurückschieben ‖ *intr*—**d. to** nachgeben (*dat*)

deference ['dɛfərəns] *s* (*courteous regard*) Ehrerbietung *f*; (*yielding*) Nachgiebigkeit *f*; **in d. to** aus Rücksicht gegen; **with all due d. to** bei aller Achtung vor (*dat*)

deferential [,dɛfə'rɛnʃəl] *adj* ehrerbietig, rücksichtsvoll

deferment [dɪ'fʌrmənt] *s* Aufschub *m*; (mil) Zurückstellung *f*

defiance [dɪ'faɪəns] *s* Trotz *m*; **in d. of s.o.** j–m zum Trotz

defiant [dɪ'faɪənt] *adj* trotzig

deficiency [dɪ'fɪʃənsi] *s* (**of**) Mangel *m* (an *dat*); (*shortcoming*) Defekt *m*; (*deficit*) Defizit *n*

deficient [dɪ'fɪʃənt] *adj* mangelhaft; **be d. in** Mangel haben an (*dat*); **mentally d.** schwachsinnig

deficit ['dɛfɪsɪt] *s* Defizit *n*

defilade [,dɛfɪ'led] *s* Deckung *f* ‖ *tr* gegen Feuer sichern

defile [dɪ'faɪl], ['dɪfaɪl] *s* Hohlweg *m* ‖ [dɪ'faɪl] *tr* beflecken

defilement [dɪ'faɪlmənt] *s* Befleckung *f*

define [dɪ'faɪn] *tr* definieren, bestimmen; (*e.g., boundaries*) festlegen

definite ['dɛfɪnɪt] *adj* bestimmt

definition [,dɛfɪ'nɪʃən] *s* Definition *f*, Bestimmung *f*; (opt) Bildschärfe *f*

definitive [dɪ'fɪnɪtɪv] *adj* endgültig

deflate [dɪ'flet] *tr* Luft ablassen aus; (*prices*) herabsetzen; (*s.o.'s ego, hopes*) e–n Stoß versetzen (*dat*)

deflation [dɪˈfleʃən] *s* (fin) Deflation *f*

deflect [dɪˈflɛkt] *tr* ablenken || *intr* (from) abweichen (von)

deflection [dɪˈflɛkʃən] *s* Ablenkung *f*; Abweichung *f*; (of an indicator) Ausschlag *m*; (of light rays) Beugung *f*; (radar, telv) Ablenkung *f*

deflower [dɪˈflau̇ər] *tr* entjungfern

defoliate [diˈfolɪ‚et] *tr* entblättern

deforest [diˈfɔrɪst] *tr* abholzen

deform [dɪˈfɔrm] *tr* entstellen

deformed' *adj* verwachsen, mißförmig

deformity [dɪˈfɔrmɪti] *s* (state of being deformed) Mißgestalt *f*; (deformed part) Verwachsung *f*; (ugliness) Häßlichkeit *f*

defraud [dɪˈfrɔd] *tr* (of) betrügen (um)

defray [dɪˈfre] *tr* tragen, bestreiten

defrock [diˈfrɑk] *tr* das Priesteramt entziehen (dat)

defrost [dɪˈfrɔst] *tr* entfrosten

defroster [dɪˈfrɔstər] *s* Entfroster *m*

deft [dɛft] *adj* flink, fingerfertig

defunct [dɪˈfʌŋkt] *adj* (person) verstorben; (no longer in operation) stillgelegt; (no longer in effect) außer Kraft (befindlich); (newspaper) eingegangen

de·fy [dɪˈfaɪ] *v* (pret & pp –fied) *tr* trotzen (dat); (challenge) herausfordern; **d. description** sich nicht beschreiben lassen

degeneracy [dɪˈdʒɛnərəsi] *s* Entartung *f*

degenerate [dɪˈdʒɛnərɪt] *adj* entartet, verkommen || [dɪˈdʒɛnə‚ret] *intr* entarten; (into) ausarten (in *acc*)

degrade [dɪˈgred] *tr* degradieren; (bring into low esteem) entwürdigen

degrad'ing *adj* entwürdigend

degree [dɪˈgri] *s* Grad *m*; (gram) Steigerungsstufe *f*; **by degrees** gradweise; **d. of latitude** Breitengrad *m*; **d. of longitude** Längengrad *m*; **take one's d.** promovieren; **to a d.** einigermaßen; **to a high d.** in hohem Maße

dehumanize [dɪˈhjumə‚naɪz] *tr* entmenschlichen

dehumidifier [‚dihjuˈmɪdɪ‚faɪ·ər] *s* Luftentfeuchter *m*

dehumidi·fy [‚dihjuˈmɪdɪ‚faɪ] *v* (pret & pp –fied) entfeuchten

dehydrate [dɪˈhaɪdret] *tr* (vegetables) dörren, das Wasser entziehen (dat); (chem) dehydrieren || *intr* das Wasser verlieren

dehy'drated *adj* (vegetables) Trocken–; (body) dehydriert

deice [dɪˈaɪs] *tr* enteisen

dei·fy [ˈdiɪ‚faɪ] *v* (pret & pp –fied) *tr* (a man) zum Gott erheben; (a woman) zur Göttin erheben

deject'ed *adj* niedergeschlagen

dejection [dɪˈdʒɛkʃən] *s* Niedergeschlagenheit *f*, Mutlosigkeit *f*

delay [dɪˈle] *s* Aufschub *m*, Verzögerung *f*; **without d.** unverzüglich || *tr* (postpone) aufschieben; (detain) aufhalten || *intr* zögern

delectable [dɪˈlɛktəbəl] *adj* ergötzlich

delegate [ˈdɛlɪ‚get], [ˈdɛlɪgɪt] *s* De-

legierte *mf* || [ˈdɛlɪ‚get] *tr* delegieren; (authority) übertragen

delegation [‚dɛlɪˈgeʃən] *s* (persons delegated) Delegation *f*; (e.g., of authority) Übertragung *f*

delete [dɪˈlit] *tr* tilgen

deletion [dɪˈliʃən] *s* Tilgung *f*

deliberate [dɪˈlɪbərɪt] *adj* (intentional) vorsätzlich, bewußt; (slow) gemessen, bedächtig || [dɪˈlɪbə‚ret] *intr* überlegen; (said of several persons) beratschlagen; **d. on** sich beraten über (acc)

deliberately [dɪˈlɪbərɪtli] *adv* mit Absicht

deliberation [dɪ‚lɪbəˈreʃən] *s* Überlegung *f*; (by several persons) Beratung *f*; (slowness) Bedächtigkeit *f*

delicacy [ˈdɛlɪkəsi] *s* Zartheit *f*; (fine food) Delikatesse *f*

delicate [ˈdɛlɪkɪt] *adj* fein, delikat; (situation) heikel; (health) zart

delicatessen [‚dɛlɪkəˈtɛsən] *s* (food) Delikatessen *pl*; (store) Delikatessengeschäft *n*

delicious [dɪˈlɪʃəs] *adj* köstlich

delight [dɪˈlaɪt] *s* Freude *f*; (high degree of pleasure) Entzücken *n*; **take d. in** Freude finden an (dat) || *tr* entzücken, erfreuen; **be delighted by** sich freuen an (dat); **I'll be delighted to come** ich komme mit dem größten Vergnügen || *intr*—**d. in** sich ergötzen an (dat)

delightful [dɪˈlaɪtfəl] *adj* entzückend

delimit [dɪˈlɪmɪt] *tr* abgrenzen

delineate [dɪˈlɪnɪ‚et] *tr* zeichnen

delinquency [dɪˈlɪŋkwənsi] *s* Pflichtvergessenheit *f*; (misdeed) Vergehen *n*

delinquent [dɪˈlɪŋkwənt] *adj* pflichtvergessen; (guilty) straffällig; (overdue) rückständig; (in default) säumig || *s* Straffällige *mf*

delirious [dɪˈlɪrɪ·əs] *adj* irre; (with) rasend (vor *dat*)

delirium [dɪˈlɪrɪ·əm] *s* Fieberwahn *m*

deliver [dɪˈlɪvər] *tr* liefern; (a message) überreichen; (free) befreien; (mail) zustellen; (a speech) halten; (a blow) versetzen; (a verdict) aussprechen; (a child) zur Welt bringen; (votes) bringen; (a ball) werfen; (relig) erlösen

deliverance [dɪˈlɪvərəns] *s* Erlösung *f*

delivery [dɪˈlɪvəri] *s* Lieferung *f*; (freeing) Befreiung *f*; (of mail) Zustellung *f*; (of a speaker, actor, singer) Vortragsweise *f*; (of a pitcher) Wurf *m*; (childbirth) Entbindung *f*

deliv'ery·man [–‚mɛn] *s* Austräger *m*

deliv'ery room' *s* Kreißsaal *m*

deliv'ery truck' *s* Lieferwagen *m*

dell [dɛl] *s* enges Tal *n*

delouse [diˈlaʊs] *tr* entlausen

delta [ˈdɛltə] *s* Delta *n*

delude [dɪˈlud] *tr* täuschen

deluge [ˈdɛljudʒ] *s* Überschwemmung *f*; (fig) Hochflut *f*; **Deluge** (Bib) Sintflut *f* || *tr* überschwemmen; (with letters, etc.) überschütten

delusion [dɪˈluʒən] *s* (state of being deluded) Täuschung *f*; (misconcep-

tion) Wahnvorstellung *f;* (psychiatry) Wahn *m; delusions of grandeur* Größenwahn *m*

deluxe [dɪˈlʊks], [dɪˈlʌks] *adj* Luxus
delve [dɛlv] *intr*—d. into sich vertiefen in (*acc*)

demagogue [ˈdɛməˌgɑg] *s* Volksverführer *–in mf*

demand [dɪˈmænd] *s* Verlangen *n;* (com) (for) Nachfrage *f* (nach); in (great) d. (sehr) gefragt; make demands on Ansprüche erheben auf (*acc*); on d. auf Verlangen ‖ *tr* (from or of) verlangen (von), fordern (von)

demand´ing *adj* anspruchsvoll; (*strict*) streng

demarca´tion line´ [ˌdimarˈkeʃən] *s* Demarkationslinie *f*

demean [dɪˈmin] *tr* erniedrigen

demeanor [dɪˈminər] *s* Benehmen *n*

demented [dɪˈmɛntɪd] *adj* wahnsinnig

demerit [diˈmɛrɪt] *s* (*fault*) Fehler *m;* (*deficiency mark*) Minuspunkt *m*

demigod [ˈdɛmɪˌgɑd] *s* Halbgott *m*

demijohn [ˈdɛmɪˌdʒɑn] *s* Korbflasche *f*

demilitarize [diˈmɪlɪtəˌraɪz] *tr* entmilitarisieren

demise [dɪˈmaɪz] *s* Ableben *n*

demitasse [ˈdɛmɪˌtæs], [ˈdɛmɪˌtɑs] *s* Mokkatasse *f*

demobilize [diˈmobɪˌlaɪz] *tr & intr* demobilisieren

democracy [dɪˈmɑkrəsɪ] *s* Demokratie *f*

democrat [ˈdɛməˌkræt] *s* Demokrat *–in mf*

democratic [ˌdɛməˈkrætɪk] *adj* demokratisch

demolish [dɪˈmɑlɪʃ] *tr* (*raze*) niederreißen; (*destroy*) zertrümmern; (*an argument*) vernichten; (*devour*) (coll) verschlingen

demolition [ˌdɛməˈlɪʃən], [ˌdiməˈlɪʃən] *s* (*act of razing*) Abbruch *m;* (*by explosives*) Sprengung *f;* **demolitions** Sprengstoff *m*

demoli´tion squad´ *s* Sprengkommando *n*

demoli´tion work´ *s* Sprengarbeiten *pl*

demon [ˈdimən] *s* Dämon *m,* böser Geist *m*

demonstrable [dɪˈmɑnstrəbəl] *adj* beweisbar

demonstrate [ˈdɛmənˌstret] *tr* (*prove*) beweisen; (*explain*) dartun; (*display*) zeigen; (*a product, process*) vorführen ‖ *intr* (pol) demonstrieren

demonstration [ˌdɛmənˈstreʃən] *s* (com) Vorführung *f;* (pol) Demonstration *f*

demonstrative [dɪˈmɑnstrətɪv] *adj* (*showing emotions*) gefühlvoll; (*illustrative*) anschaulich; (gram) hinweisend

demonstrator [ˈdɛmənˌstretər] *s* (*of products*) Vorführer *–in mf;* (*model used in demonstration*) Vorführmodell *n;* (pol) Demonstrant *–in mf*

demoralize [dɪˈmɔrəˌlaɪz] *tr* demoralisieren

demote [dɪˈmot] *tr* (*an employee*) herabstufen; (*a student*) zurückversetzen; (mil) degradieren

demotion [dɪˈmoʃən] *s* (*of an employee*) Herabstufung *f;* (*of a student*) Zurückversetzung *f;* (mil) Degradierung *f*

de·mur [dɪˈmʌr] *v* (*pret* & *pp* –murred; *ger* –murring) *intr* Einwände erheben

demure [dɪˈmjur] *adj* zimperlich

den [dɛn] *s* (*of animals; of thieves*) Höhle *f;* (*comfortable room*) Freizeitraum *m*

denaturalize [diˈnætʃərəˌlaɪz] *tr* ausbürgern

denial [dɪˈnaɪ·əl] *s* (*of an assertion*) Leugnung *f;* (*of guilt*) Leugnen *n;* (*of a request*) Ablehnung *f;* (*of faith*) Ableugnung *f;* (*of rights*) Verweigerung *f;* (*of a report*) Dementi *n*

denigrate [ˈdɛnɪˌgret] *tr* anschwärzen

denim [ˈdɛnɪm] *s* Drillich *m*

denizen [ˈdɛnɪzən] *s* Bewohner *–in mf*

Denmark [ˈdɛnmark] *s* Dänemark *n*

denomination [dɪˌnɑmɪˈneʃən] *s* Bezeichnung *f;* (*class, kind*) Klasse *f;* (*of money*) Nennwert *m;* (*of shares*) Stückelung *f;* (relig) Konfession *f,* Bekenntnis *n;* **in denominations of five and ten dollars** in Fünf- und Zehndollarnoten

denotation [ˌdinoˈteʃən] *s* Bedeutung *f*

denote [dɪˈnot] *tr* (*mean*) bedeuten; (*indicate*) anzeigen

dénouement [ˌdenuˈmɑ] *s* Auflösung *f*

denounce [dɪˈnauns] *tr* (*inform against*) denunzieren; (*condemn openly*) brandmarken, anprangern; (*a treaty*) kündigen

dense [dɛns] *adj* dicht; (coll) beschränkt

density [ˈdɛnsɪtɪ] *s* Dichte *f*

dent [dɛnt] *s* Beule *f* ‖ *tr* einbeulen

dental [ˈdɛntəl] *adj* Zahn–; (ling) dental ‖ *s* (ling) Zahnlaut *m*

den´tal hygiene´ *s* Zahnpflege *f*

den´tal sur´geon *s* Zahnarzt *m,* Zahnärztin *f*

dentifrice [ˈdɛntɪfrɪs] *s* Zahnputzmittel *n*

dentist [ˈdɛntɪst] *s* Zahnarzt *m,* Zahnärztin *f*

dentistry [ˈdɛntɪstrɪ] *s* Zahnheilkunde *f*

denture [ˈdɛntʃər] *s* künstliches Gebiß *n*

denunciation [dɪˌnʌnsɪˈeʃən] *s* (*informing against*) Denunzierung *f;* (*public condemnation*) Brandmarkung *f*

de·ny [dɪˈnaɪ] *v* (*pret* & *pp* –nied) *tr* (*a statement*) leugnen; (*officially*) dementieren; (*a request*) ablehnen; (*one's faith*) ableugnen; (*rights*) verweigern; **d. oneself s.th.** sich [*dat*] etw versagen; **d. s.o. s.th.** j–m etw aberkennen

deodorant [diˈodərənt] *s* Deodorant *n*

deodorize [diˈodəˌraɪz] *tr* desodorieren

deoxidize [diˈɑksɪˌdaɪz] *tr* desoxydieren

depart [dɪˈpɑrt] *intr* (*on foot*) fortgehen; (*in a vehicle or boat*) abfahren; (*by plane*) abfliegen; (*on horseback*) abreiten; (*on a trip*) abreisen; (*deviate*) abweichen

department [dɪˈpɑrtmənt] *s* (*subdivision*) Abteilung *f*; (*field*) Fach *n*; (*principal branch of government*) Ministerium *n*; (*government office*) Amt *n*; (*educ*) Abteilung *f*

depart′ment head′ *s* Abteilungsleiter –in *mf*

depart′ment store′ *s* Kaufhaus *n*, Warenhaus *n*

departure [dɪˈpɑrtʃər] *s* (*on foot*) Weggehen *n*; (*by car, boat, train*) Abfahrt *f*, Abreise *f*; (*by plane*) Abflug *m*; (*deviation*) Abweichung *f*

depend [dɪˈpend] *intr* (**on**) abhängen (von); (*rely on*) sich verlassen (auf *acc*); **depending on** je nach; **depending on how je nachdem**; **it all depends** (coll) es kommt darauf an

dependable [dɪˈpendəbəl] *adj* zuverlässig

dependence [dɪˈpendəns] *s* Abhängigkeit *f*

dependency [dɪˈpendənsi] *s* Schutzgebiet *n*

dependent [dɪˈpendənt] *adj* (**on**) abhängig (von) ‖ *s* Abhängige *mf*; (*for tax purposes*) Unterhaltsberechtigte *mf*

depict [dɪˈpɪkt] *tr* schildern

deplete [dɪˈplit] *tr* entleeren; (fig) erschöpfen

deplorable [dɪˈplorəbəl] *adj* (*situation*) beklagenswert; (*regrettable*) bedauerlich; (*bad*) schlecht

deplore [dɪˈplor] *tr* bedauern

deploy [dɪˈplɔɪ] *tr* entfalten ‖ *intr* sich entfalten

deployment [dɪˈplɔɪmənt] *s* Entfaltung *f*

depolarize [diˈpoləˌraɪz] *tr* depolarisieren

deponent [dɪˈponənt] *s* (gram) Deponens *n*; (jur) Deponent –in *mf*

depopulate [diˈpɑpjəˌlet] *tr* entvölkern

deport [dɪˈport] *tr* deportieren; **d. oneself** sich benehmen

deportation [ˌdiporˈteʃən] *s* Deportation *f*

deportment [dɪˈportmənt] *s* Benehmen *n*

depose [dɪˈpoz] *tr* (*from office*) absetzen; (jur) bezeugen ‖ *intr* (jur) unter Eid aussagen; (*in writing*) (jur) eidesstattlich versichern

deposit [dɪˈpɑzɪt] *s* (*partial payment*) Anzahlung *f*; (*at a bank*) Einlage *f*; (*for safekeeping*) Hinterlegung *f*; (geol) Ablagerung *f*; (min) Vorkommen *n*; **for d. only** nur zur Verrechnung ‖ *tr* (*set down*) niederlegen; (*money at a bank*) einlegen; (*a check*) verrechnen; (*as part payment*) anzahlen; (*for safekeeping*) deponieren; (geol) ablagern; (*a coin*) (telp) einwerfen

depositor [dɪˈpɑzɪtər] *s* Einzahler –in *mf*; (*of valuables*) Hinterleger –in *mf*

depos′it slip′ *s* Einzahlungsbeleg *m*

depot [ˈdipo], [ˈdepo] *s* (*bus station; storage place*) Depot *n*; (*train station*) Bahnhof *m*

depraved [dɪˈprevd] *adj* verworfen

depravity [dɪˈprævɪti] *s* Verworfenheit *f*

deprecate [ˈdeprɪˌket] *tr* mißbilligen

depreciate [dɪˈpriʃɪˌet] *tr* (*money, stocks*) abwerten; (*for tax purposes*) abschreiben; (*value or price*) herabsetzen; (*disparage*) geringschätzen ‖ *intr* im Wert sinken

depreciation [dɪˌpriʃɪˈeʃən] *s* (*decrease in value*) Wertminderung *f*; (*of currency or stocks*) Abwertung *f*; (*for tax purposes*) Abschreibung *f*

depress [dɪˈpres] *tr* niederdrücken; (*sadden*) deprimieren; (*cause to sink*) herunterdrücken

depressed′ *adj* (*saddened*) niedergeschlagen; (*market*) flau

depressed′ ar′ea *s* Notstandsgebiet *n*

depress′ing *adj* deprimierend

depression [dɪˈpreʃən] *s* (*mental state; economic crisis*) Depression *f*; (geol) Vertiefung *f*

deprive [dɪˈpraɪv] *tr*—**d. s.o. of s.th.** j–m etw entziehen; (*withhold*) j–m etw vorenthalten

depth [depθ] *s* Tiefe *f*; **go beyond one's d.** den Boden unter den Füßen verlieren; **in d.** gründlich

depth′ charge′ *s* Wasserbombe *f*

depth′ of field′ *s* (phot) Tiefenschärfe *f*

deputation [ˌdepjəˈteʃən] *s* Abordnung *f*

deputize [ˈdepjəˌtaɪz] *tr* abordnen

deputy [ˈdepjəti] *s* Vertreter –in *mf*; (pol) Abgeordnete *mf*

derail [dɪˈrel] *tr* zum Entgleisen bringen ‖ *intr* entgleisen

derailment [dɪˈrelmənt] *s* Entgleisung *f*

deranged [dɪˈrendʒd] *adj* geistesgestört

derangement [dɪˈrendʒmənt] *s* Geistesgestörtheit *f*

derby [ˈdɑrbi] *s* (*hat*) Melone *f*; (*race*) Derbyrennen *n*

derelict [ˈderɪlɪkt] *adj* (*negligent*) (**in**) nachlässig (in *dat*); (*abandoned*) herrenlos ‖ *s* (*ship; bum*) Wrack *n*

dereliction [ˌderɪˈlɪkʃən] *s* (*neglect*) Vernachlässigung *f*

deride [dɪˈraɪd] *tr* verspotten

derision [dɪˈrɪʒən] *s* Spott *m*

derivation [ˌderɪˈveʃən] *s* (gram, math) Ableitung *f*

derivative [dɪˈrɪvətɪv] *adj* abgeleitet ‖ *s* (chem) Derivat *n*; (gram, math) Ableitung *f*

derive [dɪˈraɪv] *tr* (*obtain*) gewinnen; (gram, math) ableiten; **d. pleasure from s.th.** Freude an etw finden ‖ *intr* (*from*) herstammen (von)

dermatologist [ˌdʌrməˈtɑlədʒɪst] *s* Hautarzt *m*, Hautärztin *f*

derogatory [dɪˈrɑgəˌtori] *adj* abfällig

derrick [ˈderɪk] *s* (*over an oil well*) Bohrturm *m*; (naut) Ladebaum *m*

dervish [ˈdʌrvɪʃ] *s* Derwisch *m*

desalinization [diˌselɪnɪˈzeʃən] *s* Entsalzung *f*

desalt [diˈsɔlt] *tr* entsalzen
descend [diˈsend] *tr* hinuntergehen ‖
intr (dismount, alight) absteigen;
(said of a plane) niedergehen; *(from
a tree, from heaven)* herabsteigen;
(said of a road) sich senken; *(pass
by inheritance)* **(to)** übergehen (auf
acc); **be descended from** abstammen
von; **d. upon** hereinbrechen über
(acc)
descendant [diˈsendənt] *s* Abkömmling *m*, Nachkomme *m*; **descendants**
Nachkommenschaft *f*
descendent [diˈsendənt] *adj* absteigend
descent [diˈsent] *s* Abstieg *m*; *(lineage)* Herkunft *f*; *(of a plane or parachute)* Niedergehen *n*; *(slope)* Abhang *m*; *(hostile raid)* **(on)** Überfall
m (auf *acc*)
describe [diˈskraɪb] *tr* beschreiben
description [diˈskrɪpʃən] *s* Beschreibung *f*; *(type)* Art *f*; **beyond d.** unbeschreiblich
descriptive [diˈskrɪptɪv] *adj* beschreibend
de•scry [diˈskraɪ] *v (pret & pp
–scried) tr* erspähen, erblicken
desecrate [ˈdesɪˌkret] *tr* entweihen
desecration [ˌdesɪˈkreʃən] *s* Entweihung *f*
desegregate [diˈsegrɪˌget] *tr* die Rassentrennung aufheben in *(dat)*
desegregation [diˌsegrɪˈgeʃən] *s* Aufhebung *f* der Rassentrennung
desert [ˈdezərt] *adj* öde, wüst; *(sand,
warfare, etc.)* Wüsten– ‖ *s* Wüste *f*;
(fig) Öde *f* ‖ [diˈzɜrt] *s* Verdienst
m; **get one's just deserts** seinen wohlverdienten Lohn empfangen ‖ *tr* verlassen ‖ *intr* (mil) desertieren; **(to)**
überlaufen (zu)
deserter [diˈzɜrtər] *s* Deserteur *m*
desertion [diˈzɜrʃən] *s* Verlassen *n*;
(of a party) Abfall *m*; (mil) Fahnenflucht *f*
deserve [diˈzɜrv] *tr* verdienen
deservedly [diˈzɜrvɪdlɪ] *adv* mit Recht
deserv′ing *adj* **(of)** würdig *(genit)*
design [diˈzaɪn] *s (outline)* Entwurf
m; *(pattern)* Muster *n*; *(plan)* Plan
m; *(plot)* Anschlag *m*; *(of a building, etc.)* Bauart *f*; *(aim)* Absicht *f*;
designs on böse Absichten auf *(acc)*
‖ *tr (make a preliminary sketch of)*
entwerfen; *(draw up detailed plans
for)* konstruieren; **designed for** gedacht für
designate [ˈdezɪgˌnet] *tr* **(as)** bezeichnen (als); **(to)** ernennen (zu)
designation [ˌdezɪgˈneʃən] *s (act of
designating)* Kennzeichnung *f*; *(title)*
Bezeichnung *f*; *(appointment)* Ernennung *f*
designer [diˈzaɪnər] *s (of patterns)*
Musterzeichner –in *mf*; *(of fashions)*
Modeschöpfer –in *mf*; (theat) Dekorateur –in *mf*
design′ing *adj* intrigant; *(calculating)*
berechnend
desirable [diˈzaɪrəbəl] *adj* wünschenswert, begehrenswert
desire [diˈzaɪr] *s (wish)* Wunsch *m*;
(interest) Lust *f*; *(craving)* Begierde

f; *(thing desired)* Gewünschte *n* ‖ *tr*
wünschen
desirous [diˈzaɪrəs] *adj* **(of)** begierig
(nach)
desist [diˈzɪst] *intr* **(from)** ablassen
(von)
desk [desk] *s* Schreibtisch *m*; *(of a
teacher)* Pult *n*; *(of a pupil)* Schulbank *f*; *(in a hotel)* Kasse *f*
desk′ cop′y *s* Freiexemplar *n*
desk′ lamp′ *s* Tischlampe *f*
desk′ pad′ *s* Schreibunterlage *f*
desolate [ˈdesəlɪt] *adj (barren)* öde;
(joyless) trostlos; *(deserted)* verlassen; *(delapidated)* verfallen ‖
[ˈdesəˌlet] *tr* verwüsten
desolation [ˌdesəˈleʃən] *s (devastation)* Verwüstung *f*; *(dreariness)*
Trostlosigkeit *f*
despair [dɪsˈper] *s* Verzweiflung *f* ‖
intr **(of)** verzweifeln (an *dat*)
despair′ing *adj* verweifelt
despera•do [ˌdespəˈrado], [ˌdespəˈredo] *s (–does & –dos)* Desperado *m*
desperate [ˈdespərɪt] *adj* verzweifelt
desperation [ˌdespəˈreʃən] *s* Verzweiflung *f*
despicable [ˈdespɪkəbəl] *adj* verächtlich, verachtungswürdig
despise [dɪsˈpaɪz] *tr* verachten
despite [dɪsˈpaɪt] *prep* trotz *(genit)*
despondency [dɪsˈspandənsɪ] *s* Kleinmut *m*
despondent [dɪsˈspandənt] *adj* kleinmütig
despot [ˈdespət] *s* Despot –in *mf*
despotic [desˈpatɪk] *adj* despotisch
despotism [ˈdespəˌtɪzəm] *s* Despotie
f; *(as a system)* Despotismus *m*
dessert [dɪˈzɜrt] *s* Nachtisch *m*
destination [ˌdestɪˈneʃən] *s (of a trip)*
Bestimmungsort *m*, Reiseziel *n*; *(purpose)* Bestimmung *f*
destine [ˈdestɪn] *tr* **(for)** bestimmen
(zu or für)
destiny [ˈdestɪnɪ] *s* Schicksal *n*;
(doom) Verhängnis *n*
destitute [ˈdestɪˌt(j)ut] *adj* mittellos;
d. of ohne
destitution [ˌdestɪˈt(j)uʃən] *s* äußerste
Armut *f*
destroy [dɪsˈtrɔɪ] *tr* vernichten, zerstören; *(animals, bacteria)* töten
destroyer [dɪsˈtrɔɪər] *s* (nav) Zerstörer *m*
destroy′er es′cort *s* Zerstörergeleitschutz *m*
destruction [dɪsˈtrʌkʃən] *s* Zerstörung
f; *(of species)* Ausrottung *f*
destructive [dɪsˈtrʌktɪv] *adj* zerstörend; *(criticism)* vernichtend; *(tendency)* destruktiv
desultory [ˈdesəlˌtorɪ] *adj (without
plan)* planlos; *(fitful)* sprunghaft;
(remark) deplaciert
detach [dɪsˈtætʃ] *tr* ablösen; *(along a
perforation)* abtrennen; *(mil)* abkommandieren
detachable [dɪsˈtætʃəbəl] *tr* abnehmbar,
ablösbar
detached′ *adj (building)* alleinstehend;
(objective) objektiv; *(aloof)* distanziert

detachment [dɪ'tætʃmənt] *s* Objektivität *f*; (*aloofness*) Abstand *m*; (mil) Trupp *m*, Kommando *n*

detail [dɪ'tel], ['ditel] *s* Enzelheit *f*, Detail *n*; (mil) Kommando *n*, Trupp *m*; **details** (pej) Kleinkram *m*; **in d.** ausführlich || [dɪ'tel] (*relate in detail*) ausführlich berichten; (*list*) einzeln aufzählen; (mil) abkommandieren

de'tail draw'ing *s* Detailzeichnung *f*

detailed' *adj* ausführlich; **d. work** Kleinarbeit *f*

detain [dɪ'ten] *tr* zurückhalten; (jur) in Haft behalten

detect [dɪ'tɛkt] *tr* (*discover*) entdecken; (*catch*) ertappen

detection [dɪ'tɛkʃən] *s* Entdeckung *f*

detective [dɪ'tɛktɪv] *s* Detektiv *m*

detec'tive sto'ry *s* Kriminalroman *m*

detector [dɪ'tɛktər] *s* (*e.g., of smoke*) Spürgerät *n*; (*of objects*) Suchgerät *n*; (rad) Detektor *m*

détente [de'tɑnt] *s* Entspannung *f*, Détente *f*

detention [dɪ'tɛnʃən] *s* (jur) Haft *f*

deten'tion camp' *s* Internierungslager *n*

deten'tion home' *s* Haftanstalt *f*

de·ter [dɪ'tʌr] *v* (*pret & pp* **-terred**) *ger—terring*) *tr* (from) abschrecken (von), abhalten (von)

detergent [dɪ'tʌrdʒənt] *s* Reinigungsmittel *n*; (*in a washer*) Waschmittel *n*

deteriorate [dɪ'tɪrɪ·ə‚ret] *tr* verschlechtern || *intr* sich verschlechtern

deterioration [dɪ‚tɪrɪ·ə'reʃən] *s* Verschlechterung *f*, Verfall *m*

determination [dɪ‚tʌrmɪ'neʃən] *s* Bestimmung *f*; (*resoluteness*) Entschlossenheit *f*; (*of boundaries*) Festlegung *f*

determine [dɪ'tʌrmɪn] *tr* (*fix conclusively*) bestimmen; (*boundaries*) festlegen; (*decide*) entscheiden

deter'mined *adj* entschlossen

deterrent [dɪ'tʌrənt] *adj* abschreckend || *s* Abschreckungsmittel *n*

detest [dɪ'tɛst] *tr* verabscheuen

detestable [dɪ'tɛstəbəl] *adj* abscheulich

dethrone [dɪ'θron] *tr* entthronen

detonate ['dɛtə‚net] *tr* explodieren lassen || *intr* explodieren

detour [dɪ'tur] *s* (*for cars*) Umleitung *f*; (*for pedestrians*) Umweg *m* || *tr* umleiten || *intr* e–n Umweg machen

detract [dɪ'trækt] *tr* ablenken || *intr*—**d. from** beeinträchtigen

detraction [dɪ'trækʃən] *s* Beeinträchtigung *f*

detractor [dɪ'træktər] *s* Verleumder –in *mf*

detrain [dɪ'tren] *tr* ausladen || *intr* aussteigen

detriment ['dɛtrɪmənt] *s* Nachteil *m*

detrimental [‚dɛtrɪ'mɛntəl] *adj* (to) nachteilig (für), schädlich (für)

deuce [d(j)us] *s* (*in cards or dice*) Zwei *f*; (*in tennis*) Einstand *m*; **what the d.?** was zum Teufel?

devaluate [di'vælju‚et] *tr* abwerten

devaluation [di‚vælju'eʃən] *s* Abwertung *f*

devastate ['dɛvəs‚tet] *tr* verheeren

develop [dɪ'vɛləp] *tr* entwickeln; (*one's mind*) (aus)bilden; (*a habit*) annehmen; (*a disease*) sich [*dat*] zuziehen; (*cracks*) bekommen; (*land*) nutzbar machen; (*a mine*) ausbauen; (phot) entwickeln || *intr* sich entwickeln; (*said of habits*) sich herausbilden; **d. into** sich entwickeln zu

developer [dɪ'vɛləpər] *s* (*of land*) Spekulant –in *mf*; (phot) Entwickler *m*

development [dɪ'vɛləpmənt] *s* Entwicklung *f*; (*of relations, of a mine*) Ausbau *m*; (*of land*) Nutzbarmachung *f*; (*of housing*) Siedlung *f*; (*an event*) Ereignis *n*; (educ) Ausbildung *f*; (phot) Entwicklung *f*

deviate ['divɪ‚et] *intr* abweichen

deviation [‚divɪ'eʃən] *s* Abweichung *f*

device [dɪ'vaɪs] *s* Vorrichtung *f*, Gerät *n*; (*means*) Mittel *n*; (*crafty scheme*) Kniff *m*; (*literary device*) Kunstgriff *m*; (heral) Sinnbild *n*; **leave s.o. to his own devices** j–n sich [*dat*] selbst überlassen

dev·il ['dɛvəl] *s* Teufel *m*; **a d. of a** (coll) verteufelt; **between the d. and the deep blue sea** zwischen zwei Feuern; **poor d.** armer Teufel; **the d. with you!** (coll) scher dich zum Teufel; **what** (who, *etc.*) **the d.?** was (wer, *etc.*) zum Teufel? || *v* (*pret & pp* **-il[l]ed**; *ger* **-il[l]ing**) *tr* (culin) mit viel Gewürz zubereiten

devilish ['dɛv(ə)lɪʃ] *adj* teuflisch

dev'il-may-care' *adj* (*informal*) wurstig; (*reckless*) verwegen

devilment ['dɛvɪlmənt] *s* Unfug *m*

deviltry ['dɛvɪltrɪ] *s* Unfug *m*

devious ['divɪ·əs] *adj* abweichend; (*tricky*) unredlich; (*reasoning*) abwegig

devise [dɪ'vaɪz] *tr* ersinnen; (jur) vermachen

devoid [dɪ'vɔɪd] *adj*—**d. of** ohne

devolve [dɪ'vɑlv] *intr*—**d. on** zufallen (*dat*)

devote [dɪ'vot] *tr* widmen

devot'ed *adj* (*dedicated*) ergeben; (*affectionate*) liebevoll

devotee [‚dɛvə'ti] *s* Anhänger –in *mf*

devotion [dɪ'voʃən] *s* Ergebenheit *f*; (*devoutness*) Frömmigkeit *f*; (*special prayer*) (to) Gebet *n* (zu); **devotions** Andacht *f*

devour [dɪ'vaur] *tr* verschlingen; (*said of fire*) verzehren

devout [dɪ'vaut] *adj* fromm; (*e.g., hope*) innig

dew [d(j)u] *s* Tau *m*; **dew is falling es** taut

dew'drop' *s* Tautropfen *m*

dew'lap' *s* Wamme *f*

dewy ['d(j)u·ɪ] *adj* tauig

dexterity [dɛks'tɛrɪti] *s* Geschicklichkeit *f*, Handfertigkeit *f*

dexterous ['dɛkstərəs] *adj* handfertig

dextrose ['dɛkstroz] *s* Traubenzucker *m*

diabetes [‚daɪ·ə'bitɪs] *s* Zuckerkrankheit *f*

diabetic [ˌdaɪ·ə'betɪk] *adj* zuckerkrank *mf*

diabolic(al) [ˌdaɪ·ə'balɪk(ə)l] *adj* teuflisch

diacritical [ˌdaɪ·ə'krɪtɪkəl] *adj* diakritisch

diadem ['daɪ·ə ˌdɛm] *s* Diadem *n*

diaere·sis [daɪ'erɪsɪs] *s* (-ses [ˌsiz]) Diäresis *f*; (*mark*) Trema *n*

diagnose [ˌdaɪ·əg'nos], [ˌdaɪ·əg'noz] *tr* diagnostizieren

diagno·sis [ˌdaɪ·əg'nosɪs] *s* (-ses [siz]) Diagnose *f*

diagonal [daɪ'ægənəl] *adj* diagonal || *s* Diagonale *f*

diagonally [daɪ'ægənəli] *adv*—d. across from schräg gegenüber von

diagram ['daɪ·ə ˌgræm] *s* Diagramm *n*

di·al ['daɪ·əl] *s* Zifferblatt *n*; (tech) Skalenscheibe *f*; (telp) Wählscheibe *f* || *v* (*pret* & *pp* -al[l]ed) *ger* -al[l]ing) *tr* & *intr* (telp) wählen

di'aling *s* (telp) Wählen *n* der Nummer

dialogue ['daɪ·ə ˌlɔg] *s* Dialog *m*

di'al tel'ephone *s* Selbstanschlußtelefon *n*

di'al tone' *s* Summton *m*, Amtszeichen *n*

diameter [daɪ'æmɪtər] *s* Durchmesser *m*

diamond ['daɪmənd] *adj* diamanten, (*in shape*) rautenförmig || *s* Diamant *m*; (*cut diamond*) Brillant *m*; (*rhombus*) Raute *f*; (baseball) Spielfeld *n*; (cards) Karo *n*

dia'mond ring' *s* Brillantring *m*

diaper ['daɪpər] *s* Windel *f*; change the diapers of trockenlegen, wickeln

diaphanous [daɪ'æfənəs] *adj* durchsichtig, durchscheinend

diaphragm ['daɪ·ə ˌfræm] *s* (*for birth control*) Gebärmutterkappe *f*; (anat) Zwerchfell *n*; (phot) Blende *f*; (tech, telp) Membran *f*

diarrhea [ˌdaɪ·ə'ri·ə] *s* Durchfall *m*

diary ['daɪ·əri] *s* Tagebuch *n*

diastole [daɪ'æstəli] *s* Diastole *f*

diatribe ['daɪ·ə ˌtraɪb] *s* Schmährede *f*

dice [daɪs] *spl* Würfel *pl* || *tr* in Würfel schneiden

dice'box' *s* Würfelbecher *m*

dichotomy [daɪ'katəmi] *s* Zweiteilung *f*; (bot) Gabelung *f*

dicker ['dɪkər] *intr* (about) feilschen (um)

dickey ['dɪki] *s* Hemdbrust *f*

dictaphone ['dɪktə ˌfon] *s* Diktaphon *n*

dictate ['dɪktet] *s* Diktat *n*; the dictates of conscience das Gebot des Gewissens || *tr* & *intr* diktieren

dictation [dɪk'teʃən] *s* Diktat *n*

dictator ['dɪktetər] *s* Diktator *m*

dictatorial [ˌdɪktə'tori·əl] *adj* diktatorisch; (*power*) unumschränkt

dic'tatorship' *s* Diktatur *f*

diction ['dɪkʃən] *s* Ausdrucksweise *f*

dictionary ['dɪkʃə ˌneri] *s* Wörterbuch *n*

dic·tum ['dɪktəm] *s* (-ta [tə]) (*saying*) Spruch *m*; (*pronouncement*) Ausspruch *m*

didactic [daɪ'dæktɪk] *adj* lehrhaft

die [daɪ] *s* (dice [daɪs]) Würfel *m*; the die is cast die Würfel sind gefallen || *s* (dies) (*coining die*) Prägestempel *m*; (*casting die*) Form *f*; (*forging die*) Gesenk *n*; (*threader*) Schneidkopf *m* || *v* (*pret* & *pp* died; *ger* dying) *tr*—die a natural death e-s natürlichen Todes sterben || *intr* sterben; (*said of plants and animals*) eingehen; be dying for (coll) sich sehnen nach; be dying to (*inf*) (coll) ich würde schrecklich gern (*inf*)

die'sel oil' *s* Dieselöl *n*

die'-hard' *s* Unentwegte *mf*

die'sel en'gine ['dizəl] *s* Dieselmotor *m*

die'sel oil' *s* Dieselöl *n*

die'stock' *s* Gewindeschneidkluppe *f*

diet ['daɪ·ət] *s* Kost *f*; (*special menu*) Diät *f*; (parl) Reichstag *m*; be on a d. diät leben; put on a d. auf Diät setzen || *intr* diät leben

dietary ['daɪ·ə ˌteri] *adj* Diät—; d. laws rituelle Diätvorschriften *pl*

dietetic [ˌdaɪ·ə'tetɪk] *adj* diätetisch || **dietetics** *spl* Diätetik *f*

dietitian [ˌdaɪ·ə'tɪʃən] *s* Diätspezialist —in *mf*

differ ['dɪfər] *intr* sich unterscheiden; (*said of opinions*) auseinanderweichen; d. from abweichen von; d. in verschieden sein in (dat); d. with anderer Meinung sein als

difference ['dɪfərəns] *s* Unterschied *m*; (*argument*) Streit *m*; (math) Differenz *f*; d. of opinion Meinungsverschiedenheit *f*; it makes no d. to me es ist mir gleich; split the d. den Rest teilen

different ['dɪfərənt] *adj* verschieden; a d. kind of e-n andere Art von; d. from anders als, verschieden von; d. kinds of verschiedene

differential [ˌdɪfə'renʃəl] *adj* (econ, elec, mach, math, phys) Differential— || *s* (*difference*) Unterschied *m*; (mach) Differentialgetriebe *n*; (math) Differential *n*

dif'feren'tial cal'culus *s* Differentialrechnung *f*

differentiate [ˌdɪfə'renʃɪ ˌet] *tr* unterscheiden; (math) differenzieren || *intr* —d. between unterscheiden zwischen (dat)

difficult ['dɪfɪ ˌkʌlt] *adj* schwierig, schwer

difficulty ['dɪfɪ ˌkʌlti] *s* Schwierigkeit *f*; I have d. in (ger) es fällt mir schwer zu (*inf*); with d. mit Mühe

diffuse [dɪ'fjus] *adj* (weit) zerstreut; (*style*) diffus || [dɪ'fjuz] *tr* (*spread*) verbreiten; (*pour out*) ausgießen; (phys) diffundieren || *intr* sich zerstreuen

diffusion [dɪ'fjuʒən] *s* (*spread*) Verbreitung *f*; (phys) Diffusion *f*

dig [dɪg] *s* (*jab*) Stoß *m*; (*sarcasm*)

Seitenhieb *m;* (archeol) Ausgrabung *f* || *v* (*pret & pp* dug [dʌg] & digged; *ger* digging) *tr* graben; (*a ditch*) auswerfen; (*potatoes*) ausgraben; (*understand*) (sl) kapieren; (*look at*) (sl) anschauen; (*appreciate*) (sl) schwärmen für; dig up ausgraben; (*find*) auftreiben; (*information*) ausfindig machen; (*money*) aufbringen; || *intr* graben, wühlen; dig in (*with the hands*) hineinfassen; (*work hard*) (coll) schuften; (mil) sich eingraben; dig for (*e.g., gold*) schürfen nach

digest [ˈdaɪdʒɛst] *s* Zusammenfassung *f;* (jur) Gesetzessammlung *f* || [daɪˈdʒɛst] *tr* verdauen; (*in the mind*) verarbeiten || *intr* verdauen

digestible [daɪˈdʒɛstɪbəl] *adj* verdaulich, verträglich

digestion [daɪˈdʒɛstʃən] *s* Verdauung *f*

digestive [daɪˈdʒɛstɪv] *adj* Verdauungs–; d. tract Verdauungsapparat *m*

digit [ˈdɪdʒɪt] *s* (math) Ziffer *f* (unter zehn); (math) Stelle *f*

digital [ˈdɪdʒɪtəl] *adj* digital, Digital–

dig'ital comput'er *s* digitale Rechenanlage *f*

digitalis [dɪdʒɪˈtælɪs] *s* Digitalis *n*

dignified [ˈdɪgnɪˌfaɪd] *adj* würdig

digni·fy [ˈdɪgnɪˌfaɪ] *v* (*pret & pp* –fied) *tr* ehren

dignitary [ˈdɪgnɪˌteri] *s* Würdenträger –in *mf*

dignity [ˈdɪgnɪti] *s* Würde *f;* d. of man Menschenwürde *f;* stand on one's d. sich [*dat*] nichts vergeben

digress [daɪˈgrɛs] *intr* (from) abschweifen (von)

digression [daɪˈgrɛʃən] *s* Abschweifung *f*

dike [daɪk] *s* Deich *m*

dilapidated [dɪˈlæpɪˌdetɪd] *adj* baufällig

dilate [daɪˈlet] *tr* ausdehnen || *intr* sich ausdehnen

dilation [daɪˈleʃən] *s* Ausdehnung *f*

dilatory [ˈdɪləˌtori] *adj* saumselig; (*tending to cause delay*) hinhaltend

dilemma [dɪˈlɛmə] *s* Dilemma *n*

dilettan·te [ˌdɪləˈtænti], [ˈdɪləˌtɑnt] *s* (*–tes & –ti* [ti]) Dilettant –in *mf*

diligence [ˈdɪlɪdʒəns] *s* Fleiß *m*

diligent [ˈdɪlɪdʒənt] *adj* fleißig

dill [dɪl] *s* Dill *m*

dillydal·ly [ˈdɪlɪˌdæli] *v* (*pret & pp* –lied) *intr* herumtrödeln

dilute [dɪˈlut], [daɪˈlut] *adj* verdünnt || [dɪˈlut] *tr* verdünnen; (*with water*) verwässern || *intr* sich verdünnen

dilution [dɪˈluʃən] *s* Verdünnung *f;* (*with water*) Verwässerung *f*

dim [dɪm] *adj* (dimmer; dimmest) (*light, eyesight*) schwach; (*poorly lighted*) schwach beleuchtet; (*dull*) matt; (*chances, outlook*) schlecht; (*indistinct*) undeutlich; take a dim view of (*disapprove of*) mißbilligen; (*be pessimistic about*) sich [*dat*] etw schwarz ausmalen || *v* (*pret & pp* dimmed; *ger* dimming) *tr* trüben; (*lights*) abblenden || *intr* sich ver-

dunkeln; (*said of lights, hopes*) verblassen

dime [daɪm] *s* Zehncentstück *n*

dime' nov'el *s* Groschenroman *m*

dimension [dɪˈmɛnʃən] *s* Maß *n,* Ausdehnung *f;* dimensions Ausmaß *n*

diminish [dɪˈmɪnɪʃ] *tr* (ver)mindern, verringern || *intr* sich vermindern

diminutive [dɪˈmɪnjətɪv] *adj* winzig; (gram) Verkleinerungs– || *s* Verkleinerungsform *f*

dimmer [ˈdɪmər] *s* (aut) Abblendvorrichtung *f*

dimple [ˈdɪmpəl] *s* Grübchen *n*

dim'wit' *s* Schwachsinnige *mf*

din [dɪn] *s* Getöse *n* || *v* (*pret & pp* dinned; *ger* dinning) *tr* betäuben; din s.th. into s.o. j–m etw einhämmern

dine [daɪn] *intr* speisen; d. out auswärts speisen

diner [ˈdaɪnər] *s* Tischgast *m;* (*small restaurant*) speisewagenähnliches Speiselokal *n;* (rr) Speisewagen *m*

dinette [daɪˈnet] *s* Speisenische *f*

dingbat [ˈdɪŋˌbæt] *s* (sl) (*person*) Dingsda *m;* (*thing*) Dingsda *n*

ding-dong [ˈdɪŋˌdɔŋ] *interj* bimbam!, klingklang!

dinghy [ˈdɪŋgi] *s* Beiboot *n;* rubber d. Schlauchboot *n*

dingy [ˈdɪndʒi] *adj* (*gloomy*) düster; (*shabby*) schäbig

din'ing car' *s* (rr) Speisewagen *m*

din'ing hall' *s* Speisesaal *m*

din'ing room' *s* Eßzimmer *n*

dinner [ˈdɪnər] *s* (*supper*) Abendessen *n;* (*main meal*) Hauptmahlzeit *f;* (*formal meal*) Diner *n;* after d. nach Tisch; at d. bei Tisch; before d. vor Tisch

din'ner guest' *s* Tischgast *m*

din'ner jac'ket *s* Smoking *m*

din'ner mu'sic *s* Tafelmusik *f*

din'ner par'ty *s* Tischgesellschaft *f*

din'ner time' *s* Tischzeit *f*

dinosaur [ˈdaɪnəˌsɔr] *s* Dinosaurier *m*

dint [dɪnt] *s*—by d. of kraft (*genit*)

diocesan [daɪˈɑsɪsən] *adj* Diözesan–

diocese [ˈdaɪəˌsɪs] *s* Diözese *f*

diode [ˈdaɪˌod] *s* (electron) Diode *f*

dioxide [daɪˈɑksaɪd] *s* Dioxyd *n*

dip [dɪp] *s* (*in the road*) Neigung *f;* (*short swim*) kurzes Bad *n;* (*dunk*) Eintauchen *n;* (*sauce*) Tunke *f;* (*of ice cream*) Portion *f* || *v* (*pret & pp* dipped; *ger* dipping) *tr* eintauchen; (*e.g., doughnuts*) eintunken; (*a flag*) senken || *intr* sich senken; dip into (*e.g., reserves*) angreifen; dip into one's pockets (fig) in die Tasche greifen

diphtheria [dɪfˈθɪrɪ·ə] *s* Diphtherie *f*

diphthong [ˈdɪfθɔŋ] *s* Doppelvokal *m*

diploma [dɪˈplomə] *s* Diplom *n*

diplomacy [dɪˈploməsi] *s* Diplomatie *f*

diplomat [ˈdɪpləˌmæt] *s* Diplomat –in *mf*

diplomatic [ˌdɪpləˈmætɪk] *adj* (& *fig*) diplomatisch

dipper [ˈdɪpər] *s* Schöpflöffel *m*

dipsomania [ˌdɪpsəˈmenɪ·ə] *s* Trunksucht *f*

dip′ stick′ *s* (aut) Ölstandmesser *m*

dire [daɪr] *adj* (*terrible*) gräßlich; (*need*) äußerste

direct [dɪ'rɛkt] *adj* direkt, unmittelbar; (*frank*) unverblümt; (*quotation*) wörtlich ‖ *tr* (*order*) beauftragen; (*a company*) leiten; (*traffic*) regeln; (*a movie, play*) Regie führen bei; (*an orchestra*) dirigieren; (*attention, glance*) (**to**) richten (auf *acc*); (*a person*) (**to**) verweisen (an *acc*); (*words, letter*) (**to**) richten (an *acc*)

direct′ call′ *s* Selbstwählverbindung *f*

direct′ cur′rent *s* Gleichstrom *m*

direct′ dis′course *s* direkte Rede *f*

direct′ hit′ *s* Volltreffer *m*

direction [dɪ'rɛkʃən] *s* Richtung *f*; (*order*) Anweisung *f*; (*leadership*) Leitung *f*, Führung *f*; (cin, theat) Regie *f*; (mus) Stabführung *f*; **directions** Weisungen *pl*; (*for use*) Gebrauchsanweisung *f*; **in all directions** nach allen Richtungen

directional [dɪ'rɛkʃənəl] *adj* Richt-

direc′tion find′er *s* Peilgerät *n*

direc′tion sig′nal *s* (aut) Richtungsanzeiger *m*

directive [dɪ'rɛktɪv] *s* Anweisung *f*

direct′ ob′ject *s* direktes Objekt *n*

direct′ op′posite *s* genaues Gegenteil *n*

director [dɪ'rɛktər] *s* Leiter –in *mf*, Direktor –in *mf*; (cin, theat) Regisseur –in *mf*; (mus) Dirigent –in *mf*; (rad, telv) Sendeleiter –in *mf*

direc′torship′ *s* Direktorat *n*

directory [dɪ'rɛktəri] *s* Verzeichnis *n*

dirge [dʌrdʒ] *s* Trauergesang *m*

dirigible ['dɪrɪdʒɪbəl] *s* lenkbares Luftschiff *n*

dirt [dʌrt] *s* Schmutz *m*, Dreck *m*; (*moral filth*) Schmutz *m*; (*soil*) Erde *f*

dirt′-cheap′ *adj* spottbillig

dirt′ farm′er *s* kleiner Farmer *m*

dirt′ road′ *s* unbefestigte Straße *f*

dirt·y ['dʌrti] *adj* schmutzig, dreckig; (*morally*) schmutzig; **d. business** Schweinerei *f*; **d. dog** Sauhund *m*; **d. joke** Zote *f*; **d. lie** gemeine Lüge *f*; **d. linen** schmutzige Wäsche *f*; **d. look** böser Blick *m*; **d. trick** übler Streich *m*; **that′s a d. shame** das ist e–e Gemeinheit! ‖ *v* (*pret & pp –ied*) *tr* beschmutzen

disability [,dɪsə'bɪlɪti] *s* Invalidität *f*

disable [dɪs'ebəl] *tr* (*e.g., a worker*) arbeitsunfähig machen; (*make unsuited for combat*) kampfunfähig machen; (jur) rechtsunfähig machen

disa′bled *adj* invalide; (mil) kampfunfähig; **d. veteran** Kriegsversehrte *mf*; **d. person** Invalide *mf*

disabuse [,dɪsə'bjuz] *tr*—**d. of** befreien von

disadvantage [,dɪsəd'væntɪdʒ] *s* Nachteil *m*; **place at a d.** benachteiligen

disadvantageous [dɪs,ædvən'tedʒəs] *adj* nachteilig

disagree [,dɪsə'gri] *intr* nicht übereinstimmen; (*be contradictory*) einander widersprechen; (*quarrel*) (sich) streiten; **d. with** (*said of food*) nicht bekommen (*dat*); **d. with s.o. on**

anderer Meinung über (*acc*) als j–d sein

disagreeable [,dɪsə'gri·əbəl] *adj* unangenehm

disagreement [,dɪsə'grimənt] *s* (*unlikeness*) Verschiedenheit *f*; (*dissention*) Uneinigkeit *f*; (*quarrel*) Meinungsverschiedenheit *f*

disappear [,dɪsə'pɪr] *intr* verschwinden

disappearance [,dɪsə'pɪrəns] *s* Verschwinden *n*

disappoint [,dɪsə'pɔɪnt] *tr* enttäuschen; **be disappointed at** (or **with**) enttäuscht sein über (*acc*)

disappointment [,dɪsə'pɔɪntmənt] *s* Enttäuschung *f*

disapproval [,dɪsə'pruvəl] *s* Mißbilligung *f*

disapprove [,dɪsə'pruv] *tr* mißbilligen; (*e.g., an application*) nicht genehmigen ‖ *intr*—**d. of** mißbilligen

disarm [dɪs'ɑrm] *tr* (& fig) entwaffnen; (*a bomb*) entschärfen ‖ *intr* abrüsten

disarmament [dɪs'ɑrməmənt] *s* Abrüstung *f*

disarm′ing *adj* (fig) entwaffnend

disarray [,dɪsə're] *s* Unordnung *f* ‖ *tr* in Unordnung bringen, verwirren

disassemble [,dɪsə'sɛmbəl] *tr* zerlegen

disaster [dɪ'zæstər] *s* Unheil *n*

disas′ter ar′ea *s* Katastrophengebiet *n*

disastrous [dɪ'zæstrəs] *adj* unheilvoll

disavow [,dɪsə'vaʊ] *tr* ableugnen

disavowal [,dɪsə'vaʊ·əl] *s* Ableugnung *f*

disband [dɪs'bænd] *tr* auflösen ‖ *intr* sich auflösen

dis·bar [dɪs'bɑr] *v* (*pret & pp –barred; ger –barring*) *tr* aus dem Anwaltsstand ausschließen

disbelief [,dɪsbɪ'lif] *s* Unglaube *m*

disbelieve [,dɪsbɪ'liv] *tr & intr* nicht glauben

disburse [dɪs'bʌrs] *tr* auszahlen

disbursement [dɪs'bʌrsmənt] *s* Auszahlung *f*

disc [dɪsk] *s* var of **disk**

discard [dɪs'kɑrd] *s* Ablegen *n* ‖ *tr* (*clothes, cards, habits*) ablegen; (*a plan*) verwerfen

discern [dɪ'sʌrn] *tr* (*perceive*) wahrnehmen; **be able to d. right from wrong** zwischen Gut und Böse unterscheiden können

discern′ing *adj* scharfsinnig

discernment [dɪ'sʌrnmənt] *s* Scharfsinn *m*

discharge [dɪs't'ʃɑrdʒ] *s* (*of a gun*) Abfeuern *n*; (*of a battery*) Entladung *f*; (*of water*) Abfluß *m*; (*of smoke*) Ausströmen *n*; (*of duties*) Erfüllung *f*; (*of debts*) Tilgung *f*; (*of employees, patients, soldiers*) Entlassung *f*; (*of a prisoner*) Freilassung *f*; (pathol) Ausfluß *m* ‖ *tr* (*a gun*) abfeuern; (*e.g., water*) ergießen; (*smoke*) ausstoßen; (*debts*) tilgen; (*duties*) erfüllen; (*an office*) verwalten; (*an employee, patient, soldier*) entlassen ‖ *intr* (*said of a gun*) losgehen; (*said of a battery*) sich entladen; (*pour out*) abfließen; (pathol) eitern

disciple [dɪˈsaɪpəl] *s* Jünger *m*

disciplinarian [ˌdɪsɪplɪˈnɛrɪ·ən] *s* Zuchtmeister *m*

disciplinary [ˈdɪsɪplɪˌnɛri] *adj* Disziplinar-

discipline [ˈdɪsɪplɪn] *s* Disziplin *f*; (*punishment*) Züchtigung *f* ‖ *tr* disziplinieren; (*punish*) züchtigen

disclaim [dɪsˈklem] *tr* leugnen; (jur) verzichten auf (*acc*)

disclose [dɪsˈkloz] *tr* enthüllen

disclosure [dɪsˈkloʒər] *s* Enthüllung *f*

discolor [dɪsˈkʌlər] *tr* verfärben ‖ *intr* sich verfärben

discoloration [dɪsˌkʌləˈreʃən] *s* Verfärbung *f*

discomfiture [dɪsˈkʌmfɪtʃər] *s* (*defeat*) Niederlage *f*; (*frustration*) Enttäuschung *f*; (*confusion*) Verwirrung *f*

discomfort [dɪsˈkʌmfərt] *s* Unbehagen *n* ‖ *tr* Unbehagen verursachen (*dat*)

disconcert [ˌdɪskənˈsʌrt] *tr* aus der Fassung bringen

dis'concert'ed *adj* fassungslos

disconnect [ˌdɪskəˈnɛkt] *tr* trennen; (elec) ausschalten; (mach) auskuppeln; (telp) unterbrechen

disconsolate [dɪsˈkɑnsəlɪt] *adj* trostlos

discontent [ˌdɪskənˈtɛnt] *s* Unzufriedenheit *f* ‖ *tr* unzufrieden machen

dis'content'ed *adj* (with) mißvergnügt (über *acc*)

discontinue [ˌdɪskənˈtɪnju] *tr* (*permanently*) einstellen; (*temporarily*) aussetzen; (*a newspaper*) abbestellen; **d.** (ger) aufhören zu (*inf*)

discord [ˈdɪskɔrd] *s* Mißklang *m*; (*dissention*) Zwietracht *f*

discordance [dɪsˈkɔrdəns] *s* Uneinigkeit *f*

discotheque [ˌdɪskoˈtɛk] *s* Diskothek *f*

discount [ˈdɪskaʊnt] *s* (*in price*) Rabatt *m*; (*cash discount*) Kassaskonto *n*; (*deduction from nominal value*) Diskont *m*; **at a d.** mit Rabatt; (st. exch.) unter pari ‖ *tr* (*disregard*) außer acht lassen; (*minimize*) geringen Wert beimessen (*dat*); (*for cash payment*) e-n Abzug gewähren auf (*acc*); (*e.g., a promissory note*) diskontieren

dis'count store' *s* Rabattladen *m*

discourage [dɪsˈkʌrɪdʒ] *tr* (*dishearten*) entmutigen; **d. s.o. from** (ger) (*deter*) j-n davon abschrecken zu (*inf*); (*dissuade*) j-m davon abraten zu (*inf*)

discour'aged *adj* mutlos

discouragement [dɪsˈkʌrɪdʒmənt] *s* (*act*) Entmutigung *f*; (*state*) Mutlosigkeit *f*; (*deterrent*) Abschreckung *f*

discourse [ˈdɪskors] *s* (*conversation*) Gespräch *n*; (*formal treatment*) Abhandlung *f*; (*lecture*) Vortrag *m* ‖ [dɪsˈkors] *intr* (on) sich unterhalten (über *acc*)

discourteous [dɪsˈkʌrtɪ·əs] *adj* unhöflich

discourtesy [dɪsˈkʌrtəsi] *s* Unhöflichkeit *f*

discover [dɪsˈkʌvər] *tr* entdecken

discovery [dɪsˈkʌvəri] *s* Entdeckung *f*

discredit [dɪsˈkrɛdɪt] *s* (*disrepute*) Mißkredit *m*; (*disbelief*) Zweifel *m* ‖ *tr* (*destroy confidence in*) in Mißkredit bringen; (*disbelieve*) anzweifeln; (*disgrace*) in Verruf bringen

discreditable [dɪsˈkrɛdɪtəbəl] *adj* schändlich

discreet [dɪsˈkrit] *adj* diskret

discrepancy [dɪsˈkrɛpənsi] *s* Unstimmigkeit *f*

discretion [dɪsˈkrɛʃən] *s* Diskretion *f*, Besonnenheit *f*; **at one's d.** nach Belieben; **leave to s.o.'s d.** in j-s Belieben stellen

discriminate [dɪsˈkrɪmɪˌnet] *tr* voneinander unterscheiden ‖ *intr*—**d. against** diskriminieren

discrimination [dɪsˌkrɪmɪˈneʃən] *s* (*distinction*) Unterscheidung *f*; (*prejudicial treatment*) Diskriminierung *f*

discriminatory [dɪsˈkrɪmɪnəˌtori] *adj* diskriminierend

discus [ˈdɪskəs] *s* Diskus *m*

discuss [dɪsˈkʌs] *tr* besprechen, diskutieren; (*formally*) erörtern

discussion [dɪsˈkʌʃən] *s* Diskussion *f*; (*formal consideration*) Erörterung *f*

disdain [dɪsˈden] *s* Geringschätzung *f* ‖ *tr* geringschätzen

disdainful [dɪsˈdenfəl] *adj* geringschätzig; **be d. of** geringschätzen

disease [dɪˈziz] *s* Krankheit *f*

diseased' *adj* krank, erkrankt

disembark [ˌdɪsɛmˈbɑrk] *tr* ausschiffen, landen ‖ *intr* an Land gehen, landen

disembarkation [dɪsˌɛmbɑrˈkeʃən] *s* Ausschiffung *f*

disembowel [ˌdɪsɛmˈbaʊ·əl] *v* (*pret* & *pp* -el[l]ed; *ger* -el[l]ing) *tr* ausweiden

disenchant [ˌdɪsɛnˈtʃænt] *tr* ernüchtern

disenchantment [ˌdɪsɛnˈtʃæntmənt] *s* Ernüchterung *f*

disengage [ˌdɪsɛnˈgedʒ] *tr* (*a clutch*) ausrücken; (*the enemy*) sich absetzen von; (*troops*) entflechten; **d. the clutch** auskuppeln ‖ *intr* loskommen; (mil) sich absetzen

disengagement [ˌdɪsɛnˈgedʒmənt] *s* Lösung *f*; (mil) Truppenentflechtung *f*

disentangle [ˌdɪsɛnˈtæŋgəl] *tr* entwirren

disentanglement [ˌdɪsɛnˈtæŋgəlmənt] *s* Entwirrung *f*

disfavor [dɪsˈfevər] *s* Ungunst *f*

disfigure [dɪsˈfɪgjər] *tr* entstellen

disfigurement [dɪsˈfɪgjərmənt] *s* Entstellung *f*

disfranchise [dɪsˈfræntʃaɪz] *tr* die Bürgerrechte entziehen (*dat*)

disgorge [dɪsˈgɔrdʒ] *tr* ausspeien ‖ *intr* sich ergießen

disgrace [dɪsˈgres] *s* Schande *f*; (*of a family*) Schandfleck *m* ‖ *tr* in Schande bringen; (*a girl*) schänden; **be disgraced** in Schande kommen

disgraceful [dɪsˈgresfəl] *adj* schändlich, schimpflich

disgruntled [dɪsˈgrʌntəld] *adj* mürrisch

disguise [dɪsˈgaɪz] *s* (*clothing*) Verkleidung *f*; (*insincere manner*) Ver-
stellung *f* ‖ *tr* (*by dress*) verkleiden;
(*e.g., the voice*) verstellen

disgust [dɪsˈgʌst] *s* (at) Ekel *m* (vor
dat) ‖ *tr* anekeln

disgust′ing *adj* ekelhaft

dish [dɪʃ] *s* Schüssel *f*, Platte *f*; (*food*)
Gericht *n*; do the dishes das Ge-
schirr spülen ‖ *tr*—d. out (coll) austeilen

dish′cloth′ *s* Geschirrlappen *m*

dishearten [dɪsˈhɑrtən] *tr* entmutigen

disheveled [dɪˈʃɛvəld] *adj* unordentlich

dishonest [dɪsˈɑnɪst] *adj* unehrlich

dishonesty [dɪsˈɑnɪsti] *s* Unehrlichkeit
f

dishonor [dɪsˈɑnər] *s* Unehre *f* ‖ *tr*
verunehren

dishonorable [dɪsˈɑnərəbəl] *adj* (*person*) ehrlos; (*action*) unehrenhaft

dishon′orable dis′charge *s* Entlassung
f wegen Wehrunwürdigkeit

dish′pan′ *s* Aufwaschschüssel *f*

dish′rack′ *s* Abtropfkörbchen *n*

dish′rag′ *s* Spüllappen *m*

dish′tow′el *s* Geschirrtuch *n*

dish′wash′er *s* (*person*) Aufwäscher
–in *mf*; (*appliance*) Geschirrspülmaschine *f*

dish′wa′ter *s* Spülwasser *n*

disillusion [ˌdɪsɪˈluʒən] *s* Ernüchterung *f* ‖ *tr* ernüchtern

disillusionment [ˌdɪsɪˈluʒənmənt] *s* Ernüchterung *f*

disinclination [dɪsˌɪnklɪˈneʃən] *s* Abneigung *f*, Abgeneigtheit *f*

disinclined [ˌdɪsɪnˈklaɪnd] *adj* abge-
neight

disinfect [ˌdɪsɪnˈfɛkt] *tr* desinfizieren

disinfectant [ˌdɪsɪnˈfɛktənt] *adj* des-
infizierend ‖ *s* Desinfektionsmittel *n*

disinherit [ˌdɪsɪnˈhɛrɪt] *tr* enterben

disintegrate [dɪsˈɪntɪˌgret] *tr* (& fig)
zersetzen ‖ *intr* zerfallen

disintegration [dɪsˌɪntɪˈgreʃən] *s* (&
fig) Zerfall *m*

disin-ter [ˌdɪsɪnˈtʌr] *v* (*pret & pp*
–terred; *ger* –terring) *tr* ausgraben

disinterested [dɪsˈɪntəˌrɛstɪd] *adj* (*unbiased*) unparteiisch; (*uninterested*)
desinteressiert

disjunctive [dɪsˈdʒʌŋktɪv] *adj* disjunk-
tiv

disk [dɪsk] *s* Scheibe *f*

disk′ brake′ *s* Scheibenbremse *f*

disk′ jock′ey *s* Schallplattenjockei *m*

dislike [dɪsˈlaɪk] *s* (of) Abneigung *f*
(gegen) ‖ *tr* nicht mögen

dislocate [ˈdɪsloˌket] *tr* verschieben;
(*a shoulder*) verrenken; (fig) stören

dislocation [ˌdɪsloˈkeʃən] *s* Verschie-
bung *f*; (*of a shoulder*) Verrenkung
f; (fig) Störung *f*

dislodge [dɪsˈlɑdʒ] *tr* losreißen; (mil)
aus der Stellung werfen

disloyal [dɪsˈlɔɪ.əl] *adj* untreu

disloyalty [dɪsˈlɔɪ.əlti] *s* Untreue *f*

dismal [ˈdɪzməl] *adj* trübselig, düster

dismantle [dɪsˈmæntəl] *tr* demontieren

dismay [dɪsˈme] *s* Bestürzung *f* ‖ *tr*
bestürzen

dismember [dɪsˈmɛmbər] *tr* zerstük-
keln

dismiss [dɪsˈmɪs] *tr* verabschieden; (*an
employee*) (from) entlassen (aus);
(*a case*) (jur) abweisen; (mil) wegtreten lassen; d. as abtun als; dismissed! (mil) wegtreten!

dismissal [dɪsˈmɪsəl] *s* Entlassung *f*;
(jur) Abweisung *f*

dismount [dɪsˈmaʊnt] *tr* (*throw down*)
abwerfen; (mach) abmontieren ‖ *intr*
(*from a carriage*) herabsteigen; (*from
a horse*) absitzen

disobedience [ˌdɪsəˈbidɪ.əns] *s* Ungehorsam *m*, Unfolgsamkeit *f*

disobedient [ˌdɪsəˈbidɪ.ənt] *adj* ungehorsam, unfolgsam

disobey [ˌdɪsəˈbe] *tr* nicht gehorchen
(*dat*) ‖ *intr* nicht gehorchen

disorder [dɪsˈɔrdər] *s* Unordnung *f*;
(*public disturbance*) Unruhe *f*;
(pathol) Erkrankung *f*; throw into
d. in Unordnung bringen

disorderly [dɪsˈɔrdərli] *adj* unordentlich, liederlich

disor′derly con′duct *s* ungebührliches
Benehmen *n*

disor′derly house′ *s* Bordell *n*; (*gambling house*) Spielhölle *f*

disorganize [dɪsˈɔrgəˌnaɪz] *tr* zerrütten, desorganisieren

disown [dɪsˈon] *tr* verleugnen

disparage [dɪˈspærɪdʒ] *tr* herabsetzen,
geringschätzen

disparate [ˈdɪspərɪt] *adj* ungleichartig

disparity [dɪˈspærɪti] *s* (*inequality*)
Ungleichheit *f*; (*difference*) Unterschied *m*

dispassionate [dɪsˈpæʃənɪt] *adj* leidenschaftslos

dispatch [dɪˈspætʃ] *s* Abfertigung *f*;
(*message*) Depesche *f*; with d. in Eile
‖ *tr* (*send off*) absenden; (*e.g., a
truck*) abfertigen; (*e.g., a task*)
schnell erledigen; (*kill*) töten; (*eat
fast*) (coll) verputzen

dispatcher [dɪˈspætʃər] *s* (*of vehicles*)
Fahrbereitschaftsleiter –in *mf*

dis-pel [dɪˈspɛl] *v* (*pret & pp* –pelled;
ger –pelling) *tr* vertreiben; (*thoughts,
doubts*) zerstreuen

dispensary [dɪˈspɛnsəri] *s* Arzneiaus-
gabestelle *f*; (mil) Krankenrevier *n*

dispensation [ˌdɪspənˈseʃən] *s* (eccl)
(from) Dispens *m* (von); by divine
d. durch göttliche Fügung

dispense [dɪˈspɛns] *tr* (*exempt*) (from)
entbinden (von); (pharm) zubereiten
und ausgeben; d. justice Recht
sprechen ‖ *intr*—d. with verzichten
auf (*acc*)

dispersal [dɪˈspʌrsəl] *s* Auflockerung *f*

disperse [dɪˈspʌrs] *tr* zerstreuen; (*a
crowd*) zersprengen; (*one's troops*)
auflockern; (*the enemy*) auseinander-
sprengen ‖ *intr* (said *of clouds, etc.*)
sich verziehen; (said *of crowds*) auseinandergehen

dispirited [dɪˈspɪrɪtɪd] *adj* niedergeschlagen

displace [dɪs'ples] *tr* (*people in war*) verschleppen; (*phys*) verdrängen
displacement [dɪs'plesmənt] *s* Vertreibung *f*; (*phys*) Verdrängung *f*
display [dɪ'sple] *s* (*of energy, wealth*) Entfaltung *f*; (*of goods*) Ausstellung *f*; (*pomp*) Aufwand *m*; **on d.** zur Schau ‖ *tr* (*wares*) ausstellen; (*reveal*) entfalten; (*flaunt*) protzen mit
display′ case′ *s* Vitrine *f*
display′ room′ *s* Ausstellungsraum *m*
display′ win′dow *s* Schaufenster *n*
displease [dɪs'pliz] *tr* mißfallen (*dat*); **be displeased with** Mißfallen finden an (*dat*) ‖ *intr* mißfallen
displeas′ing *adj* mißfällig
displeasure [dɪs'plɛʒər] *s* Mißfallen *n*
disposable [dɪ'spozəbəl] *adj* Einweg-
disposal [dɪ'spozəl] *s* (*riddance*) Beseitigung *f*; (*of a matter*) Erledigung *f*; (*distribution*) Anordnung *f*; **be at s.o.'s d.** j-m zur Verfügung stehen; **have at one's d.** verfügen über (*acc*); **put at s.o.'s d.** j-m zur Verfügung stellen
dispose [dɪ'spoz] *tr* (*incline*) (**to**) geneigt machen (zu); (*arrange*) anordnen ‖ *intr*—**d. of** (*a matter*) erledigen; (*get rid of*) loswerden
disposed′ *adj* gesinnt; **d. to** (*ger*) geneigt zu (*inf*)
disposition [ˌdɪspə'zɪʃən] *s* (*settlement*) Erledigung *f*; (*nature*) Gemütsart *f*; (*inclination*) Neigung *f*
dispossess [ˌdɪspə'zɛs] *tr*—**d. s.o. of s.th.** j-m etw enteignen
disproof [dɪs'pruf] *s* Widerlegung *f*
disproportionate [ˌdɪsprə'porʃənɪt] *adj* unverhältnismäßig; **be d. to** im Mißverhältnis stehen zu
disprove [dɪs'pruv] *tr* widerlegen
dispute [dɪs'pjut] *s* (*quarrel*) Streit *m*; (*debate*) Wortgefecht *n*; **beyond d.** unstreitig; **in d.** umstritten ‖ *tr* bestreiten ‖ *intr* disputieren
disqualification [dɪsˌkwɑlɪfɪ'keʃən] *s* Disqualifizierung *f*
disquali-fy [dɪs'kwɑlɪˌfaɪ] *v* (*pret & pp* **-fied**) *tr* (*make unfit*) (**for**) untauglich machen (für); (*declare ineligible*) disqualifizieren
disquiet [dɪs'kwaɪ·ət] *tr* beunruhigen
disqui′eting *adj* beunruhigend
disregard [ˌdɪsrɪ'gɑrd] *s* (*lack of attention*) Nichtbeachtung *f*; (*disrespect*) Mißachtung *f* ‖ *tr* (*not pay attention to*) nicht beachten; (*treat without due respect*) mißachten
disrepair [ˌdɪsrɪ'pɛr] *s* Verfall *m*; **fall into d.** verfallen
disreputable [dɪs'rɛpjətəbəl] *adj* verrufen
disrepute [ˌdɪsrɪ'pjut] *s* Verruf *m*
disrespect [ˌdɪsrɪ'spɛkt] *s* Nichtachtung *f*, Mißachtung *f* ‖ *tr* nicht achten
disrespectful [ˌdɪsrɪ'spɛktfəl] *adj* respektlos, unehrerbietig
disrobe [dɪs'rob] *tr* entkleiden ‖ *intr* sich entkleiden
disrupt [dɪs'rʌpt] *tr* (*throw into confusion*) in Verwirrung bringen; (*interrupt*) unterbrechen; (*cause to*

break down) zum Zusammenbruch bringen
dissatisfaction [ˌdɪssætɪs'fækʃən] *s* Unzufriedenheit *f*
dissat′isfied′ *adj* unzufrieden
dissatis-fy [dɪs'sætɪsˌfaɪ] *v* (*pret & pp* **-fied**) *tr* nicht befriedigen
dissect [dɪ'sɛkt] *tr* (*fig*) zergliedern; (*anat*) sezieren
dissection [dɪ'sɛkʃən] *s* (*fig*) Zergliederung *f*; (*anat*) Sektion *f*
dissemble [dɪ'sɛmbəl] *tr* verbergen ‖ *intr* heucheln
disseminate [dɪ'sɛmɪˌnet] *tr* verbreiten
dissension [dɪ'sɛnʃən] *s* Uneinigkeit *f*
dissent [dɪ'sɛnt] *s* abweichende Meinung *f* ‖ *intr* (**from**) anderer Meinung sein (als)
dissenter [dɪ'sɛntər] *s* Andersdenkende *mf*; (*relig*) Dissident *-in* *mf*
dissertation [ˌdɪsər'teʃən] *s* Dissertation *f*
disservice [dɪs'sʌrvɪs] *s* schlechter Dienst *m*; **do s.o. a d.** j-m e-n schlechten Dienst erweisen
dissidence [ˈdɪsɪdəns] *s* Meinungsverschiedenheit *f*
dissident [ˈdɪsɪdənt] *adj* andersdenkend ‖ *s* Dissident *-in* *mf*
dissimilar [dɪ'sɪmɪlər] *adj* unähnlich
dissimilate [dɪ'sɪmɪˌlet] *tr* (*phonet*) dissimilieren
dissimulate [dɪ'sɪmjəˌlet] *tr* verheimlichen ‖ *intr* heucheln
dissipate [ˈdɪsɪˌpet] *tr* (*squander*) vergeuden; (*scatter*) zerstreuen; (*dissolve*) auflösen ‖ *intr* (*scatter*) sich zerstreuen; (*dissolve*) sich auflösen
dis′sipat′ed *adj* ausschweifend
dissipation [ˌdɪsɪ'peʃən] *s* (*squandering*) Vergeudung *f*; (*dissolute mode of life*) Ausschweifung *f*; (*phys*) Dissipation *f*
dissociate [dɪ'soʃɪˌet] *tr* trennen; **d. oneself from** abrücken von
dissolute [ˈdɪsəˌlut] *adj* ausschweifend
dissolution [ˌdɪsə'luʃən] *s* Auflösung *f*
dissolve [dɪ'zɑlv] *s* (*cin*) Überblendung *f* ‖ *tr* auflösen; (*cin*) überblenden ‖ *intr* sich auflösen; (*cin*) überblenden
dissonance [ˈdɪsənəns] *s* Mißklang *m*
dissuade [dɪ'swed] *tr* (**from**) abbringen (von); **d. s.o. from** (*ger*) j-n davon abbringen zu (*inf*)
dissyllabic [ˌdɪsɪ'læbɪk] *adj* zweisilbig
distaff [ˈdɪstæf] *s* Spinnrocken *m*; (*fig*) Frauen *pl*
dis′taff side′ *s* weibliche Linie *f*
distance [ˈdɪstəns] *s* Entfernung *f*; (*between two points*) Abstand *m*; (*stretch*) Strecke *f*; (*of a race*) Rennstrecke *f*; **from a d.** aus einiger Entfernung; **go the d.** bis zum Ende aushalten; **in the d.** in der Ferne; **keep one's d.** zurückhalten mit; **keep your d.** bleib mir vom Leib!; **within easy d.** of nicht weit weg von; **within walking d. of** zu Fuß erreichbar von
distant [ˈdɪstənt] *adj* entfernt; (*reserved*) zurückhaltend

distaste [dɪs'test] s (for) Abneigung f (gegen), Ekel m (vor dat)

distasteful [dɪs'testfəl] adj (unpleasant) (to) unangenehm (dat); (offensive) (to) ekelhaft (dat)

distemper [dɪs'tempər] s (of dogs) Staupe f; (paint) Temperafarbe f

distend [dɪs'tend] tr (swell) aufblähen; (extend) ausdehnen || intr (swell) anschwellen; (extend) (aus)dehnen

distension [dɪs'tenʃən] s Aufblähung f; Ausdehnung f

distill [dɪ'stɪl] tr destillieren; (e.g., whiskey) brennen

distillation [ˌdɪstɪ'leʃən] s Destillation f; (of whiskey) Brennen n

distiller [dɪs'tɪlər] s Brenner m

distillery [dɪs'tɪləri] s Brennerei f

distinct [dɪ'stɪŋkt] adj (clear) deutlich; (different) verschieden; as d. from zum Unterschied von; keep d. auseinanderhalten

distinction [dɪs'tɪŋkʃən] s (difference) Unterschied m; (differentiation) Unterscheidung f; (honor) Auszeichnung f; (eminence) Vornehmheit f; have the d. of (ger) den Vorzug haben zu (inf)

distinctive [dɪs'tɪŋktɪv] adj (distinguishing) unterscheidend; (characteristic) kennzeichnend

distinguish [dɪs'tɪŋgwɪʃ] tr (differentiate) unterscheiden; (classify) einteilen; (honor) auszeichnen; (characterize) kennzeichnen; (discern) erkennen || intr (between) unterscheiden (zwischen dat)

distin'guished adj (eminent) prominent; (for) berühmt (wegen)

distort [dɪs'tort] tr verzerren; (the truth) entstellen; distorted picture Zerrbild n

distortion [dɪs'torʃən] s Verzerrung f; (of the truth) Entstellung f

distract [dɪ'strækt] tr ablenken

distraction [dɪ'strækʃən] s (diversion of attention) Ablenkung f; (entertainment) Zerstreuung f; drive s.o. to d. j-n zum Wahnsinn treiben

distraught [dɪ'strot] adj (bewildered) verwirrt; (deeply agitated) (with) aufgewühlt (von); (crazed) (with) rasend (vor dat)

distress [dɪ'stres] s (anxiety) Kummer m; (mental pain) Betrübnis f; (danger) Notstand m, Bedrängnis f; (naut) Seenot f || tr betrüben

distress'ing adj betrüblich

distress' sig'nal s Notzeichen n

distribute [dɪ'strɪbjut] tr verteilen; (divide) einteilen; (apportion) (jur) aufteilen

distribution [ˌdɪstrɪ'bjuʃən] s Verteilung f; (geographic range) Verbreitung f; (of films) Verleih m; (marketing) Vertrieb m; (of dividends) Ausschüttung f; (jur) Aufteilung f

distributor [dɪ'strɪbjətər] s Verteiler –in mf; (of films) Verleiher –in mf; (dealer) Lieferant –in mf; (aut) Verteiler m

distri'butorship' s Vertrieb m

district ['dɪstrɪkt] s Bezirk m

dis'trict attor'ney s Staatsanwalt m

distrust [dɪs'trʌst] s Mißtrauen n || tr mißtrauen (dat)

distrustful [dɪs'trʌstfəl] adj (of) mißtrauisch (gegen)

disturb [dɪs'tʌrb] tr stören; (disquiet) beunruhigen; d. the peace die öffentliche Ruhe stören

disturbance [dɪs'tʌrbəns] s (interruption) Störung f; (breach of peace) Unruhe f

disunited [ˌdɪsju'naɪtɪd] adj uneinig

disunity [dɪs'junɪti] s Uneinigkeit f

disuse [dɪs'jus] s Nichtverwendung f; fall into d. außer Gebrauch kommen

ditch [dɪtʃ] s Graben m || tr (discard) (sl) wegschmeißen; (aer) (coll) auf dem Wasser notlanden mit || intr (aer) (coll) notwassern

dither ['dɪðər] s—be in a d. verdattert sein

dit•to ['dɪto] adj (coll) dito || s (–tos) Kopie f || tr vervielfältigen

dit'to mark' s Wiederholungszeichen n

ditty ['dɪti] s Liedchen n

diva ['divə] s (mus) Diva f

divan ['darvæn], [dɪ'væn] s Diwan m

dive [daɪv] s Kopfsprung m; (coll) Spelunke f; (aer) Sturzflug m; (nav) Tauchen n; (sport) Kunstsprung m; make a d. for (fig) sich stürzen auf (acc) || v (pret & pp dived & dove [dov]) intr (submerge) tauchen; (plunge head first) e-n Kopfsprung machen; (aer) e-n Sturzflug machen; (nav) (unter)tauchen; (sport) e-n Kunstsprung machen

dive'-bomb' tr & intr im Sturzflug mit Bomben angreifen

dive' bomb'er s Sturzkampfbomber m

diver ['daɪvər] s Taucher –in mf; (orn) Taucher m; (sport) Kunstspringer –in mf

diverge [daɪ'vʌrdʒ] intr (said of roads, views) sich teilen; (from the norm) abweichen; (geom, phys) divergieren

diverse [daɪ'vʌrs] adj (different) verschieden; (of various kinds) vielförmig

diversi•fy [daɪ'vʌrsɪ͵faɪ] v (pret & pp –fied) tr abwechslungsreich gestalten

diversion [daɪ'vʌrʒən] s Ablenkung f; (recreation) Zeitvertreib m; (mil) Ablenkungsmanöver n

diversity [daɪ'vʌrsɪti] s Mannigfaltigkeit f

divert [daɪ'vʌrt] tr (attention) ablenken; (traffic) umleiten; (a river) ableiten; (money) abzweigen; (entertain) zerstreuen

divest [daɪ'vest] tr—d. oneself of sich entäußern (genit); d. s.o. of (e.g., office, power) j-n entkleiden (genit); (e.g., rights, property) j-m (seine Rechte, etc.) entziehen

divide [dɪ'vaɪd] s (geol) Wasserscheide f || tr teilen; (cause to disagree) entzweien; (math) (by) teilen (durch); d. into einteilen in (acc); d. off (a room) abteilen; d. up (among) aufteilen (unter acc) ||

(*said of a road*) sich teilen; **d. into** sich teilen in (*acc*)

dividend [′dɪvɪˌdend] *s* Dividende *f*; (math) Dividend *m*; **pay dividends** Dividenden ausschütten; (fig) sich lohnen

divid′ing line′ *s* Trennungsstrich *m*

divination [ˌdɪvɪ′neʃən] *s* Weissagung *f*

divine [dɪ′vaɪn] *adj* göttlich || *s* Geist- licher *m* || *tr* (er)ahnen

divine′ prov′idence *s* göttliche Vorse- hung *f*

divine′ right′ of kings′ *s* Königtum *n* von Gottes Gnaden

div′ing *s* Tauchen *n* (sport) Kunst- springen *n*

div′ing bell′ *s* Taucherglocke *f*

div′ing board′ *s* Sprungbrett *n*

div′ing suit′ *s* Taucheranzug *m*

divin′ing rod′ *s* Wünschelrute *f*

divinity [dɪ′vɪnɪti] *s* (*divine nature*) Göttlichkeit *f*; (*deity*) Gottheit *f*

divisible [dɪ′vɪzɪbəl] *adj* teilbar

division [dɪ′vɪʒən] *s* Teilung *f*; (*dis- sention*) Uneinigkeit *f*; (adm) Ab- teilung *f*; (math, mil) Division *f*; (sport) Sportklasse *f*

divisor [dɪ′vaɪzər] *s* (math) Teiler *m*; Divisor *m*

divorce [dɪ′vors] *s* Scheidung *f*; **apply for a d.** die Scheidungsklage ein- reichen; **get a d.** sich scheiden lassen || *tr* (*said of a spouse*) sich scheiden lassen von; (*said of a judge*) schei- den; (*separate*) trennen

divorcee [dɪvor′si] *s* Geschiedene *f*

divulge [dɪ′vʌldʒ] *tr* ausplaudern

dizziness [′dɪzɪnɪs] *s* Schwindel *m*

dizzy [′dɪzi] *adj* schwindlig; (*causing dizziness*) schwindelerregend; (*men- tally confused*) benommen; (*foolish*) damisch; (*feeling, spell*) Schwindel-

do [du] *v* (*3d pers* does [dʌz]; *pret* did [dɪd]; *pp* done [dʌn]; *ger* doing [′du·ɪŋ] *tr* tun, machen; (*damage*) anrichten; (*one's hair*) frisieren; (*an injustice*) antun; (*a favor, disservice*) erweisen; (*time in jail*) absitzen; (*miles per hour*) fahren; (*tour*) (coll) besichtigen; (*Shakespeare, etc., in class*) durchnehmen; **do duty as** die- nen als; **do in** (sl) umbringen; **do over** (*with paint*) neu anstreichen; (*with covering*) neu überziehen; **what can I do for you?** womit kann ich dienen? || *intr* tun, machen; (*suffice*) genügen; **do away with** abschaffen; (*persons*) aus dem Wege räumen; **do away with oneself** sich [*dat*] das Leben nehmen; **I am doing well** es geht mir gut; (*financially*) ich verdiene gut; (*e.g., in history*) ich komme gut voran; **I'll make it** do ich werde schon damit auskommen; **nothing doing!** ausgeschlossen! **that will do!** genug davon!; **that won't do!** das geht nicht! || *aux* used in English but not specifically expressed in Ger- man: 1) in questions, e.g., **do you speak German?** sprechen Sie deutsch?; 2) in negative sentences,

e.g., **I do not live here** ich wohne hier nicht; 3) for emphasis, e.g., **I do feel better** ich fühle mich wirk- lich besser; 4) in imperative en- treaties, e.g., **do come again** besu- chen Sie mich doch wieder!; 5) in elliptical sentences, e.g., **I like Ber- lin. So do I** Mir gefällt Berlin. Mir auch.; **he drinks, doesn't he?** er trinkt, nicht wahr?; 6) in inversions after adverbs such as hardly, rarely, scarcely, little, e.g., **little did she realize that…** sie hatte keine Ah- nung, daß… || *impers*—**it doesn't do to** (*inf*) es ist unklug zu (*inf*); **it won't do you any good to stay here** es wird Ihnen nicht viel nützen, hier zu bleiben

docile [′dɑsɪl] *adj* gelehrig; (*easy to handle*) fügsam, lenksam

dock [dɑk] *s* Anlegeplatz *m*; (jur) An- klagebank *f*; **docks** Hafenanlagen *pl*; **in the d.** (jur) auf der Anklagebank || *tr* (*a ship, space vehicle*) docken; (*a tail*) stutzen; (*pay*) kürzen; **d. an employee (for)** e-m Arbeitnehmer den Lohn kürzen (um) || *intr* (naut) (*am Kai*) anlegen; (rok) docken, koppeln

docket [′dɑkɪt] *s* (*agenda*) Tagesord- nung *f*; (jur) Prozeßliste *f*

dock′ hand′ *s* Hafenarbeiter *m*

dock′ing *s* (naut) Anlegen *n*; (rok) Andocken *n*

dock′ work′er *s* Dockarbeiter *m*

dock′yard′ *s* Werft *f*

doctor [′dɑktər] *s* Doktor *m*; (*physi- cian*) Arzt *m*, Ärztin *f* || *tr* (records) frisieren; (*adapt, e.g., a play*) zu- rechtmachen || *intr* (coll) in ärztlicher Behandlung stehen

doctorate [′dɑktərɪt] *s* Doktorwürde *f*

doctrine [′dɑktrɪn] *s* Doktrin *f*, Lehre *f*

document [′dɑkjəmənt] *s* Urkunde *f* || [′dɑkjəˌment] *tr* dokumentieren

documentary [ˌdɑkjə′mentərɪ] *adj* do- kumentarisch || *s* Dokumentarfilm *m*

documentation [ˌdɑkjəmen′teʃən] *s* Dokumentation *f*

doddering [′dɑdərɪŋ] *adj* zittrig

dodge [dɑdʒ] *s* Winkelzug *m* || *tr* (*e.g., a blow*) ausweichen (*dat*); (*e.g., a responsibility*) sich drücken vor (*dat*) || *intr* ausweichen

do-do [′dodo] *s* (**-does & -dos**) (coll) Depp *m*

doe [do] *s* Rehgeiß *f*, Damhirschkuh *f*

doer [′du·ər] *s* Täter –in *mf*

doe′skin′ *s* Rehleder *n*

doff [dɔf] *tr* (*a hat*) abnehmen; (*clothes*) ausziehen; (*habits*) ablegen

dog [dɔg] *s* Hund *m*; **dog eats dog** jeder für sich; **go to the dogs** (coll) vor die Hunde gehen; **lucky dog** (coll) Glückspitz!; **put on the dog** (coll) großtun || *v* (*pret* & *pp* **dogged**; *ger* **dogging**) *tr* nachspüren (*dat*)

dog′ bis′cuit *s* Hundekuchen *m*

dog′ days′ *spl* Hundstage *pl*

dog′-eared′ *adj* mit Eselsohren

dog′face′ *s* (mil) Landser *m*

dog'fight' s (aer) Kurbelei f
dogged ['dɔgɪd] adj verbissen
doggerel ['dɔgərəl] s Knittelvers m
doggone ['dɔg'gɔn] adj (sl) verflixt
dog'house' s Hundehütte f; in the d. (fig) in Ungnade
dog' ken'nel s Hundezwinger m
dogma ['dɔgmə] s Dogma n
dogmatic [dɔg'mætɪk] adj dogmatisch
do-gooder ['du'gudər] s Humanitäts-apostel m
dog' show' s Hundeschau f
dog's' life' s Hundeleben n
Dog' Star' s Hundestern m
dog' tag' s Hundemarke f; (mil) Er-kennungsmarke f
dog'-tired' adj hundemüde
dog'wood' s Hartriegel m
doily ['dɔɪlɪ] s Zierdeckchen n
do'ing s Werk n; doings Tun und Trei-ben n; (events) Ereignisse pl
doldrums ['dɔldrəmz] spl Kalmengür-tel m; in the d. (fig) deprimiert
dole [dol] s Spende f; be on the d. stempeln gehen ‖ tr—d. out verteilen
doleful ['dolfəl] adj trübselig
doll [dɑl] s Puppe f ‖ tr—d. up (coll) aufdonnern ‖ intr (coll) sich aufdon-nern
dollar ['dɑlər] s Dollar m
doll' car'riage s Puppenwagen m
dolly ['dɑlɪ] s Püppchen n; (cart) Schiebkarren m
dolphin ['dɑlfɪn] s Delphin m
dolt [dolt] s Tölpel m
domain [do'men] s (& fig) Domäne f
dome [dom] s Kuppel f
dome' light' s (aut) Deckenlicht n
domestic [də'mestɪk] adj (of the home) Haus-, häuslich, Haushalts-; (pro-duced at home) einheimisch, inlän-disch, Landes-; (tame) Haus-; (e.g., policy) Innen-, innere ‖ s Hausange-stellte mf
domesticate [də'mestɪ͵ket] tr zähmen
domicile ['dɑmɪ͵saɪl] s Wohnsitz m
dominance ['dɑmɪnəns] s Vorherr-schaft f
dominant ['dɑmɪnənt] adj vorherr-schend; (factor) entscheidend
dominate ['dɑmɪ͵net] tr beherrschen ‖ intr (over) herrschen (über acc)
domination [͵dɑmɪ'neʃən] s Beherr-schung f, Herrschaft f
domineer [͵dɑmɪ'nɪr] tr & intr tyran-nisieren
domineer'ing adj tyrannisch
dominion [də'mɪnjən] s (sovereignty) (over) Gewalt f (über acc); (domain) Domäne f; (of British Empire) Do-minion n
domi·no ['dɑmɪ͵no] s (-noes & nos) Dominostein m; dominoes ssg Do-minospiel n
don [dɑn] s Universitätsprofessor m ‖ v (pret & pp donned; ger donning) tr anlegen; (a hat) sich [dat] auf-setzen
donate ['donet] tr schenken, spenden
donation [do'neʃən] s Schenkung f; (small contribution) Spende f
done [dʌn] adj erledigt; (culin) gar, fertig; d. for kaputt; d. with (com-pleted) fertig; get (s.th.) d. fertigbe-kommen; well d. (culin) durchge-braten
donkey ['dʌŋkɪ] s Esel m
donor ['donər] s Spender –in mf
doodad ['dudæd] s (gadget) Dings n; (decoration) Tand m
doodle ['dudəl] s Gekritzel n ‖ tr be-kritzeln ‖ intr kritzeln
doom [dum] s Verhängnis n ‖ tr ver-dammen, verurteilen
doomed adj todgeweiht
doomsday ['dumz͵de] s der Jüngste Tag
door [dor] s Tür f; from d. to d. von Haus zu Haus; out of doors draußen, im Freien; show s.o. the d. j–m die Tür weisen; two doors away zwei Häuser weiter
door'bell' s Türklingel f; the d. is ring-ing es klingelt
door'bell but'ton s Klingelknopf m
door'frame' s Türrahmen m
door'han'dle s Türgriff m, Türklinke f
door'jamb' s Türpfosten m
door'knob' s Türknopf m
door'man' s (-men') Portier m
door'mat' s Abtreter m, Türmatte f
door'nail' s—dead as a d. mausetot
door'post' s Türpfosten m
door'sill' s Türschwelle f
door'step' s Türstufe f
door'stop' s Türanschlag m
door'-to-door' sales'man s Hausierer m
door'-to-door sel'ling s Hausieren n
door'way' s Türöffnung f; (fig) Weg m
dope [dop] s (drug) (sl) Rauschgift n; (information) (sl) vertraulicher Tip m; (fool) (sl) Trottel m; (aer) Lack m ‖ tr (a racehorse) (sl) dopen; (a person) (sl) betäuben, verdrogen; (aer) lackieren; d. out (sl) heraus-finden, ausarbeiten; d. up (sl) ver-drogen
dope' ad'dict s (sl) Rauschgiftsüchtige–mf
dope' push'er s (sl) Rauschgiftschieber –in mf
dope'sheet' s (sl) vertraulicher Bericht m
dope' traf'fic s (sl) Rauschgifthandel m
dopey ['dopɪ] adj (dopier; dopiest) (sl) dämlich; (from sleep) (coll) schlaftrunken
dormant ['dɔrmənt] adj ruhend, un-tätig; (bot) in der Winterruhe
dormer ['dɔrmər] s Bodenfenster n; (the whole structure) Mansarde f
dor'mer win'dow s Bodenfenster n
dormitory ['dɔrmɪ͵torɪ] s (building) Studentenheim n; (room) Schlafsaal m
dormouse ['dɔr͵maus] s (mice [͵maɪs]) Haselmaus f
dor'sal fin' ['dɔrsəl] s Rückenflosse f
dosage ['dosɪdʒ] s Dosierung f
dose [dos] s (& fig) Dosis f
dossier ['dɑsɪ͵e] s Dossier m
dot [dɑt] s Punkt m, Tupfen m; on the dot auf die Sekunde; three o'clock on the dot Punkt drei Uhr ‖ v (pret

& *pp* **dotted; *ger* dotting** *tr* punktieren; tüpfeln; **dot one's i's** den Punkt aufs i setzen; (fig) übergenau sein

dotage ['dotidʒ] *s*—**be in one's d.** senil sein

dotard ['dotərd] *s* kindischer Greis *m*

dote [dot] *intr*—**d. on** vernarrt sein in (*acc*)

dot'ing *adj* **(on)** vernarrt (in *acc*)

dots' and dash'es *spl* (telg) Punkte und Striche *pl*

dot'ted *adj* (*pattern*) getüpfelt; (*with flowers, etc.*) übersät; (*line*) punktiert

double ['dʌbəl] *adj* doppelt ‖ *s* Doppelte *n;* (*person*) Doppelgänger *m* (cin, theat) Double *n; doubles* (tennis) Doppel *n;* **on the d.** im Geschwindschritt ‖ *tr* (ver)doppeln; (*the fist*) ballen; (*cards*) doppeln; (naut) umsegeln ‖ *intr* sich verdoppeln; (*cards*) doppeln; **d. back** umkehren; **d. up with** sich biegen vor (*dat*)

dou'ble-bar'reled *adj* doppelläufig; (fig) mit zweifacher Wirkung

dou'ble bass' [bes] *s* Kontrabaß *m*

dou'ble bed' *s* Doppelbett *n*

dou'ble-breast'ed *adj* doppelreihig

dou'ble' chin' *s* Doppelkinn *n*

dou'ble cross' *s* Schwindel *m*

dou'ble-cross' *tr* beschwindeln

dou'ble-cross'er *s* Schwindler –in *mf*

dou'ble date' *s* Doppelrendezvous *n*

dou'ble-deal'er *s* Betrüger –in *mf*

dou'ble-deal'ing *s* Doppelzüngigkeit *f*

dou'ble-deck'er *s* (*ship, bus*) Doppeldecker *m;* (*sandwich*) Doppelsandwich *n;* (*bed*) Etagenbett *n*

dou'ble-edged' *adj* (& fig) zweischneidig

double entendre ['dʌbələn'tandrə] *s* (*ambiguity*) Doppelsinn *m;* (*ambiguous term*) doppelsinniger Ausdruck *m*

dou'ble en'try *s* (com) doppelte Buchführung *f*

dou'ble expo'sure *s* Doppelbelichtung *f*

dou'ble fea'ture *s* Doppelprogramm *n*

dou'blehead'er *s* Doppelspiel *n*

dou'ble-joint'ed *adj* mit Gummigelenken

dou'blepark' *tr* & *intr* falsch parken

dou'ble-spaced' *adj* mit doppeltem Zeilenabstand

dou'ble stand'ard *s* zweierlei Maß *n*

doublet ['dʌblɪt] *s* (*duplicate; counterfeit stone*) Dublette *f;* (hist) Wams *m;* (ling) Doppelform *f*

dou'ble take' *s* (fig) Spätzündung *f*

dou'ble-talk' *s* zweideutige Rede *f*

dou'ble time' *s* (*wage rate*) doppelter Lohn *m;* (mil) Eilschritt *m*

dou'ble track' *s* (rr) doppelgleisige Bahnlinie *f*

doubly ['dʌbli] *adv* doppelt

doubt [daut] *s* Zweifel *m;* **be still in d.** (*said of things*) noch zweifelhaft sein; **beyond d.** ohne (jeden) Zweifel; **in case of d.** im Zweifelsfalle; **no d.** zweifellos; **raise doubts** Bedenken

erregen; **there is no d. that** es unterliegt keinem Zweifel, daß ‖ *tr* bezweifeln ‖ *intr* zweifeln

doubter ['dautər] *s* Zweifler –in *mf*

doubtful ['dautfəl] *adj* zweifelhaft

doubtless ['dautlɪs] *adj* & *adv* zweifellos

douche [duʃ] *s* (*device*) Irrigator *m;* (*act of cleansing*) Spülung *f* ‖ *tr* & *intr* spülen

dough [do] *s* Teig *m;* (sl) Pinke *f*

dough'boy' *s* (sl) Landser *m*

dough'nut' *s* Krapfen *m*

doughty ['dauti] *adj* wacker

doughy ['do-i] *adj* teigig

dour [daur], [dur] *adj* mürrisch

douse [daus] *tr* eintauchen; (*with*) übergießen (mit); (*a fire*) auslöschen

dove [dʌv] *s* (& pol) Taube *f*

dovecote ['dʌv,kot] *s* Taubenschlag *m*

dove'tail' *s* (carp) Schwalbenschwanz *m* ‖ *tr* verzinken; (fig) ineinanderfügen ‖ *intr* ineinanderpassen

dowager ['dau-ədʒər] *s* Witwe *f* (von Stand); (coll) Matrone *f*

dowdy ['daudi] *adj* schlampig

dow'el ['dau-əl] *s* Dübel *m* ‖ *v* (*pret* & *pp* -el[l]ed; *ger* -el[l]ing) *s* (ein)dübeln

down [daun] *adj* (*prices*) gesunken; (*sun*) untergegangen; **be d.** für vorgemerkt sein für; **be d. on s.o.** auf j-m herumtrampeln; **be d. three points** (sport) drei Punkte zurück sein; **be d. with a cold** mit e-r Erkältung im Bett liegen; **d. and out** völlig erledigt; **d. in the mouth** niedergedrückt ‖ *adv* herunter, hinunter; **d. from** von...herab; **d. there** da unten; **d. to** bis hinunter zu; **d. to the last man** bis zum letzten Mann; **d. with...!** nieder mit...! ‖ *s* (*of fowl*) Daune *f;* (*fine hair*) Flaum *m; downs* grasbedecktes Hügelland *n* ‖ *prep* (postpositive) (*acc*) herunter, hinunter; **a little way d. the road** etwas weiter auf die Straße; **d. the river** flußabwärts ‖ *tr* niederschlagen; (*a glass of beer*) (coll) hinunterstürzen; (aer) abschießen

down'cast' *adj* niedergeschlagen

down'draft' *s* Abwind *m*, Fallwind *m*

down'fall' *s* Untergang *m*

down'grade' *s* Gefälle *n;* **on the d.** (fig) im Niedergang ‖ *tr* herabsetzen; niedriger einstufen

down'heart'ed *adj* niedergeschlagen

down'hill' *adj* bergabgehend; (*in skiing*) Abfahrts- ‖ *adv* bergab; **he's going d.** (coll) mit ihm geht es abwärts

down' pay'ment *s* Anzahlung *f*

down'pour' *s* Regenguß *m*, Sturzregen *m*

down'right' *adj* ausgesprochen; (*lie*) glatt; (*contradiction*) schroff ‖ *adv* ausgesprochen

down'spout' *s* Fallrohr *n*

down'stairs' *adj* unten befindlich ‖ *adv* (*position*) unten; (*direction*) nach unten

down'stream' *adv* stromabwärts

down′stroke′ *s* (*in writing*) Grund-
strich *m*; (*of a piston*) Abwärtshub
m

down′-the-line′ *adj* vorbehaltlos

down-to-earth′ *adj.*nüchtern

down′town′ *adj* im Geschäftsviertel
gelegen || *adv* (*position*) im Ge-
schäftsviertel; (*direction*) ins Ge-
schäftsviertel, in die Stadt || *s*
Geschäftsviertel *n*

down′trend′ *s* Baissestimmung *f*

downtrodden [′daʊn‚trɑdən] *adj* un-
terdrückt

downward [′daʊnwərd] *adj* Abwärts-
|| *adv* abwärts

downwards [′daʊnwərdz] *adv* abwärts

downy [′daʊnɪ] *adj* flaumig; (*soft*)
weich wie Flaum

dowry [′daʊrɪ] *s* Mitgift *f*

dowser [′daʊzər] *s* (*rod*) Wünschelrute *f*; (*person*) Wünschelrutengän-
ger *m*

doze [doz] *s* Schläfchen *n* || *intr* dösen

dozen [′dʌzən] *s* Dutzend *n*; **a d. times**
dutzendmal

Dr. *abbr* (**Doctor**) **Dr.**; (*in addresses:*
Drive) Str.

drab [dræb] *adj* (**drabber; drabbest**)
graubraun; (*fig*) trüb

drach·ma [′drækmə] *s* (**-mas & -mae**
[mi]) Drachme *f*

draft [dræft] *s* (*of air; drink*) Zug *m*;
(*sketch*) Entwurf *m*; (*fin*) Tratte *f*;
(*mil*) Einberufung *f*; **on d.** vom Faß
|| *tr* (*sketch*) entwerfen, abfassen;
(*mil*) einberufen

draft′ age′ *s* wehrpflichtiges Alter *n*

draft′ beer′ *s* Schankbier *n*

draft′ board′ *s* Wehrmeldeamt *n*

draft′ dodg′er [′dɑdʒər] *s* Drückeberger *m*

draftee [‚dræf′ti] *s* Dienstpflichtige
mf

draft′ing *s* (*of a document*) Abfassung
f; (*mechanical drawing*) Zeichnen *n*;
(*mil*) Aushebung *f*

draft′ing board′ *s* Zeichenbrett *n*

draft′ing room′ *s* Zeichenbüro *n*

drafts·man [′dræftsmən] *s* (**-men**)
Zeichner *m*

drafty [′dræftɪ] *adj* zugig

drag [dræg] *s* (*sledge*) Lastschlitten
m; (*in smoking*) (coll) Zug *m*; (*boring person*) langweiliger Mensch *m*;
(*s.th. tedious*) etwas langweiliges *n*
(für); (*encumbrance*) (on) Hemmschuh *m*
(aer) Luftwiderstand *m*; (*for
recovering objects*) (naut) Schleppnetz *n*; (*for retarding motion*) (naut)
Schleppanker *m* || *v* (*pret* & *pp*
dragged; *ger* **dragging**) *tr* schleppen,
schleifen; **d. one′s feet** schlurfen;
(fig) sich [*dat*] Zeit lassen; **d. out**
dahinschleppen; (*protract*) verschleppen; **d. through the mud** (fig) in den
Schmutz zerren; **d. up** (fig) aufwär-
men || *intr* (*said of a long dress,
etc.*) schleifen; (*said of time*) dahinschleichen; **d. on** (*be prolonged*) sich
hinziehen

drag′net′ *s* Schleppnetz *n*

dragon [′drægən] *s* Drache *m*

drag′onfly′ *s* Libelle *f*

dragoon [drə′gun] *s* Dragoner *m* || *tr*
(*coerce*) zwingen

drag′ race′ *s* Straßenrennen *n*; (sport)
Kurzstreckenrennen *n*

drain [dren] *s* (*sewer*) Kanal *m*; (*under a sink*) Abfluß *m*; (fig) (**on**)
Belastung *f* (*genit*); (surg) Drain *m*;
down the d. (fig) zum Fenster hin-
aus || *tr* (*land*) entwässern; (*water*)
ableiten; (*a cup, glass*) austrinken;
(fig) verzehren || *intr* ablaufen;
(culin) abtropfen

drainage [′drenɪdʒ] *s* Ableitung *f*;
(*e.g., of land*) Entwässerung *f*; (surg)
Drainage *f*

drain′age ditch′ *s* Abflußgraben *m*

drain′ cock′ *s* Entleerungshahn *m*

drain′pipe′ *s* Abflußrohr *n*

drain′ plug′ *s* Abflußstöpsel *m*

drake [drek] *s* Enterich *m*

dram [dræm] *s* Dram *n*

drama [′drɑmə] *s* Drama *n*; (*art and
genre*) Dramatik *f*

dra′ma crit′ic *s* Theaterkritiker –in *mf*

dramatic [drə′mætɪk] *adj* dramatisch
|| **dramatics** *s* Dramatik *f*; *spl* (pej)
Schauspielerei *f*

dramatist [′dræmətɪst] *s* Dramatiker
–in *mf*

dramatize [′dræmə‚taɪz] *tr* dramati-
sieren

drape [drep] *s* Vorhang *m*; (*hang of a
drape or skirt*) Faltenwurf *m* || *tr*
drapieren

drapery [′drepərɪ] *s* Vorhänge *pl*

dra′pery mate′rial *s* Vorhangstoff *m*

drastic [′dræstɪk] *adj* drastisch

draught [dræft] *s* & *tr* var *of* **draft**

draw [drɔ] *s* (*in a lottery*) Ziehen *n*;
(*that which attracts*) Schlager *m*;
(*power of attraction*) Anziehungskraft *f*; **end in a d.** unentschieden
ausgehen || *v* (*pret* **drew** [dru]; *pp*
drawn [drɔn]) *tr* (*pictures*) zeichnen;
(*a line, comparison, parallel, conclusion, lots, winner, sword, wagon*)
ziehen; (*a crowd*) anlocken; (*a distinction*) machen; (*blood*) vergießen; (*curtains*) zuziehen; (*a check*)
ausstellen; (*water*) schöpfen; (*cards*)
nehmen; (*rations*) (mil) in Empfang
nehmen; **d. a blank** (coll) e–e Niete
ziehen; **d. aside** beiseiteziehen; **d. attention to** die Aufmerksamkeit lenken auf (*acc*); **d. into** (*e.g., an argument*) hineinziehen in (*acc*); **d. lots
for** losen um; **d. out** (*protract*) in
die Länge ziehen; (*money from a
bank*) abheben; **d. s.o. out** j–n aus-
holen; **d. the line** (fig) e–e Grenze
ziehen; **d. up** (*a document*) verfas-
sen; (*plans*) entwerfen || *intr* zeich-
nen; **d. away** sich entfernen; **d. back**
sich zurückziehen; **d. near** heran-
nahen; **d. on** zurückgreifen auf (*acc*);
d. to a close sich dem Ende zuneigen

draw′back′ *s* Nachteil *m*

draw′bridge′ *s* Zugbrücke *f*

drawee [drɔ′i] *s* Trassat –in *mf*

drawer [′drɔ·ər] *s* Zeichner –in *mf*;
(com) Trassant –in *mf* & [drɔr] *s*
Schublade *f*; **drawers** Unterhose *f*

draw′ing *s* (*of pictures*) Zeichnen *n*;

(*picture*) Zeichnung *f*; (*in a lottery*) Ziehung *f*, Verlosung *f*
draw'ing board' *s* Reißbrett *n*
draw'ing card' *s* Zugnummer *f*
draw'ing room' *s* Empfangszimmer *n*
drawl [drɔl] *s* gedehntes Sprechen *n* || *intr* gedehnt sprechen
drawn [drɔn] *adj* (*face*) (**with**) verzerrt (vor *dat*); (*sword*) blank
dray [dre] *s* niedriger Rollwagen *m*; (*sledge*) Schleife *f*
dread [dred] *adj* furchtbar || *s* Furcht *f* || *tr* fürchten
dreadful ['dredfəl] *adj* furchtbar
dream [drim] *s* Traum *m*; (*aspiration, ambition*) Wunschtraum *m*; (*ideal*) (coll) Gedicht *n* || *v* (*pret & pp* **dreamed & dreamt** [dremt] *tr* träumen; **d. away** verträumen; **d. up** zusammenträumen || *intr* träumen; **d. of** (*long for*) sich [*dat*] enträumen; **I dreamt of her** mir träumte von ihr
dreamer ['drimər] *s* Träumer –in *mf*
dream'land' *s* Traumland *n*
dream'-like' *adj* traumhaft
dream'world' *s* Traumwelt *f*
dreamy ['drimi] *adj* (*place*) verträumt; (*eyes*) träumerisch
dreary ['drɪri] *adj* trüb, trist
dredge [dredʒ] *s* Bagger *m* || *tr* (aus)baggern || *intr* baggern
dredger ['dredʒər] *s* Bagger *m*
dredg'ing *s* Baggern *n*
dregs [dregz] *spl* Bodensatz *m*; (*of society*) Abschaum *m*, Auswurf *m*
drench [drentʃ] *tr* durchnässen
Dres'den chi'na ['drezdən] *s* Meißner Porzellan *n*
dress [dres] *s* Kleidung *f*; (*woman's dress*) Kleid *n* || *tr* anziehen; (*a store window*) dekorieren; (*skins*) gerben; (*a salad, goose, chicken*) zubereiten; (*vines*) beschneiden; (*stones*) behauen; (*ore*) aufbereiten; (*wounds*) verbinden; (*hair*) frisieren; (*tex*) appretieren; **d. down** (coll) ausschimpfen; **d. ranks** die Glieder ausrichten; **get dressed** sich anziehen || *intr* sich anziehen; **d. up** sich fein machen
dress' affair' *s* Galaveranstaltung *f*
dresser ['dresər] *s* Frisierkommode *f*; **be a good d.** sich gut kleiden
dress'ing *s* (*stuffing for fowl*) Füllung *f*; (*for salad*) Soße *f*; (surg) Verband *m*
dress'ing down' *s* Gardinenpredigt *f*
dress'ing room' *s* Umkleideraum *m*; (theat) Garderobe *f*
dress'ing sta'tion *s* Verbandsplatz *m*
dress'ing ta'ble *s* Frisierkommode *f*
dress'mak'er *s* Schneiderin *f*
dress'mak'ing *s* Damenschneiderei *f*
dress' rehear'sal *s* Kostümprobe *f*
dress' shirt' *s* Frackhemd *n*
dress' shop' *s* Modenhaus *n*, Modengeschäft *n*
dress' suit' *s* Frackanzug *m*, Frack *m*
dress' un'iform *s* Paradeuniform *f*
dressy ['dresi] *adj* (*showy*) geschniegelt; (*stylish*) modisch; (*for formal affairs*) elegant
dribble ['drɪbəl] *s* (*trickle*) Getröpfel

n; (sport) Dribbeln *n* || *tr & intr* tröpfeln; (sport) dribbeln
driblet ['drɪblɪt] *s* Bißchen *n*
dried [draɪd] *adj* Trocken-, Dörr-
dried' beef' *s* Dörrfleisch *n*
dried' fruit' *s* Dörrobst *n*
dried'-up' *adj* ausgetrocknet, verdorrt
drier ['draɪ·ər] *s* Trockner *m*; (*for the hair*) Haartrockenhaube *f*; (*hand model*) Fön *m*
drift [drɪft] *s* (*of sand, snow*) Wehe *f*; (*tendency*) Richtung *f*, Neigung *f*; (*intent*) Absicht *f*; (*meaning*) Sinn *m*; (aer, naut, rad) Abtrift *f*; (*flow of the ocean current*) (naut) Drift *f* || *intr* (*said of sand, snow*) sich anhäufen; (*said of a boat*) treiben; **d. away** (*said of sounds*) verwehen; (*said of a crowd*) sich verlaufen; **d. shut** verweht werden
drifter ['drɪftər] *s* zielloser Mensch *m*
drift' ice' *s* Treibeis *n*
drift'wood' *s* Treibholz *n*
drill [drɪl] *s* (*tool*) Bohrer *m*; (*exercise*) Drill *m*; (tex) Drillich *m* || *tr* bohren; (*exercise*) drillen; **d. s.th. into s.o.** j–m etw einpauken || *intr* bohren; (*exercise*) drillen
drill'mas'ter *s* (mil) Ausbilder *m*
drill' press' *s* Bohrpresse *f*
drink [drɪŋk] *s* Trunk *m* || *v* (*pret* **drank** [dræŋk]; *pp* **drunk** [drʌŋk] *tr* trinken; (*said of animals*) saufen; (pej) saufen; **d. away** (*money*) versaufen; **d. down** hinunterkippen; **d. in** (*air*) einschlürfen; (*s.o.'s words*) verschlingen || *intr* trinken; (*excessively*) saufen; **d. to** trinken auf (*acc*); **d. up** austrinken
drinkable ['drɪŋkəbəl] *adj* trinkbar
drinker ['drɪŋkər] *s* Trinker –in *mf*; **heavy drinker** Zecher –in *mf*
drink'ing foun'tain *s* Trinkbrunnen *m*
drink'ing par'ty *s* Zechgelage *n*
drink'ing song' *s* Trinklied *n*
drink'ing straw' *s* Strohhalm *m*
drink'ing trough' *s* Viehtränke *f*
drink'ing wa'ter *s* Trinkwasser *n*
drip [drɪp] *s* Tröpfeln *n* || *v* (*pret & pp* **dripped**; *ger* **dripping**) *tr & intr* tröpfeln
drip' cof'fee *s* Filterkaffee *m*
drip'-dry' *adj* bügelfrei
drip' pan' *s* Bratpfanne *f*
drip'pings *spl* Bratenfett *n*
drive [draɪv] *s* (*in a car*) Fahrt *f*; (*road*) Fahrweg *m*; (*energy*) Schwungkraft *f*; (*inner urge*) Antrieb *m*; (*campaign*) Aktion *f*; (*for raising money*) Spendeaktion *f*; (golf) Treibschlag *m*; (mach) Antrieb *m*; (mil) Vorstoß *m*; (tennis) Treibschlag *m*; **go for a d.** spazierenfahren || *v* (*pret* **drove** [drov]; *pp* **driven** ['drɪvən]) *tr* (*a car, etc.*) fahren; (*e.g., cattle*) treiben; (*a tunnel*) vortreiben; **d. a hard bargain** zäh um den Preis feilschen; **d. away** abtreiben; **d.** (*oneself, a horse*) **hard** abjagen; **d. home** nahebringen; **d. in** (*a nail*) einschlagen; **d. off course** (naut) verschlagen; **d. on** antreiben; **d. out** austreiben; **d. s.o. to** (*inf*) j–n

dazu bringen zu (inf); **d. to despair** zur Verzweiflung treiben ‖ intr fahren; **d. along** mitfahren; **d. at** abzielen auf (acc); **d. away** wegfahren; **d. by** vorbeifahren an (dat); **d. in** einfahren; **d. on** weiterfahren; **d. out** herausfahren; **d. up** anfahren

drive′ belt′ s Treibriemen m

drive′-in′ s Autorestaurant n; (cin) Autokino n

driv·el ['drɪvəl] s (slobber) Geifer m; (nonsense) Faselei f ‖ v (pret & pp -el[l]ed; ger -el[l]ing) intr sabbern; (fig) faseln

driver ['draɪvər] s (of a car) Fahrer -in mf; (of a locomotive, streetcar) Führer m; (golf) Treibschläger m; (mach) Treibhammer m

driv′er's li′cense s Führerschein m

drive′ shaft′ s Antriebswelle f

drive′way′ s Einfahrt f

drive′-yourself′ serv′ice s Autovermietung f an Selbstfahrer

driv′ing adj (rain) stürmisch ‖ s (aut) Steuerung f

driv′ing instruc′tor s Fahrlehrer -in mf

driv′ing les′son s Fahrstunde f

driv′ing school′ s Autofahrschule f

drizzle ['drɪzəl] s Nieselregen m ‖ impers—it is drizzling es nieselt

droll [drol] adj drollig

dromedary ['drɑmə‚deri] s Dromedar n

drone [dron] s (bee; loafer) Drohne f; (buzz) Gesumme n; (monotonous speech) Geleier n ‖ tr (e.g., prayers) leiern ‖ intr summen; (fig) leiern

drool [drul] intr sabbern

droop [drup] s Herabhängen n; (stoop) gebeugte Haltung f ‖ intr herabhängen; (said of flowers) zu welken beginnen; (fig) den Kopf hängen lassen

droopy ['drupi] adj (saggy) schlaff herabhängend; (dejected) mutlos; (shoulders) abfallend; (flowers) welkend

drop [drɑp] s (of liquid) Tropfen m; (candy) Fruchtbonbon m & n; (fall) Fall m; (height differential) Gefälle n; (reduction) Abnahme f; (in prices) Rückgang m; (in temperature) Sturz m; (of bombs or supplies) Abwurf m; (of paratroopers) Absprung m; a fifty-meter d. ein Fall m aus e-r Höhe von fünfzig Metern; **d. by d.** tropfenweise; **d. in the bucket** Tropfen m auf e-n heißen Stein ‖ v (pret & pp dropped; ger dropping) tr (let fall) fallenlassen; (bombs, supplies) abwerfen; (a subject, remarks, hints) fallenlassen; (the eyes, voice) senken; (anchor; young of animals) werfen; (money in gambling) (sl) verlieren; (terminate) einstellen; (from membership roll) ausschließen; (paratroopers) absetzen; **d. it!** laß das!; **d. s.o. a line** j-m ein paar Zeilen schreiben ‖ intr fallen; (drip) tropfen; (said of prices, temperature) sinken, fallen; (keel over) umfallen; (said of a curtain) niedergehen; **d. behind** zurück-

fallen; **d. dead!** (sl) laß dich begraben!; **d. in on s.o.** auf e-n Sprung bei j-m vorbeikommen; **d. off to sleep** einschlafen; **d. out** sich zurückziehen; (sport) ausscheiden; **d. out of school** von der Schule abgehen

drop′ ar′ea s (aer) Abwurfraum m

drop′ cur′tain s (bemalter) Vorhang m

drop′ ham′mer s Fallhammer m

drop′-leaf ta′ble s Tisch m mit herunterklappbaren Flügeln

drop′light′ s Hängelampe f

drop′out′ s Gescheiterte mf; (educ) Abgänger -in mf

dropper ['drɑpər] s (med) Tropfer m

drop′ping adj (prices) rückgängig ‖ s (of bombs, supplies) Abwurf m; droppings tierischer Kot m

dropsy ['drɑpsi] s Wassersucht f

drop′ ta′ble s Klapptisch m

dross [drɔs] s (slag) Schlacke f; (waste) Abfall m

drought [draut] s Dürre f

drove [drov] s Herde f

drown [draun] tr (& fig) ertränken; **d. out** übertönen ‖ intr ertrinken

drowse [drauz] intr dösen

drowsiness ['drauzɪnɪs] s Schläfrigkeit f

drowsy ['drauzi] adj schläfrig, dösig

drub [drʌb] v (pret & pp drubbed; ger drubbing) tr (flog) verprügeln; (sport) entscheidend schlagen

drudge [drʌdʒ] s Packesel m ‖ intr sich placken, schuften

drudgery ['drʌdʒəri] s Plackerei f

drug [drʌg] s Droge f, Arznei f; (narcotic) Betäubungsmittel n; (addictive narcotic) Rauschgift n ‖ v (pret & pp drugged; ger drugging) tr betäuben

drug′ ad′dict s Rauschgiftsüchtige mf

drug′ addic′tion s Rauschgiftsucht f

druggist ['drʌgɪst] s Apotheker -in mf

drug′store′ s Apotheke f, Drogerie f

drug′ traf′fic s Rauschgifthandel m

druid ['dru·ɪd] s Druide m

drum [drʌm] s (musical instrument; container) Trommel f ‖ v (pret & pp drummed; ger drumming) tr trommeln; **d. s.th. into s.o.** j-m etw einpauken; **d. the table** auf den Tisch trommeln; **d. up** zusammentrommeln ‖ intr trommeln

drum′ and bu′gle corps′ s Musikzug m

drum′beat′ s Trommelschlag m

drum′fire′ s (mil) Trommelfeuer n

drum′head′ s Trommelfell n

drum′ ma′jor s Tambourmajor m

drum′ majorette′ s Tambourmajorin f

drummer ['drʌmər] s Trommler -in mf

drum′stick′ s Trommelschlegel m; (culin) Unterschenkel m

drunk [drʌŋk] adj betrunken ‖ s Säufer -in mf

drunkard ['drʌŋkərd] s Trunkenbold m

drunken ['drʌŋkən] adj betrunken

dry [draɪ] adj trocken; (boring) trocken; (wine) herb; (thirsty) durstig; (rainless) regenarm; (wood) dürr ‖ v (pret & pp -dried) tr (ab)trocknen;

dry' bat'tery s Trockenbatterie f

dry' cell' s Tockenelement n

dry'-clean' tr (chemically) reinigen

dry' clean'er's s Reinigungsanstalt f

dry' clean'ing s chemische Reinigung f

dry' dock' s Trockendock n

dry'-eyed' adj ungerührt

dry' goods' spl Schnittwaren pl

dry' ice' s Trockeneis n

dry' land' s fester Boden m

dry' meas'ure s Trockenmaß n

dryness ['draɪnɪs] s Trockenheit f, Dürre f; (fig) Nüchternheit f

dry' nurse' s Säuglingsschwester f

dry' rot' s Trockenfäule f

dry' run' s Vorübung f; (test run) Probelauf m; (with blank ammunition) Zielübung f

dry' sea'son s Trockenzeit f

dual ['d(j)u·əl] adj Zwei-, doppelt; (tech) Doppel-

dualism ['d(j)u·ə‚lɪzəm] s Dualismus m

du'al-pur'pose adj e-m doppelten Zweck dienend

dub [dʌb] v (pret & pp dubbed; ger dubbing) tr (nickname) betiteln; (cin) synchronisieren; (golf) schlecht treffen; (hist) zum Ritter schlagen

dub'bing s (cin) Synchronisierung f

dubious ['d(j)ubɪ·əs] adj zweifelhaft

ducal ['d(j)ukəl] adj herzoglich

duchess ['dʌtʃɪs] s Herzogin f

duchy ['dʌtʃi] s Herzogtum n

duck [dʌk] s Ente f ‖ tr (the head) ducken; (in water) (unter)tauchen; (evade) sich drücken vor (dat) ‖ intr ducken; (go under the surface) untertauchen

duck'ing s—give s.o. a d. j-n untertauchen

duck' pond' s Ententeich m

duck' soup' s (sl) Kinderspiel n

ducky ['dʌki] adj (coll) nett, lieb

duct [dʌkt] s Rohr n, Kanal m, Leitung f; (anat, elec) Kanal m

duct'less gland' ['dʌktlɪs] s endokrine Drüse f

duct'work' s Rohrleitungen pl

dud [dʌd] s (sl & mil) Versager m, Blindgänger m; **duds** (coll) Klamotten pl

dude [d(j)ud] s (dandy) Geck m

dude' ranch' s Vergnügungsfarm f

due [d(j)u] adj (payment; bus, train) fällig; (proper) gehörig; (consideration) reichlich; **be due to** (as a cause) beruhen auf (dat); (said of an honor) gebühren (dat); (said of money) zustehen (dat); **be due to** (inf) sollen, müssen; **in due course** im gegebenen Moment; **in due time** zur rechten Zeit ‖ adv (just) genau ‖ s—**dues** Beitrag m; **get one's due** nach Verdienst behandelt werden; **give every-**one his **due** jedem geben, was ihm gebührt

due' date' s (of a payment) Termin m

duel ['d(j)u·əl] s Duell n; **fight a d.** sich duellieren ‖ v (pret & pp duel[l]ed; ger duel[l]ing) intr sich duellieren

dues-paying ['d(j)uz‚pe·ɪŋ] adj beitragzahlend

duet [d(j)u'ɛt] s Duett n

due' to' prep wegen (genit)

duf'fle bag' ['dʌfəl] s (mil) Kleidersack m

dug'out' s (boat) Einbaum m; (baseball, mil) Unterstand m

duke [d(j)uk] s Herzog m

dukedom ['d(j)ukdəm] s Herzogtum n

dull [dʌl] adj (not sharp) stumpf; (pain) dumpf; (not shining) glanzlos, matt; (uninteresting) nüchtern, geistlos; (stupid) stumpfsinnig; (com) flau ‖ tr stumpf machen; (fig) abstumpfen ‖ intr stumpf werden; (fig) abstumpfen

dullard ['dʌlərd] s Dummkopf m

dullness ['dʌlnɪs] s (of a blade) Stumpfheit f; (of color) Mattheit f; (of a speech, etc.) Stumpfsinn m

duly ['d(j)uli] adv ordnungsgemäß

dumb [dʌmb] adj stumm; (stupid) dumm ‖ adv—**play d.** sich unwissend stellen

dumb'bell' s Hantel f; (sl) Dummkopf m

dumbstruck ['dʌm‚strʌk] adj wie auf den Mund geschlagen

dumb' wait'er s (elevator) Speiseaufzug m; (serving table) Serviertisch m

dumdum ['dʌm‚dʌm] s Dumdumgeschoß n

dumfound ['dʌm‚faund] tr verblüffen

dummy ['dʌmi] adj (not real) Schein-; (mil) blind, Übungs- ‖ s (representation for display) Attrappe f; (clothes form) Schneiderpuppe f; (dolt) Ölgötze m; (cards) Strohmann m; (mil) Übungspatrone f; (typ) Blindband m

dump [dʌmp] s (trash heap) Schuttabladeplatz m; (sl) Bude f; (mil) Lager n; **be down in the dumps** (coll) Trübsal blasen ‖ tr (aus)kippen; (fling down) hinplumpsen; (garbage) abladen; (com) verschleudern; **be dumped** (be fired) entlassen werden; **no dumping** (public sign) Schuttabladen verboten

dumpling ['dʌmplɪŋ] s Kloß m, Knödel m

dump' truck' s Kipper m

dumpy ['dʌmpi] adj rundlich

dun [dʌn] adj schwarzbraun ‖ v (pret & pp dunned; ger dunning) tr drängen

dunce [dʌns] s Schwachkopf m

dunce' cap' s Narrenkappe f

dune [d(j)un] s Düne f

dung [dʌŋ] s Dung m, Mist m ‖ tr düngen

dungarees [‚dʌŋgə'riz] spl Drillichhose f, Drillichanzug m

dungeon ['dʌndʒən] s Verlies n; (hist) Bergfried m

dung'hill' s Düngerhaufen m

dunk [dʌŋk] tr eintunken

duo ['d(j)u·o] s (duet) Duett n; (a pair) Duo n

duode·num [ˌd(j)u·ə'dinəm] s (-na [nə]) Zwölffingerdarm m

dupe [d(j)up] s Düpierte mf || tr düpieren, übertölpeln

duplex ['d(j)uplɛks] s Doppelhaus n

duplicate ['d(j)uplɪkɪt] adj Duplikat-; (parts) Ersatz-; **d. key** Nachschlüssel m || s Duplikat n, Abschrift f; **in d.** abschriftlich || ['d(j)uplɪˌket] tr (make a copy of) kopieren; (make many copies of) vervielfältigen; (reproduce by writing) abschreiben; (repeat) wiederholen; (perform again) nachmachen

duplication [ˌd(j)uplɪ'keʃən] s Vervielfältigung f

duplicator ['d(j)uplɪˌketər] s Vervielfältigungsapparat m

duplicity [d(j)u'plɪsɪti] s Duplizität f

durable ['d(j)urəbəl] adj dauerhaft

duration [d(j)u're/ən] s Dauer f

duress ['d(j)ures] s (jur) Nötigung f

during ['d(j)urɪŋ] prep während (genit), bei (dat); **d. the meal** bei Tisch; **d. the day** tagsüber

dusk [dʌsk] s Abenddämmerung f

dust [dʌst] s Staub m; **cover with d.** bestauben; **make d.** stauben || tr (free of dust) abstauben; (sprinkle, spray with insecticides) bestäuben

dust' bowl' s Staubsturmgebiet n

dust' cloth' s Staubtuch n

dust' collec'tor s Staubfänger m

duster ['dʌstər] s (feather duster) Staubwedel m; (for insecticides) Zerstäuber m

dust'ing pow'der s Streupulver n

dust' jac'ket s Schutzumschlag m

dust' mop' s Mop m

dust'pan' s Kehrichtschaufel f

dust'proof' adj staubdicht

dust' rag' s Staublappen m

dusty ['dʌsti] adj staubig

Dutch [dʌtʃ] adj niederländisch; **go D.** (coll) getrennt bezahlen || s (language) Niederländisch n; **in D.** (coll)

in der Patsche; **the D.** die Niederländer

Dutch'man s (-men) Niederländer m

Dutch' treat' s (coll) Beisammensein n bei getrennter Kasse

dutiable ['d(j)utɪ·əbəl] adj steuerpflichtig

dutiful ['d(j)utɪfəl] adj pflichtgetreu

duty ['d(j)uti] s (to) Pflicht f (gegenüber dat); (service) Dienst m; (task) Aufgabe f; (tax) Zoll m, Abgabe f; **be in d. bound to** (inf) pflichtgemäß müssen (inf); **do d. as** (said of a thing) dienen als; (said of a person) Dienst tun als; **off d.** außer Dienst, dienstfrei; **on. d.** im Dienst; **pay d. on** verzollen

du'ty-free' adj zollfrei

du'ty ros'ter s (mil) Diensteinteilung f

dwarf [dwɔrf] adj zwergenhaft, Zwerg- || s Zwerg m || tr (stunt) in der Entwicklung behindern; (fig) in den Schatten stellen

dwell [dwɛl] v (pret & pp dwelled & dwelt [dwɛlt]) intr wohnen; **d. on** verweilen bei

dwell'ing s Wohnung f

dwell'ing house' s Wohnhaus n

dwindle ['dwɪndəl] intr schwinden, abnehmen; **d. away** dahinschwinden

dye [daɪ] s Farbe f || v (pret & pp dyed; ger dyeing) tr färben

dyed'-in-the-wool' adj (fig) in der Wolle gefärbt

dye'ing s Färben n

dyer ['daɪ·ər] s Färber –in mf

dy'ing adj (person) sterbend; (words) letzte || s Sterben n

dynamic [daɪ'næmɪk] adj dynamisch || **dynamics** s Dynamik f; **dynamics** spl (fig) Triebkraft f

dynamite ['daɪnəˌmaɪt] s Dynamit n || tr sprengen

dyna·mo ['daɪnəˌmo] s (-mos) Dynamo m

dynastic [daɪ'næstɪk] adj dynastisch

dynasty ['daɪnəsti] s Dynastie f

dysentery ['dɪsənˌteri] s Ruhr f

dyspepsia [dɪs'pɛpsɪ·ə] s Verdauungsstörung f

E

E, e [i] s fünfter Buchstabe des englischen Alphabets; (mus) E n; **E flat** Es n; **E sharp** Eis n

each [itʃ] indef adj jeder; **e. and every** jeder einzelne || adv je, pro Person, pro Stück || indef pron jeder; **e. other** einander, sich

eager ['igər] adj eifrig; **e.** for begierig nach; **e. to** (inf) begierig zu (inf)

ea'ger bea'ver s (coll) Streber –in mf

eagerness ['igərnɪs] s Eifer m

eagle ['igəl] s Adler m

ea'gle-eyed' adj adleräugig

ear [ɪr] s Ohr n; (of corn, wheat) Ähre f; (fig) Gehör n; **be all ears**

ganz Ohr sein; **bend s.o.'s ears** (sl) j–m die Ohren vollreden; **be up to one's ears in** bis über die Ohren stecken in (dat); **by ear** nach Gehör; **ear for music** musikalisches Gehör n; **fall on deaf ears** kein Gehör finden; **in one ear and out the other** zu e–m Ohr hinein und zum anderen hinaus; **turn a deaf ear to** taub sein gegen

ear'ache' s Ohrenschmerzen pl

ear'drops' spl (med) Ohrentropfen pl

ear'drum' s Trommelfell n

earl [ʌrl] s Graf m

ear'lobe' s Ohrläppchen n

early ['ʌrli] *adj* früh; *(reply)* baldig; *(far back in time)* Früh-; **at the earliest possible moment** baldigst; **at your earliest convenience** bei erster Gelegenheit; **be too e.** sich verfrühen || *adv* früh, frühzeitig; *(too soon)* zu früh; **as e. as** schon

ear'ly bird' *s* Frühaufsteher –in *mf*

ear'ly ris'er *s* Frühaufsteher –in *mf*

ear'ly warn'ing sys'tem *s* Vorwarnungssystem *n*

ear'mark' *s* (fig) Kennzeichen *n* || *tr (mark out)* kennzeichnen; *(e.g., funds)* **(for)** bestimmen (für)

ear'muffs' *spl* Ohrenschützer *m*

earn [ʌrn] *tr (money)* verdienen; *(a reputation)* sich [*dat*] erwerben; *(interest)* einbringen

earnest ['ʌrnɪst] *adj* ernst, ernsthaft || *s*—**are you in e.?** ist das Ihr Ernst?; **be in e. about** es ernst meinen mit; **in e.** im Ernst

ear'phone' *s* Kopfhörer *m*

ear'piece' *s* (earphone) Hörer *m*; *(of eyeglasses)* Bügel *m*

ear'ring' *s* Ohrring *m*

ear'shot' *s*—**within e.** in Hörweite

ear'split'ting *adj* ohrenbetäubend

earth [ʌrθ] *s* Erde *f*; **come down to e.** auf den Boden der Wirklichkeit zurückkehren; **on e.** (coll) in aller Welt

earthen ['ʌrθən] *adj* irden

earth'enware' *s* Tonwaren *pl*

earthly ['ʌrθli] *adj* irdisch; **be of no e. use** völlig unnütz sein; **e. possessions** Glücksgüter *pl*

earth'quake' *s* Erdbeben *n*

earth'shak'ing *adj* welterschütternd

earth'work' *s* Schanze *f*

earth'worm' *s* Regenwurm *m*

earthy ['ʌrθi] *adj* erdig; (fig) deftig

ear'wax' *s* Ohrenschmalz *m*

ease [iz] *s (facility)* Leichtigkeit *f*; *(comfort)* Bequemlichkeit *f*; *(informality)* Zwanglosigkeit *f*; **at e.!** (mil) rührt euch!; **feel at e. with s.o.** sich in j-s Gegenwart wohl fühlen; **put at e.** beruhigen; **with e.** mühelos || *tr (work)* erleichtern; *(pain)* lindern; *(move carefully)* lavieren; **e. out** *(of a job)* hinausmanövrieren || *intr*—**e. up** nachlassen; **e. up on** *(work)* es sich [*dat*] leichter machen mit

easel ['izəl] *s* Staffelei *f*

easement ['izmənt] *s* (jur) Dienstbarkeit *f*

easily ['izəli] *adv* leicht, mühelos; **e. satisfied** genügsam

easiness ['izinɪs] *s* Leichtigkeit *f*

east [ist] *adj* Ost–, östlich || *adv* ostwärts, nach Osten; **e. of** östlich von || *s* Osten *m*; **the East** der Osten

east'bound' *adj* nach Osten fahrend

Easter ['istər] *adj* Oster– || *s* Ostern *n & pl*

easterly ['istərli] *adj* österlich

eastern ['istərn] *adj* Ost–

East'ertide' *s* Osterzeit *f*

East'-Ger'man mark' *s* Ostmark *f*

eastward ['istwərd] *adv* ostwärts

easy ['izi] *adj* leicht; *(terms)* günstig; *(virtue)* locker; *(pace)* gemächlich; **e. on the eye** knusprig; **e. to digest** leichtverdaulich; **have an e. time of it** leichtes Spiel haben; **it's e. for you to talk** du hast gut reden!; **make e. erleichtern** || *adv*—**e. come, e. go** wie gewonnen, so zerronnen; **get off e.** gnädig davonkommen; **take it e.** *(relax)* es sich [*dat*] leicht machen; **take on'e time)** sich [*dat*] Zeit lassen; *(in parting)* mach's gut! *(remain calm)* reg dich nicht auf!; **take it e. on** *(a person)* schonend umgehen mit; *(a thing)* sparsam umgehen mit

eas'y chair' *s* Lehnsessel *m*

eas'ygo'ing *adj* ungeniert, ungezwungen

eas'y mark' *s* (coll) leichte Beute *f*

eat [it] *s*—**eats** *pl* (coll) Essen *n* || *v (pret* ate [et]; *pp* eaten ['itən]) *tr* essen; *(said of animals)* fressen; **eat away** zerfressen; **eat one's fill** sich satt essen; **eat one's heart out** sich in Kummer verzehren; **eat one's words** das Gesagte zurücknehmen; **eat up aufessen**; **what's eating him?** was hat er denn? || *intr* essen; **eat out** auswärts essen

eatable ['itəbəl] *adj* eßbar

eaves [ivz] *spl* Dachrinne *f*, Traufe *f*

eaves'drop' *v (pret & pp* –dropped; *ger* –dropping) *intr* horchen; **e. on** belauschen

eaves'drop'per *s* Horcher –in *mf*

ebb [eb] *s* Ebbe *f*; **at a low ebb** sehr heruntergekommen || *intr* ebben; (fig) nachlassen

ebb' and flow' *s* Ebbe und Flut *f*

ebb' tide' *s* Ebbe *f*

ebony ['ebəni] *s* Ebenholz *n*

ebullient [ɪ'bʌljənt] *adj* überschwenglich, hochbegeistert

eccentric [ek'sentrɪk] *adj* (& fig) exzentrisch || *s* Sonderling *m*, Kauz *m*; (mach) Exzenter *m*

eccentricity [‚eksen'trɪsɪti] *s* Verschrobenheit *f*, Tick *m*

ecclesiastic [ɪ‚klizi'æstɪk] *adj* kirchlich; *(law)* Kirchen– || *s* Geistlicher *m*

echelon ['eʃə‚lɑn] *s (level)* Befehlsebene *f*; *(group occupying a particular level)* Stabsführung *f*; *(flight formation)* Staffel *f*; **in echelons** staffelförmig || *tr* staffeln

echo ['eko] *s (*–oes*)* Echo *n* || *tr (sounds)* zurückwerfen; (fig) nachsprechen || *intr* widerhallen, echoen

éclair [e'kler] *s* Eclair *n*

eclectic [ek'lektɪk] *adj* eklektisch || *s* Eklektiker –in *mf*

eclipse [ɪ'klɪps] *s* Verfinsterung *f*; **go into e.** sich verfinstern; **in e.** im Schwinden || *tr* verfinstern; (fig) in den Schatten stellen

eclogue ['eklɔg] *s* Ekloge *f*

ecological [‚ekə'lɑdʒɪkəl] *adj* ökologisch

ecology [ɪ'kɑlədʒi] *s* Ökologie *f*

economic [‚ikə'nɑmɪk], [‚ekə'nɑmɪk] *adj* wirtschaftlich, Wirtschafts–

economical [‚ikə'nɑmɪkəl], [‚ekə'nɑmɪkəl] *adj* sparsam

economics [‚ikə'nɑmɪks], [‚ekə'nɑm-ɪks] *s* Wirtschaftswissenschaften *pl*

economist [ɪ'kanəmɪst] *s* Volkswirtschaftler –in *mf*
economize [ɪ'kanə,maɪz] *intr* sparen
economy [ɪ'kanəmi] *s* Wirtschaft *f*; *(thriftiness)* Sparsamkeit *f*; *(a saving)* Ersparnis *f*
ecstasy ['ekstəsi] *s* Verzückung *f*; **go into e.** in Verzückung geraten
ecstatic [ɛk'stætɪk] *adj* verzückt
ecumenic(al) [,ɛkjə'mɛnɪk(əl)] *adj* ökumenisch
eczema [eg'zimə] *s* Ausschlag *m*
ed·dy ['edi] *s* Strudel *m* || *v (pret & pp* –**died**) *intr* strudeln
edelweiss ['edəl,vaɪs] *s* Edelweiß *n*
edge [edʒ] *s (of a knife)* Schneide *f*; *(of a forest, town, water, road)* Rand *m*; *(e.g., of a table)* Kante *f*; *(keenness)* Schärfe *f*; (bb) Schnitt *m*; **have an e. on s.o.** den Vorteil gegenüber j–m haben; **on e.** *(said of a person or teeth)* kribbelig; *(said of nerves)* aufs äußerste gespannt; **take the e. off** abstumpfen; (fig) die Schärfe nehmen *(dat)* || *tr (a lawn)* beschneiden; *(put a border on)* einfassen; **e. out** (sport) knapp schlagen || *intr* —**e. forward** langsam vorrücken
edge'wise' *adv*—**not get a word in e.** nicht zu Worte kommen können
edg'ing *s* Umrandung *f*, Besatz *m*
edgy ['edʒi] *adj* kribbelig
edible ['edɪbəl] *adj* eßbar, genießbar
edict ['idɪkt] *s* Edikt *n*, Erlaß *m*
edification [,edɪfɪ'keʃən] *s* Erbauung *f*
edifice ['edɪfɪs] *s* Bauwerk *n*, Gebäude *n*
edi·fy ['edɪ,faɪ] *v (pret & pp* –**fied**) *tr* erbauen; **be edified by** sich erbauen an *(dat)*
ed'ifying *adj* erbaulich
edit ['edɪt] *tr (a book)* herausgeben; *(a newspaper)* redigieren; (cin) schneiden
edition [ɛ'dɪʃən] *s* Ausgabe *f*
editor ['edɪtər] *s (of a newspaper or magazine)* Redakteur –in *mf*; *(of a book)* Herausgeber –in *mf*; *(of editorials)* Leitartikler –in *mf*; (cin) Schnittmeister –in *mf*
editorial [,edɪ'torɪəl] *adj* redaktionell, Redaktions– || *s* Leitartikel *m*
editorialize [,edɪ'torɪə,laɪz] *intr* (on) seine Meinung zum Ausdruck bringen (über *acc*); *(report with a slant)* tendenziös berichten
edito'rial of'fice *s* Redaktion *f*
edito'rial staff' *s* Redaktion *f*
ed'itor in chief' *s* Chefredakteur –in *mf*
educate ['edʒu,ket] *tr* bilden, erziehen
education [,edʒu'keʃən] *s* Bildung *f*, Erziehung *f*; (educ) Pädagogik *f*
educational [,edʒu'keʃənəl] *adj* Bildungs–; **e. background** Vorbildung *f*; **e. film** Lehrfilm *m*; **e. institution** Lehranstalt *f*
educator ['edʒu,ketər] *s* Erzieher –in *mf*
educe [ɪ'd(j)us] *tr* hervorholen
eel [il] *s* Aal *m*
eerie, eery ['ɪri] *adj* unheimlich

efface [ɪ'fes] *tr* austilgen; **e. oneself** sich zurückhalten
effect [ɪ'fɛkt] *s* (on) Wirkung *f* (auf *acc*); *(consequence)* (on) Auswirkung *f* (auf *acc*); *(impression)* Eindruck *m*; **effects** *(movable property)* Habe *f*; **for e.** zum Effekt; **go into e.** in Kraft treten; **have an e. on** wirken auf *(acc)*; **in e.** praktisch; **put into e.** in Kraft setzen; **take e.** zur Geltung kommen; **to the e. that** des Inhalts, daß || *tr* bewirken
effective [ɪ'fɛktɪv] *adj* wirkungsvoll; *(actual)* effektiv; **e. against** wirksam gegen; **e. date** Tag *m* des Inkrafttretens; **e. from** mit Wirkung von; **e. immediately** mit sofortiger Wirkung; **e. strength** (mil) Iststärke *f*
effectual [ɪ'fɛkt/ʊ·əl] *adj* wirksam
effectuate [ɪ'fɛkt/ʊ,et] *tr* bewirken
effeminacy [ɪ'fɛmɪnəsi] *s* Verweichlichung *f*
effeminate [ɪ'fɛmɪnɪt] *adj* verweichlicht
effervesce [,efər'ves] *intr* aufbrausen
effervescence [,efər'vesəns] *s* Aufbrausen *n*, Moussieren *n*
effervescent [,efər'vesənt] *adj (liquid; personality)* aufbrausend
effete [ɪ'fit] *adj* entkräftet
efficacious [,efɪ'keʃəs] *adj* wirksam
efficacy ['efɪkəsi] *s* Wirksamkeit *f*, Wirkungskraft *f*
efficiency [ɪ'fɪʃənsi] *s* Tüchtigkeit *f*; (phys) Nutzeffekt *m*; (tech) Leistungsfähigkeit *f*
efficient [ɪ'fɪʃənt] *adj* tüchtig; (tech) leistungsfähig
effigy ['efɪdʒi] *s* Abbild *n*; **hang in e.** symbolisch hängen
effort ['efort] *s (exertion)* Mühe *f*; *(attempt)* Bestreben *n*; **efforts** Bemühungen *pl*; **make an honest e. to** *(inf)* sich redlich bemühen zu *(inf)*
effortless ['efortlɪs] *adj* mühelos
effrontery [ɪ'frʌntəri] *s* Frechheit *f*, Unverschämtheit *f*
effusion [ɪ'fjuʒən] *s* Erguß *m*
effusive [ɪ'fjusɪv] *adj* überschwenglich
egg [eg] *s* Ei *n*; **bad egg** (sl) übler Geselle *m*; **good egg** (sl) feiner Kerl *m*; **lay an egg** ein Ei legen; (fig) **e–e** völlige Niete sein || *tr*—**egg on** anstacheln
egg'beat'er *s* Schneeschläger *m*
egg'cup' *s* Eierbecher *m*
egg'head' *s* (coll) Intelligenzler –in *mf*
eggnog ['eg,nag] *s* Eierlikör *m*, Egg-Nog *m*
egg'plant' *s* Eierfrucht *f*
egg'shell' *s* Eierschale *f*
egg' white' *s* Eiweiß *n*
egg' yolk' *s* Eigelb *n*, Eidotter *m*
ego ['igo] *s* Ego *n*, Ich *n*; (coll) Ich-sucht *f*
egocentric [,igo'sɛntrɪk] *adj* egozentrisch
egoism ['igo,ɪzəm] *s* Selbstsucht *f*
egoist ['igo·ɪst] *s* Egoist *m*
egotism ['igo,tɪzəm] *s* Ichsucht *f*
egotistic(al) [,igo'tɪstɪk(əl)] *adj* egotistisch, geltungsbedürtig

egregious [ɪˈgridʒəs] *adj* unerhört
egress [ˈigres] *s* Ausgang *m*
Egypt [ˈidʒɪpt] *s* Ägypten *n*
Egyptian [ɪˈdʒɪp/ən] *adj* ägyptisch ‖
s Ägypter –in *mf;* (*language*) Ägyptisch *n*
eiderdown [ˈaɪdərˌdaʊn] *s* Eiderdaunen *pl;* (*cover*) Daunenbett *n*
eight [et] *adj & pron* acht ‖ *s* Acht *f*
eight'ball' *s*—be behind the e. (sl) in der Klemme sitzen
eighteen [ˈetˈtin] *adj & pron* achtzehn ‖ *s* Achtzehn *f*
eighteenth [ˈetˈtinθ] *adj* achtzehnte ‖ *s* (*fraction*) Achtzehntel *n;* the e. (*in dates or in a series*) der Achtzehnte
eighth [etθ] *adj* achte ‖ *s* (*fraction*) Achtel *n;* the e. (*in dates or in a series*) der Achte
eighth' note' *s* (mus) Achtelnote *f*
eightieth [ˈetɪˈθ] *adj* achtzigste ‖ *s* (*fraction*) Achtzigstel *n;* the e. der Achtzigste
eighty [ˈeti] *adj & pron* achtzig ‖ *s* Achtzig *f;* the eighties die achtziger Jahre *pl*
eigh'ty-one' *adj & pron* einundachtzig
either [ˈiðər], [ˈaɪðər] *adj*—e. one is correct beides ist richtig; e. way auf die e–e oder andere Art; in e. case in jedem der beiden Fälle; on e. side auf beiden Seiten ‖ *adv*—not...e. auch nicht ‖ *pron* einer von beiden; e. of you einer von euch beiden; I didn't see e. ich habe beide nicht gesehen ‖ *conj*—e....or entweder... oder
ejaculate [ɪˈdʒækjəˌlet] *tr* ausstoßen; (physiol) ejakulieren
eject [ɪˈdʒekt] *tr* ausstoßen; (*from a property*) (*from*) hinauswerfen (aus)
ejection [ɪˈdʒek/ən] *s* Ausstoßung *f*
ejec'tion seat' *s* Schleudersitz *m*
eke [ik] *tr*—eke out a living das Leben fristen
el [el] *s* (coll) Hochbahn *f*
elaborate [ɪˈlæbərɪt] *adj* (*detailed*) weitläufig; (*ornate*) kunstvoll; (*idea*) compliziert ‖ [ɪˈlæbəˌret] *tr* ausarbeiten ‖ *intr*—e. on sich verbreiten über (*acc*)
elaboration [ɪˌlæbəˈreʃən] *s* Ausarbeitung *f*
elapse [ɪˈlæps] *intr* verrinnen
elastic [ɪˈlæstɪk] *adj* elastisch; (*conscience*) weit ‖ *s* Gummiband *n*
elasticity [ˌilæsˈtɪsɪti] *s* Elastizität *f*
elated [ɪˈletɪd] *adj* freudig erregt
elation [ɪˈleʃən] *s* Hochgefühl *n*
elbow [ˈelbo] *s* Ellbogen *m;* (*of a pipe*) Rohrknie *n;* at one's e. bei der Hand; rub elbows with s.o. mit j–m in nähere Berührung kommen ‖ *tr*—e. one's way sich [*dat*] seinen Weg bahnen
el'bow grease' *s* (coll) Knochenschmalz *n*
el'bowroom' *s* Spielraum *m*
elder [ˈeldər] *adj* älter ‖ *s* Ältere *mf;* (bot) Holunder *m;* (eccl) Kirchenälteste *mf*
el'derber'ry *s* Holunderbeere *f*

elderly [ˈeldərli] *adj* ältlich
el'der states'man *s* profilierter Staatsmann *m*
eldest [ˈeldɪst] *adj* älteste
elect [ɪˈlekt] *adj* erlesen; (*elected but not yet installed*) zukünftig; (relig) auserwählt ‖ the e. *spl* die Auserwählten *pl* ‖ *tr* wählen; e. s.o. president j–n zum Präsidenten wählen
election [ɪˈlek/ən] *adj* Wahl– ‖ *s* Wahl *f*
elec'tion campaign' *s* Wahlkampf *m*
elec'tion day' *s* Wahltag *m*
electioneer [ɪˌlek/əˈnɪr] *intr* Stimmen werben
elective [ɪˈlektɪv] *adj* (educ) wahlfrei; (pol) Wahl– ‖ *s* (educ) Wahlfach *n*
electoral [ɪˈlektərəl] *adj* Wahl–
elec'toral col'lege *s* Wahlmänner *pl*
electorate [ɪˈlektərɪt] *s* Wählerschaft *f*
electric(al) [ɪˈlektrɪk(əl)] *adj* elektrisch, Elektro–
elec'trical appli'ance *s* Elektrogerät *n*
elec'trical engineer' *s* Elektroingenieur *m*
elec'trical engineer'ing *s* Elektrotechnik *f*
elec'tric blan'ket *s* Heizdecke *f*
elec'tric bulb' *s* Glühbirne *f*
elec'tric chair' *s* elektrischer Stuhl *m;* (*penalty*) Hinrichtung *f* auf dem elektrischen Stuhl
elec'tric cir'cuit *s* Stromkreis *m*
elec'tric eel' *s* Zitteraal *m*
elec'tric eye' *s* Photozelle *f*
elec'tric fan' *s* Ventilator *m*
elec'tric fence' *s* elektrisch geladener Drahtzaun *m*
electrician [ɪˌlekˈtrɪʃən] *s* Elektriker –in *mf*
electricity [ˌɪlekˈtrɪsɪti] *s* Elektrizität *f;* (current) Strom *m*
elec'tric light' *s* elektrisches Licht *n*
elec'tric me'ter *s* Stromzähler *m*
elec'tric mo'tor *s* Motorsäge *f*
elec'tric shav'er *s* elektrischer Rasierapparat *m*
elec'tric storm' *s* Gewittersturm *m*
elec'tric stove' *s* Elektroherd *m*
electri-fy [ɪˈlektrɪˌfaɪ] *v* (*pret & pp* –fied*) *tr* (& fig) elektrisieren; (*a streetcar, railroad*) elektrifizieren
electrocute [ɪˈlektrəˌkjut] *tr* durch elektrischen Strom töten; (jur) auf dem elektrischen Stuhl hinrichten
electrode [ɪˈlektrod] *s* Elektrode *f*
electrolysis [ɪˌlekˈtrɑlɪsɪs] *s* Elektrolyse *f*
electrolyte [ɪˈlektrəˌlaɪt] *s* Elektrolyt *m*
electromagnet [ɪˌlektrəˈmægnət] *s* Elektromagnet *m*
electromagnetic [ɪˌlektrəmægˈnetɪk] *adj* elektromagnetisch
electron [ɪˈlektrɑn] *s* Elektron *n*
electronic [ɪˌlekˈtrɑnɪk] *adj* elektronisch, Elektronen– ‖ electronics *s* Elektronik *f*
electron'ic flash' *s* Röhrenblitz *m;* (*device*) Blitzgerät *n*
electronic [ɪˌlekˈtrɑnɪk] *adj* elektroplattieren, galvanisieren

electrostatic [ɪ͵lɛktrə'stætɪk] *adj* elektrostatisch

electrotype [ɪ'lɛktrə͵taɪp] *s* Galvano *n* ‖ *tr* galvanoplastisch vervielfältigen

elegance ['ɛlɪgəns] *s* Eleganz *f*

elegant ['ɛlə͵gənt] *adj* elegant

elegiac [͵ɛlɪ'dʒaɪ-æk] *adj* elegisch

elegy ['ɛlɪdʒɪ] *s* Elegie *f*

element ['ɛlɪmənt] *s* (& *fig*) Element *n*; (*e.g., of truth*) Körnchen *n*

elementary [͵ɛlɪ'mɛntərɪ] *adj* elementar, grundlegend

elemen'tary school' *s* Grundschule *f*

elephant ['ɛlɪfənt] *s* Elefant *m*

elevate ['ɛlɪ͵vet] *tr* erheben, erhöhen

el'evated *adj* (*eyes*) erhoben; (*style*) erhaben ‖ *s* (coll) Hochbahn *f*

elevation [͵ɛlɪ'veʃən] *s* (*height*) Höhe *f*; (*hill*) Anhöhe *f*; (*above sealevel*) Seehöhe *f*; (*to the throne*) Erhebung *f*; (archit) Aufriß *m*; (arti) Richthöhe *f*; (astr, relig) Elevation *f*

elevator ['ɛlɪ͵vetər] *s* Aufzug *m*, Fahrstuhl *m*; (aer) Höhenruder *n*; (agr) Getreidespeicher *m*

el'evator op'erator *s* Fahrstuhlführer –in *mf*

el'evator shaft' *s* Fahrstuhlschacht *m*

eleven [ɪ'lɛvən] *adj* & *pron* elf ‖ *s* Elf *f*

eleventh [ɪ'lɛvənθ] *adj* elfte ‖ *s* (*fraction*) Elftel *n*; **the e.** (*in dates and in a series*) der Elfte

elev'enth hour' *s*—**at the e.** (fig) kurz vor Torschluß

elf [ɛlf] *s* (**elves** [ɛlvz]) Elf *m*, Elfe *f*

elicit [ɪ'lɪsɪt] *tr* hervorlocken; (*an answer*) entlocken

elide [ɪ'laɪd] *tr* elidieren

eligible ['ɛlɪdʒɪbəl] *adj* qualifiziert; (*entitled*) berechtigt; (*for office*) wählbar; (*for marriage*) heiratsfähig

el'igible bach'elor *s* Heiratskandidat *m*

eliminate [ɪ'lɪmɪ͵net] *tr* ausscheiden; (alg) eliminieren

elimination [ɪ͵lɪmɪ'neʃən] *s* Ausscheidung *f*

elimina'tion bout' *s* Ausscheidungskampf *m*

elision [ɪ'lɪʒən] *s* Auslassung *f*

elite [e'lit] *adj* Elite– ‖ *s* Elite *f*

elixir [ɪ'lɪksər] *s* Elixier *n*

elk [ɛlk] *s* Elch *m*

ellipse [ɪ'lɪps] *s* (geom) Ellipse *f*

ellip·sis [ɪ'lɪpsɪs] *s* (**-ses** [siz]) (gram) Ellipse *f*

elliptic(al) [ɪ'lɪptɪk(əl)] *adj* elliptisch

elm [ɛlm] *s* Ulme *f*

elocution [͵ɛlə'kjuʃən] *s* (*art*) Vortragskunst *f*; (*style*) Vortragsweise *f*

elope [ɪ'lop] *intr* ausreißen

elopement [ɪ'lopmənt] *s* Ausreißen *n*

eloquence ['ɛləkwəns] *s* Beredsamkeit *f*

eloquent ['ɛləkwənt] *adj* beredt

else [ɛls] *adj* sonst; **someone else's house** das Haus e–s anderen; **what e.?** was sonst?; (*in addition*) was noch? ‖ *adv* sonst, anders; **nowhere e.** sonst nirgends; **or e.** sonst, andernfalls; **where e.?** wo sonst?

else'where' *adv* (*position*) woanders;

(*direction*) sonstwohin; **from e.** anderswoher

elucidate [ɪ'lusɪ͵det] *tr* erläutern

elucidation [ɪ͵lusɪ'deʃən] *s* Erläuterung *f*

elude [ɪ'lud] *tr* entgehen (*dat*)

elusive [ɪ'lusɪv] *adj* schwer zu fassen; (*memory*) unzuverlässig

emaciated [ɪ'meʃɪ͵etɪd] *adj* abgezehrt

emanate ['ɛmə͵net] *intr*—**e. from** (*said of gases*) ausströmen aus; (*said of rays*) ausstrahlen aus; (fig) ausgehen von

emancipate [ɪ'mænsɪ͵pet] *tr* emanzipieren

emasculate [ɪ'mæskjə͵let] *tr* (& *fig*) entmannen

embalm [ɛm'bam] *tr* einbalsamieren

embankment [ɛm'bæŋkmənt] *s* Damm *m*

embar·go [ɛm'bargo] *s* (**-goes**) Sperre *f*, Embargo *n* ‖ *tr* sperren

embark [ɛm'bark] *intr* (**for**) sich einschiffen (nach); **e. upon** sich einlassen auf (*acc*)

embarkation [͵ɛmbar'keʃən] *s* Einschiffung *f*

embarrass [ɛm'bærəs] *tr* in Verlegenheit bringen

embar'rassed *adj* verlegen; **feel e.** sich genieren

embar'rassing *adj* peinlich

embarrassment [ɛm'bærəsmənt] *s* Verlegenheit *f*

embassy ['ɛmbəsɪ] *s* Botschaft *f*

em·bed [ɛm'bɛd] *v* (*pret* & *pp* **-bedded**; *ger* **-bedding**) *tr* einbetten; **e. in concrete** einbetonieren

embellish [ɛm'bɛlɪʃ] *tr* verschönern

embellishment [ɛm'bɛlɪʃmənt] *s* Verschönerung *f*

ember ['ɛmbər] *s* glühende Kohle *f*; **embers** Glut *f*

Em'ber day' *s* Quatember *m*

embezzle [ɛm'bɛzəl] *tr* unterschlagen

embezzlement [ɛm'bɛzəlmənt] *s* Unterschlagung *f*, Veruntreuung *f*

embezzler [ɛm'bɛzlər] *s* Veruntreuer –in *mf*

embitter [ɛm'bɪtər] *tr* verbittern

emblazon [ɛm'blezən] *tr* (*decorate*) verzieren; (*extol*) verherrlichen; (heral) heraldisch darstellen

emblem ['ɛmbləm] *s* Sinnbild *n*

emblematic(al) [͵ɛmblə'mætɪk(əl)] *adj* sinnbildlich

embodiment [ɛm'badɪmənt] *s* Verkörperung *f*

embod·y [ɛm'badɪ] *v* (*pret* & *pp* **-ied**) *tr* verkörpern

embolden [ɛm'boldən] *tr* ermutigen

embolism ['ɛmbə͵lɪzəm] *s* Embolie *f*

emboss [ɛm'bɔs] *tr* bossieren

embossed' *adj* getrieben

embrace [ɛm'bres] *s* Umarmung *f* ‖ *tr* umarmen; (*include*) umfassen; (*a religion, idea*) annehmen ‖ *intr* sich umarmen

embrasure [ɛm'breʒər] *s* Schießscharte *f*

embroider [ɛm'brɔɪdər] *tr* sticken

embroidery [ɛm'brɔɪdərɪ] *s* Stickerei *f*

embroi'dery nee'dle *s* Sticknadel *f*

embroil [em'brɔɪl] *tr* verwickeln
embroilment [em'brɔɪlmənt] *s* Verwicklung *f*
embry·o ['embrɪ ,o] *s* (**-os**) Embryo *m*
embryology [,embrɪ'alədʒɪ] *s* Embryologie *f*
embryonic [,æmbrɪ'anɪk] *adj* embryonal
emend [ɪ'mend] *tr* berichtigen
emendation [,imen'deʃən] *s* Berichtigung *f*
emerald ['emərəld] *adj* smaragdgrün ‖ *s* Smaragd *m*
emerge [ɪ'mʌrdʒ] *intr* (*come forth*) hervortreten; (*surface*) auftauchen; (*result*) (**from**) herauskommen (bei)
emergence [ɪ'mʌrdʒəns] *s* Hervortreten *n*; (*surfacing*) Auftauchen *n*
emergency [ɪ'mʌrdʒənsɪ] *adj* Not– ‖ *s* Notlage *f*; **in case of e.** im Notfall
emeritus [ɪ'merɪtəs] *adj* emeritiert
emersion [ɪ'mʌrʒən] *s* Auftauchen *n*
emery ['emərɪ] *s* Schmirgel *m*
em'ery cloth' *s* Schmirgelleinwand *f*
em'ery wheel' *s* Schmirgelrad *n*
emetic [ɪ'metɪk] *adj* Brech– ‖ *s* Brechmittel *n*
emigrant ['emɪgrənt] *s* Auswanderer –in *mf*
emigrate ['emɪ ,gret] *intr* auswandern
emigration [,emɪ'greʃən] *s* Auswanderung *f*
eminence ['emɪnəns] *s* (*height*) Anhöhe *f*; (*fame*) Berühmtheit *f*; **Eminence** (*title of a cardinal*) Eminenz *f*; **rise to e.** zu Ruhm und Würde gelangen
eminent ['emɪnənt] *adj* hervorragend
emissary ['emɪ ,serɪ] *s* Abgesandte *mf*
emission [ɪ'mɪʃən] *s* (biol) Erguß *m*; (phys) Austrahlung *f*, Ausströmung *f*
emis'sion control' *s* Abgasentgiftung *f*
emit [ɪ'mɪt] *v* (*pret & pp* **emitted;** *ger* **emitting**) *tr* von sich geben; (*rays*) ausstrahlen; (*gases*) ausströmen; (*sparks*) sprühen
emolument [ɪ'maljəmənt] *s* Vergütung *f*
emotion [ɪ'moʃən] *s* Gemütsbewegung *f*
emotional [ɪ'moʃənəl] *adj* (*e.g., disorder*) Gemüts–; (*person*) gefühlvoll; (*e.g., sermon*) ergreifend; (*mawkish*) rührselig
emperor ['empərər] *s* Kaiser *m*
empha·sis ['emfəsɪs] *s* (**-ses** [,siz])
Betonung *f*
emphasize ['emfə ,saɪz] *tr* betonen
emphatic [em'fætɪk] *adj* nachdrücklich
emphysema [,emfɪ'simə] *s* Emphysem *n*
empire ['empaɪr] *s* Reich *n*; (*Roman period*) Kaiserzeit *f*
Em'pire fur'niture *s* Empiremöbel *n*
empiric(al) [em'pɪrɪk(əl)] *adj* erfahrungsmäßig, empirisch
empiricist [em'pɪrɪsɪst] *s* Empiriker –in *mf*
emplacement [em'plesmənt] *s* Stellung *f*
employ [em'plɔɪ] *s* Dienst *m* ‖ *tr* (*hire*) anstellen; (*keep in employ-*

ment) beschäftigen; (*use*) verwenden; (*troops, police*) einsetzen
employee [em'plɔɪ·ɪ], [,emplɔɪ'i] *s* Arbeitnehmer –in *mf*
employer [em'plɔɪ·ər] *s* Arbeitgeber –in *mf*
employment [em'plɔɪmənt] *s* (*work*) Beschäftigung *f*, Arbeit *f*; (*use*) Verwendung *f*; (*e.g., of troops*) Einsatz *m*; **out of e.** arbeitslos
employ'ment a'gency *s* Arbeitsvermittlung *f*
empower [em'pau·ər] *tr* ermächtigen
empress ['emprɪs] *s* Kaiserin *f*
emptiness ['emptɪnɪs] *s* Leere *f*; (fig) Nichtigkeit *f*
emp·ty ['emptɪ] *adj* leer; **e. talk** leere Worte *pl*; **on an e. stomach** auf nüchternen Magen ‖ **empties** *spl* Leergut *n* ‖ *v* (*pret & pp* **-tied**) *tr* (aus)leeren ‖ *intr*—**e. into** münden in (*acc*)
emp'ty-hand'ed *adj* mit leeren Händen
emp'ty-head'ed *adj* hohlköpfig
emulate ['emjə ,let] *s* nacheifern (*dat*)
emulation [,emjə'leʃən] *s* Nacheiferung *f*
emulator [,emjə'letər] *s* Nacheiferer –in *mf*
emulsi·fy [ɪ'mʌlsɪ ,faɪ] *v* (*pret & pp* **-fied**) *tr* emulgieren
emulsion [ɪ'mʌlʃən] *s* Emulsion *f*; (phot) Schicht *f*
enable [en'ebəl] *tr* befähigen
enact [en'ækt] *tr* erlassen
enactment [en'æktmənt] *s* Erlassen *n*
enam·el [ɪ'næməl] *s* Email *n*; (dent) Zahnschmelz *m* ‖ *v* (*pret & pp* **-el[l]ed;** *ger* **-el[l]ing**) *tr* emaillieren
enam'el paint' *s* Emaillack *m*
enam'elware' *s* Emailwaren *pl*
enamored [ɛ'næmərd] *adj*—**be e. of** verliebt sein in (*acc*)
encamp [en'kæmp] *tr* in e–m Lager unterbringen ‖ *intr* lagern, sich lagern
encampment [en'kæmpmənt] *s* (*camping*) Lagern *n*; (*campsite*) Lager *n*
encase [en'kes] *tr* einschließen
enchant [en't'ænt] *tr* verzaubern; (fig) bezaubern
enchanter [en't'æntər] *s* Zauberer –in *mf*
enchant'ing *adj* bezaubernd
enchantment [en't'æntmənt] *s* (*state*) Verzauberung *f*; (*cause of enchantment*) Zauber *m*
enchantress [en't'æntrɪs] *s* Zauberin *f*
encircle [en'sʌrkəl] *tr* umgeben; (mil) einschließen
encirclement [en'sʌrkəlmənt] *s* (mil) Einschließung *f*
enclave [en'klev] *s* Enklave *f*
enclitic [en'klɪtɪk] *adj* enklitisch ‖ *s* Enklitikon *n*
enclose [en'kloz] *tr* einschließen; (*land*) umzäunen; (*in a letter*) beilegen; **e. in parentheses** einklammern; **please find enclosed in der Anlage erhalten Sie**
enclosure [en'klozər] *s* Umzäunung *f*; (*in a letter*) Anlage *f*

encomi·um [ɛnˈkomɪ·əm] s (–ums & –a [ə]) Lobpreisung f, Enkomion n

encompass [ɛnˈkʌmpəs] tr umfassen

encore [ˈɑnkor] s (performance) Zugabe f; (recall) Dakaporuf m ‖ interj da capo!; noch einmal!

encounter [ɛnˈkauntər] s Begegnung f; (hostile meeting) Zusammenstoß m; (mil) Gefecht n ‖ tr begegnen (dat)

encourage [ɛnˈkʌrɪdʒ] tr ermutigen

encouragement [ɛnˈkʌrɪdʒmənt] s Ermutigung f

encroach [ɛnˈkrotʃ] intr—e. on übergreifen auf (acc); (rights) beeinträchtigen

encroachment [ɛnˈkrotʃmənt] s Übergriff m

encrust [ɛnˈkrʌst] tr überkrusten

encumber [ɛnˈkʌmbər] tr belasten; (with debts) verschulden

encumbrance [ɛnˈkrʌmbrəns] s Belastung f

encyclical [ɛnˈsɪklɪkəl] s Enzyklika f

encyclopedia [ɛnˌsaɪkləˈpidɪ·ə] s Enzyklopädie f

encyclopedic [ɛnˌsaɪkləˈpidɪk] adj enzyklopädisch

end [ɛnd] s Ende n; (purpose) Zweck m; (goal) Ziel n; (closing) Schluß m; (outcome) Ausgang m, Ergebnis n; at the end of one's strength am Rande seiner Kraft; come to a bad end ein schlimmes Ende finden; come to an end zu Ende gehen; end in itself Selbstzweck m; gain one's ends seinen Vorsatz ausführen; go off the deep end sich unnötig aufregen; in the end schließlich; make both ends meet gerade auskommen; no end of unendlich viel(e); on end hochkant; (without letup) ununterbrochen; put an end to ein Ende machen (dat); that will be the end of me das überlebe ich nicht; to no end vergebens ‖ tr beenden ‖ intr enden; (gram) auslauten; end in a point spitz zulaufen; end up (in) (coll) landen (in dat); end up with beenden mit

end′-all′ s Schluß m vom Ganzen

endanger [ɛnˈdendʒər] tr gefährden

endear [ɛnˈdɪr] tr—e. s.o. to j-n einschmeicheln bei

endear′ing adj gewinnend

endearment [ɛnˈdɪrmənt] s Beliebtheit f

endeavor [ɛnˈdevər] s Bestreben n ‖ intr—e. to (inf) sich bestreben zu (inf), versuchen zu (inf)

endemic [ɛnˈdemɪk] adj endemisch ‖ s Endemie f, endemische Krankheit f

end′ing s Beendigung f, Abschluß m; (gram) Endung f

endive [ˈɛndaɪv] s Endivie f

endless [ˈɛndlɪs] adj endlos; an e. number of unendlich viele

end′most′ adj entfernteste

endocrine [ˈɛndoˌkraɪn] adj endokrin

endorse [ɛnˈdors] tr (confirm) bestätigen; (a check) indossieren

endorsee [ˌɛndorˈsi] s Indossat –in mf

endorsement [ɛnˈdorsmənt] s Indossament n; (approval) Bestätigung f

endorser [ɛnˈdorsər] s Indossant –in mf; (backer) Hintermann m

endow [ɛnˈdau] tr (provide with income) dotieren; (with talent) begaben

endowment [ɛnˈdaumənt] s Dotierung f; (talent) Begabung f

endow′ment fund′ s Stiftungsvermögen n

endurance [ɛnˈd(j)urəns] s Dauer f; (ability to hold out) Ausdauer f

endur′ance test′ s Dauerprobe f

endure [ɛnˈd(j)ur] tr aushalten ‖ intr fortdauern

endur′ing adj dauerhaft

enema [ˈɛnəmə] s Einlauf m

enemy [ˈɛnəmi] adj feindlich, Feind– ‖ s Feind m; become enemies sich verfeinden

energetic [ˌɛnərˈdʒetɪk] adj energisch

energy [ˈɛnərdʒi] s Energie f

enervate [ˈɛnərˌvet] tr entkräften

enfeeble [ɛnˈfibəl] tr entkräften

enfilade [ˈɛnfrˌled] s (mil) Flankenfeuer n ‖ tr mit Flankenfeuer bestreichen

enfold [ɛnˈfold] tr einhüllen

enforce [ɛnˈfors] tr durchsetzen; (obedience) erzwingen

enforcement [ɛnˈforsmənt] s Durchsetzung f

enfranchise [ɛnˈfræntʃaɪz] tr (admit to citizenship) einbürgern; (give the right to vote to) das Wahlrecht verleihen (dat)

engage [ɛnˈgedʒ] tr (hire) anstellen; (reserve) vorbestellen; (attention) fesseln; (gears) einrücken; (one's own troops) einsetzen; (the enemy) angreifen; be engaged in beschäftigt sein mit; e. in verwickeln in (acc) ‖ intr (mach) (ein)greifen; e. in sich einlassen in (acc)

engaged′ adj verlobt; get e. (to) sich verloben (mit)

engaged′ cou′ple s Brautleute pl

engagement [ɛnˈgedʒmənt] s (betrothal) Verlobung f; (appointment) Verabredung f; (obligation) Verpflichtung f; (mil) Gefecht n; have a previous e. verabredet sein

engage′ment ring′ s Verlobungsring m

engag′ing adj gewinnend

engender [ɛnˈdʒendər] tr hervorbringen

engine [ˈɛndʒɪn] s Maschine f; (aer, aut) Motor m; (rr) Lokomotive f

engineer [ˌɛndʒəˈnɪr] s Ingenieur m, Techniker m; (mil) Pionier m; (rr) Lokomotivführer m; engineers (mil) Pioniertruppe f ‖ tr errichten; (fig) bewerkstelligen

engineer′ing s Ingenieurwesen n

engineer′ing school′ s Technikum n

en′gine beam′ s Spritzenhaus n

en′gine room′ s Maschinenraum m

England [ˈɪŋglənd] s England n

English [ˈɪŋglɪʃ] adj englisch ‖ s (spin) Effet n; (language) Englisch n; in plain E. unverblümt; the E. die Engländer

Eng′lish Chan′nel s Ärmelkanal m
Eng′lish horn′ s Englischhorn n
Eng′lish·man s (–men) Engländer m
Eng′lish-speak′ing adj englischsprechend
Eng′lish-wom′an s (–wom′en) Engländerin f
engraft [ɛn′græft] tr aufpropfen; (fig) einprägen
engrave [ɛn′grev] tr gravieren
engraver [ɛn′grevər] s Graveur m
engrav′ing s Kupferstich m
engross [ɛn′gros] tr in Anspruch nehmen; (a document) mit großen Buchstaben schreiben; **become engrossed in** sich versenken in (acc)
engross′ing adj fesselnd
engulf [ɛn′gʌlf] tr (fig) verschlingen
enhance [ɛn′hæns] tr erhöhen; **be enhanced** sich erhöhen
enhancement [ɛn′hænsmənt] s Erhöhung f
enigma [ɪ′nɪgmə] s Rätsel n
enigmatic(al) [ˌɪnɪg′mætɪk(əl)] adj rätselhaft
enjoin [ɛn′dʒɔɪn] tr (forbid) (from ger) verbieten (dat) (zu inf); **e. s.o. to** (inf) j-m auferlegen zu (inf)
enjoy [ɛn′dʒɔɪ] tr (take pleasure in) Gefallen finden an (dat); (have the advantage of) genießen, sich erfreuen (genit); **e. doing s.th.** gern etw tun; **e. oneself** sich gut unterhalten; **e. to the full** auskosten; **I e. the wine** mir schmeckt der Wein
enjoyable [ɛn′dʒɔɪ·əbəl] adj erfreulich; **thoroughly e.** genußreich
enjoyment [ɛn′dʒɔɪmənt] s Genuß m
enkindle [ɛn′kɪndəl] tr entzünden
enlarge [ɛn′lɑrdʒ] tr vergrößern ‖ intr sich vergrößern; **e. upon** näher eingehen auf (acc)
enlargement [ɛn′lɑrdʒmənt] s Vergrößerung f
enlarger [ɛn′lɑrdʒər] s (phot) Vergrößerungsapparat m
enlighten [ɛn′lɑrtən] tr aufklären
enlightenment [ɛn′lɑrtənmənt] s (act) Aufklärung f; (state) Aufgeklärtheit f
enlist [ɛn′lɪst] tr (services) in Anspruch nehmen; (mil) anwerben; **e. s.o. in a cause** j–n für e-e Sache gewinnen ‖ intr (in) sich freiwillig melden (zu)
enlist′ed man′ s Soldat m; **enlisted men** Mannschaften pl
enlistment [ɛn′lɪstmənt] s Anwerbung f; (period of service) Militärdienstzeit f
enliven [ɛn′lɑɪvən] tr beleben
enmesh [ɛn′mɛʃ] tr verstricken
enmity [′ɛnmɪti] s Feindschaft f
ennoble [ɛn′nobəl] tr veredeln, adeln
ennui [′ɑnwi] s Langeweile f
enormity [ɪ′nɔrmɪti] s Ungeheuerlichkeit f
enormous [ɪ′nɔrməs] adj enorm, ungeheuer
enough [ɪ′nʌf] adj & adv genug, genügend; **be e.** genügen; **I have e. of it** ich bin es satt; **it's e. to drive one crazy** es ist zum Verrücktwerden

enounce [ɪ′nauns] tr (declare) verkünden; (pronounce) aussprechen
enrage [ɛn′redʒ] tr wütend machen
enraged′ adj (at) wütend (über acc)
enrapture [ɛn′ræptʃər] tr hinreißen
enrich [ɛn′rɪtʃ] tr (a person with money; the mind, a program) bereichern; (soil) fruchtbarer machen; (food, metals, gases) anreichern
enrichment [ɛn′rɪtʃmənt] s Bereicherung f; (of food, metals, gases) Anreicherung f
enroll [ɛn′rol] tr als Mitglied aufnehmen ‖ intr (educ) sich immatrikulieren lassen
enrollment [ɛn′rolmənt] s (in a course or school) Schülerzahl f; (of a society) Mitgliederzahl f
en route [ɑn ′rut] adv unterwegs
ensconce [ɛn′skɑns] tr verbergen
ensemble [ɑn′sɑmbəl] s Ensemble n
ensign [′ɛnsɪn] s (flag) (mil) Fahne f; (flag) (nav) Flagge f; (emblem) Abzeichen n; (nav) Leutnant m zur See
enslave [ɛn′slev] tr versklaven
enslavement [ɛn′slevmənt] s Versklavung f
ensnare [ɛn′sner] tr (fig) umgarnen
ensue [ɛn′s(j)u] intr (from) (er)folgen (aus)
ensu′ing adj darauffolgend
ensure [ɛn′ʃur] tr gewährleisten
entail [ɛn′tel] tr mit sich bringen
entangle [ɛn′tæŋgəl] tr verwickeln; **get entangled** sich verwickeln
entanglement [ɛn′tæŋgəlmənt] s Verwicklung f; (mil) Drahtverhau m
enter [′ɛntər] tr (a room) betreten, treten in (acc); (political office) antreten; (a university) beziehen; (a protest) erheben; (a career) einschlagen; (in the records) eintragen; **e. the army** Soldat werden ‖ intr eintreten, hereinkommen; (by car) einfahren; (sport) melden; (theat) auftreten; **e. into** (an agreement) treffen; (a contract) abschließen; **e. upon** anfangen; (a career) einschlagen; (an office, inheritance) antreten; (year of life) eintreten in (acc)
enterprise [′ɛntər‚praɪz] s Unternehmen n; (spirit) Unternehmungsgeist m
en′terprising adj unternehmungslustig
entertain [ˌɛntər′ten] tr unterhalten; (guests) bewirten; (doubts, hopes, suspicions) hegen ‖ intr Gäste haben
entertainer [ˌɛntər′tenər] s Unterhaltungskünstler –in mf
entertain′ing adj unterhaltsam ‖ s—**do a lot of e.** ein großes Haus führen
entertainment [ˌɛntər′tenmənt] s Unterhaltung f
entertain′ment tax′ s Vergnügungssteuer f
enthrall [ɛn′θrɔl] tr bezaubern, fesseln
enthrone [ɛn′θron] tr auf den Thron setzen; **be enthroned** thronen
enthuse [ɛn′θ(j)uz] tr (coll) begeistern
enthusiasm [ɛn′θ(j)uzɪ‚æzəm] s Begeisterung f, Schwärmerei f

enthusiast [en'θ(j)uzɪ,æst] *s* Schwärmer –in *mf*

enthusiastic [en,θ(j)uzɪ'æstɪk] *adj* (about) begeistert (über *acc* or von)

entice [en'taɪs] *tr* (ver)locken

enticement [en'taɪsmənt] *s* Verlockung *f*

entic'ing *adj* verlockend

entire [en'taɪr] *adj* ganz, gesamt; (*trust*) voll

entirely [en'taɪrlɪ] *adv* ganz, gänzlich

entirety [en'taɪrtɪ] *s*—**in its e.** in seiner Gesamtheit

entitle [en'taɪtəl] *tr* (*call*) betiteln; (to) berechtigen (zu); **be entitled to** Anspruch haben auf (*acc*); **be entitled to** (*inf*) berechtigt sein zu (*inf*)

entity ['entɪtɪ] *s* Wesen *n*

entomb [en'tum] *tr* bestatten

entombment [en'tummənt] *s* Bestattung *f*

entomology [,entə'malədʒɪ] *s* Entomologie *f*

entourage [,antu'raʒ] *s* Begleitung *f*

entrails ['entrelz] *spl* Eingeweide *pl*

entrain [en'tren] *tr* verladen || *intr* einsteigen

entrance ['entrəns] *s* Eingang *m*; (*drive*) Einfahrt *f*; (*of a home*) Flur *m*; (*upon office*) Antritt *m*; (*theat*) Auftritt *m*; **make one's e.** eintreten || [en'træns] *tr* mitreißen

en'trance examina'tion *s* Aufnahmeprüfung *f*

en'trance fee' *s* Eintrittspreis *m*

entrant ['entrənt] *s* (in) Teilnehmer –in *mf* (an *dat*)

en·trap [en'træp] *v* (*pret* & *pp* –trapped*; ger* –trapping) *tr* verleiten

entreat [en'trit] *tr* anflehen

entreaty [en'tritɪ] *s* dringende Bitte *f*; **at his e.** auf seine Bitte

entrée ['antre] *s* (*access*) Zutritt *m*; (*before main course*) Vorspeise *f*; (*between courses*) Zwischengericht *n*; (*main course*) Hauptgericht *n*

entrench [en'trentʃ] *tr* verschanzen; **be entrenched in** (fig) eingewurzelt sein in (*dat*)

entrenchment [en'trentʃmənt] *s* (*activity*) Schanzbau *m*; (*the result*) Verschanzung *f*

entrepreneur [antrəprə'nʌr] *s* Unternehmer –in *mf*

entrust [en'trʌst] *tr* (to) anvertrauen (*dat*)

entry ['entrɪ] *s* Eintritt *m*; (*by car*) Einfahrt *f*; (*door*) Eingang *m*, Eingangstür *f*; (*into a country*) Einreise *f*; (*into office*) Antritt *m*; (*in a dictionary*) Stichwort *n*; (*into a race*) Nennung *f*; (*contestant*) Bewerber –in *mf*; (com) Buchung *f*; (theat) Auftritt *m*; **unlawful e.** Hausfriedensbruch *m*

entwine [en'twaɪn] *tr* umwinden

enumerate [ɪ'n(j)umə,ret] *tr* aufzählen

enunciate [ɪ'nʌnsɪ,et] *tr* aussprechen || *intr* deutlich aussprechen

envelop [en'veləp] *tr* (*said of crowds, waves*) verschlingen; (*said of mist, clouds, darkness*) umhüllen; (mil) umfassen

envelope ['envə,lop] *s* Umschlag *m*

envelopment [en'veləpmənt] *s* Umhüllung *f*; (mil) Umfassung *f*

envenom [en'venəm] *tr* vergiften

enviable ['envɪ·əbəl] *adj* beneidenswert

envious ['envɪ·əs] *adj* (of) neidisch (auf *acc*)

environment [en'vaɪrənmənt] *s* (*ecological condition*) Umwelt *f*; (*surroundings*) Umgebung *f*

environmental [en,vaɪrən'mentəl] *adj* Umwelt–; umgebend, Umgebungs–

environmentalist [en,vaɪrən'mentəlist] *s* Umweltschützer –in *mf*

environs [en'vaɪrənz] *spl* Umgebung *f*

envisage [en'vɪzɪdʒ] *tr* ins Auge fassen

envoy ['envoɪ] *s* Gesandte *mf*

en·vy ['envi] *s* Neid *m* || *v* (*pret* & *pp* –vied) *tr* (for) beneiden (um)

enzyme ['enzaɪm] *s* Enzym *n*

epaulet, epaulette ['epə,let] *s* Epaulette *f*, Schulterstück *n*

ephemeral [ɪ'femərəl] *adj* flüchtig

epic ['epɪk] *adj* episch; **e. poetry** Epik *f* || *s* Epos *n*, Heldengedicht *n*

epicure ['epɪ,kjur] *s* Feinschmecker –in *mf*

epicurean [,epɪkju'ri·ən] *adj* genußsüchtig; (philos) epikureisch || *s* Genußmensch *m*; (philos) Epikureer *m*

epidemic [,epɪ'demɪk] *adj* epidemisch || *s* Epidemie *f*, Seuche *f*

epidermis [,epɪ'dɑrmɪs] *s* Oberhaut *f*

epigram ['epɪ,græm] *s* Epigramm *n*

epigraph ['epɪ,græf] *s* Inschrift *f*

epigraphy [e'pɪgrəfɪ] *s* Inschriftenkunde *f*

epilepsy ['epɪ,lepsɪ] *s* Epilepsie *f*

epileptic [,epɪ'leptɪk] *adj* epileptisch || *s* Epileptiker –in *mf*

epilogue ['epɪ,log] *s* Nachwort *n*

Epiphany [ɪ'pɪfənɪ] *s* Dreikönigsfest *n*

episcopal [ɪ'pɪskəpəl] *adj* bischöflich

Episcopalian [ɪ,pɪskə'pelɪ·ən] *adj* Episkopal– || *s* Episkopale *m*, Episkopalin *f*

epis'copal see' *s* Bischofssitz *m*

episcopate [ɪ'pɪskə,pet] *s* Bischofsamt *n*

episode ['epɪ,sod] *s* Episode *f*

epistemology [ɪ,pɪstə'malədʒɪ] *s* Epistemologie *f*, Erkenntnistheorie *f*

epistle [ɪ'pɪsəl] *s* Epistel *f*

epitaph ['epɪtæf] *s* Grabinschrift *f*

epithet ['epɪ,θet] *s* Beiwort *n*

epitome [ɪ'pɪtəmɪ] *s* Auszug *m*; (fig) Verkörperung *f*

epitomize [ɪ'pɪtə,maɪz] *tr*—**e–n** Auszug machen von or aus; (fig) verkörpern

epoch ['epək], ['ipɑk] *s* Epoche *f*

epochal ['epəkəl] *adj* epochal

e'poch-mak'ing *adj* bahnbrechend

Ep'som salts' ['epsəm] *spl* Bittersalz *n*

equable ['ekwəbəl] *adj* gleichmäßig; (*disposition*) gleichmütig

equal ['ikwəl] *adj* gleich; (*in birth or status*) ebenbürtig; (*in worth*) gleichwertig; (*in kind*) gleichartig; **be e. to** (*e.g., a task*) gewachsen sein (*dat*); **be on e. terms** (*be on the same level*) auf gleichem Fuß stehen; **other**

things being e. bei sonst gleichen Verhältnissen || *s* Gleiche *mfn;* **her** or **their e.(s)** ihresgleichen; **my (your,** *etc.***) e.(s)** meines- (deines-, *etc.*) gleichen || *v* (*pret* & *pp* **equal[l]ed;** *ger* **equal[l]ing** *tr* gleichkommen (*dat*); (*a record*) erreichen; (*math*) ergeben

equality [ɪ'kwɑlɪti] *s* Gleichheit *f;* (*in standing*) Gleichberechtigung *f*

equalize ['ikwə‚laɪz] *tr* gleichmachen

equally ['ikwəli] *adv* gleich, ebenso

equanimity [‚ikwə'nɪmɪti] *s* Gleichmut *m*

equate [i'kwet] *tr* (**to** or **with**) gleichsetzen (*dat* or mit)

equation [i'kweʒən] *s* Gleichung *f*

equator [i'kwetər] *s* Äquator *m*

equatorial [‚ikwə'tori‚əl] *adj* äquatorial

equestrian [ɪ'kwestrɪ‚ən] *adj* Reiter–; **e. statue** Reiterstandbild *n* || *s* Kunstreiter –in *mf*

equilateral [‚ikwɪ'lætərəl] *adj* gleichseitig

equilibrium [‚ikwɪ'lɪbrɪ‚əm] *s* Gleichgewicht *n;* (*fig*) Gleichmaß *n*

equinox ['ikwɪ‚nɑks] *s* Tagundnachtgleiche *f*

equip [ɪ'kwɪp] *v* (*pret* & *pp* **equipped;** *ger* **equipping** *tr* ausrüsten, ausstatten

equipment [ɪ'kwɪpmənt] *s* Ausrüstung *f,* Ausstattung *f*

equipoise ['ikwɪ‚pɔɪz] *s* Gleichgewicht *n*

equitable ['ɛkwɪtəbəl] *adj* gerecht

equity ['ɛkwɪti] *s* (*fairness*) Unparteilichkeit *f;* (fin) Nettowert *m*

equivalent [ɪ'kwɪvələnt] *adj* gleichwertig; (**to**) gleichbedeutend (mit) || *s* Gegenwert *m;* (**of**) Äquivalent *n* (für)

equivocal [ɪ'kwɪvəkəl] *adj* zweideutig

equivocate [ɪ'kwɪvə‚ket] *intr* zweideutig reden

equivocation [ɪ'kwɪvə‚keʃən] *s* Zweideutigkeit *f*

era ['ɪrə], ['irə] *s* Zeitalter *n*

eradicate [ɪ'rædɪ‚ket] *tr* ausrotten

erase [ɪ'res] *tr* ausradieren; (*a tape recording*) löschen; (*a blackboard*) abwischen; (fig) auslöschen

eraser [ɪ'resər] *s* Radiergummi *m;* (*for a blackboard*) Tafelwischer *m*

erasure [ɪ'reʃər], [ɪ'reʒər] *s* (*action*) Ausradieren *n;* (*erased spot*) Rasur *f*

ere [ɛr] *prep* (poet) vor (*dat*) || *conj* (poet) ehe, bevor

erect [ɪ'rɛkt] *adj* aufrecht, straff; (*hair*) gesträubt; **with head e.** erhobenen Hauptes || *tr* errichten

erection [ɪ'rɛkʃən] *s* Errichtung *f;* (*of sexual organs*) Erektion *f*

erg [ʌrg] *s* Erg *n*

ermine ['ʌrmɪn] *s* Hermelinpelz *m*

erode [ɪ'rod] *tr* (*corrode*) zerfressen; (fig) unterhöhlen; (geol) erodieren || *intr* zerfressen werden

erosion [ɪ'roʒən] *s* (*corrosion*) Zerfressen *n;* (fig) Unterhöhlung *f;* (geol) Erosion *f*

erotic [ɪ'rɑtɪk] *adj* erotisch

err [ʌr] *intr* irren, sich irren

errand ['ɛrənd] *s* Besorgung *f;* **run an e. e–e** Besorgung machen

er′rand boy′ *s* Laufbursche *m*

erratic [ɪ'rætɪk] *adj* regellos, ziellos; (geol) erratisch

erroneous [ɪ'roni‚əs] *adj* irrtümlich

erroneously [ɪ'roni‚əsli] *adv* irrtümlicherweise, versehentlich

error ['ɛrər] *s* Fehler *m,* Irrtum *m*

erudite ['ɛr(j)ʊ‚daɪt] *adj* gelehrt

erudition [‚ɛr(j)ʊ'dɪʃən] *s* Gelehrsamkeit *f*

erupt [ɪ'rʌpt] *intr* ausbrechen

eruption [ɪ'rʌpʃən] *s* Ausbruch *m;* (pathol) Ausschlag *m*

escalate ['ɛskə‚let] *tr* & *intr* eskalieren

escalation [‚ɛskə'leʃən] *s* Eskalierung *f*

escalator ['ɛskə‚letər] *s* Rolltreppe *f*

es′calator clause′ *s* Indexklausel *f*

escapade ['ɛskə‚ped] *s* Eskapade *f*

escape [ɛs'kep] *s* Flucht *f;* (*of gas or liquid*) Ausströmen *n;* **have a narrow e.** mit knapper Not davonkommen || *intr* flüchten (aus); (*said of gas or liquid*) ausströmen; (**from**) flüchten (aus)

escape′ clause′ *s* Ausweichklausel *f*

escapee [‚ɛskə'pi] *s* Flüchtling *m*

escape′ hatch′ *s* Notausstieg *m*

escapement [ɛs'kepmənt] *s* (horol) Hemmung *f*

escape′ wheel′ *s* (horol) Hemmungsrad *n*

escapism [ɛs'kepɪzəm] *s* Wirklichkeitsflucht *f*

escarpment [ɛs'kɑrpmənt] *s* (geol) Steilabhang *m;* (mil) Abdachung *f*

eschew [ɛs't∫u] *tr* (ver)meiden

escort ['ɛskort] *s* Geleit *n,* Schutzgeleit *n;* (*person*) Begleiter *m;* (mil) Begleitmannschaft *f,* Bedeckung *f;* (nav) Geleitschutz *m* || [ɛs'kort] *tr* begleiten; (mil, nav) geleiten

es′cort ves′sel *s* Geleitschiff *n*

escutcheon [ɛs'kʌt∫ən] *s* Wappenschild *m;* (*doorplate*) Schlüssellochschild *n*

Eskimo ['ɛskɪ‚mo] *adj* Eskimo– || *s* (**–mos** & **–mo**) Eskimo *m*

esopha·gus ['isəfəgəs] *s* (**–gi** [‚dʒaɪ]) Speiseröhre *f*

esoteric [‚ɛso'tɛrɪk] *adj* esoterisch

especial [ɛs'pɛʃəl] *adj* besondere

especially [ɛs'pɛʃəli] *adv* besonders

espionage [‚ɛspɪ‚ə'nɑʒ] *s* Spionage *f*

espousal [ɛs'pauzəl] *s* (**of**) Annahme *f* (von)

espouse [ɛs'pauz] *tr* annehmen

esprit de corps [ɛs'pri də 'kɔr] *s* Korpsgeist *m,* Gemeinschaftsgeist *m*

espy [ɛs'paɪ] *v* (*pret* & *pp* **espied**) *tr* erspähen

essay ['ɛse] *s* Aufsatz *m,* Essay *n* || [ɛ'se] *tr* probieren

essayist ['ɛse‚ɪst] *s* Essayist –in *mf*

essence ['ɛsəns] *s* Wesenheit *f;* (*scent*) Duft *m;* (*extract*) Essenz *f;* (philos) inneres Wesen *n;* **in e.** im wesentlichen

essential [ɛ'sɛn∫əl] *adj* (**to**) wesentlich (für) || *s* Hauptsache *f;* **the essentials** die Grundzüge *pl*

establish [ɛsˈtæblɪʃ] *tr (found)* gründen; *(a business, an account)* eröffnen; *(relations, connections)* herstellen; *(order)* schaffen; *(a record)* aufstellen; *(a fact)* feststellen

establishment [ɛsˈtæblɪʃmənt] *s (act)* Gründung *f*; *(institution)* Anstalt *f*; *(business)* Unternehmen *n*; **the Establishment** das Establishment

estate [ɛsˈtet] *s (landed property)* Landgut *n*; *(possessions)* Vermögen *n*; *(property of deceased person)* Nachlaß *m*; *(social station)* Stand *m*

esteem [ɛsˈtim] *s* Hochachtung *f*; **hold in e.** achten || *tr* achten

esthete [ˈɛsθit] *s* Ästhetiker –in *mf*

esthetic [ɛsˈθɛtɪk] *adj* ästhetisch || **esthetics** *s* Ästhetik *f*

estimable [ˈɛstɪməbəl] *adj* schätzenswert

estimate [ˈɛstɪˌmet], [ˈɛstɪmɪt] *s* Kostenanschlag *m*; *(judgment of value)* Schätzung *f*; **rough e.** Überschlag *m* || [ˈɛstɪˌmet] *tr (costs)* veranschlagen; *(the value)* abschätzen; *(homes, damages)* schätzen; **(at)** beziffern (auf *acc*); **e. roughly** überschlagen

estimation [ˌɛstɪˈmeʃən] *s* Schätzung *f*; **in my e.** nach meiner Schätzung

Estonia [ɛsˈtonɪ·ə] *s* Estland *n*

estrangement [ɛsˈtrendʒmənt] *s* Entfremdung *f*

estuary [ˈɛstʃʊˌɛri] *s (of a river)* Mündung *f*; *(inlet)* Meeresarm *m*

etch [ɛtʃ] *tr* radieren, ätzen

etcher [ˈɛtʃər] *s* Radierer –in *mf*

etch'ing *s* Radierung *f*; *(as an art)* Radierkunst *f*

eternal [ɪˈtʌrnəl] *adj* ewig

eternity [ɪˈtʌrnɪti] *s* Ewigkeit *f*

ether [ˈiθər] *s* Äther *m*

ethereal [ɪˈθɪrɪ·əl] *adj* ätherisch

ethical [ˈɛθɪkəl] *adj* ethisch, sittlich

ethics [ˈɛθɪks] *s* Ethik *f*, Sittenlehre *f*

Ethiopia [ˌiθɪˈopɪ·ə] *s* Äthiopien *n*

Ethiopian [ˌiθɪˈopɪ·ən] *adj* äthiopisch || *s* Äthiopier –in *mf*; *(language)* Äthiopisch *n*

ethnic(al) [ˈɛθnɪk(əl)] *adj* völkisch; **e. group** Volksgruppe *f*

ethnography [ɛθˈnɑɡrəfi] *s* Ethnographie *f*

ethnology [ɛθˈnɑlədʒi] *s* Völkerkunde *f*

ethyl [ˈɛθɪl] *s* Äthyl *m*

ethylene [ˈɛθɪˌlin] *s* Äthylen *n*

etiquette [ˈɛtɪˌkɛt] *s* Etikette *f*

etymology [ˌɛtɪˈmɑlədʒi] *s* Etymologie *f*

ety·mon [ˈɛtɪˌmɑn] *s (–mons & –ma [mə])* Etymon *n*

eucalyp·tus [ˌjukəˈlɪptəs] *s (–tuses & –ti [taɪ])* Eukalyptus *m*

Eucharist [ˈjukərɪst] *s*—**the E.** das heilige Abendmal, die Eucharistie *f*

eugenics [juˈdʒɛnɪks] *s* Rassenhygiene *f*

eulogize [ˈjuləˌdʒaɪz] *tr* lobpreisen

eulogy [ˈjulədʒi] *s* Lobrede *f*

eunuch [ˈjunək] *s* Eunuch *m*

euphemism [ˈjufɪˌmɪzəm] *s* Euphemismus *m*

euphemistic [ˌjufəˈmɪstɪk] *adj* euphemistisch, verblümt

euphonic [juˈfɑnɪk] *adj* wohlklingend

euphony [ˈjufəni] *s* Wohlklang *m*

euphoria [juˈforɪ·ə] *s* Euphorie *f*

euphoric [juˈforɪk] *adj* euphorisch

euphuism [ˈjufjuˌɪzəm] *s* gezierte Ausdrucksweise *f*

Europe [ˈjʊrəp] *s* Europa *n*

European [ˌjʊrəˈpi·ən] *adj* europäisch || *s* Europäer –in *mf*

Europe'an plan' *s* Hotelpreis *m* ohne Mahlzeiten

euthanasia [ˌjuθəˈneʒə] *s* Euthanasie *f*

evacuate [ɪˈvækjuˌet] *tr* evakuieren; *(med)* entleeren; *(an area)* räumen || *intr* sich zurückziehen

evacuation [ɪˌvækjuˈeʃən] *s* Evakuierung *f*; *(med)* Entleerung *f*

evade [ɪˈved] *tr* ausweichen *(dat)*; *(duties)* vernachlässigen; *(laws)* umgehen; *(prosecution, responsibility)* sich entziehen *(dat)*; *(taxes)* hinterziehen

evaluate [ɪˈvæljuˌet] *tr (e.g., jewels)* (ab)schätzen; *(e.g., a performance)* beurteilen

evaluation [ɪˌvæljuˈeʃən] *s* Abschätzung *f*; *(judgment)* Beurteilung *f*

evangelic(al) [ˌivænˈdʒɛlɪk(əl)], [ˌɛvənˈdʒɛlɪk(əl)] *adj* evangelisch

Evangelist [ɪˈvændʒəlɪst] *s* Evangelist *m*

evaporate [ɪˈvæpəˌret] *tr* eindampfen || *intr (above boiling point)* verdampfen; *(below boiling point)* verdunsten; (fig) sich verflüchtigen

eva'porated milk' *s* Kondensmilch *f*

evasion [ɪˈveʒən] *s (dodge)* Ausweichen *n*; *(of the law)* Umgehung *f*; *(of responsibility)* Vernachlässigung *f*; *(in speech)* Ausflucht *f*

evasive [ɪˈvesɪv] *adj* ausweichend

eve [iv] *s* Vorabend *m*

even [ˈivən] *adj (smooth)* eben, gerade; *(number)* gerade; *(uniform)* gleichmäßig; *(chance)* gleich; *(temperament)* ruhig, ausgeglichen; **an e. dozen** genau ein Dutzend; **be e.** (coll) quitt sein; **e. with** auf gleicher Höhe mit; **get e. with** mit j–m abrechnen || *adv* selbst, sogar; *(before comparatives)* noch; *(as intensifier before nouns and pronouns)* selbst; **break e.** gerade auf seine Kosten kommen; **e. if** selbst wenn, wenn auch; **e. so** trotzdem; **e. though** obgleich; **e. today** noch heute; **e. when** selbst wenn || *tr* ebnen; **e. up** ausgleichen

e'ven-hand'ed *adj* unparteiisch

evening [ˈivnɪŋ] *adj* Abend– || *s* Abend *m*; **in the e.** am Abend; **this e.** heute abend

eve'ning gown' *s* Abendkleid *n*

eve'ning pa'per *s* Abendblatt *n*

eve'ning school' *s* Abendschule *f*

evenly [ˈivənli] *adv* gleichmäßig; **e. matched** (sport) gleichwertig

ev'en-mind'ed *adj* gleichmütig

evenness [ˈivənnɪs] *s (smoothness)*

Ebenheit *f;* (*uniformity*) Gleichmäßigkeit *f*

event [ɪ'vent] *s* Ereignis *n;* (sport) Veranstaltung *f;* **at all events, in any e. auf jeden Fall; in the e. of** im Falle (*genit*)

eventful [ɪ'ventfəl] *adj* ereignisvoll

eventual [ɪ'ventʃʊ-əl] *adj* schließlich

eventuality [ɪ,ventʃʊ'ælɪtɪ] *s* Möglichkeit *f*

eventually [ɪ'ventʃʊ,əlɪ] *adj* schließlich

ever ['evər] *adv* je, jemals; (*before comparatives*) immer; **did you e.!** hat man schon sowas gehört!; **e. after** die ganze Zeit danach; **e. so** noch so; **e. so much** (coll) sehr; **hardly e.** fast nie

ev′ergreen′ *adj* immergrün ‖ *s* Immergrün *n*

ev′erlast′ing *adj* ewig; (*continual*) fortwährend; (iron) ewig

ev′ermore′ *adv* immer; **for e. in** Ewigkeit

every ['evrɪ] *adj* jeder; (*confidence*) voll; **e. bit** (coll) völlig; **e. now and then** ab und zu; **e. once in a while** dann und wann; **e. other day** alle zwei Tage; **e. time (that)** jedesmal (wenn)

ev′erybod′y *indef pron* jeder, jedermann

ev′eryday′ *adj* alltäglich, Alltags

ev′eryone′, ev′ery one′ *indef pron* (of) jeder (von); **e. else** alle anderen

ev′erything′ *indef pron* alles

ev′erywhere′ *adv* (*position*) überall; (*direction*) überallhin

evict [ɪ'vɪkt] *tr* delogieren

eviction [ɪ'vɪkʃən] *s* Delogierung *f*

evidence ['evɪdəns] *s* Beweismaterial *n,* Beweise *pl;* (*piece of evidence*) Beweis *m;* **as e. of** zum Beweis (*genit*); **for lack of e.** wegen Mangels an Beweisen; **give e.** aussagen; **in e.** sichtbar

evident ['evɪdənt] *adj* (*obvious*) offensichtlich; (*visible*) ersichtlich; **be e.** zutage liegen

evidently ['evɪdəntlɪ] *adv* offenbar

evil ['ivəl] *adj* übel, böse ‖ *s* Übel *n*

e′vildo′er *s* Übeltäter *–in mf*

e′vildo′ing *s* Missetat *f*

e′vil eye′ *s* böser Blick *m*

e′vil-mind′ed *adj* übelgesinnt

E′vil One′ *s* Böse *m*

evince [ɪ'vɪns] *tr* bekunden

evoke [ɪ'vok] *tr* hervorrufen

evolution [,evə'luʃən] *s* Evolution *f*

evolve [ɪ'vɑlv] *tr* entwickeln, entfalten ‖ *intr* sich entwickeln, sich entfalten

ewe [ju] *s* Mutterschaf *n*

ewer ['juər] *s* Wasserkanne *f*

exact [eg'zækt] *adj* genau (*e.g., money*) beitreiben; (*obedience*) erzwingen

exact′ing *adj* (*strict*) streng; (*task*) aufreibend; (*picky*) anspruchsvoll

exactly [eg'zæktlɪ] *adv* genau

exactness [eg'zæktnɪs] *s* Genauigkeit *f*

exact′ sci′ences *spl* Realien *pl*

exaggerate [eg'zædʒə,ret] *tr* übertreiben

exaggeration [eg,zædʒə'reʃən] *s* Übertreibung *f*

exalt [eg'zɔlt] *tr* erheben

exam [eg'zæm] *s* (coll) Prüfung *f*

examination [eg,zæmɪ'neʃən] *s* Prüfung *f,* Examen *n;* (jur) Verhör *n,* Vernehmung *f;* (med) Untersuchung *f;* **direct e.** (jur) direkte Befragung *f;* **fail an e.** bei e-r Prüfung durchfallen; **on closer e.** bei näherer Prüfung; **pass an e.** e-e Prüfung bestehen; **take an e.** e-e Prüfung ablegen

examine [eg'zæmɪn] *tr* prüfen; (jur) verhören, vernehmen; (med) untersuchen

examinee [eg,zæmɪ'ni] *s* Prüfling *m*

examiner [eg'zæmɪnər] *s* (educ) Prüfer *–in mf;* (med) Untersucher *–in mf*

example [eg'zæmpəl] *s* Beispiel *n;* **for e.** zum Beispiel; **make an e. of** ein Exempel statuieren an (*dat*); **set a good e.** mit gutem Beispiel vorangehen

exasperate [eg'zæspə,ret] *tr* reizen

excavate ['ekskə,vet] *tr* ausgraben

excavation [,ekskə'veʃən] *s* Ausgrabung *f*

excavator ['ekskə,vetər] *s* (archeol) Ausgräber *–in mf;* (mach) Trockenbagger *m*

exceed [ek'sid] *tr* überschreiten

exceedingly [ek'sidɪŋlɪ] *adv* außerordentlich

ex-cel [ek'sel] *v* (*pret & pp* **–celled;** *ger* **–celling**) *tr* übertreffen ‖ *intr* (in) sich auszeichnen (in *dat*)

excellence ['ekseləns] *s* Vorzüglichkeit *f*

excellency ['ekselənsɪ] *s* Vorzüglichkeit *f;* **Your Excellency** Eure Exzellenz

excellent ['ekselənt] *adj* ausgezeichnet

excelsior [ek'selsɪ-ər] *s* Holzwolle *f*

except [ek'sept] *adv—* **e. for** abgesehen von; **e. if** außer wenn; **e. that** außer daß; **e. when** außer wenn ‖ *prep* außer (*dat*), ausgenommen (*acc*) ‖ *tr* ausnehmen, ausschließen

exception [ek'sepʃən] *s* Ausnahme *f;* **by way of e.** ausnahmsweise; **take e. to** Anstoß nehmen an (*dat*); **without e.** ausnahmslos; **with the e. of** mit Ausnahme von

exceptional [ek'sepʃənəl] *adj* außergewöhnlich, Sonder

excerpt ['eksʌrpt] *s* Auszug *m* ‖ [ek-'sʌrpt] *tr* exzerpieren

excess ['ekses], [ek'ses] *adj* überschüssig ‖ [ek'ses] *s* (*surplus*) Überschuß *m;* (*immoderate amount*) (of) Übermaß *n* (von or an *dat*); **carry to e.** übertreiben; **excesses** Ausschreitungen *pl;* **in e. of** mehr als; **to e.** übermäßig

ex′cess bag′gage *s* Überfracht *f*

excessive [ek'sesɪv] *adj* übermäßig

ex′cess-prof′its tax′ *s* Mehrgewinnsteuer *f*

exchange [eks't′fendʒ] *s* Austausch *m;* (*e.g., of purchases*) Umtausch *m;* (*of words*) Wechselgespräch *n;* (of *money*) Geldwechsel *m*; (fin) Börse *f*; (mil) Kantine *f*; (telp) Vermittlung *f*; **e. of letters** Briefwechsel *m*; **in e.** dafür; **in e. for** für || *tr* (*trade*) tauschen; (*replace*) auswechseln; **e. for** umtauschen gegen; **e. places with s.o.** mit j—m tauschen

exchequer [ɛks't'/ɛkər] *s* Staatskasse *f*; (*department*) Schatzamt *n*

ex'cise tax' ['ɛksaɪz] *s* Verbrauchssteuer *f*

excitable [ɛk'saɪtəbəl] *adj* erregbar

excite [ɛk'saɪt] *tr* erregen, aufregen

excitement [ɛk'saɪtmənt] *s* Erregung *f*, Aufregung *f*

excit'ing *adj* erregend, aufregend

exclaim [ɛks'klem] *tr & intr* ausrufen

exclamation [,ɛksklə'meʃən] *s* Ausruf *m*

exclama'tion point' *s* Ausrufungszeichen *n*

exclude [ɛks'klud] *tr* ausschließen

exclusion [ɛks'kluʒən] *s* Ausschließung *f*, Ausschluß *m*; **to the e. of** unter Ausschluß (*genit*)

exclusive [ɛks'klusɪv] *adj* (*rights, etc.*) alleinig, ausschließlich; (*club*) exklusiv; (*shop*) teuer; **e. of** ausschließlich (*genit*)

excommunicate [,ɛkskə'mjunɪ,ket] *tr* exkommunizieren

excommunication [,ɛkskə,mjunɪ'keʃən] *s* Exkommunikation *f*, Kirchenbann *m*

excoriate [ɛks'korɪ,et] *tr* (fig) heruntermachen

excrement ['ɛkskrəmənt] *s* Exkremente *pl*

excrescence [ɛks'krɛsəns] *s* Auswuchs *m*

excruciating [ɛks'kruʃɪ,etɪŋ] *adj* qualvoll

exculpate ['ɛkskʌl,pet] *tr* entschuldigen

excursion [ɛks'kʌrʒən] *s* (*side trip*) Abstecher *m*; (*short trip*) Ausflug *m*

excusable [ɛks'kjuzəbəl] *adj* entschuldbar, verzeihlich

excuse [ɛks'kjus] *s* Ausrede *f*; **give as an e.** vorgeben; **make excuses** sich ausreden || [ɛks'kjuz] *tr* entschuldigen; **e. me!** entschuldigen Sie!; **you may be excused now** Sie können jetzt gehen

execute ['ɛksɪ,kjut] *tr* (*a condemned man*) hinrichten; (*by firing squad*) erschießen; (*perform*) durchführen, vollziehen; (*a will, a sentence*) vollstrecken; (*mus*) vortragen

execution [,ɛksɪ'kjuʃən] *s* Hinrichtung *f*; (*by firing squad*) Erschießung *f*; (*performance*) Durchführung *f*, Vollziehung *f*; (*mus*) Vortrag *m*

executioner [,ɛksɪ'kjuʃənər] *s* Scharfrichter *m*

executive [ɛg'zɛkjətɪv] *adj* vollziehend, exekutiv || *s* (*com*) Manager *m*, leitender Angestellte *mf*; **the Executive** (*pol*) die Exekutive *f*

exec'utive commit'tee *s* Vollzugsausschuß *m*, Vorstand *m*

exec'utive or'der *s* Durchführungsverordnung *f*

executor [ɛg'zɛkjətər] *s* Vollstrecker *m*

executrix [ɛg'zɛkjətrɪks] *s* Vollstreckerin *f*

exemplary [ɛg'zɛmpləri] *adj* vorbildlich, mustergültig

exempli·fy [ɛg'zɛmplɪ,faɪ] *v* (*pret & pp* –fied) *tr* (*demonstrate*) an Beispielen erläutern; (*embody*) als Beispiel dienen für

exempt [ɛg'zɛmpt] *adj* (*from*) befreit (von) || *tr* befreien; (mil) freistellen

exemption [ɛg'zɛmpʃən] *s* Befreiung *f*; (mil) Freistellung *f*

exercise ['ɛksər,saɪz] *s* Übung *f*; (*of the body*) Bewegung *f*; (*of power*) Ausübung *f*; (mil) Exerzieren *n*; **take e.** sich [*dat*] Bewegung machen || *tr* üben; (*the body, a horse*) bewegen; (*power, influence*) ausüben; (mil) exerzieren || *intr* üben; (mil) exerzieren

exert [ɛg'zʌrt] *tr* ausüben; **e. every effort** alle Kräfte rühren; **e. oneself** sich anstrengen

exertion [ɛg'zʌrʃən] *s* Anstrengung *f*; (*e.g., of power*) Ausübung *f*

exhalation [,ɛks·hə'leʃən] *s* Ausatmung *f*; (*of gases*) Gasabgabe *f*

exhale [ɛks'hel] *tr & intr* ausatmen

exhaust [ɛg'zɔst] *s* (aut) Auspuff *m* || *tr* erschöpfen

exhaust'ed *adj* erschöpft

exhaust' fan' *s* Absaugventilator *m*

exhaust' gas' *s* Abgas *n*

exhaust'ing *adj* anstrengend, mühselig

exhaustion [ɛg'zɔstʃən] *s* Erschöpfung *f*

exhaustive [ɛg'zɔstɪv] *adj* erschöpfend

exhaust' pipe' *s* Auspuffrohr *n*

exhaust' valve' *s* Auspuffventil *n*

exhibit [ɛg'zɪbɪt] *s* (*exhibition*) Ausstellung *f*; (*object exhibited*) Ausstellungsstück *n*; (jur) Beleg *m* || *tr* zur Schau stellen; (*wares*) ausstellen; (*e.g., courage*) zeigen

exhibition [,ɛksɪ'bɪʃən] *s* Ausstellung *f*

exhilarating [ɛg'zɪlə,retɪŋ] *adj* erheiternd

exhort [ɛg'zɔrt] *tr* ermahnen

exhume [ɛks'hjum] *tr* exhumieren

exigency ['ɛksɪdʒənsɪ] *s* (*demand, need*) Erfordnis *n*; (*state of urgency*) Dringlichkeit *f*

exigent ['ɛksɪdʒənt] *adj* dringlich

exile ['ɛgzaɪl] *s* Exil *n*; (*person*) Verbannte *mf* || *tr* verbannen

exist [ɛg'zɪst] *intr* existieren; (*continue to be*) bestehen; **e. from day to day** dahinleben

existence [ɛg'zɪstəns] *s* Existenz *f*, Dasein *n*; **be in e.** bestehen; **come into e.** entstehen

existential [,ɛgzɪs'tɛnʃəl] *adj* existentiell

existentialism [,ɛgzɪs'tɛnʃə,lɪzəm] *s* Existentialismus *m*

exit ['ɛgzɪt] *s* Ausgang *m*; (*by car*) Ausfahrt *f*; (theat) Abgang *m* || *intr* (theat) abtreten

exodus ['ɛksədəs] *s* Abwanderung *f*

exonerate [ɛg'zɑnə,ret] *tr* entlasten

exorbitant [eg'zɔrbɪtənt] *adj* schwindelhaft; **e. price** Wucherpreis *m*

exorcise ['eksɔr̩saɪz] *tr* exorzieren

exotic [eg'zɑtɪk] *adj* exotisch

expand [eks'pænd] *tr* (aus)dehnen; (*enlarge*) erweitern; (*math*) entwickeln ‖ *intr* sich ausdehnen

expanse [eks'pæns] *s* Weite *f*, Fläche *f*

expansion [eks'pænʃən] *s* Ausdehnung *f*; (*expanded part*) Erweiterung *f*

expansive [eks'pænsɪv] *adj* expansiv; (fig) mitteilsam

expatiate [eks'peʃɪ̩et] *intr* (**on**) sich verbreiten (über *acc*)

expatriate [eks'petrɪ̩ɪt] *adj* ausgebürgert ‖ *s* Ausgebürgerte *mf* ‖ [eks'petrɪ̩et] *tr* ausbürgern

expect [eks'pekt] *tr* erwarten ‖ *intr*— **she's expecting** (coll) sie ist in anderen Umständen

expectancy [eks'pektənsɪ] *s* Ewartung *f*

expectant [eks'pektənt] *adj* erwartungsvoll; (*mother*) werdende

expectation [‚ekspek'teʃən] *s* Erwartung *f*

expectorate [eks'pektə̩ret] *tr* & *intr* spucken

expediency [eks'pidɪ·ənsɪ] *s* Zweckmäßigkeit *f*

expedient [eks'pidɪ·ənt] *adj* zweckmäßig ‖ *s* Mittel *n*, Hilfsmittel *f*

expedite ['ekspɪ̩daɪt] *tr* beschleunigen; (*a document*) ausstellen

expedition [‚ekspɪ'dɪʃən] *s* Expedition *f*

expedi'tionary force' [‚ekspɪ'dɪʃə̩nerɪ] *s* (mil) Expeditionsstreitkräfte *pl*

expeditious [‚ekspɪ'dɪʃəs] *adj* schleunig

ex·pel [eks'pel] *v* (*pret* & *pp* **–pelled**; *ger* **–pelling**) *tr* (aus)treiben; (*a student*) (**from**) verweisen vom

expend [eks'pend] *tr* (*time, effort, etc.*) aufwenden; (*money*) ausgeben

expendable [eks'pendəbəl] *adj* entbehrlich

expenditure [eks'pendɪt/ər] *s* Aufwand *m*; (*of money*) Ausgabe *f*

expense [eks'pens] *s* Ausgabe *f*; **at s.o.'s e.** (& fig) auf j-s Kosten; **expenses** Unkosten *pl*; **go to great e.** sich in Unkosten stürzen

expense' account' *s* Spesenkonto *n*

expensive [eks'pensɪv] *adj* kostspielig

experience [eks'pɪrɪ·əns] *s* Erfahrung *f*; (*an event*) Erlebnis *n*; **no previous e. necessary** Vorkenntnisse nicht erforderlich ‖ *tr* erfahren; (*pain*) erdulden; (*loss*) erleiden

expe'rienced *adj* erfahren

experiment [eks'perɪmənt] *s* Experiment *n*, Versuch *m* ‖ [‚eks'perɪ̩ment] *intr* experimentieren, Versuche anstellen

experimental [eks‚perɪ'mentəl] *adj* experimentell, Versuchs—

expert ['ekspərt] *adj* fachmännisch, erfahren; **e. advice** Gutachten *n* ‖ *s* Fachmann *m*; (jur) Sachverständige *mf*

expertise [‚eksper'tiz] *s* (*opinion*) Gutachten *n*; (*skill*) Sachkenntnis *f*

expiate ['ekspɪ̩et] *tr* sühnen, büßen

expiation [‚ekspɪ'eʃən] *s* Sühnung *f*

expiration [‚ekspɪ'reʃən] *s* Verfall *m*

expira'tion date' *s* Verfalltag *m*

expire [eks'paɪr] *tr* ausatmen ‖ *intr* verfallen; (*die*) verscheiden

explain [eks'plen] *tr* erklären, erläutern; (*justify*) rechtfertigen

explanation [‚eksplə'neʃən] *s* Erklärung *f*, Erläuterung *f*

explanatory [eks'plænə̩torɪ] *adj* erklärend, erläuternd

expletive ['eksplɪtɪv] *s* Füllwort *n*

explicit [eks'plɪsɪt] *adj* ausdrücklich

explode [eks'plod] *tr* explodieren lassen; (*a theory*) verwerfen ‖ *intr* explodieren; (*said of a grenade*) krepieren; (**with**) platzen (vor *dat*)

exploit ['eksplɔɪt] *s* Heldentat *f*, Großtat *f* ‖ [eks'plɔɪt] *tr* ausnutzen; (pej) ausbeuten; (min) abbauen

exploitation [‚eksplɔɪ'teʃən] *s* Ausnutzung *f*; (pej) Ausbeutung *f*; (min) Abbau *m*

exploration [‚eksplə'reʃən] *s* Erforschung *f*

explore [eks'plor] *tr* erforschen

explorer [eks'plorər] *s* Forscher –in *mf*

explosion [eks'ploʒən] *s* Explosion *f*

explosive [eks'plosɪv] *adj* explosiv, Spreng– ‖ *s* (*explosive substance*) Sprengstoff *m*; (*device*) Sprengkörper *m*

explo'sive charge' *s* Sprengladung *f*

exponent [eks'ponənt] *s* Exponent *m*

export ['eksport] *adj* Ausfuhr– ‖ *s* Ausfuhr *m*, Export *m*; **exports** Ausfuhrgüter *pl* ‖ [eks'port] *tr* ausführen

exportation [‚ekspor'teʃən] *s* Ausfuhr *m*

exporter ['eksportər], [eks'portər] *s* Ausfuhrhändler –in *mf*, Exporteur –in *mf*

expose [eks'poz] *tr* (*to danger, ridicule, sun*) aussetzen; (*bare*) entblößen; (*a person*) (as) bloßstellen (als), entlarven (als); (phot) belichten

exposé [‚ekspo'ze] *s* Enthüllung *f*

exposition [‚ekspə'zɪʃən] *s* Ausstellung *f*; (rhet) Exposition *f*

expostulate [eks'pɑst/ə̩let] *intr* protestieren; **e. with s.o. about** j-m ernste Vorhaltungen machen über (*acc*)

exposure [eks'poʒər] *s* (*of a child*) Aussetzung *f*; (*laying bare*) Entblößung *f*; (*unmasking*) Entlarvung *f*; (*of a building*) Lage *f*; (phot) Belichtung *f*

expo'sure me'ter *s* Belichtungsmesser *m*

expound [eks'paund] *tr* erklären

express [eks'pres] *adj* ausdrücklich ‖ *s* (rr) Expreß *m*; **by e.** als Eilgut ‖ *tr* ausdrücken; (*feelings*) zeigen; **e. oneself** sich äußern

express' com'pany *s* Paketpostgesellschaft *f*

expression [eks'preʃən] *s* Ausdruck *m*

expressive [ɛksˈprɛsɪv] *adj* ausdrucksvoll

express′ train′ *s* Expreßzug *m*

express′way′ *s* Schnellverkehrsstraße *f*

expropriate [ɛksˈproprɪˌet] *tr* enteignen

expulsion [ɛksˈpʌlʃən] *s* Austreibung *f*; *(from school or a game)* Verweisung *f*

expunge [ɛksˈpʌndʒ] *tr* ausstreichen

expurgate [ˈɛkspərˌget] *tr* säubern

exquisite [ˈɛkskwɪzɪt], [ɛksˈkwɪzɪt] *adj* exquisit, vorzüglich

ex-service•man [ˌɛksˈsʌrvɪsˌmæn] *s* (**-men′**) ehemaliger Soldat *m*

extant [ˈɛkstənt] *adj* noch bestehend

extemporaneous [ɛksˌtɛmpəˈreni·əs] *adj* aus dem Stegreif, unvorbereitet

extempore [ɛksˈtɛmpəri] *adj* unvorbereitet ‖ *adv* aus dem Stegreif

extemporize [ɛksˈtɛmpəˌraɪz] *tr & intr* extemporieren

extend [ɛksˈtɛnd] *tr* *(expand)* ausdehnen; *(a line)* fortführen; *(time)* verlängern; *(congratulations, invitation)* aussprechen; *(one's hand)* ausstrecken; *(a building)* ausbauen ‖ *intr* **(to)** sich erstrecken (bis); **e. beyond** hinausgehen über *(acc)*

extension [ɛksˈtɛnʃən] *s* Ausdehnung *f*; *(of time, credit)* Verlängerung *f*; *(archit)* Anbau *m*; *(telp)* Nebenanschluß *m*

exten′sion cord′ *s* Verlängerungsschnur *f*

exten′sion lad′der *s* Ausziehleiter *f*

exten′sion ta′ble *s* Ausziehtisch *m*

extensive [ɛksˈtɛnsɪv] *adj* umfassend

extent [ɛksˈtɛnt] *s* Umfang *m*, Ausmaß *n*; **to some e.** eingermaßen; **to the full e.** in vollem Umfang; **to what e.** inwiefern

extenuating [ɛksˈtɛnjuˌetɪŋ] *adj* mildernd

exterior [ɛksˈtɪrɪ·ər] *adj* Außen-, äußere ‖ *s* Äußere *n*

exterminate [ɛksˈtʌrmɪˌnet] *tr* vertilgen, ausrotten

extermination [ɛksˌtʌrmɪˈneʃən] *s* Vertilgung *f*; *(of vermin)* Raumentwesung *f*

exterminator [ɛksˈtʌrmɪˌnetər] *s* Raumentweser *m*

external [ɛksˈtʌrnəl] *adj* Außen-, äußerlich ‖ **externals** *spl* Äußerlichkeiten *pl*

extinct [ɛksˈtɪŋkt] *adj* *(volcano)* erloschen; *(animal)* ausgestorben; **become e.** aussterben

extinguish [ɛksˈtɪŋgwɪʃ] *tr* auslöschen; **be extinguished** erlöschen

extinguisher [ɛksˈtɪŋgwɪʃər] *s* Löschgerät *n*

extirpate [ˈɛkstərˌpet] *tr* ausrotten

ex•tol [ɛksˈtol] *v* (*pret & pp* **-tolled;** *ger* **-tolling**) *tr* erheben, lobpreisen

extort [ɛksˈtɔrt] *tr* erpressen

extortion [ɛksˈtɔrʃən] *s* Erpressung *f*

extortionate [ɛksˈtɔrʃənɪt] *adj* überhöht

extra [ˈɛkstrə] *adj* übrig; *(special)* Sonder-, Extra-; **meals are e.** Mahlzeiten werden zusätzlich berechnet ‖ *adv* extra, besonders ‖ *s* (cin) Statist –in *mf*; *(journ)* Sonderausgabe *f*; *(theat)* Komparse *m*; **extras** *(expenses)* Nebenausgaben *pl*; *(accessories)* Zubehör *n*

extract [ˈɛkstrækt] *s* Extrakt *m*, Auszug *m*; *(excerpt)* Ausschnitt *m* ‖ [ɛksˈtrækt] *tr* extrahieren, ausziehen; *(dent, math)* ziehen

extraction [ɛksˈtrækʃən] *s* *(lineage)* Abstammung *f*; *(dent)* Zahnziehen *n*; *(min)* Gewinnung *f*

extracurricular [ˌɛkstrəkəˈrɪkjələr] *adj* außerplanmäßig

extradite [ˈɛkstrəˌdaɪt] *tr* ausliefern

extradition [ˌɛkstrəˈdɪʃən] *s* Auslieferung *f*

ex′tra in′come *s* Nebeneinkünfte *pl*

ex′tramar′ital *adj* außerehelich

extramural [ˌɛkstrəˈmjurəl] *adj* außerhalb der Schule stattfindend

extraneous [ɛksˈtreni·əs] *adj* unwesentlich

extraordinary [ˌɛksˈtrɔrdɪˌneri] *adj* außerordentlich

ex′tra pay′ *s* Zulage *f*

extrapolate [ɛksˈtræpəˌlet] *tr & intr* extrapolieren

extrasensory [ˌɛkstrəˈsɛnsəri] *adj* übersinnlich

extravagance [ɛksˈtrævəgəns] *s* Verschwendung *f*

extravagant [ɛksˈtrævəgənt] *adj* verschwenderisch, extravagant; *(idea, plan)* überspannt

extreme [ɛksˈtrim] *adj* äußerst; *(radical)* extrem; *(old age)* höchst; *(necessity)* dringend ‖ *s* Äußerste *n*; **at the other e.** am entgegengesetzten Ende; **carry to extremes** auf die Spitze treiben; **in the e.** äußerst

extremely [ɛksˈtrimli] *adj* äußerst

extreme′ unc′tion *s* die Letzte Ölung

extremist [ɛksˈtrimist] *s* Extremist –in *mf*

extremity [ɛksˈtrɛmɪti] *s* Äußerste *n*, äußerstes Ende *n*; **be reduced to extremities** aus dem letzten Loch pfeifen; **extremities** *(hands and feet)* Extremitäten *pl*

extricate [ˈɛkstrɪˌket] *tr* befreien

extrinsic [ɛksˈtrɪnsɪk] *adj* äußerlich

extrovert [ˈɛkstrəˌvʌrt] *s* Extravertierte *mf*

extrude [ɛksˈtrud] *tr* ausstoßen

exuberant [ɛgˈz(j)ubərənt] *adj* *(luxuriant)* üppig; *(lavish)* überschwenglich

exude [ɛgˈzud] *tr* ausschwitzen; (fig) ausstrahlen

exult [ɛgˈzʌlt] *intr* jauchzen

exultant [ɛgˈzʌltənt] *adj* jauchzend

eye [aɪ] *s* Auge *n*; *(of a needle)* Öhr *n*; **an eye for an eye** Auge um Auge; **be all eyes** große Augen machen; **by eye** nach dem Augenmaß; **close one's eyes to** die Augen schließen vor *(dat)*; **have an eye for** Sinn haben für; **have good eyes** gut sehen; **in my eyes** nach meiner Ansicht; **in the eyes of the law** vom Standpunkt des Gesetzes aus; **keep a close eye on s.o.** j–m auf die Finger sehen; **keep an eye on s.th.** ein wachsames Auge auf etw [*acc*] haben; **keep one's eyes peeled** scharf aufpassen; **lay eyes on** zu Gesicht bekommen; **makes eyes at** verliebte Blicke zuwerfen (*dat*); **see eye to eye with** völlig übereinstimmen mit; **with an eye to** mit Rücksicht auf (*acc*) ‖ *v* (*pret & pp* **eyed;** *ger* **eying & eyeing**) *tr* mustern, schielen nach

eye'ball' *s* Augapfel *m*

eye'brow' *s* Augenbraue *f*

eye'brow pen'cil *s* Augenbrauenstift *m*

eye' cat'cher *s* Blickfang *m*

eye' cup' *s* Augenspülglas *n*

eye' drops' *spl* Augentropfen *pl*

eyeful [ˈaɪful] *s*—**get an e.** etw Hübsches sehen

eye'glass' *s* Augenglas *n*; **eyeglasses** Brille *f*

eye'lash' *s* Wimper *f*

eyelet [ˈaɪlɪt] *s* Öse *f*

eye'lid' *s* Lid *n*, Augenlid *n*

eye'o'pener *s* (*surprise*) Überraschung *f*; (*liquor*) Schnäpschen *n*

eye'piece' *s* Okular *n*

eye'shade' *s* Augenschirm *m*

eye' shad'ow *s* Lidschatten *m*

eye'shot' *s*—**within e.** in Sehweite

eye'sight' *s* Augenlicht *n*, Sehkraft *f*; (*range*) Sehweite *f*; **have bad** (or **good**) **e.** schlechte (or gute) Augen haben

eye' sock'et *s* Augenhöhle *f*

eye'sore' *s* (fig) Dorn *m* im Auge

eye'strain' *s* Überanstrengung *f* der Augen

eye'tooth' *s* (**–teeth**) Augenzahn *m*; **cut one's eyeteeth** (fig) erfahrener werden

eye'wash' *s* Augenwasser *n*; (sl) Schwindel *m*

eye'wit'ness *s* Augenzeuge *m*, Augenzeugin *f*

F

F, f [ɛf] *s* sechster Buchstabe des englischen Alphabets; (mus) F *n*; **F flat** Fes *n*; **F sharp** Fis *n*

fable [ˈfebəl] *s* Fabel *f*, Märchen *n*

fabric [ˈfæbrɪk] *s* Gewebe *n*; (*cloth*) Stoff *m*; (fig) Gefüge *n*

fabricate [ˈfæbrɪˌket] *tr* herstellen; (*lies*) erfinden

fabrication [ˌfæbrɪˈkeʃən] *s* Herstellung *f*; (fig) Erfindung *f*

fabulous [ˈfæbjələs] *adj* fabelhaft

façade [fəˈsɑd] *s* Fassade *f*

face [fes] *s* Gesicht *n*; (dial) Zifferblatt *n*; (tex) rechte Seite *f*; (typ) Satzspiegel *m*; **f. to f. with** Auge in Auge mit; **in the f. of** angesichts (*genit*); **lose f.** sich blamieren; **make faces at s.o.** j—m Gesichter schneiden; **on the f. of it** augenscheinlich; **save f.** das Gesicht wahren; **show one's f.** sich blicken lassen ‖ *tr* (& fig) ins Auge sehen (*dat*); (*said of a building*) liegen nach; (*e.g., with brick*) verkleiden; **be faced with** stehen vor (*dat*); **facing** gegenüber (*dat*); **have to f. the music** die Suppe löffeln müssen ‖ *intr* (*in some direction*) liegen; **about f.!** (mil) kehrt!; **he faced up to it like a man** er stellte seinen Mann

face' card' *s* Bildkarte *f*, Figur *f*

face' cream' *s* Gesichtskrem *f*

face' lift'ing *s* Gesichtsstraffung *f*; (of a building) Schönheitsreparatur *f*

face' pow'der *s* Gesichtspuder *m*

facet [ˈfæsɪt] *s* Facette *f*; (fig) Aspekt *m*

facetious [fəˈsiʃəs] *adj* scherzhaft

face' val'ue *s* Nennwert *m*; **take at f.** (fig) für bare Münze nehmen

facial [ˈfeʃəl] *adj* Gesichts—; **f. expression** Miene *f*; **f.** Gesichtspflege *f*

facilitate [fəˈsɪlɪˌtet] *tr* erleichtern

facility [fəˈsɪlɪti] *s* (*ease*) Leichtigkeit

f; (*skill*) Geschicklichkeit *f*; **facilities** Einrichtungen *pl*

fac'ing *s* (archit) Verkleidung *f*; (sew) Besatz *m*

facsimile [fækˈsɪmɪli] *s* Faksimile *n*

fact [fækt] *s* Tatsache *f*; **apart from the f. that** abgesehen davon, daß; **facts of the case** Tatbestand *m*; **in f.** tatsächlich; **it is a f. that** es steht fest, daß

fact'-find'ing *adj* Untersuchungs—

faction [ˈfækʃən] *s* Clique *f*

factional [ˈfækʃənəl] *adj* klüngelhaft

factor [ˈfæktər] *s* (& math) Faktor *m*

factory [ˈfæktəri] *s* Fabrik *f*

factual [ˈfæktʃʊəl] *adj* sachlich

faculty [ˈfækəlti] *s* Vermögen *n*; (educ) Lehrkörper *m*

fad [fæd] *s* Mode *f*; **latest fad** letzter Schrei *m*

fade [fed] *tr* verblassen lassen; **f. in** einblenden; **f. out** ausblenden ‖ *intr* (*said of colors, memories*) verblassen; (*said of cloth, wallpaper, etc.*) verschießen; (*said of flowers*) verwelken; **f. away** (*said of sounds*) abklingen; **f. in** (cin, rad, telv) einblenden; **f. out** (cin, rad, telv) ausblenden

fade'-in' *s* (cin, rad, telv) Einblenden *n*

fade'-out' *s* (cin, rad, telv) Ausblenden *n*

fag [fæg] *s* (*cigarette*) (sl) Glimmstengel *m*; (*homosexual*) (sl) Schwuler *m* ‖ *v* (*pret & pp* **fagged;** *ger* **fagging**) *tr*—**fag out** (sl) auspumpen

fagged *adj* (sl) erschöpft

fagot [ˈfægət] *s* Reisigbündel *n*

fail [fel] *s*—**without f.** ganz bestimmt ‖ *tr* (*an examination*) durchfallen bei; (*a student*) durchfallen lassen; (*friends*) im Stich lassen; (*a father*) enttäuschen; **failing this** widrigenfalls; **I f. to see** ich kann nicht einsehen; **words f. me** mir fehlen die

Worte || *intr* (*said of a person or device*) versagen; (*said of a project, attempt*) fehlschlagen; (*said of crops*) schlecht ausfallen; (*said of strength*) abnehmen; (*said of health*) sich verschlechtern; (com) in Konkurs geraten

failure ['feljər] *s* Versagen *n*; (*person*) Versager –in *mf*; (*lack of success, unsuccessful venture*) Mißerfolg *m*; (*omission*) Versäumnis *n*; (*deterioration*) Schwäche *f*; (educ) ungenügende Zensur *f*; (com) Konkurs *m*

faint [fent] *adj* schwach; (*slight*) leise; **feel f.** sich schwach fühlen || *s* Ohnmacht *f* || *intr* ohnmächtig werden

faint'-heart'ed *adj* kleinmütig

faint'ing spell' *s* Ohnmachtsanfall *m*

fair [fer] *adj* (*just*) gerecht, fair; (*blond*) blond; (*complexion*) hell; (*weather*) heiter; (*chance, knowledge*) mittelmäßig; (*warning*) rechtzeitig; **f. to middling** gut bis mäßig || *s* Jahrmarkt *m*, Messe *f*

fair' game' *s* (& fig) Freiwild *n*

fair'ground' *s* Jahrmarktplatz *m*

fairly ['ferli] *adv* ziemlich

fair'-mind'ed *adj* unparteiisch

fairness ['fernis] *s* Gerechtigkeit *f*; **in f. to s.o.** um j–m Gerechtigkeit widerfahren zu lassen

fair' play' *s* fair Play *n*

fair' sex', **the** *s* das schöne Geschlecht

fair'way' *s* (golf) Spielbahn *f*; (naut) Fahrwasser *n*

fair'-weath'er *adj* (*friend*) unzuverlässig

fairy ['feri] *adj* Feen– || *s* Fee *f*; (sl) Schwule *mf*

fair'y god'mother *s* gute Fee *f*

fair'yland' *s* Märchenland *n*

fair'ytale' *s* (*f*) Märchen *n*

faith [feθ] *s* Glaube(n) *m*; (in) Vertrauen *n* (auf *acc* or zu); **on the f.** of im Vertrauen auf (*acc*); **put one's f.** in Glauben schenken (*dat*)

faithful ['feθfəl] *adj* (to) (ge)treu (*dat*); (*exact*) genau, wahrheitsgemäß || **the f.** *spl* die Gläubigen

faith' heal'er *s* Gesundbeter –in *mf*

faithless ['feθlɪs] *adj* treulos

fake [fek] *adj* verfälscht || *s* Fälschung *f*; (*person*) Simulant –in *mf* || *tr* vortäuschen, simulieren; (*forge*) fälschen

faker ['fekər] *s* Simulant –in *mf*

falcon ['fɔ(l)kən] *s* Falke *m*

falconer ['fɔ(l)kənər] *s* Falkner *m*

fall [fɔl] *adj* Herbst– || *s* Fall *m*; (*of prices, of a government*) Sturz *m*; (*moral*) Verfall *m*; (*of water*) Fall *m*; (*autumn*) Herbst *m*; (Bib) Sündenfall *m*; || *v* (*pret* **fell** [fel]; *pp* **fallen** ['fɔlən] *intr* (*said of a person, object, rain, snow, holiday, prices, temperature*) fallen; (*said of a town*) gestürzt werden; **f. apart** auseinanderfallen; **f. away** wegfallen; **f. back** zurückfallen; (mil) sich zurückziehen; **f. back on** zurückgreifen auf (*acc*); **f. behind** (in) zurückbleiben (mit); **f. below** unterschreiten; **f. down** umfallen; (*said only of per-*

sons) hinfallen; **f. down on the job** versagen; **f. due** fällig werden; **f. flat** (coll) flachfallen; **f. for** reinfallen auf (*acc*); **f. from** abfallen von; **f.. from grace** in Ungnade fallen; **f. in** (*said of a roof*) einstürzen; (mil) antreten; **f. in love with** sich verlieben in (*acc*); **f. in step** Tritt fassen; **f. into** (*e.g., a hole*) hereinfallen in (*acc*); (*e.g., trouble*) geraten in (*acc*); **f. into ruin** zerfallen; **f. in with s.o.** j–n zufällig treffen; **f. off** abfallen; (com) zurückgehen; **f. out** (*said of hair*) ausfallen; **f. out with** sich verfeinden mit; **f. over** umfallen; **f. short** knapp werden; (arti) kurz gehen; **f. short of** zurückbleiben hinter (*dat*); **f. through** durchfallen; **f. to s.o.'s share** j–m zufallen; **f. under s.o.'s influence** unter j–s Einfluß geraten; **f. upon** herfallen über (*acc*)

fallacious [fə'lefəs] *adj* trügerisch

fallacy ['fæləsi] *s* Trugschluß *m*, Fehlschluß *m*

fall' guy' *s* (sl) Sündenbock *m*

fallible ['fælɪbəl] *adj* fehlbar

fall'ing off' *s* Rückschritt *m*

fall'ing rocks' *spl* (public sign) Steinschlag *m*

fall'ing star' *s* Sternschnuppe *f*

fall'out' *s* radioaktiver Niederschlag *m*

fallow ['fælo] *adj* (agr) brach; **lie f.** (& fig) brachliegen

false [fɔls] *adj* falsch, Miß–; (*start, step*) Fehl–; (*bottom*) doppelt; (*ceiling*) Zwischen–

false' alarm' *s* blinder Alarm *m*; (fig) Schreckschuß *m*

false' face' *s* Maske *f*

false' front' *s* (fig) (coll) Mache *f*

false'-heart'ed *adj* treulos

false'hood' *s* Unwahrheit *f*

false' pretens'es *spl* Hochstapelei *f*

false' teeth' *spl* (künstliches) Gebiß *n*

falset-to [fɔl'seto] *s* (–tos) Falsett *n*

falsi-fy ['fɔlsɪ‚faɪ] *v* (*pret* & *pp* –fied) *tr* (ver)fälschen

falsity ['fɔlsɪti] *s* Falschheit *f*

falter ['fɔltər] *intr* schwanken; (*in speech*) stocken

fame [fem] *s* Ruf, *m*, Ruhm *m*

famed *adj* (*for*) berühmt (wegen, durch)

familiar [fə'mɪljər] *adj* bekannt; (*expression*) geläufig; (*e.g., sight*) gewohnt; (*close*) vertraut; **become f. with** sich bekannt machen mit

familiarity [fə‚mɪlɪ'ærɪti] *s* Vertrautheit *f*; (*closeness*) Vertraulichkeit *f*

familiarize [fə'mɪljə‚raɪz] *tr* bekannt machen

family ['fæm(ɪ)li] *adj* Familien–; **in a f. way** in anderen Umständen || *s* Familie *f*

fam'ily doc'tor *s* Hausarzt *m*

fam'ily man' *s* häuslicher Mann *m*

fam'ily name' *s* Familienname *m*

fam'ily tree' *s* Stammbaum *m*

famine ['fæmɪn] *s* Hungersnot *f*

famish ['fæmɪʃ] *tr* (ver)hungern lassen || *intr* verhungern

fam'ished *adj* ausgehungert

famous [´feməs] *adj* (**for**) berühmt (wegen, durch)

fan [fæn] *s* Fächer *m*, Wedel *m*; (*electric*) Ventilator *m*; (sl) Fan *m* ‖ *v* (*pret & pp* **fanned; *ger* fanning**) *tr* fächeln; (*a fire*) anfachen; (*passions*) entfachen ‖ *intr*—**fan out** (*said of roads*) fächerförmig auseinandergehen; (mil) ausschwärmen

fanatic [fə´nætɪk] *adj* fanatisch ‖ *s* Fanatiker –in *mf*

fanatical [fə´nætɪkəl] *adj* fanatisch

fanaticism [fə´nætɪ͵sɪzəm] *s* Fanatismus *m*

fan′ belt′ *s* (aut) Keilriemen *m*

fan′cied *adj* eingebildet

fancier [´fænsɪ·ər] *s* Liebhaber –in *mf*

fanciful [´fænsɪfəl] *adj* phantastisch

fan-cy [´fænsɪ] *adj* (extra)fein; (*e.g., dress*) Luxus–; (sport) Kunst–; (*e.g. price*) Phantasiepreis *m* ‖ *s* Phantasie *f*; passing **f.** vorübergehender Spleen *m*; **take a f. to** Gefallen finden an (*dat*) ‖ *v* (*pret & pp* –**cied**) *tr* sich [*dat*] vorstellen

fan′cy foods′ *spl* Feinkost *f*

fan′cy-free′ *adj* ungebunden

fan′fare′ *s* Fanfare *f*; (*fuss*) Tamtam *n*

fang [fæŋ] *s* Fangzahn *m*; (*of a snake*) Giftzahn *m*

fan′ mail′ *s* Verehrerbriefe *pl*

fantastic(al) [fæn´tæstɪk(əl)] *adj* phantastisch, toll

fantasy [´fæntəsɪ] *s* Phantasie *f*

far [fɑr] *adj* (& fig) weit; **at the far end** am anderen Ende; **far cry from** etw ganz anderes als; **far side** andere Seite *f*; **in the far future** in der fernen Zukunft ‖ *adv* weit; **as far as** soweit; (*up to*) bis zu, bis an (*acc*); **as far as I am concerned** was mich anbelangt; **as far as I know** soviel ich weiß; **as far as that goes** was das betrifft; **by far** weitaus, bei weitem; **far and away** weitaus; **far away** weit entfernt; **far below** tief unten; **far better** weit besser; **far from it!** weit gefehlt!; **far from ready** noch lange nicht fertig; **far into the night** tief in die Nacht hinein; **far out** (sl) ausgefallen; **from far** von weitem; (*from a distant place*) von weit her; **go far** es weit bringen; **go far towards** (*ger*) viel beitragen zu (*inf*); **go too far** das Maß überschreiten; **not far from** unweit von; **so far** soweit, bisher

far′away′ *adj* weit entfernt; (fig) träumerisch

farce [fɑrs] *s* Possenspiel *n*, Farce *f*; (fig) Posse *f*, Schwank *m*

farcical [´fɑrsɪkəl] *adj* possenhaft

fare [fɛr] *s* (*travel price*) Fahrpreis *m*; (*money for travel*) Fahrgeld *n*; (*passenger*) Fahrgast *m*; (*food*) Kost *f* ‖ *intr* (er)gehen; **how did you f., well or ill?** wie ist es Ihnen ergangen, gut oder schlecht?

Far′ East′, the *s* der Ferne Osten

Far′ East′ern *adj* fernöstlich

fare′well′ *s* Valet *n*, Lebewohl *n*; **bid s.o. f.** j–m Lebewohl sagen ‖ *interj* lebe wohl!; lebt wohl!

farewell′ din′ner *s* Abschiedsschmaus *m*

farewell′ par′ty *s* Abschiedsfeier *f*

far-fetched [´fɑr´fɛt/t] *adj* gesucht

far-flung [´fɑr´flʌŋ] *adj* weit ausgedehnt

farina [fə´rinə] *s* Grießmehl *n*

farm [fɑrm] *adj* landwirtschaftlich ‖ *s* Farm *f*, Bauernhof *m* ‖ *tr* bebauen, bewirtschaften ‖ *intr* Landwirtschaft betreiben, Bauer sein

farm′ hand′ *s* Landarbeiter *m*

farm′house′ *s* Bauernhaus *n*

farm′ing *adj* landwirtschaftlich ‖ *s* Landwirtschaft *f*

farm′land′ *s* Ackerland *n*

farm′ machin′ery *s* Landmaschinen *pl*

farm′yard′ *s* Bauernhof *m*

far′-off′ *adj* fernliegend

far′-reach′ing *adj* weitreichend; (*decision*) folgenschwer

far′-sight′ed *adj* weitsichtig; (fig) weitblickend

farther [´fɑrðər] *adj & adv* weiter

farthest [´fɑrðɪst] *adj* weiteste ‖ *adv* am weitesten

farthing [´fɑrðɪŋ] *s*—**not worth a f.** keinen Pfifferling wert

fascinate [´fæsɪ͵net] *tr* faszinieren

fas′cinating *adj* faszinierend

fascination [͵fæsɪ´ne/ən] *s* Faszination *f*

fascism [´fæ/ɪzəm] *s* Faschismus *m*

fascist [´fæ/ɪst] *s* Faschist –in *mf*

fashion [´fæ/ən] *s* Mode *f*; (*manner*) Art *f*, Weise *f*; **after a f.** in gewisser Weise; **in f.** in Mode; **out of f.** aus der Mode ‖ *tr* gestalten, bilden

fashionable [´fæ/ənəbəl] *adj* (*modern*) modisch; (*elegant*) elegant

fash′ion magazine′ *s* Modezeitschrift *f*

fash′ion plate′ *s* Modedame *f*

fash′ion show′ *s* Mode(n)schau *f*

fast [fæst] *adj* schnell; (*dye*) dauerhaft; (*company*) flott; (*life*) locker; (phot) lichtstark; **be f.** (*said of a clock*) vorgehen; **f. train** Schnellzug *m*; **pull a f. one on s.o.** (coll) j–m ein Schnippchen schlagen ‖ *adv* schnell; (*firmly*) fest; **as f. as possible** schnellstens; **be f. asleep** im tiefen Schlaf liegen; **hold f.** festhalten; **not so f.!** nicht so stürmisch! ‖ *s* Fasten *n* ‖ *intr* fasten

fast′ day′ *s* Fasttag *m*

fasten [´fæsən] *tr* festmachen, sichern; (*a buckle*) schnallen; (**to**) befestigen (an *dat*); **f. one′s seat belt** sich anschnallen; **f. the blame on die Schuld** zuschieben (*dat*) ‖ *intr*—**f. upon** sich heften an (*acc*)

fastener [´fæsənər] *s* Verschluß *m*

fastidious [fæs´tɪdɪ·əs] *adj* wählerisch

fast′ing *s* Fasten *n*

fat [fæt] *adj* (**fatter; fattest**) fett; (*plump*) dick, fett; (*profits*) reich ‖ *s* Fett *n*; **chew the fat** (sl) schwatzen

fatal [´fetəl] *adj* tödlich; (*mistake*) verhängnisvoll; **f. to** verhängnisvoll für

fatalism [´fetə͵lɪzəm] *s* Fatalismus *m*

fatalist [´fetəlɪst] *s* Fatalist –in *mf*

fatality [fə'tælɪti] s Todesfall m; (accident victim) Todesopfer n; (disaster) Unglück n

fat' cat' s (sl) Geldgeber –in mf

fate [fet] s Schicksal n, Verhängnis n; the Fates die Parzen pl

fated ['fetɪd] adj vom Schicksal bestimmt

fateful ['fetfəl] adj verhängnisvoll

fat'head' s (coll) dummes Luder n

father ['faðər] s Vater m; (eccl) Pater m || tr (beget) erzeugen; (originate) hervorbringen

fa'therhood' s Vaterschaft f

fa'ther-in-law' s (fathers-in-law) Schwiegervater m

fa'therland' s Vaterland n

fatherless ['faðərlɪs] adj vaterlos

fatherly ['faðərli] adj väterlich

Fa'ther's Day' s Vatertag m

fathom ['fæðəm] s Klafter f || tr sondieren; (fig) ergründen

fathomless ['fæðəmlɪs] adj unergründlich

fatigue [fə'tig] s Ermattung f; (mil) Arbeitsdienst m; fatigues (mil) Arbeitsanzug m || tr abmatten

fat·so ['fætso] s (-sos & -soes) (coll) Fettkloß m

fatten ['fætən] tr mästen || intr—f. up (coll) sich mästen

fatty ['fæti] adj fettig, fett; f. tissue Fettgewebe n || s (coll) Dicke mf

fatuous ['fætʃʊ·əs] adj albern

faucet ['fɔsɪt] s Wasserhahn m

fault [fɔlt] s (blame) Schuld f; (misdeed) Vergehen n, Fehler m; (deject) Defekt m; (geol) Verwerfung f; (tennis) Fehlball m; at f. schuld; find f. with etw zu tadeln finden an (dat); to a f. allzusehr || intr (geol) sich verwerfen

fault'find'er s Krittler –in mf

fault'find'ing adj tadelsüchtig || s Krittelei f

faultless ['fɔltlɪs] adj fehlerfrei

faulty ['fɔlti] adj fehlerhaft

faun [fɔn] s (myth) Faun m

fauna ['fɔnə] s Fauna f

favor ['fevər] s (kind act) Gefallen m; (good will) Gunst f; in f. of zugunsten (genit), für; in s.o.'s f. zu j–s Gunsten; lose f. with s.o. sich [dat] j–s Gunst verwirken; speak in f. of s.th. für etw aussprechen || tr begünstigen; (prefer) bevorzugen; (a sore limb) schonen

favorable ['fevərəbəl] adj günstig; (criticism) positiv; (report) beifällig

favorite ['fevərɪt] adj Lieblings– || s Liebling m; (sport) Favorit –in mf

favoritism ['fevərɪ‚tɪzəm] s Günstlingswirtschaft f

fawn [fɔn] s Rehkalb n || intr—f. on schmeicheln (dat)

fawn'ing adj schmeichlerisch

faze [fez] tr (coll) auf die Palme bringen

FBI [‚ɛf‚bi'aɪ] s (Federal Bureau of Investigation) Bundessicherheitspolizei f

fear [fɪr] s (of) Furcht f (vor dat), Angst f (vor dat); for f. of aus Angst

vor (dat); for f. of (ger) um nicht zu (inf); stand in f. of sich fürchten vor (dat) || tr fürchten, sich fürchten vor (dat); f. the worst das Schlimmste befürchten || intr sich fürchten; f. for besorgt sein um

fearful ['fɪrfəl] adj (afraid) furchtsam; (terrible) furchtbar

fearless ['fɪrlɪs] adj furchtlos

feasible ['fizɪbəl] adj durchführbar

feast [fist] s Fest n; (sumptuous meal) Schmaus m || tr—f. one's eyes on seine Augen weiden an (dat) || intr schwelgen; f. on sich gütlich tun an (dat)

feast'day' s Festtag m

feast'ing s Schmauserei f

feat [fit] s Kunststück n; f. of arms Waffentat f

feather ['fɛðər] s Feder f; a f. in his cap ein Triumph für ihn || tr mit Federn versehen; (aer) auf Segelstellung fahren; (crew) flach drehen; f. one's nest sich warm betten

feath'er bed' s Federbett n

feath'erbed'ding s Anstellung f unnötiger Arbeitskräfte

feath'erbrain' s Schwachkopf m

feath'er dust'er s Staubwedel m

feath'eredge' s feine Kante f

feath'erweight' adj Federgewichts– || s (boxer) Federgewichtler m

feathery ['fɛðəri] adj federartig; (light as feathers) federleicht

feature ['fitʃər] s (of the face) Gesichtszug m; (characteristic) Merkmal n; f. film Spielfilm m; main f. Grundzug m; (cin) Hauptfilm m || tr als Hauptschlager herausbringen; (cin) in der Hauptrolle zeigen

fea'ture writ'er s Sonderberichterstatter –in mf

February ['febru‚ɛri] s Februar m

feces ['fisiz] spl Kot m, Stuhl m

feckless ['fɛklɪs] adj (incompetent) unfähig; (ineffective) unwirksam; (without spirit) geistlos

fecund ['fikənd] adj fruchtbar

federal ['fedərəl] adj Bundes-, bundesstaatlich; f. government Bundesregierung f

federate ['fedə‚ret] adj verbündet || tr zu e–m Bund vereinigen || intr sich verbünden

federation [‚fedə'reʃən] s Staatenbund m

fed' up' [fed] adj—be f. die Nase voll haben; be f. with s.th. etw satt haben

fee [fi] s Gebühr f; (of a doctor) Honorar n

feeble ['fibəl] adj schwächlich

fee'ble-mind'ed adj schwachsinnig

feed [fid] s Futter n; (mach) Zuführung f || v (pret & pp fed [fed]) tr (animals) füttern; (persons) zu Essen geben; (in a restaurant) verpflegen; (e.g., a nation) nähren; (a fire) unterhalten; (mach) zuführen || intr fressen; f. on sich ernähren von

feed'back' s Rückwirkung f; (electron) Rückkoppelung f

feed' bag' s Futtersack m; put on the f. (sl) futtern

feeder ['fidər] s (elec) Speiseleitung f; (mach) Zubringer m

feed'er line' s (aer, rr) Zubringerlinie f

feed'ing s (of animals) Fütterung f; (& mach) Speisung f

feed' trough' s Futtertrog m

feed' wire' s (elec) Zuleitungsdraht m

feel [fil] s Gefühl n; get the f. of sich gewöhnen an (acc) || v (pret & pp felt [felt]) tr fühlen; (a pain) spüren; f. one's way sich vortasten; (fig) sondieren; f. s.o. out bei j-m vorfühlen || intr (sick, tired, well) sich fühlen; f. about for herumtasten nach; f. for s.o. mit j-m fühlen; f. like (ger) Lust haben zu (inf); f. up to sich gewachsen fühlen (dat); his head feels hot sein Kopf fühlt sich heiß an; how do you f. about it? was halten Sie davon?; I don't quite f. myself ich fühle mich nicht ganz wohl; I f. as if es ist mir, als wenn; make itself felt sich fühlbar machen

feeler ['filər] s (ent) Fühler m; put out feelers to vorfühlen bei

feel'ing s Gefühl n; bad f. Verstimmung f; good f. Wohlwollen n; have a f. for Sinn haben für; have a f. that das Gefühl haben, daß; with f. gefühlsvoll

feign [fen] tr vortäuschen; f. death sich totstellen

feint [fent] s Finte f, Scheinangriff m

feldspar ['feld,spar] s Feldspat m

feline ['filain] adj katzenartig

fell [fel] adj grausam || tr fällen

fellow ['felo] s (coll) Kerl m; (of a society) Mitglied n

fel'low be'ing s Mitmensch m

fel'low cit'izen s Mitbürger –in mf

fel'low coun'tryman s Landsmann m

fel'low crea'ture s Mitgeschöpf n

fel'lowman' s (-men') Mitmensch m

fel'low mem'ber s Mitglied m

fel'lowship' s Kameradschaft f; (educ) Stipendium n

fel'low stu'dent s Kommilitone m

fel'low trav'eler s Mitreisende mf; (pol) Mitläufer –in mf

felon ['felən] s Schwerverbrecher –in mf

felony ['feləni] s Schwerverbrechen n

felt [felt] adj Filz– || s Filz m

felt' pen' s Filzschreiber m, Faserstift m

female ['fimel] adj weiblich || s (of animals) Weibchen n; (pej) Weibsbild n

feminine ['feminin] adj weiblich

feminism ['femi,nizəm] s Feminismus m

fen [fen] s Bruch m & n

fence [fens] s Zaun m; (of stolen goods) Hehler m; on the f. (fig) unentschlossen || tr—f. in einzäunen; f. off abzäunen || intr (sport) fechten

fence' post' s Zaunpfahl m

fenc'ing s Fechten n

fend [fend] tr—f. off abwehren || intr —f. for oneself für sich selbst sorgen

fender ['fendər] s (aut) Kotflügel m

fennel ['fenəl] s Fenchel m

ferment ['fʌrment] s Gärmittel n; (fig) Unruhe f || [fər'ment] tr in Gärung bringen || intr gären

fermentation [,fʌrmən'teʃən] s Gärung f

fern [fʌrn] s Farn m

ferocious [fə'roʃəs] adj wild

ferocity [fə'rɑsiti] s Wildheit f

ferret ['ferit] s Frettchen n || tr—f. out aufspüren

Fer'ris wheel' ['feris] s Riesenrad n

ferrule ['ferul], ['ferəl] s Stockzwinge f, Zwinge f

fer·ry ['feri] s Fähre f || v (pret & pp -ried) tr übersetzen

fer'ryboat' s Fährboot n

fer'ry·man s (-men') Fährmann m

fertile ['fʌrtil] adj fruchtbar

fertility [fər'tiliti] s Fruchtbarkeit f

fertilization [,fʌrtiliˈzeʃən] s Befruchtung f; (of soil) Düng f

fertilize ['fʌrti,laiz] tr (a field) düngen; (an egg) befruchten

fertilizer ['fʌrti,laizər] s Kunstdünger m

fervent ['fʌrvənt] adj inbrünstig

fervid ['fʌrvid] adj brennend

fervor ['fʌrvər] s Inbrunst f

fester ['festər] intr schwären, eitern; (fig) nagen

festival ['festivəl] adj festlich, Fest– || s Fest n; (mus, theat) Festspiele pl

festive ['festiv] adj festlich

festivity [fes'tiviti] s Feierlichkeit f

festoon [fes'tun] s Girlande f || tr mit Girlanden schmücken

fetch [fetʃ] tr holen, abholen

fetch'ing adj entzückend

fete [fet] s Fest n

fetid ['fetid], [fitd] adj stinkend

fetish ['fetiʃ], ['fitiʃ] s Fetisch m

fetlock ['fetlak] s Köte f; (tuft of hair) Kötenzopf m

fetter ['fetər] s Fessel f || tr fesseln

fettle ['fetəl] s—in fine f. in Form

fetus ['fitəs] s Leibesfrucht f

feud [fjud] s Fehde f

feudal ['fjudəl] adj feudal

feudalism ['fjudə,lizəm] s Feudalismus m

fever ['fivər] s Fieber n

feverish ['fivəriʃ] adj fieberig; be f. fiebern

few [fju] adj & pron wenige; a few ein paar

fiancé [,fi·ɑn'se] s Verlobte m

fiancée [,fi·ɑn'se] s Verlobte f

fias·co [fɪ'æsko] s (-cos & -coes) Fiasko n

fib [fɪb] s Flunkerei f || v (pret & pp fibbed or fibbing) intr flunkern

fibber ['fɪbər] s Flunkerer –in m

fiber ['faibər] s Faser f

fibrous ['faibrəs] adj faserig

fickle ['fɪkəl] adj wankelmütig

fickleness ['fɪkəlnis] s Wankelmut m

fiction ['fɪkʃən] s Dichtung f, Romanliteratur f

fictional ['fɪkʃənəl] adj romanhaft

fic'tion writ'er s Romanschriftsteller –in mf

fictitious [fɪk'tɪʃəs] adj fingiert

fiddle ['fɪdəl] s Fiedel f, Geige f || tr fiedeln; f. away (time) vergeuden ||

intr fiedeln; **f. with** herumfingern an (*dat*)

fiddler ['fɪdlər] *s* Fiedler –in *mf*

fid'dlestick' *s* Fiedelbogen *m* || **fiddlesticks** *interj* Quatsch!

fidelity [fɪ'delɪtɪ] *s* Treue *f*

fidget ['fɪdʒɪt] *intr* zappeln; **f. with** nervös spielen mit

fidgety ['fɪdʒɪtɪ] *adj* zappelig

fiduciary [fɪ'd(j)uʃɪ‚erɪ] *adj* treuhänderisch; (*note*) ungedeckt || *s* Treuhänder –in *mf*

fief [fif] *s* (hist) Lehen *n*

field [fild] *adj* (*artillery, jacket, hospital, kitchen*) Feld– || *s* Feld *n*; (*under cultivation*) Acker *m*; (*contestants collectively*) Wettbewerbsteilnehmer *pl*; (*specialty*) Gebiet *n*; (aer) Flugplatz *m*; (elec) Feld *n*; (*of a motor*) (elec) Magnetfeld *n*; (sport) Spielfeld *n*

field' am'bulance *s* Sanitätskraftwagen *m*

field' day' *s* (fig) großer Tag *m*

fielder ['fildər] *s* Feldspieler *m*

field' ex'ercise *s* Truppenübung *f*

field' glass'es *spl* Feldstecher *m*

field' hock'ey *s* Rasenhockey *n*

field'mar'shal *s* Feldmarschall *m*

field' mouse' *s* Feldmaus *f*

field' of vi'sion *s* Blickfeld *n*

field' pack' *s* (mil) Tornister *m*

field' piece' *s* Feldgeschütz *n*

field' trip' *s* Studienfahrt *f*

field' work' *s* praktische Arbeit *f*

fiend [find] *s* (*devil*) Teufel *m*; (*wicked person*) Unhold *m*; (*addict*) Süchtige *mf*

fiendish ['findɪʃ] *adj* teuflisch

fierce [fɪrs] *adj* wild, wütend; (*vehement*) heftig; (*menacing*) drohend; (*heat*) glühend

fiery ['faɪrɪ], ['faɪ‚ərɪ] *adj* feurig

fife [faɪf] *s* Querpfeife *f*

fifteen ['fɪf'tin] *adj & pron* fünfzehn || *s* Fünfzehn *f*

fifteenth ['fɪf'tinθ] *adj & pron* fünfzehnte || *s* (*fraction*) Fünfzehntel *n*; **the f.** (*in dates or a series*) der Fünfzehnte

fifth [fɪfθ] *adj & pron* fünfte || *s* (*fraction*) Fünftel *n*; **the f.** (*in dates or a series*) der Fünfte

fifth' col'umn *s* (pol) Fünfte Kolonne *f*

fiftieth ['fɪftɪ‚rθ] *adj & pron* fünfzigste || *s* (*fraction*) Fünfzigstel *n*

fifty ['fɪftɪ] *adj & pron* fünfzig || *s* Fünfzig *f*; **the fifties** die fünfziger Jahre

fif'ty-fif'ty *adv* halbpart; **go f. with s.o.** mit j–m halbpart machen

fig [fɪg] *s* Feige *f*; (fig) Pfifferling *m*

fight [faɪt] *s* Kampf *m*, Gefecht *n*; (*quarrel*) Streit *m*; (*brawl*) Rauferei *f*; (box) Boxkampf *m*; **pick a f.** Zank suchen || *tr* bekämpfen; (*a case*) durchkämpfen; **f. back** (*tears*) niederkämpfen; **f. it out** ausfechten; **f. one's way out** sich durchkämpfen || *intr* kämpfen; (*quarrel*) streiten; (*brawl*) raufen

fighter ['faɪtər] *adj* (aer) Jagd– || *s*

fight'er pi'lot *s* Jagdflieger *m*

fight'ing *s* Schlägerei *f*; (*quarreling*) Streiten *m*; (mil) Kampfhandlungen *pl*

fig' leaf' *s* Feigenblatt *n*

figment ['fɪgmənt] *s*—**f. of the imagination** Hirngespinst *n*

fig' tree' *s* Feigenbaum *m*

figurative ['fɪgjərətɪv] *adj* bildlich; (*meaning*) übertragen

figure ['fɪgjər] *s* Figur *f*; (*personage*) Persönlichkeit *f*; (*number*) Zahl *f*; **be good at figures** ein guter Rechner sein; **cut a fine** (or **poor**) **f.** e–e gute (or **schlechte**) Figur abgeben; **run into three figures** in die Hunderte gehen || *tr* (coll) glauben, meinen; **f. out** ausknobeln || *intr*—**f. large** e–e große Rolle spielen; **f. on** rechnen mit

fig'urehead' *s* Strohmann *m*; (naut) Bugfigur *f*; **a mere f.** e–e bloße Nummer

fig'ure of speech' *s* Redewendung *f*

fig'ure skat'ing *s* Kunstlauf *m*

figurine ['fɪgjə'rin] *s* Figurine *f*

filament ['fɪləmənt] *s* Faser *f*, Faden *m*; (elec) Glühfaden *m*

filbert ['fɪlbərt] *s* Haselnuß *f*

filch [fɪltʃ] *tr* mausen

file [faɪl] *s* (*tool*) Feile *f*; (*record*) Akte *f*; (*cards*) Kartei *f*; (*row*) Reihe *f*; **put on f.** zu den Akten legen || *tr* (*with a tool*) feilen; (*letters, etc.*) ablegen, abheften; (*a complaint*) erheben; (*a report*) erstatten; (*a claim*) anmelden; (*a petition*) einreichen; **f. suit** e–n Prozeß anstrengen || *intr* —**f. for** sich bewerben um; **f. out** im Gänsemarsch herausmarschieren; **f. past** vorbeidefilieren (an *dat*)

file' cab'inet *s* Aktenschrank *m*

file' card' *s* Karteikarte *f*

filial ['fɪlɪ‚əl] *adj* kindlich

filibuster ['fɪlɪ‚bʌstər] *s* Obstruktion *f* || *intr* Obstruktion treiben

filigree ['fɪlɪ‚gri] *s* Filigran *n*

fil'ing *s* Feilen *n*; (*of records*) Ablegen *n* von Akten; (*of a claim*) Anmeldung *f*; (*of a complaint*) Erhebung *f*; (*of a petition*) Einreichung *f*; **filings** Feilspäne *pl*

Filipi·no ['fɪlɪ'pino] *adj* filipinisch || *s* (**-nos**) Filipino *m*

fill [fɪl] *s* (*fullness*) Fülle *f*; (*land fill*) Aufschüttung *f*; **eat one's f.** sich satt essen; **I have had my f. of it** ich habe es satt || *tr* füllen; (*an order*) ausführen; (*a pipe*) stopfen; (*a position*) besetzen; (dent) plombieren, füllen; **f. full** vollfüllen; **f. in** (*empty space*) ausfüllen; (*one's name*) einsetzen; (*a hole, grave*) zuwerfen; **f. it up** (aut) volltanken; **f. up** auffüllen; (*a tank*) nachfüllen; (*a bag*) anfüllen; (*a glass*) vollschenken; **f. with smoke** verräuchern || *intr* sich füllen; (*said of sails*) sich blähen; **f. in for** einspringen für; **f. out** rund werden; **f. up** sich füllen

filler ['fɪlər] *s* Füller *m*; (*of a cigar*)

Einlage *f*; (journ) Lückenbüßer *m*;
(paint) Grundierfirnis *m*
fillet ['fɪlɪt] *s* (*headband*) Kopfbinde
f; (archit) Leiste *f* || [fɪ'le] *s* (culin)
Filet *n* || *tr* filetieren
fillet' of beef' *s* Rinderfilet *n*
fillet' of sole' *s* Seezungenfilet *n*
fill'ing *s* (culin, dent) Füllung *f*
fill'ing sta'tion *s* Tankstelle *f*
fillip ['fɪlɪp] *s* Schnippchen *n*; (*on the
nose*) Nasenstüber *m*
filly ['fɪli] *s* Stutenfüllen *n*
film [fɪlm] *s* (*thin layer*) Schicht *f*;
(cin, phot) Film *m*; **f. of grease**
Fettschicht *f*
film' fes'tival *s* Filmfestspiele *pl*
film' li'brary *s* Filmarchiv *n*
film' speed' *s* Filmempfindlichkeit *f*
film' star' *s* Filmstar *m*
film'strip' *s* Bildstreifen *m*
filmy ['fɪlmi] *adj* trüb
filter ['fɪltər] *s* Filter *m*; (rad) Sieb *n*
|| *tr* filtern; (rad) sieben
fil'tering *s* Filtrierung *f*
fil'ter pa'per *s* Filterpapier *n*
fil'ter tip' *s* Filtermundstück *n*; (coll)
Filterzigarette *f*
filth [fɪlθ] *s* Schmutz *m*; (fig) Unflä-
tigkeit *f*, Zote *f*
filthy ['fɪlθi] *adj* schmutzig (*talk*) un-
flätig; (*lucre*) schnöd(e) || *adv*—**f.
rich** (sl) klotzig reich
filtrate ['fɪltret] *s* Filtrat *n* || *tr & intr*
filtrieren
filtration [fɪl'treʃən] *s* Filtrierung *f*
fin [fɪn] *s* Flosse *f*; (*of a shark or
whale*) Finne *f*; (*of a bomb*) Steuer-
schwanz *m*; (aer) Flosse *f*
final ['faɪnəl] *adj* End–, Schluß–; (*de-
finitive*) endgültig || *s* (educ) Ab-
schlußprüfung *f*; **finals** (sport) End-
runde *f*, Endspiel *n*
finale [fɪ'nɑli] *s* Finale *n*
finalist ['faɪnəlɪst] *s* Finalist –in *mf*
finality [faɪ'nælɪti] *s* Endgültigkeit *f*
finally ['faɪnəli] *adv* schließlich
finance ['faɪnæns], [fɪ'næns] *s* Finanz
f; **finances** Finanzwesen *n* || *tr* finan-
zieren
financial [fɪ'nænʃəl], [faɪ'nænʃəl] *adj*
(*e.g., policy, situation, crisis, aid*)
Finanz–; (*e.g., affairs, resources, embarrassment*) Geld–
financier [,fɪnən'sɪr], [,faɪnən'sɪr] *s*
Finanzmann *m*
financ'ing, fi'nancing *s* Finanzierung *f*
finch [fɪntʃ] *s* Fink *m*
find [faɪnd] *s* Fund *m*; (archeol) Bo-
denfund *m* || *v* (*pret & pp* found
[faʊnd]) *tr* finden; (math) bestimmen; **f. one's way** sich zurechtfinden;
f. one's way back zurückfinden; **f.
out** herausfinden; **f. s.o. guilty** j–n
für schuldig erklären || *intr*—**f. out
about s.th.** hinter etw (acc) kommen
finder ['faɪndər] *s* Finder –in *mf*
find'ing *s* Finden *n*; **findings** Tatbestand *m*
fine [faɪn] *adj* fein; (*excellent*) hervorragend; (*weather*) schön; **f.! gut!**
|| *s* Geldstrafe *f* || *tr* mit e–r Geld-
strafe belegen
fine' arts' *spl* schöne Künste *pl*

fineness ['faɪnnɪs] *s* Feinheit *f*; (*of a
coin or metal*) Feingehalt *m*
fine' point' *s* Feinheit *f*
fine' print' *s* Kleindruck *m*
finery ['faɪnəri] *s* Putz *m*, Staat *m*
fine-spun ['faɪn,spʌn] *adj* feingespon-
nen
finesse [fɪ'nes] *s* Finesse *f*; (cards)
Impaß *m* || *tr & intr* impassieren
fine-toothed ['faɪn,tuθt] *adj* feinge-
zahnt; **go over with a f. comb** unter
die Lupe nehmen
fine' touch' *s* Feinheit *f*
fine' tun'ing *s* Feineinstellung *f*
finger ['fɪŋɡər] *s* Finger *m*; **have a f.
in the pie** die Hand im Spiel haben;
keep your fingers crossed halten Sie
mir den Daumen; **not lift a f.** keinen
Finger rühren; **put the f. on s.o.** (sl)
j–n verpetzen; **snap one's fingers**
mit den Fingern schnellen; **twist
around one's little f.** um den kleinen
Finger wickeln || *tr* befingern
fin'ger bowl' *s* Fingerschale *f*
fin'gering *s* (mus) Fingersatz *m*
fin'gernail' *s* Fingernagel *m*
fin'gernail pol'ish *s* Nagellack *m*
fin'gerprint' *s* Fingerabdruck *m* || *tr*—
f. s.o. j–m die Fingerabdrücke abnehmen
fin'gertip' *s* Fingerspitze *f*; **have at
one's fingertips** parat haben
finicky ['fɪnɪki] *adj* wählerisch
finish ['fɪnɪʃ] *s* Ende *n*, Abschluß *m*;
(*polish*) Lack *m*, Politur *f*; **put a f.
on** fertig bearbeiten; **f.** beenden;
(*complete*) vollenden; (*put a finish
on*) fertig bearbeiten; (*smooth*) glätten; (*polish*) polieren; (*ruin*) kaputt
machen; **f. drinking** austrinken; **f.
eating** aufessen; **f. off** (*supplies*)
aufbrauchen; (*food*) aufessen; (*a
drink*) austrinken; (*kill*) (sl) erledi-
gen; **f. reading** (*a book*) auslesen ||
intr—**f. drinking** austrinken; **be all f.
fix und fertig sein
fin'ished *adj* beendet, fertig; **be all f.
fix und fertig sein
fin'ished pro'duct *s* Fertigprodukt *n*
fin'ishing coat' *s* Deckanstrich *m*
fin'ishing mill' *s* Nachwalzwerk *n*
fin'ishing school' *s* Mädchenpensionat
n
fin'ishing touch'es *spl*—**put the f. to**
die letzte Hand legen an (acc)
fin'ish line' *s* Ziel *n*, Ziellinie *f*
finite ['faɪnaɪt] *adj* endlich
fi'nite verb' *s* Verbum *n* finitum
fink [fɪŋk] *s* (*informer*) (sl) Verräter
–in *mf*; (*strikebreaker*) (sl) Streikbrecher –in *mf*
Finland ['fɪnlənd] *s* Finnland *n*
Finn [fɪn] *s* Finne *m*, Finnin *f*
Finnish ['fɪnɪʃ] *adj* finnisch || *s* (*lan-
guage*) Finnisch *n*
fir [fʌr] *s* Tanne *f*
fir' cone' *s* Tannenzapfen *m*
fire [faɪr] *s* Feuer *n*; (*conflagration*)
Brand *m*; (mil) Feuer *n*; **come under
f.** unter Beschuß geraten; **on f.** in
Brand; **open f.** Feuer eröffnen; **set
on f.** in Brand stecken || *tr* (*a gun,
pistol, shot*) abfeuern; (*bricks, ceramics*) brennen; (*an oven*) befeuern;
(*an employee*) entlassen; (*throw*

hard) feuern; **f. questions at s.o.**
j-n mit Fragen bombardieren; **f. up**
(& fig) anfeuern || *intr* feuern,
schießen; **f. away!** schieß los!; **f. on**
(mil) beschießen
fire′ alarm′ *s* Feuermeldung *f;* (box)
Feuermelder *m*
fire′arm′ *s* Schußwaffe *f*
fire′ball′ *s* Feuerball *m;* (hustler)
Draufgänger *m*
fire′bomb′ *s* Brandbombe *f* || *tr* mit
Brandbomben belegen
fire′brand′ *s* (fig) Aufwiegler –in *mf*
fire′break′ *s* Feuerschneise *f*
fire′ brigade′ *s* Feuerwehr *f*
fire′bug′ *m* (coll) Brandstifter –in *mf*
fire′ chief′ *s* Branddirektor *m*
fire′ com′pany *s* Feuerwehr *f*
fire′crack′er *s* Knallfrosch *m*
fire′damp′ *s* Schlagwetter *pl*
fire′ depart′ment *s* Feuerwehr *f*
fire′ drill′ *s* Feueralarmübung *f;* (by a
fire company) Feuerwehrübung *f*
fire′ en′gine *s* Spritze *f*
fire′ escape′ *s* Feuerleiter *f*
fire′ extin′guisher *s* Feuerlöscher *m*
fire′fly′ *s* Glühwurm *m*
fire′ hose′ *s* Spritzenschlauch *m*
fire′house′ *s* Feuerwache *f*
fire′ hy′drant *s* Hydrant *m*
fire′ insur′ance *s* Brandversicherung *f*
fire′ i′rons *spl* Kamingeräte *pl*
fire′lane′ *s* Feuer(schutz)schneise *f*
fire′man *s* (–men) Feuerwehrmann *m;*
(stoker) Heizer *m*
fire′place′ *s* Kamin *m,* Herd *m*
fire′plug′ *s* Hydrant *m*
fire′ pow′er *s* (mil) Feuerkraft *f*
fire′proof′ *adj* feuerfest || *tr* feuerfest
machen
fire′ sale′ *s* Ausverkauf *m* von feuer-
beschädigten Waren
fire′ screen′ *s* Feuervorhang *m*
fire′side′ *s* Kamin *m,* Herd *m*
fire′trap′ *s* feuergefährdetes Gebäude
n
fire′ wall′ *s* Brandmauer *f*
fire′wa′ter *s* (coll) Feuerwasser *n*
fire′wood′ *s* Brennholz *n*
fire′works′ *spl* Feuerwerk *n*
fir′ing *s* (of a weapon) Abfeuern *n;*
(of an employee) Entlassung *f*
fir′ing line′ *s* Feuerlinie *f*
fir′ing range′ *s* Schießstand *m*
fir′ing squad′ *s* Erschießungskom-
mando *n;* (for ceremonies) Ehren-
salutkommando *n;* **put to the f.** an
die Wand stellen
firm [fʌrm] *adj* fest || *s* (com) Firma *f*
firmament [′fʌrməmənt] *s* Firmament
n
firmness [′fʌrmnɪs] *s* Festigkeit *f*
first [fʌrst] *adj* erste; **very f. allererste**
|| *adv* erst, erstens; **f. of all** zunächst
|| *s* (aut) erster Gang *m;* **at f.** zuerst;
f. come, f. served wer zuerst kommt,
mahlt zuerst; **from the f.** von vorn-
herein; **the f.** (in dates or in a series)
der Erste
first′ aid′ *s* Erste Hilfe *f*
first′-aid′ kit′ *s* Verbandpäckchen *n*
first′-aid′ sta′tion *s* Unfallstation *f;*
(mil) Verbandsplatz *m*

first′-born′ *adj* erstgeboren
first′-class′ *adj* erstklassig || *adv* erster
Klasse
first′-class′ mail′ *s* Briefpost *f*
first′-class′ tic′ket *s* Fahrkarte *f* (or
Flugkarte *f)* erster Klasse
first′ cous′in *s* leiblicher Vetter *m,*
leibliche Cousine *f*
first′-degree′ *adj* ersten Grades
first′ draft′ *s* Konzept *n*
first′ fin′ger *s* Zeigefinger *m*
first′ floor′ *s* Parterre *n,* Erdgeschoß *n*
first′ fruits′ *spl* Erstlinge *pl*
first′ lieuten′ant *s* Oberleutnant *m*
firstly [′fʌrstli] *adv* erstens
first′ mate′ *s* Obersteuermann *m*
first′ name′ *s* Vorname *m*
first′ night′ *s* (theat) Erstaufführung *f*
first′-nigh′ter [′fʌrst′naɪtər] *s* (theat)
Premierenbesucher –in *mf*
first′ offend′er *s* noch nicht Vorbestrafte *mf*
first′ of′ficer *s* erster Offizier *m*
first′ prize′ *s* Hauptgewinn *m,* Haupt-
treffer *m*
first′-rate′ *adj* erstklassig
first′ ser′geant *s* Hauptfeldwebel *m*
fir′ tree′ *s* Tannenbaum *m*
fiscal [′fɪskəl] *adj* (period, year)
Rechnungs–; (policy) Finanz–
fish [fɪʃ] *s* Fisch *m;* **drink like a f.**
wie ein Bürstenbinder saufen; **like a**
f. out of water nicht in seinem Ele-
ment || *tr* fischen || *intr* fischen; **f.**
for angeln nach
fish′bone′ *s* Gräte *f,* Fischgräte *f*
fish′ bowl′ *s* Fischglas *n*
fisher [′fɪʃər] *s* Fischer –in *mf*
fish′er·man *s* (–men) Angler *m*
fishery [′fɪʃəri] *s* Fischerei *f*
fish′hook′ *s* Angelhaken *m*
fish′ing *adj* Fisch–, Angel– || *s* Fischen
n
fish′ing line′ *s* Angelschnur *f*
fish′ing reel′ *s* Angelschnurrolle *f*
fish′ing rod′ *s* Angelrute *f*
fish′ing tack′le *s* Fischgerät *n*
fish′ mar′ket *s* Fischmarkt *m*
fishmonger [′fɪʃ‚mʌŋgər] *s* Fisch-
händler –in *mf*
fish′pond′ *s* Fischteich *m*
fish′ sto′ry *s* Jägerlatein *n*
fish′tail′ *s* (aer) Abbremsen *n* || *intr*
(aer) abbremsen
fishy [′fɪʃi] *adj* fischig; (eyes, look)
ausdruckslos; (suspicious) anrüchig;
there′s s.th. f. about it das geht nicht
mit rechten Dingen zu
fission [′fɪʃən] *s* (phys) Spaltung *f*
fissionable [′fɪʃənəbəl] *adj* spaltbar
fissure [′fɪʃər] *s* Riß *m,* Spalt *m*
fist [fɪst] *s* Faust *f;* **make a f. die**
Faust ballen; **shake one′s f. at s.o.**
j-m mit der Faust drohen
fist′ fight′ *s* Handgemenge *n*
fisticuffs [′fɪstɪ‚kʌfs] *spl* Faustschläge
pl
fit [fɪt] *adj* (fitter; fittest) gesund;
(for) tauglich (für, zu); (sport) gut
in Form; **be fit as a fiddle** kerngesund sein; **be fit to be tied** Gift
und Galle spucken; **feel fit** auf der
Höhe sein; **fit for military service**

diensttauglich; **fit to eat** genießbar; **fit to drink** trinkbar; **keep fit in Form bleiben; see fit to** (*inf*) es für richtig halten zu (*inf*) || *s* (*of clothes*) Sitz *m*; **by fits and starts** ruckweise; **fit of anger** Wutanfall *m*; **fit of laughter** Lachkrampf *m*; **give s.o. fits** j–n auf die Palme bringen; **it is a good** (or **a bad**) **fit** es sitzt gut (or schlecht); **throw a fit** e–n Wutanfall kriegen || *v* (*pret & pp* **fitted; ger fitting**) *tr* passen (*dat*); **fit in** (*for an appointment*) einschieben; **fit out** ausrüsten, ausstatten || *intr* passen; **fit into** sich einfügen in (*acc*); **fit in with** passen zu; **fit together** zusammenpassen

fitful ['fɪtfəl] *adj* unregelmäßig

fitness ['fɪtnɪs] *s* Tauglichkeit *f*; **physical f.** gute körperliche Verfassung *f*

fit'ting *adj* passend, angemessen || *s* (*of a garment*) Anprobe *f*; (*mach*) Montage *f*; **fittings** Armaturen *pl*

five [faɪv] *adj & pron* fünf || *s* Fünf *f*

five'-year plan' *s* Fünfjahresplan *m*

fix [frks] *s* (*determination of a position*) Standortbestimmung *f*; (*position*) Standort *m*; (*injection of heroin*) (sl) Schuß *m*; **be in a fix** (coll) in der Klemme sein || *tr* befestigen; (*a price, time*) festsetzen; (*repair*) reparieren, wieder in Ordnung bringen; (*get even with*) (sl) erledigen, das Handwerk legen (*dat*); (*one's glance*) (on) heften (auf *acc*); (*the blame*) (on) zuschreiben (*dat*); (*a game*) (sl) auf unehrliche Weise beeinflussen; (*bayonets*) aufpflanzen; (phot) fixieren

fixed *adj* (*unmovable*) unbeweglich; (*stare*) starr; (*income*) fest; (*idea, cost*) fix; **f. date** Termin *m*

fixer ['frksər] *s* (phot) Fixiermittel *n*

fix'ing *s* (*making fast*) Befestigung *f*; (*of a date, etc.*) Festsetzung *f*; **fixings** (culin) Zutaten *pl*

fix'ing bath' *s* (phot) Fixierbad *n*

fixture ['frkstʃər] *s* Installationsteil *m*; **he is a permanent f.** er gehört zum Inventar

fizz [fɪz] *s* Zischen *n* || *intr* zischen

fizzle ['fɪzəl] *s* (coll) Pleite *f* || *intr* aufzischen; **f. out** verpuffen

flabbergast ['flæbər‚gæst] *tr* verblüffen

flabby ['flæbi] *adj* schlaff, schlapp

flag [flæg] *s* Fahne *f*, Flagge *f* || *v* (*pret & pp* **flagged; ger flagging**) *tr* signalisieren || *intr* nachlassen

flag'pole' *s* Fahnenmast *m*

flagrant ['flegrənt] *adj* schreiend

flag'ship' *s* Flaggschiff *n*

flag'staff' *s* Flaggenmast *m*

flag'stone' *s* Steinfliese *f*

flag' stop' *s* (rr) Bedarfshaltestelle *f*

flail [flel] *s* Dreschflegel *m* || *tr* dreschen || *intr*—**f. about** um sich schlagen

flair [fler] *s* Spürsinn *m*, feine Nase *f*

flak [flæk] *s* Flak *f*, Flakfeuer *n*

flake [flek] *s* (*thin piece*) Schuppe *f*; (*of snow, soap*) Flocke *f* || *intr* Schuppen bilden; **f. off** abblättern

flaky ['fleki] *adj* (*skin*) schuppig; (*pastry*) blätterig; (sl) überspannt

flamboyant [flæm'bɔɪ‚ənt] *adj* (*person*) angeberisch; (*style*) überladen

flame [flem] *s* Flamme *f*; **be in flames** in Flammen stehen; **burst into flames** in Flammen aufgehen || *intr* flammen

flamethrower ['flem‚θro‚ər] *s* Flammenwerfer *m*

flam'ing *adj* flammend

flamin·go [flə'mɪŋgo] *s* (**-gos &** **-goes**) (orn) Flamingo *m*

flammable ['flæməbəl] *adj* brennbar

Flanders ['flændərz] *s* Flandern *n*

flange [flændʒ] *s* (*of a pipe*) Flansch *m*; (*of a wheel*) (rr) Spurkranz *m*

flank [flæŋk] *s* (anat, mil, zool) Flanke *f* || *tr* flankieren

flank'ing move'ment *s* (mil) Umgehung *f*

flannel ['flænəl] *adj* flanellen || *s* Flanell *m*

flap [flæp] *s* Klappe *f*; **f. of the wing** Flügelschlag *m* || *v* (*pret & pp* **flapped; ger flapping**) *tr*—**f. the wings mit den Flügeln schlagen** || *intr* flattern

flare [fler] *s* Leuchtsignal *n*; (*of anger, excitement*) Aufbrausen *n*; (*of a skirt*) Glocke *f*; (mil) Leuchtrakete *f*, Leuchtbombe *f* || *intr* flackern; (*said of a skirt*) glockenförmig abstehen; **f. up** auflodern; (fig) aufbrausen

flare'-up' *s* Auflodern *n*; (*of anger*) Aufbrausen *n*

flash [flæʃ] *s* Blitz *m*; (*of a gun*) Mündungsfeuer *n*; (phot) Blitzlicht *n*; **f. of genious** Geistesblitz *m*; **f. of light** Lichtstrahl *m*; **f. of lightning** Blitzstrahl *m*; **in a f.** im Nu || *tr* (*a glance*) zuwerfen; (*a message*) funkeln; **f. a light in s.o.'s face** j–m ins Gesicht leuchten || *intr* blitzen; (*said of eyes*) funkeln; **f. by** vorbeisausen; **f. on** aufleuchten; **f. through one's mind** j–m durch den Kopf schießen

flash'back' *s* (cin) Rückblende *f*

flash' bulb' *s* Blitzlichtbirne *f*

flash' cube' *s* Blitzlichtwürfel *m*

flash' flood' *s* plötzliche Überschwemmung *f*

flash' gun' *s* Blitzlichtgerät *n*

flash'light' *s* Taschenlampe *f*

flash' pic'ture, flash' shot' *s* Blitzlichtaufnahme *f*

flashy ['flæʃi] *adj* auffällig; (*clothes*) protzig; (*colors*) grell

flask [flæsk] *s* Taschenflasche *f*; (*for laboratory use*) Glaskolben *m*

flat [flæt] *adj* (**flatter; flattest**) platt, flach; (*food*) fad(e); (*rate*) Pauschal–; (*tire*) platt; (*color*) matt; (*beer, soda*) schal; (*lie*) glatt; (*denial*) entschieden; (mus) erniedrigt; **be f.** (mus) zu tief singen || *adv* (*e.g., in exactly ten minutes*) genau; **fall f.** (fig) flachfallen; **go f.** schal werden; **lie f.** flach liegen || *s* (*apartment*) Wohnung *f*; (*tire*) Reifenpanne *f*

flat'boat' *s* Flachboot *n*

flat-broke ['flæt'brok] *adj* (coll) völlig pleite

flat'car' *s* Plattformwagen *m*

flat' feet' *spl* Plattfüße *pl*

flat'-foot'ed *adj* plattfüßig; **catch f. auf frischer Tat ertappen**

flat'i'ron *s* Bügeleisen *n*

flatly ['flætli] *adv* rundweg, reinweg

flatten ['flætən] *tr* (*paper, cloth*) glattstreichen; (*raze*) einebnen; **f. out** abplatten; (aer) abfangen ∥ *intr* sich verflachen; (aer) ausschweben

flatter ['flætər] *tr* schmeicheln (*dat*); **be flattered sich geschmeichelt fühlen; f. oneself sich** [dat] **einbilden**

flatterer ['flætərər] *s* Schmeichler –in *mf*

flat'tering *adj* schmeichelhaft

flattery ['flætəri] *s* Schmeichelei *f*

flat' tire' *s* Reifenpanne *f*

flat'top' *s* (coll) Flugzeugträger *m*

flat' trajec'tory *s* Rasanz *f*

flatulence ['flætʃələns] *s* Blähung *f*

flat'ware' *s* (*silverware*) Eßbestecke *pl*

flaunt [flɔnt] *tr* prunken mit

flavor ['flevər] *s* Aroma *n* ∥ *tr* würzen

fla'voring *s* Würze *f*

flavorless ['flevərlɪs] *adj* fad(e)

flaw [flɔ] *s* Fehler *m*; (*crack*) Riß *m*; (*in glass, precious stone*) Blase *f*

flawless ['flɔlɪs] *adj* tadellos

flax [flæks] *s* Flachs *m*, Lein *m*

flaxen ['flæksən] *adj* flachsen

flax'seed' *s* Leinsamen *m*

flay [fle] *tr* ausbalgen

flea [fli] *s* Floh *m*

flea'bag' *s* (*sleeping bag*) (coll) Flohkiste *f*; (*hotel*) (coll) Penne *f*

flea'bite' *s* Flohbiß *m*

flea'mar'ket *s*, Flohmarkt *m*

fleck [flɛk] *s* Fleck *m*

fledgling ['fledʒlɪŋ] *s* eben flügge gewordener Vogel *m*; (fig) Grünschnabel *m*

flee [fli] *v* (*pret & pp* **fled** [flɛd]) *intr* fliehen

fleece [flis] *s* Vlies *n* ∥ *tr* (coll) rupfen

fleecy ['flisi] *adj* wollig; **f. clouds** Schäfchenwolken *pl*

fleet [flit] *adj* flink ∥ *s* Flotte *f*; (aer) Geschwader *n*; (nav) Kriegsflotte *f*; **f. of cars** Wagenpark *m*

fleet'ing *adj* flüchtig

Flemish ['flemɪʃ] *adj* flämisch ∥ *s* Flämisch *n*

flesh [flɛʃ] *s* Fleisch *n*; **in the f.** leibhaftig

flesh'-col'ored *adj* fleischfarben

fleshiness ['flɛʃɪnɪs] *s* Fleischigkeit *f*

flesh' wound' *s* Fleischwunde *f*

fleshy ['flɛʃi] *adj* fleischig

flex [flɛks] *tr* biegen; (*muscles*) anspannen

flexible ['flɛksɪbəl] *adj* biegsam

flex(i)time ['flɛks(ɪ) ˌtaɪm] *s* Gleitzeit *f*

flick [flɪk] *s* Schnippen *n* ∥ *tr* (away) wegschnippen

flicker ['flɪkər] *s* (*of a flame*) Flakkern *n*; (*of eyelids*) Zucken *n* ∥ *intr* flackern

flier ['flaɪ-ər] *s* Flieger –in *mf*; (*handbill*) Flugblatt *n*

flight [flaɪt] *s* Flug *m*; (*fleeing*) Flucht *f*; (*of birds, geese*) Schar *f*; (*of stairs*) Treppe *f*; **f. of stairs** Treppenflucht *f*; **f. of the imagination** Geistesschwung *m*; **live two flights up** zwei Treppen hoch wohnen; **put to f.** in die Flucht schlagen; **take to f.** sich davonmachen

flight' bag' *s* (aer) Reisetasche *f*

flight' deck' *s* (nav) Landedeck *n*

flight' engineer' *s* Bordmechaniker *m*

flight' instruc'tor *s* Fluglehrer –in *mf*

flight' path' *s* Flugstrecke *f*

flighty ['flaɪti] *adj* leichtsinnig

film-flam ['flɪm ˌflæm] *s* (*nonsense*) Unsinn *m*; (*deception*) Betrügerei *f* ∥ *v* (*pret & pp* –flammed) *ger* –flamming) *tr* (coll) betrügen

flimsy ['flɪmzi] *adj* (*material*) hauchdünn; (*excuse, construction*) schwach

flinch [flɪntʃ] *intr* (at) zurückweichen (vor *dat*), zusammenfahren (vor *dat*)

flinch'ing *s*—**without f.** ohne mit der Wimper zu zucken

fling [flɪŋ] *s* Wurf *m*; **go on** (or **have**) **a f. sich austoben; have a f. at versuchen** ∥ *v* (*pret & pp* **flung** [flʌŋ]) *tr* schleudern; **f. off** abschleudern; **f. open aufreißen**

flint [flɪnt] *s* Feuerstein *m*

flinty ['flɪnti] *adj* steinhart; (fig) hart

flip [flɪp] *adj* leichtfertig ∥ *s* (*of a coin*) Hochwerfen *n*; (*somersault*) Purzelbaum *m* ∥ *v* (*pret & pp* **flipped**) *ger* **flipping**) *tr* schnellen; (*a coin*) hochwerfen; **f. one's lid** (sl) rasend werden; **f. over umdrehen**

flippancy ['flɪpənsi] *s* Leichtfertigkeit *f*

flippant ['flɪpənt] *adj* leichtfertig

flipper ['flɪpər] *s* Flosse *f*

flirt [flʌrt] *s* Flirt *m* ∥ *intr* kokettieren, flirten; (*with an idea*) liebäugeln

flirtation [flʌr'teʃən] *s* Liebelei *f*

flit [flɪt] *v* (*pret & pp* **flitted**) *ger* **flitting**) *intr* flitzen; **f.** by vorbeiflitzen; (*said of time*) verfliegen

float [flot] *s* Schwimmkörper *m*; (*of a fishing line*) Schwimmer *m*; (*raft*) Floß *n*; (*in parades*) Festwagen *m* ∥ *tr* (*logs*) flößen; (*a loan*) auflegen ∥ *intr* schwimmen; (*in the air*) schweben; **f. about herumtreiben**

float'ing kid'ney *s* Wanderniere *f*

float'ing mine' *s* Treibmine *f*

flock [flɑk] *s* (*of sheep*) Herde *f*; (*of birds*) Schar *f*, Schwarm *m*; (*of people*) Menge *f* ∥ *intr* herbeiströmen; **come flocking herbeigeströmt kommen; f. around sich scharen um; f. into strömen in** (*acc*); **f. to zulaufen** (*dat*); **f. together sich zusammenscharen**

floe [flo] *s* Eisscholle *f*

flog [flɑg] *v* (*pret & pp* **flogged**) *ger* **flogging**) *tr* prügeln

flood [flʌd] *s* Flut *f*; (*caused by heavy rains*) Überschwemmung *f*; (*sudden rise of a river*) Hochwasser *n*; (fig) Schwall *m*; (Bib) Sintflut *f* ∥ *tr* (& fig) überschwemmen; (*e.g., with mail*) überschütten

flood′gate′ s (& fig) Schleusentor n
flood′light′ s Flutlicht n ‖ tr anstrahlen
flood′ tide′ s Flut f; at f. zur Zeit der Flut
flood′ wa′ters spl Flutwasser n
floor [flor] s Fußboden m; (story) Stock m; (parl) Sitzungssaal m; have the f. das Wort haben; may I have the f.? ich bitte ums Wort; on the third f. im zweiten Stock ‖ tr zu Boden strecken; (coll) verblüffen
floor′board′ s Diele f
floor′ing s Fußbodenbelag m
floor′ lamp′ s Stehlampe f
floor′ plan′ s Grundriß m
floor′ pol′ish s Bohnermasse f
floor′ sam′ple s Vorführungsmuster n
floor′ show′ s Kabarett n
floor′ tile′ s Bodenfliese f
floor′walk′er s Abteilungsaufseher -in m f
floor′ wax′ s Bohnerwachs n
flop [flɑp] s (coll) Mißerfolg m; (person) Niete f; (fall) (coll) Plumps m; take a f. (coll) plumpsen ‖ v (pret & pp flopped; ger flopping) intr (fall) (coll) plumpsen; (fail) (coll) versagen; (theat) (coll) durchfallen; f. down in (coll) sich plumpsen lassen in (acc)
flora [′florə] s Pflanzenwelt f
floral [′florəl] adj Blumen-
Florence [′florəns] s Florenz n
florescence [flo′resəns] s Blüte f
florid [′florɪd] adj (ornate) überladen; (complexion) blühend
florist [′florɪst] s Blumenhändler -in m f
floss [flɔs] s Rohseide f; (of corn) Narbenfäden pl
floss′ silk′ s Florettseide f
flossy [′flɔsi] adj seidenweich
flotilla [flo′tɪlə] s Flotille f
flotsam [′flɑtsəm] s Wrackgut n
flot′sam and jet′sam s Treibgut n; (trifles) Kleinigkeiten pl
flounce [flauns] s Volant m ‖ tr mit Volants besetzen ‖ intr erregt stürmen
flounder [′flaundər] s Flunder f ‖ intr taumeln; (fig) ins Schwimmen kommen
flour [flaur] s Mehl n
flourish [′flʌrɪʃ] s (in writing) Schnörkel m; (in a speech) Floskel f; (gesture) große Geste f; (mus) Tusch m; f. of trumpets Trompetengeschmetter n ‖ tr (banners) schwenken; (swords) schwingen ‖ intr blühen, gedeihen
flour′ishing adj blühend; (business) schwunghaft
flour′ mill′ s Mühle f
floury [′flauri] adj mehlig
flout [flaut] tr verspotten ‖ intr—f. at spotten über (acc)
flow [flo] s Fluß m ‖ intr fließen, rinnen; (said of hair, clothes) wallen; f. by vorbeifließen; f. into zuströmen (dat)
flower [′flau·ər] s Blume f; cut flowers Schnittblumen pl ‖ intr blühen

flow′er bed′ s Blumenbeet n
flow′er gar′den s Blumengarten m
flow′er girl′ s Blumenmädchen n
flow′erpot′ s Blumentopf m
flow′er shop′ s Blumenladen m
flow′er show′ s Blumenausstellung f
flow′er stand′ s Blumenstand m
flowery [′flau·əri] adj blumig; (fig) geziert; f. phrase Floskel f
flu [flu] s (coll) Grippe f
flub [flʌb] v (pret & pp flubbed; ger flubbing) tr (coll) verkorksen
fluctuate [′flʌktʃu‚et] intr schwanken
fluctuation [‚flʌktʃu′eʃən] s Schwankung f
flue [flu] s Rauchrohr n
fluency [′flu·ənsi] s Geläufigkeit f
fluent [′flu·ənt] adj (speaker) redegewandt; (speech) fließend
fluently [′flu·əntli] adv fließend
fluff [flʌf] s Staubflocke f; (blunder) Schnitzer m ‖ tr verpfuschen; f. up (a pillow) schütteln; (a rug) aufrauhen
fluffy [′flʌfi] adj flaumig
fluid [′flu·ɪd] adj flüssig ‖ s Flüssigkeit f
fluke [fluk] s Ankerflügel m; (coll) Dusel m
flunk [flʌŋk] s Durchfallen n ‖ tr (a test) (coll) durchfallen in (dat); (a student) (coll) durchfallen lassen ‖ intr (coll) durchfallen
flunky [′flʌŋki] s Schranze m f
fluorescent [flo′resənt] adj fluoreszierend
fluores′cent light′ s Leuchtstofflampe f
fluores′cent tube′ s Leuchtröhre f
fluoridate [′florɪ‚det] tr mit e-m Fluorid versetzen
fluoride [′florɑɪd] s Fluorid n
fluorine [′florin] s Fluor n
fluorite [′florɑɪt] s Fluorkalzium n
fluoroscope [′florə‚skop] s Fluoroskop n
flurry [′flʌri] s (of snow) Schneegestöber m; (st. exch.) kurzes Aufflakkern n; f. of activity fieberhafte Tätigkeit f
flush [flʌʃ] adj (even) eben, glatt; (well-supplied) gut bei Kasse; (full to overflowing) übervoll ‖ adv direkt ‖ s (on the cheeks) Erröten n; (of youth) Blüte f; (of a toilet) Spülung f; (cards) Flöte f; f. of victory Siegesrausch m ‖ tr (a toilet) spülen; (hunt) auftreiben; f. down hinunterspülen; f. out (animals) auftreiben ‖ intr erröten
flush′ switch′ s Unterputzschalter m
flush′ tank′ s Spülkasten m
flush′ toi′let s Spülklosett n
fluster [′flʌstər] s Verwirrung f ‖ tr verwirren
flute [flut] s (archit) Kannelüre f; (mus) Flöte f ‖ tr riffeln
flut′ing s (archit) Kannelierung f
flutist [′flutɪst] s Flötist -in m f
flutter [′flʌtər] s Flattern n; (excitement) Aufregung f ‖ tr—f. one's eyelashes mit den Wimpern klimpern ‖ intr flattern

flux [flʌks] s (flow) Fließen n, Fluß m; (for fusing metals) Schmelzmittel n; **in f.** im Fluß

fly [flai] s Fliege f; (of trousers) Schlitz m; (angl) künstliche Fliege f; **flies** (theat) Soffitten pl; **fly in the ointment** Haar n in der Suppe || v (pret **flew** [flu]; pp **flown** [flon]) tr fliegen || intr fliegen; (rush) stürzen; (said of rumors) schwirren; (said of time) verfliegen; **fly around** umherfliegen; (e.g., the globe) umfliegen; **fly at s.o.** auf j-n losgehen; **fly away** abfliegen; **fly in all directions** nach allen Seiten zerstieben; **fly low** tief fliegen; **fly off the handle** (fig) aus der Haut fahren; **fly open** aufspringen; **fly over** überfliegen; **fly past** vorbeifliegen; (an dat); **let fly** (e.g., an arrow) schnellen

fly'-ball' s (baseball) Flugball m

fly'-by-night' adj unverläßlich || s (coll) Schwindelunternehmen n

fly' cast'ing s Fischen n mit der Wurfangel

flyer ['flai·ər] s var of flier

fly'-fish' intr mit künstlichen Fliegen angeln

fly'ing adj fliegend; (boat, field, time) Flug–; (suit, club, school) Flieger– || s Fliegen n

fly'ing but'tress s Strebebogen m

fly'ing col'ors spl—**come through with f.** e-n glänzenden Sieg erringen

fly'ing sau'cer s fliegende Untertasse f

fly'leaf' s (-leaves') Vorsatzblatt n

fly'pa'per s Fliegenfänger m

fly' rod' s Angelrute f

fly'speck' s Fliegendreck m

fly' swat'ter [ˌswatər] s Fliegenklappe f

fly'trap' s Fliegenfalle f

fly'wheel' s Schwungrad n

foal [fol] s Fohlen n || intr fohlen

foam [fom] s Schaum m; (of waves) Gischt m; (from the mouth) Geifer m || intr schäumen; (said of waves) branden

foam' rub'ber s Schaumgummi m

foamy ['fomi] adj (full of foam) schaumig; (beer) schäumend; (foamlike) schaumartig

F.O.B., f.o.b. [ˌɛf‚o'bi] adv (free on board) frei an Bord

focal ['fokəl] adj fokal; **be the f. point** im Brennpunkt stehen; **f. point** (fig & opt) Brennpunkt m

fo·cus ['fokəs] s (-cuses & -ci [sai]) (math, opt) Brennpunkt m; (pathol) Herd m; **bring into f.** richtig (or scharf) einstellen; **in f.** scharf eingestellt; **out of f.** unscharf || v (pret & pp -cus[s]ed; ger -cus[s]ing) tr (a camera) einstellen; (attention, etc.) (on) richten (auf acc) || intr sich scharf einstellen

fo'cusing s Scharfeinstellung f

fodder ['fodər] s Futter n

foe [fo] s Feind –in mf

fog [fɔg] s Nebel m; (fig) Verwirrung f; (phot) Grauschleier m || v (pret & pp **fogged;** ger **fogging**) tr ver-

nebeln; (fig) umnebeln || intr (phot) verschleiern; **fog up** beschlagen

fog' bank' s Nebelbank f

fog' bell' s Nebelglocke f

fog'-bound' adj durch Nebel festgehalten

fogey ['fogi] s Kauz m

foggy ['fogi] adj neblig, nebelhaft; (phot) verschleiert; **he hasn't the foggiest idea** er hat nicht die leiseste Ahnung

fog'horn' s Nebelhorn n

fog' light' s (aut) Nebelscheinwerfer m

foible ['fɔibəl] s Schwäche f

foil [fɔil] s (of metal) Folie f; (of a mirror) Spiegelbelag m; (fig) (to) Hintergrund m (für); (fencing) Florett n || tr (a plan) durchkreuzen; (an attempt) vereiteln

foist [fɔist] tr—**f. s.th. on s.o.** j-m etw anhängen

fold [fold] s Falte f; (in stiff material) Falz m; (for sheep) Pferch m; (flock of sheep) Schafherde f; (relig) Herde f || tr falten; (stiff material) falzen; (e.g., a chair) zusammenklappen; (the arms) kreuzen; (the wash) zusammenlegen || intr sich (zusammen) falten; (com) zusammenbrechen

folder ['foldər] s (loose-leaf binder) Schnellhefter m; (manila folder) Mappe f; (brochure) Prospekt m

fold'ing adj (bed, chair, camera, wing) Klapp–

fold'ing door' s Falttür f

fold'ing screen' s spanische Wand f

foliage ['folɪ·ɪdʒ] s Laubwerk n, Laub n

foli·o ['folɪ‚o] adj Folio–, in Folio || s (-os) (page) Folioblatt n; (book) Foliant m || tr paginieren

folk [fok] adj Volks– || **folks** spl (people) Leute pl; (family) Angehörige pl

folk' dance' s Volkstanz m

folk'lore' s Volkskunde f

folk' mu'sic s Volksmusik f

folk' song' s Volkslied n

folksy ['foksi] adj (person) leutselig; (speech, expression) volkstümlich

folk' tale' s Volkssage f

folk'ways' spl volkstümliche Lebensweise f

follicle ['falɪkəl] s Follikel n

follow ['falo] tr folgen (dat); (instructions) befolgen; (a goal, events, news) verfolgen; (in office) folgen auf (acc); (a profession) ausüben; (understand) folgen können (dat); **f. one another** aufeinanderfolgen; (said of events) sich überstürzen; **f. up** nachgehen (dat); **f. your nose!** immer der Nase nach! || intr (nach)-folgen; **as follows** folgendermaßen; **f. after** nachfolgen (dat); **f. through** (sport) ganz durchziehen; **f. upon** folgen auf (acc); **it follows that** daraus folgt, daß

follower ['falo·ər] s Anhänger –in mf

fol'lowing adj nachstehend, folgend || s Gefolgschaft f

fol'low-up' adj Nach– || s weitere Verfolgung f

folly ['fɑli] *s* Torheit *f;* **follies** (theat) Revue *f*

foment [fo'ment] *tr* schüren, anstiften

fond [fɑnd] *adj* (*hope, wish*) sehnlich; **become f.** of lieb gewinnen; **be f. of** gern haben; **be f. of reading** gern lesen

fondle ['fɑndəl] *tr* liebkosen

fondness ['fɑndnɪs] *s* Verliebtheit *f;* (**for**) Hang *m* (zu), Vorliebe *f* (für)

font [fɑnt] *s* (*for holy water*) Weihwasserbecken *n;* (*for baptism*) Taufbecken *n;* (typ) Schriftart *f*

food [fud] *adj* Nähr-, Speise- ‖ *s* (*on the table*) Essen *n;* (*in a store*) Lebensmittel *pl;* (*requirement for life*) Nahrung *f;* (*for animals*) Futter *n;* (*for plants*) Nährstoff *m;* **f. and drink** Speis' und Trank; **f. for thought** Stoff *m* zum Nachdenken

food′ poi′soning *s* Nahrungsmittelvergiftung *f*

food′stuffs′ *spl* Nahrungsmittel *pl*

food′ val′ue *s* Nährwert *m*

fool [ful] *s* Narr *m;* **born f.** Mondkalb *n;* **make a f. of oneself** sich blamieren ‖ *tr* täuschen, anführen ‖ *intr*—**f. around** herumtrödeln; **f. around with** herumspielen mit; (*romantically*) sich herumtreiben mit

fool′har′dy *adj* tollkühn

fool′ing *s* Späße *pl;* **f. around** Firlefanz *m;* **no f.!** na, so was!

foolish ['fulɪʃ] *adj* töricht, albern

foolishness ['fulɪʃnɪs] *s* Torheit *f*

fool′-proof′ *adj* narrensicher

fools′cap′ *s* Narrenkappe *f;* (*paper size*) Kanzleipapier *n*

foot [fut] *s* (feet [fit]) Fuß *m;* **be (back) on one′s feet** (wieder) auf den Beinen sein; **f. of the bed** Fußende *n* des Bettes; **on f.** zu Fuß; **put one′s best f. forward** sich ins rechte Licht setzen; **put one′s f. down** (fig) ein Machtwort sprechen; **put one′s f. in it** (coll) ins Fettnäpfchen treten; **stand on one′s own two feet** auf eigenen Füßen stehen ‖ *tr*—**f. the bill** blechen

footage ['futɪdʒ] *s* Ausmaß *n* in Fuß

foot′-and-mouth′ disease′ *s* Maul- und Klauenseuche *f*

foot′ball′ *s* Fußball *m*

foot′board′ *s* (*in a car*) Trittbrett *n;* (*of a bed*) Fußbrett *n*

foot′bridge′ *s* Steg *m*

foot′fall′ *s* Schritt *m*

foot′hills′ *spl* Vorgebirge *n*

foot′hold′ *s* (& fig) Halt *m;* **gain a f.** festen Fuß fassen

foot′ing *s* Halt *m;* **lose one′s f.** ausgleiten; **on an equal f. with** auf gleichem Fuße mit

foot′lights′ *spl* Rampenlicht *n*

foot′man *s* (-men) Lakai *m*

foot′note′ *s* Fußnote *f*

foot′path′ *s* Fußpfad *m*, Fußsteig *m*

foot′print′ *s* Fußstapfe *f*

foot′ race′ *s* Wettlauf *m*

foot′rest′ *s* Fußraste *f*

foot′ rule′ *s* Zollstock *m*

foot′ sol′dier *s* Infanterist *m*

foot′sore′ *adj* fußkrank

foot′step′ *s* Tritt *m;* **follow in s.o.'s footsteps** in j-s Fußstapfen treten

foot′stool′ *s* Schemel *m*

foot′wear′ *s* Schuhwerk *n*

foot′work′ *s* (sl) Lauferei *f;* (sport) Beinarbeit *f*

foot′worn′ *adj* abgetreten

fop [fɑp] *s* Geck *m*

for [fɔr] *prep* für; (*a destination*) nach (*dat*); (with an English present perfect tense) schon (*acc*), e.g., **I have been living here for a month** ich wohne hier schone e-n Monat (or seit e-m Monat); (with an English future tense) für or auf (*acc*); **for good** für immer; **for joy** vor Freude; **for years** jahrelang ‖ *conj* denn

forage ['fɔrɪdʒ] *s* Furage *f* ‖ *intr* furagieren

foray ['fɔre] *s* (*raid*) Raubzug *m;* (*e.g., into politics*) Streifzug *m* ‖ *intr* plündern

for-bear [fɔr'bɛr] *v* (pret –bore ['bor]; pp –borne ['born]) *tr* unterlassen ‖ *intr* ablassen

forbearance [fɔr'bɛrəns] *s* (*patience*) Geduld *f;* (*leniency*) Nachsicht *f*

for-bid [fɔr'bɪd] *v* (pret –bade ['bæd] & –bad ['bæd]; pp –bidden ['bɪdən]) *tr* verbieten

forbid′ding *adj* abschreckend; (*dangerous*) gefährlich

force [fɔrs] *s* (*strength*) Kraft *f;* (*compulsion*) Gewalt *f;* (phys) Kraft *f;* **be in f.** in Kraft sein; **by f.** gewaltsam; **come into f.** in Kraft treten; **forces** (mil) Streitkräfte *pl;* **have the f. of** gelten als; **resort to f.** zu Zwangsmaßnahmen greifen; **with full f.** mit voller Wucht ‖ *tr* zwingen; (*plants*) treiben; (*a door*) aufsprengen; (*e.g., an issue*) forcieren; (*into*) zwängen (in *acc*); **f. down** hinunterdrücken; (aer) zur Landung zwingen; **f. one′s way** sich drängen; **f. s.th. on s.o.** j-m etw aufdringen

forced′ land′ing *s* Notlandung *f*

forced′ march′ *s* Gewaltmarsch *m*

forceful ['fɔrsfəl] *adj* eindrucksvoll

for-ceps ['fɔrsɛps] *s* (–ceps & –cipes [sɪ‚piz]) (dent, surg, zool) Zange *f*

forcible ['fɔrsɪbəl] *adj* (*strong*) kräftig; (*violent*) gewaltsam

ford [fɔrd] *s* Furt *f* ‖ *tr* durchwaten

fore [fɔr] *adj* Vorder- ‖ *adv* (naut) vorn ‖ *s*—**come to the f.** hervortreten ‖ *interj* (golf) Achtung!

fore′ and aft′ *adv* längsschiffs

fore′arm′ *s* Vorderarm *m*, Unterarm *m*

fore′bears *spl* Vorfahren *pl*

forebode [fɔr'bod] *tr* vorbedeuten

forebod′ing *s* (*omen*) Vorzeichen *n;* (*presentiment*) Vorahnung *f*

fore′cast′ *s* Voraussage *f* ‖ *v* (pret & pp –cast &–casted) *tr* voraussagen

forecastle ['foksəl] *s* Back *f*

foreclose′ *tr* (*a mortgage*) für verfallen erklären; (*shut out*) ausschließen

foredoom′ *tr* im voraus verurteilen

fore′fa′thers *spl* Vorfahren *pl*

fore′fin′ger *s* Zeigefinger *m*

fore′front′ *s* Spitze *f*

fore′go′ing *adj* vorhergehend

fore'gone' conclu'sion s ausgemachte Sache f

fore'ground' s Vordergrund m

forehead ['fɔrɪd] s Stirn(e) f

foreign ['fɔrɪn] adj (e.g., aid, product) Auslands–; (e.g., body, language, word, worker) Fremd–; (e.g., minister, office, policy, trade) Außen–; (e.g., affairs, service) auswärtig

foreigner ['fɔrɪnər] s Ausländer –in mf

for'eign exchange' s Devisen pl

fore'leg' s Vorderbein n

fore'lock' s Stirnlocke f

fore'man s (–men) Vorarbeiter m; (jur) Obmann m; (min) Steiger m

foremast ['for,mæst] s Fockmast m

fore'most' adj vorderste || adv zuerst

fore'noon' s Vormittag m

fore'part' s vorderster Teil m

fore'paw' s Vorderpfote f

fore'quart'er s Vorderviertel n

fore'run'ner s Vorbote m

fore'sail' s Focksegel n

fore•see' v (pret –saw'; pp –seen') tr voraussehen

foreseeable [for'si·əbəl] adj absehbar

foreshad'ow tr ahnen lassen

foreshort'en tr verkürzen

fore'sight' s Voraussicht f

fore'sight'ed adj umsichtig

fore'skin' s Vorhaut f

forest ['fɔrɪst] s Wald m, Forst m

forestall' tr zuvorkommen (dat)

for'est fire' s Waldbrand m

for'est rang'er s Forstbeamte m

forestry ['fɔrɪstri] s Forstwirtschaft f

fore'taste' s Vorgeschmack m

fore•tell' v (pret & pp –told') tr vorhersagen, weissagen

fore'thought' s Vorsorge f, Vorbedacht m

forev'er adv ewig, für immer; **f. and ever** auf immer und ewig

forewarn' tr (of) vorher warnen (vor dat)

fore'word' s Vorwort n

forfeit ['fɔrfɪt] s Einbuße f || tr einbüßen, verwirken

forfeiture ['fɔrfɪtʃər] s Verwirkung f

forgather [for'gæðər] intr sich treffen

forge [fɔrdʒ] s Schmiede f || tr schmieden; (documents) fälschen || intr— **forge ahead** vordringen

forger ['fɔrdʒər] s Fälscher –in mf

forgery ['fɔrdʒəri] s Fälschung f; (coin) Falschgeld n

for•get' [for'gɛt] v (pret –got; pp –got & –gotten; ger –getting) tr vergessen; **f. it!** spielt keine Rolle!; **f. oneself** sich vergessen

forgetful [for'gɛtfəl] adj vergeßlich

forgetfulness [for'gɛtfəlnɪs] s Vergeßlichkeit f

forget'-me-not' s Vergißmeinnicht n

forgivable [for'gɪvəbəl] adj verzeihlich

for•give' [for'gɪv] v (pret –gave; pp –given) tr (a person) vergeben (dat); (a thing) vergeben

forgiveness [for'gɪvnɪs] s Vergebung f

forgiv'ing adj versöhnlich

for•go' [for'go] v (pret –went; pp –gone) tr verzichten auf (acc)

fork [fɔrk] s Gabel f; (in the road) Gabelung f; (of a tree) Astgabelung f || tr gabeln; **f. over** (coll) übergeben

forked adj gabelförmig; (tongue) gespalten

fork'lift truck' s Gabelstapler m

forlorn [for'lɔrn] adj (forsaken) verlassen; (wretched) elend; (attempt) verzweifelt

forlorn' hope' s aussichtsloses Unternehmen n

form [fɔrm] s Form f, Gestalt f; (paper to be filled out) Formular n || tr formen, bilden; (a plan) fassen; (a circle, alliance) schließen; (suspicions) schöpfen; (a habit) annehmen; (blisters) werfen || intr sich bilden

formal ['fɔrməl] adj formell, förmlich

for'mal call' s Höflichkeitsbesuch m

for'mal educa'tion s Schulbildung f

formality [for'mælɪti] s Formalität f; **without f.** ohne Umstände

format ['fɔrmæt] s Format n

formation [for'meʃən] s Bildung f; (aer) Verband m; (geol, mil) Formation f

former ['fɔrmər] adj ehemalig, früher; **the f.** jener

formerly ['fɔrmərli] adv ehemals, früher

form'-fit'ting adj—**be f. e–e** gute Paßform haben

formidable ['fɔrmɪdəbəl] adj (huge) gewaltig; (dreadful) schrecklich

formless ['fɔrmlɪs] adj formlos

form' let'ter s Rundbrief m

formu•la ['fɔrmjələ] s (–las & –lae [,li]) Formel f; (baby food) Kindermilch f

formulate ['fɔrmjə,let] tr formulieren

formulation [,fɔrmjə'leʃən] s Formulierung f

fornicate ['fɔrnɪ,ket] intr Unzucht treiben

fornication [,fɔrnɪ'keʃən] s Unzucht f

for•sake [for'sek] v (pret –sook ['suk]; pp –saken ['sekən]) tr verlassen

fort [fɔrt] s Burg f; (mil) Fort n

forte [fɔrt] s Stärke f

forth [forθ] adv hervor; **and so f.** und so fort; **from that day f.** von dem Tag an

forth'com'ing adj bevorstehend

forth'right' adj ehrlich, offen

forth'with' adv sofort

fortieth ['fɔrtɪ·ɪθ] adj & pron vierzigste || s (fraction) Vierzigstel n; (in a series) Vierzigste mfn

fortification [,fɔrtɪfɪ'keʃən] s Befestigung f

forti•fy ['fɔrtɪ,faɪ] v (pret & pp –fied) tr (a place) befestigen; (e.g., with liquor) kräftigen; (encourage) ermutigen

fortitude ['fɔrtɪ,t(j)ud] s Seelenstärke f

fortnight ['fɔrtnaɪt] s vierzehn Tage pl

fortress ['fɔrtrɪs] s Festung f

fortuitous [for't(j)u·ɪtəs] adj zufällig

fortunate ['fɔrtʃənɪt] adj glücklich

fortunately ['fɔrtʃənɪtli] adv glücklicherweise

fortune ['fɔrtʃən] s Glück n; (money) Vermögen n; **make a f.** sich [dat] ein Vermögen erwerben; **have one's f. told** sich [dat] wahrsagen lassen; **tell fortunes** wahrsagen

for'tune hunt'er s Mitgiftjäger –in mf

for'tunetell'er s Wahrsagerin f

forty ['fɔrti] adj & pron vierzig ‖ s Vierzig f; **the forties** die vierziger Jahre

fo·rum ['fɔrəm] s (–rums & –ra [rə]) (& fig) Forum n

forward ['fɔrwərd] adj vordere, Vor-wärts–; (person) keck; (mil) vorge-schoben ‖ adv vorwärts, nach vorn; **bring f.** (an idea) vorschlagen; (a proposal) vorbringen; **come f.** sich melden; **look f. to** sich freuen auf (acc); **put f.** vorlegen ‖ s (fb) Stür-mer m ‖ tr befördern; **please f.** bitte nachsenden ‖ interj—f., march! im Gleichschritt, marsch!

fossil ['fɑsɪl] adj versteinert ‖ s Fossil n

foster ['fɔstər] adj (child, father, mother, home) Pflege–; (brother, sis-ter) Milch– ‖ tr pflegen

foul [faʊl] adj übel; (in smell) übel-riechend; (air, weather) schlecht; (language) unflätig; (means) unfair ‖ s (sport) Foul n ‖ tr (make dirty) besudeln; (the lines) verwickeln; (sport) foulen; **f. up** durcheinander-bringen ‖ intr (sport) foulen

foul' line' s (baseball) Grenzlinie f; (basketball) Freiwurflinie f

foul-mouthed ['faʊl,maʊðd], ['faʊl,maʊθt] adj zotige Reden führend

foul' play' s unfaires Spiel n; (crime) Verbrechen n, Mord m

found [faʊnd] tr gründen; (cast) gießen

foundation [faʊn'deʃən] s (act) Grün-dung f; (of a structure) Fundament n; (fund) Stiftung f; (fig) Grundlage f; **lay the foundation of** (& fig) den Grund legen zu

founda'tion gar'ments spl Miederwaren pl

founda'tion wall' s Grundmauer f

founder ['faʊndər] s Gründer –in mf; (metal) Gießer –in mf ‖ tr intr (said of a ship) sinken; (fail) scheitern

foundling ['faʊndlɪŋ] s Findling m

foundry ['faʊndri] s Gießerei f

found'ry-man s (–men) Gießer m

fount [faʊnt] s Quelle f

fountain ['faʊntən] s Springbrunnen m

foun'tainhead' s Urquell m

foun'tain pen' s Füller m

four [fɔr] adj & pron vier ‖ s Vier f; **on all fours** auf allen vieren

four'-cy'cle adj (mach) Viertakt–

four'-en'gine adj viermotorig

fourflusher ['fɔr ,flʌʃər] s Angeber m

four'foot'ed adj vierfüßig

four' hun'dred adj & pron vierhundert ‖ spl—**the Four Hundred** die oberen Zehntausend

four'lane' adj Vierbahn–

four'-leaf' adj vierblätterig

four'-leg'ged adj vierbeinig

four'-letter word' s unanständiges Wort n

foursome ['fɔrsəm] s Viererspiel n; (group of four) Quartett n

fourteenth [for'tinθ] adj & pron vier-zehnte ‖ s (fraction) Vierzehntel n; **the f.** (in dates and in a series) der Vierzehnte

fourth [fɔrθ] adj & pron vierte ‖ s (fraction) Viertel n; **the f.** (in dates and in a series) der Vierte

fourth' estate' s Presse f

fowl [faʊl] s Huhn n, Geflügel n

fox [fɑks] s (& fig) Fuchs m

fox'glove' s (bot) Fingerhut m

fox'hole' s (mil) Schützenloch n

fox' hound' s Hetzhund m

fox' hunt' s Fuchsjagd f

fox' ter'rier s Foxterrier m

fox' trot' s Foxtrott m

foyer ['fɔɪ·ər] s (of a theater) Foyer n; (of a house) Diele f

fracas ['frekəs] s Aufruhr m

fraction ['frækʃən] s Bruchteil m; **fractions** Bruchrechnung f

fractional ['frækʃənəl] adj Bruch–

fracture ['fræktʃər] s Bruch m ‖ tr sich [dat] brechen

fragile ['frædʒɪl] adj zerbrechlich

fragment ['frægmənt] s Bruchstück n; (of writing) Fragment n

fragmentary ['frægmən ,teri] adj bruch-stückhaft; (writing) fragmentarisch

fragmenta'tion bomb' [,frægmən'te-ʃən] s Splitterbombe f

fragrance ['fregrəns] s Duft m

fragrant ['fregrənt] adj duftend; **be f.** duften

frail [frel] adj schwach, hinfällig; (fragile) zerbrechlich

frailty ['frelti] s Schwachheit f

frame [frem] s (e.g., of a picture, door) Rahmen m; (of glasses) Fassung f; (of a house) Balkenwerk n; (struc-ture) Gestell n; (anat) Körperbau m; (cin, telv) Bild n; (naut) Spant n ‖ tr (a picture) einrahmen; (a plan) ersinnen; (sl) reinhängen

frame' house' s Holzhaus n

frame' of mind' s Gemütsverfassung f

frame' of ref'erence s Bezugspunkte pl

frame'-up' s abgekartete Sache f

frame'work' s Gebälk n, Fachwerk n; (fig) Rahmen m; (aer) Aufbau m

franc [fræŋk] s Franc m; (Swiss) Franken m

France [fræns] s Frankreich n

Frances ['frænsɪs] s Franziska f

franchise ['fræntʃaɪz] s Konzession f; (right to vote) Wahlrecht n

Francis ['frænsɪs] s Franz m

Franciscan [fræn'sɪskən] adj Franzis-kaner– ‖ s Franziskaner m

frank [fræŋk] adj offen ‖ s Freiver-merk m; **Frank** (masculine name) Franz m; (medieval German person) Franke m, Frankin f ‖ tr franieren

frankfurter ['fræŋkfərtər] s Würstel n

frankincense ['fræŋkɪn ,sens] s Weih-rauch m

Frankish ['fræŋkɪʃ] adj fränkisch

frankness ['fræŋknɪs] s Offenheit f; (bluntness) Freimut m

frantic ['fræntɪk] adj (with) außer sich (vor dat); (efforts) krampfhaft

fraternal [frə'tʌrnəl] *adj* brüderlich; (*twins*) zweieiig

fraternity [frə'tʌrnɪti] *s* Bruderschaft *f*; (*educ*) Studentenverbindung *f*

fraternize ['frætər͵naɪz] *intr* (**with**) sich anfreunden (mit)

fraud [frɔd] *s* Betrug *m*; (*person*) (*coll*) Betrüger –in *mf*

fraudulent ['frɔdjələnt] *adj* betrügerisch

fraught [frɔt] *adj*—**f. with** voll mit; **f. with danger** gefahrvoll

fray [fre] *s* Schlägerei *f*; (*battle*) Kampf *m* || *tr* ausfranzen; (*the nerves*) aufreiben || *intr* (*said of edges*) sich ausfranzen; (*become threadbare*) sich durchscheuern

freak [frik] *s* Mißbildung *f*; (*whimsy*) Laune *f*; (*enthusiast*) Enthusiast –in *mf*; (*abnormal person*) verrückter Kerl *m*; **f. of nature** Monstrum *n*

freakish ['frikɪʃ] *adj* grotesk; (*capricious*) launisch

freckle ['frekəl] *s* Sommersprosse *f*

freckled ['frekəld], **freckly** ['frekli] *adj* sommersprossig

Frederick ['fredərɪk] *s* Friedrich *m*

free [fri] *adj* (**freer** ['fri·ər]; **freest** ['fri·ɪst]) frei; (*off duty*) dienstfrei; **for f.** (*coll*) gratis; **f. with** (*e.g., money, praise*) freigebig mit; **go f.** frei ausgehen; **he is f. to** (*inf*) es steht ihm frei zu (*inf*); **set f.** freilassen || *adv* umsonst, kostenlos || (*pret & pp* **freed** [frid]; *ger* **freeing** ['fri·ɪŋ]) *tr* (*liberate*) befreien; (*untie*) losmachen

free′ and **ea′sy** *adj* zwanglos

freebooter ['fri͵butər] *s* Freibeuter *m*

free′born′ *adj* freigeboren

freedom ['fridəm] *s* Freiheit *f*

free′dom of assem′bly *s* Versammlungsfreiheit *f*

free′dom of speech′ *s* Redefreiheit *f*

free′dom of the press′ *s* Pressefreiheit *f*

free′dom of wor′ship *s* Glaubensfreiheit *f*

free′ en′terprise *s* freie Wirtschaft *f*

free′-for-all′ *s* allgemeine Prügelei *f*

free′ hand′ *s* freie Hand *f*

free′-hand draw′ing *s* (*activity*) Freihandzeichnen *n*; (*product*) Freihandzeichnung *f*

free′hand′ed *adj* freigebig

free′hold′ *s* (*jur*) Freigut *n*

free′ kick′ *s* (fb) Freistoß *m*

free′-lance′ *adj* freiberuflich || *intr* freiberuflich tätig sein

free-lancer ['fri͵lænsər] *s* Freiberufliche *mf*

free′ li′brary *s* Volksbibliothek *f*

free′man *s* (-men) Ehrenbürger *m*

Free′ma′son *s* Freimaurer *m*

Free′ma′sonry *s* Freimaurerei *f*

free′ of charge′ *adj & adv* kostenlos

free′ on board′ *adv* frei an Bord

free′ play′ *s* (fig & mach) Spielraum *m*

free′ port′ *s* Freihafen *m*

free′ sam′ple *s* (*of food*) Gratiskostprobe *f*; (*of products*) Gratismuster *n*

free′ speech′ *s* Redefreiheit *f*

free′-spo′ken *adj* freimütig

free′stone′ *adj* mit leicht auslösbarem Kern

free′think′er *s* Freigeist *m*

free′ thought′ *s* Freigeisterei *f*

free′ trade′ *s* Freihandel *m*

free′way′ *s* Autobahn *f*

free′ will′ *s* Willensfreiheit *f*; **of one's own f.** aus freien Stücken

freeze [friz] *s*. Frieren *n* || *v* (*pret* **froze** [froz]; *pp* **frozen** ['frozən]) *tr* frieren; (*assets*) einfrieren; (*prices*) stoppen; (*food*) tiefkühlen; (surg) vereisen || *intr* (ge)frieren; (*e.g., with fear*) erstarren; **f. over** zufrieren; **f. to death** erfrieren; **f. up** vereisen

freeze′-dry′ *v* (*pret & pp* **-dried**) *tr* gefriertrocknen

freezer ['frizər] *s* (*chest*) Tiefkühltruhe *f*; (*cabinet*) Tiefkühlschrank *m*

freez′er compart′ment *s* Gefrierfach *n*

freez′ing *s* Einfrieren *n*; **below f.** unter dem Gefrierpunkt

freight [fret] *s* (*load*) Fracht *f*; (*cargo*) Frachtgut *n*; (*fee*) Frachtgebühr *f*; **by f.** als Frachtgut || *tr* beladen

freight′ car′ *s* Güterwagen *m*

freight′ el′evator *s* Warenaufzug *m*

freighter ['fretər] *s* Frachter *m*

freight′ of′fice *s* Güterabfertigung *f*

freight′ train′ *s* Güterzug *m*

freight′ yard′ *s* Güterbahnhof *m*

French [frentʃ] *adj* französisch || *s* (*language*) Französisch *n*; **the F.** die Franzosen

French′ doors′ *spl* Glastüre *pl*

French′ fries′ *spl* Pommes frites *pl*

French′ horn′ *s* (mus) Waldhorn *n*

French′ leave′ *s*—**take F.** sich französisch empfehlen

French′man *s* (-men) Franzose *m*

French′ roll′ *s* Schrippe *f*

French′ toast′ *s* arme Ritter *pl*

French′ win′dow *s* Flügelfenster *n*

French′ wom′an *s* (-wom′en) Französin *f*

frenzied ['frenzid] *adj* rasend

frenzy ['frenzi] *s* Raserei *f*

frequency ['frikwənsi] *s* Häufigkeit *f*; (*phys*) Frequenz *f*

fre′quency modula′tion *s* Frequenzmodulation *f*

frequent ['frikwənt] *adj* häufig || [fri'kwənt] *tr* besuchen, frequentieren

frequently ['frikwentli] *adv* häufig

fres·co ['fresko] *s* (**-coes & -cos**) Fresko *n*, Freskogemälde *n*

fresh [freʃ] *adj* frisch; (*coll*) frech || *adv* neu, kürzlich

fresh′-baked′ *adj* neugebacken

freshen ['freʃən] *tr* erfrischen; **f. up** auffrischen || *intr*—**f. up** sich auffrischen

freshet ['freʃɪt] *s* Hochwasser *n*; (*fresh-water stream*) Fluß *m*

fresh′man *s* (-men) Fuchs *m*

freshness ['freʃnɪs] *s* Frische *f*; (*coll*) Naseweisheit *f*

fresh′ wa′ter *s* Süßwasser *n*

fresh′-wa′ter *adj* Süßwasser-

fret [fret] *s* Verdruß *m*; (carp) Laubsägewerk *n*; (mus) Bund *n* || *v* (*pret*

& pp **fretted;** ger **fretting**) tr gitterförmig verzieren || intr sich ärgern

fretful ['fretfəl] adj verdrießlich

fret'work' s Laubsägewerk n

Freudian ['frɔɪdɪ-ən] adj Freudsch || s Freudianer –in mf

friar ['fraɪ-ər] s Klosterbruder m

fricassee [ˌfrɪkə'si] s Frikassee n

friction ['frɪk/ən] s Reibung f; (fig) Reiberei f, Mißhelligkeit f

fric'tion tape' s Isolierband n

Friday ['fraɪdi] s Freitag m

fried [fraɪd] adj gebraten, Brat-, Back-

fried' chick'en s Backhuhn n

fried' egg' s Spiegelei f

fried' pota'toes spl Bratkartoffeln pl

friend [frend] s Freund –in mf; **be (close) friends** (eng) befreundet sein; **make friends (with)** sich anfreunden (mit)

friendliness ['frendlɪnɪs] s Freundlichkeit f

friendly ['frendli] adj freundlich; **on f. terms with** in freundschaftlichem Verhältnis mit

friend'ship' s Freundschaft f

frieze [friz] s Fries m

frigate ['frɪgɪt] s Fregatte f

fright [fraɪt] s Schrecken m

frighten ['fraɪtən] tr schrecken; **be frightened** erschrecken; **f. away** verscheuchen, vertreiben

frightful ['fraɪtfəl] adj schrecklich

frigid ['frɪdʒɪd] adj eiskalt; (pathol) Frigid

frigidity [frɪ'dʒɪdɪti] s Kälte f; (pathol) Frigidität f

Frig'id Zone' s kalte Zone f

frill [frɪl] s (ruffle) Volant m, Krause f; (frippery) Schnörkel m; **put on frills** sich aufgeblasen benehmen; **with all the frills** mit allen Schikanen

fringe [frɪndʒ] s Franse f || tr mit Fransen besetzen; (fig) einsäumen

fringe' ar'ea s Randgebiet n

fringe' ben'efit s zusätzliche Sozialleistung f

frippery ['frɪpəri] s (cheap finery, trifles) Flitterkram m

frisk [frɪsk] tr (sl) durchsuchen || intr —f. about herumtollen

frisky ['frɪski] adj ausgelassen

fritter ['frɪtər] s Beignet m || tr—f. away vertrödeln, verzetteln

fritz [frɪts] s—on the f. kaputt

frivolous ['frɪvələs] adj leichtfertig; (object) geringfügig

friz [frɪz] s (frizzes) Kraushaar n || v (pret & pp **frizzed;** ger **frizzing**) tr kräuseln || intr sich kräuseln

frizzle ['frɪzəl] s Kraushaar n || tr (hair) kräuseln; (food) knusprig braten || intr sich kräuseln; (sizzle) zischen

frizzy ['frɪzi] adj kraus

fro [fro] adv—to and fro hin und her

frock [frɑk] s Kleid n; (eccl) Mönchskutte f

frog [frɑg] s (animal; slight hoarseness) Frosch m

frog'man' s (–men') Froschmann m

frol·ic ['frɑlɪk] s Spaß m || v (pret &

pp **–icked;** ger **–icking**) intr Spaß machen; (frisk about) herumtollen

frolicsome ['frɑlɪksəm] adj ausgelassen

from [frʌm] prep von (dat), aus (dat), von (dat) aus; **f. afar** von weitem; **f. now on** künftig; **f. . . . on** von . . . an

front [frʌnt] adj Vorder-, vordere || s (façade) Vorderseite f; (of a shirt, dress) Einsatz m; (cover-up) Aushängeschild n; (meteor, mil) Front f; **from the f.** von vorn; **in f.** vorn; **in f. of** vor (dat or acc); **in the f. of the book** vorn im Buch; **put on a bold f.** Mut zeigen; **they put on a big f.** alles Fassade! || tr gegenüberliegen (dat) || intr—**f. for s.o.** j–m als Strohmann dienen; **f. on** mit der Front liegen nach

frontage ['frʌntɪdʒ] s Straßenfront f

frontal ['frʌntəl] adj Frontal-; (anat) Stirn-

fron'tal view' s Vorderansicht f

front' door' s Haustür f

front' foot' s Vorderfuß m

frontier [frʌn'tɪr] s (border) Grenze f; (area) Grenzland n; (fig) Grenzbereich m

frontiers'man s (–men) Pionier m

frontispiece ['frʌntɪsˌpis] s Titelbild n

front' line' s Front f, Frontlinie f

front'-line' adj Front-, Gefechts-

front' page' s Titelseite f

front' porch' s Veranda f

front' rank' s (mil) vorderes Glied n; **be in the f.** (fig) im Vordergrund stehen

front' row' s erste Reihe f

front' run'ner s (pol) Spitzenkandidat –in mf

front' seat' s Vordersitz m

front' steps' spl Vordertreppe f

front' yard' s Vorgarten m, Vorplatz m

frost [frɔst] s (freezing) Frost m; (frozen dew) Reif m || tr mit Reif überziehen; (culin) glasieren

frost'bite' s Erfrierung f

frost'bit'ten adj erfroren

frost'ed glass' s Mattglas n

frost'ing s Glasur f

frost' line' s Frostgrenze f

frosty ['frɔsti] adj (& fig) frostig

froth [frɔθ] s (foam) Schaum m; (slaver) Geifer m || intr schäumen; geifern

frothy ['frɔθi] adj schäumend

froward ['frowərd] adj eigensinnig

frown [fraun] s Stirnrunzeln n || intr die Stirn runzeln; **f. at** böse anschauen; **f. on** mißbilligen

frowsy, frowzy ['frauzi] adj (slovenly) schlampig; (ill-smelling) muffig

froz'en as'sets ['frozən] spl eingefrorene Guthaben pl

froz'en foods' spl tiefgekühlte Lebensmittel pl

frugal ['frugəl] adj frugal

fruit [frut] adj (tree) Obst-, Südfrucht- || s Frucht f, Obst n, Südfrüchte pl; (fig) Frucht f

fruit' cake' s Stolle f, Stollen m

fruit′ cup′ s gemischte Früchte pl

fruit′ fly′ s Obstfliege f

fruitful [′frutfəl] adj fruchtbar

fruition [fru′ɪ/ən] s Reife f; **come to f.** zur Reife gelangen

fruit′ jar′ s Konservenglas n

fruit′ juice′ s Fruchtsaft m, Obstsaft m

fruitless [′frutlɪs] adj (& fig) fruchtlos

fruit′ sal′ad s Obstsalat m

fruit′ stand′ s Obststand m

frump [frʌmp] s Scharteke f

frumpish [′frʌmpɪ/] adj schlampig

frustrate [′frʌstret] tr (discourage) frustrieren; (an endeavor) vereiteln

frustration [frʌs′tre/ən] s Frustration f; (of an endeavor) Vereitelung f

fry [fraɪ] s Gebratenes n ‖ v (pret & pp fried) tr & intr braten

fry′ing pan′ s Bratpfanne f; **jump out of the f. into the flames** Öl ins Feuer gießen ‖ v (pret & pp fuel[l]ed) ger vom Regen unter die Traufe kommen

fuchsia [′fju/ə] s (bot) Fuchsie f

fudge [fʌdʒ] s weiches, milchhaltiges, mit Kakao versetztes Zuckerwerk n

fuel [′fju·əl] s Brennstoff m; (for engines) Treibstoff m; (fig) Nahrung f; **add f. to the flames** Öl ins Feuer gießen ‖ v (pret & pp fuel[l]ed) ger fuel[l]ing) tr mit Brennstoff versorgen ‖ intr tanken

fu′el dump′ s Treibstofflager n

fu′el gauge′ s Benzinuhr f

fu′el tank′ s Treibstoffbehälter m

fugitive [′fjudʒɪtɪv] adj flüchtig ‖ s Flüchtling m

fugue [fjug] s (mus) Fuge f

ful·crum [′fʌlkrəm] s (-crums & -cra [krə]) Stützpunkt m, Drehpunkt m

fulfill [ful′fɪl] tr erfüllen

fulfillment [ful′fɪlmənt] s Erfüllung f

full [ful] adj voll; (with food) satt; (clothes) weit; (hour) ganz; (life) inhaltsreich; (voice) wohlklingend; (professor) ordentlich; **f. of** voller, voll von; **too f.** übervoll; **work f. time** ganztägig arbeiten ‖ adv—f. **well** sehr gut ‖ s—**in f.** voll, ganz ‖ tr (tex) walken

full′back′ s (fb) Außenverteidiger m

full′-blood′ed adj vollblütig

full-blown [′ful′blon] adj (flower) voll aufgeblüht; (fig) voll erblüht

full′-bod′ied adj (wine) stark, schwer

full′ dress′ s Gesellschaftsanzug m; (mil) Paradeanzug m

full′-dress′ adj Gala–, formell

full′-faced′ adj pausbackig; (portrait) mit voll zugewandtem Gesicht

full-fledged [′ful′fledʒd] adj richtiggehend

full-grown [′ful′gron] adj voll ausgewachsen

full′ house′ s (cards) Full house n; (theat) volles Haus n

full′-length′ adj (dress) in voller Größe; (portrait) lebensgroß; (movie) abendfüllend

full′ moon′ s Vollmond m

full′-page′ adj ganzseitig

full′ pay′ s volles Gehalt n

full′ profes′sor s Ordinarius m

full′-scale′ adj in voller Größe

full′-sized′ adj in natürlicher Größe

full′ speed′ adv auf höchsten Touren

full′ stop′ s (gram) Punkt m; **come to a f.** völlig stillstehen

full′ swing′ s—**in f.** in vollem Gange

full′ throt′tle s Vollgas n

full′ tilt′ adv auf höchsten Touren

full′-time′ adj ganztägig

full′ view′ s—**in f.** direkt vor den Augen

fully [′ful(l)i] adj völlig; **be f. booked** ausverkauft sein

fulsome [′fulsəm] adj (excessive) übermäßig; (offensive) widerlich

fumble [′fʌmbəl] tr (a ball) fallen lassen ‖ intr fummeln; **f. for** umherfühlen nach

fume [fjum] s Gas n, Dampf m ‖ intr dampfen; (smoke) rauchen; **f. with rage** vor Wut schnauben

fumigate [′fjumɪ‚get] tr ausräuchern

fun [fʌn] s Spaß m; **be (great) fun** (viel) Spaß machen; **for fun** zum Spaß; **for the fun of it** spaßeshalber; **have fun!** viel Spaß!; **make fun of** sich lustig machen über (acc); **poke fun at** witzeln über (acc)

function [′fʌŋk/ən] s Funktion f; (office) Amt n; (formal occasion) Feier f ‖ intr funktionieren; (officiate) fungieren

functional [′fʌŋk/ənəl] adj (practical) Zweck–, zweckmäßig; (disorder) funktionell, Funktions–

functionary [′fʌŋk/ə‚neri] s Funktionär –in mf

fund [fʌnd] s Fonds m; (fig) Vorrat m **funds** Geldmittel pl ‖ tr fundieren

fundamental [‚fʌndə′mentəl] adj grundlegend, Grund– ‖ s Grundbegriff m

fundamentalist [‚fʌndə′mentəlɪst] s Fundamentalist –in mf

fundamentally [‚fʌndə′mentəli] adv im Grunde, prinzipiell

funeral [′fjunərəl] adj Leichen–, Trauer–, Begräbnis– ‖ s Begräbnis n

fu′neral direc′tor s Bestattungsunternehmer –in mf

fu′neral home′ s Aufbahrungshalle f

fu′neral proces′sion s Trauergefolge n

fu′neral serv′ice s Trauergottesdienst m

fu′neral wreath′ s Totenkranz m

funereal [fju′nɪrɪ·əl] adj düster

fungus [′fʌŋɡəs] s (funguses & fungi [′fʌndʒaɪ]) Pilz m, Schwamm m

funicular [fju′nɪkjələr] s Drahtseilbahn f

funk [fʌŋk] s (fear) Mordsangst f; **be in a f.** niedergeschlagen sein

fun·nel [′fʌnəl] s Trichter m; (naut) Schornstein m ‖ v (pret & pp -nel[l]ed; ger -nel[l]ing) tr durch e–n Trichter gießen; (fig) (into) konzentrieren (auf acc)

funnies [′fʌnɪz] spl Witzseite f

funny [′fʌni] adj komisch; (strange, suspicious) sonderbar; **don′t try anything f.** mach mir keine Dummheiten!

fun′ny bone′ s Musikantenknochen m

fun′ny bus′iness s dunkle Geschäfte pl

fun′ny ide′as spl Flausen pl

fun'ny pa'per s Witzblatt n
fur [fʌr] adj (coat, collar) Pelz– ‖ s Pelz m; (on the tongue) Belag m
furbish ['fʌrbiʃ] tr aufputzen
furious ['fjuri·əs] adj (at) wütend (auf acc); **be f.** wüten
furl [fʌrl] tr zusammenrollen
fur'-lined' adj pelzgefüttert
furlong ['fʌrlɔŋ] s Achtelmeile f
furlough ['fʌrlo] s (mil) Urlaub m; **go on f.** auf Urlaub kommen ‖ tr beurlauben
furnace ['fʌrnis] s Ofen m
furnish ['fʌrniʃ] tr (a room) möblieren; (e.g., an office) ausstatten; (proof) liefern; (supply) (with) versehen (mit)
fur'nished room' s möbliertes Zimmer n
furnishings ['fʌrniʃiŋz] spl Ausstattung f
furniture ['fʌrnitʃər] s Möbel pl; **piece of f.** Möbelstück n
fur'niture store' s Möbelhandlung f
furor ['fjuror] s (rage) Wut f; (uproar) Furore f; (vogue) Mode f; **cause a f.** Furore machen
furrier ['fʌri·ər] s Pelzhändler –in mf
furrow ['fʌro] s Furche f ‖ tr furchen
furry ['fʌri] adj pelzig
further ['fʌrðər] adj weiter; (particulars) näher ‖ adv weiter ‖ tr fördern
furtherance ['fʌrðərəns] s Förderung f
fur'thermore' adv überdies, außerdem
furthest ['fʌrðist] adj weiteste ‖ adv **am weitesten**
furtive ['fʌrtiv] adj verstohlen

fury ['fjuri] s Wut f; **Fury** (myth) Furie f
fuse [fjuz] s (of an explosive) Zünder m; (elec) Sicherung f; **blown f.** durchgebrannte Sicherung f ‖ tr verschmelzen ‖ intr verschmelzen; (fig) sich vereinigen
fuse' box' s Sicherungskasten m
fuselage ['fjuzəlidʒ] s (aer) Rumpf m
fusible ['fjuzibəl] adj schmelzbar
fusillade ['fjusə‚led] s Feuersalve f; (fig) Hagel m
fusion ['fjuʒən] s Verschmelzung f; (pol, phys) Fusion f
fuss [fʌs] s Getue n; **make a f. over** viel Aufhebens machen von ‖ intr sich aufregen; **f. around** herumwirtschaften; **f. over** viel Aufhebens machen von; **f. with** herumspielen mit
fuss' bud'get, fuss'pot' s Umstandskrämer m
fussy ['fʌsi] adj (given to detail) umständlich; (fastidious) heikel; (irritable) reizbar; **be f.** Umstände machen
fustian ['fʌstʃən] s (bombast) Schwulst m; (tex) Barchent m
fusty ['fʌsti] adj (musty) muffig; (old-fashioned) veraltet
futile ['fjutəl] adj vergeblich, nutzlos
futility [fju'tɪlɪti] s Nutzlosigkeit f
future ['fjutʃər] adj (zu)künftig ‖ s Zukunft f; **futures** (econ) Termingeschäfte pl; **in the f.** künftig
fuzz [fʌz] s (from cloth) Fussel f; (on peaches) Flaum m
fuzzy ['fʌzi] adj flaumig; (unclear) unklar; (hair) kraus

G

G, g [dʒi] s siebenter Buchstabe des englischen Alphabets
gab [gæb] s (coll) Geschwätz n ‖ v (pret & pp gabbed; ger gabbing) intr schwatzen
gabardine ['gæbər‚din] s Gabardine m
gabble ['gæbəl] s Geschnatter n ‖ intr schnattern
gable ['gebəl] s Giebel m
ga'ble end' s Giebelwand f
ga'ble roof' s Giebeldach n
gad [gæd] v (pret & pp gadded; ger gadding) intr—**gad about** umherstreifen
gad'about' s Bummler –in mf
gad'fly' s Viehbremse f; (fig) Störenfried m
gadget ['gædʒit] s (coll) Gerät n
Gaelic ['gelɪk] adj gälisch ‖ s (language) Gälisch n
gaff [gæf] s Fischhaken m
gag [gæg] s (something put into the mouth) Knebel m; (joke) Witz m; (hoax, trick) amüsanter Trick m ‖ v (pret & pp gagged; ger gagging) tr knebeln; (said of a tight collar) würgen; (fig) mundtot machen ‖ intr (on food) würgen

gage [gedʒ] s (challenge) Fehdehandschuh m; (pawn) Pfand m
gaiety ['ge·ɪti] s Fröhlichkeit f
gaily ['geli] adv fröhlich
gain [gen] s Gewinn m; (advantage) Vorteil m; **g. in weight** Gewichtszunahme f ‖ tr gewinnen; (pounds) zunehmen; (a living) verdienen; (a victory) erringen; **g. a footing** festen Fuß fassen; **g. ground** (mil & fig) Terrain gewinnen; **g. speed** schneller werden; **g. weight** an Gewicht zunehmen ‖ intr (said of a car) aufholen; (said of a clock) vorgehen; **g. from** Gewinn haben von; **g. in** gewinnen an (dat); **g. on s.o.** j–m den Vorteil abgewinnen
gainful ['genfəl] adj einträglich
gainfully ['genfəli] adv—**g. employed** erwerbstätig
gain'say' v (pret & pp –said [‚sed], [‚sed]) tr (a thing) verneinen; (a person) widersprechen (dat)
gait [get] s Gang m, Gangart f
gala ['gælə], ['gelə] adj festlich ‖ s (celebration) Feier f; (dress) Gala f
galaxy ['gæləksi] s Galaxis f; (fig) glänzende Versammlung f

gale [gel] s Sturm m, Sturmwind m; gales of laughter Lachensalven pl

gale' warn'ing s Sturmwarnung f

gall [gol] s Galle f; (audacity) Unverschämtheit f || tr (rub) wundreiben; (vex) ärgern, belästigen

gallant ['gælənt] adj (tapfer); (stately) stattlich || [gə'lænt] adj galant || s Galan m

gallantry ['gæləntri] s (bravery) Tapferkeit f; (courteous behavior) Ritterlichkeit f

gall' blad'der s Gallenblase f

galleon ['gælɪ-ən] s Galeone f

gallery ['gæləri] s (arcade) Säulenhalle f; (art, theat) Galerie f; (min) Stollen m; play to the g. (coll) Effekthascherei treiben

galley ['gæli] s (a ship) Galeere f; (a kitchen) Kombüse f; (typ) Setzschiff n

gal'ley proof' s (typ) Fahne f

gal'ley slave' s Galeerensklave m

Gallic ['gælɪk] adj gallisch

gall'ing adj verdrießlich

gallivant ['gælɪˌvænt] intr bummeln

gallon ['gælən] s Gallone f

galloon [gə'lun] s Tresse f

gallop ['gæləp] s Galopp m; at full g. in gestrecktem Galopp || tr in Galopp setzen || intr galoppieren

gal·lows ['gæloz] s (–lows & –lowses) Galgen m

gal'lows bird' s (coll) Galgenvogel m

gall'stone' s Gallenstein m

galore [gə'lor] adv im Überfluß

galosh [gə'lɑʃ] s Galosche f

galvanize ['gælvəˌnaɪz] tr galvanisieren

gambit ['gæmbɪt] s (fig) Schachzug m; (chess) Gambit n

gamble ['gæmbəl] s Hasardspiel n; (risk) Risiko n; (com) Spekulationsgeschäft n || tr—g. away verspielen || intr spielen, hasardieren

gambler ['gæmblər] s Spieler –in mf; (fig) Hasardeur m, Hasardeuse f

gam'bling s Spielen n, Spiel n

gam'bling house' s Spielhölle f

gam'bling ta'ble s Spieltisch m

gam·bol ['gæmbəl] s Luftsprung m || v (pret & pp —bol[l]ed; ger —bol[l]ing) intr umhertollen

gambrel ['gæmbrəl] s (hock) Hachse f; (in a butcher shop) Spriegel m

gam'brel roof' s Mansardendach n

game [gem] adj bereit; (fight) tapfer; (leg) lahm; (hunt) Wild–, Jagd– || s Spiel n; (e.g., of chess) Partie f; (fig) Absicht f; (culin) Wildbret n; (hunt) Wild n, Jagdwild n; have the g. in the bag den Sieg in der Tasche haben; play a losing g. auf verlorenem Posten kämpfen; the g. is up das Spiel ist aus

game' bird' s Jagdvogel m

game' board' s Spielbrett n

game'cock' s Kampfhahn m

gameness ['gemnɪs] f Tapferkeit f

game' of chance' s Glücksspiel n

game' preserve' s Wildpark m

game' war'den s Jagdaufseher m

gamut ['gæmət] s Skala f

gamy ['gemi] adj nach Wild riechend; g. flavor Wildgeschmack m

gander ['gændər] s Gänserich m; take a g. at (coll) e–n Blick werfen auf (acc)

gang [gæŋ] s (group of friends) Gesellschaft f; (antisocial group) Bande f; (of workers) Kolonne f || intr— g. up (on) sich zusammenrotten (gegen)

gangling ['gæŋglɪŋ] adj schlaksig

gangli·on ['gæŋglɪ-ən] s (–ons & –a [ə]) (cystic tumor) Überbein n; (of nerves) Nervenknoten m

gangly ['gæŋgli] adj schlaksig

gang'plank' s Laufplanke f, Steg m

gangrene ['gæŋgrin] s Gangrän n, Brand m || intr brandig werden

gangrenous ['gæŋgrɪnəs] adj brandig

gangster ['gæŋstər] s Gangster m

gang'way' s (passageway) Durchgang m; (naut) Laufplanke f || interj aus dem Weg!

gantlet ['gɔntlət] s (rr) Gleisverschlingung f

gantry ['gæntri] s (rok) Portalkran m; (rr) Signalbrücke f

gan'try crane' s Portalkran m

gap [gæp] s Lücke f; (in the mountains) Schlucht f; (mil) Bresche f

gape [gep] s Riß m, Sprung m; (gaping) Gaffen n || intr gaffen; (said of wounds, etc.) klaffen; g. at angaffen

garage [gə'rɑʒ] s Garage f; (repair shop) Reparaturwerkstatt f; put into the g. unterstellen

garb [gɑrb] s Tracht f

garbage ['gɑrbɪdʒ] s Müll m; (nonsense) Unsinn m

gar'bage can' s Mülltonne f

gar'bage dispos'al s Müllabfuhr f

gar'bage dump' s Müllplatz m

gar'bage man' s Müllfahrer m

gar'bage truck' s Müllabfuhrwagen m

garble ['gɑrbəl] tr verstümmeln

garden ['gɑrdən] s Garten m; gardens Gartenanlage f

gardener ['gɑrdənər] s Gärtner –in mf

gar'den hose' s Gartenschlauch m

gardenia [gɑr'din-ə] s Gardenie f

gar'dening s Gartenarbeit f

gar'den par'ty s Gartengesellschaft f

gargle ['gɑrgəl] s Mundwasser n || tr & intr gurgeln

gargoyle ['gɑrgɔɪl] s Wasserspeier m

garish ['gerɪʃ], ['gærɪʃ] adj grell

garland ['gɑrlənd] s Girlande f

garlic ['gɑrlɪk] s Knoblauch m

garment ['gɑrmənt] s Kleidungsstück n

garner ['gɑrnər] tr (grain) aufspeichern; (gather) ansammeln

garnet ['gɑrnɪt] s Granat m

garnish ['gɑrnɪʃ] s Verzierung f; (culin) Garnierung f || tr verzieren; (culin) garnieren

garret ['gærɪt] s Dachstube f

garrison ['gærɪsən] s (troops) Garnison f, Besatzung f; (fort) Festung f || tr mit e–r Garnison versehen; (troops) in Garnison stationieren

gar'rison cap' s Schiffchen n

garrote [gə'rɑt], [gə'rot] s Garrotte f || tr garrottieren

garrulous ['gær(j)ələs] *adj* schwatzhaft
garter ['gɑrtər] *s* Strumpfband *n*
gar'ter belt' *s* Strumpfhaltergürtel *m*
gas [gæs] *adj* (*e.g., generator, light, main, meter*) Gas– ‖ *s* Gas *n*; (coll) Benzin *n*, Sprit *m*; (*empty talk*) (sl) leeres Geschwätz *n*; **get gas** (coll) tanken; **step on the gas** (coll) Gas geben ‖ *v* (*pret & pp* **gassed**; *ger* **gassing**) *tr* vergasen ‖ *intr* (sl) schwatzen; **gas up** (coll) volltanken
gas' attack' *s* Gasangriff *m*
gas' burn'er *s* Gasbrenner *m*
gas' en'gine *s* Gasmotor *m*
gaseous ['gæsɪ-əs], ['gæ/əs] *adj* gasförmig
gas' fit'ter *s* Gasinstallateur *m*
gash [gæʃ] *s* tiefe Schnittwunde *f* ‖ e–e tiefe Schnittwunde beibringen (*dat*)
gas' heat' *s* Gasheizung *f*
gas'hold'er *s* Gasbehälter *m*
gasi·fy ['gæsɪ‚faɪ] *v* (*pret & pp* –**fied**) *tr* in Gas verwandeln ‖ *intr* zu Gas werden
gas' jet' *s* Gasflamme *f*
gasket ['gæskɪt] *s* Dichtung *f*
gas' mask' *s* Gasmaske *f*
gasoline [‚gæsə'lin] *s* Benzin *n*
gasoline' pump' *s* Benzinzapfsäule *f*
gasp [gæsp] *s* Keuchen *n* ‖ *tr* (out) hervorstoßen ‖ *intr* keuchen; **g. for air** nach Luft schnappen; **g. for breath** nach Atem ringen
gas' range' *s* Gasherd *m*
gas' sta'tion *s* Tankstelle *f*
gas' sta'tion attend'ant *s* Tankwart *m*
gas' stove' *s* Gasherd *m*
gas' tank' *s* Benzinbehälter *m*
gastric ['gæstrɪk] *adj* gastrisch
gas'tric juice' *s* Magensaft *m*
gastronomy [gæs'trɑnəmɪ] *s* Gastronomie *f*
gas'works' *spl* Gasanstalt *f*
gate [get] *s* Tor *n*, Pforte *f*; (rr) Sperre *f*; (sport) eingenommenes Eintrittsgeld *n*; **crash the g.** ohne Eintrittskarte durchschlupfen
gate' crash'er [‚kræʃər] *s* unberechtigter Zuschauer *m*
gate'keep'er *s* Pförtner –in *mf*
gate'post' *s* Torpfosten *m*
gate'way' *s* Tor *n*, Torweg *m*
gather ['gæðər] *tr* (*things*) sammeln; (*people*) versammeln; (*flowers, fruit, peas*) pflücken; (*courage*) aufbringen; (*the impression*) gewinnen; (*information*) einziehen; (*strength, speed*) zunehmen an (*dat*); (*conclude*) (from) schließen (aus); **g. together** versammeln; **g. up** aufheben; (*curtains, dress*) raffen ‖ *intr* sich (an)sammeln; (*said of clouds*) sich zusammenziehen; **g. around** sich scharen um
gath'ered *adj* (*skirt*) gerafft
gath'ering *s* Versammlung *f*; (sew) Kräuselfalten *pl*
gaudy ['gɔdɪ] *adj* (*overdone*) überladen; (*color*) grell
gauge [gedʒ] *s* (*instrument*) Messer *m*, Anzeiger *m*; (*measurement*) Eichmaß *n*; (*of wire*) Stärke *f*; (*of a shot-*

gun) Kaliber *n*; (fig) Maß *n*; (mach) Lehre *f*; (rr) Spurweite *f* ‖ *tr* messen; (*check for accuracy*) eichen; (fig) abschätzen
Gaul [gɔl] *s* Gallien *n*; (*native*) Gallier –in *mf*
Gaulish ['gɔlɪ/] *adj* gallisch
gaunt [gɔnt] *adj* hager
gauntlet ['gɔntlɪt] *s* Panzerhandschuh *m*; (fig) Fehdehandschuh *m*; **run the g.** Spießruten laufen
gauze [gɔz] *s* Gaze *f*
gavel ['gævəl] *s* Hammer *m*
gawk [gɔk] *s* (coll) Depp *m* ‖ *intr*—**g. at** (coll) blöde anstarren
gawky ['gɔkɪ] *adj* schlaksig
gay [ge] *adj* lustig; (*homosexual*) schwul
gay' blade' *s* lebenslustiger Kerl *m*
gaze [gez] *intr* starren; **g. at** anstarren; (*in astonishment*) anstaunen
gazelle [gə'zɛl] *s* Gazelle *f*
gazetteer [‚gæzə'tɪr] *s* Ortslexikon *n*
gear [gɪr] *s* (*equipment*) Ausrüstung *f*; (aut) Schaltgetriebe *n*, Gang *m*; (mach) Zahnrad *n*; **gears** Räderwerk *n*; **in g.** eingeschaltet; **in high g.** im höchsten Gang; (fig) auf Touren; **shift gears** umschalten; **throw into g.** einschalten; **throw out of g.** (fig) aus dem Gleichgewicht bringen ‖ *tr*—**g. to** anpassen (*dat*)
gear'box' *s* Schaltgetriebe *n*
gear'shift' *s* Gangschaltung *f*; (*lever*) Schalthebel *m*
gear'wheel' *s* Zahnrad *n*
gee [dʒi] *interj* nanu!
Geiger counter ['gaɪgər‚kauntər] *s* Geigerzähler *m*
gel [dʒɛl] *s* Gel *n* ‖ *v* (*pret & pp* **gelled**; *ger* **gelling**) *intr* gelieren; (coll) klappen
gelatin ['dʒɛlətɪn] *s* Gelatine *f*
geld [gɛld] *v* (*pret & pp* **gelded & gelt** [gɛlt]) *tr* kastrieren
geld'ing *s* Wallach *m*
gem [dʒɛm] *s* Edelstein *m*; (fig) Perle *f*
Gemini ['dʒɛmɪ‚naɪ] *s* (astr) Zwillinge *pl*
gender ['dʒɛndər] *s* Geschlecht *n*
gene [dʒin] *s* Gen *n*, Erbanlage *f*
genealogical [‚dʒinɪ·ə'lɑdʒɪkəl] *adj* genealogisch, Stamm–
genealog'ical ta'ble *s* Stammtafel *f*
genealog'ical tree' *s* Stammbaum *m*
genealogy [‚dʒinɪ'ælədʒɪ] *s* Genealogie *f*
general ['dʒɛnərəl] *adj* allgemein, Gesamt– ‖ *s* General *m*; **in g.** im allgemeinen
Gen'eral Assem'bly *s* Vollversammlung *f*
gen'eral deliv'ery *adv* postlagernd
gen'eral head'quarters *spl* Oberkommando *n*
generalissi·mo [‚dʒɛnərə'lɪsɪmo] *s* (–**mos**) Generalissimus *m*
generality [‚dʒɛnə'rælɪtɪ] *s* Allgemeingültigkeit *f*; **generalities** Gemeinplätze *pl*
generalization [‚dʒɛnərəlɪ'zeʃən] *s* Verallgemeinerung *f*

generalize ['dʒenərə‚laɪz] *tr* & *intr* verallgemeinern

generally ['dʒenərəli] *adv* im allgemeinen; (*usually*) gewöhnlich; (*mostly*) meistens

gen'eral man'ager *s* Generaldirektor –in *mf*

gen'eral plan' *s* Übersichtsplan *m*

gen'eral post' of'fice *s* Oberpostamt *n*

gen'eral practi'tioner *s* praktischer Arzt *m*

gen'eralship' *s* Führereingenschaften *pl*

gen'eral staff' *s* Generalstab *m*

gen'eral store' *s* Gemischtwarenhandlung *f*

gen'eral strike' *s* Generalstreik *m*

generate ['dʒenə‚ret] *tr* (*procreate*) zeugen; (fig) verursachen; (elec) erzeugen; (geom) bilden

gen'erating sta'tion *s* Kraftwerk *n*

generation [‚dʒenə're/ən] *s* Generation *f*; **present g.** Mitwelt *f*; **younger g.** junge Generation *f*

genera'tion gap' *s* Generationsproblem *n*

generator ['dʒenə‚retər] *s* Erzeuger *m*; (chem, elec) Generator *m*; (elec) Stromerzeuger *m*

generic [dʒɪ'nerɪk] *adj* generisch, Gattungs–; **g. name** Gattungsname *m*

generosity [‚dʒenə'rɑsɪti] *s* Freigebigkeit *f*

generous ['dʒenərəs] *adj* freigebig

gene·sis ['dʒenɪsɪs] *s* (–ses [‚siz]) Genese *f*, Entstehung *f*; **Genesis** (Bib) Genesis *f*

genetic [dʒɪ'netɪk] *adj* genetisch

genet'ic engineer' *s* Gen-Ingenieur *m*

genet'ic engineer'ing *s* Gen-Manipulation *f*

genetics [dʒɪ'netɪks] *s* Genetik *f*, Vererbungslehre *f*

Geneva [dʒɪ'nivə] *adj* Genfer ‖ *s* Genf *n*

Genevieve ['dʒenə‚viv] *s* Genoveva *f*

genial ['dʒinɪ·əl] *adj* freundlich

genie ['dʒini] *s* Kobold *m*

genital ['dʒenɪtəl] *adj* Genital– ‖ **genitals** *spl* Genitalien *pl*

genitive ['dʒenɪtɪv] *s* Genitiv *m*, Wesfall *m*

genius ['dʒinɪ·əs] *s* (**geniuses**) Genie *n* ‖ *s* (**genii** ['dʒinɪ‚aɪ]) Genius *m*

Genoa ['dʒeno·ə] *s* Genua *n*

genocidal [‚dʒeno'saɪdəl] *adj* rassenmörderisch

genocide ['dʒeno‚saɪd] *s* Rassenmord *m*

genre ['ʒɑnrə] *s* Genre *n*

genteel [dʒen'til] *adj* vornehm

gentile ['dʒentaɪl] *adj* nichtjüdisch; (*pagan*) heidnisch ‖ *s* Nichtjude *m*, Nichtjüdin *f*; (*pagan*) Heide *m*, Heidin *f*

gentility [dʒen'tɪlɪti] *s* Vornehmheit *f*

gentle ['dʒentəl] *adj* sanft, mild; (*tame*) zahm

gen'tle·man *s* (–men) Herr *m*, Gentleman *m*

gentlemanly ['dʒentəlmənli] *adj* weltmännisch

gen'tleman's agree'ment *s* Kavaliersab-

kommen *n*, Gentleman's Agreement *n*

gentleness ['dʒentəlnɪs] *s* Sanftmut *f*

gen'tle sex' *s* zartes Geschlecht *n*

gentry ['dʒentri] *s* feine Leute *pl*

genuflection [‚dʒenjʊ'flek/ən] *s* Kniebeugung *f*

genuine ['dʒenjʊ·ɪn] *adj* echt

genus ['dʒinəs] *s* (**genera** ['dʒenərə] & **genuses**) (biol, log) Gattung *f*

geographer [dʒɪ'ɑgrəfər] *s* Geograph –in *mf*

geographic(al) [‚dʒi·ə'græfɪk(əl)] *adj* geographisch

geography [dʒɪ'ɑgrəfi] *s* Geographie *f*

geologic(al) [‚dʒi·ə'lɑdʒɪk(əl)] *adj* geologisch

geolog'ical e'ra *s* Erdalter *n*

geologist [dʒɪ'ɑlədʒɪst] *s* Geologe *m*, Geologin *f*

geology [dʒɪ'ɑlədʒi] *s* Geologie *f*

geometric(al) [‚dʒi·ə'metrɪk(əl)] *adj* geometrisch

geometrician [dʒɪ‚ɑmɪ'trɪ/ən] *s* Geometer –in *mf*

geometry [dʒɪ'ɑmɪtri] *s* Geometrie *f*

geophysics [‚dʒi·ə'fɪzɪks] *s* Geophysik *f*

geopolitics [‚dʒi·ə'pɑlɪtɪks] *s* Geopolitik *f*

George [dʒɔrdʒ] *s* Georg *m*

geranium [dʒɪ'renɪ·əm] *s* Geranie *f*

geriatrics [‚dʒerɪ'ætrɪks] *s* Geriatrie *f*

germ [dʒʌrm] *s* Keim *m*

German ['dʒʌrmən] *adj* & *adv* deutsch ‖ *s* Deutsche *mf*; (*language*) Deutsch *n*; **in G.** auf deutsch

germane [dʒer'men] *adj* (**to**) passend (zu)

Germanize ['dʒʌrmə‚naɪz] *tr* eindeutschen

Ger'man mea'sles *s* & *spl* Röteln *pl*

Ger'man shep'herd *s* deutscher Schäferhund *m*

Ger'man sil'ver *s* Alpaka *n*, Neusilber *n*

Germany ['dʒʌrməni] *s* Deutschland *n*

germ' cell' *s* Keimzelle *f*

germicidal [‚dʒʌrmɪ'saɪdəl] *adj* keimtötend

germicide ['dʒʌrmɪ‚saɪd] *s* Keimtöter *m*

germinate ['dʒʌrmɪ‚net] *intr* keimen

germ' war'fare *s* bakteriologische Kriegsführung *f*

gerontology [‚dʒerən'tɑlədʒi] *s* Gerontologie *f*

gerund ['dʒerənd] *s* Gerundium *n*

gerundive [dʒɪ'rʌndɪv] *s* Gerundiv *n*

gestation [dʒes'te/ən] *s* Schwangerschaft *f*; (*in animals*) Trächtigkeit *f*

gesticulate [dʒes'tɪkjə‚let] *intr* gestikulieren, sich gebärden

gesticulation [dʒes‚tɪkjə'le/ən] *s* Gebärdenspiel *n*, Gestikulation *f*

gesture ['dʒest/ər] *s* Geste *f* ‖ *intr* Gesten machen

get [get] *v* (*pret* **got** [gɑt]; *pp* **got** & **gotten** ['gɑtən]; *ger* **getting**) *tr* (*acquire*) bekommen; (*receive*) erhalten; (*procure*) beschaffen, besorgen; (*fetch*) holen; (*understand*) (coll) kapieren; (*s.o. to do s.th.*) dazu

bringen; *(reach by telephone)* erreichen; *(make, e.g., dirty)* machen;
(convey, e.g., a message) übermitteln; **get across** klarmachen; **get back**
zurückbekommen; **get down** *(depress)* verdrießen; *(swallow)* hin-
unterwürgen; **get going** in Gang setzen; **get hold of** *(a person)* erwischen; *(a thing)* erlangen; *(grip)*
ergreifen; **get off** *(e.g., a lid)* ab-
bekommen; **get one's way** sich durchsetzen; **get out** *(e.g., a spot)* heraus-
bekommen; **get s.o. used to** j–n gewöhnen an *(acc)*; **get s.th. into one's
head** sich *dat* etw in den Kopf setzen; **get the hang of** *(coll)* wegbe-
kommen; **get the jump on s.o.** j–m
zuvorkommen; **get the worst of** it
am schlechtesten dabei wegkommen;
get *(s.th.)* **wrong** falsch verstehen;
you're going to get it! *(coll)* du wirst
es kriegen! || *intr* *(become)* werden;
get about sich fortbewegen; **get
ahead in the world** in der Welt fort-
kommen; **get along** auskommen; **get
along with** zurechtkommen mit; **get
around** herumkommen; **get around
to it** dazu kommen; **get at** herankom-
men an *(acc)*; *(e.g., the real reason)*
herausfinden; **get away** *(run away)*
entlaufen; *(escape)* entkommen; **get
away from me!** geh weg von mir!;
get away with davonkommen mit;
get back at s.o. es j–m heimzahlen;
get by *(e.g., the guards)* vorbeikommen an *(dat)*; *(on little money)*
durchkommen; **get down** *(step
down)* absteigen; **get down to brass
tacks** *(or business)* zur Sache kommen; **get going** sich auf den Weg
machen; **get going!** mach, daß du
weiter kommst!; **get into** *(a vehicle)*
einsteigen in *(acc)*; *(trouble, etc.)*
geraten in *(acc)*; **get loose** sich losmachen; **get lost** verloren gehen, abhanden kommen; *(lose one's way)*
sich verirren; **get lost!** *(sl)* hau ab!;
get off aussteigen; **get off with** *(a
light sentence)* davonkommen mit;
get on *(e.g., a train)* einsteigen (in
acc); **get on one's feet again** sich
hochrappeln; **get on with** *(s.o.)* zurechtkommen mit; **get out** aussteigen;
get out of a tight spot sich aus der
Schlinge ziehen; **get over** *(a hurdle)*
nehmen; *(a misfortune)* überwinden;
(a sickness) überstehen; **get ready**
sich fertig machen; **get through**
durchkommen; **get through to s.o.**
sich verständlich machen *(dat)*; *(telp)*
erreichen; **get to be** werden; **get together** *(meet)* sich treffen; *(agree)*
(on) sich einig werden (über *acc*);
get to the bottom of ergründen; **get
up** aufstehen; **get used to** sich gewöhnen an *(acc)*; **get well** gesund
werden; **get with it!** *(coll)* zur
Sache!

get'away' s Entkommen *n*; *(sport)*
Start *m*; **make one's g.** entkommen
get'away car' s Fluchtwagen *m*
get'-togeth'er s zwangloses Treffen *n*
get'up' s *(coll)* Aufzug *m*

get' up' and go' s Unternehmungsgeist
m
gewgaw ['g(j)uɡə] s Plunder *m*
geyser ['ɡaɪzə] s Geiser *m*
ghastly | 'ɡæstlɪ] *adj* *(ghostly)* gespen-
stisch; *(e.g., crime)* grausig; *(in-
tensely unpleasant)* schrecklich
gherkin | 'ɡʌrkɪn] s Essiggurke *f*
ghet•to ['ɡɛto] s *(-tos)* Getto *n*
ghost [ɡost] s Gespenst *n*, Geist *m*;
(telv) Doppelbild *n*; **give up the g.**
den Geist aufgeben; **not a g. of a
chance** nicht die geringsten Aussichten
ghostly ['ɡostlɪ] *adj* gespenstisch
ghost' sto'ry s Spukgeschichte *f*
ghost' town' s Geisterstadt *f*
ghost' writ'er s Ghostwriter *m*
ghoul |ɡul] s *(& fig)* Unhold *m*
ghoulish | 'ɡulɪ| *adj* teuflisch
GHQ | 'dʒi'et|'kju| s **(General Head-
quarters)** Oberkommando *n*
GI | 'dʒi'a | s **(GI's)** *(coll)* Landser *m*
giant ['dʒaɪ.ənt] *adj* riesig, Riesen– ||
s Riese *m*, Riesin *f*
giantess | 'dʒaɪ.əntɪs] s Riesin *f*
gibberish | 'dʒɪbərɪʃ], | 'ɡɪbərɪʃ] s
Klauderwelsch *f*
gibbet | 'dʒɪbɪt] s Galgen *m* || *tr* hän-
gen
gibe [dʒaɪb] s Spott *m* || *intr* spotten;
g. at verspotten
giblets | 'dʒɪblɪts] *spl* Gänseklein *n*
giddiness | 'ɡɪdɪnɪs] s Schwindelgefühl
n; *(frivolity)* Leichtsinn *m*
giddy | 'ɡɪdɪ] *adj* *(dizzy)* schwindlig;
(height) schwindelerregend; *(frivolous)* leichtsinnig
gift [ɡɪft] s Geschenk *n*; *(natural ability)* Begabung *f*
gift'ed *adj* begabt
gift'horse' s—**never look a g. in the
mouth** e–m geschenkten Gaul schaut
man nicht ins Maul
gift' of gab' s *(coll)* gutes Mundwerk *n*
gift' shop' s Geschenkartikelladen *m*
gift'-wrap' v *(pret & pp* –**wrapped***; ger*
–**wrapping)** *tr* als Geschenk verpacken
gift'wrap'ping s Geschenkverpackung
f
gigantic [dʒaɪ'ɡæntɪk] *adj* riesig
giggle | 'ɡɪɡəl] s Gekicher *n* || *intr*
kichern
gigly | 'ɡɪɡlɪ] *adj* allezeit kichernd
gigo•lo | 'dʒɪɡə.lo] s *(-los)* Gigolo *m*
gild [ɡɪld] v *(pret & pp* gilded & gilt
[ɡɪlt]) *tr* vergolden
gild'ing s Vergoldung *f*
gill [ɡɪl] s *(of a fish)* Kieme *f*; *(of a
cock)* Kehllappen *m*
gilt [ɡɪlt] *adj* vergoldet || s Vergol-
dung *f*
gilt' edge' s Goldschnitt *m*
gilt'-edged' *adj* mit Goldschnitt versehen; *(first-class)* *(coll)* erstklassig
gimlet | 'ɡɪmlɪt] s Handbohrer *m*
gimmick | 'ɡɪmɪk] s *(sl)* Trick *m*
gin [dʒɪn] s Wacholderbranntwein *m*,
Gin *m*; *(snare)* Schlinge *f* || *v* *(pret
& pp* ginned; *ger* ginning) *tr* ent-
körnen
ginger | 'dʒɪndʒər] s Ingwer *m*

gin'ger ale' s Ingwerlimonade f

gin'gerbread' s Pfefferkuchen m

gingerly ['dʒɪndʒərli] adv sacht(e)

gin'gersnap' s Ingwerplätzchen n

gingham ['gɪŋəm] s Gingham m

giraffe [dʒɪ'ræf] s Giraffe f

gird [gʌrd] v (pret & pp girt [gʌrt] & girded) tr gürten; g. oneself with a sword sich [dat] ein Schwert umgürten

girder ['gʌrdər] s Tragbalken m

girdle ['gʌrdəl] s Gürtel m

girl [gʌrl] s Mädchen n, Mädel n

girl' friend' s Freundin f, Geliebte f

girl'hood' s Mädchenzeit f

girlish ['gʌrlɪʃ] adj mädchenhaft

girl' scout' s Pfadfinderin f

girth [gʌrθ] s Umfang m; (for a horse) Sattelgurt m

gist [dʒɪst] s Kernpunkt m; g. of the matter des Pudels Kern

give [gɪv] s Elastizität f; (yielding) Nachgeben n ‖ v (pret gave [gev]; pp given ['gɪvən]) tr geben; (a gift, credence) schenken; (free of charge) verschenken; (contribute) spenden; (hand over) übergeben; (a report) erstatten; (a reason, the time) angeben; (attention, recognition) zollen; (a lecture) halten; (an award) zusprechen; (homework) aufgeben; (a headache, etc.) verursachen; (joy) machen; (a reception) veranstalten; (a blow) versetzen; g. away weggeben; (divulge) verraten; g. away the bride Brautvater sein; g. back zurückgeben; g. ground zurückweichen; g. it to 'em! (coll) hau zu!; g. off von sich geben; (steam) ausströmen lassen; g. oneself away sich verplappern; g. oneself up sich stellen; g. or take mehr oder weniger; g. out ausgeben; g. rise to Anlaß geben zu; g. up aufgeben; (a business) schließen; g. up for lost verlorengeben; g. way weichen; g. way to sich überlassen (dat) ‖ intr (yield) nachgeben; (collapse) einstürzen; g. in to nachgeben (dat), weichen (dat); g. out (said of the voice, legs) versagen; (said of strength) nachlassen; g. up aufgeben; (mil) die Waffen strecken; g. up on verzagen an (dat)

give'-and-take' s Kompromiß m & n; (exchange of opinion) Meinungsaustausch m

give'away' s (betrayal of a secret) unbeabsichtigte Preisgabe f; (promotional article) Gratisprobe f

give'away show' s Preisrätselsendung f

given ['gɪvən] adj gegeben; (time) festgesetzt; (math, philos) gegeben; g. to drinking dem Trunk ergeben

giv'en name' s Vorname m

giver ['gɪvər] s Geber –in mf; (of a contribution) Spender –in mf

gizzard ['gɪzərd] s Geflügelmagen m

gla'cial pe'riod ['gleʃəl] s Eiszeit f

glacier ['gleʃər] s Gletscher m

glad [glæd] adj (gladder; gladdest) froh; be g. (about) sich freuen (über acc); g. to (inf) erfreut zu (inf); g. to meet you sehr erfreut!, sehr angenehm!; I'll be g. to do it for you ich werde das gern für Sie tun

gladden ['glædən] tr erfreuen

glade [gled] s Waldwiese f, Waldlichtung f

gladiator ['glædɪ,etər] s Gladiator m

gladiola [,glædɪ'olə] s Gladiole f

gladly ['glædli] adv gern(e)

gladness ['glædnɪs] s Freude f

glad' rags' spl (sl) Sonntagsstaat m

glad' tid'ings spl Freundenbotschaft f

glamorous ['glæmərəs] adj bezaubernd

glamour ['glæmər] s (of a girl) Zauber m; (of an event) Glanz m

glam'our girl' s gefeierte Schönheit f; (pej) Zierpuppe f

glance [glæns] s Blick m; at a g., at first g. auf den ersten Blick; ‖ intr (at) blicken (auf acc or nach); g. around umherblicken; g. off abgleiten an (dat); g. through (or over) flüchtig durchsehen; g. up aufblicken

gland [glænd] s Drüse f

glanders ['glændərz] spl Rotzkrankheit f

glare [gler] s grelles Licht n; (look) böser Blick m ‖ intr blenden; (look) böse starren; g. at böse anstarren

glar'ing adj (light) grell; (fig) schreiend, aufdringlich

glass [glæs] adj gläsern, Glas– ‖ s Glas n; glasses Brille f

glass' bead' s Glasperle f

glass' blow'er ['blo·ər] s Glasbläser –in mf

glass' blow'ing s Glasbläserei f

glass' case' s Schaukasten m

glass' cut'ter s Glasschleifer –in mf; (tool) Glasschneider m

glassful ['glæsful] s Glas n

glass'ware' s Glaswaren pl

glass' wool' s Glaswolle f

glass'works' s Glasfabrik f, Glashütte f

glassy ['glæsi] adj (surface) spiegelglatt; (eyes) glasig

glaucoma [glau'komə] s Glaukom n, grüner Star m

glaze [glez] s (on ceramics) Glasur f; (on paintings) Lasur f; (of ice) Glatteis n ‖ tr (ceramics, baked goods) glasieren; (a window) verglasen; (a painting) lasieren

glazed adj (ceramics, baked goods) glasiert; (eyes) glasig; g. tile Kachel f

glazier ['gleʒər] s Glaser –in mf

gleam [glim] s Lichtstrahl m; g. of hope Hoffnungsschimmer m ‖ intr strahlen

glean [glin] tr & intr auflesen; (fig) zusammentragen

gleanings ['glinɪŋz] spl Nachlese f

glee [gli] s Frohsinn m

glee' club' s Gesangverein m

glen [glɛn] s Bergschlucht f

glib [glɪb] adj (glibber; glibbest) (tongue) beweglich; (person) zungenfertig

glide [glaɪd] s Gleiten n; (aer) Gleitflug m; (with a glider) (aer) Segelflug m; (ling) Gleitlaut m; (mus) Glissando n ‖ intr gleiten

glider ['glaɪdər] s (porch swing) Schaukelbett n; (aer) Segelflugzeug n

glid'er pi'lot s Segelflieger –in mf

glid'ing s Segelfliegen n

glimmer ['glɪmər] s Schimmer m; g. of hope Hoffnungsschimmer m || intr schimmern

glim'mering adj flimmernd || s Flimmern n

glimpse [glɪmps] s flüchtiger Blick m; catch a g. of flüchtig zu sehen bekommen || tr flüchtig erblicken || intr—g. at e-n flüchtigen Blick werfen auf (acc)

glint [glɪnt] s Lichtschimmer m || intr schimmern

glisten ['glɪsən] s Glanz m || intr glänzen

glitter ['glɪtər] s Glitzern n, Glanz m || intr glitzern, glänzen

gloat [glot] intr schadenfroh sein; g. over sich weiden an (dat)

gloat'ing s Schadenfreude f

global ['globəl] adj global, Welt-

globe [glob] s Erdkugel f, Globus m

globe'-trot'ter s Weltenbummler –in mf

globule ['glabjul] s Kügelchen n

glockenspiel ['glɑkən‚spil] s Glockenspiel n

gloom [glum] s Düsternis f; (fig) Trübsinn m

gloominess ['glumɪnɪs] s Düsterkeit f; (fig) Trübsinn m

gloomy ['glumi] adj düster; (depressing) bedrückend; (depressed) trübsinnig

glorification ['glorɪfɪ‚keʃən] s Verherrlichung f

glori·fy ['glorɪ‚faɪ] v (pret & pp –fied) tr verherrlichen

glorious ['glorɪ·əs] adj (full of glory) glorreich; (magnificent) herrlich

glo·ry ['glori] s Ruhm m; (magnificence) Herrlichkeit f; be in one's g. im siebenten Himmel sein || v (pret & pp –ried) intr—g. in frohlocken über (acc)

gloss [glɔs] s (shine) Glanz m; (notation) Glosse f || tr glossieren; g. over verschleiern

glossary ['glɔsəri] s Glossar n

glossy ['glɔsi] adj glänzend

glottis ['glɑtɪs] s Stimmritze f

glove [glʌv] s Handschuh m; fit like a g. wie angegossen passen

glove' compart'ment s Handschuhfach n

glow [glo] s Glühen n || intr glühen; g. with (fig) (er)glühen vor (dat)

glower ['glau·ər] s finsterer Blick m || intr finster blicken; g. at finster anblicken

glow'ing adj glühend; (account) begeistert

glow'worm' s Glühwurm m

glucose ['glukos] s Glukose f

glue [glu] s Leim m, Klebemittel n || tr (wood) leimen; (paper) kleben

gluey ['glu·i] adj leimig

glum [glʌm] adj (glummer; glummest) verdrießlich

glut [glʌt] s Übersättigung f; a g. on the market e-e Überschwemmung des Marktes || v (pret & pp glutted; ger glutting) tr übersättigen; (com) überschwemmen

glutton ['glʌtən] s Vielfraß m

gluttonous ['glʌtənəs] adj gefräßig

gluttony ['glʌtəni] s Gefräßigkeit f

glycerine ['glɪsərɪn] s Glyzerin n

gnarled [nɑrld] adj knorrig

gnash [næʃ] tr—g. one's teeth mit den Zähnen knirschen

gnat [næt] s Mücke f

gnaw [nɔ] tr zernagen; g. off abnagen || intr (on) nagen (an dat)

gnome [nom] s Gnom m, Berggeist m

go [go] s—be on the go auf den Beinen sein; have a lot of go viel Mumm in den Knochen haben; it's no go es geht nicht; let's have a go at it probieren wir's mal; make a go of it es zu e-m Erfolg machen || v (pret went [went], pp gone [gɔn]) tr—go it alone es ganz allein(e) machen || intr gehen; (depart) weggehen; (travel) fahren, reisen; (operate) arbeiten; (belong) gehören; (turn out) verlaufen; (collapse) zusammenbrechen; (fail, go out of order) kaputtgehen; (said of words) lauten; (said of bells) läuten; (said of a buzzer) ertönen; (said of awards) zugeteilt werden; (said of a road) führen; be going to, e.g., I am going to study ich werde studieren; go about umhergehen; (a task) in Angriff nehmen; go about it darangehen; go after (run after) nachlaufen; (strive for) streben nach; go against the grain gegen den Strich gehen; go ahead vorausgehen; go ahead! voran!; go along with (accompany) mitgehen mit; (agree with) zustimmen mit; go and see for yourself überzeugen Sie sich selbst davon!; go around herumgehen; (suffice) (aus)reichen; (an obstacle) umgehen; go at (a person) losgehen auf (acc); (a thing) herangehen an (acc); go away weggehen; go bad schlecht werden; go back zurückkehren; (ride back) zurückfahren; go back on (one's word) brechen; go beyond überschreiten; go by (pass by) vorbeigehen (an dat); (said of time) vergehen; (act according to) sich richten nach; go down niedergehen; (said of the sun or a ship) untergehen; (said of a swelling) zurückgehen; (said of a fever or a price) sinken; go down in history in die Geschichte eingehen; go for (fetch) holen; (apply to) gelten für; (be enthusiastic about) schwärmen für; (have a crush on) verknallt sein in (acc); (be sold for) verkauft werden für; (attack) losgehen auf (acc); go in hineingehen; (said of the sun) verschwinden; go in for schwärmen für; (sport) treiben; go into eintreten in (acc); (arith) enthalten sein in (dat); go into detail ins Detail gehen; **go in with s.o. on** sich beteiligen mit j-m an (dat); **go off** (depart) weggehen; (said of a gun) losgehen; (said of a bomb) explodieren; **go on** (happen) vorgehen; (continue) weitergehen; (with) fortfahren (mit); (theat) auftreten; **go on!** (expressing encouragement) nur zu!; (expressing disbelief) ach was!; **go on reading** weiterlesen; **go on to** (another theme) übergehen auf (acc); **go over** (check) überprüfen; (review) noch einmal durchgehen; (figures) nachrechnen; (be a success) einschlagen; **go over to** hinüberreichen zu; (the enemy) übergehen zu; **go out** (e.g., of the house) hinausgehen; (on an errand or socially; said of a light) ausgehen; **go out of one's way** sich besonders anstrengen; **go out to dinner** auswärts essen; **go through** (penetrate) durchdringen; (a traffic signal) überfahren; (endure) durchmachen; **go through with** zu Ende führen; **go to** (said of a prize) zugeteilt werden (dat); **go together** zueinanderpassen; **go to it!** los!; **go to show** ein Beweis sein für; **go with** (fit, match) passen zu; (associate with) verkehren mit; **go without** entbehren; **go under an assumed name** e-n angenommenen Namen führen; **go up to s.o.** auf j-n zugehen; **g. on** (fig) anstacheln

goad [god] s Stachel m || tr antreiben; **g. on** (fig) anstacheln

go'-ahead sig'nal n freie Bahn f

goal [gol] s Ziel n; (sport) Tor n; **make a goal** (sport) ein Tor schießen

goalie ['goli] s Torwart m

goal'keep'er s Torwart m

goal' line' s Torlinie f

goal' post' s Torpfosten m

goat [got] s Ziege f, Geiß f; (male goat) Ziegenbock m; **get s.o.'s g.** (sl) j-n auf die Palme bringen

goatee [go'ti] s Ziegenbart m, Spitzbart m

goat' herd' s Ziegenhirt m

goat'skin' s Ziegenfell n

gob [gab] s (coll) Klumpen m; (sailor) (coll) Blaujacke f; **gobs of money** (coll) ein Haufen m Geld

gobble ['gabəl] s Kollern n || tr verschlingen; **g. up** (food) herunterschlingen; (e.g., land) zusammenraffen || intr (said of a turkey) kollern

gobbledegook ['gabəldɪ‚guk] s (coll) Amtssprache f

gobbler ['gablər] s (coll) Fresser –in mf; (orn) (coll) Puter m, Truthahn m

go'-between' s Vermittler –in mf, Unterhändler –in mf

goblet ['gablɪt] s Kelchglas n

goblin ['gablɪn] s Kobold m

go'cart' s (walker) Laufstuhl m; (stroller) Sportwagen m; (small racer) Go-Kart m; (handcart) Handwagen m

god [gad] s Gott m; **God forbid!** Gott bewahre!; **God knows** weiß Gott; **my God!** du lieber Gott!; **so help me God!** so wahr mir Gott helfe!; **ye gods!** heiliger Strohsack!

god'child' s (–chil'dren) Patenkind n

goddess ['gadɪs] s Göttin f

god'fa'ther s Pate m; **be a g. Pate stehen**

God-fear'ing adj gottesfürchtig

god'forsak'en adj gottverlassen

god'head' s Göttlichkeit f; **Godhead** Gott m

godless ['gadlɪs] adj gottlos

god'like' adj göttlich

godly ['gadli] adj gottselig

god'moth'er s Patin f; **be a g. Patin stehen**

god'send' s Segen m

God'speed' s—**wish s.o. G.** j-m Lebewohl sagen

go-getter ['go‚getər] s Draufgänger m

goggle ['gagəl] intr glotzen

gog'gle-eyed' adj glotzäugig

goggles ['gagəlz] spl Schutzbrille f

go'ing adj (rate) gültig, üblich; **g. on** (e.g., six o'clock) gegen; **I'm g. to do it** ich werde es tun

go'ing concern' s schwunghaftes Geschäft n

go'ing-o'ver s Überprüfung f; (beating) Prügel pl

go'ings on' spl Treiben n, Wirtschaft f

goiter ['gɔɪtər] s Kropf m

gold [gold] adj Gold– || s Gold n

gold' bar' s Goldbarren m

gold'brick' s (mil) Drückeberger m

gold'-brick' intr faulenzen

gold'-brick'ing s (mil) Drückebergerei f

gold'crest' s Goldhähnchen n

gold' dig'ger ['dɪgər] s Goldgräber m; (sl) Vamp m

golden ['goldən] adj golden; (opportunity) günstig

gold'en age' s Glanzzeit f, Goldenes Zeitalter n

gold'en calf', the s das Goldene Kalb

gold'en ea'gle s Goldadler m

Gold'en Fleece', the (myth) das Goldene Vlies

gold'en mean' s goldene Mitte f

gold'en rule' s goldene Regel f

gold'en wed'ding s goldene Hochzeit f

gold'-filled' adj vergoldet

gold' fill'ing s (dent) Goldplombe f

gold'finch' s Goldfink m, Stieglitz m

gold'fish' s Goldfisch m

goldilocks ['goldɪ‚laks] s (bot) Hahnenfuß m

gold' leaf' s Blattgold n

gold'mine' s Goldbergwerk n

gold' nug'get s Goldklumpen m

gold' plate' s Goldgeschirr n

gold'-plate' tr vergolden

gold'smith' s Goldschmied –in mf

gold' stand'ard s Goldwährung f

golf [galf] s Golf n || intr Golf spielen

golf' bag' s Köcher m

golf' club' s Golfschläger m; (organization) Golfklub m

golf' course' s Golfplatz m

golfer ['galfər] s Golfspieler –in mf

golf' links' spl Golfplatz m

gondola ['gandələ] s Gondel f

gon'dola car' s offener Güterwagen m
gondolier [ˌgɑndəˈlɪr] s Gondelführer m
gone [gɔn] adj hin, weg; (ruined) futsch; all g. ganz weg; (sold out) ausverkauft; he is g. er ist fort
goner ['gɔnər] s (coll) verlorener Mensch m
gong [gɔŋ] s Gong m, Tamtam n
gonorrhea [ˌgɑnəˈriːə] s Tripper m
goo [gu] s (sl) klebrige Masse f
good [gud] adj (better: best) gut; (well behaved) brav, artig; (in health) gesund; (valid) gültig; as g. as so gut wie; be g. enough to (inf) so gut sein und; g. and recht, e.g., g. and cheap recht billig; g. at gut in (dat); g. for (suited to) geeignet zu; (effective against) wirksam für; (valid for) gültig für; g. for you! (serves you right!) das geschieht dir recht!; (expressing congratulations) ich gratuliere!, bravo!; make g. wiedergutmachen; (losses) vergüten; (a promise) erfüllen; || s Gut n; (welfare) Wohl n; (advantage) Nutzen m; (philos) Gut n, das Gute: be up to no g. nichts Gutes im Schilde führen; catch with the goods auf frischer Tat ertappen; do g. wohltun; for g. für immer; goods Waren pl; to the g. als Nettogewinn; what g. is it?, what's the g. of it? was nutzt es?
good'-by', good'-bye' s Lebewohl n; say g. (to) sich verabschieden (von) || interj auf Wiedersehen!; (on the telephone) auf Wiederhören!
good' day' interj guten Tag!
good' deed' s Wohltat f
good' egg' s (sl) feiner Kerl m
good' eve'ning interj guten Abend!
good' fel'low s netter Kerl m
good'-fel'lowship s gute Kameradschaft f
good'-for-noth'ing adj nichtsnutzig || s Taugenichts m, Nichtsnutz m
Good' Fri'day s Karfreitag m
good' graces spl—be in s.o.'s g. in j-s Gunst stehen
good'-heart'ed adj gutherzig
good'-hu'mored adj gutgelaunt, gutmütig
good'-look'ing adj gutaussehend, hübsch
goodly ['gudli] adj beträchtlich; a g. number of viele
good' morn'ing interj guten Morgen!
good'-na'tured adj gutmütig
goodness ['gudnis] s Güte f; for g. sake! um Himmels willen!; g. knows weiß Gott; thank g. Gott sei Dank!
good' night' interj gute Nacht!
good' sense' s Sinn m; (common sense) gesunder Menschenverstand m; make g. Sinn haben
good'-sized' adj ziemlich groß
good'-tem'pered adj ausgeglichen
good' time' s—have a g. sich gut unterhalten; keep g. taktfest sein
good' turn' s Gefallen m; one g. deserves another e-e Hand wäscht die andere

good' will' s Wohlwollen n; (com) Geschäftswert m
goody ['gudi] s Näscherei f || interj pfundig!
gooey ['guːi] adj klebrig
goof [guf] s (person) (sl) Depp m; (mistake) (sl) Schnitzer m || tr (sl) verpfuschen || intr (sl) e-n Schnitzer machen; g. off (sl) faulenzen
goof'ball' s (pill) (sl) Beruhigungspille f; (eccentric person) (sl) Sonderling m
goofy ['gufi] adj (sl) dämlich; g. about (sl) vernarrt in (acc)
goon [gun] s (sl) Dummkopf m; (in strikes) bestellter Schläger m
goose [gus] s (geese [gis]) Gans f; (culin) Gänsebraten m; cook s.o.'s g. j-n erledigen
goose'ber'ry s Stachelbeere f
goose' egg' s (sl) Null f
goose' flesh' s Gänsehaut f
goose'neck' s Schwanenhals m
goose' pim'ples spl Gänsehaut f
goose' step' s Stechschritt m
goose'-step' v (pret & pp –stepped; ger –stepping) intr im Stechschritt marschieren
gopher ['gofər] s Taschenratte f
gore [gor] s geronnenes Blut n || tr aufspießen
gorge [gɔrdʒ] s Schlucht f || tr vollstopfen || intr schlingen
gorgeous ['gɔrdʒəs] adj prachtvoll
gorilla [gəˈrɪlə] s Gorilla m
gorse [gɔrs] s Stechginster m
gory ['gori] adj blutig
gosh [gɑʃ] interj herrjeh!
Gospel ['gɑspəl] s Evangelium n
gos'pel truth' s reine Wahrheit f
gossamer ['gɑsəmər] s Sommerfäden pl
gossip ['gɑsɪp] s Klatsch m; (woman) Klatschweib n; (man) Schwätzer m || intr klatschen, tratschen
gos'sip col'umn s Klatschspalte f
gossipmonger ['gɑsɪpˌmʌŋgər] s Klatschbase f
gossipy ['gɑsɪpi] adj tratschsüchtig
Goth [gɑθ] s Gote m, Gotin f
Gothic ['gɑθɪk] adj gotisch || s (language) Gotisch n
Goth'ic arch' s Spitzbogen m
gouge [gaudʒ] s (tool) Hohlmeißel m; (hole made by a gouge) ausgemeißelte Vertiefung f || tr aushöhlen; (overcharge) übervorteilen; g. out (eyes) herausdrücken
gouger ['gaudʒər] s Wucherer –in mf
goulash ['gulaʃ] s Gulasch n
gourd [gord], [gurd] s Kürbis m
gourmand ['gurmənd] s (glutton) Schlemmer –in mf; (gourmet) Feinschmecker m
gourmet ['gurme] s Feinschmecker m
gout [gaut] s Gicht f
govern ['gʌvərn] tr regieren; (fig) beherrschen; (gram) regieren || intr regieren
governess ['gʌvərnɪs] s Gouvernante f
government ['gʌvərnmənt] adj Regierungs–, Staats– || s Regierung f

gov'ernment con'tract s Staatsauftrag m

gov'ernment control' s Zwangsbewirtschaftung f

gov'ernment employ'ee s Staatsbeamte m, Staatsbeamtin f

gov'ernment grant' s Staatszuschuß m

gov'ernment-in-ex'ile s Exilregierung f

governor ['gʌvərnər] s Statthalter m, Gouverneur m; (mach) Regler m

gov'ernorship' s Statthalterschaft f

gown [gaun] s Damenkleid n; (of a judge, professor) Robe f, Talar m

grab [græb] s—make a g. for grapschen nach || v (pret & pp grabbed; ger grabbing) tr schnappen; g. hold of anpacken || intr—g. for greifen nach

grab' bag' s Glückstopf m

grace [gres] s (mercy, divine favor) Gnade f; (charm) Grazie f; (table prayer) Tischgebet n; (charm) Grazie f; Graces (myth) Grazien pl

graceful ['gresfəl] adj graziös, anmutig

gracious ['greʃəs] adj gnädig; (living) angenehm || interj lieber Himmel

gradation [gre'deʃən] s Stufenfolge f

grade [gred] s (level) Stufe f, Grad m; (quality) Qualität f; (class year) Schulklasse f; (mark in a course, test) Zensur f; (slope) Steigung f; (mil) Dienstgrad m || tr (sort) einstufen; (evaluate) bewerten; (make level) planieren; (educ) zensieren

grade' cross'ing s (rr) Schienenübergang m

grade' school' s Grundschule f

gradient ['gredɪ·ənt] s Neigung f

gradual ['grædʒu·əl] adj allmählich

graduate ['grædʒu·ɪt] adj (student) graduiert; (course) Graduierten- || s Promovierte mf; (from a junior college) Abiturient –in mf; (from a university) Absolvent –in mf || ['grædʒu,et] tr & intr graduieren, promovieren; g. from absolvieren

grad'uated adj (tax) abgestuft; (marked by divisions of measurement) graduiert; g. scale Gradmesser m

graduation [,grædʒu'eʃən] s Graduierung f, Promotion f; (marking on a vessel or instrument) Gradeinteilung f

gradua'tion ex'ercises spl Schlußfeier f

graft [græft] s (illegal gain) Schiebung f; (money involved in graft) Schmiergeld n; (twig) (hort) Pfropfreis n; (place where scion is inserted) (hort) Propfstelle f; (organ transplanted) (surg) verpflanztes Gewebe n; (transplanting) (surg) Gewebeverpflanzung f || tr (hort) pfropfen; (surg) verpflanzen

gra'ham bread' ['gre·əm] s Grahambrot n

gra'ham crack'er s Grahamplätzchen n

gra'ham flour' s Grahammehl n

grain [gren] s Korn n; (of leather) Narbe f; (in wood, marble) Maserung f; (unit of weight) Gran n; (cereals) Getreide n; (phot) Korn n; against the g. (& fig) gegen den Strich; g. of truth Körnchen n Wahrheit

grain' el'evator s Getreidesilo m

grain'field' s Saatfeld n, Kornfeld n

gram [græm] s Gramm n

grammar | 'græmər] s Grammatik f

gram'mar school' s Grundschule f

grammatical [grə'mætɪkəl] adj grammatisch, grammatikalisch

gramophone ['græmə,fon] s Grammophon n

granary ['grenəri] s Getreidespeicher m

grand [grænd] adj großartig; (large and striking) grandios; (lofty) erhaben; (wonderful) (coll) herrlich

grand'aunt' s Großtante f

grand'child' s (-chil'dren) Enkelkind n

grand'daugh'ter s Enkelin f

grand' duch'ess s Großfürstin f, Großherzogin f

grand' duch'y s Großfürstentum n, Großherzogtum n

grand' duke' s Großfürst m, Großherzog m

grandee [græn'di] s Grande m

grandeur ['grændʒər], ['grændʒur] s Großartigkeit f, Erhabenheit f

grand'fath'er s Großvater m

grand'father's clock' s Standuhr f

grandiose ['grændɪ,os] adj grandios

grand' ju'ry s Anklagekammer f

grand' lar'ceny s schwerer Diebstahl m

grand' lodge' s Großloge f

grandma | 'græn(d),ma], ['græm,ma] s (coll) Oma f

grand'moth'er s Großmutter f

grand'neph'ew s Großneffe m

grand'niece' s Großnichte f

grandpa ['græn(d),pa], ['græm,pa] s (coll) Opa m

grand'par'ents spl Großeltern pl

grand' pian'o s Konzertflügel m

grand' slam' s Schlemm m

grand'son' s Enkel m

grand'stand' s Tribüne f

grand' to'tal s Gesamtsumme f

grand'un'cle s Großonkel m

grand' vizier' s Großwesir m

grange [grendʒ] s Farm f; (organization) Farmervereinigung f

granite ['grænɪt] adj Granit- || s Granit m

granny | 'græni] s (coll) Oma f

grant [grænt] s (of money) Beihilfe f; (of a pardon) Gewährung f; (of an award) Verleihung f || tr (permission) geben; (credit) bewilligen; (a favor) gewähren; (a request) erfüllen; (a privilege, award) verleihen; (admit) zugeben; granted that angenommen, daß; take for granted als selbstverständlich hinnehmen

grantee [græn'ti] s Empfänger –in mf

grant'-in-aid' s (grants-in-aid) (by the government) Subvention f; (educ) Stipendium n

grantor ['græntər] s Verleiher –in mf

granular ['grænjələr] adj körnig

granulate ['grænjə,let] tr körnen

gran'ulated sug'ar s Streuzucker m

granule ['grænjul] s Körnchen n

grape [grep] s Weintraube f

grape' ar'bor s Weinlaube f

grape'fruit' s Pampelmuse f

grape' juice' s Most m, Traubensaft m

grape' pick'er s Weinleser –in mf

grape'vine' s Weinstock m; **through the g.** gerüchtweise

graph [græf] s Diagramm n

graphic(al) ['græfɪk(əl)] adj gráphisch; (description) anschaulich, bildhaft

graph'ic arts' spl Graphik f

graphite ['græfaɪt] s Graphit m

graph' pa'per s Millimeterpapier n

grapnel ['græpnəl] s Wurfanker m

grapple ['græpəl] s Enterhaken m; (fight) Handgemenge n || tr packen || intr (use a grapple) (naut) e-n Enterhaken gebrauchen; **g. with** (& fig) ringen mit

grap'pling hook', grap'pling i'ron s Wurfanker m; (naut) Enterhaken m

grasp [græsp] s Griff m; (control) Gewalt f; (comprehension) Verständnis n; (reach) Reichweite f; **have a good g. of** gut beherrschen || tr (& fig) fassen || intr—g. at schnappen nach

grasp'ing adj habgierig, geldgierig

grass [græs] s Gras n; (lawn) Rasen m; (pasture land) Weide f

grass' court' s Rasenspielplatz m

grass'hop'per s Grashüpfer m

grass' land' s Weideland n, Grasland n

grass'-roots' adj (coll) volkstümlich

grass' seed' s Grassamen m

grass' wid'ow s Strohwitwe f

grassy ['græsi] adj grasig

grate [gret] s (on a window) Gitter n; (of a furnace) Rost m || tr (e.g., cheese) reiben; **g. the teeth** mit den Zähnen knirschen || intr knirschen; **g. on one's nerves** an den Nerven reißen

grateful ['gretfəl] adj dankbar

grater ['gretər] s (culin) Reibeisen n

grati·fy ['grætɪˌfaɪ] v (pret & pp –fied) tr befriedigen; **be gratified by** sich freuen über (acc)

grat'ifying adj erfreulich

grat'ing adj knirschend || s Gitter n

gratis ['grætɪs], ['gretɪs] adj & adv unentgeltlich

gratitude ['grætɪˌt(j)ud] s Dankbarkeit f

gratuitous [grə't(j)u·ɪtəs] adj unentgeltlich; (undeserving) unverdient

gratuity [grə't(j)u·ɪti] s Trinkgeld n

grave [grev] adj (face) ernst; (condition) besorgniserregend; (mistake) folgenschwer; (sound) tief || s Grab n; (accent) Gravis m

gravedigger ['grev ˌdɪgər] s Totengräber m

gravel ['grævəl] s (rounded stones) Kies m; (crushed stones) Schotter m; (pathol) Harngrieß m || tr mit Kies (or Schotter) bestreuen

gravelly ['grævəli] adj heiser

grav'el pit' s Kiesgrube f

grav'el road' s Schotterstraße f

grave'stone' s Grabstein m

grave'yard' s Friedhof m

gravitate ['grævɪˌtet] intr gravitieren; **g. towards** (fig) neigen zu

gravitation [ˌgrævɪ'teʃən] s Gravitation f, Massenanziehung f

gravitational [ˌgrævɪ'teʃənəl] adj Gravitations–, Schwer–

gravita'tional force' s Schwerkraft f

gravita'tional pull' s Anziehungskraft f

gravity ['grævɪti] s (seriousness) Ernst m; (of a situation) Schwere f; (phys) Schwerkraft f

gravy ['grevi] s Soße f; (coll) leichter Gewinn m

gra'vy boat' s Soßenschüssel f

gra'vy train' s (sl) Futterkrippe f

gray [gre] adj grau || s Grau n || intr ergrauen

gray'beard' s Graubart m

gray'-haired' adj grauhaarig

grayish ['gre·ɪʃ] adj gräulich

gray' mat'ter s graue Substanz f

graze [grez] tr (said of a bullet) streifen; (cattle) weiden lassen || intr weiden

graz'ing land' s Weide f

grease [gris] s Fett n, Schmiere f || [gris], [griz] tr (aut) schmieren

grease' gun' [gris] s Schmierpresse f

grease' paint' s Schminke f

grease' pit' s (aut) Schmiergrube f

grease' spot' s Fettfleck m

greasy ['grisi], ['grizi] adj fett(ig)

great [gret] adj groß; (wonderful) (coll) großartig; **a g. many** (of) e–e große Anzahl von; **g. fun** Heidenspaß m; **g. guy** Prachtkerl m

great'-aunt' s Großtante f

Great' Bear' s Großer Bär m

Great' Brit'ain s Großbritannien n

Great' Dane' s deutsche Dogge f

great'-grand'child' s (–chil'dren) Urenkel m

great'-grand'daugh'ter s Urenkelin f

great'-grand'fa'ther s Urgroßvater m

great'-grand'moth'er s Urgroßmutter f

great'-grand'par'ents spl Urgroßeltern pl

great'-grand'son' s Urenkel m

greatly ['gretli] adv sehr, stark

great'-neph'ew s Großneffe m

greatness ['gretnɪs] s Größe f

great'-niece' s Großnichte f

great'-un'cle s Großonkel m

Grecian ['griʃən] adj griechisch

Greece [gris] s Griechenland n

greed [grid] s Habgier f, Gier f

greediness ['gridinɪs] s Gierigkeit f

greedy ['gridi] adj (for) gierig (nach)

Greek [grik] adj griechisch; s (person) Grieche m, Griechin f; (language) Griechisch n; **that's G. to me** das kommt mir spanisch vor

green [grin] adj grün; (unripe) unreif; (inexperienced) unerfahren, neu; **become g.** grünen; **turn g. with envy** grün vor Neid werden || s (& golf) Grün n; **greens** Blattgemüse n

green'back' s (coll) Geldschein m

greenery ['grinəri] s Grün n

green'-eyed' adj grünäugig; (fig) neidisch

green'gro'cer s Obst– und Gemüsehändler –in mf

green'horn' s Ausländer –in mf

green'house' s Gewächshaus n

greenish l 'grɪnɪʃ] adj grünlich

Green'land s Grönland n

green' light' s (fig) freie Fahrt f

greenness ['grɪnnɪs] s Grün n; (inexperience) Unerfahrenheit f

green' pep'per s Paprikaschote f

green'room' s (theat) Aufenthaltsraum m

greensward ['grin‚swɔrd] s Rasen m

green' thumb' s—have a g. gärtnerisches Geschick besitzen

greet [grit] tr grüßen; (welcome) begrüßen

greet'ing s Gruß m; (welcoming) Begrüßung f; greetings Grüße pl

greet'ing card' s Glückwunschkarte f

gregarious [grɪ'gɛrɪ.əs] adj gesellig

Gregor'ian cal'endar [grɪ'gɔrɪ.ən] s Gregorianischer Kalender m

Gregor'ian chant' s Gregorianischer Gesang m

grenade [grɪ'ned] s Granate f

grenade' launch'er s Gewehrgranatgerät n

grey [gre] adj, s, & intr var of gray

grey'hound' s Windhund m

grid [grɪd] s (on a map) Gitternetz n; (culin) Bratrost m; (electron) Gitter n

griddle ['grɪdəl] s Bratpfanne f; (cookie sheet) Backblech n

grid'dlecake' s Pfannkuchen m

grid'i'ron s Bratrost m; (sport) Spielfeld n; (theat) Schnürboden m

grid' leak' s (electron) Gitterwiderstand m

grief [grif] s Kummer m; come to g. zu Fall (or Schaden) kommen, scheitern

grief'-strick'en adj gramgebeugt

grievance ['grivəns] s Beschwerde f

grieve [griv] tr bekümmern || intr (over) sich grämen (über acc)

grievous ['grivəs] adj (causing grief) schmerzlich; (serious) schwerwiegend

griffin ['grɪfɪn] s Greif m

grill [grɪl] s Grill m || tr grillen; (an accused person) scharf verhören

grille [grɪl] s Gitter n

grim [grɪm] adj (grimmer; grimmest) grimmig; g. humor Galgenhumor m

grimace ['grɪməs], [grɪ'mes] s Grimasse f || intr Grimassen schneiden

grime [graɪm] s Schmutz m, Ruß m

grimness ['grɪmnɪs] s Grimmigkeit f

grimy ['graɪmi] adj schmutzig, rußig

grin [grɪn] s Grinsen n, Schmunzeln n || v (pret & pp grinned; ger grinning) intr grinsen, schmunzeln; I had to g. and bear it ich mußte gute Miene zum bösen Spiel machen

grind [graɪnd] s (of coffee, grain) Mahlen n; (hard work) Schinderei f; (a student) (coll) Streber –in mf; the daily g. der graue Alltag || v (pret & pp ground [graund]) tr (coffee,

grain) mahlen; (glass, tools) schleifen; (meat) zermahlen; (in a mortar) stampfen; g. down zerreiben; g. one's teeth mit den Zähnen knirschen; g. out (e.g., articles) ausstoßen; (tunes) leiern

grinder ['graɪndər] s (molar) (dent) Backenzahn m; (mach) Schleifmaschine f

grind'stone' s Schleifstein m

grip [grɪp] s Griff m; (handle) Handgriff m; (handbag) Reisetasche f; (power) Gewalt f; come to grips with in Angriff nehmen; have a good g. on (fig) sicher beherrschen; lose one's g. (fig) den Halt verlieren || v (pret & pp gripped; ger gripping) tr (& fig) packen

gripe [graɪp] s Meckerei f || intr (about) meckern (über acc)

grippe [grɪp] s (pathol) Grippe f

grip'ping adj fesselnd, packend

grisly ['grɪzli] adj gräßlich

grist [grɪst] s Mahlkorn n; that's g. for his mill das ist Wasser auf seine Mühle

gristle ['grɪsəl] s Knorpel m

gristly ['grɪsli] adj knorpelig

grist'mill' s Getreidemühle f

grit [grɪt] s (abrasive particles) Grieß m; (pluck) (coll) Mumm m; grits Schrotmehl n || v (pret & pp gritted; ger gritting) tr (one's teeth) zusammenbeißen

gritty ['grɪti] adj grießig

grizzly ['grɪzli] adj gräulich

griz'zly bear' s Graubär m

groan [gron] s Stöhnen n; groans Geächze n || intr stöhnen; (grumble) (coll) brumen

grocer ['grosər] s Lebensmittelhändler –in mf

grocery ['grosəri] s (store) Lebensmittelgeschäft n; groceries Lebensmittel pl

gro'cery store' s Lebensmittelgeschäft n

grog [grɑg] s Grog m

groggy ['grɑgi] adj benommen

groin [grɔɪn] s (anat) Leiste f, Leistengegend f; (archit) Rippe f

groom [grum] s Bräutigam m; (stableboy) Reitknecht m || tr (a person, animal) pflegen; (for a position) heranziehen

groove [gruv] s Kerbe f; (for letting off water) Rinne f; (of a record) Rille f; (in a barrel) Zug m; in the g. (fig) im richtigen Fahrwasser

grope [grop] intr—g. one's way sich vorwärtstasten || intr tappen; g. about herumtappen; g. for tappen nach, tasten nach

gropingly ['gropɪŋli] adv tastend

gross [gros] adj (coarse, vulgar) roh, derb; (mistake) grob; (crass, extreme) kraß; (without deductions) Brutto– || s Gros n || tr e–n Bruttogewinn haben von

grossly ['grosli] adv sehr, stark

gross' na'tional prod'uct s Bruttosozialprodukt n

gross' receipts' *spl* Bruttoeinnahmen *pl*

grotesque [gro'tesk] *adj* grotesk

grot·to ['grɔto] *s* (–toes & –tos) Grotte *f*, Höhle *f*

grouch [grautʃ] *s* (coll) Brummbär *m*, Griesgram *m* || *intr* brummen

grouchy ['grautʃi] *adj* (coll) brummig

ground [graund] *s* Grund *m*, Boden *m*; *(reason)* Grund *m*; (elec) Erde *f*; **every inch of g.** jeder Fußbreit Boden; **grounds** (e.g., *of an estate*) Anlagen *pl*; *(reasons)* Gründe *pl*; *(of coffee)* Satz *m*; **break g.** mit dem Bau beginnen; **gain g. (an)** Boden gewinnen; **hold one's g.** seinen Standpunkt behaupten; **level to the g.** dem Erdboden gleichmachen; **lose g. (an)** Boden verlieren; **low g.** Niederung *f*; **new g.** (fig) Neuland *n*; **on the grounds that** mit der Begründung, daß; **run into the g.** (fig) bis zum Überdruß wiederholen; **stand one's g.** standhalten; **yield g.** (fig) nachgeben || *tr* *(a pilot)* Startverbot erteilen *(dat)*; *(a ship)* auflaufen lassen; (elec) erden; **be grounded by bad weather** wegen schlechten Wetters am Starten gehindert werden

ground' connec'tion *s* (elec) Erdung *f*

ground' crew' *s* (aer) Bodenmannschaft *f*

ground' floor' *s* Parterre *n*, Erdgeschoß *n*

ground' glass' *s* Mattglas *n*

ground' hog' *s* Murmeltier *n*

groundless ['graundlɪs] *adj* grundlos

ground' meat' *s* Hackfleisch *n*

ground' plan' *s* Grundriß *m*; (fig) Entwurf *m*

ground' speed' *s* Geschwindigkeit *f* über Grund

ground' swell' *s* Dünung *f*; (fig) wogende Erregung *f*

ground'-to-air' *adj* Boden-Bord-

ground' wa'ter *s* Grundwasser *n*

ground' wire' *s* (elec) Erdleitung *f*

ground'work' *s* Grundlage *f*

group [grup] *adj* Gruppen- || *s* Gruppe *f*; *(consisting of 18 aircraft)* Geschwader *n* || *tr* gruppieren || *intr* sich gruppieren

group'ing *s* Gruppierung *f*

group' insur'ance *s* Gruppenversicherung *f*

group' ther'apy *s* Gruppentherapie *f*

grouse [graus] *s* Waldhuhn *n* || *intr* (sl) meckern

grout [graut] *s* dünner Mörtel *m* || *tr* verstreichen

grove [grov] *s* Gehölz *n*, Hain *m*

grov·el ['grʌvəl], ['grɑvəl] *v* (*pret* & *pp* –el[l]ed; *ger* –el[l]ing) *intr* (& fig) kriechen; **g. in filth** in Schmutz wühlen

grow [gro] *v* (*pret* **grew** [gru]; *pp* **grown** [gron]) *tr* *(plants)* pflanzen, züchten; *(grain)* anbauen; *(a beard)* sich *(dat)* wachsen lassen; **the ram grows horns** dem Widder wachsen Hörner || *intr* wachsen; *(become)* werden; *(become bigger)* größer werden; **g. fond of** liebgewinnen; **g. luxuriantly** wuchern; **g. older** an Jahren zunehmen; **g. on s.o.** j–m ans Herz wachsen; **g. out of** *(clothes)* herauswachsen aus; (fig) entstehen aus; **g. pale** erblassen; **g. together** zusammenwachsen; *(close)* zuwachsen; **g. up** aufwachsen; **g. wild** *(luxuriantly)* wuchern; *(in the wild)* wild wachsen

grower ['gro·ər] *s* Züchter –in *mf*

growl [graul] *s* *(of a dog, stomach)* Knurren *n*; *(of a bear)* Brummen *n* || *tr* *(words)* brummen || *intr* knurren; *(said of a bear)* brummen; **g. at** anknurren

grown [gron] *adj* erwachsen

grown'-up' *adj* erwachsen || *s* (grown-ups) Erwachsene *mf*

growth [groθ] *s* Wachstum *n*; *(increase)* Zuwachs *m*; (pathol) Gewächs *n*; **full g.** volle Größe *f*

grub [grʌb] *s* Larve *f*, Made *f*; (sl) Fraß *m* || *v* (*pret* & *pp* **grubbed**; *ger* **grubbing**) *tr* ausjäten || *intr* wühlen; **g. for** graben nach

grubby ['grʌbɪ] *adj* *(dirty)* schmutzig

grudge [grʌdʒ] *s* Mißgunst *f*, Groll *m*; **bear (or have) a g. against s.o.** j–m grollen || *tr* mißgönnen

grudg'ing *adj* mißgünstig

grudg'ingly *adv* (nur) ungern

gruel ['gru·əl] *s* Haferschleim *m*

gruel'ing *adj* strapaziös

gruesome ['grusəm] *adj* grausig

gruff [grʌf] *adj* barsch

grumble ['grʌmbəl] *s* Murren *n* || *intr* (over) murren (über *acc*)

grumbler ['grʌmblər] *s* Brummbär *m*

grumpy ['grʌmpɪ] *adj* übellaunig

grunt [grʌnt] *s* Grunzen *n* || *tr* & *intr* grunzen

G′-string' *s* *(of a dancer)* letzte Hülle *f*; *(of a native)* Lendenschurz *m*

guarantee [ˌgærən'ti] *s* Garantie *f* || *tr* garantieren für

guarantor ['gærən‚tɔr] *s* Garant –in *mf*

guaranty ['gærənti] *s* Garantie *f* || *v* (*pret* & *pp* –tied) *tr* garantieren

guard [gard] *s* *(watch; watchman)* Wache *f*; *(person)* Wächter –in *mf*; (fb) Verteidiger *m*; *(mach)* Schutzvorrichtung *f*; *(soldier)* (mil) Posten *m*; *(soldiers)* (mil) Wachmannschaft *f*, Wache *f*; **be on g. against** sich hüten vor *(dat)*; **be on one's g.** auf der Hut sein; **keep under close g.** scharf bewachen; **mount g.** Wache beziehen; **relieve the g.** die Wache ablösen; **stand g.** Posten (or Wache) stehen; *(during a robbery)* Schmiere stehen || *tr* bewachen; (fig) hüten; **g. one's tongue** seine Zunge im Zaum halten || *intr—g.* **against** sich vorsehen gegen; **g. over** wachen über *(acc)*

guard' de'tail *s* Wachmannschaft *f*

guard' du'ty *s* Wachdienst *m*; **pull g.** Wache schieben

guard'house' *s* *(building used by guards)* Wache *f*; *(military jail)* Arrestlokal *n*

guardian ['gɑrdɪ-ən] s (custodian) Wächter –in mf; (jur) Vormund m

guard'ian an'gel s Schutzengel m

guard'ianship' s Obhut f; (jur) Vormundschaft f

guard'rail' s Geländer n

guard'room' s Wachstube f, Wachlokal n

guerrilla [gə'rɪlə] s Guerillakämpfer –in mf

gueril'la war'fare s Guerillakrieg m

guess [ges] s Vermutung f; anybody's g. reine Vermutung f; take a good g. gut raten || tr vermuten; you guessed it! geraten! || intr raten; g. at schätzen

guesser ['gesər] s Rater –in mf

guess'work' s Raten n, Mutmaßung f

guest [gest] adj Gast–, Gäste– || s Gast m; be a g. of zu Gaste sein bei

guest' book' s Gästebuch n

guest' perform'ance s Gastspiel n; give a g. (theat) gastieren

guest' perform'er s Gast m

guest' room' s Gästezimmer n

guest' speak'er s Gastredner –in mf

guffaw [gə'fɔ] s Gewieher n || intr wiehern

guidance ['gaɪdəns] s Leitung f, Führung f; (educ) Studienberatung f; for your g. zu Ihrer Orientierung

guid'ance coun'selor s Studienberater –in mf

guide [gaɪd] s Führer –in mf; (book) Reiseführer m; (tourist escort) Reiseführer –in mf; (for gardening, etc.) Leitfaden m || tr führen; (rok) lenken

guide'book' s Reiseführer m, Führer m

guid'ed mis'sile s Fernlenkkörper m

guid'ed tour' s Führung f

guide'line' s Richtlinie f

guide'post' s Wegweiser m

guide' word' s Stichwort n

guild [gɪld] s Zunft f, Gilde f

guile [gaɪl] s Arglist f

guileful ['gaɪlfəl] adj arglistig

guileless ['gaɪllɪs] adj arglos

guillotine ['gɪlə‚tin] s Fallbeil n, Guillotine f || tr mit dem Fallbeil (or mit der Guillotine) hinrichten

guilt [gɪlt] s Schuld f

guilt'-rid'den adj schuldbeladen

guilty ['gɪlti] adj (of) schuldig (genit); (conscience) schlecht; plead g. sich schuldig bekennen; plead not g. sich für nicht schuldig erklären

guil'ty par'ty s Schuldige mf

guil'ty ver'dict s Schuldspruch m

guin'ea fowl' ['gɪni], **guin'ea hen'** s Perlhuhn n

guin'ea pig' s Meerschweinchen n; (fig) Versuchskaninchen n

guise [gaɪz] s Verkleidung f; under the g. of unter dem Schein (genit)

guitar [gɪ'tɑr] s Gitarre f

guitarist [gɪ'tɑrɪst] s Gitarrenspieler –in mf

gulch [gʌltʃ] s Bergschlucht f

gulf [gʌlf] s Golf m; (fig) Kluft f

Gulf' Stream' s Golfstrom m

gull [gʌl] s Möwe f; (coll) Tölpel m || tr übertölpeln

gullet ['gʌlɪt] s Gurgel f, Schlund m

gullible ['gʌlɪbəl] adj leichtgläubig

gully ['gʌli] s Wasserrinne f

gulp [gʌlp] s Schluck m, Zug m; at one g. in e–m Zuge || tr schlucken; g. down schlingen || intr schlucken

gum [gʌm] s Gummi m & n; (chewing gum) Kaugummi m & n; (anat) Zahnfleisch n || v (pret & pp gummed; ger gumming) tr (e.g., labels) gummieren; gum up the works (coll) die Arbeit (or das Spiel) vermasseln

gum' ar'abic s Gummiarabikum n

gum'boil' s (pathol) Zahngeschwür n

gum'drop' s Gummibonbon m & n

gummy ['gʌmi] adj klebrig

gumption ['gʌmpʃən] s Unternehmungsgeist m, Mumm m

gun [gʌn] s Gewehr n; (handgun) Handfeuerwaffe f; (arti) Geschütz n; stick to one's guns bei der Stange bleiben || v (pret & pp gunned; ger gunning) tr—gun down niederschießen; gun the engine Gas geben || intr auf die Jagd gehen; be out gunning for auf dem Korn haben; gun for game auf die Jagd gehen

gun' bar'rel s Gewehrlauf m; (arti) Geschützrohr n

gun' bat'tle s Feuerkampf m

gun' belt' s Wehrgehänge n

gun'boat' s Kanonenboot n

gun' car'riage s Lafette f

gun'cot'ton s Schießbaumwolle f

gun' crew' s Bedienungsmannschaft f

gun' emplace'ment s Geschützstand m

gun' fight' s Schießerei f

gun'fire' s Geschützfeuer n

gun'man s (–men) bewaffneter Bandit m

gun' met'al s Geschützlegierung f

gun' mount' s Lafette f; (of swivel type) Schwenklafette f

gunner ['gʌnər] s Kanonier m; (aer) Bordschütze m

gunnery ['gʌnəri] s Geschützwesen n

gun'nery prac'tice s Übungsschießen n

gunnysack ['gʌni‚sæk] s Jutesack m

gun' per'mit s Waffenschein m

gun'point' s—at g. mit vorgehaltenem Gewehr

gun'pow'der s Schießpulver n

gun'run'ning s Waffenschmuggel m

gun'shot' s Schuß m; (range) Schußweite f

gun'shot wound' s Schußwunde f

gun'-shy' adj schußscheu

gun'sight' s Visier n

gun'smith' s Büchsenmacher m

gun'stock' s Gewehrschaft m

gun' tur'ret s Geschützturm m; (aer) Schwalbennest n

gunwale ['gʌnəl] s Schandeckel m

guppy ['gʌpi] s Millionenfisch m

gurgle ['gʌrgəl] s Glucksen n, Gurgeln n || intr glucksen, gurgeln

gush [gʌʃ] s Guß m; (fig) Erguß m || intr sich ergießen; g. out hervorströmen; g. over (fig) viel Aufhebens machen von

gusher ['gʌʃər] s Schwärmer –in mf; (oil well) sprudelnde Ölquelle f gush'ing *adj* (fig) überschwenglich

gushy ['gʌʃi] *adj* schwärmerisch

gusset ['gʌsɪt] *s* Zwickel *m*

gust [gʌst] *s* Stoß *m*; (*of wind*) Windstoß *m*, Bö *f*

gusto ['gʌsto] *s* Gusto *m*

gusty ['gʌsti] *adj* böig

gut [gʌt] *s* Darm *m*; guts Eingeweide *pl*; (coll) Schneid *m* || *v* (*pret & pp* gutted; *ger* gutting) *tr* ausbrennen; be gutted ausbrennen

gutter ['gʌtər] *s* Gosse *f*; (*of a roof*) Dachrinne *f*

gut'tersnipe' *s* (coll) Straßenjunge *m*

guttural ['gʌtərəl] *adj* kehlig; (ling) Kehl– *s* || (ling) Kehllaut *m*

guy [gaɪ] *s* Halteseil *n*; (*of a tent*) Spannschnur *f*; (coll) Kerl *m*; dirty guy (coll) Sauigel *m*; great guy Prachtkerl *m* || *tr* verspannen

guy' wire' *s* Spanndraht *m*

guzzle ['gʌzəl] *tr & intr* saufen

guzzler ['gʌzlər] *s* Säufer –in *mf*

gym [dʒɪm] *adj* (coll) Turn– || *s* (coll) Turnhalle *f*

gym' class' *s* (coll) Turnstunde *f*

gymnasi·um [dʒɪm'nezɪ·əm] *s* (–ums & –a [ə]) Turnhalle *f*

gymnast ['dʒɪmnæst] *s* Turner –in *mf*

gymnastic [dʒɪm'næstɪk] *adj* Turn–, gymnastisch; g. exercise Turnübung *f* || gymnastics *spl* Gymnastik *f*, Turnen *n*

gynecologist [,gaɪnə'kɑlədʒɪst] *s* Gynäkologe *m*, Gynäkologin *f*

gynecology [,gaɪnə'kɑlədʒi] *s* Gynäkologie *f*

gyp [dʒɪp] *s* (sl) Nepp *m*; (*person*) Nepper *m*; that's a gyp das ist Nepp! || *v* (*pret & pp* gypped; *ger* gypping) *tr* neppen

gyp' joint' *s* Nepplokal *n*

gypper ['dʒɪpər] *s* Nepper *m*

gypsy ['dʒɪpsi] *adj* Zigeuner– || *s* Zigeuner –in *mf*

gyp'sy moth' *s* Großer Schwammspinner *m*

gyrate ['dʒaɪret] *intr* sich drehen; kreiseln

gyration [dʒaɪ'reʃən] *s* Kreiselbegwegung *f*

gyroscope ['dʒaɪrə,skop] *s* Kreisel *m*

H

H, h [etʃ] *s* achter Buchstabe des englischen Alphabets

haberdasher ['hæbər,dæ/ər] *s* Inhaber –in *mf* e–s Herrenmodengeschäfts

haberdashery ['hæbər,dæ/əri] *s* Herrenmodengeschäft *n*

habit ['hæbɪt] *s* Gewohnheit *f*; (eccl) Ordenskleid *n*; be in the h. of (ger) pflegen zu (*inf*); break s.o. of that h. of smoking j–m das Rauchen abgewöhnen; from h. aus Gewohnheit; get into the h. of smoking sich [*dat*] das Rauchen angewöhnen; make a h. of it es zur Gewohnheit werden lassen

habitat ['hæbɪ,tæt] *s* Wohngebiet *n*

habitation [,hæbɪ'teʃən] *s* Wohnort *m*

habitual [hə'bɪtʃ/ʊ·əl] *adj* gewohnheitsmäßig, Gewohnheits–

hack [hæk] *s* (*blow*) Hieb *m*; (*notch*) Kerbe *f*; (*rasping cough*) trockener Husten *m*; (*worn-out horse*) Schindmähre *f*; (*hackney*) Droschke *f*; (*taxi*) (coll) Taxi *n*; (*writer*) (coll) Schreiberling *m* || *tr* hacken, hauen; (basketball) auf den Arm schlagen || *intr* Taxi fahren

hackney ['hækni] *s* (*carriage*) Droschke *f*; (*horse*) gewöhnliches Gebrauchspferd *n*

hackneyed ['hæknid] *adj* abgedroschen

hack'saw' *s* Metallsäge *f*, Bügelsäge *f*

haddock ['hædək] *s* Schellfisch *m*

haft [hæft] *s* Griff *m*

hag [hæg] *s* Vettel *f*; (*witch*) Hexe *f*

haggard ['hægərd] *adj* hager

haggle ['hægəl] *intr* (over) feilschen (um)

hag'gling *s* Feilschen *n*

Hague, the [heg] *s* den Haag *m*

hail [hel] *s* Hagel *m*; h. of bullets Kugelhagel *m* || *tr* (*a taxi, ship*) anrufen; (*acclaim*) preisen; (as) begrüßen (als) || *intr* hageln; h. from stammen aus (or von) || *interj* Heil!

Hail' Mar'y *s* Ave Maria *n*

hail'stone' *s* Hagelkorn *n*, Schloße *f*

hail'storm' *s* Hagelschauer *m*

hair [her] *s* (*single hair*) Haar *n*; (*collectively*) Haare *pl*; by a h. um ein Haar; do s.o.'s h. j–n frisieren; get in s.o.'s h. j–m auf die Nerven gehen lassen; split hairs Haarspalterei treiben

hair'breadth' *s*—by a h. um Haaresbreite

hair'brush' *s* Haarbürste *f*

hair' clip' *s* Spange *f*, Klammer *f*

hair'cloth' *s* Haartuch *n*

hair'curl'er *s* Lockenwickler *m*

hair'cut' *s* Haarschnitt *m*; get a h. sich [*dat*] die Haare schneiden lassen

hair'do' *s* (–dos) Frisur *f*

hair'dress'er *s* Friseur *m*, Friseuse *f*

hair' dri'er *s* Haartrockner *m*

hair' dye' *s* Haarfärbemittel *n*

hairiness ['herɪnɪs] *s* Behaartheit *f*

hairless ['herlɪs] *adj* haarlos

hair'line' *s* Haaransatz *m*

hair' net' *s* Haarnetz *n*

hair' oil' *s* Haaröl *n*

hair'piece' *s* Haarteil *m*

hair'pin' *s* Haarnadel *f*

hair'-pin curve' *s* Haarnadelkurve *f*

hair'-rais'ing *adj* haarsträubend

hair' rinse' *s* Spülmittel *n*

hair′roll′er s Haarwickler m
hair′ set′ s Wasserwelle f
hair′ shirt′ s Büßerhemd n
hair′split′ting s Haarspalterei f
hair′ spray′ s Haarspray m
hair′spring′ s Haarfeder f, Spirale f
hair′style′ s Frisur f
hair′ ton′ic s Haarwasser n
hairy [′hɛri] adj haarig, behaart
Haiti [′heti] s Haiti n
halberd [′hælbərd] s Hellebarde f
hal′cyon days′ [′hælsɪ-ən] spl (fig) glückliche Zeit f
hale [hel] adj gesund; **h. and hearty** gesund und munter
half [hæf] adj halb; **at h. price** zum halben Preis; **have h. a mind to** (inf) halb und halb entschlossen sein zu (inf); **one and a h.** eineinhalb ‖ adv halb; **h. as much as** nur halb so wie; **h. as much again** um die Hälfte mehr; **h. past three** halb vier; **not h.** durchaus nicht ‖ s (halves [hævz₁) Hälfte f; **cut in h.** in die Hälfte schneiden; **go halves with** halbpart machen mit
half′-and-half′ adj & adv halb und halb ‖ s Halb-und-halb-Mischung f
half′back′ s (fb) Läufer m
half′-baked′ adj halb gebacken; (plans, etc.) halbfertig; (person) unerfahren
half′-blood′ s Halbblut n
half′-breed′ s Halbblut n, Mischling m
half′ broth′er s Halbbruder m
half′-cocked′ adv (coll) nicht ganz vorbereitet
half′-day′ adv halbtags
half′-full′ adj halbvoll
half′-heart′ed adj zaghaft
half′-hour′ adj halbstündig ‖ s halbe Stunde f; **every h.** halbstündlich
half′ leath′er s (bb) Halbleder n
half′-length′ adj halblang; (portrait) in Halbfigur
half′-length por′trait s Brustbild n
half′-light′ s Halbdunkel n
half′-mast′ s—at h. auf halbmast
half′-meas′ure s Halbheit f
half′-moon′ s Halbmond m
half′ note′ s (mus) halbe Note f
half′ pay′ s Wartegeld n; **be on h.** Wartegeld beziehen
half′ pint′ s (sl) Zwerg m
half′ sis′ter s Halbschwester f
half′ sleeves′ spl halblange Ärmel pl
half′ sole′ s Halbsohle f
half′-staff′ s—at h. auf halbmast
half′-tim′bered adj Fachwerk-
half′ time′ s (sport) Halbzeit f
half′-time′ adj Halbzeit-
half′ ti′tle s Schmutztitel m
half′tone′ s (mus, paint, typ) Halbton m
half′-track′ s Halbkettenfahrzeug n
half′-truth′ s halbe Wahrheit f
half′way′ adj auf halbem Wege liegend ‖ adv halbwegs, auf halbem Wege; **meet s.o. h.** j-m auf dem halben Wege entgegenkommen
half′way meas′ure s Halbheit f
half′-wit′ s Schwachkopf m
half′-wit′ted adj blöd
halibut [′hælɪbət] s Heilbutt m

halitosis [,hælɪ′tosɪs] s Mundgeruch m
hall [hɔl] s (entranceway) Diele f, Flur m; (passageway) Gang m; (large meeting room) Saal m; (building) Gebäude n
hall′mark′ s Kennzeichen n
hal-lo [hə′lo] s (-los) Hallo n ‖ interj hallo!
hall′ of fame′ s Ruhmeshalle f
hallow [′hælo] tr heiligen
hallucination [hə,lusɪ′ne/ən] s Sinnestäuschung f, Halluzination f
hall′way′ s Flur m, Diele f; (passageway) Gang m
ha-lo [′helo] s (-los) Glorienschein m; (astr) Ring m, Hof m
halogen [′hælədʒən] s Halogen n
halt [hɔlt] s Halt m, Stillstand m; (rest) Rast f; **bring to a h.** zum Stillstand bringen; **call a h. to** halten lassen; **come to a h.** stehenbleiben ‖ tr anhalten ‖ intr halten; (rest) rasten ‖ interj halt!
halter [′hɔltər] s (for a horse) Halfter m; (noose) Strick m
halt′ing adj (gait) hinkend; (voice) stockend
halve [hæv] tr halbieren
halyard [′hæljərd] s Fall n
ham [hæm] s (pork) Schinken m; (back of the knee) Kniekehle f; (actor) (sl) Schmierenschauspieler -in m f; (rad) (sl) Funkamateur m
hamburger [′hæm,bɑrgər] s Hackfleisch n, deutsches Beefsteak n
hamlet [′hæmlɪt] s Dörfchen n
hammer [′hæmæk] s Hammer m; (of a bell) Klöppel m; (sport) Wurfhammer m ‖ tr hämmern; **h. in** (a nail) einschlagen; (e.g., rules) einhämmern; **h. out** aushämmern ‖ intr hämmern; **h. away at** (fig) herumarbeiten an (dat)
hammock [′hæmæk] s Hängematte f
hamper [′hæmpər] s Wäschebehälter m ‖ tr behindern
hamster [′hæmstər] s Hamster m
ham′string′ s Kniesehne f ‖ v (pret & pp -strung) tr (fig) lähmen
hand [hænd] s Hand f; (applause) Beifall m; (handwriting) Handschrift f; (of a clock) Zeiger m; (help) Hilfe f; **all hands on deck!** (naut) alle Mann an Deck!; **at first h.** aus erster Hand; **at h.** vorhanden, zur Hand; **at the hands of** von seiten (genit); **be on h.** zur Stelle sein; **by h.** mit der Hand; **change hands** in andere Hände übergehen; **fall into s.o.'s hands** in j-s Hände fallen; **from h. to mouth** von der Hand in den Mund; **get one's hands on** in die Hände bekommen; **get the upper h.** die Oberhand gewinnen; **give s.o. a free h.** j-m freies Spiel lassen; **give s.o. a h.** (help s.o.) j-m helfen; (applaud s.o.) j-m Beifall spenden; **go h. in h. with** (fig) Hand in Hand gehen mit; **h. and foot** eifrig; **h. in h.** Hand in Hand; **hands off!** Hände weg!; **hands up!** Hände hoch!; **have a good h.** (cards) gute Karten haben; **have a h.**

in die Hand im Spiel haben bei; **have one's hands full** alle Hände voll zu tun haben; **have well in h.** gut in der Hand haben; **hold hands** sich bei den Händen halten; **in one's own h.** eigenhändig; **I wash my hands of it** ich wasche meine Hände in Unschuld; **join hands** (fig) sich zusammenschließen; **new h.** Neuling *m*; **on all hands** auf allen Seiten; **on h.** (com) vorrätig; **on one h. ... on the other** einerseits ... andererseits; **out of h.** außer Rand und Band; **play into s.o.'s hands** j-m in die Hände spielen; **put one's h. on** (fig) finden; **show one's h.** (fig) seine Karten aufdecken; **take a h.** in mitarbeiten an (*dat*); **throw up one's hands** verzweifelt die Hände hochwerfen; **try one's h. at** versuchen; **win hands down** spielend gewinnen; **with a heavy h.** streng || *tr* (zu)reichen; **h. down** (*to s.o. below*) herunterreichen; (*e.g., traditions*) überliefern; **h. in** (*e.g., homework*) abgeben; (*an application*) einreichen; **h. out** austeilen; **h. over** übergeben; (*relinquish*) aushändigen, hergeben; **I have to h. it to you** (coll) ich muß dir recht geben

hand'bag' *s* Handtasche *f*, Tasche *f*
hand'ball' *s* Handball *m*
hand'bill' *s* Handzettel *m*
hand'book' *s* Handbuch *n*
hand' brake' *s* (aut) Handbremse *f*
hand'breadth' *s* Handbreit *f*
hand' cart' *s* Handkarren *m*
hand'clasp' *s* Händedruck *m*
hand'cuff' *s* Handschelle *f* || *tr* Handschellen anlegen (*dat*)
-handed [ˌhændɪd] *suf* -händig
handful [ˈhændˌful] *s* Handvoll *f*; (*a few*) ein paar; (fig) Nervensäge *f*
hand'glass' *s* Leselupe *f*
hand' grenade' *s* Handgranate *f*
handi·cap [ˈhændɪˌkæp] *s* Handikap *n*, Benachteiligung *f* || *v* (*pret & pp* -capped; *ger* -capping) *tr* handikapen, benachteiligen
hand'icap race' *s* Vorgaberennen *n*
handicraft [ˈhændɪˌkræft] *s* Handwerk *n*
handily [ˈhændɪlɪ] *adv* (*dexterously*) geschickt; (*easily*) mit Leichtigkeit
handiwork [ˈhændɪˌwɔrk] *s* Handarbeit *f*; (fig) Werk *n*, Schöpfung *f*
handkerchief [ˈhæŋkərtʃɪf] *s* Taschentuch *n*
handle [ˈhændəl] *s* Griff *m*; (*of a pot*) Henkel *m*; (*of a frying pan, broom, etc.*) Stiel *m*; (*of a crank*) Handkurbel *f*; (*of a pump*) Schwengel *m*; (*of a door*) Drücker *m*; (*name*) (coll) Name *m*; (*title*) (coll) Titelkram *m*; **fly off the h.** vor Wut platzen || *tr* (*touch*) berühren; (*tools, etc.*) handhaben; (*operate*) bedienen; (fig) erledigen; (com) handeln mit; **h. with care!** Vorsicht!; **know how to h. customers** es verstehen, mit Kunden umzugehen || *intr*—**h. well** sich leicht lenken lassen

han'dlebars' *spl* Lenkstange *f*, (*mustache*) (coll) Schnauzbart *m*
handler [ˈhændlər] *s* (sport) Trainer *m*
han'dling *s* (*e.g., of a car*) Lenkbarkeit *f*; (*of merchandise, theme, ball*) Behandlung *f*; (*of a tool*) Handhabung *f*
han'dling charg'es *spl* Umschlagspesen *pl*
hand' lug'gage *s* Handgepäck *n*
hand'made' *adj* handgemacht
hand'-me-downs' *spl* getragene Kleider *pl*
hand' mir'ror *s* Handspiegel *m*
hand'-op'erated *adj* mit Handbetrieb
hand' or'gan *s* Drehorgel *f*
hand'out' *s* milde Gabe *f*; (*sheet*) Handzettel *m*
hand'-picked' *adj* handgepflückt; (fig) ausgesucht
hand'rail' *s* Geländer *n*
hand'saw' *s* Handsäge *f*
hand'shake' *s* Handschlag *m*, Händedruck *m*
handsome [ˈhænsəm] *adj* schön
hand'-to-hand' fight'ing *s* Nahkampf *m*
hand'-to-mouth' *adj* von der Hand in den Mund
hand'work' *s* Handarbeit *f*
hand'writ'ing *s* Handschrift *f*
handwritten [ˈhændˌrɪtən] *adj* handschriftlich; **h. letter** Handschreiben *n*
handy [ˈhændɪ] *adj* handlich; (*practical*) praktisch; (*person*) geschickt; **come in h.** gelegen kommen; **have h. zur Hand haben**
hand'y·man' *s* (**-men'**) Handlanger *m*
hang [hæŋ] *s* (*of clothes*) Fall *m*; **get the h. of** (coll) sich einarbeiten in (*acc*); **I don't give a h. about it** (coll) es ist mir Wurst || *v* (*pret & pp* hung [hʌŋ]) *tr* hängen; (*a door*) einhängen; (*wallpaper*) ankleben; **h. one's head den Kopf hängen lassen; h. out** heraushängen; **h. up** aufhängen; (*the receiver*) (telp) auflegen; **I'll be hanged if** ich will mich hängen lassen, wenn || *intr* hängen; (*float*) schweben; **h. around** herumlungern; **h. around the bar** sich in der Bar herumtreiben; **h. around with** umgehen mit; **h. back** sich zurückhalten; **h. by** (*a thread, rope*) hängen an (*dat*); **h. down** niederhängen; **h. in the balance** in der Schwebe sein; **h. on** durchhalten; **h. on s.o.'s words** an j-s Worten hängen; **h. on to** festhalten; (*retain*) behalten; **h. together** zusammenhalten; **h. up** (telp) einhängen || *v* (*pret & pp* hanged & hung) *tr* hängen
hangar [ˈhæŋər] *s* Hangar *m*
hang'-dog look' *s* Armesündergesicht *n*
hanger [ˈhæŋər] *s* Kleiderbügel *m*
hang'er-on' *s* (**hangers-on**) Mitläufer –in *mf*
hang'ing *adj* (herab)hängend || *s* Hängen *n*
hang'man *s* (**-men**) Henker *m*
hang'nail' *s* Niednagel *m*

hang'out' s Treffpunkt m
hang'o'ver s (coll) Kater m
hank [hæŋk] s Strähne f
hanker ['hæŋkər] intr (for) sich sehnen (nach)
hanky-panky ['hæŋki'pæŋki] s (coll) Schwindel m
haphazard [,hæp'hæzərd] adj wahllos
haphazardly [,hæp'hæzərdli] adv aufs Geratewohl
hapless ['hæplɪs] adj unglücklich
happen ['hæpən] intr geschehen; **h. to see** zufällig sehen; **h. upon** zufällig stoßen auf (acc); **what happens now?** was soll nun werden?
hap'pening s Ereignis n
happily ['hæpɪli] adv glücklich
happiness ['hæpɪnɪs] s Glück n
happy ['hæpi] adj glücklich; **be h. about** s.th. über etw erfreut sein; **be h. to** (inf) sich freuen zu (inf); **h. as a lark** quietschvergnügt
Hap'py Birth'day interj Herzlichen Glückwunsch zum Geburtstag!
hap'py-go-luck'y adj unbekümmert
hap'py me'dium s—strike a h. e-n glücklichen Ausgleich treffen
Hap'py New' Year' interj Glückliches Neujahr!
harangue [hə'ræŋ] s leidenschaftliche Rede f || tr e-e leidenschaftliche Rede halten an (acc)
harass [hə'ræs], ['hærəs] tr schikanieren; (mil) stören
harass'ing fire' s (mil) Störungsfeuer n
harassment [hə'ræsmənt], ['hærəsmənt] s Schikane f; (mil) Störung f
harbinger ['hɑrbɪndʒər] s Vorbote m || tr anmelden
harbor ['hɑrbər] adj Hafen– || s Hafen m || tr (give refuge to) beherbergen; (hide) verbergen; (thoughts) hegen
har'bor mas'ter s Hafenmeister m
hard [hɑrd] adj (substance, water, words) hart; (problem) schwierig; (worker) fleißig; (blow, times, work) schwer; (life) mühsam; (fact) nackt; (rain) heftig; (winter) streng; (drinks) alkoholisch; **be h. on s.o.** j-m schwer zusetzen; **have a h. time** Schwierigkeiten haben; **h. to believe** kaum zu glauben; **h. to please** anspruchsvoll; **h. to understand** schwer zu verstehen || adv hart; (energetically) fleißig; **he was h. put to** (inf) es fiel ihm schwer zu (inf); **rain h.** stark regnen; **take h.** schwer nehmen; **try h.** mit aller Kraft versuchen
hard'-and-fast' adj fest
hard-bitten ['hɑrd,bɪtən] adj verbissen
hard'-boiled' adj (egg) hartgekocht; (coll) hartgesotten
hard' can'dy s Bonbons pl
hard' cash' s bare Münze f
hard' ci'der s Apfelwein m
hard' coal' s Steinkohle f
hard'-earned' adj schwer verdient
harden ['hɑrdən] tr & intr (er)härten
hard'ened adj (criminal) hartgesotten
hard'ening s Verhärtung f
hard'-head'ed adj nüchtern
hard'-heart'ed adj hartherzig

hardihood ['hɑrdɪ,hʊd] s Kühnheit f; (insolence) Frechheit f
hardiness ['hɑrdɪnɪs] s Ausdauer f, Widerstandsfähigkeit f
hard' la'bor s Zwangsarbeit f
hard' luck' s Pech n
hardly ['hɑrdli] adv kaum, schwerlich; **h. ever** fast gar nicht
hardness ['hɑrdnɪs] s Härte f
hard'-of-hear'ing adj schwerhörig
hard'-pressed' adj schwer bedrängt
hard'-shell' adj hartschalig; (coll) unnachgiebig
hard'ship' s Mühsal f
hard'top' s (aut) Hardtop n
hard' up' adj (for money) schlecht bei Kasse; **h. for** in Verlegenheit um
hard'ware' s Eisenwaren pl; (e.g., on doors, windows) Beschläge pl; military h. militärische Ausrüstung f
hard'ware store' s Eisenwarenhandlung f
hard'wood' s Hartholz n
hard'wood floor' s Hartholzboden m
hard'-work'ing adj fleißig
hardy ['hɑrdi] adj (plants) winterfest; (person) widerstandsfähig
hare [hɛr] s Hase m
hare'brained' adj unbesonnen
hare'lip' s Hasenscharte f
harem ['hɛrəm] s Harem m
hark [hɑrk] intr horchen; **h. back to** zurückgehen auf (acc)
harlequin ['hɑrləkwɪn] s Harlekin m
harlot ['hɑrlət] s Hure f
harm [hɑrm] s Schaden m; **do h.** Schaden anrichten; **I meant no h. by it** ich meinte es nicht böse; **out of harm's way** in Sicherheit; **there's no h. in trying** ein Versuch kann nicht schaden || tr beschädigen; (e.g., a reputation, chances) schaden (dat); **h. s.o.** (physically) j-m etw zuleide tun; (fig) schaden (dat)
harmful ['hɑrmfəl] adj schädlich
harmless ['hɑrmlɪs] adj unschädlich
harmonic [hɑr'mɑnɪk] adj harmonisch || s (mus) Oberton m
harmonica [hɑr'mɑnɪkə] s Harmonika f
harmonious [hɑr'monɪ-əs] adj harmonisch
harmonize ['hɑrmənɪz] intr harmonieren
harmony ['hɑrməni] s Harmonie f; **be in h. with** im Einklang stehen mit
harness ['hɑrnɪs] s Geschirr n; **die in the h.** in den Sielen sterben || tr anschirren; (e.g., a river, power) nutzbar machen
har'ness mak'er s Sattler m
har'ness rac'ing s Trabrennen n
harp [hɑrp] s Harfe f || intr—**h. on** herumreiten auf (dat)
harpist ['hɑrpɪst] s Harfner –in mf
harpoon [hɑr'pun] s Harpune f || tr harpunieren
harpsichord ['hɑrpsɪ,kɔrd] s Cembalo n
harpy ['hɑrpi] s (myth) Harpyie f
harrow ['hæro] s Egge f || tr eggen
har'rowing adj schrecklich

har·ry ['hæri] v (pret & pp **-ried**) tr martern

Harry ['hæri] s Heinz m

harsh [harʃ] adj (conditions) hart; (tone) schroff; (light) grell; (treatment) rauh

harshness ['harʃnis] s Härte f; Schroffheit f; Grelle f; Rauheit f

hart [hart] s Hirsch m

harum-scarum ['herəm'skerəm] adj wild || adv wie ein Wilder

harvest ['harvɪst] s Ernte f; **bad h.** Mißernte f || tr & intr ernten

harvester ['harvɪstər] s Schnitter -in mf; (mach) Mähmaschine f

har'vest moon' s Erntemond m

has-been ['hæz,bɪn] s (coll) Gestrige mf

hash [hæʃ] s Gehacktes n; **make h. of** (coll) verwursteln || tr zerhacken

hashish ['hæʃiʃ] s Haschisch n

hasp [hæsp] s Haspe f

hassle ['hæsəl] s (coll) Streit m

hassock ['hæsək] s Hocker m

haste [hest] s Hast f, Eile f; **in (all) h.** in (aller) Eile; **make h.** sich beeilen

hasten ['hesən] tr beschleunigen || intr hasten, eilen

hasty ['hesti] adj eilig; (rash) hastig

hat [hæt] s Hut m; **keep under one's h.** für sich behalten

hat'band' s Hutband n

hat'block' s Hutform f

hat'box' s Hutschachtel f

hatch [hætʃ] s (opening) (aer, naut) Luke f; (cover) (naut) Lukendeckel m || tr (eggs) ausbrüten; (a scheme) aushecken; (mark with strokes) schraffieren || intr Junge ausbrüten; (said of chicks) aus dem Ei kriechen

hat'check girl' s Garderobe(n)fräulein n

hatchet ['hætʃɪt] s Beil n; **bury the h.** die Streitaxt begraben

hatch'ing s Schraffierung f

hatch'way' s (naut) Luke f

hate [het] s Haß m || tr hassen; **I h. to** (inf) es widerstrebt mir zu (inf)

hateful ['hetfəl] adj verhaßt

hatless ['hætlɪs] adj hutlos

hat'pin' s Hutnadel f

hat'rack' s Hutständer m

hatred ['hetrɪd] s Haß m

haughtiness ['hotɪnɪs] s Hochmut m

haughty ['hoti] adj hochmütig

haul [hol] s Schleppen n; (hauling distance) Transportstrecke f; (amount caught) Fang m; **make a big h.** (fig) reiche Beute machen; **over the long h.** auf die Dauer || tr (tug) schleppen; (transport) transportieren; **h. ashore** ans Land ziehen; **h. down** (a flag) einholen; **h. into court** vor Gericht schleppen; **h. out of bed** aus dem Bett herausholen || intr—**h. off** (naut) abdrehen; **h. off and hit** ausholen um zu schlagen

haulage ['holɪdʒ] s Transport m; (costs) Transportkosten pl

haunch [hontʃ] s (hip) Hüfte f; (hind quarter of an animal) Keule f

haunt [hont] s Aufenthaltsort m || tr verfolgen; **h. a place** an e-m Ort umgehen; **this place is haunted** es spukt hier

haunt'ed house' s Haus n in dem es spukt

have [hæv] s—**the haves and the have-nots** die Besitzenden und die Besitzlosen || v (pret & pp **had** [hæd]) tr haben; (a baby) bekommen; (a drink) trinken; (food) essen; **h. back** (coll) zurückhaben; **h. in mind** vorhaben; **h. it in for s.o.** j–n auf dem Strich haben; **h. it out with s.o.** sich mit j–m aussprechen; **h. it your way** meinetwegen machen Sie es, wie Sie wollen; **h. left** übrig haben; **h. on** (clothes) anhaben; (a hat) aufhaben; (e.g., a program) vorhaben; **h. on one's person** bei sich tragen; **h. to do with s.o.** mit j–m zu tun haben; **h. what it takes** das Zeug dazu haben; **I've had it!** jetzt langt's mir aber!; **I will not h. it!** ich werde es nicht dulden!; **you had better** es wäre besser, wenn Sie; **what would you h. me do?** was soll ich machen? || intr—**h. done with it** fertig sein damit; **h. off** frei haben || aux (to form compound past tenses) haben, e.g., **he has paid the bill** er hat die Rechnung bezahlt; (to form compound past tenses of certain intransitive verbs of motion and change of condition, of the verb **bleiben,** and of the transitive verb **eingehen**) sein, e.g., **she has gone to the theater** sie ist ins Theater gegangen; **they h. become rich** sie sind reich geworden; **you h. stayed too long** Sie sind zu lange geblieben; **I h. assumed an obligation** ich bin e–e Verpflichtung eingegangen; (to express causation) lassen, e.g., **I am having a new suit made** ich lasse mir e–n neuen Anzug machen; (to express necessity) müssen, e.g., **I h. to study now** jetzt muß ich studieren; **that will h. to do** das wird genügen müssen

haven ['hevən] s Hafen m

haversack ['hævər,sæk] s Brotbeutel m

havoc ['hævək] s Verwüstung f; **wreak h. on** verwüsten

haw [ho] s (bot) Mehlbeere f; (in speech) Äh n || tr nach links lenken || intr nach links gehen || interj (to a horse) hü!

Hawaii [hə'waɪ·i] s Hawaii n

Hawaiian [hə'waɪjən] adj hawaiisch

Hawai'ian Is'lands spl Hawaii-Inseln pl

hawk [hok] s Habicht m || tr (wares) verhökern; **h. up** aushusten || intr sich räuspern

hawker ['hokər] s Straßenhändler -in mf

hawse [hoz] s (hole) (naut) Klüse f; (prow) (naut) Klüsenwand f

hawse'hole' s (naut) Klüse f

hawser ['hozər] s (naut) Trosse f, Tau n

hawthorn ['hoθorn] s Weißdorn m

hay [he] s Heu n; **hit the hay** (sl) sich

in die Falle hauen; **make hay** Heu machen

hay′fe′ver s Heufieber n

hay′field′ s Kleefeld n

hay′fork′ s Heugabel f

hay′loft′ s Heuboden m

hay′mak′er s (box) Schwinger m

hay′rack′ s Heuraufe f

hayrick [′heˌrɪk] s Heuschober m

hay′ride′ s Ausflug m in e–m teilweise mit Heu gefüllten Wagen

hay′seed′ s (coll) Bauerntölpel m

hay′stack′ s Heuschober m

hay′wire′ adj (sl) übergeschnappt; **go h.** (go wrong) schiefgehen; (go insane) überschnappen

hazard [′hæzərd] s (danger) Gefahr f; (risk) Risiko n || tr riskieren

hazardous [′hæzərdəs] adj gefährlich

haze [hez] s Dunst m; (fig) Unklarheit f || tr (students) piesacken

hazel [′hezəl] adj (eyes) nußbraun || s (bush) Hasel f

ha′zelnut′ s Haselnuß f

haziness [′hezɪnɪs] s Dunstigkeit f; (fig) Verschwommenheit f

haz′ing s (of students) Piesacken n

hazy [′hezi] adj dunstig; (recollection) verschwommen

H-bomb [′etʃ ˌbam] s Wasserstoffbombe f

he [hi] pers pron er; **he who** wer || s Männchen n

head [hed] adj Kopf–; (chief) Haupt–, Ober–, Chef– || s (of a body, cabbage, nail, lettuce, pin) Kopf m; (of a gang, family) Haupt m; (of a firm) Chef m; (of a school) Direktor –in mf; (of a department) Leiter –in mf; (of a bed) Kopfende n; (of a coin) Bildseite f; (of a glass of beer) Blume f; (of cattle) Stück m; (of stairs) oberer Absatz m; (of a river) Quelle f; (of a parade, army) Spitze f; (toilet) Klo n; **a h.** pro Person, pro Kopf; **at the h.** of an der Spitze (genit); **be at the h. of** vorstehen (dat); **be h. and shoulders above s.o.** haushoch über j–m stehen; (be far superior to s.o.) j–m haushoch überlegen sein; **be over one's h.** über j–s Verstand gehen; **bring to a h.** zur Entscheidung bringen; **by a h.** um e–e Kopflänge; **from h. to foot** von Kopf bis Fuß; **go over s.o.'s h.** über j–s Verstand gehen; (adm) über j–s Kopf hinweg handeln; **go to s.o.'s h.** j–m zu Kopfe steigen; **have a good h. for** begabt sein für; **h. over heels** kopfüber; (in love) bis über die Ohren; (in debt) bis über den Hals; **heads or tails?** Kopf oder Wappen?; **heads up!** aufpassen!; **keep one's h.** kaltes Blut behalten; **keep one's h. above water** sich über Wasser halten; **lose one's h.** den Kopf verlieren; **my h. is spinning** es schwindelt mir; **not be able to make h. or tail of** nicht klug werden aus; **out of one's h.** nicht ganz richtig im Kopf; **per h.** pro Kopf; **put heads together** die Köpfe zusammenstecken; **talk over**

s.o.'s h. über j–s Kopf hinwegreden; **talk s.o.'s h. off** j–n dumm und dämlich reden; **take it into one's h.** es sich [dat] in den Kopf setzen || tr (be in charge of) leiten; (a parade, army, expedition) anführen; (steer, guide) lenken; **h. a list** als erster auf e–r Liste stehen; **h. off** abwehren; **h. up** (a committee) vorsitzen (dat) || intr—**h.** back zurückkehren; **h. for** auf dem Wege sein nach; (aer) anfliegen; (naut) ansteuern; **h. home** sich heimbegeben; **where are you heading?** wo wollen Sie hin?

head′ache′ s Kopfweh n, Kopfschmerzen pl

head′band′ s Kopfband n

head′board′ s Kopfbrett n

head′cold′ s Schnupfen m

head′ doc′tor s Chefarzt m, Chefärztin f

head′dress′ s Kopfputz m

-headed [ˌhedɪd] suf –köpfig

head first adv kopfüber; (fig) Hals über Kopf

head′gear′ s Kopfbedeckung f

head′hunt′er s Kopfjäger m

head′ing s Überschrift f; (aer) Steuerkurs m

headland [′hedlənd] s Landspitze f

headless [′hedlɪs] adj kopflos; (without a leader) führerlos

head′light′ s (aut) Scheinwerfer m

head′line′ s (in a newspaper) Schlagzeile f; (at the top of a page) Überschrift f; **hit the headlines** (coll) Schlagzeilen liefern

head′lin′er s Hauptdarsteller –in mf

head′long′ adj stürmisch || adv kopfüber

head′man s (–men) Häuptling m, Chef m

head′mas′ter s Direktor m

head′mis′tress s Direktorin f

head′ nurse′ s Oberschwester f

head′ of′fice s Hauptgeschäftsstelle f

head′ of gov′ernment s Regierungschef m

head′ of hair′ s—**beautiful h.** schönes volles Haar n

head′ of the fam′ily s Familienoberhaupt n

head′-on′ adj Frontal– || adv frontal

head′phones′ spl Kopfhörer pl

head′piece′ s Kopfbedeckung f; (brains) (coll) Kopf m; (typ) Zierleiste f

head′quar′ters s Hauptquartier n; (of police) Polizeidirektion f; (mil) Hauptquartier n, Stabsquartier n

head′quarters com′pany s Stabskompanie f

head′rest′ s Kopflehne f; (aut) Kopfstütze f

head′ restrain′er s (aut) Kopfstütze f

head′set′ s Kopfhörer m

head′ shrink′er s (coll) Psychiater –in mf

head′stand′ s Kopfstand m

head′start′ s Vorsprung m

head′stone′ s Grabstein m

head′strong′ adj starrköpfig

head′ wait′er s Oberkellner m

head′wa′ters spl Quellflüsse pl

head′way′ s Vorwärtsbewegung f; (fig) Fortschritte pl

head′wear s Kopfbedeckung f

head′wind′ s Gegenwind m

head′work′ s Kopfarbeit f

heady ['hɛdɪ] adj (wine) berauschend; (news) spannend; (impetuous) unbesonnen

heal [hil] tr & intr heilen; **h. up** zuheilen

healer ['hilər] s Heilkundige mf

heal′ing s Heilung f

health [hɛlθ] s Gesundheit f; **drink to s.o.'s h.** auf j-s Wohl trinken; **in good h.** gesund; **in poor h.** kränklich; **to your h.!** auf Ihr Wohl!

health′ cer′tificate s Gesundheitspaß m

healthful ['hɛlθfəl] adj heilsam; (climate) bekömmlich

health′ insur′ance s Krankenversicherung f

health′ resort′ s Kurort m

healthy ['hɛlθɪ] adj gesund; (respect) gehörig; **keep h.** sich gesund halten

heap [hip] s Haufen m; **in heaps** haufenweise ‖ tr beladen; **h.** (e.g., praise) **on** s.o. j-n überhäufen mit; **h. up** anhäufen

hear [hɪr] v (pret & pp heard [hʌrd]) tr hören; (find out) erfahren; (get word) Bescheid bekommen; **h. s.o.'s lessons** j-n überhören; **h. s.o. out** j-n ganz ausreden lassen ‖ intr hören; **h. about** hören über (acc) or von; **h. from** Nachricht bekommen von; **h. of** hören von; **h. wrong** sich verhören; **he wouldn't h. of it** er wollte nichts davon hören

hearer ['hɪrər] s Hörer –in mf; **hearers** Zuhörer pl

hear′ing s Hören n, Gehör n; (jur) Verhör n; **within h.** in Hörweite

hear′ing aid′ s Hörgerät n, Hörapparat m

hear′say′ s Hörensagen n; **know s.th. by h.** etw nur vom Hörensagen kennen; **that's mere h.** das ist bloßes Gerede

hearse [hʌrs] s Leichenwagen m

heart [hɑrt] s Herz n; **after my own h.** nach meinem Herzen; **at h.** im Grunde genommen; **be the h. and soul of** die Seele sein (genit); **by h.** auswendig; **cross my h.!** Hand aufs Herz!; **cry one's h. out** sich ausweinen; **eat one's h. out** sich vor Kummer verzehren; **get to the h. of** auf den Grund kommen (dat); **have a h.** (coll) ein Herz haben; **have one's h. in s.th.** mit dem Herzen bei etw sein; **have the h. to** (inf) es übers Herz bringen zu (inf); **h. and soul** mit Leib und Seele; **hearts** (cards) Herz n; **lose h.** den Mut verlieren; **lose one's h. to** sein Herz verlieren an (acc); **set one's h. on** sein Herz hängen an (acc); **take h.** Mut fassen; **take to h.** beherzigen; **to one's heart's content** nach Herzenslust; **wear one's h. on one's sleeve** das Herz auf der Zunge tragen; **with all one's h.** mit ganzem Herzen

heart′ache′ s Herzweh n

heart′ attack′ s Herzanfall m

heart′beat′ s Herzschlag m

heart′break′ s Herzeleid n

heart′break′er s Herzensbrecher –in mf

heartbroken ['hɑrt‚brokən] adj trostlos

heart′burn′ s Sodbrennen n

heart′ disease′ s Herzleiden n

–hearted [‚hɑrtɪd] suf –herzig

hearten ['hɑrtən] tr ermutigen

heart′ fail′ure s Herzschlag m

heartfelt ['hɑrt‚fɛlt] adj herzinnig, tiefempfunden; (wishes) herzlich

hearth [hɑrθ] s Herd m

hearth′stone′ s Kaminplatte f

heartily ['hɑrtɪlɪ] adv (with zest) herzhaft; (sincerely) von Herzen

heartless ['hɑrtlɪs] adj herzlos

heart′ mur′mur s Herzgeräusch n

heart′-rend′ing adj herzzerreißend

heart′sick′ adj tief betrübt

heart′ strings′ spl—**pull at s.o.'s h.** j-m ans Herz greifen

heart′ throb′ s Schwarm m

heart′ trans′plant s Herzverpflanzung f

heart′ trou′ble s Herzbeschwerden pl

heart′wood′ s Kernholz n

hearty ['hɑrtɪ] adj herzhaft; (meal) reichlich; (eater) stark; (appetite) gut

heat [hit] s Hitze f, Wärme f; (heating) Heizung f; (sexual) Brunst f; (in the case of dogs) Läufigkeit f; (of battle) Eifer m; (sport) Rennen n, Einzelrennen n; **be in h.** brunsten; (said of dogs) läufig sein; **final h.** Schlußrennen n; **put the h. on** (sl) unter Druck setzen; **qualifying h.** Vorlauf m ‖ tr (e.g., food) wärmen; (fluids) erhitzen; (a house) heizen; **h. up** aufwärmen ‖ intr—**h. (up)** warm (or heiß) werden

heat′ed adj erhitzt; (fig) erregt

heater ['hitər] s Heizkörper m; (oven) Heizofen m

heath [hiθ] s Heide f

hea·then ['hiðən] adj heidnisch ‖ s (–then & –thens) Heide m, Heidin f

heathendom ['hiðəndəm] s Heidentum n

heather ['hɛðər] s Heiderkraut n

heat′ing s Heizung f

heat′ing pad′ s Heizkissen n

heat′ing sys′tem s Heizanlage f

heat′ light′ning s Wetterleuchten n

heat′ prostra′tion s Hitzekollaps m

heat′-resis′tant adj hitzebeständig

heat′ shield′ s (rok) Hitzeschild m

heat′stroke′ s Hitzschlag m

heat′ treat′ment s Wärmebehandlung f

heat′ wave′ s Hitzewelle f

heave [hiv] s Hub m; (throw) Wurf m; **heaves** (vet) schweres Atmen n ‖ v (pret & pp heaved & hove [hov]) tr heben; (throw) werfen; (a sigh) ausstoßen; (the anchor) lichten ‖ intr (said of the breast or sea) wogen; (retch) sich übergeben; **h. in sight** auftauchen; **h. to** (naut) stoppen

heaven ['hɛvən] *s* Himmel *m; for heaven's sake* um Himmels willen; *good heavens!* ach du lieber Himmel!; *the heavens* der Himmel

heavenly ['hɛvənlɪ] *adj* himmlisch

hea′venly bod′y *s* Himmelskörper *m*

heavenwards ['hɛvənwərdz] *adv* himmelwärts

heavily ['hɛvɪlɪ] *adv* schwer; *h. in debt* überschuldet

heavy ['hɛvɪ] *adj* schwer; *(food)* schwer verdaulich; *(fine, price)* hoch; *(walk)* schwerfällig; *(heart)* bedrückt, schwer; *(traffic, frost, rain)* stark; *(fog)* dicht; *(role)* (theat) ernst, düster; *h. drinker* Gewohnheitstrinker *–in mf; h. seas* Sturzsee *f; h. with sleep* schlaftrunken

heav′y-armed′ *adj* schwerbewaffnet

heav′y-du′ty *adj* Hochleistungs-, Schwerlast–

heav′y-du′ty truck′ *s* Schwerlastwagen *m*

heav′y-heart′ed *adj* bedrückt

heav′y in′dustry *s* Schwerindustrie *f*

heav′yset′ *adj* untersetzt

heav′y weight′ *adj* Schwergewicht– ‖ *s* Schwergewichtler *m*

Hebrew ['hibru] *adj* hebräisch ‖ *s* Hebräer *–in mf; (language)* Hebräisch *n*

hecatomb ['hɛkə‚tom] *s* Hekatombe *f*

heck [hɛk] *s*—*give s.o. h.* (sl) j–m tüchtig einheizen; *what are you doing?* (sl) was zum Teufel tust du? ‖ *interj* (sl) verflixt!

heckle ['hɛkəl] *tr* durch Zwischenrufe belästigen

heckler ['hɛklər] *s* Zwischenrufer *–in mf*

hectic ['hɛktɪk] *adj* hektisch

hectograph ['hɛktə‚græf] *s* Hektograph *m* ‖ *tr* hektographieren

hedge [hɛdʒ] *s* Hecke *f* ‖ *tr*—*h. in* (or *h. off*) einhegen ‖ *intr* sich den Rücken decken

hedge′hog′ *s* Igel *m*

hedge′hop′ *v* (*pret & pp* –hopped; *ger* hopping) *intr* (aer) heckenspringen

hedge′hop′ping *s* (aer) Heckenhüpfen *n*

hedge′row′ *s* Hecke *f*

hedonism ['hidə‚nɪzəm] *s* Hedonismus *m*

hedonist ['hidənɪst] *s* Hedonist *–in mf*

heed [hid] *s* Acht *f; pay h. to* achtgeben auf (*acc*); *take h.* achtgeben ‖ *tr* beachten ‖ *intr* achtgeben

heedful ['hidfəl] *adj* (of) achtsam (auf *acc*)

heedless ['hidlɪs] *adj* achtlos; *h. of* ungeachtet (*genit*)

heehaw ['hi‚hɔ] *s* Iah *n* ‖ *interj* iah!

heel [hil] *s* (*of the foot*) Ferse *f; (of a shoe*) Absatz *m; (of bread*) Brotende *n;* (sl) Schurke *m; down at the h.* abgerissen; *cool one's heels* sich *[dat]* die Beine in den Bauch stehen; *take to one's heels* Fersengeld geben ‖ *intr* (*said of a dog*) auf den Fersen folgen

hefty ['hɛftɪ] *adj* (*heavy*) schwer; (*muscular*) stämmig; (*blow*) zünftig

heifer ['hɛfər] *s* Färse *f*

height [haɪt] *s* Höhe *f; (e.g., of power*) Gipfel *m; h. of the season* Hochsaison *f*

heighten ['haɪtən] *tr* erhöhen; (fig) verschärfen

heinous ['henəs] *adj* abscheulich

heir [ɛr] *s* Erbe; *m; become h. to* erben; *become s.o.'s h.* j–n beerben

heir′ appar′ent *s* (*heirs apparent*) Thronerbe *m*

heiress ['ɛrɪs] *s* Erbin *f*

heir′loom′ *s* Erbstück *n*

heir′ presump′tive *s* (*heirs presumptive*) mutmaßlicher Erbe *m*

Helen ['hɛlən] *s* Helene *f*

helicopter ['hɛlɪ‚kɑptər] *s* Hubschrauber *m*

heliport ['hɛlɪ‚pɔrt] *s* Hubschrauberlandeplatz *m*

helium ['hilɪ-əm] *s* Helium *n*

helix ['hilɪks] *s* (helixes & helices ['hɛlɪ‚siz]) Spirale *f;* (archit) Schnecke *f*

hell [hɛl] *s* Hölle *f*

hell′bent′ *adj*—*h. on* (sl) erpicht auf (*acc*)

hell′cat′ *s* (*shrew*) Hexe *f*

Hellene ['hɛlin] *s* Hellene *m,* Hellenin *f*

Hellenic [hɛ'lɛnɪk] *adj* hellenisch

hell′fire′ *s* Höllenfeuer *n*

hellish ['hɛlɪʃ] *adj* höllisch

hel-lo [hɛ'lo] *s* (–los) Hallo *n* ‖ *interj* guten Tag!; (in southern Germany and Austria) Grüß Gott!; (to get s.o.'s attention and in answering the telephone) hallo!

helm [hɛlm] *s* (& fig) Steuerruder *n*

helmet ['hɛlmɪt] *s* Helm *m*

helms′man *s* (–men) Steuermann *m*

help [hɛlp] *s* Hilfe *f; (domestic*) Hilfe *f,* Hilfskraft *f; (temporary*) Aushilfe *f; h. wanted* (in *newspapers*) Stellenangebot *n; there's no h. for it* da ist nicht zu helfen; *with the h. of* mit Hilfe (*genit*) ‖ *tr* helfen (*dat*); *can I h. you?* womit kann ich (Ihnen) dienen?; *h. along* nachhelfen (*dat*); *h. down from* herunterhelfen (*dat*) von (*dat*); *h. oneself* sich bedienen; (*at table*) zugreifen; *h. oneself to* sich [*dat*] nehmen; *h. out* aushelfen (*dat*); *h. s.o. on* (or *off*) *with the coat* j–m in den (or aus dem) Mantel helfen; *I cannot h.* (ger), *I cannot h. but* (*inf*) ich kann nicht umhin zu (*inf*); *sorry, that can't be helped* es tut mir leid, aber es geht nicht anders ‖ *intr* helfen ‖ *interj* Hilfe!

helper ['hɛlpər] *s* Gehilfe *m,* Gehilfin *f*

helpful ['hɛlpfəl] *adj* (*person*) hilfsbereit; (*e.g., suggestion*) nützlich

help′ing *s* Portion *f*

help′ing hand′ *s* hilfreiche Hand *f*

helpless ['hɛlplɪs] *adj* hilflos, ratlos

helter-skelter ['hɛltər'skɛltər] *adj* wirr ‖ *adv* holterdiepolter

hem [hɛm] *s* Saum *m* ‖ *v* (*pret & pp* hemmed; *ger* hemming) *tr* säumen; *hem in* umringen ‖ *intr* stocken; *hem*

and **haw** nicht mit der Sprache her-
auswollen || *interj* hm!

hemisphere | ˈhemɪˌsfɪr | *s* Halbkugel *f*

hemistich | ˈhemɪˌstɪk] *s* Halbvers *m*

hem′line′ *s* Rocklänge *f*

hem′lock′ *s* (*conium*) Schierling *m*;
(*poison*) Schierlingsgift *n*; (*Tsuga
canadensis*) Kanadische Hemmlock-
tanne *f*

hemoglobin | ˌhiməˈglobɪn] *s* Blutfarb-
stoff *m*, Hämoglobin *n*

hemophilia | ˌhiməˈfrliˑə] *s* Bluter-
krankheit *f*, Hämophilie *f*

hemorrhage | ˈheməridʒ] *s* Blutung *f*

hemorrhoids | ˈheməˌrɔɪdz] *spl* Hämor-
rhoiden *pl*

hemostat | ˈhiməˌstæt] *s* Unterbin-
dungssklemme *f*

hemp [hemp] *s* Hanf *m*

hem′stitch′ *s* Hohlsaum *m* || *tr* mit e-m
Hohlsaum versehen

hen [hen] *s* Henne *f*, Huhn *n*

hence [hens] *adv* von hier; (*therefore*)
daher, daraus; **a year h.** in e-m Jahr

hence′forth′ *adv* hinfort, von nun an

hench·man | ˈhentʃmən] *s* (–men) An-
hänger *m*; (*gang member*) Helfers-
helfer *m*

hen′house′ *s* Hühnerstall *m*

henna | ˈhenə] *s* Henna *f*

hen′ par′ty *s* (coll) Damengesellschaft
f

hen′peck′ *tr* unter dem Pantoffel haben; **be henpecked** unter dem Pantoffel stehen; **henpecked husband**
Pantoffelheld *m*

Henry | ˈhenrɪ] *s* Heinrich *m*

hep [hep] *adj* (to) eingeweiht (in *acc*)

her [hʌr] *poss adj* ihr; (if the antece-
dent is neuter, e.g., Fräulein) sein ||
pers pron sie; (if the antecedent is
neuter) es; (indirect object) ihr; (if
the antecedent is neuter) ihm

herald | ˈherəld] *s* Herold *m*; (fig) Vor-
bote *m* || *tr* ankündigen; **h.** in ein-
führen

heraldic [heˈrældɪk] *adj* heraldisch; **h.
figure** Wappenbild *n*; **h. motto**
Wappenspruch *m*

heraldry | ˈherəldrɪ] *s* Wappenkunde *f*

herb | (h)ɜrb] *s* Kraut *n*, Gewürz *n*;
(pharm) Arzneikraut *n*

herculean [ˌhɜrkjuˈliˑən] *adj* herkulisch

herd [hʌrd] *s* Herde *f*; (of game) Rudel
n; **the common h.** der Pöbel *m* || *tr*
hüten; **h. together** zusammenpfer-
chen || *intr* in e–r Herde gehen (or
leben)

herds′man *s* (–men) Hirt *m*

here [hɪr] *adv* (*position*) hier; (*direction*) hierher, her; **h. and there**
hie(r) und da; **h. below** in diesem
Leben; **h. goes!** jetzt gilt's!; **here's
to you!** auf Ihr Wohl!; **neither h. nor
there** belanglos || *interj* hier!

hereabouts [ˈhɪrəˌbauts] *adv* hier in
der Nähe

hereaf′ter *adv* hiernach || *s* Jenseits *n*

hereby′ *adv* hierdurch

hereditary [hɪˈredɪˌteri] *adj* erblich,
Erb-; **be h.** sich vererben

heredity [hɪˈredɪti] *s* Vererbung *f*

herein′ *adv* hierin

hereof′ *adv* hiervon

hereon′ *adv* hierauf

heresy | ˈherəsi] *s* Ketzerei *f*

heretic | ˈherətɪk] *s* Ketzer –in *mf*

heretical [hɪˈretɪkəl] *adj* ketzerisch

heretofore′ | ˌhɜrtuˈfɔr] *adv* zuvor

here′upon′ *adv* daraufhin

herewith′ *adv* hiermit; (in a letter) anbei, in d… Anlage

heritage [ˈherɪtɪdʒ] *s* Erbe *n*

hermet′ically sealed′ [hʌrˈmetɪkəli]
adj hermetisch verschlossen

hermit | ˈhʌrmɪt] *s* Einsiedler –in *mf*;
(eccl) Eremit *m*

hermitage | ˈhʌrmɪtɪdʒ] *s* Eremitage *f*

herni·a | ˈhʌrnɪˑə] *s* (–as & –ae [ˌii])
Bruch *m*

he·ro [ˈhiro] *s* (–roes) Held *n*

heroic [hɪˈroˑɪk] *adj* heldenhaft,
Helden–; (pros) heroisch || **heroics**
spl Heldentaten *pl*

hero′ic age′ *s* Helden(zeit)alter *n*

hero′ic coup′let *s* heroisches Reim-
paar *n*

hero′ic verse′ *s* heroisches Vermaß *n*

heroin | ˈheroˑɪn] *s* Heroin *n*

heroine | ˈheroˑɪn] *s* Heldin *f*

heroism | ˈheroˌɪzəm] *s* Heldenmut *m*

heron | ˈherən] (orn) Fischreiher *m*

he′ro wor′ship *s* Heldenverehrung *f*

herring | ˈherɪŋ] *s* Hering *m*

her′ringbone′ *s* (*pattern*) Grätenmuster
n; (*parquetry*) Riemenparkett *n*

hers [hʌrz] *poss pron* der ihre (or
ihrige), ihrer

herself′ *reflex pron* sich; **she's not h.
today** sie ist heute gar nicht wie sonst
|| *intens pron* selbst, selber

hesitancy | ˈhezɪtənsi] *s* Zaudern *n*

hesitant | ˈhezɪtənt] *adj* zögernd

hesitate | ˈhezɪˌtet] *intr* zögern

hesitation [ˌheziˈteʃən] *s* Zögern *n*

heterodox | ˈhetərəˌdaks] *adj* anders-
gläubig, heterodox

heterodyne | ˈhetərəˌdain] *adj* Über-
lagerungs– || *tr & intr* überlagern

heterogeneous | [ˌhetərəˈdʒiniˑəs] *adj*
heterogen

hew [hju] *v* (*pret* hewed; *pp* hewed &
hewn) *tr* (stone) hauen; (trees) fällen; **hew down** umhauen

hex [heks] *s* (spell) Zauber *m*; (witch)
Hexe *f*; **put a hex on** (coll) behexen
|| *tr* (coll) behexen

hexagon | ˈheksəgən] *s* Hexagon *n*

hey [he] *interj* (coll) hei!; **hey there! hey! heda!**

hey′day′ *s* Hochblüte *f*, Glanzzeit *f*

H′-hour′ *s* (mil) X-Zeit *f*

hi [hai] *interj* he!; **hi there! hi! heda!**

hia·tus | ˈhaiˈetəs] *s* (–tuses & –tus)
Lücke *f*; (ling) Hiatus *m*

hibernate | ˈhaɪbərˌnet] *intr* (& fig)
Winterschlaf halten

hibernation [ˌhaɪbərˈneʃən] *s* Winterschlaf *m*

hibiscus [haiˈbiskəs] *s* Hibiskus *m*

hiccough, hiccup [ˈhikəp] *s* Schluckauf
m

hick [hik] *s* Tölpel *m*

hickory [ˈhikəri] *s* Hickorybaum *m*

hick′ town′ *s* Kuhdorf *n*

hidden [ˈhɪdən] *adj* verborgen, versteckt; (*secret*) geheim

hide [haɪd] *s* Haut *f*, Fell *n* ‖ *v* (*pret* hid [hɪd]; *pp* hid & hidden [ˈhɪdən] *tr* verstecken; (*a view*) verdecken; (fig) verbergen; **h. from** verheimlichen vor (*dat*) ‖ *intr* (out) sich verstecken

hide'-and-seek' *s* Versteckspiel *n*; **play h.** Verstecken spielen

hide'away' *s* Schlupfwinkel *m*

hide'bound' *adj* engherzig

hideous [ˈhɪdɪ-əs] *adj* gräßlich

hide'out' *s* (coll) Versteck *n*

hid'ing *s* Verstecken *n*; **be in h.** sich versteckt halten; **get a h.** (coll) Prügel bekommen

hid'ing place' *s* Versteck *n*

hierarchy [ˈhaɪ-ə͵rɑrki] *s* Hierarchie *f*

hieroglyphic [͵haɪ-ərə'glɪfɪk] *adj* Hieroglyphen– ‖ *s* Hieroglyphe *f*

hi-fi [ˈhaɪˈfaɪ] *adj* Hifi- ‖ *s* Hi-Fi *n*

high [haɪ] *adj* hoch; (*wind*) stark; (*hopes*) hochgespannt; (*fever*) heftig (*spirits*) gehoben; **h. and dry** auf dem Trockenen; **h. and mighty** hochfahrend; **it is h. time** es ist höchste Zeit ‖ *adv* hoch; **h. and low** weit und breit ‖ *s* (*e.g., in prices*) Hochstand *m*; (aut) höchster Gang *m*; (meteor) Hoch *n*; **on h.** oben; **shift into h.** den höchsten Gang einschalten

high' al'tar *s* Hochaltar *m*

high'ball' *s* Highball *m*

high'born' *adj* hochgeboren

high'boy' *s* hochbeinige Kommode *f*

high'brow' *adj* intellektuell ‖ *s* Intellektuelle *mf*

high' chair' *s* Kinderstuhl *m*

High' Church' *s* Hochkirche *f*

high'-class' *adj* vornehm, herrschaftlich

high' command' *s* Oberkommando *n*

high' cost' of liv'ing *s* hohe Lebenshaltungskosten *pl*

high' div'ing *s* Turmspringen *n*

high'er educa'tion *s* Hochschulbildung *f*

high'er-up' *s* (coll) hohes Tier *n*

high'est bid' [ˈhaɪ·ɪst] *s* Meistgebot *n*

high'est bid'der *s* Meistbietende *mf*

high' explo'sive *s* hochexplosiver Sprengstoff *m*

highfalutin [͵haɪfə'lutən] *adj* hochtönend

high' fidel'ity *s* äußerst getreue Tonwiedergabe *f*, High Fidelity *f*

high'-fidel'ity *adj* klanggetreu

high' fre'quency *s* Hochfrequenz *f*

high'-fre'quency *adj* hochfrequent

high' gear' *s* höchster Gang *m*; **shift into h.** den höchsten Gang einschalten; (fig) auf Hochtouren gehen

High' Ger'man *s* Hochdeutsch *n*

high'-grade' *adj* hochfein, Qualitäts–

high'-grade steel' *s* Edelstahl *m*

high'-hand'ed *adj* anmaßend

high' heel' *s* Stöckel *m*

high'-heeled shoe' *s* Stöckelschuh *m*

high' horse' *s*—**come off one's h.** klein beigeben; **get up on one's h.** sich aufs hohe Roß setzen

high' jinks' [͵dʒɪŋks] *spl* Ausgelassenheit *f*

high' jump' *s* (sport) Hochsprung *m*

highland [ˈhaɪlənd] *s* Hochland *n*; **highlands** Hochland *n*

highlander [ˈhaɪləndər] *s* Hochländer –in *mf*

high' life' *s* Prasserei *f*, Highlife *n*

high'light' *s* (*big moment*) Höhepunkt *m*; (*in a picture*) Glanzlicht *n* ‖ *tr* hervorheben; (*in a picture*) Glanzlichter aufsetzen (*dat*)

highly [ˈhaɪli] *adv* hoch, hoch–, höchst; **h. sensitive** hochempfindlich; **speak h. of** in den höchsten Tönen sprechen von; **think h. of** große Stücke halten auf (*acc*)

High' Mass' *s* Hochamt *n*

high'-mind'ed *adj* hochgesinnt

high'-necked' *adj* hochgeschlossen

highness [ˈhaɪnɪs] *s* Höhe *f*; **Highness** (*title*) Hoheit *f*

high' noon' *s*—**at h. am hellen Mittag**

high'-oc'tane *adj* mit hoher Oktanzahl

high'-pitched' *adj* (*voice*) hoch; (*roof*) steil

high'-pow'ered *adj.* starkmotorig; **h. engine** Hochleistungsmotor *m*

high' pres'sure *s* Hochdruck *m*

high'-pres'sure *adj* Hochdruck–; **h. area** Hochdruckgebiet *n* ‖ *tr* (com) bearbeiten

high'-priced' *adj* kostspielig

high' priest' *s* Hohe(r)priester *m*

high'-qual'ity *adj* Qualitäts–, hochwertig

high'-rank'ing *adj* hochgestellt

high' rise' *s* Hochbau *m*, Hochhaus *n*

high'road' *s* (fig) sicherer Weg *m*

high' school' *s* Oberschule *f*

high' sea' *s*—**on the high seas** auf offenem Meer

high' soci'ety *s* vornehme Welt *f*, High Society *f*

high'-sound'ing *adj* hochtönend

high'-speed' *adj* Schnell–; (phot) lichtstark

high'-speed steel' *s* Schnelldrehstahl *m*

high'-spir'ited *adj* hochgemut; (*horse*) feurig

high' spir'its *spl* gehobene Stimmung *f*

high-strung [ˈhaɪˈstrʌŋ] *adj* überempfindlich

high' ten'sion *s* Hochspannung *f*

high'-ten'sion *adj* Hochspannungs–

high'-test' gas'oline *s* Superbenzin *n*

high' tide' *s* Flut *f*

high' time' *s* höchste Zeit *f*; (sl) Heidenspaß *m*

high' trea'son *s* Hochverrat *m*

high' volt'age *s* Hochspannung *f*

high'-volt'age *adj* Hochspannungs–

high'-wa'ter mark' *s* Hochwassermarke *f*; (fig) Höhepunkt *m*

high'way' *s* Landstraße *f*, Chaussee *f*

high'way'man *s* (–men) Straßenräuber *m*

high'way patrol' *s* Straßenstreife *f*

high'way rob'bery *s* Straßenraub *m*

hijack [ˈhaɪ͵dʒæk] *tr* (*a truck*) überfallen und rauben; (*a plane*) entführen

hijacker [ˈhaɪ ˌdʒækər] *s* (*of a truck*) Straßenräuber –in *mf*; (*of a plane*) Entführer –in *mf*

hi'jack'ing *s* Entführung *f*

hike [haɪk] *s* Wanderung *f*; (*in prices*) Erhöhung *f* ‖ *tr* (*prices*) erhöhen ‖ *intr* wandern

hiker [ˈhaɪkər] *s* Wanderer –in *mf*

hik'ing *s* Wandern *n*

hilarious [hɪˈlɛri·əs] *adj* heiter

hill [hɪl] *s* Hügel *m*; **go over the h.** (mil) ausbüxen; **over the h.** (coll) auf dem absteigenden Ast ‖ *tr* häufeln

hill'bil'ly *adj* hinterwäldlerisch ‖ *s* Hinterwäldler –in *mf*

hill' coun'try *s* Hügelland *n*

hillock [ˈhɪlək] *s* Hügelchen *n*

hill'side' *s* Hang *m*

hilly [ˈhɪli] *adj* hügelig

hilt [hɪlt] *s* Griff *m*; **armed to the h.** bis an die Zähne bewaffnet; **to the h.** (fig) gründlich

him [hɪm] *pers pron* (*dative*) ihm; (*accusative*) ihn

himself' *reflex pron* sich; **he is not h. today** er ist heute gar nicht wie sonst ‖ *intens pron* selbst, selber

hind [haɪnd] *adj* Hinter– ‖ *s* Hirschkuh *f*

hinder [ˈhɪndər] *tr* (ver)hindern

hind'most' *adj* hinterste

hind'quar'ter *s* Hinterviertel *n*; (*of a horse*) Hinterhand *f*; (*of venison*) Ziemer *m*

hindrance [ˈhɪndrəns] *s* (to) Hindernis *n* (für)

hind'sight' *s* späte Einsicht *f*

Hindu [ˈhɪndu] *adj* Hindu– ‖ *s* Hindu *m*

hinge [hɪndʒ] *s* Scharnier *n*; (*of a door*) Angel *f* ‖ *intr*—**h. on** abhängen von

hint [hɪnt] *s* Wink *m*, Andeutung *f*; **give a broad h.** e-n Wink mit dem Zaunpfahl geben; **take the h.** den Wink verstehen ‖ *intr*—**h. at** andeuten

hinterland [ˈhɪntərˌlænd] *s* Hinterland *n*

hip [hɪp] *adj* (sl) im Bild ‖ *s* Hüfte *f*; (*of a roof*) Walm *m*

hip'bone' *s* Hüftbein *n*

hip'joint' *s* Hüftgelenk *n*

hipped *adj*—**h. on** (coll) erpicht auf (*acc*)

hippopota·mus [ˌhɪpəˈpɑtəməs] *s* (**-muses** & **–mi** [ˌmaɪ]) Nilpferd *n*

hip' roof' *s* Walmdach *n*

hire [haɪr] *s* Miete *f*; (*salary*) Lohn *m*; **for h.** zu vermieten ‖ *tr* (*workers*) anstellen; (*rent*) mieten; **h. oneself out to** sich verdingen bei; **h. out** vermieten

hired' hand' *s* Lohnarbeiter –in *mf*

hireling [ˈhaɪrlɪŋ] *s* Mietling *m*

his [hɪz] *poss adj* sein ‖ *poss pron* seiner, der seine (or seinige)

Hispanic [hɪsˈpænɪk] *adj* hispanisch

hiss [hɪs] *s* Zischen *n* ‖ *tr* auszischen ‖ *intr* zischen

hiss'ing *s* Zischen *n*, Gezisch *n*

hiss'ing sound' *s* Zischlaut *m*

hist [hɪst] *interj* st!

historian [hɪsˈtɔri·ən] *s* Historiker –in *mf*

historic [hɪsˈtɔrɪk] *adj* historisch bedeutsam

historical [hɪsˈtɔrɪkəl] *adj* historisch, geschichtlich

history [ˈhɪstəri] *s* Geschichte *f*

historionic [ˌhɪstrɪˈɑnɪk] *adj* schauspielerisch; (fig) übertrieben ‖ **histrionics** *spl* theatralisches Benehmen *n*

hit [hɪt] *s* Schlag *m*, Stoß *m*; (*a success*) Schlager *m*; (sport) Treffer *m*; (theat) Zugstück *n* ‖ *v* (*pret* & *pp* **hit**; *ger* **hitting**) *tr* (*e.g., with the fist*) schlagen; (*a note, target*) treffen; **hit bottom** (*fig*) auf dem Nullpunkt angekommen sein; **hit it off** gut miteinander auskommen; **hit one's head against** mit dem Kopf stoßen gegen; **hit s.o. hard** (*said of misfortunes, etc.*) schwer treffen; **hit the road** sich auf den Weg machen; **hit the sack** sich hinhauen ‖ *intr* schlagen; **hit on** (or **upon**) kommen auf (*acc*)

hit'-and-run' *adj* (*driver*) flüchtig; **h. accident** Unfall *m* mit Fahrerflucht; **h. attack** Zerstörangriff *m*

hitch [hɪtʃ] *s* (*difficulty*) Haken *m*; (*knot*) Stich *m*; (*term of service*) Dienstzeit *f*; **that's the h.** das ist ja gerade der Haken; **without a h.** reibungslos ‖ *tr* spannen; **h. a ride** (to) per Anhalter fahren (nach); **h. to the wagon** vor (or an) den Wagen spannen; **h. up** (*horses*) anspannen; (*trousers*) hochziehen

hitch'hike' *intr* per Anhalter fahren

hitch'ing post' *s* Pfosten *m* (zum Anbinden von Pferden)

hither [ˈhɪðər] *adv* her, hierher; **h. and thither** hierhin und dorthin

hitherto' *adv* bisher

hit' or miss' *adv* aufs Geratewohl

hit'-or-miss' *adj* planlos

hitter [ˈhɪtər] *s* Schläger *m*

hive [haɪv] *s* Bienenstock *m*; **hives** (pathol) Nesselausschlag *m*

hoard [hord] *s* Hort *m* ‖ *tr* & *intr* horten; (*food*) hamstern

hoarder [ˈhordər] *s* Hamsterer –in *mf*

hoard'ing *s* Horten *n*; (*of food*) Hamstern *n*

hoarfrost [ˈhorˌfrɔst] *s* Rauhreif *m*

hoarse [hors] *adj* heiser

hoarseness [ˈhorsnɪs] *s* Heiserkeit *f*

hoary [ˈhori] *adj* ergraut; (fig) altersgrau

hoax [hoks] *s* Schnabernack *m* ‖ *tr* anführen

hob [hɑb] *s* Kamineinsatz *m*

hobble [ˈhɑbəl] *s* Humpeln *n* ‖ *intr* humpeln

hobby [ˈhɑbi] *s* Hobby *n*

hob'byhorse' *s* (*stick with horse's head*) Steckenpferd *n*; (*rocking horse*) Schaukelpferd *n*

hob'gob'lin *s* Kobold *m*; (*bogy*) Schreckgespenst *n*

hob'nail' *s* grober Schuhnagel *m*

hob·nob ['hɑb ,nɑb] *v* (*pret & pp* **–nobbed;** *ger* **–nobbing**) *intr*—h. **with** freundschaftlich verkehren mit

ho·bo ['hobo] *s* (**–bos & –boes**) Landstreicher *m*

hock [hɑk] *s* (*of a horse*) Sprunggelenk *n;* **in h.** verpfändet ‖ *tr* (*hamstring*) lähmen; (*pawn*) (coll) verpfänden

hockey ['hɑkɪ] *s* Hockey *n*

hoc′key stick′ *s* Hockeystock *m*

hock′shop′ *s* (coll) Leihhaus *n*

hocus-pocus ['hokəs'pokəs] *s* Hokuspokus *m*

hod [hɑd] *s* Mörteltrog *m*

hodgepodge ['hɑdʒ ,pɑdʒ] *s* Mischmasch *m*

hoe [ho] *s* Hacke *f*, Haue *f* ‖ *tr* hacken

hog [hɔg] *s* Schwein *n* ‖ *v* (*pret & pp* **hogged;** *ger* **hogging**) *tr* (sl) gierig an sich reißen; **hog the road** rücksichtslos fahren

hog′back′ *s* scharfer Gebirgskamm *m*

hog′ bris′tle *s* Schweinsborste *f*

hoggish ['hɔgɪʃ] *adj* schweinisch, gefräßig

hog′wash′ *s* (*nonsense*) Quatsch *m*

hoist [hɔɪst] *s* (*apparatus for lifting*) Hebezeug *n;* (*act of lifting*) Hochwinden *n* ‖ *tr* hochwinden; (*a flag, sail*) hissen

hokum ['hokəm] *s* (*nonsense*) (coll) Quatsch *m;* (*flimflam*) (coll) Effekthascherei *f*

hold [hold] *s* Halt *m*, Griff *m;* (naut) Raum *m;* (sport) Griff *m;* **get h. of** (*catch*) erwischen; (*acquire*) erwerben; **get h. of oneself** sich fassen; **take h. of** anfassen ‖ *v* (*pret & pp* **held** [held] *tr* halten; (*contain*) enthalten; (*regard as*) halten für; (*one's breath*) anhalten; (*an audience*) fesseln; (*a meeting, election, court*) abhalten; (*an office, position*) bekleiden, innehaben; (*talks*) führen; (*a viewpoint*) vertreten; (*a meet*) (sport) veranstalten; **able to h. one's liquor** trinkfest; **h. back** zurückhalten; (*news*) geheimhalten; **h. dear** werthalten; **h. down** niederhalten; **h. in contempt** verachten; **h. it!** halt!; **h. off** abhalten; **h. office** amtieren; **h. one's ground** die Stellung halten; **h. one's own** seinen Mann stehen; **h. one's own against** sich behaupten gegen; **h. one's tongue** den Mund halten; **h. open** (*a door*) aufhalten; **h. out** (*a hand*) hinhalten; (*proffer*) vorhalten; **h. over** (*e.g., a play*) verlängern; **h. s.th. against s.o.** j–m etw nachtragen; **h. sway** walten; **h. under** niederhalten; **h. up** (*raise*) hochhalten; (*detain*) aufhalten; (*traffic*) behindern; (*rob*) räuberisch überfallen; **h. up to ridicule** dem Spott preisgeben; **h. the line** (telp) am Apparat bleiben; **h. the road well** e–e gute Straßenlage haben; **h. together** zusammenhalten; **h. water** (fig) stichhaltig sein ‖ *intr* (*said of a knot*) halten; **h. back** sich zurückhalten; **h. forth** (coll) dozieren; **h. on** warten; **h. on to** festhalten, sich

festhalten an (*dat*); **h. out** aushalten; **h. out for** abwarten; **h. true** gelten; **h. true for** zutreffen auf (*acc*); **h. up** (*wear well*) halten

holder ['holdər] *s* (*device*) Halter *m;* (*e.g., of a title*) Inhaber –in *mf*

hold′ing *s* (*of a meeting*) Abhaltung *f;* (*of an office*) Bekleidung *f;* **holdings** Besitz *m*, Bestand *m*

hold′ing com′pany *s* Holdinggesellschaft *f*

hold′ing pat′tern *s* (aer) Platzrunde *f*

hold′-o′ver *s* Überbleibsel *n*

hold′up′ *s* (*delay*) Aufenthalt *m;* (*robbery*) Raubüberfall *m;* (*in traffic*) Verkehrsstauung *f*

hold′up man′ *s* Räuber *m*

hole [hol] *s* Loch *n;* (*of animals*) Bau *m;* **h. in the wall** Loch *n;* **in a h.** in der Patsche; **in the h.** hängengeblieben, e.g., **I am ten dollars in the h.** ich bin mit zehn Dollar hängengeblieben; **pick holes in** (fig) herumkritisieren an (*dat*); **wear holes in** völlig abtragen ‖ *intr*—h. **out** (golf) ins Loch spielen; **h. up** sich vergraben; (fig) sich verstecken

holiday ['hɑlɪ ,de] *s* Feiertag *m;* (*vacation*) Ferien *pl;* **take a h.** e–n freien Tag machen, Urlaub nehmen

hol′iday mood′ *s* Ferienstimmung *f*

holiness ['holɪnɪs] *s* Heiligkeit *f;* **His Holiness** Seine Heiligkeit

Holland ['hɑlənd] *s* Holland *n*

Hollander ['hɑləndər] *s* Holländer –in *mf*

hollow ['hɑlo] *adj* hohl ‖ *s* Höhle *f*, Höhlung *f;* (geol) Talmulde *f* ‖ *tr*—h. **out** aushöhlen

hol′low-cheeked′ *adj* hohlwangig

hol′low-eyed′ *adj* hohläugig

holly ['hɑlɪ] *s* Stechpalme *f*

holm′ oak′ [hom] *s* Steineiche *f*

holocaust ['hɑlə ,kɔst] *s* Brandopfer *n;* (*disaster*) Brandkatastrophe *f*

holster ['holstər] *s* Pistolentasche *f*

holy ['holɪ] *adj* heilig; **h. smokes!** (coll) heiliger Strohsack!

Ho′ly Commu′nion *s* Kommunion *f,* das Heilige Abendmahl

ho′ly day′ *s* Feiertag *m*

Ho′ly Ghost′ *s* Heiliger Geist *m*

Ho′ly of Ho′lies *s* Allerheiligste *n*

ho′ly or′ders *spl* Priesterweihe *f*

Ho′ly Scrip′ture *s* die Heilige Schrift

Ho′ly See′ *s* Heiliger Stuhl *m*

Ho′ly Sep′ulcher *s* Heiliges Grab *n*

Ho′ly Spir′it *s* Heiliger Geist *m*

ho′ly wa′ter *s* Weihwasser *n*

Ho′ly Week′ *s* Karwoche *f*

Ho′ly Writ′ *s* die Heilige Schrift

homage ['(h)ɑmɪdʒ] *s* Huldigung *f;* **pay h. to** huldigen (*dat*)

home [hom] *adj* inländisch, Innen– ‖ *adv* nach Hause, heim; **bring h. to s.o.** j–m beibringen ‖ *s* Heim *n;* (*house*) Haus *n*, Wohnung *f;* (*place of residence*) Wohnort *m;* (*institution*) Heim *n;* **at h.** zu Hause, daheim; **at h. and abroad** im In– und Ausland; **feel at h.** sich zu Hause fühlen; **for the h.** für den Hausbedarf; **from h.** von zu Hause; **h. for the aged** Altersheim *n;* **h. for the blind** Blindenheim *n;* **h. of one's own** Zuhause *n*

home′ address′ *s* Privatadresse *f*

home′-baked′ *adj* hausbacken

home′ base′ *s* (aer) Heimatflughafen *m*

home′bod′y *s* Stubenhocker –in *mf*

homebred [′hom ‚bred] *adj* einheimisch

home′-brew′ *s* selbstgebrautes Getränk *n*

home′-brewed′ *adj* selbstgebraut

home′com′ing *s* Heimkehr *f*

home′ comput′er *s* Heimcomputer *m*

home′ coun′try *s* Heimatstaat *m*

home′ econom′ics *s* Hauswirtschafts-lehre *f*

home′-fried pota′toes *spl,* **home′ fries′** [‚fraiz] *spl* Bratkartoffeln *pl*

home′ front′ *s* Heimatfront *f*

home′-grown′ *adj* selbstgezogen

home′ guard′ *s* Landsturm *m*

home′land′ *s* Heimatland *n*

homeless [′homlɪs] *adj* obdachlos ‖ *s* Obdachlose *mf*

home′like′ *adj* anheimelnd

homely [′homli] *adj* unschön

home′made′ *adj* selbstgemacht; (culin) selbstgebacken

home′mak′er *s* Hausfrau *f*

home′ of′fice *s* Hauptbüro *n*

home′ own′er *s* Hausbesitzer –in *mf*

home′ plate′ *s* Schlagmal *n*

home′ rem′edy *s* Hausmittel *n*

home′ rule′ *s* Selbstverwaltung *f*

home′ run′ *s* (baseball) Vier-Mal-Lauf *m*

home′sick′ *adj*—**be h.** Heimweh haben

home′sick′ness *s* Heimweh *n*

homespun [′hom ‚spʌn] *adj* selbstge-macht; (fig) einfach

home′stead′ *s* Siedlerstelle *f*

home′stretch′ *s* Zielgerade *f*

home′ team′ *s* Ortsmannschaft *f*

home′town′ *adj* Heimat- ‖ *s* Heimat-stadt *f*

homeward [′homwərd] *adv* heimwärts

home′ward jour′ney *s* Heimreise *f*

home′work′ *s* Hausaufgabe *f*

homey [′homi] *adj* anheimelnd

homicidal [‚hamɪ′saɪdəl] *adj* mörde-risch

homicide [′hamɪ ‚saɪd] *s* (act) Tot-schlag *m;* (person) Totschläger –in *mf*

hom′icide squad′ *s* Mordkommission *f*

homily [′hamɪli] *s* Homilie *f*

hom′ing device′ [′homɪŋ] *s* Zielsucher *m*

hom′ing pi′geon *s* Brieftaube *f*

homogeneous [‚homə′dʒinɪˌəs] *adj* ho-mogen

homogenize [hə′madʒə ‚naɪz] *tr* homo-genisieren

homonym [′hamənɪm] *s* Homonym *n*

homosexual [‚homə′sɛkʃʊˌəl] *adj* ho-mosexuell ‖ *s* Homosexuelle *mf*

hone [hon] *s* Wetzstein *m* ‖ *tr* honen

honest [′anɪst] *adj* ehrlich, aufrecht

honestly [′anɪstli] *adv* ehrlich; **to tell you h.** offengestanden ‖ *interj* auf mein Wort!

honesty [′anɪsti] *s* Ehrlichkeit *f*

hon·ey [′hʌni] *s* Honig *m;* (as a term of endearment) Schatz *m,* Liebling *m* ‖ *v* (pret & pp **–eyed** & **–ied**) *tr* versüßen; (speak sweetly to) schmeicheln (dat)

hon′eybee′ *s* Honigbiene *f*

hon′eycomb′ *s* Honigwabe *f* ‖ *tr* (e.g., a hill) wabenartig durchlöchern

hon′eyed *adj* mit Honig gesüßt; (fig) honigsüß

hon′ey lo′cust *s* Honigdorn *m*

hon′eymoon′ *s* Flitterwochen *pl* ‖ *intr* die Flitterwochen verbringen

hon′eysuck′le *s* Geißblatt *n*

honk [hɔŋk] *s* (aut) Hupensignal *n* ‖ *tr*—**h. the horn** hupen ‖ *intr* hupen

honkytonk [′hɔŋkɪ ‚tɔŋk] *s* (sl) Tingel-tangel *m & n*

honor [′anər] *s* Ehre *f;* (award) Aus-zeichnung *f;* (chastity) Ehre *f;* **be held in h.** in Ehren gehalten werden; **consider it an h.** es sich [dat] zur Ehre anrechnen; **do the honors** die Honneurs machen; **have the h. of** (ger) sich beehren zu (inf); **in s.o.'s h.** j–m zu Ehren; **your Honor** Euer Gnaden ‖ *tr* ehren; (favor) beehren; (a check) honorieren; **feel honored** sich geehrt fühlen

honorable [′anərəbəl] *adj* (person) ehr-bar; (intentions) ehrlich; (peace treaty) ehrenvoll

honorari·um [‚anə′rerɪˌəm] *s* (**–ums &** **–a** [ə]) Honorar *n;* **give an h. to** honorieren

hon′orary degree′ *s* Ehrendoktorat *n*

honorific [‚anə′rɪfɪk] *adj* ehrend, Ehren– ‖ *s* Ehrentitel *m*

hooch [hut∫] *s* (sl) Fusel *m,* Schnaps *m*

hood [hud] *s* Haube *f;* (of a monk) Kapuze *f;* (of a baby carriage) Ver-deck *n;* (sl) Gangster *m;* (aut) Motorhaube *f;* (culin) Rauchabzug *m;* (educ) Talarüberwurf *m* ‖ *tr* mit e–r Haube versehen; (fig) verhüllen

hoodlum [′hudləm] *s* Ganove *m*

hoodoo [′hudu] *s* Unglücksbringer *m* ‖ *tr* Unglück bringen (dat)

hood′wink′ *tr* täuschen

hooey [′hu·i] *s* (sl) Quatsch *m*

hoof [huf], [hʊf] *s* Huf *m* ‖ *tr*—**h. it** auf Schusters Rappen reiten

hoof′beat′ *s* Hufschlag *m*

hook [hʊk] *s* Haken *m;* (angl) Angel-haken *m;* (baseball) Kurvball *m;* (box) Haken *m;* (golf) Hook *m;* **by h. or by crook** so oder so; **h., line, and sinker** mit allem Drum und Dran; **off the h.** (coll) aus der Schlinge; **on one's own h.** (coll) auf eigene Faust ‖ *tr* festhaken, ein-haken; (e.g., a boyfriend) angeln; (steal) schnappen; (box) e–n Haken versetzen (dat); (golf) nach links verziehen; **h. up** zuhaken; (elec) an-schließen ‖ *intr* sich krümmen; **h. up with s.o.** sich j–m anschließen

hook′ and eye′ *s* Haken *m* und Öse *f*

hook′-and-lad′der truck′ *s* Feuerwehr-fahrzeug *n* mit Drehleiter

hooked *adj* hakenförmig; **h. on drugs** rauschgiftsüchtig

hooker ['hukər] *s* (sl) Nutte *f*

hook'nose' *s* Hakennase *f*

hook'up' *s* (elec, electron) Schaltung *f*; (electron) Schaltbild *n*; (rad, telv) Gemeinschaftsschaltung *f*

hook'worm' *s* Hakenwurm *m*

hooky ['huki] *s*—**play h.** schwänzen

hooligan ['huligən] *s* Straßenlümmel *m*

hoop [hup] *s* Reifen *m* || *tr* binden

hoop' skirt' *s* Reifrock *m*

hoot [hut] *s* Geschrei *n*; **not give a h. about** keinen Pfifferling geben für || *intr* schreien; **h. at** anschreien

hoot' owl' *s* Waldkauz *m*

hop [hɑp] *s* Hopser *m*; (*dance*) Tanz *m*; **hops** (bot) Hopfen *m* || *v* (*pret & pp* **hopped**; *ger* **hopping**) *tr* (*e.g., a train*) aufspringen auf (*acc*); **hop a ride** (coll) mitfahren || *intr* hüpfen; **hop around** herumhüpfen

hope [hop] *s* (of) Hoffnung *f* (auf *acc*); **beyond h.** hoffnungslos; **not get up one's hopes** sich [*dat*] keine Hoffnungen machen || *tr* hoffen || *intr* hoffen; **h. for** hoffen auf (*acc*); **h. for the best** das Beste hoffen; **I h.** (parenthetical) hoffentlich

hope' chest' *s* Aussteuertruhe *f*

hopeful ['hopfəl] *adj* hoffnungsvoll || *s* (pol) Kandidat *-in mf*

hopefully ['hopfəli] *adv* hoffentlich

hopeless ['hoplıs] *adj* hoffnungslos

hopper ['hɑpər] *s* Fülltrichter *m*; (*in a toilet*) Spülkasten *m*; (*storage container*) Vorratsbehälter *m*; (data proc) Kartenmagazin *n*

hop'per car' *s* (rr) Selbstentladewagen *m*

hop'ping mad' *adj* fuchsteufelswild

hop'scotch' *s* Himmel und Hölle

horde [hord] *s* Horde *f*

horehound ['hor‚haund] *s* (*lozenge*) Hustenbonbon *m*; (bot) Andorn *m*

horizon [hə'raızən] *s* Horizont *m*

horizontal [‚harı'zɑntəl] *adj* horizontal, waagrecht || *s* Horizontale *f*

horizon'tal bar' *s* (gym) Reck *n*

horizon'tal controls' *spl* (aer) Seitenleitwerk *n*

horizon'tal sta'bilizer *s* (aer) Höhenflosse *f*

hormone ['hormon] *s* Hormon *n*

horn [hɔrn] *s* (*of an animal; wind instrument*) Horn *n*; (aut) Hupe *f*; **blow one's own h.** (coll) ins eigene Horn stoßen; **blow the h.** (aut) hupen; **horns** (*of an animal*) Geweih *n* || *intr*—**h. in** (on) (coll) sich eindrängen (in *acc*)

hornet ['hornıt] *s* Hornisse *f*

hor'net's nest' *s*—**stir up a h.** in ein Wespennest stechen

horn' of plen'ty *s* Füllhorn *n*

horn'-rimmed glass'es *spl* Hornbrille *f*

horny ['horni] *adj* (*callous*) schwielig; (*having horn-like projections*) verhornt; (sl) geil

horoscope ['horə‚skop] *s* Horoskop *n*; **cast s.o.'s h.** j-m das Horoskop stellen

horrible ['horıbəl] *adj* (& coll) schrecklich

horrid ['horıd] *adj* abscheulich

horri•fy ['horı‚faı] *v* (*pret & pp* **-fied**) *tr* erschrecken, entsetzen

horror ['horər] *s* Schrecken *m*, Entsetzen *n*

hor'ror sto'ry *s* Schaudergeschichte *f*

hors d'oeuvre [ɔr'dʌrv] *s* (**hors d'oeuvres** [ɔr'dʌrvz]) Vorspeise *f*

horse [hɔrs] *s* Pferd *n*; (carp) Sägebock *m*; **back the wrong h.** (fig) auf's falsche Pferd setzen; **bet on a h.** auf ein Pferd setzen; **hold your horses** immer mit der Ruhe!; **h. of another color** e-e andere Sache; **mount a h.** zu Pferd steigen; **straight from the horse's mouth** direkt von der Quelle || *intr*—**h. around** (sl) herumalbern; **stop horsing around** laß den Unsinn!

horse'back' *s*—**on h.** zu Pferd || *adv*—**ride h.** reiten

horse'back rid'ing *s* Reiten *n*

horse' blan'ket *s* Pferdedecke *f*

horse' chest'nut *s* Roßkastanie *f*

horse' col'lar *s* Kummet *n*

horse' doc'tor *s* (coll) Roßarzt *m*

horse'fly' *s* Pferdebremse *f*

horse'hair' *s* Roßhaar *n*, Pferdehaar *n*

horse'laugh' *s* wieherndes Gelächter *n*

horse'man *s* (-men) Reiter *m*

horse'manship' *s* Reitkunst *f*

horse' meat' *s* Pferdefleisch *n*

horse' op'era *s* (coll) Wildwestfilm *m*

horse'play' *s* grober Unfug *m*

horse'pow'er *s* Pferdestärke *f*

horse' race' *s* Pferderennen *n*

horse'rad'ish *s* Meerrettich *m*, Kren *m*

horse' sense' *s* gesunder Menschenverstand *m*

horse' shoe' *s* Hufeisen *n* || *tr* beschlagen

horse'shoe mag'net *s* Hufeisenmagnet *m*

horse' show' *s* Pferdeschau *f*

horse' tail' *s* Pferdeschwanz *m*

horse' trad'er *s* Pferdehändler *m*; (fig) Kuhhändler *m*

horse' trad'ing *s* Pferdehandel *m*; (fig) Kuhhandel *m*

horse'whip' *s* Reitpeitsche *f* || *v* (*pret & pp* **-whipped**; *ger* **-whipping**) *tr* mit der Reitpeitsche schlagen

horse'wom'an *s* (-wom'en) Reiterin *f*

horsy ['horsi] *adj* pferdeartig; (*horse-loving*) pferdeliebend

horticultural [‚hortı'kʌltʃərəl] *adj* Gartenbau—

horticulture ['hortı‚kʌltʃər] *s* Gartenbau *m*, Gärtnerei *f*

hose [hoz] *s* Schlauch *m* || *s* (hose) Strumpf *m*; (*collectively*) Strümpfe *pl*

hosiery ['hoʒəri] *s* Strumpfwaren *pl*; (*mill*) Strumpffabrik *f*

hospice ['hɑspıs] *s* Hospiz *n*

hospitable ['hɑspıtəbəl], [hɑs'pıtəbəl] *adj* gastlich, gastfreundlich

hospital ['hɑspıtəl] *s* Hospital *n*, Krankenhaus *n*; (mil) Lazarett *n*

hospitality [‚hɑspı'tælıti] *s* Gastfreundschaft *f*; **show s.o. h.** j-m Gastfreundschaft gewähren

hospitalize ['hɔspɪtə‚laɪz] *tr* ins Krankenhaus einweisen

hos′pital ship′ *s* Lazarettschiff *f*

hos′pital train′ *s* Sanitätszug *m*

hos′pital ward′ *s* Kranken(haus)station *f*

host [host] *s* Gastgeber *m*; (*at an inn*) Wirt *m*; (*in a television show*) Leiter *m*; (*multitude*) Heerschar *f*; (*army*) Heer *n*; **Host** (relig) Hostie *f*

hostage ['hɔstɪdʒ] *s* Geisel *mf*

hostel ['hɑstəl] *s* Herberge *f*

hostelry ['hɑstəlrɪ] *s* Gasthaus *n*

hostess ['hostɪs] *s* Gastgeberin *f*; (*at an inn*) Wirtin *f*; (*on an airplane*) Stewardeß *f*; (*in a restaurant*) Empfangsdame *f*; (*on a television show*) Leiterin *f*

hostile ['hɑstɪl] *adj* feindlich; (**to**) feindselig (gegen)

hostility [hɑs'tɪlɪtɪ] *s* Feindseligkeit *f*; **hostilities** Feindseligkeiten *pl*

hot [hɑt] *adj* heiß; (*spicy*) scharf; (*meal*) warm; (*stolen, sought by the police, radioactive; jazz, tip*) heiß; (*trail, scent*) frisch; (*in heat*) geil; **be hot** (*said of the sun*) stechen; **get into hot water** in die Patsche geraten; **hot and bothered** aufgeregt; **hot from the press** frisch von der Presse; **hot on s.o.'s trail** j-m dicht auf der Spur; **hot stuff** (sl) toller Kerl *m*; **I am hot** mir ist heiß; **I don't feel so hot** (coll) ich fühle mich nicht besonders; **she's not so hot** (coll) sie is nicht so toll

hot′ air′ *s* Heißluft *f*; (sl) blauer Dunst *m*

hot′-air heat′ *s* Heißluftheizung *f*

hot′bed′ *s* Frühbeet *n*; (fig) Brutstätte *f*

hot′-blood′ed *adj* heißblütig

hot′ cake′ *s* Pfannkuchen *m*; **sell like hot cakes** wie warme Semmeln weggehen

hotchpotch ['hɑtʃ‚pɑtʃ] *s* (coll) Mischmasch *m*

hot′ dog′ *s* warmes Würstel *n*

hotel [ho'tel] *adj* Hotel– || *s* Hotel *n*; (*small hotel*) Gasthof *m*

hotel′ busi′ness *s* Hotelgewerbe *n*

hotel′man *s* (–men) Hotelbesitzer *m*

hot′foot′ *adv* in aller Eile || *tr*—**h. it** schleunigst eilen; **h. it after s.o.** j-m nacheilen

hot′head′ *s* Hitzkopf *m*

hot′-head′ed *adj* hitzköpfig

hot′house′ *s* Treibhaus *n*, Gewächshaus *n*

hot′ line′ *s* (telp) heißer Draht *m*

hot′ mon′ey *s* (sl) Fluchtkapital *n*

hot′ pep′per *s* scharfe Paprikaschote *f*

hot′ plate′ *s* Heizplatte *f*

hot′ pota′to *s* (coll) schwieriges Problem *n*

hot′ rod′ *s* (sl) frisiertes altes Auto *n*

hot′ rod′der [‚rɑdər] *s* (sl) Fahrer *m* e-s frisierten Autos

hot′ seat′ *s* (sl) elektrischer Stuhl *m*

hot′ springs′ *spl* Thermalquellen *pl*

hot′ tem′per *s* hitziges Temperament *n*

hot′-tem′pered *adj* hitzig, hitzköpfig

hot′ war′ *s* Schießkrieg *m*

hot′ wa′ter *s* Heißwasser *n*; **be in h.** (fig) in der Tinte sitzen; **get into h.** (fig) in die Patsche geraten

hot′-wa′ter bot′tle *s* Gummiwärmflasche *f*

hot′-wa′ter heat′er *s* Heißwasserbereiter *m*

hot′-wa′ter heat′ing *s* Heißwasserheizung *f*

hot′-wa′ter tank′ *s* Heißwasserspeicher *m*

hound [haund] *s* Jagdhund *m* || *tr* hetzen

hour [aur] *s* Stunde *f*; **after hours** nach Arbeitsschluß; **at any h.** zu jeder Tageszeit; **by the h.** stundenweise; **every h.** stündlich; **for an h.** e–e Stunde lang; **for a solid h.** e-e geschlagene Stunde lang; **for hours** stundenlang; **h. of death** Todesstunde *f*; **h. overtime** Überstunde *f*; **in the small hours** in den frühen Morgenstunden; **keep late hours** spät zu Bett gehen; **keep regular hours** zur Zeit aufstehen und schlafengehen; **on the h.** zur vollen Stunde

–hour *suf* –stündig

hour′glass′ *s* Stundenglas *n*

hour′ hand′ *s* Stundenzeiger *m*

hourly ['aurlɪ] *adj* stündlich; **h. rate** Stundensatz *m*; **h. wages** Stundenlohn *m* || *adv* stündlich

house [haus] *adj* (*boat, dress*) Haus– || *s* (**houses** ['hauzɪz]) Haus *n*; **h. and home** Haus und Hof; **h. for rent** Haus *n* zu vermieten; **keep h.** (**for s.o.**) (j-m) den Haushalt führen; **on the h.** auf Kosten des Wirts; **put one's h. in order** (fig) seine Angelegenheiten in Ordnung bringen || ['hauz] *tr* unterbringen

house′ arrest′ *s* Hausarrest *m*

house′boat′ *s* Hausboot *m*

house′break′ing *s* Einbruchsdiebstahl *m*

housebroken ['haus‚brokən] *adj* stubenrein

house′ clean′ing *s* Hausputz *m*; (fig) Säuberungsaktion *f*

house′fly′ *s* Stubenfliege *f*

houseful ['haus‚ful] *s* Hausvoll *n*

house′guest′ *s* Logierbesuch *m*

house′hold′ *adj* Haushalts– || *s* Haushalt *m*

house′hold′er *s* Haushaltsvorstand *m*

house′hold fur′nishings *spl* Hausrat *m*

house′hold needs′ *spl* Hausbedarf *m*

house′hold word′ *s* Alltagswort *n*

house′ hunt′ing *s* Wohnungssuche *f*

house′keep′er *s* Haushälterin *f*

house′keep′ing *s* Hauswirtschaft *f*

house′maid′ *s* Dienstmädchen *n*

house′moth′er *s* Hausmutter *f*

house′ of cards′ *s* Kartenhaus *n*

House′ of Com′mons *s* Unterhaus *n*

house′ of corec′tion *s* Zuchthaus *n*, Besserungsanstalt *f*

house′ of ill′ repute′ *s* öffentliches Haus *n*

House′ of Lords′ *s* Oberhaus *n*

house′ physi′cian s Krankenhausarzt m; (in a hotel) Hausarzt m
house′-to-house′ adv von Haus zu Haus; **sell h.** hausieren
house′warm′ing s Einzugsfest n
house′wife′ s (wives′) Hausfrau f
house′work′ s Hausarbeit f
hous′ing s Unterbringung f, Wohnung f; (mach) Gehäuse n
hous′ing devel′opment s Siedlung f
hous′ing pro′ject s Sozialsiedlung f
hous′ing short′age s Wohnungsnot f
hous′ing un′it s Wohneinheit f
hovel [′hʌvəl], [′hɑvəl] s Hütte f
hover [′hʌvər] intr schweben; (fig) pendeln; **h. about** sich herumtreiben in der Nähe von
Hov′ercraft′ s (trademark) Schwebefahrzeug n
how [haʊ] adv wie; **and how!** und wie!; **how about ...?** (would you care for ...?) wie wäre es mit ...?; (what's the progress of ...?) wie steht es mit ...?; (what do you think of ...?) was halten Sie von ...?; **how are you?** wie befinden Sie sich?; **how beautiful!** wie schön!; **how come?** wieso?, wie kommt es?; **how do you do?** (as a greeting) guten Tag!; (at an introduction) freut mich sehr!; **how many** wie viele; **how much** wieviel; **how on earth** wie in aller Welt; **how the devil** wie zum Teufel || s Wie n
how-do-you-do [′haʊdəjə′du] s—**that's a fine h.!** (coll) das ist e-e schöne Geschichte!
however adv jedoch, aber; (with adjectives and adverbs) wie ... auch immer; **h. it may be** wie es auch sein mag
howitzer [′haʊˌɪtsər] s Haubitze f
howl [haʊl] s Geheul n, Gebrüll n || tr heulen, brüllen; **h. down** (a speaker) niederschreien; **h. out** hinausbrüllen || intr (said of a dog, wolf, wind, etc.) heulen; (in pain, anger) brüllen; **h. with laughter** vor Lachen brüllen
howler [′haʊlər] s (coll) Schnitzer m
hub [hʌb] s Nabe, f, Radnabe f
hubbub [′hʌbʌb] s Rummel m
hubby [′hʌbi] s (coll) Mann m
hub′cap′ s Radkappe f
huckleberry [′hʌkəlˌbɛri] s Heidelbeere f
huckster [′hʌkstər] s (hawker) Straßenhändler m; (peddler) Hausierer m; (adman) Reklamefachmann m || tr verhökern
huddle [′hʌdəl] s (fb) Zusammendrängen n; **go into a h.** die Köpfe zusammenstecken || intr sich zusammendrängen; (fb) sich um den Mannschaftsführer drängen
hue [hju] s Farbton m
hue′ and cry′ s Zetergeschrei n
huff [hʌf] s Aufbrausen n; **in a h.** beleidigt
huffy [′hʌfi] adj übelnehmerisch
hug [hʌg] s Umarmung f; **give s.o. a hug** j-n an sich drücken || v (pret & pp hugged; ger hugging) tr umar-

men; **hug the road** gut auf der Straße liegen; **hug the shore** sich dicht an der Küste halten || intr einander herzen
huge [hjudʒ] adj riesig, ungeheuer; **h. success** (theat) Bombenerfolg m
hulk [hʌlk] s (body of an old ship) Schiffsrumpf m; (old ship used as a warehouse, etc.) Hulk m & f; **h. of a man** Koloß m
hulk′ing adj ungeschlacht
hull [hʌl] s (of seed) Schale f; (naut) Schiffsrumpf m || tr schälen
hullabaloo [ˌhʌləbə′lu] s Heidenlärm m
hum [hʌm] s Summen n || v (pret & pp hummed; ger humming) tr summen; **hum** (e.g., a tune) **to oneself** vor sich hin summen || intr summen; (fig) in lebhafter Bewegung sein
human [′hjumən] adj menschlich, Menschen-
hu′man be′ing s Mensch m, menschliches Wesen n
humane [hju′men] adj human
humaneness [hju′mennɪs] s Humanität f
humanistic [hjumə′nɪstɪk] adj humanistisch
humanitarian [hjuˌmænɪ′terɪən] adj menschenfreundlich || s Menschenfreund –in mf
humanity [hju′mænɪti] s (mankind) Menschheit f; (humaneness) Humanität f, Menschlichkeit f; **humanities** Geisteswissenschaften pl; (Greek and Latin studies) klassische Philologie f
humanize [′hjuməˌnaɪz] tr zivilisieren
hu′mankind′ s Menschengeschlecht n
humanly [′hjumənli] adv menschlich; **h. possible** menschmöglich; **h. speaking** nach menschlichen Begriffen
hu′man na′ture s menschliche Natur f
hu′man race′ s Menschengeschlecht n
humble [′(h)ʌmbəl] adv demütig; (origins) niedrig; **in my h. opinion** nach meiner unmaßgeblichen Meinung || tr demütigen
hum′ble pie′ s—**eat h.** sich demütigen
hum′bug′ s Humbug m
hum′drum′ adj eintönig
humer·us [′hjumərəs] s (–i [ˌaɪ]) Oberarmknochen m
humid [′hjumɪd] adj feucht
humidifier [hju′mɪdɪˌfaɪ·ər] s Verdunster m
humidity [hju′mɪdɪti] s Feuchtigkeit f
humiliate [hju′mɪlɪˌet] tr erniedrigen
humil′iating adj schmachvoll
humiliation [hjuˌmɪlɪ′eʃən] s Erniedrigung f
hum′mingbird′ s Kolibri m
humor [′(h)jumər] s (comic quality) Komik f; (frame of mind) Laune f; **in bad** (or good) **h.** bei schlechter (or guter) Laune || tr bei guter Laune halten
humorist [′(h)jumərɪst] s Humorist –in mf
humorous [′(h)jumərəs] adj humorvoll
hump [hʌmp] s Buckel m; (of a camel)

Höcker *m; (slight elevation)* kleiner Hügel *m;* **over the h.** (fig) über den Berg ‖ *tr*—**h. its back** *(said of an animal)* e-n Buckel machen

hump′back′ *s* Buckel *m; (person)* Bucklige *mf*

Hun [hʌn] *s* (hist) Hunne *m*, Hunnin *f*

hunch [hʌntʃ] *s (hump)* Buckel *m;* (coll) Ahnung *f* ‖ *intr*—**h. over** sich bücken über *(acc)*

hunch′back′ *s* Bucklige *mf*

hunch′backed′ *adj* bucklig

hunched *adj*—**h. up** zusammengekauert

hundred [′hʌndrəd] *adj & pron* hundert ‖ *s* Hundert *n;* **by the h.**(s) hundertweise; **hundreds (and hundreds) of** Hunderte (und aber Hunderte) von

hun′dredfold′ *adj & adv* hundertfach

hundredth [′hʌndrədθ] *adj & pron* hundertste; **for the h. time** (fig) zum X-ten Male; **h. anniversary** Hundertjahrfeier *f* ‖ *s (fraction)* Hundertstel *n*

hun′dredweight′ *s* Zentner *n*

Hungarian [hʌŋ′gɛrɪ·ən] *adj* ungarisch ‖ *s (person)* Ungar –in *mf; (language)* Ungarisch *n*

Hungary [′hʌŋgəri] *s* Ungarn *n*

hunger [′hʌŋgər] *s* Hunger *m* ‖ *intr* hungern; **h. for** hungern nach

hun′ger strike′ *s* Hungerstreik *m*

hungry [′hʌŋgri] *adj* hungrig; **be h.** Hunger haben; **be h. for** (fig) begierig sein nach; **go h. am Hungertuch nagen; I feel h.** es hungert mich

hunk [hʌŋk] *s* großes Stück *n*

hunt [hʌnt] *s* Jagd *f; (search)* (for) Suche *f* (nach); **on the h. for** auf der Suche nach ‖ *tr* jagen; *(a horse)* jagen mit; *(look for)* suchen; **h. down** erjagen ‖ *intr* jagen; **h. for** suchen; *(game)* jagen; *(a criminal)* fahnden nach; **go hunting** auf die Jagd gehen

hunter [′hʌntər] *s* Jäger –in *mf; (horse)* Jagdpferd *n*

hunt′ing *adj (e.g., dog, knife, season)* Jagd– ‖ *s* Jägerei *f; (on horseback)* Parforcejagd *f*

hunt′ing ground′ *s* Jagdrevier *n*

hunt′ing li′cense *s* Jagdschein *m*

hunt′ing lodge′ *s* Jagdhütte *f*

huntress [′hʌntrɪs] *s* Jägerin *f*

hunts′man *s* (–men) Weidmann *m*

hurdle [′hʌrdəl] *s* Hürde *f;* (fig) Hindernis *n;* **hurdles** (sport) Hürdenlauf *m* ‖ *tr* überspringen; (fig) überwinden

hurdygurdy [′hʌrdi′gʌrdi] *s* Drehorgel *f*

hurl [hʌrl] *s* Wurf *m* ‖ *tr* schleudern; **h. abuse at s.o.** j–m Beleidigungen ins Gesicht schleudern; **h. down** zu Boden werfen

hurrah [hə′rɑ], **hurray** [hə′re] *s* Hurra *n* ‖ *interj* hurra!

hurricane [′hʌrɪˌken] *s* Orkan *m*

hur′ricane lamp′ *s* Sturmlaterne *f*

hurried [′hʌrid] *adj* eilig, flüchtig

hurriedly [′hʌridli] *adv* eilig, eilends

hur·ry [′hʌri] *s* Eile *f;* **be in too much of a h.** sich übereilen; **in a h.** in Eile; **there's no h.** es hat keine Eile ‖ *v*

(pret & pp –**ried**) *tr (prod)* antreiben; *(expedite)* beschleunigen; *(an activity)* zu schnell tun; *(to overhasty action)* drängen ‖ *intr* eilen; **h. away** wegeilen; **h. over s.th.** etw flüchtig erledigen; **h. up** sich beeilen

hurt [hʌrt] *adj (injured, offended)* verletzt; **feel h.** *(about)* sich verletzt (or gekränkt) fühlen (durch) ‖ *s* Verletzung *f* ‖ *v (pret & pp* hurt) *tr (a person, animal, feelings)* verletzen; *(e.g., a business)* schaden (dat); **it hurts him to think of it** es schmerzt ihn, daran zu denken ‖ *intr (& fig)* weh tun, schmerzen; **my arm hurts** mir tut der Arm weh; **that won't h.** das schadet nichts; **will it h. if I'm late?** macht es etw aus, wenn ich zu spät komme?

hurtle [′hʌrtəl] *tr* schleudern ‖ *intr* stürzen

husband [′hʌzbənd] *s* Ehemann *m;* **my h.** mein Mann *m* ‖ *tr* haushalten mit

hus′bandman *s* (–men) Landwirt *m*

husbandry [′hʌzbəndri] *s* Landwirtschaft *f*

hush [hʌʃ] *s* Stille *f* ‖ *tr* zur Ruhe bringen; **h. up** *(suppress)* vertuschen ‖ *intr* schweigen ‖ *interj* still!

hush′-hush′ *adj* streng vertraulich und geheim

hush′ mon′ey *s* Schweigegeld *n*

husk [hʌsk] *s* Hülse *f; (of corn)* Maishülse *f* ‖ *tr* enthülsen

husky [′hʌski] *adj* stämmig; *(voice)* belegt ‖ *s* Eskimohund *m*

hussy [′hʌsi] *s (prostitute)* Dirne *f; (saucy girl)* Fratz *m*

hustle [′hʌsəl] *s* (coll) Betriebsamkeit *f;* **h. and bustle** Getriebe *n* ‖ *tr (jostle, rush)* drängen; *(wares, girls)* an den Mann bringen; *(customers)* bearbeiten; *(money)* betteln ‖ *intr* rührig sein; *(shove)* sich drängen; *(hasten)* hasten; *(make money by fraud)* Betrügereien verüben; *(engage in prostitution)* Prostitution betreiben

hustler [′hʌslər] *s* rühriger Mensch *m*

hut [hʌt] *s* Hütte *f;* (mil) Baracke *f*

hutch [hʌtʃ] *s* Stall *m*

hyacinth [′haɪ·əsɪnθ] *s* Hyazinthe *f*

hybrid [′haɪbrɪd] *adj* hybrid ‖ *s* Kreuzung *f*

hydrant [′haɪdrənt] *s* Hydrant *m*

hydrate [′haɪdret] *s* Hydrat *n* ‖ *tr* hydratisieren, hydrieren

hydraulic [haɪ′drɒlɪk] *adj* hydraulisch ‖ **hydraulics** *s* Hydraulik *f*

hydrau′lic brakes′ *spl* Öldruckbremsen *pl*

hydrocarbon [ˌhaɪdrə′kɑrbən] *s* Kohlenwasserstoff *m*

hydrochlor′ic ac′id [ˌhaɪdrə′klɒrɪk] *s* Salzsäure *f*

hydroelectric [ˌhaɪdro·ɪ′lektrɪk] *adj* hydroelektrisch

hydroelec′tric plant′ *s* Wasserkraftwerk *n*

hydrofluor′ic ac′id [ˌhaɪdrəflu′ɒrɪk] *s* Flußsäure *f*

hydrofoil [′haɪdrəˌfɔɪl] *s* Tragflügelboot *n*

hydrogen ['haɪdrədʒən] s Wasserstoff m

hy'drogen bomb' s Wasserstoffbombe f

hy'drogen perox'ide s Wasserstoffsuperoxyd n

hydrometer [haɪ'drɑmɪtər] s Hydrometer m

hydrophobia [,haɪdrə'fobɪə] s Wasserscheu f; (rabies) Tollwut f

hydrophone ['haɪdrə,fon] s Unterwasserhorchgerät n, Hydrophon n

hydroplane ['haɪdrə,plen] s (aer) Wasserflugzeug n; (aer) Gleitfläche f; (naut) Gleitboot n; (in a submarine) (nav) Tiefenruder n

hydroxide [haɪ'drɑksaɪd] s Hydroxyd n

hyena [haɪ'inə] s Hyäne f

hygiene ['haɪdʒin] s Hygiene f; (educ) Gesundheitslehre f

hygienic [haɪ'dʒinɪk] adj hygienisch

hymn [hɪm] s Hymne f; (eccl) Kirchenlied n

hymnal ['hɪmnəl] s Gesangbuch n

hymn'book' s Gesangbuch n

hyperacidity [,haɪpərə'sɪdɪti] s Übersäuerung f

hyperbola [haɪ'pʌrbələ] s Hyperbel f

hyperbole [haɪ'pʌrbəli] s Hyperbel f

hypersensitive [,haɪpər'sɛnsɪtɪv] adj (to) überempfindlich (gegen)

hypertension [,haɪpər'tɛn/ən] s Hypertonie f

hyphen ['haɪfən] s Bindestrich m

hyphenate ['haɪfə,net] tr mit Bindestrich schreiben

hypnosis [hɪp'nosɪs] s Hypnose f

hypnotic [hɪp'nɑtɪk] adj hypnotisch

hypnotism ['hɪpnə,tɪzəm] s Hypnotismus m

hypnotist ['hɪpnətɪst] s Hypnotiseur m

hypnotize ['hɪpnə,taɪz] tr hypnotisieren

hypochondriac [,haɪpə'kɑndrɪ,æk] s Hypochonder m

hypocrisy [hɪ'pɑkrəsi] s Heuchelei f

hypocrite ['hɪpəkrɪt] s Heuchler –in mf; be a h. heucheln

hypocritical [,hɪpə'krɪtɪkəl] adj heuchlerisch

hypodermic [,haɪpə'dʌrmɪk] adj subkutan || s (injection) subkutane Spritze f

hypoderm'ic nee'dle s Injektionsnadel f

hypotenuse [haɪ'pɑtɪ,n(j)us] s Hypotenuse f

hypothe·sis [haɪ'pɑθɪsɪs] s (–ses [,siz]) Hypothese f

hypothetic(al) [,haɪpə'θɛtɪk(əl)] adj hypothetisch

hysterectomy [,hɪstə'rɛktəmi] s Hysterektomie f

hysteria [hɪs'tɪrɪ·ə] s Hysterie f

hysteric [hɪs'tɛrɪk] adj hysterisch || **hysterics** spl Hysterie f; go into hysterics e–n hysterischen Anfall bekommen

hysterical [hɪs'tɛrɪkəl] adj hysterisch

I

I, i [aɪ] s elfter Buchstabe des englischen Alphabets

I pers pron ich

iambic [aɪ'æmbɪk] adj jambisch

Iberian [aɪ'bɪrɪ·ən] adj iberisch

ibex ['aɪbɛks] s (ibexes & ibices ['ɪbɪ,siz]) Steinbock m

ice [aɪs] s Eis n; break the ice (coll) das Eis brechen; cut no ice (coll) nicht ziehen || tr (a cake) glasieren || intr—ice up vereisen

ice' age' s Eiszeit f

iceberg ['aɪs,bʌrg] s Eisberg m

ice'boat' s (sport) Segelschlitten m

ice'bound' adj (boat) eingefroren; (port, river) zugefroren

ice'box' s Eisschrank m; (refrigerator) Kühlschrank m

ice'break'er s Eisbrecher m

ice' buck'et s Sektkübel m

ice'cap' s Eiskappe f

ice' cream' s Eis n, Eiskrem f

ice'-cream cone' s Tüte f Eis

ice' cube' s Eiswürfel m

ice'-cube tray' s Eiswürfelschale f

iced' tea' s Eistee m

ice' floe' s Eisscholle f

ice' hock'ey s Eishockey n

Iceland ['aɪslənd] s Island n

Icelander ['aɪs,lændər] s Isländer –in mf

Icelandic [aɪs'lændɪk] adj isländisch || s (language) Isländisch n

ice'man' s (–men') Eismann m

ice' pack' s (geol) Packeis n; (med) Eisbeutel m

ice' pick' s Eispfriem m; (mount) Eispickel m

ice' skate' s Schlittschuh m

ice'-skate' intr eislaufen

ichthyology [,ɪkθɪ'ɑlədʒi] s Ichthyologie f, Fischkunde f

icicle ['aɪsɪkəl] s Eiszapfen m

icing ['aɪsɪŋ] s Glasur f, Zuckerguß m; (aer) Vereisung f

icon ['aɪkɑn] s Ikone f

iconoclast [aɪ'kɑnə,klæst] s Bilderstürmer –in mf

icy ['aɪsi] adj (& fig) eisig

id [ɪd] s (psychol) Es n

I.D. card ['aɪ'di'kɑrd] s Ausweis m

idea [aɪ'di·ə] s Idee f, Vorstellung f; (intimation) Ahnung f; crazy i. Schnapsidee f; have big ideas große Rosinen im Kopf haben; that's the i.! so ist's richtig!; the i.! na so was!; what's the i.? wie kommen Sie darauf?

ideal [aɪˈdi·əl] *adj* ideal ‖ *s* Ideal *n*
idealism [aɪˈdi·ə‚lɪzəm] *s* Idealismus *m*
idealist [aɪˈdi·əlɪst] *s* Idealist –in *mf*
idealistic [aɪˌdi·əlˈɪstɪk] *adj* idealistisch
idealize [aɪˈdi·ə‚laɪz] *tr* idealisieren
identical [aɪˈdentɪkəl] *adj* identisch
identification [aɪˌdentɪfɪˈkeʃən] *s* Identifizierung *f*
identifica'tion tag' *s* Erkennungsmarke *f*
identi·fy [aɪˈdentɪ‚faɪ] *v* (*pret & pp* –fied) *tr* identifizieren; **i. oneself** sich ausweisen ‖ *intr*—**i. with** sich einfühlen in (*acc*)
identity [aɪˈdentɪti] *s* Identität *f*; **prove one's i.** sich ausweisen
iden'tity card' *s* Ausweis *m*
ideological [ˌaɪdɪ·əˈlɑdʒɪkəl] *adj* ideologisch
ideology [ˌaɪdɪ·ˈɑlədʒi] *s* Ideologie *f*
idiocy [ˈɪdɪ·əsi] *s* Idiotie *f*
idiom [ˈɪdɪ·əm] *s* (*phrase*) Redewendung *f*; (*language, style*) Idiom *n*
idiomatic [ˌɪdɪ·əˈmætɪk] *adj* idiomatisch; **i. expression** (idiomatische) Redewendung *f*
idiosyncrasy [ˌɪdɪ·əˈsɪnkrəsi] *s* Idiosynkrasie *f*
idiot [ˈɪdɪ·ət] *s* Idiot *m*, Trottel *m*
idiotic [ˌɪdɪˈɑtɪk] *adj* idiotisch
idle [ˈaɪdəl] *adj* (*person, question, hours*) müßig; (*machine, factory*) stillstehend; (*capital*) tot; (*fears*) grundlos; (*talk, threats*) leer; **lie i.** stilliegen; **stand i.** stillstehen ‖ *s* (aut) Leerlauf *m* ‖ *tr* arbeitslos machen; **i. away** vertrödeln ‖ *intr* (aut) leerlaufen
idleness [ˈaɪdəlnɪs] *s* Müßiggang *m*
idler [ˈaɪdlər] *s* Müßiggänger *m*
i'dling *s* (aut) Leerlauf *m*
idol [ˈaɪdəl] *s* Abgott *m*; (fig) Idol *n*
idolatry [aɪˈdɑlətri] *s* Abgötterei *f*
idolize [ˈaɪdə‚laɪz] *tr* verhimmeln
idyll [ˈaɪdəl] *s* Idyll *n*, Idylle *f*
idyllic [aɪˈdɪlɪk] *adj* idyllisch
if [ɪf] *s* Wenn *n* ‖ *conj* wenn; (*whether*) ob
igloo [ˈɪglu] *s* Schneehütte *f*, Iglu *m & n*
ignite [ɪgˈnaɪt] *tr & intr* zünden
ignition [ɪgˈnɪʃən] *adj* Zünd– ‖ *s* Entzünden *n*; (aut) Zündung *f*
igni'tion key' *s* Zündschlüssel *m*
igni'tion switch' *s* Zündschloß *n*
ignoble [ɪgˈnobəl] *adj* unedel
ignominious [ˌɪgnəˈmɪnɪ·əs] *adj* schmachvoll, schändlich
ignoramus [ˌɪgnəˈreməs] *s* Ignorant –in *mf*
ignorance [ˈɪgnərəns] *s* Unwissenheit *f*; (*of*) Unkenntnis *f* (*genit*)
ignorant [ˈɪgnərənt] *adj* unwissend; **be i. of** nicht wissen
ignore [ɪgˈnor] *tr* ignorieren; (*words*) überhören; (*rules*) nicht beachten
ilk [ɪlk] *s*—**of that ilk** derselben Art
ill [ɪl] *adj* (*worse* [wʌrs]; *worst* [wʌrst]) krank; (*repute*) schlecht; (*feelings*) feindselig; **fall** (*or* **take**)

ill krank werden ‖ *adv* schlecht; **he can ill afford to** (*inf*) er kann es sich [*dat*] kaum leisten zu (*inf*); **take s.th. ill** etw übelnehmen
ill'-advised' *adj* (*person*) schlecht beraten; (*action*) unbesonnen
ill'-at-ease' *adj* unbehaglich
ill'-bred' *adj* ungezogen
ill'-consid'ered *adj* unbesonnen
ill'-disposed' *adj*—**be i. towards** übelgesinnt sein (*dat*)
illegal [ɪˈligəl] *adj* illegal
illegible [ɪˈledʒɪbəl] *adj* unlesbar
illegitimate [ˌɪlɪˈdʒɪtɪmɪt] *adj* unrechtmäßig; (*child*) illegitim
ill'-fat'ed *adj* unglücklich
illgotten [ˈɪl‚gɑtən] *adj* unrechtmäßig erworben
ill' health' *s* Kränklichkeit *f*
ill'-hu'mored *adj* übelgelaunt
illicit [ɪˈlɪsɪt] *adj* unerlaubt
illiteracy [ɪˈlɪtərəsi] *s* Analphabetentum *n*
illiterate [ɪˈlɪtərɪt] *adj* analphabetisch ‖ *s* Analphabet –in *mf*
ill'-man'nered *adj* ungehobelt
ill'-na'tured *adj* bösartig
illness [ˈɪlnɪs] *s* (& fig) Krankheit *f*
illogical [ɪˈlɑdʒɪkəl] *adj* unlogisch
ill'-spent' *adj* verschwendet
ill'-starred' *adj* unglücklich
ill'-suit'ed *adj* (*to*) unpassend (*dat*)
ill'-tem'pered *adj* schlechtgelaunt
ill'-timed' *adj* unpassend
ill'-treat' *tr* mißhandeln
illuminate [ɪˈlumɪ‚net] *tr* beleuchten; (*public buildings, manuscripts*) illuminieren; (*enlighten*) erleuchten; (*explain*) erklären
illumination [ɪˌlumɪˈneʃən] *s* Beleuchten *n*; Erleuchtung *f*; Illuminierung *f*
illusion [ɪˈluʒən] *s* Illusion *f*
illusive [ɪˈlusɪv] *adj* trügerisch
illusory [ɪˈlusəri] *adj* illusorisch
illustrate [ˈɪləs‚tret] *tr* (*exemplify*) erläutern; (*a book*) illustrieren; **illustrated lecture** Lichtbildervortrag *m*; **richly illustrated** bilderreich
illustration [ˌɪləsˈtreʃən] *s* Erläuterung *f*; (*in a book*) Abbildung *f*
illustrative [ɪˈlʌstrətɪv] *adj* erläuternd; **i. material** Anschauungsmaterial *n*
illustrator [ˈɪləs‚tretər] *s* Illustrator *m*
illustrious [ɪˈlʌstrɪ·əs] *adj* berühmt
ill' will' *s* Feindschaft *f*
image [ˈɪmɪdʒ] *s* Bild *n*; (*reflection*) Spiegelbild *n*; (*statue*) Standbild *n*; (*before the public*) Image *n*; (opt, phot, telv) Bild *n*; **the spitting i. of his father** ganz der Vater
imagery [ˈɪmɪdʒ(ə)ri] *s* Bildersprache *f*
imaginable [ɪˈmædʒɪnəbəl] *adj* erdenklich
imaginary [ɪˈmædʒɪ‚neri] *adj* imaginär
imagination [ɪˌmædʒɪˈneʃən] *s* Phantasie *f*, Einbildungskraft *f*; **that's pure i.** das ist pure Einbildung
imaginative [ɪˈmædʒɪnətɪv] *adj* phantasievoll
imagine [ɪˈmædʒɪn] *tr* sich [*dat*] vorstellen, sich [*dat*] denken; **i. oneself**

in sich hineindenken in (acc); **you're only imagining things** das bilden Sie sich [dat] nur ein || intr—**I can i. das läßt sich denken; you I so ich glaube schon; just i.** denken Sie nur mal!

imbecile ['ɪmbɪsɪl] adj geistesschwach || s Geistesschwache mf

imbecility [ˌɪmbɪ'sɪlɪti] s Geistesschwäche f, Blödheit f

imbibe [ɪm'barb] tr aufsaugen; (coll) trinken; (fig) (geistig) aufnehmen

imbue [ɪm'bju] tr durchfeuchten; (fig) (with) durchdringen (mit)

imitate ['ɪmɪ‚tet] tr nachahmen, nachmachen; **i. s.o. in everything** j-m alles nachmachen

imitation [ˌɪmɪ'teʃən] adj unecht, nachgemacht || s Nachahmung f; **in i. of** nach dem Muster (genit)

imita'tion leath'er s Kunstleder n

imitator ['ɪmɪ‚tetər] s Nachahmer –in mf

immaculate [ɪ'mækjəlɪt] adj makellos; (sinless) unbefkleckt

immaterial [ˌɪmə'tɪrɪ‚əl] adj immateriell, unkörperlich; (unimportant) unwesentlich; **it's i. to me** es ist mir gleichgültig

immature [ˌɪmə'tʃur] adj unreif

immaturity [ˌɪmə'tʃurɪti] s Unreife f

immeasurable [ɪ'mɛʒərəbəl] adj unermeßlich

immediacy [ɪ'midɪ‚əsi] s Unmittelbarkeit f

immediate [ɪ'midɪ‚ɪt] adj sofortig; (direct) unmittelbar

immediately [ɪ'midɪ‚ɪtli] adv sofort; **i. afterwards** gleich darauf

immemorial [ˌɪmɪ'morɪ‚əl] adj uralt; **since time i.** seit Menschengedenken

immense [ɪ'mɛns] adj unermeßlich

immensity [ɪ'mɛnsɪti] s Unermeßlichkeit f

immerse [ɪ'mʌrs] tr (unter)tauchen; **immersed in** (books, thought, work) vertieft in (acc); **i. oneself in** sich vertiefen in (acc)

immersion [ɪ'mʌrʒən] s Untertauchen n; (fig) Versunkenheit f

immigrant ['ɪmɪgrənt] adj einwandernd || s Einwanderer –in mf

immigrate ['ɪmɪ‚gret] intr einwandern

immigration [ˌɪmɪ'greʃən] s Einwanderung f

imminent ['ɪmɪnənt] adj drohend

immobile [ɪ'mobɪl] adj unbeweglich

immobilize [ɪ'mobɪ‚laɪz] tr unbeweglich machen; (tanks) bewegungsunfähig machen; (troops) fesseln; (med) ruhigstellen

immoderate [ɪ'madərɪt] adj unmäßig

immodest [ɪ'madɪst] adj unbescheiden

immolate ['ɪmə‚let] tr opfern

immoral [ɪ'mɔrəl] adj unsittlich

immorality [ˌɪmə'rælɪti] s Unsittlichkeit f

immortal [ɪ'mɔrtəl] adj unsterblich

immortality [ˌɪmɔr'tælɪti] s Unsterblichkeit f

immortalize [ɪ'mɔrtə‚laɪz] tr unsterblich machen

immovable [ɪ'muvəbəl] adj unbeweglich

immune [ɪ'mjun] adj (free, exempt) (from) immun (gegen); (not responsive) (to) gefeit (gegen); (med) (to) immun (gegen)

immunity [ɪ'mjunɪti] s Immunität f

immunization [ˌɪmjunɪ'zeʃən] s Schutzimpfung f, Immunisierung f

immunize ['ɪmjə‚naɪz] tr (against) immunisieren (gegen)

immutable [ɪ'mjutəbəl] adj unwandelbar

imp [ɪmp] s Schlingel m

impact ['ɪmpækt] s Anprall m; (of a shell) Aufschlag m; (fig) Einwirkung f

impair [ɪm'pɛr] tr beeinträchtigen

impale [ɪm'pel] tr pfählen

impan-el [ɪm'pænəl] v (pret & pp –el[l]ed; ger –el[l]ing) tr in die Geschworenenliste eintragen

impart [ɪm'pɑrt] tr mitteilen

impartial [ɪm'pɑrʃəl] adj unparteiisch

impassable [ɪm'pæsɪbəl] adj (on foot) ungangbar; (by car) unbefahrbar

impasse ['ɪmpæs] s Sackgasse f; **reach an i.** in e-e Sackgasse geraten

impassible [ɪm'pæsɪbəl] adj (to) unempfindlich (für)

impassioned [ɪm'pæʃənd] adj leidenschaftlich

impassive [ɪm'pæsɪv] adj (of person) teilnahmslos; (expression) ausdruckslos

impatience [ɪm'peʃəns] s Ungeduld f

impatient [ɪm'peʃənt] adj ungeduldig

impeach [ɪm'pitʃ] tr (an official) wegen Amtsmißbrauchs unter Anklage stellen; (a witness, motives) in Zweifel ziehen

impeachment [ɪm'pitʃmənt] s (of an official) öffentliche Anklage f; (of a witness, motives) Anzweiflung f

impeccable [ɪm'pekəbəl] adj makellos

impecunious [ˌɪmpɪ'kjunɪ‚əs] adj mittellos

impede [ɪm'pid] tr behindern, erschweren

impediment [ɪm'pedɪmənt] s Behinderung f; (of speech) Sprachfehler m

im-pel [ɪm'pel] v (pret & pp –pelled; ger –pelling) tr antreiben

impending [ɪm'pendɪŋ] adj nahe bevorstehen; (threatening) drohend

impenetrable [ɪm'penətrəbəl] adj undurchdringlich; (fig) unergründlich

impenitent [ɪm'penɪtənt] adj unbußfertig

imperative [ɪm'perətɪv] adj dringend nötig || s Imperativ m

imper'ative mood' s Befehlsform f

imperceptible [ˌɪmpər'septɪbəl] adj nicht wahrnehmbar, unmerklich

imperfect [ɪm'pʌrfɪkt] adj unvollkommen || s (gram) Imperfekt(um) n

imperfection [ˌɪmpər'fekʃən] s Unvollkommenheit f; (flaw) Fehler m

imperial [ɪm'pɪrɪ‚əl] adj kaiserlich

imperialism [ɪm'pɪrɪ‚ə‚lɪzəm] s Imperialismus m

imperialist [ɪm'pɪrɪ‚əlɪst] adj imperialistisch || s Imperialist –in mf

imper·il [ɪm'perɪl] v (*pret & pp* –il[l]ed; *ger* –il[l]ing) *tr* gefährden

imperious [ɪm'perɪ·əs] *adj* herrisch, anmaßend

imperishable [ɪm'perɪʃəbəl] *adj* unvergänglich

impersonal [ɪm'pʌrsənəl] *adj* unpersönlich

impersonate [ɪm'pʌrsə‚net] *tr* (*imitate*) nachahmen; (*e.g., an officer*) sich ausgeben als; (*theat*) darstellen

impersonator [ɪm'pʌrsə‚netər] *s* Imitator –in *mf*

impertinence [ɪm'pʌrtɪnəns] *s* Ungezogenheit *f*

impertinent [ɪm'pʌrtɪnənt] *adj* ungezogen

imperturbable [‚ɪmpʌr'tʌrbəbəl] *adj* unerschütterlich

impetuous [ɪm'petʃu·əs] *adj* ungestüm

impetus ['ɪmpɪtəs] *s* (& *fig*) Antrieb *m*

impiety [ɪm'paɪ·əti] *s* Gottlosigkeit *f*

impinge [ɪm'pɪndʒ] *intr*–i. on (an) stoßen an (*acc*); (*said of rays*) fallen auf (*acc*); (fig) eingreifen in (*acc*)

impious ['ɪmpɪ·əs] *adj* gottlos

impish ['ɪmpɪʃ] *adj* spitzbübisch

implant [ɪm'plænt] *tr* einpflanzen

implement ['ɪmplɪmənt] *s* Werkzeug *n*, Gerät *n* || ['ɪmplɪ‚ment] *tr* durchführen

implicate ['ɪmplɪ‚ket] *tr* (in) verwickeln (in *acc*)

implication [‚ɪmplɪ'keʃən] *s* (*involvement*) Verwicklung *f*; (*implying*) Andeutung *f*; **implications** Folgerungen *pl*

implicit [ɪm'plɪsɪt] *adj* (*approval*) stillschweigend; (*trust*) unbedingt

implied [ɪm'plaɪd] *adj* stillschweigend

implore [ɪm'plor] *tr* anflehen

im·ply [ɪm'plaɪ] v (*pret & pp* –plied) *tr* (*express indirectly*) andeuten; (*involve*) in sich schließen; (*said of words*) besagen

impolite [‚ɪmpə'laɪt] *adj* unhöflich

import ['ɪmport] *s* Import *m*, Einfuhr *f*; (*meaning*) Bedeutung *f*; **imports** Einfuhrwaren *pl* || [ɪm'port], ['ɪmport] *tr* importieren, einführen

importance [ɪm'portəns] *s* Wichtigkeit *f*; **a man of i.** ein Mann *m* von Bedeutung; **of no i.** unwichtig

important [ɪm'portənt] *adj* wichtig

im'port du'ty *s* Einfuhrzoll *m*

importer [ɪm'portər] *s* Importeur *m*

importune [‚ɪmpor't(j)un] *adj* aufdringlich || *tr* bestürmen

impose [ɪm'poz] *tr* (on, upon) auferlegen (*dat*) || *intr*–i. on über Gebühr beanspruchen

impos'ing *adj* imposant

imposition [‚ɪmpə'zɪʃən] *s* (*of hands, of an obligation*) Auferlegung *f*; (*taking unfair advantage*) Zumutung *f*

impossible [ɪm'pɑsɪbəl] *adj* unmöglich

impostor [ɪm'pɑstər] *s* Hochstapler *m*

imposture [ɪm'pɑstʃər] *s* Hochstapelei *f*

impotence ['ɪmpətəns] *s* Machtlosigkeit *f*; (pathol) Impotenz *f*

impotent ['ɪmpətənt] *adj* machtlos; (pathol) impotent

impound [ɪm'paund] *tr* beschlagnahmen

impoverish [ɪm'pɑvərɪʃ] *tr* arm machen; **become impoverished** verarmen

impracticable [ɪm'præktɪkəbəl] *adj* unausführbar

impractical [ɪm'præktɪkəl] *adj* unpraktisch

impregnable [ɪm'pregnəbəl] *adj* uneinnehmbar

impregnate [ɪm'pregnet] *tr* (*saturate*) imprägnieren; (& fig) schwängern

impresari·o [‚ɪmprɪ'sɑrɪ‚o] *s* (–os) Impresario *m*

impress [ɪm'pres] *tr* (*affect*) imponieren (*dat*), beeindrucken; (*emphasize*) einprägen; **i. s.th. on s.o.** j–m etw einprägen

impression [ɪm'preʃən] *s* Eindruck *m*; (*stamp*) Gepräge *n*; **try to make an i.** Eindruck schinden

impressive [ɪm'presɪv] *adj* eindrucksvoll

imprint ['ɪmprɪnt] *s* Aufdruck *m*; (fig) Eindruck *m* || [ɪm'prɪnt] *tr* aufdrucken (auf *acc*); **i. on s.o.'s memory** j–m ins Gedächtnis einprägen

imprison [ɪm'prɪzən] *tr* einsperren

imprisonment [ɪm'prɪzənmənt] *s* Haft *f*; (*penalty*) Freiheitsstrafe *f*; (*captivity*) Gefangenschaft *f*

improbable [ɪm'prɑbəbəl] *adj* unwahrscheinlich

impromptu [ɪm'prɑmpt(j)u] *adj & adv* aus dem Stegreif || *s* Stegreifstück *n*

improper [ɪm'prɑpər] *adj* ungehörig, unschicklich; (*use*) unzulässig

improve [ɪm'pruv] *tr* verbessern; (*relations*) ausbauen; (*land*) kultivieren; (*a salary*) aufbessern; **i. oneself** sich bessern; (*financially*) sich verbessern || *intr* bessern; (com) sich erholen; **i. on** Verbesserungen vornehmen an (*dat*)

improvement [ɪm'pruvmənt] *s* Verbesserung *f*; (*reworking*) Umarbeitung *f*; (*of money value*) Erholung *f*; (*of a salary*) Aufbesserung *f*; (*in health*) Besserung *f*; **be an i. on** ein Fortschritt sein gegenüber

improvident [ɪm'prɑvɪdənt] *adj* unbedacht

improvise ['ɪmprə‚vaɪz] *tr* improvisieren || *intr* improvisieren; (mus) phantasieren

imprudence [ɪm'prudəns] *s* Unklugheit *f*

imprudent [ɪm'prudənt] *adj* unklug

impudence ['ɪmpjədəns] *s* Unverschämtheit *f*

impudent ['ɪmpjədənt] *adj* unverschämt

impugn [ɪm'pjun] *tr* bestreiten

impulse ['ɪmpʌls] *s* Impuls *m*; **act on i.** impulsiv handeln

impulsive [ɪm'pʌlsɪv] *adj* impulsiv

impunity [ɪm'pjunɪti] *s* Straffreiheit *f*; **with i.** ungestraft

impure [ɪm'pjur] *adj* (& fig) unrein

impurity [ɪmˈpjʊrɪti] s (& fig) Unreinheit f
impute [ɪmˈpjut] tr (to) unterstellen (dat)
in [ɪn] adv (position) drin, drinnen; (direction away from the speaker) hinein; (direction toward the speaker) herein; **be all in** ganz erschöpft sein; **be in** da sein; (said of a political party) an der Macht sein; (be in style) in Mode sein; **be in for** zu erwarten haben; **have it in for** auf dem Strich haben || s—**the ins and outs of** die Einzelheiten (genit) || prep (position) in (dat); (direction) in (acc); (e.g., the morning, afternoon, evening) am; (a field, the country; one eye) auf (dat); (one's opinion; all probability) nach (dat); (circumstances; a reign) unter (dat); (ink; one stroke) mit (dat); (because of pain, joy, etc.) vor (dat); **he doesn't have it in him to** (inf) er hat nicht das Zeug dazu zu (inf); **in German** auf deutsch
inability [ˌɪnəˈbɪlɪti] s Unfähigkeit f; **i. to pay** Zahlungsunfähigkeit f
inaccessible [ˌɪnækˈsɛsɪbəl] adj unzugänglich
inaccuracy [ɪnˈækjərəsi] s Ungenauigkeit f
inaccurate [ɪnˈækjərɪt] adj ungenau
inaction [ɪnˈækʃən] s Untätigkeit f
inactive [ɪnˈæktɪv] adj untätig; (chem) unwirksam; (st. exch.) lustlos
inactivity [ˌɪnækˈtɪvɪti] s Untätigkeit f
inadequate [ɪnˈædɪkwɪt] adj unangemessen
inadmissible [ˌɪnədˈmɪsɪbəl] adj unstatthaft, unzulässig
inadvertent [ˌɪnədˈvɑrtənt] adj versehentlich
inadvisable [ˌɪnədˈvaɪzəbəl] adj nicht ratsam
inalienable [ɪnˈeljənəbəl] adj unveräußerlich
inane [ɪnˈen] adj leer, unsinnig
inanimate [ɪnˈænɪmɪt] adj unbeseelt
inappropriate [ˌɪnəˈproprɪ·ɪt] adj unangemessen
inarticulate [ˌɪnɑrˈtɪkjəlɪt] adj unartikuliert, undeutlich
inartistic [ˌɪnɑrˈtɪstɪk] adj unkünstlerisch, kunstlos
inasmuch as [ˌɪnæzˈmʌtʃˌæz] conj da
inattentive [ˌɪnəˈtɛntɪv] adv (to) unaufmerksam (or unachtsam) (gegenüber)
inaudible [ɪnˈɔdɪbəl] adj unhörbar
inaugural [ɪnˈɔg(j)ərəl] adj Antritts-
inaugurate [ɪnˈɔg(j)əˌret] tr feierlich eröffnen; (a new policy) einleiten
inauguration [ɪnˌɔg(j)əˈreʃən] s Eröffnung f; (of an official) Amtsantritt m
inauspicious [ˌɪnɔsˈpɪʃəs] adj ungünstig
inborn [ˈɪnˌbɔrn] adj angeboren
inbred [ˈɪnˌbred] adj angeboren, ererbt
in'breed'ing s Inzucht f

incalculable [ɪnˈkælkjələbəl] adj unberechenbar
incandescent [ˌɪnkənˈdɛsənt] adj Glüh-
incantation [ˌɪnkænˈte/ən] s Beschwörung f
incapable [ɪnˈkepəbəl] adj untüchtig; **i. of** (ger) nicht fähig zu (inf)
incapacitate [ˌɪnkəˈpæsɪˌtet] tr unfähig machen; (jur) für geschäftsunfähig erklären
incarcerate [ɪnˈkɑrsəˌret] tr einkerkern
incarnate [ɪnˈkɑrnet] adj—**God i.** Gottmensch m; **the devil i.** der Teufel in Menschengestalt
incarnation [ˌɪnkɑrˈne/ən] s (fig) Verkörperung f; (eccl) Fleischwerdung f
incendiary [ɪnˈsɛndɪˌeri] adj Brand-; (fig) aufhetzend || s Brandstifter –in mf
incense [ˈɪnsəns] s Weihrauch m || tr (eccl) beräuchern || [ɪnˈsens] tr erzürnen
in'cense burn'er s Räuchergefäß n
incentive [ɪnˈsɛntɪv] s Anreiz m
inception [ɪnˈsɛp/ən] s Anfang m
incessant [ɪnˈsɛsənt] adj unaufhörlich
incest [ˈɪnsest] s Blutschande f
incestuous [ɪnˈsest/ʊ·əs] adj blutschänderisch
inch [ɪnt/] s Zoll m; **beat within an i. of one's life** fast zu Tode prügeln; **by inches** nach und nach; **not yield an i.** keinen Fußbreit nachgeben || intr—**i. along** dahinschleichen; **i. forward** langsam vorrücken
incidence [ˈɪnsɪdəns] s Vorkommen n
incident [ˈɪnsɪdənt] s Vorfall m; (adverse event) Zwischenfall m
incidental [ˌɪnsɪˈdɛntəl] adj zufällig; **i. to** gehörig zu || **incidentals** spl Nebenausgaben pl
incidentally [ˌɪnsɪˈdɛntəli] adv übrigens
incinerate [ɪnˈsɪnəˌret] tr einäschern
incinerator [ɪnˈsɪnəˌretər] s Verbrennungsofen m
incipient [ɪnˈsɪpɪ·ənt] adv beginnend
incision [ɪnˈsɪʒən] s Schnitt m
incisive [ɪnˈsaɪsɪv] adj (biting) beißend; (penetrating) durchdringend; (sharp) scharf
incisor [ɪnˈsaɪzər] s Schneidezahn m
incite [ɪnˈsaɪt] tr aufreizen, aufhetzen
inclement [ɪnˈklemənt] adj ungünstig
inclination [ˌɪnklɪˈne/ən] s (& fig) Neigung f
incline [ˈɪnklaɪn] s Abhang m || [ɪnˈklaɪn] tr neigen || intr (towards) sich neigen (nach or zu); (fig) (towards) neigen (zu); **the roof inclines sharply** das Dach fällt steil ab
include [ɪnˈklud] tr einschließen; **i. among** rechnen unter (acc); **i. in** einrechnen in (acc)
includ'ed adj (mit) inbegriffen
includ'ing prep einschließlich (genit)
inclusive [ɪnˈklusɪv] adj umfassend, gesamt; **all i.** alles inbegriffen; **from ... to ... i.** von ... zu ... einschließlich (or inklusive); **i. of** einschließlich (genit)

incognito [ɪn'kagnɪ‚to] *adv* inkognito

incoherent [‚ɪnko'hɪrənt] *adj* unzusammenhängend; **be i.** (*said of a person*) nicht ganz bei sich sein

incombustible [‚ɪnkəm'bʌstɪbəl] *adj* unverbrennbar

income ['ɪnkʌm] *s* (**from**) Einkommen *n* (aus)

in'come tax' *s* Einkommensteuer *f*

in'come-tax return' *s* Einkommensteuererklärung *f*

in'com'ing *adj* (*e.g., tide*) hereinkommend; (*bus, train*) ankommend; (*official*) neu eintretend; **i. goods, i. mail** Eingänge *pl*

incomparable [ɪn'kampərəbəl] *adj* unvergleichlich

incompatible [‚ɪnkəm'pætɪbəl] *adj* (**with**) unvereinbar (mit); (*persons*) unverträglich

incompetent [ɪn'kampɪtənt] *adj* untauglich; (*not legally qualified*) nicht zuständig; (*not legally capable*) geschäftsunfähig; (*inadmissible*) unzulässig ‖ *s* Nichtkönner –in *mf*

incomplete [‚ɪnkəm'plit] *adj* unvollständig

incomprehensible [‚ɪnkamprɪ'hensɪbəl] *adj* unbegreiflich

inconceivable [‚ɪnkən'sivəbəl] *adj* undenkbar

inconclusive [‚ɪnkən'klusɪv] *adj* (*not convincing*) nicht überzeugend; (*leading to no result*) ergebnislos

incongruous [ɪn'kaŋgru‐əs] *adj* nicht übereinstimmend

inconsequential [ɪn‚kansɪ'kwenʃəl] *adj* belanglos

inconsiderate [‚ɪnkən'sɪdərɪt] *adj* unüberlegt; (**towards**) rücksichtslos (gegen)

inconsistency [‚ɪnkən'sɪstənsɪ] *s* (*lack of logical connection*) Inkonsequenz *f*; (*contradiction*) Unstimmigkeit *f*; (*instability*) Unbeständigkeit *f*

inconsistent [‚ɪnkən'sɪstənt] *adj* inkonsequent; (*uneven*) unbeständig

inconspicuous [‚ɪnkən'spɪkju‐əs] *adj* unauffällig

inconstant [ɪn'kanstənt] *adj* unbeständig

incontinent [ɪn'kantɪnənt] *adj* zügellos

incontrovertible [‚ɪnkantrə'vʌrtɪbəl] *adj* unwiderlegbar

inconvenience [‚ɪnkən'vini‐əns] *s* Ungelegenheit *f* ‖ *tr* bemühen, belästigen

inconvenient [‚ɪnkən'vini‐ənt] *adj* ungelegen

incorporate [ɪn'kɔrpə‚ret] *tr* einverleiben; (*an organization*) zu e–r Körperschaft machen ‖ *intr* e–e Körperschaft werden

incorporation [ɪn‚kɔrpə'reʃən] *s* Einverleibung *f*; (*jur*) Körperschaftsbildung *f*

incorrect [‚ɪnkə'rɛkt] *adj* unrichtig, falsch; (*conduct*) unschicklich

incorrigible [ɪn'kɔrɪdʒɪbəl] *adj* unverbesserlich

increase ['ɪnkris] *s* Zunahme *f*; **be on the i.** steigen; **i. in costs** Kostensteigerung *f*; **i. in pay** Gehaltserhöhung *f*; (mil) Solderhöhung *f*; **i. in population** Bevölkerungszunahme *f*; **i. in prices** Preiserhöhung *f*; **i. in rent** Mieterhöhung *f*; **i. in taxes** Steuererhöhung *f*; **i. in value** Wertsteigerung *f*; **i. in weight** Gewichtszunahme *f* ‖ [ɪn'kris] *tr* (*in size*) vergrößern; (*in height*) erhöhen; (*in quantity*) vermehren; (*in intensity*) verstärken; (*prices*) heraufsetzen ‖ *intr* zunehmen, sich vergrößern; (*rise*) sich erhöhen; (*in quantity*) sich vermehren; (*in intensity*) sich verstärken; **i. in** zunehmen an (*dat*)

increasingly [ɪn'krisɪŋli] *adv* immer mehr; **i. more difficult** immer schwieriger

incredible [ɪn'krɛdɪbəl] *adj* unglaublich

incredulous [ɪn'krɛdʒələs] *adj* ungläubig

increment ['ɪnkrɪmənt] *s* Zunahme *f*, Zuwachs *m*; (*in pay*) Gehaltszulage *f*

incriminate [ɪn'krɪmɪ‚net] *tr* belasten

incrust [ɪn'krʌst] *tr* überkrusten

incubate ['ɪnkjə‚bet] *tr & intr* brüten

incubator ['ɪnkjə‚betər] *s* Brutapparat *m*

inculcate [ɪn'kʌlket], ['ɪnkʌl‚ket] *tr* (**in**) einprägen (*dat*)

incumbency [ɪn'kʌmbənsi] *s* (*obligation*) Obliegenheit *f*; (*term of office*) Amtszeit *f*

incumbent [ɪn'kʌmbənt] *adj*—**be i. on** obliegen (*dat*) ‖ *s* Amtsinhaber –in *mf*

incunabula [‚ɪnkju'næbjələ] *spl* (typ) Wiegendrucke *pl*

in‐cur [ɪn'kʌr] *v* (*pret & pp* –**curred;** *ger* –**curring**) *tr* sich (*dat*) zuziehen; (*debts*) machen; (*a loss*) erleiden; (*a risk*) eingehen

incurable [ɪn'kjurəbəl] *adj* unheilbar ‖ *s* unheilbarer Kranke *m*

incursion [ɪn'kʌrʒən] *s* Einfall *m*

indebted [ɪn'dɛtɪd] *adj* (**to**) verschuldet (bei); **be i. to s.o. for s.th.** j–m etw zu verdanken haben

indecency [ɪn'disənsi] *s* Unsittlichkeit *f*

indecent [ɪn'disənt] *adj* unsittlich; **i. assault** Sittlichkeitsvergehen *n*

indecision [‚ɪndɪ'sɪʒən] *s* Unentschlossenheit *f*

indecisive [‚ɪndɪ'saɪsɪv] *adj* (*person*) unentschlossen; (*battle*) nicht entscheidend

indeclinable [‚ɪndɪ'klaɪnəbəl] *adj* undeklinierbar

indeed [ɪn'did] *adv* ja, zwar ‖ *interj* jawohl!

indefatigable [‚ɪndɪ'fætɪgəbəl] *adj* unermüdlich

indefensible [‚ɪndɪ'fensɪbəl] *adj* nicht zu verteidigen(d); (*argument*) unhaltbar; (*behavior*) unentschuldbar

indefinable [‚ɪndɪ'faɪnəbəl] *adj* undefinierbar

indefinite [ɪn'dɛfɪnɪt] *adj* (*unlimited*) unbegrenzt; (*not exact*) unbestimmt; (*answer*) ausweichend; (*vague*) undeutlich; (gram) unbestimmt

indelible [ɪn'delɪbəl] *adj (ink, pencil)* wasserfest; (fig) unauslöschlich

indelicate [ɪn'delɪkɪt] *adj* unzart

indemnification [ɪn,demnɪfɪ'keʃən] *s* Schadenersatzleistung *f*

indemni·fy [ɪn'demnɪ,faɪ] *v (pret & pp* –**fied**) *tr* entschädigen

indemnity [ɪn'demnɪti] *s* Schadenersatz *m*

indent [ɪn'dent] *tr (notch)* einkerben; *(the coast)* tiefe Einschnitte bilden in *(dat)*; (typ) einrücken || *intr* (typ) einrücken

indentation [,ɪnden'teʃən] *s* Kerbe *f*; (typ) Absatz *m*

indenture [ɪn'dentʃər] *s (service contract)* Arbeitsvertrag *m*; *(apprentice contract)* Lehrvertrag *m* || *tr* vertraglich binden

independence [,ɪndɪ'pendəns] *s* Unabhängigkeit *f*

independent [,ɪndɪ'pendənt] *adj (of)* unabhängig (von) || *s* Unabhängige *mf*

indescribable [,ɪndɪ'skraɪbəbəl] *adj* unbeschreiblich

indestructible [,ɪndɪ'strʌktɪbəl] *adj* unzerstörbar

index ['ɪndeks] *s* (**indexes & indices** ['ɪndɪ,siz]) *(in a book)* Register *n*; (fig) (to) Hisweis *m* (auf *acc*); Index Index *m* || *tr* registrieren; *(a book)* mit e–m Register versehen

in'dex card' *s* Karteikarte *f*

in'dex fin'ger *s* Zeigefinger *m*

India ['ɪndɪ·ə] *s* Indien *n*

In'dia ink' *s* chinesische Tusche *f*

Indian ['ɪndɪ·ən] *adj* indisch; *(e.g., chief, tribe)* Indianer– || *s (of India)* Inder –*in mf; (of North America)* Indianer –*in mf; (of Central or South America)* Indio *m*

In'dian corn' *s* Mais *m*

In'dian file' *adv* in Gänsemarsch

In'dian O'cean *s* Indischer Ozean *m*

In'dian sum'mer *s* Altweibersommer *m*

indicate ['ɪndɪ,ket] *tr* angeben, anzeigen

indication [,ɪndɪ'keʃən] *s* Angabe *f*; *(of s.th. imminent)* (of) Anzeichen *n* (für); **give i. of** anzeigen

indicative [ɪn'dɪkətɪv] *adj* (gram) indikativ; **be i. of** hindeuten auf *(acc)* || *s* (gram) Wirklichkeitsform *f*, Indikativ *m*

indicator ['ɪndɪ,ketər] *s* Zeiger *m*

indict [ɪn'daɪt] *tr* (for) anklagen (wegen)

indictment [ɪn'daɪtmənt] *s* Anklage *f*

indifference [ɪn'dɪfərəns] *s* (to) Gleichgültigkeit *f* (gegen or gegenüber)

indifferent [ɪn'dɪfərənt] *adj (mediocre)* mittelmäßig; (to) gleichgültig (gegen)

indigenous [ɪn'dɪdʒɪnəs] *adj* (to) einheimisch (in *dat)*

indigent ['ɪndɪdʒənt] *adj* bedürftig

indigestible [,ɪndɪ'dʒestɪbəl] *adj* unverdaulich

indigestion [,ɪndɪ'dʒestʃən] *s* Verdauungsstörung *f*, Magenverstimmung *f*

indignant [ɪn'dɪgnənt] *adj* (at) empört (über *acc)*

indignation [,ɪndɪg'neʃən] *s* (at) Empörung *f* (über *acc)*

indignity [ɪn'dɪgnɪti] *s* Beleidigung *f*

indigo ['ɪndɪ,go] *adj* Indigo– || *s* Indigo *m & n*

indirect [,ɪndɪ'rekt] *adj* indirekt

in'direct dis'course *s* indirekte Rede *f*

in'direct ques'tion *s* indirekter Fragesatz *m*

indiscreet [,ɪndɪs'krit] *adj* indiskret

indiscretion [,ɪndɪs'kreʃən] *s* Indiskretion *f*

indiscriminate [,ɪndɪs'krɪmɪnɪt] *adj* unterschiedslos

indispensable [,ɪndɪs'pensəbəl] *adj* unentbehrlich

indisposed *adj (ill)* unpäßlich; **i. to** abgeneigt *(dat)*

indissoluble [,ɪndɪ'saljəbəl] *adj* unauflösbar

indistinct [,ɪndɪ'stɪŋkt] *adj* undeutlich

individual [,ɪndɪ'vɪdʒu·əl] *adj* individuell, Einzel–, einzeln || *s* Individuum *n*

individ'ual case' *s* Einzelfall *m*

individuality [,ɪndɪ,vɪdʒu'ælɪti] *s* Individualität *f*

individually [,ɪndɪ'vɪdʒu·əli] *adv* einzeln

indivisible [,ɪndɪ'vɪzɪbəl] *adj* unteilbar

Indochina ['ɪndo't'faɪnə] *s* Indochina *n*

indoctrinate [ɪn'daktrɪ,net] *tr* (in) schulen (in *dat)*, unterweisen (in *dat)*

indoctrination [,ɪndaktrɪ'neʃən] *s* Schulung *f*, Unterweisung *f*

Indo–European ['ɪndo,jurə'pi·ən] *adj* indogermanisch || *s (language)* Indogermanisch *n*

indolence ['ɪndələns] *s* Trägheit *f*

indolent ['ɪndələnt] *adj* träge

Indonesia [,ɪndo'niʒə] *s* Indonesien *n*

Indonesian [,ɪndo'nɪʒən] *adj* indonesisch || *s* Indonesier –*in mf*

indoor ['ɪn,dor] *adj* Haus–, Zimmer–, Innen–; (sport) Hallen–

indoors [ɪn'dorz] *adv* innen, drin(nen)

in'door shot' *s* (phot) Innenaufnahme *f*

induce [ɪn'd(j)us] *tr* veranlassen, bewegen; *(bring about)* verursachen; (elec, phys) induzieren

inducement [ɪn'd(j)usmənt] *s* Anreiz *m*

induct [ɪn'dʌkt] *tr* (into) einführen (in *acc)*; (mil) (into) einberufen (zu)

inductee [,ɪn'dʌkti] *s* Einberufene *mf*

induction [ɪn'dʌkʃən] *s* Einführung *f*; (elec, log) Induktion *f*; (mil) Einberufung *f*

induc'tion coil' *s* Induktionsspule *f*

indulge [ɪn'dʌldʒ] *tr (a desire)* frönen *(dat)*; *(a person)* befriedigen; *(children)* verwöhnen; **i. oneself** in schwelgen in *(dat)* || *intr* (coll) trinken; **i. in s.th.** sich *[dat]* etw gestatten

indulgence [ɪn'dʌldʒəns] *s (of a desire)* Frönen *n*; *(tolerance)* Duldung *f*; (relig) Ablaß *m*; **ask s.o.'s i.** j–n um Nachsicht bitten

indulgent [ɪn'dʌldʒənt] *adj* schonend; (toward) nachsichtig (gegen)

industrial [ɪn'dʌstrɪ·əl] *adj (e.g., bank,*

center, alcohol, product, worker)
Industrie–; (e.g., accident, medicine)
Betriebs–; (e.g., revolution) industri-
ell; (e.g., school, engineering) Gewerbe–

industrialist [ɪn'dʌstrɪ·əlɪst] s In-
dustrielle mf

industrialize [ɪn'dʌstrɪ·ə‚laɪz] tr industrialisieren

indus'trial man'agement s Betriebs-
wirtschaft f

industrious [ɪn'dʌstrɪ·əs] adj fleißig

industry ['ɪndəstrɪ] s Industrie f; (energy) Fleiß m

inebriated [ɪn'ibrɪ‚etɪd] adj betrunken

inedible [ɪn'edɪbəl] adj ungenießbar

ineffable [ɪn'efəbəl] adj unaussprechlich

ineffective [‚ɪnɪ'fektɪv] adj unwirksam; (person) untüchtig

ineffectual [‚ɪnɪ'fektʃu·əl] adj unwirksam

inefficient [‚ɪnɪ'fɪʃənt] adj untüchtig;
(process, procedure) unrationell;
(mach) nicht leistungsfähig

ineligible [ɪn'elɪdʒɪbəl] adj nicht wählbar; (not suitable) ungeeignet

inept [ɪn'ept] adj ungeschickt

inequality [‚ɪnɪ'kwɑlɪti] s Ungleichheit f

inequity [ɪn'ekwɪti] s Ungerechtigkeit
f

inertia [ɪn'ʌrʃə] s Trägheit f

inescapable [‚ɪnes'kepəbəl] adj unentrinnbar, unabwendbar

inevitable [ɪn'evɪtəbəl] adj unvermeid-
lich, unausweichlich

inexact [‚ɪneg'zækt] adj ungenau

inexcusable [‚ɪneks'kjuzəbəl] adj unentschuldbar

inexhaustible [‚ɪneg'zɔstɪbəl] adj unerschöpflich

inexorable [ɪn'eksərəbəl] adj unerbittlich

inexpensive [‚ɪnek'spensɪv] adj billig

inexperience [‚ɪnek'spɪrɪ·əns] s Unerfahrenheit f

inexpe'rienced adj unerfahren

inexplicable [ɪn'eksplɪkəbəl] adj uner-
klärlich

inexpressible [‚ɪnek'spresɪbəl] adj unaussprechlich

infallibility [‚ɪnfælɪ'bɪlɪti] s Unfehl-
barkeit f

infallible [ɪn'fælɪbəl] adj unfehlbar

infamous ['ɪnfəməs] adj schändlich

infamy ['ɪnfəmɪ] s Schändlichkeit f

infancy ['ɪnfənsɪ] s Kindheit f; be still
in its i. (fig) noch in den Kinder-
schuhen stecken

infant ['ɪnfənt] adj Säuglings– ‖ s
Kleinkind n, Säugling m

infantile ['ɪnfən‚taɪl] adj infantil

in'fantile paral'ysis s Kinderlähmung f

infantry ['ɪnfəntrɪ] s Infanterie f

in'fantry·man s (–men) Infanterist m

infatuated [ɪn‚fætʃu'etɪd] adj betört

infatuation [ɪn‚fætʃu'eʃən] s Betörung
f

infect [ɪn'fekt] tr anstecken, infizieren; become infected sich anstecken

infection [ɪn'fekʃən] s Ansteckung f

infectious [ɪn'fekʃəs] adj (& fig) ansteckend

in·fer [ɪn'fʌr] v (pret & pp –ferred;
ger –ferring) tr folgern

inference ['ɪnfərəns] s Folgerung f

inferior [ɪn'fɪrɪ·ər] adj (in rank) niedriger; (in worth) minderwertig; (to)
unterlegen (dat)

inferiority [ɪn‚fɪrɪ'ɑrɪti] s Unterlegen-
heit f; (in worth) Minderwertigkeit f

inferior'ity com'plex s Minderwertig-
keitskomplex m

infernal [ɪn'fʌrnəl] adj höllisch

infest [ɪn'fest] tr in Schwärmen überfallen; be infested with wimmeln von

infidel ['ɪnfɪdəl] adj ungläubig ‖ s
Ungläubige mf

infidelity [‚ɪnfɪ'delɪti] s Untreue f

in'field' s (baseball) Innenfeld n

infiltrate [ɪn'fɪltret], ['ɪnfɪl‚tret] tr
(filter through) infiltrieren; (mil)
durchsickern durch; (pol) unterwan-
dern ‖ intr infiltrieren

infinite ['ɪnfɪnɪt] adj unendlich

infinitive [ɪn'fɪnɪtɪv] s (gram) Nennform f, Infinitiv m

infinity [ɪn'fɪnɪti] s Unendlichkeit f;
to i. endlos

infirm [ɪn'fʌrm] adj schwach; (from
age) altersschwach

infirmary [ɪn'fʌrmərɪ] s Krankenstube
f; (mil) Revier n

infirmity [ɪn'fʌrmɪti] s Schwachheit f

inflame [ɪn'flem] tr (fig & pathol) entzünden; become inflamed sich entzünden

inflammable [ɪn'flæməbəl] adj entzündbar, feuergefährlich

inflammation [‚ɪnflə'meʃən] s Entzündung f

inflammatory [ɪn'flæmə‚torɪ] adj aufrührerisch; (pathol) Entzündungs–

inflate [ɪn'flet] tr aufblasen; (tires)
aufpumpen

inflation [ɪn'fleʃən] s (econ) Inflation f

inflationary [ɪn'fleʃə‚nerɪ] adj infla-
tionistisch

inflect [ɪn'flekt] tr (the voice) modulieren; (gram) flektieren

inflection [ɪn'flekʃən] s (of the voice)
Tonfall m; (gram) Flexion f

inflexible [ɪn'fleksɪbəl] adj unbiegsam;
(person) unbeugsam; (law) unabänderlich

inflict [ɪn'flɪkt] tr (punishment) (on)
auferlegen (dat); (a defeat) (on) zufügen (dat); (a wound) (on) beibringen (dat)

influence ['ɪnflu·əns] s (on) Einfluß m
(auf acc) ‖ tr beeinflussen

influential [ɪnflu'enʃəl] adj einfluß-
reich, maßgebend

influenza [ɪnflu'enzə] s Grippe f

influx ['ɪnflʌks] s Zufluß m

inform [ɪn'fɔrm] tr (of) benachrichtigen (von) ‖ intr—i. against anzeigen

informal [ɪn'fɔrməl] adj zwanglos

informant [ɪn'fɔrmənt] s Gewährsmann m

information [‚ɪnfər'meʃən] s Nachricht
f, Auskunft f; (items of information)

Informationen *pl;* **a piece of i.** e–e Auskunft *f;* **for your i.** zu Ihrer Information

informa'tion desk' *s* Auskunftsstelle *f*

informative [ɪn'fɔrmətɪv] *adj* belehrend

informed' *adj* unterrichtet

informer [ɪn'fɔrmər] *s* Denunziant –in *mf*

infraction [ɪn'frækʃən] *s* **(of)** Verstoß *m* **(gegen)**

infrared [ˌɪnfrə'red] *adj* infrarot

infrequent [ɪn'frikwənt] *adj* selten

infringe [ɪn'frɪndʒ] *tr* verletzen || *intr* —**i. on** eingreifen in *(acc)*

infringement [ɪn'frɪndʒmənt] *s* **(of** *a law)* Verletzung *f;* **(of** *a right)* Eingriff *m* (in *acc*)

infuriate [ɪn'fjʊrɪˌet] *tr* wütend machen

infuse [ɪn'fjuz] *tr* **(& fig) (into)** einflößen *(dat)*

infusion [ɪn'fjuʒən] *s* **(& fig)** Einflößung *f;* **(med)** Infusion *f*

ingenious [ɪn'dʒinɪ·əs] *adj* erfinderisch

ingenuity [ˌɪndʒɪ'n(j)u·ɪti] *s* Erfindungsgabe *f,* Scharfsinn *m*

ingenuous [ɪn'dʒenju·əs] *adj* aufrichtig; *(naive)* naiv

ingest [ɪn'dʒest] *tr* zu sich nehmen

inglorious [ɪn'glɔrɪ·əs] *adj* *(shameful)* unrühmlich; *(without honor)* ruhmlos

ingot ['ɪŋgət] *s* Block *m;* *(of gold or silver)* Barren *m*

ingrained', **in'grained** *adj* eingewurzelt

ingrate ['ɪngret] *s* Undankbare *mf*

ingratiate [ɪn'greʃɪˌet] *tr*—**i.** oneself with sich einschmeicheln bei

ingra'tiating *adj* einschmeichelnd

ingratitude [ɪn'grætɪˌt(j)ud] *s* Undankbarkeit *f,* Undank *m*

ingredient [ɪn'gridɪ·ənt] *s* Bestandteil *m;* (culin) Zutat *f*

in'grown' *adj* eingewachsen

inhabit [ɪn'hæbɪt] *tr* bewohnen

inhabitant [ɪn'hæbɪtənt] *s* Bewohner –in *mf,* Einwohner –in *mf*

inhale [ɪn'hel] *tr* & *intr* einatmen; inhalieren

inherent [ɪn'hɪrənt] *adj* innewohnend; *(right)* angeboren

inherit [ɪn'herɪt] *tr* (biol, jur) erben

inheritance [ɪn'herɪtəns] *s* Erbschaft *f*

inher'itance tax' *s* Erbschaftssteuer *f*

inheritor [ɪn'herɪtər] *s* Erbe *m,* Erbin *f*

inhibit [ɪn'hɪbɪt] *tr* hemmen, inhibieren

inhibition [ˌɪnɪ'bɪʃən] *s* Hemmung *f*

inhospitable [ɪn'hɑspɪtəbəl] *adj* ungastlich; *(place)* unwirtlich

inhuman [ɪn'hjumən] *adj* unmenschlich

inhumane [ˌɪnju'men] *adj* inhuman

inhumanity [ˌɪnhju'mænɪti] *s* Unmenschlichkeit *f*

inimical [ɪ'nɪmɪkəl] *adj* **(to)** abträglich *(dat)*

iniquity [ɪ'nɪkwɪti] *s* Niederträchtigkeit *f,* Ungerechtigkeit *f*

ini·tial [ɪn'ɪʃəl] *adj* anfänglich || *s* Anfangsbuchstabe *m,* Initiale *f* || *v*

(pret & pp –tial[l]ed; ger –tial[l]ing) *tr* mit den Initialen unterzeichnen

initially [ɪ'nɪʃəli] *adv* anfangs

initiate [ɪ'nɪʃɪˌet] *tr* einführen; *(reforms)* einleiten; **(into)** aufnehmen in *(acc)*

initiation [ɪˌnɪʃɪ'eʃən] *s* Einführung *f;* **(into)** Aufnahme *f* (in *acc*)

initiative [ɪ'nɪʃ(ɪ)ətɪv] *s* Unternehmungsgeist *m;* **take the i.** die Initiative ergreifen

inject [ɪn'dʒekt] *tr* *(a needle)* einführen; *(a word)* dazwischenwerfen; *(e.g., bigotry into a campaign)* einfließen lassen; *(a liquid)* (med) injizieren

injection [ɪn'dʒekʃən] *s* (mach) Einspritzung *f;* (med) Injektion *f*

injudicious [ˌɪndʒu'dɪʃəs] *adj* unverständig

injunction [ɪn'dʒʌŋkʃən] *s* Gebot *n;* (jur) gerichtliche Verfügung *f*

injure ['ɪndʒər] *tr* verletzen; (fig) schädigen

injurious [ɪn'dʒʊrɪ·əs] *adj* schädlich

injury ['ɪndʒəri] *s* Verletzung *f;* **(to)** Schädigung *f* *(genit)*

injustice [ɪn'dʒʌstɪs] *s* Ungerechtigkeit *f*

ink [ɪŋk] *s* Tinte *f* || *tr* schwärzen

inkling ['ɪŋklɪŋ] *s* leise Ahnung *f*

ink' pad' *s* Stempelkissen *n*

ink' spot' *s* Tintenklecks *m*

inky ['ɪŋki] *adj* tiefschwarz

inlaid ['ɪn‿led] *adj* eingelegt

in'laid floor' *s* Parkettfußboden *m*

inland ['ɪnlənd] *adj* Binnen– || landeinwärts || *s* Binnenland *n*

in'-laws' *spl* angeheiratete Verwandte *pl*

inlay ['ɪnˌle] *s* Einlegearbeit *f;* (dent) gegossene Plombe *f*

in'let *s* Meeresarm *m;* *(opening)* Öffnung *f*

in'mate *s* Insasse *m,* Insassin *f*

inn [ɪn] *s* Gasthaus *n,* Wirtshaus *n*

innards ['ɪnərdʒ] *spl* (coll) Innere *n*

innate [ɪ'net] *adj* angeboren

inner ['ɪnər] *adj* innere, inwendig, Innen–

in'nermost' *adj* innerste

in'nerspring mat'tress *s* Federkernmatratze *f*

in'ner tube' *s* Schlauch *m*

inning ['ɪnɪŋ] *s* Runde *f*

inn'keep'er *s* Wirt *m,* Wirtin *f*

innocence ['ɪnəsəns] *s* Unschuld *f;* **(of** *a crime)* Schuldlosigkeit *f*

innocent ['ɪnəsənt] *adj* **(of)** unschuldig **(an** *dat);* *(harmless)* harmlos; *(guileless)* arglos || *s* Unschuldige *mf*

innocuous [ɪ'nɑkju·əs] *adj* harmlos

innovation [ˌɪnə've ʃən] *s* Neuerung *f*

innovative ['ɪnəˌvetɪv] *adj* *(person)* neuerungssüchtig; *(thing)* Neuerungs–

innuen·do [ˌɪnju'endo] *s* (**-does**) Unterstellung *f*

innumerable [ɪ'n(j)umərəbəl] *adj* unzählig, unzählbar

inoculate [ɪn'ɑkjəˌlet] *tr* impfen

inoculation [ɪn‿ˌɑkjə'leʃən] *s* Impfung *f*

inoffensive [ˌɪnəˈfensɪv] *adj* unschädlich

inopportune [ɪnˌapərˈt(j)un] *adj* ungelegen

inordinate [ɪnˈɔrdɪnɪt] *adj* übermäßig

inorganic [ˌɪnɔrˈgænɪk] *adj* unorganisch; (chem) anorganisch

in′put′ *adj* (data proc) Eingabe- ‖ *s* (in production) Aufwand *m*; (data proc) Eingabe *f*, Eingangsinformation *f*; (elec) Stromzufuhr *f*

inquest [ˈɪnkwest] *s* Untersuchung *f*

inquire [ɪnˈkwaɪr] *intr* anfragen; **i. about** sich erkundigen nach; **i. into** untersuchen; **i. of** sich erkundigen bei

inquiry [ɪnˈkwaɪri], [ˈɪnkwɪri] *s* Anfrage *f*; (investigation) Untersuchung *f*; **make inquiries (about)** Erkundigungen einziehen (über *acc*)

inquisition [ˌɪnkwɪˈzɪʃən] *s* Inquisition *f*

inquisitive [ɪnˈkwɪzɪtɪv] *adj* wißbegierig

in′road *s* (raid) Einfall *m*; (fig) Eingriff *m*

ins′ and outs′ *spl* alle Kniffe *pl*

insane [ɪnˈsen] *adj* wahnsinnig; (absurd) unsinnig

insane′ asy′lum *s* Irrenanstalt *f*

insanity [ɪnˈsænɪti] *s* Wahnsinn *m*

insatiable [ɪnˈseʃəbəl] *adj* unersättlich

inscribe [ɪnˈskraɪb] *tr* (a name) einschreiben; (a book) widmen; (a monument) mit e-r Inschrift versehen

inscription [ɪnˈskrɪpʃən] *s* Inschrift *f*; (of a book) Widmung *f*

inscrutable [ɪnˈskrutəbəl] *adj* unerforschlich

insect [ˈɪnsekt] *s* Insekt *n*, Kerbtier *n*

insecticide [ɪnˈsektɪˌsaɪd] *s* Insektenvertilgungsmittel *n*, Insektizid *n*

insecure [ˌɪnsɪˈkjur] *adj* unsicher

insecurity [ˌɪnsɪˈkjurɪti] *s* Unsicherheit *f*

insensitive [ɪnˈsensɪtɪv] *adj* (to) unempfindlich (gegen)

inseparable [ɪnˈsepərəbəl] *adj* untrennbar; (friends) unzertrennlich

insert [ˈɪnsʌrt] *s* Einsatzstück *n* ‖ [ɪnˈsʌrt] *tr* einfügen; (a coin) einwerfen

insertion [ɪnˈsʌrʃən] *s* Einfügung *f*; (of a coin) Einwurf *m*

in′set′ (of a map) Nebenkarte *f*; (inserted piece) Einsatz *m*

in′shore′ *adj* Küsten- ‖ *adv* auf die Küste zu

in′side′ *adj* innere, Innen-; (information) vertraulich ‖ *adv* innen, drinnen; **come i.** hereinkommen; **i. of** innerhalb von; **i. out** verkehrt; **know i. out** in- und auswendig kennen; **turn i. out** umdrehen ‖ *s* Innenseite *f*, Innere *n*; **on the i.** innen ‖ *prep* innerhalb (genit)

insider [ɪnˈsaɪdər] *s* Eingeweihte *mf*

in′side track′ *s* (sport) Innenbahn *f*; **have the i.** (fig) im Vorteil sein

insidious [ɪnˈsɪdɪəs] *adj* hinterlistig

in′sight′ *s* Einsicht *f*

insigni·a [ɪnˈsɪgnɪ·ə] *s* (-a & -as) Ab-

zeichen *n*; **i. of office** Amtsabzeichen *pl*; **i. of rank** Rangabzeichen *pl*

insignificant [ˌɪnsɪgˈnɪfɪkənt] *adj* bedeutungslos, geringfügig

insincere [ˌɪnsɪnˈsɪr] *adj* unaufrichtig

insincerity [ˌɪnsɪnˈserɪti] *s* Unaufrichtigkeit *f*

insinuate [ɪnˈsɪnjuˌet] *tr* andeuten

insipid [ɪnˈsɪpɪd] *adj* (& fig) fad(e)

insist [ɪnˈsɪst] *intr*—**i. on** bestehen auf (dat); **i. on** (ger) darauf bestehen zu (inf)

insistent [ɪnˈsɪstənt] *adj* beharrlich

insofar as [ˌɪnsoˈfar ˌæz] *conj* insoweit als

insolence [ˈɪnsələns] *s* Unverschämtheit *f*

insolent [ˈɪnsələnt] *adj* unverschämt

insoluble [ɪnˈsaljəbəl] *adj* unlösbar

insolvency [ɪnˈsalvənsi] *s* Zahlungsunfähigkeit *f*, Insolvenz *f*

insolvent [ɪnˈsalvənt] *adj* zahlungsunfähig

insomnia [ɪnˈsamnɪ·ə] *s* Schlaflosigkeit *f*

insomuch as [ˌɪnsoˈmʌt(ʃəz] *conj* insofern als

inspect [ɪnˈspekt] *tr* (view closely) besichtigen; (check) kontrollieren; (aut) untersuchen; (mil) besichtigen

inspection [ɪnˈspekʃən] *s* Besichtigung *f*; Kontrolle *f*; (aut) Untersuchung *f*; (mil) Truppenbesichtigung *f*

inspector [ɪnˈspektər] *s* Kontrolleur *m*; (of police) Inspektor *m*

inspiration [ˌɪnspɪˈreʃən] *s* Begeisterung *f*

inspire [ɪnˈspaɪr] *tr* begeistern; (feelings) erwecken

inspir′ing *adj* begeisternd

instability [ˌɪnstəˈbɪlɪti] *s* Unbeständigkeit *f*

install [ɪnˈstɔl] *tr* (appliances) installieren; (in office) einführen

installation [ˌɪnstəˈleʃən] *s* (of appliances) Installation *f*; (mil) Anlage *f*

installment [ɪnˈstɔlmənt] *s* Installation *f*; (in a serialized story) Fortsetzung *f*; (partial payment) Rate *f*; **in installments** ratenweise

install′ment plan′ *s* Teilzahlungsplan *m*

instance [ˈɪnstəns] *s* (case) Fall *m*; (example) Beispiel *n*; (jur) Instanz *f*; **for i.** zum Beispiel

instant [ˈɪnstənt] *adj* augenblicklich; (foods) gebrauchsfertig ‖ *s* Augenblick *m*; **this i.** sofort

instantaneous [ˌɪnstənˈtenɪ·əs] *adj* augenblicklich, sofortig

instead [ɪnˈsted] *adv* statt dessen

instead′ of *prep* (an)statt (genit); (ger) anstatt zu (inf)

in′step′ *s* Rist *m*

instigate [ˈɪnstɪˌget] *tr* anstiften

instigation [ˌɪnstɪˈgeʃən] *s* Anstiftung *f*

instigator [ˈɪnstɪˌgetər] *s* Anstifter -in *m*

instill [ɪnˈstɪl] *tr* einflößen

instinct [ˈɪnstɪŋkt] *s* Trieb *m*, Instinkt *m*; **by i.** instinktiv

instinctive [ɪnˈstɪŋktɪv] *adj* instinktiv

institute ['ɪnstɪ‚t(j)ut] *s* Institut *n* ‖ *tr* einleiten
institution [‚ɪnstɪ't(j)uʃən] *s* Anstalt *f*
instruct |ɪn'strʌkt] *tr* anweisen, beauftragen; (*teach*) unterrichten
instruction [ɪn'strʌkʃən] *s* (*teaching*) Unterricht *m;* **instructions** Anweisungen *pl;* **instructions for use** Gebrauchsanweisung *f*
instructive |ɪn'strʌktɪv] *adj* lehrreich
instructor |ɪn'strʌktər| *s* Lehrer –in *mf;* (*at a university*) Dozent –in *mf*
instrument ['ɪnstrəmənt] *s* Instrument *n;* (*tool*) Werkzeug *n;* (jur) Dokument *n*
instrumental [‚ɪnstrə'mentəl] *adj* (mus) instrumental; **he was i. in my getting an award** er war mir behilflich, e–n Preis zu erhalten
instrumentality [‚ɪnstrəmən'tælɪti] *s* Vermittlung *f*
in'strument land'ing *s* Instrumentenlandung *f*
in'strument pan'el *s* Armaturenbrett *n*
insubordinate [‚ɪnsə'bɔrdɪnɪt] *adj* widersetzlich
insubordination [‚ɪnsəbɔrdɪ'neʃən] *s* Widersetzlichkeit *f*
insufferable [ɪn'sʌfərəbəl] *adj* unausstehlich
insufficient [‚ɪnsə'fɪʃənt] *adj* ungenügend, unzureichend
insular |'ɪns(j)ələr| *adj* insular
insulate |'ɪnsə‚let] *tr* isolieren
insulation [‚ɪnsə'leʃən] *s* Isolierung *f;* (*insulating material*) Isolierstoff *m*
insulator |'ɪnsə‚letər| *s* Isolator *m*
insulin |'ɪnsəlɪn| *s* Insulin *n*
insult |'ɪnsʌlt] *s* Beleidigung *f* ‖ [ɪn'sʌlt] *tr* beleidigen, beschimpfen
insurance [ɪn'ʃurəns] *adj* Versicherungs– ‖ *s* Versicherung *f*
insure [ɪn'ʃur] *tr* versichern
insured' *adj* (*letter, package*) Wert– ‖ *s* Versicherungsnehmer –in *mf*
insurer [ɪn'ʃurər] *s* Versicherer –in *mf*
insurgent [ɪn'sʌrdʒənt] *adj* aufständisch ‖ *s* Aufständische *mf*
insurmountable |‚ɪnsər'mauntəbəl] *adj* unübersteigbar; (fig) unüberwindlich
insurrection [‚ɪnsə'rekʃən] *s* Aufstand *m*
intact [ɪn'tækt] *adj* unversehrt
in'take *s* (aut) Einlaß *m;* **i. of food** Nahrungsaufnahme *f*
in'take valve' *s* Einlaßventil *n*
intangible [ɪn'tændʒɪbəl] *adj* immateriell
integer ['ɪntɪdʒər] *s* ganze Zahl *f*
integral ['ɪntɪgrəl] *adj* wesentlich; (math) Integral– ‖ *s* Integral *n*
integrate ['ɪntɪ‚gret] *tr* eingliedern; (*a school*) die Rassentrennung aufheben in (*dat*); (& math) integrieren
integration [‚ɪntɪ'greʃən] *s* Integration *f;* (*of schools*) Aufhebung *f* der Rassentrennung
integrity [ɪn'tegrɪti] *s* Redlichkeit *f*
intellect ['ɪntə‚lekt] *s* Intellekt *m*
intellectual [‚ɪntə'lektʃʊ‚əl] *adj* intellektuell; (*freedom, history*) Geistes– ‖ *s* Intellektuelle *mf*

intelligence [ɪn'telɪdʒəns] *s* Intelligenz *f,* Klugheit *f;* (*information*) Nachricht *f;* (*department*) Nachrichtendienst *m;* **gather i.** Nachrichten einziehen
intel'ligence quo'tient *s* Intelligenz-Quotient *m*
intel'ligence test' *s* Begabungsprüfung *f*
intelligent [ɪn'telɪdʒənt] *adj* intelligent, klug
intelligentsia [ɪn‚telɪ'dʒentsɪ‚ə] *s* Intelligenz *f,* geistige Oberschicht *f*
intelligible |ɪn'telɪdʒɪbəl] *adj* (to) verständlich (*dat*)
intemperate |ɪn'tempərɪt] *adj* unmäßig; (*in drink*) trunksüchtig
intend |ɪn'tend] *tr* beabsichtigen; **be intended for** bestimmt sein für, gemünzt sein auf (*acc*); **i. by** bezwecken mit; **i. for s.o.** j–m zudenken
intend'ed *s* (coll) Verlobte *mf*
intense |ɪn'tens] *adj* intensiv, stark
intensi·fy [ɪn'tensɪ‚faɪ] *v* (*pret & pp* –fied) *tr* steigern, verstärken ‖ *intr* sich steigern, stärker werden
intensity [ɪn'tensɪti] *s* Stärke *f*
intensive |ɪn'tensɪv] *adj* intensiv; (gram) verstärkend
inten'sive care' *s* Intensivstation *f*
intent [ɪn'tent] *adj* (on) erpicht (auf *acc*) ‖ *s* Absicht *f;* **to all intents and purposes** praktisch genommen
intention [ɪn'tenʃən] *s* Absicht *f;* **good i.** guter Wille *m;* **have honorable intentions** es ehrlich meinen; **with the i. of** (*ger*) in der Absicht zu (*inf*)
intentional [ɪn'tenʃənəl] *adj* absichtlich
intently [ɪn'tentli] *adv* gespannt
in·ter [ɪn'tʌr] *v* (*pret & pp* –terred; *ger* –terring) *tr* beerdigen
interact [‚ɪntər'ækt] *intr* zusammenwirken, aufeinander wirken
interaction [‚ɪntər'ækʃən] *s* Wechselwirkung *f*
inter·breed [‚ɪntər'brid] *v* (*pret & pp* –bred) *tr* kreuzen ‖ *intr* sich kreuzen
intercede [‚ɪntər'sid] *intr* Fürsprache einlegen; **i. for s.o. with** Fürsprache einlegen für j–n bei
intercept [‚ɪntər'sept] *tr* (*a letter, aircraft*) abfangen; (*a radio message*) abhören; (*cut off, check*) den Weg abschneiden (*dat*)
interceptor [‚ɪntər'septər] *s* (aer) Abfangjäger *m*
intercession [‚ɪntər'seʃən] *s* Fürsprache *f;* (relig) Fürbitte *f*
interchange ['ɪntər‚tʃendʒ] *s* Wechsel *m;* (*on a highway*) Anschlußstelle *f* ‖ [‚ɪntər'tʃendʒ] *tr* auswechseln ‖ *intr* (with) abwechseln (mit)
interchangeable [‚ɪntər'tʃendʒəbəl] *adj* auswechselbar, austauschbar
intercom ['ɪntər‚kɑm] *s* Wechselsprachanlage *f*
intercourse ['ɪntər‚kors] *s* Verkehr *m;* (*sexual*) Geschlechtsverkehr *m*
interdependent [‚ɪntərdɪ'pendənt] *adj* voneinander abhängig
interdict ['ɪntər‚dɪkt] *s* Verbot *n;* (eccl) Interdikt *n* ‖ [‚ɪntər'dɪkt] *tr*

verbieten; **i. s.o. from** (*ger*) j—m verbieten zu (*inf*)

interest ['ɪnt(ə)rɪst] *s* (**in**) Interesse *n* (**an** *dat*, für); (fin) Zinsen *pl*; **at i. gegen Zinsen**; **be in s.o.'s i. in** j-s Interesse liegen; **have an i. in** beteiligt sein an (*dat*) or bei; **interests** Belange *pl*; **pay i.** (*bring in interest*) Zinsen abwerfen; (*pay out interest*) Zinsen zahlen; **take an i. in** sich interessieren für; **with i.** (& fig) mit Zinsen || *tr* (**in**) interessieren (für)

in'terested *adj*—**i. in** interessiert an (*dat*); **the i. parties** die Beteiligten *pl*

in'teresting *adj* interessant

in'terest rate' *s* Zinsfuß *m*, Zinssatz *m*

interfere [ˌɪntər'fɪr] *intr* (*said of a thing*) dazwischenkommen; (*said of a person*) eingreifen; (**in** or **with**) sich (ein)mengen (**in** *acc*); **i. with** (*dat*, *telv*) stören; **i. with s.o.'s work** j—n bei seiner Arbeit stören

interference [ˌɪntər'fɪrəns] *s* Einmischung *f*; (phys) Interferenz *f*; (rad, telv) Störung *f*

interim ['ɪntərɪm] *adj* Zwischen— || *s* Zwischenzeit *f*

interior [ɪn'tɪrɪ-ər] *adj* innere, Innen— || *s* Innere *n*; (*of a building*) Innenraum *m*; (*of a country*) Inland *n*

inte'rior dec'orator *s* Innenarchitekt —in *mf*

interject [ˌɪntər'dʒɛkt] *tr* dazwischenwerfen

interjection [ˌɪntər'dʒɛkʃən] *s* Zwischenwurf *m*; (gram) Interjektion *f*

interlard [ˌɪntər'lɑrd] *tr* (& fig) spicken

interlinear [ˌɪntər'lɪnɪ-ər] *adj* Interlinear—

interlock [ˌɪntər'lɑk] *tr* miteinander verbinden || *intr* sich ineinanderschließen

interloper [ˌɪntər'lopər] *s* Eindringling *m*

interlude ['ɪntər,lud] *s* (*interval*) Pause *f*; (fig, mus, theat) Zwischenspiel *n*

intermediary [ˌɪntər'midɪ,ɛri] *adj* vermittelnd || *s* Vermittler —in *mf*

intermediate [ˌɪntər'midɪ-ɪt] *adj* zwischenliegend, Zwischen—

interment [ɪn'tɑrmənt] *s* Beerdigung *f*

intermez-zo [ˌɪntər'metso] *s* (**-zos** & **zi** [tsi]) Intermezzo *n*

intermingle [ˌɪntər'mɪŋgəl] *tr* vermischen || *intr* sich vermischen

intermission [ˌɪntər'mɪʃən] *s* Unterbrechung *f*; (theat) Pause *f*

intermittent [ˌɪntər'mɪtənt] *adj* intermittierend

intermix [ˌɪntər'mɪks] *tr* vermischen || *intr* sich vermischen

intern ['ɪntɑrn] *s* Assistenzarzt *m*, Assistenzärztin *f*

internal [ɪn'tɑrnəl] *adj* innere, intern; (*domestic*) einheimisch; (*trade*, *rhyme*) Binnen—

inter'nal-combus'tion en'gine *s* Verbrennungsmotor *m*

inter'nal med'icine *s* innere Medizin *f*

inter'nal rev'enue *s* Steueraufkommen *n*

international [ˌɪntər'næʃənəl] *adj* international

interna'tional date' line' *s* internationale Datumsgrenze *f*

interna'tional law' *s* Völkerrecht *n*

interne'cine war' [ˌɪntər'nisɪn] *s* gegenseitiger Vernichtungskrieg *m*

internee [ˌɪntər'ni] *s* Internierte *mf*

internment [ɪn'tɑrnmənt] *s* Internierung *f*

in'ternship' *s* Pflichtzeit *f* als Assistenzarzt (or Assistenzärztin)

interoffice [ˌɪntər'ɑfɪs] *adj* Haus—

interplanetary [ˌɪntər'plænɪ,teri] *adj* interplanetarisch

interplay ['ɪntər,ple] *s* Wechselspiel *n*

interpolate [ɪn'tɑrpə,let] *tr* interpolieren

interpose [ˌɪntər'poz] *tr* (*an obstacle*) dazwischensetzen; (*a remark*) einwerfen

interpret [ɪn'tɑrprɪt] *tr* (& mus) interpretieren; (*translate*) verdolmetschen || *intr* dolmetschen

interpretation [ɪn,tɑrprɪ'teʃən] *s* (& mus) Interpretation *f*

interpreter [ɪn'tɑrprɪtər] *s* Dolmetscher —in *mf*; **act as i.** dolmetschen

interrogate [ɪn'terə,get] *tr* ausfragen; (jur) verhören, vernehmen

interrogation [ɪn,terə'geʃən] *s* Verhör *n*

interrogative [ˌɪntər'rɑgətɪv] *adj* Frage—

interrupt [ˌɪntə'rʌpt] *tr* unterbrechen

interruption [ˌɪntə'rʌpʃən] *s* Unterbrechung *f*; (*in industry*) Betriebsstörung *f*

intersect [ˌɪntər'sekt] *tr* durchschneiden || *ref* sich kreuzen

intersection [ˌɪntər'sekʃən] *s* Straßenkreuzung *f*; (math) Schnittpunkt *m*

intersperse [ˌɪntər'spɑrs] *tr* durchsetzen

interstate ['ɪntər,stet] *adj* zwischenstaatlich

interstellar [ˌɪntər'stelər] *adj* interstellar

interstice [ɪn'tɑrstɪs] *s* Zwischenraum *m*

intertwine [ˌɪntər'twaɪn] *tr* verflechten || *intr* sich verflechten

interval ['ɪntərvəl] *s* Abstand *m*; (mus) Stufe *f*, Intervall *n*

intervene [ˌɪntər'vin] *intr* dazwischenkommen; (*interfere*) eingreifen; (*intercede*) intervenieren

intervention [ˌɪntər'venʃən] *s* Dazwischenkommen *n*; Eingreifen *n*; Intervention *f*

interview ['ɪntər,vju] *s* Interview *n* || *tr* interviewen

inter-weave [ˌɪntər'wiv] *v* (*pret* **-wove** & **-weaved**; *pp* **-wove**, **-woven** & **-weaved**) *tr* durchweben, durchflechten

intestate [ɪn'testet] *adj* ohne Testament

intestine [ɪn'testɪn] *s* Darm *m*; **intestines** Gedärme *pl*

intimacy ['ɪntɪməsi] *s* Vertraulichkeit *f*; **intimacies** Intimitäten *pl*

intimate ['ɪntɪmɪt] *adj* intim, vertraut

|| *s* Vertraute *mf* || [ˈɪntɪˌmet] *tr* andeuten

intimation [ˌɪntɪˈmeʃən] *s* Andeutung *f*

intimidate [ɪnˈtɪmɪˌdet] *tr* einschüchtern

intimidation [ˌɪntɪmɪˈdeʃən] *s* Einschüchterung *f*

into [ˈɪntu], [ˈɪntu] *prep* in (*acc*)

intolerable [ɪnˈtɑlərəbəl] *adj* unerträglich

intolerance [ɪnˈtɑlərəns] *s* (**of**) Intoleranz *f* (gegen)

intolerant [ɪnˈtɑlərənt] *adj* (**of**) intolerant (gegen)

intonation [ˌɪntoˈneʃən] *s* Tonfall *m*

intone [ɪnˈton] *tr* intonieren

intoxicate [ɪnˈtɑksɪˌket] *tr* berauschen; (*poison*) vergiften

intoxication [ɪnˌtɑksɪˈkeʃən] *s* (& fig) Rausch *m*; (*poisoning*) Vergiftung *f*

intractable [ɪnˈtræktəbəl] *adj* (*person*) störrisch; (*thing*) schwer zu bearbeiten(d)

intransigent [ɪnˈtrænsɪdʒənt] *adj* unversöhnlich

intransitive [ɪnˈtrænsɪtɪv] *adj* intransitiv

intravenous [ˌɪntrəˈvinəs] *adj* intravenös

intrepid [ɪnˈtrepɪd] *adj* unerschrocken

intricate [ˈɪntrɪkɪt] *adj* verwickelt

intrigue [ɪnˈtrig], [ˈɪntrig] *s* Intrige *f* || [ɪnˈtrig] *tr* fesseln || *intr* intriguieren

intrigu'ing *adj* fesselnd

intrinsic(al) [ɪnˈtrɪnsɪk(əl)] *adj* innere, innerlich; (*value*) wirklich

introduce [ˌɪntrəˈd(j)us] *tr* einführen; (*strangers*) vorstellen

introduction [ˌɪntrəˈdʌkʃən] *s* Einführung *f*; (*of strangers*) Vorstellung *f*; (*in a book*) Einleitung *f*

introductory [ˌɪntrəˈdʌktəri] *adj* (*offer, price*) Einführungs-; (*remarks*) einleitend

introspection [ˌɪntrəˈspekʃən] *s* Selbstbeobachtung *f*

introspective [ˌɪntrəˈspektɪv] *adj* introspektiv

introvert [ˈɪntrəˌvʌrt] *s* Introvertierte *mf*

intrude [ɪnˈtrud] *intr* (**on**) sich aufdrängen (dat); **am I intruding?** störe ich?

intruder [ɪnˈtrudər] *s* Eindringling *m*

intrusion [ɪnˈtruʒən] *s* Eindrängen *n*, Stören *n*

intrusive [ɪnˈtrusɪv] *adj* störend, lästig

intuition [ˌɪnt(j)uˈɪʃən] *s* Intuition *f*

inundate [ˈɪnənˌdet] *tr* überschwemmen

inundation [ˌɪnənˈdeʃən] *s* Überschwemmung *f*

inure [ɪnˈjur] *tr* (**to**) abhärten (gegen)

invade [ɪnˈved] *tr* (*a country*) eindringen in (*acc*); (*rights*) verletzen; (*privacy*) stören

invader [ɪnˈvedər] *s* Eindringling *m*; (mil) Angreifer *m*

invalid [ɪnˈvælɪd] *adj* ungültig || [ˈɪnvəlɪd] *adj* kränklich || *s* Invalide *m*

invalidate [ɪnˈvælɪˌdet] *tr* ungültig machen; (*a law*) außer Kraft setzen

invalidity [ˌɪnvəˈlɪdɪti] *s* Ungültigkeit *f*

invaluable [ɪnˈvæljuˌəbəl] *adj* unschätzbar

invariable [ɪnˈverɪˌəbəl] *adj* unveränderlich

invasion [ɪnˈveʒən] *s* Invasion *f*

invective [ɪnˈvektɪv] *s* Schmähung *f*

inveigh [ɪnˈve] *intr*—**i. against** schimpfen über (*acc*) or auf (*acc*)

inveigle |ɪnˈvigel| *tr* verleiten; **i. s.o. into** (*ger*) j–n verleiten zu (*inf*)

invent [ɪnˈvent] *tr* erfinden; (*a story*) sich |dat| ausdenken

invention [ɪnˈvenʃən] *s* Erfindung *f*

inventive [ɪnˈventɪv] *adj* erfinderisch

inventiveness [ɪnˈventɪvnɪs] *s* Erfindungsgabe *f*

inventor [ɪnˈventər] *s* Erfinder –in *mf*

inven·to·ry [ˈɪnvənˌtɔri] *s* (*stock*) Inventar *n*; (*act*) Inventur *f*; (*list*) Bestandsverzeichnis *n*; **take i.** Inventur machen || *v* (*pret & pp* **–ried**) *tr* inventarisieren

inverse [ɪnˈvʌrs] *adj* umgekehrt

inversion [ɪnˈvʌrʒən] *s* Umkehrung *f*; (gram) Umstellung *f*

invert [ɪnˈvʌrt] *tr* umkehren; (gram) umstellen

invertebrate [ɪnˈvʌrtɪˌbret] *adj* wirbellos || *s* wirbelloses Tier *n*

invest [ɪnˈvest] *tr* (**in**) investieren (in *acc*); (mil) belagern; **i. with** ausstatten mit

investigate [ɪnˈvestɪˌget] *tr* untersuchen

investigation [ɪnˌvestɪˈgeʃən] *s* Untersuchung *f*

investigator [ɪnˈvestɪˌgetər] *s* Untersucher –in *mf*

investment [ɪnˈvestmənt] *s* Anlage *f*, Investition *f*; (*with an office*) Amtseinführung *f*; (mil) Belagerung *f*

investor [ɪnˈvestər] *s* Investor –in *mf*

inveterate [ɪnˈvetərɪt] *adj* (*habitual*) eingefleischt; (*firmly established*) eingewurzelt

invidious [ɪnˈvɪdɪ·əs] *adj* haßerregend

invigorate [ɪnˈvɪgəˌret] *tr* beleben

invig'orating *adj* belebend

invincible [ɪnˈvɪnsɪbəl] *adj* unbesiegbar

invisible [ɪnˈvɪzɪbəl] *adj* unsichtbar

invis'ible ink' *s* Geheimtinte *f*

invitation [ˌɪnvɪˈteʃən] *s* Einladung *f*

invite [ɪnˈvaɪt] *tr* einladen; **i. in** hereinbitten

invit'ing *adj* lockend

invocation [ˌɪnvəˈkeʃən] *s* Anrufung *f*; (relig) Bittgebet *n*

invoice [ˈɪnvɔɪs] *s* Faktura *f*, Warenrechnung *f*; **as per i.** laut Rechnung || *tr* fakturieren

invoke [ɪnˈvok] *tr* anrufen; (*cite*) zitieren

involuntary [ɪnˈvɑlənˌteri] *adj* (*against one's will*) unfreiwillig; (*without one's will*) unwillkürlich

invol'untary man'slaughter *s* unbeabsichtigte Tötung *f*

involve [ɪn'vɑlv] *tr* verwickeln; (*include*) einschließen; (*affect*) betreffen; (*entail*) zur Folge haben

involved' *adj* verwickelt, kompliziert; **be i. in** (*e.g., construction*) beschäftigt sein bei; (*e.g., a crime*) verwickelt sein in (*acc*); **be i. with** (*e.g., a married person*) e-e Affäre haben mit

involvement [ɪn'vɑlvmənt] *s* Verwicklung *f*

invulnerable [ɪn'vʌlnərəbəl] *adj* unverwundbar

inward ['ɪnwərd] *adj* inner(lich) ‖ *adv* nach innen

inwardly ['ɪnwərdli] *adv* innerlich

iodine ['aɪ·ə‚din] *s* (chem) Jod *n* ‖ ['aɪ·ə‚daɪn] *s* (pharm) Jodtinktur *f*

ion ['aɪ·ən], ['aɪ·ɑn] *s* Ion *n*

ionize ['aɪ·ə‚naɪz] *tr* ionisieren

IOU ['aɪ‚o'ju] *s* (**I owe you**) Schuldschein *m*

I.Q. ['aɪ'kju] *s* (**intelligence quotient**) Intelligenz-Quotient *m*

Iran [ɪ'rɑn], [ɪ'ræn] *s* Iran *m*

Iranian [aɪ'renɪ·ən] *adj* iranisch ‖ *s* Iran(i)er –in *mf*

Iraq [ɪ'rɑk] *s* Irak *m*

Ira·qi [ɪ'rɑki] *adj* irakisch ‖ *s* (**–qis**) Iraker –in *mf*

irascible [ɪ'ræsɪbəl] *adj* jähzornig

irate ['aɪret], [aɪ'ret] *adj* zornig

ire [aɪr] *s* Zorn *m*

Ireland ['aɪrlənd] *s* Irland *n*

iris ['aɪrɪs] *s* (anat, bot) Iris *f*

Irish ['aɪrɪʃ] *adj* irisch ‖ *s* (*language*) Irisch *n*; **the I.** die Iren *pl*

I'rish·man *s* (**–men**) Ire *m*

I'rish·wom'an *s* (**–wom·en**) Irin *f*

irk [ʌrk] *tr* ärgern

irksome ['ʌrksəm] *adj* ärgerlich

iron ['aɪ·ərn] *adj* (& fig) eisern ‖ *s* Eisen *n*; (*for pressing clothes*) Bügeleisen *n* ‖ *tr* bügeln; **i. out** ausbügeln; (fig) ins Reine bringen

ironclad ['aɪ·ərn‚klæd] *adj* (fig) unumstößlich

i'ron cur'tain *s* eiserner Vorhang *m*

ironic(al) [aɪ'rɑnɪk(əl)] *adj* ironisch

i'roning *s* (*act*) Bügeln *n*; (*clothes*) Bügelwäsche *f*

i'roning board' *s* Bügelbrett *n*

i'ron lung' *s* eiserne Lunge *f*

i'ron ore' *s* Eisenerz *n*

irony ['aɪrəni] *s* Ironie *f*

irradiate [ɪ'redɪ‚et] *tr* bestrahlen; (*light*) ausstrahlen; (*a face*) aufheitern

irrational [ɪ'ræʃənəl] *adj* irrational

irreconcilable [ɪ‚rekən'saɪləbəl] *adj* unversöhnlich

irredeemable [ɪrrɪ'diməbəl] *adj* (*loan, bond*) nicht einlösbar; (*hopeless*) hoffnungslos

irrefutable [ɪrrɪ'fjutəbəl] *adj* unwiderlegbar

irregular [ɪ'regjələr] *adj* unregelmäßig

irregularity [ɪ‚regjə'lærɪti] *s* Unregelmäßigkeit *f*

irrelevant [ɪ'reləvənt] *adj* (**to**) nicht anwendbar (auf *acc*)

irreligious [ɪrrɪ'lɪdʒəs] *adj* irreligiös

irreparable [ɪ'repərəbəl] *adj* unersetzlich

irreplaceable [ɪrrɪ'plesɪbəl] *adj* unersetzlich

irrepressible [ɪrrɪ'presɪbəl] *adj* unbezähmbar

irreproachable [ɪrrɪ'protʃəbəl] *adj* untadelig

irresistible [ɪrrɪ'zɪstɪbəl] *adj* unwiderstehlich

irresolute [ɪ'rezəlut] *adj* unentschlossen, unschlüßig

irrespective [ɪrrɪ'spektɪv] *adj*—**i. of** ohne Rücksicht auf (*acc*)

irresponsible [ɪrrɪ'spɑnsɪbəl] *adj* unverantwortlich

irretrievable [ɪrrɪ'trivəbəl] *adj* unwiederbringlich, unrettbar

irreverent [ɪ'revərənt] *adj* unehrerbietig

irrevocable [ɪ'revəkəbəl] *adj* unwiderruflich

irrigate ['ɪrɪ‚get] *tr* verwässern; (med) irrigieren

irrigation [ɪrrɪ'geʃən] *s* Bewässerung *f*

irritable ['ɪrrɪtəbəl] *adj* reizbar

irritant ['ɪrrɪtənt] *s* Reizstoff *m*

irritate ['ɪrrɪ‚tet] *tr* reizen, irritieren

ir'ritating *adj* ärgerlich

irritation [ɪrrɪ'teʃən] *s* Reizung *f*

irruption ['ɪrʌpʃən] *s* Einbruch *m*

isinglass ['aɪzɪŋ‚glæs] *s* Fischleim *m*; (*mica*) Glimmer *m*

Islam ['ɪsləm] *s* Islam *m*

island ['aɪlənd] *s* Insel *f*

islander ['aɪləndər] *s* Insulaner –in *mf*

isle [aɪl] *s* kleine Insel *f*

isolate ['aɪsə‚let] *tr* isolieren

isolation [‚aɪsə'leʃən] *s* Isolierung *f*

isolationist [‚aɪsə'leʃənɪst] *s* Isolationist –in *mf*

isola'tion ward' *s* Isolierstation *f*

isometric [‚aɪsə'metrɪk] *adj* isometrisch

isosceles [aɪ'sɑsə‚liz] *adj* gleichschenklig

isotope ['aɪsə‚top] *s* Isotop *n*

Israel ['ɪzrɪ·əl] *s* Israel *n*

Israe·li [ɪz'reli] *adj* israelisch ‖ *s* (**–li**) Israeli *m*

Israelite ['ɪzrɪ·ə‚laɪt] *adj* israelitisch ‖ *s* Israelit –in *mf*

issuance ['ɪʃu·əns] *s* Ausgabe *f*

issue ['ɪʃu] *s* (*of a magazine*) Nummer *f*; (*result*) Ausgang *m*; (*e.g., of securities*) Ausgabe *f*, Emission *f*; (*under discussion*) Streitpunkt *m*; (*offspring*) Nachkommenschaft *f*; **avoid the i.** der Frage ausweichen; **be at i.** zur Debatte stehen; **make an i. of it** e-e Streitfrage daraus machen; **take i. with** anderer Meinung sein als ‖ *tr* (*orders, supplies, stamps, stocks*) ausgeben; (*a pass*) ausstellen ‖ *intr* (**from**) herauskommen (aus)

isthmus ['ɪsməs] *s* Landenge *f*

it [ɪt] *pron* es; **about it** darüber, davon; **it is I** ich bin es

Italian [ɪ'tælɪ·ən] *adj* italienisch ‖ *s* (*person*) Italiener –in *mf*; (*language*) Italienisch *n*

italicize [ɪ'tælɪ‚saɪz] *tr* kursiv drucken

italics [ɪ'tælɪks] *spl* Kursivschrift *f*
Italy ['ɪtəli] *s* Italien *n*
itch [ɪtʃ] *s* Jucken *n; (*pathol) Krätze *f* ‖ *intr* jucken; **I am itching to** *(inf)* es reizt mich zu *(inf);* **my nose itches me** es juckt mich in der Nase
itchy ['ɪtʃi] *adj* juckend; (pathol) krätzig
item ['aɪtəm] *s* Artikel *m; (in a list)* Punkt *m; (*com) Posten *m; (*journ) Nachricht *f;* **hot i.** (coll) Schlager *m*
itemize ['aɪtə‚maɪz] *tr* einzeln aufführen

itinerant [aɪ'tɪnərənt], [ɪ'tɪnərənt] *adj* Wander-, reisend ‖ *s* Reisende *mf*
itinerary [aɪ'tɪnə‚reri] *s* Reiseplan *m*
its [ɪts] *poss adj* sein
itself *reflex pron* sich; **in i.** an und für sich ‖ *intens pron* selbst, selber
ivied ['aɪvɪd] *adj* efeubewachsen
ivory ['aɪvəri] *adj* elfenbeinern, Elfenbein-; *(*color) kremfarben ‖ *s* Elfenbein *n;* **tickle the ivories** in die Tasten greifen
i'vory tow'er *s* (fig) Elfenbeinturm *m*
ivy ['aɪvi] *s* Efeu *m*

J

J, j [dʒe] *s* zehnter Buchstabe des englischen Alphabets
jab [dʒæb] *s* Stoß *m; (*box) Gerade *f* ‖ *v (pret & pp* **jabbed;** *ger* **jabbing)** *tr* stoßen; (box) mit der Gerade stoßen
jabber ['dʒæbər] *tr & intr* plappern
jack [dʒæk] *s (*money) (sl) Pinke *f; (*aut) Wagenheber *m; (*cards) Bube *m; (*telp) Klinke *f;* **Jack Hans m** ‖ *tr—***j. up** (aut) heben; *(*prices) hinaufschrauben
jackal ['dʒækəl] *s* Schakal *m*
jack'ass' *s* Esel *m*
jacket ['dʒækɪt] *s* Jacke *f; (of a book)* Umschlag *m; (of a potato)* Schale *f*
Jack' Frost' *s* Herr Winter *m*
jack'ham'mer *s* Preßlufthammer *m*
jack'-in-the-box' *s* Kastenteufel *m*
jack'knife' *s* (-knives) Klappmesser *n; (*dive) Hechtbeuge *f* ‖ *intr* zusammenklappen
jack'-of-all'-trades' *s* Hansdampf *m* in allen Gassen
jack'pot' *s* Jackpot *m;* **hit the j.** das Große Los gewinnen
jack' rab'bit *s* Hase *m*
Jacob ['dʒekəb] *s* Jakob *m*
jade [dʒed] *adj* jadegrün ‖ *s (*stone) Jade *m; (*color) Jadegrün *n; (*horse) Schindmähre *f*
jad'ed *adj* ermattet
jag [dʒæg] *s* Zacke *f;* **have a jag on** (sl) e-n Schwips haben
jagged ['dʒægɪd] *adj* zackig, schartig
jaguar ['dʒægwar] *s* Jaguar *m*
jail [dʒel] *s* Gefängnis *n,* Untersuchungsgefängnis *n;* **be in j.** sitzen ‖ *tr* einsperren
jail'bird' *s* Knastbruder *m*
jailer ['dʒelər] *s* Gefängniswärter *m*
jalopy [dʒə'lapi] *s* Rumpelkasten *m*
jal'ousie win'dow ['dʒæləsi] *s* Glasjalousie *f*
jam [dʒæm] *s* Marmelade *f;* **be in a jam** (coll) in der Patsche sitzen ‖ *v (pret & pp* **jammed;** *ger* **jamming)** *tr (a room)* überfüllen; *(a street)* verstopfen; *(a finger)* quetschen; *(*rad) stören; **be jammed in** eingezwängt sein; **jam on the brakes** auf die Bremsen drücken; **jam s.th. into**

etw stopfen in *(acc)* ‖ *intr (said of a window)* klemmen; *(said of gears)* sich verklemmen; *(said of a gun)* Ladehemmung haben; **jam into** sich hineinquetschen in *(acc)*
jamb [dʒæm] *s* Pfosten *m*
jamboree [‚dʒæmbə'ri] *s* Trubel *m; (of scouts)* Pfadfindertreffen *n*
James [dʒemz] *s* Jakob *m*
jam'ming *s* (rad) Störung *f*
Jane [dʒen] *s* Johanna *f*
Janet ['dʒænɪt] *s* Hanna *f*
jangle ['dʒæŋgəl] *s* Rasseln *n* ‖ *tr* rasseln lassen; **j. s.o.'s nerves** j-m auf die Nerven gehen ‖ *intr* rasseln
janitor ['dʒænɪtər] *s* Hausmeister *m*
January ['dʒænju‚eri] *s* Januar *m*
Japan [dʒə'pæn] *s* Japan *n*
Japanese [‚dʒæpə'niz] *adj* japanisch ‖ *s* Japaner –in *mf; (*language) Japanisch *n*
Jap'anese bee'tle *s* Japankäfer *m*
jar [dʒar] *s* Krug *m; (e.g., of jam)* Glas *n; (*jolt) Stoß *m* ‖ *v (pret & pp* **jarred;** *ger* **jarring)** *tr (*jolt) anstoßen; (fig) erschüttern ‖ *intr* nicht harmonieren; **jar on the nerves** auf die Nerven gehen
jargon ['dʒargən] *s* Jargon *m*
jasmine ['dʒæzmɪn] *s* Jasmin *m*
jaundice ['dʒɔndɪs] *s* Gelbsucht *f*
jaun'diced *adj* gelbsüchtig
jaunt [dʒɔnt] *s* Ausflug *m*
jaunty ['dʒɔnti] *adj (*sprightly) lebhaft; *(clothes)* fesch
javelin ['dʒæv(ə)lɪn] *s* Speer *m*
jaw [dʒɔ] *s* Kiefer *m;* **the jaws of death** die Klauen des Todes
jaw'bone' *s* Kiefer *m* ‖ *intr* (sl) sich stark machen
jay [dʒe] *s* (orn) Häher *m*
jay'walk' *intr* verkehrswidrig die Straße überqueren
jazz [dʒæz] *s* Jazz *m* ‖ *tr—***j. up** (coll) aufmöbeln
jazz' band' *s* Jazzband *f*
jazzy ['dʒæzi] *adj* bunt, grell
jealous ['dʒeləs] *adj (*of) eifersüchtig *(*auf *acc)*
jealousy ['dʒeləsi] *s* Eifersucht *f*
jeans [dʒinz] *spl* Jeans *pl*

jeep [dʒiːp] *s* Jeep *m*

jeer [dʒɪr] *s* Hohn *m* ‖ *tr* verhöhnen ‖ *intr* höhnen; **j. at** verhöhnen

Jeffrey ['dʒefrɪ] *s* Gottfried *m*

Jehovah [dʒɪ'hovə] *s* Jehova *m*

jell [dʒel] *s* Gelee *n* ‖ *intr* gelieren; (fig) zum Klappen kommen

jellied ['dʒelɪd] *adj* geliert

jelly ['dʒelɪ] *s* Gallerte *f*

jel'lyfish' *s* Qualle *f*; (pej) Waschlappen *m*

jeopardize ['dʒepər‚daɪz] *tr* gefährden

jeopardy ['dʒepərdɪ] *s* Gefahr *f*

jerk [dʒʌrk] *s* Ruck *m*; (sl) Knülch *m* ‖ *tr* ruckweise ziehen ‖ *intr* zucken

jerky ['dʒʌrkɪ] *adj* ruckartig

jersey ['dʒʌrzɪ] *s* (material) Jersey *m*; (shirt) Jersey *n*; (sport) Trikot *n*

jest [dʒest] *s* Scherz *m*; **in j.** scherzweise ‖ *intr* scherzen

jester ['dʒestər] *s* Hofnarr *m*; (joker) Spaßvogel *m*

Jesuit ['dʒezʊ‚ɪt] *adj* Jesuiten– ‖ *s* Jesuit *m*

Jesus ['dʒizəs] *s* Jesus *m*

jet [dʒet] *adj* Düsen– ‖ *s* (stream) Strahl *m*; (nozzle) Düse *f*; (plane) Jet *m*, Düsenflugzeug *n* ‖ *v* (pret & pp **jetted**; ger **jetting**) herausströmen; (aer) jetten

jet'-black' *adj* rabenschwarz

jet' propul'sion *s* Düsenantrieb *m*

jetsam ['dʒetsəm] *s* Seewurfgut *n*

jet' stream' *s* Strahlströmung *f*

jettison ['dʒetɪsən] *s* Seewurf *m* ‖ *tr* (aer) abwerfen; (naut) über Bord werfen

jetty ['dʒetɪ] *s* (wharf) Landungsbrücke *f*; (breakwater) Hafendamm *m*

Jew [dʒu] *s* Jude *m*, Jüdin *f*

jewel ['dʒu·əl] *s* (& fig) Juwel *n*; (in a watch) Stein *m*

jew'el box' *s* Schmuckkästchen *n*

jewel(l)er ['dʒu·ələr] *s* Juwelier –in *mf*

jewelry ['dʒu·əlrɪ] *s* Juwelen *pl*; **piece of j.** Schmuckstück *n*

jew'elry store' *s* Juweliergeschäft *n*

Jewish ['dʒu·ɪʃ] *adj* jüdisch

Jew's' harp' *s* Maultrommel *f*

jib [dʒɪb] *s* Ausleger *m*; (naut) Klüver *m*

jibe [dʒaɪb] *intr* (coll) übereinstimmen

jiffy ['dʒɪfɪ] *s*—**in a j.** im Nu

jig [dʒɪg] *s* (dance) Gigue *f*; (tool) Spannvorrichtung *f*; **the jig is up** (sl) das Spiel ist aus

jigger ['dʒɪgər] *s* Schnapsglas *n*; (gadget) Dingsbums *n*; (naut) Besan *m*

jiggle ['dʒɪgəl] *tr & intr* rütteln

jig'saw' *s* Laubsäge *f*

jig'saw puz'zle *s* Puzzelspiel *n*

jilt [dʒɪlt] *tr* (a girl) sitzenlassen; (a boy) den Laufpaß geben (dat)

jim·my ['dʒɪmɪ] *s* Brecheisen *n* ‖ *v* (pret & pp **-mied**) *tr* mit dem Brecheisen aufbrechen

jingle ['dʒɪŋgəl] *s* (of coins) Klimpern *n*; (bell) Schelle *f*; (verse) Verseklingel *n* ‖ *tr* klimpern mit ‖ *intr* klimpern; (said of verses) klingeln

jin·go ['dʒɪŋgo] *s* (–goes) Chauvinist –in *mf*; **by j.!** alle Wetter!

jinx [dʒɪŋks] *s* Unglücksrabe *m* ‖ *tr* Pech bringen (dat); **be jinxed** vom Pech verfolgt sein

jitters ['dʒɪtərz] *spl*—**have the j.** wahnsinnig nervös sein; **give s.o. the j.** j-n wahnsinnig nervös machen

jittery ['dʒɪtərɪ] *adj* durchgedreht

Joan [dʒon] *s* Johanna *f*

job [dʒab] *s* (employment) Job *m*; (task, responsibility) Aufgabe *f*; **bad job** Machwerk *n*; **do a good job** gute Arbeit leisten; **fall down on the job** seine Pflicht nicht erfüllen; **know one's job** seine Sache verstehen; **on the job** bei der Arbeit; (fig) auf Draht; **out of a job** arbeitslos

jobber ['dʒabər] *s* (middleman) Zwischenhändler –in *mf*; (pieceworker) Akkordarbeiter –in *mf*

job'hold'er *s* Stelleninhaber –in *mf*

jobless ['dʒablɪs] *adj* stellungslos

jockey ['dʒaki] *s* Jockei *m* ‖ *tr* manövrieren

jog [dʒag] *s* Dauerlauf *m*; (of a horse) Trott *m* ‖ *v* (pret & pp **jogged**; ger **jogging**) *tr* (shake) rütteln; (the memory) auffrischen ‖ *intr* trotten; (for exercise) langsam rennen, Dauerlauf machen

John [dʒan] *s* Johann *m*; **john** (sl) Klo *n*

Johnny ['dʒani] *s* Hans *m*

John'ny-come-late'ly *s* Neuling *m*, Nachzügler *m*

join [dʒɔɪn] *tr* verbinden; (a club) beitreten (dat); (a person) sich anschließen (dat); (two parts) zusammenfügen; **j. the army** zum Militär gehen ‖ *intr* sich verbinden; **j. in** sich beteiligen an (dat); **j. up** (mil) einrücken

joiner ['dʒɔɪnər] *s* (coll) Vereinsmeier *m*; (carp) Tischler *m*

joint [dʒɔɪnt] *adj* (account, venture) gemeinschaftlich; (return) gemeinsam; (committee) gemischt; (heir, owner) Mit– ‖ *s* Verbindungspunkt *m*; (in plumbing) Naht *f*; (sl) Bumslokal *n*; (anat, bot, mach) Gelenk *n*; (carp) Fuge *f*; (culin) Bratenstück *n*; **throw out of j.** ausrenken

jointly ['dʒɔɪntlɪ] *adv* gemeinsam

joint'-stock' com'pany *s* Aktiengesellschaft *f*

joist [dʒɔɪst] *s* Tragbalken *m*

joke [dʒok] *s* Witz *m*; **he can't take a j.** er versteht keinen Spaß; **make a j. of** ins Lächerliche ziehen; **play a j. on** e-n Streich spielen (dat) ‖ *intr* Spaß machen; **j. about** witzeln über (acc); **j. around** schäkern; **joking aside** Spaß beiseite

joker ['dʒokər] *s* Spaßvogel *m*; (pej) Knülch *m*; (cards) Joker *m*

jolly ['dʒalɪ] *adj* lustig

jolt [dʒolt] *s* Stoß *m* ‖ *tr* stoßen ‖ *intr* holpern; **j. along** dahinholpern

Jordan ['dʒɔrdən] *s* (country) Jordanien *n*; (river) Jordan *m*

josh [dʒaʃ] *tr & intr* hänseln

jostle ['dʒasəl] *tr & intr* drängeln

jot [dʒat] *s*—**not a jot** kein Jota ‖ *tr*

(*pret & pp* **jotted; ger jotting**) *tr—* **jot down** notieren

journal ['dʒʌrnəl] *s* (*daily record*) Tagebuch *n*; (*magazine*) Zeitschrift *f*

journalism ['dʒʌrnə‚lɪzəm] *s* Journalismus *m*, Zeitungswesen *n*

journalist ['dʒʌrnəlɪst] *s* Journalist -in *mf*

journey ['dʒʌrni] *s* Reise *f*; **go on a j.** verreisen ‖ *intr* reisen

jour'ney‚man *adj* tüchtig ‖ *s* (-men) Geselle *m*

joust [dʒaust] *s* Tjost *f* ‖ *intr* turnieren

jovial ['dʒovɪ‚əl] *adj* jovial

jowls [dʒaulz] *spl* Hängebacken *pl*

joy [dʒɔɪ] *s* Freude *f*

joyful ['dʒɔɪfəl] *adj* froh, freudig

joyless ['dʒɔɪlɪs] *adj* freudlos

joy' ride' *s* (coll) Schwarzfahrt *f*

joy' stick' *s* (aer) Steuerknüppel *m*

Jr. *abbr* (**Junior**) jr., jun.

jubilant ['dʒubɪlənt] *adj* frohlockend

jubilation [‚dʒubɪ'leʃən] *s* Jubel *m*

jubilee ['dʒubɪ‚li] *s* Jubiläum *n*

Judaea [dʒu'di‚ə] *s* Judäa *n*

Judaic [dʒu'de‚ɪk] *adj* jüdisch

Judaism ['dʒudə‚ɪzəm] *s* Judaismus *m*

judge [dʒʌdʒ] *s* (*in a competition*) Preisrichter -in *mf*; (box) Punktrichter -in *mf*; (jur) Richter -in *mf* ‖ *tr* (by) beurteilen (nach); (*distances*) abschätzen; (jur) richten ‖ *intr* urteilen; (jur) richten; **judging by his words** seinen Worten nach zu urteilen

judge' ad'vocate *s* Kriegsgerichtsrat *m*

judgment ['dʒʌdʒmənt] *s* (& jur) Urteil *n*; **in my j.** meines Erachtens; **show good j.** ein gutes Urteilsvermögen haben; **sit in j. over** zu Gericht sitzen über (*acc*)

Judg'ment Day' *s* Tag *m* des Gerichts

judicial [dʒu'dɪʃəl] *adj* Rechts—

judiciary [dʒu'dɪʃɪ‚erɪ] *adj* richterlich ‖ *s* (*branch*) richterliche Gewalt *f*; (*judges*) Richterstand *m*

judicious [dʒu'dɪʃəs] *adj* klug

judo ['dʒudo] *s* Judo *n*

jug [dʒʌg] *s* Krug *m*; (*jail*) Kittchen *n*

juggle ['dʒʌgəl] *tr* jonglieren; (*accounts*) frisieren ‖ *intr* jonglieren

juggler ['dʒʌglər] *s* Gaukler -in *mf*

Jugoslav ['jugo‚slav] *adj* jugoslawisch ‖ *s* Jugoslawe *m*, Jugoslawin *f*

Jugoslavia [‚jugo'slavɪ‚ə] *s* Jugoslawien *n*

jug'ular vein' ['dʒʌgjələr] *s* Halsader *f*

juice [dʒus] *s* Saft *m*

juicy ['dʒusi] *adj* saftig

jukebox ['dʒuk‚baks] *s* Musikautomat *m*

July [dʒu'laɪ] *s* Juli *m*

jumble ['dʒʌmbəl] *s* Wust *m* ‖ *tr* durcheinanderwerfen

jumbo ['dʒʌmbo] *adj* Riesen-

jump [dʒʌmp] *s* Sprung *m*; (aer) Absprung *m*; **get the j. on** zuvorkommen (*dat*) ‖ *tr* überspringen; (*attack*) überfallen; (*a hurdle*) nehmen; (*in*

checkers) schlagen; **j. bail** die Kaution verfallen lassen; **j. channels** den amtlichen Weg nicht einhalten; **j. rope** seilspringen; **j. ship** vom Schiff weglaufen; **j. the gun** übereilt handeln; (sport) zu früh starten; **j. the track** entgleisen ‖ *intr* springen; (*be startled*) auffahren; **j. at** (*a chance*) stürzen auf (*acc*); **j. down s.o.'s throat** j-n anfahren

jump' ball' *s* (basketball) Sprungball *m*

jumper ['dʒʌmpər] *s* (*dress*) Jumper *m*; (elec) Kurzschlußbrücke *f*

jump'-off' *s* Beginn *m*; (sport) Start *m*

jump' rope' *s* Springseil *n*

jumpy ['dʒʌmpi] *adj* unruhig, nervös

junction ['dʒʌŋkʃən] *s* Verbindung *f*; (*of roads, rail lines*) Knotenpunkt *m*

juncture ['dʒʌŋktʃər] *s* Verbindungsstelle *f*; **at this j.** in diesem Augenblick

June [dʒun] *s* Juni *m*

June' bug' *s* Maikäfer *m*

jungle ['dʒʌŋgəl] *s* Dschungel *m, n & f*

junior ['dʒunjər] *adj* jünger ‖ *s* Student -in *mf* im dritten Studienjahr

juniper ['dʒunɪpər] *s* Wacholder *m*

junk [dʒʌŋk] *s* Altwaren *pl*; (*scrap iron*) Schrott *m*; (*useless stuff*) Plunder *m*; (naut) Dschunke *f*

junket ['dʒʌŋkɪt] *s* Vergnügungsreise *f* auf öffentliche Kosten

junk' mail' *s* Wurfsendung *f*

junk'yard' *s* Schrottplatz *m*

junta ['hʌntə], ['dʒʌntə] *s* Junta *f*

jurisdiction [‚dʒurɪs'dɪkʃən] *s* Zuständigkeit *f*; **have j. over** zuständig sein für

jurisprudence [‚dʒurɪs'prudəns] *s* Rechtswissenschaft *f*

jurist ['dʒurɪst] *s* Jurist -in *mf*

juror ['dʒurər] *s* Geschworene *mf*

jury ['dʒuri] *s* Geschworene *pl*

ju'ry box' *s* Geschworenenbank *f*

ju'ry tri'al *s* Schwurgerichtsverfahren *n*

just [dʒʌst] *adj* gerecht ‖ *adv* gerade; (*only*) nur; (*simply*) einfach

justice ['dʒʌstɪs] *s* Gerechtigkeit *f*; (*of a claim*) Berechtigung *f*; (*judge*) Richter *m*; **bring to j.** vor Gericht bringen; **do j. to** (*a meal*) wacker zusprechen (*dat*); (*said of a picture*) gerecht werden (*dat*)

jus'tice of the peace' *s* Friedensrichter *m*

justification [‚dʒʌstɪfɪ'keʃən] *s* Rechtfertigung *f*

justi‑fy ['dʒʌstɪ‚faɪ] *v* (*pret & pp* **-fied**) *tr* rechtfertigen

justly ['dʒʌstli] *adv* mit Recht

jut [dʒʌt] *v* (*pret & pp* **jutted; ger jutting**) *intr*—**jut out** hervorragen

juvenile ['dʒuvə‚naɪl] *adj* (*books, court*) Jugend-; (*childish*) unreif

ju'venile delin'quency *s* Jugendkriminalität *f*

ju'venile delin'quent *s* jugendlicher Verbrecher *m*

juxtapose [‚dʒʌkstə'poz] *tr* nebeneinanderstellen

K

K, k [ke] *s* elfter Buchstabe des englischen Alphabets
kale [kel] *s* Grünkohl *m*
kaleidoscopic [kə‚laɪdə'skɑpɪk]   *adj* (& fig) kaleidoskopisch
kangaroo [‚kæŋgə'ru] *s* Känguruh *n*
kangaroo court *s* Scheingericht *n*
kashmir ['kae/mɪr] *s* (tex) Kaschmir *m*
kayo ['ke'o] *s* K.o. *m* ‖ *tr* k.o. schlagen
keel [kil] *s* Kiel *m; on an even k.* (fig) gleichmäßig ‖ *intr*—k. over umkippen; (naut) kentern
keen [kin] *adj (sharp)* scharf; *(interest)* lebhaft; *k.* on scharf auf *(acc)*
keenness ['kinnɪs] *s* Schärfe *f*
keep [kip] *s* Unterhalt *m; (of a castle)* Bergfried *m; for keeps (forever)* für immer; *(seriously)* im Ernst ‖ *v (pret & pp* kept [kɛpt]) *tr (retain)* behalten; *(detain)* aufhalten; *(save for s.o.)* aufbewahren; *(a secret)* bewahren; *(a promise)* (ein)halten; *(animals)* halten; *(books)* (acct) führen; **be kept in school** nachsitzen müssen; *k.* at arm's length vom Leibe halten; *k.* at bay sich erwehren *(genit)*; *k.* away fernhalten; *k.* back zurückhalten; *(retain)* zurückbehalten; *k. (s.o.)* company Gesellschaft leisten *(dat)*; *k.* down *(one's head)* niederhalten; *(one's voice)* verhalten; *(prices)* niedrig halten; *k.* from abhalten von; *k.* from *(ger)* daran hindern zu *(inf)*; *k.* going im Gange halten; *k.* good time gut gehen; *k.* guard Wache halten; *k.* house den Haushalt führen; *k.* in good condition instand halten; *k.* in mind sich *[dat]* merken; *k.* it up! nur so weiter; *k.* on *(a garment)* anbehalten; *(a hat)* aufbehalten; *k.* oneself from *(ger)* es fertigbringen nicht zu *(inf)*; *k.* one's temper sich beherrschen; *k.* out ausschließen; *(light)* nicht durchlassen; *(rain)* abhalten; *k.* posted auf dem laufenden halten; *k.* score die Punktliste führen; *k.* secret geheimhalten; *k.* step Tritt halten; *k. s.th. from s.o.* j-m etw verschweigen; *k.* track of sich *[dat]* merken; *k.* under wraps (coll) totschweigen; *k.* up instand halten; *(appearances)* wahren; *(correspondence)* unterhalten; *k.* up the good work! arbeiten Sie weiter so gut!; *k.* waiting warten lassen; *k.* warm warm halten; *k.* your shirt on! (coll) daß du die Nase im Gesicht behältst! ‖ *intr (said of food)* sich halten; *k.* at beharren bei; *k.* at it! bleib dabei!; *k.* away sich fernhalten; *k.* cool (fig) die Nerven behalten; *k.* cool! ruhig Blut!; *k.* from sich enthalten *(genit)*; *k.* from *(ger)* es unterlassen zu *(inf)*; *k.* from laughing sich das Lachen verkneifen;

k. going weitermachen; *k.* moving weitergehen; *k.* on *(ger)* weiter *(inf)*, e.g., *k.* on driving weiterfahren; *k.* out! Eintritt verboten! *k.* out of sich fernhalten von; *k.* quiet sich ruhig verhalten; *k.* quiet! sei still!; *k.* to the right sich rechts halten; *k.* up with *(work)* nachkommen mit; *k.* up with the Joneses mit den Nachbarn Schritt halten; *k.* within bleiben innerhalb *(genit)*
keeper ['kipər] *s (of animals)* Halter –in *mf; (at a zoo)* Tierwärter –in *mf; (watchman)* Wächter *m*
keep'ing *s* Verwahrung *f;* **in k. with** in Einklang mit
keep'sake' *s* Andenken *n*
keg [kɛg] *s* Faß *n*
ken [kɛn] *s* Gesichtskreis *m*
kennel ['kɛnəl] *s* Hundezwinger *m*
kep·i ['kepi], ['kepi] *s* (–is) Kappi *n*
kerchief ['kʌrt/ɪf] *s (for the head)* Kopftuch *n; (for the neck)* Halstuch *n*
kernel ['kʌrnəl] *s (of fruit)* Kern *m; (of grain)* Korn *n;* (fig) Kern *m*
kerosene [‚kerə'sin] *s* Petroleum *n*
kerplunk [kər'plʌŋk] *interj* bums!
ketchup ['ket/əp] *s* Ketchup *m* & *n*
kettle ['ketəl] *s* Kessel *m*
ket'tledrum' *s* Kesselpauke *f*
key [ki] *adj (ring, hole, industry, position)* Schlüssel– ‖ *s* (& fig) Schlüssel *m; (of a map)* Zeichenerklärung *f; (of a typewriter, piano, organ)* Taste *f; (of a windinstrument)* Klappe *f; (reef)* Riff *n; (low island)* Insel *f;* (mus) Tonart *f;* key of C major C-dur; off key falsch ‖ *tr* (mach) festkeilen
key'board' *s* Tastatur *f*
keyed *adj*—*k.* to gestimmt auf *(acc)*; *k.* up in Hochspannung
key'man' *s* Schlüsselfigur *f*
key'note' *s* Grundgedanke *m;* (mus) Tonika *f*
key'note address' *s* programmatische Rede *f*
keynoter ['kɪ‚notər] *s* Programmatiker –in *mf*
keypuncher ['ki‚pʌntʃər] *s* Locher –in *mf*
key'stone' *s* Schlußstein *m;* (fig) Grundlage *f*
key' word' *s* Stichwort *n*
kha·ki ['kæki] *adj* Khaki– ‖ *s* (–kis) Khaki *m;* **khakis** Khakiuniform *f*
kibitz ['kɪbɪts] *intr* (coll) kiebitzen
kibitzer ['kɪbɪtsər] *s* (coll) Kiebitz *m*
kick [kɪk] *s* Fußtritt *m; (of a rifle)* Rückstoß *m; (of a horse)* Schlag *m; (final spurt)* (sport) Endspurt *m;* give **s.o. a k.** j-m e-n Fußtritt versetzen; **I get a (great) k. out of him** er macht mir (riesigen) Spaß ‖ *tr* treten, stoßen; (fb) kicken; **be kicked upstairs** (coll) die Treppe hinauffallen;

I could k. myself ich könnte mich ohrfeigen; **k. a goal** (fb) ein Tor schießen; **k.** (s.o.) **around** schlecht behandeln; (e.g., an idea) beschwatzen; **k. in** (money) beisteuern; **k. open** (a door) aufstoßen; **k. out** (coll) rausschmeißen; **k. s.o. in the shins** j–n gegen das Schienbein treten; **k. the bucket** (sl) krepieren; **k. up a storm** Krach schlagen || intr (said of a gun) stoßen; (said of a horse) ausschlagen; (complain) (about) meckern (über acc); **k. around Europe** in Europa herumbummeln; **k. off** (fb) anspielen

kick'back' s Schmiergeld n

kick'off' s (commencement) Beginn m; (fb) Anstoß m

kid [kɪd] s Zicklein n; (coll) Kind n || v (pret & pp **kidded**; ger **kidding**) tr necken || intr scherzen; **no kidding!** mach keine Witze!

kid' gloves' spl Glacéhandschuhe pl; **handle with k.** (fig) mit Glacéhandschuhen anfassen

kid'nap' v (pret & pp -nap(p)ed; ger -nap(p)ing) tr kidnappen, entführen

kidnap(p)er ['kɪd,næpər] s Kidnapper m

kid'nap(p)ing s Kidnapping s

kidney ['kɪdni] s Niere f

kid'ney bean' s rote Bohne f

kid'ney-shaped' adj nierenförmig

kid'ney stone' s Nierenstein m

kid'ney trans'plant s Nierenverpflanzung f; (transplanted kidney) verpflanzte Niere f

kid'ney trou'ble s Nierenleiden n

kid' stuff' s (coll) Kinderei f

kill [kɪl] s (aer) Abschuß m; (hunt) Jagdbeute f; (nav) Versenkung f || tr töten; (murder) ermorden, killen; (plants) zum Absterben bringen; (time) totschlagen; (a proposal, plans, competition) zu Fall bringen; (the motor) abwürgen; (the ball) stark schlagen; (a bottle) austrinken; **be killed in action** (im Felde) fallen; **it won't k. you** (coll) es wird dich nicht umbringen; **k. off** abschlachten; **k. oneself** sich umbringen; **k. two birds with one stone** zwei Fliegen mit e–r Klappe schlagen; **she is dressed to k.** sie ist totschick angezogen

killer ['kɪlər] s Totschläger –in mf, Killer m

kill'er whale' s Schwertwal m

kill'ing s Tötung f; **make a k.** e–n unerhofften Gewinn erzielen

kill'joy' s Spaßverderber m

kiln ['kɪl(n)] s Brennofen m

kilo ['kɪlo], ['kilo] s (-os) Kilo n

kilocycle ['kɪlə,saɪkəl] s Kilohertz n

kilogram ['kɪlə,græm] s Kilogramm n

kilohertz ['kɪlə,hʌrts] s Kilohertz n

kilometer [kɪ'lamɪtər] s Kilometer m; **kilometers per hour** Stundenkilometer pl

kilowatt ['kɪlə,wat] s Kilowatt n

kil'owatt'-hour' s Kilowattstunde f

kilt [kɪlt] s Kilt m

kilter ['kɪltər] s—**out of k.** nicht in Ordnung

kimono [kɪ'mono] s (-nos) Kimono m

kin [kɪn] s Sippe f; **the next of kin** die nächsten Angehörigen

kind [kaɪnd] adj liebenswürdig; (to) gütig (zu), freundlich (zu); **would you be so k. as to** (inf)? würden Sie so gefällig sein zu (inf)?; **with k. regards** mit freundlichen Grüßen || s Art f, Sorte f; **all kinds of** allerlei; **another k. of** ein anderer; **any k. of** irgendwelcher; **every k. of** jede Art von; **in. k.** (fig) auf gleiche Weise; **k. of** (coll) etwas; **nothing of the k.** nichts dergleichen; **that k. of** derartig; **two (three) kinds of** zweierlei (dreierlei); **what k. of** was für ein

kindergarten ['kɪndər,gartən] s Vorschule f, Vorschuljahr n

kind'-heart'ed adj gutmütig

kindle ['kɪndəl] tr anzünden; (fig) erwecken || intr sich entzünden

kindling ['kɪndlɪŋ] s Entzündung f; (wood) Kleinholz n

kindly ['kaɪndli] adj gütig, freundlich || adv freundlich; (please) bitte

kindness ['kaɪndnɪs] s Freundlichkeit f; (deed) Gefälligkeit f

kindred ['kɪndrɪd] adj verwandtschaftlich; (fig) verwandt || s Verwandtschaft f

kinescope ['kɪnɪ,skop] s (trademark) Fernsehempfangsröhre f

kinetic [kɪ'nɛtɪk] adj kinetisch || **kinetics** s Kinetik f

king [kɪŋ] s König m; (cards, chess) König m; (checkers) Dame f

kingdom ['kɪŋdəm] s Königreich n; (of animals, etc.) Reich n; **k. of heaven** Himmelreich n

king'fish'er s Königsfischer m

kingly ['kɪŋli] adj königlich

king'pin' s (coll) Boß m; (bowling) König m

king'ship' s Königtum n

king'-size' adj übergroß

kink [kɪŋk] s (in a wire) Knick m; (in the hair) Kräuselung f; (in a muscle) Muskelkrampf m; (flaw) Fehler m

kinky ['kɪŋki] adj gekräuselt

kin'ship' s Verwandtschaft f

kins'man s (-men) Blutsverwandte m

kins'wom'an s (-wom'en) Blutsverwandte f

kipper ['kɪpər] s Räucherhering m || tr einsalzen und räuchern

kiss [kɪs] s Kuß m || tr & intr küssen

kisser ['kɪsər] s (sl) Fresse f

kit [kɪt] s (equipment) Ausrüstung f; (tool kit) Werkzeugkasten m; (for models) Modellsatz m; (e.g., for a convention) Mappe f; **the whole kit and caboodle** (things) der ganze Kram; (persons) die ganze Sippschaft

kitchen ['kɪtʃən] s Küche f

kitchenette [,kɪtʃə'nɛt] s Kochnische f

kit'chen knife' s Küchenmesser n

kit'chen police' s (mil) Küchendienst m

kit'chen range' s Herd m, Kochherd m

kit′chen sink′ s Ausguß m

kit′chenware′ s Küchengeschirr n

kite [kaɪt] s Drachen m; (orn) Weih m; **fly a k.** e-n Drachen steigen lassen; **go fly a k.!** (coll) scher dich zum Kuckuck!

kith′ and kin′ [kɪθ] spl Freunde and Verwandte pl

kitten [′kɪtən] s Kätzchen n

kitty [′kɪti] s Kätzchen n; (cards) gemeinsame Kasse f; **Kitty** Käthchen n

kleptomaniac [,kleptə′meɪɪ ,æk] s Kleptomane m, Kleptomanin f

knack [næk] s—**have a k. for** Talent haben für; **have the k. of it** den Griff heraus haben

knapsack [′næp ,sæk] s Rucksack m

knave [nev] s Schelm m; (cards) Bube m

knavery [′nevəri] s Schelmenstreich m

knead [nid] tr kneten

knead′ing trough′ s Teigmulde f

knee [ni] s Knie n; **bring s.o. to his knees** j-n auf die Knie zwingen; **go down on one′s knees** niederknien; **on bended knees** kniefällig

knee′ bend′ s Kniebeuge f

knee′ breech′es spl Kniehose f

knee′cap′ s Kniescheibe f

knee′-deep′ adj knietief

knee′-high′ adj kniehoch

knee′ jerk′ s Patellarreflex m

kneel [nil] v (pret & pp knelt [nɛlt] & kneeled) intr knien

knee′-length′ adj kniefrei

knee′pad′ s (sport) Knieschützer m

knee′pan′ s Kniescheibe f

knee′ swell′ s (of organ) Knieschweller m

knell [nɛl] s Totengeläute n

knickers [′nɪkərz] spl Knickerbockerhosen pl

knickknack [′nɪk ,næk] s Nippsache f

knife [naɪf] s (knives [naɪvz]) Messer n || tr erstechen

knife′ sharp′ener s Messerschleifer m

knife′ switch′ s (elec) Messerschalter m

knight [naɪt] s Ritter m; (chess) Springer m || tr zum Ritter schlagen

knight′hood′ s Ritterschaft f

knightly [′naɪtli] adj ritterlich

knit [nɪt] v (pret & pp knitted & knit; ger knitting) tr stricken; **k. one′s brows** die Brauen runzeln || intr stricken; (said of bones) zusammenheilen

knit′ goods′ spl Trikotwaren pl

knit′ted dress′ s Strickkleid n

knit′ting s (act) Strickerei f; (materials) Strickzeug n

knit′ting machine′ s Strickmaschine f

knit′ting nee′dle s Stricknadel f

knit′ting yarn′ s Strickgarn n

knit′wear′ s Strickwaren pl

knob [nɑb] s (of a door) Drücker m; (lump) Auswuchs m; (in wood) Knorren m; (of a radio) Knopf m

knock [nɑk] s (& aut) Klopfen m; tr (criticize) tadeln; **k. a hole through** durchbrechen; **k. around** herumstoßen; (mistreat) unsanft behandeln;

k. down niederschlagen; (with a car) umfahren; (trees) umbrechen; (at auctions) zuschlagen; **k. it off!** (sl) hör mal auf!; **k. oneself out over** sich [dat] die Zähne ausbeißen an (dat); **k. one′s head against the wall** mit dem Kopf gegen die Wand rennen; **k. out** ausschlagen; (a tank) abschießen; (box) k.o. schlagen; **k. over** umwerfen; **k. together** (build hurriedly) schnell zusammenhauen; **k. to the ground** zu Boden schlagen; **k. up a girl** (sl) e-m Mädchen ein Kind anhängen || intr (an)klopfen; (aut) klopfen; **k. about** herumbummeln; **k. against** stoßen an (acc); **k. off** (from) (coll) aufhören (mit)

knock′down′ s (box) Niederschlag m

knocker [′nɑkər] s Türklopfer m; **knockers** (sl) Brüste pl

knock-kneed [′nɑk ,nid] adj x-beinig

knock′-knees′ spl X-Beine pl

knock′out′ s (woman) (coll) Blitzmädel n; (box) Knockout m

knock′out drops′ spl Betäubungsmittel n

knock′-out punch′ s K.O.-Schlag m

knoll [nol] s Hügel m

knot [nɑt] s Knoten m; (in wood) Knorren m; (of people) Gruppe f; (naut) Knoten m; **tie a k.** e-n Knoten machen; **tie the k.** (coll) sich verheiraten || tr e-n Knoten machen in (acc); (two ends) zusammenknoten

knot′hole′ s Astloch n

knotty [′nɑti] adj knorrig; (problem) knifflig

know [no] s—**be in the k.** Bescheid wissen || v (pret **knew** [n(j)u); pp **known**) tr (facts) wissen; (be familiar with) kennen; (a language) können; **come to k.** erfahren; **get to k.** kennenlernen; **known** bekannt; **k. one′s way around** sich auskennen; **k. the ropes** (coll) Bescheid wissen; **k. what′s what** (coll) den Rummel kennen || intr wissen; **he ought to k. better** er sollte mehr Verstand haben; **k. about** wissen über (acc); **k. of** wissen von; **not that I k. of** (coll) nicht, daß ich wüßte; **you k.** (coll) wissen Sie

knowable [′no·əbəl] adj kenntlich

know′-how′ s Sachkenntnis f

know′ing adj (glance) vielsagend

knowingly [′no·ɪŋli] adv wissentlich; (intentionally) absichtlich

know′-it-all′ s Naseweis m

knowledge [′nɑlɪdʒ] s Wissen n, Kenntnisse pl; (information) (of) Kenntnis f (von); **basic k. of** Grundkenntnisse pl in (dat); **come to s.o.′s k.** j-m zur Kenntnis kommen; **to my k.** soweit (or soviel) ich weiß; **to the best of my k.** nach bestem Wissen; **without my k.** ohne mein Mitwissen; **working k. of** praktisch verwertbare Kenntnisse pl (genit)

knowledgeable [′nɑlɪdʒəbəl] adj kenntnisreich

known [non] adj bekannt; **become k.**

kundwerden; **k. all over town** stadtbekannt; **make k.** bekanntgeben

know′-noth′ing s Nichtswisser m

knuckle [′nʌkəl] s Knöchel m, Fingerknöchel m; (mach) Gelenkstück n; **k. of ham** Eisbein n ‖ intr—**k. down to work** sich ernsthaft an die Arbeit machen; **k. under** klein beigeben

k.o. [′ke′o] s K.o. m ‖ tr k.o.-schlagen

Koran [ko′ræn] s Koran m

Korea [ko′ri·ə] s Korea n

Korean [ko′ri·ən] adj koreanisch ‖ s Koreaner –in m/; (language) Koreanisch n

kosher [′koʃər] adj (& coll) koscher

kowtow [′kau′tau] intr e–n Kotau machen; **k. to** kriechen vor (dat)

K.P. [′ke′pi] s (kitchen police) (mil) Küchendienst m

Kremlin [′krɛmlɪn] s Kreml m

kudos [′k(i)udas] s (coll) Ruhm m, Renommee n

L

L, l [el] s zwölfter Buchstabe des englischen Alphabets

lab [læb] s (coll) Labor n

la·bel [′lebəl] s Etikett n; (brand) Marke /; (fig) Bezeichnung / ‖ v (pret & pp —bel[l]ed; ger —bel[l]ing) tr etikettieren; (fig) bezeichnen

labial [′lebɪ·əl] adj Lippen– ‖ s Lippenlaut m, Labial m

labor [′lebər] adj Arbeits–, Arbeiter– ‖ s Arbeit /; (toil) Mühe /; **be in l.** in den Wehen liegen ‖ tr (a point) ausführlich eingehen auf (acc) ‖ intr sich abmühen; (at) arbeiten (an dat); (exert oneself) sich anstrengen; (aut of a ship) stampfen; **l. under** zu leiden haben unter (dat)

la′bor and man′agement spl Arbeitnehmer und Arbeitgeber pl

laboratory [′læbərə,tori] s Laboratorium n

lab′oratory techni′cian s Laborant –in m/

la′bor camp′ s Zwangsarbeitslager n

la′bor con′tract s Tarifvertrag m

la′bor dis′pute s Arbeitsstreitigkeit /

la′bored adj (e.g., breathing) mühsam; (style) gezwungen

laborer [′lebərər] s Arbeiter –in m/; (unskilled) Hilfsarbeiter –in m/

la′bor force′ s Arbeitskräfte pl

laborious [lə′borɪ·əs] adj mühsam, schwierig

la′bor law′ s Arbeitsrecht n

la′bor lead′er s Arbeiterführer –in m/

la′bor mar′ket s Arbeitsmarkt m

la′bor move′ment s Arbeiterbewegung /

la′bor pains′ spl Geburtswehen pl

la′bor-sav′ing adj arbeitssparend; **l. device** Hilfsgerät n

la′bor short′age s Mangel m an Arbeitskräften

la′bor supply′ s Arbeitsangebot n

la′bor un′ion s Gewerkschaft /

laburnum [lə′bʌrnəm] s Goldregen m

labyrinth [′læbɪrɪnθ] s Labyrinth n

lace [les] adj (collar, dress) Spitzen– ‖ s Spitze /; (shoestring) Schnürsenkel m ‖ tr (e.g., shoes) schnüren; (braid) flechten; (drinks) (coll) mit e–m Schuß Branntwein versetzen; (beat) (coll) prügeln; **l. up** zuschnüren

lacerate [′læsə,ret] tr zerfleischen

laceration [,læsə′reʃən] s Fleischwunde /

lace′ trim′ming s Spitzenbesatz m

lace′work′ s Spitzenarbeit /

lachrymose [′lækrɪ,mos] adj tränenreich

lac′ing s Schnürung /; (coll) Prügel pl

lack [læk] s (of) Mangel m (an dat); **for l. of** aus Mangel an (dat); **l. of space** Raummangel m; **l. of time** Zeitmangel m ‖ tr—**I l.** es mangelt mir an (dat) ‖ intr—**be lacking** fehlen; **he is lacking in courage** ihm fehlt der Mut

lackadaisical [,lækə′dezɪkəl] adj teilnahmslos, gleichgültig

lackey [′lækɪ] s Lakai m

lack′ing prep mangels (genit)

lack′lus′ter adj glanzlos

laconic [lə′kɑnɪk] adj lakonisch

lacquer [′lækər] s Lack m ‖ tr lackieren

lac′quer ware′ s Lackwaren pl

lacrosse [lə′krɔs] s Lacrosse n

lacu·na [lə′kjunə] s (–nas & –nae [ni]) Lücke /, Lakune /

lacy [′lesi] adj spitzenartig

lad [læd] s Bube m

la′dies′ man′ s Weiberheld m, Salonlöwe m

la′dies′ room′ s Damentoilette /

ladle [′ledəl] s Schöpflöffel m ‖ tr ausschöpfen

lady [′ledi] s Dame /; **ladies and gentlemen** meine Damen und Herren!

la′dybird′, la′dybug′ s Marienkäfer m

la′dy compan′ion s Gesellschaftsdame /

la′dyfin′ger s Löffelbiskuit m & n

la′dy-in-wait′ing s (ladies-in-waiting) Hofdame /

la′dy-kil′ler s Schwerenöter m

la′dylike′ adj damenhaft

la′dylove′ s Geliebte /

la′dy of the house′ s Hausherrin /

la′dy's maid′ s Zofe /

la′dy's man′ s var of ladies' man

lag [læg] s Zurückbleiben n; (aer) Rücktrift /; (phys) Verzögerung / ‖ v (pret & pp lagged; ger lagging) intr zurückbleiben; **l.** zurückbleiben (hinter dat)

la′ger beer′ [′lɑgər] s Lagerbier n

laggard [′lægərd] s Nachzügler m

lagoon [lə'gun] *s* Lagune *f*

laid′ up′ *adj* (with) bettlägerig (infolge von); **be l. in bed** auf der Nase liegen

lair [ler] *s* Höhle *f*, Lager *n*

laity [′leɪti] *s* Laien *pl*

lake [lek] *s* See *m*

Lake′ Con′stance [′kɑnstəns] *s* der Bodensee

lamb [læm] *s* Lamm *n*; (culin) Lammfleisch *n*

lambaste [læm′best] *tr* (berate) (coll) herunterputzen; (beat) (coll) verdreschen

lamb′ chop′ *s* Hammelrippchen *n*

lambkin [′læmkɪn] *s* Lammfell *n*

lame [lem] *adj* (person, leg; excuse) lahm; **be l. in one leg** auf e-m Bein lahm sein ‖ *tr* lähmen

lament [lə′ment] *s* Jammer *m*; (dirge) Klagelied *n* ‖ *tr* beklagen ‖ *intr* wehklagen

lamentable [′læməntəbəl] *adj* beklagenswert; (pej) jämmerlich

lamentation [‚læmə′te/ən] *s* Wehklage *f*

laminate [′læmɪ‚net] *tr* schichten

lamp [læmp] *s* Lampe *f*

lamp′ chim′ney *s* Lampenzylinder *m*

lamp′light′ *s* Lampenlicht *n*

lamp′light′er *s* Laternenanzünder *m*

lampoon [læm′pun] *s* Schmähschrift *f* ‖ *tr* mit e-r Schmähschrift verspotten

lamp′post′ *s* Laternenpfahl *m*

lamp′shade′ *s* Lampenschirm *m*

lance [læns] *s* Lanze *f*; (surg) Lanzette *f* ‖ *tr* (surg) aufstechen

lance′ cor′poral *s* (Brit) Hauptgefreite *m*

lancet [′lænsɪt] *s* Lanzette *f*

land [lænd] *s* (dry land; country) Land *n*; (ground) Boden *m*; **by l. zu Lande** ‖ *tr* (a plane, troops, punch) landen; (a ship, fish) an Land bringen; (a job) (coll) kriegen; **l. s.o. in trouble** j–n in Schwierigkeiten bringen ‖ *intr* (aer, naut, & fig) landen; (said of a blow) treffen; **l. on s.o.'s head** j–m auf den Kopf fallen; **l. on water** auf dem Wasser aufsetzen

land′ breeze′ *s* Landwind *m*

land′ed prop′erty *s* Landbesitz *m*

land′fall′ *s* (sighting of land) Sichten *n* von Land; **make l.** landen

land′ forc′es *spl* Landstreitkräfte *pl*

land′ing *s* Landung *f*; (of a staircase) Absatz *m*; **l. on the moon** Mondlandung *f*

land′ing craft′ *s* Landungsboot *n*

land′ing field′ *s* Landeplatz *m*

land′ing force′ *s* Landekorps *n*

land′ing gear′ *s* Fahrgestell *n*

land′ing par′ty *s* Landeabteilung *f*

land′ing stage′ *s* Landungssteg *m*

land′ing strip′ *s* Start- und Landestreifen *m*

land′la′dy *s* (of an apartment) Hauswirtin *f*; (of an inn) Gastwirtin *f*

land′locked′ *adj* landumschlossen

land′lord′ *s* (of an apartment) Hauswirt *m*; (of an inn) Gastwirt *m*

landlubber [′lænd‚lʌbər] *s* Landratte *f*

land′mark′ *s* Landmarke *f*; (cardinal event) Markstein *m*

land′ of′fice *s* Grundbuchamt *n*

land′-office bus′iness *s* (fig) Bombengeschäft *n*

land′own′er *s* Grundbesitzer –in *mf*

landscape [′lænd‚skep] *s* Landschaft *f*; (paint) Landschaftsbild *n* ‖ *tr* landschaftlich gestalten

land′scape ar′chitect *s* Landschaftsarchitekt –in *mf*

land′scape paint′er *s* Landschaftsmaler –in *mf*

land′slide′ *s* Bergrutsch *m*; (pol) Stimmenrutsch *m*

landward [′lændwərd] *adv* landwärts

land′ wind′ [wɪnd] *s* Landwind *m*

lane [len] *s* Bahn *f*; (country road) Feldweg *m*; (aer) Flugschneise *f*; (aut) Fahrbahn *f*; (naut) Fahrtroute *f*; (sport) Laufbahn *f*; (sport) Schwimmbahn *f*

language [′læŋgwɪdʒ] *s* Sprache *f*

lan′guage instruc′tion *s* Sprachunterricht *m*

lan′guage teach′er *s* Sprachlehrer –in *mf*

languid [′læŋgwɪd] *adj* schlaff

languish [′læŋgwɪ/] *intr* schmachten

languor [′læŋgər] *s* Mattigkeit *f*

languorous [′læŋgərəs] *adj* matt

lank [læŋk] *adj* schlank; (hair) glatt

lanky [′læŋki] *adj* schlaksig

lanolin [′lænəlɪn] *s* Lanolin *n*

lantern [′læntərn] *s* Laterne *f*

lan′tern slide′ *s* Diapositiv *n*

lanyard [′lænjərd] *s* (around the neck) Halsschnur *f*; (naut) Taljereep *n*

Laos [′le·ɑs] *s* Laos *n*

Laotian [le′o/ən] *adj* laotisch ‖ *s* Laote *m*, Laotin *f*; (language) Laotisch *n*

lap [læp] *s* (of the body or clothing) Schoß *m*; (of the waves) Plätschern *n*; (sport) Runde *f* ‖ *v* (pret & pp lapped; ger lapping) *tr* schlappen; (sport) überrunden; **lap up** auf(sch)lecken ‖ *intr*—**lap against** (e.g., a boat, shore) plätschern gegen; **lap over** hinausragen über (acc)

lap′ dog′ *s* Schoßhund *m*

lapel [lə′pel] *s* Aufschlag *m*

Lap′land′ *s* Lappland *n*

Laplander [′læp‚lændər] *s* Lappländer –in *mf*

Lapp [læp] *s* Lappe *m*, Lappin *f*; (language) Lappisch *n*

lapse [læps] *s* (error) Versehen *n*; (of time) Ablauf *m*; **after a l. of** nach Ablauf von; **l. of duty** Pflichtversäumnis *f*; **l. of memory** Gedächtnislücke *f* ‖ *intr* (said of a right, an insurance policy) verfallen; (said of time) ablaufen; **l. into** verfallen in (acc); **l. into unconsciousness** das Bewußtsein verlieren

lap′wing′ *s* Kiebitz *m*

larceny [′lɑrsəni] *s* Diebstahl *m*

larch [lɑrt/] *s* (bot) Lärche *f*

lard [lɑrd] *s* Schmalz *n* ‖ *tr* spicken

larder [′lɑrdər] *s* Speisekammer *f*

large [lɑrdʒ] *adj* groß; **at l.** (as a whole) gesamt; (at liberty) auf freiem

Fuß; (said of an official) zur beson-
deren Verfügung; **become larger** sich
vergrößern; **on a l. scale** in großem
Umfang

large' intes'tine s Dickdarm m

largely ['lɑrdʒli] adv größtenteils

largeness ['lɑrdʒnɪs] s Größe f

large'-scale' adj Groß–; (map) in großem Maßstab; (production) Serien–

largesse ['lɑrdʒes] s (generosity) Freigebigkeit f; (handout) Geldverteilung
f

lariat ['lærɪ·ət] s Lasso m & n; (for
grazing animals) Halteseil n

lark [lɑrk] s (orn) Lerche f; **for a l.**
zum Spaß

lark'spur' s (bot) Rittersporn m

lar·va ['lɑrvə] s (–vae [vi]) Larve f

laryngitis [,lærɪn'dʒaɪtɪs] s Kehlkopf-
entzündung f, Laryngitis f

larynx ['lærɪŋks] s (larynxes & laryn-
ges [lə'rɪndʒiz]) Kehlkopf m

lascivious [lə'sɪvɪ·əs] adj wollüstig

lasciviousness [lə'sɪvɪ·əsnɪs] s Wol-
lüstigkeit f

laser ['lezər] s Laser m

lash [læʃ] s Peitsche f; (as a punishment) Peitschenhieb m; (of the eye)
Wimper f || tr (whip) peitschen;
(bind) (to) anbinden (an acc); (said
of rain, storms) peitschen || intr—
l. out (at) ausschlagen (nach)

lass [læs] s Mädel m

lassitude ['læsɪ,t(j)ud] s Mattigkeit f

last [læst] adj letzte; **very l.** allerletzte
|| adv zuletzt; **l. of all** zuallerletzt ||
s Letzte mfn; (of a cobbler) Schuh-
leisten m; **at l.** schließlich; **at long l.**
zu guter Letzt; **look one's l. on** zum
letzten Mal blicken auf (acc); **see the
l. of s.o.** j–n nicht mehr wiedersehen;
to the l. bis zum Letzten || intr (re-
main unchanged) anhalten; (for a
specific time) dauern; (said of money,
supplies) reichen; (said of a person)
aushalten

last'ing adj dauerhaft, andauernd; **l.
effect** Dauerwirkung f; **l. for months**
monatelang

Last' Judg'ment s Jüngstes Gericht n

lastly ['læstli] adv zuletzt

last'-min'ute adj in letzter Minute

last'-minute news' s neueste Nachrichten pl

last' night' adv gestern abend

last' quar'ter s (astr) abnehmendes
Mondviertel n; (com) letztes Quartal
n

last' resort' s letztes Mittel n

last' sleep' s Todesschlaf m

last' straw' s—**that's the l.** das schlägt
dem Faß den Boden aus

Last' Sup'per, the s das Letzte Abendmahl

last' week' adv vorige Woche

last' will' and test'ament s letztwillige
Verfügung f

last' word' s letztes Wort n; **the l.**
(fig) der letzte Schrei

latch [lætʃ] s Klinke f || tr zuklinken
|| intr einschnappen; **l. on to** (coll)
spitzkriegen

latch'key' s Hausschlüssel m

late [let] adj (after the usual time)
spät; (at a late hour) zu später Stunde; (deceased) verstorben; **be l.** sich
verspäten; (said of a train) Verspätung haben; **keep l. hours** spät
aufbleiben || adv spät; **come l.** zu
spät kommen; **of l.** kürzlich; **see you
later** (coll) bis später!

latecomer ['let ,kʌmər] s Nachzügler m

lateen' sail' [læ'tin] s Lateinsegel n

lateen' yard' s Lateinrah f

lately ['letli] adv neulich, unlängst

lateness ['letnɪs] s Verspätung f

latent ['letənt] adj latent, verborgen

later ['letər] adj später || adv später,
nachher; **l. on** späterhin

lateral ['lætərəl] adj seitlich, Seiten–

lath [læθ] s Latte f || tr belatten

lathe [leð] s Drehbank f; **turn on a l.**
drechseln

lather ['læðər] s Seifenschaum m; (of
a horse) schäumender Schweiß m ||
tr einseifen || intr schäumen

lathing ['læθɪŋ] s Lattenwerk n

Latin ['lætɪn] adj lateinisch || s
(Romance-speaking person) Romane
m, Romanin f; (language) Lateinisch
n

La'tin Amer'ica s Lateinamerika n

La'tin-Amer'ican adj lateinamerika-
nisch || s Lateinamerikaner –in mf

latitude ['lætɪ,t(j)ud] s Breite f; (fig)
Spielraum m

latrine [lə'trin] s Latrine f

latter ['lætər] adj (later) später; (final)
End–; (recent) letzte; **in the l. part
of** (e.g., the year) in der zweiten
Hälfte (genit); **the l.** dieser

lat'ter-day' adj (later) später; (recent)
letzte

Lat'ter-day Saint' s Heilige mf der
Jüngsten Tage

lattice ['lætɪs] s Gitter n || tr vergittern

lat'ticework' s Gitterwerk n

Latvia ['lætvɪ·ə] s Lettland n

Latvian ['lætvɪ·ən] adj lettisch || s
Lette m, Lettin f; (language) Lettisch
n

laud [lɔd] tr loben, preisen

laudable ['lɔdəbəl] adj löblich

laudanum ['lɔd(ə)nəm] s Opiumtink-
tur f

laudatory ['lɔdə,tɔri] adj Lob–

laugh [læf] s Lachen n, Gelächter n;
for laughs zum Spaß || tr—**l. off** sich
lachend hinwegsetzen über (acc) || intr
lachen; **it's easy for you to l.** Sie
haben leicht lachen!; **l. about** lachen
über (acc); **l. at** (deride) auslachen;
(find amusement in) lachen über
(acc)

laughable ['læfəbəl] adj lächerlich

laugh'ing adj lachend; **it's no l. matter**
es ist nichts zum Lachen

laugh'ing gas' s Lachgas n

laugh'ingstock' s Gespött n

laughter ['læftər] s Gelächter n, Lachen n; **roar with l.** vor Lachen
brüllen

launch [lɔntʃ] s (open boat) Barkasse

ƒ ‖ *tr* (*a boat*) aussetzen; (*a ship*) vom Stapel laufen lassen; (*a plane*) katapultieren; (*a rocket*) starten; (*a torpedo*) abschießen; (*an offensive*) beginnen; **be launched** (naut) vom Stapel laufen; (rok) starten ‖ *intr*— **l. into** sich stürzen in (*acc*)

launch'ing *s* (*of a ship*) Stapellauf *m*; (*of a torpedo*) Ausstoß *m*; (*of a rocket*) Abschuß *m*, Start *m*

launch' pad' *s* (rok) Startrampe ƒ

launder ['lɔndər] *tr* waschen

laundress ['lɔndrɪs] *s* Wäscherin ƒ

laundry ['lɔndri] *s* (*clothes*) Wäsche ƒ; (*room*) Waschküche ƒ; (*business*) Wäscherei ƒ

laun'drybag' *s* Wäschebeutel *m*

laun'drybas'ket *s* Wäschekorb *m*

laun'dry list' *s* Wäschezettel *m*

laun'dry-man' *s* (*-men'*) Wäscher *m*

laun'dry-wom'an *s* (*-wom'en*) Wäscherin ƒ

laurel ['lɔrəl] *s* Lorbeer *m*

lau'rel tree' *s* Lorbeerbaum *m*

lava ['lɑvə] *s* Lava ƒ

lavatory ['lævə͵tori] *s* Waschraum *m*; (*toilet*) Toilette ƒ

lavender ['lævəndər] *adj* lavendelfarben ‖ *s* (bot) Lavendel *m*

lavish ['lævɪʃ] *adj* (*person*) verschwenderisch; (*dinner*) üppig ‖ *tr*—**l. care on** hegen und pflegen; **l. s.th. on s.o.** j-n mit etw überhäufen

lavishness ['lævɪʃnɪs] *s* Üppigkeit ƒ

law [lɔ] *s* Gesetz *n*; (*system*) Recht *n*; (*as a science*) Rechtswissenschaft ƒ; (relig) Gebot *n*; **according to law** dem Recht entsprechend; **act within the law** sich ans Gesetz halten; **against the law** gesetzwidrig; **become law** Gesetzkraft erlangen; **by law** gesetzlich; **go against the law** gegen das Gesetz handeln; **lay down the law** gebieterisch auftreten; **practice law** den Anwaltsberuf ausüben; **study law** Jura studieren; **take the law into one's own hands** sich [*dat*] selbst sein Recht verschaffen; **under the law** nach dem Gesetz

law'-abid'ing *adj* friedlich

law' and or'der *s* Ruhe und Ordnung *pl*

law'-and-or'der *adj* für Ruhe und Ordnung

law'break'er *s* Rechtsbrecher –in *mf*

law'break'ing *s* Rechtsbruch *m*

law'court' *s* Gerichtshof *m*, Gericht *n*

lawful ['lɔfəl] *adj* gesetzmäßig

lawless ['lɔlɪs] *adj* gesetzlos

lawlessness ['lɔlɪsnɪs] *s* Gesetzlosigkeit ƒ

law'mak'er *s* Gesetzgeber *m*

lawn [lɔn] *s* Rasen *m*; (tex) Batist *m*

lawn' mow'er *s* Rasenmäher *m*

lawn' par'ty *s* Gartenfest *n*

lawn' sprin'kler *s* Rasensprenger *m*

law' of dimin'ishing returns' *s* Gesetz *n* der abnehmenden Erträge

law' of'fice *s* Anwaltsbüro *n*

law' of na'tions *s* Völkerrecht *n*

law' of na'ture *s* Naturgesetz *n*

law' of probabil'ity *s* Wahrscheinlichkeitsgesetz *n*

law' of supply' and demand' *s* Gesetz *n* von Angebot und Nachfrage

law' of the land' *s* Landesgesetz *n*

law' school' *s* juristische Fakultät ƒ

law' stu'dent *s* Student –in *mf* der Rechtswissenschaft

law'suit' *s* Klage ƒ, Prozeß *m*

lawyer ['lɔjər] *s* Advokat –in *m*, Anwalt –in *mf*

lax [læks] *adj* lax, nachlässig

laxative ['læksətɪv] *s* Abführmittel *n*

laxity ['læksɪti] *s* Laxheit ƒ

lay [le] *adj* (*not of the clergy*) Laien-, weltlich; (*non-expert*) laienhaft ‖ *s* (*poem*) Lied *n* ‖ *v* (*pret & pp* laid [led]) *tr* legen; (*eggs; foundation, bricks, lineoleum*) legen; (*cables, pipes, tracks*) verlegen; (*vulg*) umlegen; **be laid up with** das Bett hüten müssen wegen (*genit*); **I'll lay you two to one** ich wette mit dir zwei zu eins; **lay aside** beiseite legen; (*save*) sparen; **lay bare** bloßlegen; **lay down** niederlegen; (*principles*) aufstellen; **lay claim to** Anspruch erheben auf (*acc*); **lay it on thick** dick auftragen; **lay low** (*said of an illness*) bettlägerig machen; **lay off** (*workers*) vorübergehend entlassen; **lay open** freilegen; **lay out** auslegen; (*a garden*) anlegen; (*money*) aufwenden; (*a corpse*) aufbahren; (surv) abstecken; **lay siege to** belagern; **lay waste** verwüsten ‖ *intr* (*said of hens*) legen; **lay for** auflauern (*dat*); **lay into** (*beat*) (coll) verdreschen; (*scold*) (coll) heruntermachen; **lay off** (*abstain from*) sich enthalten (*genit*); (*let alone*) in Ruhe lassen; **lay over** (*on a trip*) sich aufhalten; **lay to** (naut) stilliegen

lay' broth'er *s* Laienbruder *m*

layer ['le·ər] *s* Schicht ƒ; (bot) Ableger *m*; **in layers** schichtenweise; **l. of fat** Fettschicht ƒ; **thin l.** Hauch *m*

lay'er cake' *s* Schichttorte ƒ

layette [le'et] *s* Babyausstattung ƒ

lay' fig'ure *s* Gliederpuppe ƒ

lay'man *s* (*-men*) Laie *m*; **layman's** laienhaft

lay'off' *s* vorübergehende Entlassung ƒ

lay' of the land' *s* Gestaltung ƒ des Terrains; (fig) Gesichtspunkt *m* der Angelegenheit

lay'out' *s* Anlage ƒ, Anordnung ƒ; (typ) Layout *n*; **l. of rooms** Raumverteilung ƒ

laziness ['lezɪnɪs] *s* Faulheit ƒ

lazy ['lezi] *adj* faul

la'zybones' *s* (coll) Faulpelz *m*

la'zy Su'san *s* drehbares Tablett *n*

lea [li] *s* (poet) Aue ƒ

lead [led] *adj* Blei- ‖ *s* Blei *n*; (*in a pencil*) Mine ƒ; (*plumb line*) Bleilot *n* ‖ *v* (*pret & pp* leaded; *ger* leading) *tr* verbleien; (typ) durchschießen ‖ [lid] *s* Führung ƒ; (cards) Vorhand ƒ; (elec) Zuführung ƒ; (sport) Vorsprung *m*; (theat) Hauptrolle ƒ; **be in the l.** an der Spitze stehen; **have the l.** die Führung haben; **take the l.** die Führung übernehmen ‖ *v* (*pret & pp* led [lɛd]) *tr* führen, leiten; (*to error, drinking, etc.*) verleiten; (*a parade*) anführen; (*a life*) führen; **l. astray** verführen; **l. away** wegführen; (*e.g., a criminal*) abführen; **l. back** zurückführen; **l. by the nose** an der Nase herumführen; **l. on** weiterführen; (*deceive*) täuschen; **l. the way** vorangehen || *intr* führen; (*cards*) anspielen; **l. nowhere** zu nichts führen; **l. off** den Anfang machen; **l. to** hinausgehen auf (*acc*); **l. up to** hinauswollen auf (*acc*) **where will all this l. to?** wo soll das alles hinführen?

leaden ['lɛdən] *adj* bleiern; (*in color*) bleifarbig; (*sluggish*) schwerfällig; **l. sky** bleierner Himmel *m*

leader ['lidər] *s* Führer –in *mf*; (*of a band*) Dirigent –in *mf*; (*of a film*) Vorspann *m*; (*lead article*) Leitartikel *m*

lead'ership' *s* Führung *f*

leading ['lidɪŋ] *adj* (*person, position, power*) führend

lead'ing ide'a *s* Leitgedanke *m*

lead'ing la'dy *s* Hauptdarstellerin *f*

lead'ing man' *s* Hauptdarsteller *m*

lead'ing ques'tion *s* Suggestivfrage *f*

lead'ing role' *s* Hauptrolle *f*

lead'-in wire' *s* Zuleitungsdraht *m*

lead' pen'cil [lɛd] *s* Bleistift *m*

lead' pipe' [lɛd] *s* Bleirohr *n*

lead' poi'soning [lɛd] *s* Bleivergiftung *f*

leaf [lif] *s* (**leaves** [livz]) Blatt *n*; (*of a folding door*) Flügel *m*; (*of a folding table*) Tischklappe *f*; (*insertable table board*) Einlegebrett *n*; **turn over a new l.** ein neues Leben anfangen || *intr*—**l. through** durchblättern

leafage ['lifɪdʒ] *s* Laubwerk *n*

leafless ['liflɪs] *adj* blattlos

leaflet ['liflɪt] *s* Werbeprospekt *m*, Flugblatt *n*; (*bot*) Blättchen *n*

leafy ['lifi] *adj* (*abounding in leaves*) belaubt; (*e.g., vegetables*) Blatt-

league [lig] *s* Bund *m*; (*unit of distance*) Meile *f*; (*sport*) Liga *f*; **in l. with** verbündet mit || *tr* verbünden || *intr* sich verbünden

League' of Na'tions *s* Völkerbund *m*

leak [lik] *s* Leck *n*; **spring a l.** ein Leck bekommen; **take a l.** (*vulg*) schiffen || *tr* (*e.g., a story to the press*) durchsickern lassen || *intr* (*said of a container*) leck sein; (*said of a boat*) lecken; (*said of a fluid*) auslaufen; (*said of a spigot*) tropfen; **l. out** (& *fig*) durchsickern

leakage ['likɪdʒ] *s* Lecken *n*; (& *fig*) Durchsickern *n*; (*com*) Schwund *m*; (*elec*) Streuung *f*

leaky ['liki] *adj* leck

lean [lin] *adj* mager || *v* (*pret & pp* **leaned & leant** [lɛnt]) *tr* (*against*) lehnen (an *acc* or gegen) || *intr* lehnen; **l. against** sich anlehnen an (*acc*); **l. back** sich zurücklehnen; **l. forward** sich vorbeugen; **l. on** sich stützen auf (*acc*); **l. over** (*e.g., a railing*) sich neigen über (*acc*); **l. toward** (*fig*) neigen zu

lean'ing *adj* sich neigend; (*tower*) schief || *s* (*toward*) Neigung *f* (zu)

leanness ['linnɪs] *s* Magerkeit *f*

lean'-to' *s* (–**tos**) Anbau *m* mit Pultdach

lean' years' *spl* magere Jahre *pl*

leap [lip] *s* Sprung *m*, Satz *m*; **by leaps and bounds** sprungweise; **l. in the dark** (*fig*) Sprung *m* ins Ungewisse || *v* (*pret & pp* **leaped & leapt** [lɛpt]) *tr* überspringen || *intr* springen; **l. at** anspringen; **l. at an opportunity** e-e Gelegenheit beim Schopf ergreifen; **l. forward** vorspringen; **l. up** emporschnellen

leap'frog' *s* Bocksprung *m*; **play l.** Bocksprünge machen

leap' year' *s* Schaltjahr *n*

learn [lʌrn] *v* (*pret & pp* **learned & learnt** [lʌrnt]) *tr* lernen; (*find out*) erfahren; **l. s.th. from s.o.** erfahren

learned ['lʌrnɪd] *adj* (*person, word*) gelehrt; (*for or of scholars*) Gelehrten-

learn'ed jour'nal *s* Gelehrtenzeitschrift *f*

learn'ed soci'ety *s* Gelehrtenvereinigung *f*

learn'ed world' *s* Gelehrtenwelt *f*

learn'ing *s* (*act*) Lernen *n*; (*erudition*) Gelehrsamkeit *f*

lease [lis] *s* Mietvertrag *m*; (*of land*) Pachtvertrag *m* || *tr* (*in the role of landlord*) vermieten; (*land*) verpachten; (*in the role of tenant*) mieten; (*land*) pachten

lease'hold' *adj* Pacht– || *s* Pachtbesitz *m*

leash [liʃ] *s* Leine *f*, Hundeleine *f*; **keep on the l.** an der Leine führen; **strain at the l.** (*fig*) an der Leine zerren || *tr* an die Leine nehmen

leas'ing *s* Miete *f*; (*of land*) Pachtung *f*; **l. out** Vermietung *f*; (*of land*) Verpachtung *f*

least [list] *adj* mindeste, wenigste || *adv* am wenigsten; **l. of all** am wenigsten von allen || *s* Geringste *mfn*; **at l.** mindestens, wenigstens; **at the very l.** zum mindesten; **not in the l.** nicht im mindesten

leather ['lɛðər] *adj* ledern || *s* Leder *n*

leath'er bind'ing *s* Ledereinband *m*

leath'erbound' *adj* ledergebunden

leath'erneck' *s* (*sl*) Marineinfanterist *m*

leathery ['lɛðəri] *adj* (*e.g., steak*) (*coll*) lederartig

leave [liv] *s* (*permission*) Erlaubnis *f*; (*mil*) Urlaub *m*; **on l.** auf Urlaub; **take l. (from)** Abschied nehmen (von); **take l. of one's senses** (*coll*) den Verstand verlieren || *v* (*pret & pp* **left** [lɛft]) *tr* (*go away from*) verlassen; (*undone, open, etc.*) lassen; (*a message, bequest*) hinterlassen; (*a job*) aufgeben; (*a scar*) zurücklassen; (*forget*) liegenlassen, stehenlassen; (*e.g., some food for s.o.*) übriglassen; **be left** übrig sein; **l. alone** (*a thing*) bleibenlassen; (*a person*) in Frieden lassen; **l. behind** (*said of a deceased person*) hinterlassen; *(forget)* liegenlassen; **l. home** von zu Hause fortgehen; **l. it at that!** überlaß es mir!; **l. lying about** herumliegen lassen; **l. nothing to chance** nichts dem Zufall überlassen; **l. nothing undone** nichts unversucht lassen; **l. open** offen lassen; **l. out** auslassen; **l. standing** stehenlassen; **l.** *(e.g., work)* **undone** liegenlassen ‖ *intr* fortgehen; *(on travels)* abreisen; *(said of vehicles)* abfahren; (aer) abfliegen; **l. off** *(e.g., from reading)* aufhören

leaven ['levən] *s* Treibmittel *n* ‖ *tr* säuern

leav'ening *s* Treibstoff *m*

leave' of ab'sence *s* Urlaub *m*

leave'-tak'ing *s* Abschiednehmen *n*

leavings ['livɪŋz] *spl* Überbleibsel *pl*

Leba•nese [,lebə'niz] *adj* libanesisch ‖ *s* (–nese) Libanese *m*, Libanesin *f*

Lebanon ['lebənən] *s* Libanon *n*

lecher ['letʃər] *s* Lüstling *m*

lecherous ['letʃərəs] *adj* wollüstig

lechery ['letʃəri] *s* Wollust *f*

lectern ['lektərn] *s* Lesepult *n*

lector ['lektər] *s* (eccl) Lektor *m*

lecture ['lektʃər] *s* Vorlesung *f*, Vortrag *m*; (coll) Standpauke *f*; **give a l. on** e-n Vortrag halten über *(acc)*; **give s.o. a l.** j-m den Text lesen ‖ *tr* (coll) abkanzeln ‖ *intr* lesen

lecturer ['lektʃərər] *s* Vortragende *mf*; *(at a university)* Dozent –in *mf*

lec'ture room' *s* Hörsaal *m*

ledge [ledʒ] *s* Sims *m* & *n*; *(of a cliff)* Felsenriff *n*

ledger ['ledʒər] *s* (acct) Hauptbuch *n*

lee [li] *s* Lee *f*

leech [litʃ] *s* Blutegel *m*; (fig) Blutsauger –in *mf*

leek [lik] *s* (bot) Porree *m*, Lauch *m*

leer [lɪr] *s* lüsterner Seitenblick *m* ‖ *intr* lüstern schielen (nach)

leery ['lɪri] *adj* mißtrauisch; **be l. of** mißtrauen *(dat)*

lees [liz] *spl* Hefe *f*

lee' side' s Leeseite *f*

leeward ['liwərd] *adv* leewärts ‖ *s* Leeseite *f*

Lee'ward Is'lands *spl* Inseln *pl* unter dem Winde

lee'way' *s* (coll) Spielraum *m*; (aer, naut) Abtrift *f*

left [left] *adj* linke; *(left over)* übrig ‖ *adv* links; **l. face!** (mil) links um! ‖ *s* *(left hand)* Linke *f*; **on our l.** zu unserer Linken; **the l.** (pol) die Linke; **the third street to the l.** die dritte Querstraße links; **to the l.** nach links; **to the l. of** links von

left' field' *s* (baseball) linkes Außenfeld *n*

left' field'er ['fildər] *s* Spieler *m* im linken Außenfeld

left'-hand drive' *s* Linkssteuerung *f*

left'-hand'ed *adj* linkshändig; *(compliment)* fragwürdig; *(counterclockwise)* linksgängig; *(clumsy)* linkisch

left-hander ['left'hændər] *s* Linkshänder –in *mf*

leftish ['leftɪʃ] *adj* linksgerichtet

leftist ['leftɪst] *s* Linksradikaler *m*; (pol) Linkspolitiker –in *mf*

left'o•ver *adj* übriggeblieben ‖ **leftovers** *spl* Überbleibsel *pl*

left'-wing' *adj* Links-

left' wing' *s* (pol) linker Flügel *m*; (sport) Linksaußen *m*

left-winger ['left'wɪŋər] *s* (coll) Linkspolitiker –in *mf*

lefty ['lefti] *adj* (coll) linkshändig ‖ *s* (coll) Linkshänder –in *mf*

leg [leg] *s* *(of a body, of furniture, of trousers)* Bein *n*; *(stretch)* Etappe *f*; *(of a compass)* Schenkel *m*; *(of a boot)* Schaft *m*; **be on one's last legs** auf den letzten Loche pfeifen; **pull s.o.'s leg** (coll) j-n auf die Schippe nehmen; **run one's legs off** sich abrennen; **you don't have a leg to stand on** Sie haben keinerlei Beweise

legacy ['legəsi] *s* Vermächtnis *n*

legal ['ligəl] *adj* *(according to the law)* gesetzlich; legal; *(pertaining to or approved by law)* Rechts-, juristisch; **take l. action** den Rechtweg beschreiten; **take l. steps against s.o.** gerichtlich gegen j-n vorgehen

le'gal advice' *s* Rechtsberatung *f*

le'gal advis'er *s* Rechtsberater –in *mf*

le'gal age' *s* Volljährigkeit *f*; **of l.** großjährig

le'gal aid' *s* Rechtshilfe *f*

le'gal ba'sis *s* Rechtsgrundlage *f*

le'gal case' *s* Rechtsfall *m*

le'gal claim' *s* Rechtsanspruch *m*

le'gal en'tity *s* juristische Person *f*

le'gal force' *s* Rechtskraft *f*

le'gal grounds' *spl* Rechtsgrund *m*

le'gal hol'iday *s* gesetzlicher Feiertag *m*

legality [lɪ'gælɪti] *s* Gesetzlichkeit *f*, Rechtlichkeit *f*

legalize ['ligə,laɪz] *tr* legalisieren

le'gal jar'gon *s* Kanzleisprache *f*

le'gal profes'sion *s* Rechtsanwaltsberuf *m*

le'gal rem'edy *s* Rechtsmittel *n*

le'gal ten'der *s* gesetzliches Zahlungsmittel *n*; **be l.** gelten

le'gal ti'tle *s* Rechtsanspruch *m*

legate ['legɪt] *s* Legat –in *mf*

legatee [,legə'ti] *s* Legatar –in *mf*

legation [lɪ'geʃən] *s* Gesandtschaft *f*

legend ['ledʒənd] *s* Legende *f*

legendary ['ledʒən,deri] *adj* legendär

legerdemain [,ledʒərdɪ'men] *s* Taschenspielerei *f*

leggings ['legɪŋz] *spl* hohe Gamaschen *pl*

leggy ['legi] *adj* langbeinig

Leg'horn' *s* (chicken) Leghorn *n*; *(town in Italy)* Livorno *n*

legibility [,ledʒɪ'bɪlɪti] *s* Lesbarkeit *f*

legible ['ledʒɪbəl] *adj* lesbar

legion ['lidʒən] *s* Legion *f*; (fig) Heerschar *f*

legionnaire [,lidʒə'ner] *s* Legionär *m*

legislate ['ledʒɪs,let] *tr* durch Gesetzgebung bewirken ‖ *intr* Gesetze geben

legislation [,ledʒɪs'leʃən] *s* Gesetzgebung *f*

legislative ['lɛdʒɪs ˌlɛtɪv] *adj* gesetzgebend

legislator ['lɛdʒɪs ˌlɛtər] *s* Gesetzgeber –in *mf*

legislature ['lɛdʒɪs ˌlɛtʃər] *s* Legislatur *f*

legitimacy [lɪ'dʒɪtɪməsɪ] *s* Rechtmäßigkeit *f*

legitimate [lɪ'dʒɪtɪmɪt] *adj* gesetzmäßig, legitim; (*child*) ehelich ‖ [lɪ'dʒɪtɪ ˌmet] *tr* legitimieren

legit'imate the'ater *s* literarisch wertvolles Theater *n*

legitimize [lɪ'dʒɪtɪ ˌmaɪz] *tr* legitimieren

leg' of lamb' *s* Lammkeule *f*

leg' of mut'ton *s* Hammelkeule *f*

leg' room' *s* Beinfreiheit *f*

leg'work' *s* Vorarbeiten *pl*

leisure ['liʒər] *s* Muße *f*; **at l.** mit Muße; **at s.o.'s l.** wenn es j–m paßt

lei'sure class' *s* wohlhabende Klasse *f*

lei'sure hours' *spl* Mußestunden *pl*

leisurely ['liʒərlɪ] *adj & adv* gemächlich

lei'sure time' *s* Freizeit *f*

lemon ['lɛmən] *adj* Zitronen– ‖ *s* Zitrone *f*; (sl) Niete *f*

lemonade [ˌlɛmɪ'ned] *s* Zitronenlimonade *f*

lem'on squeez'er *s* Zitronenpresse *f*

lend [lɛnd] *v* (*pret & pp* **lent** [lɛnt]) *tr* leihen, borgen; **l. at five percent interest** zu fünf Prozent Zinsen anlegen; **l. itself to** sich eignen zu or für; **l. oneself to** sich hergeben zu; **l. out** ausleihen, verborgen; **l. s.o. a hand** j–m zur Hand gehen

lender ['lɛndər] *s* Verleiher –in *mf*

lend'ing li'brary *s* Leihbücherei *f*

length [lɛŋθ] *s* Länge *f*; (*of time*) Dauer *f*; (*in horse racing*) Pferdelänge *f*; **at great l.** sehr ausführlich; **at l.** ausführlich; (*finally*) schließlich; **at some l.** ziemlich ausführlich; **go to any l.** alles Erdenkliche tun; **go to great lengths** sich sehr bemühen; **keep s.o. at arm's l.** zu j–m Abstand wahren; **stretch out full l.** sich der Länge nach ausstrecken

lengthen ['lɛŋθən] *tr* verlängern; (*a vowel*) dehnen

length'ening *s* Verlängerung *f*; (ling) Dehnung *f*

length'wise' *adj & adv* der Länge nach

lengthy ['lɛŋθɪ] *adj* langwierig

leniency ['linɪ·ənsɪ] *s* Milde *f*

lens [lɛnz] *s* Linse *f*; (*combination of lenses*) Objektiv *n*

Lent [lɛnt] *s* Fastenzeit *f*

Lenten ['lɛntən] *adj* Fasten–

lentil ['lɛntɪl] *s* (bot) Linse *f*

leopard ['lɛpərd] *s* Leopard *m*

leper ['lɛpər] *s* Aussätzige *mf*

leprosy ['lɛprəsɪ] *s* Aussatz *m*, Lepra *f*

lesbian ['lɛzbɪ·ən] *adj* lesbisch ‖ *s* Lesbierin *f*

lesbianism ['lɛzbɪ·ə ˌnɪzəm] *s* lesbische Liebe *f*

lesion ['liʒən] *s* Wunde *f*

less [lɛs] *comp adj* weniger, geringer;

l. and l. immer weniger ‖ *adv* weniger, minder; **l. than** weniger als ‖ *s*—**do with l.** mit weniger auskommen; **for l.** billiger; **in l. than no time** in Null Komma nichts ‖ *prep* abzüglich (*genit* or *acc*); (arith) weniger (*acc*), minus (*acc*)

lessee [lɛ'si] *s* Mieter –in *mf*; (*of land*) Pächter –in *mf*

lessen ['lɛsən] *tr* vermindern ‖ *intr* sich vermindern, abnehmen

lesser ['lɛsər] *comp adj* minder, geringer

lesson ['lɛsən] *s* Unterrichtsstunde *f*, Stunde *f*; (*in a textbook*) Lektion *f*; (*warning*) Lehre *f*; **learn a l. from** e–e Lehre ziehen aus; **let that be l. to you!** lassen Sie sich das e–e Lehre sein

lessor ['lɛsər] *s* Vermieter –in *mf*; (*of land*) Verpächter –in *mf*

lest [lɛst] *conj* damit nicht; (after expressions of fear) daß

let [lɛt] *v* (*pret & pp* **let**; *ger* **letting**) *tr* lassen; **I really let him have it!** (coll) ich hab's ihm ordentlich gegeben!; **let alone** in Ruhe lassen; (*not to mention*) geschweige denn; **let down** herunterlassen; (*disappoint*) enttäuschen; **let drop** fallen lassen; **let fly** fliegen lassen; (coll) loslassen; **let go** fortlassen, loslassen; **let go ahead** vorlassen; **let in** hereinlassen; (*water*) zuleiten; **let in on** (*e.g., a secret*) einweihen in (*acc*); **let it go,** e.g., **I'll let it go this time** diesmal werde ich es noch hingehen lassen; **let lie** liegenlassen; **let know** wissen lassen, Bescheid geben (*dat*); **let off** (*e.g., at the next corner*) absetzen; **let off easy** noch so davonkommen lassen; **let off scot-free** straflos laufen lassen; **let one's hair down** (fig) sich gehenlassen; **let out** (*seams, air, water*) auslassen; (*e.g., a yell*) von sich geben; **let pass** durchlassen; **let s.o. have s.th.** j–m etw zukommen lassen; **let stand** (fig) gelten lassen; **let through** durchlassen; **let things slide** die Dinge laufen lassen; **let things take their course** den Dingen ihren Lauf lassen; **let's go!** los!; **let us** (or **let's**) (*inf*), e.g., **let's** (or **let us**) **sing** singen wir ‖ *intr* (*be rented out*) (**for**) vermietet werden (für); **let fly with** (coll) losgegen mit; **let go of** loslassen; **let on that** sich [*dat*] anmerken lassen, daß; **let up** nachlassen; **let up on** (coll) ablassen von

let'down' *s* Hereinfall *m*

lethal ['liθəl] *adj* tödlich

lethargic [lɪ'θɑrdʒɪk] *adj* lethargisch

lethargy ['lɛθərdʒɪ] *s* Lethargie *f*

letter ['lɛtər] *s* Brief *m*, Schreiben *n*; (*of the alphabet*) Buchstabe *m*; **by l.** brieflich, schriftlich; **to the l.** aufs Wort ‖ *tr* beschriften

let'ter box' *s* Briefkasten *m*

let'ter car'rier *s* Briefträger –in *mf*

let'ter drop' *s* Briefeinwurf *m*

let'tered *adj* gelehrt

let'ter file' *s* Briefordner *m*

let'terhead' s Briefkopf m

let'tering s (act) Beschriften n; (inscription) Beschriftung f

let'ter of condol'ence s Beileidsbrief m

let'ter of cred'it s Kreditbrief m

let'ter of recommenda'tion s Empfehlungsbrief m

letter o'pener s Brieföffner m

let'terper'fect adj buchstabengetreu

let'terpress' s (typ) Hochdruck m

let'ter scales' spl Briefwaage f

let'ter to the ed'itor s Leserbrief m

lettuce ['lɛtɪs] s Salat m

let'up' s Nachlassen n; without l. ohne Unterlaß

leukemia [lu'kimɪ·ə] s Leukämie f

Levant [lɪ'vænt] s Levante f

Levantine [lɪ'væntɪn] adj levantinisch || s Levantiner –in mf

levee ['lɛvi] s Uferdamm m

lev·el ['lɛvəl] adj eben, gerade; (flat) flach; (spoonful) gestrichen; be l. with so hoch sein wie; do one's l. best sein Möglichstes tun; have a l. head ausgeglichen sein; keep a l. head e–n klaren Kopf behalten || s (& fig) Niveau n; (tool) Wasserwaage f; at higher levels höheren Ortes; be up to the usual l. (fig) auf der gewöhnlichen Höhe sein; on a l. with (& fig) auf gleicher Höhe mit; on the l. (fig) ehrlich || v (pret & pp –el[l]ed; ger –el[l]ing tr (a street, ground) planieren; l. (e.g., a rifle) at richten auf (acc); (e.g., complaints) richten gegen; l. off nivellieren; (aer) abfangen; l. to the ground dem Erdboden gleichmachen || intr—l. off sich verflachen; (said of prices) sich stabilisieren; (aer) in Horizontalflug übergehen; l. with s.o. mit j–m offen sein

lev'elhead'ed adj besonnen, vernünftig

lever ['livər] s Hebel m, Brechstange f || tr mit e–r Brechstange fortbewegen

leverage ['livərɪdʒ] s Hebelkraft f; (fig) Einfluß m

leviathan [lɪ'vaɪ·əθən] s Leviathan m

levitate ['lɛvɪ,tet] tr schweben lassen || intr frei schweben

levitation [,lɛvɪ'teʃən] s Schweben n

levity ['lɛvɪti] s Leichtsinn m

lev·y ['lɛvi] s Truppenaushebung f; (of taxes) Erhebung f; (tax) Steuer f || v (pret & pp –vied) tr (troops) ausheben; (taxes) erheben; l. war on Krieg führen gegen

lewd [lud] adj unzüchtig

lewdness ['ludnɪs] s Unzucht f

lexical ['lɛksɪkəl] adj lexikalisch

lexicographer [,lɛksɪ'kɑgrəfər] s Lexikograph –in mf

lexicographic(al) [,lɛksɪkə'græfɪk(əl)] adj lexikographisch

lexicography [,lɛksɪ'kɑgrəfi] s Lexikographie f

lexicology [,lɛksɪ'kɑlədʒi] s Wortforschung f, Lexikologie f

lexicon ['lɛksɪkən] s Wörterbuch n

liability [,laɪ·ə'bɪlɪti] s (ins) Haftpflicht f; (jur) Haftung f; liabilities Schulden pl; (acct) Passiva pl

liabil'ity insur'ance s Haftpflichtversicherung f

liable ['laɪ·əbəl] adj (jur) (for) haftbar (für); be l. to (inf) (coll) leicht können (inf); l. for damages schadenersatzpflichtig

liaison [li'ezɑn] s Verbindung f; (illicit affair) Liaison f; (ling) Bindung f

liai'son of'ficer s Verbindungsoffizier m

liar ['laɪ·ər] s Lügner –in mf

libation [laɪ'beʃən] s Opfertrank m

li·bel ['laɪbəl] s Verleumdung f; (in writing) Schmähschrift f || v (pret & pp –bel[l]ed; ger –bel[l]ing) tr verleumden

libelous ['laɪbələs] adj verleumderisch

li'bel suit' s Verleumdungsklage f

liberal ['lɪbərəl] adj (views) liberal, freisinnig; (with money) freigebig; (gift) großzügig; (interpretation) weitherzig; (education) allgemeinbildend; (pol) liberal || s Liberale mf

lib'eral arts' spl Geisteswissenschaften pl

liberalism ['lɪbərə,lɪzəm] s Liberalismus m

liberality [,lɪbə'rælɪti] s Freigebigkeit f, Großzügigkeit f

liberate ['lɪbə,ret] tr befreien; (chem) freimachen

liberation [,lɪbə'reʃən] s Befreiung f; (chem) Freimachen n

liberator ['lɪbə,retər] s Befreier –in mf

libertine ['lɪbər,tin] s Wüstling m

liberty ['lɪbərti] s Freiheit f; take liberties sich [dat] Freiheiten herausnehmen; you are at l. to (inf) es steht Ihnen frei zu (inf)

libidinous [lɪ'bɪdɪnəs] adj wollüstig

libido [lɪ'bido] s Libido f

librarian [laɪ'brɛrɪ·ən] s Bibliothekar –in mf

library ['laɪ,brɛri] s Bibliothek f

li'brary card' s Benutzerkarte f

libret·to [lɪ'brɛto] s (–tos) Operntext m, Libretto n

Libya ['lɪbɪ·ə] s Libyen n

Libyan ['lɪbɪ·ən] adj libysch || s Libyer –in mf

license ['laɪsəns] s Lizenz f, Genehmigung f; (document) Zulassungsschein m; (for a business, restaurant) Konzession f; (to drive) Führerschein m; (excessive liberty) Zügellosigkeit f || tr konzessionieren; (aut) zulassen

li'cense num'ber s (aut) Kennzeichen n

li'cense plate' or tag' s Nummernschild n

licentious [laɪ'sɛnʃəs] adj unzüchtig

lichen ['laɪkən] s (bot) Flechte f

lick [lɪk] s Lecken n || tr lecken; (thrash) (coll) wichsen; (defeat) (coll) schlagen; (said of a flame) züngeln an (dat); l. clean auslecken; l. into shape auf Hochglanz bringen; l. off ablecken; l. one's chops sich [dat] die Lippen lecken; l. s.o.'s boots vor j–m kriechen; l. up auflecken

lick'ing s Prügel pl; give s.o. a good l. j–n versohlen

licorice [ˈlɪkərɪs] s Lakritze f
lid [lɪd] s Deckel m
lie [laɪ] s Lüge f; **give the lie to s.o.**
(or **s.th.**) j–n (or etw) Lügen strafen;
tell a lie lügen ‖ v (pret & pp **lied**;
ger **lying**) tr—**lie one's way out of**
sich herauslügen aus ‖ intr lügen;
lie like mad das Blaue vom Himmel
herunter lügen; **lie to** belügen ‖ v
(pret **lay** [le]; pp **lain** [len]; ger
lying) intr liegen; **lie down** sich hin-
legen; **lie down!** (to a dog) leg dich!;
lie in wait auf der Lauer liegen; **lie
in wait for** auflauern (dat); **lie low**
sich versteckt halten; (bide one's
time) abwarten; **take s.th. lying down**
etw widerspruchslos hinnehmen
lie′ detec′tor s Lügendetektor m
lien [lin] s Pfandrecht n
lieu [lu] s—**in l. of** statt (genit)
lieutenant [luˈtɛnənt] s Leutnant m;
(nav) Kapitänleutnant m
lieuten′ant colo′nel s Oberstleutnant m
lieuten′ant comman′der s Korvetten-
kapitän m
lieuten′ant gen′eral s Generalleutnant
m
lieuten′ant gov′ernor s Vizegouverneur
m
lieuten′ant jun′ior grade′ s (nav) Oberleutnant m zur See
lieuten′ant sen′ior grade′ s (nav) Kapitänleutnant m
life [laɪf] adj (imprisonment) lebenslänglich ‖ s (lives [laɪvz]) Leben n;
(e.g., of a car) Lebensdauer f; **all
my l.** mein ganzes Leben lang; **as big
as l.** in voller Lebensgröße; **bring
back to l.** wieder zum Bewußtsein
bringen; **bring to l.** ins Leben bringen; **for dear l.** ums liebe Leben;
for l. auf Lebenszeit; **full of l.** voller
Leben; **I can't for the l. of me** ich
kann beim besten Willen nicht; **lives
lost** Menschenleben pl; **not on your
l.** auf keinen Fall; **put l. into** beleben; **such is l.!** so ist nun mal das
Leben; **take one's l.** sich [dat] das
Leben nehmen; **upon my l.!** so wahr
ich lebe!; **you can bet your l. on
that!** darauf kannst du Gift nehmen!
life′-and-death′ adj auf Leben und Tod
life′ annu′ity s Lebensrente f
life′ belt′ s Schwimmgürtel m
life′blood′ s Lebensblut n
life′boat′ s Rettungsboot n
life′ buoy′ s Rettungsboje f
life′ expect′ancy s Lebenserwartung f
life′ guard′ s (at a pool) Bademeister
–in mf; (at the shore) Strandwärter
–in mf
life′ impris′onment s lebenslängliche
Haft f
life′ insur′ance s Lebensversicherung f
life′ jack′et s Schwimmweste f
lifeless [ˈlaɪflɪs] adj leblos; (fig)
schwunglos
life′-like′ adj naturgetreu, lebensecht
life′ line′ s Rettungsleine f; (for a
diver) Signalleine f; (supply line)
Lebensader f
life′long′ adj lebenslänglich

life′ mem′ber s Mitglied n auf Lebenszeit
life′ of lei′sure s Wohlleben n
life′ of plea′sure s Wohlleben n
life′ of Ri′ley [ˈraɪli] s Herrenleben n
life′ of the par′ty s—**be the l.** die ganze
Gesellschaft unterhalten
life′ preserv′er [prɪˈzʌrvər] s Rettungs-
ring m
lifer [ˈlaɪfər] s (sl) Lebenslängliche mf
life′ raft′ s Rettungsfloß n
lifesaver [ˈlaɪfˌsevər] s Rettungs-
schwimmer –in mf; (fig) rettender
Engel m
life′ sen′tence s Verurteilung f zu le-
benslänglicher Haft
life′-size(d)′ adj lebensgroß
life′ span′ s Lebensdauer f
life′ style′ s Lebensweise f
life′time′ adj lebenslänglich ‖ s Leben
n; **for a l.** auf Lebenszeit; **once in a
l.** einmal im Leben
life′ vest′ s Schwimmweste f
life′work′ s Lebenswerk n
lift [lɪft] s (elevator) Aufzug m; (aer
& fig) Auftrieb m; **give s.o. a l.** j–n
im Wagen mitnehmen ‖ tr heben;
(gently) lüpfen; (with effort) wuchten; (weights) stemmen; (the receiver) abnehmen; (an embargo) aufheben; (steal) (sl) klauen; **l. up** aufheben; (the eyes) erheben; **not l. a
finger** keinen Finger rühren ‖ intr
(said of a mist) steigen; **l. off** (rok)
starten
lift′-off′ s (rok) Start m
lift′ truck′ s Lastkraftwagen m mit
Hebevorrichtung
ligament [ˈlɪgəmənt] s Band n
ligature [ˈlɪgətʃər] s (mus) Bindung f;
(act) (surg) Abbinden n; (filament)
(surg) Abbindungsschnur f; (typ)
Ligatur f
light [laɪt] adj (clothing, meal, music,
heart, wine, sleep, punishment,
weight) leicht; (day, beer, color,
complexion, hair) hell; **as l. as day**
tageshell; **l. as a feather** federleicht;
make l. of auf die leichte Schulter
nehmen; (belittle) als bedeutungslos
hinstellen ‖ s Licht n; **according to
his lights** nach dem Maß seiner Einsicht; **bring to l.** ans Licht bringen;
come to l. ans Licht kommen; **do
you have a l.?** haben Sie Feuer?;
in the l. of im Lichte (genit), angesichts (genit); **put in a false l.** in ein
falsches Licht stellen; **see the l. of
day** (be born) das Licht der Welt
erblicken; **shed l. on** Licht werfen
auf (acc); **throw quite a different l.
on** ein ganz anderes Licht werfen
auf (acc) ‖ v (pret & pp **lighted** &
lit [lɪt]) tr (a fire, cigarette) anzünden; (an oven) anheizen; (a
street) beleuchten; (a hall) erleuchten; (a face) aufleuchten lassen ‖
intr sich entzünden; **l. up** (said of a
face) aufleuchten; (light a cigarette)
sich [dat] e–e Zigarette anstecken
light′-blue′ adj lichtblau, hellblau
light′ bulb′ s Glühbirne f

light-complexioned ['laɪtkəm'plɛkʃənd] *adj* von heller Hautfarbe

lighten ['laɪtən] *tr (in weight)* leichter machen; *(brighten)* erhellen; *(fig)* erleichtern || *intr (become brighter)* sich aufhellen; *(during a storm)* blitzen

lighter ['laɪtər] *s* Feuerzeug *n*; *(naut)* Leichter *m*

ligh'ter flu'id *s* Feuerzeugbenzin *n*

light'-fin'gered *adj* geschickt; *(thievish)* langfingerig

light'-foot'ed *adj* leichtfüßig

light'-head'ed *adj* leichtsinnig; *(dizzy)* schwindlig

light'-heart'ed *adj* leichtherzig

light'-heav'y·weight' *adj (box)* Halbschwergewichts- || *s* Halbschwergewichtler *m*

light'house' *s* Leuchtturm *m*

light'ing *s* Beleuchtung *f*

light'ing effects' *spl* Lichteffekte *pl*

light'ing fix'ture *s* Beleuchtungskörper *m*

lightly ['laɪtli] *adv* leicht; *(without due consideration)* leichthin; *(disparagingly)* geringschätzig

light' me'ter *s* Lichtmesser *m*

lightness ['laɪtnɪs] *s (in weight)* Leichtigkeit *f*; *(in shade)* Helligkeit *f*

lightning ['laɪtnɪŋ] *s* Blitz *m* || *impers* —**it is l.** es blitzt

light'ning arrest'er [ə‚rɛstər] *s* Blitzableiter *m*

light'ning bug' *s* Leuchtkäfer *m*

light'ning rod' *s* Blitzableiter *m*

light'ning speed' *s* Windeseile *f*

light' op'era *s* Operette *f*

light' read'ing *s* Unterhaltungslektüre *f*

light'ship' *s* Leuchtschiff *n*

light' sleep' *s* Dämmerschlaf *m*

light' switch' *s* Lichtschalter *m*

light' wave' *s* Lichtwelle *f*

light'weight' *adj (box)* Leichtgewichts- || *s (coll)* geistig Minderbemittelter *m*; *(box)* Leichtgewichtler *m*

light'-year' *s* Lichtjahr *n*

likable ['laɪkəbəl] *adj* sympathisch, lieb

like [laɪk] *adj* gleich, ähnlich; **be l.** gleichen *(dat)* || *adv*—**l. crazy** (coll) wie verrückt || *s*—**and the l.** und dergleichen; **likes and dislikes** Neigungen und Abneigungen *pl* || *tr* gern haben, mögen; **I l. him** er ist mir sympathisch; **I l. the picture** das Bild gefällt mir; **I l. the food** das Essen schmeckt mir; **l. to** *(inf)*, e.g., **I l. to read** ich lese gern || *intr*—**as you l.** wie Sie wollen; **if you l.** wenn Sie wollen || *prep* wie; **feel l.** *(ger)* Lust haben zu *(inf)*; **feel l. hell** (sl) sich elend fühlen; **it looks l.** es sieht nach ... aus; **l. greased lightning** wie geschmiert; **that's just l. him** das sieht ihm ähnlich; **there's nothing l. traveling** es geht nichts übers Reisen

likelihood ['laɪklɪ‚hʊd] *s* Wahrscheinlichkeit *f*

likely ['laɪkli] *adj* wahrscheinlich; **a l. story!** (iron) e-e glaubhafte Ge-

schichte!; **it's l. to rain** es wird wahrscheinlich regen

like'-mind'ed *adj* gleichgesinnt

liken ['laɪkən] *tr (to)* vergleichen (mit)

likeness ['laɪknɪs] *s* Ähnlichkeit *f*; **a good l.** of ein gutes Portrait *(genit)*

like'wise' *adv* gleichfalls, ebenso

lik'ing *s (for)* Zuneigung *f (zu)*; **not to my l.** nicht nach meinem Geschmack; **take a l. to** Zuneigung fassen zu

lilac ['laɪlək] *adj* lila || *s* Flieder *m*

lilt [lɪlt] *s* rhythmischer Schwung *m*; *(lilting song)* lustiges Lied *n*

lily ['lɪli] *s* Lilie *f*

lil'y·of·the·val'ley *s* Maiglöckchen *n*

lil'y pad' *s* schwimmendes Seerosenblatt *n*

lil'y-white' *adj* lilienweiß

li'ma bean' ['laɪmə] *s* Limabohne *f*

limb [lɪm] *s* Glied *n*; *(of a tree)* Ast *m*; **go out on a l.** *(fig)* sich exponieren; **limbs** Gliedmaßen *pl*

limber ['lɪmbər] *adj* geschmeidig || *tr* —**l. up** geschmeidig machen || *intr*— sich geschmeidig machen

lim·bo ['lɪmbo] *s (-bos)* Vorhölle *f*; *(fig)* Vergessenheit *f*

lime [laɪm] *s* Kalk *m*; *(bot)* Limonelle *f*

lime'kiln' *s* Kalkofen *m*

lime'light' *s (& fig)* Rampenlicht *n*

limerick ['lɪmərɪk] *s* Limerick *m*

lime'stone' *adj* Kalkstein– || *s* Kalkstein *m*

limit ['lɪmɪt] *s* Grenze *f*; **go the l.** zum Äußersten gehen; **off limits** Zutritt verboten; **set a l. to** e–e Grenze ziehen *(dat)*; **that's the l.!** das ist denn doch die Höhe!; **there's a l. to everything** alles hat seine Grenzen; **within limits** in Grenzen; **without l.** schrankenlos || *tr* begrenzen; **(to)** beschränken *(auf acc)*

limitation [‚lɪmɪ'teʃən] *s* Begrenzung *f*, Beschränkung *f*

lim'ited *adj* **(to)** beschränkt *(auf acc)*

lim'ited-ac'cess high'way *s* Autobahn *f*

lim'ited mon'archy *s* konstitutionelle Monarchie *f*

limitless ['lɪmɪtlɪs] *adj* grenzenlos

limousine ['lɪmə‚zin], [‚lɪmə'zin] *s* Limousine *f*

limp [lɪmp] *adj (& fig)* schlaff || *s* Hinken *n*; **walk with a l.** hinken || *intr (& fig)* hinken

limpid ['lɪmpɪd] *adj* durchsichtig

linchpin ['lɪntʃ‚pɪn] *s* Achsnagel *m*

linden ['lɪndən] *s* Linde *f*, Lindenbaum *m*

line [laɪn] *s* Linie *f*, Strich *m*; *(boundary)* Grenze *f*; *(of a page)* Zeile *f*; *(of verse)* Verszeile *f*; *(of a family)* Zweig *m*; *(sphere of activity)* Fach *n*; *(e.g., of a streetcar)* Linie *f*, Strecke *f*; *(wrinkle)* Furche *f*; *(of articles for sale)* Sortiment *n*; *(for wash)* Leine *f*; *(queue)* Schlange *f*; (sl) zungenfertiges Gerede *n*; (angl) Schnur *f*; (mil) Linie *f*, Front *f*; (telp) Leitung *f*; **all along the l.** *(fig)* auf der ganzen Linie; **along the lines**

of nach dem Muster von; **draw the l. (at)** (fig) e-e Grenze ziehen (bei); **fall into l.** sich einfügen; **forget one's lines** (theat) steckenbleiben; **form a l.** sich in e-r Reihe aufstellen; **get a l. on** (coll) herausklamüsern; **give s.o. a l.** (sl) j-m schöne Worte machen; **hold the l.** die Stellung halten; (telp) am Apparat bleiben; **in l. of duty** im Dienst; **in l. with** in Übereinstimmung mit; **keep in l.** in der Reihe bleiben; **keep s.o. in l.** j-n im Zaum halten; **stand in l.** Schlange stehen; **the l. is busy** (telp) Leitung besetzt! || *tr* linieren; (*e.g., a coat*) füttern; (*a face*) furchen; (*a drawer*) ausschlagen; (*a wall*) verkleiden; **l. one's purse** sich [*dat*] den Beutel spicken; **l. the streets** in den Straßen Spalier bilden; **l. up** ausrichten; (mil) aufstellen || *intr*—**l. up** Schlange stehen; (mil) antreten; **l. up for** sich anstellen nach

lineage ['lɪnɪ·ɪdʒ] *s* Abkunft *f*, Abstammung *f*

lineal ['lɪnɪ·əl] *adj* (*descent*) direkt; (*linear*) geradlinig

lineaments ['lɪnɪ·əmənts] *spl* Gesichtszüge *pl*

linear ['lɪnɪ·ər] *adj* (*arranged in a line*) geradlinig; (*involving a single dimension*) Längen-; (*using lines*) Linien-; (math) linear

lined' pa'per *s* Linienpapier *n*

line'man *s* (–men) (rr) Streckenwärter *m*; (telp) Telephonarbeiter *m*

linen ['lɪnən] *adj* Leinen– || *s* Leinen *n*; (*in the household*) Wäsche *f*; (*of the bed*) Bettwäsche *f*; **linens** Weißzeug *n*; **put fresh l. on the bed** das Bett überziehen

lin'en clos'et *s* Wäscheschrank *m*

lin'en cloth' *s* Leinwand *f*

lin'en goods' *spl* Weißwaren *pl*

line' of approach' *s* (aer) Anflugschneise *f*

line' of bus'iness *s* Geschäftszweig *m*

line' of communica'tion *s* Verbindungslinie *f*

line' of fire' *s* Schußlinie *f*

line' of sight' *s* (*of a gun*) Visierlinie *f*; (astr) Sichtlinie *f*

liner ['laɪnər] *s* Einsatz *m*; (naut) Linienschiff *n*

lines'man *s* (–men) (sport) Linienrichter *m*

line'up' *s* (*at a police station*) Gegenüberstellung *f*; (sport) Aufstellung *f*

linger ['lɪŋgər] *intr* (*tarry*) verweilen; (*said of memories*) nachwirken; (*said of a melody*) nachtönen; **l. over** verweilen bei

lingerie [,lænʒə'ri] *s* Damenunterwäsche *f*

lin'gering *adj* (*disease*) schleichend; (*tune*) nachklingend; (*memory, taste, feeling*) nachwirkend

lingo ['lɪŋgo] *s* Kauderwelsch *n*

linguist ['lɪŋgwɪst] *s* Sprachwissenschaftler –in *mf*

linguistic [lɪŋ'gwɪstɪk] *adj* (*e.g., skill*) sprachlich; (*of linguistics*) sprach-

wissenschaftlich || **linguistics** *s* Sprachwissenschaft *f*

liniment ['lɪnɪmənt] *s* Einreibemittel *n*

lin'ing *s* (*of a coat*) Futter *n*; (*of a brake*) Bremsbelag *m*; (*e.g., of a wall*) Verkleidung *f*

link [lɪŋk] *s* Glied *n*; (fig) Bindeglied *n* || *tr* verbinden; (fig) verketten; **l. to** verbinden mit; (fig) in Verbindung bringen mit || *intr*—**l. up** (rok) dokken; **l. up with** sich anschließen an (*acc*)

linnet ['lɪnɪt] *s* (orn) Hänfling *m*

linoleum [lɪ'nolɪ·əm] *s* Linoleum *n*

linotype ['laɪnə,taɪp] *s* (trademark) Linotype *f*

lin'seed oil' ['lɪn,sid] *s* Leinöl *n*

lint [lɪnt] *s* Fussel *f*

lintel ['lɪntəl] *s* Sturz *m*

lion ['laɪ·ən] *s* Löwe *m*

li'on cage' *s* Löwenzwinger *m*

lioness ['laɪ·ənɪs] *s* Löwin *f*

lionize ['laɪ·ə,naɪz] *tr* zum Helden des Tages machen

li'ons' den' *s* Löwengrube *f*

li'on's share' *s* Löwenanteil *m*

li'on tam'er *s* Löwenbändiger –in *mf*

lip [lɪp] *s* Lippe *f*; (*edge*) Rand *m*; **bite one's lips** sich auf die Lippen beißen; **smack one's lips** sich [*dat*] die Lippen lecken

lip' read'ing *s* Lippenlesen *n*

lip' serv'ice *s* Lippenbekenntnis *n*; **pay l. to** ein Lippenbekenntnis ablegen zu

lip'stick' *s* Lippenstift *m*

lique·fy ['lɪkwɪ,faɪ] *v* (*pret & pp* –fied) *tr* verflüssigen || *intr* sich verflüssigen

liqueur [lɪ'kʌr] *s* Likör *m*

liquid ['lɪkwɪd] *adj* flüssig; (*clear*) klar || *s* Flüssigkeit *f*

liq'uid as'sets *spl* flüssige Mittel *pl*

liquidate ['lɪkwɪ,det] *tr* (*a debt*) tilgen; (*an account*) abrechnen; (*a company*) liquidieren

liquidation [,lɪkwɪ'deʃən] *s* (*of a debt*) Tilgung *f*; (*of an account*) Abrechnung *f*; (*of a company*) Liquidation *f*

liquidity [lɪ'kwɪdɪtɪ] *s* flüssiger Zustand *m*; (fin) Liquidität *f*

liq'uid meas'ure *s* Hohlmaß *n*

liquor ['lɪkər] *s* Spirituosen *pl*, Schnaps *m*; **have a shot of l.** einen zwitschern

liquorice ['lɪkərɪs] *s* Lakritze *f*

li'quor li'cense *s* Schankerlaubnis *f*

Lisbon ['lɪzbən] *s* Lissabon *n*

lisp [lɪsp] *s* Lispeln *n* || *tr & intr* lispeln

lissome ['lɪsəm] *adj* biegsam, gelenkig

list [lɪst] *s* Liste *f*, Verzeichnis *n*; (naut) Schlagseite *f* **enter the lists** (& fig) in die Schranken treten; **make a l. of** verzeichnen || *tr* verzeichnen || *intr* (naut) Schlagseite haben

listen ['lɪsən] *intr* horchen, zuhören; **l. closely** die Ohren aufsperren; **l. for** achten auf (*acc*); **l. in** mithören; **l. to** zuhören (*dat*); (*a thing*) horchen auf (*acc*); (*obey*) gehorchen (*dat*); (*take advice from*) hören auf (*acc*); **l. to reason** auf e-n Rat hören; **l. to the radio** Radio hören

listener ['lɪsənər] s Zuhörer –in mf;
(rad) Rundfunkhörer –in mf
lis'tening adj Abhör-, Horch–
lis'tening post' s Horchposten m
listless ['lɪstlɪs] adj lustlos
list' price' s Listenpreis m
litany ['lɪtəni] s (& fig) Litanei f
liter ['litər] s Liter m & n
literacy ['lɪtərəsi] s Kenntnis f des
Lesens und Schreibens
literal ['lɪtərəl] adj buchstäblich; (person) pedantisch; **l. sense** wörtlicher
Sinn m
literally ['lɪtərəli] adv buchstäblich
literary ['lɪtə‚reri] adj literarisch; **l.
language** Literatursprache f; **l. reference** Schrifttumsangabe f
literate ['lɪtərɪt] adj des Lesens und
des Schreibens kundig; (educated)
gebildet || s Gebildete mf
literati [‚lɪtɪ'rɑti] spl Literaten pl
literature ['lɪtərət/ər] s Literatur f;
(com) Drucksachen pl
lithe [laɪð] adj gelenkig
lithia ['lɪθɪ·ə] s (chem) Lithiumoxyd n
lithium ['lɪθɪ·əm] s Lithium n
lithograph ['lɪθə‚græf] s Steindruck m
|| tr lithographieren
lithographer [lɪ'θɑgrəfər] s Lithograph
–in mf
lithography [lɪ'θɑgrəfi] s Steindruck
m, Lithographie f
Lithuania [‚lɪθu'enɪ·ə] s Litauen n
Lithuanian [‚lɪθu'enɪ·ən] adj litauisch || s Litauer –in mf; (language)
Litauisch n
litigant ['lɪtɪgənt] adj prozessierend;
the l. parties die streitenden Parteien
|| s Prozeßführer –in mf
litigate ['lɪtɪ‚get] tr prozessieren gegen
|| intr prozessieren
litigation [‚lɪtɪ'ge/ən] s Rechsstreit m
lit'mus pa'per ['lɪtməs] s Lackmuspapier n
litter ['lɪtər] s (stretcher) Tragbahre
f; (bedding for animals) Streu f; (of
pigs, dogs) Wurf m; (trash) herumliegender Abfall m; (hist) Sänfte f ||
tr verunreinigen || intr (bear young)
werfen; (strew litter) Abfälle wegwerfen; **no littering!** das Wegwerfen
von Abfällen ist verboten!
lit'terbug' s—**don't be a l.** wirf keine
Abfälle weg
little ['lɪtəl] adj (in size) klein; (in
amount) wenig || adv wenig; **l. by l.**
nach und nach || s—**after a l.** nach
kurzer Zeit; **a l.** ein wenig, ein
bißchen; **make l. of** wenig halten von
Lit'tle Bear' s Kleiner Bär m
Lit'tle Dip'per s Kleiner Wagen m,
Kleiner Bär m
lit'tle fin'ger s kleiner Finger m
lit'tle peo'ple s kleine Leute pl; (myth)
Heinzelmännchen pl
Lit'tle Red Rid'inghood' s Rotkäppchen n
lit'tle slam' s (cards) Klein-Schlemm
m
liturgic(al) [lɪ'tʌrdʒɪk(əl)] adj liturgisch
liturgy ['lɪtərdʒi] s Liturgie f

livable ['lɪvəbəl] adj (place) wohnlich;
(life) erträglich
live [laɪv] adj lebendig; (coals) glühend; (ammunition) scharf; (elec)
stromführend; (rad, telv) live; **l. program** Originalsendung f || adv (rad,
telv) live || [lɪv] tr leben; (a life)
führen; **l. down** durch einwandfreien
Lebenswandel vergessen machen; **l.
it up** (coll) das Leben genießen; **l.
out** (survive) überleben || intr leben;
(reside) wohnen; (reside temporarily)
sich aufhalten; **l. and learn!** man
lernt nie aus!; **l. for the moment** in
den Tag hineinleben; **l. high off the
hog** in Saus und Braus leben; **l. off
s.o.** j–m auf der Tasche liegen; **l. on**
(subsist on) sich nähren von; (continue to live) fortleben; **l. through**
durchmachen; **l. to see** erleben; **l.
up to** gerecht werden (dat)
livelihood ['laɪvlɪ‚hud] s Lebensunterhalt m
liveliness ['laɪvlɪnɪs] s Lebhaftigkeit f
livelong ['lɪv‚lɔŋ] adj—**all the l. day**
den lieben langen Tag
lively ['laɪvli] adj lebhaft; (street) belebt
liven ['laɪvən] tr aufmuntern || intr
munter werden
liver ['lɪvər] s (anat) Leber f
liverwurst ['lɪvər‚wʌrst] s Leberwurst f
livery ['lɪvəri] s Livree f
liv'ery sta'ble s Mietstallung f
live' show' [laɪv] s Originalsendung f,
Livesendung f
livestock ['laɪv‚stɑk] s Viehstand m
live' wire' [laɪv] s geladener Draht m;
(coll) energiegeladener Mensch m
livid ['lɪvɪd] adj bleifarben; (enraged)
wütend
liv'ing adj (alive) lebend, lebendig; (for
living) Wohn–; **not a l. soul** keine
Mutterseele f || s Unterhalt m; **good
l.** Wohlleben n; **make a l.** (as) sein
Auskommen haben (als); **what do
you do for a l.?** wie verdienen Sie
Ihren Lebensunterhalt?
liv'ing accommoda'tions spl Unterkunft f
liv'ing be'ing s Lebewesen n
liv'ing condi'tions spl Lebensbedingungen pl
liv'ing expens'es spl Unterhaltskosten
pl
liv'ing quar'ters spl Unterkunft f
liv'ing room' s Wohnzimmer n
liv'ing-room set' (or suite') s Polstergarnitur f
liv'ing space' s Lebensraum m
liv'ing wage' s Existenzminimum n
lizard ['lɪzərd] s Eidechse f
load [lod] s Last f, Belastung f; (in a
truck) Fuhre f; **get a l. of that!** schau
dir das mal an!; **have a l. on** (sl)
einen sitzen haben; **loads of** (coll)
Mengen von; **that's a l. off my mind**
mir ist dabei ein Stein vom Herzen
gefallen || tr (a truck, gun) laden;
(cargo on a ship) einladen; (with
work) überladen; (with worries) belasten; **l. down** belasten; **l. the cam-**

era den Film einlegen; **l. up** aufladen || *intr* das Gewehr laden

load'ed *adj* (*rifle*) scharf geladen; (*dice*) falsch; (*question*) verfänglich; (*very rich*) (sl) steinreich; (*drunk*) (sl) sternhagelvoll; **fully l.** (aut) mit allen Schikanen

loader ['lodər] *s* (*worker*) Ladearbeiter –in *mf*; (*device*) Verladevorrichtung *f*

load'ing *s* Ladung *f*, Verladung *f*

load'ing plat'form *s* Laderampe *f*

load'ing ramp' *s* Laderampe *f*

load' lim'it *s* Tragfähigkeit *f*; (elec) Belastungsgrenze *f*

load'stone' *s* Magneteisenstein *m*

loaf [lof] *s* (**loaves** [lovz]) Laib *m* || *intr* faulenzen; **l. around** herumlungern

loafer ['lofər] *s* Faulenzer *m*

loaf'ing *s* Faulenzen *n*

loam [lom] *s* Lehm *m*

loamy ['lomi] *adj* lehmig

loan [lon] *s* Anleihe *f*, Darlehe(n) *n* || *tr* (ver)leihen, borgen; **l. out** leihen

loan' com'pany *s* Leihanstalt *f*

loan' shark' *s* (coll) Wucherer *m*

loan' word' *s* Lehnwort *n*

loath [loθ] *adj*—**be l. to** (*inf*) abgeneigt sein zu (*inf*)

loathe [loð] *tr* verabscheuen

loathing ['loðɪŋ] *s* (**for**) Abscheu *m* (vor *dat*)

loathsome ['loðsəm] *adj* abscheulich

lob [lab] *s* (tennis) Lobball *m* || *v* (*pret & pp* **lobbed;** *ger* **lobbing**) *tr* lobben, hochschlagen

lob•by ['labi] *s* (*of a hotel or theater*) Vorhalle *f*, Foyer *n*; (pol) Interessengruppe *f* || *v* (*pret & pp* **-bied**) *intr* antichambrieren

lob'bying *s* Beeinflussung *f* von Abgeordneten, Lobbying *n*

lobbyist ['labi‑ɪst] *s* Lobbyist –in *mf*

lobe [lob] *s* (anat) Lappen *m*

lobster ['labstər] *s* Hummer *m*; **red as a l.** (fig) krebsrot

local ['lokal] *adj* örtlich, Orts–; (*produce*) heimisch || *s* (*group*) Ortsgruppe *f*; (rr) Personenzug *m*

lo'cal anesthe'sia *s* Lokalanästhese *f*

lo'cal call' *s* (telp) Ortsgespräch *n*

lo'cal col'or *s* Lokalkolorit *n*

lo'cal deliv'ery *s* Ortszustellung *f*

locale [lo'kæl] *s* Ort *m*

lo'cal gov'ernment *s* Gemeindeverwaltung *f*

locality [lo'kælɪti] *s* Örtlichkeit *f*

localize ['lokə‚laɪz] *tr* lokalisieren

lo'cal news' *s* Lokalnachrichten *pl*

lo'cal pol'itics *s* Kommunalpolitik *f*

lo'cal show'er *s* Strichregen *m*

lo'cal tax' *s* Gemeindesteuer *f*

lo'cal time' *s* Ortszeit *f*

lo'cal traf'fic *s* Nahverkehr *m*, Ortsverkehr *m*

locate ['loket], ['loket] *tr* (*find*) ausfindig machen; (*a ship, aircraft*) orten; (*the trouble*) finden, feststellen; (*set up, e.g., an office*) errichten; **be located** liegen, gelegen sein || *intr* sich niederlassen

location [lo'keʃən] *s* Lage *f*; **on l.** (cin) auf Außenaufnahme

lock [lak] *s* Schloß *n*; (*of hair*) Locke *f*; (*of a canal*) Schleuse *f*; **l., stock, and barrel** mit allem Drum und Dran; **under l. and key** unter Verschluß || *tr* zusperren; (*arms*) verschränken; **l. in** einsperren; **l. out** aussperren; **l. up** (*a house*) zusperren; (*imprison*) einsperren || *intr* (*said of a lock*) zuschnappen; (*said of brakes*) sperren; **l. together** (*said of bumpers*) sich ineinander verhaken

locker ['lakər] *s* (*as in a gym or barracks*) Spind *m & n*; (*for luggage*) Schließfach *n*

lock'er room' *s* Umkleideraum *m*

locket ['lakɪt] *s* Medaillon *n*

lock'jaw' *s* Maulsperre *f*

lock' nut' *s* Gegenmutter *f*

lock'out' *s* Aussperrung *f*

lock'smith' *s* Schlosser –in *mf*

lock'smith shop' *s* Schlosserei *f*

lock' step' *s* Marschieren *n* in dicht geschlossenen Gliedern

lock' stitch' *s* Kettenstich *m*

lock'up' *s* (coll) Gefängnis *n*

lock' wash'er *s* Sicherungsring *m*

locomotion [‚lokə'moʃən] *s* (*act*) Fortbewegung *f*; (*power*) Fortbewegungsfähigkeit *f*

locomotive [‚lokə'motɪv] *s* Lokomotive *f*

lo•cus ['lokəs] *s* (**-ci** [saɪ]) Ort *m*; (geom) geometrischer Ort *m*

locust ['lokəst] *s* (*black locust*) (bot) Robinie *f*; (*carob*) (bot) Johannisbrotbaum *m*; (*Cicada*) (ent) Zikade *f*

lode [lod] *s* (min) Gang *m*

lode'star' *s* Leitstern *m*

lodge [ladʒ] *s* (*of Masons*) Loge *f*; (*for hunting*) Jagdhütte *f*; (*for weekending*) Wochenendhäuschen *n*; (*summer house*) Sommerhäuschen *n* || *tr* unterbringen; **l. a complaint** e–e Beschwerde einreichen || *intr* wohnen; (*said of an arrow, etc.*) steckenbleiben

lodger ['ladʒər] *s* Untermieter –in *mf*

lodg'ing *s* Unterkunft *f*; **lodgings** Logis *n*

loft [lɔft] *s* Speicher *m*; (*for hay*) Heuboden *m*; (*of a church*) Chor *m*; (*of a golf club*) Hochschlaghaltung *f* || *tr* (*a golf club*) in Hochschlaghaltung bringen; (*a golf ball*) hochschlagen

loftiness ['lɔftɪnɪs] *s* Erhabenheit *f*

lofty ['lɔfti] *adj* (*style*) erhaben; (*high*) hochragend; (*elevated in rank*) gehoben; (*haughty*) anmaßend

log [lɔg] *s* (*trunk*) Baumstamm *m*; (*for the fireplace*) Holzklotz *m*; (*record book*) Tagebuch *n*; (aer, naut) Log *n*; **sleep like a log** wie ein Klotz schlafen || *v* (*pret & pp* **logged;** *ger* **logging**) *tr* (*trees*) fällen und abästen; (*cut into logs*) in Klötze schneiden; (*an area*) abholzen; (*enter into a logbook*) in das Logbuch eintragen; (*traverse*) zurücklegen

logarithm ['lɔgə‚rɪðəm] *s* Logarithmus *m*

log′book′ s (aer, naut) Logbuch n
log′ cab′in s Blockhaus n, Blockhütte f
logger [′lɔgər] s Holzfäller m
log′gerhead′ s—at **loggerheads** auf Kriegsfuß
log′ging s Holzarbeit f
logic [′lɑdʒɪk] s Logik f
logical [′lɑdʒɪkəl] adj logisch
logician [loˈdʒɪʃən] s Logiker –in mf
logistic(al) [loˈdʒɪstɪk(əl)] adj logistisch
logistics [loˈdʒɪstɪks] s Logistik f
log′jam′ s aufgestaute Baumstämme pl; (fig) völlige Stockung f
log′wood′ s Kampescheholz n
loin [lɔɪn] s (of beef) Lendenstück n; (anat) Lende f; gird up one's loins (fig) sich rüsten
loin′cloth′ s Lendentuch n
loin′ end′ s (of pork) Rippenstück n
loiter [′lɔɪtər] tr—l. away vertrödeln ‖ intr trödeln; (hang around) herumlungern
loiterer [′lɔɪtərər] s Bummler –in mf
loi′tering s Trödelei f; no l. Herumlungern verboten!
loll [lɑl] intr sich bequem ausstrecken
lollipop [′lɑlɪ‚pɑp] s Lutschbonbon m & n
Lombardy [′lɑmbərdi] s die Lombardei
London [′lʌndən] adj Londoner ‖ s London n
Londoner [′lʌndənər] s Londoner –in mf
lone [lon] adj (sole) alleinig; (solitary) einzelstehend
loneliness [′lonlɪnɪs] s Einsamkeit f
lonely [′lonli] adj einsam; become l. vereinsamen
loner [′lonər] s Einzelgänger m
lonesome [′lonsəm] adj einsam; be l. for sich sehnen nach
lone′ wolf′ s (fig) Einzelgänger m
long [lɔŋ] adj (longer [′lɔŋgər]; longest [′lɔŋgɪst]) lang; (way, trip) weit; (detour) groß; a l. time lange; a l. time since schon lange her, daß; in the l. run auf die Dauer ‖ adv lange; as l. as so lange wie; but not for l. aber nicht lange; l. after lange nach; l. ago vor langer Zeit; l. live ...! es lebe ...!; l. since längst; so l.! bis dann! ‖ intr—l. for sich sehnen nach; l. to (inf) sich danach sehnen zu (inf)
long′boat′ s Pinasse f
long′ dis′tance s (telp) Ferngespräch n; call l. ein Ferngespräch anmelden
long′-dis′tance adj (sport) Langstrecken-
long′-dis′tance call′ s Ferngespräch n
long′-dis′tance flight′ s Langstreckenflug m
long′-drawn′-out′ adj ausgedehnt; (story) langatmig
longevity [lɑnˈdʒɛvɪti] s Langlebigkeit f
long′ face′ s langes Gesicht n
long′hair′ adj (fig) intellektuell ‖ s (fig) Intellektueller m; (mus) (coll) konservativer Musiker m
long′hand′ s Langschrift f; in l. mit der Hand geschrieben

long′ing adj sehnsüchtig ‖ s (for) Sehnsucht f (nach)
longitude [′lɑndʒɪ‚t(j)ud] s Länge f
longitudinal [‚lɑndʒɪˈt(j)udɪnəl] adj Longitudinal-
long′ jump′ s Weitsprung m
long-lived [′lɔŋ′laɪvd] adj langlebig
long′-play′ing rec′ord s Langspielplatte f
long′-range′ adj (plan) auf lange Sicht; (aer) Langstrecken-
long′shore′man s (–men) Hafenarbeiter m
long′ shot′ s (coll) riskante Wette f; by a l. bei weitem
long′stand′ing adj althergebracht, alt
long′-suf′fering adj langmütig
long′ suit′ s (fig) Stärke f; (cards) lange Farbe f
long′-term′ adj langfristig
long-winded [′lɔŋ ′wɪndɪd] adj langatmig
look [lʊk] s (glance) Blick m; (appearance) Aussehen n; (expression) Ausdruck m; from the looks of things wie die Sache aussieht; give a second l. sich [dat] genauer ansehen; have a l. around Umschau halten; have a l. at s.th. sich [dat] etw ansehen; I don't like the looks of it die Sache gefällt mir nicht; looks pl Aussehen n; new l. verändertes Aussehen n; (latest style) neueste Mode f; take a l. at s.th. sich [dat] etw ansehen ‖ tr—he looks his age man sieht ihm sein Alter an; l. one's best sich in bester Verfassung zeigen; l. one's last at zum letzten Mal ansehen; l. s.o. in the eye j–m in die Augen sehen; l. s.o. over j–n mustern; l. s.th. over etw (über)prüfen (or durchsehen); l. up (e.g., a word) nachschlagen; (e.g., a friend) aufsuchen; l. up and down von oben bis unten mustern ‖ intr schauen; (appear, seem) aussehen; l. after (e.g., children) betreuen; (a household, business) besorgen; (a departing person) nachblicken (dat); l. ahead vorausschauen; l. around (for) sich [dat] umsehen (nach); l. at anschauen; l. back (on) zurücksehen (auf acc); l. down herabsehen; (cast the eyes down) die Augen niederschlagen; l. down on herabsehen auf (acc); (in contempt) über die Achseln ansehen; l. for suchen; (e.g., a criminal) fahnden nach; l. forward to sich freuen auf (acc); l. hard at scharf ansehen; l. into (a mirror, the future) blicken in (acc); (a matter) nachgehen (dat); l. like gleichen (dat); (e.g., rain) aussehen nach; l. on zuschauen; l. on s.o. as j–n betrachten als; l. out aufpassen; l. out for ausgehen nach; l. out on (a view) hinausgehen auf (acc); l. over hinwegsehen über (acc); l. sharp! jetzt aber hoppla!; l. through (e.g., a window) blicken durch; (s.o. or s.o.'s motives) durchschauen; l. up (raise one's gaze) aufschauen; l. up to s.o. zu j–m hinaufsehen; **things**

are beginning to l. up es wird langsam besser; **things don't l. so good for** est steht übel mit; **what does he l. like?** wie sieht er aus?

look'ing glass' s Spiegel m

look'out' s (watchman) Wachposten m; (observation point) Ausguck m; (matter of concern) Sache f; **be a l.** Schmiere stehen; **be on the l. (for)** Auschau halten (nach)

look'out man' s—**be the l.** Schmiere stehen

look'out tow'er s Aussichtsturm m

loom [lum] s Webstuhl m || intr undeutlich und groß auftauchen; **l. large** von großer Bedeutung scheinen

loon [lun] s (orn) Taucher m

loony ['luni] adj verrückt; **be l.** spinnen

loop [lup] s Schleife f, Schlinge f; (e.g., on a dress for a hook) Öse f; (aer) Looping m; **do a l.** (aer) e-n Looping drehen || tr schlingen || intr Schlingen (or Schleifen) bilden

loop'hole' s Guckloch n; (in a fortification) Schießscharte f; (in a law) Lücke f

loose [lus] adj locker, los; (wobbly) wackelig; (morally) locker, unsolid; (unpacked) unverpackt; (translation) frei; (interpretation) dehnbar; (dress, tongue) lose; (skin) schlaff; **l. connection** (elec) Wackelkontakt m || adv—**break l.** (from an enclosure) ausbrechen; (e.g., from a hitching) sich losmachen; (said of a storm, hell) losbrechen; **come l.** losgehen; **cut l.** (act up) (coll) außer Rand und Band geraten; **turn l.** befreien; **work l.** sich lockern; (said of a button) abgehen; (said of a brick, stone, shoestring) sich lösen || s—**on the l.** ungehemmt, frei || tr (a boat) losmachen; (a knot) lösen

loose' change' s Kleingeld n

loose' end' s (fig) unerledigte Kleinigkeit f; **at loose ends** im ungewissen

loose'-leaf note'book s Loseblattbuch n

loosen ['lusən] tr lockern, locker machen || intr locker werden

looseness ['lusnıs] s Lockerheit f

loot [lut] s Beute f || tr erbeuten; (plunder) plündern; (e.g., art treasures) verschleppen

lop [lap] v (pret & pp lopped; ger lopping) tr—**lop off** abhacken

lope [lop] s Trab m || intr—**l. along** in großen Schritten laufen

lop'sid'ed adj schief; (score) einseitig

loquacious [lo'kweʃəs] adj geschwätzig

lord [lord] s Herr m; (Brit) Lord m; **Lord** Herrgott m || tr—**l. it over** sich als Herr aufspielen über (acc)

lordly ['lordli] adj würdig; (haughty) hochmütig

Lord's' Day' s Tag m des Herrn

lord'ship' s Herrschaft f

Lord's' Prayer' s Vaterunser n

Lord's' Sup'per s heiliges Abendmahl n

lore [lor] s Kunde f; (traditional wisdom) überlieferte Kunde f

lorry ['lɔri] s (Brit) Lastkraftwagen m

lose [luz] v (pret & pp lost [lɔst]) tr verlieren; (several minutes, as a clock does) zurückbleiben; (in betting) verwetten; (in gambling) verspielen; (the page in a book) verblättern; **l. one's way** sich verirren; (on foot) sich verlaufen; (by car) sich verfahren || intr verlieren; (sport) geschlagen werden; **l. to** (sport) unterliegen (dat)

loser ['luzər] s Unterlegene mf; **be the l.** mit langer Nase abziehen

los'ing adj verlierend; (com) verlustbringend || **losings** spl Verluste pl

los'ing game' s aussichtsloses Spiel n

loss [lɔs] s (in) Verlust m (an dat); **at a l.** in Verlegenheit; (com) mit Verlust; **be at a l. for words** nach Worten suchen; **inflict l. on s.o.** j-m Schaden zufügen; **l. of appetite** Appetitlosigkeit f; **l. of blood** Blutverlust m; **l. of face** Blamage f; **l. of life** Verluste pl an Menschenleben; **l. of memory** Gedächtnisverlust m; **l. of sight** Erblindung f; **l. of time** Zeitverlust m; **straight l.** Barverlust m

lost [lɔst] adj verloren; **be l.** (said of a thing) verlorengehen; (not know one's way) sich verirrt haben; **be l. on s.o.** auf j-n keinen Eindruck machen; **get l.** in Verlust geraten; **get l.!** hau ab!; **l. in thought** in Gedanken versunken

lost'-and-found' depart'ment s Fundbüro n

lost' cause' s aussichtslose Sache f

lot [lat] s (fate) Los n, Schicksal n; (in a drawing) Los n; (portion of land) Grundstück n; (cin) Filmgelände n; (com) Posten m, Partie f; **a lot** viel, sehr; **a lot of** (or **lots of**) viel(e); **the lot** das Ganze

lotion ['loʃən] s Wasser n

lottery ['latəri] s Lotterie f

lot'tery tick'et s Lotterielos n

lotto ['lato] s Lotto n

lotus ['lotəs] s Lotos m

loud [laud] adj laut; (colors) schreiend

loud-mouthed ['laud,mauðd] adj laut

loud'speak'er s Lautsprecher m

lounge [laundʒ] s Aufenthaltsraum m || intr sich recken; **l. around** herumlungern

lounge' chair' s Klubsessel m

lounge' liz'ard s (sl) Salonlöwe m

louse [laus] s (lice [lais]) Laus f; (sl) Sauhund m || tr—**l. up** (sl) versauen

lousy ['lauzi] adj verlaust; (sl) lausig; **l. with** (people) wimmelnd von; **l. with money** stinkreich

lout [laut] s Lümmel m

louver ['luvər] s Jalousie f

lovable ['lʌvəbəl] adj liebenswürdig

love [lʌv] adj Liebes– || s (for, of) Liebe f (zu); **be in l. with** verliebt sein in (acc); **for the l. of God** um Gottes willen; **fall (madly) in l. with** sich (heftig) verlieben in (acc); **Love** (at the end of a letter) herzliche Grüße; **l. at first sight** Liebe f auf den ersten Blick; **make l. to** herzen;

(sl) geschlechtlich verkehren mit; **not for l. or money** nicht für Gold und gute Worte; **there's no l. lost between them** sie schätzen sich nicht || *tr* lieben; (*like*) gern haben; **l. to dance** sehr gern tanzen

love′ affair′ *s* Liebeshandel *m*, Liebesverhältnis *n*

love′birds′ *spl* (coll) Unzertrennlichen *pl*

love′ child′ *s* Kind *n* der Liebe

love′ feast′ *s* (eccl) Liebesmahl *n*

love′ game′ *s* (tennis) Nullpartie *f*

love′ knot′ *s* Liebesschleife *f*

loveless [′lʌvlɪs] *adj* lieblos

love′ let′ter *s* Liebesbrief *m*

lovelorn [′lʌv‚lɔrn] *adj* vor Liebe vergehend

lovely [′lʌvli] *adj* lieblich

love′-mak′ing *s* Geschlechtsverkehr *m*

love′ match′ *s* Liebesheirat *f*

love′ po′em *s* Liebesgedicht *n*

love′ po′tion *s* Liebestrank *m*

lover [′lʌvər] *s* Liebhaber *m*; **lovers** Liebespaar *n*

love′ scene′ *s* Liebesszene *f*

love′ seat′ *s* Sofasessel *n*

love′sick′ *adj* liebeskrank

love′ song′ *s* Liebeslied *n*

love′ to′ken *s* Liebespfand *n*

lov′ing liebevoll; **Your l. . . .** Dich liebender . . .

lov′ing-kind′ness *s* Herzensgüte *f*

low [lo] *adj* (*building, mountain, forehead, birth, wages, estimate, prices, rent*) niedrig; (*number*) nieder; (*altitude, speed*) gering; (*not loud*) leise; (*vulgar*) gemein; (*grades, company*) schlecht; (*fever*) leicht; (*pulse, pressure*) schwach; (*ground*) tiefgelegen; (*bow, voice*) tief; (*almost empty*) fast leer; (*supplies, funds*) knapp; **be low** (*said of the sun, water*) niedrigstehen; **be low in funds** knapp bei Kasse sein; **feel low** niedergeschlagen sein; **have a low opinion of** e–e geringe Meinung haben von || *adv* niedrig; **lay low** über den Haufen werfen; **lie low** sich versteckt halten; (*bide one's time*) abwarten; **run low** knapp werden; **sing low** tief singen; **sink low** tief sinken || *s* (*low point*) (fig) Tiefstand *m*; (meteor) Tief *n* || *intr* muhen, brüllen

low′ blow′ *s* (box) Tiefschlag *m*

low′born′ *adj* von niederer Herkunft

low′brow′ *s* Spießbürger *m*

low′-cost hous′ing *s* sozial geförderter Wohnungsbau *m*

Low′ Coun′tries, the *spl* die Niederlande

low′-cut′ *adj* tiefausgeschnitten

low′-down′ *adj* schurkisch || *s* (*unadorned facts*) unverblümte Wahrheit *f*; (*inside information*) Geheimnachrichten *pl*

lower [′lo·ər] *comp adj* untere; (*e.g., deck, house, jaw, lip*) Unter– || *tr* herunterlassen; (*the eyes, voice, water level, temperature*) senken; (*prices*) herabsetzen; (*a flag, sail*) streichen; (*lifeboats*) aussetzen; **l.**

oneself sich herablassen || [′laʊ·ər] *intr* finster blicken; **l. at** finster anblicken

low′er ab′domen [′lo·ər] *s* Unterbauch *m*

low′er berth′ [′lo·ər] *s* untere Koje *f*

low′er case′ [′lo·ər] *s* Kleinbuchstaben *pl*

lower-case [′lo·ər′kes] *adj* klein

low′er course′ [′lo·ər] *s* (*of a river*) Unterlauf *m*

low′er mid′dle class′ [′lo·ər] *s* Kleinbürgertum *n*

lowermost [′lo·ər‚most] *adj* niedrigste

low′er world′ [′lo·ər] *s* Unterwelt *f*

low′-fly′ing *adj* tieffliegend

low′ fre′quency *s* Niederfrequenz *f*

low′-fre′quency *adj* Niederfrequenz–

low′ gear′ *s* erster Gang *m*

low′-grade′ *adj* minderwertig

low′ing *s* Gebrüll *n*

lowland [′loland] *s* Flachland *n*; **Lowlands** (*in Scotland*) Unterland *n*

low′ lev′el *s* Tiefstand *m*

low′-lev′el attack′ *s* Tiefangriff *m*

low′-lev′el flight′ *s* Tiefflug *m*

lowly [′loli] *adj* bescheiden; (*humble in spirit*) niederträchtig

low′-ly′ing *adj* tiefliegend

Low′ Mass′ *s* stille Messe *f*

low′-mind′ed *adj* niedrig gesinnt

low′ neck′ *s* (*of a dress*) Ausschnitt *m*

low′-necked′ *adj* tief ausgeschnitten

low′-pitched′ *adj* (*sound*) tief; (*roof*) mit geringer Neigung

low′-pres′sure *adj* Tiefdruck–, Unterdruck–

low′-priced′ *adj* billig

low′ shoe′ *s* Halbschuh *m*

low′-speed′ *adj* mit geringer Geschwindigkeit; (*film*) unempfindlich

low′-spir′ited *adj* niedergeschlagen

low′ spir′its *spl* Niedergeschlagenheit *f*; **be in l.** niedergeschlagen sein

low′ tide′ *s* Ebbe *f*; (fig) Tiefstand *m*

low′ wa′ter *s* Niedrigwasser *n*

low′-wa′ter mark′ *s* (fig) Tiefpunkt *m*

loyal [′lɔɪ·əl] *adj* treu, loyal

loyalist [′lɔɪ·əlɪst] *s* Regierungstreue *mf*

loyalty [′lɔɪ·əlti] *s* Treue *f*

lozenge [′lazɪndʒ] *s* Pastille *f*

LP [′el′pi] *s* (trademark) (**long-playing record**) Langspielplatte *f*

Ltd. *abbr* (Brit) (**Limited**) Gesellschaft *f* mit beschränkter Haftung

lubricant [′lubrɪkənt] *s* Schmiermittel *n*

lubricate [′lubrɪ‚ket] *tr* (ab)schmieren

lubrication [‚lubrɪ′keʃən] *s* Schmierung *f*

lucerne [lu′sʌrn] *s* (bot) Luzerne *f*; **Lucerne** Luzern *n*

lucid [′lusɪd] *adj* (*clear*) klar, deutlich; (*bright*) hell

luck [lʌk] *s* Glück *n*; (*chance*) Zufall *m*; **as l. would have it** wie es der Zufall wollte; **be down on one's l.** an seinem Glück verzagen; **be in l.** Glück haben; **be out of l.** Unglück haben; **dumb l.** (coll) Sauglück *n*; **have tough l.** (coll) Pech haben;

rotten l. (coll) Saupech *n;* **try one's l.** sein Glück versuchen; **with l. you should win** wenn Sie Glück haben, werden Sie gewinnen

luckily [ˈlʌkɪli] *adv* zum Glück

luckless [ˈlʌklɪs] *adj* glücklos

lucky [ˈlʌki] *adj* glücklich; **be l.** Glück haben; **l. dog** (coll) Glückspilz *m;* **l. penny** Glückspfennig *m*

luck'y shot' *s* Glückstreffer *m*

lucrative [ˈlukrətɪv] *adj* gewinnbringend

ludicrous [ˈludɪkrəs] *adj* lächerlich

lug [lʌg] *s (pull, tug)* Ruck *m; (lout)* (sl) Lümmel *m; (elec)* Öse *f* || *v (pret & pp* **lugged;** *ger* **lugging)** *tr* schleppen

luggage [ˈlʌgɪdʒ] *s* Gepäck *n;* **excess l.** Mehrgepäck *n;* **piece of l.** Gepäckstück *n*

lug'gage car'rier *s* Gepäckträger *m*

lug'gage compart'ment *s* (aer) Frachtraum *m*

lug'gage rack' *s* Gepäckablage *f; (on the roof of a car)* Dachgepäckträger *m*

lug'gage receipt' *s* Aufgabeschein *m*

lugubrious [luˈg(j)ubrɪ·əs] *adj* tieftraurig

lukewarm [ˈluk‚wɔrm] *adj* lau, lauwarm

lull [lʌl] *s* Windstille *f;* (com) Flaute *f* || *tr* einlullen; *(e.g., fears)* beschwichtigen; **l. to sleep** einschläfern || *intr* nachlassen

lullaby [ˈlʌlə‚baɪ] *s* Wiegenlied *n*

lumbago [lʌmˈbego] *s* Hexenschluß *m*

lumber [ˈlʌmbər] *s* Bauholz *n* || *intr* sich schwerfällig fortbewegen

lum'berjack' *s* Holzfäller *m*

lum'ber·man' *s* (**-men'**) *(dealer)* Holzhändler *m; (lumberjack)* Holzfäller *m*

lum'beryard' *s* Holzplatz *m*

luminary [ˈlumɪ‚neri] *s* Leuchtkörper *m;* (fig) Leuchte *f*

luminescent [‚lumɪˈnesənt] *adj* lumineszierend

luminous [ˈlumɪnəs] *adj* leuchtend, Leucht-

lu'minous di'al *s* Leuchtzifferblatt *n*

lu'minous paint' *s* Leuchtfarbe *f*

lummox [ˈlʌməks] *s* Lümmel *m*

lump [lʌmp] *s (e.g., of clay)* Klumpen *m; (on the body)* Beule *f;* **have a l. in one's throat** e–n Kloß (or Knödel) im Hals haben; **l. of sugar** Würfel *m* Zucker || *tr*—**l. together** (fig) zusammenwerfen

lumpish [ˈlʌmpɪʃ] *adj* klumpig

lump' sug'ar *s* Würfelzucker *m*

lump' sum' *s* Pauschalbetrag *m*

lumpy [ˈlʌmpi] *adj* klumpig; *(sea)* bewegt

lunacy [ˈlunəsi] *s* Irrsinn *m*

lu'nar eclipse' [ˈlunər] *s* Mondfinsternis *f*

lu'nar land'ing *s* Mondlandung *f*

lu'nar mod'ule *s* (rok) Mondfähre *f*

lu'nar year' *s* Mondjahr *n*

lunatic [ˈlunətɪk] *s* Irre *mf*

lu'natic asy'lum *s* Irrenhaus *n*

lu'natic fringe' *s* Extremisten *pl*

lunch [lʌntʃ] *s (at noon)* Mittagessen *n,* Lunch *m; (light meal)* Zwischenmahlzeit *f;* **eat l.** zu Mittag essen; **have** *(s.th.)* **for l.** zum Mittagessen haben || *intr* zu Mittag essen, lunchen

lunch' coun'ter *s* Theke *f*

luncheon [ˈlʌntʃən] *s* gemeinsames Mittagessen *n*

luncheonette [‚lʌntʃəˈnet] *s* Imbißstube *f*

lunch' hour' *s* Mittagsstunde *f*

lunch'room' *s* Imbißhalle *f*

lunch'time' *s* Mittagszeit *f*

lung [lʌŋ] *s* Lunge *f;* **at the top of one's lungs** aus voller Kehle

lunge [lʌndʒ] *s* Sprung *m* vorwärts; *(fencing)* Ausfall *m* || *tr (a horse)* an der Longe laufen lassen || *intr*— e–n Sprung vorwärts machen; *(with a sword)* (at) e–n Ausfall machen (gegen); **l.** at losstürzen auf *(acc)*

lurch [lʌrtʃ] *s* Torkeln *n,* Taumeln *n;* **leave in a l.** im Stich lassen || *intr* torkeln; *(said of a ship)* zur Seite rollen

lure [lʊr] *s* Köder *m* || *tr* ködern; (fig) verlocken; **l. away** weglocken

lurid [ˈlʊrɪd] *adj (light)* gespenstisch; *(sunset)* düsterrot; *(gruesome)* grausig; *(pallid)* fahl

lurk [lʌrk] *intr* lauern

luscious [ˈlʌʃəs] *adj* köstlich; **a l. doll** (coll) ein tolles Weib

lush [lʌʃ] *adj* üppig

lust [lʌst] *s* Wollust *f;* **(for)** Begierde *f* (nach) || *intr* **(after, for)** gieren (nach)

luster [ˈlʌstər] *s* Glanz *m; (e.g., chandelier)* Lüster *m*

lusterless [ˈlʌstərlɪs] *adj* matt

lus'terware' *s* Tongeschirr *n* mit Lüster

lustful [ˈlʌstfəl] *adj* lüstern, geil

lustrous [ˈlʌstrəs] *adj* glänzend

lusty [ˈlʌsti] *adj* kräftig

lute [lut] *s* Laute *f*

Lutheran [ˈluθərən] *adj* lutherisch || *s* Lutheraner –in *mf*

luxuriance [lʌgˈʒʊrɪ·əns] *s* Üppigkeit *f*

luxuriant [lʌgˈʒʊrɪ·ənt] *adj* üppig

luxuriate [lʌgˈʒʊrɪ‚et] *intr (thrive)* gedeihen; *(delight)* **(in)** schwelgen (in *dat*)

luxurious [lʌgˈʒʊrɪ·əs] *adj* luxuriös; **l. living** Prasserei *f*

luxury [ˈlʌgʒəri] *s* Extravaganz *f,* Luxus *m; (object of luxury)* Luxusartikel *m;* **live a life of l.** im vollen leben

lye [laɪ] *s* Lauge *f*

ly'ing *adj* lügenhaft || *s* Lügen *n*

ly'ing-in' hos'pital *s* Entbindungsanstalt *f*

lymph [lɪmf] *s* Lymphe *f*

lymphatic [lɪmˈfætɪk] *adj* lymphatisch

lynch [lɪntʃ] *tr* lynchen

lynch'ing *s* Lynchen *n*

lynch' law' *s* Lynchjustiz *f*

lynx [lɪŋks] *s* Luchs *m*

lynx'-eyed' *adj* luchsäugig

lyre [laɪr] s (mus) Leier f
lyric ['lɪrɪk] adj lyrisch; **l. poetry**
Lyrik f ‖ s lyrisches Gedicht n; (of a song) Text m

lyrical ['lɪrɪkəl] adj lyrisch
lyricism ['lɪrɪˌsɪzəm] s Lyrik f
lyricist ['lɪrɪsɪst] s (of a song) Texter –in mf; (poet) lyrischer Dichter m

M

M, m [ɛm] s dreizehnter Buchstabe des englischen Alphabets
ma [mɑ] s (coll) Mama f
ma'am [mæm] s (coll) gnädige Frau f
macadam [mə'kædəm] s Makadamdecke f
macadamize [mə'kædəˌmaɪz] tr makadamisieren
maca'dam road' s Straße f mit Makadamdecke
macaroni [ˌmækə'roni] spl Makkaroni pl
macaroon [ˌmækə'run] s Makrone f
macaw [mə'kɔ] s (orn) Ara m
mace [mes] s Stab m, Amtsstab m
mace'bear'er s Träger m des Amtsstabes
machination [ˌmækɪ'neʃən] s Intrige f; **machinations** Machenschaften pl
machine [mə'ʃin] s Maschine f; (pol) Apparat m; **by m.** maschinell ‖ tr spannabhebend formen
machine'-driv'en adj mit Maschinenantrieb
machine' gun' s Maschinengewehr n
machine'-gun' v (pret & pp –gunned; ger –gunning) tr unter Maschinengewehrfeuer nehmen
machine' gun'ner s Maschinengewehrschütze m
machine'-made' adj maschinell hergestellt
machinery [mə'ʃinəri] s (& fig) Maschinerie f
machine' screw' s Maschinenschraube f
machine' shop' s Maschinenhalle f
machine' tool' s Werkzeugmaschine f
machinist [mə'ʃinɪst] s (maker and repairer of machines) Maschinenbauer m; (machine operator) Maschinenschlosser –in mf
mackerel ['mækərəl] s Makrele f
mad [mæd] adj (madder; maddest) verrückt; (angry) böse; **be mad about** vernarrt sein in (acc); **be mad at** böse sein auf (acc); **drive mad** verrückt machen; **go mad** verrückt werden
madam ['mædəm] s gnädige Frau f; (of a brothel) (sl) Bordellmutter f
mad'cap' adj ausgelassen ‖ s Wildfang m
madden ['mædən] tr verrückt machen; (make angry) zornig machen
made'-to-or'der adj nach Maß angefertigt
made'-up' adj (story) erfunden; (artificial) künstlich; (with cosmetics) geschminkt

mad'house' s Irrenhaus n, Narrenhaus n
madly ['mædli] adv (coll) wahnsinnig
mad'man' s (–men') Verrückter m
madness ['mædnɪs] s Wahnsinn m
Madonna [mə'dɑnə] s Madonna f
maelstrom ['melstrəm] s (& fig) Strudel m
magazine [ˌmægə'zin] s (periodical) Zeitschrift f; (illustrated) Illustrierte f; (warehouse for munitions; cartridge container) Magazin n; (for a camera) Kassette f
magazine' rack' s Zeitschriftenständer m
Maggie ['mægi] s Gretchen n
maggot ['mægət] s Made f
Magi ['medʒaɪ] spl—**the three M.** (Bib) die drei Weisen pl aus dem Morgenland
magic ['mædʒɪk] adj (enchanting) zauberhaft; (trick, word, wand) Zauber– ‖ s Zauberkunst f
magician [mə'dʒɪʃən] s Zauberer –in mf
ma'gic lan'tern s Laterna magica f
magisterial [ˌmædʒɪs'tɪrɪəl] adj (of a magistrate) obrigkeitlich; (authoritative) autoritativ; (pompous) anmaßend
magistrate ['mædʒɪsˌtret] s Polizeirichter m
magnanimous [mæg'nænɪməs] adj großmütig
magnate ['mægnet] s Magnat m
magnesium [mæg'niziəm] s Magnesium n
magnet ['mægnɪt] s Magnet m
magnetic [mæg'nɛtɪk] adj magnetisch; (personality) fesselnd
magnetism ['mægnɪˌtɪzəm] s Magnetismus m; (fig) Anziehungskraft f
magnetize ['mægnɪˌtaɪz] tr magnetisieren
magnificence [mæg'nɪfɪsəns] s Pracht f
magnificent [mæg'nɪfɪsənt] adj prächtig
magnifier ['mægnɪˌfaɪ·ər] s (electron) Verstärker m
magni·fy ['mægnɪˌfaɪ] v (pret & pp –fied) tr vergrößern; (fig) übertreiben
mag'nifying glass' s Lupe f
magnitude ['mægnɪˌt(j)ud] s (& astr) Größe f
magno'lia tree' [mæg'nolɪ·ə] s Magnolia f
magpie ['mægˌpaɪ] s (& fig) Elster f
mahlstick ['mɑlˌstɪk] s Malerstock m

mahogany [mə'hɔgəni] *s* Mahagoni *n*
mahout [mə'haut] *s* Elefantentreiber *m*

maid [med] *s* Dienstmädchen *n*
maiden ['medən] *s* Jungfer *f;* (poet) Maid *f*
maid'enhair' *s* (bot) Jungfernhaar *n*
maid'enhead' *s* Jungfernhäutchen *n*
maid'enhood' *s* Jungfräulichkeit *f*
maidenly ['medənli] *adj* jungfräulich
maid'en name' *s* Mädchenname *m*
maid'en voy'age *s* Jungfernfahrt *f*
maid'-in-wait'ing *s* (maids-in-waiting) Hofdame *f*
maid' of hon'or *s* erste Brautjungfer *f*
maid'serv'ant *s* Dienstmädchen *n*
mail [mel] *adj* Post– ‖ *s* Post *f;* (*armor*) Kettenpanzer *m;* by m. brieflich; by return m. postwendend ‖ *tr* (*put into the mail*) aufgeben; (*send*) abschicken; m. to zuschicken (*dat*)
mail'bag' *s* Postsack *m*
mail'boat' *s* Postschiff *n*
mail'box' *s* Briefkasten *m*
mail' car'rier *s* Briefträger –in *mf*
mail' deliv'ery *s* Postzustellung *f*
mail' drop' *s* Briefeinwurf *m*
mailer ['melər] *s* (phot) Versandbeutel *m*
mail'ing *s* Absendung *f*
mail'ing list' *s* Postversandliste *f*
mail'ing per'mit *s* Zulassung *f* zum portofreien Versand
mail'man' *s* (-men') Briefträger *m*
mail' or'der *s* Bestellung *f* durch die Post
mail'-order house' *s* Versandhaus *n*
mail' plane' *s* Postflugzeug *n*
mail' train' *s* Postzug *m*
mail' truck' *s* Postauto *n*
main [mem] *tr* verstümmeln
main [men] *adj* Haupt– ‖ *s* Hauptleitung *f;* in the main hauptsächlich
main' clause' *s* (gram) Hauptsatz *m*
main' course' *s* Hauptgericht *n*
main' deck' *s* Hauptdeck *n*
main' floor' *s* Erdgeschoß *n*
mainland ['men‚lænd] *s* Festland *n*
main' line' *s* (rr) Hauptstrecke *f*
mainly ['menli] *adv* größtenteils
mainmast ['men‚mæst] *s* Großmast *m*
main' of'fice *s* Hauptbüro *n,* Zentrale *f*
main' point' *s* springender Punkt *m*
mainsail ['men‚sel] *s* Großsegel *n*
main'spring' *s* (horol & fig) Triebfeder *f*
main'stay' *s* (fig) Hauptstütze *f;* (naut) Großtag *n*
main' street' *s* Hauptstraße *f*
maintain [men'ten] *tr* aufrechterhalten; (*e.g., a family*) unterhalten; (*assert*) behaupten; (*one's reputation*) wahren; (*e.g., in good condition*) bewahren; (*order, silence*) halten; (*a road*) instand halten
maintenance ['mentinəns] *s* (*upkeep*) Instandhaltung *f;* (*support*) Unterhalt *m;* (*e.g., of an automobile*) Wardirektor *m*
maître d'hôtel [‚metrdo'tel] *s* (*head waiter*) Oberkellner *m;* (*owner*)

Hotelbesitzer *m;* (*manager*) Hoteltung *f*
majestic [mə'dʒestik] *adj* majestätisch
majesty ['mædʒisti] *s* Majestät *f*
major ['medʒər] *adj* Haupt–; (mus) –Dur ‖ *s* (educ) Hauptfach *n;* (mil) Major *m* ‖ *intr*–m. in als Hauptfach studieren
majordomo ['medʒər'domo] *s* Haushofmeister *m*
ma'jor gen'eral *s* Generalmajor *m*
majority [mə'dʒɔriti] *adj* Mehrheits– ‖ *s* Mehrheit *f;* (*full age*) Mündigkeit *f;* (mil) Majorsrang *m;* (parl) Stimmenmehrheit *f;* be in the m. in der Mehrheit sein; in the m. of cases in der Mehrzahl der Fälle; the m. of people die meisten Menschen
major'ity vote' *s* Mehrheitsbeschluß *m*
ma'jor league' *s* Oberliga *f*
make [mek] *s* Fabrikat *n,* Marke *f* ‖ *tr* machen; (*in a factory*) herstellen; (*cause*) lassen; (*force*) zwingen; (*clothes*) anfertigen; (*money*) verdienen; (*a reputation, name*) erwerben; (*a choice*) treffen; (*a confession*) ablegen; (*a report*) erstatten; (*plans*) schmieden; (*changes*) vornehmen; (*a movie*) drehen; (*contact*) herstellen; (*a meal*) (zu)bereiten; (*conditions*) stellen; (*rules, assertions*) aufstellen; (*a bet, compromise, peace*) schließen; (*excuses, requests, objections*) vorbringen; (*a protest*) erheben; (*a goal*) schießen (or erzielen); (*a comparison*) ziehen; (*a speech*) halten; (*e.g., a good father*) abgeben; (be able to fit through, e.g., a window*) gehen durch; (*e.g., a train, bus, destination*) erreichen; (*e.g., ten miles*) zurücklegen; (*a girl*) (sl) verführen; (arith) machen; m. ... (*s.o.*) believe weismachen (*dat*); m. into verarbeiten zu; m. of halten von; m. out (*e.g., writing*) entziffern; (*e.g., a person at a distance*) erkennen; (*understand*) kapieren; (*a blank or form*) ausfüllen; (*a check, receipt*) ausstellen; m. over to (jur) überschreiben auf (*acc*); m. s.o. out to be a liar j–n als Lügner hinstellen; m. s.th. of oneself es weit bringen; m. the most of ausnutzen; m. time Zeit gewinnen; m. time with (*a woman*) (coll) flirten mit; m. up (*e.g., a list*) zusammenstellen; (*a bill*) ausstellen; (*a sentence*) bilden; (*a story*) sich [*dat*] ausdenken; m. up one's mind (about) sich [*dat*] schlüssig werden (über *acc*); m. way! Platz da!; m. way for ausweichen vor (*dat*) ‖ *intr*–m. believe schauspielern; m. believe that nur so tun, als ob; m. do with sich behelfen mit; m. for los-steuern auf (*acc*); m. off with durchbrennen mit; m. out well gut auskommen; m. sure of sich vergewissern (*genit*); m. sure that vergewissern, daß; m. up (*after a quarrel*) sich versöhnen; m. up for (*past mistakes*) wieder gutmachen; (*lost time*) wieder einbringen

make′-believe′ *adj* Schein-, vorge-
täuscht || *s* Schein *m*, Mache *f*
maker [′mekər] *s* Hersteller –in *mf;*
Maker Schöpfer *m*
make′shift′ *adj* behelfsmäßig, Behelfs-
|| *s* Notbehelf *m*
make′-up′ *s* Aufmachung *f; (cosmetic)*
Make-up *n*, Schminke *f; (of a team)*
Aufstellung *f;* (theat) Maske *f;* (typ)
Umbruch *m;* **apply m.** sich schmin-
ken
make′weight′ *s* Gewichtszugabe *f*
mak′ing *s* Herstellung *f;* **be in the m.**
im Werden sein; **have the makings
of das Zeug haben zu; this is of his
own m.** dies ist sein eigenes Werk
maladjusted [͵mælə′dʒʌstɪd] *adj* unausgeglichen
maladroit [͵mælə′drɔɪt] *adj* ungeschickt
malady [′mælədi] *s* (& fig) Krankheit
f
malaise [mæ′lez] *s (physical)* Unwohl-
sein *n; (mental)* Unbehagen *n*
malaria [mə′lerɪ·ə] *s* Malaria *f*
Malaya [mə′le·ə] *s* Malaya *n*
Malaysia [mə′leʒɪ·ə] *s* Malaysia *n*
malcontent [′mælkən͵tent] *adj* unzufrieden *s* Unzufriedene *mf*
male [mel] *adj* männlich || *s* Mann *m;*
(bot) männliche Pflanze *f;* (zool)
Männchen *n*
malediction [͵mælɪ′dɪkʃən] *s* Ver-
wünschung *f*
malefactor [′mælɪ͵fæktər] *s* Übeltäter
–in *mf*
male′ nurse′ *s* Pfleger *m*
malevolence [mæ′levələns] *s* Böswillig-
keit *f*
malevolent [mæ′levələnt] *adj* böswillig
malfeasance [mæl′fizəns] *s* strafbare
Handlung *f;* **m. in office** Amtsvergehen *n*
malfunction [mæl′fʌŋkʃən] *s* technische Störung *f*
malice [′mælɪs] *s* Bosheit *f*
malicious [mə′lɪʃəs] *adj* boshaft
malign [mə′laɪn] *adj* böswillig || *tr*
verleumden
malignancy [mə′lɪgnənsi] *s* (pathol)
Bösartigkeit *f*
malignant [mə′lɪgnənt] *adj* böswillig;
(pathol) bösartig
malinger [mə′lɪŋgər] *intr* simulieren
malingerer [mə′lɪŋgərər] *s* Simulant
–in *mf*
mall [mɔl] *s (promenade)* Lauben-
promenade *f; (shopping center)* über-
dachtes Einkaufszentrum *n*, Mall *f*
mallard [′mælərd] *s* Stockente *f*
malleable [′mælɪ·əbəl] *adj* schmiedbar
mallet [′mælɪt] *s* Schlegel *m*
mallow [′mælo] *s* Malve *f*
malnutrition [͵mæln(j)u′trɪʃən] *s* Unterernährung *f*
malodorous [mæl′odərəs] *adj* übelriechend
malpractice [mæl′præktɪs] *s* ärztlicher
Kunstfehler *m*
malt [mɔlt] *s* Malz *n*
maltreat [mæl′trit] *tr* mißhandeln
mamma [′mɑmə] *s* Mama *f*, Mutti *f*

mammal [′mæməl] *s* Säugetier *n*
mammalian [mæ′melɪ·ən] *adj* Säu-
getier- || *s* Säugetier *n*
mam′mary gland′ [′mæməri] *s* Milch-
drüse *f*
mam′ma′s boy′ *s* Muttersöhnchen *n*
mammoth [′mæməθ] *adj* ungeheuer
(groß) || *s* (zool) Mammut *n*
man [mæn] *s* (**men** [mɛn]) *(adult male)*
Mann *m; (human being)* Mensch *m;*
(servant) Diener *m; (worker)* Arbeiter *m; (mankind)* die Menschheit
f; (checkers) Stein *m;* **man alive!**
Menschenskind! || *v (pret & pp*
manned; *ger* **manning)** *tr* besetzen;
(nav, rok) bemannen
man′ about town′ *s* weltgewandter
Mann *m*
manacle [′mænəkəl] *s* Handschelle *f* ||
tr fesseln
manage [′mænɪdʒ] *tr (a business,
household)* leiten; *(an estate)* verwalten; *(tools, weapons)* handhaben;
(e.g., a boat, car) völlig in der Gewalt haben; *(children)* fertig werden
mit; **I'll m. it** ich werde es schon
schaffen; **m. the situation** die Sache
deichseln || *intr* zurechtkommen;
(**with,** on) auskommen (mit); **m. to**
(inf) es fertigbringen zu *(inf)*
manageable [′mænɪdʒəbəl] *adj* handlich; *(hair)* fügsam
management [′mænɪdʒmənt] *s* Unter-
nehmensführung *f; (group which
manages)* Direktion *f; (as opposed
to labor)* Management *n*
man′agement consult′ant *s* Unterneh-
mungsberater –in *mf*
manager [′mænədʒər] *s* Manager *m*,
Geschäftsführer –in *mf; (of a bank
or hotel)* Direktor –in *mf; (of an
estate)* Verwalter –in *mf; (of a department)* Abteilungsleiter –in *mf;
(of a star, theater, athlete)* Manager
m
managerial [͵mænə′dʒɪrɪ·əl] *adj* Lei-
tungs-, Führungs-
man′aging *adj* geschäftsführend
man′aging direc′tor *s* Geschäftsführer
–in *mf*
Manchuria [mæn′tʃurɪ·ə] *s* Mandschurei *f*
mandarin or′ange [′mændərɪn] *s*
Mandarine *f*
mandate [′mændet] *s* Mandat *n* || *tr*
(**to**) zuweisen *(dat)*
mandatory [′mændə͵tori] *adj* verbindlich
mandolin [′mændəlɪn] *s* Mandoline *f*
mandrake [′mændrek] *s* (bot) Alraune
f
mane [men] *s* Mähne *f*
maneuver [mə′nuvər] *s* Manöver *n;* **go
on maneuvers** (mil) ins Manöver zie-
hen || *tr* manövrieren; **m. s.o. into**
(ger) j–n dazubringen zu *(inf)*
maneuverability [mə͵nuvərə′bɪliti] *s*
Manövrierbarkeit *f*
maneuverable [mə′nuvərəbəl] *adj* ma-
növrierfähig
manful [′mænfəl] *adj* mannhaft
manganese [′mæŋgə͵niz] *s* Mangan *n*

mange [mendʒ] *s* Räude *f*
manger ['mendʒər] *s* Krippe *f*
mangle ['mæŋgəl] *s* Mangel *f* ‖ *tr*
(*tear apart*) zerfleischen; (*wash*)
mangeln
mangy ['mendʒi] *adj* räudig; (*fig*)
schäbig
man'han'dle *tr* grob behandeln
man'hole' *s* Kanalschacht *m*, Mann-
loch *n*
man'hole cov'er *s* Schachtdeckel *m*
man'hood' *s* (*virility*) Männlichkeit *f*;
(*age*) Mannesalter *n*
man'-hour' *s* Arbeitsstunde *f* pro Mann
man'hunt' *s* Fahndung *f*
mania ['menɪ-ə] *s* Manie *f*
maniac ['menɪ,æk] *s* Geisteskranke
mf
maniacal [mə'naɪ-əkəl] *adj* manisch
manicure ['mænɪ,kjur] *s* Maniküre *f*,
Handpflege *f* ‖ *tr* maniküren
manicurist ['mænɪ,kjurɪst] *s* Maniküre *f*
manifest ['mænɪ,fest] *adj* offenkundig,
offenbar ‖ *s* (aer, naut) Manifest *n*
‖ *tr* bekunden, bezeigen
manifestation [,mænɪfes'teʃən] *s*
(*manifesting*) Offenbarung *f*; (*indication*) Anzeichen *n*
manifes'to [,mænɪ'festo] *s* (–toes)
Manifest *n*
manifold ['mænɪ,fold] *adj* mannigfaltig ‖ *s* (aut) Rohrverzweigung *f*
manikin ['mænɪkɪn] *s* Männchen *n*;
(*for teaching anatomy*) anatomisches
Modell *n*; (*mannequin*) Mannequin *n*
man' in the moon' *s* Mann *m* im Mond
man' in the streets' *s* Durchschnitts-
mensch *m*
manipulate [mə'nɪpjə,let] *tr* manipulieren
man'kind' *s* Menschheit *f*
manliness ['mænlɪnɪs] *s* Männlichkeit
f
manly ['mænli] *adj* mannhaft, männlich
man'-made' *adj* künstlich
manna ['mænə] *s* Manna *n*, Himmels-
brot *n*
manned' space'craft *s* bemanntes
Raumfahrzeug *n*
mannequin ['mænɪkɪn] *s* (*clothes
model*) Mannequin *n*; (*in a display
window*) Schaufensterpuppe *f*
manner ['mænər] *s* Art *f*, Weise *f*;
(*custom*) Sitte *f*; **after the m. of**
nach der Art von; **by all m. of means**
auf jeden Fall; **by no m. of means**
auf keinen Fall; **in a m.** gewissermaßen; **in a m. of speaking** sozusagen; **in like m.** gleicherweise; **in
the following m.** folgendermaßen; **in
this m.** auf diese Weise; **it's bad
manners to** (*inf*) es schickt sich nicht
zu (*inf*); **m. of death** Todesart *f*;
manners Manieren *pl*
mannerism ['mænə,rɪzəm] *s* Manie-
riertheit *f*
mannerly ['mænərli] *adj* manierlich
mannish ['mænɪʃ] *adj* männisch;
(*woman*) unweiblich
man' of let'ters *s* Literat *m*

man' of the world' *s* Weltmann *m*
man' of war' *s* Kriegsschiff *n*
manor ['mænər] *s* Herrengut *n*
man'or house' *s* Herrenhaus *n*
man'pow'er *s* Arbeitskräfte *pl*; (mil)
Kriegsstärke *f*
man'serv'ant *s* (menservants) Diener *m*
mansion ['mænʃən] *s* Herrenhaus *n*
man'slaugh'ter *s* Totschlag *m*
mantel ['mæntəl] *s* Kaminsims *m* & *n*
man'telpiece' *s* Kaminsims *m* & *n*
mantilla [mæn'tɪlə] *s* Mantille *f*
mantle ['mæntəl] *s* (& fig) Mantel *m*;
(*of a gaslight*) Glühstrumpf *m*; (geol)
Mantel *m* ‖ *tr* verhüllen
manual ['mænjʊ-əl] *adj* manuell, Hand–
‖ *s* (*book*) Handbuch *n*, Leitfaden
m; (mus) Manual *n*
man'ual control' *s* Handbedienung *f*
man'ual dexter'ity *s* Handfertigkeit *f*
man'ual la'bor *s* Handarbeit *f*
man'ual of arms' *s* (mil) Dienstvor-
schrift *f*
man'ual train'ing *s* Werkunterricht *m*
manufacture [,mænjə'fæktʃər] *s* Herstellung *f*; (*production*) Erzeugnis *n*
‖ *tr* herstellen; (*clothes*) konfektionieren
manufac'tured goods' *spl* Fertigwaren
pl
manufacturer [,mænjə'fæktʃərər] *s*
Hersteller –in *mf*
manure [mə'n(j)ur] *s* Mist *m* ‖ *tr*
misten
manuscript ['mænjə,skrɪpt] *adj* handschriftlich ‖ *s* Manuskript *n*
many ['meni] *adj* viele; **a good** (or
great) **m.** sehr viele; **how m.** wieviele; **in so m. words** ausdrücklich;
m. a mancher, manch ein; **m. a person** manch einer; **m. a time** manchmal; **twice as m.** noch einmal so
viele ‖ *pron* viele; **as m. as** ten nicht
weniger als zehn; **how m.** wieviele
man'y-sid'ed *adj* vielseitig
map [mæp] *s* Karte *f*, Landkarte *f*; (*of
a city*) Plan *m*; (*of a local area*)
Spezialkarte *f*; **map of the world**
Weltkarte *f*; **put on the map** (coll)
ausposaunen ‖ *v* (*pret* & *pp* **mapped**;
ger **mapping**) *tr* kartographisch aufnehmen; **map out** planen
maple ['mepəl] *s* Ahorn *m*
ma'ple sug'ar *s* Ahornzucker *m*
ma'ple syr'up *s* Ahornsirup *m*
mar [mɑr] *v* (*pret* & *pp* **marred;** *ger*
marring) *tr* (*detract from the beauty
of*) verunzieren; (*e.g., a reputation*)
beeinträchtigen
marathon ['mærə,θɑn] *s* Dauerwett-
bewerb *m*
mar'athon race' *s* Marathonlauf *m*
maraud [mə'rɔd] *tr* & *intr* plündern
marauder [mə'rɔdər] *s* Plünderer *m*
marble ['mɑrbəl] *adj* marmorn ‖ *s*
Marmor *m*; (*little glass ball*) Murmel
f; **marbles** (*game*) Murmelspiel *n* ‖
tr marmorieren
mar'ble quar'ry *s* Marmorbruch *m*
march [mɑrtʃ] *s* Marsch *m*; (*festive
parade*) Umzug *m*; **March** März *m*;
on the m. auf dem Marsch; **steal a**

m. on s.o. j–m den Rang ablaufen; **the m. of time** der Lauf der Zeit || *tr* marschieren || *intr* marschieren; **m. by** vorbeimarschieren (an *dat*); **m. off** abmarschieren || *interj* marsch!

marchioness ['marʃənɪs] *s* Marquise *f*

mare [mɛr] *s* Stute *f*

Margaret ['margərɪt] *s* Margarete *f*

margarine ['mardʒərɪn] *s* Margarine *f*

margin ['mardʒɪn] *s* (*of a page*) Rand *m*; (*leeway*) Spielraum *m*; (fin) Spanne *f*; **by a narrow m.** mit knappem Abstand; **leave a m.** am Rande Raum lassen; **m. of profit** Gewinnspanne *f*; **m. of safety** Sicherheitsfaktor *m*; **win by a ten-second m.** mit zehn Sekunden Abstand gewinnen; **write in the m.** an dem Rand schreiben

marginal ['mardʒɪnəl] *adj* (*costs, profits, case*) Grenz–; (*in the margin*) Rand–

mar'ginal note' *s* Randbemerkung *f*

mar'gin release' *s* Randauslöser *m*

mar'gin set'ter *s* Randsteller *m*

marigold ['mærɪ‚gold] *s* Ringelblume *f*

marijuana [‚marɪ'hwanə] *s* Marihuana *n*

marinate ['mærɪ‚net] *tr* marinieren

marine [mə'rin] *adj* See–, Meer(es)– || *s* (*fleet*) Marine *f*; (*fighter*) Marineinfanterist *m*; **marines** Marinetruppen *pl*

Marine' Corps' *s* Marineinfanteriekorps *n*

mariner ['mærɪnər] *s* Seemann *m*

marionette [‚mærɪ‧ə'nɛt] *s* Marionette *f*

marital ['mærɪtəl] *adj* ehelich, Gatten–

mar'ital sta'tus *s* Familienstand *m*

maritime ['mærɪ‚taɪm] *adj* See–

marjoram ['mardʒərəm] *s* Majoran *m*

mark [mark] *s* (& fig) Zeichen *n*; (*stain, bruise*) Fleck *m*, Mal *n*; (*German unit of currency*) Mark *f*; (*educ*) Zensur *f*; **be an easy m.** (coll) leicht reinzulegen sein; **hit the m.** ins Schwarze treffen; **make one's m.** sich durchsetzen; **m. of confidence** Vertrauensbeweis *m*; **m. of favor** Gunstbezeichnung *f*; **m. of respect** Zeichen *n* der Hochachtung; **on your marks!** auf die Plätze!; **wide of the m.** am Ziel vorbei || *tr* (aus)zeichnen, bezeichnen; (*student papers*) zensieren; (*cards*) zinken; (*labels*) beschriften; (*laundry*) zeichnen; (*the score*) anschreiben; **m. down** aufschreiben, niederschreiben; (com) im Preis herabsetzen; **m. my words!** merken Sie sich, was ich sage!; **m. off** abgrenzen; (surv) abstecken; (mil & fig) auf der Stelle treten; (mus) den Takt schlagen; **m. up** (*e.g., a wall*) beschmieren; (com) im Preis heraufsetzen

mark'down' *s* Preisnachlaß *m*

marked *adj* (*difference*) merklich; **a m. man** ein Gezeichneter *m*

marker ['markər] *s* (*of scores*) Anschreiber –in *mf*; (*commemorative marker*) Gedenktafel *f*; (*on a firing range*) Anzeiger *m*; (*bombing marker*) Leuchtbombe *f*; (*felt pen*) Filzschreiber *m*

market ['markɪt] *s* Markt *m*; (*grocery store*) Lebensmittelgeschäft *n*; (*stock exchange*) Börse *f*; (*ready sale*) Absatz *m*; **be in the m. for** Bedarf haben an (*dat*); **be on the m.** zum Verkauf stehen; **put on the m.** auf den Markt bringen || *tr* verkaufen

marketable ['markɪtəbəl] *adj* marktfähig

mar'ket anal'ysis *s* Marktanalyse *f*

mar'keting *s* (econ) Marketing *n*; **do the m.** Einkäufe machen

mar'keting research' *s* Absatzforschung *f*

mar'ketplace' *s* Marktplatz *m*

mar'ket price' *s* Marktpreis *m*

mar'ket town' *s* Marktflecken *m*

mar'ket val'ue *s* Marktwert *m*; (st. exch.) Kurswert *m*

mark'ing *s* Kennzeichen *n*

marks·man ['marksmən] *s* (–men) Schütze *m*

marks'manship' *s* Schießkunst *f*

mark'up' *s* (com) Gewinnaufschlag *m*

marl [marl] *s* Mergel *m* || *tr* mergeln

marmalade ['marmə‚led] *s* Marmelade *f*

maroon [mə'run] *adj* rotbraun, kastanienbraun || *s* Kastanienbraun *n* || *tr* aussetzen; **be marooned** von der Außenwelt abgeschnitten sein

marquee [mar'ki] *s* Schutzdach *n*

marquess ['markwɪs] *s* Marquis *m*

marquis ['markwɪs] *s* Marquis *m*

marquise [mar'kiz] *s* Marquise *f*

marriage ['mærɪdʒ] *s* Heirat *f*; (*state*) Ehe *f*, Ehestand *m*; **by m.** angeheiratet, schwägerlich; **give in m.** verheiraten

marriageable ['mærɪdʒəbəl] *adj* heiratsfähig; **m. age** (*of a girl*) Mannbarkeit *f*

mar'riage brok'er *s* Heiratsvermittler –in *mf*

mar'riage cer'emony *s* Trauung *f*

mar'riage li'cense *s* Heiratsurkunde *f*

mar'riage of conven'ience *s* Vernunftehe *f*

mar'riage por'tion *s* Mitgift *f*

mar'riage propos'al *s* Heiratsantrag *m*

mar'riage vow' *s* Ehegelöbnis *n*

mar'ried cou'ple *s* Ehepaar *n*

mar'ried state' *s* Ehestand *m*

marrow ['mæro] *s* Knochenmark *n*; (fig) Mark *n*

mar·ry ['mæri] *v* (*pret & pp* –ried) *tr* heiraten; (*said of a priest or minister*) trauen; **m. off (to)** verheiraten (mit) || *intr* heiraten; **m. rich** e–e gute Partie machen

Mars [marz] *s* Mars *m*

marsh [marʃ] *s* Sumpf *m*

mar·shal ['marʃəl] *s* Zeremonienmeister *m*; (*police officer*) Bezirkspolizeichef *m*; (mil) Marschall *m* || *v* (*pret & pp* –shal[l]ed; *ger* –shal[l]ing) *tr* (*troops*) ordnungsgemäß aufstellen; (*strength*) zusammenraffen

marsh'land' s Sumpfland n

marsh' mal'low s (bot) Eibisch m

marsh'mal'low s (candy) Konfekt n aus Stärkesirup, Zucker, Stärke, Gelatine, und geschlagenem Eiweiß

marshy ['marʃi] adj sumpfig

mart [mɑrt] s Markt m

marten ['mɑrtən] s (zool) Marder m

Martha ['mɑrθə] s Martha f

martial ['mɑrʃəl] adj Kriegs–

mar'tial law' s Standrecht n; **declare m.** das Standrecht verhängen; **under m.** standrechtlich

martin ['mɑrtɪn] s Mauerschwalbe f; **Martin** Martin m

martinet [,mɑrtɪ'nɛt] s Pauker –in mf; (mil) Schleifer m

martyr ['mɑrtər] s Märtyrer –in mf || tr martern

martyrdom ['mɑrtərdəm] s Märtyrertum n

mar•vel ['mɑrvəl] s Wunder n || v (pret & pp –vel[l]ed; ger –vel[l]ing) intr (at) sich wundern (über acc)

marvelous ['mɑrvələs] adj wundervoll; (coll) pfundig

Marxist ['mɑrksɪst] adj marxistisch || Marxist –in mf

marzipan ['mɑrzɪ,pæn] s Marzipan n

mascara [mæs'kærə] s Lidtusche f

mascot ['mæskɑt] s Maskotte f

masculine ['mæskjəlɪn] adj männlich

mash [mæʃ] s Brei m; (in brewing) Maische f || tr zerquetschen; (potatoes) zerdrücken

mashed' pota'toes spl Kartoffelbrei m

mask [mæsk] s Maske f || tr maskieren

masked' ball' s Maskenball m

mason ['mesən] s Maurer m; **Mason** Freimaurer m

Masonic [mə'sɑnɪk] adj Freimaurer–

masonite ['mesə,naɪt] s Holzfaserplatte f

masonry ['mesənri] s Mauerwerk n; **Masonry** Freimaurerei f

masquerade [,mæskə'red] s (& fig) Maskerade f || intr (& fig) sich maskieren; **m. as** sich ausgeben als

mass [mæs] adj Massen– || s Masse f; (eccl) Messe; **the masses** die breite Masse f || tr massieren || intr sich ansammeln

massacre ['mæsəkər] s Massaker n || tr massakrieren, niedermetzeln

massage [mə'sɑʒ] s Massage f || tr massieren

masseur [mə'sʌr] s Masseur m

masseuse [mə'suz] s Masseuse f

massif ['mæsɪf] s Gebirgsstock m

massive ['mæsɪv] adj massiv

mass' me'dia ['midɪ-ə] spl Massenmedien pl

mass' meet'ing s Massenversammlung f

mass' mur'der s Massenmord m

mass'-produce' tr serienmäßig herstellen

mass' produc'tion s Serienherstellung f

mast [mæst] s Mast m; (food for swine) Mast f

master ['mæstər] adj (bedroom, key, switch, cylinder) Haupt– || s Herr m,

Meister m; (male head of a household) Hausherr m; (of a ship) Kapitän m || tr beherrschen

mas'ter build'er s Baumeister m

mas'ter cop'y s Originalkopie f

masterful ['mæstərfəl] adj herrisch; (masterly) meisterhaft

masterly ['mæstərli] adj meisterhaft

mas'ter mechan'ic s Schlossermeister m

mas'termind' s führender Geist m || tr planen und übernehmen

Mas'ter of Arts' s Magister m der freien Künste

mas'ter of cer'emonies s Zeremonienmeister m

mas'ter stroke' s Meisterstreich m

mas'terwork' s Meisterwerk n

mastery ['mæstəri] s (of) Beherrschung f (genit); **gain m. over** die Oberhand gewinnen über (acc)

mast'head' s (naut) Topp m; (typ) Impressum n

masticate ['mæstɪ,ket] tr zerkauen || intr kauen

mastiff ['mæstɪf] s Mastiff m

masturbate ['mæstər,bet] intr onanieren

masturbation [,mæstər'beʃən] s Onanie f

mat [mæt] s (for a floor) Matte f; (before the door) Türvorleger m; (under cups, vases, etc.) Zierdeckchen n || v (pret & pp matted; ger matting) tr (cover with matting) mit Matten belegen; (the hair) verfilzen || intr sich verfilzen

match [mætʃ] s Streichholz n; (for marriage) Partie f; (sport) Match n; **be a good m.** zueinanderpassen; **be a m. for** gewachsen sein (dat); **be no m. for** sich nicht messen können mit; **meet one's m.** seinen Mann finden || tr (fit together) zusammenstellen; (harmonize with) passen zu; (equal) (in) gleichkommen (in dat); (funds) in gleicher Höhe aufbringen; (adapt) in Übereinstimmung bringen mit; **be well matched** auf gleicher Höhe sein; **m. up** zusammenpassen; **m. wits with** sich geistig messen mit || intr zueinanderpassen

match'book' s Streichholzbrief m

match' box' s Streichholzschachtel f

match'ing adj (clothes) passend; (funds) in gleicher Höhe || s Paarung f

match'mak'er s Heiratsvermittler –in mf; (sport) Veranstalter m

mate [met] s Genosse m, Kamerad m; (in marriage) Ehepartner m; (one of a pair, e.g., of gloves) Gegenstück n; (especially of birds) Männchen n, Weibchen n; (naut) Maat m || tr paaren || intr sich paaren

material [mə'tɪrɪ,əl] adj materiell; (important) wesentlich || s Material n, Stoff m; (tex) Stoff m

materialist [mə'tırı·əlıst] *s* Materialist –in *mf*

materialistic [mə,tırı·ə'lıstık] *adj* materialistisch

materialize [mə'tırı·ə,laız] *intr* sich verwirklichen

materiel [mə,tırı'el] *s* Material *n;* (mil) Kriegsmaterial *n*

maternal [mə'tʌrnəl] *adj* mütterlich; (*relatives*) mütterlicherseits

maternity [mə'tʌrnıtı] *s* Mutterschaft *f*

mater'nity dress' *s* Umstandskleid *n*

mater'nity hos'pital *s* Wöchnerinnenheim *n*

mater'nity ward' *s* Wöchnerinnenstation *f*

math [mæθ] *s* (coll) Mathe *f*

mathematical [,mæθɪ'mætɪkəl] *adj* mathematisch

mathematician [,mæθɪmə'tɪʃən] *s* Mathematiker –in *mf*

mathematics [,mæθɪ'mætɪks] *s* Mathematik *f*

matinée [,mætɪ'ne] *s* Nachmittagsvorstellung *f*

mat'ing sea'son *s* Paarungszeit *f*

matins ['mætɪnz] *spl* Frühmette *f*

matriarch ['metrɪ,ɑrk] *s* Stammesmutter *f*

matriarchal [,metrɪ'ɑrkəl] *adj* matriarchalisch

matriarchy ['metrɪ,ɑrkɪ] *s* Matriarchat *n*

matricide ['mætrɪ,saɪd] *s* (*act*) Muttermord *m;* (*person*) Muttermörder –in *mf*

matriculate [mə'trɪkjə,let] *tr* immatrikulieren || *intr* sich immatrikulieren

matriculation [mə,trɪkjə'leʃən] *s* Immatrikulation *f*

matrimonial [,mætrɪ'monɪ·əl] *adj* Ehe-

matrimony ['mætrɪ,monɪ] *s* Ehestand *m*

ma·trix ['metrɪks] *s* (–trices [trɪ,siz] & –trixes) (*mold*) Gießform *f;* (math) Matrix *f;* (typ) Matrize *f*

matron ['metrən] *s* Matrone *f*

matronly ['metrənlɪ] *adj* matronenhaft, gesetzt

matt [mæt] *adj* (phot) matt

matter ['mætər] *s* Stoff *m;* (*affair*) Sache *f,* Angelegenheit *f;* (*pus*) Eiter *m;* (phys) Materie *f;* **as a m. of course** routinemäßig; **as matters now stand** wie die Sache jetzt liegt; **for that m.** was das betrifft; **it's a m. of** es handelt sich um; **it's a m. of life and death** es geht um Leben und Tod; **m. of opinion** Ansichtssache *f;* **m. of taste** Geschmackssache *f;* **something is the m. with his heart** er hat was am Herz; **no laughing m.** nichts zum Lachen; **no m.** ganz gleich; **what's the m. (with)?** was ist los (mit)? || *intr* von Bedeutung sein; **it doesn't m.** es macht nichts (aus); **it doesn't m. to me** es ist mir nichts daran; **it matters a great deal to me** es liegt mir sehr viel daran

mat'ter of fact' *s* Tatsache *f;* **as a m.** tatsächlich

mat'ter-of-fact' *adj* sachlich, nüchtern

Matthew ['mæθju] *s* Matthäus *m*

mattock ['mætək] *s* Breithacke *f*

mattress ['mætrɪs] *s* Matratze *f*

mature [mə'tjʊr] *adj* (& fig) reif || *tr* reifen lassen || *intr* reifen; (fin) fällig werden

maturity [mə'tjʊrɪtɪ] *s* Reife *f;* (fin) Verfall *m*

maudlin ['mɔdlɪn] *adj* rührselig

maul [mɔl] *tr* schlimm zurichten

maulstick ['mɔl,stɪk] *s* Mahlstock *m*

mausole·um [,mɔsə'li·əm] *s* (–ums & –a [ə]) Mausoleum *n*

maw [mɔ] *s* (*mouth of an animal*) Rachen *m;* (*stomach of an animal*) Tiermagen *m;* (*of birds*) Kropf *m*

mawkish ['mɔkɪʃ] *adj* rührselig

maxim ['mæksɪm] *s* Maxime *f,* Lehrspruch *m*

maximum ['mæksɪməm] *adj* Höchst-; **m. load** Höchstbelastung *f* || *s* Maximum *n*

May [me] *s* Mai *m* || **may** *v* (pret **might** [maɪt]) *aux* (expressing possibility) mögen, können; (expressing permission) dürfen; (expressing a wish) mögen; **be that as it may** wie dem auch sei; **come what may** komme, was da wolle; **it may be too late** es ist vielleicht zu spät; **that may be** das kann (or mag) sein

maybe ['mebɪ] *adv* vielleicht

May' Day' *s* der erste Mai

mayhem ['mehəm] *s* Körperverletzung *f*

mayonnaise [,me·ə'nez] *s* Mayonnaise *f*

mayor [mer] *s* Bürgermeister *m;* (*of a large city*) Oberbürgermeister *m*

May'pole' *s* Maibaum *m*

May' queen' *s* Maikönigin *f*

maze [mez] *s* Irrgarten *m;* (fig) Gewirr *n*

me [mi] *pers pron* (*direct object*) mich; (*indirect object*) mir; **this one is on me** das geht auf meine Rechnung

mead [mid] *s* (hist) Met *m;* (poet) Aue *f*

meadow ['medo] *s* Wiese *f*

mead'owland' *s* Wiesenland *n*

meager ['migər] *adj* karg, kärglich

meal [mil] *s* Mahl *n,* Mahlzeit *f;* (*grain*) grobes Mehl *n*

meal' tick'et *s* Gutschein *m* für e-e Mahlzeit

meal'time' *s* Essenszeit *f*

mealy ['milɪ] *adj* mehlig

mealy-mouthed ['milɪ,maʊðd] *adj* zurückhaltend

mean [min] *adj* (*nasty*) bösartig; (*lowly*) gemein, niedrig; (*shabby*) schäbig; (*in statistics*) mittel; **no m.** kein schlechter || *s* (log) Mittelbegriff *m;* (math) Mittel *n;* **by all means** unbedingt; **by every means** mit allen Mitteln; **by means or foul** ganz gleich wie; **by lawful means** auf dem Rechtswege; **by means of**

mittels (*genit*); **by no means** keineswegs; **live beyond one's means** über seine Verhältnisse leben; **live within one's means** seinen Verhältnissen entsprechend leben; **means** (*way*) Mittel *n;* (*resources*) Mittel *pl,* Vermögen *n;* **means of transportation** Verkehrsmittel *n;* **means to an end** Mittel *pl* zum Zweck; **of means** bemittelt ‖ *v* (*pret & pp* **meant** [ment]) *tr* (*intend, intend to say*) meinen; (*signify*) bedeuten; **be meant for** (*said, e.g., of a remark*) gelten (*dat*); (*said, e.g., of a gift*) bestimmt sein für; **it means a lot to me to** (*inf*) mir liegt viel daran zu (*inf*); **m. business** es ernst meinen; **m. little** (or **much**) wenig (or viel) gelten; **m. no harm** es nicht böse meinen; **m. s.o. no harm** j-n nicht verletzen wollen; **m. the world to s.o.** j-m alles bedeuten; **what is meant by ...?** was versteht man unter ...? ‖ *intr*—**m. well** es gut meinen

meander [mɪ'ændər] *intr* sich winden

mean'ing *s* Bedeutung *f;* **take on m.** e-n Sinn bekommen; **what's the m. of this?** was soll das heißen?

meaningful ['minɪŋfəl] *adj* sinnvoll

meaningless ['minɪŋlɪs] *adj* sinnlos

mean'-look'ing *adj* bösartig aussehend

meanness ['minnɪs] *s* Gemeinheit *f;* (*nastiness*) Bösartigkeit *f*

mean'time', mean'while' *adv* mittlerweile ‖ *s*—**in the m.** mittlerweile, in der Zwischenzeit

measles ['mizəlz] *s* Masern *pl;* (*German measles*) Röteln *pl*

measly ['mizli] *adj* kümmerlich, lumpig

measurable ['meʒərəbəl] *adj* meßbar

measure ['meʒər] *s* Maß *n;* (*step*) Maßnahme *f;* (*law*) Gesetz *n;* (*mus*) Takt *m;* **beyond m.** übermäßig; **for good m.** obendrein; **in a great m.** in großem Maß; **to some m.** gewissermaßen; **take drastic measures** durchgreifen; **take measures to** (*inf*) Maßnahmen ergreifen um zu (*inf*); **take s.o.'s m.** (*fig*) j-n einschätzen ‖ *tr* messen; **m. off** abmessen; **m. out** ausmessen ‖ *intr* messen; **m. up to** gewachsen sein (*dat*)

measurement ['meʒərmənt] *s* (*measured dimension*) Maß *n;* (*measuring*) Messung *f;* **measurements** Maße *pl;* **take s.o.'s measurements for** j-m Maß nehmen zu

meas'uring cup' *s* Meßbecher *m*

meas'uring tape' *s* Meßband *n*

meat [mit] *s* Fleisch *n;* (*of a nut, of the matter*) Kern *m*

meat'ball' *m* Fleischklößchen *n*

meat' grind'er *s* Fleischwolf *m*

meat'hook' *s* Fleischhaken *m*

meat'mar'ket *s* Fleischmarkt *m*

meat' pie' *s* Fleischpastete *f*

meaty ['miti] *adj* fleischig; (*fig*) kernig

Mecca ['mekə] *s* Mekka *n*

mechanic [mə'kænɪk] *s* Mechaniker *m,* Schlosser *m;* (*aut*) Autoschlosser *m;* **mechanics** Mechanik *f*

mechanical [mə'kænɪkəl] *adj* mechanisch

mechan'ical engineer' *s* Maschinenbauingenieur *m*

mechan'ical engineer'ing *s* Maschinenbau *m*

mechanism ['mekə,nɪzəm] *s* Mechanismus *m*

mechanize ['mekə,naɪz] *tr* mechanisieren

medal ['medəl] *s* Medaille *f,* Orden *m*

medallion [mɪ'dæljən] *s* Medaillon *n*

meddle ['medəl] *intr* sich einmischen; **m. with** sich abgeben mit

meddler ['medlər] *s* zudringliche Person *f*

meddlesome ['medəlsəm] *adj* zudringlich

media ['midɪ·ə] *spl* Medien *pl*

median ['midɪ·ən] *adj* mittlere, Mittel- ‖ *s* (arith) Mittelwert *m;* (geom) Mittellinie *f*

me'dian strip' *s* Mittelstreifen *m*

mediate ['midɪ,et] *tr & intr* vermitteln

mediation [,midɪ'e/ən] *s* Vermittlung *f*

mediator ['midɪ,etər] *s* Vermittler –in *mf*

medic ['medɪk] *s* (mil) Sanitäter *m*

medical ['medɪkəl] *adj* (*of a doctor*) ärztlich; (*of medicine*) medizinisch; (*of the sick*) Kranken-

med'ical bul'letin *s* Krankheitsbericht *m*

med'ical corps' *s* Sanitätstruppe *f*

med'ical profes'sion *s* Arztberuf *m*

med'ical school' *s* medizinische Fakultät *f*

med'ical sci'ence *s* Heilkunde *f*

med'ical stu'dent *s* Medizinstudent –in *mf*

medication [,medɪ'ke/ən] *s* Medikament *n*

medicinal [mə'dɪsɪnəl] *adj* medizinisch

medicine ['medɪsɪn] *s* Medizin *f,* Arznei *f;* (*profession*) Medizin *f;* **practice m.** den Arztberuf ausüben

med'icine cab'inet *s* Hausapotheke *f*

med'icine kit' *s* Reiseapotheke *f*

med'icine man' *s* Medizinmann *m*

medic∙o ['medɪ,ko] *s* (**–cos**) (coll) Mediziner –in *mf*

medieval [,midɪ'ivəl], [,medɪ'ivəl] *adj* mittelalterlich

mediocre [,midɪ'okər] *adj* mittelmäßig

mediocrity [,midɪ'ɑkrɪti] *s* Mittelmäßigkeit *f*

meditate ['medɪ,tet] *tr* vorhaben ‖ *intr* (**on**) meditieren (über *acc*)

meditation [,medɪ'te/ən] *s* Meditation *f*

Mediterranean [,medɪtə'reni·ən] *adj* Mittelmeer– ‖ *s* Mittelmeer *n*

medi∙um ['midɪ·əm] *adj* Mittel-, mittlere ‖ *s* (**–ums** & **–a** [ə]) Mittel *n;* (*culture*) Nährboden *m;* (*in spiritualism, communications*) Medium *n;* **through the m. of** vermittels (*genit*)

me'dium of exchange' *s* Tauschmittel *n*

me'dium-rare' *adj* halb durchgebraten

me'dium size' *s* Mittelgröße *f*

med′ium-sized′ *adj* mittelgroß

medley [′medli] *s* Mischmasch *m*; (mus) Potpourri *n*

medul·la [mɪ′dʌlə] *s* (–las & –lae [li]) Knochenmark *n*, Mark *n*

meek [mik] *adj* sanftmütig; **m. as a lamb** lammfromm

meekness [′miknɪs] *s* Sanftmut *m*

meerschaum [′mɪr/əm] *s* Meerschaum *m*

meet [mit] *adj* passend ‖ *s* (sport) Treffen *n*, Veranstaltung *f* ‖ *v* (*pret* & *pp* **met** [met]) *tr* begegnen (*dat*), treffen; (*make the acquaintance of*) kennenlernen; (*demands*) befriedigen; (*obligations*) nachkommen (*dat*); (*wishes*) erfüllen; (*a deadline*) einhalten; **m. s.o. at the train** j-n von der Bahn abholen; **m. s.o. halfway** j-m auf halbem Wege entgegenkommen; **m. the train** zum Zug gehen; **pleased to m. you** freut mich sehr, sehr angenehm ‖ *intr* (*said of persons, of two ends*) zusammenkommen; (*said of persons*) sich treffen; (*in conference*) tagen; (*said of roads, rivers*) sich vereinigen; **make both ends m.** gerade mit dem Geld auskommen; **m. again** sich wiedersehen; **m. up with s.o.** j-n einholen; **m. with** zusammentreffen mit; **m. with an accident** verunglücken; **m. with a refusal** e-e Fehlbitte tun; **m. with approval** Beifall finden; **m. with success** Erfolg haben

meet′ing *s* (*of an organization*) Versammlung *f*; (*e.g., of a committee*) Sitzung *f*; (*of individuals*) Zusammenkunft *f*

meet′ing place′ *s* Treffpunkt *m*

megacycle [′megə,saɪkəl] *s* Megahertz [′megə,hʌrts] *s* (elec) Megahertz *n*

megalomania [,megəlo′menɪ·ə] *s* Größenwahn *m*

megaphone [′megə,fon] *s* Sprachrohr *n*

megohm [′meg,om] *s* Megohm *n*

melancholy [′melən,kɑli] *adj* schwermütig ‖ *s* Schwermut *f*

melee [′mele], [′mele] *s* Gemenge *n*

mellow [′melo] *adj* (*very ripe*) mürb(e); (*wine*) abgelagert; (*voice*) schmelzend; (*person*) gereift ‖ *tr* zur Reife bringen; (fig) mildern ‖ *intr* mürb(e) werden; (fig) mild werden

melodic [mɪ′lɑdɪk] *adj* melodisch

melodious [mɪ′lodɪ·əs] *adj* melodisch

melodrama [′melo,drɑmə] *s* (& fig) Melodrama *n*

melody [′melədi] *s* Melodie *f*

melon [′melən] *s* Melone *f*

melt [melt] *tr* & *intr* schmelzen

melt′ing point′ *s* Schmelzpunkt *m*

melt′ing pot′ *s* (& fig) Schmelztiegel *m*

member [′membər] *s* Glied *n*; (*person*) Mitglied *n*, Angehörige *mf*; **m. of the family** Familienangehörige *mf*

mem′bership′ *s* Mitgliedschaft *f*; (*collectively*) Mitglieder *pl*; (*number of members*) Mitgliederzahl *f*

mem′bership card′ *s* Mitgliedskarte *f*

membrane [′membren] *s* Häutchen *n*, Membran(e) *f*

memen·to [mɪ′mento] *s* (–tos & –toes) Erinnerung *f*, Memento *n*

mem·o [′memo] *s* (–os) (coll) Notiz *f*

mem′o book′ *s* Notizbuch *n*, Agenda *f*

memoirs [′memwɑrz] *spl* Memoiren *pl*

mem′o pad′ *s* Notizblock *m*, Agenda *f*

memorable [′memərəbəl] *adj* denkwürdig

memoran·dum [,memə′rændəm] *s* (–dums & –da [də]) Notiz *f*, Vermerk *m*; (dipl) Memorandum *n*

memorial [mɪ′morɪ·əl] *adj* Gedächtnis–. Erinnerungs– ‖ *s* Denkmal *n*

Memor′ial Day′ *s* Gefallenengedenktag *m*

memorialize [mɪ′morɪ·ə,laɪz] *tr* gedenken (*genit*)

memorize [′memə,raɪz] *tr* auswendig lernen

memory [′meməri] *s* (*faculty*) Gedächtnis *n*; (of) Gedenken *n* (an *acc*), Erinnerung *f* (an *acc*); **commit to m.** auswendig lernen; **escape one′s m.** seinem Gedächtnis entfallen; **from m.** aus dem Gedächtnis; **in m. of** zur Erinnerung an (*acc*); **of blessed m.** seligen Angedenkens; **within the m. of men** seit Menschengedenken

menace [′menɪs] *s* (to) Drohung *f* (*genit*) ‖ *tr* bedrohen

menagerie [mə′nædʒəri] *s* Menagerie *f*

mend [mend] *s* Besserung *f*; **on the m.** auf dem Wege der Besserung ‖ *tr* (*clothes*) ausbessern; (*socks*) stopfen; (*repair*) reparieren

mendacious [men′deʃəs] *adj* lügnerisch

mendicant [′mendɪkənt] *adj* Bettel– ‖ *s* Bettelmönch *m*

menfolk [′men,fok] *spl* Mannsleute *pl*

menial [′minɪ·əl] *adj* niedrig ‖ *s* Diener –in *mf*

menopause [′menə,pɔz] *s* Wechseljahre *pl*

menses [′mensiz] *spl* Monatsfluß *m*

men′s′ room′ *s* Herrentoilette *f*

men′s′ size′ *s* Herrengröße *f*

men′s′ store′ *s* Herrenbekleidungsgeschäft *n*

menstruate [′menstru,et] *intr* menstruieren

menstruation [,menstru′eʃən] *s* Menstruation *f*

men′s′ wear′ *s* Herrenbekleidung *f*

mental [′mentəl] *adj* geistig, Geistes–

men′tal an′guish *s* Seelenpein *f*

men′tal arith′metic *s* Kopfrechnen *n*

men′tal capac′ity *s* Fassungskraft *f*

men′tal disor′der *s* Geistesstörung *f*

men′tal institu′tion *s* Nervenheilanstalt *f*

mentality [men′tæliti] *s* Mentalität *f*

mentally [′mentəli] *adv* geistig, Geistes–; **m. alert** geistesgegenwärtig; **m. disturbed** geistesgestört; **m. lazy** denkfaul

men′tal reserva′tion *s* geistiger Vorbehalt *m*

men′tal teleg′raphy *s* Gedankenübertragung *f*

mention [′menʃən] *s* Erwähnung *f*;

make m. of erwähnen ‖ *tr* erwähnen; nennen; **be mentioned** zur Sprache kommen; **don't m. it!** keine Ursache!; **not worth mentioning** nicht der Rede wert

menu ['menju] *s* Speisekarte *f*

meow [mi'au] *s* Miauen *n* ‖ *intr* miauen

mercantile ['mʌrkən‚til], ['mʌrkən‚tail] *adj* Handels-, kaufmännisch

mercenary ['mʌrsə‚neri] *adj* gewinnsüchtig ‖ *s* Söldner *m*

merchandise ['mʌrtʃən‚daiz] *s* Ware *f* ‖ *tr* handeln

mer'chandising *s* Verkaufspolitik *f*

merchant ['mʌrtʃənt] *s* Händler, Kaufmann *m*

mer'chant·man *s* (**-men**) Handelsschiff *n*

mer'chant marine' *s* Handelsmarine *f*

mer'chant ves'sel *s* Handelsschiff *n*

merciful ['mʌrsɪfəl] *adj* barmherzig

merciless ['mʌrsɪlɪs] *adj* erbarmungslos

mercurial [mer'kjurɪ·əl] *adj* quecksilbrig

mercury ['mʌrkjəri] *s* Quecksilber *n*

mercy ['mʌrsi] *s* Barmherzigkeit *f*; **be at s.o.'s m.** in j–s Gewalt sein; **be at the m. of** (*e.g., the wind, waves*) preisgegeben sein (*dat*); **beg for m.** um Gnade flehen; **show no m.** keine Gnade walten lassen; **show s.o. m.** sich j–s erbarmen; **throw oneself on the m. of** sich auf Gnade und Ungnade ergeben (*dat*); **without m.** ohne Gnade

mere [mir] *adj* bloß, rein

merely ['mirli] *adv* nur, lediglich

meretricious [‚meri'trɪʃəs] *adj* (*tawdry*) flitterhaft; (*characteristic of a prostitute*) dirnenhaft

merge [mʌrdʒ] *tr* verschmelzen ‖ *intr* sich verschmelzen

merger ['mʌrdʒər] *s* (com) Fusion *f*; (jur) Verschmelzung *f*

meridian [mə'rɪdɪ·ən] *s* (astr) Meridian *m*; (geog) Meridian *m*, Längenkreis *m*

meringue [mə'ræŋ] *s* (*topping*) Eierschnee *m*; (*pastry*) Schaumgebäck *n*

merit ['merɪt] *s* Verdienst *n*; **of great m.** hochverdient ‖ *tr* verdienen

meritorious [‚merə'torɪ·əs] *adj* verdienstvoll

merlin ['mʌrlɪn] *s* (orn) Merlinfalke *m*

mermaid ['mʌr‚med] *s* Seejungfer *f*

merriment ['merimənt] *s* Fröhlichkeit *f*

merry ['meri] *adj* fröhlich, heiter

Mer'ry Christ'mas *s* fröhliche Weihnachten *pl*

mer'ry-go-round' *s* Karussell *n*

mer'rymak'er *s* Zecher –in *mf*

mesh [meʃ] *s* Masche *f*; (*network*) Netzwerk *n*; (mach) Ineinandergreifen *n*; **meshes** (fig) Schlingen *pl* ‖ *intr* ineinandergreifen

mesmerize ['mesmə‚raiz] *tr* hypnotisieren

mess [mes] *s* (*disorder*) Durcheinander *n*; (*dirty condition*) Schweinerei *f*; (*for officers*) Messe *f*; **a nice m.!** e–e schöne Wirtschaft!; **get into a m.** in die Klemme geraten; **make a m.** Schmutz machen; **make a m. of** verpfuschen; **what a m.!** nette Zustände! ‖ *tr*—**m. up** (*dirty*) beschmutzen; (*put into disarray*) in Unordnung bringen ‖ *intr*—**m. around** herumtrödeln; **m. around with** herumnmurksen an (*dat*)

message ['mesidʒ] *s* Botschaft *f*

messenger ['mesəndʒər] *s* Bote *m*, Botin *f*

mess' hall' *s* Messe *f*

Messiah [mə'saɪ·ə] *s* Messias *m*

mess' kit' *s* Eßgeschirr *n*

messy ['mesi] *adj* (*disorderly*) unordentlich; (*dirty*) dreckig

metabolism [mə'tæbə‚lizəm] *s* Stoffwechsel *m*

metal ['metəl] *s* Metall *n*

metallic [mi'tælik] *adj* metallisch

metallurgy ['metə‚lʌrdʒi] *s* Hüttenwesen *n*, Metallurgie *f*

met'alwork' *s* Metallarbeit *f*

metamorpho·sis [‚metə'mɔrfəsis] *s* (**-ses** [‚siz]) Verwandlung *f*

metaphor ['metə‚fɔr] *s* Metapher *f*

metaphorical [‚metə'fɔrɪkəl] *adj* bildlich

metaphysical [‚metə'fizɪkəl] *adj* metaphysisch

metaphysics [‚metə'fizɪks] *s* Metaphysik *f*

metathe·sis [mi'tæθisis] *s* (**-ses** [‚siz]) Metathese *f*, Lautversetzung *f*

mete [mit] *tr*—**m. out** austeilen

meteor ['mitɪ·ər] *s* Meteor *m*

meteoric [‚mitɪ'ɔrik] *adj* meteorisch; (fig) kometenhaft

meteorite ['mitɪ·ə‚rait] *s* Meteorit *m*

meteorologist [‚mitɪ·ə'ralədʒist] *s* Meteorologe *m*, Meteorologin *f*

meteorology [‚mitɪ·ə'ralədʒi] *s* Meteorologie *f*, Wetterkunde *f*

meter ['mitər] *s* Meter *m* & *n*; (*instrument*) Messer *m*, Zähler *m*; (pros) Versmaß *n*

me'ter read'er *s* Zählerableser –in *mf*

methane ['meθen] *s* Methan *n*, Sumpfgas *n*

method ['meθəd] *s* Methode *f*

methodic(al) [mi'θadɪk(əl)] *adj* methodisch

Methodist ['meθədist] *s* Methodist –in *mf*

methodology [‚meθə'dalədʒi] *s* Methodenlehre *f*

Methuselah [mi'θuzələ] *s* Methusalem *m*

meticulous [mi'tikjələs] *adj* übergenau

metric(al) ['metrik(əl)] *adj* metrisch

metrics ['metriks] *s* Metrik *f*

metronome ['metrə‚nom] *s* Metronom *n*

metropolis [mi'trapəlis] *s* Metropole *f*

metropolitan [‚metrə'palitən] *adj* großstädtisch ‖ *s* (eccl) Metropolit *m*

mettle ['metəl] *s* (*temperament*) Veranlagung *f*; (*courage*) Mut *m*

mettlesome ['metəlsəm] *adj* mutig

mew [mju] s Miau n || intr miauen

Mexican ['meksɪkən] adj mexikanisch || s Mexikaner –in mf

Mexico ['meksɪ͵ko] s Mexiko n

mezzanine ['mezə͵nin] s Zwischenge-schoß n

mica ['maɪkə] s Glimmer m, Marien-glas n

Michael ['maɪkəl] s Michel m

microbe ['maɪkrob] s Mikrobe f

microbiology [͵maɪkrəbaɪ'alədʒi] s Mikrobiologie f

microcosm ['maɪkrə͵kazəm] s Mikro-kosmos m

microfilm ['maɪkrə͵fɪlm] s Mikrofilm m || tr mikrofilmen

microgroove ['maɪkrə͵gruv] s Mikro-rille f

mic'rogroove rec'ord s Schallplatte f mit Mikrorillen

microphone ['maɪkrə͵fon] s Mikro-phon n

microscope ['maɪkrə͵skop] s Mikro-skop n

microscopic [͵maɪkrə'skapɪk] adj mi-kroskopisch

microwave ['maɪkrə͵wev] s Mikro-welle f

mid [mɪd] adj mittlere

midair' s—in m. mitten in der Luft

mid'day' adj mittäglich, Mittags– || s Mittag m

middle ['mɪdəl] adj mittlere || s Mitte f, Mittel n; in the m. of inmitten (genit), mitten in (dat)

mid'dle age' s mittleres Lebensalter n; **Middle Ages** Mittelalter n

middle-aged ['mɪdəl͵edʒd] adj mitt-leren Alters

mid'dle class' s Mittelstand m

mid'dle-class' adj bürgerlich

mid'dle dis'tance s Mittelgrund m

mid'dle ear' s Mittelohr n

Mid'dle East', the s der Mittlere Osten

mid'dle fin'ger s Mittelfinger m

Mid'dle High' Ger'man s Mittelhoch-deutsch n

Mid'dle Low' Ger'man s Mittelnieder-deutsch n

mid'dle-man' s (–men') Mittelsmann m, Zwischenhändler m

mid'dleweight box'er s Mittelgewichtler m

mid'dleweight divi'sion s Mittelgewicht n

middling ['mɪdlɪŋ] adj mittelmäßig || adv leidlich, ziemlich

middy ['mɪdi] s (nav) Fähnrich m zur See

midget ['mɪdʒɪt] s Zwerg m

mid'get rail'road s Liliputbahn f

mid'get submarine' s Kleinst-U-Boot n

midland ['mɪdlənd] adj binnenländisch

mid'night' adj mitternächtlich; **burn the m. oil** bis in die tiefe Nacht arbeiten || s Mitternacht f; **at m.** um Mitter-nacht

midriff ['mɪdrɪf] s (of a dress) Mittel-teil m; (diaphragm) Zwerchfell n; (middle part of the body) Magen-grube f; **have a bare m.** die Taille frei lassen

mid'shipman' s (–men') Fähnrich m zur See

midst [mɪdst] s Mitte f; **from our m.** aus unserer Mitte; **in the m. of** mit-ten in (dat)

mid'stream' s—in m. in der Mitte des Stromes

mid'sum'mer s Mittsommer m

mid'-term' adj mitten im Semester || **midterms** spl Prüfungen pl mitten im Semester

mid'way' adj in der Mitte befindlich || adv auf halbem Weg || s Mitte f des Weges; (at a fair) Mittelstraße f

mid'week' s Wochenmitte f

mid'wife' s (–wives') Hebamme f

mid'win'ter s Mittwinter m

mid'year' adj in der Mitte des Studien-jahres || **midyears** spl Prüfungen pl in der Mitte des Studienjahres

mien [min] s Miene f

miff [mɪf] s kleine Auseinandersetzung f || tr ärgern

might [maɪt] s Macht f, Kraft f; **with m. and main** mit aller Kraft || aux used to form the potential mood, e.g., **she m. lose her way** sie könnte sich verirren; **we m. as well go** es ist wohl besser, wenn wir gehen

mightily ['maɪtəli] adv gewaltig; (coll) enorm

mighty ['maɪti] adj mächtig || adv (coll) furchtbar

migraine ['maɪgren] s Migräne f

mi'grant work'er ['maɪgrənt] s Wan-derarbeiter –in mf

migrate ['maɪgret] intr wandern, zie-hen

migration [maɪ'greʃən] s Wanderung f; (e.g., of birds) Zug m

migratory ['maɪgrə͵tori] adj Wander–

mi'gratory bird' s Zugvogel m

Milan [mɪ'læn] s Mailand n

mild [maɪld] adj mild, lind

mildew ['mɪl͵d(j)u] s Mehltau m

mildly ['maɪldli] adv leicht, schwach; **to put it m.** gelinde gesagt

mildness ['maɪldnɪs] s Milde f

mile [maɪl] s Meile f; **for miles** meilen-weit; **miles apart** meilenweit ausein-ander; **miles per hour** Stundenge-schwindigkeit

mileage ['maɪlɪdʒ] s Meilenzahl f; (charge) Meilengeld n

mile'post' s Wegweiser m mit Entfer-nungsangabe

mile'stone' s (& fig) Meilenstein m

militancy ['mɪlɪtənsi] s Kampfgeist m

militant ['mɪlɪtənt] adj militant || s Kämpfer –in mf

militarism ['mɪlɪtə͵rɪzəm] s Militaris-mus m

militarize ['mɪlɪtə͵raɪz] tr auf den Krieg vorbereiten

military ['mɪlə͵teri] adj militärisch; (academy, band, government) Mili-tär– || s Militär n

mil'itary campaign' s Feldzug m

mil'itary cem'etery s Soldatenfriedhof m

mil'itary obliga'tions spl Wehrpflicht f

mil'itary police' s Militärpolizei f

mil′itary police′man *s* (**–men**) Militär-
polizist *m*
mil′itary sci′ence *s* Kriegswissenschaft
f
militate ['mɪlɪ‚tet] *intr* (**against**) entgegenwirken (*dat*)
militia [mɪ'lɪ/ə] *s* Miliz *f*
mili′tia-man *s* (**–men**) Milizsoldat *m*
milk [mɪlk] *s* Milch *f* ‖ *tr* (& fig)
melken
milk′ bar′ *s* Milchbar *f*
milk′ car′ton *s* Milchtüte *f*
milk′maid′ *s* Milchmädchen *n*
milk′man′ *s* (**–men′**) Milchmann *m*
milk′ pail′ *s* Melkeimer *m*
milk′shake′ *s* Milchmischgetränk *n*
milk′sop′ *s* Milchbart *m*
milk′ tooth′ *s* Milchzahn *m*
milk′weed′ *s* Wolfsmilch *f*, Seiden-
pflanze *f*
milky ['mɪlkɪ] *adj* milchig
Milk′y Way′ *s* Milchstraße *f*
mill [mɪl] *s* Mühle *f*; (*factory*) Fabrik
f, Werk *n*; **put through the m.** (coll)
durch e-e harte Schule schicken ‖ *tr*
(*grain*) mahlen; (*coins*) rändeln;
(*with a milling machine*) fräsern;
(*chocolate*) quirlen ‖ *intr*—**m. around**
durcheinanderlaufen
millenial [mɪ'lenɪ-əl] *adj* tausendjährig
millenni•um [mɪ'lenɪ-əm] *s* (**–ums &
–a** [ə]) Jahrtausend *n*
miller ['mɪlər] *s* Müller *m*
millet ['mɪlɪt] *s* Hirse *f*
milligram ['mɪlɪ‚græm] *s* Milligramm
n
millimeter ['mɪlɪ‚mitər] *s* Millimeter
n
milliner ['mɪlɪnər] *s* Putzmacher –in
mf
mil′linery shop′ ['mɪlɪ‚nerɪ] *s* Damen-
hutgeschäft *n*
mill′ing *s* (*of grain*) Mahlen *n*; (*of
wood or metal*) Fräsen *n*
mill′ing machine′ *s* Fräsmaschine *f*
million ['mɪljən] *adj*—**one m. people**
e-e Million Menschen; **two m. people**
zwei Millionen Menschen ‖ *s* Million
f
millionaire [‚mɪljən'er] *s* Millionär –in
mf
millionth ['mɪljənθ] *adj* & *pron* millionste ‖ *s* (*fraction*) Millionstel *n*
mill′pond′ *s* Mühlteich *m*
mill′stone′ *s* Mühlstein *m*
mill′ wheel′ *s* Mühlrad *n*
mime [maɪm] *s* Mime *m*, Mimin *f* ‖ *tr*
mimen
mimeograph ['mɪmɪ‚ə‚græf] *s* Vervielfältigungsapparat *m* ‖ *tr* vervielfältigen
mim•ic ['mɪmɪk] *s* Mimiker –in *mf* ‖
v (*pret & pp* **–icked**; *ger* **–icking**) *tr*
nachäffen
mimicry ['mɪmɪkrɪ] *s* Nachäffen *n*;
(zool) Mimikry *f*
mimosa [mɪ'mosə] *s* Mimose *f*
minaret [‚mɪnə'ret] *s* Minarett *n*
mince [mɪns] *tr* (*meat*) zerhacken; **not
m. words** kein Blatt vor den Mund
nehmen
mince′meat′ *s* Pastetenfüllung *f*;

(*chopped meat*) Hackfleisch *n*; **make
m. of** (fig) in die Pfanne hauen
mind [maɪnd] *s* Geist *m*; **bear in m.**
denken an (*acc*); **be of one m.** ein
Herz und e-e Seele sein; **be of two
minds** geteilter Meinung sein; **be out
of one's m.** nicht bei Trost sein;
call to m. erinnern; (*remember*) sich
erinnern; **change one's m.** sich anders besinnen; **give s.o. a piece of
one's m.** j–m gründlich die Meinung
sagen; **have a good m. to** (*inf*) große
Lust haben zu (*inf*); **have in m.** im
Sinn haben zu (*inf*); **have one's m.
on s.th.** ständig an etw denken
müssen; **I can't get her out of my m.**
sie will mir nicht aus dem Sinn;
know one's own m. wissen, was man
will; **of sound m.** zurechnungsfähig;
put s.th. out of one's m. sich [*dat*]
etw aus dem Sinn schlagen; **set one's
m. on** sein Sinnen und Trachten
richten auf (*acc*); **slip s.o.'s m.** j–m
entfallen; **to my m.** meines Erachtens ‖ *tr* (*watch over*) aufpassen auf
(*acc*); (*obey*) gehorchen (*dat*); (*be
troubled by; take care of*) sich kümmern um; **do you m. if I smoke?**
macht es Ihnen etw aus, wenn ich
rauche?; **do you m. the smoke?** macht
Ihnen der Rauch etw aus?; **I don't
m. your smoking** ich habe nichts dagegen, daß (or wenn) Sie rauchen;
m. your own business! kümmere dich
um deine Angelegenheit!; **m. you!**
wohlgemerkt! ‖ *intr*—**I don't m.** es
macht mir nichts aus; **I don't m. if
I do** (coll) ja, recht gern; **never m.!**
schon gut!
–minded [‚maɪndɪd] *suf* –mütig, –gesinnt, –sinnig
mindful ['maɪndfəl] *adj* (**of**) eingedenk
(*genit*); **be m. of** achten auf (*acc*)
mind′ read′er *s* Gedankenleser –in *mf*
mind′ read′ing *s* Gedankenlesen *n*
mine [maɪn] *s* Bergwerk *n*, Mine *f*;
(fig) Fundgrube *f*; (mil) Mine *f* ‖
poss pron meiner ‖ *tr* (*e.g., coal*)
abbauen; (mil) verminen ‖ *intr*—**m.
for** graben nach
mine′ detec′tor *s* Minensuchgerät *n*
mine′field′ *s* Minenfeld *n*
minelayer ['maɪn‚le-ər] *s* Minenleger
m
miner ['maɪnər] *s* Bergarbeiter *m*
mineral ['mɪnərəl] *adj* mineralisch,
Mineral– ‖ *s* Mineral *n*
mineralogy [‚mɪnə'ralədʒɪ] *s* Mineralogie *f*
min′eral resour′ces *spl* Bodenschätze
pl
min′eral wa′ter *s* Mineralwasser *n*
mine′sweep′er *s* Minenräumboot *n*
mingle ['mɪŋgəl] *tr* vermengen ‖ *intr*
(**with**) sich mischen (unter *acc*)
miniature ['mɪnɪ-ət/ər], ['mɪnɪt/ər]
adj Miniatur–, Klein– ‖ *s* Miniatur *f*
minimal ['mɪnɪməl] *adj* minimal, Mindest–
minimize ['mɪnə‚maɪz] *tr* auf das
Minimum herabsetzen; (fig) bagatellisieren

minimum ['mɪnɪməm] *adj* minimal, Mindest– ‖ *s* Minimum *n*; (*lowest price*) untere Preisgrenze *f*

min'imum wage' *s* Mindestlohn *m*

min'ing *adj* Bergbau– ‖ *s* Bergbau *m*, Bergwesen *n*; (mil) Minenlegen *n*

minion ['mɪnjən] *s* Günstling *m*

miniskirt ['mɪnɪ͵skʌrt] *s* Minirock *m*

minister ['mɪnɪstər] *s* (eccl) Geistlicher *m*; (pol) Minister *m* ‖ *intr*—**m.** to dienen (*dat*); (*aid*) Hilfe leisten (*dat*)

ministerial [͵mɪnɪs'tɪrɪ-əl] *adj* (eccl) geistlich; (pol) ministeriell

ministry ['mɪnɪstrɪ] *s* (*office*) (eccl) geistliches Amt *n*; (*the clergy*) (eccl) geistlicher Stand *m*; (pol) Ministerium *n*

mink [mɪŋk] *s* (zool) Nerz *m*; (*fur*) Nerzfell *n*

mink' coat' *s* Nerzmantel *m*

minnow ['mɪno] *s* Pfrille *f*, Elritze *f*

minor ['maɪnər] *adj* minder, geringer, Neben– ‖ *s* (*person*) Minderjährige *mf*; (educ) Nebenfach *n*; (log) Untersatz *m*; (mus) Moll *n* ‖ *intr*—**m. in** als Nebenfach studieren

minority [mɪ'nɔrɪtɪ] *adj* Minderheits– ‖ *s* Minderheit *f*; (*of votes*) Stimmenminderheit *f*; (*ethnic group*) Minorität *f*

mi'nor key' *s* Molltonart *f*; **in a m. in** Moll

minstrel ['mɪnstrəl] *s* (hist) Spielmann *m*

mint [mɪnt] *s* Münzanstalt *f*; (bot) Minze *f* ‖ *tr* münzen

mintage ['mɪntɪdʒ] *s* Prägung *f*

minuet [͵mɪnju'et] *s* Menuett *n*

minus ['maɪnəs] *adj* negativ ‖ *prep* minus, weniger; (*without*) (coll) ohne (*acc*)

mi'nus sign' *s* Minuszeichen *n*

minute [maɪ'n(j)ut] *adj* winzig ‖ ['mɪnɪt] *s* Minute *f*; **minutes** *spl* Protokoll *n*; **take the minutes** das Protokoll führen

–minute [mɪnɪt] *suf* –minutig

min'ute hand' *s* Minutenzeiger *m*

minutiae [mɪ'n(j)uʃɪ-i] *spl* Einzelheiten *pl*

minx [mɪŋks] *s* Range *f*

miracle ['mɪrəkəl] *s* Wunder *n*

mir'acle play' *s* Mirakelspiel *n*

miraculous [mɪ'rækjələs] *adj* wunderbar; (*e.g., power*) Wunder–

mirage [mɪ'rɑʒ] *s* Luftspiegelung *f*; (fig) Luftbild *n*, Täuschung *f*

mire [maɪr] *s* Morast *m*, Schlamm *m*

mirror ['mɪrər] *s* Spiegel *m* ‖ *tr* spiegeln

mirth [mʌrθ] *s* Fröhlichkeit *f*

miry ['maɪrɪ] *adj* sumpfig, schlammig

misadventure [͵mɪsəd'ventʃər] *s* Mißgeschick *n*

misanthrope ['mɪsən͵θrop] *s* Menschenfeind *m*

misapprehension [͵mɪsæprɪ'henʃən] *s* Mißverständnis *n*

misappropriate [͵mɪsə'proprɪ͵et] *tr* sich (*dat*) widerrechtlich aneignen

misbehave [͵mɪsbɪ'hev] *intr* sich schlecht benehmen

misbehavior [͵mɪsbɪ'hevɪ-ər] *s* schlechtes Benehmen *n*

miscalculate [mɪs'kælkjə͵let] *tr* falsch berechnen ‖ *intr* sich verrechnen

miscalculation [͵mɪskælkjə'leʃən] *s* Rechenfehler *m*

miscarriage [mɪs'kærɪdʒ] *s* Fehlgeburt *f*; (fig) Fehlschlag *m*

miscar'riage of jus'tice *s* Justizirrtum *m*

miscar-ry [mɪs'kærɪ] *v* (*pret & pp* –ried) *intr* e–e Fehlgeburt haben; (*said of a plan*) scheitern, fehlschlagen

miscellaneous [͵mɪsə'lenɪ-əs] *adj* vermischt

miscellany ['mɪsə͵lenɪ] *s* Gemisch *n*; (*of literary works*) Sammelband *m*

mischief ['mɪstʃɪf] *s* Unfug *m*; **be up to m.** e–n Unfug im Kopf haben; **cause m.** Unfug treiben; **get into m.** etw anstellen

mis'chief-mak'er *s* Störenfried *m*

mischievous ['mɪstʃɪvəs] *adj* mutwillig

misconception [͵mɪskən'sepʃən] *s* falsche Auffassung *f*

misconduct [mɪs'kɑndʌkt] *s* schlechtes Benehmen *n*; **m. in office** Amtsvergehen *n* ‖ [͵mɪskən'dʌkt] *tr* schlecht verwalten; **m. oneself** sich schlecht benehmen

misconstrue [͵mɪskən'stru] *tr* falsch auffassen

miscount [mɪs'kaunt] *s* Rechenfehler *m* ‖ *tr* falsch zählen ‖ *intr* sich verzählen

miscreant ['mɪskrɪ-ənt] *s* Schurke *m*

miscue [mɪs'kju] *s* (fig) Fehler *m*; (billiards) Kicks *m* ‖ *intr* (billiards) kicksen; (theat) den Auftritt verpassen

mis-deal ['mɪs͵dil] *s* falsches Geben *n* ‖ [mɪs'dil] *v* (*pret & pp* –delt [delt]) *tr* falsch geben ‖ *intr* sich vergeben

misdeed [mɪs'did] *s* Missetat *f*

misdemeanor [͵mɪsdɪ'minər] *s* Vergehen *n*

misdirect [͵mɪsdɪ'rekt], [͵mɪsdaɪ'rekt] *tr* (& fig) fehlleiten

misdoing [mɪs'du-ɪŋ] *s* Missetat *f*

miser ['maɪzər] *s* Geizhals *m*

miserable ['mɪzərəbəl] *adj* elend; **feel m.** sich elend fühlen; **make life m. for s.o.** j–m das Leben sauer machen

miserly ['maɪzərlɪ] *adj* geizig

misery ['mɪzərɪ] *s* Elend *n*

misfeasance [mɪs'fizəns] *s* (jur) Amtsmißbrauch *m*

misfire [mɪs'faɪr] *s* Versagen *n* ‖ *intr* versagen

misfit ['mɪsfɪt] *s* (*clothing*) schlecht sitzendes Kleidungsstück *n*; (*person*) Gammler *m*

misfortune [mɪs'fɔrtʃən] *s* Unglück *n*

misgiving [mɪs'gɪvɪŋ] *s* böse Ahnung *f*; **full of misgivings** ahnungsvoll

misgovern [mɪs'gʌvərn] *tr* schlecht verwalten

misguidance [mɪs'gaɪdəns] *s* Irreführung *f*

misguide [mɪs'gaɪd] *tr* irreleiten

misguid'ed *adj* irregeleitet

mishap ['mɪshæp] s Unfall m

mishmash ['mɪʃ‚mæʃ] s Mischmasch m

misinform [‚mɪsɪn'fɔrm] tr falsch informieren, falsch unterrichten

misinterpret [‚mɪsɪn'tʌrprɪt] tr mißdeuten, falsch auffassen

misjudge [mɪs'dʒʌdʒ] tr (e.g., a person, situation) falsch beurteilen; (distance) falsch schätzen

mis‧lay [mɪs'le] v (pret & pp –laid) tr verlegen, verkramen

mis‧lead [mɪs'lid] v (pret & pp –led) tr irreführen

mislead′ing adj irreführend

mismanage [mɪs'mænɪdʒ] tr schlecht verwalten; (funds) verwirtschaften

mismanagement [mɪs'mænɪdʒmənt] s Mißwirtschaft f, schlechte Verwaltung f

mismarriage [mɪs'mærɪdʒ] s Mißheirat f

misnomer [mɪs'nomər] s Felhbezeichnung f

misplace [mɪs'ples] tr verlegen

misprint ['mɪs‚prɪnt] s Druckfehler m ‖ [mɪs'prɪnt] tr verdrucken

mispronounce [‚mɪsprə'naʊns] tr falsch aussprechen

mispronunciation [‚mɪsprənʌnsɪ'eʃən] s falsche Aussprache f

misquote [mɪs'kwot] tr falsch zitieren

misread [mɪs'rid] v (pret & pp –read ['red]) tr falsch lesen ‖ intr sich verlesen

misrepresent [‚mɪsrɛprɪ'zɛnt] tr falsch darstellen; m. the facts to s.o. j–m falsche Tatsachen vorspiegeln

miss [mɪs] s Fehlschlag m, Versager m; **Miss Fräulein** n; **Miss America** die Schönheitskönigin von Amerika ‖ tr (a target; one's calling; a person, e.g., at the station; a town along the road; one's way) verfehlen; (feel the lack of) verpassen; (school, a train, an opportunity) versäumen; **m. one's step** fehltreten; **m. the mark** vorbeischießen; (fig) sein Ziel verfehlen; **m. the point** die Pointe nicht verstanden haben ‖ intr fehlen; (in shooting) vorbeischießen

missal ['mɪsəl] s Meßbuch n

misshapen [mɪs'ʃepən] adj mißgestaltet

missile ['mɪsɪl] s Geschoß n; (rok) Rakete f

missing ['mɪsɪŋ] adj—**be m.** fehlen; (said, e.g., of a child) vermißt werden; **m. in action** vermißt

miss′ing per′son s Vermißte mf

miss′ing-per′sons bu′reau s Suchdienst m

mission ['mɪʃən] s Mission f; **m. in life** Lebensaufgabe f

missionary ['mɪʃən‚ɛri] adj Missions– ‖ s Missionar –in mf

missis ['mɪsɪz] s—**the m.** (the wife) die Frau; (of the house) (coll) die Frau des Hauses

missive ['mɪsɪv] s Sendschreiben n

mis‧spell [mɪs'spɛl] v (pret & pp –spelled & –spelt) tr & intr falsch schreiben

misspell′ing s Schreibfehler m

misspent [mɪs'spɛnt] adj vergeudet

misstate [mɪs'stet] tr falsch angeben

misstatement [mɪs'stetmənt] s falsche Angabe f

misstep [mɪs'stɛp] s (& fig)Fehltritt m

mist [mɪst] s feiner Nebel m ‖ tr umnebeln ‖ intr (said of the eyes) sich trüben; **mist over** nebeln

mis‧take [mɪs'tek] s Fehler m; **by m.** aus Versehen ‖ v (pret –took ['tʊk]; pp –taken) tr verkennen; **m. s.o. for s.o. else** j–n mit e–m anderen verwechseln

mistaken [mɪs'tekən] adj falsch, irrig; **be m.** (about) sich irren (in dat); **unless I'm m.** wenn ich mich nicht irre

mistak′en iden′tity s Personenverwechslung f

mistakenly [mɪs'tekənli] adv versehentlich

mister ['mɪstər] s Herr m ‖ interj (pej) Herr!

mistletoe ['mɪsəl‚to] s Mistel f

mistreat [mɪs'trit] tr mißhandeln

mistreatment [mɪs'tritmənt] s Mißhandlung f

mistress ['mɪstrɪs] s Herrin f; (lover) Mätresse f, Geliebte f

mistrial [mɪs'traɪ‧əl] s fehlerhaft geführter Prozeß m

mistrust [mɪs'trʌst] s Mißtrauen n ‖ tr mißtrauen (dat)

misty ['mɪsti] adj neblig; (eyes) umflort; (fig) unklar

misunder‧stand [‚mɪsʌndər'stænd] v (pret & pp –stood) tr & intr mißverstehen

misunderstanding [‚mɪsʌndər'stændɪŋ] s Mißverständnis n

misuse [mɪs'jus] s Mißbrauch m ‖ [mɪs'juz] tr mißbrauchen; (mistreat) mißhandeln

misword [mɪs'wʌrd] tr in falsche Worte fassen

mite [maɪt] s (ent) Milbe f

miter ['maɪtər] s Bischofsmütze f ‖ tr auf Gehrung verbinden

mi′ter box′ s Gehrlade f

mitigate ['mɪtɪ‚get] tr lindern

mitigation [‚mɪtɪ'geʃən] s Linderung f

mitt [mɪt] s Fausthandschuh m; (sl) Flosse f; (baseball) Fängerhandschuh m

mitten ['mɪtən] s Fausthandschuh m

mix [mɪks] s Mischung f, Gemisch n ‖ tr (ver)mischen; (a drink) mixen; (a cake) anrühren; **mix in** beimischen; **mix up** vermischen; (confuse) verwirren ‖ intr sich (ver)mischen; **mix with** vekehren mit

mixed adj vermischt; (feelings, company, doubles) gemischt

mixed′ drink′ s Mixgetränk n

mixed′ mar′riage s Mischehe f

mixer ['mɪksər] s Mischer –in mf; (of cocktails) Mixer –in mf; (mach) Mischmaschine f; **a good m.** ein guter Gesellschafter

mixture ['mɪkstʃər] s (e.g., of gases)

Gemisch *n*; (*e.g., of tobacco, coffee*) Mischung *f*; (pharm) Mixtur *f*

mix'-up' *s* Wirrwar *m*, Verwechslung *f*

mizzen ['mɪzən] *s* Besan *m*

mnemonic [nə'manɪk] *s* Gedächtnishilfe *f*

moan [mon] *s* Stöhnen *n* ‖ *intr* stöhnen; **m. about** jammern über (*acc*) or um

moat [mot] *s* Schloßgraben *m*

mob [mab] *s* (*populace*) Pöbel *m*; (*crush of people*) Andrang *m*; (*gang of criminals*) Verbrecherbande *f* ‖ *v* (*pret & pp* mobbed; *ger* mobbing) *tr* (*crowd into*) lärmend eindringen in (*acc*); (*e.g., a consulate*) angreifen; (*a celebrity*) umringen

mobile ['mobɪl] *adj* fahrbar; (mil) motorisiert

mo'bile home' *s* Wohnwagen *m*

mobility [mo'bɪlɪti] *s* (& mil) Beweglichkeit *f*

mobilization [,mobɪlɪ'zeʃən] *s* Mobilisierung *f*

mobilize ['mobɪ,laɪz] *tr* mobilisieren; (*strength*) aufbieten

mob' rule' *s* Pöbelherrschaft *f*

mobster ['mabstər] *s* Gangster *m*

moccasin ['makəsɪn] *s* Mokassin *m*; (*snake*) Mokassinschlange *f*

Mo'cha cof'fee ['mokə] *s* Mokka *m*

mock [mak] *adj* Schein– ‖ *tr* verspotten; (*imitate*) nachäffen ‖ *intr* spotten; **m. at** sich lustig machen über (*acc*); **m. up** improvisieren

mocker ['makər] *s* Spötter –in *mf*

mockery ['makəri] *s* Spott *m*, Spöttelei *f*; **make a m. of** hohnsprechen (*dat*)

mock'ing *adj* spöttisch

mock'ingbird' *s* Spottdrossel *f*

mock' tri'al *s* Schauprozeß *m*

mock' tur'tle soup' *s* falsche Schildkrötensuppe *f*

mock'-up' *s* Schaumodell *n*

modal ['modəl] *adj* modal, Modal–

mode [mod] *s* Modus *m*; (mus) Tonart *f*

mod-el ['madəl] *adj* vorbildlich; (*student, husband*) Muster– ‖ *s* (*e.g., of a building*) Modell *n*; (*at a fashion show*) Vorführdame *f*; (*for art or photography*) Modell *n*; (*example for imitation*) Vorbild *n*, Muster *n*; (*make*) Typ *m*, Bauart *f* ‖ *v* (*pret & pp* -el[l]ed; *ger* -el[l]ing) *tr* (*clothes*) vorführen; **m. oneself on** sich (*dat*) ein Muster nehmen an (*dat*); **m. s.th. on** etw formen nach; (fig) etw gestalten nach ‖ *intr* (**for**) Modell stehen (zu *dat*)

mod'el air'plane *s* Flugzeugmodell *n*

mod'el num'ber *s* (aut) Typennummer *f*

moderate ['madərɪt] *adj* (*climate*) gemäßigt; (*demand*) maßvoll; (*price*) angemessen; (*e.g., in drinking*) mäßig; **of m. means** minderbemittelt ‖ ['madə,ret] *tr* mäßigen; (*a meeting*) den Vorsitz führen über (*acc*) or bei; (*a television show*) moderieren ‖ *intr* sich mäßigen

moderation [,madə'reʃən] *s* Mäßigung

f, Maß *n*; **in m.** mit Maß; **observe m.** Maß halten

moderator ['madə,retər] *s* Moderator *m*

modern ['madərn] *adj* modern, zeitgemäß

mod'ern Eng'lish *s* Neuenglisch *n*

mod'ern his'tory *s* Neuere Geschichte *f*

modernize ['madər,naɪz] *tr* modernisieren

mod'ern lan'guages *spl* neuere Sprachen *pl*

mod'ern times' *spl* die Neuzeit *f*

modest ['madɪst] *adj* bescheiden

modesty ['madɪsti] *s* Bescheidenheit *f*

modicum ['madɪkəm] *s* bißchen *n*; **a m. of truth** ein Körnchen Wahrheit

modification [,madɪfɪ'keʃən] *s* Abänderung *f*

modifier ['madɪ,faɪ-ər] *s* (gram) nähere Bestimmung *f*

modi-fy ['madɪ,faɪ] *tr* (*pret & pp* -fied) *tr* abändern; (gram) näher bestimmen

modish ['modɪʃ] *adj* modisch

modulate ['madjə,let] *tr & intr* modulieren

modulation [,madjə'leʃən] *s* Modulation *f*

mohair ['mo,her] *s* Mohair *m*

Mohammedan [mo'hæmɪdən] *adj* mohammedanisch ‖ *s* Mohammedaner –in *mf*

Mohammedanism [mo'hæmɪdə,nɪzəm] *s* Mohammedanismus *m*

moist [mɔɪst] *adj* feucht; (*eyes*) tränenfeucht

moisten ['mɔɪsən] *tr* anfeuchten; (*lips*) befeuchten ‖ *intr* feucht werden

moisture ['mɔɪstʃər] *s* Feuchtigkeit *f*

molar ['molər] *s* Backenzahn *m*

molasses [mə'læsɪz] *s* Melasse *f*

mold [mold] *s* Form *f*; (*mildew*) Schimmel *m*; (typ) Matrize *f* ‖ *tr* formen ‖ *intr* (ver)schimmeln

molder ['moldər] *s* Former –in *mf*; (fig) Bildner –in *mf* ‖ *intr* modern

mold'ing *s* Formen *n*; (carp) Gesims *n*

moldy ['moldi] *adj* mod(e)rig, schimmlig

mole [mol] *s* (*breakwater*) Hafendamm *m*; (*blemish*) Muttermal *n*; (zool) Maulwurf *m*

molecular [mə'lekjələr] *adj* molekular

molecule ['malɪ,kjul] *s* Molekül *n*

mole'skin' *s* (fur) Maulwurfsfell *n*; (tex) Englischleder *n*

molest [mə'lest] *tr* belästigen

molli-fy ['malɪ,faɪ] *v* (*pret & pp* -fied) *tr* besänftigen

mollusk ['maləsk] *s* Weichtier *n*

mollycoddle ['malɪ,kadəl] *s* Weichling *m* ‖ *tr* verweichlichen

Mol'otov cock'tail ['malətəf] *s* Flaschengranate *f*

molt [molt] *s intr* sich mausern

molten ['moltən] *adj* schmelzflüssig

molybdenum [mə'lɪbdɪnəm] *s* Molybdän *n*

mom [mam] *s* (coll) Mama *f*, Mutti *f*

moment ['momənt] *s* Moment *m*, Au-

genblick *m;* **a m. ago** nur eben; **at a
moment's notice** jeden Augenblick;
at any m. jederzeit; **at the m.** im
Augenblick, zur Zeit; **of great m.**
von großer Tragweite; **the very m.
I spotted her** sobald ich sie erblickte
momentarily ['moumən,terɪli] *adv* momentan; *(in a moment)* gleich
momentary ['moumən,tɛri] *adj* vorübergehend
momentous [mo'mɛntəs] *adj* folgenschwer
momen·tum [mo'mɛntəm] *s* (**–tums &
–ta** [tə]) (phys) Moment *n;* (fig)
Schwung *m;* **gather m.** Schwung bekommen
monarch ['mɑnərk] *s* Monarch *m*
monarchical [mə'nɑrkɪkəl] *adj* mo-
narchisch
monarchy ['mɑnərki] *s* Monarchie *f*
monastery ['mænəs,tɛri] *s* Kloster *n*
monastic [mə'næstɪk] *adj* Kloster–,
Mönchs–
monasticism [mə'næsti,sɪzəm] *s*
Mönchswesen *n*
Monday ['mʌndi], ['mʌnde] *s* Montag
m; **on M.** am Montag
monetary ['mɑni,tɛri] *adj (e.g., crisis,
unit)* Währungs–; *(e.g., system,
value)* Geld–
mon'etary stand'ard *s* Münzfuß *m*
money ['mʌni] *adj* Geld– ‖ *s* Geld *n;*
big m. schweres Geld; **get one's
money's worth** reell bedient werden;
make m. (on) Geld verdienen (an
dat); **put m. on** Geld setzen auf *(acc)*
mon'eybag' *s* Geldbeutel *m;* **money-
bags** (coll) Geldsack *m*
mon'ey belt' *s* Geldgürtel *m*
moneychanger ['mʌni,tʃendʒər] *s*
Wechsler –in *mf*
moneyed ['mʌnid] *adj* vermögend
mon'ey exchange' *s* Geldwechsel *m*
mon'eylend'er *s* Geldverleiher –in *mf*
mon'eymak'er *s* (fig) Goldgrube *f*
mon'ey or'der *s* Postanweisung *f*
Mongol ['mɑŋgəl] *adj* mongolid ‖ *s*
Mongole *m,* Mongolin *f*
Mongolian [mɑŋ'goli·ən] *adj* mongolisch ‖ *s (language)* Mongolisch *n*
mon·goose ['mɑŋgus] *s* (**–gooses**)
Mungo *m*
mongrel ['mʌŋgrəl] *s* Bastard *m*
monitor ['mɑnɪtər] *s (at school)* Klas-
senordner *m;* (rad, telv) Über-
wachungsgerät *n,* Monitor *m* ‖ *tr*
überwachen
monk [mʌŋk] *s* Mönch *m*
monkey ['mʌŋki] *s* Affe *m; (female)*
Äffin *f;* **make a m. of** zum Narren
halten ‖ *intr*—**m. around** *(trifle idly)*
herumalbern; **m. around with s.o.** es
mit j–m treiben; **m. around with s.th.**
an etw *[dat]* herummurksen
mon'keybusi'ness *s (underhanded conduct)* Gaunerei *f; (frivolous behavior)* (sl) Unfug *m*
mon'keyshine' *s* (sl) Possen *m*
mon'key wrench' *s* Engländer *m*
monocle ['mɑnəkəl] *s* Monokel *n*
monogamous [mə'nɑgəməs] *adj* mono-
gam

monogamy [mə'nɑgəmi] *s* Einehe *f*
monogram ['mɑnə,græm] *s* Monogramm *n*
monograph ['mɑnə,græf] *s* Monogra-
phie *f*
monolithic [,mɑnə'lɪθɪk] *adj* (& fig)
monolithisch
monologue ['mɑnə,lɔg] *s* Monolog *m*
monomania [,mɑnə'meni·ə] *s* Mono-
manie *f*
monoplane ['mɑnə,plen] *s* Eindecker
m
monopolize [mə'nɑpə,laɪz] *tr* monopolisieren
monorail ['mɑnə,rel] *s* Einschienen-
bahn *f*
monosyllable ['mɑnə,sɪləbəl] *s* einsil-
biges Wort *n*
monotheism [,mɑnə'θi·ɪzəm] *s* Mono-
theismus *m*
monotonous [mə'nɑtənəs] *adj* eintönig
monotony [mə'nɑtəni] *s* Eintönigkeit *f*
monotype ['mɑnə,taɪp] *s* Monotype *f*
monoxide [mə'nɑksaɪd] *s* Monoxyd *n*
monsignor [mɑn'sinjər] *s* (**monsignors
& monsignori** [,mɑnsi'njori]) (eccl)
Monsignore *m*
monsoon [mɑn'sun] *s* Monsun *m*
monster ['mɑnstər] *s* (& fig) Ungeheuer *n*
monstrance ['mɑnstrəns] *s* Monstranz
f
monstrosity [mɑns'trɑsɪti] *s* Monstrosität *f,* Ungeheuerlichkeit *f*
monstrous ['mɑnstrəs] *adj* ungeheuer-
(lich)
month [mʌnθ] *s* Monat *m*
monthly ['mʌnθli] *adj* & *adv* monat-
lich ‖ *s* Monatszeitschrift *f*
monument ['mɑnjəmənt] *s* Denkmal *n*
monumental [,mɑnjə'mɛntəl] *adj*
monumental
moo [mu] *s* Muhen *n* ‖ *intr* muhen
mood [mud] *s* Laune *f,* Stimmung *f;*
(gram) Aussageweise *f,* Modus *m;*
be in a bad m. schlechtgelaunt sein;
be in the m. for s.th. zu etw gelaunt
sein
moody ['mudi] *adj* launisch
moon [mun] *s* Mond *m* ‖ *intr*—**m.
about** herumlungern
moon'beam' *s* Mondstrahl *m*
moon'light' *s* Mondschein *m* ‖ *intr*
schwarzarbeiten
moon'light'er *s* Doppelverdiener –in *mf*
moon'light'ing *s* Schwarzarbeit *f*
moon'lit' *adj* mondhell
moon'shine' *s* Mondschein *m;* (sl)
schwarz gebrannter Whisky *m*
moonshiner ['mun,ʃaɪnər] *s* Schwarz-
brenner –in *mf*
moon'shot' *s* Mondgeschoß *n*
moor [mur] *s* Moor *n,* Heidemoor *n;*
Moor Mohr *m* ‖ *tr* (naut) vertäuen
‖ *intr* (naut) festmachen
moor'ing *s* (act) Festmachen *n;* **moor-
ings** *(cables)* Vertäuung *f; (place)*
Liegeplatz *m*
Moorish ['murɪʃ] *adj* maurisch
moose [mus] *s* (**moose**) amerikanischer
Elch *m*
moot [mut] *adj* umstritten

mop [mɑp] *s* Mop *m; (of hair)* Wust *m* ‖ *v (pret & pp* **mopped;** *ger* **mopping)** *tr* mit dem Mop wischen; **mop up** mit dem Mop aufwischen; (mil) säubern

mope [mop] *intr* Trübsal blasen

moped ['mopəd] *s* Moped *n*

mop/ping-up/ opera'tion *s* (mil) Säuberungsaktion *f*

moral ['mɔrəl] *adj* moralisch ‖ *s* Moral *f;* **morals** Sitten *pl*

morale [mə'ræl] *s* Moral *f*

morality [mə'rælti] *s* Sittlichkeit *f*

moralize ['mɔrə͵laɪz] *intr* moralisieren

morass [mə'ræs] *s* Morast *m*

moratori·um [͵mɔrə'tɔri·əm] *s* (**–ums** & a– [ə]) Moratorium *n*

Moravia [mə'revɪ·ə] *s* Mähren *n*

morbid ['mɔrbɪd] *adj* krankhaft, morbid

mordacious [mɔr'deʃəs] *adj* bissig

mordant ['mɔrdənt] *adj* beißend

more [mɔr] *comp adj* mehr; **one m. minute** noch e–e Minute ‖ *comp adv* mehr; **all the m.** erst recht; **all the m. because** zumal, da; **m. and m.** immer mehr; **m. and m. expensive** immer teurer; **m. or less** gewissermaßen; **m. than anything** über alles; **no m.** nicht mehr; **not any m.** nicht mehr; **once m.** noch einmal; **the more ... the** (expressing quantity) je mehr ... desto; (expressing frequency) je öfter ... desto ‖ *s* mehr; **see m. of s.o.** j–n noch öfter sehen; **what's m.** außerdem ‖ *pron* mehr

more/o'ver *adv* außerdem, übrigens

morgue [mɔrg] *s* Leichenschauhaus *n;* (journ) Archiv *n,* Zeitungsarchiv *n*

morning ['mɔrnɪŋ] *adj* Morgen– ‖ *s* Morgen *m;* **from m. till night** von früh bis spät; **in the early m.** in früher Morgenstunde; **in the m.** am Morgen; **this m.** heute morgen; **tomorrow m.** morgen früh

morn'ing-af'ter pill' *s* Pille *f* danach

morn'ing-glo'ry *s* Trichterwinde *f*

morn'ing sick'ness *s* morgendliches Erbrechen *n*

morn'ing star' *s* Morgenstern *m*

Moroccan [mə'rɑkən] *adj* marokkanisch ‖ *s* Marokkaner –in *mf*

morocco [mə'rɑko] *s (leather)* Saffian *m;* **Morocco** Marokko *n*

moron ['mɔrɑn] *s* Schwachsinnige *mf*

morose [mə'ros] *adj* mürrisch

morphine ['mɔrfin] *s* Morphium *n*

morphology [mɔr'fɑlədʒi] *s* Morphologie *f*

morrow ['mɔro] *s*—**on the m.** am folgenden Tag

Morse' code' [mɔrs] *s* Morsealphabet *n*

morsel ['mɔrsəl] *s* Bröckchen *n*

mortal ['mɔrtəl] *adj* sterblich ‖ *s* Sterbliche *mf*

mor'tal dan'ger *s* Lebensgefahr *f*

mor'tal en'emy *s* Todfeind *m*

mor'tal fear' *s* Heidenangst *f*

mortality [mɔr'tælti] *s* Sterblichkeit *f*

mortally ['mɔrtəli] *adv* tödlich

mor'tal remains' *spl* irdische Überreste *pl*

mor'tal sin' *s* Todsünde *f*

mor'tal wound' *s* Todeswunde *f*

mortar ['mɔrtər] *s (vessel)* Mörser *m;* (archit) Mörtel *m;* (mil) Granatwerfer *m*

mor'tarboard' *s* Mörtelbrett *n*

mor'tar fire' *s* Granatwerferfeuer *n*

mor'tar shell' *s* Granate *f*

mortgage ['mɔrgɪdʒ] *s* Hypothek *f* ‖ *tr* mit e–r Hypothek belasten

mortgagee [͵mɔrgɪ'dʒi] *s* Hypothekengläubiger –in *mf*

mortgagor ['mɔrgɪdʒər] *s* Hypothekenschuldner –in *mf*

mortician [mɔr'tɪʃən] *s* Leichenbestatter –in *mf*

morti·fy ['mɔrtɪ͵faɪ] *v (pret & pp* **–fied)** *tr (the flesh)* abtöten; *(humiliate)* demütigen; **m. oneself** sich kasteien

mortise ['mɔrtɪs] *s* (carp) Zapfenloch *n* ‖ *tr* (carp) verzapfen

mortuary ['mɔrt/ʊ͵eri] *s* Leichenhalle *f*

mosaic [mo'ze·ɪk] *adj* mosaisch ‖ *s* Mosaik *n*

Moscow ['mɑsko], ['mɑskaʊ] *s* Moskau *n*

Moses ['mozɪz], ['mozɪs] *s* Moses *m*

mosey ['mozi] *intr* (coll) dahinschlürfen

Mos·lem ['mɑzləm] *adj* muselmanisch ‖ *s* (**–lems** & **–lem)** Moslem –in *mf*

mosque [mɑsk] *s* Moschee *f*

mosqui·to [məs'kito] *s* (**–toes** & **–tos)** Moskito *m,* Mücke *f*

mosqui'to net' *s* Moskitonetz *n*

moss [mɔs] *s* Moos *n*

mossy ['mɔsi] *adj* bemoost

most [most] *super adj* meist ‖ *super adv* am meisten; *(very)* höchst; **m. of all** am allermeisten ‖ *s*—**at (the) m.** höchstens; **make the m. of** möglichst gut ausnützen; **m. of** die meisten; **m. of the day** der größte Teil des Tages; **the m.** das meiste, das Höchste ‖ *pron* die meisten

mostly ['mostli] *adv* meistens

motel [mo'tel] *s* Motel *n*

moth [mɔθ] *s* Nachtfalter *m;* (clothes moth) Motte *f*

moth'ball' *s* Mottenkugel *f;* **put into mothballs** (nav) stillegen, einmotten ‖ *tr* (& fig) einmotten

moth-eaten ['mɔθ͵itən] *adj* mottenzerfressen

mother ['mʌðər] *s* Mutter *f* ‖ *tr (produce)* gebären; *(take care of as a mother)* bemuttern

moth'er coun'try *s* Mutterland *n*

moth'erhood' *s* Mutterschaft *f*

moth'er-in-law' *s* (**mothers-in-law)** Schwiegermutter *f*

motherless ['mʌðərlɪs] *adj* mutterlos

motherly ['mʌðərli] *adj* mütterlich

mother-of-pearl ['mʌðərəv'pʌrl] *adj* perlmuttern ‖ *s* Perlmutter *f*

Moth'er's Day' *s* Muttertag *m*

moth'er's help'er *s* Stütze *f* der Hausfrau

moth′er supe′rior *s* (Schwester) Oberin *f*

moth′er tongue′ *s* Muttersprache *f*

moth′ hole′ *s* Mottenfraß *m*

mothy [′mɔθi] *adj* mottenzerfressen

motif [mo′tif] *s* (mus, paint) Motiv *n*

motion [′moʃən] *s* Bewegung *f*; (parl) Antrag *m*; **make a m.** e-n Antrag stellen; **set in m.** in Bewegung setzen ‖ *tr* zuwinken (*dat*); **m. s.o. to** (*inf*) j-n durch e-n Wink auffordern zu (*inf*)

motionless [′moʃənlɪs] *adj* bewegungslos

mo′tion pic′ture *s* Film *m*; **be in motion pictures** beim Film sein

mo′tion-pic′ture *adj* Film—

mo′tion-pic′ture the′ater *s* Kino *n*

motivate [′motɪ,vet] *tr* begründen, motivieren

motive [′motɪv] *s* Anlaß *m*, Beweggrund *m*

mo′tive pow′er *s* Triebkraft *f*

motley [′matlɪ] *adj* bunt zusammengewürfelt

motor [′motər] *adj* Motor— ‖ *s* Motor *m*

motorcade [′motər,ked] *s* Wagenkolonne *f*

mo′torcy′cle *s* Motorrad *n*

mo′torcyc′list *s* Motorradfahrer —in *mf*

mo′toring *s* Autofahren *n*

motorist [′motərɪst] *s* Autofahrer —in *mf*

motorize [′motə,raɪz] *tr* motorisieren

mo′tor launch′ *s* Motorbarkasse *f*

mo′tor-man *s* (**–men**) Straßenbahnführer *m*

mo′tor pool′ *s* Fahrbereitschaft *f*

mo′tor scoot′er *s* Motorroller *m*

mo′tor ve′hicle *s* Kraftfahrzeug *n*

mottle [′matəl] *tr* sprenkeln

mot·to [′mato] *s* (**–toes & –tos**) Motto *n*

mound [maʊnd] *s* Wall *m*, Erdhügel *m*

mount [maʊnt] *s* (*mountain*) Berg *m*; (*riding horse*) Reittier *n* ‖ *tr* (*a horse, mountain*) besteigen; (*stairs*) hinaufgehen; (*e.g., a machinegun*) in Position bringen; (*a precious stone*) fassen; (*photographs in an album*) einkleben; (*photographs on a backing*) aufkleben; **m.** (*e.g., a gun*) **on** montieren auf (*acc*)

mountain [′maʊntən] *s* Berg *m*; **down the m.** bergab; **up the m.** bergauf

moun′tain climb′er *s* Bergsteiger —in *mf*

moun′tain climb′ing *s* Bergsteigen *n*

mountaineer [,maʊmtə′nɪr] *s* Bergbewohner —in *mf*

mountainous [′maʊntənəs] *adj* gebirgig

moun′tain pass′ *s* Gebirgspaß *m*, Paß *m*

moun′tain rail′road *s* Bergbahn *f*

moun′tain range′ *s* Gebirge *n*

moun′tain scen′ery *s* Berglandschaft *f*

mountebank [′maʊntə,bæŋk] *s* Quacksalber *m*; (*charlatan*) Scharlatan *m*

mount′ing *s* Montage *f*; (*of a precious stone*) Fassung *f*

mourn [morn] *tr* betrauern ‖ *intr*

trauern; **mourn for** betrauern, trauern um

mourner [′mornər] *s* Leidtragende *mf*

mournful [′mornfəl] *adj* traurig

mourn′ing *s* Trauer *f*; **be in m.** Trauer tragen

mourn′ing band′ *s* Trauerflor *m*

mourn′ing clothes′ *spl* Trauerkleidung *f*; **wear m.** Trauer tragen

mouse [maʊs] *s* (**mice** [maɪs]) Maus *f*

mouse′hole′ *s* Mauseloch *n*

mouse′trap′ *s* Mausefalle *f*

moustache [məs′tæʃ] *s* Schnurrbart *m*

mouth [maʊθ] *s* (**mouths** [maʊðz]) Mund *m*; (*of an animal*) Maul *n*; (*of a gun, bottle, river*) Mündung *f*; (sl) Maul *n*; **keep one's m. shut** den Mund halten; **make s.o.'s m. water** j-m das Wasser im Munde zusammenlaufen lassen

mouthful [′maʊθ,ful] *s* Mundvoll *m*; (sl) großes Wort *n*

mouth′ or′gan *s* Mundharmonika *f*

mouth′piece′ *s* (*of an instrument*) Ansatz *m*; (box) Mundstück *n*; (fig) Sprachrohr *n*

mouth′wash′ *s* Mundwasser *n*

movable [′muvəbəl] *adj* beweglich, mobil ‖ **movables** *spl* Mobilien *pl*

move [muv] *s* (*movement*) Bewegung *f*; (*step, measure*) Maßnahme *f*; (*resettlement*) Umzug *m*; (checkers) Zug *m*; (parl) Vorschlag *m*; **be on the m.** unterwegs sein; **don't make a m.!** keinen Schritt!; **get a m. on** (coll) sich rühren; **it's your m.** (& fig) du bist am Zug; **she won't make a m. without him** sie macht keinen Schritt ohne ihn ‖ *tr* bewegen; (*emotionally*) rühren; (*shove*) rücken; (checkers) e-n Zug machen mit; (parl) beantragen; **m. the bowels** abführen; **m. up** (mil) vorschieben ‖ *intr* (*stir*) sich bewegen; (*change residence*) umziehen; (*in society*) verkehren; (checkers) ziehen; (com) Absatz haben; **m. away** wegziehen; **m. back** zurückziehen; **m. for** (*e.g., a new trial*) beantragen; **m. in** zuziehen; **m. into** (*a home*) beziehen; **m. on** fortziehen; **m. out** (of) ausziehen (aus); **m. over** (*make room*) zur Seite rücken; **m. up** (*to a higher position*) vorrücken; (*into a vacated position*) nachrücken; (*said of a team*) aufsteigen

movement [′muvmənt] *s* (& fig) Bewegung *f*; (mus) Satz *m*

mover [′muvər] *s* Möbeltransporteur *m*; (parl) Antragsteller —in *mf*

movie [′muvi] *adj* (*actor, actress, camera, projector*) Film— ‖ *s* (coll) Film *m*; **movies** Kino *n*; **go to the movies** ins Kino gehen

mov′ie cam′era *s* Filmkamera *f*

moviegoer [′muvi,go·ər] *s* Kinobesucher —in *mf*

mov′ie house′ *s* Kino *n*

mov′ie screen′ *s* Filmleinwand *f*

mov′ie set′ *s* Filmkulisse *f*

mov′ie the′ater *s* Kino *n*

mov′ing *adj* beweglich; (*force*) treibend; (fig) herzergreifend ‖ s (change of residence) Umzug m

mov′ing pic′ture s Lichtspiel n, Film m

mov′ing spir′it s führender Kopf m

mow [mo] v (pret **mowed;** pp **mowed & mown**) tr mähen; **mow down** (enemies) niedermähen

mower ['mo·ər] s Mäher m

m.p.h. ['em'pi'et∫] spl (**miles per hour**) Stundenmeilen; **drive sixty m.p.h.** mit sechzig Stundenmeilen fahren

Mr. [mɪstər] s Herr m

Mrs. ['mɪsɪz] s Frau f

Ms. [mɪz] s Fräulein n

much [mʌt∫] adj, adv & pron viel; **as m. again** noch einmal soviel; **how m.** wieviel; **m. less** (not to mention) geschweige denn; **not so m.** as nicht einmal; **so m. so** so sehr; **so m. the better** um so besser; **very m.** sehr

mucilage ['mjusɪlɪdʒ] s Klebstoff m

muck [mʌk] s (& fig) Schmutz m

muck′rake′ intr (coll) Korruptionsfälle enthüllen

muckraker ['mʌk‚rekər] s (coll) Korruptionsschnüffler -in mf

mucky ['mʌki] adj schmutzig

mucous ['mjukəs] adj schleimig

muc′ous mem′brane s Schleimhaut f

mucus ['mjukəs] s Schleim m

mud [mʌd] s Schlamm m; **drag through the mud** (fig) in den Schmutz ziehen

mud′ bath′ s Schlammbad n, Moorbad n

muddle ['mʌdəl] s Durcheinander n ‖ tr durcheinanderbringen ‖ intr—**m. through** sich durchwursteln

mud′dlehead′ s Wirrkopf m

mud·dy ['mʌdi] adj schlammig; (fig) trüb ‖ v (pret & pp –died) trüben

mud′hole′ s Schlammloch n

mudslinging ['mʌd‚slɪŋɪŋ] s (fig) Verleumdung f

muff [mʌf] s Muff m ‖ tr (coll) verpfuschen

muffin ['mʌfɪn] s Teekuchen m aus Backpulverteig

muffle ['mʌfəl] tr (sounds) dämpfen; **m. up** (wrap up) einhüllen

muf′fled adj dumpf

muffler ['mʌflər] s (scarf) Halstuch n; (aut) Auspufftopf m

mufti ['mʌfti] s Zivil n

mug [mʌg] s Krug m; (for beer) Seidel n; (thug) (sl) Rocker m; (face) (sl) Fratze f ‖ v (pret & pp **mugged;** ger **mugging**) tr (sl) photographieren; (assault) (sl) überfallen ‖ intr (sl) Gesichter schneiden

muggy ['mʌgi] adj schwül

mug′ shot′ s (sl) Polizeifoto n

mulat·to [mə'læto] s (–toes) Mulatte m, Mulattin f

mulberry ['mʌl‚beri] s Maulbeere f

mul′berry tree′ s Maulbeerbaum m

mulch [mʌlt∫] s Streu n

mulct [mʌlkt] tr (of) betrügen (um)

mule [mjul] s Maulesel m, Maultier n

mulish ['mjulɪ∫] adj störrisch

mull [mʌl] intr—**m. over** nachgrübeln über (acc)

mullion ['mʌljən] s Mittelpfosten m

multicolored ['mʌlti‚kələrd] adj bunt

multigraph ['mʌlti‚græf] s (trademark) Vervielfältigungsmaschine f ‖ tr vervielfältigen

multilateral [‚mʌlti'lætərəl] adj mehrseitig

multimillionaire ['mʌlti‚mɪljə'ner] s vielfacher Millionär m

multiple ['mʌltɪpəl] adj mehrfach, Vielfach– ‖ s (math) Vielfaches n

multiplication [‚mʌltɪplɪ'ke∫ən] s Vermehrung f; (arith) Multiplikation f

multiplica′tion ta′ble s Einmaleins n

multiplicity [‚mʌlti'plɪsɪti] s Vielfältigkeit f

multi·ply ['mʌlti‚plaɪ] v (pret & pp –plied) tr vervielfältigen; (biol) vermehren; (math) multiplizieren ‖ intr sich vervielfachen; (biol) sich vermehren

multistage ['mʌlti‚stedʒ] adj mehrstufig

multistory ['mʌlti‚stori] adj mehrstöckig

multitude ['mʌlti‚t(j)ud] s (large number) Vielheit f; (of people) Masse f

mum [mʌm] adj still; **keep mum about** Stillschweigen beobachten über (acc); **mum's the word!** Mund halten!

mumble ['mʌmbəl] tr & intr murmeln

mummery ['mʌmərɪ] s Hokuspokus m

mummy ['mʌmi] s Mumie f

mumps [mʌmps] s Ziegenpeter m, Mumps m

munch [mʌnt∫] tr & intr geräuschvoll kauen

mundane [mʌn'den] adj irdisch

municipal [mju'nɪsɪpəl] adj städtisch

muni′cipal bond′ s Kommunalobligation f

municipality [mju‚nɪsɪ'pælɪti] s Stadt f, Gemeinde f; (governing body) Stadtverwaltung f

munificent [mju'nɪfɪsənt] adj freigebig

munificence [mju'nɪfɪsəns] s Freigebigkeit f

munitions [mju'nɪ∫əns] s Kriegsmaterial n, Munition f

muni′tions dump′ s Munitionsdepot n

muni′tions fac′tory s Rüstungsfabrik f

mural ['mjurəl] s Wandgemälde n

murder ['mʌrdər] s Mord m ‖ tr (er)morden; (a language) radebrechen

murderer ['mʌrdərər] s Mörder m

murderess ['mʌrdərɪs] s Mörderin f

mur′der mys′tery s Krimi m

murderous ['mʌrdərəs] adj mörderisch

mur′der plot′ s Mordanschlag m

murky ['mʌrki] adj düster

murmur ['mʌrmər] s Gemurmel n ‖ tr & intr murmeln

muscle ['mʌsəl] s Muskel m; **muscles** Muskulatur f

muscular ['mʌskjələr] adj muskulös

Muse [mjuz] s Muse f ‖ **muse** intr (over) nachsinnen (über acc)

museum [mju'zi·əm] s Museum n

mush [mʌ∫] s (corn meal) Maismehlbrei m; (soft mass) Matsch m; (sentimental talk) Süßholzraspeln n

mush′room′ s Pilz m, Champignon m

|| *intr* wie Pilze aus dem Boden schießen

mushy ['mʌʃi] *adj* matschig; *(sentimental)* rührselig

music ['mjuːzɪk] *s* Musik *f;* *(score)* Noten *pl;* **face the m.** die Sache ausbaden; **set to m.** vertonen

musical ['mjuːzɪkəl] *adj* musikalisch || *s (cin)* Singspielfilm *m;* *(theat)* Musical *n,* Singspiel *n*

mu'sical in'strument *s* Musikinstrument *n*

musicale [ˌmjuːzɪˈkæl] *s* Musikabend *m*

mu'sic box' *s* Spieldose *f*

musician [mjuˈzɪʃən] *s* Musikant –in *mf;* *(accomplished artist)* Musiker –in *mf*

musicology [ˌmjuːzɪˈkalədʒi] *s* Musikwissenschaft *f*

mu'sic stand' *s* Notenständer *m*

mus'ing *s* Grübelei *f*

musk [mʌsk] *s* Moschus *m*

musket ['mʌskɪt] *s* Muskete *f*

musk'rat' *s* Bisamratte *f*

muslin ['mʌzlɪn] *s* Musselin *m*

muss [mʌs] *tr (hair)* zerzausen; *(dirty)* schmutzig machen; *(rumple)* zerknittern

mussel ['mʌsəl] *s* Muschel *f*

mussy ['mʌsi] *adj (hair)* zerzaust; *(clothes)* zerknittert

must [mʌst] *s (a necessity)* Muß *n;* *(new wine)* Most *m;* *(mold)* Moder *m* || **mod—I m.** *(inf)* ich muß *(inf)*

mustache [mʌsˈtæʃ] *s* Schnurrbart *m*

mustard ['mʌstərd] *s* Senf *m*

mus'tard plas'ter *s* Senfpflaster *n*

muster ['mʌstər] *s* Appell *m;* **pass m.** die Prüfung bestehen || *tr (troops)* antreten lassen; *(courage, strength)* aufbringen; **m. out** ausmustern

musty ['mʌsti] *adj* mod(e)rig

mutation [mjuˈteʃən] *s (biol)* Mutation *f*

mute [mjut] *adj (& ling)* stumm || *s (ling)* stummer Buchstabe *m;* *(mus)* Dämpfer *m* || *tr (mus)* dämpfen

mutilate ['mjutɪˌlet] *tr* verstümmeln

mutineer [ˌmjutɪˈnɪr] *s* Meuterer *m*

mutinous ['mjutɪnəs] *adj* meuterisch

muti·ny ['mjutɪni] *s* Meuterei *f* || *v (pret & pp* –**nied)** *intr* meutern

mutt [mʌt] *s (coll)* Köter *m*

mutter ['mʌtər] *s* Gemurmel *n* || *tr & intr* murmeln

mutton ['mʌtən] *s (culin)* Hammel *m*

mut'ton-head' *s (sl)* Hammel *m*

mutual ['mjutʃu·əl] *adj* gegenseitig; *(friends)* gemeinsam

mu'tual fund' *s* Investmentfond *m*

mu'tual insur'ance com'pany *s* Versicherungsgesellschaft *f* auf Gegenseitigkeit

mutually ['mjutʃu·əli] *adv* gegenseitig

muzzle ['mʌzəl] *s* Maulkorb *m;* *(of a gun)* Rohrmündung *f;* *(snout)* Schnauze *f* || *tr (an animal)* e–n Maulkorb anlegen *(dat);* *(e.g., the press)* mundtot machen

muz'zle flash' *s* Mündungsfeuer *n*

my [maɪ] *poss adj* mein

myopic [maɪˈapɪk] *adj* kurzsichtig

myriad ['mɪrɪ·əd] *adj* Myriade *f*

myrrh [mʌr] *s* Myrrhe *f*

myrtle ['mʌrtəl] *s* Myrte *f*

myself [maɪˈsɛlf] *reflex pron* mich; *(indirect object)* mir || *intens pron* selbst, selber

mysterious [mɪsˈtɪrɪ·əs] *adj* mysteriös

mystery ['mɪstəri] *s* Geheimnis *n;* *(fi)* Rätsel *n;* *(relig)* Mysterium *n*

mys'tery nov'el *s* Kriminalroman *m*

mys'tery play' *s* Mysterienspiel *n*

mystic ['mɪstɪk] *adj* mystisch || *s* Mystiker –in *mf*

mystical ['mɪstɪkəl] *adj* mystisch

mysticism ['mɪstɪˌsɪzəm] *s* Mystik *f*

mystification [ˌmɪstɪfɪˈkeʃən] *s* Verwirrung *f*

mysti·fy ['mɪstɪˌfaɪ] *v (pret & pp* –**fied)** *tr* verwirren

myth [mɪθ] *s* Mythe *f,* Mythos *m;* *(ill-founded belief)* Märchen *n*

mythical ['mɪθɪkəl] *adj* mythisch

mythological [ˌmɪθəˈladʒɪkəl] *adj* mythologisch

mythology [mɪˈθalədʒi] *s* Mythologie *f*

N

N, n [ɛn] *s* vierzehnter Buchstabe des englischen Alphabets

nab [næb] *v (pret & pp* nabbed; *ger* –**nabbing)** *tr (coll)* schnappen

nadir ['nedɪr] *s (fig)* Tiefpunkt *m;* *(astr)* Nadir *m*

nag [næg] *s* Gaul *m;* **old nag** Schindmähre *f* || *v (pret & pp* nagged; *ger* nagging) *tr* zusetzen *(dat)* || *intr* nörgeln; **nag at** herumnörgeln an *(dat)*

nag'ging *adj* nörgelnd || *s* Nörgelei *f*

naiad ['naɪˌæd] *s* Najade *f*

nail [nel] *s* Nagel *m;* **hit the n. on the head** den Nagel auf den Kopf treffen || *tr (to)* annageln (an *acc);* *(catch)*

(coll) erwischen; *(box) (coll)* treffen; **n. down** (fig) festnageln; **n. shut** zunageln

nail' clip'pers *spl* Nagelzange *f*

nail' file' *s* Nagelfeile *f*

nail' pol'ish *s* Nagellack *m*

nail' scis'sors *s & spl* Nagelschere *f*

naïve [nɑˈiv] *adj* naiv

naked ['nekɪd] *adj* nackt; *(eye)* bloß

nakedness ['nekɪdnɪs] *s* Nacktheit *f*

name [nem] *s* Name *m;* *(reputation)* Name *m,* Ruf *m;* **by n.** dem Namen nach; **by the n. of** namens; **in n. only** nur dem Namen nach; **of the same n.** gleichnamig; **spell one's n.** sich schreiben; **what is your n.?** wie heißen Sie? ∥ *tr* nennen; *(nominate)* ernennen; **be named after** heißen nach; **n. after** nennen nach; **named** namens

name'-call'ng *s* Beschimpfung *f*

name' day' *s* Namenstag *m*

nameless ['nemlɪs] *adj* namenlos

namely ['nemlɪ] *adv* nämlich, und zwar

name'plate' *s* Namensschild *n*

name'sake' *s* Namensvetter *m*

nanny ['næni] *s* Kindermädchen *n*

nan'ny goat' *s* (coll) Ziege *f*

nap [næp] *s* Schläfchen *n;* (tex) Noppe *f;* **take a nap** ein Schläfchen machen ∥ *v* (*pret* & *pp* **napped;** *ger* **napping**) *intr* schlummern; **catch s.o. napping** (fig) j–n überrumpeln

napalm ['nepam] *s* Napalm *n*

nape [nep] *s*—**n. of the neck** Nacken *m*

naphtha ['næfθə] *s* Naphtha *f* & *n*

napkin ['næpkɪn] *s* Serviette *f*

nap'kin ring' *s* Serviettenring *m*

narcissism ['narsɪ ˌsɪzəm] *s* Narzißmus *m*

narcissus [nar'sɪsəs] *s* (bot) Narzisse *f*

narcotic [nar'kɑtɪk] *adj* narkotisch ∥ *s* (med) Betäubungsmittel *n,* Narkotikum *n;* *(addictive drug)* Rauschgift *n;* *(addict)* Rauschgiftsüchtige *mf*

narrate [næ'ret] *tr* erzählen

narration [næ're/ən] *s* Erzählung *f*

narrative ['nærətɪv] *adj* erzählend ∥ *s* Erzählung *f*

narrator [næ'retər] *s* Erzähler *m;* (telv) Moderator *m*

narrow ['næro] *adj* eng, schmal; *(e.g., margin)* knapp ∥ **narrows** *spl* Meerenge *f* ∥ *tr* verengen ∥ *intr* sich verengen

nar'row escape' *s*—**have a n.** mit knapper Not entkommen

nar'row-gauge rail'road *s* Schmalspurbahn *f*

narrowly ['næroli] *adv* mit knapper Not

nar'row-mind'ed *adj* engstirnig

nasal ['nezəl] *adj* *(of the nose)* Nasen–; *(sound)* näselnd ∥ *s* (phonet) Nasenlaut *m*

nasalize ['nezə ˌlaɪz] *tr* nasalieren ∥ *intr* näseln

na'sal twang' *s* Näseln *n*

nascent ['nesənt] *adj* werdend

nastiness ['næstɪnɪs] *s* Ekligkeit *f*

nasturtium [nə'stʌrʃəm] *s* Kapuzinerkresse *f*

nasty ['næsti] *adj* *(person, smell, taste)* ekelhaft; *(weather)* scheußlich; *(dog, accident, tongue)* böse; **n. to** garstig zu or gegen

nation ['ne/ən] *s* Nation *f,* Volk *n*

national ['næ/ənəl] *adj* national, Landes– ∥ *s* Staatsangehörige *mf*

na'tional an'them *s* Nationalhymne *f*

na'tional defense' *s* Landesverteidigung *f*

nationalism ['næ/ənə ˌlɪzəm] *s* Nationalismus *m*

nationality [ˌnæ/ə'nælɪti] *s* (citizen-

ship) Staatsangehörigkeit *f;* *(ethnic identity)* Nationalität *f*

nationalization [ˌnæ/ənəlɪ'ze/ən] *s* Verstaatlichung *f*

nationalize ['næ/ənə ˌlaɪz] *tr* verstaatlichen

na'tional park' *s* Naturschutzpark *m*

na'tional so'cialism *s* Nationalsozialismus *m*

na'tionwide' *adj* im ganzen Land

native ['netɪv] *adj* eingeboren; *(products)* heimisch, Landes– ∥ *s* Eingeborene *mf;* **be a n. of** beheimatet sein in *(dat)*

na'tive coun'try *s* Vaterland *n*

na'tive land' *s* Heimatland *n*

na'tive tongue' *s* Muttersprache *f*

nativity [nə'tɪvɪti] *s* Geburt *f;* (astrol) Nativität *f;* **the Nativity** die Geburt Christi

NATO ['neto] *s* (**North Atlantic Treaty Organization**) NATO *f*

natty ['næti] *adj* elegant

natural ['næt/ərəl] *adj* natürlich; *(behavior)* ungezwungen ∥ *s* (mus) weiße Taste *f; (symbol)* (mus) Auflösungszeichen *n;* **a n.** *(person)* (coll) ein Naturtalent *n; (thing)* (coll) e–e totsichere Sache *f*

na'tural his'tory *s* Naturgeschichte *f*

naturalism ['næt/ərə ˌlɪzəm] *s* Naturalismus *m*

naturalist ['næt/ərəlɪst] *s* *(student of natural history)* Naturforscher –in *mf;* (paint, philos) Naturalist –in *mf*

naturalization [ˌnæt/ərəlɪ'ze/ən] *s* Einbürgerung *f*

naturalize ['næt/ərə ˌlaɪz] *tr* einbürgern

na'tural law' *s* Naturgesetz *n*

na'tural phenom'enon *s* *(occurring in nature)* Naturereignis *n; (not supernatural)* natürliche Erscheinung *f*

na'tural re'sources *spl* Bodenschätze *pl*

na'tural sci'ence *s* Naturwissenschaft *f*

na'tural state' *s* Naturzustand *m*

nature ['net/ər] *s* die Natur; *(qualities)* Natur *f,* Beschaffenheit *f;* **by n.** von Natur aus

naught [nɔt] *s* Null *f;* **all for n.** ganz umsonst; **bring to n.** zuschanden machen; **come to n.** zunichte werden

naughty ['nɔti] *adj* unartig, ungezogen

nausea ['nɔ/ɪ-ə], ['nɔsɪ-ə] *s* Übelkeit *f*

nauseate ['nɔ/ɪ ˌet], ['nɔsɪ ˌet] *tr* Übelkeit erregen *(dat)*

naus'eating *adj* Übelkeit erregend

nauseous ['nɔ/ɪ-əs], ['nɔsɪ-əs] *adj* *(causing nausea)* Übelkeit erregend; **I feel n.** mir ist übel

nautical ['nɔtɪkəl] *adj* See–, nautisch

nau'tical mile' ['nɔtɪkəl] *s* Seemeile *f*

nau'tical term' *s* Ausdruck *m* der Seemannssprache *f*

naval ['nevəl] *adj* *(e.g., battle, blockade, cadet, victory)* See–; *(unit)* Flotten–; *(academy, officer)* Marine–

na'val base' *s* Flottenstützpunkt *m*

na'val cap'tain *s* Kapitän *m* zur See

na'val engage'ment *s* Seegefecht *n*

na'val forc'es *s* Seestreitkräfte *pl*

na'val suprem'acy *s* Seeherrschaft *f*

nave [nev] *s* (*of a church*) Schiff *n;* (*of a wheel*) Nabe *f*

navel ['nevəl] *s* Nabel *m*

na'vel or'ange *s* Navelorange *f*

navigable ['nævɪgəbəl] *adj* schiffbar

navigate ['nævɪ‚get] *tr* (*traverse*) befahren; (*steer*) steuern ‖ *intr* (aer, naut) navigieren

navigation [‚nævɪ'geʃən] *s* (*plotting courses*) Navigation *f;* (*sailing*) Schiffahrt *f*

naviga'tion chart' *s* Navigationskarte *f*

naviga'tion light' *s* (aer, naut) Positionslicht *n*

navigator ['nævɪ‚getər] *s* Seefahrer *m;* (aer) Navigator *m*

navy ['nevi] *adj* Marine– ‖ *s* Kriegsmarine *f*

na'vy bean' *s* Weiße Bohne *f*

na'vy blue' *adj* marineblau ‖ *s* Marineblau *n*

na'vy yard' *s* Marinewerft *f*

nay [ne] *adv* nein ‖ *s* Nein *n;* (parl) Neinstimme *f;* **the nays have it** die Mehrheit stimmt dagegen

Nazarene [‚næzə'rin] *adj* aus Nazareth ‖ *s* Nazarener *m*

Nazi ['natsi] *adj* Nazi– ‖ *s* Nazi *m*

Nazism ['natsɪzəm] *s* Nazismus *m*

N.C.O. ['en'si'o] *s* (**noncommissioned officer**) Unteroffizier *m*

neap' tide' [nip] *s* Nippflut *f*

near [nɪr] *adj* nahe(liegend); (*escape*) knapp; **n. at hand** zur Hand ‖ *adv* nahe; **draw n.** (**to**) sich nähern (*dat*); **live n.** (*e.g., a church*) in der Nähe wohnen (*genit*) ‖ *prep* nahe (*dat*), nahe an (*dat*), bei (*dat*); **n. here** hier in der Nähe

near'by' *adj* nahe(gelegen) ‖ *adv* in der Nähe

Near' East', **the** *s* der Nahe Osten

nearly ['nɪrli] *adv* beinahe, fast

nearness ['nɪrnɪs] *s* Nähe *f*

near'-sight'ed *adj* kurzsichtig

near'-sight'edness *s* Kurzsichtigkeit *f*

neat [nit] *adj* sauber, ordentlich; (*simple but tasteful*) nett; (*cute*) niedlich; (*tremendous*) (coll) prima

neatness ['nitnɪs] *s* Sauberkeit *f*

nebu-la ['nebjələ] *s* (**-lae** [‚li] **& -las**) (astr) Nebelfleck *m*

nebulous ['nebjələs] *adj* nebelhaft; (astr) Nebel–

necessarily [‚nesɪ'serɪli] *adv* notwendigerweise, unbedingt

necessary ['nesɪ‚seri] *adj* notwendig, nötig; (*consequence*) zwangsläufig; **if n.** notfalls

necessitate [nɪ'sesɪ‚tet] *tr* notwendig machen, enfordern

necessity [nɪ'sesɪti] *s* (*state of being necessary*) Notwendigkeit *f;* (*something necessary*) Bedürfnis *n;* (*poverty*) Not *f;* **in case of n.** im Notfall; **necessities of life** Lebensbedürfnisse *pl;* **of n.** notwendigerweise

neck [nɛk] *s* Hals *m;* (*of a dress*) Halsausschnitt *m;* **break one's n.** (& fig) sich ¦dat¦ den Hals brechen; **get it in the n.** (sl) eins aufs Dach kriegen; **get s.o. off one's n.** sich ¦dat¦ j–n

vom Halse schaffen; **n. and n.** Seite an Seite ‖ *intr* (coll) sich knutschen

–necked [‚nɛkt] *suf* –halsig, –nackig

neckerchief ['nɛkərtʃɪf] *s* Halstuch *n*

neck'ing *s* Abknutscherei *f*

necklace ['nɛklɪs] *s* Halsband *n;* (*metal chain*) Halskette *f*

neck'line' *s* Halsausschnitt *m;* **with a low n.** tief ausgeschnitten

neck'tie' *s* Krawatte *f*, Schlips *m*

necrology [nɛ'krɑlədʒi] *s* (*list of the dead*) Totenliste *f;* (*obituary*) Nekrolog *m*

necromancer ['nɛkrə‚mænsər] *s* Geistesbeschwörer –in *mf*

necromancy ['nɛkrə‚mænsi] *s* Geistesbeschwörung *f*

necropolis [nɛ'krɑpəlɪs] *s* Nekropolis *f*

nectar ['nɛktər] *s* (bot, myth) Nektar *m*

nectarine [‚nɛktə'rin] *s* Nektarine *f*

nee [ne] *adj* geborene, e.g., **Mrs. Mary Schmidt, nee Müller** Frau Maria Schmidt, geborene Müller

need [nid] *s* Bedarf *m*, Bedürfnis *n;* **be in n.** in Not sein; **be in n. of repair** reparaturbedürftig sein; **be in n. of s.th.** etw nötig haben; **if n. be** erforderlichenfalls; **meet s.o.'s needs** j–s Bedarf decken; **needs** Bedarfsartikel *pl* ‖ *tr* benötigen, brauchen; **as needed** nach Bedarf

needful ['nidfəl] *adj* nötig

needle ['nidəl] *s* Nadel *f* ‖ *tr* (*prod*) anstacheln; **n. s.o. about** gegen j–n sticheln wegen

nee'dlepoint', **nee'dlepoint lace'** *s* Nadelspitze *f*

needless ['nidlɪs] *adj* unnötig; **n. to say** es erübrigt sich zu sagen

nee'dlework' *s* Näharbeit *f*

needy ['nidi] *adj* bedürftig

ne'er [ner] *adv* nie

ne'er'-do-well' *s* Tunichtgut *m*

nefarious [nɪ'ferɪ‚əs] *adj* ruchlos

negate [nɪ'get] *tr* verneinen

negation [nɪ'geʃən] *s* Verneinung *f*

negative ['negətɪv] *adj* negativ ‖ *s* Verneinung *f;* (elec) negativer Pol *m;* (gram) Verneinungswort *n;* (phot) Negativ *n*

neglect [nɪ'glɛkt] *s* Vernachlässigung *f* ‖ *tr* vernachlässigen; **n. to** (*inf*) unterlassen zu (*inf*)

négligée, **negligee** [‚nɛglɪ'ʒe] *s* Negligé *n*

negligence ['nɛglɪdʒəns] *s* Fahrlässigkeit *f*

negligent ['nɛglɪdʒənt] *adj* fahrlässig

negligible ['nɛglɪdʒɪbəl] *adj* geringfügig

negotiable [nɪ'goʃɪ‚əbəl] *adj* diskutierbar; (fin) übertragbar, bankfähig

negotiate [nɪ'goʃɪ‚et] *tr* (*a contract*) abschließen; (*a curve*) nehmen ‖ *intr* verhandeln

negotiation [nɪ‚goʃɪ'eʃən] *s* Verhandlung *f;* **carry on negotiations with** in Verhandlungen stehen mit; **enter negotiations with** in Verhandlungen treten mit

negotiator [nɪˈgoʃɪ͵etər] s Unterhändler –in mf

Ne·gro [ˈnigro] s (-groes) Neger –in mf

neigh [ne] s Wiehern n ‖ intr wiehern

neighbor [ˈnebər] s Nachbar –in mf; (fellow man) Nächste m ‖ tr angrenzen an (acc) ‖ intr—n. on angrenzen an (acc)

neigh′borhood′ s Nachbarschaft f; (vicinity) Umgebung f; **in the n. of** (coll) etwa

neigh′boring adj benachbart, Nachbar–, angrenzend

neighborliness [ˈnebərlɪnɪs] s gutnachbarliche Beziehungen pl

neighborly [ˈnebərli] adj (gut)nachbarlich

neither [ˈniðər] indef adj keiner ‖ indef pron (of) keiner (von); **n. of them** keiner von beiden ‖ conj noch, ebensowenig; auch nicht, e.g., **n. do I** ich auch nicht; **neither … nor** weder … noch; **that's n. here nor there** das hat nichts zu sagen

neme·sis [ˈnɛməsɪs] s (-ses [͵siz]) Nemesis f

Neolith′ic Age′ [͵ni·əˈlɪθɪk] s Neusteinzeit f

neologism [niˈɑlə͵dʒɪzəm] s Neubildung f, Neologismus m

neon [ˈni·ɑn] s Neon n

ne′on light′ s Neonröhre f

ne′on sign′ s Neonreklame f

neophyte [ˈni·ə͵faɪt] s Neuling m; (relig) Neubekehrte mf

nephew [ˈnɛfju] s Neffe m

nepotism [ˈnɛpə͵tɪzəm] s Nepotismus m

Neptune [ˈnɛpt(j)un] s Neptun m

neptunium [nɛpˈt(j)uni·əm] s Neptunium n

nerve [nʌrv] adj Nerven– ‖ s Nerv m; (courage) Wagemut m; (gall) (coll) Unverfrorenheit f; **get on s.o.'s nerves** j–m auf die Nerven gehen; **lose one's n.** die Nerven verlieren; **nerves of steel** Nerven pl wie Drahtseile

nerve′ cen′ter s Nervenzentrum n

nerve′-rack′ing adj nervenaufreibend

nervous [ˈnʌrvəs] adj nervös; (system) Nerven–; (horse) kopfscheu; **be a n. wreck** mit den Nerven herunter sein

ner′vous break′down s Nervenzusammenbruch m

nervousness [ˈnʌrvəsnɪs] s Nervosität f

nervy [ˈnʌrvi] adj (brash) unverschämt; (courageous) mutig

nest [nɛst] s Nest n ‖ intr nisten

nest′ egg′ s (fig) Sparpfennig m

nestle [ˈnɛsəl] intr (up to) sich anschmiegen (an acc)

net [nɛt] adj Rein– ‖ s Netz n; (for fire victims) Sprungtuch n ‖ v (pret & pp netted; ger netting) tr (e.g., fish, butterflies) mit dem Netz fangen; (said of an enterprise) rein einbringen; (said of a person) rein verdienen

net′ball′ s (tennis) Netzball m

Netherlander [ˈnɛðər͵lændər] s Niederländer –in mf

Netherlands, the [ˈnɛðərləndz] s & spl die Niederlande

net′ting s Netzwerk n

nettle [ˈnɛtəl] s Nessel f ‖ tr reizen

net′work′ s Netzwerk n; (rad, telv) Sendergruppe f

neuralgia [n(j)uˈrældʒə] s Neurologie f

neuritis [n(j)uˈraɪtɪs] s Nervenentzündung f

neurologist [n(j)uˈralədʒɪst] s Nervenarzt m, Nervenärztin f

neurology [n(j)uˈralədʒi] s Nervenheilkunde f, Neurologie f

neuron [ˈn(j)urɑn] s Neuron n

neuro·sis [n(j)uˈrosɪs] s (-ses [siz]) Neurose f

neurotic [n(j)uˈrɑtɪk] adj neurotisch ‖ s Neurotiker –in mf

neuter [ˈn(j)utər] adj (gram) sächlich ‖ s (gram) Neutrum n

neutral [ˈn(j)utrəl] adj neutral ‖ s Neutrale mf; (aut) Leerlauf m

neutrality [n(j)uˈtrælɪti] s Neutralität f

neutralize [ˈn(j)utrə͵laɪz] tr (a bomb) entschärfen; (& chem) neutralisieren; (troops) lahmlegen; (an attack) unterbinden

neutron [ˈn(j)utrɑn] s Neutron n

never [ˈnɛvər] adv nie(mals); **n. again** nie wieder; **n. before** noch nie; **n. mind!** spielt keine Rolle!

ne′vermore′ adv nimmermehr

ne′verthe·less′ adv nichtsdestoweniger

new [n(j)u] adj neu; (wine) jung; (inexperienced) unerfahren; **what's new?** was gibt's Neues?

new′ arriv′al s Neuankömmling m

new′born′ adj neugeboren

New′cas′tle s—carry coals to N. Eulen nach Athen tragen

newcomer [ˈn(j)u͵kʌmər] s Neuankömmling m

newel [ˈn(j)u·əl] s Treppenspindel f

new′el post′ s Geländerpfosten m

newfangled [ˈn(j)u͵fæŋgəld] adj neumodisch

Newfoundland [ˈn(j)ufənd͵lænd] s Neufundland n ‖ [n(j)uˈfaundlənd] s (dog) Neufundländer m

newly [ˈn(j)uli] adv neu, Neu–

new′lyweds′ spl Neuvermählten pl

new′ moon′ s Neumond m

new-mown [ˈn(j)u ͵mon] adj frischgemäht

newness [ˈn(j)unɪs] s Neuheit f

news [n(j)uz] s Nachricht f; (rad, telv) Nachrichten pl; **that's not n. to me** das ist mir nicht neu; **piece of n.** Neuigkeit f

news′ a′gency s Nachrichtenagentur f

news′boy′ s Zeitungsjunge m

news′ bul′letin s Kurznachricht f

news′cast′ s Nachrichtensendung f

news′cast′er s Nachrichtensprecher –in mf

news′deal′er s Zeitungshändler –in mf

news′ ed′itor s Nachrichtenredakteur –in mf

news'let'ter s Rundschreiben n
news'man' s (–men') Journalist m; (dealer) Zeitungshändler m
news'pa'per adj Zeitungs– || s Zeitung f
news'paper clip'ping s Zeitungsausschnitt m
news'paper·man' s (–men') Journalist m; (dealer) Zeitungshändler m
news'paper se'rial s Zeitungsroman m
news'print' s Zeitungspapier n
news'reel' s Wochenschau f
news' report' s Nachrichtensendung f
news' report'er s Zeitungsreporter –in mf
news' room' s Nachrichtenbüro n
news'stand' s Zeitungskiosk m
news'wor'thy adj berichtenswert
New' Tes'tament s Neues Testament n
New' World' s Neue Welt f
New' Year' s Neujahr n; happy N.! glückliches Neues Jahr!
New' Year's' Eve' s Silvesterabend m
New' Zea'land ['zilənd] s Neuseeland n
next [nekst] adj nächste; be n. an der Reihe sein; come n. folgen; in the n. place darauf; n. best nächstbeste; n. time das nächste Mal; n. to (locally) gleich neben (dat); (almost) sogut wie; the n. day am nächsten Tag || adv dann, danach; what should I do n.? was soll ich als Nächstes tun?
next'-door' adj—n. neighbor unmittelbarer Nachbar m || next'-door' adv nebenan; n. to direkt neben (dat)
next' of kin' s (pl: next of kin) nächster Angehöriger m
niacin ['naɪ·əsɪn] s Niacin n
Niag'ara Falls' [naɪ'ægrə] s Niagarafall m
nib [nɪb] s Spitze f; (of a pen) Federspitze f
nibble ['nɪbəl] tr knabbern || intr (on) knabbern (an dat)
Nibelung ['nibəlʊŋ] s (myth) Nibelung m
nice [naɪs] adj nett; (pretty) hübsch; (food) lecker; (well-behaved) artig; (distinction) fein; have a n. time sich gut unterhalten; n. and warm schön warm
nicely ['naɪsli] adv nett; he's doing n. es geht ihm recht gut; that will do n. das paßt gut
nicety ['naɪsəti] s Feinheit f; niceties of life Annehmlichkeiten pl des Lebens
niche [nɪtʃ] s Nische f; (fig) rechter Platz m
nick [nɪk] s Kerbe f, Scharte f; in the n. of time gerade im rechten Augenblick || tr kerben
nickel ['nɪkəl] s Nickel n; (coin) Fünfcentstück n || tr vernickeln
nick'el-plate' tr vernickeln
nick'name' s Spitzname m || tr e–n Spitznamen geben (dat)
nicotine ['nɪkə,tin] s Nikotin n; low in n. nikotinarm
niece [nis] s Nichte f
nifty ['nɪfti] adj (coll) fesch, prima

niggard ['nɪgərd] s Knauser –in mf
niggardly ['nɪgərdli] adj knauserig
night [naɪt] adj (light, shift, train, watch) Nacht– || s Nacht f; all n. (long) die ganze Nacht (über); at n. nachts; last n. gestern abend; n. after n. Nacht für Nacht; n. before last vorgestern abend
night' cap' s Nachtmütze f; (drink) Schlummertrunk m
night' club' s Nachtklub m
night'fall' s Anbruch m der Nacht; at n. bei Anbruch der Nacht
night'gown' s Damennachthemd n
nightingale ['naɪtən,gel] s Nachtigall f
night'light' s Nachtlicht n
night'long' adj & adv die ganze Nacht dauernd
nightly ['naɪtli] adj & adv allnächtlich
night'mare' s Alptraum m
nightmarish ['naɪt,merɪʃ] adj alpartig
night' owl' s (coll) Nachteule f
night' school' s Abendschule f
night'time' s Nachtzeit f; at n. zur Nachtzeit
night' watch'man s Nachtwächter m
nihilism ['naɪ·ɪ,lɪzəm] s Nihilismus m
nil [nɪl] s Nichts n, Null f
Nile [naɪl] s Nil m
nimble ['nɪmbəl] adj flink
nincompoop ['nɪnkəm,pup] s Trottel m
nine [naɪn] adj & pron neun || s Neun f
nineteen ['naɪn'tin] adj & pron neunzehn || s Neunzehn f
nineteenth ['naɪn'tinθ] adj & pron neunzehnte || s (fraction) Neunzehntel n; the nineteenth (in dates or in a series) der Neunzehnte
ninetieth ['naɪntɪ·ɪθ] adj & pron neunzigste || s (fraction) Neunzigstel n
ninety ['naɪnti] adj & pron neunzig || s Neunzig f; the nineties die neunziger Jahre
nine'ty-first' adj & pron einundneunzigste
nine'ty-one' adj & pron einundneunzig
ninny ['nɪni] s (coll) Trottel m
ninth [naɪnθ] adj & pron neunte || s (fraction) Neuntel n; the n. (in dates or in a series) der Neunte
nip [nɪp] s (pinch) Kneifen n; (of cold weather) Schneiden n; (of liquor) Schluck m || v (pret & pp nipped; ger nipping) tr (pinch) kneifen; (alcohol) nippen; nip in the bud im Keime ersticken
nippers ['nɪpərz] spl Zwickzange f
nipple ['nɪpəl] s (of a nursing bottle) Lutscher m; (anat) Brustwarze f; (mach) Schmiernippel m
nippy ['nɪpi] adj schneidend
nirvana [nɪr'vɑnə] s Nirwana n
nit [nɪt] s (ent) Nisse f
niter ['naɪtər] s Salpeter m
nit'pick'er s (coll) Pedant –in mf
nitrate ['naɪtret] s Nitrat n || tr nitrieren
ni'tric ac'id ['naɪtrɪk] s Salpetersäure f

nitride ['naɪtraɪd] s Nitrid n
nitrogen ['naɪtrədʒən] s Stickstoff m
nitroglycerin [ˌnaɪtrə'glɪsərɪn] s Nitroglyzerin n
ni'trous ac'id ['naɪtrəs] s salpetrige Säure f
ni'trous ox'ide s Stickstoffoxydul n
nit'wit' s Trottel m
no [no] adj kein; **no admittance** Zutritt verboten; **no ... of any kind** keinerlei; **no offense!** nichts für ungut!; **no parking** Parkverbot; **no smoking** Rauchen verboten; **no thoroughfare** Durchgang verboten; **no ... whatever** überhaupt kein ‖ adv nein; **no?** nicht wahr?; **no longer** (or **no more**) nicht mehr ‖ s Nein n; **give no for an answer** mit (e-m) Nein antworten
No'ah's Ark' ['no·əz] s Arche f Noah(s)
nobility [no'bɪlɪti] s (nobleness; aristocracy) Adel m; (noble rank) Adelsstand m; **n. of mind** Seelenadel m
noble ['nobəl] adj (rank) ad(e)lig; (character, person) edel ‖ s Adliger m; **nobles** Edelleute pl
no'ble·man s (–men) Edelmann m
no'blemind'ed adj edelgesinnt
nobleness ['nobəlnɪs] s Vornehmheit f
no'ble·wom'an s (–wom'en) Edelfrau f
nobody ['no‚badi] s indef pron niemand, keiner; **n. else** sonst keiner ‖ s (coll) Null f
nocturnal [nak'tʌrnəl] adj nächtlich
nod [nad] s Kopfnicken n ‖ v (pret & pp **nodded**; ger **nodding**) tr—**nod one's head** mit dem Kopf nicken ‖ intr nicken; **nod to** zunicken (dat)
node [nod] s (anat, astr, math, phys) Knoten m
nodule ['nadʒul] s Knötchen n; (bot) Knollen m
noise [nɔɪz] s Geräusch n; (disturbingly loud) Lärm m ‖ tr—**n. abroad** ausposaunen
noiseless ['nɔɪzlɪs] adj geräuschlos
noisy ['nɔɪzi] adj lärmend, geräuschvoll
nomad ['nomæd] s Nomade m, Nomadin f
no' man's' land' s Niemandsland n
nomenclature ['nomən‚klet/ər] s Nomenklatur f
nominal ['namɪnəl] adj nominell
nominate ['namɪ‚net] tr ernennen; **n. as candidate** als Kandidaten aufstellen
nomination [ˌnamɪ'ne/ən] s Ernennung f; (of a candidate) Aufstellung f
nominative ['namɪnətɪv] s Nominativ m
nominee [ˌnamɪ'ni] s Designierte mf
non– [nan] pref Nicht–, nicht–
non'accept'ance s Nichtannahme f
non'belli'gerent adj nicht am Krieg teilnehmend
non'break'able adj unzerbrechlich
non'-Cath'olic adj nichtkatholisch ‖ s Nichtkatholik –in mf
nonchalant [ˌnan/ə'lant] adj zwanglos

noncom ['nan‚kam] s (coll) Kapo m
non'com'batant s Nichtkämpfer m
non'commis'sioned of'ficer s Unteroffizier m
noncommittal [ˌnankə'mɪtəl] adj nichtssagend; (person) zurückhaltend
nondescript ['nandɪ‚skrɪpt] adj unbestimmbar
none [nʌn] adv—**n. too** keineswegs zu ‖ indef pron keiner; **that's n. of your business** das geht dich nichts an
nonen'tity s Nichts n; (fig) Null f
non'exis'tent adj nichtexistent
nonfic'tion s Sachbücher pl
nonfulfill'ment s Nichterfüllung f
non'interven'tion s Nichteinmischung f
non'met'al s Nichtmetall n, Metalloid n
non'nego'tiable adj unübertragbar; (demands) unabdingbar
nonpar'tisan adj überparteilich
nonpay'ment s Nichtbezahlung f
non'polit'ical adj unpolitisch
non-plus [nan'plʌs] s Verlegenheit f ‖ v (pret & pp –plus[s]ed; ger –plus[s]ing) tr verblüffen
nonprof'it adj gemeinnützig
nonres'ident adj nich ansässig ‖ s Nichtansässige mf
non'return'able adj (bottles, etc.) Einweg–; (merchandise) nicht rücknehmbar
non'scienti'fic adj nichtwissenschaftlich
non'sectar'ian adj keiner Sekte angehörend
nonsense ['nansəns] s Unsinn m
nonsen'sical adj unsinnig, widersinnig
non'skid' adj rutschsicher
nonsmok'er s Nichtraucher –in mf
non'stop' adj & adv ohne Zwischenlandung
nonvi'olence s Gewaltlosigkeit f
nonvi'olent adj gewaltlos
noodle ['nudəl] s Nudel f; (head) (coll) Birne f
noo'dle soup' s Nudelsuppe f
nook [nuk] s Ecke f; (fig) Winkel m
noon [nun] s Mittag m; **at n.** zu Mittag
no' one', **no'-one'** indef pron niemand, keiner; **n. else** kein anderer
noon' hour' s Mittagsstunde f
noon'time' adj mittäglich ‖ s Mittagszeit f
noose [nus] s Schlinge f
nor [nɔr] conj (after **neither**) noch; auch nicht, e.g., **nor do I** ich auch nicht
Nordic ['nɔrdɪk] adj nordisch
norm [nɔrm] s Norm f
normal ['nɔrməl] adj normal
normalcy ['nɔrməlsi] s Normalzustand m
normalize ['nɔrmə‚laɪz] tr normalisieren
Norman ['nɔrmən] adj normannisch ‖ s Normanne m, Normannin f
Normandy ['nɔrməndi] s die Normandie
Norse [nɔrs] adj altnordisch ‖ s (language) Altnordisch n; **the N.** die Skandinavier pl
Norse'man s (–men) Nordländer m

north [nɔrθ] *adj* nördlich, Nord– ‖ *adv* nach Norden ‖ *s* Norden *m;* **to the n. of** im Norden von

North′ Amer′ica *s* Nordamerika *n*

North′ Amer′ican *adj* nordamerikanisch ‖ *s* Nordamerikaner –in *mf*

north′east′ *adj & adv* nordöstlich ‖ *s* Nordosten *m*

north′east′er *s* Nordostwind *m*

northerly [′nɔrðərli] *adj* nördlich

northern [′nɔrðərn] *adj (direction)* nördlich; *(race)* nordisch

north′ern expo′sure *s* Nordseite *f*

North′ern Hem′isphere *s* nördliche Halbkugel *f*

north′ern lights′ *spl* Nordlicht *n*

nor′thernmost′ *adj* nördlichst

North′ Pole′ *s* Nordpol *m*

North′ Sea′ *s* Nordsee *f*

northward [′nɔrθwərd] *adv* nach Norden

north′west′ *adj & adv* nordwestlich ‖ *s* Nordwesten *m*

north′ wind′ *s* Nordwind *m*

Norway [′nɔrwe] *s* Norwegen *n*

Norwegian [nɔr′widʒən] *adj* norwegisch ‖ *s* Norweger –in *mf; (language)* Norwegisch *n*

nose [noz] *s* Nase *f;* (aer) Nase *f,* Bug *m;* **by a n.** (sport) um e–e Nasenlänge; **blow one's n.** sich schneuzen; **lead around by the n.** an der Nase herumführen; **pay through the n.** e–n zu hohen Preis bezahlen; **turn one's n. up at** die Nase rümpfen über *(acc)* ‖ *tr* **–n. out** (fig) mit knappem Vorsprung besiegen; (sport) um e–e Nasenlänge schlagen ‖ *intr* **–n. about** herumschnüffeln; **n. over** (aer) sich überschlagen

nose′bleed′ *s* Nasenbluten *n*

nose′ cone′ *s* (rok) Raketenspitze *f*

nose′ dive′ *s* (aer) Sturzflug *m*

nose′-dive′ *intr* e–n Sturzflug machen

nose′ drops′ *spl* Nasentropfen *pl*

nose′gay′ *s* Blumenstrauß *m*

nose′-heav′y *adj* (aer) vorderlastig

nostalgia [nɑ′stældʒə] *s* Heimweh *n*

nostalgic [nɑ′stældʒɪk] *adj* wehmütig

nostril [′nɑstrɪl] *s* (anat) Nasenloch *n;* (zool) Nüster *f*

nostrum [′nɑstrəm] *s* Allheilmittel *n*

nosy [′nozi] *adj* neugierig

not [nɑt] *adv* nicht; **not at all** überhaupt nicht; **not even** nicht einmal; **not one** keiner; **not only ... but also** nicht nur ... sondern auch

notable [′notəbəl] *adj* bemerkenswert ‖ *s* Standesperson *f*

notarial [no′tɛri·əl] *adj* notariell

notarize [′notə‚raɪz] *tr* notariell beglaubigen

no′tary pub′lic [′notəri] *s* (**notaries public**) Notar *m,* Notarin *f*

notation [no′teʃən] *s (note)* Aufzeichnung *f; (system of symbols)* Bezeichnung *f; (method of noting)* Schreibweise *f*

notch [nɑtʃ] *s* Kerbe *f; (in a belt)* Loch *n; (degree, step)* Grad *m; (of a wheel)* Zahn *m* ‖ *tr* einkerben

note [not] *s* Notiz *f; (to a text)* An-

merkung *f; (slip)* Zettel *m; (e.g., of doubt)* Ton *m;* (mus) Note *f;* **jot down notes** sich *[dat]* Notizen machen; **make a n. of** sich *[dat]* notieren; **take n. of** zur Kenntnis nehmen; **take notes** sich *[dat]* Notizen machen ‖ *tr* beachten; **n. down** notieren; **n. in passing** am Rande bemerken

note′book′ *s* Heft *n,* Notizbuch *n*

note′ pad′ *s* Schreibblock *m*

note′wor′thy *adj* beachtenswert

nothing [′nʌθɪŋ] *indef pron* nichts; **be for n.** vergebens sein; **come to n.** platzen; **for n.** (gratis) umsonst; **have n. to go on** keine Unterlagen haben; **next to n.** soviel wie nichts; **n. at all** gar nichts; **n. but** lauter; **n. doing!** kommt nicht in Frage!; **n. else** sonst nichts; **n. new** nichts Neues; **there is n. like** es geht nichts über *(acc)*

nothingness [′nʌθɪŋnɪs] *s (nonexistence)* Nichts *n; (utter insignificance)* Nichtigkeit *f*

notice [′notɪs] *s (placard)* Anschlag *m; (in the newspaper)* Anzeige *f; (attention)* Beachtung *f; (announcement)* Ankündigung *f; (notice of termination)* Kündigung *f;* **at a moment's n.** jeden Moment; **escape s.o.'s n.** j–m entgehen; **give s.o. a week's n.** j–m acht Tage vorher kündigen; **take n. of** Notiz nehmen von; **until further n.** bis auf weiteres ‖ *tr* (be)merken, wahrnehmen; **be noticed by s.o.** j–m auffallen; **n. s.th. about s.o.** j–m etw anmerken

noticeable [′notɪsəbəl] *adj* wahrnehmbar

notification [‚notɪfɪ′keʃən] *s* Benachrichtigung *f*

noti·fy [′notɪ‚faɪ] *v (pret & pp* **–fied)** *tr (about)* benachrichtigen (von)

notion [′noʃən] *s (idea)* Vorstellung *f;* **I have a good n. to** (inf) ich habe gute Lust zu (inf); **notions** Kurzwaren *pl*

notoriety [‚notə′raɪ·ɪti] *s* Verruf *m*

notorious [no′tori·əs] *adj* (for) notorisch (wegen)

no′-trump′ *adj* ohne Trumpf ‖ *s* Ohne Trumpf-Ansage *f*

notwithstanding [‚nɑtwɪθ′stændɪŋ] *adv* trotzdem ‖ *prep* trotz (genit)

noun [naun] *s* Hauptwort *n*

nourish [′nʌrɪʃ] *tr* (er)nähren

nour′ishing *adj* nahrhaft, Nähr–

nourishment [′nʌrɪʃmənt] *s (feeding)* Ernährung *f; (food)* Nahrung *f*

Nova Scotia [′novə′skoʃə] *s* Neuschottland *n*

novel [′nɑvəl] *adj* neuartig ‖ *s* Roman *m*

novelist [′nɑvəlɪst] *s* Romanschriftsteller –in *mf*

novelty [′nɑvəlti] *s* Neuheit *f*

November [no′vembər] *s* November *m*

novena [no′vinə] *s* Novene *f*

novice [′nɑvɪs] *s* Neuling *m;* (eccl) Novize *m,* Novizin *f*

novitiate [no′vɪʃi·ɪt] *s* Noviziat *n*

novocaine [′novə‚ken] *s* Novokain *n*

now [nau] *adv* jetzt; *(without tem-*

poral force) nun; **before now** schon früher; **by now** nachgerade; **from now on** von nun ab, fortan; **now and then** dann und wann; **now ... now** bald ... bald; **now or never** jetzt oder nie

nowadays ['nau·ə‚dez] *adv* heutzutage

no'way', **no'ways'** *adv* keineswegs

no'where' *adv* nirgends

noxious ['nakʃəs] *adj* schädlich

nozzle ['nazəl] *s* Düse *f;* (*on a can*) Schnabel *m*

nth [enθ] *adj* —**nth times** zig mal; **to the nth degree** (fig) im höchsten Maße

nuance ['n(j)u·ɑns] *s* Nuance *f*

nub [nʌb] *s* Knoten *m;* (*gist*) Kernpunkt *m*

nuclear ['n(j)uklɪ·ər] *adj* nuklear; (*energy, fission, fusion, physics, reactor, weapon*) Kern—

nu'clear pow'er *s* Atomkraft *f*

nu'clear pow'er plant' *s* Atomkraftwerk *n*

nucleolus [n(j)u'kli·ələs] *s* Nukleolus *m*

nucleon ['n(j)ukli·an] *s* Nukleon *n*

nucle·us ['n(j)uklɪ·əs] *s* (—**uses** & **i-** [‚aɪ]) Kern *m*

nude [n(j)ud] *adj* nackt ‖ *s* (*nude figure*) Akt *m;* **in the n.** nackt

nudge [nʌdʒ] *s* Stups *m* ‖ *tr* stupsen

nudist ['n(j)udɪst] *s* Nudist —*in mf*

nudity ['n(j)udɪti] *s* Nacktheit *f*

nugget ['nʌgɪt] *s* Klumpen *m*

nuisance ['n(j)usəns] *s* Ärgernis *n;* **be a n.** lästig sein

nui'sance raid' *s* Störungsangriff *m*

null' and void' [nʌl] *adj* null und nichtig

nulli·fy ['nʌlɪ‚faɪ] *v* (*pret & pp* —**fied**) *tr* (*e.g., a law*) für ungültig erklären; (*e.g., the effects*) aufheben

numb [nʌm] *adj* taub; (*with*) starr (vor *dat*); (fig) betäubt; **grow n.** erstarren ‖ *tr* (& fig) betäuben; (*said of cold*) starr machen

number ['nʌmbər] *s* Nummer *f;* (*count*) Zahl *f*, Anzahl *f;* (*article*) (com) Artikel *m;* (gram) Zahl *f;* (mus) Stück *n;* **in n.** der Zahl nach; **get s.o.'s n.** (coll) j–m auf die Schliche kommen ‖ *tr* (*e.g., pages*) numerieren; (*amount to*) zählen; **be numbered among** zählen zu; **n. among** zählen zu

numberless ['nʌmbərlɪs] *adj* zahllos

num'bers game' *s* Zahlenlotto *n*

numbness ['nʌmnɪs] *s* Taubheit *f;* (*from cold*) Starrheit *f*

numeral ['n(j)umərəl] *adj* Zahl— ‖ *s* Zahl *f*, Ziffer *f;* (gram) Zahlwort *n*

numerator ['n(j)umə‚retər] *s* Zähler *m*

numerical [n(j)u'merɪkəl] *adj* numerisch; **n. order** Zahlenfolge *f;* **n. superiority** Überzahl *f;* **n. value** Zahlenwert *m*

numerous ['n(j)umərəs] *adj* zahlreich

numismatic [‚n(j)umɪz'mætɪk] *adj* numismatisch ‖ **numismatics** *s* Münzkunde *f*

numskull ['nʌm‚skʌl] *s* Dummkopf *m*

nun [nʌn] *s* Nonne *f*

nunci·o ['nʌnʃɪ·o] *s* (—**os**) Nuntius *m*

nuptial ['nʌpʃəl] *adj* Braut—, Hochzeits— ‖ **nuptials** *spl* Trauung *f*

Nuremberg ['n(j)urəm‚bʌrg] *s* Nürnberg *n*

nurse [nʌrs] *s* Krankenschwester *f;* (*male*) Krankenpfleger *m;* (*wet nurse*) Amme *f* ‖ *tr* (*the sick*) pflegen; (*a child*) stillen; (*hopes*) hegen; **n. a cold** e–e Erkältung kurieren

nurse'maid' *s* Kindermädchen *n*

nursery ['nʌrsəri] *s* Kinderstube *f;* (*for day care*) Kindertagesstätte *f;* (hort) Baumschule *f*, Pflanzschule *f*

nurs'ery·man *s* (—**men**) Kunstgärtner *m*

nurs'ery rhyme' *s* Kinderlied *n*

nurs'ery school' *s* Kindergarten *m*

nurs'e's aide' *s* Schwesternhelferin *f*

nurs'ing *s* (*as a profession*) Krankenpflege *f;* (*of a person*) Pflege *f;* (*of a baby*) Stillen *n*

nurs'ing home' *s* Pflegeheim *n*

nurture ['nʌrtʃər] *s* Nahrung *f* ‖ *tr* (er)nähren

nut [nʌt] *s* Nuß *f;* (sl) verrückter Kerl *m;* (mach) Mutter *f*, Schraubenmutter *f;* **be nuts** (sl) verrückt sein; **be nuts about** (sl) vernarrt sein in (*acc*); **go nuts** (sl) e–n Klaps kriegen

nut'crack'er *s* Nußknacker *m*

nutmeg ['nʌt‚meg] *s* (*spice*) Muskatnuß *f;* (*tree*) Muskat *m*

nutrient ['nutri·ənt] *s* Nährstoff *m*

nutriment ['n(j)utrɪmənt] *s* Nährstoff *m*

nutrition [n(j)u'trɪʃən] *s* Ernährung *f*

nutritious [n(j)u'trɪʃəs] *adj* nahrhaft

nutritive ['n(j)utrɪtɪv] *adj* nahrhaft, Nähr—

nut'shell' *s* Nußschale *f;* **in a n.** mit wenigen Worten

nutty ['nʌti] *adj* nußartig; (sl) spleenig, verrückt

nuzzle ['nʌzəl] *tr* sich mit der Schnauze (or Nase) reiben an (*dat*) ‖ *intr* (*burrow*) mit der Schnauze wühlen; **n. up to** sich anschmiegen an (*acc*)

nylon ['naɪlɑn] *s* Nylon *n*

nymph [nɪmf] *s* Nymphe *f*

nymphomaniac [‚nɪmfə'meni·æk] *s* Nymphomanin *f*

O

O, o [o] fünfzehnter Buchstabe des englischen Alphabets

oaf [of] *s* Tölpel *m*

oak [ok] *adj* eichen ‖ *s* Eiche *f*

oak' leaf' clus'ter *s* Eichenlaub *n*

oak' tree' *s* Eichbaum *m*

oakum ['okəm] *s* Werg *n*

oar [or], [ər] *s* Ruder *n*, Riemen *m*

oar'lock' s Ruderdolle f
oars'man' s (**-men'**) Ruderer m
oa·sis [o'esɪs] s (**-ses** [siz] Oase f
oath [oθ] s (**oaths** [oðz]) Eid m; **o. of
allegiance** Treueid m; **o. of office**
Amtseid m; **under o.** eidlich
oat'meal' s Hafergrütze f, Hafermehl
n
oats [ots] spl Hafer m; **he's feeling
his o.** (coll) ihn sticht der Hafer;
sow one's wild o. (coll) sich [dat]
die Hörner ablaufen
obbligato [,ɑblɪ'gɑto] adj hauptstim-
mig || s Obligato m
obdurate ['ɑbdjərɪt] adj verstockt
obedience [o'bidɪ·əns] s (**to**) Gehorsam
m (gegenüber dat, gegen); **blind o.**
Kadavergehorsam m
obedient [o'bidɪ·ənt] adj (**to**) gehorsam (dat)
obeisance [o'bisəns] s Ehrerbietung f
obelisk ['ɑbəlɪsk] s Obelisk m
obese [o'bis] adj fettleibig
obesity [o'bisɪti] s Fettleibigkeit f
obey [o'be] tr gehorchen (dat); (a
law, order) befolgen || intr gehor-
chen
obfuscate [ɑb'fʌsket] tr verdunkeln
obituary [o'bɪtʃu,ɛri] adj Todes- || s
Todesanzeige f, Nachruf m
object ['ɑbdʒɪkt] s Gegenstand m;
(aim) Ziel n, Zweck m; (gram) Ergänzung f, Objekt n; **money is no o.**
Geld spielt keine Rolle || [ɑb'dʒɛkt]
intr (**to**) Einwände erheben (gegen)
objection [ɑb'dʒɛkʃən] s Einwand m;
I have no o. to his staying ich habe
nichts dagegen (einzuwenden), daß
er bleibe
objectionable [ɑb'dʒɛkʃənəbəl] adj
nicht einwandfrei
objective [ɑb'dʒɛktɪv] adj sachlich,
objektiv || s Ziel n
objec'tive case' s Objektsfall m
ob'ject les'son s Lehre f
obligate ['ɑblɪ,get] tr verpflichten; **be
obligated to s.o.** j—m zu Dank verbunden sein
obligation [,ɑblɪ'geʃən] s Verpflichtung f
obligatory ['ɑblɪgə,tori], [ə'blɪgə,to-
ri] adj verpflichtend, obligatorisch
oblige [ə'blaɪdʒ] tr (bind) verpflichten;
(do a favor to) gefällig sein (dat);
be obliged to (inf) müssen (inf); **feel
obliged to** (inf) sich bemüßigt fühlen
zu (inf); **I'm much obliged to you**
ich bin Ihnen sehr verbunden
oblig'ing adj gefällig
oblique [ə'blik] adj schief
obliterate [ə'blɪtə,ret] tr auslöschen;
(traces) verwischen; (writing) unleserlich machen
oblivion [ə'blɪvɪ·ən] s Vergessenheit f
oblivious [ə'blɪvɪ·əs] adj—**be o.** of
sich [dat] nicht bewußt sein (genit)
oblong ['ɑblɔŋ] adj länglich || s Recht-
eck n
obnoxious [əb'nɑkʃəs] adj widerlich
oboe ['obo] s Oboe f
oboist ['obo·ɪst] s Oboist –in mf
obscene [ɑb'sin] adj obszön

obscenity [ɑb'sɛnɪti] s Obszönität f
obscure [əb'skjur] adj dunkel, obskur
|| tr verdunkeln
obscurity [əb'skjurɪti] s Dunkelheit f
obsequies ['ɑbsɪkwiz] spl Totenfeier f
obsequious [əb'sikwɪ·əs] adj unterwürfig
observance [əb'zʌrvəns] s Beachtung f,
Befolgung f; (celebration) Feier f
observant [əb'zʌrvənt] adj beobachtend
observation [,ɑbzər'veʃən] s Beobachtung f; **keep under o.** beobachten
observa'tion tow'er s Aussichtsturm m
observatory [əb'zʌrvə,tori] s Stern-
warte f, Observatorium n
observe [əb'zʌrv] tr (a person, rules)
beobachten; (a holiday) feiern; **o.
silence** Stillschweigen bewahren
obsess [əb'sɛs] tr verfolgen; **obsessed
(by)** besessen (von)
obsession [əb'sɛʃən] s Besessenheit f
obsolescent [,ɑbsə'lɛsənt] adj veral-
tend
obsolete ['ɑbsə,lit] adj veraltet; **become o.** veralten
obstacle ['ɑbstəkəl] s Hindernis n
ob'stacle course' s Hindernisbahn f
obstetrical [ɑb'stɛtrɪkəl] adj Geburtshilfe–, Entbindungs–
obstetrician [,ɑbstə'trɪʃən] s Geburts-
helfer –in mf
obstetrics [ɑb'stɛtrɪks] s Geburtshilfe f
obstinacy ['ɑbstɪnəsi] s Starrheit f
obstinate ['ɑbstɪnɪt] adj starr
obstreperous [əb'strɛpərəs] adj (clamorous) lärmend; (unruly) widerspenstig
obstruct [əb'strʌkt] tr (e.g., a pipe)
verstopfen; (a view, way) versperren;
(traffic) behindern; **o. justice** die
Rechtspflege behindern
obstruction [əb'strʌkʃən] s (of a view,
way) Versperrung f; (of traffic) Behinderung f; (obstacle) Hindernis n;
(parl, pathol) Obstruktion f
obtain [əb'ten] tr erhalten, erlangen ||
intr bestehen
obtrusive [əb'trusɪv] adj aufdringlich
obtuse [əb't(j)us] adj (& fig) stumpf
obviate ['ɑbvɪ,et] tr erübrigen
obvious ['ɑbvɪ·əs] adj naheliegend; **it
is o.** es liegt auf der Hand
occasion [ə'keʒən] s Gelegenheit f;
(reason) Anlaß m; **on o.** gelegentlich; **on the o. of** anläßlich (genit)
|| tr veranlassen
occasional [ə'keʒənəl] adj gelegentlich
occasionally [ə'keʒənəli] adv gelegentlich, zuweilen
occident ['ɑksɪdənt] s Abendland n
occidental [,ɑksɪ'dɛntəl] adj abend-
ländisch || s Abendländer –in mf
occlusion [ə'kluʒən] s Okklusion f
occult [ə'kʌlt] adj geheim, okkult
occupancy ['ɑkjəpənsi] s Besitz m, Besitzergreifung f; (of a home) Einzug
m
occupant ['ɑkjəpənt] s Besitzer –in
mf; (of a home) Inhaber –in mf;
(of a car) Insasse m, Insassin f
occupation [,ɑkjə'peʃən] s (employ-

ment) Beruf *m*, Beschäftigung *f*; (mil) Besetzung *f*, Besatzung *f*

occup'ational disease' [ˌʌkjə'peʃənəl] *s* Berufskrankheit *f*

occupa'tional ther'apy *s* Beschäftigungstherapie *f*

occupa'tion troops' *spl* Besatzungstruppen *pl*

occu·py ['ʌkjəˌpaɪ] *v* (*pret & pp* **–pied**) *tr* in Besitz nehmen; (*a house*) bewohnen; (*time*) in Anspruch nehmen; (*keep busy*) beschäftigen; (mil) besetzen; **occupied** (*said of a seat or toilet*) besetzt; (*said of a person*) beschäftigt; **o. oneself with** sich befassen mit

oc·cur [ə'kʌr] *v* (*pret & pp* **–curred**; *ger* **–curring**) *intr* sich ereignen; (*come to mind*) (**to**) einfallen (*dat*)

occurrence [ə'kʌrəns] *s* Ereignis *n*; (*e.g., of a word*) Vorkommen *n*

ocean ['oʃən] *s* Ozean *m*

oceanic [ˌoʃɪ'ænɪk] *adj* Ozean-, ozeanisch

o'cean lin'er *s* Ozeandampfer *m*

oceanography [ˌoʃən'ɑɡrəfi] *s* Ozeanographie *f*

ocher ['okər] *s* Ocker *m & n*

o'clock [ə'klɑk] *adv* Uhr; **at . . . o'clock** um . . . Uhr

octane ['okten] *s* Oktan *n*

oc'tane num'ber *s* Oktanzahl *f*

octave ['ɑktɪv], ['ɑktev] *s* Oktave *f*

October [ɑk'tobər] *s* Oktober *m*

octogenarian [ˌɑktədʒɪ'nerɪ·ən] *s* Achtzige *mf*

octo·pus ['ɑktəpəs] *s* (**–puses &** **–pi** [ˌpaɪ]) Seepolyp *m*

ocular ['ɑkjələr] *adj* Augen-

oculist ['ɑkjəlɪst] *s* Augenarzt *m*, Augenärztin *f*

odd [ɑd] *adj* (*strange*) seltsam, eigenartig; (*number*) ungerade; (*e.g., glove*) einzeln; **two hundred odd pages** etwas über zweihundert Seiten ‖ **odds** *spl* (*probability*) Wahrscheinlichkeit *f*; (*advantage*) Vorteil *m*; (*in gambling*) Vorgabe *f*; **at odds** uneinig; **lay** (*or* **give**) **odds** vorgeben; **the odds are two to one** die Chancen stehen zwei zu eins

odd' ball' *s* (sl) Sonderling *m*

oddity ['ɑdɪti] *s* Seltsamkeit *f*

odd' jobs' *spl* Gelegenheitsarbeit *f*; (*chores*) kleine Aufgaben *pl*

odds' and ends' *spl* Kleinkram *m*

ode [od] *s* Ode *f*

odious ['odɪ·əs] *adj* verhaßt

odor ['odər] *s* Duft *m*, Geruch *m*; **be in bad o.** in schlechtem Ruf stehen

odorless ['odərlɪs] *adj* geruchlos

odyssey ['ɑdɪsi] *s* Irrfahrt *f*; **Odyssey** Odyssee *f*

of [ʌv], [əv] *prep* von (*dat*); genit, e.g., **the name of the dog** der Name des Hundes

off [ɔf] *adj* (*free from work*) dienstfrei; (*poor, bad*) schlecht; (*electric current*) ausgeschaltet, abgeschaltet; **be badly off** in schlechten Verhältnissen sein; **be off** (*said of a clock*) nachgehen; (*said of a measurement*)

---

falsch sein; (*said of a person*) im Irrtum sein; (*be crazy*) nicht ganz richtig im Kopf sein; **be well off** in guten Verhältnissen sein; **the deal** (*or* **party**) **is off** es ist aus mit dem Geschäft (or mit der Party) ‖ *adv* (*distant*) weg; **he was off in a flash** er war im Nu weg; **I must be off** ich muß fort ‖ *prep* von (*dat*); **off duty** außer Dienst; **off limits** Zutritt verboten

offal ['ɔfəl] *s* (*refuse*) Abfall *m*; (*of butchered meat*) Innereien *pl*

off' and on' *adv* ab und zu

off'beat' *adj* (sl) ungewöhnlich

off' chance' *s* geringe Chance *f*

off'-col'or *adj* schlüpfrig

off'-du'ty *adj* außerdienstlich

offend [ə'fend] *tr* beleidigen ‖ *intr*—**o. against** verstoßen gegen

offender [ə'fendər] *s* Missetäter –in *mf*; **first o.** nicht Vorbestrafte *mf*; **second o.** Vorbestrafte *mf*

offense [ə'fens] *s* (*against*) Vergehen *n* (*gegen*); **give o.** Anstoß geben; **no o.!** nichts für ungut!; **take o.** (**at**) Anstoß nehmen (an *dat*)

offensive [ə'fensɪv] *adj* anstößig; (*odor*) ekelhaft; (*action*) offensiv ‖ *s* Offensive *f*; **take the o.** die Offensive ergreifen

offer ['ɔfər] *s* Angebot *n* ‖ *tr* anbieten; (*a price*) bieten; (*help, resistance*) leisten; (*friendship*) schenken; **o. an excuse** o e Entschuldigung vorbringen; **o. as an excuse** als Entschuldigung vorbringen; **o. for sale** feilbieten; **o. one's services** sich anbieten; **o. up** aufopfern ‖ *intr*—**o. to** (*inf*) sich erbieten zu (*inf*)

of'fering *s* (*act*) Opferung *f*; (*gift*) Opfergabe *f*

offertory ['ɔfərˌtori] *s* Offertorium *n*

off'hand' *adj* (*excuse*) unvorbereitet; (*manner*) lässig ‖ *adv* kurzerhand

office ['ɔfɪs] *s* (*room*) Büro *n*, Amt *n*; (*position*) Amt *n*; (*of a doctor*) Sprechzimmer *n*; **be in o.** amtieren; **through the good offices of** durch die freundliche Vermittlung (*genit*); **run for o.** für ein Amt kandidieren

of'fice boy' *s* Bürojunge *m*

of'fice build'ing *s* Bürogebäude *n*

of'ficehold'er *s* Amtsträger –in *mf*

of'fice hours' *spl* Dienststunden *pl*; (*of a doctor, lawyer*) Sprechstunde *f*

officer ['ɔfrsər] *s* (adm) Beamte *m*, Beamtin *f*; (com) Direktor –in *mf*; (mil) Offizier –in *mf*

of'ficer can'didate *s* Offiziersanwärter –in *mf*

of'ficers' mess' *s* Offizierskasino *n*; (nav) Offiziersmesse *f*

of'fice seek'er *s* Amtsbewerber –in *mf*

of'fice supplies' *spl* Bürobedarf *m*

of'fice work' *s* Büroarbeit *f*

official [ə'fɪʃəl] *adj* amtlich; (*in line of duty*) Dienst-; (*visit*) offiziell; (*document*) öffentlich; **on o. business** dienstlich ‖ *s* Beamte *m*, Beamtin *f*; **top officials** Spitzenkräfte *pl*

offi'cial busi'ness *s* Dienstsache *f*

offi'cial call' *s* (telp) Dienstgespräch *n*
officialdom [ə'fɪʃəldəm] *s* Beamtentum *n*
officialese [ə͵fɪʃə'liz] *s* Amtssprache *f*
officially [ə'fɪʃəli] *adv* offiziell
offi'cial use' *s* Dienstgebrauch *m*
officiate [ə'fɪʃɪ͵et] *intr* amtieren; **o. at a marriage** e-n Trauuntesdienst halten
officious [ə'fɪʃəs] *adj* dienstbeflissen
offing ['ɔfɪŋ] *s—***in the o.** in Aussicht
off'-lim'its *adj* gesperrt
off'print' *s* Abdruck *m*, Sonderdruck *m*
off'-seas'on *adj—***o. prices** Preise *pl* während der Vor– und Nachsaison || *s* Vor– und Nachsaison *f*
offset' *s* (compensation) Ausgleich *m*; (typ) Offsetdruck *m* || **off'set'** *v* (pret –set; ger –setting) *tr* ausgleichen
off'set press' *s* Offsetdruck *m*
off'shoot' *s* Ableger *m*
off'shore' *adj* küstennah
off'side' *adv* (sport) abseits
off'spring' *s* Sprößling *m*
off'stage' *adj* hinter der Bühne befindlich || *adv* hinter der Bühne
off'-the-cuff' *adj* aus dem Stegreif
off'-the-rec'ord *adj* im Vertrauen
often ['ɔfən] *adv* oft, häufig; **every so o.** von Zeit zu Zeit; **quite o.** öfters
of'tentimes' *adv* oftmals
ogive ['odʒaɪv] *s* (diagonal vaulting rib) Gratrippe *f*; (pointed arch) Spitzbogen *m*
ogle ['ogəl] *tr* liebäugeln mit || *intr* liebäugeln
ogre ['ogər] *s* Scheusal *n*; (myth) Menschenfresser *m*
oh [o] *interj* oh!; **oh, dear!** o weh!
ohm [om] *s* Ohm *n*
oil [ɔɪl] *s* Öl *n*; **strike oil** auf Öl stoßen || *tr* ölen
oil' burn'er *s* Ölbrenner *m*
oil'can' *s* Ölkanne *f*
oil'cloth' *s* Wachsleinwand *f*
oil' col'or *s* Ölfarbe *f*
oil' drum' *s* Ölfaß *n*
oil' field' *s* Ölfeld *n*
oil' gauge' *s* Ölstandsanzeiger *m*
oil' heat' *s* Ölheizung *f*
oil' lev'el *s* Ölstand *m*
oil'man' *s* (–men') Ölhändler *m*
oil' paint'ing *s* Ölgemälde *n*
oil' pres'sure *s* Öldruck *m*
oil' rig' *s* Ölbohrinsel *f*
oil' shale' *s* Ölschiefer *m*
oil' slick' *s* Öllache *f*
oil' tank' *s* Ölbehälter *m*
oil' tank'er *s* Öltanker *m*
oil' well' *s* Ölquelle *f*
oily ['ɔɪli] *adj* ölig; (unctious) salbungsvoll
ointment ['ɔɪntmənt] *s* Salbe *f*
O.K. ['o'ke] *adj* in Ordnung, okay || *s* Billigung *f* || *v* (pret & pp O.K.'d; ger O.K.'ing) *tr* billigen || *intr* okay!
old [old] *adj* alt; **as old as the hills** uralt; (said of a person) steinalt
old' age' *s* Alter *n*, Greisenalter *n*
old'-age' home' *s* Altersheim *n*
old' coun'try *s* Heimatland *n*
olden ['oldən] *adj* alt

old'-fash'ioned *adj* altmodisch
old' fog'(e)y ['fogi] *s* alter Kauz *m*
Old' Glo'ry *s* Sternenbanner *n*
old' hand' *s* alter Hase *m*
old' hat' *adj* bärtig
old' la'dy *s* Greisin *f*; (wife) (pej) Alte *f*
old' maid' *s* alte Jungfer *f*
old' man' *s* Greis *m*; (mil) Alter *m*
old' mas'ter *s* (paint) alter Meister *m*
old' moon' *s* letztes Viertel *n*
old' salt' *s* alter Seebär *m*
oldster ['oldstər] *s* alter Knabe *m*
Old' Tes'tament *s* Altes Testament *n*
old'-time' *adj* altväterisch
old'-tim'er *s* (coll) alter Hase *m*
old' wives'' tale' *s* Altweibergeschichte *f*
Old' World' *s* alte Welt *f*
oleander [͵olɪ'ændər] *s* Oleander *m*
olfactory [al'fæktori] *adj* Geruchs–
oligarchy ['alɪ͵garki] *s* Oligarchie *f*
olive ['alɪv] *s* Olive *f*
ol'ive branch' *s* Ölzweig *m*
ol'ive grove' *s* Olivenhain *m*
ol'ive oil' *s* Olivenöl *n*
ol'ive tree' *s* Ölbaum *m*, Olivenbaum *m*
olympiad [o'lɪmpɪ͵æd] *s* Olympiade *f*
Olympian [o'lɪmpɪ͵ən] *adj* olympisch
Olympic [o'lɪmpɪk] *adj* olympisch || **the Olympics** *spl* die Olympischen Spiele
omelet, omelette ['amə͵lɛt] *s* Eierkuchen *m*, Omelett *n*
omen ['omən] *s* Omen *n*, Vorzeichen *n*
ominous ['amɪnəs] *adj* ominös, unheilvoll
omission [o'mɪʃən] *s* Auslassung *f*; (of a deed) Unterlassung *f*
omit [o'mɪt] *v* (pret & pp omitted; ger omitting) *tr* (a word) auslassen; (a deed) unterlassen; **be omitted** ausfallen; **o.** (ger) es unterlassen zu (inf)
omnibus ['amnɪ͵bʌs] *adj* Sammel–, Mantel– || *s* Omnibus *m*, Autobus *m*
omnipotent [am'nɪpətənt] *adj* allmächtig
omnipresent [͵amnɪ'prezənt] *adj* allgegenwärtig
omniscient [am'nɪʃənt] *adj* allwissend
on [ɑn] *adj* (in progress) im Gange; (light, gas, water) an; (radio, television) angestellt; (switch) eingeschaltet; (brakes) angezogen; **be on to s.o.** j–n durchsehen; **be on to s.th.** über etw [acc] im Bilde sein || *adv* weiter; **on and off** dann und wann; **on and on** in e–m fort || *prep* auf (dat or acc), an (dat or acc); (concerning) über (acc)
once [wʌns] *adv* einmal; (formerly) einst; **at o.** auf einmal; (immediately) sofort; **not o.** nicht ein einziges Mal; **o. and for all** ein für allemal; **o. before** früher einmal; **o. in a while** ab und zu; **o. more** noch einmal; **o. upon a time there was** es war einmal || *s—***this o.** dieses (eine) Mal || *conj* sobald
once'-o'ver *s—***give** (s.o. or s.th.) **the o.** rasch mustern
one [wʌn] *adj* ein; (one certain, e.g.,

Mr. Smith) ein gewisser; **for one thing** zunächst; **her one care** ihre einzige Sorge; **it's all one to me** es ist mir ganz gleich; **one and a half hours** anderthalb Stunden; **one day** e–s Tages; **one more** noch ein; **one more thing** noch etwas; **one o'clock** ein Uhr, eins; **on the one hand ... on the other** einerseits ... andererseits ‖ *s* Eins *f* ‖ *pron* einer; **I for one** was mich betrifft, ich jedenfalls; **one after another** einer nach dem anderen; **one after the other** nacheinander; **one another** einander, sich; **one at a time, please!** einer nach dem anderen, bitte!; **one behind the other** hintereinander; **one by one** einer nach dem anderen; **one of these days** früher oder später; **one on top of the other** übereinander, aufeinander; **one to nothing** eins zu Null; **this one** dieser da, der da; **with one another** miteinander ‖ *indef pron* man; **one's** sein

one'-armed' *adj* einarmig
one'-eyed' *adj* einäugig
one'-horse town' *s* Kuhdorf *n*
one'-leg'ged *adj* einbeinig
onerous [ˈɒnərəs] *adj* lästig
oneself' *reflex pron* sich; **be o.** sein, wie man immer ist; **by o.** allein; **to o.** vor sich [*acc*] hin
one'-sid'ed *adj* (& fig) einseitig
one'-track' *adj* eingleisig; (fig) einseitig
one'-way street' *s* Einbahnstraße *f*
one'-way tick'et *s* einfache Fahrkarte *f*
one'-week' *adj* achttägig
onion [ˈʌnjən] *s* Zwiebel *f*; **know one's onions** (coll) Bescheid wissen
on'ionskin' *s* Durchschlagpapier *n*
on'look'er *s* Zuschauer –in *mf*
only [ˈonli] *adj* (son, hope) einzig ‖ *adv* nur; **not only ... but also** nicht nur ... sondern auch; **o. too** nur (all)zu; **o. too well** zur Genüge; **o. yesterday** erst gestern ‖ *conj* aber; **o. that** nur daß
on'ly-begot'ten *adj* eingeboren
onomatopoeia [ˌɒnəˌmætəˈpiə] *s* Lautmalerei *f*
on'-ramp' *s* Zufahrtsrampe *f*
on'rush' *s* Ansturm *m*
on'set' *s* Anfang *m*; (attack) Angriff *m*
onslaught [ˈɒnˌslɔt] *s* Angriff *m*
on'to *prep* auf [*acc*] hinauf; **be o. s.o.** hinter j–s Schliche kommen; **be o. s.th.** über etw [*acc*] im Bilde sein
onus [ˈonəs] *s* Last *f*; **o. of proof** Beweislast *f*
onward(s) [ˈɒnwərd(z)] *adv* vorwärts
onyx [ˈɒniks] *s* Onyx *m*
oodles [ˈudəlz] *spl* (coll) (of) Unmengen *pl* (von)
ooze [uz] *s* Sickern *n*; (mud) Schlamm *m* ‖ *tr* ausschwitzen ‖ *intr* sickern; **o. out** durchsickern
opal [ˈopəl] *s* Opal *m*
opaque [oˈpek] *adj* undurchsichtig; (stupid) stumpf
open [ˈopən] *adj* (window, position, sea, question, vowel) offen; (air, field, seat) frei; (business, office)

geöffnet; (seam) geplatzt; (account) laufend; (meeting) öffentlich; **be o.** offenstehen; **get o.** aufbekommen; **have an o. mind about s.th.** sich noch nicht auf etw [*acc*] festgelegt haben; **keep o.** offenhalten; **lay oneself o. to** sich aussetzen (*dat*); **o. to** (the public) zugänglich (*dat*); (criticism) ausgesetzt (*dat*); (doubt) unterworfen (*dat*); **o. to bribery** bestechlich; **o. to question** strittig ‖ *s*—**come out into the o.** (fig) mit seinen Gedanken herauskommen; **in the o.** im Freien ‖ *tr* öffnen, aufmachen; (a business, account, meeting, hostilities, fire) eröffnen; (a book) aufschlagen; (eyes in surprise) aufreißen; (a box, bottle) anbrechen; (an umbrella) aufspannen; **o. the attack** losschlagen; **o. to traffic** dem Verkehr übergeben; **o. wide** weit aufreißen ‖ *intr* sich öffnen, aufgehen; (said of a school, speech, play) beginnen; **o. into** ausgehen auf (*acc*); **o. up** sich auftun; **o. with hearts** (cards) Herz ausspielen
o'pen-air' Freiluft–; (theat) Freilicht–; **o. concert** Konzert *n* im Freien
opener [ˈopənər] *s* Öffner *m*, **for openers** (coll) für den Anfang
o'pen-eyed' *adj* mit offenen Augen
o'pen-hand'ed *adj* freigebig
o'pen-heart'ed *adj* offenherzig
o'pen house' *s* allgemeiner Besuchstag *m*
o'pening *adj* (scene) erste; (remarks Eröffnungs– ‖ *s* Öffnung *f*; (of a speech, play) Anfang *m*; (of a store, etc.) Eröffnung *f*; (vacant job) freie (or offene) Stelle *f*; (in the woods) Lichtung *f*; (good opportunity) günstige Gelegenheit *f*; (theat) Erstaufführung *f*
o'pening night' *s* Eröffnungsvorstellung *f*, Premiere *f*
o'pening num'ber *s* erstes Stück *n*
o'pen-mind'ed *adj* aufgeschlossen
openness [ˈopənnis] *s* Offenheit *f*
o'pen sea'son *s* Jagdzeit *f*
o'pen se'cret *s* offenes Geheimnis *n*
o'pen shop' *s* offener Betrieb *m* (für den kein Gewerkschaftszwang besteht)
opera [ˈɒpərə] *s* Oper *f*
op'era glass'es *spl* Opernglas *n*
op'era house' *s* Opernhaus *n*
operate [ˈɒpəˌret] *tr* (a machine, gun) bedienen; (a tool) handhaben; (a business) betreiben; **be operated by electricity** elektrisch betrieben werden ‖ *intr* (said of a device, machine) funktionieren, laufen; (surg) operieren; **o. on** (surg) operieren
operatic [ˌɒpəˈrætɪk] *adj* opernhaft
op'erating costs' *spl* Betriebskosten *pl*
op'erating instruc'tions *spl* Bedienungsanweisung *f*
op'erating room' *s* Operationssaal *m*
op'erating ta'ble *s* Operationstisch *m*
operation [ˌɒpəˈreʃən] *s* (process) Verfahren *n*; (of a machine) Bed.

nung *f*; (*of a business*) Leitung *f*; (mil) Operation *f*, Aktion *f*; (surg) Operation *f*; **be in o.** (*said of a machine*) in Betrieb sein; (*said of a law*) in Kraft sein; **have** (or **undergo**) **an o.** sich e-r Operation unterziehen; **in a single o.** in e-m einzigen Arbeitsgang; **put into o.** in Betrieb setzen

operational [ˌɑpəˈreʃənəl] *adj* (*ready to be used*) betriebsbereit; (*pertaining to operations*) Betriebs– Arbeits–; (mil) Einsatz–, Operations–

opera'tions room' *s* (aer) Bereitschaftsraum *m*

operative [ˈɑpərətɪv] *adj* funktionsfähig, wirkend; **become o.** in Kraft treten || *s* Agent –in *mf*

operator [ˈɑpəˌretər] *s* (*of a machine*) Bedienende *mf*; (*of an automobile*) Fahrer –in *mf*; (sl) Schieber –in *mf*; (telp) Telephonist –in *mf*; **o.!** (telp) Zentrale!

op'erator's li'cense *s* Führerschein *m*

operetta [ˌɑpəˈretə] *s* Operette *f*

ophthalmologist [ˌɑfθəlˈmɑlədʒɪst] *s* Augenarzt *m*, Augenärztin *f*

ophthalmology [ˌɑfθəlˈmɑlədʒi] *s* Augenheilkunde *f*, Ophthalmologie *f*

opiate [ˈopɪˌet] *s* Opiat *n*; (fig) Betäubungsmittel *n*

opinion [əˈpɪnjən] *s* Meinung *f*; **be of the o.** der Meinung sein; **give an o. on** begutachten; **have a high o. of** große Stücke halten auf (*acc*); **in my o.** meiner Meinung nach, meines Erachtens

opinionated [əˈpɪnjəˌnetɪd] *adj* von sich eingenommen

opin'ion poll' *s* Meinungsumfrage *f*

opium [ˈopɪəm] *s* Opium *n*

o'pium den' *s* Opiumhöhle *f*

o'pium pop'py *s* Schlafmohn *m*

opossum [əˈpɑsəm] *s* Opossum *n*

opponent [əˈponənt] *s* Gegner –in *mf*

opportune [ˌɑpərˈt(j)un] *adj* gelegen

opportunist [ˌɑpərˈt(j)unɪst] *s* Opportunist –in *mf*

opportunity [ˌɑpərˈt(j)unɪti] *s* Gelegenheit *f*

oppose [əˈpoz] *tr* sich widersetzen (*dat*); (*for comparison*) gegenüberstellen; **be opposed to s.th.** gegen etw sein

oppos'ing *adj* (*team, forces*) gegnerisch; (*views*) entgegengesetzt

opposite [ˈɑpəsɪt] *adj* (*side, corner*) gegenüberliegend; (*meaning*) entgegengesetzt; (*view*) gegenteilig; **o. angle** (geom) Gegenwinkel *m*; **o. to** gegenüber (*dat*) || *s* Gegensatz *m*, Gegenteil *n* || *prep* gegenüber (*dat*)

op'posite num'ber *s* Gegenstück *n*, Gegenspieler –in *mf*

opposition [ˌɑpəˈzɪʃən] *s* Widerstand *m*; (pol) Opposition *f*; **meet with stiff o.** auf heftigen Widerstand stoßen; **offer o.** Widerstand leisten

oppress [əˈpres] *tr* unterdrücken

oppression [əˈpreʃən] *s* Unterdrückung *f*

oppressive [əˈpresɪv] *adj* bedrückend

oppressor [əˈpresər] *s* Unterdrücker –in *mf*

opprobrious [əˈprobrɪ·əs] *adj* schändlich

opprobrium [əˈprobrɪ·əm] *s* Schande *f*

opt [ɑpt] *intr*—**opt for** optieren für

optic [ˈɑptɪk] *adj* Augen– || **optics** *s* Optik *f*

optical [ˈɑptɪkəl] *adj* optisch

op'tical illus'ion *s* optische Täuschung *f*

optician [ɑpˈtɪʃən] *s* Optiker –in *mf*

op'tic nerve' *s* Augennerv *m*

optimism [ˈɑptɪˌmɪzəm] *s* Optimismus *m*

optimist [ˈɑptɪmɪst] *s* Optimist –in *mf*

optimistic [ˌɑptɪˈmɪstɪk] *adj* optimistisch

option [ˈɑpʃən] *s* (*choice*) Wahl *f*; (*alternative*) Alternative *f*; (ins) Option *f*

optional [ˈɑpʃənəl] *adj* wahlfrei; **be o.** freistehen

optometrist [ɑpˈtɑmɪtrɪst] *s* Augenoptiker –in *mf*

optometry [ɑpˈtɑmɪtri] *s* Optometrie *f*

opulent [ˈɑpjələnt] *adj* (*wealthy*) reich; (*luxurious*) üppig

or [ɔr] *conj* oder

oracle [ˈɔrəkəl] *s* Orakel *n*

oracular [oˈrækjələr] *adj* orakelhaft

oral [ˈɔrəl] *adj* mündlich

o'ral hygiene' *s* Mundpflege *f*

orange [ˈɔrɪndʒ] *adj* orange || *s* Orange *f*, Apfelsine *f*

orangeade [ˌɔrɪndʒˈed] *s* Orangeade *f*

or'ange blos'som *s* Orangenblüte *f*

or'ange grove' *s* Orangenhain *m*

or'ange tree' *s* Orangenbaum *m*

orang-outang [oˈræŋuˌtæŋ] *s* Orang-Utan *m*

oration [oˈreʃən] *s* Rede *f*

orator [ˈɔrətər] *s* Redner –in *mf*

oratorical [ˌɔrəˈtɔrɪkəl] *adj* rednerisch

oratori·o [ˌɔrəˈtɔri·o] *s* (–os) Oratorium *n*

oratory [ˈɔrəˌtori] *s* Redekunst *f*

orb [ɔrb] *s* Kugel *f*; (*of the moon* or *sun*) Scheibe *f*

orbit [ˈɔrbɪt] *s* Umlaufbahn *f*; **send into o.** in die Umlaufbahn schicken || *tr* umkreisen

orbital [ˈɔrbɪtəl] *adj* Kreisbahn–

orchard [ˈɔrtʃərd] *s* Obstgarten *m*

orchestra [ˈɔrkɪstrə] *s* Orchester *n*

or'chestra pit' *s* Orchesterraum *m*

orchestrate [ˈɔrkɪˌstret] *tr* orchestrieren

orchid [ˈɔrkɪd] *s* Orchidee *f*

ordain [ɔrˈden] *tr* verordnen; (eccl) ordinieren, zum Priester weihen

ordeal [ɔrˈdil] *s* Qual *f*; (hist) Gottesurteil *n*; **o. by fire** Feuerprobe *f*

order [ˈɔrdər] *s* (*command*) Befehl *m*; (*decree*) Verordnung *f*; (*order, arrangement*) Ordnung *f*; (*medal*) Orden *m*; (*sequence*) Reihenfolge *f*; (archit, bot, zool) Ordnung *f*; (com) (**for**) Auftrag *m* (auf *acc*), Bestellung *f* (auf *acc*); (eccl) Orden *m*; (jur) Beschluß *m*; **according to orders** befehlsgemäß; **be in good o.** in gutem

Zustand sein; **be the o. of the day** (coll) an der Tagesordnung sein; **be under orders to** (inf) Befehl haben zu (inf); **by o. of** auf Befehl von (or genit); **call to o.** (a meeting) für eröffnet erklären; (reestablish order) zur Ordnung rufen; **in o.** (functioning) in Ordnung; (proper, in place) angebracht; **in o. of** geordnet nach; **in o. that** damit; **in o. to** (inf) um ... zu (inf); **make to o.** nach Maß machen; **of a high o.** von ausgezeichneter Art; **on o.** (com) im Auftrag; **o.!, o.!** zur Ordnung! **out of o.** (defective) außer Betrieb; (not functioning at all) nicht in Ordnung; (disarranged) in Unordnung; (parl) im Widerspruch zur Geschäftsordnung, unzulässig; **put in o.** in Ordnung bringen; **restore to o.** die Ordnung wiederherstellen; **you are out of o.** Sie haben nicht das Wort ‖ tr (command) befehlen, anordnen; (decree) verordnen; (com) bestellen; **as ordered** auftragsgemäß; **o. around** herumkommandieren; **o. more of** nachbestellen; **o. s.o. off** (e.g., the premises) j-n weisen von

or′der blank′ s Auftragsformular n

orderliness [′ɔrdərlınıs] s (of a person) Ordnungsliebe f; (of a room, etc.) Ordnung f

orderly [′ɔrdərli] adj ordentlich ‖ s (med) Krankenwärter m; (mil) Bursche m

or′derly room′ s (mil) Schreibstube f

or′der slip′ s Bestellzettel m

ordinal [′ɔrdınəl] adj Ordnungs– ‖ s Ordnungszahl f

ordinance [′ɔrdınəns] s Verfügung f; (of a city) Verordnung f

ordinary [′ɔrdı‚neri] adj gewöhnlich; (member) ordentlich; **o. person** Alltagsmensch m ‖ s Gewöhnliche n; (eccl) Ordinarius m; **nothing out of the o.** nichts Ungewöhnliches; **out of the o.** außerordentlich

ordination [‚ɔrdı′neʃən] s Priesterweihe f

ordnance [′ɔrdnəns] s Waffen und Munition pl; (arti) Geschützwesen n

ore [ɔr] s Erz n

organ [′ɔrgən] s (means) Werkzeug n; (publication) Organ n; (adm, biol) Organ n; (mus) Orgel f

organdy [′ɔrgəndi] s Organdy m

or′gan grind′er s Drehorgelspieler m

organic [ɔr′gænık] adj organisch

organism [′ɔrgə‚nızəm] s Organismus m

organist [′ɔrgənıst] s Organist –in mf

organization [‚ɔrgənı′zeʃən] s Organisation f

organizational [‚ɔrgənı′zeʃənəl] adj organisatorisch

organize [′ɔrgə‚naız] tr organisieren

organizer [′ɔrgə‚naızər] s Organisator –in mf

or′gan loft′ s Orgelbühne f

orgasm [′ɔrgæzəm] s Orgasmus m

orgy [′ɔrdʒi] s Orgie f

Orient [′ɔrı‚ent] s Orient m ‖ **orient** [′ɔrı‚ent] tr orientieren

oriental [‚ɔrı′entəl] adj orientalisch ‖ **Oriental** s Orientale m, Orientalin f

orientation [‚ɔrı‚ən′teʃən] s Orientierung f; (of new staff members) Einführung f

orifice [′ɔrıfıs] s Öffnung f

origin [′ɔrıdʒın] s Ursprung m; (of a person or word) Herkunft f

original [ə′rıdʒınəl] adj ursprünglich; (first) Ur–; (novel, play) originell; (person) erfinderisch ‖ s Original n

originality [ə‚rıdʒı′nælıti] s Originalität f

ori′ginal research′ s Quellenstudium n

ori′ginal sin′ s Erbsünde f, Sündenfall m

originate [ə′rıdʒı‚net] tr hervorbringen ‖ intr (from) entstehen (aus); **o.** in seinen Ursprung haben in (dat)

originator [ə′rıdʒı‚netər] s Urheber –in mf

oriole [′ɔrı‚ol] s Goldamsel f, Pirol m

ormolu [′ɔrmə‚lu] s Malergold n

ornament [′ɔrnəmənt] s Verzierung f, Schmuck m ‖ [′ɔrnə‚ment] tr verzieren

ornamental [‚ɔrnə′mentəl] adj Zier–

ornamentation [‚ɔrnəmən′teʃən] s Verzierung f

ornate [ɔr′net] adj überladen; (speech) bilderreich

ornery [′ɔrnəri] adj (cantankerous) mürrisch; (vile) gemein

ornithology [‚ɔrnı′θalədʒi] s Vogelkunde f, Ornithologie f

orphan [′ɔrfən] s Waise f; **become an o.** verwaisen

orphanage [′ɔrfənıdʒ] s Waisenhaus n

or′phaned adj verwaist; **be o.** verwaisen

or′phans′ court′ s Vormundschaftsgericht n

orthodox [′ɔrθə‚daks] adj orthodox

orthography [ɔr′θagrəfi] s Orthographie f, Rechtschreibung f

orthopedist [‚ɔrθə′pidıst] s Orthopäde m, Orthopädin f

oscillate [′ası‚let] intr schwingen

oscillation [‚ası′leʃən] s Schwingung f

oscillator [′ası‚letər] s Oszillator m

osier [′oʒər] s Korbweide f

osmosis [as′mosıs] s Osmose f

osprey [′aspri] s Fischadler m

ossi·fy [′ası‚faı] v (pret & pp –fied) tr verknöchern lassen ‖ intr verknöchern

ostensible [as′tensıbəl] adj vorgeblich

ostentation [‚asten′teʃən] s Zurschaustellung f, Prahlerei f

ostentatious [‚asten′teʃəs] adj prahlerisch, prunksüchtig

osteopath [′astı‚ə‚pæθ] s Osteopath –in mf

osteopathy [‚astı′apəθi] s Osteopathie f

ostracism [′astrə‚sızəm] s Ächtung f; (hist) Scherbengericht n

ostracize [′astrə‚saız] tr verfemen

ostrich [′astrıtʃ] s Strauß m

Ostrogoth [′astrə‚gaθ] s Ostgote m

other [´ʌðər] *adj* andere, sonstig; **among o. things** unter anderem; **every o. day** jeden zweiten Tag; **none o. than he** kein anderer als er; **on the o. hand** andererseits; **o. things being equal** unter gleichen Voraussetzungen; **someone or o.** irgend jemand; **some ... or o.** irgendein; **the o. day** unlängst || *adv*—**o. than** anders als || *indef pron* andere; **the others** die anderen

otherwise [´ʌðər͵waɪz] *adj* sonstig || *adv* sonst; **I can't do o.** ich kann nicht umhin; **o. engaged** anderweitig beschäftigt; **think o.** anders denken

otter [´ɑtər] *s* Otter *m*; (*snake*) Otter *f*

Ottoman [´ɑtəmən] *adj* osmanisch || **ottoman** *s* (*couch*) Ottomane *m*; (*cushioned stool*) Polsterschemel *m*; **O.** Osmane *m*

ouch [aʊtʃ] *interj* au!

ought [ɔt] *aux* used to express obligation, e.g., **you o. to tell her** Sie sollten es ihr sagen; **they o. to have been here** sie hätten hier sein sollen

ounce [aʊns] *s* Unze *f*

our [aʊr] *poss adj* unser

ours [aʊrz] *poss pron* der uns(e)rige, der uns(e)re, uns(e)rer; **a friend of o.** ein Freund von uns; **this is o.** das gehört uns

ourselves [aʊr´sɛlvz] *reflex pron* uns; **we are by o.** wir sind doch unter uns || *intens pron* selbst, selber

oust [aʊst] *tr* (**from**) verdrängen (aus); **o. from office** seines Amtes entheben

ouster [´aʊstər] *s* Amtsenthebung *f*

out [aʊt] *adj*—**an evening out** ein Ausgehabend *m*; **be out** (*of the house*) ausgegangen sein; (*said of a light, fire*) aus sein; (*said of a new book*) erschienen sein; (*said of a secret*) enthüllt sein; (*said of flowers*) aufgeblüht sein; (*said of a dislocated limb*) verrenkt sein; (*be out of style*) aus der Mode sein; (*be at an end*) aus sein; (*be absent from work*) der Arbeit fernbleiben; (*be on strike*) streiken; **be out after s.o.** hinter j-m her sein; **be out for a good time** dem Vergnügen nachgehen; **be out on one's feet** (coll) erledigt sein; **be out ten marks** zehn Mark eingebüßt haben; **be out to** (*inf*) darauf ausgehen (or aus sein) zu (*inf*); **that's out** das kommt nicht in Frage; **the best thing out** das Beste, was es gibt || *adv* (*gone forth; ended, terminated*) aus; **out of** (*curiosity, pity, etc.*) aus (*dat*); (*fear*) vor (*dat*); (*a certain number*) von (*dat*); (*deprived of*) beraubt (*genit*); **out of breath** außer Atem; **out of money** ohne Geld; **out of place** verlegt; (*not appropriate or proper*) unpassend; **out of the window** zum Fenster hinaus || *s* (*pretext*) Ausweg *m*; **be on the outs with s.o.** mit j-m auf gespanntem Fuße sein || *prep* aus (*dat*) || *interj* (sport) aus!; **out with it!** heraus damit!

out′ and away′ *adv* bei weitem

out′-and-out′ *adj* abgefeimt

out′-ar′gue *tr* in Grund und Boden argumentieren

out′bid′ *v* (*pret* **–bid;** *pp* **–bid & –bidden;** *ger* **–bidding**) *tr* überbieten

out′board mo′tor *s* Außenbordmotor *m*

out′bound′ *adj* nach auswärts bestimmt; (*traffic*) aus der Stadt fließend

out′break′ *s* Ausbruch *m*

out′build′ing *s* Nebengebäude *n*

out′burst′ *s* Ausbruch *m*; **o. of anger** Zornausbruch *m*

out′cast′ *adj* ausgestoßen || *s* Ausgestoßene *mf*

out′come′ *s* Ergebnis *n*

out′cry′ *s* Ausruf *m*; **raise an o.** ein Zetergeschrei erheben

out-dat′ed *adj* zeitlich überholt

out′dis′tance *tr* hinter sich [*dat*] lassen

out′do′ *v* (*pret* **–did;** *pp* **–done**) *tr* überbieten, übertreffen; **not to be outdone by s.o.** in zeal j-m nichts an Eifer nachgeben; **o. oneself** in sich überbieten in (*dat*)

out′door′ *adj* Außen—

out′doors′ *adv* draußen, im Freien || *s*—**in the outdoors** im Freien

out′door shot′ *s* (*phot*) Außenaufnahme *f*

out′door swim′ming pool′ *s* Freibad *n*

out′door the′ater *s* Naturtheater *n*

out′door toil′et *s* Abtritt *m*

outer [´aʊtər] *adj* äußere, Außen—

out′er ear′ *s* Ohrmuschel *f*

out′er gar′ment *s* Überkleid *n*

out′ermost′ *adj* äußerste

out′er space′ *s* Weltall *n*, Weltraum *m*

out′field′ *s* (baseball) Außenfeld *n*

out′fit′ *s* (*equipment*) Ausrüstung *f*; (*set of clothes*) Ausstattung *f*; (*uniform*) Kluft *f*; (*business firm*) Gesellschaft *f*; (mil) Einheit *f* || *v* (*pret* **–fitted;** *ger* **–fitting**) *tr* (*with equipment*) ausrüsten; (*with clothes*) neu ausstaffieren

out′flank′ *tr* überflügeln, umfassen

out′flow′ *s* Ausfluß *m*

out′go′ing *adj* (*sociable*) gesellig; (*officer*) bisherig; (*tide*) zurückgehend; (*train, plane*) abgehend

out′grow′ *v* (*pret* **–grew;** *pp* **–grown**) *tr* herauswachsen aus; (fig) entwachsen (*dat*)

out′growth′ *s* Auswuchs *m*; (fig) Folge *f*

out′ing *s* Ausflug *m*

outlandish [aʊt´lændɪʃ] *adj* fremdartig; (*prices*) überhöht

out′last′ *tr* überdauern

out′law′ *s* Geächtete *mf* || *tr* ächten

out′lay′ *s* Auslage *f*, Kostenaufwand *m* || **out′lay′** *v* (*pret* & *pp* **–laid**) *tr* auslegen

out′let′ *s* (*for water*) Abfluß *m*, Ausfluß *m*; (fig) (**for**) Ventil *n* (für); (com) Absatzmarkt *m*; (elec) Steckdose *f*; **find an o. for** (fig) Luft machen (*dat*); **no o.** Sackgasse *f*

out′line′ *s* (*profile*) Umriß *m*; (*sketch*) Umrißzeichnung *f*; (*summary*) Grundriß *m*; **rough o.** knapper Umriß *m* || *tr* umreißen

out'live' *tr* überleben

out'look' *s* (*place giving a view*) Ausguck *m*; (*view from a place*) Ausblick *m*; (*point of view*) Anschauung *f*; (*prospects*) Aussichten *pl*

out'ly'ing *adj* Außen–

out'maneu'ver *tr* ausmanövrieren; (fig) überlisten

outmoded [‚aʊt'moʊdɪd] *adj* unmodern

out'num'ber *tr* an Zahl übertreffen

out'-of-bounds' *adj* (fig) nicht in den Schranken; (sport) im Aus

out'-of-court' set'tlement *s* außergerichtlicher Vergleich *m*

out'-of-date' *adj* veraltet

out'-of-door' *adj* Außen–

out'-of-doors' *adj* Außen– || *adv* im Freien, draußen || *s*—**in the o.** im Freien

out'-of-pock'et *adj*—**o. expenses** Barauslagen *pl*

out' of print' *adj* vergriffen

out'-of-the-way' *adj* abgelegen

out' of tune' *adj* verstimmt

out' of work' *adj* arbeitslos, erwerbslos

out'pace' *tr* überholen

out'pa'tient *s* ambulant Behandelte *mf*

out'patient clin'ic *s* Ambulanz *f*

out'play' *tr* überspielen

out'point' *tr* (sport) nach Punkten schlagen

out'post' *s* (mil) Vorposten *m*

out'pour'ing *s* (& fig) Erguß *m*

out'put' *s* (*of a machine or factory*) Arbeitsleistung *f*; (*of a factory*) Produktion *f*; (mech) Nutzleistung *f*; (min) Förderung *f*

out'rage' *s* Unverschämtheit *f*; (against) Verletzung *f* (genit) || *tr* gröblich beleidigen

outrageous [aʊt'redʒəs] *adj* unverschämt

out'rank' *tr* im Rang übertreffen

out'rid'er *s* Vorreiter *m*

outrigger [‚aʊt'rɪgər] *s* Ausleger *m*; (*of a racing boat*) Outrigger *m*

out'right' *adj* (*lie, refusal*) glatt; (*loss*) total; (*frank*) offen || *adv* (*completely*) völlig; (*without reserve*) ohne Vorbehalt; (*at once*) auf der Stelle; **buy o.** per Kasse kaufen; **refuse o.** glatt ablehnen

out'run' *v* (*pret* **–ran;** *pp* **–run;** *ger* **–running**) *tr* hinter sich [*dat*] lassen

out'sell' *v* (*pret* & *pp* **–sold**) *tr* e–n größeren Umsatz haben als

out'set' *s* Anfang *m*

out'shine' *v* (*pret* & *pp* **–shone**) *tr* überstrahlen

out'side' *adj* (*help, interference*) von außen; (*world, influence, impressions*) äußere; (*lane, work*) Außen– || *adv* draußen || *s* Außenseite *f*, Äußere *n*; **at the** (*very*) **o.** (aller–)höchstens; **from the o.** von außen || *prep* außerhalb (genit)

outsider [‚aʊt'saɪdər] *s* Außenstehende *mf*; (sport) Außenseiter *m*

out'size' *adj* übergroß || *s* Übergröße *f*

out'skirts' *spl* Randgebiet *n*, Stadtrand *m*

out'smart' *tr* überlisten

out'spo'ken *adj* freimütig

out'spread' *adj* (*legs*) gespreizt; (*arms, wings*) ausgebreitet

out'stand'ing *adj* hervorragend, profiliert; (*money, debts*) ausstehend

out'strip' *v* (*pret* & *pp* **–stripped;** *ger* **–stripping**) *tr* (& fig) hinter sich [*dat*] lassen

out'vote' *tr* überstimmen

outward ['aʊtwərd] *adj* äußerlich, äußere || *adv* auswärts, nach außen

outwardly ['aʊtwərdli] *adv* äußerlich

outwards ['aʊtwərdz] *adv* auswärts

out'weigh' *tr* an Gewicht übertreffen; (fig) überwiegen

out'wit' *v* (*pret* & *pp* **–witted;** *ger* **–witting**) *tr* überlisten

oval ['oʊvəl] *adj* oval || *s* Oval *n*

ovary ['oʊvəri] *s* Eierstock *m*

ovation [o'veʃən] *s* Huldigung *f*, Ovation *f*

oven ['ʌvən] *s* Ofen *m*; (*for baking*) Backofen *m*

over ['oʊvər] *adj* (*ended*) vorbei, aus; **it's all o. with him** es ist vorbei mit ihm; **o. and done with** total erledigt || *adv*—**all o.** (*everywhere*) überall; (*on the body*) über und über; **children of twelve and o.** Kinder von zwölf Jahren und darüber; **come o.!** komm herüber!; **o.!** (*turn the page*) bitte wenden!; **o. again** noch einmal; **o. against** gegenüber (*dat*); **o. and above** obendrein; **o. and out!** (rad) Ende!; **o. and o. again** immer wieder; **o. in Europe** drüben in Europa; **o. there** dort, da drüben || *prep* (*position*) über (*dat*); (*motion*) über (*acc*); (*because of*) wegen (genit); (*in the course of, e.g., a cup of tea*) bei (*dat*); (*during; more than*) über (*acc*); **all o. town** (*position*) in der ganzen Stadt; (*direction*) durch die ganze Stadt; **be o. s.o.** über j–m stehen; **b. o. s.o.'s head** j–m zu hoch sein; **from all o. Germany** aus ganz Deutschland; **o. and above** außer (genit); **o. the radio** im Radio

o'veract' *tr* & *intr* (theat) übertreiben

o'verac'tive *adj* übermäßig tätig

overage ['oʊvər'edʒ] *adj* über das vorgeschriebene Alter hinaus

o'verall' *adj* Gesamt– || **o'veralls'** *spl* Monteuranzug *m*; (*trousers*) Überziehhose *f*

o'verambi'tious *adj* allzu ehrgeizig

o'veranx'ious *adj* überängstlich; (*over-eager*) übereifrig

o'verawe' *tr* einschüchtern

o'verbear'ing *adj* überheblich

o'verboard' *adv* über Bord; **go o. about** sich übermäßig begeistern für

o'vercast' *adj* bewölkt, bedeckt; **become o.** sich bewölken || *s* Bewölkung *f*

o'vercharge' *s* Überteuerung *f*; (elec) Überladung *f* || **o'vercharge'** *tr* e–n Überpreis abverlangen (*dat*); (elec) überladen

o'vercoat' *s* Mantel *m*, Überrock *m*

o'ver·come' *v* (*pret* **–came;** *pp* **–come**)

tr überwältigen; **be o. with joy** vor
Freude hingerissen sein

o'vercon'fidence *s* zu großes Selbstvertrauen *n*

o'vercon'fident *adj* zu vertrauensvoll

o'vercook' *tr* (*overboil*) zerkochen;
(*overbake*) zu lange backen, zu lange
braten

o'vercrowd' *tr* überfüllen; (*a room,
hotel, hospital*) überbelegen

o'ver·do' *v* (*pret* –did; *pp* –done) *tr*
übertreiben; **o. it** sich überanstrengen

o'verdone' *adj* (culin) übergar

o'verdose' *s* Überdosis *f*

o'verdraft' *s* Überziehung *f*

o'ver·draw' *v* (*pret* –drew; *pp* –drawn)
tr überziehen

o'verdress' *intr* sich übertrieben kleiden

o'verdrive' *s* (aut) Schongang *m*

o'verdue' *adj* überfällig

o'ver·eat' *v* (*pret* –ate; *pp* –eaten) *intr*
sich überessen

o'verem'phasis *s* Überbetonung *f*

o'verem'phasize *tr* überbetonen

o'veres'timate *tr* überschätzen

o'verexcite' *tr* überreizen

o'verexert' *tr* überanstrengen

o'verexer'tion *s* Überanstrengung *f*

o'verexpose' *tr* (phot) überbelichten

o'verexpo'sure *s* Überbelichtung *f*

o'verextend' *tr* übermäßig ausweiten

o'verflow' *s* (*inundation*) Überschwemmung *f*; (*surplus*) Überschuß *m*; (*outlet for surplus liquid*) Überlauf *m*;
filled to o. bis zum Überfließen gefüllt ‖ o'verflow' *tr* überfluten; **o.
the banks** über die Ufer treten ‖
intr überfließen

o'ver·fly' *v* (*pret* –flew; *pp* –flown) *tr*
überfliegen

o'verfriend'ly *adj* katzenfreundlich

o'vergrown' *adj* überwachsen; (*child*)
lang aufgeschossen; **become o.** (*said
of a garden*) verwildern; **become o.
with** überwuchert werden von

o'verhang' *s* Überhang *m* ‖ o'ver·hang'
v (*pret & pp* –hung) *tr* hervorragen
über (*acc*); (*threaten*) bedrohen ‖
intr überhängen

o'verhaul' *s* Überholung *f* ‖ o'verhaul'
tr (*repair; overtake*) überholen

o'verhead' *adj* (*line*) oberirdisch;
(*valve*) obengesteuert ‖ *adv* droben
‖ *s* (econ) Gemeinkosten *pl*, laufende
Unkosten *pl*

o'verhead door' *s* Federhubtor *n*

o'verhead line' *s* (*of a trolley*) Oberleitung *f*

o'ver·hear' *v* (*pret & pp* –heard) *tr*
mitanhören; **be o.** belauscht werden

o'verheat' *tr* überhitzen; (*a room*)
überheizen ‖ *intr* heißlaufen

o'verindulge' *tr* verwöhnen ‖ *intr* (in)
sich allzusehr ergehen (in *dat*)

o'verkill' *s* Overkill *m*

overjoyed [ˌovərˈdʒɔɪd] *adj* überglücklich

overland [ˈovərˌlænd] *adj* Überland–;
o. route Landweg *m* ‖ *adv* über Land

o'verlap' *s* Überschneiden *n* ‖ o'verlap'
v (*pret & pp* –lapped) *ger* –lapping)

tr sich überschneiden mit ‖ *intr* (&
fig) sich überschneiden

o'verlap'ping *s* (& fig) Überschneidung
f

o'verlay' *s* Auflage *f*; (*for a map*)
Planpause *f*; **o. of gold** Goldauflage
f

o'verload' *s* Überbelastung *f*; (elec)
Überlast *f* ‖ o'verload' *tr* überlasten;
(*a truck*) überladen; (*in radio communications*) übersteuern; (elec)
überlasten

o'verlook' *tr* (*by mistake*) übersehen;
(*a mistake*) hinwegsehen über (*acc*);
(*a view*) überblicken

overly [ˈovərli] *adv* übermäßig

o'vernight' *adj*—**o. stop** Aufenthalt *m*
von e–r Nacht; **o. things** Nachtzeug
n ‖ *adv* über Nacht; **stay o.** übernachten

o'vernight' bag' *s* Nachtzeugtasche *f*

o'verpass' *s* Überführung *f*

o'ver·pay' *v* (*pret & pp* –paid) *tr* &
intr überbezahlen

o'verpay'ment *s* Überbezahlung *f*

o'verpop'ulat'ed *adj* übervölkert

o'verpop'ula'tion *s* Übervölkerung *f*

o'verpow'er *tr* (& fig) überwältigen

o'verproduc'tion *s* Überproduktion *f*

o'verrate' *tr* zu hoch schätzen

o'verreach' *tr* (*extend beyond*) hinausragen über (*acc*); (*an arm*) zu weit
ausstrecken; **o. oneself** sich übernehmen

o'verrefined' *adj* überspitzt

o'verripe' *adj* überreif

o'verrule' *tr* (*an objection*) zurückweisen; (*a proposal*) verwerfen; (*a person*) überstimmen

o'verrun' *s* Überproduktion *f* ‖ o'verrun' *v* (*pret* –ran; *pp* –run; *ger*
–running) *tr* überrennen; (*said of a
flood*) überschwemmen; **o. with**
(*weeds*) überwuchert von; (*tourists*)
überlaufen von; (*vermin*) wimmeln
von

o'versalt' *tr* versalzen

o'versea(s)' *adj* Übersee– ‖ *adv* nach
Übersee

o'ver·see' *v* (*pret & pp* –saw; *pp* –seen)
tr beaufsichtigen

o'verse'er *s* Aufseher –in *mf*

o'versen'sitive *adj* überempfindlich

o'vershad'ow *tr* überschatten; (fig) in
den Schatten stellen

o'vershoe' *s* Überschuh *m*

o'ver·shoot' *v* (*pret & pp* –shot) *tr* (&
fig) hinausschießen über (*acc*)

o'versight' *s* Versehen *n*; **through an o.**
aus Versehen

o'versimplifica'tion *s* allzu große Vereinfachung *f*

o'versize' *adj* übergroß ‖ *s* Übergröße
f

o'ver·sleep' *v* (*pret & pp* –slept) *tr* &
intr verschlafen

o'verspe'cialized *adj* überspezialisiert

o'verstaffed' *adj* (mit Personal) übersetzt

o'verstay' *tr* überschreiten

o'ver·step' *v* (*pret & pp* –stepped; *ger*
–stepping) *tr* überschreiten

o'verstock' *tr* überbevorraten

o'verstrain' *tr* überanstrengen

o'verstuffed' *adj* überfüllt; (*furniture*) überpolstert

o'versupply' *s* zu großer Vorrat *m*; (com) Überangebot *n* || o'versup·ply' *v* (*pret & pp* –plied) *tr* überreichlich versehen; (com) überreichlich anbieten

overt ['ovərt], [o'vʌrt] *adj* offenkundig

o'ver·take' *v* (*pret* –took; *pp* –taken) *tr* (*catch up to*) einholen; (*pass*) überholen; (*suddenly befall*) überfallen

o'vertax' *tr* überbesteuern; (fig) überfordern, übermäßig in Anspruch nehmen

o'ver-the-coun'ter *adj* (pharm) rezeptfrei; (st. exch.) freihändig

o'verthrow' *s* Sturz *m* || o'ver·throw' (*pret* –threw; *pp* –thrown) *tr* stürzen

o'vertime' *adj* Überstunden– || *adv*—work o. Überstunden arbeiten; work five hours o. fünf Überstunden machen || *s* Überstunden *pl*; (sport) Spielverlängerung *f*

o'vertired' *adj* übermüdet

o'vertone' *s* (fig) Nebenbedeutung *f*; (mus) Oberton *m*

o'vertrump' *tr* überstechen

overture ['ovərtʃər] *s* Antrag *m*; (mus) Ouvertüre *f*

o'verturn' *tr* umstürzen || *intr* umkippen; (aut) sich überschlagen

overweening [,ovər'winɪŋ] *adj* hochmütig

o'verweight' *adj* zu schwer || *s* Übergewicht *n*; (*of freight*) Übertracht *f*

overwhelm [,ovər'whelm] *tr* (*with some feeling*) überwältigen; (*e.g., with questions, gifts*) überschütten; (*with work*) überbürden

o'verwhelm'ing *adj* überwältigend

overwind [,ovər'waɪnd] *v* (*pret & pp* –wound) *tr* überdrehen

o'verwork' *s* Überarbeitung *f*, Überanstrengung *f* || o'verwork' *tr* überfordern || *intr* sich überarbeiten

o'verwrought' *adj* überreizt

o'verzeal'ous *adj* übereifrig

ow [au] *interj* au!

owe [o] *tr* schulden (*dat*), schuldig sein (*dat*); he owes her everything er verdankt ihr alles

ow'ing *adj*—it is o. to you that es ist dein Verdienst, daß; o. to infolge (*genit*)

owl [aul] *s* Eule *f*; (barn owl, screech owl) Schleiereule *f*

own [on] *adj* eigen || *s*—be left on one's own sich [*dat*] selbst überlassen sein; be on one's own auf eigenen Füßen stehen; come into one's own zu seinem Recht kommen; hold one's own sich behaupten; of one's own für sich allein; on one's own (*initiative*) aus eigener Initiative; (*responsibility*) auf eigene Faust || *tr* besitzen; (*acknowledge*) anerkennen; who owns this house? wem gehört dieses Haus? || *intr*—own to sich bekennen zu; own up to zugeben (*dat*)

owner ['onər] *s* Eigentümer –in *mf*

own'ership' *s* Eigentum *n*; (*legal right of possession*) Eigentumsrecht *n*; under new o. unter neuer Leitung

ox [aks] *s* (oxen ['aksən]) Ochse *m*

ox'cart' *s* Ochsenkarren *m*

oxfords ['aksfərdz] *spl* Halbschuhe *pl*

oxide ['aksaɪd] *s* Oxyd *n*

oxidize ['aksɪˌdaɪz] *tr & intr* oxydieren

oxydation [,aksɪ'deʃən] *s* Oxydation *f*

oxygen ['aksɪdʒən] *s* Sauerstoff *m*

oxygenate ['aksɪdʒəˌnet] *tr* mit Sauerstoff anreichern

ox'ygen mask' *s* Sauerstoffmaske *f*

ox'ygen tank' *s* Sauerstofflasche *f*

ox'ygen tent' *s* Sauerstoffzelt *n*

oxytone ['aksɪˌton] *adj* oxytoniert || *s* Oxytonon *n*

oyster ['ɔɪstər] *s* Auster *f*

oys'ter bed' *s* Austernbank *f*

oys'ter farm' *s* Austernpark *m*

oys'ter·man *s* (–men) Austernfischer *m*

oys'tershell' *s* Austernschale *f*

oys'ter stew' *s* Austernragout *n*

ozone ['ozon] *s* Ozon *n*

O'zone layer' *s* Ozonschicht *f*

P

P, p [pi] *s* sechzehnter Buchstabe des englischen Alphabets

pace [pes] *s* Schritt *m*; (speed) Tempo *n*; at a fast p. in schnellem Tempo; keep p. with Schritt halten mit; put s.o. through his paces j–n auf Herz und Nieren prüfen; set the p. das Tempo angeben; (sport) Schrittmacher sein || *tr* (the room, floor) abschreiten; p. off abschreiten || *intr*—p. up and down (in) auf und ab schreiten (in *dat*)

pace'mak'er *s* Schrittmacher *m*

pacific [pə'sɪfɪk] *adj* pazifisch; the

Pacific Ocean der Pazifische (or Stille) Ozean || *s*—the Pacific der Pazifik

pacifier ['pæsɪˌfaɪ·ər] *s* Friedensvermittler –in *mf*; (for a baby) Schnuller *m*

pacifism ['pæsɪˌfɪzəm] *s* Pazifismus *m*

pacifist ['pæsɪfɪst] *s* Pazifist –in *mf*

paci·fy ['pæsɪˌfaɪ] *v* (*pret & pp* –fied) *tr* (a country) befrieden; (a person) beruhigen

pack [pæk] *s* Pack *m*, Packen *m*; (of a soldier) Gepäck *n*; (of wolves, submarines) Rudel *n*; (of hounds) Meute

f; (*of cigarettes*) Päckchen *n,* Schachtel *f;* (*on pack animals*) Last *f;* (med) Packung *f;* **p. of cards** Spiel *n* Karten; **p. of lies** Lug und Trug || *tr* (*a trunk*) packen; (*clothes*) einpacken; (*seal*) abdichten; **p. in** (*above normal capacity*) einpferchen; **p. up** zusammenpacken || *intr* packen; **send s.o. packing** j-m Beine machen
package ['pækɪdʒ] *adj* (*price, tour, agreement*) Pauschal– || *s* Paket *n* || *tr* (ver)packen
pack'age deal' *s* Koppelgeschäft *n*
pack' an'imal *s* Packtier *n*
packet ['pækɪt] *s* Paket *n,* Päckchen *n;* (naut) Postschiff *n*
pack'ing *s* (*act*) Packen *n;* (*seal*) Dichtung *f;* (*wrapper*) Verpackung *f*
pack'ing case' *s* Packkiste *f*
pack'ing house' *s* Konservenfabrik *f*
pack'sad'dle *s* Packsattel *m*
pact [pækt] *s* Pakt *m;* **make a p.** paktieren
pad [pæd] *s* (*of writing paper*) Block *m;* (*ink pad*) Stempelkissen *n;* (*cushion*) Kissen *n;* (*of butter*) Stück *n;* (*under a rug*) Unterlage *f;* (*living quarters*) Bude *f;* (rok) Abschußrampe *f;* (sport) Schützer *m;* (surg) Bausch *m* || *v* (*pret & pp* **padded;** *ger* **padding**) *tr* (*e.g., the shoulders*) wattieren; (*writing*) ausbauschen
pad'ded cell' *s* Gummizelle *f*
pad'ding *s* Wattierung *f;* (coll) Ballast *m*
paddle ['pædəl] *s* (*of a canoe*) Paddel *n;* (*for table tennis*) Schläger *m* || *tr* paddeln; (*spank*) prügeln || *intr* paddeln
pad'dle wheel' *s* Schaufelrad *n*
paddock ['pædək] *s* Pferdekoppel *f;* (*at the races*) Sattelplatz *m*
pad'dy wag'on *s* ['pædi] *s* (sl) Grüne Minna *f*
pad'lock' *s* Vorhängeschloß *n* || *tr* mit e-m Vorhängeschloß verschließen
paean ['piːən] *s* Siegeslied *n*
pagan ['pegən] *adj* heidnisch || *s* Heide *m,* Heidin *f*
paganism ['pegəˌnɪzəm] *s* Heidentum *n*
page [pedʒ] *s* Seite *f;* (*in a hotel or club; at court*) Page *m* || *tr* (*summon*) über den Lautsprecher (or durch Pagen) holen lassen || *intr*— **p. through** durchblättern
pageant ['pædʒənt] *s* Festspiel *n;* (*procession*) Festzug *m*
pageantry ['pædʒəntri] *s* Schaugepränge *n*
page'boy' *s* Pagenfrisur *f*
page' proof' *s* Umbruchabzug *m*
pagoda [pə'godə] *s* Pagode *f*
paid' in full' [ped] *adj* voll bezahlt
paid'-up' *adj* (*debts*) abgezahlt; (*policy, capital*) voll eingezahlt
pail [pel] *s* Eimer *m*
pain [pen] *s* Schmerz *m;* **on p. of death** bei Todesstrafe; **take pains** sich bemühen || *tr & intr* schmerzen || *impers*—**it pains me to** (*inf*) es fällt mir schwer zu (*inf*)

painful ['penfəl] *adj* schmerzhaft; (fig) peinlich
pain' in the neck' *s* (coll) Nervensäge *f*
pain'kill'er *s* schmerzstillendes Mittel *n*
painless ['penlɪs] *adj* schmerzlos
pains'tak'ing *adj* (*work*) mühsam; (*person*) sorgfältig
paint [pent] *s* Farbe *f;* (*for a car*) Lack *m* || *tr* (be)malen; (*e.g., a house*) (an) streichen; (*a car*) lackieren; (*with watercolors*) aquarellieren; (fig) schildern; **p. the town red** tüchtig auf die Pauke hauen || *intr* malen; (*with house paint*) überstreichen
paint'box' *s* Malkasten *m*
paint'brush' *s* Pinsel *m*
paint' can' *s* Farbendose *f*
painter ['pentər] *s* Maler –in *mf;* (*of houses, etc.*) Anstreicher –in *mf*
paint'ing *s* Malerei *f;* (*picture*) Gemälde *n*
paint' remov'er *s* Farbenabbeizmittel *n*
paint' spray'er *s* Farbspritzpistole *f*
pair [per] *s* Paar *n;* **a p. of glasses** e–e Brille *f;* **a p. of gloves** ein Paar *n* Handschuhe; **a p. of pants** e–e Hose *f;* **a p. of scissors** e–e Schere *f;* **a p. of twins** ein Zwillingspaar *n;* **in pairs** paarweise || *tr* paaren; **p. off** paarweise ordnen; (coll) verheiraten || *intr*—**p. off** sich paarweise absondern
pajamas [pə'dʒɑməz] *s* Pyjama *m*
Pakistan ['pækɪˌstæn] *s* Pakistan *n*
Pakista·ni [ˌpækɪ'stɑni] *adj* pakistanisch || *s* (–nis) Pakistaner –in *mf*
pal [pæl] *s* Kamerad *m* || *v* (*pret & pp* **palled;** *ger* **palling**) *intr*—**pal around with** dick befreundet sein mit
palace ['pælɪs] *s* Palast *m*
palatable ['pælətəbəl] *adj* (& fig) mundgerecht
palatal ['pælətəl] *adj* Gaumen– || *s* (phonet) Gaumenlaut *m*
palate ['pælɪt] *s* Gaumen *m*
palatial [pə'leʃəl] *adj* palastartig
Palatinate [pə'lætɪˌnet] *s* Rheinpfalz *f*
pale [pel] *adj* (*face, colors, recollection*) blaß; **turn pale** erblassen, erbleichen || *s* Pfahl *m* || *intr* erblassen; **pale beside** (fig) verblassen neben (*dat*)
pale'face' *s* Bleichgesicht *n*
Palestine ['pælɪsˌtaɪn] *s* Palästina *n*
palette ['pælɪt] *s* Palette *f*
palisade [ˌpælɪ'sed] *s* Palisade *f;* (*line of cliffs*) Flußklippen *pl*
pall [pɔl] *s* Bahrtuch *n;* (*of smoke, gloom*) Hülle *f* || *intr* (on) zuviel werden (*dat*)
pall'bear'er *s* Sargträger *m*
pallet ['pælɪt] *s* Lager *n*
palliate ['pælɪˌet] *tr* lindern; (fig) bemänteln
pallid ['pælɪd] *adj* blaß, bleich
pallor ['pælər] *s* Blässe *f*
palm [pɑm] *s* (*of the hand*) Handfläche *f;* (*tree*) Palme *f;* **grease s.o.'s palm** j-n schmieren; **palm of victory** Siegespalme *f* || *tr* (*a card*) in der Hand verbergen; **palm s.th. off on s.o.** j-m etw andrehen

palmette [pæl'mɛt] s Palmette f
palmet·to [pæl'mɛto] s (-tos & -toes) Fächerpalme f
palmist ['pɑmɪst] s Wahrsager -in mf
palmistry ['pɑmɪstri] s Handlesekunst f
palm' leaf' s Palmblatt n
Palm' Sun'day s Palmsonntag m
palm' tree' s Palme f
palpable ['pælpəbəl] adj greifbar
palpitate ['pælpɪˌtet] intr klopfen
palsied ['pɔlzɪd] adj lahm, gelähmt
palsy ['pɔlzi] s Lähmung f
paltry ['pɔltri] adj armselig
pamper ['pæmpər] tr verwöhnen
pamphlet ['pæmflɪt] s Flugschrift f
pan [pæn] s Pfanne f; (sl) Visage f || tr (gold) waschen; (a camera) schwenken; (criticize sharply) (coll) verreißen || intr (cin) panoramieren; **pan out** glücken, klappen
panacea [ˌpænə'si·ə] s Allheilmittel n
Panama ['pænəmɑ] s Panama n
Pan'ama Canal' s Panamakanal m
Pan-American [ˌpænə'mɛrɪkən] adj panamerikanisch
pan'cake' s (flacher) Pfannkuchen m || intr (aer) absacken, bumslanden
pan'cake land'ing s Bumslandung f
panchromatic [ˌpænkro'mætɪk] adj panchromatisch
pancreas ['pænkrɪ·əs] s Bauchspeicheldrüse f
pandemic [pæn'dɛmɪk] adj pandemisch
pandemonium [ˌpændə'monɪ·əm] s Höllenlärm m
pander ['pændər] s Kuppler m || intr kuppeln; **p. to** Vorschub leisten (dat)
pane [pen] s Scheibe f
panegyric [ˌpænɪ'dʒɪrɪk] s Lobrede f
pan·el ['pænəl] s Tafel f, Feld n; (in a door) Füllung f; (for instruments) Schlattafel f; (of experts) Diskussionsgruppe f; (archit) Paneel n; (jur) Geschworenenliste f || v (pret & pp -el[l]ed; ger -el[l]ing) tr täfeln
pan'el discus'sion s Podiumsdiskussion f
pan'eling s Täfelung f
panelist ['pænəlɪst] s Diskussionsteilnehmer -in mf
pang [pæŋ] s stechender Schmerz m; (fig) Angst f; **pangs of conscience** Gewissensbisse pl; **pangs of hunger** nagender Hunger m
pan'han'dle s Pfannenstiel m; (geog) Landzunge f || intr (sl) betteln
pan'han'dler s (sl) Bettler -in mf
pan·ic ['pænɪk] s Panik f || v (pret & pp -icked; ger -icking) tr in Panik versetzen || intr von panischer Angst erfüllt werden
pan'ic-strick'en adj von panischem Schrecken erfaßt
panicky ['pæniki] adj übernervös
panoply ['pænəpli] s Pracht f; (full suit of armor) vollständige Rüstung f
panorama [ˌpænə'ræmə] s Panorama n
pansy ['pænzi] s Stiefmütterchen n
pant [pænt] s Keuchen n; **pants** Hose f, Hosen pl || intr keuchen; **p. for or after** gieren nach
pantheism ['pænθɪˌɪzəm] s Pantheismus m
pantheon ['pænθɪˌɑn] s Pantheon n
panther ['pænθər] s Panther m
panties ['pæntiz] spl Schlüpfer m
pantomime ['pæntəˌmaɪm] s Pantomime f
pantry ['pæntri] s Speisekammer f
pap [pæp] s Brei m, Kleister m
papa ['pɑpə] s Papa m, Vati m
papacy ['pepəsi] s Papsttum n
papal ['pepəl] adj päpstlich
Pa'pal State' s Kirchenstaat m
paper ['pepər] adj (money, plate, towel) Papier- || s Papier n; (before a learned society) Referat n; (newspaper) Zeitung f; **papers** (documents) Papiere pl || tr tapezieren
pa'perback' s Taschenbuch n, Pappband m
pa'per bag' s Papiertüte f, Tüte f
pa'perboy' s Zeitungsjunge m
pa'per clip' s Büroklammer f
pa'per cone' s Tüte f
pa'per cup' s Papierbecher m
pa'per cut'ter s Papierschneidemaschine f
pa'perhang'er s Tapezierer -in mf
pa'perhang'ing s Tapezierarbeit f
pa'pering s Tapezieren n
pa'per mill' s Papierfabrik f
pa'per nap'kin s Papierserviette f
pa'perweight' s Briefbeschwerer m
pa'perwork' s Schreibarbeit f
papier-mâché [ˌpepərmə'ʃe] s Papiermaché n, Pappmaché n
paprika [pə'prikə] s Paprika m
papy·rus [pə'paɪrəs] s (-ri [raɪ]) Papyrus m
par [pɑr] s (fin) Pari n; (golf) festgesetzte Schlagzahl f; **at par** pari, auf Pari; **on a par with** auf gleicher Stufe mit; **up to par** (coll) auf der Höhe
parable ['pærəbəl] s Gleichnis n
parabola [pə'ræbələ] s Parabel f
parachute ['pærə ˌʃut] s Fallschirm m || tr mit dem Fallschirm abwerfen || intr abspringen
par'achute jump' s Fallschirmabsprung m
parachutist [ˌpærə ˌʃutɪst] s Fallschirmspringer -in mf
parade [pə'red] s Parade f || tr zur Schau stellen || intr paradieren; (mil) aufmarschieren
paradigm ['pærədɪm], ['pærə ˌdaɪm] s Musterbeispiel n, Paradigma n
paradise ['pærə ˌdaɪs] s Paradies n
paradox ['pærə ˌdɑks] s Paradox n
paradoxical [ˌpærə'dɑksɪkəl] adj paradox
paraffin ['pærəfɪn] s Paraffin n
paragon ['pærə ˌgɑn] s Musterbild n
paragraph ['pærə ˌgræf] s Absatz m, Paragraph m
parakeet ['pærə ˌkit] s Sittich m
paral·lel ['pærə ˌlɛl] adj parallel; **be (or run) p. to** parallel verlaufen zu || s Parallele f; (of latitude) Breiten-

kreis *m;* (fig) Gegenstück *n;* **without p.** ohnegleichen ‖ *v* (*pret & pp* **-lel[l]ed;** *ger* **-lel[l]ing**) *tr* parallel verlaufen zu; (*match*) gleichkommen (*dat*); (*correspond to*) entsprechen (*dat*)

par′allel bars′ *spl* Barren *m*

paraly·sis [pə′rælɪsɪs] *s* (**-ses** [ˌsiz]) Lähmung *f*, Paralyse *f*

paralytic [ˌpærə′lɪtɪk] *adj* paralytisch ‖ *s* Paralytiker –in *mf*

paralyze [′pærəˌlaɪz] *tr* lähmen, paralysieren; (*traffic*) lahmlegen

parameter [pə′ræmɪtər] *s* Parameter *m*

paramilitary [ˌpærə′mɪlɪˌteri] *adj* halbmilitärisch

paramount [′pærəˌmaunt] *adj* oberste; **be p.** an erster Stelle stehen; **of p. importance** von äußerster Wichtigkeit

paranoia [ˌpærə′nɔɪ·ə] *s* Paranoia *f*

paranoiac [ˌpærə′nɔɪ·æk] *adj* paranoisch ‖ *s* Paranoiker –in *mf*

paranoid [′pærəˌnɔɪd] *adj* paranoid

parapet [′pærəˌpet] *s* (*of a wall*) Brustwehr *f;* (*of a balcony*) Geländer *n*

paraphernalia [ˌpærəfər′neli·ə] *s* Zubehör *n,* Ausrüstung *f*

paraphrase [′pærəˌfrez] *s* Umschreibung *f* ‖ *tr* umschreiben

parasite [′pærəˌsaɪt] *s* (& fig) Parasit *m*

parasitic(al) [ˌpærə′sɪtɪk(əl)] *adj* parasitisch

parasol [′pærəˌsɔl] *s* Sonnenschirm *m*

paratrooper [′pærəˌtrupər] *s* Fallschirmjäger *m*

par·cel [′parsəl] *s* Paket *n;* (com) Posten *m* ‖ *v* (*pret & pp* **-cel[l]ed;** *ger* **-cel[l]ing**) *tr*—**p. out** aufteilen

par′cel post′ *s* Paketpost *f*

parch [partʃ] *tr* ausdörren; **my throat is parched** mir klebt die Zunge am Gaumen

parchment [′partʃmənt] *s* Pergament *n*

pardon [′pardən] *s* Verzeihung *f;* (jur) Begnadigung *f;* **I beg your p.** ich bitte um Entschuldigung; **p.?** wie, bitte? ‖ *tr* (*a person*) verzeihen (*dat*); (*an act*) verzeihen; (*officially*) begnadigen

pardonable [′pardənəbəl] *adj* verzeihlich

pare [per] *tr* (*nails*) schneiden; (*e.g., potatoes*) (ab)schälen; (*costs*) beschneiden

parent [′perənt] *s* Elternteil *m;* **parents** Eltern *pl*

parentage [′perəntɪdʒ] *s* Abstammung *f*

parental [pə′rentəl] *adj* elterlich

parenthe·sis [pə′renθɪsɪs] *s* (**-ses** [ˌsiz]) Klammer *f;* (*expression in parentheses*) Parenthese *f*

parenthetic(al) [ˌpærən′θetɪk(əl)] *adj* parenthetisch

parenthood [′perənt,hud] *s* Elternschaft *f*

pariah [pə′raɪ·ə] *s* Paria *m*

par′ing knife′ *s* Schälmesser *n*

Paris [′pærɪs] *s* Paris *n*

parish [′pærɪʃ] *adj* Pfarr– ‖ *s* Pfarrgemeinde *f*

parishioner [pə′rɪʃənər] *s* Gemeindemitglied *n,* Pfarrkind *n*

Parisian [pə′rɪʒən] *adj* Pariser ‖ *s* Pariser –in *mf*

parity [′pærɪti] *s* Parität *f*

park [park] *s* Park *m* ‖ *tr* abstellen, parken ‖ *intr* parken

park′ing *s* Parken *n;* **no p.** (public sign) Parken verboten

park′ing light′ *s* Parklicht *n*

park′ing lot′ *s* Parkplatz *m*

park′ing lot′ atten′dant′ *s* Parkplatzwärter –in *mf*

park′ing me′ter *s* Parkuhr *f*

park′ing place′, park′ing space *s* Parkplatz *m,* Parkstelle *f*

park′ing tick′et *s* gebührenpflichtige Verwarnung *f* (wegen falschen Parkens)

park′way′ *s* Aussichtsautobahn *f*

parley [′parli] *s* Unterhandlung *f* ‖ *intr* unterhandeln

parliament [′parləmənt] *s* Parlament *n*

parliamentary [ˌparlə′mentəri] *adj* parlamentarisch

parlor [′parlər] *s* Salon *m;* (*living room*) Wohnzimmer *n*

par′lor game′ *s* Gesellschaftsspiel *n*

parochial [pə′roki·əl] *adj* Pfarr–; (fig) beschränkt

paro′chial school′ *s* Pfarrschule *f*

paro·dy [′pærədi] *s* Parodie *f* ‖ *v* (*pret & pp* **-died**) *tr* parodieren

parole [pə′rol] *s* bedingte Strafaussetzung *f;* **be out on p.** bedingt entlassen sein ‖ *tr* bedingt entlassen

par·quet [par′ke], [par′ket] *v* (*pret & pp* **-queted** [′ked]; *ger* **-queting** [′ke·ɪŋ]) *tr* parkettieren

parquetry [′parkɪtri] *s* Parkettfußboden *m*

parrot [′pærət] *s* Papagei *m* ‖ *tr* nachplappern

par·ry [′pæri] *s* Parade *f* ‖ *v* (*pret & pp* **-ried**) *tr* parieren

parse [pars] *tr* zergliedern

parsimonious [ˌparsɪ′moni·əs] *adj* sparsam

parsley [′parsli] *s* Petersilie *f*

parsnip [′parsnɪp] *s* Pastinak *m*

parson [′parsən] *s* Pfarrer *m*

parsonage [′parsənɪdʒ] *s* Pfarrhaus *n*

part [part] *adv*—**p. ... p.** zum Teil ... zum Teil ‖ *s* Teil *m & n;* (*section*) Abschnitt *m;* (*spare part*) Ersatzteil *m;* (*of a machine, etc.*) Bestandteil *m;* (*share*) Anteil *m;* (*of the hair*) Scheitel *m;* (mus) Partie *f;* (theat) Rolle *f;* **do one's p.** das Seinige tun; **for his p.** seinerseits; **for the most p.** größtenteils; **have a p. in** Anteil haben an (*dat*); **in p.** zum Teil, teilweise; **make a p.** (*in the hair*) e-n Scheitel ziehen; **on his p.** seinerseits; **p. and parcel** ein wesentlicher Bestandteil *m;* **take p. (in)** teilnehmen (*an dat*); **take s.o.'s p.** j-s Partei ergreifen ‖ *tr* (ab)scheiden; (*the hair*) scheiteln; **p. company** von einander scheiden ‖ *intr* sich trennen; **p. with** hergeben

par·take [parˈtek] *v* (*pret* **–took;** *pp* **taken**) *intr*—**p. in** teilnehmen an (*dat*); **p. of** zu sich nehmen

partial [ˈparʃəl] *adj* Teil-, partiell; (*prejudiced*) parteiisch; **be p. to** bevorzugen

partiality [ˌparʃɪˈælɪti] *s* Parteilichkeit *f*, Befangenheit *f*

partially [ˈparʃəli] *adv* teilweise

participant [parˈtɪsɪpənt] *s* Teilnehmer –in *mf*

participate [parˈtɪsɪˌpet] *intr* (**in**) teilnehmen (an *dat*)

participation [paɪˌtɪsɪˈpeʃən] *s* (**in**) Teilnahme *f* (an *dat*)

participle [ˈpartɪˌsɪpəl] *s* Mittelwort *n*, Partizip *n*

particle [ˈpartɪkəl] *s* Teilchen *n*; (gram, phys) Partikel *f*

particular [parˈtɪkjələr] *adj* (*specific*) bestimmt; (*individual*) einzeln; (*meticulous*) peinlich genau; (*especial*) peinlich genau; (*choosy*) heikel ‖ *s* Einzelheit *f*; **in p.** insbesondere

partisan [ˈpartɪzən] *adj* parteiisch ‖ *s* (mil) Partisan –in *mf*; (pol) Parteigänger –in *mf*

partition [parˈtɪʃən] *s* Teilung *f*; (*wall*) Scheidewand *f* ‖ *tr* (auf)teilen; **p. off** abteilen

partly [ˈpartli] *adv* teils, teilweise

partner [ˈpartnər] *s* Partner –in *mf*

part′nership′ *s* Partnerschaft *f*

part′ of speech′ *s* Wortart *f*

part′-time′ *adj* & *adv* nicht vollzeitlich

part′-time work′ *s* Teilzeitarbeit *f*

party [ˈparti] *s* Gesellschaft *f*, Party *f*; (jur) Partei *f*; (mil) Kommando *n*; (pol) Partei *f*; (telp) Teilnehmer –in *mf*; **be a p.** to sich hergeben zu

par′ty affilia′tion *s* Parteizugehörigkeit *f*

par′ty line′ *s* (pol) Parteilinie *f*; (telp) Gemeinschaftsanschluß *m*

par′ty mem′ber *s* Parteigenosse *m*, Parteigenossin *f*

par′ty pol′itics *s* Parteipolitik *f*

paschal [ˈpæskəl] *adj* Oster-

pass [pæs] *s* (*over a mountain; permit*) Paß *m*; (*erotic advance*) Annäherungsversuch *m*; (fencing) Stoß *m*; (fb) Paßball *m*; (mil) Urlaubsschein *m*; (theat) Freikarte *f*; **make a p. at** (*flirt with*) e–n Annäherungsversuch machen bei; (aer) vorbeifliegen an (*dat*) ‖ *tr* (*go by*) vorbeigehen an (*dat*), passieren; (*a test*) bestehen; (*a student in a test*) durchlassen; (*a bill*) verabschieden; (*hand over*) reichen; (*judgment*) abgeben; (*sentence*) sprechen; (*time*) verbringen; (*counterfeit money*) in Umlauf bringen; (*a car*) überholen; (*e.g., a kidney stone*) ausscheiden; (*a ball*) weitergeben; (**to**) zuspielen (*dat*); **p. around** herumgehen lassen; **p. away** (*time*) vertreiben; **p. in** einhändigen; **p. off as** ausgeben als; **p. on** weiterleiten; (*e.g., news*) weitersagen; **p.**

out ausgeben; **p. over in silence** unerwähnt lassen; **p. up** verzichten auf (*acc*) ‖ *intr* (by) vorbeikommen (an *dat*), vorbeigehen (an *dat*); (*in a car*) (by) vorbeifahren (an *dat*); (*in a test*) durchkommen; (*e.g., from father to son*) übergehen; (cards) passen; (parl) zustandekommen; **bring to p.** herbeiführen; **come to p.** geschehen; **p.!** (cards) passe!; **p. away** verscheiden; **p. for** gelten als; **p. on** abscheiden; **p. out** ohnmächtig werden; **p. over** (*disregard*) hinweggehen über (*acc*); **p. through** durchgehen (*durch*); (*said of an army*) durchziehen (*durch*); (*said of a train*) berühren

passable [ˈpæsəbəl] *adj* (*road*) gangbar; (*by car*) befahrbar; (*halfway good*) leidlich, passabel

passage [ˈpæsɪdʒ] *s* Korridor *m*, Gang *m*; (*crossing*) Überfahrt *f*; (*in a book*) Stelle *f*; (*of a law*) Annahme *f*; (*of time*) Ablauf *m*; **book p. for** e–e Schiffskarte bestellen nach

pas′sageway′ *s* Durchgang *m*, Passage *f*

pass′book′ *s* Sparbuch *n*

passenger [ˈpæsəndʒər] *s* Passagier –in *mf*; (*in public transportation*) Fahrgast *m*; (*in a car*) Insasse *m*, Insassin *f*

pas′senger car′ *s* Personenkraftwagen *m*

pas′senger plane′ *s* Passagierflugzeug *n*

pas′senger train′ *s* Personenzug *m*

passer-by [ˈpæsərˌbaɪ] *s* (**passers-by**) Passant –in *mf*

pass′ing *adj* vorübergehend; **a p. grade** die Note „befriedigend“ ‖ *s* (*act of passing*) Vorbeigehen *n*; (*of a law*) Verabschiedung *f*; (*of time*) Verstreichen *n*; (*dying*) Hinscheiden *n*; **in p.** im Vorbeigehen; (*as understatement*) beiläufig; **no p.** (public sign) Überholen verboten

passion [ˈpæʃən] *s* Leidenschaft *f*; (*of Christ*) Passion *f*; **fly into a p.** in Zorn geraten; **have a p. for** e–e Vorliebe haben für

passionate [ˈpæʃənɪt] *adj* leidenschaftlich

pas′sion play′ *s* Passionsspiel *n*

passive [ˈpæsɪv] *adj* (& gram) passiv ‖ *s* Passiv(um) *n*

pass′key′ *s* (*master key*) Hauptschlüssel *m*; (*skeleton key*) Nachschlüssel *m*

Pass′o′ver *s* Passah *n*

pass′port *s* Paß *m*, Reisepaß *m*

pass′port of′fice *s* Paßamt *n*

pass′word′ *s* (mil) Kennwort *n*

past [pæst] *adj* (*e.g., week*) vergangen; (*e.g., president*) ehemalig, früher; (*gone*) vorbei; **for some time p.** seit einiger Zeit ‖ *s* Vergangenheit *f* ‖ *prep* (*e.g., one o'clock*) nach; (*beyond*) über (*acc*) hinaus; **get p.** (*an opponent*) (sport) umspielen; **go p.** vorbeigehen an (*dat*); **it's way p. bedtime** es ist schon längst Zeit zum Schlafengehen

paste [pest] *s* (*glue*) Kleister *m*; (culin) Brei *m*, Paste *f* ‖ *tr* (*e.g., a wall*) (with) bekleben (mit); **p. on** aufkleben auf (acc); **p. together** zusammenkleben

paste'board' s Pappe f

pastel [pæs'tel] adj pastellfarben ‖ s Pastell n

pastel' col'or s Pastellfarbe f

pasteurize ['pæstə‚raɪz] tr pasteurisieren

pastime ['pæs‚taɪm] s Zeitvertreib m

past' mas'ter s Experte m

pastor ['pæstər] s Pastor m

pastoral ['pæstərəl] adj Schäfer–, Hirten–; (eccl) Hirten–, pastoral ‖ s Schäfergedicht n

pas'toral let'ter s Hirtenbrief m

pastorate ['pæstərɪt] s Pastorat n

pastry ['pestri] s Gebäck n; **pastries** Backwaren pl

pas'try shop' s Konditorei f

past' tense' s Vergangenheit f

pasture ['pæst/ər] s Weide f ‖ tr & intr weiden

pas'ture land' s Weideland n

pasty ['pesti] adj (sticky) klebrig; (complexion) bläßlich

pat [pæt] adj (answer) treffend; **have s.th. down pat** etw in– und auswendig wissen ‖ adv—**stand pat** bei der Stange bleiben ‖ s Klaps m; (of butter) Klümpchen n ‖ tr tätscheln; **pat s.o. on the back** j–m auf die Schulter klopfen; (fig) j–n beglückwünschen

patch [pæt/] s (of clothing, land, color) Fleck m; (garden bed) Beet n; (for clothing, inner tube) Flicken m; (over the eye) Binde f; (for a wound) Pflaster n ‖ tr flicken; **p. together** (& fig) zusammenflicken; **p. up** (a friendship) kitten; (differences) beilegen

patch'work' s Flickwerk n; (fig) Stückwerk n

patch'work quilt' s Flickendecke f

pate [pet] s (coll) Schädel m

patent ['petənt] adj öffentlich ‖ ['pætənt] adj Patent–, e.g., **p. lawyer** Patentanwalt m ‖ s Patent n; **p. pending** Patent angemeldet ‖ tr patentieren

pa'tent leath'er ['pætənt] s Lackleder n

pa'tent-leath'er shoe' s Lackschuh m

pat'ent med'icine ['pætənt] s rezeptfreies Medikament n

pat'ent rights' ['pætənt] spl Schutzrechte pl

paternal [pə'tʌrnəl] adj väterlich

paternity [pə'tʌrnɪti] s Vaterschaft f

path [pæθ] s Pfad m; (astr) Lauf m; **clear a p.** e–n Weg bahnen; **cross s.o.'s p.** j–s Weg kreuzen

pathetic [pə'θetɪk] adj (moving) rührend; (evoking contemptuous pity) kläglich

path'find'er s Pfadfinder m; (aer) Beleuchter m

pathologist [pə'θalədʒɪst] s Pathologe m, Pathologin f

pathology [pə'θalədʒi] s Pathologie f

pathos ['peθas] s Pathos n

path'way' s Weg m, Pfad m

patience ['pe/əns] s Geduld f

patient ['pe/ənt] adj geduldig ‖ s Patient –in mf

pati·o ['pætɪ‚o] s (–os) Terasse f

patriarch ['petri‚ɑrk] s Patriarch m

patrician [pə'trɪ/ən] adj patrizisch ‖ s Patrizier –in mf

patricide ['pætrɪ‚saɪd] s (act) Vatermord m; (person) Vatermörder –in mf

patrimony ['pætrɪ‚moni] s väterliches Erbe n

patriot ['petrɪ‚ət] s Patriot –in mf

patriotic [‚petrɪ'ɑtɪk] adj patriotisch

patriotism ['petrɪ‚ə‚tɪzəm] s Patriotismus m

pa·trol [pə'trol] s Patrouille f, Streife f ‖ v (pret & pp **–trolled;** ger **–trolling)** tr & intr patrouillieren

patrol' car' s Streifenwagen m

patrol'man s (–men) Polizeistreife f

patrol' wag'on s Gefangenenwagen m

patron ['petrən] s Schutzherr m; (com) Kunde m, Kundin f; (eccl) Schutzpatron m

patronage ['petrənɪdʒ] s Patronat n

patroness ['petrənɪs] s Schutzherrin f; (eccl) Schutzpatronin f

patronize ['petrə‚naɪz] tr beschützen, protegieren; (com) als Kunde besuchen; (theat) regelmäßig besuchen

pa'tronizing adj gönnerhaft

pa'tron saint' s Schutzheilige mf

patter ['pætər] s (of rain) Prasseln n; (of feet) Getrappel n ‖ intr (said of rain) prasseln; (said of feet) trappeln

pattern ['pætərn] s Muster n; (sew) Schnittmuster n

patty ['pæti] s Pastetchen n

paucity ['pɔsɪti] s Knappheit f

paunch [pɔnt/] s Wanst m

paunchy ['pɔn/i] adj dickbäuchig

pauper ['pɔpər] s Arme mf; (person on welfare) Unterstützte mf

pause [pɔz] s Pause f; (mus) Fermate f ‖ intr pausieren

pave [pev] tr pflastern; **p. the way for** (fig) anbahnen

pavement ['pevmənt] s Pflaster n; (sidewalk) Bürgersteig m, Trottoir n

pavilion [pə'vɪljən] s Pavillon m

pav'ing s Pflasterung f

pav'ing stone' s Pflasterstein m

paw [pɔ] s Pfote f ‖ tr (scratch) kratzen; (coll) befummeln; **paw the ground** auf dem Boden scharren ‖ intr (said of a horse) mit dem Huf scharren

pawl [pɔl] s Sperrklinke f

pawn [pɔn] s Pfand n; (fig) Schachfigur f; (chess) Bauer m ‖ tr verpfänden

pawn'brok'er s Pfandleiher –in mf

pawn'shop' s Pfandhaus n

pawn' tick'et s Pfandschein m

pay [pe] s Lohn m; (mil) Sold m ‖ v (pret & pp **paid** [ped]) tr bezahlen; (a visit) abstatten; (a dividend) ausschütten; (a compliment) machen; **pay back** zurückzahlen; **pay damages** Schadenersatz leisten; **pay down** anzahlen; **pay extra** nachzahlen; **pay in advance** vorausbezahlen; **pay in full**

begleichen; **pay interest on** verzinsen; **pay off** (*a debt*) abbezahlen; (*a person*) entlohnen; **pay one's way** ohne Verlust arbeiten; **pay out** auszahlen; **pay s.o. back for s.th.** j-m etw heimzahlen; **pay taxes on** versteuern; **pay up** (*a debt*) abbezahlen; (*ins*) voll einzahlen ‖ *intr* zahlen; (*be worthwhile*) sich lohnen; **pay extra** zuzahlen; **pay for** (*a purchase*) (be)zahlen für; (*suffer for*) büßen

payable ['pe·əbəl] *adj* fällig, zahlbar
pay' check' *s* Lohnscheck *m*
pay'day' *s* Zahltag *m*
pay' dirt' *s*—**hit p.** sein Glück machen
payee [pe'i] *s* (*of a draft*) Zahlungsempfänger –in *mf*; (*of a check*) Wechselnehmer –in *mf*
pay' en'velope *s* Lohntüte *f*
payer ['pe·ər] *s* Zahler –in *mf*
pay'load' *s* Nutzlast *f*; (*explosive energy*) Sprengladung *f*
pay'mas'ter *s* Zahlmeister *m*
payment ['pemənt] *s* Zahlung *f*; **in p. of** zur Bezahlung (*genit*)
pay' phone' *s* Münzfernsprecher *m*
pay' raise' *s* Gehaltserhöhung *f*
pay' rate' *s* Lohnsatz *m*
pay'roll' *s* Lohnliste *f*; (*money paid*) gesamte Lohnsumme *f*
pay' sta'tion *s* Telephonautomat *m*
pea [pi] *s* Erbse *f*
peace [pis] *s* Friede(n) *m*; (*quiet*) Ruhe *f*; **be at p. with** in Frieden leben mit; **keep the p.** die öffentliche Ruhe bewahren
peaceable ['pisəbəl] *adj* friedfertig
Peace' Corps' *s* Friedenskorps *n*
peace'-lov'ing *adj* friedliebend
peace'mak'er *s* Friedenstifter –in *mf*
peace' nego'tia'tions *spl* Friedensverhandlungen *pl*
peace' of mind' *s* Seelenruhe *f*
peace'pipe' *s* Friedenspfeife *f*
peace'time' *adj* Friedens– ‖ *s*—**in p.** in Friedenszeiten
peace' trea'ty *s* Friedensvertrag *m*
peach [pitʃ] *s* Pfirsich *m*
peach' tree' *s* Pfirsichbaum *m*
peachy ['pitʃi] *adj* (coll) pfundig
pea'cock' *s* Pfau *m*
pea'hen' *s* Pfauenhenne *f*
pea' jack'et *s* (nav) Matrosenjacke *f*
peak [pik] *s* Spitzen– ‖ *s* (& fig) Gipfel *m*; (*of a cap*) Mützenschirm *m*; (elec) Leistungsspitze *f*; (phys) Scheitelwert *m*
peak' hours' *spl* (*of traffic*) Hauptverkehrszeit *f*; (elec) Stoßzeit *f*
peak' load' *s* (elec) Spitzenlast *f*
peak' vol'tage *s* (elec) Spitzenspannung *f*
peal [pil] *s* Geläute *n* ‖ *intr* erschallen
peal' of laugh'ter *s* Lachsalve *f*
peal' of thun'der *s* Donnergetöse *n*
pea'nut' *s* Erdnuß *f*; **peanuts** (coll) kleine Fische *pl*
pea'nut but'ter *s* Erdnußbutter *f*
pear [per] *s* Birne *f*
pearl [pʌrl] *adj* Perlen– ‖ *s* Perle *f*
pearl' neck'lace *s* Perlenkette *f*
pearl' oys'ter *s* Perlenauster *f*
pearl' tree' *s* Birnbaum *m*

peasant ['pezənt] *adj* Bauern–, bäuerlich ‖ *s* Bauer *m*, Bäuerin *f*
peasantry ['pezəntri] *s* Bauernstand *m*
pea'shoot'er *s* Blasrohr *n*
pea' soup' *s* Erbsensuppe *f*; (fig) Waschküche *f*
peat [pit] *s* Torf *m*
peat' moss' *s* Torfmull *m*
pebble ['pebəl] *s* Kiesel *m*; **pebbles** Geröll *n*
peck [pek] *s* (*measure*) Viertelscheffel *m*; (*e.g., of a bird*) Schnabelhieb *n*; (*kiss*) (coll) flüchtiger Kuß *m*; (*of trouble*) (coll) Menge *f* ‖ *tr* hacken; (*food*) aufpicken ‖ *intr* hacken, picken; (*eat food*) picken; **p. at** hacken nach; (*food*) (coll) herumstochern in (*dat*)
peculation [ˌpekjə'leʃən] *s* Geldunterschlagung *f*
peculiar [pɪ'kjuljər] *adj* eigenartig, absonderlich; **p. to** eigen (*dat*)
peculiarity [ˌpɪkjulɪ'ærɪti] *s* Eigenheit *f*, Absonderlichkeit *f*
pedagogic(al) [ˌpedə'gadʒɪk(əl)] *adj* pädagogisch, erzieherisch
pedagogue ['pedəˌgag] *s* Pädagoge *m*, Erzieher *m*
pedagogy ['pedəˌgadʒi] *s* Pädagogik *f*, Erziehungskunde *f*
ped·al ['pedəl] *s* Pedal *n* ‖ *v* (*pret & pp* –al[l]ed; *ger* –al[l]ing) *tr* fahren ‖ *intr* die Pedale treten
pedant ['pedənt] *s* Pedant –in *mf*
pedantic [pɪ'dæntɪk] *adj* pedantisch
pedantry ['pedəntri] *s* Pedanterie *f*
peddle ['pedəl] *tr* hausieren mit ‖ *intr* hausieren
peddler ['pedlər] *s* Hausierer –in *mf*
pedestal ['pedɪstəl] *s* Sockel *m*, Postament *n*; **put s.o. on a p.** (fig) j-n aufs Podest erheben
pedestrian [pɪ'destrɪ·ən] *adj* Fußgänger–; (fig) schwunglos ‖ *s* Fußgänger –in *mf*
pediatrician [ˌpidɪ·ə'trɪʃən] *s* Kinderarzt *m*, Kinderärztin *f*
pediatrics [ˌpidɪ'ætrɪks] *s* Kinderheilkunde *f*
pediment ['pedɪmənt] *s* Giebelfeld *n*
peek [pik] *s* schneller Blick *m* ‖ *intr* gucken; **p. at** angucken
peekaboo ['pikəˌbu] *adj* durchsichtig ‖ *interj* guck, guck!
peel [pil] *s* Schale *f* ‖ *tr* schälen; **p. off** abschälen ‖ *intr* sich schälen; (*said of paint*) abbröckeln; **p. off** (aer) sich aus dem Verband lösen
peep [pip] *s* schneller Blick *m*; heimlicher Blick *m*; **not another p. out of you!** kein Laut mehr aus dir! ‖ *intr* gucken; (*look carefully*) lugen; **p. out** hervorlugen
peep'hole' *s* Guckloch *n*
peep' show' *s* Fleischbeschau *f*
peer [pɪr] *s* Gleichgestellte *mf* ‖ *intr* blicken; **p. at** mustern
peerless ['pɪrlɪs] *adj* unvergleichlich
peeve [piv] *s* (coll) Beschwerde *f* ‖ *tr* (coll) ärgern
peeved *adj* verärgert
peevish ['pivɪʃ] *adj* sauertöpfisch

peg [peg] *s* Pflock *m;* (*for clothes*)
Haken *m;* (*e.g., of a violin*) Wirbel
m; **take down a peg or two** ducken
|| *v* (*pret & pp* **pegged**; *ger* **pegging**)
tr festpflocken; (*prices*) festlegen;
(*throw*) (sl) schmeißen; (*identify*)
(sl) erkennen

peg'board' *s* Klammerplatte *f*

Peggy ['pegɪ] *s* Gretchen *n,* Gretl *f & n*

peg' leg' *s* Stelzbein *n*

Pekin·ese [,pikɪ'niz] *s* (**–ese**) Pekine-
se *m*

pelf [pelf] *s* (pej) Mammon *m*

pelican ['pelɪkən] *s* Pelikan *m*

pellet ['pelɪt] *s* Kügelchen *n;* (*bullet*)
Schrotkugel *f,* Schrotkorn *n*

pell-mell ['pel'mel] *adj* verworren ||
adv durcheinander

pelt [pelt] *s* Fell *n,* Pelz *m;* (*whack*)
Schlag *m* || *tr* (**with**) bewerfen (mit);
(*with questions*) bombardieren

pelvis ['pelvɪs] *s* Becken *n*

pen [pen] *s* Feder *f;* (*fountain pen*)
Füllfederhalter *m;* (*enclosure*) Pferch
m; (*prison*) (sl) Kittchen *n* || *v* (*pret
& pp* **penned**; *ger* **penning**) *tr* (*a
letter*) verfassen || (*pret & pp* **penned
& pent**; *ger* **penning**) *tr*—**pen in**
pferchen

penal ['pinəl] *adj* strafrechtlich, Straf–

pe'nal code' *s* Strafgesetzbuch *n*

penalize ['pinə,laɪz] *tr* bestrafen;
(*box*) mit Strafpunkten belegen

penalty ['penəltɪ] *s* Strafe *f;* (*point
deducted*) (sport) Strafpunkt *m;*
under p. of death bei Todesstrafe

pen'alty ar'ea *s* (sport) Strafraum *m*

pen'alty box' *s* Strafbank *f*

pen'alty kick' *s* Strafstoß *m*

penance ['penəns] *s* Buße *f*

penchant ['penʃənt] *s* (**for**) Hang *m*
(zu)

pen·cil ['pensəl] *s* Bleistift *m* || *v* (*pret
& pp* **–cil[l]ed**; *ger* **–cil[l]ing**) *tr* mit
Bleistift anzeichnen

pen'cil push'er *s* (coll) Schreiberling *m*

pen'cil sharp'ener *s* Bleistiftspitzer *m*

pendant ['pendənt] *s* Anhänger *m;*
(*electrical fixture*) Hängeleuchter *m*

pendent ['pendənt] *adj* (herab)hängend

pend'ing *adj* schwebend; **be p.** in (der)
Schwebe sein || *prep* (*during*) wäh-
rend (*genit*); (*until*) bis zu (*dat*)

pendulum ['pendʒələm] *s* Pendel *n*

pen'dulum bob' *s* Pendelgewicht *n*

penetrate ['penɪ,tret] *tr* eindringen in
(*acc*) || *intr* eindringen

penetration [,penɪ'treʃən] *s* Durchdringen *n;* (*of, e.g., a country*) Eindringen *n* (in *acc*); (*in ballistics*)
Durchschlagskraft *f*

penguin ['peŋgwɪn] *s* Pinguin *m*

penicillin [,penɪ'sɪlɪn] *s* Penizillin *n*

peninsula [pə'nɪnsələ] *s* Halbinsel *f*

pe·nis ['pinɪs] *s* (**–nes** [niz] & **–nises**)
Penis *m*

penitence ['penɪtəns] *s* Bußfertigkeit *f*

penitent ['penɪtənt] *adj* bußfertig || *s*
Büßer –in *mf;* (eccl) Beichtkind *n*

penitentiary [,penɪ'tenʃərɪ] *s* Zuchthaus *n*

pen'knife' *s* (**–knives'**) Federmesser *n*

penmanship ['penmən,ʃɪp] *s* Schreib-
kunst *f*

pen' name' *s* Schriftstellername *m*

pennant ['penənt] *s* Wimpel *m;* (nav)
Stander *m*

penniless ['penɪlɪs] *adj* mittellos

penny ['penɪ] *s* Pfennig *m;* (*U.S.A.*)
Cent *m*

pen'ny pinch'er [,pɪntʃər] *s* Pfennigfuchser *m*

pen' pal' *s* Schreibfreund –in *mf*

pension ['penʃən] *s* Pension *f,* Rente
f; **put on p.** pensionieren || *tr* pen-
sionieren

pensioner ['penʃənər] *s* Pensionär –in
mf; (ins) Rentenempfänger –in *mf*

pen'sion fund' *s* Pensionskasse *f*

pensive ['pensɪv] *adj* sinnend

pentagon ['pentə,gan] *s* Fünfeck *n;*
the Pentagon das Pentagon

Pentecost ['pentɪ,kost] *s* Pfingsten *n*

penthouse ['pent,haus] *s* Wetterdach
n; (*exclusive apartment*) Penthouse *n*

pent-up ['pent'ʌp] *adj* verhalten

penult ['pinʌlt] *s* vorletzte Silbe *f*

penurious [pɪ'nurɪ·əs] *adj* karg

penury ['penjərɪ] *s* Kargheit *f*

peony ['pi·ənɪ] *s* Pfingstrose *f*

people ['pipəl] *spl* Leute *pl,* Menschen
pl; **his p.** die Seinen; **p. like him**
seinesgleichen; **p. say** man sagt, die
Leute sagen || *s* (**peoples**) Volk *n* ||
tr bevölkern

pep [pep] *s* (coll) Schwungkraft *f* || *v*
(*pret & pp* **pepped**; *ger* **pepping**) *tr*—
pep up aufpulvern

pepper ['pepər] *s* (*spice*) Pfeffer *m;*
(*plant*) Paprika *f;* (*vegetable*) Papri-
kaschote *f* || *tr* pfeffern

pep'per mill' *s* Pfeffermühle *f*

pep'permint' *adj* Pfefferminz– || *s* Pfef-
ferminze *f*

pep'per shak'er *s* Pfefferstreuer *m*

peppery ['pepərɪ] *adj* pfefferig

per [pʌr] *prep* pro (*acc*); **as per** laut
(*genit & dat*)

perambulator [pər'æmbjə,letər] *s* Kinderwagen *m*

per capita [pər'kæpɪtə] pro Kopf

perceivable [pər'sivəbəl] *adj* wahrnehmbar

perceive [pər'siv] *tr* wahrnehmen

percent [pər'sent] *s* Prozent *n*

percentage [pər'sentɪdʒ] *s* Prozentsatz
m; **p. of** (*e.g., the profit*) Anteil *m*
an (*dat*); (*e.g., of a group*) Teil *m*
(*genit*)

perceptible [pər'septəbəl] *adj* wahrnehmbar

perception [pər'sepʃən] *s* Wahrneh-
mung *f*

perch [pʌrtʃ] *s* Stange *f;* (ichth)
Barsch *m* || *tr* setzen || *intr* sitzen

percolate ['pʌrkə,let] *tr* durchseihen;
(*coffee*) perkolieren || *intr* durch-
sickern

percolator ['pʌrkə,letər] *s* Perkolator
m

percussion [pər'kʌʃən] *s* Schlag *m;*
(med) Perkussion *f*

percus'sion in'strument *s* Schlaginstru-
ment *n*

per di′em allow′ance [pər′daɪ-əm] s Tagegeld n

perdition [pər′dɪʃən] s Verdammnis f

perennial [pə′rɛnɪ-əl] adj immerwährend; (bot) ausdauernd ‖ s ausdauernde Pflanze f

perfect [′pʌrfɪkt] adj perfekt, vollkommen; **he is a p. stranger to me** er ist mir völlig fremd ‖ s (gram) Perfekt(um) n ‖ [pər′fɛkt] tr vervollkommnen

perfection [pər′fɛkʃən] s Vollkommenheit f; **to p.** vollkommen

perfectionist [pər′fɛkʃənɪst] s Perfektionist –in mf

perfectly [′pʌrfɪktlɪ] adv völlig, durchaus; **p. well** ganz genau

perfidious [pər′fɪdɪ-əs] adj treulos

perfidy [′pʌrfɪdɪ] s Treubruch m

perforate [′pʌrfə‚ret] tr durchlöchern

per′forated line′ s durchlochte Linie f

perforation [‚pʌrfə′reʃən] s gelochte Linie f

perforce [pər′fɔrs] adv notgedrungen

perform [pər′fɔrm] tr ausführen; (an operation) vornehmen; (theat) aufführen ‖ intr (öffentlich) auftreten; (mach) funktionieren

performance [pər′fɔrməns] s Ausführung f; (mach) Leistung f; (theat) Aufführung f

performer [pər′fɔrmər] s Künstler –in mf

perform′ing arts′ spl darstellende Künste pl

perfume [pər′fjum] s Parfüm n ‖ tr parfümieren

perfunctorily [pər′fʌŋktərɪlɪ] adv oberflächlich

perfunctory [pər′fʌŋktərɪ] adj oberflächlich

perhaps [pər′hæps] adv vielleicht

per hour′ pro Stunde, in der Stunde

peril [′perɪl] s Gefahr f; **at one's own p.** auf eigene Gefahr

perilous [′perɪləs] adj gefährlich

perimeter [pə′rɪmɪtər] s (math) Umfang m; (mil) Rand m

period [′pɪrɪ-əd] s Periode f, Zeitabschnitt m; (menstrual period) Periode f; (educ) Stunde f; (gram) Punkt m; (sport) Viertel n; **extra p.** (sport) Verlängerung f; **for a p. of** für die Dauer von; **p.!** und damit punktum!; **p. of grace** Frist f; **p. of life** Lebensalter n; **p. of time** Zeitdauer pl

pe′riod fur′niture s Stilmöbel pl

periodic [‚pɪrɪ′ɑdɪk] adj zeitweilig

periodical [‚pɪrɪ′ɑdɪkəl] s Zeitschrift f

peripheral [pə′rɪfərəl] adj peripher

periphery [pə′rɪfərɪ] s Peripherie f

periscope [′perɪ‚skop] s Periskop n

perish [′perɪʃ] intr umkommen; (said of wares) verderben

perishable [′perɪʃəbəl] adj vergänglich; (food) leicht verderblich

perjure [′pʌrdʒər] tr—**p. oneself** Meineid begehen

perjury [′pʌrdʒərɪ] s Meineid m; **commit p.** e–n Meineid leisten

perk [pʌrk] tr—**p. up** (the head) aufwerfen; (the ears) spitzen ‖ intr

(percolate) (coll) perkolieren; **p. up** lebhaft werden

permanence [′pʌrmənəns] s Dauer f

permanent [′pʌrmənənt] adj (fort)dauernd, bleibend ‖ s Dauerwelle f

per′manent address′ s ständiger Wohnort m

per′manent job′ s Dauerstellung f

per′manent wave′ s Dauerwelle f

permeable [′pʌrmɪ-əbəl] adj durchlässig

permeate [′pʌrmɪ‚et] tr durchdringen ‖ intr durchsickern

permissible [pər′mɪsɪbəl] adj zulässig

permission [pər′mɪʃən] s Erlaubnis f; **with your p.** mit Verlaub

permissive [pər′mɪsɪv] adj nachsichtig

per·mit [′pʌrmɪt] s Erlaubnis f; (document) Erlaubnisschein m ‖ [pər′mɪt] v (pret & pp –mitted; ger –mitting) tr erlauben, gestatten; **be permitted to** (inf) dürfen (inf)

permute [pər′mjut] tr umsetzen; (math) permutieren

pernicious [pər′nɪʃəs] adj (to) schädlich (für)

perox′ide blonde′ [pə′rɑksaɪd] s Wasserstoffblondine f

perpendicular [‚pʌrpən′dɪkjələr] adj senkrecht ‖ s Senkrechte f

perpetrate [′pʌrpɪ‚tret] tr verüben

perpetual [pər′petʃʊ-əl] adj (everlasting) ewig; (continual) unaufhörlich

perpetuate [pər′petʃʊ‚et] tr verewigen

perplex [pər′pleks] tr verblüffen

perplexed′ adj verblüfft

perplexity [pər′pleksɪtɪ] s Verblüffung f

persecute [′pʌrsɪ‚kjut] tr verfolgen

persecution [‚pʌrsɪ′kjuʃən] s Verfolgung f

persecutor [′pʌrsɪ‚kjutər] s Verfolger –in mf

perseverance [‚pʌrsɪ′vɪrəns] s Ausdauer f, Beharrlichkeit f

persevere [‚pʌrsɪ′vɪr] intr ausdauern; **p. in** (cling to) beharren auf (acc); (e.g., efforts, studies) fortfahren mit

Persia [′pʌrʒə] s Persien n

Persian [′pʌrʒən] adj persisch ‖ s Perser –in mf; (language) Persisch n

Per′sian rug′ s Perserteppich m

persimmon [pər′sɪmən] s Persimone f

persist [pər′sɪst] intr andauern; **p. in** verbleiben bei

persistent [pər′sɪstənt] adj andauernd

person [′pʌrsən] s Person f; **in p.** persönlich; **per p.** pro Person

personable [′pʌrsənəbəl] adj (attractive) ansehnlich; (good-natured) verträglich

personage [′pʌrsənɪdʒ] s Persönlichkeit f

personal [′pʌrsənəl] adj persönlich; (private) Privat–; **become p.** anzüglich werden

per′sonal da′ta spl Personalien pl

per′sonal hygiene′ s Körperpflege f

per′sonal in′jury s Personenschaden m

personality [‚pʌrsə′nælɪtɪ] s Persönlichkeit f

personally [′pʌrsənəlɪ] adv persönlich

per'sonal pro'noun s Personalpronomen n

personi·fy [pər'sɑnɪ ˌfaɪ] v (pret & pp –fied) tr personifizieren, verkörpern

personnel [ˌpʌrsə'nɛl] s Personal n

per'son-to-per'son call' s Gespräch n mit Voranmeldung

perspective [pər'spɛktɪv] s Perspektive f

perspicacious [ˌpʌrspɪ'keʃəs] adj scharfsinnig

perspiration [ˌpʌrspɪ'reʃən] s Schweiß m; (perspiring) Schwitzen n

perspire [pər'spaɪr] intr schwitzen

persuade [pər'swed] tr überreden

persuasion [pər'sweʒən] s Überredung f

persuasive [pər'swesɪv] adj redegewandt

pert [pʌrt] adj keck; (sprightly) lebhaft

pertain [pər'ten] intr—p. to betreffen, sich beziehen auf (acc)

pertinacious [ˌpʌrtɪ'neʃəs] adj beharrlich

pertinent ['pʌrtɪnənt] adj einschlägig; **be p.** to sich beziehen auf (acc)

perturb [pər'tʌrb] tr beunruhigen

peruse [pə'ruz] tr sorgfältig durchlesen

pervade [pər'ved] tr durchdringen

perverse [pər'vʌrs] adj (abnormal) pervers; (obstinate) verstockt

perversion [pər'vʌrʒən] s Perversion f; (of truth) Verdrehung f

perversity [pər'vʌrsɪti] s Perversität f

pervert ['pʌrvərt] s perverser Mensch m ‖ [pər'vʌrt] tr (corrupt) verderben; (twist) verdrehen; (misapply) mißbrauchen

pesky ['pɛski] adj (coll) lästig

pessimism ['pɛsɪ ˌmɪzəm] s Pessimismus m

pessimist ['pɛsɪmɪst] s Pessimist –in mf

pessimistic [ˌpɛsɪ'mɪstɪk] adj pessimistisch

pest [pɛst] s (insect) Schädling m; (annoying person) Plagegeist· m; (pestilence) Pest f

pest' control' s Schädlingsbekämpfung f

pester ['pɛstər] tr piesacken; (with questions) belästigen

pesticide ['pɛstɪ ˌsaɪd] s Pestizid n

pestilence ['pɛstɪləns] s Pestilenz f

pestle ['pɛsəl] s Stößel m

pet [pɛt] adj Lieblings– ‖ s (animal) Haustier n; (person) Liebling m; (favorite child) Schoßkind n ‖ v (pret & pp petted; ger petting) tr streicheln ‖ intr sich abknutschen

petal ['pɛtəl] s Blumenblatt n

Peter ['pitər] s Peter m ‖ intr—peter out im Sande verlaufen

pet' ide'a s Lieblingsgedanke m

petition [pɪ'tɪʃən] s Eingabe f; (jur) Gesuch n ‖ tr (s.o.) ersuchen

pet' name' s Kosename m

petri·fy ['pɛtrɪ ˌfaɪ] v (pret & pp –fied) tr (& fig) versteinern; **be petrified** versteinern; (fig) zu Stein werden

petroleum [pə'trolɪ·əm] s Petroleum n

pet' shop' s Tierhandlung f

petticoat ['pɛtɪ ˌkot] s Unterrock m

pet'ting s Petting n

petty ['pɛti] adj klein, geringfügig; (narrow) engstirnig

pet'ty cash' s Handkasse f

pet'ty lar'ceny s geringer Diebstahl m

pet'ty of'ficer s (nav) Bootsmann m

petulant ['pɛtjələnt] adj verdrießlich

petunia [pə't(j)unɪ·ə] s Petunie f

pew [pju] s Bank f, Kirchenstuhl m

pewter ['pjutər] s Weißmetall n

Pfc. ['pi'ɛf'si] s (private first class) Gefreiter m

phalanx ['fælæŋks] s Phalanx f

phantasm ['fæntæzəm] s Trugbild n

phantom ['fæntəm] s Phantom n

Pharaoh ['fero] s Pharao m

Pharisee ['færɪ ˌsi] s Pharisäer m

pharmaceutical [ˌfɑrmə'sutɪkəl] adj pharmazeutisch

pharmacist ['fɑrməsɪst] s Apotheker –in mf

pharmacy ['fɑrməsi] s Apotheke f; (science) Pharmazie f

pharynx ['færɪŋks] s Rachenhöhle f

phase [fez] s Phase f ‖ tr in Phasen einteilen; **p. out** abwickeln

pheasant ['fɛzənt] s Fasan m

phenobarbital [ˌfino'bɑrbɪ ˌtæl] s Phenobarbital n

phenomenal [fɪ'nɑmɪnəl] adj phänomenal

phenome·non [fɪ'nɑmɪ ˌnɑn] s (–na [nə]) (& fig) Phänomen n, Erscheinung f

phial ['faɪ·əl] s Phiole f

philanderer [fɪ'lændərər] s Schürzenjäger m

philanthropist [fɪ'lænθrəpɪst] s Menschenfreund –in mf, Philanthrop –in mf

philanthropy [fɪ'lænθrəpi] s Menschenliebe f, Philanthropie f

philately [fɪ'lætəli] s Briefmarkenkunde f

Philippine ['fɪlɪ ˌpin] adj philippinisch ‖ **the Philippines** spl die Philippinen

Philistine ['fɪlɪstin] adj (& fig) philisterhaft ‖ s (& fig) Philister m

philologist [fɪ'lɑlədʒɪst] s Philologe m, Philologin f

philology [fɪ'lɑlədʒi] s Philologie f

philosopher [fɪ'lɑsəfər] s Philosoph m

philosophic(al) [ˌfɪlə'sɑfɪk(əl)] adj philosophisch

philosophy [fɪ'lɑsəfi] s Philosophie f

phlebitis [flɪ'baɪtɪs] s Venenentzündung f

phlegm [flɛm] s Schleim m

phlegmatic(al) [flɛg'mætɪk(əl)] adj phlegmatisch

phobia ['fobɪ·ə] s Phobie f

Phoenicia [fɪ'nɪʃə] s Phönizien n

Phoenician [fɪ'nɪʃən] adj phönizisch ‖ s Phönizier m

phoenix ['finɪks] s Phönix m

phone [fon] s (coll) Telephon n; **on the p.** am Apparat ‖ tr (coll) anrufen ‖ intr telephonieren

phone' call' s (coll) Anruf m

phonetic [fo'nɛtɪk] *adj* phonetisch, Laut– ‖ **phonetics** *s* Lautlehre *f*, Phonetik *f*

phonograph ['fonə,græf] *s* Grammophon *n*

pho'nograph rec'ord *s* Schallplatte *f*

phonology [fə'nɑlədʒi] *s* Lautlehre *f*

phony ['foni] *adj* falsch, Schein– ‖ *s* Schwindler –in *mf*

phosphate ['fasfet] *s* Phosphat *n*

phosphorescent [,fasfə'rɛsənt] *adj* phosphoreszierend

phospho·rus ['fasfərəs] *s* (**-ri** [,raɪ]) Phosphor *m*

pho·to ['foto] *s* (**-tos**) (coll) Photo *n*

pho'tocop'y *s* Photokopie *f* ‖ *v* (*pret & pp* **-ied**) *tr* photokopieren

pho'toengrav'ing *s* Lichtdruckverfahren *n*

pho'to fin'ish *s* Zielphotographie *f*

photogenic [,foto'dʒɛnɪk] *adj* photogen

photograph ['fotə,græf] *s* Photographie *f* ‖ *tr & intr* photographieren

photographer [fə'tɑgrəfər] *s* Photograph –in *mf*

photography [fə'tɑgrəfi] *s* Photographie *f*

photostat ['fotə,stæt] *s* (trademark) Photokopie *f* ‖ *tr* photokopieren

phrase [frez] *s* Sinngruppe *f* ‖ *tr* formulieren; (mus) phrasieren

phrenology [frə'nɑlədʒi] *s* Schädellehre *f*

physic ['fɪzɪk] *s* Abführmittel *n*; **physics** *s* Physik *f*

physical ['fɪzɪkəl] *adj* körperlich, physisch ‖ *s* (*examination*) ärztliche Untersuchung *f*

phys'ical condi'tion *s* Gesundheitszustand *m*

phys'ical de'fect *s* körperliches Gebrechen *n*

phys'ical educa'tion *s* Leibeserziehung *f*

phys'ical ex'ercise *s* Leibesübungen *pl*; (*calisthenics*) Bewegung *f*

phys'ical hand'icap *s* Körperbehinderung *f*

physician [fɪ'zɪʃən] *s* Arzt *m*, Ärztin *f*

physicist ['fɪzɪsɪst] *s* Physiker –in *mf*

physics ['fɪzɪks] *s* Physik *f*

physiognomy [,fɪzɪ'ɑgnəmi] *s* Gesichtsbildung *f*, Physiognomie *f*

physiological [,fɪzɪ-ə'lɑdʒɪkəl] *adj* physiologisch

physiology [,fɪzɪ'ɑlədʒi] *s* Physiologie *f*

physique [fɪ'zɪk] *s* Körperbau *m*

pi [paɪ] *s* (math) Pi *n* ‖ *tr* (typ) zusammenwerfen

pianist ['pi·ənɪst] *s* Pianist –in *mf*

pian·o [pɪ'æno] *s* (**-os**) Klavier *n*

pian'o stool' *s* Klavierschemel *m*

picayune [,pɪkə'jun] *adj* (*paltry*) geringfügig; (*person*) kleinlich

picco·lo ['pɪkəlo] *s* (**-los**) Pikkoloflöte *f*

pick [pɪk] *s* (*tool*) Spitzhacke *f*; (*choice*) Auslese *f*; **the p. of the crop** das Beste von allem ‖ *tr* (*choose*) sich [*dat*] aussuchen; (*e.g., fruit*)

pflücken; (*one's teeth*) stochern in (*dat*); (*one's nose*) bohren in (*dat*); (*a lock*) mit e–m Dietrich öffnen; (*a quarrel*) suchen; (*a bone*) abnagen; **p. off** abpflücken; (*shoot*) (coll) abknallen; **p. out** auswählen; **p. s.o.'s brains** j–s Ideen klauen; **p. s.o.'s pocket** j–m die Tasche ausräumen; **p. up** (*lift up*) aufheben; (*a girl*) (coll) aufgabeln; (*a suspect*) aufgreifen; (*with a car*) abholen; (*passengers; the scent*) aufnehmen; (*a language; news*) aufschnappen; (*a habit*) annehmen; (*a visual object*) erkennen; (*strength*) wieder erlangen; (*weight*) zunehmen an (*dat*); **p. up speed** in Fahrt kommen ‖ *intr*–**p. and choose** wählerisch suchen; **p. at** herumstochern in (*dat*); **p. on** herumreiten auf (*dat*); **p. up** (*improve in health or business*) sich (wieder) erholen

pick'ax' *s* Picke *f*, Pickel *m*

picket ['pɪkɪt] *s* Holzpfahl *m*; (*of strikers*) Streikposten *m* ‖ *tr* durch Streikposten absperren, Streikposten stehen vor (*dat*) ‖ *intr* Streikposten stehen

pick'et fence' *s* Lattenzaun *m*

pick'et line' *s* Streikkette *f*

pickle ['pɪkəl] *s* Essiggurke *f*; **be in a p.** (coll) im Schlamassel sitzen ‖ *tr* (ein)pökeln

pick'led *adj* (sl) blau

pick'led her'ring *s* Rollmops *m*

pick'pock'et *s* Taschendieb *m*

pick'up' *s* (*of a car*) Beschleunigungsvermögen *n*; (*girl*) Straßenbekanntschaft *f*; (*restorative*) Stärkungsmittel *n*, Erfrischung *f*; (*a stop to pick up*) Abholung *f*; (*of a phonograph*) Schalldose *f*

pick'up truck' *s* offener Lieferwagen *m*

picky ['pɪki] *adj* wählerisch

pic·nic ['pɪknɪk] *s* Picknick *n* ‖ *v* (*pret & pp* **-nicked**; *ger* **-nicking**) *intr* picknicken

pictorial [pɪk'torɪ·əl] *adj* illustriert ‖ *s* Illustrierte *f*

picture ['pɪktʃər] *s* Bild *n*; (fig) Vorstellung *f*; **look the p. of health** kerngesund aussehen ‖ *tr* sich [*dat*] vorstellen

pic'ture gal'lery *s* Gemäldegalerie *f*

pic'ture post'card *s* Ansichtspostkarte *f*

picturesque [,pɪktʃə'rɛsk] *adj* malerisch, pittoresk; (*language*) bilderreich

pic'ture tube' *s* Bildröhre *f*

pic'ture win'dow *s* Panoramafenster *n*

piddling ['pɪdlɪŋ] *adj* lumpig

pie [paɪ] *s* Torte *f*; (*meat-filled*) Pastete *f*; **pie in the sky** Luftschloß *n*

piece [pis] *s* Stück *n*; (checkers) Stein *m*; (chess) Figur *f*; (mil) Geschütz *n*; (mus, theat) Stück *n*; **a p. of advice** ein Rat *m*; **a p. of bad luck** ein unglücklicher Zufall *m*; **a p. of furniture** ein Möbelstück *n*; **a p. of luggage** ein Gepäckstück *n*; **a p. of**

news e–e Neuigkeit *f;* **a p. of paper** ein Blatt Papier; **a p. of toast** e–e geröstete Brotscheibe *f;* **say one's p. seine Meinung sagen**

piece'meal' *adv* stückweise

piece'work' *s* Akkordarbeit *f;* **do p. in Akkord arbeiten**

piece'work'er *s* Akkordarbeiter –in *mf*

pier [pɪr] *s* Landungsbrücke *f,* Pier *m* & *f; (of a bridge)* Pfeiler *m*

pierce [pɪrs] *tr* durchstechen, durchbohren

pierc'ing *adj (look, pain)* scharf, stechend; *(cry)* gellend; *(cold)* schneidend

piety ['paɪ·əti] *s* Frömmigkeit *f*

pig [pɪg] *s* Schwein *n*

pigeon ['pɪdʒən] *s* Taube *f*

pi'geonhole' *s* Fach *n* || *tr* auf die lange Bank schieben

pi'geon loft' *s* Taubenschlag *m*

pi'geon-toed' *adj* & *adv* mit einwärts gerichteten Zehen

piggish ['pɪgɪʃ] *adj* säuisch

piggyback ['pɪgɪ‚bæk] *adv* huckepack

pig'gy bank' *s* Sparschweinchen *n*

pig'head'ed *adj* dickköpfig

pig' i'ron *s* Roheisen *n*

pigment ['pɪgmənt] *s* Pigment *n*

pig'pen' *s* Schweinekoben *m*

pig'skin' *s* Schweinsleder *n; (sport)* (coll) Fußball *m*

pig'sty' *s* Schweinestall *m*

pig'tail' *s (hair style)* Rattenschwanz *m*

pike [paɪk] *s* Pike *f,* Spieß *m; (highway)* Landstraße *f; (ichth)* Hecht *m*

piker ['paɪkər] *s* (coll) Knicker *m*

pilaster [pɪ'læstər] *s* Wandpfeiler *m*

pile [paɪl] *s (heap)* Haufen *m; (e.g., of papers)* Stoß *m; (stake)* Pfahl *m; (fortune)* (coll) Menge *f; (atom. phys)* Meiler *m,* Reaktor *m; (elec, phys)* Säule *f; (tex)* Flor *m; (pathol)* Hämorrhoiden *pl;* **piles of money** (coll) Heidengeld *n* || *tr* anhäufen, aufhäufen; **p. it on** (coll) dick auftragen || *intr*—**p. into** sich drängen in *(acc);* **p. on** sich übereinander stürzen; **p. out of** sich hinausdrängen aus; **p. up** sich (an)häufen

pile' driv'er *s* Pfahlramme *f,* Rammbär *m*

pilfer ['pɪlfər] *tr* mausen, stibitzen

pilgrim ['pɪlgrɪm] *s* Pilger –in *mf*

pilgrimage ['pɪlgrɪmɪdʒ] *s* Pilgerfahrt *f;* **go on a p.** pilgern

pill [pɪl] *s* (& fig) Pille *f*

pillar ['pɪlər] *s* Pfeiler *m,* Säule *f*

pill'box' *s* Pillenschachtel *f;* (mil) Bunker *m*

pillo·ry ['pɪləri] *s* Pranger *m* || *v (pret & pp* –**ried)** *tr* an den Pranger stellen; (fig) anprangern

pillow ['pɪlo] *s* Kopfkissen *n*

pil'lowcase' *s* Kopfkissenbezug *m*

pilot ['paɪlət] *adj (experimental)* Versuchs– || *s* (aer) Pilot *m,* Flugzeugführer –in *mf;* (naut) Lotse *m* || *tr* (aer) steuern, führen; (naut) steuern, lotsen

pi'lothouse' *s* (naut) Ruderhaus *n*

pi'lot light' *s* Sparflamme *f*

pi'lot's li'cense *s* Flugzeugführerschein *m*

pimp [pɪmp] *s* Zuhälter *m* || *intr* kuppeln

pimp'ing *s* Zuhälterei *f*

pimple ['pɪmpəl] *s* Pickel *m*

pimply ['pɪmpli] *adj* pickelig

pin [pɪn] *s* Stecknadel *f; (ornament)* Anstecknadel *f; (bowling)* Kegel *m;* (mach) Pinne *f,* Zapfen *m;* **be on pins and needles** wie auf Nadeln sitzen || *v (pret & pp* **pinned;** *ger* **pinning)** *tr (fasten with a pin)* mit e–r Nadel befestigen; *(e.g., a dress)* abstecken; *(e.g., under a car)* einklemmen; *(e.g., against the wall)* drücken; *(in wrestling)* auf die Schultern legen; **pin down** *(a person)* festlegen; *(troops)* niederhalten; **pin one's hopes on** seine Hofnungen setzen auf *(acc);* **pin s.th. on s.o.** (fig) j–m etw anhängen; **pin up** *(a sign)* anschlagen; *(the hair, a dress)* aufstecken

pinafore ['pɪnə‚for] *s* Latz *m*

pin'ball machine' *s* Spielautomat *m*

pin' boy' *s* Kegeljunge *m*

pincers ['pɪnsərs] *s* & *spl* Kneifzange *f*

pinch [pɪntʃ] *s* Kneifen *n; (of salt)* Prise *f;* **give s.o. a p.** j–n kneifen; **in a p.** zur Not, in der Not || *tr* kneifen, zwicken; *(steal)* (sl) klauen; *(arrest)* (coll) schnappen; **I got my finger pinched in the door** ich habe mir den Finger in der Tür geklemmt; **p. and scrape every penny** sich *[dat]* jeden Groschen vom Munde absparen; **p. off** abzwicken || *intr (said of shoe)* (& fig) drücken

pinchers ['pɪntʃərz] *s* & *spl* Kneifzange *f*

pinch'-hit' *v (pret & pp* –**hit;** *ger* –**hitting)** *intr* einspringen

pinch' hit'ter *s* Ersatzmann *m*

pin'cush'ion *s* Nadelkissen *n*

pine [paɪn] *adj* Kiefern– || *s* Kiefer *f* || *intr*—**p. away** sich abzehren; **p. for** sich sehnen nach

pine'ap'ple *s* Ananas *f*

pine' cone' *s* Kiefernzapfen *m*

pine' nee'dle *s* Kiefernnadel *f*

ping [pɪŋ] *s* Päng *n; (of a motor)* Klopfen *n* || *intr* (aut) klopfen

ping-pong ['pɪŋ‚pɑŋ] *s* Ping-pong *n*

pin'head' *s* (& fig) Stechnadelkopf *m*

pink [pɪŋk] *adj* rosa || *s* Rosa *n*

pin' mon'ey *s* Nadelgeld *n*

pinnacle ['pɪnəkəl] *s* Zinne *f*

pin'point' *adj* haarscharf; **p. landing** Ziellandung *f* || *tr* markieren

pin'prick' *s* Nadelstich *m*

pint [paɪnt] *s* Schoppen *m,* Pinte *f*

pin'up girl' *s* Pin-up-Girl *n*

pin'wheel' *s (toy)* Windmühle *f; (fireworks)* Feuerrad *n*

pioneer [‚paɪ·ə'nɪr] *s* Bahnbrecher –in *mf;* (fig & mil) Pionier *m* || *tr* (fig) den Weg freimachen für || *intr* (fig) Pionierarbeit leisten

pious ['paɪ·əs] *adj* fromm

pip [pɪp] *s (in fruit)* Kern *m; (on dice)* Punkt *m; (on a radarscope)* Leuchtpunkt *m; (of chickens)* Pips *m*

pipe [paɪp] *s* Rohr *n*; *(for smoking; of an organ)* Pfeife *f* ‖ *tr* durch ein Rohr (weiter)leiten ‖ *intr* pfeifen; **p. down** (sl) das Maul halten; **p. up** (coll) anfangen zu sprechen, loslegen

pipe′ clean′er *s* Pfeifenreiniger *m*

pipe′ dream′ *s* Wunschtraum *m*

pipe′ joint′ *s* Rohranschluß *m*

pipe′ line′ *s* Rohrleitung *f*, Pipeline *f*; *(of information)* Informationsquelle *f*

pipe′ or′gan *s* Orgel *f*

piper [′paɪpər] *s* Pfeifer –in *mf*

pipe′ wrench′ *s* Rohrzange *f*

piping [′paɪpɪŋ] *adv*—**p. hot** siedend heiß ‖ *s* Rohrleitung *f*; *(on uniforms)* Biese *f*; (sew) Paspel *f*

piquancy [′pikənsɪ] *s* Pikanterie *f*

piquant [′pikənt] *adj* pikant

pique [pik] *s* Pik *m* ‖ *tr* verärgern; **be piqued at** pikiert sein über *(acc)*

piracy [′paɪrəsɪ] *s* Seeräuberei *f*

pirate [′paɪrɪt] *s* Seeräuber *m* ‖ *tr (a book)* (ungesetzlich) nachdrucken

pirouette [ˌpɪru′et] *s* Pirouette *f*

pista′chio nut′ [pɪs′tæʃɪ·o] *s* Pistaziennuß *f*

pistol [′pɪstəl] *s* Pistole *f*

pis′tol point′ *s*—**at p.** mit vorgehaltener Pistole

piston [′pɪstən] *s* Kolben *m*

pis′ton ring′ *s* Kolbenring *m*

pis′ton rod′ *s* Kolbenstange *f*

pis′ton stroke′ *s* Kolbenhub *m*

pit [pɪt] *s* Grube *f*; *(in fruit)* Kern *m*; *(trap)* Fallgrube *f*; *(in the skin)* Narbe *f*; *(from corrosion)* Rostgrübchen *n*; *(in auto racing)* Box *f*; *(for cockfights)* Kampfplatz *m*; (min) Schacht *m*; (theat) Parkett *n*; (mus) Orchester *n*; **pit of the stomach** Magengrube *f* ‖ *v (pret & pp* **pitted**) *ger* **pitting**) *tr (a face)* mit Narben bedecken; *(fruit)* entkernen; *(through corrosion)* anfressen; **pit A against B** A gegen B ausspielen; **pit one's strength against s.th.** seine Kraft mit etw messen

pitch [pɪtʃ] *s* Pech *n*; *(of a roof)* Dachschräge *f*; *(downward slope)* Gefälle *n*; *(of a ship)* Stampfen *n*; *(of a screw, thread)* Teilung *f*; *(of a propeller)* Steigung *f*; *(throw)* Wurf *m*; *(sales talk)* Verkaufsgespräch *n*; (mus) Tonhöhe *f* ‖ *tr (seal with pitch)* verpichen; *(a tent)* aufschlagen; *(a ball)* dem Schläger zuwerfen; *(hay)* mit der Heugabel werfen ‖ *intr* (naut) stampfen; **p. and toss** schlingern; **p. in** mithelfen

pitch′ ac′cent *s* musikalischer Tonakzent *m*

pitch′-black′ *adj* pechrabenschwarz

pitcher [′pɪtʃər] *s* (jug) Krug *m*

pitch′fork′ *s* Heugabel *f*

pitch′ing *s* (naut) Stampfen *n*

pit′fall′ *s* Fallgrube *f*; (fig) Falle *f*

pith [pɪθ] *s* (& fig) Mark *n*

pithy [′pɪθɪ] *adj* (& fig) markig

pitiable [′pɪtɪ·əbəl] *adj* erbarmenswert

pitiful [′pɪtɪfəl] *adj* erbärmlich

pitiless [′pɪtɪlɪs] *adj* erbarmungslos

pit′ted *adj* (by corrosion) angefressen; *(fruit)* entkernt

pit·y [′pɪtɪ] *s* Erbarmen *n*, Mitleid *n*; **have p. on** Mitleid haben mit; **it's a p. that** (es ist) schade, daß; **move to p.** jammern; **what a p.!** wie schade! ‖ *v (pret & pp* **–ied**) *tr* sich erbarmen *(genit)*, bemitleiden

pivot [′pɪvət] *s* Drehpunkt *m* ‖ *intr* **(on)** sich drehen (um); (mil) schwenken

placard [′plækɑrd] *s* Plakat *n*

placate [′pleket] *tr* begütigen

place [ples] *s* (seat; room) Platz *m*; *(area, town, etc.)* Ort *m*, Ortschaft *f*; *(in a book; in a room)* Stelle *f*; *(situation)* Lage *f*; *(spot to eat in, dance in, etc.)* Lokal *n*; **all over the p.** überall; **at your p.** (coll) bei Ihnen; **in my p.** an meiner Stelle; **in p. of** anstelle von (or genit); **in the first p.** erstens; **know one's p.** wissen, wohin man gehört; **out of p.** (& fig) nicht am Platz; **p. to stay** Unterkunft *f*; **put s.o. in his p.** j–n in seine Schranken verweisen; **take one's p.** antreten; **take p.** stattfinden; **take s.o.'s p.** an j–s Stelle treten ‖ *tr* setzen, stellen; *(an advertisement)* aufgeben; *(an order)* erteilen; *(find a job for)* unterbringen; **I can't p. him** ich weiß nicht, wo ich ihn hintun soll; **p. a call** (telp) ein Gespräch anmelden ‖ *intr (in horseracing)* sich als Zweiter placieren, (sport) sich placieren

place·bo [plə′sibo] *s* (**–bos** & **–boes**) Placebo *n*

place′ card′ *s* Tischkarte *f*

place′ mat′ *s* Tischmatte *f*

placement [′plesmənt] *s* Unterbringung *f*

place′-name′ *s* Ortsname *m*

place′ of birth′ *s* Geburtsort *m*

place′ of employ′ment *s* Arbeitsstätte *f*

place′ of res′idence *s* Wohnsitz *m*

placid [′plæsɪd] *adj* ruhig, sanftmütig

plagiarism [′pledʒəˌrɪzəm] *s* Plagiat *n*

plagiarist [′pledʒərɪst] *s* Plagiator –in *mf*

plagiarize [′pledʒəˌraɪz] *intr* ein Plagiat begehen

plague [pleg] *s* Seuche *f* ‖ *tr* heimsuchen

plaid [plæd] *adj* buntkariert ‖ *s* Schottenkaro *n*

plain [plen] *adj* (simple) einfach; *(clear)* klar; *(fabric)* einfarbig; *(homely)* unschön; *(truth)* rein; *(food)* bürgerlich; *(paper)* unlin(i)iert; *(speech)* unverblümt; *(alcohol)* unverdünnt ‖ *s* Ebene *f*

plain′ clothes′ *spl*—**in p.** in Zivil

plain′-clothes′ man′ *s* Geheimpolizist *m*

plaintiff [′plentɪf] *s* Kläger –in *mf*

plaintive [′plentɪv] *adj* Klage–, klagend

plait [plet] *s* Flechte *f*; **p. of hair** Zopf *m* ‖ *tr* flechten

plan [plæn] *s* Plan *m*; *(intention)* Vorhaben *n*; **according to p.** planmäßig

what are your plans for this evening?
was haben Sie für heute abend vor?
|| *v* (*pret* & *pp* **planned**; *ger* **planning**) *tr* planen; (*one's time*) einteilen; **p. to** (*inf*) vorhaben zu (*inf*) || *intr*—**p. for** Pläne machen für; **p. on** rechnen mit

plane [plen] *s* (*airplane*) Flugzeug *n*, Maschine *f*; (*airfoil*) Tragfläche *f*; (*carp*) Hobel *m*; (*geom*) Ebene *f*; **on a high p.** (fig) auf e—m hohen Niveau || *tr* hobeln; **p. down** abhobeln

plane′ connec′tion *s* Fluganschluß *m*
plane′ geom′etry *s* Planimetrie *f*
planet [ˈplænɪt] *s* Planet *m*
planetari·um [ˌplænɪˈterɪ·əm] *s* (**-a** [ə] & **-ums**) Planetarium *n*
planetary [ˈplænə‚teri] *adj* Planeten-
plane′ tick′et *s* Flugkarte *f*
plane′ tree′ *s* Platane *f*
plank [plæŋk] *s* Brett *n*, Planke *f*; (pol) Programmpunkt *m*
planned′ par′enthood *s* Familienplanung *f*
plant [plænt] *s* (*factory*) Anlage *f*; (*spy*) Spion –in *mf*; (bot) Pflanze *f* || *tr* (an)pflanzen; (*a field*) bepflanzen; (*a colony*) gründen; (*as a spy*) als Falle aufstellen; (*a bomb*) verstecken; **p. oneself** sich hinstellen
plantation [plænˈteʃən] *s* Plantage *f*
planter [ˈplæntər] *s* (*person who plants; plantation owner*) Pflanzer –in *mf*; (*decorative container*) Blumentrog *m*; (mach) Pflanzmaschine *f*
plasma [ˈplæzmə] *s* Plasma *n*
plaster [ˈplæstər] *s* Verputz *m*; (med) Pflaster *m* || *tr* verputzen; (*e.g., with posters*) bepflastern; **be plastered** (sl) besoffen sein
plas′terboard′ *s* Gipsdiele *f*
plas′ter cast′ *s* (med) Gipsverband *m*; (sculp) Gipsabguß *m*
plasterer [ˈplæstərər] *s* Stukkateur *m*
plas′tering *s* Verputz *m*
plas′ter of Par′is *s* Gips *m*
plastic [ˈplæstɪk] *adj* Plastik– || *s* Plastik *n*
plas′tic sur′gery *s* Plastik *f*
plas′tic wood′ *s* Holzpaste *f*
plate [plet] *s* (*dish*) Teller *m*; (*of metal*) Platte *f*; (*in a book*) Tafel *f*; (elec, phot, typ) Platte *f*; (electron) Plattenelektrode *f* || *tr* plattieren
plateau [plæˈto] *s* Plateau *n*
plate′ glass′ *s* Tafelglas *n*
platen [ˈplætən] *s* Schreibmaschinenwalze *f*
platform [ˈplæt‚fɔrm] *s* Plattform *f*; (*for a speaker*) Bühne *f*; (*for loading*) Rampe *f*; (pol) Programm *n*; (rr) Bahnsteig *m*
plat′form shoes′ *spl* Plateauschuhe *pl*
plat′ing *s* (*e.g., of gold*) Plattierung *f*; (*armor*) Panzerung *f*
platinum [ˈplætɪnəm] *s* Platin *n*
plat′inum blonde′ *s* Platinblondine *f*
platitude [ˈplætɪ‚t(j)ud] *s* Gemeinplatz *m*
Plato [ˈpleto] *s* Plato *m*

Platonic [pləˈtɑnɪk] *adj* platonisch
platoon [pləˈtun] *s* Zug *m*
platter [ˈplætər] *s* Platte *f*
plausible [ˈplɔzɪbəl] *adj* plausibel
play [ple] *s* Spiel *n*; (mach) Spielraum *m*; (sport) Spielzug *m*; (theat) Stück *n*; **in p.** im Spiel; **out of p.** aus dem Spiel || *tr* spielen; (*a card*) ausspielen; (*an opponent*) spielen gegen; **p. back** (*a tape, record*) abspielen; **p. down** bagatellisieren; **p. the horses** bei Pferderennen wetten || *intr* spielen; (*records, tapes*) abspielen; **p. about** (*the lips*) umspielen; **p. along** mitspielen; **p. around with** herumspielen mit; **p. for** (*stakes*) spielen um; (*a team*) spielen für; **p. into s.o.'s hands** j–m in die Hände spielen; **p. safe** auf Nummer Sicher gehen; **p. up to** schmeicheln (*dat*)
play′back′ *s* (*reproduction*) Wiedergabe *f*; (*device*) Abspielgerät *n*
play′boy′ *s* Playboy *m*
player [ˈple·ər] *s* Spieler –in *mf*; (sport) Sportler –in *mf*; (theat) Schauspieler –in *mf*
playful [ˈplefəl] *adj* spielerisch
play′ground′ *s* Spielplatz *m*
play′house′ *s* Theater *n*; (*for children*) Spielhaus *n*
play′ing card′ *s* Spielkarte *f*
play′ing field′ *s* Spielfeld *n*
play′mate′ *s* Spielkamerad –in *mf*
play′-offs′ *spl* Vorrunde *f*
play′ on words′ *s* Wortspiel *n*
play′pen′ *s* Laufgitter *n*
play′room′ *s* Spielzimmer *n*
play′school′ *s* Kindergarten *m*
play′thing′ *s* (& fig) Spielzeug *n*
playwright [ˈple‚raɪt] *s* Schauspieldichter –in *mf*
plea [pli] *s* Bitte *f*; (jur) Plädoyer *n*
plead [plid] *v* (*pret* & *pp* **pleaded** & **pled** [pled]) *tr* (*ignorance*) vorschützen || *intr* plädieren; **p. guilty** sich schuldig bekennen; **p. not guilty** sich als nichtschuldig erklären; **p. with s.o.** j–n anflehen
pleasant [ˈplezənt] *adj* angenehm
pleasantry [ˈplezəntri] *s* Heiterkeit *f*; (*remark*) Witz *m*
please [pliz] *tr* gefallen (*dat*); **be pleased to** (*inf*) sich freuen zu (*inf*); **be pleased with** sich freuen über (*acc*); **pleased to meet you!** sehr angenehm || *intr* gefallen; **as one pleases** nach Gefallen; **do as you p.** tun Sie, wie Sie wollen; **if you p.** wenn ich bitten darf; (iron) gefälligst; **p.!** bitte!
pleas′ing *adj* angenehm, gefällig
pleasure [ˈpleʒər] *s* Vergnügen *n*
pleas′ure trip′ *s* Vergnügungsreise *f*
pleat [plit] *s* Plissee *n* || *tr* plissieren
pleat′ed skirt′ *s* Plisseerock *m*
plebeian [plɪˈbi·ən] *adj* plebejisch || *s* Plebejer –in *mf*
plect·rum [ˈplektrəm] *s* (**-rums** & **-ra** [rə]) Plektron *n*; (*for zither*) Schlagring *m*
pledge [pledʒ] *s* (*solemn promise*) Gelübde *n*; (*security for a payment*)

Pfand *n;* (fig) Unterpfand *n* ‖ *tr* geloben; (*money*) zeichnen

plenary ['pliːnəri] *adj* Plenar–, Voll–

ple'nary indul'gence *s* vollkommener Ablaß *m*

ple'nary ses'sion *s* Plenum *n*

plenipotentiary [ˌplenɪpə'tenʃɪˌeri] *adj* bevollmächtigt ‖ *s* Bevollmächtigte *mf*

plentiful ['plentɪfəl] *adj* reichlich

plenty ['plenti] *s* Fülle *f;* **have p. of** Überfluß haben an (*dat*); **have p. to do** vollauf zu tun haben ‖ *adv* (coll) reichlich

pleurisy ['plʊrɪsi] *s* Brustfellentzündung *f*

plexiglass ['pleksɪˌglæs] *s* Plexiglas *n*

pliant ['plaɪ·ənt] *adj* biegsam; (fig) gefügig

pliers ['plaɪ·ərz] *s & spl* Zange *f*

plight [plaɪt] *s* Notlage *f*

plod [plɑd] *v* (*pret & pp* **plodded**; *ger* **plodding**) *intr* stapfen; **p. along** mühsam weitermachen

plop [plɑp] *v* (*pret & pp* **plopped**; *ger* **plopping**) *tr* plumpsen lassen ‖ *intr* plumpsen ‖ *interj* plumps!

plot [plɑt] *s* (*conspiracy*) Komplott *n;* (*of a story*) Handlung *f;* (*of ground*) Grundstück *n* ‖ *v* (*pret & pp* **plotted**; *ger* **plotting**) *tr* (*a course*) abstecken; (*intrigues*) schmieden; (*e.g., murder*) planen ‖ *intr* sich verschwören

plough [plaʊ] *s, tr & intr* var of **plow**

plow [plaʊ] *s* Pflug *m* ‖ *tr* pflügen; **p. up** umpflügen; **p. under** unterpflügen ‖ *intr* pflügen; **p. through the waves** durch die Wellen streichen

plow'man *s* (**–men**) Pflüger *m*

plow'share *s* Pflugschar *f*

pluck [plʌk] *s* (*tug*) Ruck *m;* (fig) Schneid *m* ‖ *tr* (*e.g., a chicken*) rupfen; (*flowers, fruit*) pflücken; (*eyebrows*) auszupfen; (*mus*) zupfen ‖ *intr*—**p. up** Mut fassen

plug [plʌg] *s* (*for a sink*) Pfropfen *m;* (*of tobacco*) Priem *m;* (*old horse*) alter Klepper *m;* (*advertising*) Befürwortung *f;* (*aut*) Zündkerze *f;* (*elec*) Stecker *m* ‖ *v* (*pret & pp* **plugged**; *ger* **plugging**) *tr* (*a hole*) zustopfen; **p. in** an die Steckdose anschließen ‖ *intr*—**p. away** (*work hard*) schuften; (*study hard*) pauken

plum [plʌm] *s* Pflaume *f*

plumage ['pluːmɪdʒ] *s* Gefieder *n*

plumb [plʌm] *adj* lotrecht ‖ *adv* (coll) völlig ‖ *s* Lot *n;* **out of p.** aus dem Lot ‖ *tr* loten, sondieren

plumb' bob' *s* Lot *n*

plumber ['plʌmər] *s* Installateur *m*

plumb'ing *s* (*plumbing work*) Installateurarbeit *f;* (*pipes*) Rohrleitung *f*

plumb' line' *s* Lotschnur *f*

plume [pluːm] *s* Feder *f;* (*on a helmet*) Helmbusch *m;* **p. of smoke** Rauchfahne *f* ‖ *tr* (*adorn with plumes*) mit Federn schmücken; **p. itself** sich putzen

plummet ['plʌmɪt] *s* Lot *n* ‖ *intr* stürzen

plump [plʌmp] *adj* rundlich ‖ *tr* plumpsen; **p. oneself down** sich schwerfällig hinwerfen

plum' tree' *s* Pflaumenbaum *m*

plunder ['plʌndər] *s* (*act*) Plünderung *f;* (*booty*) Beute *f* ‖ *tr & intr* plündern

plunderer ['plʌndərər] *s* Plünderer *m*

plunge [plʌndʒ] *s* Sturz *m* ‖ *tr* stürzen ‖ *intr* (*fall*) stürzen; (*throw oneself*) sich stürzen

plunger ['plʌndʒər] *s* Saugglocke *f*

plunk [plʌŋk] *adv* (*squarely*) (coll) genau ‖ *tr* (*e.g., a guitar*) zupfen; **p. down** klirrend auf den Tisch legen

pluperfect [ˌpluː'pʌrfɛkt] *s* Vorvergangenheit *f*, Plusquamperfekt(um) *n*

plural ['plʊrəl] *adj* Plural– ‖ *s* Mehrzahl *f*, Plural *m*

plurality [plʊ'rælɪti] *s* Mehrheit *f;* (pol) Stimmenmehrheit *f*

plus [plʌs] *adj* Plus–; (elec) positiv ‖ *s* Plus *n* ‖ *prep* plus (*acc*)

plush [plʌʃ] (coll) luxuriös

plus' sign' *s* Pluszeichen *n*

plutonium [pluː'toni·əm] *s* Plutonium *n*

ply [plaɪ] *s* (*of wood, etc.*) Schicht *f;* (*of yarn*) Strähne *f* ‖ *v* (*pret & pp* **plied**) *tr* (*e.g., a needle*) (eifrig) handhaben; (*a trade*) betreiben; (*with questions*) bestürmen; (*a waterway*) regelmäßig befahren ‖ *intr* (*between*) verkehren (zwischen *dat*)

ply'wood' *s* Sperrholz *n*

pneumatic [n(j)u'mætɪk] *adj* pneumatisch

pneumat'ic drill' *s* Preßluftbohrer *m*

pneumonia [n(j)u'moni·ə] *s* Lungenentzündung *f*

poach [potʃ] *tr* (*eggs*) pochieren ‖ *intr* wildern

poached' egg' *s* verlorenes Ei *n*

poacher ['potʃər] *s* Wilderer *m*

pock [pɑk] *s* Pocke *f*, Pustel *f*

pocket ['pɑkɪt] *adj* (*comb, flap, knife, money, watch*) Taschen– ‖ *s* Tasche *f;* (*billiards*) Loch *n;* (mil) Kessel *m* ‖ *tr* in die Tasche stecken; (*billiards*) ins Loch spielen

pock'etbook' *s* Handtasche *f;* (*book*) Taschenbuch *n*

pock'et cal'culator *s* Taschenrechner *m*

pock'mark' *s* Pockennarbe *f*

pock'marked' *adj* pockennarbig

pod [pɑd] *s* Hülse *f*

podi·um ['podi·əm] *s* (**–ums & –a** [ə]) Podium *n*

poem ['po·ɪm] *s* Gedicht *n*

poet ['po·ɪt] *s* Dichter *m*, Poet *m*

poetaster ['po·ɪˌæstər] *s* Dichterling *m*

poetess ['po·ɪtɪs] *s* Dichterin *f*

poetic [po'etɪk] *adj* dichterisch, poetisch ‖ **poetics** *s* Poetik *f*

poetry ['po·ɪtri] *s* Dichtung *f;* **write p.** dichten, Gedichte schreiben

poignant ['pɔɪn(j)ənt] *adj* (*touching*) ergreifend; (*pungent*) scharf; (*cutting*) beißend

point [pɔɪnt] *s* (*dot, score*) Punkt *m;*

(tip) Spitze *f; (of a joke)* Pointe *f; (of a statement)* Hauptpunkt *m; (side of a character)* Seite *f; (purpose)* Sinn *m; (matter, subject)* Sache *f; (of a compass)* Kompaßstrich *m; (to show decimals)* Komma *n;* (aut) Zündkontakt *m;* (geog) Landspitze *f;* (typ) Punkt *m;* **at this p.** in diesem Augenblick; **be on the p. of** (ger) gerade im Begriff sein zu (inf); **come to the p.!** zur Sache! **get the p.** verstehen; **in p. of fact** tatsächlich; **make a p. of** bestehen auf (dat); **make it a p. to** (inf) es sich (dat) zur Pflicht machen zu (inf); **not to the p.** nicht zur Sache gehörig; **off the p.** unzutreffend; **on points** (sport) nach Punkten; **p. at issue** strittiger Punkt *m;* **p. of order!** zur Tagesordnung!; **p. of time** Zeitpunkt *m;* **score a p.** (fig) e-n Punkt für sich buchen; **that's beside the p.** darum handelt es sich nicht; **there's no p. to it** es hat keinen Zweck; **to the p.** zutreffend; **up to a certain p.** bis zu e-m gewissen Grade ‖ *tr (e.g., a gun)* (at) richten (auf acc); **p. out** (auf)zeigen; **p. s.th. out to s.o.** j-n auf etw (acc) hinweisen; **p. the finger at** mit dem Finger zeigen auf (acc) ‖ *intr* mit dem Finger zeigen; **p. to** deuten auf (acc); (fig) hinweisen auf (acc)

point'-blank' *adj (refusal)* glatt; *(shot)* rasant, Kernschuß *f;* **at p. range** auf Kernschußweite ‖ *adv (at close range)* aus nächster Nähe; (fig) glatt; (arti) auf Kernschußweite

point'ed *adj* spitzig; *(remark)* anzüglich; *(gun)* gerichtet; *(arch, nose)* Spitz–

pointer ['pɔɪntər] *s (of a meter)* Zeiger *m; (stick)* Zeigestock *m; (advice)* Tip *m; (hunting dog)* Vorstehhund *m*

pointless ['pɔɪntlɪs] *adj* zwecklos

point' of hon'or *s* Ehrensache *f*

point' of law' *s* Rechtsfrage *f*

point' of view' *s* Gesichtspunkt *m*

poise [pɔɪz] *s* sicheres Auftreten *n* ‖ *tr* im Gleichgewicht halten ‖ *intr* schweben

poison ['pɔɪzən] *s* Gift *n* ‖ *tr* (& fig) vergiften

poi'son gas' *s* Giftgas *n*

poi'son i'vy *s* Giftsumach *m*

poisonous ['pɔɪzənəs] *adj* giftig

poke [pok] *s* Stoß *m,* Knuff *m* ‖ *tr* anstoßen, knuffen; *(the fire)* schüren; *(head, nose)* stecken; **p. fun at** sich lustig machen über (acc); **p. out** *(an eye)* ausstechen; **p. s.o. in the ribs** j-m e-n Rippenstoß geben ‖ *intr* bummeln; **p. around** herumstochern; *(be slow)* herumbummeln; *(in another's business)* herumstöbern

poker ['pokər] *s* Schürhaken *m; (cards)* Poker *n*

pok'er face' *s* Pokergesicht *n*

poky ['poki] *adj* bummelig

Poland ['polənd] *s* Polen *n*

polar ['polər] *adj* Polar–

po'lar bear' *s* Eisbär *m*

polarity [po'lærɪti] *s* Polarität *f*

polarize ['polə‚raɪz] *tr* polarisieren

pole [pol] *s (rod)* Stange *f; (for telephone lines, flags, etc.)* Mast *m;* (astr, geog, phys) Pol *m;* **Pole Pole** *m,* Polin *f* ‖ *tr (a raft, boat)* staken

pole'cat' *s* Iltis *m*

polemic(al) [pə'lɛmɪk(əl)] *adj* polemisch

polemics [pə'lɛmɪks] *s* Polemik *f*

pole'star' *s* Polarstern *m*

pole'-vault' *intr* stabhochspringen

pole'-vault'ing *s* Stabhochsprung *m*

police [pə'lis] *adj* polizeilich ‖ *s* Polizei *f* ‖ *tr* polizeilich überwachen; *(clean up)* (mil) säubern

police' es'cort *s* Polozeibedeckung *f*

police'man *s* (–men) Polizist *m*

police' of'ficer *s* Polizeibeamte *m,* Polizeibeamtin *f*

police' pre'cinct *s* Polizeirevier *n*

police' state' *s* Polizeistaat *m*

police' sta'tion *s* Polizeiwache *f*

police'wom'an *s* (–wom'en) Polizistin *f*

policy ['pɑlɪsi] *s* Politik *f;* (ins) Police *f*

polio ['polɪ‚o] *s* Polio *f*

polish ['pɑlɪʃ] *s (material; shine)* Politur *f; (for shoes)* Schuhcreme *f;* (fig) Schliff *m* ‖ *tr* polieren; *(fingernails)* lackieren; *(shoes, silver, etc.)* putzen; *(floors)* bohnern; (fig) abschleifen; **p. off** *(eat)* (sl) verdrücken; *(an opponent)* (sl) erledigen; *(work)* (sl) hinhauen ‖ *intr—***p. up on** auf-polieren ‖ **Polish** ['polɪʃ] *adj* polnisch ‖ *s* Polnisch *n*

polite [pə'laɪt] *adj* höflich

politeness [pə'laɪtnɪs] *s* Höflichkeit *f*

politic ['pɑlɪtɪk] *adj* diplomatisch

political [pə'lɪtɪkəl] *adj* politisch

poli'tical econ'omy *s* Volkswirtschaft *f*

poli'tical sci'ence *s* Staatswissenschaften *pl*

politician [‚pɑlɪ'tɪʃən] *s* Politiker –in *mf*

politics ['pɑlɪtɪks] *s* Politik *f;* **be in p.** sich politisch betätigen; **talk p.** politisieren

polka ['po(l)kə] *s* Polka *f*

pol'ka-dot' *adj* getupft

poll [pol] *s (voting)* Abstimmung *f; (of public opinion)* Umfrage *f;* **be defeated at the polls** e-e Wahlniederlage erleiden; **go to the polls** zur Wahl gehen; **polls** *(voting place)* Wahllokal *n;* **take a p.** e-e Umfrage halten ‖ *tr* befragen

pollen ['pɑlən] *s* Pollen *m*

poll'ing booth' *s* Wahlzelle *f*

pollster ['polstər] *s* Meinungsforscher –in *mf*

poll' tax' *s* Kopfsteuer *f*

pollute [pə'lut] *tr* verunreinigen

pollution [pə'luʃən] *s* Verunreinigung *f*

polo ['polo] *s* (sport) Polo *n*

po'lo shirt' *s* Polohemd *n*

polygamist [pə'lɪgəmɪst] *s* Polygamist *m*

polygamy [pə'lɪgəmi] *s* Polygamie *f*

polyglot ['pɑlɪ‚glɑt] *s* Polyglott *m*

polygon ['pɑlɪ ˌgɑn] s Vieleck n
polyp ['pɑlɪp] s Polyp m
polytheism [ˌpɑlɪ'θiˌɪzəm] s Vielgötterei f, Polytheismus m
polytheistic [ˌpɑlɪθi'ɪstɪk] adj polytheistisch
pomade [pə'med] s Pomade f
pomegranate ['pɑmˌgrænɪt] s Granatapfel m; (tree) Granatapfelbaum m
Pomerania [ˌpɑmə'renɪ·ə] s Pommern n
pom·mel ['pʌməl] s (of a sword) Degenkopf m; (of a saddle) Sattelknopf m || v (pret & pp –mel[l]ed; ger –el[l]ing) tr mit der Faust schlagen
pomp [pɑmp] s Pomp m, Prunk m
pompous ['pɑmpəs] adj hochtrabend
pon·cho ['pɑntʃo] s (–chos) Poncho m
pond [pɑnd] s Teich m
ponder ['pɑndər] tr erwägen; (words) abwägen || intr (over) nachsinnen (über acc)
ponderous ['pɑndərəs] adj schwerfällig
pontiff ['pɑntɪf] s (eccl) Papst m; (hist) Pontifex m
pontifical [pɑn'tɪfɪkəl] adj pontifikal
pontoon [pɑn'tun] s Ponton m; (aer) Schwimmer m
pony ['poni] s (small horse; hair style) Pony n; (crib) Eselsbrücke f
poodle ['pudəl] s Pudel m
pool [pul] s (small pond) Tümpel m; (of blood) Lache f; (swimming pool) Schwimmbecken n; (in betting) Pool m; (game) Billiard n; (fin) Pool m || tr zusammenlegen
pool′room′ s Billardsalon m
pool′ ta′ble s Billardtisch m
poop [pup] s Heck n || tr (sl) erschöpfen; be pooped (out) erschöpft sein
poor [pur] adj arm; (e.g., in spelling) schwach; (soil, harvest) schlecht; (miserable) armselig; p. in arm an (dat)
poor′ box′ s Opferstock m
poor′house′ s Armenhaus n
poorly ['purli] adv schlecht
pop [pɑp] adj (concert, singer, music) Pop– || s Puff m, Knall m; (dad) Vati m; (soda) Brauselimonade f; (mus) Popmusik f || v (pret & pp popped; ger popping) tr (corn) rösten; (cause to pop) knallen lassen; pop the question (coll) e-n Heiratsantrag machen || intr (make a popping noise) knallen; (said of popcorn) aufplatzen; pop in (visit unexpectedly) (coll) hereinplatzen; pop off (sl) das Maul aufreißen; pop up (appear) (coll) auftauchen; (jump up) hochfahren
pop′corn′ s Puffmais m
pope [pop] s Papst m
pop′eyed′ adj glotzäugig
pop′gun′ s Knallbüchse f
poplar ['pɑplər] s Pappel f
poppy ['pɑpi] s Mohnblume f, Mohn m
pop′pycock′ s (coll) Quatsch m
pop′pyseed′ s Mohn m
popsicle ['pɑpˌsɪkəl] s Eis n am Stiel
populace ['pɑpjələs] s Pöbel m

popular ['pɑpjələr] adj populär; (e.g., music, expression) volkstümlich; p. with beliebt bei
popularity [ˌpɑpjə'lærɪti] s Popularität f, Beliebtheit f
popularize ['pɑpjələˌraɪz] tr popularisieren
populate ['pɑpjəˌlet] tr bevölkern
population [ˌpɑpjə'leʃən] s Bevölkerung f
popula′tion explo′sion s Bevölkerungsexplosion f
populous ['pɑpjələs] adj volkreich
porcelain ['pɔrs(ə)lɪn] s Porzellan n
porch [pɔrtʃ] s Vorbau m, Veranda f
porcupine ['pɔrkjəˌpaɪn] s Stachelschwein n
pore [pɔr] s Pore f || intr—p. over eifrig studieren
pork [pɔrk] adj Schweine– || s Schweinefleisch n
pork′chop′ s Schweinekotelett n
pornography [pɔr'nɑgrəfi] s Pornographie f
porous ['pɔrəs] adj porös
porphyry ['pɔrfrɪi] s Porphyr m
porpoise ['pɔrpəs] s Tümmler m
porridge ['pɔrɪdʒ] s Brei m
port [pɔrt] s Hafen m; (wine) Portwein m; (slit for shooting) Schießscharte f; (naut) Backbord m & n; to p. (naut) backbord
portable ['pɔrtəbəl] adj tragbar; (radio, television, typewriter) Koffer–
portal ['pɔrtəl] s Portal n
portend [pɔr'tend] tr vorbedeuten
portent ['pɔrtənt] s schlimmes Vorzeichen n, böses Omen n
portentous [pɔr'tentəs] adj unheildrohend
porter ['pɔrtər] s (in a hotel) Hausdiener m; (at a station) Gepäckträger m; (doorman) Portier m
portfoli·o [pɔrt'folɪˌo] s (–os) Aktenmappe f; (fin) Portefeuille n; without p. ohne Geschäftsbereich
port′hole′ s (for shooting) Schießscharte f; (naut) Bullauge n
portico ['pɔrtɪˌko] s (–coes & –cos) Säulenvorbau m, Portikus m
portion ['pɔrʃən] s Anteil m; (serving) Portion f; (dowry) Heiratsgut n || tr —p. out austeilen, einteilen
portly ['pɔrtli] adj wohlbeleibt
port′ of call′ s Anlaufhafen m
port′ of en′try s Einfuhrhafen m
portrait ['pɔrtret] s Porträt n
portray [pɔr'tre] tr porträtieren; (fig) beschreiben; (theat) darstellen
portrayal [pɔr'tre·əl] s Porträtieren n; (fig) Beschreibung f; (theat) Darstellung f
port′side′ s Backbord m & n
Portugal ['pɔrtʃəgəl] s Portugal n
Portuguese ['pɔrtʃə·ˌgiz] adj portugiesisch || s Portugiese m, Portugiesin f; (language) Portugiesisch n
port′ wine′ s Portwein m
pose [poz] s Haltung f, Pose f || tr (a question, problem) stellen || intr posieren; p. as sich ausgeben als; p. for an artist e-m Künstler Modell ste-

hen; **p. for a picture** sich e-m Photographen stellen

posh [paʃ] *adj* (sl) großartig

position [pə'ziʃən] *s* Stellung *f*; (*situation, condition*) Lage *f*; (*job; place of defense*) Stellung *f*; (*point of view*) Standpunkt *m*; (aer, naut) Standort *m*; (astr, mil, naut) Position *f*; **be in a p. to** (*inf*) in der Lage sein zu (*inf*); **in p.** am rechten Platz; **p. wanted** (*as in an ad*) Stelle gesucht; **take a p. on** Stellung nehmen zu; **take one's p.** sich aufstellen

positive ['pazɪtɪv] *adj* (*reply, result, attitude*) positiv; (*answer*) zustimmend; (*sure*) sicher; (*offer*) fest; (elec, math, med, phot, phys) positiv ‖ *s* (gram) Positiv *m*; (phot) Positiv *n*

posse ['pasɪ] *s* Polizeiaufgebot *n*

possess [pə'zes] *tr* besitzen; **be possessed by the devil** von dem Teufel besessen sein

possession [pə'zeʃən] *s* Besitz *m*; (*property*) Eigentum *n*; **be in p. of s.th.** etw besitzen; **take p. of s.th.** etw in Besitz nehmen

possessive [pə'zesɪv] *adj* eifersüchtig; (gram) besitzanzeigend, Besitz-

possibility [,pasɪ'bɪlɪti] *s* Möglichkeit *f*

possible ['pasɪbəl] *adj* möglich; **make p.** ermöglichen

possibly ['pasɪbli] *adv* möglicherweise

possum ['pasəm] *s* Opossum *n*; **play p.** sich verstellen; (*play dead*) sich tot stellen

post [post] *s* (*pole*) Pfahl *m*; (*job; of a sentry*) Posten *m*; (*military camp*) Standort *m* ‖ *tr* (*a notice*) anschlagen; (*a guard*) aufstellen; **p. bond** Kaution stellen; **p. no bills** Plakatankleben verboten

postage ['postɪdʒ] *s* Porto *n*

post'age due' *s* Nachporto *n*

post'age stamp' *s* Briefmarke *f*

postal ['postəl] *adj* Post-

post'al mon'ey or'der *s* Postanweisung *f*

post'card' *s* Ansichtskarte *f*

post'date' *tr* nachdatieren

post'ed *adj*—**keep s.o. p.** j-n auf dem laufenden halten

poster ['postər] *s* Plakat *n*

posterity [pas'terɪti] *s* Nachkommenschaft *f*, Nachwelt *f*

postern ['postərn] *s* Hintertür *f*

post' exchange' *s* Marketenderei *f*

post'haste' *adv* schnellstens

posthumous ['pastʃuməs] *adj* posthum

post'man *s* (**-men**) Briefträger *m*

post'mark' *s* Poststempel *m* ‖ *tr* abstempeln

post'mas'ter *s* Postmeister *m*

post'mas'ter gen'eral *s* Postminister *m*

post-mortem [,post'mortəm] *s* Obduktion *f*

post' of'fice *s* Post *f*, Postamt *n*

post'-office box' *s* Postschließfach *n*

post'paid' *adv* frankiert

postpone [post'pon] *tr* (till, to) aufschieben (auf acc)

postponement [post'ponmənt] *s* Aufschub *m*

post'script' *s* Nachschrift *f*

posture ['pastʃər] *s* Haltung *f*

post'war' *adj* Nachkriegs-

posy ['pozi] *s* Sträußchen *n*

pot [pat] *s* Topf *m*; (*for coffee, tea*) Kanne *f*; (*in gambling*) Einsatz *m*; **go to pot** (sl) hops gehen; **pots and pans** Kochgeschirr *n*

potash ['pat,æʃ] *s* Pottasche *f*, Kali *n*

potassium [pə'tæsɪəm] *s* Kalium *n*

pota·to [pə'teto] *s* (**-toes**) Kartoffel *f*

pota'to chips' *spl* Kartoffelchips *pl*

potbellied ['pat,belid] *adj* dickbäuchig

pot'bel'ly *s* Spitzbauch *m*

potency ['potənsi] *s* Stärke *f*; (physiol) Potenz *f*

potent ['potənt] *adj* (*powerful*) mächtig; (*persuasive*) überzeugend; (*e.g., drugs*) wirksam; (physiol) potent

potentate ['potən,tet] *s* Potentat *m*

potential [pə'tenʃəl] *adj* möglich; (phys) potentiell ‖ *s* (& elec, math, phys) Potential *n*

pot'hold'er *s* Topflappen *m*

pot'hole' *s* Schlagloch *n*

potion ['poʃən] *s* Trank *m*

pot'luck' *s*—**take p.** mit dem vorliebnehmen, was es gerade gibt

pot' roast' *s* Schmorbraten *m*

pot'sherd' *s* Topfscherbe *f*

pot' shot' *s* müheloser Schuß *m*; **take a p. at** unfair bekritteln

pot'ted *adj* Topf-

potter ['patər] *s* Töpfer *m*

pot'ter's clay' *s* Töpferton *m*

pot'ter's wheel' *s* Töpferscheibe *f*

pottery ['patəri] *s* Tonwaren *pl*

potty ['pati] *s* (coll) Töpfchen *n*

pouch [pautʃ] *s* Beutel *m*

poultice ['poltɪs] *s* Breiumschlag *m*

poultry ['poltri] *s* Geflügel *n*

poul'try-man *s* (**-men**) Geflügelzüchter *m*; (*dealer*) Geflügelhändler *m*

pounce [pauns] *intr*—**p. on** sich stürzen auf (acc)

pound [paund] *s* Pfund *n*; (*for animals*) Pferch *m* ‖ *tr* (zer)stampfen; (*meat*) klopfen; **p. the sidewalks** Pflaster treten ‖ *intr* (*said of the heart*) klopfen; **p. on** (*e.g., a door*) hämmern an (acc)

-pound *suf* -pfündig

pound' ster'ling *s* Pfund *n* Sterling

pour [por] *tr* gießen; (*e.g., coffee*) einschenken; **p. away** wegschütten ‖ *intr* (meteor) gießen; **p. out of** (*e.g., a theater*) strömen aus ‖ *impers*—**it's pouring** es gießt

pout [paut] *s* Schmollen *n* ‖ *intr* schmollen

pout'ing *adj* (lips) aufgeworfen ‖ *s* Schmollen *n*

poverty ['pavərti] *s* Armut *f*

pov'erty-strick'en *adj* verarmt

POW ['pi'o'dʌbl,ju] *s* (**prisoner of war**) Kriegsgefangener *m*

powder ['paudər] *s* Pulver *n*; (*cosmetic*) Puder *m* ‖ *tr* (*e.g., the face*) pudern; (*plants*) stäuben; (*a cake*) bestreuen ‖ *intr* zu Pulver werden

pow'der box' s Puderdose f
pow'dered milk' s Milchpulver n
pow'dered sug'ar s Staubzucker m
pow'der keg' s Pulverfaß n
pow'der puff' s Puderquaste f
pow'der room' s Damentoilette f
powdery ['paudərɪ] adj pulverig
power ['pau‐ər] s Macht f; (personal control) Gewalt f; (electricity) Strom m; (math) Potenz f; (opt) Vergrößerungskraft f; (phys) Leistung f; (pol) Macht f; be in p. an der Macht sein; be in s.o.'s p. in j‐s Gewalt sein; be within s.o.'s p. in j‐s Macht liegen; come to p. an die Macht gelangen; have the p. (inf) vermögen zu (inf); more p. to you! viel Erfolg!; the powers that be die Obrigkeit f || tr antreiben
pow'er brake' s (aut) Servobremse f
pow'er dive' s (aer) Vollgassturzflug m
pow'er drill' s Elektrobohrer m
pow'er-driv'en adj mit Motorantrieb
pow'er fail'ure s Stromausfall m
powerful ['pau‐ərfəl] adj mächtig; (opt) stark
pow'erhouse' s Kraftwerk n; (coll) Kraftprotz m
pow'erhun'gry adj herrschsüchtig
powerless ['pau‐ərlɪs] adj machtlos
pow'er line' s Starkstromleitung f
pow'er mow'er s Motorrasenmäher m
pow'er of attorn'ey s Vollmacht f
pow'er plant' s (powerhouse) Kraftwerk n; (aer, aut) Triebwerk n
pow'er shov'el s Löffelbagger m
pow'er sta'tion s Kraftwerk n
pow'er steer'ing s Servolenkung f
pow'er supply' s Stromversorgung f
practicable ['præktɪkəbəl] adj praktikabel, durchführbar
practical ['præktɪkəl] adj praktisch
prac'tical joke' s Streich m
practically ['præktɪkəlɪ] adv praktisch; (almost) fast, so gut wie
prac'tical nurse' s praktisch ausgebildete Krankenschwester f
practice ['præktɪs] s (exercise) Übung f; (habit) Gewohnheit f; (of medicine, law) Praxis f; in p. (in training) in der Übung; (in reality) in der Praxis; make it a p. to (inf) es sich [dat] zur Gewohnheit machen zu (inf); out of p. aus der Übung || tr (a profession) tätig sein als; (patience, reading, dancing, etc.) sich üben in (dat); (music, gymnastics) treiben; (piano, etc.) üben || intr üben; (said of a doctor) praktizieren; p. on (e.g., the violin, piano, parallel bars) üben auf (dat)
prac'tice game' s Übungsspiel n
prac'tice teach'er s Studienreferendar –in mf
practitioner [præk'tɪʃənər] s Praktiker –in mf
pragmatic [præg'mætɪk] adj pragmatisch
pragmatism ['prægmə,tɪzəm] s Sachlichkeit f; (philos) Pragmatismus m
Prague [prɑg] s Prag n
prairie ['prerɪ] s Steppe f, Prärie f

praise [prez] s Lob n || tr (for) loben (wegen); p. to the skies verhimmeln
praise'wor'thy adj lobenswert
prance [præns] intr tänzeln
prank [præŋk] s Schelmenstreich m
prate [pret] intr schwätzen
prattle ['prætəl] s Geplapper n || intr plappern, schwätzen
prawn [prɔn] s Garnele f
pray [pre] tr & intr beten
prayer [prer] s Gebet n; say a p. ein Gebet sprechen
prayer' book' s Gebetbuch n
preach [pritʃ] tr & intr predigen
preacher ['pritʃər] s Prediger m
preamble ['pri,æmbəl] s Präambel f
precarious [prɪ'kerɪ‐əs] adj prekär
precaution [prɪ'kɔʃən] s Vorsichtsmaßnahme f; as a p. vorsichtshalber; take precautions Vorkehrungen treffen
precede [prɪ'sid] tr vorausgehen (dat) || intr vorangehen
precedence ['presɪdəns] s Vorrang m; take p. over den Vorrang haben vor (dat)
precedent ['presɪdənt] s Präzedenzfall m; set a p. e‐n Präzedenzfall schaffen
preced'ing adj vorhergehend
precept ['prisept] s Vorschrift f
precinct ['prisɪŋkt] s Bezirk m
precious ['preʃəs] adj (expensive) kostbar; (valuable) wertvoll; (excessively refined) geziert; (child) lieb || adv p. few (coll) herzlich wenige
pre'cious stone' s Edelstein m
precipice ['presɪpɪs] s Abgrund m
precipitate [prɪ'sɪpɪ,tet] adj jäh abfallend || s (chem) Niederschlag m || tr (hurl) (into) stürzen (in acc); (bring about) heraufbeschwören; (vapor) (chem) niederschlagen; (from a solution) (chem) ausfällen || intr (chem, meteor) sich niederschlagen
precipitation [prɪ,sɪpɪ'teʃən] s (meteor) Niederschlag m
precipitous [prɪ'sɪpɪtəs] adj jäh
precise [prɪ'saɪs] adj präzis, genau
precision [prɪ'sɪʒən] s Präzision f
preclude [prɪ'klud] tr ausschließen
precocious [prɪ'koʃəs] adj frühreif
preconceived [,prikən'sivd] adj vorgefaßt
predatory ['predə,tori] adj Raub–
predecessor ['predɪ,sesər] s Vorgänger –in mf
predestination [,pridestɪ'neʃən] s Prädestination f
predicament [prɪ'dɪkəmənt] s Mißliche Lage f
predicate ['predɪkɪt] s (gram) Aussage f, Prädikat n || ['predɪ,ket] tr (of) aussagen (über acc); (base) (on) gründen (auf acc)
predict [prɪ'dɪkt] tr voraussagen
prediction [prɪ'dɪkʃən] s Voraussage f
predispose [,pridɪs'poz] tr (to) im voraus geneigt machen (zu); (pathol) empfänglich machen (für)
predominant [prɪ'dɑmɪnənt] adj vorwiegend

preeminent [prɪˈemɪnənt] *adj* hervorragend
preempt [prɪˈempt] *tr (a program)* ersetzen; *(land)* durch Vorkaufsrecht
erwerben
preen [prin] *tr* putzen
prefabricated [priˈfæbrɪ ˌketɪd] *adj*
Fertig–
preface [ˈprefɪs] *s* Vorwort *n*, Vorrede
f ‖ *tr* einleiten
prefer [prɪˈfʌr] *v (pret & pp* –**ferred**;
ger –**ferring)** *tr* bevorzugen; *(charges)*
vorbringen; **I p. to wait** ich warte
lieber
preferable [ˈprefərəbəl] *adj* (to) vorzu-
ziehen(d) *(dat)*
preferably [ˈprefərəbli] *adv* vorzugs-
weise
preferred' stock' *s* Vorzugsaktie *f*
prefix [ˈprifɪks] *s* Vorsilbe *f*, Präfix *n*
‖ *tr* vorsetzen
pregnancy [ˈpregnənsi] *s* Schwangerschaft *f*; *(of animals)* Trächtigkeit *f*
pregnant [ˈpregnənt] *adj* schwanger;
(animals) trächtig; *(fig)* inhalts-
schwer
prehistoric [ˌprihɪsˈtɔrɪk] *adj* vorge-
schichtlich, prähistorisch
prejudice [ˈpredʒədɪs] *s* Voreingeno-
menheit *f*; *(detriment)* Schaden *m* ‖
tr beeinträchtigen; **p. s.o. against**
j–n einnehmen gegen
pre'judiced *adj* voreingenommen
prejudicial [ˌpredʒəˈdɪʃəl] *adj* (to)
schädlich (für)
prelate [ˈprelɪt] *s* Prälat *m*
preliminary [prɪˈlɪmɪ ˌneri] *adj* einleitend, Vor– ‖ *s* Vorbereitung *f*
prelude [ˈprel(j)ud] *s* (fig, mus, theat)
Vorspiel *n*
premarital [priˈmærɪtəl] *adj* vorehelich
premature [ˌpriməˈt(j)ur] *adj* verfrüht;
p. birth Frühgeburt *f*
premeditated [priˈmedɪ ˌtetɪd] *adj* vorbedacht; *(murder)* vorsätzlich
premier [prɪˈmɪr] *s* Premier *m*
premiere [prɪˈmɪr] *s* Erstaufführung *f*
premise [ˈpremɪs] *s* Voraussetzung *f*;
on the premises an Ort und Stelle;
the premises das Lokal
premium [ˈprimɪ ˌəm] *s* Prämie *f*; **at a
p.** *(in demand)* sehr gesucht; *(at a
high price)* über pari
premonition [ˌpriməˈnɪʃən] *s* Vorahnung *f*
preoccupation [pri ˌakjəˈpeʃən] *s* (with)
Beschäftigtsein *n* (mit)
preoccupied [priˈakjəˌpaɪd] *adj* ausschließlich beschäftigt
preparation [ˌprepəˈreʃən] *s* Vorbereitung *f*; (med) Präparat *n*
preparatory [prɪˈpærə ˌtori] *adj* vorbe-
reitend; **p. to** vor *(dat)*
prepare [prɪˈper] *tr* vorbereiten; *(a
meal)* zubereiten; *(a prescription)*
anfertigen; *(a document)* abfassen
preparedness [prɪˈperɪdnɪs] *s* Bereitschaft *f*; (mil) Einsatzbereitschaft *f*
pre-pay [priˈpe] *v (pret & pp* –**paid)**
tr im voraus bezahlen
preponderant [prɪˈpɑndərənt] *adj* überwiegend

preposition [ˌprepəˈzɪʃən] *s* Präposition *f*, Verhältniswort *n*
prepossessing [ˌpripəˈzesɪŋ] *adj* ein-
nehmend
preposterous [prɪˈpɑstərəs] *adj* lächerlich
prep' school' [prep] *s* Vorbereitungs-
schule *f*
prerecorded [ˌpririˈkɔrdɪd] *adj* vorher aufgenommen
prerequisite [priˈrekwɪzɪt] *s* Voraussetzung *f*, Vorbedingung *f*
prerogative [prɪˈrɑgətɪv] *s* Vorrecht *n*
presage [ˈpresɪdʒ] *s* Vorzeichen *n* ‖
[prɪˈsedʒ] *tr* ein Vorzeichen sein für
Presbyterian [ˌprezbɪˈtɪrɪ ˌən] *adj*
presbyterianisch ‖ *s* Presbyterianer
–in *mf*
prescribe [prɪˈskraɪb] *tr* vorschreiben;
(med) verordnen
prescription [prɪˈskrɪpʃən] *s* Vorschrift
f; (med) Rezept *n*, Verordnung *f*
presence [ˈprezəns] *s* Anwesenheit *f*
pres'ence of mind' *s* Geistesgegenwart
f
present [ˈprezənt] *adj (at this place)*
anwesend; *(of the moment)* gegenwärtig ‖ *s (gift)* Geschenk *n*; *(present time or tense)* Gegenwart *f*; **at p.**
zur Zeit; **for the p.** vorläufig ‖
[prɪˈzent] *tr* bieten; *(facts)* darstellen; *(introduce)* vorstellen; (theat)
vorführen; **p. s.o. with s.th.** j–m etw
verehren
presentable [prɪˈzentəbəl] *adj* presen-
tabel
presentation [ˌprezənˈteʃən] *s* Vorstellung *f*; (theat) Aufführung *f*
pres'ent-day' *adj* heutig, aktuell
presentiment [prɪˈzentɪmənt] *s* Ahnung
f
presently [ˈprezəntli] *adv* gegenwärtig;
(soon) alsbald
preservation [ˌprezərˈveʃən] *s* Erhaltung *f*; *(from)* Bewahrung *f* (vor *dat)*
preservative [prɪˈzɜrvətɪv] *s* Konser-
vierungsmittel *n*
preserve [prɪˈzɜrv] *s* Revier *n*; **preserves** Konserven *pl* ‖ *tr* konservieren; **p. from** schützen vor *(dat)*
preside [prɪˈzaɪd] *intr* (over) den Vorsitz führen (über *acc* oder bei)
presidency [ˈprezɪdənsi] *s* Präsident-
schaft *f*
president [ˈprezɪdənt] *s* Präsident –in
mf; *(of a university)* Rektor –in *mf*;
(of a board) Vorsitzende *mf*
presidential [ˌprezɪˈdentʃəl] *adj* Präsidenten–
press [pres] *s (agency, agent, conference, gallery, report, secretary)*
Presse– ‖ *s (wine press; printing
press; newspapers)* Presse *f*; **go to p.**
in Druck gehen ‖ *tr* drucken; *(a
suit)* (auf)bügeln; *(a person)* bedrängen; *(fruit)* ausdrücken; **be
pressed for** knapp sein an *(dat)*; **p.
s.o. to** *(inf)* j–n dringend bitten zu
(inf); **p. the button** auf den Knopf
drücken ‖ *intr (said of time)* drängen; **p. for** drängen auf *(acc)*; **p.
forward** sich vorwärtsdrängen

press' box' s Pressekabine f
press' card' s Presseausweis m
press'ing adj dringend, dringlich
press' release' s Pressemitteilung f
pressure ['prɛʃər] s Druck m; (of work) Andrang m; (aut) Reifendruck m; **put p. on** unter Druck setzen || tr drängen
pres'sure cook'er s Schnellkochtopf m
pres'sure group' s Interessengruppe f
pressurize ['prɛʃə‚raɪz] tr druckfest machen
prestige [prɛs'tiʒ] s Prestige n
presumably [prɪ'z(j)uməbli] adv vermutlich
presume [prɪ'z(j)um] tr vermuten || intr vermuten; **p. on** pochen auf (acc)
presumption [prɪ'zʌmpʃən] s Vermutung f; (presumptuousness) Anmaßung f
presumptuous [prɪ'zʌmptʃʊ‑əs] adj anmaßend
presuppose [‚prisə'poz] tr voraussetzen
pretend [prɪ'tɛnd] tr vorgeben; **he pretended that he was a captain** er gab sich für e-n Hauptmann aus || intr so tun, als ob
pretender [prɪ'tɛndər] s Quaksalber m; **p. to the throne** Thronbewerber m
pretense [prɪ'tɛns], ['prɪtɛns] s Schein m; **under false pretenses** unter Vorspiegelung falscher Tatsachen; **under the p. of** unter dem Vorwand (genit)
pretentious [prɪ'tɛnʃəs] adj (person) anmaßend; (home) protzig
pretext ['pritɛkst] s Vorwand m
pretty ['prɪti] adj hübsch || adv (coll) ziemlich
pretzel ['prɛtsəl] s Brezel f
prevail [prɪ'vel] intr (predominate) (vor)herrschen; (triumph) (against) sich behaupten (gegen); **p. on** überreden
prevail'ing adj (fashion, view) (vor)herrschend; (situation) obwaltend
prevalence ['prɛvələns] s Vorherrschen n
prevalent ['prɛvələnt] adj vorherrschend; **be p.** herrschen
prevaricate [prɪ'værɪ‚ket] intr Ausflüchte machen
prevent [prɪ'vɛnt] tr verhindern; (war, danger) abwenden; **p. s.o. from** j-n hindern an (dat); **p. s.o. from** (ger) j-n daran hindern zu (inf)
prevention [prɪ'vɛnʃən] s Verhütung f
preventive [prɪ'vɛntɪv] adj vorbeugend || s Schutzmittel n
preview ['pri‚vju] s Vorschau f
previous ['priviəs] adj vorhergehend, vorig; Vor‑, e.g., **p. conviction** Vorstrafe f; **p. day** Vortag m; **p. record** Vorstrafenregister n
previously ['priviəsli] adv vorher
prewar ['pri‚wɔr] adj Vorkriegs‑
prey [pre] s Beute f, Raub m; (fig) Opfer n; **fall p. to** (& fig) zum Opfer fallen (dat) || intr—**p. on** erbeuten; (exploit) ausbeuten; **p. on s.o.'s mind** an j-s Gewissen nagen

price [praɪs] s Preis m; **(st. exch.)** Kurs m; **at any p.** um jeden Preis; **at the p. of** im Wert von || tr mit Preisen versehen; (inquire about the price of) nach dem Preis fragen (genit)
price' control' s Preiskontrolle f
price' fix'ing s Preisbindung f
price' freeze' s Preisstopp m
priceless ['praɪslɪs] adj unbezahlbar; (coll) sehr komisch
price' range' s Preislage f
price' rig'ging s Preistreiberei f
price' tag' s Preiszettel m, Preisschild n
price'-wage' spi'ral s Preis-Lohn-Spirale f
price' war' s Preiskrieg m
prick [prɪk] s (& fig) Stich m || tr stechen; **p. up** (ears) spitzen
prickly ['prɪkli] adj stachelig, Stech‑
prick'ly heat' s Hitzepickel pl
pride [praɪd] s Stolz m; (pej) Hochmut m; **swallow one's p.** seinen Stolz in die Tasche stecken; **take p. in** stolz sein auf (acc) || tr—**p. oneself on** sich viel einbilden auf (acc)
priest [prist] s Priester m
priestess ['pristɪs] s Priesterin f
priest'hood' s Priestertum n
priestly ['pristli] adj priesterlich
prig [prɪg] s Tugendbold m
prim [prɪm] adj (primmer; primmest) spröde
primacy ['praɪməsi] s Primat m & n
primarily [praɪ'mɛrɪli] adv vor allem
primary ['praɪ‚mɛri] adj primär, Haupt‑; (e.g., color, school) Grund‑ || s (pol) Vorwahl f
primate ['praɪmet] s (zool) Primat m
prime [praɪm] adj (chief) Haupt‑; (best) erstklassig || s Blüte f; (math) Primzahl f; **p. of life** Lenz m des Lebens || tr (a pump) ansaugen lassen; (ammunition) scharfmachen; (a surface for painting) grundieren; (with information) vorher informieren
prime' min'ister s Ministerpräsident m; (in England) Premierminister m
primer ['primər] s Fibel f || ['praɪmər] s (for painting) Grundierfarbe f; (of an explosive) Zündsatz m; (aut) Einspritzpumpe f
prime' time' s schönste Zeit f
primeval [praɪ'mivəl] adj urweltlich, Ur‑; **p. world** Urwelt f
primitive ['prɪmɪtɪv] adj primitiv || s Primitive mf, Urmensch m
primp [prɪmp] tr aufputzen || intr sich aufputzen, sich zieren
prim'rose' s Himmelschlüssel m
prince [prɪns] s Prinz m, Fürst m
Prince' Al'bert s Gehrock m
princely ['prɪnsli] adj prinzlich
princess ['prɪnsɪs] s Prinzessin f, Fürstin f
principal ['prɪnsɪpəl] adj Haupt‑ || s (educ) Schuldirektor ‑in mf; (fin) Kapitalbetrag m, Kapital n
principality [‚prɪnsɪ'pælɪti] s Fürstentum n

principally [ˈprɪnsɪpəli] *adv* größtenteils

principle [ˈprɪnsɪpəl] *s* Grundsatz *m*, Prinzip *n*; **in p.** im Prinzip

print [prɪnt] *s* (*lettering; design on cloth*) Druck *m*; (*printed dress*) bedrucktes Kleid *n*; (phot) Abzug *m*; **in cold p.** schwarz auf weiß; **out of p.** vergriffen || *tr* drucken; (*e.g., one's name*) in Druckschrift schreiben; (phot) kopieren; (tex) bedrucken

print′ed mat′ter *s* Drucksache *f*

printer [ˈprɪntər] *s* Drucker *m*; (phot) Kopiermaschine *f*

prin′ter's ink′ *s* Druckerschwärze *f*

print′ing *s* Drucken *n*; (*of a book*) Buchdruck *m*; (*subsequent printing*) Abdruck *m*; (phot) Kopieren *n*, Abziehen *n*

print′ing press′ *s* Druckerpresse *f*

print′ shop′ *s* Druckerei *f*

prior [ˈpraɪ·ər] *adj* vorherig; **p. to** vor (*dat*) || *s* (eccl) Prior *m*

priority [praɪˈɔrɪti] *s* Priorität *f*

prism [ˈprɪzəm] *s* Prisma *n*

prison [ˈprɪzən] *s* Gefängnis *n*

pris′on camp′ *s* Gefangenenlager *n*

prisoner [ˈprɪz(ə)nər] *s* Gefangene *mf*; (*in a concentration camp*) Häftling *m*; **be taken p.** in Gefangenschaft geraten; **take p.** gefangennehmen

pris′oner of war′ *s* Kriegsgefangene *mf*

prissy [ˈprɪsi] *adj* zimperlich

privacy [ˈpraɪvəsi] *s* Zurückgezogenheit *f*; **disturb s.o.'s p.** j-s Ruhe stören

private [ˈpraɪvɪt] *adj* privat; (*personal*) persönlich; **keep p.** geheimhalten || *s* (mil) Gemeine *m*; **in p.** privat(im); **privates** Geschlechtsteile *pl*

pri′vate cit′izen *s* Privatperson *f*

pri′vate eye′ *s* (coll) Privatdetektiv *m*

pri′vate first′ class′ *s* Gefreite *mf*

privately [ˈpraɪvɪtli] *adv* privat(im)

privet [ˈprɪvɪt] *s* Liguster *m*

privilege [ˈprɪvɪlɪdʒ] *s* Privileg *n*

privy [ˈprɪvi] *adj*—**p. to** eingeweiht in (*acc*) || *s* Abtritt *m*

prize [praɪz] *s* Preis *m*, Prämie *f*; (nav) Prise *f* || *tr* schätzen

prize′ fight′ *s* Preisboxkampf *m*

prize′ fight′er *s* Berufsboxer *m*

prize′ ring′ *s* Boxring *m*

pro [pro] *s* (**pros**) (coll) Profi *m*; **the pros and the cons** das Für und Wider || *prep* für (*acc*)

probability [ˌprɑbəˈbɪlɪti] *s* Wahrscheinlichkeit *f*; **in all p.** aller Wahrscheinlichkeit nach

probable [ˈprɑbəbəl] *adj* wahrscheinlich

probate [ˈprobet] *s* Testamentsbestätigung *f* || *tr* bestätigen

pro′bate court′ *s* Nachlaßgericht *n*

probation [proˈbeʃən] *s* Probe *f*; (jur) Bewährungsfrist *f*; **on p.** auf Probe; (jur) mit Bewährung

proba′tion of′ficer *s* Bewährungshelfer –in *mf*

probe [prob] *s* (jur) Untersuchung *f*;

(mil) Sondierungsangriff *m*; (rok) Versuchsrakete *f*; (surg) Sonde *f* || *tr* (*with the hands*) abtasten; (fig & surg) sondieren

problem [ˈprɑbləm] *s* Problem *n*; (math) Aufgabe *f*

prob′lem child′ *s* Sorgenkind *n*

procedure [proˈsidʒər] *s* Verfahren ·*n*

proceed [proˈsid] *intr* (*go on*) fortfahren; (*act*) verfahren; **p. against** (jur) vorgehen gegen; **p. from** kommen von; **p. to** (*inf*) darangehen zu (*inf*)

proceed′ing *s* Vorgehen *n*; **proceedings** (*of a society*) Sitzungsberichte *pl*; (jur) Verfahren *n*

proceeds [ˈprosidz] *spl* Erlös *m*

process [ˈprɑsɛs] *s* Verfahren *n*, Prozeß *m*; **be in p.** im Gang sein; **in the p.** dabei || *tr* (*raw materials*) verarbeiten; (*applications*) bearbeiten; (*persons*) abfertigen; (phot) entwickeln und vervielfältigen

procession [proˈsɛʃən] *s* Prozession *f*

proclaim [proˈklem] *tr* ankündigen; (*a law*) bekanntmachen; **p. (as) a holiday** zum Feiertag erklären

proclamation [ˌprɑkləˈmeʃən] *s* Aufruf *m*, Proklamation *f*

procrastinate [proˈkræstɪˌnet] *intr* zaudern

proctor [ˈprɑktər] *s* Aufsichtsführende *mf* || *tr* beaufsichtigen

procure [proˈkjur] *tr* besorgen, verschaffen; (*said of a pimp*) verkuppeln

procurement [proˈkjurmənt] *s* Besorgung *f*

procurer [proˈkjurər] *s* Kuppler *m*

prod [prɑd] *s* Stoß *m*; (*stick*) Stachelstock *m* || *v* (*pret & pp* **prodded**) *ger* **prodding**) *tr* stoßen; **prod s.o. into** (*ger*) j–n dazu anstacheln zu (*inf*)

prodigal [ˈprɑdɪgəl] *adj* verschwenderisch

prod′igal son′ *s* verlorener Sohn *m*

prodigious [proˈdɪdʒəs] *adj* großartig

prodigy [ˈprɑdɪdʒi] *s* Wunderzeichen *n*; (*talented child*) Wunderkind *n*

produce [ˈprod(j)us] *s* (*product*) Erzeugnis *n*; (*amount produced*) Ertrag *m*; (*fruits and vegetables*) Bodenprodukte *pl* || [proˈd(j)us] *tr* produzieren; (*manufacture*) herstellen; (*said of plants, trees*) hervorbringen; (*interest, profit*) abwerfen; (*proof*) beibringen; (*papers*) vorlegen; (cin) produzieren; (theat) inszenieren || *intr* (bot) tragen; (econ) Gewinne abwerfen

pro′duce depart′ment *s* Obst– und Gemüseabteilung *f*

producer [proˈd(j)usər] *s* Hersteller *m*; (cin, theat) Produzent –in *mf*

product [ˈprɑdʌkt] *s* Erzeugnis *n*, Produkt *n*

production [proˈdʌkʃən] *s* Erzeugung *f*, Produktion *f*; (fa, lit) Werk *n*

productive [proˈdʌktɪv] *adj* produktiv

profane [proˈfen] *adj* profan; **p. language** Fluchen *n* || *tr* profanieren

profanity [proˈfænɪti] *s* Fluchen *n*; **profanities** Flüche *pl*

profess [pro'fes] *tr* gestehen
profession [pro'feʃən] *s* Beruf *m;* *(of faith)* Bekenntnis *n;* **by p.** von Beruf
professional [pro'feʃənəl] *adj* berufsmäßig, professionell ‖ *s (expert)* Fachmann *m; (sport)* Profi *m*
profes′sional jea′lousy *s* Brotneid *m*
professor [pro'fesər] *s* Professor –in *mf*
profes′sorship′ *s* Professur *f*
proffer ['profər] *s* Angebot *n* ‖ *tr* anbieten
proficient [pro'fiʃənt] *adj* tüchtig
profile ['profaɪl] *s* Profil *n; (biographical sketch)* Kurzbiographie *f*
profit ['profɪt] *s* Gewinn *m;* **show a p. e-n Gewinn** abwerfen ‖ *tr* nutzen ‖ *intr* **(by)** Nutzen ziehen aus
profitable ['profɪtəbəl] *adj* einträglich
profiteer [ˌprofɪ'tɪr] *s* Wucherer *m,* Schieber *m* ‖ *intr* wuchern, schieben
prof′it shar′ing *s* Gewinnbeteiligung *f*
profligate ['proflɪgɪt] *adj* verkommen; *(extravagant)* verschwenderisch ‖ *s* verkommener Mensch *m; (spendthrift)* Verschwender –in *mf*
profound [pro'faund] *adj (knowledge)* gründlich; *(change)* tiefgreifend
profuse [prə'fjus] *adj* überreichlich
progeny ['prodʒəni] *s* (& bot) Nachkommenschaft *f; (of animals)* Junge *pl*
progno·sis [prag'nosɪs] *s* (**–ses** [siz]) Prognose *f*
prognosticate [prag'nastɪˌket] *tr* voraussagen
pro·gram ['progræm] *s* Programm *n; (radio or television show)* Sendung *f* ‖ *v (pret & pp* **–grammed;** *ger* **–gramming)** *tr* programmieren
progress ['progres] *s* Fortschritt *m;* **be in progress** im Gang sein ‖ [prə'gres] *intr (make progress)* fortschreiten; *(develop)* sich fortentwickeln
progressive [prə'gresɪv] *adj* fortschrittlich; *(party)* Fortschritts– ‖ *s* Fortschrittler –in *mf*
prog′ress report′ *s* Tätigkeitsbericht *m*
prohibit [pro'hɪbɪt] *tr* verbieten
prohibition [ˌpro·ə'bɪʃən] *s* Verbot *n; (hist)* Prohibition *f*
prohibitive [pro'hɪbɪtɪv] *adj (costs)* unertragbar; *(prices)* unerschwinglich
project ['prodʒekt] *s* Project *n,* Vorhaben *n* ‖ [prə'dʒekt] *tr (light, film)* projizieren; *(plan)* vorhaben ‖ *intr* vorspringen, vorragen
projectile [prə'dʒektɪl] *s (fired from a gun)* Projektil *n; (thrown object)* Wurfgeschoß *n*
projection [prə'dʒekʃən] *s (jutting out)* Vorsprung *m,* Vorbau *m; (cin)* Projektion *f*
projector [prə'dʒektər] *s* Projektor *m*
proletarian [ˌprolɪ'terɪ·ən] *adj* proletarisch ‖ *s* Proletarier –in *mf*
proletariat [ˌprolɪ'terɪ·ət] *s* Proletariat *n*
proliferate [prə'lɪfəˌret] *intr* sich stark vermehren
prolific [prə'lɪfɪk] *adj* fruchtbar
prolix [pro'lɪks] *adj* weitschweifig

prologue ['prolɔg] *s* Prolog *m*
prolong [pro'lɔŋ] *tr* verlängern
promenade [ˌpramɪ'ned] *s* Promenade *f* ‖ *intr* promenieren
promenade′ deck′ *s* Promenadendeck *n*
prominent ['pramɪnənt] *adj* hervorragend, prominent; *(chin)* vorstehend
promiscuity [ˌpramɪs'kju·ɪti] *s* Promiskuität *f*
promiscuous [pro'mɪskju·əs] *adj* unterschiedslos; *(sexually)* locker
promise ['pramɪs] *s* Versprechen *n* ‖ *tr* versprechen
prom′ising *adj (thing)* aussichtsreich; *(person)* vielversprechend
prom′issory note′ ['pramɪˌsori] *s* Eigenwechsel *m*
promontory ['pramənˌtori] *s* Landspitze *f*
promote [prə'mot] *tr (in rank)* befördern; *(a cause)* fördern; *(a pupil)* versetzen; *(wares)* werben für
promoter [prə'motər] *s* Förderer –in *mf; (sport)* Veranstalter –in *mf*
promotion [prə'moʃən] *s (in rank)* Beförderung *f; (of a cause)* Förderung *f; (of a pupil)* Versetzung *f*
prompt [prampt] *adj* prompt ‖ *tr* veranlassen; *(theat)* soufflieren *(dat)*
prompter ['pramptər] *s* Souffleur *m,* Souffleuse *f*
prompt′er's box′ *s* Souffleurkasten *m*
promptness ['pramptnɪs] *s* Pünktlichkeit *f*
promulgate [pro'mʌlget] *tr* bekanntmachen
prone [pron] *adj*—**be p. to** neigen zu; **in the p. position** auf Anschlag liegend
prong [prɔŋ] *s (of a fork)* Zinke *f; (of a deer)* Sprosse *f*
pronoun ['pronaun] *s* Fürwort *n*
pronounce [prə'nauns] *tr (enunciate)* aussprechen; **p. sentence** das Strafausmaß festsetzen; **p. s.o.** *(e.g., guilty, insane, man and wife)* erklären für
pronouncement [prə'naunsmənt] *s (announcement)* Erklärung *f; (of a sentence)* (jur) Verkündung *f*
pronunciation [prəˌnʌnsɪ'eʃən] *s* Aussprache *f*
proof [pruf] *adj*—**p. against** (fig) gefeit gegen; **90 p. 45** prozentig ‖ *s* Beweis *m; (phot)* Probebild *n; (typ)* Korrekturbogen *m*
proof′read′er *s* Korrektor –in *mf*
prop [prap] *s* Stütze *f;* **props** (coll) Beine *pl; (theat)* Requisiten *pl* ‖ *v (pret & pp* **propped;** *ger* **propping)** *tr* stützen; **p. oneself up** sich aufstemmen; **p. up** abstützen
propaganda [ˌprapə'gændə] *s* Propaganda *f*
propagate ['prapəˌget] *tr* fortpflanzen; *(fig)* propagieren ‖ *intr* sich fortpflanzen
pro·pel [prə'pel] *v (pret & pp* **–pelled;** *ger* **–pelling)** *tr* antreiben
propeller [prə'pelər] *s* (aer) Propeller *m; (naut)* Schraube *f*
propensity [prə'pensɪti] *s* Neigung *f*

proper ['prɑpər] *adj* passend; (*way, time*) richtig; (*authority*) zuständig; (*strictly so-called*) selbst, e.g., **Germany p.** Deutschland selbst

properly ['prɑpərli] *adj* gehörig

prop'er name' *s* Eigenname *m*

property ['prɑpərti] *s* Eigentum *n;* (*land*) Grundstück *n;* (*quality*) Eigenschaft *f*

prop'erty dam'age *s* Sachschaden *m*

prop'erty tax' *s* Grundsteuer *f*

prophecy ['prɑfɪsi] *s* Prophezeiung *f*

prophe·sy ['prɑfɪ‚saɪ] *v* (*pret & pp -sied*) *tr* prophezeien

prophet ['prɑfɪt] *s* Prophet *m*

prophetess ['prɑfɪtɪs] *s* Prophetin *f*

prophylactic [‚profɪ'læktɪk] *adj* prophylaktisch || *s* Prophylaktikum *n;* (*condom*) Präservativ *n*

propitiate [prə'pɪʃɪ‚et] *tr* versöhnen

propitious [prə'pɪʃəs] *adj* günstig

prop'jet' *s* Flugzeug *n* mit Turboprop

proportion [prə'porʃən] *s* Verhältnis *n;* **in p.** to im Verhältnis zu; **out of p.** to in keinem Verhältnis zu; **proportions** Proportionen *pl* || *tr* bemessen; **well proportioned** gut proportioniert

proposal [prə'pozəl] *s* Vorschlag *m;* (*of marriage*) Heiratsantrag *m*

propose [prə'poz] *tr* vorschlagen; (*intend*) beabsichtigen; **p. a toast** to e–n Toast ausbringen auf (*acc*) || *intr* (**to**) e–n Heiratsantrag machen (*dat*)

proposition [‚prɑpə'zɪʃən] *s* Vorschlag *m;* (*log, math*) Lehrsatz *m* || *tr* ansprechen

propound [prə'paʊnd] *tr* vortragen

proprietor [prə'praɪ‚ətər] *s* Inhaber *m*

proprietress [prə'praɪ‚ətrɪs] *s* Inhaberin *f*

propriety [prə'praɪ‚əti] *s* Anstand *m;* **proprieties** Anstandsformen *pl*

propulsion [prə'pʌlʃən] *s* Antrieb *m*

prorate [pro'ret] *tr* anteilmäßig verteilen

prosaic [pro'ze‚ɪk] *adj* prosaisch

proscribe [pro'skraɪb] *tr* proskribieren

prose [proz] *adj* Prosa– || *s* Prosa *f*

prosecute ['prɑsɪ‚kjut] *tr* verfolgen

prosecutor ['prɑsɪ‚kjutər] *s* Ankläger –in *mf*

proselytize ['prɑsɪlə‚taɪz] *intr* Anhänger gewinnen

prose' writ'er *s* Prosaiker –in *mf*

prosody ['prɑsədi] *s* Silbenmessung *f*

prospect ['prɑspekt] *s* Aussicht *f;* (*person*) Interessent –in *mf;* **hold out the p. of s.th.** etw in Aussicht stellen || *intr* (**for**) schürfen (nach)

prospector ['prɑspektər] *s* Schürfer *m*

prospectus [prə'spektəs] *s* Prospekt *m*

prosper ['prɑspər] *intr* gedeihen

prosperity [prɑs'perɪti] *s* Wohlstand *m*

prosperous ['prɑspərəs] *adj* wohlhabend

prostitute ['prɑstɪ‚t(j)ut] *s* Prostituierte *f* || *tr* prostituieren

prostrate ['prɑstret] *adj* hingestreckt; (*exhausted*) erschöpft || *tr* niederwerfen; (*fig*) niederzwingen

prostration [prɑs'treʃən] *s* Niederwerfen *n;* (*abasement*) Demütigung *f*

protagonist [pro'tægənɪst] *s* Protagonist *m,* Hauptfigur *f*

protect [prə'tekt] *tr* (be)schützen; (*interests*) wahrnehmen; **p. from** schützen vor (*dat*)

protection [prə'tekʃən] *s* (**from**) Schutz *m* (vor *dat*)

protector [prə'tektər] *s* Beschützer *m*

protein ['protin] *s* Protein *n*

protest ['protest] *s* Protest *m* || [pro'test] *tr & intr* protestieren

Protestant ['prɑtɪstənt] *adj* protestantisch || *s* Protestant –in *mf*

protocol ['protə‚kal] *s* Protokoll *n*

proton ['protan] *s* Proton *n*

protoplasm ['protə‚plæzəm] *s* Protoplasma *n*

prototype ['protə‚taɪp] *s* Prototyp *m*

protozo·an [‚protə'zo‚ən] *s* (**-a** [ə]) Einzeller *m*

protract [pro'trækt] *tr* hinziehen

protrude [pro'trud] *intr* hervorstehen

proud [praʊd] *adj* (**of**) stolz (auf *acc*)

prove [pruv] *v* (*pret* **proved**; *pp* **proved & proven** ['pruvən]) *tr* beweisen; **p. a failure** sich nicht bewähren; **p. one's worth** sich bewähren || *intr*—**p. right** zutreffen; **p. to be** sich erweisen als

proverb ['prɑvərb] *s* Sprichwort *n*

proverbial [prə'vʌrbɪ‚əl] *adj* sprichwörtlich

provide [prə'vaɪd] *tr* (*s.th.*) besorgen; **p. s.o. with s.th.** j–n mit etw versorgen || *intr*—**p. for** (*e.g., a family*) sorgen für; (*e.g., a special case*) vorsehen; (*the future*) voraussehen

provid'ed *adj* (**with**) versehen (mit) || *conj* vorausgesetzt, daß

Providence ['prɑvɪdəns] *s* Vorsehung *f*

providential [‚prɑvɪ'dentʃəl] *adj* von der Vorsehung beschlossen

provid'ing *conj* vorausgesetzt, daß

province ['prɑvɪns] *s* (*district*) Provinz *f;* (*special field*) Ressort *n*

provision [prə'vɪʒən] *s* (*providing*) Versorgung *f;* (*stipulation*) Bestimmung *f;* **make p. for** Vorsorge treffen für; **provisions** Lebensmittelvorräte *pl* || *tr* (mil) verpflegen

provisional [prə'vɪʒənəl] *adj* vorläufig

provi·so [prə'vaɪzo] *s* (**-sos & -soes**) Vorbehalt *m*

provocation [‚prɑvə'keʃən] *s* Provokation *f*

provocative [prə'vakətɪv] *adj* aufreizend

provoke [prə'vok] *tr* (*a person*) provozieren; (*e.g., laughter*) erregen

provok'ing *adj* ärgerlich

prow [praʊ] *s* Bug *m*

prowess ['praʊ‚ɪs] *s* Tapferkeit *f*

prowl [praʊl] *intr* herumschleichen

prowl' car' *s* Streifenwagen *m*

prowler ['praʊlər] *s* mutmaßlicher Einbrecher *m*

proximity [prak'sɪmɪti] *s* Nähe *f*

proxy ['prɑksi] *s* Stellvertreter –in *mf;* **by p.** in Vertretung

prude [prud] *s* prüde Person *f*
prudence [ˈprudəns] *s* Klugheit *f*; *(caution)* Vorsicht *f*
prudent [ˈprudənt] *adj* klug; *(cautious)* umsichtig
prudish [ˈprudɪʃ] *adj* prüde
prune [prun] *s* Zwetschge *f* ‖ *tr* stuzen
Prussia [ˈprʌʃɪ·ə] *s* Preußen *n*
Prussian [ˈprʌʃən] *adj* preußisch ‖ *s* Preuße *m*, Preußin *f*
pry [praɪ] *v* (*pret & pp* pried) *tr*—pry open aufbrechen; **pry s.th. out of s.o.** etw aus j-m herauspressen ‖ *intr* herumschnüffeln; **pry into** seine Nase stecken in (*acc*)
P.S. [ˈpiˈes] *s* (*postscript*) NS
psalm [sɑm] *s* Psalm *m*
pseudo– [ˈsudo] *adj* Pseudo–, falsch
pseudonym [ˈsudənɪm] *s* Deckname *m*
psyche [ˈsaɪki] *s* Psyche *f*
psychiatrist [saɪˈkaɪ·ətrɪst] *s* Psychiater –in *mf*
psychiatry [saɪˈkaɪ·ətri] *s* Psychiatrie *f*
psychic [ˈsaɪkɪk] *adj* psychisch ‖ *s* Medium *n*
psychoanalysis [ˌsaɪko·əˈnælɪsɪs] *s* Psychoanalyse *f*
psychoanalyze [ˌsaɪkoˈænəˌlaɪz] *tr* psychoanalytisch behandeln
psychologic(al) [ˌsaɪkoˈlɑdʒɪk(əl)] *adj* psychologisch
psychologist [saɪˈkɑlədʒɪst] *s* Psychologe *m*, Psychologin *f*
psychology [saɪˈkɑlədʒi] *s* Psychologie *f*
psychopath [ˈsaɪko ˌpæθ] *s* Psychopath –in *mf*
psycho·sis [saɪˈkosɪs] *s* (**–ses** [siz]) Psychose *f*
psychotic [saɪˈkɑtɪk] *adj* psychotisch ‖ *s* Psychosekranke *mf*
pto'main poi'soning [ˈtomen] *s* Fleischvergiftung *f*
pub [pʌb] *s* Kneipe *f*
puberty [ˈpjubərti] *s* Pubertät *f*
public [ˈpʌblɪk] *adj* öffentlich ‖ *s* Öffentlichkeit *f*, Publikum *n*
pub'lic address' sys'tem *s* Lautsprecheranlage *f*
publication [ˌpʌblɪˈkeʃən] *s* Veröffentlichung *f*
pub'lic domain' *n*—**in the p. d.** gemeinfrei
publicity [pʌbˈlɪsɪti] *s* Publizität *f*
publicize [ˈpʌblɪ ˌsaɪz] *tr* bekanntmachen
pub'lic opin'ion *s* öffentliche Meinung *f*
pub'lic-opin'ion poll' *s* öffentliche Meinungsumfrage *f*
pub'lic pros'ecutor *s* Staatsanwalt *m*
pub'lic rela'tions *spl* Kontaktpflege *f*
pub'lic serv'ant *s* Staatsangestellte *mf*
pub'lic util'ity *s* öffentlicher Versorgungsbetrieb *m*
publish [ˈpʌblɪʃ] *tr* veröffentlichen
publisher [ˈpʌblɪʃər] *s* Verleger –in *mf*
pub'lishing house' *s* Verlag *m*
puck [pʌk] *s* Puck *m*
pucker [ˈpʌkər] *tr* (*the lips*) spitzen ‖ *intr*—**p. up** den Mund spitzen
pudding [ˈpudɪŋ] *s* Pudding *m*

puddle [ˈpʌdəl] *s* Pfütze *f*, Lache *f*
pudgy [ˈpʌdʒi] *adj* dicklich
puerile [ˈpjuˌərɪl] *adj* knabenhaft
puff [pʌf] *s* (*on a cigarette*) Zug *m*; (*of smoke*) Rauchwölkchen *n*; (*on sleeves*) Puff *m* ‖ *tr* (*e.g., a cigar*) paffen; **p. oneself up** sich aufblähen; **p. out** ausblasen ‖ *intr* keuchen; **p. on** (*a pipe, cigar*) paffen an (*dat*)
pugilist [ˈpjudʒɪlɪst] *s* Faustkämpfer *m*
pugnacious [pʌgˈneʃəs] *adj* kampflustig
pug-nosed [ˈpʌg ˌnozd] *adj* stupsnasig
puke [pjuk] *s* (sl) Kotze *f* ‖ *intr* (sl) kotzen
pull [pul] *s* Ruck *m*; (*influence*) Beziehungen *pl*; (*of gravity*) Anziehungskraft *f* ‖ *tr* ziehen; (*a muscle*) zerren; (*proof*) (typ) abziehen; **p. down** (*e.g., a shade*) herunterziehen; (*a building*) niederreißen; **p. off** (coll) zuwegebringen; **p. oneself together** sich zusammennehmen; **p. out** (*weeds*) herausreißen; **p. up** (*e.g., a chair*) heranrücken ‖ *intr* (on) ziehen (an *dat*); **p. back** sich zurückziehen; **p. in** (*arrive*) ankommen; **p. out** (*depart*) abfahren; **p. over to the side** an den Straßenrand heranfahren; **p. through** durchkommen; **p. up** (*e.g., in a car*) vorfahren
pullet [ˈpulɪt] *s* Hühnchen *n*
pulley [ˈpuli] *s* Rolle *f*; (*pulley block*) Flaschenzug *m*
pull'o'ver *s* Pullover *m*
pulmonary [ˈpʌlmə ˌneri] *adj* Lungen–
pulp [pʌlp] *s* Brei *m*; (*to make paper*) Papierbrei *m*; **beat to a p.** windelweich schlagen
pulpit [ˈpulpɪt] *s* Kanzel *f*
pulsate [ˈpʌlset] *intr* pulsieren
pulsation [pʌlˈseʃən] *s* Pulsieren *n*
pulse [pʌls] *s* Puls *m*; **take s.o.'s p.** j–m den Puls fühlen
pulverize [ˈpʌlvə ˌraɪz] *tr* pulverisieren
pum'ice stone' [ˈpʌmɪs] *s* Bimsstein *m*
pum·mel [ˈpʌməl] *v* (*pret & pp* **–mel[l]ed;** *ger* **–mel[l]ing**) *tr* mit der Faust schlagen
pump [pʌmp] *s* Pumpe *f*; (*shoe*) Pump *m* ‖ *tr* pumpen; (*for information*) ausfragen; **p. up** (*a tire*) aufpumpen
pump'han'dle *s* Pumpenschwengel *m*
pumpkin [ˈpʌmpkɪn] *s* Kürbis *m*
pun [pʌn] *s* Wortspiel *n* ‖ *v* (*pret & pp* **punned;** *ger* **punning**) *intr* ein Wortspiel machen
punch [pʌntʃ] *s* Faustschlag *m*; (*to make holes*) Locher *m*; (*drink*) Punsch *m* ‖ *tr* mit der Faust schlagen; (*a card*) lochen; (*a punch clock*) stechen
punch' bowl' *s* Punschschüssel *f*
punch' card' *s* Lochkarte *f*
punch' clock' *s* Kontrolluhr *f*
punch'-drunk' *adj* von Faustschlägen betäubt
punch'ing bag' *s* Punchingball *m*
punch' line' *s* Pointe *f*
punctilious [pʌŋkˈtɪlɪ·əs] *adj* förmlich
punctual [ˈpʌŋktʃʊ·əl] *adj* pünktlich
punctuate [ˈpʌŋktʃu ˌet] *tr* interpunktieren

punctuation [ˌpʌŋktʃuˈeʃən] s Interpunktion f

punctua′tion mark′ s Satzzeichen n

puncture [ˈpʌŋktʃər] s Loch n ‖ tr durchstechen; **p. a tire** e–e Reifenpanne haben

punc′ture-proof′ adj pannensicher

pundit [ˈpʌndɪt] s Pandit m

pungent [ˈpʌndʒənt] adj beißend, scharf

punish [ˈpʌnɪʃ] tr (be)strafen

punishment [ˈpʌnɪʃmənt] s Strafe f, Bestrafung f; (educ) Strafarbeit f

punk [pʌŋk] adj (sl) mies; **I feel p.** mir ist mies ‖ s (sl) Rocker m

punster [ˈpʌnstər] s Wortspielmacher m

puny [ˈpjuni] adj kümmerlich, winzig

pup [pʌp] s junger Hund m

pupil [ˈpjupəl] s Schüler –in mf; (of the eye) Pupille f

puppet [ˈpʌpɪt] s Marionette f

pup′pet gov′ernment s Marionettenregierung f

pup′pet show′ s Marionettentheater n

puppy [ˈpʌpi] s Hündchen n

pup′py love′ s Jugendliebe f

purchase [ˈpʌrtʃəs] s Kauf m; (leverage) Hebelwirkung f ‖ tr kaufen

pur′chasing pow′er s Kaufkraft f

pure [pjur] adj (& fig) rein

purgative [ˈpʌrgətɪv] s Abfuhrmittel n

purgatory [ˈpʌrgəˌtori] s Fegefeuer n

purge [pʌrdʒ] s (pol) Säuberungsaktion f ‖ tr reinigen; (pol) säubern

puri·fy [ˈpjurɪˌfaɪ] v (pret & pp –fied) tr reinigen, läutern

puritan [ˈpjurɪtən] adj puritanisch ‖ **Puritan** s Puritaner –in mf

purity [ˈpjurɪti] s Reinheit f

purloin [pərˈlɔɪn] tr entwenden

purple [ˈpʌrpəl] adj purpurn ‖ s Purpur m

purport [ˈpʌrport] s Sinn m ‖ [pərˈport] tr vorgeben; (imply) besagen

purpose [ˈpʌrpəs] s Absicht f; (goal) Zweck m; **on p.** absichtlich; **to no p.** ohne Erfolg

purposely [ˈpʌrpəsli] adv absichtlich

purr [pʌr] s Schnurren n ‖ intr schnurren

purse [pʌrs] s Beutel m; (handbag) Handtasche f ‖ tr—**p. one's lips** den Mund spitzen

purse′ strings′ spl—**hold the p.** über das Geld verfügen

pursue [pərˈs(j)u] tr (a person; a plan, goal) verfolgen; (studies, profession) betreiben; (pleasures) suchen

pursuit [pərˈs(j)ut] s Verfolgung f; **in hot p.** hart auf den Fersen

pursuit′ plane′ s Jäger m

purvey [pərˈve] tr liefern, versorgen

pus [pʌs] s Eiter m

push [puʃ] s Schub m; (mil) Offensive f ‖ tr (e.g., a cart) schieben; (jostle) stoßen; (a button) drücken auf (acc); **p. around** (coll) schlecht behandeln; **p. aside** beiseite schieben; (curtains) zurückschlagen; **p. one's way through** sich durchdrängen; **p. through** durchsetzen ‖ intr drängen

push′ but′ton s Druckknopf m

push′ cart′ s Verkaufskarren m

push′o′ver s (snap) (coll) Kinderspiel n; (sucker) Gimpel m; (easy opponent) leicht zu besiegender Gegner m

push′-up′ s (gym) Liegestütz m

pushy [ˈpuʃi] adj zudringlich

puss [pus] s (cat) Mieze f; (face) (sl) Fresse f

pussy [ˈpʌsi] adj eit(e)rig ‖ [ˈpusi] s Mieze f

puss′y wil′low s Salweide f

put [put] v (pret & pp **put**; ger **putting**) tr (stand) stellen; (lay) legen; (set) setzen; **feel put out** ungehalten sein; **put across to** beibringen (dat); **put down** (a load) abstellen; (a rebellion) niederschlagen; (in writing) aufschreiben; **put in** (e.g., a windowpane) einsetzen; (e.g., a good word) einlegen; (time) (on) verwenden (auf acc); **put off** (a person) hinhalten; (postpone) aufschieben; **put on** (clothing) anziehen; (a hat) aufsetzen; (a ring) anstecken; (an apron) umbinden; (the brakes) betätigen; (to cook) ansetzen; (a play) aufführen; **put on an act** sich in Szene setzen; **put oneself into** sich hineindenken in (acc); **put oneself out** sich [dat] Umstände machen; **put on its feet again** (com) auf die Beine stellen; **put s.o. on to s.th.** j–n auf etw [acc] bringen; **put out** (a fire) löschen; (lights) auslöschen; (throw out) herauswerfen; (a new book) herausbringen; **put out of action** kampfunfähig machen; **put over on s.o.** j–n übers Ohr hauen; **put through** durchsetzen; (a call) (telp) herstellen; **put (s.o.) through to** (telp) j–n verbinden mit; **put to good use** gut verwenden; **put up** (erect) errichten; (bail) stellen; (for the night) unterbringen; **put up a fight** sich zur Wehr setzen; **put up to** anstiften zu; **to put it mildly** gelinde gesagt ‖ intr—**put on** sich verstellen; **put out to sea** (said of a ship) in See gehen; **put up with** sich abfinden mit

put′-on′ adj vorgetäuscht ‖ s (affectation) Affektiertheit f; (parody) Jux m

put-put [ˈpʌtˈpʌt] s Tacktack n ‖ intr—**p. along** knattern

putrid [ˈpjutrɪd] adj faul(ig)

putt [pʌt] tr & intr (golf) putten

putter [ˈpʌtər] s (golf) Putter m ‖ intr—**p. around** herumwursteln

put·ty [ˈpʌti] s Kitt m ‖ v (pret & pp –tied) tr (ver)kitten

put′ty knife′ s Spachtel m & f

put′-up job′ s abgekartete Sache f

puzzle [ˈpʌzəl] s Rätsel n; (game) Geduldspiel n ‖ tr verwirren; **be puzzled** verwirrt sein; **p. out** enträtseln ‖ intr—**p. over** tüfteln an (dat)

puzzler [ˈpʌzlər] s Rätsel n

puz′zling adj rätselhaft

PW [ˈpiˈdʌbəlˌju] s (**prisoner of war**) Kriegsgefangene mf

pygmy ['pɪgmɪ] s Pygmäe m, Pygmäin f

pylon ['paɪlən] s (entrance to Egyptian temple) Pylon m; (aer) Wendemarke f; (elec) Leitungsmast m

pyramid ['pɪrəmɪd] s Pyramide f

pyre [paɪr] s Scheiterhaufen m

Pyrenees [,pɪrɪ'niz] spl Pyrenäen pl

pyrotechnics [,paɪrə'tekmks] spl Feuerwerkskunst f, Pyrotechnik f

python ['paɪθən] s Pythonschlange f

pyx [pɪks] s (eccl) Pyxis f

Q

Q, q [kju] s siebzehnter Buchstabe des englischen Alphabets

quack [kwæk] s Quacksalber m, Kurpfuscher m || intr schnattern

quadrangle ['kwɑd,ræŋgəl] s Viereck n; (inner yard) Innenhof m, Lichthof m

quadrant ['kwɑdrənt] s Quadrant m

quadratic [kwɑd'rætɪk] adj quadratisch

quadruped ['kwɑdrʊ,ped] s Vierfüßer m

quadruple [kwɑd'rupəl] adj vierfach || s Vierfache n || tr vervierfachen || intr sich vervierfachen

quadruplets [kwɑd'ruplets] spl Vierlinge pl

quaff [kwɑf] tr in langen Zügen trinken

quagmire ['kwæg,maɪr] s Morast m

quail [kwel] s Wachtel f || intr verzagen

quaint [kwent] adj seltsam

quake [kwek] s Zittern n; (geol) Beben n || intr zittern; (geol) beben

Quaker ['kwekər] s Quäker –in mf

qualification [,kwɑlɪfɪ'keʃən] s (for) Qualifikation f (für)

quali-fy ['kwɑlɪ,faɪ] v (pret & pp –fied) tr qualifizieren; (modify) einschränken || intr sich qualifizieren

quality ['kwɑlɪtɪ] s (characteristic) Eigenschaft f; (grade) Qualität f

qualm [kwɑm] s Bedenken n

quandary ['kwɑndərɪ] s Dilemma n

quantity ['kwɑntɪtɪ] s Menge f, Quantität f; (math) Größe f; (pros) Silbenmaß n; **buy in q.** auf Vorrat kaufen

quan'tum the'ory ['kwɑntəm] s Quantentheorie f

quarantine ['kwɔrən,tin] s Quarantäne f || tr unter Quarantäne stellen

quar-rel ['kwɔrəl] s Streit m; **pick a q.** Händel suchen || v (pret & pp –rel[l]ed; ger –el[l]ing) intr (over) streiten (über acc or um)

quarrelsome ['kwɔrəlsəm] adj streitsüchtig, händelsüchtig

quar-ry ['kwɔrɪ] s Steinbruch m; (hunt) Jagdbeute f || v (pret & pp –ried) tr brechen

quart [kwɔrt] s Quart n

quarter ['kwɔrtər] s Viertel n; (of a city) Stadtviertel n; (of the moon) Mondviertel n; (of the sky) Himmelsrichtung f; (coin) Vierteldollar m; (econ) Quartal n; (sport) Viertelzeit f; **a q. after one** (ein) Viertel nach

eins; **a q. of an hour** e–e Viertelstunde f; **a q. to eight** dreiviertel acht, (ein) viertel vor acht; **at close quarters** im Nahkampf; **from all quarters** von überall; **give no q.** keinen Pardon geben; **quarters** (& mil) Unterkunft f, Quartier n || tr (lodge) einquartieren; (divide into four, tear into quarters) vierteilen || intr im Quartier liegen

quar'ter-deck' s Quarterdeck n

quar'terfi'nal s Zwischenrunde f

quar'ter-hour' s Viertelstunde f

quarterly ['kwɔrtərlɪ] adj vierteljährig; (econ) Quartals– || s Vierteljahresschrift f

quar'termas'ter s Quartiermeister m

Quar'termaster Corps' s Versorgungstruppen pl

quar'ter note' s (mus) Viertelnote f

quar'ter rest' s (mus) Viertelpause f

quartet [kwɔr'tet] s Quartett n

quartz [kwɔrts] s Quarz m

quash [kwɑʃ] tr niederschlagen

quatrain ['kwɑtren] s Vierzeiler m

quaver ['kwevər] s Zittern n; (mus) Triller m || intr zittern; (mus) trillern, tremolieren

queasy ['kwizɪ] adj übel

queen [kwin] s Königin f; (cards) Dame f

queen' bee' s Bienenkönigin f

queen' dow'ager s Königinwitwe f

queenly ['kwinlɪ] adj königlich

queen' moth'er s Königinmutter f

queer [kwɪr] adj sonderbar; (homosexual) schwul || s (homosexual) Schwule mf

queer' duck' s (coll) Unikum n

quell [kwel] tr unterdrücken

quench [kwentʃ] tr (thirst) löschen; (a fire) (aus)löschen

que-ry ['kwɪrɪ] s Frage f || v (pret & pp –ried) tr befragen; (cast doubt on) bezweifeln

quest [kwest] s Suche f; **in q. of** auf der Suche nach

question ['kwestʃən] s Frage f; **ask (s.o.) a q.** (j–m) e–e Frage stellen; **be out of the q.** außer Frage sein; **beyond q.** außer Frage; **call into q.** in Frage stellen; **call the q.** (parl) um Abstimmung bitten; **in q.** betreffend; **it is a q. of** (ger) es handelt sich darum zu (inf); **q. of time** Zeitfrage f; **that's an open q.** darüber läßt sich streiten; **there's no q. about it** darüber besteht kein Zweifel || tr be-

fragen; (said of the police) verhören; (cast doubt on) bezweifeln
questionable ['kwest/ənəbəl] adj fraglich, fragwürdig; (doubtful) zweifelhaft; (character) bedenklich
ques'tioning s Verhör n, Vernehmung f
ques'tion mark' s Fragezeichen n
questionnaire [‚kwest/ə'ner] s Frage-
bogen m
queue [kju] s Schlange f || intr—q. up
sich anstellen
quibble ['kwɪbəl] s Deutelei f || intr
(about) deuteln (an dat)
quibbler ['kwɪblər] s Wortklauber m
quick [kwɪk] adj schnell, fix || s—cut
to the q. bis ins Mark treffen
quicken ['kwɪkən] tr beschleunigen ||
intr sich beschleunigen
quick'lime' s gebrannter ungelöschter
Kalk m
quick' lunch' s Schnellimbiß m
quick'sand' s Treibsand m
quick'sil'ver s Quecksilber n
quick'-tem'pered adj jähzornig
quick'-wit'ted adj scharfsinnig
quiet ['kwaɪ-ət] adj ruhig; (person)
schweigsam; (still) still; (street) un-
belebt; **be q.!** sei still!; **keep q.**
schweigen || s Stille f || tr beruhigen
|| intr—q. down sich beruhigen; (said
of excitement, etc.) sich legen
quill [kwɪl] s Feder f, Federkiel m;
(of a porcupine) Stachel m
quilt [kwɪlt] s Steppdecke f || tr step-
pen
quince [kwɪns] s Quitte f
quince' tree' s Quittenbaum m
quinine ['kwaɪnaɪn] s Chinin n
quintessence [kwɪn'tesəns] s Inbegriff
m
quintet [kwɪn'tet] s Quintett n
quintuplets [kwɪn'tʌplets] spl Fünf-
linge pl
quip [kwɪp] s witziger Seitenhieb m ||
v (pret & pp quipped; ger quipping)
tr witzig sagen || intr witzeln

quire [kwaɪr] s (bb) Lage f
quirk [kwark] s Eigenart f; (subterfuge) Ausflucht f; (sudden change)
plötzliche Wendung f
quit [kwɪt] adj quitt; **let's call it quits!**
(coll) Strich drunter! || v (pret & pp
quit & quitted; ger quitting) tr aufgeben; (e.g., a gang) abspringen von;
q. it! hören Sie damit auf! || intr
aufhören; (at work) seine Stellung
aufgeben
quite [kwaɪt] adv recht, ganz; **q. a disappointment** e-e ausgesprochene Enttäuschung f; **q. recently** in jüngster
Zeit; **q. the reverse** genau das Gegenteil
quitter ['kwɪtər] s Schlappmacher m
quiver ['kwɪvər] s Zittern n; (to hold
arrows) Köcher m || intr zittern
quixotic [kwɪks'atɪk] adj überspannt
quiz [kwɪz] s Prüfung f; (game) Quiz
n || v (pret & pp quizzed; ger quiz-
zing) tr ausfragen; **q. s.o. on s.th.**
j-n etw abfragen
quiz'mas'ter s Quizonkel m
quiz' show' s Quizshow f
quizzical ['kwɪzɪkəl] adj (puzzled)
verwirrt; (strange) seltsam; (mocking) spöttisch
quoit [kwɔɪt] s Wurfring m
quondam ['kwandæm] adj ehemalig
Quon'set hut' ['kwɑnsət] s Nissen-
hütte f
quorum ['kworəm] s beschlußfähige
Anzahl f
quota ['kwotə] s Quote f, Anteil m;
(work) Arbeitsleistung f
quotation [kwo'te/ən] s Zitat n; (price)
Notierung f
quota'tion marks' spl Anführungszei-
chen pl
quote [kwot] s Zitat n; (of prices)
Notierung f || tr zitieren; (prices)
notieren || interj—q. ... unquote Be-
ginn des Zitats! ... Ende des Zitats!
quotient ['kwo/ənt] s Quotient m

R

R, r [ɑr] s achtzehnter Buchstabe des
englischen Alphabets
rabbet ['ræbɪt] s Falz m || tr falzen
rabbi ['ræbaɪ] s Rabbiner m
rabbit ['ræbɪt] s Kaninchen n
rabble ['ræbəl] s Pöbel m
rab'ble-rous'er s Volksaufwiegler –in
mf
rabid ['ræbɪd] adj rabiat; (dog) toll-
wütig
rabies ['rebiz] s Tollwut f
raccoon [ræ'kun] s Waschbär m
race [res] s Rasse f; (contest) Wettren-
nen n; (fig) Wettlauf m || tr um die
Wette laufen mit; (in a car) um die
Wette fahren mit; (a horse) rennen
lassen; (an engine) hochjagen || intr

rennen; (on foot) um die Wette laufen; (in a car) um die Wette fahren
race' driv'er s Rennfahrer –in mf
race' horse' s Rennpferd n
racer ['resər] s (person) Wettfahrer
–in mf; (car) Rennwagen m; (in
speed skating) Schnelläufer –in mf
race' ri'ot s Rassenaufruhr m
race' track' s Rennbahn f
racial ['re/əl] adj rassisch, Rassen-
rac'ing s Rennsport m
racism ['resɪzəm] s Rassenhaß m
rack [ræk] s (shelf) Regal n, Ablage f;
(for clothes, bicycles, hats) Ständer
m; (for luggage) Gepäcknetz n; (for
fodder) Futterraufe f; (for torture)
Folter f; (toothed bar) Zahnstange f;

go to r. and ruin völlig zugrunde gehen; put to the r. auf die Folter spannen || *tr (with pain)* quälen; r. one's brains (over) sich *[dat]* den Kopf zerbrechen (über *acc)*

racket ['rækɪt] *s (noise)* Krach *m; (illegal business)* Schiebergeschäft *n;* (tennis) Rakett *n*

racketeer [ˌrækɪ'tɪr] *s* Schieber –in *mf*

racketeer'ing *s* Schiebertum *n*

rack' rail'way *s* Zahnradbahn *f*

racy ['resi] *adj (off-color)* schlüpfrig; *(vivacious, pungent)* rassig

radar ['redɑr] *s* Radar *n*

ra'darscope' *s* Radarschirm *m*

radial ['redɪ-əl] *adj* radial

radiance ['redɪ-əns] *s* Strahlung *f*

radiant ['redɪ-ənt] *adj (with)* strahlend (vor *dat); (phys)* Strahlungs-

radiate ['redɪ‚et] *tr & intr* ausstrahlen

radiation [ˌredɪ'eʃən] *s* Strahlung *f*

radia'tion belt' *s* Strahlungsgürtel *m*

radia'tion treat'ment *s* Bestrahlung *f;* give r. treatment to bestrahlen

radiator ['redɪ‚etər] *s* Heizkörper *m;* (aut) Kühler *m*

ra'diator cap' *s* Kühlerverschluß *m*

radical ['rædɪkəl] *adj* radikal || *s* Radikale *mf*

radically ['rædɪkəli] *adv* von Grund auf

radi·o ['redɪ‚o] *s* (–os) Radio *n,* Rundfunk *m;* go on the r. im Rundfunk sprechen || *tr* funken

ra'dioac'tive *adj* radioaktiv

ra'dio announc'er *s* Rundfunkansager –in *mf*

ra'dio bea'con *s* (aer) Funkfeuer *n*

ra'dio beam' *s* Funkleitstrahl *m*

ra'dio broad'cast *s* Rundfunksendung *f*

radiocar'bon dat'ing *s* Radiokarbonmethode *f*

ra'diofre'quency *s* Hochfrequenz *f*

radiogram ['redɪ‚o‚græm] *s* Radiogramm *n*

radiologist [ˌredɪ'alədʒɪst] *s* Röntgenologe *m,* Röntgenologin *f*

radiology [redɪ'alədʒi] *s* Röntgenologie *f*

ra'dio net'work *s* Rundfunknetz *n*

ra'dio op'erator *s* Funker –in *mf*

radioscopy [ˌredɪ'askəpi] *s* Durchleuchtung *f*

ra'dio set' *s* Radioapparat *m*

ra'dio sta'tion *s* Rundfunkstation *f*

radish ['rædɪʃ] *s* Radieschen *n*

radium ['redɪ‚əm] *s* Radium *n*

radi·us ['redɪ‚əs] *s* (–i [‚aɪ] & –uses) Halbmesser *m;* (anat) Speiche *f;* within a r. of in e–m Umkreis von

raffish ['ræfɪʃ] *adj* gemein, niedrig

raffle ['ræfəl] *s* Tombola *f* || *tr*—r. off in e–r Tombola verlosen

raft [ræft] *s* Floß *n;* a r. of (coll) ein Haufen *m*

rafter ['ræftər] *s* Dachsparren *m;* rafters Sparrenwerk *n*

rag [ræg] *s* Lumpen *m;* chew the rag (sl) quasseln

ragamuffin ['rægə‚mʌfɪn] *s* Lump *m*

rag' doll' *s* Stoffpuppe *f*

rage [redʒ] *s* Wut *f;* all the r. letzter

Schrei *m;* be the r. die große Mode sein; fly into a r. in Wut geraten || *intr* wüten, toben

ragged ['rægɪd] *adj* zerlumpt, lumpig

rag'man *s* (–men) Lumpenhändler *m*

ragout [ræ'gu] *s* Ragout *n*

rag'weed' *s* Ambrosiapflanze *f*

raid [red] *s* Beutezug *m; (by police)* Razzia *f;* (mil) Überfall *m* || *tr* überfallen; e–e Razzia machen auf *(acc)*

raider ['redər] *s* (naut) Kaperkreuzer *m;* raiders (mil) Kommandotruppe *f*

rail [rel] *s* Geländerstange *f;* (naut) Reling *f;* (rr) Schiene *f;* by r. per Bahn ||—r. at beschimpfen

rail'head' *s* Schienenkopf *m*

rail'ing *s* Geländer *n;* (naut) Reling *f*

rail'road' *s* Eisenbahn *f* || *tr (a bill)* durchpeitschen

rail'road cross'ing *s* Bahnübergang *m*

rail'road embank'ment *s* Bahndamm *m*

rail'road sta'tion *s* Bahnhof *m*

rail'road tie' *s* Schwelle *f*

rail'way' *adj* Eisenbahn- || *s* Eisenbahn *f*

raiment ['remənt] *s* Kleidung *f*

rain [ren] *s* Regen *m;* it looks like r. es sieht nach Regen aus; r. or shine bei jedem Wetter || *tr*—r. cats and dogs Bindfäden regnen; r. out verregnen || *intr* regnen

rainbow ['ren‚bo] *s* Regenbogen *m*

rain'coat' *s* Regenmantel *m*

rain'drop' *s* Regentropfen *m*

rain'fall' *s* Regenfall *m; (amount of rain)* Regenmenge *f*

rain' gut'ter *s* Dachrinne *f*

rain' pipe' *s* Fallrohr *n*

rain'proof' *adj* regenfest, regendicht

rainy ['reni] *adj* regnerisch; *(e.g., day, weather)* Regen–; save money for a r. day sich *[dat]* e–n Notpfennig aufsparen

rain'y sea'son *s* Regenzeit *f*

raise [rez] *s* Lohnerhöhung *f;* (in poker) Steigerung *f* || *tr (lift)* heben, erheben; *(increase)* erhöhen, steigern; *(erect)* aufstellen; *(children)* großziehen; *(a family)* ernähren, *(grain, vegetables)* anbauen; *(animals)* züchten; *(dust)* aufwirbeln; *(money, troops)* aufbringen; *(blisters)* ziehen; *(a question)* aufwerfen; *(hopes)* erwecken; *(a laugh, smile)* hervorrufen; *(the ante)* steigern; *(a siege)* aufheben; *(from the dead)* auferwecken; r. Cain (or hell) Krach schlagen; r. the arm *(before striking)* mit dem Arm ausholen; r. the price of verteuern; r. to a higher power potenzieren || *intr (in poker)* höher wetten

raisin ['rezən] *s* Rosine *f*

rake [rek] *s* Rechen *m; (person)* Wüstling *m* || *tr* rechen; *(with gunfire)* bestreichen; r. in *(money)* kassieren; r. together (or up) zusammenrechen

rake'-off' *s* (coll) Gewinnanteil *m*

rakish ['rekɪʃ] *adj (dissolute)* liederlich; *(jaunty)* schmissig

ral·ly ['ræli] *s (meeting)* Massenversammlung *f; (recovery)* Erholung *f;*

(mil) Umgruppierung *f* ‖ *v* (*pret & pp* –lied) *tr* (wieder) sammeln ‖ *intr* sich (wieder) sammeln; (*recover*) sich erholen

ram [ræm] *s* Schafbock *m* ‖ *v* (*pret & pp* **rammed;** *ger* **ramming**) *tr* rammen; **ram s.th. down s.o.'s throat** j–m etw aufdrängen

ramble ['ræmbəl] *intr*—**r. about** herumwandern; **r. on** daherreden

ramification [‚ræmɪfɪ'keʃən] *s* Verzweigung *f*

ramp [ræmp] *s* Rampe *f*

rampage ['ræmpedʒ] *s* Toben *n*, Wüten *n*; **go on a r.** toben, wüten

rampant ['ræmpənt] *adj*—**be r.** grassieren

rampart ['ræmpart] *s* Wall *m*, Ringwall *m*

ram'rod' *s* Ladestock *m*; (*cleaning rod*) Reinigungsstock *m*

ram'shack'le *adj* baufällig

ranch [rænt∫] *s* Ranch *f*

rancid ['rænsɪd] *adj* ranzig

random ['rændəm] *adj* zufällig, Zufalls–; **at r.** aufs Geratewohl

range [rendʒ] *s* (row) Reihe *f*; (*mountains*) Bergkette *f*; (*stove*) Herd *m*; (*for firing practice*) Schießplatz *m*; (*of a gun*) Schießweite *f*; (*distance*) Reichweite *f*; (*mus*) Umfang *m*; **at a r. of** in e–r Entfernung von; **at close r.** auf kurze Entfernung; **come within s.o.'s r.** j–m vor den Schuß kommen; **out of r.** außer Reichweite; (*in shooting*) außer Schußweite; **within r.** in Reichweite; (*in shooting*) in Schußweite ‖ *tr* reihen ‖ *intr*—**r. from ... to** sich bewegen zwischen (*dat*) ... und

range' find'er *s* Entfernungsmesser *m*

ranger ['rendʒər] *s* Förster *m*; **rangers** Stoßtruppen *pl*

rank [ræŋk] *adj* (*rancid*) ranzig; (*smelly*) stinkend; (*absolute*) kraß; (*excessive*) übermäßig; (*growth*) üppig ‖ *s* Rang *m*; **according to r.** standesgemäß; **person of r.** Standesperson *f* ‖ *tr* einreihen, rangieren; **be ranked as** gelten als ‖ *intr* rangieren; **r. above** stehen über (*dat*); **r. among** zählen zu; **r. below** stehen unter (*dat*); **r. with** mitzählen zu

rank' and file' *s* die breite Masse

rank'ing of'ficer *s* Rangälteste *mf*

rankle ['ræŋkəl] *tr* nagen an (*dat*) ‖ *intr* nagen

ransack ['rænsæk] *tr* durchstöbern

ransom ['rænsəm] *s* Lösegeld *n* ‖ *tr* auslösen

rant [rænt] *intr* schwadronieren

rap [ræp] *s* (*on the door*) Klopfen *n*; (*blow*) Klaps *m*; **not give a rap for** husten auf (*acc*); **take the rap den** Kopf hinhalten; **there was a rap on the door** es klopfte an der Tür ‖ *v* (*pret & pp* **rapped;** *ger* **rapping**) *tr* (*strike*) schlagen; (*criticize*) tadeln ‖ *intr* (*talk freely*) offen reden; (*on*) klopfen (an *dat*)

rapacious [rə'peʃəs] *adj* raffgierig; (*animal*) raubgierig

rape [rep] *s* Vergewaltigung *f* ‖ *tr* vergewaltigen

rapid ['ræpɪd] *adj* rapid(e); (*river*) reißend ‖ **rapids** *spl* Stromschnelle *f*

rap'id-fire' *adj* Schnell–; (mil) Schnellfeuer–

rap'id trans'it *s* Nahschnellverkehr *m*

rapier ['repɪ.ər] *s* Rapier *n*

rapist ['repɪst] *s* sexueller Gewaltverbrecher *m*

rap' ses'sion *s* zwanglose Diskussion *f*

rapt [ræpt] *adj* (*attention*) gespannt; (*in thought*) vertieft

rapture ['ræptʃər] *s* Entzückung *f*; **go into raptures** in Entzücken geraten

rare [rer] *adj* selten; (culin) halbgar

rare' bird' *s* (fig) weißer Rabe *m*

rare•fy ['rerɪ‚faɪ] *v* (*pret & pp* –**fied**) *tr* verdünnen

rarely ['rerli] *adv* selten

rarity ['rerrti] *s* Rarität *f*

rascal ['ræskəl] *s* Bengel *m*

rash [ræʃ] *adj* vorschnell, unbesonnen ‖ *s* Ausschlag *m*

rasp [ræsp] *s* (*sound*) Kratzlaut *m*; (*tool*) Raspel *f* ‖ *tr* raspeln

raspberry ['ræz‚beri] *s* Himbeere *f*

rat [ræt] *s* Ratte *f*; (*deserter*) (sl) Überläufer –in *mf*; (*informer*) (sl) Spitzel *m*; (*scoundrel*) (sl) Gauner *m*; **smell a rat** (coll) den Braten riechen ‖ *intr*—**rat on** (sl) verpetzen

ratchet ['ræt∫ɪt] *s* (*wheel*) Sperrad *n*; (*pawl*) Sperrklinke *f*

rate [ret] *s* Satz *m*; (*for mail, freight*) Tarif *m*; **at any r.** auf jeden Fall; **at the r. of** (*a certain speed*) mit der Geschwindigkeit von; (*a certain price*) zum Preis von; **at the r. of a dozen per week** ein Dutzend pro Woche; **at this** (or **that**) **r.** bei diesem Tempo ‖ *tr* bewerten ‖ *intr* (coll) hochgeschätzt sein

rate' of exchange' *s* Kurs *m*

rate' of in'terest *s* Zinssatz *m*

rather ['ræðər] *adv* ziemlich; **I would r. wait** ich würde lieber warten; **r. ... than lieber ... als** ‖ *interj* na ob!

rati•fy ['rætɪ‚faɪ] *v* (*pret & pp* –**fied**) *tr* ratifizieren, bestätigen

rat'ing *s* Beurteilung *f*; (mach) Leistung *f*; (mil) Dienstgrad *m*; (sport) Bewertung *f*

ra•tio ['reʃ(ɪ)‚o] *s* (–**tios**) Verhältnis *n*

ration ['ræʃən], ['reʃən] *s* Ration *f*; **rations** (mil) Verpflegung *f* ‖ *tr* rationieren

ra'tion card' *s* Bezugsschein *m*

ra'tioning *s* Rationierung *f*

rational ['ræʃənəl] *adj* vernünftig

rationalize ['ræʃənə‚laɪz] *tr & intr* rationalisieren

rat' poi'son *s* Rattengift *n*

rat' race' *s* (fig) Hetzjagd *f*

rattle ['rætəl] *s* Geklapper *n*; (*toy*) Klapper *f*, Schnarre *f* ‖ *tr* (*confuse*) verwirren; **get s.o. rattled** j–n aus dem Konzept bringen; **r. off** herunterschnarren; **r. the dishes** mit dem Geschirr klappern ‖ *intr* klappern; (*said of a machine gun*) knattern;

(*said of windows*) klirren; **r.** on daherplappern

rat'tlebrain' *s* Hohlkopf *m*

rat'tlesnake' *s* Klapperschlange *f*

rat'tletrap' *s* (coll) Kiste *f*, Karre *f*

rat'trap' *s* Rattenfalle *f*

raucous [ˈrɔkəs] *adj* heiser

ravage [ˈrævɪdʒ] *s* Verwüstung *f*, Verheerung *f* || *tr* verwüsten, verheeren

rave [rev] *s* (coll) Modeschrei *m* || *intr* irrereden; **r.** about schwärmen von

raven [ˈrevən] *adj* (*black*) rabenschwarz || *s* Kolkrabe *m*, Rabe *m*

ravenous [ˈrævənəs] *adj* rasend

ravine [rəˈvin] *s* Bergschlucht *f*

rav'ing *adj* (coll) toll || *adv*—**r.** mad tobsüchtig

ravish [ˈrævɪʃ] *tr* vergewaltigen

rav'ishing *adv* entzückend

raw [rɔ] *adj* roh; (*weather*) naßkalt; (*throat*) rauh; (*recruit*) unausgebildet; (*skin*) wundgerieben; (*leather*) ungegerbt; (*wool*) ungesponnen

raw'-boned' *adj* hager

raw' deal' *s* (sl) unfaire Behandlung *f*

raw'hide' *s* Rohhaut *f*

raw' mate'rial *s* Rohstoff *m*

ray [re] *s* Strahl *m*; (ichth) Rochen *m*; **ray of hope** Hoffnungsstrahl *m*

rayon [ˈre-ɑn] *adj* kunstseiden || *s* Kunstseide *f*, Rayon *s*

raze [rez] *tr* abtragen; **r. to the ground** dem Erdboden gleichmachen

razor [ˈrezər] *s* Rasiermesser *n*; (*safety razor*) Rasierapparat *m*

ra'zor blade' *s* Rasierklinge *f*

razz [ræz] *tr* (sl) aufziehen

re [ri] *prep* betreffs (*genit*)

reach [ritʃ] *s* Reichweite *f*; **beyond the r.** of s.o. für j—n unerreichbar; **out of r.** unerreichbar; **within easy r.** leicht zu erreichen; **within r.** in Reichweite || *tr* (*a goal, person, city, advanced age, an understanding*) erreichen; (*a certain amount*) sich belaufen auf (*acc*); (*a compromise*) schließen; (*an agreement*) treffen; (*e.g., the ceiling*) heranreichen an (*acc*); **r. out** ausstrecken || *intr* (*extend*) reichen, sich erstrecken; **r. for** greifen nach; **r. into one's pocket** in die Tasche greifen

react [riˈækt] *intr* (to) reagieren (auf *acc*); **r. upon** zurückwirken auf (*acc*)

reaction [riˈækʃən] *s* Reaktion *f*

reactionary [riˈækʃənˌɛri] *adj* reaktionär || *s* Reaktionär –in *mf*

reac'tion time' *s* Reaktionszeit *f*

reactor [riˈæktər] *s* Reaktor *m*

read [rid] *v* (*pret & pp* read [red]) *tr* lesen; **r. a paper on** referieren über (*acc*); **r. off** verlesen; **r. over** durchlesen; **r. to** vorlesen (*dat*) || *intr* lesen; (*said of a passage*) lauten; (*said of a thermometer*) zeigen; **r. up on** studieren

readable [ˈridəbəl] *adj* lesbar

reader [ˈridər] *s* (*person*) Leser –in *mf*; (*book*) Lesebuch *m*

readily [ˈrɛdɪli] *adv* gern(e)

readiness [ˈrɛdɪnɪs] *s* Bereitwilligkeit *f*; (*preparedness*) Bereitschaft *f*

read'ing *s* (*act*) Lesen *n*; (*material*) Lektüre *f*; (*version*) Lesart *f*; (eccl, parl) Lesung *f*

read'ing glass'es *spl* Lesebrille *f*

read'ing lamp' *s* Leselampe *f*

read'ing room' *s* Lesesaal *m*

readjustment [ˌri-əˈdʒʌstmənt] *s* Umstellung *f*

read-y [ˈrɛdi] *adj* (*done*) fertig; **be r.** (*stand in readiness*) in Bereitschaft stehen; **get r.** sich fertig (or bereit) machen; **get s.th. r.** etw fertigstellen; **r. for** bereit zu; **r. for use** gebrauchsfertig; **r. to** (*inf*) bereit zu (*inf*) || *v* (*pret & pp* –ied) *tr* fertigmachen

read'y cash' *s* flüssiges Geld *n*

read'y-made' *adj* von der Stange

read'y-made' clothes' *spl* Konfektion *f*

reaffirm [ˌri-əˈfʌrm] *tr* nochmals beteuern

real [ˈri-əl] *adj* wirklich; (*genuine*) echt; (*friend*) wahr

re'al estate' *s* Immobilien *pl*

re'al-estate' a'gent *s* Immobilienmakler –in *mf*

re'al-estate tax' *s* Grundsteuer *f*

realist [ˈri-əlɪst] *s* Realist –in *mf*

realistic [ri-əˈlɪstɪk] *adj* wirklichkeitsnah, realistisch

reality [riˈælɪti] *s* Wirklichkeit *f*; **in r.** wirklich; **realities** (*facts*) Tatsachen *pl*

realize [ˈri-əˌlaɪz] *tr* einsehen; (*a profit*) erzielen; (*a goal*) verwirklichen; (*a good*) realisieren

really [ˈri-əli] *adv* wirklich; **not r.** eigentlich nicht

realm [rɛlm] *s* Königreich *n*; (fig) Reich *n*, Gebiet *n*; **within the r. of possibility** im Rahmen des Möglichen

Realtor [ˈri-əltər] *s* Immobilienmakler –in *mf*

ream [rim] *s* Ries *n* || *tr* ausbohren

reamer [ˈrimər] *s* Reibahle *f*

reap [rip] *tr* (*cut*) mähen; (& fig) ernten

reaper [ˈripər] *s* Mäher –in *mf*; (mach) Mähmaschine *f*

reappear [ˌri-əˈpɪr] *intr* wiederauftauchen, wiedererscheinen

rearmament [riˈɑrməmənt] *s* Wiederscheinen *s*

reappoint [ˌri-əˈpɔɪnt] *tr* wieder anstellen

rear [rir] *adj* hintere, rückwärtig || *s* Hinterseite *f*; (*of an army*) Nachhut *f*; (sl) Hintern *m*; **bring up the r.** den Schluß bilden; (mil) den Zug beschließen; **from the r.** von hinten; **to the r.** nach hinten; **to the r. march!** kehrt, marsch! || *tr* (*children*) aufziehen; (*animals*) züchten; (*a structure, one's head*) aufrichten || *intr* sich bäumen

rear' ad'miral *s* Konteradmiral *m*

rear' ax'le *s* Hinterachse *f*

rear' end' *s* (sl) Hintern *m*

rear' guard' *s* (mil) Nachhut *f*

rear' gun'ner *s* Heckschütze *m*

rearm [ri'ɑrm] *tr* wieder aufrüsten

rearmament [ri'ɑrməmənt] *s* Wiederaufrüstung *f*

rearrange [,ri·ə'rendʒ] *tr* umstellen

rear′ seat′ *s* Hintersitz *m*

rear′-view mir′ror *s* Rückspiegel *m*

rear′-wheel drive′ *s* Hinterradantrieb *m*

rear′ win′dow *s* (aut) Heckfenster *n*

reason ['rizən] *s* Vernunft *f*; (*cause*) Grund *m*; **by r.** of auf Grund (*genit*); **for this r.** aus diesem Grund; **listen to r.** sich belehren lassen; **not listen to r.** sich [*dat*] nichts sagen lassen; **not without good r.** nicht umsonst || **tr—r.** out durchdenken || **intr—r. with** vernünftig reden mit

reasonable ['rizənəbəl] *adj* (*person*) vernünftig; (*price*) solid; (*wares*) preiswert

reassemble [,ri·ə'sembəl] *tr* (*people*) wieder versammeln; (mach) wieder zusammenbauen || *intr* sich wieder sammeln

reassert [,ri·ə'sert] *tr* wieder behaupten

reassurance [,ri·ə'ʃurəns] *s* Beruhigung *f*

reassure [ri·ə'ʃur] *tr* beruhigen

reawaken [,ri·ə'wekən] *tr* wieder erwecken || *intr* wieder erwachen

rebate ['ribet] *s* Rabatt *m*

re·bel ['rebəl] *adj* Rebellen- || *s* Rebell -in *mf* || ['rɪ'bɛl] *v* (*pret* & *pp* -belled; *ger* -belling) *intr* rebellieren

rebellion [rɪ'bɛljən] *s* Aufstand *m*, Rebellion *f*

rebellious [rɪ'bɛljəs] *adj* aufständisch

rebirth ['ribʌrθ] *s* Wiedergeburt *f*

rebore [ri'bor] *tr* nachbohren

rebound ['rɪ,baʊnd] *s* Rückprall *m* || [ri'baʊnd] *intr* zurückprallen

rebroad·cast [ri'brɔd,kæst] *s* Wiederholungssendung *f* || *v* (*pret* & *pp* -cast & -casted) *tr* nochmals übertragen

rebuff [rɪ'bʌf] *s* Zurückweisung *f* || *tr* schroff abweisen

re·build [ri'bɪld] *v* (*pret* & *pp* -built) *tr* wiederaufbauen; (mach) wiederherholen; (*confidence*) wiederherstellen

rebuke [rɪ'bjuk] *s* Verweis *m* || *tr* verweisen

re·but [rɪ'bʌt] *v* (*pret* & *pp* -butted; *ger* -butting) *tr* widerlegen

rebuttal [rɪ'bʌtəl] *s* Widerlegung *f*

recall [rɪ'kɔl], ['rikɔl] *s* (*recollection*) Erinnerungsvermögen *n*; (com) Zurücknahme *f*; (dipl, pol) Abberufung *f*; **beyond r.** unwiderruflich || [rɪ'kɔl] *tr* (*remember*) sich erinnern an (*dat*); (*an ambassador*) abberufen; (*workers*) zurückrufen; (mil) wiedereinberufen

recant [rɪ'kænt] *tr* & *intr* (öffentlich) widerrufen

re·cap ['ri,kæp] *s* Zusammenfassung *f* || *v* (*pret* & *pp* -capped; *ger* -capping) *tr* zusammenfassen; (*a tire*) runderneuern

recapitulate [,rikə'pɪtʃə,let] *tr* zusammenfassen

recapitulation [,rikə,pɪtʃə'leʃən] *s* Rekapitulation *f*, Zusammenfassung *f*

re·cast ['ri,kæst] *s* Umguß *m* || [ri'kæst] *v* (*pret* & *pp* -cast) *tr* umgießen; (*a sentence*) umarbeiten; (theat) neubesetzen

recede [rɪ'sid] *intr* zurückgehen; (*become more distant*) zurückweichen

reced′ing *adj* (*forehead, chin*) fliehend

receipt [rɪ'sit] *s* Quittung *f*; acknowledge r. of den Empfang bestätigen (*genit*); **receipts** Eingänge *pl* || *tr* quittieren

receive [rɪ'siv] *tr* bekommen, erhalten; (*a guest*) empfangen; (*pay*) beziehen; (rad) empfangen

receiver [rɪ'sivər] *s* Empfänger -in *mf*; (jur) Zwangsverwalter -in *mf*; (telp) Hörer *m*

receiv′ership′ *s* Zwangsverwaltung *f*

recent ['risənt] *adj* neu, jung; **in r. years** in den letzten Jahren; **of r. date** neueren Datums

recently ['risəntli] *adv* kürzlich

receptacle [rɪ'septəkəl] *s* Behälter *m*; (elec) Steckdose *f*

reception [rɪ'sepʃən] *s* (& rad) Empfang *m*

recep′tion desk′ *s* Empfang *m*

receptionist [rɪ'sepənɪst] *s* Empfangsdame *f*; (med) Sprechstundenhilfe *f*

receptive [rɪ'septɪv] *adj* (**to**) aufgeschlossen (für)

recess [rɪ'ses], ['rises] *s* (*alcove*) Nische *f*; (*cleft*) Einschnitt *m*; (at school) Pause *f*; (jur) Unterbrechung *f*; (parl) Ferien *pl* || [rɪ'ses] *tr* (*place in a recess*) versenken || *intr* (until) sich vertagen (auf acc)

recession [rɪ'seʃən] *s* Rezession *f*, Rückgang *m*

recharge [rɪ'tʃɑrdʒ] *tr* wieder aufladen

recipe ['resɪ,pi] *s* Rezept *n*

recipient [rɪ'sɪpɪ·ənt] *s* Empfänger -in *mf*

reciprocal [rɪ'sɪprəkəl] *adj* gegenseitig

reciprocate [rɪ'sɪprə,ket] *tr* sich erkenntlich zeigen für || *intr* sich erkenntlich zeigen

reciprocity [,resɪ'prɑsɪti] *s* Gegenseitigkeit *f*

recital [rɪ'saɪtəl] *s* Vortrag *m*

recite [rɪ'saɪt] *tr* vortragen

reckless ['reklɪs] *adj* (*careless of consequences*) unbekümmert; (*lacking caution*) leichtsinnig; (*negligent*) fahrlässig

reck′less driv′ing *s* rücksichtsloses Fahren *n*

reckon ['rekən] *tr* (*count*) rechnen; (*compute*) (coll) schätzen || *intr* rechnen; (coll) schätzen; **r. on** rechnen auf (*acc*); **r. with** (*deal with*) abrechnen mit; (*take into consideration*) rechnen mit

reck′oning *s* (*accounting*) Abrechnung *f*; (*computation*) Berechnung *f*; (aer, naut) Besteck *n*

reclaim [rɪ'klem] *tr* (*demand back*) zurückfordern; (*from wastes*) rückgewinnen; (*land*) urbar machen

reclamation [ˌrɛklə'meʃən] *s* (*of land*) Urbarmachung *f*

recline [rɪ'klaɪn] *intr* ruhen; **r. against** sich lehnen an (*acc*); **r. in** (*a chair*) sich zurücklehnen in (*dat*)

recluse ['rɛklus] *s* Einsiedler –in *mf*

recognition [ˌrɛkəg'nɪʃən] *s* Wiedererkennung *f*; (*acknowledgement*) Anerkennung *f*; **gain r.** zur Geltung kommen

recognizable [ˌrɛkəg'naɪzəbəl] *adj* erkennbar

recognize ['rɛkəg,naɪz] *tr* (**by**) erkennen (an *dat*); **r. as** anerkennen als

recoil ['rɪkɔɪl] *s* (*of a rifle*) Rückstoß *m*; (arti) Rücklauf *m* ‖ [rɪ'kɔɪl] *intr* (*in fear*) zurückfahren; (*from, e.g., a challenge*) zurückschrecken vor (*dat*); (*said of a rifle*) zurückstoßen; (arti) zurücklaufen

recoilless [rɪ'kɔɪllɪs] *adj* rückstoßfrei

recollect [ˌrɛkə'lɛkt] *tr* sich erinnern an (*acc*)

recollection [ˌrɛkə'lɛkʃən] *s* Erinnerung *f*

recommend [ˌrɛkə'mɛnd] *tr* empfehlen

recommendation [ˌrɛkəmən'deʃən] *s* Empfehlung *f*

recompense ['rɛkəm,pɛns] *s* (**for**) Vergütung *f* (für) ‖ *tr* vergüten

reconcile ['rɛkən,saɪl] *tr* (**with**) versöhnen (mit); **become reconciled** sich versöhnen; **r. oneself to** sich abfinden mit

reconciliation [ˌrɛkən,sɪlɪ'eʃən] *s* Versöhnung *f*, Aussöhnung *f*

recondite ['rɛkən,daɪt] *adj* (*deep*) tiefgründig; (*obscure*) dunkel

recondition [ˌrikən'dɪʃən] *tr* wiederinstandsetzen

reconnaissance [rɪ'kɑnɪsəns] *s* Aufklärung *f*

reconnoiter [ˌrɛkə'nɔɪtər] *tr* erkunden ‖ *intr* aufklären

reconquer [ri'kɑŋkər] *tr* zurückerobern

reconquest [ri'kɑŋkwɛst] *s* Zurückeroberung *f*

reconsider [ˌrikən'sɪdər] *tr* noch einmal erwägen

reconstruct [ˌrikən'strʌkt] *tr* (*rebuild*) wiederaufbauen; (*make over*) umbauen; (*e.g., events of a case*) rekonstruieren

record ['rɛkərd] *adj* Rekord– ‖ *s* (*highest achievement*) Rekord *m*; (*document*) Akte *f*, Protokoll *n*; (*documentary evidence*) Aufzeichnung *f*; (mus) Schallplatte *f*; **have a criminal r.** vorbestraft sein; **keep a r. of** Buch führen über (*acc*); **make a r. of** zu Protokoll nehmen; **off the r.** inoffiziell; **on r.** bisher registriert; **set a r.** e–n Rekord aufstellen ‖ [rɪ'kɔrd] *tr* (*in writing*) aufzeichnen; (*officially*) protokollieren; (*on tape or disk*) aufnehmen ‖ *intr* Schallplatten aufnehmen

rec'ord chang'er *s* Plattenwechsler *m*

recorder [rɪ'kɔrdər] *s* Protokollführer –in *mf*; (*device*) Zähler *m*; (*on tape*

or disk) Aufnahmegerät; (mus) Blockflöte *f*

rec'ord hold'er *s* Rekordler –in *mf*

record'ing *adj* aufzeichnend; (*on tape or disk*) Aufnahme– ‖ *s* Aufzeichnung *f*; (*on tape or disk*) Tonaufnahme *f*

rec'ord play'er *s* Plattenspieler *m*

recount ['ri,kaunt] *s* Nachzählung *f* ‖ [ri'kaunt] *tr* (*count again*) nachzählen ‖ [rɪ'kaunt] *tr* (*relate*) im einzelnen erzählen

recoup [rɪ'kup] *tr* (*losses*) wieder einbringen; (*a fortune*) wiedererlangen; (*reimburse*) entschädigen

recourse [rɪ'kors], ['rikors] *s* (**to**) Zuflucht *f* (zu); (jur) Regreß *m*; **have r. to** seine Zuflucht nehmen zu

recover [rɪ'kʌvər] *tr* (*get back*) wiedererlangen; (*losses*) wiedereinbringen; (*e.g., a spent rocket*) bergen; (*one's balance*) wiederfinden; (*e.g., a chair*) neu beziehen ‖ *intr* (**from**) sich erholen (von)

recovery [rɪ'kʌvəri] *s* Wiedererlangung *f*, Rückgewinnung *f*; (*of health*) Genesung *f*; (*of a rocket*) Bergung *f*

recreation [ˌrɛkri'eʃən] *s* Erholung *f*

recrea'tion room' *s* Unterhaltungsraum *m*

recruit [rɪ'krut] *s* Rekrut *m* ‖ (& mil) rekrutieren; **be recruited from** sich rekrutieren aus

recruit'ing of'ficer *s* Werbeoffizier *m*

recruitment [rɪ'krutmənt] *s* Rekrutierung *f*; (mil) Rekrutenaushebung *f*

rectangle ['rɛk,tæŋgəl] *s* Rechteck *n*

rectangular [rɛk'tæŋgjələr] *adj* rechteckig

rectifier ['rɛktə,faɪər] *s* Berichtiger *m*; (elec) Gleichrichter *m*

recti·fy ['rɛktɪ,faɪ] *v* (*pret & pp* –fied) *tr* berichtigen; (elec) gleichrichten

rector ['rɛktər] *s* Rektor *m*

rectory ['rɛktəri] *s* Pfarrhaus *n*

rec·tum ['rɛktəm] *s* (–ta [tə]) Mastdarm *m*

recumbent [rɪ'kʌmbənt] *adj* liegend

recuperate [rɪ'k(j)upə,ret] *intr* sich (wieder) erholen

re·cur [rɪ'kʌr] *v* (*pret & pp* –curred; *ger* –curring) *intr* wiederkehren

recurrence [rɪ'kʌrəns] *s* Wiederkehr *f*

red [rɛd] *adj* (**redder; reddest**) rot ‖ *s* Rot *n*, Röte *f*; **be in the red** in den Roten Zahlen stecken; **Red** (pol) Rote *mf*; **see red** wild werden

red' ant' *s* rote Waldameise *f*

red'bird' *s* Kardinal *m*

red'blood'ed *adj* lebensprühend

red'breast' *s* Rotkehlchen *n*

red' cab'bage *s* Rotkohl *m*

red' car'pet *s* (fig) roter Teppich *m*

red' cent' *s*—**not give a r. for** keinen roten Heller geben für

red'-cheeked' *adj* rotbäckig

Red' Cross', **the** *s* das Rote Kreuz

redden ['rɛdən] *tr* röten, rot machen ‖ *intr* erröten, rot werden

reddish ['rɛdɪʃ] *adj* rötlich

redecorate [ri'dɛkə,ret] *tr* neu dekorieren

redeem [rɪ'dim] *tr* zurückkaufen; (*a pawned article, promise*) einlösen; **r. oneself** seine Ehre wiederherstellen

redeemable [rɪ'diməbəl] *adj* (fin) ablösbar, kündbar

Redeemer [rɪ'dimər] *s* Erlöser *m*

redemption [rɪ'dempʃən] *s* Rückkauf *m*, Wiedereinlösung *f*; (relig) Erlösung *f*

red'-haired' *adj* rothaarig

red'-hand'ed *adj*—**catch s.o. r.** j–n auf frischer Tat ertappen

red'head' *s* Rotkopf *m*

red' her'ring *s* Bückling *m*; (fig) Ablenkungsmanöver *n*

red'-hot' *adj* glühend heiß, rotglühend

redirect [,ridɪ'rɛkt] *tr* umdirigieren

rediscover [,ridɪs'kʌvər] *tr* wiederentdecken

red'-let'ter day' *s* Glückstag *m*

red' light' *s* rotes Licht *n*

red'-light' dis'trict *s* Bordellviertel *n*

red' man' *s* Rothaut *f*

redness ['rednɪs] *s* Röte *f*

re·do ['ri'du] *v* (*pret* –**did**; *pp* –**done**) *tr* neu machen; (*redecorate*) renovieren

redolent ['redələnt] *adj* (**with**) duftend (**nach**)

redoubt [rɪ'daut] *s* Redoute *f*

redound [rɪ'daund] *intr*—**r. to** gereichen zu

red' pep'per *s* spanischer Pfeffer *m*

redress [rɪ'drɛs] *s* Wiedergutmachung *f* || *tr* wiedergutmachen

Red' Rid'inghood' *s* Rotkäppchen *n*

red'skin' *s* Rothaut *f*

red' tape' *s* Amtsschimmel *m*

reduce [rɪ'd(j)us] *tr* reduzieren, verringern; (*prices*) herabsetzen; (math) (ab)kürzen

reduction [rɪ'dʌkʃən] *s* Verminderung *f*; (*gradual reduction*) Abbau *m*; (*in prices*) Absetzung *f*; (*in weight*) Abnahme *f*

redundant [rɪ'dʌndənt] *adj* überflüssig

red' wine' *s* Rotwein *m*

red'wing' *s* Rotdrossel *f*

red'wood' *s* Rotholz *n*

reecho [ri'ɛko] *tr* wiederhallen lassen || *intr* wiederhallen

reed [rid] *s* Schilf *n*; (*in mouthpiece*) Rohrblatt *n*; (*of metal*) Zunge *f*; (*pastoral pipe*) Hirtenflöte *f*

reedit [ri'ɛdɪt] *tr* neu herausgeben

reeducate [ri'ɛdʒu,ket] *tr* umerziehen

reef [rif] *s* Riff *n*; (naut) Reff *n* || *tr* (naut) reffen

reek [rik] *intr* (**of**) riechen (**nach**)

reel [ril] *s* (*sway*) Taumeln *n*; (*for cables*) Trommel *f*; (angl, cin) Spule *f*; (min, naut) Haspel *f* || *tr* (angl, cin) spulen; (min, naut) haspeln; **r. in** (*a fish*) einholen; **r. off** abhaspeln; (fig) herunterrasseln || *intr* taumeln

reelect [,ri·ɪ'lɛkt] *tr* wiederwählen

reelection [,ri·ɪ'lɛkʃən] *s* Wiederwahl *f*

reenlist [,ri·ɛn'lɪst] *tr* wieder anwerben || *intr* sich weiterverpflichten

reenlistment [,ri·ɛn'lɪstmənt] *s* Weiterverpflichtung *f*

reentry [ri'ɛntri] *s* Wiedereintritt *m*

reexamination [,ri·ɛg,zæmɪ'neʃən] *s* Nachprüfung *f*

re·fer [,rɪ'fʌr] *v* (*pret* & *pp* –**ferred**; *ger* –**ferring**) *tr*—**r. s.o. to** j–n verweisen an (*acc*) || *intr*—**r. to** hinweisen auf (*acc*); (*e.g., to an earlier correspondence*) sich beziehen auf (*acc*)

referee [,rɛfə'ri] *s* (box) Ringrichter *m*; (sport) Schiedsrichter *m* || *tr* als Schiedsrichter fungieren bei || *intr* als Schiedsrichter fungieren

reference ['rɛfərəns] *s* (**to**) Hinweis *m* (auf *acc*); (*person or document*) Referenz *f*; **in r. to** in Bezug auf (*acc*); **make r. to** hinweisen auf (*acc*)

ref'erence li'brary *s* Handbibliothek *f*

ref'erence work' *s* Nachschlagewerk *n*

referen·dum [,rɛfə'rɛndəm] *s* (–**da** [də]) Volksentscheid *m*

referral [rɪ'fʌrəl] *s* (**to**) Zuweisung *f* (**an** *acc*, **auf** *acc*); **by r.** auf Empfehlung

refill ['rifɪl] *s* Nachfüllung *f*; (*for a pencil, ball-point pen*) Ersatzmine *f* || [ri'fɪl] *tr* nachfüllen

refine [rɪ'faɪn] *tr* (*metal*) läutern; (*oil, sugar*) raffinieren; (fig) verfeinern

refinement [rɪ'faɪnmənt] *s* Läuterung *f*; (*of oil, sugar*) Raffination *f*; (fig) Verfeinerung *f*

refinery [rɪ'faɪnəri] *s* Raffinerie *f*

reflect [rɪ'flɛkt] *tr* (& fig) widerspiegeln || *intr* (*throw back rays*) reflektieren; (**on**) nachdenken (über *acc*); **r. on** (*comment on*) sich äußern über (*acc*); (*bring reproach on*) ein schlechtes Licht werfen auf (*acc*)

reflection [rɪ'flɛkʃən] *s* (*e.g., of light*) Reflexion *f*; (*reflected image*) Spiegelbild *n*; (*thought*) Überlegung *f*; **that's no r. on you** das färbt nicht auf Sie ab

reflector [rɪ'flɛktər] *s* Reflektor *m*

reflex ['riflɛks] *s* Reflex *m*

reflexive [rɪ'flɛksɪv] *adj* (gram) reflexiv || *s* Reflexivform *f*

reforestation [,rifɔrɪs'teʃən] *s* Aufforstung *f*

reform [rɪ'fɔrm] *s* Reform *f* || *tr* reformieren, verbessern || *intr* sich bessern

reformation [,rɛfər'meʃən] *s* Besserung *f*; **Reformation** Reformation *f*

reformatory [rɪ'fɔrmə,tori] *s* Besserungsanstalt *f*

reformer [rɪ'fɔrmər] *s* Reformator –in *m*

reform' school' *s* Besserungsanstalt *f*

refraction [rɪ'frækʃən] *s* Ablenkung *f*

refrain [rɪ'fren] *s* Kehrreim *m* || *intr*—**r. from** sich enthalten (*genit*); **r. from** (*ger*) es unterlassen zu (*inf*)

refresh [rɪ'frɛʃ] *tr* erfrischen; (*the memory*) auffrischen

refresh'er course' [rɪ'frɛʃər] *s* Auffrischungskurs *m*

refresh'ing *adj* erfrischend

refreshment [rɪ'freʃmənt] *s* Erfrischung *f*

refresh'ment stand' *s* Erfrischungsstand *m*

refrigerant [rɪ'frɪdʒərənt] *s* Kühlmittel *n*

refrigerate [rɪ'frɪdʒə‚ret] *tr* kühlen

refrigerator [rɪ'frɪdʒə‚retər] *s* Kühlschrank *m*; *(walk-in type)* Kühlraum *m*

refrig'erator car' *s* (rr) Kühlwagen *m*

re•fuel [ri'fjul] *v (pret & pp* **–fuel[l]ed;** *ger* **–fuel[l]ing)** *tr* auftanken ‖ *intr* tanken

refuge ['refjudʒ] *s* Zuflucht *f*; **take r. in** *(in)* (sich) flüchten in *(acc)*

refugee [‚refju'dʒi] *s* Flüchtling *m*

refugee' camp' *s* Flüchtlingslager *n*

refund ['rifʌnd] *s* Zurückzahlung *f* ‖ [rɪ'fʌnd] *tr (pay back)* zurückzahlen ‖ [rɪ'fʌnd] *tr (fund again)* neu fundieren

refurnish [rɪ'fʌrnɪʃ] *tr* neu möblieren

refusal [rɪ'fjuzəl] *s* Ablehnung *f*

refuse ['refjus] *s* Abfall *m* ‖ [rɪ'fjuz] *tr* ablehnen; **r. to** *(inf)* sich weigern zu *(inf)*

refutation [‚refju'teʃən] *s* Widerlegung *f*

refute [rɪ'fjut] *tr* widerlegen

regain [rɪ'gen] *tr* zurückgewinnen

regal ['rigəl] *adj* königlich

regale [rɪ'gel] *tr (delight)* ergötzen; *(entertain)* reichlich bewirten

regalia [rɪ'gelɪ‚ə] *spl* Insignien *pl*

regard [rɪ'gɑrd] *s (for)* Rücksicht *f (auf acc);* **best regards to** herzlichster Gruß an *(acc);* **have little r. for** wenig achten; **in every r.** in jeder Hinsicht; **in (or with) r. to** in Hinsicht auf *(acc);* **in this r.** in dieser Hinsicht; **without r. for** ohne Rücksicht auf *(acc)* ‖ *tr* betrachten; **as regards** in Bezug auf *(acc)*

regard'ing *prep* hinsichtlich *(genit)*

regardless [rɪ'gɑrdlɪs] *adv* (coll) ungeniert; **r. of** ungeachtet *(genit)*

regatta [rɪ'gætə] *s* Regatta *f*

regency ['ridʒənsi] *s* Regentschaft *f*

regenerate [rɪ'dʒenə‚ret] *tr* regenerieren

regent ['ridʒənt] *s* Regent –in *mf*

regicide ['redʒɪ‚saɪd] *s (act)* Königsmord *m; (person)* Königsmörder –in *mf*

regime [re'ʒim] *s* Regime *n*

regiment ['redʒɪmənt] *s* (mil) Regiment *n* ‖ ['ʒredʒɪ‚ment] *tr* reglementieren

regimental [‚redʒɪ'mentəl] *adj* Regiments–

region ['ridʒən] *s* Gegend *f*, Region *f*

regional ['ridʒənəl] *adj* regional

register ['redʒɪstər] *s* Register *n*, Verzeichnis *n* ‖ *tr* registrieren; *(students)* immatrikulieren; *(feelings)* erkennen lassen ‖ *intr* sich einschreiben lassen; *(at a hotel)* sich eintragen lassen

reg'istered let'ter *s* eingeschriebener Brief *m*

reg'istered nurse' *s* (staatlich) geprüfte Krankenschwester *f*

registrar ['redʒɪstrɑr] *s* Registrator –in *mf*

registration [‚redʒɪs'treʃən] *s (e.g., of firearms)* Registrierung *f; (for a course; at a hotel)* Anmeldung *f; (of a trademark)* Eintragung *f;* (aut) Zulassung *f;* (educ) Einschreibung *f*

registra'tion blank' *s* Meldeformular *n*

registra'tion fee' *s* Anmeldegebühr *f*

registra'tion num'ber *s* Registriernummer *f*

regression [rɪ'greʃən] *s* Rückgang *m*

regret [rɪ'gret] *s* (over) Bedauern *n* (über *acc*) ‖ *v (pret & pp* **–gretted;** *ger* **regretting)** *tr* bedauern; **I r. to say** es tut mir leid, sagen zu müssen

regrettable [rɪ'gretəbəl] *adj* bedauerlich

regroup [rɪ'grup] *tr* umgruppieren

regular ['regjələr] *adj (usual)* gewöhnlich; *(pulse, breathing, features, intervals)* regelmäßig; **r. army** stehendes Heer *n;* **r. guy** (coll) Pfundskerl *m;* **r. officer** Berufsoffizier –in *mf*

regularity [‚regjə'lærɪti] *s* Regelmäßigkeit *f*

regulate ['regjə‚let] *tr* regeln

regulation [‚regjə'leʃən] *s* Regelung *f; (rule)* Vorschrift *f*, Bestimmung *f;* **against regulations** vorschriftswidrig

regulator ['regjə‚letər] *s* Regler *m*

rehabilitate [‚rihə'bɪlɪ‚tet] *tr* rehabilitieren

rehash [rɪ'hæʃ] *tr* (coll) aufwärmen

rehearsal [rɪ'hɑrsəl] *s* Probe *f*

rehearse [rɪ'hɑrs] *tr & intr* proben

rehire [rɪ'haɪr] *tr* wiedereinstellen

reign [ren] *s* Regierung *f; (period of rule)* Regierungszeit *f* ‖ *intr* regieren; **r. over** herrschen über *(acc)*

reimburse [ri‚ɪm'bʌrs] *tr (costs)* rückerstatten; **r. s.o. for s.th.** j–m etw vergüten

rein [ren] *s* Zügel *m;* **give free r. to** die Zügel schießen lassen *(dat)* ‖ *tr* **—r. in** *(a horse)* parieren

reincarnation [‚ri‚ɪnkɑr'neʃən] *s* Reinkarnation *f*, Wiedergeburt *f*

rein'deer' *s* Rentier *n*

reinforce [‚ri‚ɪn'fors] *tr* verstärken

reinforced' concrete' *s* Stahlbeton *m*

reinforcement [‚ri‚ɪn'forsmənt] *s* Verstärkung *f; reinforcements* (mil) Verstärkungen *pl*

reinstate [‚ri‚ɪn'stet] *tr* (in) wiedereinsetzen (in *acc*)

reiterate [ri'ɪtə‚ret] *tr* wiederholen

reject ['ridʒekt] *s* Ausschußware *f* ‖ [rɪ'dʒekt] *tr* ablehnen, zurückweisen; *(a request, appeal)* abweisen

rejection [rɪ'dʒekʃən] *s* Ablehnung *f; (of a request, appeal)* Abweisung *f*

rejoice [rɪ'dʒɔɪs] *intr* frohlocken

rejoin [rɪ'dʒɔɪn] *tr (answer)* erwidern; *(a group)* sich wieder anschließen *(dat)*

rejoinder [rɪ'dʒɔɪndər] *s* Erwiderung *f;* (jur) Duplik *f*

rejuvenate [rɪ'dʒuvɪ‚net] *tr* verjüngen

rekindle [ri'kɪndəl] *tr* wieder anzünden; (fig) wieder entzünden

relapse [rɪ'læps] *s (& pathol)* Rückfall

m ‖ *intr* (**into**) wieder verfallen (in *acc*)

relate [rɪ'let] *tr* (*a story*) erzählen; (*connect*) verknüpfen; **r. s.th. to s.th.** etw auf etw [*acc*] beziehen ‖ *intr*—**r. to** in Beziehung stehen mit

relat'ed *adj* (*by blood*) verwandt; (*by marriage*) verschwägert; (*subjects*) benachbart

relation [rɪ'leʃən] *s* Beziehung *f*, Verhältnis *n*; (*relative*) Verwandte *mf*; **in r. to** in Bezug auf (*acc*); **relations** (*sex*) Verkehr *m*

rela'tionship' *s* (*connection*) Beziehung *f*; (*kinship*) Verwandtschaft *f*

relative ['relətɪv] *adj* relativ, verhältnismäßig; **r. to** bezüglich (*genit*) ‖ *s* Verwandte *mf*

rel'ative clause' *s* Relativsatz *m*

rel'ative pro'noun *s* Relativpronomen *n*

relativity [ˌrelə'tɪvɪti] *s* Relativität *f*

relax [rɪ'læks] *tr* auflockern; (*muscles*) entspannen ‖ *intr* sich entspannen

relaxation [ˌrilæk'seʃən] *s* Entspannung *f*; **r. of tension** Entspannung *f*

relay ['rile] *s* Relais *n*; (sport) Staffel *f* ‖ [rɪ'le] *v* (*pret & pp* **-layed**) *tr* übermitteln; (*through relay stations*) übertragen

re'lay race' *s* Staffellauf *m*

re'lay team' *s* Staffel *f*

release [rɪ'lis] *s* (**from**) Entlassung *f* (aus); (*of bombs*) Abwurf *m*; (*of news*) Mitteilung *f* ‖ *tr* entlassen; (*a film, book*) freigeben; (*bombs*) abwerfen; (*energy*) freisetzen; (*brakes*) lösen; **r. the clutch** auskuppeln

relegate ['relɪˌget] *tr* (**to**) verweisen (an *acc*); **r. to second position** auf den zweiten Platz verweisen

relent [rɪ'lent] *intr* (*let up*) nachlassen; (*yield*) sich erweichen lassen

relentless [rɪ'lentlɪs] *adj* (*tireless*) unermüdlich; (*unappeasable*) unerbittlich; (*never-ending*) unaufhörlich

relevant ['relɪvənt] *adj* sachdienlich

reliable [rɪ'laɪ-əbəl] *adj* zuverlässig

reliance [rɪ'laɪ-əns] *s* Vertrauen *n*

relic ['relɪk] *s* Reliquie *f*; **r. of the past** Zeuge *m* der Vergangenheit

relief [rɪ'lif] *s* Erleichterung *f*; (*for the poor*) Armenunterstützung *f*; (*replacement*) Ablösung *f*; (*sculpture*) Relief *n*; **on r.** von Sozialhilfe lebend; **bring r.** Linderung schaffen; **go on r.** stempeln gehen

relief' map' *s* Reliefkarte *f*

relieve [rɪ'liv] *tr* erleichtern; (*from guard duty*) ablösen; **r. oneself** seine Notdurft verrichten

religion [rɪ'lɪdʒən] *s* Religion *f*

religious [rɪ'lɪdʒəs] *adj* religiös; (*order*) geistlich

relinquish [rɪ'lɪŋkwɪʃ] *tr* aufgeben; **r. the right to s.th. to s.o.** j-m das Recht auf etw [*acc*] überlassen

relish ['relɪʃ] *s* (**for**) Genuß *m* (an *acc*); (*condiment*) Würze *f* ‖ *tr* genießen

reluctance [rɪ'lʌktəns] *s* Widerstreben *n*

reluctant [rɪ'lʌktənt] *adj* widerstrebend; **be r. to do s.th.** etw ungern tun

reluctantly [rɪ'lʌktəntli] *adv* ungern

re·ly [rɪ'laɪ] *v* (*pret & pp* **-lied**) *intr*—**r. on** sich verlassen auf (*acc*)

remain [rɪ'men] *s*—**remains** Überreste *pl*; (*corpse*) sterbliche Reste *pl* ‖ *intr* bleiben; (*at end of letter*) verbleiben; **r. behind** zurückbleiben; **r. seated** sitzenbleiben; **r. steady** (*said of prices*) sich behaupten

remainder [rɪ'mendər] *s* Restbestand *m*, Rest *m* ‖ *tr* verramschen

remark [rɪ'mark] *s* Bemerkung *f* ‖ *tr* bemerken

remarkable [rɪ'markəbəl] *adj* markant, bemerkenswert

remar·ry [ri'mæri] *v* (*pret & pp* **-ried**) *tr* sich wiederverheiraten mit ‖ *intr* sich wiederverheiraten

reme·dy ['remɪdi] *s* (**for**) Heilmittel *n* (für); (fig) (**for**) Gegenmittel *n* (gegen) ‖ *v* (*pret & pp* **-died**) *tr* abhelfen (*dat*); (*damage, shortage*) abheben

remember [rɪ'membər] *tr* sich erinnern an (*acc*); **r. me to** empfehlen Sie mich (*dat*) ‖ *intr* sich erinnern

remembrance [rɪ'membrəns] *s* Erinnerung *f*; **in r. of** zum Andenken an (*acc*)

remind [rɪ'maɪnd] *tr* (**of**) erinnern (an *acc*); **r. s.o. to** (*inf*) j-n mahnen zu (*inf*)

reminder [rɪ'maɪndər] *s* (*note*) Zettel *m*; (*from a creditor*) Mahnung *f*

reminisce [ˌremɪ'nɪs] *intr* in Erinnerungen schwelgen

remiss [rɪ'mɪs] *adj* nachlässig

remission [rɪ'mɪʃən] *s* Nachlaß *m*

re·mit [rɪ'mɪt] *v* (*pret & pp* **-mitted;** *ger* **-mitting**) *tr* (*in cash*) übersenden; (*by check*) überweisen; (*forgive*) vergeben

remittance [rɪ'mɪtəns] *s* (*in cash*) Übersendung *f*; (*by check*) Überweisung *f*

remnant ['remnənt] *s* Rest *m*; (*of cloth*) Stoffrest *m*

remod·el [rɪ'madəl] *v* (*pret & pp* **-el[l]ed;** *ger* **-el[l]ing**) *tr* umgestalten; (*a house*) umbauen

remonstrate [rɪ'manstret] *intr* protestieren; **r. with s.o.** j-m Vorwürfe machen

remorse [rɪ'mɔrs] *s* Gewissensbisse *pl*

remorseful [rɪ'mɔrsfəl] *adj* reumütig

remote [rɪ'mot] *adj* fern; (*possibility*) vage; (*idea*) blaß; (*resemblance*) entfernt; (*secluded*) abgelegen

remote' control' *s* Fernsteuerung *f*; (telv) Fernbedienung *f*; **guide by r.** fernlenken

removable [rɪ'muvəbəl] *adj* entfernbar

removal [rɪ'muvəl] *s* Entfernung *f*; (*by truck*) Abfuhr *f*; (*from office*) Absetzung *f*

remove [rɪ'muv] *tr* entfernen; (*clothes*) ablegen; (*one's hat*) abnehmen; (*e.g., dishes from the table*) abräumen; (*a stain*) entfernen; (*from office*) absetzen; (*furniture*) ausräumen

remuneration [rɪ̩mjunə'reʃən] *s* Vergütung *f*

renaissance [ˌrenə'sɑns] *s* Renaissance *f*

rend [rend] *v* (*pret & pp* **rent** [rent]) *tr* (& *fig*) zerreißen

render ['rendər] *tr* (*give*) geben; (*a service*) leisten; (*honor*) erweisen; (*thanks*) abstatten; (*a verdict*) fällen; (*translate; play, e.g., on the piano*) wiedergeben; **r. harmless** unschädlich machen

rendez-vous ['rɑndə̩vu] *s* (**-vous** [ˌvuz]) Rendezvous *n*, Treffpunkt *m*; (*mil*) Sammelplatz *m* ‖ *v* (*pret & pp* **-voused** [ˌvud]; *ger* **-vousing** [ˌvuˌɪŋ]) *intr* sich treffen; (*mil*) sich versammeln

rendition [ren'dɪʃən] *s* Wiedergabe *f*

renegade ['renɪ̩ged] *s* Renegat –in *mf*

renege [rɪ'nɪg] *s* Renonce *f* ‖ *intr* (*cards*) nicht bedienen; **r. on** nicht einhalten

renew [rɪ'n(j)u] *tr* erneuern; (*e.g., a passport*) verlängern lassen

renewable [rɪ'n(j)u-əbəl] *adj* erneuerbar

renewal [rɪ'n(j)u-əl] *s* Erneuerung *f*; (*e.g., of a passport*) Verlängerung *f*

renounce [rɪ'naʊns] *tr* verzichten auf (*acc*)

renovate ['renə̩vet] *tr* renovieren; (*fig*) erneuern

renovation [ˌrenə'veʃən] *s* Renovierung *f*

renown [rɪ'naʊn] *s* Ruhm *m*

renowned [rɪ'naʊnd] *adj* (**for**) berühmt (*wegen*)

rent [rent] *adj* zerrissen ‖ *s* Miete *f*; (*tear*) Riß *m* ‖ *tr* mieten; **r. out** vermieten

rental ['rentəl] *s* Miete *f*

rent'al serv'ice *s* Verleih *m*

rent'ed car' *s* Mietwagen *m*, Mietauto *n*

renter ['rentər] *s* Mieter –in *mf*

renunciation [rɪ̩nʌnsɪ'eʃən] *s* (**of**) Verzicht *m* (auf *acc*)

reopen [ri'opən] *tr* wieder öffnen; (*a business*) wieder eröffnen; (*an argument; school year*) wieder beginnen ‖ *intr* (*said of a shop or business*) wieder geöffnet werden; (*said of a school year*) wieder beginnen

reopening [ri'opənɪŋ] *s* (*of a business*) Wiedereröffnung *f*; (*of school*) Wiederbeginn *m*; (*jur*) Wiederaufnahme *f*

reorder [ri'ɔrdər] *tr* nachbestellen

reorganization [ˌri·ɔrgənɪ'zeʃən] *s* Reorganisation *f*, Neuordnung *f*

reorganize [ri'ɔrgə̩naɪz] *tr* reorganisieren; (*an administration*) umbilden

repack [ri'pæk] *tr* umpacken

repair [rɪ'per] *s* Ausbesserung *f*, Reparatur *f*; **in bad r.** in schlechtem Zustand; **keep in good r.** im Stande halten ‖ *tr* ausbessern, reparieren ‖ *intr* (**to**) sich begeben (nach, zu)

repair' gang' *s* Störungstrupp *m*

repair' shop' *s* Reparaturwerkstatt *f*

repaper [ri'pepər] *tr* neu tapezieren

reparation [ˌrepə're̩ʃən] *s* Wiedergutmachung *f*; **reparations** Reparationen *pl*, Kriegsentschädigung *f*

repartee [ˌrepɑr'ti] *s* schlagfertige Antwort *f*

repast [rɪ'pæst] *s* Mahl *n*

repatriate [ri'petrɪ̩et] *tr* repatriieren

re·pay [rɪ'pe] *v* (*pret & pp* **–paid**) *tr* (*e.g., a loan*) zurückzahlen; (*a person*) entschädigen; **r. a favor** e–n Gefallen erwidern

repayment [rɪ'pemənt] *s* Rückzahlung *f*; (*reprisal*) Vergeltung *f*

repeal [rɪ'pil] *s* Aufhebung *f* ‖ *tr* aufheben, außer Kraft setzen

repeat [rɪ'pit] *tr* wiederholen; (*a story, gossip*) weitererzählen; **r. s.th. after s.o.** j–m etw nachsagen

repeat'ed *adj* abermalig, mehrmalig

repeatedly [rɪ'pitdli] *adv* wiederholt

re·pel [rɪ'pel] *v* (*pret & pp* **–pelled**; *ger* **–pelling**) *tr* (*an enemy, an attack*) zurückschlagen; (*e.g., water*) abstoßen

repellent [rɪ'pelənt] *s* Bekämpfungsmittel *n*

repent [rɪ'pent] *tr* bereuen ‖ *intr* Reue empfinden; **r. of** bereuen

repentance [rɪ'pentəns] *s* Reue *f*

repentant [rɪ'pentənt] *adj* reuig

repercussion [ˌripər'kʌʃən] *s* Rückwirkung *f*

repertory ['repər̩tori] *s* Repertoire *n*

repetition [ˌrepɪ'tɪʃən] *s* Wiederholung *f*

replace [rɪ'ples] *tr* (**with**) ersetzen (*durch*)

replaceable [rɪ'plesəbəl] *adj* ersetzbar

replacement [rɪ'plesmənt] *s* (*act*) Ersetzen *n*; (*substitute part*) Ersatz *m*; (*person*) Ersatzmann *m*

replay ['riple] *s* (*sport*) Wiederholungsspiel *n* ‖ [ri'ple] *tr* nochmals spielen

replenish [rɪ'plenɪʃ] *tr* wieder auffüllen

replete [rɪ'plit] *adj* angefüllt

replica ['replɪkə] *s* Replik *f*

re·ply [rɪ'plaɪ] *s* Erwiderung *f*; (*letter*) Antwortschreiben *n*; **in r. to your letter** in Beantwortung Ihres Schreibens ‖ *v* (*pret & pp* **–plied**) *tr & intr* erwidern

report [rɪ'port] *s* Bericht *m*; (*rumor*) Gerücht *n*; (*e.g., of a gun*) Knall *m* ‖ *tr* (*give an account of*) berichten; (*give notice of*) melden; **r. s.o. to the police** j–n bei der Polizei anzeigen ‖ *intr* (**to**) sich melden (bei); **r. in** sich anmelden

report' card' *s* Zeugnis *n*

reportedly [rɪ'portdli] *adv* angeblich

reporter [rɪ'portər] *s* Reporter –in *mf*

repose [rɪ'poz] *s* Ruhe *f* ‖ *intr* ruhen

repository [rɪ'pazɪ̩tori] *s* Verwahrungsort *m*; (*of information*) Fundgrube *f*

represent [ˌreprɪ'zent] *tr* vertreten; (*depict*) darstellen

representation [ˌreprɪzen'teʃən] *s* Vertretung *f*; (*depiction*) Darstellung *f*

representative [ˌreprɪ'zentətɪv] *adj* (*function*) stellvertretend; (*government*) parlamentarisch; (*typical*) (**of**) typisch (für) || *s* Vertreter –in *mf;* (pol) Abgeordnete *mf*

repress [rɪ'pres] *tr* unterdrücken; (psychoanal) verdrängen

repression [rɪ'preʃən] *s* Unterdrückung *f;* (psychoanal) Verdrängung *f*

reprieve [rɪ'priv] *s* Strafaufschub *m;* (fig) Gnadenfrist *f,* Atempause *f*

reprimand ['reprɪˌmænd] *s* Verweis *m;* **give s.o. a r.** j–m e–n Verweis erteilen || *tr* (for) zurechtweisen (wegen, für), rügen (wegen, für)

reprint ['riprɪnt] *s* Nachdruck *m* || [ri'prɪnt] *tr* nachdrucken

reprisal [rɪ'praɪzəl] *s* Vergeltung *f;* **take reprisals against** or **on** Repressalien ergreifen gegen

reproach [rɪ'protʃ] *s* Vorwurf *m* || *tr* (for) tadeln (wegen); **r. s.o. with s.th.** j–m etw vorwerfen

reproduce [ˌriprə'd(j)us] *tr* reproduzieren; *(copies)* vervielfältigen; *(an experiment)* wiederholen; *(a play)* neuaufführen; *(a sound)* wiedergeben; *(a lost limb)* regenerieren || *intr* sich fortpflanzen

reproduction [ˌriprə'dʌkʃən] *s* Reproduktion *f;* *(making copies)* Vervielfältigung *f;* *(of sound)* Wiedergabe *f;* (biol) Fortpflanzung *f*

reproductive [ˌriprə'dʌktɪv] *adj* Fortpflanzungs-

reproof [rɪ'pruf] *s* Rüge *f*

reprove [rɪ'pruv] *tr* rügen

reptile ['reptaɪl] *s* Kriechtier *n*

republic [rɪ'pʌblɪk] *s* Republik *f*

republican [rɪ'pʌblɪkən] *adj* republikanisch || *s* Republikaner –in *mf*

repudiate [rɪ'pjudɪˌet] *tr* *(disown)* verleugnen; *(a charge)* zurückweisen; *(a debt)* nicht anerkennen; *(a treaty)* für unverbindlich erklären; *(a woman)* verstoßen

repugnant [rɪ'pʌgnənt] *adj* widerwärtig

repulse [rɪ'pʌls] *s* *(refusal)* Zurückweisung *f;* *(setback)* Rückschlag *m* || *tr* zurückweisen; (mil) zurückschlagen

repulsive [rɪ'pʌlsɪv] *adj* abstoßend

reputable ['repjətəbəl] *adj* anständig

reputation [ˌrepjə'teʃən] *s* Ruf *m,* Ansehen *n;* **have the r. of being** im Rufe stehen zu sein

repute [rɪ'pjut] *s*—**be held in high r.** hohes Ansehen genießen; **bring into bad r.** in üble Nachrede bringen; **of r.** von Ruf || *tr*—**she is reputed to be a beauty** sie soll e–e Schönheit sein

reputedly [rɪ'pjutɪdli] *adv* angeblich

request [rɪ'kwest] *s* Bitte *f,* Gesuch *n;* **at his r.** auf seine Bitte; **on r.** auf Wunsch || *tr* *(a person)* bitten; *(a thing)* bitten um, ersuchen

Requiem ['rekwɪˌem] *s* *(Mass)* Seelenmesse *f;* *(chant, composition)* Requiem *n*

require [rɪ'kwaɪr] *tr* erfordern; **if required** erforderlichenfalls

requirement [rɪ'kwaɪrmənt] *s* Anforderung *f*

requisite ['rekwɪzɪt] *adj* erforderlich ||

s Erfordernis *n;* *(required article)* Requisit *n*

requisition [ˌrekwɪ'zɪʃən] *s* Anforderung *f;* (mil) Requisition *f* || *tr* anfordern; (mil) beschlagnahmen

requital [rɪ'kwaɪtəl] *s* *(retaliation)* Vergeltung *f;* *(for a kindness)* Belohnung *f*

requite [rɪ'kwaɪt] *tr* vergelten; **r. s.o. for a favor** sich j–m für e–n Gefallen erkenntlich zeigen

re·read [ri'rid] *v* *(pret & pp* –**read** [red]) *tr* nachlesen

rerun ['rirʌn] *s* (cin) Reprise *f*

resale ['ri ˌsel] *s* Wiederverkauf *m*

rescind [rɪ'sɪnd] *tr* *(an order)* rückgängig machen; *(a law)* aufheben

rescue ['reskju] *s* Rettung *f,* Bergung *f* || *tr* retten, bergen

rescuer ['reskju·ər] *s* Retter –in *mf*

research [rɪ'sʌrtʃ], ['risʌrtʃ] *s* Forschung *f;* **do r. on** Forschungen betreiben über *(acc)* || *intr* forschen

researcher ['risʌrtʃər] *s* Forscher –in *mf*

re·sell [ri'sel] *v* *(pret & pp* –**sold**) *tr* wiederverkaufen, weiterverkaufen

resemblance [rɪ'zembləns] *s* (to) Ähnlichkeit *f* (mit); **bear a close r. to s.o.** große Ähnlichkeit mit j–m haben

resemble [rɪ'zembəl] *tr* ähneln *(dat)*

resent [rɪ'zent] *tr*—**I r. your remark** Ihre Bemerkung paßt mir nicht

resentful [rɪ'zentfəl] *adj* grollend

resentment [rɪ'zentmənt] *s* Groll *m;* **feel r. toward** Groll hegen gegen

reservation [ˌrezər've∫ən] *s* Vorbestellung *f;* *(Indian land)* Reservation *f;* **do you have a r.?** haben Sie vorbestellt?; **make reservations** vorbestellen

reserve [rɪ'zʌrv] *s* *(discretion)* Zurückhaltung *f;* (econ, mil) Reserve *f;* **without r.** rückhaltlos || *tr* *(e.g., seats)* reservieren, belegen; **r. judgment** mit seinem Urteil zurückhalten

reserved' *adj* *(place)* belegt; *(person)* zurückhaltend

reserve' of'ficer *s* Reserveoffizier *m*

reservist [rɪ'zʌrvɪst] *s* Reservist –in *mf*

reservoir ['rezərˌvwɑr] *s* Staubecken *m*

re·set [ri'set] *v* *(pret & pp* –**set;** *ger* –**setting)** *tr* *(a gem)* neu fassen; (mach) nachstellen; (typ) neu setzen

resettle [ri'setəl] *tr & intr* umsiedeln

reshape [ri'ʃep] *tr* umformen

reshuffle [ri'ʃʌfəl] *tr* *(cards)* neu mischen; (pol) umgruppieren

reside [rɪ'zaɪd] *intr* wohnen

residence ['rezɪdəns] *s* Wohnsitz *m;* *(for students)* Studentenheim *n*

resident ['rezɪdənt] *adj* wohnhaft || *s* Einwohner –in *mf*

residential [ˌrezɪ'dentʃəl] *adj* Wohn-

residue ['rezɪˌd(j)u] *s* Rest *m;* (chem) Rückstand *m*

resign [rɪ'zaɪn] *tr* *(an office)* niederlegen; **r. oneself to** sich ergeben in *(acc)* || *intr* zurücktreten

resignation [ˌrezɪg'neʃən] *s* *(from an office)* Rücktritt *m;* *(submissive* *state*) Ergebung *f;* **hand in one's r.** sein Entlassungsgesuch einreichen

resilience [rɪˈzɪlɪ·əns] *s* Elastizität *f;* (fig) Spannkraft *f*

resilient [rɪˈzɪlɪ·ənt] *adj* elastisch; (fig) unverwüstlich

resin [ˈrezɪn] *s* Harz *m*

resist [rɪˈzɪst] *tr* widerstehen (*dat*) ‖ *intr* Widerstand leisten

resistance [rɪˈzɪstəns] *s* (& elec) Widerstand *m*

resole [riˈsol] *tr* neu besohlen

resolute [ˈrezə‚lut] *adj* entschlossen

resolution [‚rezəˈluʃən] *s* (*resoluteness*) Entschlossenheit *f;* (parl) Beschluß *m;* **make good resolutions** gute Vorsätze fassen

resolve [rɪˈzɑlv] *s* Vorsatz *m* ‖ *tr* auflösen; (*a question, problem*) lösen; **r. to** (*inf*) beschließen zu (*inf*) ‖ *intr* —**r. into** sich auflösen in (*acc*); **r. upon s.th.** sich [*dat*] etw vornehmen

resonance [ˈrezənəns] *s* Resonanz *f*

resort [rɪˈzɔrt] *s* (*refuge*) Zuflucht *f;* (*for health*) Kurort *m;* (*for vacation*) Ferienort *m,* Sommerfrische *f;* **as a last r.** als letztes Mittel ‖ *intr*—**r. to** greifen zu

resound [rɪˈzaund] *intr* widerhallen

resource [ˈrisors] *s* Mittel *n;* **resources** (fin) Geldmittel *pl*

resourceful [rɪˈsorsfəl] *adj* findig

respect [rɪˈspekt] *s* (*esteem*) Achtung *f,* Respekt *m;* (*reference*) Hinsicht *f;* **in every r.** in jeder Hinsicht; **pay one's respects to s.o.** j-m seine Aufwartung machen; **with r. to** mit Bezug auf (*acc*) ‖ *tr* achten

respectable [rɪˈspektəbəl] *adj* achtbar; (*e.g., firm*) angesehen

respect'ed *adj* angesehen

respectful [rɪˈspektfəl] *adj* ehrerbietig

respectfully [rɪˈspektfəlɪ] *adv*—**r. yours** hochachtungsvoll, Ihr … or Ihre …

respective [rɪˈspektɪv] *adj* jeweilig

respectively [rɪˈspektɪvlɪ] *adv* beziehungsweise

respiration [‚respɪˈreʃən] *s* Atmung *f*

respirator [ˈrespɪ‚retər] *s* Atemgerät *n*

respiratory [ˈrespɪrə‚tori] *adj* Atmungs-

respite [ˈrespɪt] *s* (*pause*) Atempause *f;* (*reprieve*) Aufschub *m;* **without r.** ohne Unterlaß

resplendent [rɪˈsplendənt] *adj* glänzend

respond [rɪˈspɑnd] *tr* antworten ‖ *intr* (*reply*) (**to**) antworten (auf *acc*); (*react*) (**to**) ansprechen (auf *acc*)

response [rɪˈspɑns] *s* Antwort *f;* (*reaction*) Reaktion *f;* (fig) Widerhall *m;* **in r. to** als Antwort auf (*acc*)

responsibility [rɪ‚spɑnsɪˈbɪlɪtɪ] *s* Verantwortung *f*

responsible [rɪˈspɑnsɪbəl] *adj* (*position*) verantwortlich; (*person*) verantwortungsbewußt; **be held r.** for verantwortlich gemacht werden für; **be r. for** (*be answerable for*) verantwortlich sein für; (*be to blame for*) schuld sein an (*dat*); (*be the cause of*) die Ursache sein (*genit*); (*be liable for*) haften für

responsive [rɪˈspɑnsɪv] *adj*—**be r. to** ansprechen auf (*acc*)

rest [rest] *s* (*repose*) Ruhe *f;* (*from work*) Ruhepause *f;* (*e.g., from walking*) Rast *f;* (*remainder*) Rest *m;* (*support*) Stütze *f;* (mus) Pause *f;* **all the r.** (*in number*) alle andern; (*in quantity*) alles übrige; **be at r.** (*be calm*) beruhigt sein; (*be dead*) ruhen; (*not be in motion*) sich in Ruhelage befinden; **come to r.** stehenbleiben; **put one's mind to r.** sich beruhigen; **take a r.** sich ausruhen; **the r. of the boys** die übrigen (or andern) Jungen ‖ *tr* ruhen lassen, ausruhen; (*support, e.g., one's elbow*) stützen ‖ *intr* sich ausruhen; **r. on** lasten auf (*dat*); (*be based on*) beruhen auf (*dat*); **r. with** liegen bei

restaurant [ˈrestərənt] *s* Restaurant *n*

restful [ˈrestfəl] *adj* ruhig

rest' home' *s* Erholungsheim *n*

rest'ing place' *s* Ruheplatz *m;* **final r.** letzte Ruhestätte *f*

restitution [‚restɪˈt(j)uʃən] *s* Wiedergutmachung *f;* **make r.** Genugtuung leisten

restive [ˈrestɪv] *adj* (*restless*) unruhig; (*balky*) störrisch

restless [ˈrestlɪs] *adj* ruhelos

restock [rɪˈstɑk] *tr* wieder auffüllen; (*waters*) wieder mit Fischen besetzen

restoration [‚restəˈreʃən] *s* (*of a work of art or building*) Restaurierung *f*

restore [rɪˈstor] *tr* (*order*) wiederherstellen; (*a painting, building*) restaurieren; (*stolen goods*) zurückerstatten; **r. to health** wiederherstellen

restrain [rɪˈstren] *tr* zurückhalten; (*feelings; a horse*) zügeln; (*e.g., trade*) einschränken; **r. s.o. from** (*ger*) j-n davon abhalten zu (*inf*)

restrain'ing or'der *s* Unterlassungsurteil *n*

restraint [rɪˈstrent] *s* Zurückhaltung *f;* (*force*) Zwang *m*

restrict [rɪˈstrɪkt] *tr* begrenzen; **r. to** beschränken auf (*acc*)

restrict'ed ar'ea *s* Sperrgebiet *n*

rest' room' *s* Abort *m,* Toilette *f*

result [rɪˈzʌlt] *s* Ergebnis *n,* Resultat *n;* (*consequence*) Folge *f;* **as a r. of** als Folge (*genit*); **without r.** ergebnislos ‖ *intr*—**r. from** sich ergeben aus; **r. in** führen zu

result' clause' *s* Folgesatz *m*

resume [rɪˈzum] *tr* wieder aufnehmen; (*a journey*) fortsetzen

résumé [ˈrezu‚me] *s* Zusammenfassung *f*

resumption [rɪˈzʌmpʃən] *s* Wiederaufnahme *f*

resurface [riˈsʌrfɪs] *tr*—**r. the road** with die Straßendecke erneuern von ‖ *intr* (naut & fig) wiederauftauchen

resurrect [‚rezəˈrekt] *tr* (*the dead*) wieder zum Leben erwecken; (fig) wieder aufleben lassen

resurrection [‚rezəˈrekʃən] *s* Auferstehung *f*

resuscitate [rɪˈsʌsɪ‚tet] *tr* wiederbeleben

retail ['ritel] *adj* Kleinhandels- || *adv* im Kleinhandel || *tr* im Kleinhandel verkaufen || *intr*—**r. at two dollars** im Kleinverkauf zwei Dollar kosten

re'tail busi'ness *s* Kleinhandel *m*

retailer ['ritelər] *s* Kleinhändler –in *mf*

retain [rɪ'ten] *tr* (zurück)behalten; (*a lawyer*) sich [*dat*] nehmen

retainer [rɪ'tenər] *s* (hist) Gefolgsmann *m*; (jur) Honorarvorschuß *m*

retain'ing wall' *s* Stützmauer *f*

retake ['ritek] *s* (cin) Neuaufnahme *f* || [ri'tek] *tr* (*a town*) zurückerobern; (cin) nochmals aufnehmen

retaliate [rɪ'tælɪ‚et] *intr* (**against**) Vergeltung üben (an *dat*)

retaliation [rɪ‚tælɪ'eʃən] *s* Vergeltung *f*

retaliatory [rɪ'tælɪ‚ə‚tori] *adj* Vergeltungs–

retard [rɪ'tard] *tr* verzögern

retard'ed *adj* zurückgeblieben

retch [retʃ] *intr* würgen

retch'ing *s* Würgen *n*

retell [rɪ'tel] *tr* wiedererzählen

retention [rɪ'tenʃən] *s* Beibehaltung *f*

re‧think [rɪ'θɪŋk] *v* (*pret & pp* –**thought**) *tr* umdenken

reticence ['retɪsəns] *s* Verschwiegenheit *f*

reticent ['retɪsənt] *adj* verschwiegen

retina ['retɪnə] *s* Netzhaut *f*, Retina *f*

retinue ['retɪ‚n(j)u] *s* Gefolge *n*

retire [rɪ'taɪr] *tr* pensionieren || *intr* (*from employment*) in den Ruhestand treten; (*withdraw*) sich zurückziehen; (*go to bed*) sich zur Ruhe begehen

retired' *adj* pensioniert

retirement [rɪ'taɪrmənt] *s* Ruhestand *m*; **go into r.** in den Ruhestand treten, sich pensionieren lassen

retire'ment pay' *s* Pension *f*

retire'ment plan' *s* Pensionsplan *m*

retir'ing *adj* zurückhaltend

retort [rɪ'tort] *s* schlagfertige Erwiderung *f*; (chem) Retorte *f* || *tr & intr* erwidern

retouch [ri'tʌtʃ] *tr* retuschieren

retrace [rɪ'tres] *tr* zurückverfolgen

retract [rɪ'trækt] *tr* (*a statement*) widerrufen; (*claws; landing gear*) einziehen

retract'able land'ing gear' [rɪ'træktəbəl] *s* Verschwindfahrgestell *n*

retrain [ri'tren] *tr* umschulen

retread ['ri‚tred] *s* (aut) runderneuerter Reifen *m* || *tr* runderneuern

retreat [rɪ'trit] *s* (*quiet place*) Ruhesitz *m*; (mil) Rückzug *m*; (rel) Exerzitien *pl*; **beat a hasty r.** eilig den Rückzug antreten || *intr* sich zurückziehen

retrench [rɪ'trentʃ] *tr* einschränken || *intr* sich einschränken

retribution [‚retrɪ'bju(j)ən] *s* Vergeltung *f*

retrieval [rɪ'trivəl] *s* Wiedererlangung *f*

retrieve [rɪ'triv] *tr* wiedererlangen; (*a loss*) wettmachen; (hunt) apportieren

retriever [rɪ'trivər] *s* Apportierhund *m*

retroactive [‚retro'æktɪv] *adj* (**from**) rückwirkend von … an

retrogressive [‚retrə'gresɪv] *adj* rückläufig

retrorocket ['retro‚rakɪt] *s* Bremsrakete *f*

retrospect ['retrə‚spekt] *s*—**in r.** rückblickend

re‧try [ri'traɪ] *v* (*pret & pp* –**tried**) *tr* (jur) nochmals verhandeln

return [rɪ'tʌrn] *s* Rückkehr *f*; (*giving back*) Rückgabe *f*; (*the way back*) Rückweg *m*; (*tax form*) Steuererklärung *f*; (*profit*) Umsatz *m*; (tennis), Rückschlag *m*; **in r.** dafür; **in r. for** als Entgelt für; **returns** (*profits*) Ertrag *m*; (*of an election*) Ergebnisse *pl* || *tr* zurückgeben; (*send back*) zurücksenden; (*put back*) zurückstellen; (*thanks*) abstatten; (*a verdict*) fällen; (*a favor, love, gun fire*) erwidern; (tennis) zurückschlagen || *intr* zurückkehren; **r. to** (e.g., *a topic*) zurückkommen auf (*acc*)

return' address' *s* Rückadresse *f*

return' flight' *s* Rückflug *m*

return' match' *s* Revanchepartie *f*

return' tick'et *s* Rückfahrkarte *f*; (aer) Rückflugkarte *f*

reunification [ri‚junɪfɪ'keʃən] *s* (pol) Wiedervereinigung *f*

reunion [ri'junjən] *s* Treffen *n*

rev [rev] *v* (*pret & pp* **revved;** *ger* **revving**) *tr* (**up**) auf Touren bringen || *intr* auf Touren kommen

revamp [ri'væmp] *tr* umgestalten

reveal [rɪ'vil] *tr* offenbaren

reveille ['revəli] *s* Wecken *s*

rev‧el ['revəl] *s* Gelage *n* || *v* (*pret & pp* –el[l]ed; *ger* –el[l]ing) *intr* ein Gelage halten; **r. in** (fig) schwelgen in (*dat*)

revelation [‚revə'leʃən] *s* Offenbarung *f*; **Revelations** (Bib) Offenbarung *f*

reveler ['revələr] *s* Zecher –in *mf*

revelry ['revəlri] *s* Zechgelage *n*

revenge [rɪ'vendʒ] *s* Rache *f*; **take r. on s.o. for s.th.** sich an j–m für etw rächen || *tr* rächen

revengeful [rɪ'vendʒfəl] *adj* rachsüchtig

revenue ['revə‚n(j)u] *s* (*yield*) Ertrag *m*; (*internal revenue*) Steueraufkommen *n*

rev'enue stamp' *s* Banderole *f*

reverberate [rɪ'vʌrbə‚ret] *intr* widerhallen

revere [rɪ'vɪr] *tr* verehren

reverence ['revərəns] *s* (*respect given or received*) Ehrerbietung *f*; (*respect felt*) Ehrfurcht *f*

reverend ['revərənd] *adj* ehrwürdig; **the Reverend** … Hochwürden …

reverie ['revəri] *s* Träumerei *f*; **be lost in r.** in Träumen versunken sein

reversal [rɪ'vʌrsəl] *s* Umkehrung *f*; (*of opinion*) Umschwung *m*

reverse [rɪ'vʌrs] *adj* umgekehrt; (*side*) linke || *s* (*back side*) Rückseite *f*; (*opposite*) Gegenteil *n*; (*setback*) Rückschlag *m*; (*of a coin*) Revers *m*;

(aut) Rückwärtsgang m ‖ tr umkehren, umdrehen; (a decision) umstoßen ‖ intr sich rückwärts bewegen

reverse′ side′ s Rückseite f, Kehrseite f

reversible [rɪ'vʌrsɪbəl] adj (decision) umstoßbar; (material) zweiseitig; (chem, phys) umkehrbar; (mach) umsteuerbar

revert [rɪ'vʌrt] intr—r. to zurückkommen auf (acc); (jur) zurückfallen an (acc)

review [rɪ'vju] s (of) Überblick m (über acc); (of a lesson) Wiederholung f; (of a book) Besprechung f; (periodical) Rundschau m; (mil) Besichtigung f; pass in r. mustern ‖ tr (a lesson) wiederholen; (a book) besprechen; (e.g., the events of the day) überblicken; (mil) besichtigen

reviewer [rɪ'vju‧ər] s Besprecher –in mf

revile [rɪ'vaɪl] tr schmähen

revise [rɪ'vaɪz] tr (a book) umarbeiten; (one's opinion) revidieren

revised′ edi′tion s verbesserte Auflage f

revision [rɪ'vɪʒən] s Neubearbeitung f

revival [rɪ'vaɪvəl] s Wiederbelebung f; (rel) Erweckung f; (theat) Reprise f

reviv′al meet′ing s Erweckungsversammlung f

revive [rɪ'vaɪv] tr wieder aufleben lassen; (memories) aufrühren; (a victim) wieder zu Bewußtsein bringen ‖ intr wieder aufleben

revoke [rɪ'vok] tr widerrufen

revolt [rɪ'volt] s Aufstand m ‖ tr abstoßen ‖ intr revoltieren

revolt′ing adj abstoßend

revolution [,revə'luʃən] s Revolution f; (turn) Umdrehung f; **revolutions per minute** Drehzahl f

revolutionary [,revə'luʃə,neri] adj revolutionär ‖ s Revolutionär –in mf

revolve [rɪ'valv] intr (around) sich drehen (um)

revolver [rɪ'valvər] s Revolver m

revolv′ing adj Dreh-

revue [rɪ'vju] s (theat) Revue f

revulsion [rɪ'vʌlʃən] s Abscheu m

reward [rɪ'wɔrd] s Belohnung f ‖ tr belohnen

reward′ing adj lohnend

re‧wind [ri'waɪnd] v (pret & pp -wound) tr (a tape, film) umspulen; (a clock) wieder aufziehen

rewire [ri'waɪr] tr Leitungen neu legen in (dat)

rework [ri'wʌrk] tr umarbeiten

re‧write [ri'raɪt] v (pret -wrote; pp -written) tr umschreiben

rhapsody ['ræpsədɪ] s Rhapsodie f

rheostat ['ri‧ə,stæt] s Rheostat m

rhetoric ['retərɪk] s Redekunst f

rhetorical [rɪ'tɔrɪkəl] adj rhetorisch

rheumatic [ru'mætɪk] adj rheumatisch

rheumatism ['rumə,tɪzəm] s Rheumatismus m

Rhine [raɪn] s Rhein m

Rhineland ['raɪn,lænd] s Rheinland n

rhine′stone′ s Rheinkiesel m

rhinoceros [raɪ'nasərəs] s Nashorn n

rhubarb ['rubarb] s Rhabarber m; (sl) Krach m

rhyme [raɪm] s Reim m ‖ tr & intr reimen

rhythm ['rɪðəm] s Rhythmus m

rhythmic(al) ['rɪðmɪk(əl)] adj rhythmisch

rib [rɪb] s Rippe f ‖ v (pret & pp ribbed; ger ribbing) tr (coll) sich lustig machen über (acc)

ribald ['rɪbəld] adj zotig

ribbon ['rɪbən] s Band n; (decoration) Ordensband n; (for a typewriter) Farbband n

rice [raɪs] s Reis m

rich [rɪtʃ] adj reich; (voice) volltönend; (soil) fruchtbar; (funny) (coll) köstlich; r. in reich an (dat) ‖ **riches** spl Reichtum n

rickets ['rɪkɪts] s Rachitis f

rickety ['rɪkɪtɪ] adj (building) baufällig; (furniture) wackelig

rid [rɪd] v (pret & pp rid; ger ridding) tr (of) befreien (von); **get rid of** losriten

riddance ['rɪdəns] s Befreiung f; **good r.!** den (or die or das) wäre ich glücklich los!

riddle ['rɪdəl] s Rätsel n

ride [raɪd] s Fahrt f; **give s.o. a r.** j—n im Auto mitnehmen; **take for a r.** (murder) entführen und umbringen; (dupe) hochnehmen ‖ v (pret rode [rod]; pp ridden ['rɪdən]) tr (a bicycle) fahren; (a horse) reiten; (a train, bus) fahren mit; (harass) hetzen; **r. out** (a storm) gut überstehen ‖ intr (e.g., in a car) fahren; (on a horse) reiten; **let s.th. r.** sich mit etw abfinden

rider ['raɪdər] s (on horseback) Reiter –in mf; (on a bicycle) Radfahrer –in mf; (in a vehicle) Fahrer –in mf; (to a document) Zusatzklausel f

ridge [rɪdʒ] s (of a hill; of the nose) Rücken m; (of a roof) Dachfirst m

ridge′pole′ s Firstbalken m

ridicule ['rɪdɪ,kjul] s Spott m ‖ tr verspotten

ridiculous [rɪ'dɪkjələs] adj lächerlich; **look r.** lächerlich wirken

rid′ing acad′emy s Reitschule f

rid′ing boot′ s Reitstiefel m

rid′ing breech′es spl Reithose f

rid′ing hab′it s Reitkostüm n

rife [raɪf] adj häufig; **r. with** voll von

riffraff ['rɪf,ræf] s Gesindel n

rifle ['raɪfəl] s Gewehr n ‖ tr ausplündern

rift [rɪft] s (& fig) Riß m

rig [rɪg] s (gear) Ausrüstung f; (horse and carriage) Gespann n; (truck) Laster m; (oil drill) Bohrturm m; (getup) (coll) Aufmachung f; (naut) Takelung f ‖ v (pret & pp rigged; ger rigging) tr (auf)takeln; (prices, elections, accounts) manipulieren

rig′ging s Takelung f

right [raɪt] adj (side, glove, angle) recht; (just) gerecht; (correct) richtig; (moment) richtig; **do you have the r. time?** können Sie mir die genaue Uhrzeit sagen?; **be in one's r. mind** bei klarem Verstand sein; **it is all r.** es ist schon gut; **r.?** nicht wahr?; **that's r.!** eben!; **the r. thing** das Richtige; **you are r.** Sie haben recht || *adv* direkt; *(to the right)* rechts; **r. along** durchaus; **r. away** sofort, gleich; **r. behind the door** gleich hinter der Tür; **r. glad** (coll) recht froh; **r. here** gleich hier; **r. now** *(at the moment)* momentan; *(immediately)* sofort; **r. through** durch und durch || *s* Recht *n*; (box) Rechte *f*; **all rights reserved** alle Rechte vorbehalten; **by rights** von Rechts wegen; **in the r.** im Recht; **on the r.** rechts, zur Rechten || *tr* aufrichten; *(an error)* berichtigen; *(a wrong)* wiedergutmachen || *interj* stimmt!

righteous ['raɪtʃəs] *adj* gerecht, rechtschaffen; *(smug)* selbstgerecht

rightful ['raɪtfəl] *adj (owner)* rechtmäßig; *(claim, place)* berechtigt

right'-hand' *adj* zur Rechten; *(glove)* recht

right'-hand'ed *adj* rechtshändig

right-hander ['raɪt'hændər] *s* Rechtshänder –in *mf*

right'-hand man' *s* rechte Hand *f*

rightist ['raɪtɪst] *adj* rechtsstehend || *s* Rechtspolitiker –in *mf*

rightly ['raɪtli] *adv* richtig; *(rightfully)* rechtmäßig

right' of way' *s (in traffic)* Vorfahrtsrecht *n*; *(across another's land)* Grunddienstbarkeit *f*

right' wing' *s* rechter Flügel *m*

rigid ['rɪdʒɪd] *adj* steif, starr

rigmarole ['rɪgmə‚rol] *s (meaningless talk)* Geschwafel *n*; *(fuss)* Getue *n*

rigorous ['rɪgərəs] *adj* hart, streng

rile [raɪl] *tr* aufbringen

rill [rɪl] *s* Bächlein *n*

rim [rɪm] *s* Rand *m*; *(of eyeglasses)* Fassung *f*; *(of a wheel)* Felge *f*

rind [raɪnd] *s* Rinde *f*

ring [rɪŋ] *s (for the fingers; for boxing; of criminals or spies; of a circus; circle under the eyes)* Ring *m*; *(of a bell, voice, laughter)* Klang *m*; **give s.o. a r.** (telp) j–n anrufen; **run rings around s.o.** j–n in die Tasche stecken || *v (pret & pp ringed) tr* umringen; **r. in** einschließen || *v (pret rang* [ræŋ]; *pp rung* [rʌŋ]) *tr* läuten; **r. the bell** läuten, klingeln; **r. out** ausläuten; **r. up** anrufen || *intr* läuten, klingeln; **my ears are ringing** mir klingen die Ohren; **r. for s.o.** nach j–m klingeln; **r. out** laut schallen; **the bell is ringing** es läutet

ring'ing *adj* schallend || *s* Läuten *n*; *(in the ears)* Klingen *n*

ring'lead'er *s* Rädelsführer *m*

ring'mas'ter *s* Zirkusdirektor *m*

ring'side' *s* Ringplatz *m*

ring'worm' *s* Scherpilzflechte *f*

rink [rɪŋk] *s* Eisbahn *f*; *(for rollerskating)* Rollschuhbahn *f*

rinse [rɪns] *s* Spülen *n* || *tr* ausspülen

riot ['raɪ‚ət] *s* Aufruhr *m*; **r. of colors**

Farbengemisch *n*; **run r.** sich austoben; *(said of plants)* wuchern || *intr* sich zusammenrotten

ri'ot act' *s*—**read the r. to s.o.** j–m die Leviten lesen

rioter ['raɪ‚ətər] *s* Aufrührer –in *mf*

rip [rɪp] *s* Riß *m* || *v (pret & pp ripped; ger ripping) tr* (zer)reißen; **rip off** abreißen; *(the skin)* abziehen; *(cheat)* betrügen || *intr* reißen

rip' cord' *s* Reißlinie *f*

ripe [raɪp] *adj* reif

ripen ['raɪpən] *tr (& fig)* reifen lassen || *intr (& fig)* reifen

rip' off' *s* (sl) Wucher *m*

ripple ['rɪpəl] *s* leichte Welle *f* || *intr* leichte Wellen schlagen

rise [raɪz] *s* Aufsteigen *n*; *(in prices)* Steigerung *f*; *(of heavenly bodies)* Aufgang *m*; *(increase, e.g., in population)* Zunahme *f*; *(in the ground)* Erhebung *f*; **get a r. out of s.o.** j–n zu e–r Reaktion veranlassen; **give r. to** veranlassen || *v (pret rose* [roz]; *pp risen* ['rɪzən]) *intr (said of the sun, of a cake)* aufgehen; *(said of a river, prices, temperature, barometer)* steigen; *(said of a road)* ansteigen; *(get out of bed)* aufstehen; *(stand up)* sich erheben; *(from the dead)* auferstehen; *(said of anger)* hochsteigen; **r. to the occasion** sich der Lage gewachsen zeigen; **r. up from the ranks** von der Pike auf dienen

riser ['raɪzər] *s (of a staircase)* Futterbrett *n*; **early r.** Frühaufsteher –in *mf*; **late r.** Langschläfer –in *mf*

risk [rɪsk] *s* Risiko *n*; **run the r. of** *(ger)* Gefahr laufen zu *(inf)* || *tr* wagen, aufs Spiel setzen

risky ['rɪski] *adj* riskant, gewagt

risqué [rɪs'ke] *adj* schlüpfrig

rite [raɪt] *s* Ritus *m*; **last rites** Sterbesakramente *pl*

ritual ['rɪt/u‚əl] *adj* rituell || *s* Ritual *n*

ri·val ['raɪvəl] *adj* rivalisierend || *s* Rivale *m*, Rivalin *f* || *v (pret & pp -val[l]ed; ger -val[l]ing) tr* rivalisieren, wetteifern mit

rivalry ['raɪvəlri] *s* Rivalität *f*

river ['rɪvər] *adj* Fluß– || *s* Fluß *m*

riv'er ba'sin *s* Flußgebiet *n*

riv'erfront' *s* Flußufer *n*

riv'erside' *adj* am Flußufer gelegen || *s* Flußufer *n*

rivet ['rɪvɪt] *s* Niet *m* || *tr* nieten

riv'et gun' *s* Nietmaschine *f*

riv'eting *s (act)* Vernieten *n*; *(connection)* Nietnaht *f*

rivulet ['rɪvjəlɪt] *s* Flüßchen *n*

R.N. ['ɑr'en] *s (registered nurse)* staatlich geprüfte Krankenschwester *f*

roach [rotʃ] *s (ent)* Schabe *f*; *(ichth)* Plötze *f*

road [rod] *s (& fig)* Weg *m*; **be (much) on the r.** (viel) auf Reisen sein; **go on the r.** auf Tour gehen; *(theat)* auf Tournee gehen

road'bed' *s* Bahnkörper *m*

road'block' *s* Straßensperre *f*

road′ hog′ s rücksichtsloser Autofahrer m

road′ house′ s Wirtshaus n, Rasthaus n

road′ map′ s Straßenkarte f, Autokarte f

road′side′ adj Straßen– || s Straßenrand m

road′side inn′ s Rasthaus n

road′sign′ s Wegweiser m

road′stead′ s Reede f

road′ test′ s (aut) Probefahrt f

road′way′ s Fahrweg m

roam [rom] tr durchstreifen || intr herumstreifen

roar [ror] s Gebrüll n; (of a waterfall, sea, wind) Brausen n; (of an engine) Dröhnen n; (laughter) schallendes Gelächter n || intr brüllen; (said of a waterfall, sea, wind) brausen; **r. at** anbrüllen; (e.g., a joke) schallend lachen über (acc); **r. by** vorbeibrausen; **r. with** brüllen vor (dat)

roast [rost] adj gebraten || s Braten m || tr (meat, fish) braten, rösten; (coffee, chestnuts) rösten; (a person) (coll) durch den Kakao ziehen || intr braten

roast′ beef′ s Roastbeef n

roaster [′rostər] s (appliance) Röster m, Röstapparat m; (fowl) Brathuhn n

roast′ pork′ s Schweinsbraten m

rob [rɑb] v (pret & pp robbed; ger robbing) tr (a thing) rauben; (a person) (of) berauben (genit)

robber [′rɑbər] s Räuber –in mf

robbery [′rɑbəri] s Raubüberfall m

robe [rob] s Robe f; (house robe) Hausrock m || tr feierlich ankleiden || intr sich feierlich ankleiden

robin [′rɑbɪn] s Rotkehlchen n

robot [′robat] s Roboter m

robust [ro′bʌst] adj robust

rock [rɑk] adj (mus) Rock– || s Fels m; (one that is thrown) Stein m; (mus) Rockmusik f; **on the rocks** mit Eiswürfeln; (ruined) kaputt || tr schaukeln, wiegen; **r. the boat** (fig) die Sache ins Wanken bringen; **r. to sleep** in den Schlaf wiegen || intr schwanken, wanken; (said of a boat) schaukeln

rock′-bot′tom adj äußerst niedrig || s Tiefpunkt m

rock′ can′dy s Kandiszucker m

rock′ crys′tal s Bergkristall m

rocker [′rɑkər] s Schaukelstuhl m; **go off one's r.** (coll) den Verstand verlieren

rocket [′rɑkɪt] s Rakete f

rock′et launch′er s Raketenwerfer m

rocketry [′rɑkətri] s Raketentechnik f

rock′et ship′ s Raketenflugkörper m

rock′ gar′den s Steingarten m

rock′ing chair′ s Schaukelstuhl m

rock′ing horse′ s Schaukelpferd n

rock-′n′-roll [′rɑkən′rol] s Rock 'n Roll m

rock′ salt′ s Steinsalz n

rocky [′rɑki] adj felsig; (shaky) wacklig

rod [rɑd] s Stab m, Stange f; (whip)

Zuchtrute f; (of the retina; of a microorganism) Stäbchen n; (revolver) (sl) Schießeisen n; (angl) Angelrute f; (Bib) Reis n; (mach) Pleuelstange f; (surg) Absteckpfahl m

rodent [′rodənt] s Nagetier n

roe [ro] s (deer) Reh n; (ichth) Rogen m

rogue [rog] s Schuft m, Schurke m

rogues′ gal′lery s Verbrecheralbum n

roguish [′rogɪʃ] adj schurkisch

role, rôle [rol] s Rolle f

roll [rol] s Rolle f; (bread) Brötchen n; (of thunder, of a ship) Rollen n; (of drums) Wirbel m; (of fat) Wulst m; **call the r.** die Namen verlesen; (mil) Appell halten || tr rollen; (cigarettes) drehen; (metals, roads) walzen; **r. over** überrollen; **r. up** zusammenrollen; (sleeves) zurückstreifen || intr sich wälzen; **be rolling in money** im Geld wühlen

roll′back′ s (com) Senkung f

roll′call′ s Namensverlesung f; (mil) Appell m

roll′er bear′ing s Rollenlager n

roll′er coast′er s Berg-und-Tal-Bahn f

roll′er skate′ s Rollschuh m

roll′er-skate′ intr rollschuhlaufen

roll′er tow′el s Rollhandtuch n

roll′ing mill′ s Walzwerk n

roll′ing pin′ s Nudelholz n, Teigrolle f

roll′ing stock′ s (rr) rollendes Material n

roly-poly [′roli′poli] adj dick und rund

roman [′romən] adj (typ) Antiqua–; **Roman** römisch || s (typ) Antiqua f; **Roman** Römer –in mf

Ro′man can′dle s Leuchtkugel f

Ro′man Cath′olic adj römisch-katholisch || s Katholik –in mf

romance [ro′mæns] adj (ling) romanisch || s Romanze f

Romanesque [,romə′nɛsk] adj romanisch || s das Romanische

Ro′man nose′ s Römernase f

Ro′man nu′meral s römische Ziffer f

romantic [ro′mæntɪk] adj romantisch

romanticism [ro′mæntɪ,sɪzəm] s Romantik f

romp [rɑmp] intr umhertollen

rompers [′rɑmpərz] spl Spielanzug m

roof [ruf] s Dach n; (aut) Verdeck n; **raise the r.** (coll) Krach machen; **r. of the mouth** Gaumendach n

roofer [′rufər] s Dachdecker m

roof′ gar′den s Dachgarten m

roof′ tile′ s Dachziegel m

rook [ruk] s (chess) Turm m; (orn) Saatkrähe f || tr (coll) (out of) beschwindeln (um)

rookie [′ruki] s (coll) Neuling m

room [rum] s Zimmer n; (space) Raum m, Platz m; **make r.** Platz machen; **r. for complaint** Anlaß m zur Klage; **take up too much r.** zu viel Platz in Anspruch nehmen || intr wohnen

room′ and board′ s Kost und Quartier

room′ clerk′ s Empfangschef m

roomer [′rumər] s Mieter –in mf

room'ing house' s Pension f
room'mate' s Zimmergenosse m
room' serv'ice s Bedienung f aufs Zimmer
roomy ['rumi] adj geräumig
roost [rust] s Hühnerstange f; **rule the r.** Hahn im Korb sein || intr auf der Stange sitzen
rooster ['rustər] s Hahn m
root [rut] s Wurzel f; **get to the r. of s.th.** etw [dat] auf den Grund gehen; **take r.** Wurzel schlagen; (fig) sich einbürgern || tr—**be rooted in** wurzeln in (dat); **rooted to the spot** festgewurzelt; **r. out** ausrotten || intr —**r. about** wühlen; **r. for** zujubeln (dat)
rope [rop] s Strick m, Seil n; **know the ropes** alle Kniffe kennen || tr mit e-m Seil festbinden; (a steer) mit e-m Lasso einfangen; **r. in** (coll) einwickeln; **r. off** absperren
rosary ['rozəri] s Rosenkranz m
rose [roz] adj rosenrot || s Rose f
rose'bud' s Rosenknospe f
rose'bush' s Rosenstock m
rose'-col'ored adj rosenfarbig; (fig) rosa(rot)
rosemary ['roz‚meri] s Rosmarin m
rosin ['razɪn] s Harz n; (for violin bow) Kolophonium n
roster ['rustər] s Namenliste f; (educ) Stundenplan m; (mil, naut) Dienstplan m
rostrum ['rastrəm] s Rednerbühne f
rosy ['rozi] adj (& fig) rosig
rot [rat] s Fäulnis f; (sl) Quatsch m || v (pret & pp **rotted**; ger **rotting**) tr faulen lassen || intr verfaulen
rotate ['rotet] tr rotieren lassen; (tires) auswechseln; (agr) wechseln || intr rotieren; (take turns) sich abwechseln
rotation [ro'tefən] s Rotation f; **in r.** wechselweise; **r. of crops** Wechselwirtschaft f
rote [rot] s—**by r.** mechanisch
rotisserie [ro'tɪsəri] s Fleischbraterei f
rotten ['ratən] adj faul; (trick) niederträchtig; **feel r.** (sl) sich elend fühlen
rotund [ro'tʌnd] adj rundlich
rotunda [ro'tʌndə] s Rotunde f
rouge [ruʒ] s Rouge n || tr schminken
rough [rʌf] adj (hands, voice, person) rauh; (piece of wood) roh; (work, guess, treatment) grob; (water, weather) stürmisch; (road) uneben; **have it r.** viel durchmachen || tr— **r. in** roh entwerfen; (carp) grob bearbeiten; **r. it** primitiv leben; **r. up** grob behandeln
rough' draft' s Konzept n
roughen ['rʌfən] tr aufrauhen
rough'house' s Radau m || intr Radau machen
roughly ['rʌfli] adv grob; (about) etwa
rough'neck' s (coll) Rauhbein n
roulette [ru'let] s Roulett n
round [raund] adj rund || s Runde f; (of applause) Salve f; (shot) Schuß m; (of drinks) Lage f; (of a sentinel,

policeman, inspector, mailman) Rundgang m; **daily r.** Alltag m || prep um (acc) herum || tr (make round) runden; (a corner) herumgehen (or herumfahren) um (acc); **r. off** abrunden; (finish) vollenden; **r. up** (animals) zusammentreiben; (persons) zusammenbringen; (criminals) ausheben
round'house' s (rr) Lokomotivschuppen m
round'-shoul'dered adj mit runden Schultern
round' steak' s Kugel f
round'-ta'ble adj am runden Tisch
round' trip' s Hin-und Rückfahrt f; (aer) Hin- und Rückflug m
round'-trip' tick'et s Rückfahrkarte f
round'up' s (of cattle) Zusammentreiben n; (of criminals) Aushebung f
rouse [rauz] tr (from) aufwecken (aus)
rout [raut] s völlige Niederlage f; (mil) wilde Flucht f; **put to r.** in die Flucht schlagen || tr (mil) zersprengen
route [rut], [raut] s Route f, Weg m || tr leiten
routine [ru'tin] adj routinemäßig || s Routine f; **be r.** die Regel sein
rove [rov] intr umherwandern
row [rau] s Krach m; **raise a row** (coll) Krach machen || [ro] Reihe f; **in a row** hintereinander || tr rudern
rowboat ['ro‚bot] s Ruderboot n
rowdy ['raudi] adj flegelhaft || s Flegel m
rower ['ro‚ər] s Ruderer –in mf
rowing ['ro‚ɪŋ] s Rudersport m
royal ['rɔɪ‚əl] adj königlich
royalist ['rɔɪ‚əlɪst] adj königstreu || s Königstreue mf
royalty ['rɔɪ‚əlti] s (royal status) Königswürde f; (personage) fürstliche Persönlichkeit f; (collectively) fürstliche Persönlichkeiten pl; (author's compensation) Tantieme f; (inventor's compensation) Lizenzgebühr f
r.p.m. ['ar'pi'em] spl (revolutions per minute) Drehzahl f
R.S.V.P. abbr u.A.w.g. (um Antwort wird gebeten)
rub [rʌb] s Reiben n; **there's the rub** (coll) da sitzt der Haken || v (pret & pp **rubbed**; ger **rubbing**) tr reiben; **rub down** abreiben; **rub elbows with** verkehren mit; **rub in** einreiben; **rub it in** (sl) es (j-m) unter die Nase reiben; **rub out** ausradieren; (sl) umbringen; **rub s.o. the wrong way** j-m auf die Nerven gehen || intr reiben; **rub against** sich reiben an (dat); **rub off on** (fig) abfärben auf (acc)
rubber ['rʌbər] adj Gummi– || s Gummi m & n; (cards) Robber m; **rubbers** Gummischuhe pl
ru'ber band' s Gummiband n
rubberize ['rʌbə‚raɪz] tr gummieren
rub'ber plant' s Kautschukpflanze f
rub'ber stamp' s Gummistempel m
rub'ber-stamp' tr abstempeln; (coll) automatisch genehmigen
rubbery ['rʌbəri] adj gummiartig
rub'bing al'cohol s Franzbranntwein m

rubbish ['rʌbɪʃ] s (trash) Abfall m; (nonsense) dummes Zeug n
rubble ['rʌbəl] s Schutt m; (used in masonry) Bruchstein m
rub'down' s Abreibung f
rubric ['rubrɪk] s Rubrik f
ruby ['rubi] adj rubinrot || s Rubin m
ruckus ['rʌkəs] s (coll) Krawall m
rudder ['rʌdər] s (aer) Seitenruder n; (naut) Steuerruder n
ruddy ['rʌdi] adj rosig
rude [rud] adj grob
rudeness ['rudnɪs] s Grobheit f
rudiments ['rudɪmənts] spl Grundlagen pl
rue [ru] tr bereuen
rueful ['rufəl] adj reuig; (pitiable) kläglich; (mournful) wehmütig
ruffian ['rʌfɪ·ən] s Raufbold m
ruffle ['rʌfəl] s Rüsche f; (in water) Kräuseln f; (of a drum) gedämpfter Trommelwirbel m || tr kräuseln; (feathers, hair) sträuben
rug [rʌg] s Teppich m
rugged ['rʌgɪd] adj (country) wild; (robust) kräftig; (life) hart
ruin ['ru·ɪn] s Ruine f; (undoing) Ruin m; go to r. zugrunde gehen; lie in ruins in Trümmern liegen; ruins (debris) Trümmer pl || tr ruinieren
rule [rul] s (reign) Herrschaft f; (regulation) Regel f; as a r. in der Regel; become the r. zur Regel werden || tr beherrschen; (paper) linieren; r. out ausschließen || intr (over) herrschen (über acc)
rule' of law' s Rechtsstaatlichkeit f
rule' of thumb' s Faustregel f; by r. über den Daumen gepeilt
ruler ['rulər] s Herrscher –in mf; (for measuring) Lineal n
rul'ing adj herrschend || s Regelung f
rum [rʌm] s Rum m
Rumania [ru'menɪ·ə] s Rumänien n
Rumanian [ru'menɪ·ən] adj rumänisch || s Rumäne m, Rumänin f; (language) Rumänisch n
rumble ['rʌmbəl] s (of thunder) Rollen n; (of a truck) Rumpeln n || intr rollen; rumpeln
ruminate ['rumɪ‚net] tr & intr wiederkäuen
rummage ['rʌmɪdʒ] intr—r. through durchsuchen
rum'mage sale' s Ramschverkauf m
rumor ['rumər] s Gerücht n || tr—it is rumored that es geht das Gerücht, daß
rump [rʌmp] s (of an animal) Hinterteil m & n; (buttocks) Gesäß n
rumple ['rʌmpəl] tr (clothes) zerknittern; (hair) zerzausen
rump' steak' s Rumpsteak n
rumpus ['rʌmpəs] s (coll) Krach m; raise a r. (coll) Krach machen
rum'pus room' s Spielzimmer n
run [rʌn] s Lauf m; (in stockings) Laufmasche f; (fin) Run m; (theat) Laufzeit f; be on the run auf der Flucht sein; in the long run auf die Dauer; run of bad luck Pechsträhne f; run of good luck Glücksträhne f ||

v (pret ran [ræn]; pp run; ger running) tr (a machine) bedienen; (a business, household) führen; (a distance) laufen; (a blockade) brechen; (a cable) verlegen; run a race um die Wette laufen; run down (with a car) niederfahren; (clues) nachgehen (dat); (a citation) nachschlagen; (through gossip) schlechtmachen; run off (typ) Abzüge machen von; run over (with a vehicle) überfahren; (rehearse) nochmal durchgehen; run through (with a sword) erstechen; run up (bills) auflaufen lassen; (prices) in die Höhe treiben; (a flag) hissen || intr laufen, rennen; (flow) fließen; (of buses, etc.) verkehren; (said of the nose) laufen, e.g., ihm läuft die Nase his nose is running; (said of colors) auslaufen; (said of a meeting) dauern; (said of a lease) (for) gelten (auf acc); run across zufällig treffen; run after nachlaufen (dat); run around herumlaufen; run around with sich herumtreiben mit; run away weglaufen; (said of a spouse) durchgehen; run down (said of a clock) ablaufen; run dry austrocknen; run for kandidieren für; run high, e.g., feelings ran high die Gemüter waren erhitzt; run in the family in der Familie liegen; run into (e.g., a tree) fahren gegen; (e.g., trouble, debt) geraten in (acc); (e.g., a friend) unerwartet treffen; run into the thousands in die Tausende gehen; run low knapp werden; run out (said of liquids) ausgehen; (said of supplies, time) zu Ende gehen; run out of ausgehen, e.g., they ran out of supplies die Vorräte gingen ihnen aus; run over (said of a pot) überlaufen; run up against stoßen auf (acc); run up to s.o. j–m entgegenlaufen; run wild verwildern
run'-around' s—give s.o. the r. j–n von Pontius zu Pilatus schicken
run'away' adj flüchtig; (horse) durchgegangen || s Ausreißer m; (horse) Durchgänger m
run'down' s kurze Zusammenfassung f
run'-down' adj (condition) heruntergekommen; (clock) abgelaufen; (battery) entladen
rung [rʌŋ] s (of a ladder) Sprosse f; (of a chair) Querleiste f
run-in' s (coll) Zusammenstoß m
runner ['rʌnər] s Läufer –in mf; (of a sled or skate) Kufe f; (of a sliding door) Laufschiene f; (rug) Läufer m; (bot) Ausläufer m; (mil) Meldegänger m
run'ner-up' s (runners-up) Zweitbeste mf; (sport) Zweite mf
run'ning adj (water) fließend; (debts, expenses, sore) laufend || s Laufen n, Lauf m; be in the r. gut im Rennen liegen; be out of the r. (out of the race) aus dem Rennen ausgeschieden sein; (not among the front runners) keine Aussichten haben

run′ning board′ s Trittbrett n
run′ning start′ s fliegender Start m
run′off′ s (sport) Entscheidungslauf m
run′off′ elec′tion s entscheidende Vor-
wahl f
run′-of-the-mill′ adj Durchschnitts–
runt [rʌnt] s Dreikäsehoch m
run′way′ s Startbahn f
rupture [′rʌpt/ər] s Bruch m || tr (re-
lations) abbrechen; **be ruptured** e–n
Bruch (or Riß) bekommen; **r. one-
self** [dat] e–n Bruch zuziehen ||
intr platzen
rural [′rurəl] adj ländlich
ruse [ruz] s List f
rush [rʌʃ] adj dringend || s Eile f; (for)
Ansturm m (auf acc); (bot) Binse f;
be in a r. es eilig haben; **what's your
r.?** wozu die Eile? || tr (a person)
hetzen; (a defensive position) im
Sturm nehmen; (work) schnell erledigen; (goods) schleunigst schicken;
(e.g., to a hospital) schleunigst schaffen; **be rushed for time** sehr wenig
Zeit haben; **r. through** (a bill) durch-
peitschen; **r. up** (reinforcements)
schnell herbeischaffen || intr eilen,
sich stürzen; **r. at** zustürzen auf

(acc); **r. forward** vorstürmen; **r. into**
stürzen in (acc); **r. up to** zuschießen
auf (acc); **the blood rushed to his
head** ihm stieg das Blut in den Kopf
rush′ hours′ spl Hauptverkehrszeit f
rush′ or′der s Eilauftrag m
russet [′rʌsɪt] adj rotbraun
Russia [′rʌʃə] s Rußland n
Russian [′rʌʃən] adj russisch || s Russe
m, Russin f; (language) Russisch n
rust [rʌst] s Rost m || tr rostig machen
|| intr (ver)rosten
rustic [′rʌstɪk] adj (rural) ländlich;
(countryish) bäuerlich || s Bauer m
rustle [′rʌsəl] s Rauschen n; (of silk)
Knistern n || tr rascheln mit; (cattle)
stehlen || intr rauschen; (said of silk)
knistern
rust′proof′ adj rostfrei
rusty [′rʌstɪ] adj rostig; (fig) einge-
rostet
rut [rʌt] s Geleise n, Spur f; (fig) alter
Trott m
ruthless [′ruθlɪs] adj erbarmungslos
rye [raɪ] s (grain) Roggen m; (whiskey)
Roggenwhisky m
rye′ bread′ s Roggenbrot n
rye′ grass′ s Raigras n

S

S, s [es] s neunzehnter Buchstabe des
englischen Alphabets
Sabbath [′sæbəθ] s Sabbat m
sabbat′ical year′ [sə′bætɪkəl] s ein-
jähriger Urlaub m (e-s Professors)
saber [′sebər] s Säbel m
sable [′sebəl] adj schwarz || s (fur)
Zobelpelz m; (zool) Zobel m
sabotage [′sæbə ̗tɑʒ] s Sabotage f || tr
sabotieren
saboteur [̗sæbə′tʌr] s Saboteur –in
mf
saccharin [′sækərɪn] s Saccharin n
sachet [sæ′ʃe] s Duftkissen n
sack [sæk] s Sack m; (bed) (coll) Falle
f; **hit the s.** (coll) in die Falle gehen
|| tr einsacken; (dismiss) (coll) an
die Luft setzen; (mil) ausplündern
sack′cloth′ s Sacktuch n; **in s. and ashes**
in Sack und Asche
sacrament [′sækrəmənt] s Sakrament n
sacramental [̗sækrə′mentəl] adj sakra-
mental
sacred [′sekrəd] adj heilig; **s. to** geweiht (dat)
sacrifice [′sækrɪ ̗faɪs] s Opfer n; **at a
s.** mit Verlust || tr opfern
sacrilege [′sækrɪlɪdʒ] s Sakrileg n
sacrilegious [̗sækrɪ′lɪdʒəs] adj frevel-
haft, gotteslästerlich
sacristan [′sækrɪstən] s Sakristan m
sacristy [′sækrɪsti] s Sakristei f
sad [sæd] adj traurig; (plight) schlimm
sadden [′sædən] tr traurig machen
saddle [′sædəl] s Sattel m || tr satteln;
be saddled with auf dem Halse haben

sad′dlebag′ s Satteltasche f
sadism [′sedɪzəm] s Sadismus m
sadistic [se′dɪstɪk] adj sadistisch
sadness [′sædnɪs] s Traurigkeit f
sad′ sack′ s (sl) Trauerkloß m
safe [sef] adj (from) sicher (vor dat);
(arrival) glücklich; **s. and sound** heil
und gesund; (said of a thing) unversehrt; **to be on the s. side** vorsichts-
halber || s Geldschrank m
safe′-con′duct s sicheres Geleit n
safe′-depos′it box′ s Schließfach n
safe′ dis′tance s Sicherheitsabstand m
safe′guard′ s Schutz m || tr schützen
safe′keep′ing s sicherer Gewahrsam m
safety [′sefti] adj Sicherheits– || s
Sicherheit f
safe′ty belt′ s Sicherheitsgurt m
safe′ty pin′ s Sicherheitsnadel f
safe′ty ra′zor s Rasierapparat m
safe′ty valve′ s Sicherheitsventil n
saffron [′sæfrən] adj safrangelb || s
Safran m
sag [sæg] s Senkung f || v (pret & pp
sagged; ger sagging) intr sich senken;
(said of a cable) durchhängen; (fig)
sinken
sagacious [sə′geʃəs] adj scharfsinnig
sage [sedʒ] adj weise, klug || s Weise
m; (plant) Salbei f
sage′brush′ s Beifuß m
sail [sel] s Segel n; **set s. for** in See
stechen nach || tr (a boat) segeln;
(the sea) segeln über (acc) || intr
segeln; (depart) abfahren; **s. across**
übersegeln; **s. along the coast** an der

Küste entlangsegeln; **s. into** (coll) herunterputzen

sail'boat' s Segelboot n

sail'cloth' s Segeltuch n

sail'ing s Segelfahrt f; (sport) Segelsport m; **it will be smooth s.** (fig) es wird alles glattgehen

sail'ing ves'sel s Segelschiff n

sailor ['selər] s Matrose m

Saint [sent] s Heilige mf; **S. George** der heilige Georg, Sankt Georg

Saint' Bernard' s (dog) Bernhardiner m

sake [sek] s—**for her s.** ihretwegen; **for his s.** seinetwegen; **for my s.** meinetwegen; **for our s.** unsertwegen; **for their s.** ihretwegen; **for the s. of** um (genit) willen; **for your s.** deinetwegen, Ihretwegen

salable ['seləbəl] adj verkäuflich

salacious [sə'leʃəs] adj (person) geil; (writing, pictures) obszön

salad ['sæləd] s Salat m

sal'ad bowl' s Salatschüssel f

sal'ad dress'ing s Salatsoße f

sal'ad oil' s Salatöl n

salami [sə'lɑmi] s Salami f

salary ['sæləri] s Gehalt n

sale [sel] s Verkauf m; (special sale) Ausverkauf m; **be up for s.** zum Kauf stehen; **for s.** zu verkaufen; **sales** (com) Absatz m, Umsatz m; **put up for s.** zum Verkauf anbieten

sales'' clerk' s Verkäufer –in mf

sales'girl' s Ladenmädchen n

sales'la'dy s Verkäuferin f

sales'man s (–men) Verkäufer m

sales'man'ship s Verkaufstüchtigkeit f

sales' promo'tion s Verkaufsförderung f

sales' slip' s Kassenzettel m, Bon m

sales' tax' s Umsatzsteuer f

saliva [sə'laɪvə] s Speichel m

sallow ['sælo] adj bläßlich

sal·ly ['sæli] s (side trip) Abstecher m; (mil) Ausfall m || v (pret & pp –lied) intr (mil) ausfallen; **s. forth** sich aufmachen

salmon ['sæmən] adj lachsfarben || s Lachs m

saloon [sə'lun] s Kneipe f; (naut) Salon m

salt [sɔlt] s Salz n || tr salzen; **s. away** (coll) auf die hohe Kante legen

salt'cel'lar s Salzfaß n

salt'ed meat' s Salzfleisch n

salt' mine' s Salzbergwerk n; **back to the salt mines** zurück zur Tretmühle

salt'pe'ter s Salpeter m

salt' shak'er s Salzfaß n

salty ['sɔlti] adj salzig

salutary ['sæljə,teri] adj heilsam

salute [sə'lut] s Salut m || tr & intr salutieren

salvage ['sælvɪdʒ] s (saving by ship) Bergung n; (property saved by ship) Bergungsgut n; (discarded material) Altmaterial n || tr bergen; (discarded material) verwerten

salvation [sæl've/ən] s Heil n

Salva'tion Ar'my s Heilsarmee f

salve [sæv] s Salbe f || tr (one's conscience) beschwichtigen

sal·vo ['sælvo] s (–vos & –voes) Salve f

Samaritan [sə'mærɪtən] s Samariter –in mf; **good S.** barmherziger Samariter m

same [sem] adj—**at the s. time** gleichzeitig; **it's all the s. to me** es ist mir ganz gleich; **just the s.** trotzdem; **thanks, s. to you!** danke, gleichfalls!; **the s.** derselbe

sameness ['semnɪs] s Eintönigkeit f

sample ['sæmpəl] s Muster n, Probe f || tr (aus)probieren

sancti·fy ['sæŋktɪ,faɪ] v (pret & pp –fied) tr heiligen

sanctimonious [,sæŋktɪ'monɪ-əs] adj scheinheilig

sanction ['sæŋkʃən] s Sanktion f || tr sanktionieren

sanctity ['sæŋktɪti] s Heiligkeit f

sanctuary ['sæŋktʃʊ,eri] s (shrine) Heiligtum n; (of a church) Altarraum m; (asylum) Asyl n

sand [sænd] s Sand m || tr mit Sandpapier abschleifen; (a road, sidewalk) mit Sand bestreuen

sandal ['sændəl] s Sandale f

san'dalwood' s Sandelholz n

sand'bag' s Sandsack m

sand'bank' s Sandbank f

sand' bar' s Sandbank f

sand'blast' tr sandstrahlen

sand'box' s Sandkasten m

sand' cas'tle s Strandburg f

sand' dune' s Sanddüne f

sand'glass' s Sanduhr f

sand'man s (–men) (fig) Sandmann m

sand'pa'per s Sandpapier n || tr mit Sandpapier abschleifen

sand'stone' s Sandstein m

sand'storm' s Sandsturm m

sandwich ['sændwɪtʃ] s belegtes Brot n, Sandwich n || tr (in between) einzwängen (zwischen dat)

sandy ['sændi] adj sandig; (color) sandfarben

sane [sen] adj geistig gesund; (e.g., advice) vernünftig

sanguine ['sæŋgwɪn] adj (about) zuversichtlich (in Bezug auf acc)

sanitarium [,sænɪ'terɪ-əm] s Heilanstalt f, Sanatorium n

sanitary ['sænɪ,teri] adj sanitär

san'itary nap'kin s Damenbinde f

sanitation [,sænɪ'teʃən] s Gesundheitswesen n; (in a building) sanitäre Einrichtungen pl

sanity ['sænɪti] s geistige Gesundheit f

Santa Claus ['sæntə ,klɔz] s der Weihnachtsmann m, der Nikolaus

sap [sæp] s Saft m; (coll) Schwachkopf m || v (pret & pp sapped; ger sapping) tr (strength) erschöpfen

sapling ['sæplɪŋ] s junger Baum m

sapphire ['sæfaɪr] s Saphir m

Saracen ['særəsən] adj sarazenisch || s Sarazene m, Sarazenin f

sarcasm ['sɑrkæzəm] s Sarkasmus m

sarcastic [sɑr'kæstɪk] adj sarkastisch

sarcophagus [sɑr'kɑfəgəs] s Sarkophag m

sardine [sɑr'din] s Sardine f; **packed**

in like sardines zusammengedrängt wie die Heringe
Sardinia [sɑrˈdɪnɪ·ə] s Sardinien n
Sardinian [sɑrˈdɪnɪ·ən] adj sardinisch || s Sardinier –in m; (language) Sardinisch n
sash [sæʃ] s Schärpe f; (of a window) Fensterrahmen m
sass [sæs] s (coll) Revolverschnauze f || tr (coll) (off) patzig antworten (dat)
sassy [ˈsæsi] adj (coll) patzig
Satan [ˈsetən] s Satan m
satanic(al) [səˈtænɪk(əl)] adj satanisch
satchel [ˈsætʃəl] s Handtasche f
sate [set] tr übersättigen
satellite [ˈsætəˌlaɪt] s Satellit m
sat'ellite coun'try s Satellitenstaat m
satiate [ˈseʃɪˌet] tr sättigen
satin [ˈsætɪn] s Seidenatlas m
satire [ˈsætaɪr] s Satire f
satiric(al) [səˈtɪrɪk(əl)] adj satirisch
satirize [ˈsætɪˌraɪz] tr verspotten
satisfaction [ˌsætɪsˈfækʃən] s Befriedigung f, Genugtuung f
satisfactory [ˌsætɪsˈfæktəri] adj friedenstellend, genügend
satis·fy [ˈsætɪsˌfaɪ] v (pret & pp –fied) tr (desires, needs) befriedigen; (requirements) genügen (dat); (a person) zufriedenstellen; **be satisfied with** zufrieden sein mit || intr befriedigen
saturate [ˈsætʃəˌret] tr (& chem) sättigen, saturieren
satura'tion bomb'ing s Bombenteppich m
satura'tion point' s Sättigungspunkt m
Saturday [ˈsætərˌde] s Samstag m; **on S.** am Samstag
sauce [sɔs] s Soße f; (coll) Frechheit f || tr mit Soße zubereiten; (season) würzen
sauce'pan' s Stielkasserolle f
saucer [ˈsɔsər] s Untertasse f
saucy [ˈsɔsi] adj (impertinent) frech; (amusingly flippant) keß; (trim) flott
sauerkraut [ˈsaʊrˌkraʊt] s Sauerkraut n
saunter [ˈsɔntər] s Schlendern n || intr schlendern
sausage [ˈsɔsɪdʒ] s Wurst f
saute [soˈte] v (pret & pp sauteed) tr sautieren
savage [ˈsævɪdʒ] adj wild || s Wilde mf
savant [ˈsævənt] s Gelehrte m
save [sev] tr (rescue) retten; (money, fuel) sparen; (keep, preserve) aufheben; (trouble) ersparen; (time) gewinnen; (stamps) sammeln; **s. face** das Gesicht wahren; **s. from** bewahren vor (dat) || prep außer (dat)
sav'ing adj (grace) seligmachend; (quality) ausgleichend || s (of souls) Rettung f; (in) Ersparnis f (an dat); **savings** Ersparnisse pl
sav'ings account' s Sparkonto n
sav'ings bank' s Sparkasse f
sav'ings certi'ficate s Sparbon m
sav'ings depos'it s Spareinlage f
savior [ˈsevjər] s Retter –in mf; **Saviour** Heiland m

savor [ˈsevər] s Wohlgeschmack m || tr auskosten || intr—**s. of** (smell of) riechen nach; (taste of) schmecken nach
savory [ˈsevəri] adj wohschmeckend
saw [sɔ] s Säge f; (saying) Sprichwort n || tr sägen; **saw up** zersägen
saw'dust' s Sägespäne pl
saw'horse' s Sägebock m
saw'mill' s Sägemühle f
Saxon [ˈsæksən] adj sächsisch || s Sachse m, Sachsin f
Saxony [ˈsæksəni] s Sachsen n
saxophone [ˈsæksəˌfon] s Saxophon n
say [se] s—**have a** (or no) **say in etw** (or nichts) zu sagen haben bei; **have one's say** (about) seine Meinung äußern (über acc) || v (pret & pp said [sed]) tr sagen; (Mass) lesen; (a prayer) sprechen; (one's prayers) verrichten; (said of a newspaper article, etc.) besagen; **it says in the papers** in der Zeitung steht; (let's) **say** sagen wir; **no sooner said than done** gesagt, getan; **say!** (to draw attention) sag mall; (to elicit agreement) gelt!; **say s.th. behind s.o.'s back** j–m etw nachsagen; **she is said to be** to be clever sie soll klug sein; **that is not to say** das will nicht sagen; **that is to say** das heißt; **they say** man sagt; **to say nothing of** ganz zu schweigen von; **you don't say so!** tatsächlich!
say'ing s Sprichwort n; **as the s. goes** wie man zu sagen pflegt; **it goes without s.** das versteht sich von selbst
say'-so' s (assertion) Behauptung f; (order) Anweisung f; (final authority) letztes Wort n
scab [skæb] s Schorf m; (sl) Streikbrecher –in mf
scabbard [ˈskæbərd] s Schwertscheide f
scabby [ˈskæbi] adj schorfig
scads [skædz] spl (sl) e–e Menge f
scaffold [ˈskæfəld] s Gerüst n; (for executions) Schafott n
scaf'folding s Baugerüst n
scald [skɔld] tr verbrühen; (milk) aufkochen
scale [skel] s (on fish, reptiles) Schuppe f; (pan of a balance) Waagschale f; (of a thermometer, wages) Skala f; (mus) Tonleiter f; **on a grand s.** im großen Stil; **on a large** (or **small**) **s.** in großem (or kleinem) Maßstab; **s. 1:1000** Maßstab 1:1000; **scales** Waage f; **to s.** maßstabgerecht || tr erklettern; **s. down** maßstäblich verkleinern; (prices) herabsetzen
scallop [ˈskæləp] s Kammuschel f; (sew) Zacke f || tr auszacken; (culin) überbacken
scalp [skælp] s Kopfhaut f; (Indian trophy) Skalp m || tr skalpieren
scalpel [ˈskælpəl] s Skalpell n
scaly [ˈskeli] adj schuppig
scamp [skæmp] s Fratz m, Wildfang m
scamper [ˈskæmpər] intr herumtollen; **s. away** davonlaufen
scan [skæn] v (pret & pp scanned; ger

scanning) *tr* (*a page*) überfliegen; (*a verse*) skandieren; (*examine*) genau prüfen; (radar, telv) abtasten

scandal ['skændəl] *s* Skandal *m*

scandalize ['skændə‚laɪz] *tr* schockieren

scandalmonger ['skændəl‚mʌŋgər] *s* Lästermaul *n*

scandalous ['skændələs] *adj* skandalös

scan'dal sheet' *s* Sensationsblatt *n*

Scandinavia [‚skændɪ'nevɪ‚ə] *s* Skandinavien *n*

Scandinavian [‚skændɪ'nevɪ‚ən] *adj* skandinavisch ‖ *s* Skandinavier –in *mf*; (*language*) Skandinavisch *n*

scansion ['skænʃən] *s* Skandieren *n*

scant [skænt] *adj* gering; **a s. two hours** knapp zwei Stunden

scantily ['skæntɪli] *adv*—**s. clad** leicht bekleidet

scanty ['skænti] *adj* kärglich, knapp

scapegoat ['skep‚got] *s* Sündenbock *m*

scar [skɑr] *s* Narbe *f*; (fig) Makel *m* ‖ *v* (*pret & pp* scarred; *ger* scarring) *tr* (*e.g., a face*) entstellen; (*e.g., a tabletop*) verschrammen; (fig) beinträchtigen

scarce [skers] *adj* knapp, rar; **make oneself s.** (coll) das Weite suchen

scarcely ['skersli] *adv* kaum; **be s. able to** (*inf*) Not haben zu (*inf*)

scarcity ['skersɪti] *s* (**of**) Knappheit *f* (an *dat*), Mangel *m* (an *dat*)

scare [sker] *s* Schrecken *m*; **be scared** erschrecken; **be scared stiff** e-e Hundeangst haben; **give s.o. a s.** j–m e–n Schrecken einjagen ‖ *tr* erschrecken; **s. away** verscheuchen; **s. up** (*money*) auftreiben ‖ *intr* erschrecken

scare'crow' *s* Vogelscheuche *f*

scarf [skɑrf] *s* (**scarfs & scarves** [skɑrvz]) Schal *m*

scarlet ['skɑrlɪt] *adj* scharlachrot ‖ *s* Scharlachrot *n*

scar'let fe'ver *s* Scharlach *m*

scarred *adj* narbig, schrammig

scary ['skeri] *adj* schreckenerregend

scat [skæt] *interj* weg!

scathing ['skeðɪŋ] *adj* vernichtend

scatter ['skætər] *tr* zerstreuen ‖ *intr* sich zerstreuen

scat'terbrain' *s* Wirrkopf *m*

scat'tered show'ers *spl* einzelne Schauer *pl*

scenari·o [sɪ'nerɪ·o] *s* (**–os**) Drehbuch *n*

scene [sin] *s* Szene *f*; **be on the s.** zur Stelle sein; **behind the scenes** hinter den Kulissen; **make a s.** e–e Szene machen; **s. of the crime** Tatort *m*

scenery ['sinəri] *s* Landschaft *f*; (theat) Bühnenausstattung *f*

scenic ['sinɪk] *adj* landschaftlich; (theat) szenisch

scent [sent] *s* Duft *m*; (*of a dog*) Witterung *f*; (hunt) Spur *f*; **have a s. duften** ‖ *tr* wittern

scepter ['septər] *s* Zepter *n*

sceptic ['skeptɪk] *s* Skeptiker –in *mf*

scepticism ['skeptɪ‚sɪzəm] *s* (*doubt*) Skepsis *f*; (*doctrine*) Skeptizismus *m*

schedule ['skedjʊl] *s* Plan *m*; (*for work*) Arbeitsplan *m*; (*in travel*) Fahrplan *m*; (*at school*) Stundenplan *m*; (*appendix to a tax return*) Einkommensteuerformular *n*; (*table*) Einkommensteuertabelle *f*; **on s.** fahrplanmäßig ‖ *tr* ansetzen; **the plane is scheduled to arrive at six** nach dem Flugplan soll die Maschine um sechs Uhr ankommen

scheme [skim] *s* (*schematic*) Schema *n*; (*plan, program*) Plan *m*; (*intrigue*) Intrige *f* ‖ *tr* planen ‖ *intr* Ränke schmieden

schemer ['skimər] *s* Ränkeschmied *m*

schilling ['ʃɪlɪŋ] *s* (Aust) Schilling *m*

schism ['sɪzəm] *s* (fig) Spaltung *f*; (eccl) Schisma *n*

schizophrenia [‚skɪtso'frinɪ·ə] *s* Schizophrenie *f*, Bewußtseinsspaltung *f*

schizophrenic [‚skɪtso'frenɪk] *adj* schizophren

schmaltzy ['ʃmɔltsi] *adj* schmalzig

scholar ['skɑlər] *s* Gelehrte *mf*

scholarly ['skɑlərli] *adj* gelehrt

schol'arship' *s* Gelehrsamkeit *f*; (*award*) Stipendium *n*

scholastic [skə'læstɪk] *adj* Schul–, Bildungs–; (hist) scholastisch

school [skul] *adj* (*book, house, master, room, teacher, yard, year*) Schul–' ‖ *s* Schule *f*; (*of a university*) Fakultät *f*; (*of fish*) Schwarm *m*; **s. is over** die Schule ist aus ‖ *tr* schulen

school' age' *s* schulpflichtiges Alter *n*; **of s.** schulpflichtig

school'bag' *s* Schulranzen *m*

school' board' *s* Schulausschuß *m*

school'boy' *s* Schüler *m*

school'girl' *s* Schülerin *f*

school'ing *s* (*formal education*) Schulbildung *f*; (*training*) Schulung *f*

school'mate' *s* Mitschüler –in *mf*

schooner ['skunər] *s* Schoner *m*

sciatica [saɪ'ætɪkə] *s* Hüftschmerz *m*

science ['saɪ·əns] *s* Wissenschaft *f*; **the sciences** die Naturwissenschaften *pl*

sci'ence fic'tion *s* Science-fiction *f*

scientific [‚saɪ·ən'tɪfɪk] *adj* wissenschaftlich

scientist ['saɪ·əntɪst] *s* Wissenschaftler –in *mf*

scimitar ['sɪmɪtər] *s* Türkensäbel *m*

scintillate ['sɪntɪ‚let] *intr* funkeln

scion ['saɪ·ən] *s* Sprößling *m*; (bot) Pfropfreis *n*

scissors ['sɪzərz] *s & spl* Schere *f*; (*in wrestling*) Zangengriff *m*

scoff [skɔf] *s* Spott *m* ‖ *intr* (**at**) spotten (über *acc*)

scold [skold] *tr & intr* schelten

scold'ing *s* Schelte *f*; **get a s.** Schelte bekommen

sconce [skɑns] *s* Wandleuchter *m*

scoop [skup] *s* (*ladle*) Schöpfkelle *f*; (*for sugar, flour*) Schaufel *f*; (*amount scooped*) Schlag *m*; (journ) Knüller *m* ‖ *tr* schöpfen; **s. out** ausschaufeln; **s. up** scheffeln

scoot [skut] *intr* (coll) flitzen

scooter ['skutər] *s* Roller *m*

scope [skop] *s* (*extent*) Umfang *m*;

(*range*) Reichweite *f;* **give free s. to the imagination** der Phatasie freien Lauf lassen; **give s.o. free s.** j—m freie Hand geben; **within the s. of** im Rahmen (*genit*) or von

scorch [skɔrt∫] *tr* versengen

scorched'-earth' pol'icy *s* Politik *f* der verbrannten Erde

scorch'ing *adj & adv* sengend

score [skor] *s* (*of a game*) Punktzahl *f;* (*final score*) Ergebnis *n;* (*notch*) Kerbe *f;* (*mus*) Partitur *f;* **a s. of** zwanzig; **have an old s. to settle with s.o.** mit j—m e—e alte Rechnung zu begleichen haben; **keep s.** die Punktzahl anschreiben; **know the s.** (*coll*) auf Draht sein; **on that s.** diesbezüglich; **what's the s.?** wie steht das Spiel? ‖ *tr* (*points*) erzielen; (*goals*) schießen; (*notch*) einkerben; (*mus*) in Partitur setzen ‖ *intr* e—n Punkt erzielen

score'board' *s* Anzeigetafel *f*

score'card' *s* Punktzettel *m*

score'keep'er *s* Anschreiber –in *mf*

score'sheet' *s* Spielberichtsbogen *m*

scorn [skɔrn] *s* Verachtung *f;* **laugh to s.** auslachen ‖ *tr* verachten

scornful ['skɔrnfəl] *adj* verächtlich

scorpion ['skɔrpɪ·ən] *s* Skorpion *m*

Scot [skɑt] *s* Schotte *m,* Schottin *f*

Scotch [skɑt∫] *adj* schottisch; (*sl*) geizig ‖ *s* schottischer Whisky *m;* (*dialect*) Schottisch *n* ‖ *tr* (*a rumor*) ausrotten; (*with a chock*) blockieren; (*render harmless*) unschädlich machen

Scotch'man *s* (**–men**) Schotte *m*

Scotch' pine' *s* gemeine Kiefer *f*

Scotch' tape' *s* (*trademark*) durchsichtiger Klebstreifen *m*

scot'-free' *adj* ungestraft

Scotland ['skɑtlənd] *s* Schottland *n*

Scottish ['skɑtɪ∫] *adj* schottisch ‖ *s* (*dialect*) Schottisch *n;* **the S.** die Schotten *pl*

scoundrel ['skaundrəl] *s* Lump *m*

scour [skaur] *tr* scheuern; (*the city*) absuchen

scourge [skʌrdʒ] *s* Geißel *f* ‖ *tr* geißeln

scout [skaut] *s* Pfadfinder *m;* (*mil, sport*) Kundschafter *m* ‖ *tr* aufklären ‖ *intr* kundschaften

scout'mas'ter *s* Pfadfinderführer *m*

scowl [skaul] *s* finsterer Blick *m* ‖ *intr* finster blicken; **s. at** grollend ansehen

scram [skræm] *v* (*pret & pp* **scrammed;** *ger* **scramming**) *intr* (*coll*) abhauen

scramble ['skræmbəl] *s* (**for**) Balgerei *f* (um) ‖ *tr* (*mix up*) durcheinandermischen; (*a message*) unverständlich machen; **s. eggs** Rührei machen ‖ *intr* (*e.g., over rocks*) klettern; **s. for s.th.** um etw reißen; **s. to one's feet** sich aufrappeln

scram'bled eggs' *spl* Rührei *n*

scrap [skræp] *s* (*of metal*) Schrott *m;* (*of paper*) Fetzen *m;* (*of food*) Rest *m;* (*refuse*) Abfall *m;* (*quarrel*) (*coll*) Zank *m;* (*fight*) (*coll*) Rauferei *f* ‖ *v* (*pret & pp* **scrapped;** *ger*

scrapping) *tr* ausrangieren ‖ *intr* (*quarrel*) (*coll*) zanken; (*fight*) (*coll*) raufen

scrap'book' *s* Einklebebuch *n*

scrape [skrep] *s* Kratzer *m;* (*coll*) Patsche *f* ‖ *tr* schaben; (*the skin*) abscheuern; **s. off** abschaben; **s. together** (or **up**) zusammenkratzen

scrap' heap' *s* Schrotthaufen *m;* (*refuse heap*) Abfallhaufen *m*

scrap' i'ron *s* Schrott *m,* Alteisen *n*

scrapper ['skræpər] *s* Zänker –in *mf*

scrappy ['skræpi] *adj* (*made of scraps*) zusammengestoppelt; (*coll*) rauflustig

scratch [skræt∫] *s* Kratzer *m,* Schramme *f;* **start from s.** wieder ganz von vorne anfangen ‖ *tr* kratzen; (*sport*) streichen; **s. open** aufkratzen; **s. out** (*a line*) ausstreichen; (*eyes*) aushacken; **s. the surface of** nur streifen ‖ *intr* kratzen; (*scratch oneself*) sich kratzen

scratch' pad' *s* Notizblock *m*

scratch' pa'per *s* Schmierpapier *n*

scrawl [skrɔl] *s* Gekritzel *n* ‖ *tr & intr* kritzeln

scrawny ['skrɔni] *adj* spindeldürr

scream [skrim] *s* Aufschrei *m;* **he's a s.!** er ist zum Schreien! ‖ *tr & intr* schreien

screech [skrit∫] *s* Kreischen *n* ‖ *intr* (*said of tires, brakes*) kreischen; (*said of an owl*) schreien

screech' owl' *s* Kauz *m*

screen [skrin] *s* Wandschirm *m;* (*for a window*) Fliegengitter *n;* (*camouflage*) Tarnung *f;* (*aer*) (**of**) Abschirmung *f* (durch); (*cin*) Leinwand *f;* (*nav*) Geleitschutz *m;* (*radar, telv*) Leinwand *f* ‖ *tr* (*sand, gravel, coal; applications*) durchsieben; (*applicants*) überprüfen; (*a porch, windows*) mit Fliegengittern versehen; (*mil*) verschleiern; **s. off** abschirmen

screen'play' *s* Filmdrama *n;* (*scenario*) Drehbuch *n*

screen' test' *s* Probeaufnahme *f*

screw [skru] *s* Schraube *f;* **he has a s. loose** (*coll*) bei ihm ist e—e Schraube locker ‖ *tr* schrauben; (*cheat*) (*sl*) hereinlegen; (*vulg*) vögeln; **s. tight** festschrauben; **s. up** (*courage*) aufbringen; (*bungle*) (*coll*) verpfuschen

screw'ball' *adj* (*coll*) verrückt ‖ *s* (*coll*) Wirrkopf *m*

screw'driv'er *s* Schraubenzieher *m*

screw'-on cap' *s* Schraubendeckel *m*

screwy ['skru·i] *adj* (*sl*) verrückt

scribble ['skrɪbəl] *s* Gekritzel *n* ‖ *tr & intr* kritzeln

scribe [skraib] *s* Schreiber *m;* (*Bib*) Schriftgelehrte *m*

scrimmage ['skrɪmɪdʒ] *s* (*fb*) Übungsspiel *n*

scrimp [skrɪmp] *tr* knausern mit ‖ *intr* (**on**) knausern (mit)

scrimpy ['skrɪmpi] *adj* knapp

script [skrɪpt] *s* (*handwriting*) Handschrift *f;* (*cin*) Drehbuch *n;* (*rad*) Textbuch *n;* (*typ*) Schreibschrift *f*

scriptural ['skrɪpt∫ərəl] *adj* biblisch; **s. passage** Bibelstelle *f*

Scripture ['skrɪptʃər] s die Heilige Schrift; *(Bible passage)* Bibelzitat n
script'writ'er s (cin) Drehbuchautor m
scrofula ['skrɑfjələ] s Skrofeln pl
scroll [skrol] s Schriftrolle f; (archit) Schnörkel m
scroll'work' s Schnörkelverzierung f
scro·tum ['skrotəm] s (-ta [tə] or -tums) Hodensack m
scrounge [skraundʒ] tr stibitzen || intr —s. around for herumstöbern nach
scrub [skrʌb] s Schrubben n; *(shrubs)* Buschwerk n; (sport) Ersatzmann m || v *(pret & pp* scrubbed; ger scrubbing) tr schrubben
scrub'bing brush' s Scheuerbürste f
scrub'wom'an s (-wom'en) Scheuerfrau f
scruff [skrʌf] s—s. of the neck Genick n
scruple ['skrupəl] s Skrupel m
scrupulous ['skrupjələs] adj skrupulös
scrutinize ['skrutɪ‚naɪz] tr genau prüfen; *(a person)* mustern
scrutiny ['skrutɪni] s genaue Prüfung f
scud [skʌd] s Wolkenfetzen m
scuff [skʌf] tr *(a shoe, waxed floor)* abschürfen || intr *(shuffle)* schlurfen
scuffle ['skʌfəl] s Rauferei f || intr raufen
scuff' mark' s Schmutzfleck m
scull [skʌl] s (sport) Skull m || intr (sport) skullen
scullery ['skʌləri] s Spülküche f
scul'lery maid' s Spülerin f
sculptor ['skʌlptər] s Bildhauer m
sculptress ['skʌlptrɪs] s Bildhauerin f
sculptural ['skʌlptʃərəl] adj bildhauerisch
sculpture ['skʌlptʃər] s (art) Bildhauerei f; *(work of art)* Skulptur f || tr meißeln || intr bildhauern
scum [skʌm] s (& fig) Abschaum m
scummy ['skʌmi] adj schaumig; (fig) niederträchtig
scurrilous ['skʌrɪləs] adj skurril
scur·ry ['skʌri] v *(pret & pp* -ried) intr huschen
scurvy ['skʌrvi] adj gemein || s Skorbut m
scuttle ['skʌtəl] s (naut) Springluke f || tr *(hopes, plans)* vernichten; (naut) selbst versenken
scut'tlebutt' s (coll) Latrinenparole f
scut'tling s Selbstversenkung f
scythe [saɪð] s Sense f
sea [si] s See f, Meer n; at sea zur See; go to sea zur See gehen; heavy seas hoher (or schwerer) Seegang m
sea'board' s Küstenstrich m
sea' breeze' s Seebrise f
sea'coast' s Seeküste f, Meeresküste f
seafarer ['si‚ferər] s Seefahrer m
seafaring ['si‚ferɪŋ] s Seefahrt f
sea'food' s Fischgerichte pl
sea'go'ing adj seetüchtig
sea' gull' s Seemöwe f, Möwe f
seal [sil] s Siegel n; (zool) Seehund m || tr *(a document)* siegeln; *(a deal, s.o.'s fate)* besiegeln; *(against leakage)* verschließen, abdichten; s. off (mil) abriegeln; s. up abdichten

sea' legs' spl—get one's s. seefest werden
sea'lev'el s Meereshöhe f
seal'ing wax' s Siegellack m
seal'skin' s Seehundsfell n
seam [sim] s *(groove)* Fuge f; (geol) Lager n; (min) Flöz n; (sew) Naht f
sea'man s (-men) Seemann m; (nav) Matrose m
sea' mile' s Seemeile f
seamless ['simlɪs] adj nahtlos
sea' mon'ster s Meeresungeheuer n
seamstress ['simstrɪs] s Näherin f
seamy ['simi] adj verrufen; s. side (fig) Schattenseite f
séance ['se·ɑns] s Séance f
sea'plane' s Seeflugzeug n
sea'port' s Seehafen m
sea'port town' s Hafenstadt f
sea' pow'er s Seemacht f
sear [sɪr] tr versengen
search [sʌrtʃ] s Durchsuchung f; *(for a person)* (for) Fahndung f (nach); in s. of auf der Suche nach || tr durchsuchen || intr suchen; s. for suchen, fahnden nach
search'ing adj gründlich; *(glance)* forschend
search'light' s Scheinwerfer m
search' war'rant s Haussuchungsbefehl m
seascape ['si‚skep] s Seegemälde n
sea' shell' s Muschel f
sea'shore' s Strand m
sea'shore resort' s Seebad n
sea'sick' adj seekrank
sea'sick'ness s Seekrankheit f
sea'side' adj Meeres–, See–
season ['sizən] s Jahreszeit f; *(appropriate period)* Saison f; closed s. (hunt) Schonzeit f; dry s. Trockenzeit f; in and out of s. jederzeit; in s. zur rechten Zeit; out of s. *(game)* außerhalb der Saison; *(fruits, vegetables)* nicht auf dem Markt; peak s. Hochsaison f || tr *(food)* würzen; *(wine)* lagern; *(wood)* austrocknen lassen; *(tobacco)* reifen lassen; *(soldiers)* abhärten || intr *(e.g., said of wine)* (ab)lagern
seasonal ['sizənəl] adj jahreszeitlich; *(caused by seasons)* saisonbedingt
sea'sonal work' s Saisonarbeit f
sea'soned adj erfahren; *(troops)* kampfgewohnt, fronterfahren
sea'soning s Würze f
sea'son's greet'ings spl Festgrüße pl
sea'son tick'et s Dauerkarte f
seat [sit] s Sitz m, Platz m; *(of trousers)* Gesäß n; have a s. Platz nehmen; keep one's s. sitzenbleiben || tr *(a person)* e–n Platz anweisen (dat); *(said of a room)* Sitzplätze bieten für; be seated sich hinsetzen
seat' belt' s (aer, aut) Sicherheitsgurt m; fasten seat belts! bitte anschnallen!
seat' cov'er s (aut) Auto-Schonbezug m
seat'ing capac'ity s (for) Sitzgelegenheit f (für); have a s. of fassen
seat' of gov'ernment s Regierungssitz m
sea'wall' s Strandmauer f

sea'way' s Seeweg m; (heavy sea) schwerer Seegang m

sea'weed' s Alge f, Seetang m

sea'wor'thy adj seetüchtig

secede [sɪ'sid] intr sich trennen

secession [sɪ'sɛʃən] s Sezession f

seclude [sɪ'klud] tr abschließen

seclud'ed adj abgeschieden; (life) zurückgezogen; (place) abgelegen

seclusion [sɪ'kluʒən] s Zurückgezogenheit f, Abgeschiedenheit f

second ['sɛkənd] adj zweite; be s. to none niemandem nachstehen; in the s. place zweitens; s. in command stellvertretender Kommandeur m ‖ s (unit of time) Sekunde f; (moment) Augenblick m; (in boxing or duelling) Sekundant m; George the Second Georg der Zweite; the s. (of the month) der zweite ‖ pron zweite ‖ tr unterstützen

secondary ['sɛkən,dɛri] adj sekundär, Neben– ‖ s (elec) Sekundärwicklung f; (fb) Spieler pl in der zweiten Reihe

sec'ondary school' s Oberschule

sec'ondary-school teach'er s Oberlehrer –in mf

sec'ondary sourc'es spl Sekundärliteratur f

sec'ondary tar'get s Ausweichziel n

sec'ond best' s Zweitbeste mfn

sec'ond-best' adj zweitbeste; come off s. den kürzeren ziehen

sec'ond-class' adj zweitklassig; s. ticket Fahrkarte f zweiter Klasse

sec'ond cous'in s Cousin m (or Kusine f) zweiten Grades

sec'ond fid'dle s—play s. die zweite Geige spielen

sec'ond hand' s (horol) Sekundenzeiger m

sec'ondhand' adj (car) gebraucht (information) aus zweiter Hand; (books) antiquarisch

sec'ondhand book'store s Antiquariat n

sec'ondhand deal'er s Altwarenhändler –in mf

sec'ond lieuten'ant s Leutnant m

secondly ['sɛkəndli] adv zweitens

sec'ond mate' s (naut) zweiter Offizier m

sec'ond na'ture s zweite Natur f

sec'ond-rate' adj zweitklassig

sec'ond sight' s zweites Gesicht n

sec'ond thought' s—have second thoughts Bedenken hegen; on s. bei weiterem Nachdenken

sec'ond wind' s—get one's s. wieder zu Kräften kommen

secrecy ['sikrəsi] s Heimlichkeit f

secret ['sikrɪt] adj geheim ‖ s Geheimnis n; in s. insgeheim; keep no secrets from keine Geheimnisse haben vor (dat); keep s. geheimhalten; make no s. of kein Hehl machen aus

secretary ['sɛkrə,dɛri] s (man, desk, bird) Sekretär m; (female) Sekretärin f; (in government) Minister m

sec'retary-gen'eral s Generalsekretär m

sec'retary of com'merce s Handelsminister m

sec'retary of defense' s Verteidigungsminister m

sec'retary of la'bor s Arbeitsminister m

sec'retary of state' s Außenminister m

sec'retary of the inter'ior s Innenminister m

sec'retary of the treas'ury s Finanzminister n

se'cret bal'lot s geheime Abstimmung f

secrete [sɪ'krit] tr (hide) verstecken; (physiol) absondern, ausscheiden

secretive ['sikrɪtɪv] adj verschwiegen

se'cret police' s Geheimpolizei f

se'cret serv'ice s Geheimdienst m

sect [sɛkt] s Sekte f

sectarian [sɛk'tɛrɪ·ən] adj sektiererisch; (school) Konfessions–

section ['sɛkʃən] s (segment, part) Teil m; (of a newspaper, chapter) Abschnitt m; (of a city) Viertel n; (group) Abteilung f; (cross section; thin slice, e.g., of tissue) Schnitt m; (jur) Paragraph m; (mil) Halbzug m; (rr) Strecke f; (surg) Sektion f ‖ tr— s. off abteilen

sectional ['sɛkʃənəl] adj (view) Teil–; (pride) Lokal–

sec'tional fur'niture s Anbaumöbel n

sec'tion hand' s Schienenleger m

sector ['sɛktər] s Sektor m

secular ['sɛkjələr] adj weltlich ‖ s Weltpriester m, Weltgeistlicher m

secularism ['sɛkjələ,rɪzəm] s Weltlichkeit f, Säkularismus m

secure [sɪ'kjur] adj sicher ‖ tr (make fast) sichern; (obtain) sich [dat] beschaffen

security [sɪ'kjurɪti] s (& jur) Sicherheit f; securities Wertpapiere pl

sedan [sɪ'dæn] s Limousine f

sedan' chair' s Sänfte f

sedate [sɪ'det] adj gesetzt

sedation [sɪ'deʃən] s Beruhigung f

sedative ['sɛdətɪv] s Beruhigungsmittel n

sedentary ['sɛdən,tɛri] adj sitzend

sedge [sɛdʒ] s (bot) Segge f

sediment ['sɛdɪmənt] s Bodensatz m; (geol) Ablagerung f, Sediment n

sedition [sɪ'dɪʃən] s Aufruhr m

seditious [sɪ'dɪʃəs] adj aufrührerisch

seduce [sɪ'd(j)us] tr verführen

seducer [sɪ'd(j)usər] s Verführer –in mf

seduction [sɪ'dʌkʃən] s Verführung f

seductive [sɪ'dʌktɪv] adj verführerisch

sedulous ['sɛdʒələs] adj emsig

see [si] s (eccl) (erz)bischöflicher Stuhl m ‖ v (pret saw [sɔ]; pp seen [sin]) tr sehen; (comprehend) verstehen; (realize) einsehen; (by a doctor) gehen zu; see red rasend werden; see s.o. off j–n an den Zug (aus Flugzeug) bringen; see s.o. to the door j–n zur Tür geleiten; see s.th. through etw durchstehen; that remains to be seen das wird man erst sehen ‖ intr sehen; see through (fig) durchschauen; see to sich kümmern um; see to it that sich darum kümmern,

daß; **you see** (*parenthetical*) wissen
Sie

seed [sid] *s* Samen *m*; (*collective &*
fig) Saat *f*; (*in fruit*) Kern *m*;
(*physiol*) Samen *m*; **go to s.** in Samen schießen; **seeds** (*fig*) Keim *m* ‖
tr besäen

seed'bed' *s* Samenbeet *n*

seed'ed rye' bread' *s* Kümmelbrot *n*

seedless ['sidlɪs] *adj* kernlos

seedling ['sidlɪŋ] *s* Sämling *m*

seedy ['sidi] *adj* (*person*) heruntergekommen; (*thing*) schäbig

see'ing *s* Sehen *n* ‖ *conj*—**s. that** in
Anbetracht dessen, daß

See'ing Eye' dog' *s* Blindenhund *m*

seek [sik] *v* (*pret & pp* **sought** [sɔt])
tr suchen; **s. s.o.'s advice** j-s Rat er-
bitten; **s. to** (*inf*) versuchen zu (*inf*)
‖ *intr*—**s. after** suchen nach

seem [sim] *intr* scheinen ‖ *impers*—**it**
seems to me es kommt mir vor

seemingly ['simɪŋli] *adv* anscheinend

seemly ['simli] *adj* schicklich

seep [sip] *intr* sickern

seepage ['sipɪdʒ] *s* Durchsickern *n*

seer [sɪr] *s* Seher *m*

seeress ['sɪrɪs] *s* Seherin *f*

see'saw' *s* Schaukelbrett *n*, Wippe *f* ‖
intr wippen; (*fig*) schwanken

seethe [sið] *intr* sieden; **s. with** (*fig*)
sieden vor (*dat*)

segment ['sɛgmənt] *s* Abschnitt *m*

segregate ['sɛgrɪˌget] *tr* trennen, absondern

segregation [ˌsɛgrɪ'geʃən] *s* Absonde-
rung *f*; (*of races*) Rassentrennung *f*

seismograph ['saɪzməˌgræf] *s* Erdbe-
benmesser *m*, Seismograph *m*

seismology [saɪz'malədʒi] *s* Erdbeben-
kunde *f*, Seismologie *f*

seize [siz] *tr* anfassen; (*a criminal*)
festnehmen; (*a town, fortress*) einnehmen; (*an opportunity*) ergreifen;
(*power*) an sich reißen; (*confiscate*)
beschlagnahmen

seizure ['siʒər] *s* Besitzergreifung *f*;
(*confiscation*) Beschlagnahme *f*;
(*pathol*) plötzlicher Anfall *m*

seldom ['sɛldəm] *adv* selten

select [sɪ'lɛkt] *adj* erlesen ‖ *tr* auslesen, auswählen

select'ed *adj* ausgesucht

selection [sɪ'lɛkʃən] *s* Auswahl *f*

selective [sɪ'lɛktɪv] *adj* Auswahl-;
(*rad*) trennscharf

selec'tive serv'ice *s* allgemeine Wehrpflicht *f*

self [sɛlf] *s* (**selves** [sɛlvz]) Selbst *n*,
Ich *n*; **be one's old s. again** wieder
der alte sein; **his better s.** sein bes-
seres Ich ‖ *pron*—**payable to s.** auf
Selbst ausgestellt

self'-addressed' en'velope *s* mit Anschrift versehener Freiumschlag *m*

self'-assur'ance *s* Selbstbewußtsein *n*

self'-cen'tered *adj* ichbezogen

self'-conceit'ed *adj* eingebildet

self'-con'fident *adj* selbstsicher

self'-con'scious *adj* befangen

self'-control' *s* Selbstbeherrschung *f*

self'-decep'tion *s* Selbsttäuschung *f*

self'-defense' *s* Selbstverteidigung *f*; **in**
s. aus Notwehr

self'-deni'al *s* Selbstverleugnung *f*

self'-destruc'tion *s* Selbstvernichtung *f*

self'-determina'tion *s* Selbstbestim-
mung *f*

self'-dis'cipline *s* Selbstzucht *f*

self'-ed'ucated per'son *s* Autodidakt
–in *mf*

self'-employed' *adj* selbständig

self'-esteem' *s* Selbsteinschätzung *f*

self'-ev'ident *adj* selbstverständlich

self'-explan'ator'y *adj* keiner Erklärung
bedürftig

self'-gov'ernment *s* Selbstverwaltung *f*

self'-impor'tant *adj* eingebildet

self'-indul'gence *s* Genußsucht *f*

self'-in'terest *s* Eigennutz *m*

selfish ['sɛlfɪʃ] *adj* eigennützig

selfishness ['sɛlfɪnɪs] *s* Eigennutz *m*

selfless ['sɛlflɪs] *adj* selbstlos

self'-love' *s* Selbstliebe *f*

self'-made man' *s* Selfmademan *m*

self'-por'trait *s* Selbstbildnis *n*

self'-possessed' *adj* selbstbeherrscht

self'-praise' *s* Eigenlob *n*

self'-preserva'tion *s* Selbsterhaltung *f*

self'-reli'ant *adj* selbstsicher

self'-respect' *s* Selbstachtung *f*

self'-right'eous *adj* selbstgerecht

self'-sac'rifice *s* Selbstaufopferung *f*

self'same' *adj* ebenderselbe

self'-sat'isfied *adj* selbstzufrieden

self'-seek'ing *adj* selbstsüchtig

self'-serv'ice *adj* mit Selbstbedienung
‖ *s* Selbstbedienung *f*

self'-styled' *adj* von eigenen Gnaden

self'-suffi'cient *adj* selbstgenügsam

self'-support'ing *adj* finanziell unab-
hängig

self'-taught' *adj* autodidaktisch

self'-willed' *adj* eigenwillig

self'-wind'ing *adj* automatisch

sell [sɛl] *v* (*pret & pp* **sold** [sold]) *tr*
verkaufen; (*at auction*) versteigern;
(*wares*) führen; **be sold on** (*coll*) begeistert sein von; **s. dirt cheap** verramschen; **s. s.o. on s.th.** (*coll*) j-n
zu etw überreden; **s. out** ausverkaufen; (*betray*) verraten; **s. short** (*st.*
exch.) in blanko verkaufen ‖ *intr*
sich verkaufen; **s. for** verkauft werden für; **s. short** fixen

seller ['sɛlər] *s* Verkäufer –in *mf*; **good**
s. (*com*) Reißer *m*

Seltzer ['sɛltsər] *s* Selterswasser *n*

selvage ['sɛlvɪdʒ] *s* (*of fabric*) Salleiste
f; (*of a lock*) Eckplatte *f*

semantic [sɪ'mæntɪk] *adj* semantisch
‖ **semantics** *s* Wortbedeutungslehre *f*

semaphore ['sɛməˌfor] *s* Winkzeichen
n; (*rr*) Semaphor *m* ‖ *intr* winken

semblance ['sɛmbləns] *s* Anschein *m*

semen ['simən] *s* Samen *m*

semicircle ['sɛmɪˌsʌrkəl] *s* Halbkreis
m

semicolon ['sɛmɪˌkolən] *s* Strichpunkt
m

semiconductor [ˌsɛmɪkən'dʌktər] *s*
Halbleiter *m*

semiconscious [ˌsɛmɪ'kanʃəs] *adj* halb-
bewußt

semifinal [ˌsemɪ'faɪnəl] *adj* Halbfinale– ‖ *s* Halbfinale *n*, Vorschluß-
runde *f*
seminar ['semɪ ˌnɑr] *s* Seminar *n*
seminarian [ˌsemɪ'nerɪ-ən] *s* Seminarist *m*
seminary ['semɪ ˌnerɪ] *s* Seminar *n*
semiprecious [ˌsemɪ'preʃəs] *adj* halb-
edel
Semite ['semaɪt] *s* Semit –in *mf*
Semitic [sɪ'mɪtɪk] *adj* semitisch
semitrailer ['semɪ ˌtreɪlər] *s* Schleppan-
hänger *m*
senate ['senɪt] *s* Senat *m*
senator ['senətər] *s* Senator *m*
senatorial [ˌsenə'torɪ-əl] *adj* (*of one
senator*) senatorisch; (*of the senate*)
Senats–
send [send] *v* (*pret & pp* sent [sent])
tr schicken, senden; (*rad, telv*) senden; **s. back** zurückschicken; **s. back
word** zurücksagen lassen; **s. down**
(*box*) niederschlagen; **s. forth**
(*leaves*) treiben; **s. off** absenden; **s.
on** (*forward*) weiterbefördern; **s.
word** that benachrichtigen, daß ‖
intr—**s. for** (*e.g., free samples*) bestellen; (*e.g., a doctor*) rufen lassen
sender ['sendər] *s* Absender –in *mf*;
(*telg*) Geber –in *mf*
send'-off' *s* Abschiedsfeier *f*
senile ['sinaɪl] *adj* senil
senility [sɪ'nɪlɪti] *s* Senilität *f*
senior ['sinjər] *adj* (*in age*) älter; (*in
rank*) ranghöher; (*class*) oberste;
Mr. John Smith Senior Herr John
Smith senior ‖ *s* Älteste *mf*; (*student*) Student –in *mf* im letzten
Studienjahr
sen'ior cit'izen *s* bejahrter Mitbürger
m
seniority [sin'jɑrɪti] *s* Dienstalter *n*
sen'ior of'ficer *s* Vorgesetzte *mf*
sen'ior part'ner *s* geschäftsführender
Partner *m*
sen'ior year' *s* letztes Studienjahr *n*
sensation [sen'seʃən] *s* (*feeling*) Gefühl *n*; (*cause of interest*) Sensation *f*
sensational [sen'seʃənəl] *adj* sensationell
sensationalism [sen'seʃənə ˌlɪzəm] *s*
Sensationsgier *f*
sense [sens] *s* (*e.g., of sight; meaning*)
Sinn *m*; (*feeling*) Gefühl *n*; (*common sense*) Verstand *m*; **be out of
one's senses** von Sinnen sein; **bring
s.o. to his senses** j–n zur Vernunft
bringen; **in a s.** in gewissem Sinne;
in the broadest s. im weitesten Sinne;
make s. Sinn haben; **there's no s. to
it** da steckt kein Sinn drin ‖ *tr*
spüren, fühlen
senseless ['senslɪs] *adj* sinnlos; (*from
a blow*) bewußtlos
sense' of direc'tion *s* Ortssinn *m*
sense' of du'ty *s* Pflichtgefühl *n*
sense' of guilt' *s* Schuldgefühl *n*
sense' of hear'ing *s* Gehör *n*
sense' of hon'or *s* Ehrgefühl *n*
sense' of hu'mor *s* Humor *m*
sense' of jus'tice *s* Gerechtigkeits-
gefühl *n*

sense' of responsibil'ity *s* Verantwor-
tungsbewußtsein *n*
sense' of sight' *s* Gesichtssinn *m*
sense' of smell' *s* Geruchssinn *m*
sense' of taste' *s* Geschmackssinn *m*
sense' of touch' *s* Tastsinn *m*
sense' or'gan *s* Sinnesorgan *n*
sensibility [ˌsensɪ'bɪlɪti] *s* Empfindlichkeit *f*
sensible ['sensɪbəl] *adj* vernünftig
sensitive ['sensɪtɪv] *adj* (**to**, *e.g., cold*)
empfindlich (**gegen**); (*touchy*) überempfindlich; **s. post** Vertrauensposten
m; **very s.** überempfindlich
sensitize ['sensɪ ˌtaɪz] *tr* (phot) licht-
empfindlich machen
sensory ['sensəri] *adj* Sinnes–
sen'sory depriva'tion *s* Reizentzug *m*
sensual ['sen(ʊ-əl] *adj* sinnlich
sensuality [ˌsen(ʊ'ælɪti] *s* Sinnlichkeit
f, Sinnenlust *f*
sensuous ['sen(ʊ-əs] *adj* sinnlich
sentence ['sentəns] *s* (gram) Satz *m*;
(*jur*) Urteil *n*; **pronounce s.** das Urteil verkünden ‖ *tr* verurteilen
sentiment ['sentɪmənt] *s* Empfindung
f
sentimental [ˌsentɪ'mentəl] *adj* sentimental, rührselig
sentinel ['sentɪnəl] *s* Posten *m*; **stand
s.** Wache stehen
sentry ['sentri] *s* Wachposten *m*
sen'try box' *s* Schilderhaus *n*
separable ['sepərəbəl] *adj* trennbar
separate ['sepərɪt] *adj* getrennt; **under
s. cover** separat ‖ ['sepə ˌret] *tr*
trennen; (*segregate*) absondern;
(*scatter*) zerstreuen; (*discharge*) entlassen; **s. into** teilen in (*acc*) ‖ *intr*
sich trennen, sich scheiden
sep'arated *adj* (*couple*) getrennt
separation [ˌsepə'reʃən] *s* Trennung *f*
September [sep'tembər] *s* September
m
sep'tic tank' ['septɪk] *s* Kläranlage *f*
sepulcher ['sepəlkər] *s* Grabmal *n*
sequel ['sikwəl] *s* Fortsetzung *f*; (fig)
Nachspiel *n*
sequence ['sikwəns] *s* Reihenfolge *f*
se'quence of tens'es *s* Zeitenfolge *f*
sequester [sɪ'kwestər] *tr* (*remove*) entfernen; (*separate*) absondern; (jur)
sequestrieren
sequins ['sikwɪnz] *spl* Flitter *m*
ser-aph ['seræf] *s* (**-aphs & –aphim**
[əfɪm]) Seraph *m*
Serb [sʌrb] *adj* serbisch ‖ *s* Serbe *m*,
Serbin *f*
Serbia ['sʌrbɪ-ə] *s* Serbien *n*
serenade [ˌserə'ned] *s* Ständchen *n* ‖
tr ein Ständchen bringen (*dat*)
serene [sɪ'rin] *adj* heiter; (*sea*) ruhig
serenity [sɪ'renɪti] *s* Heiterkeit *f*
serf [sʌrf] *s* Leibeigene *mf*
serfdom ['sʌrfdəm] *s* Leibeigenschaft
f
serge [sʌrdʒ] *s* (tex) Serge *f*
sergeant ['sɑrdʒənt] *s* Feldwebel *m*
ser'geant-at-arms' *s* (**sergeants-at-arms**)
Ordnungsbeamter *m*
ser'geant first' class' *s* Oberfeldwebel
m

ser'geant ma'jor s (sergeant majors) Hauptfeldwebel m

serial ['sɪrɪ-əl] s Fortsetzungsroman m, Romanfolge f

serialize ['sɪrɪ-ə,laɪz] tr in Fortsetzungen veröffentlichen

se'rial num'ber s laufende Nummer f; (of a product) Fabriknummer f

se·ries ['sɪriz] s (–ries) Serie f, Reihe f; in s. reihenweise; (elec) hintereinandergeschaltet

serious ['sɪrɪ-əs] adj ernst; (mistake) schwerwiegend; (illness) gefährlich

seriously ['sɪrɪ-əsli] adv ernstlich; s. wounded schwerverwundet; take s. ernst nehmen

seriousness ['sɪrɪ-əsnɪs] s Ernst m

sermon ['sʌrmən] s Predigt f

sermonize ['sʌrmə,naɪz] intr e-e Moralpredigt halten

serpent ['sʌrpənt] s Schlange f

serrated ['sɛretɪd] adj sägeartig

se·rum ['sɪrəm] s (–rums & –ra [rə]) Serum n

servant ['sʌrvənt] s Diener –in mf; (domestic) Hausdiener –in mf

serv'ant girl' s Dienstmädchen n

serve [sʌrv] s (tennis) Aufschlag m ‖ tr (a master, God) dienen (dat); (food) servieren; (a meal) anrichten; (guests) bedienen; (time in jail) verbüßen; (one's term in the service) abdienen; (the purpose) erfüllen; (tennis) aufschlagen; s. mass (eccl) zur Messe dienen; s. notice on s.o. j–n vorladen; s. up (food) auftragen ‖ intr (& mil) dienen; (at table) servieren; s. as dienen als; s. on a committe e–m Ausschuß angehören

server ['sʌrvər] s (eccl) Ministrant m; (tennis) Aufschläger m

service ['sʌrvɪs] s (diplomatic, secret, foreign, public, etc.) Dienst m; (in a restaurant) Bedienung f; (set of table utensils) Besteck n; (set of dishes) Service n; (assistance at a repair shop) Service m; (maintenance) Wartung f; (transportation) Verkehr m; (relig) Gottesdienst m; (tennis) Aufschlag m; at your s. zu Ihren Diensten; be in s. (mach) in Betrieb sein; be in the s. (mil) beim Militär sein; be of s. behilflich sein; do s.o. a s. j–m e–n Dienst erweisen; essential services lebenswichtige Betriebe pl; fit for active s. kriegsverwendungsfähig; see s. Kriegsdienst tun; the services die Waffengattungen pl ‖ tr (mach) warten

serviceable ['sʌrvɪsəbəl] adj (usable) verwendungsfähig; (helpful) nützlich; (durable) haltbar

serv'ice club' s (mil) Soldatenklub m

serv'ice en'trance s Dienstboteneingang m

serv'ice·man' s (–men') Monteur m; (at a gas station) Tankwart m; (mil) Soldat m

serv'ice rec'ord s Wehrpaß m

serv'ice sta'tion s Tankstelle f

serv'ice-station atten'dant s Tankwart m

serv'ice troops' spl Versorgungstruppen pl

servile ['sʌrvaɪl] adj kriecherisch

serv'ing s Portion f; (e.g., of a subpoena) Zustellung f

serv'ing cart' s Servierwagen m

servitude ['sʌrvɪ,t(j)ud] s Knechtschaft f

ses'ame seed' ['sɛsəmi] s Sesamsamen m

session ['sɛʃən] s Sitzung f, Tagung f; (educ) Semester n; be in session tagen

set [sɛt] adj (price, time) festgesetzt; (rule) festgelegt; (speech) wohlüberlegt; be all set fix und fertig sein; be set in one's ways festgefahren sein ‖ s (group of things belonging together) Satz m, Garnitur f; (of chess or checkers) Spiel n; (clique) Sippschaft f; (rad, telv) Apparat m; (tennis) Satz m; (theat) Bühnenbild n; younger set Nachwuchs m ‖ v (pret & pp set; ger setting) tr (put) setzen; (stand) stellen; (lay) legen; (a clock, a trap) stellen; (the hair) legen; (a record) aufstellen; (an example) geben; (a time, price) festsetzen; (the table) decken; (jewels) (ein)fassen; (a camera) einstellen; (surg) einrenken; (typ) setzen; set ahead (a clock) vorstellen; set back (a clock) nachstellen; (a patient) zurückwerfen; set down niedersetzen; set down in writing schriftlich niederlegen; set foot in (or on) betreten; set forth (explain) erklären; set free freilassen; set in order in Ordnung bringen; set limits to Schranken setzen (dat); set off (a bomb) sprengen lassen; set (s.o.) over (j–n) überordnen (dat); set right wieder in Ordnung bringen; set store by Gewicht beimessen (dat); set straight (on) aufklären (über acc); set the meeting for two die Versammlung auf zwei Uhr ansetzen; set up (at the bar) (coll) zu e–m Gläschen einladen; (mach) montieren; (typ) (ab)setzen; set up housekeeping Wirtschaft führen; set up in business etablieren ‖ intr (said of cement) abbinden; (astr) untergehen; set about (ger) darangehen zu (inf); set in einsetzen; set out (for) sich auf den Weg machen (nach); set out on (a trip) antreten; set to work sich an die Arbeit machen

set'back' s Rückschlag m, Schlappe f

set'screw' s Stellschraube f

settee [sɛ'ti] s Polsterbank f

setter ['sɛtər] s Vorstehhund m

set'ting s (of the sun) Niedergang m; (of a story) Ort m der Handlung; (of a gem) Fassung f; (theat) Bühnenbild n

settle ['sɛtəl] tr (conclude) erledigen; (decide) entscheiden; (an argument) schlichten; (a problem) erledigen; (an account) begleichen; (one's affairs) in Ordnung bringen; (a creditor's claim) befriedigen; (a lawsuit) durch Vergleich beilegen; (a region) besiedeln; (*people*) ansiedeln || *intr* (*in a region*) sich niederlassen; (*said of a building*) sich senken; (*said of a ship*) absacken; (*said of dust*) sich legen; (*said of a liquid*) sich klären; (*said of suspended particles*) sich setzen; (*said of a cold*) (**in**) sich festsetzen (in *dat*); **s. down** (*in a chair*) sich niederlassen; (*calm down*) sich beruhigen; **s. down to** (*e.g., work*) sich machen an (*acc*); **s. for** sich einigen auf (*acc*); **s. on** sich entscheiden für; **s. up** (fin) die Verbindlichkeit vergleichen

settlement ['sɛtəlmənt] *s* (*colony*) Siedlung *f*; (*agreement*) Abkommen *n*; (*of an argument*) Beilegung *f*; (*of accounts*) Abrechnung *f*; (*of a debt*) Begleichung *f*; **reach a s.** e-n Vergleich schließen

settler ['sɛtlər] *s* Ansiedler –in *mf*

set'up' *s* Aufbau *m*, Anlage *f*

seven ['sɛvən] *adj & pron* sieben || *s* Sieben *f*

seventeen ['sɛvən'tin] *adj & pron* siebzehn || *s* Siebzehn *f*

seventeenth ['sɛvən'tinθ] *adj & pron* siebzehnte || *s* (*fraction*) Siebzehntel *n*; **the s.** (*in dates or a series*) der Siebzehnte

seventh ['sɛvənθ] *adj & pron* sieb(en)te || *s* (*fraction*) Sieb(en)tel *n*; **the s.** (*in dates or a series*) der Sieb(en)te

seventieth ['sɛvəntɪ·ɪθ] *adj & pron* siebzigste || *s* (*fraction*) Siebzigstel *n*

seventy ['sɛvəntɪ] *adj & pron* siebzig || *s* Siebzig *f*; **the seventies** die siebziger Jahre

sev'enty-first' *adj & pron* einundsiebzigste

sev'enty-one' *adj* einundsiebzig

sever ['sɛvər] *tr* (ab)trennen; (*relations*) abbrechen

several ['sɛvərəl] *adj & indef pron* mehrere; **s. times** mehrmals

severance ['sɛvərəns] *s* Trennung *f*; (*of relations*) Abbruch *m*

sev'erance pay' *s* (& mil) Abfindungsentschädigung *f*

severe [sɪ'vɪr] *adj* (*judge, winter, cold*) streng; (*blow, sentence, winter*) hart; (*illness, test*) schwer; (*criticism*) scharf

severity [sɪ'vɛrɪtɪ] *s* Strenge *f*; Härte *f*; Schärfe *f*

sew [so] *v* (*pret* **sewed**; *pp* **sewed & sewn**) *tr & intr* nähen

sewage ['su·ɪdʒ] *s* Abwässer *pl*

sew'age-dispos'al plant' *s* Kläranlage *f*

sewer ['su·ər] *s* Kanal *m* || ['so·ər] *s* Näher –in *mf*

sewerage ['su·ərɪdʒ] *s* Kanalisation *f*

sew'er pipe' ['su·ər] *s* Abwasserleitung *f*

sew'ing *s* Näharbeit *f*

sew'ing bas'ket *s* Nähkasten *m*

sew'ing kit' *s* Nähzeug *n*

sew'ing machine' *s* Nähmaschine *f*

sex [sɛks] *adj* (*crime, education, harmone*) Sexual– || *s* Geschlecht *n*; (*intercourse*) Sex *m*

sex appeal' *s* Sex-Appeal *m*

sex' pot' *s* (coll) Sexbombe *f*

sextent ['sɛkstənt] *s* Sextant *m*

sexton ['sɛkstən] *s* Küster *m*

sexual ['sɛkʃʊ·əl] *adj* geschlechtlich, Geschlechts–, sexuell

sex'ual in'tercourse *s* Geschlechtsverkehr *m*

sexuality [sɛkʃʊ'ælɪtɪ] *s* Sexualität *f*

sexy ['sɛksɪ] *adj* sexy

shabbily ['ʃæbɪlɪ] *adv* schäbig; (*in treatment*) stiefmütterlich

shabby ['ʃæbɪ] *adj* schäbig

shack [ʃæk] *s* Bretterbude *f*

shackle ['ʃækəl] *s* (naut) Schäkel *m*; **shackles** Fesseln *pl* || *tr* fesseln

shad [ʃæd] *s* Shad *m*, Alse *f*

shade [ʃed] *s* Schatten *m*; (*for a window*) Rollo *n*; (*of a lamp*) Schirm *m*; (*hue*) Schattierung *f*; **throw into the s.** (fig) in den Schatten stellen || *tr* beschatten; (paint) schattieren

shad'ing *s* Schattierung *f*

shadow ['ʃædo] *s* Schatten *m* || *tr* (*a person*) beschatten

shad'ow box'ing *s* Schattenboxen *n*

shadowy ['ʃædo·i] *adj* (*like a shadow*) schattenhaft; (*indistinct*) verschwommen; (*shady*) schattig

shady ['ʃedɪ] *adj* schattig; (coll) dunkel; **s. character** Dunkelmann *m*; **s. deal** Lumperei *f*; **s. side** (& fig) Schattenseite *f*

shaft [ʃæft] *s* Schaft *m*; (*of an elevator*) Schacht *m*; (*handle*) Stiel *m*; (*of a wagon*) Deichsel *f*; (*of a column*) Säulenschaft *m*; (*of a transmission*) Welle *f*

shaggy ['ʃægɪ] *adj* zottig, struppig

shake [ʃek] *s* Schütteln *n*; **he's no great shakes** mit ihm ist nicht viel los || *v* (*pret* **shook** [ʃuk]; *pp* **shaken**) *tr* schütteln; **s. a leg!** (coll) rühr dich ein bißchen; **s. before using** vor Gebrauch schütteln; **s. down** (sl) erpressen; **s. hands** sich [*dat*] die Hand geben; **s. hands with s.o.** j–m die Hand drücken; **s. off** (& fig) abschütteln; **s. one's head** mit dem Kopf schütteln; **s. out** (*a rug*) ausschütteln; **s. up** aufschütteln; (fig) aufrütteln || *intr* (**with**) zittern (vor *dat*), beben (vor *dat*)

shake'down' *s* (sl) Erpressung *f*

shake'down cruise' *s* Probefahrt *f*

shaker ['ʃekər] *s* (*for salt*) Streuer *m*; (*for cocktails*) Shaker *m*

shake'-up' *s* Umgruppierung *f*

shaky ['ʃekɪ] *adj* (& fig) wacklig

shale [ʃel] *s* Schiefer *m*

shale' oil' *s* Schieferöl *n*

shall [ʃæl] *v* (*pret* **should** [ʃud]) *aux* (*to express future tense*) werden, e.g., **I s. go** ich werde gehen; (*to express obligation*) sollen, e.g., **s. I stay?** soll ich bleiben?

shallow ['ʃælo] *adj* (*river, person*) seicht; (*water, bowl*) flach || **shallows** *spl* Untiefe *f*

sham [ʃæm] *adj* Schein– || *s* Schein *m* || *v* (*pret & pp* **shammed** || *ger* **shamming**) *tr* vortäuschen

sham′ bat′tle s Scheingefecht n
shambles [′ʃæmbəlz] s Trümmerhaufen m
shame [ʃem] s Schande f; (feeling of shame) Scham f; **put s.o. to s.** (outdo s.o.) j–n in den Schatten stellen; **s. on you!** schäm dich!; **what a s.!** wie schade! || tr beschämen
shame′faced′ adj verschämt
shameful [′ʃemfəl] adj schändlich
shameless [′ʃemlɪs] adj unverschämt
shampoo [ʃæm′pu] s Shampoo n || tr shampoonieren
shamrock [′ʃæmrak] s Kleeblatt n
Shanghai [ʃæŋ′haɪ] s Schanghai n || **shanghai** [′ʃæŋhaɪ] -tr schanghaien
shank [ʃæŋk] s Unterschenkel m; (of an anchor, column, golf club) Schaft m; (cut of meat) Schenkel m
shanty [′ʃænti] s Bude f
shan′tytown′ s Bretterbudensiedlung f
shape [ʃep] s Form f, Gestalt f; **in bad s.** (coll) in schlechter Form; **in good s.** in gutem Zustand; **out of s.** aus der Form; **take s.** sich gestalten || tr formen, gestalten || intr—**s. up** (coll) sich zusammenfassen
shapeless [′ʃeplɪs] adj formlos
shapely [′ʃepli] adj wohlgestaltet
share [ʃer] s Anteil m; (st. exch.) Aktie f; **do one′s s.** das Seine tun || tr teilen || intr—**s. in** teilhaben an (dat)
share′hold′er s Aktionär –in mf
shark [ʃark] s Hai m, Haifisch m
sharp [ʃarp] adj scharf; (pointed) spitzig; (keen) pfiffig || adv pünktlich || s (mus) Kreuz n
sharpen [′ʃarpən] tr schärfen; (a pencil) spitzen
sharply [′ʃarpli] adv scharf
sharp′shoot′er s Scharfschütze m
shatter [′ʃætər] tr zersplittern; (the nerves) zerrütten; (dreams) zerstören || intr zersplittern
shat′terproof′ adj splittersicher
shave [ʃev] s—**get a s.** sich rasieren lassen || tr rasieren || intr sich rasieren
shav′ing brush′ s Rasierpinsel m
shav′ing cream′ s Rasierkrem m
shav′ing mug′ s Rasiernapf m
shawl [ʃɔl] s Schal m
she [ʃi] s Weibchen n || pers pron sie
sheaf [ʃif] s (sheaves [ʃivz]) Garbe f
shear [ʃɪr] s—**shears** Schere f || v (pret sheared; pp sheared & shorn [ʃorn]) tr scheren; **s. off** abschneiden
sheath [ʃiθ] s Scheide f
sheathe [ʃið] tr in die Scheide stecken
shed [ʃed] s Schuppen m || v (pret & pp shed; ger shedding) tr (leaves) abwerfen; (tears) vergießen; (hair, leaves) verlieren; (peace) verbreiten; **s. light on** (fig) Licht werfen auf (acc)
sheen [ʃin] s Glanz m
sheep [ʃip] s (sheep) Schaf n
sheep′dog′ s Schäferhund m
sheep′fold′ s Schafhürde f, Schafpferch m
sheepish [′ʃipɪʃ] adj (embarrassed) verlegen; (timid) schüchtern

sheep′skin′ s Schaffell n; (coll) Diplom n
sheep′skin coat′ s Schafpelz m
sheer [ʃɪr] adj rein; (tex) durchsichtig; **by s. force** durch bloße Gewalt || intr—**s. off** (naut) abscheren
sheet [ʃit] s (for the bed) Leintuch n; (of paper) Blatt n, Bogen m; (of metal) Blech n; (naut) Segelleine f; **come down in sheets** (fig) in Strömen regnen; **s. of ice** Glatteis n; **s. of flame** Feuermeer n
sheet′ i′ron s Eisenblech n
sheet′ mu′sic s Notenblatt n
she′-goat′ s Ziege f
sheik [ʃik] s Scheich m
shelf [ʃelf] s (shelves [ʃelvz]) Regal n; **put on the s.** (fig) auf die lange Bank schieben
shell [ʃel] s Schale f; (conch) Muschel f; (of a snail) Gehäuse n; (of a tortoise) Panzer m; (explosive) Granate f; (bullet) Patrone f || tr (eggs) schälen; (nuts) aufknacken; (mil) beschießen; **s. out money** (coll) mit dem Geld herausrücken || intr—**s. out** (coll) blechen
shel·lac [ʃə′læk] s Schellack m || v (pret & pp -lacked; ger -lacking) tr mit Schellack streichen; (sl) verdreschen
shell′fish′ s Schalentier n
shell′ hole′ s Granattrichter m
shell′ shock′ s Bombenneurose f
shelter [′ʃeltər] s Obdach n; (fig) Schutz m || tr schützen
shelve [ʃelv] tr auf ein Regal stellen; (fig) auf die lange Bank schieben
shenanigans [ʃɪ′nænɪgənz] spl Possen pl
shepherd [′ʃepərd] s Hirt m; (fig) Seelenhirt m || tr hüten
shep′herd dog′ s Schäferhund m
shepherdess [′ʃepərdɪs] s Hirtin f
sherbet [′ʃʌrbət] s Speiseeis n
sheriff [′ʃerɪf] s Sheriff m
sherry [′ʃeri] s Sherry m
shield [ʃild] s Schild m; (fig) Schutz m; (rad) Röhrenabschirmung f || tr (from) schützen (vor dat); (elec, mach) abschirmen
shift [ʃɪft] s (of worker, work) Schicht f; (change) Verschiebung f; (loose-fitting dress) Kittelkleid n || tr (a meeting) verschieben; (the blame) (on) (ab)schieben (auf acc); **s. gears** umschalten || intr (said of the wind) umspringen; **s. for oneself** sich allein durchschlagen; **s. into second gear** in den zweiten Gang umschalten
shift′ key′ s Umschalttaste f
shiftless [′ʃɪftlɪs] adj träge
shifty [′ʃɪfti] adj schlau, gerissen
shimmer [′ʃɪmər] s Schimmer m || intr schimmern, flimmern
shin [ʃɪn] s Schienbein n
shin′bone′ s Schienbein n
shine [ʃaɪn] s Schein m, Glanz m || v (pret & pp shined) tr polieren; (shoes) wichsen || v (pret & pp shone [ʃon]) intr scheinen; (said of the

eyes) leuchten; (*be outstanding*) (**in**) glänzen (in *dat*)

shiner ['ʃaɪnər] *s* (sl) blaues Auge *n*

shingle ['ʃɪŋgəl] *s* (*for a roof*) Schindel *f;* (*e.g., of a doctor*) Aushängeschild *n* ‖ *tr* mit Schindeln decken

shin'ing *adj* (*eyes*) leuchtend, strahlend; (*example*) glänzend

shiny ['ʃaɪnɪ] *adj* blank, glänzend

ship [ʃɪp] *s* Schiff *n* ‖ *v* (*pret & pp* **shipped;** *ger* **shipping**) *tr* senden; **s. water** e–e Sturzsee bekommen ‖ *intr*—**s. out** absegeln

ship'board' *s* Bord *m;* **on s.** an Bord

ship'build'er *s* Schiffbauer *m*

ship'build'ing *s* Schiffbau *m*

shipment ['ʃɪpmənt] *s* Lieferung *f*

ship'ping *s* Absendung *f*, Verladung *f;* (*ships*) Schiffe *pl*

ship'ping clerk' *s* Expedient *m*

ship'ping depart'ment *s* Versandabteilung *f*

ship'shape' *adj* ordentlich

ship'wreck' *s* Schiffbruch *m* ‖ *tr* scheitern lassen; **be s.** schiffbrüchig sein ‖ *intr* Schiffbruch erleiden

ship'yard' *s* Werft *f*

shirk [ʃɜrk] *tr* sich drücken vor (*dat*) ‖ *intr* (**from**) sich drücken (vor *dat*)

shirt [ʃʌrt] *s* Hemd *n;* **keep your s. on!** (sl) regen Sie sich nicht auf!

shirt'col'lar *s* Hemdkragen *m*

shirt'sleeve' *s* Hemdsärmel *m*

shirttail' *s* Hemdzipfel *m*

shit [ʃɪt] *s* (vulg) Scheiße *f* ‖ *v* (*pret & pp* **shit**) *tr & intr* (vulg) scheißen

shiver ['ʃɪvər] *s* Schauder *m* ‖ *intr* (**at**) schaudern (vor *dat*); (**with**) zittern (vor *dat*)

shoal [ʃol] *s* Untiefe *f*

shock [ʃɑk] *s* Schock *m;* (*of hair*) Schopf *m;* (agr) Schober *m;* (elec) Schlag *m* ‖ *tr* schockieren; (elec) e–n Schlag versetzen (*dat*)

shock'absorb'er [æb,sɔrbər] *s* Stoßdämpfer *m*

shock'ing *adj* schockierend

shock'troops' *spl* Stoßtruppen *pl*

shock'wave' *s* Stoßwelle *f*

shoddy ['ʃɑdɪ] *adj* schäbig

shoe [ʃu] *s* Schuh *m* ‖ *v* (*pret & pp* **shod** [ʃɑd]) *tr* beschlagen

shoe'horn' *s* Schuhlöffel *m*

shoe'lace' *s* Schuhband *n*, Schnürsenkel *m*

shoe'mak'er *s* Schuster *m*

shoe'pol'ish *s* Schuhwichse *f*

shoe'shine' *s* Schuhputzen *n*

shoe'store' *s* Schuhladen *m*

shoe'string' *s* Schuhband *m;* **on a s.** mit ein paar Groschen

shoe'tree' *s* Schuhspanner *m*

shoo [ʃu] *tr* (**away**) wegscheuchen ‖ *interj* sch!

shook-up ['ʃuk'ʌp] *adj* (coll) verdattert

shoot [ʃut] *s* Schößling *m* ‖ *v* (*pret & pp* **shot** [ʃɑt]) *tr* (an)schießen, (ab)schießen; (*kill*) erschießen; (*dice*) werfen; (cin) drehen; (phot) aufnehmen; **s. down** (aer) abschießen; **s. the breeze** zwanglos plaudern; **s. up** (*e.g., a town*) zusammenschie-

ßen ‖ *intr* schießen; **s. at** schießen auf (*acc*); **s. by** vorbeisausen an (*dat*); **s. up** (*in growth*) aufschießen; (*said of flames*) emporschlagen; (*said of prices*) emporschnellen

shoot'ing *s* Schießerei *f;* (*execution*) Erschießung *f;* (*of a film*) Drehen *n*

shoot'ing gal'lery *s* Schießbude *f*

shoot'ing match' *s* Preisschießen *n*

shoot'ing star' *s* Sternschnuppe *f*

shoot'ing war' *s* heißer Krieg *m*

shop [ʃɑp] *s* Laden *m*, Geschäft *n;* **talk s.** fachsimpeln ‖ *v* (*pret & pp* **shopped;** *ger* **shopping**) *intr* einkaufen; **go shopping** einkaufen gehen; **s. around** for sich in einigen Läden umsehen nach

shop'girl' *s* Ladenmädchen *n*

shop'keep'er *s* Ladeninhaber –in *mf*

shoplifter ['ʃɑp,lɪftər] *s* Ladendieb –in *mf*

shop'lift'ing *s* Ladendiebstahl *m*

shopper ['ʃɑpər] *s* Einkäufer –in *mf*

shop'ping *s* Einkaufen *n;* (*purchases*) Einkäufe *pl*

shop'ping bag' *s* Einkaufstasche *f*

shop'ping cen'ter *s* Einkaufcenter *n*

shop'ping dis'trict *s* Geschäftsviertel *n*

shop'ping spree' *s* Einkaufsorgie *f*

shop'talk' *s* Fachsimpelei *f*

shop'win'dow *s* Schaufenster *n*

shop'worn' *adj* (fig) abgerissen

shore [ʃor] *s* Küste *f;* (*beach*) Strand *m;* (*of a river*) Ufer *n;* **go to the s.** ans Meer fahren ‖ *tr*—**s. up** abstützen

shore'leave' *s* Landurlaub *m*

shore'line' *s* Küstenlinie *f;* (*of a river*) Uferlinie *f*

shore'patrol' *s* Küstenstreife *f*

short [ʃɔrt] *adj* kurz; (*person*) klein; (*loan*) kurzfristig; **a s. time ago** vor kurzem; **be s. of,** *e.g.,* **I am s. of bread** das Brot geht mir aus; **be s. with s.o.** j–n kurz abfertigen; **cut s.** abbrechen; **fall s. of** zurückbleiben hinter (*dat*); **get the s. end** das Nachsehen haben; **I am three marks s.** es fehlen mir drei Mark; **in s.** kurzum; **s. of breath** außer Atem; **s. of cash** knapp bei Kasse ‖ *s* (cin) Kurzfilm *m;* (elec) Kurzschluß *m* ‖ *tr* (elec) kurzschließen

shortage ['ʃɔrtɪdʒ] *s* (**of**) Mangel *m* (an *dat*); (com) Minderbetrag *m*

short'cake' *s* Mürbekuchen *m*

short'-change' *tr* zu wenig Wechselgeld herausgeben (*dat*); (fig) betrügen

short'cir'cuit *s* Kurzschluß *m*

short'-cir'cuit *tr* kurzschließen

short'com'ing *s* Fehler *m*, Mangel *m*

short'cut' *s* Abkürzung *f;* **take a s.** den Weg abkürzen

shorten ['ʃɔrtən] *tr* abkürzen

short'ening *s* Abkürzung *f;* (culin) Backfett *n*

short'hand' *adj* stenographisch ‖ *s* Stenographie *f;* **in s.** stenographisch; **take down in s.** stenographieren

short-lived ['ʃɔrt'laɪvd] *adj* kurzlebig

shortly ['ʃɔrtlɪ] *adv* in kurzem; **s. after** kurz nach

short′-or′der cook′ s Schnellimbißkoch m, Schnellimbißköchin f
short′-range′ adj Nah-, auf kurze Sicht
shorts [ʃɔrts] s (underwear) Unterhose f; (walking shorts) kurze Hose f; (sport) Sporthose f
short′-sight′ed adj kurzsichtig
short′ sto′ry s Novelle f
short′-tem′pered adj leicht aufbrausend
short′-term′ adj kurzfristig
short′wave′ adj Kurzwellen– || s Kurzwelle f
short′wind′ed adj kurzatmig
shot [ʃɑt] adj (sl) kaputt; (drunk) (sl) besoffen; **my nerves are s.** ich bin mit meinen Nerven ganz herunter || s Schuß m; (shooter) Schütze m; (pellets) Schrot m; (injection) Spritze f; (snapshot) Aufnahme f; (of liquor) Gläschen n; **be a good s.** gut schießen; **s. in the arm** (fig) Belebungsspritze f; **s. in the dark** Sprung m ins Ungewisse; **take a s.** at e–n Schuß abgeben auf (acc); (fig) versuchen; **wild s.** Schuß m ins Blaue
shot′gun′ s Schrotflinte f
shot′gun wed′ding s Mußehe f
shot′-put′ s (sport) Kugelstoßen n
should [ʃʊd] aux (to express softened affirmation) **I s. like to know** ich möchte wissen; **I s. think so** das will ich meinen; (to express obligation) **how s. I know?** wie sollte ich das wissen?; **you shouldn't do that** Sie sollten das nicht tun; (in conditional clauses) **if it s. rain tomorrow** wenn es morgen regnen sollte
shoulder [′ʃoldər] s Schulter f, Achsel f; (of a road) Bankett n; **have broad shoulders** e–n breiten Rücken haben || tr (a rifle) schultern; (responsibility) auf sich nehmen
shoul′der bag′ s Umhängetasche f
shoul′der blade′ s Schulterblatt n
shoul′der strap′ s (of underwear) Trägerband n; (mil) Schulterriemen m
shout [ʃaʊt] s Schrei m, Ruf m || tr schreien, rufen; **s. down** (coll) niederschreien || intr schreien, rufen
shove [ʃʌv] s Stoß m; **give s.o. a s.** j–m e–n Stoß versetzen || tr stoßen; (e.g., furniture) rücken; **s. around** (coll) herumschubsen; **s. forward** vorschieben || intr drängeln; **s. off** (coll) abschieben; (naut) vom Land abstoßen
shov·el [′ʃʌvəl] s Schaufel f || v (pret & pp -el[l]ed; ger -el[l]ing) tr schaufeln
show [ʃo] s (exhibition) Ausstellung f; (outer appearance) Schau f; (spectacle) Theater n; (cin, theat) Vorstellung f; **by s. of hands** durch Handzeichen; **make a s. of s.th.** mit etw Staat machen; **only for s.** nur zur Schau || v (pret showed; pp shown [ʃon] & showed) tr zeigen; (prove) beweisen, nachweisen; (said of evidence, tests) ergeben; (tickets, passport, papers) vorweisen; **s. around** (a person) herumführen; (a thing) herumzeigen || intr zu sehen sein;

(said of a slip) vorgucken; **s. off** (with) großtun (mit); **s. up** erscheinen
show′ busi′ness s Unterhaltungsindustrie f
show′case′ s Schaukasten m, Vitrine f
show′down′ s entscheidender Wendepunkt m; (e.g., in a western) Kraftprobe f; (cards) Aufdecken n der Karten
shower [′ʃaʊ·ər] s (rain) Schauer m; (bath) Dusche f; (shower room) Duschraum m; (of stones, arrows) Hagel m; (of bullets, sparks) Regen m; (for a bride) Party f zur Überreichung der Brautgeschenke; **take a s.** (sich) duschen || tr (with gifts) überschütten || intr duschen; (meteor) schauern
show′er bath′ s Dusche f, Brausebad n
show′ girl′ s Revuegirl n
show′ing s Zeigen n; (cin) Vorführung f
show′ing off′ s Großtuerei f
show′man s (–men) s Schauspieler m
show′-off′ s Protz m
show′piece′ s Schaustück n
show′room′ s Ausstellungsraum m
show′ win′dow s Schaufenster n
showy [′ʃo·i] adj prunkhaft
shrapnel [′ʃræpnəl] s Schrapnell n
shred [ʃred] s Fetzen m; (least bit) Spur f; **tear to shreds** in Fetzen reißen; (an argument) gründlich widerlegen || v (pret & pp shredded & shred; ger shredding) tr zerfetzen; (paper) in Streifen schneiden; (culin) schnitzeln
shredder [′ʃredər] s (of paper) Reißwolf m; (culin) Schnitzelmaschine f
shrew [ʃru] s böse Sieben f
shrewd [ʃrud] adj schlau
shriek [ʃrik] s Gekreische n, gellender Schrei m || intr kreischen
shrill [ʃrɪl] adj schrill
shrimp [ʃrɪmp] s Garnele f; (coll) Knirps m
shrine [ʃraɪn] s Heiligtum n
shrink [ʃrɪŋk] v (pret shrank [ʃræŋk] & shrunk [ʃrʌŋk]; pp shrunk & shrunken) tr einlaufen lassen || intr schrumpfen; **s. back from** zurückschrecken vor (dat); **s. from** sich scheuen vor (dat); **s. up** einschrumpfen
shrinkage [′ʃrɪŋkɪdʒ] s Schrumpfung f
shriv·el [′ʃrɪvəl] s (pret & pp -el[l]ed; ger -el[l]ing) intr schrumpfen; **s. up** zusammenschrumpfen
shriv′eled adj schrumpelig
shroud [ʃraʊd] s Leichentuch n; (fig) Hülle f; (naut) Want f || tr (in) einhüllen (in acc)
shrub [ʃrʌb] s Strauch m
shrubbery [′ʃrʌbəri] s Strauchwerk n
shrug [ʃrʌg] s Zucken n || v (pret & pp shrugged; ger shrugging) tr zucken; **s. off** mit e–m Achselzucken abtun; **s. one's shoulders** mit den Achseln zucken || intr mit den Achseln zucken
shuck [ʃʌk] tr enthülsen
shudder [′ʃʌdər] s Schau(d)er m ||

intr (at) schau(d)ern (vor *dat*); **s. at the thought of s.th.** bei dem Gedanken an etw [*acc*] zittern

shuffle [ˈʃʌfəl] *s* Schlurfen *n;* (cards) Mischen *n;* **get lost in the s.** (fig) unter den Tisch fallen ‖ *tr* (cards) mischen; (*the feet*) schleifen; ‖ *intr* die Karten mischen; (*walk*) schlurfen; **s. along** latschen

shun [ʃʌn] *v* (*pret & pp* **shunned;** *ger* **shunning**) *tr* (*a person*) meiden; (*a thing*) (ver)meiden

shunt [ʃʌnt] *s* (elec) Nebenschluß *m* ‖ *tr* (*shove aside*) beiseite schieben; (**across**) parallelschalten (zu); (rr) rangieren

shut [ʃʌt] *adj* zu ‖ (*pret & pp* **shut;** *ger* **shutting**) *tr* schließen, zumachen; **be s. down** stilliegen; **s. down** stillegen; **s. off** absperren; **s. one's eyes to** hinwegsehen über (*acc*); **s. out** aussperren; **s. s.o. up** j-m den Mund stopfen ‖ *intr* sich schließen; **s. up!** (coll) halt's Maul!

shut′down′ *s* Stillegung *f*

shutter [ˈʃʌtər] *s* Laden *m;* (phot) Verschluß *m*

shuttle [ˈʃʌtəl] *s* Schiffchen *n* ‖ *intr* pendeln, hin- und herfahren

shut′tle bus′ *s* Pendelbus *m*

shut′tlecock′ *s* Federball *m*

shut′tle serv′ice *s* Pendelverkehr *m*

shut′tle train′ *s* Pendelzug *m*

shy [ʃaɪ] *adj* (**shyer; shyest**) schüchtern; **be a dollar shy** e-n Dollar los sein ‖ *intr* (*said of a horse*) stutzen; **shy at** zurückscheuen vor (*dat*); **shy away from** sich scheuen vor (*dat*)

shyness [ˈʃaɪnɪs] *s* Scheu *f*

shyster [ˈʃaɪstər] *s* Winkeladvokat *m*

Siamese′ twins′ [ˌsaɪ·əˈmiz] *spl* Siamesische Zwillinge *pl*

Siberia [saɪˈbɪrɪ·ə] *s* Sibirien *n*

Siberian [saɪˈbɪrɪ·ən] *adj* sibirisch ‖ *s* Sibirier –in *mf*

sibilant [ˈsɪbɪlənt] *s* Zischlaut *m*

siblings [ˈsɪblɪŋz] *spl* Geschwister *pl*

sibyl [ˈsɪbɪl] *s* Sibylle *f*

sic [sɪk] *adv* sic ‖ *v* (*pret & pp* **sicked;** *ger* **sicking**) *tr*—**sic 'em!** (coll) faß!; **sic the dog on s.o.** den Hund auf j-n hetzen

Sicilian [sɪˈsɪljən] *adj* sizilianisch ‖ *s* Sizilianer –in *mf*

Sicily [ˈsɪsɪli] *s* Sizilien *n*

sick [sɪk] *adj* krank; **be s. and tired of s.th.** etw gründlich satt haben; **be s. as a dog** sich hundeelend fühlen; **I am s. to my stomach** mir ist übel; **play s.** krankfeiern

sick′ bay′ *s* Schiffslazarett *n*

sick′bed′ *s* Krankenbett *n*

sicken [ˈsɪkən] *tr* krank machen; (*disgust*) anekeln ‖ *intr* krank werden

sick′ening *adj* (fig) ekelhaft

sick′ head′ache *s* Kopfschmerzen *pl* mit Übelkeit

sickle [ˈsɪkəl] *s* Sichel *f*

sick′ leave′ *s* Krankenurlaub *m*

sickly [ˈsɪkli] *adj* kränklich; (*smile*) erzwungen

sickness [ˈsɪknɪs] *s* Krankheit *f*

sick′ room′ *s* Krankenzimmer *n*

side [saɪd] *adj* Neben–, Seiten– ‖ *s* Seite *f;* (*of a team, government*) Partei *f;* (*edge*) Rand *m;* **at my s.** mir zur Seite; **dark s.** Schattenseite *f;* **off sides** (sport) abseits; **on the father's s.** väterlicherseits; **on the s.** (coll) nebenbei; **this s. up** Vorsicht, nicht stürzen; **to be on the safe s.** um ganz sicher zu gehen ‖ *intr*— **s. with s.o.** j–s Partei ergreifen

side′ aisle′ *s* Seitengang *m;* (*of a church*) Seitenschiff *n*

side′ al′tar *s* Nebenaltar *m*

side′arm′ *s* Seitengewehr *n*

side′board′ *s* Anrichte *f*, Büffet *n*

side′burns′ *spl* Koteletten *pl*

side′ dish′ *s* Nebengericht *n*

side′ door′ *s* Seitentür *f*

side′ effect′ *s* Nebenwirkung *f*

side′ en′trance *s* Seiteneingang *m*

side′ glance′ *s* Seitenblick *m*

side′ is′sue *s* Nebenfrage *f*

side′ job′ *s* Nebenverdienst *m*

side′kick′ *s* (coll) Kumpel *m*

side′line′ *s* (*occupation*) Nebenbeschäftigung *f;* (fb) Seitenlinie *f* ‖ *tr* (coll) an der aktiven Teilnahme hindern

side′ of ba′con *s* Speckseite *f*

side′ road′ *s* Seitenweg *m*

side′sad′dle *adv*—**ride s.** im Damensattel reiten

side′ show′ *s* Nebenvorstellung *f;* (fig) Episode *f*

side′split′ting *adj* zwerchfellerschütternd

side′-step′ *v* (*pret & pp* **-stepped;** *ger* **-stepping**) *tr* ausweichen (*dat*)

side′ street′ *s* Seitenstraße *f*

side′stroke′ *s* Seitenschwimmen *n*

side′track′ *s* Seitengeleise *n* ‖ *tr* (& fig) auf ein Seitengeleise schieben

side′ trip′ *s* Abstecher *m*

side′ view′ *s* Seitenansicht *f*

side′walk′ *s* Bürgersteig *m*, Gehsteig *m*

sideward [ˈsaɪdwərd] *adj* nach der Seite gerichtet ‖ *adv* seitwärts

side′ways′ *adv* seitlich, seitwärts

sid′ing *s* (*of a house*) Verkleidung *f;* (rr) Nebengeleise *n*

sidle [ˈsaɪdəl] *intr*—**s. up to s.o.** sich heimlich an j–n heranmachen

siege [sidʒ] *s* Belagerung *f;* **lay s. to** belagern

siesta [si·ˈɛstə] *s* Mittagsruhe *f*

sieve [sɪv] *s* Sieb *n* ‖ *tr* durchsieben

sift [sɪft] *tr* (durch)sieben; (fig) sichten; **s. out** aussieben

sigh [saɪ] *s* Seufzer *m;* **with a s.** seufzend ‖ *intr* seufzen

sight [saɪt] *s* Anblick *m;* (*faculty*) Sehvermögen *n;* (*on a weapon*) Visier *n;* **at first s.** auf den ersten Blick; **at s.** sofort; **be a s.** (coll) unmöglich aussehen; **by s.** vom Sehen; **catch s. of** erblicken; **in s.** in Sicht; **lose s. of** aus den Augen verlieren; **out of s.** außer Sicht; **s. for sore eyes** Augentrost *m;* **sights** Sehenswürdigkeiten *pl;* **s. unseen** unbesehen; **within s.** in Sehweite ‖ *tr* sichten

sight'see'ing s Besichtigung f; **go s.** sich [dat] die Sehenswürdigkeiten ansehen

sight'seeing tour' s Rundfahrt f

sightseer ['saɪtˌsi·ər] s Tourist –in mf

sign [saɪn] s (signboard) Schild n; (symbol, omen, signal) Zeichen n; (symptom, indication) Kennzeichen n; (trace) Spur f; (math, mus) Vorzeichen n; **s. of life** Lebenszeichen n || tr unterschreiben; **s. away** aufgeben; **s. over (to)** überschreiben (auf acc) || intr unterschreiben; **s. for** zeichnen für; **s. in** sich eintragen; **s. off** (rad) die Sendung beenden; **s. out** sich austragen; **s. up** (mil) sich anwerben lassen; **s. up for** (e.g., courses, work) sich anmelden für

sig·nal ['sɪgnəl] adj auffallend || s (by gesture) Zeichen n, Wink m; (aut, rad, rr, telv) Signal n || v (pret & pp –nal[l]ed; ger –nal[l]ing) tr signalisieren; (a person) ein Zeichen geben (dat)

sig'nal corps' s Fernmeldetruppen pl

sig'nal·man s (–men) (nav) Signalgast m; (rr) Bahnwärter m

signatory ['sɪgnəˌtori] s Unterzeichner –in mf

signature ['sɪgnətʃər] s Unterschrift f

sign'board' s Aushängeschild n

signer ['saɪnər] s Unterzeichner –in mf

sig'net ring' ['sɪgnɪt] s Siegelring m

significance [sɪg'nɪfɪkəns] s Bedeutung f

significant [sɪg'nɪfɪkənt] adj bedeutsam

signi·fy ['sɪgnɪˌfaɪ] v (pret & pp –fied) bedeuten, bezeichnen

sign' lan'guage s Zeichensprache f

sign' of the cross' s Kreuzzeichen n; **make the s.** sich bekreuzigen

sign'post' s Wegweiser m

silence ['saɪləns] s Ruhe f, Stille f; (reticence) Schweigen n; **in s.** schweigend || tr zum Schweigen bringen; (a conscience) beschwichtigen

silent ['saɪlənt] adj (night, partner) still; (movies) stumm; (person) schweigend; **be s.** stillschweigen; **keep s.** schweigen

silhouette [ˌsɪlu'ɛt] s Schattenbild n, Silhouette f || tr silhouettieren

silicon ['sɪlɪkən] s Silizium n

silicone ['sɪlɪkon] s Silikon n

silk [sɪlk] adj seiden || s Seide f

silken ['sɪlkən] adj seiden

silk' hat' s Zylinder m

silk' mill' s Seidenfabrik f

silk' worm' s Seidenraupe f

silky ['sɪlki] adj seiden, seidenartig

sill [sɪl] s (of a window) Sims m & n; (of a door) Schwelle f

silliness ['sɪlɪnɪs] s Albernheit f

silly ['sɪli] adj albern, blöd(e)

si·lo ['saɪlo] s (–los) Getreidesilo m; (rok) Raketenbunker m, Silo m

silt [sɪlt] s Schlick m || intr—**s. up** verschlammen

silver ['sɪlvər] adj silbern || s Silber n; (for the table) Silberzeug n; (money) Silbergeld n

sil'verfish' s Silberfischchen n

sil'ver foil' s Silberfolie f

sil'ver lin'ing s (fig) Silberstreifen m

sil'ver plate' s Silbergeschirr n

sil'ver-plat'ed adj versilbert

sil'versmith' s Silberschmied m

sil'ver spoon' s—**be born with a s. in one's mouth** ein Sonntagskind sein

sil'verware' s Silbergeschirr n

silvery ['sɪlvəri] adj silbern

similar ['sɪmɪlər] adj (to) ähnlich (dat)

similarity [ˌsɪmɪ'lærɪti] s Ähnlichkeit f

simile ['sɪmɪli] s Gleichnis n

simmer ['sɪmər] tr leicht kochen lassen || intr brodeln; **s. down** (coll) sich abreagieren

simper ['sɪmpər] s selbstgefälliges Lächeln n || intr selbstgefällig lächeln

simple ['sɪmpəl] adj einfach; (truth) rein; (fact) bloß

sim'ple-mind'ed adj einfältig

simpleton ['sɪmpəltən] s Einfaltspinsel m

simpli·fy ['sɪmplɪˌfaɪ] v (pret & pp –fied) tr vereinfachen

simply ['sɪmpli] adv einfach

simulate ['sɪmjəˌlet] tr (illness) simulieren; (e.g., a rocket flight) am Modell vorführen

sim'ulated adj unecht

simultaneous [ˌsaɪməl'teni·əs] adj gleichzeitig, simultan

sin [sɪn] s Sünde f || v (pret & pp sinned; ger sinning) intr sündigen; **sin against** sich versündigen an (dat)

since [sɪns] adv seitdem, seither || prep seit (dat); **s. then** seither; **s. when** seit wann || conj (temporal) seitdem); (causal) da

sincere [sɪn'sɪr] adj aufrichtig

sincerely [sɪn'sɪrli] adv aufrichtig, ehrlich; **Sincerely yours** Ihr ergebener, Ihre ergebene

sincerity [sɪn'sɛrɪti] s Aufrichtigkeit f

sinecure ['saɪnɪˌkjur] s Sinekure f

sinew ['sɪnju] s Sehne f, Flechse f; (fig) Muskelkraft f

sinewy ['sɪnju·i] adj sehnig; (fig) kräftig, nervig

sinful ['sɪnfəl] adj sündhaft

sing [sɪŋ] v (pret sang [sæŋ] & sung [sʌŋ]; pp sung) tr & intr singen

singe [sɪndʒ] v (singeing) tr sengen; (the hair) versengen

singer ['sɪŋər] s Sänger –in mf

single ['sɪŋgəl] adj einzeln; (unmarried) ledig; **not a s. word** kein einziges Wort || tr—**s. out** herausgreifen

sin'gle bed' s Einzelbett n

sin'glebreast'ed adj einreihig

sin'gle file' s Gänsemarsch m

sin'gle-hand'ed adj einhändig

sin'gle-lane' adj einspurig

sin'gle life' s Ledigenstand m

sin'gle-mind'ed adj zielstrebig

sin'gle room' s Einzelzimmer n

sin'gle-track' adj (rr) eingleisig

sing'song' adj eintönig || s Singsang m

singular ['sɪŋgjələr] adj (outstanding) ausgezeichnet; (unique) einzig; (odd) seltsam || s (gram) Einzahl f

sinister ['sɪnɪstər] adj unheimlich

sink [sɪŋk] s (in the kitchen) Ausguß m; (in the bathroom) Waschbecken n || v (pret sank [sæŋk] & sunk [sʌŋk]; pp sunk) tr (a ship; a post) versenken; (money) investieren; (min) abteufen; s. a well e–n Brunnen bohren || intr sinken; (said of a building) sich senken; he is sinking fast seine Kräfte nehmen rapide ab; s. in (coll) einleuchten; s. into (an easychair) sich fallen lassen in (acc); (poverty) geraten in (acc); (unconsciousness) fallen in (acc)

sink'ing feel'ing s Beklommenheit f

sink'ing fund' s Schuldentilgungsfonds m

sinless ['sɪnlɪs] adj sünd(en)los

sinner ['sɪnər] s Sünder –in mf

sinuous ['sɪnju·əs] adj gewunden

sinus ['saɪnəs] s Stirnhöhle f

sip [sɪp] s Schluck m || v (pret & pp sipped; ger sipping) tr schlürfen

siphon ['saɪfən] s Siphon m, Saugheber m || tr entleeren; s. off absaugen; (profits) abschöpfen

sir [sɪr] s Herr m; yes sir! jawohl!; **Dear Sir** Sehr geehrter Herr

sire [saɪr] s (& zool) Vater m || tr zeugen

siren ['saɪrən] s (& myth) Sirene f

sirloin ['sʌrlɔɪn] s Lendenbraten m

sissy ['sɪsɪ] s Schlappschwanz m

sister ['sɪstər] s Schwester f

sis'ter-in-law' s (sisters-in-law) Schwägerin f

sisterly ['sɪstərlɪ] adj schwesterlich

sit [sɪt] v (pret & pp sat [sæt]; ger sitting) intr sitzen; sit down sich (hin)setzen; sit for a painter e–m Maler Modell stehen; sit in on (a meeting) dabeisein bei; sit up and beg Männchen machen

sit'down strike' s Sitzstreik m

site [saɪt] s (position, location) Lage f; (piece of ground) Gelände n

sit'ting s—at one s. auf e–n Sitz

sit'ting duck' s wehrloses Ziel n

sit'ting room' s Gemeinschaftsraum m

situated ['sɪtʃu,etɪd] adj gelegen; be s. liegen

situation [,sɪtʃu'eʃən] s Lage f; s. wanted Stelle gesucht

six [sɪks] adj & pron sechs || s Sechs f

sixteen ['sɪks'tin] adj & pron sechzehn || s Sechzehn f

sixteenth ['sɪks'tinθ] adj & pron sechzehnte || s (fraction) Sechzehntel n; **the s.** (in dates or in series) der Sechzehnte

sixth [sɪksθ] adj & pron sechste || s (fraction) Sechstel n; **the s.** (in dates or in series) der Sechste

sixtieth ['sɪkstɪ·ɪθ] adj & pron sechzig || s (fraction) Sechzigstel n

sixty ['sɪkstɪ] adj & pron sechzig || s Sechzig f; the sixties die sechziger Jahre

six'ty-four dol'lar ques'tion s Preisfrage f

sizable ['saɪzəbəl] adj beträchtlich

size [saɪz] s Größe f; (of a book,

paper) Format n || tr grundieren; **s. up** einschätzen

sizzle ['sɪzəl] s Zischen n || intr zischen

skate [sket] s Schlittschuh m || intr Schlittschuh laufen

skat'ing rink' s Eisbahn f

skein [sken] s Strähne f

skeleton ['skɛlɪtən] s Gerippe n

skel'eton crew' s Minimalbelegschaft f

skel'eton key' s Dietrich m

skeptic ['skɛptɪk] s Zweifler –in mf

skeptical ['skɛptɪkəl] adj skeptisch

skepticism ['skɛptɪ,sɪzəm] s (doubt) Skepsis f; (philos) Skeptizismus m

sketch [skɛtʃ] s Skizze f; (theat) Sketch m || tr & intr skizzieren

sketch'book' s Skizzenbuch n

sketchy ['skɛtʃɪ] adj skizzenhaft

skewer ['skju·ər] s Fleischspieß m

ski [ski] s Schi m || intr schilaufen

ski' boot' s Schistiefel m

skid [skɪd] s Rutschen n, Schleudern n; go into a s. ins Schleudern geraten || v (pret & pp skidded; ger skidding) intr rutschen, schleudern

skid' mark' s Bremsspur f

skid'proof' adj bremssicher

skid' row' [ro] s Elendsviertel n

skiff [skɪf] s Skiff n

ski'ing s Schilaufen n

ski' jack'et s Anorak m

ski' jump' s Schisprung m; (chute) Sprungschanze f

ski' jump'ing s Schispringen n

ski' lift' s Schilift m

skill [skɪl] s Fertigkeit f

skilled adj gelernt

skillet ['skɪlɪt] s Bratpfanne f

skillful ['skɪlfəl] adj geschickt

skim [skɪm] v (pret & pp skimmed; ger skimming) tr (milk) abrahmen; (a book) überfliegen; **s. off** abschöpfen || intr—s. over the water über das Wasser streichen; **s. through** (a book) flüchtig durchblättern

skim' milk' s entrahmte Milch f

skimp [skɪmp] intr (on) knausern (mit)

skimpy ['skɪmpɪ] adj (person) knauserig; (thing) knapp, dürftig

skin [skɪn] s Haut f; (fur) Fell n; (of fruit) Schale f; by the s. of one's teeth mit knapper Not; get under s.o.'s s. j–m auf die Nerven gehen || v (pret & pp skinned; ger skinning) tr (an animal) enthäuten; (a knee) aufschürfen; (fleece) das Fell über die Ohren ziehen (dat); (defeat) schlagen; **s. alive** zur Sau machen

skin'-deep' adj oberflächlich

skin' div'er s Schwimmtaucher –in mf

skin'flint' s Geizhals m

skin' graft' s Hautverpflanzung f

skinny ['skɪnɪ] adj spindeldürr, mager

skin'tight' adj hauteng

skip [skɪp] s Sprung m || v (pret & pp skipped; ger skipping) tr (omit) auslassen; (a page) überblättern; **s. it!** Schwamm drüber!; **s. rope** Seil springen; **s. school** Schule schwänzen || intr springen; **s. out** abhauen

ski' pole' s Schistock m

skipper ['skɪpər] s Kapitän m
skirmish ['skɜːrmɪʃ] s Scharmützel n ||
intr scharmützeln
skir'mish line' s (mil) Schützenlinie f
skirt [skɜːrt] s Rock m || tr (border)
umsäumen; (pass along) sich ent-
langziehen (an dat)
ski' run' s Schipiste f
skit [skɪt] s Sket(s)ch m
skittish ['skɪtɪʃ] adj (lively) lebhaft;
(horse) scheu
skull [skʌl] s Schädel m
skull' and cross'bones s Totenkopf m
skull'cap' s Käppchen n
skunk [skʌŋk] s Stinktier n; (sl) Saukerl m
sky [skaɪ] s Himmel m; out of the
clear blue sky wie aus heiterem Himmel; praise to the skies über den
grünen Klee loben
sky'-blue' adj himmelblau
sky'div'er s Fallschirmspringer –in mf
sky'div'ing s Fallschirmspringen n
sky'lark' s Feldlerche f
sky'light' s Dachluke f
sky'line' s Horizontlinie f; (of a city)
Stadtsilhouette f
sky'rock'et s Rakete f || intr in die
Höhe schießen
sky'scrap'er s Wolkenkratzer m
sky'writ'ing s Himmelsschrift f
slab [slæb] s Platte f, Tafel f
slack [slæk] adj schlaff; (period) flau
|| s Spielraum m; slacks Herrenhose
f, Damenhose f || intr—s. off nach-
lassen
slacken ['slækən] tr (slow down) ver-
langsamen; (loosen) lockern || intr
nachlassen
slack' per'iod s Flaute f
slack' sea'son s Sauregurkenzeit f
slag [slæg] s Schlacke f
slag' pile' s Schlackenhalde f
slake [slek] tr (thirst, lime) löschen
slalom ['slɑləm] s Slalom m
slam [slæm] s Knall m; (cards)
Schlemm m || v (pret & pp slammed;
ger slamming) tr zuknallen; s. down
hinknallen || intr knallen
slander ['slændər] s Verleumdung f ||
tr verleumden
slanderous ['slændərəs] adj verleumderisch
slang [slæŋ] s Slang m
slant [slænt] s Schräge f; (view) Einstellung f; (personal point of view)
Tendenz f || tr abschrägen; (fig)
färben
slap [slæp] s Klaps m; s. in the face
Ohrfeige f || v (pret & pp slapped;
ger slapping) tr schlagen; (s.o.'s face)
ohrfeigen; s. together zusammen-
hauen
slap'stick' adj Radau– || s Radauko-
mödie f
slash [slæʃ] s Schnittwunde f || tr auf-
schlitzen; (prices) drastisch herabsetzen
slat [slæt] s Stab m
slate [slet] s Schiefer m; (to write on)
Schiefertafel f; (of candidates) Vor-
schlagsliste f || tr (a roof) mit Schie-

fer decken; (schedule) planen; he is
slated to speak er soll sprechen
slate' roof' s Schieferdach n
slattern ['slætərn] s (slovenly woman)
Schlampe f; (slut) Dirne f
slaughter ['slɔtər] s Schlachten n;
(massacre) Metzelei f || tr schlachten;
(massacre) niedermetzeln
slaugh'terhouse' s Schlachthaus n
Slav [slɑv], [slæv] adj slawisch || s
(person) Slawe m, Slawin f
slave [slev] s Sklave m, Sklavin f ||
intr (coll) schuften; s. at a job sich
mit e-r Arbeit abquälen
slave' driv'er s (fig) Leuteschinder m
slaver ['slævər] s Geifer m
slavery ['slevəri] s Sklaverei f
slave' trade' s Sklavenhandel m
Slavic ['slɑvɪk], ['slævɪk] adj slawisch
slavish ['slevɪʃ] adj sklavisch
slay [sle] v (pret slew [slu]; pp slain
[slen]) tr erschlagen
slayer ['sle·ər] s Totschläger –in mf
sled [slɛd] s Schlitten m || v (pret &
pp sledded; ger sledding) intr Schlitten fahren
sledge [slɛdʒ] s Schlitten m
sledge' ham'mer s Vorschlaghammer m
sleek [slik] adj (hair) glatt; (cattle)
fett || tr glätten
sleep [slip] s Schlaf m; get enough s.
sich ausschlafen || v (pret & pp slept
[slɛpt]) tr (accommodate) Schlafge-
legenheiten bieten für; s. off a hang-
over seinen Kater ausschlafen || intr
schlafen; I didn't s. a wink ich habe
kein Auge zugetan; s. like a log wie
ein Murmeltier schlafen; s. with (a
woman) schlafen mit
sleeper ['sliper] s Schläfer –in mf;
(sleeping car) Schlafwagen m; (fig)
überraschender Erfolg m
sleepiness ['slipɪnɪs] s Schläfrigkeit f
sleep'ing bag' s Schlafsack m
Sleep'ing Beau'ty s Dornröschen n
sleep'ing car' s Schlafwagen m
sleep'ing compart'ment s Schlafabteil
n
sleep'ing pill' s Schlaftablette f
sleep'ing sick'ness s Schlafkrankheit f
sleepless ['slɪplɪs] adj schlaflos
sleep'walk'er s Nachtwandler –in mf
sleepy ['slipi] adj schläfrig
sleep'yhead' s Schlafmütze f
sleet [slit] s Schneeregen m; (on the
ground) Glatteis n || impers—it is
sleeting es gibt Schneeregen, es graup-
pelt
sleeve [sliv] s Ärmel m; (mach) Muffe
f; have s.th. up one's s. etw im
Schilde führen; roll up one's sleeves
die Ärmel hochkrempeln
sleeveless ['slivlɪs] adj ärmellos
sleigh [sle] s Schlitten m
sleigh' bell' s Schlittenschelle f
sleigh' ride' s Schlittenfahrt f; go for
sleight' of hand' [slaɪt] s Taschenspie-
lertrick m
slender ['slɛndər] adj schlank; (means)
gering
sleuth [sluθ] s Detektiv m
slice [slaɪs] s Scheibe f, Schnitte f;

(tennis) Schnittball *m* || *tr* aufschneiden

slicer ['slaɪsər] *s* Schneidemaschine *f*

slick [slɪk] *adj* glatt; (*talker*) raffiniert

slicker ['slɪkər] *s* Regenmantel *m*

slide [slaɪd] *s* (*slip*) Rutsch *m*; (*chute*) Rutschbahn *f*; (*of a microscope*) Objektträger *m*; (*phot*) Diapositiv *n* || *v* (*pret & pp* **slid** [slɪd]) *tr* schieben || *intr* rutschen; **let things s.** die Dinge laufen lassen

slide′ rule′ *s* Rechenschieber *m*

slide′ valve′ *s* Schieberventil *n*

slide′ view′er *s* Bildbetrachter *m*

slid′ing door′ *s* Schiebetür *f*

slid′ing scale′ *s* gleitende Skala *f*

slight [slaɪt] *adj* gering(fügig); (*illness*) leicht; (*petite*) zart || *tr* mißachten

slim [slɪm] *adj* schlank; (*chance*) gering || *intr*—**s. down** abnehmen

slime [slaɪm] *s* Schlamm *m*; (*e.g., of fish, snakes*) Schleim *m*

slimy ['slaɪmi] *adj* schleimig; (*muddy*) schlammig

sling [slɪŋ] *s* (*to hurl stones*) Schleuder *f*; (*for a broken arm*) Schlinge *f* || *v* (*pret & pp* **slung** [slʌŋ]) *tr* schleudern; **s. over the shoulders** umhängen

sling′shot′ *s* Schleuder *f*

slink [slɪŋk] *v* (*pret & pp* **slunk** [slʌŋk]) *intr* schleichen; **s. away** wegschleichen

slip [slɪp] *s* (*slide*) Ausrutschen *n*; (*cutting*) Ableger *m*; (*underwear*) Unterrock *m*; (*paper*) Zettel *m*; (*pillowcase*) Kissenbezug *m*; (*error*) Flüchtigkeitsfehler *m*; (*for ships*) Schlippe *m*; **give s.o. the s.** j-m entwischen; **s. of the pen** Schreibfehler *m*; **s. of the tongue** Sprechfehler *m* || *v* (*pret & pp* **slipped**; *ger* **slipping**) *tr*—**s. in** (*a remark*) einfließen lassen; (*poison*) heimlich schütten; **s. on** (*a glove*) überstreifen; (*a coat*) überziehen; (*a ring*) auf den Finger streifen; **s. s.o. money** j-m etw Geld zustecken; **s.o.'s mind** j-m entfallen || *intr* rutschen; (*e.g., out of or into a room*) schlüpfen; (*lose one's balance*) ausgleiten; **let s. slip** [dat] entgehen lassen; **s. by** verstreichen; **s. in** (*said of errors*) unterlaufen; **s. through one's fingers** durch die Finger gleiten; **s. out on s.o.** j-m entschlüpfen; **s. up (on)** danebenhauen (bei); **you are slipping** (coll) Sie lassen in der Leistung nach

slip′cov′er *s* Schonbezug *m*

slip′knot′ *s* Schleife *f*

slipper ['slɪpər] *s* Pantoffel *m*

slippery ['slɪpəri] *adj* glatt

slipshod ['slɪp ˌʃɑd] *adj* schlampig; **do s. work** schludern

slip′stream′ *s* Luftschraubenstrahl *m*

slip′-up′ *s* (coll) Flüchtigkeitsfehler *m*

slit [slɪt] *s* Schlitz *m* || *v* (*pret & pp* **slit**; *ger* **slitting**) *tr* schlitzen; **s. open** aufschlitzen

slit′-eyed′ *adj* schlitzäugig

slither ['slɪðər] *intr* gleiten

slit′ trench′ *s* (mil) Splittergraben *m*

sliver ['slɪvər] *s* Splitter *m*, Span *m*

slob [slɑb] *s* (sl) Schmutzfink *m*

slobber ['slɑbər] *s* Geifer *m* || *intr* geifern

sloe [slo] *s* (bot) Schlehe *f*

sloe′-eyed′ *adj* schlitzäugig

slog [slɑg] *v* (*pret & pp* **slogged**; *ger* **slogging**) *intr* stapfen

slogan ['slogən] *s* Schlagwort *n*

sloop [slup] *s* Schaluppe *f*

slop [slɑp] *s* Spülicht *n*; (*bad food*) (sl) Fraß *m* || *v* (*pret & pp* **slopped**; *ger* **slopping**) *tr* (*hogs*) füttern; (*spill*) verschütten

slope [slop] *s* Abhang *m*; (*of a road*) Gefälle *n*; (*of a roof*) Neigung *f* || *tr* abschrägen || *intr* sich neigen; (*said of a road*) abfallen

sloppy ['slɑpi] *adj* schlampig; (*weather*) matschig

slosh [slɑʃ] *intr* schwappen

slot [slɑt] *s* Schlitz *m*

sloth [sloθ] *s* Faulheit *f*, Trägheit *f*; (zool) Faultier *n*

slothful ['sloθfəl] *adj* faul, träge

slot′ machine′ *s* Spielautomat *m*

slouch [slaʊtʃ] *s* nachlässige Haltung *f*; (*person*) Schlappschwanz *m* || *intr* in schlechter Haltung sitzen; **s. along** latschen

slouch′ hat′ *s* Schlapphut *m*

slough [slaʊ] *s* Sumpf *m* || [slʌf] *s* (*of a snake*) abgestreifte Haut *f*; (pathol) Schorf *m* || *tr* (& fig) abstreifen || *intr* (*said of a snake*) sich häuten

Slovak ['slovak], ['slovæk] *adj* slowakisch || *s* (*person*) Slowake *m*, Slowakin *f*; (*language*) Slowakisch *n*

slovenly ['slʌvənli] *adj* schlampig

slow [slo] *adj* langsam; (*dawdling*) bummelig; (*mentally*) schwer von Begriff; (com) flau; **be s.** (horol) nachgehen || *adv* langsam || *tr*—**s. down** verlangsamen || *intr*—**s. down** (in driving) langsamer fahren; (in working) nachlassen; **s. down** (public sign) Schritt fahren

slow′down′ *s* Bummelstreik *m*

slow′ mo′tion *s* (cin) Zeitlupe *f*; **in s.** (cin) im Zeitlupentempo

slow′-mo′tion *adj* Zeitlupen-

slow′poke′ *s* (coll) langsamer Mensch *m*

slow′-wit′ted *adj* schwer von Begriff

slug [slʌg] *s* Rohling *m*; (*drink*) Zug *m*; (zool) Wegschnecke *f* || *v* (*pret & pp* **slugged**; *ger* **slugging**) *tr* (coll) hart mit der Faust treffen

sluggard ['slʌgərd] *s* Faulpelz *m*

sluggish ['slʌgɪʃ] *adj* träge

sluice [slus] *s* Schleuse *f*

sluice′ gate′ *s* Schleusentor *n*

slum [slʌm] *s* Elendsviertel *n*

slumber ['slʌmbər] *s* Schlummer *m* || *intr* schlummern

slum′ dwell′ing *s* Elendsquartier *n*

slump [slʌmp] *s* (st. exch.) Baisse *f*; **s. in sales** Absatzstockung *f* || *intr* zusammensacken; (*said of prices*) stürzen

slur [slʌr] *s* (*insult*) Verleumdung *f*; (mus) Bindezeichen *n* || *v* (*pret & pp* **slurred**; *ger* **slurring**) *tr* (*words*) verschleifen; (mus) binden; **s. over** hinweggehen über (acc)

slurp [slʌrp] s Schlürfen n ‖ tr & intr schlürfen

slush [slʌʃ] s Matsch m, Schneematsch m

slush' fund' s Schmiergeld n

slushy ['slʌʃi] adj matschig

slut [slʌt] s Nutte f

sly [slaɪ] adj (slyer & slier; slyest & sliest) schlau ‖ s—**on the sly** im Verborgenen

sly' fox' s Pfiffikus m

smack [smæk] s (blow) Klaps m; (sound) Klatsch m; (kiss) Schmatz m; **s. in the face** Backpfeife f ‖ tr klapsen; **s. one's lips** schmatzen ‖ intr—**s. of** riechen nach

small [smɔl] adj klein; (difference) gering; (comfort) schlecht; (petty) kleinlich

small' arms' spl Handwaffen pl

small' busi'ness s Kleinbetrieb m

small' cap'ital s (typ) Kapitälchen n

small' change' s Kleingeld n

small' fry' s kleine Fische pl

small' intes'tine s Dünndarm m

small'-mind'ed adj engstirnig

small' of the back' s Kreuz n

smallpox ['smɔl͵pɑks] s Pocken pl

small' print' s Kleindruck m

small' talk' s Geplauder n

small'-time' adj klein

small'-town' adj kleinstädtisch

smart [smɑrt] adj (bright) klug; (neat, trim) schick; (car) schneidig; (pej) überklug ‖ s Schmerz m ‖ intr weh tun; (burn) brennen

smart' al'eck s [͵ælɪk] s Neunmalkluge mf

smart'-look'ing adj schnittig

smart' set' s elegante Welt f

smash [smæʃ] s (hit) (coll) Bombe f; (tennis) Schmetterschlag m ‖ tr zerschmettern; (e.g., a window) einschlagen; (sport) schmettern; **s. up** zerknallen ‖ intr zerbrechen; **s. into** krachen gegen

smash' hit' s (theat) Bombenerfolg m

smash'-up' s (aut) Zusammenstoß m

smattering ['smætərɪŋ] s (of) oberflächliche Kenntnis f (genit)

smear [smɪr] s Schmiere f; (smudge) Schmutzfleck m; (vilification) Verunglimpfung f; (med) Abstrich m ‖ tr (spread) schmieren; (make dirty) beschmieren; (vilify) verunglimpfen; (trounce) vollständig fertigmachen

smear' campaign' s Verleumdungsfeldzug m

smell [smel] s Geruch m; (aroma) Duft m; (sense) Geruchssinn m ‖ v (pret & pp smelled & smelt [smelt]) tr riechen; (danger, trouble) wittern ‖ intr (of) riechen (nach)

smell'ing salts' pl Riechsalz n

smelly ['smeli] adj übelriechend

smelt [smelt] s (fish) Stint m ‖ tr schmelzen, verhütten

smile [smaɪl] s Lächeln n ‖ intr lächeln; **s. at** anlächeln; (clandestinely) zulächeln (dat); **s. on** lächeln (dat)

smirk [smɪrk] s Grinsen n ‖ intr grinsen

smite [smaɪt] v (pret smote [smot]; pp smitten ['smɪtən] & smit [smɪt]) tr schlagen; (said of a plague) befallen; **smitten with** hingerissen von

smith [smɪθ] s Schmied m

smithy ['smɪθi] s Schmiede f

smock [smɑk] s Kittel m, Bluse f

smog [smɑg] s Smog m

smoke [smok] s Rauch m; (heavy smoke) Qualm m; **go up in s.** (fig) in Dunst und Rauch aufgehen ‖ tr rauchen; (meat) räuchern ‖ intr rauchen; (said of a chimney) qualmen

smoke' bomb' s Rauchbombe f

smoked' ham' s Räucherschinken m

smoker ['smokər] s Raucher –in mf; (sl) obszöner Film m

smoke' screen' s Rauchvorhang m

smoke'stack' s Schornstein m

smok'ing s Rauchen n; **no s.** (public sign) Rauchen verboten

smok'ing car' s Raucherwagen m

smok'ing jack'et s Hausjacke f

smoky ['smoki] adj rauchig

smolder ['smoldər] intr (& fig) schwelen

smooch [smutʃ] intr sich abknutschen

smooth [smuð] adj (surface; talker; landing, operation) glatt; (wine) mild ‖ tr glätten; **s. away** (difficulties) beseitigen; **s. out** glätten; **s. over** beschönigen

smooth'-faced' adj glattwangig

smooth-shaven ['smuð'ʃevən] adj glattrasiert

smooth'-talk'ing adj schönrednerisch

smoothy ['smuði] s Schönredner –in mf

smother ['smʌðər] tr ersticken; **s. with kisses** abküssen

smudge [smʌdʒ] s Schmutzfleck m ‖ tr beschmutzen ‖ intr schmutzig werden

smug [smʌg] adj (smugger; smuggest) selbstgefällig

smuggle ['smʌgəl] tr & intr schmuggeln

smuggler ['smʌglər] s Schmuggler –in mf

smug'gling s Schmuggel m

smut [smʌt] s Schmutz m

smutty ['smʌti] adj schmutzig, obszön

snack [snæk] s Imbiß m

snack' bar' s Imbißstube f, Snack Bar f

snaffle ['snæfəl] s Trense f

snag [snæg] s—**hit a s.** auf Schwierigkeiten stoßen ‖ v (pret & pp snagged; ger snagging) tr hängenbleiben mit

snail [snel] s Schnecke f; **at a snail's pace** im Schneckentempo

snake [snek] s Schlange f ‖ intr sich schlängeln

snake'bite' s Schlangenbiß m

snake' in the grass' s heimtückischer Mensch m

snap [snæp] s (sound) Knacks m; (on clothes) Druckknopf m; (of a dog) Biß m; (liveliness) Schwung m; (easy work) Kinderspiel n ‖ v (pret & pp snapped; ger snapping) tr (break) zerreißen, entzweibrechen; (a picture) knipsen; **s. a whip** mit der

Peitsche knallen; **s. back** (*words*) hervorstoßen; (*the head*) zurückwerfen; **s. off** abbrechen; **s. one's fingers** mit den Fingern schnalzen; **s. s.o.'s head off** j-n zusammenstauchen; **s. up** gierig an sich reißen; (*buy up*) aufkaufen ‖ *intr* (*tear*) zerreißen; (*break*) entzweibrechen; **s. at** schnappen nach; (fig) anfahren; **s. out of it!** komm zu dir!; **s. shut** zuschnappen; **s. to it!** mach zu!

snap'drag'on *s* (bot) Löwenmaul *n*
snap' fas'tener *s* Druckknopf *m*
snap' judg'ment *s* vorschnelles Urteil *n*
snap'per soup' ['snæpər] *s* Schildkrötensuppe *f*
snappish ['snæpiʃ] *adj* bissig
snappy ['snæpi] *adj* (*caustic*) bissig; (*lively*) energisch; **make it s.!** mach schnell!
snap'shot' *s* Schnappschuß *m*
snare [sner] *s* Schlinge *f* ‖ *tr* mit e-r Schlinge fangen; (fig) fangen
snare' drum' *s* Schnarrtrommel *f*
snarl [snɑrl] *s* (*tangle*) Verwicklung *f*; (*sound*) Knurren *n* ‖ *tr* verwickeln; **s. traffic** e-e Verkehrsstockung verursachen ‖ *intr* knurren
snatch [snætʃ] *s*—**in snatches** ruckweise; **snatches** (*of conversation*) Bruchstücke *pl* ‖ *tr* schnappen; **s. away from** entreißen (*dat*); **s. up** schnappen
snazzy ['snæzi] *adj* (sl) schmissig
sneak [snik] *s* Schleicher –in *mf* ‖ *tr* (*e.g., a drink*) heimlich trinken; **s. in** einschmuggeln ‖ *intr* schleichen; **s. away** sich davonschleichen; **s. in** sich einschleichen; **s. out** sich herausschleichen; **s. up on s.o.** an j-n heranschleichen
sneaker ['snikər] *s* Tennisschuh *m*
sneaky ['sniki] *adj* heimtückisch
sneer [snɪr] *s* Hohnlächeln *n* ‖ *intr* höhnisch grinsen; **s. at** spötteln über (*acc*)
sneeze [sniz] *s* Niesen *n* ‖ *tr*—**not to be sneezed at** nicht zu verachten ‖ *intr* niesen
snicker ['snɪkər] *s* Kichern *n* ‖ *intr* kichern
snide' remark' [snaɪd] *s* Anzüglichkeit *f*
sniff [snɪf] *s* Schnüffeln *n* ‖ *tr* (be)riechen; **s. out** ausschnüffeln ‖ *intr* (**at**) schnüffeln (*an dat*)
sniffle ['snɪfəl] *s* Geschnüffel *n*; **sniffles** Schnupfen *m* ‖ *intr* schniefen
snip [snɪp] *s* (*cut*) Einschnitt *m*; (*small piece snipped off*) Schnippel *m* ‖ *v* (*pret & pp* **snipped;** *ger* **snipping**) *tr & intr* schnippeln
snipe [snaɪp] *intr*—**s. at** aus dem Hinterhalt schießen auf (*acc*)
sniper ['snaɪpər] *s* Heckenschütze *m*
snippet ['snɪpɪt] *s* Schnippelchen *n*; (*small person*) Knirps *m*
snippy ['snɪpi] *adj* schroff, barsch
snitch [snɪtʃ] *tr* (coll) klauen ‖ *intr* (coll) petzen; **s. on** (coll) verpfeifen
sniv·el ['snɪvəl] *s* (*whining*) Gewimmer *n*; (*mucus*) Nasenschleim *m* ‖ *v*

(*pret & pp* **–el[l]ed;** *ger* **–el[l]ing**) *intr* (*whine*) wimmern; (*cry with sniffling*) schluchzen; (*have a runny nose*) e-e tropfende Nase haben
snob [snɑb] *s* Snob *m*
snob' appeal' *s* Snobappeal *m*
snobbery ['snɑbəri] *s* Snobismus *m*
snobbish ['snɑbɪʃ] *adj* snobistisch
snoop [snup] *s* (coll) Schnüffler –in *mf* ‖ *intr* (coll) schnüffeln
snoopy ['snupi] *adj* schnüffelnd
snoot [snut] *s* (sl) Rüssel *m*; **make a s.** e-e Schnute ziehen
snooty ['snuti] *adj* hochnäsig
snooze [snuz] *s* (coll) Nickerchen *n* ‖ *intr* (coll) ein Nickerchen machen
snore [snor] *s* Schnarchen *n* ‖ *intr* schnarchen
snort [snɔrt] *s* Schnauben *n* ‖ *tr* wütend schnauben ‖ *intr* prusten; (*said of a horse*) schnauben; (*with laughter*) vor Lachen prusten
snot [snɑt] *s* (sl) Rotz *m*
snotty ['snɑti] *adj* (sl & fig) rotzig
snout [snaʊt] *s* Schnauze *f*, Rüssel *m*
snow [sno] *s* Schnee *m* ‖ *tr* (sl) einwickeln; **s. in** einschneien; **s. under** mit Schnee bedecken ‖ *impers*—**it is snowing** es schneit
snow'ball' *s* Schneeball *m* ‖ *intr* (fig) lawinenartig anwachsen
snow'bank' *s* Schneeverwehung *f*
snow'bird' *s* Schneefink *m*
snow' blind'ness *s* Schneeblindheit *f*
snow' blow'er *s* Schneefräse *f*
snow'bound' *adj* eingeschneit
snow'-capped' *adj* schneebedeckt
snow' chain' *s* (aut) Schneekette *f*
snow'-clad' *adj* verschneit
snow'drift' *s* Schneeverwehung *f*
snow'fall' *s* Schneefall *m*
snow'flake' *s* Schneeflocke *f*
snow' flur'ry *s* Schneegestöber *n*
snow' job' *s*—**give s.o. a s.** (sl) j-n hereinlegen
snow'man' *s* (**-men**) Schneemann *m*
snow'mobile' *s* Motorschlitten *m*
snow'plow' *s* Schneepflug *m*
snow'shoe' *s* Schneeteller *m*
snow' shov'el *s* Schneeschaufel *f*
snow'storm' *s* Schneesturm *m*
snow' tire' *s* Winterreifen *m*
Snow' White' *s* Schneewittchen *n*
snow'-white' *adj* schneeweiß
snowy ['sno·i] *adj* schneeig
snub [snʌb] *s* verächtliche Behandlung *f* ‖ *v* (*pret & pp* **snubbed;** *ger* **snubbing**) *tr* (*ignore*) schneiden; (*treat contemptuously*) verächtlich behandeln
snubby ['snʌbi] *adj* (*nose*) etwas abgestumpft; (*person*) abweisen
snub'-nosed' *adj* stumpfnasig
snuff [snʌf] *s* Schnupftabak *m*; (*of a candle*) Schnuppe *f*; **up to s.** (sl) auf Draht ‖ *tr*—**s. out** (*a candle*) auslöschen; (*suppress*) unterdrücken
snuff'box' *s* Schnupftabakdose *f*
snug [snʌg] *adj* (**snugger; snuggest**) behaglich; (*fit*) eng angeschmiegt; **s. as a bug in a rug** wie die Made im Speck

snuggle ['snʌgəl] *intr*—**s. up** (**to**) sich schmiegen (an *acc*)
so [so] *adv* (with adjectives or adverbs) so; (*thus*) so; (*for this reason*) daher; (*then*) also; **and so forth** und so weiter; **or so** etwa, e.g., **ten miles or so** etwa zehn Meilen; **so as to** (*inf*) um zu (*inf*); **so far** bisher; **so far as** soviel; **so far, so good** soweit ganz gut; **so I see!** das seh' ich!; **so long!** (coll) bis bald!; **so much** soviel; **so much the better** um so besser; **so that** damit; **so what?** na, und?
soak [sok] *s* Einweichen *n* || *tr* einweichen; (*soak through and through*) durchnässen; (*overcharge*) (sl) schröpfen; **soaked to the skin** bis auf die Haut durchnäßt || *intr* weichen
so'-and-so' *s* (–**sos**) Soundso *mf*
soap [sop] *s* Seife *f* || *tr* einseifen
soap'box der'by *s* Seifenkistenrennen *n*
soap'box or'ator *s* Straßenredner –in *mf*
soap' bub'ble *s* Seifenblase *f*
soap' dish' *s* Seifenschale *f*
soap' flakes' *spl* Seifenflocken *pl*
soap' op'era *s* (rad) rührselige Hörspielreihe *f*; (telv) rührselige Fernsehspielreihe *f*
soap' pow'der *s* Seifenpulver *n*
soap'stone' *s* Seifenstein *m*
soap'suds' *spl* Seifenlauge *f*
soapy ['sopi] *adj* seifig; (*like soap*) seifenartig
soar [sor] *intr* schweben, (auf)steigen, (*prices*) steigen
sob [sab] *s* Schluchzen *n* || *v* (*pret & pp* **sobbed;** *ger* **sobbing**) *intr* schluchzen
sober ['sobər] *adj* nüchtern || *tr* (**up**) ernüchtern || *intr*—**s. up** wieder nüchtern werden
sobriety [so'braɪ·əti] *s* Nüchternheit *f*
sob' sto'ry *s* Schmachtfetzen *pl*
so'-called' *adj* sogenannt
soccer ['sakər] *s* Fußball *m*
soc'cer play'er *s* Fußballer *m*
sociable ['soʃəbəl] *adj* gesellig
social ['soʃəl] *adj* gesellschaftlich || *s* geselliges Beisammensein *s*
so'cial climb'er *s* Streber –in *mf*
socialism ['soʃə‚lɪzəm] *s* Sozialismus *m*
socialist ['soʃəlɪst] *s* Sozialist –in *mf*
socialistic [‚soʃə'lɪstɪk] *adj* sozialistisch
socialite ['soʃə‚laɪt] *s* Prominente *mf*
socialize ['soʃə‚laɪz] *intr* (**with**) verkehren (mit)
so'cialized med'icine *s* staatliche Gesundheitspflege *f*
so'cial reg'ister *s* Register *n* der prominenten Mitglieder der oberen Gesellschaftsklasse
so'cial sci'ence *s* Sozialwissenschaft *f*
so'cial secu'rity *s* Sozialversicherung *f*
so'cial wel'fare *s* Sozialfürsorge *f*
so'cial work'er *s* Sozialfürsorger –in *mf*
society [sə'saɪ·əti] *s* Gesellschaft *f*; (*an organization*) Verein *m*
soci'ety col'umn *s* Gesellschaftsspalte *f*

soci'ety for the preven'tion of cru'elty to an'imals *s* Tierschutzverein *m*
sociological [‚sosɪ·ə'lɑdʒɪkəl] *adj* sozialwissenschaftlich, soziologisch
sociologist [‚sosɪ'ɑlədʒɪst] *s* Soziologe *m*, Soziologin *f*
sociology [‚sosɪ'ɑlədʒi] *s* Soziologie *f*
sock [sak] *s* Socke *f*; (sl) Faustschlag *m* || *tr*—**s. it to him!** gib's ihm!; **s. s.o.** j–m eine 'runterhauen
socket ['sakɪt] *s* (anat) Höhle *f*; (elec) Steckdose *f*; (mach) Muffe *f*
sock'et joint' *s* (anat) Kugelgelenk *n*
sock'et wrench' *s* Steckschlüssel *m*
sod [sad] *s* Rasenstück *n* || *v* (*pret & pp* **sodded;** *ger* **sodding**) *tr* mit Rasen bedecken
soda ['sodə] *s* (*refreshment*) Limonade *f*; (*in mixed drinks*) Selterswasser *n*; (chem) Soda *f & n*
so'da crack'er *s* Keks *m*
so'da wa'ter *s* Sodawasser *n*
sodium ['sodɪ·əm] *s* Natrium *n*
sofa ['sofə] *s* Sofa *n*
soft [sɔft] *adj* (*not hard or tough*) weich; (*not loud*) leise; (*light, music*) sanft; (*sleep, breeze*) leicht; (*effeminate*) verweichlicht; (*muscles*) schlaff; **be s. on** weich sein gegenüber (dat)
soft'-boiled egg' *s* weichgekochtes Ei *n*
soft' coal' *s* Braunkohle *f*
soft' drink' *s* alkoholfreies Getränk *n*
soften ['sɔfən] *tr* aufweichen; (*palliate*) lindern; (*water*) enthärten; **s. up** (mil) zermürben || *intr* (& fig) weich werden
soft'-heart'ed *adj* weichherzig
soft' job' *s* Druckposten *m*
soft' land'ing *s* (rok) weiche Landung *f*
soft' pal'ate *s* Hintergaumen *m*
soft'-ped'al *v* (*pret & pp* **-al[l]ed;** *ger* **-al[l]ing**) *tr* zurückhaltender vorbringen
soft'-soap' *tr* (coll) schmeicheln (dat)
soggy ['sagi] *adj* (*soaked*) durchnäßt; (*ground*) sumpfig
soil [sɔɪl] *s* Boden *m* || *tr* beschmutzen || *intr* schmutzen
soil' pipe' *s* Abflußrohr *n*
sojourn ['sodʒʌrn] *s* Aufenthalt *m* || *intr* sich vorübergehend aufhalten
solace ['salɪs] *s* Trost *m* || *tr* trösten
solar ['solər] *adj* Sonnen–
so'lar plex'us ['plɛksəs] *s* (anat) Sonnengeflecht *n*
solder ['sɔdər] *s* Lötmetall *n* || *tr* löten
sol'dering i'ron *s* Lötkolben *m*
soldier ['soldʒər] *s* Soldat *m*
sole [sol] *adj* einzig, alleinig || *s* (*of a shoe, foot*) Sohle *f*; (*fish*) Scholle *f* || *tr* (be)sohlen
solely ['soli] *adv* einzig und allein
solemn ['saləm] *adj* feierlich; (*expression*) ernst
solemnity [sə'lɛmnɪti] *s* Feierlichkeit *f*
solicit [sə'lɪsɪt] *tr* (*beg for*) dringend bitten um; (*accost*) ansprechen; (*new members, customers*) werben
solicitor [sə'lɪsɪtər] *s* (com) Agent –in *mf*; (jur) Rechtsanwalt *m*

solicitous [sə'lɪsɪtəs] *adj* fürsorglich
solid ['salɪd] *adj* (*hard, firm, e.g., ice, ground*) fest; (*sturdy, e.g., person, furniture; firm, e.g., foundation, learning; financially sound*) solid(e); (*compact*) kompakt, massiv; (*durable*) dauerhaft; (*gold*) gediegen; (*meal, blow*) kräftig; (*hour*) ganz, geschlagen; (*of one color*) einfarbig; (*color*) getönt; (*of one mind*) einmütig; (*grounds, argument*) stichhaltig; (*row of houses*) geschlossen; (*clouds, fog*) dicht; (*geom*) Raum– ‖ *s* (geom, phys) Körper *m*
solidarity [ˌsalɪ'dærɪti] *s* Solidarität *f*, Verbundenheit *f*
sol'id food' *s* feste Nahrung *f*
sol'id geo'metry *s* Stereometrie *f*
solidi·fy [sə'lɪdɪˌfaɪ] *v* (*pret & pp* –fied) *tr* fest werden lassen; (fig) konsolidieren ‖ *intr* fest werden
solidity [sə'lɪdɪti] *s* (*state*) Festigkeit *f*; (*soundness*) Solidität *f*
solidly ['salɪdli] *adv*—**be s. behind s.o.** sich mit j-m solidarisch erklären
sol'id-state' *adj* Transistor–
soliloquy [sə'lɪləkwi] *s* Selbstgespräch *n*
solitaire ['salɪˌter] *s* Solitär *m*
solitary ['salɪˌteri] *adj* allein; (*life*) zurückgezogen; (*exception*) einzig; (*lonely*) einsam
sol'itary confine'ment *s* Einzelhaft *f*
solitude ['salɪˌt(j)ud] *s* Einsamkeit *f*; (*lonely spot*) abgelegener Ort *m*
so·lo ['solo] *adj & adv* solo ‖ *s* (–los) Solo *n*
so'lo flight' *s* Soloflug *m*
soloist ['solo·ɪst] *s* Solist –in *mf*
so'lo part' *s* (mus) Solostimme *f*
solstice ['salstɪs] *s* Sonnenwende *f*
soluble ['saljəbəl] *adj* (fig) (auf)lösbar; (chem) löslich
solution [sə'luʃən] *s* Lösung *f*
solvable ['salvəbəl] *adj* (auf)lösbar
solve [salv] *tr* (auf)lösen
solvency ['salvənsi] *s* Zahlungsfähigkeit *f*
solvent ['salvənt] *adj* zahlungsfähig; (chem) (auf)lösend ‖ *s* Lösungsmittel *n*
somber ['sambər] *adj* düster, trüb(e)
some [sʌm] *indef adj* (*with singular nouns*) etwas; (*with plural nouns*) manche; (*sometimes not translated*) e.g., **I am buying s. stockings** ich kaufe Strümpfe; (coll) toll, e.g., **s. girl!** tolles Mädchen!; **at s. time or other** irgendeinmal, irgendwann; **s. ... or other** irgendein; **s. other way** sonstwie ‖ *adv* (*with numerals*) etwa, ungefähr ‖ *indef pron* manche; (*part of*) ein Teil *m*; **s. of these people** einige Leute; **s. of us** manche von uns
some'bod'y *indef pron* jemand, irgendwer; **s. else** jemand anderer ‖ *s*—**be a s.** etwas Besonderes sein
some'day' *adv* e–s Tages
some'how' *adv* irgendwie; (*for some reason or other*) aus irgendeinem Grunde

some'one' *indef pron* jemand, irgendwer; **s. else** jemand anderer; **s. else's** fremd, e.g., **s. else's property** fremdes Eigentum
some'place' *adv* irgendwo; (*direction*) irgendwohin
somersault ['sʌmərˌsɔlt] *s* Purzelbaum *m*; (gym) Überschlag *m*; **do a s.** e–n Purzelbaum schlagen ‖ *intr* sich überschlagen
some'thing' *indef pron* etwas; **he is s. of an expert** er ist e–e Art Experte; **s. else** etwas anderes; **s. or other** irgend etwas
some'time' *adv* einmal; **s. today** irgendwann heute
some'times' *adv* manchmal; **sometimes ... sometimes ...** mal ... mal ...
some'way', **some'ways'** *adv* irgendwie
some'what' *adv* etwas
some'where' *adv* irgendwo; (*direction*) irgendwohin; **from s. else** sonstwoher; **s. else** sonstwo
somnambulist [sam'næmbjəlɪst] *s* Nachtwandler –in *mf*
somnolent ['samnələnt] *adj* schläfrig
son [sʌn] *s* Sohn *m*
sonar ['sonar] *s* Sonar *n*
sonata [sə'natə] *s* Sonate *f*
song [sɔŋ] *s* Lied *n*; (*of birds*) Gesang *m*; **for a s.** (coll) um ein Spottgeld
Song' of Songs' *s* (Bib) Hohelied *n*
sonic ['sanɪk] *adj* Schall–
son'ic boom' *s* Kopfwellenknall *m*
son'-in-law' *s* (sons-in-law) Schwiegersohn *m*
sonnet ['sanɪt] *s* Sonett *n*
sonny ['sʌni] *s* Söhnchen *n*, Kleiner *m*
Son' of Man', **the** *s* (Bib) der Menschensohn
sonorous [sə'norəs] *adj* sonor
soon [sun] *adv* bald; **as s. as** sobald; **as s. as possible** sobald wie möglich; **just as s.** (*expressing preference*) genauso gern(e); **no sooner said than done** gesagt, getan; **sooner** (*expressing time*) früher, eher; (*expressing preference*) lieber, eher; **sooner or later** über kurz oder lang; **the sooner the better** je eher, je besser; **too s.** zu früh
soot [sut] *s* Ruß *m*
soothe [suð] *tr* beschwichtigen, beruhigen; **have a soothing effect on** beruhigend wirken auf (*acc*)
soothsayer ['suθˌse·ər] *s* Wahrsager *m*
sooty ['suti] *adj* rußig
sop [sap] *s* eingetunktes Stück *n* Brot; (*something given to pacify*) Beschwichtigungsmittel *n*; (*bribe*) Schmiergeld *n*; (*spineless person*) Waschlappen *m* ‖ *v* (*pret & pp* **sopped**; *ger* **sopping**) *tr* (*dip*) eintunken; **sop up** aufsaugen
sophist ['safɪst] *s* Sophist –in *mf*
sophisticated [sə'fɪstɪˌketɪd] *adj* (*person*) weltklug; (*way of life*) verfeinert; (*highly developed*) hochentwickelt
sophistication [səˌfɪstɪ'keʃən] *s* Weltklugheit *f*
sophistry ['safɪstri] *s* Sophisterei *f*

sophomore ['sɑfə‚mor] *s* Student –in *mf* im zweiten Studienjahr

sop'ping *adj* klatschnaß || *adv—s.* **wet** klatschnaß

sopran‧o [sə'præno] *adj* Sopran– || *s* (–os) (*uppermost voice*) Sopran *m*; (*soprano part*) Sopranpartie *f*; (*singer*) Sopranist –in *mf*

sorcerer ['sɔrsərər] *s* Zauberer *m*

sorceress ['sɔrsərɪs] *s* Zauberin *f*

sorcery ['sɔrsəri] *s* Zauberei *f*

sordid ['sɔrdɪd] *adj* schmutzig; (*improper*) unlauter

sore [sor] *adj* wund; (*sensitive*) empfindlich; (*coll*) (at) bös (auf *acc*); **be s.** weh tun; **s. spot** (& *fig*) wunder Punkt *m* || *s* Wunde *f*

sore'head' *s* (coll) Verbitterte *mf*

sorely ['sorli] *adv* sehr

soreness ['sornɪs] *s* Empfindlichkeit *f*

sore' throat' *s* Halsweh *n*

sorority [sə'rɔrɪti] *s* Studentinnenvereinigung *f*

sorrel ['sɔrəl] *adj* fuchsrot || *s* Fuchs *m*; (bot) Sauerampfer *m*

sorrow ['sɔro] *s* Kummer *m* || *intr* (for *or* over) Kummer haben (um)

sorrowful ['sɔrəfəl] *adj* betrübt

sorry ['sɔri] *adj* traurig, betrübt; (*appearance*) armselig; **I am s.** es tut mir leid; **I am** (*or* feel) **s. for him** er tut mir leid

sort [sɔrt] *s* Art *f*, Sorte *f*; **all sorts of** alle möglichen; **nothing of the s.** nichts dergleichen; **out of sorts** unpäßlich; **s. of** (coll) (with adjectives) etwas; (with verbs) irgendwie; (with nouns) so 'n, e.g., **I had a s. of feeling that** ich hatte so 'ne Ahnung, daß; **these sorts of** derartige; **what s. of** was für ein || *tr* sortieren; **s. out** aussortieren; (fig) sichten

sortie ['sɔrti] *s* (from a fortress) Ausfall *m*; (aer) Einzeleinsatz *m* || *intr* e–n Ausfall machen

so'-so' *adj* & *adv* soso, leidlich

sot [sɑt] *s* Trunkenbold *m*

soul [sol] *s* (spiritual being; inhabitant) Seele *f*; **not a s.** (coll) keine Seele *f*; **upon my s.!** meiner Seele!

sound [saund] *adj* Schall–, Ton–; (*healthy*) gesund; (*valid*) einwandfrei; (*basis*) tragfähig; (*sleep*) fest; (*beating*) (coll) tüchtig; (*business*) solid; (*judgment*) treffsicher || *s* Laut *m*, Ton *m*; (*noise*) Geräusch *n*; (of one's voice) Klang *m*; (narrow body of water) Sund *m*; (phys) Schall *m*; (surg) Sonde *f* || *adv—be* **s. asleep** fest schlafen || *tr* ertönen lassen; (med) sondieren; (naut) loten; **s. s.o. out** (coll) j–m auf den Zahn fühlen; **s. the alarm** Alarm schlagen; **s. the all-clear** entwarnen || *intr* (er)klingen, (er)tönen; (*seem*) klingen; (naut) loten; **it sounds good to me** es kommt mir gut vor; **s. off** (coll) sich laut beschweren

sound' bar'rier *s* Schallgrenze *f*, Schallmauer *f*

sound' effects' *spl* Klangeffekte *pl*

sound' film' *s* Tonfilm *m*

sound'ing *s* Lotung *f*; **take soundings** loten

sound'ing board' *s* (on an instrument) Resonanzboden *m*; (over an orchestra or speaker) Schallmuschel *f*; (board for damping sounds) Schalldämpfungsbrett *n*

soundly ['saundli] *adv* tüchtig

sound'proof' *adj* schalldicht || *tr* schalldicht machen

sound' stu'dio *s* (cin) Tonatelier *n*

sound' techni'cian *s* Tontechniker *m*

sound' track' *s* (cin) Tonstreifen *m*

sound' truck' *s* Lautsprecherwagen *m*

sound' wave' *s* Schallwelle *f*

soup [sup] *s* Suppe *f*; (thick fog) (coll) Waschküche *f*; **in the s.** (coll) in der Patsche || *tr—s.* **up** (aut) frisieren

soup' kitch'en *s* Volksküche *f*

soup' meat' *s* Suppenfleisch *n*

soup' plate' *s* Suppenteller *m*

soup'spoon' *s* Suppenlöffel *m*

sour [saur] *adj* (& fig) sauer || *tr* säuern; (fig) verbittern || *intr* säuern; (fig) versauern

source [sors] *s* Quelle *f*

source' lan'guage *s* Ausgangssprache *f*

source' mate'rial *s* Quellenmaterial *n*

sour' cher'ry *s* Weichsel *f*

sour' grapes' *spl* (fig) saure Trauben *pl*

sour' note' *s* (& fig) Mißklang *m*

sour'puss' *s* (sl) Sauertopf *m*

souse [saus] *s* (sl) Säufer –in *mf*

soused *adj* (sl) besoffen

south [sauθ] *adj* Süd–, südlich || *adv* (direction) nach Süden; **s. of** südlich von || *s* Süd(en) *m*

South' Amer'ica *s* Südamerika *n*

south'east' *adj* Südost– || *adv* (direction) südöstlich; **s. of** südöstlich von || *s* Südost(en) *m*

southerly ['sʌðərli] *adj* südlich

southern ['sʌðərn] *adj* südlich

southerner ['sʌðərnər] *s* Südländer –in *mf*; (in the U.S.A.) Südstaatler –in *mf*

south'paw' *adj* (coll) linkshändig || *s* (coll) Linkshänder –in *mf*

South' Pole' *s* Südpol *m*

South' Seas' *spl* Südsee *f*

southward ['sauθwərd] *adv* südwärts

south'west' *adj* Südwest– || *adv* südwestlich; **s. of** südwestlich von || *s* Südwest(en) *m*

south'west'ern *adj* südwestlich

souvenir [‚suvə'nɪr] *s* Andenken *n*

sovereign ['sɑvrɪn] *adj* souverän || *s* Souverän *m*, Landesfürst *m*

sov'ereign rights' *spl* Hoheitsrechte *pl*

sovereignty ['sɑvrɪnti] *s* Souveränität *f*

soviet ['sovi‚ɛt] *adj* sowjetisch || *s* Sowjet *m*; **the Soviets** die Sowjets *pl*

So'viet Rus'sia *s* Sowjetrußland *n*

So'viet Un'ion *s* Sowjetunion *f*

sow [sau] *s* Sau *f* || [so] *v* (pret sowed; pp sowed & sown) *tr* & *intr* säen

soybean ['sɔɪ‚bin] *s* Sojabohne *f*

spa [spɑ] *s* Bad *n*, Badekurort *m*

space [spes] *s* Raum *m*; (between ob-

jects) Zwischenraum *m;* (typ) Spatium *n;* **take up s.** Platz einnehmen ‖ *tr* in Abständen anordnen; (typ) spationieren

space′ age′ *s* Weltraumzeitalter *n*

space′ bar′ *s* (typ) Leertaste *f*

space′ cap′sule *s* (rok) Raumkapsel *f*

space′craft′ *s* Weltraumfahrzeug *n*

space′ flight′ *s* Raumflug *m*

space′man′ *s* (**-men**) Raumfahrer *m*

space′ probe′ *s* Sonde *f*

space′ship′ *s* Raumschiff *n*

space′ shot′ *s* Weltraumabschuß *m*

space′ shut′tle *s* Raumfähre *f*

space′ suit′ *s* Raumanzug *m*

space′ trav′el *s* Raumfahrt *f*

spacious ['speʃəs] *adj* geräumig

spade [sped] *s* Spaten *m;* (cards) Pik *n;* **call a s. a s.** das Kind beim richtigen Namen nennen

spade′work′ *s* (fig) Pionierarbeit *f*

spaghetti [spə'gɛti] *s* Spahetti *pl*

Spain [spen] *s* Spanien *n*

span [spæn] *s* (& fig) Spanne *f;* (*of a bridge*) Joch *n;* **s. of time** Zeitspanne *f* ‖ *v* (*pret* & *pp* **spanned**) *ger* **spanning**) *tr* (*e.g., the waist*) umspannen; (*a river*) überbrücken; (*said of a bridge*) überspannen

spangle ['spæŋgəl] *s* Flitter *m* ‖ *tr* mit Flitter besetzen

Spaniard ['spænjərd] *s* Spanier –in *mf*

spaniel ['spænjəl] *s* Wachtelhund *m*

Spanish ['spænɪʃ] *adj* spanisch ‖ *s* Spanisch *n;* **the S.** die Spanier

Span′ish-Amer′ican *adj* spanischamerikanisch ‖ *s* Amerikaner –in *mf* mit spanischer Muttersprache

Span′ish moss′ *s* Moosbärte *pl*

spank [spæŋk] *tr* (ver)hauen

spank′ing *adj* (*quick*) flink; (*breeze*) frisch ‖ *adv*—**s. new** funkelnagelneu ‖ *s* Schläge *pl*

spar [spɑr] *s* (aer) Holm *m;* (mineral) Spat *m;* (naut) Spiere *f* ‖ *v* (*pret* & *pp* **sparred**; *ger* **sparring**) *intr* sparren

spare [sper] *adj* Ersatz–; (*thin*) mager; (*time*) frei; (*leftover*) übrig ‖ *s* (aut) Ersatzreifen *m* ‖ *tr* (*a person*) schonen; (*time, money*) erübrigen; (*expense*) scheuen; (*do without*) entbehren; **have to s.** übrig haben; **s. s.o. s.th.** j–m etw ersparen

spare′ bed′ *s* Gastbett *n*

spare′ part′ *s* Ersatzteil *n*

spare′ rib′ *s* Rippenspeer *n*

spare′ time′ *s* Freizeit *f*

spare′-time′ *adj* nebenberuflich

spare′ tire′ *s* Ersatzreifen *m*

spar′ing *adj* sparsam; **be s. with** sparsam umgehen mit

spark [spɑrk] *s* Funke(n) *m* ‖ *tr* (*set off*) auslösen; (*stimulate*) anregen ‖ *intr* Funken sprühen

spark′ gap′ *s* Funkenstrecke *f*

sparkle ['spɑrkəl] *s* Funkeln *n* ‖ *intr* funkeln; (*said of wine*) moussieren

spark′ plug′ *s* Zündkerze *f*

spar′ring part′ner *s* Übungspartner *m*

sparrow ['spæro] *s* Spatz *m,* Sperling *m*

spar′row hawk′ *s* Sperber *m*

sparse [spɑrs] *adj* spärlich

Spartan ['spɑrtən] *adj* spartanisch ‖ *s* Spartaner –in *mf*

spasm ['spæzəm] *s* Krampf *m,* Zuckung *f*

spasmodic [spæz'mɑdɪk] *adj* sprunghaft; (pathol) krampfartig

spastic ['spæstɪk] *adj* spastisch

spat [spæt] *s* (coll) Wortwechsel *m*

spatial ['speʃəl] *adj* räumlich

spatter ['spætər] *s* Spritzen *n;* (*stain*) Spritzfleck *m* ‖ *tr* verspritzen

spatula ['spætʃələ] *s* Spachtel *m* & *f*

spawn [spɔn] *s* Fischlaich *m* ‖ *tr* hervorbringen ‖ *intr* (*said of fish*) laichen

spay [spe] *tr* die Eierstöcke entfernen aus

speak [spik] *v* (*pret* **spoke** [spok]; *pp* **spoken**) *tr* sprechen; **s. one's mind** sich aussprechen ‖ *intr* (**about**) sprechen (über *acc,* von); **generally speaking** im allgemeinen; **so to s.** sozusagen; **speaking!** (telp) am Apparat!; **s. to** sprechen mit; (*give a speech to*) sprechen zu; **s. up** lauter sprechen; (*say something*) den Mund aufmachen; **s. up!** heraus mit der Sprache!; **s. up for** eintreten für

speak′-eas′y *s* Flüsterkneipe *f*

speaker ['spikər] *s* Sprecher –in *mf;* (*before an audience*) Redner –in *mf;* (parl) Sprecher –in *mf;* (rad) Lautsprecher *m*

spear [spɪr] *s* Speer *m* ‖ *tr* durchbohren; (*a piece of meat*) aufspießen; (*fish*) mit dem Speer fangen

spear′head′ *s* Speerspitze *f;* (mil) Stoßkeil *m* ‖ *tr* an der Spitze stehen von

spear′mint′ *s* Krauseminze *f*

special ['speʃəl] *adj* besonder, Sonder– ‖ *s* (rr) Sonderzug *m;* **today's s.** Stammgericht *n*

spe′cial deliv′ery *s* Eilzustellung *f;* (*tab on envelope*) Eilsendung *f*

spec′ial-deliv′ery let′ter *s* Eilbrief *m*

specialist ['speʃəlɪst] *s* Spezialist –in *mf*

specialization [ˌspeʃəlɪ'zeʃən] *s* Spezialisierung *f*

specialize ['speʃəˌlaɪz] *intr* sich spezialisieren; **specialized knowledge** Fachkenntnisse *pl*

spe′cial of′fer *s* (com) Sonderangebot *n*

specialty ['speʃəlti] *s* Spezialität *f;* (*special field*) Spezialfach *n*

spe′cialty shop′ *s* Spezialgeschäft *n*

specie ['spisi] *s*—**in s.** in der Art nach

spe-cies ['spisiz] *s* (**-cies**) Gattung *f*

specific [spɪ'sɪfɪk] *adj* spezifisch

specification [ˌspesɪfɪ'keʃən] *s* Spezifizierung *f;* **specifications** (tech) technische Beschreibung *f*

specif′ic grav′ity *s* spezifisches Gewicht *n*

speci-fy ['spesɪˌfaɪ] *v* (*pret* & *pp* **-fied**) *tr* spezifizieren; (*stipulate*) bestimmen

specimen ['spesɪmən] *s* (*example*) Exemplar *n;* (*test sample*) Probe *f*

specious ['spiʃəs] *adj* Schein–

speck [spek] *s* Fleck *m; (in the distance)* Pünktchen *n;* **s. of dust** Stäubchen *n;* **s. of grease** Fettauge *n*

speckle ['spɛkəl] *s* Sprenkel *m* ‖ *tr* sprenkeln

spectacle ['spɛktəkəl] *s* Schauspiel *n,* Anblick *m;* **spectacles** Brille *f*

spec′tacle case′ *s* Brillenfutteral *n*

spectacular [spɛk'tækjələr] *adj* sensationell ‖ *s* (cin) Monsterfilm *m*

spectator ['spɛktetər] *s* Zuschauer –in *mf*

specter ['spɛtər] *s* Gespenst *n*

spec·trum ['spɛktrəm] *s* (**–tra** [trə]) Spektrum *n*

speculate ['spɛkjə‚let] *intr* spekulieren; **s. in** spekulieren in (*dat*); **s. on** Überlegungen anstellen über (*acc*)

speculation [‚spɛkjə'leʃən] *s* Spekulation *f*

speculative ['spɛkjələtɪv] *adj* (com) Spekulations–; (philos) spekulativ

speculator ['spɛkjə‚letər] *s* Spekulant –in *mf*

speech [spitʃ] *s* Sprache *f; (address)* Rede *f;* **give a s.** e–e Rede halten

speech′ defect′ *s* Sprachfehler *m*

speech′ imped′iment *s* Sprachstörung *f*

speechless ['spitʃlɪs] *adj* sprachlos

speed [spid] *s* Geschwindigkeit *f; (gear)* Gang *m;* **at top s.** mit Höchstgeschwindigkeit; **pick up s.** auf Touren kommen ‖ *v* (*pret & pp* **speeded** & **sped** [spɛd]) *tr* beschleunigen; **s. up** forcieren; **s. it up** (coll) ein scharfes Tempo vorlegen ‖ *intr* (aut) rasen; *(above the speed limit)* (aut) zu schnell fahren

speed′boat′ *s* Schnellboot *n*

speed′ing *s* (aut) Schnellfahren *n;* **be arrested for s.** wegen Überschreitung der Höchstgeschwindigkeit verhaftet werden; **no s.** *(public sign)* Schnellfahren verboten

speed′ lim′it *s* Geschwindigkeitsgrenze *f*

speed′ of light′ *s* Lichtgeschwindigkeit *f*

speed′ of sound′ *s* Schallgeschwindigkeit *f*

speedometer [spi'dɑmɪtər] *s* Tachometer *n; (mileage indicator)* Meilenzähler *m,* Kilometerzähler *m*

speed′ rec′ord *s* Geschwindigkeitsrekord *m*

speed′ trap′ *s* Autofalle *f*

speed′way′ *s* (aut) Rennstrecke *f*

speedy ['spidɪ] *adj* schnell, schleunig; *(reply)* baldig

speed′ zone′ *s* Geschwindigkeitsbeschränkung *f*

spell [spɛl] *s (short period)* Zeitlang *f; (attack)* Anfall *m; (magical influence)* Bann *m;* **be under s.o.'s s.** in j–s Bann stehen; **cast a s.** bannen ‖ *v* (*pret & pp* **spelled** & **spelt** [spɛlt]) *tr* buchstabieren; *(in writing)* schreiben; **s. out** Buchstaben für Buchstaben lesen; (fig) auseinanderklamüsern; **s. trouble** Schwie-

rigkeiten bedeuten ‖ *intr* buchstabieren

spell′bind′er *s* faszinierender Redner *m*

spell′bound′ *adj* gebannt

spell′ing *s* Schreibweise *f; (orthography)* Rechtschreibung *f*

spell′ing bee′ *s* orthographischer Wettbewerb *m*

spelt [spɛlt] *s* Spelz *m*

spelunker [spɪ'lʌŋkər] *s* Höhlenforscher –in *mf*

spend [spɛnd] *v (pret & pp* **spent** [spɛnt]) *tr (money)* ausgeben; *(time)* verbringen; **s. the night** übernachten; **s. time and effort on** Zeit und Mühe verwenden auf (*acc*)

spend′thrift′ *s* Verschwender –in *mf*

spent [spɛnt] *adj (exhausted)* erschöpft; *(cartridge)* leergeschossen

sperm [spʌrm] *s* Sperma *n*

sperm′ whale′ *s* Pottwal *m*

spew [spju] *tr* erbrechen; (fig) ausspeien ‖ *intr* sich erbrechen; (fig) herausströmen

sphere [sfɪr] *s* Kugel *f,* Sphäre *f;* (fig) Bereich *m;* **s. of influence** Einflußsphäre *f*

spherical ['sfɛrɪkəl] *adj* sphärisch, kugelförmig

sphinx [sfɪŋks] *s* (**sphinxes & sphinges** ['sfɪndʒiz]) Sphinx *f*

spice [spaɪs] *s* Gewürz *n,* Würze *f;* (fig) Würze *f* ‖ *tr* würzen

spick-and-span ['spɪkənd'spæn] *adj* blitzblank

spicy ['spaɪsi] *adj* würzig; (fig) pikant

spider ['spaɪdər] *s* Spinne *f*

spi′derweb′ *s* Spinnengewebe *n*

spiffy ['spɪfi] *adj* (sl) fesch

spigot ['spɪɡət] *s* Wasserhahn *m*

spike [spaɪk] *s (nail)* langer Nagel *m; (in volleyball)* Schmetterball *m;* (bot) Ähre *f;* (rr) Schwellenschraube *f;* (sport) Dorn *m* ‖ *tr (a drink)* e–n Schuß Alkohol tun in (*acc*); *(in volleyball)* schmettern

spill [spɪl] *s (spilling)* Vergießen *n; (stain)* Fleck *m,* Klecks *m; (fall)* Sturz *m;* **take a s.** stürzen ‖ *v (pret & pp* **spilled** & **spilt** [spɪlt]) *tr* verschütten; *(a rider)* abwerfen; **s. out** ausschütten; **s. the beans** (sl) alles ausplaudern ‖ *intr* überlaufen; **s. over into** (fig) übergreifen auf (*acc*)

spill′way′ *s* Überlauf *m*

spin [spɪn] *s (rotation)* Umdrehung *f; (short ride)* kurze Fahrt *f;* (aer) Trudeln *n;* **go for a s.** e–e Spritztour machen; **go into a s.** (aer) ins Trudeln kommen ‖ *v (pret & pp* **spun** [spʌn]; *ger* **spinning**) *tr (rotate)* drehen; (tex) spinnen; **s. out** *(a story)* ausspinnen; **s. s.o. around** j–n im Kreise herumwirbeln ‖ *intr* kreiseln, sich drehen; (tex) spinnen; **my head is spinning** mir dreht sich alles im Kopf

spinach ['spɪnɪtʃ] *s* Spinat *m*

spi′nal col′umn ['spaɪnəl] *s* Wirbelsäule *f*

spi′nal cord′ *s* Rückenmark *n*

spi′nal flu′id s Rückenmarksflüssigkeit f

spindle ['spɪndəl] s Spindel f

spin′-dry′ v (pret & pp **-dried**) tr schleudern

spin′-dry′er s Trockenschleuder m

spine [spaɪn] s Rückgrat n, Wirbelsäule f; (bb) Buchrücken m

spineless ['spaɪnlɪs] adj (& fig) rückgratlos

spinet ['spɪnɪt] s Spinett n

spinner ['spɪnər] s Spinner –in mf; (mach) Spinnmaschine f

spin′ning adj (rotating) sich drehend; (tex) Spinn– || s (tex) Spinnen n

spin′ning wheel′ s Spinnrad n

spinster ['spɪnstər] s alte Jungfer f

spi·ral ['spaɪrəl] adj spiralig || s Spirale f; **s. of rising prices and wages** Lohn-Preis-Spirale f || v (pret & pp **-ral[l]ed;** ger **-ral[l]ing**) intr sich in die Höhe schrauben

spi′ral stair′case s Wendeltreppe f

spire [spaɪr] s Spitze f

spirit ['spɪrɪt] s Geist m; (enthusiasm) Schwung m; (ghost) Geist m; **in high spirits** in gehobener Stimmung; **in low spirits** in gedrückter Stimmung; **spirits** Spirituosen pl; **that′s the right s.!** das ist die richtige Einstellung! || tr—**s. away** wegzaubern

spir′ited adj lebhaft; (horse) feurig

spiritless ['spɪrɪtlɪs] adj schwunglos

spiritual ['spɪrɪt/u·əl] adj (incorporeal) geistig; (of the soul) seelisch; (religious) geistlich || s geistliches Negerlied n

spiritualism ['spɪrɪt/uə‚lɪzəm] s Spiritismus m

spiritualist ['spɪrɪt/u·əlɪst] s Spiritist –in mf

spir′itual life′ s Seelenleben n

spit [spɪt] s Spucke f; (culin) Spieß m || v (pret & pp **spat** [spæt] & **spit;** ger **spitting**) tr & intr spucken

spite [spaɪt] s Trotz m; **for s. aus** Trotz; **in s. of** trotz (genit) || tr kränken; **he did it to s. me** er hat es mir zum Trotz getan

spiteful ['spaɪtfəl] adj gehässig

spit′fire′ s (coll) Sprühteufel m

spit′ting im′age s (coll) Ebenbild n

spittoon [spɪ'tun] s Spucknapf m

splash [splæʃ] s Platschen n; (noise of falling into water) Klatschen n; **make a s.** (coll) Aufsehen erregen || tr (a person, etc.) bespritzen; (e.g., water) spritzen || intr klatschen, patschen; **s. about** planschen; **s. down** (rok) wassern || interj schwaps!, platsch!

splash′down′ s (rok) Wasserung f

splatter ['splætər] tr & intr kleckern

spleen [splin] s Milz f; (fig) schlechte Laune f; **vent one′s s. on** seiner schlechten Laune Luft machen gegenüber (dat)

splendid ['splendɪd] adj prächtig, herrlich; (coll) großartig

splendor ['splendər] s Herrlichkeit f

splice [splaɪs] s Spleiß || tr (a rope) spleißen; (film) zusammenkleben

splint [splɪnt] s Schiene f; **put in splints** schienen

splinter ['splɪntər] s Splitter m || tr (zer)splittern

splin′ter group′ s Splittergruppe f

split [splɪt] adj rissig || s Riß m, Spalt m; (fig) Spaltung f; (gym) Spagat m || v (pret & pp **split;** ger **splitting**) tr (asunder; (pants) platzen; (profits, the difference) sich teilen in (acc); **s. hairs** Haarspalterei treiben; **s. one′s sides laughing** vor Lachen platzen; **s. open** aufbrechen || intr (into) sich spalten (in acc); **splitting headache** rasende Kopfschmerzen pl; **s. up** (said of a couple) sich trennen

split′ infin′itive s gespaltener Infinitiv m

split′-lev′el adj mit Zwischenstockwerk versehen

split′ personal′ity s gespaltene Persönlichkeit f

split′ sec′ond s Sekundenbruchteil m

splotch [splat/] s Klecks m || tr kleckern

splotchy ['splat/i] adj fleckig

splurge [splʌrdʒ] s—**go on a s.** verschwenderischen Aufwand treiben || tr verschwenden || intr (on) verschwenderische Ausgaben machen (für)

splutter ['splʌtər] s Geplapper n || tr (words) herausprudeln; (besplatter) bespritzen || intr plappern; (said, e.g., of grease) spritzen

spoil [spɔɪl] s—**spoils** Beute f || v (pret & pp **spoiled & spoilt** [spɔɪlt]) tr (perishable goods; fun) verderben; (a child) verziehen, verwöhnen || intr verderben, schlecht werden; **spoiling for a fight** zanksüchtig

spoilage ['spɔɪlɪdʒ] s Verderb m

spoil′ sport′ s Spielverderber –in mf

spoils′ sys′tem s Futterkrippensystem n

spoke [spok] s Speiche f

spokes′man s (–men) Wortführer –in mf

sponge [spʌndʒ] s Schwamm m || tr schnorren || intr schnorren; **s. on** (coll) schmarotzen bei

sponge′ cake′ s Sandtorte f

sponger ['spʌndʒər] s Schmarotzer –in mf

sponge′ rub′ber s Schaumgummi m & n

spongy ['spʌndʒi] adj schwammig

sponsor ['spansər] s Förderer –in mf; (of a program) Sponsor m; (of an immigrant) Bürge m, Bürgin f; (at baptism or confirmation) Pate m, Patin f || tr fördern; (a program) finanziell fördern

spontaneity [spantə'ni·ɪti] s Spontaneität f

spontaneous [span'teni·əs] adj spontan

sponta′neous combus′tion s Selbstverbrennung f

spontaneously [span'teni·əsli] adv von selbst, unaufgefordert

spoof [spuf] *s (hoax)* Jux *m; (parody)*
(on) Parodie *f (auf acc)* ‖ *intr*
albern

spook [spuk] *s (coll)* Spuk *m*

spooky ['spuki] *adj* spukhaft

spool [spul] *s* Spule *f*, Rolle *f*

spoon [spun] *s* Löffel *m;* **wooden s.**
Kochlöffel *m* ‖ *tr (out)* löffeln

spoonerism ['spunə‚rızəm] *s* Schüttel-
reim *m*

spoon'-feed' *v (pret & pp* —fed) *tr (fig)*
es leicht machen *(dat)*

spoonful ['spunful] *s* Löffel *m*

sporadic [spə'rædık] *adj* vereinzelt

spore [spor] *s* Spore *f*

sport [sport] *adj* Sport— ‖ *s* Sport *m;*
(biol) Spielart *f;* **a good s.** ein
Pfundskerl *m;* **go in for sports** spor-
teln; **in s.** im Spaß; **make s. of** sich
lustig machen über *(acc);* **play
sports** Sport treiben; **poor s.** Spielverderber —in *mf;* **sports** Sport *m;*
(sportscast) Sportbericht *m* ‖ *intr*
sich belustigen

sport'ing event' *s* Sportveranstaltung *f*

sport'ing goods' *spl* Sportwaren *pl*

sport' jac'ket *s* Sportjacke *f*

sports' car' *s* Sportwagen *m*

sports'cast' *s* Sportbericht *m*

sports'cast'er *s* Sportberichterstatter *m*

sports' fan' *s* Sportfreund —in *mf*

sport' shirt' *s* Sporthemd *n*

sports'man *s* (—men) Sportsmann *m*

sports'manlike *adj* sportlich

sports'manship' *s* sportliches Verhalten
n

sports' news' *s* Sportnachrichten *pl*

sports'wear' *s* Sportkleidung *f*

sports' world' *s* Sportwelt *f*

sports' writ'er *s* Sportjournalist —in *mf*

sporty ['sporti] *adj* auffallend

spot [spat] *s (stain)* Fleck(en) *m;*
(place) Platz *m,* Ort *m; (as on a
leopard)* Tüpfel *m & n;* **be on the s.**
(be present) zur Stelle sein; *(be in
difficulty)* in der Klemme sein; **hit
the s.** gerade das Richtige sein; **on
the s.** auf der Stelle; **put on the s.**
in Verlegenheit bringen ‖ *v (pret &
pp* spotted; *ger* spotting) *tr (stain)*
beflecken; *(espy)* erblicken; *(points
in betting)* vorgeben

spot' announce'ment *s* Durchsage *f*

spot' cash' *s* ungebundene Barmittel
pl

spot' check' *s* Stichprobe *f*

spot'-check' *tr* stichprobenweise prüfen

spotless ['spatlıs] *adj* makellos

spot'light' *s* Scheinwerfer *m;* **in the s.**
(fig) im Rampenlicht der Öffentlichkeit ‖ *tr (fig)* in den Vordergrund
stellen

spot' remov'er [rı‚muvər] *s* Fleckputz-
mittel *n*

spotty ['spati] *adj* fleckig; *(uneven)*
ungleichmäßig

spot' weld'ing *s* Punktschweißung *f*

spouse [spaus] *s* Gatte *m,* Gattin *f*

spout [spaut] *s (of a pot)* Tülle *f;*
(jet of water) Strahl *m* ‖ *tr (& fig)*
hervorsprudeln ‖ *intr* spritzen; *(coll)*
große Reden schwingen

sprain [spren] *s* Verstauchung *f* ‖ *tr*
verstauchen; **s. one's ankle** sich *[dat]*
den Fuß vertreten

sprat [spræt] *s (ichth)* Sprotte *f*

sprawl [sprol] *intr (out)* alle viere von
sich ausstrecken; *(said of a city)*
sich weit ausbreiten

spray [spre] *s (of ocean)* Gischt *m;*
(from a can) Spray *n; (from a fountain)* Sprühwasser *n;* **s. of flowers**
Blütenzweig *m* ‖ *tr* spritzen; *(liquids)*
zerstäuben; *(plants)* besprühen

sprayer ['spre‚ər] *s* Zerstäuber *m; (for
a garden)* Gartenspritze *f*

spray' gun' *s* Spritzpistole *f*

spray' paint' *s* Spritzfarbe *f*

spread [spred] *s (act of spreading)*
Ausbreitung *f; (extent)* Verbreitung
f; (e.g., of a tree) Umfang *m; (on
bread)* Aufstrich *m; (bedspread)* Bettdecke *f; (large piece of land)* weite
Fläche *f; (of a shot)* Streubereich
m & n; (sumptuous meal) Gelage *n*
‖ *v (pret & pp* spread) *tr (warmth,
light, news, rumors)* verbreiten; *(mortar, glue)* auftragen; *(e.g., butter)*
aufstreichen; *(the legs)* spreizen;
(manure) streuen; **s. oneself too thin**
sich verzetteln; **s. out over** sich auf
über ein Jahr verteilen ‖ *intr* sich
verbreiten; *(said of margarine)* sich
aufstreichen lassen

spree [spri] *s* Bummel *m; (carousal)*
Zechgelage *n;* **go on a buying s.** sich
in e-e Kauforgie stürzen

sprig [sprıg] *s* Zweiglein *n*

sprightly ['spraıtli] *adj* lebhaft; *(gait)*
federnd

spring [sprıŋ] *adj* Frühlings— ‖ *s (of
water)* Quelle *f; (season)* Frühling
m; (resilience) Sprungkraft *f; (of
metal)* Feder *f; (jump)* Sprung *m;*
springs (aut) Federung *f* ‖ *v (pret*
sprang [spræŋ] *&* sprung [sprʌŋ];
pp sprung [sprʌŋ]) *tr (a trap)* zuschnappen lassen; *(a leak)* bekommen; *(a question) (on)* plötzlich
stellen *(dat); (a surprise) (on)* bereiten *(dat);* **s. the news on s.o.** j-n
mit der Nachricht überraschen ‖ *intr*
springen; **s. back** zurückschnellen;
s. from entspringen *(dat);* **s. up** aufspringen; *(said of industry, towns)*
aus dem Boden schießen

spring'board' *s (& fig)* Sprungbrett *n*

spring' chic'ken *s* Hähnchen *n;* **she's
no s.** (sl) sie ist nicht die Jüngste

spring' fe'ver *s* Frühlingsmüdigkeit *f*

spring'time' *s* Frühlingszeit *f*

spring' wa'ter *s* Quellwasser *n*

springy ['sprıŋi] *adj* federnd

sprinkle ['sprıŋkəl] *s* Spritzen *n;*
(light rain) Sprühregen *m* ‖ *tr
(water, streets, lawns, laundry)*
sprengen; *(e.g., sugar)* streuen ‖ *intr*
sprühen

sprinkler ['sprıŋklər] *s (truck)* Spreng-
wagen *m; (for the lawn)* Rasensprenger *m; (eccl)* Sprengwedel *m*

sprin'kling *s* Sprengung *f;* **a s. of** *(e.g.,
sugar)* ein bißchen *f; (e.g., of people)*
ein paar

sprin'kling can' s Gießkanne f
sprin'kling sys'tem s Feuerlöschanlage f
sprint [sprɪnt] s Sprint m ‖ intr sprinten
sprinter ['sprɪntər] s Sprinter –in mf
sprite [spraɪt] s Kobold m, Elfe f
sprocket ['sprakɪt] s Zahnrad n
sprout [spraut] s Sproß m ‖ intr sprießen
spruce [sprus] adj schmuck ‖ s (bot) Fichte f ‖ intr—s. up sich schmücken
spry [spraɪ] adj (spryer & sprier; spryest & spriest) flink
spud [spʌd] s (for weeding) Jäthacke f; (potatoe) (coll) Kartoffel f
spume [spjum] s Schaum m
spun' glass' s Glasfaser f
spunk [spʌŋk] s (coll) Mumm m
spunky ['spʌŋki] adj (coll) feurig
spur [spʌr] s (on riding boot; on a rooster) Sporn m; (of a mountain) Ausläufer m; (fig) Ansporn m; (archit) Strebe f; (bot) Stachel m; (rr) Seitengleis n; **on the s. of the moment** der Eingebung des Augenblicks folgend ‖ v (pret & pp **spurred**; ger **spurring**) tr die Sporen geben (dat); **s. on** anspornen
spurious ['spjʊri-əs] adj unecht
spurn [spʌrn] tr verschmähen
spurt [spʌrt] s Ruck m; (sport) Spurt m; **in spurts** ruckweise ‖ tr speien ‖ intr herausspritzen; (sport) spurten
sputnik ['spʌtnɪk] s Sputnik m
sputter ['spʌtər] s Stottern n ‖ tr umherspritzen; (words) hervorsprudeln ‖ intr (said of a person, engine) stottern; (said of a candle, fire) flackern
sputum ['spjutəm] s Sputum n
spy [spaɪ] s Spion –in mf ‖ v (pret & pp **spied**) tr—**spy out** ausspionieren ‖ intr spionieren
spy'glass' s Fernglas n
spy'ing s Spionage f
spy' ring' s Spionageorganization f
squabble ['skwabəl] s Zank m ‖ intr zanken
squad [skwad] s (gym) Riege f; (mil) Gruppe f; (sport) Mannschaft f
squad' car' s Funkstreifenwagen m
squad' lead'er s (mil) Gruppenführer m
squadron ['skwadrən] s (aer) Staffel f; (nav) Geschwader n
squalid ['skwalɪd] adj verkommen
squall [skwɔl] s Bö f
squander ['skwandər] tr verschwenden
square [skwer] adj quadratisch; (mile, meter, foot) Quadrat–; (fellow; meal) anständig; (even) quitt; **ten meters** s. zehn Meter im Quadrat; **ten s. meters** zehn Quadratmeter ‖ s Quadrat n; (city block) Häuserblock m; (open area) Platz m; (of a checkerboard or chessboard) Feld n; (carp) Winkel m; (math) zweite Potenz f ‖ tr quadrieren; (a number) ins Quadrat erheben; (accounts) abrechnen ‖ intr—s. off in Kampfstellung gehen; **s. with** (agree with)

übereinstimmen mit; (be frank with) aufrichtig sein zu
square' dance' s Reigen m
square' deal' s reelles Geschäft n
square' root' s Quadratwurzel f
squash [skwaʃ] s (bot) Kürbis m ‖ tr (a hat) zerdrücken; (a finger, grape) quetschen; (fig) unterdrücken ‖ intr zerdrückt (or zerquetscht) werden
squashy ['skwaʃi] adj weich, matschig
squat [skwat] adj gedrungen, untersetzt ‖ s Hocken f ‖ v (pret & pp **squatted**; ger **squatting**) intr hocken; **s. down** sich (hin)hocken
squatter ['skwatər] s Ansiedler –in mf ohne Rechtstitel
squaw [skwɔ] s Indianerin f
squawk [skwɔk] s Geschrei n; (sl) Schimpferei f ‖ intr schreien; (sl) schimpfen
squeak [skwik] s (of a door) Quietschen n; (of a mouse) Pfeifen n ‖ intr quietschen; (said of a mouse) pfeifen
squeal [skwil] s Quieken n ‖ intr (said of a pig) quieken; (said of a mouse) pfeifen; (sl) petzen; **s. for joy** vor Vergnügen quietschen; **s. on** (sl) (a pupil) verpetzen; (to the police) verpfeifen
squealer ['skwilər] s (sl) Petze f
squeamish ['skwimɪʃ] adj zimperlich
squeeze [skwiz] s Druck m; **s. of the hand** Händedruck m ‖ tr drücken; (oranges) auspressen; **s. into** (e.g., a trunk) hineinquetschen; **s. out** auspressen; **s. together** zusammenpressen; (e.g., people) zusammenpferchen ‖ intr—s. in sich eindrängen; **s. through** sich durchzwängen (durch)
squelch [skwɛltʃ] s schlagfertige Antwort f ‖ tr niederschmettern
squid [skwɪd] s Tintenfisch m
squill [skwɪl] s (bot) Meerzwiebel f; (zool) Heuschreckenkrebs m
squint [skwɪnt] s Schielen n ‖ intr (look with eyes partly closed) blinzeln; (be cross-eyed) schielen; (look askance) (at) argwöhnisch blicken (auf acc)
squint'-eyed' adj schielend
squire [skwaɪr] s (hist) Knappe m; (jur) Friedensrichter m
squirm [skwʌrm] intr (through) sich winden (durch); (be restless) zappeln; **s. out of** sich herauswinden aus
squirrel ['skwʌrəl] s Eichhörnchen n
squirt [skwʌrt] s Spritzer m; (boy) (coll) Stöpsel m ‖ tr (ver)spritzen ‖ intr spritzen; **s. out** herausspritzen
S'S' troops' ['es'es] spl Schutzstaffel f
stab [stæb] s Stich m; (wound) Stichwunde f; **make a s. at** (coll) probieren ‖ v (pret & pp **stabbed**; ger **stabbing**) tr stechen; (kill) erstechen; (a pig) abstechen; **s.s.o. in the back** j–m in den Rücken fallen
stability [stə'bɪlɪti] s Stabilität f
stabilization [ˌstebɪlɪ'zeʃən] s (e.g., of prices) Stabilisierung f; (aer) Dämpfung f

stabilize ['sterbɪ͵laɪz] *tr* stabilisieren
stabilizer ['sterbɪ͵laɪzər] *s* (aer) Flosse *f*
stab' in the back' *s* Stoß *m* aus dem Hinterhalt
stable ['sterbəl] *adj* stabil ‖ *s* Stall *m* ‖ *tr* unterbringen
sta'ble boy' *s* Stalljunge *m*
stack [stæk] *s* (*of papers, books*) Stapel *m*; (*of wheat*) Schober *m*; (*of a ship*) Schornstein *m*; (*of rifles*) Pyramide *f*; **stacks** (libr) Bücherregale *pl* ‖ *tr* (*wood, wheat*) aufstapeln; (*rifles*) zusammensetzen; (*cards*) packen
stadi·um ['sterdɪ·əm] *s* (**-ums** & **-a** [ə]) Stadion *n*
staff [stæf] *s* (*rod*) Stab *m*; (*personnel*) Personal *n*; (*of a newspaper*) Redaktion *f*; (mil) Stab *m*; (mus) Notensystem *n* ‖ *tr* mit Personal besetzen
staff' of'ficer *s* Stabsoffizier *m*
staff' ser'geant *s* Feldwebel *m*
stag [stæg] *adj* Herren– ‖ *adv*—**go s.** ohne Damenbegleitung sein ‖ *s* Hirsch *m*
stage [stedʒ] *s* (*of a theater*) Bühne *f*; (*phase*) Stadium *n*; (*stretch*) Strecke *f*; (*of life*) Etappe *f*; (*of a rocket*) Stufe *f*; (*scene*) Szene *f*; **at this s.** in diesem Stadium; **by easy stages** etappenweise; **final stages** Endstadien *pl* ‖ *tr* (*a play*) inszenieren; (*a comeback*) veranstalten
stage'coach' *s* Postkutsche *f*
stage'craft' *s* Bühnenkunst *f*
stage' direc'tion *s* Bühnenanweisung *f*
stage' door' *s* Bühneneingang *m*
stage' effect' *s* Bühnenwirkung *f*
stage' fright' *s* Lampenfieber *n*
stage' hand' *s* Bühnenarbeiter –in *mf*
stage' light'ing *s* Bühnenbeleuchtung *f*
stage' man'ager *s* Bühnenleiter –in *mf*
stage' play' *s* Bühnenstück *n*
stage' prop'erties *spl* Theaterrequisiten *pl*
stagestruck ['stedʒ͵strʌk] *adj* theaterbegeistert
stagger ['stægər] *s* Taumeln *n* ‖ *tr* (*e.g., lunch hours*) staffeln; (& fig) erschüttern ‖ *intr* taumeln
stag'gering *adj* taumelnd; (*blow, loss*) vernichtend; (*news*) erschütternd
stagnant ['stægnənt] *adj* (*water*) stillstehend; (*air*) schlecht; (fig) träge
stagnate ['stægnet] *intr* stagnieren
stag' par'ty *s* Herrenabend *m*
staid [sted] *adj* gesetzt
stain [sten] *s* Fleck *m*; (*paint*) Beize *f* ‖ *tr* beflecken; (*wood*) beizen
stained'-glass win'dow *s* buntes Glasfenster *n*
stainless ['stenlɪs] *adj* rostfrei
stair [ster] *s* Stufe *f*; **stairs** Treppe *f*
stair'case' *s* Treppenhaus *n*
stair'way' *s* Treppenaufgang *m*
stair'well' *s* Treppenschacht *m*
stake [stek] *s* Pfahl *m*; (*bet*) Einsatz *m*; **be at s.** auf dem Spiel stehen; **die at the s.** auf dem Scheiterhaufen sterben; **play for high stakes** viel riskieren; **pull up stakes** (coll) ab-

hauen ‖ *tr* (*plants*) mit e–m Pfahl stützen; **s. off** abstecken; **s. out a claim** (fig) e–e Forderung umreißen
stake'-out' *s* polizeiliche Überwachung *f*
stalactite [stə'læktaɪt] *s* Stalaktit *m*
stalagmite [stə'lægmaɪt] *s* Stalagmit *m*
stale [stel] *adj* (*baked goods*) altbacken; (*e.g., beer*) schal; (*air*) verbraucht; (*joke*) abgedroschen; **get s.** abstehen
stale'mate' *s* (fig) Sackgasse *f*; (chess) Patt *n* ‖ *tr* (fig) in e–e Sackgasse treiben; (chess) patt setzen
stalk [stɔk] *s* (*of grain*) Halm *m*; (*of a plant*) Stiel *m* ‖ *tr* beschleichen; **s. game** pirschen
stall [stɔl] *s* (*for animals*) Stall *m*; (*booth*) Bude *f*; (sl) Vorwand *m* ‖ *tr* (*a motor*) abwürgen; (*a person*) aufhalten ‖ *intr* ausweichen; (aut) absterben; **s. for time** Zeit zu gewinnen suchen
stallion ['stæljən] *s* Hengst *m*
stalwart ['stɔlwərt] *adj* stämmig; (*supporter*) treu
stamen ['stemən] *s* Staubfaden *m*
stamina ['stæmɪnə] *s* Ausdauer *f*
stammer ['stæmər] *s* Stammeln *n* ‖ *tr* & *intr* stammeln
stammerer ['stæmərər] *s* Stammler –in *mf*
stamp [stæmp] *s* (*mark*) Gepräge *n*; (*device for stamping*) Stempel *m*; (*for postage*) Briefmarke *f* ‖ *tr* (*e.g., a document*) stempeln; (*a letter*) freimachen; (*the earth*) stampfen; **s. one's foot** mit dem Fuß aufstampfen; **s. out** (*a fire*) austreten; (*a rebellion*) niederschlagen
stampede [stæm'pid] *s* panische Flucht *f* ‖ *tr* in die Flucht jagen ‖ *intr* in wilder Flucht davonrennen
stamped' en'velope *s* Freiumschlag *m*
stamp'ing grounds' *spl* Lieblingsplatz *m*
stamp' machine' *s* Briefmarkenautomat *m*
stamp' pad' *s* Stempelkissen *n*
stance [stæns] *s* Haltung *f*, Stellung *f*
stanch [stɔntʃ] *tr* stillen
stand [stænd] *s* (*booth*) Stand *m*; (*platform*) Tribüne *f*; (*e.g., for bicycles*) Ständer *m*; (*view, position*) Standpunkt *m*; (*piece of furniture*) Ständer *m*; **take a s. (on)** Stellung nehmen (zu); **take one's s.** (*e.g., near the door*) sich stellen; **s. of timber** Waldbestand *m*; **stands** (sport) Tribüne *f*; **take the s.** (jur) als Zeuge auftreten ‖ *v* (*pret & pp* **stood** [stud]) *tr* (*put*) stellen; (*the cold, hardships*) aushalten; (*a person*) leiden; **s. a chance** e–e Chance haben; **s. guard** Posten stehen; **s. one's ground** sich behaupten; **s. s.o. up** j–n aufsitzen lassen; **s. the test** sich bewähren ‖ *intr* stehen; (*have validity*) gelten; **she wants to know where she stands** sie will wissen, wie sie daran ist; **s. aside** auf die Seite treten; **s. at attention** stillstehen; **s.**

back zurückstehen; **s. behind** s.o. (fig) hinter j-m stehen; **s. by** (in readiness) in Bereitschaft stehen; (a decision) bleiben bei; (e.g., for the latest news) am Apparat bleiben; **s. by** s.o. j-m beistehen; **s. firm** fest bleiben; **s. for** (champion) eintreten für; (tolerate) sich [dat] gefallen lassen; (mean) bedeuten; **s. good for** gutstehen für; **s. idle** stillstehen; **s. on end** sich sträuben, e.g., **my hair stood on end** mir sträubten sich die Haare; **s. on one's head** kopfstehen; **s. out** (project) abstehen; (be conspicuous) hervorstechen; **s. out against** sich abzeichnen gegen; **s.o. in good stead** j-m zugute kommen; **s. up** aufstehen; **s. up against** aufkommen gegen; **s. up for** (a thing) verfechten; (a person) die Stange halten (dat); **s. up to** s.o. j-m die Stirn bieten; **s. up under** aushalten
standard ['stændərd] adj Standard-, Normal– || s Standard m; (banner) Banner n
stand'ard-bear'er s Bannerträger m
stand'ard-gauge track' s Normalspur f
standardize ['stændər‚daɪz] tr normen
stand'ard of liv'ing s Lebensstandard m
stand'ard time' s Normalzeit f
stand'-by' adj Reserve– || s—**on s. in** Bereitschaft
standee [stæn'di] s Stehplatzinhaber –in mf
stand'in' s (coll) Ersatzmann m; (cin, theat) Double n
stand'ing adj (army, water, rule) stehend; (committee) ständig; (jump) aus dem Stand || s Stehen n; (social) Stellung f; (of a team) Stand m; **in good s.** treu; **of long s.** langjährig
stand'ing or'der s (com) Dauerauftrag m
stand'ing room' s Stehplatz m; **s. only** nur noch Stehplätze
stand'-off' s Unentschieden n
stand-offish ['stænd'ɔfɪʃ] adj zurückhaltend
stand'out' s Blickfang m
stand'point' s Standpunkt m
stand'still' s Stillstand m; **come to a s.** zum Stillstand kommen
stanza ['stænzə] s Strophe f
staple ['stepəl] adj Haupt–, Stapel– || s (food) Hauptnahrungsmittel n; (product) Hauptprodukt n; (clip) Heftklammer f || tr mit Draht heften
stapler ['steplər] s Heftmaschine f
star [star] adj Spitzen–; (astr) Stern– || s Stern m; (cin, rad, telv, theat) Star m; **I saw stars** (fig) Sterne tanzten mir vor den Augen || v (pret & pp **starred**; ger **starring**) tr (cin, rad, sport, telv, theat) als Star herausstellen; (typ) mit Sternchen kennzeichnen || intr Star sein
starboard ['starbərd] adj Steuerbord– || s Steuerbord n
starch [startʃ] s Stärke f || tr stärken
starchy ['startʃi] adj stärkenhaltig
stare [ster] s starrer Blick m || tr—

s. down durch Anstarren aus der Fassung bringen || intr starren; **s. at** anstarren; **s. into space** ins Leere blicken, ins Blaue starren
star'fish' s Seestern m
stargazer ['star‚gezər] s Sterngucker –in mf
stark [stark] adj (landscape) kahl; (sheer) völlig || adv völlig
stark'-na'ked adj splitter(faser)nackt
starlet ['starlət] s Sternchen n
star'light' s Sternenlicht n
starling ['starlɪŋ] s (orn) Star m
star'lit' adj sternhell
Star' of Da'vid s David(s)stern m
starry ['stari] adj gestirnt; (night) sternklar; (sky) Stern–
star'ry-eyed' adj verträumt
Stars' and Stripes' spl Sternenbanner n
Star'-Spangled Ban'ner s Sternenbanner n
start [start] s Anfang m; (sudden springing movement) plötzliches Hochfahren n; (lead, advantage) Vorgabe f, Vorsprung m; (of a race) Start m; **give s.o. a s.** j-m auf die Beine helfen || tr anfangen; (a motor) anlassen; (a rumor) in die Welt setzen; (a conversation) anknüpfen; **s. a fire** ein Feuer anmachen; (said of an arsonist) e-n Brand legen || intr anfangen; **s. in to** (inf) anfangen zu (inf); **s. out** (begin) anfangen; (start walking) losgehen; **s. out on** (a trip) antreten; **to s.** with zunächst
start'ing gate' s Startmaschine f
start'ing gun' s Startpistole f; **at the s.** beim Startschuß
start'ing point' s Ausgangspunkt m
startle ['startəl] tr erschrecken; **be startled** zusammenfahren
starvation [star've∫ən] s Hunger m; **die of s.** verhungern
starva'tion di'et s Hungerkur f
starva'tion wag'es spl Hungerlohn m
starve [starv] tr verhungern lassen; **s. out** aushungern || intr hungern; (coll) furchtbaren Hunger haben; **s. to death** verhungern
state [stet] adj staatlich, Staats–; (as opposed to federal) bundesstaatlich || s (condition) Zustand m; (government) Staat m; (of the U.S.A.) Bundesstaat m || tr angeben; (a rule, problem) aufstellen; **as stated above** wie oben angegeben
State' Depart'ment s Außenministerium n
stateless ['stetlɪs] adj staatenlos
stately ['stetli] adj stattlich
statement ['stetmənt] s Angabe f; (from a bank) Abrechnung f; (jur) Aussage f
state' of affairs' s Lage f
state' of emer'gency s Notstand m
state' of health' s Gesundheitszustand m
state' of mind' s Geisteszustand m
state' of war' s Kriegszustand m
state'-owned' adj staatseigen; (in communistic countries) volkseigen
state' police' s Staatspolizei f

state′room′ s (*in a palace*) Prunkzimmer n; (*on a ship*) Passagierkabine f

states′man s (**-men**) Staatsmann m

states′manlike′ adj staatsmännisch

states′manship′ s Staatskunst f

static [′stætɪk] adj statisch ‖ s (rad) Nebengeräusche pl

station [′steɪʃən] s (*social*) Stellung f; (*of a bus, rail line*) Bahnhof m; (mil) Standort m ‖ tr aufstellen; (mil) stationieren

stationary [′steɪʃə͵nerɪ] adj stationär

sta′tion break′ s Werbepause f

stationer [′steɪʃənər] s Schreibwarenhändler –in mf

stationery [′steɪʃə͵nerɪ] s Briefpapier n

sta′tionery store′ s Schreibwarenhandlung f

sta′tion house′ s Polizeiwache f

sta′tion identifica′tion s (rad) Pausenzeichen n

sta′tionmas′ter s Bahnhofsvorsteher m

sta′tions of the cross′ spl Kreuzweg m

sta′tion wag′on s Kombiwagen m

statistic [stə′tɪstɪk] s Angabe f; **statistics** (*science*) Statistik f ‖ spl (*data*) Statistik f

statistical [stə′tɪstɪkəl] adj statistisch

statistician [͵stætɪs′tɪʃən] s Statistiker –in mf

statue [′stætʃʊ] s Statue f

statuesque [͵stætʃʊ′esk] adj statuenhaft

stature [′stætʃər] s Gestalt f; (fig) Format m

status [′steɪtəs] s (*in society*) Stellung f; (*e.g., mental*) Stand m

sta′tus quo′ [kwo] s Status m quo

sta′tus sym′bol s Statussymbol n

statute [′stætʃʊt] s Satzung f, Statut n

statutory [′stætʃʊ͵torɪ] adj statutenmäßig

staunch [stɔntʃ] adj unentwegt

stave [stev] s (*of a barrel*) Daube f; (*of a chair*) Steg m; (*of a ladder*) Sprosse f; (mus) Notensystem n ‖ tr—s. off abwenden

stay [ste] s (*visit*) Aufenthalt m; (prop) Stütze f; (*of execution*) Aufschub m ‖ intr bleiben; **have to s. in** (*after school*) nachsitzen müssen; **s. away** wegbleiben; **s. behind** zurückbleiben; (*of a child*) sitzenbleiben

stay′-at-home′ s Stubenhocker –in mf

stead [sted] s Statt f; **in s.o.'s s.** an j-s Statt

stead′fast′ adj standhaft

stead·y [′stedɪ] adj fest, beständig; (*hands*) sicher; (*ladder*) fest; (*pace*) gleichmäßig; (*progress*) ständig; (*nerves*) stark; (*prices*) stabil; (*work*) regelmäßig; **s. customer** Stammkunde m, Stammkundin f; **s. now!** immer langsam! ‖ v (pret & pp **-ied**) tr festigen

steak [stek] s Beefsteak n

steal [stil] s—**it's a s.** (coll) das ist geschenkt ‖ v (pret **stole** [stol]; pp **stolen**) tr stehlen; (*a kiss*) rauben; **s. s.o.'s thunder** j–m den Wind aus den Segeln nehmen; **s. the show** den Vogel abschießen ‖ intr stehlen; **s.**

away wegstehlen; **s. up on s.o.** sich an j–n heranschleichen

stealth [stelθ] s—**by s.** heimlich

stealthy [′stelθɪ] adj verstohlen

steam [stim] s Dampf m; (vapor) Dunst m; (fig) Kraft f; **full s. ahead!** Volldampf voraus!; **let off s.** Dampf ablassen; (fig) sich [*dat*] Luft machen; **put on s.** (fig) Dampf dahinter machen ‖ tr dämpfen; (culin) dünsten; **s. up** beschlagen ‖ intr dampfen; (culin) dünsten; **s. up** sich beschlagen

steam′ bath′ s Dampfbad n

steam′boat′ s Dampfer m

steam′ en′gine s Dampfmaschine f

steamer [′stimər] s Dampfer m

steam′ heat′ s Dampfheizung f

steam′ i′ron s Dampfbügeleisen n

steam′ roll′er s (& fig) Dampfwalze f ‖ tr glattwalzen; (fig) niederwalzen

steam′ship′ s Dampfschiff n

steam′ship line′ s Dampfschiffahrtslinie f

steam′ shov′el s Dampflöffelbagger m

steamy [′stimɪ] adj dampfig, dunstig

steed [stid] s Streitroß n

steel [stil] adj stählern, Stahl– ‖ s Stahl m ‖ tr stählen; **s. oneself against s.th.** sich gegen etw wappnen

steel′ wool′ s Stahlwolle f

steel′works′ spl Stahlwerk n

steely [′stilɪ] adj (fig) stählern

steelyard [′stiljərd] s Schnellwaage f

steep [stip] adj steil; (*prices*) happig ‖ tr (*immerse*) eintauchen; (*soak*) einweichen; **be steeped in** (*e.g., prejudice*) durchdrungen sein von; (*be expert in*) ein Kenner sein (genit); **s. oneself in** sich versenken in (acc)

steeple [′stipəl] s Kirchturm m

stee′plechase′ s Hindernisrennen n

steer [stɪr] s Stier m ‖ tr lenken, steuern; **s. a middle course** e–n Mittelweg einschlagen ‖ intr lenken, steuern; **s. clear of** vermeiden

steerage [′stɪrɪdʒ] s Zwischendeck n

steer′ing wheel′ s Steuerrad n

stellar [′stelər] adj (*role*) Star–; (*attraction*) Haupt–; (astr) Stern(en)–

stem [stem] s (*of a plant*) Halm m; (*of a word; of a tree*) Stamm m; (*of a leaf, fruit; of a glass; of a smoke pipe*) Stiel m; (*of a watch*) Aufziehwelle f; (naut) Steven m; **from s. to stern** von vorn bis achtern ‖ v (pret & pp **stemmed**; ger **stemming**) tr (*check*) hemmen; (*fruit*) entstielen; (*the flow*) (an)stauen; (*the blood*) stillen; (*in skiing*) stemmen ‖ intr— **s. from** (ab)stammen von

stench [stentʃ] s Gestank m

sten·cil [′stensɪl] s (*for printing*) Schablone f; (*for typing*) Matrize f ‖ v (pret & pp **-cil[l]ed**; ger **-cil[l]ing**) tr mittels Schablone aufmalen

stenographer [stə′nɑgrəfər] s Stenograph –in mf

stenography [stə′nɑgrəfɪ] s Stenographie f

step [stɛp] s Schritt m; (*of a staircase*) Stufe f; (*footprint*) Fußtritt m;

(measure) Maßnahme f; **be out of s.**
nicht Schritt halten; **in. s.** im Takt;
keep in s. with the times mit der
Zeit Schritt halten; **s. by s.** schritt-
weise; **watch your s.!** Vorsicht! || v
(pret & pp **stepped**; ger **stepping**)
tr—**s. down** (elec) heruntertransfor-
mieren; **s. off** abschreiten || intr
schreiten, treten; **s. aside** beiseite-
treten; **s. back** zurücktreten; **s. forward** vortreten; **s. on** betreten; **s.
on it** (coll) sich beeilen; **s. on s.o.'s
toes** (fig) j-m auf die Zehen treten;
s. out hinausgehen; **s. out on** (a marriage partner) betrügen

step′broth′er s Stiefbruder m

step′child′ s (-chil′dren) Stiefkind n

step′daugh′ter s Stieftochter f

step′fa′ther s Stiefvater m

step′lad′der s Stehleiter f

step′moth′er s Stiefmutter f

steppe [stɛp] s Steppe f

step′ping stone′ s Trittstein m; (fig)
Sprungbrett n

step′sis′ter s Stiefschwester f

step′son′ s Stiefsohn m

stere•o [′stɛri‿o] adj Stereo— || s (-os)
(sound) Stereoton m, Raumton m;
(reproduction) Raumtonwiedergabe
f; (set) Stereoapparat m

stereotyped [′stɛri‿ə‿taipt] adj (& fig)
stereotyp

sterile [′stɛril] adj keimfrei

sterility [stɛ′riliti] s Sterilität f

sterilize [′stɛri‿laiz] tr sterilisieren

sterling [′stʌrliŋ] adj (fig) gediegen ||
s (currency) Sterling m; (sterling silver) Sterlingsilber n; (articles of
sterling silver) Sterlingsilberwaren pl

stern [stʌrn] adj streng; (look) finster
|| s (naut) Heck n

stethoscope [′stɛθə‿skop] s Stethoskop
n

stevedore [′stivə‿dor] s Stauer m

stew [st(j)u] s Ragout m, Stew n || tr &
intr dünsten; (& fig) schmoren

steward [′st(j)u‿ərd] s (aer, naut)
Steward m; (of an estate) Gutsverwalter m; (of a club) Tafelmeister m

stewardess [′st(j)u‿ərdis] s (aer, naut)
Stewardeß f

stewed′ fruit′ s Kompott n

stick [stik] s Stecken m, Stock m; (for
punishment) Prügel pl; (of candy or
gum) Stange f; **the sticks** (coll) die
Provinz f || tr (with a sharp point; into
one's pocket) stecken; (paste) (on)
ankleben (an acc); **s. it out** durchhalten; **s. one's finger** sich in den
Finger stecken; **s. out** herausstrecken;
s. up (sl) überfallen und berauben ||
intr (adhere) kleben; (be stuck, be
tight) klemmen; **nothing sticks in his
mind** (coll) bei ihm bleibt nichts
haften; **s. around** (coll) in der Nähe
bleiben; **s. by** (coll) bleiben bei; **s.
close to** sich heften an (acc); **s. out**
(said of ears) abstehen; (be visible)
heraushängen; **s. to** (fig) beharren
auf (dat); **s. together** zusammenkleben; (fig) zusammenhalten; **s. up
for** sich einsetzen für

sticker [′stikər] s Klebezettel m

stick′-in-the-mud′ s (coll) Schlafmütze
f

stickler [′stiklər] s (for) Pedant m (in
dat)

stick′pin′ s Krawattennadel f

stick′-up′ s (sl) Raubüberfall m

sticky [′stiki] adj klebrig; (air) schwül;
(ticklish) heikel

stiff [stif] adj steif; (difficult) schwer;
(drink) stark; (opposition) hartnäckig; (sentence) streng; (bearing)
steif; (price) hoch; **s. as a board**
stocksteif || s (corpse) (sl) Leiche f;
big s. (sl) blöder Kerl m

stiffen [′stifən] tr versteifen || intr
sich versteifen

stiffly [′stifli] adv gezwungen

stiff′-necked′ adj mit steifem Hals; (fig)
eigensinnig

stifle [′staifəl] tr (a yawn) unterdrücken; (a person) ersticken

stig•ma [′stigmə] s (-mas & **mata**
[mətə]) Brandmal n; **stigmata** Wund-
male pl Christi

stigmatize [′stigmə‿taiz] tr brandmarken

stile [stail] s Stiege f

stilet•to [sti′lɛto] s (-os) Stilett n

still [stil] adj still, ruhig || adv (up to
this time, as yet, even) noch; (yet,
nevertheless) dennoch; **keep s.** still-
bleiben || s (stillness) Stille f; (for
whiskey) Brennapparat m; (cin) Ein-
zelphotographie f; (phot) Standphoto
n || tr stillen

still′born′ adj totgeboren

still′ life′ s (still lifes & **still lives**)
Stilleben n

stilt [stilt] s Stelze f

stilt′ed adj (style) geschraubt; (archit)
auf Pfeilern ruhend

stimulant [′stimjələnt] s Reizmittel n;
act as a s. anregend wirken

stimulate [′stimjə‿let] tr anregen

stimulation [‿stimjə′leʃən] s Anregung
f

stimu•lus [′stimjələs] s (-li [‿lai])
(& fig) Reizmittel n; (fig) Ansporn
m

sting [stiŋ] s Biß m, Stich m; (sting-
ing organ) Stachel m || v (pret & pp
stung [stʌŋ]) tr & intr stechen

stingy [′stindʒi] adj geizig

stink [stiŋk] s Gestank m; (sl) Krach
m || v (pret **stank** [stæŋk]; **stunk**
[stʌŋk]) tr—**s. up** verstänkern || intr
stinken

stinker [′stiŋkər] s (sl) Stinker m

stinky [′stiŋki] adj stinkend, stinkig

stint [stint] s bestimmte Arbeit f; **with-
out s.** freigebig || tr einschränken ||
intr (on) knausern (mit)

stipend [′staipənd] s (salary) Gehalt
n; (of a scholarship) Zuwendung f

stipple [′stipəl] tr punktieren

stipulate [′stipjə‿let] tr bedingen; **as
stipulated** wie vertraglich festgelegt

stipulation [‿stipjə′leʃən] s Bedingung
f

stir [stʌr] s (movement) Bewegung f;
(unrest) Unruhe f; (commotion, ex-

citement) Aufsehen *n;* **create quite a s.** großes Aufsehen erregen || *v (pret & pp* **stirred;** *ger* **stirring)** *tr e.g., with a spoon)* (um)rühren; *(said of a breeze)* (the fire) schüren; **s. up** *(hatred)* entfachen; *(trouble)* stiften; *(people)* aufhetzen || *intr* sich rühren

stir'ring *adj* erregend; *(times)* bewegt; *(speech)* mitreißend; *(song)* schwungvoll

stirrup ['stʌrəp] *s* Steigbügel *m*

stitch [stɪtʃ] *s* Stich *m;* *(in knitting)* Masche *f;* **stitches** (surg) Naht *f;* **s. in the side** Seitenstechen *n* || *tr* heften; (surg) nähen

stock [stɑk] *s* *(supplies)* Lager *n;* *(of a gun)* Schaft *m;* *(lineage)* Zucht *f;* *(of paper)* Papierstoff *m;* (culin) Fond *m;* (st. exch.) Aktie *f;* **in s.** vorrätig, auf Lager; **not put much s. in** nicht viel Wert legen auf *(acc);* **out of s.** nicht (mehr) vorrätig; *(books)* vergriffen; **stocks** (hist) Stock *m;* **take s.** den Bestand aufnehmen; **take s. of** (fig) in Betracht ziehen || *tr* auf Lager halten; *(a stream)* (mit Fischen) besetzen; *(a farm)* ausstatten || *intr*—**s. up (on)** sich eindecken (mit)

stockade [stɑˈked] *s* Palisade *f;* (mil) Gefängnis *n*

stock'breed'er *s* Viehzüchter·-in *mf*

stock'brok'er *s* Börsenmakler –in *mf*

stock' car' *s* (aut) Serienwagen *m;* (sport) als Rennwagen hergerichteter Personenkraftwagen *m*

stock' com'pany *s* (com) Aktiengesellschaft *f;* (theat) Repertoiregruppe *f*

stock' div'idend *s* Aktiendividende *f*

stock' exchange' *s* Börse *f*

stock'hold'er *s* Aktionär –in *mf*

stock'ing *s* Strumpf *m*

stock' in trade' *s* Warenbestand *m;* (fig) Rüstzeug *n*

stock'pile' *s* Vorrat *m* || *tr* aufstapeln

stock'room' *s* Lagerraum *m*

stocky ['stɑki] *adj* untersetzt

stock'yard' *s* Viehhof *m*

stodgy ['stɑdʒi] *adj* gezwungen

stogy ['stogi] *s* (coll) Glimmstengel *m*

stoic ['sto·ɪk] *adj* stoisch ·|| *s* Stoiker *m*

stoke [stok] *tr* *(a fire)* schüren; *(a furnace)* heizen

stoker ['stokər] *s* Heizer *m*

stole [stol] *s* *(woman's fur piece)* Pelzstola *f;* (eccl) Stola *f*

stolid ['stɑlɪd] *adj* unempfindlich

stomach ['stʌmək] *s* Magen *m;* (fig) **(for)** Lust *f* (zu) || *tr* *(food)* verdauen; (fig) vertragen

stom'ach ache' *s* Magenschmerzen *pl*

stone [ston] *adj* steinern || *s* Stein *m;* *(of fruit)* Kern *m;* (pathol) Stein *m* || *tr* steinigen; *(fruit)* entsteinen

stone' age' *s* Steinzeit *f*

stone'-broke' *adj* (coll) völlig abgebrannt

stone'-deaf' *adj* stocktaub

stone' ma'son *s* Steinmetz *m*

stone' quar'ry *s* Steinbruch *m*

stone's' throw' *s* Katzensprung *m*

stony ['stoni] *adj* steinig

stooge [studʒ] *s* Lakai *m*

stool [stul] *s* Schemel *m;* *(e.g., at a bar)* Hocker *m;* *(bowel movement)* Stuhl *m*

stool' pi'geon *s* Polizeispitzel *m*

stoop [stup] *s* Beugung *f;* *(condition of the body)* gebeugte Körperhaltung *f;* *(porch)* kleine Verande *f* || *intr* sich bücken; *(demean oneself)* sich erniedrigen

stoop'-shoul'dered *adj* gebeugt

stop [stɑp] *s* *(for a bus or streetcar)* Haltestelle *f;* *(layover)* Aufenthalt *m;* *(station)* Station *f;* *(of an organ)* Register *n;* (ling) Verschlußlaut *m;* **bring to a s.** zum Halten bringen; **come to a s.** anhalten; **put a s. to** ein Ende machen *(dat)* || *v* *(pret & pp* **stopped;** *ger* **stopping)** *tr (an activity)* aufhören mit; *(ger)* aufhören (zu *inf);* *(e.g., a thief, car)* anhalten; *(bring to a stop with difficulty)* zum Halten bringen; *(delay, detain)* aufhalten; *(a leak)* stopfen; *(a check)* sperren; *(payment)* einstellen; *(the blood)* stillen; *(traffic)* lahmlegen; **s. down** (phot) abblenden; **s. s.o. from** *(ger)* j–n davonhalten zu *(inf)* || *intr (cease)* aufhören; *(come to a stop; break down)* stehenbleiben; *(said of a person stopping for a short time or of a vehicle at an unscheduled stop)* anhalten; *(said of a vehicle at a scheduled stop)* halten; **s. at nothing** vor nichts zurückschrecken; **s. dead** plötzlich stehenbleiben; **s.** in vorbeikommen; **s. off at** e–n kurzen Halt machen bei

stop'gap' *adj* Not–, Behelfs– || *s* Notbehelf *m*

stop'light' *s* *(on a car)* Bremslicht *n;* *(traffic light)* Verkehrsampel *f*

stop'o'ver *s* Fahrtunterbrechung *f;* (aer) Zwischenlandung *f*

stoppage ['stɑpɪdʒ] *s* *(of a pipe)* Verstopfung *f;* *(of payment, of work)* Einstellung *f;* (pathol) Verstopfung *f*

stopper ['stɑpər] *s* Stöpsel *m;* *(made of cork)* Korken *m*

stop' sign' *s* Haltezeichen *n*

stop'watch' *s* Stoppuhr *f*

storage ['stɔrɪdʒ] *s* Lagerung *f*

stor'age bat'tery *s* Akkumulator *m*

stor'age charge' *s* Lagergebühr *f*

stor'age room' *s* Rumpelkammer *f;* (com) Lagerraum *m*

stor'age tank' *s* Sammelbehälter *m*

store [stor] *s* *(small shop)* Laden *m;* *(large shop)* Geschäft *n;* *(supply)* Vorrat *m;* **be in s. for** bevorstehen *(dat);* **have in s. for** bereithalten *f;* **set great s. by** viel Wert legen auf *(acc);* **s. of knowledge** Wissenschaft *m* || *tr* einlagern; *(in the attic)* auf den Speicher stellen; **s. up** aufspeichern

store'house' *s* Lagerhaus *n;* (fig) Schatz *m,* Fundgrube *f*

store'keep'er *s* Ladeninhaber –in *mf*

store'room' s Lagerraum m, Vorrats- raum m

stork [stork] s Storch m

storm [storm] s Sturm m; (thunder- storm) Gewitter n; (fig) Sturm m; **take by s.** (& fig) im Sturm nehmen || tr (er)stürmen || intr stürmen

storm' cloud' s Gewitterwolke f

storm' door' s Doppeltür f

storm' warn'ing s Sturmwarnung f

storm' win'dow s Doppelfenster n

stormy ['stormi] adj stürmisch

story ['stori] s Geschichte f; (floor) Stock m, Stockwerk n; **that's another s.** das ist e–e Sache für sich

sto'rybook' s Geschichtenbuch n

sto'rytell'er s Erzähler –in mf

stout [staut] adj beleibt; (heart) tapfer || s Starkbier n

stout'-heart'ed adj beherzt

stove [stov] s Ofen m, Küchenherd m

stove'pipe' s Ofenrohr n; (coll) Angst- röhre f

stow [sto] tr stauen; **s. away** verstauen || intr—**s. away** als blinder Passagier mitreisen

stowage ['sto·idʒ] s Stauen n; (costs) Staugebühr f

stow'away' s blinder Passagier m

straddle ['strædəl] tr mit gespreizten Beinen sitzen auf (dat)

strafe [stref] tr im Tiefflug mit Bord- waffen angreifen

straggle ['strægəl] intr abschweifen

straggler ['stræglər] s Nachzügler –in mf; (mil) Versprengte m

straight [stret] adj gerade; (honest) aufrecht; (candid) offen; (hair) glatt; (story) wahr; (uninterrupted) un- unterbrochen; (whiskey) unverdünnt || adv (directly) direkt; (without in- terruption) ununterbrochen; **give it to s.o. s.** j–m die ungeschminkte Wahrheit sagen; **go s.** (fig) seinen geraden Weg gehen; **is my hat on s.?** sitzt mein Hut richtig?; **make s. for** zuhalten auf (acc); **set the record s.** den Sachverhalt klarstellen; **s. ahead** (immer) geradeaus; **s. as an arrow** pfeilgerade; **s. from the horse's mouth** (coll) aus erster Hand; **s. home** schnurstracks nach Hause; **s. off** ohne weiteres || s (cards) Buch n

straight'away' adv geradewegs, sofort || s (sport) Gerade f

straighten ['stretən] tr gerade machen; (e.g., a tablecloth) glattziehen; **s. out** (fig) wieder in Ordnung bringen; **s. s.o.'s tie** j–m die Krawatte zurecht- rücken; **s. up** (a room) aufräumen || intr gerade werden; **s. up** sich auf- richten

straight' face' s—**keep a s.** keine Miene verziehen

straight'for'ward adj aufrichtig

straight' left' s (box) linke Gerade f

straight' man' s Stichwortgeber m

straight' ra'zor s Rasiermesser n

straight' right' s (box) rechte Gerade f

straight'way' adv quer an der Stelle

strain [stren] s Belastung f; (of a mus- cle or tendon) Zerrung f; (task re-

quiring effort) (coll) Strapaze f; (stock, family) Linie f; (trait) Erbei- genschaft f; (bot) Art f; **without s.** mühelos || tr (filter) durchseihen; (the eyes, nerves) überanstrengen; **s. oneself** (make a great effort) sich überanstrengen; (in lifting) sich überheben; **s. the truth** übertreiben || intr sich anstrengen; **s. after** sich abmühen um; **s. at** ziehen an (dat), zerren an (dat)

strained adj (smile) gezwungen; (rela- tions) gespannt

strainer ['strenər] s Seiher m, Filter m

strait [stret] s Straße f; **financial straits** finanzielle Schwierigkeiten pl; **straits** Meerenge f

strait' jack'et s Zwangsjacke f

strait'-laced' adj sittenstreng

strand [strænd] s Strähne f; (beach) Strand m; **s. of pearls** Perlenschnur f || tr auf den Strand setzen; (fig) stranden lassen; **be stranded** (fig) in der Patsche sitzen; **get stranded** auf- laufen; **leave s.o. stranded** j–n im Stich lassen

strange [strendʒ] adj (quaint) sonder- bar; (foreign) fremd; **s. character** Sonderling m || adv—**s. to say** merk- würdigerweise

stranger ['strendʒər] s Fremde mf

strangle ['stræŋgəl] tr erwürgen || intr ersticken

stran'glehold' s Würgegriff m

strap [stræp] s Riemen m, Gurt m; (of metal) Band n || v (pret & pp strapped; ger strapping) tr (to) an- schnallen (an acc); (a razor) abziehen

strap'ping adj stramm

stratagem ['strætədʒəm] s Kriegslist f

strategic(al) [strə'tidʒɪk(əl)] adj strate- gisch

strategist ['strætɪdʒɪst] s Stratege m

strategy ['strætɪdʒi] s Strategie f

stratification [ˌstrætɪfɪ'keʃən] s Schich- tung f

strati·fy ['strætɪˌfaɪ] v (pret & pp –fied) tr schichten || intr Schichten bilden

stratosphere ['strætəˌsfɪr] s Strato- sphäre f

stra·tum ['stretem], ['strætəm] s (–ta [tə] & –tums) Schicht f

straw [stro] s (e.g., hat, man, mat) Stroh– || s Stroh n; (single stalk; for drinking) Strohhalm m; **that's the last s.!** das schlägt dem Faß den Boden aus!

straw'ber'ry s Erdbeere f

straw'berry blond' adj rotblond

straw' mat'tress s Strohsack m

straw' vote' s Probeabstimmung f

stray [stre] adj (e.g., bullet) verirrt; (cat, dog) streunend; **s. shell** (mil) Ausreißer m || s verirrtes Tier n || intr herumirren; (fig) abschweifen

streak [strik] s Streifen m; **like a s.** wie der Blitz; **s. of bad luck** Pech- strähne f; **s. of luck** Glückssträhne f; **s. of light** Lichtstreifen m || tr streifen || intr streifig werden; **s. along** vorbeisausen

streaky ['striki] *adj* gestreift; (*uneven*) (coll) ungleich(mäßig)

stream [strim] *s* Fluß *m*; (*of people, cars, air, blood, lava*) Strom *m*; (*of words*) Schwall *m*; (*of tears*) Flut *f*; (*of a liquid*) Strahl *m* ‖ *intr* (aus-)strömen

streamer ['strimər] *s* (*pennant*) Wimpel *m*; (*ribbon*) herabhängendes Band *n*; (*rolled crepe paper*) Papierschlange *f*

stream'line' *tr* in Stromlinienform bringen; (fig) reorganizieren

stream'lined' *adj* stromlinienförmig

street [strit] *s* Straße *f*

street'car' *s* Straßenbahn *f*

street' clean'er *s* Straßenkehrer –in *mf*; (*truck*) Straßenkehrmaschine *f*

street' fight' *s* Straßenschlacht *f*

street'light' *s* Straßenlaterne *f*

street' sign' *s* Straßenschild *n*

street' ven'dor *s* Straßenhändler –in *mf*

street'walk'er *s* Straßendirne *f*

strength [streŋθ] *s* Kraft *f*; (*strong point; potency of alcohol; moral or mental power*) Stärke *f*; (mil) Kopfstärke *f*; bodily *s.* Körperkraft *f*; on the *s.* of auf Grund (*genit*)

strengthen ['streŋθən] *tr* stärken; (fig) bestärken ‖ *intr* stärker werden

strenuous ['strenju·əs] *adj* anstrengend; *s.* effort Kraftanstrengung *f*

stress [stres] *s* (*emphasis, weight*) Nachdruck *m*; (*mental*) Belastung *f*; (mus, pros) Ton *m*, Betonung *f*; (phys) Beanspruchung *f*, Spannung *f* ‖ *tr* (& mus, pros) betonen

stress' ac'cent *s* Betonungsakzent *m*

stress' mark' *s* Betonungszeichen *n*

stretch [stretʃ] *s* (*of road*) Strecke *f*; (*of the limbs*) Strecken *n*; (*of water*) Fläche *f*; (*of a racetrack*) Gerade *f*; (*of years*) Zeitspanne *f*; do a *s.* (sl) brummen; in one *s.* in e–m Zug ‖ *tr* (*a rope*) spannen; (*one's neck*) rekken; (*shoes, gloves*) ausdehnen; (*wire*) ziehen; (*strings of an instrument*) straffziehen; *s.* a point es nicht allzu genau nehmen; *s.* oneself sich strecken; *s.* one's legs sich [*dat*] die Beine vertreten; *s.* out (*e.g., hands*) ausstrecken ‖ *intr* sich (aus-)dehnen; (*said of a person*) sich strecken; *s.* out on sich ausstrecken auf (*dat*)

stretcher ['stretʃər] *s* Tragbahre *f*

stretch'erbear'er *s* Krankenträger *m*

strew [stru] *v* (*pret* strewed; *pp* strewed & strewn) *tr* (aus)streuen; *s.* with bestreuen mit

stricken ['strɪkən] *adj* (with *e.g., misfortune*) heimgesucht (von); (with *e.g., fear, grief*) ergriffen (von); (with *a disease*) befallen (von)

strict [strɪkt] *adj* streng; in *s.* confidence streng vertraulich

strictly ['strɪktli] *adv* streng; *s.* speaking genau genommen

stricture ['strɪktʃər] *s* (on) kritische Bemerkung *f* (über *acc*)

stride [straɪd] *s* Schritt *m*; hit one's *s.* auf Touren kommen; make great

strides große Fortschritte machen; take in *s.* ruhig hinnehmen ‖ *v* (*pret* strode [strod]; *pp* stridden ['strɪdən]) *intr* schreiten; *s.* along tüchtig ausschreiten

strident ['straɪdənt] *adj* schrill

strife [straɪf] *s* Streit *m*, Hader *m*

strike [straɪk] *s* (*work stoppage*) Streik *m*; (*blow*) Schlag *m*; (*discovery, e.g., of oil*) Fund *m*; (baseball) Fehlschlag *m*; go on *s.* in Streik treten ‖ *v* (*pret* & *pp* struck [strʌk]) *tr* (*a person, the hours, coins, strings of an instrument*) schlagen; (*a match*) anstreichen; (*a bargain*) schließen; (*a note*) greifen; (go on strike against) bestreiken; (*a tent*) abbrechen; (*oil*) stoßen auf (*acc*); (*run into*) auffahren auf (*acc*); (*s.o. blind, dumb*) machen; (*s.o. with fear*) erfüllen; (*a blow*) versetzen; (*a pose*) einnehmen; (*seem to s.o.*) erscheinen (*dat*); *s.* it rich auf e–e Goldader stoßen; *s.* fear into s.o. j–m e–n Schrecken einjagen; *s.* up (*a conversation, an acquaintance*) anknüpfen; (*a song*) anstimmen ‖ *intr* schlagen; (*said of a person or clock*) schlagen; (*said of workers*) streiken; (*said of lightning*) einschlagen; *s.* home Eindruck machen; *s.* out (& fig) fehlschlagen

strike'break'er *s* Streikbrecher –in *mf*

striker ['straɪkər] *s* Streikende *mf*

strik'ing *adj* auffallend; (*example*) treffend; (*workers*) streikend

strik'ing pow'er *s* Schlagkraft *f*

string [strɪŋ] *s* Bindfaden *m*; (*row, series*) Reihe *f*; (*of a bow*) Sehne *f*; (*of a musical instrument*) Saite *f*; pull strings (fig) der Drahtzieher sein; *s.* of pearls Perlenkette *f*; strings (mus) Streicher *pl*; with no strings attached ohne einschränkende Bedingungen ‖ *v* (*pret* & *pp* strung [strʌŋ]) *tr* (*pearls*) auf e–e Schnur (auf)reihen; (*a bow*) spannen; *s.* along hinhalten; *s.* up (coll) aufknüpfen

string' band' *s* Streichorchester *n*

string' bean' *s* grüne Bohne *f*; (*tall, thin person*) Bohnenstange *f*

stringed' in'strument *s* Saiteninstrument *n*

stringent ['strɪndʒənt] *adj* streng

string' quartet' *s* Streichquartett *n*

stringy ['strɪŋi] *adj* (*vegetables*) holzig; (*meat*) sehnig; (*hair*) zottelig

strip [strɪp] *s* Streifen *m* ‖ *v* (*pret* & *pp* stripped; *ger* stripping) *tr* (off) abziehen; (*clothes*) (off) abstreifen; (*a thread*) überdrehen; (*gears*) beschädigen; *s.* down abmontieren; *s.* s.o. of office j–n seines Amtes entkleiden ‖ *intr* sich ausziehen

stripe [straɪp] *s* Streifen *m*; (*elongated welt*) Striemen *m*; (mil) Tresse *f* ‖ *tr* streifen

strip' mine' *s* Tagebau *m*

stripper ['strɪpər] *s* Stripperin *f*

strip'tease' *s* Entkleidungsnummer *f*

stripteaser ['strɪp.tizər] *s* Stripperin *f*

strive [straɪv] *v* (*pret* strove [strov])

pp **striven** [ˈstrɪvən]) *intr* (for) streben (nach); s. to (*inf*) sich bemühen
zu (*inf*)
stroke [strok] *s* Schlag *m*; (*caress with
the hand*) Streicheln *n*; (*of a piston*)
Hub *m*; (*of a pen, brush*) Strich *m*;
(*of a sword*) Hieb *m*; (*in swimming*)
Schwimmstoß *m*; (*of the leg*) Bein-
stoß *m*; (*of an oar*) Schlag *m*; (pathol)
Schlaganfall *m*; **at a single s.** mit
e-m Schlag; **at the s. of twelve**
Schlag zwölf Uhr; **not do a s. of
work** keinen Strich tun; **she'll have
a s.** (coll) dann trifft sie der Schlag;
s. of genius Genieblitz *m*; **s. of luck**
Glücksfall *m*; **with a s. of the pen**
mit e-m Federstrich || *tr* streicheln
stroll [strol] *s* Spaziergang *m* || *intr*
spazieren
stroller [ˈstrolər] *s* Spaziergänger –in
mf; (*for a baby*) Kindersportwagen
m
strong [strɔŋ] *adj* kräftig; (*firm*) fest;
(*smell, light, wind, feeling*) stark; (*glasses*) scharf; (*wine*) schwer;
(*suspicion*) dringend; (*memory*) gut;
(*candidate*) aussichtsreich; (*argument*) triftig
strong′-arm′ *adj* (e.g., *methods*)
Zwangs–
strong′box′ *s* Geldschrank *m*
strong′hold′ *s* Feste *f*; (fig) Hochburg
f
strong′ lan′guage *s* Kraftausdrücke *pl*
strongly [ˈstrɔŋli] *adv* nachdrücklich;
feel s. about sich sehr einsetzen für
strong′-mind′ed *adj* willensstark
strontium [ˈstrʌnʃ/ɪ·əm] *s* Strontium *n*
strop [strap] *s* Streichriemen *m* || *v*
(*pret & pp* **stropped;** *ger* **stropping**)
tr abziehen
strophe [ˈstrofi] *s* Strophe *f*
structural [ˈstrʌkt/ərəl] *adj* strukturell,
Bau–
structure [ˈstrʌkt/ər] *s* Struktur *f*;
(*building*) Bau *m*
struggle [ˈstrʌɡəl] *s* Kampf *m* || *intr*
(for) kämpfen (um); **s. against** an-
kämpfen gegen; **s. to one's feet** sich
mit Mühe erheben
strum [strʌm] *v* (*pret & pp* **strummed;**
ger **strumming**) *tr* klimpern auf (*dat*)
strumpet [ˈstrʌmpɪt] *s* Dirne *f*
strut [strʌt] *s* (brace) Strebebalken *m*;
(*haughty walk*) stolzer Gang *m* || *v*
(*pret & pp* **strutted;** *ger* **strutting**)
intr stolzieren
strychnine [ˈstrɪknaɪn] *s* Strychnin *n*
stub [stʌb] *s* (*of a checkbook*) Abschnitt *m*; (*of a ticket*) Kontroll-
abschnitt *m*; (*of a candle, pencil,
cigarette*) Stummel *m* || *v* (*pret &
pp* **stubbed;** *ger* **stubbing**) *tr*—**s. one's
toe** sich an der Zehe stoßen
stubble [ˈstʌbəl] *s* Stoppel *f*; (*facial
hair*) Bartstoppeln *pl*
stubbly [ˈstʌbli] *adj* stopp(e)lig
stubborn [ˈstʌbərn] *adj* eigensinnig;
(e.g., *resistance*) hartnäckig; (*hair*)
widerspenstig
stubby [ˈstʌbi] *adj* kurz und dick;
(*person*) untersetzt

stuc·co [ˈstʌko] *s* (–coes & –cos) Ver-
putz *m* || *tr* verputzen
stuc′co work′ *s* Verputzarbeit *f*
stuck [stʌk] *adj*—**be s.** feststecken;
(*said, e.g., of a lock*) klemmen; **be
s. on** vernarrt sein in (*acc*); **get s.**
steckenbleiben
stuck′-up′ *adj* (coll) hochnäsig
stud [stʌd] *s* (*ornament*) Ziernagel *m*;
(*horse*) Zuchthengst *m*; (archit)
Wandpfosten *m* || *v* (*pret & pp*
studded; *ger* **studding**) *tr* mit Zier-
nägeln verzieren
stud′ bolt′ *s* Schraubenbolzen *m*
student [ˈst(j)udənt] *s* Studenten– ||
s (*in college*) Student –in *mf*; (*in
grammar or high school*) Schüler
–in *mf*; (*scholar*) Gelehrte *mf*
stu′dent bod′y *s* Studentenschaft *f*
stu′dent nurse′ *s* Krankenpflegerin *f* in
Ausbildung
stud′ farm′ *s* Gestüt *n*
stud′horse′ *s* Zuchthengst *m*
stud′ied *adj* gesucht
studi·o [ˈst(j)udɪˌo] *s* (–os) (fa, phot)
Atelier *n*; (cin, fa, phot, telv) Studio
n
studious [ˈst(j)udɪ·əs] *adj* fleißig
stud·y [ˈstʌdi] *s* Studium *n*; (*room*)
Studierzimmer *n*; (paint) Studie *f* ||
v (*pret & pp* –**ied**) *tr & intr* studieren
stuff [stʌf] *s* Stoff *m*; (coll) Kram *m*;
do your s.! (coll) schieß los!; **know
one's s.** (coll) sich auskennen || *tr*
(*animals*) ausstopfen; (*a cushion*)
polstern; (*e.g., cotton in the ears*)
sich [*dat*] stopfen; (culin) füllen;
s. oneself sich vollstopfen
stuffed′ shirt′ *s* steifer, eingebildeter
Mensch *m*
stuff′ing *s* Polstermaterial *n*; (culin)
Fülle *f*
stuffy [ˈstʌfi] *adj* (*room*) stickig; (*nose*)
verstopft; (*person*) steif
stumble [ˈstʌmbəl] *intr* stolpern; (*in
reading*) holpern; **s. across** stoßen
auf (*acc*)
stum′bling block′ *s* Stein *m* des An-
stoßes
stump [stʌmp] *s* (*of an arm, tree, ciga-
rette, pencil*) Stummel *m* || *tr* (*a ciga-
rette*) ausdrücken; (*nonplus*) verblüffen; (*a district, state*) als Wahlredner bereisen
stump′ speak′er *s* Wahlredner –in *mf*
stun [stʌn] *v* (*pret & pp* **stunned;** *ger*
stunning) *tr* betäuben
stun′ning *adj* (coll) phantastisch
stunt [stʌnt] *s* Kunststück *n*; **do stunts**
Kunststücke vorführen || *tr* hemmen
stunt′ed *adj* verkümmert
stunt′ fly′ing *s* Kunstflug *m*
stunt′ man′ *s* (**men′**) Sensationsdarstel-
ler *m*
stupe·fy [ˈst(j)upɪˌfaɪ] *v* (*pret & pp*
–**fied**) *tr* verblüffen
stupendous [st(j)uˈpendəs] *adj* erstaunlich
stupid [ˈst(j)upɪd] *adj* dumm, blöd
stupidity [stˈ(j)dɪti] *s* Dummheit *f*
stupor [ˈst(j)upər] *s* Stumpfsinn *m*
sturdy [ˈstʌrdi] *adj* (*person*) kräftig;

(*thing*) stabil; (*resolute*) standhaft; (*plant*) widerstandsfähig

sturgeon ['stɑrdʒən] *s* Stör *m*

stutter ['stʌtər] *s* Stottern *n* || *tr & intr* stottern

sty [staɪ] *s* Schweinestall *m;* (*pathol*) Gerstenkorn *n*

style [staɪl] *s* Stil *m;* (*manner*) Art *f;* (*fashion*) Mode *f;* (*cut of suit*) Schnitt *m;* **be in s. in** Mode sein; **go out of s.** veralten; **live in s.** auf großem Fuße leben || *tr* (*title*) betiteln; (*e.g., clothes*) gestalten; (*hair*) nach der Mode frisieren

stylish ['staɪlɪʃ] *adj* modisch; (*person*) modisch gekleidet

stylistic [staɪ'lɪstɪk] *adj* stilistisch

stymie ['staɪmi] *tr* vereiteln

styp'tic pen'cil ['stɪptɪk] *s* Alaunstift *m*

suave [swɑv] *adj* verbindlich

sub [sʌb] *s* (naut) U-boot *n;* (sport) Ersatzspieler –in *mf*

sub'chas'er *s* U-bootjäger *m*

sub'commit'tee *s* Unterausschuß *m*

subconscious [sʌb'kɑnʃəs] *adj* unterbewußt || *s* Unterbewußtsein *n*

sub'con'tinent *s* Subkontinent *m*

sub'con'tract *s* Nebenvertrag *m* || *tr* e–n Nebenvertrag abschließen über (*acc*)

sub'con'tractor *s* Unterlieferant –in *mf*

sub'divide', sub'divide' *tr* unterteilen || *intr* sich unterteilen

sub'divi'sion *s* (*act*) Unterteilung *f;* (*unit*) Unterabteilung *f*

subdue [səb'd(j)u] *tr* (*an enemy*) unterwerfen; (*one who is struggling*) überwältigen; (*light, sound*) dämpfen; (*feelings, impulses*) bändigen

sub'floor' *s* Blindboden *m*

sub'head' *s* Untertitel *m*

subject ['sʌbdʒɪkt] *adj* (**to**) untertan (*dat*); **be s. to** (*e.g., approval, another country*) abhängig sein von; (*e.g., colds*) neigen zu; (*laws of nature, change*) unterworfen sein (*dat*); **s. to change without notice** Änderungen vorbehalten || *s* Thema *n;* (*of a kingdom*) Untertan –in *mf;* (*educ*) Fach *n;* (fa) Vorwurf *m;* (gram) Satzgegenstand *m,* Subjekt *n;* (libr) Stichwort *n;* **change the s.** das Thema wechseln; **get off the s.** vom Thema abkommen || [səb'dʒɛkt] *tr* (& fig) unterwerfen (*dat*)

subjection [səb'dʒɛkʃən] *s* Unterwerfung *f*

subjective [səb'dʒɛktɪv] *adj* subjektiv; **s. case** Werfall *m*

sub'ject mat'ter *s* Inhalt *m*

subjugate ['sʌdʒə‚get] *tr* unterjochen

subjunctive [səb'dʒʌŋktɪv] *adj* konjunktiv(isch) || *s* Konjunktiv *m*

sub'lease' *s* Untermiete *f* || **sub'lease'** *tr & intr* (*to s.o.*) untervermieten; (*from s.o.*) untermieten

sublet [səb'lɛt] *v* (*pret & pp* **–let;** *ger* **–letting**) *tr & intr* (*to s.o.*) untervermieten; (*from s.o.*) untermieten

sublimate ['sʌblɪmət] *s* (chem) Sublimat *n* || ['sʌblɪ‚met] *tr* sublimieren

sublime [sə'blaɪm] *adj* erhaben || *s* Erhabene *n*

submachine' gun' *s* Maschinenpistole *f*

sub'marine' *adj* U-boot– || *s* U-boot *n*

sub'marine' base' *s* U-bootstützpunkt *m*

submerge [səb'mʌrdʒ] *tr & intr* untertauchen; **ready to s.** tauchklar

submersion [səb'mʌrʒən] *s* Untertauchen *n*

submission [səb'mɪʃən] *s* (**to**) Unterwerfung *f* (unter *acc*); (*of a document*) Vorlage *f;* (*of a question*) Unterbreitung *f*

submissive [səb'mɪsɪv] *adj* unterwürfig

sub-mit [səb'mɪt] *v* (*pret & pp* **–mitted;** *ger* **–mitting**) *tr* (*a question*) unterbreiten; (*a document*) vorlegen; (*suggest*) der Ansicht sein || *intr* (**to**) sich unterwerfen (*dat*)

subordinate [səb'ɔrdɪnɪt] *adj* (*lower in rank*) untergeordnet; (*secondary*) Neben– || *s* Untergebene *mf* || [səb'ɔrdɪ‚net] *tr* (**to**) unterordnen (*dat*)

subor'dinate clause' *s* Nebensatz *m*

suborn [sə'bɔrn] *tr* verleiten; (*bribe*) bestechen

sub'plot' *s* Nebenhandlung *f*

subpoena [sʌb'pinə] *s* Vorladung *f* || *tr* (unter Strafandrohung) vorladen

subscribe [səb'skraɪb] *tr* unterschreiben; (*money*) zeichnen || *intr*—**s. to** (*a newspaper*) abonnieren; (*to a series of volumes*) subskribieren; (*an idea*) billigen

subscriber [səb'skraɪbər] *s* Abonnent –in *mf*

subscription [səb'skrɪpʃən] *s* (**to**) Abonnement *n* (auf *acc*); (*to a series of volumes*) Subskription *f* (auf *acc*); **take out a s.** to sich abonnieren auf (*acc*)

sub'sec'tion *s* Unterabteilung *f*

subsequent ['sʌbsɪkwənt] *adj* (nach)folgend; **s. to** anschließend an (*acc*)

subsequently ['sʌbsɪkwəntli] *adv* anschließend

subservient [səb'sʌrvɪ‚ənt] *adj* (**to**) unterwürfig (gegenüber *dat*)

subside [səb'saɪd] *intr* nachlassen; (geol) sich senken

subsidiary [səb'sɪdɪ‚eri] *adj* Tochter– || *s* Tochtergesellschaft *f*

subsidize ['sʌbsɪ‚daɪz] *tr* subventionieren

subsidy ['sʌbsɪdi] *s* Subvention *f*

subsist [səb'sɪst] *intr* (*exist*) existieren; **s. on** leben von

subsistence [səb'sɪstəns] *s* (*existence*) Dasein *n;* (*livelihood*) Lebensunterhalt *m;* (philos) Subsistenz *f*

subsis'tence allow'ance *s* Unterhaltszuschuß *m*

sub'soil' *s* Untergrund *m*

subsonic [səb'sɑnɪk] *adj* Unterschall–

sub'spe'cies *s* Unterart *f*

substance ['sʌbstəns] *s* Substanz *f,* Stoff *m;* **in s.** im wesentlichen

substand'ard *adj* unter dem Niveau

substantial [səb'stænʃəl] *adj* (*sum, amount*) beträchtlich; (*difference*) wesentlich; (*meal*) kräftig; **be in s. agreement** im wesentlichen übereinstimmen

substantiate [səb'stænʃɪ,et] *tr* begründen, nachweisen

substantive ['sʌbstəntɪv] *adj* wesentlich ‖ *s* (*gram*) Substantiv *m*

sub'sta'tion *s* Nebenstelle *f*; (*post-office*) Zweigpostamt *n*; (*elec*) Umspannwerk *n*

substitute ['sʌbstɪ,t(j)ut] *s* (*person*) Stellvertreter –in *mf*; (*material*) Austauschstoff *m*; (*pej*) Ersatz *m*; (*sport*) Ersatzspieler – in *mf*; **act as a s. for** vertreten; **beware of substitutes** vor Nachamung wird gewarnt ‖ *tr*—**A for B** B durch A ersetzen ‖ *intr*— **s. for** einspringen für

sub'stitute teach'er *s* Aushilfslehrer –in *mf*

substitution [,sʌbstɪ't(j)uʃən] *s* Einsetzung *f*; (*chem, math, ling*) Substitution *f*; (*sport*) Auswechseln *n*

sub'stra'tum *s* (–ta [tə] & –tums) Unterlage *f*; (*biol*) Nährboden *m*

sub'struc'ture *s* Unterbau *m*

subsume [sʌb'sjum] *tr* unterordnen

subterfuge ['sʌbtər,fjudʒ] *s* Winkelzug *m*

subterranean [,sʌbtə'reni·ən] *adj* unterirdisch

sub'ti'tle *s* Untertitel *m*

subtle ['sʌtəl] *adj* fein; (*poison*) schleichend; (*cunning*) raffiniert

subtlety ['sʌtəlti] *s* Feinheit *f*

subtract [səb'trækt] *tr* subtrahieren

subtraction [səb'trækʃən] *s* Subtraktion *f*

suburb ['sʌbʌrb] *s* Vorstadt *f*, Vorort *m*; **the suburbs** der Stadtrand

suburban [sə'bʌrbən] *adj* Vorstadt-

suburbanite [sə'bʌrbə,naɪt] *s* Vorstadtbewohner –in *mf*

subvention [səb'venʃən] *s* Subvention *f*

subversion [səb'vʌrʒən] *s* Umsturz *m*

subversive [səb'vʌrsɪv] *adj* umstürzlerisch ‖ *s* Umstürzler –in *mf*

subver'sive activ'ity *s* Wühlarbeit *f*

subvert [səb'vʌrt] *tr* (*a government*) stürzen; (*the law*) umstoßen; (*corrupt*) (sittlich) verderben

sub'way' *s* U-Bahn *f*, Untergrundbahn *f*

succeed [sək'sid] *tr* folgen (*dat*) ‖ *intr* (*said of persons*) (**in**) Erfolg haben (mit); (*said of things*) gelingen; **I succeeded in** (*ger*) es gelang mir zu (*inf*); **not s.** mißglücken; **s. to the throne** die Thronfolge antreten

success [sək'ses] *s* Erfolg *m*; (*play, song, piece of merchandise*) Knüller *m*; **be a s.** Erfolg haben; **without s.** erfolglos

successful [sək'sesfəl] *adj* erfolgreich

succession [sək'sesən] *s* Reihenfolge *f*; (*as heir*) Erbfolge *f*; **in s.** nacheinander; **s. to** (e.g., *an office, estate*) Übernahme *f* (*genit*)

successive [sək'sesɪv] *adj* aufeinanderfolgend

successor [sək'sesər] *s* Nachfolger –in

mf; **s. to the throne** Thronfolger –in *mf*

succor ['sʌkər] *s* Beistand *m* ‖ *tr* beistehen (*dat*)

succotash ['sʌkə,tæʃ] *s* Gericht *n* aus Süßmais und grünen Bohnen

succulent ['sʌkjələnt] *adj* saftig

succumb [sə'kʌm] *intr* (**to**) erliegen (*dat*)

such [sʌt(ʃ)] *adj* solch; **as s.** als solcher; **no s. thing** nichts dergleichen; **some s. thing** irgend so (et)was; **s. and s.** der und der; **s. as** wie (etwa); **s. a long time** so lange; **s. as it is** wie es nun einmal ist

suck [sʌk] *s* Saugen *n*; (*licking*) Lutschen *n* ‖ *tr* saugen; **s. in** einsaugen; (*sl*) reinlegen ‖ *intr* saugen; **s. on** (e.g., *candy*) lutschen

sucker ['sʌkər] *s* (*coll*) Gimpel *m*; (*carp*) Karpfenfisch *m*; (*bot*) Wurzelschößling *m*; (*zool*) Saugröhre *f*

suckle ['sʌkəl] *tr* stillen; (*animals*) säugen

suck'ling *s* Säugling *m*

suck'ling pig' *s* Spanferkel *n*

suction ['sʌkʃən] *s* Saugen *n*, Sog *m*

suc'tion cup' *s* Saugnapf *m*

suc'tion pump' *s* Saugpumpe *f*

sudden ['sʌdən] *adj* plötzlich, jäh; **all of a s.** (ganz) plötzlich

suddenly ['sʌdənli] *adv* plötzlich

suds [sʌdz] *spl* Seifenschaum *m*

sudsy ['sʌdzi] *adj* schaumig

sue [s(j)u] *tr* (**for**) verklagen (auf *acc*) ‖ *intr* (**for**) klagen (auf *acc*)

suede [swed] *adj* Wildleder– ‖ *s* Wildleder *n*

suet ['s(j)u·ɪt] *s* Talg *m*

suffer ['sʌfər] *tr* erleiden; (*damage*) nehmen; (*put up with*) ertragen ‖ *intr* (**from**) leiden (an *dat*)

sufferance ['sʌfərəns] *s* stillschweigende Einwilligung *f*

suf'fering *s* Leiden *n*

suffice [sə'faɪs] *intr* ausreichen

sufficient [sə'fɪʃənt] *adj* (**for**) ausreichend (für)

suffix ['sʌfɪks] *s* Nachsilbe *f*

suffocate ['sʌfə,ket] *tr* & *intr* ersticken

suffrage ['sʌfrɪdʒ] *s* Stimmrecht *n*

suffuse [sə'fjuz] *tr* übergießen

sugar ['ʃugər] *s* Zucker *m* ‖ *tr* zuckern

sug'ar beet' *s* Zuckerrübe *f*

sug'ar bowl' *s* Zuckerdose *f*

sug'ar cane' *s* Zuckerrohr *n*

sug'ar-coat' *tr* (& *fig*) überzuckern

sug'ar dad'dy *s* Geldonkel *m*

sug'ar ma'ple *s* Zuckerahorn *m*

sug'ar tongs' *spl* Zuckerzange *f*

sugary ['ʃugəri] *adj* zuckerig

suggest [səg'dʒest] *tr* vorschlagen; (*hint*) andeuten

suggestion [səg'dʒestʃən] *s* Vorschlag *m*

suggestive [səg'dʒestɪv] *adj* (*remark*) zweideutig; (*thought-provoking*) anregend; (e.g., *dress*) hauteng; **be s. of** erinnern an (*acc*)

suicidal [,su·ɪ'saɪdəl] *adj* selbstmörderisch

suicide ['su·ɪ,saɪd] *s* Selbstmord *m*;

(*person*) Selbstmörder –in *mf*; commit s. Selbstmord begehen

suit [sut] *s* (*men's*) Anzug *m*; (*women's*) Kostüm *n*; (cards) Farbe *f*; (jur) Prozeß *m*; bring s. (against) e–e Klage einbringen (gegen); follow s. Farbe bekennen; (fig) sich nach den anderen richten ‖ *tr* (*please*) passen (*dat*); (*correspond to*) entsprechen (*dat*); (*said, e.g., of colors, style*) gut passen (*dat*); be suited for sich eignen für; s. s.th. to etw anpassen (*dat*); s. yourself! wie Sie wollen!

suitable ['sutəbəl] *adj* (to) geeignet (für)

suit'case' *s* Handkoffer *m*

suit' coat' *s* Sakko *m & n*

suite [swit] *s* (*series of rooms*) Zimmerflucht *f*; (*set of furniture*) Zimmergarnitur *f*; (mus) Suite *f*

suitor ['sutər] *s* Freier *m*

sul'fa drug' *s* Sulfonamid *n*

sulfate ['sʌlfet] *s* Sulfat *n*

sulfide ['sʌlfaɪd] *s* Sulfid *n*

sulfur ['sʌlfər] *adj* Schwefel– ‖ *s* Schwefel *m* ‖ *tr* einschwefeln

sulfur'ic ac'id [sʌl'f(j)ʊrɪk] *s* Schwefelsäure *f*

sul'fur mine' *s* Schwefelgrube *f*

sulk [sʌlk] *intr* trotzen

sulky ['sʌlki] *adj* trotzend, mürrisch ‖ *s* (sport) Traberwagen *m*

sulk'y race' *s* Trabrennen *n*

sullen ['sʌlən] *adj* mißmutig

sul·ly ['sʌli] *v* (*pret & pp* –lied) *tr* besudeln

sulphur ['sʌlfər] *var of* sulfur

sultan ['sʌltən] *s* Sultan *m*

sultry ['sʌltri] *adj* schwül

sum [sʌm] *s* Summe *f*, Betrag *m*; in sum kurz gesagt ‖ *v* (*pret & pp* summed; *ger* summing)—sum up summieren; (*summarize*) zusammenfassen; (*make a quick estimate of*) kurz abschätzen

sumac, sumach ['ʃʊmæk] *s* Sumach *m*

summarize ['sʌmə‚raɪz] *tr* zusammenfassen

summary ['sʌməri] *adj* summarisch ‖ *s* Zusammenfassung *f*

sum'mary court'mar'tial *s* summarisches Militärgericht *n*

summer ['sʌmər] *s* Sommer *m*

sum'mer cot'tage *s* Sommerwohnung *f*

sum'mer resort' *s* Sommerfrische *f*

sum'mer school' *s* Sommerkurs *m*

sum'mertime' *s* Sommerzeit *f*

summery ['sʌməri] *adj* sommerlich

summit ['sʌmɪt] *s* (& fig) Gipfel *m*

sum'mit con'ference *s* Gipfelkonferenz *f*

sum'mit talks' *spl* Gipfelgespräche *pl*

summon ['sʌmən] *tr* (e.g., *a doctor*) kommen lassen; (*a conference*) einberufen; (jur) vorladen; s. up (*courage, strength*) aufbieten

summons ['sʌmənz] *s* (jur) Vorladung *f*

sumptuous ['sʌmptʃu‑əs] *adj* üppig

sun [sʌn] *s* Sonne *f* ‖ *v* (*pret & pp* sunned; *ger* sunning) *tr* sonnen; sun oneself sich sonnen

sun' bath' *s* Sonnenbad *n*

sun'beam' *s* Sonnenstrahl *m*

sun'burn' *s* Sonnenbrand *m*

sun'burned' *adj* sonnverbrannt

sundae ['sʌnde] *s* Eisbecher *m* mit Sirup, Nüssen, Früchten und Schlagsahne

Sunday ['sʌnde] *adj* sonntäglich; dressed in one's S. best sonntäglich gekleidet ‖ *s* Sonntag *m*; on S. am Sonntag

Sun'day driv'er *s* Sonntagsfahrer –in *mf*

Sun'day school' *s* Sonntagsschule *f*

sunder ['sʌndər] *tr* trennen

sun'di'al *s* Sonnenuhr *f*

sun'down' *s* Sonnenuntergang *m*

sun'-drenched' *adj* sonnenüberflutet

sundries ['sʌndriz] *pl* Diverses *n*

sundry ['sʌndri] *adj* verschiedene

sun'fish' *s* Sonnenfisch *m*

sun'flow'er *s* Sonnenblume *f*

sun'glass'es *pl* Sonnenbrille *f*

sun' hel'met *s* Tropenhelm *m*

sunken ['sʌŋkən] *adj* (ship) gesunken; (*eyes; garden*) tiefliegend; (*treasure*) versunken; (*cheeks*) eingefallen; s. rocks blinde Klippe *f*

sun' lamp' *s* Höhensonne *f*

sun'light' *s* Sonnenlicht *n*

sunny ['sʌni] *adj* sonnig

sun'ny side' *s* Sonnenseite *f*

sun' par'lor *s* Glasveranda *f*

sun'rise' *s* Sonnenaufgang *m*

sun' roof' *s* (aut) Schiebedach *n*

sun'set' *s* Sonnenuntergang *m*

sun'shade' *s* Sonnenschirm *m*; (*awning*) Sonnendach *n*; (phot) Gegenlichtblende *f*

sun'shine' *s* Sonnenschein *m*

sun'spot' *s* Sonnenfleck *m*

sun'stroke' *s* Sonnenstich *m*

sun'tan' *s* Sonnenbräune *f*

sun'tanned' *adj* sonnengebräunt

sun' vis'or *s* (aut) Sonnenblende *f*

sup [sʌp] *v* (*pret & pp* supped; *ger* supping) *intr* zu Abend essen

super ['supər] *adj* (*oversized*) Super–; (sl) prima ‖ *s* (theat) Komparse *m*

su'perabun'dance *s* (of) Überfülle *f* (an *dat*)

su'perabun'dant *adj* überreichlich

superannuated [‚supər'ænju‚etɪd] *adj* (*person*) pensioniert; (*thing*) veraltet

superb [sʊ'pʌrb] *adj* prachtvoll, herrlich

su'perbomb' *s* Superbombe *f*

su'perbomb'er *s* Riesenbomber *m*

supercilious [‚supər'sɪli‑əs] *adj* hochnäsig

superficial [‚supər'fɪʃəl] *adj* oberflächlich

superfluous [sʊ'pʌrflu‑əs] *adj* überflüssig

su'perhigh'way' *s* Autobahn *f*

su'perhu'man *adj* übermenschlich

su'perimpose' *tr* darüberlegen; (elec, phys) überlagern

su'perintend' *tr* die Aufsicht führen über (*acc*), beaufsichtigen

superintendent [‚supərɪn'tendənt] *s* Oberaufseher –in *mf*; (*in industry*)

Betriebsleiter –in *mf*; (*of a factory*) Werksleiter –in *mf*; (*of a building*) Hausverwalter –in *mf*; (*educ*) Schulinspektor –in *mf*

superior [sə'pɪrɪ-ər] *adj* (*physically*) höher; (*in rank*) übergeordnet; (*quality*) hervorragend; **s.** in überlegen an (*dat*); **s. to** überlegen (*dat*) || *s* Vorgesetzte *mf*

supe′rior court′ *s* Obergericht *n*

superiority [sə͵pɪrɪ'ɑrɪti] *s* (**in**) Überlegenheit *f* (in *dat*, an *dat*); (*mil*) Übermacht *f*

superlative [su'pʌrlətɪv] *adj* hervorragend; (*gram*) superlativisch, Superlativ– || *s* (*gram*) Superlativ *m*

su′perman′ *s* (**–men**) Übermensch *m*

su′permar′ket *s* Supermarkt *m*

su′pernat′ural *adj* übernatürlich || *s* Übernatürliche *n*

supersede [͵supər'sid] *tr* ersetzen

su′persen′sitive *adj* überempfindlich

su′person′ic *adj* Überschall–

superstition [͵supər'stɪʃən] *s* Aberglaube *m*; (*superstitious idea*) abergläubische Vorstellung *f*

superstitious [͵supər'stɪʃəs] *adj* abergläubisch

su′perstruc′ture *s* Überbau *m*; (*of a bridge*) Oberban *m*; (*of a building or ship*) Aufbauten *pl*

supervise ['supər͵vaɪz] *tr* beaufsichtigen

supervision [͵supər'vɪʒən] *s* Beaufsichtigung *f*

supervisor ['supər͵vaɪzər] *s* Vorgesetzte *mf*

su′pine posi′tion ['supaɪn] *s* Rückenlage *f*

supper ['sʌpər] *s* Abendessen *n*; **eat s.** zu Abend essen

sup′pertime′ *s* Abendbrotzeit *f*

supplant [sə'plænt] *tr* ersetzen

supple ['sʌpəl] *adj* geschmeidig; (*mind*) beweglich

supplement ['sʌplɪmənt] *s* (*e.g., to a diet*) (**to**) Ergänzung *f* (*genit*); (*to a writing*) Anhang *m*; (*to a newspaper*) Beilage *f* || ['sʌplɪ͵ment] *tr* ergänzen

supplementary [͵sʌplɪ'mentəri] *adj* ergänzend

suppliant ['sʌplɪ-ənt] *adj* flehend || *s* Bittsteller –in *mf*

supplicant ['sʌplɪkənt] *s* Bittsteller –in *mf*

supplicate ['sʌplɪ͵ket] *tr* flehen

supplication [͵sʌplɪ'keʃən] *s* Flehen *n*

supplier [sə'plaɪ-ər] *s* Lieferant –in *mf*

sup•ply [sə'plaɪ] *s* (*supplying*) Versorgung *f*; (*stock*) (**of**) Vorrat *m* (an *dat*); (*com*) Angebot *n*; **supplies** Vorräte *pl*; (*e.g., office supplies, dental supplies*) Bedarfsartikel *pl*; (*mil*) Nachschub *m* || *v* (*pret & pp* **–plied**) *tr* (**with**) versorgen (mit); (*deliver*) liefern; (*procure*) beschaffen; (*with a truck*) zuführen; (*equip*) (**with**) versehen (mit); (*a demand*) befriedigen; (*a loss*) ausgleichen; (*missing words*) ergänzen; (*mil*) mit Nachschub versorgen

supply′ and demand′ *spl* Angebot *n* und Nachfrage *f*

supply′ base′ *s* Nachschubstützpunkt *m*

supply′ line′ *s* Versorgungsweg *m*; (*mil*) Nachschubweg *m*

support [sə'port] *adj* Hilfs– || *s* (*prop, brace, stay; person*) Stütze *f*; (*of a family*) Unterhalt *m*; **in s. of** zur Unterstützung (*genit*); **without s.** (*unsubstantiated*) haltlos; (*unprovided*) unversorgt; **with the s. of** mit dem Beistand von || *tr* stützen, tragen; (*back*) unterstützen; (*a family*) erhalten; (*a charge*) erhärten; (*a claim*) begründen

supporter [sə'portər] *s* (*of a family*) Ernährer –in *mf*; (*backer*) Förderer –in *mf*; (*jockstrap*) Suspensorium *n*

support′ing role′ *s* Nebenrolle *f*

suppose [sə'poz] *tr* annehmen; **be supposed to** sollen; **I s. so** ich glaube schon; **s. it rains** gesetzt den Fall (or angenommen) es regnet; **s. we take a walk** wie wäre es, wenn wir e–n Spaziergang machten?; **what is that supposed to mean?** was soll das bedeuten? || *intr* vermuten

supposed′ *adj* mutmaßlich

supposedly [sə'pozɪdli] *adv* angeblich

supposition [͵sʌpə'zɪʃən] *s* Annahme *f*

suppository [sə'pɑzɪ͵tori] *s* Zäpfchen *n*

suppress [sə'pres] *tr* unterdrücken; (*news, scandal*) verheimlichen

suppression [sə'preʃən] *s* Unterdrükkung *f*; (*of news, truth, scandal*) Verheimlichung *f*

suppurate ['sʌpjə͵ret] *intr* eitern

supremacy [sə'preməsi] *s* Oberherrschaft *f*

supreme [sə'prim] *adj* Ober–, höchste

supreme′ author′ity *s* Obergewalt *f*

Supreme′ Be′ing *s* höchstes Wesen *n*

supreme′ command′ *s* Oberkommando *n*; **have s. command** den Oberbefehl führen

supreme′ command′er *s* oberster Befehlshaber *m*

Supreme′ Court′ *s* Oberster Gerichtshof *m*

surcharge ['sʌr͵tʃɑrdʒ] *s* (**on**) Zuschlag *m* (zu)

sure [ʃur] *adj* sicher, gewiß; (*shot, cure*) unfehlbar; (*shot, footing, ground, way, proof*) sicher; **are you s. you won't come?** kommen Sie wirklich nicht?; **be s. of** sicher sein (*genit*); **be s. to** (*inf*) vergiß nicht zu (*inf*); **feel s. of oneself** s–r selbst sicher sein; **for s.** sicherlich; **she is s. to come** sie wird sicher(lich) kommen; **s. enough** wirklich; **to be s.** (*parenthetically*) zwar

sure′-foot′ed *adj* trittsicher

surely ['ʃurli] *adv* sicher(lich), gewiß

surety ['ʃur(ɪ)ti] *s* Bürgschaft *f*; **stand s. (for)** bürgen (für)

surf [sʌrf] *s* Brandung *f* || *intr* wellenreiten

surface ['sʌrfɪs] *adj* (*superficial*) oberflächlich; (*apparent rather than real*)

Schein- ‖ *s* Oberfläche *f*; *(of a road)* Belag *m*; (aer) Tragfläche *f*; **on the s.** oberflächlich (betrachtet) ‖ *tr* (a road) mit e-m Belag versehen ‖ *intr* auftauchen

sur'face mail' *s* gewöhnliche Post *f*

sur'face-to-air' mis'sile *s* Boden-Luft-Rakete *f*

sur'face-to-sur'face mis'sile *s* Boden-Boden-Rakete *f*

surf'board' *s* Wellenreiterbrett *n*

surf'board'ing *s* Wellenreiten *n*

surfeit ['sʌrfɪt] *s* Übersättigung *f* ‖ *tr* übersättigen

surfer ['sʌrfər] *s* Wellenreiter –in *mf*

surf'ing *s* Wellenreiten *n*

surge [sʌrdʒ] *s* *(forward rush of a wave or crowd)* Wogen *n*; *(swelling wave)* Woge *f*; *(swelling sea)* Wogen *n*; (elec) Stromstoß *m* ‖ *intr* wogen; *(said of waves or a crowd)* wogen; *(said of emotions, blood)* **(up)** (auf)wallen

surgeon ['sʌrdʒən] *s* Chirurg –in *mf*

surgery ['sʌrdʒəri] *s* Chirurgie *f*; *(room)* Operationssaal *m*; **undergo s.** sich e-r Operation unterziehen

surgical ['sʌrdʒɪkəl] *adj* chirurgisch; *(resulting from surgery)* Operations-

surly ['sʌrli] *adj* bärbeißig

surmise [sər'maɪz] *s* Vermutung *f* ‖ *tr & intr* vermuten

surmount [sər'maʊnt] *tr* überwinden

surname ['sʌr,nem] *s* *(family name)* Zuname *m*; *(epithet)* Beiname *m* ‖ *tr* e-n Zunamen (oder Beinamen) geben *(dat)*

surpass [sər'pæs] *tr* **(in)** übertreffen *(an dat)*

surplice ['sʌrplɪs] *s* Chorhemd *n*

surplus ['sʌrplʌs] *adj* überschüssig, Über- ‖ *s* **(of)** Überschuß *m* *(an dat)*

surprise [sər'praɪz] *adj* Überraschungs- ‖ *s* Überraschung *f*; **take by s.** überraschen; **to my (great) s.** zu meiner (großen) Überraschung ‖ *tr* überraschen; **be surprised at** sich wundern über *(acc)*; **be surprised to see how** staunen, wie; **I am surprised that** es wundert mich, daß

surpris'ing *adj* überraschend

surrealism [sə'ri·ə‚lɪzəm] *s* Surrealismus *m*

surrender [sə'rendər] *s* *(e.g., of a fortress)* Übergabe *f*; *(of an army or unit)* Kapitulation *f*; *(of rights)* Aufgabe *f*; *(of a prisoner)* Auslieferung *f* ‖ *tr* übergeben; *(rights)* aufgeben; *(a prisoner)* ausliefern ‖ *intr* sich ergeben

surreptitious [‚sʌrep'tɪʃəs] *adj* heimlich; *(glance)* verstohlen

surround [sə'raʊnd] *tr* umgeben; *(said of a crowd, police)* umringen; (mil) einschließen

surround'ing *adj* umliegend ‖ **surroundings** *spl* Umgebung *f*

surtax ['sʌr‚tæks] *s* Steuerzuschlag *m*

surveillance [sər'vel(j)əns] *s* Überwachung *f*; **keep under s.** unter Polizeiaufsicht halten

survey ['sʌrve] *s* **(of)** Überblick *m* *(über acc)*; *(of opinions)* Umfrage *f*; *(of land)* Vermessung *f*; *(plan or description of the survey)* Lageplan *m* ‖ [sʌr've] *tr* überblicken; *(a person)* mustern; *(land)* vermessen; *(people for their opinion)* befragen

sur'vey course' *s* Einführungskurs *m*

survey'ing *s* Landvermessung *f*

surveyor [sər've·ər] *s* Landmesser *m*

survival [sər'vaɪvəl] *s* Überleben *n*; *(after death)* Weiterleben *n*

surviv'al of the fit'test *s* Überleben *n* des Tüchtigsten

survive [sər'vaɪv] *tr* *(a person)* überleben; *(a thing)* überstehen; **be survived by** hinterlassen ‖ *intr* am Leben bleiben

surviv'ing *adj* überlebend

survivor [sər'vaɪvər] *s* Überlebende *mf*

susceptible [sə'septɪbəl] *adj* *(impressionable)* eindrucksfähig; **be s. of** zulassen; **be s. to** *(disease, infection)* anfällig sein für; *(flattery)* empfänglich sein für

suspect ['sʌspekt] *adj* verdächtig ‖ *s* Verdächtige *mf* ‖ [səs'pekt] *tr* in Verdacht haben; *(surmise)* vermuten; *(have a hint)* ahnen; **s. s.o. of** j-n verdächtigen *(genit)*

suspend [səs'pend] *tr* *(from a job, office)* suspendieren; *(payment, hostilities, proceedings, a game)* einstellen; *(a rule)* zeitweilig aufheben; *(a sentence)* aussetzen; *(a player)* sperren; *(from a club)* zeitweilig ausschließen; **(from)** hängen *(an dat)*

suspenders [səs'pendərz] *spl* Hosenträger *pl*

suspense [səs'pens] *s* Spannung *f*; **hang in s.** in der Schwebe sein; **keep in s.** im ungewissen lassen

suspension [səs'penʃən] *s* Aufhängung *f*; *(of a sentence)* Aussetzung *f*; *(of work)* Einstellung *f*; *(e.g., of telephone service)* Sperrung *f*; (aut) Federung *f*; (chem) Suspension *f*; **s. of driver's license** Führerscheinentzug *m*

suspen'sion bridge' *s* Hängebrücke *f*

suspen'sion points' *spl* *(indicating unfinished thoughts)* Gedankenpunkte *pl*; *(indicating omission)* Auslassungspunkte *pl*

suspicion [səs'pɪʃən] *s* Verdacht *m*; **above s.** über jeden Verdacht erhaben; **be under s.** unter Verdacht stehen; **on s. of murder** unter Mordverdacht

suspicious [səs'pɪʃəs] *adj* *(person)* verdächtig; *(e.g., glance)* argwöhnisch; *(character)* zweifelhaft

sustain [səs'ten] *tr* aufrechterhalten; *(a loss, defeat, injury)* erleiden; *(a family)* ernähren; *(an army)* verpflegen; *(a motion, an objection)* stattgeben *(dat)*; *(a theory, position)* erhärten; *(a note)* dehnen

sustenance ['sʌstɪnəns] *s* *(nourishment)* Nahrung *f*; *(means of livelihood)* Unterhalt *m*

swab [swɑb] *s* (med, surg) Tupfer *m*;

(*matter collected on a swab*) Abstrich *m;* (naut) Schwabber *m* ‖ *v* (*pret & pp* **swabbed; ger swabbing**) *tr* (med, surg) abtupfen; (naut) schrubben

Swabia ['swebɪ-ə] *s* Schwaben *n*

Swabian ['swebɪ-ən] *adj* schwäbisch ‖ *s* Schwabe *m,* Schwäbin *f;* (*dialect*) Schwäbisch *n*

swad'dling clothes' ['swɑdlɪŋ] *spl* Windeln *pl*

swagger ['swægər] *s* (*strut*) Stolzieren *n;* (*swaggering manner*) Prahlerei *f* ‖ *intr* stolzieren; (*show off*) prahlen

swain [swen] *s* (*lover*) Liebhaber *m;* (*country lad*) Bauernbursche *m*

swallow ['swɑlo] *s* Schluck *m;* (orn) Schwalbe *f* ‖ *tr* schlucken; (fig) hinunterschlucken ‖ *intr* schlucken; **s. the wrong way** sich verschlucken

swamp [swɑmp] *s* Sumpf *m,* Moor *n* ‖ *tr* überfluten; (*with work*) überhäufen

swamp'land' *s* Moorland *n*

swampy ['swɑmpi] *adj* sumpfig

swan [swɑn] *s* Schwan *m*

swan' dive' *s* Schwalbensprung *m*

swank [swæŋk]**, swanky** ['swæŋki] *adj* (*luxurious*) schick; (*ostentatious*) protzig

swan's'-down' *s* Schwanendaunen *pl*

swan' song' *s* Schwanengesang *m*

swap [swɑp] *s* (coll) Tauschgeschäft *n* ‖ *v* (*pret & pp* **swapped; ger swapping**) *tr & intr* (coll) tauschen

swarm [swɑrm] *s* Schwarm *m;* (*of children*) Schar *f* ‖ *intr* schwärmen; **s. around** umschwärmen; **s. into** sich drängen in (*acc*); **s. with** (fig) wimmeln von

swarthy ['swɔrði] *adj* dunkelhäutig

swashbuckler ['swɑʃ ˌbʌklər] *s* Eisenfresser *m*

swastika ['swɑstɪkə] *s* Hakenkreuz *n*

swat [swɑt] *s* Schlag *m* ‖ (*pret & pp* **swatted; ger swatting**) *tr* schlagen

swath [swɑθ] *s* Schwaden *m*

swathe [sweð] *tr* umwickeln, einwickeln

sway [swe] *s* Schwanken *n,* Schwingen *n;* (*domination*) Herrschaft *f* ‖ *tr* (*e.g., tree*) hin- und herbewegen; (*influence*) beeinflussen; (*cause to vacillate*) ins Wanken bringen ‖ *intr* schwanken

sway'-back' *s* Senkrücken *m*

swear [swer] *v* (*pret* **swore** [swor]; *pp* **sworn** [sworn]) *tr* schwören; **s. in** vereidigen; **s. s.o. to secrecy** j-n auf Geheimhaltung vereidigen ‖ *intr* schwören; (coll) fluchen; **s. at** schimpfen über (*acc*) or auf (*acc*); **s. by** schwören bei; **s. off** abschwören (*dat*); **s. on a stack of Bibles** Stein und Bein schwören; **s. to** (*a statement*) beschwören; **s. to it** darauf schwören

swear'ing-in' *s* Vereidigung *f*

swear'word' *s* Fluchwort *n*

sweat [swet] *s* Schweiß *m;* **break out in s.** in Schweiß geraten ‖ *v* (*pret & pp* **sweat & sweated**) *tr* (*blood*) schwitzen; (*metal*) seigern; (*a horse*) in Schweiß bringen; **s. off** abschwitzen; **s. out** (sl) geduldig abwarten; **s. up** durchschwitzen ‖ *intr* schwitzen

sweater ['swetər] *s* Sweater *m,* Pullover *m*

sweat'er girl' *s* vollbusiges Mädchen *n*

sweat' shirt' *s* Trainingsbluse *f*

sweat' shop' *s* (sl) Knochenmühle *f*

sweaty ['sweti] *adj* verschwitzt; (*hand*) schweißig

Swede [swid] *s* Schwede *m,* Schwedin *f*

Swedish ['swidɪʃ] *adj* schwedisch ‖ *s* Schwedisch *n*

sweep [swip] *s* (*sweeper*) Kehrer –in *mf;* (*of the arm, scythe, weapon*) Schwung *m;* (*of an oar*) Schlag *m;* (*range*) Reichweite *f;* (*continuous stretch*) ausgedehnte Strecke *f;* **in one clean s.** mit e-m Schlag; **make a clean s. of it** reinen Tisch machen ‖ *v* (*pret & pp* **swept** [swept]) *tr* kehren, fegen; (*mines*) räumen; (*with machine-gun fire*) bestreichen; (*with a searchlight*) absuchen; **he swept her off her feet** er hat sie im Sturm erobert; **s. clean** reinemachen ‖ *intr* kehren, fegen

sweeper ['swipər] *s* Kehrer –in *mf;* (*carpet sweeper*) Teppichkehrer *m*

sweep'ing *adj* weitreichend ‖ **sweepings** *spl* Kehricht *m & n*

sweep'-sec'ond *s* Zentralsekundenzeiger *m*

sweep'stakes' *s & spl* Lotterie *f;* (sport) Toto *m & n*

sweet [swit] *adj* süß; (*person*) lieb; (*butter*) ungesalzen; **be s. on** scharf sein auf (*acc*) ‖ **sweets** *spl* Süßigkeiten *pl*

sweet'bread' *s* Bries *n*

sweet'bri'er *s* Heckenrose *f*

sweet' corn' *s* Zuckermais *m*

sweeten ['switən] *tr* süßen; (fig) versüßen ‖ *intr* süß(er) werden

sweet'heart' *s* Liebste *mf,* Schatz *m*

sweetish ['switɪʃ] *adj* süßlich

sweet' mar'joram *s* Gartenmajoran *m*

sweet'meats' *spl* Zuckerwerk *n*

sweetness ['switnɪs] *s* Süßigkeit *f*

sweet' pea' *s* Gartenwicke *f*

sweet' pep'per *s* grüner Paprika *m*

sweet' pota'to *s* Süßkartoffel *f*

sweet'-scent'ed *adj* wohlriechend

sweet' tooth' *s*—**have a s.** gern naschen

sweet' wil'liam *s* Fleischnelke *f*

swell [swel] *adj* (coll) prima ‖ *s* (*of the sea*) Wellengang *m;* (*of an organ*) Schweller *m* ‖ *v* (*pret* **swelled;** *pp* **swelled & swollen** ['swolən]) *tr* zum Schwellen bringen; (*the number*) vermehren; (*a musical tone*) anschwellen lassen ‖ *intr* schwellen

swell'ing *s* Schwellung *f*

swelter ['sweltər] *intr* unter der Hitze leiden

swept'-back' *adj* (aer) keilförmig

swerve [swʌrv] *s* Abweichung *f* ‖ *tr* ablenken ‖ *intr* scharf abbiegen

swift [swɪft] *adj* geschwind, rasch

swig [swɪg] *s* (coll) kräftiger Schluck

m ‖ *v* (*pret & pp* **swigged***; ger* **swigging**) *tr* in langen Zügen trinken

swill [swɪl] *s* Spülicht *n;* (*for swine*) Schweinefutter *n;* (*deep drink*) tüchtiger Schluck *m* ‖ *tr & intr* gierig trinken

swim [swɪm] *s* Schwimmen *n;* **take a s.** schwimmen ‖ *v* (*pret* **swam** [swæm]*; pp* **swum** [swʌm]*; ger* **swimming**) *tr* (*e.g., a lake*) durchschwimmen; (*cause to swim*) schwimmen lassen; (*challenge in swimming*) um die Wette schwimmen mit ‖ *intr* schwimmen; **my head is swimming** mir schwindelt der Kopf

swimmer [ˈswɪmər] *s* Schwimmer –in *mf*

swim′ming *adj* Schwimm– ‖ *s* Schwimmen *n;* (sport) Schwimmsport *m*

swim′ming pool′ *s* Schwimmbecken *n*

swim′ming suit′ *s* Badeanzug *m*

swim′ming trunks′ *spl* Badehose *f*

swindle [ˈswɪndəl] *s* Schwindel *m* ‖ *tr* gaunern; **s. s.th. out of** etw erschwindeln von

swindler [ˈswɪndlər] *s* Schwindler –in *mf*

swind′ling *s* Schwindelei *f*

swine [swaɪn] *s* Schwein *n*

swine′herd′ *s* Schweinehirt *m*

swing [swɪŋ] *s* (*for children*) Schaukel *f;* (*swinging movement*) Hin– und Herschwingen *n;* (box) Schwinger *m;* (mus) Swing *m;* **in full s.** in vollem Gang; **take a s. at s.o.** nach j–m schlagen ‖ *v* (*pret & pp* **swung** [swʌŋ]) *tr* schwingen; (*children on a swing*) schaukeln; (*an election*) entscheidend beeinflussen; **s.** (*e.g., a car*) **around** herumdrehen; **we'll s. it somehow** (coll) wir werden es schon schaffen ‖ *intr* pendeln; (*on a swing*) schaukeln; **s. around** sich umdrehen; **s. into action** in Schwung kommen; **things are swinging around here** (coll) hier geht es lustig zu

swing′ing door′ *s* Pendeltür *f*

swinish [ˈswaɪnɪʃ] *adj* schweinisch

swipe [swaɪp] *s* (coll) Hieb *m;* **take a s. at** (coll) schlagen nach ‖ *tr* (*hit with full force*) (coll) kräftig schlagen; (*steal*) (sl) mausen

swirl [swʌrl] *s* Wirbel *m* ‖ *tr* (**about**) herumwirbeln ‖ *intr* wirbeln; (*said of water*) Strudel bilden

swish [swɪʃ] *s* (*e.g., of a whip*) Sausen *n;* (*of a dress*) Rauschen *n* ‖ *tr* (*a whip*) sausen lassen; **s. its tail** mit dem Schwanz wedeln ‖ *intr* (*said of a whip*) sausen; (*said of a dress*) rauschen

Swiss [swɪs] *adj* schweizerisch ‖ *s* Schweizer –in *mf*

Swiss′ cheese′ *s* Schweizer Käse *m*

Swiss′ franc′ *s* Schweizerfranken *m*

Swiss′ Guard′ *s* Schweizergarde *f*

switch [swɪtʃ] *s* (*exchange*) Wechsel *m,* Umschwung *m;* (*stick*) Rute *f;* (elec) Schalter *m;* (rr) Weiche *f* ‖ *tr* wechseln; (*e.g., coats by mistake*) verwechseln; (rr) rangieren; **s. off** (elec, rad, telv) ausschalten; **s. on**

(elec, rad, telv) einschalten ‖ *intr* Plätze wechseln

switch′-blade knife′ *s* feststellbares Messer *n*

switch′board′ *s* Schaltbrett *n,* Zentrale *f*

switch′board op′erator *s* Telephonist –in *mf*

switch′ box′ *s* Schaltkasten *m*

switch′man *s* (–men) (rr) Weichensteller *m*

switch′ tow′er *s* (rr) Blockstation *f*

switch′yard′ *s* Rangierbahnhof *m*

Switzerland [ˈswɪtsərlənd] *s* die Schweiz

swiv·el [ˈswɪvəl] *s* Drehlager *n* ‖ *v* (*pret & pp* **-el[l]ed***; ger* **-el[l]ing**) *tr* herumdrehen ‖ *intr* sich drehen

swiv′el chair′ *s* Drehstuhl *m*

swiz′zle stick′ [ˈswɪzəl] *s* Rührstäbchen *n*

swollen [ˈswolən] *adj* (an)geschwollen; (*eyes*) verquollen

swoon [swun] *s* Ohnmacht *f* ‖ *intr* ohnmächtig werden

swoop [swup] *s* Herabstoßen *n;* **in one fell s.** mit e–m Schlag ‖ *intr*—**s. down** (**on**) herabstoßen (auf *acc*)

sword [sord] *s* Schwert *n;* **put to the s.** mit dem Schwert hinrichten

sword′ belt′ *s* Schwertgehenk *n*

sword′fish′ *s* Schwertfisch *m*

swords′man *s* (–men) Fechter *m*

sworn [sworn] *adj* (*statement*) eidlich; **s. enemy** Todfeind *m*

sycamore [ˈsɪkəmor] *s* Platane *f*

sycophant [ˈsɪkəfənt] *s* Sykophant *m*

syllabary [ˈsɪləˌbɛri] *s* Silbenschrift *f*

syllabification [sɪˌlæbɪfɪˈkeʃən] *s* Silbentrennung *f*

syllable [ˈsɪləbəl] *s* Silbe *f*

sylla·bus [ˈsɪləbəs] *s* (**–bi** [ˌbaɪ] & **–buses**) Lehrplan *m*

syllogism [ˈsɪləˌdʒɪzəm] *s* Syllogismus *m*

sylvan [ˈsɪlvən] *adj* Wald–

symbol [ˈsɪmbəl] *s* Sinnbild *n,* Symbol *n*

symbolic(al) [sɪmˈbɑlɪk(əl)] *adj* sinnbildlich, symbolisch

symbolism [ˈsɪmbəˌlɪzəm] *s* Symbolik *f*

symbolize [ˈsɪmbəˌlaɪz] *tr* symbolisieren

symmetric(al) [sɪˈmɛtrɪk(əl)] *adj* symmetrisch

symmetry [ˈsɪmɪtri] *s* Symmetrie *f*

sympathetic [ˌsɪmpəˈθɛtɪk] *adj* mitfühlend; (physiol) sympathisch

sympathize [ˈsɪmpəˌθaɪz] *intr*—**s. with** mitfühlen mit; (*be in accord with*) sympathisieren mit

sympathizer [ˈsɪmpəˌθaɪzər] *s* Sympathisant –in *mf*

sympathy [ˈsɪmpəθi] *s* Mitleid *n;* **be in s. with** inr Einverständnis sein mit; **offer one's sympathies to s.o.** j–m sein Beileid bezeigen

sym′pathy card′ *s* Beileidskarte *f*

sym′pathy strike′ *s* Sympathiestreik *m*

symphonic [sɪmˈfɑnɪk] *adj* sinfonisch

symphony [ˈsɪmfəni] *s* Sinfonie *f*

symposi·um [sɪm'pozi·əm] *s* (-a [ə] & -ums) Symposion *n*

symptom ['sɪmptəm] *s* (of) Symptom *n* (für)

symptomatic [ˌsɪmtə'mætɪk] *adj* (of) symptomatisch (für)

synagogue ['sɪnə͵gog] *s* Synagoge *f*

synchronize ['sɪŋkrə͵naɪz] *tr* synchronisieren

synchronous ['sɪŋkrənəs] *adj* synchron; (elec) Synchron–

syncopate ['sɪŋkə͵pet] *tr* synkopieren

syncopation [ˌsɪŋkə'peʃən] *s* Synkope *f*

syncope ['sɪŋkə͵pi] *s* Synkope *f*

syndicate ['sɪndɪkɪt] *s* Interessengemeinschaft *f*, Syndikat *n* || ['sɪndɪ͵ket] *tr* zu e–m Syndikat zusammenschließen; (a column) in mehreren Zeitungen zugleich veröffentlichen || *intr* ein Syndikat bilden

synod ['sɪnəd] *s* Synode *f*

synonym ['sɪnənɪm] *s* Synonym *n*

synonymous [sɪ'nɑnəməs] *adj* sinnverwandt; **s. with** gleichbedeutend mit

synop·sis [sɪ'nɑpsɪs] *s* (-ses [siz]) Zusammenfassung *f*

synoptic [sɪ'nɑptɪk] *adj* synoptisch

syntax ['sɪntæks] *s* Satzlehre *f*, Syntax *f*

synthe·sis ['sɪnθɪsɪs] *s* (-ses [ˌsiz]) Synthese *f*

synthesize ['sɪnθɪ͵saɪz] *tr* (& chem) zusammenfügen

synthetic [sɪn'θetɪk] *adj* künstlich, Kunst– || *s* Kunststoff *m*

syphilis ['sɪfɪlɪs] *s* Syphilis *f*

Syria ['sɪrɪ·ə] *s* Syrien *n*

Syrian ['sɪrɪ·ən] *adj* syrisch || *s* Syrer –in *mf*; (language) Syrisch *n*

syringe [sɪ'rɪndʒ] *s* Spritze *f* || *tr* (inject) einspritzen; (wash) ausspritzen

syrup ['sɪrəp] *s* Sirup *m*

system ['sɪstəm] *s* System *n*; (bodily system) Organismus *m*

systematic(al) [ˌsɪstə'mætɪk(əl)] *adj* systematisch, planmäßig

systematize ['sɪstəmə͵taɪz] *tr* systematisieren, systematisch ordnen

systole ['sɪstəli] *s* Systole *f*

T

T, t [ti] *s* zwanzigster Buchstabe des englischen Alphabets

tab [tæb] *s* (label) Etikett *n*; (on file cards) Karteireiter *m*; **keep tabs on** (coll) genau kontrollieren; **pick up the tab** (coll) die Zeche bezahlen || *v* (pret & pp tabbed; ger tabbing) *tr* (designate) ernennen

tabby ['tæbi] *s* getigerte Katze *f*

tabernacle ['tæbər͵nækəl] *s* Tabernakel *n*

table ['tebəl] *s* Tisch *m*; (list, chart) Tafel *f*, Tabelle *f*; (geol) Tafel *f*; **at t.** bei Tisch; **the tables have turned** das Blatt hat sich gewendet || *tr* (parl) verschieben

tab·leau ['tæblo] *s* (-leaus & leaux [loz]) Tableau *n*

ta'blecloth' *s* Tischtuch *n*

ta'bleland' *s* Tafelland *n*

ta'ble man'ners *spl* Tischmanieren *pl*

ta'ble of con'tents *s* Inhaltsverzeichnis *n*

ta'ble salt' *s* Tafelsalz *n*

ta'ble set'ting *s* Gedeck *n*

ta'blespoon' *s* Eßlöffel *m*

tablespoonful ['tebəl͵spun͵ful] *s* Eßlöffel *m*

tablet ['tæblɪt] *s* (writing pad) Schreibblock *m*; (med) Tablette *f*

ta'ble talk' *s* Tischgespräch *n*

ta'ble ten'nis *s* Tischtennis *n*

ta'bletop' *s* Tischplatte *f*

ta'bleware' *s* Tafelgeschirr *n*

ta'ble wine' *s* Tafelwein *m*

tabloid ['tæblɔɪd] *adj* konzentriert || *s* Bildzeitung *f*; (pej) Sensationsblatt *n*

taboo [tə'bu] *adj* tabu || *s* Tabu *n* || *tr* für Tabu erklären

tabular ['tæbjələr] *adj* tabellarisch

tabulate ['tæbjə͵let] *tr* tabellarisieren

tabulator ['tæbjə͵letər] *s* Tabelliermaschine *f*

tacit ['tæsɪt] *adj* stillschweigend

taciturn ['tæsɪtərn] *adj* schweigsam

tack [tæk] *s* (nail) Zwecke *f*, Stift *m*; (stitch) Heftstich *m*; (stickiness) Klebrigkeit *f*; (course of action) Kurs *m*; (gear for a riding horse) Reitgeschirr *n*; (course run obliquely to the wind) Schlag *m*; **be on the wrong t.** (fig) auf dem Holzweg sein || *tr* (down) mit Zwecken befestigen; (sew) heften; **t. on** (to) anfügen (an acc) || *intr* (fig & naut) lavieren

tackle ['tækəl] *s* (gear) Ausrüstung *f*; (for lifting) Flaschenzug *m*; (fb) Halbstürmer *m*; (naut) Takelwerk *n* || *tr* (a problem) anpacken; (fb) packen

tacky ['tæki] *adj* klebrig; (gaudy) geschmacklos

tact [tækt] *s* Takt *m*, Feingefühl *n*

tactful ['tæktfəl] *adj* taktvoll

tactical ['tæktɪkəl] *adj* taktisch

tac'tical u'nit *s* Kampfeinheit *f*

tactician [tæk'tɪʃən] *s* Taktiker *m*

tactics ['tæktɪks] *spl* (& fig) Taktik *f*

tactless ['tæktlɪs] *adj* taktlos

tadpole ['tæd͵pol] *s* Kaulquappe *f*

taffeta ['tæfɪtə] *s* Taft *m*

taffy ['tæfi] *s* Sahnebonbon *m*

tag [tæg] *s* (label) Etikett *n*; (loose end) loses Ende *n*; (on a shoestring) Stift *m*; (loop for hanging up a coat) Aufhänger *m*; (on a fish hook) Glitzerschmuck *m*; (game) Haschen *n*; **play tag** sich haschen; **tags** (aut)

Nummernschild *n* ‖ *v* (*pret & pp* **tagged**; *ger* **tagging**) *tr* (*mark with a tag*) mit e–m Etikett versehen; (*touch*) haschen; (*hit solidly*) heftig schlagen; (*give a traffic ticket to*) e–n Strafzettel geben (*dat*) ‖ *intr*—**tag after** s.o. sich an j–s Sohlen heften

tag′ line′ *s* (*e.g., of a play*) Schlußworte *pl*; (*favorite phrase*) stehende Redensart *f*

tail [tel] *s* Schwanz *m*; (*of a horse, comet*) Schweif *m*; (*of a shirt*) Schoß *m*; (*aer*) Heck *n*; tails ein Frack *m*; (*of a coin*) Rückseite *f*; **turn t.** ausreißen; **wag its t.** mit dem Schwanz wedeln ‖ *tr* (coll) beschatten ‖ *intr*—**t. after** nachlaufen (*dat*); **t. off** abflauen

tail′ end′ *s* (*e.g., of a conversation*) Schlußteil *n*; **come in at the t. end** als letzter durchs Ziel gehen

tail′gate′ *s* (*of a station wagon*) Hecktür *f*; (*of a truck*) Ladeklappe *f* ‖ *intr* dicht hinter e–m anderen fahren

tail′ gun′ner *s* (aer) Heckschütze *m*

tail′-heav′y *adj* schwanzlastig

tail′light′ *s* (aer) Hecklicht *n*; (aut) Rücklicht *n*

tailor ['telər] *s* Schneider *m* ‖ *tr & intr* schneidern

tai′loring *s* Schneiderarbeit *f*

tai′lor-made suit′ *s* Maßanzug *m*

tai′lor shop′ *s* Schneiderei *f*

tail′piece′ *s* (*appendage*) Anhang *m*; (*of a stringed instrument*) Saitenhalter *m*; (typ) Zierleiste *f*

tail′ pipe′ *s* (aut) Auspuffrohr *n*

tail′skid′ *s* (aer) Sporn *m*

tail′spin′ *s*—**go into a t.** abtrudeln

tail′ wheel′ *s* (aer) Spornrad *n*

tail′wind′ *s* Rückenwind *m*

taint [tent] *s* Fleck *m*; (fig) Schandfleck *m* ‖ *tr* beflecken; (*food*) verderben

take [tek] *s* (*income*) (sl) Einnahmen *pl*; (*loot*) (sl) Beute *f*; (angl) Fang *m*; (cin) Szenenaufnahme *f*; **be on the t.** (sl) sich bestechen lassen ‖ *v* (*pret & pp* [tuk]; *pp* **taken**) *tr* nehmen; (*in a car*) mitnehmen; (*bring, carry*) bringen; (*subtract*) abziehen; (*require*) erfordern; (*insults, criticism*) hinnehmen; (*bear, stand*) ertragen; (*with a camera*) aufnehmen; (*food, pills*) einnehmen; (s.o.'s *temperature*) messen; (*courage*) schöpfen; (*a deep breath*) holen; (*precautions*) treffen; (*responsibility*) übernehmen; (*an oath, test*) ablegen; (*inventory*) aufnehmen; (*a walk, trip, examination, turn, notes*) machen; (*the consequences*) tragen; (*measures*) ergreifen; (*a certain amount of time to travel*) in Anspruch nehmen; (*a step*) tun; (*advice*) befolgen; (*a game*) gewinnen; (*e.g., third place*) belegen; (*a trick*) (cards) stechen; (gram) regieren; **be able to t. a lot** e–n breiten Rücken haben; **be taken in by** s.o. j–m auf den Leim gehen; **I'm not going to t. that**

das lasse ich nicht auf mir sitzen; **t. along** mitnehmen; **t. aside** beiseitenehmen; **t. at one's word** beim Wort nehmen; **t. away** wegschaffen; **t. away from** wegnehmen (*dat*); **t. back** zurücknehmen; **t.** (*e.g., s.o.'s hat*) **by mistake** verwechseln; **t. down** herunternehmen; (*in writing*) aufschreiben; (*dictation*) aufnehmen; (*minutes*) zu Protokoll nehmen; **t. in** (*money*) einnehmen; (*washing*) ins Haus nehmen; (*as guest*) beherbergen; (*deceive*) täuschen; (*encompass*) umfassen; (*observe*) beobachten; (*sightsee*) besichtigen; (*sew*) enger machen; **t. it out on** s.o. seinen Zorn an j–m auslassen; **t. it that** annehmen, daß; **taken** (*occupied*) besetzt; **t. off** (*subtract*) abziehen; (*clothes*) ausziehen; (*a coat*) ablegen; (*gloves*) abstreifen; (*a hat*) abnehmen; (*a tire, wheel*) abmontieren; (*e.g., a day from work*) sich [*dat*] freinehmen; **t.** (*e.g., wares*) **off** s.o.'s **hands** j–m abnehmen; **t. on** (*hire*) anstellen; (*passengers*) aufnehmen; **t. out** (*from a container*) herausnehmen; (*a spot*) entfernen; (*a girl*) ausführen; (*a mortgage, loan*) aufnehmen; (ins) abschließen; (libr) sich [*dat*] ausleihen; **t. over** übernehmen; **t. s.o. for** j–n halten für; **t. up** aufnehmen; (*absorb*) aufsaugen; (*a profession*) ergreifen; (*room, time*) wegnehmen; (*a collection*) veranstalten; (*a skirt*) kürzer machen; **t. upon oneself** auf sich nehmen; **t. up** (*a matter*) with besprechen mit ‖ *intr* (*said of an injection*) anschlagen; (*said of seedlings, skin transplants*) anwachsen; **how long does it t.?** wie lange dauert es?; **how long does it t. to** (*inf*)? wie lange braucht man, um zu (*inf*)?; **t. after** nachgeraten (*dat*); **t. off** (*depart*) (coll) abhauen; (*from work*) wegbleiben; (aer, rok) starten; (aut) abfahren; **t. over for** s.o. für j–n einspringen; **t. to** (*a person*) warm werden mit; (*an idea*) aufgreifen; **t. up with** sich abgeben mit

take′-home pay′ *s* Nettolohn *m*

take′-off′ *s* Karikatur *f*; (aer) Start *m*

take′-off ramp′ *s* (in skiing) Schanzentisch *m*

take′o′ver *s* Übernahme *f*

tal′cum pow′der ['tælkəm] *s* Federweiß *n*

tale [tel] *s* Geschichte *f*; **tell tales out of school** aus der Schule plaudern

tale′bear′er *s* Zuträger –in *mf*

talent ['tælənt] *s* Talent *n*

tal′ented *adj* talentiert, begabt

talisman ['tælɪsmən] *s* Talisman *m*

talk [tɔk] *s* Gespräch *n*; (*gossip*) Geschwätz *n*; (*lecture*) Vortrag *m*; (*speech*) Rede *f*; **cause t.** von sich reden machen; **give a t. on** e–n Vortrag halten über (*acc*); **t. of the town** Stadtgespräch *n* ‖ *tr* reden; (*business, politics, etc.*) sprechen über (*acc*); **t. down** zum Schweigen bringen; (aer) heruntersprechen; **t. one-**

self hoarse sich heiser reden; **t. one's way out of** sich herausreden aus; **t. over** besprechen; **t. sense** vernünftig reden; **t. s.o. into** (ger) j-n überreden zu (inf); **t. up** Reklame machen für ‖ intr reden; (chat) schwätzen; **t. back** scharf erwidern; **t. big** große Töne reden; **t. dirty** Zoten reißen; **t. down to** herablassend reden zu; **talking of food** a propos Essen; **t. on** (a topic) e-n Vortrag halten über (acc); **t. to the walls** in den Wind reden

talkative ['tɔkətɪv] adj redselig

talker ['tɔkər] s Plauderer –in mf; **big t.** Schaumschläger m

talkie ['tɔki] s (cin) Sprechfilm m

talk'ing-to' s Denkzettel m

tall [tɔl] adj hoch; (person) hochgewachsen; **t. story** Mordsgeschichte f

tallow ['tælo] s Talg m

tal·ly ['tæli] s (reckoning) Rechnung f; (game score) Punktzahl f ‖ v (pret & pp –lied) tr (up) berechnen ‖ intr (with) übereinstimmen (mit)

tallyho [,tæli'ho] interj hallo!

tal'ly sheet' s Zählbogen m

talon ['tælən] s Klaue f

tambourine [,tæmbə'rin] s Tamburin n

tame [tem] adj zahm; (docile) gefügig; (dull) langweilig ‖ tr zähmen; (e.g., lions) bändigen ‖ intr—**t. down** (said of a person) gesetzter werden

tamp [tæmp] tr (a tobacco pipe) stopfen; (earth, cement) stampfen; (a drill hole) zustopfen

tamper ['tæmpər] s Stampfer m ‖ intr—**t. with** sich einmischen in (acc); (machinery) herumbasteln an (dat); (documents) frisieren

tampon ['tæmpɑn] s Damenbinde f; (surg) Tampon m ‖ tr (surg) tamponieren

tan [tæn] adj gelbbraun ‖ v (pret & pp tanned; ger tanning) tr (the skin) bräunen; (leather) gerben ‖ intr sich bräunen

tandem ['tændəm] adj & adv hintereinander (geordnet) ‖ s Tandem n; **in t.** hintereinander

tang [tæŋ] s Herbheit f; (sound) Geklingel n

tangent ['tændʒənt] adj—**be t. to** tangieren ‖ s Tangente f; **fly off on a t.** plötzlich vom Thema abschweifen

tangerine [,tændʒə'rin] s Mandarine f

tangible ['tændʒɪbəl] adj (& fig) greifbar

tangle ['tæŋgəl] s Verwicklung f; (twisted strands; confused jumble) Gewirr n; (conflict) Auseinandersetzung f ‖ tr verwirren; **get tangled** sich verfilzen ‖ intr sich verwirren; **t. with** sich in e-n Kampf einlassen mit

tango ['tæŋgo] s Tango m ‖ intr Tango tanzen

tangy ['tæŋi] adj herb

tank [tæŋk] s Behälter m; (of a toilet) Spülkasten m; (mil) Panzer m

tank' attack' s Panzerangriff m

tank' car' s (rr) Kesselwagen m, Tankwagen m

tanker ['tæŋkər] s (truck) Tankwagen m; (ship) Tanker m; (plane) Tankflugzeug n

tank' trap' s Panzersperre f

tank' truck' s Tankwagen m

tanned adj gebräunt

tanner ['tænər] s Gerber –in mf

tannery ['tænəri] s Gerberei f

tantalize ['tæntə,laɪz] tr quälen

tantamount ['tæntə,maʊnt] adj—**be t. to** gleichkommen (dat)

tantrum ['tæntrəm] s Koller m; **throw a t.** e-n Koller kriegen

tap [tæp] s (light blow) Klaps m; (on a window or door) Klopfen n; (faucet) Wasserhahn m; (in a cask) Faßhahn m; (elec) Anzapfung f; (mach) Gewindebohrer m; (surg) Punktion f; **on tap** vom Faß; **play taps** (mil) den Zapfenstreich blasen ‖ v (pret & pp tapped; ger tapping) tr (a cask, powerline, telephone) anzapfen; (fluids) abzapfen; (a person on the shoulder) antippen; (a hole) mit e–m Gewinde versehen; **tap one's foot** (to mark time) Takt treten; **tap s.o. for** (money) (coll) j-n anpumpen um; **tap s.o.'s spine** j-n punktieren; **tap the window** am Fenster klopfen ‖ intr tippen

tap' dance' s Steptanz m

tap'-dance' intr steppen

tap' dan'cer s Stepper –in mf

tape [tep] s Band n; (electron) Tonband n; (friction tape) Isolierband n; (of paper) Papierstreifen m; (med) Klebstreifen m; (sport) Zielband n ‖ tr (mit Band) umwickeln; (electron) auf Tonband aufnehmen

tape' meas'ure s Meßband n

taper ['tepər] s Wachsfaden m ‖ tr zuspitzen ‖ intr spitz zulaufen; **t. off** langsam abnehmen

tape' record'er s Tonbandgerät n

ta'pered adj kegelförmig, Keil-

tapestry ['tæpɪstri] s Wandteppich m

tape'worm' s Bandwurm m

tapioca [,tæpɪ'okə] s Tapioka f

tappet ['tæpɪt] s (mach) Stößel m

tap'room' s Ausschank m

tap'root' s Pfahlwurzel f

tap' wa'ter s Leitungswasser n

tap' wrench' s Gewindeschneidkluppe f

tar [tɑr] s Teer m ‖ v (pret & pp tarred; ger tarring) tr teeren

tardy ['tɑrdi] adj säumig

target ['tɑrgɪt] s Ziel n; (on a firing range; of ridicule) Zielscheibe f

tar'get ar'ea s Zielraum m

tar'get date' s Zieltag m

tar'get lan'guage s Zielsprache f

tar'get prac'tice s Scheibenschießen n

tariff ['tærɪf] s Tarif m

tarnish ['tɑrnɪʃ] tr matt (or blind) machen; (fig) beflecken ‖ intr matt (or blind) werden

tar'pa'per s Teerpappe f

tarpaulin ['tɑrpəlɪn] s Plane f

tar·ry ['tɑri] adj teerig ‖ ['tæri] v

(*pret & pp* **–ried**) *intr* verweilen; (*stay*) bleiben

tart [tɑrt] *adj* sauer; (*reply*) scharf || *s* Törtelett *n*

tartar ['tɑrtər] *s* (dent) Zahnstein *m*

tar'tar sauce' *s* pikante Soße *f*

task [tæsk] *s* Aufgabe *f*; **take to t.** zur Rede stellen

task' force' *s* Sonderverband *m*

task'mas'ter *s* Zuchtmeister *m*

tassel ['tæsəl] *s* Quaste *f*; (*on corn*) Narbenfäden *pl*

taste [test] *s* (& *fig*) Geschmack *m*; **develop a t. for** Geschmack gewinnen an (*dat*); **have a bad t.** schlecht || *intr*—**t.** like (or of) schmecken schmecken; **have bad t.** e-n schlechten Geschmack haben; **in bad t.** geschmacklos; **in good t.** geschmackvoll; **to t.** (*culin*) nach Gutdünken || *tr* schmecken; (*try out*) kosten; (*e.g., the pepper in soup*) herausschmecken; **t. blood** (*fig*) Blut lecken nach

taste' bud' *s* Geschmacksknospe *f*

tasteful ['testfəl] *adj* geschmackvoll

tasteless ['testlɪs] *adj* (& *fig*) geschmacklos

tasty ['testi] *adj* schmackhaft

tatter ['tætər] *s* Lumpen *m* || *tr* zerfetzen

tat'tered *adj* zerlumpt

tattle ['tætəl] *intr* petzen

tattler ['tætlər] *s* Petze *f*

tat'tletale' *s* Petze *f*

tattoo [tæ'tu] *s* Tätowierung *f* || *tr* tätowieren

taunt [tɔnt] *s* Stichelei *f* || *tr* sticheln gegen

taut [tɔt] *adj* straff, prall

tavern ['tævərn] *s* Schenke *f*

tawdry ['tɔdri] *adj* aufgedonnert

tawny ['tɔni] *adj* gelbbraun

tax [tæks] *s* Steuer *f* || *tr* besteuern; (*fig*) beanspruchen; **tax s.o. with** j–n rügen wegen

taxable ['tæksəbəl] *adj* steuerpflichtig

tax' assess'ment *s* Steuereinschätzung *f*

taxation [tæk'seʃən] *s* Besteuerung *f*

tax' brac'ket *s* Steuerklasse *f*

tax' collec'tor *s* Steuereinnehmer –in *mf*

tax' cut' *s* Steuersenkung *f*

tax' eva'sion *s* Steuerhinterziehung *f*

tax' exemp'tion *s* steuerfreier Betrag *m*

tax-i ['tæksi] *s* Taxi *n*; **go by t.** mit e–m Taxi fahren || *v* (*pret & pp* **–ied**) *ger* **–iing** & **–ying**) *tr* (aer) rollen lassen || *intr* mit e–m Taxi fahren; (aer) rollen

tax'icab' *s* Taxi *n*

tax'i danc'er *s* Taxigirl *n*

taxidermist ['tæksɪ,dʌrmɪst] *s* Tierpräparator –in *mf*

tax'i driv'er *s* Taxifahrer –in *mf*

tax'ime'ter *s* Taxameter *m*

tax'i stand' *s* Taxistand *m*

tax'pay'er *s* Steuerzahler –in *mf*

tax' rate' *s* Steuersatz *m*

tax' return' *s* Steuererklärung *f*

tea [ti] *s* Tee *m*

tea' bag' *s* Teebeutel *m*

tea' cart' *s* Teewagen *m*

teach [titʃ] *v* (*pret & pp* **taught** [tɔt]) *tr* lehren; (*instruct*) unterrichten; **t. school** an e–r Schule unterrichten; **t. s.o. manners** j–m Manieren beibringen; **t. s.o. music** j–n in Musik unterrichten; **t. s.o.** (**to play**) **tennis** j–m das Tennisspielen beibringen || *intr* lehren, unterrichten

teacher ['titʃər] *s* Lehrer –in *mf*

teach'er's pet' *s* Liebling *m* des Lehrers (or der Lehrerin)

teach'ing *s* Lehren *n*; (*profession*) Lehrberuf *m*

teach'ing aid' *s* Lehrmittel *n*

teach'ing staff' *s* Lehrkörper *m*

tea'cup' *s* Teetasse *f*

teak [tik] *s* Teakholz *n*

tea'ket'tle *s* Teekessel *m*

tea' leaves' *spl* Teesatz *m*

team [tim] *s* Team *n*; (*of draught animals*) Gespann *n*; (*sport*) Mannschaft *f* || *tr* (*draft animals*) zusammenspannen || *intr*—**t. up with** sich vereinigen mit

team' cap'tain *s* Spielführer –in *mf*

team'mate' *s* Mannschaftskamerad –in *mf*

teamster ['timstər] *s* Fuhrmann *m*; (*trucker*) Lastwagenfahrer *m*

team'work' *s* Gemeinschaftsarbeit *f*; (sport) Zusammenspiel *n*

tea'pot' *s* Teekanne *f*

tear [tɪr] *s* Träne *f*; **bring tears to the eyes** Tränen in die Augen treiben; **burst into tears** in Tränen ausbrechen || [ter] *s* Riß *m* || *v* (*pret* **tore** [tor]; *pp* **torn** [torn]) *tr* (zer)reißen; **t. apart** (*meat*) zerreißen; (*a speech*) zerpflücken; **t. away** wegreißen; **t. down** (*a building*) abreißen; (*mach*) zerlegen; (*a person*) sich [*dat*] das Maul zerreißen über (*acc*); **t. off** abreißen; **t. open** aufreißen; **t. oneself away** sich losreißen; **t. out** ausreißen; **t. up** (*a street*) aufreißen; (*e.g., letter*) zerreißen || *intr* (zer)reißen; **t. along** (*at high speed*) dahinsausen

teardrop ['tɪr,drɑp] *s* Träne *f*

tear' gas' [tɪr] *s* Tränengas *n*

tear-jerker ['tɪr,dʒʌrkər] *s* (sl) Schnulze *f*

tea'room' *s* Teestube *f*

tease [tiz] *tr* necken; (*e.g., a dog*) quälen; (*hair*) auflockern

teas'ing *s* Neckerei *f*

tea'spoon' *s* Teelöffel *m*

teaspoonful ['ti,spun,ful] *s* Teelöffel *m*

teat [tit] *s* Zitze *f*

technical ['tɛknɪkəl] *adj* technisch, Fach–

tech'nical in'stitute *s* technische Hochschule *f*

technicality [,tɛknɪ'kælɪti] *s* technische Einzelheit *f*

tech'nical school' *s* Technikum *n*

tech'nical term' *s* Fachausdruck *m*

technician [tek'nɪʃən] *s* Techniker –in *mf*

technique [tɛk'nik] *s* Technik *f*

technocrat ['tɛknə‚kræt] s Technokrat m

technological [‚tɛknə'lɑdʒɪkəl] adj technologisch

technology [tɛk'nɑlɪdʒɪ] s Technologie f

ted'dy bear' ['tedɪ] s Teddybär m

tedious ['tidɪ‚əs] adj langweilig

tee [ti] s (mound) Abschlagplatz m; (wooden or plastic peg) Aufsatz m; **to a tee** aufs Haar || tr—**tee off** (sl) aufregen; **tee up** (golf) auf den Aufsatz stellen || intr—**tee off** (golf) abschlagen

teem [tim] intr (with) wimmeln (von)

teem'ing adj wimmelnd; (rain) strömend

teen-age ['tin ‚edʒ] adj halbwüchsig

teen-ager ['tin ‚edʒər] s Teenager m

teens [tinz] spl Jugendalter n (vom dreizehnten bis neunzehnten Lebensjahr); **in one's t.** in den Jugendjahren

teeny ['tini] adj (coll) winzig

tee' shot' (golf) Abschlag m

teeter ['titər] s Schaukeln n || intr schaukeln

teethe [tið] intr zahnen

teeth'ing ring' s Beißring m

teetotaler [ti'totələr] s Abstinenzler –in mf

tele·cast ['tɛlɪ ‚kæst] s Fernsehsendung f || v (pret & pp –cast & –casted) tr im Fernsehen übertragen

telecommunications [‚tɛlɪkə ‚mjunɪ'keʃəns] spl Fernmeldewesen n

telegram ['tɛlɪ ‚græm] s Telegramm n

telegraph ['tɛlɪ ‚græf] s Telegraph m || tr & intr telegraphieren

telegrapher [tɪ'lɛɡrəfər] s Telegraphist –in mf

tel'egraph pole' s Telegraphenstange f

telemeter [tɪ'lɛmɪtər] s Telemeter n

telepathy [tɪ'lɛpəθɪ] s Telepathie f

telephone ['tɛlɪ ‚fon] s Telephon n, Fernsprecher m; **be on the t.** am Apparat sein; **by t.** telephonisch; **speak on the t.** telephonieren mit || tr & intr anrufen

tel'ephone booth' s Telephonzelle f

tel'ephone call' s Telephonanruf m

tel'ephone direc'tory s Teilnehmerverzeichnis n

tel'ephone exchange' s Telephonzentrale f

tel'ephone num'ber s Telephonnummer f

tel'ephone op'erator s Telephonist –in f

tel'ephone receiv'er s Telephonhörer m

tel'ephoto lens' ['tɛlɪ ‚foto] s Teleobjektiv n

telescope ['tɛlɪ ‚skop] s Fernrohr n, Perspektiv n || tr ineinanderschieben; (fig) verkürzen || intr sich ineinanschieben

telescopic [‚tɛlɪ'skɑpɪk] adj teleskopisch

telescop'ic sight' s Zielfernrohr n

Teletype ['tɛlɪ ‚taɪp] s (trademark) Fernschreiber m || **teletype** tr durch Fernschreiber übermitteln || intr fernschreiben

tel'etype'writ'er s Fernschreiber m

televiewer ['tɛlɪ ‚vju·ər] s Fernsehteilnehmer –in mf

televise ['tɛlɪ ‚vaɪz] tr im Fernsehen übertragen (or senden)

television ['tɛlɪ ‚vɪʒən] adj Fernseh– || s Fernsehen n; **watch t.** fernsehen

tel'evision net'work s Fernsehnetz n

tel'evision screen' s Bildschirm m

tel'evision set' s Fernsehapparat m; **color t.** Farbfernsehapparat m

tel'evision show' s Fernschau f

telex ['tɛlɛks] s Fernschreiber m; (message) Telex n || tr fernschreiben

tell [tɛl] v (pret & pp **told** [told]) tr (the truth, a lie) sagen; (relate) erzählen; (a secret) anvertrauen; (let know) Bescheid sagen (dat); (inform) bestellen; (express) ausdrücken; (the reason) angeben; (distinguish) auseinanderhalten; **be able to t. time** die Uhr lesen können; **t. apart** auseinanderhalten; **t. me another!** (sl) das machst du mir nicht weis!; **t. s.o. off** j–n abkanzeln; **t. s.o. that** (assure s.o. that) j–m versichern, daß; **t. s.o. to** (inf) j–m sagen, daß er (inf) soll; **t. s.o. where to get off** (sl) j–m e–e Zigarre verpassen; **to t. the truth** ehrlich gesagt; **you can t. by looking at her** that man sieht es ihr an, daß || intr—**don't t. me!** na, so was!; **t. on** (betray) verraten; (produce a marked effect on) sehr mitnehmen; **you're telling me!** wem sagst du das!

teller ['tɛlər] s (of a bank) Kassierer –in mf; (of votes) Zähler –in mf

tell'ing adj (blow) wirksam

tell'-tale' adj verräterisch

temper ['tɛmpər] s (anger) Zorn m; (of steel) Härtegrad m; **bad t.** großer Zorn m; **even t.** Gleichmut m; **lose one's t.** in Wut geraten || tr (with) mildern (durch); (steel) härten; (mus) temperieren

temperament ['tɛmpərəmənt] s Temperament n

temperamental [‚tɛmpərə'mentəl] adj launisch, temperamentvoll

temperance ['tɛmpərəns] s Mäßigkeit f

temperate ['tɛmpərɪt] adj mäßig; (climate) gemäßigt

Tem'perate Zone' s gemäßigte Zone f

temperature ['tɛmərət/ər] s Temperatur f

tempest ['tɛmpɪst] s Sturm m; **a t. in a teapot** ein Sturm im Wasserglas

tempestuous [tɛm'pɛst/ʊ·əs] adj stürmisch

temple ['tɛmpəl] s Tempel m; (of glasses) Bügel m; (anat) Schläfe f

tem·po ['tɛmpo] s (–pos & –pi [pi]) Tempo n

temporal ['tɛmpərəl] adj zeitlich

temporary ['tɛmpə ‚rɛrɪ] adj zeitweilig; (credit, solution) Zwischen–

temporize ['tɛmpə ‚raɪz] intr Zeit zu gewinnen suchen

tempt [tɛmpt] tr versuchen; (said of things) reizen, locken

temptation [temp'teʃən] *s* Versuchung *f*

tempter ['temptər] *s* Versucher *m*

tempt'ing *adj* verlockend

temptress ['temptrıs] *s* Versucherin *f*

ten [ten] *adj & pron* zehn ‖ *s* Zehn *f*

tenable ['tenəbəl] *adj* haltbar

tenacious [tɪ'neʃəs] *adj* (*obstinate*) nartnäckig; (*memory*) verläßlich

tenacity [tɪ'næsɪti] *s* Hartnäckigkeit *f*

tenant ['tenənt] *s* Mieter –in *mf*

ten'ant farm'er *s* Pächter –in *mf*

tend [tend] *tr* (*flocks*) hüten; (*the sick*) pflegen; (*a machine*) bedienen ‖ *intr*—t. to (*attend to*) sich kümmern um; (*inf*) dazu neigen zu (*inf*); **t. toward(s)** neigen zu

tendency ['tendənsi] *s* Tendenz *f*

tender ['tendər] *adj* zart ‖ *s* Angebot *n*; (*nav*, *rr*) Tender *m* ‖ *tr* anbieten

ten'derfoot' *s* Neuankömmling *m*; (*boyscout*) neu aufgenommener Pfadfinder *m*

ten'derheart'ed *adj* zartfühlend

ten'derloin' *s* Rindslendenstück *n*

tenderness ['tendərnıs] *s* Zartheit *f*

tendon ['tendən] *s* Sehne *f*

tendril ['tendrıl] *s* Ranke *f*

tenement ['tenımənt] *s* (*dwelling*) Wohnung *f*; (*rented dwelling*) Mietwohnung *f*

ten'ement house' *s* Mietskaserne *f*

tenet ['tenɪt] *s* Grundsatz *m*, Lehrsatz *m*

ten'fold' *adj & adv* zehnfach

tennis ['tenɪs] *s* Tennis *n*

ten'nis court' *s* Tennisplatz *m*

ten'nis rack'et *s* Tennisschläger *m*

tenor ['tenər] *s* (*drift*, *meaning*; *singer*; *voice range*) Tenor *m*

ten'pin' *s* Kegel *m*

tense [tens] *adj* gespannt, straff; **make t.** spannen ‖ *s* (gram) Tempus *n*, Zweitform *f*

tension ['tenʃən] *s* (& elec) Spannung *f*; (phys) Spannkraft *f*

tent [tent] *s* Zelt *n*

tentacle ['tentəkəl] *s* Fühler *m*; (bot) Tentakel *m*

tentative ['tentətıv] *adj* vorläufig

tenth [tenθ] *adj & pron* zehnte ‖ *s* (*fraction*) Zehntel *n*; **the t.** (*in dates and in series*) der Zehnte

tent' pole' *s* Zeltstange *f*

tenuous ['tenju·əs] *adj* (*thin*) dünn; (*rarefied*) verdünnt; (*insignificant*) unbedeutend; (*weak*) schwach

tenure ['tenjər] *s* (*possession*) Besitz *m*; (educ) Anstellung *f* auf Lebenszeit; **t. of office** Amtsdauer *f*

tepid ['tepɪd] *adj* lauwarm

term [tʌrm] *s* (*expression*) Ausdruck *m*; (*time period*) Frist *f*; (*of office*) Amtszeit *f*; (jur) Sitzungsperiode *f*; (math) Glied *n*; (log) Begriff *m*; **be on good terms with** in guten Beziehungen stehen mit; **come to terms with** handelseinig werden mit; **in plain terms** unverblümt; **in terms of** im Sinne von; **in terms of praise** mit lobenden Worten; **on easy terms** zu günstigen Bedingungen; **on equal terms** auf gleichem Fuß; **on t.** (com) auf Zeit; **not be on speaking terms with** nicht sprechen mit; **tell s.o. in no uncertain terms** j–m gründlich die Meinung sagen; **terms** (*of a contract*, *treaty*, *payment*) Bedingungen *pl* ‖ *tr* bezeichnen

termagant ['tʌrməgənt] *s* Xanthippe *f*

terminal ['tʌrmɪnəl] *adj* End–; (*disease*) unheilbar ‖ *s* (aer) Flughafenempfangsgebäude *n*; (*pole*) (elec) Pol *m*; (rr) Kopfbahnhof *m*

terminate ['tʌrmɪˌnet] *tr* (*end*) beenden; (*limit*) begrenzen ‖ *intr* enden, endigen; (gram) (**in**) auslauten (auf *acc*)

termination [ˌtʌrmɪ'neʃən] *s* Beendigung *f*; (gram) Endung *f*

terminology [ˌtʌrmɪ'nɑlɪdʒi] *s* Terminologie *f*

term' insur'ance *s* Versicherung *f* auf Zeit

terminus ['tʌrmɪnəs] *s* (*end*) Endpunkt *m*; (*boundary*) Grenze *f*; (rr) Endstation *f*

termite ['tʌrmaɪt] *s* Termite *f*

term' pa'per *s* Referat *n*

terrace ['terəs] *s* Terrasse *f* ‖ *tr* abstufen, terrassieren

terra cotta ['terə'kɑtə] *s* Terrakotta *f*

ter'ra-cot'ta *adj* Terrakotta–

terrain [te'ren] *s* Gelände *n*, Terrain *n*

terrestrial [tə'restrı·əl] *adj* irdisch

terrible ['terɪbəl] *adj* furchtbar

terribly ['terɪbli] *adv* (coll) furchtbar

terrier ['terı·ər] *s* Terrier *m*

terrific [tə'rɪfɪk] *adj* (*frightful*) fürchterlich; (*intense*) (coll) gewaltig; (*splendid*) (coll) prima

terri·fy ['terɪˌfaɪ] *v* (*pret & pp* –**fied**) *tr* Entsetzen einjagen (*dat*)

ter'rifying *adj* schrecklich

territorial [ˌterɪ'torı·əl] *adj* territorial; **t. waters** Hoheitsgewässer *pl*

territory ['terɪˌtori] *s* Gebiet *n*, Territorium *n*; (*of a salesman*) Absatzgebiet *n*; (pol) Hoheitsgebiet *n*; (sport) Spielhälfte *f*

terror ['terər] *s* Schrecken *m*; **in t. vor** Schrecken

terrorism ['terəˌrɪzəm] *s* Terrorismus *m*

terrorist ['terərɪst] *s* Terrorist –in *mf*

terrorize ['terəˌraɪz] *tr* terrorisieren

ter'ror-strick'en *adj* schreckerfüllt

ter'ry cloth' ['teri] *s* Frottee *m & n*

terse [tʌrs] *adj* knapp

tertiary ['tʌrʃɪˌeri] *adj* Tertiär–

test [test] *s* Probe *f*, Prüfung *f*; (*criterion*) Prüfstein *m*; (med) Probe *f*; **put to the t.** auf die Probe stellen ‖ *tr* (**for**) prüfen (auf *acc*); (chem) (**for**) analysieren (auf *acc*); **t. out** (coll) ausprobieren

testament ['testəmənt] *s* Testament *n*

testator [tes'tetər] *s* Erblasser –in *mf*

test' ban' *s* Atomstopp *m*

test' case' *s* Probefall *m*; (jur) Präzedenzfall *m*

test'flight' *s* Probeflug *m*

testicle ['testɪkəl] *s* Hoden *m*

testi·fy ['testɪˌfaɪ] *v* (*pret & pp* –**fied**)

intr **(against)** zeugen (gegen), aussagen (gegen); **t. to** bezeugen
testimonial [ˌtɛstɪˈmonɪ·əl] *adj* (*dinner*) Ehren– ‖ *s* Anerkennungsschreiben *n*
testimony [ˈtɛstɪˌmoni] *s* Zeugnis *n*
test′ pa′per *s* Prüfungsarbeit *f*
test′ pi′lot *s* Versuchsflieger –in *mf*
test′ tube′ *s* Reagenzglas *n*
testy [ˈtɛsti] *adj* reizbar
tetanus [ˈtɛtənəs] *s* Starrkrampf *m*
tether [ˈtɛðər] *s* Haltestrick *m;* **be at the end of one's t.** nicht mehr weiter wissen ‖ *tr* anbinden
Teuton [ˈt(j)utən] *s* Teutone *m,* Teutonin *f*
Teutonic [t(j)uˈtɑnɪk] *adj* teutonisch
text [tɛkst] *s* Text *m*
text′book′ *s* Lehrbuch *n*
textile [ˈtɛkstaɪl] *adj* Textil– ‖ *s* Webstoff *m;* **textiles** Textilien *pl*
textual [ˈtɛkstʃʊ·əl] *adj* textlich
texture [ˈtɛkstʃər] *s* (*structure*) Gefüge *n;* (*of a fabric*) Gewebe *n;* (*of a play*) Aufbau *m*
Thai [taɪ] *adj* Thai– ‖ *s* (*person*) Thai –in *mf*; (*language*) Thai *n*
Thailand [ˈtaɪlənd] *s* Thailand *n*
Thames [tɛmz] *s* Themse *f*
than [ðæn] *conj* als; **t. ever** denn je
thank [θæŋk] *adj* (*offering*) Dank– ‖ **thanks** *spl* Dank *m;* **give thanks to** danken (*dat*); **many thanks!** vielen Dank!; **return thanks** danksagen; **thanks a lot!** danke vielmals!; **thanks to her, I** ich verdanke es ihr, daß ich ‖ *tr* danken (*dat*); **t. God!** Gott sei Dank!; **t. goodness!** gottlob!; **t. you!** danke schön!; **t. you ever so much!** verbindlichsten Dank!; **you have only yourself to t. for that** das hast du dir nur selbst zu verdanken
thankful [ˈθæŋkfəl] *adj* dankbar
thankless [ˈθæŋklɪs] *adj* undankbar
Thanksgiv′ing Day′ *s* Danksagungstag *m*
that [ðæt] *adj* jener, der; **t. one** der da, jener ‖ *adv* (coll) so, derart ‖ *rel pron* der, welcher; (after indefinite pronouns) was ‖ *dem pron* das; **about t.** darüber; **after t.** danach; **and that's t.** und damit punktum!; **at t.** so, dabei; **by t.** dadurch; **for all t.** trotz alledem; **for t.** dafür; **from t.** daraus; **in t.** darin, daran; **on t.** darauf, drauf; **t. is** das heißt; **that's out** das kommt nicht in Frage!; **t. will do!** das reicht! ‖ *conj* daß
thatch [θætʃ] *s* Dachstroh *n*
thatched′ roof′ *s* Strohdach *n*
thaw [θɔ] *s* Tauwetter *n* ‖ *tr* & *intr* (auf)tauen
the [ðə], [ði] *def art* der, die, das ‖ *adv*—**so much the better** um so besser; **the ... the** je ... desto, je ... um so
theater [ˈθi·ətər] *s* Theater *n*
the′atergo′er *s* Theaterbesucher –in *mf*
the′ater of war′ *s* Kriegsschauplatz *m*
theatrical [θɪˈætrɪkəl] *adj* (& fig) theatralisch
thee [ði] *pers pron* dich; **to t.** dir
theft [θɛft] *s* Diebstahl *m*
their [ðɛr] *poss adj* ihr
theirs [ðɛrz] *poss pron* ihrer
them [ðɛm] *pron* sie; **to t.** ihnen
theme [θim] *s* Thema *n;* (*essay*) Aufsatz *m;* (mus) Thema *n*
theme′ song′ *s* Kennmelodie *f*
themselves′ *intens pron* selbst, selber ‖ *reflex pron* sich
then [ðɛn] *adv* (*next; in that case*) dann; (*at that time*) damals; **by t.** bis dahin; **from t. on** von da an; **t. and there** auf der Stelle; **till t.** bis dahin; **what t.?** was dann?
thence [ðɛns] *adv* von da, von dort; (*from that fact*) daraus
thence′forth′ *adv* von da an
theologian [ˌθi·əˈlodʒən] *s* Theologe *m,* Theologin *f*
theological [ˌθi·əˈlɑdʒɪkəl] *adj* theologisch
theology [θiˈɑlədʒi] *s* Theologie *f*
theorem [ˈθi·ərəm] *s* Lehrsatz *m*
theoretical [ˌθi·əˈrɛtɪkəl] *adj* theoretisch
theorist [ˈθi·ərɪst] *s* Theoretiker –in *mf*
theorize [ˈθi·əˌraɪz] *intr* theoretisieren
theory [ˈθi·əri] *s* Theorie *f,* Lehre *f*
the′ory of relativ′ity *s* Relativitätstheorie *f*
therapeutic [ˌθɛrəˈpjutɪk] *adj* therapeutisch ‖ **therapeutics** *s* Therapeutik *f*
therapy [ˈθɛrəpi] *s* Therapie *f*
there [ðɛr] *adv* (*position*) da; (*direction*) dahin; **down t.** da unten; **not be all t.** (coll) nicht ganz richtig sein; **over t.** da drüben; **t. are** es gibt, es sind; **t. is** es gibt, es ist; **t., t.!** sachte, sachte!; **up t.** da (or dort) oben
there′abouts′ *adv* daherum; **ten people or t.** so ungefähr zehn Leute
there′af′ter *adv* danach
there′by′ *adv* dadurch, damit
therefore [ˈðɛrˌfor] *adv* deshalb, darum
there′in′ *adv* darin
there′of′ *adv* davon
there′to′ *adv* dazu
there′upon′ *adv* daraufhin, danach
there′with′ *adv* damit
thermal [ˈθʌrməl] *adj* Thermal–, Wärme–
thermodynamic [ˌθʌrmodaɪˈnæmɪk] *adj* thermodynamisch ‖ **thermodynamics** *s* Thermodynamik *f,* Wärmelehre *f*
thermometer [θɛrˈmɑmɪtər] *s* Thermometer *n*
thermonuclear [ˌθɛrmoˈn(j)uklɪ·ər] *adj* thermonuklear
ther′mos bot′tle [ˈθʌrməs] *s* Thermosflasche *f*
thermostat [ˈθʌrməˌstæt] *s* Thermostat *m*
thesau•rus [θɪˈsɔrəs] *s* (**–ri** [raɪ]) Thesaurus *m*
these [ðiz] *dem adj & pron* diese
the•sis [ˈθisɪs] *s* (–ses [siz]) These *f*
they [ðe] *pers pron* sie; **t. say** man sagt
thick [θɪk] *adj* dick; (*dense*) dicht;

(*stupid*) stumpfsinnig; (*lips*) wulstig; (*intimate*) (coll) dick; **t. with dust** dick bedeckt mit Staub ‖ *adv*—**be in t. with** (coll dicke Beziehungen haben mit; **come t. and fast** Schlag auf Schlag gehen; **lay it on t.** (coll) dick auftragen ‖ *s*—**in the t. of** mitten in (*dat*); **through t. and thin** durch dick und dünn

thicken ['θɪkən] *tr* verdicken; (*make denser*) verdichten; (*a sauce*) eindicken ‖ *intr* sich verdicken; (*become denser*) sich verdichten; (*said of liquids*) sich verfestigen; (*said of a sauce*) eindicken; **the plot thickens** der Knoten schürzt sich

thicket ['θɪkɪt] *s* Dickicht *n*

thick'head' *s* (coll) Dickkopf *m*

thick'-head'ed *adj* (coll) dickköpfig

thickness ['θɪknɪs] *s* Dicke *f*

thick'-set' *adj* stämmig

thick'skinned' *adj* (coll) dickfellig

thief [θif] *s* (**thieves** [θivz] Dieb –in *mf*

thieve [θiv] *intr* stehlen

thievery ['θivəri] *s* Dieberei *f*

thievish ['θivɪʃ] *adj* diebisch

thigh [θaɪ] *s* Schenkel *m*, Oberschenkel *m*

thighbone' *s* Oberschenkelknochen *m*

thimble ['θɪmbəl] *s* Fingerhut *m*

thin [θɪn] *adj* (**thinner; thinnest**) dünn; (*hair*) schütter; (*lean*) mager; (*excuse*) schwach; (*soup*) wäßrig ‖ *v* (*pret & pp* **thinned**) *ger* **thinning**) *tr* (*a liquid*) verdünnen; (*a forest*) lichten; **t. out** (*plants*) vereinzeln ‖ *intr* (*said of hair*) sich lichten; **t. out** (*said of a crowd*) sich verlaufen

thing [θɪn] *s* Ding *n*, Sache *f*; **among other things** unter anderem; **first t.** zu allererst; **how are things?** wie geht's?; **I'll do no such t.!** ich werde mich schön hüten; **of all things!** na sowas!; **the real t.** das Richtige; **things** (*the situation*) die Lage *f*; (*belongings*) Sachen *pl*

think [θɪŋk] *v* (*pret & pp* **thought** [θɔt]) *tr* denken; (*regard*) halten; (*believe*) glauben, denken; **he thinks he's clever** er hält sich für klug; **that's what you t.!** ja, denkste!; **t. better of it** sich e–s Besseren besinnen; **t. it best to** (*inf*) es für das Beste halten zu (*inf*); **t. little of** nicht viel halten von; **t. nothing of it!** es ist nicht der Rede wert!; **t. over** sich [*dat*] überlegen; **t. up** sich [*dat*] ausdenken; **what do you t. you're doing?** was soll das? ‖ *intr* denken; **be thinking of** (*ger*) beabsichtigen zu (*inf*); **do you t. so?** meinen Sie?; **t. about** (*call to consciousness*) denken an (*acc*); (*reflect on*) nachdenken über (*acc*); (*be concerned about*) bedacht sein auf (*acc*); **t. twice before** es sich [*dat*] zweimal überlegen, bevor

thinker ['θɪŋkər] *s* Denker –in *mf*

thin'-lipped' *adj* dünnlippig

thinner ['θɪnər] *s* Verdünnungsmittel *n*

third [θɪrd] *adj & pron* dritte ‖ *s* (*fraction*) Drittel *n*; (mus) Terz *f*; **the third** (*in dates and in series*) der Dritte

third'-class' *adj & adv* dritter Klasse

third' degree' *s*—**give s.o. the t.** j–n e–m Folterverhör unterwerfen

third' par'ty *s* Dritter *m*, dritte Seite *f*

third'-rate' *adj* drittrangig

thirst [θʌrst] *s* (**for**) Durst *m* (nach); **t. for knowledge** Wissensdurst *m*; **t. for power** Herrschsucht *f* ‖ *intr* (**for**) dürsten (nach)

thirsty ['θʌrsti] *adj* durstig; **be t.** Durst haben

thirteen ['θʌr'tin] *adj & pron* dreizehn ‖ *s* Dreizehn *f*

thirteenth ['θʌr'tinθ] *adj & pron* dreizehnte ‖ *s* (*fraction*) Dreizehntel *n*; **the t.** (*in dates and in series*) der Dreizehnte

thirtieth ['θʌrtɪ·əθ] *adj & pron* dreißigste ‖ *s* (*fraction*) Dreißigstel *n*; **the t.** (*in dates and in series*) der Dreißigste

thirty ['θʌrti] *adj & pron* dreißig ‖ *s* Dreißig *f*; **the thirties** die dreißiger Jahre

thir'ty-one' *adj & pron* einunddreißig

this [ðɪs] *dem adj* dieser; **t. afternoon** heute nachmittag; **t. evening** heute abend; **t. minute** augenblicklich; **t. one** dieser ‖ *adv* (coll) so ‖ *dem pron* dieser, der; **about t.** hierüber; (*concerning this*) davon; **t. and that** dies und jenes

thistle ['θɪsəl] *s* Distel *f*

thither ['θɪðər] *adv* dorthin, hinzu

thong [θɔŋ] *s* Riemen *m*; (*sandal*) Sandale *f*

tho•rax ['θɔræks] *s* (**–raxes & –races** [rə‚siz]) Brustkorb *m*

thorn [θɔrn] *s* Dorn *m*; **t. in the side** Dorn *m* im Fleisch

thorny ['θɔrni] *adj* dornig; (fig) heikel

thorough ['θʌro] *adj* gründlich; (coll) tüchtig

thor'oughbred' *adj* reinrassig ‖ *s* Vollblut *n*; (*horse*) Vollblutpferd *n*, Rassepferd *n*

thor'oughfare' *s* Durchgang *m*; **no t.** (public sign) Durchgang verboten

thor'oughgo'ing *adj* gründlich

thoroughly ['θʌroli] *adv* gründlich

those [ðoz] *dem adj & pron* jene, die da

thou [ðaʊ] *pers pron* du

though [ðo] *adv* immerhin ‖ *conj* obwohl

thought [θɔt] *s* Gedanke(n) *m*; **be lost in t.** in Gedanken versunken sein; **give some t. to** sich [*dat*] Gedanken machen über (*acc*); **have second thoughts** sich [*dat*] eines Besseren besinnen; **on second t.** nach reiflicher Überlegung; **the mere t.** schon der Gedanke

thoughtful ['θɔtfəl] *adj* (*reflective*) nachdenklich; (*e.g., essay*) gedankenvoll; (*considerate*) aufmerksam; (*gift*) sinnig; **t. of** bedacht auf (*acc*)

thoughtless ['θɔtlɪs] *adj* gedankenlos

thought'-provok'ing *adj* anregend

thousand ['θauzənd] *adj & pron* tausend; **a t. times** tausendmal ‖ *s* Tausend *f;* **by the t.** zu Tausenden

thousandth ['θauzəndθ] *adj & pron* tausendste ‖ *s (fraction)* Tausendstel *n*

thrash [θræʃ] *tr (& fig)* dreschen; **t. out** *(debate)* gründlich erörten ‖ *intr* dreschen; **t. about** sich hin– und herwerfen

thrash'ing *s* Dreschen *n; (beating)* Dresche *f*

thread [θred] *s* Faden *m; (of a screw)* Gewinde *n; (of a story)* Faden *m;* **hang by a t.** an e–m Faden hängen ‖ *tr (a needle)* einfädeln; *(pearls)* aufreihen; *(mach)* Gewinde schneiden in *(acc)*

thread'bare' *adj* fadenscheinig

threat [θret] *s* Drohung *f*

threaten ['θretən] *tr* drohen *(dat),* bedrohen; **t. so. with s.th.** j–m etw androhen ‖ *intr* drohen

three [θri] *adj & pron* drei ‖ *s* Drei *f;* **in threes** zu dritt

three' cheers' *spl* ein dreimaliges Hoch *n*

three'-dimen'sional *adj* dreidimensional

three'-en'gine *adj* dreimotorig

three'-piece' *adj (suit)* dreiteilig

three'-ply' *adj* dreischichtig

three'-point land'ing *s* Dreipunktlandung *f*

threnody ['θrenədi] *s* Klagelied *n*

thresh [θreʃ] *tr* dreschen; **t. out** *(debate)* gründlich erörten ‖ *intr* dreschen

thresh'ing floor' *s* Dreschtenne *f*

thresh'ing machine' *s* Dreschmaschine *f*

threshold ['θreʃold] *s* Türschwelle *f; (psychol)* Schwelle *f*

thrice [θraɪs] *adv* dreimal

thrift [θrɪft] *s* Sparsamkeit *f*

thrifty ['θrɪfti] *adj* sparsam

thrill [θrɪl] *s* Nervenkitzel *m* ‖ *tr* erregen, packen

thriller ['θrɪlər] *s* Thriller *m*

thrill'ing *adj* packend, spannend

thrive [θraɪv] *v (pret* **thrived** *&* **throve** [θrov]; *pp* **thrived** *&* **thriven** ['θrɪvən]) *intr* gedeihen

throat [θrot] *s* Kehle *f;* **clear one's t.** sich räuspern; **cut one another's t.** (fig) sich gegenseitig kaputt machen; **cut one's own t.** (fig) sich [*dat*] sein eigenes Grab schaufeln; **jump down s.o.'s t.** j–m an die Gurgel fahren; **sore t.** Halsweh *n*

throb [θrab] *s* Schlagen *n; (of a motor)* Dröhnen *n* ‖ *v (pret & pp* **throbbed;** *ger* **throbbing)** *intr* schlagen; *(said of a motor or head)* dröhnen

throes [θroz] *spl* Schmerzen *pl;* **be in the t. of death** im Todeskampf liegen

thrombosis [θram'bosɪs] *s* Thrombose *f*

throne [θron] *s* Thron *m*

throng [θrɔŋ] *s* Menschenmenge *f* ‖ *tr* umdrängen; *(the streets)* sich drängen in *(acc)* ‖ *intr (around)* sich drängen (um)

throttle ['θratəl] *s* Drossel(klappe) *f*

‖ *tr* drosseln; *(a person)* erwürgen ‖ *intr*—**t. back** *(aut)* das Gas zurücknehmen

through [θru] *adj (traffic, train)* Durchgangs–; *(street)* durchgehend; *(finished)* fertig; *(coll)* quitt ‖ *adv*— **t. and t.** durch und durch ‖ *prep* durch *(acc)*

throughout' *adv* durch und durch ‖ *prep* hindurch *(acc)* (postpositive), e.g., **t. the summer** den ganzen Sommer hindurch; **t. the world** in der ganzen Welt

throw [θro] *s* Wurf *m; (scarf)* Überwurf *m* ‖ *v (pret* **threw** [θru]; *pp* **thrown** [θron]) *tr* werfen; *(a rider)* abwerfen; *(sparks)* sprühen; *(a party, banquet)* geben; *(a game)* absichtlich verlieren; *(into confusion)* bringen; **t. away** wegwerfen; **t. down** niederwerfen; *(overturn)* umwerfen; **t. in** *(e.g., a few extras)* als Zugabe geben; **t. off** *(fig)* aus dem Gleichgewicht bringen; **t. out** hinauswerfen; *(a person)* vor die Tür setzen; *(the chest)* herausdrücken; **t. out of the game** vom Platz verweisen; **t. the book at s.o.** (fig) j–n zur Höchststrafe verurteilen; **t. up to s.o.** j–m vorwerfen ‖ *intr* werfen; **t. up** sich erbrechen

throw'away' *adj* Einweg–

throw'back' *s* (to) Rückkehr *f* (zu)

throw' rug' *s* Vorleger *m*

thrum [θrʌm] *v (pret & pp* **thrummed;** *ger* **thrumming)** *intr* (on) mit den Fingern trommeln (auf *acc*)

thrush [θrʌʃ] *s* (orn) Drossel *f*

thrust [θrʌst] *s (shove)* Stoß *m; (stab)* Hieb *m;* (aer, archit, geol, rok) Schub *m;* (mil) Vorstoß *m* ‖ *v (pret & pp* **thrust)** *tr* stoßen

thud [θʌd] *s* Bums *m* ‖ *v (pret & pp* **thudded;** *ger* **thudding)** *tr & intr* bumsen ‖ *interj* bums!

thug [θʌg] *s* Rocker *m*

thumb [θʌm] *s* Daumen *m;* **be all thumbs** zwei linke Hände haben; **be under s.o.'s t.** unter j–s Fuchtel stehen; **thumbs down!** pfui!; **thumbs up!** Kopf hoch! ‖ *tr (a book)* abgreifen; **t. a ride** per Anhalter fahren; **t. one's nose at s.o.** j–m e–e lange Nase machen ‖ *intr*—**t. through** durchblättern

thumb' in'dex *s* Daumenindex *m*

thumb'print' *s* Daumenabdruck *m*

thumb'screw' *s* Flügelschraube *f*

thumb'tack' *s* Reißnagel *m*

thump [θʌmp] *s* Bums *m* ‖ *tr & intr* bumsen ‖ *interj* bums!

thump'ing *adj* (coll) enorm

thunder ['θʌndər] *s* Donner *m* ‖ *tr & intr* donnern

thun'derbolt' *s* Donnerkeil *m*

thun'derclap' *s* Donnerschlag *m*

thunderous ['θʌndərəs] *adj* donnernd

thun'dershow'er *s* Gewitterregen *m*

thun'derstorm' *s* Gewitter *n*

thunderstruck ['θʌndər,strʌk] *adj* (fig) wie vom Schlag getroffen

Thursday ['θʌrzde] *s* Donnerstag *m;* **on T.** am Donnerstag

thus [ðʌs] *adv* so; (*consequently*) also; **t. far** soweit

thwack [θwæk] *s* heftiger Schlag *m* ‖ *tr* klatschen

thwart [θwɔːt] *adj* Quer– ‖ *s* (naut) Ruderbank *f* ‖ *tr* (*plans*) durchkreuzen; (*a person*) in die Quere kommen (*dat*)

thy [ðaɪ] *poss adj* dein

thyme [taɪm] *s* Thymian *m*

thy'roid gland' ['θaɪrɔɪd] *s* Schilddrüse *f*

thyself [ðaɪ'self] *intens pron* selbst, selber ‖ *reflex pron* dich

tiara [taɪ'erə] *s* Tiara *f*; (*lady's headdress*) Diadem *n*

tibia ['tɪbɪ·ə] *s* Schienbein *n*

tic [tɪk] *s* (pathol) Tick *m*

tick [tɪk] *s* (*of a clock*) Ticken *n*; (*mattress case*) Überzug *m*; (ent) Zecke *f*; **on t.** (coll) auf Pump ‖ *tr*—**be ticked off (at)** (sl) verärgert sein (über *acc*); **t. off** (*names, items*) abhaken; (*the minutes*) ticken ‖ *intr* ticken; **t. by** vergehen

ticker ['tɪkər] *s* (*watch*) (sl) Uhr *f*, Armbanduhr *f*; (*heart*) (sl) Herz *n*; (st. exch.) Börsentelegraph *m*

tick'er tape' *s* Papierstreifen *m* (des Börsentelegraphen)

tick'er-tape parade' *s* Konfettiregenparade *f*

ticket ['tɪkɪt] *s* Karte *f*; (*for travel*) Fahrkarte *f*; (*by air*) Flugkarte *f*; (*for admission*) Eintrittskarte *f*; (*in a lottery*) Los *n*; (*for a traffic violation*) Strafzettel *m*; (pol) Wahlliste *f* ‖ *tr* etikettieren; (*aut*) mit e–m Strafzettel versehen

tick'et a'gency *s* Vorverkaufsstelle *f*

tick'et a'gent *s* Fahrkartenverkäufer –in *mf*

tick'et of'fice *s* Kartenverkaufsstelle *f*

tick'et win'dow *s* Schalter *m*

tick'ing *s* Ticken *n*

tickle ['tɪkəl] *s* Kitzel *m* ‖ *tr* kitzeln ‖ *intr* jucken

ticklish ['tɪklɪʃ] *adj* kitzlig; (*touchy*) heikel

ticktock ['tɪk‚tak] *adv*—**go t.** ticktack machen ‖ *s* Ticken *n*

tid'al wave' ['taɪdəl] *s* Flutwelle *f*

tidbit ['tɪd‚bɪt] *s* Leckerbissen *m*

tiddlywinks ['tɪdlɪ‚wɪŋks] *s* Flohhüpfspiel *n*

tide [taɪd] *s* Gezeiten *pl*; **against the t.** (fig) gegen den Strom; **the t. is coming in** die Flut steigt; **the t. is going out** die Flut fällt ‖ *tr*—**t. s.o. over** j–n über Wasser halten

tide'land' *s* Watt *n*

tide'wa'ter *s* Flutwasser *n*

tidings ['taɪdɪŋz] *spl* Botschaft *f*

ti·dy ['taɪdi] *adj* ordentlich; (*sum*) hübsch ‖ *v* (*pret & pp* **–died**) *tr* in Ordnung bringen; **t. up** aufräumen ‖ *intr*—**t. up** aufräumen

tie [taɪ] *adj* (sport) unentschieden ‖ *s* (cord) Schnur *f*; (*ribbon*) Band *n*; (*necktie*) Krawatte *f*; (*knot*) Schleife *f*; (mus) Ligatur *f*; (parl) Stimmengleichheit *f*; (rr) Schwelle *f*; (sport)

Unentschieden *n*; **end in a tie** punktgleich enden; **ties** (e.g., *of friendship*) Bande *pl* ‖ *v* (*pret & pp* **tied**; *ger* **tying**) *tr* binden; **be tied up** (*said of a person or telephone*) besetzt sein; **get tied up** (*in traffic*) steckenbleiben; **my hands are tied** mir sind die Hände gebunden; **tie in with** verknüpfen mit; **tie oneself down** sich festlegen; **tie to** festbinden an (*dat*); **tie up** (*a wound*) verbinden; (*traffic*) lahmlegen; (*money*) fest anlegen; (*production*) stillegen; (*the telephone*) blockieren; (*a boat*) festmachen

tie'back' *s* Gardinenhalter *m*

tie'clasp' *s* Krawattenhalter *m*

tie'pin' *s* Krawattennadel *f*

tier [tɪr] *s* Reihe *f*; (theat) Rang *m*

tie'-up' *s* (*of traffic*) Stockung *f*

tiger ['taɪgər] *s* Tiger *m*

ti'ger shark' *s* Tigerhai *m*

tight [taɪt] *adj* (*firm*) fest; (*clothes*) eng; (*taut*) straff; (*scarce*) knapp; (*container*) dicht; (*drunk*) beschwipst; (*with money*) knaus(e)rig; **feel t. in** the chest sich beengt fühlen ‖ *adv* fest; **hold t.** festhalten; **sit t.** sich nicht rühren; **pull t.** strammziehen ‖ **tights** *spl* Trikot *m* & *n*

tighten ['taɪtən] *tr* (*a rope*) straff spannen; (*a belt*) enger schnallen; (*a jar lid*) festziehen; (*a screw*) anziehen; (*a spring*) spannen; (*a knot*) zuziehen

tight'-fist'ed *adj* knaus(e)rig

tight'-fit'ting *adj* eng anliegend

tight'-lipped' *adj* verschlossen

tight'rope' *s* Drahtseil *n*; **walk a t.** auf e–m festgespannten Drahtseil gehen

tight' spot' *s* (coll) Klemme *f*

tight' squeeze' *s* (coll) Zwickmühle *f*

tight'wad' *s* Geizkragen *m*

tigress ['taɪgrɪs] *s* Tigerin *f*

tile [taɪl] *s* (*for the floor or wall*) Fliese *f*; (*for the roof*) Dachziegel *m*; (*glazed tile*) Kachel *f* ‖ *tr* (*a roof*) mit Ziegeln decken; (*a floor*) mit Fliesen auslegen; (*a bathroom*) kacheln

tile' roof' *s* Ziegeldach *n*

till [tɪl] *s* Kasse *f* ‖ *tr* ackern ‖ *prep* bis (*acc*); **t. now** bisher ‖ *conj* bis

tiller ['tɪlər] *s* (naut) Pinne *f*

tilt [tɪlt] *s* Kippen *n*; **full t.** mit voller Wucht ‖ *tr* kippen; (*a bottle, the head*) neigen; **t. back** (e.g., *a chair*) zurücklehnen; **t. over** umkippen ‖ *intr* kippen; **t. over** umkippen

timber ['tɪmbər] *s* Holz *n*; (*for structural use*) Bauholz *n*; (*rafter*) Balken *m*

tim'berland' *s* Waldland *n*

tim'ber line' *s* Baumgrenze *f*

timbre ['tɪmbər] *s* Klangfarbe *f*

time [taɪm] *s* Zeit *f*; (*limited period*) Frist *f*; (*instance*) Mal *n*; (mus) Takt *m*; **all the t.** ständig; **all this t.** die ganze Zeit; **any number of times** x-mal; **at no t.** nie; **at one t.** einst; **at some t.** irgendwann; **at that t.**

damals; **at the present t.** derzeit; **at times** manchmal; **at what t.?** um wieviel Uhr?; **by this t.** nunmehr; **do t.** (sl) sitzen; **do you have the t.?** können Sie mir sagen, wie spät es ist?; **for a t.** e-e Zeitlang; **for the last t.** zum letzten Mal; **for the t. being** vorläufig; **give s.o. a hard t.** j–m das Leben schwer machen; **have a good t.** sich gut unterhalten; **have a hard t.** (ger) es schwer haben zu (inf); **in no t.** im Nu; **in t.** zur rechten Zeit; (in the course of time) mit der Zeit; **make good t.** Fortschritte machen; **on one's own t.** in der Freizeit; **on t.** pünktlich; (on schedule) fahrplanmäßig; (com) auf Raten; **several times** mehrmals; **take one's t.** sich [dat] Zeit lassen; **there's t. for that** das hat Zeit; **this t. tomorrow** morgen um diese Zeit; **t.!** (sport) Zeit!; **t. is up!** die Zeit ist um!; **t. of life** Lebensalter n; **times** Zeiten pl; (math) mal, e.g., **two times two** zwei mal zwei; **t. will tell** die Zeit wird es lehren; **what t. is it?** wieviel Uhr ist es? **t** (mit der Uhr) messen; **t. s.th. right** die richtige Zeit wählen für

time' bomb' s Zeitbombe f
time' card' s Stechkarte f
time' clock' s Stechuhr f
time'-consum'ing adj zeitraubend
time' expo'sure s (phot) Zeitaufnahme f
time' fuse' s Zeitzünder m
time'-hon'ored adj altehrwürdig
time'keep'er s Zeitnehmer –in mf
time'-lag' s Verzögerung f
timeless ['taɪmlɪs] adj zeitlos
time' lim'it s Frist f; **set a t. on** befristen
timely ['taɪmli] adj zeitgerecht; (topic) aktuell
time' pay'ment s Ratenzahlung f
time'piece' s Uhr f
timer ['taɪmər] s (person) Zeitnehmer –in mf; (device) Schaltuhr f; (aut) Zündunterbrecher m; (phot) Zeitauslöser m
time' sig'nal s Zeitzeichen n
time' stud'y s Zeitstudien pl
time'ta'ble s Zeittabelle f; (aer) Flugplan m; (rr) Fahrplan m
time'work' adj Zeitlohnarbeit f
time'worn' adj abgenutzt
time' zone' s Zeitzone f
timid ['tɪmɪd] adj ängstlich
tim'ing s genaue zeitliche Berechnung f; (aut) Zündeinstellung f
timorous ['tɪmərəs] adj furchtsam
tin [tɪn] adj Zinn– || s (element) Zinn n; (tin plate) Weißblech n
tin' can' s Blechdose f
tincture ['tɪŋktʃər] s Tinktur f
tinder ['tɪndər] s Zunder m
tin'derbox' s (fig) Pulverfaß n
tin' foil' s Zinnfolie f
ting-a-ling ['tɪŋə,lɪŋ] s Klingeling m
tinge [tɪndʒ] s (of color) Stich m; (fig) Spur f || v (pret **tingeing** & **tinging**) tr leicht färben

tingle ['tɪŋgəl] s Kribbeln n, Prickeln n || intr kribbeln, prickeln
tinker ['tɪŋkər] s (bungler) Pfuscher m || intr basteln
tinkle ['tɪŋkəl] s Klingeln n || intr klingeln
tin' mine' s Zinnbergwerk n
tinsel ['tɪnsəl] s Lametta f; (fig) Flitterkram m
tin'smith' s Klempner m
tin' sol'dier s Zinnsoldat m
tint [tɪnt] s Farbton m || tr tönen, leicht färben
tint'ed glass' s (aut) blendungsfreies Glas n
tiny ['taɪni] adj winzig
tip [tɪp] s Spitze f; (gratuity) Trinkgeld n; (hint) Tip m; **it's on the tip of my tongue** es schwebt mir auf der Zunge || v (pret & pp **tipped**; ger **tipping**) tr schief halten; (a waiter) ein Trinkgeld geben (dat); **tip off** e–n Tip geben (dat); **tip one's hat** auf den Hut tippen || intr—**tip over** umtippen
tip'-off' s Tip m, rechtzeitiger Wink m
tipple ['tɪpəl] tr & intr süffeln
tippler ['tɪplər] s Säufer –in mf
tipster ['tɪpstər] s Wettberater m
tipsy ['tɪpsi] adj beschwipst
tip'toe' s—**on t.** auf den Zehenspitzen || v (pret & pp **–toed**; ger **–toeing**) intr auf den Zehenspitzen gehen
tip'top' adj tipptopp
tirade ['taɪred] s Tirade f
tire [taɪr] s Reifen m || tr ermüden; **t. out** strapazieren || intr ermüden
tired adj müde; **be t. of** (ger) es satt haben zu (inf); **be t. of coffee** den Kaffee satt haben; **t. out** abgespannt
tire' gauge' s Reifendruckmesser m
tireless ['taɪrlɪs] adj unermüdlich
tire' pres'sure s Reifendruck m
tiresome ['taɪrsəm] adj (tiring) ermüdend; (boring) langweilig
tissue ['tɪ/ju] s Gewebe n; (thin paper) Papiertaschentuch n; **t. of lies** Lügengewebe n
tis'sue pa'per s Seidenpapier n
tit [tɪt] s (sl) Brust f; **tit for tat** wie du mir, so ich dir
Titan ['taɪtən] s Titan(e) m
titanic [taɪ'tænɪk] adj titanisch
titanium [taɪ'tenɪ–əm] s Titan n
tithe [taɪð] s Kirchenzehnt m || tr (pay one tenth of) den Zehnten bezahlen von; (exact a tenth from) den Zehnten erheben von
Titian ['tɪ/ən] adj tizianrot
titillate ['tɪtɪ,let] tr & intr kitzeln, (angenehm) reizen
title ['taɪtəl] s Titel m; (to a property) Eigentumsrecht n; (claim) Rechtstitel m; (of a chapter) Überschrift f; (honor) Würde f; (aut) Kraftfahrzeugbrief m || tr titulieren
ti'tle bout' s (box) Titelkampf m
ti'tled adj ad(e)lig
ti'tle deed' s Eigentumsurkunde f
ti'tle hold'er s Titelverteidiger –in mf
ti'tle page' s Titelblatt n
ti'tle role' s Titelrolle f

titter ['tɪtər] s Gekicher n ‖ intr kichern

titular ['tɪtələr] adj Titular–

to [tu], [tʊ] adv—to and fro hin und her ‖ prep zu (dat); (a city, country, island) nach (dat); (as far as) bis (acc); (in order to) um ... zu (inf); (against, e.g., a wall) an (dat or acc); **a quarter to eight** viertel vor acht; **how far is it to the town?** wie weit ist es bis zur Stadt?; **to a T** haargenau

toad [tod] s Kröte f

toad'stool' s Giftpilz m

toad·y ['todi] s Schranze m & f ‖ v (pret & pp –ied) intr (to) scharwenzeln (um)

to-and-fro ['tu·ənd'fro] adj Hin– und Her– ‖ adv hin und her

toast [tost] s (bread; salutation) Toast m; **drink a t. to** e–n Toast ausbringen auf (acc) ‖ tr (bread) rösten

toaster ['tostər] s Toaster m

toast'mas'ter s Spitzentanz m

tobac·co [tə'bæko] s (–cos) Tabak m

tobac'co pouch' s Tabaksbeutel m

toboggan [tə'bagən] s Rodel m & f ‖ intr rodeln

tocsin ['taksɪn] s Alarmglocke f

today [tʊ'de] adv heute ‖ s—from t. on von heute an; **today's** heutig

toddle ['tadəl] s Watscheln n ‖ intr watscheln

toddler ['tadlər] s Kleinkind n

toddy ['tadi] s Toddy m

to-do [tə'du] s Getue n

toe [to] s Zehe f; **be on one's toes** auf Draht sein; **step on s.o.'s toes** j–m auf die Zehen treten ‖ v (pret & pp toed; ger toeing) tr—**toe the line** nicht aus der Reihe tanzen

toe' dance' s Spitzentanz m

toe'-in' s (aut) Spur f

toe'nail' s Zehennagel m

together [tʊ'geðər] adv zusammen; **t. with** mitsamt (dat), samt (dat)

togetherness [tʊ'geðərnɪs] s Zusammengehörigkeit f

tog'gle switch' ['tagəl] s (elec) Kippschalter m

togs [tagz] spl Klamotten pl

toil [tɔɪl] s Mühe f; **toils** Schlingen pl ‖ intr sich mühen

toilet ['tɔɪlɪt] s (room) Toilette f; (bathroom fixture) Klosett n

toi'let ar'ticle s Toilettenartikel m

toi'let bowl' s Klosettschüssel f

toi'let pa'per s Klosettpapier n

toi'let seat' s Toilettenring m

token ['tokən] adj (payment) symbolisch; (strike) Warn– ‖ Zeichen n; (proof) Beweis m; **by the same t.** aus dem gleichen Grund; **as** (or **in**) **t. of** zum Beweis (genit)

tolerable ['talərəbəl] adj erträglich

tolerably ['talərəbli] adv leidlich

tolerance ['talərəns] s Duldsamkeit f; (mach) Toleranz f

tolerant ['talərənt] adj (of) duldsam (gegen), tolerant (gegen)

tolerate ['talə ˌret] tr dulden

toleration [ˌtalə'reʃən] s Duldung f

toll [tol] adj (road) gebührenpflichtig ‖ s Wegezoll m; (at a bridge) Brückenzoll m; (of bells) Läuten n; (number of victims) Zahl f der Opfer; (fig) Tribut m; (telp) Gebühr f für ein Ferngespräch; **take a heavy t. of** life viele Menschenleben kosten ‖ tr & intr läuten

toll' booth' s Zahlkasse f

toll' bridge' s Zollbrücke f

toll' call' s Ferngespräch n

toll' collec'tor s Zolleinnehmer –in mf

toma·to [tə'meto] s (–toes) Tomate f

toma'to juice' s Tomatensaft f

tomb [tum] s Grab n, Grabmal n

tomboy ['tam ˌbɔɪ] s Wildfang m

tomb'stone' s Grabstein m

tomcat ['tam ˌkæt] s Kater m

tome [tom] s Band m

tomfoolery [tam'fuləri] s Albernheit f

Tom'my gun' ['tami] s Maschinenpistole f

tom'myrot' s Blödsinn m

tomorrow [tʊ'moro] adv morgen; **t.** evening morgen abend; **t. morning** morgen früh; **t. night** morgen abend; **t. noon** morgen mittag ‖ s morgen; **tomorrow's** morgig

tom-tom ['tam ˌtam] s Hindutrommel f

ton [tʌn] s Tonne f

tone [ton] s Ton m; (of color) Farbton m; (phot) Tönung f ‖ tr tönen; (phot) tönen; **t. down** dämpfen ‖ intr milder werden

tone'-control knob' s (rad) Klangregler m

tongs [taŋz] spl Zange f

tongue [tʌŋ] s Zunge f; (language) Sprache f; (of a shoe) Zunge f; (of a buckle) Dorn m; (of a bell) Klöppel m; (of a wagon) Deichsel f; (carp) Feder f; **hold one's t.** den Mund halten

tongue'-tied' adj zungenlahm; (fig) sprachlos

tongue' twist'er s Zungenbrecher m

tonic ['tanɪk] adj tonisch ‖ s (med) Tonikum n; (mus) Tonika f

tonight [tʊ'naɪt] adv heute nacht; (this evening) heute abend

tonnage ['tʌnɪdʒ] s Tonnage f

tonsil ['tansɪl] s Mandel f

tonsilitis [ˌtansɪ'laɪtɪs] s Mandelentzündung f

tonsure ['tanʃər] s Tonsur f

too [tu] adv (also) auch; (excessively) zu; **too bad!** Schade!

tool [tul] s (& fig) Werkzeug n ‖ tr (with tools) bearbeiten

tool'box' s Werkzeugkasten m

tool'mak'er s Werkzeugmacher m

tool' shed' s Geräteschuppen m

toot [tut] s (aut) Hupen n ‖ tr (a trumpet) blasen; **t. the horn** (aut) hupen ‖ intr (aut) hupen

tooth [tuθ] s (teeth [tiθ]) Zahn m; (of a rake) Zinke f; **t. and nail** mit aller Gewalt

tooth'ache' s Zahnschmerz m, Zahnweh n

tooth'brush' s Zahnbürste f
tooth' decay' s Zahnfäule f
toothless ['tuθlɪs] adj zahnlos
tooth'paste' s Zahnpaste f
tooth'pick' s Zahnstocher m
tooth' pow'der s Zahnpulver n
top [tap] adj oberste; (speed, price, form) Höchst–; (team) Spitzen–; (first-class) erstklassig || s Spitze f; (of a mountain) Gipfel m; (of a tree) Wipfel m; (of a car) Verdeck n; (of a box) Deckel m; (of a garment) Oberteil m & n; (of a bottle) Verschluß m; (of an object) obere Seite f; (of the water) Oberfläche f; (of a turnip) Kraut n; (toy) Kreisel m; at the top of one's voice aus voller Kehle; at the top of the page oben auf der Seite; be tops with s.o. (coll) bei j–m ganz groß angeschrieben sein; from top to bottom von oben bis unten; on top (& fig) obenauf; on top of (position) auf (dat); (direction) auf (acc); on top of that obendrein || v (pret & pp topped; ger topping) tr (a tree) kappen; (surpass) übertreffen; that tops everything das übersteigt alles; top off (a meal, an evening) abschließen; to top it off zu guter Letzt
topaz ['topæz] s Topas m
top' brass' s (mil) hohe Tiere pl
top'coat' s Überzieher m
top' dog' s (coll) Erste mf
top' ech'elon s Führungsspitze f
top' hat' s Zylinder m
top'-heav'y adj oberlastig
topic ['tapɪk] s Gegenstand m, Thema n
topical ['tapɪkəl] adj aktuell
top' kick' s (mil) Spieß m
topless ['taplɪs] adj Oben-ohne–
topmast ['tap ˌmɛst] s Toppmast m
top'most' adj oberste
top'notch' adj erstklassig
top' of the head' s Scheitel m
topography [tə'pagrəfi] s Topographie f
topple ['tapəl] tr & intr stürzen
topsail ['tapsəl] s Toppsegel n
top'-se'cret adj streng geheim
top' ser'geant s Hauptfeldwebel m
top'side' adv auf Deck || s Oberseite f
top'soil' s Mutterboden m
topsy-turvy ['tapsi'tʌrvi] adj drunter und drüber || adv—turn t. durcheinanderbringen
torch [tɔrtʃ] s Fackel f; (Brit) Taschenlampe f; carry the t. for (coll) verknallt sein in (acc)
torch'bear'er s (& fig) Fackelträger m
torch'light' s Fackelschein m
torch'light parade' s Fackelzug m
torment ['tɔrment] s Qual f || [tɔr'ment] tr quälen
tormentor [tɔr'mɛntər] s Quäler –in mf
torn [tɔrn] adj zerrissen, rissig
torna·do [tɔr'nedo] s (–does & –dos) Tornado m, Windhose f
torpe·do [tɔr'pido] s (–does) Torpedo m || tr torpedieren

torpe'do boat' s Torpedoboot n
torpe'do tube' s Ausstoßrohr n
torpid ['tɔrpɪd] adj träge
torque [tɔrk] s Drehmoment n
torrent ['tɔrənt] s Sturzbach m; (of words) Schwall m; in torrents stromweise
torrential [tə'rɛntʃəl] adj—t. rain Wolkenbruch m
torrid ['tɔrɪd] adj brennend
Tor'rid Zone' s heiße Zone f
tor·so ['tɔrso] s (–sos) (of a statue) Torso m; (of a human body) Rumpf m
tortoise ['tɔrtəs] s Schildkröte f
tor'toise shell' s Schildpatt n
torture ['tɔrtʃər] s Folter f, Qual f || tr foltern, quälen
toss [tɔs] s Wurf m; (of the head) Zurückwerfen n; (of a ship) Schlingern n; (of a coin) Loswurf m || tr (throw) werfen; (the head) zurückwerfen; (a ship) hin- und herwerfen; (a coin) hochwerfen; t. off (work) hinhauen; t. s.o. for j–m losen um || intr (naut) schlingern; t. for e–e Münze hochwerfen um; t. in bed sich im Bett hin –und herwerfen
toss'up' s Loswurf m; it's a t. whether es hängt ganz vom Zufall ab, ob
tot [tat] s Knirps m
to·tal ['totəl] adj Gesamt–, total || s Gesamtsumme f || v (pret & pp –tal[l]ed; ger –tal[l]ing) tr (add up) zusammenrechnen; (amount to) sich belaufen auf (acc); (sl) (Wagen) ganz kaputt machen
totalitarian [to ˌtæli'tɛrɪˌən] adj totalitär
tote [tot] tr schleppen
totem ['totəm] s Totem n
totter ['tatər] intr schwanken
touch [tʌtʃ] s Berührung f; (sense of touch) Tastsinn m; (e.g., of a fever) Anflug m; (trace, small bit) Spur f; (of a pianist) Anschlag m; get in t. with in Verbindung treten mit; keep in t. with in Verbindung bleiben mit; put in t. with in Verbindung setzen mit; with sure t. mit sicherer Hand || tr berühren; (fig) rühren; he's a little touched (coll) er hat e–n kleinen Klaps; t. bottom anstoßen; t. glasses mit den Gläsern anstoßen; t. off auslösen; t. s.o. for (coll) j–n anpumpen um; t. up (with cosmetics) auffrischen; (paint, phot) retuschieren || intr sich berühren; t. down (aer) aufsetzen; t. on (a topic) berühren; (e.g., arrogance) grenzen an (acc)
touch' and go' s—be t. auf der Kippe stehen
touch'ing adj rührend, herzergreifend
touch'stone' s (fig) Prüfstein m
touch'-type' tr blindschreiben
touchy ['tʌtʃi] adj (spot, person) empfindlich; (situation) heikel
tough [tʌf] adj (strong) derb; (meat) zäh; (life) mühselig; (difficult) schwierig || s Gassenjunge m
toughen ['tʌfən] tr zäher machen; t.

up (*through training*) ertüchtigen ‖ *intr* (up) zäher werden

tough′ luck′ *s* Pech *n*

tour [tur] *s* (*of a country*) Tour *f*; (*of a city*) Rundfahrt *f*; (*of a museum*) Führung *f*; (*mus, theat*) Tournee *f*; **go on t.** auf Tournee gehen ‖ *tr* besichtigen; (*a country*) bereisen ‖ *intr* auf der Reise sein; (*theat*) auf Tournee sein

tour′ guide′ *s* Reiseführer *-in mf*

tourism [′turɪzəm] *s* Touristik *f*

tournament [′turnəmənt] *s* Turnier *n*

tourney [′turni] *s* Turnier *n*

tourniquet [′turnɪˌket] *s* Aderpresse *f*

tousle [′tauzəl] *tr* (*zer*)zausen

tow [to] *s*—**have in tow** im Schlepptau haben; **take in tow** ins Schlepptau nehmen ‖ *tr* schleppen; **tow away** abschleppen

toward(s) [tord(z)] *prep* (*with respect to*) gegenüber (*dat*); (*a goal, direction*) auf (*acc*), zu; (*shortly before*) gegen (*acc*); (*for*) für (*acc*); (*facing*) zugewandt (*dat*)

tow′boat′ *s* Schleppschiff *n*

tow-el [′tau-əl] *s* Handtuch *n* ‖ *v* (*pret & pp* -el[l]ed; *ger* -el[l]ing) *tr* mit e-m Handtuch abtrocknen

tow′el rack′ *s* Handtuchhalter *m*

tower [′tau-ər] *s* Turm *m*; **t. of strength** starker Hort *m* ‖ *intr* ragen; **t. over** überragen

tow′ering *adj* hochragend; (*rage*) rasend

tow′ing serv′ice *s* Schleppdienst *m*

tow′line′ *s* Schlepptau *n*

town [taun] *adj* städtisch, Stadt– ‖ *s* Stadt *f*; **in t.** in der Stadt; **out of t.** verreist; **go to t. on** Feuer und Flamme sein für

town′ coun′cil *s* Stadtrat *m*

town′ hall′ *s* Rathaus *n*

town′ house′ *s* Stadthaus *n*

town′ship′ *s* Gemeinde *f*

tow′rope′ *s* Schlepptau *n*; (*for a glider*) Startseil *n*

tow′ truck′ *s* Abschleppwagen *m*

toxic [′taksɪk] *adj* Gift–, toxisch ‖ *s* Giftstoff *m*

toy [tɔɪ] *adj* Spielzeug– ‖ *s* Spielzeug *n*; **toys** Spielsachen *pl*; (*com*) Spielwaren *pl* ‖ *intr* spielen; **toy with** (*fig*) herumspielen mit

toy′ dog′ *s* Schoßhund *m*

toy′ shop′ *s* Spielwarengeschäft *n*

toy′ sol′dier *s* Spielzeugsoldat *m*

trace [tres] *s* Spur *f*; (*of a harness*) Strang *m*; **without a t.** spurlos ‖ *tr* (*a drawing*) durchpausen; (*lines*) nachziehen; (*track*) ausfindig machen; **t.** (*back*) **to** zurückführen auf (*acc*)

tracer [′tresər] *s* Suchzettel *m*

trac′er bul′let *s* Leuchtspurgeschoß *n*

trac′ing pa′per *s* Pauspapier *n*

track [træk] *s* Spur *f*; (*of a foot*) Fußspur *f*; (*of a wheel*) Radspur *f*; (*chain of a tank*) Raupenkette *f*; (*parallel rails*) Geleise *n*, (*single rail*) Gleis *n*, Schiene *f*; (*station platform*) Bahnsteig *m*; (*path*) Pfad *m*; (*course*

for running) Laufbahn *f*; (*course for motor and horse racing*) Rennbahn *f*; (*running as a sport*) Laufen *n*; **be off the t.** (fig) auf dem Holzweg sein; **go off the t.** (*derail*) entgleisen; **in one's tracks** mitten auf dem Weg; **jump the t.** aus den Schienen springen ‖ *tr* verfolgen; **t. down** (*game, a criminal*) zur Strecke bringen; (*a rumor, reference*) nachgehen (*dat*); **t. up** (*a rug*) schmutzig treten

track′-and-field′ *adj* Leichtathletik–

trackless [′træklɪs] *adj* pfadlos; (*vehicle*) schienenlos

track′ meet′ *s* Leichtathletikwettkampf *m*

tract [trækt] *s* Strich *m*; (*treatise*) Traktat *m*; *s* of land Grundstück *n*

traction [′trækʃən] *s* (*med*) Ziehen *n*; (*of the road*) Griffigkeit *f*

tractor [′træktər] *s* Traktor *m*; (*of a tractor-trailer*) Zugmaschine *f*

trac′tor-trail′er *s* Sattelschlepper *m* mit e-m Anhänger

trade [tred] *s* Handel *m*; (*calling, job*) Gewerbe *n*; (*exchange*) Tausch *m*; **by t.** von Beruf ‖ *tr* (aus)tauschen; **t. in** (*e.g., a used car*) in Zahlung geben ‖ *intr* Handel treiben

trade′ agree′ment *s* Handelsabkommen *n*

trade′ bar′riers *spl* Handelsschranken *pl*

trade′-in val′ue *s* Handelswert *m*

trade′mark′ *s* Warenzeichen *n*

trade′ name′ *s* (*of products*) Handelsbezeichnung *f*; (*of a firm*) Firmenname *m*

trader [′tredər] *s* Händler *-in mf*

trade′ school′ *s* Gewerbeschule *f*

trade′ se′cret *s* Geschäftsgeheimnis *n*

trades′man *s* (–men) Handelsmann *m*

trade′ un′ion *s* Gewerkschaft *f*

trade′wind′ *s* Passatwind *m*

trad′ing post′ *s* Handelsniederlassung *f*

trad′ing stamp′ *s* Rabattmarke *f*

tradition [trə′dɪʃən] *s* Tradition *f*

traditional [trə′dɪʃənəl] *adj* herkömmlich, traditionell

traf·fic [′træfɪk] *s* Verkehr *m*; (*trade*) (in) Handel *m* (in *dat*) ‖ *v* (*pret & pp* –ficked; *ger* –ficking) *intr*—**t. in** handeln in (*dat*)

traf′fic ac′cident *s* Verkehrsunfall *m*

traf′fic cir′cle *s* Kreisverkehr *m*

traf′fic is′land *s* Verkehrsinsel *f*

traf′fic jam′ *s* Verkehrsstockung *f*

traf′fic lane′ *s* Fahrbahn *f*

traf′fic light′ *s* Verkehrsampel *f*; **go through a t.** bei Rot durchfahren

traf′fic sign′ *s* Verkehrszeichen *n*

traf′fic tick′et *s* Strafzettel *m*

traf′fic viola′tion *s* Verkehrsdelikt *n*

tragedian [trə′dʒidɪ·ən] *s* Tragiker *m*

tragedy [′trædʒɪdi] *s* (& *fig*) Tragödie *f*

tragic [′trædʒɪk] *adj* tragisch

trail [trel] *s* (*path*) Fährte *f*; **be on s.o.'s t.** j–m auf der Spur sein; **t. of smoke** Rauchfahne *f* ‖ *tr* (*on foot*) nachgehen (*dat*); (*in a vehicle*) nachfahren (*dat*); (*in a race*) nachhinken (*dat*) ‖ *intr* (*said of a robe*) schleifen

trailer ['treilər] s Anhänger m; (mobile home) Wohnwagen m
trail'er camp' s Wohnwagenparkplatz m
train [tren] s (of railway cars) Zug m; (of a dress) Schleppe f; (following) Gefolge n; (of events) Folge f; **go by t.** mit dem Zug fahren; **t. of thought** Gedankengang m || tr ausbilden; (for a particular job) anlernen; (the memory) üben; (plants) am Spalier aufziehen; (an animal) dressieren; (a gun) (on) zielen (auf acc); (sport) trainieren || intr üben; (sport) trainieren
trained adj geschult, ausgebildet
trainee [tre'ni] s Anlernling m
trainer ['trenər] s (of domestic animals) Dresseur m, Dresseuse f; (of wild animals) Dompteur m, Dompteuse f; (aer) Schulflugzeug n; (sport) Sportwart –in mf
train'ing s Ausbildung f; (of animals) Dressur f; (sport) Training n
train'ing school' s (vocational school) Berufsschule f; (reformatory) Erziehungsanstalt f
trait [tret] s Charakterzug m
traitor ['tretər] s Verräter –in mf; (of a country) Hochverräter –in mf
trajectory [trə'dʒɛktəri] s Flugbahn f
tramp [træmp] s Landstreicher –in mf; (loose woman) Frauenzimmer n || tr trampeln; (traverse on foot) durchstreifen || intr vagabundieren; **t. on** herumtrampeln auf (dat)
trample ['træmpəl] s Getrampel n || tr trampeln; **t. to death** tottreten; **t. under foot** (fig) mit Füßen treten || intr—**t. on** herumtrampeln auf (dat); (fig) mit Füßen treten
trampoline ['træmpə,lin] s Trampolin n
trance [træns] s Trance f
tranquil ['træŋkwɪl] adj ruhig
tranquilize ['træŋkwɪ,laɪz] tr beruhigen
tranquilizer ['træŋkwɪ,laɪzər] s Beruhigungsmittel n
tranquillity [træn'kwɪlɪti] s Ruhe f
transact [træn'zækt] tr abwickeln
transaction [træn'zækʃən] s Abwicklung f; **transactions** (of a society) Sitzungsbericht m
transatlantic [,trænsət'læntɪk] adj transatlantisch
transcend [træn'sɛnd] tr übersteigen
transcendental [,trænsɛn'dɛntəl] adj übersinnlich; (philos) transzendental
transcribe [træn'skraɪb] tr (copy) umschreiben; (dictated or recorded material) übertragen; (mus) transkribieren; (phonet) in Lautschrift wiedergeben; (rad) auf Band aufnehmen
transcript ['trænskrɪpt] s Transkript n
transcription [træn'skrɪpʃən] s Umschrift f; (mus) Transkription f
transept ['trænsɛpt] s Querschiff n
trans-fer ['trænsfər] s (of property) Übertragung f; (of money) Überweisung f; (of an employee) Versetzung f; (of a passenger) Umsteigen n; (ticket) Umsteigefahrschein

m || [træns'fʌr], ['trænsfər] v (pret & pp –ferred; ger –ferring) tr (property) übertragen; (money) überweisen; (to another account) umbuchen; (an employee) versetzen || intr (to) versetzt werden (nach, zu); (said of a passenger) umsteigen
transfix [træns'fɪks] tr durchbohren
transform [træns'fɔrm] tr (a person) verwandeln; (into) umwandeln (in acc); (elec) umspannen
transformer [træns'fɔrmər] s (elec) Stromwandler m, Transformator m
transfusion [træns'fjuʒən] s (med) Übertragung f, Transfusion f
transgress [træns'grɛs] tr überschreiten
transgression [træs'grɛʃən] s Vergehen n
transient ['trænʃənt] adj vorübergehend; (fleeting) flüchtig || s Durchreisende mf
transistor [træn'sɪstər] adj Transistor– || s Transistor m
transistorize [træn'sɪstə,raɪz] tr transistorisieren
transit ['trænzɪt] s (astr) Durchgang m; (com) Transit m; **in t.** unterwegs
transition [træn'zɪʃən] s Übergang m
transitional [træn'zɪʃənəl] adj Übergangs–
transitive ['trænsɪtɪv] adj transitiv
transitory ['trænsɪ,tori] adj vergänglich
translate [træns'let] tr übersetzen; **t. into action** in die Tat umsetzen
translation [træns'leʃən] s Übersetzung f
translator [træns'letər] s Übersetzer –in mf
transliterate [træns'lɪtə,ret] tr transkribieren
translucent [træns'lusənt] adj durchscheinend, lichtdurchlässig
transmigration [,trænsmaɪ'greʃən] s— **t. of the soul** Seelenwanderung f
transmission [træns'mɪʃən] s (of a text) Textüberlieferung f; (of news, information) Übermittlung f; (aut) Getriebe n; (rad, telv) Sendung f
trans-mit [træns'mɪt] v (pret & pp –mitted; ger –mitting) tr (send forward) übersenden; (disease, power, light, heat) übertragen; (e.g., customs) überliefern; (by inheritance) vererben; (rad, telp, telv) senden
transmitter [træns'mɪtər] s (rad, telg, telv) Sender m
transmutation [,trænsmu'teʃən] s Umwandlung f; (biol) Transmutation f; (chem, phys) Umwandlung f
transmute [træns'mjut] tr umwandeln
transoceanic [,trænzoʃɪ'ænɪk] adj überseeisch, Übersee–
transom ['trænsəm] s (crosspiece) Querbalken m; (window over a door) Oberlicht n mit Kreuzsprosse; (of a boat) Spiegel m
transparency [træns'pɛrənsi] s Durchsichtigkeit f, Transparenz f; (phot) Diapositiv n
transparent [træns'pɛrənt] adj durchsichtig, transparent

transpire [træns'paɪr] *intr* (*happen*) sich ereignen; (*leak out*) (fig) durchsickern

transplant ['træns,plænt] *s* (bot, surg) Verpflanzung *f* || [træns'plænt] *tr* (bot, surg) verpflanzen

transport ['trænsport] *s* Beförderung *f*, Transport *m*; (nav) Truppentransporter *m* || [træns'port] *tr* befördern

transportation [,trænspor'teʃən] *s* Beförderung *f*; (*public transportation*) Verkehrsmittel *n*; **do you need t.?** brauchen Sie e-e Fahrgelegenheit?

trans′port plane′ *s* Transportflugzeug *n*

transpose [træns'poz] *tr* umstellen; (math, mus) transponieren

trans·ship [træns'ʃɪp] *v* (*pret & pp* -shipped; *ger* -shipping) *tr* (com, naut) umladen

trap [træp] *s* (& fig) Falle *f*; (*snare*) Schlinge *f*; (*pit*) Fallgrube *f*; (*under a sink*) Geruchsverschluß *m*; (*mouth*) (sl) Klappe *f*; (chem) Abscheider *m*; (golf) Sandbunker *m*; **fall** (or **walk**) **into a t.** in die Falle gehen; **set a trap** e-e Falle stellen || *v* (*pret & pp* trapped; *ger* trapping) *tr* mit e-r Falle fangen; (fig) erwischen; (mil) einfangen

trap′ door′ *s* Falltür *f*, Klapptür *f*; (theat) Versenkung *f*

trapeze [trə'piz] *s* Trapez *n*; (gym) Schwebereck *n*

trapezoid ['træpɪ,zɔɪd] *s* Trapez *n*

trapper ['træpər] *s* Fallensteller *m*

trappings ['træpɪŋz] *spl* Staat *m*; (*caparison*) Staatsgeschirr *n*

trap′shoot′ing *s* Tontaubenschießen *n*

trash [træʃ] *s* Abfälle *pl*; (*junk*) Schund *m*; (*artistically inferior material*) Kitsch *m*; (*worthless people*) Gesindel *n*

trash′ can′ *s* Mülleimer *m*, Abfalleimer *m*

trashy ['træʃi] *adj* kitschig; (*literature*) Schund-

travail [trə'vel] *s* Plackerei *f*; (*labor of childbirth*) Wehen *pl*

trav·el ['trævəl] *s* Reisen *n*; (*trip*) Reise *f*; (*e.g., of a bullet, rocket*) Bewegung *f*; (*of moving parts*) Lauf *m*; **travels** Reiseerlebnisse *pl* || *v* (*pret & pp* -el[l]ed; *ger* -el[l]ing) *tr* bereisen || *intr* reisen; (*said of a vehicle or passenger*) fahren; (astr, aut, mach, phys) sich bewegen

trav′el a′gency *s* Reisebüro *n*

traveler ['trævələr] *s* Reisende *mf*

trav′eler's check′ *s* Reisescheck *m*

trav′el·fold′er *s* Reiseprospekt *m*

trav′eling bag′ *s* Reisetasche *f*

trav′eling sales′man *s* (-men) Geschäftsreisende *m*

travelogue ['trævə,log] *s* Reisebericht *m*; (cin) Reisefilm *m*

traverse [trə'vʌrs] *tr* durchqueren || *intr* (*said of a gun*) sich drehen

traves·ty ['trævɪsti] *s* Travestie *f* || *v* (*pret & pp* -tied) *tr* travestieren

trawl [trɔl] *s* Schleppnetz *n* || *tr* mit dem Schleppnetz fangen || *intr* mit dem Schleppnetz fischen

trawler ['trɔlər] *s* Schleppnetzboot *n*

tray [tre] *s* Tablett *n*; (phot) Schale *f*

treacherous ['tretʃərəs] *adj* verräterisch; (*e.g., ice*) trügerisch

treachery ['tretʃəri] *s* Verrat *m*

tread [tred] *s* (*step*) Tritt *m*; (*imprint*) Spur *f*; (*on a tire*) Profil *n* || *v* (*pret* trod [trɑd]; *pp* trodden ['trɑdən] & trod) *tr* betreten || *intr* (on) treten (*auf acc*)

treadle ['tredəl] *s* Trittbrett *n*

tread′mill′ *s* (& fig) Tretmühle *f*

treason ['trizən] *s* Verrat *m*

treasonable ['trizənəbəl] *adj* verräterisch

treasure ['treʒər] *s* Schatz *m* || *tr* sehr schätzen

treasurer ['treʒərər] *s* Schatzmeister -in *mf*

treasury ['treʒəri] *s* Schatzkammer *f*; (*chest*) Tresor *m*; (*public treasury*) Staatsschatz *m*; **Treasury** Finanzministerium *n*

treat [trit] *s* Hochgenuß *m* || *tr* behandeln; (*regard*) (as) betrachten (als); **t. oneself to s.th.** sich [*dat*] etw genehmigen; **t. s.o. to s.th** j-n bewirten mit

treatise ['tritɪs] *s* Abhandlung *f*

treatment ['tritmənt] *s* Behandlung *f*

treaty ['triti] *s* Vertrag *m*

treble ['trebəl] *adj* (*threefold*) dreifach; (mus) Diskant- || *s* Diskant *m*; (*voice*) Diskantstimme *f* || *tr* verdreifachen || *intr* sich verdreifachen

tre′ble clef′ *s* Violinschlüssel *m*

tree [tri] *s* Baum *m*

treeless ['trilɪs] *adj* baumlos

tree′top′ *s* Baumwipfel *m*

tree′ trunk′ *s* Baumstamm *m*

trellis ['trelɪs] *s* Spalier *n*; (*gazebo*) Gartenhäuschen *n*

tremble ['trembəl] *s* Zittern *n* || *intr* zittern; (geol) beben; **t. all over** am ganzen Körper zittern

tremendous [trɪ'mendəs] *adj* ungeheuer

tremor ['tremər] *s* Zittern *n*; (geol) Beben *n*

trench [trentʃ] *s* Graben *m*; (mil) Schützengraben *m*

trenchant ['trentʃənt] *adj* schneidend; (*policy*) durchschlagend

trench′ war′fare *s* Stellungskrieg *m*

trend [trend] *s* Richtung *f*, Trend *m*

trespass ['trespəs] *s* unbefugtes Betreten *n*; (*sin*) Sünde *f* || *intr* unbefugt fremdes Eigentum betreten; **no trespassing** (*public sign*) Betreten verboten; **t. on** unbefugt betreten

trespasser ['trespəsər] *s* Unbefugte *mf*

tress [tres] *s* Flechte *f*

trestle ['tresəl] *s* Gestell *n*; (*of a bridge*) Brückenbock *m*

trial ['traɪəl] *s* (*attempt*) Versuch *m*; (*hardship*) Beschwernis *f*; (jur) Prozeß *m*; **a week's t.** e-e Woche Probezeit; **be on t. for** vor Gericht stehen wegen; **be brought up** (or **come up**) **for t.** zur Verhandlung kommen; **new t.** Wiederaufnahmeverfahren *n*; **on t.** (com) auf Probe; **put on t.** vor Gericht bringen

tri'al and er'ror s—by t. durch Ausprobieren

tri'al balloon' s Versuchsballon m

tri'al by ju'ry s Verhandlung f vor dem Schwurgericht

tri'al or'der s Probeauftrag m

tri'al run' s Probelauf m

triangle ['traɪ͵æŋgəl] s Dreieck n

triangular [traɪ'æŋgjələr] adj dreieckig

tribe [traɪb] s Stamm m; (pej) Sippschaft f

tribunal [traɪ'bjunəl] s Tribunal n

tributary ['trɪbjə͵teri] adj zinspflichtig || s Nebenfluß m

tribute ['trɪbjut] s Tribut m, Zins m; **pay t. to** Anerkennung zollen (dat)

trice [traɪs] s—**in a t.** im Nu

trick [trɪk] s Trick m; (prank) Streich m; (technique) Kniff m; (artifice) Schlich m; (cards) Stich m; **be on to s.o.'s tricks** j-s Schliche kennen; **be up to one's old tricks** sein Unwesen treiben; **do the t.** die Sache schaffen; **play a dirty t. on s.o.** j-m e-n gemeinen Streich spielen || tr reinlegen; **t. s.o. into** (ger) j-n durch Kniffe dazu bringen zu (inf)

trickery ['trɪkəri] s Gaunerei f

trickle ['trɪkəl] s Tröpfeln n || intr tröpfeln, rieseln

trickster ['trɪkstər] s Gauner m

tricky ['trɪki] adj (wily) listig; (touchy) heikel; (difficult) verzwickt

trident ['traɪdənt] s Dreizack m

tried [traɪd] adj bewährt, probat

trifle ['traɪfəl] s Kleinigkeit f; **a t.** (e.g., too big) ein bißchen || tr— **t. away** vertändeln || intr tändeln

trif'ling adj geringfügig || s Tändelei f

trigger ['trɪgər] s Abzug m; **pull the t.** abdrücken || tr auslösen

trig'ger-hap'py adj schießwütig

trigonometry [͵trɪgə'nɑmətri] s Trigonometrie f

trill [trɪl] s Triller m || tr & intr trillern

trillion ['trɪljən] s Billion f; (Brit) Trillion f

trilogy ['trɪlədʒi] s Trilogie f

trim [trɪm] adj (trimmer; trimmest) (figure) schick; (well-kept) gepflegt || s (e.g., of a hat) Zierleiste f; (naut) Trimm m; **be in t.** in Form sein || v (pret & pp trimmed; ger trimming) tr (clip) stutzen; (decorate) dekorieren; (a Christmas tree) schmücken; (beat) (coll) schlagen; (naut) trimmen

trim'ming s (e.g., of a dress) Besatz m; (of hedges) Stutzen n; **take a t.** (coll) e-e Niederlage erleiden; **trimmings** (decorations) Verzierungen pl; (food) Zutaten pl; (scraps) Abfälle pl; **with all the trimmings** (fig) mit allen Schikanen

trinity ['trɪnɪti] s Dreiheit f; **Trinity** Dreifaltigkeit f

trinket ['trɪŋkɪt] s Schmuckgegenstand m

tri-o ['tri-o] s (-os) (& mus) Trio n

trip [trɪp] s Reise f; (on drugs) Trip m; **go on** (or **take**) **a t.** e-e Reise

machen || v (pret & pp tripped; ger tripping) tr ein Bein stellen (dat); **t. up** (fig) zu Fall bringen || intr stolpern

tripartite [traɪ'pɑrtaɪt] adj Dreiparteien–; (of three powers) Dreimächte–

tripe [traɪp] s Kutteln pl; (sl) Schund m

trip'ham'mer s Schmiedehammer m

triple ['trɪpəl] adj dreifach || s Dreifache n || tr verdreifachen

triplet ['trɪplɪt] s (offspring) Drilling m; (mus) Triole f

triplicate ['trɪplɪkɪt] adj dreifach || s—**in t.** in dreifacher Ausfertigung

tripod ['traɪpɑd] s Dreifuß m; (phot) Stativ n

triptych ['trɪptɪk] s Triptychon n

trite [traɪt] adj abgedroschen

triumph ['traɪ.əmf] s Triumph m || intr (over) triumphieren (über acc)

triumphal [traɪ'ʌmfəl] adj Sieges–

triumphant [traɪ'ʌmfənt] adj triumphierend

trivia ['trɪvɪ-ə] spl Nichtigkeiten pl

trivial ['trɪvɪ-əl] adj trivial, alltäglich; (person) oberflächlich

triviality [͵trɪvɪ'ælɪti] s Trivialität f, Nebensächlichkeit f

Trojan ['trodʒən] adj trojanisch || s Trojaner –in mf

troll [trol] s (myth) Troll m || tr & intr mit der Schleppangel fischen

trolley ['trɑli] s Straßenbahn f

trollop ['trɑləp] s (slovenly woman) Schlampe f; (prostitute) Dirne f

trombone ['trɑmbon] s Posaune f

troop [trup] s Trupp m; (mil) Truppe f

trooper ['trupər] s Kavallerist m; **swear like a t.** fluchen wie ein Kutscher

troop'ship' s Truppentransporter m

trophy ['trofi] s Trophäe f; (sport) Pokal m

tropical ['trɑpɪkəl] adj Tropen–

tropics ['trɑpɪks] spl Tropen pl

trot [trɑt] s Trab m || v (pret & pp trotted; ger trotting) tr—**t. out** (coll) zur Schau stellen || intr traben

troubadour ['trubə͵dor] s Minnesänger m

trouble ['trʌbəl] s (inconvenience, bother) Mühe f; (difficulty) Schwierigkeit f; (physical distress) Leiden n; (civil disorder) Unruhe f; **ask for t.** das Schicksal herausfordern; **be in t.** in Schwierigkeiten sein; (be pregnant) schwanger sein; **cause s.o. a lot of t.** j-m viel zu schaffen machen; **get into t.** in Schwierigkeiten geraten; **go to a lot of t.** sich [dat] viel Mühe machen; **it was no t. at all!** gern geschehen!; **make t.** Geschichten machen; **take the t. to** (inf) sich der Mühe unterziehen zu (inf); **that's the t.** da liegt die Schwierigkeit; **what's the t.?** was ist los? || tr (worry) beunruhigen; (bother) belästigen; (distrurb) stören; (said of ills) plagen

trou'blemak'er s Unruhestifter –in mf

troubleshooter ['trʌbəl͵ʃutər] s Störungssucher –in *mf*; (*in disputes*) Friedensstifter –in *mf*

troublesome ['trʌbəlsəm] *adj* lästig

trough [trɔf] *s* Trog *m*; (*of a wave*) Wellental *n*

troupe [trup] *s* Truppe *f*

trousers ['trauzərz] *spl* Hose *f*

trous·seau [tru'so] *s* (–seaux & –seaus) Brautausstattung *f*

trout [traut] *s* Forelle *f*

trowel ['trau·əl] *s* Kelle *f*

truant ['tru·ənt] *adj* schwänzend || *s—* **play t.** die Schule schwänzen

truce [trus] *s* Waffenruhe *f*

truck [trʌk] *s* Last(kraft)wagen *m*; (*for luggage*) Gepäckwagen *m* || *tr* mit Lastkraftwagen befördern

truck'driv'er *s* Lastwagenfahrer *m*

trucker ['trʌkər] *s* (*driver*) Lastwagenfahrer *m*; (*owner of a trucking firm*) Fuhrunternehmer –in *mf*

truck' farm'ing *s* Gemüsebau *m*

truculent ['trʌkjələnt] *adj* gehässig

trudge [trʌdʒ] *intr* stapfen

true [tru] *adj* wahr; (*loyal*) (ge)treu; (*genuine*) echt; (*sign*) sicher; **come t.** sich verwirklichen; **prove t.** sich als wahr erweisen; **that's t.** das stimmt

truffle ['trʌfəl] *s* Trüffel *f*

truism ['tru·ɪzəm] *s* Binsenwahrheit *f*

truly ['truli] *adv* wirklich; **Yours t.** Hochachtungsvoll

trump [trʌmp] *s* Trumpf *m* || *tr* trumpfen; **t. up** erdichten || *intr* trumpfen

trumpet ['trʌmpɪt] *s* Trompete *f* || *intr* (*said of an elephant*) trompeten

truncheon ['trʌntʃən] *s* Gummiknüppel *m*

trunk [trʌŋk] *s* (*chest*) Koffer *m*; (*of a tree*) Stamm *m*; (*of a living body*) Rumpf *m*; (*of an elephant*) Rüssel *m*; (*aut*) Kofferraum *m*; **trunks** (sport) Sporthose *f*

trunk' line' *s* Fernverkehrsweg *m*

truss [trʌs] *s* (*archit*) Tragwerk *n*; (*med*) Bruchband *n* || *tr* (*archit*) stützen; (*bind*) festbinden

trust [trʌst] *s* (**in**) Vertrauen *n* (*auf acc*); (*com*) Trust *m*; (*jur*) Treuhand *f* || *tr* trauen (*dat*); (*hope*) hoffen || *intr*—**t. in** vertrauen auf (*acc*)

trust' com'pany *s* Treuhandgesellschaft *f*

trustee [trʌs'ti] *s* Aufsichtsrat *m*; (*jur*) Treuhänder –in *mf*

trustee'ship *s* Treuhandverwaltung *f*

trustful ['trʌstfəl] *adj* zutraulich

trust' fund' *s* Treuhandfonds *m*

trust'wor'thy *adj* vertrauenswürdig

trusty ['trʌsti] *adj* treu *s* Kalfaktor *m*

truth [truθ] *s* Wahrheit *f*; **in t.** wahrlich

truthful ['truθfəl] *adj* (*person*) ehrlich; (*e.g., account*) wahrheitsgemäß

try [traɪ] *s* Versuch *m* || *v* (*pret & pp* **tried**) *tr* versuchen; (*one's patience*) auf e–e harte Probe stellen; (*a case*) verhandeln; **be tried for** vor Gericht kommen wegen; **try on** anprobieren; (*a hat*) aufprobieren; **try out** erproben; (*new food*) kosten; **try s.o. for**

gegen j–n verhandeln wegen || *intr* versuchen

try'ing *adj* anstrengend

try'out' *s* (sport) Ausscheidungskampf *m*

T'-shirt' *s* T-Shirt *n*

tub [tʌb] *s* Wanne *f*; (*boat*) Kasten *m*

tubby ['tʌbi] *adj* (coll) kugelrund

tube [t(j)ub] *s* (*pipe*) Rohr *n*, Röhre *f*; (*e.g., of toothpaste*) Tube *f*; (*of rubber*) Schlauch *m*; (*rad*) Röhre *f*

tuber ['t(j)ubər] *s* (bot) Knolle *f*

tubercle ['t(j)ubərkəl] *s* Tuberkel *m*

tuberculosis [t(j)u,bʌrkjə'losɪs] *s* Lungenschwindsucht *f*

tuck [tʌk] *s* (sew) Abnäher *m* || *tr* (*into one's pocket, under a mattress*) stecken; (*under one's arm*) klemmen; (*into bed*) packen; **t. in** reinstecken; **t. up** (*trousers*) hochkrempeln; (*a skirt, dress*) hochschürzen

Tuesday ['t(j)uzde] *s* Dienstag *m*; **on T. am** Dienstag

tuft [tʌft] *s* Büschel *m & n* || *tr* (*e.g., a mattress*) durchheften

tug [tʌg] *s* (*pull*) Zug *m*; (*boat*) Schlepper *m* || *v* (*pret & pp* **tugged**; *ger* **tugging**) *tr* schleppen || *intr* (*at*) zerren (*an dat*)

tug'boat' *s* Schleppdampfer *m*

tug' of war' *s* Tauziehen *n*

tuition [t(j)u'ɪʃən] *s* Schuldgeld *n*

tulip ['t(j)ulɪp] *s* Tulpe *f*

tumble ['tʌmbəl] *s* (*fall*) Sturz *m*; (*gym*) Purzelbaum *m* || *intr* (*fall*) stürzen; (*gym*) Saltos machen; **t. down the stairs** die Treppe henunterpurzeln

tum'ble-down' *adj* baufällig

tumbler ['tʌmblər] *s* (*glass*) Trinkglas *n*; (*of a lock*) Zuhaltung *f*; (*acrobat*) Akrobat –in *mf*

tumor ['t(j)umər] *s* Geschwulst *f*

tumult ['t(j)umʌlt] *s* Getümmel *m*

tuna ['tunə] *s* Thunfisch *m*

tune [t(j)un] *s* Melodie *f*; **be in t.** richtig gestimmt sein; **be out of t.** falsch singen; (*said of a piano*) verstimmt sein; **change one's t.** e–n anderen Ton anschlagen || *tr* stimmen; **t. up** (aut) neu einstellen || *intr*—**t. in** on (rad) einstellen; **t. up** (*said of an orchestra*) stimmen

tungsten ['tʌŋstən] *s* Wolfram *n*

tunic ['t(j)unɪk] *s* Tunika *f*

tun'ing fork' *s* Stimmgabel *f*

tun·nel ['tʌnəl] *s* Tunnel *m*; (min) Stollen *m* || *v* (*pret & pp* **–nel[l]ed**; *ger* **–nel[l]ing**) *intr* e–n Tunnel bohren

turban ['tʌrbən] *s* Turban *m*

turbid ['tʌrbɪd] *adj* trüb(e)

turbine ['tʌrbɪn] *s* Turbine *f*

turboprop ['tʌrbo,prɑp] *s* Turboprop *m*

turbulence ['tʌrbjələns] *s* Turbulenz *f*

tureen [t(j)u'rin] *s* Terrine *f*

turf [tʌrf] *s* Rasendecke *f*; (*of a gang*) (sl) Gebiet *n*; **the t.** der Turf

Turk [tʌrk] *s* Türke *m*, Türkin *f*

turkey ['tʌrki] *s* Truthahn *m*; (*female*) Truthenne *f*; **Turkey** die Türkei

Turkish ['tɜrkɪʃ] *adj* türkisch ‖ *s* Türkisch *n*

Tur'kish tow'el *s* Frottiertuch *n*

turmoil ['tɜrmɔɪl] *s* Getümmel *n*

turn [tɜrn] *s* (*rotation*) Drehung *f*; (*change of direction or condition*) Wendung *f*; (*curve*) Kurve *f*; (*by a driver*) Abbiegen *n*; (*of a century*) Wende *f*; (*of a spool*) Windung *f*; **at every t.** bei jeder Gelegenheit; **good t.** Gunst *f*; **it's his t.** er ist dran; **out of t.** außer der Reihe; **take turns** sich abwechseln ‖ *tr* drehen; (*the page*) umblättern; (*one's head*) wenden; **t. down** (*refuse*) ablehnen; (*a radio*) leiser stellen; (*a bed*) aufdecken; (*a collar*) umschlagen; (*an appeal*) (*jur*) verwerfen; **t. in** (*an application, resignation*) einreichen; (*lost articles*) abgeben; (*a person*) anzeigen; **t. into** verwandeln in (*acc*); **t. loose** frei lassen; **t. off** (*light, gas*) abdrehen; (*rad, telv*) abstellen; (*a collar*) umschlagen; (*an appeal*) (*jur*) verwerfen; **t. on** (*gas, light*) andrehen; (*excite*) (coll) in Erregung versetzen; (*rad, telv*) anstellen; **t. out** produzieren; (*pockets*) umkehren; (*eject*) vor die Tür setzen; **t. over** (*property*) abtreten; (*a business*) übertragen; (*e.g., weapons*) abliefern; **t. up** (*a card, sleeve*) aufschlagen ‖ *intr* (*rotate*) sich drehen; (*in some direction*) sich wenden; **it turned out that es** stellte sich heraus, daß; **t. against** (fig) sich wenden gegen; **t. around** sich herumdrehen; **t. back** umdrehen; **t. down** (*a street*) einbiegen in (*acc*); **t. in** (*go to bed*) zu Bett gehen; **t. into** werden zu; **t. out** ausfallen; **t. out for** sich einfinden zu; **t. out for the best** sich zum Guten wenden; **t. out in force** vollzählig erscheinen; **t. out to be** sich erweisen als; **t. over** (*tip over*) umkippen; (aut) anspringen; **t. to s.o. for help** sich an j-n um Hilfe wenden; **t. towards** sich wenden gegen; **t. up** auftauchen

turn'coat' *s* Überläufer –in *mf*

turn'ing point' *s* Wendepunkt *m*

turnip ['tɜrnɪp] *s* Steckrübe *f*

turn'out' *s* Beteiligung *f*

turn'o'ver *s* Umsatz *m*

turn'pike' *s* Autobahn *f*

turnstile ['tɜrn‚staɪl] *s* Drehkreuz *n*

turn'ta'ble *s* Plattenteller *m*; (rr) Drehscheibe *f*

turpentine ['tɜrpən‚taɪn] *s* Terpentin *n*

turpitude ['tɜrpɪ‚t(j)ud] *s* Verworfenheit *f*

turquoise ['tɜrk(w)ɔɪz] *adj* türkisfarben ‖ *s* Türkis *m*

turret ['tɜrɪt] *s* Turm *m*

turtle ['tɜrtəl] *s* Schildkröte *f*

tur'tledove' *s* Turteltaube *f*

tur'tleneck' *s* Rollkragen *m*

tusk [tʌsk] *s* (*of an elephant*) Stoßzahn *m*; (*of a boar*) Hauer *m*

tussle ['tʌsəl] *s* Rauferei *f* ‖ *intr* raufen

tutor ['t(j)utər] *s* Hauslehrer –in *mf*

tuxe•do [tʌk'sido] *s* (**–dos**) Smoking *m*

twang [twæŋ] *s* (*of a musical instrument*) Schwirren *n*; (*of the voice*) Näseln *n* ‖ *intr* schwirren; näseln

tweed [twid] *adj* aus Tweed ‖ *s* Tweed *m*

tweet [twit] *s* Gezwitscher *n* ‖ *intr* zwitschern

tweezers ['twizərz] *spl* Pinzette *f*

twelfth [twelfθ] *adj & pron* zwölfte ‖ *s* (*fraction*) Zwölftel *n*; **the t.** (*in dates or in series*) der Zwölfte

twelve [twelv] *adj & pron* zwölf ‖ *s* Zwölf *f*

twentieth ['twentɪ‚ɪθ] *adj & pron* zwanzigste ‖ *s* (*fraction*) Zwanzigstel *n*; **the t.** (*in dates or in series*) der Zwanzigste

twenty ['twenti] *adj & pron* zwanzig ‖ *s* Zwanzig *f*; **the twenties** die zwanziger Jahre

twen'ty-one' *adj & pron* einundzwanzig

twice [twaɪs] *adv* zweimal

twiddle ['twɪdəl] *tr* müßig herumdrehen; **t. one's thumbs** Daumen drehen

twig [twɪg] *s* Zweig *m*

twilight ['twaɪ‚laɪt] *adj* dämmerig ‖ *s* Abenddämmerung *f*

twin [twɪn] *adj* (*brother, sister*) Zwillings–; (*double*) Doppel– ‖ *s* Zwilling *m*

twine [twaɪn] *s* (*for a package*) Bindfaden *m*; (sew) Zwirn *m* ‖ *tr*–**t. around** winden um

twin'-en'gine *adj* zweimotorig

twinge [twɪndʒ] *s* stechender Schmerz *m*

twinkle ['twɪŋkəl] *s* Funkeln *n*; **in a t.** im Nu ‖ *intr* funkeln

twirl [twɜrl] *s* Wirbel *m* ‖ *tr* herumwirbeln ‖ *intr* wirbeln

twist [twɪst] *s* (*turn*) Drehung *f*; (*distortion*) Verdrehung *f*; (*strand*) Flechte *f*; (*bread roll*) Zopf *m*; (*dance*) Twist *m* ‖ *tr* (*revolve*) drehen; (*wind*) winden; (*an arm, words*) verdrehen; **t. one's ankle** sich [*dat*] den Knöchel vertreten ‖ *intr* sich drehen; (*wind*) sich winden

twister ['twɪstər] *s* (coll) Windhose *f*

twit [twɪt] *s* (sl) Depp *m* ‖ *v* (*pret & pp* **twitted**; *ger* **twitting**) *tr* verspotten; (*upbraid*) rügen

twitch [twɪtʃ] *s* Zucken *n* ‖ *intr* zucken

twitter ['twɪtər] *s* Zwitschern *n* ‖ *intr* zwitschern

two [tu] *adj & pron* zwei ‖ *s* Zwei *f*; **by twos** zu zweit; **in two** entzwei; **put two and two together** Schlußfolgerungen ziehen

two'-edged' *adj* zweischneidig

two'-faced' *adj* doppelzüngig

two' hun'dred *adj & pron* zweihundert

two'-piece' *adj* (*suit*) zweiteilig

twosome ['tusəm] *s* (*of lovers*) Liebespaar *n*; (golf) Einzelspiel *n*

two'-time' *tr* untreu sein (*dat*)

two'-tone' *adj* zweifarbig

two'-way traf'fic *s* Gegenverkehr *m*

tycoon [taɪ'kun] *s* Industriekapitän *m*

type [taɪp] *s* (*kind*) Art *f*; (*of person; of manufacture*) Typ *m*; (typ) Drucktype *f*, Letter *f* ‖ *tr & intr* tippen

type′face′ s Schriftbild n
type′script′ s Maschinenschrift f
type′set′ter s Schriftsetzer –in mf
type′write′ v (pret –wrote; pp –written) tr & intr mit der Maschine schreiben
type′writ′er s Schreibmaschine f
type′writer rib′bon s Farbband n
ty′phoid fe′ver [′taɪfɔɪd] s Typhus m
typhoon [taɪ′fun] s Taifun m
typical [′tɪpɪkəl] adj (of) typisch (für)
typi‧fy [′tɪpɪ,faɪ] v (pret & pp –fied) tr (characterize) typisch sein für; (exemplify) ein typisches Beispiel sein für
typ′ing er′ror s Tippfehler m

typist [′taɪpɪst] s Maschinenschreiber –in mf
typographic(al) [,taɪpə′græfɪk(əl)] adj typographisch; (error) Druck–
typography [taɪ′pɑgrəfi] s (the skill) Buchdruckerkunst f; (the work) Buchdruck m
tyrannical [tɪ′rænɪkəl] adj tyrannisch
tyrannize [′tɪrə,naɪz] tr tyrannisieren
tyranny [′tɪrəni] s Tyrannei f
tyrant [′taɪrənt] s Tyrann m
ty‧ro [′taɪro] s (–ros) Neuling m
Tyrol [tɪ′rol] s Tirol n
Tyrolean [tɪ′roli‧ən] adj tirolerisch ‖ s Tiroler –in mf

U

U, u [ju] s einundzwanzigster Buchstabe des englischen Alphabets
ubiquitous [ju′bɪkwɪtəs] adj allgegenwärtig
udder [′ʌdər] s Euter n
ugliness [′ʌglɪnɪs] s Häßlichkeit f
ugly [′ʌgli] adj häßlich
Ukraine [ju′kren] s Ukraine f
Ukrainian [ju′krenɪ‧ən] adj ukrainisch ‖ s (person) Ukrainer –in mf; (language) Ukrainisch n
ulcer [′ʌlsər] s Geschwür n
ulcerate [′ʌlsə,ret] intr eitern
ulte′rior mo′tive [ʌl′tɪrɪ‧ər] s Hintergedanke m
ultimate [′ʌltɪmɪt] adj äußerste; (goal) höchst; (result) End– ‖ s Letzte n
ultima‧tum [,ʌltɪ′metəm] s (–tums & –ta [tə]) Ultimatum n
ul′trahigh fre′quency [′ʌltrə,haɪ] s Ultrahochfrequenz f
ultramodern [,ʌltrə′mɑdərn] adj ultramodern
ultraviolet [,ʌltrə′vaɪ‧əlɪt] adj ultraviolett ‖ s Ultraviolett n
ultravi′olet lamp′ s Höhensonne f
umbil′ical cord′ [ʌm′bɪlɪkəl] adj Nabelschnur f
umbrage [′ʌmbrɪdʒ] s—take u. at Anstoß nehmen an (dat)
umbrella [ʌm′brelə] s Regenschirm m; (aer) Abschirmung f
umlaut [′umlaut] s Umlaut m ‖ tr umlauten
umpire [′ʌmpaɪr] s Schiedsrichter –in mf ‖ tr als Schiedsrichter leiten ‖ intr Schiedsrichter sein
umpteen [ʌmp′tin] adj zig; u. times zigmal
UN [′ju′en] s (United Nations) UNO f
unable [ʌn′ebəl] adj unfähig
unabridged [ʌnə′brɪdʒd] adj ungekürzt
unaccented [,ʌnæk′sentɪd] adj unbetont
unacceptable [,ʌnæk′septɪbəl] adj unannehmbar
unaccountable [,ʌnə′kauntəbəl] adj

nicht verantwortlich; (strange) seltsam
unaccounted-for [,ʌnə′kauntɪd ,fɔr] adj unerklärt; (acct) nicht belegt
unaccustomed [,ʌnə′kʌstəmd] adj (to) nicht gewöhnt (an acc)
unaffected [,ʌnə′fektɪd] adj nicht affektiert; u. by unbeeinflusst von
unafraid [,ʌnə′fred] adj—be u. (of) sich nicht fürchten (vor dat)
unalterable [ʌn′ɔltərəbəl] adj unabänderlich
unanimity [,junə′nɪmɪti] s Stimmeneinheit f
unanimous [ju′nænɪməs] adj (persons) einmütig; (vote) einstimmig
unannounced [,ʌnə′naunst] adj unangemeldet
unanswered [ʌn′ænsərd] adj (question) unbeantwortet; (claim, statement) unwiderlegt; (request) nicht erhört
unappreciative [,ʌnə′priʃɪ‧ətɪv] adj (of) unempfänglich (für)
unapproachable [,ʌnə′protʃəbəl] adj unzugänglich
unarmed [ʌn′ɑrmd] adj unbewaffnet
unasked [ʌn′æskt] adj (advice) unerbeten; (uninvited) ungeladen
unassailable [,ʌnə′seləbəl] adj unangreifbar
unassuming [,ʌnə′s(j)umɪŋ] adj nicht anmaßend
unattached [,ʌnə′tætʃt] adj (to) nicht befestigt (an dat); (person) ungebunden; (mil) zur Verfügung stehend
unattainable [,ʌnə′tenəbəl] adj unerreichbar
unattended [,ʌnə′tendɪd] adj unbeaufsichtigt
unattractive [,ʌnə′træktɪv] adj reizlos
unauthorized [ʌn′ɔθəraɪzd] adj unberechtigt
unavailable [,ʌnə′veləbəl] adj (person) unabkömmlich; (thing) nicht verfügbar
unavenged [,ʌnə′vendʒd] adj ungerächt
unavoidable [,ʌnə′vɔɪdəbəl] adj unvermeidlich

unaware [ˌʌnəˈwɛr] *adj* (**of**) nicht bewußt (*genit*)

unawares [ˌʌnəˈwɛrz] *adv* (*unexpectedly*) unversehens; (*unintentionally*) versehentlich; **catch u.** überraschen

unbalanced [ʌnˈbælənst] *adj* nicht im Gleichgewicht; (*fig*) unausgeglichen

un·bar [ʌnˈbɑr] *v* (*pret & pp* **–barred;** *ger* **–barring**) *tr* aufriegeln

unbearable [ʌnˈbɛrəbəl] *adj* unerträglich

unbeaten [ʌnˈbitən] *adj* (& *fig*) ungeschlagen

unbecoming [ˌʌnbɪˈkʌmɪŋ] *adj* (*improper*) ungeziemend; (*clothing*) unkleidsam

unbelievable [ˌʌnbɪˈlivəbəl] *adj* unglaublich

unbeliever [ˌʌnbɪˈlivər] *s* Ungläubige *mf*

unbending [ʌnˈbɛndɪŋ] *adj* unbeugsam

unbiased [ʌnˈbaɪəst] *adj* unvoreingenommen

unbidden [ʌnˈbɪdən] *adj* ungebeten

un·bind [ʌnˈbaɪnd] *v* (*pret & pp* **–bound**) *tr* losbinden

unbleached [ʌnˈblitʃt] *adj* ungebleicht

unbolt [ʌnˈbolt] *tr* aufriegeln

unborn [ˈʌnbɔrn] *adj* ungeboren

unbosom [ʌnˈbuzəm] *tr* –**u. oneself to** sich offenbaren (*dat*)

unbowed [ʌnˈbaud] *adj* ungebeugt

unbreakable [ʌnˈbrekəbəl] *adj* unzerbrechlich

unbridled [ʌnˈbraɪdəld] *adj* ungezügelt

unbroken [ʌnˈbrokən] *adj* (*intact*) ungebrochen; (*line, series*) ununterbrochen; (*horse*) nicht zugeritten

unbuckle [ʌnˈbʌkəl] *tr* aufschnallen

unburden [ʌnˈbʌrdən] *tr* entlasten; **u. oneself** sein Herz ausschütten

unburied [ʌnˈbɛrɪd] *adj* unbeerdigt

unbutton [ʌnˈbʌtən] *adj* aufknöpfen

uncalled-for [ʌnˈkɔld ˌfɔr] *adj* unangebracht

uncanny [ʌnˈkæni] *adj* unheimlich

uncared-for [ʌnˈkɛrd ˌfɔr] *adj* verwahrlost

unceasing [ʌnˈsisɪŋ] *adj* unaufhörlich

unceremonious [ˌʌnsɛrɪˈmoni·əs] *adj* (*informal*) ungezwungen; (*rude*) unsanft

uncertain [ʌnˈsʌrtən] *adj* unsicher

uncertainty [ʌnˈsʌrtənti] *s* Unsicherheit *f*

unchain [ʌnˈtʃen] *tr* losketten; (*fig*) entfesseln

unchangeable [ʌnˈtʃendʒəbəl] *adj* unveränderlich

uncharacteristic [ˌʌnkærɪktəˈrɪstɪk] *adj* wesensfremd

uncharted [ʌnˈtʃɑrtɪd] *adj* auf keiner Karte verzeichnet

unchaste [ʌnˈtʃest] *adj* unkeusch

unchecked [ʌnˈtʃɛkt] *adj* ungehemmt

unchristian [ʌnˈkrɪstʃən] *adj* unchristlich

uncivilized [ʌnˈsɪvɪˌlaɪzd] *adj* unzivilisiert

unclad [ʌnˈklæd] *adj* unbekleidet

unclaimed [ʌnˈklemd] *adj* nicht abgeholt

unclasp [ʌnˈklæsp] *tr* loshaken; (*the arms, hands*) öffnen

unclassified [ʌnˈklæsɪ ˌfaɪd] *adj* nicht klassifiziert; (*not secret*) nicht geheim

uncle [ˈʌnkəl] *s* Onkel *m*

unclean [ʌnˈklin] *adj* unsauber; (*relig*) unrein

unclear [ʌnˈklɪr] *adj* unklar

un·clog [ʌnˈklɑg] *v* (*pret & pp* **–clogged;** *ger* **–clogging**) *tr* von e–m Hindernis befreien

uncombed [ʌnˈkomd] *adj* ungekämmt

uncomfortable [ʌnˈkʌmfərtəbəl] *adj* unbequem; **feel u.** sich nicht recht wohl fühlen

uncommitted [ˌʌnkəˈmɪtɪd] *adj* (*troops*) nicht eingesetzt; (*delegates, nations*) unentschieden

uncommon [ʌnˈkɑmən] *adj* ungewöhnlich; (*outstanding*) außergewöhnlich

uncomplaining [ˌʌnkʌmˈplenɪŋ] *adj* klaglos

uncompromising [ʌnˈkɑmprəˌmaɪzɪŋ] *adj* unbeugsam

unconcealed [ˌʌnkənˈsild] *adj* unverholen

unconcerned [ˌʌnkənˈsʌrnd] *adj* (**about**) unbesorgt (um)

unconditional [ˌʌnkənˈdɪʃənəl] *adj* bedingungslos

unconfirmed [ˌʌnkənˈfɪrmd] *adj* unbestätigt, unverbürgt

unconquerable [ʌnˈkɑŋkərəbəl] *adj* unüberwindlich

unconquered [ʌnˈkɑŋkərd] *adj* unbezwungen

unconscious [ʌnˈkɑnʃəs] *adj* bewußtlos; (*of*) nicht bewußt (*genit*) ‖ *s*–**the u.** das Unbewußte

unconstitutional [ˌʌnkɑnstɪˈt(j)uʃənəl] *adj* verfassungswidrig

uncontested [ˌʌnkənˈtɛstɪd] *adj* unbestritten

uncontrollable [ˌʌnkənˈtroləbəl] *adj* unkontrollierbar; (*fig*) unbändig

unconventional [ˌʌnkənˈvɛntʃənəl] *adj* unkonventionell

uncork [ʌnˈkɔrk] *tr* entkorken

uncouple [ʌnˈkʌpəl] *tr* abkoppeln

uncouth [ʌnˈkuθ] *adj* ungehobelt; (*appearance*) ungeschlacht

uncover [ʌnˈkʌvər] *tr* aufdecken

unctuous [ˈʌŋktʃu·əs] *adj* salbungsvoll

uncultivated [ʌnˈkʌltɪˌvetɪd] *adj* unbebaut

uncultured [ʌnˈkʌltʃərd] *adj* (*fig*) unkultiviert

uncut [ʌnˈkʌt] *adj* nicht abgeschnitten; (*gem*) ungeschliffen; (*grain*) ungemäht

undamaged [ʌnˈdæmɪdʒd] *adj* unbeschädigt, unversehrt

undaunted [ʌnˈdɔntɪd] *adj* unverzagt

undecided [ˌʌndɪˈsaɪdɪd] *adj* (*person*) unschlüssig; (*thing*) unentschieden

undefeated [ˌʌndɪˈfitɪd] *adj* unbesiegt

undefended [ˌʌndɪˈfɛndɪd] *adj* unverteidigt

undefiled [ˌʌndɪˈfaɪld] *adj* unbefleckt

undefined [ˌʌndɪˈfaɪnd] *adj* unklar

undeliverable [ˌʌndɪˈlɪvərəbəl] *adj* unbestellbar

undeniable [ˌʌndɪˈnaɪ·əbəl] *adj* unleugbar
under [ˈʌndər] *adj* Unter– ‖ *adv*
unter–, e.g., go u. untergehen ‖ *prep*
unter (*position*) (*dat*); (*direction*)
unter (*acc*)
un'derage' *adj* unmündig
un·der·bid' *v* (*pret & pp* **–bid**; *ger*
–bidding) *tr* unterbieten
un'derbrush' *s* Unterholz *n*
un'dercar'riage *s* Fahrgestell *n*
un'derclothes' *spl* Unterwäsche *f*
un'dercov'er *adj* Geheim–; **u. agent**
Spitzel *m*
un'dercur'rent *s* (& *fig*) Unterströ-
mung *f*
un'dercut' *v* (*pret & pp* **–cut**; *ger* **–cutting**) *tr* unterbieten
un'derdevel'oped *adj* unterentwickelt
un'derdog' *s* (coll) Unterlegene *mf*
un'derdone' *adj* nicht durchgebraten
un'deres'timate *tr* unterschätzen
un'derexpose' *tr* (phot) unterbelichten
un'dergar'ment *s* Unterkleidung *f*
un'dergo' *v* (*pret* **–went**; *pp* **–gone**)
durchmachen; (*an operation*) sich
unterziehen (*dat*)
un'dergrad'uate *s* Collegestudent –in
mf
un'derground' *adj* unterirdisch; (fig)
Untergrund–; (*water*) Grund–; (min)
unter Tage ‖ **un'derground'** *s* (*secret
movement*) Untergrundbewegung *f*;
go u. untertauchen
un'dergrowth' *s* Buschholz *n*, Unterholz
n
un'derhand' *adj* (*throw*) unter Schulter-
höhe (ausgeführt)
un'derhand'ed *adj* hinterhältig
un'derline', **un'derline'** *tr* unterstreichen
underling [ˈʌndərlɪŋ] *s* Handlanger *m*
un'dermine' *tr* (& *fig*) untergraben
underneath [ˌʌndərˈniθ] *adj* Unter– ‖
adv unten ‖ *s* Unterseite *f* ‖ *prep*
(*position*) unter (*dat*), unterhalb
(*genit*); (*direction*) unter (*acc*)
un'dernour'ished *adj* unterernährt
un'dernour'ishment *s* Unterernährung *f*
un'derpad' *s* (*of a rug*) Unterlage *f*
un'derpaid' *adj* unterbezahlt
un'derpass' *s* Straßenunterführung *f*
un'derpin' *v* (*pret & pp* **–pinned**; *ger*
–pinning) *tr* untermauern
un'derplay' *tr* unterspielen
un'derpriv'ileged *adj* benachteiligt
un'derrate' *tr* unterschätzen
un'derscore' *tr* (& *fig*) unterstreichen
un'dersea' *adj* Unterwasser–
un'dersec'retar'y *s* Untersekretär –in
mf
un·der·sell' *v* (*pret & pp* **–sold**; *ger*
–selling) *tr* (*a person*) unterbieten;
(*goods*) verschleudern
un'dershirt' *s* Unterhemd *n*
un'derside' *s* Unterseite *f*
un'dersigned' *adj* unterschrieben ‖
un'dersigned' *s* Unterzeichnete *mf*
un'derstand' *v* (*pret & pp* **–stood**) *tr*
verstehen; **it's understood that** es ist
selbstverständlich, daß; **make oneself
understood** sich verständlich machen

understandable [ˌʌndərˈstændəbəl] *adj*
verständlich
understandably [ˌʌndərˈstændəbli] *adv*
begreiflicherweise
un'derstand'ing *adj* verständnisvoll ‖ *s*
(**of**) Verständnis *n* (für); (*between
persons*) Einvernehmen *n*; (*agreement*) Übereinkommen *n*; **come to an
u. with s.o.** sich mit j–m verständigen; **it is my u. that** wie ich verstehe
un'derstud'y *s* Ersatzmann *m*; (cin,
theat) Ersatzschauspieler –in *mf*
un·der·take' *v* (*pret* **–took**; *pp* **–taken**)
tr unternehmen
undertaker ‖ˈʌndərˌtekər‖ *s* Leichenbestatter –in *mf*
un'dertak'ing *s* Unternehmen *n*
un'dertone' *s* leise Stimme *f*; (fig)
Unterton *m*
un'dertow' *s* Sog *m*
un'derwa'ter *adj* Unterwasser–
un'derwear' *s* Unterwäsche *f*
un'derweight' *adj* untergewichtig
un'derworld' *s* (**of** *criminals*) Unterwelt *f*; (myth) Totenreich *n*
un·der·write', **un'derwrite'** *v* (*pret*
–wrote; *pp* **–written**) *tr* unterschrei-
ben; (ins) versichern
un'derwrit'er *s* Unterzeichner –in *mf*;
(ins) Versicherer –in *mf*; (st. exch.)
Wertpapiermakler –in *mf*; **under-
writers** Emissionsfirma *f*
undeserved [ˌʌndɪˈzɑrvd] *adj* unverdient
undeservedly [ˌʌndɪˈzɑrvidli] *adv* un-
verdientermaßen
undesirable ‖ˌʌndɪˈzaɪrəbəl‖ *adj* unerwünscht ‖ *s* Unerwünschte *mf*
undeveloped [ˌʌndɪˈveləpt] *adj* unent-
wickelt; (*land*) unerschlossen
undies [ˈʌndiz] *spl* (coll) Unterwäsche
f
undigested [ˌʌndɪˈdʒestɪd] *adj* (& *fig*)
unverdaut
undignified [ʌnˈdɪgnɪˌfaɪd] *adj* wür-
delos
undiluted [ˌʌndɪˈlutɪd] *adj* unverdünnt
undiminished [ˌʌndɪˈmɪnɪʃt] *adj* unvermindert
undisciplined [ʌnˈdɪsəplɪnd] *adj* un-
diszipliniert, zuchtlos
undisputed ‖ˌʌndɪsˈpjutɪd‖ *adj* unbestritten, unangefochten
undisturbed [ˌʌndɪsˈtʌrbd] *adj* ungestört
undivided [ˌʌndɪˈvaɪdɪd] *adj* ungeteilt
un·do' [ʌnˈdu] *v* (*pret* **–did**; *pp* **–done**)
tr (*a knot*) aufschnüren; (*a deed*) un-
geschehen machen
undo'ing *s* Ruin *m*
undone [ʌnˈdʌn] *adj* (*not done*) un-
getan; (*ruined*) ruiniert; **come u.**
sich lösen; **leave nothing u.** nichts
unversucht lassen
undoubtedly [ʌnˈdautidli] *adv* zweifellos
undramatic [ˌʌndrəˈmætɪk] *adj* undra-
matisch
undress [ʌnˈdres] *s*—**in a state of u.**
(*nude*) in unbekleidetem Zustand; (*in
a negligee*) im Negligé ‖ *tr* ausziehen
‖ *intr* sich ausziehen

undrinkable [ʌnˈdrɪŋkəbəl] adj nicht trinkbar

undue [ʌnˈd(j)u] adj (inappropriate) unangemessen; (excessive) übermäßig

undulate [ˈʌndjəˌlet] intr wogen

undulating [ˈʌndjəˌletɪŋ] adj wellenförmig

unduly [ʌnˈd(j)uli] adv übermäßig

undying [ʌnˈdaɪ·ɪŋ] adj unsterblich

un'earned in'come [ˈʌnˌʌrnd] s Kapitalrente f

unearth [ʌnˈʌrθ] tr ausgraben; (fig) aufstöbern

unearthly [ʌnˈʌrθli] adj unirdisch; (cry) schauerlich; at an u. hour (early) in aller Herrgottsfrühe

uneasy [ʌnˈizi] adj (worried) ängstlich; (ill at ease) unbehaglich

uneatable [ʌnˈitəbəl] adj ungenießbar

uneconomic(al) [ˌʌnekəˈnɑmɪk(əl)] adj unwirtschaftlich

uneducated [ʌnˈedjəˌketɪd] adj ungebildet

unemployed [ˌʌnemˈplɔɪd] adj arbeitslos ‖ s Arbeitslose mf

unemployment [ˌʌnemˈplɔɪmənt] s Arbeitslosigkeit f

unemploy'ment compensa'tion s Arbeitslosenunterstützung f; collect u. (sl) Stempeln gehen

unencumbered [ˌʌnənˈkʌmbərd] adj unbelastet

unending [ʌnˈendɪŋ] adj endlos

unequal [ʌnˈikwəl] adj ungleich; u. to nicht gewachsen (dat)

unequaled [ʌnˈikwəld] adj ohnegleichen

unequivocal [ˌʌnəˈkwɪvəkəl] adj eindeutig

unerring [ʌnˈerɪŋ] adj unfehlbar

UNESCO [juˈnesko] s (United Nations Educational, Scientific, and Cultural Organization) UNESCO f

unessential [ˌʌneˈsenʃəl] adj unwesentlich

uneven [ʌnˈivən] adj (not smooth) uneben; (unbalanced) ungleich; (not uniform) ungleichmäßig; (number) ungerade

uneventful [ˌʌnɪˈventfəl] adj ereignislos

unexceptional [ˌʌnekˈsepʃənəl] adj nicht außergewöhnlich

unexpected [ˌʌnekˈspektɪd] adj unerwartet

unexplained [ˌʌnekˈsplend] adj unerklärt

unexplored [ˌʌnekˈsplord] adj unerforscht

unexposed [ˌʌnekˈspozd] adj (phot) unbelichtet

unfading [ʌnˈfedɪŋ] adj unverwelklich

unfailing [ʌnˈfelɪŋ] adj unfehlbar

unfair [ʌnˈfer] adj unfair; (competition) unlauter

unfaithful [ʌnˈfeθfəl] adj treulos

unfamiliar [ˌʌnfəˈmɪljər] adj unbekannt

unfasten [ʌnˈfæsən] tr losbinden; (e.g., a seat belt) aufschnallen

unfathomable [ʌnˈfæðəməbəl] adj unergründlich

unfavorable [ʌnˈfevərəbəl] adj ungünstig

unfeasible [ʌnˈfizəbəl] adj unausführbar

unfeeling [ʌnˈfilɪŋ] adj unempfindlich

unfilled [ʌnˈfɪld] adj ungefüllt; (post) unbesetzt

unfinished [ʌnˈfɪnɪʃt] adj unfertig; (business) unerledigt

unfit [ʌnˈfɪt] adj (for) ungeeignet (für); (not qualified) (for) untauglich (für); u. for military service wehrdienstuntauglich

unfold [ʌnˈfold] tr (a chair) aufklappen; (cloth, paper) entfalten; (ideas, plans) offenbaren

unforeseeable [ˌʌnforˈsi·əbəl] adj unabsehbar

unforeseen [ˌʌnforˈsin] adj unvorhergesehen

unforgettable [ˌʌnforˈgetəbəl] adj unvergeßlich

unfortunate [ʌnˈfortʃənɪt] adj unglücklich

unfortunately [ʌnˈfortʃənɪtli] adv leider

unfounded [ʌnˈfaundɪd] adj unbegründet

un-freeze [ʌnˈfriz] v (pret –froze; pp –frozen) tr auftauen; (prices) freigeben

unfriendly [ʌnˈfrendli] adj unfreundlich

unfruitful [ʌnˈfrutfəl] adj unfruchtbar

unfulfilled [ˌʌnfəlˈfɪld] adj unerfüllt

unfurl [ʌnˈfʌrl] tr (a flag) entrollen; (sails) losmachen

unfurnished [ʌnˈfʌrnɪʃt] adj unmöbliert

ungainly [ʌnˈgenli] adj plump

ungentlemanly [ʌnˈdʒentəlmənli] adj unfein, unedel

ungodly [ʌnˈgɑdli] adj (hour) ungehörig

ungracious [ʌnˈgreʃəs] adj ungnädig

ungrammatical [ˌʌngrəˈmætɪkəl] adj ungrammatisch

ungrateful [ʌnˈgretfəl] adj undankbar

ungrudgingly [ʌnˈgrʌdʒɪŋli] adv gern

unguarded [ʌnˈgɑrdɪd] adj unbewacht; (moment) unbedacht

unguent [ˈʌngwent] s Salbe f

unhandy [ʌnˈhændi] adj unhandlich; (person) unbeholfen

unhappy [ʌnˈhæpi] adj unglücklich

unharmed [ʌnˈhɑrmd] adj unversehrt

unharness [ʌnˈhɑrnɪs] tr abschirren

unhealthful [ʌnˈhelθfəl] adj ungesund

unhealthy [ʌnˈhelθi] adj ungesund

unheard-of [ʌnˈhɑrd ˌɑv] adj unerhört

unheated [ʌnˈhitɪd] adj ungeheizt

unhesitating [ʌnˈhezɪˌtetɪŋ] adj (immediate) unverzüglich; (unswerving) unbeirrbar; (support) bereitwillig

unhinge [ʌnˈhɪndʒ] tr (fig) aus den Angeln heben

unhitch [ʌnˈhɪtʃ] tr (horses) ausspannen; (undo) losmachen

unholy [ʌnˈholi] adj unheilig

unhook [ʌnˈhuk] tr losmachen; (a dress) aufhaken; (the receiver) abnehmen

unhoped-for [ˌʌn'hopt ˌfər] *adj* unverhofft

unhurt [ʌn'hʌrt] *adj* unbeschädigt; (*person*) unversehrt

unicorn [ˈjunɪ ˌkɔrn] *s* Einhorn *n*

unification [ˌjunɪfɪ'keʃən] *s* Vereinigung *f*

uniform [ˈjunɪ ˌfɔrm] *adj* gleichförmig ‖ *s* Uniform *f*

uniformity [ˌjunɪ'fɔrmɪti] *s* Gleichförmigkeit *f*

uni-fy [ˈjunɪ ˌfaɪ] *v* (*pret & pp* –**fied**) *tr* vereinigen

unilateral [ˌjunɪ'lætərəl] *adj* einseitig

unimpaired [ˌˌʌnɪm'perd] *adj* ungeschwächt

unimpeachable [ˌˌʌnɪm'pitʃəbəl] *adj* unantastbar

unimportant [ˌʌnɪm'pɔrtənt] *adj* unwichtig

uninflected [ˌʌnɪn'flektɪd] *adj* (gram) unflektiert

uninhabited [ˌʌnɪn'hæbɪtɪd] *adj* unbewohnt

uninspired [ˌʌnɪn'spaɪrd] *adj* schwunglos

unintelligible [ˌˌʌnɪn'telɪdʒəbəl] *adj* unverständlich

unintentional [ˌʌnɪn'tenʃənəl] *adj* unabsichtlich

uninterested [ʌn'ɪntə ˌrestɪd] *adj* (in) uninteressiert (an *dat*)

uninteresting [ʌn'ɪntə ˌrestɪŋ] *adj* uninteressant

uninterrupted [ˌˌʌnɪntə'rʌptɪd] *adj* ununterbrochen

uninvited [ˌʌnɪn'vaɪtɪd] *adj* ungeladen

union [ˈjunjən] *adj* Gewerkschafts– ‖ *s* Vereinigung *f*; (*harmony*) Eintracht *f*; (*of workers*) Gewerkschaft *f*; (pol) Union *f*

unionize [ˈjunjə ˌnaɪz] *tr* gewerkschaftlich organisieren ‖ *intr* sich gewerkschaftlich organisieren

un'ion shop' *s* Betrieb *m*, der nur Gewerkschaftsmitglieder beschäftigt

unique [ju'nik] *adj* einzigartig

unison [ˈjunɪsən] *s* Einklang *m*

unit [ˈjunɪt] *s* (& mil) Einheit *f*

unite [ju'naɪt] *tr* vereinigen; (chem) verbinden ‖ *intr* sich vereinigen; (chem) sich verbinden

Unit'ed King'dom *s* Vereinigtes Königreich *n*

Unit'ed Na'tions *spl* Vereinte Nationen *pl*

Unit'ed States' *s* Vereinigte Staaten *pl*

unity [ˈjunɪti] *s* (*harmony*) Einigkeit *f*; (*e.g., of a nation*) Einheit *f*; (fa) Einheitlichkeit *f*

universal [ˌjunɪ'vʌrsəl] *adj* universal, allgemein ‖ *s* Allgemeine *n*; (philos) Allgemeinbegriff *m*

u'niver'sal joint' *s* Kardangelenk *n*

u'niver'sal mil'itary train'ing *s* allgemeine Wehrpflicht *f*

universe [ˈjunɪ ˌvʌrs] *s* Universum *n*

university [ˌjunɪ'vʌrsɪti] *adj* Universitäts– ‖ *s* Universität *f*

unjust [ʌn'dʒʌst] *adj* ungerecht

unjustified [ʌn'dʒʌstɪ ˌfaɪd] *adj* ungerechtfertigt

unjustly [ʌn'dʒʌstli] *adv* zu Unrecht

unkempt [ʌn'kempt] *adj* ungekämmt; (fig) verwahrlost

unkind [ʌn'kaɪnd] *adj* unfreundlich

unknown [ʌn'non] *adj* unbekannt

un'known quan'tity *s* Unbekannte *f*

Un'known Sol'dier *s* Unbekannter Soldat *m*

unlatch [ʌn'lætʃ] *tr* aufklinken

unlawful [ʌn'lɔfəl] *adj* gesetzwidrig

unleash [ʌn'liʃ] *tr* losbinden; (fig) entfesseln

unleavened [ʌn'levənd] *adj* ungesäuert

unless [ʌn'les] *conj* wenn ... nicht

unlettered [ʌn'letərd] *adj* ungebildet

unlicensed [ʌn'laɪsənst] *adj* unerlaubt

unlike [ʌn'laɪk] *adj* (*unequal*) ungleich; (*dissimilar*) unähnlich ‖ *prep* im Gegensatz zu (*dat*); **be u. s.o.** anders als jemand sein

unlikely [ʌn'laɪkli] *adj* unwahrscheinlich

unlimited [ʌn'lɪmɪtɪd] *adj* unbeschränkt

unlined [ʌn'laɪnd] *adj* (*clothes*) ungefüttert; (*paper*) unliniert; (*face*) faltenlos

unload [ʌn'lod] *tr & intr* ausladen

unload'ing *s* Ausladen *n*; (naut) Löschen *n*

unlock [ʌn'lak] *tr* aufsperren

unloose [ʌn'lus] *tr* lösen

unloved [ʌn'lʌvd] *adj* ungeliebt

unlucky [ʌn'lʌki] *adj* unglücklich

un-make [ʌn'mek] *v* (*pret & pp* –**made**) *tr* rückgängig machen; (*a bed*) abdecken

unmanageable [ʌn'mænɪdʒəbəl] *adj* (*person, animal*) widerspenstig; (*thing*) unhandlich

unmanly [ʌn'mænli] *adj* unmännlich

unmanned [ʌn'mænd] *adj* (rok) unbemannt

unmannerly [ʌn'mænərli] *adj* unmännlich

unmarketable [ʌn'markɪtəbəl] *adj* nicht marktgängig

unmarriageable [ʌn'mærɪdʒəbəl] *adj* nicht heiratsfähig

unmarried [ʌn'mærɪd] *adj* unverheiratet

unmask [ʌn'mæsk] *tr* (& fig) demaskieren ‖ *intr* sich demaskieren

unmatched [ʌn'mætʃt] *adj* (*not matched*) ungleichartig; (*unmatchable*) unvergleichlich

unmerciful [ʌn'mʌrsɪfəl] *adj* unbarmherzig

unmesh [ʌn'meʃ] *tr* (mach) ausrücken

unmindful [ʌn'maɪndfəl] *adj* uneingedenk

unmistakable [ˌˌʌnmɪs'tekəbəl] *adj* unmißverständlich

unmitigated [ʌn'mɪtɪ ˌgetɪd] *adj* ungemildert (*liar*) Erz–

unmixed [ʌn'mɪkst] *adj* ungemischt

unmoor [ʌn'mur] *tr* losmachen ‖ *intr* sich losmachen

unmoved [ʌn'muvd] *adj* (fig) ungerührt

unmuzzle [ʌn'mʌzəl] *tr* den Maulkorb abnehmen (*dat*)

unnatural [ʌn'nætʃərəl] *adj* unnatür-
lich; (*forced*) gezwungen
unnecessary [ʌn'nesə‚seri] *adj* unnötig
unneeded [ʌn'nidid] *adj* nutzlos
unnerve [ʌn'nɑrv] *tr* entnerven
unnoticeable [ʌn'notisəbəl] *adj* unbe-
merkbar
unnoticed [ʌn'notist] *adj* unbemerkt
unobserved [‚ʌnəb'zʌrvd] *adj* unbeob-
achtet
unobtainable [‚ʌnəb'tenəbəl] *adj* nicht
erhältlich
unobtrusive [‚ʌnəb'trusiv] *adj* unauf-
dringlich
unoccupied [ʌn'ɑkjə‚paid] *adj* (*room,
house*) leerstehend; (*seat*) unbesetzt;
(*person*) unbeschäftigt
unofficial [‚ʌnə'fiʃəl] *adj* inoffiziell
unopened [ʌn'opənd] *adj* ungeöffnet
unopposed [‚ʌnə'pozd] *adj* (*without
opposition*) widerspruchslos; (*unre-
sisted*) unbehindert
unorthodox [ʌn'ɔrθə‚dɑks] *adj* unorthodox; (relig) nicht orthodox
unpack [ʌn'pæk] *tr* auspacken
unpalatable [ʌn'pælətəbəl] *adj* unschmackhaft; (fig) widerlich
unparalleled [ʌn'pærə‚leld] *adj* unvergleichlich
unpardonable [ʌn'pɑrdənəbəl] *adj* un-
verzeihlich
unpatriotic [‚ʌnpetri'ɑtik] *adj* unpatri-
otisch
unpaved [ʌn'pevd] *adj* ungepflastert
unperceived [‚ʌnpər'sivd] *adj* unbemerkt
unpleasant [ʌn'plezənt] *adj* unangenehm; (*person*) unsympathisch
unpopular [ʌn'pɑpjələr] *adj* unbeliebt
unpopularity [ʌn‚pɑpjə'læriti] *s* Unbe-
liebtheit *f*
unprecedented [ʌn'presi‚dentid] *adj*
unerhört; (jur) ohne Präzedenzfall
unpredictable [‚ʌnpri'diktəbəl] *adj* unberechenbar; (*weather*) wechselhaft
unprejudiced [ʌn'predʒədist] *adj* unvoreingenommen
unprepared [‚ʌnpri'perd] *adj* unvorbereitet
unpresentable [‚ʌnpri'zentəbəl] *adj*
nicht präsentabel
unpretentious [‚ʌnpri'tenʃəs] *adj* an-
spruchslos
unprincipled [ʌn'prinsipəld] *adj* haltlos
unproductive [‚ʌnprə'dʌktiv] *adj* un-
produktiv; (of) unergiebig (an *dat*)
unprofessional [‚ʌnprə'feʃənəl] *adj*
(*work*) unfachmännisch; (*conduct*)
berufswidrig
unprofitable [ʌn'prɑfitəbəl] *adj* (*useless*) nutzlos; (fi) unrentabel
unpronounceable [‚ʌnprə'naunsəbəl]
adj unaussprechlich
unprotected [‚ʌnprə'tektid] *adj* (*place*)
ungeschützt; (*person*) unbeschützt
unpropitious [‚ʌnprə'piʃəs] *adj* ungünstig
unpublished [ʌn'pʌbliʃt] *adj* unveröf-
fentlicht
unpunished [ʌn'pʌniʃt] *adj* ungestraft
unqualified [ʌn'kwɑlə‚faid] *adj* un-

qualifiziert; (*full, complete*) unbedingt
unquenchable [ʌn'kwentʃəbəl] *adj* un-
stillbar
unquestionably [ʌn'kwestʃənəbli] *adv*
fraglos, unbezweifelbar
unquestioning [ʌn'kwestʃəniŋ] *adj*
(*obedience*) bedingungslos
unquiet [ʌn'kwai‚ət] *adj* unruhig
unrav-el [ʌn'rævəl] *v* (*pret & pp*
–el[l]ed; *ger* –el[l]ing) *tr* (*a knitted
fabric*) auftrennen; (fig) entwirren ‖
intr sich fasern; (fig) sich entwirren
unreachable [ʌn'ritʃəbəl] *adj* unerreichbar
unreal [ʌn'ri‚əl] *adj* unwirklich
unreality [‚ʌnri'æliti] *s* Unwirklich-
keit *f*
unreasonable [ʌn'rizənəbəl] *adj* unver-
nünftig
unrecognizable [ʌn'rekəg‚naizəbəl] *adj*
unerkennbar
unreel [ʌn'ril] *tr* abspulen
unrefined [‚ʌnri'faind] *adj* roh
unrelated [‚ʌnri'letid] *adj* (to) ohne
Beziehung (zu)
unrelenting [‚ʌnri'lentiŋ] *adj* unerbittlich
unreliable [‚ʌnri'lai‚əbəl] *adj* unzuverlässig; (fin) unsolid(e)
unremitting [‚ʌnri'mitiŋ] *adj* unabläs-
sig
unrepentant [‚ʌnri'pentənt] *adj* unbußfertig
unrequited [‚ʌnri'kwaitid] *adj* uner-
widert
unreserved [‚ʌnri'zʌrvd] *adj* vorbehaltlos
unresponsive [‚ʌnri'spɑnsiv] *adj* (to)
unempfänglich (für)
unrest [ʌn'rest] *s* Unruhe *f*
unrestricted [‚ʌnri'striktid] *adj* uneingeschränkt
unrewarded [‚ʌnri'wɔrdid] *adj* unbe-
lohnt
unrhymed [ʌn'raimd] *adj* ungereimt
un-rig [ʌn'rig] *v* (*pret & pp* –rigged;
ger –rigging) *tr* abtakeln
unripe [ʌn'raip] *adj* unreif
unrivaled [ʌn'raivəld] *adj* unübertreff-
lich
unroll [ʌn'rol] *tr* aufrollen; (*e.g., a
cable*) abrollen ‖ *intr* sich aufrollen;
sich abrollen
unromantic [‚ʌnro'mæntik] *adj* unro-
mantisch
unruffled [ʌn'rʌfəld] *adj* unerschüttert
unruly [ʌn'ruli] *adj* ungebärdig
unsaddle [ʌn'sædəl] *tr* (*a horse*) ab-
satteln; (*a rider*) aus dem Sattel
werfen
unsafe [ʌn'sef] *adj* unsicher
unsaid [ʌn'sed] *adj* ungesagt
unsalable [ʌn'seləbəl] *adj* unverkäuf-
lich
unsanitary [ʌn'sæni‚teri] *adj* unhygie-
nisch
unsalted [ʌn'sɔltid] *adj* ungesalzen
unsatisfactory [ʌn‚sætis'fæktəri] *adj*
unbefriedigend
unsatisfied [ʌn'sætis‚faid] *adj* unbe-
friedigt

unsavory [ʌn'sevəri] *adj* unschmackhaft; (fig) widerlich

unscathed [ʌn'skeðd] *adj* unversehrt

unscientific [ˌʌnsaɪən'tɪfɪk] *adj* unwissenschaftlich

unscramble [ʌn'skræmbəl] *tr* (a message) entziffern; (fig) entflechten

unscrew [ʌn'skru] *tr* aufschrauben

unscrupulous [ʌn'skrupjələs] *adj* skrupellos

unseal [ʌn'sil] *tr* entsiegeln; (eyes, lips) öffnen

unseasonable [ʌn'sizənəbəl] *adj* unzeitig; (weather) nicht der Jahreszeit entsprechend

unseasoned [ʌn'sizənd] *adj* ungewürzt

unseat [ʌn'sit] *tr* (a rider) aus dem Sattel heben; (an official) aus dem Posten verdrängen

unseemly [ʌn'simli] *adj* ungehörig

unseen [ʌn'sin] *adj* ungesehen

unselfish [ʌn'selfɪʃ] *adj* selbstlos

unsettle [ʌn'setəl] *tr* beunruhigen

unsettled [ʌn'setəld] *adj* (matter, bill) unerledigt; (without a residence) ohne festen Wohnsitz; (restless) unruhig; (life) unstet

unshackle [ʌn'ʃækəl] *tr* die Fesseln abnehmen (dat)

unshakable [ʌn'ʃekəbəl] *adj* unerschütterlich

unshapely [ʌn'ʃepli] *adj* mißgestaltet

unshaven [ʌn'ʃevən] *adj* unrasiert

unsheathe [ʌn'ʃið] *tr* aus der Scheide ziehen

unshod [ʌn'ʃad] *adj* unbeschuht

unsightly [ʌn'saɪtli] *adj* unansehnlich

unsinkable [ʌn'sɪŋkəbəl] *adj* nicht versenkbar

unskilled [ʌn'skɪld] *adj* ungelernt; u. laborer Hilfsarbeiter –in *mf*

unskillful [ʌn'skɪlfəl] *adj* ungewandt

unsnarl [ʌn'snarl] *tr* entwirren

unsociable [ʌn'soʃəbəl] *adj* ungesellig

unsolicited [ˌʌnsə'lɪsɪtɪd] *adj* unverlangt

unsold [ʌn'sold] *adj* unverkauft

unsophisticated [ˌʌnsə'fɪstɪˌketɪd] *adj* unverfälscht; (naive) arglos

unsound [ʌn'saʊnd] *adj* ungesund; (sleep) unruhig; **of u. mind** geisteskrank

unspeakable [ʌn'spikəbəl] *adj* unsagbar

unspoiled [ʌn'spɔɪld] *adj* unverdorben

unsportsmanlike [ʌn'sportsmən ˌlaɪk] *adj* unsportlich

unstable [ʌn'stebəl] *adj* unbeständig; (e.g., ladder) wacklig; (hand) zittrig; (market, walk) schwankend; (inconstant) unbeständig; (chem) unbeständig

unstinted [ʌn'stɪntɪd] *adj* uneingeschränkt

unstinting [ʌn'stɪntɪŋ] *adj* freigebig

unstitch [ʌn'stɪtʃ] *tr* auftrennen

unstressed [ʌn'strest] *adj* unbetont

unsuccessful [ˌʌnsək'sesfəl] *adj* erfolglos

unsuitable [ʌn'sutəbəl] *adj* ungeeignet; (inappropriate) unangemessen

unsullied [ʌn'sʌlid] *adj* unbefleckt

unsung [ʌn'sʌŋ] *adj* unbesungen

unsuspected [ˌʌnsəs'pektɪd] *adj* unverdächtig; (not known to exist) ungeahnt

unsuspecting [ˌʌnsəs'pektɪŋ] *adj* arglos

unswerving [ʌn'swɜrvɪŋ] *adj* unentwegt

unsympathetic [ˌʌnsɪmpə'θetɪk] *adj* teilnahmslos

unsystematic(al) [ˌʌnsɪstə'mætɪk(əl)] *adj* unsystematisch

untactful [ʌn'tæktfəl] *adj* taktlos

untalented [ʌn'tæləntɪd] *adj* unbegabt

untamed [ʌn'temd] *adj* ungezähmt

untangle [ʌn'tæŋgəl] *tr* (& fig) entwirren

untenable [ʌn'tenəbəl] *adj* unhaltbar

untested [ʌn'testɪd] *adj* ungeprüft

unthankful [ʌn'θæŋkfəl] *adj* undankbar

unthinking [ʌn'θɪŋkɪŋ] *adj* gedankenlos

untidy [ʌn'taɪdi] *adj* unordentlich

un·tie [ʌn'taɪ] *v* (pret & pp –tied; ger –tying) *tr* aufbinden; (a knot) lösen; **my shoe is untied** mein Schuh ist aufgegangen

until [ʌn'tɪl] *prep* bis (acc); **u. further notice** bis auf weiteres || *conj* bis

untimely [ʌn'taɪmli] *adj* frühzeitig; (at the wrong time) unzeitgemäß

untiring [ʌn'taɪrɪŋ] *adj* unermüdlich

untold [ʌn'told] *adj* (suffering) unsäglich; (countless) zahllos

untouched [ʌn'tʌtʃt] *adj* unangetastet; (fig) ungerührt

untoward [ʌn'tord] *adj* (unfavorable) ungünstig; (unruly) widerspenstig

untrained [ʌn'trend] *adj* unausgebildet; (eye) ungeschult; (sport) untrainiert

untried [ʌn'traɪd] *adj* (unattempted) unversucht; (untested) unerprobt; (case) (jur) nicht verhandelt

untroubled [ʌn'trʌbəld] *adj* (mind, times) ruhig; (peace) ungestört

untrue [ʌn'tru] *adj* unwahr; (unfaithful) un(ge)treu; (not exact) ungenau

untrustworthy [ʌn'trʌst ˌwɜrði] *adj* unglaubwürdig

untruth [ʌn'truθ] *s* Unwahrheit *f*

untruthful [ʌn'truθfəl] *adj* (statement) unwahr; (person) unaufrichtig

untwist [ʌn'twɪst] *tr* aufflechten || *intr* aufgehen

unusable [ʌn'juzəbəl] *adj* nicht verwendbar; (unconsumable) unbenutzbar

unusual [ʌn'juʒʊ·əl] *adj* ungewöhnlich

unutterable [ʌn'ʌtərəbəl] *adj* unaussprechlich

unvarnished [ʌn'varnɪʃt] *adj* nicht gefirnißt; (truth) ungeschminkt

unveil [ʌn'vel] *tr* (a monument) enthüllen; (a face) entschleiern

unventilated [ʌn'ventɪ ˌletɪd] *adj* ungelüftet

unvoiced [ʌn'vɔɪst] *adj* (ling) stimmlos

unwanted [ʌn'wantɪd] *adj* unerwünscht

unwarranted [ʌn'warəntɪd] *adj* ungerechtfertigt

unwary [ʌn'weri] *adj* unvorsichtig

unwavering [ʌn'wevərɪŋ] *adj* standhaft
unwelcome [ʌn'welkəm] *adj* unwillkommen
unwell [ʌn'wel] *adj* unwohl
unwept [ʌn'wept] *adj* unbeweint
unwholesome [ʌn'holsəm] *adj* schädlich; (& *fig*) unbekömmlich
unwieldy [ʌn'wildi] *adj* (*person*) schwerfällig; (*thing*) unhandlich
unwilling [ʌn'wɪlɪŋ] *adj* (*involuntary*) unfreiwillig; (*reluctant*) widerwillig; (*obstinate*) eigensinnig; **be u. to** (*inf*) nicht (*inf*) wollen
unwillingly [ʌn'wɪlɪŋli] *adv* ungern
un·wind [ʌn'waɪnd] *v* (*pret & pp* —**wound**) *tr* abwickeln ‖ *intr* sich abwickeln; (*fig*) sich entspannen
unwise [ʌn'waɪz] *adj* unklug
unwished-for [ʌn'wɪ/t,fɔr] *adj* unerwünscht
unwitting [ʌn'wɪtɪŋ] *adj* unwissentlich
unworkable [ʌn'wʌrkəbəl] *adj* (*plan*) unausführbar; (*material*) nicht zu bearbeiten(d)
unworldly [ʌn'wʌrldli] *adj* nicht weltlich; (*naive*) weltfremd
unworthy [ʌn'wʌrði] *adj* unwürdig
un·wrap [ʌn'ræp] *v* (*pret & pp* —**wrapped**; *ger* —**wrapping**) *tr* auspacken ‖ *intr* aufgehen
unwrinkled [ʌn'rɪŋkəld] *adj* faltenlos
unwritten [ʌn'rɪtən] *adj* ungeschrieben; (*agreement*) mündlich
unyielding [ʌn'jildɪŋ] *adj* unnachgiebig
up [ʌp] *adj & adv* (*at a height*) oben; (*to a height*) hinauf; **be up** (*be out of bed; said of a shade*) aufsein; (*baseball*) am Schlag sein; **be up and around again** wieder auf dem Damm sein; **be up to** (*be ready for*) gewachsen sein (*dat*); (*e.g., mischief*) vorhaben; **from ten dollars and up** von zehn Dollar aufwärts; **it's up to you** es hängt von Ihnen ab; **prices are up** die Preise sind gestiegen; **up and down** (*back and forth*) auf und ab; (*from head to toe*) von oben bis unten; **up there** da oben; **up to** (*e.g., one hour*) bis zu; **up to the ears in debt** bis über die Ohren in Schulden ‖ *v* (*pret & pp* **upped**; *ger* **upping**) *tr* erhöhen ‖ *prep* (*acc*) hinauf (*postpositive*)
up-and-coming [‚ʌpən'kʌmɪŋ] *adj* (*coll*) unternehmungslustig
up-and-up [‚ʌpən'ʌp] *s*—**be on the u.** aufrichtig sein
upbraid' *tr* Vorwürfe machen (*dat*)
upbringing ['ʌp,brɪŋɪŋ] *s* Erziehung *f*
update' *tr* aufs laufende bringen
up'draft' *s* Aufwind *m*
upend' *tr* hochkant stellen
up'grade' *s* Steigung *f*; **on the u.** (*fig*) im Aufsteigen ‖ **up'grade'** *tr* (*reclassify*) höher einstufen; (*improve*) verbessern
upheaval [ʌp'hivəl] *s* Umbruch *m*
up'hill' *adj* ansteigend; (*fig*) mühsam; **u. struggle** harter Kampf *m* ‖ *adv* bergauf
uphold' *v* (*pret & pp* —**held**) *tr* (*the law*) unterstützen; (*a verdict*) bestätigen

upholster [ʌp'holstər] *tr* (auf)polstern
upholsterer [ʌp'holstərər] *s* Polsterer –in *mf*
upholstery [ʌp'holstəri] *s* Polsterung *f*
up'keep' *s* Instandhaltung *f*; (*maintenance costs*) Instandhaltungskosten *pl*
upland ['ʌplənd] *adj* Hochlands-, Berg– ‖ **the uplands** *spl* das Hochland
up'lift' *s* (*fig*) Aufschwung *m*; **moral u.** moralischer Auftrieb *m* ‖ **up'lift'** *tr* (*fig*) geistig (*or* moralisch) erheben
upon [ə'pɑn] *prep* (*position*) an (*dat*), auf (*dat*); (*direction*) an (*acc*), auf (*acc*); **u. my word!** auf mein Wort!
upper ['ʌpər] *adj* obere, Ober– ‖ **uppers** *spl* Oberleder *n*
up'per-case' *adj* in Großbuchstaben gedruckt (*or* geschrieben)
up'per class'es *spl* Oberschicht *f*
up'per·cut' *s* (box) Aufwärtshaken *m*
up'per deck' *s* Oberdeck *n*
up'per hand' *s* Oberhand *f*
up'per lip' *s* Oberlippe *f*
up'permost' *adj* oberste
uppish ['ʌpɪʃ] *adj* (*coll*) hochnäsig
uppity ['ʌpiti] *adj* (*coll*) eingebildet
upraise' *tr* erheben
up'right' *adj* aufrecht; (*fig*) redlich ‖ *s* (fb) Torpfosten *m*
up'ris'ing *s* Aufstand *m*
up'roar' *s* Aufruhr *m*
uproarious [ʌp'rori·əs] *adj* (*noisy*) lärmend; (*laughter*) schallend; (*applause*) tosend; (*very funny*) zwerchfellerschütternd
uproot' *tr* entwurzeln
ups' and downs' *spl* Auf und Ab *n*
upset' *adj* (*over*) verstimmt (über *acc*) ‖ **up'set'** *s* unerwartete Niederlage *f* ‖ **up'set'** *v* (*pret & pp* —**set**; *ger* —**setting**) *tr* (*throw over*) umwerfen; (*tip over*) umkippen; (*plans*) umstoßen; (*a person*) aufregen; (*the stomach*) verderben
up'shot' *s* Ergebnis *n*
up'side down' *adv* verkehrt; **turn u.** auf den Kopf stellen
up'stage' *adv* in den (*or* im) Hintergrund der Bühne ‖ *tr* (*coll*) ausstechen
up'stairs' *adj* im oberen Stockwerk ‖ *adv* (*position*) oben; (*direction*) nach oben ‖ *s* oberes Stockwerk *n*
upstanding *adj* aufrecht; (*sincere*) aufrichtig
up'start' *s* Emporkömmling *m*
up'stream' *adj* weiter stromaufwärts gelegen ‖ *adv* stromaufwärts
up'stroke' *s* Aufstrich *m*; (mach) Hub *m*
up'surge' *s* Aufwallung *f*
up'sweep' *s* Hochfrisur *f*
up'swing' *s* (fig) Aufschwung *m*
upsy-daisy ['ʌpsi'dezi] *interj* hopsasa!
up-to-date ['ʌptə'det] *adj* (*modern*) zeitgemäß; (*with latest information*) auf dem neuesten Stand
up'-to-the-min'ute news' ['ʌptəðə-'mɪnɪt] *s* Zeitfunk *m*
up'trend' *s* steigende Tendenz *f*

up'turn' *s* Aufschwung *m*

upturned' *adj* nach oben gebogen; **u. nose** Stupsnase *f*

upward ['ʌpwərd] *adj* nach oben ge-richtet; *(tendency)* steigend ‖ *adv* aufwärts

U'ral Moun'tains ['jurəl] *spl* Ural *m*

uranium [ju'rɛnɪ·əm] *adj* Uran– ‖ *s* Uran *n*

urban ['ʌrbən] *adj* städtisch, Stadt–

urbane [ʌr'ben] *adj* weltgewandt

urbanite ['ʌrbə‚naɪt] *s* Städter –in *mf*

urbanize ['ʌrbə‚naɪz] *tr* verstädtern

ur'ban renew'al *s* Altstadtsanierung *f*

urchin ['ʌrtʃɪn] *s* Bengel *m*

ure·thra [ju'riθrə] *s* (–thras & –thrae [θri]) Harnröhre *f*

urge [ʌrdʒ] *s* Drang *m*, Trieb *m* ‖ *tr* drängen; **u. on** antreiben

urgency ['ʌrdʒənsi] *s* Dringlichkeit *f*

urgent ['ʌrdʒənt] *adj* dringend

urinal ['jurɪnəl] *s* *(in a toilet)* Urin-becken *n*; *(in a sick bed)* Urinflasche *f*

urinary ['jurɪ‚nɛri] *adj* Harn–, Urin–

urinate ['jurɪ‚nɛt] *intr* harnen

urine ['jurɪn] *s* Harn *m*, Urin *m*

urn [ʌrn] *s* Urne *f*; *(for coffee)* Kaf-feemaschine *f*

urology [jɪ'rɑlədʒi] *s* Urologie *f*

us [ʌs] *per pron* uns

U.S.A. ['ju'ɛs'e] *s* **(United States of America)** USA *pl*

usable ['juzəbəl] *adj* *(consumable items)* verwendbar; *(non-consumable items)* benutzbar

usage ['jusɪdʒ] *s* *(using)* Gebrauch *m*; *(treatment)* Behandlung *f*; *(ling)* Sprachgebrauch *m*; **rough u.** starke Beanspruchung *f*

use [jus] *s* *(of consumable items)* Ver-wendung *f*, Gebrauch *m*; *(of non-consumable items)* Benutzung *f*; *(ap-plication)* Anwendung *f*; *(advantage)* Nutzen *m*; *(purpose)* Zweck *m*; *(con-sumption)* Verbrauch *m*; **I have no use for him** ich habe nichts für ihn übrig; **in use** in Gebrauch; **it's no use** es nützt nichts; **make use of** aus-nutzen; **of use** von Nutzen; **there's no use in** *(ger)* es hat keinen Zweck zu *(inf)* ‖ [juz] *tr* (ge)brauchen, ver-wenden; *(non-consumable items)* be-nutzen; *(apply)* anwenden; *(e.g.,*

troops) einsetzen; **use up** verbrau-chen ‖ *intr*—**he used to live here** er wohnte früher hier

used [juzd] *adj* gebraucht; *(car)* Ge-braucht–; **be u. to** gewöhnt sein an *(acc)*; **be u. to** *(ger)* gewöhnt sein zu *(inf)*; **get s.o. u. to** j–n gewöhnen an *(acc)*; **get u. to** sich gewöhnen an *(acc)*

useful ['jusfəl] *adj* nützlich

usefulness ['jusfəlnɪs] *s* Nützlichkeit *f*; *(usability)* Brauchbarkeit *f*

useless ['juslɪs] *adj* nutzlos; *(not us-able)* unbrauchbar

user ['juzər] *s* *(of gas, electric)* Ver-braucher –in *mf*; *(e.g., of a book)* Benutzer –in *mf*

usher ['ʌʃər] *s* Platzanweiser –in *mf* ‖ *tr*—**u. in** hereinführen; *(a new era)* einleiten

U.S.S.R. ['ju'ɛs'ɛs'ɑr] *s* **(Union of Soviet Socialist Republics)** UdSSR *f*

usual ['juʒʊ·əl] *adj* gewöhnlich; **as u.** wie gewöhnlich

usually ['juʒʊ·əli] *adv* gewöhnlich

usurp [ju'zʌrp] *tr* usurpieren

usurper [ju'zʌrpər] *s* Usurpator –in *mf*

usury ['juʒəri] *s* Wucher *m*

utensil [ju'tɛnsɪl] *s* Gerät *n*; **utensils** Utensilien *pl*

uter·us ['jutərəs] *s* (–i [‚aɪ]) Gebär-mutter *f*

utilitarian [‚jutɪlɪ'tɛrɪ·ən] *adj* utili-taristisch, Nützlichkeits-

utility [ju'tɪlɪti] *s* *(usefulness)* Nütz-lichkeit *f*; *(company)* öffentlicher Versorgungsbetrieb *m*; **apartment with all utilities** Wohnung *f* mit allem Zubehör; **utilities** Gas, Wasser, Strom *pl*

utilize ['jutɪ‚laɪz] *tr* verwerten

utmost ['ʌt‚most] *adj* äußerste, höchste ‖ *s*—**do one's u.** sein Äußerstes tun; **to the u.** auf äußerste; **to the u. of one's power** nach besten Kräften

utopia [ju'topɪ·ə] *s* Utopie *f*

utopian [ju'topɪ·ən] *adj* utopisch

utter ['ʌtər] *adj* völlig, Erz– ‖ *tr* *(a sigh)* ausstoßen; *(a sound)* hervor-bringen; *(feelings)* ausdrücken; *(words)* äußern

utterance ['ʌtərəns] *s* Äußerung *f*

utterly ['ʌtərli] *adv* ganz und gar, völlig

V

V, v [vi] *s* zweiundzwanzigster Buch-stabe des englischen Alphabets

vacancy ['vekənsi] *s* *(emptiness)* Leere *f*; *(unfilled job)* freie Stelle *f*; **no v.** (public sign) kein freies Zimmer

vacant ['vekənt] *adj* frei; *(stare)* gei-stesabwesend; *(lot)* unbebaut

vacate [ve'ket] *tr* *(a home)* räumen; *(a seat)* freimachen ‖ *intr* ausziehen

vacation [ve'keʃən] *s* Urlaub *m*; *(educ)*

Ferien *pl*; **on v.** auf Urlaub ‖ *intr* Urlaub machen

vacationer [ve'keʃənər] *s* Urlauber –in *mf*

vaccinate ['væksɪ‚net] *tr* impfen

vaccination [‚væksɪ'neʃən] *s* Impfung *f*

vaccina'tion certi'ficate *s* Impfschein *m*

vaccine [væk'sin] *s* Impfstoff *m*

vacillate ['væsɪ‚let] *intr* schwanken
vacuous ['vækju‚əs] *adj* nichtssagend
vacu·um ['vækju‚əm] *s* (-ums & –a [ə]) Vakuum *n* ‖ *tr* & *intr* staubsaugen
vac'uum clean'er *s* Staubsauger *m*
vac'uum pump' *s* Absaugepumpe *f*
vac'uum tube' *s* Vakuumröhre *f*
vagabond ['væɡə‚bɑnd] *s* Landstreicher –in *mf*
vagary ['veɡərɪ] *s* Laune *f*
vagina [və'dʒaɪnə] *s* Scheide *f*
vagrancy ['veɡrənsɪ] *s* Landstreicherei *f*
vagrant ['veɡrənt] *adj* vagabundierend ‖ *s* Landstreicher –in *mf*
vague [veɡ] *adj* unbestimmt, vage
vain [ven] *adj* (*proud*) eitel; (*pointless*) vergeblich; **in v.** vergebens
vainglo'rious *adj* prahlerisch
valance ['væləns] *s* Quervolant *m*
vale [vel] *s* Tal *n*
valedictory [‚vælɪ'dɪktərɪ] *s* Abschiedsrede *f*
valence ['veləns] *s* Wertigkeit *f*
valentine ['vælən‚taɪn] *s* Valentinsgruß *m*
vale' of tears' *s* Jammertal *n*
valet ['vælɪt] *s* Kammerdiener *m*
valiant ['væljənt] *adj* tapfer
valid ['vælɪd] *adj* (*law, ticket*) gültig; (*argument, objection*) wohlbegründet; (*e.g., contract*) rechtsgültig; **be v.** gelten
validate ['vælɪ‚det] *tr* bestätigen
validation [‚vælɪ'deʃən] *s* Bestätigung *f*
validity [və'lɪdrtɪ] *s* Gültigkeit *f*
valise [və'lis] *s* Reisetasche *f*
valley ['vælɪ] *s* Tal *n*
valor ['vælər] *s* Tapferkeit *f*
valorous ['vælərəs] *adj* tapfer
valuable ['væljʊ‚əbəl] *adj* wertvoll ‖ **valuables** *spl* Wertsachen *pl*
value ['vælju] *s* Wert *m* ‖ *tr* (at) schätzen (auf *acc*)
val'ue judg'ment *s* Werturteil *n*
valueless ['væljʊlɪs] *adj* wertlos
valve [vælv] *s* (*anat, mach, zool*) Klappe *f*; (*mach, mus*) Ventil *n*
vamp [væmp] *s* (coll) Vamp *m*
vampire ['væmpaɪr] *s* Vampir *m*
van [væn] *s* Möbelwagen *m*; (*panel truck*) Kastenwagen *m*; (fig) Avantgarde *f*; (mil) Vorhut *f*
vandal ['vændəl] *s* Vandale *m*; **Vandal** Vandale *m*
vandalism ['vændə‚lɪzəm] *s* Vandalismus *m*
vane [ven] *s* (*of a windmill, fan, propeller*) Flügel *m*; (*in a turbine*) Schaufel *f*
vanguard ['væn‚ɡɑrd] *s* (fig) Spitze *f*; (mil) Vorhut *f*
vanilla [və'nɪlə] *s* Vanille *f*
vanish ['vænɪʃ] *intr* (ver)schwinden; **v. into thin air** sich in blauen Dunst auflösen
van'ishing cream' *s* Tagescreme *f*
vanity ['vænɪtɪ] *s* (*arrogance*) Anmaßung *f*; (*emptiness*) Nichtigkeit *f*; (*furniture*) Frisiertisch *m*

van'ity case' *s* Kosmetikköfferchen *n*
vanquish ['væŋkwɪʃ] *tr* besiegen
van'tage point' ['væntɪdʒ] *s* (*advantage*) günstiger Ausgangspunkt *m*; (*view*) Aussichtspunkt *m*
vapid ['væpɪd] *adj* schal, fad(e)
vapor ['vepər] *s* Dampf *m*, Dunst *m*
vaporize ['vepə‚raɪz] *tr* & *intr* verdampfen
vaporizer ['vepə‚raɪzər] *s* Inhalationsapparat *m*
va'por trail' *s* Kondensstreifen *m*
variable ['verɪ‚əbəl] *adj* veränderlich; (*wind*) aus wechselnden Richtungen ‖ *s* (math) Veränderliche *f*
variance ['verɪ‚əns] *s* Veränderung *f*; (*difference*) Abweichung *f*; (*argument*) Streit *m*; **be at v. with** (*a person*) in Zwiespalt sein mit; (*a thing*) in Widerspruch stehen zu
variant ['verɪ‚ənt] *adj* abweichend ‖ *s* Variante *f*
variation [‚verɪ'eʃən] *s* Veränderung *f*; (alg, biol, mus) Variation *f*
var'icose vein' ['verɪ‚kos] *s* Krampfader *f*
varied ['verɪd] *adj* abwechslungsreich; (*diverse*) verschieden
variegated ['verɪ‚ə‚ɡetɪd] *adj* (*diverse*) verschieden; (*in color*) bunt
variety [və'raɪ‚ətɪ] *s* (*choice*) Auswahl *f*; (*difference*) Verschiedenheit *f*; (*sort*) Art *f*; (biol) Spielart *f*; **for a v. of reasons** aus verschiedenen Gründen
vari'ety show' *s* Varietévorstellung *f*
various ['verɪ‚əs] *adj* verschieden; (*several*) mehrere
varnish ['vɑrnɪʃ] *s* Firnis *m*, Lack *m* ‖ *tr* firnissen
varsity ['vɑrsɪtɪ] *adj* Auswahl– ‖ *s* Auswahlmannschaft *f*
var·y ['verɪ] *v* (*pret & pp* –ied) *tr* & *intr* abwechseln, variieren
vase [ves, vez] *s* Vase *f*
vaseline ['væsə‚lin] *s* (trademark) Vaseline *f*
vassal ['væsəl] *s* Lehensmann *m*
vast [væst] *adj* riesig; (*majority*) überwiegend; **v. amount** Unmasse *f*
vastness ['væstnɪs] *s* Unermeßlichkeit *f*
vat [væt] *s* Bottich *m*
Vatican ['vætɪkən] *adj* vatikanisch; (*city*) Vatikan– ‖ *s* Vatikan *m*
Vat'ican Coun'cil *s* Vatikanisches Konzil *n*
vaudeville ['vodvɪl] *s* Varieté *n*
vaude'ville show' *s* Varietévorstellung *f*
vault [vɔlt] *s* (*underground chamber*) Gruft *f*; (*of a bank*) Tresor *m*; (*archit*) Gewölbe *n*; **v. of heaven** Himmelsgewölbe *n* ‖ *tr* überspringen
vaunt [vɔnt] *s* Prahlerei *f* ‖ *tr* sich rühmen (*genit*) ‖ *intr* sich rühmen
veal [vil] *s* Kalbfleisch *n*
veal' cut'let *s* Kalbskotelett *n*
veer [vɪr] *intr* drehen, wenden
vegetable ['vedʒɪtəbəl] *adj* pflanzlich; (*garden, soup*) Gemüse–; (*kingdom, life, oil, dye*) Pflanzen– ‖ *s* Gemüse *n*; **vegetables** Gemüse *n*

vegetarian [ˌvedʒɪ'terɪ·ən] *adj* vegetarisch ‖ *s* Vegetarier –in *mf*

vegetate ['vedʒɪ.tet] *intr* vegetieren

vegetation [ˌvedʒɪ'teʃən] *s* Vegetation *f*

vehemence ['vi·ɪməns] *s* Heftigkeit *f*

vehement ['vi·ɪmənt] *adj* heftig

vehicle ['vi·ɪkəl] *s* Fahrzeug *n*

veil [vel] *s* Schleier *m* ‖ *tr* (& *fig*) verschleiern

veiled *adj* verschleiert; (*threat*) verhüllt

vein [ven] *s* Vene *f*; (*geol, min*) Ader *f*

vellum ['veləm] *s* Velin *n*

velocity [vɪ'lɑsɪti] *s* Geschwindigkeit *f*

velvet ['velvɪt] *adj* Samt– ‖ *s* Samt *m*

velveteen [ˌvelvɪ'tin] *s* Baumwollsamt *m*

velvety ['velvɪti] *adj* samtartig

vend [vend] *tr* verkaufen

vend′ing machine′ *s* Automat *m*

vendor ['vendər] *s* Verkäufer –in *mf*

veneer [və'nɪr] *s* Furnier *n*; (*fig*) Tünche *f* ‖ *tr* furnieren

venerable ['venərəbəl] *adj* ehrwürdig

venerate ['venə.ret] *tr* verehren

veneration [ˌvenə'reʃən] *s* Verehrung *f*

Venetian [vɪ'niʃən] *adj* venezianisch ‖ *s* Venezianer –in *mf*

Vene′tian blind′ *s* Fensterjalousie *f*

vengeance ['vendʒəns] *s* Rache *f*; take v. on sich rächen an (*dat*); with a v. mit Gewalt

vengeful ['vendʒfəl] *adj* rachsüchtig

venial ['vinɪ·əl] (*sin*) lässlich

Venice ['venɪs] *s* Venedig *n*

venison ['venɪsən] *s* Wildbret *n*

venom ['venəm] *s* Gift *n*; (*fig*) Geifer *m*

venomous ['venəməs] *adj* giftig

vent [vent] *s* Öffnung *f*; give v. to Luft machen (*dat*) ‖ *tr* auslassen

ventilate ['ventɪ.let] *tr* ventilieren

ventilation [ˌventɪ'leʃən] *s* Ventilation *f*

ventilator ['ventɪ.letər] *s* Ventilator *m*

ventricle ['ventrɪkəl] *s* Ventrikel *m*

ventriloquist [ven'trɪləkwɪst] *s* Bauchredner –in *mf*

venture ['ventʃər] *s* Unternehmen *n* ‖ *tr* wagen ‖ *intr* (on) sich wagen (an *acc*); v. out sich hinauswagen; v. to (*inf*) sich vermessen zu (*inf*)

venturesome ['ventʃərsəm] *adj* (*person*) wagemutig; (*deed*) gewagt

venue ['venju] *s* zuständiger Gerichtsort *m*; change of v. Änderung *f* des Gerichtsstandes

Venus ['vinəs] *s* Venus *f*

veracity [vɪ'ræsɪti] *s* Wahrhaftigkeit *f*

veranda [və'rændə] *s* Veranda *f*

verb [vɜrb] *s* Verb *n*, Zeitwort *n*

verbal ['vɜrbəl] *adj* (*oral*) mündlich; (*gram*) verbal

verbatim [vər'betɪm] *adj* wortgetreu

verbiage ['vɜrbɪ·ɪdʒ] *s* Wortschwall *m*

verbose [vər'bos] *adj* weitschweifig

verdant ['vɜrdənt] *adj* grün

verdict ['vɜrdɪkt] *s* Urteilsspruch *m* (der Geschworenen); give a v. e–n Spruch fällen

verdigris ['vɜrdɪ.gris] *s* Grünspan *m*

verge [vɜrdʒ] *s* (*fig*) Rand *m*; on the v. of (*ger*) nahe daran zu (*inf*) ‖ *intr*—v. on grenzen an (*acc*)

verifiable [ˌverɪ'faɪ·əbəl] *adj* nachprüfbar

verification [ˌverɪfɪ'keʃən] *s* Nachprüfung *f*

verify ['verɪ.faɪ] *v* (*pret & pp* **–fied**) *tr* nachprüfen

verily ['verɪli] *adv* (Bib) wahrlich

veritable ['verɪtəbəl] *adj* echt

vermilion [vər'mɪljən] *adj* zinnoberrot

vermin ['vɜrmɪn] *s* (*objectionable person*) Halunke *m*; v. *spl* Schädlinge *pl*; (*objectionable persons*) Gesindel *n*

vermouth [vər'muθ] *s* Wermut *m*

vernacular [vər'nækjələr] *adj* volkssprachlich ‖ *s* Volkssprache *f*

ver′nal e′quinox ['vɜrnəl] *s* Frühlingstagundnachtgleiche *f*

versatile ['vɜrsətɪl] *adj* beweglich

verse [vɜrs] *s* (& Bib) Vers *m*; (*stanza*) Strophe *f*

versed [vɜrst] *adj* (in) bewandert in (*dat*)

versification [ˌvɜrsɪfɪ'keʃən] *s* (*metrical structure*) Versbau *m*; (*versifying*) Verskunst *f*; (*metrical version*) Versfassung *f*

versifier ['vɜrsɪ.faɪ·ər] *s* Verseschmied *m*

version ['vɜrʒən] *s* Version *f*

ver·so ['vɜrso] *s* (**–sos**) (*of a coin*) Revers *m*; (*typ*) Verso *n*

versus ['vɜrsəs] *prep* gegen (*acc*)

verte·bra ['vɜrtɪbrə] *s* (**–brae** [ˌbri] & **–bras**) Rückenwirbel *m*, Wirbel *m*

vertebrate ['vɜrtɪ.bret] *s* Wirbeltier *n*

ver·tex ['vɜrteks] *s* (**–texes** & **–tices** [tɪˌsiz]) Scheitelpunkt *m*

vertical ['vɜrtɪkəl] *adj* senkrecht ‖ *s* Vertikale *f*

ver′tical hold′ *s* (telv) Vertikaleinstellung *f*

ver′tical take′off *s* Senkrechtstart *m*

vertigo ['vɜrtɪ.go] *s* Schwindel *m*, Schwindelgefühl *n*

very ['veri] *adj*—**that v. day** an demselben Tag; **the v. thought** der bloße Gedanke; **the v. truth** die reine Wahrheit; **the v. man** genau der Mann ‖ *adv* sehr; **the v. best** der allerbeste; **the v. same** ebenderselbe

vesicle ['vesɪkəl] *s* Bläschen *n*

vespers ['vespərz] *spl* Vesper *f*

vessel ['vesəl] *s* (*ship*) Schiff *n*; (*container*) Gefäß *n*

vest [vest] *s* Weste *f*; (*for women*) Leibchen *n* ‖ *tr* (with) bekleiden (mit); **be vested in** zustehen (*dat*)

vest′ed in′terest *s* (*for personal benefits*) persönliches Interesse *n*; (*jur*) rechtmäßiges Interesse *n*

vestibule ['vestɪ.bjul] *s* Vestibül *n*

vestige ['vestɪdʒ] *s* Spur *f*

vestment ['vestmənt] *s* Gewand *n*

vest′-pock′et *adj* Westentaschen–

vestry ['vestri] *s* Sakristei *f*; (*committee*) Gemeindevertretung *f*

vetch [vetʃ] *s* Wicke *f*

veteran ['vetərən] s Veteran m; (sport) Senior m

veterinarian [,vetərɪ'nerɪ·ən] s Tierarzt m, Tierärztin f

veterinary ['vetərɪ ,nerɪ] adj (college) tierärztlich; **v. medicine** Tierheilkunde f

ve·to ['vito] s (–toes) Veto n || tr ein Veto einlegen gegen

vex [veks] tr ärgern

vexation [vek'seʃən] s Ärger m

V′-forma′tion s (aer) Staffelkeil m

via ['vɪ·ə] prep über (acc)

viable ['vaɪ·əbəl] adj lebensfähig

viaduct ['vaɪ·ə ,dʌkt] s Viadukt m

vial ['vaɪ·əl] s Phiole f

viands ['vaɪ·əndz] spl Lebensmittel pl

vibrate ['vaɪbret] intr vibrieren; **cause to v.** in Schwingung versetzen

vibration [vaɪ'breʃən] s Schwingung f

vicar ['vɪkər] s Vikar m

vicarage ['vɪkərɪdʒ] s Pfarrhaus n

vicarious [vaɪ'kerɪ·əs] adj (pleasure) nachempfunden; (taking the place of another) stellvertretend; **v. experience** Ersatzbefriedigung f

vice [vaɪs] s Laster n

vice′-ad′miral s Vizeadmiral m

vice′-con′sul s Vizekonsul m

vice′-pres′ident s Vizepräsident –in mf

viceroy ['vaɪsrɔɪ] s Vizekönig m

vice′ squad′ s Sittenpolizei f

vice versa ['vaɪsə'vʌrsə] adv umgekehrt

vicinity [vɪ'sɪnɪti] s Umgebung f; **in the v. of** in der Nähe (genit)

vicious ['vɪʃəs] adj (temper) bösartig; (dog) bissig; (person, gossip) heimtückisch

vi′cious cir′cle s Zirkelschluß m

vicissitudes [vɪ'sɪsɪ ,tjudz] spl Wechselfälle pl

victim ['vɪktɪm] s Opfer n; (animal) Opfertier n; **fall v. to** zum Opfer fallen (dat)

victimize ['vɪktɪ ,maɪz] tr (make a victim of) benachteiligen; (dupe) hereinlegen

victor ['vɪktər] s Sieger –in mf

victorious [vɪk'torɪ·əs] adj siegreich

victory ['vɪktəri] adj Sieges– || s Sieg m; (myth) Siegesgöttin f; **flushed with v.** siegestrunken

victuals ['vɪtəlz] spl Viktualien pl

vid′eo sig′nal ['vɪdɪ ,o] s Bildsignal n

vid′eo tape′ s Bildband n

vid′eo tape′ record′er s Bildbandgerät n

vid′eo tape′ record′ing s Bildbandaufnahme f

vie [vaɪ] v (pret & pp vied; ger vying) intr (with) wetteifern (mit)

Vienna [vɪ'enə] s Wien n

Vien·nese [,vɪ·ə'niz] adj wienerisch || s (–nese) Wiener –in mf

Vietnam [,vɪ·et'nam] s Vietnam n

Vietnam·ese [vɪ ,etnə'miz] adj vietnamesisch || s (–se) Vietnamese m, Vietnamesin f

view [vju] s Aussicht f; (opinion) Ansicht f; **come into v.** in Sicht kommen; **in my v.** meiner Ansicht nach;

in v. of angesichts (genit); **with a v. to** (ger) in der Absicht zu (inf) || tr betrachten; (sights) besichtigen

viewer ['vju·ər] s Zuschauer –in mf

view′find′er s Bildsucher m

view′point′ s Standpunkt m

vigil ['vɪdʒɪl] s Nachtwache f; **keep v.** wachen

vigilance ['vɪdʒɪləns] s Wachsamkeit f

vigilant ['vɪdʒɪlənt] adj wachsam

vignette [vɪn'jet] s Vignette f

vigor ['vɪgər] s (physical) Kraft f; (mental) Energie f; (intensity) Wucht f

vigorous ['vɪgərəs] adj (strong) kräftig; (act) energisch

vile [vaɪl] adj gemein; (coll) scheußlich

vileness ['vaɪlnɪs] s Gemeinheit f

vili·fy ['vɪlɪ ,faɪ] v (pret & pp –fied) tr verleumden

villa ['vɪlə] s Villa f

village ['vɪlɪdʒ] s Dorf n, Ort m

villager ['vɪlɪdʒər] s Dorfbewohner –in mf

villain ['vɪlən] s Bösewicht m, Schurke m

villainous ['vɪlənəs] adj schurkisch

villainy ['vɪləni] s Schurkerei f

vim [vɪm] s Mumm m

vindicate ['vɪndɪ ,ket] tr rechtfertigen

vindictive [vɪn'dɪktɪv] adj rachsüchtig

vine [vaɪn] s Rebe f; (creeper) Ranke f

vinegar ['vɪnɪgər] s Essig m

vine′ grow′er [,gro·ər] s Winzer m

vineyard ['vɪnjərd] s Weinberg m

vintage ['vɪntɪdʒ] adj Qualitäts– || s Weinernte f

vin′tage year′ s Weinjahr n

vintner ['vɪntnər] s Weinbauer –in mf

vinyl ['vaɪnɪl] adj Vinyl–

viola [vaɪ'olə] s Bratsche f, Viola f

violate ['vaɪ·ə ,let] tr (a law) verletzen; (a promise) brechen; (the peace) stören; (a custom, shrine) entweihen; (a girl) vergewaltigen

violation [,vaɪ·ə'leʃən] s (of the law) Verletzung f; (of a shrine) Entweihung f; (of a girl) Vergewaltigung f

violence ['vaɪ·əlɪns] s Gewalt f

violent ['vaɪ·ələnt] adj (person) gewalttätig; (deed) gewaltsam; (anger, argument) heftig

violet ['vaɪ·əlɪt] adj violett || s Veilchen n

violin [,vaɪ·ə'lɪn] s Geige f

violinist [,vaɪ·ə'lɪnɪst] s Geiger –in mf

violoncel·lo [,vaɪ·ələn't∫elo] s (–los) Violoncello n

viper ['vaɪpər] s Natter f, Viper f

virgin ['vʌrdʒɪn] adj Jungfern–; (land) unberührt || s Jungfrau f

virginity [vər'dʒɪnɪti] s Jungfräulichkeit f

virility [vɪ'rɪlɪti] s Zeugungskraft f

virology [vaɪ'ralədʒi] s Virusforschung f

virtual ['vʌrt∫u·əl] adj faktisch; (opt, tech) virtuell

virtue ['vʌrt∫u] s Tugend f; **by v. of** kraft (genit), vermöge (genit)

virtuosity [ˌvɑrtʃuˈɑsɪti] *s* Virtuosität *f*

virtuo·so [ˌvɑrtʃuˈoso] *s* (**-sos** & **-si** [si]) Virtuose *m*, Virtuosin *f*

virtuous [ˈvɑrtʃuˑəs] *adj* tugendhaft

virulence [ˈvɪrjələns] *s* Virulenz *f*

virulent [ˈvɪrjələnt] *adj* virulent

virus [ˈvaɪrəs] *s* Virus *n*

visa [ˈvizə] *s* Visum *n*

visage [ˈvɪzɪdʒ] *s* Antlitz *n*

viscera [ˈvɪsərə] *s* Eingeweide *pl*

viscosity [vɪsˈkɑsɪti] *s* Viskosität *f*

viscount [ˈvaɪkaunt] *s* Vicomte *m*

viscountess [ˈvaɪkauntɪs] *s* Vicomtesse *f*

viscous [ˈvɪskəs] *adj* zähflüssig

vise [vaɪs] *s* Schraubstock *m*

visibility [ˌvɪziˈbɪlɪti] *s* Sichtbarkeit *f*; (*meteor*) Sicht *f*

visible [ˈvɪzɪbəl] *adj* sichtbar

visibly [ˈvɪzɪbli] *adv* zusehends

vision [ˈvɪʒən] *s* (*faculty*) Sehvermögen *n*; (*appearance*) Vision *f*; **of great v.** von großem Weitblick

visionary [ˈvɪʒəˌnɛri] *adj* visionär ‖ *s* Visionär –in *mf*

visit [ˈvɪzɪt] *s* Besuch *m*; (*official*) Visite *f* ‖ *tr* besuchen; (*a museum, town*) besichtigen

visitation [ˌvɪzɪˈteʃən] *s* Visitation *f*; **Visitation of our Lady** Heimsuchung *f* Mariä

vis'iting hours' *spl* Besuchszeit *f*

vis'iting nurse' *s* Fürsorgerin *f*

visitor [ˈvɪzɪtər] *s* Besucher –in *mf*; **have visitors** Besuch haben

visor [ˈvaɪzər] *s* Schirm *m*; (*on a helmet*) Visier *n*

vista [ˈvɪstə] *s* (& *fig*) Ausblick *m*

Vistula [ˈvɪstʃulə] *s* Weichsel *f*

visual [ˈvɪʒuˑəl] *adj* visuell

vis'ual aids' *spl* Anschauungsmaterial *n*

visualize [ˈvɪʒuˑəˌlaɪz] *tr* sich [*dat*] vorstellen

vital [ˈvaɪtəl] *adj* (lebens)wichtig; (*signs, functions*) Lebens– ‖ **vitals** *spl* edle Teile *pl*

vitality [vaɪˈtælɪti] *s* Lebenskraft *f*

vitalize [ˈvaɪtəˌlaɪz] *tr* beleben

vitamin [ˈvaɪtəmɪn] *s* Vitamin *n*

vi'tamin defi'ciency *s* Vitaminmangel *m*

vitiate [ˈvɪʃɪˌet] *tr* verderben

vitreous [ˈvɪtrɪˑəs] *adj* glasartig

vitriolic [ˌvɪtrɪˈɑlɪk] *adj* (fig) beißend; (chem) Vitriol–

vituperate [vaɪˈt(j)upəˌret] *tr* schelten

vivacious [vɪˈveʃəs] *adj* lebhaft

vivid [ˈvɪvɪd] *adj* lebhaft

vivi·fy [ˈvɪvɪˌfaɪ] *v* (*pret* & *pp* **–fied**) *tr* beleben

vivisection [ˌvɪvɪˈsɛkʃən] *s* Vivisektion *f*

vixen [ˈvɪksən] *s* Füchsin *f*

viz. *abbr* nämlich

vizier [vɪˈzɪr] *s* Vezier *m*, Wesir *m*

vocabulary [voˈkæbjəˌlɛri] *s* (*word range*) Wortschatz *m*; (*list*) Wörterverzeichnis *n*

vocal [ˈvokəl] *adj* stimmlich, Stimm–; (*outspoken*) redselig

voc'al cord' *s* Stimmband *n*

vocalist [ˈvokəlɪst] *s* Sänger –in *mf*

vocalize [ˈvokəˌlaɪz] *tr* (phonet) vokalisieren ‖ *intr* singen; (phonet) in e–n Vokal verwandelt werden

vocation [voˈkeʃən] *s* Beruf *m*; (relig) Berufung *f*

voca'tional guid'ance [voˈkeʃənəl] *s* Berufsberatung *f*

voca'tional school' *s* Berufsschule *f*

voca'tional train'ing *s* Berufsausbildung *f*

vocative [ˈvɑkətɪv] *s* Vokativ *m*

vociferous [voˈsɪfərəs] *adj* laut

vodka [ˈvɑdkə] *s* Wodka *m*

vogue [vog] *s* (herrschende) Mode *f*; **be in v.** Mode sein

voice [vɔɪs] *s* Stimme *f*; **in a low v.** mit leiser Stimme ‖ *tr* äußern; (phonet) stimmhaft aussprechen

voiced *adj* (phonet) stimmhaft

voiceless [ˈvɔɪslɪs] *adj* stimmlos

void [vɔɪd] *adj* leer; (*invalid*) ungültig ‖ *s* Leere *f* ‖ *tr* für ungültig erklären; (*the bowels*) entleeren

volatile [ˈvɑlətɪl] *adj* (*explosive*) jähzornig; (*changeable*) unbeständig; (chem) flüchtig

volcanic [vɑlˈkænɪk] *adj* vulkanisch

volca·no [vɑlˈkeno] *s* (**-noes** & **-nos**) Vulkan *m*

volition [voˈlɪʃən] *s* Wollen *n*; **of one's own v.** aus eigenem Antrieb

volley [ˈvɑli] *s* (*of gunfire*) Salve *f*; (*of stones*) Hagel *m*; (sport) Flugschlag *m*

vol'leyball' *s* Volleyball *m*

volt [volt] *s* Volt *n*

voltage [ˈvoltɪdʒ] *s* Spannung *f*

voluble [ˈvɑljəbəl] *adj* redegewandt

volume [ˈvɑljəm] *s* (*book*) Band *m*; (*of a magazine series*) Jahrgang *m*; (*of sound*) Lautstärke *f*; (*amount*) Ausmaß *n*; (*of a container*) Rauminhalt *m*; **speak volumes** Bände sprechen; **v. of sales** Umsatz *m*

vol'ume control' *s* Lautstärkeregler *m*

voluminous [vəˈlumɪnəs] *adj* (*writer*) produktiv; (*of great extent or size*) umfangreich

voluntary [ˈvɑlənˌtɛri] *adj* freiwillig

volunteer [ˌvɑlənˈtɪr] *adj* Freiwilligen– ‖ *s* Freiwillige *mf* ‖ *tr* freiwillig anbieten ‖ *intr* (**for**) sich freiwillig erbieten (für, zu)

voluptuary [vəˈlʌptʃuˌɛri] *s* Wollüstling *m*

voluptuous [vəˈlʌptʃuˑəs] *adj* wollüstig

vomit [ˈvɑmɪt] *s* Erbrechen *n* ‖ *tr* (er)brechen; (*smoke*) ausstoßen; (*fire*) speien; (*lava*) auswerfen ‖ *intr* sich erbrechen

voodoo [ˈvudu] *adj* Wudu– ‖ *s* Wudu *m*

voracious [vəˈreʃəs] *adj* gefräßig

voracity [vəˈræsɪti] *s* Gefräßigkeit *f*

vor·tex [ˈvɔrteks] *s* (**-texes** & **-tices** [tɪˌsiz]) (& fig) Wirbel *m*

votary [ˈvotəri] *s* Verehrer –in *mf*

vote [vot] *s* Stimme *f*; (*act of voting*) Abstimmung *f*; (*right to vote*) Stimmrecht *n*; **put to a v.** zur Abstimmung

bringen ‖ *tr (approve of, e.g., money)* (for) bewilligen (für); **v. down** niederstimmen ‖ *intr* stimmen; **v. by acclamation** durch Zuruf stimmen; **v. for** wählen; **v. on** abstimmen über *(acc)*
vote′ get′ter [ˌgetər] *s* Wahllokomotive *f*
vote′ of con′fidence *s* Vertrauensvotum *n*
vote′ of no′ con′fidence *s* Mißvertrauensvotum *n*
voter [ˈvotər] *s* Wähler –in *mf*
vot′ing booth′ *s* Wahlzelle *f*
vot′ing machine′ *s* Stimmenzählapparat *m*
votive [ˈvotɪv] *adj* Votiv-, Weih-
vo′tive of′fering *s* Weihgabe *f*
vouch [vautʃ] *tr* bezeugen ‖ *intr*—**v. for** bürgen für
voucher [ˈvautʃər] *s* Beleg *m*
vouchsafe′ *tr* gewähren

vow [vau] *s* Gelübde *n;* **take a vow of** geloben ‖ *tr* geloben; *(revenge)* schwören; **vow to** *(inf)* sich *[dat]* geloben zu *(inf)*
vowel [ˈvau‧əl] *s* Selbstlaut *m*, Vokal *m*
voyage [ˈvɔɪ‧ɪdʒ] *s* Reise *f; (by sea)* Seereise *f* ‖ *intr* reisen
voyager [ˈvɔɪ‧ɪdʒər] *s* Reisende *mf; (by sea)* Seereisende *mf*
V′-shaped′ *adj* keilförmig
V′-sign′ *s* Siegeszeichen *n*
vulcanize [ˈvʌlkəˌnaɪz] *tr* vulkanisieren
vulgar [ˈvʌlgər] *adj* vulgär
vulgarity [vʌlˈgærɪti] *s* Gemeinheit *f*
Vul′gar Lat′in *s* Vulgärlatein *n*
Vulgate [ˈvʌlget] *s* Vulgata *f*
vulnerable [ˈvʌlnərəbəl] *adj* verwundbar; *(position)* ungeschützt; *(fig)* angreifbar; **v. to** anfällig für
vulture [ˈvʌltʃər] *s* Geier *m*

W

W, w [ˈdʌbəl ˌju] *s* dreiunzwanzigster Buchstabe des englischen Alphabets
wad [wad] *s (of cotton)* Bausch *m; (of money)* Bündel *n; (of papers)* Stoß *m; (of tobacco)* Priem *m*
waddle [ˈwadəl] *s* Watscheln *n* ‖ *intr* watscheln
wade [wed] *intr* waten; **w. into** *(fig)* anpacken; **w. through** *(fig)* sich mühsam durcharbeiten durch
wafer [ˈwefər] *s* Oblate *f*
waffle [ˈwafəl] *s* Waffel *f*
waf′fle i′ron *s* Waffeleisen *n*
waft [wæft], [waft] *tr & intr* wehen
wag [wæg] *s (nod)* Nicken *n; (shake)* Schütteln *n; (of the tail)* Wedeln *n; (mischievous person)* Schalk *m* ‖ *v (pret & pp* **wagged**) *ger* **wagging**) *tr (the tail)* wedeln mit; *(nod)* nicken mit; *(shake)* schütteln ‖ *intr (said of a tail)* wedeln; *(said of tongues)* nicht still sein
wage [wedʒ] *adj* Lohn- ‖ *s* Lohn *m;* **wages** Lohn *m* ‖ *tr (war)* führen
wage′ cut′ *s* Lohnabbau *m*
wage′ freeze′ *s* Lohnstopp *m*
wager [ˈwedʒər] *s* Wette *f;* **lay a w.** e-e Wette eingehen ‖ *tr & intr* wetten
waggish [ˈwægɪʃ] *adj* schalkhaft
wagon [ˈwægən] *s* Wagen *m*
wag′on load′ *s* Wagenladung *f*
waif [wef] *s (child)* verwahrlostes Kind *n; (animal)* verwahrlostes Tier *n*
wail [wel] *s* Wehklage *f* ‖ *intr (over)* wehklagen (über *acc*)
wain‧scot [ˈwenskət] *s* Täfelung *f* ‖ *v (pret & pp* **-scot[t]ed**) *ger* **-scot-[t]ing**) *tr* täfeln
waist [west] *s* Taille *f;* **strip to the w.** den Oberkörper freimachen
waist′-deep′ *adj* bis an die Hüften (reichend)

waist′line′ *s* Taille *f;* **watch one's w.** auf die schlanke Linie achten
wait [wet] *s* Warten *n;* **an hour's w.** e-e Stunde Wartezeit ‖ *intr* warten; **that can w.** das hat Zeit; **w. for** *(a person)* warten auf *(acc); (e.g., an answer)* abwarten; **w. on** bedienen; **w. up for** aufbleiben und warten auf *(acc)*
wait′-and-see′ pol′icy *s* Politik *f* des Abwartens
waiter [ˈwetər] *s* Kellner *m;* **w.!** Herr Ober!
wait′ing line′ *s* Schlange *f*
wait′ing list′ *s* Warteliste *f*
wait′ing room′ *s* Warteraum *m; (e.g., in a railroad station)* Wartesaal *m*
waitress [ˈwetrɪs] *s* Kellnerin *f*
waive [wev] *tr* verzichten auf *(acc)*
waiver [ˈwevər] *s* Verzicht *m*
wake [wek] *s (at a funeral)* Totenwache *f; (naut)* Kielwasser *n;* **in the w. of** im Gefolge *(genit)* ‖ *v (pret* **waked &** **woke** [wok]; *pp* **waked**) *tr* wecken; **w. up** aufwecken ‖ *intr* erwachen; **w. up** aufwachen; **w. up to** *(fig)* bewußt werden *(genit)*
wakeful [ˈwekfəl] *adj* wachsam
waken [ˈwekən] *tr* (auf)wecken ‖ *intr* erwachen
walk [wɔk] *s* Spaziergang *m; (gait)* Gang *m; (path)* Spazierweg *m;* **a five-minute w. to** fünf Minuten zu Fuß zu; **from all walks of life** aus allen Ständen; **go for a w.** spazierengehen; **take for a w.** spazierenführen ‖ *tr (a dog)* spazierenführen; *(a person)* begleiten; *(a horse)* führen; *(the streets)* ablaufen ‖ *intr (zu Fuß)* gehen, laufen; **w. off with** klauen; **w. out on** sitzenlassen; **w. up to** zugehen auf *(acc)*
walk′-away′ *s* (coll) leichter Sieg *m*

walker ['wɔkər] s Fußgänger –in mf
walkie-talkie ['wɔkɪ'tɔkɪ] s Sprechfunkgerät n
walk′-in′ adj (closet) begehbar
walk′ing pa′pers spl Laufpaß m
walk′ing shoes′ spl Straßenschuhe pl
walk′ing stick′ s Spazierstock m
walk′-on′ s (theat) Statist –in mf
walk′out′ s Ausstand m
walk′-o′ver s (sport) leichter Sieg m
walk′-up′ s Mietwohnung f ohne Fahrstuhl
wall [wɔl] s Mauer f; (between rooms) Wand f || tr—w. up vermauern
wall′ brack′et s Konsole f
wall′ clock′ s Wanduhr f
wallet ['wɑlɪt] s Brieftasche f
wall′flow′er s (coll) Wandblümchen n
wall′ map′ s Wandkarte f
wallop ['wɑləp] s Puff m; have a w. Schlagkraft haben || tr verprügeln; (defeat) schlagen
wal′loping adj (sl) mordsgroß
wallow ['wɑlo] intr sich wälzen; w. in (fig) schwelgen in (dat)
wall′pa′per s Tapete f || tr tapezieren
walnut ['wɔlnət] s Walnuß f; (wood) Walnußholz n; (tree) Walnußbaum m
walrus ['wɔlrəs] s Walroß n
waltz [wɔlts] s Walzer m || intr Walzer tanzen
wan [wɑn] adj (wanner; wannest) bleich; (smile) schwach, matt
wand [wɑnd] s Stab m; (in magic) Zauberstab m
wander ['wɑndər] intr wandern; (from a subject) abschweifen
wanderer ['wɑndərər] s Wanderer –in mf
wan′derlust′ s Wanderlust f
wane [wen] s—be on the w. abnehmen || intr abnehmen
wangle ['wæŋgəl] tr sich [dat] erschwindeln
want [wɔnt] s Bedürfnis n; for w. of mangels (genit) || tr wollen; wanted (sought, desired) gesucht
want′ ad′ s Kleinanzeige f
want′ing adj—be w. in ermangeln (genit)
war [wɔr] s Krieg m; at war im Kriege; go to war with e-n Krieg beginnen gegen; make war on Krieg führen gegen || v (pret & pp warred; ger warring) intr kämpfen
warble ['wɑrbəl] s Trillern n || intr trillern
war′ bond′ s Kriegsanleihe f
war′ cry′ s Schlachtruf m
ward [wɔrd] s (in a hospital) Station f; (of a city) Bezirk m; (person under protection) Schützling m; (person under guardianship) Mündel n; (guardianship) Vormundschaft f || tr—w. off abwehren
warden ['wɔrdən] s Gefängnisdirektor m
ward′robe′ s Garderobe f
ward′room′ s (nav) Offiziersmesse f
ware [wer] s Ware f
ware′house′ s Lagerhaus n, Warenlager n

ware′house′man s (–men) Lagerist m
war′fare′ s Kriegsführung f, Krieg m
war′ foot′ing s Kriegsbereitschaft f
war′head′ s Gefechtskopf m
war′-horse′ s (coll) alter Kämpe m
war′like′ adj kriegerisch
war′ lord′ s Kriegsherr m
warm [wɔrm] adj warm; (friends) intim || tr wärmen; w. up aufwärmen || intr—w. up warm werden; (sport) warmlaufen
warm′-blood′ed adj warmblütig
warm′front′ s Warmfront f
warm′-heart′ed adj warmherzig
warmonger ['wɔr‚mʌŋgər] s Kriegshetzer –in mf
warmth [wɔrmθ] s Wärme f
warm′-up′ s (sport) Lockerungsübungen pl
warn [wɔrn] tr (against) warnen (vor dat)
warn′ing s Warnung f; let this be a w. to you lassen Sie sich das zur Warnung dienen
warn′ing shot′ s Warnschuß m
war′ of attri′tion s Zermürbungskrieg m
warp [wɔrp] s (of a board) Verziehen n || tr (wood) verziehen; w. s.o.'s mind j–n verschroben machen || intr sich verziehen
war′path′ s Kriegspfad m
warped adj (wood) verzogen; (mind, opinion) verschroben
war′plane′ s Kampfflugzeug n
warrant ['wɔrənt] s (justification) Rechtfertigung f; (authorization) Berechtigung f; w. for arrest Haftbefehl m || tr (justify) rechtfertigen; (guarantee) garantieren
war′rant of′ficer s (mil) Stabsfeldwebel m; (nav) Deckoffizier m
warranty ['wɔrəntɪ] s Gewährleistung f
war′ranty serv′ice s Kundendienst m
warren ['wɔrən] s Kaninchengehege n
war′ring adj kriegsführend
warrior ['wɔrɪ‚ər] s Krieger m
Warsaw ['wɔrsɔ] s Warschau n
war′ship′ s Kriegsschiff n
wart [wɔrt] s Warze f
war′time′ adj Kriegs– || s Kriegszeit f
war′-torn′ adj vom Krieg verwüstet
wary ['werɪ] adj vorsichtig
war′ zone′ s Kriegsgebiet n
wash [wɑʃ] adj Wasch– || s Wäsche f; (aer) Luftstrudel m; (paint) dünner Farbüberzug m; do the w. die Wäsche waschen || tr waschen; (metal) schlämmen; (paint) tuschen; (phot) wässern; w. ashore anschwemmen; w. away wegspülen; w. off abwaschen; w. out auswaschen; (a bridge) wegreißen; w. up aufwaschen || intr waschen; w. ashore ans Land spülen
washable ['wɑʃəbəl] adj waschbar
wash′-and-wear′ adj bügelfrei
wash′ba′sin s Waschbecken n
wash′bas′ket s Wäschekorb m
wash′board′ s Waschbrett n
wash′bowl′ s Waschbecken n
wash′cloth′ s Waschlappen m

wash'day' s Waschtag m
washed'-out' adj verwaschen; (tired) schlapp
washer ['wɔʃər] s Waschmaschine f; (of rubber) Dichtungsring m; (of metal) Unterlegscheibe f
washed'-up' adj (coll) erledigt
wash'er·wom'an s (-wom'en) Waschfrau f
wash'ing s Waschen n; (clothes) Wäsche f
wash'ing machine' s Waschmaschine f
wash'out' s Auswaschung f; (failure) Pleite f; (person who fails) Versager –in mf
wash'rag' s Waschlappen m
wash'room' s Waschraum m
wash'stand' s Waschtisch m
wash'tub' s Waschtrog m
wasp [wɑsp] s Wespe f
wasp' waist' s Wespentaille f
waste [west] adj (superfluous) überflüssig; (land) öde || s (of material goods, time, energy) Verschwendung f; (waste material) Müll m; (wilderness) Wildnis f; go to w. vergeudet werden || tr verschwenden, vergeuden || intr—w. away verfallen
waste'bas'ket s Papierkorb m
wasteful ['westfəl] adj verschwenderisch
waste'land' s Ödland n
waste'pa'per s Makulatur f
waste'pipe' s Abflußrohr n
waste'prod'uct s Abfallprodukt n
wastrel ['westrəl] s Verschwender –in mf
watch [wɑtʃ] s Uhr f; (lookout) Wache f; be on the w. for acht haben auf (acc) || tr (observe) beobachten; (guard) bewachen; (oversee) aufpassen auf (acc); w. how I do it passen Sie auf, wie ich es mache; w. your step! Vorsicht, Stufe! || intr (keep guard) wachen; (observe) zuschauen; w. for abwarten; w. over überwachen; w. out! Vorsicht!; w. out for ausschauen nach; (some danger) sich hüten vor (dat); w. out for oneself sich vorsehen
watch'band' s Uhrarmband n
watch'case' s Uhrgehäuse n
watch' crys'tal s Uhrglas n
watch'dog' s Wachhund m
watch'dog committee s Überwachungsausschuß m
watchful ['wɑtʃfəl] adj wachsam
watchfulness ['wɑtʃfəlnɪs] s Wachsamkeit f
watch'mak'er s Uhrmacher –in mf
watch'man s (-men) Wächter m
watch' pock'et s Uhrtasche f
watch' strap' s Uhrarmband n
watch'tow'er s Wachturm m
watch'word' s Kennwort n, Parole f
water ['wɔtər] s Wasser n; (body of water) Gewässer n; pass w. Wasser lassen || tr (e.g., flowers) begießen; (fields) bewässern; (animals) tränken; (the garden, streets) sprengen; w. down (& fig) verwässern || intr (said of the eyes) tränen; my mouth

waters das Wasser läuft mir im Mund zusammen
wa'ter boy' s Wasserträger m
wa'ter clos'et s Wasserklosett n
wa'tercol'or s (paint) Aquarellfarbe f; (painting) Aquarell n
wa'tercourse' s Wasserlauf m
wa'tercress' s Brunnenkresse f
wa'terfall' s Wasserfall m
wa'terfront' s Hafenviertel n
wa'ter heat'er s Warmwasserbereiter m
wa'tering can' s Wasserkanne f
wa'tering place' s (for cattle) Tränke f; (for tourists) Badeort m
wa'ter lev'el s Wasserstand m
wa'terlogged' adj vollgesogen
wa'ter main' s Wasserleitung f
wa'termark' s Wasserzeichen n
wa'ter mat'tress s Wasserbett n
wa'termel'on s Wassermelone f
wa'ter me'ter s Wasserzähler m
wa'ter pipe' s Wasserrohr n
wa'ter po'lo s Wasserball m
wa'ter pow'er s Wasserkraft f
wa'terproof' adj wasserdicht || tr imprägnieren
wa'ter-repel'lent adj wasserabstoßend
wa'tershed' s Wasserscheide f
wa'ter-ski' intr wasserschifahren
wa'terspout' s (orifice) Wasserspeier m; (pipe) Ablaufrohr n
wa'ter supply' s Wasserversorgung f
wa'ter ta'ble s Grundwasserspiegel m
wa'ter tank' s Wasserbehälter m
wa'tertight' adj wasserdicht; (fig) eindeutig
wa'ter wag'on s—be on the w. Abstinenzler sein
wa'terway' s Wasserstraße f
wa'ter wheel' s (for raising water) Schöpfwerk n; (water-driven) Wasserrad n
wa'ter wings' spl Schwimmkissen n
wa'terworks' s Wasserwerk n
watery ['wɔtəri] adj wäss(e)rig
watt [wɑt] s Watt n
wattage ['wɑtɪdʒ] s Wattleistung f
wattles ['wɑtəlz] spl Flechtwerk s
watt'me'ter s Wattmeter m
wave [wev] s (fig, meteor, mil, phys, rad) Welle f; w. of the hand Wink m mit der Hand || tr (a hat, flag) schwenken; (a hand, handkerchief) winken mit; (hair) wellen; w. one's hands about mit den Händen herumfuchteln; w. s.o. away j–n abwinken || intr (said of a flag) wehen; (said of grain) wogen; (with the hand) winken; w. to zuwinken (dat)
wave'length' s Wellenlänge f
waver ['wevər] intr schweben, wanken
wavy ['wevi] adj wellenförmig; w. line Wellenlinie f
wax [wæks] adj Wachs– || s Wachs n || tr (the floor) bohnern; (skis) wachsen || intr werden; (said of the moon) zunehmen; wax and wane zu– und abnehmen
wax' muse'um s Wachsfigurenkabinett n
wax' pa'per s Wachspapier n
way [we] adv weit; **way ahead** weit

voraus ‖ *s* Weg *m*; *(manner)* Art *f*; *(means)* Mittel *n*; *(condition)* Verfassung *f*; *(direction)* Richtung *f*; **across the way** gegenüber; **a long way from** weit weg von; **a long way off** weit weg; **by the way** übrigens; **by way of** über *(acc)*; **by way of comparison** vergleichsweise; **get s.th. out of the way** etw aus dem Wege schaffen; **get under way** in Gang kommen; **go all the way** aufs Ganze gehen; **go one's own way** aus der Reihe tanzen; **have a way with s.o.** mit j-m umzugehen verstehen; **have in the way of** *(merchandise)* haben an *(dat)*; **have it both ways** es sich *[dat]* aussuchen können; **have one's own way** seinen Willen durchsetzen; **I'm on my way!** ich komme schon!; **in a way** gewissermaßen; **in no way** keineswegs; **in the way** im Weg; **in this way** auf diese Weise; **in what way** in welcher Hinsicht; **make one's way through the crowd** sich *[dat]* e-n Weg durch die Menge bahnen; **one way or another** irgendwie; **on the way out** unterwegs; **on the way out** *(fig)* im Begriff unmodern zu werden; **see one's way clear** bereit sein; **that way** auf diese Weise; *(in that direction)* in jener Richtung; **the way it looks** voraussichtlich; **way back** Rückweg *m*; **way here** Herweg *m*; **way out** Ausgang *m*; *(fig)* Ausweg *m*; **way there** Hinweg *m*

wayfarer ['we‚ferər] *s* Wanderer *m*
way'lay' *v (pret & pp* -laid*) tr* auflauern *(dat)*
way' of life' *s* Lebensweise *f*
way' of think'ing *s* Denkweise *f*
ways' and means' *spl* Mittel und Wege *pl*
way'side' *adj* an der Straße gelegen ‖ *s* Wegrand *m*; **fall by the w.** dem Untergang anheimfallen
wayward ['wewərd] *adj* ungeraten
we [wi] *pers pron* wir
weak [wik] *adj* schwach
weaken ['wikən] *tr* (ab)schwächen ‖ *intr* schwach werden
weakling ['wiklɪŋ] *s* Schwächling *m*
weak'-mind'ed *adj* willenlos
weakness ['wiknɪs] *s* (& fig) Schwäche *f*
weak' spot' *s* schwache Stelle *f*
weal [wil] *s* Strieme *f*, Striemen *m*
wealth [welθ] *s (of)* Reichtum *m* (an *dat*)
wealthy ['welθi] *adj* wohlhabend
wean [win] *tr (from)* entwöhnen *(genit)*
weapon ['wepən] *s* Waffe *f*
weaponry ['wepənri] *s* Bewaffnung *f*
wear [wer] *s (use)* Gebrauch *m*; *(durability)* Haltbarkeit *f*; *(clothing)* Kleidung *f*; *(wearing down)* Verschleiß *m* ‖ *v (pret* wore [wor]*; pp* worn [worn]*)tr* tragen; **w. down** *(a heel)* abtreten; *(a person)* zermürben; **w. out** abnützen; *(tires)* abfahren; *(a person)* erschöpfen; **w. the pants in the family** die Hosen anhaben ‖ *intr* sich tragen; **w. off** sich abtragen; **w.**

out sich abnützen; **w. thin** *(said of clothes)* fadenscheinig werden; *(said of patience)* zu Ende gehen
wearable ['werəbəl] *adj* tragbar
wear' and tear' [ter] *s* Verschleiß *m*; **takes a lot of w.** strapazierfähig sein
weariness ['wɪrɪnɪs] *s* Müdigkeit *f*
wearisome ['wɪrɪsəm] *adj* mühsam
wea•ry ['wɪri] *adj* müde ‖ *v (pret & pp* -ried*) tr* ermüden ‖ *intr (of)* müde werden *(genit)*
weasel ['wizəl] *s* Wiesel *n* ‖ *intr*—**w. out** of sich herauswinden aus
weather ['weðər] *s* Wetter *n*; **be under the w.** unpäßlich sein; **w. permitting** bei günstiger Witterung ‖ *tr* dem Wetter aussetzen; *(the storm)* (fig) überstehen ‖ *intr* sich herausbilden *f*
weath'erbeat'en *adj* verwittert
weath'er bu'reau *s* Wetterdienst *m*
weath'er condi'tions *spl* Wetterverhältnisse *pl*
weath'er fore'cast *s* Wettervoraussage *f*
weath'erman' *s* (-men') Wetteransager *m*
weath'er report' *s* Wetterbericht *m*
weath'erstrip'ping *s* Dichtungsstreifen *pl*
weath'er vane' *s* (& fig) Wetterfahne *f*
weave [wiv] *s* Webart *f* ‖ *v (pret* wove [wov] & **weaved**; *pp* woven ['wovən]*) tr* weben; *(a rug)* wirken; *(a basket)* flechten; *(a wreath)* winden; **w. one's way through traffic** sich durch den Verkehr schlängeln ‖ *intr* weben
weaver ['wivər] *s* Weber –in *mf*
web [web] *s (of a spider)* Spinngewebe *n*; *(of ducks)* Schwimmhaut *f*; **web of lies** Lügengewebe *n*
web'-foot'ed *adj* schwimmfüßig
wed [wed] *v (pret & pp* wed & **wedded**; *ger* wedding*) tr & intr* heiraten
wed'ding *adj (cake, present, day, reception)* Hochzeits–; *(ring)* Trau– ‖ *s* Hochzeit *f*; *(ceremony)* Trauung *f*
wedge [wedʒ] *s* Keil *m* ‖ *tr*—**w.** in einkeilen
wed'lock' *s* Ehestand *m*; **out of w.** unehelich
Wednesday ['wenzde] *s* Mittwoch *m*; **on W.** am Mittwoch
wee [wi] *adj* winzig; **a wee bit** ein klein wenig
weed [wid] *s* Unkraut *n*; *(marijuana)* (sl) Marihuana *n*; *(cigarette)* (sl) Zigarette *f*; **pull weeds** jäten ‖ *tr* jäten; **w. out** (fig) aussondern
weed' kill'er *s* Unkrautvertilgungsmittel *n*
week [wik] *s* Woche *f*; **a w. from today** heute in e-r Woche; **a w. ago today** heute vor acht Tagen; **for weeks** wochenlang
week'day' *s* Wochentag *m*
week'end' *s* Wochenende *n*
weekender ['wik‚endər] *s* Wochenendausflügler –in *mf*
weekly ['wikli] *adj* wöchentlich; *(wages)* Wochen– ‖ *s* Wochenblatt *n*
weep [wip] *v (pret & pp* wept [wept]*) tr & intr* weinen

weep'ing wil'low *s* Trauerweide *f*

weevil ['wivəl] *s* Rüsselkäfer *m*

weft [weft] *s* (tex) Schußfaden *m*

weigh [we] *tr* wiegen; (*ponder*) wägen; (*anchor*) lichten || *intr* wiegen; **w. heavily on** schwer lasten auf (*dat*)

weight [wet] *s* Gewicht *n*; (*burden*) Last *f*; (*influence*) Einfluß *m*; (*importance*) Bedeutung *f*; **carry great w.** sehr ins Gewicht fallen; **lift weights** Gewichte heben; **pull one's w.** das Seine tun; **throw one's w. about** sich breitmachen

weightless ['wetlɪs] *adj* schwerelos

weightlessness ['wetlɪsnɪs] *s* Schwerelosigkeit *f*

weighty ['weti] *adj* (& fig) gewichtig

weird [wɪrd] *adj* unheimlich

weir·do ['wɪrdo] *s* (–dos) (sl) Kauz *m*

welcome ['welkəm] *adj* willkommen; (*news*) erfreulich; **you're w.!** bitte sehr!; **you're w. to** (*inf*) es steht Ihnen frei zu (*inf*) || *s* Empfang *m*, Willkomm *m* || *tr* empfangen; (*an opportunity*) mit Freude begrüßen || *interj* (to) willkommen! (*in dat*)

weld [weld] *s* Schweißnaht *n* || *tr* & *intr* schweißen

welder ['weldər] *s* Schweißer –in *mf*

weld'ing *s* Schweißung *f*, Schweißarbeit *f*

welfare ['wel ˌfer] *s* Wohlfahrt *f*

wel'fare work'er *s* Wohlfahrtspfleger –in *mf*

well [wel] *adj* gesund; **all is w.** alles ist in Ordnung; **feel w.** sich wohl fühlen || *adv* gut, wohl; **as w.** ebenso; **as w.** as so gut wie; (*in addition to*) sowohl ... als auch; **he is doing w.** es geht ihm gut; **his company is doing w.** seine Firma geht gut; **leave w. enough alone** es gut sein lassen; **w. on in years** schon bejahrt; **w. on the way** mitten auf dem Wege; (fig) auf dem besten Wege; **w. over** weit über || *s* Brunnen *m*; (*hole*) Bohrloch *n*; (*source*) Quelle *f* || *intr*—**w. up** hervorquellen || *interj* na!; (*in surprise*) nanu!

well'-behaved' *adj* artig

well'-be'ing *s* Wohlergehen *n*

well'born' *adj* aus guter Familie

wellbred ['wel'bred] *adj* wohlerzogen

well'-deserved' *adj* wohlverdient

well'-disposed' *adj* (toward) wohlgesinnt (*dat*)

well-done ['wel'dʌn] *adj* (culin) durchgebraten || *interj* gut gemacht!

well'-dressed' *adj* gut angezogen

well'-found'ed *adj* wohlbegründet

well'-groomed' *adj* gut gepflegt

well'-heeled' *adj* (coll) steinreich

well'-informed' *adj* wohlunterrichtet

well'-inten'tioned *adj* wohlmeinend

well-kept ['wel'kept] *adj* gut gepflegt; (*secret*) gut gehütet

well'-known' *adj* wohlbekannt

well'-mean'ing *adj* wohlmeinend

well'-nigh' *adv* fast

well'-off' *adj* wohlhabend, vermögend

well'-preserved' *adj* gut erhalten

well-read ['wel'red] *adj* belesen

well'-spent' *adj* (*money*) gut verwendet; (*time*) gut verbracht

well'spring' *s* Brunnquell *m*

well'-thought'-of' *adj* angesehen

well'-timed' *adj* wohl berechnet

well-to-do ['weltə'du] *adj* wohlhabend

well-wisher ['wel'wɪʃər] *s* Gratulant –in *mf*

well'-worn' *adj* (*clothes*) abgetragen; (*phrase, subject*) abgedroschen

Welsh [welʃ] *adj* walisisch || *s* Walisisch *n*; **the W.** die Waliser *pl* || **welsh** *intr*—**welsh on** (*a promise*) brechen

Welsh' rab'bit or **rare'bit** ['rerbɪt] *s* geröstete Käseschnitte *f*

welt [welt] *s* Striemen *m*

welter ['weltər] *s* Durcheinander *n* || *intr* sich wälzen

wel'terweight *s* Weltergewichtler *m*

we'lterweight divi'sion *s* Weltergewicht *n*

wench [wentʃ] *s* Dirne *f*, Weibsbild *n*

wend [wend] *tr*—**w. one's way** seinen Weg nehmen

werewolf ['wer ˌwʌlf] *s* Werwolf *m*

west [west] *adj* westlich || *adv* nach Westen || *s* Westen *m*

western ['westərn] *adj* westlich || *s* (cin) Wildwestfilm *m*

West' Ger'many *s* Westdeutschland *n*

West' In'dies, the ['ɪndiz] *spl* Westindien *n*

Westphalia [ˌwest'felɪ·ə] *s* Westfalen *n*

westward ['westwərd] *adv* westwärts

wet [wet] *adj* (wetter; wettest) naß; **all wet** (coll) auf dem Holzwege || *v* (*pret* & *pp* **wet** & **wetted**; *ger* **wetting**) *tr* naß machen

wet' blan'ket *s* (fig) Miesepeter *m*

wet' nurse' *s* Amme *f*

whack [wæk] *s* (coll) Klaps *m* || *tr* (coll) klapsen

whale [wel] *s* Wal(fisch) *m*; **have a w. of a time** sich großartig unterhalten

whaler ['welər] *s* Walfänger *m*

wharf [wɔrf] *s* (wharves [wɔrvz]) Kaianlage *f*

what [wɑt] *interr adj* welcher, was für ein || *interr pron* was; **so w.?** na und?; **w. about me?** und was geschieht mit mir?; **w. if** was geschieht, wenn; **w. is more** außerdem; **w. next?** was noch?; **w. of it?** was ist da schon dabei?; **what's new?** was gibt es Neues? **what's that to you?** was geht Sie das an? || *interj* was für ein

whatev'er *adj* welch ... auch immer; **no ... w.** überhaupt kein || *pron* was auch immer; **w. I have** alles, was ich habe; **w. you please** was Sie wollen

what'not' *s*—**and w.** und was weiß ich noch (alles)

what's-his-name' *s* (coll) Dingsda *m*

wheal [wil] *s* Pustel *f*; (welt) Striemen *m*

wheat [wit] *s* Weizen *m*

wheedle ['hwidəl] *tr*—**w. s.o. into** (*ger*) j–n beschwatzen zu (*inf*); **w. s.th. out of s.o.** j–m etw abschwatzen

wheel [wil] *s* Rad *n;* **at the w.** (aut) am Steuer || *tr* fahren || *intr* sich drehen; **w. around** sich umdrehen

wheelbarrow ['wil,bæro] *s* Schubkarre *f*

wheel'chair' *s* Krankenfahrstuhl *m*

wheeler-dealer ['wilər 'dilər] *s* Drahtzieher –in *mf*

wheeze [wiz] *s* Schnaufen *n* || *intr* schnaufen

whelp [wɛlp] *s* Welpe *m* || *tr* werfen

when [wɛn] *adv* wann || *conj* (*once in the past*) als; (*whenever; at a future time*) wenn

whence [wɛns] *adv & conj* woher

whenev'er *conj* wenn, wann immer

where [wɛr] *adv & conj* wo; (*whereto*) wohin; **from w.** woher

whereabouts ['wɛrə,bauts] *adv* wo ungefähr || *s & spl* Verbleib *m*

whereas' *conj* während, wohingegen

whereby' *conj* wodurch

where'fore' *adv & conj* weshalb

wherefrom' *adv* woher

wherein' *adv & conj* worin

whereof' *adv & conj* wovon

whereto' *adv* wohin

where'upon' *adv* worauf, wonach

wherever [wɛr'ɛvər] *conj* wo auch

wherewith' *adv* womit

wherewithal ['wɛrwið,ɔl] *s* Geldmittel *pl*

whet [wɛt] *v* (*pret & pp* **whetted;** *ger* **whetting**) *tr* wetzen, schleifen; (*the appetite*) anregen

whether ['wɛðər] *conj* ob

whet'stone' *s* Wetzstein *m,* Schleifstein *m*

whew [hwju] *interj* huil; uil

which [wɪtʃ] *interr adj* welcher || *interr pron* welcher || *rel pron* der, welcher

whichev'er *rel adj & rel pron* welcher

whiff [wɪf] *s* Geruch *m,* Nasevoll *f*

while [waɪl] *s* Weile *f* || *conj* während || *tr*—**w. away** sich (*dat*) vertreiben

whim [wɪm] *s* Laune *f,* Grille *f*

whimper ['wɪmpər] *s* Wimmern *n* || *tr & intr* wimmern

whimsical ['wɪmzɪkəl] *adj* schrullig

whine [waɪn] *s* Wimmern *n;* (*of a siren, engine, storm*) Heulen *n* || *intr* wimmern; heulen

whin·ny ['wɪni] *s* Wiehern *n* || *v* (*pret & pp* –**nied**) *intr* wiehern

whip [wɪp] *s* Peitsche *f* || *v* (*pret & pp* **whipped;** *ger* **whipping**) *tr* peitschen; (*egg whites*) zu Schaum schlagen; (*defeat*) schlagen; **w. out** blitzschnell ziehen; **w. up** (*a meal*) hervorzaubern; (*enthusiasm*) erregen

whip'lash' *s* Peitschenhieb *m;* (fig) Peitschenhiebeffekt *m*

whipped' cream' *s* Schlagsahne *f*

whipper-snapper ['wɪpər ,snæpər] *s* Frechdachs *m*

whip'ping *s* Prügel *pl*

whip'ping boy' *s* Prügelknabe *m*

whip'ping post' *s* Schandpfahl *m*

whir [wʌr] *s* Schnurren *n* || *v* (*pret & pp* **whirred**) *intr* schnurren

whirl [wʌrl] *s* Wirbel *m;* **give s.th. a w.** (coll) etw ausprobieren || *tr* wirbeln || *intr* wirbeln; **my head is whirling** mir ist schwindlig

whirl'pool' *s* Strudel *m,* Wirbel *m*

whirl'wind' *s* Wirbelwind *m*

whirlybird ['wʌrli ,bʌrd] *s* (coll) Hubschrauber *m*

whisk [wɪsk] *s* Wedel *m;* (culin) Schneebesen *m* || *tr* wischen; **w. away** (fig) eilends mitnehmen; **w. off** wegfegen

whisk' broom' *s* Kleiderbesen *m*

whiskers ['wɪskərz] *spl* Bart *m;* (*on the cheeks*) Backenbart *m;* (*of a cat*) Barthaare *pl*

whiskey ['wɪski] *s* Whisky *m*

whisper ['wɪspər] *s* Flüsterton *m* || *tr & intr* flüstern

whistle ['wɪsəl] *s* (*sound*) Pfiff *m;* (*device*) Trillerpfeife *f;* **wet one's w.** sich (*dat*) die Nase begießen || *tr* pfeifen || *intr* pfeifen; (*said of the wind, bullet*) sausen; **w. for** (coll) vergeblich warten auf (*acc*)

whit [wɪt] *s*—**not care a w. about** sich keinen Deut kümmern um

white [waɪt] *adj* weiß; **w. as a sheet** kreidebleich || *s* Weiß *n;* (*of the eye*) Weiße *f*

white' caps' *spl* Schaumkronen *pl*

white'-col'lar work'er *s* Angestellte *mf*

white'fish' *s* Weißfisch *m*

white'-haired' *adj* weißhaarig

white'-hot' *adj* weißglühend

white' lie' *s* Notlüge *f*

white' meat' *s* weißes Fleisch *n*

whiten ['waɪtən] *tr* weiß machen || *intr* weiß werden

whiteness ['waɪtnɪs] *s* Weiße *f*

white' slav'ery *s* Mädchenhandel *m*

white' tie' *s* Frackschleife *f;* (*formal*) Frack *m*

white'wash' *s* Tünche *f;* (fig) Beschönigung *f* || *tr* tünchen; (fig) beschönigen

whither ['wɪðər] *adv* wohin

whitish ['waɪtɪʃ] *adj* weißlich

whittle ['wɪtəl] *tr* schnitzeln; **w. away** (*or down*) verringern || *intr*—**w. away at** herumschnitzeln an (*dat*); (fig) verringern

whiz(z) [wɪz] *s* Zischen *n;* (fig) Kanone *f* || *v* (*pret & pp* **whizzed;** *ger* **whizzing**) *intr* zischen; **w. by** flitzen

who [hu] *interr pron* wer; **who the devil** wer zum Teufel || *rel pron* der; **he who** wer

whoa [wo] *interj* halt!

whoev'er *rel pron* wer, wer auch immer

whole [hol] *adj* ganz || *s* Ganze *n;* **as a w.** im großen und ganzen

whole'-heart'ed *adj* ernsthaft

whole' note' *s* (mus) ganze Note *f*

whole' rest' *s* (mus) ganze Pause *f*

whole'sale' *adj* Massen–; (com) Großhandels– || *adv* en gros || *s* Großhandel *m* || *tr* en gros verkaufen || *intr* im großen handeln

wholesaler ['hol ,selər] *s* Großhändler –in *mf*

wholesome ['holsəm] *adj* gesund; (*food*) zuträglich
whole'-wheat' bread' *s* Vollkornbrot *n*
wholly ['holi] *adv* ganz, völlig
whom [hum] *interr pron* wen; **to w. wem** ‖ *rel pron* den, welchen; **to w. dem, welchem**
whomev'er *rel pron* wen auch immer; **to w. wem** auch immer
whoop [hup], [hwup] *s* Ausruf *m* ‖ *tr*—**w. it up** Radau machen
whoop'ing cough' *s* Keuchhusten *m*
whopper ['wɑpər] *s* Mordsding *n*; (*lie*) (coll) faustdicke Lüge *f*
whop'ping *adj* (coll) enorm, Riesen-
whore [hor] *s* Hure *f* ‖ *intr*—**w. around** huren
whose [huz] *interr pron* wessen ‖ *rel pron* dessen
why [waɪ] *adv* warum; **that's why** deswegen; **why, there you are!** da sind Sie ja!; **why, yes!** aber ja! ‖ *s* Warum *n*; **the whys and the wherefores** das Warum und Weshalb
wick [wɪk] *s* Docht *m*
wicked ['wɪkɪd] *adj* (*evil*) böse; (*roguish*) boshaft; (*vicious*) bösartig; (*unpleasant*) ekelhaft; (*cold, pain, storm, wound*) (coll) schlimm; (*fantastic*) (coll) großartig
wicker ['wɪkər] *adj* (*basket, chair*) Weiden- ‖ *s* (*wickerwork*) Flechtwerk *n*
wide [waɪd] *adj* breit; (*selection*) reich ‖ *adv* weit
wide'-an'gle lens' *s* Weitwinkelobjektiv *n*
wide'-awake' *adj* hellwach
wide'-eyed' *adj* mit weit aufgerissenen Augen; (*innocence*) naiv
widely ['waɪdli] *adv* weit
widen ['waɪdən] *tr* ausweiten, verbreiten ‖ *intr* sich ausweiten
wide'-o'pen *adj* weit geöffnet
wide' screen' *s* (cin) Breitleinwand *f*
wide'spread' *adj* weitverbreitet; (*damage*) weitgehend
widow ['wɪdo] *s* Witwe *f*
widower ['wɪdo·ər] *s* Witwer *m*
wid'owhood' *s* Witwenstand *m*
width [wɪdθ] *s* Breite *f*; **in w.** breit
wield [wild] *tr* (*a weapon*) führen; (*power, influence*) ausüben
wife [waɪf] *s* (**wives** [waɪvz]) Frau *f*
wig [wɪg] *s* Perücke *f*
wiggle ['wɪgəl] *s* Wackeln *n* ‖ *tr* wackeln mit
wigwag ['wɪg‚wæg] *s* Winksignal *n*
wigwam ['wɪgwɑm] *s* Wigwam *m* & *n*
wild [waɪld] *adj* wild; **w. about** scharf auf (*acc*); **go w.** verwildern; **grow w.** (*become neglected*) verwildern; **make s.o. w.** (coll) j-n rasend machen ‖ *adv*—**grow w.** (*grow in the wild*) wild wachsen; **run w.** verwildern
wild' boar' *s* Wildschwein *n*
wild' card' *s* wilde Karte *f*
wild'cat' *s* Wildkatze *f*
wild'cat strike' *s* wilder Streik *m*
wilderness ['wɪldərnɪs] *s* Wildnis *f*
wild'fire' *s*—**like w.** wie Lauffeuer
wild' flow'er *s* Feldblume *f*

wild'-goose' chase' *s*—**go on a w.** sich [*dat*] vergeblich Mühe machen
wild'life' *s* Wild *n*
wild' oats' *spi*—**sow one's w.** sich [*dat*] die Hörner abstoßen
wile [waɪl] *s* List *f* ‖ *tr*—**w. away** sich [*dat*] vertreiben
will [wɪl] *s* Wille(n) *m*; (jur) Testament *n*; **at w.** nach Belieben ‖ *tr* (*bequeath*) vermachen ‖ *v* (*pret & cond* **would** [wʊd]) *aux* werden
willful ['wɪlfəl] *adj* absichtlich; (*stubborn*) eigensinnig
William ['wɪljəm] *s* Wilhelm *m*
will'ing *adj* bereitwillig; **be w. to** (*inf*) bereit sein zu (*inf*)
willingly ['wɪlɪŋli] *adv* gern
willingness ['wɪlɪŋnɪs] *s* Bereitwilligkeit *f*
will-o'-the-wisp ['wɪləðə'wɪsp] *s* (& fig) Irrlicht *n*
willow ['wɪlo] *s* Weide *f*
willowy ['wɪlo·i] *adj* biegsam
will' pow'er *s* Willenskraft *f*
willy-nilly ['wɪli'nɪli] *adv* wohl oder übel
wilt [wɪlt] *tr* verwelken lassen ‖ *intr* verwelken
wilt'ed *adj* welk
wily ['waɪli] *adj* schlau, listig
wimple ['wɪmpəl] *s* Kinntuch *n*
win [wɪn] *s* Gewinn *m*; (sport) Sieg *m* ‖ *v* (*pret & pp* **won** [wʌn]; *ger* **winning**) *tr* gewinnen; **win over to one's side** auf seine Seite ziehen ‖ *intr* gewinnen, siegen
wince [wɪns] *s* Zucken *n* ‖ *intr* zucken
winch [wɪntʃ] *s* (*windlass*) Winde *f*; (*handle*) Kurbel *f*; (min, naut) Haspel *f* & *m*
wind [wɪnd] *s* Wind *m*; **break w.** e-n Darmwind lassen; **get w. of** Wind bekommen von; **take the w. out of s.o.'s sails** j-m den Wind aus den Segeln nehmen; **there is s.th. in the w.** es liegt etw in der Luft ‖ [waɪnd] *v* (*pret & pp* **wound** [waʊnd]) *tr* wickeln, winden; (*a timepiece*) aufziehen; **w. up** aufwickeln; (*affairs*) abwickeln; (*a speech*) abschließen ‖ *intr* (*said of a river, road*) sich winden; **w. around** (*said of a plant*) sich ranken um
windbag ['wɪnd‚bæg] *s* (coll) Schaumschläger –in *mf*
windbreak ['wɪnd‚brek] *s* Windschutz *m*
windbreaker ['wɪnd‚brekər] *s* Windjacke *f*
winded ['wɪndɪd] *adj* außer Atem, atemlos
windfall ['wɪnd‚fɔl] *s* (*fallen fruit*) Fallobst *n*; (fig) Glücksfall *m*
wind'ing road' ['waɪndɪŋ] *s* Serpentinenstraße *f*; (public sign) kurvenreiche Straße *f*
wind'ing sheet' ['waɪndɪŋ] *s* Leichentuch *n*
wind' in'strument [wɪnd] *s* Blasinstrument *n*
windlass ['wɪndləs] *s* Winde *f*
windmill ['wɪnd‚mɪl] *s* Windmühle *f*

window ['wɪndo] *s* Fenster *n; (of a ticket office)* Schalter *m; (for display)* Schaufenster *n*

win'dow display' *s* Schaufensterauslage *f*

win'dow dress'er *s* Schaufensterdekorateur –in *mf*

win'dow dress'ing *s* Schaufensterdekoration *f*

win'dow en'velope *s* Fensterumschlag *m*

win'dow frame' *s* Fensterrahmen *m*

win'dowpane' *s* Fensterscheibe *f*

win'dow screen' *s* Fliegengitter *n*

win'dow shade' *s* Rollvorhang *m*, Rollo *n*

win'dow-shop' *v (pret & pp –shopped; ger –shopping) intr* e-n Schaufensterbummel machen

win'dow shut'ter *s* Fensterladen *m*

win'dow sill' *s* Fensterbrett *n*

windpipe ['wɪnd,paɪp] *s* Luftröhre *f*

windshield ['wɪnd,ʃild] *s* Windschutzscheibe *f*

wind'shield wash'er *s* Scheibenwäscher *m*

wind'shield wip'er *s* Scheibenwischer *m*

windsock ['wɪnd,sak] *s* Windsack *m*

windstorm ['wɪnd,stɔrm] *s* Sturm *m*

wind' tun'nel [wɪnd] *s* Windkanal *m*

wind-up ['waɪnd,ʌp] *s (of affairs)* Abwicklung *f; (of a speech)* Schluß *m*

windward ['wɪndwərd] *adj (side)* Wind– || *adv* windwärts || *s* Windseite *f;* **turn to w.** anluven

windy ['wɪndi] *adj* windig; *(speech)* weitschweifig; *(person)* redselig

wine [waɪn] *s* Wein *m* || *tr* mit Wein bewirten

wine' cel'lar *s* Weinkeller *m*

wine'glass' *s* Weinglas *n*

winegrower ['waɪn,groˑər] *s* Weinbauer –in *mf*

wine'grow'ing *s* Weinbau *m*

wine' list' *s* Weinkarte *f*

wine' press' *s* Weinpresse *f*

winery ['waɪnəri] *s* Weinkellerei *f*

wine'skin' *s* Weinschlauch *m*

wing [wɪŋ] *s (of a bird, building, party)* Flügel *m; (unit of three squadrons)* Geschwader *n; (theat)* Kulisse *f* || *tr (shoot)* in den Flügel treffen; **w. one' way** dahinfliegen

wing' chair' *s* Ohrensessel *m*

wing' nut' *s* Flügelmutter *f*

wing'spread' *s* Spannweite *f*

wink [wɪŋk] *s* Augenwink *m;* **quick as a w.** im Nu || *intr* blinzeln; **w. at** zublinzeln *(dat); (overlook)* ein Auge zudrücken bei *(dat)*

winner ['wɪnər] *s* Gewinner –in *mf*, Sieger –in *mf; (e.g., winning ticket)* Treffer *m*

win'ning *adj (e.g., smile)* gewinnend; *(sport)* siegreich || **winnings** *spl* Gewinn *m*

winsome ['wɪnsəm] *adj* reizend

winter ['wɪntər] *s* Winter *m* || *intr* überwintern

winterize ['wɪntə,raɪz] *tr* winterfest machen

wintry ['wɪntri] *adj* winterlich; *(fig)* frostig

wipe [waɪp] *tr* wischen; **w. clean** abwischen; **w. out** auswischen; *(e.g., a debt)* tilgen; *(destroy)* vernichten; *(fin)* ruinieren; **w.** up aufwischen

wire [waɪr] *s* Draht *m; (telg)* Telegramm *n;* **get in under the w.** es gerade noch schaffen || *tr* mit Draht versehen; *(a house)* (elec) elektrische Leitungen legen in *(dat); (a message)* drahten; *(a person)* telegraphieren *(dat)*

wire' cut'ter *s* Drahtschere *f*

wire'draw' *v (pret –drew; pp –drawn) tr* drahtziehen

wire' entan'glement *s* Drahtverhau *m*

wire' gauge' *s* Drahtlehre *f*

wire'-haired' *adj* drahthaarig

wireless ['waɪrlɪs] *adj* drahtlos

wire' nail' *s* Drahtnagel *m*

Wire'pho'to *s (–tos)* (trademark) Bildtelegramm *n*

wire' record'er *s* Drahttonaufnahmegerät *n*

wire'tap' *s* Abhören *n* || *v (pret & pp –tapped; ger –tapping) tr* abhören

wir'ing *s* Leitungen *pl;* **do the w.** die elektrischen Leitungen legen

wiry ['waɪri] *adj* drahtig

wisdom ['wɪzdəm] *s* Weisheit *f*

wis'dom tooth' *s* Weisheitszahn *m*

wise [waɪz] *adj (person, decision)* klug; *(impertinent)* naseweis; **be w. to** sich [dat] klar werden über *(acc);* **put s.o. w. to** j–n einweihen in *(acc)* || *s*—**in no w.** keineswegs || *intr*— **w.** up endlich mal vernünftig werden

wise'a'cre *s* Neunmalkluge *mf*

wise'crack' *s* schnippische Bemerkung *f*

wise' guy' *s* (sl) Naseweis *m*

wisely ['waɪzli] *adv* wohlweislich

wish [wɪʃ] *s* Wunsch *m* || *tr* wünschen || *intr*— **w. for** sich [dat] wünschen

wish'bone' *s* Gabelbein *n*

wish'ful think'ing ['wɪʃfəl] *s* ein frommer Wunsch *m*

wishy-washy ['wɪʃi,waʃi] *adj* charakterlos; **be w.** ein Waschlappen sein

wisp [wɪsp] *s (of hair)* Strähne *f*

wistful ['wɪstfəl] *adj* versonnen

wit [wɪt] *s* Geist *m; (person)* geistreicher Mensch *m;* **be at one's wit's end** sich [dat] keinen Rat mehr wissen; **keep one's wits** about one e–n klaren Kopf behalten; **live by one's wits** sich durchschlagen

witch [wɪtʃ] *s* Hexe *f*

witch'craft' *s* Hexerei *f*

witch' doc'tor *s* Medizinmann *m*

witch' ha'zel *s* Zaubernuß *f; (ointment)* Präperat *n* aus Zaubernuß

witch' hunt' *s* Hexenjagd *f*

with [wɪð], [wɪθ] *prep* mit *(dat); (at the house of)* bei *(dat); (because of)* vor *(dat),* e.g., **green w. envy** grün vor Neid; *(despite)* trotz *(genit);* **not be w. it** nicht bei der Sache sein

with'draw' *v (pret –drew; pp –drawn) tr* zurückziehen; *(money)* abheben || *intr* sich zurückziehen withdrawal [wɪð'drɔ·əl] s Zurückziehung f; (retraction) Zurücknahme f; (from a bank) Abhebung f; (mil) Rückzug m

withdraw'al slip' s Abhebungsformular n

wither ['wɪðər] intr verwelken

with·hold' v (pret & pp –held) tr (pay) einbehalten; (information) (from) vorenthalten (dat)

withhold'ing tax' s einbehaltene Steuer f

within' adv drin(nen); from w. von innen || prep (time) binnen (dat), innerhalb von (dat); (place) innerhalb (genit); w. walking distance in Gehweite

without' adv draußen || prep ohne (acc); w. (ger) ohne zu (inf), ohne daß; w. reason ohne allen Anlaß

with·stand' v (pret & pp –stood) tr widerstehen (dat)

witness ['wɪtnɪs] s Zeuge m, Zeugin f; (evidence) Zeugnis n; bear w. to Zeugnis ablegen von; in w. whereof zum Zeugnis dessen; w. for the defense Entlastungszeuge m; w. for the prosecution Belastungszeuge m || tr (an event) anwesend sein bei; (an accident, crime) Augenzeuge sein (genit); (e.g., a contract, will) als Zeuge unterschreiben

wit'ness stand' s Zeugenstand m

witticism ['wɪtɪ‚sɪzəm] s Witzelei f

wittingly ['wɪtɪŋlɪ] adv wissentlich

witty ['wɪtɪ] adj geistreich, witzig

wizard ['wɪzərd] s Hexenmeister m

wizardry ['wɪzərdrɪ] s (& fig) Hexerei f

wizend ['wɪzənd] adj runzelig

wobble ['wɑbəl] intr wackeln

wobbly ['wɑblɪ] adj wackelig

woe [wo] s Weh n || interj—woe is me! weh mir!

woebegone ['wobɪ‚gɑn] adj jammervoll

woeful ['wofəl] adj jammervoll

wolf [wʊlf] s (wolves [wʊlvz]) Wolf m; (coll) Schürzenjäger m; cry w. blinden Alarm schlagen; keep the w. from the door sich über Wasser halten || tr—w. down verschlingen

wolf'pack' s Wolfsrudel n; (nav) U-bootrudel n

wolfram ['wʊlfrəm] s (chem) Wolfram n; (mineral) Wolframit n

woman ['wʊmən] s (women ['wɪmən]) Frau f

wom'an doc'tor s Ärztin f

wom'anhood' s Frauen pl; reach w. e-e Frau werden

womanish ['wʊmənɪʃ] adj weibisch

wom'ankind' s Frauen pl

womanly ['wʊmənlɪ] adj fraulich

womb [wʊm] s Mutterleib m

wom'enfolk' spl Weibsvolk n

wom'en's dou'bles spl (tennis) Damendoppelspiel n

wom'en's sin'gles spl (tennis) Dameneinzelspiel n

wonder ['wʌndər] s Wunder n || intr (be surprised) sich wundern; (ask oneself) sich fragen; (reflect) überlegen; wonder at sich verwundern über (acc)

wonderful ['wʌndərfəl] adj wunderbar

won'derland' s Wunderland n

won'der work'er s Wundertäter –in mf

wont [wʌnt], [wont] adj—be w. to (inf) pflegen zu (inf) || s Gepflogenheit f

wont'ed adj gewöhnlich, üblich

woo [wu] tr den Hof machen (dat)

wood [wʊd] s Holz n; out of the woods (fig) über den Berg; woods Wald m

wood' al'cohol s Methylalkohol m

woodbine ['wʊd‚baɪn] s Geißblatt n; (Virginia creeper) wilder Wein m

wood' carv'ing s Holzschnitzerei f

wood'chuck' s Murmeltier n

wood'cock' s Holzschnepfe f

wood'cut' s (block) Holzplatte f; (print) Holzschnitt m

wood'cut'ter s Holzfäller m

wood'ed adj bewaldet

wooden ['wʊdən] adj (& fig) hölzern

wood' engrav'ing s Holzschnitt m

wood'en peg' s Stelzbein n

wood'en shoe' s Holzschuh m

woodland ['wʊdlənd] adj Wald– || s Waldland n

wood'man s (–men) Holzhauer m

woodpecker ['wʊd‚pekər] s Specht m

wood' pi'geon s Ringeltaube f

wood'pile' s Holzhaufen m

wood'pulp' s Holzfaserstoff m

wood' screw' s Holzschraube f

wood'shed' s Holzschuppen m

woods'man s (–men) Förster m; (lumberman) Holzhauer m

wood'winds' spl Holzblasinstrumente pl

wood'work' s Holzarbeit f; (structure in wood) Gebälk n

wood'work'er s Holzarbeiter –in mf

wood'worm' s (ent) Holzwurm m

woody ['wʊdɪ] adj waldig; (woodlike) holzig

wooer ['wu·ər] s Verehrer m

woof [wʊf] s (of a dog) unterdrücktes Bellen n; (tex) Gewebe n

woofer ['wʊfər] s (rad) Tieftöner m

wool [wʊl] adj wollen || s Wolle f

woolen ['wʊlən] adj wollen, Woll– || woolens spl Wollwaren pl

woolly ['wʊlɪ] adj wollig; (e.g., thinking) verschwommen

woozy ['wuzɪ] adj benebelt

word [wʌrd] s Wort n; be as good as one's w. zu seinem Wort stehen; by w. of mouth mündlich; get w. from Nachricht haben von; give one's w. sein Wort geben; have a w. with ein ernstes Wort sprechen mit; have words e-n Wortwechsel haben; in a w. mit e-m Wort; in other words mit anderen Worten; in so many words ausdrücklich; leave w. Bescheid hinterlassen; not another w.! kein Wort mehr!; not a w. of truth in it kein wahres Wort daran; put in a good w. for s.o. ein gutes Wort für j–n einlegen; put into words in

Worte kleiden; **put words in s.o.'s mouth** j-m Worte in den Mund legen; **send w. to s.o.** j-n benachrichtigen; **take s.o.'s w. for it** j-n beim Wort nehmen; **w. for w.** Wort für Wort ‖ *tr* formulieren
word'-for-word' *adj* wörtlich
word'ing *s* Formulierung *s*
word' of hon'or *s* Ehrenwort *n;* **w.!** auf mein Wort!
word' or'der *s* Wortfolge *f*
wordy ['wʌrdi] *adj* wortreich
work [wʌrk] *s* Arbeit *f;* (*production, book*) Werk *n;* **be in the works** (coll) im Gang sein; **get to w.** sich an die Arbeit machen; (*travel to work*) zum Arbeitsplatz kommen; **give s.o. the works** (coll) j-n fertigmachen; **have one's w.** cut out zu tun haben; **it took a lot of w. to** (*inf*) es hat viel Arbeit gekostet zu (*inf*); **make short w.** of kurzen Prozeß machen mit; **out of w.** arbeitslos; **works** (horol) Uhrwerk *n* ‖ *tr* (*a machine*) bedienen; (*a pedal*) treten; (*a mine*) abbauen; (*the soil*) bearbeiten; (*metal*) treiben; (*dough*) kneten; (*wonders*) wirken; **w. in** einarbeiten; **w. off** (*a debt*) abarbeiten; **w. oneself to death** sich totarbeiten; **w. one's way up** sich hocharbeiten; **w. out** (*a solution*) ausarbeiten; (*a problem*) lösen; **w. to death** abhetzen; **w. up an appetite** sich [*dat*] Appetit machen ‖ *intr* arbeiten; (*junction*) funktionieren; (*succeed*) klappen; **w. against** wirken gegen; **w. away at** losarbeiten auf (*acc*); **w. at** (*a trade*) ausüben; **w. both ways** für beide Fälle gelten; **w. loose** sich lockern; **w. on** (*a person*) bearbeiten; (*a patient, car*) arbeiten an (*dat*); **w. out** (sport) trainieren; **w. out well** gut ausgehen
workable ['wʌrkəbəl] *adj* brauchbar; (*plan*) durchführbar
work'bench' *s* Werkbank *f*
work'book' *s* Übungsheft *n*
work' camp' *s* Arbeitslager *n*
work'day' *s* Arbeitstag *m*
work' detail' *s* (mil) Arbeitskommando *n*
worked'-up' *adj* erregt; **get s.o. w.** j-n erregen; **get w.** sich erregen
worker ['wʌrkər] *s* Arbeiter –in *mf*
work' force' *s* Belegschaft *f*
work'horse' *s* Arbeitspferd *n*
work'ing day' *s* Arbeitstag *m*
work'ing girl' *s* Arbeiterin *f*
work'ing hours' *spl* Arbeitsstunden *pl*
work'ingman' *s* (**-men'**) Arbeiter *m*
work'ing or'der—in w. betriebsfähig
work'ingwom'an *s* (**-wom'en**) Arbeiterin *f;* (*professionally*) berufstätige Frau *f*
work'man *s* (**-men**) Arbeiter *m*
work'manship' *s* Ausführung *f*
work'men's compensa'tion insur'ance *s* Arbeiterunfallversicherung *f*
work' of art' *s* Kunstwerk *n*
work'out' *s* Training *n*
work' per'mit *s* Arbeitsgenehmigung *f*
work'room' *s* Arbeitszimmer *n*

work' sche'dule *s* Dienstplan *m*
work'shop' *s* Werkstatt *f*
work' stop'page *s* Arbeitseinstellung *f*
world [wʌrld] *adj* Welt– ‖ *s* Welt *f;* **a w. of** groß; **from all over the w.** aus aller Herren Ländern; **not for all the w.** nicht um die Welt; **see the w.** in der Welt herumkommen; **they are worlds apart** es liegen Welten zwischen den beiden; **think the w. of** große Stücke halten auf (*acc*); **who (where) in the w.** wer (wo) in aller Welt
world' affairs' *spl* internationale Angelegenheiten *pl*
world'-fa'mous *adj* weltberühmt
worldly ['wʌrldli] *adj* (*goods, pleasures*) irdisch; (*person*) weltlich; (*wisdom*) Welt–
world'ly-wise' *adj* weltklug
world's' fair' *s* Weltausstellung *f*
world'-shak'ing *adj* weltbewegend
world'-wide' *adj* weltweit
worm [wʌrm] *s* Wurm *m* ‖ *tr*—**w. one's way** sich schlängeln; **w. secrets out of s.o.** j-m die Würmer aus der Nase ziehen
worm-eaten ['wʌrm‚itən] *adj* (& fig) wurmstichig
wormy ['wʌrmi] *adj* wurmig
worn [worn] *adj* (*clothes*) getragen; (*tires*) abgenutzt; (*wearied*) müde
worn'-out' *adj* (*clothes*) abgetragen; (*tires*) abgenutzt; (*exhausted*) erschöpft
worrisome ['wʌrisəm] *adj* (*causing worry*) beunruhigend; (*inclined to worry*) sorgenvoll
wor-ry ['wʌri] *s* Sorge *f;* (*source of worry*) Ärger *m* ‖ *v* (*pret & pp* **-ried**) *tr* beunruhigen; **be worried** besorgt sein ‖ *intr* (about) sich [*dat*] Sorgen machen (um); **don't w.!** keine Sorge!
worse [wʌrs] *comp adj* schlechter, schlimmer; **be w. off** schlimmer daran sein; **he's none the w. for it** es hat ihm nichts geschadet; **what's w.** was noch schlimmer ist
worsen ['wʌrsən] *tr* verschlimmern ‖ *intr* sich verschlimmern
wor-ship ['wʌrʃɪp] *s* Anbetung *f;* (*services*) Gottesdienst *m* ‖ *v* (*pret & pp* **-ship[p]ed;** *ger* **-ship[p]ing**) *tr* (& fig) anbeten ‖ *intr* seine Andacht verrichten
worship(p)er ['wʌrʃɪpər] *s* Anbeter –in *mf;* (*in church*) Andächtige *mf*
worst [wʌrst] *super adj* schlimmste ‖ *super adv* am schlimmsten ‖ *s* Schlimmste *n;* **at the w.** schlimmstenfalls; **get the w. of** den kürzeren ziehen bei; **if w. comes to w.** wenn alle Stricke reißen; **the w. is yet to come** das dicke Ende kommt noch ‖ *tr* schlagen
worsted ['wustɪd] *adj* Kammgarn–
worth [wʌrθ] *adj* wert; **it is w.** (*ger*) es lohnt sich zu (*inf*); **it is w. the trouble** es ist der Mühe wert; **ten dollars' w.** of meat für zehn Dollar Fleisch; **w. seeing** sehenswert ‖ *s* Wert *m*

worthless ['wʌrθlɪs] *adj* wertlos; (*person*) nichtsnutzig
worth'while' *adj* lohnend
worthy ['wʌrði] *adj* (**of**) würdig (*genit*)
would [wʊd] *aux* used to express 1) indirect statements, e.g., **he said he w. come** er sagte, er würde kommen; 2) the present conditional, e.g., **he w. do it if he could** er würde es tun, wenn er könnte; 3) past conditional, e.g., **he w. have paid, if he had had the money** er würde gezahlt haben, wenn er das Geld gehabt hätte; 4) habitual action in the past, e.g., **he w. always buy the morning paper** er kaufte immer das Morgenblatt; 5) polite requests, e.g., **w. you please pass me the butter?** würden Sie mir bitte die Butter reichen; 6) a wish, e.g., **w. that I had never seen it** wenn ich es nur nie gesehen hätte!; **w. rather** möchte lieber, e.g., **I w. rather go on foot** ich möchte lieber zu Fuß gehen
would'-be' *adj* angeblich, Möchtegern-
wound [wund] *s* Wunde *f* || *tr* verwunden
wound'ed *adj* verwundet || **the w.** *spl* die Verwundeten *pl*
wow [wau] *s* (coll) Bombenerfolg *m* || *tr* (coll) erstaunen || *interj* nanu!
wrack [ræk] *s*—**go to w. and ruin** untergehen, in Brüche gehen
wraith [reθ] *s* (*apparition*) Erscheinung *f*; (*spirit*) Geist *m*
wrangle ['ræŋɡəl] *s* Streit *m* || *intr* streiten
wrap [ræp] *s* Überwurf *m* || *v* (*pret & pp* **wrapped**; *ger* **wrapping**) *tr* wickeln; (*a package*) einpacken; **be wrapped up in** (*e.g., thoughts*) versunken sein in (*dat*); **wrapped in darkness** in Dunkelheit gehüllt; **w. up** (*a deal*) abwickeln
wrapper ['ræpər] *s* Verpackung *f*; (*for mailing newspapers*) Streifband *n*
wrap'ping *s* Verpackung *f*
wrap'ping pa'per *s* Packpapier *n*
wrath [ræθ] *s* Zorn *m*, Wut *f*
wrathful ['ræθfəl] *adj* zornig, wütend
wreak [rik] *tr* (*vengeance*) üben; **w. havoc** schlimm hausen
wreath [riθ] *s* (**wreaths** [riðz]) Kranz *m*; **w. of smoke** Rauchfahne *f*
wreathe [rið] *tr* bekränzen, umwinden
wreck [rek] *s* (*of a car or train*) Unglück *n*; (*wrecked ship, car, person*) Wrack *n* || *tr* (*e.g., a car*) zertrümmern; (*a building*) in Trümmer legen; (*a marriage*) zerrütten; (fig) zum Scheitern bringen; **be wrecked** (fig & naut) scheitern
wreckage ['rekɪdʒ] *s* Wrackgut *n*; (*of an accident*) Trümmer *pl*
wrecker ['rekər] *s* Abschleppwagen *m*
wren [ren] *s* (orn) Zaunkönig *m*
wrench [rentʃ] *s* (*tool*) Schraubenschlüssel *m*; (*of a muscle*) Verrenkung *f* || *tr* verrenken
wrest [rest] *tr* (from) entreißen (*dat*)
wrestle ['resəl] *tr* ringen mit || *intr* ringen

wrestler ['reslər] *s* Ringer *m*; (*professional wrestler*) Catcher *m*
wrestling ['reslɪŋ] *s* Ringen *n*; (*professional wrestling*) Catchen *n*
wres'tling match' *s* Ringkampf *m*
wretch [retʃ] *s* armer Kerl *m*; (*vile person*) Schuft *m*
wretched ['retʃɪd] *adj* elend; (*terrible*) scheußlich
wriggle ['rɪɡəl] *s* Krümmung *f*; (*of a worm*) schlängelnde Bewegung *f* || *tr* hin– und herbewegen; **w. one's way** sich dahinschlängeln || *intr* sich winden
wring [rɪŋ] *v* (*pret & pp* **wrung** [rʌŋ]) *tr* (*the hands*) ringen; **w. out** (*the wash*) auswinden; **w. s.o.'s neck** j–m den Hals umdrehen
wringer ['rɪŋər] *s* Wringmaschine *f*
wrinkle ['rɪŋkəl] *s* Falte *f*; **new w.** (fig) neuer Kniff *m*; **take out the wrinkles** (fig) den letzten Schliff geben || *tr* falten, runzeln; (*paper, clothes*) zerknittern || *intr* Falten werfen
wrin'kle-proof' *adj* knitterfrei
wrinkly ['rɪŋkli] *adj* faltig, runzelig
wrist [rɪst] *s* Handgelenk *n*
wrist'band' *s* Armband *n*
wrist' watch' *s* Armbanduhr *f*
writ [rɪt] *s* gerichtlicher schriftlicher Befehl *m*
write [raɪt] *v* (*pret* **wrote** [rot]; *pp* **written** ['rɪtən]) *tr* schreiben; (*compose*) verfassen; **it is written** (*in the Bible*) es steht geschrieben; **it is written all over his face** es steht ihm im Gesicht geschrieben; **w. down** aufschreiben; **w. off** abschreiben; **w. out** ausschreiben; (*a check*) ausstellen || *intr* schreiben; **w. for information** Informationen anfordern
write'-off' *s* Abschreibung *f*
writer ['raɪtər] *s* Schreiber –in *mf*; (*author*) Schriftsteller –in *mf*
writ'er's cramp' *s* Schreibkrampf *m*
write'-up' *s* Pressebericht *m*
writhe [raɪð] *intr* (**in**) sich krümmen (vor *dat*)
writ'ing *s* Schreiben *n*; (*handwriting*) Schrift *f*; **in w.** schriftlich; **put in w.** niederschreiben
writ'ing desk' *s* Schreibtisch *m*
writ'ing pad' *s* Schreibblock *m*
writ'ing pa'per *s* Schreibpapier *n*; (*stationery*) Briefpapier *n*
written ['rɪtən] *adj* schriftlich; (*law*) geschrieben; (*language*) Schrift-
wrong [rɔŋ] *adj* (*incorrect*) falsch; (*unjust*) unrecht; **be w.** (*be incorrect*) nicht stimmen; (*be in error*) Unrecht haben; (*said of a situation*) nicht in Ordnung sein; **be w. with** fehlen (*dat*); **sorry, w. number!** (telp) falsch verbunden! || *s* Unrecht *n*; **be in the w.** im Unrecht sein; **do w.** ein Unrecht begehen; **do w. to s.o.** j–m ein Unrecht zufügen; **get in w. with s.o.** es sich (*dat*) mit j–m verderben || *adv* falsch, unrecht; **go w.** (*morally*) auf Abwege geraten; (*in walking*) sich verirren; (*in reckoning*)

irregehen; (*in driving*) sich verfahren; (*said of plans*) schief gehen
wrongdoer ['rɔŋ ‚du·ər] *s* Missetäter –in *mf*

wrong′do′ing *s* Missetat *f*
wrought′ i′ron [rɔt] *s* Schmiedeeisen *n*
wrought′-up′ *adj* aufgebracht
wry [raɪ] *adj* schief

X

X, x [ɛks] *s* vierundzwanzigster Buchstabe des englischen Alphabets
xenophobia [‚zɛnə′fobɪ·ə] *s* Fremdenhaß *m*
Xerox ['zɪrɑks] *s* (*trademark*) Xerographie *f* ‖ **xerox** *tr* ablichten
Xer′ox-cop′y *s* Ablichtung *f*

Xmas ['krɪsməs] *adj* Weihnachts– ‖ *s* Weihnachten *pl*
x′-ray′ *adj* Röntgen– ‖ *s* (*picture*) Röntgenbild *n*; x-rays Röntgenstrahlen *pl* ‖ *tr* röntgen
x′-ray ther′apy *s* Röntgentherapie *f*
xylophone ['zaɪlə ‚fon] *s* Xylophon *n*

Y

Y, y [waɪ] *s* fünfundzwanzigster Buchstabe des englischen Alphabets
yacht [jɑt] *s* Jacht *f*
yacht′ club′ *s* Jachtklub *m*
yam [jæm] *s* Yamwurzel *f*
yank [jæŋk] *s* Ruck *m*; **Yank** Ami *m* ‖ *tr*—y. s.th. out of reißen aus ‖ *intr* —y. on heftig ziehen an (*dat*)
Yankee ['jæŋki] *s* Yankee *m*
yap [jæp] *s* (*talk*) (sl) Geschwätz *n*; (*mouth*) (sl) Maul *n*; (*bark*) Gekläff *n* ‖ *v* (*pret & pp* yapped; *ger* yapping) *intr* (*bark*) kläffen; (*talk*) (sl) schwätzen
yard [jɑrd] *s* (*measure*) Yard *n*; (*ground adjoining a building*) Hof *m*; (naut) Rahe *f*; (rr) Rangierbahnhof *m*
yard′arm′ *s* (naut) Nock *f & n*
yard′ mas′ter *s* (rr) Rangiermeister *m*
yard′stick′ *s* Yardmaß *n*; (fig) Maßstab *m*
yarn [jɑrn] *s* (*thread; story*) Garn *n*; spin yarns (fig) Garne spinnen
yaw [jɔ] *s* (aer, rok) Schwanken *n*; (naut) Gieren *n* ‖ *intr* (aer, rok) schwanken; (naut) gieren
yawl [jɔl] *s* (naut) Jolle *f*
yawn [jɔn] *s* Gähnen *n* ‖ *intr* gähnen; (*said, e.g., of a gorge*) klaffen
ye [ji] *pers pron* ihr
yea [je] *s* Jastimme *f* ‖ *adv* ja
yeah [jɛ] *adv* ja
year [jɪr] *s* Jahr *n*; all y. round das ganze Jahr hindurch; a y. from today heute übers Jahr; for years seit Jahren; jahrelang; in years seit Jahren; y. in y. out jahraus jahrein
year′book′ *s* Jahrbuch *n*
yearling ['jɪrlɪŋ] *s* Jährling *m*
yearly ['jɪrli] *adj & adv* jährlich
yearn [jʌrn] *intr*—y. for sich sehnen nach; y. to (*inf*) sich danach sehnen zu (*inf*)
yearn′ing *s* Sehnsucht *f*

yeast [jist] *s* Hefe *f*
yell [jel] *s* Ruf *m*, Aufschrei *m*; (sport) Kampfruf *m* ‖ *tr* (gellend) schreien; y. one′s lungs out sich tot schreien ‖ *intr* schreien; y. at anschreien
yellow ['jelo] *adj* gelb; (sl) feige ‖ *s* Gelb *n* ‖ *tr* gelb machen ‖ *intr* vergilben
yellowish ['jelo·ɪʃ] *adj* gelblich
yel′lowjack′et *s* Wespe *f*
yel′low jour′nalism *s* Sensationspresse *f*
yel′low streak′ *s* Zug *m* von Feigheit
yelp [jelp] *s* Gekläff *n* ‖ *intr* kläffen
yen [jen] *s* (*Japanese money*) Yen *m*; (*for*) brennendes Verlangen *n* (nach)
yeo·man ['joman] *s* (–men) (nav) Verwaltungsunteroffizier *m*
yeo′man′s serv′ice *s* großer Dienst *m*
yes [jes] *adv* ja; yes, Sir jawohl ‖ *s* Ja *n*; say yes to bejahen
yes′ man′ *s* Jasager *m*
yesterday ['jestər ‚de] *adv* gestern; y. morning gestern früh ‖ *s* Gestern *n*; yesterday′s gestrig
yet [jet] *adv* (*still*) noch; (*however*) doch; (*already*) schon; and yet trotzdem, dennoch; as yet schon; not yet noch nicht ‖ *conj* aber
yew [ju] *s* Eibe *f*
Yiddish ['jɪdɪʃ] *adj* jiddisch ‖ *s* Jiddisch *n*
yield [jild] *s* Ertrag *m* ‖ *tr* (*profit*) einbringen; (*interest*) tragen; (*crops*) hervorbringen; (*give up*) überlassen ‖ *intr* (to) nachgeben (*dat*)
yo·del ['jodəl] *s* Jodler *m* ‖ *v* (*pret & pp* –del[l]ed; *ger* –del[l]ing) *intr* jodeln
yodeler ['jodələr] *s* Jodler –in *mf*
yogurt ['jogurt] *s* Yoghurt *m & n*
yoke [jok] *s* (*part of harness; burden*) Joch *n*; pass under the y. sich in ein Joch fügen; y. of oxen Ochsengespann *n* ‖ *tr* ins Joch spannen

yokel [ˈjokəl] s Bauerntölpel m
yolk [jok] s Dotter m & n
yonder [ˈjandər] adv dort drüben
yore [jor] s—of y. vormals
you [ju] pers pron du; (plural form) ihr; (polite form) Sie; to you dir; (plural form) euch; (polite form) Ihnen; **you of all people!** ausgerechnet Sie! || indef pron man
young [jʌŋ] adj (younger [ˈjʌŋgər]; youngest [ˈjʌŋgɪst]) jung; **y. for one's age** jugendlich für sein Alter || spl (of animals) Jungen pl; **the y.** die Jungen, die Jugend; **with y.** (pregnant) trächtig
young′ la′dy s Fräulein n
young′ man′ s junger Mann m; (boyfriend) Freund m
youngster [ˈjʌŋstər] s Jugendliche mf
your [jur] poss adj dein; (plural form) euer; (polite form) Ihr
yours [jurz] poss pron deiner; (plural

form) euerer; (polite form) Ihrer; **y. truly** hochachtungsvoll
your·self [jurˈsɛlf] intens pron (–selves [ˈsɛlvz]) selbst, selber || reflex pron dich; (plural form) euch; (polite form) Sich; to y. dir; (polite form) Sich; **to yourselves** euch; (polite form) Sich
youth [juθ] s (youths [juθs], [juðz]) (age) Jugend f; (person) Jugendliche mf
youthful [ˈjuθfəl] adj jugendlich
youth′ hos′tel s Jugendherberge f
yowl [jaul] s Gejaule n || tr & intr jaulen
Yugoslav [ˈjugoˈslav] adj jugoslawisch || s Jugoslawe m, Jugoslawin f
Yugoslavia [ˈjugoˈslavɪ·ə] s Jugoslavien n
yule′ log′ [jul] s Weihnachtsscheit n
yule′tide′ s Weihnachtszeit f

Z

Z, z [zi] s sechsundzwanzigster Buchstabe des englischen Alphabets
zany [ˈzeni] adj närrisch || s Hanswurst m
zeal [zil] s Eifer m
zealot [ˈzɛlət] s Zelot –in mf
zealous [ˈzɛləs] adj eifrig
zebra [ˈzibrə] s Zebra n
zenith [ˈzinɪθ] s Scheitelpunkt m, Zenit m
zephyr [ˈzɛfər] s Zephir m
zeppelin [ˈzɛpəlɪn] s Zeppelin m
ze·ro [ˈziro] s (–ros & –roes) Null f || tr—z. **in a rifle** Visier e–s Gewehrs justieren || intr—z. **in on** zielen auf (acc)
ze′ro hour′ s Stunde f Null
zest [zɛst] s Würze f
Zeus [zus] s Zeus m
zig·zag [ˈzɪgˌzæg] adj Zickzack– || adv im Zickzack || s Zickzack m || (pret & pp –zagged; ger –zagging) intr im Zickzack fahren
zinc [zɪŋk] s Zink n
Zionism [ˈzaɪ·əˌnɪzəm] s Zionismus m

zip [zɪp] s (coll) Schmiß m || v (pret & pp zipped; ger zipping) tr (convey with speed) mit Schwung befördern; (fasten with a zipper) mit e–m Reißverschluß schließen || intr sausen; **zip by** vorbeisausen || interj wuppdich!
zip′ code′ s Postleitzahl f
zipper [ˈzɪpər] s Reißverschluß m
zircon [ˈzʌrkan] s Zirkon m
zither [ˈzɪθər] s Zither f
zodiac [ˈzodɪˌæk] s Tierkreis m
zombie [ˈzɔmbi] s (sl) Depp m
zone [zon] s (& geol) Zone f; (postal zone) Postbezirk m; (mil) Bereich m
zoo [zu] s Zoo m, Tiergarten m
zoologic(al) [ˌzo·əˈladʒɪk(əl)] adj zoologisch
zoologist [zoˈalədʒɪst] s Zoologe m, Zoologin f
zoology [zoˈalədʒi] s Zoologie f
zoom [zum] s lautes Summen n; (aer) Hochreißen n || intr laut summen; **z. up** (aer) hochreißen
zoom′ lens′ s Gummilinse f

	To Obtain
	lbs./sq. ft.
	lbs./sq. in.
	cm./sec.
	cm./hr.
	knots
	millimeters
	feet

METRIC CONVERSIONS

Multiply:	By:	To Obtain:
acres	43,560	sq. ft.
	0.4047	hectares
	0.0015625	sq. mi.
ampere-hours	3600	coulombs
atmospheres	76.0	cm. of mercury
	33.90	ft. of water
	14.70	lbs./sq. in.
British thermal units	1054	joules
	777.5	ft.-lbs.
	252.0	gram calories
	0.0003927	horsepower-hrs.
	0.0002928	kilowatt-hrs.
B.T.U./hr.	0.2928	watts
B.T.U./min.	12.96	ft.-lbs./sec.
	0.02356	horsepower
bushels	3523.8	hectoliters
	2150.42	cu. ins.
	35.238	liters
°C + 17.78	1.8	°F
centimeters	0.3937	inches
cm-grams	980.1	cm.-dynes
chains	66	ft.
circumference	6.2832	radians
cubic centimeters	0.0610	cu. ins.
cu. feet	1728	cu. ins.
	62.43	lbs. of water
	7.481	gals. (liq.)
	0.0283	cu. m.
cu. ft./min.	62.43	lbs. water/min.
cu. ft./sec.	448.831	gals./min.
cu. inches	16.387	cu. cm.
	0.0005787	cu. ft.
cu. meters	264.2	gals. (liq.)
	35.3147	cu. ft.
	1.3079	cu. yds.
cu. yards	27	cu. ft.
	0.765	cu. m.
days	86,400	seconds
degrees/sec.	0.1667	revolutions/min.
°F − 32	0.5556	°C
faradays/sec.	96,500	amperes
feet	30.48	cm.
	0.3048	meters
	0.0001894	mi. (stat.)
	0.0001645	mi. (Brit. naut.)

Multiply:	By:	To Obtain
ft. of water	62.43	lbs./sq. ft.
	0.4335	lbs./sq. in.
ft./min.	0.5080	cm./sec.
ft./sec.	0.6818	mi./hr.
	0.5921	knots
fluid ounces	29.573	milliliters
furlongs	660	feet
	0.125	mi.
gallons	231	cu. ins.
	8.345	lbs. of water
	8	pts.
	4	qts.
	3.785	liters
	0.003785	cu. m.
gals./min.	8.0208	cu. ft./hr.
grains	0.0648	grams
grams	980.1	dynes
	15.43	grains
	0.0353	oz. (avdp.)
	0.0022	lbs. (avdp.)
hectares	107,600	sq. ft.
	2.47	acres
hectoliters	2.838	bushels
horsepower	33,000	ft.-lbs./min.
	2545	B.T.U./hr.
	745.7	watts
	42.44	B.T.U./min.
	0.7457	kilowatts
inches	25.40	mm.
	2.540	cm.
	0.00001578	mi.
ins. of water	0.03613	lbs./sq. in.
kilograms	980,100	dynes
	2.2046	lbs. (avdp.)
kg. calories	3086	ft.-lbs.
	3.968	B.T.U.
kg. cal./min.	51.43	ft.-lbs./sec.
	0.06972	kilowatts
kilometers	3280.8	ft.
	0.621	mi.
km./hr.	0.621	mi./hr.
	0.5396	knots
kilowatts	737.6	ft.-lbs./sec.
	56.92	B.T.U./min.
	1.341	horsepower
kilowatt-hrs.	2,655,000	ft.-lbs.
	3415	B.T.U.
	1.341	horsepower-hrs.
knots	6080	ft./hr.
	1.151	stat. mi./hr.
	1	(Brit.) naut. mi./hr.
liters	61.02	cu. ins.
	2.113	pts. (liq.)
	1.057	qts. (liq.)
	0.264	gals. (liq.)
	1.816	pts. (dry)
	0.908	qts. (dry)
	0.1135	pecks
	0.0284	bushels

Multiply:	By:	To Obtain:
meters	39.37	inches
	3.2808	ft.
	1.0936	yds.
	0.0006215	mi. (stat.)
	0.0005396	mi. (Brit. naut.)
miles		
statute	5280	ft.
	1.609	km.
	0.8624	mi. (Brit. naut.)
nautical (Brit.)	6080	ft.
	1.151	mi. (stat.)
mi./hr.	1.467	ft./sec.
milligrams/liter	1	parts/million
milliliters	0.0338	fluid oz.
millimeters	0.03937	inches
ounces		
avoirdupois	28.349	grams
	0.9115	oz. (troy)
	0.0625	lbs. (avdp.)
troy	31.103	grams
	1.0971	oz. (avdp.)
pecks	8.8096	liters
pints		
liquid	473.2	cu. cm.
	28.875	cu. ins.
	0.473	liters
dry	0.550	liters
pounds		
avoirdupois	444,600	dynes
	453.6	grams
	32.17	poundals
	14.58	oz. (troy)
	1.21	lbs. (troy)
	0.4536	kg.
troy	0.373	kg.
lbs. (avdp.)/sq. in.	70.22	g./sq. cm.
	2.307	ft. of water
quarts		
liquid	57.75	cu. ins.
	32	fluid oz.
	2	pts.
	0.946	liters
dry	67.20	cu. ins.
	1.101	liters
quires	25	sheets
radians	3437.7	minutes
	57.296	degrees
reams	500	sheets
revolutions/min.	6	degrees/sec.
rods	16.5	ft.
	5.5	yds.
	5.029	meters
slugs	32.17	lbs. (mass)
square centimeters	0.155	sq. ins.
sq. feet	0.093	sq. m.
sq. inches	6.451	sq. cm.
sq. kilometers	247.1	acres
	0.3861	sq. mi.

Multiply:	By:	To Obtain:
sq. meters	10.76	sq. ft.
	1.1960	sq. yds.
sq. miles	27,878,400	sq. ft.
	640	acres
	2.5889	sq. km.
sq. yards	0.8361	sq. m.
tons		
long	2240	lbs. (avdp.)
	1.12	short tons
	1.0160	metric tons
metric	2204.6	lbs. (avdp.)
	1000	kg.
	1.1023	short tons
	0.9842	long tons
short	2000	lbs. (avdp.)
	0.9072	metric tons
	0.8929	long tons
watts	3.415	B.T.U./hr.
	0.001341	horsepower
yards	36	inches
	3	ft.
	0.9144	meters
	0.0005682	mi. (stat.)
	0.0004934	mi. (Brit. naut.)

LABELS AND ABBREVIATIONS

BEZEICHNUNGEN DER SACHGEBIETE UND ABKÜRZUNGEN

abbr abbreviation—Abkürzung
acc accusative—Akkusativ
(acct) accounting—Rechnungswesen
adj adjective—Adjektiv
(adm) administration—Verwaltung
adv adverb—Adverb
(aer) aeronautics—Luftfahrt
(agr) agriculture—Landwirtschaft
(alg) algebra—Algebra
(Am) American—amerikanisch
(anat) anatomy—Anatomie
(angl) angling—Angeln
(archeol) archeology—Archäologie
(archit) architecture—Architektur
(arith) arithmetic—Rechnen
art article—Artikel
(arti) artillery—Artillerie
(astr) astronomy—Astronomie
(atom. phys.) Atomic physics—Atomphysik
(Aust) Austrian—österreichisch
(aut) automobile—Automobile
aux auxiliary verb—Hilfsverb
(bact) bacteriology—Bakteriologie
(baseball) Baseball
(basketball) Korbball
(bb) bookbinding—Buchbinderei
(Bib) Biblical—biblisch
(billiards) Billard
(biochem) biochemistry—Biochemie
(biol) biology—Biologie
(bowling) Kegeln
(bot) botany—Botanik
(box) boxing—Boxen
(Brit) British—britisch
(cards) Kartenspiel
(carp) carpentry—Zimmerhandwerk
(checkers) Damespiel

(chem) chemistry—Chemie
(chess) Schachspiel
(cin) cinematography—Kinematographie
(coll) colloquial—umgangssprachlich
(com) commercial—Handels-
comb.fm. combining form—Wortbildungselement
comp comparative—Komparativ
conj conjunction—Konjunktion
(crew) Rudersport
(culin) culinary—kulinarisch
(data proc.) data processing—Datenverarbeitung
dem demonstrative—hinweisend
(dent) dentistry—Zahnheilkunde
(dial) dialectical—dialektisch
(dipl) diplomacy—Diplomatie
(eccl) ecclesiastical—kirchlich
(econ) economics—Wirtschaft
(educ) education—Schulwesen
e–e a(n)—eine
e.g. for example—zum Beispiel
(elec) electricity—Elektrizität
(electron) electronics—Elektronik
e–m to a(n)—einem
e–n a(n)—einen
(eng) engineering—Technik
(ent) entomology—Entomologie
e–r of a(n), to a(n)—einer
e–s of a(n)—eines
etw something—etwas
f feminine noun—Femininum
(fa) fine arts—schöne Künste
fem feminine—weiblich
(fencing) Fechtkunst
(fig) figurative—bildlich
(& fig) literal and figurative—buchstäblich und bildlich
(fin) finance—Finanzwesen
(fb) football, soccer—Fußball
fut future—Zukunft
genit genitive—Genitiv
(geog) geography, Geographie
(geol) geology—Geologie
(geom) geometry—Geometrie
ger gerund—Gerundium
(golf) Golf
(gram) grammar—Grammatik
(gym) gymnastics—Gymnastik
(heral) heraldry—Wappenkunde
(hist) history—Geschichte
(horol) horology—Zeitmessung
(hort) horticulture—Gartenbau
(hum) humorous—scherzhaft
(hunt) hunting—Jagdwesen
(ichth) ichthyology—Ichthyologie

373

imperf imperfect—Imperfekt
impers impersonal—unpersönlich
ind indicative—Indikativ
indecl indeclinable—undeklinierbar
indef indefinite—unbestimmt
(indust) industry—Industrie
inf infinitive—Infinitiv
(ins) insurance—Versicherungswesen
insep inseparable—untrennbar
intens intensive—verstärkend
interj interjection—Interjektion
interr interrogative—Frage-
intr intransitive—intransitiv
invar invariable—unveränderlich
(iron) ironical—ironisch
j—m to someone—jemandem
j—n someone—jemanden
(journ) journalism—Zeitungswesen
j—s someone's—jemand(e)s
(jur) jurisprudence—Rechtswissenschaft
(libr) library science—Bibliothekswissenschaft
(ling) linguistics—Linguistik
(lit) literary—literarisch
(log) logic—Logik
m masculine noun—Maskulinum
(mach) machinery—Maschinen
(mech) mechanics—Mechanik
(med) medicine—Medizin
(metal) metallurgy—Metallurgie
(meteor) meteorology—Meteorologie
mf masculine or feminine noun according to sex—Maskulinum
    oder Femininum je nach Geschlecht
(mil) military—Militär-
(min) mining—Bergwerkswesen
(mineral) mineralogy—Mineralogie
mod aux modal auxiliary—Modalverb
(mount) mountain climbing—Bergsteigerei
(mus) music—Musik
(myth) mythology—Mythologie
m & f masculine and feminine noun without regard to sex—
    Maskulinum oder Femininum ohne Rücksicht auf Geschlecht
(naut) nautical—nautisch
(nav) navy—Kriegsmarine
neut neuter—sächlich
(obs) obsolete—veraltet
(obstet) obstetrics—Geburtshilfe
(opt) optics—Optik
(orn) ornithology—Ornithologie
(paint) painting—Malerei
(parl) parliamentary—parlamentarisch
(pathol) pathology—Pathologie
(pej) pejorative—pejorativ
pers personal—Personal-

374

(pharm) pharmacy—Pharmazie
(philos) philosophy—Philosophie
(phonet) phonetics—Phonetik
(phot) photography—Photographie
(phys) physics—Physik
(physiol) physiology—Physiologie
pl plural—Plural
(poet) poetical—dichterisch
(pol) politics—Politik
poss possessive—besitzanzeigend
pp past participial—Partizip Perfekt
pref prefix—Präfix
prep preposition—Präposition
pres present—Gegenwart
pret preterit—Präteritum
pron pronoun—Pronomen
pros prosody—Prosodie
(Prot) Protestant—protestantisch
(psychol) psychology—Psychologie
(public sign) Hinweisschild
(rad) radio—Radio
(radar) Radar
recip reciprocal—wechselseitig
ref reflexive verb—Reflexivverb
reflex reflexive—reflexiv
rel relative—relativ
(relig) religion—Religion
(rhet) rhetoric—Rhetorik
(rok) rocketry—Raketen
(rr) railroad—Eisenbahn
s substantive—Substantiv
(sculp) sculpture—Bildhauerkunst
sep separable—trennbar
(sewing) Näherei
sg singular—Einzahl
(sl) slang—Slang
s.o. someone—jemand
s.o.'s someone's—jemand(e)s
spl substantive plural—pluralisches Substantiv
(sport) sports—Sports
(st. exch.) stock exchange—Börse
subj subjunctive—Konjunktiv
suf suffix—Suffix
super superlative—Superlativ
(surg) surgery—Chirurgie
(surv) surveying—Vermessungswesen
(tech) technical—Fachsprache
(telg) telegraphy—Telegraphie
(telp) telephone—Fernsprechwesen
(telv) television—Fernsehen
(tennis) Tennis
(tex) textiles—Textilien
(theat) theater—Theater

(theol) theology—Theologie
tr transitive—transitiv
(typ) typography—Typographie
usw. and so forth—und so weiter
v verb—Verb
var variant—Variante
(vet) veterinary medicine—Veterinärmedizin
(vulg) vulgar—vulgär
(zool) zoology—Zoologie